AMERICAN CONSTITUTIONAL LAW

SECOND EDITION

By

LAURENCE H. TRIBE
Ralph S. Tyler, Jr. Professor of Constitutional Law,
Harvard University

Mineola, New York
THE FOUNDATION PRESS, INC.
1988

Library of Congress Cataloging in Publication Data

Tribe, Laurence H.
  American constitutional law / Laurence H. Tribe.—2nd ed.
    p. cm. — (University textbook series)
  Includes bibliographical references and index.
  ISBN 0–88277–601–0
  1. United States—Constitutional law. I. Title. II. Series.
KF4550.T785 1988
342.73——dc19
[347.302]

87–27798
CIP

PREFACE TO THE SECOND EDITION

It is a great pleasure for me to be publishing this second edition at the time of the Constitution's Bicentennial—and on the fiftieth anniversary of the constitutional revolution of 1937. If I shared the sense of some on the left that constitutional discourse in the United States is but an apology for the status quo—a facade calculated to deflect any real critique of prevailing patterns of power—I would have long since set this enterprise aside. And if I shared the belief of others on the right that the sorts of constitutional arguments I advance are but a cover for whatever liberal political views I might hold, I would likewise have found other uses for my energy: a scholarly treatise—one providing ammunition to all combatants in the constitutional controversies of the day—is hardly the most effective way to fight political or legal views I would like to see rejected. My commitment to constitutional analysis is, in truth, neither particularly instrumental nor reflective of any specific philosophy beyond this: the Constitution is an endlessly intriguing object of study, and represents the best effort of its kind in the history of the world. Hence this edition.

Although completely updating the book (covering developments through August, 1987), I have left the basic organization of the work unchanged. Still, much of what has occurred in the intervening years has called for substantive revisions throughout. In the decade or so that has passed since the first edition was published, there have been a great many relevant developments for me to take into account—including hundreds of Supreme Court decisions and scores of pertinent articles and books, many of these opinions or other writings commenting upon or quoting the original edition, sometimes approvingly and sometimes not. I have been affected as well by a shift in my own experience. Having taught constitutional law for another decade and, perhaps more crucially, having argued around a dozen cases in the Supreme Court between the first edition and this, I have both broadened my perspective and sharpened my sense of the bridges that need to be built linking theory, teaching, and practice, gaining in the process a deeper appreciation of the very great difference between *reading* the Constitution we have and *writing* the Constitution some of us might wish to have.

Rather than focusing directly on the character of that difference in this edition, I leave such broader speculations to my other writings and structure this new edition, as I did its predecessor, in terms of doctrinal and historical models designed to shed some light on what courts have done with constitutional language and structure, to explore the themes and tensions within and among lines of decisions sometimes decades long, and to suggest possible lines of development yet to come.

If the result is generally informative and even eye-opening from time to time, I have a great many people to thank. In addition to those listed in the preface to the first edition, which is reproduced after this preface even though its rather grand tone is now a source of some embarrassment to me—and in addition to my wife Carolyn, my son Mark, and my daughter Kerry—there is a group of dedicated and tireless students and former students whose names appear, with much more gratitude than a marginal acknowledgement can display, in an appreciative footnote.[1] Then there are my secretaries Leslie Sterling and Pamela Massey, who helped in all the usual secretarial ways [2] but, even more important, kept me from either going crazy or taking myself too seriously.

There are two colleagues—both of them, distinguished former students of mine—whose encouragement and criticism also helped more than I can say: Professors Kathleen Sullivan and Susan Estrich. Kathleen is among the most remarkable members of the Harvard Law School faculty; as a teacher of constitutional law here, she has taught me at least as much as I ever taught her. And Susan, apart from being an enormously powerful lawyer, teacher, and writer, somehow got me over my deathly fear of the word processor—no mean feat, and one utterly indispensable to moving this project to completion.

Finally, there is my truly extraordinary associate and collaborator, Brian Koukoutchos, J.D. 1983, who returned to Cambridge after a year's clerkship with a federal district judge and who worked closely with me, both in the library and at the keyboard, to help me produce a work that

---

1. In addition to students too numerous to name who taught me as I tried to teach them, and many who assisted me on various research matters from time to time, the students who helped most notably with this edition—some of them on research projects they might long since have thought I had forgotten—include, from the Harvard Law School class of 1977, Carl Bryant Rogers; from the class of 1978, Steven Smith; from the class of 1982, Thomas Rollins; from the class of 1983, James G. Pope; from the class of 1984, Joan I. Greco, David A. Hoffman, William A. Hunter, and David A. Sklansky; from the class of 1985, Chai R. Feldblum; from the class of 1986, John Q. Barrett, Brian S. Bix, Kenneth J. Chesebro, Dan Gordon, Elena Kagan, and Jeffrey R. Toobin; from the class of 1987, Michael Abney, Stephen G. Bates, John Burchett, Clifford A. Cantor, Scott D. Deatherage, Robert D. Denious, Paul A. Engelmayer, Kenneth J. Hansen, Valerie Johnson, Michael D. Landry, Bennett W. Lasko, Nina T. Pillard, Michael D. Ricciuti, Michael L. Selmi, and Rona Wittels; from the class of 1988, Jonathan S. Massey and Peter J. Rubin. Also very helpful was Kristina Bielenberg, a 1986 graduate of Vermont Law School, who spent many hours proofreading and suggesting corrections.

To all of these talented individuals go my sincere thanks. And I want to single out for special appreciation, for work especially well done, and for help above and beyond the call of duty, a few of those named above: John Barrett (for work on Chapters 4 and 15), Stephen Bates (for especially extensive work on Chapter 14), Brian Bix (for work on Chapters 6 and 15), Kenneth Chesebro (for especially extensive work on Chapter 3), Paul Engelmayer (for work on Chapters 3 and 9), Kenneth Hansen (for work on Chapters 10 and 17), Elena Kagan (for work on Chapter 13), Jonathan Massey (for especially extensive work on Chapter 12), Nina Pillard (for work on Chapters 15 and 16), and Jeffrey Toobin (for work on Chapter 5 and especially extensive work on Chapter 12).

2. The combination of meticulousness, unflappability, and sheer intelligence such help has required in the case of this edition is almost beyond imagining.

almost certainly could not have been completed without him—and that would, even if completed, have been completed much less well.[3] Brian's combination of a searching mind and a sterling pen have made my long association with him among the few real pleasures of an effort that has entailed more struggle than joy.

If there is anyone to whom I really want to dedicate this edition, though, it is my parents. My mother continues to love and encourage me, even if only from afar. My father has helped from an even greater distance. He died two years after the first edition was published, just before my first Supreme Court argument—in the *Richmond Newspapers* case [4]—and just as I began to give thought to beginning this edition. He was a wonderful man, and I know how good this book would have made him feel.

LAURENCE H. TRIBE

Cambridge, Mass.
September, 1987

3. That is especially true of Chapters 4, 6, 15, and 16.

4. See § 12–20, infra. Throughout this edition, so as to alert readers to possible bias, I mention my role in Supreme Court cases that I argued.

*

PREFACE TO THE FIRST EDITION

This treatise ventures a unified analysis of constitutional law.* I have been tempted to state a more modest purpose, hoping to be measured by a more generous standard than this claim sets for the work, but that just wouldn't wash. The book has been too long in the making, its scope too obviously embracing, for me to offer it as merely a collection of tentative, disconnected observations on constitutional topics (though parts of it are tentative) or as only a student guide (though it certainly is designed to guide students).

I believe that another extended outline, a largely non-critical summary of leading cases and black-letter rules, would not serve the real needs even of beginning students, let alone of scholars, practitioners, and officials sworn to uphold the Constitution. My conclusion, after a number of years of teaching and talking about constitutional law with all these groups, is that their needs are more shared than divergent, and that only a systematic treatment, rooted in but not confined to the cases, sensitive to but not centered on social and political theory, can offer a clear perspective on how the doctrines and themes of our constitutional law have been shaped, what they mean, how they interconnect, and where they are moving. I also think only such a treatment can provide a coherent foundation for an active, continuing, and openly avowed effort to construct a more just constitutional order.

To achieve coherence without sacrificing nuance, I have relied heavily upon Supreme Court decisions and less upon the decisions of other courts and non-judicial tribunals. Yet I do not regard the rulings of the Supreme Court as synonymous with constitutional truth. As Justice Robert Jackson once observed of the Court, "We are not final because we are infallible, but we are infallible only because we are final." And the Courts that held slaves to be non-persons, separate to be equal, and pregnancy to be non sex-related can hardly be deemed either final *or* infallible. Such passing finality as judicial pronouncements possess is an essential compromise between constitutional order and chaos: the Constitution is an intentionally incomplete, often deliberately indeterminate structure for the participatory evolution of political ideals and governmental practices. This process cannot be the special province of any single entity. Thus my central topic is the Constitution itself, not the Supreme Court as an institution. While addressing relevant issues of institutional capacities and roles, I do not stop at discussing the Court as the right or wrong forum to review a particular issue and render judgment; the more crucial question for me is whether the judgment

---

* Criminal procedure, however, is considered only in conjunction with other topics rather than as a unified and complete whole.

vii

itself was right or wrong as an element in the living development of constitutional justice.

While conceding the courts a less exclusive role as constitutional oracles, this book cedes them a greater authority—and duty—to advance that justice overtly. Judicial neutrality inescapably involves taking sides. The judgment of the Court, though it may be to elude an issue, in effect settles the substance of the case. Judicial authority to determine when to defer to others in constitutional matters is a procedural form of substantive power; judicial restraint is but another form of judicial activism. In advocating a more candidly creative role than conventional scholarship has accorded the courts, I see myself as a proponent more of self-awareness than of an altered balance of governmental power. Most of the worry about how far judges may go, however genuine it may be and however fashionable it is again becoming, strikes me as rote unreality, profoundly misconceived in light of the inevitable social and cultural constraints on judicial intention and impact. Those constraints are perennially strong; they explain why the Supreme Court's decisions, even those universally rejected in a later era, may be controversial when they are rendered but never seem *unthinkable* at that time. The inescapable boundaries of societal context and consciousness argue not that judges should restrain themselves still further, but that they must raise distinctive voices of principle. Though I express occasional reservations about judicial initiative in specific settings, I reject the assumptions characteristic of Justices like Felix Frankfurter and scholars like Alexander Bickel: the highest mission of the Supreme Court, in my view, is not to conserve judicial credibility, but in the Constitution's own phrase, "to form a more perfect Union" between right and rights within that charter's necessarily evolutionary design.

It should be plain by now that I do not shrink from offering forthright opinions in this book. For me, the morality of responsible scholarship points not at all to the classic formula of supposedly value-free detachment and allegedly unbiased description. Instead such morality points to an avowal of the substantive beliefs and commitments that necessarily inform any account of constitutional arguments and conclusions. I am convinced that attempts to treat constitutional doctrine neutrally elide important questions and obscure available answers. Therefore the reader will find this book taking explicit positions on the most troublesome problems in constitutional law. To understand the structure of those problems, as it is set forth here, and to understand the principles that bear on the solutions, one need not share my views— either about the proper role of judges or about the correct resolution of substantive constitutional controversies. Because such views are openly presented, and because I believe that contrary views are fairly considered, the decision to forego an illusory neutrality can enhance the value of the book to all readers, who whether they agree, dissent, or wonder at any given point will know more of the values that may have influenced a particular judgment, which at bottom can never stand solely on a neutral base.

Having said I would be open about my own views, I should state at the outset that I perceive in recent decisions of the Supreme Court a distressing retreat from an appropriate defense of liberty and equality. Given its remarkable activism in constraining the President vis-a-vis Congress and the courts and in limiting Congress vis-a-vis the States, the current Supreme Court cannot be understood as pursuing a modest institutional role. In truth no less activist than its predecessors, the Burger Court has been animated by a specific substantive vision of the proper relationship between individuals and government—a vision I regard as bordering on the authoritarian, unduly beholden to the status quo, and insufficiently sensitive to human rights and needs. I believe that the course of the Burger Court, at least in its first years, will eventually be marked not as the end of an era of exaggerated activism on behalf of individuals and minorities, but as a sad period of often opposite activism, cloaked in the worn-out if well-meant disguise of judicial restraint. Because I understand and respect other assessments, I do not take the correctness of my own view for granted, but rather undertake the case for it. Indeed, my reactions to the Burger Court are not uniformly negative. I reject the thesis that the Court is engaged merely in the dismantling of Warren Court doctrines, and I see much to commend in the current Court's resurrection of economic rights through such provisions as the contract clause and in its efforts to enhance state and local autonomy and responsibility. Admittedly, though, I am more a critic than an admirer of the Burger Court—and in the end, differences of opinion on matters of this sort must turn on different axioms about issues too irreducible to be explored at length in a work on constitutional law. Still I prefer postulates honestly expressed to analyses whose underlying assumptions are obscured by the jargon of neutral principles and the language of "objective" legal description.

Equally fundamental is my belief that the conventional ways even of *stating* the choices between greater freedom or equality, on the one hand, and greater governmental power, on the other hand—and particularly the conventional emphasis on "balancing interests" as the statesmanlike method of making such choices—are remarkably unilluminating as well as misleadingly ahistorical. I think that the evolution of constitutional doctrine can be far better understood in terms of a division of the subject into distinct models of constitutional argument that I believe have shaped, and continue to shape, that fundamental body of law. I introduce seven such models in Chapter 1; they are the central organizing idea of the entire work. By showing how constitutional analysis has been structured over time, I hope not only to clarify otherwise confusing aspects of technical constitutional doctrine but also to expose otherwise concealed doctrinal connections and to reveal possibilities of freedom, equality, and fraternity latent in doctrinal alternatives. In short, I hope to provide not just a summary of constitutional rulings, but a system of thought about constitutional law. This should serve simultaneously to explicate the traditional approaches and to introduce ideas that go beyond them.

If the pages that follow begin to offer an alternative to the habit of reading the final words of constitutional wisdom solely in the entrails of specific Supreme Court opinions, I will be deeply gratified. But even if this book succeeds only in making more transparent the ideas and tensions that have directed our constitutional development, my investment of years will have been rewarded.

ACKNOWLEDGMENTS

No one not in an author's position can appreciate the full truth of the traditional disclaimer: it would be impossible to acknowledge adequately all those who have helped. Many Harvard colleagues—including Paul Bator, Derrick Bell, Abe Chayes, John Ely, Morton Horwitz, Milton Katz, Duncan Kennedy, Frank Michelman, and Richard Parker—have played roles for which I am deeply grateful. There were many research assistants and associates at Harvard and elsewhere whose energy and talent eased my burdens as the work progressed: Joseph Angland, Wynne Carvill, Michael Dell, Ruth Epstein, Ira Karasick, Arvid Roach, Dinah Seiver—and also Greg Ballard, Paul Berman, Richard Briffault, Paul Brown, Steven Calkins, Irwin Chemerinsky, Wayne Cypen, Chris Edley, Leslie Espinoza, Susan Estrich, Charles Garvin, Lisa Goldberg, Jeff Gordon, Allen Kenyon, John Koeltl, Michael Lampert, Joseph Loveland, Elliot Mincberg, Barbara O'Connor, David Oppenheimer, Jeffrey Pash, Dallas Perkins, Whit Peters, Bryant Rogers, Tom Rollins, Faith Shapiro, Steven Sirianni, Michael Sussman, Marc Temin, David Wade, and Tom Welch. I wish also to thank those in the Harvard Law School administration whose generous help made so large an undertaking possible; Dean Albert Sacks, Vice Dean William Bruce, and Elizabeth Stout were especially forthcoming with assistance. My former secretary, Linda Heinsohn, was a great help with the book's earliest drafts. My administrative assistant and secretary, Cathy Durovich, deserves special mention for the extraordinary way in which she combined a wonderful tolerance and intelligence with thoroughness, competence, and plain hard work.

I must single out four people in particular whose aid proved truly indispensable. One helped with so many chapters, and at so many stages of this undertaking, that his role was plainly more that of colleague than that of assistant: Patrick Gudridge, without whom this enterprise would have faltered often, contributed more than any routine acknowledgment could possibly suggest; his power and insight truly transformed the ambition and depth of the entire work. Likewise, David Drueding, Lisa Goldberg, and John Sexton, as my research associates during the final phases of the project, gave extensive and invaluable assistance as both intellectual collaborators and untiring aides; they deserve special thanks for their extraordinarily perceptive contributions, as well as for their generously helping the entire effort along in some of its most discouraging moments.

Finally, I add an expression of special gratitude to the several people whose forbearance and encouragement persuaded me to persist in those gloomy periods when I genuinely doubted that I had the will. Chief among those to whom I owe such very special thanks are my parents, my wife Carolyn, and my friend Sargent Shriver. It was a conversation with him one winter morning that convinced me not to abandon this project. It is to him, as well as to my parents, my wife, and my children Mark and Kerry, that I dedicate this book.

LAURENCE TRIBE

Cambridge, Mass.
November, 1977

*

SUMMARY OF CONTENTS

*

TABLE OF CONTENTS

CHAPTER 1. APPROACHES TO CONSTITUTIONAL ANALYSIS

CHAPTER 2. MODEL I—THE MODEL OF SEPARATED AND DIVIDED POWERS

CHAPTER 3. FEDERAL JUDICIAL POWER

CHAPTER 4. FEDERAL EXECUTIVE POWER

CHAPTER 5. FEDERAL LEGISLATIVE POWER: CONGRESSIONAL AUTHORITY AND THE IMPLICATIONS OF STATE SOVEREIGNTY

CHAPTER 6. FEDERALISM–BASED LIMITS ON STATE AND LOCAL POWER: REGULATION AND TAXATION OF COMMERCE, FEDERAL SUPREMACY, AND PROBLEMS OF INTERSTATE DISCRIMINATION

CHAPTER 7. DIRECT PROTECTION OF INDIVIDUALS AND GROUPS: MODELS BEYOND THE SEPARATION AND DIVISION OF POWER

CHAPTER 8. MODEL II—THE MODEL OF IMPLIED LIMITATIONS ON GOVERNMENT: THE RISE AND FALL OF CONTRACTUAL LIBERTY

CHAPTER 9. MODEL III—THE MODEL OF SETTLED EXPECTATIONS: UNCOMPENSATED TAKINGS AND CONTRACT IMPAIRMENTS

CHAPTER 10. MODEL IV—THE MODEL OF GOVERNMENTAL REGULARITY: EX POST FACTO LAWS, BILLS OF ATTAINDER, AND PROCEDURAL DUE PROCESS

CHAPTER 11. MODEL V—THE MODEL OF PREFERRED RIGHTS: LIBERTY BEYOND CONTRACT

CHAPTER 12. RIGHTS OF COMMUNICATION AND EXPRESSION

CHAPTER 13. RIGHTS OF POLITICAL PARTICIPATION

CHAPTER 14. RIGHTS OF RELIGIOUS AUTONOMY

CHAPTER 15. RIGHTS OF PRIVACY AND PERSONHOOD

CHAPTER 17. MODEL VII—TOWARD A MODEL OF STRUCTURAL JUSTICE?

CHAPTER 18. THE PROBLEM OF STATE ACTION

*

THE CONSTITUTION OF THE UNITED STATES OF AMERICA

We the People of the United States, in Order to form a more perfect Union, establish Justice, insure domestic Tranquility, provide for the common defence, promote the general Welfare, and secure the Blessings of Liberty to ourselves and our Posterity, do ordain and establish this Constitution for the United States of America.

ARTICLE I

Section 1. All legislative Powers herein granted shall be vested in a Congress of the United States, which shall consist of a Senate and House of Representatives.

Section 2. [1] The House of Representatives shall be composed of Members chosen every second Year by the People of the several States, and the Electors in each State shall have the Qualifications requisite for Electors of the most numerous Branch of the State Legislature.

[2] No Person shall be a Representative who shall not have attained to the Age of twenty five Years, and been seven Years a Citizen of the United States, and who shall not, when elected, be an Inhabitant of that State in which he shall be chosen.

[3] Representatives and direct Taxes shall be apportioned among the several States which may be included within this Union, according to their respective Numbers, which shall be determined by adding to the whole Number of free Persons, including those bound to Service for a Term of Years, and excluding Indians not taxed, three fifths of all other Persons. The actual Enumeration shall be made within three Years after the first Meeting of the Congress of the United States, and within every subsequent Term of ten Years, in such Manner as they shall by Law direct. The Number of Representatives shall not exceed one for every thirty Thousand, but each State shall have at Least one Representative; and until such enumeration shall be made, the State of New Hampshire shall be entitled to chuse three, Massachusetts eight, Rhode Island and Providence Plantations one, Connecticut five, New York six, New Jersey four, Pennsylvania eight, Delaware one, Maryland six, Virginia ten, North Carolina five, South Carolina five, and Georgia three.

[4] When vacancies happen in the Representation from any State, the Executive Authority thereof shall issue Writs of Election to fill such Vacancies.

[5] The House of Representatives shall chuse their Speaker and other Officers; and shall have the sole Power of Impeachment.

Section 3. [1] The Senate of the United States shall be composed of two Senators from each State, chosen by the Legislature thereof, for six Years; and each Senator shall have one Vote.

[2] Immediately after they shall be assembled in Consequence of the first Election, they shall be divided as equally as may be into three Classes. The Seats of the Senators of the first Class shall be vacated at the Expiration of the second Year, of the second Class at the Expiration of the fourth Year, and of the third Class at the Expiration of the sixth Year, so that one third may be chosen every second Year; and if Vacancies happen by Resignation, or otherwise, during the Recess of the Legislature of any State, the Executive thereof may make temporary Appointments until the next Meeting of the Legislature, which shall then fill such Vacancies.

[3] No Person shall be a Senator who shall not have attained to the Age of thirty Years, and been nine Years a Citizen of the United States, and who shall not, when elected, be an Inhabitant of that State for which he shall be chosen.

[4] The Vice President of the United States shall be President of the Senate, but shall have no Vote, unless they be equally divided.

[5] The Senate shall chuse their other Officers, and also a President pro tempore, in the Absence of the Vice President, or when he shall exercise the Office of President of the United States.

[6] The Senate shall have the sole Power to try all Impeachments. When sitting for that Purpose, they shall be on Oath or Affirmation. When the President of the United States is tried, the Chief Justice shall preside: And no Person shall be convicted without the Concurrence of two thirds of the Members present.

[7] Judgment in Cases of Impeachment shall not extend further than to removal from Office, and disqualification to hold and enjoy any Office of honor, Trust, or Profit under the United States: but the Party convicted shall nevertheless be liable and subject to Indictment, Trial, Judgment, and Punishment, according to Law.

Section 4. [1] The Times, Places and Manner of holding Elections for Senators and Representatives, shall be prescribed in each State by the Legislature thereof; but the Congress may at any time by Law make or alter such Regulations, except as to the Places of chusing Senators.

[2] The Congress shall assemble at least once in every Year, and such Meeting shall be on the first Monday in December, unless they shall by Law appoint a different Day.

Section 5. [1] Each House shall be the Judge of the Elections, Returns, and Qualifications of its own Members, and a Majority of each shall constitute a Quorum to do Business; but a smaller Number may adjourn from day to day, and may be authorized to compel the Attendance of absent Members, in such Manner, and under such Penalties as each House may provide.

[2] Each House may determine the Rules of its Proceedings, punish its Members for disorderly Behaviour, and, with the Concurrence of two thirds, expel a Member.

[3] Each House shall keep a Journal of its Proceedings, and from time to time publish the same, excepting such Parts as may in their Judgment require Secrecy; and the Yeas and Nays of the Members of either House on any question shall, at the Desire of one fifth of those Present, be entered on the Journal.

[4] Neither House, during the Session of Congress, shall, without the Consent of the other, adjourn for more than three days, nor to any other Place than that in which the two Houses shall be sitting.

Section 6. [1] The Senators and Representatives shall receive a Compensation for their Services, to be ascertained by Law, and paid out of the Treasury of the United States. They shall in all Cases, except Treason, Felony and Breach of the Peace, be privileged from Arrest during their Attendance at the Session of their respective Houses, and in going to and returning from the same; and for any Speech or Debate in either House, they shall not be questioned in any other Place.

[2] No Senator or Representative shall, during the Time for which he was elected, be appointed to any civil Office under the Authority of the United States, which shall have been created, or the Emoluments whereof shall have been encreased during such time; and no Person holding any Office under the United States, shall be a Member of either House during his Continuance in Office.

Section 7. [1] All Bills for raising Revenue shall originate in the House of Representatives; but the Senate may propose or concur with Amendments as on other Bills.

[2] Every Bill which shall have passed the House of Representatives and the Senate, shall, before it become a Law, be presented to the President of the United States; If he approves he shall sign it, but if not he shall return it, with his Objections to that House in which it shall have originated, who shall enter the Objections at large on their Journal, and proceed to reconsider it. If after such Reconsideration two thirds of that House shall agree to pass the Bill, it shall be sent together with the Objections, to the other House, by which it shall likewise be reconsidered, and if approved by two thirds of that House, it shall become a Law. But in all such Cases the Votes of both Houses shall be determined by Yeas and Nays, and the Names of the Persons voting for and against the Bill shall be entered on the Journal of each House respectively. If any Bill shall not be returned by the President within ten Days (Sundays excepted) after it shall have been presented to him, the Same shall be a Law, in like Manner as if he had signed it, unless the Congress by their Adjournment prevent its Return in which Case it shall not be a Law.

[3] Every Order, Resolution, or Vote, to Which the Concurrence of the Senate and House of Representatives may be necessary (except on a question of Adjournment) shall be presented to the President of the United States; and before the Same shall take Effect, shall be approved by him, or being disapproved by him, shall be repassed by two thirds of

the Senate and House of Representatives, according to the Rules and Limitations prescribed in the Case of a Bill.

Section 8. [1] The Congress shall have Power To lay and collect Taxes, Duties, Imposts and Excises, to pay the Debts and provide for the common Defence and general Welfare of the United States; but all Duties, Imposts and Excises shall be uniform throughout the United States;

[2] To borrow Money on the credit of the United States;

[3] To regulate Commerce with foreign Nations, and among the several States, and with the Indian Tribes;

[4] To establish an uniform Rule of Naturalization, and uniform Laws on the subject of Bankruptcies throughout the United States;

[5] To coin Money, regulate the Value thereof, and of foreign Coin, and fix the Standard of Weights and Measures;

[6] To provide for the Punishment of counterfeiting the Securities and current Coin of the United States;

[7] To Establish Post Offices and Post Roads;

[8] To promote the Progress of Science and useful Arts, by securing for limited Times to Authors and Inventors the exclusive Right to their respective Writings and Discoveries;

[9] To constitute Tribunals inferior to the supreme Court;

[10] To define and punish Piracies and Felonies committed on the high Seas, and Offences against the Law of Nations;

[11] To declare War, grant Letters of Marque and Reprisal, and make Rules concerning Captures on Land and Water;

[12] To raise and support Armies, but no Appropriation of Money to that Use shall be for a longer Term than two Years;

[13] To provide and maintain a Navy;

[14] To make Rules for the Government and Regulation of the land and naval Forces;

[15] To provide for calling forth the Militia to execute the Laws of the Union, suppress Insurrections and repel Invasions;

[16] To provide for organizing, arming, and disciplining, the Militia, and for governing such Part of them as may be employed in the Service of the United States, reserving to the States respectively, the Appointment of the Officers, and the Authority of training the Militia according to the discipline prescribed by Congress;

[17] To exercise exclusive Legislation in all Cases whatsoever, over such District (not exceeding ten Miles square) as may, by Cession of particular States, and the Acceptance of Congress, become the Seat of the Government of the United States, and to exercise like Authority over all Places purchased by the Consent of the Legislature of the State in which the Same shall be, for the Erection of Forts, Magazines, Arsenals, dock-Yards, and other needful Buildings;—And

[18] To make all Laws which shall be necessary and proper for carrying into Execution the foregoing Powers, and all other Powers vested by this Constitution in the Government of the United States, or in any Department or Officer thereof.

Section 9.   [1] The Migration or Importation of Such Persons as any of the States now existing shall think proper to admit, shall not be prohibited by the Congress prior to the Year one thousand eight hundred and eight, but a Tax or duty may be imposed on such Importation, not exceeding ten dollars for each Person.

[2] The Privilege of the Writ of Habeas Corpus shall not be suspended, unless when in Cases of Rebellion or Invasion the public Safety may require it.

[3] No Bill of Attainder or ex post facto Law shall be passed.

[4] No Capitation, or other direct, Tax shall be laid, unless in Proportion to the Census or Enumeration herein before directed to be taken.

[5] No Tax or Duty shall be laid on Articles exported from any State.

[6] No Preference shall be given by any Regulation of Commerce or Revenue to the Ports of one State over those of another: nor shall Vessels bound to, or from, one State be obliged to enter, clear, or pay Duties in another.

[7] No Money shall be drawn from the Treasury, but in Consequence of Appropriations made by Law; and a regular Statement and Account of the Receipts and Expenditures of all public Money shall be published from time to time.

[8] No Title of Nobility shall be granted by the United States: And no Person holding any Office of Profit or Trust under them, shall, without the Consent of the Congress, accept of any present, Emolument, Office, or Title, of any kind whatever, from any King, Prince, or foreign State.

Section 10.   [1] No State shall enter into any Treaty, Alliance, or Confederation; grant Letters of Marque and Reprisal; coin Money; emit Bills of Credit; make any Thing but gold and silver Coin a Tender in Payment of Debts; pass any Bill of Attainder, ex post facto Law, or Law impairing the Obligation of Contracts, or grant any Title of Nobility.

[2] No State shall, without the Consent of the Congress, lay any Imposts or Duties on Imports or Exports, except what may be absolutely necessary for executing its inspection Laws: and the net Produce of all Duties and Imposts, laid by any State on Imports or Exports, shall be for the Use of the Treasury of the United States; and all such Laws shall be subject to the Revision and Controul of the Congress.

[3] No State shall, without the Consent of Congress, lay any Duty of Tonnage, keep Troops, or Ships of War in time of Peace, enter into any Agreement or Compact with another State, or with a foreign

Power, or engage in War, unless actually invaded, or in such imminent Danger as will not admit of delay.

ARTICLE II

Section 1. [1] The executive Power shall be vested in a President of the United States of America. He shall hold his Office during the Term of four Years, and, together with the Vice President, chosen for the same Term, be elected, as follows:

[2] Each State shall appoint, in such Manner as the Legislature thereof may direct, a Number of Electors, equal to the whole Number of Senators and Representatives to which the State may be entitled in the Congress; but no Senator or Representative, or Person holding an Office of Trust or Profit under the United States, shall be appointed an Elector.

[3] The Electors shall meet in their respective States, and vote by Ballot for two Persons, of whom one at least shall not be an Inhabitant of the same State with themselves. And they shall make a List of all the Persons voted for, and of the Number of Votes for each; which List they shall sign and certify, and transmit sealed to the Seat of the Government of the United States, directed to the President of the Senate. The President of the Senate shall, in the Presence of the Senate and House of Representatives, open all the Certificates, and the Votes shall then be counted. The Person having the greatest Number of Votes shall be the President, if such Number be a Majority of the whole Number of Electors appointed; and if there be more than one who have such Majority, and have an equal Number of Votes, then the House of Representatives shall immediately chuse by Ballot one of them for President; and if no Person have a Majority, then from the five highest on the List the said House shall in like Manner chuse the President. But in chusing the President, the Votes shall be taken by States, the Representation from each State having one Vote; A quorum for this Purpose shall consist of a Member or Members from two thirds of the States, and a Majority of all the States shall be necessary to a Choice. In every Case, after the Choice of the President, the Person having the greater Number of Votes of the Electors shall be the Vice President. But if there should remain two or more who have equal Votes, the Senate shall chuse from them by Ballot the Vice President.

[4] The Congress may determine the Time of chusing the Electors, and the Day on which they shall give their Votes; which Day shall be the same throughout the United States.

[5] No person except a natural born Citizen, or a Citizen of the United States, at the time of the Adoption of this Constitution, shall be eligible to the Office of President; neither shall any Person be eligible to that Office who shall not have attained to the Age of thirty five Years, and been fourteen Years a Resident within the United States.

[6] In case of the removal of the President from Office, or of his Death, Resignation or Inability to discharge the Powers and Duties of

the said Office, the Same shall devolve on the Vice President, and the Congress may by Law provide for the Case of Removal, Death, Resignation or Inability, both of the President and Vice President, declaring what Officer shall then act as President, and such Officer shall act accordingly, until the Disability be removed, or a President shall be elected.

[7] The President shall, at stated Times, receive for his Services, a Compensation, which shall neither be encreased nor diminished during the Period for which he shall have been elected, and he shall not receive within that Period any other Emolument from the United States, or any of them.

[8] Before he enter on the Execution of his Office, he shall take the following Oath or Affirmation: "I do solemnly swear (or affirm) that I will faithfully execute the Office of President of the United States, and will to the best of my Ability, preserve, protect and defend the Constitution of the United States."

Section 2. [1] The President shall be Commander in Chief of the Army and Navy of the United States, and of the militia of the several States, when called into the actual Service of the United States; he may require the Opinion, in writing, of the principal Officer in each of the executive Departments, upon any Subject relating to the Duties of their respective Offices, and he shall have Power to grant Reprieves and Pardons for Offenses against the United States, except in Cases of Impeachment.

[2] He shall have Power, by and with the Advice and Consent of the Senate, to make Treaties, provided two thirds of the Senators present concur; and he shall nominate, and by and with the Advice and Consent of the Senate, shall appoint Ambassadors, other public Ministers and Consuls, Judges of the supreme Court, and all other Officers of the United States, whose Appointments are not herein otherwise provided for, and which shall be established by Law; but the Congress may by Law vest the Appointment of such inferior Officers, as they think proper, in the President alone, in the Courts of Law, or in the Heads of Departments.

[3] The President shall have power to fill up all Vacancies that may happen during the Recess of the Senate, by granting Commissions which shall expire at the End of their next Session.

Section 3. He shall from time to time give to the Congress Information of the State of the Union, and recommend to their Consideration such Measures as he shall judge necessary and expedient; he may, on extraordinary Occasions, convene both Houses, or either of them, and in Case of Disagreement between them, with Respect to the Time of Adjournment, he may adjourn them to such Time as he shall think proper; he shall receive Ambassadors and other public Ministers; he shall take Care that the Laws be faithfully executed, and shall Commission all the Officers of the United States.

Section 4. The President, Vice President and all civil Officers of the United States, shall be removed from Office on Impeachment for, and Conviction of, Treason, Bribery, or other high Crimes and Misdemeanors.

ARTICLE III

Section 1. The judicial Power of the United States, shall be vested in one supreme Court, and in such inferior Courts as the Congress may from time to time ordain and establish. The Judges, both of the supreme and inferior Courts, shall hold their Offices during good Behaviour, and shall, at stated Times, receive for their Services a Compensation, which shall not be diminished during their Continuance in Office.

Section 2. [1] The judicial Power shall extend to all Cases, in Law and Equity, arising under this Constitution, the Laws of the United States, and Treaties made, or which shall be made, under their Authority;—to all Cases affecting Ambassadors, other public Ministers and Consuls;—to all Cases of admiralty and maritime Jurisdiction;—to Controversies to which the United States shall be a Party;—to Controversies between two or more States;—between a State and Citizens of another State;—between Citizens of different States;—between Citizens of the same State claiming Lands under the Grants of different States, and between a State, or the Citizens thereof, and foreign States, Citizens or Subjects.

[2] In all Cases affecting Ambassadors, other public Ministers and Consuls, and those in which a State shall be a Party, the supreme Court shall have original Jurisdiction. In all the other Cases before mentioned, the supreme Court shall have appellate Jurisdiction, both as to Law and Fact, with such Exceptions, and under such Regulations as the Congress shall make.

[3] The trial of all Crimes, except in Cases of Impeachment, shall be by Jury; and such Trial shall be held in the State where the said Crimes shall have been committed; but when not committed within any State, the Trial shall be at such Place or Places as the Congress may by Law have directed.

Section 3. [1] Treason against the United States, shall consist only in levying War against them, or, in adhering to their Enemies, giving them Aid and Comfort. No Person shall be convicted of Treason unless on the Testimony of two Witnesses to the same overt Act, or on Confession in open Court.

[2] The Congress shall have Power to declare the Punishment of Treason, but no Attainder of Treason shall work Corruption of Blood, or Forfeiture except during the Life of the Person attained.

ARTICLE IV

Section 1. Full Faith and Credit shall be given in each State to the public Acts, Records, and judicial Proceedings of every other State.

And the Congress may by general Laws prescribe the Manner in which such Acts, Records and Proceedings shall be proved, and the Effect thereof.

Section 2. [1] The Citizens of each State shall be entitled to all Privileges and Immunities of Citizens in the several States.

[2] A Person charged in any State with Treason, Felony, or other Crime, who shall flee from Justice, and be found in another State, shall on demand of the executive Authority of the State from which he fled, be delivered up, to be removed to the State having Jurisdiction of the Crime.

[3] No Person held to Service or Labour in one State, under the Laws thereof, escaping into another, shall, in Consequence of any Law or Regulation therein, be discharged from such Service or Labour, but shall be delivered up on Claim of the Party to whom such Service or Labour may be due.

Section 3. [1] New States may be admitted by the Congress into this Union; but no new State shall be formed or erected within the Jurisdiction of any other State; nor any State be formed by the Junction of two or more States, or Parts of States, without the Consent of the Legislatures of the States concerned as well as of the Congress.

[2] The Congress shall have Power to dispose of and make all needful Rules and Regulations respecting the Territory or other Property belonging to the United States; and nothing in this Constitution shall be so construed as to Prejudice any Claims of the United States, or of any particular State.

Section 4. The United States shall guarantee to every State in this Union a Republican Form of Government, and shall protect each of them against Invasion; and on Application of the Legislature, or of the Executive (when the Legislature cannot be convened) against domestic Violence.

ARTICLE V

The Congress, whenever two thirds of both Houses shall deem it necessary, shall propose Amendments to this Constitution, or, on the Application of the Legislatures of two thirds of the several States, shall call a Convention for proposing Amendments, which, in either Case, shall be valid to all Intents and Purposes, as part of this Constitution, when ratified by the Legislatures of three fourths of the several States, or by Conventions in three fourths thereof, as the one or the other Mode of Ratification may be proposed by the Congress; Provided that no Amendment which may be made prior to the Year One thousand eight hundred and eight shall in any Manner affect the first and fourth Clauses in the Ninth Section of the first Article; and that no State, without its Consent, shall be deprived of its equal Suffrage in the Senate.

ARTICLE VI

[1] All Debts contracted and Engagements entered into, before the Adoption of this Constitution, shall be as valid against the United States under this Constitution, as under the Confederation.

[2] This Constitution, and the Laws of the United States which shall be made in Pursuance thereof; and all Treaties made, or which shall be made, under the Authority of the United States, shall be the supreme Law of the Land; and the Judges in every State shall be bound thereby, any Thing in the Constitution or Laws of any State to the Contrary notwithstanding.

[3] The Senators and Representatives before mentioned, and the Members of the several State Legislatures, and all executive and judicial Officers, both of the United States and of the several States, shall be bound by Oath or Affirmation, to support this Constitution; but no religious Test shall ever be required as a Qualification to any Office or public Trust under the United States.

ARTICLE VII

The Ratification of the Conventions of nine States shall be sufficient for the Establishment of this Constitution between the States so ratifying the Same.

ARTICLES IN ADDITION TO, AND AMENDMENT OF, THE CONSTITUTION OF THE UNITED STATES OF AMERICA, PROPOSED BY CONGRESS, AND RATIFIED BY THE LEGISLATURES OF THE SEVERAL STATES PURSUANT TO THE FIFTH ARTICLE OF THE ORIGINAL CONSTITUTION.

AMENDMENT I [1791]

Congress shall make no law respecting an establishment of religion, or prohibiting the free exercise thereof; or abridging the freedom of speech, or of the press; or the right of the people peaceably to assemble, and to petition the Government for a redress of grievances.

AMENDMENT II [1791]

A well regulated Militia, being necessary to the security of a free State, the right of the people to keep and bear Arms, shall not be infringed.

AMENDMENT III [1791]

No Soldier shall, in time of peace be quartered in any house, without the consent of the Owner, nor in time of war, but in a manner to be prescribed by law.

AMENDMENT IV [1791]

The right of the people to be secure in their persons, houses, papers, and effects, against unreasonable searches and seizures, shall not be violated, and no Warrants shall issue, but upon probable cause, supported by Oath or affirmation, and particularly describing the place to be searched, and the persons or things to be seized.

AMENDMENT V [1791]

No person shall be held to answer for a capital, or otherwise infamous crime, unless on a presentment or indictment of a Grand Jury, except in cases arising in the land or naval forces, or in the Militia, when in actual service in time of War or public danger; nor shall any person be subject for the same offence to be twice put in jeopardy of life or limb; nor shall be compelled in any criminal case to be a witness against himself, nor be deprived of life, liberty, or property, without due process of law; nor shall private property be taken for public use, without just compensation.

AMENDMENT VI [1791]

In all criminal prosecutions, the accused shall enjoy the right to a speedy and public trial, by an impartial jury of the State and district wherein the crime shall have been committed, which district shall have been previously ascertained by law, and to be informed of the nature and cause of the accusation; to be confronted with the witnesses against him; to have compulsory process for obtaining witnesses in his favor, and to have the Assistance of Counsel for his defence.

AMENDMENT VII [1791]

In Suits at common law, where the value in controversy shall exceed twenty dollars, the right of trial by jury shall be preserved, and no fact tried by jury, shall be otherwise re-examined in any Court of the United States, than according to the rules of the common law.

AMENDMENT VIII [1791]

Excessive bail shall not be required, nor excessive fines imposed, nor cruel and unusual punishments inflicted.

AMENDMENT IX [1791]

The enumeration in the Constitution, of certain rights, shall not be construed to deny or disparage others retained by the people.

AMENDMENT X [1791]

The powers not delegated to the United States by the Constitution, nor prohibited by it to the States, are reserved to the States respectively, or to the people.

AMENDMENT XI [1798]

The Judicial power of the United States shall not be construed to extend to any suit in law or equity, commenced or prosecuted against one of the United States by Citizens of another State, or by Citizens or Subjects of any Foreign State.

AMENDMENT XII [1804]

The Electors shall meet in their respective states and vote by ballot for President and Vice-President, one of whom, at least, shall not be an inhabitant of the same state with themselves; they shall name in their ballots the person voted for as President, and in distinct ballots the person voted for as Vice-President, and they shall make distinct lists of all persons voted for as President, and of all persons voted for as Vice-President, and of the number of votes for each, which lists they shall sign and certify, and transmit sealed to the seat of the government of the United States, directed to the President of the Senate;—The President of the Senate shall, in the presence of the Senate and House of Representatives, open all the certificates and the votes shall then be counted;—The person having the greatest number of votes for President, shall be the President, if such number be a majority of the whole number of Electors appointed; and if no person have such majority, then from the persons having the highest numbers not exceeding three on the list of those voted for as President, the House of Representatives shall choose immediately, by ballot, the President. But in choosing the President, the votes shall be taken by states, the representation from each state having one vote; a quorum for this purpose shall consist of a member or members from two-thirds of the states, and a majority of all the states shall be necessary to a choice. And if the House of Representatives shall not choose a President whenever the right of choice shall devolve upon them before the fourth day of March next following, then the Vice-President shall act as President, as in the case of the death or other constitutional disability of the President.—The person having the greatest number of votes as Vice-President, shall be the Vice-President, if such number be a majority of the whole number of Electors appointed, and if no person have a majority, then from the two highest numbers on the list, the Senate shall choose the Vice-President; a quorum for the purpose shall consist of two-thirds of the whole number of Senators, and a majority of the whole number shall be necessary to a choice. But no person constitutionally ineligible to the office of President shall be eligible to that of Vice-President of the United States.

AMENDMENT XIII [1865]

Section 1. Neither slavery nor involuntary servitude, except as a punishment for crime whereof the party shall have been duly convicted, shall exist within the United States, or any place subject to their jurisdiction.

Section 2. Congress shall have power to enforce this article by appropriate legislation.

AMENDMENT XIV [1868]

Section 1. All persons born or naturalized in the United States, and subject to the jurisdiction thereof, are citizens of the United States and of the State wherein they reside. No State shall make or enforce any law which shall abridge the privileges or immunities of citizens of the United States; nor shall any State deprive any person of life, liberty, or property, without due process of law; nor deny to any person within its jurisdiction the equal protection of the laws.

Section 2. Representatives shall be apportioned among the several States according to their respective numbers, counting the whole number of persons in each State, excluding Indians not taxed. But when the right to vote at any election for the choice of electors for President and Vice President of the United States, Representatives in Congress, the Executive and Judicial officers of a State, or the members of the Legislature thereof, is denied to any of the male inhabitants of such State, being twenty-one years of age, and citizens of the United States, or in any way abridged, except for participation in rebellion, or other crime, the basis of representation therein shall be reduced in the proportion which the number of such male citizens shall bear to the whole number of male citizens twenty-one years of age in such State.

Section 3. No person shall be a Senator or Representative in Congress, or elector of President and Vice President, or hold any office, civil or military, under the United States, or under any State, who having previously taken an oath, as a member of Congress, or as an officer of the United States, or as a member of any State legislature, or as an executive or judicial officer of any State, to support the Constitution of the United States, shall have engaged in insurrection or rebellion against the same, or given aid or comfort to the enemies thereof. But Congress may by a vote of two-thirds of each House, remove such disability.

Section 4. The validity of the public debt of the United States, authorized by law, including debts incurred for payment of pensions and bounties for services in suppressing insurrection or rebellion, shall not be questioned. But neither the United States nor any State shall assume or pay any debt or obligation incurred in aid of insurrection or rebellion against the United States, or any claim for the loss or emancipation of any slave; but all such debts, obligations and claims shall be held illegal and void.

Section 5. The Congress shall have power to enforce, by appropriate legislation, the provisions of this article.

AMENDMENT XV [1870]

Section 1. The right of citizens of the United States to vote shall not be denied or abridged by the United States or by any State on account of race, color, or previous condition of servitude.

Section 2. The Congress shall have power to enforce this article by appropriate legislation.

AMENDMENT XVI [1913]

The Congress shall have power to lay and collect taxes on incomes, from whatever source derived, without apportionment among the several States, and without regard to any census or enumeration.

AMENDMENT XVII [1913]

[1] The Senate of the United States shall be composed of two Senators from each State, elected by the people thereof, for six years; and each Senator shall have one vote. The electors in each State shall have the qualifications requisite for electors of the most numerous branch of the State legislatures.

[2] When vacancies happen in the representation of any State in the Senate, the executive authority of such State shall issue writs of election to fill such vacancies: *Provided*, That the legislature of any State may empower the executive thereof to make temporary appointments until the people fill the vacancies by election as the legislature may direct.

[3] This amendment shall not be so construed as to affect the election or term of any Senator chosen before it becomes valid as part of the Constitution.

AMENDMENT XVIII [1919]

Section 1. After one year from the ratification of this article the manufacture, sale, or transportation of intoxicating liquors within, the importation thereof into, or the exportation thereof from the United States and all territory subject to the jurisdiction thereof for beverage purposes is hereby prohibited.

Section 2. The Congress and the several States shall have concurrent power to enforce this article by appropriate legislation.

Section 3. This article shall be inoperative unless it shall have been ratified as an amendment to the Constitution by the legislatures of the several States, as provided in the Constitution, within seven years from the date of the submission hereof to the States by the Congress.

AMENDMENT XIX [1920]

[1] The right of citizens of the United States to vote shall not be denied or abridged by the United States or by any State on account of sex.

[2] Congress shall have power to enforce this article by appropriate legislation.

AMENDMENT XX [1933]

Section 1. The terms of the President and Vice President shall end at noon on the 20th day of January, and the terms of Senators and Representatives at noon on the 3d day of January, of the years in which such terms would have ended if this article had not been ratified; and the terms of their successors shall then begin.

Section 2. The Congress shall assemble at least once in every year, and such meeting shall begin at noon on the 3d day of January, unless they shall by law appoint a different day.

Section 3. If, at the time fixed for the beginning of the term of the President, the President elect shall have died, the Vice President elect shall become President. If the President shall not have been chosen before the time fixed for the beginning of his term, or if the President elect shall have failed to qualify, then the Vice President elect shall act as President until a President shall have qualified; and the Congress may by law provide for the case wherein neither a President elect nor a Vice President elect shall have qualified, declaring who shall then act as President, or the manner in which one who is to act shall be selected, and such person shall act accordingly until a President or Vice President shall have qualified.

Section 4. The Congress may by law provide for the case of the death of any of the persons from whom the House of Representatives may choose a President whenever the right of choice shall have devolved upon them, and for the case of the death of any of the persons from whom the Senate may choose a Vice President whenever the right of choice shall have devolved upon them.

Section 5. Sections 1 and 2 shall take effect on the 15th day of October following the ratification of this article.

Section 6. This article shall be inoperative unless it shall have been ratified as an amendment to the Constitution by the legislatures of three-fourths of the several States within seven years from the date of its submission.

AMENDMENT XXI [1933]

Section 1. The eighteenth article of amendment to the Constitution of the United States is hereby repealed.

Section 2. The transportation or importation into any State, Territory, or possession of the United States for delivery or use therein of intoxicating liquors, in violation of the laws thereof, is hereby prohibited.

Section 3. This article shall be inoperative unless it shall have been ratified as an amendment to the Constitution by conventions in the several States, as provided in the Constitution, within seven years from the date of the submission hereof to the States by the Congress.

AMENDMENT XXII [1951]

Section 1. No person shall be elected to the office of the President more than twice, and no person who has held the office of President, or acted as President, for more than two years of a term to which some other person was elected President shall be elected to the office of President more than once. But this Article shall not apply to any person holding the office of President when this Article was proposed by the Congress, and shall not prevent any person who may be holding the office of President, or acting as President, during the term within which this Article becomes operative from holding the office of President or acting as President during the remainder of such term.

Section 2. This article shall be inoperative unless it shall have been ratified as an amendment to the Constitution by the legislatures of three-fourths of the several States within seven years from the date of its submission to the States by the Congress.

AMENDMENT XXIII [1961]

Section 1. The District constituting the seat of Government of the United States shall appoint in such manner as the Congress may direct:

A number of electors of President and Vice President equal to the whole number of Senators and Representatives in Congress to which the District would be entitled if it were a State, but in no event more than the least populous state; they shall be in addition to those appointed by the states, but they shall be considered, for the purposes of the election of President and Vice President, to be electors appointed by a state; and they shall meet in the District and perform such duties as provided by the twelfth article of amendment.

Section 2. The Congress shall have power to enforce this article by appropriate legislation.

AMENDMENT XXIV [1964]

Section 1. The right of citizens of the United States to vote in any primary or other election for President or Vice President, for electors for President or Vice President, or for Senator or Representative in Congress, shall not be denied or abridged by the United States or any State by reason of failure to pay any poll tax or other tax.

Section 2. The Congress shall have power to enforce this article by appropriate legislation.

AMENDMENT XXV [1967]

Section 1. In case of the removal of the President from office or of his death or resignation, the Vice President shall become President.

Section 2. Whenever there is a vacancy in the office of the Vice President, the President shall nominate a Vice President who shall take office upon confirmation by a majority vote of both Houses of Congress.

Section 3. Whenever the President transmits to the President pro tempore of the Senate and the Speaker of the House of Representatives his written declaration that he is unable to discharge the powers and duties of his office, and until he transmits to them a written declaration to the contrary, such powers and duties shall be discharged by the Vice President as Acting President.

Section 4. Whenever the Vice President and a majority of either the principal officers of the executive departments or of such other body as Congress may by law provide, transmit to the President pro tempore of the Senate and the Speaker of the House of Representatives their written declaration that the President is unable to discharge the powers and duties of his office, the Vice President shall immediately assume the powers and duties of the office as Acting President.

Thereafter, when the President transmits to the President pro tempore of the Senate and the Speaker of the House of Representatives his written declaration that no inability exists, he shall resume the powers and duties of his office unless the Vice President and a majority of either the principal officers of the executive department or of such other body as Congress may by law provide, transmit within four days to the President pro tempore of the Senate and the Speaker of the House of Representatives their written declaration that the President is unable to discharge the powers and duties of his office. Thereupon Congress shall decide the issue, assembling within forty-eight hours for that purpose if not in session. If the Congress, within twenty-one days after receipt of the latter written declaration, or, if Congress is not in session, within twenty-one days after Congress is required to assemble, determines by two-thirds vote of both Houses that the President is unable to discharge the powers and duties of his office, the Vice President shall continue to discharge the same as Acting President; otherwise, the President shall resume the powers and duties of his office.

AMENDMENT XXVI [1971]

Section 1. The right of citizens of the United States, who are eighteen years of age or older, to vote shall not be denied or abridged by the United States or by any State on account of age.

Section 2. The Congress shall have power to enforce this article by appropriate legislation.

*

TABLE OF CASES

References are to Pages

TABLE OF CASES

AMERICAN CONSTITUTIONAL LAW

*

Chapter 1

APPROACHES TO CONSTITUTIONAL ANALYSIS

§ 1–1. Overview: Seven Models of Constitutional Law

There was a time not long ago when constitutional law seemed in danger of becoming essentially anecdotal and fragmentary—an occasion for some welcome wit and even a bit of hard-won wisdom, but seldom more. Lately, constitutional law seems in equal danger of being submerged in political and legal and even literary theory—with the law of the Constitution becoming little more than a setting for the ventilation of favored views about the meaning of lawmaking and of legal interpretation and about the relation of both to politics, history, language, and society. Much intriguing theorizing has gone on over the past decade or so. Imaginative contributions have included those that defend constitutional review by an independent judiciary as an activity serving the "prophetic function" of seeking objectively correct answers to moral and political questions;[1] those that justify such judicial review as an enterprise designed to repair defective processes of participation and representation;[2] those that support it as an undertaking in "interpreting" certain social practices in such a way as to give them the greatest possible integrity;[3] those that seek to ground judicial review in the avoidance of governmental actions justified solely by "naked preferences";[4] and even some that aim to link judicial enforcement of the Constitution to common-law "principles of property, contract, and tort law."[5]

How much can be gained by seeking *any* single, unitary theory for construing the Constitution is unclear. It may be that all efforts at such reduction or simplification, however suggestive, are ultimately more misleading than informative. For the Constitution is an historically discontinuous composition; it is the product, over time, of a series of not altogether coherent compromises; it mirrors no single vision or philosophy but reflects instead a set of sometimes reinforcing and sometimes conflicting ideals and notions.[6]

§ 1–1

1. See M. Perry, The Constitution, The Courts, and Human Rights (1982). Cf. S. Barber, On What the Constitution Means 9 (1984) (explicating constitutionalism as the "best thinking" of what Americans "stand for as a people").

2. See J. Ely, Democracy and Distrust (1980).

3. See R. Dworkin, Law's Empire (1986).

4. See Sunstein, "Naked Preferences and the Constitution," 84 Colum.L.Rev. 1689, 1732 (1984).

5. See R. Epstein, Takings 331–32 (1985). Strikingly different (but still individualistically rights-based) theories are set forth in D. Richards, Toleration and the Constitution (1986), and in R. Dworkin, Taking Rights Seriously (1977). Both of the latter owe much of their inspiration to J. Rawls, A Theory of Justice (1971).

6. This thesis is put forward by Kaufman, "Judges or Scholars: To Whom Shall We Look for Our Constitutional Law?," 37 J. Legal Educ. 184 (1987), and by Tribe, "The Idea of the Constitution: A Metaphor-morphosis," 37 J. Legal Educ. 170 (1987). See also Aleinikoff, "Constitutional

With this in mind, I have continued to organize the constitutional principles, rules, and theories that are this book's subject in terms of the seven basic models that, as the first edition of this treatise suggested, have represented the major alternatives for constitutional argument and decision in American law from the early 1800's to the present. The models to be described are those of (I) separated and divided powers; (II) implied limitations on government; (III) settled expectations; (IV) governmental regularity; (V) preferred rights; (VI) equal protection; and (VII) structural justice.

Representing approximate tendencies, emphases, and approaches rather than precise formal systems, these models are not put forth as mutually exclusive; constitutional discourse in any given period can thus be expected to draw on ideas and categories characteristic of more than one model. The models reflect neither entirely self-conscious patterns of thought nor wholly unconscious explanatory structures; they combine elements at both levels of awareness. Their main function, as will emerge, is heuristic; the hope is that they can enlarge understanding while drawing on lines of thought genuinely implicit in the doctrinal and historical materials. This grounding in the materials is important. The thought is that the models have specific historical roots and concrete reflections in legal and political experience; they are not purely imposed mental constructs but grow out of immersion in judicial decisions and lawyers' arguments themselves. For that reason, the models should startle no one. Far from being idiosyncratic, they should represent quite familiar themes, however unconventional might be the decision to structure the exposition and critique of constitutional law through the lenses that these seven models provide.

§ 1–2. The Basic Pattern: Model I and the Roots of Models III and IV

That all lawful power derives from the people and must be held in check to preserve their freedom is the oldest and most central tenet of American constitutionalism. At the outset, only a small number of explicit substantive limitations on the exercise of governmental authority were thought essential; in the main, it was believed that personal freedom could be secured more effectively by decentralization than by express command. From the thought of seventeenth century English liberals, particularly as elaborated in eighteenth century France by Montesquieu, the Constitution's framers had derived the conviction that human rights could best be preserved by inaction and indirection—shielded behind the play of deliberately fragmented centers of countervailing power, in a vision almost Newtonian in its inspiration. In this first model, the centralized accumulation of power in any man or single group of men meant tyranny; the division and separation of powers, both vertically (along the axis of federal, state and local authority) and horizontally (along the axis of legislative, executive, and judicial authority) meant liberty.[1] It was thus essential that no depart-

1. See, e.g., The Federalist Nos. 10, 28, 41, 47, 51; B. Bailyn, The Ideological Ori-

ment, branch, or level of government be empowered to achieve dominance on its own. If the legislature would punish, it must enlist the cooperation of the other branches—the executive to prosecute, the judicial to try and convict.[2] So too with each other center of governmental power: exercising the mix of functions delegated to it by the people in the social compact that was the Constitution, each power center would remain dependent upon the others for the final efficacy of its social designs.

Although exerting continuing influence to the present day (as Chapters 2 through 6 will attest), Model I played its most pervasive role from the era of the Marshall Court to the Civil War. While "kicking upstairs" those governmental powers, primarily over commerce, that the individual states could not be relied upon to exercise without undue parochialism or factionalism, Model I relied heavily upon the vitality and autonomy of the states in most other respects to furnish, in the words of the 46th Federalist, a "barrier against the enterprises of ambition." Interestingly, this reliance on state autonomy did not take the form of judicially declaring Acts of Congress *ultra vires* in the name of state sovereignty. On the contrary, every such challenge was defeated in the pre-Civil War Supreme Court, with the sole exception of *Dred Scott's* ill-fated invalidation of the Missouri compromise.[3] Instead, reliance on state autonomy as a major source of individual rights and security in Model I took the indirect form of preserving state sovereignty by rejecting all but a handful of individual challenges to exercises of state authority said to violate the Constitution. Witness, for example, the refusal by the Supreme Court in 1833,[4] and by the Senate nearly half a century earlier,[5] to extend the Bill of Rights into a general charter of liberty against the states and municipalities.

In part, this refusal reflected a concession to state power as such, and a degree of ambivalence about the actual content of the personal freedom that merited protection. But also implicit in the refusal to extend the Bill of Rights against the states seems to have been a view that, just as the states were by and large adequately represented in the Congress, so individuals were likely for most purposes to be sufficiently represented in their own states, whose obliteration or serious erosion would leave individuals exposed to oppression by private violence and national tyranny alike.[6] Thus it was largely through the preservation

gins of the American Revolution 273–80 (1967); G. Wood, The Creation of the American Republic 151, 604 (1969); J. Rakove, The Beginnings of National Politics (1979). For a comparison with the continental variant of functionally separated rather than mutually checking powers, see 2 C. de Malberg, Contribution à la Théorie Générale de L'Etat § 1, at 23–34 (1922).

2. This theme surfaces most powerfully in United States v. Brown, 381 U.S. 437, 442–44 (1965), discussed in Chapter 10, infra.

3. Dred Scott v. Sandford, 60 U.S. (19 How.) 393 (1857).

4. Barron v. Mayor of Baltimore, 32 U.S. (7 Pet.) 243 (1833) (holding first eight amendments inapplicable to the states; had "congress engaged in the extraordinary occupation of improving the constitutions of the several states, by affording the people additional protection from the exercise of power by their own governments, in matters which concerned themselves alone, they would have declared this purpose in plain and intelligible language").

5. See Brennan, "State Constitutions and the Protection of Individual Rights," 90 Harv.L.Rev. 489, 503–04 (1977).

6. See, e.g., The Federalist No. 28 (A. Hamilton), at 228 (J. Hamilton ed. 1892):

of boundaries between and among institutions in Model I that the rights of persons were to be secured.

Two qualifications must be noted. First, a Bill of Rights directed against federal abuses was thought necessary in addition to the separation and division of powers; [7] although actual Bill-of-Rights invalidation of congressional legislation is a fairly recent phenomenon, [8] institutional boundaries in the absence of such a list of liberties were not deemed quite sufficient to preserve individual rights. Indeed, two supplementary models—that of settled expectations (Model III, expressed through guarantees like those against contract impairment and uncompensated takings, discussed in Chapter 9), and that of governmental regularity (Model IV, expressed through guarantees like those against ex post facto laws, bills of attainder, and procedurally arbitrary deprivations, discussed in Chapter 10)—are directly traceable to the earliest decisions of the federal judiciary. Built on the leanest of substantive premises

"The state governments will, in all possible contingencies, afford complete security against invasions of the public liberty by the national authorities."

7. The Constitutional Convention decided against including a Bill of Rights largely in the belief that Congress was in any event delegated none of the powers such a bill would seek to deny. See The Federalist No. 84; 2 M. Farrand, The Records of the Federal Convention of 1787, at 587–88, 617–18 (rev.ed. 1937). Opponents of ratification made the absence of a Bill of Rights a major objection, see 1 B. Schwartz, The Bill of Rights: A Documentary History 435–620; 2 id. at 627–980 (1971), and leading proponents such as Jefferson urged amendment of the Constitution to include such a bill. See 12 The Papers of Thomas Jefferson 438, 440 (J. Boyd ed. 1958). Even many who, like Madison, did not regard the omission of a Bill of Rights as "a material defect" nonetheless favored its inclusion by amendment. See 5 The Writings of James Madison 269 (G. Hunt ed. 1904) (expressing doubt, however, that such inclusion would do much good when it would be most needed). The winning argument, for some who most doubted the efficacy of a Bill of Rights, was Jefferson's stress upon "the legal check which [such a Bill would put] into the hands of the judiciary," as "a body, which if rendered independent, and kept strictly to their own department merits great confidence for their learning and integrity." 14 The Papers of Thomas Jefferson 659 (J. Boyd ed. 1958). The final version of the Bill of Rights, in which the Senate accepted twelve of the seventeen amendments proposed by the House, was adopted on Sept. 24 and 25, 1789. Of the twelve amendments sent to the states, ten were ratified; the two that failed of ratification dealt with the ratio of population to representatives and with compensation of

Members of Congress. See H. Ames, The Proposed Amendments to the Constitution 184–85 (1896).

It is also noteworthy that art. I, § 9, forbade suspension of "the Writ of Habeas Corpus" except when required by public safety "in Cases of Rebellion or Invasion," see Ex parte Milligan, 71 U.S. (4 Wall.) 2 (1866), and that art. III, § 2, secured a right to trial, for "all crimes, except in Cases of Impeachment," by "Jury . . . in the State where the said crimes shall have been committed." See Callan v. Wilson, 127 U.S. 540 (1888).

8. Two early cases invalidated contractual impairments under the fifth amendment. Reichert v. Felps, 73 U.S. (6 Wall.) 160 (1868) (annulment of titles previously conferred by governors of Northwest Territory); Hepburn v. Griswold, 75 U.S. (8 Wall.) 603 (1870) (attempt to make non-interest-bearing United States notes legal tender in payment of debts previously contracted), overruled in Knox v. Lee (Legal Tender Cases), 79 U.S. (12 Wall.) 457 (1870). Boyd v. United States, 116 U.S. 616 (1886), invoked the fourth and fifth amendments to hold unconstitutional the federally required production of certain documents, but successful invocation of the Bill of Rights to protect from Congress what would today be called "civil rights" or "civil liberties" dates from the 1950's. See, e.g., Bolling v. Sharpe, 347 U.S. 497 (1954) (holding segregated schools in District of Columbia violative of fifth amendment due process); Trop v. Dulles, 356 U.S. 86 (1958) (holding loss of citizenship for desertion a cruel and unusual punishment violative of the eighth amendment). The first time an Act of Congress was held violative of the first amendment, for example, was Lamont v. Postmaster General, 381 U.S. 301 (1965).

that could be teased from the basic model of separated and divided powers, these additional models posited judicially enforceable guarantees for vested rights and for the interest in having government proceed in accord with settled rules of law. Although their independent significance was not to be demonstrated until many decades later, those two models plainly went beyond notions of checks and balances from the very beginning.

Second, although the effort was finally rejected in the Senate, the House was sufficiently persuaded by James Madison's fear of state and local oppression across a wide spectrum of issues to approve a constitutional amendment which would have provided that "no State shall infringe the equal rights of conscience, nor the freedom of speech or of the press, nor of the right of trial by jury in criminal cases." [9] Not until well after the adoption of the fourteenth amendment itself some 79 years later was Madison's aim accomplished. [10] For purposes of this introduction, it is noteworthy both that he came close to succeeding in 1789, and that it took a Civil War to make the difference.

§ 1–3. The Civil War's Impact: The Rise of Model II

That Madison nearly succeeded even in 1789 suggests that the willingness to trust each state to shield its people's rights was more qualified even in the late eighteenth century than might be inferred from the Constitution's initial inclusion of no explicit shields beyond the contract clause, the ex post facto clause, and the bill of attainder clause. And that the Civil War made the crucial difference points to a key weakness in Model I's linkage between individual rights and federal-state institutional boundaries: the linkage relied heavily upon an identity of interests between the states, as the level of government closest to the people, and the primary corpus of civil rights and liberties of the people themselves—an identity incomplete from the start, and quite impossible to maintain after the great battle over slavery had been fought.

Leaving largely intact Model I's connection between individual rights and the tripartite separation of powers, the Civil War necessarily challenged the Model's connection between individual rights and the federal-state division of governmental responsibility. Yet the Supreme Court, as we will see in Chapters 7 and 8, persisted in defending that linkage between freedom and geography for more than a decade beyond the war's end. Thus the Court reiterated the state-shield idea as late as 1873, when it refused to hold Louisiana's slaughterhouse monopoly a violation of the then recently-enacted fourteenth amendment on the primary ground that the amendment was not meant to displace the central role of the states as protectors of their own citizens. [1] And even in controversies involving race, the Court was slow to treat the Civil

---

9. 1 Annals of Congress 783 (Aug. 17, 1789).

10. The fourteenth amendment was certified by Secretary Seward as ratified on July 28, 1868.

§ 1–3

1. Slaughterhouse Cases, 83 U.S. (16 Wall.) 36 (1873), discussed in Chapters 7 and 8, infra.

War Amendments as fundamentally realigning federal-state relations.[2] But it was only a matter of time until the weakened link would be more fully severed.

A major stumbling block to its severance was the persistent fear of national tyranny. However great the supposed need to use the four-teenth amendment as a shield for citizens against their own states, the cure was feared by many to be worse than the disease, since it seemed to mean that Congress could deploy the amendment as a sword against the only governments close enough to the people to provide enduring protection for their interests.

Yet Justice Miller's opinion for the Court in the *Slaughterhouse Cases* [3] appears to have contained the seeds of its own decisive refuta-tion: General principles of common law—the very principles that Miller unhesitatingly applied two years later in a diversity case to strike down a local tax as a disguised instance of robbery [4]—would enable the Court to distinguish between national legislation *remedying* state infringements upon common-law rights (state actions which were not "true" exercises of the police, taxing, and eminent domain powers reserved to the states) and national legislation *invading* the proper sphere of reserved state authority. Once the possibility of such a distinction was clearly perceived by the mid-1880's,[5] and forcefully articulated at the federal bench by the allies of property and contract by the 1890's,[6] it became possible—or so it seemed—to employ the fourteenth amendment as a federal shield without transforming it into a fatal sword.

The synthesis embodying that vision was Model II, the model of implied limitations on government, which held sway through the first quarter of the twentieth century. By defining the spheres of private, state, and national power in terms of the essential character and hence the implied limitations of each, federal judges believed they had derived a science of rights in which congressional laws intruding upon the state domain would be invalidated just as state laws invading the private domain would be struck down.[7] Probably more coherent than it has been fashionable to admit in the long era of lamentation over *Lochner v. New York* [8] and its progeny, Model II—whose rise and fall is traced in Chapter 8—tied its own knot between individual and institutional concerns. It was a knot more complex than that of Model I, since it no longer leaned heavily upon the presumed trustworthiness of state and local governments in dealing with their own citizens. But it was a knot with its own difficulties, since it appeared to presuppose instead an objective judicial method for defining the limitations of state power and

---

2. In re Civil Rights Cases, 109 U.S. 3 (1883), discussed in Chapter 18, infra.

3. Note 1, supra.

4. Loan Ass'n v. Topeka, 87 U.S. (20 Wall.) 655 (1875). See Chapter 8, infra.

5. See, e.g., Barbier v. Connolly, 113 U.S. 27 (1885).

6. See A. Paul, Conservative Crisis and the Rule of Law (1969).

7. See Kennedy, "Form and Substance in Private Law Adjudication," 89 Harv.L. Rev. 1685, 1745–55 (1976); Kennedy, "To-ward an Understanding of Legal Con-sciousness: The Case of Classical Legal Thought in America, 1850–1940," 3 Re-search in Law & Sociology 3–24 (1980).

8. 198 U.S. 45 (1905) (invalidating maxi-mum-hours legislation for bakers).

hence filling out, by a reciprocal process, the contents and contours of personal liberty.

§ 1–4. The Depression: Collapse of Model II

Major signs of doubt as to the existence of any such objective method appeared in federal judicial decisions by the early 1920's,[1] but it was the Great Depression, the New Deal, and the intellectual movements to which both contributed, that finally severed Model II's peculiar linkage between institutional boundaries and personal rights. The crucial impact of that national economic upheaval, and of the conceptual revolution that attended it, was to devastate the belief that property and its contractually realizable advantages were attributable to some natural order of things implicit in a revealed structure of common-law rights. Who had property and who did not, who enjoyed contractual freedom and who had to be satisfied with what was offered, became a function of whom government had chosen to protect through its legal rules and whom it had decided to abandon to the strength of others. Liberty of any meaningful sort came to be seen by growing numbers as a function of positive action by the state—not simply a function of leaving undisturbed the economic results of blind social forces and adventitious circumstance. In such a universe, the conduct of federal judges in policing preconceived limitations on governmental powers came to be viewed ever more broadly as an exercise in will rather than a study in logic, and the invisible hand of reason became instead the all too visible hand of entrenched wealth and power.[2]

Although the Court-packing plan may have fixed the precise timing of Model II's fall, it was the general rise of the positive state that made some alternative model or models inevitable. No longer content with securing justice by defining the inherent limits and internal boundaries of governmental institutions, judges and advocates were consumed by the search for an alternative conception of the just in matters of governmental power. The years since 1937 are best understood in terms of that search; its triumphs and failures mark the history of modern constitutional thought.

§ 1–5. The Post-Depression Models: III through VII

From time to time after the fall of Model II, lawyers have had recourse to either or both of the two models with the clearest antecedents in Model I—Model III, that of settled expectations; and Model IV, that of governmental regularity. The continuing appeal of those models traces largely to their appearance of neutrality and objectivity. In Chapters 9 and 10, it will be argued that this appearance has for the most part been an illusion, and that the edifice of doctrine built on the ideals of respecting expectations and acting with regularity has been defensible only in terms of rarely articulated substantive beliefs. To

---

§ 1–4

1. See, e.g., Pennsylvania Coal Co. v. Mahon, 260 U.S. 393 (1922); Miller v. Schoene, 276 U.S. 272 (1928), both discussed in Chapters 8 and 9, infra.

2. See M. Weber, Law in Economy and Society 188–91 (1954 ed.); R. Wolff, The Poverty of Liberalism 89–93 (1968).

the extent that the models genuinely avoid reliance on such beliefs, they prove circular, or empty, or both.

Squarely confronting the need to defend constitutional principles in substantive terms is Model V, the model of preferred rights, introduced in Chapter 11. Expressed through doctrines involving rights of communication and expression (Chapter 12), rights of political participation (Chapter 13), rights of religious autonomy (Chapter 14), and rights of privacy and personhood (Chapter 15), this model does not seek to define inherent internal limits on the power of all governmental institutions but aims more modestly to exclude governmental power from certain spheres, by identifying islands of "preferred freedoms" and immunizing choices within those islands from all but the most compellingly justified instances of governmental intrusion. Broad limitations on economic intervention once thought to be derived from the internal structure of governmental powers in Model II were thus replaced in Model V by more selective limitations imposed from without.

Throughout the same post-1937 period, a competing Model VI, that of equal protection, has offered alluring alternatives for constitutional argument; it is examined in Chapter 16. Decisions under Model VI have sought to identify both those fundamental aspects of the social and legal structure which should be equally open to all, and those criteria of government classification most likely to reflect prejudiced reactions against various types of persons and thus most likely to deny the basic right of all persons to be treated as equals.

Spurred partly by general social change and partly by the appointment of judges unsympathetic to how their recent predecessors had resolved the substantive controversies inescapable in Models V and VI, the Supreme Court in recent years has significantly cut back on avenues, both substantive and procedural, for growth in these two models. We will trace such retrenching developments and will attempt to analyze their premises and implications at a number of levels— primarily at the level of federal judicial and legislative power (Chapters 3 and 5), at the level of preferred rights and equality (Chapters 11 through 16), and at the level of state action doctrine (Chapter 18). We will also examine the contemporary emergence of a new model of constitutional argument, composed almost entirely of ideas already present in Models I through VI, but nonetheless distinctive in its way of linking structural concerns about governmental decision-making with substantive concerns about individual and community rights. This is Model VII, the model of structural justice; it is taken up in Chapter 17.

§ 1–6. The Tension Between Containing Government and Harnessing Its Capacities

In the twentieth century era of increasingly accepted, and indeed often demanded, affirmative governance, there has emerged an inescapable tension between Model I's ideal of dividing, separating, and checking powers so as to *contain* government, and the conviction that real freedom requires governmental *action* rather than passivity. But given our dominant constitutional heritage of containment, it should not seem surprising that even affirmative governmental duties have tended to find expression in the older language and theory of legal limitations upon the state. Not only is this the case with Models III and IV (settled expectations and governmental regularity); it is the case as well with Model V, the model of preferred rights; with Model VI, the model of equal protection; and with Model VII, the model of structural justice. The idea that government must facilitate opportunities for free expression has appeared as a prohibition upon governmental abridgements of speech and assembly.[1] The emerging idea that government must consider the many interests that its omissions as well as its positive actions will affect has been expressed in terms of a requirement that the target of public choice must be heard before government intrudes upon certain expectations, even by simply failing to renew a relationship where an entitlement exists.[2] And the still more far-reaching idea that government must secure at least some minimal level of human subsistence and shelter has been clothed in the language of prohibitions against unjustified governmental discrimination and procedurally unfair governmental deprivation.[3]

At this introductory stage, having very roughly sketched the models themselves, it suffices to observe that, whatever the language employed, and without in the least disparaging the deep significance of the still incomplete shift from the minimal state to the affirmative state, the continuing perception of many Americans over two centuries has been unshaken: whatever the model, government cannot be relied upon to behave voluntarily as the Constitution demands. Neither the effective maintenance of structural checks and balances, nor the adequate discharge of government's affirmative obligations, have been thought likely without some form of intervention from a point at least partially outside of ordinary majoritarian politics.

With respect to the limitation of governmental power in the original minimal-state conception, the formative experiences of our colonial and post-independence periods were not calculated to instill trust in legislative or executive fidelity, even among our own governments, to constitutionally established boundaries on authority.[4] Unless the federal judiciary was empowered to police those boundaries in proper cases, it was thought, they would be honored more in the breach than the observance.[5] And in the more affirmative if unfinished conception of the positive state whose eventual acceptance was probably assured by the Great Depression and its aftermath, it has been feared by many that, without judicial prodding, whatever positive constitutional duties might exist would too often and too easily be ignored by public authorities short-sightedly wedded to the status quo.

§ 1–6

1. See Chapter 12, infra.

2. See Chapter 10, infra.

3. See Chapters 10, 15, and 16, infra.

4. See generally G. Wood, The Creation of the American Republic (1969).

5. Hamilton voiced a widely felt belief when he argued that, absent federal judicial review, "all the reservations of particular rights or privileges would amount to nothing." The Federalist No. 78. See also Jefferson's views in § 1–2, note 7, supra.

§ 1–7. The Antimajoritarian Difficulty

Whether imposed by unelected judges or by elected officials conscientious and daring enough to defy popular will in order to do what they believe the Constitution requires, choices to ignore the majority's inclinations in the name of a higher source of law invariably raise questions of legitimacy in a nation that traces power to the people's will. As common-law developments increasingly draw upon constitutional principles to displace legislative choices in a curious inversion of Model II,[1] such questions of legitimacy extend well beyond constitutional law narrowly conceived. But those questions are sharpest when the room for legislative revision is narrowest. In its most basic form, the question in such cases is why a nation that rests legality on the consent of the governed would choose to constitute its political life in terms of commitments to an original agreement—made by the people, binding on their children, and deliberately structured so as to be difficult to change. Since that question would arise, albeit less dramatically, even without the institution of judicial review, its answer must be sought at a level more fundamental than is customary in discussions of why judges, appointed for life, should wield great power. For even without such judges, it must be stressed, lawmakers and administrators sworn to uphold the Constitution must from time to time ask themselves, if they take their oath seriously, why its message should be heeded over the voices of their constituents.[2]

For some years now, I have sought the outlines of an answer in the parable of the pigeon, drawn from an ingeniously designed experiment reported in the *Journal of the Experimental Analysis of Behavior*.[3] Pigeons were given a small but immediate food reinforcement for pecking a certain key, and a larger but delayed reinforcement for not pecking it. Most of the pigeons tested pecked the key in over 95% of

---

§ 1–7

1. For the role of common-law conceptions in Model II, see Chapters 7 and 8, infra.

2. Asking why *our* Constitution in particular should be deemed binding—given, among other things, the highly limited constituency of white property owners whose "consent" it represented even when adopted and amended, see Simon, "The Authority of the Framers of the Constitution," 73 Cal.L.Rev. 1482, 1498 & n. 44 (1985)—is different from asking why persons in the present should *ever* be deemed bound by "the compromises of another age." Brest, "The Misconceived Quest for the Original Understanding," 60 B.U.L.Rev. 234, 229 n. 96 (1980). Ultimately, this treatise is premised on the *axiom* that the Constitution—what it *says*, although not necessarily what some of its authors or ratifiers *intended* or *assumed*—is binding law; making that axiom seem plausible, while instructive, is not essential to the enterprise this book represents. It is also a premise of this work that, although the Constitution of 1787 was

deeply flawed—most profoundly, of course, by its acceptance of slavery—it remains a radical overstatement to say, as Justice Thurgood Marshall did in remarks he made to a group of attorneys in Maui, Hawaii, on May 6, 1987, that, "[w]hile the Union survived the civil war, the Constitution did not." This treatise treats the Constitution as it stands in 1987 as the contemporary, amended version of a text traceable to 1787—not in an unbroken line, to be sure, but in a historically connected set of processes. That those processes were anything but smooth, and that they pose deep puzzles of continuity and linkage, renders dubious any notion that the Constitution "as a whole" may be regarded as expressing any single, coherent vision or philosophy (see § 1–1, supra)—but does *not* require abandoning the view that it is to the *entire* Constitution, and not just some parts, that we owe our allegiance.

3. G. W. Ainslie, "Impulse Control in Pigeons," 21 J.Exper.Anal.Behavior 485 (1974).

the trials. But they regretted their choice. So anthropomorphic an observation is possible because the experimenters offered the impulsive pigeons the option of pecking a differently colored key at an earlier time. Those pigeons that pecked the differently colored key found, upon waddling into the test chamber, that the temptation of the small, immediate food reinforcement had been removed. They were thereby forced to wait for the larger, delayed reward—something that over 95% of them could not bring themselves to do when the temptation was immediately present. Significantly, 30% of those same pigeons learned to peck the earlier key when it operated to foreclose the later temptation. In their article on "Impulse Control in Pigeons," the experimenters conclude that even pigeons seem capable of learning to bind their "own future freedom of choice" in order to reap the rewards of acting in ways that would elude them under the pressures of the moment.

In a traditional or tightly-knit community, religious or other enduring sources of adherence to deep beliefs serve purposes analogous to those of the pigeons' differently-colored key. In a heterogeneous modern society, it may well be that nothing short of explicit agreements of a constitutional sort can serve those purposes.[4] Moreover, it may be necessary to create mechanisms for enforcing such constitutional agreements in a setting carefully insulated from momentary pressures, just as the pigeon experimenters concluded that any "effective device for getting the later, larger reinforcement must include a means of either preventing preference from changing as the smaller, earlier reward comes close, or keeping the subject from acting on this change."[5]

Within the American constitutional system of separated and divided powers, the means offered was a complex interplay of mutually checking institutions—institutions created, literally "constituted," by the founding document as drafted in 1787, and as amended from time to time thereafter. As will appear in Chapter 3, the often-asserted

---

4. In the decade or so since the pigeon parable first struck me as an apt model for constitutionalism, its limitations have impressed themselves on me as no less illuminating than its positive uses. Most crucially, the pigeon parable overlooks the role of the Constitution, and perhaps of any similarly structured constitution, in affirmatively *constituting* the institutions that would thereafter act out the constitutional plan—and in providing the *language* through which those institutions would thereafter direct and challenge one another and the society at large. See generally J. B. White, When Words Lose Their Meaning (1984). Without moving beyond a focus on constitutional text as the principal if partly indeterminate guide—contrast, e.g., Ackerman, "The Storrs Lectures: Discovering the Constitution," 93 Yale L.J. 1013 (1984); Grey, "Do We Have an Unwritten Constitution," 27 Stan.L. Rev. 702 (1975)—one can recognize that the Constitution's role is better captured in notions of discourse and dialogue than in

conceptions of mechanical or physical power and constraint.

5. G. W. Ainslie, supra note 3. Compare Homer, The Odyssey, Book XII (Scylla and Charybdis), lines 141–200 (Harper Colophon ed. 1975). Analysis of constitution-like rules regarded as mechanisms for forcing oneself to abide by a set of preferences that one fears one may abandon—a set of "second-order preferences," Sunstein, "Legal Interference with Private Preferences," 53 U.Chic.L.Rev. 1129, 1141 (1986)—has reached a considerable level of sophistication since this perspective was initially suggested in the first edition of this treatise. See, e.g., J. Elster, Ulysses and the Sirens 94–96 (1984); Schelling, "Enforcing Rules on Oneself," 1 J. L., Econ., & Org. 357 (1985); Schelling, "The Intimate Contest for Self-Command," 60 Pub. Interest 94 (1980). For a perceptive prior discussion of the theme, see Sen, "Rational Fools: A Critique of the Behavioral Foundations of Economic Theory," 6 Phil. & Pub. Affairs 317 (1977).

supremacy of the federal judiciary in that interplay of institutions is something of an exaggeration, given the significant constitutional roles assigned to other actors within the system. The fact remains, however, that remarkable power, often decisive, has been ceded by that system to federal judges generally and the Justices of the Supreme Court in particular. It is this specific phenomenon, quite apart from the general puzzle of why majority will should be constitutionally constrained,[6] that has been the focus of the most persistent theorizing, its conclusions ranging from extravagant praise to angry condemnation, throughout our constitutional history.[7]

§ 1–8. The Worry About Judicial Legitimacy: Guarding the Guardians

To the danger that the judges themselves might stray beyond their constitutionally delegated sphere of authority and thereby serve personal impulse rather than the Constitution, leaders of post-Revolutionary opinion replied by arguing that the judiciary would "be bound down by strict rules and precedents."[1] They added that, lacking ultimate "influence over either the sword or the purse," the federal judiciary "may truly be said to have neither FORCE nor WILL but merely judgment" and may thus be expected to remain "the least dangerous" branch.[2] It was for this reason that courts could be trusted to serve as "an intermediate body between the people and the legislature."

6. One general approach to this "puzzle" is to deny that it is all that puzzling— either by denying that supposedly representative processes in fact reflect majority will very accurately or meaningfully, see § 3–6, infra, or, much more fundamentally, by denying that there exists any meaningful sense in which *any* process could even hope to "reflect" any such thing as the will of the majority, given the well-known theorem for which Kenneth Arrow received his Nobel Prize in Economics, see K. Arrow, Social Choice and Individual Values (1951). Stated roughly, the theorem holds that *there can exist no method at all* for combining or aggregating individual preferences into a "social choice function" without violating one or more of several entirely natural and elementary conditions. Those conditions include such requirements as *transitivity* (the requirement that, if X is socially preferred to Y and Y is socially preferred to Z then X must be socially preferred to Z); *unanimity* (the requirement that, if every individual prefers X to Y, then the social choice is for X over Y); and *non-dictatorship* (the requirement that there be no individual whose preferences automatically dictate the social preference regardless of what everyone else prefers). The ramifications and significance of Arrow's so-called Impossibility Theorem are intriguingly explored in Plott, "Axiomatic Social Choice Theory: An Overview and Interpretation," in Rational Man and Irra-

tional Society? (B. Barry & R. Hardin, eds. 1982) at 231–51. I am indebted to Professor Cass Sunstein, visiting Harvard in 1986–87 from Chicago Law School, for reminding me of Arrow's theorem in this connection. Whether the theorem might be circumvented by suitably relaxing one or more of its constraints in such a way as to make it possible to speak meaningfully of "majority will" involves issues beyond the scope of this analysis. At the least, however, the analysis puts the burden of persuasion on those who assert that legislatures (or executives) deserve judicial deference as good aggregators of individual preference.

7. Compare, e.g., C. Black, The People and the Court (1960), with e.g., L. Lusky, By What Right? (1975), and R. Berger, Government by Judiciary (1977). See J. Ely, Democracy and Distrust (1980); J. Choper, Judicial Review and the National Political Process (1980); cf. M. Perry, The Constitution, the Courts and Human Rights (1982). See generally A. Bickel, The Least Dangerous Branch (1962); L. Hand, The Spirit of Liberty (3d ed. 1960); Rostow, "The Democratic Character of Judicial Review," 66 Harv.L.Rev. 193 (1952).

§ 1–8

1. The Federalist No. 78 (A. Hamilton).

2. Id.

To appreciate how natural a notion that might once have seemed, it is helpful to note that the idea of judicial review was born in the 1600's, in opposing the will of the Crown at a time when legislature and court alike were perceived as the voices of reason.[3] By the 1780's, colonial legislation had slipped from its early-seventeenth century pinnacle as an expression of reason, into a posture closely resembling that of the executive.[4] It was not until the late 1820's, however, that adjudication joined legislation in the subjective pit of will and power.[5] The breathing space, or fault line, between those two great slides—the brief period around the turn of the century, reaching into the early 1800's—provided a uniquely auspicious moment for the designers of our constitutional structure to treat federal judges as the logical guardians of our deepest commitments, and for the Supreme Court in *Marbury v. Madison* [6] to assert the power to review the constitutional validity of actions taken by coordinate branches of the national government.[7]

With the decline of faith in reason generally,[8] and with the growing perception that, particularly in giving content to the more open-ended of the Constitution's commands, judges could not hope to liberate themselves from the need to make substantive choices,[9] emphasis has shifted from the unique institutional characteristics of courts, or the unique characteristics of the method employed by them to fill the holes

3. See Jaffe & Henderson, "Judicial Review and the Rule of Law: Historical Origins," 72 Law.Q.Rev. 345 (1956).

4. See Horwitz, "Separation of Powers and Judicial Review: The Development of Post-Revolutionary Constitutional Theory," Thomas Cooley Lecture, Univ. of Michigan, 1975.

5. Id.

6. 5 U.S. (1 Cranch) 137 (1803) (Marshall, C.J.).

7. Martin v. Hunter's Lessee, 14 U.S. (1 Wheat.) 304 (1816) (Story, J.), was the first Supreme Court decision holding that federal courts may review the actions of state governments for their constitutional validity. However debatable one finds the conclusion of Marbury v. Madison, supra note 6, the holding of Martin v. Hunter's Lessee was quite plainly compelled by the structure of the federal system. See, e.g., Holmes, Collected Legal Papers 295 (1920): "I do not think the United States would come to an end if [the Court] lost [its] power to declare an act of Congress void. I do think that the Union would be imperiled if we could not make that declaration as to the laws of the several states." See also C. Black, Structure and Relationship in Constitutional Law 74 (1969): "On the whole, there is nothing in our entire governmental structure which has a more leak-proof claim to legitimacy than the function of the courts in reviewing state acts for federal unconstitutionality." It is striking that, over the past century and a

half, the great majority of politically controversial Supreme Court decisions have involved the largely incontrovertible power recognized by Martin v. Hunter's Lessee, rather than the more debatable power assumed in Marbury v. Madison, the power to review the validity of actions by a coordinate federal branch. Id. at 67–77.

8. See M. Horkheimer, Eclipse of Reason (1947).

9. On the inescapability of such choice, see generally L. Tribe, Constitutional Choices (1985). Although a general theory of what such choice entails and how it is constrained is beyond the scope of this work, it should be stressed that neither that 1985 book, nor this treatise, accepts the perspective of those theorists who deem constitutional text in particular, or language in general, to be so radically indeterminate that any text is capable of meaning virtually anything one wants it to mean. See, e.g., Tushnet, "A Note on the Revival of Textualism in Constitutional Theory," 58 S.Cal.L.Rev. 683, 685 (1985). "The theorists who matter least are those who find language so indeterminate that any text can mean almost anything. These theorists seem to assume that a statute is not essentially different from a poem. They deny one of the fundamental premises of the polity, and consequently make themselves irrelevant." Laycock, "Constitutional Theory Matters," 65 Texas L.Rev. 767, 773–74 (1987) (footnotes omitted).

left by constitutional text and history, to more modest claims about the sociological and professional milieu in which judges operate, the numerous indirect checks constraining their independent authority, and the necessarily interstitial role occupied by institutions lacking either the affirmative power to command the truly unwilling, or the agenda-setting authority to act outside the context of actual controversies brought to them by others.[10] But as a growing tradition of reverence for judicial supremacy has reduced the significance of the Court's lack of armies and appropriations, and as broader and more managerial notions of the judicial role in shaping and controlling controversies have partly displaced narrower and more passive concepts,[11] problems of judicial legitimacy have become increasingly acute.[12]

Louis Hartz has suggested that the task of defending judicial review becomes more difficult as fundamental beliefs and values cease to be widely shared: "When half of a nation believes in Locke and half in Filmer or Marx, the result is not law but philosophy. *Inter arma leges silent*. . . . America's famous legalism is thus the reverse side of its philosophic poverty in politics. . . .."[13] Paul Freund replies that the real meaning of judicial review is to be found "in the introduction of mediating principles between the large constitutional or philosophical concepts to which some or all of a community pay tribute and the common problems of reconciliation which beset the modern state."[14] Both Hartz and Freund appear to take for granted that an institution like judicial review, or a process like legal argument, must founder in the face of the most ultimate challenges of principle and purpose—that such challenges must in the end be met with silence or civil war. To dispute their shared starting point in detail would require another sort of book entirely; this one, by setting forth doctrinal frameworks for future discussion, can at most hope to clear the ground for the work that still remains. In broad outline, however, the difficulty with such conventional wisdom about the political limits of constitutional law is that it undervalues the place of vigorously contested constitutional discourse and decision in political dialogue. By debating our deepest differences in the shared language of constitutional rights and responsibilities and in the terms of an enacted constitutional *text*, we create the possibility of persuasion and even moral

---

10. See generally Deutsch, "Neutrality, Legitimacy, and the Supreme Court. Some Intersections Between Law and Political Science," 20 Stan.L.Rev. 169 (1968); Grey, "The Constitution as Scripture," 37 Stan.L. Rev. 1 (1984).

11. See Chayes, "The Role of the Judge in Public Law Litigation," 89 Harv.L.Rev. 1281 (1976).

12. Despite pleas to move beyond the legitimacy debate—see, e.g., Parker, "The Past of Constitutional Theory—And Its Future," 42 Ohio St.L.J. 223 (1981)—the volume of contemporary comment on the subject shows no sign of abating. See, e.g.,

Bryden, "Politics, the Constitution, and the New Formalism," 3 Const.Comm. 415 (1986); Simon, "The Authority of the Constitution and Its Meaning: A Preface to a Theory of Constitutional Interpretation," 58 S.Cal.L.Rev. 603 (1985); Sedler, "The Legitimacy Debate in Constitutional Adjudication: An Assessment and a Different Perspective," 44 Ohio St.L.J. 93 (1983).

13. Hartz, "The Whig Tradition in America and Europe," 46 Am.Pol.Sci.Rev. 989, 997 n.10 (1952).

14. Freund, "Umpiring the Federal System," 54 Colum.L.Rev. 561 (1954).

education in our national life [15]—looking not toward any one, permanent reconciliation of conflicting impulses but toward a judicially modulated unending struggle.[16]

Although the non-judicial branches, too, are sworn to uphold the Constitution, the independent judiciary has a unique capacity and commitment to engage in constitutional discourse—to explain and justify its conclusions about governmental authority in a dialogue with those who read the same Constitution even if they reach a different view. This is a commitment that only a dialogue-engaging institution, insulated from day-to-day political accountability but correspondingly burdened with oversight by professional peers and vigilant lay critics, can be expected to maintain. The enemies of this commitment are those, whether on the constitutional right or on the constitutional left, whose principal mode of argument consists in self-righteous appeals to ideas beyond argument, whether expressed as principles of fairness to minorities or as calls of fidelity to aspiration or as certitudes about original intent, whether derived from modern sensibility or from ancient tradition. The price we pay for allowing judges to discharge this commitment is that, for various periods of time, an enlightened consensus may be blocked by blind judicial adherence to constitutional views we will later come to regret. But the price of the alternative course is that, for other periods, the enlightened consensus that judges might help to catalyze in the name of the Constitution may be blocked by more self-interested or short-sighted majorities.

§ 1–9. The Limited Relevance of Institutional Questions

If this argument yields but two and one half cheers for a mild form of judicial supremacy, the reader will detect little inclination here to push the theme further. For it seems in truth a close question, in the long pull of time, whether the Constitution's implicit vision of a just society, or indeed any decent vision of justice couched in terms of our Constitution's partly indeterminate categories and phrases, would be more or less advanced by a greater or lesser role for the federal judiciary. This book will proceed on the premise of a relatively large judicial role more because it has become an historical given than because any ineluctable logic would have made an alternative course of history unthinkable or patently unwise. Not even the "judicial passivists" would seriously oppose federal judicial rescue from a state law or city ordinance authorizing the burning of unpopular books, or from a congressional or presidential reinstatement of racial apartheid, and a

---

15. See A. Cox, The Role of the Supreme Court in American Government 117 (1976).

16. See Seidman, "Public Principle and Private Choice: The Uneasy Case for a Boundary Maintenance Theory of Constitutional Law," 96 Yale L.J. 1006, 1007 (1987): "Instead of offering reconciliation, constitutional law allows us to live with contradiction by establishing a shifting, uncertain, and contested boundary between distinct public and private spheres within which conflicting values can be separately nurtured." See id. at 1042–59, for a provocative sketch of this picture of constitutional debate and adjudication, and a thoughtful if tentative account of why judges in particular are needed to make such a picture function.

serious exposition of constitutional doctrine might as well take such starting points for granted.[1]

But there is a deeper reason than habit, or the desire to get on with things, for not pausing overly long to discuss issues of judicial capacity and legitimacy. The United States Constitution addresses its commands not only to federal judges but to all public authorities in the United States.[2] It is at least ironic that generations of students and lawyers preoccupied with lamenting judicial excess have paid so much less attention to the substantive meaning of the Constitution as a guide to choice by nonjudicial actors.[3] Grant for the moment that judges should not employ the due process clause to strike down a state intrusion upon a woman's decision whether or not to bear a child. That is not my conclusion,[4] but grant it: What follows? Must not a state legislator, voting on a proposed regulation of contraception or abortion, ask whether the regulation would deprive women of liberty without due process of law in violation of the legislator's oath under article VI?[5] Surely that question is not reducible to a measure of constituents' preferences. Equally surely, it is not answerable by any geometry of indisputable reference to an agreed text. That the question is to be taken seriously *whether or not judges threaten to offer binding answers of their own*, and that its depth is underscored rather than refuted by the nonexistence of incontestable replies,[6] seems to me axiomatic. Throughout this book, therefore, I will attempt to address the *substance* of constitutional issues without always reducing them to their institutional components. That the best answer to a question

§ 1–9

1. This is not to deny that the half-decade or so preceding the Constitution's Bicentennial gave rise to a highly vocal theory holding, roughly, that "the Bill of Rights and similar provisions restricting the powers of government are unimportant." Laycock, "Constitutional Theory Matters," 65 Texas L.Rev. 767 (1987) (describing, and roundly rejecting, this theory). Such provisions, according to that theory, "were aimed only at the most egregious offenses of George III and the Confederate States. Perhaps they were a meaningless sop to the opposition, or an extra safeguard against a monarchist coup. But they do not forbid anything a democratic government might plausibly do." Id. Professor Douglas Laycock collects the proponents of this quite extreme perspective in id. at 767–69 & nn. 2–13. An interested reader might wish to consult such samples as Easterbrook, "Substance and Due Process," 1982 Sup.Ct.Rev. 85, 94–95 (1982); Graglia, "The Constitution, Community, and Liberty," 8 Harv.J.L. & Pub. Pol'y 291, 294 (1985); Graglia, "Was the Constitution a Good Idea?," Nat'l Rev., July 13, 1984, at 34; Meese, "The Supreme Court of the United States: Bulwark of a Limited Constitution," 27 S.Tex.L.J. 455, 463–64 (1986); Meese, "Construing the Constitution," 19

U.C. Davis L.Rev. 22 (1985). See also R. Bork, Tradition and Morality in Constitutional Law (1984). Such views have been propounded with enough vigor to induce responses even from several sitting Supreme Court Justices—see, e.g., Brennan, "The Constitution of the United States: Contemporary Ratification," 27 S.Tex.L.J. 433 (1986); Stevens, "The Supreme Court of the United States: Reflections After a Summer Recess," 27 S.Tex.L.J. 447 (1986).

2. See e.g., art. VI: "The Senators and Representatives before mentioned, and the Members of the several State Legislatures, and all executive and judicial Officers, both of the United States and of the several States, shall be bound by Oath or Affirmation, to support this Constitution. . . ."

3. For a notable exception, see Linde, "Judges, Critics, and the Realist Tradition," 82 Yale L.J. 227 (1972). See also Brest, "The Conscientious Legislator's Guide to Constitutional Interpretation," 27 Stan.L.Rev. 586 (1975).

4. See Chapter 15, infra.

5. See L. Tribe, Constitutional Choices 19–20 (1985).

6. See R. Nozick, Philosophical Explanations 1–24 (1981).

undeniably depends in significant part upon who is being asked to address it, and that institutional concerns are thus inescapably relevant to substantive ones, cannot be allowed to obscure indefinitely the great truth that it is, after all, a *constitution*, and not merely its judicial management, that we are expounding.[7]

7. Cf. McCulloch v. Maryland, 17 U.S. (4 Wheat.) 316 (1819).

Chapter 2

MODEL I—THE MODEL
OF SEPARATED AND
DIVIDED POWERS

§ 2–1. Constitutional Law's Interplay of Structure and Substance

An incisive cartoon depicts a tall ship, perhaps the Mayflower, with two pilgrims leaning pensively over its side. As they scan the horizon, one says to the other: "Religious freedom is my immediate goal, but my long-range plan is to go into real estate." The remark nicely portrays a basic duality in constitutional history. For that history has embraced two dramatically different strands: the first, concerned with intensely human and humane aspirations of personality, conscience, and freedom; the second, concerned with vastly more mundane and mechanical matters like geography, territorial boundaries, and institutional arrangements. It was in what I will call Model I, the model of separated and divided powers, that those two strands were first intertwined in a single, grand fabric of law and politics. The Madisonian clockwork would enable the forces and counterforces of government to mesh as needed to execute the purposes of the nation in the community of nations, and to check one another as needed to shield the individual and community from governmental oppression and discrimination. The concerns that inspired the system's design were human; the design itself, mechanical. Structure would thus serve substance, in a framework ultimately supervised by a disinterested judiciary.

§ 2–2. The Persistence of Model I: Independence and Interdependence

Although its primacy and its perfection have both been questioned as the nation has encountered the inevitable crises and changes of a maturing society, Model I has always remained important in constitutional thought and argument. It has taught students, practitioners, courts, commentators, and legislators to focus on the degree to which various governmental arrangements comport with, or threaten to undermine, either the *independence* and *integrity* of one of the branches or levels of government, or the ability of each to fulfill its mission in checking the others so as to preserve the *interdependence* without which independence can become domination.[1]

Although the late nineteenth century Supreme Court expressed a wooden notion that each branch must "be limited to the exercise of the

---

§ 2–2

1. On the evolution of separation-of-powers concepts, see Friedrich, "Separation of Powers," 13 Encyc.Soc.Sci. 663–66 (1934). On the evolution of federalism ideas, see Elazar, "Federalism," 5 Int'l.En-cyc.Soc.Sci. 353, 361–65 (1968); Roche, "Distribution of Powers," 3 id. at 300. For a less reverent view, see C. McIlwain, Constitutionalism: Ancient and Modern 142–43 (1947 ed.)

powers appropriate to its own department and no other," [2] that view has since been properly understood as indefensibly extreme. After all, the Constitution on its face contemplates that the Executive will perform a "legislative" function when exercising the power to veto legislation; [3] that the House will indict and the Senate adjudicate in cases of impeachment; [4] and that the Supreme Court will "make" such law as it must in expounding or modifying the corpus of federal legal principle pursuant to its exercise of the judicial power under article III. More recent expressions accordingly stress that the "separation of powers . . . did not make each branch . . . autonomous . . . [but] left each . . . dependent upon the others, as it left to each . . . [the exercise of] functions in their nature executive, legislative and judicial." [5] The upshot is to require, in most instances, that at least two full branches of the federal government cooperate before governmental choices potentially hostile to individual rights or needs can be effected. Passage of a federal law, for example, requires the concurrence of both Houses of Congress and the agreement of the Executive unless Congress can muster a special bicameral majority to override an executive veto; [6] enforcement of the law in turn requires cooperation of the Judiciary and the Executive but no further action by Congress. [7]

It is particularly worth noting the dual character of a typical Model I argument: such an argument focuses both on those aspects of a scheme that threaten to *swell* governmental power in politically unaccountable ways, and on those facets that threaten to *reduce* the necessary range of authority or flexibility within any particular center of governmental power. This duality is somewhat less characteristic of arguments about the federal-state division of power than of arguments about the legislative-executive-judicial separation of powers. In arguments about federalism, it has been less common to consider the degree to which complicity between and among levels of government may yield damaging choices for which no one is adequately answerable, than to address the degree to which action at one level may render another incapable of fulfilling its mission in the constitutional design. Yet the danger that federal-state cooperation may threaten individual rights in insufficiently accountable ways should not be overlooked, [8] and not even

2. Kilbourn v. Thompson, 103 U.S. 168, 191 (1881). See also Kendall v. United States ex rel. Stokes, 37 U.S. (12 Pet.) 524 (1838).

3. Art. I, § 7.

4. Art. I, §§ 2–3.

5. Myers v. United States, 272 U.S. 52, 291 (1926) (Brandeis, J., dissenting). Accord, United States v. Nixon, 418 U.S. 683, 703–05 (1974).

6. Art. I, § 7. See INS v. Chadha, 462 U.S. 919 (1983), in § 4–3, infra.

7. Indeed, attempts by Congress to control enforcement by appointing the enforcing officer violate art. II, § 2. Buckley v. Valeo, 424 U.S. 1 (1976).

8. In Shapiro v. Thompson, 394 U.S. 618 (1969), for example, state actions (one-year waiting periods for welfare to new arrivals) invalidated as unduly burdening the right to interstate travel had been defended by the states in part on the ground that Congress had authorized and even encouraged the imposition of such burdens, id. at 638; although the Court indicated that such authorization would not validate an otherwise impermissible state violation of a personal right, id. at 641, its doubt that Congress in fact meant to authorize the burdens in question, id. at 639–41, suggests an independent basis for finding the resulting deprivations objectionable: the locus of responsibility for those deprivations was unduly attenuated.

doctrinal developments reinforcing state autonomy [9] are likely to alter the central realities that the federal and state governments will have to depend upon one another in virtually every significant area of endeavor, and that such mutual dependence must continue to provide the primary assurance that neither level of government will achieve a threatening hegemony over all of our public life. Thus, along both dimensions, that of federalism as well as that of separation of powers, it is *institutional interdependence* rather than *functional independence* that best summarizes the American idea of protecting liberty by fragmenting power.[10]

§ 2–3. The Link Between Separation-of-Powers Considerations and Controversies Over Federal-State Division

Separation-of-powers considerations and issues of federal-state division ordinarily arise in separate spheres of controversy. Thus, whether Congress may appoint officers to enforce its own statutes raises exclusively a separation issue; whether a state may pass judgment on a foreign government or its citizens in administering decedents' estates raises exclusively a federalism issue.[1]

9. See National League of Cities v. Usery, 426 U.S. 833 (1976), overruled in Garcia v. San Antonio Metropolitan Transit Auth., 469 U.S. 528 (1985), discussed in § 5–22, infra. For praise of federalism generally, see Acton, History of Freedom 98 (1907); 1 Bryce, The American Commonwealth 318–19 (2d rev.ed. 1891); 1 Tocqueville, Democracy in America 158–59 (Bradley ed. 1945). In 1962, Nelson Rockefeller found "highly exaggerated" the "reports of the death of federalism, so authoritatively asserted in the nineteen-thirties. . . ." The Future of Federalism 29 (1962). In his 1969 Cooley Lectures, Philip Kurland insisted that Rockefeller had erred, claiming flatly: "Federalism is dead." Politics, the Constitution, and the Warren Court 96 (1970); see id. at 54–57. Kurland was wrong.

10. See Damaška, "Structures of Authority and Comparative Criminal Procedure," 84 Yale L.J. 480, 533 (1975). See generally Maass, "Division of Powers: An Areal Analysis," in Area and Power 9–14 (Maass ed. 1959).

The limits of such interdependence became crucial in the quite unusual recent case of Young v. United States ex rel. Vuitton et Fils S.A., 107 S.Ct. 2124 (1987). In that case, while every Justice except Justice White agreed that counsel for a party that is the beneficiary of a court order may not be appointed to undertake a contempt prosecution for alleged violation of that order (see § 10–16, infra, at note 17), the Court, with only Justice Scalia dissenting on the point, concluded that an article III court must "possess inherent authority to initiate contempt proceedings for disobedi-

ence to [its] orders, authority which necessarily encompasses the ability to appoint a private attorney to prosecute the contempt," id. at 2130, because "[c]ourts cannot be at the mercy of another branch in deciding whether such proceedings should be initiated." Id. at 2131. Although the Court saw in this limited argument "no principle that can be wielded to eradicate fundamental separation-of-powers boundaries," id. at 2134 n.10, Justice Scalia saw the matter otherwise, stressing his view that *every* branch of the Federal Government not only *can* but *must* be at the mercy of the other branches to effectuate its purposes: "Such dispersion of power was central to the scheme of forming a government with enough power to serve the expansive purposes set forth in the preamble of the Constitution, yet one that would 'secure the blessings of liberty' rather than use its power tyrannically. Congress, for example, is dependent on the Executive and the courts for enforcement of the laws it enacts. Even complete failure by the Executive to prosecute law violators, or by the courts to convict them, has never been thought to authorize congressional prosecution and trial." Id. at 2143. It is noteworthy that no other Member of the Court subscribed to Justice Scalia's analysis as applied to the issue of inherent judicial authority to appoint contempt prosecutors—authority that only Justice Scalia denied.

§ 2–3

1. See Zschernig v. Miller, 389 U.S. 429 (1968), answering the question in the negative.

But it will be important to remember in the chapters that follow that many disputes implicate more complex combinations of separation and federalism concerns. Thus, the limits on federal judicial intrusion into state and local governments reflect both notions about the role of federal courts vis-a-vis the other branches of the national government, and notions about the role of the national government in matters of intensely state and local concern. And it is largely principles of federalism, for example, that prevent federal courts or agents from imposing federal separation-of-powers notions on states choosing to structure themselves along different lines.[2]

Ordinarily, as will appear in the eleventh amendment immunity of states from federal citizen suits (discussed in Chapter 3), Congress is trusted to strike the federal-state balance, and the emerging doctrine appears primarily as a limit on federal judicial action. In the law of federal immunity from state taxation (discussed in Chapter 6), the balance is again entrusted to Congress, and the doctrine operates primarily to limit the federal executive. In one notable modern instance, however, *National League of Cities v. Usery*,[3] the federalism balance was for a time taken from the unilateral control of Congress, and federal judicial doctrine briefly emerged as a nominally state-protecting limit on the national government as a whole.

§ 2–4. Plan of the Model I Chapters

Given the complexities referred to in § 2–3, it is not possible cleanly to separate federalism issues from separation-of-powers issues in the four succeeding chapters that explicate Model I. However, the bulk of Chapter 3 on Federal Judicial Power and Chapter 4 on Federal Executive Power will be concerned with the separation of powers, while the bulk of Chapter 5 on Federal Legislative Power and Chapter 6 on Federalism-Based Limits on State and Local Power will be concerned with federal-state division.

Throughout these chapters, it will be vital not to forget that all of these "checks and counterpoises, which Newton might readily have recognized as suggestive of the mechanism of the heavens,"[1] can represent only the scaffolding of a far more subtle "vehicle of life."[2] The great difficulty of any theory less rich, Woodrow Wilson once warned, "is that government is not a machine, but a living thing. It falls, not under the theory of the universe, but under the theory of organic life. It is accountable to Darwin, not to Newton. It is . . . shaped to its functions by the sheer pressure of life. No living thing can have its organs offset against each other as checks, and live."[3] Yet

---

2. See Mayor of Philadelphia v. Educational Equality League, 415 U.S. 605, 615 (1974) (dictum); Sweezy v. New Hampshire, 354 U.S. 234, 256 (1957) (Frankfurter, J., concurring).

3. 426 U.S. 833 (1976). See § 5–22, infra.

§ 2–4

1. W. Wilson, Constitutional Government in the United States 56 (1908).

2. Id. at 192: "The Constitution cannot be regarded as a mere legal document, to be read as a will or a contract would be. It must, of the necessity of the case, be a vehicle of life."

3. Id. at 56. See generally M. Kammen, A Machine That Would Go of Itself: The Constitution in American Culture (1986).

because no complex society can have its centers of power *not* "offset against each other as checks," and resist tyranny, the model of separated and divided powers offers continuing testimony to the undying dilemmas of progress and justice.[4]

4. See Youngstown Sheet & Tube Co. v. Sawyer, 343 U.S. 579, 593–94 (1952) (Frankfurter, J., concurring in the Court's invalidation of President Truman's steel seizure): "Not so long ago it was fashionable to find our system of checks and balances obstructive to effective government. It was easy to ridicule that system as outmoded—too easy. The experience through which the world has passed in our own day has made vivid the realization that the Framers of our Constitution were not inexperienced doctrinaires. These long-headed statesmen had no illusion that our people enjoyed biological or psychological or sociological immunities from the hazards of concentrated power. It is absurd to see a dictator in a representative product of the sturdy democratic traditions of the Mississippi Valley. The accretion of dangerous power does not come in a day. It does come, however slowly, from the generative force of unchecked disregard of the restrictions that fence in even the most disinterested assertion of authority."

Chapter 3

FEDERAL JUDICIAL POWER

§ 3–1. Structuring the Inquiry into Federal Judicial Power

An account of the constitutional characteristics of federal judicial power involves three distinct inquiries, which this chapter will take up in turn. First, such an account must address the most remarkable aspect of the power of federal courts, their power to interpret and enforce the Constitution as law.[1] Second, an account of federal judicial power must describe the chief limitation which article III itself imposes upon the federal judiciary: the requirement that federal courts exercise their power only to resolve "cases" or "controversies." The Supreme Court has developed an elaborate body of justiciability doctrine in an effort to give meaning to the case-or-controversy requirement. The doctrine incorporates both constitutional and nonconstitutional elements; a chief task of constitutional analysis is to provide some explanation for this uniquely amalgamated state of the law.[2] Finally, an account of federal judicial power must describe the constraints which the existence of the states as distinct institutions places upon the power of federal courts. A number of these federalism constraints, associated with the eleventh amendment and related considerations of state sovereignty, are longstanding; others, limiting the availability of federal equitable remedies, are of relatively recent origin.[3]

§ 3–2. Overview—Marbury v. Madison: Judicial Review as Axiom

In *Marbury v. Madison*,[1] the Supreme Court held that Congress acted unconstitutionally in conferring upon the Court authority to issue original writs of mandamus in cases not "affecting Ambassadors, other public Ministers and Consuls [or] those in which a State [is] Party": article III, in defining the extent of the Supreme Court's original jurisdiction,[2] did not include among its grants of power the authority to issue such writs. *Marbury* is the first case in which the Supreme Court asserted that a federal court has power to refuse to give effect to congressional legislation if it is inconsistent with the Court's interpretation of the Constitution.[3] The Constitution does not expressly confer

§ 3–1

1. See §§ 3–2 to 3–6, infra.

2. See §§ 3–7 to 3–21, infra.

3. See §§ 3–22 to 3–30, infra.

§ 3–2

1. 5 U.S. (1 Cranch) 137 (1803).

2. The Supreme Court's original jurisdiction is discussed in § 3–5, infra.

3. Earlier, in the opinions reported in connection with Hayburn's Case, 2 U.S. (2 Dall.) 409 (1792), the Justices of the Su-

preme Court, in their capacity as Circuit Justices, had agreed, albeit in separate decisions, that Congress could not require federal courts to provide the executive branch with advisory opinions as to the validity of pension claims. In Hylton v. United States, 3 U.S. (3 Dall.) 171 (1796), the Supreme Court considered whether, in taxing carriages, Congress had unconstitutionally enacted an unapportioned direct tax. See U.S. Const., art. I, § 9. The Court concluded that the tax was not a direct tax, and thus did not have to decide

such a power upon the federal courts.[4] In *Marbury*, however, Chief Justice Marshall, although acknowledging that "[t]he question, whether an act, repugnant to the constitution, can become the law of the land, is a question deeply interesting to the United States," nonetheless concluded that the issue is "not of an intricacy proportioned to its interest." [5]

Marshall rested his defense of federal judicial review of the constitutionality of acts of Congress chiefly upon the following propositions. (1) "[A]ll those who have framed written constitutions contemplate them as forming the fundamental and paramount law of the nation, and consequently the theory of every such government must be, that an act of the legislature, repugnant to the constitution, is void." [6] (2) "It is, emphatically, the province and duty of the judicial department, to say what the law is. Those who apply the rule to particular cases, must of necessity expound and interpret that rule. If two laws conflict with each other, the courts must decide on the operation of each. . . . If then, the courts are to regard the constitution, and the constitution is superior to any ordinary act of the legislature, the constitution, and not such ordinary act, must govern the case to which they both apply." [7] (3) "Those, then, who controvert the principle, that the constitution is to be considered, in court, as a paramount law, are reduced to the necessity of maintaining that courts must close their eyes on the constitution, and see only the law. This doctrine . . . would declare, that if the legislature shall do what is expressly forbidden, such act,

whether it could declare an act of Congress unconstitutional. See also Calder v. Bull, 3 U.S. (3 Dall.) 386 (1798) (challenge to state law as unconstitutional ex post facto law). For discussion of these early cases, see J. Goebel, History of the Supreme Court of the United States: Antecedents and Beginnings to 1801, 554–68, 580–84 (1971).

4. Herbert Wechsler attempted to ground the power of federal courts to engage in judicial review in the supremacy clause. See Wechsler, "Toward Neutral Principles of Constitutional Law," 73 Harv. L.Rev. 1, 3–5 (1959). The supremacy clause provides, in pertinent part, that "[t]his Constitution . . . shall be the supreme Law of the Land; and the Judges in every State shall be bound thereby, any Thing in the Constitution or Laws of any State to the Contrary notwithstanding." U.S. Const. art. VI, § 2. Wechsler argued: (1) that the supremacy clause requires state courts to interpret and apply the Constitution; (2) that article III authorizes the Supreme Court to review state court judgments as to federal constitutionality; (3) that Congress need not create lower federal courts; (4) that state courts would in such an event hear challenges to the constitutionality of federal statutes and the Supreme Court would then review the state court judgments; and (5) that it is absurd to suppose, if state courts can re-

view the constitutionality of federal statutes, and the Supreme Court review such state court judgments, that federal courts, should they come into existence, cannot similarly engage in judicial review, and the Supreme Court scrutinize their judgments. As Alexander Bickel noted, however, nothing in the supremacy clause in fact authorizes state courts to strike down federal statutes which they regard as unconstitutional; the supremacy clause is perfectly consistent with a view that treats congressional enactment as conclusive of constitutionality. See A. Bickel, The Least Dangerous Branch 11–12 (1962). State court review of the federal constitutionality of state law, and Supreme Court review of such state court action, see § 3–4, infra, does not imply judicial power to declare acts of Congress unconstitutional. The two powers are arguably quite distinct in consequence. Justice Holmes observed that "I do not think the United States would come to an end if we lost our power to declare an Act of Congress void. I do think the Union would be imperiled if we could not make that declaration as to the laws of the several States." O. Holmes, "Law and the Court," in Collected Legal Papers 295–96 (1920).

5. 5 U.S. at 176.

6. Id. at 177.

7. Id. at 177–78.

notwithstanding the express prohibition, is in reality effectual. It would be giving to the legislature a practical and real omnipotence, with the same breath which professes to restrict their powers within narrow limits." [8]

As critics have repeatedly noted,[9] Marshall's justification for his assertion of federal judicial power to interpret and apply the Constitution is not conclusive. The premise of a written Constitution would not be disserved, and legislative power would not necessarily be unbounded, if Congress itself judged the constitutionality of its enactments. Under such a system, courts would not ignore the Constitution; rather, they would simply treat the legislative interpretation as definitive, and thus leave to Congress the task of resolving apparent conflicts between statute and Constitution.[10] It is not clear, however, what significance should be attached to the fact that neither Marshall nor anyone else has successfully established that independent judicial review, but no alternative, is consistent with constitutional text and structure. No one has formulated a stronger textual argument for the proposition that congressional interpretation is final, or for any other alternative. On this fundamental issue, therefore, the Constitution is indeterminate. Marshall resolved the indeterminancy, in essence, by *postulating* that federal courts have the power independently to interpret and apply the Constitution; it is no argument against Marshall's postulate to point out (correctly) that it is not a corollary.

Of course, if *Marbury v. Madison* does not state a corollary but rather asserts a postulate, the question arises why Marshall chose to make the particular assumption that he did. That question can be answered at any number of levels. No doubt Marshall had a personal interest in increasing his own power. No doubt also, Marshall's politics were relevant: judicial review provided Federalist judges like Marshall with a means of checking whatever excesses might result from Jefferson's triumph in the "Revolution of 1800." Perhaps more significantly, Marshall decided *Marbury* at a time when the idea that legislatures would ignore principle in order to please controlling "factions" was widely shared but the idea that courts were similarly political was not yet current (although it would be within a few decades).[11] In the

---

8. Id. at 178.

9. E.g., L. Hand, The Bill of Rights 1–11 (1958); A. Bickel, supra note 4, at 1–14; Van Alstyne, "A Critical Guide to Marbury v. Madison," 1969 Duke L.J. 1.; J. Ely, Democracy and Distrust 186 n. 11 (1980). For an overview of arguments regarding the propriety of federal judicial invalidation of legislative enactments, see L. Levy, Judicial Review and the Supreme Court (1967).

10. In England, France, and most socialist states, courts ordinarily take this approach. See Cappalletti, "Fundamental Guarantees of the Parties in Civil Litigation: Comparative Constitutional, International, and Social Trends," 25 Stan.L.Rev. 651, 654–59 (1973). See also E. McWhin-

ney, Supreme Courts and Judicial Law-Making: Constitutional Tribunals and Constitutional Review xi–xvi, 18–20 (1986). Sharp contrast to the American system is provided by section 59(2) of the 1961 Constitution of South Africa, which expressly provides that, with very few exceptions, "[n]o court of law shall be competent to enquire into or to pronounce upon the validity of any Act passed upon by Parliament"; observers point to this exclusion of judicial review as a key feature of the legislature's ability "to ride roughshod over individual liberty." J. Dugard, Human Rights and the South African Legal Order 35 (1978).

11. See § 1–8, supra.

context of the time, therefore, *Marbury* represented no novel seizure of power; indeed, the records of the Constitutional Convention itself suggest to at least some scholars that the Framers did not explicitly grant federal courts the power of judicial review because they took that power for granted.[12]

Despite the fact that *Marbury*'s historical significance is the result of Marshall's assertion of the power of judicial review, in a sense it may be anachronistic to see the establishment of judicial review as the chief object of Marshall's opinion. Robert McCloskey has said that *Marbury*'s holding that Congress could not constitutionally expand the Supreme Court's jurisdiction put the Court "in the delightful position . . . of rejecting and assuming power in a single breath." [13] Marshall and his fellow Justices, however, probably would not have described their situation as "delightful." Congress had canceled the Supreme Court's 1802 Term as part of its effort to undo President Adams' packing of the federal bench; moreover, there was much sentiment in Congress favoring impeachment of Marshall and his fellow Federalist Justices, for purely political reasons.[14] By declaring the jurisdictional statute unconstitutional, Marshall was able to avoid a direct confrontation with Jefferson, although Marshall structured the *Marbury* opinion in a way which allowed for an extended dictum proclaiming the illegality of Madison's conduct and asserting the power of the judiciary to remedy lawless executive action.[15] Paradoxically, therefore, *Marbury v. Madison* not only reflects its own era's sense that adjudication was somehow free from politics but also helps to account for why the next generation would find that view to be naive.

§ 3–3. Judicial Review and Debate Over the Normative Breadth and Retroactive Reach of a Judgment of Unconstitutionality: Defining *Marbury*'s Assumption

If, as a matter of constitutional law, the power of federal courts independently to interpret and apply the Constitution is an assumption and not a deduction, attention must be paid not only to the historical plausibility of that assumption but also to its internal structure. The concept of judicial review, as Marshall articulated it in *Marbury v. Madison*, is by no means a simple one. Marshall first had to postulate

12. See, e.g., R. Berger, Congress v. The Supreme Court (1969).

13. R. McCloskey, The American Supreme Court 42 (1960).

14. See G. Gunther, Constitutional Law 11–12 (11th ed. 1985).

15. See generally Chapter 4, infra. Marshall's inclination to lecture Jefferson may have stemmed in part from his own political involvement in the controversy. The dispute in Marbury arose from efforts of the outgoing Federalists to pack the federal bench with loyalist judges in the period between President Jefferson's election and his inauguration, during which President Adams made a series of appoint-

ments—those of the so-called "Midnight Judges" being the best known. William Marbury was confirmed on the last day of the Adams administration as one of 42 new justices of the peace for the District of Columbia. Marshall, then serving as both the outgoing Secretary of State *and* the new Chief Justice, signed and sealed the commissions, but Marshall's brother did not have time to deliver Marbury's commission before Jefferson took office. Jefferson's Secretary of State, James Madison, refused to deliver the commission, leading Marbury to bring his suit for mandamus in the Supreme Court. See also G. Gunther, supra note 14, at 10–12.

that the Constitution was "the fundamental and paramount law of the nation," and not merely the statement of an ideal political structure to which American government should aspire, or an initial distribution of rights and responsibilities which defined the starting point for bargaining among political institutions and individuals. Unless Marshall postulated that the Constitution was in some sense regulatory, he could not assume "that an act of the legislature, repugnant to the constitution, is void." Second, Marshall had to assume that the Constitution is the sort of law which courts can recognize and apply. Unless courts can determine whether Constitution and statute "conflict with each other," unless courts can identify "the rule" to "apply . . . to particular cases," they cannot, regardless of their "province and duty," "say what the law is."

The twin assumptions that the Constitution is law and that the Constitution is law which courts can expound are quite easily and mistakenly collapsed into one. It is possible, for example, to equate the process of constitutional adjudication with the task of identifying the content of the Constitution, without any regard for the constraints which the institutional characteristics of courts put on the adjudicatory process. Alternatively, it is possible to identify the content of the Constitution with the results of the process of constitutional adjudication, ignoring any possibility that constitutional norms may be capable of statement in vocabularies other than that available to courts. A proper analysis of judicial review, therefore, must be careful to distinguish the dancer from the dance; put otherwise, the task is to avoid the extremes of both natural law and positivist analysis.[1]

The practical implications of this distinction between the Constitution and judicial enforcement of its commands can be illuminated by considering a traditional issue associated with the exercise of judicial review: the effect of a judgment of unconstitutionality. Historically, the approach of the courts to this question has reflected the interaction of two points of view. One position, perhaps the dominant view in the era between the Civil War and the Great Depression,[2] holds, in Cooley's words, that "the term unconstitutional law, as employed in American jurisprudence, is a misnomer, and implies a contradiction; that enactment which is opposed to the constitution being in fact no law at all."[3] Or, as Justice Field declared in *Norton v. Shelby County*: "An unconstitutional act is not a law; it confers no rights; it imposes no duties; it affords no protection; it creates no office; it is, in legal contemplation, as inoperative as though it had never been passed."[4] The opposite position refuses to grant such import to a judicial pronouncement of unconstitutionality in a given case, and asserts that "[t]he parties to

---

§ 3–3

1. See §§ 3–4, 3–7 infra. For an analysis of this tension, as well as an argument that the federal judiciary should concern itself forthrightly with the exposition of fundamental values rather than pretend simply to resolve discrete disputes, see Spann, "Expository Justice," 131 U.Pa.L. Rev. 585 (1983). Spann's emphasis would require a substantial rethinking of current justiciability doctrine, discussed in §§ 3–7 to 3–21, infra. See id. at 617–60.

2. See O. Field, The Effect of an Unconstitutional Statute 2 (1935).

3. T. Cooley, Constitutional Limitations 4 (5th ed. 1883).

4. 118 U.S. 425, 442 (1886).

that suit are concluded by the judgment, but no one else is bound." [5] Adherents of this view argue that in future cases involving the allegedly unconstitutional act, "[p]rima facie, and upon the face of the act itself, nothing will generally appear to show that the act is not valid; and it is only when some person attempts to resist its operation, and calls on the aid of the judicial power, to pronounce it void, as to him, his property, or his rights, that the objection of unconstitutionality can be presented and sustained." [6] Thus, "the courts have no real power to repeal or abolish a statute, and . . . notwithstanding a decision holding it unconstitutional a statute continues to remain on the statute books." [7]

Plainly, these two perspectives correlate closely with the twin assumptions underlying judicial review. The first approach emphasizes what is supposed to be a corollary of the fact of unconstitutionality itself: the Constitution operates of its own force; it is only judicial recognition of this fact which might be delayed. The second approach focuses on the fact that a finding of unconstitutionality comes in the context of adjudication; the result of a judgment of unconstitutionality is not the invalidation of a statute, but the resolution of a particular dispute between particular parties. Equally plainly, therefore, an appropriate resolution of the question of the effect of a judgment of unconstitutionality would be one which acknowledges both that such a judgment involves the statement of a constitutional norm and that the norm is, in the end, stated in an adjudicatory context.

Such a resolution can be achieved in part by recognizing that the two perspectives blur into one another with the passage of time. In handing down an opinion, it is true that "[u]nder *Marbury* the Court decides a case; it does not pass a statute calling for obedience by all within the purview of the rule that is declared." [8] But although the decision immediately binds only the parties to the lawsuit, as word of it spreads—and assuming that it withstands attack to gain general acceptance [9]—it eventually establishes a norm of broad applicability that cannot be ignored by future litigants. [10] At that point in time, it may be

---

5. Shepherd v. Wheeling, 30 W.Va. 479, 4 S.E. 635, 637 (1887).

6. In re Wellington, 33 Mass. (6 Pick) 87, 96 (1834). See also A. Bickel, The Morality of Consent 111 (1975) ("The general practice is to leave the enforcement of judge-made constitutional law to private initiative, and to enforce it case by case, so that no penalties attach to failure to abide by it before completion of a successful enforcement litigation. This means quite literally that no one is under any legal obligation to carry out a rule of constitutional law announced by the Supreme Court until someone else has conducted a successful litigation and obtained a decree directing him to do so.").

7. 39 Ops.Atty.Gen. 22 (1937).

8. Wechsler, "The Court and the Constitution," 65 Colum.L.Rev. 1001, 1008 (1965).

9. There is always, of course, "the 'chance' that the decision 'may be overruled and never become a precedent for other cases.'" Id. (quoting Abraham Lincoln's first inaugural address, referring to the *Dred Scott* case). For example, in West Coast Hotel Co. v. Parrish, 300 U.S. 379 (1937), the Supreme Court dramatically reversed itself in upholding minimum wage legislation essentially indistinguishable from legislation struck down only the year before in Morehead v. New York ex rel. Tipaldo, 298 U.S. 587 (1936); see § 8–7, infra.

10. On a purely pragmatic level, the remedies available against parties who insist on flouting the clear principles laid down by the Court's decisions, barring definitive litigation against them, are substantial. Public officials are especially at risk; the availability of damage actions,

said that "acceptance is demanded, without insisting on repeated litigation . . . both as the necessary implication of our constitutional tradition and to avoid the greater evils that will otherwise ensue." [11]

Of course, such acceptance is demanded only to the extent that the constitutional norm comes to bear in future situations in which its applicability is sufficiently clear. The degree to which a constitutional norm announced in an individual case will bind those involved in future situations calling for a constitutional choice thus depends in large part on issues to be addressed in the remainder of this chapter: for example, the degree to which the internal structure of the norm admits of value judgments contrary to the thrust of the Court's opinion; [12] the degree to which the Supreme Court views differing interpretations by other courts and branches as a threat to its judicial supremacy; [13] whether future courts will have jurisdiction to reinforce the norm; [14] whether the norm is properly presented in a justiciable lawsuit; [15] and whether future courts will refrain, for equitable reasons, from imposing the norm on parties to other lawsuits.[16]

In recent years, the Supreme Court has considered the effect of judgments of unconstitutionality chiefly in the context of determining the retroactive reach of its criminal procedure decisions.[17] If an unconstitutional statute or practice effectively never existed as a lawful justification for state action, individuals convicted under the statute or

injunctive relief mandating wide-ranging reform, and other collateral measures serve to remedy the effects of past violations and to deter future ones. See Farber, "The Supreme Court and the Rule of Law: *Cooper v. Aaron* Revisited," 1982 U.Ill.L. Rev. 387, 405–08.

11. Wechsler, supra note 8. The United States Government in particular is not bound by the doctrine of nonmutual offensive collateral estoppel, see United States v. Mendoza, 464 U.S. 154 (1984). The Government may therefore selectively relitigate statutory or constitutional issues in a succession of cases involving different parties—e.g., when it is attempting to generate a circuit conflict or otherwise to create a suitable test case to take to the Supreme Court. But it does not follow that the United States could simply choose to flout the settled law of a particular circuit (or, *a fortiori*, the law as settled by the Supreme Court) in order to limit the benefit of a definitive ruling (obtained, presumably, outside the context of a sufficiently broad class action) to those litigants with the time, energy, and resources to litigate the issue through the courts in their own behalf. See, e.g., Lopez v. Heckler, 725 F.2d 1489, 1503 (9th Cir. 1984) (concluding that such wanton flouting of applicable law, in addition to unfairly exploiting the circumstances of litigants unprotected by prior rulings, is inconsistent with Marbury v. Madison), vacated and remanded with directions to enter decree crafted in light of

intervening congressional legislation, 469 U.S. 1082 (1984); Note, "Administrative Agency Intracircuit Nonacquiescence," 85 Colum.L.Rev. 582 (1985). Cf. note 26, infra. For a perceptive argument that a broad reading of Mendoza should give way to a flexible balancing test for determining the preclusive effect of judgments against the United States, see Note, "Collateral Estoppel and Nonacquiescence: Precluding Government Relitigation in the Pursuit of Litigant Equality," 99 Harv.L.Rev. 847 (1986).

12. See §§ 3–4, 3–24, infra.

13. See § 3–4, infra.

14. See §§ 3–5, 3–25 to 3–30, infra.

15. See §§ 3–7 to 3–21, infra.

16. See §§ 3–28 to 3–30, infra. See generally Shapiro, "Jurisdiction and Discretion," 60 N.Y.U.L.Rev. 543 (1985).

17. But the question of "the nonretroactive application of judicial decisions . . . is by no means limited to that area. The earliest instances of nonretroactivity in the decisions of [the] Court [arose outside the criminal context, and] . . . in the last few decades, [the Court] has recognized the doctrine of nonretroactivity outside the criminal area many times, in both constitutional and nonconstitutional cases." Chevron Oil Co. v. Huson, 404 U.S. 97, 105–06 (1971) (citations omitted). For an analysis of the factors relied on in gauging nonretroactivity in the civil context, see id. at 106–07.

in trials which tolerated the practice were convicted unlawfully even if their trials took place before the declaration of unconstitutionality; such a declaration should have a fully retroactive effect, and previously convicted individuals should be able to win their freedom through the writ of habeas corpus. Alternatively, if a judgment of unconstitutionality affects only the case at hand, the legality of the convictions of individuals previously tried is not affected.

In *Linkletter v. Walker*, the Court rejected both extremes: "the Constitution neither prohibits nor requires retrospective effect." [18] Quoting Justice Cardozo for the proposition that " 'the federal constitution has no voice upon the subject,' " [19] the *Linkletter* Court treated the question of retroactivity as purely a matter of policy, to be decided anew in each case.[20] The Supreme Court codified the *Linkletter* approach in *Stovall v. Denno*: "The criteria guiding resolution of the question implicate (a) the purpose to be served by the new standards, (b) the extent of the reliance by law enforcement authorities on the old standards, and (c) the effect on the administration of justice of a retroactive application of the new standards." [21]

Formally, *Linkletter* and *Stovall*, by treating retroactivity as purely a matter of policy, adopt a point of view which treats the effect of a judgment of unconstitutionality as purely a question of remedy, thus emphasizing the adjudicatory rather than the constitutional aspect of constitutional adjudication. In practice, however, the Supreme Court's approach has been more complex. Although generally continuing to adhere to the *Stovall* standards in its collateral review of criminal convictions,[22] the Court has focused on whether "the major purpose of new constitutional doctrine is to overcome an aspect of the criminal trial that substantially impairs its truth-finding function and so raises serious questions about the accuracy of guilty verdicts in past trials . . . . ." [23] Under this inquiry, the prospect of "arbitrary or unreliable results" generally leads to "complete retroactive effect"; [24] the absence

---

18. 381 U.S. 618, 629 (1965).

19. Id., quoting Great Northern Ry. v. Sunburst Oil & Refining Co., 287 U.S. 358, 364 (1932).

20. See 381 U.S. at 629. By contrast, before Linkletter, "both the common law and [the Court's] own decisions recognized a general rule of retrospective effect for the constitutional decisions of [the] Court . . . subject to [certain] limited exceptions." Robinson v. Neil, 409 U.S. 505, 507 (1973). This rule derived from the belief "that the duty of the court was not to 'pronounce a new law, but to maintain and expound the old one.' " Linkletter, 381 U.S. at 622–23 (1965), citing 1 W. Blackstone, Commentaries 69 (15th ed. 1809). Outside the criminal justice field, however, the rule still holds force, as "a legal system based on precedent has a built-in presumption of retroactivity." Solem v. Stumes, 465 U.S. 638, 642 (1984). For guidance on exceptions in civil cases, see note 17, supra.

21. 388 U.S. 293 (1967). In formulating this approach the Court also relied heavily on its decisions in Johnson v. New Jersey, 384 U.S. 719 (1966), and Tehan v. United States ex rel. Shott, 382 U.S. 406 (1966).

22. See, e.g., United States v. Leon, 468 U.S. 897, 912–13 n.10 (1984); Solem v. Stumes, 465 U.S. 638, 642 (1984); Brown v. Louisiana, 447 U.S. 323, 327–28 (1980) (plurality opinion).

23. Williams v. United States, 401 U.S. 646, 653 (1971) (plurality opinion).

24. See, e.g., id. at 653 n.6; Brown v. Louisiana, 447 U.S. 323, 328–30 (1980) (plurality opinion); Hankerson v. North Carolina, 432 U.S. 233, 243 (1977); United States v. Peltier, 422 U.S. 531, 535 (1975); Gosa v. Mayden, 413 U.S. 665, 679 (1973) (plurality opinion); Ivan V. v. New York, 407 U.S. 203, 205 (1972) (per curiam); Arsenault v. Massachusetts, 393 U.S. 5 (1968). The Supreme Court also gives full retroactive effect to decisions which would safeguard

of such a concern generally warrants only prospective application of the decision.[25] Moreover, the Court has departed from the *Stovall* approach in certain circumstances so as to accord the benefit of new and generally nonretroactive decisions to *all* defendants with cases pending on direct review at the time of the decision, in an attempt to minimize the unfairness of treating similarly situated litigants differently.[26]

This concern to minimize unfairness plainly reflects not so much a judicial balancing of policies—the apparent approach of *Stovall*—as a recognition of a hierarchy of constitutional values, however controversial. Justice Stevens has articulated this hierarchy with the suggestion that the retroactivity precedents are premised on two levels of constitutional error. Decisions will be limited to prospective application when the constitutional errors implicated "are important enough to require reversal on direct appeal but do not reveal the kind of fundamental unfairness to the accused that will support a collateral attack on a final judgment." But decisions will enjoy retroactive application when the constitutional errors "are so fundamental that they infect the validity of the underlying judgment itself, or the integrity of the process by which that judgment was obtained." [27] That not all criminal procedure

defendants from being put to trial at all. See, e.g., Robinson v. Neil, 409 U.S. 505, 509 (1973) (double jeopardy protection); United States v. United States Coin & Currency, 401 U.S. 715, 723 (1971) (fifth amendment prohibition of laws punishing gamblers for failing to register and pay special taxes).

25. See, e.g., Solem v. Stumes, 465 U.S. 638, 643–45 (1984); Michigan v. Payne, 412 U.S. 47, 52–55 (1973); Halliday v. United States, 394 U.S. 831, 832–33 (1969) (per curiam); Johnson v. New Jersey, 384 U.S. 719, 727–31 (1966); Stovall, 388 U.S. at 297–99.

26. The Court announced this approach in United States v. Johnson, 457 U.S. 537 (1982), where it imposed a flat rule that any decision interpreting the fourth amendment that does not represent a "clear break" with the past must be applied to all defendants whose convictions were pending on direct review or not final when the decision was announced. Id. at 553–54, 562. The five-member majority adopted the approach to such cases that had been advocated for years by a shifting minority of Justices and most stridently by the second Justice Harlan, concluding that a blanket rule was needed to prevent inconsistency and to combat the violation of the judicial role and the unfairness to individuals occasioned by the alternative practice of applying a decision retroactively only to the particular litigant involved in the case. See id. at 545–48. The Court extended its approach beyond the fourth amendment context in Shea v. Louisiana, 470 U.S. 51 (1985); see note 27, infra. In Griffith v. Kentucky, 107 S.Ct. 708 (1987),

the Johnson and Shea majority added the sixth vote of newly named Justice Scalia in applying retroactively the rule of Batson v. Kentucky, 106 S.Ct. 1712 (1986) (barring racially discriminatory use by prosecutors of peremptory challenges), and declaring generally that new rules for the conduct of criminal prosecutions will be applied retroactively to all pending or non-final cases even if they constitute a "clear break" with the past. Stovall still governs the retroactivity of decisions applied to convictions that are final at the time of decision and are attacked on collateral review, see 388 U.S. at 563–64 (Brennan, J., concurring); see also Solem v. Stumes, 465 U.S. 638, 643 n.3 (1984).

27. Rose v. Lundy, 455 U.S. 509, 543–44 & n.8 (1982) (Stevens, J., dissenting). Compare, e.g., Solem v. Stumes, 465 U.S. 638, 643–50 (1984) (declining to apply fifth amendment rule of Edwards v. Arizona, 451 U.S. 477 (1981), retroactively on collateral review), with Shea v. Louisiana, 470 U.S. 51, 55–61 (1985) (applying Edwards retroactively to all cases not final at the time decision was announced). Justice Stevens thus concluded that, "[i]n ruling that a constitutional principle is not to be applied retroactively, the Court implicitly suggests that the right is not necessary to ensure the integrity of the underlying judgment; the Court certainly would not allow claims of such magnitude to remain unremedied." Rose, 455 U.S. at 544 n.8. But see Johnson v. New Jersey, 384 U.S. 719, 728 (1966) ("we do not disparage a constitutional guarantee in any manner by declining to apply it retroactively").

decisions are applied retroactively therefore reveals that "the Court's constitutional jurisprudence has expanded beyond the concept of ensuring fundamental fairness to the accused." [28] Thus it appears that, despite its rhetorical emphasis on the remedial, "adjudicative" aspects of a judgment of unconstitutionality, the Supreme Court has attempted to take into account the specific "constitutional" status of such a judgment as well.

§ 3–4. Judicial Review and the Problem of "Other Minds": The Legitimacy of Differing Interpretations of the Constitution

In both *Hayburn's Case*[1] and *Marbury v. Madison*,[2] the Supreme Court exercised the power of judicial review defensively—to prevent Congress and the Executive Branch, in *Hayburn's Case*, and Congress alone in *Marbury*, from enlarging the jurisdiction of the federal courts beyond the scope fixed by the case-or-controversy and subject-matter limits of article III. Since *Marbury*, however, the Supreme Court has not restricted the exercise of its authority to enforce the Constitution to cases in which the federal courts' own constitutional sphere was threatened. Thus, the Court has engaged in constitutional adjudication in cases in which private individuals asserted that congressional or executive action had infringed their rights,[3] in controversies between Congress and the Executive as to the scope of their constitutional powers relative to each other,[4] and in cases in which a dispute was entirely internal to Congress[5] or to the Executive Branch.[6]

The Supreme Court's power to review state action has undergone a similar transformation. In view of the obvious need for a means of policing state compliance with the supremacy clause,[7] as well as the

---

28. Rose, 455 U.S. at 544 n.8. Compare, e.g., Wellington, "Common Law Rules and Constitutional Double Standards: Some Notes on Adjudication," 83 Yale L.J. 221, 258–61 (1973), and Mishkin, "The Supreme Court, 1964 Term, Foreword: The High Court, The Great Writ and the Due Process of Time and Law," 79 Harv.L.Rev. 56, 77–92 (1965) (essentially justifying the Court's approach), with Schwartz, "Retroactivity, Reliability, and Due Process: A Reply to Professor Mishkin," 33 U.Chi.L.Rev. 719, 740–42 (1966) (challenging hierarchy which singles out accuracy as value deserving of special protection). See also § 10–7, infra (sketching noninstrumental conception of procedural due process).

§ 3–4

1. 2 U.S. (2 Dall.) 409 (1792), discussed in § 3–2, supra.

2. 5 U.S. (1 Cranch) 137 (1803), discussed in § 3–2, supra.

3. See, e.g., Immigration and Naturalization Serv. v. Chadha, 462 U.S. 919 (1983), discussed in §§ 4–3, 4–9, infra; United States v. Robel, 389 U.S. 258 (1967), discussed in § 12–30, infra; Youngstown Sheet & Tube Co. v. Sawyer, 343 U.S. 579 (1952), discussed in § 4–8, infra.

4. See, e.g., Bowsher v. Synar, 106 S.Ct. 3181 (1986); Buckley v. Valeo, 424 U.S. 1 (1976); Myers v. United States, 272 U.S. 52 (1926). These cases are discussed in §§ 4–9 and 4–10, infra.

5. See, e.g., Powell v. McCormack, 395 U.S. 486 (1969), discussed in § 3–13, infra.

6. See, e.g., United States v. Nixon, 418 U.S. 683 (1974), discussed in §§ 3–9, 3–12, 4–15, infra.

7. U.S.Const., art. VI, cl. 2. See, e.g., 1 C. Warren, The Supreme Court in United States History 14–15 (rev. ed. 1932) (arguing that "a supremacy of the Constitution and laws of the Union 'without a supremacy in the exposition and execution of them would be as much a mockery as a scabbard put into the hands of a soldier without a sword in it'" (quoting James Madison)); Baucus & Kay, "The Court Stripping Bills: Their Impact on the Constitution, the Courts, and Congress," 27 Vill.L.Rev. 988, 997 (1982) (noting Framers' intention that the Court enforce the supremacy clause,

need to ensure the uniform interpretation of federal law, the first Congress not surprisingly granted the Supreme Court appellate jurisdiction to review federal question decisions of state courts.[8] Not surprisingly, the Court also concluded that the Constitution in fact authorized it to accept such a power of review under article III, and that such power included authority to engage in constitutional adjudication.[9]

Read narrowly, the supremacy clause binds only state judges. But other provisions of the Constitution, most notably the fourteenth amendment, directly constrain the action of all state officials, often without regard to whether state courts have ruled on the validity of officials' acts;[10] moreover, article VI declares that "the Members of the several State Legislatures, and all executive and judicial Officers . . . of the several states, shall be bound by Oath or Affirmation, to support this Constitution. . . ." Accordingly, the Court has not limited to state judges its demand for compliance with the federal Constitution. In *Cooper v. Aaron*,[11] a school desegregation case decided against the background of Governor Faubus's resistance to the desegregation of public schools in Little Rock, Arkansas, the Supreme Court asserted what is probably its broadest definition of its power: "*Marbury v. Madison* . . . declared the basic principle that the federal judiciary is supreme in the exposition of the law of the Constitution, and that principle has ever since been respected by this Court and the country as a permanent and indispensable feature of our constitutional system. It follows that the interpretation of the Fourteenth Amendment enunciated by this Court in the *Brown* case is the supreme law of the land. . . . Every state legislator and executive and judicial officer is solemnly committed by oath . . . 'to support this Constitution.' "[12]

The directness of the Court's claim of supremacy in *Cooper*— uniquely punctuated by the Justices' individual signatures of the opinion—is quite understandable given the open state resistance to the principles announced in *Brown*.[13] Although subsequent assertions of ultimate authority have tended to be more restrained,[14] it remains important to consider the effect of *Cooper* on the Court's role as announced in *Marbury*. A broad reading of *Cooper* would seem to embody two central assumptions. The first is that the Court, in

given the failure of the Articles of Confederation, which contained a similar clause, to provide an enforcement mechanism).

8. Judiciary Act of 1789, § 25, 1 Stat. 73, 85. The supremacy rationale was clearly dominant, for the 1789 Act conferred jurisdiction only when a federal law had been held invalid or a federal claim against a state statute had been rejected. Jurisdiction over decisions relying on federal claims to invalidate state statutes was conferred on the Court in 1914. See Act of Dec. 23, 1914, ch. 2, 38 Stat. 790; see also § 3–5, infra.

9. See Martin v. Hunter's Lessee, 14 U.S. (1 Wheat.) 304 (1816). For a review of both the Framers' understanding of the role of the Court in fostering supremacy

and uniformity, and of the development of the Court's view of its role, see Ratner, "Majoritarian Constraints on Judicial Review: Congressional Control of Supreme Court Jurisdiction," 27 Vill.L.Rev. 929, 942–52 (1982).

10. See § 18–4, infra.

11. 358 U.S. 1 (1958).

12. Id. at 18.

13. See generally Farber, "The Supreme Court and the Rule of Law: Cooper v. Aaron Revisited," 1982 U.Ill.L.Rev. 387, 309–403.

14. See, e.g., United States v. Nixon, 418 U.S. 683, 703–05 (1974); Powell v. McCormack, 395 U.S. 486, 549 (1969); Baker v. Carr, 369 U.S. 186, 211 (1962).

rendering a constitutional decision, announces a general norm of wide applicability. This viewpoint ignores the competing conception that the Court, in making constitutional determinations pursuant to its responsibility under *Marbury*, simply resolves the claims of the parties before it.[15] But an expansive view of the judicial function was clearly warranted in *Brown*; the Court's unanimous opinion was couched in the most general terms and was perceived at the time as applying to all schools.[16] If any constitutional principle stands out with unique clarity in our time, it is the fourteenth amendment prohibition of racial discrimination—the prohibition that the Supreme Court invoked in *Brown* and reiterated in *Cooper*.[17]

The second possible assumption—that the Court's interpretation is *itself* the "supreme law of the land" and that state officials are directly bound by oath to support that interpretation—is more troubling. This view has been criticized as wrongly equating the Constitution with the Court's interpretation of it—as saying that *Marbury* means that the Constitution is what the Court says it is, and no more.[18] So construed, *Cooper* ignores the reality that, at least so long as the manner in which our nation's fundamental document is to be interpreted remains open to question,[19] the "meaning" of the Constitution is subject to legitimate dispute,[20] and the Court is not alone in its responsibility to address that

15. See § 3–3, supra.

16. School officials both in Little Rock and throughout the country generally perceived Brown as the law of the land, to which they must adhere whatever their doubts as to its wisdom. See Farber, supra note 13, at 391–92.

17. See Allen v. Wright, 468 U.S. 737, 756 (1984). See generally §§ 16–14 to 16–21, infra.

18. See, e.g., A. Bickel, The Least Dangerous Branch: The Supreme Court at the Bar of Politics 264 (1962) (characterizing opinion as mandating that "[w]hatever the Court lays down is right, even if wrong, because the Court and only the Court speaks in the name of the Constitution"); Monaghan, "Constitutional Adjudication: The Who and When," 82 Yale L.J. 1363, 1363 n. 2 (1973). See also "Meese Says Rulings By U.S. High Court Don't Establish Law," New York Times, Oct. 23, 1986, at A1 (noting Attorney General's admonition to governmental officials to be guided by their own views of the Constitution, rather than always deferring to those expounded by the Supreme Court). To the extent that politicians like Mr. Meese, in criticizing the equation of the Supreme Court with the supreme law of the land, have meant to reiterate the elementary proposition that Justices are fallible, their views are unexceptionable. See "Review and Outlook: The Irrepressible Mr. Meese," Wall St. Journal, Oct. 29, 1986, at 28 (interpreting the Attorney General's remarks as endorsing this unremarkable

proposition and quoting the admonitions in the first edition of this treatise that there is a "distinction between the Constitution and judicial enforcement of its commands" and thus that "we must distinguish the dancer from the dance"). But to the extent that such statements instead encourage defiance of settled Supreme Court doctrine, it is doubtful they represent a responsible exercise of executive power.

19. See, e.g., Carter, "Constitutional Adjudication and Indeterminate Text: A Preliminary Defense of an Imperfect Muddle," 94 Yale L.J. 821, 823–31 (1985); see generally § 3–6, infra.

20. See, e.g., Graves v. New York, 306 U.S. 466, 491–92 (1939) (Frankfurter, J., concurring) (although "[judicial exegesis is unavoidable . . . the ultimate touchstone of constitutionality is the Constitution itself and not what we have said about it"); E. Corwin, Court Over Constitution 68 (1938) (contrary view "supposes a kind of transubstantiation whereby the Court's opinion of the Constitution . . . becomes the very body and blood of the Constitution"); R. Dworkin, Taking Rights Seriously 211, 214–15 ("We cannot assume . . . that the Constitution is always what the Supreme Court says it is. . . . Sometimes, even after a contrary Supreme Court decision, an individual may still reasonably believe that the law is on his side."). Contrast Chief Justice Hughes' admonition: "We are under a Constitution, but the Constitution is what the judges say it is." The Autobiographical Notes of

meaning. Rather, a variety of actors must make their own constitutional judgments, and possess the power to develop interpretations of the Constitution which do not necessarily conform to the judicially enforced interpretation articulated by the Supreme Court: the president,[21] legislators,[22] state courts [23] and the public at large.[24]

The *Cooper* opinion as a whole, however, does not require so literal a reading of its invocation of absolute judicial supremacy; conceived with sufficient subtlety, it is readily compatible with American democracy. Plainly, in *Cooper* the Court does say that its *Brown* decision is binding law under the supremacy clause. But the Court need not be understood to say anything more than that *Brown* and its progeny, including the case at hand, are binding in the same way that any other judicial decision is binding, so that state officials who interfere with enforcement of a judgment, or act to undermine its goals, are acting unlawfully. On this view, *Brown* need not be seen as itself "part" of the Constitution, but as a constitutional judgment, an exercise of judicial power entitled to respect under the supremacy clause not because it *is* the Constitution but because it is an exercise of power *under* the Constitution—just as the Court's imposition of a federal common-law rule,[25] or interpretation of a federal statute, is binding.[26] On this view, to declare that "the federal judiciary is *supreme* in the exposition of the law of the Constitution" is to make a statement more about the role of the federal judiciary than about the content of the Constitution's commands.

Accepting that the Court's interpretations of the Constitution are binding on other government actors in this sense, it becomes vital to determine, at every occasion for constitutional choice, the parameters of those interpretations. On one level, the practical power of other governmental actors to employ differing constitutional interpretations is obvious: so long as they do not involve themselves in justiciable controversies coming within the subject-matter limits of article III, the

Charles Evans Hughes 144 (D. Danelski & J. Tulchin eds. 1973).

For an interesting perspective on the controversy, drawing an analogy between debate over the ultimate authority of the Supreme Court and the dispute over religious authority between adherents of Protestantism and Roman Catholicism, see Levinson, " 'The Constitution' in American Civil Religion," 1979 Sup.Ct.Rev. 123, 137–47. For other approaches to the analogy, see, e.g., Burt, "Constitutional Law and the Teaching of the Parables," 93 Yale L.J. 455 (1984); Grey, "The Constitution as Scripture," 37 Stan.L.Rev. 1 (1984).

21. See, e.g., G. Gunther, Constitutional Law 26–29 (11th ed. 1985); see generally Chapter 4, infra. But while the executive branch is free to articulate its own views of the Constitution—and indeed, to relitigate constitutional issues in different circuit courts, or in a series of cases involving different parties—it may not properly use

this discretion to flout the law of a given circuit or of the Supreme Court. See § 3–3, supra, at note 11.

22. See, e.g., Levinson, supra note 20, at 146–47; Sager, "Fair Measure: The Legal Status of Underenforced Constitutional Norms," 91 Harv.L.Rev. 1212, 1215–20 (1978); Brest, "The Conscientious Legislator's Guide to Constitutional Interpretation," 27 Stan.L.Rev. 586 (1975).

23. See, e.g., Bator, "The State Courts and Federal Constitutional Litigation," 22 Wm. & Mary L.Rev. 605 (1981).

24. See, e.g., L. Tribe, Constitutional Choices vii, 19–20 (1985); L. Tribe, God Save This Honorable Court: How the Choice of Supreme Court Justices Shapes Our History (1985).

25. See § 3–23, infra.

26. See, e.g., Farber, supra note 13, at 405–11.

Supreme Court's view of the Constitution cannot be brought to bear, and those other governmental actors will be free to interpret and apply the Constitution as they deem best. Thus, members of Congress and state legislators can vote for or against proposed legislation on the basis of their own theories of constitutional law, and Presidents and governors can similarly invoke their own constitutional views in signing or vetoing legislation and in granting or denying pardons.

This answer, however, is ultimately unsatisfactory, unless we wish to sanction in this context Holmes's "bad man" theory of the law.[27] Because of their oaths, government officials would be under at least a moral obligation to adopt the Supreme Court's view of the Constitution, if that view were entitled to be seen as always dispositive, even if the acts of such officials happened not to be judicially reviewable.[28] The more fundamental question is therefore whether, consistent with the concept of judicial review assumed in *Marbury* and subsequently articulated in *Cooper*, the Supreme Court should itself tolerate interpretations of the Constitution other than its own, even in situations where it has ample jurisdiction to review what other governmental actors have done. If so, legislators and executives are to that degree free, notwithstanding their oaths, to interpret the Constitution differently from the Supreme Court.

In *Katzenbach v. Morgan*,[29] the Supreme Court held that Congress could prohibit the use of certain literacy tests for voter eligibility even though the Supreme Court had held that such tests did not violate the fourteenth amendment equal protection clause; the Court rested its holding in part on the proposition that nothing in the Constitution prohibited Congress, at least in this instance, from acting under § 5 of the fourteenth amendment, on the basis of an interpretation of the equal protection clause more expansive than that enforced by the Supreme Court. As the discussion in Chapter 5 will demonstrate,[30] subsequent Court decisions reveal substantial uncertainty as to *Morgan's* validity; similarly, the commentators are undecided as to whether the opinion is or is not heresy. The fundamental issue is *Morgan's* consistency with *Marbury v. Madison*.

Many efforts to justify *Morgan* seek to portray it as something other than recognition of congressional authority to interpret the Constitution itself. *Morgan*, it is argued, really turned on judicial deference to legislative factfinding or remedy-making, or merely involved the Supreme Court's usual acquiescence in congressional judgments as to essentially political questions of federalism. These interpretations will be discussed in Chapter 5.[31] Of more interest here is another response to *Morgan* developed most fully by Professor Henry Monaghan.[32] Monaghan would preserve a sphere of "pure" constitu-

27. See O. W. Holmes, Collected Legal Papers 172–73 (1920) ("The prophecies of what the courts will do in fact, and nothing more pretentious, are what I mean by the law").

28. See Brest, supra note 22, at 587–89.

29. 384 U.S. 641 (1966).

30. See §§ 5–12 to 5–15, infra.

31. See id.

32. Monaghan, "The Supreme Court, 1974 Term—Foreword: Constitutional Common Law," 89 Harv.L.Rev. 1 (1975). See also Burt, "Miranda and Title II: A

tional law, within which only one interpretation, that of the Supreme Court, would be permissible. But he would also postulate another sphere, that of "constitutional common law," concerned with such questions as the specific accommodations of conflicting rights, the need for prophylactic rules, and the precise content of the procedures required by due process, within which Congress would not merely participate as the Supreme Court's equal, but would hold the power to substitute its own views for those of the Court.

As a practical matter, Monaghan's distinction suffers from a formidable defect which he himself acknowledges: "It is obviously crucial to the theory . . . that satisfactory criteria exist for distinguishing between *Marbury*-shielded constitutional exegesis and congressionally reversible constitutional law."[33] Monaghan is nonetheless forced to conclude that "any distinction between constitutional exegesis and common law cannot be analytically precise, representing, as it does, differences of degree."[34] Because of the uncertain line along which it must balance, Monaghan's distinction would complicate the process of constitutional adjudication and would exacerbate the tension between Congress and the Court.[35]

If flawed, however, Monaghan's analysis is nonetheless significant: it acknowledges the need to find some place for Congress, and thus by implication for other nonjudicial actors, in the process of constitutional interpretation. Moreover, the limits of Monaghan's approach are instructive: analysis of its defects may provide the basis for construction of a more satisfactory alternative. Ultimately, the difficulty with Monaghan's approach is the result of a failure to follow *Katzenbach v. Morgan* out to its conclusion: the theory of constitutional common law continues to insist that there must be an ultimate arbiter of the content of constitutional law; the theory's novelty lies in its division of the task of oracle between Congress and the Supreme Court, with each accorded control over its own sector of the constitutional terrain. This insistence on a determinate constitutional law, however, reflects a confusion of the concept of constitutional law with judicial enforcement of that law—the sort of confusion, in fact, discussed in the preceding section.[36] The adjudicatory process, as a matter of necessity, must yield but a single result in any single case. Judges, therefore, must treat the law as determinate. But law itself, and thus constitutional law, need not be viewed through the judicial lens, and thus need not always be conceived as determinate.[37]

Morganatic Marriage," 1969 Sup.Ct.Rev. 81.

33. Monaghan, supra note 32, at 30–31.

34. Id. at 31.

35. For a general criticism of Monaghan's thesis, see Schrock & Welsh, "Reconsidering the Constitutional Common Law," 91 Harv.L.Rev. 1117 (1978). Compare Monaghan, "Third Party Standing," 84 Colum.L.Rev. 277, 314–15 & n. 201 (1984).

36. See § 3–3, supra.

37. Jurisprudential discussions of open-textured rules or of a distinction between determinate rules and open-ended standards or principles are commonplace. For an account and analysis of jurisprudential writing on these questions, see Soper, "Legal Theory and the Obligation of a Judge: The Hart/Dworkin Dispute," 75 Mich.L. Rev. 473 (1977).

It is not difficult to reconcile indeterminate constitutional law—constitutional law which recognizes, within limits, the equal legitimacy of differing interpretations—with a determinate adjudicatory process; indeed, so long as the Supreme Court is not distracted by the fact that Congress or a state legislature has its own theory of the Constitution, the doctrinal frameworks upon which the Court currently relies in the main accomplish just such a reconciliation. The Court may hold, to suggest just two examples, that the Constitution does not compel prior hearings in public school corporal punishment cases,[38] and that the Constitution does not require public funding for abortions,[39] without implying that a legislature which acts on a larger view of its federal constitutional duty is therefore in error. If the Court were to conclude that prior hearings are *forbidden* in some situations (perhaps because of the added anxiety they inflict), or that public funding of certain practices is *prohibited* (perhaps because of the religious character of the proposed expenditures), then—but not until then—governmental hearings or expenditures premised on disagreement with such holdings could not be tolerated by a Court serious about its own constitutional conclusions. But each such conclusion has its own internal structure, and it is that structure—rather than an invariable principle that constitutional provisions must always lead all governmental actors to the same result—which determines, in any given case, the degree to which the Supreme Court's theory of the Constitution operates to bind others.[40]

Consideration of the internal structure of a constitutional norm must involve a determination of how the Court, in formulating the norm, might have been constrained in its analysis by institutional factors. Often, it is quite apparent that the Supreme Court's exposition of a constitutional norm does not exhaust the possibilities of the concepts on which the norm rests. Rather, constitutional claims may be denied on the basis of related federalism concerns, or a perceived lack of competence to develop judicially workable standards to regulate a sphere of government conduct. This tendency is prominent with equal protection challenges to state-fashioned taxing programs, business regulation, or various bureaucratic regimes, and is evident in fifth-amendment takings law and fourteenth-amendment due process jurisprudence as well.[41] Professor Lawrence Sager has described such norms as "underenforced" by the federal courts and has argued convincingly that judicial exposition of a norm "should be understood as delineating only the boundaries of the federal courts' role in enforcing the norm" and that "the unenforced margins of underenforced norms

---

38. See Ingraham v. Wright, 430 U.S. 651 (1977), discussed in §§ 10–14, 15–9, infra.

39. See Harris v. McRae, 448 U.S. 297 (1980); Maher v. Roe, 432 U.S. 464 (1977), discussed in § 15–10, infra.

40. For an interesting example of this principle, arguing that apparently unconstitutional intrusions by the states on federal power can be validated by Congress,

see Cohen, "Congressional Power to Validate Unconstitutional State Laws," 35 Stan.L.Rev. 387 (1983). See generally § 6–33, infra.

41. See Sager, supra note 22, at 1215–20. For a survey of the due process issues, see Note, "Congressional Power to Enforce Due Process Rights," 80 Colum.L.Rev. 1265 (1980).

should have the full status of positive law" under the Constitution "save only that the federal judiciary will not enforce these margins." [42]

Some of the most troublesome constitutional issues arise in settings in which judges may be incapable of addressing all aspects of controversy; these issues can be addressed, if at all, only by responsible legislators.[43] And the increasingly frequent invocation of arguments founded on separation of powers, federalism and equitable restraint to deny justiciability of constitutional disputes in federal courts [44] requires that the public recognize that constitutional law cannot be simply what the courts, from time to time, say it is. Congress must thus be recognized as having the power and the duty to interpret the document in a way that may command the respect of others. This argument is among the many answers to the charge that constitutional interpretation is a disturbingly anti-democratic enterprise. Although the Constitution in a sense stands beyond ordinary politics—and perhaps even beyond the Supreme Court's interpretations of the Constitution as text and as history—democracy is surely less threatened by a system of constitutional interpretation in which many may share significant and respected roles than by a system with but one authoritative voice.

This perspective resolves the most basic problem posed by *Morgan*: where, for institutional reasons, it appears that the Court has stopped short in its analysis of the implications of the fourteenth amendment, Congress is free under § 5 to add to that analysis.[45] But in the absence of such constraints, where it appears that norms have been "fully enforced" to their analytical limits, Congress may not offer its own interpretation.[46] For this reason, the "underenforcement" thesis bars Congress from enforcing rights in a manner that would diminish the force of other rights recognized by Supreme Court interpretations.[47]

42. Sager, supra note 22, at 1221; see also id. at 1221–28. Sager finds in the political question doctrine, see § 3–13, infra, recognition that constitutional norms are perceived as constraining government action even where the judiciary itself will decline to apply the Constitution. See id. at 1224–26. For an earlier, less fully elaborated exposition of this view, see Tribe, "Unraveling National League of Cities: The New Federalism and Affirmative Rights to Essential Government Services," 90 Harv.L.Rev. 1065, 1084–91 (1977).

43. For example, effectuation of the government's duty to minimize the conflict between the constitutional interests of women and those of their unborn children would require an uncertain commitment of resources and use of a variety of approaches; it is implausible that judges could justify imposing these requirements on their own. See Tribe, "The Abortion Funding Conundrum: Inalienable Rights, Affirmative Duties, and the Dilemma of Dependence," 99 Harv.L.Rev. 330, 340–43 (1985).

44. See § 3–8, infra.

45. See Sager, supra note 22, at 1239–42. For an alternative view of Morgan, see Carter, "The Morgan 'Power' and the Forced Reconsideration of Constitutional Decisions," 53 U.Chi.L.Rev. 818, 824 (1986) (arguing that the Morgan power "is best understood as a tool that permits the Congress to use its power to enact ordinary legislation to engage the Court in a dialogue about our fundamental rights, thereby 'forcing' the Justices to take a fresh look at their own judgments").

46. See Sager, supra note 22, at 1239–42; but cf. Note, supra note 41, at 1272–74.

47. See Sager, supra note 22, at 1240–41. Thus § 5 could not be used, for example, to enhance the rights of the fetus by restricting abortions, as set out in the Human Life Bill, S. 158, 97th Cong., 1st Sess. (1981). See § 5–14, note 87, infra. Morgan warrants extension of rights only where the Court has stopped short of their full analysis; in Roe v. Wade, see Chapter 15 infra, the Court articulated the maximum enforcement of the fetus's rights. See Emerson, "The Power of Congress to

It might be argued that state courts should be allowed as well to flesh out the full contours of an underenforced constitutional norm.[48] This possibility was addressed in *Oregon v. Hass*.[49] There, the Oregon Supreme Court had held that, under the fifth amendment, statements which a defendant made in response to continued police interrogation which followed his assertion of his *Miranda* rights[50] could not be introduced at trial to impeach his testimony. Earlier, in *Harris v. New York*,[51] the United States Supreme Court had held that the fifth amendment did not bar use of such statements for impeachment purposes. In *Hass*, the United States Supreme Court reversed the Oregon judgment, on the ground that "a State may not impose . . . greater restrictions [on its police] *as a matter of federal constitutional law* when this Court specifically refrains from imposing them."[52] State courts were thereby compelled to treat the federal Constitution as setting both a ceiling and a floor on the extent of protection that can be accorded in its name.

The first edition of this treatise argued that *Hass* was wrongly decided because the Oregon court had done no more than conclude that the Supreme Court's solicitude for state law enforcement processes nationwide was unnecessary in Oregon, and because *Cooper* should not be read so broadly as to preclude that kind of determination.[53] Although those observations do fit firmly within the underenforcement thesis discussed above, and although state courts do have a vital role to play in the exposition of federal constitutional norms,[54] on further reflection it seems clear that the *Hass* rule serves on balance to advance rather than retard responsible constitutional decisionmaking. If Congress chooses to pursue a broader view of its responsibilities by supplementing a constitutional norm not fully enforced by the Court, citizens have a ready means of opposing that decision. By contrast, if the state court's interpretation of federal law in *Hass* had remained in

Change Constitutional Decisions of the Supreme Court: The Human Life Bill," 77 Nw.L.Rev. 129, 136–42 (1982).

For other views, compare Note, "Toward Limits on Congressional Enforcement Power Under the Civil War Amendments," 34 Stan.L.Rev. 453 (1982) (arguing that Morgan threatens contraction of individual rights), with Nathanson, "Congressional Power to Contradict the Supreme Court's Constitutional Decisions: Accommodation of Rights in Conflict," 27 Wm. & Mary L.Rev. 331 (1986) (arguing that Morgan embodies Congress's special role in moderating conflicts between fundamental rights such as those involved in Roe).

48. See Welsh, "Whose Federalism?— The Burger Court's Treatment of State Civil Liberties Judgments," 10 Hastings Const.L.Q. 819 (1983); Sager, supra note 22, at 1242–50.

49. 420 U.S. 714 (1975).

50. See Miranda v. Arizona, 384 U.S. 436, 467–73 (1966).

51. 401 U.S. 222 (1971).

52. 420 U.S. at 719 (emphasis added in part). Justice Blackmun's majority opinion did not elaborate upon this assertion, and the two decisions of the U.S. Court of Appeals which the majority cited declare only that state interpretations of federal law do not bind federal courts. See Smayda v. United States, 352 F.2d 251, 253 (9th Cir. 1965), cert. denied 382 U.S. 981 (1966); Aftanase v. Economy Baler Co., 343 F.2d 187, 192–93 (8th Cir. 1965). In subsequent cases the Court has reaffirmed the doctrine with little explanation. See, e.g., Minnesota v. Clover Leaf Creamery Co., 449 U.S. 456, 461–63 n. 6 (1981); Fare v. Michael C., 442 U.S. 707, 717 (1979); North Carolina v. Butler, 441 U.S. 369, 376 (1979).

53. See L. Tribe, American Constitutional Law § 3–4, at 31–33 (1st ed. 1978).

54. See Bator, supra note 23.

place, it could not have been overturned through the state's political processes.[55] To encourage state courts to rely on the federal Constitution in such cases would stifle the independent development of state constitutional law as a means of enhancing favored rights.[56] But, even if *Hass* is therefore correct on the merits, it is not clear whether the Court should devote the considerable resources it has at times invested in undertaking review of such cases.[57]

In summary: *Cooper v. Aaron* need not bear as literal a reading as some might accord it. Properly understood, both *Cooper* and *Marbury v. Madison* are consistent with *Katzenbach v. Morgan*. And it is clear that, despite the growth of federal judicial power, the Constitution remains in significant degree a democratic document—not only written, ratified and amended through essentially democratic processes but

55. As Judge Ruth Bader Ginsburg pointed out in her review of the first edition, "[t]he state court's federal law determination could not be overturned by Oregon's legislature or electorate," and "[u]nless the Oregon court itself changed position, nothing short of a *federal* constitutional amendment could undo the decision." Ginsburg, "Book Review," 92 Harv. L.Rev. 340, 343–44 (1978) (emphasis in the original). For replies to this objection, as well as to others, see Sager, supra note 22, at 1250–60. The Court's view in Hass is consistent with its approach to determining whether independent and adequate state grounds support state court decisions, thereby rendering any federal determinations irrelevant, see § 3–24, infra, but conflicts somewhat with its apparent willingness to allow state court interpretations of federal constitutional law to go unreviewed in cases where federal justiciability standards are not met, see § 3–15, infra.

56. See § 3–24, infra. And, when a state court turns to its own constitution— see, e.g., PruneYard Shopping Center v. Robins, 447 U.S. 74 (1980)—the fact that federal norms governing the matter are "underenforced" provides a powerful rationale for interpreting similarly worded state provisions more expansively. Professor Lawrence Sager in particular has argued that state courts interpreting state constitutional provisions need not be bound by Supreme Court interpretations of like-worded federal provisions. See Sager, "Foreword: State Courts and the Strategic Space Between Norms and Rules of Constitutional Law," 63 Tex.L.Rev. 959 (1985). Sager contends that constitutional interpretation is often advanced, or impeded, by what he terms "pragmatic" or "strategic" considerations: for example, the preference in many doctrinal areas for categorical rules reflects merely a pragmatic unwillingness to engage in case-by-case inquiries. Id. at 964. Because state courts are distanced from the "homogenized na-

tional vision from which the Supreme Court is forced to operate," id. at 976, but instead act against the backdrop of divergent state histories and practices, Sager argues that it is permissible for them to arrive at different "strategic" interpretations of like-worded provisions. For further analysis of what Sager terms "the renaissance of active and independent state judicial implementation of state constitutional law," id., see generally "Symposium: The Emergence of State Constitutional Law," 63 Tex.L.Rev. 959–1318 (1985); McGraw (ed.), Developments in State Constitutional Law: The Williamsburg Conference (1985). See also "State Constitutional Law," Natl. L.J., Sept. 29, 1986 (special section devoted to the subject). See also § 3–24, note 27, infra.

57. Several Justices have attacked the Court for adding to its " 'burdensome' workload" by aggressively seeking out isolated fourth amendment cases "presenting fact-bound errors of minimal significance" upholding individual rights, thus resolving conflicting interests without the benefit of other courts' approaches. California v. Carney, 471 U.S. 386, 396–401 (1985) (Stevens, J., joined by Brennan and Marshall, JJ., dissenting); see also Florida v. Meyers, 466 U.S. 380, 383–387 (1984) (same). Justice Stevens has been most vocal in arguing against review of state court decisions upholding individual rights on federal grounds, particularly where state grounds also exist to support the judgment. See, e.g., Connecticut v. Barrett, 107 S.Ct. 828, 836 (1987) (Stevens, J., joined by Marshall, J., dissenting); Delaware v. Van Arsdall, 106 S.Ct. 1431, 1441–1450 (1986) (Stevens, J., dissenting); Ponte v. Real, 471 U.S. 491, 501–03 (1985) (Stevens, J., concurring in part); City of Revere v. Massachusetts General Hospital, 463 U.S. 239, 246–47 (1983) (Stevens, J., concurring in the judgment). See also discussion of Michigan v. Long, 463 U.S. 1032 (1983), in § 3–24, infra; Welsh, supra note 48.

indeed open at any given time to competing interpretations limited only by the values which inform the Constitution's provisions themselves, and by the complex political processes that the Constitution creates— processes which on various occasions give the Supreme Court, Congress, the President, or the states, the last word in constitutional debate.

§ 3–5. Judicial Review in an Institutional Setting: The Paradox of Congressional Control of Federal Court Jurisdiction

Whatever the extent to which Congress, the Executive Branch, and the states may participate in the process of constitutional interpretation, it is clear that the federal courts, through the power of constitutional review, possess a power to *govern*—to regulate other actors—that they would not possess if the federal judicial business consisted of nothing but statutory interpretation and interstitial common lawmaking. At the same time, however, the fact that federal courts possess a power of constitutional review paradoxically underscores their ultimate dependence on Congress: outside the Supreme Court's original jurisdiction, federal courts cannot *use* their power to review the constitutionality of any government action unless Congress first authorizes the federal courts to exercise jurisdiction.

The language of article III, § 1 makes it apparent that, while the Constitution itself provides for a Supreme Court, it does not similarly mandate lower federal courts: "The judicial Power of the United States, shall be vested in one Supreme Court, and in such inferior Courts as the Congress may from time to time ordain and establish." Moreover, article III, § 2, by mandating Supreme Court *original* jurisdiction only "[i]n all Cases affecting Ambassadors, other public Ministers and Consuls, and those in which a State shall be Party," makes the full exercise of federal judicial power dependent upon congressional creation of lower federal courts. By implication, § 2 thus acknowledges that federal judicial power might not in fact be exercisable to its limits, since the creation of lower federal courts rests with Congress. Justice Story argued in dictum in *Martin v. Hunter's Lessee* that, if Congress created any lower federal courts, it had to confer full federal jurisdiction.[1] The language of article III, however, seems inconsistent with this limitation of congressional discretion: since § 2 provides that "the Supreme Court shall have appellate Jurisdiction, both as to Law and Fact," only "with such Exceptions, and under such Regulations as the Congress shall make," it would be anomalous to hold that Congress lacked a similar power of "exception" in dealing with courts of its own creation.[2]

---

§ 3–5

1. 14 U.S. (1 Wheat.) 304, 330–31 (1816).

2. Some commentators, however, interpret Story's opinion as arguing that Congress is obligated to create inferior federal courts with full federal judicial power. See, e.g., Clinton, "A Mandatory View of Federal Court Jurisdiction: A Guided Quest for the Original Understanding of Article III," 132 Pa.L.Rev. 741, 750–52 & n.

21 (1984). Likewise, Professor Akhil Amar has argued that focus on Story's ultimate conclusion—either that Congress must create lower federal courts with plenary jurisdiction, see supra note 1, or that if created such courts must have full jurisdiction— obscures broader implications of Story's emphasis on mandatory federal jurisdiction. See Amar, "A Neo-Federalist View of Article III: Separating the Two Tiers of

The first Congress acted on the assumption that it had power to decide whether the jurisdiction of the lower federal courts, and the appellate jurisdiction of the Supreme Court, would in practice extend to the limits defined by article III, § 2's enumeration of federal judicial power.[3] The Supreme Court, apart from Justice Story's dictum, has not questioned this assumption. With the sole exception of the Supreme Court's original jurisdiction,[4] the enumeration in article III, § 2, of the heads of federal judicial power limits Congress more than the Supreme Court. For the federal courts generally, the relevant limits are those that are fixed by congressional jurisdictional statutes, enacted within the boundaries set by article III.[5]

A detailed description of the federal courts' current statutory jurisdiction, encompassing the original jurisdiction of the federal district courts and the appellate jurisdiction of the Courts of Appeals and of the Supreme Court, is obviously beyond the scope of this book.[6] The remainder of this section considers the two chief methods by which

---

Federal Jurisdiction," 65 B.U.L.Rev. 205, 210–19 (1985). Professor Amar views Story's argument as resting on three premises: (1) under article III, federal judicial power *must* be vested in certain cases in *some* article III court, in either original or appellate form; (2) some such cases, for example federal criminal prosecutions, were not within the original jurisdiction of state courts; and (3) the Supreme Court's original jurisdiction could not be expanded to hear these exclusively federal cases. Id. at 211–12. Amar argues that only the second premise is flawed, and that focus on the other two premises reveals problems with any congressional attempt to remove jurisdiction of any class of cases from both the Supreme Court and lower federal courts. Id. at 212–16.

3. Judiciary Act of 1789, 1 Stat. 73. The Act, for example, did not grant lower federal courts civil jurisdiction to hear "federal question" cases, cases arising under the Constitution or laws of the United States.

4. The importance of the grant of original jurisdiction to the Supreme Court is verified by its self-executing nature: "[I]t has been the established doctrine . . . ever since the [Judiciary Act of 1789], that in all cases where original jurisdiction is given by the Constitution, [the Supreme Court] has authority to exercise it without any further act of Congress to . . . confer jurisdiction . . . ." Kentucky v. Dennison, 65 U.S. (24 How.) 66, 98 (1861). The basic holding of Marbury v. Madison, 5 U.S. (1 Cranch) 137 (1803), was of course that the original jurisdiction of the Supreme Court could not be *expanded* by mere act of Congress. But *within* the categories enumerated in article III, the Court has discretion to accept or decline original jurisdiction as it deems convenient. See,

e.g., Massachusetts v. Missouri, 308 U.S. 1 (1939).

The established authority of Congress to allow suits enumerated in the Court's grant of original jurisdiction to be brought in lower federal courts as well derives not from the language of the Constitution but from "the practical construction put on [article III] by Congress at the very first moment of the organization of the government, . . . [evidencing a purpose] to open and keep open the highest court of the nation for the determination, in the first instance, of suits involving a State or a diplomatic or commercial representative of a foreign government" but not to require that *all* such suits, many of which might involve petty offenses or grievances, be brought in the Supreme Court. Ames v. Kansas, 111 U.S. 449, 464, 469 (1884). The current statutory provisions allocating the original jurisdiction of the Supreme Court thus reflect the Court's important national role. *Exclusive* original jurisdiction is provided only with respect to (a) "controversies between two or more States," and (b) "actions or proceedings *against* ambassadors or other public ministers of foreign states or their domestics or domestic servants, not inconsistent with the law of nations." 28 U.S.C. § 1251(a) (emphasis added). The need to provide a federal forum to try these two classes of cases was among the primary considerations that motivated the Framers in their design of article III.

5. "Courts created by statute can have no jurisdiction but such as the statute confers." Sheldon v. Sill, 49 U.S. (8 How.) 441, 449 (1850). Absent congressional authorization, federal courts even lack power to issue writs of habeas corpus. See Ex parte Bollman, 8 U.S. (4 Cranch) 75 (1807).

6. See generally C. Wright, A. Miller & E. Cooper, Federal Practice and Procedure,

Congress controls the jurisdiction of federal courts: through regulation of jurisdiction as such, and through creation of so-called "legislative courts," tribunals which replace article III courts as primary adjudicators of questions over which article III courts would otherwise exercise jurisdiction.

Congressional regulation of federal court jurisdiction may take either of two broad forms. The first form concerns the jurisdictional framework of trial and appeal within which federal cases will ordinarily proceed. The current tripartite division of responsibility among the federal district courts, the U.S. Courts of Appeals, and the Supreme Court, is largely the product of two acts, the Evarts Act of 1891,[7] which fixed the basic outline, and the Judges' Bill of 1925,[8] drafted by a committee of Supreme Court Justices, which established the ordinarily discretionary character of Supreme Court review.[9] The second form,

vols. 13–17 (1977–87). For an excellent general discussion of Supreme Court jurisdiction, see R. Stern, E. Gressman & S. Shapiro, Supreme Court Practice 40–187 (6th ed. 1986).

7. 26 Stat. 826.

8. 43 Stat. 936.

9. See generally P. Bator, D. Shapiro, P. Mishkin & H. Wechsler, Hart and Wechsler's The Federal Courts and the Federal System 40–41 (2d ed. 1973) [hereinafter Hart & Wechsler]. A brief word about Supreme Court jurisdiction, however, is necessary. The Court exercises its appellate jurisdiction either by writ of certiorari or on appeal. Review on certiorari is not a matter of right, but one of judicial discretion, and will be granted only where special reasons exist. Thus, considerations of prudence and politics guide the Court in its decisions whether to grant or deny a petition for certiorari. See Maryland v. Baltimore Radio Show, Inc., 338 U.S. 912, 917–19 (1950) (opinion of Frankfurter, J.); R. Stern, E. Gressman & S. Shapiro, supra note 6, at 188–239; Gressman, "Much Ado About Certiorari," 52 Geo.L.J. 742 (1964). Because the writ is discretionary, a denial of certiorari ordinarily "carries with it no implication whatever regarding the Court's views on the merits of a case which it has declined to review." Maryland v. Baltimore Radio Show, Inc., supra, at 919. Although *appeals*, unlike writs of certiorari, are mandatory, the Supreme Court follows much the same procedure in processing appeals as in dealing with petitions for writs of certiorari; based on a number of prudential considerations it determines whether the issues presented warrant plenary consideration and oral argument. See Ohio ex rel. Eaton v. Price, 360 U.S. 246 (1959) (opinion of Brennan, J.); R. Stern, E. Gressman & S. Shapiro, supra note 6, at 239–46 & n. 95. But appeals differ from petitions for certiorari in that

they are "of right"; if the Court properly has jurisdiction, it may not exercise "the discretionary power to refuse to decide the merits" in resolving the case. Graves v. Barnes, 405 U.S. 1201, 1203 (1972) (Powell, Circuit Justice). Thus, any judgment rendered—including a summary affirmance of an appeal, or the dismissal of an appeal for want of a substantial federal question—necessarily expresses a view by the Supreme Court on the legal issues presented by the case. And such a view, although entitled to less precedential weight in the determination of future cases before the Court when its grounds remain unrevealed than if the matter had received full consideration and had been disposed of in a full opinion, see, e.g., Edelman v. Jordan, 415 U.S. 651, 670–71 (1974), is nonetheless fully binding on lower courts. See Hicks v. Miranda, 422 U.S. 332, 343–45 (1975). At times, however, it may be exceedingly difficult for lower courts to divine the substantive content behind a summary disposition, see R. Stern, E. Gressman & S. Shapiro, supra note 6, at 249–52.

In practice, the distinction between mandatory and discretionary jurisdiction may often hinge on little more than the skill of the adversary involved in framing the issues. For example, 28 U.S.C. § 1257(2) authorizes appeal when the "validity" of a state statute has been sustained against an attack based on federal law. A careful litigant will recognize that the validity of a state statute is sustained not just when a state court holds that it is consistent with federal law, but also when a state court *applies* the state statute to a given factual situation *against* the claim that the statute, as so applied, is invalid on federal grounds. For example, in Dahnke-Walker Milling Co. v. Bondurant, 257 U.S. 282 (1921), the state court had evaluated a commerce clause claim, holding that a particular transaction was intrastate, not in-

not surprisingly, encompasses legislation which alters the "normal" jurisdictional structure insofar as certain kinds of cases are concerned. Most of this legislation has not been constitutionally controversial. Congress, for example, until 1976 required suits seeking an interlocutory or permanent injunction restraining the enforcement, operation, or execution of a federal or state statute on grounds of unconstitutionality to be first heard by special three judge federal district courts; [10] even at present, actions challenging the constitutionality of the apportionment of congressional districts or the apportionment of any statewide legislative body must be heard by such courts.[11]

On occasion, however, such special congressional regulation is more troublesome. The Reconstruction Congress in 1868 withdrew Supreme Court jurisdiction to review lower federal courts' denials of the writ of habeas corpus "on appeals which have been, or may hereafter be taken" [12] in order to prevent the Court from deciding a case as to which it had already heard oral argument, a case seemingly raising the question of the constitutionality of Reconstruction military government in the South. Somewhat similarly, the Portal-to-Portal Act of 1947 [13] provided that no federal court should have jurisdiction after a given date to decide any action, whether filed before or after that date, which sought to enforce rights under the Fair Labor Standards Act for overtime pay for underground travel to and from various mines; at the same time, Congress amended the Fair Labor Standards Act to exclude time spent in such travel from the employee's "work week." [14]

The Emergency Price Control Act of 1942 [15] took a different if equally controversial tack: Congress denied individuals who were criminally prosecuted for price control violations the right to challenge the validity of the price control regulations in that trial; instead, regulations could be challenged only by bringing an action before a special Emergency Court of Appeals within 30 days after an unsuccessful administrative challenge to the regulations. So too, the Voting Rights Act of 1965 [16] requires a state seeking judicial review of a decision of the Attorney General suspending the state's voting regulations to bring its action only in the District Court for the District of Columbia. Finally, the Selective Training and Service Act of 1940 [17] placed a particularly draconian limitation on federal jurisdiction: in a suit in which an individual was prosecuted for failing to report for induction, the federal court could not hear the individual's defense that he had been wrongly classified; he could raise this argument only by submit-

---

terstate, and hence that the state statute could be applied and enforced; it thus upheld the validity of the statute. The litigant had made clear that, if construed to allow application to the specific circumstances involved, the statute would be void under federal law; the litigant would not have enjoyed a right to appeal if it had merely claimed that the particular application of the statute would work to violate its federal rights. See generally R. Stern, E. Gressman & S. Shapiro, supra note 6, at 112–14.

10. See former 28 U.S.C. §§ 2281, 2282, repealed, Pub.L. 94–381, 90 Stat. 1119 (1976).

11. See 28 U.S.C. § 2284, as amended, Pub.L. 94–381, 90 Stat. 1119 (1976).

12. 15 Stat. 44.

13. 29 U.S.C. §§ 251–62.

14. Id. § 252(a).

15. 56 Stat. 23.

16. 42 U.S.C. § 1973 et seq.

17. 54 Stat. 885.

ting to induction and proceeding through administrative and judicial remedies while in the service.

Federal courts held none of these jurisdictional regulations to be unconstitutional.[18] But it would be a mistake to attach too much significance to the results of these decisions when evaluating the kinds of jurisdiction-stripping proposals that have been advocated in recent years. For although Congress has granted federal courts broad jurisdiction over federal claims, the fact that federal jurisdiction over constitutional questions is not self-executing poses a continuing danger that Congress may seek to circumvent the federal judiciary's accepted role as constitutional guardian by silencing it through removal of its jurisdiction over whole classes of cases. Recent proposals to effect such limitations have addressed particular areas of substantive law—including abortion, busing and school prayer—in which, it has been urged, federal courts have overstepped their authority. Accordingly, these proposals have been designed, through jurisdictional manipulation or gerrymandering, to undo developed substantive constitutional principles—reaching a result that would otherwise require amendment of the Constitution.[19] Such proposals pose a danger not only to the federal

18. The Supreme Court upheld the 1868 act in Ex parte McCardle, 74 U.S. (7 Wall.) 506 (1868). The Court never reviewed the constitutionality of the Portal-to-Portal Act, but lower federal courts unanimously upheld its constitutionality. See, e.g., Battaglia v. General Motors Corp., 169 F.2d 254 (2d Cir. 1948). The Supreme Court did review the constitutionality of the jurisdictional restriction included in the Emergency Price Control Act of 1942, sustaining it against due process, sixth amendment, and separation of powers challenges. See Yakus v. United States, 321 U.S. 414 (1944). The Court affirmed the constitutionality of other jurisdictional limitations included in the Act, not discussed above, in Lockerty v. Phillips, 319 U.S. 182 (1943), and Bowles v. Willingham, 321 U.S. 503 (1944). Relying upon Yakus, Lockerty, and Bowles, the Court upheld the Voting Rights Act's jurisdictional limitation in South Carolina v. Katzenbach, 383 U.S. 301, 331 (1966). Finally, the Court upheld the 1940 Selective Service Act in Falbo v. United States, 320 U.S. 549, 554 (1944): "Even if there were, as the petitioner argues, a constitutional requirement that judicial review must be available to test the validity of the decision of the local board, it is certain that Congress was not required to provide for judicial intervention before final acceptance of an individual for national service." See also Estep v. United States, 327 U.S. 114 (1946). The Military Selective Service Act of 1967, which authorized the system of conscription in use during the Vietnam War, allowed individuals to obtain judicial review of classification or processing by raising these issues as a defense to crimi-

nal prosecution, but denied any judicial review except in criminal proceedings. See 50 U.S.C.App. § 460(b)(3). In Clark v. Gabriel, 393 U.S. 256 (1968) (per curiam), the Supreme Court found "no constitutional objection" to this provision. But the Court narrowed the reach of this provision by statutory construction. See, e.g., Oestereich v. Selective Service System Local Board No. 11, 393 U.S. 233, 238 (1968): "To hold that a person deprived of his statutory exemption in . . . a blatantly lawless manner must either be indicted and raise his protest through habeas corpus or defy induction and defend his refusal in a criminal proceeding is to construe the Act with unnecessary harshness." See Donahue, "The Supreme Court vs. Section 10(b)(3) of the Selective Service Act: A Study in Ducking Constitutional Issues," 17 U.C. L.A.L.Rev. 908 (1970).

19. For arguments supporting this strategy, see, e.g., Berger, "Insulation of Judicial Usurpation: A Comment on Lawrence Sager's 'Court-Stripping' Polemic," 44 Ohio St.L.J. 611 (1983); Conference, "A Symposium on Judicial Activism: Problems and Responses," 7 Harv.J. Law & Pub. Pol'y 1 (1984); Rice, "Congress and the Supreme Court's Jurisdiction," 27 Vill. L.Rev. 959 (1982). A large number of such proposals were pending before Congress during the early 1980s. For a review and criticism of selected proposals, albeit one that may focus too heavily on the external limits imposed by the Constitution as opposed to the internal limits imposed by article III and discussed in the ensuing text, see Tribe, "Jurisdictional Gerrymandering: Zoning Disfavored Rights Out of

judiciary, but also to Congress: they threaten to challenge its legitimacy by removing the faith that people would otherwise have in the lawfulness of what Congress does when they know that its actions are constrained by an independent branch's reading of the Constitution's demands.

As the cases noted above involving past jurisdictional withdrawals illustrate, federal courts clearly have jurisdiction to determine whether such withdrawals comport with the commands of the Constitution. Although it might appear that no court could undertake such a review on the ground that jurisdiction-restricting laws lift cases out of the judicial system entirely, this view—which cedes literally boundless power to Congress—ignores the way in which a federal court operates.[20] A federal litigant urges dismissal of the case, or denial of a remedy, on the basis of a statute limiting or eliminating a court's jurisdiction. The court then looks at the statute—it has jurisdiction, all agree, to do at least that.[21] And when the court looks, it necessarily sees not only that statute but, standing behind it, the Constitution: that, among other things, is what the supremacy clause of the Constitution has come to mean.[22] So the court must decide whether the statute is valid in light of whatever the Constitution seems to say on the subject. Two quite distinct kinds of limits on congressional power readily appear: *internal limits* set by article III's definition of Congress's authority to control jurisdiction; and *external limits* set by the constitutional terrain Congress has chosen (or happened) to traverse.

The question whether a federal court has jurisdiction to review the constitutionality of a congressional withdrawal of jurisdiction is distinct from the question of what limitations the Constitution in fact imposes upon such legislation. Plainly, the usual limitations of the Bill of Rights and of article I, § 9, apply: the paradigmatic example of an external constitutional limitation would be the undisputed prohibitions imposed by the due process and free speech clauses on legislation that would, say, restrict access to the federal courts on the basis of a litigant's race, religion, gender or political affiliation or viewpoint. Moreover, laws *designed* to hinder the exercise of constitutional rights are, to that degree, unconstitutional. Likewise, even those jurisdictional statutes which unintentionally *burden* the exercise of such rights

the Federal Courts," 16 Harv.C.R.-C.L.Rev. 129 (1981).

20. The argument that Congress can wholly preclude review even of preliminary jurisdictional issues may flow from an incomplete reading of Ex parte McCardle, 74 U.S. (7 Wall.) 506, 514 (1868), where the Supreme Court, in complying with an 1868 act of Congress by dismissing a habeas appeal before it for want of jurisdiction, declared: "Without jurisdiction the court cannot proceed at all in any case. Jurisdiction is power to declare the law, and when it ceases to exist, the only function remaining to the court is that of announcing the fact and dismissing the cause." But even in McCardle it appears that the Court did indeed decide whether the congressional action was consistent with the Constitution. The Court noted, for example, in a preceding paragraph: "We are not at liberty to inquire into the motives of the legislature. We can only examine into its powers under the Constitution; and the power to make exceptions to the appellate jurisdiction of this court is given by express words." Id. at 514.

21. See, e.g., Hart, "The Power of Congress to Limit the Jurisdiction of Federal Courts: An Exercise in Dialectic," 66 Harv.L.Rev. 1362, 1387 (1953).

22. Marbury v. Madison, 5 U.S. (1 Cranch) 137, 178 (1803).

warrant strict scrutiny;[23] thus, if busing were demonstrably the only remedy to effectuate one's right not to attend a segregated school, federal legislation limiting judicial power to order busing as a remedy would appear highly suspect. Even the withdrawal of a gratuity— whether in the form of a welfare payment that a state is not independently required to make[24] or in the form of an extension of court jurisdiction that Congress is not independently compelled to provide— may be forbidden if it penalizes a separately secured right.[25] Congress, in short, is not entirely at liberty to create free-fire zones around currently unpopular constitutional rights.[26] Nevertheless, while these external constitutional precepts do constrain congressional jurisdictional manipulation to a considerable degree, those who would construe the analysis of jurisdictional limitation enactments as a mere subset of substantive constitutional analysis overlook the formidable—and in many cases, more relevant—internal limitations presented by article III itself.[27]

23. Shapiro v. Thompson, 394 U.S. 618, 629–31 (1969); United States v. Jackson, 390 U.S. 570, 581 (1968).

24. Thomas v. Review Bd. of Indiana Employment Security Div., 450 U.S. 707, 717–18 (1981); Memorial Hospital v. Maricopa County, 415 U.S. 250, 256–69 (1974); Shapiro v. Thompson, 394 U.S. 618, 634 (1969); Sherbert v. Verner, 374 U.S. 398, 404–07 (1963).

25. See, e.g., Frost v. Railroad Comm'n, 271 U.S. 583, 593–94 (1926) (terming it "inconceivable that guarantees embedded in the Constitution . . . may thus be manipulated out of existence"), quoted with approval in Western & So. Life Ins. Co. v. State Bd. of Equal. of Calif., 451 U.S. 648, 664–65 (1981). See § 11–5, infra.

26. Just as it would be impermissible for Congress to restrict access to federal courts to whites or to Democrats, so Congress may neither create special obstacles to those who assert certain rights nor steal the levers of federal judicial power from those who want to assert rights Congress disfavors. Cf. Hunter v. Erickson, 393 U.S. 385 (1969) (invalidating a city charter amendment that required special approval of all open housing ordinances). Indeed, withdrawing the protection of the federal government from some few rights may impermissibly *invite* private and even state actors, who know that federal relief cannot be obtained against them, to make the exercise of those rights more difficult. Such an attempt to insulate certain rights from meaningful vindication is clearly unconstitutional. See, e.g., Lynch v. United States, 189 F.2d 476, 479–80 (5th Cir. 1951), cert. denied 342 U.S. 831 (1951) (police guilty of "culpable official inaction" and held responsible for beating administered to prisoner by mob while police looked on passively); cf. Reitman v. Mulkey, 387 U.S.

369, 376–80 (1967) (state responsible for private discrimination that state had expressly immunized "from [official] censure or interference"); NAACP v. Alabama, 357 U.S. 449, 462–63 (1958) (state responsible for private injuries likely to be triggered when it withdraws protection of anonymity); Feiner v. New York, 340 U.S. 315, 326–27 (1951) (Black, J., dissenting) (state abridges speech if it fails to give speaker reasonable police protection from hostile audience); Miller v. Schoene, 276 U.S. 272, 279 (1928) (state failure to cut down diseased trees to protect more valuable crop, although an omission, would have been "none the less a choice").

27. In an essay written in the midst of the early 1980s jurisdiction-stripping campaign spearheaded by right wing legislators and lobbyists, the author of this treatise argued that most such legislation was vulnerable under the Bill of Rights because it burdened specified rights or rightholders. See Tribe, "Jurisdictional Gerrymandering: Zoning Disfavored Rights Out of the Federal Courts," 16 Harv.C.R.-C.L.Rev. 129 (1981). While that essay's external-limits challenge to that era's specific ideologically tinged bills seeking to restrict federal court jurisdiction in the areas of abortion, busing and school prayer may remain persuasive, the essay's broader attempt to impeach jurisdictional statutes under various Bill of Rights provisions seems in retrospect to have been somewhat overreaching. A congressional attempt to limit jurisdiction in a particular substantive area—say, abortion—seems less akin to a clearly unconstitutional decision to cut off food-stamp funding or other such benefits from those who receive abortions than to the more constitutionally ambiguous determination not to fund abortions while funding other childbirth

The limitations imposed by article III on the extent of permissible congressional jurisdictional regulation operate as a corollary of the separation of powers. Professor Henry Hart argued, for example, that with respect to the Supreme Court's appellate jurisdiction, article III prohibits Congress from making such exceptions "as will destroy the essential role of the Supreme Court in the constitutional plan." [28] Hart's thesis, of course, has never been put to the test. Most constitutional litigation in this context concerns a less dramatic issue: whether Congress, rather than withdrawing the jurisdiction of article III courts, may control the exercise of that jurisdiction by limiting the power of article III courts to judge independently the questions of law and fact in cases which come before them. [29]

options. For an elaboration on this distinction, see L. Tribe, Constitutional Choices 55–58 (1985). For a provocative critique of "Jurisdictional Gerrymandering," albeit one according Congress unduly sweeping powers, see Gunther, "Congressional Power to Curtail Federal Court Jurisdiction: An Opinionated Guide to the Ongoing Debate," 36 Stan.L.Rev. 895, 917–22 (1984). But cf. Bator, "Withdrawing Jurisdiction From Federal Courts," 7 Harv. J. Law & Pub. Pol'y 31 (1984) (arguing that, whatever the constitutionality of jurisdiction withdrawal, proposals like those of the early 1980s would strip the nation of the "authoritative law-giver" needed for a "viable society" and predicting that most state courts would continue to accept pre-existing Supreme Court decisions—even in areas like abortion from which federal jurisdiction had been removed—as binding precedent).

28. Hart, "The Power of Congress to Limit the Jurisdiction of Federal Courts: An Exercise in Dialectic," 66 Harv.L.Rev. 1362, 1402 (1953). Professor Hart's article is reprinted, and discussed in light of subsequent developments, in Hart & Wechsler, supra note 9 at 330–75.

29. A number of recent articles have provided a useful elaboration of various internal (and external) limitations on congressional control of federal court jurisdiction. See, e.g., Amar, supra note 2; Gunther, supra note 27; Ratner, "Majoritarian Constraints on Judicial Review: Congressional Control of Supreme Court Jurisdiction," 27 Vill.L.Rev. 929 (1982); Redish, "Constitutional Limitations on Congressional Power to Control Federal Jurisdiction: A Reaction to Professor Sager," 77 Nw.U.L.Rev. 143 (1982); Sager, "The Supreme Court, 1980 Term—Foreword: Constitutional Limitations on Congress' Authority to Regulate the Jurisdiction of the Federal Courts," 95 Harv.L.Rev. 17 (1981). See also Gunther, supra, at 896 n. 3 (collecting sources).

For a particularly provocative thesis on the limits set by article III on congressional jurisdiction withdrawal, see Brilmayer and Underhill, "Congressional Obligation to Provide a Forum for Constitutional Claims: Discriminatory Jurisdictional Rules and the Conflict of Laws," 69 Va.L. Rev. 819 (1983). Brilmayer's theory—one of the few original views advanced in recent years in this heavily written-about area—is that congressional statutes excluding from federal courts some or all claims *arising under the Constitution*, while including substantively parallel claims *arising under Acts of Congress*, discriminate against claims arising from a co-equal or higher source of law within the federal system in violation of a basic axiom requiring full interjurisdictional cooperation in that system: "[I]t is not clear why all independent sources of law within our federal system whose mandates are insulated from the control of the jurisdiction-determining legislature should not be protected in the same way as federal legislation or the legislation of another state. It is not dispositive that the independent source of rights is a text and not a legislative body because states must afford equal access to federal constitutional claims. Moreover, if a source of 'sovereignty' must be found before constitutional claims are entitled to equal access, one need only allude to the sovereignty of the people of the United States, which predates the sovereignty of Congress and is the foundation of *Marbury* itself." Id. at 832. One weakness of this intriguing conflict-of-laws approach to the jurisdictional gerrymandering issue is that it would leave Congress free to take such steps as "creat[ing] a federal statutory right to abortion in order [then] to strip federal courts of jurisdiction to hear abortion claims generally" without running afoul of the interjurisdictional-nondiscrimination axiom. Id. at 846 n. 133. The answer that Congress would be reluctant to "create a new [statutory] right to abortion enforceable in state courts" as a prel-

  Consistent with constitutional limitations, Congress clearly has authority to fix the rules of procedure, including rules of evidence, which article III courts must apply.[30] Again consistent with constitutional limitations, Congress also has authority to define by statute the substantive law which such courts are to enforce.[31] Nonetheless, the separation of powers does limit congressional regulation of the decision-making processes of article III courts at least this much: if Congress does not purport to alter the governing procedural and substantive law, Congress cannot force its interpretation of that law upon the federal courts in particular cases. The leading decision is *United States v. Klein*,[32] a case that arose in the cockpit of Reconstruction politics. By issuing a general pardon in 1868, President Johnson, among other things, made it possible for former adherents of the Confederacy to file claims with the federal government under a statute which authorized loyal citizens to obtain compensation for property abandoned to federal troops during the Civil War. Congress, not wishing to repeal the statute but desirous of denying its benefits to unreconstructed southerners, passed legislation which ordered the Court of Claims and the Supreme Court, in applying the statute, to treat the fact that an individual had accepted the pardon as conclusive evidence that the individual had given aid "to the Rebellion," but to ignore the pardon in deciding whether the individual affirmatively satisfied the loyalty requirement. Congress further provided that, on proof of pardon, a court should summarily dismiss for want of jurisdiction. The Supreme Court held the statute unconstitutional. Carefully distinguishing a case in which the Court had previously upheld a congressional statute legalizing a bridge that the court had declared illegal under prior law,[33] Chief Justice Chase's majority opinion concluded: "No arbitrary rule of decision was prescribed in that case, but the court was left to apply its ordinary rules to the new circumstances created by the act. In the case before us no new circumstances have been created by the legislation. But the court is forbidden to give the effect to evidence which, in its own judgment, such evidence should have, and is directed to give it an effect precisely the contrary. We must think that Congress has inadvertently passed the limit which separates the legislative from the judicial power."[34]

ude to excising abortion cases from federal courts, id., erroneously assumes that the hypothesized federal statutory right would not be limited from the outset to enforcement exclusively in federal courts. And the further answer that congressional enactment of federal statutory rights followed by jurisdiction-stripping measures would be subject to invalidation as impermissibly motivated, id., seems far too optimistic given the difficulty of establishing forbidden motive as a basis for invalidating congressional legislation. Cf. United States v. O'Brien, 391 U.S. 367 (1968).

30. See Hanna v. Plumer, 380 U.S. 460, 471–72 (1965): "the constitutional provision for a federal court system (augmented by the Necessary and Proper Clause) car-

ries with it congressional power to make rules governing the practice and pleading in those courts, which in turn includes a power to regulate matters which, though falling within the uncertain area between substance and procedure, are rationally capable of classification as either."

31. See generally Chapter 5, infra.

32. 80 U.S. (13 Wall.) 128 (1871).

33. Pennsylvania v. Wheeling & Belmont Bridge Co., 59 U.S. (18 How.) 421, 431–32 (1855).

34. 80 U.S. at 146–47. The legislation could not be upheld as a redefinition of the consequences of a pardon; as the Court noted, if viewed as such, "[t]he rule prescribed is also liable to just exception as

The exercise of jurisdiction can also be substantively controlled by channeling certain issues through non-article III tribunals. The Supreme Court has never definitively resolved how far Congress, in the exercise of the authority granted it by such provisions as article I, § 8, may create tribunals to resolve questions falling within the subject-matter jurisdiction of article III courts unencumbered by the tenure limitations and justiciability requirements of article III. Several early cases indicated that Congress possessed at least some flexibility. In *American Insurance Co. v. Canter*,[35] Chief Justice Marshall held that, "[a]lthough admiralty jurisdiction can be exercised in the states, in those courts only which are established in pursuance of the third article of the constitution," Congress could, in providing for a judicial system for the Florida territory, rely upon its power under article IV, § 3,[36] and allow the territorial legislature to lodge admiralty jurisdiction in courts not meeting article III tenure requirements. Justice Curtis, writing for a unanimous Court in *Murray's Lessee v. Hoboken Land and Improvement Co.*,[37] looked not to the terms of article III as such, but to the differing natures of the rights which federal courts enforced in the exercise of their jurisdiction, in order to define the scope of congressional power to substitute other tribunals for article III courts: "there are matters, involving public rights, which may be presented in such form that the judicial power is capable of acting on them, and which are susceptible of judicial determination, but which congress may or may not bring within the cognizance of the courts of the United States, as it may deem proper." But, Justice Curtis added, "we do not consider congress can either withdraw from judicial cognizance any matter which, from its nature, is the subject of a suit at common law, or in equity, or admiralty; nor on the other hand, can it bring under the judicial power a matter which, from its nature, is not a subject for judicial determination." [38]

Later cases, however, took as their premise a rigorous theory of the separation of powers: "a power definitely assigned by the Constitution to one department can neither be surrendered nor delegated by that department, nor vested by *statute* in another department or agency." [39] Accordingly, if judicial power fell within the ambit of an article III court, Congress could confer it only upon an article III court. "The provision of [article III, section 2] is that the 'judicial power shall extend' to the cases enumerated, and it logically follows that where jurisdiction over these cases is conferred upon the courts . . ., the judicial power . . . is, ipso facto, vested in such courts as inferior courts of the United States." [40] Conversely, if Congress could confer a judicial authority "upon an executive officer or administrative board, or an existing or specially constituted court, or retain [such authority] for

. . . infringing the constitutional power of the Executive." Id. at 147. See § 4–11, infra. Cf. § 10–4, infra.

35. 26 U.S. (1 Pet.) 511, 546 (1828).

36. "The Congress shall have Power to dispose of and make all needful Rules and Regulations respecting the Territory . . . belonging to the United States. . . ."

37. 59 U.S. (18 How.) 272, 284 (1855).

38. Id.

39. Williams v. United States, 289 U.S. 553, 580 (1933).

40. O'Donoghue v. United States, 289 U.S. 516, 545 (1933).

itself," it "follows indubitably that such power, in whatever guise or by whatever agency exercised, is no part of the judicial power vested in the constitutional courts by the third article." [41] Thus, while in *Canter* and *Murray's Lessee* the Supreme Court acknowledged the possibility of Congress at its discretion conferring certain judicial power within article III upon either article III courts or "legislative courts," these later decisions denied this possibility: "whether a court is of one class or the other" does not depend "on the intention of Congress"; "the true test lies in the power under which the court was created and the jurisdiction conferred." [42]

The Supreme Court's most recent decisions leave uncertain the extent to which this vision of a strict dichotomy between article III authority, exercised only by article III courts, and non-article III power, exercised almost always [43] by only "legislative" tribunals, continues to command the support of a majority of the Court. One line of modern cases returns to the approach of *Canter* and *Murray's Lessee*, at least insofar as it acknowledges the possibility that Congress may at its option confer judicial authority falling within the rubrics of article III upon either article III courts or legislative tribunals.[44] *Murray's Lessee*, however, also indicated that there were limits to congressional discretion, that at least certain kinds of cases arising under article III *had* to be decided by article III courts if they were to be decided at all. Accordingly, many of the Supreme Court's modern decisions continue to acknowledge that such a limitation constrains Congress,[45] although

41. Williams v. United States, 289 U.S. 553, 580–81 (1933); accord, Ex parte Bakelite Corp., 279 U.S. 438, 458–59 (1929).

42. Id. at 459.

43. In O'Donoghue v. United States, 289 U.S. 516 (1933), the Supreme Court had held that District of Columbia judges were article III judges, and thus exempt from a congressional pay reduction. The Court had little difficulty in finding that District of Columbia courts exercised article III power; unfortunately, however, these courts equally clearly performed various administrative functions. The Supreme Court accordingly ruled that District of Columbia courts, because Congress possessed both ordinary federal power and a general legislative authority within the district, could exercise simultaneously the powers of an article III court and of a state court—the latter powers including authority to act in a non-judicial capacity. See id. at 545–48. The other decisions of this era were more straightforward. See, e.g., Williams v. United States, 289 U.S. 553 (1933); Ex parte Bakelite Corp., 279 U.S. 438 (1929).

44. See, e.g., Palmore v. United States, 411 U.S. 389, 397–408 (1973); Glidden Co. v. Zdanok, 370 U.S. 530, 549–51 (1962) (opinion of Harlan, J.). In Palmore, the Supreme Court upheld the constitutionality of a reorganized District of Columbia court system, insofar as the reorganization conferred jurisdiction in some criminal matters upon article I courts. Accord, Swain v. Pressley, 430 U.S. 372 (1977). In Glidden, the Court held that the Court of Claims and the Court of Customs and Patent Appeals were indeed courts created under article III, and thus that their judges could validly sit by designation on United States District Courts and Courts of Appeals. Justice Harlan's plurality opinion treated the question as conceptually quite straightforward: "whether a tribunal is to be recognized as one created under Article III depends basically upon whether its establishing legislation complies with the limitations of that article; whether, in other words, its business is the federal business there specified and its judges and judgments are allowed the independence there expressly or impliedly made requisite." 370 U.S. at 552.

45. See, e.g., Northern Pipeline Construction Co. v. Marathon Pipe Line Co., 458 U.S. 50 (1982) (invalidating Bankruptcy Reform Act of 1978 because it unconstitutionally conferred article III judicial power upon bankruptcy court judges who lacked life tenure and protection against salary diminution), discussed infra; Glidden Co. v. Zdanok, 370 U.S. 530, 549 (1962) (opinion of Harlan, J.). The Palmore Court seemed to suggest a somewhat differ-

the precise nature and extent of that limitation remains a matter of considerable dispute.

The Court's first such modern case, *Crowell v. Benson*,[46] reinterpreted *Murray's Lessee* in a way which significantly limits the earlier case's contemporary significance. *Crowell* accomplished its limitation in two stages. *Murray's Lessee* defined those cases which were capable of adjudication only by article III courts as cases involving "any matter which, from its nature, is the subject of a suit at common law, or in equity, or in admiralty." The focus was on the subject-matter of the suit: if the dispute was one which a common law, equity, or admiralty court could hear, Congress had to confer federal jurisdiction to resolve the dispute on an article III court. In *Crowell*, however, Chief Justice Hughes redefined *Murray's Lessee's* core cases as those involving adjudication "of liability of one individual to another under the law as defined."[47] Form thus replaced substance: Congress could avoid conferring jurisdiction upon an article III court simply by altering the party structure in its new action, by replacing the private plaintiff with a government prosecutor.[48] Yet judicial review of agency determinations of questions of law is said to be constitutionally required.[49] This limitation is not universally observed in practice: there is no article III judicial review, for example, of most questions of law decided by military courts.[50] Moreover, the issue has not been recently litigated since the principal administrative procedure statutes provide for such review.[51] Nonetheless, the consensus remains.

In *Crowell*, Chief Justice Hughes said that article III required federal courts to retain power of review over two kinds of factual questions: questions of jurisdictional fact, facts whose "existence is a condition precedent to the operation of the statutory scheme";[52] and questions of constitutional fact, facts which courts, in order to insure protection of constitutional rights, must independently determine. The Hughes opinion, although initially treating the "jurisdictional fact" and "constitutional fact" limitations as distinct, blurred the two limitations

ent limitation: "the requirements of Art. III, which are applicable where laws of national applicability and affairs of national concern are at stake, must in proper circumstances give way to accommodate plenary grants of power to Congress to legislate with respect to specialized areas having particularized needs and warranting distinctive treatment." Palmore v. United States, 411 U.S. 389, 407–08 (1973).

46. 285 U.S. 22 (1932).

47. Id. at 51.

48. Cf. Atlas Roofing Co., Inc. v. Occupational Safety and Health Review Comm'n, 430 U.S. 442 (1977) (no seventh amendment right to jury trial in government initiated penalty proceeding paralleling common law private litigation remedies).

49. "The supremacy of law demands that there shall be an opportunity to have some court decide whether an erroneous rule of law was applied. . . ." St. Joseph Stock Yards Co. v. United States, 298 U.S. 38, 84 (1936) (Brandeis, J., concurring).

50. The writ of habeas corpus provides the chief vehicle for article III judicial review in this area; on habeas, federal courts reviewing the judgments of military courts concern themselves with questions of jurisdiction, and also with questions of constitutionality to which the military court did not give fair consideration. See Burns v. Wilson, 346 U.S. 137 (1953); "Developments in the Law—Habeas Corpus," 83 Harv.L.Rev. 1058, 1216–26 (1970).

51. See, e.g., 5 U.S.C. § 706.

52. 285 U.S. at 54.

in subsequent discussion.[53]   Since *Crowell*, the idea that article III requires federal courts to review de novo agency determinations of questions of "jurisdictional fact" has fallen into desuetude.[54]   The alternative view which Justice Brandeis developed in dissent appears more accurately to reflect the present state of the law: "If there be any controversy to which the judicial power extends that may not be subjected to the conclusive determination of administrative bodies or federal legislative courts, it is not because of any prohibition against the diminution of the jurisdiction of the federal district courts as such, but because, under certain circumstances, the constitutional requirement of due process is a requirement of judicial process." [55]   Independent judicial fact-finding is generally seen as mandatory today only insofar as it is implied by those constitutional rights, such as the right of free speech,[56] in which administrative discretion may itself be an impediment to the right's exercise.[57]

The 1982 case of *Northern Pipeline Construction Co. v. Marathon Pipe Line Co.*[58] strongly echoed *Crowell*'s admonition that the Constitution channels certain types of cases exclusively to article III courts.   At the time it was handed down, *Marathon* clearly seemed to signal that the Court was adopting a formalistic conception of the limits imposed by article III, § 1—one that would threaten to hamstring, in the name of separation of powers, politically innovative schemes of the sort that may well be essential to the functioning of an ambitious government. In *Marathon*, the Supreme Court invalidated the Bankruptcy Act of 1978, holding that the act unconstitutionally granted article III judicial power to bankruptcy court judges who lacked life tenure and protection against salary diminution.   The Court found itself of two minds.   The plurality, led by Justice Brennan,[59] attempted to impose order on the confused and confusing constitutional history of article III by cramming exceptions to article III into three pigeonholes and invalidating any legislation (like the Bankruptcy Act) that did not fit.   Justice White, writing for the three dissenters,[60] surveyed the Court's scattered precedents and found them to be little more than "landmarks on a judicial 'darkling plain' where ignorant armies have clashed by night." [61]   Accordingly, the dissenters advocated a more functional application of article III, concluding that the Court should read Article III "as expressing one value that must be balanced against competing constitutional values and legislative responsibilities." [62]

The plurality opinion took as its touchstone the "inexorable command" of article III, § 1, that the judicial power of the United States

53. See id. at 56.

54. See 4 K. Davis, Administrative Law Treatise, § 29.08 (1958).

55. 285 U.S. at 86–87 (Brandeis, J., dissenting).

56. See § 12–37, infra.

57. Cf. § 10–18, infra.

58. 458 U.S. 50 (1982).

59. He was joined by Justices Marshall, Blackmun and Stevens.   Justices Rehn-

quist and O'Connor concurred in the result.

60. He was joined by Chief Justice Burger and Justice Powell.

61. Justice Rehnquist so characterized the dissent in his concurring opinion, 458 U.S. at 91.

62. 458 U.S. at 113 (White, J., dissenting).

may be exercised only by judges having both life tenure and irreducible salaries.[63] By retreating to the Constitution's text and even the Declaration of Independence [64] for pristine proclamations of judicial independence which had long since been sullied,[65] the plurality overlooked the confusion that has reigned in this field since Chief Justice Marshall's problematic opinion in *Canter*. Justice Brennan refused to acknowledge that any significant erosion of the tenure and salary protections had occurred since the "late colonial period," [66] and insisted that all of the cases in which the Court has sanctioned exceptions to article III belong to three narrow categories of "exceptional" grants of power to the executive and legislative branches.[67] The non-article III courts of the territories [68] and the District of Columbia [69] are authorized by the "extraordinary control" over these geographical areas given Congress by article IV, § 3, Cl. 2, and article I, § 8, Cl. 17, respectively.[70] And the establishment by Congress and the executive of courts-martial [71] is authorized by the special military powers conferred by article I, § 8, Cl. 13 and 14, and article II, § 2, Cl. 1.[72] Finally, the legislative courts and administrative agencies that adjudicate matters involving public rather than private rights [73] are created pursuant to the "exceptional power[ ] bestowed upon Congress by . . . historical consensus." [74]

The plurality argued that, since the bankruptcy courts "do not lie exclusively outside the States of the Federal Union," nor "bear any resemblance to courts-martial," they do not fit into either of the first two pigeonholes.[75] And, since the substantive legal right at issue in the *Marathon* case was not the "restructuring of debtor-creditor relations" under the federal bankruptcy clause [76]—which the plurality said is arguably a matter of "public" rights—but, rather, Northern's *state*-created right to sue Marathon for breaches of contract and warranty in order to augment its estate, the public rights exception provides no

---

63. 458 U.S. at 58–59.

64. Id. at 60.

65. It is settled, for example, that Congress may decide, in its unfettered discretion, whether or not to award cost-of-living salary increases to federal judges so as to prevent inflation from working de facto reductions in the salaries of such judges— so long as, having enacted a salary increase, Congress does not then repeal any such increase after the date on which it was scheduled to go into effect. See United States v. Will, 449 U.S. 200 (1980) (striking down retroactive repeals but upholding repeals whose effective date fell *prior* to the effective date of the scheduled salary increase). Arguably, the bill of attainder clause, article I, § 9, cl. 3, as well as article III, continue to protect *individual* federal judges even from *prospective* repeals targeted at identifiable judges; but the holding of *Will*, in which the Court's justices were required to rule on the validity of measures affecting their own compensation, leaves Congress free—both by calculated omission and by prospective rescission—to retaliate against the federal

judiciary as a whole for a corpus of decisions with which Congress is displeased.

66. 458 U.S. at 59.

67. Id. at 64.

68. See American Insurance Co. v. Canter, 26 U.S. (1 Pet.) 511 (1828).

69. See, e.g., Palmore v. United States, 411 U.S. 389 (1973).

70. 458 U.S. at 64–65.

71. See, e.g., Dynes v. Hoover, 61 U.S. (20 How.) 65 (1857); Burns v. Wilson, 346 U.S. 137 (1953).

72. 458 U.S. at 66.

73. See, e.g., Murray's Lessee v. Hoboken Land & Improvement Co., 59 U.S. (18 How.) 272 (1855); Ex parte Bakelite Corp., 279 U.S. 438 (1929); Crowell v. Benson, 285 U.S. 22 (1932); Atlas Roofing Co. v. Occupational Safety & Health Comm'n., 430 U.S. 442 (1977).

74. 458 U.S. at 70.

75. Id. at 71.

76. U.S. Const., art. I, § 8, cl. 4.

haven either.[77] Therefore, Justice Brennan concluded, the exercise of jurisdiction over Northern's contract claims by the "adjunct" bankruptcy court violated article III.[78]

The dissent argued that the principles underlying the three categories of exceptions to article III complement each other; "together they cover virtually the whole domain of possible areas of adjudication." [79] A major problem is that, because the *Marathon* plurality adduced no unifying principle for its three exceptions, there is no reason to assume that its laundry list of acceptable non-article III courts is exhaustive— that the list may not sprout additions on command.

The plurality sought to link its three pigeonholes into a single unit by arguing that exceptions to article III's "inexorable command" are recognized by the Court in the three situations it identified only because of "certain exceptional powers bestowed upon Congress by the Constitution or by historical consensus." [80] Justice Brennan admitted that these extraordinary grants are nowhere to be found in the constitutional text, but insisted that they are "firmly established in our historical understanding of the constitutional structure." [81] But the plurality's "historical consensus" is little more than a grudging acceptance of precedents too ingrained in our governmental apparatus to be exorcised at this late date, and its "unifying principle" is but an adamant refusal to tolerate still more exceptions to article III. The plurality simply put its foot down and cried, "Enough!" If the bankruptcy courts will not fit comfortably into the plurality's procrustean bed, then they must be dismissed.[82]

In the years since *Marathon*, the Court has twice handed down decisions dealing with "legislative courts" that strongly questioned the formalistic approach of Justice Brennan's opinion in *Marathon*. In the 1985 case of *Thomas v. Union Carbide Agricultural Products Co.*,[83] a unanimous Court upheld the 1978 amendments to the Federal Insecti-

---

77. 458 U.S. at 71.

78. The plurality found it significant that Congress constituted the bankruptcy courts as "adjuncts" to the district courts and not as legislative courts, 458 U.S. at 63 n. 13, and chided the dissenters for not appreciating the distinction. Id. at 77 n. 29. The plurality concluded that the bankruptcy court was in fact a "non-Art. III adjunct." Id. at 87. It may be ill-advised to take the plurality's taxonomic distinctions too seriously, since it had difficulty in using its own vocabulary precisely; the administrative entity in Crowell v. Benson, 285 U.S. 22 (1932), is variously referred to as a "legislative court," id. at 72, an "administrative agency," id. at 78, and an "adjunct," id. at 77. For an amusing variation on the immortal question, "What's in a name?" see "Federal Jurisdiction Haiku," 32 Stan.L.Rev. 229, 230 (1979): "Legislative Courts/Are but agencies in drag;/Glidden is but paint" (K. Karst).

79. 458 U.S. at 105. If one adds the three exceptions together, rather than subtracting them seriatim from article III, one discovers that the plurality has put its stamp of approval on article I courts which "operate throughout the country" (administrative agencies), "adjudicate both private and public rights" (courts of the territories and the District of Columbia), and adjudicate matters in "areas in which congressional control is 'extraordinary'" (courts-martial and the D.C. courts). Id. Justice White found it impossible to distinguish the last category from "the general 'arising under' jurisdiction of Art. III courts." Id.

80. Id. at 70.

81. Id. at 70 n. 25. This reliance on history seems ironic in an opinion that goes to such lengths to paper over inconsistencies and reversals in the case law.

82. For a more detailed discussion of the formalism seemingly enshrined by Marathon, see L. Tribe, Constitutional Choices 84–98 (1985).

83. 473 U.S. 568 (1985).

cide, Fungicide, and Rodenticide Act against a claim—accepted by a federal district court below—that the statute's binding arbitration provision violated article III. Justice O'Connor's opinion for the Court held that article III does not prevent Congress from selecting binding arbitration with only limited judicial review as the mechanism for resolving disputes among participants in the act's pesticide registration scheme.[84] The Court in *Thomas* pointedly limited *Marathon* as a case involving a "traditional contract action[ ] arising under state law, without consent of the litigants," [85] and further observed that Justice Brennan's dichotomy in *Marathon* between public and private rights did not command a majority of the Court in that case.[86] In short, the Court concluded, "practical attention to substance rather than doctrinaire reliance on formal categories should inform application of Article III." [87] Accordingly, the insecticide act's important public purpose of safeguarding health, its pragmatic attempt to contain burgeoning litigation costs, and the internal sanctions built into the act, militated in favor of its validity.[88]

A more damaging salvo was fired at *Marathon* the next year in *Commodity Futures Trading Commission (CFTC) v. Schor*.[89] In *CFTC*, the Court, again speaking through Justice O'Connor, upheld against an article III challenge the Commodity Exchange Act's delegation to the Commodity Futures Trading Commission of power to entertain state law counterclaims in reparation proceedings. Besides affirming *Thomas'* rejection of the use of "formal categories," [90] the *CFTC* majority also concluded that article III's guarantee "serves to protect primarily personal, rather than structural interests" [91]—a refutation of a key tenet of Justice Brennan's *Marathon* opinion. Under the facts of *CFTC*, the majority held that the particular claimant, a futures customer, had "indisputably waived" any right to a full trial of his broker's counterclaims against him in an article III court.[92] Moreover, to the extent that article III does serve as an element in the constitutional system of checks and balances, the Court concluded that the congressional scheme allocating powers between the CFTC and article III courts "does not impermissibly intrude on the province of the judiciary." [93] In particular, the Court observed, the CFTC's adjudicatory

---

84. Id. at 582–93.

85. Id. at 584.

86. Id. at 585–86.

87. Id.

88. Id. at 589–93. The Court also noted that the insecticide act did not fully preclude review by an article III tribunal, asserting that "at a minimum" the act permitted review of an arbitrator's findings for fraud, misconduct, or misrepresentation, id. at 592, and to correct constitutional errors. Id.

Justice Brennan's concurrence, joined by Justices Marshall and Blackmun, reaffirmed his Marathon analysis. He distinguished Thomas as a "public rights" case "arising entirely within the confines" of a federal regulatory statute, noting that "a

proper interpretation of article III affords the federal government substantial flexibility to rely on administrative tribunals." Id. at 599.

89. 106 S.Ct. 3245 (1986).

90. Id. at 3256, 3258.

91. Id.

92. Id. at 3258.

93. Id. Justice O'Connor emphasized that courts evaluating article III challenges should look to a variety of factors, including "the extent to which the 'essential attributes of judicial power' are reserved to article III courts," the extent to which the non-article III forum exercises the range of jurisdiction and powers normally vested only in article III courts, the origins and importance of the right to be

powers were strikingly similar to those embodied in the "traditional agency model," differing only in that the CFTC possessed jurisdiction over common law counterclaims. While conceding that giving agencies wholesale control of pendent or ancillary jurisdiction could create constitutional difficulties, the *CFTC* Court held that the "single deviation" in the particular case—the counterclaim jurisdiction—carried with it "little practical reason" for judicial invalidation.[94] The Court also emphasized that the choice of the CFTC forum was not statutorily required but rather "left entirely to the parties"—a situation in which the Court deemed separation of powers concerns to be diminished.[95] Finally, the Court observed the practical value of the CFTC's counterclaim jurisdiction, which, it emphasized, "is incidental to, and completely dependent upon, adjudications of reparations claims created by federal law."[96] Justice Brennan's dissent, joined by Justice Marshall, charged the majority with eroding article III's mandate and of "abdicat[ing] to claims of legislative convenience."[97] The dissent charged that the Court's balancing test "pits an interest the benefits of which are immediate, concrete and easily understood against one, the benefits of which are almost entirely prophylactic, and thus often seem remote and not worth the cost in any single case."[98]

The Supreme Court's decisions concerning the relationship between article III courts and the military justice system illustrate the "rights"-based approach sanctioned in *Crowell* and perpetuated in *Marathon*. Article I, § 8 authorizes Congress "[t]o make Rules for the Government and Regulation of the land and naval Forces." As the Supreme Court long ago recognized in *Dynes v. Hoover*,[99] this constitutional grant of authority empowers Congress "to provide for the trial and punishment of military and naval officers in the manner then and now practiced by civilized nations; . . . the power to do so is given without any connection between it and the 3rd article of the Constitution defining the judicial power of the United States." Congress has exercised this power to establish a system of military justice which in many ways "exists separate and apart from the law which governs in our federal judicial establishment."[100] Because "it is the primary business of armies and navies to fight or be ready to fight wars should the occasion arise,"[101] inevitably the military has become "a specialized society separate from civilian society."[102] As the Supreme Court noted in *Parker v. Levy*, the Code of Military Justice "cannot be equated to a

---

adjudicated, and the concerns animating Congress's departure from the requirements of article III. Id.

94. Id.

95. Id. at 3260.

96. Id.

97. Id. at 3264 (Brennan, J., dissenting).

98. Id. The dissent added that "[t]he danger of the Court's balancing approach is, of course, that as individual cases accumulate in which the Court finds that the short-term benefits of efficiency outweigh the long-term benefits of judicial independence, the protections of article III may well be eviscerated." Id. See Strauss, "Formal and Functional Approaches to Separation-of-Powers Questions—A Foolish Consistency?" 72 Cornell L.Rev. 488, 502–26 (1987).

99. 61 U.S. (20 How.) 65, 79 (1858).

100. Burns v. Wilson, 346 U.S. 137, 140 (1953).

101. United States ex rel. Toth v. Quarles, 350 U.S. 11, 17 (1955).

102. Parker v. Levy, 417 U.S. 733, 743 (1974).

civilian criminal code. . . . While a civilian criminal code carves out a relatively small segment of potential conduct and declares it criminal, the Uniform Code of Military Justice essays more varied regulation of a much larger segment of the activities of the more tightly knit military community." [103]

The distinct character of military justice is reflected not only substantively but procedurally. The fifth amendment exempts "cases arising in the land or naval forces, or in the Militia, when in actual service in time of War or public danger" from its requirement of grand jury indictment as a condition precedent to federal criminal prosecution. The Supreme Court stated in *Ex parte Milligan* that "the framers of the Constitution, doubtless, meant to limit the right of trial by jury, in the Sixth Amendment, to those persons who were subject to indictment or presentment in the fifth." [104] More generally, the Court suggested in *Ex parte Quirin* that " 'cases arising in the land or naval forces' . . . are deemed excepted by implication" from the sixth amendment. [105] The Court has not in recent years confirmed the *Milligan* and *Quirin* dicta, but it has held, in *Middendorf v. Henry*, [106] that there is no sixth amendment right to counsel in summary court-martial proceedings notwithstanding the fact that, under *Argersinger v. Hamlin*, [107] such a right would exist in a civilian misdemeanor trial if that trial, like a summary court-martial proceeding, would result in a defendant's imprisonment. The fifth amendment due process clause does apply in the military context. But as the *Middendorf* Court demonstrated, the procedural limitations imposed by due process are flexible, and thus subject to relaxation when courts find the need for procedural protections outweighed by the exigencies of military life. [108] Although the Supreme Court has not yet decided what procedural rights due process requires in the military context, the Court's current interest-balancing approach [109] may yield a constitutional requirement which would tolerate the traditionally "rough form of justice" which has characterized military justice, "emphasizing summary procedures, speedy convictions and stern penalties with a view to maintaining obedience and fighting fitness in the ranks." [110]

Until 1983, Congress had never granted the Supreme Court "appellate jurisdiction to supervise the administration of criminal justice in the military." [111] Nor do any other article III courts directly review the judgments of military courts. In any event, "[t]he valid, final judg-

103. Id. at 749–51. For a discussion of this case and others treating the closed nature of military society as a justification for restricting first amendment rights, see §§ 12–24, 12–32, infra.

104. 71 U.S. (4 Wall.) 2, 123 (1867) (dictum).

105. 317 U.S. 1, 40 (1942) (dictum).

106. 425 U.S. 25 (1976).

107. 407 U.S. 25 (1972).

108. See 425 U.S. at 43–48.

109. See § 10–13, infra.

110. Reid v. Covert, 354 U.S. 1, 35–36 (1957).

111. Noyd v. Bond, 395 U.S. 683, 694 (1969). The Military Justice Act of 1983, P.L. 28–209, provides in 28 U.S.C. § 1259 for certiorari review by the Supreme Court in certain cases from the Court of Military Appeals. See Boskey & Gressman, "The Supreme Court's New Certiorari Jurisdiction Over Military Appeals," 102 F.R.D. 329 (1984). The new provision is limited in scope and works no basic alteration in the basic fabric of the pre-1983 law, as set forth infra.

ments of military courts, like those of any court of competent jurisdiction not subject to direct review for errors of fact or law, have res judicata effect and preclude further litigation of the merits." [112] Article III courts, however, do have jurisdiction to hear collateral attacks on the jurisdiction of military courts-martial. The writ of habeas corpus is the ordinary procedural vehicle for such collateral attack, but the Supreme Court has held that military jurisdiction may also be questioned in a suit for damages or for equitable relief.[113] Indeed, the Court has repeatedly held that there are constitutional limits on the jurisdiction of courts-martial, restrictions which draw their force from the fact that courts-martial do not afford defendants the procedural rights which the Constitution guarantees in article III proceedings. Thus, the Court has held that, even in wartime, military officials cannot try civilians in military courts for offenses committed within the United States and its territories if civilian courts are operating.[114] "Martial rule can never exist where courts are open, and in the proper and unobstructed exercise of their jurisdiction. It is also confined to the locality of actual war." [115]

In peacetime, there are further constitutional limits on the jurisdiction of military courts. Courts-martial cannot be given jurisdiction, even abroad, over civilian dependents of military personnel [116] or over civilian employees of the military forces.[117] Moreover, at least in peacetime, courts-martial do not even possess complete jurisdiction over military personnel. Courts-martial cannot try individuals for violations of military law, even if the individuals were members of the military at the time of such violations, if by the time military officials initiate proceedings the individuals have returned to civilian life.[118] However, courts-martial may exercise jurisdiction over members of the armed forces, even in peacetime, whether or not the crime is "service-connected," i.e., involves a "question of the flouting of military authority, the security of a military post, or the integrity of military property." [119]

Until recently, the Supreme Court had not required individuals who challenge the constitutional jurisdiction of military courts to exhaust military remedies before seeking collateral relief in article III

---

112. Schlesinger v. Councilman, 420 U.S. 738, 746 (1975).

113. See id. at 747–48.

114. See Duncan v. Kahanamoku, 327 U.S. 304 (1946); Ex parte Milligan, 71 U.S. (4 Wall.) 2 (1866).

115. Id. at 127. The only exception to this rule concerns enemy combatants. During wartime, court-martial jurisdiction extends to acts of espionage and sabotage by enemy agents, even if the agents are American citizens. Ex parte Quirin, 317 U.S. 1 (1942). At least if enemy combatants are not American citizens, military courts may retain jurisdiction to try such combatants for wartime activities even after hostilities cease. In re Yamashita, 327 U.S. 1 (1946).

116. Kinsella v. United States ex rel. Singleton, 361 U.S. 234 (1960); Reid v. Covert, 354 U.S. 1 (1957).

117. McElroy v. United States ex rel. Guagliardo, 361 U.S. 281 (1960); Grisham v. Hagen, 361 U.S. 278 (1960).

118. United States ex rel. Toth v. Quarles, 350 U.S. 11 (1955).

119. O'Callahan v. Parker, 395 U.S. 258, 274 (1969) (requiring service connection), was overruled in Solorio v. United States, 107 S.Ct. 2924 (1987), in an opinion by Chief Justice Rehnquist, over the dissents of Justices Brennan, Marshall, and Blackmun.

courts.[120] This departure from usual exhaustion rules is not surprising: in raising the question of constitutional jurisdiction, individuals are invoking limits which have their origin in a constitutional recognition of the defects of military procedure; it would thus be "especially unfair to require exhaustion of military remedies when the complainants raised substantial arguments denying the right of the military to try them at all." [121] The Supreme Court's decision in *Schlesinger v. Councilman*,[122] however, indicates that the Court may no longer adhere to the traditional approach in these matters. There, a serviceman subject to court-martial for possession of marijuana sought a federal district court injunction halting the court-martial proceedings on the then relevant ground that his offense was not service-connected. The Supreme Court, drawing by analogy on the doctrine limiting the power of federal courts to enjoin *state* judicial proceedings,[123] held that the serviceman could seek collateral relief in an article III court only after exhausting remedies within the military justice system. Justice Powell's majority opinion distinguished prior cases which found no need for exhaustion on the ground that there "petitioners were *civilians* who contended that Congress had no constitutional power to subject them to the jurisdiction of courts-martial." [124] In such cases the question was constitutional as well as jurisdictional and "turned on the status of the persons as to whom the military asserted its power." [125]

§ 3–6. The Antimajoritarian Difficulty Reexamined

As we saw in Chapter 1, arguments about the legitimacy of judicial review are ultimately metaconstitutional: the relevant considerations are political, philosophical, and historical in the broadest sense. It would be remarkable if factors of so inevitably general and speculative a nature could be fully represented within the parameters of constitutional argument as such. Constitutional law is not mathematics—but one must wonder why, if mathematicians in this post-Gödelian age treat as inevitable the fact that interesting logical systems are open-ended,[1] constitutional lawyers continue to demand that their universe of discourse be closed. It is nonetheless a fact that, particularly at one point in our constitutional history, in the late 1950s and early 1960s, many of the most prominent, and most skillful, constitutional theorists treated the question of the legitimacy of judicial review as itself the central problem of constitutional law.[2] The conclusions about constitu-

---

120. See McElroy v. United States ex rel. Guagliardo, 361 U.S. 281 (1960); Reid v. Covert, 354 U.S. 1 (1957); United States ex rel. Toth v. Quarles, 350 U.S. 11 (1955).

121. Noyd v. Bond, 395 U.S. 683, 696 n. 8 (1969).

122. 420 U.S. 738 (1975).

123. See § 3–30, infra.

124. 420 U.S. at 738.

125. Id. After Solorio, see note 119 supra, the constitutional irrelevance of service-connection makes personal status the *only* relevant factor. When Councilman was decided, however, service-connection

was no less a constitutional requirement than was military status. The Court's rationale was therefore unconvincing.

§ 3–6

1. See E. Nagel & J. Newman, Gödel's Proof (1958).

2. See, e.g., L. Hand, The Bill of Rights (1958); A. Bickel, The Least Dangerous Branch (1962); Wechsler, "Toward Neutral Principles of Constitutional Law," 73 Harv. L.Rev. 1 (1959). For a critical account of the ideas of these theorists, see Deutsch, "Neutrality, Legitimacy, and the Supreme Court: Some Intersections Between Law

tional law which these scholars drew from their analyses of the propriety of judicial review shaped their often critical response to the decisions
of the Warren Court.[3] These decisions, as subsequent chapters will
show, define the core of much of contemporary constitutional doctrine;
the Burger Court worked no counter-revolution.[4] Analysis of the
fundamental arguments of the classical critics is thus worthwhile both
for its own sake and as a preliminary step in the process of understanding current constitutional debate. But the analysis that follows will be
brief indeed; the subject is beyond the scope of an essentially doctrinal
treatise.

The critics start from the assumption that, in a political society
which aspires to representative democracy or at least to popular representation, exercises of power which cannot find their justification in the
ultimate consent of the governed are difficult, if not impossible, to
justify. Judicial review is thus immediately and doubly suspect. The
judges who declare statutes and executive actions to be unconstitutional
do not acquire their positions through popular election; once appointed,
they cease to be accountable even to the elected officials who nominated
and confirmed them but rather are secured in their independence by
life tenure and guaranteed salary.[5] Perhaps even more significantly,
judicial review is itself said to be antidemocratic since its result is the
invalidation of government action, legislative or executive—action that,
however indirectly, did have the sanction of the electorate. It is
obvious, the critics argue, that if judicial review cuts against the grain
of representative democracy, judges should invoke their power to strike
down legislative and executive action only sparingly. Programmatic
and protracted courses of constitutional adjudication are to be avoided;
such campaigns, as the history of the Supreme Court's economic due
process era shows, call public attention to the judiciary's antidemocratic character and inevitably transform a theoretical problem of legitimacy into a real one, a problem for which the political process suggests no
obvious solution and thus a problem which ultimately ends in crisis.
And, even when crisis is avoided, the most far-reaching decisions of the
Court are said to sap the body politic of the will to seek truly meaningful reform: symbolic victories in the Court replace real victories in life.

and Political Science," 20 Stan.L.Rev. 169
(1968). The 1980s have witnessed a rebirth of interest in these matters—a renaissance more voluminous than illuminating. The literature is ably canvassed in
Fallon, "A Constructivist Coherence Theory of Constitutional Interpretation," 100
Harv.L.Rev. 1189, 1194–1231 (1987).

3. See, e.g., A. Bickel, The Supreme
Court and the Idea of Progress (1970);
Wechsler, supra note 2, at 26–35. The
critical reaction to the Warren Court is
also notably revealed in the Forewords accompanying the annual surveys of Supreme Court decisions found in volumes 73
to 79 of the Harvard Law Review and in
the volumes of the Supreme Court Review
edited by Professor Philip Kurland during

the Warren era. The response of these
critics to the Warren Court is itself criti-
cized in Wright, "Professor Bickel, The
Scholarly Tradition, and the Supreme
Court," 84 Harv.L.Rev. 769 (1971), and in
Linde, "Judges, Critics, and the Realist
Tradition," 82 Yale L.J. 227 (1972). The
Burger Court, especially because of Roe v.
Wade, 410 U.S. 113 (1973), has not escaped
similar criticism. See, e.g., J. Ely, Democ-
racy and Distrust (1980).

4. See, e.g., The Burger Court: The
Counter-Revolution That Wasn't (1983) (V.
Blasi ed.).

5. See generally L. Tribe, God Save
This Honorable Court (1985).

One school of thought among the critics also holds that, if judicial review is not itself democratic, it should nonetheless link itself to public consent in some way. The medium, it turns out, is the Constitution itself: the constitutional text, even if not put to the test of repeated public approval, is nonetheless a product of a political process of ratification. If constitutional decisions are truly grounded in the Constitution, therefore, they may claim a measure of democratic legitimacy notwithstanding the antidemocratic character of the judiciary responsible for these decisions. This point of view seeks to reduce the role of judges in the process of constitutional review by holding judges to a method of reasoning which, as much as possible, moves from constitutional text and history to the result in the case at hand without intervening value judgments.

Another school of thought likewise seeks to assimilate judicial review to a political consensus, but there the resemblance ends. This alternative point of view would ground constitutional adjudication in a present consensus, and not in the historical consent of "We the People" which underlies the Constitution itself. On this view, judges should constantly maneuver to minimize the discrepancy between their decisions and the popular will. Plainly, there will be times when unpopular constitutional adjudication is necessary; but courts should husband their reserves of good will in order to provide for such rare occasions. Courts should treat their dockets as discretionary in order to be in a position to avoid adjudicating a series of unpopular constitutional cases, and to seize whatever opportunities exist for popular adjudication. Moreover, even in deciding the merits of constitutional cases, courts should exercise discretion in order to take advantage of opportunities for resolving issues on nonconstitutional grounds or on constitutional bases which render unnecessary the articulation of controversial principles.

The foregoing, of course, is at best a cartoon; the arguments outlined here are, for the most part, stated in too stylized a form to be attributed to particular authors. The critics themselves developed their arguments in greater detail, in a more nuanced form, and in ways which combined aspects of the several divergent tendencies noted above. Nonetheless, even if a caricature, the summary just completed provides a basis for identifying the characteristic assumptions of the critics' arguments, and thus for developing a "criticism of the critics" which does not purport to be anything like a final evaluation but seeks at least to put the critics' arguments in context, and to suggest the foundations for alternative points of view.

Initially, the critics may be evaluated in their own terms. Their arguments rest ultimately upon a dichotomy between a democratic political process and an antidemocratic adjudicatory process.[6] It is this dichotomy which creates the problem of legitimacy for judicial review, and it is this dichotomy which the critics seek to bridge. A realistic analysis of judicial and political institutions, however, might suggest that the dichotomy is more metaphorical than real. Certainly, the

6. See Deutsch, supra note 2, at 185–87.

Constitution does provide for an independent judiciary, by granting article III judges a fixed salary and life tenure, and by making congressional removal, at least, quite difficult.[7] The process of appointment, however, is entirely political,[8] and the sometimes quite rapid turnover in the Supreme Court's membership suggests that the federal judiciary may be more capable of adapting to changes in the political consensus than the notion of an independent judiciary would immediately suggest. Moreover, it is not ultimately true that constitutional decisions are beyond the reach of democratic politics: there is, after all, the process of constitutional amendment, a process which is again almost purely political,[9] and which has in fact been used successfully on four (or

7. Judges sitting on courts constituted pursuant to article III are "civil officers of the United States" for purposes of article II, § 4, and thus may "be removed from office on Impeachment [by the House of Representatives] for and Conviction [by the Senate] of, Treason, Bribery, or other high Crimes and Misdemeanors." In the special case of federal judges, the Constitution additionally provides that such officers "shall hold their offices during good Behaviour." U.S. Const. article III, § 1. Both the historical bases, see R. Berger, Impeachment: The Constitutional Problems 130 (1973), and the current perceptions, see, e.g., 116 Cong.Rec. 11913 (1970) (remarks of then Representative Ford), of this special provision indicate that the "good behaviour" standard imposed by the Constitution on federal judges is higher than that constitutionally demanded of other civil officers. However, the only remedy explicitly provided by the Constitution for the removal of judges is the same procedurally cumbersome impeachment process as for other civil officers. See Note, "Removal of Judges—New Alternatives to an Old Problem: Chandler v. Judicial Council of the Tenth Circuit," 13 U.C.L.A.L.Rev. 1385, 1389 (1966). The impracticality of enforcing the "good behaviour" standard through the impeachment process has led to several suggestions of procedures less drastic and cumbersome by which to discipline federal judges. See, e.g., Stolz, "Disciplining Federal Judges: Is Impeachment Hopeless?" 57 Cal.L.Rev. 659 (1969); R. Berger, supra, at 174; Note, supra, at 1396; Shartel, "Federal Judges—Appointment, Supervision and Removal—Some Possibilities under the Constitution," 28 Mich.L.Rev. 870 (1930), discussed in Comment, 118 U.Pa.L. Rev. 1064, 1085–87 (1970). The debate over whether the Framers intended that the judiciary be able to discipline its own members continues. Compare R. Berger, supra, ch. III, with Ervin, "Separation of Powers: Judicial Independence," 35 Law & Contemp.Prob. 1081 (1970). But whatever the original intent, the continuing reluctance of Congress to attempt to provide any mode of removal other than impeach-

ment, see Kurland, "The Constitution and the Tenure of Federal Judges: Some Notes from History," 26 U.Chi.L.Rev. 665 (1969), may well indicate that the exclusivity of the impeachment process for removing federal judges sitting on article III courts is today regarded as a central constitutional safeguard of federal judicial independence. See id.

8. Initial responsibility for filling the judicial offices created by Congress is constitutionally delegated to the President who, according to article II, § 2, "shall nominate, and by and with the Advice and Consent of the Senate, shall appoint . . . Judges of the Supreme Court, and all other Officers of the United States, whose appointments are not herein otherwise provided for, and which shall be established by Law. . . ." It has generally been accepted that the Senate's power of "advice and consent" is formally limited to a veto. See 3 Ops.Atty.Gen'l. 188 (1837). But of course a formal power of veto increases presidential susceptibility to advice. See L. Tribe, God Save This Honorable Court (1985).

9. Article V provides in part: "The Congress, whenever two thirds of both Houses shall deem it necessary, shall propose Amendments to this Constitution or, on the Application of the Legislatures of two thirds of the several States, shall call a Convention for proposing Amendments, which, in either Case, shall be valid to all Intents, and Purposes, as Part of this Constitution, when ratified by the Legislatures of three fourths of the several States, or by Conventions in three fourths thereof, as the one or the other Mode of Ratification may be proposed by the Congress; Provided . . . that no State, without its Consent, shall be deprived of its equal Suffrage in the Senate." To date only Congress has proposed amendments to the Constitution, and all but one, the twenty-first, were ratified by the state legislature mode, rather than by conventions called in the states. See Special Constitutional Convention Study Committee of the American Bar Association, Amendment of the Constitution

perhaps five) occasions to override Supreme Court decisions.[10] More fundamentally if less dramatically, the Court's power to move beyond a current consensus is circumscribed by its institutional incapacity to lead where others are too reluctant to follow. If judicial review thus may be somewhat more democratic than its stereotype, it may also be true that the democracy of legislative and executive politics is overstated. The point does not require much development: the ways in which representative democracy in practice diverges from the ideal are well-known.[11] The result then is an imperfectly antidemocratic judicial process and an imperfectly democratic political process; the conclusion which this result suggests is that, *contra* the critics, it cannot be consent which is the sole touchstone of legitimacy.

Perhaps most fundamentally, the very idea of grounding the legitimacy of constitutional claims in the "consent" of the governed is problematically circular—and ungrounded. It is circular because it

By the Convention Method Under Article V (1971). But numerous state requests for conventions have been made to Congress at various times since 1789; for a full compilation and discussion, see id. at 59–77.

The Supreme Court has indicated that the process by which an amendment is proposed and ratified is committed exclusively to the control of Congress, and therefore that the constitutional validity of particular elements of that process are not ordinarily susceptible to judicial determination by an article III court. Thus, in Coleman v. Miller, 307 U.S. 433 (1939), the efficacy of ratification of a proposed amendment by a state legislature which had previously rejected the proposal was deemed a "political question" for Congress and not the Supreme Court to resolve. See § 3–13, infra. It should be noted, however, that even "exclusive" control by Congress over the process of ratification (and presumably that of convention-calling) need not preclude congressional provision for Supreme Court review of challenged procedures or actions in order to lend legitimacy and impartiality to amendment processes, particularly with respect to the not-yet used convention mode of amendment. See Special Study, supra, at 24. A few Supreme Court decisions have already passed on aspects of the amendment process. In United States v. Sprague, 282 U.S. 716 (1931), the Court rejected a claim that, because the eighteenth amendment conferred "on the United States new direct powers over individuals," the amendment could be ratified only by state conventions, rather than by state legislatures: "The choice . . . of the mode of ratification lies within the sole discretion of Congress." Id. at 730. Similarly, in Hawke v. Smith, 253 U.S. 221 (1920), the Court held that, where Congress has required that an amendment be ratified by the state legislatures, a provision of a state constitution requiring that the amendment be submitted to a general referendum is without effect. Finding that an amendment's "ratification must be within some reasonable time after the proposal," the Supreme Court, in Dillon v. Gloss, 256 U.S. 368 (1921), held that Congress could limit the time for ratification of the eighteenth amendment to seven years. To the extent that Dillon implies a judicial power to review congressional determination of "subsidiary matters of detail," the Court's dictum that the time limit must be "reasonable" is open to doubt in the wake of Coleman v. Miller, supra.

10. See U.S. Const. amend. XI (limiting jurisdiction of federal courts, contra prior broad interpretation in Chisholm v. Georgia, 2 U.S. (2 Dall.) 419 (1793), to hear suits brought against states without states' consent); id. amend. XIV, § 1 (nullifying decision in Scott v. Sandford, 60 U.S. (19 How.) 393 (1856), that Americans of African descent, whether slave or free, could not be deemed citizens of United States); id. amend. XVI (nullifying decision in Pollock v. Farmers' Loan and Trust Co., 157 U.S. 429 (1895), holding federal income tax unconstitutional unless apportioned); id. amend. XXVI (nullifying decision in Oregon v. Mitchell, 400 U.S. 112 (1970), that Congress was without power to set voting age in state elections; the amendment set the age itself—eighteen). See also id. amend. XIX (reversing decision in Minor v. Happersett, 88 U.S. (21 Wall.) 162 (1874), that women may be denied the vote). Unlike the other amendments noted here, the 19th, ratified in 1920, was not widely perceived as a reaction to a specific court decision.

11. See, e.g., M. Shapiro, Freedom of Speech: The Supreme Court and Judicial Review 32 (1966). On the non-existence of *any* satisfactory form of representation, see § 1–7, note 6, supra.

leaves unanswered the question of *whose* consent counts [12] and *what* the consent encompasses. And it is ungrounded because it *assumes*, without any necessary basis in the Constitution itself, that "consent" is what matters.

The implications of these conclusions can be developed by assessing the critics' position in light of this chapter's preceding sections. The fact of congressional control of the jurisdiction of article III courts, considered in § 3–5, further blurs the distinction between an antidemocratic judiciary and a democratic political process: the federal courts are in a position to exercise their antimajoritarian power because a majoritarian Congress put them there. The idea of an indeterminate Constitution—the necessary corollary of the fact, considered in § 3–4, that constitutional adjudication is not an inevitable bar to congressional, executive, or state constitutional interpretations differing from the interpretation of the courts—suggests a further point: some of the critics, at least, assume that constitutional interpretation is the unique prerogative of the judiciary; if instead the political branches may participate in the process of constitutional interpretation,[13] then such interpretation must be allowed to share in whatever legitimacy the democratic character of political processes creates.

Finally, there is the dual character of *Marbury v. Madison's* core assumption: the postulate, considered in § 3–2, that the Constitution is first of all law and only secondarily law which courts are capable of interpreting. It is noteworthy that the critics' responses to the asserted antidemocratic character of judicial review seek to solve the problem of legitimacy by focusing more on the judiciary than on the Constitution itself: although one approach emphasizes a process of reasoning which enables the judiciary to pierce the Constitution and thereby share in the political consensus which underlies it, this way of linking adjudication to the constitutional text generates legitimacy not because of what the text *says*, but because adherence to text provides the only means of making contact with the consensus.

Nothing in the Constitution itself, of course, specifies that a search for consensus must play a paramount constitutional role. In significant part, the Constitution creates a process less of consensus than of controlled conflict. The regime it creates gives a central place to a judiciary that speaks not always in one voice but often in many, and whose pronouncements are best understood not as final answers but as parts of an ongoing discourse—a discourse with the other levels and branches of government, with the people at large, with courts that have gone before and courts yet to be appointed. It is this constitutional discourse, and the role it plays in subjecting governmental practices to continuing critique in terms of our fundamental law, that gives the institution of judicial review such legitimacy as it may enjoy.

---

12. See, e.g., Remarks of Justice Marshall (Maui, Hawaii, May 6, 1987) (criticizing the 1787 Constitution for its exclusion of "the majority of America's citizens" from its notion of who "We the People" are).

13. See § 3–4, supra; § 3–13, infra.

§ 3–7. Overview—Limits on the Exercise of Federal Judicial Power: The Requirement of a "Case" or "Controversy" as Defined by the Doctrines of Justiciability

Article III limits the scope of federal judicial power in two ways. First, the Constitution limits the jurisdiction of the federal courts to cases which either raise certain subjects or involve certain parties.[1] Except for the Supreme Court's original jurisdiction,[2] however, this initial limitation operates upon federal courts only indirectly. Federal courts are dependent for their jurisdiction upon acts of Congress;[3] accordingly, article III's restrictions of federal jurisdiction are more limitations on Congress than on the courts.

Article III's second set of limitations, by contrast, immediately affect the federal judiciary. The article's grants of subject-matter jurisdiction extend only to "cases" and "controversies." The Supreme Court has derived from these two words a substantial body of doctrine prescribing the circumstances in which federal courts may or may not exercise their subject-matter jurisdiction. "Embodied in the words 'cases' and 'controversies' are two complementary but somewhat different limitations. In part those words limit the business of federal courts to questions presented in an adversary context and in a form historically viewed as capable of resolution through the judicial process. And in part those words define the role assigned to the judiciary in a tripartite allocation of power to assure that the federal courts will not intrude into areas committed to the other branches of government. *Justiciability* is the term of art employed to give expression to this dual limitation placed upon federal courts by the case-and-controversy doctrine."[4]

These concerns—both of keeping the power exercised by the judicial branch within proper bounds and of preventing its intrusion on the prerogatives of the coordinate branches—are typical ones in a constitutional jurisprudence marked by the central concepts of limited government and the separation of powers. But in operation the justiciability rules are unlike most constitutional doctrine—indeed, unlike most *law*—in that they are self-regarding. In deciding whether a justiciable case or controversy exists, federal courts necessarily speak to their *own* power.[5] Moreover, in doing so they often move beyond a bare analysis of the constitutional authority vested in them to evaluate, on largely prudential grounds, the appropriateness of deciding the question which the litigants press upon them.[6] This enterprise reflects the view that,

§ 3–7

1. See § 3–5, supra.

2. See id.

3. Id.

4. Flast v. Cohen, 392 U.S. 83, 94–95 (1968) (emphasis added).

5. See Monaghan, "Constitutional Adjudication: The Who and When," 82 Yale L.J. 1363, 1364, 1397 (1973).

6. See § 3–8, infra, as well as analysis of the prudential factors underlying the specific justiciability doctrines discussed in §§ 3–9 to 3–21, infra. For an enlightening debate about the content and appropriateness of the Court's approach to justiciability, see Brilmayer, "The Jurisprudence of Article III: Perspectives on the 'Case or Controversy' Requirement," 93 Harv.L. Rev. 207 (1979); Tushnet, "The Sociology of Article III: A Response to Professor Brilmayer," 93 Harv.L.Rev. 1698 (1980); Brilmayer, "A Reply," 93 Harv.L.Rev. 1727 (1980), summarized at § 3–8, note 25, infra.

for largely institutional reasons, judges should employ substantial discretion in exercising their subject-matter jurisdiction—a view that has come under sharp attack in recent years as the Supreme Court has articulated avoidance of clashes with coordinate branches as the keystone of justiciability doctrine,[7] and has enforced other self-made jurisdictional limits,[8] with a fervor matching or surpassing its efforts in policing many explicit constitutional commandments.[9] The next series of sections,[10] therefore, involves in an important sense the description of an institutional psychology: an account of how the federal courts, or more accurately the Justices of the Supreme Court, view their own role.[11]

In order for a claim to be justiciable as an article III matter, it must "present a real and substantial controversy which unequivocally calls for adjudication of the rights" asserted.[12] In part, the extent to which there is a "real and substantial controversy" is determined under the doctrine of "standing" by an examination of the sufficiency of the stake of the person making the claim, to ensure the litigant has suffered an actual injury which is fairly traceable to challenged action and likely to be redressed by the judicial relief requested.[13] The substantiality of the controversy is also in part a feature of the controversy itself—an aspect of "the appropriateness of the issues for [judicial] decision . . . and the actual hardship . . . of denying [litigants] the relief sought."[14] Examination of the contours of the controversy is regarded as necessary to ensure that courts do not overstep their constitutional authority by issuing "advisory opinions."[15] The ban on advisory opinions is further articulated and reinforced by judicial consideration of two supplementary doctrines: that of "ripeness," which requires that the factual claims underlying the litigation be concretely presented, and not based on speculative future contingencies;[16] and that of "mootness," which reflects the complementary

---

7. See Allen v. Wright, 468 U.S. 737, 750 (1984). See generally Floyd, "The Justiciability Decisions of the Burger Court," 60 Notre Dame L.Rev. 862 (1985).

8. See generally Shapiro, "Jurisdiction and Discretion," 60 N.Y.U.L.Rev. 543 (1985) (cataloging and approving of broad judicial discretion in the exercise of jurisdiction). See, e.g., §§ 3-25 to 3-27 (eleventh amendment sovereign immunity) and 3-28 to 3-30 (abstention doctrines).

9. See, e.g., Fallon, "Of Justiciability, Remedies and Public Law Litigation: Notes on the Jurisprudence of Lyons," 59 N.Y.U.L.Rev. 1 (1984) (criticizing the Court's increasing use of justiciability doctrine to curtail the role of the federal judiciary in public law litigation); Redish, "Abstention, Separation of Powers, and the Limits of the Judicial Function," 94 Yale L.J. 71 (1984) (criticizing the Court's federalism-based abstention doctrine as a usurpation of the legislative authority embodied in jurisdictional and civil rights statutes); Reinhardt, "Limiting Access to

the Federal Courts: Round Up the Usual Victims," 6 Whittier L.Rev. 967 (1984); Tushnet, supra note 6 (criticizing standing doctrine as both manipulable and too restrictive of substantive rights).

10. See §§ 3-8 to 3-21, infra.

11. See generally Spann, "Expository Justice," 131 U.Pa.L.Rev. 585, 617-60 (1983) (noting intimate relation of justiciability doctrine to debate over whether courts should serve primarily in the resolution of disputes or in the exposition of fundamental norms).

12. Poe v. Ullman, 367 U.S. 497, 509 (1961) (Brennan, J., concurring in the judgment).

13. See discussion in §§ 3-14 to 3-21, infra.

14. Poe v. Ullman, 367 U.S. 497, 509 (1961) (plurality opinion).

15. See § 3-9, infra; see also § 3-12, infra.

16. See § 3-10, infra.

concern of ensuring that the passage of time or succession of events has not destroyed the previously live nature of the controversy.[17] Finally related to the nature of the controversy is the "political question" doctrine, barring decision of certain disputes best suited to resolution by other governmental actors.[18]

§ 3–8. Nonconstitutional Aspects of Justiciability Doctrine

Because it is self-regarding, the Supreme Court's justiciability doctrine, although constitutional in origin, is quite different from most other aspects of constitutional law. The Court has at times applied under the rubric of justiciability both rules which state the furthest reaches of constitutional power and policies which suggest when that power should not be exercised. This amalgam of the constitutional and the political would be superfluous in other contexts. The Supreme Court properly leaves to Congress and the Executive the task of deciding whether and when to exercise their constitutional authority. In defining the extent of its own authority and that of subordinate federal judicial tribunals, however, the Court cannot avoid expressly considering both the limits of power and the wisdom of its exercise.

The concept of justiciability is thus not exhausted by the set of specific limitations which the Court derives from it. "Justiciability is of course not a legal concept with a fixed content or susceptible to scientific verification. Its utilization is the resultant of many subtle pressures, including the appropriateness of the issues for decision . . . and the actual hardship to the litigants of denying them the relief sought." [1] Indeed, it is not truly possible to analyze specific justiciability limits as though they were islands in a sea of discretion: the constitutional and the political interpenetrate. Before considering the more conventionally constitutional aspects of justiciability, therefore, it is necessary to describe generally the factors and circumstances which prompt the Supreme Court to prevent federal judicial power from reaching its constitutional limits.

The place to begin is where the Supreme Court's exercise of discretion is most obvious: the cases in which the Court refuses to accept constitutionally and statutorily authorized jurisdiction. Early in the history of the Supreme Court, Chief Justice Marshall declared: "It is most true that this court will not take jurisdiction if it should not; but it is equally true, that it must take jurisdiction if it should." [2] Yet despite this dictum, the Court has on occasion refused to hear even cases over which its jurisdiction was ostensibly mandatory—for example, cases in which a state judgment is appealable "as of right." [3]

17. See § 3–11, infra.

18. See § 3–13, infra.

§ 3–8

1. Poe v. Ullman, 367 U.S. 497, 509 (1961) (plurality opinion).

2. Cohens v. Virginia, 19 U.S. (6 Wheat.) 264, 404 (1821).

3. See 28 U.S.C. § 1257(1) & (2). See generally R. Stern, E. Gressman & S. Sha-

piro, Supreme Court Practice 106–44 (6th ed. 1986). 28 U.S.C. §§ 1252, 1253 & 1254(2) provide other avenues of formally "obligatory" appeal jurisdiction. By contrast, the more usual mode of review, by writ of certiorari under 28 U.S.C. §§ 1254(1) and 1257(3), is completely discretionary in function. See also § 3–5, supra, note 9.

In *Rescue Army v. Municipal Court of Los Angeles*,[4] for example, the Supreme Court refused to review a California decision denying a claim under the first amendment's establishment clause because the Court was unable to determine with certainty how much of the questioned statute was implicated in the case: "jurisdiction here should be exerted only when the jurisdictional question presented by the proceeding . . . tenders the underlying constitutional issues in clean-cut and concrete form, unclouded by any serious problem of construction relating either to the terms of the questioned legislation or to its interpretation by the state courts."[5] And in *Socialist Labor Party v. Gilligan*,[6] the Supreme Court refused, after other issues in the case had become moot, to review a constitutional challenge to a state requirement that a political party must file a loyalty oath in order to obtain a position on the ballot: "All issues litigated below have become moot except for one that received scant attention in appellants' complaint and was treated not at all in the affidavits filed in support of the cross-motions for summary judgment. Nothing in the record shows that appellants have suffered any injury thus far, and the law's future effect remains wholly speculative."[7] Similarly, the Supreme Court has refused to reach the merits of a case "[b]ecause of the inadequacy of the record";[8] because the Court found that "resolution of the constitutional issues presented . . . would not be appropriate;"[9] "[b]ecause of an ambiguity in the record;"[10] or because the federal issue was not "properly" presented.[11]

The policies which explain particular decisions of the Supreme Court refusing jurisdiction are many and varied. The *stated* bases for declining to adjudicate, reflecting the Court's conception of its role in the constitutional system, "lie in all that goes to make up the unique place and character, in our scheme, of judicial review of governmental action for constitutionality. They are found in the delicacy of that function . . .; the comparative finality of [its] consequences; the consideration due to the judgment of other repositories of constitutional power concerning the scope of their authority; the necessity . . . for each to keep within its power, including the courts; [and] the inherent limitations of the judicial process, arising especially from its largely negative character and limited resources of enforcement. . . ."[12]

It is also true, however, that unarticulated institutional considerations may figure heavily in the Court's refusal to accept jurisdiction in a particular case. For example, in *Naim v. Naim*,[13] the Court dismissed

---

4. 331 U.S. 549 (1947).

5. Id. at 584. Compare reasons stated for declining to proceed to the merits of cases falling within the "Pullman" abstention doctrine, discussed in § 3–29, infra.

6. 406 U.S. 583 (1972).

7. Id. at 589. But cf. Communist Party of Indiana v. Whitcomb, 414 U.S. 441 (1974) (reaching merits to invalidate loyalty oath similar to that involved in *Gilligan*).

8. International Bhd. of Teamsters v. Denver Milk Producers, 334 U.S. 809 (1948) (mem).

9. DeBacker v. Brainard, 396 U.S. 28, 29 (1969).

10. Simmons v. West Haven Hous. Auth., 399 U.S. 510, 511 (1970).

11. Mattiello v. Connecticut, 395 U.S. 209 (1969) (per curiam); Naim v. Naim, 350 U.S. 985 (1956) (per curiam).

12. Rescue Army v. Municipal Court of Los Angeles, 331 U.S. 549, 571 (1947).

13. 350 U.S. 891 (1955), 985 (1956) (per curiam).

outright a case raising the constitutionality of the Virginia antimiscegenation statutes. In light of the Court's then recently decided school segregation cases, the Court could not have meant to legitimate the Virginia statute. Rather, the Court probably thought it unwise to decide the first case of this sort on an issue "that the Negro community as a whole [could] hardly be said to be pressing hard at the moment," at the very time that the Court was subject "to scurrilous attack by men who predicted that integration of the schools would lead directly to 'mongrelization of the race' and that this was the result the Court had really willed. . . ." [14] Of course, refusing to accept jurisdiction because of the supposed "wisdom" of doing so in a particular case necessarily abrogates the "obligatory" nature of the appeal jurisdiction.[15] If, as has been argued, there is thus no truly obligatory appeal, but instead a general "power to decline the exercise of jurisdiction that is given," [16] then in every appeal the Court may be faced with the dilemma of either reaching an unwelcome or ill-timed decision on the merits or declining the exercise of statutorily mandated jurisdiction in seeming disregard of the rule of law.[17]

A means of resolving this apparent conflict between prudence and legality is suggested by commentators who view the very concept of jurisdiction as intimately linked to judicial discretion. Professor David Shapiro, for example, describes discretion over jurisdictional matters as rooted both in a wide variety of recognized discretionary doctrines built on legislative grants of jurisdiction, and in our common law tradition more generally.[18] "Far from amounting to judicial usurpation," he argues, "open acknowledgement of reasoned discretion is wholly consistent with the Anglo-American legal tradition," and the exercise of such discretion "has much to contribute to the easing of interbranch and intergovernmental tensions in our complex system of government." [19]

The policies underlying the justiciability doctrine long ago led the Supreme Court to develop an elaborate body of devices for avoiding difficult questions, sketched prominently by Justice Brandeis in his concurring opinion in *Ashwander v. Tennessee Valley Authority*.[20] There, he noted that the Court had developed, "for its own governance in the cases confessedly within its jurisdiction, a series of rules under which it has avoided passing upon a large part of all the constitutional

---

14. A. Bickel, The Least Dangerous Branch 174 (1962).

15. Cf. Cohens v. Virginia, 19 U.S. (6 Wheat.) 264, 404 (1821).

16. A. Bickel, supra note 14, at 127. But see Gunther, "The Subtle Vices of the 'Passive Virtues'—A Comment on Principle and Expediency in Judicial Review," 64 Colum.L.Rev. 1, 16–17 (1964) (vigorously disputing this position). For an interesting study of Bickel's viewpoint and reactions to it, see Kronman, "Alexander Bickel's Philosophy of Prudence," 94 Yale L.J. 1567, 1573–90 (1985).

17. See, e.g., Wechsler, "Toward Neutral Principles of Constitutional Law," in Principles, Politics, and Fundamental Law 47 (1961) (describing Court's action in Naim v. Naim, see supra note 13, as "wholly without basis in law").

18. See Shapiro, "Jurisdiction and Discretion," 60 N.Y.U.L.Rev. 543, 545–74 (1985).

19. Id. at 545. Compare sources cited in § 3–7, note 9, supra.

20. 297 U.S. 288, 341 (1936) (Brandeis, J. concurring).

questions pressed upon it for decision." [21]   These rules are part of a broader general prescription that courts "do not review issues, especially constitutional issues, until they have to." [22]   Or more particularly, one is tempted to add, until they want to badly enough. [23]   For in recent years, particularly in the area of standing, [24] the Court at times has gone to extraordinary lengths in manipulating justiciability doctrine to achieve its substantive goals. [25]

21. Id. at 346. In his classic summary of the doctrine, Justice Brandeis explained that, for example, the Court refuses unnecessarily to anticipate constitutional questions, formulates rules only as broad as necessary for the case at hand, prefers decision on nonconstitutional grounds, and construes statutes where possible to avoid constitutional problems. See id. at 346–48.

22. Joint Anti-Fascist Refugee Comm. v. McGrath, 341 U.S. 123, 154–55 (1951) (Frankfurter, J., concurring). See, e.g., Kremens v. Bartley, 431 U.S. 119, 133–34 & n. 15 (1977) (relying on "discretionary considerations" to refuse review of "important constitutional issues," despite "[t]he availability of thoroughly prepared attorneys to argue both sides . . . and of numerous *amici curiae* ready to assist in the decisional process, . . . all of them 'stand[ing] like greyhounds in the slips, straining upon the start' ").

23. See, e.g., Marbury v. Madison, 5 U.S. (1 Cranch) 137 (1803), discussed in § 3–2, supra; Epperson v. Arkansas, 393 U.S. 97 (1968), a declaratory judgment action in which Justice Fortas, writing for a Court evidently anxious to invalidate a 1928 law forbidding the teaching of evolution, noted the absence of any real threat of prosecution and observed that the law might be "more of a curiosity than a vital fact of life." He disposed of all doubts as to justiciability, however, with the remarkable statement that "the present case was brought, the appeal as of right is properly here, and it is our duty to decide the issues presented." Id. at 102. Cf. § 3–10, infra.

24. See §§ 3–14 to 3–21, infra; L. Tribe, "Choke Holds, Church Subsidies and Nuclear Meltdowns: Problems of Standing?," in Constitutional Choices 99–120 (1985).

25. See, e.g., City of Los Angeles v. Lyons, 461 U.S. 95 (1983), discussed in § 3–16, infra; Valley Forge Christian College v. Americans United for Separation of Church and State, Inc., 454 U.S. 464 (1982), discussed in § 3–17, infra; Duke Power Co. v. Carolina Envtl. Study Group, Inc., 438 U.S. 59 (1978). See generally Tushnet,

"The Sociology of Article III: A Response to Professor Brilmayer," 93 Harv.L.Rev. 1699, 1705–06 & nn. 31–33 (1980); § 3–7, note 9, supra.

In a provocative article, Professor Lea Brilmayer argues that the Court's explanations for its justiciability doctrines "have not been sufficiently persuasive to deflect the cynical suggestion that the Court has manipulated justiciability questions to mask hostility to the merits of constitutional claims," but suggests that these doctrines can nonetheless be rationalized by reference to three policies purportedly underlying article III's grant of judicial power. Brilmayer, "The Jurisprudence of Article III: Perspectives on the 'Case or Controversy' Requirement," 93 Harv.L. Rev. 297, 298 (1979). First is that of "restraint," requiring that courts avoid deciding legal issues sooner than necessary so as to allocate judicial power smoothly over time, since premature decisionmaking would result in either an outmoded body of law or a high rate of precedent-overturning. See id. at 302–06. Second is the policy of "representation," helping to ensure fairness for injured individuals by barring ideological plaintiffs who may attempt to assert others' rights from litigating cases that may create adverse precedent. See id. at 306–10. Closely related is the final principle of "self-determination," designed to enhance the liberal ideal of self-definition by barring even good representatives from paternalistically asserting claims for the "benefit" of others. See id. at 310–15.

Professor Mark Tushnet has criticized Brilmayer's approach, arguing that it inadequately explains existing doctrine, invites extreme doctrinal manipulation, and is blind to the realities of public interest litigation in which most clients are essentially ideological and function mainly as fronts for activist lawyers—making traditional justiciability doctrines inapposite. See Tushnet, supra. Compare Brilmayer, "A Reply," 93 Harv.L.Rev. 1727 (1980).

§ 3–9. The Ban on Advisory Opinions and the Problems of Declaratory and Partially Circumventable Judgments

The federal courts created pursuant to article III are barred by the case-or-controversy requirement from deciding "abstract, hypothetical or contingent questions."[1] Because of this bar, it is said that these article III courts will not "give opinions in the nature of advice concerning legislative [or executive] action. . . ."[2] The ban on advisory opinions traces from the Supreme Court's celebrated refusal under Chief Justice Jay to advise President Washington informally on questions relating to the neutral status of the United States in the European war of 1793,[3] and from the earlier refusal by members of that same Court to give extrajudicial advice to Congress and the Secretary of War on pension applications:[4] " '[N]either the Legislature nor the Executive branches can constitutionally assign to the judicial any duties, but such as are properly judicial, and to be performed in a judicial manner.' "

The earliest cases of judicial refusal to issue advisory opinions were justified primarily in terms of the need to maintain the constitutional separation of powers.[5] The refusal to give advice has more recently been explained in terms of the character of the judicial function. For example, in *United States v. Freuhauf*,[6] the Supreme Court refused to give what it deemed an advisory opinion in a matter of federal statutory construction: "Such opinions, such advance expressions of legal judgment upon issues which remain unfocused because they are not pressed before the Court with that clear concreteness provided when a question emerges precisely framed and necessary for decision from a clash of adversary argument exploring every aspect of a multi-faced situation embracing conflicting and demanding interests, we have con-

---

§ 3–9

1. Alabama State Fed. of Labor v. McAdory, 325 U.S. 450, 461 (1945). Accord, United States v. Evans, 213 U.S. 297, 300 (1909).

2. Muskrat v. United States, 219 U.S. 346, 362 (1911). But cf. South Carolina v. Katzenbach, 383 U.S. 301 (1966) (holding justiciable a claim under § 5 of the Voting Rights Act of 1965 which provided that whenever any state, or subdivision of any state, "shall enact or seek to administer any voting qualification or prerequisite to voting, or standard, practice or procedure with respect to voting different from that in force or effect on November 1, 1964," such state or subdivision must submit the change to the Attorney General or alternatively "may institute an action in the United States District Court for the District of Columbia for a declaratory judgment that such qualification, prerequisite, standard, practice, or procedure does not have the purpose and will not have the effect of denying or abridging the right to vote on account of race or color").

3. Correspondence of the Justices, Letter from Chief Justice John Jay and the Associate Justices to President George Washington, August 8, 1793.

4. Hayburn's Case, 2 U.S. (2 Dall.) 409, 410 n. (a) (1792) (quoting circuit court opinion). Note that even in those states in which advisory opinions are allowed (Colorado, Florida, Massachusetts, Maine, New Hampshire, Rhode Island and South Dakota), the judges who render such opinions often maintain the notion that, in so doing, they are performing an extrajudicial function, and that such opinions should consequently have dramatically limited *stare decisis* effect. That limitation, however, severely restricts the utility of advisory opinions, whose most important function is to reduce debilitating uncertainty as to the constitutionality of contemplated legislative or executive action. See Note, "Advisory Opinions on the Constitutionality of Statutes," 69 Harv.L.Rev. 1302 (1956).

5. Correspondence of the Justices, supra note 3.

6. 365 U.S. 146 (1961).

sistently refused to give." [7]   Indeed, the presence of unmistakable concreteness and vigorous adversary argument in a dispute can be enough to avoid an advisory opinion even when the nominal parties to the lawsuit agree with each other on the legal issues.[8]

Despite Justice Brandeis' dictum that granting or reviewing declaratory judgments "is beyond the power conferred upon the federal judiciary," [9] it is now settled that congressionally authorized declaratory judgments [10] may be obtained in federal courts, and state declaratory judgments reviewed there,[11] if the requirements of the justiciability doctrine are otherwise met: "Where there is . . . a concrete case admitting of an immediate and definite determination of the legal rights of the parties in an adversary proceeding upon the facts alleged, the judicial function may be appropriately exercised although the adjudication of the rights of the litigants may not require the award of process or the payment of damages." [12]

Nonjusticiable declaratory actions are usually characterized as "hypothetical"—as presenting "abstract" questions because of suppositions contrary to fact or because of wholly speculative assumptions. For example, when doctors and their patients sought to challenge the constitutionality of a Connecticut anti-birth control law by seeking declaratory relief, the Supreme Court refused to assume that the statute, which had been enforced only once, twenty-one years past,

---

7. Id. at 157. This formulation rests on assumptions about the nature of the adversary process which may not be wholly realistic and do not in any event necessarily inhere in adjudication. Most generic problems with advisory opinions stem from the fact that they are usually issued without briefs and arguments of counsel and have no assurances of addressing a narrowly framed question. See Note, supra note 4. These problems need not prove insuperable; suggestions have been made to remedy them through such techniques as liberal intervention rules, see Note, "Judicial Determinations in Nonadversary Proceedings," 72 Harv.L.Rev. 723, 735–37 (1959), to provide a necessary concreteness by analogy to legislative or administrative rulemaking hearings, where the advisory apparatus is quite well developed.

8. For example, in Immigration and Naturalization Serv. v. Chadha, 462 U.S. 919 (1983), discussed in Chapter 4, infra, the INS agreed before the Court, in principle, with Chadha's circuit court victory. Nevertheless, the Court rejected the argument that the suit was " 'a friendly, nonadversary, proceeding.' " Id. at 939. It noted that the lower court ruling would necessarily force the INS to refrain from action (i.e., deporting Chadha) it otherwise would have taken, thereby assuring that something concrete turned on the decision. See id. Similarly, in Bob Jones Univ. v. United States, 461 U.S. 574 (1983), discussed in §§ 16–15, note 32, infra, the gov-

ernment largely agreed with the schools' position, but was nevertheless adverse because it intended to enforce the challenged statute against the schools in compliance with a court order. See 461 U.S. at 585 n. 9. Compare the standards governing "collusive" suits, discussed in § 3–12, infra.

9. Willing v. Chicago Auditorium Ass'n, 277 U.S. 274, 289 (1928). See also Piedmont & Northern Ry. Co. v. United States, 280 U.S. 469 (1930); Arizona v. California, 283 U.S. 423 (1931); Alabama v. Arizona, 291 U.S. 286 (1934) (all suggesting constitutional barriers to declaratory judgments).

10. See 28 U.S.C. § 2201.

11. E.g., Nashville, C. & St. L. Ry. v. Wallace, 288 U.S. 249 (1933).

12. Aetna Life Ins. Co. v. Haworth, 300 U.S. 227, 241 (1937). The unanimous Court in Haworth included Justice Brandeis, who had stated in Willing that declaratory judgments were not within the judicial power to grant. Chief Justice Hughes, writing for the Court in Haworth, firmly stated that the congressional provision for declaratory judgments in no way altered the justiciability requirements of article III. Rather, the legislation merely provided the courts with a new remedy: "Thus the operation of the Declaratory Judgment Act is procedural only . . . . Exercising [its] control of [federal court] practice and procedure the Congress is not confined to traditional forms or traditional remedies." Id. at 240.

would be applied to the claimants' conduct, especially since the particular kind of conduct in which they were engaging had not been the target of the law's previous application.[13]

Similarly, in *United Public Workers of America v. Mitchell*,[14] government employees sought declaratory relief from allegedly unconstitutional restrictions imposed on their political activities by the Hatch Act. The employees described in highly general terms the future conduct in which they planned to engage. The Court's refusal to grant the relief sought turned in part upon the speculative nature of the claim: "A hypothetical threat is not enough. We can only speculate as to the kinds of political activity the appellants desire to engage in or as to the contents of their proposed public statements or the circumstances of their publication."[15]

Moreover, although declaratory judgments are not *per se* "advisory," those declaratory actions characterized by "double contingency," in that *both* the activity suggested *and* the reaction to it are merely hypothesized, are typically found nonjusticiable either because the decision requested would be purely advisory or because the issues are not yet "ripe for review," a closely related ground of decision discussed more fully below.[16] In the context of anticipatory challenges to criminal statutes, for example, *either* a demonstrable threat of enforcement directed personally to the plaintiff (in the case of a statute whose applicability to the plaintiff's intended acts might seem unclear)[17] *or* the existence of a non-moribund[18] prohibition which applies "particularly and unambiguously to activities in which the plaintiff regularly engaged or sought to engage"[19] (in the absence of any actual threat of enforcement directed to the plaintiff), is necessary to avoid double contingency. Once the purely hypothetical character of an anticipatory challenge is removed by a showing that the challenged prohibition clearly forbids the conduct plaintiff seeks to undertake, the challenge becomes justiciable even without an actual threat.[20]

13. Poe v. Ullman, 367 U.S. 497, 501–02 (1961) (plurality opinion). But compare, as to the effect of non-enforcement, Epperson v. Arkansas, 393 U.S. 97 (1968), in which the Court found justiciable a declaratory challenge to an anti-evolution statute for which there was no record of any prosecution, but for which, *if* a prosecution were to be brought, someone in the position of the declaratory plaintiff would necessarily be its target.

14. 330 U.S. 75 (1947). See also the discussion of this case in § 3–10, infra.

15. Id. at 90. See also Babbitt v. United Farm Workers, 442 U.S. 289, 303–05 (1979) (holding nonjusticiable a farmworkers' union challenge to two provisions in Arizona's farm labor statute—one permitting employers to deny unions access to their information, time and facilities, and another requiring compulsory arbitration in the event of the entry of a temporary order restraining a labor strike;

the Court emphasized that the employers had yet to deny access to employees or sought to enjoin a strike).

16. See § 3–10, infra.

17. See Steffel v. Thompson, 415 U.S. 452, 456, 459 (1974); id. at 476 (Stewart, J., concurring).

18. See note 13, supra.

19. Ellis v. Dyson, 421 U.S. 426, 447 (1975) (Powell, J., dissenting).

20. See, e.g., Doe v. Bolton, 410 U.S. 179, 188–89 (1973); Lake Carriers Ass'n v. MacMullan, 406 U.S. 498, 506–08 (1972); Epperson v. Arkansas, 393 U.S. 97 (1968). See also Bowers v. Hardwick, 106 S.Ct. 2841 (1986) (adjudicating merits of challenge—ultimately, an unsuccessful one—to Georgia statute criminalizing sodomy despite history of non-enforcement because plaintiff had already been arrested, though not prosecuted, for sodomy). But see § 3–30, infra.

Note that a decision to grant or deny declaratory relief, while to an extent regulated by the constitutional prohibition of "advisory opinions," is in addition governed by the law of equitable remedies, detailed consideration of which is beyond the scope of this book.[21]

In an otherwise justiciable controversy, the fact that a judgment adverse to one of the litigants removes only one of the lawful options available to that litigant does not render such a judgment impermissibly advisory. For example, in *United States v. Nixon*,[22] the Supreme Court obviously thought it could render a decision that would not be merely "advisory", even though a judgment adverse to the President in that case could have been partly circumvented by steps culminating in the discharge of the Watergate Special Prosecutor, the subordinate who brought the suit on behalf of the United States, thus denying the subordinate of the fruits of his legal victory. That fact alone, however, did not reduce the Court's role to one of merely advising the parties. For, assuming the controversy to be a real one in all other respects, a judgment in favor of the subordinate definitively removed at least one rather tempting Presidential option—namely, that of retaining his subordinate as prosecutor while refusing to comply with the subordinate's demand for designated items of evidence needed in a pending prosecution of former Presidential aides.[23] In fact, the President chose to submit the demanded evidence in response to the Court's holding; had he chosen instead to find an Attorney General who would revoke the regulations assuring the Special Prosecutor's independence and tenure, the President would have sacrificed the politically useful image of an independent prosecution. In either event, the decision dramatically altered the courses of action open to the President; it could be circumvented, but not ignored.

Similarly, in *Larson v. Valente*,[24] the Court upheld a claim by the Unification Church that Minnesota's charitable solicitations law violated the establishment clause [25] in exempting from certain onerous requirements of the act only those "religious organizations" that received more than half of their total contributions from their membership. The state had proceeded against the Unification Church on the assumption that it was a religious organization but that it was not entitled to an exemption because it raised most of its funds from outside sources. The Court's judgment thus benefited the Unification Church by ensuring exemptions for all organizations classified as "religious." The Court ruled for the Unification Church even though it recognized that the organization could not "be assured of a continued religious-organization exemption even in the absence of the fifty per cent rule" and

21. Among the factors bearing on whether a declaratory judgment is an appropriate remedy in the particular case are the degree to which such a judgment will terminate the uncertainty or controversy giving rise to the action, convenience to the parties, the strength of the interest in settlement, and the availability of other appropriate remedies. See "Developments in the Law: Declaratory Judgments—1941–1949," 62 Harv.L.Rev. 787, 805–17 (1949).

22. 418 U.S. 683 (1974).

23. This case is also discussed from the perspective of collusive suits in § 3–12, infra, and of political questions in § 3–13, infra. See also the discussion in Chapter 4, infra.

24. 456 U.S. 228 (1982).

25. See Ch. 14, infra.

that it "may indeed be compelled, ultimately to register under the Act" on another ground—in particular, because it might ultimately be determined to be a *non*-religious organization not entitled to an exemption.[26] But the decision nonetheless awarded "substantial and meaningful relief" because it "put the State to the task of demonstrating" the Unification Church's non-religious nature, a requirement "surely more burdensome than that of demonstrating that the Church's proportion of non-member contributions exceeds fifty per cent." [27]

§ 3–10. Ripeness

The prohibition of advisory opinions [1] derives directly from the case-or-controversy requirement of article III. A closely related limitation imposed by justiciability doctrine, further defining the policy against decision of abstract or hypothetical questions, is that of *ripeness*. Judicial refusal to issue an advisory opinion ordinarily stresses an essentially *retrospective* finding that the process by which a matter has reached a federal court has failed to crystallize that matter so as to render it justiciable. In contrast, the conclusion that an issue is not ripe for adjudication ordinarily emphasizes a *prospective* examination of the controversy which indicates that future events may affect its structure in ways that determine its present justiciability, either by making a later decision more apt or by demonstrating directly that the matter is not yet appropriate for adjudication by an article III court.

Ripeness doctrine highlights two central concerns for examination by federal courts. In *Abbott Laboratories v. Gardner*,[2] the Supreme Court, in its "leading discussion of the doctrine . . . indicated that the question of ripeness turns on 'the fitness of the issues for judicial decision' and 'the hardship to the parties of withholding court consideration.' " [3] The fitness of the issues for federal adjudication embodies both constitutional and prudential concerns. "[I]ssues of ripeness involve, at least in part, the existence of a live 'Case or Controversy' "; [4]

---

26. See 456 U.S. at 242–43.

27. Id. at 243. Duke Power Co. v. Carolina Envtl. Study Group, Inc., 438 U.S. 59 (1978), also involved a potential avenue for circumvention of the outcome suggested by the Court's ruling. If the plaintiffs had succeeded in invalidating the $560 million liability limit of the federal law they challenged, their victory could have been easily overcome: Congress could simply have guaranteed government compensation of any nuclear damages exceeding the limit— a not implausible option, given that Congress had originally promised to consider such compensation in the event of an accident—or could have built in extra incentives for power plant construction and operation to offset any negative effect of the decision. It was sufficient to avoid an advisory opinion, however, that the plaintiffs would have obtained immediate relief, for however short a time. Compare the justiciability of equal protection challenges to the award of benefits to similarly situated

persons, where a favorable judgment may lead only to denial of benefits to all, discussed in § 3–16, note 77, infra.

§ 3–10

1. See § 3–12, supra.

2. 387 U.S. 136 (1967).

3. Pacific Gas & Elec. Co. v. State Energy Resources Conservation and Development Comm'n, 461 U.S. 190, 201 (1983) (quoting Abbott Laboratories, 387 U.S. at 149).

4. Regional Rail Reorganization Act Cases, 419 U.S. 102, 138 (1974). See also Babbitt v. United Farm Workers Nat'l Union, 442 U.S. 289, 297–98 (1979); Steffel v. Thompson, 415 U.S. 452, 459 & n. 10 (1974). The constitutional underpinnings of ripeness doctrine are often emphasized through reference to the prohibition on advisory opinions, see, e.g., Babbitt, 442 U.S. at 305; EPA v. Brown, 431 U.S. 99, 103–04 (1977); United Public Workers v.

as such, "ripeness is peculiarly a question of timing"[5]—"its basic rationale is to prevent the courts, through premature adjudication, from entangling themselves in abstract disagreements . . . ."[6] Even when a dispute is adequately mature in a constitutional sense, however, subsequent events may sharpen the controversy or remove the need for decision of at least some aspects of the matter. Thus, ripeness doctrine also furthers the prudential policy of "judicial restraint from unnecessary decision of constitutional issues"[7] by allowing a determination that a resolution of the dispute should come at a later date, if at all. By contrast, the second concern of ripeness doctrine as articulated by *Abbott Laboratories*, requiring a consideration of the hardship of withholding decision, is wholly prudential in operation.

In gauging the fitness of the issues in a case for judicial resolution, courts are centrally concerned with "whether the case involves uncertain or contingent future events that may not occur as anticipated, or indeed may not occur at all."[8] Findings of nonjusticiability based on this concern typically arise when a litigant has challenged at an early stage, often in a suit for declaratory relief,[9] the constitutionality of a statutory or regulatory scheme. In such cases the litigant may have a plausible claim that the challenged provision, by somehow limiting his available legal options, threatens him with direct injury sufficient to confer standing to sue.[10] But standing doctrine discusses only "*what issues* a litigant might raise, not *when* he might raise them. That a proper party is before [a] court is no answer to the objection that he is there prematurely"[11]—that he raises unduly "hypothetical" or "abstract" issues.[12]

Mitchell, 330 U.S. 75, 89 (1947). Ripeness as a constitutional minimum cannot be conceded or stipulated by the parties to a lawsuit. See Regional Rail Reorganization Act Cases, supra, 419 U.S. at 138; Poe v. Ullman, 367 U.S. 497, 501 (1961) (plurality opinion).

5. Regional Rail Reorganization Act Cases, 419 U.S. at 140.

6. Abbott Laboratories, 387 U.S. at 148.

7. Regional Rail Reorganization Act Cases, 419 U.S. at 138. On the justiciability policy counseling restraint on nonconstitutional grounds, see generally § 3–8, supra.

8. 13A C. Wright, A. Miller & E. Cooper, Federal Practice and Procedure: Jurisdiction 2d § 3532, at 112 (1984).

9. See § 3–9, supra.

10. See §§ 3–14 to 3–18, infra.

11. Communist Party of the United States v. Subversive Activities Control Bd., 367 U.S. 1, 79 (1961) (emphasis added).

12. It should be noted, however, that with the lack of any general requirement in standing doctrine that a litigant show a "nexus" between a concrete injury in fact and the legal right asserted, see § 3–19, note 67, infra, a litigant may be quite premature in asserting his particular legal challenge but still present a ripe controversy on other grounds. Most notably, for example, in Duke Power Co. v. Carolina Env. Study Group, 438 U.S. 59 (1978), the event underlying the constitutional due process claim presented—a full-scale nuclear power plant meltdown followed by inadequate compensation because of the statutory liability limit at issue—was obviously unripe. The Court, however, deemed the constitutional function of the ripeness requirement to have been satisfied by plaintiffs' showing of article III standing based on the incidental environmental injury currently caused by the plants; it considered the ripeness of the constitutional claim only prudentially. See 438 U.S. at 81–82. Thus, the Court collapsed the two doctrines: regardless of how speculative the contingency underlying the right asserted, a case is constitutionally ripe given the existence of an injury in fact. Although this departure from traditional analysis has been criticized as unwarranted, see Varat, "Variable Justiciability and the Duke Power Case," 58 Tex.L.Rev. 273, 296–98, 303–07 (1980), it is seems a necessary incident to the wise rejection of the nexus requirement—and a doctrinal twist

In *United Public Workers of America v. Mitchell*,[13] for example, government employees, seeking declaratory relief from allegedly unconstitutional restrictions imposed by the Hatch Act on their political activities, described the future conduct in which they planned to engage in terms so general that the Supreme Court could not accept their claim, as tendered, without imposing what were deemed unacceptable limits on the power of Congress. It explained that "[a]ppellants want to engage in 'political management and political campaigns,' to persuade others to follow appellants' views by discussion, speeches, articles and other acts . . . . Such generality of objection is really an attack on the political expediency of the Hatch Act, not the presentation of legal issues." The Court concluded that it was "beyond the competence of courts to render such a decision" because judges are empowered to make constitutional determinations "only when the interests of litigants require the use of this judicial authority for their protection against actual interference. A hypothetical threat is not enough." [14]

Constitutional concerns of ripeness must be applied to every aspect of a lawsuit. For example, ripeness must be evaluated for each legal provision implicated by a challenge, given that "[e]ven where some of the provisions of a comprehensive legislative enactment are ripe for adjudication, portions of the enactment not immediately involved are not thereby thrown open for a judicial determination of constitutionality." [15] Ripeness requirements also constrain a court's power over

relevant only to cases in which such a nexus is lacking.

13. 330 U.S. 75 (1947). See also discussion in § 3–9, supra.

14. Id. at 89–90. Similarly, in International Longshoremen's and Warehousemen's Union, Local 37 v. Boyd, 347 U.S. 222 (1954), a group of resident alien workers sought on constitutional grounds to bar any interpretation of a new labor statute that would imperil their right to return to their homes after their seasonal work in Alaskan fish canneries. The Supreme Court overruled the lower court's grant of relief, which was announced "in advance of [an] immediate adverse effect in the context of a concrete case [and thus had involved] too remote and abstract an inquiry for the proper exercise of the judicial function." Id. at 224. See also Roe v. Wade, 410 U.S. 113, 127–29 (1973) (affirming dismissal of "speculative" complaint by married couple, the woman not being pregnant, that statute prohibiting abortion had a "detrimental effect upon [their] marital happiness"); Laird v. Tatum, 408 U.S. 1, 13–15 (1972) (reinstating dismissal of complaint that Army data-gathering system chilled first amendment rights as impermissibly based on respondents' "speculative apprehension that the Army may at some future date misuse the information in some way that would cause direct harm to respondents"); Socialist Labor Party v. Gilligan, 406 U.S. 583 (1972), discussed in § 3–

8, supra; Communist Party of the United States v. Subversive Activities Control Bd., 367 U.S. 1, 70–81 (1961); Rescue Army v. Municipal Court of Los Angeles, 331 U.S. 549 (1947), discussed in § 3–8, supra. Anticipatory review of unclear criminal statutes can be obtained, however, if the litigant can show a demonstrable threat of enforcement against him personally; alternatively, if the statute clearly applies to his activities, such a threat is generally not required. See § 3–9, supra; note 20, infra.

15. Communist Party of the United States v. Subversive Activities Control Bd., 367 U.S. 1, 71 (1961). For example, Babbitt v. United Farm Workers Nat'l Union, 442 U.S. 289 (1979), which upheld the justiciability of select provisions of a state farm labor statute challenged by farmworkers, found not justiciable a provision allowing employers to bar unions from campaign access to business property; a unanimous Court concluded that it was "conjectural to anticipate that access will be denied," and therefore that an opinion "would be patently advisory," id. at 304. Provisions empowering employers to obtain injunctions against employee strikes and thereafter to submit disputes to compulsory arbitration were similarly found not justiciable, on the assumption that the employers might well elect other responses to labor strife. See id. at 304–05. Likewise, in Pacific Gas & Electric Co. v. State Energy Resources Conservation & Devel.

remedies: even plaintiffs previously injured by a challenged exercise of governmental power may be be foreclosed from relief sought to prevent speculative *future* harm.[16]

In some cases, the constitutional ripeness of the issues presented depends more upon a specific contingency needed to establish a concrete controversy than upon the general development of the underlying facts. For example, litigants alleging that a governmental action has effected an unconstitutional "taking" without "just compensation" [17] are normally obliged to exhaust all avenues for obtaining compensation before the issue is deemed ripe.[18]

Cases in which early legal challenges *are* held to be ripe normally present either or both of two features: significant *present* injuries produced by contemplation of a future event; or legal questions that do not depend for their resolution on an extensive factual background. Both factors are heavily laced with prudential considerations. As the Court explained in the *Regional Rail Reorganization Act Cases*, the first concern recognizes that "[w]here the inevitability of the operation of a statute against certain individuals is patent, it is irrelevant to the existence of a justiciable controversy that there will be a time delay before the disputed provisions will come into effect. . . . 'One does not have to await the consummation of threatened injury to obtain preventive relief. If the injury is certainly impending that is enough.' " [19] Moreover, a claim may be ripe even though it is clear that the threatened injury will *never* occur because the litigant has disclaimed exercise of a right in the face of reasonably certain enforcement against any such exercise.[20] Still, even in "situations where . . .

Comm'n, 461 U.S. 190 (1983), the Court held ripe for review a California moratorium on the certification of new nuclear plants; at the same time, however, it held not ripe a provision of the same statute conditioning construction of nuclear plants on a decision by a state energy commission that adequate facilities are available for interim storage of their nuclear waste. The Court reasoned that, because the energy commission had never found such storage facilities to be inadequate, "a court should not stretch to reach an early, and perhaps premature, decision" on that question. Id. at 203.

16. In O'Shea v. Littleton, 414 U.S. 488 (1974), for example, plaintiffs alleging that they had suffered from discriminatory criminal procedure practices were found not to present a ripe case for injunctive relief against such practices; the possibility that the presumably law-abiding plaintiffs would again be arrested, charged and subjected to the same practices was wholly speculative. See id. at 495–99. See also City of Los Angeles v. Lyons, 461 U.S. 95, 101–10 (1983), discussed in § 3–16, infra; Ashcroft v. Mattis, 431 U.S. 171, 172–73 (1977) (per curiam); Rizzo v. Goode, 423 U.S. 362, 372 (1976); Golden v. Zwickler, 394 U.S. 103, 109 (1969).

17. See Chapter 9, infra.

18. However, if a challenge is to the complete absence of any public purpose, that challenge is ripe without resolution of the "just compensation" issue. See Hawaii Housing Authority v. Midkiff, 467 U.S. 229 (1984). But cf. §§ 8–5, 9–2, infra (explaining how absence of provision for compensation may itself suggest absence of public purpose).

19. 419 U.S. at 143, quoting Pennsylvania v. West Virginia, 262 U.S. 553, 593 (1923) (citations omitted). In the railroad cases, for example, failing railroads facing future compulsion to transfer their property to a new private reorganization corporation attacked the plan under the fifth amendment's just compensation clause; although the transfer was "virtually a certainty," doubt over *when* Congress would trigger the mechanism created the ripeness concern but did not suffice to render the claim unripe. See also Buckley v. Valeo, 424 U.S. 1, 114–17 (1976); Carter v. Carter Coal Co., 298 U.S. 238, 287 (1936); Pierce v. Society of Sisters, 268 U.S. 510, 530, 536 (1925).

20. Such a person "should not be required to await and undergo a criminal prosecution as the sole means of seeking

an allegedly injurious event is certain to occur, [a court] may delay resolution of constitutional questions until a time closer to the actual occurrence of the disputed event, when a better factual record might be available." [21]

The chief feature of the second category of cases is that additional facts are not particularly useful to resolution of the pending challenge, so that such cases can be resolved as well at an early stage. Sometimes, the issues presented are "purely legal, and will not be clarified by further factual development." [22] More often, the issues are "predominantly legal," such that further factual development, while helpful, is not essential.[23] Of course, whether an issue is a "legal" one admitting of decision on a sparse factual record may itself engender sharp—and illuminating—disagreement.[24]

relief." Doe v. Bolton, 410 U.S. 179, 188 (1973). See Babbitt v. United Farm Workers Nat'l Union, 442 U.S. 289, 298–99 (1979). Cf. Steffel v. Thompson, 415 U.S. 452, 459 (1974) (finding ripeness based on explicit threat of police arrest); Clements v. Fashing, 457 U.S. 957, (1982) (finding ripeness based on automatic civil enforcement); Bantam Books, Inc. v. Sullivan, 372 U.S. 58, 67 (1963) (finding ripe a constitutional challenge to a state agency's informal exhortation urging book distributors to stop selling books that the agency, which officially could only recommend prosecution, considered obscene).

21. Regional Rail Reorganization Cases, 419 U.S. at 143.

22. Thomas v. Union Carbide Agricultural Products Co., 473 U.S. 568, 581 (1985). See also Abbott Laboratories, 387 U.S. at 149.

23. Pacific Gas & Elec. Co. v. State Energy Resources Conservation and Development Comm'n, 461 U.S. 190, 201 (1983). For example, in evaluating the ripeness of a constitutional challenge to a federal limit on private liability for nuclear power plant accidents, the Court noted that to wait for such an event "would eliminate much of the existing scientific uncertainty surrounding this subject [but] would not . . . significantly advance [the Court's] ability to deal with the legal issues presented nor aid [it] it their resolution." Duke Power Co. v. Carolina Envtl. Study Group, Inc., 438 U.S. 59, 81–82 (1978).

24. See Scharpf, "Judicial Review and the Political Question: A Functional Analysis," 75 Yale L.J. 517, 531–33 (1966). Professor Scharpf employs Adler v. Board of Education, 342 U.S. 485 (1952), to illustrate the dramatic effect of substantive doctrine on ripeness conclusions. In arguing against the majority's facial approval of a New York law providing for dismissal of all teachers who were members of subversive organizations, Justice Frankfurter

alone concluded that the issue lacked ripeness; he saw "equally legitimate interests" on both sides requiring further factual development for decision. The majority needed no further facts; the law was constitutional because it merely put to the teachers the choice between freedom of private association and access to public employment. The dissenters on the merits could just as easily see that the statute infringed "absolute" first amendment freedoms. See Scharpf, supra, at 532. Much of the dissenters' view ultimately prevailed fifteen years later, see Keyishian v. Board of Regents, 385 U.S. 589 (1967), discussed in § 12–2, infra.

Disagreement about the legitimacy of reviewing legislative enactments at an early stage of events would seem most likely to arise in cases like Adler implicating the most fundamental individual rights. Compare Thornburgh v. American College of Obstetricians and Gynecologists, 106 S.Ct. 2169 (1986) (invalidating as an attempt "to intimidate women into continuing pregnancies" an entire state abortion regulation scheme, never put into operation, in preliminary injunction posture), with id. at 2206–07 (O'Connor, J., dissenting) (criticizing majority for making it "painfully clear" that no state regulation of abortion "is safe from ad hoc nullification" through premature decision of "serious constitutional questions on an inadequate record, in contravention of settled principles of constitutional adjudication and procedural fairness").

Sometimes further factual developments, rather than simply providing the backdrop for detailed constitutional analysis, are themselves viewed as essential operative facts in triggering ripeness. See, e.g., Goldwater v. Carter, 444 U.S. 996, 997–98 (1979) (Powell, J., concurring in the judgment) (finding treaty termination question not ripe until Congress has confronted the

A final prudential factor underlying the determination of ripeness, comprising the second concern of the *Abbott Laboratories* test, is the extent that a delay in judgment will cause hardship. Delay may do so by imposing a continuing harm of uncertainty and expense flowing from doubt about the authority of legal rules governing relations between private parties;[25] by failing to provide clear guidelines needed for effective long-term investment;[26] or by failing to honor explicit legislative goals of certainty.[27]

As even this brief summary should make clear,[28] the categorization of a case as unripe for federal adjudication cannot be reduced to an orderly, much less a highly principled and predictable, process. That realization cannot sit well with anyone concerned to cabin the power of courts to duck controversy without candor. But it is unclear whether judicial discretion to engage in such avoidance of decision could be significantly constrained without unduly restricting the flexibility needed to discharge the article III function wisely.

§ 3–11. Mootness

In contrast to the future-oriented ripeness requirement, the bar on consideration of "moot" cases looks primarily to the relationship between past events and the present challenge in order to determine whether there remains a "case" or "controversy" which meets the article III test of justiciability and satisfies related prudential concerns.[1] Whereas ripeness doctrine focuses on the presence of a possibility or contingency in the place of an actual litigable event, mootness doctrine centers on the succession of events themselves, to ensure that a person

President over the issue), discussed in § 3–13, infra. See also note 18, supra.

25. See, e.g., Thomas v. Union Carbide Agricultural Products Co., 473 U.S. 568, 581 (1986).

26. See, e.g., Pacific Gas & Elec. Co. v. State Energy Resources Conservation and Development Comm'n, 461 U.S. 190, 201–02 (1983).

27. See, e.g., Bowsher v. Synar, 106 S.Ct. 3181 (1986); Duke Power Co. v. Carolina Envtl. Study Group, Inc., 438 U.S. 59, 82 (1978); Buckley v. Valeo, 424 U.S. 1, 117 (1976).

28. For further elaboration of the ripeness doctrine, see Nichol, "Ripeness and the Constitution," 54 U.Chi.L.Rev. 153 (1987).

§ 3–11

1. See, e.g., United States Parole Comm'n v. Geraghty, 445 U.S. 388, 395–97 (1980); North Carolina v. Rice, 404 U.S. 244, 246 (1971); Powell v. McCormack, 395 U.S. 486, 496 n. 7 (1969). As a constitutional prerequisite to exercise of jurisdiction, the question of mootness must be considered even if ignored by the parties, see, e.g., St. Paul Fire & Marine Ins. Co. v. Barry, 438 U.S. 531, 537 (1978). Although

now firmly rooted in article III, the mootness doctrine was not given constitutional status in a Supreme Court decision, apart from a dictum in Aetna Life Ins. Co. v. Haworth, 300 U.S. 227, 240 (1937), until 1964. See Liner v. Jafco, Inc., 375 U.S. 301, 306 n. 3 (1964). Prior to 1964, the mootness doctrine was treated simply as a rule of economy and good sense in judicial administration. See, e.g., Mills v. Green, 159 U.S. 651, 653 (1895); Searcy v. Fayette Home Tel., 143 Ky. 811, 812, 137 S.W. 777 (1911); Note, "Mootness on Appeal in the Supreme Court," 83 Harv.L.Rev. 1672, 1675 (1970). The nonconstitutional discretionary elements of justiciability doctrine, see § 3–8, supra, remain at work in mootness issues as well. See, e.g., Kremens v. Bartley, 431 U.S. 119, 134 n. 15 (1977).

Note the difficulties that may arise on Supreme Court review of a state court decision where state and federal concepts of mootness, or of justiciability generally, are not congruent. See, e.g., Princeton Univ. v. Schmid, 455 U.S. 100, 102 n. * (1982) (per curiam); Richardson v. Ramirez, 418 U.S. 24, 34–40 (1974); L. Tribe, Constitutional Choices 99, 328 & n. 3 (1985). See also § 3–15, infra.

or group mounting a constitutional challenge confronts continuing harm or a significant prospect of future harm. A case is moot, and hence not justiciable, if the passage of time has caused it completely to lose "its character as a present, live controversy of the kind that must exist if [the Court is] to avoid advisory opinions on abstract propositions of law." [2] Thus, the Supreme Court has recognized that mootness can be viewed "as 'the doctrine of standing set in a time frame: The requisite personal interest that must exist at the commencement of the litigation (standing) must continue throughout its existence (mootness).' " [3] A federal trial court, of course, may not hear a moot case; and if mootness evolves later on appeal, "the judgment below normally is vacated with directions to dismiss the complaint." [4]

A dispute may become moot for any of a variety of reasons. The underlying legal framework may change in a manner rendering the plaintiff's claims irrelevant. For example, in *Hall v. Beals*,[5] a challenge to a state voter residency requirement of six months was adjudged mooted by the legislature's reduction of the requirement to two months: "We review the judgment below in the light of the Colorado statute as it now stands, not as it once did. . . . And under the statute as currently written, the appellants could have voted in the . . . presidential election [in question]." [6] Lawsuits for injunctive relief may become moot when the condition challenged is of limited duration and ceases to exist before final review: for example, a prisoner

---

2. Hall v. Beals, 396 U.S. 45, 48 (1969) (per curiam). See also Powell v. McCormack, 395 U.S. 486, 496 (1969) ("Simply stated, a case is moot when the issues presented are no longer 'live' or the parties lack a legally cognizable interest in the outcome"); SEC v. Medical Comm. for Human Rights, 404 U.S. 403, 407 (1972).

3. United States Parole Comm'n v. Geraghty, 445 U.S. 388, 397 (1980) (quoting Monaghan, "Constitutional Adjudication: The Who and When," 82 Yale L.J. 1363, 1384 (1973)). See also Preiser v. Newkirk, 422 U.S. 395, 401–02 (1975), and sources cited; Steffel v. Thompson, 415 U.S. 452, 459 n. 10 (1974) ("an actual controversy must be extant at all stages of review, not merely at the time the complaint is filed").

4. City of Mesquite v. Aladdin's Castle, Inc., 455 U.S. 283, 288 n. 9 (1982). An order to vacate a federal judgment below with directions to dismiss the complaint because mootness has evolved on appeal is known as a "Munsingwear order," after United States v. Munsingwear, Inc., 340 U.S. 36, 39–40 & n. 2 (1950), in which the Supreme Court vacated a judgment and directed dismissal of a price-fixing action because the commodity in question had been decontrolled during the course of the appeal. The effect of a Munsingwear order is to deprive the decision below of any precedential value. See R. Stern, E. Gressman & S. Shapiro, Supreme Court Practice

722–24 (6th ed. 1986). For a recent case of unusual significance disposed of by such an order, see Burke v. Barnes, 107 S.Ct. 734, 737 (1987) (vacating judgment of court of appeals and directing that district court dismiss as moot congressmen's suit challenging presidential "pocket veto" of bill linking military aid to El Salvador to that country's human rights record, on the ground that the bill by its own terms had expired during the appeal, whether or not it had previously been properly enacted into law). See also National Organization for Women v. Idaho, 459 U.S. 809 (1982) (vacating decision striking down as unconstitutional a congressional joint resolution extending time to ratify the proposed Equal Rights Amendment, after the extension had passed without the requisite number of state ratifications, and directing dismissal of complaint as moot). When late-developing mootness appears on appeal from a state court decision, the Supreme Court typically vacates and remands for whatever further proceedings the state court deems proper. See, e.g., DeFunis v. Odegaard, 416 U.S. 312, 320 (1974).

5. 396 U.S. 45 (1969).

6. Id. at 48. See also United States Dep't of Justice v. Provenzano, 469 U.S. 14, 15 (1984) (per curiam) (issue on which certiorari granted mooted by passage of new legislation, though underlying case remained alive).

may be released from custody;[7] a war may end, mooting the legality of restraints on an individual's previous desire to protest it;[8] a business may close, mooting the effect of legal restrictions on it.[9] During the course of a lawsuit an opponent may provide full relief,[10] or the parties may dispose of their claims through consent judgment or simple settlement.[11] Each issue in a case must be examined for mootness; "[w]here one of the several issues presented becomes moot, the remaining live issues supply the constitutional requirement of a case or controversy" with respect to those live issues.[12] Often, a claim for damages will keep a case from becoming moot where equitable relief no longer forms the basis of a live controversy.[13]

The basic concept of mootness is thus straightforward. The complexities of the doctrine generally center on whether any reasons exist for hearing a case which is seemingly moot. Specifically, courts ask: (1) whether an issue is a recurring one which will nonetheless evade ordinary review; (2) whether a plaintiff whose claim is moot nevertheless may continue suit as the representative of a broad class of individuals with a continuing interest; (3) whether plaintiff's claim has been mooted only because defendant has voluntarily, but not necessarily permanently, acquiesced; or (4) whether a case appears to be moot only because collateral consequences of challenged action have been ignored. This section will take up each of these considerations in turn.

In *Southern Pacific Terminal Co. v. ICC*,[14] the Supreme Court announced that an issue is not deemed moot if it is "capable of repetition, yet evading review,"[15] either for the individual originally making the challenge or for others in the group represented.[16] Under this doctrine, in the absence of a claim for class treatment, a litigant

7. See, e.g., Lane v. Williams, 455 U.S. 624 (1982); North Carolina v. Rice, 404 U.S. 244 (1971).

8. See, e.g., Steffel v. Thompson, 415 U.S. 452, 460 (1974) (reviewing three-year-old proposed Vietnam War protest near time of settlement of hostilities).

9. See, e.g., Board of License Commissioners v. Pastore, 469 U.S. 238 (1985).

10. See, e.g., Honig v. Students of the Calif. School for the Blind, 471 U.S. 148 (1985) (full compliance with affirmative requirements of preliminary injunction); Deposit Guaranty Nat'l Bank v. Roper, 445 U.S. 326 (1980) (full payment of money damages mooting individual claims of class representatives); Commissioner v. Shapiro, 424 U.S. 614, 622 n. 7 (1976) (procedural objections cured by intervening action complying with requirements).

11. See, e.g., Lake Coal Co., Inc. v. Roberts & Schaefer Co., 474 U.S. 120 (1985). It is permissible, however, for parties to settle fully the *consequences* of court review through agreement on non-trivial liquidated damages, without thereby mooting the case. See, e.g., Nixon v. Fitzgerald, 457 U.S. 731, 743–44 (1982); Havens Realty

Corp. v. Coleman, 455 U.S. 363, 371 (1982). See also § 3–12, infra.

12. Powell v. McCormack, 395 U.S. 486, 497 (1969).

13. In Powell, id., for example, a congressman's injunctive demand to be seated as a member of the 90th Congress became moot with the termination of that Congress and his seating in the 91st Congress; he was allowed to continue his suit, however, on his claim for back salary. See also Ellis v. Brotherhood of Clerks, 466 U.S. 435, 442 (1984).

14. 219 U.S. 498 (1911).

15. Id. at 515 (holding that the validity of the short-term ICC order challenged by railroad could not be considered moot, despite the order's expiration, as otherwise the issue would avoid review altogether because future orders would likely expire as well before the Supreme Court could be expected to hear the case).

16. The issue may repeat either in the sense that one individual will confront it more than once or in the sense that all the members of a group may each confront it. See United States Parole Comm'n v. Geraghty, 445 U.S. 388, 398–400 (1980).

must establish that: "(1) the challenged action [is] in its duration too short to be fully litigated prior to its cessation or expiration, and (2) there [is] a reasonable expectation that the same complaining party [will] be subjected to the same action again." [17]

This doctrine is often invoked in suits challenging election laws. In *Moore v. Ogilvie*,[18] for example, the Supreme Court found justiciable rather than moot a constitutional challenge to Illinois' petition requirement for independent candidates, even though the claim was based on conduct that had occurred in connection with the completed 1968 election. The Court explained that although there was "no possibility of granting any relief" to the candidates because "the 1968 election is over, the burden . . . placed on the nomination of candidates for statewide offices remains and controls future elections, as long as Illinois maintains her present system as she has done since 1935." [19] Other events are also of predictably short duration; for example, in *Roe v. Wade*,[20] where a pregnant woman's class action challenging the constitutionality of state anti-abortion statutes reached the Supreme Court only *post partum*, the Court held that termination of the plaintiff's pregnancy did not render the case moot: "Pregnancy often comes more than once to the same woman, and in the general population, if man is to survive, it will always be with us." [21] *Roe* was thus a classic case in which an issue was "capable of repetition, yet evading review." [22]

If a lawsuit is properly brought as a class action,[23] the moot claim of the named plaintiff need not even be capable of repetition, yet evading review; the Supreme Court has held that in some situations a mooted plaintiff may continue to pursue the class claim in a representative capacity.[24] The Court's line of significant class action mootness cases begins with *Sosna v. Iowa*.[25] *Sosna* involved a challenge brought

17. Weinstein v. Bradford, 423 U.S. 147, 149 (1975) (per curiam). See also Murphy v. Hunt, 455 U.S. 478, 482 (1982) (per curiam) (noting that "[t]he Court has never held that a mere physical or theoretical possibility was sufficient to satisfy the test stated in *Weinstein*.").

18. 394 U.S. 814 (1969).

19. Id. at 816. See also Anderson v. Celebrezze, 460 U.S. 780, 786–87 (1983); Democratic Party of the United States v. Wisconsin ex rel. LaFollette, 450 U.S. 107, 115 n. 13 (1981); American Party v. White, 415 U.S. 767, 770 n. 1 (1974); Storer v. Brown, 415 U.S. 724, 737 n. 8 (1974); Rosario v. Rockefeller, 410 U.S. 752, 756 n. 3 (1973) (all allowing review of challenges pertaining to past elections).

20. 410 U.S. 113 (1973).

21. Id. at 125.

22. See also, e.g., Press-Enterprise Co. v. Superior Court, 106 S.Ct. 2735, 2739 (1986); Globe Newspaper Co. v. Superior Court, 457 U.S. 596, 603 (1982); Richmond Newspapers, Inc. v. Virginia, 448 U.S. 555,

563 (1980); Reeves, Inc. v. Stake, 447 U.S. 429, 434 n. 5 (1980); Gannett Co. v. DePasquale, 443 U.S. 368, 377–78 (1979); SEC v. Sloan, 436 U.S. 103, 108–10 (1978); United States v. New York Telephone Co., 434 U.S. 159, 165 n. 6 (1977); Nebraska Press Ass'n v. Stuart, 427 U.S. 539, 546–47 (1976); Carroll v. President & Commr's, 393 U.S. 175, 178–79 (1968) (all rejecting claims of mootness). Compare Lane v. Williams, 455 U.S. 624, 633–34 (1982); Murphy v. Hunt, 455 U.S. 478, 482–83 (1982) (per curiam); Weinstein v. Bradford, 423 U.S. 147, 149 (1975) (per curiam) (all finding mootness).

23. See Fed.R.Civ.P. 23.

24. Compare, e.g., DeFunis v. Odegaard, 416 U.S. 312, 317 (1974) (per curiam) (noting failure to bring class action as ground for finding of mootness).

25. 419 U.S. 393 (1975). Earlier, more preliminary cases include Richardson v. Ramirez, 418 U.S. 24 (1974) (ex-felons allowed to challenge voting restrictions as representatives of larger class despite full

in the federal courts to the constitutionality of a state divorce law's one-year durational residency requirement. After the federal district court certified the case as a proper class action and ruled on the merits, the named plaintiff's individual claim was mooted by her satisfaction of the residency requirement.[26] The Supreme Court, however, ruled that the case as a whole was not moot because she had brought the challenge "in a representative capacity." Upon certification, it held, the class had "acquired a legal status separate from the interest asserted by" her that presented a continuing controversy.[27] In finding the case not moot, the Court relief heavily on the conclusion that, given the one-year term involved, *for the class as a whole* the issue was capable of repetition yet evading review.[28] Despite the apparent importance of this factor in *Sosna,*[29] it was subsequently declared, in *Franks v. Bowman Transportation Company,*[30] to be merely a prudential factor informing mootness determinations rather than a constitutional prerequisite to exercise of jurisdiction. *Franks* involved a Title VII class action in which it developed during the litigation that the named plaintiff's own racial discrimination claim was unfounded and that his ability to benefit from any relief was thereby mooted. The Court declined to find mootness even though, unlike *Sosna,* the claim was not of an inherently transitory nature that might frustrate review,[31] concluding that the personal stake of the unnamed class members in the litigation—who had been identified and who were clearly interested in the litigation [32]—guaranteed that "an adversary relationship sufficient to [assure concrete adverseness] exists," preventing mootness.[33]

relief as to them), and Dunn v. Blumstein, 405 U.S. 330, 333 n. 2 (1972) (class challenge to durational voting residence requirement by mooted plaintiff allowed, distinguishing Hall v. Beals, discussed supra). Both are discussed in Note, "The Mootness Doctrine in the Supreme Court," 88 Harv. L.Rev. 373, 387, 390–95 (1974).

26. The case was also mooted by her success in obtaining a divorce in another state. See Sosna, 419 U.S. at 398–99 & n. 7.

27. Id. at 399.

28. Because the Court was unwilling to speculate that the named plaintiff would leave the state and later return to seek another divorce, it ruled that as to her the issue was not capable of repetition yet evading review. See id. at 400. But as to the remaining class members, the Court noted that although the challenged statute would continue to be enforced, "because of the passage of time, no single challenger [would] remain subject to its restrictions for the period necessary to see such a lawsuit to its conclusion." Id. at 400.

This mootness exception, the Court made clear, left unaffected the requirement that the named plaintiff have a live claim at the time the suit was filed and that a live

controversy between defendant and at least one member of the class remain at the time of review. See id. at 402.

29. The Sosna Court explicitly cautioned that "[i]n cases in which the alleged harm would not dissipate during the normal time required for resolution of the controversy, the general principles of Article III jurisdiction require that the plaintiff's personal stake in the litigation continue throughout the entirety of the litigation." Id. at 402.

30. 424 U.S. 747 (1976).

31. The Court stated that "nothing in [Sosna] . . . holds or even intimates that the fact that the named plaintiff no longer has a personal stake in the outcome of a certified class action renders the class action moot unless there remains an issue 'capable of repetition, yet evading review.' " Id. at 754.

32. See id. at 756. By contrast, in Sosna, in which the class members were unidentified and their interests unknown, the Court simply presumed that all members of the class would desire invalidation of the statute. See 419 U.S. at 403 n. 13.

33. 424 U.S. at 755–56.

Sosna and *Franks* therefore established, through emphasis on the continuing interest of class *members* as opposed to the class *representative*, that the mooting of the named plaintiff's individual claim does not moot the entire controversy. A separate question, however, is whether the same result obtains when the named plaintiff is mooted out before the class is even certified. The *Sosna* and *Franks* cases would suggest that the inquiry properly focuses on the unnamed class members rather than the mooted named plaintiff—on whether the putative class has a continuing dispute with the defendant. If such a dispute exists, it is difficult to see why the lack of class certification is in any way relevant to the existence of an article III case or controversy.[34] Accordingly, it seems reasonable to conclude that an uncertified class should be deemed part of the case for purposes of litigating the certification question, and that the mooted class representative should be allowed to press that question, just as the named plaintiff in *Sosna* was allowed to press the class claim on the merits.[35]

However, when squarely presented with the mootness problem posed by uncertified class actions, the Court, in *Deposit Guaranty National Bank v. Roper*[36] and *United States Parole Commission v. Geraghty*,[37] focused on the personal interest of the mooted class representative in arguing the certification issue rather than on the interests of the putative class itself. In *Roper*, the named plaintiffs were credit card holders whose individual usury claims were mooted by the defendant's tender of full payment after denial of class certification.[38] In a 7–2 decision, the Court held that the named plaintiffs were nevertheless entitled to appeal the denial of certification based on their "*individual* interest in the litigation" in shifting their litigation costs to other class members, "as distinguished from whatever may be their representative

---

34. See, e.g., Deposit Guaranty Nat'l Bank v. Roper, 445 U.S. 326, 342–44 & n. 3 (1980) (Stevens, J., concurring) ("no question of mootness arises simply because the remaining adversary parties are unnamed"); Greenstein, "Bridging the Mootness Gap in Federal Court Class Actions," 35 Stan.L.Rev. 897, 922–23 (1983). But see United States Parole Comm'n v. Geraghty, 445 U.S. 388, 413, 415 & n. 8 (1980) (Powell, J., dissenting).

Moreover, to find the entire class action moot in situations where the district court has erroneously withheld certification and the named plaintiff has been mooted out, or where the issue could not be presented in time for the court to rule on it before that event, is unreasonable. Indeed, in the latter situation, the Court early on recognized that the certification question can remain live for decision. In Gerstein v. Pugh, 420 U.S. 103 (1975), pretrial detainees jailed without a probable cause hearing challenged by class action the state's authority to so detain them; the case was not moot, despite the lack of evidence that any

of them were pretrial detainees at the time of certification, because the Court did not doubt "the constant existence of a class of persons suffering the deprivation," id. at 111 n. 11. See also Sosna, 419 U.S. at 402 n. 11 (noting that subsequent certification can "relate back" to date complaint was filed so as to avoid mootness gap).

35. See Deposit Guaranty Nat'l Bank v. Roper, 445 U.S. 326, 342–44 (1980) (Stevens J., concurring); Greenstein, supra note 34, at 908–09, 920, 925; Note, "Class Standing and the Class Representative," 94 Harv.L. Rev. 1637, 1647–50 (1981).

36. 445 U.S. 326 (1980).

37. 445 U.S. 388 (1980).

38. The settlement was imposed on plaintiffs by the district court, see Roper, 445 U.S. at 329–30. The Court expressed concern that to deny an appeal on the certification question would allow defendants to "buy off" individual claims to forstall class adjudication, and encourage forum shopping by plaintiffs. See id. at 339–40.

responsibilities to the putative class. . . ." [39]   More creative reasoning was required in *Geraghty*, which involved a prisoner who had been refused parole and who filed a class action challenging the validity of the applicable federal parole guidelines. The trial court denied class action certification and ruled against him on the merits; during appeal of both issues the prisoner was released, mooting his individual claim. The Court, by a 5–4 margin, concluded that the issue of class certification was not moot and could be appealed by the ex-prisoner, deeming him to possess the required "personal stake" in the certification issue.[40]

In *Geraghty* the Court justified looking beyond the mootness of the individual claim for a personal stake by adopting an "issue by issue" approach to interpreting the requirements of article III and eschewing reliance on "the strict, formalistic perception" of article III urged by the dissent—a perception which it argued had been "riddled with exceptions." [41]   It explained that, in addition to a claim on the merits, a named plaintiff presents for judicial resolution a wholly separate "claim that he is entitled to represent the class." This claim, it said, is created by Rule 23 of the Federal Rules of Civil Procedure, which guarantees named plaintiffs "the right to have a class certified if the Rules are met." [42]   The Court acknowledged that "[t]his 'right' is more analogous to the private attorney general concept than to the type of interest traditionally thought to satisfy the 'personal stake' requirement," [43] but argued that such a traditional interest was unnecessary given the "concrete, sharply presented" certification issue and *Sosna's* recognition that "vigorous advocacy can be assured through means other than the traditional requirement . . . ." [44]

As the dissent pointed out, it seems obvious that a litigant—or more accurately, perhaps, the lawyer involved [45]—will press a certification claim not for its intrinsic value, but because of an interest in the merits.[46]   By permitting such continued challenge, the *Geraghty* decision, although in a limited manner,[47] defines a class of persons allowed

---

39. Id. at 340; see also id. at 334 n. 6, 336. One dissenter argued that the record was devoid of proof that litigation costs would be shifted, given the contingent fee agreement used by plaintiffs' lawyers. See id. at 349–52 (Powell, J., dissenting).

40. See Geraghty, 445 U.S. at 396–97, 404. Justice Blackmun wrote for the Court, joined by Justices Brennan, White, Marshall, and Stevens.

41. Id. at 401, 404–06 n. 11.

42. Id. at 402–03.

43. Id. at 403. The dissent argued that neither Rule 23 nor the private attorney general concept could supply such a substantive right. See id. at 420–21 (Powell, J., joined by Burger, C.J., and Stewart and Rehnquist, JJ., dissenting). Deriding the Court's creation of "a substantive right out of a procedural claim," one commentator has argued that because *every* named plaintiff has such a stake, Geraghty is "an abandonment of the personal stake re-

quirement masquerading as its application." Note, supra note 35, at 1647. See also id. at 1650–52.

44. Geraghty, 445 U.S. at 403–04. In countering the dissent's claim that the Court was opening the judicial process to claims by "concerned bystanders," the Court suggested that its holding merely prevented an erroneous certification decision from being insulated from review, allowing any subsequent reversal to "relate back" to the time of the initial denial of certification. See id. at 407 n. 11. On the roots of the relation-back doctrine, see supra note 34.

45. See, e.g., Tushnet, "The Sociology of Article III: A Response to Professor Brilmayer," 93 Harv.L.Rev. 1698, 1706–07 (1980).

46. See Geraghty, 445 U.S. at 422 n. 17 (Powell, J., dissenting).

47. The majority made clear that mooted plaintiffs are guaranteed *only* the right

to assert the rights of third parties—in contravention of general policy underlying the law of standing.[48] But this exception is entirely unproblematic given Congress's sanction of the class action device at issue, and the reasonable conclusion that the *Geraghty* rule furthers the purposes underlying the class action.[49] Congress's purposes could have been more frankly served, however, had the Court, in avoiding mootness, relied on the interest of absent class members in having a class certified.

Turning from the case of repeated harm, we look next to problems of voluntary cessation. "It is well settled that a defendant's voluntary cessation of a challenged practice does not deprive a federal court of its power to determine the legality of the practice"[50]—although courts may give such voluntary cessation emphasis in determining appropriate relief.[51] Such acquiescence would necessarily be without effect if a plaintiff were seeking damages for past wrongs. But voluntary cessation will generally not moot even an action for an injunction, or for other relief with continuing force; "if it did, the courts would be compelled to leave '[t]he defendant . . . free to return to his old ways.' "[52] As long as there is a possibility that the challenged practice may resume, and even though the controversy is not one that would otherwise evade review,[53] the case is not moot. For example, the Court has refused to consider moot a claim for injunctive relief against allegedly illegal police practices which had been banned for an indeterminate period by administrative moratorium;[54] a challenge on vagueness grounds to a city ordinance that was repealed during litigation;[55] and antitrust suits in which defendants for various reasons ceased their

to press the certification issue, leaving who will represent the class on the merits as a separate issue. See id. at 404–07.

48. See § 3–19, infra. See also Rohr, "Fighting for the Rights of Others: The Troubled Law of Third-Party Standing and Mootness in the Federal Courts," 35 U. Miami L.Rev. 393, 447–50 (1981); Note, "Article III Justiciability and Class Actions: Standing and Mootness," 59 Tex.L. Rev. 297, 316–19 (1981).

49. Cf. § 3–15, notes 6 & 7, infra. The Court's willingness to take a fresh look at the dictates of article III when presented with novel means of structuring litigation is not new. See, e.g., § 3–9, supra (discussing declaratory judgment actions).

50. City of Mesquite v. Aladdin's Castle, Inc., 455 U.S. 283, 289 (1982). See also, e.g., County of Los Angeles v. Davis, 440 U.S. 625, 631 (1979); Allee v. Medrano, 416 U.S. 802, 810–11 (1974); DeFunis v. Odegaard, 416 U.S. 312, 318 (1974).

51. See, e.g., City of Mesquite, 455 U.S. at 289 (it "is an important factor bearing on the question whether a court should exercise its power to enjoin the defendant

from renewing the practice"); United States v. Concentrated Phosphate Export Ass'n, 393 U.S. 199, 203 (1968) (noting challenged party may show "that the likelihood of further violations is sufficiently remote to make injunctive relief unnecessary"); United States v. W. T. Grant Co., 345 U.S. 629, 633 (1953) (stating "it is one of the factors to be considered in determing the appropriateness of granting an injunction against the now-discontinued acts").

52. United States v. Concentrated Phosphate Export Ass'n, 393 U.S. 199, 203 (1968) (quoting United States v. W. T. Grant Co., 345 U.S. 629, 632 (1953)).

53. See Note, supra note 25, at 385–86.

54. See City of Los Angeles v. Lyons, 461 U.S. 95, 100–01 (1983) (noting that "the moratorium by its terms is not permanent"), discussed in § 3–16, infra.

55. See City of Mesquite v. Aladdin's Castle, Inc., 455 U.S. 283, 288–89 and n. 11 (1982) (noting that repeal did not preclude the city "from reenacting precisely the same provision if the [injunction] were vacated" and that "the city [had] announced just such an intention").

challenged actions and disclaimed any intent to commit future violations.[56]

Although "[d]efendants face a heavy burden to establish mootness in such cases because otherwise they would simply be free to 'return to [their] old ways' after the threat of a lawsuit had passed,"[57] in certain circumstances voluntary cessation can dispose of a case. A case will be mooted, the Court indicated in *County of Los Angeles v. Davis*,[58] when: (1) "it can be said with assurance that 'there is no reasonable expectation . . . .' that the alleged violation will recur"; and (2) "interim relief or events have completely and irrevocably eradicated the effects of the alleged violation."[59] For example, in *Davis* the Court, by a 5–4 vote, found moot a racial discrimination case in which a federal district court had invalidated a 1972 firefighter hiring plan (and issued affirmative relief) based solely on the disparate racial impact of the plan; it regarded any future attempt by defendants to implement the never-enacted plan implausible under apparently unusual circumstances, and found no lingering effects.[60]

Most cases in this area finding mootness depend to some degree on events or aspects of a factual situation independent of a defendant's simple intent to cease challenged conduct which indicate that continuation of the conduct is unlikely.[61] For example, in *DeFunis v. Odegaard*,[62] the Supreme Court declared moot a challenge to the constitutionality of "benign" discrimination imposed by the University of Washington Law School's admissions procedures; the plaintiff had been denied admission and after prevailing at the trial level had obtained an injunction ordering his admission pending appellate review. When the Court announced its decision the plaintiff was only a few weeks from graduation, and the school had recognized the plaintiff's right, under regular policy, to finish the term; mootness was based on this policy

---

56. See St. Paul Fire & Marine Ins. Co. v. Barry, 438 U.S. 531, 537–38 (1978) (challenge to malpractice insurance companies' allegedly illegal refusal to deal, discontinued but not barred under state's collective insurance-pooling scheme); United States v. Concentrated Phosphate Ass'n, 393 U.S. 199, 202–03 (1968) (complaint against organization whose members had disbanded and forsworn future violations); United States v. W. T. Grant Co., 345 U.S. 629, 632–33 (1953) (challenge to interlocking directorates which the defendants dissolved and disclaimed any interest in reviving).

57. Iron Arrow Honor Soc'y v. Heckler, 464 U.S. 67, 72 (1983) (per curiam) (quoting United States v. W. T. Grant Co., 345 U.S. 629, 632 (1953)).

58. 440 U.S. 625 (1979).

59. Id. at 631 (citations omitted); see also United States v. Concentrated Phosphate Export Ass'n, 393 U.S. 199, 203 (1968).

60. See Davis, 440 U.S. at 627–34. The Court noted first that there "was no reason to believe that [defendants] would replace

their present hiring procedures with procedures that they regarded as unsatisfactory even before the commencement of this litigation"—the 1972 plan that had been proposed in response to a "unique" temporary workforce shortage "unlikely to recur." Id. at 632–33. It found the second condition for mootness met given that the district court's affirmative action decree, over a five-year period, "had completely cured any discriminatory effect of the 1972 proposal"—although the Court was "extremely doubtful" that the plan, never implemented, had ever produced discriminatory effects. Id. at 633–34. But see id. at 637, 641–45 (Powell, J., dissenting) (finding majority's conclusion "a questionable means of avoiding" the important question of whether racial discrimination could be found absent "proof of racially discriminatory intent or purpose," and manifestly at odds with the record in the case and defendants' articulated wishes).

61. See Note, supra note 25, at 384–85.

62. 416 U.S. 312 (1974).

rather than on any ad hoc promise by the school to change its admissions practices.[63] Similarly, in reviewing a student group's request to enjoin a government agency from pressuring the university to ban the group's activities as sexually discriminatory, a bare majority of the Court found the controversy moot because the university had unequivocally decided to exclude the group regardless of the government's position.[64] And, in a suit by shareholders of a company to force a vote on continuation of Vietnam War napalm sales in which the company had consented to one vote, the Court found the controversy moot on the assumption that, given the trivial support for the measure evidenced by the vote already held, the company would allow another vote when next asked rather than repeat the litigation.[65]

We turn finally to the matter of collateral consequences, mandating an inquiry into the possible continuing effects of a challenged but completed action. Although the collateral consequences doctrine will on occasion constitute a ground for avoiding mootness in a civil case,[66]

---

63. The Court noted that, since "all parties agree that DeFunis is now entitled to complete his legal studies . . . and to receive his degree . . . [a] determination by this Court of the legal issues . . . is no longer necessary," id. at 317. Cf. discussion of collusive suits, § 3–12, infra. It concluded that "mootness in the present case depends not at all upon a 'voluntary cessation' of the admissions practices" but "depends, instead, upon the simple fact that DeFunis is now in the final quarter of the final year of his course of study, and the settled and unchallenged policy of the Law School is to permit him to complete the term for which he is now enrolled." Id. at 318. By contrast, in urging that the case was not moot, the dissent suggested that "unexpected events," such as "illness, economic necessity, [or] academic failure," could result in DeFunis failing to finish the academic term and being forced to request readmission to the school. Id. at 348 (Brennan, J., dissenting). In dismissing the case as moot the Court avoided addressing divisive issues which it later encountered in Regents of the Univ. of California v. Bakke, 438 U.S. 265 (1978), discussed in § 16–22, infra.

64. See Iron Arrow Honor Soc'y v. Heckler, 464 U.S. 67, 70–72 (1983) (per curiam). Justices Brennan and Stevens dissented; Justices Marshall and Blackmun would have denied certiorari. The Court's reasoning ignored the fact that, even if a decision barring the federal interference would not necessarily have reinstated the group's relationship with the university, it would have removed one justification for the university's adverse action, requiring that a decision be made solely on other grounds; it would also have removed a financial penalty to reconsideration of the decision, see id. at 75–77 (Ste-

vens, J., dissenting). Compare Larson v. Valente, 456 U.S. 228 (1982), discussed in § 3–9, supra.

65. See SEC v. Medical Comm'n for Human Rights, 404 U.S. 403, 405–06 (1972).

66. See, e.g., Super Tire Engineering Co. v. McCorkle, 416 U.S. 115 (1974) (issue of striking workers' eligibility for welfare assistance not moot post-strike given continuing effect on bargaining dynamics); Carroll v. President & Comm'rs, 393 U.S. 175 (1968) (state court's sanction of ten-day restraining order of rally presents live issue given officials' reliance on decision in continuing dispute). See also Note, supra note 25, at 379–80; Note, supra note 1, at 1680–81. An unusually expansive application of the collateral consequences doctrine appears in Justice Stevens' dissent, joined by Justice White, in Burke v. Barnes, 107 S.Ct. 734 (1987), in which the Supreme Court held that a challenge by congressmen to a presidential "pocket veto" of a bill conditioning American military aid to El Salvador on that country's human rights record had been mooted by the bill's expiration by its own terms shortly after the court of appeals had handed down its decision in the case. Justice Stevens urged that legislators have an institutional interest in "protecting [their] work product from nullifcation," regardless of whether a particular enactment had lapsed. Id. at 737. As Justice Stevens' opinion seemed to imply, see id., acknowledging a lawmaker interest in the *enforcement* of the laws—as opposed to the more typical case for legislative legal intervention, in which a lawmaker's own role in the enactment of legislation had been compromised or circumvented, see, e.g., Goldwater v. Carter, 444 U.S. 996, 997 (1979) (Powell, J.,

its primary function is to allow an individual to challenge a criminal conviction even when the resulting sentence has been completely served.[67] "[A] criminal case is moot only if it is shown that there is no possibility that any collateral legal consequences will be imposed on the basis of the challenged conviction." [68] Collateral legal consequences include the prospects of disenfranchisement, consideration in sentencing for any future conviction, character impeachment at a future trial, inability to hold office or serve as a juror, and ineligibility for municipal licenses.[69] When collateral consequences are present, a case may be pressed either on direct appeal or through a federal habeas corpus action,[70] and continuing review is available to the state as well as the individual.[71] Pending review of a conviction, a number of events might nonetheless lead to dismissal of the case. For example, the death of the appellant will moot the case,[72] and the appellant's flight from the jurisdiction will bar further attempts at relief.[73]

concurring in the judgment)—would substantially expand the doctrine of legislator standing and make the issues of mootness and standing indistinguishable in the case in question. The Burke majority opinion, written by Chief Justice Rehnquist, pointedly rejected the contention that "the questions of mootness and standing are necessarily intertwined," 107 S.Ct. at 736 n. **, arguing that a legislator's interest in seeing the law carried out extends no farther than his interest in seeing his vote effectuated.

67. Although the Supreme Court has termed this an "exception," see Sibron v. New York, 392 U.S. 40, 51, 53, 54 (1968), it might more satisfactorily be regarded as an instance where the defendant's continuing interest in reversal of a past conviction shows the existence of a live rather than moot controversy. See Note, supra note 25, at 381 n. 34.

68. Sibron v. New York, 392 U.S. 40, 57 (1968).

69. See, e.g, Evitts v. Lucey, 469 U.S. 387, 391 n. 4 (1985); Pennsylvania v. Mimms, 434 U.S. 106, 108 n. 3 (1977) (per curiam); North Carolina v. Rice, 404 U.S. 244, 247 n. 1 (1977) (per curiam); Sibron v. New York, 392 U.S. 40, 55–56 (1968); Carafas v. LaVallee, 391 U.S. 234, 238 (1968). Under the definition of collateral consequences articulated in Sibron, supra, 392 U.S. at 57, it would seem that nearly any interest in removing a conviction will avoid mootness. Even such purely personal impacts as possible loss of employment may suffice, see Street v. New York, 394 U.S. 576, 579–80 n. 3 (1969); Ginsberg v. New York, 390 U.S. 629, 634 n.2 (1968). However, the Court has at times suggested limitations to the scope of the consequences that will be considered sufficient.

See, e.g., Lane v. Williams, 455 U.S. 624, 631–33 (1982) (case found moot because no "civil disabilities" flow from potential discretionary consideration by future employer or sentencing judge of challenged parole violation); Rice, supra, 404 U.S. at 247–48 (challenge to *length* of sentence served held moot given failure to articulate benefits of sentence correction). Cf. Ginsberg v. New York, 390 U.S. 629, 634 n. 2 (1968) (distinguishing earlier cases failing to allege substantial collateral consequences).

70. See Carafas v. LaVallee, 391 U.S. 234 (1968) (overruling Parker v. Ellis, 362 U.S. 574 (1960) (per curiam)).

71. Just as a defendant has an interest in avoiding collateral consequences, the government's interest in imposing such consequences entitles it to continued review of a decision favorable to a defendant. See Pennsylvania v. Mimms, 434 U.S. 106, 108 n. 3 (1977) (per curiam).

72. See Dove v. United States, 423 U.S. 325 (1976) (per curiam) (death moots appeal but does not require that indictment be vacated) (overruling Durham v. United States, 401 U.S. 481 (1971) (per curiam)). But cf. Robinson v. California, 370 U.S. 660 (1962), petition to dismiss appeal as moot denied, 371 U.S. 905 (1962) (prejudgment death does not moot appeal when noticed after judgment).

73. Such a case is technically not moot; rather, the defendant is "disentitled" from seeking relief from a conviction. See, e.g., United States v. Sharpe, 470 U.S. 675, 681 n. 2 (1985); Molinaro v. New Jersey, 396 U.S. 365 (1970). By contrast, governmental officials may continue any attempt to overturn a decision favorable to the defendant. See, e.g., Sharpe, supra, at id.

Many of the exceptions to the mootness prohibition suggest the mootness doctrine's implicit concern with practical considerations of judicial economy and political flexibility, as distinct from the basic elements of the "case or controversy" requirement of article III.[74] Specifically, the cases evidence reluctance to stretch exceptions to the mootness ban when doing so would have limited value in obviating future litigation, or when doing so would be likely to cause a premature restriction in policymaking by the legislative or executive branches.[75] Conversely, when judicial resources can be conserved by clearly settling an issue that is not within an area of current flux—or when it is perceived as unfair to refuse the power of the judiciary to a litigant who has suffered past harm and who faces some risk if denied review [76]—the cases suggest a greater willingness to overlook mootness difficulties.[77]

§ 3–12. Collusive Suits

A suit is collusive and hence not justiciable in "the absence of a genuine adversary issue between the parties, without which a court may not safely proceed to judgment, especially when it assumes the grave responsibility of passing on the validity of legislative action." [1] Thus, in *United States v. Johnson*,[2] the Supreme Court dismissed a civil suit that had been filed at the request of the defendant, who had also paid all of the costs: "Here an important public interest is at stake— the validity of an Act of Congress. . . . That interest has been adjudicated in a proceeding in which the plaintiff has no active participation, over which he has exercised no control, and the expense of which he has not borne." Similarly, if one party agrees with the position taken by the other, there is no case or controversy within the meaning of article III.[3]

---

74. See Kates & Barker, "Mootness in Judicial Proceedings: Toward a Coherent Theory," 62 Calif.L.Rev. 1385, 1412 (1974). See, e.g., United States v. W. T. Grant Co., 345 U.S. 629, 632 (1953). Of course, the public interest in efficient and flexible judicial administration cannot alone confer article III jurisdiction absent a real "case" or "controversy," see Richardson v. Ramirez, 418 U.S. 24, 36 (1974) (suggesting that the "purely practical consideration" of an important issue evading review cannot control article III mootness issue), but it can be relevant in shaping a satisfactory conception of what *counts* as such an event. Cf. Note, supra note 1; Note, "Cases Moot on Appeal: A Limit on the Judicial Power," 103 U.Pa.L.Rev. 772 (1955).

75. See, e.g., Kremens v. Bartley, 431 U.S. 119, 134 n. 15 (1977); DeFunis v. Odegaard, 416 U.S. 312 (1974), discussed supra note 63.

76. In such situations—for example, where a party relies on voluntary cessation of the challenged behavior to defeat review, or when the case presents a claim "capable of repetition but evading review"—the Court has sometimes, in effect,

"lowered the ripeness threshold so as to preclude manipulation of the parties or the mere passage of time from frustrating judicial review." Vitek v. Jones, 445 U.S. 480, 503 (1980) (Blackmun, J., dissenting).

77. See Note, supra note 25, at 394–95.

§ 3–12

1. United States v. Johnson, 319 U.S. 302, 304 (1943). The first such case was Lord v. Veazie, 49 U.S. (8 How.) 251 (1850), where the Supreme Court denounced "the whole proceeding" (in which a suit was instituted to decide whether Veazie in fact had the rights that he asserted he had in a deed executed to Lord) as "in contempt of the court, and highly reprehensible." Id. at 254–55.

2. 319 U.S. 302, 304–05 (1943). But cf. Hylton v. United States, 3 U.S. (3 Dall.) 171 (1796).

3. But see § 3–9, supra, note 8. Cf. Kentucky v. Indiana, 281 U.S. 163 (1930); Young v. United States, 315 U.S. 257, 258– 59 (1942); Sibron v. New York, 392 U.S. 40, 58–59 (1968). The mere fact, however, that parties may have conditioned terms of a settlement on the legal resolution by a

The prohibition of collusive suits does not bar claims which arise out of conduct designed by the litigant to provoke litigation while minimizing possible adverse consequences, but in which the litigant nonetheless retains an adversary interest. For example, in *Evers v. Dwyer*,[4] the Supreme Court allowed a challenge to bus segregation even though the individual who was threatened with arrest for failing to sit in the appropriate place had so acted in order to be able to instigate the litigation without actually incurring arrest: "A resident of a municipality who cannot use transportation facilities therein without being subjected by statute to special disabilities necessarily has . . . a substantial, immediate, and real interest in the validity of the statute which imposes the disability."

But parties seeking access to a judicial decision by an article III court may not so plan their conduct as to eliminate all conflict except a disagreement over a general principle. Thus, in *Muskrat v. United States*,[5] the Supreme Court found nonjusticiable an action challenging the constitutionality of federal laws regulating Indian lands. The action was brought under a statute conferring jurisdiction in the federal courts over the claim of the particular plaintiffs only to the extent of allowing recovery of the costs of bringing the claim. Although the plaintiffs in *Muskrat* were found to lack the requisite adversary interest because of how Congress had defined the right of action that could be brought against the United States, the mere fact that a suit against the United States requires Congressional approval because of sovereign immunity does not by itself render a case nonjusticiable as "collusive." This result occurs in part because such approval, once given as to a particular case, might not be freely retractable in the course of litigation,[6] but also in part because a legal controversy is not necessarily illusory simply because one of the parties retains options for circumvention of the judgment.[7] The Supreme Court has thus rejected Chief Justice Taney's confining view that the "award of execution is a part, and an essential part of every judgment passed by a court exercising the judicial power." [8]

The Supreme Court has found justiciable, for purposes of its own appellate review, decisions of the Court of Claims, whose awards are entirely the consequence of legislative action. In *La Abra Silver*

---

court of a bona fide legal question does not render the case impermissibly collusive. Thus, in the case of Nixon v. Fitzgerald, 457 U.S. 731 (1982), former President Nixon and the plaintiff—a management analyst fired from the executive branch—had agreed to alternative settlement figures depending on the Supreme Court's resolution of the issue of executive immunity, but the suit remained justiciable. Id. at 743–44 n. 24. Cf. id. at 798 (Blackmun, J., joined by Brennan and Marshall, JJ., dissenting) ("had the details of this agreement been known at the time the petition for certiorari came before the Court, certiorari would have been denied"). By contrast, had Nixon and Fitzgerald merely, say, "bet" on the resolution of the abstract legal question of the scope of executive immunity unconnected to a concrete dispute, the stakes for each would have been purely artificial and the case thus nonjusticiable. Cf. id. at 798–799 (dissenters "cannot escape the feeling that [the] long-undisclosed agreement [between Nixon and Fitzgerald] comes close to being a wager on the outcome of the case").

4. 358 U.S. 202, 204 (1958).

5. 219 U.S. 346 (1911).

6. See § 3–5, supra.

7. See the discussion in § 3–9, supra.

8. Gordon v. United States, 117 U.S. 697, 702 (1886) (report of undelivered 1864 opinion).

Mining Co. v. United States,[9] for example, the Court held justiciable the review of a declaratory judgment obtained by the United States in the Court of Claims in a controversy over liability for payment of an award that had been procured by the claimant, allegedly by fraudulent means, from an international arbitration panel. Similarly, Justice Harlan, writing for a plurality of the Court in *Glidden Co. v. Zdanok,*[10] stated that "[i]f [the Supreme] Court may rely on the good faith of state governments or other public bodies to respond to its judgments, there seems to be no sound reason why the Court of Claims may not rely on the good faith of the United States."[11] Analogously, in *United States v. Nixon,*[12] the Supreme Court rejected the contention that Watergate Special Prosecutor Jaworski's claim of authority to subpoena evidence from President Nixon "was nonjusticiable because it was between the Special Prosecutor and the Chief Executive and hence 'intra-executive' in character. . . ." Writing for a unanimous Court, Chief Justice Burger observed that "the production or nonproduction of specified evidence deemed by the Special Prosecutor to be relevant and admissible in a pending criminal case" presents "issues . . . 'of a type which are traditionally justiciable.'"[13] Further, the Court concluded that "the fact that both parties are officers of the Executive Branch cannot be viewed as a barrier to justiciability" since congressional and administrative actions blocked the President from directly and immediately ordering the Special Prosecutor to cease his investigations. Congress had granted the Attorney General "the power to appoint subordinate officers to assist him in the discharge of his duties." Acting under this congressionally granted authority, the Attorney General had promulgated a regulation having, as the Court observed, "the force of law," which gave the Special Prosecutor "unique authority and tenure" as well as "explicit power to contest the invocation of executive privilege in the process of seeking evidence. . . ."[14] The Supreme Court held that, so long as the Attorney General did not "amend or revoke the regulation defining the special prosecutor's authority . . . the Executive Branch is bound by [the regulation], and indeed the United States as the sovereign composed of the three branches is bound to respect and enforce it." Therefore, "[in] light of the uniqueness of the setting in which the conflict arises, the fact that both parties are officers of the Executive Branch cannot be viewed as a barrier to justiciability."[15] It is in this sense that the Court in *United States v. Nixon* rejected the extravagant claim that the President "is" the Executive Branch.[16]

---

9. 175 U.S. 423 (1899).

10. 370 U.S. 530 (1962).

11. Id. at 571. See discussion of Glidden in § 3–5, supra. See also the discussion of United States v. Nixon, 418 U.S. 683 (1974), in § 3–12, supra.

12. 418 U.S. 683 (1974).

13. Id. at 697. See also the discussion of political questions in § 3–13, infra.

14. 418 U.S. at 697, 694, 695. The Special Prosecutor could not be removed except for cause, and then only with "the 'consensus' of eight designated leaders of Congress."

15. Id. at 697.

16. See the discussion of the merits of the case, in the context of executive privilege, in § 4–15, infra.

§ 3–13. The Political Question Doctrine

The political question doctrine is in a state of some confusion.[1] The confusion is perhaps most clearly revealed in the Supreme Court's purportedly "definitive" statement of the political question doctrine in *Baker v. Carr*:[2] "Prominent on the surface of any case held to involve a political question is found" either: (1) "a textually demonstrable constitutional commitment to a coordinate political department"; (2) "a lack of judicially discoverable and manageable standards for resolving it"; (3) "the impossibility of deciding without an initial policy determination of a kind clearly for nonjudicial discretion"; (4) "the impossibility of a court's undertaking independent resolution without expressing lack of the respect due coordinate branches of government"; (5) "an unusual need for unquestioning adherence to a political decision already made"; or (6) "the potentiality of embarrassment from multifarious pronouncements by various departments on one question."

Even this "definitive" statement contains strands of at least three different theories of the role of the Court (as well as federal courts generally) with regard to the other branches of the government. A *classical* view would take the Court's role as announced in *Marbury v. Madison*[3] quite rigidly, and would impose on the Court the requirement of deciding all cases and issues before it unless the Court finds, purely as a matter of constitutional interpretation, that the Constitution itself has committed the determination of the issue to the autonomous decision of another agency of government.[4] A *prudential* view of the Court's role would treat the political question doctrine as a means to avoid passing on the merits of a question when reaching the merits would force the Court to compromise an important principle or would undermine the Court's authority.[5] Unlike the classical or prudential views, a *functional* approach to the role of the Court would have it consider such factors as the difficulties in gaining judicial access to relevant information, the need for uniformity of decision, and the wider responsibilities of the other branches of government, when determining whether or not to decide a certain issue or case.[6]

§ 3–13

1. See, e.g., Redish, "Judicial Review and the 'Political Question'," 79 Nw.U.L. Rev. 1031, 1022–55 (1985); Tigar, "The 'Political Question' Doctrine and Foreign Relations," 17 U.C.L.A.L.Rev. 1135 (1970); Note, The Supreme Court, 1968 Term," 83 Harv.L.Rev. 7, 62 (1969). For a discussion of some of the problems caused by the unstable nature of the doctrine, see Hughes, "Civil Disobedience and the Political Question Doctrine," 48 N.Y.U.L.Rev. 1 (1968).

2. 369 U.S. 186, 217 (1962).

3. 5 U.S. (1 Cranch) 137 (1803), discussed in § 3–2, supra.

4. See, e.g., Wechsler, "Toward Neutral Principles of Constitutional Law," 73 Harv. L.Rev. 1, 7 (1959); Weston, "Political Questions," 38 Harv.L.Rev. 296 (1925).

5. See, e.g, A. Bickel, The Least Dangerous Branch 23–28, 69–71 (1962); Finkelstein, "Judicial Self-Limitation," 37 Harv. L.Rev. 338, 361 (1924), and "Some Further Notes on Judicial Self-Limitation," 39 Harv.L.Rev. 221 (1926).

6. See, e.g., Scharpf, "Judicial Review and the Political Question: A Functional Analysis," 75 Yale L.J. 517, 566–82 (1966).

Returning to the factors listed in Baker v. Carr, it is evident that the first, "a textually demonstrable constitutional commitment to a coordinate political department," reflects essentially classical concerns. The last three factors—"the impossibility of a court's undertaking independent resolution without expressing lack of the respect due coordinate branches of government"; "an unusual need for unquestioning adherence to a political decision already made"; and "the potentiality

One conventional view of the doctrine grounds it in the assumption that there are certain constitutional questions which are *inherently* non-justiciable. These "political questions," it is said, concern matters as to which departments of government other than the courts, or perhaps the electorate as a whole, must have the final say. With respect to these matters, the judiciary does not define constitutional limits.[7] Professor Louis Henkin, however, has forcefully criticized the idea that there are parts of the Constitution to which the judiciary must be blind.[8] The political question cases, he argues, do not support such a proposition. In these cases, the Supreme Court concluded or could have concluded that a particular legislative or executive action fell within a constitutional grant of authority and without the scope of any constitutional limitation, and thus that the action at issue, because constitutionally proper, was open only to political challenge.[9] Alternatively, Henkin urges, the Court ruled or could have ruled that a particular constitutional restriction was unenforceable because it did not confer standing to sue upon the parties who sought to invoke it or because it required for its enforcement remedies which were judicially unmanageable or equitably unwise.[10]

Professor Henkin is clearly right that one should not accept lightly the proposition that there are provisions of the Constitution which the courts may not independently interpret, since it is plainly inconsistent with *Marbury v. Madison's* basic assumption that the Constitution is judicially declarable law.[11] In order to account for the political question doctrine, however, it is not necessary to postulate that there are parts of the Constitution to which the judiciary is blind. The Supreme Court does not surrender its power of judicial review by holding that, while a particular provision may grant Congress or the Executive authority to act, it is not susceptible of an interpretation which would yield judicially enforceable rights, rights whose enforcement would either constrain congressional or executive action or alternatively provide the basis for an exercise of judicial power parallel to the actions of the political branches. Such a holding does not deprive the Court of all power to interpret a constitutional provision: the Court retains the power to determine whether a particular congressional or executive action comes within the terms of the constitutional grant of authority. Moreover, such a holding is not simply a ruling on standing or on the propriety of equitable remedies. In rendering such a holding, Supreme

---

of embarrassment from multifarious pronouncements by various departments on one question"—all partake of prudential considerations. The second two—"a lack of judicially discoverable and manageable standards for resolving [the issue]," and "the impossibility of deciding without an initial policy determination of a kind clearly for nonjudicial discretion"—incorporate functional criteria.

7. On this, the "classical," "political," and "functional" theories agree. See, e.g., Wechsler, supra note 4, at 7–9; A. Bickel, supra note 5, at 183–98; Scharpf, supra note 6, at 596–97.

8. Henkin, "Is There a 'Political Question' Doctrine," 85 Yale L.J. 597 (1976).

9. See id. at 607–17.

10. See id. at 617–22. But see Redish, supra note 1, at 1033–39 (challenging Henkin's argument but ultimately concluding that the doctrine should be abandoned completely).

11. See § 3–2, supra. Marbury v. Madison, 5 U.S. (1 Cranch) 137 (1803), expressly contemplated, however, that at least some seemingly "constitutional" issues would be committed to political discretion. See id. at 165–66.

Court is not concerned with the character of a litigant's injury or the shape of potential remedies as such, but rather with the possibility of deriving *rights* from the provision of the Constitution at issue. It is possible to test putative rights by imagining the sorts of injury their asserted infringement would bring about or by considering the sorts of remedies their enforcement would require, but the ultimate issue is whether it is possible to translate the principles underlying the constitutional provision at issue into restrictions on government or affirmative definitions of individual liberty which courts can articulate and apply.

The political question cases themselves suggest that it is this inquiry—the inquiry into whether particular constitutional provisions yield judicially enforceable rights—which has concerned the Supreme Court. Because this inquiry ultimately focuses on the limits of judicial competency, the political question doctrine is plainly a part of justiciability doctrine as a whole.

The central line of political question cases runs from *Luther v. Borden* [12] to *Baker v. Carr.* [13] *Luther* arose out of Dorr's Rebellion: an ultimately successful attempt by Rhode Island citizens who were disenfranchised under the original colonial charter to force the adoption of a new and more democratic constitution despite the opposition of the government established under the charter. [14] The specific issue *Luther* raised was whether soldiers of the charter government committed a trespass by breaking into plaintiff's home at a point in the rebellion when the rebels had prematurely proclaimed the adoption of a new constitution notwithstanding the charter government's continued insistence on the governing power of the charter. In resolving this issue, the Supreme Court had to consider two questions: whether a federal court could independently determine which of two competing governments was the "true" government of Rhode Island; and, even if the charter government was in power, whether that government, by proclaiming martial law, had acted unlawfully by departing from principles of republican government in contravention of the guaranty clause of article IV, § 4. [15]

The Court concluded that a federal court could not independently decide which state government was in power. The question was not one which fell within the judicial competence: the evidentiary problems would be staggering. [16] Congress, moreover, did possess such a power under the guaranty clause, which in this case it had delegated to the President, who had exercised it. The fact that Congress possessed the power confirmed that the power was lacking in the judiciary: this was not the sort of question which would admit of conflicting answers, a possibility if more than one branch of government could pass on it. [17]

---

12. 48 U.S. (7 How.) 1 (1849).

13. 369 U.S. 186 (1962).

14. See 48 U.S. at 34–37.

15. The guaranty clause provides: "The United States shall guarantee to every State in this Union a Republican Form of Government, and shall protect each of them against invasion; and on Application of the Legislature, or of the Executive (when the Legislature cannot be convened) against domestic violence."

16. See 48 U.S. at 41–42.

17. See id. at 42–44.

With respect to the question of whether, even if it were the lawful government, the charter government had acted unlawfully in adopting martial law, the Court took a more activist approach: it assumed that a federal court could decide whether a state government had violated the guaranty clause, but held that in this case, since the period of martial law was of only temporary duration, Rhode Island had not acted unconstitutionally.[18]

A number of nineteenth century cases in which litigants invoked the protection of the guaranty clause follow the pattern of *Luther v. Borden*: the Supreme Court did not doubt that the guaranty clause could be applied to protect individual rights but held that, on the facts of the particular case, the challenged state action did not constitute a departure from principles of republican government.[19] In *Pacific States Tel. & Tel. Co. v. Oregon*,[20] however, the Supreme Court held that the question whether a state government is "republican," like the question of which of two competing governments in fact governs, is one which federal courts are not competent to answer; thus, the guaranty clause is not a source of judicially enforceable private rights.[21] Chief Justice White colorfully assumed that if one feature of a state government— there, Oregon's initiative mechanism—caused the structure of state government of depart from principles of republican government, then a federal court would have to treat the state government as a nullity, "practically award a decree absolving from all obligation to contribute to the support or obey the laws" of the outlaw government, and "build by judicial action upon the ruins of the previously established government a new one . . . ."[22] Such action would be different in kind from the steps a federal court would ordinarily take in protecting individual rights, since ordinarily an individual challenges specific government action and not the government itself. Accordingly, the Court concluded, to recognize federal judicial power under the guaranty clause would be to recognize a judicial power so great as to "obliterate the division between judicial authority and legislative power . . . ."[23]

Chief Justice White's decisive assumption was dubious: if a court found that a particular feature of state government rendered the government unrepublican, why could not the court simply declare that feature invalid?[24] White's basic approach, however, is characteristic of political question jurisprudence. An issue is political not because it is one of particular concern to the political branches of government but because the constitutional provisions which litigants would invoke as guides to resolution of the issue do not lend themselves to judicial application. A plurality of the Supreme Court departed from this

---

18. See id. at 45.

19. See, e.g., Attorney General ex rel. Kies v. Lowery, 199 U.S. 233, 239 (1905); Forsyth v. Hammond, 166 U.S. 506, 519 (1897); Minor v. Happersett, 88 U.S. (21 Wall.) 162, 175–76 (1875). But see Taylor v. Beckham, 178 U.S. 548, 579 (1900).

20. 223 U.S. 118 (1912).

21. See generally Bonfield, "The Guaranty Clause of Article IV, § 4: A Study of Congressional Desuetude," 46 Minn.L.Rev. 513 (1962). It might nonetheless be a source of judicially enforceable *states'* rights. See §§ 5–23, infra.

22. 223 U.S. at 142.

23. Id.

24. See Henkin, supra note 8, at 609 n. 36.

approach in *Colegrove v. Green*.[25] There, litigants challenged the constitutionality of a state's malapportioned congressional districts. Justice Frankfurter, joined by three other Justices, wrote the principal opinion, holding that "appellants ask of this Court what is beyond its competence to grant": "due regard for the effective working of our Government reveal[s] this issue to be of a peculiarly political nature and therefore not meet for judicial determination." [26] Justice Frankfurter noted his view that a court was without remedial power to reapportion voting districts by itself,[27] and further observed that the Constitution plainly granted authority to Congress to deal with the problem.[28] Frankfurter, however, never identified the "various provisions of the United States Constitution" which the litigants invoked,[29] and accordingly did not ground his analysis in any conclusion that the particular provisions which the litigants would have the Court enforce did not suggest criteria which courts could apply to protect individual rights. Instead, the Justice treated the issue itself as beyond judicial competence: "Courts ought not to enter this political thicket." [30]

The Supreme Court, however, decisively repudiated Justice Frankfurter's analysis in *Baker v. Carr*.[31] This was another apportionment case, involving a constitutional challenge to a state's districting of its state legislature.[32] Justice Brennan's majority opinion unequivocally rejected the *Colegrove* formulation of the political question doctrine: "The doctrine of which we treat is one of 'political questions,' not one of 'political cases.' The courts cannot reject as 'no lawsuit' a bona fide controversy as to whether some action denominated 'political' exceeds constitutional authority." [33] Instead, Justice Brennan returned to the traditional approach, asking whether the constitutional provision which the litigants invoked could be successfully translated into judicially enforceable rights. Plaintiffs had argued that because the populations of the various legislative districts differed, the votes of residents of the more populous districts were "debased" relative to the votes of residents of less populous districts. This inequality of treatment, plaintiffs claimed, violated the fourteenth amendment equal protection clause. The Court had little difficulty in finding the equal protection clause to be judicially enforceable: "Judicial standards under the Equal Protection Clause are well developed and familiar . . . ." [34]

25. 328 U.S. 549 (1946).

26. Id. at 552. Justices Reed and Burton concurred in the opinion; Justice Rutledge wrote separately, concurring in the result.

27. See id. at 553.

28. 328 U.S. at 554–56.

29. See id. at 550. It appears that plaintiffs were chiefly claiming a violation of the fourteenth amendment equal protection clause. See id. at 568 (Black, J., dissenting).

30. Id. at 556.

31. 369 U.S. 186 (1962).

32. Only from the perspective of the political question doctrine is it possible to speak of Baker v. Carr as "another" apportionment case. Baker is, of course, the Supreme Court's landmark reapportionment case, the initial decision in a long series of cases in which the Court effectively restructured most of the nation's legislatures. See Chapter 13, infra.

33. 369 U.S. at 217.

34. Id. at 226. The Tennessee apportionment involved in Baker was plainly illegal under state law and had been so for sixty years. But the malapportioned legislature was also the body charged by Tennessee law with the task of reapportionment—a fact that made proper apportionment exceedingly unlikely. See Pollak, "Judicial Power and the Politics of

The theme of these central cases, that the political question doctrine involves an inquiry into the ability of courts to derive enforceable rights from the constitutional provisions which the litigants invoke, echoes in the Supreme Court's other political question decisions. In *Coleman v. Miller*,[35] three Justices of the Supreme Court, in announcing the Court's decision, held that the questions of whether a state could ratify a proposed constitutional amendment it had once rejected, and whether a proposed amendment lapses into oblivion if not ratified within a reasonable period of time, were political questions. With respect to the first issue, the plurality found "no basis in either Constitution or statute for . . . judicial action." [36] As to the second, the plurality asked: "Where are to be found the criteria for such a judicial determination?" [37] *Coleman*, however, is not fully consistent with *Baker v. Carr*. Four Justices were prepared to adopt the radical view of the political question doctrine criticized by Professor Henkin: "Congress has sole and complete control over the amending process, subject to no judicial review . . . ." [38] That *Coleman* can be presently read to require an absolute bar on judicial review of the amendment process is doubtful,[39] and commentators on the subject tend to disagree mainly on the *scope* of judicial review that is appropriate in governing the process by which amendments proposed by Congress are ratified by the states.[40] The need for an active judicial role in supervising the process of calling and conducting a new constitutional convention, on

the People," 72 Yale L.J. 81, 88 (1962). Thus the Supreme Court's invocation of the equal protection clause provided the only realistic path to conforming the state's actions with norms that were not themselves in serious dispute. See Bonfield, "Baker v. Carr: New Light on the Constitutional Guarantee of Republican Government," 50 Calif.L.Rev. 245, 253–55 (1963).

35. 307 U.S. 433 (1939).

36. Id. at 450 (Hughes, C.J., joined by Stone and Reed, JJ.).

37. Id. at 453.

38. Id. at 459 (Black, J., concurring, joined by Roberts, Frankfurter, and Douglas, JJ.).

39. See Uhler v. AFL–CIO, 468 U.S. 1310, 1312 (1984) (Rehnquist, Circuit Justice) (noting this "position did not command a majority" in Coleman and suggesting that Coleman in any event cannot be read expansively to shut out all judicial review of the amending process). But cf. Goldwater v. Carter, 444 U.S. 996, 1002–03 (1979) (Rehnquist, J., joined by Burger, C.J., Stewart and Stevens, JJ., concurring in the judgment) (relying on Coleman to support absolute bar on judicial review of the Senate's role in the treaty-termination process), discussed infra.

40. Professor Walter Dellinger, for example, has argued that the plurality opinion in Coleman is profoundly misguided, and that an active judicial role in governing the constitutional amendment process is essential to ensuring that its legitimacy is supported by agreement on basic rules which operate with reasonable certainty. See Dellinger, "The Legitimacy of Constitutional Change: Rethinking the Amendment Process," 97 Harv.L.Rev. 386 (1983). Dellinger proposes, as formal rules resolving most of the major current ambiguities, that whether a state's approval is counted toward ratification should be unaffected by: (1) a state's rejection of an amendment prior to approval, (2) subsequent rescission of an approved amendment, or (3) eventual approval of an amendment after a substantial time delay where Congress has not set a ratification period in the amendment text. See id. at 419–27. For an opposing view, arguing that broad judicial oversight risks interference with the one clear check on the federal judiciary's constitutional lawmaking and that the appropriate procedural rules may well vary with the circumstances underlying a given ratification question, see Tribe, "*A Constitution* We Are Amending: In Defense of a Restrained Judicial Role," 97 Harv.L.Rev. 433 (1983). Compare Dellinger, "Constitutional Politics: A Rejoinder," 97 Harv.L.Rev. 446 (1983).

the application of two-thirds of the states pursuant to article V, seems considerably clearer.[41] The constitutional appropriateness of the *substance* of proposed amendments, however, is undoubtedly a matter entirely committed to judicially unreviewable resolution by the political branches of government.[42]

Turning to perhaps less fundamental matters, in *Chicago & S. Air Lines v. Waterman S.S. Corp.*,[43] the Court held that federal courts could not apply ordinary procedures for judicial review of administrative action in dealing with presidential orders concerning international air routes: "[T]he very nature of executive decisions as to foreign policy is political, not judicial. Such decisions . . . are delicate, complex, and involve large elements of prophecy . . . . They are decisions of a kind for which the Judiciary has neither aptitude, facilities nor responsibility . . . ."[44] Again, despite emphasis on judicially manageable standards, *Waterman* is something of a deviant case. Perhaps because

41. Because the *function* of this provision for a constitutional convention is to permit the states to deal with a recalcitrant Congress, substantial judicial inquiry into procedural determinations by Congress on whether a convention has been properly called seems justified. See, e.g., Comment, "A Constitutional Convention: Scouting Article Five's Undiscovered Country," 134 U.Pa.L.Rev. 939, 947–57 (1986). How both procedural and substantive questions concerning a convention would be resolved cannot be determined in advance; attempting to call such a convention in this state of uncertainty may well be a prescription for constitutional chaos, suggesting that a second convention (none has been held since 1787) should be avoided unless compelling circumstances manifestly warrant taking the drastic step of calling one, or unless article V is itself first amended to clarify the process of amendment by convention. See Tribe, "Issues Raised by Requesting Congress to Call a Constitutional Convention to Propose a Balanced Budget Amendment," 10 Pac.L.J. 627, 632–40 (1979).

42. "Constitutional" principles of a sort must no doubt be applied in evaluating the substantive merit of a proposed amendment; as long as we understand the Constitution as embodying fundamental norms and purport to be amending rather than discarding it, abrogation of those norms by amendment must be a prospect of considerable concern. Yet any intrusion by courts into this evaluation, however principled, would clearly threaten the integrity of the overall constitutional structure by vitiating the mechanism for peaceful constitutional change embodied in the amendment process. See Tribe, supra note 41, at 438–43. Even more fundamentally, the notion that "the Constitution" embodies an immanent, unitary, changeless set of underlying values or principles—whether procedural

or substantive or structural—seems an intellectual conceit inconsistent with the character of the Constitution's various provisions as concrete political enactments that represent historically contingent, and not always wholly coherent, compromises.

43. 333 U.S. 103 (1948).

44. Id. at 111. As the Supreme Court subsequently noted, "it is error to suppose that every case or controversy which touches foreign relations lies beyond judicial cognizance." Baker v. Carr, 369 U.S. 186, 211 (1962) (dictum). Thus, for example, while the Executive is immune from judicial oversight while engaged in the negotiation of treaties on behalf of the United States, the Supreme Court will construe such treaties and will assess their validity in cases properly challenging them as inconsistent with the constitutional rights of adversely affected individuals. See generally L. Henkin, Foreign Affairs and the Constitution 210–16 (1972).

The "act of state" cases provide perhaps the best illustration both of the Supreme Court's use and of its rejection of political question analysis in the foreign policy context. The "act of state" doctrine declares that "the courts of one nation will not sit in judgment on the acts of another nation within [the latter's] own territory . . . ." Banco Nacional de Cuba v. Sabbatino, 376 U.S. 398, 416 (1964), quoting Underhill v. Hernandez, 168 U.S. 250, 252 (1897). Three important Supreme Court decisions, Banco Nacional de Cuba v. Sabbatino, 376 U.S. 398 (1964), First National City Bank v. Banco Nacional de Cuba, 406 U.S. 759 (1972), and Alfred Dunhill of London, Inc. v. Republic of Cuba, 425 U.S. 682 (1976), have dealt with the applicability of the doctrine to federal court determinations of the consequences of Cuban expropriations that occurred soon after the Castro government's rise to power in the late 1950's.

the application of no constitutional provision was at issue, the Court
emphasized the political nature of the question as much as the absence

In Sabbatino, the Supreme Court reversed a judgment that had been entered
for the receiver of proceeds from a sugar
sale. The courts below had ruled for the
defendant receiver as a matter of law on
the ground that plaintiff's claim to the
proceeds was negated by the illegality, under customary international law as construed by the lower federal courts, of the
expropriation through which Cuba, plaintiff's assignor, had acquired the sugar.
The Supreme Court, in reversing defendant's victory, declared the validity of the
expropriation to be a nonjusticiable issue
for the federal courts: "[The] Judicial
Branch will not examine the validity of a
taking of property within its own territory
by a foreign sovereign government, extant
and recognized by this country at the time
of suit, in the absence of a treaty or other
unambiguous agreement regarding controlling legal principles, even if the complaint
alleges that the taking violates customary
international law." 376 U.S. at 428. The
Court did not suggest that the validity of
the Cuban expropriation was not fit for
determination by *any* court: "We do not, of
course, mean to say that there is no international standard in this area; we conclude only that the matter is not meet for
adjudication by *domestic* tribunals." Id. at
429 n. 26 (emphasis added). Nor did the
Court hold article III tribunals without
constitutional *power* to adjudicate the issue. See id. at 423, 427–28. What concerned the Court in Sabbatino was in part
the separation of powers, see id., but, even
more centrally, the apparent illegitimacy
of federal judicial resolution in such cases.
After noting that "[t]here are few if any
issues in international law today on which
opinion seems to be so divided as the limitations on a state's power to expropriate
the property of aliens," id. at 428, the
Court concluded that "[i]t is difficult to
imagine the courts of this country embarking on adjudication in an area which
touches more sensitively the practical and
ideological goals of the various members of
the community of nations." Id. at 430.

Sabbatino was not a political question
case. Justice Harlan's analysis, however,
plainly paralleled the political question approach advanced here: the central question was whether a federal court could
formulate standards of law appropriate for
judicial application. By contrast, in First
National City Bank, the Court took an
approach more consistent with traditional
political question analysis—reasoning that
certain problems, not issues, fall outside
judicial responsibility. Although the issue
was again the validity of Cuban expropria-

tions, the Executive Branch expressly took
the position, unlike its posture in Sabbatino (see 376 U.S. at 407), that the "act of
state" doctrine should not be applied. A
plurality of the Court acceded in the Executive's request: "We conclude that where
the Executive Branch, charged as it is with
primary responsibility for the conduct of
foreign affairs, expressly represents to the
Court that application of the act of state
doctrine would not advance the interests of
American foreign policy, that doctrine
should not be applied by the courts." 406
U.S. at 768 (plurality opinion of Rehnquist,
J., joined by Chief Justice Burger and Justice White). The plurality opinion in First
National City Bank would have replaced
the Sabbatino principle, which had limited
the judiciary to areas resolvable by accepted standards of decision, with a crude, prudential rule to avoid conflict between the
federal judiciary and executive departments by having the former simply defer
to the judgment of the latter in a pending
case. "[The] Court becomes a mere errand
boy for the Executive Branch which may
choose to pick some people's chestnuts
from the fire, but not others." 406 U.S. at
773 (Douglas, J., concurring in result). In
Dunhill, the Supreme Court finally returned at least part of the way to the
Sabbatino approach, although a majority
could agree only that there was not sufficient evidence of action by the Cuban government to justify application of the act of
state doctrine. See 425 U.S. at 690–95.
See also id. at 704 (White, J., joined by
Burger, C.J., and Rehnquist and Powell,
JJ.); see generally "The Supreme Court,
1975 Term," 90 Harv.L.Rev. 56, 265–75
(1976). For a comprehensive critique and
proposed rejection of the "act of state doctrine", see Bazyler, "Abolishing the Act of
State Doctrine," 134 U.Pa.L.Rev. 325 (1986)
(concluding that the doctrine allows courts
to evade difficult questions; rewards politically influential litigants; dilutes important federal laws; arrests development of
international law in the United States;
creates considerable confusion generally;
and should be supplanted by a variety of
more established doctrines, including the
political-question doctrine). For more limited proposals for legislative change, see,
e.g., Note, "Limiting the Act of State Doctrine: A Legislative Initiative," 23 Va.J.
Int'l L. 103 (1982); Mathias, "Restructuring the Act of State Doctrine: A Blueprint
for Legislative Reform," 12 Law & Pol'y
Int'l Bus. 369 (1980). Congress has acted
once on the issue. In 1964, reacting to
Sabbatino and attempting to restrict the
scope of the act of state doctrine by requir-

of judicial standards: in this context, however, because the judicial rule at stake was one governing review of factfinding, the two inquiries really amounted to the same thing.

The Supreme Court's decisions since *Baker v. Carr* more clearly reflect the approach to the political question doctrine which *Baker* exemplifies. In *United States v. Nixon*,[45] for example, the Supreme Court held that the intra-executive nature of the dispute between President Nixon and Special Prosecutor Jaworski did not give rise to a political question: because the President had himself restricted his discretion to deal with Jaworski, the President, until he repealed the regulations limiting his discretion, could refuse Jaworski's demands only by asserting a valid claim of privilege; the issue of privilege, of course, was " 'of a type which [is] traditionally justiciable.' "[46] Moreover, in *Powell v. McCormack*,[47] the Supreme Court concluded that the political question doctrine did not bar its review of the House of Representatives' exercise of the article I, § 5, power to judge the qualifications of its members: article I, § 5, did not grant the House unreviewable discretion, the Court concluded, but rather authorized the House to exclude only those members who did not meet the three standing qualifications of article I, § 2, or several other qualifications not there relevant. Thus, the Court held that judicial review was possible at least to determine if the House had in fact acted on the basis of the article I, § 2, criteria, which the defendants conceded that Congressman Powell met.

In *Davis v. Bandemer*[48] the Court, in an opinion written by Justice White, applied *Baker* to find a legislative districting case justiciable in a context substantially more problematic than that involved in the *Baker* challenge. *Davis* reviewed the constitutionality of political "gerrymandering" conducted by Republican state legislators in Indiana, who redrew state legislative districts subsequent to the 1980 Census to hamper the electoral prospects of Democratic candidates. Evaluating the Democrats' claim that, despite the equivalence of population in each district, the redistricting plan impermissibly diluted the strength of Democratic votes as a *group*, the Court discounted the lack of standards for adjudicating such claims, reading *Baker* as holding generally that "legislative line-drawing in the districting context [is] susceptible of adjudication under the applicable constitutional criteria."[49] Given its past acceptance of racial gerrymandering claims, the Court viewed such claims by political groups as entitled in principle to similar treatment.[50] Three Justices, through Justice O'Connor's opinion, de-

ing adjudication of title claims to property before the courts, it passed the Hickenlooper Amendment, codified as amended at 22 U.S.C. § 2370(e)(2). The amendment has been construed narrowly, however, to cover only American-owned property taken in violation of international law by a foreign sovereign. See Note, "The Act of State Doctrine: Resolving Debt Situs Confusion," 86 Colum.L.Rev. 594, 595 n. 4 (1986).

45. 418 U.S. 683 (1974). See § 4–15, infra.

46. Id. at 697.

47. 395 U.S. 486 (1969).

48. 106 S.Ct. 2797 (1986). See § 13–9, infra.

49. Id. at 2805.

50. See id. at 2806. The Court thus characterized as a justiciable plea for fair representation the claim "that each politi-

cried this abstract analysis and the lack of any judicially manageable standards to resolve the claims of the multitude of societal groups thereby invited to fight heatedly partisan redistricting battles in federal court, and could perceive no basis for a group right of equal political power underlying the fourteenth amendment.[51] These Justices also noted that, unlike deviations from the one person-one vote principle, political gerrymanders have a built-in tendency to be self-limiting, inasmuch as their deployment requires a political party to sacrifice *safe* seats in a strategic bid for *more* seats.[52] For this reason, the need to relax justiciability constraints seems weaker in this context than in that of *Baker*. Adopting the somewhat implausible posture that such "political" considerations should not count in applying the political question doctrine, Justice White's opinion saw no need to address Justice O'Connor's shrewd analysis on its merits.[53]

Gilligan v. Morgan [54] is the only case since *Baker v. Carr* in which the Surpeme Court has invoked the political question doctrine to hold an issue nonjusticiable. Plaintiffs had asked the federal courts to evaluate the training of the Ohio National Guard under the fourteenth amendment due process clause; if that training was found constitutionally deficient, they sought appropriate injunctive relief. The Supreme Court's decision that the issue was nonjusticiable turned on a number of factors. Chief among them, however, were the facts that article I, § 8, authorized Congress to engage in just such supervision, and that judicial review in this area would be essentially standardless: "[I]t is difficult to conceive of an area of governmental activity in which the courts have less competence. The complex, subtle, and professional decisions as to the composition, training, equipping, and control of a military force are essentially professional military judgments, subject *always* to civilian control of the Legislative and Executive Branches." [55]

Four Justices of the Court sought to invoke the doctrine again in *Goldwater v. Carter*,[56] which summarily vacated a court of appeals

cal group in a State should have the same chance to elect representatives of its choice as any other political group." Id.

51. See id. at 2817–22 (O'Connor, J., joined by Burger, C.J., and Rehnquist, J., concurring in the judgment). On the merits, Justice White's plurality opinion, joined by Justices Brennan, Marshall and Blackmun, minimized the impact of its justiciability holding by holding that political gerrymandering could be invalidated only when it works to "consistently degrade a voter's or a group of voters' influence on the political process as a whole" and refused to invalidate the Indiana plan involved in Davis. Id. at 2810. Justices Powell and Stevens, joining the justiciability analysis, argued for application of stricter substantive standards, concluding based on these standards that the plan was impermissible. See id. at 2835–38 (Powell, J., dissenting).

52. See id. at 2820–21 (O'Connor, J. concurring in the judgment).

53. See id. at 2806–07.

54. 413 U.S. 1 (1973).

55. Id. at 10. Contrast Scheuer v. Rhodes, 416 U.S. 232 (1974) (permitting, despite claim of official immunity, lawsuits against Ohio and National Guard officials for killing students on the campus of Kent State University during May 1970 protests). In addition, the Court has undoubtedly relied on the policies underlying the political question doctrine in denying review of lower court decisions finding challenges to foreign military operations nonjusticiable. See, e.g., Crockett v. Reagan, 720 F.2d 1355 (D.C. Cir. 1983) (per curiam), cert. denied 467 U.S. 1251 (1984) (challenge to military activities in El Salvador); Mora v. McNamara, 387 F.2d 862 (D.C. Cir. 1967), cert. denied 389 U.S. 934 (1967) (challenge to Vietnam War involvement). See also § 4–7, infra.

56. 444 U.S. 996 (1979). The Court declined to hear argument but granted certi-

decision that the President had power to terminate a treaty with Taiwan without the approval of the Senate. The plurality took the view that the President's power to abrogate a treaty was a question that was "'political' and therefore nonjusticiable" and accordingly should be left for resolution by the President and Congress.[57] Likening the case to *Coleman v. Miller*,[58] the plurality argued that only political standards could resolve the matter—that the Constitution specifies the process by which treaties are to be created but says nothing about how, or by whom, they may be ended, just as it details procedures for the adoption but not the rejection of constitutional amendments.[59] Justice Powell concurred in the judgment on the ground that the suit, brought by a few individual Members of Congress, was not ripe[60] because neither the Senate nor the House had created a "constitutional impasse" through direct challenge on the issue.[61] Justice Brennan persuasively argued for affirmance of the lower court's decision on the merits, stating that, although the political question doctrine bars review of foreign policy judgments entrusted to another branch of government, it "does not pertain when a court is faced with the *antecedent* question whether a particular branch has been constitutionally designated as the repository of political decisionmaking power."[62]

There is, thus, a political question doctrine. It does not mark certain provisions of the Constitution as off-limits to judicial interpretation. But it does require federal courts to determine whether constitutional provisions which litigants would have judges enforce do in fact lend themselves to interpretation as guarantees of enforceable rights.[63]

orari, vacated the judgment of the Court of Appeals for the District of Columbia Circuit, and remanded with orders to dismiss the complaint. Justice Rehnquist wrote for the plurality concurring in the judgment, joined by Chief Justice Burger and Justices Stewart and Stevens. Justice Powell concurred separately on ripeness grounds as noted in text. Justice Marshall concurred in the result. Justice Brennan would have affirmed the judgment below as noted in text. Justices Blackmun and White would have given the case plenary consideration.

57. See id. at 1002–03 (Rehnquist, J., concurring in the judgment).

58. See the discussion in notes 35–40, supra.

59. See 444 U.S. at 1002–03. Given this constitutional silence, the plurality argued that the political branches were meant to establish their own rules, which had in the past varied from treaty to treaty. See id. at 1003–04 & n. 1. It added that the two other branches of the federal government have sufficient "resources available to protest and assert [their] interests, resources not available to private litigants outside the judicial forum." Id. at 1004. The case was even more compelling for the plurality than Coleman because the

Goldwater question "involve[d] foreign relations." Id. at 1003.

60. See § 3–10, supra.

61. See id. at 997–98 (Powell, J., concurring in the judgment). Justice Powell explained that prudential concerns dictated "that a dispute between Congress and the President is not ready for judicial review unless and until each branch has taken action asserting its constitutional authority." Id. at 997. He argued that judicial review of such a mutual challenge "would eliminate, rather than create, multiple constitutional interpretations" and noted that the Court in the past had shown its willingness to fulfill its duty to resolve such disputes. Id. at 1001–02.

62. Id. at 1006–07 (Brennan, J., dissenting) (emphasis in original). Similarly, Justice Powell argued that the plurality's approach was inconsistent with the three central concerns articulated in Baker v. Carr. See id. at 998–1001 (Powell, J., dissenting). On the standing of Senator Goldwater and his fellow plaintiffs in this case, see § 3–20, infra.

63. In this regard, the political question doctrine bears a close resemblance to the zone-of-interest test in standing doctrine, see § 3–19, infra: both, in a sense, are concerned with the larger question of

To make such a determination, a court must first of all construe the relevant constitutional text, and seek to identify the purposes the particular provision serves within the constitutional scheme as a whole. At this stage of the analysis, the court would find particularly relevant the fact that the constitutional provision by its terms grants authority to another branch of government; if the provision recognizes such authority, the court will have to consider the possibility of conflicting conclusions, and the actual necessity for parallel judicial and political remedies. But ultimately, the political question inquiry turns as much on the court's conception of judicial competence as on the constitutional text. Thus the political question doctrine, like other justiciability doctrines, at bottom reflects the mixture of constitutional interpretation and judicial discretion which is an inevitable by-product of the efforts of federal courts to define their own limitations.

§ 3–14. Standing: A Summary

The doctrine most central to defining article III's requirement of a "case" or "controversy"[1] is that of standing, which addresses the question whether "a party has a sufficient *stake* in an otherwise justiciable controversy to obtain judicial resolution of that controversy."[2] Standing differs, in theory, from all other elements of justiciability[3] by its primary focus "on the *party* seeking to get his complaint before a federal court" and only secondarily "on the *issues* he wishes to have adjudicated."[4] Standing questions arise principally in challenges to government conduct, where litigants often lack the obvious stake normally present in most lawsuits between private parties;[5] standing doctrine thus defines the framework for "judicial control of public officers"[6] and is therefore of special significance in constitutional law.

Although the Supreme Court's view of standing has evolved considerably in recent years and currently presents substantial confusion at a number of points, the doctrinal categories that must be examined are clear. Standing doctrine "subsumes a blend of constitutional requirements and prudential considerations,"[7] which are explored in turn in subsequent sections. The constitutional requirements were pointedly emphasized by the Supreme Court's recapitulation of standing doctrine in *Valley Forge Christian College v. Americans United for Separation of*

whether the Constitution provides a cause of action a litigant can assert to obtain the requested judicial relief. But while the political question doctrine seeks to answer that question by asking whether a particular constitutional provision lends itself to judicial application, the nexus requirement asks whether the litigant asserts the sort of interest which the constitutional provision was meant to protect. See § 3–19, infra.

§ 3–14

1. See § 3–7, supra.

2. Sierra Club v. Morton, 405 U.S. 727, 731 (1972) (emphasis added).

3. See §§ 3–9 to 3–13, supra.

4. Flast v. Cohen, 392 U.S. 83, 99 (1968) (emphasis added).

5. See C. Wright, Law of Federal Courts 60 (4th ed. 1984); Chayes, "The Supreme Court, 1981 Term—Foreword: Public Law Litigation and the Burger Court," 96 Harv. L.Rev. 4, 8–9 (1982).

6. L. Jaffe, Judicial Control of Administrative Action 459 (1965).

7. Valley Forge Christian College v. Americans United for Separation of Church and State, 454 U.S. 464, 471 (1982).

Church and State,[8] which stated that, as an "irreducible minimum," article III requires a litigant invoking the authority of a federal court to demonstrate: (1) " 'that he personally has suffered some actual or threatened injury as a result of the putatively illegal conduct of the defendant,' " (*injury in fact*); [9] (2) "that the injury 'fairly can be traced to the challenged action' " (*causation*); [10] and (3) that the injury " 'is likely to be redressed by a favorable decision' " (*redressability*).[11]

Even if injury in fact, causation and redressability are established, a litigant "may still lack standing under the prudential principles by which the judiciary seeks to avoid deciding questions of broad social import where no individual rights would be vindicated and to limit access to the federal courts to those litigants best suited to assert a particular claim." [12] As summarized in *Valley Forge*,[13] standing may be denied where a litigant: (1) presents " 'abstract questions of wide public significance' which amount to '*generalized grievances*,' pervasively shared and most appropriately addressed in the representative branches"; [14] or (2) rests his claim " 'on the legal rights or interests of *third parties*' " rather than on his own; [15] or (3) does not present a claim arguably falling "within 'the *zone of interests* to be protected or regulated by the statute or constitutional guarantee in question.' " [16] Additional doctrinal complexities, of both a constitutional and a prudential nature, are introduced when a state or organization asserts legal claims, or when the litigant is a legislator suing in connection with his official duties.[17]

The Burger Court dramatically altered the constitutional focus of standing inquiry through its reassessment of how separation-of-powers concerns guide and shape the doctrine. Two decades ago these concerns appeared relevant only to ensuring that federal courts do not exceed their article III powers by entertaining claims of litigants pressing solely abstract interests founded on ill-defined facts, creating a danger that a judicial pronouncement would constitute a prohibited "advisory opinion." [18] "The 'gist of the question of standing,' " as summarized in *Flast v. Cohen* [19] in the final year of the Warren Court, involved whether the litigant's personal stake in a lawsuit assured " 'that concrete adverseness which sharpens the presentation of issues upon which the court so largely depends for illumination of difficult

---

8. Id. at 472 (1982) (citations omitted); see also Allen v. Wright, 468 U.S. 737, 751 (1984) ("[a] plaintiff must allege [1] personal injury [2] fairly traceable to the defendant's allegedly unlawful conduct and [3] likely to be redressed by the requested relief").

9. See §§ 3–15 to 3–17, infra.

10. See § 3–18, infra.

11. See id.

12. Gladstone, Realtors v. Bellwood, 441 U.S. 91, 99–100 (1979). See also Secretary of State of Maryland v. J. H. Munson Co., 467 U.S. 947, 955 n. 5 (1984). On nonconstitutional aspects of justiciability doctrine generally, see § 3–8, supra.

13. 454 U.S. at 474–75 (emphasis added) (citations omitted); see also Allen v. Wright, 468 U.S. 737, 751 (1984); Gladstone, Realtors v. Bellwood, 441 U.S. 91, 99–100 (1979).

14. See § 3–17, infra.

15. See § 3–19, infra.

16. See id.

17. See § 3–20, infra.

18. See § 3–9, supra.

19. 392 U.S. 83, 99 (1968) (quoting Baker v. Carr, 369 U.S. 186, 204 (1962)).

constitutional questions.'" Whether a litigant had standing did not, "by its own force, raise separation of powers problems" by threatening intrusion on coordinate branches of government, inasmuch as such problems arose "if at all, only from the substantive issues the individual seeks to have adjudicated." [20] In subsequent decisions, however, the Court suggested—at first somewhat obliquely,[21] and then more directly [22]—that standing doctrine must be employed to prevent litigants from drawing federal courts into unnecessary conflict with coordinate branches. The focus of *Flast* was discarded formally near the end of the Burger Court in *Allen v. Wright*,[23] which announced that standing doctrine now was "built on a single basic idea—the idea of separation of powers," recognizing "'the proper—and properly limited—role of the courts in a democratic society.'" [24]

Precisely how separation-of-powers analysis advances doctrinal application of the standing inquiry may be difficult to fathom.[25] This difficulty is characteristic of the Court's standing doctrine, which as a

---

20. Flast, 392 U.S. at 100–01.

21. See, e.g., Warth v. Seldin, 422 U.S. 490, 498–500 (1975); Schlesinger v. Reservists Comm. to Stop the War, 418 U.S. 208, 220–27 (1974); United States v. Richardson, 418 U.S. 166, 188–92 (1974) (Powell, J., concurring), all discussed in § 3–17, infra.

22. See Valley Forge, 454 U.S. at 473–74. Valley Forge did not clearly signal the Court's change in direction; compare, e.g., Vander Jagt v. O'Neill, 699 F.2d 1166, 1169 (D.C. Cir. 1983) ("If the Court had meant to expand its standing doctrines to make room for a whole set of analytically-unrelated theories about the roles of the separate branches of government, it could have said so"), with id. at 1179 (Bork, J., concurring) (Valley Forge "reads separation-of-powers concepts back into that part of the standing requirement which rests upon a constitutional, rather than a prudential, foundation"). See also Moore v. United States House of Representatives, 733 F.2d 946, 957 (D.C. Cir. 1984) (Scalia, J., concurring in result). Judge Bork's prescience was noted by the Court by quotation in Allen, supra, 468 U.S. at 750.

23. 468 U.S. 737, 752 (1984).

24. Id. at 752, 750 (quoting Warth v. Seldin, 422 U.S. 490, 498 (1975)). See generally Scalia, "The Doctrine of Standing as an Essential Element of the Separation of Powers," 17 Suffolk L.Rev. 881 (1983).

Allen relied on separation-of-powers concerns to deny standing to parents of black public school students in school districts undergoing desegregation, who brought a nationwide class action seeking injunctive relief and alleging that the Internal Revenue Service had harmed them by failing to enforce its policy of denying tax-exempt status to racially discriminatory private schools. Because the parents did not claim that they or their children had personally been denied equal treatment, Justice O'Connor, writing for the Court, rejected as an overly abstract, "generalized grievance," see § 3–17 and note 32, infra, their claim of direct dignitary harm from the allegedly illegal and insulting government practice. 468 U.S. at 752–56. The Court also rejected as too speculative to meet the causation requirement, see § 3–18 and notes 7 & 10, infra, their claim that IRS inaction, by tolerating unlawful subsidization of the private schools, diminished their own children's ability to receive a desegregated public education. 468 U.S. at 756–61. Justices Brennan, Blackmun and Stevens dissented; Justice Marshall took no part.

25. See, e.g., Allen, 468 U.S. at 783, 789–95 (Stevens, J., dissenting); Nichol, "Abusing Standing: A Comment on Allen v. Wright," 133 U.Pa.L.Rev. 635, 642–49 (1985); Note, "The Supreme Court, 1983 Term—Leading Cases," 98 Harv.L.Rev. 236, 241–46 (1984). Despite Allen's assumption that separation-of-powers principles would help clarify determination of standing issues, see note 29, infra, significant elaboration by the Supreme Court will undoubtedly be necessary to provide guidance to lower courts. Compare, e.g., Haitian Refugee Center v. Gracey, 809 F.2d 794 (D.C. Cir. 1987) (per Bork, J.) (arguing that Allen prohibits any showing that governmental action causes interference with a litigant's relationship with third party, unless interference is purposeful), with id. at 820 (Buckley, J., concurring) (questioning Judge Bork's reliance "on inferences to be drawn from recent Supreme Court cases rather than on their explicit holdings"). See also id. at 826–27 (Edwards, J., concurring in part and dissenting in part).

whole is one of the most criticized aspects of constitutional law.[26] Beyond attacking the Court's revised separation-of-powers analysis, critics have charged the Court with habitually manipulating announced standing doctrine to pursue extraneous, often unacknowledged ends— such as advancing its view of the merits, resolving problems of entertaining broad equitable relief, and serving federalism concerns.[27] The inconsistent and often obtuse nature of the Court's standing rulings is of special concern because lower courts must apply the doctrine by assuming the truth of a litigant's allegations [28] and analogizing the claims made to those previously accepted or rejected by the Supreme Court.[29]

It is clear, therefore, that the Court has selectively employed standing doctrine, and justiciability doctrines generally,[30] to constrict the expansive access to federal courts previously enjoyed by litigants challenging governmental action. Although its *method* of doing so deserves the ample criticism it has received, the *legitimacy* of the overall result the Court is achieving is far harder to discredit. In changing its interpretation of the impact of the separation of powers on standing requirements, and of the definition of a constitutionally cognizable "case" or "controversy" generally, it is arguable that the Court has simply shifted somewhat its stance between two plausible but polar interpretations of the meaning of judicial review as established by the seminal case of *Marbury v. Madison*.[31] The Court's current formulation presents one aspect of the continuing debate over whether federal courts exist primarily to resolve concrete disputes among individual litigants, with the power to make constitutional decisions only a necessary incident to this role, or whether federal courts have a special responsibility, as the branch of government best able to develop a coherent interpretation of the Constitution, to engage in the exposition of constitutional norms, limited primarily by the requirement that they do so in the context of reasonably concrete disputes presented to them for review.[32]

---

26. See, e.g., Fallon, "Of Justiciability and Public Law Litigation: Notes on the Jurisprudence of *Lyons*," 59 N.Y.U.L.Rev. 1, 17 & n. 91 (1984); Nichol, "Rethinking Standing," 72 Calif.L.Rev. 68, 68 n. 3 (1984) (collecting sources).

27. See generally Nichol, supra note 25, at 649–59. See, e.g., L. Tribe, "Choke Holds, Church Subsidies, and Nuclear Meltdowns: Problems of Standing?," in Constitutional Choices 99–120, 327–62 (1985); Fallon, supra note 26; Tushnet, "The Sociology of Article III: A Response to Professor Brilmayer," 93 Harv.L.Rev. 1698 (1980), summarized in § 3–8, note 25, supra.

28. Because a litigant's standing is normally evaluated on the pleadings, before evidence has been amassed, a court is required to assume their truth and construe them in the litigant's favor—although it may require more specific pleading if necessary, and an initial determination of

standing may later be reversed on proof ultimately produced. See Gladstone, Realtors v. Bellwood, 441 U.S. 91, 109 & n. 22, 115 & n. 31 (1979); Warth v. Seldin, 422 U.S. 490, 501–02 (1975). This admonition has been disregarded by the Court where convenient. See, e.g., Allen, 468 U.S. at 774–76 & n. 6 (Brennan, J., dissenting); City of Los Angeles v. Lyons, 461 U.S. 95, 120–22 (1983) (Marshall, J., dissenting).

29. See Allen, 468 U.S. at 751–52 (noting that, given the Court's precedents, lower courts are not "at sea" and that often a decision can be made "chiefly by comparing the allegations of the particular complaint to those made in prior standing cases," although consideration of separation-of-powers principles is also essential).

30. See §§ 3–7 and 3–8, supra.

31. See § 3–2, supra.

32. See §§ 3–3, 3–4 and 3–7 supra. See generally Spann, "Expository Justice," 131

The aspect of the Court's standing jurisprudence most open to criticism, therefore, is less the underlying view of the role of the federal judiciary this new jurisprudence embodies, than the Court's lack of candor in articulating and justifying the basic choice it has made. The Court has replaced careful focus on the fundamental issues involved with an emphasis on artificial and confusing questions such as whether injuries are "distinct" and "palpable," or whether is it fair to say they are "caused" by the complained-of conduct; this tendency has obscured rather than clarified the role of the federal courts in our constitutional system and the instances in which persons may seek relief from those courts. Unless the Court modifies or attempts to clarify its approach, standing doctrine will likely remain a mystery to litigants and lower courts.

Moreover, by using the various concepts of standing doctrine as verbal proxies for conclusions about the most important questions of federal judicial power, the Court has overburdened the doctrine with concerns that bear little relation to whether a particular litigant is properly before a court. In so doing, it has supplanted well-recognized doctrines that are far better suited to the issues at stake—such as other justiciability doctrines [33] and a variety of discretionary jurisdictional doctrines flowing from legislative grants of jurisdiction and common law traditions.[34]

§ 3–15. Injury in Fact as the Constitutional Core of the Standing Requirement: Its Application in Federal and State Courts

In its requirement that a litigant "must allege personal injury fairly traceable to the . . . allegedly unlawful conduct and likely to be redressed by the requested relief," [1] the core of standing doctrine is generally regarded as part of the case-or-controversy limitation of article III,[2] which defines "with respect to the Judicial Branch the idea of separation of powers on which the Federal Government is founded." [3] Although the necessity for insisting on injury in fact, so defined, is not obvious,[4] the view that such injury is mandated by article III reveals

U.Pa.L.Rev. 585 (1983). Compare Barnes v. Kline, 759 F.2d 21, 41, 52–53 (D.C. Cir. 1984) (Bork, J., dissenting) (arguing that dispute-resolution conception underlies standing doctrine), vacated as moot, sub nom. Burke v. Barnes, 107 S.Ct. 734 (1987), with Spann, supra, at 592–617 (arguing for emphasis on norm-exposition).

33. See §§ 3–9 to 3–13, supra.

34. See, e.g., Shapiro, "Jurisdiction and Discretion," 60 N.Y.U.L.Rev. 543, 545–74 (1985); Nagel, "Separation of Powers and the Scope of Federal Equitable Remedies," 30 Stan.L.Rev. 661 (1978).

§ 3–15

1. Allen v. Wright, 468 U.S. 737, 751 (1984); see also § 3–17, infra.

2. See § 3–7, supra.

3. Allen v. Wright, 468 U.S. 737, 750 (1984); see also Valley Forge Christian College v. Americans United for Separation of Church and State, 454 U.S. 464, 471–72, 475–76 (1982).

4. Were the case-or-controversy inquiry focused on the existence of a concrete dispute and vigorous advocacy, see Baker v. Carr, 369 U.S. 186, 204 (1962), a litigant alleging *no* injury to his own "interests," whether statutory or otherwise, might nonetheless have standing. A number of commentators have advocated this approach. See, e.g., Tushnet, "The Sociology of Article III: A Response to Professor Brilmayer," 93 Harv.L.Rev. 1698, 1706–07 (1980); Jaffe, "The Citizen as Litigant in Public Actions: The Non-Hohfeldian or Ideological Plaintiff," 116 U.Pa.L.Rev. 1033, 1037 (1968), and history does not

much about the character of standing doctrine. Specifically, because the requirement is addressed only to federal judges, it does not limit congressional power to define interests whose infringement will confer injury in fact, nor does it impose an obligation that state courts require injury in fact before addressing federal claims.

The article III-based injury requirement serves only to limit the ability of federal courts to confer standing in the absence of statute;[5] it does not limit Congress's power to designate categories of individuals or groups as sufficiently aggrieved by particular actions to warrant federal judicial intervention at their behest.[6] The Supreme Court has made clear that "[t]he actual or threatened injury required by article III may exist solely by virtue of 'statutes creating legal rights, the invasion of which creates standing,'"[7] and has accordingly heard litigants who would have lacked standing absent such statutes.[8] Whether a given statute actually does create such a legal right may be open to debate.[9]

Similarly, state courts, if consistent with their own constitutions, may hear the federal claims of litigants who would not have standing to adjudicate them in federal court.[10] This reflects the conclusion that federal standing requirements, whether dictated by article III or sug-

clearly bar it, see Berger, "Standing to Sue in Public Actions: Is it a Constitutional Requirement?," 78 Yale L.J. 816, 825–27 (1969).

5. Compare the discussion of the eleventh amendment as a similar limit on federal judicial action only when unaided by an otherwise valid congressional enactment, § 3–26, infra.

6. See Fallon, "Of Justiciability, Remedies, and Public Law Litigation: Notes on the Jurisprudence of Lyons," 59 N.Y.U.L. Rev. 1, 48–56 (1984); Monaghan, "Third Party Standing," 84 Colum.L.Rev. 277, 313 n. 195 (1984); Monaghan, "Constitutional Adjudication: The Who and When," 82 Yale L.J. 1363, 1375–79 (1973). Nor does it limit the power of *state* legislatures in this respect, see Diamond v. Charles, 106 S.Ct. 1697, 1705 n. 17 (1986). However, City of Los Angeles v. Lyons, 461 U.S. 95 (1983), can be read to suggest limits to Congress's power, see Fallon, supra, at 31–35, 47–48, 56–59. Such a reading would be undesirable and would itself conflict with the separation of powers. See Spann, "Expository Justice," 131 U.Pa.L.Rev. 585, 643–44 (1983). This power, of course, does not allow Congress to compel adjudication that would violate the role of the federal courts as defined by other justiciability doctrines, see §§ 3–9 to 3–13. Fallon, supra, at 51–54. In any event, Congress has the independent power to establish courts under article I that may operate free of the restrictions of article III. See § 3–5, supra.

7. Warth v. Seldin, 422 U.S. 490, 500 (1975) (quoting Linda R. S. v. Richard D., 410 U.S. 614, 617 n. 3 (1973)). See also

§ 3–16, note 29, infra. Congress may grant a party a substantive right not to be subjected to the act complained of, or a procedural right to invoke judicial process to redress an alleged illegality that might not involve a breach of a substantive duty to the complaining party. Such a procedural right was recognized in United States Parole Comm'n v. Geraghty, 445 U.S. 388, 402–03 (1980) (finding Fed.R.Civ.P. 23 grants named plaintiff in class action right to pursue certification of class), discussed in § 3–11, supra, and is evident in statutes authorizing persons to serve as private attorneys general, see Fallon, supra note 6, at 54–56. Statutes providing that certain people's views or interests be taken into account administratively may imply either or both kinds of rights. See Stewart, "The Reformation of American Administrative Law," 88 Harv.L.Rev. 1667, 1727 & n. 286 (1975).

8. See § 3–16, note 29, infra.

9. See, e.g., Gladstone, Realtors v. Bellwood, 441 U.S. 91, 122–29 (1979) (Rehnquist, J., dissenting).

10. See City of Los Angeles v. Lyons, 461 U.S. 95, 113 (1983). See also Princeton Univ. v. Schmid, 455 U.S. 100, 102 n.* (1982) (per curiam); City of Revere v. Massachusetts Gen. Hosp., 463 U.S. 239, 243 (1983). The Court's first recognition of this principle appeared in Doremus v. Board of Educ., 342 U.S. 429, 434 (1952): "We do not undertake to say that a state court may not render an opinion on a federal constitutional question even under such circumstances that it can be regarded only as advisory."

gested by policy, all arise out of institutional concerns peculiar to the federal judiciary and its special role [11] and are therefore irrelevant to the question of what more generous standing rules a state may adopt if it chooses to do so.[12]   In certain cases, however, a state court may not be free to apply standing rules *less* generous than those applied in federal courts.[13]

When a litigant lacking minimum article III-based standing appeals from a state judgment, the practice of the Supreme Court is therefore to dismiss the appeal for want of a justiciable controversy, rather than vacating the judgment entirely.[14]   For example, in *Doremus v. Board of Education*,[15] the Supreme Court concluded: "because our own jurisdiction is cast in terms of 'case or controversy,' we cannot accept as the basis for review, nor as the basis for conclusive disposition of an issue of federal law without review, any procedure which does not constitute such." [16]

This approach, however, may leave the Court powerless to correct state court decisions of federal statutory or constitutional law that may be erroneous, a result the Court has worked to prevent in other doctrinal areas.[17]   One solution would regard a litigant's standing to raise a federal question as itself a federal question, allowing the Supreme Court to find the state court lacked jurisdiction over the substantive federal question involved and to vacate the judgment.[18]

11. See Arlington Heights v. Metropolitan Housing Corp., 429 U.S. 252, 262 n. 8 (1977).

12. But cf. Coleman v. Miller, 307 U.S. 433, 460 (1939) (plurality opinion of Frankfurter, J.). The argument is analogous to the functional arguments about whether a *federal* court sitting in a diversity case and thereby compelled to apply state substantive law, see § 3–23, infra, should decline to apply state door-closing rules reflecting concerns only about state judicial operation rather than about primary conduct, see, e.g., Woods v. Interstate Realty Co., 337 U.S. 535 (1949); Cohen v. Beneficial Indus. Loan Corp., 337 U.S. 541 (1949); Szantay v. Beech Aircraft Corp., 349 F.2d 60 (4th Cir. 1965); Atkins v. Schmutz Mfg. Co., 435 F.2d 527 (4th Cir. 1970), and thereby entertain cases that a state court could not.

13. At minimum, states may not limit standing to assert federal claims *more* than the federal courts would if in so doing they offer narrower access to federal claimants than they do to parties with analogous state claims, Testa v. Katt, 330 U.S. 386 (1947); see also FERC v. Mississippi, 456 U.S. 742, 760–63 (1982) (elaborating Testa), or where in so doing they "impose unnecessary burdens upon" federal rights. Brown v. Western Ry. of Alabama, 338 U.S. 294, 298 (1949). For an argument that state courts are obligated to hear federally justiciable issues and grant federally allowable remedies regardless of whether similar

state claims would be heard, see Gordon & Gross, "Justiciability of Federal Claims in State Court," 59 Notre Dame L.Rev. 1145 (1984). See also Monaghan "Third Party Standing," 84 Colum.L.Rev. 277, 292–310 (1984) (identifying possible obligation to recognize certain third-party standing claims).

14. However, where a litigant would be barred in federal court by *prudential* aspects of standing doctrine, the Supreme Court may review the case. See City of Revere v. Massachusetts Gen. Hosp., 463 U.S. 239, 243 (1983), discussed in Monaghan, supra note 13, at 290–92.

15. 342 U.S. 429 (1952).

16. Id. at 434.

17. See § 3–4, supra and § 3–24, infra. Moreover, regardless of the correctness of a constitutional judgment, there may be cases, particularly those which present "generalized grievances" better suited for resolution in the national legislature, see § 3–17, infra, whose mere consideration by a state court would seem anomolous. But see § 3–5, supra (noting independent obligation of states to vindicate federal rights especially where federal jurisdiction has been closed off).

18. See P. Freund, Supreme Court and Supreme Law 31, 38 (E. Cahn ed. 1954). The Court has taken this approach where a state has entertained a federal claim and then on appeal it is adjudged moot. See

This would intrude greatly on state procedures for the formulation and adjudication of rights,[19] however, and such a general approach appears unnecessarily extreme compared with the potential problem.[20]

§ 3–16. Injury in Fact: Defining Judicially Cognizable Harms

The first of three elements of standing doctrine imposed by article III's requirement of a "case" or "controversy" is the requirement of an "injury in fact": "at an irreducible minimum, article III requires the party who invokes the court's authority to 'show that he personally has suffered some actual or threatened injury as a result of the putatively illegal conduct' of the other party . . . ."[1] In the past the *injury in fact* requirement was thought primarily to ensure that the litigant had a personal stake in the outcome of the lawsuit that would ensure adequate presentation of the case, though such a requirement is not, of course, the only way to ensure such presentation.[2] In recent years, however, the Supreme Court, moved by a changing vision of how separation-of-powers concerns impact on standing analysis, has rejected that emphasis.[3] In theory, a litigant must now demonstrate, regardless of the actual existence of a claimed injury or its subjective importance, an individuated harm impacting specifically upon him and of a tangible, concrete nature.

The Court's formal articulation of this standard is decidedly amorphous, for apart from introducing a few verbalisms the Supreme Court has done little to describe or justify the content of the required injury. The keystone for defining injury in fact is the requirement that it be "distinct and palpable"[4]—and conversely that it not be " 'abstract' or 'conjectural' or 'hypothetical'."[5] Although the Court has done little to explain how this conception of injury in fact promotes a proper view of the separation of powers, and indeed has commented that the terms "cannot be defined so as to make application of the constitutional standing requirement a mechanical exercise,"[6] it appears that the test

---

Liner v. Jafco, Inc., 375 U.S. 301, 304 (1964).

19. Compare, e.g., state provisions for advisory opinions, see § 3–9, note 4, supra.

20. Because much of the restrictiveness of federal standing requirements is prudentially based, in most cases the Supreme Court enjoys review power, see note 14, supra. Federal determinations in other cases would constitute only the weakest source of authority outside the state and Congress could avoid them entirely by conditioning state jurisdiction on an undertaking to apply federal rules of standing. Moreover, in extreme cases presenting the prospect that an erroneous decision of federal law would create significant disruption at the state level, the Supreme Court arguably could vacate the state judgment. Doremus, in which the state court took no action favoring the party found to have standing, may not be inconsistent with such a result. See Barnes v. Kline, 759

F.2d 21, 63 n.16 (D.C. Cir. 1985) (Bork, J., dissenting), vacated as moot, sub nom. Burke v. Barnes, 107 S.Ct. 734 (1987). Cf. DeFunis v. Odegaard, 416 U.S. 312, 320 (1974) (per curiam) (vacating state court judgment upon finding of mootness without explanation).

§ 3–16

1. Valley Forge Christian College v. Americans United for Separation of Church and State, 454 U.S. 464, 472 (1982) (quoting Gladstone, Realtors v. Village of Bellwood, 441 U.S. 91, 99 (1979)).

2. See § 3–15, note 4, supra.

3. See § 3–14, supra.

4. Warth v. Seldin, 422 U.S. 490, 501 (1975).

5. Allen v. Wright, 468 U.S. 737, 751 (1984) (citations omitted).

6. Id.

screens out certain injuries that are not viewed as "judicially cognizable" because their recognition and protection would unduly enhance the role of the judiciary in relation to other branches.[7] In any event, no general definition of the requirement is truly satisfactory. As the Supreme Court has recognized,[8] only through immersion in the various cases raising questions of injury in fact is it possible to come to some understanding of what the requirement entails. This section therefore essentially collects the various claims of injury which the Court has held are or are not proper injury-in-fact assertions.[9]

A person subject to criminal prosecution, or faced with its imminent prospect,[10] has clearly established the requisite "injury in fact" to oppose such prosecution by asserting any relevant constitutional or federal rights. Thus, in *Wisconsin v. Yoder*,[11] a parent convicted and fined five dollars for failure to send a child to school was allowed to challenge the state compulsory attendance law under the free exercise clause of the first amendment.[12]

Economic injury (or its prospect) from action of another is also such a "personal stake in the outcome" as to confer standing. Injury in fact is established, for example, by an employee's claim that the operation of a challenged law will necessarily result in a loss of employment, even though the law's criminal sanctions directly affect only the employer. In *Truax v. Raich*,[13] an Arizona statute making it illegal for an employer to include within his work force more than a given percentage of aliens was successfully challenged under the equal protection clause of the fourteenth amendment by a soon-to-be-discharged alien employee.

Adverse changes in economic relationships less dramatic than a complete deprivation of employment have also been found to create the required personal stake in the outcome of a controversy. In *Association of Data Processing Service Organizations v. Camp*,[14] the Supreme Court found that the prospect of competition with regulated national banks was so adverse to existing data processors' economic interests as to create the required personal stake for the processors to challenge the validity of agency rulings allowing the banks to enter the field. The same result was obtained in *Hardin v. Kentucky Utilities Co.*,[15] in which a private utility enjoying an almost complete monopoly of two markets was allowed to challenge the legality of a plan of the Tennessee Valley Authority to offer cheaper power in those areas. Similarly, tenant farmers have been held to have sufficient economic stake to challenge a decision by the Secretary of Agriculture broadening, in alleged viola-

---

7. See, e.g., Vander Jagt v. O'Neil, 699 F.2d 1166, 1177–80 (D.C. Cir. 1982) (Bork, J., concurring); Scalia, "The Doctrine of Standing as an Essential Element of the Separation of Powers," 17 Suffolk U.L.Rev. 881, 894–97 (1983). See also § 3–17, infra.

8. See § 3–14, note 29, supra.

9. For a more expansive treatment, see generally 13 C. Wright, A. Miller & E. Cooper, Federal Practice and Procedure § 3531.4 (1984 & Supp. 1987).

10. For "ripeness" aspects of this situation, see § 3–10, supra.

11. 406 U.S. 205 (1972).

12. See the discussion of "test cases" in § 3–12, supra.

13. 239 U.S. 33 (1915).

14. 397 U.S. 150 (1970).

15. 390 U.S. 1 (1968).

tion of a federal statute, the opportunity of landlords to condition leases upon the assignment of the tenants' federal crop subsidies, thereby depriving the tenants of cash needed to purchase supplies from anyone but the landlord.[16] And businesses have been granted standing to challenge laws barring or otherwise interfering with prospective business activities.[17]

A taxpayer of course has standing to challenge the validity or application of a taxing statute in determining his or her tax obligation.[18] Less obviously, perhaps, an individual may have a sufficient interest, in his or her capacity as a taxpayer, to challenge *spending* programs of the taxing government, on the theory—or more candidly, the fiction—that a successful suit against such a program can result in some decrease in the litigant's taxes. The Supreme Court has placed heavy restrictions on recognition of such standing in relation to the federal government, because of the concern that broad availability of taxpayer standing would invite judicial consideration of litigants' generalized ideological interests in the operation of government.[19] A number of cases have recognized such standing, however. For example, in *Flast v. Cohen*,[20] a federal income taxpayer was allowed to challenge a federal aid-to-education program in federal court; in *United States v. Butler*,[21] federal agricultural process taxpayers were accorded standing to question a federal program of purchasing reduced acreage allotments from farmers. It appears that local taxpayers, as long as they bring "a good-faith pocketbook action" [22] attacking the validity of a direct expenditure of funds, are granted more expansive standing than federal taxpayers on the theory that their interest is more direct and immediate.[23] The Court has been particularly generous in entertaining challenges under the establishment clause of the first amendment to state or local aid to church-related schools. For example, in *Everson v. Board of Education*,[24] a local taxpayer was held to have standing to invoke the Supreme Court's appellate jurisdiction in a suit originally brought to protest school district expenditures reimbursing parents for money spent in transporting their children to parochial schools.[25]

16. Barlow v. Collins, 397 U.S. 159 (1970).

17. See, e.g., Bacchus Imports, Ltd. v. Dias, 468 U.S. 263, 267 (1984); Secretary of State of Maryland v. Joseph H. Munson Co., Inc., 467 U.S. 947, 954–55 (1984); Bryant v. Yellen, 447 U.S. 352, 366–68 (1980); Village of Arlington Heights v. Metropolitan Housing Development Corp., 429 U.S. 252, 262 (1977).

18. See, e.g., Bacchus Imports, Ltd. v. Dias, 468 U.S. 263 (1984); Regan v. Taxation With Representation, 461 U.S. 540, 547 n. 8 (1983) (assuming successful challenge to veterans' tax preference would extend preference to plaintiff organizations).

19. See §§ 3–17 and 3–19, note 66, infra.

20. 392 U.S. 83 (1968) (establishment clause challenge).

21. 297 U.S. 1 (1936) (states' rights challenge).

22. Doremus v. Board of Education, 342 U.S. 429, 434 (1952).

23. Id. at 433–34. See, e.g., Marsh v. Chambers, 463 U.S. 783, 786 n. 4 (1983).

24. 330 U.S. 1 (1947).

25. See also Grand Rapids School Dist. v. Ball, 473 U.S. 373, 380 n. 5 (1985) (citing "the numerous cases in which [the Court has] adjudicated Establishment Clause challenges by state taxpayers to programs for aiding nonpublic schools").

Cases in which environmental injury is alleged again illustrate the Supreme Court's refusal to confer standing so broad that only the assertion of generalized grievances is involved. Thus, environmental injury has been recognized as sufficient to confer standing, but only if such injury represents an individuated interest of the litigant as distinguished from the polity as a whole. To be individuated, an interest need only be expressible in terms of the individual's concrete satisfactions or experiences; but such satisfactions or experiences need not be *unique* to the litigant: "Aesthetic and environmental well-being, like economic well-being, are important ingredients of the quality of life in our society, and the fact that particular environmental interests are shared by the many rather than the few does not make them less deserving of legal protection through the judicial process." [26]

Yet the decision in *Sierra Club v. Morton*,[27] which validated environmental injury as a basis for standing, construed Section 10 of the Administrative Procedure Act [28] as failing to confer standing on a private association challenging federal action which permitted commercial exploitation of the Mineral King Valley, part of the Sequoia National Forest in California, since the association had not asserted that its members were users of the Valley and hence among those materially injured by the alleged "change in the aesthetics and ecology of the area." Thus, the Court held that, absent a federal statute to the contrary,[29] purely "public" or ideological interests in the environment—including the interests of those who oppose its "use" by anyone [30]—are insufficient to confer standing.[31]

26. Sierra Club v. Morton, 405 U.S. 727, 734 (1972).

27. Id.

28. 5 U.S.C. § 702.

29. If a congressional statute had defined the members of nature-protecting organizations as among those entitled to invoke the judicial process against nature-threatening agency action, the Court would quite properly have regarded such members as meeting the injury-in-fact requirement of article III despite their inability to assert concrete, individuated, material harm, Sierra Club, 405 U.S. at 732 & n. 3, since injury to a litigant's own statutory rights affects interests sufficiently palpable and individuated to meet whatever requirements article III imposes with respect to standing. See also Singleton v. Wulff, 428 U.S. 106, 124–25 n. 3 (1976) (opinion of Powell, J.); Warth v. Seldin, 422 U.S. 490, 500–01, 509–10 (1975); Linda R. S. v. Richard D., 410 U.S. 614, 617 n. 3 (1973); § 3–15, notes 6 and 7, supra. The Court has entertained claims on this basis on a number of occasions, see, e.g., Havens Realty Corp. v. Coleman, 455 U.S. 363, 375–78 & n. 16 (1982); Gladstone, Realtors v. Village of Bellwood, 441 U.S. 91, 103–07 & n. 9 (1979); Trafficante v. Metropolitan Life Ins. Co., 409 U.S. 205, 212 (1972) (White, J., concurring). Perhaps the clearest example

of the effect of congressional authorization of suit is TVA v. Hill, 437 U.S. 153, 164 n. 15 (1978), which recognized a litigant's standing under the Endangered Species Act to preserve the snail darter, a three-inch fish of no evident tangible value.

30. See Sierra Club, 405 U.S. at 741–43 (Douglas, J., dissenting); Stone, "Should Trees Have Standing?—Toward Legal Rights for Natural Objects," 45 S.Cal.L. Rev. 450 (1972); Tribe, "Ways Not to Think About Plastic Trees: New Foundations for Environmental Law," 83 Yale L.J. 1315 (1974); Sagoff, "On Preserving the Natural Environment," 84 Yale L.J. 205 (1974); Tribe, "From Environmental Foundations to Constitutional Structures: Learning from Nature's Future," 84 Yale L.J. 545 (1975).

31. Actually, the Sierra Club case does not test squarely the question whether a clearly defined and well-documented interest in preserving a particular wilderness area against all current use would suffice to confer standing absent a statute, since the Court evidently believed that members of the Club had in fact utilized the Mineral King Valley for recreational purposes and had refrained from alleging such use in their complaint not because they opposed use on principle but rather because they sought a way to challenge environmental

The procedural legitimacy afforded environmental interests by *Sierra Club* was given effect in *United States v. SCRAP*,[32] a case in which the Supreme Court found that the plaintiff, an association of law student users of environmental resources (such as parks) in the Washington, D.C. area, had asserted the "specific and perceptible harm" necessary to distinguish them from citizens who had a purely ideological concern for the natural resources that the students claimed were affected by the action they challenged. SCRAP, the ad hoc student group formed for the purpose of instituting the litigation in question,[33] had contended that a railroad rate increase permitted by the ICC would "cause increased use of nonrecyclable commodities as compared to recyclable goods," which would eventually divert natural resources out of the Washington area and into the manufacturing process, which would ultimately cause more litter everywhere, including Washington.[34] Even as the Court accepted the plaintiffs' "but-for-a-nail" claim of standing, it noted the "attenuated line of causation to the eventual injury of which [they] complained," and warned that "pleading must be something more than an ingenious academic exercise in the conceivable."[35]

Interests sufficient to raise questions under the establishment clause of the first amendment may be asserted not only by criminal defendants[36] and by taxpayers,[37] but by all who can show a *direct and concrete impact* upon themselves from the action questioned. Thus, the Supreme Court reached the merits in an establishment clause challenge to the constitutionality of Bible-reading in public schools in *Abington School District v. Schempp*,[38] finding that plaintiffs had standing to raise the issue because they sued in their capacity as students and parents of students, and thus were "directly affected by the laws and practices against which their complaints [were] directed."[39]

---

degradation wherever it might occur. See Sierra Club, 405 U.S. at 735–36 n. 8.

32. 412 U.S. 669, 689 (1973).

33. For a suggestion that federal courts should be more responsive to focused claims for standing by organizations with an established history of concern with a particular principle than to claims by such ad hoc groups even when only the latter can claim material injury, see Stewart, "The Reformation of American Administrative Law," 88 Harv.L.Rev. 1667, 1738 n. 334 (1975).

34. 412 U.S at 688.

35. Id. SCRAP's attempt to require the ICC to take greater account of environmental concerns ultimately failed on the merits. See Aberdeen & Rockfish R.R. Co. v. SCRAP, 422 U.S. 289 (1975). Even though SCRAP is reflective of a liberal approach to standing currently out of favor, see § 3–14, supra, the vitality of early decisions entertaining noneconomic injuries was reaffirmed in Valley Forge Christian College v. Americans United for Separation of Church and State, 454 U.S. 464, 486 (1982).

See also Duke Power Co. v. Carolina Envt'l Study Group, Inc., 438 U.S. 59, 73–74 (1978) (concluding thermal pollution and emission of non-natural radiation into the environment from nuclear power plant constitutes injury in fact); Village of Arlington Heights v. Metropolitan Housing Development Corp., 429 U.S. 252, 262–63 (1977) (holding nonprofit corporation's interest in building low-cost housing satisfies injury standard).

36. See, e.g., McGowan v. Maryland, 366 U.S. 420 (1961) (challenge to Sunday Closing Law by persons convicted and fined five dollars for violating that law).

37. See, e.g., Flast v. Cohen, 392 U.S. 83 (1968); Everson v. Board of Education, 330 U.S. 1 (1947).

38. 374 U.S. 203 (1963).

39. Id. at 224 n. 9. The distinction between the standing requirements of the free exercise clause and those of the establishment clause is also relevant to Chapter 14, infra. Briefly, the difference arises from the free exercise clause's concern with coercion, so that only persons alleged-

As with establishment clause cases, plaintiffs who claim violation of civil liberties in actions brought or reviewed in federal courts must show that they were directly affected, in the capacity in which they raise the claim, by the action they challenge. Thus, in *Baker v. Carr*,[40] plaintiffs were deemed to have standing to challenge as unconstitutional the particular districting system apportioning representation in the Tennessee General Assembly because they claimed that malapportionment impaired the relative effectiveness of their own votes, thereby injuring them in their capacity as voters registered in allegedly underrepresented districts.[41] And, in *Trafficante v. Metropolitan Life Insurance Co.*,[42] the Supreme Court held that two tenants had standing to attack the discriminatory practices of their landlord as violative of the Fair Housing Act of 1968: "[T]he alleged injury to existing tenants by exclusion of minority persons from the apartment complex is the loss of important benefits from interracial associations [with the excluded tenants]." [43]

The Court has recognized allegations of future injuries as sufficient to confer standing. Stating that " '[o]ne does not have to await the consummation of threatened injury to obtain preventive relief,' " the Court allowed nursing home residents to sue to prevent threatened transfers to other facilities.[44] The Court has likewise allowed officeholders to challenge prohibitions and penalties on their running for other state offices without actually defying those limits.[45] And a union intending "conduct arguably affected with a constitutional interest" [46]

ly coerced by a rule or practice are "directly affected" by it for free exercise purposes. See also Grand Rapids School Dist. v. Ball, 473 U.S. 373, 380 n. 5 (1985) (taxpayers have standing to challenge school district's shared-time program); Aguilar v. Felton, 473 U.S. 402, 407 (1985) (taxpayers have standing to challenge distribution of funds to programs involving instruction by public employees on premises of parochial schools); Wallace v. Jaffree, 472 U.S. 38 (1985) (parent has standing to challenge school prayer statute); Lynch v. Donnelly, 465 U.S. 668 (1984) (Pawtucket residents have standing to challenge city's inclusion of a creche in its annual display).

40. 369 U.S. 186 (1962).

41. The Court found it unnecessary to decide whether "voters in counties allegedly overrepresented in the General Assembly also have standing to complain." Id. at 205 n. 24. Under the theory that limits standing to cases where the litigant's own material interests are adversely affected, such voters quite plainly would *not* have standing. See also Davis v. Bandemer, 106 S.Ct. 2797, 2805–06 (1986).

42. 409 U.S. 205, 209–10 (1972).

43. See also Havens Realty Corp. v. Coleman, 455 U.S. 363, 375–78 (1982) (opinion for a unanimous Court by Brennan, J.) (allowing white and black residents of the Richmond, Virginia, metropolitan area and an organization providing "counseling and referral services for low- and moderate-income homeseekers" to challenge one realtor's alleged steering in suburban Richmond because of the individuals' alleged losses of "the important social, professional, business and economic, political and aesthetic benefits of interracial associations that arise from living in integrated communities free from discriminatory housing practices" and the impairment or frustration of the organization's activities); Gladstone, Realtors v. Bellwood, 441 U.S. 91, 103–07 (1979) (opinion for the Court by Powell, J., joined by Burger, C.J., Brennan, White, Marshall, Blackmun, and Stevens, JJ.) (granting standing to challenge realtors' alleged racial steering to municipality fearing loss of stable, integrated neighborhoods and to white residents of the "target area" fearing loss of the "social and professional benefits of living in an integrated society"). Compare Warth v. Seldin, 422 U.S. 490, 512–14 (1975) (rejecting similar associational claim, distinguishing Trafficante on ground that no statutory right was involved).

44. Blum v. Yaretsky, 457 U.S. 991, 1000 (1982) (quotation omitted).

45. Clements v. Fashing, 457 U.S. 957 (1982).

46. Babbitt v. United Farm Workers National Union, 442 U.S. 289, 298 (1979)

and showing a "credible threat of prosecution" for that conduct was allowed to attack regulations on labor representation elections, consumer publicity, and boycotts.[47]

Nevertheless, the Supreme Court has not always conferred standing upon litigants concerned about future injuries, and on those occasions where the Justices have thus denied standing, they have often seemed to be influenced by the substantive merits of the lawsuit in question. In *City of Los Angeles v. Lyons*,[48] for example, the Court rejected on standing grounds a challenge to the Los Angeles Police Department's use of "choke holds" against suspects not threatening violence. The allegations of the complainant, a 24-year-old black man by the name of Adolph Lyons, were hardly ethereal, for Lyons himself had been the victim of a choke hold. That incident took place after city police, having spotted a burned-out taillight on Lyons' car, pulled him over to the curb and proceeded to search him and (despite his compliance with the search) slam his head and apply a forearm against his throat until he blacked out.[49] Lyons' larynx was damaged, but he might have considered himself lucky: since 1975, at least sixteen other people subjected to choke holds, twelve of them black males, had been killed.[50] Lyons sued for both damages and injunctive relief against the city's use of choke holds except in limited circumstances involving deadly force, and after a series of procedural twists, the case reached the Supreme Court.[51]

The Court, while conceding Lyons' right to sue for damages,[52] held that he had no right to seek an injunction against the police department's use of chokeholds. It discarded or disregarded without comment "[t]he fundamental aspect of standing . . . that it focuses on the *party* seeking to get his complaint before a federal court and not on the *issues* he wants to have adjudicated,"[53] or "on the precise nature of the relief sought."[54] Writing for a five-to-four majority,[55] Justice White's opinion for the Court held that Lyons' allegations fell "far short of the allegations" necessary for standing to seek an injunction. It demanded that Lyons show, apparently to a certainty, that he would again be choked without provocation or that the city had ordered or authorized that he

(conduct specifically protected by the first and fourteenth amendments).

47. Id. at 297–303.

48. 461 U.S. 95 (1983). Justice White wrote for the Court, joined by Chief Justice Burger and Justices Powell, Rehnquist, and O'Connor.

49. Id. at 114–15 (Marshall, J., joined by Brennan, Blackmun, and Stevens, JJ. dissenting). No evidence was offered that Lyons ever menaced or provoked the officers. See also id. at 106 n. 7 (opinion of the Court). According to uncontradicted evidence in the record before the Court, when Lyons regained consciousness, he was lying face down on the ground, choking, gasping for air, and spitting up blood and dirt. He had urinated and defecated. Id. at 115 (Marshall, J., dissenting).

50. Id. at 115–16 (Marshall, J., dissenting).

51. The procedural history of the case, along with considerably more detailed analysis, is presented in L. Tribe, "Choke Holds, Church Subsidies, and Nuclear Meltdowns: Problems of Standing?," in Constitutional Choices 99–120, 327–62 (1985).

52. 461 U.S. at 106 n. 7, 111.

53. Flast v. Cohen, 392 U.S. 83, 99 (1968) (emphasis added).

54. Jenkins v. McKeithen, 395 U.S. 411, 423 (1969) (plurality opinion of Marshall, J., joined by Warren, C.J., and Brennan, J.).

55. Justice Marshall dissented in an opinion joined by Justices Brennan, Blackmun and Stevens.

be.[56] This bears stark contrast to the convoluted chains of contingencies the Court has been willing to follow in commercial cases,[57] and the Court gave no indication why this level of certainty was necessary. Indeed, it noted that the assertions it insisted upon would be "unbelievable" and "incredible." [58]

A survey of the cases where standing would have been denied under the *Lyons* approach demonstrates the extreme and unprecedented nature of the Court's rejection of completed harm as constituting an "injury in fact" and of its demand for certainty of future injuries before a party may seek injunctive relief. Most ballot access cases seeking prospective relief would have to be dismissed after the election at issue was held since no one could ever prove with certainty that the candidates indeed would seek access in a future election,[59] would meet all legitimate access requirements,[60] and would be denied access for illegitimate reasons.[61] Yet *Clements v. Fashing*,[62] decided only a Term before and nowhere cited in *Lyons*, allows standing to obtain declaratory and injunctive relief on a far less substantial showing. Likewise, under the analysis deployed by the *Lyons* Court, voting rights cases would probably suffer a similar fate,[63] and abortion cases would probably have to be filed during the subject pregnancy—indeed, during the trimester of the alleged deprivation of rights.[64] Most durational residency requirement cases would dissolve once the plaintiff had completed the specified period, especially since the plaintiff would be hard-pressed to "make [a] showing that he is realistically threatened by a repetition of his experience." [65] The landmark affirmative action case of *Regents of the*

56. "Lyons would have had not only to allege that he would have another encounter with the police but also to make the incredible assertion either, (1) that *all* police officers in Los Angeles *always* choke any citizen with whom they happen to have an encounter, whether for purposes of arrest, issuing a citation or for questioning or, (2) that the City ordered or authorized police officers to act in such a manner." 461 U.S. at 105–06 (emphasis in original).

57. See, e.g., Duke Power Co. v. Carolina Environmental Study Group, Inc., 438 U.S. 59 (1978), and Watt v. Energy Action Educational Foundation, 454 U.S. 151 (1981). Both cases are discussed in L. Tribe, Constitutional Choices 99–120 (1985).

58. 461 U.S. at 106–07 & n. 7. The Court also sought to justify its denial of standing by invoking traditional equitable theories urging restraint. For a critique of this rationale, see L. Tribe, supra note 57, at 102–03; Fallon, "Of Justiciability, Remedies, and Public Law Litigation: Notes on the Jurisprudence of *Lyons*," 59 N.Y.U.L. Rev. 1, 59–74 (1984).

59. Compare Lyons, 461 U.S. at 105–06: "to establish an actual controversy in this case, Lyons would have had not only to allege that he would have another encounter with the police. . . ."

60. Compare id. at 105–07 & n. 7: "it is no more than conjecture to suggest . . . that the police will act unconstitutionally and inflict injury without legal provocation or excuse." "[A]ny future threat to Lyons . . . would be no more real than the possibility that he would again have an encounter with the police and . . . illegally resist arrest or detention."

61. Compare id.

62. 457 U.S. 957 (1982) (officeholders who would be forced by state constitutional provision to resign in order to run for higher office, or prevented by state constitutional provision from running for state legislature before the end of their elected term, have standing to challenge such provisions even though they are not now candidates).

63. See generally Chapter 13, infra. See also Tribe, Constitutional Choices 115, 349–50 (1985).

64. The Court explicitly rejected this view in Roe v. Wade, 410 U.S. 113, 125 (1973), see Chapter 15, infra, and has not been troubled by it since. See L. Tribe, supra note 63, at 115, 350 nn. 194–96.

65. Lyons, 461 U.S. at 109. For an elaboration of the Court's approach to standing questions in such cases, see L. Tribe, supra note 63, at 351 n. 197.

University of California v. Bakke [66] would also almost certainly have required dismissal on standing grounds had the Court rigorously applied *Lyons.* [67] The fact that in none of these areas has standing proven the insuperable barrier that it did in *Lyons* suggests that *Lyons* must be understood in large part as a decision of substantive law. [68] In particular, the case seems to represent a further extension and reification of the Court's general, sweeping respect and deference for men in uniform [69] that has overridden a wide range of substantive law claims. [70]

Another striking example of the manipulability of the Court's standing doctrine [71] is the case of *Laird v. Tatum,* [72] in which the Court ruled that standing is not conferred in a federal court by a claim "that the exercise of . . . First Amendment rights is being chilled by the mere existence, without more, of a governmental investigative and data-gathering activity that is alleged to be broader in scope than is reasonably necessary for the accomplishment of a valid governmental purpose. . . . Allegations of a subjective 'chill' are not an adequate substitute for a claim of specific present objective harm or a threat of specific future harm [e.g., imprisonment or its prospect] . . . ." But this language may plausibly be regarded as dictum inasmuch as the Court noted the respondents' apparent concession that they were not *themselves* "chilled." This concession, if accepted, would leave the Court only with claims that the government action was unlawful, not that anyone before the Court had been "injured in fact" in *any* sense. [73]

66. 438 U.S. 265 (1978), discussed in Chapter 16, infra.

67. In Bakke, the plaintiff, an unsuccessful applicant for admission to the University of California at Davis Medical School, never demanded that he be allowed to join either of the classes to which he had been denied entry. Like Lyons, Bakke did not and probably could not claim redress that would have undone the alleged wrong against him, and thus his claim was for future, preventive relief only: he sought an order forbidding Davis to again deny him admission to later entering classes for the allegedly unconstitutional reasons that caused his prior rejections. If Bakke's continuing lack of a medical education resulting from the consummated acts of the past supplied him standing to demand admission to a future class, then surely Lyons' continuing throat injury and continuing fear of police chokings gave him standing to have the police prevented from choking him again. For further discussion of the rather striking inconsistency between the standing analyses of Bakke and Lyons, see L. Tribe, supra note 63, at 115–17, 351–53.

68. Indeed, the Court's opinion in Lyons is sprinkled with comments assuming various substantive conclusions. In finding that fear of choking did not constitute an injury in fact, it assumed a definition of the substantive rights that the first, fourth, eighth and fourteenth amendments protect. Lyons, 461 U.S. at 107 n. 8. The

Court's repeated equation of legality and constitutionality, and its assumption that the police could only "act unconstitutionally" if they "inflict injury without provocation or legal excuse," implies that the Los Angeles Police Department's policy is coextensive with the applicable constitutional parameters. Id. at 108.

69. See L. Tribe, supra note 63, at 355 n. 240 (listing cases noting Court's deference to military and police judgments and its related preference for *men*, as opposed to women, in uniform).

70. See id. at 355 n. 241; see also id. at 118–19 (arguing that the Court in Lyons in effect treated "the issues Lyons raised as ones constitutionally committed to the discretion of the police and thus immune from judicial review, except insofar as an after-the-fact damages action may be available") (footnotes omitted).

71. For an argument that the Supreme Court's standing decisions in general have come to reflect the Court's views on the underlying substantive issues in question, see L. Tribe, supra note 63, at 99–120.

72. 408 U.S. 1, 10, 13–14 (1972).

73. Perhaps for this reason, the Supreme Court has recently characterized narrowly the standing barrier imposed by Laird. In Meese v. Keene, 107 S.Ct. 1862 (1987), the Court upheld the standing of a would-be exhibitor of foreign films to challenge the Department of Justice's designa-

A citizen's general interest in the fair enforcement of the law by government agencies or administrators presents a particularly troubling claim as a basis for standing.[74] Even if one assumes, as seems reasonable, that proper enforcement of the law maintains public security and provides an environment for individual productivity and tranquility, the connection between this general premise and any particular person's material interests is highly attenuated. Indeed, the general interest in fair law enforcement can quite plausibly be seen as a purely "ideological attachment to the principle that the law be obeyed for its own sake." [75] These perspectives manifest themselves in stringent limits on standing to challenge allegedly discriminatory administration of the criminal laws.

First, the class of "victims" of discriminatory criminal administration is very narrowly defined. Thus, while discriminatory enforcement of criminal laws may be challenged by those against whom such laws are *enforced*, persons injured by criminal conduct which goes *unpunished* because of discriminatory law enforcement do not ordinarily have standing to challenge the discrimination: a victim of an undeterred crime is not automatically a victim of nonenforcement. For example, in *Linda R. S. v. Richard D.*,[76] the Supreme Court held that an unwed mother who was not receiving child support payments from the father of her child did not have standing to seek an injunction against state law enforcement officials for their refusal to enforce a "child neglect" law against unwed fathers. The Court found "no injury in fact" because "appellant has made no showing that her failure to secure support payments *results* from the nonenforcement, as to her child's father, of [the criminal statute]." [77] Justice Marshall's majority opinion

tion of those films as "political propaganda" under the Foreign Agents Registration Act. The Court emphasized that the exhibitor, a member of the California State Senate, "has alleged and demonstrated more than a 'subjective chill;' he establishes that the term 'political propaganda' threatens to cause him cognizable injury." Id. at 1867. The Court based this determination solely on the exhibitor's statements and detailed affidavits—including those from a pollster and a political analyst, id.—suggesting, perhaps, that a conscientious plaintiff, by proffering enough "hard" data, can often sidestep Laird's bar on those who merely allege a "subjective chill."

For a further discussion of "chilling effects," see Chapter 12, infra.

74. See Stewart, supra note 33, at 1739–40.

75. Id. at 1739.

76. 410 U.S. 614 (1973). See § 3–18, infra.

77. Id. at 618 (emphasis added). Although this result might at first glance seem both harsh and bizarre given the apparent consequences to the unwed mother of the nonenforcement of support laws, the case becomes somewhat more comprehensible if one notes that a successful challenge by an unwed mother might result not in enforcement against *all* fathers but in enforcement against *none*, a consequence that could simultaneously (a) put in doubt the sense in which the unwed mother's interest had been affected by discriminatory enforcement after all, and (b) lead one to question the propriety of risking such harm to married mothers in a lawsuit where they are not represented. However, it should be noted that a great many equal protection claims regularly entertained by federal courts are subject to the same criticism since equalization may often be achieved by depriving third parties of benefits instead of awarding the benefits to the litigant. This possibility has not ordinarily triggered doubts as to justiciability or representation adequacy. See, e.g., Heckler v. Mathews, 465 U.S. 728, 739–40 & n. 8 (1984) ("when the 'right invoked is that to equal treatment,' the appropriate remedy is a *mandate* of equal treatment, a result that can be accomplished by withdrawal of benefits from the favored class as well as by extension of benefits to the excluded

concluded by observing that "in American jurisprudence at least, a private citizen lacks a judicially cognizable interest in the prosecution or nonprosecution of another." [78]

Second, in dealing with claims of discriminatory criminal law administration, the Supreme Court has in effect narrowly defined the class of "offenders." Discriminatory enforcement of criminal laws cannot be challenged, for example, by those who do not claim to be the subjects of present or future criminal prosecutions. Thus, in *O'Shea v. Littleton* [79], the Court found that the plaintiffs had failed to show the requisite injury in fact in a class action brought to enjoin what plaintiffs claimed was the racially discriminatory administration of the Cairo, Illinois, system of criminal justice: "[Claimants] here have not pointed to any imminent prosecutions contemplated against any of their number and they naturally do not suggest that any one of them expects to violate valid criminal laws. Yet their vulnerability to the alleged threatened injury from which relief is sought is necessarily contingent upon the bringing of prosecutions against one or more of them." [80]

The upshot of *Linda R. S.* and *O'Shea* is that the interest in the just administration of the laws, including the interest in nondiscriminatory criminal enforcement, is presumptively deemed nonjusticiable even if invoked by persons with something beyond a generalized bystander's concern; only if the litigant is immediately affected as a target of enforcement can that presumption be overcome. But it would be a mistake to suppose that this principle represents a doctrinal quirk unique to the field of criminal law administration. Rather, it is part of a broader insistence on a clear showing that the action challenged has in fact *caused* an injury, and that a judicial pronoucement of rights be likely to redress the injury, as a subsequent section will indicate.[81]

§ 3–17. Injury in Fact: Citizen and Taxpayer Standing, and the Policy Against Assertion of "Generalized Grievances"

In 1974, in an elaborate review of standing doctrine, the Supreme Court attempted to define the point at which there ceases to exist that "personal stake in the outcome of the controversy" necessary for a claim of "injury in fact." [1] In *Schlesinger v. Reservists Committee to*

class") (citation omitted) (emphasis in original); Orr v. Orr, 440 U.S. 268, 271–73 (1979). Cf. Allen v. Wright, 468 U.S. 737, 757 n. 22 (1984). There seems no sound reason for Linda R.S. to have turned on such considerations if other similar cases do not. See also discussion of partially circumventable judgments in § 3–9, supra.

78. 410 U.S. at 619. See also Diamond v. Charles, 106 S.Ct. 1697, 1704–05 (1986) (rejecting attempt of private citizen to appeal invalidation of state abortion statute given state's acquiescence); Leeke v. Timmerman, 454 U.S. 83, 87 (1981) (per curiam) (holding a private citizen has no judicially cognizable right to prevent state officials from presenting information to as-

sist a magistrate in determining whether to issue an arrest warrant).

79. 414 U.S. 488 (1974).

80. Id. at 498. See also § 3–10, note 16, supra; Rizzo v. Goode, 423 U.S. 362, 372 (1976) (holding that even those plaintiffs previously injured by police mistreatment did not have the requisite personal stake in the outcome of a federal suit seeking an overhaul of police disciplinary procedures to satisfy the case or controversy requirement). See also § 3–30, infra.

81. See § 3–18, infra.

§ 3–17

1. Baker v. Carr, 369 U.S. 186, 204 (1962).

Stop the War,[2] the Supreme Court ruled, over the dissents of Justices Douglas, Brennan and Marshall, that individuals acting *in their capacity as United States citizens* [3] lacked standing to raise the claim that the incompatibility clause of article I, § 6, "renders a member of Congress ineligible to hold a commission in the Armed Forces Reserve during his [or her] continuance in office." [4] The incompatibility clause states: "no person holding any Office under the United States, shall be a Member of either House during his Continuance in Office." Similarly, in *Ex parte Levitt*,[5] the Court had ruled that a citizen lacked standing to raise the claim that Justice Black, who had voted while a Senator to increase Supreme Court Justices' retirement benefits, was improperly appointed to the Court inasmuch as article I, § 6, also provides that "No Senator . . . shall, during the Time for which he was elected, be appointed to any civil Office . . . the Emoluments whereof shall have been increased during such time." The Court in *Levitt* declared that "to entitle a private individual to invoke the judicial power . . . he must show . . . a direct injury . . . and it is not sufficient that he has merely a general interest common to all members of the public." [6]

In *Schlesinger*, Chief Justice Burger's majority opinion held that "the generalized interest of all citizens in constitutional governance," which was the interest alleged to be adversely affected, is too "abstract" to give rise to "concrete injury" of the sort which constitutes "injury in fact." [7] The *Schlesinger* majority equated this distinction between "abstract" and "concrete" injuries with another distinction, that between "generalized" and "particular" interests. According to the Court, an injury involves a "generalized interest" and is thus "too abstract" for federal judicial concern if the class of those claiming injury cannot express their alleged collective injury as an aggregation of "specific claims of interests peculiar" to particular individuals. The case established that, "while standing is not to be denied simply because many people [each] suffer the same injury," citing *United States v. SCRAP*,[8] a citizen cannot claim standing if his or her adversely affected interest is " 'undifferentiated' from that of all other citizens." [9] The majority defended its distinction in terms of the values served by standing limitations generally: (1) a "personal stake . . . enables a complainant authoritatively to present to a court a complete perspective upon the adverse consequences flowing from the specific set of facts undergirding his grievance"; and (2) "the requirement of concrete injury further serves the function of insuring that such adjudication does not take place unnecessarily." [10] But it is anything but clear that a plaintiff whose interest is wholly "abstract" or "general" is peculiarly incapable of presenting a court with a "complete perspective" upon the

2. 418 U.S. 208 (1974).

3. Standing in a taxpayer capacity was denied on the authority of Flast v. Cohen, 392 U.S. 83, 102–10 (1968). See 418 U.S. at 227–28.

4. Id. at 209.

5. 302 U.S. 633 (1937).

6. Id. at 634.

7. The Supreme Court subsequently indicated that Schlesinger's standing decision was nonetheless prudential rather than constitutionally mandated. See Warth v. Seldin, 422 U.S. 490, 499 (1975).

8. 412 U.S. 669 (1973).

9. 418 U.S. at 217.

10. Id. at 221.

adverse consequences flowing from the action or inaction that is the subject of the complaint. Further, the Court has developed a whole panoply of tests under the general rubric of justiciability precisely to insure that adjudiciation, especially that involving constitutional issues, "does not take place unnecessarily." [11] Why it was thought necessary to turn the "injury in fact" requirement to the same end is obscure at best, particularly since standing doctrine generally stresses the identity of the litigant rather than the nature of the issue in dispute.

The *Schlesinger* majority stressed separation-of-powers considerations in reaching its decision: since "every provision of the Constitution was meant to serve the interests of all," recognition of "citizen" standing "has no boundaries" and would therefore "distort the role of the Judiciary in its relationship to the Executive and the Legislature and open the Judiciary to an arguable charge of providing 'government by injunction.' " [12] Crucially, the Court treated as irrelevant to the question of standing the argument "that if respondents could not obtain judicial review of petitioners' action, 'then as a practical matter no one can.' " [13] The Court justified its willingness to tolerate this possible outcome by relying on its statement in *United States v. Richardson*,[14] that "the absence of any particular individual or class to litigate these claims gives support to the argument that the subject matter is committed to the surveillance of Congress, and ultimately to the political process." [15]

In *Richardson*, the Court had denied standing to a federal citizen and taxpayer to raise the claim that "certain provisions . . . under the Central Intelligence Agency Act" [16] violate article I, § 9's requirement that "a regular Statement and Account of the Receipts and Expenditures of all public Money shall be published from time to time." [17] As further articulated by Justice Powell in his concurring

11. See §§ 3–7 to 3–13, supra.

12. 418 U.S. at 226–27, 222.

13. Id. at 227. Professor Stewart suggests that, as a practical matter, someone else *could* raise the issue of the incompatibility clause in the context of Congresspersons serving in the armed forces. He argues that the issue might arise if a member of Congress were to sue the United States for his or her statutory Reserve compensation. Stewart, "The Reformation of American Administrative Law," 88 Harv.L.Rev. 1667, 1742 n. 351 (1975). One must wonder, however, why the armed services would ever find it in their interest *not* to pay the members of Congress in their ranks, or what budget officials would be likely to take it upon themselves to withhold such payment.

14. 418 U.S. 166, 179 (1974).

15. See Scalia, "The Doctrine of Standing as an Essential Element of the Separation of Powers," 17 Suffolk L.Rev. 881 (1983) (interpreting these cases as part of the Court's general drift since Flast toward a vision of standing focused on the separation-of-powers implications of the doctrine).

16. Id. at 167.

17. Id. at 175. In refusing to construe the public accounts provision of article I, § 9, as protecting *taxpayers* as such from allegedly inadequate controls on federal spending, the Richardson Court implicitly decided *either* that the inadequacy of a control system could be fully tested by a defense to a prosecution under the system (e.g., for disclosure of accounts in violation of the system's prohibitions) *or* that any inadequacy could be best corrected through the political process. See 418 U.S. at 188–89 (Powell, J., concurring). Had the requirement of public accounting for CIA funds been statutory rather than constitutional in origin, it seems likely that the Supreme Court's more liberal standing principles for statutory challenges to agency or executive action would have allowed federal taxpayers to challenge violations of the requirement. See Stewart, "The Reformation of American Administrative Law," supra note 13, at 1740 & n. 346.

opinion in *Richardson*, "taxpayer or citizen advocacy, given its potentially broad base, is precisely the type of leverage that in a democracy ought to be employed against the branches that were intended to be responsive to public attitudes." [18]

Dissenting in *United States v. Richardson*,[19] Justice Stewart, joined by Justice Marshall, conceded that the requirements for taxpayer standing set out in *Flast v. Cohen* [20] had not been satisfied, but argued that Richardson had nonetheless established an "injury in fact" by claiming that "the Statement and Account Clause imposes upon the Government *an affirmative duty* to supply the information requested." [21]   Justice Stewart would have held that standing is conferred whenever the claimed affirmative duty "related to a very particularized and explicit performance by the asserted obligor, such as the payment of money or the rendition of specific items of information," since "under such circumstances, the duty itself, running as it does from the defendant to the plaintiff, provides fully adequate assurance that the plaintiff is not seeking to 'employ a federal court as a forum in which to air his generalized grievances.' " [22]   But why a duty to undertake "a very particularized and explicit performance" should have this consequence any more than does a duty to refrain from a highly specific and clearly designated act—as in *Schlesinger*—remains unclear.

The extent to which *Richardson* signalled not merely a justifiable reluctance to transform the federal judiciary into an ombudsman for general citizen grievances but rather a generally parsimonious judicial view of taxpayer standing became evident in the 1982 case of *Valley Forge Christian College v. Americans United for Separation of Church and State.*[23]   The case arose after the Department of Health, Education and Welfare (HEW) gave a 77-acre tract of land with an Army hospital on it to the Valley Forge Christian College, free of charge.[24]   The college, whose faculty members are required to be " 'baptized in the Holy Spirit and [to live] consistent Christian lives' " and whose administrators must all be affiliated with the Assemblies of God, said it planned to use the property to expand its program of " 'systematic training . . . to men and women for Christian service as either ministers or laymen.' " [25]   Americans United then sought a federal district court declaration that the transfer was null and void and an order compelling the return of the property to the United States. The group claimed standing under *Flast*, in which the Court had held that— despite the general rule that citizens have no right to bring suits seeking the enforcement of laws against others who may have violated

---

18. 418 U.S. at 189.

19. 418 U.S. 166, 202 (1974) (Stewart, J., dissenting). Justice Stewart concurred in Schlesinger.

20. 392 U.S. 83 (1968), summarized in § 3–19, note 66, infra.

21. 418 U.S. at 202 (emphasis added).

22. Id. at 203–04 (quoting Flast v. Cohen, 392 U.S. 83, 106 (1968)).

23. 454 U.S. 464 (1982).

24. Although HEW appraised the land alone at $577,500, it transferred the entire property without charge after applying a 100 percent "public benefit allowance." Id. at 468. The property may have been worth as much as $1.3 million with buildings. See Americans United v. United States Dept. of Health, Education and Welfare, 619 F.2d 252, 253 (3d Cir. 1980). The federal government spent an estimated $10.4 million to acquire the property. Id.

25. 454 U.S. at 468–69.

them—taxpayers have standing to challenge congressional exercises of the taxing and spending power allegedly in violation of the establishment clause. The *Flast* Court had reasoned that that clause had been intended as a specific limitation on the power to tax and spend in that one of the prime evils against which its proponents sought to guard was taxation to support favored religions or religion in general [26]—reasoning that seemed to apply to the facts of *Valley Forge.*

Nevertheless, in *Valley Forge* the Supreme Court sought to avoid *Flast* by pointing to all available factual distinctions between the two cases without regard to whether anything of consequence turned on those distinctions. The earlier case did not control, the Court held, because in *Flast* the transfer was made under article I, § 8's *spending* power, whereas Valley Forge had received its land under the *disposition of property* clause of article IV, § 3, Cl. 2.[27] The Court also held that taxpayer standing extended only to actions of Congress itself, not to actions of administrative agencies authorized by Congress.[28] Yet these distinctions are artificial in the extreme.[29] The Court in evaluating the legitimacy of congressional enactments long ago stopped examining legislation with respect only to the specific clause under which Congress thought it was acting: legislation, rather, is upheld based on the actual legitimacy of its means and ends pursuant to the totality of the grant of, and limits on, legislative power.[30] Likewise, by recognizing taxpayer standing to challenge acts of Congress but not congressionally authorized acts of administrative agencies, the Court turned the usual hierarchy of presumptions of legitimacy on its head. Under *Valley Forge,* anonymous civil servants in HEW now receive more protection for their actions than the elected and politically accountable Congress does for its. The choice to classify the transfer as one by HEW rather than by Congress also seems totally whimsical, for while Congress may not be able to execute either spending or property transfers on its own, neither may executive officials make disbursements without congressional authorization.[31] The Court's efforts to distinguish *Valley Forge* from *Flast* appear particularly perverse in

26. Flast, 392 U.S. at 103–04.

27. Valley Forge, 454 U.S. at 480. Article IV, § 3, Cl. 2 provides, in relevant part, "The Congress shall have Power to dispose of and make all needful Rules and Regulations respecting the Territory or other Property belonging to the United States."

28. Id. at 479. Justice Rehnquist wrote for the Court. Justice Brennan, joined by Justices Blackmun, Marshall, and Stevens, dissented.

29. As Professor Choper has said, "those are certainly accurate distinctions. Indeed, this case was called *Valley Forge* and the other was called Flast v. Cohen. [T]hat is an accurate distinction as well. But . . . the Court's distinctions in respect to *Flast* are quite formalistic and ephemeral." Choper, "The Establishment Clause: Taxpayer Standing," in J. Choper, Y. Kamisar, and L. Tribe, The Supreme

Court: Trends and Developments 1981–1982, at 68 (1983).

30. See Chapter 5, supra; cf. Heart of Atlanta Motel, Inc. v. United States, 379 U.S. 241 (1964); Katzenbach v. McClung, 379 U.S. 294 (1964). Indeed, under McCulloch v. Maryland's view of the necessary and proper clause, see 17 U.S. (4 Wheat.) 316, 421–23 (1819), both "spending" and "disposition of property" could probably be accomplished under either clause. In the context of a taxpayer's challenge, the distinction makes particularly little sense: before land, buildings or cash could be spent or disposed of, they had to be acquired, almost invariably with federal tax dollars.

31. Indeed, Flast itself was an action against the Secretary of HEW and others to enjoin the allegedly unconstitutional expenditure of public funds under an autho-

light of the concern animating the *Flast* majority about attempts to evade by subterfuge the establishment clause and the Court's decisions prohibiting public aid to religion. A license to fund religion merely by invoking the "property" clause—and perhaps giving in-kind aid or setting aside the funds a year in advance so that they become "property"—is almost more than the architects of these "numerous" and "notorious . . . subterfuges" could have imagined.

In short, even if decisions such as those in *Richardson, Schlesinger* and *Valley Forge* are animated by an understandable desire not to open the federal judiciary to ethereal citizen grievances, the opinions in those cases represent inadequately sensitive judicial applications of the principles underlying such a desire. To be sure, injuries affecting interests shared by all citizens in common, unlike harms visited upon insular minorities,[32] ordinarily present the weakest case for judicial intervention. But a court applying that rule of thumb should not forget to inquire whether the nature of the particular injury, however widely inflicted, is such as to impede the effective operation of majoritarian processes. Concealing CIA expenditures at least arguably blunts public opposition to a degree that weakens *all* political efforts at reform, an act counseling a recognition of taxpayer standing in *Richardson*. On the other hand, although the presence of numerous reservists in the halls of Congress reduces the likelihood of congressional action to require a severance of military-legislative connections, there seems no similar impediment to direct *electoral* action on the *Schlesinger* issue.

§ 3–18. Causation and Redressability: Tracing the Connection Between the Litigant and the Litigation

The Supreme Court has emphasized that the injury-in-fact requirement includes as a corollary a requirement that a litigant show that the challenged government action *caused* the litigant's injury. Sometimes this requirement is stated in a relaxed form: "In sum, when a plaintiff's standing is brought into issue the relevant inquiry is whether, assuming justiciability of the claim, the plaintiff has shown an injury to himself *that is likely to be redressed by a favorable decision.*" [1] On other occasions, the requirement is phrased more rigorously: "[T]o meet the minimum requirement of Art. III," plaintiff must "establish that, *in fact*, the asserted injury was the consequence of the defendants'

---

rizing statute—like Valley Forge, an as-applied, rather than a facial, challenge to an authorizing enactment itself.

32. See United States v. Carolene Products Co., 304 U.S. 144, 152 n. 4 (1938). See generally Chapter 16, infra. For example, in Allen v. Wright, 468 U.S. 737, 753–54 (1984), discussed in § 3–14, note 24, supra, the plaintiffs' "interest" in having the IRS halt its alleged tolerance of racial discrimination so as to "avoid the violation of law" seems to be an interest that all citizens (or at least all taxpayers), regardless of race, share. By contrast, the Allen plaintiffs' claim that they suffered racial stigma as

blacks—rejected by the Court as too abstract because they had not personally been denied equal treatment inasmuch as their children had not applied to and been rejected by the discriminatory private schools—represents an interest arguably personal to them and, as such, more suited to judicial cognizance. See id. at 770–71 n. 3 (Brennan, J., dissenting).

§ 3–18

1. Simon v. Eastern Ky. Welfare Rights Org., 426 U.S. 26, 38 (1976) (emphasis added).

actions, or that prospective relief *will remove* the harm." [2] On its face, such a causation requirement appears to be innocuous: if there were no requirement of causation whatsoever, plaintiffs could claim judicial relief even when the relief would not change their situation at all; "exercise of its power by a federal court would be gratuitous and thus inconsistent with the Art. III limitation." [3] But, as Dean Prosser noted, "[t]here is perhaps nothing in the entire field of law which has called forth more disagreement, or upon which the opinions are in such welter of confusion" [4] than the issue of causation. The causation requirement is thus highly manipulable; [5] its isolation by the Supreme Court as a separate element of the injury-in-fact requirement poses a serious risk that, in the guise of causality analysis, federal courts will engage in an unprincipled effort to screen from their dockets claims which they substantively disfavor. [6] Indeed, the causation requirement has come under increasing attack from commentators for being what Justice Brennan has termed "no more than a poor disguise for the Court's view of the merits of the underlying claims." [7]

Emphasis on causality also raises the risk of introducing a double standard into the law of injury in fact. Consider the situation in *Linda R. S. v. Richard D.*, [8] for example. If the father of Linda R. S.'s child, fearful of enforcement of the child neglect law and wishing to continue to provide no support for the child, had brought a declaratory judgment action to challenge the law's constitutionality on some theory which would void its enforcement against him, a federal court might closely examine the father's claim to see if it was sufficiently ripe, but would no doubt give short shrift to any argument by the state that the father was without standing inasmuch as he might elect to pay child support

2. Warth v. Seldin, 422 U.S. 490, 505 (1975) (emphasis added).

3. Simon, 426 U.S. at 38.

4. W. Prosser, Handbook of the Law of Torts § 41, at 236 (4th ed. 1971).

5. See "The Supreme Court, 1975 Term," 90 Harv.L.Rev. 56, 212 (1976).

6. When the relief requested is the cessation of allegedly illegal conduct, the causation and redressability components of the constitutional standing inquiry in practice perform generally similar functions. However, as the Supreme Court observed in Allen v. Wright, 468 U.S. 737, 758 (1984), when the relief requested by litigants is more sweeping, the two prongs may diverge. See id. ("[c]ases such as this, in which the relief requested goes well beyond the violation of law alleged, illustrate why it is important to keep the inquiries separate if the 'redressability' component is to focus on the requested relief"); see also Larson v. Valente, 456 U.S. 228, 269–70 (1982) (Rehnquist, J., dissenting) (arguing that plaintiffs do not have standing to lodge establishment clause challenge against charitable-solicitation law because they failed to demonstrate that "a favorable decision of this Court will redress the injuries of which they complain"). See generally Nichol, "Causation as a Standing Requirement: The Unprincipled Use of Judicial Restraint," 69 Ky.L.J. 185, 198–201 (1980).

For a discussion of the Supreme Court's fluctuating characterizations of how certain a showing a litigant must make of each element, see Nichol, "Rethinking Standing," 72 Calif.L.Rev. 68, 73–73 nn. 25 & 27 (1984). For analysis of the interaction of causality analysis with the injury in fact standard, see Nichol, "Rethinking Standing," supra, at 79–82; L. Tribe, Constitutional Choices 344–46 nn. 156, 158, 160, 161 (1985) (citing examples).

7. Allen v. Wright, 468 U.S. 737, 782 (1984) (Brennan, J., dissenting); id. at 782 n. 10 (collecting sources). The facts of Allen are summarized in § 3–14, note 24, supra. For further commentary on the manipulability of the causation requirement to serve substantive ends, see Nichol, "Abusing Standing: A Comment on Allen v. Wright," 133 U.Pa.L.Rev. 635, 639–41 & n. 27 (1985); L. Tribe, Constitutional Choices 107 & nn. 86, 88 (1985).

8. 410 U.S. 614 (1973), discussed in § 3–16, supra.

even in the absence of the law. Yet, the assumption upon which the father's standing rests is identical with that which Linda R. S. invoked: that the criminal sanction in fact alters conduct. If the father of the child could claim the benefit of that assumption in order to void a statute requiring him to provide support, it seems palpably unfair to hold that the mother of the child cannot invoke the very same assumption in order to show that a judicial decree requiring enforcement of the law will alter the father's conduct and thus confer a benefit upon her.

Again, in *Simon v. Eastern Ky. Welfare Rights Org.*,[9] the Supreme Court held that indigents lacked standing to challenge the validity of IRS regulations reducing the amount of free medical care hospitals must provide in order to obtain tax benefits conferred upon charities. The Court thought it "purely speculative whether denials of service specified in the complaint fairly can be traced to [the IRS regulations'] 'encouragement' or instead result from decisions made by hospitals without regard to the tax implications."[10] Yet if the IRS had moved in the opposite direction, and had required hospitals to provide more free care in order to win "charity" tax breaks, the hospitals would surely have standing to challenge the change in regulations notwithstanding any argument by the IRS that the new regulations might not be the cause of any increased services the hospitals might offer in the future.

It thus seems clear that an autonomous causation requirement need not be a desirable part of injury in fact doctrine. Nor is any such doctrine necessary. Where plaintiff claims that defendant's unlawful conduct has caused a third party to do plaintiff injury, a federal court need only inquire: (1) whether the third party's conduct would have provided plaintiff with the basis for a claim of injury in fact if plaintiff had directly sued the third party; and (2) whether, if defendant had required the third party to abstain from the conduct to which plaintiff objects, the third party would be able to show a sufficient injury in fact to justify an action against defendant. This approach simply involves repeated applications of the basic injury-in-fact requirement, and yet describes a way of dealing with the causation issue which satisfies the constitutional core of standing doctrine. Moreover, the Supreme Court's recent emphasis on an autonomous causation requirement is a departure from prior law. This fact does not make it any less likely that the current Court will continue in its causation analysis. But should the composition of the Court change, awareness of the aberrant character of the present approach may increase the speed with which

9. 426 U.S. 26 (1976).

10. Id. at 42–43. Similarly, in Allen v. Wright, 468 U.S. 737 (1984), discussed in § 3–14, note 24, supra, the Court, relying on Simon, denied the parents standing to complain of their children's decreased access to a desegregated public education on the ground that "[t]he links in the chain of causation between the challenged Government conduct and the asserted injury are far too weak for the chain as a whole to sustain respondents' standing." Id. at 759. For a powerful argument to the contrary,

relying on "elementary economics," see id. at 784–95 (Stevens, J., dissenting). Contrast Simon and Allen with Duke Power Co. v. Carolina Envt'l Study Group, Inc., 438 U.S. 59 (1978), discussed in §§ 3–9, note 27 and 3–10, notes 12 & 23, supra, in which the Court avoided any focus on troublesome causation questions, in its evident zeal to reach the merits, by seizing on a minor aspect of the case claimed to present actionable injury. See L. Tribe, supra note 7, at 106–08, 112–14.

the new Court repudiates its predecessor's decisions. That aberrant character is best seen by examining one case—*Warth v. Seldin*[11]—in detail. *Warth* dealt with a suit challenging an exclusionary zoning ordinance. In this area, the prior case law suffices to provide an ample backdrop against which to view the novelty of the Court's current causation approach.

Exclusionary zoning ordinances, limits on the enforceability of fair housing provisions, and other governmentally imposed restrictions on the allowable uses of land or the allowable means of broadening land's availability, may affect a wide variety of different groups with varying degrees of immediacy: owners of the property subject to restriction; persons with restricted opportunities to move into or acquire interests in the area and to use their newly acquired property as they wish; developers with a reduced chance to serve such persons; residents of nearby communities burdened by groups that might otherwise move to the restricted area. Because land use restrictions and restrictions on the means of making land more broadly available generate such a broad range of consequences, they make highly instructive test cases for the strength and character of the causal link required by the federal law of standing between the governmental action complained of and the factual injury alleged.

If a particular property transaction or project is demonstrably prevented by nothing but a challenged restriction,[12] or would be completed pursuant to statute but for a challenged state limitation on the statute's enforcement,[13] or would subject a participant in the transaction or project to civil or criminal liability only because of a challenged restriction or limitation,[14] there is of course no difficulty in identifying the restriction as the "cause" of the injury alleged. In all of these cases, the structure of the controversy assures that judicial relief from the restriction or limitation challenged by the litigant would immediately remove the injury of which the litigant complains. But the Supreme Court has not generally required identification of the specific transaction or project that would proceed unhindered but for a challenged rule or practice. Any contrary rule would confront excluded groups with a kind of Catch 22: the more severely and successfully exclusionary a challenged scheme is, the more difficult it would be to find insiders or developers willing to incur the inconvenience and

11. 422 U.S. 490 (1975).

12. See Village of Arlington Heights v. Metropolitan Housing Development Corp., 429 U.S. 252, 261–264 (1977); Cusack Co. v. Chicago, 242 U.S. 526, 527 (1917) (billboard restriction); Buchanan v. Warley, 245 U.S. 60 (1917) (racial restriction on real estate purchase); Washington ex rel. Seattle Trust Co. v. Roberge, 278 U.S. 116 (1928) (denial of permit for old-age home); Shelley v. Kraemer, 334 U.S. 1 (1948) (racially restrictive covenant).

13. See Reitman v. Mulkey, 387 U.S. 369 (1967) (ruling for plaintiffs whose stat-utory fair housing actions had been met by invocation of state constitutional amendment precluding fair housing enforcement).

14. See Eubank v. Richmond, 226 U.S. 137 (1912) (reversing fine imposed on owner for violating building set-back requirement); Barrows v. Jackson, 346 U.S. 249 (1953) (ruling for defendant in a damage action for conveying property in violation of racially restrictive covenant). Barrows also involved a separate third-party standing issue, id. at 256–60, discussed in § 3–19, infra.

expense of joining outsiders in designing a project or transaction that could meet any judicial test of specific identification.

Not surprisingly, therefore, owners have been permitted to complain of restrictions on the uses that purchasers or lessees might make of their property without identifying specific buyers or renters [15] and indeed without showing any decline in the sale or rental value of the restricted property.[16] Occupants have been permitted to complain that restrictions deprived them of association with excluded groups without identifying particular persons who would move in but for the restrictions, and indeed without proving that removal of the restrictions would in fact lead to an influx of such persons.[17] Persons alleging exclusion from an area because of a restriction have not been required to identify specific willing sellers or lessors, or even to allege that such willing parties could definitely be found.[18] And groups claiming inability to purchase or rent low-cost housing because of a rule restricting development or construction have been required neither to claim that a specific project would be built but for the rule nor to allege that any particular person would be able to occupy such new housing if it were built.[19] In all of these cases, the Supreme Court may be understood as having applied the traditional requirement of but/for causation—but to a rather broadly defined injury: not deprivation with respect to already identified property, but deprivation of the *opportunity to persuade others* to permit or to support desired purchase, lease, or construction in an area. There is no doubt in any of the cases described above that the restriction challenged is a but/for cause of *that* injury, and there can be

15. See Village of Euclid v. Ambler Realty Co., 272 U.S. 365, 384–85 (1926) (owner of tract subject to challenged zoning scheme permitted to refer generally to unidentified "prospective buyers of land" who were "deterred from buying" by the zoning provisions); Village of Belle Terre v. Boraas, 416 U.S. 1, 9–10 (1974) (owner of home subject to challenged zoning restriction not required to aver that specific renters would lease house but for the restriction).

16. See Euclid, 272 U.S. at 397; Belle Terre, 416 U.S. at 10–12 (Brennan, J., dissenting). Indeed in Belle Terre the appellees' own brief, at pp. 54–55, specifically negated any claimed injury to rental value.

17. See Trafficante v. Metropolitan Life Ins. Co., 409 U.S. 205, 208, 211 (1972). Although plaintiffs there relied on a federal statutory right to sue, see 409 U.S. at 212 (White, J., concurring), the Court's opinion did not suggest a contrary result on the standing issue in the statute's absence.

18. See Hunter v. Erickson, 393 U.S. 385 (1969) (ruling for plaintiff in an action arising out of the latter's fair housing complaint, dismissed pursuant to a challenged restriction on fair housing enforcement, where the complaint had averred only that

a real estate agent had refused to show plaintiff "whites only" listings; no claim was made that plaintiff could have purchased a house but for the complaint's dismissal).

19. See James v. Valtierra, 402 U.S. 137, 139 (1971) (citizens of San Jose and San Mateo "eligible for low cost public housing" permitted to challenge state's referendum requirement as a prerequisite to local housing authorities' applications for federal assistance). Although the relevant local housing authorities had submitted very general low-cost housing plans for referenda, there was (1) no allegation or proof that detailed plans would in fact have been developed or federal applications filed had the referenda succeeded (e.g., of the 6 San Jose council members who had voted to submit a plan for referendum, all but 5 had resigned by the time of the suit, see San Jose Jurisdictional Statement at 7); (2) no claim or evidence that federal assistance would be forthcoming even if applications were filed; and (3) no demonstration or even suggestion "that any particular . . . plaintiff would be able to occupy new housing if such housing were built." 313 F.Supp. 1, 3 (N.D.Cal.1970), rev'd (on the merits), 402 U.S. 137 (1971).

no doubt that such an injury is sufficiently material and individuated to escape classification as purely generalized or ideological.[20]

Against this background, one can only regard as aberrational in the extreme the decision in *Warth v. Seldin*,[21] in which a closely divided Supreme Court [22] was forced to ignore [23] such major cases as *Village of Euclid v. Ambler Realty Co.*,[24] *Hunter v. Erickson*,[25] *James v. Valtierra*,[26] and *Village of Belle Terre v. Boraas*,[27] in order to hold that a well-pleaded federal complaint in a case claiming intentionally exclusionary zoning [28] must somehow identify specific housing that the complaining parties would in fact occupy or build but for the exclusionary scheme.[29] Justice Brennan's dissent properly noted that the Court had never "required such unachievable specificity in standing cases in the past," [30] and correctly observed that the complainants could hardly "be expected, prior to discovery and trial, to know the future plans of building companies, the precise details of the housing market . . ., or everything which has transpired in . . . years of application of the . . . zoning ordinance, including every housing plan suggested and refused." [31] There seems little escape from the conclusion that the *Warth* Court "turn[ed] the very success of the allegedly unconstitutional scheme into a barrier to a lawsuit seeking its invalidation." [32] Nothing in article III, in the canons of sound judicial administration, or in the judicial precedents, required so harsh and bizarre a result.

§ 3–19. The Policy Against Third-Party Standing and the Related Zone-of-Interests Test Favoring a Nexus Between the Party Seeking Standing and the Right Asserted

Two of the three prudential policies that must be weighed in assessing standing are closely related: "the general prohibition on a

20. In each case, the injury of constricted housing opportunity is certainly more personal and palpable than that of risk to the complainants' environment held sufficient in United States v. SCRAP, 412 U.S. 669, 686 (1973). See also Everson v. Board of Education, 330 U.S. 1 (1947).

21. 422 U.S. 490 (1975).

22. Justice Powell's majority opinion was joined by Chief Justice Burger and Justices Stewart, Blackmun, and Rehnquist. Justice Brennan's dissenting opinion was joined by Justices White and Marshall. Justice Douglas dissented separately.

23. Oddly, the dissents ignored the cases as well.

24. See note 15, supra.

25. See note 18, supra.

26. See note 19, supra.

27. See notes 15 and 16, supra.

28. The complaint in Warth alleged that Penfield, a suburb of Rochester, N.Y., had adopted a zoning ordinance which, by its terms and as enforced by defendant board members, made "practically and economically impossible the construction of sufficient numbers of low and moderate income . . . housing"; that this result was *intended* to prevent low- and moderate-income people and non-whites from living in Penfield; and that the effect was in fact to exclude "persons of minority racial and ethnic groups." 422 U.S. at 496.

29. Although the majority did not hold that "the plaintiff who challenges a zoning ordinance or zoning practices must have a present contractual interest in a particular project," id. at 508 n. 18, it required essentially as much by treating allegations of prior fruitless efforts to locate housing as insufficient, id. at 503–04 & n. 14, and by attributing to "the economics of the area housing market, rather than . . . respondents' assertedly illegal acts," id. at 506, the undisputed inability of named complainants to purchase housing in the zoned area. Yet as the main dissent pointed out, the "causation theory which the Court [found] improbable . . . was adopted by a Task Force of the Town Board itself." Id. at 528 n. 7 (Brennan, J., dissenting).

30. Id. at 528.

31. Id. at 527–28.

32. Id. at 523.

litigant's raising another person's legal rights," and "the requirement that a plaintiff's complaint fall within the zone of interests protected by the law invoked." [1]   The third-party standing rule and the zone-of-interests test both address, from opposite directions, whether a litigant before a federal court who has satisfied the minimum standing requirements of article III [2] should be allowed to raise particular legal claims in the course of litigation.   The third-party standing rule focuses on screening out claims that protect only the interests of *others* (and not of the litigant);   conversely, the zone-of-interests test is concerned with claims that do not appear to protect the interests asserted by the *litigant* (but only of others), given the litigant's failure to show that the claims fall within the zone of interests arguably protected by the relevant statute or constitutional guarantee.

These doctrines hardly present monumental or inherent obstacles to the typical federal court litigant: the third-party standing rule as conventionally understood is riddled with exceptions, and the zone-of-interests test is relevant primarily where a claim of federal taxpayer standing in involved [3] or the litigant seeks review of administrative action.   The doctrines, in any event, are wholly subject to supplantation by Congress,[4] as long as disputes thus allowed remain of an otherwise justiciable character.[5]   But taken together the two doctrines reveal much of the Court's view of its role in governing access to the federal courts, and thereby illuminate other standing doctrines.

The third-party standing rule, often referred to as the policy against *jus tertii* standing,[6] holds that a litigant "generally must assert his own legal rights and interests, and cannot rest his claim to relief on the legal rights or interests of third parties." [7]   Although a coherent

§ 3–19

1. Allen v. Wright, 468 U.S. 737, 751 (1984). For a summary of the prudential requirements see § 3–14, supra.

2. The requirement of a showing of injury in fact fairly traceable to the challenged action and likely to be redressed by the judicial relief sought, see § 3–14, supra, cannot be eliminated through appeal to prudential factors. Absent such a showing, even compelling advantages of allowing a litigant to protect the rights of third parties that might be demonstrated will not allow suit; the Supreme Court appears never to have heard a case where the litigant's *only* basis for suit (absent legislative authorization) was to vindicate a third party's rights. Note, "Standing to Assert Constitutional Jus Tertii," 88 Harv. L.Rev. 423, 429–30 (1974). Similarly, the constitutional requirements are both: (a) anterior to the third-party or zone-of-interests test, in that no degree of nexus between the litigant and the protections of the law invoked will confer standing absent a proper showing of injury; and (b) more rigid than the third-party or zone-of-interests test, in that exceptions have been made to the latter but not to the former.

3. See § 3–17, supra.

4. See Singleton v. Wulff, 428 U.S. 106, 124–25 n. 3 (1976) (opinion of Powell, J.); see also § 3–15, note 7, supra.

5. See § 3–15, note 6, supra.

6. See Monaghan, "Third Party Standing," 84 Colum.L.Rev. 277, 278 n. 6 (1984).

7. Warth v. Seldin, 422 U.S. 490, 499 (1975) (citations omitted). See also Phillips Petroleum Co. v. Shutts, 472 U.S. 797, 804 (1985); Secretary of State of Maryland v. Joseph H. Munson Co., Inc., 467 U.S. 947, 955 (1984). At first blush, the Supreme Court's overbreadth doctrine in the first amendment area might appear an exception to the third-party standing rule, for the first amendment is thought by some analysts "to free litigants from the general limitations of as-applied challenges in permitting them to challenge the 'facial' validity of a statute by raising the 'rights' of 'hypothetical' third parties." Monaghan, supra note 6, at 282. Nevertheless, as Professor Monaghan has argued, the claim that a "special third party standing rule" had been established for first amendment cases has only fragmentary case support. Id. at 283. Professor Monaghan instead construes overbreadth doctrine as wholly consonant with the third-party standing rule: a litigant is asserting not the rights

theory explaining cases dealing with the rule is difficult to formulate,[8] several assumptions have been articulated in its support: (1) that unnecessary or premature decisions of constitutional issues should be avoided; (2) that, as a matter closely related to the necessity for decision, courts should respect the apparent judgment of absent third parties who have failed to come forward that their rights are not threatened, or that they do not wish to assert them; and (3) that third parties can best represent their own rights and thereby ensure concrete and sharp presentation of the issues.[9]

Like any general prescription, the third-party standing rule has not been applied "where its underlying justifications are absent"[10]. And, in recent years, concurrent with the general expansion by both Congress and the Supreme Court of the sorts of personal interests whose impairment may confer standing,[11] the Court has also recognized a growing number of supposed exceptions to the third-party rule.[12] Indeed, a review of the cases suggests that, considered at face value, these are "exceptions" in name only, appearing to have nearly swallowed the underlying "rule." Yet closer examination reveals that most,[13] if not all,[14] of these exceptions are most persuasively rationalized as *sub silentio* recognitions of *first-party* rights—of the interests of the *litigant* that are purportedly interfered with by the challenged action.[15] This reformulation of third-party standing emphasizes how closely the doctrine correlates with the inquiry framed by the zone-of-interests test.

The third-party standing rule is frequently relaxed in cases "[w]here practical obstacles prevent a party from asserting rights on behalf of itself" and where the litigant "can reasonably be expected properly to frame the issues and present them with the necessary adversary zeal";[16] in such cases it is obvious that the second and third assumptions underlying the rule, noted above, do not apply. In *Bar-*

---

of hypothetical others, but rather his own right to be judged in accordance with a valid rule. Id. at 282–86. See also Sedler, "The Assertion of Constitutional Jus Tertii: A Substantive Approach," 70 Calif.L. Rev. 1308, 1323–27 (1982) (interpreting first amendment facial challenges as involving litigants who themselves "had substantive rights to be free from the laws in question"). See §§ 12–27, 12–32 infra.

8. Useful recent efforts include Monaghan, supra note 6; Rohr, "Fighting for the Rights of Others: The Troubled Law of Third-Party Standing and Mootness in the Federal Courts," 35 U. Miami L.Rev. 393 (1981); and Sedler, "The Assertion of Constitutional Jus Tertii: A Substantive Approach," 70 Calif.L.Rev. 1308 (1982).

9. See Secretary of State of Maryland v. Joseph H. Munson Co., Inc., 467 U.S. 947, 955 & n. 5 (1984); Singleton v. Wulff, 428 U.S. 106, 113–14 (1976) (plurality opinion of Blackmun, J.); id. at 124 n. 3 (opinion of Powell, J.). Professor Lea Brilmayer has argued that these policies, labelled respectively "restraint," "self-determination",

and "representation," underlie justiciability law generally. See Brilmayer, "The Jurisprudence of Article III: Perspectives on the 'Case or Controversy' Requirement," 93 Harv.L.Rev. 297 (1979), discussed in § 3–8, note 25, supra.

10. Singleton v. Wulff, 428 U.S. 106, 114 (1976) (plurality opinion of Blackmun, J.).

11. See §§ 3–16, supra; but note the restrictive trend discussed in § 3–14, supra.

12. See Monaghan, supra note 6, at 288–89; Sedler, supra note 8, at 1312–14, 1321.

13. See Monaghan, supra note 6, at 297–316.

14. See Sedler, supra note 8, at 1322–44; compare Monaghan, supra note 6, at 304 n. 148.

15. See also note 7, supra.

16. Secretary of State of Maryland v. Joseph H. Munson Co., Inc., 467 U.S. 947, 956 (1984).

rows v. Jackson,[17] for example, the predicament of the litigant seeking to assert the third-party claim was itself the impediment to the third parties' assertion of their own constitutional rights. The question before the Supreme Court was whether white *sellers* of housing had standing to challenge *their* damage liability for violation of a racially restrictive covenant on the ground that the covenant violated the fourteenth amendment rights of black *buyers* who were the target of the covenant's restrictions. The Court held that the sellers could raise the claim on the buyers' behalf. The state action doctrine[18] barred a fourteenth amendment challenge to the discriminatory covenants by prospective buyers if the potential sellers "voluntarily" complied with the restrictions.[19] Because the threatened enforcement of damage liability against sellers would be likely to induce *seemingly* voluntary compliance with the covenants whenever it did not result in higher housing prices for the targeted buyers, the buyers could be deprived of any opportunity to assert their rights. Similarly, in *Eisenstadt v. Baird,*[20] a distributor of contraceptives challenging the constitutionality of a state law banning the distribution of such devices to unmarried persons was allowed standing to assert the rights of the unmarried users on the ground that "unmarried persons denied access to contraceptives in Massachusetts . . . are not themselves subject to prosecution and, to that extent, are denied a forum in which to assert their own rights."[21]

But even if the third parties (the buyers in *Barrows* and the unmarried persons in *Baird*) would not be "denied a forum" if federal courts were to refuse standing to the sellers or distributors, the result should be the same. Just as a litigant should always have standing to claim that he is being penalized for asserting his own constitutional rights,[22] a litigant's claim that complying with a duty imposed upon him would prevent another from exercising a constitutional right[23] presents a clearly justiciable issue about the permissibility of the choice the government seeks to impose upon the litigant—an issue involving the litigant's interests, not those of a third party.[24] Thus, although

17. 346 U.S. 249 (1953).

18. See the discussion in Chapter 18, infra.

19. Barrows, 346 U.S. at 245, 257–59. Cf. Shelley v. Kraemer, 334 U.S. 1 (1948). See also § 3–18; supra; Monaghan, supra note 6, at 288 n. 61.

20. 405 U.S. 438, 446 (1972).

21. Of course, to say that someone is "denied a forum" simply because he is not subject to prosecution is to underestimate the avenues for affirmative relief through, for example, declaratory judgment actions, see § 3–9, supra, although ripeness problems suggest that such avenues in this situation may be rather narrow, see § 3–10, supra.

22. See, e.g., North Carolina v. Pearce, 395 U.S. 711, 724 (1969) (penalty on appeal); Shapiro v. Thompson, 394 U.S. 618,

631 (1969) (penalty on travel); United States v. Jackson, 390 U.S. 570, 583 (1968) (penalty on defendant's silence at trial).

23. See, e.g., Maness v. Meyers, 419 U.S. 449, 468 (1975) (advocate held not punishable for good faith advice that his client assert the fifth amendment privilege against self-incrimination).

24. Cf. Simmons v. United States, 390 U.S. 377, 394 (1968) (impermissible choice between fourth and fifth amendment rights). The question whether enforcement of the duty would *in fact* have that effect becomes a question on the merits, whose answer will depend on the scope of the substantive rights held by the third parties in question and the strength of the causation theory argued by the litigant-dutyholder. See Note, supra note 2, at 431–33. Such a distinction between the third-party interests involved in a case and

cases like *Barrows* and *Baird* are often classified under the category of "obstacles to the assertion of constitutional rights," that view of the decisions understates the principle for which they should be read to stand. Indeed, the Supreme Court endorsed a broader reading of the cases in *Craig v. Boren*,[25] upholding the standing of a beer vendor to invoke the rights of male beer buyers in challenging a state law forbidding sale of 3.2% beer to males younger than 21 but permitting such sale to all females older than 18; the Court deemed it decisive that the challenged law placed the vendor under a legal duty compliance with which would " 'result indirectly in the violation of third parties' rights.' "[26]

Craig is part of a line of cases in which "vendors and those in like positions have been uniformly permitted to resist efforts at restricting their operations by acting as advocates of the rights of third parties who seek access to their market or function."[27] The protection of the vendor-vendee relationship is only one example of another general exception to the third-party rule, which stresses, beyond any inability of third parties to raise their claims, the existence of a *special relationship* between the litigant invoking the right and the third party who is alleged to possess it—an exception which suggests that the third party presumably wishes assertion of the right and that the litigant is capable of raising it effectively.[28] In *Griswold v. Connecticut*,[29] for example, the Supreme Court held that a doctor and an official of a birth control clinic who had distributed contraceptives had standing to assert the constitutional privacy rights of married users of birth control devices in challenging their own criminal convictions as accessories to the unlawful use: "We think that appellants have standing to raise the constitutional rights of the married people with whom they had a

the litigant's *own* interest in adjudicating them was noted in Phillips Petroleum Co. v. Shutts, 472 U.S. 797 (1985), in which the defendant in a state class action was granted standing to challenge the state court's jurisdiction over out-of-state class members as a violation of such litigants' due process rights. The Court held that the third-party standing issue was irrelevant because the defendant, by testing jurisdiction, was seeking "to vindicate its own interests" by ensuring that, whatever the outcome of the state lawsuit on the merits, it would have a valid "defense of res judicata in a later suit for damages by class members." Id. at 805.

25. 429 U.S. 190 (1976).

26. Id. at 195 (quoting Warth v. Seldin, 422 U.S. 490, 510 (1975)). A similar argument can be asserted persuasively in a case like NAACP v. Alabama ex rel. Patterson, 357 U.S. 449 (1958), in which the NAACP was permitted to rely on violations of its members' rights in order to bar a state court's attempt to compel disclosure of its membership list: "If petitioner's rank-and-file members are constitutionally entitled to withhold their connection with the

[NAACP] despite the production order, it is manifest that this right is properly assertable by [it]. To require that it be claimed by the members themselves would result in nullification of the right at the very moment of its assertion." Id. at 459. Again, the NAACP's standing as a dutyholder-litigant should not depend on anything beyond its claim that the choice between governmentally imposed injury to itself and impairment of the constitutional rights of third parties (its members) is an impermissible one. Cf. Joint Anti-Fascist Refugee Comm. v. McGrath, 341 U.S. 123, 183–87 (1951) (Jackson, J., concurring). The special rule formulated in the NAACP case has been supplanted by general recognition of an association's standing to assert the interests of its members, as well as its own interests. See § 3–20, infra.

27. Craig, 429 U.S. at 195. See also Carey v. Population Servs., Intn'l, 431 U.S. 678, 683–84 (1977).

28. See Monaghan, supra note 6, at 297–304.

29. 381 U.S. 479 (1965).

professional relationship . . . . Certainly the accessory should have standing to assert that the offense which he is charged with assisting is not, or cannot constitutionally be, a crime." [30] But since the target of a criminal prosecution should *always* have standing to argue that his compliance with the law would have deprived others of their constitutional rights, the Court's reliance on "relationship" in *Griswold* might plausibly be dismissed as a makeweight.[31]

More to the point is *Pierce v. Society of Sisters*,[32] where the plaintiff private schools won an injunction against enforcement of a state statute which would have made parents criminally liable for not sending their children to public school. In invalidating the statute, the Court permitted the private schools to assert the substantive due process rights of the parents and children as third parties.[33] The soundest rationale for the Court's decision is that the third parties' enjoyment of their rights in *Pierce* depended on the litigants' (the schools') *freedom from derivative injury*—the injury of having to shut down for want of students.[34] Because of the out-of-court relationship between the litigants (schools) and the rights-holders (parents and children), the litigants *had* to be allowed to assert third-party rights in order that those rights be fully protected: if private schools, deprived of students whose parents feared prosecution and lacked the desire or ability to litigate the issue, were forced to shut down, then a particular parent's successful assertion of his or her own "rights" in court would win a ticket only to an empty building—not to a private school.[35]

More generally, whenever a denial of third-party standing to a derivatively injured litigant (one who is injured because of a legal duty imposed on the third party) can be shown likely to impair the third

---

30. Id. at 481 (emphasis added). See also Secretary of State of Maryland v. Joseph H. Munson Co., Inc., 467 U.S. 947, 958 (1984); Eisenstadt v. Baird, 405 U.S. 438, at 443–46 (1972).

31. Cheaney v. Indiana, 410 U.S. 991 (1973), is not to the contrary. There, the Supreme Court denied, "for want of standing of the petitioner," a petition for writ of certiorari by a non-physician abortionist who sought to challenge her criminal conviction by asserting the right of all women to have abortions. Since Roe v. Wade, 410 U.S. 113 (1973), had already held that states may forbid all abortions by persons other than licensed physicians, it was clear that petitioner's compliance with Indiana's criminal law would *not* have deprived women of protected rights. See, e.g., id. at 991 (Douglas, J., concurring) (treating the denial of certiorari as a decision on the merits rather than a ruling of no standing).

32. 268 U.S. 510 (1925), discussed in Chapter 15, infra.

33. 268 U.S. at 534–35; see also Barrows v. Jackson, 346 U.S. 249, 257 (1953). Cf. Miles v. City Council of Augusta, Georgia, 710 F.2d 1542, 1544 n. 5 (11th Cir. 1983).

34. See Note, supra note 2, at 434. The case was therefore like Truax v. Raich, 239 U.S. 33 (1915), except that in Truax the employee who was allowed to challenge the criminal prohibition directed against his employer was relying not on the third-party employer's rights but his own. It should be conceded that some language in Pierce suggests that the statute violated the schools' own liberty of property and contract. See L. Jaffe, Judicial Control of Administrative Action 498 n. 142 (1965).

35. To be sure, a successful parent suit filed early enough to facilitate planned operations by the private school could obviate this difficulty. But when the school seeks to litigate the matter prior to any such successful suit, there is no assurance that a parent's suit will promptly enough follow. Denying the school standing would then make the rights of some parents depend on the willingness and ability of others to bear litigational hardships. In effect, access to the private school is thus a "public good" that can be protected only collectively or derivatively.

party's enjoyment of an allegedly protected right, standing should be granted and the allegations decided on the merits. A specific relationship of interdependence between the litigant and the third party will typically provide the causal link between derivative injury to the litigant and impairment of the third party's rights.[36] Where such a relationship is present, as Professor Henry Monaghan has argued,[37] the interests of the litigant cannot be adequately assessed without reference to those of the third party, and the claim should be understood in a *first-party* sense: "a litigant asserts his own rights (not those of a third person) when he seeks to void restrictions that directly impair his freedom to interact with a third person who himself could not be legally prevented from engaging in the interaction," so that "the litigant's claim is dependent upon and symmetrical with the substantive reach of the third party rights." [38] Analysis should therefore focus, as under the zone-of-interests test, on whether the law invoked by the litigant arguably protects the third party's interest in the interaction.[39]

Cases involving "true" assertions of third-party standing, then, are those in which it is not plausible to view the challenged official action as directly impairing the litigant's interaction with the third party and thus creating a first-party interest. In these cases, a litigant is essentially asking to be treated as a "private attorney general" to vindicate the interests of others who either lack litigating resources or are not sufficiently motivated to seek vindication of these interests through judicial review themselves.[40] As a matter of policy this authorization is

36. But the presence or absence of such a relationship should not otherwise be relevant, see Note, supra note 2, at 441; see also note 24, supra; Rohr, supra note 8, at 420 and n. 133. Nor should a relationship's "importance" or character matter for third-party standing except as it bears on the causal link or on the issue of the litigant's ability adequately to represent the interests of the third party.

37. See Monaghan, supra note 6, at 297–304; see also Sedler, supra note 8, at 1328–39.

38. Monaghan, supra note 6, at 299, 304.

39. Cf. Singleton v. Wulff, 428 U.S. 106, 123 n. 2 (1976) (opinion of Powell, J.). Under this analyis, interference with the interaction cannot be justified "unless it serves a legitimate governmental end," which becomes more difficult to demonstrate as the strength of the third party's right grows, see Monaghan, supra note 6, at 303–04. Where direct interference with an important right is shown, the hurdle posed by the injury-in-fact requirement to any abstract claim to a right to interact is surmounted, see id. at 309–10.

Of course, the substantive law invoked may not even arguably protect the third party's interest in the interaction. For example, in United States v. Reidel, 402 U.S. 351, 355–56 (1971), the Court ruled that a mail-order distributor of obscene materials could not bar prosecution of its activities by reliance on the right of consumers of such materials to possess and peruse it, recognized in Stanley v. Georgia, 394 U.S. 557 (1969); Stanley, the Court in effect held, did not encompass a right to *receive* the materials in any particular manner. Similarly, the Court has insisted that fourth amendment rights are strictly personal in nature, barring criminal defendants from challenging admission of evidence seized from others, see United States v. Payner, 447 U.S. 727, 731–32 (1980), and thereby indicating in effect that the fourth amendment does not protect any right of interaction, see Monaghan, supra note 6, at 305 n. 149.

When the typical "third-party standing" case is viewed in first-party terms, it becomes clear that the claims of such litigants may not be denied on prudential grounds, see id. at 301, and that the obligation to hear them applies to state as well as federal courts, see § 3–15, note 13, supra.

40. See Monaghan, supra note 6, at 310–15.

frequently sensible, and Congress has statutorily authorized such suit in a wide variety of situations.[41]

Although there may be ground for judicial authorization of such suits to protect third-party rights that are constitutional in origin, even in the absence of congressional action,[42] the Supreme Court has so far refused to go this far—reflecting the continued vitality of the prudential policies underlying the third-party standing rule. In *Singleton v. Wulff*,[43] however, Justice Blackmun's plurality opinion took a major step in this direction [44] by concluding that a pregnant woman's desire for anonymity, as well as the likely mootness of any suit she might bring concerning her pregnancy, justified a decision to allow her doctor to assert the woman's right to an abortion even though the statute involved merely denied doctors income and did not put them under a duty not to perform the abortion [45]—and such a woman could sue under a pseudonym [46] and could make use of class action procedures to guard against mootness.[47] Justice Blackmun appeared to imply that, in this context, a woman might be deterred from suit in practice even if not in theory. Justice Blackmun's opinion, however, won the support of only three other Justices,[48] with Justice Stevens concurring only in the result.[49] Justice Powell, also joined by three Justices,[50] sharply dissented from Justice Blackmun's argument, positing that only if the state "directly interfered with the abortion decision"[51] by forbidding the

---

41. See § 3-15, note 7, supra; Monaghan, supra note 6, at 313 & n. 195. The leading case is FCC v. Sanders Bros. Radio Station, 309 U.S. 470 (1940), holding that, under a statute according the right of judicial review to those "aggrieved or whose interests are adversely affected by any decision by the [Federal Communications] Commission granting or refusing [a broadcast license application]," id. at 476–77, an existing broadcaster had standing to challenge a license grant to a potential rival. The Court expressly rejected the argument that the existing broadcaster's standing was based on its own interest in freedom from competition under the statutory and administrative scheme. Id. at 473–76. Rather, the Court afforded the broadcaster standing in order to vindicate the interest of the "public" in compliance with the requirements of the Act. Id. at 476–77. Motivated by its own economic injury at the hands of the agency, the existing broadcaster's action as a "private attorney general" brought to judicial attention the interests directly protected by the statute—those of listeners, who might lack the means or motivation to challenge what the agency had done. See also Havens Realty Corp. v. Coleman, 455 U.S. 363 (1982); Gladstone, Realtors v. Bellwood, 441 U.S. 91 (1979).

42. See Monaghan, supra note 6, at 313–15. Professor Monaghan suggests such rules might be a form of "constitu-

tional common law," see § 3–4, supra. In some respects, the Court's reluctance to articulate formally a theory of "standing by necessity" tracks its increasing unwillingness to imply private rights of action from federal regulatory statutes. See L. Tribe, Constitutional Choices 112 & 342–43 n. 145 (1985) (analogizing between these two doctrinal areas); see also § 3–23, infra.

43. 428 U.S. 106 (1976).

44. See Monaghan, supra note 6, at 307 n. 163 ("*Wulff* is one of the few good examples of a genuine jus tertii case, and its correctness depends on the limits on judicial authorization of private attorneys general").

45. See 428 U.S. at 117–18 (plurality opinion of Blackmun, J.). Justice Blackmun argued that "an impecunious woman cannot easily secure an abortion without the physician's being paid by the State." Id. at 117.

46. Id. at 117; see, e.g., Roe v. Wade, 410 U.S. 113 (1973).

47. 428 U.S. at 117; see § 3–11, supra.

48. Justices Brennan, Marshall and White.

49. See 428 U.S. at 121–22.

50. Chief Justice Burger, Justice Stewart, and Justice Rehnquist.

51. Id. at 128 (opinion of Powell, J.).

procedure [52] could a physician assert a woman's rights.[53] Justice Powell thus appeared to follow the duty approach suggested above; but besides insisting on a duty, he also appeared to require a "relationship." [54] *Wulff*, therefore, hardly stands as firm precedent—one way or the other.

Four Terms after *Wulff*, however, an identical 4–4 tie over an analogous issue was broken by Justice Stevens, who joined the *Singleton* plurality to recognize a right of the named plaintiff in a class action to continue to pursue class certification after the mooting of his individual claim. In *United States Parole Commission v. Geraghty*,[55] Justice Blackmun, now writing for the Court, inferred a right "analogous to the private attorney general concept" from the applicable procedural rules.[56] Justice Powell, in dissent, argued that even if this inference were correct, Congress could not authorize such suit by a litigant lacking an independent personal stake satisfying the requirements of article III.[57] Although *Geraghty* suggests a potentially expansive definition of judicially cognizable injury in fact, the sharp division displayed even in the face of arguable congressional authorization, as well as the specialized procedural context involved, limit its practical importance.

The last of the three prudential policies which may be involved in an issue of standing is closely related to the third-party standing rule: "the requirement that a plaintiff's complaint fall within the zone of interests protected by the law invoked." [58] The zone-of-interests test was first articulated in the context of judicial review of agency action under § 10 of the Administrative Procedure Act ("APA"),[59] in *Association of Data Processing Service Organizations, Inc. v. Camp*,[60] in which the Supreme Court ruled that a person can qualify for review under § 10 as one "aggrieved by agency action within the meaning of a relevant statute" if "the interest sought to be protected by the complainant is arguably within the zone of interests to be protected or regulated by the statute or constitutional guarantee in question." [61]

---

52. Although not necessary for his argument, Justice Powell appeared to assume that only a criminal statute would constitute such direct interference. See id.

53. See also id. at 126 ("The plurality virtually concedes, as it must, that the two alleged 'obstacles' to the women's assertion of their rights are chimerical").

54. See id. Nothing in the law or policy of standing appears to support such a requirement as long as adequate advocacy seems independently assured. Justice Blackmun, although recognizing the intimate involvement of the physician in the woman's abortion decision, see id. at 117, appeared to emphasize the causal link— the fact that the denial of benefits to the physician would deny the right to the woman.

55. 445 U.S. 388 (1980), discussed in § 3–11, supra.

56. Id. at 403.

57. See id. at 421–24.

58. Allen v. Wright, 468 U.S. 737, 751 (1984).

59. 5 U.S.C. § 702.

60. 397 U.S. 150 (1970).

61. Id. at 153. See also Clarke v. Securities Industry Ass'n, 107 S.Ct. 750, 754–59 (1987) (reviewing Data Processing test); id. at 756 n. 11 (citing scholarly criticism). In Data Processing, the Court allowed data processing companies to challenge agency action authorizing national banks to compete against the companies by providing data processing services to other banks and bank customers, allegedly in violation of federal statute; the companies claimed injury in fact from the enhanced competition. The companies were permitted to defend the broad purposes of the statute even though it did not specify that such companies were to be considered "ag-

The test operates as "a guide for deciding whether, in view of Congress' evident intent to make agency action presumptively reviewable, a particular plaintiff should be heard to complain of a particular agency decision," and, where the plaintiff is not the subject of the challenged action, the test "denies a right of review if the plaintiff's interests are so marginally related to or inconsistent with the purposes implicit in the statute that it cannot reasonably be assumed that Congress intended to permit the suit." [62]

In other contexts, the zone-of-interests test is a doctrine of uneven application and uncertain meaning. The Supreme Court noted recently that the test "is most usefully understood as a gloss on the meaning of § 702" and that, "[w]hile inquiries into reviewability or prudential standing in other contexts may bear some resemblance to a zone of interest inquiry under the APA, it is not a test of universal application." [63] One related inquiry, developed by the Court even before *Data Processing* in addressing whether persons may sue in their capacity as taxpayers, involves whether plaintiffs should be required to show "a logical nexus between the status asserted and the claim sought to be adjudicated." [64] In *Flast v. Cohen*,[65] the Court, in removing an earlier established, absolute bar against taxpayers challenging government expenditures in favor of religion, imposed the nexus test as an expedient limit on this extension of standing.[66] Addressing the claim that

grieved persons." See Data Processing, 397 U.S. at 156–57.

62. Clarke v. Securities Industry Ass'n, 107 S.Ct. 750, 757 (1987). Cf. note 71, infra.

63. Id. at 758 n. 16. Justice Stevens, joined by Chief Justice Rehnquist and Justice O'Connor, did not join in what he viewed as the majority's "wholly unnecessary exegesis on the 'zone of interest' test." Id. at 763.

64. Flast v. Cohen, 392 U.S. 83, 102 (1968). The subject of taxpayer standing is discussed in § 3–16, supra.

65. Id.

66. The Court required persons suing as federal taxpayers to establish a dual nexus, establishing both: (1) "a logical link between that status and the type of legislative enactment attacked"; and (2) "a nexus between that status and the precise nature of the constitutional infringement alleged." Id. at 102.

Imposition of the nexus requirement enabled the Court to distinguish Flast from Frothingham v. Mellon, 262 U.S. 447 (1923), which had been understood to bar federal taxpayer suits. In that case, Mrs. Frothingham, suing as a federal taxpayer, sought to restrain as violative of the tenth amendment expenditures under the federal Maternity Act of 1921, which provided conditional financial grants to the states to reduct infant mortality. In Flast, Mrs. Flast, also suing as a federal taxpayer,

sought to restrain as a violation of the first amendment's establishment clause expenditures of federal funds under Titles I and II of the Elementary and Secondary Education Act of 1965, which aided religious schools. Since both plaintiffs challenged spending programs in their capacities as federal taxpayers, both met the preliminary standing requirement of injury in fact and satisfied the first prong of the nexus test. However, while the Supreme Court allowed Mrs. Flast standing to make her claim, it refused standing to Mrs. Frothingham. The difference between the two cases was explained in Flast by reference to the second prong of the nexus requirement. Mrs. Flast's claim that the challenged spending program violated the establishment clause successfully located the interest she asserted within the scope of the right she claimed: Because "[o]ur history vividly illustrates that one of the specific evils feared by those who drafted the Establishment Clause and fought for its adoption was that the taxing and spending power would be used to favor one religion over another or to support religion in general, . . . that clause of the First Amendment operates as a specific constitutional limitation upon the exercise by Congress of the taxing and spending power conferred by Art. I, § 8." 392 U.S. at 103–04. However, Mrs. Frothingham had sought to invoke the tenth amendment, which was not shown to be one of the "specific constitutional limitations imposed upon an exercise of the taxing and spending power":

such a nexus should be required in cases not involving federal taxpayers, the Court concluded that the concerns underlying the nexus test operate only as prudential factors in resolving standing questions.[67]

Largely as a label for its inquiry into these concerns, the Court has accordingly used the "zone-of-interests" pigeonhole to describe the last of the three prudential factors to be used in assessing standing generally. It is nonetheless clear that general application of the test in the constitutional context differs from its use in the administrative law context.[68] In non-administrative litigation, the zone-of-interests test is simply a restatement of the general rule against third-party standing: to say that a plaintiff's claim does not fall within the zone of interests of the law invoked is but another way of saying that the right claimed is one possessed not by the party claiming it but by others, and that, under usual principles, the plaintiff will not have standing to claim a violation of the rights of these absent third parties, whose claims *would* fall within the applicable zone of interests.[69] As such, the zone-of-interests test in non-administrative-law settings implicates the same difficulty of determining the content of the substantive rights invoked,[70]

"In essence, Mrs. Frothingham was [a third party] attempting to assert the States' interest in their legislative prerogatives and not a federal taxpayer's interest in being free of taxing and spending in contravention of specific constitutional limitations." Id. at 105. The Flast exception to taxpayer standing has been narrowly construed. See Valley Forge Christian College v. Americans United for Separation of Church and State, Inc., 454 U.S. 464 (1982), discussed in § 3–17, supra.

67. See Duke Power Co. v. Carolina Envt'l Study Group, Inc., 438 U.S. 59, 78–81 (1978). Whether establishment of a nexus is constitutionally required even in taxpayer standing cases is unclear. Id. at 79–80 n. 25. For an argument that the nexus test "was from the start misguided, productive of unfortunate results and still less fortunate rationales," and an analysis of the related issues presented in the Duke Power case, including the function of the nexus test in addressing whether the litigant before the Court is an adequate representative for absent parties benefited by the legal rule invoked, see L. Tribe, Constitutional Choices 335–36 n. 93; 347–58 n. 174 (1985).

68. See Clarke v. Securities Industry Ass'n, 107 S.Ct. 750, 758 n. 16 (1987) (noting that the Court has "occasionally listed the zone of interest inquiry among general prudential considerations bearing on standing . . . and ha[s] on one occasion conducted a zone of interest inquiry in a case brought under the Commerce Clause," but that this practice "should not be taken to mean that the standing inquiry under whatever constitutional or statutory provision a plaintiff asserts is the same as it

would be if the 'generous review provisions' of the APA apply") (citations omitted). Cf. Haitian Refugee Center v. Gracey, 809 F.2d 794, 828–29 n. 64 (D.C. Cir. 1987) (Edwards, J., concurring in part and dissenting in part). There was no mention of the zone-of-interests label when the Court granted third-party standing to certain Sioux Indians who challenged congressional restrictions on their decedents' rights to pass property at death. Hodel v. Irving, 107 S.Ct. 2076 (1987).

69. See, e.g., Singleton v. Wulff, 428 U.S. 106, 123 & n. 2 (1976) (Powell, J., concurring in part and dissenting in part) (noting that inquiry into whether "a party may argue that [challenged state action] contravenes someone else's constitutional rights . . . also has been framed, in appropriate cases, as whether a person with Art. III standing is asserting an interest arguably within the zone of interests intended to be protected by the constitutional or statutory provision in which he relies"). See also Valley Forge Christian College v. Americans United for Separation of Church and State, Inc., 454 U.S. 464, 492–93 n. 4 (1982) (Brennan, J., dissenting); Duke Power Co. v. Carolina Envt'l Study Group, Inc., 438 U.S. 59, 80–81 (1978); Monaghan, "Third Party Standing," 84 Colum.L.Rev. 277, 313 n. 193 (1984).

70. This substantive analysis parallels the inquiries required to decide such matters as whether Congress has granted persons standing to sue in federal court, see § 3–15, note 7, supra; whether an implied cause of action should be found to allow vindication of statutory or constitutional rights, see § 3–23, infra; and whether Con-

as well as the same problems of assessing the circumstances in which litigants can be said adequately to represent the interests of absent parties.

§ 3–20. Standing of Organizations, States, and Legislators: The Question of Capacity

Special questions of standing doctrine arise when the litigant seeking access to federal court possesses some supra-individual legal capacity—where the litigant might plausibly be said to be asserting, rather than or in addition to the litigant's *own* interests, the interests of *others* whom the litigant purports to have a special role in representing. The primary examples of such litigants are organizations (or associations), who may assert either institutional interests or those of their members; states, which may litigate either to protect sovereign or proprietary interests *or* on behalf of their citizens; and legislators, who when suing in connection with their official duties may be thought either to protect their own interest in exercising their official prerogatives or the broader interest of those they represent in effective performance of those duties.

In each such case, it is crucial to determine in what *capacity* a litigant is suing. Where such litigants are advancing their own interests, they are typically judged by the normal rules of standing, even though the interests might be unusual. Where standing is sought in a representative capacity, however, special rules apply to ensure that the controversy is indeed genuine and the interests of the individuals alleged to be represented are indeed protected. These rules draw force from the general policy against litigants asserting the interests of third parties.[1]

Where an *organization* is suing on its own behalf, the key question is whether it has alleged "a concrete and demonstrable injury to [its] activities . . . ."[2] A variety of injuries have been recognized in this context. For example, an organization has standing to sue on its own behalf if the defendant's actions impose economic harm, thereby draining its resources.[3] Injury to the active pursuit of noneconomic objectives, such as the encouragement of racially nondiscriminatory housing through counseling and referral service for non-wealthy home-seekers free of racial steering practices,[4] or the building of low-cost housing free of intrusive zoning restrictions,[5] will also confer standing. However, in line with the general policy against assertion of generalized grievances,[6]

---

gress has in a particular instance abrogated the sovereign immunity of the states against suit, see § 3–26, infra.

§ 3–20

1. See § 3–19, supra.

2. Havens Realty Corp. v. Coleman, 455 U.S. 363, 379 (1982). The ability of an organization to sue in this capacity was first noted in Warth v. Seldin, 422 U.S. 490, 511 (1975).

3. See, e.g, Havens Realty Corp. v. Coleman, 455 U.S. 363, 378–79 (1982); Village

of Arlington Heights v. Metropolitan Housing Dev. Corp., 429 U.S. 252, 262 (1977). Cf. Hunt v. Washington State Apple Advertising Comm'n, 432 U.S. 333, 345 (1977) (dictum).

4. Havens Realty Corp. v. Coleman, 455 U.S. 363, 378–79 (1982).

5. Village of Arlington Heights v. Metropolitan Housing Dev. Corp., 429 U.S. 252, 262–63 (1977).

6. See § 3–17, supra.

an organizational litigant must allege "more than simply a setback to [its] abstract social interests . . . ." [7]

Even where an organization itself has suffered no injury in fact, it may sue in certain cases on behalf of its members.[8] In *Hunt v. Washington State Apple Advertising Commission*,[9] the Supreme Court established a three-part test for such standing, allowing an organization to sue in a representative capacity where: "(a) its members would otherwise have standing to sue in their own right; (b) the interests it seeks to protect are germane to the organization's purpose; and (c) neither the claim asserted nor the relief requested requires the participation of individual members in the lawsuit." [10] Thus, in *Hunt* a state agency established to promote and protect the state's apple industry was granted standing to represent the interests of apple growers and dealers in challenging restrictive apple-marketing regulations of another state as imposing an unconstitutional burden on interstate commerce.[11]

Cases in which organizational standing is denied often revolve around the third prong of the *Hunt* test, for it is often not clear that the mere presence of the organization in the litigation ensures adequate representation of the members' interests. The Court has noted that an

7. Havens Realty Corp. v. Coleman, 455 U.S. 363, 379 (1982) (citing Sierra Club v. Morton, 405 U.S. 727, 739 (1972)). For example, in Sierra Club the organization alleged a special, longstanding interest in preserving wilderness areas. See also Simon v. Eastern Kentucky Welfare Rights Org., 426 U.S. 26, 40 (1976) (organization with "special interest in the health problems of the poor" could not assert standing in its own right) (dictum).

8. See, e.g., Simon v. Eastern Ky. Welfare Rights Org., 426 U.S. 26, 40 (1976); Warth v. Seldin, 422 U.S. 490, 511 (1975). A precursor of the organizational standing doctrine, styled as an exception to the rule against the assertion of the rights of third parties, is found in NAACP v. Alabama ex rel. Patterson, 357 U.S. 449 (1958), discussed in § 3–19, note 26, supra. Although an organization's representation is discussed in terms of its "members," it appears a single member may be represented, see Warth, supra, 422 U.S. at 511 (dictum).

9. 432 U.S. 333, 343 (1977).

10. Id. at 343. The Court reaffirmed the Hunt test and explicated its justification in International Union, UAW v. Brock, 106 S.Ct. 2523, 2532–34 (1986), against the claim that absent a showing of special need, members of an organization wishing litigation of common questions of law or fact in federal court should be required to bring a class action and meet the safeguards on representation adequacy imposed by Fed.R.Civ.P. 23. The Court noted that "special features, advantageous to both the individuals represented and to the judicial system as a whole . . . distinguish suits by associations on behalf of their members from class actions," in that such organizations "can draw upon a preexisting reservoir of expertise and capital," that "the primary reason people join an organization is often to create an effective vehicle for vindicating interests that they share with others" and that "[t]he very forces that cause individuals to band together in an association will thus provide some guarantee that the association will work to promote their interests." The Court did hint that if an association is not an adequate representative, "a judgment won against it might not preclude subsequent claims by the association's members without offending due process principles." Id. Cf. Phillips Petroleum v. Schutts, 472 U.S. 797, 805 (1985), discussed in § 3–19, note 24, supra; see also § 3–8, note 25, supra. For an analysis of this final point and argument that organizational standing should be allowed only if the organization can demonstrate that it is likely to adequately represent its members, see Note, "Associational Standing and Due Process: The Need for an Adequate Representation Scrutiny," 61 B.U.L.Rev. 174 (1981).

11. See id. at 342–45. The Court granted standing even though the agency technically had no members at all, on the ground that it performed "the functions of a traditional trade association" and the growers and dealers, by electing the agency's officials and financing its activities, possessed "all the indicia of membership" in the organization. Id. at 344.

organization's standing "depends in substantial measure on the nature of the relief sought," and has denied standing where monetary damages have been sought but "whatever injury might have been suffered is peculiar to the individual members concerned, and both the fact and extent of injury would require individualized proof." [12] The Court has also required the participation of individual members where conflicts of interests may be present within the organization or where specific facts are required to clarify the issues presented.[13]

Similarly, the question of whether a *state* is suing on its own behalf or rather on behalf of others (i.e., its citizens) is central to whether it has standing to sue in federal court. Article III accords special treatment to the states in their relationships with the federal judicial system, especially with regard to the original jurisdiction of the Supreme Court.[14] Any discussion of the problem of a state's standing must begin with this inquiry: has the state made its claim in a capacity that jusitifies the inference of an injury in fact to the state's own interests—or is it merely acting as a conduit for the claims of its citizens? In the latter case, in which a state is merely suing on behalf of its citizens without possessing any independent injury to itself, the standing requirement is ordinarily thought not to have been satisfied.[15]

Whether a state has standing to sue on its own behalf depends on whether the ordinary rules of standing are satisfied; no special *standing* rules are applied.[16] A state is clearly entitled to sue to protect its sovereign interests, such as "the exercise of sovereign power over individuals and entities," involving "the power to create and enforce a legal code, both civil and criminal," or to demand "recognition from other sovereigns," most frequently involving the recognition of borders.[17] Moreover, certain nonsovereign interests will allow suit. In recognition of the fact that a state, "like other associations and private parties . . . is bound to have a variety of proprietary interests," it is allowed, like other proprietors, to bring suit to protect these interests. Thus, a state may sue private parties under the federal antitrust laws "to redress wrongs suffered by [it] as the owner of a railroad and as the

---

12. Warth v. Seldin, 422 U.S. 490, 515–16 (1975). Cf. International Union, UAW v. Brock, 106 S.Ct. 2523, 2532 (1986).

13. See, e.g., Harris v. McRae, 448 U.S. 297, 320–21 (1980) (holding that "the participation of individual members" of the organization was "essential to the proper understanding" of the claim that the challenged ban on Medicaid funding of abortions on ground that is impaired the free exercise of religion of some of the organization's members); but cf. International Union, UAW v. Brock, 106 S.Ct. 2523 (1986) (giving union standing to challenge a federal policy allegedly resulting in the denial of unemployment benefits to large numbers of its members despite the fact that a legal ruling favorable to it would require later proceedings by each member for specific benefits).

14. See § 3–5, supra; see also Maryland v. Louisiana, 451 U.S. 725, 735–36 (1981).

15. Cf. Hunt, 432 U.S. at 343 (limiting standing on part of private organizations to situations where the interests such organizations seek to protect are germane to their purposes).

16. See Watt v. Energy Action Educ. Found., 454 U.S. 151, 161 (1981); Maryland v. Louisiana, 451 U.S. 725, 736 (1981).

17. Alfred L. Snapp & Sons, Inc. v. Puerto Rico, 458 U.S. 592, 601 (1982). A classic example of the former interest is the state's interest in defending the constitutionality of its laws in federal court, see, e.g., Maine v. Taylor, 106 S.Ct. 2440, 2447 (1986); Diamond v. Charles, 106 S.Ct. 1697, 1705 (1986).

owner and operator of various [public] institutions." [18] It is equally free
to sue other states for injurious action, for example, for burdening
interstate commerce through regulation of the natural gas industry in
a manner raising the costs of states purchasing gas for their own use; [19]
federal officials have also been held suable, for example, for injuries
resulting from failure to comply with federal law protecting a state's
exploitation of its natural resources.[20]

   In certain situations a state may also sue on the behalf of its
residents. Although a state may not act in a nonsovereign capacity as
the nominal party in a lawsuit "to pursue the interests of a private
party," [21] it may sue in its capacity as *parens patriae* to promote "quasi-
sovereign" interests—which "consist of a set of interests . . . in the
well-being of its populace . . . . sufficiently concrete to create an actual
controversy between the State and the defendant." [22] Two kinds of
such interests have been articulated. First is a state's "quasi-sovereign
interest in the health and well-being—both physical and economic—of
its residents in general." [23] Here, "more must be alleged than injury to
an identifiable group of individual residents," and whether the injury is
quasi-sovereign is influenced by whether it is "one that the State, if it
could, would likely attempt to address through its sovereign lawmaking
powers." [24] Thus, a state may challenge the constitutionality of congressional action implementing a treaty, where that action interferes
with state regulation of migratory birds to which the state has asserted
title.[25] Similarly, as a quasi-sovereign, a state may seek damages or
equitable relief against another state—for example, where the latter
has caused flooding in the plaintiff state by modifying the flow of a
river.[26] Its quasi-sovereign capacity also entitles a state to bring suit
against a private individual to enjoin a corporation from discharging
noxious gases from its out-of-state plant into the suing state's territory,[27] and to challenge allegedly illegal business activities on behalf of
citizen consumers, who may lack a sufficient economic stake to justify
suit.[28]

   Secondly, a state has a "quasi-sovereign interest in not being
discriminatorily denied its rightful status within the federal system,"

---

18. Georgia v. Pennsylvania Ry., 324
U.S. 439, 443 (1945); see also Hawaii v.
Standard Oil of Calif., 405 U.S. 251 (1972)
(permitting treble damage suit by state as
owner and operator of public institutions).

19. Maryland v. Louisiana, 451 U.S.
725, 736–37 (1981).

20. Watt v. Energy Action Educ.
Found., 454 U.S. 151, 160–62 (1981).

21. Alfred L. Snapp & Son, Inc. v. Puerto Rico, 458 U.S. 592, 602 (1982).

22. Id.

23. Id. at 607.

24. Id.

25. Missouri v. Holland, 252 U.S. 416
(1920).

26. North Dakota v. Minnesota, 263
U.S. 365 (1923).

27. Georgia v. Tennessee Copper Co.,
206 U.S. 230 (1907); see also id. at 237
(noting a state has an interest "independent of and behind the titles of its citizens,
in all the earth and air within its domain").

28. Maryland v. Louisiana, 451 U.S.
725, 737–39 (1981). Other cases involving
quasi-sovereign interests include Pennsylvania v. West Virginia, 262 U.S. 553
(1923); and Missouri v. Illinois, 180 U.S.
208 (1901).

ensuring that "the State and its residents are not excluded from the benefits that are to flow from participation in the federal system." [29]

Where a state's capacity as *parens patriae* is not negated by the federal structure,[30] the protection of the general health, comfort and welfare of the state's inhabitants has been held to give the state itself an interest sufficient for article III purposes to justify litigation,[31] especially in light of the provision for original Supreme Court jurisdiction in all cases in which a State is a party.[32]

But a state, as representative of its residents, is deemed to lack sufficient interest to challenge the constitutionality of a *federal* statute. Thus, in *Massachusetts v. Mellon*,[33] the Court declared that "a State, as *parens patriae*, may [not] institute judicial proceedings to protect citizens of the United States from the operation of the statutes thereof . . . . [It] is not part of [the State's] duty or power to enforce [its citizens'] rights in respect of their relations with the Federal Government. In that field it is the United States, and not the State, which represents them as *parens patriae* . . . ." [34] The Court later relied on this language in *South Carolina v. Katzenbach* [35] to hold that the state as *parens patriae* could not invoke the bill of attainder clause of article I and the due process clause of the fifth amendment. The Court in that case did, however, pass upon the merits of the state's fifteenth amendment challenge to the Voting Rights Act of 1965, given the state's argument that the statute invaded the explicitly reserved power of the states to determine voter qualifications and to regulate elections and hence exceeded the power of Congress. Similarly, Justice Douglas, dissenting from a summary refusal to grant original jurisdiction in a suit challenging the President's power to wage undeclared war in Vietnam, argued that, where the Constitution specifically prescribes

29. Alfred L. Snapp & Son, Inc. v. Puerto Rico, 458 U.S. 592, 607–08 (1982). In Snapp, the Court held that Puerto Rico, which had sued a private company alleging that it had violated provisions of two federal statutes giving United States workers a preference over temporary foreign workers for jobs that become available within the United States, had standing to bring suit. The Court reasoned that Puerto Rico had articulated an interest apart from that of particular private parties—namely, its "interest in securing residents from the harmful effects of discrimination," an interest particularly acute in Puerto Rico, which had a history of invidious discrimination along ethnic lines. Id. at 609. The Court also noted that Puerto Rico's interest in combatting unemployment constituted another "benefit" supporting its standing. Id. at 609–10.

30. See, e.g., Louisiana v. Texas, 176 U.S. 1, 19 (1900): "Inasmuch as the vindication of the freedom of interstate commerce is not committed to the State of Louisiana, and that State is not engaged in

such commerce, the cause of action must be regarded not as involving any infringement of the powers of the State . . . ."

31. E.g., Missouri v. Illinois, 180 U.S. 208 (1901); Georgia v. Tennessee Copper Co., 206 U.S. 230 (1907); Pennsylvania v. West Virginia, 262 U.S. 553 (1923).

32. Compare Hawaii v. Standard Oil Co. of Calif., 405 U.S. 251 (1972) (although allowing the state standing to sue in district court to vindicate its proprietary interests, the state's interest as *parens patriae* was not deemed sufficient to support standing to complain there of damages to the "general economy").

33. 262 U.S. 447 (1923).

34. Id. at 485–86. However, a state may *rely* on a federal statute in a suit "to secure the federally created interests of its residents against private defendants." Alfred L. Snapp & Son, Inc. v. Puerto Rico, 458 U.S. 592, 610 n. 16 (1982).

35. 383 U.S. 301, 324 (1966).

the manner in which the federal government is to act as *parens patriae*, the states may challenge nonconforming federal action.[36]

The interests that may be asserted by a state or federal *legislator* suing in connection with legislative activities [37] in federal court are more varied than those involved in suits by organizations or by states. The contours of legislator standing remain substantially undefined, largely because the Supreme Court has never comprehensively or definitively addressed the subject.[38] However, available Supreme Court and lower court decisions suggest at least four distinct capacities in which a legislator may bring suit: (1) as an advocate of a traditional individual interest that happens to be connected with legislative activities; (2) as a representative of his or her constituents; (3) as an officially designated representative of a legislative body, typically challenging allegedly unlawful executive action; or (4) as a vindicator of his or her alleged personal interest in full exercise of official legislative powers.

The principles governing the first two categories are relatively well defined. When a legislator is asserting an ordinarily recognized individual interest connected with official duties, his or her status as a legislator does not deny standing or implicate any unusual concerns. For example, in *Powell v. McCormack*,[39] the Supreme Court allowed review of a congressman's claim, challenging as unlawful his exclusion from service in the 89th Congress, which was founded on his interest in receiving back pay for the session.[40] A similar interest was advanced, although not decided upon, in *Bowsher v. Synar*,[41] where legislators attacked the Gramm-Rudman Act's automatic deficit-reduction machin-

---

36. Massachusetts v. Laird, 400 U.S. 886, 888 (1970).

37. Most significant cases involving legislator standing involve suits by Members of Congress, but the principles of standing articulated in those cases apply as well to suits by state legislators—except that such cases do not raise federal separation-of-powers considerations. See Harrington v. Bush, 553 F.2d 190, 204–05 n. 67 (D.C. Cir. 1977). For cases considering the standing of state legislators, see Dessem, "Congressional Standing to Sue: Whose Vote is This, Anyway?," 62 Notre Dame L.Rev. 1, 6 n. 31 (1986).

38. The Court's 1986 Term appeared likely to produce such a decision when the Court accepted Barnes v. Kline, 759 F.2d 21 (D.C.Cir. 1984), for review. *Barnes* had upheld a legislator's claim of standing to challenge the validity of a pocket veto by President Reagan. However, the Supreme Court, in a brief opinion, vacated and remanded the case as moot, over strenuous dissents by Justices Stevens and White. See Burke v. Barnes, 107 S.Ct. 734 (1987). In previous cases implicating legislator standing, the Court has issued opinions

without comment on the subject or affirmed lower court decisions without opinion. See Dessem, supra note 37, at 3 n. 9.

39. 395 U.S. 486 (1969).

40. See id. at 498–500. See also Bond v. Floyd, 385 U.S. 116, 128 n. 4 (1966) (upholding similar claim of state legislator). The permissibility of suit in Powell and Bond was so evident that the Court's opinion nowhere discusses standing. Likewise, the Court has accorded similar standing in connection with the coordinate branches. See, e.g., Nixon v. Administrator of General Services, 433 U.S. 425, 431, 435–36 (1977) (upholding standing of former president to raise the constitutional prerogatives of the executive branch in seeking invalidation of federal statute disposing of plaintiff's alleged personal property).

41. 106 S.Ct. 3181, 3186 (1986). The lower court found legislator standing based on a separate theory, see Synar v. United States, 626 F.Supp. 1374, 1378, 1381 (D.D.C. 1986) (three-judge court) (per curiam), whereas the Court relied solely on the standing of a co-plaintiff private organization.

ery for the reduction it threatened for their salaries and for their staff and office budgets.[42]

Just as clearly, however, a legislator's suit in the second capacity—purely as a representative of constituents' interests—falls short of minimal standing requirements. On occasion legislators have invoked this theory to challenge alleged infringements of their powers based on their constituents' interest in these powers.[43] Such an approach does not fall within recognized exceptions to the general ban on the assertion of the rights of absent third parties,[44] nor does it meet the more generous standards governing organizational or *parens patriae* suits discussed earlier in this section.[45] Moreover, recognition of any such constituent interest might violate the bar on assertion of "generalized grievances";[46] interested constituents should therefore be required to intervene if this theory is advanced, to allow careful examination of their asserted interest.[47]

The issues become more complex when a legislator is suing against infringement of constitutionally based legislative prerogatives, often alleging illegal executive action, and normally involving the claim that the right to an effective vote on a given issue has been denied. This form of suit is least troublesome when the legislature (or one of its houses, if both houses are not implicated) has officially designated the legislator to sue on its behalf or has intervened,[48] or where a number of legislators are suing collectively on a legal theory that, if upheld, will enable them to remove the challenged interference. The Supreme Court's only direct consideration of standing in this third capacity came in *Coleman v. Miller*,[49] which upheld the standing of twenty of the forty members of the Kansas state senate who argued that the state's lieutenant governor, who had cast a tie-breaking vote against their position on a resolution to ratify a proposed constitutional amendment, had no authority to do so and thereby defeat the measure. Writing for himself and two other Justices, Chief Justice Hughes explained that the

42. Conversely, a federal legislator may have standing to raise certain aspects of his legislative prerogatives as a shield to legal action by another—for example, in a libel action arguably conflicting with the immunity conferred by the speech or debate clause of article I, § 6.

43. See, e.g., Vander Jagt v. O'Neill, 699 F.2d 1166, 1167 (D.C. Cir. 1982), cert. denied, 464 U.S. 823 (1983); Synar v. United States, 626 F.Supp. 1374, 1378 (D.D.C. 1986) (three-judge court) (per curiam), aff'd sub nom. Bowsher v. Synar, 106 S.Ct. 3181 (1986).

44. See § 3–19, supra; see also Dessem, supra note 37, at 18–19 n. 112.

45. See Dessem, supra note 37, at 19–22.

46. See § 3–17, supra.

47. Such intervention is quite practicable and has been employed on occasion. See Dessem, supra note 37, at 22 n. 130.

48. See, e.g., Barnes v. Kline, 759 F.2d 21, 23 n. 3 (D.C. Cir. 1984), vacated as moot sub. nom. Burke v. Barnes, 107 S.Ct. 734 (1987); In re Application of the United States Senate Permanent Subcommittee on Investigations (Cammisano), 655 F.2d 1232 (D.C. Cir.), cert. denied 454 U.S. 1084 (1981); Goldwater v. Carter, 617 F.2d 697 n. 6 (D.C. Cir. 1979) (en banc) (opinion of Wright, J.), vacated on other grounds 444 U.S. 996 (1979) (mem.). The Senate authorizes its legal counsel to bring suit by vote pursuant to statute, see 2 U.S.C. §§ 288–288n; the House presents its institutional position by decision of the Speaker and the Bipartisan Leadership Group, see Brief for the Speaker and Bipartisan Leadership Group at 16–17 n. 15, Burke v. Barnes, supra.

49. 307 U.S. 433 (1939), discussed in § 3–13, supra.

defeated senators' votes had been "overridden and virtually held for naught" and that they had "a plain, direct and adequate interest in maintaining the effectiveness of their votes."[50] On the federal level, the Court has evinced a similar "willingness . . . to decide whether one branch of our Government has impinged upon the power of another" in order to clarify, where a "constitutional impasse" has developed, the respective responsibilities of each.[51] Where Congress has acted directly to press such issues and they are otherwise justiciable, federal courts should defer to its judgment and recognize its standing to sue.[52]

The reasonableness of suit in this capacity only highlights the problematic nature of suit in the fourth capacity, that by individual legislators—unsupported by one or both houses of Congress—claiming injury to their personally held rights to full exercise of their legislative powers. Although some commentators have argued that recognition of such rights is inconsistent with accepted understandings of the nature of official powers and that these powers may not provide the basis for a showing of cognizable injury in fact,[53] the more serious objection is that,

---

50. Id. at 438. Chief Justices Hughes avoided ruling on the merits, however, by resort to the political question doctrine. Id. at 446–56; see also § 3–13, supra. Justices Butler and McReynolds assumed the existence of standing without discussing it, see 307 U.S. at 470–74. Four Justices, led by Justice Frankfurther, argued that the legislators lacked standing. See id. at 465–70. The continued relevance of the result in Coleman was implied in Bender v. Williamsport Area School Dist., 106 S.Ct. 1326, 1333 n. 7 (1986). See also Dyer v. Blair, 390 F.Supp. 1291, 1297 n. 12 (N.D. Ill. 1975) (three-judge court) (Stevens, J.).

51. Goldwater v. Carter, 444 U.S. 996, 997, 1001 (1979) (mem.) (opinion of Powell, J.), discussed in § 3–13, supra. Although the Goldwater decision did not discuss standing, Justice Powell's opinion demonstrates that, had the Senate clearly confronted President Carter on his decision unilaterally to abrogate the mutual defense treaty with Taiwan and authorized suit accordingly, senatorial standing would have been obvious. The appropriateness of resolving such interbranch controversies generally is clear. See, e.g., Bowsher v. Synar, 106 S.Ct. 3181 (1986), discussed in Chapter 4, infra; Nixon v. Administrator of Gen. Servs., 433 U.S. 425, 439 (1977). See also Barnes v. Kline, 759 F.2d 21, 28 (D.C. Cir. 1984), vacated as moot sub. nom. Burke v. Barnes, 107 S.Ct. 734 (1987). But see id. at 41 (Bork, J., dissenting) (arguing that neither the members or houses of Congress, nor governmental actors generally, can have standing to vindicate their prerogatives in federal court).

52. See Note, "Congressional Access to the Federal Courts," 90 Harv.L.Rev. 1632, 1647–48 (1977); Note, "Should Congress Defend Its Own Interests Before the Courts?," 33 Stan.L.Rev. 715, 724–32 (1981). Because Congress has the power to negate nonconstitutional, prudential aspects of standing doctrine, see § 3–15, supra, at notes 6 and 7, its standing need only meet the constitutional minimum.

53. 18 See, e.g., Barnes v. Kline, 759 F.2d 21, 50 (D.C. Cir. 1984) (Bork, J., dissenting) (arguing "that elected representatives have a separate private right, akin to a property interest, in the powers of their offices . . . is a notion alien to the concept of a republican government"), vacated as moot sub nom. Burke v. Barnes, 107 S.Ct. 734 (1987); Moore v. United States House of Representatives, 733 F.2d 946, 959 (D.C. Cir. 1984) (Scalia, J., concurring) (stating that "no officers of the United States, of whatever Branch, exercise their governmental powers as personal prerogatives in which they have a judicially cognizable private interest . . . . [T]he powers of the office belong to the people and not to them"); Dessem, supra note 37, at 25–26. However, this objection ignores the fact that such legislators allege not a possessory *personal* injury, but injury occurring in their *official* capacities on a *personal basis*. The allowance of suit in an official capacity is commonplace in American jurisprudence. See, e.g., Bender v. Williamsport Area School Dist., 106 S.Ct. 1326, 1332–33 (1986); Note, "Congressional Access to the Federal Courts," supra note 52, at 1636. The permissibility of such suit is firmly established in the opinions of the U.S. Court of Appeals for the District of Columbia Circuit. See Synar v. United States, 626 F.Supp. 1374, 1381–82 (D.D.C. 1986) (three-judge court) (per curiam), aff'd sub nom. Bowsher v. Synar, 106 S.Ct. 3181 (1986).

where potential legislative alternatives to individual suit are available—such as direct suit or political action by Congress to rectify the alleged harm—the individual legislator is really only complaining of a failure to persuade fellow colleagues.[54] Allowance of such suits, it is argued, would only lead to unnecessary involvement by federal courts in political controversies and limit the opportunity for legislative solutions to emerge.[55] However, interpreting the silence of Congress's failure to act is always a hazardous enterprise, and denial of standing on the basis of such silence, given the numerous practical barriers to securing such action by Congress which have nothing to do with the merits of a legislator's claim, might allow fundamental shifts in the separation of powers to go unreviewed.[56] Regardless of whether such concerns may support dismissal of legislator suits on non-standing grounds,[57] they should therefore have no bearing on the standing inquiry.

Thus, a finding of standing is proper at least where a legislator demonstrates nullification of a past or future vote that is fairly traceable to the challenged action,[58] and is arguably proper where other core aspects of legislative prerogatives are implicated.[59] However, short of

54. See Barnes v. Kline, 759 F.2d 21, 28 (D.C. Cir. 1984), vacated as moot sub nom. Burke v. Barnes, 107 S.Ct. 734 (1987).

55. See id.; McGowan, "Congressmen in Court: The New Plaintiffs," 15 Ga.L. Rev. 241, 250–51 (1981); Note, "Congressional Access to the Federal Courts," supra note 52, at 1648–52.

56. See Note, "The Justiciability of Congressional-Plaintiff Suits," 82 Colum.L. Rev. 526, 536–39 (1982).

57. The U.S. Court of Appeals for the District of Columbia Circuit took this approach in Riegle v. Federal Open Market Comm., 656 F.2d 873 (D.C. Cir. 1981), cert. denied 454 U.S. 1082 (1981), where it announced a doctrine of "circumscribed equitable discretion", designed to address separation-of-powers concerns, under which a legislator's action should be dismissed where the legislator "could obtain substantial relief from his fellow legislators," unless "a private plaintiff would not likely qualify for standing," id. at 880–81. Application of this doctrine has been uncertain and sharply criticized. See Dessem, supra note 37, at 9–13.

58. The leading case is Kennedy v. Sampson, 511 F.2d 430 (D.C. Cir. 1974), which upheld the standing of a U.S. Senator to challenge a purported pocket veto on the ground that it had unconstitutionally "nullified" his vote in favor of the legislation involved, id. at 433, even though this injury was merely "derivative" of an injury to Congress as a whole and his suit had not been authorized. Id. at 436. Compare Barnes v. Kline, 759 F.2d 21, 25–30 (D.C. Cir. 1985), vacated as moot sub nom. Burke

v. Barnes, 107 S.Ct. 734 (1987) (involving similar pocket-veto challenge with participation by both houses of Congress, and reaffirming analysis in Kennedy). Unlike pocket-veto cases tracing the injury to independent executive action, other cases alleging nullification of a voting opportunity involve more directly a challenge to the actions of Congress itself. For example, in Riegle v. Federal Open Market Comm., 656 F.2d 873 (D.C. Cir. 1981), a Senator alleged that the Federal Open Market Committee had members acting as Officers of the United States who had not been confirmed by the Senate; he was accorded standing even though executive appointments to the Committee were made in accordance with statute. And in Moore v. United States House of Representatives, 733 F.2d 946 (D.C. Cir. 1984), members of the House were accorded standing to challenge the constitutionality of a tax bill on the ground that it had not been introduced initially in the House and House members' rights to originate and debate all legislation related to raising revenues had been violated, although the House as a whole had made no objection to the procedure employed. Suit in both Riegle and Moore, however, was dismissed on equitable grounds, see note 57, supra.

59. For example, in Vander Jagt v. O'Neill, 699 F.2d 1166 (D.C. Cir. 1982), cert. denied 464 U.S. 823 (1983), members of the House of Representatives were accorded standing to challenge the House leadership's adoption of certain rules purportedly implemented to further entrench the majority party, although the suit was dis-

such situations, a legislator has no greater claim than any other citizen to complain of governmental action which may interfere indirectly with the legislative process. Thus, a legislator does not have standing to challenge actions that may deprive him or her of information helpful in exercising constitutional powers.[60] Nor does a legislator have any special interest in challenging allegedly improper executive enforcement of laws,[61] or in challenging the constitutionality of a law duly passed over his or her objection.[62]

§ 3–21. Triangulating Standing: A Schematic Summary

The triangular relationship depicted below helps to focus the considerations which, although forming the underlying basis for the general bar on third-party standing and the zone-of-interests inquiry, are often left unarticulated or blurred by the application of the rule or the invocation of an exception:

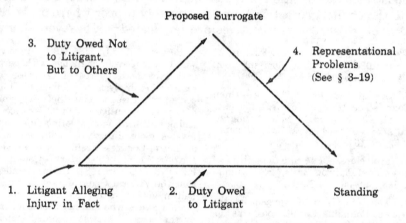

Proposed Surrogate

3. Duty Owed Not to Litigant, But to Others

4. Representational Problems (See § 3–19)

1. Litigant Alleging Injury in Fact

2. Duty Owed to Litigant

Standing

To meet the case or controversy requirement of article III as currently understood, we have seen that a litigant seeking to raise a federal claim must link himself or herself, in the capacity asserted, with an injury in fact that has been caused by the action complained of and is likely to be redressed by the relief sought. The litigant thus qualifies at the first point on the triangle. "Injury in fact," as that term is used in this context, refers to a harm of the material and individuated sort that federal courts deem themselves capable of re-

missed on grounds of equitable discretion, see note 57, supra.

whether to impeach defendants" and on other duties).

60. See Harrington v. Bush, 553 F.2d 190 (D.C. Cir. 1977) (rejecting challenge to certain activities of the Central Intelligence Agency despite claim that declaratory judgment would "bear upon" exercise of congressional duties). Compare Mitchell v. Laird, 488 F.2d 611, 614 (D.C. Cir. 1973) (upholding standing of Members of Congress to challenge U.S. involvement in Vietnam because relief sought "would bear upon the duties of plaintiffs to consider

61. See Harrington v. Schlesinger, 528 F.2d 455, 459 (4th Cir. 1975) (noting that "[o]nce a bill has become law . . . [a legislator's] interest is indistinguishable from that of any other citizen").

62. Such an abstract objection almost certainly constitutes a "generalized grievance" barred under clearly established principles of standing, see § 3–17, supra.

dressing in the limited role the constitutional scheme assigns to the judiciary.[1]

After it has been ascertained that the litigant has adequately alleged an injury in fact caused by the act against which judicial relief is sought, it must be ascertained whether the act constituted a breach of a duty arguably owed to the litigant, by analogy to the law of torts.[2] Such a duty brings the litigant to the point of standing at the lower right vertex. In this regard, the trend in the past two decades has been to identify an expanded set of interests which officials are bound to take into account, and a correspondingly expanded class of litigants who are entitled to complain that actions taken have violated duties owed to them.

In some cases, a litigant injured by another's action may presumptively lack standing to represent his own interests because the action has violated no duty, as a matter either of constitutional or of statutory law, to the litigant. In those cases, however, the litigant may be given the status of a surrogate—a "private attorney general"—to represent the interests of persons not before the court, under any of several classes of exceptions to the rule against third-party standing.[3] These exceptions take the litigant to the top of the triangle. It should be clear, however, that determining who owes what duty to whom, especially with nebulous constitutional commands, antiquated statutes, and frequent legislative buck-passing to administrators,[4] is a slippery business at best. Thus, when total denial of standing to an injured litigant rests on fine calculations of duty or its absence, the prudential purposes of standing doctrine should probably be deemed satisfied by resolving threshold doubts in favor of hearing the litigant on the merits (assuming all other elements of justiciability are present), particularly if government's overriding duty to act lawfully is accorded serious weight.

§ 3–22. Overview: Constitutional Limits on Federal Judicial Power to Review or Control State Action

The Constitution presumes the existence of the states as lawmakers and governmental institutions distinct from the federal government.[1] Thus it is not surprising that, although only the eleventh amendment explicitly limits federal judicial power in the interest of the states as independent entities, there nonetheless exists a substantial body of law which restricts the authority of the federal judiciary in order to preserve state autonomy. Much of this law is statutory; its detailed elaboration is therefore beyond the scope of this book.[2] A substantial

§ 3–21

1. See §§ 3–14 to 3–17, supra.

2. See §§ 3–16, 3–17, 3–19, supra.

3. See § 3–19, supra. Such other persons might themselves lack standing because they are not yet injured in fact. Thus the word "surrogate" may be misleading; if X has standing as a surrogate for Y, it may be the case that Y has no standing in his own right.

4. See Jaffe, "The Illusion of the Ideal Administration," 86 Harv.L.Rev. 1183 (1973).

§ 3–22

1. The tenth amendment is perhaps the most explicit constitutional acknowledgment of this presumption. See §§ 5–20 to 5–23, infra.

2. For such an elaboration, see P. Bator, D. Shapiro, P. Mishkin and H. Wechsler, Hart and Wechsler's The Federal

part, however, is judge-made.[3] These judicially developed limits generally do not purport to be "constititutional" in the sense of being beyond the reach of Congress. But they are constitutional in a broader sense: at least in part, they reflect conceptions of the proper relationship between the federal and state governments, conceptions which lie behind the governmental structures that the Constitution creates.

The next series of sections explores four doctrinal areas in which the Supreme Court has elaborated significant federalism-based restrictions on the power of the federal courts. Considered first is the general prohibition, absent congressional authorization, on creation of federal common law that would supplant state common law or legislation.[4] Second is the doctrine protecting state court judgments from federal court review provided they rest on an "adequate and independent state ground"—a rule crucial to furthering the development of state constitutional jurisprudence and to safeguarding reasonable procedural requirements of state judicial systems.[5] Third is the eleventh amendment, which the Supreme Court has interpreted as embodying a conception of sovereign immunity barring litigants from suing states, at least directly, in federal court without their consent or a clear congressional decision to override state immunity.[6] Explored finally are the "abstention" doctrines: various exceptions to the responsibility of the federal courts to exercise the jurisdiction they possess, requiring them to abstain in favor of state proceedings where necessary to protect the integrity of state law or to minimize friction with state judicial systems by respecting their institutional autonomy—central examples of the Supreme Court's renewed emphasis on the ambiguous but powerful policy of "judicial federalism" that unites much of the doctrine discussed in this chapter.[7]

§ 3–23. Limits on the Power of Federal Courts to Make Common Law

Unlike their English counterparts and state courts, federal courts are not essentially common-law tribunals—they do not, for the most part, engage themselves with a body of customary law, collected and defined in prior court decisions, in order to resolve the cases which come before them.[1] Limits on the ability of federal courts to bind states under the supremacy clause by announcing federal common law rules encompassing more than simple interpretation of constitutional and statutory provisions were first established by the Supreme Court in

Courts and the Federal System 962–79 (2d ed. 1973 and Supp. 1981).

3. Because only the impulses underlying these judge-made rules, and not the rules themselves, are of constitutional origin, the discussion of these rules in this chapter does not purport to be complete. Again, for more elaborate treatment, see id. at 926–1050. See also C. Wright, Law of Federal Courts 268–397 (4th ed. 1983); M. Redish, Federal Jurisdiction: Tensions

in the Allocation of Judicial Power 79–321 (1980).

4. See § 3–23, infra.

5. See § 3–24, infra.

6. See §§ 3–25 to 3–27, infra.

7. See §§ 3–28 to 3–30, infra.

§ 3–23

1. See Milwaukee v. Illinois, 451 U.S. 304, 312 (1981).

the case of *United States v. Hudson & Goodwin*.[2] In *Hudson* the specific question was whether federal circuit courts could exercise common law jurisdiction in criminal cases. Justice Johnson's opinion for a unanimous if troubled Court answered that question in the negative. Apart from the Supreme Court's original jurisdiction, Justice Johnson noted, federal courts are tribunals of limited jurisdiction, possessing the power to act only if Congress confers it.[3] More fundamentally, "[t]he powers of the general government are made up of concessions from the several states—whatever is not expressly given to the former, the latter expressly reserve."[4] In view of this premise, Justice Johnson concluded, it would not be proper for a federal court to "assume to itself a jurisdiction, . . . in its nature very indefinite, applicable to a great variety of subjects, varying in every state of the Union."[5]

This is not to say that federal courts are entirely lacking in common law powers. Although the Constitution does not grant federal courts general common law power, a few constitutional provisions do recognize limited spheres of federal common law authority, notably in contexts in which, for widely varying reasons, the usual federalism concerns are not relevant. Article III, § 2, for example, states that "[t]he judicial Power shall extend . . . to all Cases of admiralty and maritime jurisdiction . . . ." As with almost all other heads of federal judicial power, Congress must grant federal courts admiralty jurisdiction before they may exercise it; but once federal courts possess admiralty jurisdiction, they are not dependent upon Congress for rules of decision. "A case in admiralty does not, in fact, arise under the constitution or laws of the United States. These cases are as old as navigation itself; and the law admiralty and maritime, as it existed for ages, is applied by our courts to the cases as they arise."[6]

Article III also provides that "[t]he judicial Power shall extend . . . to Controversies . . . between Citizens of different States . . . ." The Constitution authorizes such federal diversity jurisdiction, it is usually thought, in order to protect nonresidents of a state from whatever local favoritism distorts the state's court system.[7] For

2. 11 U.S. (7 Cranch) 32 (1812). Cf. United States v. Coolidge, 14 U.S. (1 Wheat.) 415 (1816). For an exhaustive consideration of the political context of the Hudson decision, reflecting the heated partisan battle between the Republicans and Federalists over the issue at our nation's founding, as well as a broader historical view of limits on federal common law doctrine, see Jay, "Origins of Federal Common Law," 133 U.Pa.L.Rev. 1003–1116, 1231–1325 (1985).

3. Hudson & Goodwin, 11 U.S. (7 Cranch) at 32.

4. Id.

5. Id. See also § 17–1, infra.

6. See American Ins. Co. v. Canter, 26 U.S. (1 Pet.) 511, 545–46 (1828). The substantive law of admiralty is, of course, beyond the compass of this book. See generally G. Gilmore and C. Black, The Law of Admiralty (2d ed. 1975). Congress can, of course, modify admiralty law, see, e.g., In re Garnett, 141 U.S. 1 (1891), although not without limit; in the first instance, however, legislative responsibility in this area lies with the federal courts. On the nineteenth century development of congressional power to regulate admiralty, see Note, "From Judicial Grant to Legislative Power: The Admiralty Clause in the Nineteenth Century," 67 Harv.L.Rev. 1214 (1954).

7. See, e.g., Bank of United States v. Deveaux, 9 U.S. (5 Cranch) 61, 87 (1809) ("However true the fact may be, that the tribunals of the states will administer justice as impartially as those of the nation, to the parties of every description, it is not

nearly a century the Supreme Court took an expansive view of the role of federal courts under this grant of jurisdiction, beginning with *Swift v. Tyson*.[8] In *Swift*, Justice Story, reviewing a diversity case addressing whether a preexisting debt constitutes a valuable consideration, initially noted that the courts of New York, the state in which the federal diversity court sat, "do not found their decisions upon this point upon any local statute, or positive, fixed or ancient local usage; but they deduce the doctrine from the general principles of commercial law."[9] The Rules of Decision Act,[10] Story concluded, did not prevent a federal court from doing likewise;[11] Story thus proceeded to decide the case by looking not to New York precedents as such, but to "the general principles and doctrines of commercial jurisprudence"[12] which the state courts, like other common law courts, endeavored to apply.

Justice Story apparently envisioned that the *Swift* approach would promote nationwide uniformity in the common law by establishing persuasive federal decisional law for adoption by state courts,[13] but in practice this never developed. *Swift* was overruled in *Erie R. Co. v. Tompkins*,[14] in which the Supreme Court recognized the changed realities of state common law theory and practice: the chief constitutional difficulty with *Swift* was not that it was necessarily wrong but that it had become anachronistic. As *Erie* recognizes, in performing their common law functions, state courts do not truly look to a "general" law as contemplated by *Swift*, but rather persist "in their own opinions on questions of common law."[15] As a result, by the time of *Erie*, federal

less true, that the constitution itself either entertains apprehensions on this subject, or views with such indulgence the possible fears and apprehensions of suitors, that it has established national tribunals for the decision of controversies between . . . citizens of different states"). See also Jay, supra note 2, at 1267–70. For a survey of the arguments over whether the diversity jurisdiction is really necessary, see P. Bator, D. Shapiro, P. Mishkin & H. Wechsler, Hart and Wechsler's The Federal Courts and the Federal System 1051–59 (2d ed. 1973).

8. 41 U.S. (16 Pet.) 1 (1842).

9. Id. at 17.

10. Judiciary Act of 1789, § 34, currently codified as 28 U.S.C. § 1652: "The laws of the several states, except where the Constitution or treaties of the United States or Acts of Congress otherwise require or provide, shall be regarded as rules of decision in civil actions in the courts of the United States, in cases where they apply."

11. See 41 U.S. at 17. Story argued that the Act's reference to state "laws" did not refer to state judicial decisions: "They are, at most, only evidence of what the laws are, and are not, of themselves, laws." Id. Swift's critics find in this statement the basis for ascribing to Story an unrealistic declaratory theory of law, a theory

which sees the common law as "transcendental," Black and White Taxicab and Transfer Co. v. Brown and Yellow Taxicab and Transfer Co., 276 U.S. 518, 533 (1928) (Holmes, J., dissenting)—as some form of "brooding omnipresence." The Swift opinion's next sentence, however, indicates that Story adopted no such theory: "They are often re-examined, reversed and qualified by the courts themselves, whenever they are found to be either defective, or illfounded, or otherwise incorrect." 41 U.S. at 17. Story simply recognized that common law is as much a process as a set of results. See also Note, "Swift v. Tyson Exhumed," 79 Yale L.J. 284, 294–95 (1969). Ironically, since Swift followed the same approach as the New York courts, Story could have assumed that the Rules of Decision Act controlled, and yet have reached the same result.

12. 41 U.S. at 18.

13. By contrast, modern federal common law is binding on the states under the supremacy clause. See, e.g., Local 174, Teamsters v. Lucas Flour Co., 369 U.S. 95, 103 (1962); see also Field, "Sources of Law: The Scope of Federal Common Law," 99 Harv.L.Rev. 883, 897 & n. 64 (1986).

14. 304 U.S. 64, 78 (1938).

15. 304 U.S. at 74. The shift from Swift to Erie parallels that from the Loch-

courts following *Swift* had developed a body of common law which had no necessary connection with the common law of the various states. This divergence had led to "injustice and confusion." [16]

Erie's admonition that "[t]here is no federal general common law" [17] must not be read for more than it is worth. The holding of *Erie* is narrow though important: in following the "laws" of a state when sitting in diversity, federal courts must adhere to the decisional law of the state's judges as long as those precedents are consistent with federal constitutional and statutory provisions, and may not infer from the grant of diversity jurisdiction the power to override those precedents by imposing binding rules of federal common law. [18] Together with *Murdock v. Memphis*, [19] which indicates that the Supreme Court will not review issues of state law, *Erie* defines what "state law" *is* by ensuring that the pronouncements of the highest courts of the states will be respected by all federal courts. [20]

Erie, however, in no way bars federal courts from adopting rules of federal common law in specialized situations where they appear to be particularly warranted. [21] Indeed, federal common law rules have been developed in a variety of areas where a consistent federal rule has been thought to be justified—as in interstate boundary disputes, [22] cases raising questions of essentially international law, [23] cases involving the proprietary interests of the United States, [24] the property rights of Native Americans, [25] and others. [26] Despite occasional Supreme Court statements to the contrary, [27] there is no reason to conclude that the operation of federal common law is limited to these so-called "enclaves"—which are merely examples of situations raising important federal interests and calling for the development of judicial rules to cover gaps in the existing framework of federal constitutional and statutory law.

Indeed, the scope of federal common law, defined to include "any rule of federal law created by a court (usually but not invariably a federal court) when the substance of that rule is not clearly suggested by federal enactments—constitutional or congressional," [28] as suggested

---

ner Era to the post-1937 jurisprudence. See Chapter 8, infra.

16. Id. at 77. See Field, supra note 13, at 900–02.

17. 304 U.S. at 78.

18. See Field, supra note 13, at 915–27. The rule must also be followed in federal question cases involving state law issues, see id. at 912 n. 141.

19. 87 U.S. (20 Wall.) 590 (1874), discussed in § 3–24, infra.

20. See Field, supra note 13, at 919–23 & nn. 180–82. In a similar manner, the eleventh amendment has been construed to protect the states' institutional sovereignty against any claim that the grants of diversity or federal question jurisdiction override traditional state sovereign immunity. See § 3–25, infra.

21. See Field, supra note 13, at 887–99, 950–53.

22. See, e.g., Vermont v. New York, 417 U.S. 270, 277 (1974).

23. See, e.g., Banco Nacional De Cuba v. Sabbatino, 376 U.S. 398, 421–27 (1964), discussed in § 3–13, note 44, supra.

24. See, e.g., Clearfield Trust Co. v. United States, 318 U.S. 363, 366–67 (1943).

25. See, e.g., County of Oneida v. Oneida Indian Nation, 470 U.S. 226 (1985).

26. See Field, supra note 13, at 909–13.

27. See, e.g., Texas Industries, Inc. v. Radcliff Materials, Inc., 451 U.S. 630, 641 (1981); cf. Field, supra note 13, at 911–12 n. 140.

28. Field, supra note 13, at 890. "In formulating the rule, the judiciary chooses the 'best rule' based upon its own notions

by Professor Martha Field in an exhaustive study of subject,[29] is potentially quite broad. Professor Field argues that a court is limited in its power to create federal common law only by the requirement that it point "to a federal enactment, constitutional or statutory, that it interprets as authorizing the federal common law rule." [30] In recognition of the serious threat to values of federalism posed by such judicial power,[31] even where a federal common law rule is permissible, federal courts always have discretion to adopt the applicable state rule as adequate to serve federal purposes,[32] so that a federal rule should be imposed only where a federal need for it exists that outweighs the normal presumption that a state's law should ordinarily apply.[33]

Because Congress as a general rule is free to supplant federal common law,[34] the subject is not usually thought to raise separation of powers concerns.[35] A prominent exception is the issue of when it is appropriate for the judiciary to recognize a cause of action for persons injured by the violation of a congressional statute where Congress has not explicitly provided for one. Since the 1975 decision of *Cort v. Ash*,[36] this question has been addressed by a four-factor inquiry into the "intent" of Congress, as measured by both legislative history and the extent to which the background legal framework suggests that a right of action is sensible.[37] For the most part, the *Cort* test has been applied

of policy and upon whatever policies it finds implicit in the constitutional and statutory provisions it does have an obligation to follow." Id. at 893. This definition, of course, "includes much we think of as interpretation," id., and narrower definitions are therefore readily available, see id. at 892–96 & nn. 39, 54. For discussion of the desirability of recognizing a sphere of "constitutional common law" distinct from constitutional interpretation binding on Congress, see § 3–4 and notes 32–35, supra.

29. Field, supra note 13. For another recent but briefer analysis, see Merrill, "The Common Law Powers of Federal Courts," 52 U.Chi.L.Rev. 1 (1985).

30. Field, supra note 13, at 887–88; see also id. at 927–30. In the case of a federal court, of course, this enactment must be other than the grant of diversity jurisdiction or the Rules of Decision Act, id. at 929. As to what constitutes "authorization" of a federal common law rule, Professor Field explains that "[c]urrent cases do not support a requirement of any special form of words in the authorizing enactment or any specific sanction from the framers of the authorizing enactment. They require only that the rule created fit best with the scheme of the authorizing enactment and with the intent of its framers, insofar as we know that intent." Id. at 929.

31. Id. at 924–26, 931.

32. Id. at 885–86 & n. 12, 950–53.

33. See id. at 953–62. Other ways of attempting to limit judicial discretion, such as requiring a clear directive or need for federal common law rules, would seriously intrude on the judicial function and raise separation of powers concerns. See id. at 934–46.

34. Some federal common law rules, under Professor Field's definition, may be constitutionally compelled. See Field, supra note 13, at 896 n. 60.

35. See id. at 890 n. 29, 924–25, 931–34 & n. 220.

36. 422 U.S. 66 (1975).

37. These four factors are: (1) whether the plaintiff is "one of the class for whose especial benefit the statute was enacted"; (2) whether there exists "any indication of legislative intent, explicit or implicit, either to create such a remedy or to deny one"; (3) whether it is "consistent with the underlying purposes of the legislative scheme to imply such a remedy"; and (4) whether "the cause of action [is] one traditionally relegated to state law . . . so that it would be inappropriate to infer a cause of action based solely on federal laws." Cort, 422 U.S. at 78. See also Texas Industries, Inc. v. Radcliff Materials, Inc., 451 U.S. 630, 639 (1981). For discussion of the Cort test, see Field, supra note 13, at 929–30 n. 213. This analysis is quite similar to the questions of whether Congress has conferred standing on a particular individual by statute, see § 3–15, note 7, supra; and

to deny implication of a cause of action except where the text or legislative history suggests that Congress specifically intended one.[38]

When a plaintiff asserts constitutional rather than statutory rights the Court is more willing to imply a private right to sue, on the theory that defining the means for the enforcement of constitutional rights is the federal judiciary's special focus.[39] The landmark case is *Bivens v. Six Unknown Named Agents*,[40] recognizing an implied right of action

whether the claim of a particular litigant is within the zone of interests of the statutory or constitutional provision relied on, see § 3–19, *supra*.

Before Cort, civil statutes enacted to protect a special class of persons were presumed to grant an implied cause of action. See Merrill Lynch, Pierce, Fenner & Smith, Inc. v. Curran, 456 U.S. 353, 374–77 (1982). But see Cannon v. University of Chicago, 441 U.S. 677, 731–39 (1979) (Powell, J., dissenting) (challenging this characterization).

38. See Middlesex County Sewerage Auth. v. National Sea Clammers Assoc., 453 U.S. 1, 13 (1981) (citing cases); cf. id. at 25 (Stevens, J., joined by Blackmun, J., concurring in the judgment and dissenting in part) (noting that "recently some Members of the Court have been inclined to deny relief with little more than a perfunctory nod to the Cort v. Ash factors"). See also Field, supra note 13, at 887 n. 20, 942–44. Cases finding a cause of action include Herman & MacLean v. Huddleston, 459 U.S. 375, 380–87 (1983) (allowing implied cause of action to defrauded securities purchasers under one section of the securities laws despite existence of an express, but limited, remedy under another section); Merrill Lynch, Pierce, Fenner & Smith v. Curran, 456 U.S. 353, 374–88 (1982) (holding that a commodity futures investor injured by fraudulent conduct in violation of the Commodity Exchange Act has a private cause of action for damages); and Cannon v. University of Chicago, 441 U.S. 677, 688–709 (1979) (holding that victims of sex discrimination in federally assisted educational institutions could litigate alleged violations of Title IX).

Justice Powell has been quite vocal in arguing that the Court's implication of a cause of action without a clear indication of specific congressional intent unconstitutionally infringes on Congress's prerogatives. See Merrill Lynch, 456 U.S. at 396–409 (Powell, J., joined by Burger, C.J., and Rehnquist and O'Connor, JJ., dissenting); Cannon v. University of Chicago, 441 U.S. 677, 742–45, 749 (1979) (Powell, J., dissenting). He has argued that the Cort test "allows the Judicial Branch to assume policymaking authority vested by the Constitution in the Legislative Branch," and invites Congress "to shirk its constitutional obliga-

tion" to decide the remedies for federal rights it creates, and that therefore the Court should not imply a private right of action "absent the most compelling evidence that Congress in fact intended such an action to exist." Cannon, 441 U.S. at 743, 749. Yet this view ignores that Congress enacts legislation against a background practice by courts of devising appropriate remedies for violations of rights. See Merrill Lynch, supra, 456 at 375–78; National Sea Clammers Assoc., 453 U.S. at 23–24 and n. 7 (Stevens, J., joined by Blackmun, J., concurring in the judgment and dissenting in part); Field, supra note 13, at 931–32 n. 220. There is no basis in this context for presuming against the existence of a judicial remedy, as there is where a different background rule—such as the eleventh amendment's protection of state sovereign immunity, see § 3–26, infra, or the need to protect executive functions by recognizing absolute or qualified immunity of executive officers from suit, see § 4–14, infra—operates to sharply limit judicial power. Indeed, if anything, courts should be more free, given their great discretion in the area of remedies, to construct implied rights of action than they are in developing federal common law rules generally. See Field, supra note 13, at 910–11 n. 138; cf. id. at 897–98 n. 69.

39. See Davis v. Passman, 442 U.S. 228, 241–42 (1979). See also Bush v. Lucas, 462 U.S. 367, 374 & n. 12, 378 (1983); Bivens v. Six Unknown Named Agents of Federal Bureau of Narcotics, 403 U.S. 388, 399–402 (1971) (Harlan, J., concurring in the judgment). For an argument against this dichotomy between statutory and constitutional remedies, see Field, supra note 13, at 889 n. 26.

40. 403 U.S. 388 (1971). For a discussion of whether the result in Bivens and similar cases is constitutionally required or simply "constitutional common law," see Steinman, "Backing Off Bivens and the Ramifications of This Retreat for the Vindication of Federal Rights," 83 Mich.L.Rev. 269, 279 (1984); Note, "Two Approaches to Determine Whether an Implied Cause of Action Under the Constitution is Necessary: The Changing Scope of the Bivens Action," 19 Ga.L.Rev. 683 (1985). Cf. § 3–4, notes 32–35, supra.

for damages against a federal official alleged to have violated the fourth amendment. The Court has also authorized damage actions for sex discrimination in federal employment in violation of the fifth amendment,[41] and for neglect of the medical needs of a prisoner in violation of the eighth amendment's prohibition of cruel and ususual punishment.[42] Although the Court will therefore "presume that justiciable constitutional rights are to be enforced through the courts," [43] it will decline to create a remedy where there are "special factors counselling hesitation in the absence of affirmative action by Congress" or where Congress has explicitly declared an equally effective remedy as a substitute for an action under the Constitution.[44]

§ 3–24.   The Policy Against Federal Court Review of State Court Decisions Resting on "Adequate and Independent State Grounds"

The Supreme Court's appellate jurisdiction is a creation of statute.[1] From the Judiciary Act of 1789 to the present Judicial Code,[2] the Court's power to review state court decisions has been congressionally limited to the federal questions decided by the state courts. Only once did Congress even appear to have repealed that limitation: the Act of February 5, 1867, deleted this sentence from the Judiciary Act of 1789, which followed a listing of the grounds on which review could be granted: "But no other error shall be assigned or regarded as a ground of reversal . . . than such as . . . immediately respects the before mentioned questions of validity or construction of the [federal] constitution, treaties, statutes, commissions, or authorities in dispute." In *Murdock v. Memphis,*[3] however, the Supreme Court, intimating that grave constitutional questions lurked in the background,[4] applied a rule of clear statement[5] and held that, if Congress intended that the Court

---

41. Davis v. Passman, 442 U.S. 228 (1979).

42. Carlson v. Green, 446 U.S. 14 (1980).

43. Davis v. Passman, 442 U.S. 228, 242 (1979).

44. Bivens, 403 U.S. at 396–97. See also Carlson v. Green, 446 U.S. 14, 18–19 (1980); Davis v. Passman, 442 U.S. 228, 245–47 (1979). For example, in Bush v. Lucas, 462 U.S. 367, 380–90 (1983), a federal civil service employee was denied a damage remedy under the first amendment given the comprehensive scheme of remedies made available by Congress to aggrieved employees; similarly, in Chappell v. Wallace, 462 U.S. 296, 299–304 (1983), military personnel were denied a damage action for racial discrimination against their superiors given other available remedies within the military and the harmful effects of such lawsuits on military discipline. For a criticism of these decisions, see Steinman, supra note 40, at 285–97. Other disruptive aspects of creating rights

of action under the Constitution are addressed by doctrines granting certain federal officials absolute or qualified immunity against suit. See § 4–14, infra.

The arguments for and against the creation of implied rights of action and immunity for federal officials are reflected in the parallel inquiry under 42 U.S.C. § 1983 of the extent to which *state* officers or municipalities should be subject to suit and enjoy immunity for "constitutional torts". For a recent discussion see Wells, "The Past and Future of Constitutional Torts: From Statutory Interpretation to Common Law Rules," 19 Conn.L.Rev. 53 (1986).

§ 3–24

1. See § 3–5, supra, on congressional control of the Supreme Court's jurisdiction.

2. 28 U.S.C. § 1257.

3. 87 U.S. (20 Wall.) 590 (1874).

4. Id. at 626, 633.

5. Id. at 619. Compare §§ 5–7 to 5–8, infra.

review questions of state law, Congress would have to do more than suggestively repeal portions of the Judiciary Act.[6]

Since Congress has never responded to the *Murdock* Court's dare, the Supreme Court has never had to decide whether Congress could in fact constitutionally authorize it to review both the federal and state questions raised in the state cases which come before it. It nonetheless seems likely that, if Congress were to try to grant the Supreme Court such power, and if Congress further declared that the Court's decisions as to questions of state law would bind the states under the supremacy clause, the Supreme Court would declare such an extension of its jurisdiction to be unconstitutional under the tenth amendment and related principles of state autonomy.[7] For such a grant of power would effectively deny the states their lawmaking autonomy. By contrast, if Congress did not wrap the Supreme Court's state law decisions in the mantle of federal supremacy, but rather declared that any such decision simply fixed the law of the case and provided state courts with an additional precedent, it is doubtful that the Supreme Court could find that state sovereignty had been infringed.[8]

Murdock does far more than simply prevent the Supreme Court from expounding its view of state law. By its inability to review the correctness of state court resolution of state issues, the Court is also barred from reviewing *federal* issues in those cases which also contain state issues dispositive of the case. It is "the settled rule that where the judgment of a state court rests upon two grounds, one of which is federal and the other non-federal in character, [Supreme Court] jurisdiction fails if the non-federal ground is independent of the federal ground and adequate to support the judgment."[9] A state ground is "adequate" where the judgment would have to be upheld even if the federal ground were reversed; this requires as a threshhold that the state ground is permissible under federal law. A state ground is "independent" where its resolution is not tied to federal issues in the case.

The "adequate and independent state ground" doctrine prevents unjustifiable interference by the Supreme Court with a state's interest in developing and applying its own law—both substantive and procedural, as will be explored in turn. Substantive principles are most commonly involved where a state court relies on completely indepen-

6. For a critique of Murdock and of reliance on it as the basis for the "adequate and independent state ground" doctrine, see, e.g., Field, "Sources of Law: The Scope of Federal Common Law," 99 Harv. L.Rev. 883, 920–21 & nn. 180–81 (1986); Matasar & Bruch, "Procedural Common Law, Federal Jurisdictional Policy, and Abandonment of the Adequate and Independent State Grounds Doctrine," 86 Colum.L.Rev. 1291, 1317–22 (1986).

7. See Field, supra note 6, at 919 n. 174; see also §§ 5–20 to 5–23, infra.

8. Even so, this design would strip state supreme courts of their power to define state law, as "the content of 'state law' would vary according to whether it was reviewed by the Supreme Court," Field, supra note 6, at 921, preventing any authoritative resolution of its requirements, id. at 921–22 n. 182.

9. Fox Film Corp. v. Muller, 296 U.S. 207, 210 (1935); see also Henry v. Mississippi, 379 U.S. 443, 446–47 (1965). For further elaboration of the doctrine, see, e.g., C. Wright, A. Miller & E. Cooper, Federal Practice and Procedure §§ 4019–32 (1977 & Supp. 1986); M. Redish, Federal Jurisdiction: Tensions in the Allocation of Judicial Power 216–32 (1980).

dent state and federal grounds in rendering a judgment—for example, where it rules in favor of a criminal defendant based on both the state and federal constitutions.[10] In such situations, Supreme Court review is barred by "the partitioning of power between the state and federal judicial systems and in the limitations of [the Court's] jurisdiction," as its article III "power is to correct wrong judgments, not to revise opinions." [11]

A state substantive ground is clearly adequate if the ground is itself constitutionally permissible.[12] More commonly at issue is whether the state ground is independent of the federal ground—so that reversal of the federal ground will not undermine the state basis. The issue typically arises where a state court opinion discusses both state and federal constitutional grounds for a decision without making clear whether the court meant to expand the state guarantee beyond what it believed to be the federal standard. Until recently the Supreme Court addressed such problems in any of three ways: [13] (1) by examining the state's theory of state constitutional law in an attempt to discern whether the state's rule operates independently; [14] (2) by sending the case back to state court for clarification of the opinion; [15] or (3) by dismissing the case whenever the ground for decision is unclear.[16]

In its 1983 opinion in *Michigan v. Long*,[17] the Supreme Court undertook a pragmatic and thoughtful analysis of the independence issue, rejecting the three-part ad hoc approach as "antithetical to the doctrinal consistency that is required when sensitive issues of federal-

10. Less commonly, substantive principles are involved where a state has provided a state cause of action for a violation of federal law; or in designing the substantive content of state legislation or common law has incorporated by reference standards contained in a parallel federal law; or through its courts has construed state law as consistent with relevant federal law on the belief that it is required to do so under the supremacy clause. The availability of Supreme Court review in such situations is often ambiguous. See Redish, "Supreme Court Review of State Court 'Federal' Decisions: A Study in Interactive Federalism," 19 Ga.L.Rev. 861, 899–901 (1985).

11. Herb v. Pitcairn, 324 U.S. 117, 125–26 (1945).

12. For example, a state constitutional ground is adequate if it is more protective of a right than an analogous provision of the federal constitution—provided, of course, that protection of the state constitutional right does not infringe a competing federal guarantee, see, e.g., Pruneyard Shopping Center v. Robins, 447 U.S. 74, 82–88 (1980), discussed in § 12–25, infra.

State grounds relying on factual findings are also open to examination; the Court is not deprived of all power to review state court decisions on questions of state law where possibly arbitrary findings may operate to defeat federal rights. In applying the contract clause, for example, the Court has independently reviewed a state court's decision as to whether state legislation created a contract, see, e.g., Indiana ex rel. Anderson v. Brand, 303 U.S. 95 (1938); see also § 9–10, infra. Somewhat similarly, in applying the first amendment, the Court has claimed the power to substitute its own findings of fact for those of a state trial court. See, e.g., §§ 12–9, 12–16, infra.

13. For a description and analysis of the three mechanisms, see Althouse, "How to Build a Separate Sphere: State Courts and Federal Power," 100 Harv.L.Rev. 1485, 1496–1500 (1987).

14. See Michigan v. Long, 463 U.S. 1032, 1039 (1983) (citing Texas v. Brown, 460 U.S. 730 (1983) (plurality opinion)).

15. See id. at 1038 (citing Minnesota v. National Tea Co., 309 U.S. 551, 556–57 (1940); Herb v. Pitcairn, 324 U.S. 117 (1945); California v. Krivda, 409 U.S. 33, 34 (1972)).

16. See Michigan v. Long, 463 U.S. 1032, 1038 (1983) (citing Lynch v. New York, 293 U.S. 52 (1934)).

17. 463 U.S. 1032 (1983).

state relations are involved." [18] The approach was found to be unsatisfactory because it required, in each case, either interpretation of unfamiliar state law; or imposition of special burdens on state courts through clarification requests; or sacrifice of uniformity in federal law through outright dismissal of cases containing federal determinations.[19]

The Court replaced this approach with a presumption in favor of Supreme Court review, where: (1) "a state court decision fairly appears to rest primarily on federal law, or to be interwoven with the federal law," and (2) "the adequacy and independence of any possible state law ground is not clear from the face of the opinion"; in such cases the Court will assume "that the state court decided the case the way it did because it believed that federal law required it to do so." [20] The Court also specified that a state court may immunize its discussion of federal law from review by indicating, "clearly and expressly" by "a plain statement in its judgment or opinion that the federal cases are being used only for the purpose of guidance, and do not themselves compel the result reached." [21]

Justice Stevens, dissenting in *Long* and offering the only serious opposition to the new doctrine,[22] criticized it and argued for a contrary presumption—against exercise of jurisdiction where it is not clear a federal pronouncement will change the result of the case. Review in *Long* was improper, he suggested, because it involved at most the "overprotection" of the criminal defendant involved by the Michigan Supreme Court, which had suppressed evidence based on the fourth amendment of the federal constitution and an analogous provision of the state constitution.[23] Such cases, he argued, "should not be of inherent concern to [the] Court," whose primary role "is to make sure that persons who seek to *vindicate* federal rights have been fairly heard." [24]

Yet by making clear that state courts may avoid Supreme Court review by clearly separating their discussion of state and federal law, *Long* advances interests which lie at the root of our federal system. It protects essential *federal* interests by allowing the Court to maintain the supremacy and uniformity of federal law by reaching and removing erroneous state determinations of federal grounds.[25] *Long* also protects the autonomy of *state* law. It helps state judges by granting access to federal review in cases where they may mistakenly construe state law

---

18. Id. at 1039.

19. Id. at 1039–40.

20. Id. at 1040–42.

21. Id. at 1041.

22. Justice Blackmun found jurisdiction in Long, noting only that the new approach offered "little efficacy and an increased danger of advisory opinions," 463 U.S. at 1054; Justice Brennan, joined by Justice Marshall, agreed jurisdiction was present on his understanding of Michigan law, id. at 1054 n. 1.

23. 463 U.S. at 1066–68 (Stevens, J., dissenting).

24. Id. at 1068. In subsequent cases Justice Stevens has reiterated and expanded his opposition to the Court's practice of reaching out to reverse state court judgments upholding individual rights under the federal constitution. See, e.g., cases cited at § 3–4, supra, note 57. For criticism of his view, see Long, 463 U.S. at 1043 n. 8; Althouse, supra note 13, at 1506–11.

25. See Althouse, supra note 13, at 1504–08; see also § 3–4, supra.

in line with an erroneous view of federal law,[26] and by assuring them a firm basis for expounding their state constitutions, which may contain unexplored grounds for rights reaching beyond those contained in the federal constitution.[27] Most importantly, it benefits the state political branches by ensuring that they are not bound by judgments of federal law that may be erroneous but are beyond their power to alter;[28] such judgments, when accompanied by a "clear statement" and hence beyond the Supreme Court's review, are entitled to no precedential weight.[29]

The adequate and independent state ground doctrine also serves to protect the viability of reasonable procedural requirements imposed by states on litigants. State procedural grounds and federal substantive grounds are often intermixed on Supreme Court review. Of necessity, state procedural law determines the manner in which a federal question is to be presented in state court, unless federal substantive law defines its own procedural matrix. Absent such a matrix, state procedural law subtly influences the way in which a state court perceives a federal question. More dramatically, a litigant's failure to comply with state procedures may cause a state court to rule against the litigant without ever reaching the merits of the litigant's federal claim. In such cases, it is usually clear that the state procedural ground for decision is independent of the litigant's federal claim. The Supreme Court, asked to review the federal claim regardless of the litigant's

26. See Althouse, supra note 13, at 1508–11.

27. In 1977 Justice Brennan published the seminal statement advocating such inquiry. See "State Constitutions and the Protection of Individual Rights," 90 Harv. L.Rev. 489 (1977). The ability of state courts to overcome judgments of the Supreme Court limiting the scope of federal constitutional rights by resort to their own constitutions has on occasion been highlighted in Justices' opinions. See, e.g., Connecticut v. Johnson, 460 U.S. 73, 81 n. 9 (1983) (opinion of Blackmun, J.); id. at 91 (Powell, J., dissenting); Oregon v. Kennedy, 456 U.S. 667, 680–81 (1982) (Brennan, J., concurring in the judgment); South Dakota v. Opperman, 428 U.S. 364, 396 (1976) (Marshall, J., dissenting). The volume of cases and commentary addressing these issues is large and growing. See Collins, Galie & Kincaid, "State High Courts, State Constitutions, and Individual Rights Litigation Since 1980: A Judicial Survey," 13 Hastings Const.L.Q. 599 (1986); sources cited in § 3–4, note 56, supra. A central concern within the debate is the extent to which state court judges can or should, in interpreting state constitutional provisions linguistically identical or similar to federal constitutional provisions, depart from the Supreme Court's pronouncements. For discussion of one approach

legitimating such departure, see § 3–4, note 56, supra. See also Collins & Galie, "Models of Post-Incorporation Judicial Review: 1985 Survey of State Constitutional Individual Rights Decisions," 55 U.Cin.L. Rev. 317, 322–39 (1986); Note, "Developments in the Law: The Interpretation of State Constitutional Rights," 95 Harv.L. Rev. 1324, 1331–67 (1982); Williams, "In the Supreme Court's Shadow: Legitimacy of State Rejection of Supreme Court Reasoning and Result," 35 S.Car.L.Rev. 353 (1984).

28. See § 3–4, supra, note 55; see also Florida v. Casal, 462 U.S. 637, 639 (1983) (Burger, C.J., concurring) ("when state courts interpret state law to require *more* than the Federal Constitution requires, the citizens of the state must be aware that they have the power to amend state law to ensure rational law enforcement").

29. The argument that Long did not extend jurisdiction far enough, and that the Court should exercise jurisdiction to review determinations of federal grounds, even where an adequate and independent state ground is present, to prevent unreviewable judgments of federal law, incorrectly assumes that binding force will be given such determinations. See, e.g., Matasar & Bruch, supra note 6, at 1381–82.

procedural failure, must therefore reach its jurisdictional conclusion by deciding whether the state ground is "adequate".

Because the Supreme Court is the final arbiter of its own jurisdiction, the "issue whether a federal question was sufficiently and properly raised in the state courts is itself ultimately a federal question, as to which [the] Court is not bound by the decision of the state courts." [30] In resolving this issue, the Court is engaged in accommodating state interests while always insuring that appropriate consideration will be given to the federal interests involved.[31] Automatically precluding all Supreme Court review upon a state court's mere recital of procedural grounds would unacceptably endanger the vindication of important federal rights. The perspective from which the Supreme Court inquires into the "adequacy" of state procedures which purport to bar its consideration of federal questions was generally stated in *Lawrence v. State Tax Commission of Mississippi*: [32] "[T]he Constitution, which guarantees rights and immunities to the citizen, likewise insures to him the privilege of having those rights and immunities judicially declared and protected when such judicial action is properly invoked. Even though the claimed constitutional protection be denied on non-federal grounds, it is the province of this Court to inquire whether the decision of the state court rests upon a fair or substantial basis." As Justice Stone's opinion in *Lawrence* suggests, the Supreme Court's constitutional authority to override a state procedural barrier to its exercise of article III appellate jurisdiction does not itself derive from article III, but rather from the substantive character of the claim asserted.

At *minimum*, a state procedure which bars state or federal judicial consideration of *any* question, federal or state, must meet the "fundamental fairness" requirement of the fourteenth amendment due process clause. Of course, a claim that the operation of state procedure does not comport with due process is itself a federal question conferring jurisdiction on the Supreme Court. But the due process clause is not the only source of the Supreme Court's authority to set aside state procedural rules which would otherwise block its consideration of federal questions presented in state courts. Any refusal by any court to enforce a federal right obviously restricts that right to some degree. A state court's enforcement of its procedural rules in order to bar assertion of a federal claim is therefore in effect a substantive judgment: a decision that the state interest in its procedure takes priority over the federal interest in enforcement of the federal claim.[33] The extent to

---

30. Street v. New York, 394 U.S. 576, 583 (1969). Even so, the burden of demonstrating that the federal question was properly raised rests on the appellant or petitioner, who must establish that the Supreme Court has jurisdiction. See, e.g., Memphis Natural Gas Co. v. Beeler, 315 U.S. 649, 651 (1942).

31. See Sandalow, "Henry v. Mississippi and the Adequate State Ground: Proposals for a Revised Doctrine," 1965 Sup. Ct.Rev. 187, 218.

32. 286 U.S. 276, 282 (1932).

33. See Sandalow, supra note 31, at 218; Hill, "The Inadequate State Ground," 65 Colum.L.Rev. 943, 959 (1969). An extreme formulation of this interest-balancing principle was that of Justice Holmes, in Davis v. Wechsler, 263 U.S. 22, 24 (1923): "Whatever [traps] the State may set for those who are endeavoring to assert rights that the State confers, the assertion of federal rights, when plainly and reasonably made, is not to be defeated under the name of local practice."

which state law may limit the impact of federal law is, under the supremacy clause of article VI, a federal question, and jurisdiction to review the state court's striking of the balance is thus acquired by the Supreme Court.[34]

Although they are presupposed by the Supreme Court's conclusion that it has jurisdiction to decide the federal questions in a case, the substantive analyses set forth above are usually carried out *sub silentio*, with the exception of clear violations of due process.[35] It may nonetheless be helpful to make the Court's approach more transparent. To begin with, as already indicated, the existence of an independent state procedural ground does not bar the Court's consideration of substantive federal questions if the underlying application of the state's procedural rule was itself in violation of fourteenth amendment due process. For example, in *Reece v. Georgia*,[36] the Court examined a state rule requiring that objections to the composition of grand juries be made by criminal defendants *before* their indictment and concluded that such a rule could not bar state court consideration, and thus eventual Supreme Court review, of a federal claim brought by a "semi-illiterate" defendant "of low mentality" for whom counsel was not appointed until *after* the defendant was indicted: "The assignment of counsel in a state prosecution at such time and under such circumstances as to preclude the giving of effective aid in the preparation and trial of a capital case is a denial of due process of law." [37]   Similarly, in *Brinkerhoff-Faris Trust & Savings Co. v. Hill*,[38] the Court observed that the "state court refused to hear the plaintiff's complaint and denied it relief, not because of lack of power or because of any demerit in the complaint, but because, assuming power and merit, the plaintiff did not seek an administrative remedy which, in fact, was never available and which is not now open to it. Thus, by denying to it the only remedy ever available for the enforcement of its right to prevent the seizure of its property, the judgment deprives the plaintiff of its property [without due process of law]."

More commonly, however, the Court has not framed its analysis in due process terms, but has simply identified certain peculiarities in the state procedures.[39] The Court has found procedural rulings inadequate where the procedural requirements are not strictly followed and the result in a particular case is inconsistent with past practice. For example, in *James v. Kentucky*,[40] the Court reached the merits of the defendant's claim that the jury was not properly charged to ignore his

---

34. Cf. Testa v. Katt, 330 U.S. 386 (1947) (state cannot discriminate procedurally against federal claims).

35. See Brinkerhoff-Faris Trust & Savings Co. v. Hill, 281 U.S. 673 (1930). Cf. Sandalow, supra note 31, at 239.

36. 350 U.S. 85 (1955).

37. Id. at 90; but cf. Michel v. Louisiana, 350 U.S. 91 (1955) (upholding state's bar to challenges to the composition of the grand jury presented more than three days after the term of the grand jury expired; petitioner's counsel, appointed by the trial court on the day of the expiration of the term of the grand jury, filed the challenge to the composition of the grand jury five days after the grand jury's term expired).

38. 281 U.S. 673, 679 (1930).

39. For a general review of the grounds on which the Court has found state procedural rulings inadequate, see Meltzer, "State Court Forfeitures of Federal Rights," 99 Harv.L.Rev. 1128, 1137–45 (1986).

40. 466 U.S. 341 (1984).

failure to testify; the state defended on the ground that the defendant's lawyer had requested only an "admonition" rather than an "instruction" to the jury to that effect. The Court found that the requirement had not been consistently applied in prior cases and was "not the sort of firmly established and regularly followed state practice that can prevent implementation of federal constitutional rights." [41] Similarly, a procedural ruling will not bar review where it appears to be so novel that the litigant involved did not have a fair chance to comply with it. Thus, the Court has held that it is not barred from considering a first amendment claim by a state court decision that failed to reach the federal question because the claimant had not complied with a procedural rule purportedly implicit in past decisions, but of which "petitioner could not fairly be deemed to have been appraised": "Novelty in procedural requirements cannot be permitted to thwart review in this Court applied for by those who, in justified reliance upon prior decisions, seek vindication in state courts of their federal constitutional rights." [42]

The Supreme Court will also take jurisdiction of a case despite the presence of an independent state procedural ground if the application of the procedural rule is at the discretion of the state court. Thus, in *Williams v. Georgia*,[43] the Court concluded that a state court's refusal to exercise discretion "is, in effect, an avoidance of the federal right." The Court found that, while "Georgia courts have indicated many times that motions for new trial after verdict are not favored, . . . [the] general rule [evident from an examination of state decisions] is that the granting or denying of an extraordinary motion for new trial rests . . . in the discretion of the trial court." [44] In *Williams*, state court discretion to waive the procedural requirement was evident from the face of the relevant state court decisions. In *Sullivan v. Little Hunting Park, Inc.*,[45] the Court went a step beyond *Williams* (without referring to the earlier decision), engaged in a more extensive analysis of the state precedents, and inferred discretion from a state rule of reasonableness governing notice of trial transcript corrections: "[A review of prior decisions does] not enable us to say that the Virginia court has so consistently applied its notice requirement as to amount to a self-denial of the *power* to entertain the federal claim here presented if the Supreme Court of Appeals desires to do so." [46] In contrast, in *Wolfe v. North Carolina*,[47] the Court held that the state ground was adequate: "the present case is not of a pattern with *Williams v. Georgia, supra*. Even if the North Carolina Supreme Court has power to make independent inquiry as to evidence proffered in the trial court but not included

41. Id. at 345–49.

42. NAACP v. Alabama ex rel. Patterson, 357 U.S. 449, 457–58 (1958). But cf. Herndon v. Georgia, 295 U.S. 441 (1935) (requiring appellant to have knowledge of a state supreme court construction of the statute applicable to the appellant, to anticipate the probability of a similar ruling in his own case, and to take steps in the state court system to preserve the federal right).

43. 349 U.S. 375, 383 (1955).

44. Id. at 383–84.

45. 396 U.S. 229 (1969).

46. Id. at 233–34.

47. 364 U.S. 177 (1960).

in the case on appeal, its decisions make clear that it has without exception refused to do so." [48]

Finally, on a limited number of occasions the Court has allowed review where a litigant has failed to comply with state procedural rules that, "even if fairly and consistently applied, heavily burden the assertion of federal rights without significantly advancing any important state policy." [49]   *Henry v. Mississippi* embodies the most expansive application of this principle—and represents the Supreme Court's most ambitious and its most tentative confrontation with the problem of state procedural grounds in general.[50]   In *Henry*, the Court reversed and remanded a state supreme court decision denying a hearing on a criminal defendant's fourth amendment challenge to the admission at his trial of illegally seized evidence.   The defendant's appeal in the state courts on that issue was barred because he had failed to comply with the state's "contemporaneous objection" rule, which required an initial objection to the admission of evidence to be made at the time the evidence is introduced, and not at some point later in the trial.[51]   Although the Supreme Court overturned the state court judgment, it made no conclusive decision as to the "adequacy" of the Mississippi Supreme Court's reason for refusing to reach the federal question,

48. Id. at 191.

49. Meltzer, supra note 39, at 1142; see id. at 1142–45. For example, in Staub v. Baxley, 355 U.S. 313 (1958), the Supreme Court held that its review of a first amendment challenge to a licensing requirement for union organizers was not barred by a state court declaration that the challenger had failed to comply with a rule requiring constitutional attacks on state statutes and ordinances to specify the sections of the legislation questioned. The Court found that the "several sections of the ordinance are interdependent in their application to one in appellant's position."   Therefore, since Staub had "in her objections used language challenging . . . all [the] sections, . . . to require her, in these circumstances, to count off, one by one, the several sections of the ordinance would be to force resort to an arid ritual of meaningless form." Id. at 320.

50. 379 U.S. 443 (1965). Henry, in particular, is the case that most clearly raises the question of the source of the Court's power to exempt litigants before it from compliance with state procedural rules, and of the effect of the law so generated. Because it is difficult to characterize cases in the field as turning mainly on statutory or constitutional interpretation, see Meltzer, supra note 39, at 1159–67, it seems most sensible to regard them as rules growing out of federal common lawmaking, see § 3–23, supra. For contrasting views of this characterization, compare Meltzer at 1176–1202 (arguing that the rules excusing procedural defaults developed on both Supreme Court and habeas corpus review are

federal common law fully binding in all state proceedings), with Field, supra note 6, at 964–73 (arguing that the rules represent a system of "hybrid" state and federal law in which the impact of state procedural rules on federal rights is minimized by case-by-case scrutiny, without thereby imposing a generalized binding federal rule for other cases).

51. The state supreme court handed down two opinions in Henry. In the first, a slip opinion, the state court held that Henry had not waived his objection by waiting until the close of the prosecution's case because, the court found, Henry had been represented by out-of-state counsel presumably unfamiliar with local procedure, which required contemporaneous objections in order to exclude evidence. The court additionally relied on the ground that "[e]rrors affecting fundamental rights are exceptions to the rule that questions not raised in the trial court cannot be raised for the first time on appeal." Henry v. State, 253 Miss. 263, 154 So.2d 289, 296 (1963). After that opinion had been handed down, a suggestion of error was filed by the state indicating that Henry had been represented by local as well as out-of-state counsel. The state court then withdrew the advance opinion and issued another one, concluding that the omission of a contemporaneous objection was a waiver of the right to object. Moreover, the exception regarding fundamental rights was narrowed to apply only in the context of incompetent counsel. State v. Henry, 253 Miss. 263, 154 So.2d at 296 (final opinion).

instead finding a possibility that the defendant, through counsel, may have waived his right to object regardless of the impact of the state rule. The Supreme Court therefore remanded the case to allow a hearing on the waiver issue.[52] But Justice Brennan's majority opinion in *Henry* was so written that it could be construed as a first tentative move in the direction of a general program of increased Supreme Court scrutiny of state procedures affecting the assertion of federal claims.

Before disposing of the case on the waiver basis, the Court in *Henry* advanced the general proposition that, in balancing federal and state interests, the state may not place any undue procedural burden on the assertion of federal rights: "a litigant's procedural defaults in state proceedings do not prevent vindication of his federal rights unless the State's insistence on compliance with its procedural rule serves a legitimate state interest."[53] The Court then suggested that the legitimacy of the state interest allegedly served is to be determined not only by an analysis of the general policies underlying the state rule at issue, but also by an examination of the utility of the procedure in the context of the particular case in which its validity is questioned. The legitimacy of a state procedural rule may therefore be open to attack by way of a demonstration of a *less restrictive alternative*: "But on the record before [the Court] it appears that this [economizing] purpose of the contemporaneous-objection rule may have been *substantially served* by petitioner's motion at the close of the State's evidence asking for a directed verdict. . . ."[54] After discussing the manner in which the "adequacy" of a state procedural ground might be determined, Justice Brennan declared the issue irrelevant: "For even assuming the making of the objection on the motion for a directed verdict satisfied the state interest served by the contemporaneous-objection rule, the record suggests a possibility that petitioner's counsel deliberately bypassed the opportunity to make timely objection in the state court, and thus that the petitioner should be deemed to have forfeited his state court remedies."[55]

To appreciate the full implications of *Henry v. Mississippi*, it is necessary first to consider the interrelations between Supreme Court procedural grounds doctrine and federal habeas corpus procedure.[56] Although the existence of an adequate and independent state procedural ground bars direct Supreme Court appellate review of federal questions otherwise presented by a state court decision, it does not necessarily limit the collateral availability of federal writs of habeas corpus. In *Fay v. Noia*,[57] decided two years before *Henry*, the Supreme

---

52. After proceedings in the state court system, the conviction was reinstated, 202 So.2d 40 (1967), and certiorari was denied, "without prejudice to the bringing of a proceeding for relief in federal habeas corpus." 392 U.S. 931 (1968). A federal district court, in a habeas corpus proceeding, subsequently found that there had been no waiver, and granted habeas corpus. Henry v. Williams, 299 F.Supp. 36 (N.D.Miss. 1969).

53. 379 U.S. at 447.

54. Id. at 448 (emphasis added).

55. Id. at 449–50.

56. The discussion here of the largely statutory question of habeas corpus does not purport to be complete. For a general guide to the area, see P. Bator, D. Shapiro, P. Mishkin & H. Wechsler, Hart and Wechsler's The Federal Courts and the Federal System 1424–1538 (2d ed. 1973).

57. 372 U.S. 391, 399 (1963).

Court held that the federal statute requiring an applicant for federal habeas corpus to exhaust the remedies available in the courts of his state denies access to the writ of habeas corpus only for "failure to exhaust state remedies still open to the habeas applicant at the time he files his application in federal court." The Court thus decided "that the jurisdiction of the federal courts on habeas corpus is not affected by procedural defaults incurred by the applicant during the [prior] state court proceedings." [58]

Fay v. Noia did not entirely free the potential habeas applicant from any need to comply with state procedural rules: "We . . . hold that the federal habeas judge may in his discretion deny relief to an applicant who has deliberately by-passed the orderly procedure of the state courts and in so doing has forfeited his state court remedies." [59] Although this "deliberate by-pass" rule appears to require a personal waiver by defendant, while *Henry*'s deliberate by-pass rule also allows for waiver by counsel, the connection between *Henry* and *Fay* is apparent: by strictly scrutinizing state procedural grounds, *Henry* sought to restore the symmetry between the Supreme Court's jurisdiction on direct review and the federal district courts' collateral jurisdiction on habeas corpus. *Henry*, of course, restored symmetry to federal jurisdiction by reducing the Supreme Court's tolerance for state procedural systems which did not fit the Court's conception of fair procedure. *Fay* had almost immediately become a source of "irritation between the federal and state judiciaries" [60] because it signaled a lack of respect by federal courts for state procedures and at least potentially encouraged litigants in state courts not to worry about whether they had complied with state rules. In *Henry*, Justice Brennan somewhat strangely suggested that greater hostility on the part of the Supreme Court to state procedural grounds would reduce that irritation since it would increase the pressure upon the state courts to abandon procedures which did not allow for "the full airing of federal claims." [61] But *Henry* promised to have precisely the opposite effect: by increasing the pressure on state courts to abandon their own procedures, it reduced state autonomy and thus increased state resistance.

Henry's connection with *Fay v. Noia*, and its insensitivity to state procedural autonomy, may explain why its promise of a radical reformulation of state procedural grounds doctrine has not been fulfilled. In the past decade the Supreme Court has chosen to narrow the gap between direct and habeas corpus review by retreating from *Fay*, in line with its more general hostility to broad availability of habeas corpus relief.[62] In *Wainwright v. Sykes*,[63] the Court ruled that habeas corpus

---

58. Id. at 438.

59. Id.

60. Henry, 379 U.S. at 453.

61. Id.

62. Stone v. Powell, 428 U.S. 465 (1976), first signaled this change in attitude, denying habeas jurisdiction over fourth amendment claims—which rarely involve issues of guilt or innocence—where the petitioner was afforded a full and fair opportunity to litigate the search or seizure issue in the state courts. This analysis could be used to close off review of a wide variety of constitutional claims. See Cover & Aleinikoff, "Dialectical Federalism: Habeas Corpus and the Court," 86 Yale L.J. 1035, 1086–88 (1977).

63. 433 U.S. 72 (1977).

review of a state court judgment resting on the failure to heed the state's contemporaneous-objection rule was barred absent the petitioner's showing of "cause" for the procedural default and "prejudice" resulting from it.

The *Sykes* Court refused to articulate the "precise content" of the cause-and-prejudice rule or to say whether it would apply in all cases,[64] but subsequent cases make clear that it applies broadly.[65] Rejecting the view of some Justices that cause and prejudice should serve only as factors in a balancing analyis of whether review is appropriate—particularly where procedural defaults have occurred not at the trial but at the appellate stage, in which the state's interest in procedural integrity is arguably less weighty[66]—the Court has made clear that, regardless of the prejudice resulting from a procedural default—short of that resulting from a " 'fundamental miscarriage of justice' " suggesting the probable "conviction of one who is actually innocent"[67]—cause for the default must always be shown. Moreover, the Court will refuse to find cause for defaults occurring through attorney ignorance or inadvertence,[68] and will not find prejudice absent a showing that the default "worked to [a defendant's] *actual* and substantial disadvantage, infecting his entire trial with error of constitutional dimensions."[69]

§ 3–25. Limits on the Power of Federal Courts to Entertain Suits Against States: The Eleventh Amendment and Its Supposed Exemplification of Sovereign Immunity

At this point, our emphasis shifts to an explicit constitutional limit on the power of the federal courts to frame remedies for state violations of federal rights: the eleventh amendment, which has been interpreted to define the extent to which the states' sovereign immunity constrains federal efforts to provide relief for victims of state action. The eleventh amendment lies at the center of the tension between state sovereign immunity and the desire to have in place mechanisms for the effective vindication of federal rights. The Supreme Court has negotiated this tension both by resort to legal fictions and through complex and often counterintuitive interpretations of the eleventh amendment that have made that amendment far more controversial than its language would, on its face, suggest.

---

64. See id. at 91, 88 n. 12.

65. For a general discussion, see Meltzer, supra note 39, at 1147–50; Note, "The Supreme Court, 1986 Term—Leading Cases," 100 Harv.L.Rev. 100, 240–49 (1986).

66. See Murray v. Carrier, 106 S.Ct. 2639, 2651–56 (1986) (Stevens, J., joined by Blackmun, J., concurring in the judgment); Smith v. Murray, 106 S.Ct. 2661, 2669–75 (1986) (Stevens, J., joined in relevant part by Marshall & Blackmun, JJ., dissenting); id. at 2678–83 (Brennan, J., joined by Marshall, J., dissenting in both Carrier and Smith). See also Note, "Procedural Defaults at the Appellate Stage and Habeas Corpus Review," 38 Stan.L.Rev. 463 (1986) (arguing that the concerns addressed by

the Sykes rule are not present on appellate review).

67. Carrier, 106 S.Ct. at 2650 (citation omitted); see also Smith, 106 S.Ct. at 2668.

68. See Carrier, 106 S.Ct. at 2645–46; Smith, 106 S.Ct. at 2666. See also Engle v. Isaac, 456 U.S. 107, 129–34 & n. 34 (1982); cf. Reed v. Ross, 468 U.S. 1, 13–16 (1984). In such cases one may press only a claim of ineffective assistance of counsel, as an independent matter itself subject to exhaustion in state court, see Carrier, 106 S.Ct. at 2646, and governed by the standards announced in Strickland v. Washington, 466 U.S. 668 (1984).

69. United States v. Frady, 456 U.S. 152, 170 (1982) (emphasis in original).

In *Chisholm v. Georgia*[1], the Supreme Court accepted original jurisdiction of a suit brought against the State of Georgia by two South Carolina citizens to collect a debt owed an estate. The Court took article III literally, refusing to condition the constitutional grant of authority to the federal courts to adjudicate "Controversies . . . between a State and Citizens of another State"[2] on the defendant state's consent to suit. Response to *Chisholm* was not mixed. The Georgia House of Representatives was so exercised by the decision that it made any attempt to carry out the Supreme Court's mandate a felony punishable by hanging without benefit of clergy.[3] Other reactions were only less extreme. At least part of the anti-*Chisholm* clamor sounded in self-interest: the states feared ruinous suits on Revolutionary War debts.[4] Contemporary critics, jealous and perhaps fearful of the newly created power of the federal judiciary, must also have heard the whisper of betrayal, for the most ardent constitutionalists had given positive assurances that article III did not work a surrender of state sovereign immunity.[5] Within five years, *Chisholm* could claim the distinction of being the first Supreme Court case to be overruled by a constitutional amendment.

Eleventh amendment[6] jurisprudence has left no doubt that the amendment not only reversed *Chisholm*, but also countermanded any judicial inclination to interpret article III as a self-executing abrogation of state immunity from suit, thereby reinstating the original understanding that the states surrendered sovereign immunity only to the extent inherent "in the acceptance of the constitutional plan."[7] Based

§ 3-25

1. 2 U.S. (2 Dall.) 419 (1793).

2. U.S. Const. article III, § 2.

3. See G. Gunther, Cases and Materials on Constitutional Law 39 (11th ed. 1985).

4. See Cullison, "Interpretation of the Eleventh Amendment," 5 Houston L.Rev. 1, 7, 9, 16 (1967): Jaffe, "Suits Against Governments and Officers: Sovereign Immunity," 77 Harv.L.Rev. 1, 19 (1963). Other pecuniary motives included the desire to avoid suits seeking restitution of confiscated Loyalist property and the desire to retain lands placed in the public domain by legislative fiat. See C. Jacobs, The Eleventh Amendment and Sovereign Immunity 57–62, 178 n. 72 (1972).

5. "It is inherent in the nature of sovereignty, not to be amenable to the suit of an individual without [the Sovereign's] consent. This is the general sense, and the general practice of mankind; and the exemption, as one of the attributes of sovereignty, is now enjoyed by the government of every State in the Union. Unless, therefore, there is a surrender of this immunity in the plan of the convention, it will remain with the States . . . ." The Federalist No. 81, at 487–88 (C. Rossiter ed. 1961) (A. Hamilton). This Blackstonian rhetoric, compare W. Blackstone, Commentaries on

the Laws of England. Book 1, ch. 7, at 235 (1765), may have been as much political expedient as political theory. Pollock and Maitland found sovereign immunity in England to be an historical "accident" caused by the pyramidal structure of feudal courts, and not a basic idea implicit in any concept of sovereignty. See 1 F. Pollock & F. Maitland, History of English Law 518 (2d ed. 1898).

6. The eleventh amendment provides that: "The Judicial power of the United States shall not be construed to extend to any suit in law or equity, commenced or prosecuted against any one of the United States by Citizens of another State, or by Citizens or Subjects of any Foreign State." U.S. Const. amend. XI.

7. Principality of Monaco v. Mississippi, 292 U.S. 313–330 (1934). The quoted language is a paraphrase of Hamilton's language in The Federalist No. 81, quoted in note 5, supra. Hamilton's understanding that the states had not surrendered their sovereign immunity by ratifying article III is corroborated by statements of Madison and Marshall before the Virginia Convention. See 3 Elliot's Debates 533 (2d ed. 1901) (Madison); id. at 557 (Marshall), quoted in Monaco v. Mississippi, supra. at 323–24. The Monaco Court adopted Hamilton's view that the structure of the feder-

on this understanding, the Supreme Court, in deciding eleventh amendment cases, has focused not on the language of the eleventh amendment, but on the concept of sovereign immunity of which it is a reminder and "exemplification." [8] Thus, unlike the identical reference to "the judicial Power of the United States" in article III—a power which cannot be expanded by legislation [9] or by consent of the parties to a lawsuit [10]—the language of the eleventh amendment has been interpreted to allow a suit if a state has given its consent.[11] Under a similarly flexible interpretation, suits against nonconsenting states brought by foreign nations are barred,[12] even though the amendment on its face speaks only to suits by citizens of a sister state.

The Supreme Court's understanding of the principle of sovereign immunity has, however, recognized that "acceptance of the constitutional plan" puts some limitations on the power of a state to avoid suit. Suits brought by sister states [13] or by the United States [14] are thus not prohibited. The eleventh amendment also does not shield a state from suits in the courts of a sister state; the immunity applies only in federal court.[15] And neither sovereign immunity nor the eleventh amendment bars Supreme Court review of state court judgments in suits in which a state is a party, since supremacy of federal law requires review of the federal questions presented by such judgments.[16]

al union implied that state sovereign immunity was limited in at least two cases: suits against a state by another state, see id. at 327–28; and suits by the United States against a state, see id. at 328–29.

8. See, e.g., Pennhurst State School & Hosp. v. Halderman (II), 465 U.S. 89, 98 (1984); Ex parte New York, 256 U.S. 490, 497 (1921). See also H. Hart & A. Sacks, The Legal Process: Basic Problems in the Making and Application of Law 806–07 (tent. ed. 1958) (court has treated eleventh amendment "as if it were a precedent to the opposite of Chisholm").

A powerful argument has been advanced that the eleventh amendment should not be read as a constitutionalization of state sovereign immunity at all. Rather, it is argued, the amendment was intended only to restrict party identity as a basis of federal court jurisdiction. See, e.g., Field, "The Eleventh Amendment and Other Immunity Doctrines," 126 U.Pa.L.Rev. 515, 1203 (1978); Fletcher, "A Historical Interpretation of the Eleventh Amendment: A Narrow Construction of an Affirmative Grant of Jurisdiction Rather Than a Prohibition Against Jurisdiction," 35 Stan.L.Rev. 1033 (1983); Gibbons, "The Eleventh Amendment and State Sovereign Immunity: A Reinterpretation," 83 Colum.L.Rev. 1889 (1983); C. Jacobs, The Eleventh Amendment and Sovereign Immunity (1972); Orth, The Judicial Power of the United States: The Eleventh Amendment in American History (1987); Shapiro, "Wrong Turns: The Eleventh Amendment and the

Pennhurst Case," 98 Harv.L.Rev. 61 (1984). See also Atascadero State Hospital v. Scanlon, 473 U.S. 234, 247–302 and n. 11 (1985) (Brennan, J., joined by Marshall, Blackmun, and Stevens, JJ., dissenting). This thesis is well-supported, but it seems unlikely that the Supreme Court will rewrite its eleventh amendment jurisprudence anytime soon. To do so, while perhaps restoring an historically correct understanding of the eleventh amendment, would inevitably disrupt the entire complex of doctrines, of which the eleventh amendment is one, surrounding the balance of power between the states and the federal government. See note 19, infra.

9. Marbury v. Madison, 5 U.S. (1 Cranch) 137 (1803).

10. See Louisville & N.R.R. v. Mottley, 211 U.S. 149 (1908); Mansfield, C. & L.M. Ry. v. Swan, 111 U.S. 379 (1884).

11. See Clark v. Barnard, 108 U.S. 436, 447 (1883) ("immunity from suit belonging to a State . . . is a personal privilege which it may waive at pleasure").

12. Principality of Monaco v. Mississippi, 292 U.S. 313 (1934).

13. E.g., North Dakota v. Minnesota, 263 U.S. 365, 372–73 (1923).

14. E.g., United States v. Mississippi, 380 U.S. 128, 140–41 (1965).

15. Nevada v. Hall, 440 U.S. 410 (1979).

16. Cohens v. Virginia, 19 U.S. (6 Wheat.) 264, 379–83, 407 (1821); accord, Smith v. Reeves, 178 U.S. 436, 445 (1900)

If concerns of federalism are not present, however, a different result follows. Where the plaintiff is nominally another state but the suit is actually for the benefit of a discrete group of private citizens, eleventh amendment immunity can be invoked by the defendant state.[17]

A consistent vision of the eleventh amendment and state sovereign immunity is most severely tested by suits in which a plaintiff seeks relief on the basis of an asserted federal constitutional right. It is at least arguable that, in ratifying the constitutional plan, the states surrendered sovereign immunity from suits testing the constitutional limits of state action.[18] As a doctrinal matter, however, the law is settled the other way, for *Hans v. Louisiana* [19] is conventionally thought to stand for the proposition that sovereign immunity bars even suits arising under the Constitution or laws of the United States.[20] In *Hans*, a citizen of Louisiana sued to recover damages, alleging that the state's failure to pay its bonds violated the contract clause of the Constitution.[21] Although *Hans* might easily be limited on the ground that an opposite holding would have resurrected *Chisholm* to the extent of making states legally liable on their debts, it has not been so narrowed.

The rule of *Hans* has not, however, totally frustrated attempts to use the federal judiciary to protect individual rights from unconstitutional state action. Instead, the courts have distinguished suits against the state [22] from suits against an individual officer even though compliance by the officer will often be compliance by the state and the costs of

(although state may limit consent to suits in its own courts, supremacy clause requires that federal questions decided be reviewable in the Supreme Court), discussed in § 3–26, note 66, infra.

17. E.g., New Hampshire v. Louisiana, 108 U.S. 76 (1883) (eleventh amendment bars suit where plaintiff state is actually bringing suit for individual citizens); Hawaii v. Standard Oil Co., 405 U.S. 251, 258–59 n. 12 (1972) (same). Compare Employees of Dept. of Public Health and Welfare, Missouri v. Department of Pub. Health & Welfare, 411 U.S. 279, 286 (1973) (eleventh amendment does *not* bar suits by the Secretary of Labor on behalf of employees to collect back pay under Fair Labor Standards Act because suits by the United States are not barred by the amendment). See § 3–26 at note 65, infra.

18. See, e.g., Cohens v. Virginia, 19 U.S. (6 Wheat.) 264, 379–83, 407 (1821).

19. 134 U.S. 1 (1890). Hans has recently been widely criticized as wrongly decided. See note 8, supra. In Welch v. State Dept. of Highways and Public Transportation, 107 S.Ct. 2941, 2948–57 (1987), the Court expressly rejected the urging of four Justices (Brennan, Marshall, Blackmun, and Stevens, JJ.) that Hans be overruled. But Justice Scalia concurred on a narrow ground that left the future status of Hans open. See id. at 2957.

20. See e.g., Pennhurst State School & Hosp. v. Halderman (II), 465 U.S. 89, 98–99 (1984); Parden v. Terminal Ry. of Alabama State Docks Dept., 377 U.S. 184, 186 (1964); accord, Duhne v. New Jersey, 251 U.S. 311, 313 (1920) (mem.) (suit to enjoin enforcement of eighteenth amendment barred); Smith v. Reeves, 178 U.S. 436, 446–48 (1900) (eleventh amendment bars suits arising under constitution); Fitts v. McGhee, 172 U.S. 516, 524–25 (1899) (suit alleging violation of due process clause barred).

21. See 134 U.S. at 1–2.

22. Counties and municipalities do not enjoy eleventh amendment immunity. See, e.g., Mt. Healthy School District v. Doyle, 429 U.S. 274 (1977); Lincoln County v. Luning, 133 U.S. 529 (1890). In determining whether an entity is "one of the United States" entitled to invoke the eleventh amendment shield, the Court has drawn a distinction between political subdivisions of the state—which do not receive eleventh amendment protection—and "arms" or departments of the state, which do receive protection. See, e.g., Lake Country Estates, Inc. v. Tahoe Regional Planning Agency, 440 U.S. 391, 401–403 (1979) (treating an agency formed by interstate compact as a non-immune political subdivision rather than an immune arm of the state based on its function, structure, and composition).

compliance will be borne by the state treasury.[23]   Under this distinction, two principal types of cases have been allowed to proceed.   First, suits for money damages against an agent of the state in the agent's individual capacity are not barred: the damages are payable by the officer, provided primary and remedial law gives the plaintiff a cause of action against the officer for the specific actions contested.[24]   Second, if the plaintiff does not make the gross pleading error of naming the state as defendant, prospective injunctive relief against a state officer is not prohibited.[25]

That the Court has thought it necessary to continue the unsatisfactory and conceptually unruly distinction between actions against a

---

23. The nature of the distinction drawn is most clearly articulated in Edelman v. Jordan, 415 U.S. 651 (1974), where the Court reversed a district court order requiring state welfare officials to pay out illegally withheld welfare benefits: "[The order] requires payments of state funds, not as a necessary consequence of compliance in the future with a substantive federal-question determination, but as a form of compensation." Id. at 668. See § 3–27, infra.

24. See, e.g., Scheuer v. Rhodes, 416 U.S. 232, 237–38 (1974); Great Northern Life Ins. Co. v. Read, 322 U.S. 47, 50–51 (1944); In re Ayers, 123 U.S. 443, 500–01 (1887) ("the defendants, though professing to act as officers of the State, are threatening a violation of the personal or property rights of the complainant"). See also United States v. Lee, 106 U.S. (16 Otto) 196 (1882) (action in ejectment against United States officers not barred by sovereign immunity) (superceded by statute, 28 U.S.C. § 2409a). See generally P. Bator, P. Mishkin, D. Shapiro & H. Wechsler, Hart and Wechsler's The Federal Courts and the Federal System 930–37 (2d ed. 1973).

One court has suggested that damage awards against an individual officer might violate the eleventh amendment if the officer were indemnified by the state. See Hallmark Clinic v. North Carolina Dep't of Human Res., 380 F.Supp. 1153, 1159–60 & n. 12 (E.D.N.C. 1974) (three-judge court), aff'd. 519 F.2d 1315 (4th Cir. 1975). See also Edelman v. Jordan, 415 U.S. 651, 664 (1974) ("These funds will obviously not be paid out of the pocket of petitioner Edelman"). Such a voluntary assumption of an officer's liability ought to be insufficient to create eleventh amendment immunity. In the parallel case of intergovernmental tax immunities, assumption by the federal executive of state taxes levied against a private party is not enough to create tax immunity. See chapter 6, infra. For the same reasons, a state should not be able to turn a purely intramural arrangement with its officers into an extension of

sovereign immunity. Alternatively, the state's voluntary extension of indemnification could be construed as a waiver of eleventh amendment immunity. See § 3–26, infra.

25. Thus the seminal importance of Ex parte Young, 209 U.S. 123 (1908), which established an equitable cause of action against state officers in their individual capacities, the eleventh amendment notwithstanding, for violations of constitutional rights, and of Home Tel. & Tel. Co. v. Los Angeles, 227 U.S. 278 (1913), which established the fourteenth amendment as a substantive rule of conduct binding on state officials individually regardless of whether or not the state had officially sanctioned their actions. Young and Home Telephone thus enabled plaintiffs to allege "state action" sufficient to trigger the fourteenth amendment without automatically raising the bar of the eleventh. Edelman v. Jordan, 415 U.S. 651 (1974), expressly confined the Young rule to suits requesting prospective injunctive relief. Actions for retroactive relief, even when styled as requests for an injunction and even if nominally directed against state officers and not the state itself, will ordinarily be barred by the eleventh amendment if the effect of the judgment is to burden the state treasury. See 415 U.S. at 668; § 3–27, infra. The Young rule was narrowed further in Pennhurst State School & Hosp. v. Halderman (II), 465 U.S. 89 (1984). Pennhurst held that the eleventh amendment prohibited federal courts from issuing injunctions against state officers based on state law. In sum, plaintiffs in general may avoid the strictures of the eleventh amendment by satisfying three requirements—alleging a violation of federal law, naming a state official and not the state as a defendant, and requesting prospective injunctive relief. It should be noted that even though Edelman and Pennhurst interpret the Young rule narrowly, the core of the Young principle remains intact. See § 3–27, infra.

state officer individually and actions against the state [26] is itself testimony to the vitality of the states' sovereign immunity in the constitutional scheme. Although the effect of sovereign immunity on the availability of judicial review has been narrowed by fiction, the operational concept of a sovereign immunity that is secure against judicial inroads has been retained in at least the core area of damage suits and of injunctions against the state as such. It is thus not surprising that, when the Supreme Court began to consider the power of Congress to authorize damage suits against the states under article I, it found itself fenced between two conflicting premises: on the one hand, the states had retained a sovereign immunity which could be sacrificed only by a subsequent waiver. On the other, the states had ceded part of their sovereignty to the national government in ratifying article I, thereby creating a limitation on sovereign immunity inhering in "the acceptance of the constitutional plan." [27]

§ 3–26. Removing the Eleventh Amendment Shield: The Conundrum of Constructive Waiver, and an Alternative Theory of Eleventh Amendment Abrogation

Prior to 1964, eleventh amendment cases imposed an exacting requirement of proof of state consent to suit: "express language or . . . such overwhelming implication from the text [of the state statute claimed to waive immunity] as would leave no room for any other reasonable construction." [1] But in *Parden v. Terminal Railway,*[2] the Supreme Court employed a new concept of "constructive waiver" to remove the eleventh amendment bar to a negligence action brought by Alabama citizens under the Federal Employers Liability Act (FELA) against a railway owned by the State of Alabama and operated by it in interstate commerce. The Alabama Constitution and Alabama Supreme Court decisions foreclosed the possibility that the state had actually "consented" to the suit under traditional standards. The FELA, however, specifically provided that "[e]very common carrier by railroad" engaged in interstate commerce would be liable in damages to injured employees in "an action . . . brought in a district court of the United States. . . ." [3] The *Parden* Court held that this legislation transmuted the state's operation of the railroad into a constructive

26. Compare, e.g., In re Ayers, 123 U.S. 443 (1887) (contract clause action; suit by owners of tax coupons to enjoin state officials from allegedly destroying market for coupons by bringing actions against all persons attempting to use the coupons; held, eleventh amendment bars suit), with, e.g., Georgia R.R. & Banking Co. v. Redwine, 342 U.S. 299 (1952) (contract clause action; plaintiff sought injunction to prevent assessment of ad valorem taxes contrary to legislative charter; held, eleventh amendment is no bar).

27. An excellent example of these conflicting premises can be found in Parden v. Terminal Ry. of Alabama State Docks Dept., 377 U.S. 184, 192 (1964): "By em-

powering Congress to regulate commerce, then, the States necessarily surrendered any portion of their sovereignty that would stand in the way of such regulation. . . . Our conclusion is simply that Alabama, when it began operation of an interstate railroad approximately 20 years after enactment of the FELA, necessarily consented to such suit as was authorized by that Act."

§ 3–26

1. Murray v. Wilson Distilling Co., 213 U.S. 151, 171 (1909).

2. 377 U.S. 184 (1964).

3. 45 U.S.C. §§ 51, 56.

"waiver" of eleventh amendment immunity.[4] It insisted that Congress'
power to regulate interstate commerce, delegated by the states in
article I, is plenary and thus necessarily brooks no restraint by the
states on its exercise.[5] When Congress has authorized federal courts to
entertain suits in the necessary and proper furtherance of the regulation of interstate commerce, sovereign immunity can be no bar.[6] For
this reason, Alabama by its actions in operating a railroad subject to
national regulation had "necessarily consented to such suit as was
authorized by" the FELA.[7] The *Parden* Court refused to make state
law dispositive of the waiver question, fearing that Congress' article I
power would be rendered "meaningless if the State . . . could conclusively deny the waiver . . . ."[8] Thus, *Parden* clearly indicated that
even a contemporaneous state expression of nonconsent could be disregarded: "Where a State's consent . . . is alleged to arise from an act
. . . within a sphere . . . subject to the constitutional power of the
Federal Government, the question whether the State's act constitutes
the alleged consent is one of federal law."[9]

In the 1973 case of *Employees v. Department of Public Health and
Welfare*,[10] the Supreme Court reaffirmed Congress' power to bring "the
States to heel, in the sense of lifting their immunity from suit in a
federal court," but signaled that exercise of such power would not be
presumed without clear evidence of congressional purpose.[11] Thus,
although section 16(b) of the Fair Labor Standards Act (FLSA) made
employers liable to private damage suits "in any court of competent
jurisdiction,"[12] the Court declined to construe a 1966 amendment
extending the Act's coverage to state hospitals and schools[13] as enforcing a corresponding waiver of eleventh amendment immunity.[14] The
Court indicated that the authority of the Secretary of Labor to bring
suit to enjoin further violation and recover unpaid wages adequately
safeguarded federal interests in FLSA enforcement.[15] The stark result
in *Employees*, however, was that the remedies available for FLSA
violations affecting public employees were limited by the preexisting
presumption that "a federal court is not competent to render judgment
against a nonconsenting State."[16]

Edelman v. Jordan,[17] decided in 1974, continued the Court's chary
approach to constructive waiver. The *Edelman* Court held that a
federal district court could not order Illinois officials to "release and

---

4. 377 U.S. at 190–92.

5. Id. at 192.

6. Id.

7. Id.

8. Id. at 196.

9. Id.

10. 411 U.S. 279, 283 (1973); see id. at
284–85.

11. Id. at 285.

12. 29 U.S.C. § 216(b).

13. See id. §§ 203(d), (r), (s).

14. See 411 U.S. at 285. The Court
seemed influenced by two notions: first,
that the schools and hospitals in Employees were somehow more an expression of
"sovereign" power and less an extension of
"proprietary" state interests than the railroad in Parden, see 411 U.S. at 284–85;
Parden v. Terminal Ry., 377 U.S. 184, 196
(1964) (semble) ("when a State leaves the
sphere that is exclusively its own"); and
second, that the double damages provision
of § 16(b) appeared inconsistent with a
"harmonious federalism," 411 U.S. at 286.

15. 411 U.S. at 285–86.

16. Id. at 284.

17. 415 U.S. 651 (1974).

remit" federally-subsidized welfare benefits illegally withheld from Illinois citizens.[18] The Court concluded that state participation in a federal program could not in itself be taken to signify "consent on the part of the State to be sued in the federal courts." [19] State officers may be sued in federal court to compel future compliance with welfare regulations,[20] but the Court declined to find constructive waiver where the "only language in the [federal legislation] which purported to provide a federal sanction against a State [by cutting off future funds] . . . by its terms did not authorize suit against anyone . . . ." [21]

In *Fitzpatrick v. Bitzer*,[22] the Court found the clear evidence of congressional purpose that was lacking in *Employees* and *Edelman*. Congress, in adopting the Equal Employment Opportunity Act of 1972,[23] had amended Title VII of the Civil Rights Act of 1964 [24] to include "governments, governmental agencies [and] political subdivisions" [25] among the employers subject to Title VII's prohibition of discriminatory employment practices and its corollary authorization of employee back-pay actions. Such congressional action, the *Fitzpatrick* Court concluded, revealed "congressional intent to abrogate the immunity conferred by the eleventh amendment" to be "clearly present." [26]

Once the necessary intent had been found, the *Fitzpatrick* Court turned to the question of whether Congress in this case indeed possessed the *power* to roll back the states' eleventh admendment immunity. Treating the 1972 Act as an exercise of congressional authority under § 5 of the fourteenth amendment, the Court held that Congress could in fact require the states to provide back pay to victims of the states' discrimination: "When Congress acts pursuant to § 5, not only is it exercising legislative authority that is plenary within the terms of the constitutional grant, it is exercising that authority under one section of a constitutional amendment whose other sections by their own terms embody limitations on state authority." [27] Despite occasional suggestions to the contrary, Congress should be understood to have precisely the same powers under its other constitutional grants of authority.[28]

---

18. Federal regulations provided that benefits under the Aid to the Aged, Blind and Disabled categorical grant program should be paid within a prescribed period following submission of a qualifying application. Illinois paid benefits only after applications were approved, even if state application review procedures overran the federal deadlines. Id. at 653–55 and nn. 3, 4.

19. 415 U.S. at 673.

20. See, e.g., Graham v. Richardson, 403 U.S. 365 (1971); Goldberg v. Kelly, 397 U.S. 254 (1970). They may also be sued to compel them to share future costs of compliance with a decree remedying violations for which they shared responsibility. Milliken v. Bradley (II), 433 U.S. 267 (1977).

21. 415 U.S. at 674.

22. 427 U.S. 445 (1976).

23. 86 Stat. 103.

24. 42 U.S.C. § 2000 et. seq.

25. Id. § 2000e(a); see 427 U.S. at 449 n. 2.

26. 427 U.S. at 451–52.

27. Id at 452. See § 5–22, infra.

28. In Pennhurst State School & Hosp. v. Halderman (II), 465 U.S. 89, 99 (1983), and in Atascadero State Hosp. v. Scanlon, 473 U.S. 234, 238–40, 243 (1985), the Court hinted that Congress' power to abrogate the state's eleventh amendment immunity may be limited to enactments under § 5 of the fourteenth amendment. Later, however, Justice Rehnquist's opinion for the Court in Green v. Mansour, 106 S.Ct. 423 (1985), discussed Congress' power to abrogate the states' immunity but did not suggest that that power was restricted to en-

The Court emphatically reasserted the clear statement approach of *Employees* and *Edelman* in *Atascadero State Hospital v. Scanlon*,[29] stating that it would not impute to Congress any intent to abrogate the states' eleventh amendment immunity that was not apparent on the face of the relevant statute. At issue in *Atascadero* was § 504 of the Rehabilitation Act, which provides remedies for handicapped persons who are discriminated against in any program or activity receiving federal funds.[30] A sharply divided Court [31] held that the Act did not abrogate the states' eleventh amendment immunity, despite the statute's provision that remedies be available in federal court "to any person aggrieved by any act or failure to act by any recipient of federal assistance . . . ." [32] The Court stated that because the states, given

actments under the fourteenth amendment, stating only that Congress must act "pursuant to a valid exercise of power." Id. at 425–26. Edelman, it should be noted, establishes that under the spending clause Congress may condition state receipt of funds on consent to suit. Edelman, 415 U.S. at 672–73. See also Pennhurst State School & Hosp. v. Halderman (I), 451 U.S. 1, 17 (1981); Atascadero, 473 U.S. at 245–46 & n. 5. And Parden found that Congress had conditioned state operation of railroads on consent to suit under the FELA, a commerce clause enactment. 377 U.S. at 190–92.

Although it is true that the fourteenth amendment "by [its] own terms embod[ies] limitations on state authority," Fitzpatrick, 427 U.S. at 452, *all* of the Constitution's affirmative grants of power to Congress should equally be viewed as in derogation of state sovereignty. That the Framers certainly took this view is indicated by the language of the tenth amendment: "The powers not *delegated* to the United States by the Constitution . . . are reserved to the states . . . ." (emphasis added). See generally Garcia v. San Antonio Metropolitan Transit Authority, 469 U.S. 528, 548–49 (1985) ("[the] states do retain a significant measure of sovereign authority," but "[t]hey do so only to the extent that the Constitution has not divested them of their original powers and transferred those powers to the Federal Government"). To the extent that the states are in need of protection from undue congressional intrusion on their sovereignty, such protection is now afforded almost exclusively by the states' representation in Congress. See Garcia, 469 U.S. at 550–51; Brown, "State Sovereignty Under the Burger Court—How the Eleventh Amendment Survived the Death of the Tenth: Some Broader Implications of Atascadero State Hospital v. Scanlon," 74 Geo.L.J. 363, 365, 393–94 (1985); note 54, infra. But see § 5–23, infra, and compare City of Rome v. United States, 446 U.S. 156, 181 & n. 15 (1980) (citing Fitzpatrick for the proposi-

tion that "principles of federalism that might otherwise be an obstacle to congressional authority are necessarily overridden by the power to enforce the Civil War Amendments 'by appropriate legislation.'"). See also note 41, infra.

29. 473 U.S. 234 (1985).

30. 29 U.S.C. § 794.

31. Justice Powell delivered the opinion of the Court, in which Chief Justice Burger and Justices White, Rehnquist, and O'Connor joined. Justice Brennan filed an exhaustive dissent joined by Justices Marshall, Blackmun, and Stevens. Justice Brennan first argued that the Rehabilitation Act and its legislative history left no question that Congress had intended to make the states answerable in federal court for violations of the statute, and attacked the Court's "relentless" application of the clear statement rule as "serv[ing] no purpose but obstructing the will of Congress." 473 U.S. at 252–55 & n. 7. Justice Brennan then launched a lengthy historical critique of the Court's eleventh amendment jurisprudence, arguing that the amendment was never intended to constitutionalize "anachronistic" sovereign immunity doctrine, but only to prevent the federal courts from taking jurisdiction over suits against states solely on the basis of party identity. Id. at 258–302. Justice Brennan relied on the arguments of a number of recent commentators calling for reinterpretation of the eleventh amendment. See id. at 258 n. 11 (collecting commentary). Justice Brennan's view of the eleventh amendment would have the effect of reversing the presumption against state amenability to suit in federal courts embodied in the clear statement rule: If the eleventh amendment is read as a limitation only on the federal courts' diversity jurisdiction, a state would presumptively be suable in federal court on any federal question cause of action, unless exempted from suit by Congress. See § 3–25, note 8, supra.

32. 29 U.S.C. § 794.

their special constitutional role, "are not like any other class of recipients of federal aid," the "general authorization" contained in the Act was not sufficient to demonstrate congressional intent to abrogate the states' immunity.[33]   Rather, when Congress wants to subject the states to suit in federal court, it must express that intent "in unmistakable language in the statute itself." [34]

The *Atascadero* decision illustrates how far the Supreme Court's stance on eleventh amendment issues had shifted by 1985.   The *Parden* majority posited no distinction between the states and other entities that might be regulated by federal legislation and thus would make states amenable to suit in federal court whenever they undertake an activity for which a private person could potentially be held liable under a valid federal law.[35]   *Employees, Edelman,* and *Atascadero,* on the other hand, treat states as distinguished from other entities by federalism considerations.[36]   For this reason, the amenability of states to suit must be specifically addressed by federal legislation, and Congress must make its intention to treat states like private parties unmistakably clear.[37]   This policy of clear statement had been rejected by the *Parden* majority, but Justice White's formulation of the policy in

33. 473 U.S. at 245–56.

34. Id. at 243. In response to the argument that the state had constructively waived its immunity by accepting federal funding under the Rehabilitation Act, the Court also held, on virtually identical reasoning, that the Act "falls far short of manifesting a clear intent to condition participation in the programs funded under the Act on a State's consent to waive its constitutional immunity." Id. at 247. The Court also rejected the argument that California had waived its immunity, stating that "[i]n the absence of an unequivocal waiver specifically applicable to federal court jurisdiction, we decline to find that [a state] has waived its constitutional immunity." Id. at 241.

35. See Employees, 411 U.S. at 300 (Brennan, J., dissenting); accord, Edelman, 415 U.S. at 687–88 (Brennan, J., dissenting).

36. "[W]e decline to extend Parden to cover every exercise by Congress of its commerce power, where the purpose of Congress to give force to the supremacy clause by lifting the sovereignty of the States and putting the States on the same footing as other employers is not clear." Employees, 411 U.S. at 286–87. Atascadero, 473 U.S. at 242 (the "Eleventh Amendment serves to maintain" the " 'constitutionally mandated balance of power' between the States and the Federal Government [that] was adopted by the Framers to ensure the protection of 'our fundamental liberties,' " (citations omitted)). See also Brown, "State Sovereignty Under the Burger Court—How the Eleventh Amendment Survived the

Death of the Tenth: Some Broader Implications of Atascadero State Hospital v. Scanlon," 74 Geo.L.J. 363, 365 (1985) (arguing that the eleventh amendment affords the states "a form of process federalism" which substitutes for the substantive protections of National League of Cities v. Usery, 426 U.S. 833 (1976), that proved unworkable and led to the case's being overruled in Garcia, see § 5–22, infra).

37. See Edelman, 415 U.S. at 672; Employees, 411 U.S. at 285 (unless Congress indicates "in some way by clear language that the constitutional immunity [is to be] swept away," the Court will not infer that Congress "desired silently to deprive the States" of immunity); Atascadero, 473 U.S. at 243 ("Congress may abrogate the state's constitutionally secured immunity from suit in federal court only by making its intention unmistakably clear in the language of the statute."). See also Pennhurst State School & Hosp. v. Halderman (II), 465 U.S. 89, 99 (1984) (abrogation of the states' eleventh amendment immunity requires "an unequivocal expression of congressional intent"); Florida Dept. of Health and Rehabilitative Services v. Florida Nursing Home Ass'n, 450 U.S. 147 (1981) (per curiam) (holding that Florida had not waived its eleventh amendment immunity with respect to suits against the Department of Health and Rehabilitative Services by making the Department a "body corporate" with the capacity to "sue and be sued" and by agreeing under the Medicaid program to "recognize and abide by all [applicable] State and Federal Laws, Regulations, and Guidelines . . . .").

his *Parden* dissent eventually prevailed: [38] One should not lightly infer that Congress, in legislating pursuant to one article of the Constitution, intended to effect an automatic and compulsory waiver of rights arising under another. Only when Congress has clearly considered the problem and expressly declared that any State which undertakes given regulatable conduct will be deemed thereby to have waived its immunity should courts disallow the invocation of this defense. Thus in *Employees*, Justice Douglas searched the FLSA legislative history in vain for "a word . . . to indicate a purpose of Congress to make it possible for a citizen . . . to sue the State in the federal courts." [39] And in *Edelman*, the Court indicated that, in the absence of waiver, it could not find an abrogation of eleventh amendment immunity unless satisfied that the "threshold fact of congressional authorization to sue a class of defendants which literally includes States" had been established. [40] *Fitzpatrick* also took the clear statement tack: although he invoked *Parden*, Justice Rehnquist did not actually rely upon *Parden*'s broad rule, but rather grounded his approval of the congressional action in the fourteenth amendment's specific limitations on state sovereignty. Finally, in *Atascadero*, the Court refused to find abrogation absent "unmistakable language in the statute itself." [41]

Justice Marshall has charted yet another course. [42] On his view, the original grant of federal judicial power in article III did not authorize federal courts to entertain suits against non-consenting states; *Chisholm* was an unfortunate mistake; and the eleventh amendment was necessary to reestablish one of the bedrock political

---

38. Parden, 377 U.S. at 198–99. To the extent it held the contrary, Parden was formally overruled, 5–4, in Welch v. State Dept. of Highways and Public Transportation, 107 S.Ct. 2941, 2947–48 (1987) (state employee cannot sue state in federal court under Jones Act).

39. 411 U.S. at 285.

40. 415 U.S. at 672.

41. 473 U.S. at 243. At first blush, the Court in Hutto v. Finney, 437 U.S. 678 (1978) (permitting award of attorney's fees against the Alabama Department of Corrections in prisoners' suit under the eighth amendment and 42 U.S.C. § 1983), may appear to have retreated somewhat from the clear statement rule, but the Court's willingness to find abrogation was influenced by the particularly clear legislative history of the Civil Rights Attorney's Fee Awards Act, and by deference to the federal courts' traditional equitable power to award costs and attorney's fees. Id. at 695–96. The Court also suggested that Congress' historically demonstrable intent to abrogate the states' immunity need not be expressed in the language of the statute because the Act was enacted pursuant to Congress' enforcement powers under § 5 of the fourteenth amendment, rather than as an exercize of its article I powers. Id. at 698 n. 31. While there may be some justi-

fication for requiring a facially clearer statement of intent when Congress acts pursuant to its plenary powers under article I, but see note 28, supra, the danger of making too much turn on recitals as to which power Congress undertakes to exercise is amply illustrated by Justice Rehnquist's ingenious but implausible suggestion in dissent: He argued that Congress may not have the same enforcement powers under § 5 of the fourteenth amendment with respect to rights judicially "incorporated" into the fourteenth amendment as with respect to rights derived directly from the amendment itself. The Finney decision is also discussed in § 3–27, infra.

42. See Employees, 411 U.S. at 287 (Marshall, J., concurring). See also Edelman, 415 U.S. at 688 (Marshall, J., dissenting); Florida Dept. of Health and Rehabilitation Services v. Florida Nursing Home Ass'n, 450 U.S. at 150 (1981) (Marshall, J., dissenting). Justice Marshall did not file an opinion in Atascadero, but joined Justice Blackmun's dissent, which relied on Justice Marshall's dissenting opinion in Edelman. Justice Marshall also joined Justice Brennan's dissent, which rested on a somewhat different ground. See note 31, supra.

conceptions underlying article III.[43] Because eleventh amendment immunity thus reaffirms a right retained by the states, it can be relinquished only by "the sort of voluntary choice which we generally associate with the concept of constitutional waiver." [44] Absent such a choice, Justice Marshall would deny that even the most explicit congressional specification of state amenability to suit can empower a federal court to hear a case.[45] Justice Marshall was, however, willing to find waiver in the circumstances of *Parden* where Alabama had "legal notice" of the FELA prior to beginning its railroad operations.[46] The difficulty with Justice Marshall's position, however, is that it proves too much. For if states have a right under article III and the eleventh amendment not to be subjected to unconsented suits in federal court, then it would seem that Congress lacks the power to condition even their subsequent entry into various activities upon state forfeiture of that right, however knowing and voluntary.[47] Even a state that "chose to participate in an unconstitutionally conditioned program with its eyes wide open" [48] would presumably be protected against imposition

43. Edelman, 411 U.S. at 290–91. In discussing *Parden*, however, Justice Marshall has indicated that he may consider the eleventh amendment as a restoration of power surrendered in the original constitutional scheme. See id. at 288–89. This, of course, would mean that *Chisholm* was right, and that the eleventh amendment corralled, rather than corrected, the federal judiciary.

44. Id. at 296. Although Justice Marshall's opinion in *Employees* used the idiom of private rights, he wisely did not posit a complete congruence between state immunities and private rights, concepts at best tenuously connected.

45. Id. at 293–97. Justice Marshall argued that, although Congress could not compel a state to submit to a § 16(b) suit in a federal court, it could compel such submission in state courts. See id. at 297–98. It is not clear, however, whether Justice Marshall based his assertion that the eleventh amendment is "nothing more than a regulation of the forum," id. at 298, in which a federal-question plaintiff may sue a state, on an analysis of Congress' article I powers or on an analogy to *Testa v. Katt*, 330 U.S. 386 (1947), which established a general constitutional duty for states to vindicate federal claims in their own courts to the extent they would entertain parallel state claims. The former proposition presents no difficulty, but the latter is too sanguine a reading of *Testa*, which required state courts to award multiple damages as prescribed by federal law where state law provided for multiple damage remedies. It is well established that a state may not discriminate against federal claims. Compare *Douglas v. New York, N.H. & H.R.R.*, 279 U.S. 377 (1929) (state is not obliged to entertain nonresident's FE-

LA claim against foreign corporation where state law denies jurisdiction in similar state cause of action suits), with *McKnett v. St. Louis & S.F. Ry.*, 292 U.S. 230 (1934) (if state entertains all other suits against foreign corporations, it may not decline to hear FELA claim against foreign corporation). But Justice Marshall would apparently require state courts to entertain FLSA suits against the state whenever the state law includes an analogous wage-and-hour statute, even though state law gives no cause of action against the state itself. See 411 U.S. at 297–98 & n. 12. This clearly oversteps *Testa's* bounds: How can a state be charged with discrimination against a federal claim when it allows no suits in state courts against the sovereign?

46. 411 U.S. at 296.

47. See, e.g. *Terral v. Burke Const. Co.*, 257 U.S. 529 (1922) (corporation cannot be compelled to waive right to resort to federal courts in order to do business in state); cf. *Shapiro v. Thompson*, 394 U.S. 618 (1969) (durational residency requirement for receipt of welfare benefits invalidated as burden on right to travel); *United States v. Jackson*, 390 U.S. 570 (1968) (unconstitutional to force defendant to choose between guilty plea and trial by jury where jury, but not judge, could impose death penalty). See generally Hale, "Unconstitutional Conditions and Constitutional Rights," 35 Colum.L.Rev. 321 (1935); Note, "Unconstitutional Conditions," 73 Harv.L.Rev. 1595 (1960); Note, "Another Look at Unconstitutional Conditions", 117 U.Pa.L.Rev. 144 (1968). But see note 44, supra. See generally § 11–5, infra.

48. Edelman, 415 U.S. at 693 (Marshall J., dissenting).

of an independently offensive condition. The only ready escape from that conclusion is to deny that the state in fact has a right, in the sense that private persons have rights, against congressionally compelled amenability to suit in federal court.[49] This possibility in turn suggests a broader reformulation of the theory underlying the congressional power recognized not only by *Parden* but by all its progeny.

The only satisfying reconciliation of the cases with a conception of the eleventh amendment as either conferring a category of rights upon the states or at least confirming the states' retention of rights against unconsented suit, is to distinguish *rights conferred against the federal judiciary* from *rights conferred against Congress*. Nothing in the language or the history of the eleventh amendment suggests that it must be construed to limit congressional power under the commerce clause or under any other head of affirmative legislative authority. A better account of the relationship between the substantive lawmaking competence delegated by article I and the federal judicial power delimited by article III is available.

Article III permits federal adjudication of suits against states that are properly authorized pursuant to article I, or pursuant to another grant of lawmaking power to Congress, but article III does not of its own force abrogate whatever defense of sovereign immunity would otherwise be cognizable in federal court. Five years after *Chisholm v. Georgia*[50] had erroneously construed article III to the contrary, the eleventh amendment, in declaring that the federal "Judicial power . . . shall not be [so] construed," restored the original understanding. But in scuttling the notion that article III had the self-executing effect of abrogating state sovereign immunity in federal tribunals, the eleventh amendment carved no new limits for the permissible reach of otherwise valued federal legislation. On this view, it remains true after the eleventh amendment, just as it was true prior to *Chisholm*, that Congress, acting in accordance with its article I powers as augmented by the necessary and proper clause, or acting pursuant to the enforcement clauses of various constitutional amendments,[51] can effec-

49. Another possible alternative would be to approve enforced waiver only when the need is "compelling." Cf. Storer v. Brown, 415 U.S. 724, 728–37 (1974) (statute burdening right to vote upheld because of compelling state interest). Such an approach, however, partakes of the difficulty inherent in distinguishing between measures that are merely rationally related to achieving a legitimate federal purpose and those that are absolutely necessary. See Note, "The First Amendment Overbreadth Doctrine," 83 Harv.L.Rev. 844, 914 (1970). Moreover, a case-by-case search for "compelling" federal interests in coerced waivers of state immunity would enable the federal courts to deny sovereign immunity on the basis of their independent evaluation of federal interests; this would be tantamount to using the article III grant of federal question jurisdiction to abrogate sovereign immunity, a result against which

the eleventh amendment surely argues. See, e.g. Employees v. Department of Pub. Health & Welfare, 411 U.S. 279 (1973) (federal question jurisdiction insufficient to prevent successful plea of sovereign immunity): Duhne v. New Jersey, 251 U.S. 311 (1920) (same): Hans v. Louisiana, 134 U.S. 1, 15 (1890) (same).

50. 2 U.S. (2 Dall.) 419 (1793), discussed in § 3–25, supra.

51. U.S. Const. amend. XIII, § 2; id. amend. XIV, § 5; id. amend. XV, § 2; id. amend. XIX, cl. 2; id. amend. XXIV, § 2; id. amend. XXVI, § 2; see Katzenbach v. Morgan, 384 U.S. 641 (1966); cf. United States v. Mississippi, 380 U.S. 128 (1965) (suit in federal court by United States on behalf of individuals authorized under congressional implementation powers granted by § 2 of the fifteenth amendment).

tuate the valid substantive purposes of federal law by (1) compelling states to submit to adjudication in federal courts and/or (2) compelling states to entertain designated federal claims in their own courts.

The soundness of the approach advocated here depends in large measure upon the justifiability of treating congressional decisions to make jurisdictional inroads upon state sovereignty as different in kind from judicial decisions to do so. Such a difference in treatment is clearly not prohibited by the language of the eleventh amendment, which literally limits only the judicial power. It is also consistent with limitations on sovereignty inhering in the constitutional plan. Article I envisions that the national government will have plenary power to regulate certain subjects when, in the clearly expressed opinion of Congress, such regulation would serve the nation's interests. Moreover, as *Fitzpatrick v. Bitzer* [52] explicitly recognizes, the fourteenth amendment, also an important source of congressional power, is itself framed as a limit on state action. To the extent that sovereign immunity would free a state from such national controls, that immunity is inconsistent with the constitutional plan.[53] In addition, it has generally been perceived that the states are well represented in Congress, so that Congress will be particularly attentive to concerns of state governments as separate sovereigns.[54] Subject to whatever state sovereignty limits may be implied in the tenth amendment or elsewhere,[55] this analysis merely extends that perception into a means of assessing the proper reach of state litigational immunity in the federal system.

As a corollary, the clear statement approach of *Employees, Edelman,* and *Atascadero* [56] would be retained under the view advocat-

52. 427 U.S. 445 (1976).

53. See Parden v. Terminal Ry., 377 U.S. 184, 190, 192 (1964) (sovereign immunity would frustrate national legislation). See also Pennhurst State School & Hosp. v. Halderman (II), 465 U.S. 89, 105 (1984) ("the Young doctrine [Ex parte Young, 209 U.S. 123 (1908) (permitting prospective relief running against the states in suits against state officers), discussed in § 3–27, infra] rests on the need to promote the vindication of federal rights").

54. See Garcia v. San Antonio Metropolitan Transit Authority, 469 U.S. 528, 550–51 (1985) ("the principal means chosen by the Framers to ensure the role of the states in the federal system lies in the structure of the federal government itself"); The Federalist No. 45, at 291 (C. Rossiter ed. 1961) (J. Madison) (federal power checked by state influence over President, Senate, and House of Representatives); id., No. 46, at 296 (tendency will be for Congress to have a local bias because of state representation); Wechsler, "The Political Safeguards of Federalism: The Role of the States in the Composition and Selection of the National Government," 54 Colum.L.Rev. 543, 546 (1954). See also Cohen, "Congressional Power to Interpret

Due Process and Equal Protection," 27 Stan.L.Rev. 603 (1975) (using states' representation in Congress to justify congressional power under U.S. Const. amend. XIV, § 5, to limit state power more severely than a court implementing id. § 1); Mishkin, "Some Further Last Words on Erie—The Thread." 87 Harv.L.Rev. 1682, 1683, 1685 (1974) ("That Congress may have constitutional power to make federal law displacing state substantive policy does *not* imply an equal range of power for federal judges . . . [in part because] the states, and their interests as such, are represented in the Congress but not in the federal courts."). Even if some of the means state governments could originally employ to influence Congress are no longer available, e.g., U.S. Const. amend. XVII (state legislatures no longer choose U.S. Senators), the comparative proposition that the interests of state governments are more likely to find voice in Congress than in the other two federal branches continues to remain persuasive. See Garcia, supra, 469 U.S. at 554.

55. See §§ 5–21 to 5–23, infra.

56. Employees v. Department of Public Health & Welfare, 411 U.S. 279, 285 (1973); Edelman v. Jordan, 415 U.S. 651, 672

ed here, albeit for the somewhat different reason that courts should not abrogate state immunity unless they are sure that Congress has considered, and has clearly chosen to override, the federalism interests compromised by federal suits against states. By making a law unenforceable in federal courts against the states unless a contrary intent is apparent in the language of the statute, the clear statement rule would further ensure that attempts to limit state power will be unmistakable, thereby structuring the legislative process to allow the centrifugal forces in Congress the greatest opportunity to protect the states' interests.[57] Thus a recognition of the peculiar institutional competence of Congress in adjusting federal power relationships makes this an appropriate and useful approach to reconciling national power with state litigational immunity.[58]

Congressional power to abrogate the states' sovereign immunity is not, however, completely unfettered. Three limiting principles seem to follow from the constitutional plan. First, Congress cannot confer upon

(1974); Atascadero State Hospital v. Scanlon, 473 U.S. 234 (1985), discussed supra. See also Pennhurst State School & Hosp. v. Halderman (II), 465 U.S. 89, 99 (1984); Welch, supra note 38.

57. It is instructive that the Supreme Court has imposed such a clear statement requirement where state institutional interests would have been undermined by a judgment construing a federal statute's reach as coextensive with the commerce power. Thus, the Court has narrowly construed federal laws criminally punishing "conduct readily denounced as criminal by the States," United States v. Bass, 404 U.S. 336, 349 (1971), on the ground that, "unless Congress conveys its purposes clearly, it will not be deemed to have significantly changed the federal-state balance." Accord, United States v. Enmons, 410 U.S. 396 (1973); Rewis v. United States, 401 U.S. 808 (1971); United States v. Five Gambling Devices Labeled in Part Mills & Bearing Serial Nos. 593–221, 346 U.S. 441 (1953) (Jackson, J., plurality opinion). Similarly, the Court stated in Pennhurst State School & Hosp. v. Halderman (I), 451 U.S. 1, 17 (1981), that it will not find congressional intent to impose conditions on states participating in cooperative state-federal programs enacted under the spending clause unless Congress imposes such conditions "unambiguously:" "By insisting that Congress speak with a clear voice," the Court stated, "we enable the States to exercize their choice knowingly . . . ." Id. Once it is admitted that Congress can abrogate state sovereign immunity, a subsidiary question arises: Why must a court wait for Congress to act when Congress can always reverse what a court has done? The answer seems two-fold. First, the only operational meaning one can attribute to the concept of sovereign immunity is that, as with a political question, a court must accept another body's determination of an

issue without reweighing the substantive balance to see if the court agrees. Thus, allowing courts to "go first" would dilute the concept of immunity into virtual meaninglessness. Second, ratification by congressional silence is scarcely consistent with the considerations underlying the clear statement requirement. The point of that requirement is to make sure that state concerns are given an adequate airing in congressional processes of decision. Ex post consideration of sovereign immunity seems to depart from this attention to process, and is thus deficient, both (1) because it seems unlikely that Congress will actually take up a sovereign immunity complaint given the low emotive power of abstract sovereignty concerns, see Wechsler, supra note 54, at 547–48; and (2) because, even if sovereign immunity is considered, it seems unlikely that Congress can be persuaded to reopen debate on the policy balance struck in a program already passed in order to "fine tune" that policy with respect to the states. There is, however, one situation in which judicial abrogation of sovereign immunity, subject to congressional veto, might be justified. When a court implies a remedy under a constitutional rule that limits *both* national *and* state power (e.g., due process), it seems more likely that the court will in the first instance consider the claims of the states since those may largely parallel those of the federal government. It also seems more likely that a decision infringing state interests in such a case might be overturned by Congress because "the interests of the states and nation in removing unduly intrusive common law would overlap, thereby maximizing the 'clout' which the states enjoy in Congress." Monaghan, "The Supreme Court, 1974 Term—Foreword: Constitutional Common Law," 89 Harv.L.Rev. 1, 37 (1975).

58. See § 2–3, supra.

an article III court any authority to resolve disputes outside the textual confines of that article.[59]   Second, any congressional attempt to confer jurisdiction and abrogate immunity must be reasonably ancillary to an otherwise valid substantive exercise of federal lawmaking power. Third, the tenth amendment, although it may not delineate specific substantive limits on Congress' power to regulate the states,[60] demands recognition of the states' special constitutional role,[61] and suggests that the Supreme Court should not lightly infer serious congressional inroads upon state autonomy.   In particular, the clearer the history of state attempts to immunize institutions and activities from accountability in a federal forum, and the more onerous the restriction on state options represented by a coerced waiver of immunity,[62] the more courts should insist that Congress act in a fashion demonstrating full appreciation of the consequences for federalism.   Perhaps a sufficiently "drastic invasion of state sovereignty" [63] could be invalidated notwithstanding even the clearest possible expression of congressional purpose, but any such invalidation would rest ultimately on grounds outside the eleventh amendment.[64]

The theory suggested here would certainly lead to the same result in *Fitzpatrick*; it could have led to the same results in *Parden* and *Hutto v. Finney*,[65] in light of the relative clarity of the FELA and the proprietary character of the railroad activity involved in *Parden*, and because of the relatively clear legislative history and inherent limitations of fee awards in *Finney*. *Employees, Edelman*, and *Atascadero* probably also would yield the same results in light of the governmental character of the activities involved in the three cases and the lack of a sufficiently clear congressional statement in any of them.[66]   But in

---

59. Marbury v. Madison, 5 U.S. (1 Cranch) 137 (1803). But see National Mut. Ins. Co. v. Tidewater Transfer Co., 337 U.S. 582, 591–92 (1949) (plurality opinion) ("It is too late to hold that judicial functions incidental to Art. I powers of Congress cannot be conferred on courts existing under Art. III . . . .").

60. Garcia v. San Antonio Metropolitan Transit Authority, 469 U.S. 528 (1985). See § 5–22, infra.

61. Id. at 556.

62. The restriction on options is greatest when the state is put to the choice, as it would have been in Employees, between being dragooned into federal court by a private party and "ceasing operation of . . . vital [preexisting] public services," Employees v. Department of Pub. Health & Welfare, 411 U.S. 279, 296 (1973) (Marshall, J., concurring). These concerns are often encapsulated in the labels "sovereign" and "proprietary", see, e.g., Fry v. United States, 421 U.S. 542, 549 (1975) (Rehnquist, J., dissenting); Employees v. Department of Pub. Health & Welfare, 411 U.S. at 284–85, but unfortunately the boundary between the proprietary and the sovereign is both difficult to mark conceptually and difficult to locate over time. Indeed, the Court in Garcia v. San Antonio Metropolitan Transit Authority, 469 U.S. 528 (1985), rejected this distinction as an "unworkable" basis for limiting Congress' power to regulate states under commerce clause enactments. However, if this guideline is used not as a limit on congressional power to abrogate eleventh amendment immunity, but as a factor to be considered in determining how clearly Congress must express its purpose to abrogate state immunity with respect to the activity in question, the indefinite nature of the distinction might be less problematic.

63. Fry, 421 U.S. at 547–48 n. 7.

64. See § 5–23, infra.

65. 437 U.S. 678 (1978), discussed in note 41, supra.

66. Employees, however, permitted the Secretary of Labor to bring suit for back pay on behalf of aggrieved employees. The Court strangely did not apply the same standard of clear statement to language in the FLSA authorizing suit by the Secretary as it did to language providing for private damage actions. The Court may have assumed that such suits were automatically

other situations the theory could well produce different results from those indicated by a search for constructive waiver; [67] it would comport better with the notion that waivers of constitutional rights cannot be demanded as a condition of receiving a government benefit; and it seems more faithful to the history of the eleventh amendment itself.[68]

§ 3–27. The Limits of the Eleventh Amendment: The Significance of Ex parte Young

As the previous discussion noted in passing, although the eleventh amendment does ordinarily bar federal courts from ordering states as defendants to give monetary relief,[1] it does not ordinarily prevent federal courts, even in the absence of express congressional authorization, from requiring states, through their officers, to comply with prospective federal injunctions. This distinction is accomplished by fiction: an injunction, so the courts say, simply requires a state officer to act within the scope of his duty; the injunction's prohibitory force, therefore, is felt only when an officer exceeds the scope of his powers, and thus is not acting on behalf of the state; the state, therefore, is not affected by the federal injunction. The leading case is Ex parte Young.[2] There, the Supreme Court held that the eleventh amendment's partial recognition of state sovereign immunity did not bar a federal injunction restraining a state attorney general from enforcing a state law violative of the fourteenth amendment due process clause. The Court's theory was that, if it is a state officer who acts unconstitutionally, and not the state itself, the officer cannot claim the state's sovereign immunity: "[The] use of the name of the State to enforce an unconstitutional act . . . is a proceeding without . . . authority . . . which does not

authorized because suits by the United States are not within the ban of the eleventh amendment, but it does seem anomalous that when a state brings suit on behalf of individuals (rather than in its sovereign capacity), the suit is barred, but is not barred when the federal government undertakes a similar enterprise.

67. This interpretation of the eleventh amendment suggests that the doctrine of Smith v. Reeves, 178 U.S. 436 (1900), be reconsidered. In Smith, the Court held that the eleventh amendment allowed a state to consent to suit in its own courts but to retain eleventh amendment immunity in federal courts. This doctrine has been applied in later cases without consideration of the qualifications imposed in Smith—that the legislation waiving sovereign immunity not evince any hostility toward the federal government, and that it not trench upon any federal right, see id. at 445. See, e.g., Murray v. Wilson Distilling Co., 213 U.S. 151, 172 (1909). If the eleventh amendment stands for no more than the proposition that article III is not a self-executing abrogation of state sovereign immunity, then the amendment alone should provide no justification for a state consent which discriminates against a fed-

eral instrumentality. Cf. United States v. Detroit, 355 U.S. 466, 473–74 (1958) (dictum) (state may not discriminate against United States in setting tax rates); Chicago & N.W. Railway Co. v. Whitton's Adm'r, 80 U.S. (13 Wall.) 270 (1871) (state may not restrict general wrongful death cause of action to state courts). As was recognized in Smith itself, however, other factors— such as the necessities of administering a state tax system—may negate any inference of hostility, thereby validating the state's partial consent.

68. See Nowak, "The Scope of Congressional Power to Create Causes of Action Against State Governments and the History of the Eleventh and Fourteenth Amendments," 75 Colum.L.Rev. 1413 (1975). See also § 3–25, note 8, supra.

§ 3–27

1. But see Hutto v. Finney, 437 U.S. 678 (1978) (affirming federal court's award of attorney's fees, to be paid out of the state's Department of Corrections funds, on the ground that the monetary relief was ancillary to the court's power to impose injunctive relief).

2. 209 U.S. 123 (1908).

affect the State in its sovereign or governmental capacity. It is simply an illegal act upon the part of a state official in attempting to use the name of the State to enforce a legislative enactment which is void because unconstitutional." [3]

3. 209 U.S. at 159. Although the idea that a state officer who acts unconstitutionally does so personally and not on behalf of the state is the idea which today is most closely associated with Ex parte Young, the passage quoted in text does not appear until the close of the opinion, at a point at which it is apparent that the Court is tying up loose ends. Indeed, the notion that the government is not responsible for actions of its agents which are ultra vires is commonplace in sovereign immunity doctrine, was mentioned frequently in nineteenth century cases, see, e.g., In re Ayers, 123 U.S. 443, 500–01 (1887), and is one of the principal creations of nineteenth century sovereign immunity law. See Engdahl, "Immunity and Accountability for Positive Governmental Wrongs," 44 U.Colo.L.Rev. 1, 14–21 (1972). In Pennhurst State School & Hospital v. Halderman, 465 U.S. 89 (1984) (Pennhurst II), Justice Stevens, joined by Justices Marshall, Brennan, and Blackmun, dissented from the majority's holding that the eleventh amendment barred federal courts from issuing injunctions against state officers based on violations of state law. The dissent argued that traditional ultra vires principles relied upon in Ex parte Young and its progeny clearly contradicted the majority's position. Justice Powell, writing for the majority, not only accused the dissent of an unprecedented, over-broad reading of ultra vires doctrine, but questioned "the continued vitality of the ultra vires doctrine in the Eleventh Amendment context." Id. at 114 n. 25.

It has been suggested that Ex parte Young's innovation, see 209 U.S. at 166, lay in the "body of unwritten federal law which the Supreme Court [was] newly developing in the light of felt exigencies of effective constitutional administration." P. Bator, P. Mishkin, D. Shapiro, and H. Wechsler, Hart and Wechsler's The Federal Courts and the Federal System 935 (2d ed. 1973). On this view, Ex parte Young "abandoned the use of general principles of common-law liability as the measure of the content of this judicially created federal equitable cause of action" and instead implied a right of action under the Constitution itself, in this case the fourteenth amendment. Id. This theory, as will become apparent, does recognize the innovation, but incorrectly identifies the innovation's precise direction.

One may begin by noting that Justice Peckham's working premise in Ex parte Young was the same one upon which Chief Justice Marshall ultimately relied in Osborn v. Bank of the United States, 22 U.S. (9 Wheat.) 738 (1824): whether an action is that of an individual officer or the state depends upon whether the injury of which plaintiff complains was done by the officer or the state. In Osborn, Marshall applied common law forms of action (trespass, detinue, etc.) to determine whether the acts complained of were those of the officer or of the state. See id. at 853–54, 858. Osborn is best remembered for its holding that the eleventh amendment applies only if the state is a party of record. See id. at 857. After disposing of the eleventh amendment, however, Marshall did not drop the question of responsibility, but restated it in terms of whether the state officers should be held liable or dismissed as only nominal parties. See id. at 858–59. By contrast, in Young, Peckham did not invoke the forms of action to identify the responsible party. The injury which he attributed to Young, the state attorney general, was the threat of criminal prosecution. Perhaps this injury could have been assimilated to a common law category, but Peckham proceeded otherwise, establishing Young's responsibility through an analysis of his statutory and common law obligations under state law. See 209 U.S. at 160–61. It is in Peckham's way of distinguishing the leading contrary cases that the similarity of his approach to that of Marshall becomes clear. Peckham distinguished In re Ayers, supra, on the ground that, if the Court there had enjoined the state lawsuits which plaintiff sought to halt, plaintiff would have succeeded in holding the state to a contract it had entered into with plaintiff; thus the real injury at issue was not the commencement of suit by the officers but the breach of contract by the state. See 209 U.S. at 152. In Fitts v. McGhee, 172 U.S. 516 (1899), Peckham said, the prosecutions at issue were not brought under the statute plaintiff sought to challenge; the prosecutors had no responsibility for enforcing the challenged statute, and were thus merely nominal parties; the controversy plaintiff raised was not with them. See id. at 156–57. In Ex parte Young, Peckham thus broke with traditional common law categories, establishing the state prosecutor as responsible for the individual's injury by resort to *state positive law*. But Peckham did not treat this connection as a constitutional one: his federal question analysis

"State action" is thus more narrowly defined for the procedural purpose of delimiting the scope of a state's eleventh amendment immunity from judicial interference than for the substantive purpose of making federal constitutional provisions apply.[4] If the notion that a state official who is acting unconstitutionally is not acting with state authority for purposes of the eleventh amendment were to be applied to such constitutional provisions governing state action as the fourteenth amendment, a difficult dilemma would be presented. For if illegal "acts of state officials . . . could not be treated as acts of the state within the Fourteenth Amendment . . . until, by final action of an appropriate state court, it was decided that such acts were [in fact] authorized by the state,"[5] then the very circumstance making something state action for purposes of the fourteenth amendment would immunize it from redress by virtue of the eleventh amendment. That result would have left the fourteenth amendment as a purely defensive weapon rather than a potential source of affirmative relief against state infringements upon federal rights.

Despite its evident necessity, *Ex parte Young*'s theory remains a fiction, and not only from the perspective of substantive constitutional law; more importantly, it is fictional from the point of view of the sovereign immunity principle, and thus from the perspective of the eleventh amendment itself. Compliance with a federal injunction always puts some burden upon a state. A state may have to abandon a legislative program; on occasion, as in the school desegregation or contract clause contexts, the state may have to increase its expenditures substantially. To the extent, therefore, that the eleventh amendment reflects the proposition that federal courts, in the absence of specific congressional authorization, should not burden state governments, *Ex parte Young*'s restriction of the amendment's application leaves a fundamental constitutional policy unsatisfied.

The Court has itself manifested discomfort with *Ex parte Young*'s imperfect reflection of the state sovereign immunity principles that at least a majority of the Court believes were constitutionalized by the eleventh amendment.[6] It is clear that neither a requirement that the plaintiff name a state official (but not the state) as defendant, nor a

---

and cause of action analysis were quite distinct, compare id. at 143–45 with id. at 149–68, and his analysis of the federal question issue suggests that he did not regard an action directly under the Constitution as particularly novel. See id. at 144. Instead, the issue appears to have been one of equity, one which today would be treated as a question of standing. In finding standing, Peckham did innovate, but it would appear that his innovation lay in his escape from common law categories to state law, cf. Chicago Junction Case, 264 U.S. 258 (1924), and not in any reference to the Constitution.

4. See Chapter 18, infra.

5. Home Tel. & Tel. Co. v. Los Angeles, 227 U.S. 278, 282 (1913).

6. Although the Court has not always clearly identified the nature of the eleventh amendment bar, its most recent pronouncements suggest that the Court reads the amendment as a constitutionalization of state sovereign immunity. See, e.g., Pennhurst State School & Hospital v. Halderman (II), 465 U.S. 89 (1984); Green v. Mansour, 106 S.Ct. 423 (1985) (notice relief and declaratory judgment prohibited absent a continuing violation of federal law which can be enjoined by a federal court).

At the same time, the Court's most recent cases tend to treat Ex parte Young not simply as a jurisdictional fiction but as part of a basic recognition that, insofar as decisions of the early 1860s (and earlier) deemed the federal judiciary to be without power to compel state officers to perform

rule that the plaintiff receive relief only for that which can be articulated in an injunctive order, would substantially protect state treasuries. Recognizing that an expansive reading of *Young* would undercut much of the eleventh amendment's protective value, the Court in *Edelman v. Jordan* [7] struck down an injunction which ordered state officials to release benefits which had been illegally withheld from recipients of a federal-state aid program. Rejecting the Court of Appeals' characterization of the injunction as an exercise of "equitable restitution" consistent with the eleventh amendment, the Court drew a distinction between prospective and retroactive injunctive relief. According to the Court, the principle of *Young* applied only to prospective injunctive relief. Since the injunction in *Edelman* addressed past violations of federal law, and ordered disbursement of funds illegally withheld in the past, it was tantamount to a direct money judgment against the state. Thus, as an instance of retroactive relief, the injunction violated the eleventh amendment.

Edelman's distinction between prospective and retroactive relief continues at the center of the court's eleventh amendment jurisprudence. In *Hutto v. Finney*,[8] the Court upheld an award of attorney's fees, to be paid out of funds of the state's Department of Corrections, in part on the theory that the eleventh amendment does not limit the array of enforcement powers which are ancillary to the federal courts' power to impose injunctive relief.[9] The lawsuit in *Hutto v. Finney* followed earlier judicial proceedings in which a federal court had determined that conditions in the Arkansas penal system violated the eighth amendment. The district court based its award of attorney's fees upon a finding that state officials had acted in "bad faith" in their official capacities when they failed to cure the violations identified in the earlier litigation. The Supreme Court considered the award to be analogous to a remedial fine for civil contempt since it vindicated the district court's authority over a recalcitrant litigant. Since this relief gave content to the district court's power to issue prospective injunctive relief against state officials, the Court categorized it as ancillary relief beyond eleventh amendment challenge.[10]

duties under the United States Constitution—see, e.g., Kentucky v. Dennison, 65 U.S. (24 How.) 66 (1861) (federal courts may not compel states to perform their duty under extradition clause, art. IV, § 2, cl. 2, to deliver up fugitives upon proper demand)—those early decisions were "the product of another time" and rested on a "conception of the relation between the States and the Federal Government . . . fundamentally incompatible with more than a century of constitutional development." Puerto Rico v. Branstad, 107 S.Ct. 2802, 2809 (1987) (overruling Kentucky v. Dennison). See id. at 2808, treating Ex parte Young as reflecting the "settled principle that federal courts may enjoin unconstitutional action by state officials."

7. 415 U.S. 651 (1974).

8. 437 U.S. 678 (1978). See § 3–26, note 41, supra.

9. Id. at 689–93.

10. "The line between retroactive and prospective relief cannot be so rigid that it defeats the effective enforcement of prospective relief," id. at 690. Only Justice Rehnquist, joined by Justice White, dissented from this part of the holding. Id. at 714–717. The Court also rejected an objection to the "form" of the district court's order; the district court's direction that the award be paid out of Department funds was not reversible error. Id. at 692–693.

In Quern v. Jordan, 440 U.S. 332 (1979), the Court again faced the issue of whether relief ordered by a federal court constituted "permissible prospective relief or a retroactive award which requires the pay-

While the prospective/retroactive distinction and its emphasis on the nature of the relief has been prominent in the Court's analysis, another line of cases makes clear that, although *Edelman* narrowed *Young* and its progeny, it did not necessarily repudiate *Young's* theoretical underpinnings. *Cory v. White* [11] reaffirmed an earlier precedent which held that a suit nominally against a state officer would be considered a suit against the state in the absence of an allegation that the state officer had violated either state or federal law. The holding in *Cory* connects with the theory in *Young* that suits which require state officers to act in compliance with the law cannot be viewed as suits against the state insofar as the injunction's force is felt only when an officer exceeds the scope of his power, and thus is not acting on behalf of the state. *Cory* demonstrated that, in distinguishing permissible suits against state officers from impermissible suits against the state itself, *Edelman* had not meant to abandon entirely the *Young* fiction in favor of a functional test concerned solely with the nature of the relief requested by the plaintiff.[12] But if this much was clear after *Cory*, the Court had not explained when it would choose to emphasize the functional approach of *Edelman*, and when it would instead rely primarily on the ultra vires logic of *Young* and its progeny.[13]

The presence of two strands in eleventh amendment jurisprudence—one preoccupied with the nature of the relief and the other

ment of funds from the state treasury," id. at 346–47. After the Supreme Court remand in Edelman v. Jordan, 415 U.S. 651 (1974), the district court directed state officials to send members of the plaintiff class notice informing them that they were entitled to pursue state proceedings to receive public assistance which had been improperly withheld from them in the past. Although it regarded this particular form of notice relief as contrary to the eleventh amendment, the Court of Appeals modified the district court's order, suggesting that state officials could lawfully be directed to send a "mere explanatory notice" that a state administrative apparatus was available which would determine whether benefits had been improperly withheld. In Quern, the Supreme Court upheld the notice relief, as modified by the Court of Appeals, against eleventh amendment attack.

As in Hutto, the Court concluded that the relief approved by the Court of Appeals was "more properly viewed as ancillary to the prospective relief already ordered by the court" than as an award of retroactive benefits. Id. at 349. Although the availability of notice relief was narrowed somewhat in Green v. Mansour, note 6, supra, the Court continues to subscribe to the principle that relief which can be successfully characterized as "ancillary" to an exercise of prospective relief is not barred by the eleventh amendment—even if the ancillary relief directly burdens the state

treasury (as in Hutto) or addresses past violations of federal law (as in Quern). This doctrinal possibility of ancillary relief suggests that a fair measure of play remains in the Young fiction even after the narrowing the Court performed in Edelman.

11. 457 U.S. 85 (1982).

12. "Edelman did not hold that suits against state officers who are not alleged to be acting against federal or state law are permissible under the eleventh amendment if only prospective relief is sought," id. at 91.

13. For another example of an ultra vires approach, see Florida Department of State v. Treasure Salvors, Inc., 458 U.S. 670 (1982) (process issued by a federal district court to secure possession of property from state officials in an admiralty in rem action not barred by eleventh amendment). Justice Stevens, writing for a plurality of the Court, asserted that the logic of Ex parte Young governed the case. Since the state officials lacked a colorable claim to possession of the artifacts, their possession was ultra vires. Accordingly, the federal court could direct the officials to surrender possession of the artifacts without violating the eleventh amendment. Justice Stevens reiterated that suits against state officers acting beyond their statutory authority would not be considered suits against the state for purposes of the eleventh amendment. Id. at 696–97.

centered on the scope of authorized action—contributed by the early 1980s to a growing sense that the Court's analysis in this area was incoherent, technical, and removed from first principles. And indeed it was. The Court had realized that, without some narrowing of the ultra vires reasoning spun out in *Young*, the states would, in practice, be left defenseless because of the broad range of actions against the state which could be reformulated as suits against state officers for injunctive relief. But although the need to narrow *Young* was apparent, the Court had accomplished that objective by drawing a prospective/retroactive line that did not smoothly comport with the traditional ultra vires concepts which, however tenuously, provided the rationale for the holding in *Ex parte Young*. Although fictional, the *Young* rule could claim some grounding in traditional sovereign immunity principles.[14] After *Edelman* this grounding was eroded, leaving the Court even more vulnerable to the charge that its approach toward these issues rested on arbitrary, ad hoc line-drawing rather than principled elaboration.

It was in this context that the Court rendered perhaps its most significant eleventh amendment decision since *Ex parte Young*. *Pennhurst State School & Hospital* v. *Halderman* (II)[15] attempted to furnish the rigorous conceptual framework that had been conspiciously absent in the Court's decisions since *Edelman*. Justice Powell announced the sharply split, 5–4 decision. He set out to show that *Young* and *Edelman* had not been exercises in arbitrary line-drawing, but rather struck the proper balance between the state sovereignty principles embodied in the eleventh amendment and the vindication of federal rights envisioned in the constitutional plan.[16] Having cast *Young* and *Edelman* in these terms, Justice Powell concluded that an allegation that a state officer had violated state law would not suffice to remove the eleventh amendment bar—since, without a violation of federal law, there was no federal constitutional predicate for limiting the eleventh amendment immunity. Moreover, even if plaintiff's state law claims were brought into federal court under pendent jurisdiction, the majority concluded that the eleventh amendment prohibited a federal court from issuing injunctions against state officers based on state law violations.[17] In short, the *Young* fiction would apply only if plaintiff could successfully demonstrate that a state officer had violated federal law.[18]

---

14. See note 3, supra.

15. 465 U.S. 89 (1984).

16. In Green v. Mansour, 474 U.S. 64 (1985), the Court explicitly formulated its eleventh amendment inquiry as involving a balance between the supremacy clause and the eleventh amendment.

17. 465 U.S. at 121. The Court acknowledged that its holding might have unsavory "policy" ramifications since plaintiffs would be required to bifurcate their claims, bringing state claims in state court and federal claims in federal court. The Court responded with the observation that "considerations of policy cannot override the constitutional limitation on the

authority of the federal judiciary to adjudicate suits against a state." Id. at 123.

18. Justice Powell also addressed the dissent's elaborately documented claim that the majority had overruled a significant body of case law and wilfully misread ultra vires doctrine. Justice Powell labeled the dissent's approach a "fiction" and "wrong on the law". 465 U.S. at 106. However, the dissent's position probably adheres more closely to the Court's earlier understanding of ultra vires than does the majority's gloss. At the very least, the holding in Pennhurst (II) dramatically expands the restrictive reading of ultra vires doctrine in Larson v. Domestic & Foreign

Although *Pennhurst* has received anything but a warm reception from most quarters of the academic community, one can identify aspects of the holding which would probably elicit favorable reactions from many audiences. For example, the Court faced the fact that the *Young* fiction had become even more attenuated after *Edelman* and subsequent decisions. A reconceptualization was needed, and the Court responded. Furthermore, the Court acknowledged, as it had in the past that the measure of state sovereignty afforded by the eleventh amendment was limited by other elements of the constitutional plan—namely, the supremacy of federal law.

What is much less clear is whether *Pennhurst* described a balance between competing constitutional values that can be justified in terms of the language and history of the eleventh amendment and the Court's own understanding of that amendment. On this score, the decision is far less satisfying. By severely restricting the scope of ultra vires doctrine, Justice Powell effectively transformed the eleventh amendment into an absolute bar against federal court jurisdiction.[19] According to *Pennhurst*, the *Young* and *Edelman* decisions reflect limitations on this bar that are derived from other parts of the constitutional scheme, not from within the amendment itself. Whatever might be said about such a reading of the eleventh amendment, the idea that the amendment stands for a broad, unqualified immunity that is restrained only by other parts of the Constitution conflicts with the majority's own explanation of the amendment as a constitutionalization of state sovereign immunity principles, principles which themselves were never so broad and unqualified as to constitute an internally absolute bar against all actions where the state might be considered the real party in interest.

In light of these inconsistencies, the need for a reexamination of the Court's fundamental premises about the eleventh amendment has never been more pressing. The interpretation of the amendment offered above in § 3–26 promises a more coherent approach—one which squares with the text of the amendment, with the clear statement principle to which the Court has attached so much weight in its constructive waiver doctrine, and with the values of state sovereignty which the Court has emphasized in its recent decisions.

§ 3–28. Judicial Federalism: The Twin Policies of Preserving the Integrity of State Law and Respecting the Institutional Autonomy of State Judicial Systems

Many of the topics previously addressed in this chapter are important to the moderation of conflict between the federal and state judiciaries and to preventing federal courts from intruding excessively on

Commerce Corp., 337 U.S. 682 (1949). See generally, Shapiro, "Wrong Turns: The Eleventh Amendment and the Pennhurst Case," 98 Harv.L.Rev. 61 (1984) (highly critical of the Pennhurst decision); but cf. Althouse, "How to Build a Separate Sphere: Federal Courts and State Power," 100 Harv.L.Rev. 1485, 1512–37 (1985).

19. The majority went so far as to suggest that ultra vires doctrine might ultimately be abandoned altogether. See 465 U.S. at 114 n. 25.

the constitutional role of the states.[1] The evolution of these doctrines today is guided in large part by the Supreme Court's renewed emphasis on what may be termed "judicial federalism"—a view that federal courts must regard their power as tempered by a keen appreciation of the essential role of the states and their judicial systems in our constitutional universe.[2] The rhetoric and result of judicial federalism is perhaps best exemplified by the rather amorphous "abstention" doctrines, defining exceptions to "the virtually unflagging obligation of the federal courts to exercise the jurisdiction given them"[3] by requiring them to abstain in certain cases where necessary to promote the integrity of state law and respect the autonomy of state judicial officers.[4]

The Supreme Court has developed, without express congressional approval,[5] three distinct forms of abstention, which bear the names of early cases in each area.[6] The first two abstention doctrines evince a desire to limit federal-court interpretation of ambiguous state law where special concerns are present. In brief, under *"Pullman"*[7] abstention, "federal courts should abstain from decision when difficult and unsettled questions of state law must be resolved before a substantial federal constitutional question can be decided"; such abstention avoids "both unnecessary adjudication of federal questions and 'needless friction with state policies'" from possibly erroneous state law interpretation."[8] Animated by a similar concern is the requirement that litigants generally exhaust state administrative remedies prior to seeking federal court review.[9] A second, somewhat related abstention doctrine, only vaguely developed and of far less practical significance, does not require the presence of a federal constitutional question but rather counsels federal courts to abstain in cases where decision of state

§ 3–28

1. See especially §§ 3–5 (statutory limitations on federal jurisdiction); 3–10 (ripeness); 3–14 to 3–21 (standing); 3–23 (power to make federal common law); 3–24 ("independent and adequate state grounds" doctrine and particularly the limits on habeas corpus review); and 3–25 to 3–27 (eleventh amendment), supra.

2. For commentary favorable of this development see, e.g., Bator, "The State Courts and Federal Constitutional Litigation," 22 Wm. & Mary L.Rev. 605 (1981); O'Connor, "Our Judicial Federalism," 35 Case W.L.Rev. 1 (1984); Shapiro, "Jurisdiction and Discretion," 60 N.Y.U.L.Rev. 543 (1985). For critical commentary, see, e.g., Neuborne, "The Myth of Parity," 90 Harv. L.Rev. 1105 (1977); Weinberg, "The New Judicial Federalism," 29 Stan.L.Rev. 1191 (1977), and "The New Judicial Federalism: Where We Are Now," 19 Ga.L.Rev. 1075 (1985); Wisdom, "Foreword: The Ever-Whirling Wheels of American Federalism," 59 Notre Dame L.Rev. 1063, 1069–78 (1984).

3. Colorado River Water Conservation Dist. v. United States, 424 U.S. 800, 817 (1976).

4. For a brief survey of the doctrines, see note 10, infra; §§ 3–29 and 3–30, infra. For a more detailed review, see C. Wright, A. Miller & E. Cooper, 17 Federal Practice and Procedure §§ 4241 to 4255 (1978 and Supp. 1987); M. Redish, Federal Jurisdiction: Tensions in the Allocation of Judicial Power 233–321 (1980).

5. For commentary addressing the validity of the Court's independent development of abstention doctrine, see § 3–30, infra, note 18.

6. See Colorado River Water Conservation Dist. v. United States, 424 U.S. 800, 813–17 (1976).

7. Railroad Comm'n of Texas v. Pullman Co., 312 U.S. 496 (1941).

8. Hawaii Housing Auth. v. Midkiff, 467 U.S. 229, 236 (1984), quoting id. at 500. See also § 3–29, infra.

9. See § 3–29, infra.

law issues would intrude greatly on especially important state interests considered particularly well-suited to state court consideration.[10]

The abstention doctrine that most directly promotes judicial federalism and has the broadest potential scope is *"Younger"* [11] abstention, designed to help preserve the institutional autonomy of state judicial processes by limiting attempts by litigants to obtain federal declaratory or injunctive relief on constitutional grounds where such relief may interfere with certain types of ongoing state proceedings they are involved in, and where the state proceedings provide an adequate opportunity to raise the constitutional claims.[12] Such interference is doubly offensive: it not only hinders state efforts to maintain a smoothly running judicial system but also denies the principle of comity—the fundamental premise of judicial federalism which holds that, since both federal and state courts have a duty to enforce the Constitution, there is no constitutional basis, in the absence of some infirmity in the state judicial process itself, for preferring federal courts to state courts as adjudicators of federal constitutional claims.[13]

These twin considerations are relevant not only in the context of federal district court injunctive or declaratory relief against unconstitutional state action, but also in the context of Supreme Court review of

10. See Colorado River Water Conservation Dist. v. United States, 424 U.S. 800, 814 (1976). The major but still relatively little-used form of this abstention doctrine is known as "Burford" abstention, after Burford v. Sun Oil Co., 319 U.S. 315 (1943), which involved federal review of a complex state regulatory scheme. See also Alabama Pub. Serv. Comm'n v. Southern Ry. Co., 341 U.S. 341 (1951). Burford abstention is said to apply where federal review of a state question "in a case and in similar cases would be disruptive of state efforts to establish a coherent policy with respect to a matter of substantial public concern," Colorado River, supra, 424 U.S. at 814, but its rationale and operation are unclear. See generally Comment, "Abstention by Federal Courts in Suits Challenging State Administrative Decisions: The Scope of the Burford Doctrine," 46 U.Chi.L.Rev. 971 (1979); see also Wells, "Why Professor Redish is Wrong About Abstention," 19 Ga. L.Rev. 1097, 1115–18 (1985). Another form of this doctrine, sometimes referred to as "Thibodaux" abstention, see Louisiana Power & Light Co. v. Thibodaux, 360 U.S. 25 (1959), applies in cases presenting "difficult questions of state law bearing on policy problems of substantial public import whose importance transcends the result in the case then at bar." Colorado River, supra, 424 U.S. at 814. For a comparison of the Burford and Thibodaux variants, see id. at 815 n. 21; see also Comment, supra, at 978–79 n. 43, 992–95.

A final doctrine, termed "abstention" by some commentators but not viewed as such

by the Supreme Court because it does not rest on "considerations of state-federal comity or on avoidance of constitutional decisions," see Moses H. Cone Memorial Hosp. v. Mercury Construction Co., 460 U.S. 1, 14–15 (1983), is that established by Colorado River. It allows a federal court, in certain exceptional circumstances, to decline exercise of its jurisdiction in favor of a concurrent state proceeding to ameliorate the effects of duplicative jurisdiction. See Colorado River, supra, 424 U.S. at 817–20; Moses H. Cone, supra, 460 U.S. at 15–19. See generally Note, "Preclusion Concerns as an Additional Factor When Staying a Federal Suit in Deference to a Concurrent State Proceeding," 53 Fordham L.Rev. 1183 (1985).

11. Younger v. Harris, 401 U.S. 37 (1971).

12. See § 3–30, infra.

13. See generally Wells, "The Role of Comity in the Law of Federal Courts," 60 N.Car.L.Rev. 59 (1981). For representative expressions of the value of comity, see, e.g., Younger v. Harris, 401 U.S. 37, 43–45, 52–53 (1971); Bator, supra note 2; O'Connor, supra note 2. For especially trenchant criticism of its applications, see Fair Assessment in Real Estate Ass'n, 454 U.S. 100, 117–25 (Brennan, J., concurring in the judgment); Neuborne, supra note 2; Redish, "The Doctrine of Younger v. Harris: Deference in Search of a Rationale," 63 Cornell L.Rev. 463 (1978).

state court decisions. Like the federal district courts, the Supreme Court can mistakenly construe ambiguous state law and, by hearing a case that has not yet finished its progress through the state judicial system, can disrupt the processes of that system and violate the premises of comity. At least in theory, however, the statutory requirement of a final judgment which conditions the Supreme Court's jurisdiction to review state court decisions,[14] as well as the Court's own discretionary powers,[15] protect the Court from itself sinning against federalism values. Accordingly, the Court's chief doctrinal concern has focused on controlling lower federal courts.

§ 3–29. Preserving the Integrity of State Law: Exhaustion of State Administrative Remedies and Pullman Abstention

As noted previously,[1] the first policy strain animating abstention doctrine is the protection of the integrity of state law from potentially erroneous or highly intrusive federal judicial scrutiny. This concern arose initially in the context of whether litigants alleging state infringement of constitutional rights should be required to ask the state for relief before turning to the federal courts. Such litigants, as a general matter, are not required to exhaust state judicial remedies.[2]

---

14. Under 28 U.S.C. § 1257, the Supreme Court may review only state judgments which are "[f]inal judgments or decrees rendered by the highest court of a State in which a decision could be had." To meet this requirement, a state court decision must be "final" rather than "intermediate" in two senses. First, the decision must be subject to no further review or correction in any other state tribunal," Market St. Ry. v. Railroad Comm'n, 324 U.S. 548, 551 (1945). If further appellate review is possible, it must be sought even if the reviewing court may deny review on discretionary grounds, see, e.g., Gotthilf v. Sills, 375 U.S. 79, 80 (1963) (per curiam). But cf. Market St. Ry., supra. Second, the state court decision must also be "an effective determination of the litigation and not of merely interlocutory or intermediate steps," id. at 551, and must ordinarily encompass all the issues involved in the case. See, e.g., Republic Natural Gas Co. v. Oklahoma, 334 U.S. 62, 68 (1948). Whether a judgment is final under the applicable state law is relevant, but not controlling; the ultimate result turns on the Court's interpretation of the finality requirement as embodied by § 1257. See Richfield Oil Corp. v. State Bd. of Equalization, 329 U.S. 69, 72 (1946); Department of Banking v. Pink, 317 U.S. 264, 268 (1942). For further elaboration of the doctrine, see R. Stern, E. Gressman & S. Shapiro, Supreme Court Practice 120–39 (6th ed. 1986); Note, "The Finality Rule for Supreme Court Review of State Court Orders," 91 Harv.L.Rev. 1004 (1978). Section 1257's finality requirement

"serves several ends: (1) it avoids piecemeal review by federal courts of state court decisions; (2) it avoids giving advisory opinions in cases where there may be no real 'case' or 'controversy' in the sense of art. III; (3) it limits federal review of state court determinations of federal constitutional issues to leave at a minimum federal intrusion in state affairs." North Dakota State Bd. of Pharmacy v. Snyder's Drug Stores, Inc., 414 U.S. 156, 159 (1973). With these policies in mind the Court has been willing to develop pragmatic exceptions to the finality requirement to protect important federal interests, see Bradley v. Richmond School Bd., 416 U.S. 696, 722–23 n. 28 (1974): allowing, for example, speedy adjudication of separate and independent matters too important to await eventual appellate review, see National Socialist Party v. Skokie, 432 U.S. 43 (1977), and adjudication of federal issues where future state proceedings will not affect their nature or might prevent their review, see Cox Broadcasting Corp. v. Cohn, 420 U.S. 469, 479–85 (1975). On exceptions generally, see R. Stern, E. Gressman & S. Shapiro, supra, at 122–33.

15. See § 3–8, supra.

§ 3–29

1. See § 3–28, supra.

2. Some federal statutes require such exhaustion, most prominently the federal habeas corpus statute, 28 U.S.C. § 2254, see § 3–24, supra. Preiser v. Rodriguez, 411 U.S. 475 (1973). See also 28 U.S.C.

The Supreme Court rejected such an exhaustion requirement first as a matter of "state action" law [3] and second as a matter of statutory law under 42 U.S.C. § 1983,[4] the primary federal statute making constitutional violations by state officials federally actionable.[5] The Court has nonetheless held that litigants must first exhaust state administrative remedies,[6] unless they are suing under § 1983,[7] and such exhaustion may sometimes require litigants to resort to state courts if they participate in the state administrative process in a lawmaking capacity.[8]

A primary purpose of the exhaustion requirement is to ensure that a litigant's representations as to the content of allegedly unconstitutional state legislative action are in fact correct: "[i]t seems . . . only a just recognition of the solicitude with which the [litigant's] rights have been guarded [by the State] that [the litigant] should make sure that the State in its final . . . action would not respect what they think their rights to be, before resorting to the courts of the United States." [9] Absent such assurance, it is not clear that the litigant needs judicial relief at all. However, the exhaustion requirement cannot ensure final elaboration of the meaning of ambiguous policy in the large number of lawsuits brought under § 1983, given the exception constructed by the Supreme Court for such cases. But this purpose is now advanced by another mechanism that has supplanted the exhaustion requirement in importance, one which is both broader and more finely tuned: *"Pullman"* abstention.

In *Railroad Commission of Texas v. Pullman Co.*,[10] the Supreme Court held that a federal district court erred in *immediately* granting the injunctive relief sought by Pullman porters who had claimed that a Texas regulation, requiring Pullman sleeping cars previously under the supervision of black porters to be placed under the care of white conductors, violated the equal protection clause of the fourteenth amendment. Noting that if "there was no warrant in state law" for the regulation, then "the constitutional issue does not arise," and that any federal examination of the state law question could necessarily give only "a tentative answer which may be displaced tomorrow by a state adjudication," the Court found the "resources of equity . . . equal to

§§ 1341 (state-tax collections), 1342 (utility-rate orders).

3. Home Tel. & Tel. Co. v. Los Angeles, 227 U.S. 278 (1913), discussed in § 18–4, infra.

4. Monroe v. Pape, 365 U.S. 167 (1961). Chief Justice Rehnquist has urged imposition of an exhaustion requirement where the state can demonstrate an adequate judicial remedy is available. See City of Columbus v. Leonard, 443 U.S. 905, 911 (1979) (Rehnquist, J., dissenting from denial of certiorari). Note that on occasion the availability of state remedies has been employed to justify limiting the *substantive* reach of § 1983. See Eisenberg, "Section 1983: Doctrinal Foundations and an Empirical Study," 67 Cornell L.Rev. 482, 513–14 (1982). See also § 10–14, infra.

5. See generally Note, "Developments in the Law—Section 1983 and Federalism," 90 Harv.L.Rev. 1133, 1135–1250 (1977).

6. See, e.g., McKart v. United States, 395 U.S. 185 (1969); Myers v. Bethlehem Shipbuilding Corp., 303 U.S. 41 (1938).

7. Patsy v. Board of Regents of Florida, 457 U.S. 496 (1982). However, even in § 1983 cases the abstention doctrines, summarized in § 3–28, supra, may require exhaustion of a pending state administrative proceeding. See id. at 518–19 (White, J., concurring in part). See also § 3–30, infra, note 10.

8. See Prentis v. Atlantic Coast Line Co., 211 U.S. 210, 229–30 (1908).

9. Id. at 230.

10. 312 U.S. 496 (1941).

an adjustment that will avoid the waste of a tentative decision as well as the friction of premature constitutional adjudication." [11]   The Supreme Court ordered the district court to retain jurisdiction of the case, but not to rule on the merits, pending proceedings in the state courts which would clarify the state law question.

The *Pullman* doctrine therefore requires that "when a federal constitutional claim is premised on an unsettled question of state law, the federal court should stay its hand in order to provide the state courts an opportunity to settle the underlying state law question and thus avoid the possibility of unnecessarily deciding a constitutional question." [12]   Absent *Pullman* abstention, federal courts, obliged to avoid federal constitutional decisions if possible,[13] particularly where they have pendent jurisdiction over state claims that could independently resolve the litigation,[14] would risk interfering with the role of the state courts as "the principal expositors of state law." [15]   Thus, the *Pullman* doctrine, by preventing federal courts from straying unduly

---

11. Id. at 500.

12. Harris County Comm'rs Court v. Moore, 420 U.S. 77, 83 (1975). The Court will not order abstention when there is only a federal statutory, rather than constitutional, issue at stake. Propper v. Clark, 337 U.S. 472, 490 (1949). Nor will abstention be ordered unless the state law issue is so unclear and obviously susceptible to limitation as to render premature a decision reaching the federal constitutional issue. See Hawaii Housing Auth. v. Midkiff, 467 U.S. 229, 236–37 (1984). Abstention may be ordered to clarify a state constitutional issue, but not if the state constitutional provision parallels the federal provision involved. See id. at 237 n. 4; see also Examining Board of Engineers, Architects & Surveyors v. Flores De Otero, 426 U.S. 572, 598 (1976) (to do so "would convert abstention from an exception into a general rule"). This latter exception to Younger abstention appears premised on the assumption that states will interpret state constitutional provisions as coextensive with like-worded federal constitutional provisions—a premise that appears shaky in light of the considerable growth of independent state constitutional law in recent years.

For an incisive and detailed account of Pullman abstention, see Field, "Abstention in Constitutional Cases: The Scope of the Pullman Abstention Doctrine," 122 U.Pa. L.Rev. 1071 (1974).

The Younger doctrine (discussed in § 3–30, infra), which bars unnecessary intrusion by federal courts into ongoing state judicial processes, also works to prevent decision of unnecessary federal constitutional questions. It provides the best chance of finding a state ground for a decision, without erroneously stretching state law, in recognition that "[a]lmost every constitutional challenge . . . offers the opportunity for narrowing constructions that might obviate the constitutional problem and intelligently mediate federal constitutional concerns and state interests." Moore v. Sims, 442 U.S. 415, 429–30 (1979).

13. See § 3–8 & note 21, supra.

14. See Siler v. Louisville & N.R.R., 213 U.S. 175 (1909). The inability to include such pendent claims in federal lawsuits against states or state officers, created by the Supreme Court's interpretation of the eleventh amendment in Pennhurst State School Hosp. v. Halderman, 465 U.S. 89 (1984), discussed in § 3–27, supra, thus creates a great danger of unnecessary constitutional decisions. Use of Pullman abstention in such situations would more flexibly resolve the special concerns involved in such cases. See Werhan, "Pullman Abstention After Pennhurst: A Comment on Judicial Federalism," 27 Wm. & Mary L.Rev. 449 (1986).

15. Moore v. Sims, 442 U.S. 415, 429 (1979). Even when a state law question may not be sufficiently unsettled to warrant the application of Pullman abstention, the rapidly expanding doctrine of Younger abstention—counseling federal courts to abstain from enjoining pending state court proceedings—may offer succor to the litigant seeking to avoid federal court review. See § 3–30, infra; see also Pennzoil Co. v. Texaco, Inc., 107 S.Ct. 1519, 1526 n. 9 (1987) (abstaining on Younger, not Pullman, grounds and declining to address concurring argument by Justice Blackmun that Pullman abstention was appropriate, but justifying Younger abstention in part on the basis that state court might dispose of case without even reading the federal issues).

from their area of expertise in federal law and enhancing the role of state courts in interpreting state issues that arise in federal lawsuits, promotes judicial federalism by allocating issues for decision in a way that best respects the abilities of each forum.[16]

Although litigants are not barred from federal court under *Pullman* abstention,[17] the doctrine imposes substantial costs on them through the delay in the resolution of federal constitutional issues common where a definitive state court resolution of the state issues in the case must be obtained.[18] Aware of these burdens, the Court has "repeatedly warned . . . that because of the delays inherent in the abstention process and the danger that valuable federal rights might be lost in the absence of expeditious adjudication in the federal court, abstention must be invoked only in 'special circumstances', and only upon careful consideration of the facts of each case." [19]

§ 3–30. Preserving State Institutional Autonomy: The Younger Doctrine

Beginning in 1971 with *Younger v. Harris*,[1] the Supreme Court quite rapidly developed a series of rules designed to protect the institutional autonomy of state governments by limiting the power of federal courts to grant declaratory or injunctive relief against unconstitutional state action in circumstances where parallel state proceedings involving the federal litigants provide them with an adequate forum for airing

16. See Werhan, supra note 14, at 470–74. On the desirability of structuring doctrines to encourage states to perform an independent function within our federal judicial structure, see generally Althouse, "How to Build a Separate Sphere: Federal Courts and State Power," 100 Harv.L.Rev. 1485 (1987).

17. Federal courts ordering Pullman abstention generally retain jurisdiction but stay the federal suit pending state law clarification, except where state law prevents state courts from proceeding while the federal court retains jurisdiction, in which case the federal court orders the case dismissed without prejudice to later reinstatement of the federal claims. See Harris County Comm'rs Court v. Moore, 420 U.S. 77, 83 (1975). Moreover, a litigant submitting his state law issue to a state court under the Pullman doctrine cannot be compelled to submit his federal claims for binding resolution; the right to a federal determination of federal legal issues, and of the facts on which decision of those issues depends, is retained, though a litigant can waive it. See England v. Louisiana State Bd. of Medical Examiners, 375 U.S. 411 (1964).

18. Delay can be substantially diminished under a promising alternative to Pullman abstention, allowing the direct submission of state law questions to an authoritative state tribunal, thereby removing the need to file a separate state action and speeding ultimate disposition of the case; a significant number of states have passed statutes allowing such certification. See generally Note, Certification Statutes: Engineering a Solution to Pullman Abstention Delay," 59 Notre Dame L.Rev. 1339 (1985); see also Field, "The Abstention Doctrine Today," 125 U.Pa.L. Rev. 590, 605–09 (1977).

19. Harris County Comm'rs Court v. Moore, 420 U.S. 77, 83 (1975). In elaborating the guidelines it follows in considering "the facts of each case," the Supreme Court has noted that Pullman abstention is regularly required "[w]here there is an action pending in state court that will likely resolve the state law questions underlying the federal claim," and that abstention is more desirable where the state law question "concerns matters peculiarly within the province of the local courts . . . ." However, "where the litigation has already been long delayed," or where it seems "unlikely that resolution of the state law question would significantly affect the federal claim," abstention is generally not required. Id.

§ 3–30

1. 401 U.S. 37 (1971).

their constitutional claims.[2] In combination with applicable rules of res judicata [3] as well as the bar on federal district court review of state court judgments,[4] *Younger* abstention effectively bars most state litigants from obtaining a full federal hearing of their federal claims.[5] The *Younger* rules developed so quickly that, within a few years, their general operation and boundaries—although not necessarily their underlying rationale—had become reasonably clear, and subsequent cases have added comparatively little to the doctrine. The basic outline of the rules is as follows:

(1) A federal court may grant declaratory or injunctive relief against unconstitutional state action if the federal litigant is not involved in a state court proceeding in which he may raise the constitutional issue and if, before proceedings of substance on the merits have begun in the federal suit, he does not become a party to such a state proceeding.[6] To this extent, the traditional rule—that a federal constitutional litigant need not first exhaust state remedies [7]—survives.

(2) If, at the time the litigant initiates a federal proceeding to challenge unconstitutional state action, he is a defendant in an already initiated state *criminal proceeding*, and if he can raise the constitutional issue in that proceeding, he will ordinarily not be able to obtain federal declaratory or injunctive relief.[8]

2. These rules, of course, did not spring full-blown from the brow of the Burger Court. Indeed, they draw upon equitable rules, predating even Ex parte Young, 209 U.S. 123 (1908), which limited the power of courts of equity to enjoin criminal prosecutions, as well as the federalism-based constraints which the Supreme Court began to develop in order to blunt Ex parte Young's effect. But the doctrine sketched here remains unusual because, unlike other abstention doctrines discussed in § 3–28, note 10, and § 3–29, supra, although not without antecedents it draws its force so much from the most recent cases that earlier decisions truly are of only historical concern. For an account of these earlier cases, see M. Redish, Federal Jurisdiction: Tensions in the Allocation of Judicial Power 291–96 (1980).

3. The federal full faith and credit statute, 28 U.S.C. § 1738, requires federal courts to give state judgments the same res judicata effect that the state in which the prior proceeding was held would give it. See Migra v. Warren City Sch. Dist. Board of Educ., 465 U.S. 75, 80–85 (1984) (barring subsequent federal-court litigation of federal claim that might have been raised in state proceeding); Allen v. McCurry, 449 U.S. 90, 96–105 (1980) (barring relitigation in federal court of issues decided in state-court proceeding). See also Smith, "Full Faith and Credit and Section 1983: A Reappraisal," 63 N.Car.L.Rev. 59 (1984).

4. See District of Columbia Court of Appeals v. Feldman, 460 U.S. 462 (1983);

Rooker v. Fidelity Trust Co., 263 U.S. 413 (1923). This doctrine, although technically only a derivation of a current structure for appellate review that is not mandated by the Constitution, see Amar, "A New-Federalist View of Article III: Separating the Two Tiers of Federal Jurisdiction," 65 B.U.L.Rev. 205, 220–21 & nn. 59–60, 234–35 n. 100, 258–59 & nn. 169–70 (1985), is of great importance in protecting fundamental principles of federalism. See Chang, "Rediscovering the Rooker Doctrine: Section 1983, Res Judicata and the Federal Courts," 31 Hastings L.J. 1337 (1980).

5. Federal review of state court judgments is available only through the Supreme Court under 28 U.S.C. § 1257, see § 3–28, supra, at note 14, which rejects the vast majority of cases presented to it on discretionary grounds. See § 3–5, note 9, supra. The effect of the Younger rules, then, is even more drastic than that of an administrative exhaustion requirement, examined in § 3–29, supra, which allows ultimate resort to a federal forum.

6. See Doran v. Salem Inn, Inc., 422 U.S. 922 (1975) (injunctive relief); Steffel v. Thompson, 415 U.S. 452 (1974) (declaratory relief).

7. See § 3–29, supra.

8. Samuels v. Mackell, 401 U.S. 66 (1971) (declaratory relief); Younger v. Harris, 401 U.S. 37 (injunctive relief).

(3) If, at the time the litigant initiates federal proceedings, he is a party in a state *civil proceeding initiated by state officials, or* some other state civil proceeding *involving important state interests,* (or, potentially, *any* state civil proceeding), and if he is not barred from raising the constitutional issue in that proceeding, he will again ordinarily be denied federal declaratory or injunctive relief.[9]

9. Of the rules summarized here, this one is the least settled. Huffman v. Pursue, Ltd., 420 U.S. 592 (1975), extended the Younger doctrine to civil proceedings, in Huffman a state-prosecuted obscenity abatement action to which the principles of Younger were deemed applicable because the case was: (1) brought by state officials and (2) was in aid of, and closely related to, a criminal statute. Even though the equitable principle against interference with a state criminal proceeding that in part supported the result in Younger was not present, abstention was warranted by the central importance of comity, id. at 600–01, and by the quasi-criminal nature of the proceeding, id. at 604. However, the Court has refused to limit application of Younger abstention to such situations. See Juidice v. Vail, 430 U.S. 327, 334 (1977) (emphasizing that "[t]he policies underlying Younger are fully applicable to noncriminal judicial proceedings when important state interests are involved"); Middlesex County Ethics Comm. v. Garden State Bar Ass'n, 457 U.S. 423, 432 (1982); see also Pennzoil v. Texaco, 107 S.Ct. 1519, 1526–27 (1987); Ohio Civil Rights Comm'n v. Dayton Christian Schools, Inc., 106 S.Ct. 2718, 2723 (1986); Hawaii Housing Authority v. Midkiff, 467 U.S. 229, 237–39 (1984) (dictum). The interests that have satisfied this test are diverse. See Moore v. Sims, 442 U.S. 415 (1979) (protection of abused children through suit by state for child custody); Trainor v. Hernandez, 431 U.S. 434 (1977) (combating of welfare fraud through suit to recover wrongfully retained payments); Juidice v. Vail, 430 U.S. 327 (1977) (safeguarding of litigants' enjoyment of regular operation of state judicial system through application of civil contempt power for failure to respond to court orders); Pennzoil Co. v. Texaco, supra, 107 S.Ct. at 1527 (noting "importance to the States of enforcing the orders and judgments of their courts" through the application of lien and bond provisions to a litigant appealing an adverse civil decision).

The Court also applies Younger to "state administrative proceedings in which important state interests are vindicated, so long as in the course of those proceedings the federal plaintiff would have a full and fair opportunity to litigate his constitutional claim," and the pendency of such proceedings is enough to trigger Younger even though no state *court* proceeding is pending. Ohio Civil Rights Comm'n, supra, 106 S.Ct. at 2723 & n. 2. See, e.g., id. at 2723–24 (elimination of sex discrimination); Middlesex County Ethics Comm., supra, 457 U.S. at 432–34 (regulation of attorney ethics); Gibson v. Berryhill, 411 U.S. 564, 576–77 (1973) (revocation of physician licenses).

As to whether Younger applies to all civil litigation, the Court has expressly reserved the question, saving it "for another day," Juidice, supra, 430 U.S. at 336 n. 13; cf. id. at 345 n. (Brennan, J., dissenting) (calling disclaimer a "tongue in cheek . . . signal that merely the formal announcement is being postponed"). See also Moore, supra, 442 U.S. at 423 n. 8; Trainor, supra, 431 U.S. at 445 n. 8; cf. Pennzoil Co. v. Texaco, Inc., 107 S.Ct. 1519, 1527 (1987) (extending Juidice to lien and bond requirements imposed in private civil proceedings, reasoning that "[t]here is little difference between the State's interest in forcing persons to transfer property in response to a court's judgment and in forcing persons to respond to the court's process on pain of contempt"); but see id. at 1530 (Brennan, J., joined by Marshall, J., concurring on other grounds) (advocating, and citing authority for, limitation of Younger doctrine to criminal proceedings); id. at 1534–35 (Blackmun, J., concurring on other grounds) (application of Younger to Pennzoil case "expand[s] the Younger doctrine to an unprecedented extent and . . . effectively allow[s] the invocation of *Younger* abstention whenever any State proceeding is ongoing, no matter how attenuated the State's interests are"); id. at 1536 & n. 2 (Stevens, J., joined by Marshall, J., concurring on other grounds) (no state interest sufficient to support abstention where state's only "interest [is] . . . its interest as adjudicator of wholly private disputes"). Pennzoil's extension of Younger and Juidice, in the majority opinion of Justice Powell, joined by Chief Justice Rehnquist and by Justices White, O'Connor, and Scalia, was denounced by the separately concurring Justices as "cut[ting] the *Younger* doctrine adrift from its original . . . moorings" in the equitable reluctance to interfere with criminal processes. Id.

If it had not been clear before Pennzoil, it is certainly clear now that the most basic underpinning of the Younger doctrine is

(4) Even if, at the time a litigant initiates a federal action, no parallel state judicial proceedings are already under way, the litigant will ordinarily be denied federal declaratory or injunctive relief if parallel state proceedings commence before the federal court has become involved in proceedings of substance on the merits of his claim.[10]

(5) These rules apply only in the ordinary case. They do not apply if parallel state proceedings have been initiated as part of a program of harassment or are otherwise brought in bad faith.[11] The ordinary rules also do not apply if a federal litigant's constitutional claim concerns the fairness of the very state proceedings which the ordinary rules would treat as an adequate constitutional forum.[12] And, repeating a key

not any special equity concept but, rather, a federalism-based notion of comity. That notion is fully applicable even when a suit is filed under 42 U.S.C. § 1983, and thereby escapes the absolute statutory bar of the Anti-Injunction Act, 28 U.S.C. § 2283, which for nearly two centuries has barred all but specifically exempted federal court injunctions against state court proceedings. See Mitchum v. Foster, 407 U.S. 225, 243 (1972) (although § 1983 suits are exempt from the flat bar of § 2283, that fact does not "qualify in any way the principles of equity, *comity* and *federalism* that must restrain a federal court when asked to enjoin a state court proceeding") (emphasis added). It is noteworthy that, even if a § 1983 suit is filed against a private party allegedly exercising public powers "under color of" state law, as Texaco alleged Pennzoil was, the state's interest in the operations of its judicial system suffices to trigger the Younger doctrine despite the absence of any state agency or official from the § 1983 litigation. Texaco's argument to the contrary was squarely rejected by the Court in Pennzoil. The author of this treatise argued Pennzoil's case in the Supreme Court.

The Court has also expressly reserved the question whether Younger applies to damage actions where declaratory or injunctive relief has not been sought. See Juidice, supra, 430 U.S. at 339 n. 16. However, in considering taxpayer damage actions brought to redress allegedly unconstitutional administration of the state tax system, the Court has relied on a separate comity doctrine to require abstention in a suit solely for an award of damages, viewed as being as intrusive as equitable relief, see Fair Assessment in Real Estate Ass'n Inc. v. McNary, 454 U.S. 100, 111–15 (1981), while avoiding consideration of the Younger's application to such suits, see id. at 112. Compare id. at 120–21 n. 4 (Brennan, J., concurring in the judgment) (arguing that abstention should apply only in equity actions).

10. Hicks v. Miranda, 422 U.S. 332 (1975). Pendency of certain state adminis-

trative proceedings may meet this requirement even if a state judicial proceeding is not pending, see supra note 9.

11. See Younger, 401 U.S. at 47–48, 54. Typical examples of this vice include those state prosecutions under obscenity laws, see, e.g., Perez v. Ledesma, 401 U.S. 82, 85 (1971), or anarchy or public disorder statutes, see, e.g., Younger, 401 U.S. at 47–48; Boyle v. Landry, 401 U.S. 77, 80–81 (1971); Dombrowski v. Pfister, 380 U.S. 479, 482 (1965), in which no conviction is hoped for and in which it is the prosecution in and of itself that constitutes a constitutionally cognizable injury to first amendment rights.

12. See Gibson v. Berryhill, 411 U.S. 564, 577 (1973) (pending proceedings before state board of optometry did not bar federal suit since plaintiffs alleged, and district court found, that the bias in the board's makeup precluded a fair hearing). The Court has interpreted this exception quite narrowly; in cases since Gibson, it has closely scrutinized state procedures to determine if mechanisms exist to deal with problems of unfairness, see Kugler v. Helfant, 421 U.S. 117, 127–29 (1975), refusing to accept the view "that a constitutional attack on state procedures automatically vitiates the adequacy of those procedures." Moore v. Sims, 442 U.S. 415, 427 (1979); see also Ohio Civil Rights Comm'n v. Dayton Christian Schools, Inc., 106 S.Ct. 2718, 2724 (1986).

Younger also suggested that deference to state procedures might not be necessary if a state statute is " 'flagrantly and patently violative of express constitutional prohibitions in every clause, sentence and paragraph, and in whatever manner and against whomever an effort might be made to apply it.' " 401 U.S. at 53–54 (quoting Watson v. Buck, 313 U.S. 387, 402 (1941)). The Supreme Court has interpreted this exception so literally as to deprive it of any practical significance. Compare Trainor v. Hernandez, 431 U.S. 434, 446–47 (1977) with id. at 461–63 (Stevens, J., dissenting). Finally, there may be "other exceptional

component of rules two and three, the federal litigant must be able to raise the constitutional claim in the pending state proceeding.[13]

It is possible to state the framework of the *Younger* doctrine so schematically not only because the Supreme Court has quickly filled out the doctrinal structure, but also because little beyond the *results* of the Court's *Younger* cases is relevant. Beyond largely conclusory references to comity, equity, and federalism, the Court has not seriously attempted to articulate the norms or policies which shape its rules, although it is clear that a concern for protecting the ability of state courts independently to function as adjudicators of federal constitutional claims, subject of course to ultimate Supreme Court review, lies at the core of the doctrine.[14]

This lack of clarity has engendered considerable debate about the legitimacy of the *Younger* doctrine. Both sides present reasonable viewpoints, differing mainly on the proper interpretation of congressional grants of jurisdiction to the federal courts. Critics of the *Younger* doctrine allege that it impermissibly undermines the proposition recognized in a long line of cases interpreting 42 U.S.C. § 1983— the federal statute under which most litigants challenge state action— that persons enjoy the right to a federal forum to vindicate federal claims against persons acting under color of state law,[15] without any requirement that state judicial remedies be exhausted as a precondition

circumstances" sufficient to bar abstention, but these must "render the state court incapable of fairly and fully adjudicating the federal issues before it . . . creating an extraordinarily pressing need for immediate federal equitable relief," Moore, supra, 442 U.S. at 433 (quoting Kugler, supra, 421 U.S. at 124–25).

13. The burden of proof is on the federal litigant who asserts an inability to raise the constitutional claim in the ongoing state proceeding. Unless it "plainly appears" that this cannot be done, Younger applies. Middlesex County Ethics Comm. v. Garden State Bar Ass'n, 457 U.S. 423, 435 (1982). The litigant must do more than document a high probability that the state courts will *reject* the federal constitutional claim; to avoid Younger, the federal litigant must show that "state procedural law barred presentation" of its federal claim in some suitable state judicial forum in which the litigant was then appearing. Moore v. Sims, 442 U.S. 415, 432 (1979); id. at 430 & nn. 12, 13. Inability to press the federal claim in a special proceeding, tailor-made to entertain challenges to the very laws or procedures the litigant wishes to attack, meets this burden only when the state has set up a scheme whereby those laws or procedures may be enforced against the federal litigant outside the context of any ongoing state court suit, see Hernandez v. Finley, 471 F.Supp. 516, 519– 20 (N.D. Ill. 1978), summarily aff'd sub nom. Quern v. Hernandez, 440 U.S. 951

(1979), but *not* when enforcement is part and parcel of ongoing state court litigation. In Pennzoil Co. v. Texaco, Inc., 107 S.Ct. 1519 (1987), for example, the Court held that *Younger* abstention was required in Texaco's challenge to the state's rules for securing civil judgments by liens and bonds pending the losing party's appeal—notwithstanding the absence of any provision in state law expressly permitting the lien and bond rules to be suspended or relaxed in response to a federal challenge to their validity, whether facially or as applied. So long as the Texas courts in which the underlying civil judgment was rendered (and was being appealed) had general jurisdiction to consider constitutional challenges to the judgment's immediate enforcement, "the lower [federal] courts should have deferred on principles of comity to the pending state proceedings." Id. at 107 S.Ct. at 1529. That prompt relief was urgently needed to stave off Texaco's bankruptcy was irrelevant. Id. See the discussion of Pennzoil in note 9, supra.

14. See Althouse, "How to Build a Separate Sphere: Federal Courts and State Power," 100 Harv.L.Rev. 1485, 1488–89, 1531–34 (1987). For discussion of the relative merits of such comity, see sources cited in § 3–28, note 13, supra.

15. See, e.g., Mitchum v. Foster, 407 U.S. 225, 238–42 (1972); Monroe v. Pape, 365 U.S. 167, 171–87 (1961).

to federal suit.[16]   Section 1983, it is argued, was intended by the Reconstruction Congress to ensure that federal courts would exist as fully independent alternatives to state court systems.[17]   The pendency of state proceedings where the federal litigant *could* raise the claim is, under this view, simply an interesting fact, but cannot overcome the need for independent access to federal court.[18]

The contrary view recognizes the powerful constitutional principle in favor of respecting state sovereignty, and refuses to read into jurisdictional statutes—which have been interpreted to allow expansive federal jurisdiction only in recent decades—an intent by Congress to intrude excessively into state proceedings absent a *clear statement* to that effect.[19]   Moreover, § 1983 must not be read in a manner that wholly displaces pending state proceedings; the Court's decision in 1972 to treat § 1983 as an "expressly authorized" exception to the flat ban on judicial interference with such proceedings imposed by the Anti-Injunction Act,[20] presupposed *Younger's* 1971 premise that the policies of judicial federalism underlying that statute would continue to have effect in § 1983 actions.   Use of *Younger* abstention is also functionally justified because it recognizes that, in practice, given the volume of federal issues raised in state proceedings, to deny state courts the right to decide these issues would cause severe disruption.[21]   And, it is argued, Congress can always modify jurisdictional doctrine with the requisite clear statement if it wishes.[22]

For the present, *Younger* is firmly rooted in the law of judicial federalism underlying the Constitution.   Although *Younger* happened

---

16. Home Tel. & Tel. Co. v. Los Angeles, 227 U.S. 278 (1913); see also Monroe v. Pape, 365 U.S. 167, 183 (1961).

17. See Zeigler, "A Reassessment of the Younger Doctrine in Light of the Legislative History of Reconstruction," 1983 Duke L.J. 987.

18. For a detailed challenge to the legitimacy of *Younger* and other abstention doctrines, arguing that abstention to limit exercise of congressionally provided jurisdiction violates the separation of powers, see Redish, "Abstention, Separation of Powers, and the Limits of the Judicial Function," 94 Yale L.J. 71 (1984).   For an argument that the abstention doctrines are an entirely proper exercise of federal common law power, discussed in § 3–23, supra, see Wells, "Why Professor Redish is Wrong About Abstention," 19 Ga.L.Rev. 1097 (1985).   See also Shapiro, "Jurisdiction and Discretion," 60 N.Y.U.L.Rev. 543, 544–45, 580–81 (1985) (arguing that Redish fails to recognize the degree of wide-ranging discretion employed in a variety of jurisdictional doctrines).

19. See §§ 5–7, 5–8, 5–22, 6–25, supra, discussing "clear statement" rules as protections for state sovereignty, and § 3–26, supra, discussing such rules in the eleventh amendment context.

20. 28 U.S.C. § 2283.   See the discussion of Mitchum v. Foster, 407 U.S. 225 (1972), in note 9, supra.   See also Althouse, supra note 14, at 1487 n. 14.

21. See Bator, "The State Courts and Federal Constitutional Litigation," 22 Wm. & Mary L.Rev. 605, 608–22 (1981) (describing the burdens of ensuring access to a federal court in criminal and civil enforcement proceedings by allowing in each case either removal of the entire case to federal court, subsequent relitigation of the federal issues, or piecemeal litigation of the case in separate courts).   See also Althouse, supra note 14, at 1533 (arguing that "[t]he autonomous operation of state court criminal and other enforcement proceedings at the trial level is functionally superior (unless it is for some reason defective . . .) to the commencement of a secondary litigation in federal court," which "would both overburden federal courts and delay state proceedings," "express distrust of the willingness of state courts to adequately enforce federal law, and deny them the opportunity to develop expertise and sensitivity in applying that law").

22. For a more detailed argument in favor of the Younger and other abstention doctrines, see Wells, supra note 18; compare other sources cited, id.

to involve deference to pending state criminal proceedings, the *Younger* doctrine has been extended to the civil realm on each occasion presented to the Court,[23] and there now appears to be no principled way to prevent the application of the *Younger* doctrine to preclude federal litigation of any threatened federal interest where the litigant is involved in a pending state judicial proceeding that is adequate to ventilate the federal claim[24]—keeping in mind the *nature* of that federal claim in the event that the very pendency of the state procedure irreparably threatens the federal interest at stake.

But *Younger* should not be extended beyond a context where deference to a state *judicial* system is owed. If the background principle of federalism justifying *Younger* abstention is indeed trust in the state's ability fairly to adjudicate the federal claim given the provision of an adequate forum,[25] then it is wrong to rely on *Younger*'s invocation of inchoate principles of federalism in situations where the *Younger* rules themselves would suggest that these principles are not relevant. The Supreme Court first suggested the contrary in *O'Shea v. Littleton*,[26] where Justice White, writing for a majority of the Court, indicated in elaborate dictum[27] that the principles underlying *Younger* would bar a federal district court from responding to claims of systematically racially discriminatory bail and sentencing practices in a municipal court system by framing continuing injunctive relief which would involve the federal court in periodic monitoring of local judicial processes.[28] As Justice White also noted, it may very well have been the case that the *O'Shea* injunction was not appropriate on traditional grounds: the injunction appeared to be impractical;[29] and plaintiffs had neither shown substantial and immediate irreparable injury nor the inadequacy of legal remedies.[30] But it is quite clear that *Younger* was not relevant in this context: the injunction would not have prevented or disrupted any state judicial proceeding.[31] Moreover, plaintiffs' allegations challenged the constitutionality of the very judicial processes to which the ordinary *Younger* rules would remand them, so that the case fell within an otherwise well-established exception to the *Younger* doctrine.[32]

If *O'Shea* is an aberration, it is unfortunately not unique. Relying upon *O'Shea*, Justice Rehnquist's majority opinion in *Rizzo v. Goode*,[33] again in dictum,[34] invoked the principles underlying *Younger* in disapproving another federal district court injunction, this one requiring a

23. See note 9, supra.

24. On whether a given proceeding is "adequate," see note 13, supra.

25. See sources cited in note 14, supra.

26. 414 U.S. 488 (1974).

27. See id. at 504–05 (Blackmun, J., concurring in part).

28. Before reaching the question of relief, Justice White's majority opinion held that plaintiffs had not alleged an actual case or controversy. See id. at 493–90.

29. See id. at 500–02.

30. See id. at 502.

31. See Allee v. Medrano, 416 U.S. 802, 814 (1974).

32. See note 12, supra.

33. 423 U.S. 362 (1976).

34. Although initially suggesting the absence of a case or controversy, see id. at 371–73, the majority reached the merits and concluded that plaintiffs' attempt to demonstrate statistically the fact of the police department's failure to supervise did not succeed in establishing a basis for relief. See id. at 373–77.

municipal police force to set up formal internal administrative procedures to deal with citizen complaints of police brutality. The injunction in this case rested on sounder remedial grounds than those available in *O'Shea*: the police had themselves proposed this form of relief, and thus the injunction was presumably workable.[35] Even more clearly than in *O'Shea*, the Court's reference to *Younger* was not appropriate: the injunction was not even addressed to the state judicial system as such, the institution which *Younger's* principles of comity require federal courts to respect; even if considerations of federalism require federal courts to respect the autonomy of *all* state institutions, here, as in *O'Shea*, the substantive challenge was to the fairness of the state agency's own processes for protecting plaintiffs' rights, and thus the *Younger* rules by their own terms did not apply.

O'Shea and Rizzo no doubt reflect a concern on the part of the Supreme Court that some limits be placed on the power of federal district courts to put into effect broad structural injunctions of the sort which have become more commonplace in recent years.[36] But while principles of federalism certainly have a place in shaping and limiting such law, the relationship between federalism and equity is far too complex to be captured by analogies to the literally inapplicable *Younger* rules:[37] to explain the relationship, the Court will actually have to articulate its conception of federalism. In so doing, it would not only make a significant advance in the process of developing a comprehensible contemporary law of equitable remedies, but could also provide a basis for justifying the *Younger* doctrine itself. Pending such an effort, the inappropriateness of blind deference on federalism grounds to nonjudicial organs of the state in the face of federal challenges to them [38]— as well as the Court's inconsistency in deciding when to abstain in the face of pending quasi-judicial administrative proceedings [39]—indicates that there is as yet no principled basis for extending *Younger* beyond contexts that involve the state courts.

35. See id. at 381 (Blackmun, J., dissenting).

36. See also City of Los Angeles v. Lyons, 461 U.S. 95, 111–13 (1983), discussed in § 3–16, supra; Pennhurst State Sch. & Hosp. v. Halderman, 465 U.S. 89, 104 n. 13 (1984), discussed in § 3–27, supra. For a criticism of this trend, see Fallon, "Of Justiciability, Remedies, and Public Law Litigation: Notes on the Jurisprudence of Lyons," 59 N.Y.U.L.Rev. 1, 59–74 (1985).

37. See generally Shapiro, supra note 18.

38. See Althouse, supra note 14, at 1528–35.

39. Compare Ohio Civil Rights Comm'n v. Dayton Christian Schools, 106 S.Ct. 2718, 2723 & n. 2 (1986) (requiring abstention in favor of pending administrative proceeding) (discussed in note 9, supra), with Hawaii Housing Auth. v. Midkiff, 467 U.S. 229, 238–39 (1984) (essentially ignoring the case for Younger abstention despite the existence of relevant pending administrative proceedings; the Court relied on the assertion that the state statute itself deemed the administrative proceedings neither judicial nor "part of . . . a judicial proceeding" and did not reply to the HHA's arguments that the statute meant no such thing and that, in any event, the relevant administrative agency was capable of hearing, and had been asked to hear, the federal plaintiff's constitutional claims).

Chapter 4

FEDERAL EXECUTIVE POWER

§ 4-1. The Puzzle of the Presidency: Its Uneasy Truce With Constitutionalism

Whether imperial or simply magisterial—or as "close to the people" as ambition and the media can make it—the American Presidency will never be easy to locate within our constitutional framework. Although the most recent major collision between the Chief Executive and the Fundamental Law—that over Watergate—resulted in a bare, de facto victory for law, the very magnitude and drama of the conflict testified to the reality that the President occupies a place that cannot readily be assimilated to that of the other branches. For unlike them, the President is a person as well as an institution; and, unlike other institutions, the Presidency is led by an individual elected by the entire Nation to secure its survival, to represent it to the world, and to voice its aspirations to all the people. Thus it is only by an extraordinary triumph of constitutional imagination that the Commander in Chief is conceived as commanded by law.

To be reminded that it was not meant to be so—that the Framers envisioned a vastly more modest chief magistrate—is only to recall that, had the blueprint been incapable of expanding beyond the Framers' designs, the Nation could not have persisted through two centuries of turmoil.[1] No act of imagination, constitutional or otherwise, can recapture the Presidency's past. We are, and must remain, a society led by three equal branches, with one permanently "more equal" than the others: as the Supreme Court and Congress are preeminent in constitutional theory, so the President is preeminent in constitutional fact.

These things being as they are, it is not surprising that the triumph of legality over Presidential abuse in the Watergate episode should have been so widely regarded as proof of the constitutional system's continuing vitality. More accurately, it was proof of the people's commitment, in the end, to a system that could not, without such commitment, have withstood the challenge to its authority.[2] But it was only "in the end": it is worth recalling that, without a quite extraordinary confluence of circumstances, the challenge to the Constitution might well have succeeded.[3] And so it must be when law, even the greatest law on earth (if that is one's view of the American Constitution), confronts in one individual the greatest concentration of

§ 4-1

1. See W. Wilson, Constitutional Government in the United States 59–60 (1908); A. Schlesinger, The Imperial Presidency 1–34 (1973).

2. See The Federalist No. 48 (J. Madison); C. Furness, Walt Whitman's Workshop 58 (1928).

3. A. Schlesinger, supra note 1, at 273–77; Linde, "Replacing a President: Rx for a 21st Century Watergate," 43 Geo.Wash. L.Rev. 384, 387 (1975).

power in human history. To expect any abstract structure to equal that power is to be a dreamer. But to forget that even the greatest power may be felled by an idea when it is believed deeply enough by a large enough multitude is to ignore one of the deepest lessons of modern times.

One mundane implication of these introductory remarks is that there is no entirely natural way of locating this chapter on presidential power in a work on constitutional law. Initially, the plan was to put these pages on the Presidency after the chapter on Congress, if only to stress that Congress' role ought to become more prominent than it has long been in all but theory. But that would have interrupted the logical and historical flow between Chapter 5 on congressional power and its federalism-based limits, and Chapter 6 on federalism-based limits on state authority. Placing the chapter here, after the treatment of the federal judiciary but before the analysis of Congress, has its own difficulties—not least of which is a requirement of frequent reference forward to Chapter 5, as the complex interplay of presidential and congressional authority is explored. In the end, the problem was resolved in favor of giving a prior place to the topic that would in any event prove hardest to integrate into all that must come after—the constitutional sources and limits of federal executive authority.

§ 4-2. The Constitutional and Extra-Constitutional Character of Presidential Power: An Overview of its Interactions With Legislative Authority and an Introduction to Issues of Delegation

Article II, § 1, provides that "The executive Power shall be vested in a President of the United States of America." In Alexander Hamilton's widely accepted view, this statement cannot be read as mere shorthand for the specific executive authorizations that follow it in §§ 2 and 3.[1] Hamilton stressed the difference between the sweeping language of article II, § 1, and the conditional language of article I, § 1: "All legislative Powers *herein granted* shall be vested in a Congress of the United States. . . . ." Hamilton submitted that "[t]he [article II] enumeration [in §§ 2 and 3] ought therefore to be considered, as intended merely to specify the principal articles implied in the definition of executive power; leaving the rest to flow from the general grant of that power, interpreted in conformity with other parts of the Constitution. . . . ."[2]

In *Myers v. United States*, the Supreme Court accepted Hamilton's proposition, concluding that the federal executive, unlike the Congress,

---

§ 4-2

1. Although widely accepted, Hamilton's view has not won universal agreement. See 6 J. Madison, Writings 138, 147–50 (Hunt ed. 1910); Register of Debates in Congress, XI, Pt. I, 462–63 (reporting comments of Senator Webster). See also, Corwin, "The Steel Seizure Case: A Judicial Brick Without Straw," 53 Colum. L.Rev. 53 (1953) (maintaining that the purpose of the clause was simply to give the executive a title and to settle upon a single executive).

2. 7 Works of Alexander Hamilton 76, 80–81 (C. Hamilton ed. 1851).

could exercise power from sources not enumerated, so long as not forbidden by the constitutional text: "The executive power was given in general terms, strengthened by specific terms where emphasis was regarded as appropriate, and was limited by direct expressions where limitation was needed. . . ." [3] The language of Chief Justice Taft in *Myers* makes clear that the constitutional concept of inherent power is not a synonym for power without limit; rather, the concept suggests only that not all powers granted in the Constitution are themselves exhausted by internal enumeration, so that, within a sphere properly regarded as one of "executive" power, authority is implied unless there or elsewhere expressly limited. [4]

Although the Constitution provides that in matters of foreign relations the President and Congress share concurrent power, the Supreme Court has held that the Constitution's separation of powers and its arrangement of checks and balances are less precise in this area than a survey of the text might suggest. Consequently, the Court has permitted Congress to make broad delegations of its foreign policy powers to the Executive Branch at times when it might not have permitted similarly expansive delegations with regard to domestic affairs. [5]

The theoretical justification for legislative deference to executive action in the international arena was supplied by Justice Sutherland in *United States v. Curtiss-Wright Export Corp.* [6] The case involved a Joint Resolution enacted by Congress empowering the President to declare illegal the provision of arms to nations involved in the Chaco conflict if, in his opinion, such provision would prolong the hostilities. The defendants had provided arms despite an embargo declared by the President pursuant to the Joint Resolution. The question before the Court was the legality of this congressional delegation of authority to the President. The Court unequivocally held the delegation proper. Although the decision might have been bottomed upon narrower grounds, Justice Sutherland accepted the case as an invitation to propound certain of his long-held convictions about the source and distribution of the federal government's foreign affairs power. [7] Critical to his argument was an identification of executive power as the most appropriate medium for the international expression of American sovereignty.

---

3. 272 U.S. 52, 118 (1926).

4. The Myers Court thus stopped short of embracing the "stewardship theory" of Theodore Roosevelt, which insisted that the President had not only a right, but a duty, to take any action essential to the nation's well-being—even if it could not be rooted explicitly or implicitly in a constitutional provision—so long as it was not violative of an explicit constitutional proscription or contrary to an enactment of Congress within the sphere of its enumerated powers. See T. Roosevelt, An Autobiography 371–72 (MacMillan ed. 1914). The

decision thus comported with the opinions articulated by Taft prior to his appointment to the Court. See W. Taft, Our Chief Magistrate and His Powers 143–47 (1916).

5. See §§ 4–4, 5–17, infra.

6. 299 U.S. 304 (1936). Compare Panama Refining Co. v. Ryan, 293 U.S. 388 (1935), discussed in § 5–17, infra.

7. Sutherland's views on this subject were first expounded in an article written in 1909: "The Internal and External Powers of the National Government," S.Doc. No. 417, 61st Cong., 2d Sess. (1910).

Sutherland contended that the international prerogatives of the federal government need not spring exclusively from the Constitution, but may instead be the inevitable incidents of a claim of sovereignty. He reasoned that since the trappings of sovereignty passed from the British Crown to the states in their collective, rather than individual, capacity, the Constitution, which merely allocates between the federal government and the states *those powers previously lodged in the separate states*, should not be deemed an exhaustive catalogue of the federal government's powers in the realm of foreign affairs.[8] But ascribing the concomitants of nationhood to the federal government says nothing about their allocation among its three coordinate branches. Sutherland continued pragmatically by stressing the President's role as the nation's exclusive agent in foreign affairs: "[P]articipation in the exercise of the power is significantly limited. In this vast external realm, with its important, complicated, delicate and manifold problems, the President alone has the power to speak or listen as a representative of the nation." [9] He then concluded for the Court that, where Congress' constitutionally enumerated authority is itself part of the broader, inherent sovereign power to conduct foreign relations, Congress may delegate its authority to the Executive more broadly than it could where its power as enumerated in article I defines the totality of federal authority: "It is quite apparent that if, in the maintenance of our international relations, embarrassment—perhaps serious embarrassment—is to be avoided and success for our aims achieved, congressional legislation which is to be made effective through negotiation and inquiry within the international field must often accord to the President a degree of discretion and freedom from statutory restriction which would not be admissible were domestic affairs alone involved." [10]

While *Curtiss-Wright* stands for the proposition that relatively broad delegations of congressional authority to the Executive Branch are permissible in the area of foreign affairs,[11] the powers vested in the

---

8. Perhaps no other tenet of this controversial opinion has been so critically assayed as the proposition that foreign relations powers are, to an extent, extraconstitutional in character. In particular, the notion that the federal government inherited the incidents of sovereignty directly from the British Crown has been vehemently denied by several commentators. See, e.g., Berger, "The Presidential Monopoly of Foreign Relations," 71 Mich. L.Rev. 1 (1972); Levitan, "The Foreign Relations Power: An Analysis of Mr. Justice Sutherland's Theory," 55 Yale L.J. 467 (1946). It has been suggested, however, that the doctrine of the case is valid even if its historical premises are suspect. See L. Henkin, Foreign Affairs and the Constitution 24 (1972). Quite apart from American Constitutional history, the conception of distinct domestic and foreign dimensions of the executive power has deep support in

theoretical writings. John Locke, for example, deemed the executive power distinct from the "federative power" although he envisioned their being wielded by the same magistrate. See J. Locke, The Second Treatise of Civil Government, Chapter XII, §§ 143–48 (Gateway ed. 1968).

9.   299 U.S. at 319.

10.   Id. at 320.

11.   It has been argued that the delegation involved in Curtiss-Wright could have been sustained under the standards employed to test delegations of Congress' domestic authority and, consequently, that the better part of the opinion is dictum. See Bickel, "Congress, the President and the Power to Wage War," 48 Chicago-Kent L.R. 131, 137 (1971). Cf. Youngstown Sheet & Tube Co. v. Sawyer, 343 U.S. 579, 635–36 n. 2 (1952) (Jackson J., concurring).

President plainly are not unlimited. Congress is permitted to delegate its foreign relations power, but it is not required to do so. Because acquired executive power may be exercised only so long as Congress does not object, Congress retains the power to limit executive action in areas which were previously wholly discretionary with the Executive, so long as Congress acts within its constitutional grants of enumerated authority.[12]

If requirements of sovereignty dictate that power to conduct foreign relations must lie with the national government, and if requirements of expediency encourage predominant executive control in that sphere, the pattern in the domestic realm is quite different. The federal regulation of domestic affairs has its constitutional origins in the people and the states,[13] and its initiation is allocated primarily to Congress. The limitation of congressional authority, and the direct electoral responsibility of Congress to the people [14] provided some assurance to the social institutions that created the Constitution that they would not be devoured by it.

The constitutional role for the Executive in domestic matters is thus largely ancillary to that of Congress. And the more the foreign and domestic spheres tend to merge, the more this principle will apply to *all* executive action. Article II, § 3, instructs the President only that "[he] shall from time to time give to Congress Information of the State of the Union, and recommend to their Consideration such Measures as he shall judge necessary and expedient; . . . [and] he shall take Care that the Laws be faithfully executed. . . ." [15] Apart from the authority to appoint various federal officers,[16] the President was given no further sources of affirmative power over purely domestic matters.[17]

§ 4–3. The Legislative Veto: A Case Study In The Separation of Powers

The Great Depression exposed what many perceived to be Congress' deficiencies as an initiator of domestic policy, whether in matters of governmental organization or in matters of substantive regulation and fiscal direction. The congressional response was the advent of the regulatory state, as embodied in legislative delegation to the President or to various agencies of broad powers of domestic initiative. But these delegations did not entail unrestricted executive or administrative license. Since 1932, Congress has enacted a wide range of so-called legislative veto measures allowing it, or one of its Houses or commit-

12. See §§ 5–1 to 5–3, 5–16 to 5–17, infra.

13. See §§ 5–4, 5–7 to 5–8, 5–15, 5–20 to 5–22, infra.

14. When the Constitution was ratified, of course, only the House of Representatives was directly accountable to the electorate.

15. That article also authorizes the President, "on extraordinary Occasions, [to] convene both Houses, or either of them," and instructs that, "in Case of Disagreement between them, with Respect to the time of Adjournment, he may adjourn them to such Time as he shall think proper. . . ."

16. See § 4–9, infra.

17. See § 4–5, infra.

tees, to review and revoke the actions of federal agencies and executive departments.[1] Some 200 statutes containing legislative veto provisions have been enacted—most of them since 1970.[2]

The veto offered lawmakers a way to delegate vast power to the executive branch or to independent agencies while retaining the option to cancel particular exercises of such power—and, most importantly, to exercise this oversight without having to pass new legislation or to repeal existing laws. Thus presidential authority, from the power to reorganize the executive branch to the power to order American troops into foreign conflicts, has been statutorily constrained by the purported authority of one or of both Houses of Congress to exercise what may loosely be called a legislative veto.[3]

The constitutionality of the legislative veto was determined not on the battlefield of so momentous a presidential prerogative as the power to wage war, but in a skirmish over the authority to suspend the deportation of a small class of aliens. Congress had delegated to the Immigration and Naturalization Service (INS) limited discretion to suspend deportations, subject to veto within a specified period by either the Senate or the House of Representatives. A foreign graduate student named Jagdish Chadha persuaded the INS to let him remain in the United States after his visa had expired, only to have this suspension of deportation vetoed by a House resolution.

In *I.N.S. v. Chadha*,[4] the Supreme Court held that *all* action taken by Congress that is "legislative" in "character"[5] must be taken in accord with the "single, finely wrought and exhaustively considered procedure"[6] set forth in the "explicit and unambiguous provisions" of article I.[7] In his opinion for the Court,[8] Chief Justice Burger explained

§ 4–3

1. The first legislative veto provision was included in the Legislative Appropriations Act for fiscal 1933. Act of June 30, 1932, ch. 314, § 407, 47 Stat. 382, 414 (repealed 1966).

2. See Abourezk, "The Congressional Veto: A Contemporary Response to Executive Encroachments on Legislative Prerogative," 52 Ind.L.J. 323, 324 (1977).

3. See 128 Cong.Rec. S2575 (daily ed. Mar. 23, 1982) (listing 33 laws containing legislative veto provisions enacted by the 96th Congress).

4. 462 U.S. 919 (1983).

5. Id. at 952.

6. Id. at 951.

7. Id. at 945.

8. Chief Justice Burger's opinion was joined by Justices Brennan, Marshall, Blackmun, Stevens and O'Connor. Justice Powell wrote separately to concur in the judgment. Justice White took issue with the majority's analysis in a vigorous dissent.

Justice Rehnquist, joined by Justice White, dissented on the narrow ground that the presence of a boilerplate severability clause was not sufficient to allow the remainder of the immigration law to survive invalidation of the legislative veto provision. The Court reasoned that an express severability clause creates a presumption that Congress did not intend the validity of the law as a whole to depend upon the validity of any provision thereof, and that such a presumption is strengthened if what remains after severance is "fully operative" as a law. 462 U.S. at 931–35. Justice Rehnquist accused the majority of confusing the question of Congress' power to make such a delegation with the question of whether Congress intended to do so. 462 U.S. at 1016 (Rehnquist, J., dissenting). He argued that since the legislative history—and the inclusion of the veto provision itself—revealed a Congress consistently unwilling to give the executive branch unilateral power to suspend deportation, id. at 1015, it made no sense for the judiciary to sever that provision and cede to the executive a discretion-

that the presentment clause [9] and the bicamerality requirement [10] constitute crucial structural restraints on the "hydraulic pressure inherent within [the legislature] to exceed the outer limits of its power." [11] If the separation of powers is to be more than "an abstract generalization," [12] the Court must enforce the bicamerality and presentment rules not only when Congress *purports* to be legislating but whenever it takes action that must be *deemed* "legislative." [13] Since the legislative veto of Chadha's status as a permanent resident alien was neither approved by both Houses of Congress, nor presented to the President for signature or veto, it followed inexorably that it was unconstitutional.[14]

The Court explained that the veto of Chadha's suspension of deportation was "essentially legislative" because it "had the purpose and effect of altering the legal rights, duties and relations of persons . . . outside the legislative branch." [15] Without Congress' exercise of the legislative veto in his case, Chadha would have remained in America; without the veto provision in the immigration statute, the change in Chadha's legal status could have been wrought only by legislation requiring his deportation.[16]

ary power that Congress had intended to withhold. Id. at 1014. Likewise, it would make no sense to sever the one-house veto provision from the Impoundment Control Act of 1974, since the legislative history—not to mention the very title of the statute—makes clear that Congress would never have ceded impoundment authority to the President if it had known that its primary means of reining in the White House was unconstitutional. See § 4–12 infra, discussing City of New Haven, Conn. v. United States, 809 F.2d 900 (D.C.Cir. 1987) (declining to sever and instead invalidating entire impoundment scheme).

The problems inherent in such heavily intent-based approaches to severability, see L. Tribe, Constitutional Choices 79–83 (1985), might be avoided by viewing the Court's decision in Chadha not as enforcing the law "minus" the invalidated provision, but as giving effect to the entire enactment to the extent that the Constitution—in this case the bicamerality and presentment requirements—permits. See id. at 81–82. Thus, congressional exercise of an unconstitutional legislative veto against Chadha is to be treated as a nullity, as incapable of abridging whatever rights Chadha otherwise enjoys under the immigration law Congress enacted. Under this approach, it is immaterial whether Congress might not have conferred such rights on Chadha had it anticipated this outcome. Cf. Alaska Airlines, Inc. v. Brock, 107 S.Ct. 1476 (1987) (legislative veto provision covering regulations applicable to statutory employee "first-hire" rights is severable because statute itself imposed such strong affirmative duties on air carriers that first-hire

provisions scarcely need the adoption of regulations). Invalidation of the entire law is in order only if it is shown that the meaning of the entire law Congress enacted would be so thoroughly and radically compromised by the invalidation of the law's veto device that, as a matter of ordinary statutory construction, the stump that remains after the veto branch has been cut off ought to be given no legal effect at all. See City of New Haven v. United States, supra (since "raison d'etre" of the Impoundment Control Act was to assert control over presidential impoundments and such control was obtained only by means of the legislative veto, invalidation of that provision requires treating entire law as void).

9.   Art. I, § 7, cl. 2.

10.   Art. I, §§ 1, 7.

11.   462 U.S. at 951.

12.   Id. at 946.

13.   Id. at 952.

14.   It appears that the lack of presentment would in itself have been sufficient to doom the law. In United States Senate v. Federal Trade Comm'n, 463 U.S. 1216 (1983), the Court summarily affirmed a lower court judgment which had invalidated a two-House veto provision—a legislative device that obviously satisfies the bicamerality requirement.

15.   462 U.S. at 952.

16.   Id. at 952–54. In his concurring opinion, Justice Powell argued that Congress' action instead trenched upon the *judicial* power, since the veto of the INS

To be sure, the same observations apply with equal validity to nearly *all* exercises of delegated authority, whether by a House of Congress or by an executive department or an administrative agency. Both through rule-making and through case-by-case adjudication, exercises of delegated authority change legal rights and privileges no less than do full-fledged laws. But unlike laws, these clearly law-altering administrative actions need not meet the bicamerality or presentment requirements. So far at least, it is only when Congress delegates power *to itself or its members* that the Court insists on squeezing such power into one of the three pigeonholes envisioned by the Framers, labeling that power "executive," "judicial," or "legislative." [17]

It might seem arbitrary to require Congressmen to act according to the rules applicable to their lawmaking capacity even when discharging duties delegated to them by statute, while not insisting that members of the executive or judicial branches be deemed to be acting purely in their executive or judicial capacities when they exercise delegated power.[18] Yet even if the Court has failed to explain fully its return to a form of constitutional exegesis that appears to deal in "legislative" and "executive" essences, the decision in *Chadha* is not without considerable intuitive appeal. The Framers regarded the legislature as the most dangerous branch, and even two centuries later it remains a plausible proposition to many that there is more to fear when Congress—which is the source of all statutorily-delegated authority—delegates not to the other branches, but to itself.[19]

The ruling in *Chadha* undoubtedly "[struck] down in one fell swoop provisions in more laws enacted by Congress than the Court had

decision to suspend Chadha's deportation constituted review of the application of the law in an individual setting. Such legislative action adversely affecting the legal status of a specific individual, Justice Powell opined, offends "not only . . . [the Constitution's] general allocation of power, but also . . . the Bill of Attainder Clause," which concretely embodies "the Framers' concern that trial by a legislature lacks the safeguards necessary to prevent the abuse of power." Id. at 962. This argument divorces the Chadha decision from any objection to legislative vetoes as such, for if the real problem is that a veto usurps the article III function of construing pre-existing law in a way that is binding on the federal courts, that objection remains even if such usurpation is carried out by *both* Houses of Congress with the approval of the President. And a bill of attainder is still unconstitutional even if enacted by both Houses and signed by the President, as Justice Powell himself seemed to recognize. See id. 966 n. 9 (Powell, J., concurring). But see id. at 935 n. 8, 954 n. 17 (opinion of the Court) (purporting to leave this question open). See generally §§ 10–4, 10–5, 10–6, infra.

17. Expansion of this category-conscious analysis to the independent regulatory agencies that constitute the so-called "fourth branch" of the federal government could ultimately require wholesale reorganization of the executive branch and the overruling of Humphrey's Executor v. United States, 295 U.S. 602 (1935), discussed in § 4–10, infra. Justice White saw in the majority's holding in Chadha "a profoundly different conception of the Constitution than that held by the Courts which sanctioned the modern administrative state." 462 U.S. at 1002 (White, J., dissenting). For further discussion of this issue in the aftermath of Bowsher v. Synar, 106 S.Ct. 3181 (1986), see § 4–10, infra.

18. A critical analysis, along these lines, of the Court's legislative veto decision can be found in L. Tribe, Constitutional Choices 66–83 (1985). This treatise reaches a more charitable conclusion about the decision.

19. See § 4–9, infra, for a discussion of the view that the real textual bases of the Chadha decision are the Constitution's appointments (art. II, § 2, cl. 2) and incompatibility (art. I, § 6, cl. 2) clauses.

cumulatively invalidated in its history." [20]   But the degree to which *Chadha* will change the way the government does business is less clear.[21] Both academic speculation [22] and empirical review [23] suggest that legislative vetoes may not have substantially enhanced government efficiency, but may instead have simply given special interest groups that lose battles before agencies ways to win favors from committees of Congress. And there exist other legislative methods for containing, after the fact, the power delegated to agencies, commissions and executive departments that do not implicate the holding of *Chadha* in the least. Although the Court has indicated its willingness to read *Chadha* for all it is worth,[24] even the broadest reading contains nothing that would prevent Congress from enacting "report and wait" provisions.[25] The Federal Rules of Evidence and of Civil Procedure are

20. 462 U.S. at 1002 (White, J., joined by Rehnquist, J., dissenting). These provisions began to fall like dominoes almost immediately, as the Court began summarily affirming lower court judgments that invalidated a variety of legislative veto devices. See, e.g., Process Gas Consumers Group v. Consumer Energy Council of America, 463 U.S. 1216 (1983).

21. Many of the 200 or so legislative veto provisions may be largely superfluous if the underlying substantive statutes to which they are appended give little discretion to the executive branch. See, e.g., Alaska Airlines, Inc. v. Brock, 107 S.Ct. 1476 (1987) (legislative veto provision covering regulations applicable to statutory employee "first-hire" rights is severable because statute itself imposes such strong affirmative duties on air carriers that first-hire provisions scarcely need the adoption of regulations). Therefore, the inability to rein in the executive branch by legislative veto may simply induce Congress to devote more care to circumscribing executive conduct *before* the fact through the imposition of nondiscretionary statutory duties. Without a legislative veto, some congressional delegations of power to the executive are probably out of the question. See City of New Haven, Conn. v. United States, 809 F.2d 900 (D.C.Cir. 1987) (declining to sever legislative veto provision and instead invalidating entire Impoundment Control Act, since Congress would never have ceded any impoundment power to President if Congress were prohibited from regulating exercise of that power).

22. See, e.g., Scalia, "The Legislative Veto: A False Remedy for System Overload," Regulation 19 (Nov.–Dec. 1979).

23. See, e.g., Bruff & Gellhorn, "Congressional Control of Administrative Regulation: A Study of Legislative Vetoes," 90 Harv.L.Rev. 1369, 1432–33 (1977).

24. Judging from summary dispositions subsequent to the decision in Chadha, a wide range of variations on the legislative

veto theme are apparently doomed under the Court's broad holding. For example, the Court summarily affirmed the invalidation of the two-house veto at issue in United States Senate v. Federal Trade Comm'n, 463 U.S. 1216 (1983), even though the provision obviously satisfied at least the bicamerality requirement. This device, enacted as part of the Federal Trade Comm'n Improvements Act of 1980, provided that an FTC trade regulation would become effective unless both Houses of Congress voted to disapprove it. 15 U.S.C. § 57a–1 (1982). Any infringement of executive prerogative posed by such a provision is distinct from that at issue in Chadha. Unlike the INS, which operates within the executive branch at the direction of the Attorney General, the FTC is an independent agency—FTC regulations have the force of law without presidential concurrence, and the President has no authority to veto regulations with which he disagrees or to discharge FTC commissioners without cause. Yet the Supreme Court apparently did not deem these differences significant enough to warrant further explication of the principles recognized in Chadha.

25. Thus it seems plain that nothing in Chadha casts doubt on those provisions of the War Powers Resolution that impose reporting requirements on the President, War Powers Resolution § 4(a), 50 U.S.C. § 1543(a) (1976), and set durational limits of 60 to 90 days on the presense of American armed forces in "hostilities" abroad unless Congress has declared war or otherwise authorized such use of military power, War Powers Resolution § 5(b), 50 U.S.C. § 1544(b) (1976 & Supp. V. 1981). See Chadha, 462 U.S. at 955 n. 19. It follows from Chadha, however, that such reporting requirements must be triggered by objective events—such as "hostilities"—whose presence or absence a court can itself ascertain, and *not* by a congressional "resolution" that such events have indeed occurred. If Congress could trigger the application of laws restraining executive

already governed by such provisions—mandating that rule changes proposed pursuant to delegated authority shall not take effect as law until after the legislative session in which they have been reported to Congress by the Attorney General.[26] Such laws broaden Congress' opportunity to pass otherwise valid legislation denying legal effect to those executive, agency, or court actions with which it disagrees.[27]

As new patterns of interaction between the executive and legislative branches [28] are proposed, they must, in the wake of *Chadha*, be assessed not only for their practical virtues and for the degree to which they tend to swell total federal power in politically unaccountable ways or to leave either branch with diminished flexibility and independence, but also with an eye to their congruence with the Framers' assumptions about how power must be shared. An unduly severe application of the separation of powers concept may needlessly threaten pragmatic government, but the Court remains firm in its belief that the Constitution, for better or for worse, has made much of that choice for us. Bertrand Russell once warned that "pragmatism is like a warm bath that heats up so imperceptibly that you don't know when to scream." [29] The Supreme Court has made it clear that the decision to "scream"—to invoke the Constitution in resisting at least some new roles for the respective branches—will be made with strict regard for the Constitution's most fundamental architectural principles.

power by resolutions, whether bi- or unicameral, that are not subject to presidential veto, then Congress would be playing a continuing role in the implementation of extant laws—the one thing Chadha clearly forbids. It follows that § 5(c) of the War Powers Resolution, 50 U.S.C. § 1544(c) (1976 & Supp. V. 1981), is invalid insofar as it purports to require the withdrawal of American forces in specified circumstances "if the Congress so directs by concurrent resolution." See also § 4–7, infra, at notes 29–31.

26. See 28 U.S.C. § 2072 (1976) (Rules of Civil Procedure take effect 90 days after reported to Congress); 28 U.S.C. § 2076 (1976) (Rules of Evidence take effect 180 days after reported to Congress); see also Sibbach v. Wilson & Co., 312 U.S. 1 (1941), cited with approval in Chadha, 462 U.S. at 935 n. 9.

27. Likewise, a law declaring that no administrative agency rule would take effect until affirmatively approved by joint resolution and presented to the President would certainly be constitutional, if perhaps unwise. Nothing in the Court's reading of the Constitution in Chadha prevents Congress from reducing the regulatory agencies to the status of advisory study commissions.

28. The relationship between the judicial and legislative branches is also affected by the principles underlying Chadha: according constitutionally mandated respect to the structure of the legislative process places limits on the latitude afforded courts when they engage in statutory construction. If there is tension between what the judiciary believes Congress might have intended and what the judiciary concludes Congress in fact enacted, the latter must be deemed dispositive. "Judges interpret laws rather than reconstruct legislators' intentions. Where the language of those laws is clear, we are not free to replace it with an unenacted legislative intent." I.N.S. v. Cardoza-Fonseca, 107 S.Ct. 1207, 1224 (1987) (Scalia, J., concurring) (agreeing with Court that congressional legislation requires attorney general to withhold deportation of alien who shows a "well-founded fear" that her life or freedom would be threatened, but chiding Court for undertaking a needlessly exhaustive search of the legislative history to justify rejection of the Reagan administration's narrower reading of the law).

29. Quoted in Kass, "Implications of Prenatal Diagnosis for the Human Right to Life," in Biomedical Ethics and the Law 327 (J. Humber & R. Almeder eds. 1976).

§ 4-4. The Limits of Executive Authority in Foreign Affairs: The "Domestication" of International Policy

With respect to presidential power generally, constitutional text and history are commonly thought to be "almost as enigmatic as the dreams Joseph was called upon to interpret for Pharaoh." [1] In the area of foreign affairs, however, there is wide agreement at least that the President is invested with great power. In an era that could quite sharply distinguish action abroad from action at home, the unique posture of the President with regard to foreign affairs was proclaimed by the then Representative John Marshall: "The President is the sole organ of the nation in its external relations, and its sole representative with foreign nations." [2]

But even apart from the contemporary difficulty of defining any area as wholly "external," this "plenary and exclusive power of the President" [3] would be limited: although the President alone can act in foreign affairs, the content of presidential options is defined partly—and increasingly—by congressional enactments and limited by constitutional strictures. Hence, while it may be symbolically correct to say that the President is the sole national "actor" in foreign affairs, it is not accurate to label the President the sole national policy maker.[4] It would be equally inaccurate, however, to cast the role of the Executive in foreign affairs as exclusively instrumental; the President is surely accorded a more vital role in foreign relations than that of a mere medium whose charge it is to effect exogenuously posited ends.[5]

Thus the Constitution plainly grants the President the initiative in matters directly involved in the conduct of diplomatic and military affairs. Article II, § 2, provides that "[t]he President shall be Commander in Chief of the Army and Navy . . .;" that "[h]e shall have Power, by and with the Advice and Consent of the Senate, to make Treaties, provided two thirds of the Senators present concur;" and that

§ 4-4

1. Youngstown Sheet & Tube Co. v. Sawyer, 343 U.S. 579, 634 (1952) (Jackson, J., concurring). Justice Jackson continued: "A century and a half of partisan debate and scholarly speculation yields no net result but only supplies more or less apt quotations from respected sources on each side of any question. They largely cancel each other." Id. at 634–35. "A Hamilton may be matched against a Madison . . . Professor Taft is counterbalanced by Theodore Roosevelt . . . It even seems that President Taft cancels out Professor Taft . . . ." Id. at 635 n. 1.

2. Marshall's comment was made before the House of Representatives when he was defending the actions of President John Adams in regard to the extradition of one Jonathan Robbins. Robbins, who was charged with murder by the British government, was surrendered to the British authorities, without judicial process, pursuant to an order of President Adams, acting under the Jay Treaty. See generally E. Corwin, The President: Office and Powers 1787–1957, at 177–78 (1957). Doctrines recognizing greater presidential power in the foreign sphere rest on an increasingly dubious separation between foreign and domestic policy and an increasingly false premise that steps taken abroad have little impact at home and vice versa. See generally Manning, "The Congress, the Executive and Intermestic Affairs: Three Proposals," 55 Foreign Aff. 306 (1977); Nye, "Independence and Interdependence," 22 For.Pol. 129 (1976).

3. United States v. Curtiss-Wright Export Corp., 299 U.S. 304, 320 (1936).

4. Nor does Marshall's statement imply the contrary: "Clearly, what Marshall had foremost in mind was simply the President's role as *instrument of communication* with other governments." Corwin, supra note 2, at 178 (emphasis in original).

5. See L. Henkin, Foreign Affairs and the Constitution 47 (1972).

the President "shall nominate, and by and with the Advice and Consent of the Senate, shall appoint Ambassadors, other public Ministers and Consuls . . ." Similarly, Article II, § 3, states that the President "shall receive Ambassadors and other public Ministers . . ."

Taken together with the command of article II, § 3, that the President "shall take Care that the Laws be faithfully executed," these constitutional provisions have come to be regarded as explicit textual manifestations of the inherent presidential power to administer, if not necessarily to formulate, the foreign policy of the United States. Although influenced (often decisively) by congressional action or constitutional restraint, the President thus has exclusive responsibility for announcing and implementing military policy; [6] for negotiating, administering, and terminating treaties or executive agreements; for establishing and breaking relations with foreign governments; [7] and generally for applying the foreign policy of the United States.

But this set of presidential powers and responsibilities, however broad, is clearly bounded even in the absence of congressional constriction. For example, President Nixon was held to have acted unconstitu-

6. One constitutional draft had provided that the Congress should have the power to "make war." The phrase was changed to "declare war" in order to ensure that, while no one person could commit the nation to war, the conduct of an ongoing war would not be hamstrung by the need for consensus over tactics and strategy. See Bickel, "Congress, the President and the Power to Wage War," 48 Chicago-Kent L.Rev. 131, 132 (1971). Of course, Congress retains a residuum of control even here because of its command of the appropriations process. See § 5–10, infra.

7. It has not always been conceded that the power of recognizing other governments reposed exclusively with the President. Generally, the President's prerogative in this sphere is said to derive from his article II, § 3, power to "receive Ambassadors." It was suggested early by Alexander Hamilton that this power "was more a matter of dignity than of authority." The Federalist No. 69 at 451 (Mod. Lib. ed. 1941). Hamilton soon reversed ground, however, and deemed the power conferred by that clause one of substance, not just form. See generally Berger, "The Presidential Monopoly of Foreign Relations," 71 Mich.L.Rev. 1 (1972).

Although it is generally understood that the President has the substantive power to determine the recognition policies of the United States and that this power is effectively immune from congressional regulation, see L. Henkin, Foreign Affairs and the Constitution 93 (1972), it has proven difficult in practice to obtain a definitive judicial resolution of the issue. When President Carter unilaterally terminated the nation's mutual defense treaty with Taiwan in order to improve relations with the People's Republic of China, several members of the Senate filed suit, claiming that such action deprived them of their constitutional role. Although the Court of Appeals for the District of Columbia Circuit, en banc, held that the President had not exceeded his authority, Goldwater v. Carter, 617 F.2d 697 (D.C. Cir.1979) (per curiam), the Supreme Court granted certiorari two weeks later and summarily vacated the judgment below and remanded with directions to dismiss the complaint. Goldwater v. Carter, 444 U.S. 996 (1979) (mem.). Justice Rehnquist's plurality opinion, joined by Chief Justice Burger and Justices Stewart and Stevens, reasoned that the role of the Senate, if any, in the abrogation of a treaty was a nonjusticiable political question, since the Constitution was silent on the matter, and since appropriate treaty termination procedures might well vary from case to case in the sensitive field of foreign relations. 444 U.S. at 1003. Justice Powell concurred in the judgment on the ground that the controversy was not ripe, but disagreed with Justice Rehnquist's political question analysis. Id. at 997–1002. Only Justice Brennan, in his dissent, expressed an opinion on the merits: abrogation of the treaty was "a necessary incident to Executive recognition of the Peking government," id. at 1006, and thus clearly within the President's power, since it is "firmly establish[ed] that the Constitution commits to the President alone the power to recognize, and withdraw recognition from, foreign regimes," id. See § 3–13, supra.

tionally when he purported by Presidential Proclamation to impose a 10% surcharge on most articles imported into the United States from the date following his proclamation:[8] since the laying of import duties necessarily operated both to tax domestic consumers[9] and to regulate foreign commerce, it could not be sustained absent a clearly applicable and intelligibly confined congressional delegation:[10] "[N]either need or national emergency will justify the exercise of a power by the Executive not inherent in his office nor delegated by the Congress."[11] Thus, although Congress may authorize the President to adjust imports as necessary upon a finding by the Secretary of the Treasury that an "article is being imported into the United States in such quantities or under such circumstances as to threaten to impair the national security"[12] as defined by a statutorily enumerated list of factors,[13] the power of the President to take any such step unilaterally would almost certainly be denied.

In several crucial respects—most notably, article II, § 2's requirement of Senatorial "Advice and Consent" in treaty-making and ambassadorial appointments—it is the Constitution's text that expressly forecloses unilateral presidential conduct of foreign policy. More commonly, that result comes about either through an underlying notion that Congress shares in the "unenumerated foreign affairs power,"[14] or through the Constitution's grants to Congress of the power to determine the financial resources and to shape the economic and legal devices that are available for use in presidential action, whether in foreign affairs or domestically.

Article I, § 9, cl. 7, for example, provides that "[n]o money shall be drawn from the Treasury, but in Consequence of Appropriations made by Law . . . ."[15] Congress may simply refuse to appropriate funds for

8. Yoshida International, Inc. v. United States, 378 F.Supp. 1155 (Cust.Ct.1974), rev'd, 526 F.2d 560 (C.C.P.A.1975).

9. Compare National Cable Television Ass'n, Inc. v. United States, 415 U.S. 336 (1974) (holding, in order to avoid facing the validity of a delegation of taxing power, that fees to be imposed by the FCC on community antenna television systems should be measured by the value to the recipient rather than by more general policy considerations).

10. Yoshida, 378 F.Supp. at 1167, 1170–73. The Court of Customs and Patent Appeals found such a delegation, however, in the Trading With the Enemy Act. 526 F.2d at 579–80.

11. 378 F.Supp. at 1175.

12. FEA v. Algonquin SNG, Inc., 426 U.S. 548, 559 (1976) (sustaining imposition of license fees by Presidents Nixon and Ford for oil and petroleum imports).

13. The Court noted, id. at 550–51 n. 1, and relied upon, id. at 559–60, the statute's careful enumeration of over a dozen specific factors such as "loss of skills or investment . . . resulting from the displace-

ment of any domestic products by excessive imports . . . ." Id. at 551 n. 1.

14. L. Henkin, Foreign Affairs and the Constitution 68 (1972).

15. That clause goes on to require that "a regular Statement and Account of the Receipts and Expenditures of all public Money shall be published from time to time." Although the Supreme Court has held that citizens and taxpayers lack standing to challenge the failure of Congress to comply with the statement and account clause and that the issues posed by uncontrolled executive spending are therefore nonjusticiable, see United States v. Richardson, 418 U.S. 166 (1974), discussed in Chapter 3, supra, it seems clear that the congressional practice of permitting intelligence activities to be carried on with no accounting for how federal funds are expended violates the clause. See generally Note, "Cloak and Ledger: Is CIA Funding Constitutional?" 2 Hastings Const'l. Law Q. 717 (1975); Note, "The CIA's Secret Funding and the Constitution," 84 Yale L.J. 608 (1975); "Fiscal Oversight of the Central Intelligence Agency: Can Account-

policies it deems unsound. Moreover, Congress may condition appropriations in ways that limit presidential foreign policy choices. For example, the first Hickenlooper Amendment required the President to terminate foreign aid if "the government of any country has nationalized or expropriated or seized ownership or control of property owned by any United States citizen" without providing the "speedy compensation" required by international law.[16]

Perhaps the most prominent recent examples of congressional attempts to determine the substance of United States foreign policy through the use of the appropriations power have been the increasingly detailed restrictions imposed on aid to the "contras" seeking to overthrow the Nicaraguan government. The original Boland Amendment in 1982, a rider to a continuing appropriations act, forbade the use of funds by the CIA or the Department of Defense to furnish "support for military activities" to the contras.[17] Congress later made available $24 million in 1983, but more tightly prohibited the expenditure of funds beyond that amount by "any . . . agency or entity of the United States involved in intelligence activities," for the purpose of "supporting, directly or indirectly, military or paramilitary operations" of the contras.[18] Congress also directed the President to report on the results of his actions by the following March.[19] By 1984, congressional sentiment had once again swung against the contras,[20] and no funds were allowed to be spent—but this time buttressed by the tighter wording.[21]

In 1985, Congress decided to provide $27 million to the "Nicaraguan democratic resistance," but only for "humanitarian assistance." [22] This assistance could not include "weapons, weapons systems, ammunition, or other equipment, vehicles, or material which can be used to inflict serious bodily harm or death," and could not be provided by the CIA or the Department of Defense.[23] At the same time, the restrictions on the provision of any other support to the contras were further tightened, and the President was required to submit reports every 90

ability and Confidentiality Co-Exist?" 7 N.Y.U.J. Int'l Law & Politics 493 (1974).

16. 22 U.S.C. § 2370(e)(1).

17. Department of Defense Appropriations Act, 1983, Pub.L. 97–377, § 793, 96 Stat. 1865, Dec. 21, 1982.

18. Intelligence Authorization Act for Fiscal Year 1984, Pub.L. 98–215, § 108, 97 Stat. 1475, Dec. 9, 1983; see also Department of Defense Appropriations Act, 1984, Pub.L. 98–212, § 775, 97 Stat. 1452, Dec. 8, 1983.

19. Pub.L. 98–215, § 109(f).

20. The Deficit Reduction Act of 1984, Pub.L. 98–369, § 2907, 98 Stat. 1210, July 18, 1984, stated that "[i]t is the sense of Congress that no funds heretofore or hereafter appropriated in any Act of Congress shall be obligated or expended for the purpose of planning, directing, executing, or

supporting the mining of ports or territorial waters of Nicaragua."

21. Department of Defense Appropriations Act, 1985, § 8066(a), Pub.L. 98–473, § 101, 98 Stat. 1935, Oct. 12, 1984; see also Intelligence Authorization Act for Fiscal Year 1985, Pub.L. 98–618, § 801, 98 Stat. 3304, Nov. 8, 1984. In May 1985, however, the President imposed a trade embargo between the United States and Nicaragua. Executive Order 12513 of May 1, 1985.

22. International Security and Development Cooperation Act of 1985, Pub.L. 99–83, § 722(g)(1), 99 Stat. 254, Aug. 8, 1985; see also Supplemental Appropriations Act, 1985, Pub.L. 99–88, 99 Stat. 324, Aug. 15, 1985.

23. Pub.L. 99–83, § 722(g); Pub.L. 99–88, 99 Stat. 324.

days thereafter "on any actions taken" in spending the money Congress had appropriated.[24]

By the fall of 1986, Congress was willing to allocate $100 million for support to the contras, including some military activities.[25] Certain sums were reserved for humanitarian assistance and human rights programs,[26] while overall the aid was subject to the fulfillment of various specified conditions, as certified by Presidential reports.[27] For example, detailed requirements regarding the course of the fighting, the prospects of the negotiations, and the headway made by the contras in carrying out internal reforms determined whether all of the money would be provided and what types of military assistance could be given.[28] Overriding all other conditions, however, Congress insisted that no United States personnel "may enter Nicaragua," or even go "within 20 miles of the border with Nicaragua," to provide assistance to the contras.[29]

Beyond the appropriations power, article I, § 8 confers upon Congress a variety of ways in which it may control the structure of the devices and institutions available to the President in the conduct of foreign policy. Congress is empowered in article I, § 8, to "lay and collect . . . Duties, Imposts and Excises;" to "regulate Commerce with Foreign Nations"; to "establish an uniform Rule of Naturalization;" to "define and punish . . . Felonies committed on the high seas, and Offences against the Law of Nations;" to "declare War;" to "raise and support Armies;" to "provide and maintain a Navy;" to "make Rules for the Government and Regulation of the land and naval Forces;" to "provide for calling forth the Militia to . . . repel Invasions"; and to "provide for organizing, arming, and disciplining, the Militia, and for

24. Pub.L. 99–83, § 722(d); see also Pub.L. 99–88, § 102(a). Beyond the humanitarian assistance, no funds were to be used "to provide assistance of any kind, either directly or indirectly" to the contras. The U.S. Government could, however, exchange information with the contras. Pub. L. 99–88, § 102(b).

25. Military Construction Appropriations Act, 1987, § 206(a)(2), Pub.L. 99–591, Oct. 30, 1986; see also id., § 209 and the Intelligence Authorization Act for Fiscal Year 1986, § 105(a), Pub.L. 99–169, 99 Stat. 1003, Dec. 4, 1985.

26. Military Construction Appropriations Act, 1987, § 208.

27. Id., § 211.

28. Id.

29. Id., §§ 203(e) and 216(a). As this treatise goes to press in mid-1987, both Congress and an independent counsel are conducting extensive investigations into what may be serious violations of these restrictions, allegedly undertaken at White House direction with the aid of private groups and several foreign nations.

For Fiscal 1985, the Boland Amendment, see note 21, supra, provided that "no funds available to the Central Intelligence Agency, the Department of Defense, or any other agency or entity of the United States involved in intelligence activities may be obligated or expended for the purpose or which would have the effect of supporting, directly or indirectly, military or paramilitary operations in Nicaragua by any nation, group, organization, movement, or individual." The White House position initially appears to have been that the President was involved in, and aware of, no effort by his National Security Council to obtain private or foreign support for the Nicaraguan contras; as testimony in Congress made that position increasingly difficult to maintain, the White House shifted to the claim that the Boland Amendment did not, and could not constitutionally, restrict the President's secret use of National Security Council staff to solicit funds to support the military efforts of the contras. See generally Time Magazine, Vol. 129, No. 22, June 1, 1987, at 24–26. For a brief rejoinder to the statutory and constitutional views put forward by the White House as this treatise goes to press, see Tribe, "Reagan Ignites a Constitutional Crisis," The New York Times, May 20, 1987, at A31.

governing such Part of them as may be employed in the Service of the United States. . . ." [30]

As it has done with the appropriations power, Congress has often exercised these other article I, § 8, powers in ways that have either determined the nature of the devices available for presidential use, as in the area of import quotas and fees, or conditioned presidential use of particular institutions or devices upon compliance with Congress' substantive foreign policy predilections. For example, the 1987 controversy over sales of arms to Iran brought to the fore congressional restrictions on arms sales to countries involved with "international terrorism." In 1977, Congress utilized its power to regulate foreign commerce to prohibit the President from making arms sales to "any government which aids or abets, by granting sanctuary from prosecution to, any individual or group which has committed an act of international terrorism." [31] Congress extended its influence in the Export Administration Act of 1979 by requiring 30-day notification to various congressional committees prior to the approval of any license for the export of goods or technology valued at more than $7 million to any country that the Secretary of State had determined "has repeatedly provided support for acts of international terrorism." [32] Subsequently, in the Omnibus Diplomatic Security and Antiterrorism Act of 1986, Congress forbade the export of arms to any such country, unless the President submitted to the Congress a report justifying a waiver and

30. Judicial relief under such restrictions on Presidential power may be difficult to obtain, however. Sanchez-Espinoza v. Reagan, 770 F.2d 202 (D.C. Cir. 1985), dealt with a suit by Nicaraguan citizens and twelve members of the House of Representatives against federal officials for various claims arising from alleged support of the contras. Justice (then Judge) Scalia, writing for the D.C. Circuit, found that it would be an abuse of judicial discretion to provide equitable relief to the Nicaraguans "where the authority for our interjection into so sensitive a foreign affairs matter as this are statutes no more specifically addressed to such concerns than the Alien Tort Statute and the APA." Id. at 208. The war powers issue brought by the representatives was held to be a nonjusticiable political question. Id. at 210. On the other hand, indictable or impeachable offenses may arise from executive violations of duly enacted congressional restrictions; anyone charged with violating such restrictions or conspiring to do so would be free to interpose a constitutional defense—although the defense of inherent executive prerogative to conduct foreign and military policy free of all congressional restraint should be rejected on the merits.

31. 22 U.S.C. § 2753(f)(1). Such arms sales may be made, however, if the President "finds that the national security re-quires otherwise," id., in which case the President must report such finding to the Speaker of the House of Representatives and the Senate Committee on Foreign Relations. Id., § 2753(f)(2). In 1976, Congress had exercised its appropriations power to require the President to terminate assistance to all such countries, under similar provisions. 22 U.S.C. § 2371. These provisions were changed in 1985, expanding the coverage to include countries that support terrorism, but subject to an initial Presidential determination, and allowing for Presidential waiver on national security or humanitarian grounds, subject to prior notification to the House Committee on Foreign Affairs and the Senate Committee on Foreign Relations. Id.

32. 50 U.S.C.App. § 2405(j). It is also required that the Secretary of State have determined that "[s]uch exports would make a significant contribution to the military potential of such country, including its military logistics capability, or would enhance the ability of such country to support acts of international terrorism." Id., 2405(j)(1)(B). Such determinations may not be rescinded unless, 30 days previously, the President submits to the Congress a report justifying the rescission and making certain certifications regarding the country's recent and future conduct. Id., § 2405(j)(2).

describing the proposed export.[33] In addition to being subject to these restrictions specifically imposed on relations with countries supporting international terrorism, the President generally has been required to report to Congress on government-to-government sales, commercial exports, and third-country transfers of major U.S.-origin defense equipment valued at $14 million or more.[34]

Finally, foreign policy choices and their implementation, whether by the President or by Congress or by the joint action of both political branches, are fully constrained by the Constitution's protections for individuals in article I, § 9, and the Bill of Rights.[35]

§ 4–5. Treaties and Executive Agreements

Although the Supreme Court has culled from the Constitution no specific legal definition of the *process* whereby Congress and the President jointly formulate American foreign policy, the Court has declared that foreign policy, when implemented through presidentially negotiated treaties and executive agreements, does entail specific legal *consequences*.

A treaty negotiated and, with the consent of two thirds of the Senators present, ratified by the President, must "be regarded in courts of justice as equivalent to an act of the legislature . . ."[1] This

33. 22 U.S.C. § 2780. Only the determination of repetitious support for acts of international terrorism is relevant for the Act. Id., § 2780(a). For a waiver, the President must determine that the particular export is "important to the national interests of the United States." Id., § 2780(b). The waiver automatically expires at the end of 90 days after it is made, unless extended by Congress. Id. The Act also reduced the notification threshold for the export of goods or technology from $7 million to $1 million. 50 U.S.C.App. § 2405(j)(1).

34. International Security and Development Cooperation Act of 1981, § 101, Pub. L. 97–113, § 1, 95 Stat. 1519. See 22 U.S.C. §§ 2753, 2768, and 2776.

As this treatise goes to press in mid-1987, the investigations mentioned in note 29, supra, are also concerned with possible violations of these and other similar restrictions.

35. See generally L. Henkin, Foreign Affairs and the Constitution 251–70 (1972).

§ 4–5

1. Foster v. Neilson, 27 U.S. (2 Pet.) 253, 314 (1829) (Marshall, C.J.). Although the President may, of course, terminate a treaty in accord with its terms, cf. Goldwater v. Carter, 444 U.S. 996 (1979) (refusing to adjudicate validity of treaty termination without Senate consent), discussed in § 3–13, supra, he is not free to treat a treaty as though it meant something entirely different from what it says, and was presented

to the Senate as meaning at the time the Senate was asked to give its consent under article II, § 2. See Testimony of L. Tribe Before Joint Hearing of the Senate Foreign Relations and Senate Judiciary Committees, 100th Congress, March 11, 1987, "Constitutional Principles Constraining the President's Reinterpretation of the ABM Treaty." The Legal Adviser to the State Department under President Reagan testified, in contrast, that when the Senate gives its consent to a treaty, it accepts whatever international agreement was in fact negotiated between the President and the foreign power; if the secret negotiating record shows the agreement to be something other than what the Senate was led by the President to believe when Senate consent was sought, the Legal Adviser reasoned, the Senate may have consented in error, but it consented nonetheless. See Statement of Abraham D. Sofaer Before the Senate Foreign Relations and Judiciary Committees, March 26, 1987. But this presumes that the President unilaterally "makes" treaties with foreign nations which the Senate subsequently is asked to ratify. The Constitution provides otherwise, giving the President the power to "make Treaties" only "by and with the Advice and Consent of the Senate." Art. II, § 2. No treaty is "made" until the Senate has given its consent; when such consent is given, the treaty to which the Senate consented becomes part of "the supreme Law of the Land," art. VI, which the President is then bound to "faithfully

conclusion had been said to derive from the language of the supremacy clause of article VI, § 2: "This Constitution, and the Laws of the United States which shall be made in Pursuance thereof; and all Treaties made, or which shall be made, under the authority of the United States, shall be the supreme Law of the Land. . . ."[2] While the supremacy clause provides that treaties are the law of the land— even without any congressional initiative—some treaties are so drafted that they require congressional action before they have domestic legal entailments.[3]   A treaty which requires the appropriation of funds, for example, cannot be self-executing; subsequent congressional appropriation of the funds is required.[4]

Whether or not a given treaty is self-executing turns of course upon a construction of its terms; whether Congress can properly decline to take action necessary to implement a non-self-executing treaty is unresolved.

The Supreme Court, treating acts of Congress and treaties as legal equivalents, has held that, when a conflict arises between a valid treaty and a valid act of Congress, "the last expression of the sovereign will must control."[5]   Thus, legislative enactments that conflict with prior treaty obligations are given effect by the courts.[6]   Similarly, a treaty may supersede an earlier act of Congress. If the subsequent treaty is not self-executing, however, its conflict with the earlier statute may be illusory, for the statute remains the law of the land until legislation is enacted implementing the treaty. At that point, the earlier statute would be superseded by the later statute, rather than by the treaty itself.

Under the supremacy clause, it is indisputable that a valid treaty overrides any conflicting state law, even on matters otherwise within state control.[7]   Indeed, the treaty controls whether it is ratified before or after the enactment of the conflicting state law.[8]

execute[ ]." Art. II, § 3. Because it is unlikely that the Senate, or any individual Senator or group of Senators, would have standing to challenge the President's construction of a treaty, see § 3–20, supra, the resolution of such disputes as this, whether with respect to the ABM treaty or any other, is likely to be left to the political process.

2. But see L. Henkin, Foreign Affairs and the Constitution 163 (1972): "As an original matter, the equality as law of treaties and federal statutes seems hardly inevitable."

3. See Foster v. Neilson, 27 U.S. (2 Pet.) 253, 314 (1829). Of course such a treaty may be binding upon the United States as a matter of international law even before Congress acts.

4. Turner v. American Baptist Missionary Union. 24 F.Cas. 344 (No. 14251) (C.C. Mich.1852).

5. Chae Chan Ping v. United States (The Chinese Exclusion Case), 130 U.S. 581

(1889). See also Whitney v. Robertson, 124 U.S. 190, 194 (1888).

6. This is not, however, tantamount to a congressional repeal of the treaty since the underlying international obligations of the United States are left unaffected. Rather, such legislation compels the United States to go into default. Edye v. Robertson (Head Money Cases), 112 U.S. 580, 598–600 (1884).

7. See Ware v. Hylton, 3 U.S. (3 Dall.) 199 (1796) (Treaty of Peace between United States and Britain voids state law confiscating British property). See also Hauenstein v. Lynham, 100 U.S. 483 (1880) (treaty providing inheritance rights for aliens prevails over state law disqualifying aliens from inheriting).

Although the power to make treaties with the Indian tribes is constitutionally coextensive with the power to make treaties with foreign nations, Holden v. Joy, 84

8. See note 8 on page 227.

By negotiating a treaty and obtaining the requisite consent of the Senate, the President not only may effectively repeal preceding congressional legislation and preempt conflicting state law, but also may endow Congress with a source of legislative authority independent of the powers enumerated in article I (although, of course, still limited by the Constitution's explicit constraints on federal action). In *State of Missouri v. Holland*,[9] the Supreme Court, speaking through Justice Holmes, held that, even if the absence of appropriate enumerated power otherwise blocked Congress from enacting legislation to protect the migrations of wild birds, the Migratory Bird Treaty of 1916, an agreement between the United States and Canada, provided a valid basis for congressional action under the necessary and proper clause [10] adopting the protective legislation: "It is obvious that there may be matters of the sharpest exigency for the national well being that an act of Congress could not deal with but that a treaty followed by such an act could . . . ." [11] *Missouri v. Holland* thus views the treaty power as a delegation of authority to federal treaty-makers independent of the delegations embodied in the enumeration of Congress' own powers. The decision thus sanctions a legal regime wherein certain subjects may be exclusively within the ambit of the states with respect to domestic legislation, but not with respect to international agreements and laws enacted by Congress pursuant thereto. The importance of treaties as independent sources of congressional power has waned substantially in the years since *Missouri v. Holland*, however; the Supreme Court in the intervening period has so broadened the scope of Congress' constitutionally enumerated powers as to provide ample basis for most imaginable legislative enactments quite apart from the treaty power.[12]

Presidential exercise of the treaty-making power is limited not only by the procedural requirements of article II, § 2, but also by substantive constitutional restrictions. First, the Constitution may well import at least the core of the Framers' conception of what a treaty is. Thomas Jefferson, in his *Manual of Parliamentary Practice* prepared for the United States Senate, wrote that a treaty "must concern the foreign-nation party to the contract, or it would be a mere nullity. . . ." [13] The Supreme Court, in dictum, has embraced Jefferson's view as a constitutional limitation: a treaty must deal with questions

U.S. (17 Wall.) 211, 242 (1872); Worcester v. Georgia, 31 U.S. (6 Pet.) 515, 558 (1832), and although states may not undermine such treaties, The New York Indians, 72 U.S. (5 Wall.) 761 (1867), a rider inserted in an 1871 Indian appropriation act provided that "no Indian nation or tribe within the territory of the United States" would thereafter "be acknowledged . . . as an independent nation . . . with whom the United States may contract by treaty." 16 Stat. 566, Rev. Stat. 2079, now codified as 25 U.S.C. § 71. After 1871, United States-Indian relations were instead embodied in bilateral agreements which have also been given supremacy status over conflicting state law. See Antoine v. Washington, 420 U.S. 194, 203–05 (1975).

8. Nielsen v. Johnson, 279 U.S. 47 (1929).

9. 252 U.S. 416 (1920).

10. See § 5–3, infra.

11. 252 U.S. at 433.

12. See §§ 5–4 to 5–6, 5–9 to 5–12 infra.

13. See S/Doc. No. 92–1, 92d Cong., 1st Sess. 435, 516–18 (1971).

"properly the subject of negotiation with a foreign country." [14]   With global interdependence reaching across an ever broadening spectrum of issues, however, this seems unlikely to prove a serious limitation.

The treaty power is more significantly limited by the panoply of non-federalistic constitutional restrictions, restrictions independent of the Framers' conception of what constituted a proper topic for treaty-making. In *Missouri v. Holland*, Justice Holmes suggested in dictum that "[i]t is open to question" whether the treaty-making power might be constitutionally unlimited except for the procedural requirements of article II, § 2 [15]. *How* open the question was at that point was the only real issue; the Supreme Court had previously submitted that "a treaty cannot change the Constitution or be held valid if it be in violation of that instrument." [16]   In any event, the question was closed resoundingly in *Reid v. Covert*, where a plurality of the Supreme Court, in holding American civilian dependents of overseas military personnel entitled to civilian trial, stated that neither a treaty nor an executive agreement "can confer power on the Congress, or on any other branch of Government, which is free from the restraints of the Constitution." [17]

Although the Constitution explicitly invests the President with the power to negotiate and ratify only "treaties," Presidents have historically expressed the results of their international negotiations in other forms as well, forms subsumed beneath the generic rubric "executive agreements." Since the Constitution prescribes no procedure regarding such agreements, Presidents have long maintained that they may conclude executive agreements without paying heed to the procedural niceties that govern formal treaties—in particular, the requirement of obtaining the support of two-thirds of the Senate.

The precise scope of the President's power to conclude international agreements without the consent of the Senate is unresolved. [18]   At one extreme, the proposition that the treaty is the exclusive medium for effecting foreign policy goals and, consequently, that executive agreements are *ultra vires*, seems adequately refuted. The Constitution, while expounding procedural requirements for treaties alone,

---

14. De Geofroy v. Riggs, 133 U.S. 258, 267 (1890). Cf. Fort Leavenworth R. Co. v. Lowe, 114 U.S. 525, 541 (1885).

15. 252 U.S. at 433.

16. The Cherokee Tobacco, 78 U.S. (11 Wall.) 616, 620–21 (1871) (dictum).

17. 354 U.S. 1, 16 (1957).

Thus, it has been suggested that the federal government may not, by treaty, cede the territory of a state to a foreign country without that state's consent, or deny to a state a republican form of government. See De Geofroy v. Riggs, 133 U.S. 258, 267 (1890). But cf. Worcester v. Georgia, 31 U.S. (6 Pet.) 515 (1832) (grant to Indians of rights in reservations within state boundaries held valid).

18. But it does appear settled that a hybrid form of international agreement—that in which the President is supported by a Joint Resolution of Congress—is coextensive with the treaty power. Such Congressional-Executive agreements are the law of the land, superseding inconsistent state or federal laws. See Von Cotzhausen v. Nazro, 107 U.S. 215 (1882) (postal conventions have the same status as treaties); B. Altman & Co. v. United States, 224 U.S. 583 (1912) (Congressional-Executive agreement deemed a "treaty" within the meaning of a federal statute); Weinberger v. Rossi 456 U.S. 25 (1982) (executive agreement deemed a "treaty" within meaning of a federal statute, to the end that the agreement is exempt from compliance with other prior congressional enactments).

apparently contemplated alternate modes of international agreement.[19] At the very least, the President is empowered to employ executive agreements within the penumbras of enumerated presidential powers as, for example, when invoking the Commander in Chief power to justify an armistice agreement.[20]

At the other extreme the notion that executive agreements know no constitutional bounds proves equally bankrupt. Executive agreements, no less than treaties, must probably be limited to appropriate subject matter. The more difficult question is whether there exist species of international accord that may take the form of a treaty, but not that of an executive agreement. *United States v. Belmont*[21] has been read as intimating that the permissible scope of executive agreements is largely, if not completely, coextensive with that of treaties.[22] That the power to conclude executive agreements coincides perfectly with the treaty power seems untenable, since such a conclusion would emasculate the Senatorial check on executive discretion that the Framers so carefully embodied in the Constitution.[23] At a minimum, it seems clear that an executive agreement, unlike a treaty, cannot override a prior act of Congress.[24] In *United States v. Guy W. Capps, Inc.* the Fourth Circuit emphasized that "[t]he executive may not bypass congressional limitations regulating . . . [imports] by entering into an agreement with [a] foreign country that the regulation be exercised by that country through its control over exports".[25]

19. Article I, § 10, provides that "No State shall enter into any Treaty, Alliance or Confederation" and that "No State shall, without the consent of Congress, . . . enter into any Agreement or Compact with . . . a foreign Power." There thus appears to be a distinction between treaties, which are wholly denied the states, and agreements which are only conditionally proscribed. It seems highly unlikely that the states, but not the federal government, would be permitted to employ such an international device. See McDougal & Lans, "Treaties and Congressional—Executive or Presidential Agreements: Interchangeable Instruments of National Policy," 54 Yale L.J. 181, 221 (1945). Contrast Borehard, "Shall the Executive Agreement Replace the Treaty?" 53 Yale L.J. 664 (1944). It has been argued that the clause is of doubtful relevance because it was merely designed to encompass agreements between states. See Berger, "The Presidential Monopoly of Foreign Relations," 71 Mich.L.Rev. 1 (1972). The better reading appears to be that the clause was directed at more than inter-state agreements. See Note, "Self-Executing Executive Agreements: A Separation of Powers Problem," 24 Buff.L.Rev. 137 (1974). See generally, Weinfeld, "What Did the Framers of the Federal Constitution Mean By 'Agreements or Compacts'?" 3 U.Chi.L. Rev. 453 (1936).

20. L. Henkin, Foreign Affairs and the Constitution 177 (1972).

21. 301 U.S. 324 (1937).

22. See Mathews, "The Constitutional Power of the President to Conclude International Agreements," 64 Yale L.J. 345, 370 (1955); Wright, "The United States and International Agreements," 38 Am.J. Int'l L. 341, 348 (1944). Cf. United States v. Pink, 315 U.S. 203, 229 (1942).

23. See Kurland, "The Impotence of Reticence," 1968 Duke L.J. 619, 626; Berger, "The Presidential Monopoly of Foreign Relations," 71 Mich.L.Rev. 1, 39 (1972). The Framers' hesitance to imbue the President with unchecked treaty-making power is well reflected by Hamilton's admonition, in regard to that power, that "the joint possession of the power in question, by the President and the Senate, would afford a greater prospect of security, than the separate possession of it by either of them." The Federalist No. 75, at 488 (Mod.Lib.Ed. 1941).

24. See United States v. Guy W. Capps, Inc., 204 F.2d 655 (4th Cir. 1953) (invalidating an agreement with Canada regarding the importation of potatoes on the ground that the agreement conflicted with a prior law enacted by Congress in an exercise of its power to regulate foreign commerce), aff'd on other grounds 348 U.S. 296 (1955).

25. 204 F.2d at 660.

But executive agreements have the same weight as formal treaties in their effect upon conflicting state laws. The Supreme Court held in *United States v. Belmont* that "in the case of all international compacts and agreements . . . complete power over international affairs is in the national government and is not and cannot be subject to any curtailment or interference on the part of the several states." [26]

§ 4–6. The Impact of Federal Foreign Affairs Supremacy on State Action

Just as federal treaties and executive agreements prevail over conflicting state law,[1] so "[p]ower over external affairs is not shared by the States; it is vested in the national government exclusively." [2] The declaration of article I, § 10, that "[n]o State shall enter into any Treaty, Alliance, or Confederation," or, "without the consent of the Congress, lay any imposts or duties on imports or exports," is thus but one manifestation of a general constitutional principle that, whatever the division of foreign policy responsibility *within* the national government, *all* such responsibility is reposed at the national level rather than dispersed among the states and localities. "For local interests the several States of the Union exist, but for national purposes, embracing our relations with foreign nations, we are but one people, one nation, one power." [3]

It follows that all state action, whether or not consistent with current federal foreign policy, that distorts the allocation of responsibility to the national government for the conduct of American diplomacy is void as an unconstitutional infringement upon an exclusively federal sphere of responsibility. Thus, in *Zschernig v. Miller*,[4] the Supreme Court struck down, as "an intrusion by the State into the field of foreign affairs which the Constitution entrusts to the President and the Congress," an Oregon statute which required probate courts to make a three-leveled inquiry "into the type of governments that obtain in particular foreign nations" before permitting citizens of those nations to receive property left them by Oregon residents.[5]

§ 4–7. The President as Commander in Chief: Constitutional Control of the "Dogs of War"

Article II, § 2, declares that "The President shall be Commander in Chief of the Army and Navy of the United States, and of the Militia of the several States, when called into the actual Service of the United States. . . ." The Framers, in all likelihood, thought that bestowing

---

26. 301 U.S. at 331.

§ 4–6

1. See § 4–4, supra.

2. United States v. Pink, 315 U.S. 203, 233 (1942). See also Goldwater v. Carter, 444 U.S. 996, 1005 n. 2 (1979) (Rehnquist, J., concurring in the judgment) (state courts may not "trench upon exclusively federal questions of foreign policy") (dictum).

3. The Chae Chan Ping v. United States (Chinese Exclusion Case), 130 U.S. 581, 606 (1889).

4. 389 U.S. 429 (1968).

5. Id. at 432, 434. Justice Stewart, concurring separately in an opinion joined by Justice Brennan, would have held the Oregon law void on its face rather than inquiring, as the majority thought it necessary to do, into how the state probate courts were in fact administering the law. See id. at 441. See generally §§ 5–16, 6–20, infra.

this title upon the Chief Executive did little more than place him at the apex of the military hierarchy—that is, make him the First General and Admiral.[1] As late as 1866, it was declared that the President's power as Commander in Chief affected only "the command of the forces and the conduct of [military] campaigns." [2] More recently, it has become the practice to refer to the Commander in Chief Clause for whatever inherent martial authority the Executive may possess.

Article I, § 8, reposes in Congress the power to declare war. Our military history, however, is replete with instances of executively ordained uses of military force abroad in the absence of prior congressional approval.[3] Our legal history, in contrast, is almost barren of judicial pronouncements regarding the legitimacy of such executive behavior. The acquiescence of Congress in many of these executively initiated military campaigns,[4] and the reluctance of most courts to embroil themselves in the resolution of "political" disputes between the other branches of government in the United States' Indochina intervention,[5] have combined to leave meager elucidation in the cases. What scant authority that does exist recognizes the constitutionality of execu-

§ 4–7

1. See, e.g., the comment of Alexander Hamilton: "In this respect his authority would be nominally the same as that of the King of Great Britain, but in substance much inferior to it. It would amount to nothing more than the supreme command and direction of the military and naval forces, as first General and Admiral of the Confederacy; while that of the British King extends to the *declaring* of war and to the *raising* and *regulating* of fleets and armies,—all which, by the Constitution under consideration, would appertain to the legislature." The Federalist, No. 69.

2. Ex parte Milligan, 71 U.S. (4 Wall.) 2, 139 (1866) (Chase, C.J., concurring). See also Fleming v. Page, 50 U.S. (9 How.) 603, 615 (1850) (the Commander in Chief clause did not "extend the operation of our institutions and laws beyond the limits before assigned to them by the legislative power").

3. See Office of the Legal Advisor, U.S. Dept. of State, The Legality of the United States Participation in the Defense of Viet Nam, reprinted in 75 Yale L.J. 1085, 1101 (1966). It has been argued that this history of executively initiated hostilities may itself bear on the constitutionality of an executively ordained conflict. See Monaghan, "Presidential War-Making," 50 B.U.L.Rev. 19, 31 (Spring 1970, Special Issue). But see Berger, "War-Making and the President," 121 U.Pa.L.Rev. 29, 54–69 (1972).

4. See generally L. Henkin, Foreign Affairs and the Constitution 100–01 (1972); A. Sofaer, War, Foreign Affairs and Constitutional Power (1976).

5. See, e.g., Mora v. McNamara, 387 F.2d 862 (D.C.Cir. 1967), cert. denied 389 U.S. 934 (1967). See also McArthur v. Clifford, 393 U.S. 1002 (1968); Holmes v. United States, 391 U.S. 936 (1968); Velvel v. Nixon, 396 U.S. 1042 (1970); Commonwealth of Massachusetts v. Laird, 400 U.S. 886 (1970); DaCosta v. Laird, 405 U.S. 979 (1972); Holtzman v. Schlesinger, 414 U.S. 1304 (1973) (Marshall, Circuit Justice); Holtzman v. Schlesinger, 414 U.S. 1321 (1973) (Marshall, Circuit Justice). But see Holtzman v. Schlesinger, 414 U.S. 1316 (1973) (Douglas, Circuit Justice) (effectively staying, for less than one day, the bombing of Cambodia). It is by no means clear that federal courts should have refrained from addressing the issue. See, e.g., Orlando v. Laird, 443 F.2d 1039 (2d Cir. 1971) (finding challenges partly justiciable but rejecting them on the merits), cert. denied 404 U.S. 869 (1971). See generally D'Amato & O'Neil, "The Judiciary and Vietnam," 51–59 (1972); Henkin, "Viet-Nam in the Courts of the United States," 63 Am.J.Int'l. L. 284 (1969); Mora v. McNamara, 389 U.S. 934 at 935 (1967) (Douglas, J., dissenting from denial of certiorari); id. at 934 (Stewart, J., dissenting from denial of certiorari). An extensive discussion may be found in Atlee v. Laird, 347 F.Supp. 689 (E.D.Pa.1972) (dismissing a challenge to the constitutionality of the war in Southeast Asia on political question grounds), aff'd sub nom. Atlee v. Richardson, 411 U.S. 911 (1973) (mem.). Justices Douglas, Brennan, and Stewart were prepared to set the case for oral argument.

tively initiated uses of force in foreign territory where Congress has manifested some form of acquiescence.[6]

The least controversial justification for executive use of military force even before congressional acquiescence is that such force is required to defend the United States or its forces militarily. The debates of the Constitutional Convention indicate that some of the Framers contemplated that the executive might, without seeking congressional approval, use military force to repel sudden attacks.[7] Even if this prerogative were beyond the compass of the Commander in Chief clause as envisioned by the Framers, it might still be justified as a necessary concomitant of sovereignty.[8]

The legitimacy of defensive war waged by the executive was acknowledged by a narrow majority of the Supreme Court in the *Prize Cases*.[9] In upholding President Lincoln's blockade of Southern ports following the attack on Fort Sumter in April 1861, the Court there recognized an inherent executive power, exercised derivatively through the Commander in Chief clause, to repel an invasion or rebellion without first seeking legislative approval. Particular uses of this power to deal with internal insurrection or invasion were found to pose "political questions" not subject to judicial review: "This Court must be governed by the decisions and acts of the political department of the Government to which this power was entrusted." [10]

While the existence of presidential authority to wage defensive war is widely acknowleged, the breadth of such authority commands far less consensus. The President may probably deploy troops abroad in defense of American lives and property.[11] But does the President's right to repel sudden attacks embrace a right to respond without congressional approval to sudden attacks upon our allies? There is no evidence that the Framers contemplated any such presidential power.[12] But if they bestowed martial authority upon the President grudgingly, they did so in proportion to the military needs of their day. In the 18th century, a direct attack upon the United States was probably the only contingency that truly demanded instantaneous action; in the 20th, an attack on a strategically important ally might require similar dispatch. Conceivably, then, the Constitution might be read as allowing execu-

---

6. In DaCosta v. Laird, 471 F.2d 1146, 1157 (2d Cir. 1973), cert. denied 405 U.S. 979 (1972), for example, the Second Circuit held itself to be "without power to resolve the issue narrowly presented in this case" (i.e., the legality of President Nixon's directive ordering the mining of North Vietnamese ports and harbors and the continuation of air and naval strikes against North Vietnamese military targets) once it had "determined . . . that the Vietnamese War has been constitutionally authorized by the mutual participation of Congress [by not cutting off appropriations] and the President. . . ." Tactical military judgments within a lawful war, the court concluded, posed purely political questions since "no judicially discoverable

or manageable standards" were available. Id. at 1153.

7. See M. Farrand, 2 Records of the Federal Convention of 1787, 318–19 (1911).

8. See generally United States v. Curtiss-Wright Export Corp., 299 U.S. 304, 316–318 (1936).

9. 67 U.S. (2 Black) 635 (1863).

10. Id. at 670. Accord, Martin v. Mott, 25 U.S. (12 Wheat.) 19, 32–33 (1827). See also note 5, supra.

11. See Note, "Congress, the President, and the Power to Commit Forces to Combat," 81 Harv.L.Rev. 1771, 1787–94 (1968).

12. See id. at 1782.

tively initiated military action, without congressional consent, in the event of a surprise attack upon an important ally.[13]

The executive's use of force in anticipation of an enemy attack implicates similar concerns. The Framers no doubt imagined that Congress would have time to evaluate the military options, albeit hurriedly, when an attack was imminent. In the nuclear era, such sober deliberation might prove too costly a procedural luxury. Fortunately, the courts have had no occasion to pass on the propriety of a presidentially ordered preemptive strike.

Turning to the issues posed when Congress *has* acted, we observe first that the Constitution clearly empowers the President to supervise the conduct of any congressionally declared war. This paradigm, the one contemplated by the Framers, should be distinguished from the executive use of military force subsequent to some congressional action short of a formal declaration of war.

Collective defense treaties have become the way of military life in this century. These treaties, ratified by the President pursuant to the consent of the Senate, generally commit the United States to come to the aid of any signatory that is militarily attacked. Whether these treaties can serve as a predicate for executive deployment of military force has not been resolved.[14] It seems unlikely that, in the absence of a declaration of war by Congress, a prolonged military operation would be sanctioned by such a treaty. Even if the treaty is, in a sense, an inchoate declaration of war, it is one formulated by the treatymakers— that is, the President and the *Senate*—not by the *Congress* as the Constitution demands.[15] More plausible, however, is the suggestion that a collective defense treaty justifies presidential use of force in support of a harried ally until Congress has had ample time to deter-

---

13. See generally id. at 1783. It has been argued that the fact that our security is implicated by an attack upon an ally does not, in itself, justify unilateral action. Presumably *all* deployments of troops to combat are designed to realize some security interest, yet the Framers clearly vested in Congress some say in the matter. The key question should be whether waiting for congressional action would do irreparable harm to the vital interests that executive intervention is designed to serve.

14. Beyond the constitutional question whether these treaties *can* commit the United States to war, there remains the question whether, as a matter of construction, they *purport* to so commit us. As a rule, these treaties do not appear to be self-executing. See § 4–4, supra. The NATO treaty, for example, commits each member to "such action as it deems necessary." North Atlantic Treaty, April 4, 1949, art. 5, 63 Stat. 2244 (1949), T.I.A.S. No. 1964. When the treaty was submitted to the Senate for ratification, the Secretary of State disavowed any implication that the treaty committed the United States to go to war.

See McLaughlin, "The Scope of the Treaty Power in the United States," 42 Minn.L. Rev. 709 (1958). Subsequent treaties have been even more careful in stressing that they do not purport to alter the internal distribution of military decision-making in the member states. See, e.g., Southeast Asia Collective Defense Treaty, Feb. 4, 1955, art. IV, para. 1 [1953], 1 U.S.T. 81, T.I.A.S. No. 3170 (in case of an armed attack upon any signatory, each member will "act to meet the common danger *in accordance with its constitutional process*") (emphasis supplied). If a treaty did commit the United States to lend military assistance to an attacked ally, the President might justify his deployment of force by reference to his responsibility under article II, § 2, to "take Care that the Laws be faithfully executed," since mutual defense treaties have the force of law.

15. "The Congress shall have power . . . to declare war." U.S. Const., art. I, § 8. See Van Alstyne, "Congress, the President, and the Power to Declare War: A Requiem for Vietnam," 121 U.Pa.L.Rev. 1, 14–15 (1972).

mine whether it favors American military involvement in the conflict.[16] While the President may be so empowered even in the absence of a treaty, the existence of a treaty mitigates the spectre of a President thrusting the nation into a war against the wishes of the Congress.

Similar problems obtain when Congress explicitly delegates to the President the discretion to employ military forces in particular situations. The Tonkin Gulf Resolution provides a case in point. This joint resolution, passed by the Congress on August 10, 1964, provided in part that "the United States is . . . prepared, *as the President determines*, to take all necessary steps, including the use of armed force, to assist any member or protocol state of the Southeast Asia Collective Defense Treaty. . . ." [17] Assuming the resolution in fact delegated Congress' war-making power to the President with respect to Southeast Asia—a point disputed in subsequent years [18]—would such a delegation comport with the Constitution's allocation of power and responsibility? Arguably, one should resort to the standards usually employed to test the legitimacy of congressional delegations.[19] Thus a generic grant to the President of Congress' war-making power, unaccompanied by any articulated standards, would be unconstitutional as an overbroad delegation of congressional authority.[20]

To say that in certain cases the Constitution "inherently" permits a President unilaterally to make war at his or her discretion is not to say that the Constitution prohibits congressional regulation of the exercise of such discretion. To the extent that presidential action is rooted in a congressional delegation, Congress can, of course, always withdraw that delegation.[21] But Congress may also impose strictures of a more general character. For example, in the War Powers Resolution of 1973, [22] Congress linked its power under the necessary and proper clause [23] with the Commander in Chief clause so as to restrain executive deployment of United States armed forces. It did so by enumerating the circumstances in which deployment abroad is permitted, and by

---

16. See Note, "Congress, the President, and the Power to Commit Forces to Combat," 81 Harv.L.Rev. 1771, 1794–95 (1968). Cf. Van Alstyne, supra note 15, at 13 (President may wage defensive war, without congressional approval, until Congress has had opportunity to convene and take action). Cf. Prize Cases, 67 U.S. (2 Black) 635, 688–89 (1863).

17. Pub.L. No. 88–408, H.J.Res. 1145, 73 Stat. 384 (1964) (emphasis added). The Gulf of Tonkin Resolution was repealed in January 1971. See 84 Stat. 2053. For an earlier example of such congressional delegation, see Act of Feb. 6, 1802, Ch. 4, 2 Stat. 129–130, empowering the President to take action against Tripoli.

18. See Bickel, "Congress, the President, and the Power to Wage War," 48 Chicago-Kent L.Rev. 131, 137–39 (1971). For the background of the resolution's debate and passage, see A. Schlesinger, The Imperial Presidency 159–63 (1973). For a

careful analysis of how the Gulf of Tonkin Resolution of 1964, the Cuba Resolution of 1962, and the Middle East Resolution of 1957, together marked a major shift toward Executive war-making, see National Commitments, Sen.Rep. No. 797, 90th Cong., 1st Sess. (Nov. 20, 1967). See also Sen.Rep. No. 91–129, 91st Cong., 1st Sess. (Apr. 16, 1969).

19. See § 4–2, supra; § 5–17, infra.

20. See Van Alstyne, supra note 15, at 16; see also Bickel, supra note 18, at 137.

21. When Congress repealed the Gulf of Tonkin Resolution in 1971, see note 17, supra, the Administration shifted its reliance largely to the President's Commander in Chief authority.

22. 87 Stat. 555, Public Law 93–148, 93d Cong. (H.J. Res. 542, adopted over presidential veto on November 7, 1973).

23. See id., § 2(b).

limiting such deployment in any situation to sixty days unless Congress, in the interim, passes authorizing legislation.[24] The Resolution, which became law on November 7, 1973, upon receiving the two-thirds vote necessary to override President Nixon's veto,[25] announced that its purpose was "to fulfill the intent of the framers of the Constitution of the United States and insure that the collective judgment of both the Congress and the President will apply to the introduction of United States armed forces into hostilities." [26] Such "collective judgment" is to be effected by heightened consultation between the President and Congress. In "every possible instance" the consultation is to occur before American forces are introduced into hostilities; [27] when the President is required to act without prior consultation, however, he "shall submit within 48 hours [to Congress] a report, in writing, setting forth (a) the circumstances necessitating the introduction of United States Armed Forces; (b) the constitutional and legislative authority under which such introduction took place; and (c) the estimated scope and duration of the hostilities or involvement." [28]

The heart of the Resolution is in its command that: "Within sixty calendar days after a report is submitted . . . the President shall terminate any use of United States Armed Forces . . . unless the Congress (1) has declared war or has enacted a specific authorization for such use of United States Armed Forces, (2) has extended by law such sixty-day period, or (3) is physically unable to meet as a result of an armed attack upon the United States." [29]

The Resolution introduces some flexibility into the time limit by providing that the "sixty-day period shall be extended for not more than an additional thirty days if the President determines and certifies to the Congress in writing that unavoidable military necessity respecting the safety of United States Armed Forces requires the continued use of such armed forces in the course of bringing about a prompt removal of such forces." [30] But this flexibility cuts both ways, because Congress can shorten the sixty-day period as well as lengthen it; despite the provisions noted above, whenever American forces are engaged in hostilities abroad without specific congressional authoriza-

24. Compare the Impoundment Control Act of 1974, discussed in § 4–11, infra. See also § 4–2, supra.

25. See Veto Message of October 23, 1973, H.Doc. No. 93–171, 119 Cong.Rec. 34990 (1973).

26. § 2(a).

27. In late 1983, a significant majority in each house of Congress declared that the War Powers Resolution governed President Reagan's unilateral decision to invade Grenada, ostensibly to rescue American medical students endangered by civil strife and a domestic power struggle on the island. See generally N.Y. Times, A1, col. 6 (Nov. 2, 1983). President Ford's use of armed forces to evacuate Americans and South Vietnamese from Saigon without congres-

sional consultation in late April 1975 was regarded by some as an exercise of inherent presidential authority despite the War Powers Resolution's silence.

28. § 4. On May 15, 1975, President Ford reported to Congress, in accordance with § 4, his unilateral use of military force to rescue the American merchant ship S.S. Mayagüez and its crew. It seems doubtful that the lack of prior consultaion in this case was warranted; the venture's purported success is of course irrelevant to that conclusion.

29. § 5(b). On the validity of § 5(b) even after I.N.S. v. Chadha, 462 U.S. 919 (1983), see § 4–3, supra, note 25.

30. Id.

tion, "such forces shall be removed by the President if the Congress so directs by concurrent resolution." [31]

The War Powers Resolution relegates the description of the exclusive circumstances under which the President can introduce American forces into hostilities without a declaration of war to a section entitled "Purpose and Policy." The "Purpose and Policy" provisions conclude with the following paragraph: [32] "The constitutional powers of the President as Commander-in-Chief to introduce United States Armed Forces into hostilities, or into situations where imminent involvement in hostilities is clearly indicated by the circumstances, are exercised only pursuant to (1) a declaration of war, (2) specific statutory authorization, or (3) a national emergency created by attack upon the United States, its territories or possessions, or its armed forces." Senators who criticized the Resolution as too weak insisted that the "Purpose and Policy" section could have no statutory effect; critics also urged that, rather than restraining the President, the Resolution actually licensed him to engage in brief military actions inasmuch as Congress seems unlikely, after American forces are engaged, to terminate such actions before the sixty (or ninety) day periods expire.[33]

Among the provisions of most lasting significance may be the Resolution's mandate that presidential authority to use military force "shall not be inferred" from any law, treaty, or appropriation unless it "specifically authorizes" such use and "states that it is intended to constitute specific . . . authorization within the meaning of this joint resolution." [34]

President Nixon's insistence that the War Powers Resolution of 1973 unconstitutionally constrained the Commander-in-Chief power [35] seems misguided; although the Resolution may plausibly be challenged as insufficiently restoring Congress' constitutionally contemplated role in war-making, it can hardly be said to take from the Executive Branch any power delegated to it by the Constitution or to enlarge upon the powers constitutionally delegated to Congress.

The Constitution, indeed, *mandates* at least some congressional supervision of executive military operations: article I, § 8, cl. 12, limits military appropriations to a maximum of two years. Although congressional reviews of military appropriations have often been perfunctory, Congress has not always taken its duty so lightly. For example, after unsuccessful earlier efforts to cut off Vietnam appropriations,[36] and after an unsuccessful attempt by 13 members of Congress to enjoin the

---

31. § 5(c). Note that a concurrent resolution requires only a majority vote; it neither requires Presidential approval nor is subject to Presidential veto. As a result, § 5(c) is probably invalid under I.N.S. v. Chadha, 462 U.S. 919 (1983), see § 4–3, supra, note 25.

32. § 2(c).

33. But see § 8(d)(2), providing that nothing in the joint resolution "shall be construed as granting any authority to the President with respect to the introduction [of military forces] . . . which authority he would not have had in the absence of this joint resolution."

34. § 8(a)(1), (2).

35. See his Veto Message, supra note 25, focusing particularly on § 5(b)–(c) of the Resolution.

36. In June 1970, for example, the Senate adopted the Cooper-Church Amendment, but it was later dropped in conference.

President and the Secretaries of State, Defense, Army, Navy and the Air Force,[37] Congress sought to force an end to the Nixon Administration's 1973 bombing of Cambodia by passing a rider to an appropriations bill cutting off all funds for the bombing. In June, 1973, the Senate started to attach fund cut-offs to supplemental appropriations bills. After President Nixon vetoed the first such attempt, and the House failed to override, Senate Majority Leader Mansfield threatened to attach such cut-offs to successive appropriations until "the will of the people" was carried out. To avert a fiscal deadlock, the Administration was forced to agree to a compromise under which the President did not veto a provision attached to the Social Security Act that, effective August 15, 1973, prohibited "use of any past or present appropriations for financing U.S. combat activities in or over or from off the shores of North Vietnam, South Vietnam, Laos or Cambodia." [38]

The inception of major hostilities has almost always been followed by an executive arrogation of what would ordinarily be deemed exclusively congressional authority.[39] The constitutional basis for these assertions of executive authority has not always been clear. Almost invariably, Congress has acquiesced in the executive action, so there has existed no ostensible conflict between the executive and legislative branches which demanded judicial resolution.[40] Presumably, a President would base a claim of expanded domestic power upon the implied right, under the Commander in Chief clause, to regulate the domestic consequences and concomitants of a war. Within limits, this argument has appeal. However, the constitutional scheme of separation of powers mandates that some limits be recognized.

First, while a war emergency might sanction unilateral presidential action when dispatch is required and the Congress is not prepared to act, subsequent congressional disapproval of the President's course of action should require its termination.[41] In the same vein, the President should not be entitled to rely upon his augmented wartime powers when, without peculiar difficulty, he could have submitted his proposals to Congress for their consideration as would have been required in peacetime. Second, the President's new-found powers should be limited to those that impinge directly upon the war effort or its domestic entailments. The mere existence of a war should not automatically sanction presidential behavior so divorced from that war, whether

---

37. See Mitchell v. Laird, to have been reported at 476 F.2d 533 (D.C. Cir. 1973), but withdrawn by order of the court prior to publication.

38. See 87 Stat. 99. For the background of the provision's enactment see 29 Cong.Q.Almanac 792 (1973).

39. During the Civil War, for example, President Lincoln added men to the Army and Navy, spent unappropriated funds, closed the post offices to treasonable correspondence, took over the railroad between Washington and Baltimore, and suspended the writ of habeas corpus in various places. During World War I, President Wilson, beyond exercising vast discretion pursuant to broad congressional delegations, created a host of administrative boards and closed German wireless stations. World War II saw President Franklin Roosevelt create numerous presidential offices and exercise substantial control over labor relations. See E. Corwin. The President: Office and Powers 1787–1957, at 227–42 (1958).

40. See id. at 237.

41. See generally Youngstown Sheet & Tube Co. v. Sawyer, 343 U.S. 579, 634 (1952) (Jackson, J., concurring in the Court's invalidation of President Truman's seizure of steel mills in order to avert a steel strike during the Korean War).

during or after hostilities, as to suggest a boundless source of power.[42] "Even though 'theater of war' be an expanding concept," it does not suffice, for example, to permit the President, acting as Commander in Chief, "to take possession of private property in order to keep labor disputes from stopping production." [43]

Finally, the President, as Commander in Chief, bears ultimate responsibility for the enforcement, through courts-martial, of the congressionally-adopted rules and regulations governing the military forces. Whether or not the nation is at war, the sweep of this authority includes the right, independent of particular statutes, to convene courts-martial and to review their decisions.[44] In time of war this executive authority swells, permitting presidential action outside the legislatively-defined contours of the military justice system; the President's position as Commander in Chief justifies at least some unilateral amendments to Congress' rules.[45]

As we have seen, executive domestic authority is most expansive in time of war. Where, however, the President seeks directly to supplant the judiciary in the resolution of particular cases, the Supreme Court will subject the military justifications for such action to close scrutiny. Thus, in *Ex parte Milligan* the Court held that martial law during the Civil War could not "be applied to citizens in states which have upheld the authority of the government, and where the courts are open and their process unobstructed." [46] Employing a similar analysis, the Court held in 1946 that the declaration of martial law in Hawaii subsequent to the attack upon Pearl Harbor was unconstitutional.[47]

It is noteworthy if sobering that both of these decisions limiting the power of the President to declare and enforce martial law were handed down after hostilities had subsided; one may doubt that the Court would have been so courageous had war still been underway.[48]

---

42. The Supreme Court has recognized in dictum that "if the war power can be used in days of peace to treat all the wounds which war inflicts on our society, it may not only swallow up all other powers of Congress but largely obliterate the Ninth and Tenth Amendments as well." Woods v. Cloyd W. Miller Co., 333 U.S. 138, 144 (1948), (upholding post-World War II congressional provisions for rent control in areas where the war had exacerbated housing shortages). See § 5–16, infra.

43. Youngstown Sheet & Tube Co. v. Sawyer, 343 U.S. 579, 587 (1952), discussed in § 4–8, infra.

44. See Swaim v. United States, 165 U.S. 553 (1897). The relationship between military tribunals and Article III courts is discussed in Chapter 3, supra.

45. See Ex parte Quirin, 317 U.S. 1 (1942) (dictum). In response to a contention by captured Nazi saboteurs that their trial was not in accord with applicable congressional rules, the Supreme Court suggested, but found it unnecessary to rely upon, purely presidential authority: "An

important incident to the conduct of war is the adoption of measures by the military command not only to repel and defeat the enemy, but to seize and subject to disciplinary measures those enemies who in their attempt to thwart or impede our military effort have violated the law of war." Id. at 28–29.

46. 71 U.S. (4 Wall.) 2, 121 (1866). But four of the Justices indicated that Congress could have authorized military trials if it deemed them a military necessity. See id. at 136–42 (Chase, C.J., joined by Wayne, Swayne, and Miller, JJ., concurring in part and dissenting in part).

47. Duncan v. Kahanamoku, 327 U.S. 304 (1946).

48. Thus Justice Burton, dissenting in an opinion which Justice Frankfurter joined, voiced skepticism that, while the war raged, the Court would have "ordered such relief or could and then . . . attempted to enforce [it] . . . in the theater of military operations." 327 U.S. at 357. Indeed, the unusual delay between the grant of certiorari and the handing down

§ 4-8. The "Silent" Limits of "Inherent" Executive Authority

Although it has been possible for the Executive to achieve political predominance in the management of domestic affairs despite the secondary constitutional role assigned to the President, domestic executive power remains limited—even during times of national crisis—whenever its exercise must be justified in a constitutional setting. Thus, when an injunction was sought against President Truman (although nominally only his Secretary of Commerce was brought before the courts) for seizing steel mills, and operating them under federal direction, in order to avert a strike during the Korean War without first seeking congressional authorization, the Supreme Court ruled his action an unconstitutional usurpation of legislative authority in *Youngstown Sheet & Tube Co. v. Sawyer*.[1]

While it is clear that the Steel Seizure decision rebuffs any contention that the President is invested with unbridled discretion to act in the area of domestic affairs, even in furtherance of international military policy, divining the precise doctrine of the case is decidedly more difficult. The Justices apparently agreed that Congress could properly have ordered or authorized the seizure of the steel mills. Justice Black's opinion for the Court elaborated a sweeping theory that the seizure of property is an inherently congressional power and, therefore, that any effort by the President to seize property is illegitimate unless mandated by Congress. Justice Black,[2] as well as four of the Justices who filed separate concurring opinions,[3] stressed that Congress had previously refused to give the President the power to seize industrial facilities as a means of resolving labor disputes. As Justice Frankfurter proclaimed, "[i]n formulating legislation for dealing with industrial conflicts, Congress could not more clearly and emphatically have withheld authority [for seizure] than it did in 1947." [4] To these Justices, then, the President appeared to have acted in direct conflict with the articulated desire of Congress—the type of action where the executive power "is at its lowest ebb." [5]

of the opinion in Duncan v. Kahanamoku—from February 12, 1945 until February 25, 1946—has been ascribed to the Court's aversion to impinging upon the President's discretion while the war was in progress. See E. Corwin, Total War and the Constitution 104–05 (1947). The " 'war power' . . . usually is invoked in haste . . . when calm legislative consideration of constitutional limitation is difficult. It is executed in a time of patriotic fervor that makes moderation unpopular. And, worst of all, it is interpreted by judges under the influence of the same passions and pressures." Woods v. Cloyd W. Miller Co., 333 U.S. 138, 146 (1948) (Jackson, J., concurring).

§ 4-8

1. 343 U.S. 579 (1952). But see Justice Rehnquist's interesting observation in "The Notion of a Living Constitution." 54 Tex.L.Rev. 693, 704 (1976): "Within the limits of our Constitution, the representatives of the people in the executive branches of the state and national governments enact laws."

2. 343 U.S. at 586.

3. Justices Frankfurter, Jackson, Burton and Clark. The former three Justices joined Justice Black's opinion for the Court in addition to writing separately. Justice Clark concurred in the judgment.

4. 343 U.S. at 602. Cf. New York Times Co. v. United States, 403 U.S. 713 (1971) (per curiam) (Pentagon Papers Case), in which Justice Marshall, among others, stressed that "[o]n at least two occasions Congress has refused to enact legislation that would have . . . given the President the power he seeks in this case." Id. at 746 (concurring opinion).

5. 343 U.S. at 637 (Jackson, J., concurring).

Thus a decisive majority of five Justices treated Congress' *silence*—its *non*enactment of authorizing legislation—as a legally binding expression of intent to forbid the seizure at issue. It was not an Act of Congress that bound President Truman's hands, but the *inaction* of Congress. Judicial reasoning that allows Congress to legislate by silence is constitutionally dubious: the internal system of checks and balances is thwarted because legislative silences are not subject to presidential veto, and external political accountability is diminished since Congress cannot realistically be held accountable by the electorate for laws it "enacts" by silence.[6]

A less troublesome rationale for the Court's decision in the *Steel Seizure Case*, as well as the makings of a more sound approach to congressional silence, may be implicit in Justice Douglas' concurring opinion. He reasoned that, although the federal government undoubtedly had the power to condemn the steel mills, it also had the constitutional duty to pay just compensation.[7] And "[t]he branch of government that has the power to pay compensation for a seizure is the only one able to authorize a seizure or make lawful one that the President has effected."[8] Since article I, § 8, of the Constitution unambiguously gives Congress exclusive power to raise revenues,[9] it followed that only Congress could authorize seizure of the steel mills, and it had not done so.

Justice Douglas' understanding of the import of congressional silence contrasts sharply with the majority's. Congress' silence barred the challenged action by President Truman *not* because it constituted evidence of congressional will that Truman act otherwise, but because the *underlying constitutional rule*, as Justice Douglas would have had the Court announce it, made the sort of thing Truman did void absent explicit prior consent by Congress. In Justice Douglas' opinion, the Executive must not be allowed to confront Congress with a *fait accompli*—a situation in which Congress is bound by the Constitution to raise revenues it might have chosen not to raise in order to pay off just compensation obligations that it might have chosen not to incur. In light of this constitutional rule, congressional silence is a legal *fact* operating to bar unilateral executive seizure, not mere *evidence* that Congress *meant* to disapprove such seizures.

One major lesson to be drawn from the *Steel Seizure Case* is thus a rule about how to read the Constitution's allocation of power and how to read congressional silences. If the Constitution has assigned the

---

6. The problem of construing congressional and constitutional silence is more fully explored in L. Tribe, Constitutional Choices 29–44 (1985).

7. The fifth amendment dictates that private property may not "be taken for public use, without just compensation."

8. 343 U.S. at 631–32 (Douglas, J., concurring).

9. As a practical matter, some aspects of this exclusivity are difficult if not impossible to adjudicate. In Moore v. United States House of Representatives, 733 F.2d 946 (D.C.Cir. 1984), the court of appeals held that a congressman had standing to challenge a tax bill, allegedly initiated in the Senate, as a violation of the origination clause, art. I, § 7, cl. 1, which provides that "[a]ll bills for raising revenue shall originate in the House of Representatives," but dismissed the case nevertheless because of prudential concerns about the separation of powers. The Supreme Court denied certiorari. 469 U.S. 1106 (1985).

power to take actions of a particular sort—such as raising revenue to compensate for public takings—to the legislature, that grant of power is exclusive,[10] and the President has no "inherent" power to take such actions on his own. As Justice Jackson put it, the President's inherent authority consists of "his own constitutional powers *minus* any constitutional powers of Congress over the matter." [11] And if Congress has not spoken to authorize the President to take acts of a sort that article I enumerates as within the legislative sphere, then that silence is an operative fact that, against the background of the Constitution's allocation of power, must be understood to deny such authority to the executive. Similarly, against the background of a constitutional rule in the field of foreign policy that the President may make treaties only with the advice and consent of the Senate, senatorial silence—a failure to ratify the treaty—is an operative fact that must be understood as depriving the treaty of legal force.

When analyzing presidential assertions of inherent authority under this approach to congressional silence, courts cannot properly avoid the necessary first step of articulating the relevant constitutional norm that determines what effect silence as such is to have. In *Dames & Moore v. Regan*,[12] the Supreme Court sidestepped that requirement when it claimed to hear a different sound than the *Steel Seizure* Court had heard in a similar congressional silence decades before.

In December of 1979, Dames & Moore sued Iran and several of its banks in a federal district court to recover money on a contract, and, pursuant to conditional authorization contained in President Carter's order freezing Iranian assets, attached the banks' property to secure whatever judgment Dames & Moore might be awarded. To obtain the release of dozens of American hostages held in Tehran, President Carter issued executive orders nullifying all such attachments and suspending the underlying claims—relegating Dames and Moore and many other parties to an Iran-United States claims tribunal. Given the crisis and the national celebration at the hostages' safe return, it came as no surprise when the Supreme Court unanimously upheld the President's acts.[13] After all, the validity of broad congressional delegations of foreign policy power to the executive, as well as the President's inherent primacy in that sphere, had been settled for nearly half a century.[14]

The Court brushed aside objections that the President's suspension of preexisting claims against Iran constituted a taking of private

---

10. See, e.g., Consumers Union of United States, Inc. v. Kissinger, 506 F.2d 136, 142 (D.C. Cir. 1974) (without a delegation from Congress, the President has no inherent power to adjust tariffs or to regulate foreign commerce, since that is among Congress' enumerated powers); Yoshida Int'l, Inc. v. United States, 378 F.Supp. 1155 (Cust.Ct.1974) (holding presidential imposition of a supplemental tariff to be an invalid exercise of legislative power in absence of clear delegation), rev'd 526 F.2d 560 (C.C.P.A. 1975) (finding such a delegation), discussed in § 4-3 supra.

11. 343 U.S. at 637 (concurring opinion) (emphasis added).

12. 453 U.S. 654 (1981).

13. 453 U.S. at 674, 686.

14. See United States v. Curtiss-Wright Export Corp., 299 U.S. 304 (1936), discussed in § 4-2 supra.

property without just compensation.[15] Such an argument, the Court said, was premature: even if the international claims tribunal had insufficient assets to satisfy the claims, Dames & Moore could always sue the United States government in the Court of Claims to collect the balance.[16] But the Court seems to have overlooked the fact that this would present Congress with precisely the sort of *fait accompli* that the Court had implicitly ruled out in *Steel Seizure*: only the branch that holds the purse strings may constitutionally take action that could drain the purse; and Congress, as the Court conceded, had not expressly authorized the President's acts.[17] But in contrast to the demand for explicit congressional authorization for President Truman's seizure of the steel mills, the Court in *Dames & Moore* found it sufficient that Congress, in several pieces of not-quite-applicable legislation, had indirectly "indicat[ed] [its] acceptance of a broad scope for executive action in circumstances such as those presented in this case." [18]

The *Steel Seizure Case* is not the only precedent from whose standard of explicit legislative authorization the Court has strayed in recent years. In *Kent v. Dulles*,[19] the Supreme Court held that the Secretary of State had no authority to deny passports on the basis of Communist Party membership. While purporting not to reach "the question of constitutionality," [20] the Court nevertheless held that the sort of liberty the Secretary claimed authority to restrict could not be abridged without a clear delegation from Congress, and that such permission could not be "*silently* granted." [21] Yet the Court relied upon precisely the opposite presumption in *Haig v. Agee*,[22] where it found in Congress' silence implicit approval of executive power to revoke passports on national security grounds. The Court declared that "in the areas of foreign policy and national security, . . . congressional silence is not to be equated with congressional disapproval." [23] Indeed, the Court found it significant that Congress had remained silent in the face of long-standing administrative practice and never expressly denied the executive branch such broad, discretionary powers of revocation. The record of this "administrative practice" consisted of the fact that similar State Department regulations had been around for years

15. The takings issue with respect to the nullification of attachments made *after*—and indeed pursuant to—the President's freeze order was even more quickly resolved. Since Dames & Moore's prejudgment attachments were " 'revocable,' 'contingent,' and 'in every sense subordinate to the President's power under [federal law],' " the Court held that Dames & Moore "did not acquire any 'property' interest in the attachment of the sort that would support a constitutional claim for compensation." 453 U.S. at 674 n. 4. See Chapter 9, infra.

16. Id. at 688–89.

17. Although the Court has held that the Tucker Act, 28 U.S.C. § 1491, is always available as a means for seeking compensation for a taking so long as Congress has not specifically withdrawn its availability,

Ruckelshaus v. Monsanto Co., 467 U.S. 986, 1016–19 (1984), Congress' creation of a general mechanism for providing just compensation should not be construed as a blanket authorization, in advance, for any and all takings which the executive branch might care to effect.

18. 453 U.S. at 677; see id. at 669–88.

19. 357 U.S. 116 (1958).

20. Id. at 129.

21. Id. at 130 (emphasis added). See also New York Times Co. v. United States, 403 U.S. 713 (1971) (per curiam); id. at 718 (Black, J., concurring); id. at 720 (Douglas, J., concurring); id. at 742 (Marshall, J., concurring).

22. 453 U.S. 280 (1981).

23. Id. at 291.

and the fact that perhaps a half dozen passports—the government confessed that its records were so poor that it could not pin the number down—had been revoked on such grounds over the preceding half century.[24] The inconsistent prior holding in *Kent* made sense only as a constitutional ruling about the operative significance of the absence of any expressly applicable authorizing statute, not as a ruling about the then extant state of congressional intent—for in *Kent* Congress had actually enacted a law that specifically denied passports to Communists, but the law could not be applied to Kent at that time because it had not "yet become effective." [25] But the *Agee* Court, mired in an inevitably indeterminate approach to legislative silence, dismissed *Kent* as a mere effort at mindreading in the face of congressional silence.[26]

Although the notion of inherent presidential power has not regained the vigor it knew at the turn of the century,[27] the continuing failure to develop a more consistent and less easily manipulated approach to congressional silence creates the risk that the legislative reins on executive authority will grow ever looser, especially when held by a Court that seems eager to indulge presidential aggrandizement.[28]

24. Id. at 317–18 n. 8 (Brennan, J., dissenting). As Justice Brennan observed, "One wonders, then, how the [government] can argue that *Congress* was aware of any administrative practice, when the data is unavailable even to the executive." Id.

25. Kent v. Dulles, 357 U.S. 116, 130 (1958).

26. 453 U.S. at 303–06. Even the dissent in Agee protested only that the majority might have misread Congress' intent. See id. at 315–18 (Brennan, J., dissenting). Perhaps some of the inconsistency between the two cases can be explained by the singular unattractiveness of the position espoused by the plaintiff in the later case. Philip Agee was a former C.I.A. employee whose declared purpose in travelling abroad was to expose the identities of C.I.A. agents, thereby rendering them ineffective or, worse still, subjecting them to assassination by foreign intelligence operatives.

27. See, e.g., In re Debs, 158 U.S. 564, 586 (1895) (upholding President Cleveland's power to obtain an injunction against the Pullman Strike—which threatened interstate commerce and impeded the U.S. mail—even in the absence of any statutory warrant, on the grounds that "the wrongs complained of [by the President were] such . . . as affect the public at large"). See also Cunningham v. Neagle, 135 U.S. 1 (1890), where Justice Miller, in his opinion for the Court, suggested that the President's duty to take care that the laws be faithfully executed encompassed not only "the enforcement of acts of Congress or of treaties of the United States according to their *express terms*," but also

"the rights, duties and obligations growing out of the Constitution itself, our international relations, and all the protections implied by the nature of the government under the Constitution." Id. at 64 (original emphasis). Cf. United States v. Midwest Oil Co., 236 U.S. 459 (1915) (by repeated assertion from early date without congressional repudiation, President acquired right to withdraw public lands from private acquisition).

28. See, e.g., Regan v. Wald, 468 U.S. 222 (1984), in which five Justices purported to find, in a factual situation that should probably have been deemed at best ambiguous, clear congressional authorization for the Reagan administration's summary ban on travel to Cuba. The 1977 International Emergency Economic Powers Act imposed strict procedural requirements, including congressional consultation, on various executive powers over international trade and travel. The Act exempted from these requirements any previously conferred authorities which the President may have been exercising on July 1, 1977. The Court conceded that "most travel-related transactions with Cuba and Cuban nationals were permitted" on that date, but nevertheless concluded that the President's travel ban fell within the statutory "grandfather" clause because some trade restrictions—such as those on cigars—remained in effect on July 1, 1977. Id. at 234–35. The Court apparently saw no reason why expansion of the pre-existing ban on trade in cigars to include a ban on travel should be characterized as anything other than an insignificant shift in commodities—from tobacco to people.

§ 4–9. The President as Chief Executive: Powers of Appointment

As head of the executive establishment, one of the President's chief powers is that of appointing federal officers. Article II, § 2, cl. 2, provides in pertinent part: "[The President] shall nominate, and by and with the Advice and Consent of the Senate, shall appoint . . . all other Officers of the United States, whose Appointments are not herein otherwise provided for, and which shall be established by Law: but the Congress may by Law vest the Appointment of such inferior Officers, as they think proper, in the President alone, in the Courts of Law, or in the Heads of Departments." [1]

It is typical of the Constitution's scheme for separating legislative and executive authority that the *offices* in question are to be "established by Law"—that is, by act of Congress—while the *officers* are to be chosen by the President subject to the Senate's confirmation. In *Springer v. Government of the Philippine Islands*,[2] the Supreme Court indicated that Congress may not control the law enforcement process by retaining a power to appoint the individual who will execute its laws. Much as the bill of attainder clause of Article I, § 9, prevents Congress from circumventing the checks of the executive and judicial branches by identifying the individuals who are to be burdened by federal statutes,[3] so the appointments clause, rather than "merely dealing with etiquette or protocol," [4] seeks to preserve an executive check upon legislative authority in the interest of avoiding an undue concentration of power in Congress.

The 1974 amendments to the Federal Election Campaign Act of 1971, for example, established an eight-member Federal Election Commission and vested in it primary responsibility for administering and enforcing the Act by bringing civil actions against violators, making rules for carrying out the Act's provisions, temporarily disqualifying federal candidates for failing to file required reports, and authorizing convention expenditures in excess of the Act's specified limits. Because such powers of enforcement, rule making, and adjudication could not "be regarded as merely in aid of the legislative function of Congress," [5] they could be "exercised only by persons who are Officers of the United States." [6] But four of the six voting members of the Commission were appointed by the President *pro tempore* of the Senate and by the Speaker of the House although the appointments clause requires all "Officers of the United States" to be appointed by the President, the head of an Executive Department, or the Judiciary.[7] Thus the Court

§ 4–9

1. Art. II, § 2, cl. 2, also provides for the President's appointment, with the advice and consent of the Senate, of "Ambassadors, other public Ministers and Consuls, [and] Judges of the Supreme Court . . ." Although these appointment powers, particularly the power to appoint Justices, are of great significance, see L. Tribe, God Save This Honorable Court: How the Choice of Supreme Court Justices Shapes Our History (1985), they do not bear upon the President as head of the domestic executive establishment and hence are not addressed here.

2. 277 U.S. 189 (1928).

3. See § 10–5, infra.

4. Buckley v. Valeo, 424 U.S. 1, 125 (1976) (per curiam).

5. Id. at 138.

6. Id. at 141.

7. Id. at 127. Article II, § 2, cl. 2 provides that Congress may vest the appointment of "inferior Officers, as they think

held in *Buckley v. Valeo* that the Federal Election Commission was unconstitutionally composed,[8] stressing that "Congress could not, merely because it concluded that such a measure was 'necessary and proper' to the discharge of its substantive legislative authority, . . . vest in itself, or in its officers, the authority to appoint officers of the United States" any more than it could "pass a bill of attainder or *ex post facto* law contrary to the prohibitions contained in § 9 of Art. I".[9]

The clear impermissibility of Congress's efforts to bestow the appointment power on itself should be distinguished from the more complex issue of whether Congress should be allowed to delegate substantive power to itself; the difference illuminates the animating principle of the appointments clause. A conclusion that legislative self-reference is unconstitutional seems to underlie the Court's analysis of the legislative veto in *I.N.S. v. Chadha*.[10] Although the *Chadha* majority never voiced the premise that Congress may delegate authority to others but not to itself, it seemed to recognize that the decision's pivotal rationale is indeed to be found in this unspoken assumption.[11] In a somewhat cryptic footnote, the Court admitted that agencies and executive officers commonly wield "quasi-legislative" power [12] without the safeguards of presentment and bicamerality. The Court distinguished these exercises of power by noting that those who wield it are executive officers appointed by the President or his subordinates and subject in significant degree to judicial control.

Thus the objection in *Chadha* to the exercise of statutorily delegated power by all or part of Congress—as opposed to such exercise by an

proper, . . . in the Courts of Law, or in the Heads of Departments." Obviously, cabinet members and other "Heads of Departments" are not "inferior Officers," but the Constitution leaves to Congress the task of deciding which other officials to deem "inferior" in this sense. See Ex parte Siebold, 100 U.S. 371 (1879) (Congress may deem election supervisors "inferior Officers" subject to appointment by Circuit Courts); Rice v. Ames, 180 U.S. 371 (1901) (Congress may deem extradition commissioners "inferior officers" subject to appointment by lower federal courts); United States v. Solomon, 216 F.Supp. 835 (S.D. N.Y. 1963) (Congress may empower lower federal courts to appoint interim United States Attorneys to serve until vacancies are filled by the President); Hobson v. Hansen, 265 F.Supp. 902 (D.D.C. 1967) (Congress may empower District Court for District of Columbia to appoint members of District of Columbia board of education). To be sure, the Siebold Court did hold that Congress' power in this regard is limited by the requirement that there be "no incongruity" between the judicial function and the nature of the office being filled by the courts pursuant to congressional delegation, 100 U.S. at 398, but that proviso, as the cases cited above demonstrate, has not been read to impose much of a limitation.

Plainly, the Constitution does not restrict Congress to any fixed category of obviously judicial officers (such as magistrates and court clerks) for appointment by federal judges. In particular, there is no reason to question the constitutionality of federal laws providing for the appointment, by a panel of federal judges, of independent counsel to investigate and prosecute suspected crimes committed by, or in alleged complicity with, officers in the executive branch.

8. 424 U.S. 1 at 140 (1976). All nine of the Justices agreed on this aspect of the decision.

9. Id. at 135.

10. 462 U.S. 919 (1983). § 4–3, supra, assesses the Court's separation of powers analysis in Chadha.

11. In his dissent, Justice White suggested that this was the majority's animating principle. 462 U.S. at 986–89. See also Bowsher v. Synar, 106 S.Ct. 3181, 3203 (1986) (Stevens, J., concurring in the judgment) (relying on Chadha for the proposition that Congress may not delegate its "policymaking authority to one of its components, or to one of its agents").

12. 462 U.S. at 953 n. 16.

agent or agency external to Congress—may be restated as the proposition that entrusting members of Congress with such power confers upon federal lawmakers the mantle of "officers" of the United States government, in violation of the appointments clause and of the incompatibility clause.[13]

The core concern of these two clauses—concern tied closely to the Constitution's Madisonian rejection of parliamentary government—is to ensure that federal executive power remain independent of Congress and of the congressional power base. The executive power is not to be dispersed among a series of ministries selected from or subordinate to the national legislature, each headed by a congressman or similar officer representing a discrete state or local constituency within Congress' ambit.[14] Therefore, the Constitution requires certain specially mentioned officers—primarily Ambassadors and Supreme Court Justices—to be nominated by the President and confirmed by the Senate, and all inferior officers to be appointed not *by* Congress but *through* congressionally fixed procedures, by "the President alone, . . . the courts of law, or . . . the Heads of Departments." [15] This arrangement leaves Congress free to designate its own agents to exercise "powers . . . essentially of an investigative and informative nature" [16] but assures that, with the possible exception of judicially-appointed court officers, "any appointee exercising significant authority pursuant to the laws of the United States" [17] will be selected by the President or by a department head answerable to the President. It is through subordinates, and only through them, that the President can "take Care that the Laws be faithfully executed . . ." [18]

§ 4–10. The President as Chief Executive: Powers of Removal

The Constitution nowhere explicitly indicates whether Congress or the President or both possess the power to remove appointed officers

13. Art. I, § 6, cl. 2. For a fuller discussion of Chadha's implications for appointments clause analysis, see L. Tribe, Constitutional Choices 71–74 (1985).

14. See The Federalist No. 76 (A. Hamilton). See also J. Story, Commentaries on the Constitution of the United States Section 1523 (Boston 1833). This theme permeates the Court's opinion in Bowsher v. Synar, 106 S.Ct. 3181 (1986), discussed in § 4–10, infra, where the Court struck down those portions of the Gramm-Rudman Act that delegated executive power to the Comptroller General, who can be removed from office by Congress.

15. See United States v. Germaine, 99 U.S. 508, 509–10 (1879).

16. Buckley, 424 U.S. at 137, Cf. Kilbourn v. Thompson, 103 U.S. 168 (1881); McGrain v. Daugherty, 273 U.S. 135 (1927). See § 5–19, infra.

17. Buckley, 424 U.S. at 126.

18. U.S. Const., art. II, § 3. See Myers v. United States, 272 U.S. 52, 117, 163–64

(1926), discussed in § 4–10, infra. It does not follow, of course, that significant roles in the implementation of federal statutes, or of congressionally approved interstate compacts, may not be entrusted to private persons appointed by quasi-public entities, by state governors, or by others outside the executive branch. See, e.g., Seattle Master Builders Ass'n v. Pacific Northwest Electric Power and Conservation Planning Council, 786 F.2d 1359 (9th Cir. 1986) (appointments clause does not bar appointment of interstate compact agency's members by state governors because agency's members perform duties pursuant to an interstate compact which, even if authorized by federal law, is created by state law), cert. denied, 107 S.Ct. 939 (1987); Melcher v. Federal Open Market Committee, 644 F.Supp. 510 (D.D.C. 1986) (private persons appointed by directors of federal reserve banks may serve on Federal Reserve Board's Open Market Committee and may engage in trading of government securities as element of national monetary policy).

other than federal judges [1] and subordinate employees.[2] However, the Supreme Court has attempted to fill this constitutional void by linking the power of removal to the power of appointment explicitly defined in Article II, § 2.[3]

Congressional assertion of the power to limit presidential removal of executive officers dates from the Tenure of Office Act of 1867, which forbade presidential removal of designated Cabinet members without the consent of the Senate.[4] The Tenure of Office Act (even though repealed in 1887) and subsequent related legislation were declared unconstitutional by the Supreme Court in 1926 in *Myers v. United States*.[5] The Court there struck down a congressional provision that certain postmasters, appointed by the President with the approval of the Senate, could not be removed by the President without the Senate's consent.

Chief Justice Taft's majority opinion in *Myers*, delivered over the dissents of Justices Holmes, Brandeis, and McReynolds, is the primary source of the modern theory of removal. Taft concluded that "the power of removal of executive officers [is] incident to the power of appointment," and therefore that "the President has the exclusive power of removing executive officers of the United States whom he has appointed by and with the advice and consent of the Senate."[6] He found further support for his conclusion that removal was the peculiar

---

§ 4–10

1. The Constitution does explicitly circumscribe the power of all branches of government to remove federal judges from office. Article III, § 1, provides: "The Judges, both of the supreme and inferior Courts, shall hold their Offices during good Behaviour." Federal judges appointed to article III courts cannot, therefore, be removed at the President's will even though such judges are appointed by the President. Of course, these judges, like other "Officers of the United States," can be removed through the impeachment mechanism.

2. Indeed, it is not clear from the face of the document that *anyone* can remove a government officer other than by impeachment. In In re Hennen, 38 U.S. (13 Pet.) 230 (1839), the Supreme Court, in holding that the presiding judge of a federal district court could dismiss a clerk whom he had appointed without the approval of the Senate, apparently assumed that impeachment was not an exclusive medium of removal. The Court explicitly rejected the proposition that the Constitution made impeachment the sole vehicle of removal in Shurtleff v. United States, 189 U.S. 311 (1903).

3. See, e.g. In re Hennen, 38 U.S., (13 Pet.) 230, 259 (1839) ("It would seem to be a sound and necessary rule, to consider the power of removal as incident to the power of appointment").

4. This statute was the proximate cause of President Johnson's impeachment and near conviction. See § 4–17, infra.

5. 272 U.S. 52 (1926).

6. Id. at 119, 106. Taft's conclusion that the removal power reposed exclusively in the Executive was premised largely on the debates of the First Congress on the issue of removal. Taft's construction of these debates, however, has been strongly criticized. See, e.g., Corwin, "Tenure of Office and the Removal Power Under the Constitution," 27 Col.L.Rev. 353, 360–69 (1927); C. Miller, The Supreme Court and the Uses of History, 64–68 (1969). Even more telling is the likelihood that, even if the debates suggested a broad presidential power of removal, such a conclusion would be of less than constitutional dimension. Congress was probably saying no more than that, as a matter of policy, the President should be given substantial latitude. See Corwin, supra at 370; R. Berger, Impeachment 139–40 (1973). Perhaps the earliest available hint of the intent of the Framers is provided by Hamilton: "The consent of [the Senate] would be necessary to displace as well as to appoint." The Federalist No. 77, at 511 (P. Ford ed. 1898). In Myers, Taft submitted that the debates of the First Congress indicated that Hamilton had reversed his position. 272 U.S. at 136–39. But see Corwin, supra at 371.

province of the President in the Chief Executive's charge to ensure that the laws "be faithfully executed." [7]

The Court's exegesis in *Myers* went so far beyond what was necessary to dispose of the case before it that it was susceptible of either of two fundamentally distinct readings. *Myers* could be understood to mean that Congress may not place any limits on the President's power to remove executive officers; or it could be read as embodying the proposition that, whatever the limits of presidential removal power, Congress could not cede to *itself* any role in removing government officials. The former reading was repudiated in *Humphrey's Executor v. United States*,[8] where the Court drastically narrowed the application of the *Myers* rule.[9] Specifically, the Court ruled that the President could not, at his pleasure, remove from office, before the expiration of his statutory term, a Federal Trade Commissioner where Congress had sought to deny such discretion to the President.[10] The Court reasoned that the necessary and proper clause endowed Congress with the power to create federal offices independent of the President in order to implement congressional statutes and to safeguard that independence by insulating the holders of such officers from dismissal at the caprice of the Chief Executive: "The authority of Congress, in creating quasi-legislative or quasi-judicial agencies, to require them to act in discharge of their duties independently of executive control, cannot well be doubted; and that authority includes, as an appropriate incident, power to fix the period during which they shall continue in office, and to forbid their removal except for cause in the meantime." [11] The *Myers* proposition was explicitly limited: it was held to apply only to the removal of "purely executive officers." [12]

7. "Article II grants to the President the executive power of the government, . . . including the power of appointment and removal of executive officers—a conclusion confirmed by his obligation to take care that the laws be faithfully executed . . . ." 272 U.S. at 163–64. Taft's reliance upon the "faithfully executed" clause appears suspect. "The language of duty rather than of power was employed advisedly in this clause of the Constitution . . . ." Corwin, supra at 384. While the clause creates an executive obligation to enforce the laws, such an obligation plainly does not *require* limitless removal power and does not leave the President's choice of means unfettered. For example, the President surely may not spend unappropriated funds in order to "execute the laws". In large part, then, it is up to Congress to provide the means whereby the President can discharge his duty; the President may not arrogate congressional powers by reference to this clause.

8. 295 U.S. 602 (1935).

9. "[T]he narrow point actually decided was only that the President had power to remove a postmaster . . . ., without the advise and consent of the Senate as required by act of Congress. In the course of the opinion of the court, expressions occur which tend to sustain [the contention that the President's power of removal is uncircumscribed], but these are beyond the point involved and, therefore, do not come within the rule of stare decisis." 295 U.S. at 626.

10. Congress had provided that the President could dismiss a Commissioner for "inefficiency, neglect of duty, or malfeasance in office." Federal Trade Commission Act, 15 U.S.C. § 41.

11. 295 U.S. at 629. The Court took note of the fact that, if the President could remove quasi-legislative officials at will, their independence would be illusory: "[I]t is quite evident that one who holds his office only during the pleasure of another, cannot be depended upon to maintain an attitude of independence against the latter's will." Id. at 629.

12. 295 U.S. at 631–32.

The difference in emphasis of the *Myers* and *Humphrey's Executor* cases is striking. In *Myers*, the Court assumed that the exclusive locus of the removal power was identical to that of the appointment power. Although the Court's premise that the President alone possesses the power of appointment is dubious—he may *nominate* officers by himself, but he can *appoint* them only "by and with the Advice and Consent of the Senate" [13]—it is clear that the moving force in *Myers* was the allure of constitutional symmetry. In *Humphrey's Executor*, the Court pursued a more functional, if less elegant, approach: the character of the office rather than the locus of its appointment determined whether the President was to enjoy unrestricted removal power.[14]

The Supreme Court subsequently underscored the distinction between these two cases. In *Wiener v. United States*, the Court posited that the difference in outcomes of *Myers* and *Humphrey's Executor* derived from "the difference in functions between those who are part of the Executive establishment and those whose tasks require absolute freedom from Executive interference." [15] In other words, those whose decisions the Executive cannot alter, the Executive cannot remove on his own authority.[16] The Court therefore held that since "the War Claims Act precluded the President from influencing the Commission in passing on a particular claim," the President could not remove, on his own authority, War Claims Commissioner Wiener.[17]

The functional test, as articulated in *Humphrey's Executor* and elucidated in *Wiener*, is hardly free from ambiguity. It will not always be clear whether Congress intended that a particular office operate independent of the President, especially if Congress neither prescribes nor proscribes a procedure for removal. Presumably, such a case should turn upon statutory construction: if Congress intended to insulate the officer from presidential control, for example, a court should give effect to this legislative design.[18]

---

13. Const., article II, § 2, cl. 2. See Comment, "Abolition of Federal Offices as an Infringement of the President's Power to Remove Federal Executive Officers: A Reassessment of Constitutional Doctrines," 42 Fordham L.Rev. 562, 567 (1974); Myers v. United States, 272 U.S. 52, 283 (1926) (Brandeis, J., dissenting).

14. See Comment, supra note 13, at 582; Cross, "The Removal Power of the President and the Test of Responsibility," 40 Cornell L.Q. 81 (1954). That the character of the office should be the decisive factor was implicit in Marbury v. Madison, 5 U.S. (1 Cranch) 137, 165–66 (1803).

15. 357 U.S. 349, 353 (1958).

16. This is not to say, however, that Congress could not *permit* the President to remove such quasi-legislative or quasi-judicial officers.

17. 357 U.S. at 356. It has been suggested that Wiener did far more than merely clarify Humphrey's Executor. In Wiener, the discharged commissioner had

an indefinite term and the statute was silent on removal; in Humphrey's Executor, the commissioner had a specified statutory term, and the statute specified the causes for removal. Barring presidential removal is arguably more potent in the former case since it might be tantamount to granting the commission life tenure. See 1 K. Davis, Administrative Law Treatise 22 n. 18 (1958). The holding of Wiener, however, might be limited to temporary agencies such as the War Claims Commission. See Parker, "The Removal Power of the President and Independent Administrative Agencies," 36 Ind.L.J. 63, 67 (1960).

18. Wiener alleviated the problem of construction somewhat through a burden-of-proof device: As to officers who are not purely executive, power to remove exists "only if Congress may fairly be said to have conferred it." 357 U.S. at 353. But deciding whether an officer is "purely executive" requires an inquiry into the degree of independence Congress seems to have

The predicament is even more troubling when a given officer is charged with some quasi-judicial or quasi-legislative chores and some purely executive obligations.[19] Nor has this ambiguity escaped notice by the Court. Indeed, in *Humphrey's Executor* the Justices admonished: "To the extent that, between the decision in the *Myers* case, which sustains the unrestrictable power of the President to remove purely executive officers, and our present decision that such power does not extend to an office such as that here involved, there shall remain a field of doubt, we leave such cases as may fall within it for future consideration and determination as they may arise." [20]

In *Bowsher v. Synar*,[21] the Supreme Court embraced the second possible reading of *Myers*: while Congress may *limit* the scope of presidential removal power by enacting restrictions on the discharge of officers of independent agencies—or *expand* it by delegating to "the President alone . . . or [to] the Heads of Departments" power to remove inferior executive officers [22]—Congress may not *itself* play any role in the removal of those charged with execution of the laws.

intended, or at least the degree of independence the substantive scheme created by Congress seems to require.

19. See Donovan & Irvine, "The President's Power to Remove Members of Administrative Agencies," 21 Cornell L.Q. 215, 224 (1936).

20. Humphrey's Ex'r v. United States, 295 U.S. 602, 632 (1935). It is noteworthy that the President has never been judicially compelled to *reinstate* a government official whose removal he ordered. In both Humphrey's Executor and Wiener the claim was for lost wages, not reinstatement. And A. Ernest Fitzgerald, the Defense Department "whistleblower" whose 1970 dismissal triggered extensive federal litigation, see § 4–14, infra, obtained reinstatement through a settlement agreement with the United States Air Force, see Nixon v. Fitzgerald, 457 U.S. 731, 738–39 n. 17 (1982). Although President Nixon claimed initially that Fitzgerald had been fired at Nixon's direct request, his statements to that effect were soon retracted, see id. at 737, as inoperative. It seems likely, however, that an injunction could issue to bar unlawful removal and that the President or an appropriate subordinate could be required by mandamus to reinstate an unlawfully removed officer. Cf. Vitarelli v. Seaton, 359 U.S. 535 (1959) (wrongfully dismissed government employee is entitled to reinstatement). The Supreme Court evidently assumed that the President could be required to install an officer when it decided Marbury v. Madison, 5 U.S. (1 Cranch) 137 (1803). The usual reluctance of courts to "specifically enforce" contracts of employment should pose little problem in this context. Such reluctance stems from a recognition of the friction that would normally exist between employer and employ-

ee were such a contract enforced, and the impact of such friction upon their interaction. By hypothesis, however, an officer who cannot be removed at the President's pleasure is one who is essentially independent of the President, thus rendering any friction that does exist irrelevant to the discharge of duties by the officer or by the President. And, insofar as reluctance to enforce the employment contract stems also from concerns about involuntary servitude, it is obviously inapposite to an *employee's* suit for reinstatement.

21. 106 S.Ct. 3181 (1986).

22. Congress, for example, might delegate its removal power to the executive. Thus, Congress could explicitly make certain quasi-legislative officials removable by the President or by another officer. Article II, § 2, authorizes Congress to "vest the Appointment of such inferior Officers, as they think proper, in the President alone, in the Courts of Law, or in the Heads of Departments." See § 4–9, supra. In Myers, Chief Justice Taft argued that "[t]he power to remove inferior executive officers, like that to remove superior executive officers, is an incident of the power to appoint them," and therefore concluded in dictum that "[t]he authority of Congress given by the excepting clause to vest the appointment of such inferior officers in the heads of departments carries with it authority incidentally to invest the heads of departments with power to remove." Myers v. United States, 272 U.S. 52, 161 (1926). The Chief Justice did not address the question whether *courts* vested with the power of appointment could similarly be vested with the power of removal. Cf. Nader v. Bork, 366 F.Supp. 104, 109 (D.D.C.1973) (suggesting, on the level of policy rather than of constitutional law,

Synar involved a challenge to the Balanced Budget and Emergency Deficit Control Act of 1985,[23] popularly known as the "Gramm-Rudman Act." The Act ceded to the Comptroller General the ultimate power to forecast the federal deficit and to determine and dictate the precise budget cuts, program by program, that would be made to meet the statutory deficit-reduction schedule.[24] The flaw was that the Comptroller General was removable not by the President, but only for cause by a joint resolution of Congress (or, of course, by impeachment). In his opinion for the Court, Chief Justice Burger [25] relied on *Myers* for the proposition "that congressional participation in the removal of executive officers is unconstitutional," [26] and declared that "[t]o permit the execution of the laws to be vested in an officer answerable only to Congress would, in practical terms, reserve in Congress control over the execution of the laws." [27]

Like the Burger Court's previous essays on the separation of powers in *Northern Pipeline Construction Co. v. Marathon Pipe Line Co.*[28] and *I.N.S. v. Chadha*,[29] the analysis in *Synar* is a bit wooden. There can be little doubt that Gramm-Rudman indeed endowed the Comptroller General with significant power to implement the legislative mandate to reduce the federal deficit,[30] but it is less than obvious why Congress' long-forgotten enactment some sixty years ago of a limited removal power over that officer, which it has never even threatened to exercise, is sufficient without more to create the sort of "here-and-now subservience" to the legislature that imperils the separation of powers. In this respect, the concurring [31] and dissenting [32]

that a congressional decision to give federal courts "responsibility for the appointment and *supervision* of a new Watergate Special Prosecutor" would be "most unfortunate": "The Courts must remain neutral. Their duties are not prosecutorial.") (emphasis added).

23. 2 U.S.C. § 901 et seq. (Supp. 1986).

24. 106 S.Ct. at 3192 (opinion of the Court). Contrast the far more limited grant of authority to the Comptroller General to suspend the procurement process pending bid protest investigations—a grant that the Third Circuit held proper after Synar. Ameron, Inc. v. United States Army Corps of Engineers, 809 F.2d 979 (3d Cir. 1986).

25. Chief Justice Burger was joined by Justices Brennan, Powell, Rehnquist and O'Connor. Justice Stevens, joined by Justice Marshall, concurred in the judgment, and Justices White and Blackmun filed dissenting opinions.

26. 106 S.Ct. at 3188.

27. Id.

28. 458 U.S. 50 (1982). See § 3–5, supra.

29. 462 U.S. 919 (1983), discussed in § 4–3, supra. The Court in Synar expressly relied on Chadha: since "Congress could

simply remove, or threaten to remove, an officer for executing the laws in any fashion found to be unsatisfactory to Congress," it follows that "[t]o permit an officer controlled by Congress to execute the laws would be, in essence, to permit a congressional veto." 106 S.Ct. at 3189.

30. The Comptroller had discretion to exercise his judgment as to the deficit estimates, and the President was required to carry out the Comptroller's budget reductions "without the slightest variation." Id. at 3192. Attempts to depict the Comptroller as a ministerial clerk wearing a "green eye shade," id. at 3199 (Stevens, J., joined by Marshall, J., concurring in the judgment), were unavailing. Even Justice Stevens, who saw no merit in the contest over labels such as "executive" or "legislative" power, agreed that "[u]nless we make the naive assumption that the economic destiny of the Nation could be safely entrusted to a mindless bank of computers, the powers that this Act vests in the Comptroller General must be recognized as having transcendent importance." Id. at 3200.

31. 106 S.Ct. at 3194–95 (Stevens, J., joined by Marshall, J., concurring in the judgment).

32. Id. at 3209–13 (White, J.).

opinions in *Synar* seem to have had the better of the argument. Congress can remove the Comptroller General from office only for statutorily specified, if generic, reasons [33]—and only by a joint resolution that would be subject to presidential veto. Since the Comptroller is thus insulated from congressional intimidation short of the two-thirds vote of both houses necessary to override a veto, by no means is he uniquely a captive of the legislature. Even the general power of impeachment, which does not require a concurrent two-thirds vote, is arguably a more potent whip. And it is no easier for Congress to fire the Comptroller General than to abolish the office entirely, to repeal Gramm-Rudman, or to do anything else that Congress and the President can do together by passing a law.[34]

But Justice White, who took the majority to task for neglecting "[r]ealistic consideration of the nature of the Comptroller General's relation to Congress," [35] was himself properly chided for overlooking the realities of the traditional and institutional ties between the Comptroller and Congress. As Justice Stevens demonstrated, the General Accounting Office, which the Comptroller General commands, functions much less as an executive department or independent agency than "virtually as a permanent staff for Congress." [36] The Comptroller General has not only always been statutorily designated an "agent of the Congress," [37] but in actual practice he has, by and large, acted as and been treated as such.[38] Against this background, Congress' power to remove the Comptroller, even if not decisive of the separation of powers issue, nevertheless constitutes important evidence that the Comptroller lacks the necessary independence from Congress to execute the law.

This is not to say that enactment of a congressional power to remove an officer charged with implementing the law could *never* be sufficient ground for declaring a particular statutory delegation unconstitutional. If Congress were to cede to itself the power to remove members of the Federal Trade Commission or the Federal Reserve Board, for example, such a move, in light of the long tradition of independence surrounding those two bodies, could only be understood as an impermissible attempt to subjugate them to the will of the legislature.

Furthermore, a particular structural interference with the Constitution's allocation of power, such as the congressional removal power at issue in *Synar*, should probably be a necessary predicate to any separation-of-powers challenge. Otherwise, the judiciary could too readily be dragged into a slugging match between the political branches any time one branch perceived its prerogatives as being threatened in a practical way by the acts of the other. The power of the purse leaves Congress free to cut off funding to the GAO until the Comptroller quits; the

33. See id. at 3189 (opinion of the Court); id. at 3194 (Stevens, J., concurring); id. at 3211 (White, J., dissenting).

34. Id. at 3211–12 (White, J., dissenting).

35. Id. at 3213 (White, J., dissenting).

36. Id. at 3199 n. 11 (Stevens, J. concurring).

37. Id. at 3198 & nn. 6, 7.

38. See id. at 3191 (opinion of the Court).

Senate could then refuse to confirm any nominee deemed insufficiently compliant to congressional will.[39] Unless some specific trespass on the designated sphere of another branch is held to be necessary, if not always sufficient, to strike down a law as violative of the separation of powers, appropriation bills and laws restricting or altering the substantive power of executive agencies would be subject to routine challenge.

The result in *Synar*, if not the precise route by which the Court reached it, therefore seems correct. Perhaps *Synar* is best understood as reaffirming the Framers' aversion to parliamentary government, with its "mingling of the Executive and Legislative branches." [40] As the three-judge district court expressed it, executive powers "cannot be conferred upon an officer who lacks the degree of *independence from Congress* that their exercise constitutionally requires." [41] The Constitution's command that the President "take Care that the Laws be faithfully executed," [42] operates as a *negative* principle: it requires that executive officers have a measure of independence from Congress, not necessarily a degree of dependence upon the President. What our scheme of separation of powers forbids is an agency that is primarily dependent on one branch of government but that exercises the powers of another.

Nothing in *Synar* suggests that executive powers of the sort delegated to the Comptroller may be exercised only by officers removable at will by the President.[43] Thus the decision comports perfectly with the Court's prior holding in *Humphrey's Executor* and casts no doubt on the status of independent agencies. Since in matters of executive power the Constitution mandates a "hands-off" role for Congress, rather than a "hands-on" role for the President, there is nothing to stop the legislature from vesting executive authority in officers substantially independent of the White House. As Justice White observed, that Congress may deem it "necessary and proper" to insulate government officers from direct political influence by the White House "does not imply derogation of the President's . . . duty to 'take Care that the Laws be faithfully executed,' for any such duty is necessarily limited" by the substantive and structural content of the laws Congress enacts.[44] Absent substantive congressional action, there is no executive authority to regulate trade practices as in *Humphrey* or to pay out war claims as in *Wiener*. And if Congress were to structure its trade laws as a flat ban on certain mergers or acquisitions, rather than imposing a regulatory regime, the President's power would be significantly altered. In the former case, enforcing the law would involve only the decision to

39. Of course, such a plan of action could be challenged as a bill of attainder forbidden by article I, § 9. See United States v. Lovett, 328 U.S. 303 (1946), further discussed in Ch. 10, infra. See generally, "Abolition of Federal Offices as an Infringement on the President's Power to Remove Federal Executive Officers: A Reassessment of Constitutional Doctrines," 42 Fordham L.Rev. 562 (1974).

40. 1 Annals of Congress 380 (1789) (J. Madison), quoted by the Court in Synar, 106 S.Ct. at 3187.

41. Synar v. United States, 626 F.Supp. 1374, 1391 (D.D.C.1986) (emphasis added).

42. Art. II, § 3.

43. Both Chief Justice Burger for the Court, 106 S.Ct. at 3188 n. 4, and Justice White in dissent, id. at 3206, expressly disavowed any such holding.

44. Id. at 3207 (White, J., dissenting).

prosecute or not; in the latter, execution of the law entails the exercise of discretion in a wide range of rule-making and adjudication settings. In the same way, Congress may confine the scope of the President's discretion in executing the law by limiting the Executive's power to remove the Federal Trade Commissioners charged with implementing the legislative mandate.[45] So long as Congress itself has no say in how a bill is executed after it becomes law, the prerogatives of the executive branch are not threatened, and there is no constitutional infirmity.

The doctrinal framework laid out from *Humphrey's Executor* to *Synar* justifies not only limits on the President's removal power which restrain presidential interference with the exercise of congressionally-derived authority, but also limits on removal which effectuate congressionally-authorized supervision of the President's *own* constitutional responsibilities. For example, it seems likely that Congress could validly limit presidential power to remove a special prosecutor charged by Congress with responsibility for investigating presidential abuses of power and abuses by presidential aides, even if such a prosecutor were appointed by the President subject to Senate confirmation. Congress certainly has authority under the necessary and proper clause [46] to create such a prosecutor: Legislation establishing a tenured prosecutor responsible for identifying abuses of high executive authority is a rational way to ensure that the President, and those answerable to him, "take Care that the Laws be faithfully executed." [47] And, whether or not the prosecutor in question would be presidentially appointed, the *Wiener* test would permit the limitation of the President's removal power: Such a prosecutor would necessarily "require absolute freedom from Executive interference." [48]

45. Statutes that permit removal of agency officers for such "causes" as "neglect of duty" might, in any event, be construed to "sustain removal . . . for any number of actual or perceived transgressions of the [removing authority's] will," 106 S.Ct. at 3190 (opinion of the Court), thereby avoiding the question whether Congress could constitutionally insulate such officers from all political accountability by making them removable only for such politically "neutral" causes as dishonesty.

46. See § 5-3, infra.

47. Executive officials, including the President and members of the Cabinet, may also limit their own authority to remove subordinates by issuing regulations describing the conditions under which employment has been granted. Such regulations must be complied with unless and until they have been amended or repealed in accord with the governing statutory and regulatory framework. See Nader v. Bork, 366 F.Supp. 104, 108 (D.D.C. 1973) (holding that then Acting Attorney General Robert Bork had illegally discharged Watergate Special Prosecutor Archibald Cox: the dismissal was not preceded by a "finding of extraordinary impropriety" as required by the regulations creating Cox's position). Although Nader was later vacated as moot, the decision's theory is in accord with United States v. Nixon, 418 U.S. 683, 695–96 (1974).

48. Wiener v. United States, 357 U.S. 349, 353 (1958). The delegation of investigative and prosecutorial power to persons or agencies independent of the President would be constitutionally justified at least in those extraordinary circumstances where, because of inherent conflicts of interest, independence from the Chief Executive is required to assure that constitutionally assigned responsibilities are being faithfully carried out. The only significant contrary argument—that impeachment is the exclusive remedy for situations in which the President is deemed untrustworthy, see § 4-17, infra—would fly in the face of the Constitution's pervasive assumption that *no* government officer is *ever* entitled to complete trust. Moreover, the Court has recognized, in the bill of attainder context, a significant difference between identifying *situations* of conflicting interest and singling out *individuals* as unworthy. See § 10–4, infra.

§ 4–11.　The President as Chief Executive:　Powers of Prosecution and Pardon

The President's power and duty under article II, § 3, to "take care that the Laws be faithfully executed," encompasses a special role in the prosecution of crimes, a role augmented by the power conferred on the President by article II, § 2, "to grant reprieves and pardons for offenses against the United States, except in Cases of Impeachment". The "Executive Branch has exclusive authority and absolute discretion to decide whether to prosecute a case . . . ."[1] But under article II, § 2, cl. 2,[2] Congress may vest in a department head like the Attorney General "the power to conduct the criminal litigation of the United States Government,"[3] and may vest in the Attorney General "the power to appoint subordinate officers to assist him in the discharge of his duties."[4] When, "[a]cting pursuant to those statutes, the Attorney General has delegated the authority to represent the United States in . . . particular matters to a Special Prosecutor with unique authority and tenure,"[5] the regulation embodying this delegation has "the force of law" until duly revoked.[6] As long as the "regulation is extant," the "Executive Branch is bound by it, and indeed the United States as the sovereign composed of the three branches is bound to respect and enforce it."[7] It was for this reason that the Court in *United States v. Nixon* treated the dispute between the Special Prosecutor, who wished to produce specified evidence in a pending criminal case, and the President, who, as Chief Executive, resisted production of such evidence,[8] as more than "an intra-branch dispute between a subordinate and superior officer of the Executive Branch . . . analog[ous] to a dispute between . . . congressional committees."[9] Thus the Executive Branch is not an indivisible entity with a single head even for

§ 4–11

1. United States v. Nixon, 418 U.S. 683, 693 (1974) (dictum), citing the Confiscation Cases, 74 U.S. (7 Wall.) 454 (1869), and United States v. Cox, 342 F.2d 167, 176 (5th Cir. 1965), cert. denied sub nom. Cox v. Hauberg, 381 U.S. 935 (1965).

2. See § 4–9, supra.

3. United States v. Nixon, 418 U.S. at 694, referring to 28 U.S.C.A. § 516.

4. 418 U.S. at 694. After President Nixon's and acting Attorney General Bork's unlawful firing of Special Prosecutor Archibald Cox in October 1973, see § 4–10, supra, proposals were advanced for congressional establishment of a special prosecutor who would be beyond presidential control with respect to appointment as well as removal. Although such proposals might be challenged on the ground that prosecutorial activities are "purely executive," and although cogent objections might be made to lodging powers of prosecutorial appointment or supervision in federal judges, the fact that a prosecutor charged with pursuing executive illegality could constitutionally be insulated from presidential *removal*, see § 4–10, supra, suggests that insisting on presidential participation in *appointment* would make no constitutional sense. See generally § 4–9, supra. Thus a special judicial commission could properly be created and charged with the duty of selecting an independent agent for the investigation and prosecution of illegal acts by the President or the President's subordinates.

5. 418 U.S. at 694. See id. at 694–95 n. 8 for a description of the special authority delegated to the Special Prosecutor with respect to "all offenses arising out of the 1972 Presidential Election" by 38 Fed.Reg. 30739, as amended by 38 Fed.Reg. 32805 (1973).

6. 418 U.S. at 695. See also United States ex rel. Accardi v. Shaughnessy, 347 U.S. 260 (1954). Accord, Vitarelli v. Seaton, 359 U.S. 535 (1959); Service v. Dulles, 354 U.S. 363, 388 (1957).

7. 418 U.S. at 695, 696.

8. Id. at 697.

9. Id. at 692–93.

prosecutorial purposes; even the core executive mission of enforcing federal law may be internally fragmented pursuant to congressional delegations and executive subdelegations. Given the President's sweeping power "to grant reprieves and pardons for offenses against the United States" in non-impeachment cases,[10] however, any instance of non-prosecution in which Congress or the nation deeply mistrusts the motives for the President's reluctance to enforce the law may prove impossible to deal with by methods short of impeachment.

§ 4–12. The President as Chief Executive: The Power to Spend or Not to Spend

If the President's is the power of the sword, then at least in theory the power of the purse belongs to Congress. Under article I, § 7, all "Bills for raising Revenue" must "originate in the House of Representatives;" under article I, § 8, the powers of Congress include the "Power to lay and collect Taxes, Duties, Imposts and Excises, to pay the Debts and provide for the common Defence and general Welfare;" to "borrow Money on the credit of the United States;" and to "coin Money." And

10. Although the President's pardon power does not include authority to pardon in anticipation of offenses—an authority to dispense with the laws the claim to which led to James II's forced abdication, see F. Maitland, Constitutional History of England 302–06 (1920)—and although that power does not exclude a concurrent congressional authority "to pass acts of general amnesty," Brown v. Walker, 161 U.S. 591, 601 (1896); cf. The Laura, 114 U.S. 411 (1885), it *does* extend to all offenses against federal laws; it includes the power to pardon whole classes by a proclamation of amnesty, United States v. Klein, 80 U.S. (13 Wall.) 128, 147 (1871); see, e.g., 42 Fed. Reg. 4391 (Jan. 24, 1977) (Pres. Proc. No. 4483, pardoning all Vietnam-era violators of the Military Selective Service Act); it may be exercised at any time subsequent to the commission of an offense, even prior to indictment, Ex parte Garland, 71 U.S. (4 Wall.) 333 (1866); it "restores all . . . civil rights" to the pardoned offender, id. at 380; it may be granted either absolutely or conditionally, see Ex parte Wells, 59 U.S. 307, 314 (1855); Ex parte Grossman, 267 U.S. 87, 120 (1925), so long as the "condition . . . does not otherwise offend the Constitution," Schick v. Reed, 419 U.S. 256, 266 (1974); and it "cannot be modified, abridged, or diminished by the Congress." Id. Pardons must be distinguished from commutations, another form of executive clemency grantable under the pardon clause. Pardons are acts of mercy which wipe away all punishment for the original crime; commutations, on the other hand, merely substitute lighter for heavier punishment. See Biddle v. Perovich, 274 U.S. 480 (1927); Chapman v. Scott, 10 F.2d 156 (D.Conn.1925), affirmed 10 F.2d 690 (2d Cir.), cert. denied 270 U.S. 657 (1926). Even a pardon, it should be noted, does not "affect any rights [already] vested in others directly by the execution of the judgment for the offense," or "impose upon the government any obligation to give . . . compensation for what has been done or suffered," Knote v. United States, 95 U.S. 149, 153–54 (1877), nor does it prevent courts from taking the pardoned offense into account in sentencing for a subsequent conviction, see Carlesi v. People of State of New York, 233 U.S. 51, 59 (1914). See also Burdick v. United States, 236 U.S. 79, 95 (1915) (whereas amnesty "overlooks offense," pardon merely "remits punishment"). Indeed, far from wiping out guilt, the acceptance of an executive pardon may imply a confession of guilt. Id. at 90–91, 94.

Despite arguments that President Ford's pardon of ex-President Nixon for all crimes the latter might have committed against the United States during his Presidency, see Proclamation 4311, F.R.Doc. 74–21059, 39 Fed.Reg. 32601–02 (1974), went beyond the proper reach of the pardoning power, see, e.g., I. F. Stone, "On Pardons and Testimony," N.Y. Times, Oct. 9, 1974, p. 43, col. 2; P. Kurland, N.Y. Times, Sept. 13, 1974, p. 1, col. 6; R. Sprague, N.Y. Times, Oct. 5, 1975, § 4, p. 17, col. 1; Firmage and Mangrum, "Removal of the President: Resignation and the Procedural Law of Impeachment", 1974 Duke L.J. 1023, 1094–1102; Macgill, "The Nixon Pardon: Limits on the Benign Prerogative," 7 Conn.L.Rev. 56 (1974), attacks on the Nixon pardon have nonetheless proven unavailing in court. See Murphy v. Ford, 390 F.Supp. 1372 (W.D.Mich.1975).

article I, § 9, provides that "[n]o Money shall be drawn from the Treasury, but in Consequence of Appropriations made by Law," requiring further that "a regular Statement and Account of the Receipts and Expenditures of all public Money shall be published from time to time." Properly exercised, this combination of powers might have sufficed, even in the hands of a collective body like Congress, to wield substantial control over the actual expenditure, as well as the raising and appropriation, of federal funds. In theory, then, just as "the legislative department alone has access to the pockets of the people," [1] so that department might have maintained a grip over what became of the money those pockets yielded up.

But at least since the initiation in 1921 of presidential responsibility for formulation of a national budget,[2] theory and reality have parted. Clearly, the President and the Executive Branch have become preeminent in the all-important process of planning and programming federal expenditures. Yet, just as political science has focused far more attention on the process of congressional appropriation, and on the interaction between Congress and the agencies in the formulation of a budget, than on the actual spending of the people's money,[3] so also constitutional law has been more concerned with taxation and appropriation than with expenditure. The emphasis is not altogether surprising: although taxation without representation has been the occasion of many a revolution, expenditure without authorization has been the cause of few,[4] and the transfer, reprogramming, or impoundment of funds already authorized and appropriated has been the occasion of none. The brevity of this section of Chapter 4 will reflect that historic emphasis, but without meaning to endorse it; eventually, we will need a more complete theory of how constitutional law and political power have interacted, and should interact, in this vital terrain.

Although such a theory will have to address a wider range of issues than presidential impoundment, that issue provides a convenient lens through which to focus on the executive's spending power. Impoundments of congressionally appropriated sums have been of many types. When President Jefferson informed Congress that the funds it had appropriated for gunboats need not be spent since the Louisiana Purchase had averted the emergency contemplated by Congress, his action was taken in response to unforeseen events—and in fact proved temporary; President Nixon's impoundments in the early 1970's, on the other hand, were plainly designed to terminate congressionally created programs and policies which the President could not successfully veto but with which he disagreed.[5]

§ 4–12

1. The Federalist No. 48 (J. Madison).

2. It was in 1921 that the Budget and Accounting Act created the Bureau of the Budget, initially located in the Treasury Department, and authorized the President to appoint his own budget director. Both the shift of budgetary power to the President that began by the mid-19th century if not earlier, and the impact of the 1921 law, are carefully traced in L. Fisher, Presidential Spending Power 7–58 (1975).

3. See id. at 3.

4. P. Einzig, The Control of the Purse 71–72 (1959), could find only one—that of Robin of Redesdale, in 1469.

5. See L. Fisher, supra note 2, at 150–51, 169–70.

The federal courts have traditionally rejected the argument that the President possesses inherent power to impound funds and thus halt congressionally authorized expenditures. The Supreme Court issued its first major pronouncement on the constitutional basis of executive impoundment in *Kendall v. United States ex rel. Stokes*.[6] There, in order to resolve a contract dispute, Congress ordered the Postmaster General to pay a claimant whatever amount an outside arbitrator should decide was the appropriate settlement. Presented with a decision by the arbitrator in a case arising out of a claim for services rendered to the United States in carrying the mails, President Jackson's Postmaster General ignored the congressional mandate and paid, instead, a smaller amount that he deemed the proper settlement. The Supreme Court held that a writ of mandamus could issue directing the Postmaster General to comply with the congressional directive.[7] In reaching this conclusion, the Court held that the President, and thus those under his supervision, did not possess inherent authority, whether implied by the faithfully executed clause or otherwise, to impound funds that Congress had ordered to be spent: "To contend that the obligation imposed on the President to see the laws faithfully executed, implies a power to forbid their execution, is a novel construction of the constitution, and entirely inadmissible."[8]

Any other conclusion would have been hard to square with the care the Framers took to limit the scope and operation of the veto power, and quite impossible to reconcile with the fact that the Framers assured Congress the power to override any veto by a two-thirds vote in each House.[9] For presidential impoundments to halt a program would, of course, be tantamount to a veto that no majority in Congress could override.[10] To quote Justice Rehnquist, speaking in his former capacity as Assistant Attorney General in 1969: "With respect to the suggestion that the President has a constitutional power to decline to spend appropriated funds, we must conclude that existence of such a broad power is supported by neither reason nor precedent. . . . It is in our view extremely difficult to formulate a constitutional theory to justify a refusal by the President to comply with a Congressional directive to spend. It may be agreed that the spending of money is inherently an executive function, but the execution of any law is, by definition, an executive function, and it seems an anomalous proposition that because the Executive branch is bound to execute the laws, it is free to decline to execute them."[11]

---

6. 37 U.S. (12 Pet.) 524 (1838).

7. The Court stressed how "purely ministerial," or mechanical, was the task involved. 37 U.S. at 613.

8. Id. at 611.

9. See § 4–13, infra.

10. See Note, "Protecting the Fisc: Executive Impoundment and Congressional Power," 82 Yale L.J. 1616, 1638 (1974); Note, "Presidential Impounding of Funds: The Judicial Response," 40 U.Chi.L.R. 328, 330 (1973); Stassen, "Separation of Powers and the Uncommon Defense: The Case

Against Impounding of Weapons System Appropriations," 57 Geo.L.J. 1159, 1183–84 (1969). See also Note, "Presidential Impoundment: Constitutional Theories and Political Realities," 61 Geo.L.J. 1295 (1973); Mikva and Hertz, "Impoundment of Funds—The Courts, the Congress and the President: A Constitutional Triangle," 69 N'Western L.Rev. 335 (1974).

11. Then Assistant Attorney General Rehnquist added that he deemed Kendall v. United States "authority against the asserted Presidential power." The Rehnquist statement is reprinted in Hearings on

On the other hand, to deny the President, either as Commander in Chief or as Chief Executive, any discretion whatever in the expenditure of funds would arguably "convert the [President] into a Chief Clerk," [12] since intelligent management of vast resources according to a set recipe is simply inconceivable. It does not follow, however, that the President should enjoy a roving commission to pick and choose among congressional mandates, carrying out only those programs that seem, from the President's perspective, to be consistent with the national interest— whether the President purports to divine that interest from goals articulated by Congress in other statutes,[13] or from an assessment of how best to stay within congressionally mandated debt or budget ceilings.[14]

Congress has taken a number of steps designed to undermine executive justifications for the impoundment of legislatively appropriated funds. The Impoundment Control Act of 1974[15] effects broad reforms in the process whereby legislative appropriations decisions are made. One portion of the Act deals with impoundment and prescribes two different procedures through which Congress can frustrate executive impoundment attempts: first, if the President wishes to *terminate* programs or cut total spending, approval of an appropriations recision must first be obtained from both the House of Representatives and the

the Executive Impoundment of Appropriated Funds Before the Subcommittee on Separation of Powers of the Senate Committee on the Judiciary, 92d Cong. 1st Sess. 279 (1971).

12. Testimony of Deputy Attorney General Sneed in Joint Hearings on S. 373 before the Senate Committee on Government Operations and the Senate Committee on the Judiciary, 93d Cong. 1st Sess. 369 (1973). See also Fisher, "Presidential Tax Discretion and Eighteenth Century Theory," 23 West.Pol.Q. 151 (1971); Fisher, "The Efficiency Side of Separated Powers," 5 J.Am.Stud. 113 (1971).

13. See, e.g., State Highway Commission of Missouri v. Volpe, 347 F.Supp. 950 (W.D.Mo.1972), aff'd 479 F.2d 1099 (8th Cir. 1973) (holding that anti-inflationary goals expressed in other statutes cannot justify executive defiance of specific spending legislation); cf. Local 2677 v. Phillips, 358 F.Supp. 60 (D.D.C.1973) (rejecting a claim of presidential discretion under the Constitution); Williams v. Phillips, 360 F.Supp. 1363, 1368–69 (D.D.C.1973) (same), aff'd 482 F.2d 669 (D.C.Cir.1973) (per curiam). See Note, "Protecting the Fisc: Executive Impoundment and Congressional Power," 82 Yale L.J. 1616, 1649–50 (1974). Of course, the language and purpose of a particular appropriations bill involved may permit the conclusion that impoundment is consistent with the legislative will. In some cases, the appropriations bill very clearly invests the Executive Branch with wide discretion regarding the spending lev-

el. In other cases, the use of mandatory language indicates that Congress has not sanctioned impoundment. Needless to say, the vast majority of cases fall somewhere between these two poles. The Supreme Court has indicated that it will study the legislative history of the appropriations statute and carefully dissect its language in order to determine whether impoundment is permissible. See, e.g., Train v. New York, 420 U.S. 35, 42–48 (1975) (rejecting the argument that Congress intended to grant wide discretion to the Executive to control amounts spent under the Federal Water Pollution Control Act Amendments of 1972). The key, however, is that nothing extrinsic to the statute and the policies *it* was designed to effect is relevant to the calculus. Thus, monies appropriated to clean up dirty rivers might be impounded by the President because there were no more dirty rivers; they could not be impounded to stabilize the consumer price index.

14. See, e.g., Note, "Impoundment of Funds," 86 Harv.L.Rev. 1505, 1521–22 (1973), concluding that surpassing the debt ceiling did not justify President Nixon's impoundments in the early 1970's since he had alternate means of staying within the congressionally prescribed limit.

15. P.L. 93–344, 88 Stat. 297, 31 U.S.C. § 1301 et seq. The Act was signed by President Nixon on July 12, 1974, during the impeachment proceedings pending against him.

Senate within 45 days; [16] second, if a presidential impoundment is designed simply to *delay* the expenditure of appropriated funds, the President may act unilaterally, but Congress may subsequently compel the release of the funds if either the House of Representatives or the Senate passes a resolution calling for their expenditure.[17]

Congress also repealed that portion of the Anti-Deficiency Act which had authorized federal administrators "to effect savings whenever savings are made possible . . . through . . . developments subsequent to the date on which such appropriation was made available." [18] It had been argued by some that this language justified executive impoundment for reasons unrelated to the legislative purposes of the specific appropriations withheld.[19]

Unfortunately, the Impoundment Act contained the seeds of its own destruction. Unilateral presidential impoundment of appropriated funds was allowed by the Act only because Congress reserved to each of its houses the power to veto the impoundment by resolution. The Supreme Court's invalidation of such legislative veto devices in *I.N.S. v. Chadha* [20] meant that the Act would long survive only if the courts could fairly conclude that Congress would have preferred the statute, after severance of the veto provision, to no statute at all.

The very title of the Act describes a congressional search for means to wrest "control" over the budget from the White House. A clearer case of legislative intent would be hard to imagine. Indeed, the debates that preceded enactment reveal nearly unanimous consensus for total congressional control over the impoundment process and the one-house veto was specifically extolled as an integral component of the control apparatus. Were a court to sever the veto provision and uphold the remaining deferral authority, it would confirm in the President the very power that Congress has never acknowledged him to have. More-

---

16. Cf. § 5(b) of the War Powers Resolution of 1973, discussed in § 4–7, supra.

17. See § 4–3, supra. The Act also requires the President to report all impoundment actions, requires the Comptroller General to inform Congress of any unreported impoundments, and empowers him to bring civil enforcement suits. For a thoughtful critique of these anti-impoundment provisions, by a scholar sympathetic to more effective congressional control, see L. Fisher, supra note 2, at 198–201. Fisher observes that ambiguities in the provisions, coupled with their mistaken assumption that Congress could deal meaningfully with reports about literally dozens of impoundment-related actions in a brief period, created a situation in which "the number of policy impoundments under President Ford had actually increased", id. at 200, over the number under President Nixon. "[T]he Act was interpreted by the Ford Administration to allow more than a hundred policy impoundments a year, generally directed against congressional initiatives. The sheer volume of the requests,

together with the fact that they were prejudicial to programs added or augmented by Congress, undermined the prospect for careful congressional review and deliberation." Id. at 201.

18. 31 U.S.C. § 665(1). Moreover, to guard against the possibility that a statute will be construed as *permitting* rather than *mandating* spending, Congress has also incorporated, within at least some spending legislation, language which makes explicit the denial of impoundment authority. See, e.g., P.L. 93–269 (1974) ("Nothing in this section shall be construed to approve of the withholding from expenditure or the delay in expenditure of any funds appropriated to carry out any applicable program . . .").

19. The better reading, however, would have limited the scope of the provision to changes directly related to the policies the act served. See Note, 82 Yale L.J. 1636, 1650 (1973).

20. 462 U.S. 919 (1983), discussed in § 4–3, supra.

over, such judicial surgery would effectively confer upon the President a "line-item" veto power, since he could sign an appropriations bill and later indefinitely "defer" any specific appropriations for programs he thought undeserving. Since such line-by-line veto power is anathema to Congress and may well be unconstitutional,[21] the Impoundment Act in all probability is not long for this world.[22]

But the full title of the legislation enacted in 1974 is the Congressional Budget Impoundment and Control Act and, as the label indicates, it went far beyond merely curbing presidential impoundment abuses. As if in response to claims that some impoundment authority was necessary in light of Congress' institutional inability to deal comprehensively and systematically with budget issues, the 1974 Act established new budget committees in each house charged with preparing tentative budget recommendations to be adopted as concurrent resolutions each May so as to furnish targets to guide other congressional committees; a Congressional Budget Office (CBO) was created to give Congress the staff assistance for coordination that the Office of Management and Budget (OMB), successor to the Budget Bureau, provides for the President; and the schedule ordinarily to be followed for committee actions on spending and appropriations bills was revised to include an early September completion date, at which time a second concurrent resolution might be passed adjusting the targets initially set.

This ambitious mechanism may have put the federal budget process on a schedule, but it failed to put it on a diet. Congress became so disillusioned with its own ability to control government spending that it attempted to tie its own—and the President's—hands with the passage of the Balanced Budget and Emergency Deficit Control Act of 1985,[23] popularly known as the Gramm-Rudman Act. The act sets a maximum deficit level for federal spending for each fiscal year from 1986 through 1991, with the size of the maximum deficit progressively declining to zero by 1991. Each year, the Directors of OMB and CBO independently estimate the deficit for the upcoming year and submit reports to the Comptroller General. If in any fiscal year the federal budget deficit exceeds the target level by more than a specified sum, the Act mandates across-the-board spending cuts to reach the statutory maximum. The Comptroller General reviews the CBO and OMB reports and budget cut recommendations, and then issues a report to the President indicating specific budget cuts on a program-by-program basis. The Act then required the President to issue a "sequestration order" implementing those spending cuts.[24] The past tense is appropriate in the preceding sentence, of course, because the Supreme Court invalidated the Comptroller's role in the Gramm-Rudman plan in *Bowsher v. Synar*.[25]

---

21. See § 4–13, infra.

22. In City of New Haven, Conn. v. United States, 809 F.2d. 900, 909 (D.C.Cir. 1987), the veto provision was ruled inseverable for just these reasons and the entire Impoundment Act was invalidated.

23. 2 U.S.C. § 901 et seq. (Supp.1986).

24. The sequestration order was automatically suspended for a statutory period during which Congress could preclude the Comptroller's designated cuts by enacting sufficient reductions to meet the Act's target deficit level.

25. 106 S.Ct. 3181 (1986), discussed in § 4–10, supra.

Since it was the Comptroller's report—which was to be prepared independent of the executive branch and which gave orders to the President—which constituted "the engine that g[ave] life to the ambitious budget reduction process," [26] the *Synar* decision sent Congress back to the drawing board to design new legislative means for regaining the pre-eminent role in fiscal matters that the Framers envisioned. [27]

§ 4–13. A Further Study in Negation: Analyzing, "Pocket"-ing, and "Item"-izing The Presidential Veto

Article I, § 7, cl. 2, provides that every bill passed by the House of Representatives and the Senate "shall, before it become a Law, be presented to the President" for signature or veto. If the bill is vetoed, it can become law only if repassed by a two-thirds vote in each House. [1] Article I, § 7, cl. 3, extends the same scheme to "[e]very Order, Resolution, or Vote to which the Concurrence of the Senate and House . . . may be necessary (except on a question of Adjournment). . . ." [2] In purely practical terms, it is difficult to overstate the importance of the presidential veto in the constitutional scheme of separated powers. [3] The Framers were well aware of what executive veto power portends, and they endeavored to contrast the "qualified negative of the President" with the "absolute negative of the British sovereign." [4] Although the Constitutional Convention explicitly resolved to deny the President any absolute veto over legislation [5] article I, § 7, cl. 2, allows a President to "pocket veto" legislation in special circumstances so as to avoid the possibility of an absolute congressional override: The President is given "ten Days (Sunday excepted)" after

---

26. Id. at 3203 (Stevens, J., concurring).

27. Congress anticipated the possibility of a successful constitutional challenge to the Gramm-Rudman Act by including "fallback provisions." § 274(f) of the Act provided that, in the event the delegation to the Comptroller were invalidated, the budget-cutting suggestions of OMB and CBO would automatically be referred to a joint congressional committee that would compile a report which, upon enactment, would have the same legal consequences as if it had been issued by the Comptroller General. The Supreme Court stayed its judgment for 60 days to allow Congress to implement these fallback provisions.

§ 4–13

1. The requirement is that the bill be passed by two-thirds of those present, if the number present constitutes a quorum. Missouri Pacific Railway Co. v. Kansas, 248 U.S. 276 (1919).

2. All final actions of Congress having public effect are covered. See, e.g., United States v. California, 332 U.S. 19, 28 (1947). The purpose of maintaining the accountability of the executive while retaining an effective check on legislative excess led the Framers to reject proposals that the veto power be shared, as well as proposals that

its invocation be limited to particular legislative occasions. See generally 1 M. Farrand, Records of the Federal Convention of 1787 (1966 ed.) at 139–40, 144; 2 M. Farrand, at 301–02, 304, 587; The Federalist, Nos. 51, 73.

3. Professor Charles Black's depiction of the veto power remains the most vivid: "[I] ask[ed] myself, 'To what state could Congress, without violating the Constitution, reduce the President?' I arrived at a picture of a man living in a modest apartment, with perhaps one secretary to answer mail; that is where one appropriations bill could put him, at the beginning of a new term. I saw this man as negotiating closely with the Senate, and from a position of weakness, on every appointment, and as conducting diplomatic relations with those countries where Congress would pay for an embassy. But he was still vetoing bills." Black, "Some Thoughts on the Veto," 40 Law & Contemp.Prob. 87, 89 (1976).

4. The Federalist, No. 69 (Hamilton). See also McGowan, "The President's Veto Power: An Important Instrument of Conflict in Our Constitutional System," 23 San Diego L.Rev. 791, 793–96 (1986).

5. See 1 M. Farrand, at 96–99.

legislation "shall have been presented to him," either to sign the legislation into law or to veto the legislation and return it to the House in which it originated for a possible override attempt. Ordinarily, if the President fails to act within the ten day period, the legislation becomes law without his or her signature. But if the Constitution said nothing more on the subject, Congress—which controls its own calendar [6]—could vitiate the President's qualified veto by abbreviating or altogether eliminating, through adjournment, the period allotted to the President to return a bill with his objections. It is that abuse which the pocket veto clause precludes by withholding the status of law from a bill whose return Congress has prevented: [7] if "the Congress by their Adjournment prevent . . . Return" of vetoed legislation, that legislation cannot go into effect unless the President signs it into law; presidential inaction in the context of such congressional adjournment has the effect of an *absolute* veto. Thus the pocket veto clause contains not an affirmative grant of power to the President, but a *limitation* on the prerogative of Congress to reconsider a bill upon the President's refusal to sign it.

A pocket veto opportunity thus exists whenever a congressional adjournment prevents return of the vetoed legislation. But what manner of adjournment satisfies this constitutional language? Beyond doubt, the final adjournment of a Congress after its second session [8] gives rise to a pocket veto opportunity, and the Supreme Court so declared in *The Pocket Veto Case*,[9] holding further that a Congress' adjournment at the end of its first annual session also creates such an opportunity. The Court reasoned that the House to which the bill must be returned must be a House in session, since the Constitution provides that such House "proceed to reconsider" the bill.[10] Presidential delivery of veto messages to designated congressional agents was deemed inconsistent with "the object" of article I, § 7—that "there should be a timely return . . ., [enabling] Congress to proceed immediately with its reconsideration"—if Congress' adjournment is so long that delivery of veto messages to such agents places legislation "in a state of suspended animation" depriving the public of "certain and prompt knowledge as to the [ultimate] status" of vetoed legislation.[11]

The scope of the pocket veto prerogative was subsequently delimited in *Wright v. United States*.[12] There, a bill was returned to the Senate, where it had originated, during a three day adjournment of that body. The House of Representatives was still in session. The Court held that this affirmative veto was effective in triggering congressional reconsideration, concluding that during a recess of the originat-

---

6. The only exception to Congress' control over its own adjournments is in case of a disagreement between the two houses "with Respect to the Time of Adjournment," in which event the President "may adjourn them to such Time as he shall think proper." Art. II, § 3.

7. See Edwards v. United States, 286 U.S. 482, 486 (1932); J. Story, Commentaries on the Constitution of the United States § 891 (1833).

8. Each Congress lasts only two years, since that is the term of members of the House of Representatives. U.S. Const. art. I, § 2.

9. 279 U.S. 655 (1929).

10. Id. at 682.

11. Id. at 684–85.

12. 302 U.S. 583 (1938).

ing house for not greater than three days [13] a bill may be returned to an officer of the Congress designated to act in such capacity. *The Pocket Veto Case* was distinguished on the ground that the dangers there implicated were unique to a prolonged adjournment. After all, the Court observed, only the Senate, not "the Congress," had adjourned, and only adjournment by "the Congress" can prevent return of a bill.[14] More importantly, the Secretary of the Senate was still available to receive the bill, and "[t]he Constitution does not define what shall constitute a return of a bill or deny the use of appropriate agencies in effecting the return." [15]

By way of dictum, the Court submitted that an adjournment of both houses ten or more days (Sundays excepted) following presentation of a bill to the President would constitute an article I, § 7, adjournment but that an adjournment of only the nonoriginating house would not constitute an adjournment within the scope of article I, § 7, unless final. It remains unclear whether an adjournment of the originating house or both houses for greater than three days but running to less than ten days after presentation to the President gives rise to a pocket veto opportunity. But the functional approach endorsed by the Court in *Wright* suggests a negative answer.

In *Wright* the Court stressed that the Constitution's veto provisions are to be interpreted in light of their "two fundamental purposes[: (1)] the President shall have suitable opportunity to consider the bills presented to him . . . . [and (2)] the Congress shall have suitable opportunity to consider his objections to bills and on such consideration to pass them over his veto provided there are the requisite votes." [16] The Court counseled against adopting any construction "which would frustrate either of these purposes." [17] In all likelihood, neither intrasession adjournments,[18] nor even the typical month-long intersession adjournments of Congress, present pocket veto opportunities.[19] Modern congressional adjournment practice simply does not pose the hazards of

---

13. The fact that the recess was for a period not in excess of three days was perhaps important to the Court, which noted that article I, § 5, cl. 4, provides that neither House of Congress shall adjourn for *more than three days* without the consent of the other House.

14. 302 U.S. at 587.

15. Id. at 589.

16. Id. at 596.

17. Id.

18. Kennedy v. Sampson, 511 F.2d 430, 440 (D.C.Cir.1974), held that return of a bill is not prevented by an intrasession adjournment of any length by one or both houses, so long as the originating house arranged for receipt of veto messages. The case involved a five day adjournment of the originating house which extended until the third day after the expiration of the ten day period.

19. In Barnes v. Kline, 759 F.2d 21 (D.C.Cir.1984), vacated with directions to dismiss for mootness, sub nom. Burke v. Barnes, 107 S.Ct. 734 (1987), the circuit court invalidated a pocket veto that the President had predicated on a two-month intersession adjournment of both houses. Since both the House and the Senate had expressly authorized agents to receive veto messages during adjournment, the court found it "difficult to understand how Congress could be said to have prevented return of [the bill] simply by adjourning. Rather, . . . Congress affirmatively *facilitated* return of the bill. . . ." 759 F.2d at 30 (original emphasis). Because the bill had lapsed by its own terms before the Supreme Court could resolve either the merits of the pocket-veto issue or the standing of the congressional plaintiffs, the Court vacated the circuit court's ruling and directed dismissal of the complaint as moot.

long delay and public uncertainty perceived in *The Pocket Veto Case*.[20] Congress can easily arrange for the receipt of veto messages during adjournment, and adjournment resolutions typically provide that the legislature can be reassembled at any time. Moreover, reconsideration of a bill returned during an intersession adjournment is not even necessarily delayed for the duration of the adjournment, since the rules of both houses permit the convening of congressional committees during adjournments. And committees, "in the legislative scheme of things, [are] for all practical purposes Congress itself." [21]

Whatever uncertainty attends presidential *inaction* in the face of congressional adjournment, the law is clear as to the impact of presidential *action* during such adjournment. Although the constitutional text is silent on this point, a bill signed by the President within the allotted ten days becomes law even if Congress is adjourned at the time of the signing, and this is so whether it be an interim recess or a final adjournment.[22]

Whether exercised through action or inaction, the President's veto power applies to "every Bill . . ., Every Order, Resolution, or Vote to which the Concurrence of the Senate and House of Representatives may be necessary." [23] This means that the President may wield his veto on the legislative product *only* in the form in which Congress chooses to send it to the White House: be the bill small or large, its concerns focused or diffuse, its form particular or omnibus, the President must accept or reject the entire thing, swallowing the bitter with the sweet.[24] The politics of representative democracy being what they

20. See Kennedy, "Congress, the President, and the Pocket Veto," 63 Va.L.Rev. 355, 378–82 (1977). The adjournment in The Pocket Veto Case preceded a long "lame duck" session—a biennial phenomenon prior to the passage of the twentieth amendment, which rolled the start of new congressional terms back from March 3 to January 3—and that case thus involved problems of congressional reconsideration unparalleled in modern times. See Barnes v. Kline, 759 F.2d at 36 n. 26.

21. Doe v. McMillan, 412 U.S. 306, 344 (1973) (Rehnquist, J., concurring and dissenting).

22. La Abra Silver Mining Co. v. United States, 175 U.S. 423 (1899) (a bill signed within the ten day period but during a two week Christmas adjournment became law); Edwards v. United States, 286 U.S. 482 (1932) (a bill signed within the ten day period but subsequent to a final adjournment of Congress became law). Although this issue is now well settled, it was long thought that the President must approve a bill while the Congress that enacted it was still in session. See, e.g., Gauss, The American Government 14 (1908). There thus arose the practice of the President's going to the Capital on the final day of each session in order to sign whatever bills Congress had passed on that final day that

met with his approval. See Zinn, The Veto Power of the President, 12 F.R.D. 207, 222 (1952).

23. Art. I, § 7, cls. 2, 3. Questions of adjournment are expressly excepted. Id.

24. Another avenue pursued by the executive for altering the thrust of bills submitted by Congress is the issuance of a presidential signing statement, wherein the Chief Executive interprets in a favorable way objectionable provisions in legislation that he feels compelled to sign into law. For example, in signing an immigration bill barring discrimination against legal aliens, President Ronald Reagan opined that an alien seeking relief under the law would have to prove that an employer acted with discriminatory intent. See "In Signing Bills, Reagan Tries to Write History," The New York Times, Dec. 9, 1986, p. 14, col. 3. Although the President may have a right to give some direction to executive officials charged with administering the statute, this does not encompass giving advice to the judiciary in how to interpret the law. The only meaningful form of presidential disapproval is the veto. The relevant legislative history is restricted to statements and reports of Members of Congress. See Kelly v. Robinson, 107 S.Ct. 353, 362 n. 13 (1986).

are, this legislative regime inevitably leads to the appropriation of a lot of money for "pork barrel" projects and the enactment of a lot of bills encrusted with non-germane riders. Occupants of the Oval Office have long sought to enhance their control over the budget process in particular by asking Congress for a power of line-item veto, which would enable the Executive to "trim the fat" from congressional appropriations.[25] The governors of 43 states hold such power,[26] but—putting aside differences between state and federal fiscal processes that might render a line-item veto unworkable at the federal level [27]—the constitutionality of a line-item veto is dubious.

The core issue is whether Congress may statutorily expand the meaning of the term "Bill"—which denotes a singular piece of legislation in the form in which it was approved by Congress—by defining as a separate "Bill" each and every item, paragraph, or section contained within a single bill that has passed both Houses as an entirety. The method would be to direct the enrolling clerk of the House where the bill originates to disassemble a bill and enroll each numbered section and unnumbered paragraph as a separate bill or joint resolution for presentation to the President in compliance with clauses 2 and 3 of § 7 of article I.[28] But it is far from certain whether the myriad bills thus presented to the President could be said to have been considered, voted on, and passed by the two Houses in accord with the Constitution's "single, finely wrought and exhaustively considered procedure." [29] The choice of whether to adopt and submit one appropriations bill or a hundred, and the decision as to the form the bill or bills should take, might well be deemed the "kind of decision[s] that can be implemented

---

25. Ronald Reagan was only the most recent Chief Executive to ask for a line-item veto power. See 20 Weekly Comp. Pres.Doc. 87, 90 (Jan. 30, 1984) (1984 State of the Union address). Presidents Grant, Hayes, Arthur, Franklin Roosevelt, Truman, and Eisenhower made similar requests. See Abscal & Kramer, "Presidential Impoundment Part I: Historical Genesis and Constitutional Framework," 62 Geo.L.J. 1549, 1565 (1974). Proposals have been introduced but none has ever passed. E.g., S. 43, 99th Cong. 1st Sess. (1985) (later withdrawn from consideration after filibuster).

26. See 20 Weekly Comp.Pres.Doc. 87, 90 (Jan. 30, 1984).

27. The item veto works at the state level because specific budget items are included in the bills presented to the governor. Federal appropriations bills, in contrast, usually are not itemized. A typical water projects bill, for example—the archetype of pork barrel—contains few earmarked funds: the bulk of the appropriation is in the form of a huge lump sum which is to be spent by the executive branch on projects authorized by law which are identified only in the conference report on the bill. There are thus no dis-

crete "items" to veto. See Fisher, "The Item Veto—A Misconception," The Washington Post, Feb. 23, 1987, page A11, col. 3. The latitude and flexibility that lump-sum appropriations build into the budget process allow federal departments and agencies to respond to unforeseen circumstances by transferring funds within budget accounts in order to preserve congressionally-authorized programs. See Note, "Is a Presidential Item Veto Constitutional?" 96 Yale L.J. 838, 849 & nn. 56, 57 (1987).

28. See S. 43, 99th Cong. 1st Sess. (1985).

29. I.N.S. v. Chadha, 462 U.S. 919, 951 (1983). See Gressman, "Is the Item Veto Constitutional?" 64 N.C.L.Rev. 819, 820–21 (1986). But see Field v. Clark, 143 U.S. 649, 669–73 (1892) (the "respect due to coequal and independent departments" requires a conclusive presumption that an enrolled bill passed both houses of Congress if the houses attest to that fact); United States v. Ballin, 144 U.S. 1, 4–5 (1892) (rejecting challenge to revenue act as invalid on account of lack of quorum in the House; the House is free to set its own rules for determining the existence of quorum).

only in accordance with the procedures set out in article I." [30]   And delegation to an enrolling clerk in either house of the power to make decisions which would otherwise be part and parcel of the political, deliberative, and legislative process is constitutionally suspect.[31]

To the extent that the parsing and reformulating of bills by an enrolling clerk might be deemed ministerial rather than legislative tasks, it is questionable whether the enactment of a law directing the clerk to perform such duties could bind either house of Congress in any particular instance. Such changes in the internal procedures of the House and Senate might be considered matters of legislative self-governance, in which the Constitution expressly makes each house a law unto itself.[32]   The power that an item veto law would give the President could therefore be gutted, unilaterally and without opportunity for presidential veto, by either the House or the Senate as an exercise of its rules power.[33]

Finally, empowering the President to veto appropriations bills line by line would profoundly alter the Constitution's balance of power. The President would be free not only to nullify new congressional spending initiatives and priorities, but to wipe out previously enacted programs that receive their funding through the annual appropriations process. Congress, which the Constitution makes the master of the public purse,[34] would be demoted to the role of giving fiscal advice that the executive would be free to disregard. The Framers granted the President no such special veto over appropriation bills, despite their awareness that the insistence of colonial assemblies that their spending bills could not be amended once thay had passed the lower house had greatly enhanced the growth of legislative power.[35]

The wisdom in leaving the power of the purse in legislative hands, as a means of checking the executive,[36] is buttressed by the recognition that pork barrel appropriations—the *bete noir* of item-veto advocates— are but unattractive examples of legislating for diverse interests, which is the very stuff of representative government.[37]   Apportioning the

30. I.N.S. v. Chadha, 462 U.S. at 954.

31. See id. at 948–59; Gressman, supra note 29, at 822.

32. Art. I, § 5, cl. 2 ("Each House may determine the Rules of its Proceedings"). This clause has been construed to give the houses wide discretion. See, e.g., United States v. Ballin, 144 U.S. 1, 5 (1892).

33. The Supreme Court's construction of other ancillary powers held by the houses of Congress have established that Congress cannot abridge those powers by statute. See, e.g., Sinclair v. United States, 279 U.S. 263, 295 (1929) (Senate free to conduct own investigation of Teapot Dome scandal, even after enacting law requiring President to investigate, because statute could not "exhaust" Senate's ancillary investigative power); In re Chapman, 166 U.S. 661, 671–72 (1897) (enactment of criminal statute to punish contempt of Congress did not withdraw from houses their

ancillary power to punish contempt). See Note, "Is a Presidential Item Veto Constitutional?" 96 Yale L.J. 838, 855–57 (1987).

34. Art. I, § 9, cl. 7.

35. See Note, "Is a Presidential Item Veto Constitutional?" 96 Yale L.J. 838, 841–44 (1987).

36. See, e.g., The Federalist No. 58 (J. Madison).

37. It must be remembered that one legislator's "pork barrel" is another's "essential governmental initiative." And it is not beyond the realm of possibility that what the people really want from the federal government *is* pork barrel. See D. Stockman, The Triumph of Politics (1986) (arguing that the "Reagan Revolution" failed to achieve fiscal discipline because Congress correctly understood that the nation had opted for a spending regime built around government subsidies and largesse).

public fisc in a large and diverse nation requires degrees of coordination and compromise that might be unavailable under a line-item veto regime.

Log-rolling has likewise played a venerable role in the life of the republic, despite the legitimacy of complaints about its excesses. One of the earliest nongermane riders to a congressional bill was a resolution to admit Missouri to statehood, which was attached by amendment to the bill granting statehood to Maine.[38] An inelegant and irrational way to decide the merits of two completely different petitions for statehood, to be sure, but certainly an aid to preservation of the union: that rider became the Missouri Compromise of 1820.[39]

§ 4–14. The "Privileges and Immunities" of Executive Leadership: Limiting Criminal and Civil Liability

Power may be made accountable to the people and to the Constitution both by voting out of office those who abuse their power and by punishing them for specific offenses. The first of these sanctions, enforced directly by the voters at election time, obviously provides only a limited check on executive abuses. Denying re-election may at turns be too lenient or too harsh: allowing wrongdoers to escape with no more penalty than a compulsory return to private life may provide an insufficient deterrent, yet specific acts of wrongdoing may be tolerated by the electorate in exchange for a performance in office that is, on the whole, acceptable. Moreover, there are the intrinsic limitations that an electoral check has no impact in a Chief Executive's second term and, even in the first, has only an indirect impact on appointed officials and confers no compensation on those they have injured. In any event, the electorate may choose not to punish officeholders who commit offenses against groups or persons disfavored by a majority of the electorate itself.

It is thus vitally significant that political sanctions for official wrongdoing are supplemented by legal means of containing executive power. In general, there is *no* executive immunity—common law or otherwise—from *criminal* prosecution. It has nonetheless been argued that the Constitution's provision of impeachment as a means of removing "civil Officers" bars any indictment or prosecution of impeachable officials until after their removal.[1] With respect to the Vice President, this argument has been quite properly rejected in practice, although it has not been authoritatively adjudicated: prior to his 1973 resignation,

---

38. Note, "Separation of Powers: Congressional Riders and the Veto Power," 6 U.Mich.J.L.Ref. 735, 738 & n. 22 (1973).

39. On February 17, 1820, Illinois Senator Jesse Thomas proposed the Missouri rider to the Maine admission bill—which had already passed the House—in order to maintain the balance in the union between free and slave states. Almanac of American History 208 (1983) (A. Schlesinger, ed.). The virtue of a legislative process that allows for eccentric legislative bedfellows has been recognized since antiquity. A

Roman law prohibiting legislation containing unrelated subjects led to an outbreak of civil war in 91 B.C. when omnibus reform legislation on land ownership, grain prices, and citizenship was declared void by the Senate because of the defect in form. See R. Luce, Legislative Procedure 548–49 (1922).

§ 4–14

1. See, e.g., Bickel, "The Constitutional Tangle," The New Republic, pp. 14–15 (Oct. 6, 1973).

Vice President Spiro Agnew was indicted by a federal grand jury on charges of bribery and income tax evasion. With respect to the President, some commentators have assumed that the Chief Executive's unique role mandates immunity from criminal process prior to removal.[2] However, in *United States v. Nixon*, in ruling on the question whether President Nixon could appeal an order denying a motion to quash a subpoena without first being cited for contempt, the Supreme Court did *not* hold the President immune to such criminal citation but rather noted only that "issuing a citation to a President simply in order to invoke review" would be "unseemly, and would present an unnecessary occasion for constitutional confrontation between two branches of the Government."[3] Arguably, the *Nixon* decision supports, by implication, the proposition that there might be instances in which a sitting President *could* be cited for contempt or otherwise criminally charged,[4] but not even that reading of *Nixon* would imply presidential amenability to criminal proceedings generally. The question must be regarded as an open one, but the burden should be on those who insist that a President is immune from criminal trial prior to impeachment and removal from office.

The law is clearer with respect to civil liability for executive transgressions. The Supreme Court has long recognized a federal common law immunity protecting executive officials, in the absence of congressionally-created exceptions, from civil liability to private plaintiffs arising out of acts performed "in the discharge of duties imposed upon [such officials] by law."[5] In more recent cases the Court has reaffirmed the importance of containing power through judicial as well as electoral means, but has shown caution in framing remedies without express congressional authorization.

The Court stressed the principle that federal executive officials are not above the law when it refused them absolute immunity from damages liability in *Butz v. Economou*.[6] A commodities merchant there sued the Secretary of Agriculture and several other Agriculture Department officials for issuing a complaint against him without following the proper procedures; he claimed his business and reputation were injured by the complaint.[7] The Court extended to federal execu-

---

2. Id.

3. 418 U.S. 683, 692 (1974).

4. The Court granted President Nixon's cross-petition for certiorari before judgment, see Nixon v. United States, 417 U.S. 960 (1974), to decide whether the grand jury acted within its authority in naming the President as an unindicted co-conspirator in the Watergate trial, but that cross-petition was ultimately dismissed as improvidently granted, see 418 U.S. at 687 n. 2.

5. Spalding v. Vilas, 161 U.S. 483, 498 (1896). See also Barr v. Matteo, 360 U.S. 564, 572 (1959) (plurality opinion) (Vilas rule extends beyond "executive officers of cabinet rank," protecting executive officers generally).

6. 438 U.S. 478 (1978).

7. Curiously, the Court's opinion made no reference to Paul v. Davis, 424 U.S. 693 (1976) (no protected interest implicated when false criminal accusation is circulated by police), discussed infra in § 10–11. Although Economou was actually "prosecuted" before an administrative board, his deprivation was no more serious than that of the plaintiff in Paul v. Davis, suggesting again that the latter case should be read as relying on available state remedies to defeat a federal claim, and not as defining the protection of a person's interest in his reputation.

tive officials the qualified, "good faith" immunity previously provided [8] to state executive officials.[9] For agency officials performing adjudicatory or prosecutorial functions, however, the *Butz* Court recognized an absolute immunity,[10] similar to the immunity earlier accorded state judicial [11] and prosecutorial [12] officials.[13]

The limits on executive immunity were relaxed in *Harlow v. Fitzgerald* [14] and *Nixon v. Fitzgerald*,[15] two cases arising out of the discharge in 1970 of Air Force management analyst A. Ernest Fitzgerald. Fitzgerald lost his job after his testimony before Congress about Air Force cost overruns embarrassed his superiors and the Nixon Administration. Strong evidence suggested White House involvement in the decision to sack Fitzgerald as part of an ostensible Air Force "reorganization." After the Civil Service Commission ruled the discharge improper and ordered Fitzgerald reinstated with backpay, he brought suit against former President Nixon and several of Nixon's former aides.

In *Harlow v. Fitzgerald*, the Court overwhelmingly rejected the claims of absolute immunity made by Nixon's aides.[16] Reaffirming the *Butz* principle that executive officials are generally entitled to only a qualified, "good faith" immunity,[17] the Court held that a presidential aide can claim *absolute* immunity only upon a showing that he or she committed the purported violation in the course of discharging an official function so sensitive that it requires complete shielding from liability.[18] The Court went on, however, to broaden significantly the

8. Scheuer v. Rhodes, 416 U.S. 232 (1974) (State Governor, President of State University, Commander of State National Guard and other officials enjoy qualified immunity in § 1983 suit for damages arising from their actions in suppressing disturbance at Kent State University).

9. Butz v. Economou, 438 U.S. at 496–508.

10. Id. at 515–17.

11. Stump v. Sparkman, 435 U.S. 349 (1978).

12. Imbler v. Pachtman, 424 U.S. 409 (1976). But see Malley v. Briggs, 475 U.S. 335 (1986) (police officers entitled only to qualified immunity from damages liability under 42 U.S.C. § 1983 even when acting pursuant to an arrest warrant which they have obtained from a magistrate).

13. Officials conducting adjudicatory and prosecutorial functions are granted more extensive protection from civil suits for three reasons. See Imbler v. Pachtman, 424 U.S. 409, 508–17 (1976). First, such officials are especially susceptible to harassment by litigation: the prosecution and resolution of a lawsuit or administrative proceeding are likely to spur nuisance suits by vindictive losers. Second, if they are to perform effectively, administrative law judges and government attorneys—like judges and prosecutors—

must be able to exercise independent judgment free from pressure by those with stakes in the outcomes of particular contests. Finally, the review and appeals available both in the courts and in administrative proceedings guard against abuses of authority. Recognizing that these rationales warrant broad protection only for exercises of adjudicatory or prosecutorial discretion, the Butz Court limited absolute immunity of agency officials to specific functions: administrative law judges, for example, are not immune for actions taken outside their judicial roles. See id. at 515–17. And the lower federal courts generally have denied prosecutors absolute immunity for acts taken in their administrative or investigatory capacities. See Harlow v. Fitzgerald, 457 U.S. 800, 811 n. 16 (1982).

14. 457 U.S. 800 (1982).

15. 457 U.S. 731 (1982).

16. Justice Powell delivered the opinion of the Court, from which Chief Justice Burger alone dissented.

17. 457 U.S. at 807.

18. Id. at 812–13. The Court suggested in dictum that absolute immunity "might well be justified to protect the unhesitating performance" of aides "entrusted with discretionary authority in such sensitive areas as national security or foreign policy." Id. at 812. But see Mitchell v. Forsyth,

qualified immunity to which all executive officials are entitled as a minimum. The standard adopted in *Butz* had two parts: a "subjective" requirement that the official did not act maliciously or with knowledge that his or her conduct was illegal, and an "objective" requirement that the official had reasonable grounds for believing that the action violated no statutory or constitutional prohibition.[19] Noting that an immunity that depends in part on a defendant's state of mind typically cannot be successfully invoked on a motion for summary judgment,[20] the *Harlow* Court abandoned the subjective half of the standard as providing insufficient protection from the burden of defending at trial against insubstantial claims.[21] The Court viewed that burden as such a threat to efficient and fearless public service that it held judicial orders denying claims of qualified immunity to be immediately appealable, despite "any factual overlap" between this collateral issue and the merits of a plaintiff's claim;[22] executive immunity is not a mere defense to liability, but an *"immunity from suit"* itself.[23]

The Court's concern for quick disposal of frivolous and harassing claims was appropriate,[24] but purging qualified immunity doctrine of its subjective components created certain risks. As Justice Brennan pointed out, a subjective test helps to ensure that unusually well-informed officials do not escape liability for what they know are culpable offenses;[25] an objective test gratuitously excuses those who need not have known better but did. In addition, by making immunity turn

---

472 U.S. 511, 520 (1985) (Attorney General lacks absolute immunity for ordering warrantless "national security" wiretaps).

19. See also Wood v. Strickland, 420 U.S. 308, 321–22 (1975) (applying "good faith" immunity in § 1983 suit against state school officials).

20. But see Anderson v. Liberty Lobby, Inc., 106 S.Ct. 2505 (1986), discussed in note 24, infra.

21. 457 U.S. at 817–18. Justice Brennan's reading of the Court's opinion as imposing liability when an official *"knew or should have known"* that his or her conduct was illegal, id. at 821 (Brennan, J., concurring), seems strained. The Court unambiguously announced its intent to rely on "the objective reasonableness of an official's conduct," and explicitly immunized officials whose acts violated no "clearly established" prohibitions. Id. at 818 (opinion of the Court). See also Mitchell v. Forsyth, 472 U.S. 511, 535 (1985) ("Harlow teaches that officials performing discretionary functions are not subject to suit when such questions are resolved against them only after they have acted"). The same standard governs the immunity from damages liability of state officials sued under § 1983. Davis v. Scherer, 468 U.S. 183, 194 n. 12 (1984). It is only when the law is clearly established and the official pleads "extraordinary circumstances" that the Court will allow immunity to turn

on whether the official "can prove that he neither knew nor should have known of the relevant legal standard." Harlow v. Fitzgerald, 457 U.S. at 818.

22. Mitchell v. Forsyth, 472 U.S. 511, 529 n. 10 (1985).

23. Id. at 526 (emphasis in original).

24. Anthony Lewis has argued along similar lines that the "actual malice" standard of New York Times Co. v. Sullivan, 376 U.S. 254 (1964), should be modified to allow insubstantial libel claims to be defeated before imposition of the burdens of discovery and trial. See Lewis, "New York Times v. Sullivan Reconsidered: Time to Return to 'The Central Meaning of the First Amendment,'" 83 Colum.L.Rev. 603 (1983). In Anderson v. Liberty Lobby, Inc., 106 S.Ct. 2505 (1986), the Court ruled that "public-figure" libel plaintiffs, in order to fend off summary judgment motions, must produce evidence such that a reasonable jury might find that actual malice had been shown with convincing clarity. Like the Butz standard, the actual malice rule often requires inquiry into the defendant's state of mind and may therefore be difficult to invoke successfully on a motion for summary judgment. See §§ 12–12, 12–13, infra.

25. Harlow v. Fitzgerald, 457 U.S. at 821 (Brennan, J., concurring).

entirely on what a defendant could "reasonably" believe, the Court not only required lower courts to develop a much more sophisticated notion of what knowledge officials should be expected to possess, but also weakened substantially the *Butz* standard by declaring that immunity should attach so long as an official's conduct does not violate "clearly established statutory or constitutional rights of which a reasonable person would have known." [26]   Yet it is strongly arguable that government officials charged with executing the laws should be held to a significantly higher standard of legal acumen than the average citizen. A wiser course might have been to allow the defense of qualified immunity only when officials could prove that, *given their positions and status*, they could not reasonably have been expected to know that their conduct was illegal.

In *Nixon v. Fitzgerald*,[27] a bitterly divided Court [28] painted with a much broader brush.   In upholding the former President's claim of *absolute* protection from damages liability, the Court refused to limit that immunity to particular functions of the Presidency.[29]   The majority acknowledged that presidential immunity is not expressly prescribed by the Constitution, in contrast to congressional immunity, which has specific textual roots in the speech and debate clause.[30]   Nevertheless, the Court termed absolute presidential immunity "a functionally mandated incident of the President's unique office, rooted in the constitutional tradition of separation of powers and supported by our history." [31]   Invoking the same arguments used in *Butz* to justify absolute immunity for executive officials acting in adjudicatory or prosecutorial capacities, the Court stressed the visibility and influence of the Oval Office, which make its occupant an easy and tempting target for lawsuits; the importance of insulating presidential judgment and energy from the distractions and pressures that potential damages liability would create; and the availability of alternative checks on presidential action, such as media scrutiny, congressional oversight, and the threat

26. Id. at 818 (opinion of the Court). See also Mitchell v. Forsyth, 472 U.S. at 535.

27. 457 U.S. 731 (1982).

28. Justice White wrote a blistering dissent in which Justices Brennan, Blackmun and Marshall joined. Id. at 764. Justice Blackmun, joined by Justices Brennan and Marshall, also filed a separate dissenting opinion arguing that the Court should have dismissed the case. Id. at 797. After certiorari had been granted, it was disclosed that Nixon and Fitzgerald had agreed to liquidate damages: in exchange for $128,000, Fitzgerald agreed to accept additional damages of only $28,000 in the event that the Court denied Nixon's claim of absolute immunity. Id. at 743–44 (opinion of the Court). Because the parties still had what it termed "a considerable financial stake" in the outcome of the litigation, the majority found the controversy sufficiently live to warrant exercise of jurisdiction. Id. at 744.

29. With respect to presidential aides and other executive officials, even those endowed with significant discretionary authority, absolute immunity, if it exists at all, is limited to "special functions," such as national security or foreign policy. Harlow v. Fitzgerald, 457 U.S. at 812 (dictum). But see Mitchell v. Forsyth, 472 U.S. 511, 520 (1985) (Attorney General lacks absolute immunity for ordering warrantless "national security" wiretaps).

30. 457 U.S. at 750 n. 31. In part because of this conspicuous constitutional silence, the Court of Appeals for the District of Columbia Circuit had earlier ruled that the President enjoys no special immunity from civil liability. Halperin v. Kissinger, 606 F.2d 1192, 1211 (1979), aff'd in relevant part by an equally divided Court, 452 U.S. 713 (1981).

31. 457 U.S. at 749.

of impeachment.[32]   Given the diverse and open-ended nature of presidential duties, the majority added, the President's absolute immunity cannot workably be limited to specific functions of his office, but must extend to all "acts within the 'outer perimeter' of his official responsibility." [33]

Despite the dissenting charge that the decision "places the President above the law . . . [and] is a reversion to the notion that the King can do no wrong," [34] the majority in *Nixon v. Fitzgerald* did *not* rule that the Constitution flatly forbids assessment of damages against the President.   The Court held only that such liability could not be imposed without explicit congressional direction.[35] Fitzgerald had sued for damages under the Constitution [36] and under two causes of action "implied" by federal statutes of general applicability; the Court was thus not confronted by a damages claim expressly authorized against the Presidency by Congress.[37] Because the Court was careful to limit its holding to the rule of immunity to be applied in such circumstances of legislative silence, *Nixon v. Fitzgerald* does not directly impose any substantive limits on federal legislative power.

Four Justices claimed that the court unnecessarily broadened its holding by basing its analysis on constitutional requirements of separation of powers: if absolute immunity is constitutionally required, they argued, it cannot be modified by legislation.[38] But this view rests on the erroneous assumption that *all* separation-of-powers rules necessarily restrict national legislative—as well as judicial, or executive, or state—authority.   In fact, however, in addition to setting the contours of congressional power, the Constitution provides background rules— rules that apply in the absence of affirmative federal legislative action.[39] The "dormant" commerce clause [40] and the eleventh amendment [41] are two such background rules which Congress may override, and there is no *a priori* reason why presidential immunity from suits for damages cannot be another.

Thus understood, the Court's holding in *Nixon v. Fitzgerald* warrants little alarm: the Court *held* only that presidential liability for civil damages could not properly be *inferred* by courts from statutory or constitutional prohibitions of general applicability, at least when Congress has not expressly legislated such liability.   With respect to *statutory* causes of action, the decision sets forth a manifestly defensible

---

32. Id. at 749–58.

33. Id. at 756.

34. Id. at 766 (White, J., dissenting).

35. Id. at 748–49 (opinion of the Court). Likewise, the Court in Harlow v. Fitzgerald suggested that Congress might be able to override the qualified immunity the Court had recognized. See 457 U.S. at 818 n. 31 ("This case involves no claim that Congress has expressed its intent to impose 'no fault' tort liability on high federal officials for violations of particular statutes or the Constitution").

36. See Bivens v. Six Unknown Named Agents of Federal Bureau of Narcotics, 403 U.S. 388 (1971).

37. 457 U.S. at 748.

38. 457 U.S. at 770 & n. 4 (White, J., joined by Brennan, Marshall and Blackmun, JJ., dissenting); id. at 798 (Blackmun, J., dissenting). Accord, id. at 763 n. 7 (Burger, C.J., concurring).

39. See L. Tribe, Constitutional Choices 29–44 (1985).

40. See id. at 521–22, 525–26; Chapter 6, infra.

41. See §§ 3–25, 3–26, 3–27, supra.

rule of construction: given the serious effects that damages liability could have on presidential leadership, the constitutional scheme of separation of powers can reasonably be understood to preclude the courts from inferring imposition of presidential liability from ambiguous legislative enactments. The case for requiring express congressional authorization for *constitutional* causes of action may be less obvious, but it is consistent with the prudential nature of constitutional remedies. With rare exceptions,[42] the Court has not read the Constitution to require particular remedies for violations of its express prohibitions; the choice of remedies is peculiarly a matter of policy, which requires the exercise of legislative judgment or equitable discretion.[43] Accordingly, the Court has described the imposition of damages liability for constitutional torts as an act of judicial prudence, and has repeatedly suggested that courts should decline to fashion such a remedy when confronted with "special factors counseling hesitation in the absence of affirmative action by Congress."[44] The majority in *Nixon v. Fitzgerald* implicitly found such "special factors" in the extraordinary powers and responsibilities conferred on the President by the Constitution. In any event, the presidential immunity recognized by the Court, even if it could *not* be modified by Congress, would not be unlimited: "absolute" immunity extends only to acts that are within the "outer perimeter" of presidential responsibility. And, as the Court has demonstrated in such cases as *Youngstown Sheet & Tube Co. v. Sawyer*,[45] even that predictably amorphous perimeter is susceptible to judicial delineation.

42. See Weeks v. United States, 232 U.S. 383 (1914) (excluding from federal criminal trials evidence obtained in violation of the fourth amendment); cf. Mapp v. Ohio, 367 U.S. 643 (1961) (extending exclusionary rule to state trials absent adequate alternative remedy), discussed in Monaghan, "Constitutional Common Law," 89 Harv.L.Rev. 1 (1975).

43. The Court's opinion in City of Revere v. Massachusetts General Hospital, 463 U.S. 239 (1983), illustrates the broad principle that the Constitution is in general indifferent to the precise manner in which its substantive guarantees are fulfilled. The Court there held that the Constitution does not require government to compensate private hospitals for care they provide to persons who are injured while being apprehended by the police. The Court reasoned that, although the Constitution's eighth amendment requires the state to provide necessary medical care to those in its custody, how the treatment is obtained or assured is not a federal constitutional question. Cf. Daniels v. Williams, 106 S.Ct. 677, 678–80 (1986) (Stevens, J., concurring).

44. Bush v. Lucas, 462 U.S. 367, 387–90 (1983) (given comprehensive statutory protection for Civil Service employees from arbitrary action by supervisors, court should not tamper with the scheme by creating nonstatutory damages remedy for first amendment violations); Chappell v. Wallace, 462 U.S. 296, 303–05 (1983) (historic separation between military and civilian justice systems, in conjunction with special needs of military, counsels hesitation in making nonstatutory action available to military personnel absent congressional authorization); Carlson v. Green, 446 U.S. 14, 18–19 (1980) (no "special factors" militate against allowing nonstatutory damages action under eighth amendment); Davis v. Passman, 442 U.S. 228, 245 (1979) (nonstatutory constitutional tort suit allowed for discriminatory discharge of congressional assistant); Bivens v. Six Unknown Named Agents of Federal Bureau of Narcotics, 403 U.S. 388, 396 (1971) (damage award for violation of fourth amendment rights authorized in part because no "special factors" present).

45. 343 U.S. 579 (1952). See § 4–8, supra.

§ 4–15. The "Privileges and Immunities" of Executive Leadership: Secrets of State and Presidential Privacy

Executive privilege is mentioned neither in the Constitution nor in the constitutional debates.[1] That fact notwithstanding, Presidents have often invoked such a privilege when, for better reasons or worse, they wished to don the shroud of secrecy.[2] In *United States v. Nixon*,[3] the Supreme Court lent its imprimatur to this executive right to withhold certain information—and accorded it constitutional dimension—when, in holding the privilege inapposite to the facts of that case, it concluded that the privilege devolved from the constitutionally prescribed separation of powers.[4] Although it is customary to employ the phrase "executive privilege," it is perhaps more accurate to speak of executive *privileges*, for presidential refusals to furnish information may be actuated by any of at least three distinct kinds of considerations, and may be asserted, with differing degrees of success, in the context of either judicial or legislative investigations.

Presidents of the United States beginning with George Washington have invoked executive privilege on the ground that disclosure of the desired information would subvert crucial military or diplomatic objectives.[5] The Supreme Court's decision in *Totten v. United States*,[6] holding that suit could not be brought upon a contract between the government and a spy, is sometimes cited as the first judicial recognition of the state secrets doctrine. But it seems most plausible to read *Totten* as holding only that, since nondisclosure of the spy's status was an implicit term of the espionage contract, disclosure would be violative *of that contract*.[7] The Supreme Court more clearly relied upon an executive right to withhold information in *Chicago & Southern Air Lines v. Waterman Steamship Corp.* when, in declaring unreviewable a presidential decree approving a C.A.B. order which had denied an

---

§ 4–15

1. See Berger, "The Incarnation of Executive Privilege," 22 U.C.L.A.L.Rev. 4 (1974).

2. See Younger, "Congressional Investigations and Executive Secrecy: A Study in the Separation of Powers," 20 U.Pitt.L.Rev. 755, 756–69 (1959); 40 Op.Atty.Gen. 45 (1941).

3. 418 U.S. 683 (1974).

4. Id. at 705–06, 708. Although the privilege, being for the benefit of the nation rather than the incumbent, survives the individual President's tenure, entrusting President Nixon's papers to his successors with safeguards carefully designed to prevent unwarranted disclosure neither violated the privilege nor constituted an invasion of Presidential autonomy. Nixon v. Administrator of General Services, 433 U.S. 425 (1977). Whether the Constitution creates any executive privilege at all spawned no small controversy in the waning days of the Nixon Administration. The Court in United States v. Nixon correctly perceived that it did. But see R.

Berger, Executive Privilege: A Constitutional Myth (1974). For a critique of Berger's historical exegesis, see, e.g., Sofaer, Book Review, 88 Harv.L.Rev. 281 (1974); Winter, "The Seedlings for the Forest," 83 Yale L.J. 1730 (1974). Whatever may be the correct resolution of the historical debate, it is unfortunate that the Court paid it no heed. See Mishkin, "Great Cases and Soft Law: A Comment on United States v. Nixon," 22 U.C.L.A.L.Rev. 76 (1974).

5. See L. Henkin, Foreign Affairs and the Constitution 112 (1972).

6. 92 U.S. (2 Otto) 105 (1876).

7. The decision nonetheless remains somewhat mysterious in that the suit was brought by the administrator of the estate of the deceased spy several years after the termination of hostilities and the extinction of the Confederacy, thus making it difficult to see what government interest could have been subverted by the revelation of the contract's existence. See Bishop, "The Executive's Right of Privacy: An Unresolved Constitutional Question," 66 Yale L.J. 477, 480 n. 14 (1957).

overseas route, the Court proclaimed that "[t]he President has available intelligence services whose reports are not and ought not to be published to the world."[8]   Against this rather spare background, the Court has seen fit to pronounce that the "privilege against revealing military secrets . . . is well established in the law of evidence."[9]   More generally, a President can successfully claim that a measure of secrecy, and thus a qualified executive privilege from required disclosure, is a necessary condition for the successful conduct of foreign affairs.[10]

The law of evidence has also long recognized an informer's privilege—that is, "the Government's privilege to withhold from disclosure the identity of persons who furnish information of violations of law to officers charged with enforcement of that law."[11]   While the range of circumstances in which the informer's privilege can be successfully asserted has at times been judicially restricted,[12] this privilege has spawned a more general claim of executive confidentiality resting upon a denial of "unlimited license to rummage in the files of [for example] the Department of Justice."[13]

Finally, a generic privilege for internal deliberations has been said to attach to "intragovernmental documents reflecting advisory opinions, recommendations and deliberations comprising part of a process by which governmental decisions and policies are formulated."[14]   Two policies underlie this privilege: encouraging candid intragovernmental communications and honoring the justified expectations of privacy of governmental advisors and decisionmakers.   That an enforceable promise of secrecy may well be the cost of candor[15] has been recognized by the Supreme Court: "Human experience teaches that those who expect public dissemination of their remarks may well temper candor with a concern for appearances and for their own interests to the detriment of the decisionmaking process."[16]

8. 333 U.S. 103, 111 (1948).

9. United States v. Reynolds, 345 U.S. 1, 6–7 (1953). See also United States v. Curtiss-Wright Export Corp., 299 U.S. 304, 320 (1936) ("Secrecy in respect of information gathered . . . may be highly necessary, and the premature disclosure of it productive of harmful results"); New York Times Co. v. United States, 403 U.S. 713, 728–30 (1971) (Stewart, J. concurring) (Pentagon Papers Case).

10. See United States v. Reynolds, 345 U.S. 1 (1953).

11. Roviaro v. United States, 353 U.S. 53, 59 (1957). Accord, McCray v. Illinois, 386 U.S. 300 (1967). The informer's privilege has always been premised upon the notion that secrecy was an essential condition for inducing informers to talk. For indications that this proposition may not be accurate, see McKay, "The Right of Confrontation," 1959 Wash.U.L.Q. 122, 146–60.

12. See, e.g., Smith v. Illinois, 390 U.S. 129 (1968) (informer's true identity cannot be withheld from accused once prosecution

has used informer as government witness in criminal trial).

13. Alderman v. United States, 394 U.S. 165, 185 (1969) (dictum).

14. Carl Zeiss Stiftung v. V.E.B. Carl Zeiss, Jena, 40 F.R.D. 318, 324–26 (D.D.C.1966), aff'd on opinion below 384 F.2d 979 (D.C.Cir.), cert. denied 389 U.S. 952 (1967).

15. Another cost of such candor is the qualified immunity from civil damages liability that executive aides and officials enjoy. See § 4–14, supra, discussing Harlow v. Fitzgerald, 457 U.S. 800 (1982).

16. United States v. Nixon, 418 U.S. 683, 705 (1974). As a special case of this privilege, the Court held that the President's conversations and correspondence were presumptively privileged. See id. at 706, 708. In general, courts will not always indulge the assumption that disclosure to Congress is tantamount to disclosure to the public. See, e.g., Exxon Corp. v. FTC, 589 F.2d 582, 589 (D.C.Cir. 1978); Ashland Oil Corp. v. FTC, 409 F.Supp. 297, 308 (D.D.C. 1976), aff'd 548 F.2d 977, 979

Of course, the mere fact that the Executive claims that requested information falls within the compass of one of the privileges discussed above does not dispose of the question whether the information may be demanded for purposes of a judicial or other proceeding. Two questions must be answered. First, does the requested information actually fall within one of the traditional privileges? Second, should that privilege be honored in this procedural setting? Clearly, the Executive's refusal to tender the information combined with an assertion of privilege indicates that the Executive would answer these two questions affirmatively. But the Executive's is not the last word. Because "[i]t is emphatically the province and the duty of the judicial department to say what the law is," [17] executive officials are not generally allowed to judge the appropriateness of their own claims of privilege.[18] The right of the Judiciary to evaluate the propriety of an assertion of privilege embraces both the determination whether the facts of the case implicate the concerns discussed above and whether these concerns should predominate over any competing considerations that the context makes applicable.

Although respect for the Presidency and concern for the political implications of a confrontation with a co-equal branch of government doubtless induce the courts to tread more circumspectly when the President, rather than a subordinate executive official, asserts a privilege, the Judiciary is nonetheless responsible for determining whether a privilege obtains.[19] As the Supreme Court put the matter in *United States v. Nixon*, "Notwithstanding the deference each branch must accord the others, the 'judicial Power of the United States' vested in the federal courts by Art. III, § 1, of the Constitution can no more be shared with the Executive Branch than the Chief Executive, for example, can share with the Judiciary the veto power, or the Congress share with the Judiciary the power to override a presidential veto. Any other

(D.C.Cir. 1976). Indeed, the discretion conferred by the journal clause of the Constitution—requiring each house of Congress to publish "a Journal of its Proceedings . . . excepting such Parts as may in their Judgment require Secrecy," article I, § 5, cl. 3—appears to have been provided by the Framers specifically to permit sharing of the most sensitive material with Congress.

17. Marbury v. Madison, 5 U.S. (1 Cranch) 137, 177 (1803). In United States v. Nixon, 418 U.S. 683 (1974), the Court relied expressly upon this pronouncement by Chief Justice Marshall. See id. at 703. Marshall's assertion, however, could be harmonized with a regime wherein the executive branch itself decided whether information was privileged. For while the Judiciary must decide "what the law is," the "law" might *be* executive discretion. See § 3–16, supra. The Supreme Court's opinion simply rejects without extended discussion any notion that, as a general rule, executive discretion *is* the applicable rule of law in matters of evidentiary privilege. See Black, "Mr. Nixon, the Tapes

and Common Sense," N.Y. Times, Aug. 3, 1973, at 31 col. 1; Gunther, "Judicial Hegemony and Legislative Autonomy: The Nixon Case and the Impeachment Process," 22 U.C.L.A.L.Rev. 30 (1974). There may nonetheless be particular areas in which the Judiciary would accord the Executive a less reviewable power to determine whether a privilege exists. See 418 U.S. at 706, 710–11, suggesting that "military or diplomatic secrets" might be so treated. But see id. at 715 n. 21.

18. See, e.g., Committee for Nuclear Responsibility, Inc. v. Seaborg, 463 F.2d 788 (D.C.Cir. 1971). In response to an assertion of absolute privilege by the Atomic Energy Commission, the court submitted that "[a]ny claim to executive absolutism cannot override the duty of the court to assure that an official has not exceeded his charter or flouted the legislative will."

19. Or at least determining *who* is to determine whether a privilege obtains. See note 17, supra.

conclusion would be contrary to the basic concept of separation of powers and the checks and balances that flow from the scheme of a tripartite government." [20]

The leading case prior to *United States v. Nixon* was *United States v. Burr*.[21] There, Chief Justice Marshall, on circuit duty, had issued a *subpoena duces tecum* demanding of President Jefferson a letter thought by defense counsel to be relevant to the treason trial of Aaron Burr, declaring: "The propriety of introducing any paper into a case, as testimony, must depend on the character of the paper, not on the character of the person who holds it." President Jefferson then supplied the letter, although insisting that he was doing so voluntarily.[22] The position taken by Chief Justice Marshall in *United States v. Burr* was not undermined by the subsequent decision of the Supreme Court in *Mississippi v. Johnson* where, in holding that it could not enjoin the President from enforcing a law, the Court announced that neither the Congress nor the President "can be restrained in its action by the judicial department." [23] Commentators who have seen in that broad language an indication that the President was beyond the pale of judicial direction have overlooked the fact that the *Johnson* Court expressly did not reach the question whether the judiciary could order a President to perform a non-discretionary or ministerial task, since it found the act there sought to be enjoined "purely executive and political." [24]

Whether a task is ministerial may well turn upon the character of the subpoena which demands the information. For example, in *Senate Select Committee v. Nixon (I)*,[25] a district court declared that the supplying of information (in the words of the subpoena) "relating directly or indirectly to [an] attached list of individuals and to their activities, participation, responsibilities or involvement in any alleged criminal acts related to the Presidential elections of 1972" [26] was too discretionary for purposes of giving the court mandamus jurisdiction.[27] On the other hand, the Supreme Court in *United States v. Nixon* upheld the issuance by a federal district court of a *subpoena duces tecum* ordering the President, in advance of a then pending criminal trial of seven named individuals charged with conspiracy to defraud the United States and to obstruct justice, to produce "certain tapes, memoranda, papers, transcripts, or other writings relating to certain precisely identified meetings between the President and others." [28] After a process of review which it described as "particularly meticulous" in "deference to a coordinate branch of government," [29] the Court unanimously conclud-

20. 418 U.S. 683, 704 (1974).

21. 25 Fed.Cas. 30, 34 (No. 14,692) (C.C.D.Va.1807) (Marshall, C.J.).

22. For a discussion of this case and its implications, see Freund, "The Supreme Court, 1973 Term—Foreword: On Presidential Privilege," 88 Harv.L.Rev. 13, 23–31 (1974).

23. 71 U.S. (4 Wall.) 475, 500 (1867).

24. Id. at 499.

25. 366 F.Supp. 51 (D.D.C.1973).

26. Id. at 54.

27. See id. at 57. But see In re Subpoena to Nixon, 360 F.Supp. 1 (D.D.C.1973), aff'd sub nom. Nixon v. Sirica, 487 F.2d 700 (D.C.Cir. 1973) (granting Special Prosecutor Cox's demand for designated materials sought by the grand jury investigating Watergate matters).

28. 418 U.S. 683, 688 (1974).

29. Id. at 702.

ed that the challenged subpoena met all pertinent requirements, both statutory and constitutional, of relevancy, admissibility, and specificity, and was therefore properly issued, subject to any substantively valid claims of privilege.

Although the "issue whether a President can be cited for contempt" (much less fined or jailed while in office) has not been authoritatively resolved and "could itself engender protracted litigation," [30] judicial power to command compliance does not depend on the outcome of such litigation: "[Whatever] difference may exist with respect to the power to compel the same obedience to the process, as if it had been directed to a private citizen, there exists no difference with respect to the right to obtain it." [31] In any event, courts have assumed that they have the power to effectuate mandatory orders to executive officials to compel production of evidence, and history has borne that assumption out: all three presidents who are known to have been subpoenaed (Jefferson, Monroe, and Nixon) have substantially complied with the judicial orders directed to them. [32]

In deciding whether information is privileged, a court must balance the moving party's need for the information in the litigation against the reasons which are asserted in defending confidentiality. But acknowledging that a claim of privilege must be tested by balancing the virtues of disclosure against its vices sheds meager light upon the precise role of the courts, for there are several ways to implement such a balancing process. The courts could remit the process to the President, thus rendering an assertion of privilege tantamount to a finding that the balance of policy considerations favors it. Or the President might be vested with exclusive authority to balance the policies embodied in a claim of privilege against those which favor disclosure, but only when the courts have satisfied themselves that the policy considerations legitimating executive privilege are, at least to some degree, actually implicated. For example, courts might accord the President final authority to balance the harms of disclosing a state secret against the benefits that would attend such disclosure *once they were satisfied that a state secret was, in fact, involved.* To pass on this threshold question, the courts might require the disclosure of the requested information to the judge, *in camera,* or they might satisfy themselves on the basis of extrinsic evidence. [33] On the other hand, the courts

---

30. Id. at 692. See § 4–14, supra.

31. United States v. Burr, 25 Fed.Cas. 30 (No. 14,692) (C.C.D.Va.1807). Cf. Glidden Co. v. Zdanok, 370 U.S. 530 (1962) (that the Court of Claims cannot enforce its judgments against the United States does not make its decisions any less judicial in the sense of article III).

32. Note the aftermath of the Steel Seizure Case, discussed in § 4–8, supra, where President Truman complied with the Supreme Court's decision holding unconstitutional his seizure of the steel mills (the judicial order had there been directed to the Secretary of Commerce) and of United States v. Nixon, where President Nix-

on's compliance with the Supreme Court decision ordering his submission of taped White House conversations led to public disclosures of presidential misconduct and, thereafter, to the President's forced resignation. The Supreme Court's decision was rendered on July 24, 1974; eight hours later, President Nixon's office stated he would comply. On August 5, Nixon released transcripts of certain conversations held on June 23, 1972, six days after the Watergate burglary. On August 9, President Nixon resigned.

33. Compare Environmental Protection Agency v. Mink, 410 U.S. 73, 84 (1973) (district court not required, by statute as

might declare *themselves* the arbiters of the balance and proclaim either that the privilege never attaches or that they will decide, on a case by case basis, how to accommodate the conflicting policies. Finally, the courts might permit Congress to define the boundaries of executive privilege.[34]

Deciding which of these balancing processes should be employed itself requires that a balance of sorts be struck among the relevant competing considerations. For example, in deciding whether extrinsic proof is sufficient to establish that a state secret is involved in a given case, a court should seek to compare the likely harm of disclosing the secret to a judge *in camera*, with the systemic benefits that would flow from the increased confidence, created by *in camera* inspection, that the privilege was not being abused, as well as from the increased likelihood that no abuse was in fact occurring.

In "balancing" the values and interests implicated by *United States v. Nixon*, the Court acknowledged the importance of maintaining the confidentiality of high-level executive discussions.[35] The Court emphasized "the necessity for protection of the public interest in candid, objective, and even blunt or harsh opinions in presidential decision making." [36] It was largely this necessity that underlay the Court's conclusion that Oval Office presidential deliberations were presumptively privileged. But the Court evidenced appropriate skepticism that failure to honor executive privilege in the context of the *Nixon* case would much impair the candor of executive communications: "[W]e cannot conclude that advisers will be moved to temper the candor of their remarks by the infrequent occasions of disclosure because of the possibility that such conversations will be called for in the context of a criminal prosecution." [37]

construed, to make *in camera* inspection of documents labeled "secret" or "top-secret"), with United States v. Nixon, 418 U.S. 683, 713–14 (1974) (documents defended only by broad claim of confidentiality must be turned over to district court for *in camera* inspection to assess relevance).

34. See generally Van Alstyne. "A Political and Constitutional Review of United States v. Nixon," 22 U.C.L.A.L.Rev. 116, 118–19 (1974); Committee on Civil Rights of the Association of the Bar of the City of New York, "Executive Privilege: Analysis and Recommendations for Congressional Legislation," 29 Record of N.Y.C.B.A. 177 (1974).

35. The need for "confidentiality" for high level communications and exchanges, the Court concluded, "is too plain to require further discussion." United States v. Nixon, 418 U.S. 683, 705 (1974). See also id. at 715.

36. Id. at 708.

37. Id. at 712. The Court evidently believed that, the lesson of Watergate notwithstanding (or perhaps because of that lesson), very few executive conversations in the future could have any conceivable relevance to a criminal trial. It is noteworthy that, even if the privilege were found to be "absolute," full candor could not be ensured; the asserted privilege is the President's and could be invoked only by him, not by those with whom he had communicated. See, e.g., United States v. Reynolds, 345 U.S. 1, 7–8 (1953). Insofar as the presumptive privilege recognized by the Court in United States v. Nixon was aimed at encouraging the President to speak candidly to associates without fear of coerced disclosure, it is noteworthy that the President's statements will ordinarily constitute admissible evidence at another person's trial only if there is an independent showing that the President conspired with the other person to commit a crime (because of the hearsay rule and the co-conspirators' exception). See 418 U.S. at 701. Thus the Court's exception to the presidential privilege should have little if any inhibiting effect upon a President not engaged in criminal conspiracy.

Against this contextually diluted executive interest in the confidentiality of high level discussions, the Court weighed the need of the criminal justice system for the requested information. It insisted that the integrity of that system would be compromised if judgments could be founded on patently incomplete factual foundations.[38] Consequently, it concluded that the President's legitimate interest in confidentiality "cannot prevail over the fundamental demands of due process of law in the fair administration of criminal justice. . . . [I]t must yield to the demonstrated, specific need for evidence in a pending criminal trial." [39] The Court thus ordered that the materials be turned over to the trial judge for inspection *in camera* to determine whether they were in fact relevant and admissible apart from the alleged privilege.[40]

Ostensibly, *United States v. Nixon* suggests that, while presidential conversations are presumptively privileged, the presumption will always be overcome by a showing that the information is relevant to a pending criminal trial in federal court. So construed, the decision portrays the privilege for confidential communications as extremely shallow; since evidence not otherwise relevant and admissible would be excluded even without the privilege, the privilege appears to add nothing of substance. But in fact the opinion may not so completely enervate the privilege. First, it is possible that, in indicating that the trial judge should demand a showing that the materials are "essential to the justice of the [pending criminal] case," [41] the Court was suggesting that a rather stringent test be applied. Since relevance, admissibility, and necessity must in any event be shown in order to require production of evidence prior to trial,[42] the Court's allusion to the trial judge's special responsibility when the Executive refuses to comply with the subpoena may indicate that an even greater showing must be made to overcome the claim of privilege.[43] Second, the conclusion that "justice" will always—or even most often—favor disclosure seems suspect. Any such notion would point to the abolition of *all* evidentiary privileges,[44] but the Court has never intimated that the doctor-patient, lawyer-client, or priest-penitent privileges are vulnerable because they occasionally prevent valuable evidence from getting into court. The Court's decision makes more sense when its proclamations are put in

38. 418 U.S. at 709.

39. Id. at 713. The Court had earlier emphasized that "the ends of criminal justice would be defeated if judgments were to be founded on a partial or speculative presentation of the facts." Id. at 709.

40. "Statements that meet the test of admissibility and relevance must be isolated; all other material must be excised." Id. at 714.

41. Id. at 713 (brackets in original).

42. See the Court's treatment of Fed. Rule Crim.Proc. 17(c), governing issuance of subpoenas *duces tecum* in federal criminal proceedings, in 418 U.S. at 698–700.

43. See "The Supreme Court, 1973 Term," 88 Harv.L.Rev. 41, 61 (1974). Arguably, however, the Court may merely have been introducing one additional procedural filter into the evidentiary process. There are certainly occasions where, despite a preliminary showing of relevance, the evidence eventually turns out to be irrelevant. Normally, such evidence would be disclosed but would be kept from the jury upon proper motion. The Court may simply have been inviting the trial judge to make the second-level decision on relevance—that normally made at the trial—in a preliminary setting.

44. See 418 U.S. at 709; Kurland, "United States v. Nixon: Who Killed Cock Robin?," 22 U.C.L.A.L.Rev. 68, 73–74 (1974).

the context of the peculiar facts of the *Nixon* case. Although the opinion carefully avoided the issue of possible wrongdoing on the part of the President,[45] that possibility was of course perceived and may have affected the Court's conclusion. And, although the language of the opinion gives no hint of it,[46] the *Nixon* decision may eventually be construed as dealing only with the scope of presidential privilege when the President may have a conflict of interest,[47] hence posing no threat to privileges in a more traditional setting.

What of the applicability of the executive privilege in judicial proceedings of a different character? In *United States v. Nixon*, the information was sought by the prosecution. If anything, the case for compelled disclosure is stronger when a criminal defendant seeks the putatively privileged information.[48] Beyond the fact that the plight of a defendant seeking such information is more compelling than the impact of any single case upon the integrity of the criminal justice system, it must be stressed that the government can always preserve the confidentiality of information sought by the accused by dropping the charge against the defendant.[49]

---

45. In basing its holding upon the need for evidence in a pending criminal trial, the Court eschewed a legally narrower, but politically far more controversial, ground for decision: Since a grand jury had named President Nixon as an unindicted co-conspirator in the Watergate coverup, the Supreme Court could have held that the presidential privilege does not extend to conversations identified by extrinsic evidence as likely to be part of a criminal conspiracy. If it had rested its judgment on this seemingly narrow theory, the Court would have found it difficult to avoid either the thorny issue of the President's likely guilt or the controversial question whether a grand jury can lawfully brand a President as a co-conspirator. In fact, while the Court had granted certiorari on this issue, 417 U.S. 960 (1974), it subsequently dismissed the writ as improvidently granted. 418 U.S. 683, 687 n. 2 (1974). A Supreme Court finding that a grand jury could so act, or that in any event the President was probably a co-conspirator, and that the presidential privilege was consequently inapplicable, would have been widely construed as a Supreme Court decision that the President was in fact guilty of participation in the criminal conspiracy. Thus the Court's adoption of the legally broader position narrowed the political consequences of its decision.

46. Something of a hint may be seen in the Court's suggestion that its opinion will give little cause for advisers "to temper [their] candor" unless they have reason to fear "criminal prosecution." 418 U.S. at 712.

47. Absent a presidential conflict, the chief executive's judgment about what evidence to produce in a criminal case could well be deemed conclusive. Even if the case is not so construed, however, the privilege may still turn out to be quite broad if the President is not implicated in criminal activity. Were there no extrinsic evidence of presidential involvement in the criminal undertakings, the President's statements at least would not fall under the rubric of admissions by a party to a conspiracy, and consequently might be excluded as inadmissible hearsay if sought to be used substantively against alleged conspirators. See 418 U.S. at 701. And, as to the statements of others, the privilege fashioned by the Court cannot be understood as centrally concerned with them. See note 37, supra.

48. The language of the Court supports no lesser privilege when it is a defendant who seeks the disclosure: "We address . . . . the constitutional need for relevant evidence in criminal trials." 418 U.S. at 712 n. 19. Moreover, the Court's references to a *defendant's* right to the production of evidence, id. at 711, bears *only* on cases where disclosure is sought by the defendant.

49. In the extraordinary setting of United States v. Nixon, that option was constricted initially by the independence established for the Special Prosecutor by the Attorney General at the direction of the President, and secondarily by the President's evident unwillingness to name a new Attorney General to revoke the regulations that secured such independence.

The applicability of the rule to civil suits is less obvious. Arguably, there is less at stake here than in the criminal justice system; "all" that is involved is the transfer of resources. Such an argument, however, smacks of the person-property distinction that has wheathered neither the test of time nor that of reasoned criticism.[50] Thus, a showing that presumptively privileged information is needed in a civil trial should be sufficient to overcome the presumption. In *Dellums v. Powell*,[51] for example, the court of appeals ruled that executive privilege was outweighed by the needs of civil plaintiffs who claimed that they were unconstitutionally harassed and arrested as part of an executive conspiracy to disrupt "May Day" demonstrations in 1971. The court granted access to White House tapes and documents because it found "sufficient evidentiary substantiation to avoid the inference that the demand reflects mere harassment." [52]

The district court in *Halperin v. Kissinger* [53] went even further and held that the plaintiffs, in a civil suit seeking damages from former President Nixon and several other officials for illegal wiretapping of plaintiffs' home telephone, were entitled to take the former President's deposition.[54] In reaching that conclusion, the court noted that Mr. Nixon had "on several occasions . . . personally accepted responsibility for the surveillance program challenged by plaintiffs," [55] and therefore found that Mr. Nixon would be "uniquely capable of clarifying certain . . . issues" that remained unclear despite the deposition of "[m]ore than twenty [other] witnesses." [56] The court emphasized that the deposition was narrowly enough delineated to avoid "a fishing expedition into Mr. Nixon's presidency," [57] and observed that, given the character of the information sought,[58] "[r]obust government debate will not suffer if Mr. Nixon must submit to an oral deposition. . . ." [59] The argument for disclosure is of course even stronger when information is requested by a civil *defendant* against whom the government has brought suit, since it seems decidedly unfair for the government to recover from an individual to whom it has denied information relevant to the government's case.[60]

---

50. See, e.g., § 15–14, *infra*.

51. 561 F.2d 242, 247 (D.C.Cir.1977), cert. denied 434 U.S. 880 (1977).

52. Id. at 247.

53. 401 F.Supp. 272 (D.D.C.1975).

54. The court assumed *arguendo* that a former President could claim executive privilege where the current President does not invoke the privilege on his predecessor's behalf. Id. at 274. The Supreme Court subsequently entertained a claim of executive privilege by former President Nixon, expressing the view that the privilege cannot be limited to incumbents. See note 4, *supra*.

55. 401 F.Supp. at 275.

56. Id.

57. Id.

58. "Facts rather than opinions or policies are primarily sought . . . [and] [t]he decision to wiretap was made over six years ago." Id. at 274.

59. Id. at 275.

60. See Henkin, "Executive Privilege: Mr. Nixon Loses But the Presidency Largely Prevails," 22 U.C.L.A.L.Rev. 40, 42 (1974). Indeed, in Sun Oil Co. v. United States, 514 F.2d 1020 (Ct.Cl. 1975) (per curiam), in a suit against the United States alleging a breach of contract and a taking in connection with the government's denial of a permit to construct an off-shore drilling platform, the Court of Claims upheld the right of plaintiff oil companies to inspect certain memoranda between former presidential aides and other memoranda to the former President himself, where the papers sought "might well lead to the dis-

What of *state* criminal trials? Although the *Nixon* opinion speaks only of pending *federal* trials, many of the policies isolated by the Court seem no less operative simply because the criminal case is brought in a state forum.[61] If the information is sought by a criminal defendant in such a forum, however, the fact that the President would not be in a position to choose between disclosure and dismissal may suggest a slightly different rule: if the material seems potentially relevant to the defendant's innocence, failure of the President to release it even after a judicial order compelling its release should require the state to halt its prosecution even though the defendant's plight is not the state's fault.

Finally, although the *Nixon* Court did not have to consider the scope to be accorded the state secrets privilege, dicta in the opinion suggest that assertions of such a privilege might be treated more deferentially than those based solely upon the executive's need for confidentiality.[62] The Court quoted with approval its pronouncement in *United States v. Reynolds*: "It may be possible to satisfy the court, from all the circumstances of the case, that there is a reasonable danger that compulsion of the evidence will expose military matters which, in the interest of national security, should not be divulged. When this is the case, the occasion for the privilege is appropriate, and the court should not jeopardize the security which the privilege is meant to protect by insisting upon an examination of the evidence, even by the judge alone, in chambers."[63] It seems prudent, however, to read that language as limited by the factual context of the *Reynolds* case. There, the Supreme Court reversed a lower court order which had required the government to produce documents relating to the crash of a military aircraft which had been engaged in a secret mission pertaining to the testing of electronic equipment. The fact that the plane was concededly involved in a secret military mission was enough to induce the Court to forego *in camera* inspection: the extrinsic evidence that a state secret was in fact involved was unusually strong. *Reynolds* did *not* suggest that a district court was automatically prevented from inspecting documents by the mere assertion of a state secrets privilege; weaker extrinsic evidence might justify *in camera* inspection. A court might reasonably conclude, for example, that documents pertaining to the testing of military equipment were so likely to implicate *bona fide* state secrets that *in camera* inspection could be dispensed with, while documents germane to the presidentially-inspired burglary of a psychiatrists' files should be examined by a judge in chambers to determine whether their secrecy is somehow crucial to the national well-being.

It should also be noted that *Reynolds* involved a request for information by a civil plaintiff who was bringing suit against the government, a judicial setting relatively favorable to honoring a govern-

covery of . . . evidence . . . that the President or someone on his White House staff turned the [ ] application down and did so for impermissible, extraneous, political, or other reasons which they think, if shown, would make their case," id. at 1025.

61. See Mishkin, "Great Cases and Soft Law: A Comment on United States v. Nixon," 22 U.C.L.A.L.Rev. 76, 85 (1974).

62. See 418 U.S. at 706, 710–11.

63. 345 U.S. 1, 10 (1953), quoted in 418 U.S. at 711.

mental assertion of privilege. Only an unjustifiably expansive reading of *Reynolds*, then, would permit the conclusion that an assertion of military or diplomatic privilege automatically puts the requested documents entirely beyond the reach of the courts. Since *United States v. Nixon* did not itself involve a claim of privilege bottomed on military or diplomatic necessity, it should not be read as extending *Reynolds*, despite the fact that some of its language appears broader than that of the earlier holding. Particularly is this so in light of the *Nixon* Court's explicit suggestion that even material claimed to be confidential under cases involving the state secrets doctrine is to be "delivered to the District Judge . . . for *in camera* consideration of the validity of particular excisions. . . ." [64]

§ 4-16. Remedies for Presidential Abuse of Privilege: Congress' Power to Say No

The constitutional limits of executive privilege in the face of legislative inquiry have not been judicially defined.[1] Because congressional requests for information, and executive refusals to comply with such requests, generally spring from the essentially political concerns that comprise much of the ordinary business of those two branches, the disputants themselves do not always regard judicial intervention as appropriate to the resolution of the privilege controversy. And even when they do look to the judiciary, it is not always clear that such intervention could constitutionally be effected, given the protection afforded the separation of powers by the "political question" doctrine.[2]

However, even if the characteristics and consequences of executive privilege claims in legislative settings cannot be expressed in doctrinal terms as specific as might be possible when those claims are made in the course of judicial proceedings,[3] it is possible to identify the legislative environments in which claims of executive privilege are usually advanced, and to describe the primary political devices that the Constitution provides for their resolution.

Executive privilege was first asserted by President Washington, who refused in 1796 to furnish the House of Representatives with requested correspondence, documents, and instructions to John Jay in relation to the negotiation of the Jay Treaty. Washington made no claim that the provision of the requested material to the House of Representatives would compromise the public interest; he contended merely that the House of Representatives had *no right* to the materials since the Constitution afforded the House no role in the treaty-making process. Washington did make the materials available to the Senate.[4]

---

64. 418 U.S. at 715 n. 21.

§ 4-16

1. In United States v. Nixon, 418 U.S. 683, 712 n. 19 (1974), the Court explicitly rejected any notion that it was incidentally passing upon the propriety of assertions of executive privilege in a legislative setting. The opinion nonetheless lends some support to the proposition that the President may, in certain instances, withhold infor-

mation from the Congress. See Henkin, "Executive Privilege: Mr. Nixon Loses But the Presidency Largely Prevails," 22 U.C. L.A.L.Rev. 40, 43 (1974).

2. See generally § 3-13, supra.

3. See § 4-15, supra.

4. This was not the only occasion on which President Washington considered the propriety of denying Congress informa-

Given the Senate's constitutionally prescribed role in treaty making,[5] presidential claims of unilateral authority to invoke national security interests and unfettered discretion to suppress documents in that context are dubious; the Constitution does not give the Executive complete hegemony over national security.[6] In any event, the exact compass of the Executive's legal right to withhold information is likely to be of tangential importance in this context, since the constitutional requirement of article II, § 2, cl. 2, that treaties be approved by "two thirds of the Senators present" severely limits the efficacy of executive privilege in the treaty ratification process: senatorial disapproval of particular assertions of privilege is likely to be expressed in the form of a vote against treaty ratification on the ground that the disapproving Senators lack the information they would need in order to vote affirmatively.

The Constitution similarly encourages executive candor with regard to those presidential appointments which are required by article II, § 2, cl. 2, to be submitted to the Senate for approval.[7] Unless the refusal to provide pertinent information can be persuasively justified, a claim of privilege may properly jeopardize the approval prospects of the President's preferred appointee. The practical and political consequences of rejecting presidential nominees may often render this a cumbersome weapon at best, but it has been successfully deployed on occasion.[8]

Such senatorial tactics are in no sense an abuse of the Constitution's separation of power. As Justice Jackson wrote in the *Steel Seizure Case*, the Constitution "contemplates [the] integrat[ion of] the dispersed powers into a workable government. It enjoins upon its branches separateness but interdependence, autonomy but *reciprocity*." [9] That dictate of reciprocity is most starkly implicated in the areas of making treaties and of appointing federal officers, responsibilities that the Constitution expressly confers *jointly* upon the Senate and the

tion. At one point, Congress requested information regarding Major General St. Clair's ill-starred 1792 mission against the Indians. Washington summoned his Cabinet to advise him on the question whether he should withhold the relevant papers from Congress. The Cabinet concluded that the President should provide "such papers as the public good would permit." Since Washington concluded that delivering these papers to Congress would not compromise the public interest, he complied with Congress' request. See 1 T. Jefferson, Writings 189–90 (Ford ed. 1892).

5. See § 4–5, supra.

6. See United States v. AT & T, 567 F.2d 121, 128 (D.C.Cir.1977) (requiring political branches to work out a dispute over access to AT & T records of "national security" wiretaps in context of congressional investigation, because Congress, particularly the Senate, has constitutional duties and powers "equally inseparable from the national security").

7. See § 4–9, supra.

8. Senator Sam Ervin successfully argued in 1972 and 1973 that nominations should be delayed by the Judiciary Committee so long as assertions of executive privilege barred the Senators from relevant testimony and information. The nomination of Richard Kleindienst as Attorney General, ultimately approved, was stalled until President Nixon relented and permitted a White House aide to testify on particular Justice Department affairs. The confirmation of L. Patrick Gray as FBI Director was derailed, and ultimately withdrawn by the President, when Nixon refused to allow aides to testify about alleged abuses of FBI memoranda. "Executive Privilege and the Congressional Right of Inquiry", 10 Harv.J.Leg. 621, 649 (1973).

9. 343 U.S. 579, 635 (1952) (concurring opinion) (emphasis added), quoted in United States v. Nixon, 418 U.S. at 707; see also Nixon v. Administrator of General Services, 433 U.S. 425, 443 (1977).

President.[10] There is no reciprocity where a President demands confirmation of his nominees or ratification of his treaty proposals while refusing to divulge the information the Senate reasonably deems necessary to performance of its half of the process.[11]

Outside the treaty ratification and appointments approval contexts, the constitutional setting for congressional investigations does not necessarily make available a direct political device by which executive claims of privilege can be legislatively regulated. Certainly, if Congress' investigation concerns legislation proposed by the President, executive decisions to withhold information will be affected by the possibility that a claim of privilege could cause the defeat of the desired legislation.[12] However, if an investigation focuses on legislation to which executive officials are opposed or indifferent, or emphasizes matters only remotely connected with the enactment of legislation, executive officials will ordinarily have little if any institutional incentive for furnishing requested information.

Executive noncompliance with congressional subpoenas can be addressed in the way other recalcitrant witnesses are treated: by citation for criminal contempt of Congress. In 1983, a congressional committee with responsibility for oversight of the Environmental Protection Agency's Superfund program for dealing with toxic wastes sought documents relating to the administration of the Superfund; the investigators were interested in whether the EPA was properly and vigorously enforcing the law by all available means, including the institution of lawsuits to recover the costs of cleaning up abandoned toxic waste dumps. The EPA refused to comply fully with the committee's subpoena, claiming that documents from open "law enforcement" files assembled as part of the executive's responsibility to enforce the Superfund were protected by the doctrine of executive privilege.[13] The full House of Representatives cited the Administrator of the EPA for contempt and duly referred the matter to the United States Attorney for prosecution under the criminal contempt statute.[14] Instead of presenting the matter to a

10. Art. II, § 2, cl. 2.

11. In declining to release FBI files on investigations of labor disturbances and subversive activities to the House Committee on Naval Affairs, Attorney General (later Justice) Robert Jackson contrasted that decision with his policy on executive privilege when appointments are involved: "I have taken the position that committees called upon to pass on the confirmation of persons recommended for appointment by the Attorney General would be afforded confidential access to *any* information that we have—because no candidate's name is submitted without his knowledge and the department does not intend to submit the name of any person whose entire history will not stand light." 40 Op.Atty.Gen. 45 (1941) (emphasis added). When Justice Rehnquist, one of Justice Jackson's former law clerks, was nominated in 1986 to be Chief Justice, the Justice Department invoked executive privilege to deny the Sen-

ate Judiciary Committee access to memoranda written in 1969–71 by then Assistant Attorney General Rehnquist. The memoranda related to domestic surveillance and other means of dealing with anti-war protesters, civil rights groups, and other "subversives." When a bi-partisan majority of the Senate committee scheduled a vote to issue a subpoena for the documents—a move that threatened to delay action on the nomination—the Reagan administration backed down and negotiated release of the material on August 4, 1986. See N.Y.Times, Aug. 6, 1986, at A1, col. 6.

12. Arguably, the power of the purse is an exceedingly awkward vehicle for compelling disclosure. See 10 Harv.J.Leg. 621, 654–60 (1973).

13. United States v. House of Representatives, 556 F.Supp. 150, 151 (D.D.C. 1983).

14. 2 U.S.C. § 192.

grand jury, as required by law, the Justice Department sued the House in federal court, seeking injunctive and declaratory relief against enforcement of the subpoena.[15] The action was dismissed and the executive branch was told to seek resolution of its claim of privilege in the orderly course of the criminal contempt proceedings.[16] Negotiations between the executive branch and Congress promptly resumed and the committee was allowed access to the "enforcement-sensitive" documents under executive session safeguards.[17]

Legislative investigators stymied by a lack of executive cooperation have occasionally eshewed the contempt sanction and instead initiated civil judicial proceedings in an effort to obtain injunctive and declaratory relief.[18] Even if such efforts are not barred by the "political question" doctrine, practical obstacles, most notably the length of time often required to complete the judicial proceedings if the executive does not cave in at once, inhibit automatic resort to the courts to decide the validity of executive privilege claims raised in the context of legislative investigations.[19]

The political efficacy of presidential assertions of executive privilege is perhaps most limited in the context of congressional impeachment proceedings. It would be a "mockery" indeed, to quote John Quincy Adams, "to say that the House should have the power of impeachment extending even to the President . . . himself, and yet to say that the House had not the power to obtain the evidence and proofs on which their impeachment was based."[20] The same could of course

15. United States v. House of Representatives, 556 F.Supp. 150 (D.D.C. 1983).

16. Id. at 153. Although the district court did not address the issue, the speech and debate clause, art. I, § 6, cl. 1, has been construed to prevent congressional subpoenas from being questioned in civil actions brought by those resisting the subpoenas. See Eastland v. United States Servicemen's Fund, 421 U.S. 491 (1975).

17. The House Judiciary Committee subsequently declared that "the [Justice] Department misserved not only the Congress, but the executive and judicial branches as well" in its handling of the Superfund case. Report of the House Comm. on the Judiciary: "Investigation of the Role of the Department of Justice in the Withholding of EPA Documents from Congress in 1982–83," H.R.Rep. No. 435, 99th Cong., 1st Sess., Vol I. iii (1985). The report determined that the Justice Department's Office of Legal Counsel misled the President and the courts. A special prosecutor was subsequently appointed to investigate whether the head of the OLC lied to Congress in connection with the assertion of executive privilege. See In re Theodore Olson, 818 F.2d 34 (D.C.Cir. 1987).

18. See, e.g., Senate Select Comm. v. Nixon (II), 370 F.Supp. 521 (D.D.C. 1974) (holding that a congressional subpoena of information from the President, issued in

the context of an investigation of apparently criminal acts, is as justifiable as a subpoena issued in judicial proceedings, but ultimately declining to enforce the subpoena because of the need, advanced by the Watergate Special Prosecutor himself, "to safeguard pending criminal prosecutions from the possible prejudicial effect of pretrial publicity"), aff'd 498 F.2d 725 (D.C. Cir. 1974).

19. See, e.g., AT & T v. F.C.C., 539 F.2d 767 (D.C.Cir. 1976) (where district court had granted request of Justice Department to enjoin AT & T from complying with a House subcommittee's subpoena directing AT & T to disclose certain information on warrantless "national security" wiretaps, severity of "nerve-center" constitutional confrontation between executive and legislative branches warrants judicial suggestion of compromise and pendente lite treatment to allow for further efforts at settlement).

20. Cong.Globe, 27th Cong., 2d Sess. 580 (1842). See also In re Report and Recommendation of June 5, 1972 Grand Jury, 370 F.Supp. 1219, 1230 (D.D.C.1974) (holding that Fed.R.Crim.P. 6(e), which bars disclosure of matters occurring before a grand jury except in connection with a judicial proceeding, does not prohibit transmitting grand jury report to House Judiciary Committee: "it seems incredible that grand

be said of the Senate's power to try impeachments.[21] Indeed, assertions of executive privilege which thwart impeachment investigations or trials can themselves quite properly become the basis for an article of impeachment.

For example, prior to President Nixon's resignation in August 1974, the Judiciary Committee of the House of Representatives recommended to the full House an Article of Impeachment (Article III) charging that President Nixon's repeated refusal to comply with Judiciary Committee subpoenas issued in the course of the impeachment investigation was "subversive of constitutional government," since such refusal involved a presidential usurpation of "functions and judgments necessary to the exercise of the sole power of impeachment vested by the Constitution in the House of Representatives."

Although the House Judiciary Committee voted not to seek judicial enforcement of its subpoenas to the President but sought instead to submit the validity of those subpoenas to the House and Senate, it has been suggested in plausible dictum that, if and when judicial enforcement is properly requested, federal courts possess constitutional power to review the validity of congressional impeachment subpoenas answered by claims of executive privilege, and further that the congressional interest in judicially enforcing such subpoenas (if otherwise valid) is substantial enough to outweigh any danger that the prejudicial publicity associated with the impeachment investigation might frustrate the impaneling of unbiased juries in ancillary criminal trials.[22]

§ 4–17. The Ultimate Remedy: Impeachment for High Crimes and Misdemeanors

Although the impeachment process has been used periodically since 1789,[1] there has been no judicial attempt to define its limits. This is attributable, in part, to the constitutional language ostensibly confining the issue of impeachment to the legislative branch of government, and thus arguably barring judicial review of impeachments under the political question doctrine.[2] What follows, therefore, is not a discussion

jury matters should be lawfully available to disbarment committees and police disciplinary investigations and yet be unavailable to the House of Representatives in a proceeding of so great import as an impeachment investigation."); 40 Op.Atty. Gen. 45 (1941) (executive privilege would not be invoked in impeachment proceedings).

21. See § 4–17, infra.

22. See Senate Select Committee v. Nixon (II), 370 F.Supp. 521, 522–23 (D.D.C. 1974), aff'd, 998 F.2d 725 (D.C.Cir. 1974).

§ 4–17

1. For a survey of impeachments in the United States, see "Impeachment and the U.S. Congress," Cong.Q. (March 1974).

2. See Ritter v. United States, 84 Ct.Cl. 293 (1936), cert. denied 300 U.S. 668 (1937) (dismissing suit of a judge who contended

that the Senate had tried him for nonimpeachable offenses: "the Senate was the sole tribunal that could take jurisdiction of the articles of impeachment presented to that body against the plaintiff and its decision is final"). See generally C. Black, Impeachment: A Handbook 53–55 (1974) (urging that it would be absurd to reinstate a President whose legitimacy had been stripped through impeachment by the House of Representatives and conviction by the Senate, legislative bodies presumably reflecting the sense of polity); Broderick, "A Citizen's Guide to Impeachment of a President: Problem Areas", 23 Catholic U.L.Rev. 205 (1973). See also H. Black, Constitutional Law 121–22 (1897); 1 J. Story, Commentaries § 805, at 587; 3 W. Willoughby, The Constitutional Law of the United States 1451 (2d ed. 1929). That impeachments are entirely beyond the pur-

of a judicially articulated law of impeachment, but is instead an independent analysis, buttressed as appropriate by conclusions that can be drawn from the attempt to impeach President Nixon,[3] as well as from earlier impeachment proceedings.[4]

Article II, § 4, provides that "[t]he President, Vice-President and all Civil Officers of the United States, shall be removed from Office on Impeachment for, and Conviction of, Treason, Bribery, or other high Crimes and Misdemeanors." Members of Congress are not "civil officers" for purposes of impeachment. But although Senators and Representatives thus cannot be impeached, they can be removed from office. Article I, § 5 provides: "Each House shall be the Judge of the Elections, Returns and Qualifications of its own Members. . . . Each House may . . . punish its members for disorderly behavior, and, with the concurrence of two thirds, expel a member.[5]

Although of course private citizens are not subject to impeachment, the resignation of a "civil officer" does not give immunity from impeachment for acts committed while in office.[6] Congress might wish to continue an impeachment proceeding after its target has resigned from office in order to deprive the resigned officer of any retirement benefits affected by the fact of impeachment or conviction; to solidify the lesson of the officer's misconduct in the form of clear precedent; or simply to make plain to the public and for the future that the resigned officer's withdrawal from office was the result not of unjust persecution but rather of the way in which the officer had abused an official position.

Under the provisions of article II, § 4, the President, Vice President, or any other civil officer may be impeached for, and convicted of, "Treason, Bribery, or other high Crimes and Misdemeanors." Of these impeachable offences, only treason is expressly defined by the Constitution. Article III, § 3 states that "Treason against the United States, shall consist only in levying War against them, or in adhering to their Enemies, giving them Aid and Comfort." Despite then-Congressman Gerald Ford's well-known assertion that "an impeachable offence is whatever a majority of the House of Representatives considers [it] to be",[7] there is now wide agreement that the phrase "high Crimes and

---

view of the courts is not always conceded, however. See R. Berger, Impeachment 108 (1973); I. Bryant, Impeachment, Trials and Errors 182–97 (1972); Goldberg, "Question of Impeachment," 1 Hastings Con.L.Q. 5, 8 (1974); Rezneck, "Is Judicial Review of Impeachment Coming?", 60 A.B.A.J. 681 (1974); Cf. Powell v. McCormack, 395 U.S. 486 (1969), discussed in § 3–6, supra. Given the decision of the Constitutional Convention to transfer impeachment trials from the Supreme Court, where they were initially to have been conducted, to the Senate, the more defensible view appears to be the traditional one of non-reviewability.

3. The impeachment effort was terminated after the President's resignation on August 9, 1974.

4. Although impeachment has been used primarily as a way of removing federal judges, the special characteristics of judicial impeachments are not discussed here, but rather in Chapter 3, supra.

5. See Powell v. McCormack, 395 U.S. 486 (1969).

6. See Firmage and Mangrum, "Removal of the President: Resignation and the Procedural Law of Impeachment," 1974 Duke L.J. 1023, 1089–95.

7. 116 Cong.Rec. 11913 (1970). The falsity of that position is evident from an examination of the debates on impeachment at the Constitutional Convention. In response to a suggestion by Colonel Mason that impeachments not be limited to cases of bribery and treason, but include as well instances of "maladministration," Madison

Misdemeanors" was intended by the Framers to connote a relatively limited category closely analagous to the "great offences" impeachable in common law England.[8] In addition to treason and bribery, the "great offences" included misapplication of funds, abuse of official power, neglect of duty, encroachment on or contempt of legislative prerogatives, and corruption.[9]

There have been only two serious attempts to impeach American Presidents. In both instances, the offenses charged reflected the impact of the common law tradition discussed here: offenses have been regarded as impeachable if and only if they involve serious abuse of official power.

President Andrew Johnson was impeached by the House of Representatives in 1867 on the ground that he had attempted to dismiss Secretary of War Stanton in apparent defiance of the Tenure of Office Act of 1867.[10] Johnson escaped conviction in the Senate by one vote.

Representative John Bingham, leader of the House Managers of Impeachment, defined an impeachable offence in the traditional manner: "An impeachable high crime or misdemeanor is one in its nature or consequences subversive of some fundamental or essential principle of government or highly prejudicial to the public interest, and this may consist of a violation of the Constitution, of law, of an official oath, or of duty, by an act committed or omitted, or, without violating a positive law, by the abuse of discretionary powers from improper motives or for an improper purpose." [11]

History has not dealt kindly with the impeachment of Andrew Johnson. The procedural arbitrariness of the Johnson trial, and the fact that the law Johnson ignored was widely regarded as unconstitutional even before the Supreme Court so declared in *Myers v. United States*,[12] have together contributed to a fairly broad agreement that the congressional attempt to oust Johnson was itself an abuse of power.[13]

admonished that "so vague a term [would] be equivalent to tenure during the pleasure of the Senate." Mason then substituted the current constitutional language—"other high crimes and misdemeanors"—for "maladministration," apparently to ensure that mere congressional disapproval of the policies of a President could not serve as a basis for impeachment. See M. Farrand, The Records of the Constitutional Convention of 1787 (1911).

8. See, e.g., R. Berger, Impeachment 53–102 (1973); C. Black, Impeachment: A Handbook 39–40 (1974); Broderick, "A Citizen's Guide to Impeachment of a President: Problem Areas," 23 Catholic U.L. Rev. 205 (1973). Our law of impeachment has also been said to derive from the Roman law of infamy. See Franklin, "Romanist Infamy and the American Constitutional Concept of Impeachment," 23 Buff.L. Rev. 313 (1974). See generally "The Legal Aspects of Impeachment: An Overview," prepared by the Office of Legal Counsel of the Department of Justice (February 1974).

For an unusual argument that the impeachment clause makes impeachment and conviction *mandatory* in cases of "high crimes and misdemeanors" but *optional* in other cases, see Note, "The Scope of the Power to Impeach," 84 Yale L.J. 1316 (1975).

9. See R. Berger, Impeachment 70–71 (1973).

10. The act was ultimately declared unconstitutional. See Myers v. United States, 272 U.S. 52 (1926), discussed in § 4–10, supra.

11. 1 Trial of Andrew Johnson 157 (1868).

12. See note 10, supra.

13. There appears, however, to be a growing revisionist view that the "real" reason for Johnson's impeachment—his systematic subversion of congressional reconstruction efforts—was a proper basis for conviction and removal from office. See

Richard Nixon was the second President to become the subject of serious impeachment proceedings. Mr. Nixon resigned from office as the thirty-seventh President on August 9, 1974, after his compliance with the Supreme Court's decision in *United States v. Nixon* [14] disclosed information which, when added to evidence already accumulated by the House Judiciary Committee, made virtually inevitable the President's impeachment, conviction, and removal from office. The invocation of the impeachment process in the Nixon case has led to a widespread re-evaluation of the thesis, embraced by many after the Johnson acquittal, that impeachment is of little practical significance as a check on the Chief Executive. [15]

Even before the final revelations, the House Judiciary Committee had found that three proposed articles of impeachment were supported by "clear and convincing" evidence. The Committee had accordingly voted to recommend impeachment by the House and trial by the Senate. These three proposed impeachment articles, voted by the Committee on July 27, 29 and 30, 1974, provide specific illustrations of the contemporary understanding of what constitutes "high crimes and misdemeanors." The Judiciary Committee first found that President Nixon warranted "impeachment and trial, and removal from office" because he had "prevented, obstructed, and impeded the administration of justice" by engaging "personally and through his subordinates and agents in a course of conduct or plan to delay, impede, and obstruct the investigation of [the Watergate break-in]; to cover up, conceal and protect those responsible; and to conceal the existence and scope of other unlawful covert activities." [16] Under a second Article of Impeachment, the Judiciary Committee determined that President Nixon, "in violation of his constitutional oath . . . and in disregard of his constitutional duty to take care that the laws be faithfully executed," "endeavored to obtain from the Internal Revenue Service in violation of the constitutional rights of citizens, confidential information contained in income tax returns for purposes not authorized by law. . . .;" "misused" the FBI, Secret Service, and "other executive personnel in violation or disregard of the constitutional rights of citizens. . . .;" "authorized . . . a secret investigative unit . . . within the office of the President, financed in part with money derived from campaign contributions, which . . . engaged in covert and unlawful activities, and attempted to prejudice the constitutional right of an accused . . . to a fair trial;" "failed. . . . to act when he knew or had reason to know that his close subordinates endeavored to impede and frustrate lawful inquiries by duly constituted executive, judicial and legislative

M. Benedict, The Impeachment and Trial of Andrew Johnson (1973).

14. 418 U.S. 683 (1974) discussed in § 4–15, supra.

15. See, e.g., Firmage and Mangrum, supra note 6, at 1025–26. But the critical thesis has not been abandoned, and proposals of a more parliamentary or quasi-parliamentary substitute for impeachment continue to be advanced. See, e.g., H.

Joint Res. No. 903, 93d Cong., 2d Sess. 1111 (1974); Linde, "Replacing a President: Rx for 21st Century Watergate," 43 Geo.Wash. L.Rev. 384 (1975); Havighurst, "Doing Away With Presidential Impeachment: The Advantages of Parliamentary Government," 1974 Ariz.L.Rev. 223.

16. Article I specified nine "means used to implement this course of conduct or plan".

entities . . . ;" "knowingly misused the executive power by interfering with agencies of the executive branch . . . in violation of his duty to take care that the laws be faithfully executed."

In a third Article of Impeachment, the Judiciary Committee found that President Nixon "failed without lawful cause or excuse to produce papers and things as directed by duly authorized subpoenas issued by the [Judiciary] Committee . . . and wilfully disobeyed such subpoenas," contrary to "his oath faithfully to execute the office of the President." The Committee stated that the subpoenaed information was needed "to resolve by direct evidence fundamental, factual questions relating to Presidential direction, knowledge, or approval of actions demonstrated by other evidence to be substantial grounds for impeachment of the President [who] thereby assum[ed] to himself functions and judgments necessary to the exercise of the sole power of impeachment vested by the Constitution in the House of Representatives." [17]

A number of independently plausible conclusions about the character of impeachable offences are reinforced by the proposed Nixon impeachment articles. The first of these is the limited usefulness of "criminality" as a measure of "high crimes and misdemeanors". Only the first of the three Nixon impeachment articles voted by the House Judiciary Committee (and limited portions of the second) dealt with alleged presidential violations of federal criminal law.[18] At the same time, the Committee rejected an additional proposed article of impeachment based on evidence of possible criminal irregularities in presidential tax returns and in expenditures of public funds to enhance the value of President Nixon's personal property.[19]

The House Judiciary Committee's proposal of the Nixon Impeachment Articles therefore appears to confirm the view of most commentators: [20] *A showing of criminality is neither necessary nor sufficient for*

---

17. Article III was adopted by a smaller majority (21–17) than Article I (27–11) or Article II (28–10), in part because of doubts as to the propriety of congressional, rather than judicial, resolution of the Committee's right to subpoena the information from the President. See Final Report on the Impeachment of Richard M. Nixon, President of the United States, H.R. Rep. No. 1035, 93d Cong., 2d Sess., in 120 Cong.Rec. H9103 (daily ed. Aug. 22, 1974). Those doubts were perhaps understandable in light of some of the Supreme Court's needlessly extravagant if stirring language, claiming for itself the role of "ultimate interpreter of the Constitution," in United States v. Nixon, 418 U.S. 683, 704 (1974). It has never been the law, however, that only the Supreme Court can authoritatively resolve constitutional disputes. The whole thrust of the political question doctrine is in fact to the contrary. For an argument that the Judiciary would nonetheless have provided a better forum for deciding whether the President was obliged

to submit the requested information to the House, see Pollak, "The Constitution as an Experiment," 123 U.Penn.L.Rev. 1318, 1323–28 (1975).

18. See 18 U.S.C. § 1510 (1970) (making it a felony "willfully [to endeavor] . . . to obstruct, delay, or prevent the communication of information relating to a violation of any criminal statute of the United States by any person to a criminal investigator").

19. Also rejected was an article based on the administration's secret-bombing of Cambodia in 1969 and 1970. A useful discussion of the issue posed by that article and its rejection appears in Pollak, supra note 17, at 1329–39.

20. Among the most thoughtful studies, one that reaches this conclusion is particularly worth consulting: Committee on Federal Legislation, Association of the Bar of the City of New York, The Law of Presidential Impeachment (released Jan. 21, 1974).

the specification of an impeachable offense.[21] That non-criminal activities may constitute impeachable offenses is hardly surprising. A deliberate presidential decision to emasculate our national defenses, or to conduct a private war in circumvention of the Constitution, would probably violate no criminal code, but it should surely be deemed a ground of impeachment. And there is little doubt that, despite the want of criminality, such an action would fall within the compass of the common law's "great offenses."[22] In contrast, a President's technical violation of a law making jay-walking a crime obviously would not be an adequate basis for presidential removal.[23] With respect to the question of criminality, then, Edmund Burke's opening statement at the impeachment trial of Warren Hastings remains definitive: "It is by this tribunal that statesmen who abuse their power . . . are tried . . . not upon the niceties of a narrow [criminal] jurisprudence, but upon the enlarged and solid principles of morality."[24] Nor could the desire to insure that impeachment not be turned into a partisan political weapon be satisfied by a mechanical rule tying impeachable offenses to enumerated crimes, and it does not in fact require such a rule. A commitment to principle can better be secured, insofar as any verbal formula can help secure it, by accepting and acting on the proposition that "Congress may properly impeach and remove a President only for conduct amounting to a gross breach of trust or serious abuse of power, and only if it would be prepared to take the same action against any President who engaged in comparable conduct in similar circumstances."[25]

A second conclusion to which the Nixon affair points is that an inductive approach to defining impeachable offenses makes substantial sense. The House Judiciary Committee notably refrained from stating any precise definition of "high crimes and misdemeanors" against which particular proposed impeachment articles could be measured. This approach minimized the possibility of serious partisan division prior to consideration of the actual evidence. In many cases, it may not

---

21. See R. Berger, Impeachment 56–57 (1973); C. Black, Impeachment: A Handbook 33–35 (1974); C. Hughes, The Supreme Court of the United States 19 (1928); Goldberg, "Question of Impeachment", 1 Hastings Const.L.Q. 5 (1974); S. Boutwell, The Constitution of the United States at the End of the First Century (1895); Fenton, "The Scope of the Impeachment Power," 65 Nw.U.L.Rev. 719 (1970). But see Thompson & Pollit, "Impeachment of Federal Judges: An Historical Overview," 49 N.C.L.Rev. 87, 106 (1970); C. Warren, The Supreme Court in United States History 293 (1922); I, Brait, Impeachment: Trial and Errors (1972).

22. See generally Staff Report, House Judiciary Committee, "Constitutional Grounds for Presidential Impeachment" (released Feb. 22, 1974).

23. Some crimes that do not relate directly to the President's official duties may

nevertheless be impeachable offenses if their character is such as to taint the office of the presidency. For example, a President's murder of a personal enemy, while not bearing directly upon official presidential duties, would so malign the holder of the office that the President, stripped of legitimacy, would be unable effectively to discharge presidential duties. See C. Black, Impeachment: A Handbook 39 (1974). "At the heart of the matter is the determination [that] the officeholder has demonstrated by his actions that he is unfit to continue in the office in question." Committee on Federal Legislation, supra note 20.

24. 7 E. Burke, Works 11, 14 (1839).

25. Committee on Federal Legislation, supra note 20.

be until such evidence is known that legislators will perceive the need to abandon their ordinary partisan or personal loyalties. In this special context, the usual equation between ignorance and impartiality plainly makes little sense. Moreover, deciding whether impeachable conduct has occurred primarily on the basis of the conduct's factual context, rather than in terms of the application of some general rule, is more in keeping with the necessarily political—but *not* necessarily partisan—character of the impeachment process.

We turn finally to a brief consideration of the *process* of impeachment and trial. Article I, § 2, cl. 5, declares that "[t]he House of Representatives . . . shall have the sole Power of Impeachment." [26] But what *is* impeachment? In many senses, it is analogous to a grand jury indictment in the criminal justice system.[27] The House of Representatives decides by majority vote whether charges raised against "civil officers" are sufficiently serious, and are supported by sufficient evidence, to warrant holding a Senate trial.

With respect to federal grand jury proceedings, the Supreme Court has refused to establish a rule permitting defendants to challenge indictments as supported by inadequate or incompetent evidence: in the subsequent "trial on the merits, defendants are entitled to a strict observance of all the rules designed to bring about a fair verdict." [28] However this may be in the grand jury setting, in the context of impeachment the institutional costs of a Senate trial, as well as the extraordinary damage done to a civil officer's reputation by the "mere" fact of impeachment, have caused the House of Representatives to impose restraints on its impeachment decisions that the Supreme Court has not imposed on federal grand juries. For example, in 1974 the House Judiciary Committee, charged by the full House with responsibility for making a preliminary (and probably definitive) decision as to whether articles of impeachment should be voted against President Nixon, imposed upon itself the requirement that any impeachment article must be supported by "clear and convincing evidence" before it could be favorably reported out of committee. It seems likely that the House of Representatives itself would have applied the same standard in voting on the articles of impeachment if President Nixon had not resigned before such a vote could be taken.

Article I, § 3, cl. 6, governs the conduct of a trial of impeachment: "The Senate shall have the sole Power to try all Impeachments. When sitting for that Purpose, they shall be on Oath or Affirmation. When the President of the United States is tried the Chief Justice shall preside: and no person shall be convicted without the concurrence of

---

26. For an analysis of impeachment procedure in the House, see Firmage and Mangrum, supra note 6, at 1032–50. The place (if any) of executive privilege in House impeachment investigations is discussed in § 4–16, supra.

27. See C. Black, Impeachment: A Handbook (1974).

28. Costello v. United States, 350 U.S. 359 (1956) (holding that a defendant in a federal criminal case may be required to stand trial, and that his conviction may be sustained, where only hearsay evidence was presented to the grand jury which indicted him).

two thirds of the members present." [29]   Although the Chief Justice presides when the President is on trial, the Senate, possessor of "the sole Power to try all Impeachments," decides the procedural and evidentiary rules which govern such trials.   Under the prevailing rules, the Senate can overrule decisions of the Chief Justice concerning the admissibility of evidence, and, by passing questions to the Chief Justice, individual Senators may interrogate witnesses. [30]

Article I, § 3, cl. 7, limits the effect of impeachment and conviction by providing that "Judgement in Cases of Impeachment shall not extend further than to removal from Office, and disqualification to hold and enjoy any Office of Honor, Trust or Profit under the United States: but the party convicted shall nevertheless be liable and subject to Indictment, Trial, Judgement and Punishment, according to Law". Such criminal liability is absolute; Congress cannot eliminate it by a grant of immunity, nor the President by an exercise of the pardon power. [31]

It is widely thought that article I, § 9, cl. 3, [32] evidences the intention of the Framers that the English practice of directing criminal punishments against specific offenders as part of the legislative process should not be adopted in the United States.   At the same time, those who drafted article I, § 3, cl. 7, did not wish to immunize office-holders from criminal prosecution; the clause was designed in part to make clear that criminal prosecutions subsequent to removal from office would not constitute double jeopardy of the sort explicitly prohibited by the fifth amendment. [33]

---

29. For an analysis of impeachment procedure in the Senate, see Firmage and Mangrum, supra note 6, at 1050–62, 1073–78. The place (if any) of executive privilege in Senate impeachment trials is discussed in § 4–16, supra.

30. See "Impeachment and the U.S. Congress." Cong.Q. 12–13 (March, 1974).

31. U.S. Const., art. II, § 2, cl. 1, gives the President the "power to grant . . . pardons . . . except in cases of impeachment." See § 4–11, supra.

32. "No Bill of Attainder . . . shall be passed." See §§ 10–4, 10–5, infra.

33. This interpretation gives the impeachment judgment clause significance as something other than a specification of time sequence. Indictment of "civil officers" prior to impeachment and removal is not necessarily prohibited. See Firmage & Mangrum, supra note 6, at 1094–1102; Berger, "The President, Congress, and the Courts," 83 Yale L.J. 1111, 1133, 1136 (1974). See § 4–14, supra. This construction of the impeachment judgment clause also reinforces the proposition that, since impeachment is an ultimately political process, impeachable offenses must be defined politically, and are not limited to indictable crimes.

Chapter 5

FEDERAL LEGISLATIVE POWER: CONGRESSIONAL AUTHORITY AND THE IMPLICATIONS OF STATE SOVEREIGNTY

§ 5-1. The Scope and Limits of Congressional Power

It is noteworthy that article I, § 1 endows Congress not with "all legislative power," but only with the "legislative powers herein granted." In theory, Congress is thus a legislative body possessing only *limited* powers—those granted to it by the Constitution. This chapter is concerned chiefly with how well the theory of limited congressional powers corresponds with constitutional practice. The Supreme Court has in recent years largely abandoned any effort to articulate and enforce *internal* limits on congressional power—limits inherent in the grants of power themselves. Rather, the Court has been concerned chiefly with developing *external* limits on congressional power—limits which derive from particular aspects of the separation of powers taken up in Chapters 2 through 4, or from the constitutional structure as a whole, or from specific constraints on congressional power such as those contained in article I, § 9, and in the Bill of Rights. Such explicit constraints, designed to secure individual rights against Congress, will be taken up in Chapters 9 through 16; this chapter will discuss two sets of *structural* limits: those corollaries of the separation of powers which both recognize and limit congressional freedom of action; and the principles of federalism from which the Supreme Court has at least occasionally derived judicially enforceable constraints on congressional authority in order to protect state sovereignty.

Unavoidably, this chapter will focus on Supreme Court decisions and the doctrines those decisions suggest. This might suggest that the Constitution's meaning is revealed only in adjudication, and that the Constitution is without force except to the extent that courts enforce it. Clearly, however, Congress is bound by its oath to look to the Constitution in the course of legislating, and is free to formulate its own conclusions as to what the Constitution requires; even if the Supreme Court cannot or will not develop interpretations which limit the scope of the Constitution's grants of power to Congress, the political processes through which Congress reaches its conclusions, as well as custom and tradition, may fix limits on congressional power no less real simply because they cannot be found on the pages of the United States Reports. This chapter seeks to describe what the Supreme Court sees; but what the Court sees—and says—is not all there is.

§ 5–2. The Doctrine of Enumerated Powers

Although the delegates to the Constitutional Convention seriously considered describing the scope of congressional authority in a simple, inclusive statement of national legislative power,[1] the final version instead followed the format of article IX of the Articles of Confederation by specifically enumerating the powers granted to the national government.[2] The Constitution, in granting congressional power, thus simultaneously limits it: *an act of Congress is invalid unless it is affirmatively authorized under the Constitution.*[3] State actions, in contrast, are valid as a matter of federal constitutional law unless *prohibited*, explicitly or implicitly, by the Constitution. The tenth amendment makes the doctrine of enumerated powers an explicit part of the Constitution: "The powers not delegated to the United States by the Constitution, nor prohibited by it to the States, are reserved to the States respectively, or to the people."[4]

The chief powers of Congress are listed in article I, § 8. This section grants Congress the power, among other things, to levy taxes; to make expenditures for national defense and the general welfare; to borrow money; to regulate interstate and foreign commerce; to establish national rules regarding naturalization and bankruptcy; to coin and regulate currency, and punish counterfeiting; to establish post offices and roads; to grant patents and copyrights; to establish lower federal courts; to declare war, support armies and a navy, establish military law, and provide for a national militia; and to govern the District of Columbia and all federal enclaves and establishments.

Other sections of the 1787 Constitution grant Congress certain powers in addition to those granted by article I, § 8. In addition to requiring that "Full Faith and Credit shall be given in each State to the public Acts, Records, and judicial Proceedings of every other State," article IV, § 1, provides that "Congress may by general laws prescribe the Manner in which such Acts, Records and Proceedings shall be proved, and the Effect thereof."[5]

§ 5–2

1. The delegates at the Convention voted twice for a simple description such as that embodied in the Virginia Plan: ". . . the National Legislature ought to be empowered to enjoy the Legislative Rights vested in Congress by the Confederation, and moreover to legislate in all cases to which the separate states are incompetent, or in which the harmony of the United States may be interrupted by the exercise of individual Legislation." See 1 M. Farrand, Records of the Federal Convention of 1787, 53 (1911).

2. The most significant delegations of national power not contained in Article IX were the grants of the power to tax and the power to regulate interstate and foreign commerce, powers whose absence in the central government had been widely blamed for the failures of the Articles of Confederation.

3. The fact that no single state may have effective power to deal with a problem does not of itself extend congressional power beyond that granted by the Constitution. See Kansas v. Colorado, 206 U.S. 46 (1907) (mere fact that state lacks power to reclaim arid land beyond its borders does not give Congress that power).

4. Note the contrast between the current tenth amendment and the reservation of powers to the states contained in Article IX of the Articles of Confederation under which the states retained "every power, jurisdiction and right, which is not by this confederation *expressly* delegated to the United States." (emphasis added). See § 5–3, infra.

5. Acting under the full faith and credit clause and article III, Congress has enacted a law that not only establishes a requirement that legislation, records, and judicial decisions be authenticated before being ex-

Article IV, § 3, provides that "New States may be admitted by the Congress into this Union . . . ." However, this power is limited by a guarantee of territorial integrity to existing states: "No new States shall be formed or erected within the Jurisdiction of any other State . . . without the Consent of the Legislatures of the States concerned. . . ." [6] And the power to admit new states may not be invoked so as to condition a state's admission into the Union upon compliance with a substantive congressional directive that unduly limits the state's autonomy.[7] Article IV, § 3 also provides that "Con-

tended full faith and credit, but also imposes upon federal courts the same full faith and credit obligation that article IV, § 1, had imposed upon state courts. See 28 U.S.C. § 1738. The Supreme Court has held that, because this statute in effect requires federal courts to treat state courts as equals, a complementary obligation devolves upon state courts to grant res judicata effect to federal decisions. See Stoll v. Gottlieb, 305 U.S. 165, 170 (1938).

6. Note also the article V limitation on the power, even by constitutional amendment, to disenfranchise any state: ". . . no State, without its Consent, shall be deprived of its equal Suffrage in the Senate." And note the guarantee of the second amendment: "a well regulated Militia being necessary to the security of a free State, the right of the people to keep and bear Arms shall not be infringed." The congressional debates, see I Annals of Congress 750 (1789), indicate that the central concern of the second amendment's framers was to prevent such federal interferences with the state militia as would permit the establishment of a standing national army and the consequent destruction of local autonomy. Thus the inapplicability of the second amendment to purely private conduct, United States v. Cruikshank, 92 U.S. 542, 553 (1876), to state action, Presser v. Illinois, 116 U.S. 252, 265 (1886), to congressional firearms controls not shown to interfere with the preservation of state militia, United States v. Miller, 307 U.S. 174 (1939), and to gun control generally comports with the narrowly limited aim of the amendment as ancillary to other constitutional guarantees of state sovereignty.

The Court has cited Miller for the proposition that Congress is free to prohibit gun ownership provided it does not impair a state's ability to have a militia—i.e., a national guard unit, as we now think of it. See Lewis v. United States, 445 U.S. 55, 65 n. 8 (1980) (upholding congressional ban on ownership by a convicted felon of any firearm that had been in interstate commerce). On this "states' rights" view of the second amendment, it seems unlikely that the Court's 1886 refusal in Presser to "incorporate" that amendment into the

fourteenth as a protection of privacy or of individual self-protection would be revised as part of the trend (see Chapter 11, infra) toward incorporating bill of rights provisions earlier deemed inapplicable to the states. Accord, Quilici v. Morton Grove, 695 F.2d 261 (7th Cir. 1982) (upholding city ban on all hand guns as consistent with due process, and holding second amendment irrelevant), cert. denied 464 U.S. 863 (1983).

To be sure, the debates surrounding congressional approval of the second amendment do contain references to individual self-protection as well as to states' rights, and Congress did vote against a motion to qualify the "right to bear arms" with the phrase "for the common defense," see J. Goebel, Antecedents and Beginnings to 1801, 1 History of the Supreme Court of the United States 249 (P. Freund ed. 1971). But the nearly unique inclusion of a purposive preamble—the only other such language appears in the copyright clause of article I, § 8, cl. 8—strongly supports the view that "the framers and ratifiers . . . opted against leaving to the future the attribution of [other] purposes" to the second amendment, J. Ely, Democracy and Distrust 95 (1980), "choosing instead explicitly to legislate the goal in terms of which the provision was to be interpreted." Id. Thus, even if the homespun character of the "militia" in colonial times might otherwise support a less exclusively states'-rights focus in construing this right, and even if an individual-rights focus were otherwise supportable, see Kates, "Handgun Prohibition and the Original Meaning of the Second Amendment," 82 Mich.L.Rev. 204 (1983), the use in the amendment's preamble of the qualifying phrase "well regulated" makes any invocation of the amendment as a restriction on state or local gun control measures extremely problematic. See J. Ely, supra, at 227 n. 76.

7. See Coyle v. Smith, 221 U.S. 559 (1911) (1910 Oklahoma law removing the state's capital to Oklahoma City sustained despite federal law purporting to condition Oklahoma's admission to the Union on proviso that the state capital remain at Guthrie until 1913).

gress shall have Power to dispose of and make all needful Rules and Regulations respecting the Territory or other Property belonging to the United States. . . ."

Article V gives Congress the central role in the process by which constitutional amendments are proposed and ratified; that process is considered in Chapter 3.

A number of constitutional amendments also grant affirmative authority to Congress. Under the sixteenth amendment, for example, Congress is granted power "to lay and collect taxes on incomes, from whatever source derived, without apportionment among the several States, and without regard to any census or enumeration." [8] Several constitutional amendments recognizing individual rights authorize Congress to enforce their provisions through "appropriate legislation." The rights Congress is thereby empowered to enforce include the right to be free from slavery or involuntary servitude, except as a punishment for crime, established by the thirteenth amendment; the rights to enjoy the privileges or immunities of national citizenship, due process of law, and equal protection of the laws, established by the fourteenth amendment; the right not to be deprived of the vote on account of race, color, or previous condition of servitude, established by the fifteenth amendment; the right not to be deprived of the vote on account of sex, established by the nineteenth amendment; the right of residents of the District of Columbia to participate in presidential and vice-presidential elections, established by the twenty-third amendment; the right not to be deprived of the vote in federal elections on account of failure to pay any poll tax or other tax, established by the twenty-fourth amendment; and the right not to be deprived of the vote on account of age (if the voter is eighteen years of age or older), established by the twenty-sixth amendment.[9]

§ 5–3. The Doctrine of Implied Powers: All Laws Which Shall Be "Necessary and Proper"

In addition to listing the primary powers of Congress, Article I, § 8 also empowers Congress to "make all Laws which shall be necessary and proper for carrying into Execution" both the specific legislative powers granted to Congress by Article I, § 8 itself, and "all other Powers vested by this Constitution in the Government of the United States, or in any Department or Officer thereof." In one sense, the necessary and proper clause may be superfluous. As James Madison noted in the 44th Federalist: [1] "Had the Constitution been silent on this head, there can be no doubt that all the particular powers requisite as means of executing the general powers would have resulted to the

8. Although article I, § 8 gives Congress the power to lay and collect taxes, an income tax was held to be a "direct" tax and thus was required by § 8 to be apportioned among the states according to population. See Pollock v. Farmers' Loan & Trust Co., 157 U.S. 429 (1895) (income tax of 2% on individual and corporate incomes held unconstitutional). The sixteenth amendment was passed and ratified in 1913 to dispense with the requirement of apportionment.

9. See §§ 5–12 through 5–15, infra.

§ 5–3

1. The Federalist No. 44, at 285 (C. Rossiter ed. 1961) (Madison).

government by unavoidable implication. No axiom is more clearly established in law, or in reason, than that wherever the end is required, the means are authorized; wherever a general power to do a thing is given, every particular power necessary for doing it is included." But it is by no means a certainty that this view would have prevailed. And, even if the necessary and proper clause is structurally unnecessary, it remains important as an explicit incorporation within the language of the Constitution of the doctrine of implied power: *The exercise by Congress of power ancillary to an enumerated source of national authority is constitutionally valid, so long as the ancillary power does not conflict with external limitations such as those of the Bill of Rights and of federalism.* Moreover, the necessary and proper clause provided a focus for one of the great debates of early constitutional law—the controversy over the standard for judging whether an asserted congressional power is in fact "implied" by the Constitution.

The contours of the debate were drawn definitively in the 1790–91 dispute between Thomas Jefferson, then Secretary of State, and Alexander Hamilton, then Secretary of the Treasury, over the constitutionality of the bill creating the first Bank of the United States. Jefferson held that the Constitution allows Congress to exercise only those implied powers that are *necessary* for the effectuation of enumerated federal powers. If Congress were allowed the power to enact laws merely *convenient* to the exercise of enumerated powers, Congress' implied power "would swallow up all the delegated powers, and reduce the whole to one power"—a result inconsistent with the constitutional scheme.[2] Jefferson thus defined as "necessary" only those implied powers—those means to the enumerated constitutional ends—without which the explicit grants of power would be nugatory. Hamilton, in contrast, argued that "[t]he only question must be . . . whether the means to be employed . . . has a natural relation to any of the acknowledged objects or lawful ends of the government."[3] The Jefferson-Hamilton dispute was thus in form a disagreement over a definition of terms: whether "necessary" meant "absolutely or indispensably necessary," or meant only that the means must be "needful, incidental, useful, or conducive to" an expressly delegated end of power.

Hamilton's view ultimately prevailed. In *McCulloch v. Maryland*[4] the Court upheld the power of Congress to charter a second Bank of the United States, in an opinion by Chief Justice Marshall authoritatively construing the necessary and proper clause[5] and thus the basic limits of implied congressional power: "Let the end be legitimate, let it be

2. G. Gunther, Constitutional Law 101 (1975).

3. Id.

4. 17 U.S. (4 Wheat.) 316 (1819).

5. Marshall, like Madison, did not regard the necessary and proper clause as the source of the implied congressional power recognized in McCulloch: "A reasonably careful reading shows that Marshall does not place principal reliance on [the Necessary and Proper Clause] as a ground of decision; that before he reaches it he has already decided, on the basis of far more general implications, that Congress possesses the power, not expressly named, of establishing a bank and (chartering corporations; that he addresses himself to the necessary and proper clause only in response to counsel's arguing its restrictive force . . . .)". C. Black, Structure and Relationship in Constitutional Law 14 (1969).

within the scope of the constitution, and all means which are appropriate, which are plainly adapted to that end, which are not prohibited, but consistent with the letter and spirit of the constitution, are constitutional." [6] Marshall rested this interpretation in part upon separation-of-powers principles: "[W]here the law is not prohibited, and is really calculated to effect any of the objects entrusted to the government, to undertake here to inquire into the degree of its necessity, would be to pass the line which circumscribes the judicial department, and to tread on legislative ground." [7]

In *McCulloch*, Chief Justice Marshall spoke not only of a required nexus between means and ends, but also of a requirement that Congress not abuse its authority by enacting laws beyond its constitutionally entrusted powers "under the pretext" of exercising powers actually granted to it.[8] In subsequent years, however, the Supreme Court has ordinarily refused to inquire into a statute's "real" purposes or its drafters' "true" motives when inquiring into Congress' affirmative authority to enact the statute—so long as it can rationally be thought to promote legitimate ends that Congress might have been pursuing.[9]

6. 17 U.S. (4 Wheat.) at 421. Marshall had made a similar point in an earlier decision: "Congress must possess the choice of means, and must be empowered to use any means which are in fact conducive to the exercise of a power granted by the constitution." United States v. Fisher, 6 U.S. (2 Cranch) 358, 396 (1805) (upholding a law giving debts owed to the United States priority in insolvency cases).

7. 17 U.S. (4 Wheat.) at 423. Marshall's decision in McCulloch was attacked by some of his contemporaries, most prominently Judge Spencer Roane of Virginia, as a threat to states' rights. Marshall responded to the attacks in a series of nine essays published under the pseudonym, "A Friend of the Constitution." See G. Gunther, John Marshall's Defense of McCulloch v. Maryland (1969).

The spiritual heirs of Marshall's opponents included a majority of the Justices during the Lochner era. In striking down a child labor prohibition in Hammer v. Dagenhart, 247 U.S. 251, 275 (1918), Justice Day wrote for the Court: "In interpreting the Constitution, it must never be forgotten that the Nation is made up of States to which are entrusted the powers of local government. And to them and to the people the powers not *expressly* delegated to the National Government are reserved." (emphasis added). This passage plainly misstates the words—as well as the meaning—of the tenth amendment. Article IX of the Articles of Confederation *did* reserve to the states all powers not "expressly" delegated to the national government, but the tenth amendment deliberately omitted any requirement of an *express* articulation of the national government's powers. For

further discussion of Hammer, see § 5–6 infra.

8. See 17 U.S. (4 Wheat.) at 423.

9. See e.g., United States v. Darby, 312 U.S. 100, 115 (1941) ("The motive and purpose of a regulation of interstate commerce are matters for the legislative judgment upon the exercise of which the Constitution places no restriction and over which the courts are given no control"). The reasons for this refusal were canvassed in Chief Justice Warren's majority opinion in United States v. O'Brien: "Inquiries into congressional motives or purposes are a hazardous matter. . . . What motivates one legislator to make a speech about a statute is not necessarily what motivates scores of others to enact it, and the stakes are sufficiently high for us to eschew guesswork. We decline to void essentially on the ground that it is unwise legislation which Congress had the undoubted power to enact and which could be reenacted in its exact form if the same or another legislator made a 'wiser' speech about it." 391 U.S. 367, 383–84 (1968).

The Court's reluctance to inquire into Congress' actual reasons for passing a particular statute found one of its most extreme incarnations in United States Railroad Retirement Bd. v. Fritz, 449 U.S. 166 (1980). The Railroad Retirement Act of 1974 had phased out certain benefits to which many workers had been previously entitled. The district court found—and the Supreme Court did not seriously dispute—that Fritz and his colleagues had been short-changed by a Congress that *had no idea* that it was depriving *any* class of retirees of earned and promised benefits. Thus, there was every reason to believe

If one legislative end is proper, the fact that other ends not within the enumerated powers of Congress might *also* be achieved through the legislation does not invalidate the derivative exercise of an enumerated power. Motive is frequently of greater relevance in assessing whether legislation or administrative action that is concededly within the *affirmative* reach of government's power transgresses some *prohibition* on how such power is to be exercised.[10]

Chief Justice Marshall's standard for judging the scope of the implied power of Congress—permitting Congress to employ all means not prohibited by the Constitution and rationally related to ends within the compass of constitutionally enumerated national powers—is the primary standard for judicial review of legislative action. Modified slightly, it frames judicial inquiry under many constitutional provisions in addition to the necessary and proper clause.[11] But Marshall's rational connection requirement, although primary, is not definitive: *it sets a minimum standard only*; in many circumstances, legislation must pass more rigorous tests in order to survive constitutional challenge.[12]

that the law was simply an accident— neither a deliberate legislative approximation of a dividing line, nor a well-informed policy decision by Congress to aid one group at the expense of another. See id. at 188–89 (Brennan, J., dissenting). Justice Rehnquist's opinion for the seven-member majority, however, upheld the scheme against an equal protection challenge, see § 16–3, infra, and went so far as to say that the *real* facts and reasons behind the Act were constitutionally irrelevant. As Justice Rehnquist put the matter for the Court, "the plain language of the [statute] marks the beginning and end of our inquiry." 449 U.S. at 176 (footnote omitted). Writing for the majority, Justice Rehnquist rejected "the District Court's conclusion that Congress was unaware of what it accomplished or . . . was misled by the groups that appeared before it," id. at 179, *not* on the basis that this conclusion was ill-founded but out of concern that applying "this test . . . literally to every member of any legislature" would leave "very few laws" standing. Id. See § 17–3, infra.

10. It has been forcefully argued, for example, that judicial inquiry into motive is proper in contexts where governmental choices are properly either random or discretionary, and thus in which the rational connection of McCulloch is inapposite because invariably confirmatory of legislative power. See Ely, Legislative and Administrative Motivation in Constitutional Law, 79 Yale L.J. 1205 (1970). In Professor Ely's scheme, a showing of an improper motive (for example, a desire to suppress speech protected by the first amendment), where government's obligation is measured

by a duty to act randomly, or to exercise a discretion unaffected by constitutionally proscribed considerations (such as race), would shift to government the burden of proof to demonstrate that the challenged legislative action was rationally connected to a legitimate objective. See id. at 1269. Cf. Brest, Palmer v. Thompson: An Approach to the Problem of Unconstitutional Legislative Motive, 1971 Sup.Ct.Rev. 95 (demonstrated motive should be judged by the same standard as an explicit legislative criterion would be); but cf. Ely, supra, at 1262. The Supreme Court has itself acknowledged the need for motive analysis in the establishment clause context, see Epperson v. Arkansas, 393 U.S. 97 (1968); in the uniformity clause context, see United States v. Ptasynski, 462 U.S. 74, 84–86 (1983); and in situations where the due process clause, see Kennedy v. Mendoza-Martinez, 372 U.S. 144 (1963), the bill of attainder clause, see Flemming v. Nestor, 363 U.S. 603 (1960), or the fifteenth amendment, see Gomillion v. Lightfoot, 364 U.S. 339 (1960), require an inquiry into Congress' possible punitive intent, or into a state's possible intention to impair voting opportunities "on account of race, color, or previous condition of servitude." See also §§ 12–5 to 12–6 (relevance of motive in first amendment cases), § 16–20 (relevance of motive in equal protection cases), infra.

11. See, e.g., Chapters 6 (negative implications of commerce clause), 8 (due process), and 16 (equal protection), infra.

12. See, e.g., Chapters 11 (preferred rights) and 16 (equal protection), infra.

The necessary and proper clause attaches not only to the enumerated congressional powers of Article I, § 8, but also to "all other Powers vested by this Constitution in the Government of the United States, or in any Department or Officer thereof." Thus it broadens the legitimate ends of congressional action well beyond those ancillary to the explicit legislative grants of Article I. For example, although the Constitution does not grant express power to Congress to legislate concerning admiralty and maritime matters, Congress has constitutional authority to enact such legislation: Article III, § 2, extends the federal judicial power to "all cases of admiralty and maritime jurisdiction," and the Supreme Court has held that the legislative power "is co-extensive . . . ." [13]

Finally, certain peripheral congressional powers, plainly legitimate but not easily classified under the usual heads of federal legislative authority, are said to "result from," or to be implied by, the aggregate

13. In re Garnett, 141 U.S. 1, 12 (1891). At least at the start of the 19th century, federal judicial power to develop the law of admiralty, let alone congressional power to change judge-made law, was far from settled. For an account of the prestidigitatious process through which the Supreme Court developed first judicial power and then congressional power, see Note, "From Judicial Grant to Legislative Power: The Admiralty Clause in the Nineteenth Century," 67 Harv.L.Rev. 1214 (1954).

The apparently changing nature of constitutional limits on congressional admiralty power reveals in microcosm a master theme of this chapter: the decline of limits on congressional power which the Supreme Court implies from the constitutional grants of power themselves, and the consequent rise in the Court's deference to Congress' judgments as to the limits of its own affirmative authority. For a substantial period, the Court confidently accepted the proposition that the constitutional grant of admiralty jurisdiction placed limits on Congress' ancillary powers to legislate within the scope of that jurisdiction. "[I]n amending and revising the maritime law the Congress necessarily acts within a sphere restricted by the concept of the admiralty and maritime jurisdiction." Detroit Trust Co. v. Barlum S.S. Co., 293 U.S. 21, 44 (1934). "[T]he judicial power, which among other things, extends to all cases of admiralty and maritime jurisdiction, was conferred upon the Federal government by the Constitution, and Congress cannot enlarge it. . . ." The Belfast, 74 U.S. (7 Wall.) 624, 641 (1869). For example, the Court understood the chief impulse underlying the Constitution's grant of admiralty jurisdiction to the federal courts to be the need for uniformity, see, e.g., The Genesee Chief, 53 U.S. (12 How.) 443, 453–454 (1852); accordingly, the Court implied a

requirement of uniformity limiting Congress' exercise of its admiralty power. See, e.g., Knickerbocker Ice Co. v. Stewart, 253 U.S. 149, 164 (1920) (Congress cannot authorize federal courts to apply state workmens' compensation laws in cases arising in admiralty). In recent years, however, the Court has not questioned the power of Congress to "[extend] admiralty jurisdiction beyond the boundaries contemplated by the Framers," Askew v. American Waterways Operators, 411 U.S. 325, 341 (1973), and has cast doubt upon the continued validity of Knickerbocker Ice by holding that, within the areas of congressional extension, state legislation is not preempted insofar as it does not actually conflict with congressional regulation. See id. at 343 (upholding state environmental regulation of sea-to-shore pollution).

Formally, of course, congressional power—even now—is not without judicially enforceable limits: presumably, the McCulloch rationality standard constrains congressional interpretations of the scope of admiralty, and presumably there are some interpretations which would be so far removed from traditional conceptions of admiralty as to fail that test. Moreover, at least for the moment, Knickerbocker Ice is not, to borrow an apt phrase, "a derelict on the waters of the law": in Askew, the Court confined Knickerbocker Ice "to [its] facts," 411 U.S. at 344, but in so doing acknowledged its application "to suits relating to the relationship of vessels, plying the high seas and our navigable waters, and to their crews." Id. at 344.

A full description of the present extent of federal admiralty jurisdiction, legislative and judicial, is beyond the scope of this book. See G. Gilmore & C. Black, The Law of Admiralty (2d ed. 1975).

of national powers and the "nature of a political society"—for example, the power to authorize construction of national monuments. Other governmental powers, typically shared by Congress and the Executive, have been held to be "inherently inseparable from the conception of nationality," [14] and thus do not "depend upon the affirmative grant of the Constitution." [15] The chief example of an inherent federal power is the power to conduct foreign affairs. The division of responsibility between Congress and the Executive in the exercise of this power was discussed in Chapter 4. It should be noted here, however, that while the doctrine of inherent power may largely free Congress from the usual internal limits on the scope of its power in the foreign affairs field,[16] this doctrine does not free Congress, even in the realm of foreign affairs, from such external constraints as those of the Bill of Rights.[17]

§ 5–4. The Power to Regulate Interstate Commerce: Decline and Rebirth of the "Substantial Economic Effect" Principle

Article I, § 8, gives Congress the authority to "regulate Commerce . . . among the several states." [1] The commerce clause is both the

14. United States v. Curtiss-Wright Export Co., 299 U.S. 304, 318 (1936), discussed in Chapter 4, supra.

15. Id. at 318.

16. See United States v. Curtiss-Wright Export Co., 299 U.S. 304, 321–22 (1936) (Congress permitted to delegate broader responsibilities to Executive Branch in foreign affairs context than in domestic matters), discussed in § 4–2 supra.

17. See Reid v. Covert, 354 U.S. 1 (1957).

§ 5–4

1. The Commerce Clause also grants Congress power to "regulate Commerce with foreign Nations, . . . and with the Indian Tribes." Congressional power to regulate foreign commerce has traditionally been broadly construed to encompass all "transactions which either immediately, or at some stage of their progress, must be extraterritorial." Veazie v. Moor, 55 U.S. (14 How.) 568, 573 (1852). "Foreign commerce", for example, has been held to include shipment by sea from one port to another in the same state. See Lord v. Goodall Steamship Co., 102 U.S. (12 Otto) 541 (1880). Although the regulation of foreign commerce has been called "necessarily national in its character," id. at 544, not all state regulation of foreign commerce is necessarily preempted. See § 6–21, infra. Finally, the power of Congress to regulate commerce with Indian tribes has been rendered partly superfluous by the Supreme Court's extension of the treaty power to encompass federal treaties with Indian tribes, Worcester v. Georgia, 31 U.S. (6 Pet.) 515 (1832); Holden v. Joy, 84 U.S. (17 Wall.) 211, 242 (1872); Williams

v. Lee, 358 U.S. 217, 219 n. 4 (1959), and by the Court's recognition of an inherent federal power to govern Indian affairs. See United States v. Kagama, 118 U.S. 375, 384 (1886), a power in some respects limited but in most respects augmented by the recognition of "Indian tribes [as] unique aggregations possessing attributes of sovereignty over both their members and their territory," United States v. Mazurie, 419 U.S. 544, 557 (1975) (upholding congressional delegation to Indian tribes, with approval of Secretary of the Interior, of power to regulate the introduction of liquor into Indian country in conformity with state laws).

For example, the Court has held that "Indian tribes are prohibited from exercising both those powers of autonomous states that are expressly terminated by Congress and those powers 'inconsistent with their status'." Oliphant v. Suquamish Indian Tribe, 435 U.S. 191 (1978) (Indian tribe's criminal jurisdiction over non-Indians must come from affirmative congressional authorization or treaty provision, not from its "retained inherent powers") (citation omitted) (emphasis omitted). See also, e.g., Washington v. Yakima Indian Nation, 439 U.S. 463, 500–501 (1979) ("It is settled that 'the unique legal status of Indian tribes under federal law' permits the Federal Government to enact legislation singling out tribal Indians, legislation that might otherwise be constitutionally offensive . . . It is well established that Congress, in the exercise of its plenary power over Indian affairs, may restrict the retained sovereign powers of the Indian tribes.") (citations omitted). For a fuller discussion of federal control of Indians see Newton,

chief source of congressional regulatory power and, implicitly, a limitation on state legislative power. This section and §§ 5–5 through 5–8 consider the commerce clause as a grant of congressional power; the implied limits imposed on state action by the commerce clause are the major topic of Chapter 6.

The scope of the power the commerce clause delegates to Congress was first suggested by Chief Justice Marshall in *Gibbons v. Ogden*.[2] The actual *holding* of *Gibbons* was a narrow one: a New York grant of a steamboat monopoly affecting navigation between New York and New Jersey conflicted with a federal statute licensing such interstate commerce and was therefore held void under the supremacy clause.[3] But, in an elaborate preliminary discussion, Marshall indicated that, in his view, congressional power to regulate "commercial intercourse" extended to all activity having any interstate impact—however indirect. Acting under the commerce clause, Congress could legislate with respect to all "commerce which concerns more states than one."[4] This power would be plenary: absolute within its sphere, subject only to the Constitution's affirmative prohibitions on the exercise of federal authority.[5]

Until Congress enacted the Interstate Commerce Act in 1887 and the Sherman Antitrust Act in 1890, commerce clause litigation only rarely involved the Supreme Court in the review of congressional action.[6] Most cases in the early period concerned the validity of state

Federal Power Over Indians: Its Sources, Scope and Limitations, 132 U.Pa.L.Rev. 195 (1984). For a general discussion of federal Indian law, see F. Cohen, Handbook of Federal Indian Law (1982 ed.); M. Price, Law and the American Indian (1973); U.S. Dept. of Interior, Federal Indian Law (1958). See also § 16–14, infra.

2. 22 U.S. (9 Wheat.) 1 (1824).

3. The holding of Gibbons is discussed in Chapter 6, infra.

4. 22 U.S. (9 Wheat.) at 194.

5. See id. at 196. "The wisdom and the discretion of Congress, their identity with the people, and the influence which their constituents possess at elections, are, in this, as in many other instances, . . . the sole restraints on . . . its abuse." Id. at 197.

6. The Supreme Court's commerce clause decisions after Gibbons but before passage of the Sherman Act reflect inconsistent doctrinal themes. On the one hand, some cases continue to suggest, with Gibbons, that the primary limits on congressional commerce power are legislative and political rather than judicial and constitutional. In United States v. Marigold, for example, the Court held that the power to regulate commerce—in this instance, foreign commerce—entailed the power to exclude commerce, and thus that Congress had the power to prohibit the importation of counterfeit coins: ". . . it can scarcely, at this day, be open to doubt, that every subject falling within the legitimate sphere of commercial regulation may be partially or wholly excluded, where either measure shall be demanded by the safety or by the important interests of the entire nation. . . . The power once conceded, it may operate on any and every subject of commerce to which the legislative discretion may apply it." 50 U.S. (9 How.) 560, 566–67 (1850). And in The Daniel Ball, 77 U.S. (10 Wall.) 557, 565 (1871), the Court held, over the objection that it was granting Congress limitless authority, that Congress could require the licensing of ships operating exclusively intrastate if the ships were involved in the transportation of goods ultimately destined for other states, or of goods originally brought from out of state: "The fact that several different and independent agencies are employed in transporting the commodity, some acting entirely in one State, and some acting through two or more States, does in no respect affect the character of the transaction. To the extent in which each agency acts in that transportation, it is subject to the regulation of Congress."

In other cases, however, the Supreme Court took early steps toward articulating the theory of dual sovereignty in the name of which it would later substantially limit the power granted Congress by the com-

action arguably conflicting with "dormant" congressional power.[7] From 1887 to 1937, however, the Supreme Court was repeatedly required to judge the limits of congressional power.[8] The view of the commerce clause developed by the Court during this period contrasted sharply with the approach of Marshall in *Gibbons v. Ogden*. In place of the empirical test suggested in *Gibbons*, the Court substituted a formal

merce clause. An Act of Congress was, for the first time, held to be beyond the power granted by the commerce clause in United States v. DeWitt, 76 U.S. (9 Wall.) 41 (1870). Congress had prohibited all sales of naptha and illuminating oils inflammable at less than 110 degrees fahrenheit. Arguing that "this express grant of power to regulate commerce among the States has always been understood . . . as a virtual denial of any power to interfere with the internal trade and business of the separate States," id. at 43–44, Chief Justice Chase, writing for a unanimous Supreme Court, concluded that the law was "a police regulation, relating exclusively to the internal trade of the States," and thus that it could "only have effect where the legislative authority of Congress excludes, territorially, all State legislation, as for example, in the District of Columbia." Id. at 45. Nine years later, in the Trade-Mark Cases, 100 U.S. 82 (1879), the Court again held that Congress had exceeded its commerce power, this time in setting up a trademark registration scheme. Justice Miller's opinion for an again unanimous Supreme Court found it unnecessary to define the exact limits of congressional power under the commerce clause, since the "broad purpose" of the statute in question "was to establish a universal system of trade-mark registration," id. at 98, and since, "if it be apparent" that a statute "is designed to govern the commerce wholly between citizens of the same state, it is obviously the exercise of a power not confided to Congress." Id. at 96–97.

The Trade-Mark Cases are notable in part because of Justice Miller's expressed reluctance to find that Congress was attempting to exercise its commerce power inasmuch as Congress had not *said* it was making such an attempt.

An otherwise valid exercise of congressional authority is not, of course, invalidated if Congress happens to recite the wrong clause of article I as the source of its power—or, indeed, if Congress recites no clause at all. See, e.g., Woods v. Cloyd W. Miller Co., 333 U.S. 138, 144 (1948) ("The question of the constitutionality of action taken by Congress does not depend on recitals of the power which it undertakes to exercise").

On the other hand, an otherwise invalid exercise of congressional authority—e.g., a law dealing with the relationship between

a particular debtor and its creditors, and hence violating the uniformity requirement applicable to bankruptcy laws (see § 5–11, infra)—cannot be saved by invoking a clause that does not contain the stricture rendering that exercise invalid. See, e.g., Railway Labor Executives' Ass'n v. Gibbons, 455 U.S. 457, 468–69 (1982) ("if we were to hold that Congress had the power to enact nonuniform bankruptcy laws pursuant to the Commerce Clause, we would eradicate from the Constitution a limitation on the power of Congress to enact bankruptcy laws"), discussed in § 5–11, infra, at note 4.

For discussions of early Supreme Court decisions concerning congressional power under the commerce clause, see F. Ribble, State and National Power Over Commerce 61–65 (1937); G. Reynolds, The Distribution of Power to Regulate Interstate Carriers Between the Nation and the States 59–76 (1928).

7. See Chapter 6, infra.

8. This half-century is usually remembered as one in which the Court repeatedly struck down congressional action as unauthorized under the commerce clause. In fact, the Supreme Court held on only eight occasions prior to 1937—and only once since that time—that Congress had exceeded the limits of its commerce power. See In re Heff, 197 U.S. 488 (1905); The Employers' Liability Cases, 207 U.S. 463 (1908); Adair v. United States, 208 U.S. 161 (1908); Keller v. United States, 213 U.S. 138 (1909); Hammer v. Dagenhart, 247 U.S. 251 (1918); A.L.A. Schechter Poultry Corp. v. United States, 295 U.S. 495 (1935); Railroad Retirement Board v. Alton R.R. Co., 295 U.S. 330 (1935); Carter v. Carter Coal Co., 298 U.S. 238 (1936); National League of Cities v. Usery, 426 U.S. 833 (1976), discussed in § 5–22, infra. See also Ashton v. Cameron County Dist., 298 U.S. 513 (1936) (exceeding limits of bankruptcy power); United States v. Butler, 297 U.S. 1 (1936) (exceeding limits of spending power); Panama Refining Co. v. Ryan, 293 U.S. 388 (1935) (excessive delegation to executive); Pollock v. Farmers' Loan & Trust Co., 157 U.S. 429 (1895) (exceeding limits of taxing power). Of course, the relative paucity of such cases could easily understate their total impact whether on lower courts or on the Congress itself.

classification of economic activity far more restrictive of congressional power. This classification, for example, distinguished "commerce" from "mining" and "manufacturing," denying Congress the power to regulate the latter activities even if the *products* of those activities would subsequently enter "interstate commerce." [9]

Despite the narrow formalism of its doctrine, the Supreme Court of this era occasionally ratified important congressional exercises of the commerce power. In the *Shreveport Rate Case*, for example, the Court upheld the action of a congressional delegatee, the Interstate Commerce Commission, in regulating the rates of intrastate railroads in competition with interstate railroads. Justice Hughes reasoned that the power of Congress to regulate the rates of interstate railroads included the power "to control . . . all matters having such a close and substantial relation to interstate traffic that the control is essential or appropriate to the security of that traffic, to the efficiency of the interstate service, and to the maintenance of conditions under which interstate commerce may be conducted upon fair terms and without molestation or hindrance." [10]

Such willingness on the part of the pre-1937 Supreme Court to see the interconnectedness of formally interstate and intrastate activities was unusual. The Great Depression conclusively established for many Americans the interdependence of economic factors and the mutability of traditional economic relationships. [11] Until 1937, however, a majority of the Court stood by the formal distinctions drawn by its traditional doctrines, holding in the process that the commerce clause did not authorize several important pieces of New Deal legislation. [12] But with

9. For example, in United States v. E. C. Knight Co., 156 U.S. 1 (1895), the Supreme Court construed the Sherman Anti-Trust Act, in light of constitutional principles, not to reach stock purchases by which the American Sugar Refining Co. had acquired nearly complete control of the manufacture of refined sugar within the United States. "Commerce succeeds to manufacture, and is not part of it." Id. at 12. The Court's distinction between "commerce" and "manufacture" reflected a perceived need to preserve a distinction between the "essentially exclusive" police power of the states and the "also exclusive" power of Congress to regulate interstate commerce. Id. at 11. "It is vital that the independence of the commercial power and of the police power, and the delimitation between them, however sometimes perplexing, should always be recognized and observed, for while the one furnishes the strongest bond of union, the other is essential to the preservation of the autonomy of the States as required by our dual form of government . . . ." Id. at 13. Although direct restraints on interstate commerce remained vulnerable to antitrust attack, see Addyston Pipe & Steel Co. v. United States, 175 U.S. 211 (1899); Northern Securities Co. v. United States, 193

U.S. 197 (1904), the E. C. Knight decision substantially weakened the force of the Sherman Act. However, in Swift & Co. v. United States, 196 U.S. 375 (1905), the Supreme Court to a degree revitalized the statute, holding that price fixing in livestock markets could be prohibited under the Sherman Act since the markets, although themselves each located in a single state, were part of "a current of commerce among the States . . . ." Id. at 399.

10. 234 U.S. 342, 351 (1914).

11. See § 8–6, infra.

12. See Railroad Retirement Board v. Alton R. R. Co., 295 U.S. 330 (1935) (holding unconstitutional a compulsory retirement and pension system for all interstate railroads in part because objectives of the pension scheme "have no reasonable relation to the business of interstate transportation"); A.L.A. Schechter Poultry Corp. v. United States, 295 U.S. 495 (1935) (provisions of National Industrial Recovery Act of 1933 held unconstitutional in part because activities regulated under Live Poultry Code authorized by NIRA took place after "the flow in interstate commerce had ceased" and because the effect of the regulated activities upon interstate commerce was "merely indirect"); Carter v. Carter

its watershed decision in *NLRB v. Jones & Laughlin Steel Corp.*,[13] the Court acceded to political pressure and to its own recognition of its doctrine's irrelevance and manipulability, abandoning the formally analytical approach to the commerce clause, and returning to Chief Justice Marshall's original empiricism.

Jones & Laughlin held that Congress could regulate labor relations at any manufacturing plant operated by an integrated manufacturing and interstate sales concern because a work stoppage at any such plant "would have a most serious effect upon interstate commerce." [14] Since 1937, in applying the factual test of *Jones & Laughlin* to hold a broad range of activities sufficiently related to interstate commerce to justify congressional action, the Supreme Court has exercised little independent judgment, choosing instead to defer to the expressed or implied findings of Congress to the effect that regulated activities have the requisite "substantial economic effect." Such "findings" have been upheld whenever they could be said to rest upon some rational basis.[15]

The "substantial economic effect" test makes irrelevant any determination of what is "in" or "out" of the "current of commerce." [16] An activity which takes place wholly intrastate may now be subjected to congressional regulation entirely because of the activity's impact in other states—regardless of whether the activity itself occurs before, during or after interstate movement.[17] Thus the Supreme Court has found the commerce power broad enough to encompass the extension of federal wage and hour protection to all workers in places producing goods for interstate commerce, whether or not the goods used or produced by any particular worker were themselves destined for such commerce.[18] "[T]here is a basis in logic and experience for the conclu-

Coal Co., 298 U.S. 238 (1936) (holding unconstitutional the bituminous Coal Conservation Act of 1935 in part because the Act regulated incidents "of production, not of trade").

13. 301 U.S. 1 (1937). For a definitive account of the doctrinal transformation initiated by Jones & Laughlin, see Stern, "The Commerce Clause and the National Economy," 59 Harv.L.Rev. 645–93, 883–947 (1946).

14. 301 U.S. at 41.

15. See, e.g., Heart of Atlanta Motel, Inc. v. United States, 379 U.S. 241, 258–59 (1964) (upholding power of Congress, exercised in Title II of the Civil Rights Act of 1964, to prohibit racial discrimination in places of public accommodation: "The only questions are: (1) whether Congress had a rational basis for finding that racial discrimination by motels affected commerce, and (2) if it had such a basis, whether the means it selected to eliminate that evil are reasonable and appropriate"); United States v. Wrightwood Dairy Co., 315 U.S. 110, 119 (1942) (upholding power of Congress to regulate marketing of milk produced and sold intrastate but in competition with milk marketed interstate: "The

commerce power . . . extends to those activities intrastate which so affect interstate commerce . . . as to make regulation of them appropriate means to the attainment of a legitimate end, the effective execution of the granted power to regulate interstate commerce. See McCulloch v. Maryland. . . .").

16. Contrast, e.g., Swift & Co. v. United States, 196 U.S. 375, 399 (1905).

17. See, e.g., United States v. Rock Royal Co-operative, Inc., 307 U.S. 533, 569 (1939) ("Activities conducted within State lines do not by this fact alone escape the sweep of the Commerce Clause. Interstate commerce may be dependent upon them"). Accord, Shreveport Rate Cases, 234 U.S. 342 (1914).

18. Maryland v. Wirtz, 392 U.S. 183 (1968). In National League of Cities v. Usery, 426 U.S. 833 (1976), the Supreme Court overruled a second holding in Wirtz, that Congress could properly regulate the wages and hours of *state* employees. See id. at 840. The National League of Cities Court, however, did not repudiate the Wirtz commerce clause analysis. See id. at 841. Rather, in National League of Cities, the Court found that, in regulating the

sion that substandard labor conditions among any group of employees, whether or not they are personally engaged in commerce or production, may lead to strife disrupting an entire enterprise." [19]

§ 5–5. Contemporary Commerce Clause Analysis: The "Cumulative Effect" Principle

It is now established that Congress has the power to regulate not only acts which taken *alone* would have substantial economic effect on interstate commerce, such as a steel industry work stoppage, but also acts which might reasonably be deemed nationally significant in their *aggregate* economic effect; the triviality of an *individual* act's impact is irrelevant so long as the *class* of such acts might reasonably be deemed to have substantial national consequences. The Supreme Court decision that established this principle was *Wickard v. Filburn,* holding that Congress could control a farmer's production of wheat for home consumption because the cumulative effect of home consumption of wheat by many farmers might reasonably be thought to alter the supply-and-demand relationships of the interstate commodity market.[1] "The maintenance by government regulation of a price for wheat undoubtedly can be accomplished as effectively by sustaining or increasing the demand as by limiting the supply. The effect of the statute before us is to restrict the amount which may be produced for market and the extent . . . to which one may forestall resort to the market by producing to meet his own needs. That appellee's own contribution to the demand for wheat may be trivial by itself is not enough to remove him from the scope of federal regulation where, as here, his contribution, taken together with that of many others similarly situated, is far from trivial."

In recent years, Congress has relied in part upon the "cumulative effect" principle as its constitutional justification for civil rights legislation,[2] certain criminal statutes,[3] regulatory measures affecting the sale of foods and additives,[4] and a registration law for drug producers.[5] In each case, congressional fact-findings stressed that the regulation of local incidents of an activity was necessary to abate a cumulative evil affecting national commerce.[6] The Supreme Court has without fail

wages and hours of state employees, Congress had impermissibly infringed upon state sovereignty, and accordingly violated an external, if implicit, limitation upon congressional power analogous to limits found in the Bill of Rights. That holding was in turn overruled in Garcia v. San Antonio Metropolitan Transit Authority, 469 U.S. 528 (1985). See § 5–22, infra.

19. Maryland v. Wirtz, 392 U.S. 183, 192 (1968).

§ 5–5

1. 317 U.S. 111, 127–28 (1942).

2. See, e.g., 42 U.S.C. § 2000a, upheld in Katzenbach v. McClung, 379 U.S. 294 (1964).

3. See, e.g., 18 U.S.C. § 1891 et seq., upheld in Perez v. United States, 402 U.S. 146 (1971).

4. See, e.g., 21 U.S.C. §§ 347, 347a (oleomargarine).

5. See 21 U.S.C. § 360; Public Law 87–781, Section 301 (1962).

6. Chief Justice Rehnquist has expressed his discomfort—if not outright disagreement—with the Court's willingness to accept Congress' word on a statute's connection to interstate commerce. In his opinion concurring in the judgment in Hodel v. Virginia Surface Mining & Reclamation Assn., Inc., 452 U.S. 264 (1981), he stated that "it would be a mistake to conclude that Congress' power to regulate pursuant to the Commerce Clause is unlimit-

given effect to such congressional findings. In *Katzenbach v. McClung*,[7] for example, the Court upheld the enforcement against a small restaurant of a congressional prohibition of racial discrimination, relying upon the combined effect of *all* such segregated restaurants in inhibiting the sale of interstate goods, obstructing interstate travel, and hindering the establishment of new businesses. Similarly, after Congress found that loan sharking in general substantially affected interstate commerce, the Court in *Perez v. United States* held that Congress could make criminal any of loan sharking's individual, purely intrastate, manifestations: "Where the class of activities is regulated and that class is within the reach of federal power, the courts have no power to excise, as trivial, individual instances of the class."[8]

§ 5–6. Contemporary Commerce Clause Analysis: The Power to Prohibit Interstate Commerce Under the "Protective" Principle

One permissible and particularly potent form of federal commerce regulation is the imposition of *protective conditions* on the privilege of engaging in an activity that affects interstate commerce or utilizes the channels or instrumentalities of such commerce. Although this principle suffered one early defeat,[1] it is now settled that Congress may

---

ed. Some activities may be so private or local in nature that they simply may not be *in* commerce. Nor is it sufficient that the person or activity reached have *some* nexus with interstate commerce." Id. at 310. Then, curiously, in light of his nearly total deference to congressional judgment in the equal protection context of United States Railroad Retirement Board v. Fritz, 449 U.S. 166 (1980), see § 5–3, supra, then Justice Rehnquist stated: "simply because Congress may conclude that a particular activity substantially affects interstate commerce does not necessarily make it so." 452 U.S. at 311. He concluded by stating that, in his view, the commerce power "does not reach activity which merely 'affects' interstate commerce. There must instead be a showing that a regulated activity has a *substantial effect* on that commerce." 452 U.S. at 312. Exactly what significance Chief Justice Rehnquist's more restrictive view of the commerce clause would have in application is unclear; in any event, none of his fellow Justices have shown any inclination to plow with him territory that the Court tilled so fruitlessly from 1887 to 1937.

7. 379 U.S. 294 (1964).

8. 402 U.S. 146, 154 (1971), quoting Maryland v. Wirtz, 392 U.S. 183, 193 (1968).

§ 5–6

1. In Hammer v. Dagenhart, 247 U.S. 251 (1918), the Supreme Court held that Congress could not prohibit interstate commerce in the products of child labor. Noting that the case was not one in which "the use of interstate transportation was necessary to the accomplishment of harmful results," id. at 271, Justice Day's majority opinion found that "[t]he act in its effect does not regulate transportation among the States, but aims to standardize the ages at which children may be employed in mining and manufacturing within the States," id. at 271–72, and thus invalidated the congressional action upon the then familiar ground that "[o]ver interstate transportation, or its incidents, the regulatory power of Congress is ample, but the production of articles, intended for interstate commerce, is a matter of local regulation." Id. at 272. See §§ 5–2, 5–3, supra. Justice Holmes dissented: "It is not for this Court to pronounce when prohibition is necessary to regulation if it ever may be necessary— to say that it is permissible as against strong drink but not as against the product of ruined lives." 247 U.S. at 280.

Hammer v. Dagenhart highlights the tension that existed between the Supreme Court's taxonomic approach to the commerce clause in the early 20th century—an approach grounded in the theory of dual sovereignty and sustained by a faith in the market as the proper mechanism for distributing wealth—and the increasingly undeniable consequences of economic interdependence. Arguing the Hammer case, Solicitor General John W. Davis demonstrated that the theoretical autonomy of the states was in this context practically meaningless: "The shipment of child-made goods outside of one State directly induces similar employment of children in compet-

impose whatever conditions it wishes, *so long as the conditions themselves violate no independent constitutional prohibition*, on the privilege of producing for, serving customers in, or otherwise "sitting astride the channels of," interstate commerce.

For example, despite dissenting views that congressional exercise of the commerce power should be confined to strictly "commercial" regulation, the Supreme Court has consistently upheld congressional use of "protective conditions" to combat activities disfavored for largely noncommercial reasons. For example, in *Champion v. Ames*,[2] the celebrated 1903 *Lottery Case*, the Court upheld the constitutionality of legislation banning the interstate transportation of lottery tickets. Title II of the Civil Rights Act of 1964 presents a more contemporary illustration of how, through use of the "protective principle", Congress may invoke the commerce clause to achieve ends not strictly commercial. Title II prohibits "discrimination or segregation on the ground of race, color, religion, or national origin" in the operation of "a place of public accommodation . . . if its operations affect commerce. . . ."[3] Although the Supreme Court noted congressional findings of "substantial economic effect" in affirming the constitutionality of Title II,[4] the congressional action could have been more straightforwardly justified along "protective principle" lines: Congress attached the nondiscrimination requirement as a valid condition on the privilege of serving travelers "in" interstate commerce.[5]

Legislation designed to regulate aspects of economic life not directly a part of interstate commerce may also take the form of "protective conditions." The Fair Labor Standards Act of 1938, for example, excluded from interstate commerce goods manufactured in plants

ing states. It is not enough to answer that each State theoretically may regulate conditions of manufacturing within its own borders. As Congress saw the situation, the States were not entirely free agents. For salutary statutes had been repealed, legislative action on their part had been defeated and postponed time and again, solely by reason of the argument (valid or not) that interstate competition would not be withstood." Id. at 256–57. For the Court to have accepted Davis' argument, it would have had to concede that the axioms of its doctrinal scheme were internally inconsistent and that state autonomy could be threatened by the market as well as by congressional action. The Court could not go so far in 1918, but it is clear from Justice Day's rhetoric that it knew it had been asked: "The far-reaching result of upholding the act cannot be more plainly indicated than by pointing out that if Congress can thus regulate matters intrusted to local authority by prohibition of the movement of commodities in interstate commerce, all freedom of commerce will be at an end, and the power of the states over local matters may be eliminated, and thus our system of government practically destroyed." Id. at 276. Hammer was overruled in United States v. Darby, 312 U.S. 100 (1941).

2. 188 U.S. 321 (1903). Following Champion v. Ames, Congress increasingly resorted to its power to exclude, and, except for Hammer v. Dagenhart, 247 U.S. 251 (1918), the Supreme Court approved the congressional action. See, e.g., Hipolite Egg Co. v. United States, 220 U.S. 45 (1911) (upholding ban on interstate transportation of impure food); Hoke v. United States, 227 U.S. 308 (1913) (upholding ban on interstate transportation of women for immoral purposes); Brooks v. United States, 267 U.S. 432 (1925) (upholding ban on interstate transportation of kidnap victims).

3. 42 U.S.C. § 2000a.

4. See Heart of Atlanta Motel v. United States, 379 U.S. 241 (1964); Katzenbach v. McClung, 379 U.S. 294 (1964).

5. See C. Black, Structure and Relationship in Constitutional Law 55–57 (1969).

whose employees' wages and hours did not meet federal standards.[6] In *United States v. Darby*, the Supreme Court affirmed the validity of Congress' exclusionary approach: "Congress, following its own conception of public policy concerning the restrictions which may appropriately be imposed on interstate commerce, is free to exclude from [such] commerce articles whose use in the states for which they are destined it may conceive to be injurious to the public health, morals, or welfare, even though the state has not sought to regulate their use."[7]

§ 5–7. Internal Limits on the Power of Congress to Regulate Interstate Commerce: The Politics of Federalism

The doctrinal rules courts currently employ to determine whether federal legislation is affirmatively authorized under the commerce clause do not themselves effectively limit the power of Congress. Even an activity so peculiarly "local" that its repeated performance cannot rationally be said to have a "substantial economic effect" in more than one state is theoretically open to congressional commerce regulation under the "protective principle" and the necessary and proper clause: entirely local performances of an activity may be prohibited as a rational means to the fair and effective exclusion of the activity or its incidents from interstate commerce.[1]

Congressional power under the commerce clause is nonetheless limited. All congressional exercises of legislative authority are, of course, subject to judicially enforceable external restrictions such as those of the Bill of Rights. But Congress is also subject to internal political restraints—restraints reinforced by the federal structure which the Constitution created and by the practices of courts called upon to interpret congressional action.[2]

---

6. The Fair Labor Standards Act of 1938 is currently codified as 29 U.S.C. § 200 et seq.

7. 312 U.S. 100, 114 (1941). Darby overruled Hammer v. Dagenhart, 247 U.S. 251 (1918).

A still more recent application of the protective principle came in Hodel v. Virginia Surface Mining & Reclamation Assn., Inc., 452 U.S. 264 (1981), where the Court upheld against a commerce clause challenge a federal program that required states either to adopt their own regulatory structure to control surface coal mining or to participate in a federal program. Justice Marshall's opinion for the Court stated: "Here, Congress rationally determined that regulation of surface coal mining is necessary to protect interstate commerce from adverse effects that may result from that activity. This Congressional finding is sufficient to sustain the Act as a valid exercise of Congress' power under the commerce clause." Id. at 281. In a companion case, Hodel v. Indiana, 452 U.S. 314 (1981), the Court gave similar reasons for upholding the statute's "prime farmland" provisions, which required property owners to

obtain permits if they wanted to open surface mines on certain lands traditionally used for raising crops.

§ 5–7

1. See, e.g., United States v. Sullivan, 332 U.S. 689 (1948) (upholding power of Congress to prohibit relabeling by retail druggist of pills previously shipped correctly labeled in interstate commerce); McDermott v. Wisconsin, 228 U.S. 115, 133 (1913) (upholding regulations, issued pursuant to congressional authorization, requiring seizures of mislabeled goods following shipment in interstate commerce: "as a practical matter, at least, the first time the opportunity of inspection by the Federal authorities arises . . . is when the goods . . . are delivered to the consignee, unboxed, and placed by him upon the shelves of his store for sale").

2. A number of commentators have suggested that there exist, or ought to exist, judicially enforceable limits, apart from Bill of Rights restraints, on congressional power under the commerce clause. See, e.g., C. Black, Perspectives in Constitutional Law 29 (1970). In a similar vein, Justice

The political restraints on congressional activity under the commerce clause are a byproduct of the pluralist character of the federal legislative process.[3] Ordinarily, the process of legislation in Congress is one of compromise—interests of affected groups are accommodated to the extent necessary for legislation to obtain the support of a legislative coalition large enough to secure passage.[4] Limiting the scope of its legislation short of the reach constitutionally permitted is one way for Congress to accommodate otherwise conflicting interests, and thus to forge necessary coalitions. For example, in restricting the scope of the public accommodations provisions of the commerce clause-based Civil Rights Act of 1964, Congress apparently acted to compromise the interests of groups denied associational freedom by reason of racial discrimination and groups whose associational freedom would be limited by more sweeping prohibitions against discrimination.

Harlan's majority opinion in Maryland v. Wirtz, 392 U.S. 183 (1968), implied in dictum that the commerce clause might not justify congressional use of "a relatively trivial impact on commerce as an excuse for broad general regulation of state or private activities." Id. at 197 n. 27. This emphasis on the necessity for judicial limits on congressional power might be thought to slight the competence of Congress to interpret and enforce the Constitution. It is not the case, after all, that *only* courts are capable of taking legal considerations into account in their decision processes. See, e.g., Chayes, "An Inquiry Into the Workings of Arms Control Agreements," 85 Harv.L.Rev. 905, 935–42 (1972). At one level, congressional awareness of commerce clause limits may be anachronistic and self-limiting, lasting only so long as members of Congress remain who studied constitutional law at a time when courts still applied doctrines significantly limiting congressional power. Cf. R. Pound, The Formative Era of American Law 98 (1938). See also Stern, "The Commerce Clause Revisited—The Federalization of Intrastate Crime," 15 Ariz.L.Rev. 271 (1973). But more fundamentally, the interests that would be served by a judicial doctrine limiting the commerce power are also interests likely to be represented in ordinary congressional processes of decision. See § 5–20, infra. If there is a role for the judiciary here, it ought to be defined primarily as one of encouraging the legislative processes autonomously to set the limits of congressional power. And it is largely this role that the Supreme Court has assumed. But see § 5–22, infra.

In any event, if meaningful judicial limits on congressional power are to be devised to backstop legislative processes, it is not clear that the commerce clause provides an appropriate doctrinal context. To the extent that doctrine shapes the Supreme Court's perceptions, it is unlikely that congressional abuse of the commerce power could be reliably "seen" from the commerce clause perspective, given the multiple rationality standards of contemporary commerce clause doctrine. A more appropriate doctrinal form is suggested by the paradigm of the Bill of Rights, the source of those limitations that are currently most often enforced by the courts. Instead of attempting to fence Congress *in*—in the pre-1937 manner but with a little more running room—courts would do better to protect the values threatened by congressional abuse of the commerce power by fencing Congress *out*—denying the validity of particular congressional acts without altering the general shape of commerce clause doctrine. The beginnings of such a doctrinal form, linked to the tenth amendment, are discussed in §§ 5–21 to 5–22, infra.

3. Justice Blackmun's opinion for the Court in Garcia v. San Antonio Metropolitan Transit Auth., 469 U.S. 528 (1985), catalogues at length the varied political checks that the states supposedly retain on the actions of the federal legislature. See 469 U.S. at 547–55. For further discussion of Garcia, see § 5–22, infra.

4. For discussions of legislative pluralism from the perspectives of both political science and constitutional law, see Choper, "The Supreme Court and the Political Branches: Democratic Theory and Practice," 122 U.Pa.L.Rev. 810, 817–46 (1974); Auerbach, "The Reapportionment Cases: One Person, One Vote—One Vote, One Value," 1964 Sup.Ct.Rev. 1, 52. See also Stewart, "The Reformation of American Administrative Law," 88 Harv.L.Rev. 1667 (1975).

The degree to which the institutional interests of the states are among the interests recognized and accommodated in congressional processes is a matter of particular constitutional significance. If the institutional interests of state governments in limiting federal intrusion into hitherto local spheres of concern are ordinarily taken into account in congressional actions, then the political process of federal legislation may be counted on to incorporate a consistent check against the full use of congressional power. Conversely, since federalism is one of the postulates of the constitutional structure, if state institutional interests prove to be inadequately represented in Congress, then the Supreme Court's contemporary commerce clause doctrine would have to be considered deficient to the extent that it leaves state autonomy unprotected.

Congressional theorists have traditionally reasoned that certain features of the governmental structure defined by the Constitution insure that state institutional interests will indeed be taken into account in congressional processes.[5] But a number of the means state governments were formerly able to use to make their presence felt in Congress are no longer available. State legislatures, for example, no longer choose United States Senators[6] and no longer utilize such devices as the poll tax[7] and the malapportioned election district[8] to define the electorate of United States Representatives. Other points of contact between the states and congressional processes, such as the definition of the Senate electorate in terms of states,[9] guarantee only that federal legislators will take heed of the substantive interests of groups influential in particular states, not that Congress will necessarily make allowance in its exercise of power for the institutional interests of state governments as such.

Most likely, if state institutional interests are represented in congressional processes, it is for reasons other than the specific structural connections of Congress to the states. State institutional interests may be protected by proxy, either because they are brought to the attention of Congress by groups seeking to augment their more substantive arguments for limited use of congressional power, or because the success of interest groups in persuading Congress to limit its legislation for other reasons simultaneously furthers the state interests *sub silentio*. More fundamentally, as Henry Hart and Herbert Wechsler notably argued, the institutional interests of state governments may be protected by the very fact of these governments' constitutionally secured existence. Because the states exist "as governmental entities and . . . sources of . . . law,"[10] the federal legislation that interest groups demand of Congress, and that Congress enacts, tends to be

5. See The Federalist No. 45, at 291 (C. Rossiter ed. 1961) (Madison); Wechsler, "The Political Safeguards of Federalism: The Role of the States in the Composition and Selection of the National Government," 54 Col.L.Rev. 543, 547–52 (1954).

6. See U.S.Const. amend. XVII.

7. See U.S.Const. amend. XXIV; Harper v. Virginia Bd. of Elections, 383 U.S. 663 (1966).

8. See Wesberry v. Sanders, 376 U.S. 1 (1964).

9. See U.S.Const. art. I, § 3.

10. Wechsler, note 5, supra, at 546.

"generally interstitial in its nature":[11] "Federal legislation, on the whole, has been conceived and drafted on an *ad hoc* basis to accomplish limited objectives. It builds upon legal relationships established by the states, altering or supplanting them only so far as necessary for the special purpose. Congress acts, in short, against the background of the total *corpus juris* of the states in much the way that a state legislature acts against the background of the common law, assumed to govern unless changed by legislation."

§ 5–8. Judicial Review as Shaping the Politics of the Commerce Clause

Contemporary commerce clause doctrine grants Congress such broad power that judicial review of the affirmative authorization for congressional action is largely a formality. Nonetheless, federal legislation under the commerce clause may be subject to close judicial scrutiny from several angles. Legislation, even if authorized by the commerce clause, must be consistent with the Bill of Rights and other external restrictions of congressional power, restrictions which operate to protect not only individual interests but state interests as well.[1] Moreover, congressional exercises of the commerce power trigger a judicial approach to statutory construction which reinforces the political checks of pluralism and federalism discussed above.

The Supreme Court pays particularly close heed to statutory language and legislative history in judging the reach of laws enacted under the commerce clause. A law will not be held to affect all the activities Congress in theory can control unless statutory language or legislative history constitutes a *clear statement* that Congress intended to exercise its commerce power in full.[2]

The Supreme Court has invoked the clear statement requirement most notably where a judgment that a federal statute reached to the outer limits of the commerce power would be obviously inconsistent with state institutional interests. Thus, in a series of cases,[3] the Court has narrowly interpreted federal laws criminally punishing "conduct readily denounced as criminal by the States"[4] on the ground that, "unless Congress conveys its purpose clearly, it will not be deemed to have significantly changed the federal-state balance."[5] Similarly, in *Employees v. Department of Public Health and Welfare of Missouri,*[6] a

11. Hart and Wechsler's The Federal Courts and the Federal System 470–71 (P. Bator, P. Mishkin, D. Shapiro, H. Wechsler eds., 2d ed. 1973).

§ 5–8

1. See §§ 5–20 to 5–22, infra.

2. Professor Begen has argued: ". . . where the relationship of the law to interstate commerce is not readily apparent, the Court should require Congress to relate the law to its impact on interstate transactions. This could assist in focusing Congressional concern on the proper issues." Begen, "The Hunting of the Shark: An Inquiry Into the Limits of Congressional Power Under the Commerce Clause," 8 Wake Forest L.Rev. 187, 198 (1972).

3. United States v. Enmons, 410 U.S. 396 (1973); United States v. Bass, 404 U.S. 336 (1971); Rewis v. United States, 401 U.S. 808 (1971); United States v. Five Gambling Devices, 346 U.S. 441 (1953) (Jackson, J., plurality opinion).

4. United States v. Bass, 404 U.S. 336, 349 (1971).

5. Id. See also Frankfurter, "Some Reflections on the Reading of Statutes," 47 Col.L.Rev. 527, 539–40 (1947).

6. 411 U.S. 279 (1973).

majority of the Supreme Court refused to read the 1966 amendments to the Fair Labor Standards Act of 1938 as granting state employees covered by the amendments a federal cause of action against state governments in federal district courts. Such a cause of action would have been inconsistent with eleventh amendment principles of state sovereign immunity from citizen suits in federal tribunals, and the Court "found not a word in the history of the 1966 amendments to indicate a purpose of Congress to make it possible for a citizen of that State or another State to sue the State in the federal courts." [7]

At first glance, the clear statement requirement may seem to limit Congress only minimally: if Congress wishes to utilize the full reach of its power, it need only say so. The rule, however, is an important complement to the political check on congressional exercise of the commerce power. Legislative coalitions need not rest on definitive compromises of conflicting interests if the legislation a coalition secures is sufficiently ambiguous. For in that case, competing interests retain a full opportunity to press their claims anew to the courts that are called upon to interpret the law.[8] Such an outcome is unsatisfactory in the commerce clause context, however, since contemporary doctrine provides courts with no trenchant criteria for striking the balance that Congress managed to avoid. A rule like the clear statement requirement is therefore essential: Congress must be prevented from resorting to ambiguity as a cloak for its failure to accommodate the competing interests bearing on the federal-state balance.[9]

7. Id. at 285. See §§ 3–26 and 3–27, supra.

8. Cf. Jaffe, "The Illusion of the Ideal Administration," 86 Harv.L.Rev. 1183 (1973).

9. See also the analysis of federal preemption in § 6–29, infra. Not surprisingly, the Supreme Court will also limit the reach of a federal statute enacted under the commerce clause if the statutory language clearly suggests that Congress stopped short of exercising its full constitutional power. Deference to statutory language, however, creates special problems in cases involving the construction of laws enacted before the Supreme Court liberalized commerce clause doctrine: in such cases it may be unclear whether Congress deliberately limited its exercise of power or instead simply described the reach of its statute in terms that it thought were suggestive of the constitutional limits then applicable. In Gulf Oil Corp. v. Copp Paving Co., Inc., 419 U.S. 186 (1974), for example, the Supreme Court held that sections of the Robinson-Patman and Clayton Acts did not cover alleged anti-trust violations by firms "engaged in entirely intrastate sales of asphaltic concrete, a product that can be marketed only locally," even though sales of asphaltic concrete were made "for use in construction of interstate highways." Id. at 188. Both statutes were framed to reach "only persons or activities within the flow of interstate commerce," id. at 195, and Justice Powell's majority opinion concluded that sales of asphalt for use in constructing interstate highways could not be said to be part of the "flow of commerce" without radically broadening the scope of the statutes and overly formalizing their interpretation. See id. at 198–99. Despite legislative history suggesting—somewhat weakly in the case of the Robinson-Patman Act, see Recent Case, 86 Harv.L.Rev. 765, 770–72 (1973), and more strongly with respect to the Clayton Act—that Congress, in enacting these pre-1937 laws, meant to exercise its full power under the commerce clause, the Court strained in Gulf Oil to avoid "radical expansion" of the scope of the laws "beyond that which the statutory language defines," 419 U.S. at 202, by relying, in the case of the Robinson-Patman Act, on continued congressional silence despite nearly four decades of narrow statutory interpretation by the courts, see id. at 200–01, and, in the case of the Clayton Act, upon a narrow interpretation of the pleadings to take the issue out of the particular case. See id. at 202; id. at 204 (Douglas, J. dissenting).

§ 5–9. The Taxing Power

Article I, § 8, declares that "Congress shall have Power to lay and collect Taxes, Duties, Imposts and Excises. . . ." This power to tax is an independent source of federal authority: Congress may tax subjects that it may not be authorized to regulate directly under any of its enumerated regulatory powers. An extended discussion of limitations on the use of federal taxes to raise revenue is beyond the scope of this work. The specific focus here is on the use of taxes as an indirect regulatory device. Nonetheless, it is helpful to note briefly the limitations of congressional taxing power incorporated in the body of the Constitution.

Article I, § 8, requires that "all Duties, Imposts and Excises shall be uniform throughout the United States . . . ." This requirement is one of geographic uniformity only; so long as the tax structure does not discriminate among the states [1] it does not matter that a tax may not be "uniform" as it applies to particular individuals.[2] The uniformity requirement applies to all "indirect" taxes—those that (1) tax the privilege of doing business or of performing some act, and (2) are ordinarily imposed on persons other than the consumers ultimately bearing the burden of the tax.[3]

Article I, § 9, states that "[n]o Capitation, or other direct, Tax shall be laid, unless in Proportion to the Census . . . ." Article I, § 2, provides that "direct Taxes shall be apportioned among the several States which may be included within this Union, according to their respective Numbers. . . ." A direct tax is one imposed upon property as such, rather than on the performance of an act. Because of the impractical apportionment requirement attaching to direct taxes, the fate of federal income taxation in the nineteenth century turned on the content the Supreme Court gave to the distinction between direct and indirect taxes. In *Springer v. United States*,[4] the Court held a Civil War income tax to be an indirect excise tax. But in *Pollock v. Farmers' Loan & Trust Co.*,[5] a majority of the Justices ruled that, insofar as the source of income is property, and income tax is a direct tax, and is therefore invalid unless apportioned. By 1911, however, the Supreme

---

§ 5–9

1. See also art. I, § 9: "No Tax or Duty shall be laid on Articles exported from any State." Only goods shipped to other countries are deemed exports. Neither Congress nor the states can levy an export tax. United States v. Hvoslef, 237 U.S. 1 (1915).

2. Knowlton v. Moore, 178 U.S. 41 (1900).

3. E.g., license or sales taxes. See Bromley v. McCaughn, 280 U.S. 124, 136 (1929) ("a tax imposed upon a particular use of property or the exercise of a single power over property incidental to ownership, is an [indirect] excise [tax] . . . .").

The Court in 1983 considered for the first time whether the uniformity clause prohibits Congress from defining in geographic terms the class of objects to be taxed. In United States v. Ptasynski, 462 U.S. 74 (1983), the Court upheld the Crude Oil Windfall Profit Tax of 1980, which exempted some but not all Alaskan oil from its provisions. Justice Powell's opinion for the unanimous Court held that, when Congress frames a tax in geographic terms, "we will examine the classification closely to see if there is actual geographic discrimination." 462 U.S. at 85. But because Congress' action was based on a recognition of the high risks and costs peculiar to far-north oil exploration and other "neutral factors," and not on "reasons that would offend the purpose of the Clause," id. at 85–86, the geographic specificity of the tax was held not to render it invalid.

4. 102 U.S. (12 Otto) 586 (1880).

5. 158 U.S. 601 (1895).

Court had again reversed direction, holding in *Flint v. Stone Tracy Co.*[6] that a tax on corporations measured by income was not a direct tax but an excise tax on the privilege of doing business in the corporate form. The confusion was put to an end in 1913[7] with the ratification of the sixteenth amendment, which provides: "Congress shall have power to lay and to collect taxes on incomes, from whatever source derived, without apportionment among the several States, and without regard to any census or enumeration."

Almost any tax will achieve an ancillary regulatory effect by increasing the costs of the taxed activities for individuals or corporations. If Congress has authority independent of its taxing power to regulate the taxed subject, this regulatory effect is not constitutionally troublesome. In such cases, even if the tax is plainly regulatory in purpose and effect, it may be upheld under the necessary and proper clause as a means of regulating an activity properly the subject of congressional regulation. Thus, in *Veazie Bank v. Fenno*,[8] for example, the Supreme Court upheld a federal tax on banknotes issued by state banks, even though the effect of the tax was to drive such notes out of circulation, since Congress had the power under article I, § 8, to regulate currency through taxation as well as by other means.

However, if no independent source of federal regulatory authority justifies a congressional tax, classification of the tax as a regulatory or revenue measure may be determinative of its constitutionality. The classification rules on which the Supreme Court has traditionally relied can be briefly summarized: (1) A tax is a valid revenue measure if it achieves its regulatory effect through its rate structure[9] or if its regulatory provisions bear a "reasonable relation" to its enforcement.[10]

---

6. 220 U.S. 107 (1911).

7. But see Eisner v. Macomber, 252 U.S. 189 (1920) (stock dividend issued against corporate surplus is not "income" in the stockholder's hands prior to sale or conversion, and hence is not taxable without apportionment under sixteenth amendment); cf. United States v. Phellis, 257 U.S. 156 (1921) (distinguishing dividend distribution of stock of transferee in a corporate reorganization).

8. 75 U.S. (8 Wall.) 533 (1869).

9. In McCray v. United States 195 U.S. 27 (1904), for example, a tax of 10¢ per pound on yellow oleomargarine was upheld as a revenue tax even though the corresponding tax on white oleomargarine was only ¼¢ per pound. See also United States v. Sanchez, 340 U.S. 42 (1950) (upholding marijuana tax of $100 per ounce).

10. In United States v. Doremus, 249 U.S. 86 (1919), the Supreme Court upheld the Narcotics Drug Act of 1914 as a valid exercise of the congressional taxing power although, in addition to requiring payment of a special tax, the Act required those subject to the tax to register with the federal government, and to make sales only

on specified forms required to be kept for two years subject to inspection: "If the legislation enacted has some reasonable relation to the exercise of the taxing authority conferred by the Constitution, it cannot be invalidated because of the supposed [regulatory] motives which induced it." Id. at 93. Similarly, in United States v. Kahriger, 345 U.S. 22 (1953), the Court affirmed the constitutionality of provisions of the Revenue Act of 1951 levying a special tax on bookmakers and requiring persons subject to the tax to register with federal officials: "Unless there are provisions extraneous to any tax need, courts are without authority to limit the exercise of the taxing power." Id. at 31.

Kahriger was later overruled, but on the sole ground that the registration requirement violated the fifth amendment privilege against compulsory self-incrimination. See Marchetti v. United States, 390 U.S. 39 (1968) (availability to state law enforcement officials of registration information required by federal wagering tax justified invocation of fifth amendment privilege). Accord, Grosso v. United States, 390 U.S. 62 (1968). The fifth amendment privilege against compelled self-incrimination is at

(2) A tax is a regulatory tax—and hence invalid if not otherwise authorized—if its very application presupposes taxpayer violation of a series of specified conditions promulgated along with the tax.[11]

The present relevance of the distinction between revenue and regulatory taxes is not clear. The Supreme Court, in its more recent decisions, has given a broad reading to the "revenue" standards, and has refused to supplement these standards by inquiries into congressional motive.[12] Moreover, the Court's expansive modern interpretation of the commerce clause substantially reduces the likelihood that a tax, even if found to be regulatory, would be held to be beyond congressional power.[13]

present the primary restraint on congressional use of registration requirements in connection with taxes on activities possibly illegal under state laws. Compare Haynes v. United States, 390 U.S. 85 (1968) (registration requirement incident to taxes imposed by National Firearms Act inconsistent with fifth amendment privilege), with United States v. Freed, 401 U.S. 601 (1971) (revised Firearms Act not inconsistent with fifth amendment since registration information under new law may not be used as evidence, or as a lead to evidence, in state or federal criminal prosecutions). Indeed, federal tax prosecutions have provided a primary setting for the Supreme Court's contemporary redefinition of the fifth amendment privilege. See, e.g., Fisher v. United States, 425 U.S. 391 (1976) (fifth amendment does not privilege business records obtained without compelling testimony). See generally Note, "Formalism, Legal Realism and Constitutionally Protected Privacy Under the Fourth and Fifth Amendments," 90 Harv.L.Rev. 945 (1977).

11. Thus, in Bailey v. Drexel Furniture Co., 259 U.S. 20 (1922), the Supreme Court concluded that, because the duty to pay the excise tax at issue was conditioned upon an employer's noncompliance with federal regulations of the use of child labor, the tax's "prohibitory and regulatory effect and purpose are palpable," id. at 37, and the tax was thus invalid, since congressional power under the commerce clause was not at that time thought to reach the regulation of child labor. Similarly, in Hill v. Wallace, 259 U.S. 44 (1922), the Court held invalid a tax not limited in its application to interstate commerce because the tax's incidence depended upon noncompliance with federal regulations controlling the operation of grain boards of trade. See also United States v. Constantine, 296 U.S. 287 (1935) (holding invalid heavy federal tax on liquor dealers not operating in compliance with state laws); United States v. Butler, 297 U.S. 1 (1936) (holding beyond the taxing power a congressional provision for imposing processing taxes on agricultural

commodities and for making payments therefrom to farmers). Drexel Furniture and Hill highlight the relevance of constitutional grants of power other than the taxing power insofar as the validity of federal taxes is concerned. The child labor tax would be valid today. In United States v. Darby, 312 U.S. 100 (1941), the Supreme Court overruled Hammer v. Dagenhart, 247 U.S. 251 (1918), its earlier decision that Congress could not regulate child labor under the commerce clause. And within a year of its decision in Hill v. Wallace, the Court held that Congress could, by limiting its regulation to interstate commerce, achieve substantially the same results as those it sought to obtain through the tax struck down in Hill. City of Chicago Board of Trade v. Olsen, 262 U.S. 1 (1923).

12. As long as a tax produces some revenue, the Court is "not free to speculate as to the motives which moved Congress to impose it or as to the extent to which it may operate to restrict the activities taxed. . . . [I]f it is not attended by an offensive regulation and . . . operates as a tax, it is within the national taxing power." Sonzinsky v. United States, 300 U.S. 506, 514 (1937) (upholding license tax on firearms dealers). Compare the greater degree of scrutiny in United States v. Constantine, 296 U.S. 287 (1935): "the indicia which [the liquor excise tax section] exhibits of an intent to prohibit and to punish violations of state law as such are too strong to be disregarded, remove all semblance of a revenue act, and stamp the sum it exacts as a penalty." Id. at 295. Justice Cardozo dissented in Constantine: "the process of psychoanalysis has spread to unaccustomed fields." Id. at 299.

13. See, e.g., Minor v. United States, 396 U.S. 87, 98 n. 13 (1969) (responding to dissenting argument that narcotics tax was not a revenue tax by noting independent congressional power to achieve the tax's regulatory results under the commerce clause).

§ 5–10. The Spending Power

Article I, § 8, provides that "Congress shall have Power . . . to pay the debts and provide for the common Defence and general Welfare of the United States. . . ." Through use of conditional appropriations, the power to spend becomes a power to regulate. The use of conditional appropriations, therefore, raises a constitutional question similar to that presented by the problem of regulatory taxation discussed in § 5–9: to what extent may Congress achieve indirectly, through its exercise of the spending power, that which it could not legislate directly, through regulatory provisions enacted pursuant to any of its other enumerated grants of power under article I, § 8? Naturally, as the Supreme Court has construed the scope of congressional power under the commerce clause more expansively, this question has become less pressing since Congress ordinarily has the power to regulate directly, with or without the aid of conditional grants, the objects of its concern.

Article I, § 8, groups the spending power with the taxing power: "The Congress shall have Power to lay and collect Taxes, Duties, Imposts and Excises, to pay the Debts and provide for the common Defence and general Welfare of the United States. . . ." As a matter of semantics, the power of Congress to "provide for the . . . general Welfare" could be interpreted as unconnected to the power to "lay and collect Taxes" and "pay the Debts." But if the general welfare clause were thus a separate grant of congressional power, the remainder of article I, § 8, would seem to be superfluous: any exercise of congressional power, in whatever form, could be justified as being "for the . . . general Welfare" if it could be justified at all. Formally, this broad reading of the general welfare clause remained open through the first third of the twentieth century, since the Supreme Court was not required to interpret the clause until 1936.[1] By that date, however, extra-judicial analysis of the spending power had focused matters to such an extent that the Court, in *United States v. Butler*,[2] was able to adopt positions already set forth by recognized authorities.

The *Butler* Court adopted the view, earlier espoused by Justice Story, that the general welfare clause does *not* grant Congress power to provide for the general welfare by any means it chooses: "the only thing granted is the power to tax for the purpose of providing funds for

§ 5–10

1. Congressional spending programs as such have rarely been subjected to courtroom challenge, in part because federal taxpayers have been held to lack standing in that capacity to question the constitutionality of federal expenditures unless they (1) are resisting payment of a tax earmarked for the allegedly unconstitutional expenditure, see, e.g., United States v. Butler, 297 U.S. 1, 57–61 (1936), or (2) can show that the contested expenditure "exceeds specific constitutional limitations imposed upon the exercise of the congressional taxing and spending power", Flast v. Cohen, 392 U.S. 83, 102–03 (1968). See § 3–17, supra. A state, however, may have standing to challenge the constitutionality of a conditional grant offered to it. See Oklahoma v. United States Civil Service Comm'n, 330 U.S. 127 (1947) (rejecting challenge to Hatch Act provision prohibiting state employees in federally-funded jobs from taking an active part in political activities). Accord, South Dakota v. Dole, 107 S.Ct. 2793 (1987) (rejecting challenge to congressional provision withholding federal highway funds from states permitting persons under 21 to buy liquor).

2. 297 U.S. 1 (1936).

the payment of the nation's debts and . . . for the general welfare." [3] The general welfare clause thus confers only a power to spend; it confers no independent power to regulate. The *Butler* Court then proceeded to delineate the limits of congressional spending power. It rejected as "mere tautology" the Madisonian position that "the grant of power to tax and spend for the general national welfare must be confined to the enumerated legislative fields committed to Congress." [4] Instead, the Court endorsed a thesis derived from Hamilton's *Report on Manufactures to the House of Representatives*: [5] "the power of Congress to authorize expenditure of public moneys for public purposes is not limited by the direct grants of legislative power found in the Constitution"; rather, "its confines are set in the clause which confers it. . . ." [6]

In *Butler*, the Court attempted to set internal limits on the independent congressional power that it recognized by adopting the Hamiltonian thesis. The Court distinguished between *a coercive purchase of compliance which Congress could not command directly*— impermissible under *Butler*—and *an appropriation of funds conditioned on the undertaking of certain acts*—action appropriate even in areas over which Congress would have no direct regulatory authority.[7] This distinction proved unworkable, and since its decisions upholding the Social Security Act,[8] the Supreme Court has effectively ignored *Butler* in judging the limits of congressional spending power.[9]

Since the collapse of the *Butler* distinction, the Court has occasionally referred to a requirement that federal spending be "general." This "limit" on the power of Congress to achieve its regulatory objectives indirectly derives largely from the language of the general welfare clause—"provide for the . . . *general* Welfare." [10] Congressional expenditures must be made "for the common benefit as distinguished from some mere local purpose." [11] But the Court has declared that, in

---

3. Id. at 64.

4. Id. at 65.

5. See 3 Works of Alexander Hamilton 372 (Lodge ed. 1885).

6. 297 U.S. at 66.

7. See id. at 70–74. In Butler, the Court held unconstitutional the Agricultural Adjustment Act of 1933, which authorized the Secretary of Agriculture to levy a tax on agricultural processors and to use the revenue to purchase crop reduction agreements from farmers.

8. Chas. C. Steward Machine Co. v. Davis, 301 U.S. 548 (1937) (unemployment compensation); Helvering v. Davis, 301 U.S. 619 (1937) (old age benefits).

9. A recent example of the Court's disregard for Butler was its summary affirmance, during the National League of Cities era, see § 5–22, infra, in the case of North Carolina ex rel. Morrow v. Califano, 435 U.S. 962 (1979). The lower court had held that state sovereignty did not limit Congress' ability to condition federal health

aid on the state's imposition of certain standards for its health care facilities. See 445 F.Supp. 532 (E.D.N.C. 1977).

10. It derives as well from pervasive notions of the allowable limits of government coercion: public taxation to provide for a concededly private benefit would offend substantive due process. See Loan Ass'n v. Topeka, 87 U.S. (20 Wall.) 655 (1875), discussed in Chapter 8 infra. Vis-a-vis the nation as a whole, an entirely local benefit might in theory be deemed "private" in the application of this principle.

11. United States v. Gerlach Live Stock Co., 339 U.S. 725, 738 (1950). In Cincinnati Soap Co. v. United States, 301 U.S. 308 (1937), the Court, although upholding a special tax to raise revenue for the government of the then federally-ruled Philippine Islands, assumed in dictum that "a federal tax levied for the express purpose of paying the debts or providing for the welfare of a state might be invalid . . ." Id. at 317. This dictum might appear to stand in the way of federal assistance to any single

deciding whether the objective of a particular expenditure program is the national interest rather than merely the interest of the directly benefited locality, "discretion belongs to Congress, unless the choice is clearly wrong, a display of arbitrary power [rather than] an exercise of judgment." [12] Such judicial deference is understandable in an era lacking any coherent theory of the public good as more than an aggregate of private needs and wants. Judgments concerning the generality of the benefits conferred by federal expenditures require determinations of fact that Congress is better equipped to make than the Supreme Court. Given such judicial deference, the generality limit on congressional spending power is more apparent than real.

In the absence of effective limits derived from the general welfare clause itself, the primary limits on congressional expenditures are external, like the Bill of Rights or the Constitution's implicit protections of state sovereignty,[13] or political.[14] Political restraints may be reinforced by a clear statement requirement if conditional congressional expenditures, although not unconstitutional, nonetheless threaten state institutional interests.[15]

municipality threatened with bankruptcy. If Congress granted such aid today, however, it seems most unlikely that the action would or should be constitutionally invalidated. The Cincinnati Soap dictum rested upon the assumption that a state has "full powers of taxation and full power to appropriate the revenues derived therefrom," id., but Congress would be unlikely to aid a particular municipality without first concluding that a state lacked the economic capacity to rescue its city. Moreover, the national economic consequences of a particular municipal bankruptcy might themselves be sufficient to provide congressional action with the needed general justification. Cf. United States v. Bekins, 304 U.S. 27 (1938) (affirming power of Congress to allow state subdivisions to petition for bankruptcy). Note that even if the aid came out of general tax revenues, taxpayer plaintiffs might have standing to challenge the expenditure. Cf. Flast v. Cohen, 392 U.S. 83 (1968).

12. Helvering v. Davis, 301 U.S. 619, 640 (1937).

13. See §§ 5–20 to 5–22, infra. In South Dakota v. Dole, 107 S.Ct. 2793 (1987), in a 7–2 opinion by Chief Justice Rehnquist, the Court had no difficulty finding that neither general concerns of state sovereignty, nor the twenty-first amendment (see also § 6–24, infra), prevented Congress from conditioning federal highway funds on state compliance with a 21-year-old minimum drinking age—inasmuch as the condition was neither (a) "unrelated 'to the federal interest in [the] particular national projects or programs,'" id. at 2796 (citing Massachusetts v. United States, 435 U.S. 444, 461 (1978) (plurality

opinion)), nor (b) unduly coercive, given that a noncomplying state would "lose a relatively small percentage of certain federal highway funds." 107 S.Ct. at 2798. Justices Brennan and O'Connor dissented. That the challenged condition is quite closely related to highway safety, and thus to the aims of the federal program at issue, resolves the apparent paradox of at least some "states'-rights" Justices (see § 5–22, infra) voting against South Dakota here. Cf. § 11–5, note 12, infra.

14. For a discussion of the political processes limiting the exercise of congressional power, see § 5–7, supra.

15. See Pennhurst State School & Hosp. v. Halderman (I), 451 U.S. 1, 17 (1981). In Employees v. Missouri Dept. of Public Health and Welfare, 411 U.S. 279 (1973), the Supreme Court invoked the clear statement rule in holding that certain congressional commerce regulations had not deprived the states of their eleventh amendment immunity. See § 5–8, supra. Justice Rehnquist's majority opinion in Edelman v. Jordan, 415 U.S. 651 (1974), assumed that the Employees holding applied with respect to federal welfare assistance to the states allegedly conditioned upon waiver of immunity, see id. at 672, but concluded that "the threshold fact of congressional authorization to sue a class of defendants which literally includes the States is wholly absent" Id. Accord, Pennhurst State School & Hosp. v. Halderman (II), 465 U.S. 89, 99 (1984); Quern v. Jordan, 440 U.S. 332, 342 (1979) (holding that 42 U.S.C. § 1983 does not evince Congress' intent to override eleventh amendment immunity of states).

§ 5–11. Other Domestic Powers Granted Congress by Article I, Section 8

Other than the commerce, taxing and spending powers, only three of the domestic powers which article I, § 8, grants Congress have provoked sufficient legislation and litigation to generate significant bodies of constitutional doctrine. These three—the bankruptcy power, the postal power, and the property power—are of interest here primarily because each illustrates a different approach to limiting congressional authority. The primary limit upon congressional power under the bankruptcy clause is internal—the requirement of uniformity. By contrast, the most important restraints upon congressional exercise of the postal power are the external limits imposed by the Bill of Rights, chiefly the first amendment. Finally, the most interesting issue raised by congressional exercise of the property power is an issue of federalism—the extent to which the United States' ownership of property exempts uses of that property from state law.

Article I, § 8, authorizes Congress to establish "uniform Laws on the subject of Bankruptcies throughout the United States." The bankruptcy power has been broadly construed; Justice Catron's statement of its scope, made on circuit in *In re Klein*, remains definitive: [1] "[The

---

The clear statement rule received further elaboration in Atascadero State Hospital v. Scanlon, 473 U.S. 234 (1985). First analyzing the Rehabilitation Act as an exercise of congressional power pursuant to § 5 of the Fourteenth Amendment, the Court held that "Congress may abrogate the States' constitutionally secured immunity from suit in federal court only by making its intention unmistakably clear in the language of the statute," id. at 242—a requirement not met here. The Court also held that, if the Act were viewed as an exercise of the spending power, it "fell far short of manifesting a clear intent to condition participation in the programs funded under the Act on a State's consent to waive its constitutional immunity." Id. at 247. Under both prongs of its analysis, the Court apparently required that the congressional intent be clearly expressed in the provisions of the statute itself rather than displayed, however convincingly, in the legislative history. Justice Brennan, joined in dissent by Justices Marshall, Blackmun and Stevens, described the majority's requirement that the congressional intent be expressed in the *language* of the statute as an unwarranted stiffening of the clear statement rule. See id. at 254. At the least, it seems plain that there is no such requirement when Congress is imposing "retroactive liability [*not*] for prelitigation conduct [but for] expenses incurred in litigation seeking only prospective relief." Hutto v. Finney, 437 U.S. 678, 695, 696–97 & n. 27 (1978) (upholding award of attorneys fees against a state, under 42 U.S.C. § 1988, inasmuch as "it would be absurd to

require an express reference to state litigants whenever a filing fee, or a new item such as an expert witness' fee, is added to the category of taxable costs," in part because the fiscal burdens entailed are likely to be limited, citing Tribe, "Intergovernmental Immunities in Litigation, Taxation and Regulation," 89 Harv.L.Rev. 682, 695 (1976)).

§ 5–11

1. 42 U.S. (1 How.) 277 (C.C.D.Mo. 1843). See also Continental Ill. Nat'l Bank & Trust Co. v. Chicago, R.I. & Pac. Ry. Co., 294 U.S. 648, 669–75 (1935); 1 Collier on Bankruptcy § 0.02, at 5 (14th ed. 1974). Only once has the Supreme Court held that congressional action exceeded the affirmative reach of the bankruptcy power. See Ashton v. Cameron County Water Improvement Dist., 298 U.S. 513 (1936) (tenth amendment violated by federal law allowing state subdivisions to declare bankruptcy). That decision was effectively overruled two years later. See United States v. Bekins, 304 U.S. 27 (1938).

In an early case, United States v. Fox, 95 U.S. (5 Otto) 670 (1878), the Supreme Court held that a federal law penalizing frauds by persons who subsequently entered bankruptcy unconstitutionally invaded the reserved powers of the states. The Court implied that, if the statute had applied only to frauds committed in contemplation of bankruptcy, it would have been constitutional. See id. at 672–73. Since the statute was not so limited, however, it could not be held a rational exercise of the bank-

bankruptcy power] extends to all cases where the law causes to be distributed the property of the debtor among his creditors; this is its least limit. Its greatest is a discharge of the debtor from his contracts. And all intermediate legislation, affecting substance and form, but tending to further the great end of the subject—distribution and discharge—are in the competency and discretion of congress."

The power the bankruptcy clause grants Congress, however, is internally limited by the uniformity requirement.[2] The uniformity required is geographic: a federal bankruptcy law need not cover all debtors and creditors, and it may "define classes of debtors and . . . structure relief accordingly,"[3] but it may not be written so as to apply only to one identified debtor in the manner of a private bill[4] and may not discriminate among the debtors and creditors covered on the basis of location.[5] Thus, in the *Regional Rail Reorganization Act Cases,*[6] the Supreme Court upheld a federal law setting up special bankruptcy arrangements for insolvent railroads, even though the statute "operates only in a single statutorily defined region," because "the Rail Act in fact operates uniformly upon all bankrupt railroads . . . operating in the United States and uniformly with respect to all creditors of each of these railroads."[7] The fact that all of the bankrupt railroads happened to operate in one part of the country was deemed irrelevant. Furthermore, geographic uniformity is not disturbed if the federal bankruptcy

ruptcy power: "an act which is not an offense at the time it is committed cannot become such by any subsequent independent act of the party with which it has no connection." Id. at 671. Fox thus was not so much as adjudication of the limits of the bankruptcy power as an early invalidation of conclusive presumptions. See § 16–34, infra.

2. Uniformity does not imply the absence of state legislation. The grant of congressional power does not by itself deprive the states of power to act. "It is not the right to establish these uniform laws, but their actual establishment, which is inconsistent with the partial acts of the states." Sturges v. Crowninshield, 17 U.S. (4 Wheat.) 122, 196 (1819). Nor does congressional action necessarily preempt state legislation if the state legislation is not in actual conflict with federal law. "It is only state laws which conflict with the bankruptcy laws of Congress that are suspended. . . ." Stellwagen v. Clum, 245 U.S. 605, 615 (1918). See, e.g., Reitz v. Mealey, 314 U.S. 33, 37 (1941) (state suspension of driver's licenses of persons negligently involved in automobile accidents and unable to pay compensation held not inconsistent with federal bankruptcy law even though state law recognized no exemption for bankrupts), significantly limited in Perez v. Cambell, 402 U.S. 637 (1971), discussed in Chapter 6, infra.

3. Railway Labor Executives' Assn. v. Gibbons, 455 U.S. 457, 473 (1982).

4. Id. at 470–71. (invalidating the 1980 Rock Island Railroad Transition and Employee Assistance Act, a measure that would have reorganized one specific railroad and distributed its property among its debtors, and expressly distinguishing private spending bills or highly specific exercises of the commence power).

5. The classic definition of geographic uniformity is that given in the Head Money Cases, 112 U.S. 580, 594 (1884), to describe the uniformity requirement that article I, § 8, imposes upon federal excise taxes: "The tax is uniform when it operates with the same force and effect in every place where the subject of it is found."

6. 419 U.S. 102, 158, 160 (1974).

7. Id. at 160. Justice Douglas dissented: "security holders of rail carriers who now or in the future are in . . . reorganization in the South or West will receive more considerate treatment than plaintiffs below in these cases." Id. at 182 (Douglas, J., dissenting). But see id. at 161 ("The definition of the region does not obscure the reality that the legislation applies to all railroads under reorganization . . . during the time the Act applies").

law relies upon state law for the definition of debtors' property exempt from the bankruptcy proceedings.[8]

Congressional power under the bankruptcy clause, of course, is also limited by such restraints as those of article III,[9] and of the Bill of Rights.[10] And, to turn from bankruptcy to an area of power with *chiefly* external limits, we consider the clause of article I, § 8, which authorizes Congress "To establish Post Offices and Post Roads." By 1878, despite earlier controversy over the meaning of the word "establish," [11] the Supreme Court regarded it as settled that congressional postal power includes "not merely the designation of the routes over which the mail shall be carried, and the offices where letters and other documents shall be received to be distributed or forwarded," but also authority to arrange for "the carriage of the mail, and all measures necessary to secure its safe and speedy transit, and the prompt delivery of its contents;" the "power possessed by Congress embraces the regulation of the entire postal system of the country." [12]

The postal power that article I, § 8, grants Congress includes the power to exclude material from the mails.[13] This power of exclusion is obviously a sensitive one; as the Supreme Court long ago recognized in *Ex parte Jackson*, it must be exercised "consistently with rights reserved to the people, of far greater importance than the transportation of the mail." [14] Thus, the fourth amendment protection against unrea-

8. See Stellwagen v. Clum, 245 U.S. 605, 613 (1918); Hanover Nat'l Bank v. Moyses, 186 U.S. 181, 190 (1902); Vanston Bondholders Protective Comm. v. Green, 329 U.S. 156, 172 (1946) (Frankfurter, J., concurring).

9. For example, in Northern Pipeline Construction Co. v. Marathon Pipe Line Co., 458 U.S. 50 (1982), discussed in § 3–5, supra, the Court held that the 1978 Bankruptcy Reform Act was unconstitutional under article III insofar as it granted certain broad powers of adjudication to bankruptcy judges not enjoying the independence of article III judges.

10. Those Bill of Rights restraints prominently include the limits that the fifth amendment's due process and just compensation clauses impose upon retroactive destruction of property rights, see § 9–2, infra. See, e.g., Louisville Joint Stock Land Bank v. Radford, 295 U.S. 555, 589 (1935). Even when such restraints are not invoked to invalidate bankruptcy legislation, they remain relevant inasmuch as they discourage enactment of problematic provisions and encourage judicial interpretation of bankruptcy measures along lines that avoid constitutionally troublesome retroactivity. See, e.g., United States v. Security Industrial Bank, 459 U.S. 70, 75, 82 (1982). At least one commentator has suggested that Justice Brandeis' opinion for the Court in the 1935 Radford case marked a shift from emphasis on internal limits in the bankruptcy power to the use

of such external limits as those of the fifth amendment. See Rogers, "The Impairment of Secured Creditors' Rights in Reorganization: A Study of the Relationship Between the Fifth Amendment and the Bankruptcy Clause," 96 Harv.L.Rev. 973 (1983).

11. Compare United States v. Railroad Bridge Co., 27 Fed.Cas. 686, 689 (No. 16,114) (C.C.N.D.Ill.1855) (postal power "has generally been considered as exhausted in the designation of roads on which the mails are to be transported"), with Kohl v. United States, 91 U.S. (1 Otto) 367, 372 (1876) (postal power includes power to obtain sites for post offices by eminent domain).

12. Ex parte Jackson, 96 U.S. (6 Otto) 727, 732 (1878).

13. See, e.g., Electric Bond & Share Co. v. SEC, 303 U.S. 419, 442 (1938) (upholding power of Congress to deny use of the mails to holding companies unregistered with the SEC: "when Congress lays down a valid regulation pertinent to the use of the mails, it may withdraw the privilege of that use from those who disobey"); Public Clearing House v. Coyne, 194 U.S. 497, 508 (1904) (dictum) (noting power of Congress to exclude obscenity from the mails); Ex parte Jackson, 96 U.S. (6 Otto) 727, 736–37 (1878) (affirming congressional power to exclude lottery material from the mails).

14. 96 U.S. at 732.

sonable searches and seizures limits the power of postal officials to inspect the mails for forbidden matter.[15] And since, as Justice Holmes noted, "the use of the mails is almost as much a part of free speech as the right to use our tongues,"[16] the first amendment also restrains congressional exercise of the power to exclude.[17] Congress may not, for example, require recipients of politically unpopular but constitutionally protected material to request in writing that the material be delivered to them.[18] Even if material which Congress seeks to exclude from the mails is not protected by the first amendment because, for example, it is obscene, the procedures set up for accomplishing the exclusion must "include built-in safeguards against curtailment of constitutionally protected expression. . . ."[19] Although Congress cannot authorize postal officials to deny access to the mails to materials protected by the first amendment, Congress may constitutionally allow postal officials to take steps making it possible for unwilling recipients of protected material to avoid receiving it.[20]

Turning finally to an area of congressional authority limited primarily by considerations of federalism, we will examine the clause of article I, § 8, which authorizes Congress "To exercise exclusive Legislation in all Cases whatsoever" over the District of Columbia and "over all Places purchased by the Consent of the Legislature of the State in which the Same shall be, for the Erection of Forts, Magazines, Arsenals, dock-Yards, and other needful Buildings. . . ." We will be concerned also with article IV, § 3, which provides that "The Congress shall have Power to dispose of and make all needful Rules and Regulations

---

15. Id. at 733.

16. United States ex rel. Milwaukee Social Democratic Publishing Co. v. Burleson, 255 U.S. 407, 437 (1921) (Holmes, J., dissenting).

17. Early Supreme Court decisions discussing the limits placed by the first amendment on the congressional postal power may be read to suggest that, if Congress denies access to the mails to certain materials, then Congress must permit some *other* form of interstate transportation of those materials. See Ex parte Rapier, 143 U.S. 110, 133 (1892); Ex parte Jackson, 96 U.S. (6 Otto) 727, 733, 735 (1878). This view has not been followed. See, e.g., 18 U.S.C. § 1461 (prohibiting the mailing of obscene matter), upheld in Roth v. United States, 354 U.S. 476 (1957); 18 U.S.C. § 1462 (prohibiting use of interstate carriers to transport obscene material), upheld in United States v. Orito, 413 U.S. 139 (1973); 18 U.S.C. § 1465 (prohibiting interstate transportation of obscene material).

18. Lamont v. Postmaster General, 381 U.S. 301 (1965). The federal statute struck down in Lamont—the first federal law the Supreme Court ever held to be violative of the first amendment—authorized the Post Office to destroy material the statute labeled as "communist political propaganda" unless the intended recipients of the mate-

rial, after notification by the Post Office, affirmatively indicated their wish to receive the material. This decision is discussed from the first amendment perspective in Chapter 12, infra.

19. Blount v. Rizzi, 400 U.S. 410, 416 (1971). The safeguards the Constitution requires, first set out in Freedman v. Maryland, 380 U.S. 51 (1965), are discussed in Chapter 12.

20. Rowan v. United States Post Office Dept., 397 U.S. 728 (1970) (upholding a federal law providing that a person who has received a "pandering" advertisement may request the Postmaster General to order the sender of the advertisement to refrain from further mailings to the complainant). Under the law upheld in Rowan, the recipient is the sole judge of what is "pandering." "Congress provided this sweeping power not only to protect privacy but to avoid possible constitutional questions that might arise from vesting the power to make any discretionary evaluation of the material in a government official." 397 U.S. at 728. See also Hannegan v. Esquire, Inc., 327 U.S. 146, 156 (1946) ("grave constitutional questions are immediately raised once it is said that the use of the mails is a privilege which may be extended or withheld [by Congress or the Post Office] on any grounds whatsoever").

respecting the Territory or other property belonging to the United States. . . . ."

Article I, § 8's property clause is susceptible of either of two narrow readings which would place important internal limits on this grant of congressional power. The Supreme Court, however, has adopted neither interpretation.

The first narrow reading would treat article I, § 8's recognition of the power to purchase lands with the consent of the relevant state as a denial of the power to purchase lands *without* that state's consent. The Supreme Court, however, long ago rejected this interpretation.[21] Indeed, the Court has held that the federal government need not be frustrated by either a state legislature's or a private property holder's refusal to sell. Congress possesses the power of eminent domain as an inherent "attribute of sovereignty"[22] or as "the offspring of political necessity."[23]

The second narrow reading would recognize the power of Congress to acquire property without the states' consent, but would hold that, in the absence of such consent, the federal government's only rights over the property it holds are the rights of an ordinary proprietor—as those rights are defined by state law. This reading would narrowly circumscribe article IV, § 3's grant of power to make "all needful Rules and Regulations," at least with respect to lands obtained without state consent. In dictum in *Paul v. United States*, the Supreme Court apparently accepted this view.[24] More recently, however, in *Kleppe v. New Mexico*,[25] the Court repudiated the *Paul* dictum: regardless of state consent or nonconsent, under article IV, § 3, in all cases "Congress exercises the powers of both a proprietor and of a legislature over the public domain."[26] "The power over the public land thus entrusted to Congress is without limitations."[27]

The presence or absence of state consent thus does not affect the quantum of congressional power. It is, however, relevant for purposes of determining the extent to which state law governs federal property after federal acquisition. If the federal government acquires land in a state without the state's consent, state law governs the use of federal land much as it would govern use of any other land, except insofar as Congress adopts legislation preempting state regulation, or insofar as state regulation would "affect the title of the United States or embarrass it in using the lands or interfere with its right of disposal."[28]

---

21. See Kohl v. United States, 91 U.S. (1 Otto) 367, 371 (1876).

22. Mississippi & Rum River Boom Co. v. Patterson, 98 U.S. (8 Otto) 403, 406 (1879).

23. Kohl v. United States, 91 U.S. (1 Otto) 367, 371 (1876). The power of eminent domain extends to all private property interests, subject to the just compensation requirement of the fifth amendment. See Chapter 9, infra. Congress may take property only "for public use," but the definition of "public use" is within the discretion of Congress, at least unless the

congressional decision is shown to "involve an impossibility." Old Dominion Land Co. v. United States, 269 U.S. 55, 66 (1925).

24. 371 U.S. 245, 264 (1963).

25. 426 U.S. 529 (1976).

26. Id. at 540.

27. United States v. San Francisco, 310 U.S. 16, 29 (1940).

28. James v. Dravo Contracting Co., 302 U.S. 134, 142 (1937), quoting Surplus Trading Co. v. Cook, 281 U.S. 647, 650 (1930). Of course, a state may regulate only property within its jurisdiction. Federal juris-

Even if the state does consent to federal acquisition, state law continues to govern use of federal property if the state, in giving consent, reserved a right of regulation; obviously the state's right is limited by the extent of the reservation.[29]

The unconditioned consent of a state does not necessarily mean that state law ceases to regulate uses of federally-acquired property. The exclusive jurisdiction that article I, § 8, grants Congress over federal property bars state regulation only of those activities or transactions involving the federal enclaves in which "nothing occurs within the State that gives it jurisdiction to regulate. . . ." [30] Moreover, congressional jurisdiction over federal enclaves is exclusive only if exercised. State law enacted prior to federal acquisition of property continues to govern uses of the property if the state law is "not inconsistent with federal policy" and if it is not "altered by national legislation." [31] "This assures that no area however small will be left without a developed legal system for private rights." [32] Absent congressional action, the state law applied within federal enclaves is *static*. "Since only the law in effect at the time of the transfer of jurisdiction continues in force, future statutes of the state are not part of the body of laws in the ceded area." [33] Congress, however, may validly legislate a policy of *dynamic* conformity under which all state laws enacted subsequent to creation of a federal enclave will apply within the enclave unless they directly conflict with federal legislation.[34]

The federal government's use of its property is "left to the discretion of Congress." [35] The Supreme Court upheld congressional establishment of the Tennessee Valley Authority, for example, on the theory that the potential electrical energy resulting from the construction of federally-owned dams is federal property which Congress is authorized to reduce to possession through the construction of turbines and other equipment, and to dispose of through the construction of transmission lines and sale of the electricity to private parties.[36] Similarly, the Court upheld congressional protection of free-roaming wild burros on federal land: "In our view, the 'complete power' that Congress has over public lands necessarily includes the power to regulate and protect the wildlife living there." [37] Changes in the use of federal property, howev-

diction is necessarily exclusive with respect to territory not within state boundaries, such as the District of Columbia, overseas possessions, and the offshore seabed, see United States v. Maine, 420 U.S. 515 (1975). Federal immunity from state regulation and taxation is discussed in Chapter 6, infra.

29. See Paul v. United States, 371 U.S. 245, 268 (1963).

30. United States v. Mississippi State Tax Comm'n, 412 U.S. 363, 371 (1973).

31. Pacific Coast Dairy v. California Dept. of Agriculture, 318 U.S. 285, 294 (1943).

32. James Stewart & Co. v. Sadrakula, 309 U.S. 94, 100 (1940).

33. Id.

34. See, e.g., United States v. Sharpnack, 355 U.S. 286 (1958) (upholding the Assimilative Crimes Act of 1948, making applicable in federal enclaves state criminal laws enacted after federal acquisition of the property).

35. United States v. Gratiot, 39 U.S. (14 Pet.) 526, 538 (1840).

36. See Ashwander v. TVA, 297 U.S. 288, 335–40 (1936).

37. Kleppe v. New Mexico, 426 U.S. 529, 540–541 (1976); see also Hunt v. United States, 278 U.S. 96 (1928).

er, may deprive Congress of exclusive jurisdiction if state consent had been tied to a particular federal use.[38] Moreover, once federal property is sold to a private party, the state reacquires jurisdiction.[39]

§ 5–12. Congressional Power to Enforce the Civil War Amendments: Overview

Between 1865 and 1870, the Constitution was three times amended, as Congress repeatedly acted to safeguard private rights inadequately protected prior to the Civil War.[1] The thirteenth amendment outlawed slavery and involuntary servitude, except as duly administered punishment for crime. The fourteenth amendment guaranteed all persons the privileges or immunities of United States citizenship, due process of law, and the equal protection of the laws. The fifteenth amendment denied both the federal government and the states power to deprive United States citizens of the right to vote on account of race, color, or previous condition of servitude.

Each of these amendments authorized Congress to enforce "by appropriate legislation" the rights the amendment recognized. Immediately after each amendment's ratification, Congress adopted enforcing legislation.[2] The Supreme Court restrictively construed or simply invalidated much of this legislation,[3] acting to preserve in law the autonomy that the states had largely lost politically in the wake of the Civil War.[4] Following its initial flurry of legislation, Congress, reflecting the changed political climate of the post-Reconstruction era, ceased for three quarters of a century its efforts to enforce the Civil War

---

38. See, e.g., Palmer v. Barrett, 162 U.S. 399 (1896) (federal exclusive jurisdiction terminated by federal lease of land for use as market since state consent to federal jurisdiction had been conditioned upon use of land for navy yard or navy hospital).

39. S.R.A., Inc. v. Minnesota, 327 U.S. 558, 564 (1946); Fort Leavenworth R.R. v. Lowe, 114 U.S. 525, 542 (1885).

§ 5–12

1. See generally C. Fairman, Reconstruction and Reunion 1117–1300 (1971).

2. To enforce the thirteenth amendment, Congress adopted the Civil Rights Act of 1866, 14 Stat. 27, and the Anti-Peonage Act of 1867, 14 Stat. 546. Congress reenacted the Civil Rights Act of 1866 as § 18 of the Enforcement Act of 1870, 16 Stat. 141, as a measure also enforcing the fourteenth amendment. The Civil Rights Act of 1875, 18 Stat. 336, likewise sought to enforce thirteenth and fourteenth amendment rights. Through provisions of the Enforcement Act and the Force Act of 1871, 16 Stat. 433, Congress acted to enforce the fifteenth amendment. The Ku Klux Klan Act of 1871, 17 Stat. 15, chiefly enforced fourteenth and fifteenth amendment rights. See generally 1 B. Schwartz, Statutory History of the United States: Civil Rights (1970).

3. See Hodges v. United States, 203 U.S. 1 (1906) (Civil Rights Act of 1866); James v. Bowman, 190 U.S. 127 (1903) (Enforcement Act); Civil Rights Cases, 109 U.S. 3 (1883) (Civil Rights Act of 1875); United States v. Harris, 106 U.S. (16 Otto) 629 (1883) (Ku Klux Klan Act); United States v. Reese, 92 U.S. (2 Otto) 214 (1876) (Enforcement Act).

4. "The law in question, without any reference to adverse State legislation on the subject, declares that all persons shall be entitled to equal accommodations and privileges of inns, public conveyances, and places of public amusement, and imposes a penalty upon any individual who shall deny to any citizen such equal accommodations and privileges. This is not corrective legislation; it is primary and direct; it takes immediate and absolute possession of the subject of the right of admission to inns, public conveyances, and places of amusement. It supersedes and displaces State legislation on the same subject or only allows it permissive force. It ignores such legislation, and assumes that the matter is one that belongs to the domain of national regulation." Civil Rights Cases, 109 U.S. 3, 18–19 (1883).

amendments.[5]   In the 1960's, however, there was a resurgence of congressional interest in protecting individual rights.   The first major legislation, drafted with an eye to avoiding constitutional controversy, took the form of regulation of interstate commerce.[6]   Subsequent legislation [7] triggered a Supreme Court re-evaluation of doctrines limiting congressional power under the Civil War amendments.   A series of decisions appeared to hold that the power of Congress to enforce the thirteenth, fourteenth, and fifteenth amendments was without significant internal limits,[8] being restricted only by the rationality standard of *McCulloch v. Maryland*,[9] and of course by the Bill of Rights.   But a 1970 decision, holding without majority opinion that Congress exceeded its fourteenth amendment power in legislating a lowered voting age for state elections,[10] signaled that congressional power to enforce the Civil War amendments may not be entirely free of internal constraints.

§ 5–13. Congressional Power to Enforce the Thirteenth Amendment

The thirteenth amendment provides in § 1 that "[n]either slavery nor involuntary servitude, except as a punishment for crime whereof the party shall have been duly convicted, shall exist within the United States, or any place subject to their jurisdiction."   Section 2 provides that "Congress shall have power to enforce this article by appropriate legislation."   Initially, the Supreme Court read § 2 as a narrow grant of power.   In the *Civil Rights Cases*, the Court concluded that the amendment authorized Congress to regulate not only state action, but private conduct as well.[1]   Such legislation, however, could concern itself only "with slavery and its incidents." [2]   "The long existence of African slavery in this country," the Court concluded, "gave us very distinct notions of what it was, and what were its necessary incidents." [3]   In "abolishing all badges and incidents of slavery," [4] Congress could not "adjust what may be called the social rights of men and races in the community; but only . . . declare and vindicate those fundamental rights which appertain to the essence of citizenship, and the enjoyment or deprivation of which constitutes the essential distinction between freedom and slavery." [5]   "It would be running the slavery argument into the ground to make it apply to every act of discrimination which a person may see fit to make as to the guests he will entertain, or as to

---

5. Indeed, in 1894, Congress repealed the most important of the Reconstruction civil rights statutes which the Supreme Court had not struck down, the suffrage protections of the Enforcement Act and the Force Act. See B. Schwartz, supra note 2, at 803–34.

6. See Civil Rights Act of 1964, 42 U.S.C. § 2000a et seq., upheld in Katzenbach v. McClung, 379 U.S. 294 (1964), discussed in §§ 5–5 and 5–6, supra.

7. See Voting Rights Act of 1965, 42 U.S.C. § 1973 et seq.; Voting Rights Act Amendments of 1970, id.

8. See, e.g., Jones v. Alfred H. Mayer Co., 392 U.S. 409 (1968) (thirteenth amend-

ment); Katzenbach v. Morgan, 384 U.S. 641 (1966) (fourteenth amendment); South Carolina v. Katzenbach, 383 U.S. 301 (1966) (fifteenth amendment).

9. See § 5–3, supra.

10. Oregon v. Mitchell, 400 U.S. 112 (1970).

§ 5–13

1. 109 U.S. 3, 23 (1883).

2. Id.

3. Id. at 22.

4. Id. at 20.

5. Id. at 22.

the people he will take into his coach or cab or car, or admit to his concert or theatre, or deal with in other matters of intercourse or business." [6]

Subsequent decisions further restricted congressional power. In *Hodges v. United States*, the Supreme Court held that Congress could proscribe only those private acts which created a "state of entire subjection of one person to the will of another." [7] "No mere personal assault or trespass or appropriation operates to reduce the individual to a condition of slavery." [8] Moreover, in *Corrigan v. Buckley* [9] and *Hurd v. Hodge*,[10] the Court indicated that the thirteenth amendment did not grant Congress power to prohibit agreements among whites to refuse to deal with blacks (e.g., racially restrictive covenants).[11]

In *Jones v. Alfred H. Mayer Co.*,[12] however, the Supreme Court redefined the scope of congressional power under the thirteenth amendment. Overruling *Hodges v. United States*,[13] the Court rejected the notion that any judicially defined concept of slavery significantly limited the scope of congressional power. "Congress has the power under the Thirteenth Amendment rationally to determine what are the badges and incidents of slavery, and the authority to translate that determination into effective legislation." [14]

If *Jones* is read literally, Congress possesses a power to protect individual rights under the thirteenth amendment which is as open-ended as its power to regulate interstate commerce. Seemingly, Con-

6. Id. at 24–25.

7. 203 U.S. 1, 17 (1906).

8. Id. at 18.

9. 271 U.S. 323, 330–31 (1926).

10. 334 U.S. 24, 31 (1948).

11. But see note 16, infra. Supreme Court decisions of this era were not uniformly hostile to thirteenth amendment claims. In the Civil Rights Cases, 109 U.S. 3, 20 (1883), the Court acknowledged that the amendment's prohibitions were "undoubtedly self-executing." Moreover, Hodges v. United States, 203 U.S. 1 (1906), despite its restrictive reading of the rights protected by the thirteenth amendment, echoed dicta in the Slaughterhouse Cases, 83 U.S. (16 Wall.) 36, 72 (1873), in declaring that the thirteenth amendment protected persons of all races: "While the inciting cause of the Amendment was the emancipation of the colored race, yet it is not an attempt to commit that race to the care of the Nation. It is the denunciation of a condition and not a declaration in favor of a particular people. It reaches every race and every individual, and if in any respect it commits one race to the Nation it commits every race and every individual thereof. Slavery or involuntary servitude of the Chinese, of the Italian, of the Anglo-Saxon are as much within its compass as slavery or involuntary servitude of the African" 203 U.S. at 16–17.

In a number of cases, the Supreme Court in fact invoked the thirteenth amendment in declaring state legislation to be unconstitutional. The Court held that states could not punish mere breach of a labor contract as a crime. See, e.g., Pollock v. Williams, 322 U.S. 4 (1944); Taylor v. Georgia, 315 U.S. 25 (1942); Bailey v. Alabama, 219 U.S. 219 (1911). "[I]n general the defense against oppressive hours, pay, working conditions, or treatment is the right to change employers. When the master can compel and the laborer cannot escape the obligation to go on, there is no power below to redress and no incentive above to relieve a harsh overlordship or unwholesome conditions of work." Pollock v. Williams, 322 U.S. at 18. The Court also held unconstitutional a state statute allowing private employers to hire convicts as laborers without fixing any limits on the power of the employers over the convicts. United States v. Reynolds, 235 U.S. 133 (1914). Finally, the Court upheld the constitutionality of the federal Anti-Peonage Act, see 42 U.S.C. § 1994, as a measure designed to enforce the thirteenth amendment. See United States v. Gaskin, 320 U.S. 527 (1944); Clyatt v. United States, 197 U.S. 207 (1905).

12. 392 U.S. 409 (1968).

13. Id. at 442–43 n. 78.

14. Id. at 440.

gress is free, within the broad limits of reason, to recognize whatever rights it wishes, define the infringement of those rights as a form of domination and thus an aspect of slavery, and proscribe such infringement as a violation of the thirteenth amendment. On this view, Congress would possess plenary authority under the thirteenth amendment to protect all but the most trivial individual rights from both governmental and private invasion.

The Supreme Court, however, has had no occasion to consider whether *Jones* means what it says. Since the immediate post-Civil War era, Congress has enacted little legislation which relies upon the thirteenth amendment for constitutional authorization.[15] The Court's recent thirteenth amendment decisions are the result of efforts to resurrect long-ignored post-Civil War statutes.[16] Because these statutes are concerned almost entirely with racial discrimination, they raise few questions about the limits of Congress' thirteenth amendment power;[17] instead, because they were so long ignored, the statutes raise thorny problems of construction given the inherent difficulties of reconciling ambiguous century-old legislative history with contemporary conceptions of individual rights.[18]

15. Some lower federal courts have upheld provisions of Title VIII of the Civil Rights Act of 1968 which prohibit "blockbusting" and discrimination in advertising as legislation enforcing the thirteenth amendment. See Note, "Federal Power to Regulate Private Discrimination: The Revival of the Enforcement Clauses of the Reconstruction Era Amendments," 74 Col.L.Rev. 449, 500 n. 301 (1974).

16. Thus, for example, the Supreme Court has held that 42 U.S.C. § 1982, which grants "[a]ll citizens of the United States . . . the same right . . . as is enjoyed by white citizens . . . to inherit, purchase, lease, sell, hold, and convey real and personal property," prohibits racial discrimination in the sale of private homes, Jones v. Alfred H. Mayer Co., 392 U.S. 409 (1968), a private corporation's racially discriminatory refusal to assign a lease, Sullivan v. Little Hunting Park, Inc., 396 U.S. 229 (1969), and a private association's restriction of use of a community swimming pool to white members, Tillman v. Wheaton-Haven Recreation Assn., Inc., 410 U.S. 431 (1973). Similarly, the Court has held that 42 U.S.C. § 1981, which grants "[a]ll persons . . . the same right . . . to make and enforce contracts," prohibits, inter alia, racially restricted private schools, Runyon v. McCrary, 427 U.S. 160 (1976), as well as racial discrimination by private employers, McDonald v. Santa Fe Trail Transp. Co., 427 U.S. 273 (1976); Johnson v. Railway Express Agency, 421 U.S. 454 (1975). Finally, the Court has held that 42 U.S.C. § 1985(3), which grants a right of action to persons injured by "two or more persons" who "conspire or go in disguise

. . . for the purpose of depriving . . . any person or class of persons of the equal protection of the laws," includes private conspiracies within its prohibition. Griffin v. Breckenridge, 403 U.S. 88 (1971).

17. The lower federal courts have considered the applicability of these statutes, particularly 42 U.S.C. § 1985(3), to private infringements of rights not grounded in racial discrimination. These cases, however, have not generally looked beyond the statutory language to the question of the limits, if any, upon the thirteenth amendment's reach. See generally Note, "The Scope of Section 1985(3) Since Griffin v. Breckenridge," 45 Geo.Wash.L.Rev. 239 (1977).

18. In Jones v. Alfred H. Mayer Co., 392 U.S. 409 (1968), for example, Justice Harlan contributed an extended dissent arguing that the legislative history surrounding the enactment of what is now 42 U.S.C. § 1982, while ambiguous, appears to suggest that the statute was not in fact intended to reach private discrimination. See 392 U.S. at 454–76. A number of distinguished commentators, agreeing with Justice Harlan, have criticized the contrary conclusion of the Jones majority. See, e.g., C. Fairman, Reconstruction and Reunion 1207–58 (1971); Casper, "Jones v. Mayer: Clio, Bemused and Confused Muse," 1968 Sup.Ct.Rev. 89. Apart from whatever value it may have as an analysis of the Court's craftsmanship, however, the implications of this historical critique are not clear. "For even if Jones did not accurately reflect the sentiments of the Reconstruction Congress, it surely accords with the

The Supreme Court has indicated in a few recent decisions that it has not yet truly decided how extensive Congress' thirteenth amendment powers are. To be sure, the Court has not repudiated those of its early decisions, plainly grounded in the language of the thirteenth amendment, which declare that persons of all races, and not blacks alone, may claim the benefits of the thirteenth amendment's proscription of slavery and its incidents.[19] Indeed, the Court has recently held that whites victimized by racial discrimination are entitled to the protections of a civil rights statute enacted by Congress shortly after the Civil War in the exercise of its thirteenth amendment powers.[20] In at least two cases, however, the Supreme Court has indicated in dictum its doubts as to whether the thirteenth amendment does indeed grant Congress general authority to protect *all* individual rights against *all* invasions whatever. In *Norwood v. Harrison*, in discussing the thirteenth amendment, the Court was willing to say no more than that "*some* private discrimination is subject to special remedial legislation *in certain circumstances* under § 2 of the Thirteenth Amendment."[21] More significantly, in *Griffin v. Breckenridge*, Justice Stewart, author of the Court's opinion in *Jones*, spoke for the Court about "[t]he constitutional shoals that would be in the path of interpreting [42 U.S.C. § 1985(3)] as a general federal tort law,"[22] and further observed that "we need not find the language of § 1985(3) now before us constitutional in all its possible applications"[23]—words of caution which would have made little sense if *Jones'* recognition of plenary congressional power could be taken literally.[24] To see what might trouble the Court, it is necessary to look to its treatment of congressional power to enforce the fourteenth and fifteenth amendments.

§ 5–14. Congressional Power to Enforce the Fourteenth and Fifteenth Amendments

Although Congress has not acted to take advantage of the thirteenth amendment's grant of power in recent years, contemporary

prevailing sense of justice today." Runyon v. McCrary, 427 U.S. 160, 191 (1976) (Stevens, J., concurring). Although agreeing with those who thought Jones wrongly decided as an original matter, id. at 189–90, Justice Stevens thoughtfully observed that Jones had become "an important part of the fabric of our law," id. at 190, and that "[f]or the Court [in 1976] to overrule Jones would be a significant step backwards, with effects that would not have arisen from a correct decision in the first instance." Id. at 191. Thus he thought the Court "entirely correct in adhering to Jones." Id. at 192. My own view—that Jones was in fact correct *when decided*—may be affected by my role at that time as law clerk to Justice Stewart, the opinion's author.

19. See note 11, supra.

20. McDonald v. Santa Fe Trail Transp. Co., 427 U.S. 273, 285–96 (1976). The Court stressed that the actions challenged were not claimed to be "any part of an affirmative action program," and that it was not considering "the permissibility of such a program, whether judicially required or otherwise prompted." Id. at 281 n. 8. See § 16–22, infra.

21. 413 U.S. 455, 470 (1973).

22. 403 U.S. 88, 102 (1971).

23. Id. at 104.

24. The Griffin opinion was plainly concerned not simply with external, Bill of Rights' limits on congressional power under the Civil War amendments, see Runyon v. McCrary, 427 U.S. 160, 175–79 (1976) (considering, but rejecting on the facts of the case, challenges to the congressional ban on segregated private schools based on freedom of association, parental rights, and the right of privacy), but with the possible need for internal, federalism-based limits on congressional enforcement authority.

Congresses have repeatedly sought to enforce what they understand to be the commands of the fourteenth and fifteenth amendments. As a result, the Supreme Court has found itself confronting, at the level of constitutional power, the issue that it has been able to treat largely as a matter of statutory construction in the thirteenth amendment context: to what extent does Congress have authority to define for itself violations of constitutional guarantees; alternatively, to what extent do the limits which confine judicial enforcement of those guarantees' self-executing provisions also restrict congressional legislation?

The discussion which follows reflects the path of history rather than the logic of the Constitution's own ordering. Analysis begins with the fifteenth amendment rather than the fourteenth because that is the sequence in which the Supreme Court has considered the amendments in recent years. Analysis ends, rather than begins, with the state action question because, although constitutional texts and early decisions make that question paramount, recent Supreme Court decisions render it less central in this context.

The fifteenth amendment's guarantee of a racially unconditioned right to vote, like the various guarantees of the fourteenth amendment, is self-executing.[1] On a number of occasions, litigants have persuaded the Supreme Court that states have violated the limitation the fifteenth amendment imposes upon them even in the absence of implementing federal legislation.[2] Apart from several early statutes,[3] Congress has

§ 5–14

1. Guinn v. United States, 238 U.S. 347, 363 (1915).

2. The Supreme Court has held that the fifteenth amendment prohibits state action which on its face discriminates against black voters. See, e.g. Neal v. Delaware, 103 U.S. (13 Otto) 370, 389 (1881) (statute granting franchise to "free white male citizens" rendered "inoperative" by adoption of fifteenth amendment); see also Nixon v. Herndon, 273 U.S. 536 (1927) (state statute denying blacks right to vote in primary violates fourteenth amendment). The fifteenth amendment also prohibits state action which, although nondiscriminatory on its face, reveals a forbidden discriminatory purpose through its operation. "The Amendment nullifies sophisticated as well as simple-minded modes of discrimination." Lane v. Wilson, 307 U.S. 268 (1939). See also Hunter v. Underwood, 471 U.S. 222 (1985), discussed in § 16–20, infra. See generally Chapters 13, 16 and 18, infra. Indeed, because the fifteenth amendment so squarely prohibits racially-based denials of the right to vote, the Court's fifteenth amendment cases focus almost exclusively on whether racially uneven effects sufficiently establish inferences of state racial discrimination. See, e.g., Guinn v. United States, 238 U.S. 347 (1915) (grandfather clause exempting from literacy test all lineal descendants of persons entitled to vote or residing in some foreign nation on January 1, 1866, violates fifteenth amendment); Lane v. Wilson, supra (statute granting voters not qualifying under grandfather clause only 12 days within which to register unconstitutionally discriminates between black and white voters); Nixon v. Condon, 286 U.S. 73 (1932) (party executive committee authorized by state law to determine qualifications for voters in primary election violates fourteenth amendment when it excludes voters on racial grounds); Grovey v. Townsend, 295 U.S. 45 (1935) (political party convention is organ of a private association and therefore is not constitutionally restricted in deciding who may vote in its primary), overruled in Smith v. Allwright, 321 U.S. 649 (1944) (state which makes primary elections an integral part of the state's electoral process cannot treat political party which determines voter eligibility as private actor free from fifteenth amendment constraints); Terry v. Adams, 345 U.S. 461 (1953) (state violates fifteenth amendment by allowing operation of all-white preprimary election which effectively determines outcome of Democratic primary elections); Gomillion v. Lightfoot, 364 U.S. 339 (1960) (redefinition of city boundaries to exclude almost all black voters violates fifteenth amendment); Wright v. Rockefeller, 376 U.S. 52 (1964) (no fifteenth amendment violation shown where legislative design of congres-

3. See note 3 on page 336.

until recently confined its legislation enforcing the fifteenth amendment largely to procedural measures designed to facilitate judicial enforcement of the constitutional guarantee.[4] The Supreme Court had little difficulty upholding such measures as "appropriate legislation."[5] By 1965, however, Congress had concluded that judicial remedies were too time-consuming and piecemeal, and could too readily be circumvented to provide effective enforcement for fifteenth amendment rights.[6] Accordingly, Congress enacted the Voting Rights Act of 1965,[7] probably the most radical piece of civil rights legislation since Reconstruction. The Voting Rights Act had two principal features of relevance to fifteenth amendment jurisprudence. First, the Act authorized the Attorney General to suspend voting tests, and to send federal voting examiners into any state whose voter registration pattern met certain criteria.[8] Although the Attorney General's determinations were subject to a narrow form of after-the-fact judicial review,[9] this first provision largely substituted administrative remedies for judicial relief as the principal means of enforcing the fifteenth amendment. Second, the Voting Rights Act did not require the Attorney General to make the detailed determination a court would make before acting, but rather authorized enforcement procedures wherever the use of certain "tests" or "devices" in registering voters coincided with the circumstance that less than 50% of voting age residents were in fact registered.[10] The states could seek a judicial finding of no racial discrimination in order to block enforcement of the Voting Rights Act,[11] but administrative rules of thumb essentially replaced the fact-finding criteria that courts had previously developed in the course of constitutional adjudication.[12]

The constitutionality of the Voting Rights Act was settled in *South Carolina v. Katzenbach*, where the Court rejected the argument that "Congress may do no more than to forbid violations of the Fifteenth Amendment in general terms—that the task of fashioning specific remedies or of applying them to particular localities must necessarily be left entirely to the courts"; "Congress is not circumscribed by any

sional districts was plausibly explained by nonracial as well as racial considerations); Louisiana v. United States, 380 U.S. 145 (1965) (state violates fifteenth amendment through use of "interpretation" test granting registrars unreviewable discretion to decide who understands state or federal constitutional provision and thus who may vote, where such discretion had been exercised to deny blacks right to vote).

3. See § 5–12, supra.

4. The Civil Rights Act of 1957, 71 Stat. 634, authorized the Attorney General to seek injunctions against interference with the right to vote on racial grounds. The Civil Rights Act of 1960, 74 Stat. 86, permitted joinder of states as parties defendant, gave the Attorney General access to local voting records, and authorized courts to register voters in areas of systematic discrimination. The Civil Rights Act of

1964, 78 Stat. 241, expedited the hearing of voting cases before three-judge courts and outlawed certain tests used to disqualify black voters in federal elections. See generally 42 U.S.C. § 1971.

5. See, e.g., United States v. Raines, 362 U.S. 17 (1960) (Civil Rights Act of 1957); Hannah v. Larche, 363 U.S. 420 (1960) (same); United States v. Mississippi, 380 U.S. 128 (1965) (Civil Rights Act of 1960).

6. See South Carolina v. Katzenbach, 383 U.S. 301, 314–15 (1966).

7. 42 U.S.C. § 1973 et seq.

8. See 42 U.S.C. §§ 1973b, 1973d.

9. See 42 U.S.C. § 1973b(a), (d).

10. See 42 U.S.C. § 1973b(b).

11. See note 9, supra.

12. See cases cited in note 2, supra.

such artificial rules under § 2 of the Fifteenth Amendment." [13]   Instead, the fifteenth amendment left "Congress . . . chiefly responsible for implementing the rights created." [14]   To this end, congressional power must be measured by the generous standard fixed by Chief Justice Marshall in *McCulloch v. Maryland*: "Let the end be legitimate, let it be within the scope of the constitution, and all means which are appropriate, which are plainly adapted to the end, which are not prohibited, but consistent with the letter and spirit of the constitution, are constitutional." [15]   The Supreme Court readily found that the remedial and factfinding provisions of the Voting Rights Act met this traditional rationality test.[16]

The contrast between the jurisprudence of outright fourteenth and fifteenth amendment violations and the permitted power of Congress to enforce those amendments is highlighted by a comparison of *City of Mobile v. Bolden* [17] and *City of Rome v. United States*,[18] decided the

---

13. 383 U.S. 301, 327 (1966).

14. Id. at 326.

15. Id., quoting 17 U.S. (4 Wheat.) 316, 421 (1819); see § 5–3, supra.

16. See 383 U.S. at 327–37. In Oregon v. Mitchell, 400 U.S. 112 (1970), the Supreme Court unanimously upheld the constitutionality of a provision of the Voting Rights Act Amendments of 1970 which imposed a national ban on literacy tests of voter eligibility for five years; all but one of the Justices treated this legislation as enforcing the fifteenth amendment. But see 400 U.S. at 144–47 (opinion of Douglas, J.) (relying upon fourteenth amendment as source of congressional power).

With the exception of City of Mobile v. Bolden, 446 U.S. 55 (1980) and City of Rome v. United States, 446 U.S. 156 (1980), most voter discrimination cases since South Carolina v. Katzenbach, 383 U.S. 301 (1966), have been wholly statutory; the Supreme Court has focused on interpreting the Voting Rights Act and not on the power of Congress to enact the provisions in question. See, e.g., Beer v. United States, 425 U.S. 130 (1976); City of Richmond v. United States, 422 U.S. 358 (1975). In 1977, however, the Court had occasion to consider the question of congressional power in United Jewish Organizations of Williamsburgh v. Carey, 430 U.S. 144 (1977). In this case, Hasidic Jews whose neighborhood the New York legislature had formerly included in a single election district brought suit challenging the constitutionality of a redistricting which divided the Hasidic neighborhood between two districts. It was undisputed that the redistricting took race into account in attempting to guarantee the voting strength of black voters. Plaintiffs alleged that such race-conscious districting violated the fourteenth and fifteenth amendments. Although the Supreme Court decided by a 7–

1 margin that New York had not acted unconstitutionally, the Court could not agree on a majority opinion. Chief Justice Burger was the sole dissenter. Id. at 180. Justice White, joined by Justices Brennan, Blackmun, and Stevens, held that New York acted constitutionally because it took the steps it did in order to comply with the Voting Rights Act, which could constitutionally require states subject to the Act to take race into account in redistricting in order to avoid diluting the strength of black voters. See id. at 155–65. See also id. at 168–79 (Brennan, J., concurring in part). In any event, Justices White, Stevens, and Rehnquist concluded, even if New York had not acted under the compulsion or even the authority of the Voting Rights Act, it did not act unconstitutionally. See id. at 165–68. Justices Stewart and Powell, in a separate concurring opinion, argued that New York had not violated the fourteenth and fifteenth amendments whether or not the Voting Rights Act was properly construed to compel the acts that New York took in purported compliance with the Act. See id. at 179–80. Thus, four Justices (White, Brennan, Blackmun, Stevens) were prepared to say that congressionally-required benign discrimination with respect to voting is constitutional. But because two of these Justices (White and Stevens) agreed with another (Rehnquist) that benign racial discrimination in the voting context would have been constitutional even if New York had acted *without* federal prodding, the case in the end says little about the full reach of congressional power to authorize remedies for racial discrimination in voting or otherwise. See § 16–22, infra, on affirmative action with respect to race.

17. 446 U.S. 55 (1980).

18. 446 U.S. 156 (1980).

same day in 1980. In *Mobile,* a black resident challenged the constitutionality of a state legislative apportionment plan which utilized at-large elections of multiple representatives from a single district, effectively blocking the election of black candidates by Mobile's sizable black minority. Justice Stewart's plurality opinion held that the Mobile election scheme violated neither the fourteenth nor the fifteenth amendment because, although it drastically diluted black voting strength, there was insufficient evidence to establish that the scheme was adopted or maintained with intent to discriminate.[19] Mobile's electoral scheme was not challenged under the Voting Rights Act— which applies only to changes in voting procedures made since 1965— because it had been in place since 1911.

The *Rome* litigation challenged the city's annexation of 60 outlying areas and a change to a system of electing members of the city commission at large; both changes had transpired since 1965. Although this is virtually the same kind of system which the Court upheld in *Mobile,* and even though the district court explicitly found that none of the *Rome* electoral changes were made for discriminatory purposes, the changes were disallowed under the Voting Rights Act. The district court had concluded that the Voting Rights Act required the court to invalidate the changes if they had either the purpose *or* the effect of diluting black voting strength. In a 6–3 decision, the Supreme Court agreed, and found that Congress had the power under Section 2 of the fifteenth amendment to prohibit these electoral changes and annexations even though they were not intentionally discriminatory.

Justice Marshall's opinion for the Court held that Congress could conclude that "because electoral changes by jurisdictions with a demonstrable history of intentional racial discrimination in voting create the *risk* of purposeful discrimination, it was proper [for Congress] to prohibit changes that have a discriminatory impact." [20] Thus the Court held that Congress may establish a prophylactic rule—almost a rule of evidence—by deciding that certain types of changes in electoral law which have the effect of burdening minorities should be forbidden because, many of them may have been discriminatorily motivated.

19. Justice Stewart's opinion was joined by Chief Justice Burger and Justices Powell and Rehnquist. Justice Blackmun, concurring in the result, agreed with the dissenters that the findings of the district court "amply support an inference of purposeful discrimination," but felt that the district court's remedy—the imposition of a mayor-council system—was "not commensurate with the sound exercise of judicial discretion." 446 U.S. at 80. Justice Stevens, concurring in the judgment, agreed with the plurality that no constitutional violation had been proved, but applied a three-part test that sought to measure the "objective effects of the political decision rather than the subjective motivation of the decisionmaker." 446 U.S. at 90. Justice Stevens' standard tested whether the political configuration (1) was the product of a routine or traditional political decision; (2) had a significant adverse impact on a minority group; and (3) was unsupported by any neutral justification and thus was either totally irrational or entirely motivated by a desire to curtail the political strength of the minority. See id. Justices Brennan, White and Marshall, dissenting, argued that the black citizens had met the burden of showing discriminatory purpose. In addition, Justice Marshall, with whom Justice Brennan agreed, argued that the black voters could prove a violation of the fourteenth and fifteenth amendments simply by proving a discriminatory impact on their right to vote. See 446 U.S. at 94, 116–17, 126–129.

20. 446 U.S. at 177 (emphasis added; footnote omitted).

Justice Rehnquist charged in dissent that this holding amounted to allowing Congress an independent right to interpret the substance of the fifteenth amendment itself.[21] His reading, however, overstated the majority's position in *Rome*. Because district courts may take years to examine all the evidence relevant to the issue of discriminatory purpose in a voting rights case, and because the local government may too easily disguise the real reason for its actions, the Court held that Congress may simply choose to circumvent the problems of proof. To do so Congress created a general rule based on its own finding that certain practices are so likely to have been adopted for discriminatory reasons that they should be prohibited altogether. Justice Rehnquist argued that, while Congress did have the power to establish a presumption that certain kinds of electoral changes were undertaken for discriminatory reasons, Congress may not establish an "irrebuttable presumption," which he believed the Court applied in *Rome*.[22] Such a presumption, he argued, amounted to a substantive change in the fifteenth amendment, one the Court itself has not viewed as compelled by that amendment. But, as Professor Choper has cogently argued, "Congress had the right not to trust [the] findings of a single Federal District judge as to what the motivation of the legislature was. The problems of proof are too difficult, too complex for a case by case adjudication. Since electoral changes and annexations have been used in the past for purposes of discrimination, Congress can outlaw them all."[23] In addition, a ban on particular election practices that are themselves constitutionally inoffensive could be justified instrumentally—to add to the political clout that such a ban would give to a traditionally powerless group seeking to press for equality under the law.[24] Thus, while *Rome* asserts a broad congressional power to *enforce* the fifteenth amendment, it need not be read as an independent assertion of congressional power to *interpret* it.

After the decisions in *Mobile* and *Rome*, Congress amended the Voting Rights Act to make challenges easier and to move the courts towards an effects rather than an intent test. At the time of *Mobile*, section 2 of the Act stated that "no voting qualification or prerequisite to voting or standard, practice or procedure shall be imposed or applied by any State or political subdivision *to deny or abridge* the right of any citizen of the United States to vote on account of race or color." (emphasis added). *Mobile* interpreted section 2 as "intended to have an effect no different from that of the Fifteenth Amendment itself."[25] In

21. See 446 U.S. at 206 (Rehnquist, J., dissenting). Justice Stewart joined Justice Rehnquist's opinion. Justice Powell also dissented, on the ground that the Court read the Voting Rights Act incorrectly. See 446 U.S. at 193. (Powell, J., dissenting).

22. 446 U.S. at 215 (Rehnquist, J., dissenting).

23. J. Choper, Y. Kamisar & L. Tribe, 2 The Supreme Court: Trends and Developments 1979–1980 38 (National Practice Institute 1981). See also Choper, "Congressional Power to Expand Judicial Definitions of the Substantive Terms of the Civil War Amendments," 67 Minn.L.Rev. 299, 331–32 (1982).

24. See Katzenbach v. Morgan, 384 U.S. 641, 652–53 (1966) (Congress may outlaw use of English literacy tests as prerequisite to right to vote in order to give Puerto Ricans the political power necessary to end discriminatory treatment in areas other than voting).

25. 446 U.S. at 61 (plurality opinion).

1982, Congress substituted the words "in a manner which results in a denial or abridgement of" for those words italicized above.[26] The Voting Rights Act Amendment of 1982 added: "The extent to which members of a protected class have been elected to office in the State or political subdivision is one circumstance which may be considered: Provided, That nothing in this section establishes a right to have members of a protected class elected in numbers equal to their proportion in the population." [27]

The Court has not yet settled whether, with this change, Congress put itself in conflict with the Court's reading of the fifteenth amendment.[28] The Supreme Court did summarily affirm a district court decision which found the 1982 amendments constitutional.[29] The affirmance, however, drew strong dissent from Justice Rehnquist, who argued that several issues relating to the amendments should be fully aired.[30] In *Thornburg v. Gingles*,[31] the full Court did apply the 1982 amendments for the first time, holding, in part, that the Senate "Report dispositively rejects the position of the plurality in *Mobile v. Bolden*, which required proof that the contested electoral practice or mechanism was adopted or maintained with the intent to discriminate against minority voters." [32] The question of Congress' authority essentially to reverse *Mobile*—which was, after all, a purely constitutional holding—was not briefed or argued by the parties, nor raised by any of the Justices. When and if the question does come before the Court, the supporters of Congress' action will argue that the legislature had the right to use its fact-finding abilities to recognize that discriminatory effects in voting amount to overwhelming proof of discriminatory intent, and to adjust the law accordingly. The members of the *Mobile* majority may well contend that Congress had no such right. Notwithstanding the Court's treatment of the 1982 amendments in *Thornburg*, the matter should not be seen as settled. But the approach taken by the Court in *Rome*, which seems eminently sound, provides strong support for the constitutional validity of Congress' 1982 action.

Congressional power to enforce the fourteenth amendment has consistently been the source of even more pronounced and persistent constitutional controversy. That amendment recognizes a number of broad protections that the Supreme Court has never succeeded in defining in any limited way. The guarantees of due process and equal protection, at various times since the Civil War, have been construed to affect many of the most important aspects of the nation's economic, political, and social life. Because the fourteenth amendment's phrases are so open to interpretation, they invite not only remedial congressional legislation, but congressional definition of the very rights themselves. In this regard, the fourteenth amendment resembles the thirteenth.

---

26. 42 U.S.C. § 1973(a).

27. 42 U.S.C. § 1973(b).

28. The one circuit court to pass on the 1982 statute's constitutionality has upheld it. See United States v. Marengo County Comm'n, 731 F.2d 1546 (11th Cir. 1984), cert. denied 469 U.S. 976 (1984).

29. See Mississippi Republican Executive Comm. v. Brooks, 469 U.S. 1002 (1984), aff'g 604 F.Supp. 807 (N.D. Miss. 1984).

30. See 469 U.S. at 1005. Chief Justice Burger joined Justice Rehnquist's opinion.

31. 106 S.Ct. 2752 (1986).

32. Id. at 2763.

Unlike the thirteenth amendment's grant of congressional authority, however, the fourteenth amendment's analogous enforcement provision has not lain dormant in recent years. In reviewing legislation enacted under § 5 of the fourteenth amendment, the Supreme Court has had to confront certain fundamental questions: Does Congress possess a power to define constitutional rights unencumbered by judicial conceptions of those rights, at least insofar as the congressional definitions rationally relate to the language of the fourteenth amendment and violate none of the restrictions which the Bill of Rights imposes on Congress? Or do judicially defined rights instead fix the limits of the congressionally possible by serving as relatively detailed descriptions of the ends that congressional action protecting fourteenth amendment rights must further?

Katzenbach v. Morgan [33] remains the leading case. Section 4(e) of the Voting Rights Act of 1965 provides in essence that no person who has successfully completed the sixth grade in an accredited Spanish-language Puerto Rican school may be denied the right to vote because of an inability to read or write English.[34] New York voters, protesting section 4(e)'s nullification of the state's English literacy requirement, brought suit claiming that section 4(e) could not be justified as a measure enforcing the fourteenth amendment since the Supreme Court had previously held that such a literacy requirement did not violate that amendment's equal protection clause.[35] The Supreme Court disagreed. Justice Brennan's majority opinion held that § 5 of the fourteenth amendment, authorizing "appropriate" enforcement legislation, "is a positive grant of legislative power authorizing Congress to exercise its discretion in determining whether and what legislation is needed to secure the guarantees of the Fourteenth Amendment." [36] Accordingly, fourteenth amendment legislation is "appropriate" so long as it meets the rationality standard of *McCulloch v. Maryland*,[37] which the Court had previously applied in *South Carolina v. Katzenbach*.[38]

Justice Brennan specifically rested the Court's conclusion on two alternative theories. First, Congress could reasonably conclude that, by granting Puerto Ricans the right to vote, it would be providing this group with a political weapon which its members could use to gain nondiscriminatory treatment in the distribution of political services.[39] On this view, section 4(e)'s protection of the right to vote was a remedy designed to shield Puerto Ricans from unconstitutional acts not directly connected with voting. This theory drew on the acknowledged congressional power to find facts and frame remedies; thus, although it attributed to Congress a somewhat novel remedial program, it marked no doctrinal advance beyond *South Carolina v. Katzenbach*. The second theory was more radical. Justice Brennan suggested that Congress could reasonably have concluded that the English language literacy test itself violated the fourteenth amendment's equal protection clause,

33. 384 U.S. 641 (1966).

34. See 42 U.S.C. § 1973b(e)(1), (2).

35. See Lassiter v. Northampton County Bd. of Elections, 360 U.S. 45 (1959).

36. 384 U.S. at 651.

37. 17 U.S. (4 Wheat.) 316 (1819).

38. 383 U.S. 301 (1966).

39. See 384 U.S. at 652–53.

notwithstanding the previously stated contrary view of the Supreme Court.[40] Under this theory, section 4(e) was remedially quite straight-forward; its novelty lay in the assumed claim of Congress to the post of constitutional interpreter.

Katzenbach v. Morgan, although the leading case, is not the last word. For a time at least, that honor belonged to *Oregon v. Mitchell*.[41] In enacting the Voting Rights Act Amendments of 1970, Congress granted 18-year olds the right to vote in both federal and state elections, justifying this legislation apparently on the theory, at least with regard to the voting age in state elections, that the fourteenth amendment equal protection clause prohibits discrimination in suffrage between individuals aged 18 to 21 and all individuals over 21. In *Oregon v. Mitchell*, the Supreme Court held that, while Congress could lower the voting age to 18 in federal elections, it could not similarly lower the voting age in state elections.[42] Five Justices wrote opinions in *Oregon v. Mitchell*; no one opinion commanded the support of a majority. Four Justices concluded that Congress could lower the voting age in *both* federal *and* state elections; four Justices concluded that Congress could lower the voting age in *neither* federal *nor* state elections; Justice Black concluded that, while Congress could lower the voting age in federal elections, it could not similarly regulate state elections, a proposition which all eight of the other Justices rejected.[43] The Court's major post-*Morgan* "pronouncement" on this issue is thus quite literally incomprehensible. But even if *Oregon v. Mitchell* says nothing in itself, it points mutely to the controversy surrounding *Katzenbach v. Morgan's* second theory.

The proposition that Congress may define the content of fourteenth amendment rights within the broad limits fixed by the rational relationship text excites controversy for two reasons. First, as one commentator has put it, the *Morgan* majority appears to have "stood *Marbury v. Madison* on its head by judicial deference to congressional interpretation of the Constitution."[44] Justice Harlan elaborated this argument in *Oregon v. Mitchell*:[45] ". . . Congress' expression of [its] view . . . cannot displace the duty of this Court to make an independent determination whether Congress has exceeded its powers. The reason for this goes beyond Marshall's assertion that: 'It is emphatically the province and duty of the judicial department to say what the law is.' *Marbury v. Madison* . . . It inheres in the structure of the constitutional system itself. Congress is subject to none of the institutional restraints imposed on judicial decisionmaking; it is controlled only by the political process. In Article V, the Framers expressed the view that the political restraints on Congress alone were an insufficient

---

40. See id. at 653–56; see note 35, supra.

41. 400 U.S. 112 (1970); but cf. United Jewish Organizations of Williamsburgh v. Carey, 430 U.S. 144 (1977), discussed in note 16, supra.

42. See 400 U.S. at 117–18.

43. Quite remarkably, Justice Black therefore announced the Court's judgment but did so "in an opinion expressing [only] his own view of the cases. . . ." Id. at 117.

44. Cohen, "Congressional Power to Interpret Due Process and Equal Protection," 27 Stan.L.Rev. 603, 606 (1975).

45. 400 U.S. at 204–05 (separate opinion of Harlan, J.).

control over the process of constitution making. The concurrence of two-thirds of each House and of three-fourths of the States was needed for the political check to be adequate. To allow a simple majority of Congress to have final say on matters of constitutional interpretation is therefore fundamentally out of keeping with the constitutional structure."

Second, if Congress can define the content of fourteenth amendment guarantees subject only to the relatively toothless limits of the rational relationship requirement, then perhaps Congress can not only extend such guarantees beyond their judicially-given scope, but also narrow them. As Justice Harlan noted in dissent in *Katzenbach v. Morgan*, "[i]n all such cases there is room for reasonable men to differ as to whether or not a denial of equal protection or due process has occurred, and the final decision is one of judgment." [46]

In *Morgan*, Justice Brennan's majority opinion responded to the second of these difficulties by fixing a ratchet-like restraint on the power of Congress to interpret the fourteenth amendment substantively: "We emphasize that Congress' power under § 5 is limited to adopting measures to enforce the guarantees of the Amendment; § 5 grants Congress no power to restrict, abrogate, or dilute these guarantees." [47] Justice Brennan's opinion did not fully explain, however, *why* congressional power was so limited; nor did it attempt to reconcile with the principle of judicial review even a one-way power authoritatively to construe the Constitution.

Indeed, four Justices have recently taken great exception to the notion that Congress may expand the guarantees secured by the fourteenth amendment beyond those recognized by the Supreme Court. A narrow majority of five Justices upheld the extension of the Age Discrimination in Employment Act to cover state and local governments in *EEOC v. Wyoming*.[48] Chief Justice Burger's dissenting opinion not only attacked the majority position as a violation of the tenth amendment,[49] but stated that Congress lacked the affirmative power under the fourteenth amendment to extend the Age Act to the states.[50] The dissent viewed Congress' action as a naked usurpation of the judicial power to interpret the fourteenth amendment. The Chief Justice argued that Congress simply has no constitutional authority to legislate against age discrimination until and unless the Supreme Court guarantees a right against such action.[51] The dissenters did not explicitly propose a limitation of *Morgan*; they said only that Congress, in

46. 384 U.S. at 668.

47. Id. at 651 n. 10.

48. 460 U.S. 226 (1983). Justice Brennan's opinion was joined by Justices White, Marshall, Blackmun and Stevens. The majority did not reach the fourteenth amendment issue in the case, preferring to uphold Congress' authority to pass the statute under the commerce clause. See 460 U.S. at 243 & n. 18.

49. See 460 U.S. at 251–59 (Burger, C.J., dissenting). For a discussion of the place of EEOC v. Wyoming in the National League of Cities v. Usery, 426 U.S. 833 (1976), line of cases, see § 5–22, infra.

50. See 460 U.S. at 259–65 (Burger, C.J., dissenting). The Chief Justice's opinion was joined by Justices Powell, Rehnquist and O'Connor.

51. See 460 U.S. at 260 (Burger, C.J., dissenting).

expanding the Age Act, "did not use, as it did in *Katzenbach v. Morgan*, its 'specially informed legislative competence' to decide that the state law it invalidated was too intrusive on federal rights." [52] Thus it seems that Justice Brennan's first justification for the *Morgan* holding—that Congress may devise its own remedies to shield individuals from violations of federal rights [53]—remains secure. [54]

But Chief Justice Burger's dissent took great exception to Justice Brennan's one-way ratchet theory [55]—the idea that Congress may create a more (but not less) expansive definition of the fourteenth amendment than the Court. Chief Justice Burger accused Congress of "defin[ing] rights wholly independently of our case law" and thereby "fundamentally alter[ing] our scheme of government." [56] The Chief Justice's narrow view of the national legislature's power to implement equal protection of the laws hardly comports with history. Congress, after all, passed the first civil rights acts pursuant to the thirteenth and fourteenth amendments before any *court* had held that blacks had a right to be free of invidious discrimination. Congress' authority to enact legislation to implement civil rights derives from the constitutional text itself. Moreover, the way Chief Justice Burger would carve up the equal protection clause and sort it into pigeon-holes labeled "race," "gender" and "age" is inimical to the fourteenth amendment's goal of making all citizens equal under law.

The dissent asserted that the Age Discrimination Act could not be justified as a congressional attempt to provide further safeguards for a constitutionally protected class because the Court had never held that age discrimination was forbidden by the fourteenth amendment. [57] Although it is true that the two cases that have considered the constitutionality of mandatory retirement schemes, *Vance v. Bradley*, [58] and *Massachusetts Bd. of Retirement v. Murgia*, [59] both applied the deferential rationality standard, neither suggested that all discrimination

---

52. 460 U.S. at 262 (Burger, C.J., dissenting) (quoting Katzenbach v. Morgan, 384 U.S. 641, 656 (1966)).

53. See 384 U.S. at 652–53.

54. This assumption is reinforced by the Court's opinion in Fullilove v. Klutznick, 448 U.S. 448 (1980), a case challenging the constitutionality of Congress' mandatory 10% set-aside in federal construction grants for minority-owned businesses. The Court upheld the set-aside in Fullilove, finding in that affirmative action program no violation of the equal protection component of the fifth amendment. Chief Justice Burger's opinion for the six-member majority had little trouble concluding that Congress had the right to authorize this program using its powers under § 5 of the fourteenth amendment: "With respect to the [set-asides], Congress had abundant evidence from which it could conclude that minority businesses have been denied effective participation in public contracting opportunities by procurement practices that perpetuate the effects

of prior discrimination. Congress, of course, may legislate without compiling the kind of 'record' appropriate with respect to judicial or administrative proceedings." Id. at 477–78. The Court fashioned an especially broad conception of Congress' fact-finding power. To exercise its § 5 powers, the Court wrote, Congress need not have recited any "preambulary 'findings' on the subject. . . . [W]e are satisfied that Congress had abundant historical basis from which it could conclude that traditional procurement practices, when applied to minority businesses, could perpetuate the effects of prior discrimination." Id. at 478.

55. See 384 U.S. at 651 n. 10.

56. 460 U.S. at 262.

57. See 460 U.S. at 259–61 (Burger, C.J., dissenting).

58. 440 U.S. 93 (1979) (foreign service officers), discussed in § 16–31, infra.

59. 427 U.S. 307 (1976) (police), discussed in § 16–31, infra.

against the aged is necessarily—or even presumptively—constitutional. Surely *some* age discrimination—such as a mandatory retirement age of 30—would violate the fourteenth amendment. Indeed, while declining to consider police officers over 50 as a suspect class, the Court in *Murgia* admitted that the treatment of older citizens in our society has often been discriminatory.[60]

While conceding that Congress has the power to prohibit practices not themselves unconstitutional in order "to guard against encroachment of guaranteed rights or to rectify past discrimination," Chief Justice Burger claimed that there had been no finding that the Wyoming mandatory retirement law infringed federal rights.[61] Yet, in his own opinion for the Court in *Fullilove v. Klutznick*,[62] the Chief Justice had found sufficient evidence to uphold the explicit racial classification in a federal affirmative action program even though it had been adopted as a floor amendment without any congressional hearings or investigation whatsoever. The Court justified Congress' act by reference to legislative and administrative findings of discrimination which were made long before and without specific concern for the minority set-aside which was before the Court.[63] With such a low standard, there can be little doubt that the record underlying the congressional effort to prohibit age discrimination—which spans three decades and includes numerous hearings and detailed legislative and administrative findings—suffices to justify remedial legislation.[64]

But even if one accepts the view that Congress did not cut its constitutional authority to address age discrimination out of whole cloth, one cannot regard the broader issue of Justice Brennan's one-way ratchet as fully resolved. In the absence of definitive Supreme Court treatment of the one-way ratchet idea,[65] commentators have sought either to justify it or elaborate the implications of Justice Harlan's and Chief Justice Burger's criticisms. One defense of Justice Brennan's theory, developed most prominently by Archibald Cox, grounds both the reach and the limits of congressional power under the fourteenth amendment on Congress' alleged superiority over the Supreme Court as a fact-finder. "[T]he Court has long been committed both to the presumption that facts exist which sustain congressional legislation and also to deference to congressional judgment upon questions of degree

---

60. See 427 U.S. at 313.

61. 460 U.S. at 261 (Burger, C.J., dissenting).

62. 448 U.S. 448 (1980).

63. See 448 U.S. at 465–67.

64. 460 U.S. at 229–30 (opinion of Brennan, J.).

65. In Mississippi Univ. for Women v. Hogan, 458 U.S. 718, 732–33 (1982), Justice O'Connor's opinion for the five-member majority stated that section " '5 grants Congress no power to restrict, abrogate, or dilute these guarantees.' Katzenbach v. Morgan, 384 U.S. 641, 651 n. 10 (1966). Although we give deference to congressional decisions and classifications, neither Congress nor a state can validate a law that denies the rights guaranteed by the Fourteenth Amendment." This apparent adoption by a majority of the Court of Justice Brennan's one-way ratchet notion should be taken with more than the usual quantity of salt, for Justice O'Connor herself joined Chief Justice Burger's dissent in EEOC v. Wyoming. In light of the Court's workload, a law clerk's passing references to marginally relevant cases should not always be assumed to have been carefully examined by all the concurring Justices; nor should those Justices necessarily be expected to subscribe to them in the future.

and proportion." [66] Judgments about the conformity of state laws with fourteenth amendment requirements of due process and equal protection depend "to a large extent upon finding and appraisal of the practical importance of relevant facts . . . There is often room for differences of opinion in interpreting the available data." [67] If the congressional power is seen to be one of fact-finding, the "one-way ratchet" limit on the power is implicit in the recognition of the power itself: "According to the conventional theory . . . the Court has invalidated state statutes under the due process and equal protection clauses only when no state of facts which can reasonably be conceived would sustain them. Where that is true, a congressional effort to withdraw the protection granted by the clause would lack the foundation of a reasonably conceivable set of facts and would therefore be just as invalid as the state legislation." [68]

On this view, *Katzenbach v. Morgan* does not threaten *Marbury v. Madison* since congressional action involves less the interpretation of law than the finding of fact. *Katzenbach v. Morgan*, accordingly, is neither more nor less a radical decision than *South Carolina v. Katzenbach*. In both cases, so the argument goes, the Supreme Court simply acknowledged Congress' right to find facts for itself, and the Court's responsibility to defer to these findings.

Of any of the theories of congressional power under the fourteenth amendment, this fact-finding theory comes closest to having received the Supreme Court's imprimatur. Some of the language of *Katzenbach v. Morgan* itself strongly suggests the theory.[69] And Justice Brennan, in *Oregon v. Mitchell*, adopted as his own the fact-finding theory of the ratchet.[70]

A second theory draws on the fact that, because Congress need not explain its conclusions as must a court, it can devise an "appropriate adjustment of directly conflicting principles" [71] where the Supreme

---

66. Cox, "Foreword: Constitutional Adjudication and the Promotion of Human Rights," 80 Harv.L.Rev. 91, 107 (1966). See also Cox, "The Role of Congress in Constitutional Adjudication," 40 U.Cin.L. Rev. 199, 205–11 (1970).

67. See Cox, 80 Harv.L.Rev. at 106.

68. Id. at 106 n. 86. Professor Cox was not entirely persuaded by his own argument: "But while that is true in the realm of economic regulation, the Court has often substituted its own evaluation of actual conditions in reviewing legislation dealing with 'preferred rights.' It is hard to see how the Court can consistently give way to the congressional judgment in expanding the definition of equal protection in the area of human rights but refuse to give it weight in narrowing the definition when the definition depends upon appraisal of the facts." Id.

Chief Justice Burger's dissenting opinion in EEOC v. Wyoming also rejected Professor Cox's justification for congressional ac-

tion, at least on the facts of that case. The Chief Justice found that the argument that the Court should defer to Congress on questions of "legislative facts" had "no place in deciding between the legislative judgments of Congress and that of the Wyoming Legislature. Congress is simply not as well equipped as state legislators to make decisions involving purely local needs." 460 U.S. at 263 n. 8 (Burger, C.J., dissenting).

69. See 384 U.S. at 654–55; but see id. ("Congress might have also questioned whether denial of a right deemed so precious and fundamental in our society was a necessary or appropriate means of encouraging persons to learn English, or of furthering the goal of an intelligent exercise of the franchise": these are hardly factual judgments).

70. See 400 U.S. at 249 n. 31 (opinion of Brennan, White, and Marshall, JJ.).

71. Burt, "Miranda and Title II: A Morganatic Marriage," 1969 Sup.Ct.Rev. 81, 112.

Court could not do so without articulating a theory which would commit the Court to deciding future cases in ways which it did not wish. "Congress can . . . examine the problem context by context and need give no precedential effect to its decisions from one to the next." [72] Congress thus "has the ability to make either rough or finely tuned distinctions, justified by practical considerations though perhaps not by principle, in a manner not generally thought open to a court." [73] On this view, Congress has power under the fourteenth amendment to define the limits of rights which the Supreme Court has previously recognized, to fix the periphery of a right's application within the zone where the force of the value that the right protects is offset by the force of conflicting values, and where the Court could invoke no principled criteria to resolve the conflict.[74]

This view, too, need pose no great threat to judicial supremacy and *Marbury v. Madison.* "[T]he Court will set the basic terms. Congress can only fill in the blanks." [75] This view also allows for a one-way ratchet, albeit one which recognizes some power on the part of Congress to supplant the Supreme Court. Congress may use its authority, so this theory holds, "only to serve as an adjunct to the purposes the Court itself has been pursuing under the Fourteenth Amendment . . . ." [76] Accordingly, Congress has no power to substitute its views for those of the Supreme Court as to the core content of the rights which Congress may enforce. Where the Court has itself acted at the periphery, however, by drawing lines or stating rules for purposes of uniformity or administrability, in order to distinguish clearly between situations where rights are violated and situations where they are not, Congress may overrule this "constitutional common law," by substituting its own view as to the proper cutoff lines.[77]

A third approach, advanced by William Cohen, draws a distinction between decisions as to the contents of rights, preeminently within the prerogative of courts, and decisions as to the division of responsibility between federal and state governments, allegedly the peculiar province of Congress. "A congressional judgment rejecting a judicial interpretation of the due process or equal protection clauses . . . is entitled to no more deference than the identical decision of a state legislature . . . But a congressional judgment resolving at the national level an issue that could—without constitutional objection—be decided in the same way at the state level, ought normally to be binding on the courts, since Congress presumably reflects a balance between both national and state interests and hence is better able to adjust such conflicts." [78] This theory preserves judicial supremacy by limiting its subject-matter to the definition of rights; the theory creates its one-way ratchet by rigorously enforcing a presumed division of competencies: Congress is

72. Id.

73. Monaghan, "Foreword: Constitutional Common Law." 89 Harv.L.Rev. 1, 28–29 (1975).

74. This theory is thus but a specific application of the more general notion that, under a rights-based jurisprudence, courts should be reluctant to overturn legislative accommodations of rights in conflict.

75. Burt, supra note 71, at 118.

76. Id. at 114.

77. See Monaghan, supra note 73 at 26–30; see generally § 3–4, supra.

78. Cohen, supra note 44, at 614.

without power to decide for itself anything other than federalism questions.

A fourth approach was put forward by Justice Harlan in dissent in *Katzenbach v. Morgan*: "When recognized state violations of federal constitutional standards have occurred, Congress is of course empowered by § 5 to take appropriate remedial measures to redress and prevent the wrongs . . . But it is a judicial question whether the condition with which Congress has thus sought to deal is in truth an infringement of the Constitution, something that is the necessary prerequisite to bringing the § 5 power into play at all." [79] The Harlan approach preserves judicial supremacy and precludes any need for a ratchet by simply denying Congress any area of decision within which it may substitute its judgment for that of the Supreme Court concerning the content of constitutional provisions. This approach thus differs in kind from the first three, all of which suggest some form of shared legislative and judicial responsibility for articulating the meaning of the fourteenth amendment.

Each of the four approaches outlined above is not free of difficulty, even on its own terms. The fact-finding theory, for example, can supply a one-way ratchet only by assuming that the Supreme Court upholds legislation whenever any conceivable set of facts can be imagined to justify the legislation; but this assumption is inconsistent with contemporary doctrine: where "strict scrutiny" is mandated—in contexts of preferred rights [80] or suspect classifications [81] or otherwise— the Supreme Court often acts as an independent fact-finder, and always refuses to imagine facts which defenders of legislation do not demonstrate.[82] The federalism theory may also be inconsistent with Supreme Court practice: it has not always been clear that the Court regards questions of federal-state relations as essentially political matters best left to Congress.[83]

More fundamentally, although all of the above approaches are descriptions of possible internal limits on congressional power to enforce the fourteenth amendment, none is fully plausible even on its own terms. Law and fact are not distinct categories; often, neither the core nor the periphery can be identified apart from the other; [84] questions about the limits on state governmental power are inevitably questions as to both the content of rights and the meaning of federalism; rights suggest remedies and the character of remedies provided is evidence of the content of the rights.[85]

---

79. 384 U.S. at 666; see also Bickel, "The Voting Rights Cases," 1966 Sup.Ct. Rev. 79, 97.

80. See Chapters 11–15, infra.

81. See Chapter 16, infra.

82. See note 68, supra.

83. See §§ 5–20 to 5–22, infra.

84. Moreover, it is by no means clear that cases in which rights conflict are not the very cases we think courts should take primary responsibility for resolving; it may be in the context of these "hard cases"

that the politically independent status of the judiciary is most welcome.

85. The "benign discrimination" controversy, see § 16–22, infra, provides perhaps the best illustration of the truth of this proposition: at least in part, the question of whether so-called affirmative racial discrimination is proper turns on whether one regards the fourteenth amendment right as a right to color-blind government, or as a right to government which does not discriminate *against* racial minorities.

In addition, the very notion of a "one-way" ratchet may be problematic in areas where competing rights are at stake. It is now well-established, for example, that the states may interpret their own constitutions to provide more protection of individual rights than the federal constitution.[86] But the "expansion" of rights is by no means a self-defining term. For instance, the "Human Life Bill"[87] seeks to increase the amount of congressional protection given to unborn "persons"—or, at the very least, to beings that will *become* "persons"—by making abortion more difficult. Congress' claim that it is protecting the fourteenth amendment rights of these present or future "persons" more broadly than the Court may be plausible, but the rights of pregnant women secured by the Court's decision in *Roe v. Wade*[88] would be intolerably endangered by such a move. To resolve such a controversy, the Court would be forced to evaluate the *content*, not just the assertion, of the constitutional guarantees at issue. In the end, then, the judicial role is unchanged—not to forbid Congress from asserting itself in the constitutional dialogue of the day, but rather to insist that Congress do so within the outside limits established by the Court.

In fact, a plausible set of limits implicit in the grant of power itself may not be essential to a proper theory of congressional power under § 5 of the fourteenth amendment. For upon closer analysis, neither of the concerns which Justice Harlan articulated in *Oregon v. Mitchell*[89] and *Katzenbach v. Morgan*[90]—the concerns which have prompted efforts to develop theories of internal limits—turns out to be well-founded.

It is not difficult to reconcile congressional power to define the content of fourteenth amendment rights with *Marbury v. Madison* and judicial review. Judicial review does not require that the Constitution always be equated with the Supreme Court's view of it.[91] It is the Court's responsibility, under *Marbury*, to strike down acts of Congress which the Court concludes to be unconstitutional—nothing more. *Marbury* implies nothing about the criteria by which the Court should determine whether an act of Congress is constitutional; it requires only that such criteria should exist. Criteria which invalidate all legislation founded upon interpretations of the fourteenth amendment different from those of the Supreme Court, therefore, are no more consistent with *Marbury* than criteria which allow Congress to adopt any plausible interpretation of the fourteenth amendment: since both sets of criteria fix limits on congressional power, albeit of differing degrees of severity, both do justice to *Marbury*, and neither jeopardizes the principle of judicial review.

---

86. See, e.g., Pruneyard Shopping Center v. Robins, 447 U.S. 74 (1980) (California may permit individuals to exercise free speech rights in private shopping centers, even though the federal constitution protects no such right). See also Brennan, State Constitutions and the Protection of Individual Rights, 90 Harv.L.Rev. 489 (1977) (applauding the trend towards more expansive interpretations of state constitutional protections).

87. S. 158; H.R. 900, 97th Cong., 1st Sess. (1981).

88. 410 U.S. 113 (1973), discussed in § 15–10, infra.

89. See 400 U.S. at 204–05 (separate opinion of Harlan, J.).

90. See 384 U.S. at 668 (Harlan, J., dissenting).

91. See § 3–4, supra.

The real issue, then, is not judicial review, but the more substantive question of whether Congress should be allowed to depart from the Supreme Court's interpretation of the fourteenth amendment. Justice Harlan's fear in this regard was largely a fear of dilution: that Congress might enact legislation reinterpreting the fourteenth amendment to give less protection to individual rights than Supreme Court holdings had recognized. The various efforts to justify a one-way ratchet are responses to this concern. Again, however, the concern is misplaced. Congressional legislation, whether grounded in legislative interpretation of the fourteenth amendment, in the commerce clause, or in any other constitutional grant of congressional power, must be consistent with the Bill of Rights, with article I, § 9,[92] and with all other limits on federal authority. Thus, congressional legislation authorizing racial segregation of state public schools, even if it rested on a "rational" interpretation of the fourteenth amendment, would be open to challenge as purposeful racial discrimination violative of principles of equality implicit in the fifth amendment's due process clause, just as congressional legislation authorizing racial segregation in the District of Columbia schools was in fact invalidated.[93] Similarly, to the extent that the *Miranda* rule is constitutionally grounded,[94] congressional legislation authorizing the states not to comply with *Miranda* would be open to fifth and sixth amendment challenge.[95]

The Bill of Rights limits Congress when Congress grants the states power they would not otherwise possess just as much as it limits Congress when Congress grants powers to a federal agency.[96] The fourteenth amendment recognizes no limits on state authority which the Bill of Rights and other constitutional provisions do not place on Congress.[97] Concern for individual rights, therefore, does not justify creating artificial internal limits on congressional power to enforce the fourteenth amendment.[98] Indeed, in an era when Congress may in some cases exhibit a greater sensitivity to individual rights than the Court, it will be all the more important that Congress be permitted to exercise the full range of its constitutional prerogatives.

§ 5–15. Congressional Power and the State Action Limit on Fourteenth and Fifteenth Amendment Guarantees

By their terms, the due process and equal protection clauses of the fourteenth amendment, like the provisions of the fifteenth amendment,

92. See Chapter 10 on bills of attainder and ex post facto laws.

93. See Bolling v. Sharpe, 347 U.S. 497 (1954).

94. See Miranda v. Arizona, 384 U.S. 436 (1966).

95. Cf. Burt, supra note 71, at 118–34.

96. See, e.g., Shapiro v. Thompson, 394 U.S. 618, 641 (1969).

97. Indeed, certain protections of the Bill of Rights which limit Congress do not limit the states. See Chapter 11, infra.

98. The approach suggested here is essentially that followed in Katzenbach v. Morgan itself: an inquiry first into whether congressional legislation rationally relates to the purposes and objectives of the fourteenth amendment, and second into whether such legislation is consistent with the Bill of Rights and other external restraints. See 384 U.S. at 652–56; id. at 656–57; see also Runyon v. McCrary, 427 U.S. 160, 175–79 (1976); Fullilove v. Klutznick, 448 U.S. 448, 465–67 (1980).

restrict only governmental action.[1] In a series of post-Civil War cases, most notably the *Civil Rights Cases*, the Supreme Court invalidated much Reconstruction civil rights legislation on the ground that, because this legislation purported to regulate the conduct of private citizens in addition to state action, it was not authorized by the fourteenth amendment, and hence was unconstitutional.[2] Given the background and progeny of the *Civil Rights Cases*, when the Supreme Court began to reconsider the extent of congressional power under the fourteenth amendment in the 1960's a principal issue was thought to be whether, under a new theory of congressional power, Congress would be able to subject private conduct to fourteenth amendment limitations.

During the same Term in which it decided *Katzenbach v. Morgan*, the Supreme Court intimated that Congress could in fact regulate at least some private conduct under the fourteenth amendment. In *United States v. Guest*,[3] six Justices joined one or the other of two concurring opinions declaring that Congress possessed the power under § 5 of the fourteenth amendment "to enact laws punishing *all* conspiracies to interfere with the exercise of Fourteenth Amendment rights, whether or not state officers or others acting under the color of state law are implicated in the conspiracy."[4] Justice Brennan's opinion, which dealt with the question in the greatest detail, utilized an approach identical to that which Justice Brennan would subsequently apply in writing for the Court in *Katzenbach v. Morgan*: "§ 5 authorizes Congress to make laws that it concludes are reasonably necessary to protect a right created by and arising under that Amendment; and Congress is thus fully empowered to determine that punishment of private conspiracies interfering with the exercise of such a right is necessary to its full protection."[5]

In dictum in *District of Columbia v. Carter*, a unanimous Supreme Court subsequently reaffirmed the proposition that to say that "[t]he Fourteenth Amendment itself 'erects no shield against merely private conduct' . . . is not to say . . . that Congress may not proscribe purely private conduct under § 5 of the Fourteenth Amendment."[6] However, since *Guest*, and since the development of the *Katzenbach v. Morgan* controversy, the Court has had no occasion to confront the extent to which the state action requirement limits congressional power to enforce the fourteenth amendment. Nonetheless, it seems fairly clear that, at least in cases like *Guest*, congressional power exists to

§ 5–15

1. See Chapter 18, infra.

2. See Civil Rights Cases, 109 U.S. 3 (1883); United States v. Harris, 106 U.S. 629 (1883); see also James v. Bowman, 190 U.S. 127 (1903) (fifteenth amendment).

3. 383 U.S. 745 (1966).

4. Id. at 782 (opinion of Brennan, J., joined by Warren, C.J., and Douglas, J.); accord, id. at 762 (Clark, J., concurring, joined by Black and Fortas, JJ.) Justice Stewart's opinion for the Court upheld congressional power to punish the conspiracy in question by treating the statute, as applied, as protecting the right to travel, a right of national citizenship which Congress can protect from both governmental and private interference. See id. at 757–60; see also note 13, infra.

5. 383 U.S. at 782 (opinion of Brennan, J.).

6. 409 U.S. 418, 423, 424 n. 8 (1973). The question before the Court was whether the District of Columbia is a "State or Territory" for purposes of 42 U.S.C. § 1983; the Court held that it is not.

reach private conduct.[7] In *Guest*, Justice Brennan treated the regulation of private conduct as a means which Congress adopted in order to insure that individuals would in fact be able to exercise their right to equal treatment *by government*;[8] proscription of private conduct, in other words, was treated as an ancillary remedy, and thus was proper even under the narrowest reading of § 5's grant of power to Congress to enforce the fourteenth amendment.[9]

If *Katzenbach v. Morgan* survives in full, congressional authority to reach private conduct is clear: Congress could reasonably adopt the view that the states had an affirmative obligation to regulate certain forms of private conduct and that, where the states failed to do so, Congress could substitute its own regulation under the fourteenth amendment.[10] In any event, the issue today is largely academic. Congress can regulate private conduct under the commerce clause [11] and the thirteenth amendment; [12] it can also proscribe private interference with the privileges or immunities of national citizenship which derive from the constitutional structure as a whole and which § 1 of

---

7. Justice Stevens began to explore this point in his concurring opinion in Great American Federal Savings & Loan Assn. v. Novotny, 442 U.S. 366 (1979). Justice Stewart's opinion for the 6–3 majority in Novotny held that 42 U.S.C. § 1985(3) could not be invoked to redress violations of Title VII. Justice Stevens noted in his concurrence that certain rights guaranteed by the fourteenth amendment—such as the privileges and immunities of national citizenship—were protected against interference by private action, and certain other rights—such as the right to due process and equal protection—shielded individuals only from government action. "Thus, while § 1985(3) does not require that a defendant act under color of state law, there still can be no claim for relief based on a violation of the Fourteenth Amendment if there has been no involvement by the State. The requirement of state action, in this context, is no more than a requirement that there be a constitutional violation." 442 U.S. at 384–85 (Stevens, J., concurring).

8. "No one would deny that Congress could enact legislation directing state officials to provide Negroes with equal access to state schools, parks, and other facilities owned or operated by the State. Nor could it be denied that Congress has the power to punish state officers who, in excess of their authority and in violation of state law, conspire to threaten, harass and murder Negroes for attempting to use these facilities. And I can find no principle of federalism nor word of the Constitution that denies Congress power to determine that in order adequately to protect the right to equal utilization of state facilities, it is also appropriate to punish other individuals— not state officers themselves and not acting

in concert with state officers—who engage in the same brutal conduct for the same misguided purpose." 383 U.S. at 784 (opinion of Brennan, J.) (footnotes omitted).

9. Cf. Brewer v. Hoxie School District No. 46, 238 F.2d 91 (8th Cir. 1956) (federal court has power to enjoin private action designed to prevent school boards from furnishing unsegregated education). The analogy between Guest and Hoxie was developed most persuasively by Professor Cox: "It makes little difference to the Negro child or his parents whether white thugs overwhelm the janitor and bar the child at the schoolhouse door or stand a block down the street threatening violence to children on the way to school. The case is the same when parents are threatened with loss of their homes, credit, or employment if their child attends a desegregated school. The practical objective of the constitutional guarantee is that Negroes should receive equal opportunities for the use of facilities that the state provides. The national interest is equally in the provision and the enjoyment of the state facilities. From this standpoint there is just as much reason for Congress to have power to deal with conspiracies and other private activities aimed at defeating enjoyment of the constitutional right as there is for it to proscribe private interference with the state's performance of its duty." Cox, "Foreword: Constitutional Adjudication and the Promotion of Human Rights," 80 Harv.L.Rev. 91, 112 (1966).

10. Cf. Michelman, "The Supreme Court and Litigation Access Fees: The Right to Protect One's Rights—Part II," 1974 Duke L.J. 527, 568–70.

11. See §§ 5–4 to 5–6, supra.

12. See § 5–13, supra.

the fourteenth amendment acknowledges.[13] In this regard at least, as a grant of legislative power, the fourteenth amendment may be almost wholly redundant.

§ 5–16. Congressional Powers in Foreign Affairs: War, Immigration, and Citizenship

Fully eleven of the powers that article I, § 8, grants Congress deal in some way with foreign affairs. This section does not attempt to survey all these grants of authority. Instead it focuses on the constitutional limits of two forms of congressional action: domestic legislation enacted under Congress' war powers, and regulation of aliens and of naturalized citizens. With respect to both of these subjects, the object of the inquiry is the same: to describe the extent to which the peculiarly "national" character of the power granted Congress [1] limits judicial review of legislation seemingly inconsistent with the usual restraints on congressional power. Congressional foreign policymaking as such, largely concerned with the limits of executive action, is considered above in Chapter 4.

Article I, § 8, gives Congress the powers to "declare War," "raise and support Armies" through appropriations lasting no longer than two years, "provide and maintain a Navy," "make Rules for the Government and Regulation of the land and naval Forces," and "provide for organizing, arming, and disciplining, the Militia, and for governing such Part of them as may be employed in the Service of the United States. . . ." The Supreme Court has held that these war powers, in conjunction with the necessary and proper clause, grant Congress authority to take actions in wartime which would be unconstitutional in peacetime. Such congressional action may both assume responsibilities ordinarily left to the states and restrict the scope of private rights.

13. See, e.g., Griffin v. Breckenridge, 403 U.S. 88, 105–06 (1971) (right to travel); United States v. Guest, 383 U.S. 745, 757–60 (1966) (same); United States v. Classic, 313 U.S. 299, 314–15 (1941) (right to vote in congressional primary election); Ex parte Yarbrough, 110 U.S. 651, 662 (1884) (right to vote in congressional general election); In re Quarles, 158 U.S. 532, 536 (1895) (right of citizen to inform federal authorities of violation of federal laws); Logan v. United States, 144 U.S. 263, 284 (1892) (right to protection from violence while in federal custody); United States v. Cruikshank, 92 U.S. (2 Otto) 542, 552 (1876) (right to petition Congress for redress of grievances) (dictum). See generally Chapter 7, infra.

§ 5–16

1. The view that federal foreign affairs powers belong to the national government as incidents of national sovereignty, and thus do not trace from the Constitution, but are only recognized by it, was adopted by the Supreme Court in United States v. Curtiss-Wright Export Corp.: ". . . the investment of the federal government with the powers of external sovereignty did not depend upon the affirmative grants of the Constitution. The powers to declare and wage war, to conclude peace, to make treaties, to maintain diplomatic relations with other sovereignties, if they had never been mentioned in the Constitution, would have vested in the federal government as necessary concomitants of nationality." 299 U.S. 304, 318 (1936). One corollary of the "inherent foreign affairs power" conception is the irrelevance of state interests as limits upon congressional power, since "the states severally never possessed international powers. . . ." Id. at 316. External restraints such as those of the Bill of Rights, however, remain relevant. For criticism of Curtiss-Wright and its theory of inherent power, see Lofgren, "United States v. Curtiss-Wright Export Corporation: An Historical Reassessment." 82 Yale L.J. 1 (1973).

In World War I, for example, Congress enacted, and the Supreme Court subsequently upheld, a national prohibition law—justified as a wartime efficiency measure—prior to the ratification of the eighteenth amendment.[2] And in World War II, the Supreme Court affirmed the power of Congress to authorize federal control of prices and rents, as well as other allocation regulations, even though the congressional action severely restricted access to procedural channels for testing the validity of the government's actions: "In total war it is necessary that a civilian make sacrifices of his property and profits with at least the same fortitude as that with which a drafted soldier makes his traditional sacrifices of comfort, security and life itself." [3] In both world wars, congressional domestic regulation undertaken as part of the war effort was notable for its duration; wartime laws persisted in force after hostilities terminated, and after both wars the Supreme Court upheld that persistence as falling within the discretion of Congress in the exercise of its war powers.[4]

Congressional action in World War I and World War II also illustrates the sorts of direct war-time restrictions of private rights the Supreme Court has understood the Constitution to permit. In World War I, Congress passed laws punishing seditious utterances: the Supreme Court upheld their enforcement.[5] Justice Holmes noted in *Schenck v. United States*—a case usually remembered for its rhetorical protection of free speech but not for its result—that "[w]hen a nation is at war many things that might be said in time of peace are such a hindrance to its effort that their utterance will not be endured so long as men fight and . . . no Court could regard them as protected by any constitutional right." [6] In World War II, Congress authorized the detention and relocation of Japanese residents in the western United States, including persons of Japanese ancestry who were native-born American citizens. Although the congressional action involved the use of an ordinarily forbidden racial criterion, the Supreme Court refused to intervene: "when under conditions of modern warfare our shores are threatened by hostile forces, the power to protect must be commensurate with the threatened danger." [7]

2. See Hamilton v. Kentucky Distilleries & Warehouse Co., 251 U.S. 146 (1919).

3. Lichter v. United States, 334 U.S. 742, 754 (1948) (upholding Renegotiation Act authorizing recovery of excess profits). See Bowles v. Willingham, 321 U.S. 503 (1944) (upholding rent controls); Yakus v. United States, 321 U.S. 414 (1944) (upholding price controls). For an elaborate contemporaneous discussion of World War II economic legislation, see Note, "American Economic Mobilization: A Study in the Mechanism of War," 55 Harv.L.Rev. 427 (1942).

4. See Woods v. Cloyd W. Miller Co., 333 U.S. 138, 144 (1948) (upholding post-war rent control: "Congress was invoking its war power to cope with a current condition of which the war was a direct and immediate cause"); Hamilton v. Kentucky Distilleries & Warehouse Co., 251 U.S. 146, 163 (1919) (upholding post-war continuation of prohibition). See also Stewart v. Kahn, 78 U.S. (11 Wall.) 493, 507 (1871): "[The war] power is not limited to victories in the field. . . . It carries with it inherently the power to guard against the immediate renewal of the conflict, and to remedy the evils which have arisen from its rise and progress."

5. See, e.g., Debs v. United States, 249 U.S. 211 (1919); Frohwerk v. United States, 249 U.S. 204 (1919); Schenck v. United States, 249 U.S. 47 (1919).

6. 249 U.S. 47, 52 (1919), discussed in Chapter 12, infra.

7. Korematsu v. United States, 323 U.S. 214, 220 (1944); see also Hirabayashi v. United States, 320 U.S. 81 (1943) (holding

In retrospect, the Supreme Court's tolerance of the war-time excesses of Congress seems wrong, but in retrospect it is also clear that the Court saw no reasonable alternative to deference. This is the paradox of the war powers: because they are exercised in emergency, they are the constitutional grants of authority that the Supreme Court is least likely to limit—out of deference to superior legislative factfinding, out of prudent awareness of the limits of judicial power, and out of simple unfamiliarity with the issues raised. The judicially illimitable character of the war powers, especially during war itself,[8] is ultimately one of the strongest arguments for strict judicial enforcement of private rights in peacetime. If the judiciary does not remind Congress of its constitutional obligations when such reminder is possible, it is less than likely that Congress will remember to restrain itself when the courts see no practical alternative to silence.

Sweeping as are Congress' war-related powers, the Court has emphasized time and again that " 'over no conceivable subject is the legislative power of Congress more complete than it is over' the admission of aliens."[9] Authorized under article I, § 8, "to establish a uniform Rule of Naturalization," Congress plays a central role in defining the processes through which citizenship is acquired or lost, in determining the criteria by which citizenship is judged, and in fixing the consequences citizenship or noncitizenship entail. The limits of Congress' role in this sphere reflect the interaction of two contradictory conceptions of the relationship between the individual and the state. The first view, positivist in character, sees government as prior to the individual, and thus sees the rights of individuals as nonexistent except as recognized by government. It surfaces, for example, in the Supreme Court's insistence that the naturalization process is internally unlimited:[10] "Naturalization is a privilege, to be given, qualified, or withheld as Congress may determine, and which the alien may claim as of right only upon compliance with the terms which Congress imposes." A second, more individualistic view regards the proper sphere of government activity as limited by pre-existing personal rights. This view underlies the Constitution's limitations upon the powers of Congress to withdraw citizenship once recognized and to govern the affairs of resident aliens.

The Constitution, although repeatedly using the term "citizen," did not define United States citizenship prior to the Civil War. This absence of definition may have reflected a desire on the part of the Framers to avoid fixing the status of slaves. Moreover, to persons

constitutional the imposition of a curfew governing all persons of Japanese ancestry in certain areas). These cases are discussed in § 16–14, infra.

8. In post-war situations, exercises of war powers inconsistent with civil liberties have been struck down. See, e.g., Ex parte Milligan, 71 U.S. (4 Wall.) 2 (1866) (habeas corpus may not be suspended and citizens subjected to military justice except in areas where armed hostilities have made enforcement of civil law impossible).

9. Fiallo v. Bell, 430 U.S. 787, 792 (1977), quoting from Oceanic Navigation Co. v. Stranahan, 214 U.S. 320, 339 (1909). Accord, Kleindienst v. Mandel, 408 U.S. 753, 766 (1972); Shaughnessy v. United States ex rel. Mezei, 345 U.S. 206, 210 (1953); The Chinese Exclusion Case, 130 U.S. 581 (1889).

10. United States v. Macintosh, 283 U.S. 605, 615 (1931).

strongly influenced by natural law thinking, "citizenship" may have seemed too narrow a concept in terms of which to define rights naturally belonging to all; it is noteworthy, for example, that the Bill of Rights speaks exclusively of "persons", not of "citizens." Heedless of the Constitution's tactful silence, and evidently unpersuaded by the Bill of Rights' implicit distinction, the Supreme Court, in *Scott v. Sandford (the Dred Scott Case)*,[11] defined the scope of United States citizenship negatively, holding that such citizenship could not extend to a freed slave.[12] Following the Civil War it helped provoke, *Scott v. Sandford* was overruled by constitutional amendment. The fourteenth amendment provides: "All persons born or naturalized in the United States, and subject to the jurisdiction thereof, are citizens of the United States and of the State wherein they reside."

United States citizenship, as the fourteenth amendment defines it, is an individual right. In *Afroyim v. Rusk*, the Supreme Court held unconstitutional a federal law withdrawing American citizenship from persons voting in foreign elections, and concluded: "the [fourteenth amendment] can most reasonably be read as defining a citizenship which a citizen keeps unless he voluntarily relinquishes it." [13] The two kinds of citizenship the fourteenth amendment recognizes—citizenship by birth and citizenship through naturalization—are equal. Starting from "the premise that the rights of citizenship of the native born and of the naturalized person are of the same dignity and co-extensive," the Supreme Court held in *Schneider v. Rusk* that Congress could not withdraw citizenship from naturalized citizens who maintained continuous residence for three years in the countries to which they formerly owed allegiance: "Living abroad, whether the citizen be naturalized or native born, is no badge of lack of allegiance and in no way evidences a voluntary renunciation of nationality and allegiance." [14]

Not all forms of citizenship, however, fall within the scope of the fourteenth amendment. The citizenship clause of that amendment grants citizenship only to "persons born or naturalized *in* the United States, and subject to the jurisdiction thereof . . ." [15] Congress nonetheless has granted citizenship at birth to persons born abroad if one parent is an American citizen, subject to the condition subsequent that citizens thus recognized must live continuously in the United States for at least five years between the ages of 14 and 28.[16] In *Rogers v. Bellei*,[17]

11. 60 U.S. (19 How.) 393 (1857).

12. Scott, held as a slave by Sandford in Missouri, brought a diversity suit in federal court claiming that he was entitled to freedom because a previous owner had taken him to Illinois, a free state, and from there to parts of the Louisiana Territory made free under the Missouri Compromise. Chief Justice Taney's opinion announcing the Supreme Court's decision held that no federal jurisdiction existed to hear Scott's claim since no Negro, free or slave, could be a "citizen" of a state or of the United States in the required constitutional sense, and thus no Negro could take advantage of the federal courts' "diversity of citizen-

ship" jurisdiction. 60 U.S. at 404–05. See Bickel, "Citizenship in the American Constitution," 15 Ariz.L.Rev. 369 (1973). After finding no federal jurisdiction, the Court nonetheless proceeded gratuitously and irresponsibly to reach the merits, concluding that the Missouri Compromise was unconstitutional, id. at 452.

13. 387 U.S. 253, 262 (1967).

14. 377 U.S. 163, 165, 169 (1964).

15. U.S.Const. amend. XIV, § 1 (emphasis added).

16. 8 U.S.C. § 1401(b).

17. 401 U.S. 815 (1971).

the Supreme Court upheld the power of Congress on a prospective basis to confer this conditional citizenship. Despite forceful argument to the contrary by Justice Black in dissent,[18] Justice Blackmun's majority opinion concluded that fourteenth amendment citizenship did not extend to persons not literally naturalized *in* the United States,[19] and thus upheld the congressional condition as "not unreasonable, arbitrary, or unlawful." [20]

Arguably, the narrow interpretation of the fourteenth amendment citizenship clause offered in *Bellei* was unnecessary to the result in that case. The "rights" conception of citizenship embraced by the fourteenth amendment holds only that acceptance or renunciation of citizenship is a decision for the individual, not for government. Acceptance or renunciation may be signified by action as well as by express declaration: from the "rights" perspective, the issue in *Bellei* was thus whether Congress could properly infer a renunciation of citizenship from the decision of an individual, a citizen of the United States at birth but also a citizen of the land of his birth, not to reside in the United States for any substantial length of time in the early years of his maturity. On its face, the congressional inference is not implausible.[21] Less plausible, and thus distinguishable from *Bellei*, is the congressional inference at issue in *Afroyim*: that an individual who emigrated to the United States, and who successfully undertook to obtain naturalized American citizenship, renounced his American citizenship by deciding to vote in a foreign election. The two cases are distinguished by the degree to which the individuals involved, before taking the action from which Congress inferred renunciation, had

18. Justice Black concluded the fourteenth amendment traditionally had been understood to deal with *all* types of United States citizenship, see id. at 839–42, 843 (Black, J., dissenting), and insisted, therefore, that the majority's "narrow and extraordinarily technical reading of the Fourteenth Amendment" was artificial, without connection to the purpose of the amendment. See id. at 843.

19. 401 U.S. at 827.

20. Id. at 831. In addition to noting the problems dual nationality creates for the affected governments, id. at 831–32, Justice Blackmun's majority opinion observed that, given the discretionary power of Congress to define conditions precedent to naturalization, and thus the power of Congress to reenact the condition at issue in Bellei in the form of a condition precedent, "it does not make good constitutional sense, or comport with logic, to say . . . that Congress may . . . yet be powerless" to impose the restriction in the form of a condition subsequent, id. at 834, especially since the use of the condition subsequent form benefited the naturalized citizen by granting the protections of citizenship (albeit provisionally) at an earlier stage in the naturalization process. See id. at 835–36. The latter argument, although superfi-

cially appealing, is ultimately unpersuasive given the demise of the right-privilege distinction. Not infrequently, a purely discretionary legislative decision to accord individuals some benefit imposes upon the legislature an obligation to respect constitutional rights in fixing the conditions of eligibility for the benefit. Tolerance for discretion in the granting of benefits does not imply tolerance for their discretionary termination. See, e.g., Arnett v. Kennedy, 416 U.S. 134 (1974), discussed in Chapter 10, infra.

21. The congressional decision to employ what is in effect a conclusive presumption of waiver is defensible not only on the ground (1) that a clear rule is required by international comity to minimize friction and uncertainty, see Rogers v. Bellei, 401 U.S. 815, 832 (1971), but also on the ground (2) that an individual's rights as an American citizen may not be recognized under international law if the individual possesses multiple citizenship, see McDougal, Lasswell & Chen, "Nationality and Human Rights: The Protection of the Individual in External Arenas," 83 Yale L.J. 900, 981–93 (1974), so that a clear rule of choice is required if the right of American citizenship is to be fully meaningful.

affirmatively acted to link themselves with the nation whose citizenship they claimed; the constitutionality of congressional inferences of renounced citizenship, therefore, may be judged in terms of a standard of review set by the sliding scale of individual commitment—citizenship is protected to the degree that the individual has chosen it.[22]

The Supreme Court has traditionally viewed the power of Congress to regulate the entry and stay of aliens, as well as the process through which aliens become naturalized citizens, as an inherent incident of national sovereignty, committed exclusively to national, as opposed to state or local control.[23] "It is an accepted maxim of international law, that every sovereign nation has the power, as inherent in sovereignty, and essential to self-preservation, to forbid the entrance of foreigners within its dominions, or to admit them only in such cases and upon such conditions as it may see fit to prescribe." [24] As a result, the Court has consistently held that the substantive requirements an alien must meet to enter this country, to stay, or to become a citizen, are virtually political questions, matters within the discretion of Congress and outside the scope of all but the most limited judicial review.[25] Congress, in the exercise of this judicially-granted discretion, has periodically conditioned the entry, stay, and naturalization of aliens upon compliance with requirements courts would hold violative of constitutional limits if applied to American citizens.[26]

This is not to say that the power of Congress to regulate aliens is completely unlimited. Resident aliens are "persons" for purposes, at least, of the fifth amendment's due process clause.[27] Although courts

22. From this perspective, the result reached by the Supreme Court in Schneider v. Rusk may seem troublesome. Schneider, a German national by birth, came to the United States as a child, and automatically acquired citizenship at age 16 when her mother was naturalized. 377 U.S. at 164. Arguably, at least, American citizenship resulted not from her own choice, but from that of her mother. After reaching maturity, Schneider returned to Germany married a German national, and maintained residence in Germany. From the pattern of her activity, an inference of waiver might appear rational. The decision in Schneider may nonetheless be correct: the statutory classification, and not Schneider's own conduct, was at issue. In the event of foreign residence, the statute stripped of citizenship *all* naturalized citizens—including those who had emigrated to the United States and had been naturalized as adults. Unlike the situation in Bellei, moreover, the statute could not be closely linked to the problem of multi-nationality, perhaps justifying the use of a per se rule.

23. See § 16–23, infra.

24. Nishimura Ekiu v. United States, 142 U.S. 651, 659 (1892). Accord, The Chinese Exclusion Case, 130 U.S. 581, 603–04 (1889). See generally Hesse, "The Consti-

tutional Status of the Lawfully Admitted Permanent Resident Alien: The Pre-1917 Cases," 68 Yale L.J. 1578 (1959). The view that congressional power to regulate the admission, stay, and naturalization of aliens is inherent rather than enumerate continues to surface in the modern cases. See, e.g., Kleindienst v. Mandel, 408 U.S. 753, 762 (1972); Boutilier v. INS, 387 U.S. 118, 123 (1967); Carlson v. Landon, 342 U.S. 524, 537 (1952); United States ex rel. Knauf v. Shaughnessy, 338 U.S. 537, 542 (1950).

25. See, e.g., Fiallo v. Bell, 430 U.S. 787, 792–95 (1977); Galvan v. Press, 347 U.S. 522, 530–32 (1954); United States ex rel. Knauf v. Shaughnessy, 338 U.S. 537, 543 (1950); Bugajewitz v. Adams, 228 U.S. 585, 591 (1913).

26. Compare, e.g., 8 U.S.C. §§ 1182(a) (28)(C), 1251(a)(6)(c), 1424(a)(2) (providing for exclusion or deportation of, or denial of naturalization to, alien members of Communist Party), with Chapter 12, infra (first amendment limits government regulation of Communist Party outside immigration and naturalization context). See also Mathews v. Diaz, 426 U.S. 67, 80–82 (1976).

27. Kwong Hai Chew v. Colding, 344 U.S. 590, 596 (1953). At least formally, the substantive protections afforded individu-

generally will listen only half-heartedly to claims that the substantive grounds for congressionally-authorized expulsions of resident aliens are inconsistent with constitutional guarantees, courts do require that the procedures Congress sets for the expulsion of resident aliens comply with due process.[28] Similarly, the procedures Congress provides for the naturalization of resident aliens must meet minimum standards of fairness; because Congress has traditionally regarded naturalization as a judicial process, there has been no need for the courts to establish the procedural minimum required by the Constitution.[29] Nonresident aliens, however, do not benefit from even the procedural protections of the Bill of Rights.[30] The procedures Congress fixes for regulating their entry into the United States, therefore, need not meet constitutional standards of due process. "Whatever the procedure authorized by Congress is, it is due process as far as an alien denied entry is

als under the Bill of Rights extend to aliens threatened with deportation as well. The Supreme Court, for example, has judged deportation proceedings in light of the first amendment, see Harisiades v. Shaughnessy, 342 U.S. 580, 591–92 (1952), the fourth amendment, see Abel v. United States, 362 U.S. 217 (1960), and the eighth amendment, see Carlson v. Landon, 342 U.S. 524, 544–46 (1952). In general, however, the Court's deference to the discretion of Congress in assessing the necessity for deporting classes of aliens has led to extremely relaxed scrutiny of challenged government action. The discretionary character of Congress' substantive power has essentially vitiated the usual constitutional protections of individual rights. For example, the Supreme Court has consistently held that, given its origins in congressional discretion, see Bugajewitz v. Adams, 228 U.S. 585, 591 (1913), deportation is not punishment, and thus the limitations of article I, § 9, do not apply to congressional deportation legislation. See Galvan v. Press, 347 U.S. 522, 531 (1954); Harisiades v. Shaughnessy, 342 U.S. 580, 593–96 (1952), discussed in Chapter 10, infra.

28. Wong Yang Sung v. McGrath, 339 U.S. 33, 49–50 (1950); Yamataya v. Fisher, 189 U.S. 86, 100–01 (1903). Due process does not require that a deportation hearing be judicial in character; an administrative hearing suffices. The Supreme Court has, at times, granted Congress great leeway in fixing the form of the hearing. In Fong Yue Ting v. United States, 149 U.S. 698 (1893), the Court held that, consistent with due process, Congress could require noncitizen Chinese laborers to register, deport those laborers who did not obtain a certificate of registration, and enforce the deportation requirement through a hearing procedure shifting to the alien laborer the burden of showing that "unavoidable

cause" precluded his obtaining a certificate, and of showing, through the testimony of "at least one credible white witness," that he was in fact a lawful resident of the United States. Noting that Congress failed to provide the alien who bore this burden of proof any means of compelling the testimony of needed witnesses, Justice Brewer eloquently dissented: "In view of this enactment of the highest legislative body of the foremost Christian nation, may not the thoughtful Chinese disciple of Confucius fairly ask, Why do they send missionaries here?" 149 U.S. at 744 (Brewer, J., dissenting). More recently, in Kimm v. Rosenberg, 363 U.S. 405 (1960) (per curiam), a majority of the Supreme Court held that, because an alien bore the burden of proof in a deportation hearing, the alien's invocation of the fifth amendment privilege during the course of the hearing meant that the alien failed to satisfy his burden with respect to the matters as to which the constitutional privilege was claimed. As Justice Douglas noted in dissent, the burden of proof rule thus penalized the exercise of a fifth amendment right that the Court had implicitly acknowledged to be relevant. Id. at 410–11 (Douglas, J., dissenting).

29. See 8 U.S.C. § 1421.

30. Shaughnessy v. United States ex rel. Mezei, 345 U.S. 206, 212 (1953). This rule has been explained on the ground that the Constitution has no extraterritorial reach, see Fong Yue Ting v. United States, 149 U.S. 698, 738 (1893) (Brewer, J., dissenting), and thus that, in its dealings with aliens not lawfully within the United States, the federal government possesses the full discretionary power accorded it under international law. See Nishimura Ekiu v. United States, 142 U.S. 651, 659 (1892).

concerned." [31]   Congress, however, has established procedures for dealing with nonresident aliens which, despite the absence of constitutional pressure, often appear to comply with the requirements of due process.[32]

Outside the context of entry, stay, and naturalization, congressional authority to regulate the activities of aliens, and to draw lines both between aliens and citizens and among aliens in the distribution of benefits, loses its clear connection to considerations of national sovereignty and foreign policy;[33] outside those limited contexts courts should thus feel freer to limit congressional power both substantively and procedurally.[34]   To date, the Supreme Court has not had occasion to define the full impact of the Bill of Rights on congressional regulations of alien activities and opportunities.   However, even though education is not a "fundamental right" granted to individuals by the Constitution,[35] the Court has held that a state may not deprive the children of undocumented aliens of the right to a free public education.[36]   Justice Brennan's opinion for the 5–4 majority noted that the fourteenth amendment provides that " '[n]o State . . . shall deprive any person of life, liberty or property, without due process of law; nor deny to *any person within its jurisdiction* the equal protection of the laws.' (Emphasis added.) . . . Whatever his status under the immigration laws, an alien is surely a 'person' in any ordinary sense of that term." [37]   Further, "Use of the phrase 'within its jurisdiction' . . . confirms[ ] the understanding that the protection of the Fourteenth Amendment extends to anyone, citizen or stranger, who *is* subject to the law of a State, and reaches into every corner of a State's territory. That a person's initial entry into a State, or into the United States, was unlawful, and that he may for that reason be expelled, cannot negate the simple fact of his presence within the State's territorial perime-

31. United States ex rel. Knauf v. Shaughnessy, 338 U.S. 537, 544 (1950). But more recent cases cast at least some doubt on any rule so absolute: exclusions of aliens on grounds of ideology, see Kleindienst v. Mandel, 408 U.S. 753 (1972), or illegitimacy and gender, see Fiallo v. Bell, 430 U.S. 787 (1977), have been scrutinized, albeit under a standard that "turns out to be completely 'toothless.' " Id. at 805 (Marshall, J., joined by Brennan, J., dissenting).

32. See 8 U.S.C. § 1226. For detailed discussion of exclusion procedures, see C. Gordon & H. Rosenfield, Immigration Law and Procedure (rev. ed. 1966).

33. But in Fiallo v. Bell, supra note 31, the Court found "no indication in [its] prior cases that the scope of judicial review is a function of the nature of the policy choice at issue. To the contrary, '[s]ince decisions in these matters may implicate our relations with foreign powers, and since a wide variety of classifications must be defined in

light of changing political and economic circumstances, . . . [t]he reasons that preclude judicial review of political questions also dictate a narrow standard of review of decisions made by the Congress or the President in the area of immigration and naturalization.' Mathews v. Diaz, 426 U.S. 67, 81–82 (1976)."   430 U.S. at 796.

34. See, e.g., Hampton v. Mow Sun Wong, 426 U.S. 88 (1976), discussed in §§ 16–22 and 16–30, infra. See generally Dash, "Discrimination in Employment Against Aliens—The Impact of the Constitution and Federal Civil Rights Laws," 35 U.Pitt.L.Rev. 499, 536–40 (1974).

35. See San Antonio Independent School Dist. v. Rodriguez, 411 U.S. 1, 35 & n. 78 (1973), discussed in §§ 16–9, 16–58, infra.

36. See Plyler v. Doe, 457 U.S. 202 (1982).

37. Id. at 210.

ter. . . . [U]ntil he leaves the jurisdiction—either voluntarily, or involuntarily in accordance with the Constitution and laws of the United States—he is entitled to the equal protection of the laws that a State may choose to establish." [38]

In addition, given the Court's sometime treatment of alienage as a suspect criterion of classification in the context of state legislation,[39] it would seem that, with only a few exceptions, resident aliens ought to enjoy the same constitutional rights secure from congressional abridgement as are possessed by American citizens.

The positivist theory of sovereignty underlying the Supreme Court's grant of substantively unlimited power to Congress with regard to regulation of the entry, stay, and naturalization of aliens is hard to square with the Court's treatment of citizenship, once acquired, as an individual right. The conflict is likely to be resolved in the long run through extension of the "rights" thesis. The traditional international perspective, that internal limits on the powers of national governments are without significance to foreign affairs, is ultimately unrealistic [40] and cannot be the perspective of the Constitution. Yet it is the Constitution that is the lens through which American government must judge its authority; [41] the Supreme Court's traditional view, that with respect to foreign affairs the Constitution must give way to the perspective of international law, thus reflects an error of vision. Not only commentators,[42] but the Court itself, seem to be reaching this conclusion. Writing in *Rogers v. Bellei* that the fourteenth amendment's citizenship clause did not protect the congressionally conditioned citizenship in that case, Justice Blackmun's majority opinion did not blindly accept Congress' conditions, as the positivist theory of sovereignty would seem to require, but instead scrutinized the substance of those conditions at some length before upholding them as "not unreasonable, arbitrary, or unlawful. . . ." [43] Eventually, such scrutiny will have to be transformed from rhetoric into reality; but even as rhetoric, it stands as a refutation of the thesis that the Constitution, like politics, must stop at the water's edge.

38. Id. at 215.

39. See § 16–23, infra.

40. See, e.g., Chayes, "An Inquiry into the Workings of Arms Control Agreements," 85 Harv.L.Rev. 905 (1972).

41. Clarence Darrow said it well in 1904, in connection with the first amendment: "The inhibition of the First Amendment goes to the very competency of Congress itself to pass any . . . law, independent of whether such law relates to a citizen or an alien." Argument for Appellants, United States ex rel. Turner v. Williams, 194 U.S. 279, 286 (1904). Accord, Downes v. Bidwell, 182 U.S. 244, 277 (1901).

42. See, e.g., C. Gordon & H. Rosenfield, Immigration Law and Procedure (rev. ed. 1966); Note, "Constitutional Limitations on the Naturalization Power," 80 Yale L.J. 769 (1971). See also Lofgren, "United States v. Curtiss-Wright Export Corporation: An Historical Reassessment," 83 Yale L.J. 1 (1973). For an attempt to incorporate protection of individual rights into international law, see McDougal, Lasswell & Chen, "Nationality and Human Rights: The Protection of the Individual in External Arenas," 83 Yale L.J. 900 (1974).

43. 401 U.S. 815, 831–36 (1971).

§ 5–17. Congressional Action and the Separation of Powers: The Problem of Delegation

The separation of powers principles underlying the Constitution simultaneously limit and protect congressional power. This section considers the primary separation of powers *limitation* apart from the limits that constrain congressional usurpation of judicial or executive authority (discussed in Chapters 3 and 4): the delegation doctrine. Section 5–18 proceeds to discuss the principal separation of powers *protection* of congressional action, the legislative immunity conferred by the speech or debate clause; § 5–19 concludes by examining the interaction of limitation and protection in the context of judicial supervision of congressional investigations.

Under the necessary and proper clause of article I, § 8, any constitutionally-granted congressional power "implies a power [to delegate] authority under it sufficient to effect its purposes."[1] The delegation may take the form either of interstitial administrative action or of contingent legislation. Thus, Congress may grant authority to an administrative agency to specify rules in areas where Congress itself has declared only general principles. In the early case of *Wayman v. Southard*, for example, the Court upheld a congressional delegation of power to the Supreme Court to modify "in their discretion" certain procedural rules followed by the federal courts: "[A] general provision may be made, and power given to those who are to act under such general provisions to fill up the details."[2] Alternatively, Congress may condition the operation of legislation upon an administrative agency official's determination of certain facts. In *The Brig Aurora*,[3] for example, the Supreme Court upheld congressional legislation keying the suspension of a trade embargo to the President's finding and proclamation of certain facts concerning the conduct of foreign nations. These forms of congressional delegation are not mutually exclusive: most modern instances of delegation by Congress involve both contingent legislation and interstitial administrative action.[4]

Because Congress can give away only what is its to give, the most obvious limits on legislative delegation are those on all legislation: the constitutional prohibition of federal legislative action either not affirmatively authorized by the Constitution or inconsistent with constitutional prohibitions against congressional action. Moreover, certain congressional powers are simply not delegable—as when it is clear from the language of the Constitution that the purposes underlying certain powers would not be served if Congress delegated its responsibility.

§ 5–17

1. Lichter v. United States, 334 U.S. 742, 778 (1948).

2. 23 U.S. (10 Wheat.) 1, 43 (1825) (Marshall, C.J.).

3. 11 U.S. (7 Cranch) 382 (1813).

4. For example, under the Agricultural Marketing Agreement Act of 1937, upheld in United States v. Rock Royal Co-op., Inc., 307 U.S. 533 (1939), the Secretary of Agriculture was authorized, in specific circumstances, to create "milk marketing areas" (contingent legislation) and thereupon to fix milk prices within those areas consistent with a declared congressional policy (interstitial administration). See also FEA v. Algonquin SNG, Inc., 426 U.S. 548 (1976) (upholding delegation of authority to President to "adjust . . . imports" of an article found by him to be imported in quantities or circumstances threatening the national security; this delegation sufficed to sustain imposition of license fees on imported oil).

For example, if the Senate, by a two-thirds vote, set up a special agency outside Congress to approve or veto all future treaties, such action would almost surely fail to satisfy the requirement of article II, § 2, that presidentially negotiated treaties become effective only upon "the Advice and Consent of the Senate . . . provided two thirds of the Senators present concur . . ." Similarly, Congress could not set up a Federal Court of Impeachment to try all impeachments: according to article I, § 3, "The Senate shall have the sole Power to try all Impeachments." [5]

Beyond the fact that specific congressional powers may be nondelegable, the "legislative powers" as a whole are similarly nontransferable. An agency exercising delegated authority is not free, as is Congress itself, to exercise its authority to pursue any and all ends within the affirmative reach of federal authority. Rather, an agency can assert as its objectives only those ends which are connected with the task that Congress created it to perform. The open-ended discretion to choose ends is the essence of legislative power; it is this power which Congress possesses but its agents lack.

The leading case supporting these propositions is *Hampton v. Mow Sun Wong*.[6] There, the primary issue was whether the Civil Service Commission violated fifth amendment due process in promulgating a regulation denying civil service jobs to resident aliens. Resolution of this issue did not turn on whether Congress had in fact granted the Commission sufficient authority to issue the regulation, or whether the delegation was properly structured; no one disputed the validity of the delegation as such, and that the regulation fell within the power delegated proved ultimately undeniable. Instead, the decisive issue was whether the regulation was sufficiently justified, given its impact on the aliens. The Commission argued that the regulation was justified by various considerations plainly within the foreign affairs authority of Congress and the President, the delegators of the Commission's authority; the Commission also pointed to its own interests in excluding aliens from sensitive positions for reasons of efficiency and in adopting a broad exclusion for purposes of administrative convenience. The Supreme Court held that the Commission could not assert foreign policy objectives in defense of its regulation: "That agency has no responsibility for foreign affairs, for treaty negotiations, for establishing immigration quotas or conditions of entry, or for naturalization policies." [7] Instead, the Court found that "[i]t is the business of the Civil Service Commission to adopt and enforce regulations which will best promote the efficiency of the federal civil service." [8] Having narrowed the range of relevant objectives, the Court finally concluded that, because

5. In the admiralty context, for example, the Supreme Court has held that Congress may not delegate responsibility for formulating admiralty law to the states because to do so would be inconsistent with the concern for uniformity which prompted the grant of responsibility for admiralty law to the federal government in the first place. See § 5–3, supra. See also Zschernig v. Miller, 389 U.S. 429, 443 (1968) (Stewart, J., concurring) (State Department cannot permit local probate officials to conduct American foreign policy).

6. 426 U.S. 88 (1976).

7. Id. at 114.

8. Id.

there was nothing "to indicate that the Commission actually made any considered evaluation of the relative desirability of a simple exclusionary rule," not even the administrative convenience argument survived.[9]

In general, limits on congressional capacity to delegate responsibility derive from the implicit constitutional requirements of consensual government under law. Under any theory that finds legitimacy in the supposed consent of the governed within a framework of constitutional limitations, the cooperative exercise of accountable power presupposes the possibility of tracing every such exercise to a choice made by one of the "representative" branches, a choice for which someone can be held both politically and legally responsible. Put otherwise, since the contractarian political theory underlying much of American constitutional law deems consent the only legitimate basis for governmental intrusion into private autonomy, and since a representative democracy locates consent in the election of legislators and of the chief executive, it follows that every act taken under color of federal authority, whether undertaken by Congress itself or by one of its agents, must be meaningfully traceable to a specific exercise of constitutionally granted legislative or executive power. Thus, the valid exercise of congressionally delegated power depends upon the prior "adoption of [a] declared policy by Congress and its definition of the circumstances in which its command is to be effective . . ."[10]

This requirement that delegated power include at least roughly intelligible "standards" to guide the delegated party preserves, at least theoretically, both sets of constitutional checks—judicial and political—on the exercise of coercive authority in a "government of laws." So far as judicial checks are concerned, the theory has been that, if the recipient of delegated power may exercise that power only within judicially cognizable boundaries, then courts can determine (1) whether any given action falls within the scope of delegated power and is thus defensible against a charge of complete lawlessness; (2) whether the power thus delegated is one constitutionally possessed by Congress in the first place; and (3) whether the power in question is one which is delegable or rests only in Congress. If the legislative policies and standards guiding the agency are at least roughly understandable, judicial review of the means chosen by the agency in exercising its delegated power provides a safeguard of sorts against statutory or constitutional excesses.[11]

---

9. Id. at 115. This case is discussed from the substantive due process perspective in § 15–13; from the equal protection perspective in §§ 16–23, 16–31, 16–32, and 16–33; and from the perspective of structural justice in Chapter 17.

10. Opp Cotton Mills, Inc. v. Administrator, 312 U.S. 126, 144 (1941). For example, in Panama Refining Co. v. Ryan, 293 U.S. 388 (1935), the first case in which the Supreme Court invalidated a congressional delegation, the Court's decision was said to follow from its conclusion that Congress had stated no policy, nor fixed any triggering circumstances, to guide the President

in deciding whether to authorize NIRA codes regulating interstate shipment of oil: "The Congress left the matter to the President without standard or rule, to be dealt with as he pleased." Id. at 418.

11. In American Power & Light Co. v. SEC, 329 U.S. 90 (1946), the Supreme Court upheld a provision of the Public Utility Holding Company Act of 1935 authorizing the SEC to regulate the corporate structure of holding companies whose organization was "unduly or unnecessarily" complex or would "unfairly or inequitably distribute voting power among security holders." The Court reasoned that the

Often, to be sure, the primary mode of governmental accountability is political rather than legal. To the degree that this is so, limits on delegation of power serve less to facilitate judicial review than to foster the political processes ordinarily checking congressional action. From the political perspective, broad delegations of power are objectionable because they permit responsibility for government action to pass out of the hands of Congress. To a certain degree, therefore, broad delegations undermine the electoral check on congressional power. As Justice Brennan has noted: [12] "[F]ormulation of policy is a legislature's primary responsibility, entrusted to it by the electorate, and to the extent Congress delegates authority under indefinite standards, this policy-making function is passed on to other agencies, often not answerable or responsive in the same degree to the people." Moreover, apart from their effect on the electoral check—and thus apart from the question of whether the governmental decisions masked by broad delegations would have influenced the votes of a significant portion of the congressional electorate—broad delegations are politically objectionable because, by enabling Congress to pass the buck on hard choices, and to leave such choices to administrative or executive processes less open to inputs from affected groups, such delegations may short-circuit the pluralist processes of interest accommodation usually structuring legislative decisionmaking.[13]

The Supreme Court is most likely to reject broad delegations of congressional power, typically on statutory grounds, when the action of the government agency claiming delegated power touches constitutionally sensitive areas of substantive liberty. In *Greene v. McElroy*, for example, the Court refused to find an implicit congressional delegation of authority of the Department of Defense to administer a constitutionally questionable security clearance program: "Without explicit action by lawmakers, decisions of great constitutional import and effect would be relegated by default to administrators who, under our system of

specific authorization should be judged in its statutory context, and found in other provisions of the statute "a veritable code of rules . . . for the Commission to follow in giving effect" to the standards at issue. Id. at 105. More significantly, the Court emphasized that private rights were protected less by legislative guidance to the administrative agency than by "access to the courts to test the application of the policy in the light of . . . legislative declarations." Id. Satisfied that the legislative policies and standards were sufficiently clear from the judicial perspective, the Court upheld the delegation, since "judicial review of the remedies adopted by the Commission [would safeguard] against statutory or constitutional excesses." Id. at 106.

This focus on judicial review as a continuing check on agency discretion distinguishes American Power & Light from the Panama Oil case discussed in note 10, supra. In the earlier case, the Supreme Court concentrated on the extent to which the congressional delegation would itself guide executive action, essentially ignoring the possibility that the courts could act as an intermediary, giving specific content through judicial review to broad congressional directives. The difference in approach perhaps bespeaks differing models of judicial review: on the one hand, an extraordinary act correcting extraordinary abuses of the political process; on the other, an ordinary and continuing process of defining the framework in which political decisions are made.

12. United States v. Robel, 389 U.S. 258, 276 (1967) (concurring opinion).

13. See generally Cooper, "Foreword: Strengthening the Congress: An Organizational Analysis," 12 Harv.J.Legis. 307, 311 (1975).

government, are not endowed with authority to decide them." [14] *Greene v. McElroy* also illustrates a second feature of the Supreme Court's contemporary delegation doctrine. Typically, the Court "narrowly construes" federal statutes to avoid broad delegations, thus finding administrative action unauthorized as a statutory matter instead of holding congressional action constitutionally unjustified.[15]

Federal courts at least since 1937 have ordinarily tolerated those congressional delegations of responsibility to administrative agencies which do not quite clearly encroach upon constitutionally protected private rights. If necessary, courts have looked to administrative practice to infer definitions of the standards conditioning particular delegations.[16] Courts have also relied upon the procedural safeguards of agency decisionmaking, noting that such safeguards, if adequate to insure articulation of the policy being applied, and to guarantee the policy's accurate application, protect "against an arbitrary use" of delegated power.[17]

14. 360 U.S. 474, 507 (1959). A year earlier, the Supreme Court had taken a similar approach in Kent v. Dulles, 357 U.S. 116 (1958), refusing to construe federal legislation as delegating to the Secretary of State power to deny passports to persons refusing to disclose whether they had ever been Communists: "Where activities . . . natural and often necessary to the well-being of an American citizen, such as travel, are involved, we will construe narrowly all delegated powers that curtail or dilute them." Id. at 129. Unlike a general delegation doctrine triggered by a concern that Congress, unchecked, would abdicate its interest-accommodation responsibilities, "clear-statement" rules triggered only by government action threatening the exercise of certain rights or the activities of certain groups may create problems of conflict. The effect of refusing to recognize a delegation which would impair the exercise of right A may be to impair the exercise of right B, a right which itself would have triggered a clear statement rule if it had been threatened by the delegation. Rather than attempt to reconcile the conflict itself, a court in this situation would likely defer to the congressional judgment, recognizing the absence of a determinate legal solution to the problem of conflicting rights.

Separately noteworthy is the dubious suggestion in Greene v. McElroy that administrative agencies and appointed officials, "under our system of government, are not endowed with authority to decide" large constitutional questions. 360 U.S. at 507.

15. This approach is also illustrated by the Supreme Court's decision in National Cable Television Assn., Inc. v. United States, 415 U.S. 336 (1974). In order to avoid the constitutional questions it

thought would be raised by a congressional delegation of general taxing authority to an administrative agency, the Court narrowly construed a federal statute so as to restrict the FCC's collection of fees from regulated cable operators to amounts measured exclusively by the benefit the operators received from the federal regulation. This decision is particularly notable because the policy of clear statement was triggered not by some threatened infringement of a constitutionally-protected substantive right or liberty—except perhaps a freedom from "taxation without representation"—but by the delegation doctrine itself. See id. at 342. The Court's delegation concern in this case was a plausible one. Exercises of general taxing power are, as a practical matter, not susceptible to ordinary methods of judicial review. See generally Ely, "Legislative and Administrative Motivation in Constitutional Law," 79 Yale L.J. 1205, 1235 (1970). The same discretionary character of taxation that ordinarily shields it from effective judicial review would also make legislative oversight of a delegate difficult. Therefore, it seems likely that the taxation power, if it is to be exercised legitimately, may be exercised only by Congress itself.

16. See, e.g., Lichter v. United States, 334 U.S. 742, 783 (1948) (holding standard of "excessive profits" a sufficient congressional limitation of administrative discretion in part because "administrative practices currently developed under the Act . . . appear to have come well within the scope of congressional policy").

17. United States v. Rock Royal Co-op., Inc., 307 U.S. 533, 576 (1939). Procedural safeguards not only limit administrative abuse in themselves, but also do so indirectly by increasing the practicality of judicial review. See note 11, supra.

This is not to say that judicial scrutiny of administrative action has lessened. Indeed, it is at least arguable that the contrary is the case. As Professor Richard Stewart has noted,[18] once courts acknowledged the inevitability of broad congressional delegations of power, they had to acknowledge also that administrative and legislative action could not be equated, and that the legitimacy of administrative actions thus could not be presumed in quite the same way that the legitimacy of electorally-checked legislative action could be. Accordingly, courts have closely scrutinized at least some administrative decisions, seeking to insure the fairness of administrative procedures by insisting that agencies take all relevant interests into account. It was a broad delegation to an administrative agency that prompted one noteworthy recent appearance of the delegation doctrine in Supreme Court discourse. The Occupational Safety and Health Act of 1970 instructed that the Secretary of Labor, "in promulgating standards dealing with toxic materials or harmful physical agents, . . . shall set the standard which most adequately assures, to the extent feasible, . . . that no employee will suffer material impairment of health." [19] The Secretary interpreted the statute as requiring him to reduce the permissible limit on exposure to the cancer-causing agent benzene from 10 parts per million of air to 1 part per million, and to ban all dermal contact with benzene. An industry group challenged the regulation, and a sharply divided Supreme Court held that the new standard was invalid.[20] The plurality of Justices found that Congress was not concerned with absolute safety for employees, but rather with the elimination of significant harm; accordingly, the Secretary's decision to impose the burden on industry to prove the existence of a safe level of exposure was improper.[21]

While the other Justices jousted over whether Congress intended that the Secretary engage in cost-benefit analysis, Justice Rehnquist took a dramatically different approach. He wrote: "[M]y colleagues manifest a good deal of uncertainty, and ultimately divide over whether the Secretary produced sufficient evidence that the proposed standard for benzene will result in any appreciable benefits at all. This uncertainty, I would suggest, is eminently justified. . . . I would also suggest that the widely varying opinions of [my colleagues] demonstrate, perhaps better than any other fact, that Congress, the governmental body best suited and most obligated to make the choice confronting us in this litigation, has improperly delegated that choice to the Secretary of Labor and, derivatively, to this Court." [22] Canvassing the legislative history, Justice Rehnquist concluded that it "contains

18. See Stewart, "The Reformation of American Administrative Law," 88 Harv. L.Rev. 1667 (1975).

19. 29 U.S.C. § 655(b)(5).

20. See Industrial Union Dep't, AFL–CIO v. American Petroleum Institute, 448 U.S. 607 (1980). Justice Stevens wrote a plurality opinion, in which the Chief Justice and Justice Stewart joined in full and Justice Powell joined in predominate part. Justice Rehnquist concurred in the judgment. Justice Marshall, in an opinion joined by Justices Brennan, White and Blackmun, dissented.

21. See id. at 658–59.

22. Id. at 672 (Rehnquist, J., concurring in the judgment). Justice Rehnquist described what he called the three important functions of the delegation doctrine: "First, and most abstractly, it ensures to the extent consistent with orderly governmental administration that important choices of social policy are made by Congress, the branch of our Government most

nothing to indicate that the language 'to the extent feasible' does anything other than render what had been a clear, if somewhat unrealistic, standard largely, if not entirely, precatory." [23]   While one may disagree with Justice Rehnquist's conclusion about the statute in question, his opinion was a timely and wise reminder that Congress may not with impunity pass the buck to the executive and the courts on difficult policy issues.   As Justice Rehnquist recognized, congressional lawmaking by delphic command discredits the legislature, overtaxes the judiciary and prevents the prompt and predictable administration of justice.

Prior to 1937, the Supreme Court had upheld the legitimacy of broad delegations of congressional power to executive officials in the special context of joint congressional-executive exercise of foreign affairs powers.   In *United States v. Curtiss-Wright Export Corp.*,[24] the Court theorized that federal foreign affairs power derived less from the Constitution as such than from the inherent attributes of sovereignty and thus concluded that ordinary separation-of-powers principles did not govern the validity of a broad congressional delegation of power to the President to prohibit the sale of weapons to countries engaged in armed conflict: "[C]ongressional legislation which is to be made effective through negotiation and inquiry within the international field must often accord to the President a degree of discretion and freedom from statutory restriction which would not be admissible were domestic affairs alone involved." [25]

The final problem to be considered with respect to delegation is that posed by attempts to endow private decisionmaking with coercive authority over others.[26]   In 1935 and 1936, the Supreme Court struck down federal legislation giving the force of law to regulatory codes drawn up by industry associations.[27]   The Court ruled that "since, in the very nature of things, one person may not be entrusted with the power to regulate the business of another, and especially of a competi-

responsive to the popular will. Second, the doctrine guarantees that, to the extent that Congress finds it necessary to delegate authority, it provides the recipient of that authority with an 'intelligible principle' to guide the exercise of the delegated discretion.   Third, . . . the doctrine ensures that courts charged with reviewing the exercise of delegated legislative discretion will be able to test that exercise against ascertainable standards." Id. at 685–86 (citations omitted).

23. Id. at 681–82. Justice Rehnquist repeated his belief that section 6(b)(5) was an improper delegation in his dissenting opinion in American Textile Manufacturers Institute, Inc. v. Donovan, 452 U.S. 490, 543 (1981).

24. 299 U.S. 304 (1936). This case is discussed in greater detail in Chapter 4, supra.

25. 299 U.S. at 320. Accord, Zemel v. Rusk, 381 U.S. 1, 17 (1965) ("Congress—in

giving the Executive authority over matters of foreign affairs—must of necessity paint with a brush broader than that it customarily wields in domestic areas").

26. Even the institutions of contract and property can of course be understood as such delegations. A great deal about any legal system's premises may be discerned by observing which exercises of coercive power are regarded in that system as intrinsic to private ordering and which are viewed in the system as delegated by the public. The classic essay on the subject is Jaffe, "Law Making by Private Groups," 51 Harv.L.Rev. 201 (1937). See generally Liebmann, "Delegation to Private Parties in American Constitutional Law," 50 Indiana L.J. 650 (1975).

27. Carter v. Carter Coal Co., 298 U.S. 238 (1936); A. L. A. Schechter Poultry Corp. v. United States, 295 U.S. 495 (1935).

tor," [28] such legislative delegation of law-making responsibility to private groups "is unknown to our law and is utterly inconsistent with the constitutional prerogatives and duties of Congress." [29] That was an exaggeration even in 1935 and was flatly false by 1975, but delegations to private groups continue to be disfavored. The Court is especially reluctant to sanction any delegation of governmental or quasi-governmental power to religious organizations. In *Larkin v. Grendel's Den, Inc.*,[30] the Court readily struck down a Massachusetts law that allowed each church to prevent issuance of liquor licenses within a 500-foot radius of the church. As Chief Justice Burger's opinion for the eight-member majority stated, "The Framers did not set up a system of government in which important, discretionary governmental powers would be delegated to or shared with religious institutions." [31] In addition, it is noteworthy that, in the case of *United States v. Mazurie*,[32] where the Supreme Court rejected a claim that a congressional delegation to Indian tribes of authority to regulate liquor sales on Indian lands unconstitutionally transferred governmental authority to private groups, the Court's rejection of the delegation attack rested *not* on the ground that delegations to private groups are generally appropriate, but on the basis that Indian tribes "are unique aggregations possessing attributes of *sovereignty* over both their members and their territory," and thus "are a good deal more than 'private, voluntary organizations.' " [33] The judicial hostility to private lawmaking—even more apparent, perhaps, in the context of state delegations—thus represents a persistent theme in American constitutional law.[34]

28. Carter v. Carter Coal Co., 298 U.S. 238, 311 (1936).

29. A. L. A. Schechter Poultry Corp. v. United States, 295 U.S. 495, 537 (1935). Accord, Washington ex rel. Seattle Title & Trust Co. v. Roberge, 278 U.S. 116 (1928); Eubank v. Richmond, 226 U.S. 137 (1912), both cited approvingly, but distinguished, in Eastlake v. Forest City Enterprises, 426 U.S. 668, 677–78 (1976), discussed in § 10–5, infra.

30. 459 U.S. 116 (1982).

31. Id. at 127. Justice Rehnquist alone dissented, on the ground that the Massachusetts law did not "sponsor or subsidize any religious group or activity." Id. at 129 (Rehnquist, J., dissenting). For further discussion of Grendel's Den, see § 14–14, infra.

32. 419 U.S. 544 (1975).

33. Id. at 557 (emphasis added). See § 16–14, infra.

34. In the modern period, that hostility may take a variety of indirect forms. A striking example was provided by Florida Lime & Avocado Growers, Inc. v. Paul, 373 U.S. 132 (1963), discussed in § 6–25, infra, where the Supreme Court upheld a California law regulating the marketing of avocados sold in California on the basis of oil content notwithstanding the law's exclusion from the California market of a significant number of Florida-grown avocados meeting federal marketing regulations that looked to factors other than oil content in determining suitability for sale. A significant, and perhaps decisive, role was played by the fact that the federal regulations had not been drafted "by impartial experts in Washington or even in Florida, but rather by the South Florida Avocado Administrative Committee," id. at 150–51, a self-interested group of Florida growers and handlers who sought to promote their economic position in the exercise of their federally-delegated authority. Even if the "federal" regulations could not plausibly be held invalid, their origin in a private delegation plainly contributed to the Court's unwillingness to give them preemptive effect.

§ 5–18. Congressional Action and the Separation of Powers: The Speech or Debate Clause

We move in this section from separation of powers *limits* on Congress, considered in § 5–17, to separation of powers *protections* for Congress. The primary such protection is contained in article I, § 6, which provides that, "for any Speech or Debate in either House, [members of Congress] shall not be questioned in any other Place." The speech or debate clause protects Congress from two kinds of threats to its deliberative autonomy. First, it blocks attempts by executive officials to use grand jury investigations and criminal prosecutions as means of calling into question "the legislative acts of . . . members of Congress".[1] Second and more generally, the clause insures "that legislators are not distracted from or hindered in the performance of their legislative tasks by being called into court to defend their actions."[2] The speech or debate clause may be invoked in either civil or criminal proceedings.[3] Its protection extends both to members of Congress and to their aides, insofar as the aides perform "services that would be immune legislative conduct if performed" by a member of Congress.[4]

By its terms, the immunity the speech or debate clause confers is absolute.[5] The Supreme Court has nonetheless limited the *kinds* of congressional actions protected by the immunity. In the first case to construe the speech or debate clause, *Kilbourn v. Thompson*, the Court held that the immunity extends to all "things generally done in a session of [Congress] by one of its members in relation to the business before it."[6] Congressional "business", the Supreme Court has subse-

---

§ 5–18

1. United States v. Johnson, 383 U.S. 169, 185 (1966).

2. Powell v. McCormack, 395 U.S. 486, 505 (1969).

3. See Eastland v. United States Servicemen's Fund, 421 U.S. 491 (1975). The Supreme Court has been called upon to judge the limits of the speech or debate clause in a number of civil proceedings initiated by private individuals. See, e.g., Eastland v. United States Servicemen's Fund, supra; Doe v. McMillan, 412 U.S. 306 (1973); Powell v. McCormack, 395 U.S. 486 (1969); Dombrowski v. Eastland, 387 U.S. 82 (1967) (per curiam); Kilbourn v. Thompson, 103 U.S. (13 Otto) 168 (1881). Other cases have required the Court to review aspects of criminal law enforcement. See, e.g., Gravel v. United States, 408 U.S. 606 (1972) (grand jury investigation); United States v. Brewster, 408 U.S. 501 (1972) (indictment); United States v. Johnson, 383 U.S. 169 (1966) (conviction). For an argument that the scope of the speech or debate clause ought to differ depending upon whether the privilege is asserted in privately-initiated civil proceedings or executive-run criminal prosecutions, see Reinstein & Silverglate, "Legislative Privilege and the Separation of Power," 86 Harv.L.Rev. 1113 (1973) (privilege should give broader protection against criminal proceedings).

4. Gravel v. United States, 408 U.S. 606, 622 (1972). Gravel's equation of the privilege for aides to members of Congress with that of the members themselves marked a departure at least from the rhetoric of previous decisions suggesting that the speech or debate clause gave legislative aides weaker protection. See, e.g., Dombrowski v. Eastland, 387 U.S. 82, 85 (1967) (per curiam) (doctrine of legislative immunity "less absolute, although applicable, when applied to officers or employees of a legislative body"). However, the narrow construction Gravel gave to the scope of the speech or debate clause largely undermined its extension of full protection to legislative aides.

5. Eastland v. United States Servicemen's Fund, 421 U.S. 491, 509–10 (1975). The speech or debate clause extends no protection to state legislators from introduction of evidence of state legislative acts in a federal criminal prosecution. See United States v. Gillock, 445 U.S. 360 (1980).

6. 103 U.S. (13 Otto) 168, 204 (1881). The Court, in thus extending protection of the speech or debate clause beyond the

quently ruled, does not include every act performed by a member of Congress. Thus, although a former member of the House of Representatives could not be prosecuted on a conspiracy charge where conviction on the charge required proof that the legitimately legislative act of making a speech before Congress was the result of bribery,[7] a former United States Senator was properly convicted for simply *taking* a bribe, "obviously no part of the legislative process or function. . . ."[8]

The line separating protected from unprotected congressional action is ultimately one between "purely legislative activities" and "political matters."[9] Legislative activities include all congressional actions that are "an integral part of the deliberative and communicative processes by which members participate in committee and House proceedings with respect to the consideration and passage or rejection of proposed legislation or with respect to other matters which the Constitution places within the jurisdiction of either House."[10] Thus, in addition to literally speaking or debating, a range of other acts—voting, preparing committee reports, and conducting committee hearings, for example—are clearly protected by the speech or debate clause. Unprotected political matters include providing constituent services, aiding

scope of its literal language, took as persuasive the argument of Chief Justice Parsons in Coffin v. Coffin, 4 Mass. 1 (1808), a decision construing an analogous clause of the Massachusetts Constitution: "These privileges are thus secured, not with the intention of protecting the members against prosecutions for their own benefit but to support the rights of the people, by enabling their representatives to execute the functions of their office without fear of prosecutions, civil or criminal. I therefore think that the article ought not to be construed strictly, but liberally, that the full design of it may be answered. I will not confine it to delivering an opinion, uttering a speech, or haranguing in debate; but will extend it to the giving of a vote, to the making of a written report, and to every other act resulting from the nature, and in the execution, of the office; and I would define the article as securing to every member exemption from prosecution for everything said or done by him as a representative in the exercise of the functions of that office, without inquiring whether the exercise was regular according to the rules of the house, or irregular and against their rules." Id. at 27.

7. United States v. Johnson, 383 U.S. 169, 184–85 (1966).

8. United States v. Brewster, 408 U.S. 501, 526 (1972).

9. Id. at 512. "Political matters," of course, are not the only activities of members of Congress that fall outside the scope of the speech or debate clause. The physical assault of one member of Congress upon another, for example, could certainly

trigger a criminal prosecution—at least if prosecution need not involve judicial inquiry into legislative acts (for example, inquiry into whether a speech by one member provoked the other's attack). Similarly, there is no reason to suppose that members of Congress are free to ignore civil rights statutes in hiring and firing staff members. Chief Justice Burger's dissenting opinion, therefore, in Davis v. Passman, 442 U.S. 228 (1979), seems wide of the mark. The 5–4 majority in Davis held that there was an implied cause of action under the fifth amendment for a woman who claimed that she was discriminated against on the basis of sex by her employer, a United States Congressman. The majority did not reach the speech or debate clause issue, as it was not raised in the lower court. However, the Chief Justice wrote, in an opinion joined by Justices Powell and Rehnquist, that "in the performance of constitutionally defined functions, each Member of the House or Senate occupies a position in the Legislative Branch comparable to that of the President in the Executive Branch; and for the limited purposes of selecting personal staffs, their authority should be uninhibited except as Congress itself, or the Constitution, expressly provides otherwise." Id. at 250. But discrimination in hiring seems clearly divorced from any legislative act; judicial inquiry into such decisions would, it seems, invade no province the speech or debate clause is designed to protect.

10. Gravel v. United States, 408 U.S. 606, 625 (1972).

individuals seeking government contracts and arranging appointments with government agencies, as well as communicating directly with the public through such media as constituent newsletters, press releases, speeches delivered outside of Congress, and book publishing.[11] Such outside publication is not protected by the speech or debate clause even if the material published was previously communicated in the course of protected legislative activity.[12]

Although perhaps inconsistent with "[t]he realities of the American political system," [13] the Supreme Court's distinction between legislative and political acts (or some other similarly formal distinction) seems inevitable if not all congressional activity is to be privileged under the speech or debate clause. Like any privilege, the one the speech or debate clause grants Congress would be virtually worthless if courts judging its applicability had to scrutinize closely the acts ostensibly shielded. Judicial consideration of alleged improper motivation is thus necessarily an inappropriate mode of analysis for determining the limits of legislative immunity.[14] Similarly, since judgments of legality or constitutionality obviously involve "questioning" of legislative acts, courts may not strip acts taken in the legislative process of their constitutional immunity by finding that the acts are substantively illegal or unconstitutional.[15] If courts are to distinguish between privi-

11. See United States v. Brewster, 408 U.S. 501, 512 (1972). The Court elaborated on the distinction between protected and unprotected activities in Hutchinson v. Proxmire, 443 U.S. 111 (1979), holding that the speech or debate clause does not protect Members of Congress' press releases or newsletters. The Court held that Senator Proxmire could be sued for libel by a disgruntled recipient of his "Golden Fleece Award," which the Senator bestowed to publicize what he saw as wasteful government spending. See id. at 123–33. Justice Stewart dissented in part, stating his belief that the clause protected "telephone calls to federal officials." Id. at 136. Justice Brennan dissented, on the ground that "public criticism by legislators of unnecessary governmental expenditures, whatever its form," was protected by the speech or debate clause. Id.

12. Doe v. McMillan, 412 U.S. 306 (1973) (holding that the speech or debate clause did not automatically immunize printers, acting at the order of a congressional committee, who prepared for public distribution a committee report previously circulated in Congress and allegedly invading the privacy of individuals discussed in the report; but congressional committee members, members of their staff, their consultant, and their investigator were all absolutely immune from suit for the legislative acts of compiling the report, referring it to the House, or voting for its publication); Gravel v. United States, 408 U.S. 606 (1972) (speech or debate clause does not extend immunity to legislative aide called before federal grand jury to testify about

Senator Gravel's arrangement to commercially publish transcripts of the Pentagon Papers which he had previously made public at a Senate subcommittee hearing).

13. United States v. Brewster, 408 U.S. 501, 556 (1972) (White, J., dissenting).

14. Eastland v. United States Servicemen's Fund, 421 U.S. 491, 508–09 (1975); United States v. Johnson, 383 U.S. 169, 180 (1966). See also Tenney v. Brandhove, 341 U.S. 367, 377–78 (1951) (interpreting limits of state legislative immunity as analogous to speech or debate clause privilege).

15. Except where substantive constitutionality would be determined through strict scrutiny, however, the standard used to judge substantive constitutionality may be essentially the standard used to determine whether congressional action falls within the speech or debate clause. In Eastland v. United States Servicemen's Fund, 421 U.S. 491 (1975), the Supreme Court held that the speech or debate clause barred a suit brought by an anti-war group's financial backers against various members of the Senate and a Senate committee's chief counsel, seeking to quash a subpoena directed to the bank where the anti-war group maintained an account. The Court rejected an argument that because, under first amendment strict scrutiny, the subpoena would be unconstitutional, it therefore fell outside the scope of the speech or debate clause. See id. at 509–11. But the Court, in determining whether this congressional investigation fell within the legislative sphere protected by the speech or debate clause, applied the same ration-

leged and unprivileged congressional activity, therefore, they have no recourse but to classifications based on the surface characteristics of the activity at issue. But such considerations hardly support the extreme view of congressional privilege taken in *United States v. Helstoski*,[16] holding "that references to past legislative acts of a Member [of Congress] cannot [even] be admitted" as evidence in a bribery prosecution of a former Congressman.[17] As Justice Stevens pointed out in his opinion concurring in part and dissenting in part,[18] there seems no reason why "evidence that merely *refers* to legislative acts" should be excluded.[19] He continued, "If the evidentiary references to legislative acts are merely incidental to a proper purpose, the judge should admit the evidence and instruct the jury as to its limited relevance. The Constitution mandates that legislative acts 'shall not be questioned'; it does not say they shall not be mentioned."[20]

However this evidentiary matter is resolved, there are two principal justifications for interpreting the speech or debate clause to exclude altogether at least *some* congressional activity. First, although article I, § 5, empowers Congress to discipline its own members, it in fact "is ill-equipped to investigate, try and punish its Members" in connection with conduct only "incidentally related to the legislative process."[21] Except in extraordinary or partisan circumstances, Congress may be expected to be reluctant to punish its own.[22] And if Congress should act, there is no guarantee that the targets of its action would benefit from the procedural safeguards against injustice available in judicial proceedings.[23] A less than encompassing construction of the speech or debate clause is justified, second, by the mutual coexistence of legislative immunity and judicial review. "The purpose of the protection afforded legislators is not to forestall judicial review of legislative action."[24] The enforcement of legislation inevitably requires action by noncongressional officials;[25] judicial review of legislation threatening to particular individuals is thus always possible. Legislation, however, is not the only form of congressional action capable of crossing constitutional boundaries. In fact, many congressional acts requiring neither executive nor judicial assistance for completion may in substance be unconstitutional, illegal, or both. The speech or debate clause would significantly limit judicial review, therefore, if the immunity the clause

ality standard it generally uses to judge the substantive constitutionality of congressional investigations in the absence of first amendment challenge. See id. at 509.

16. 442 U.S. 477 (1979).

17. Id. at 489.

18. Justice Stevens was joined by Justice Stewart. Justice Brennan dissented, based on his view, first expressed in United States v. Brewster, 408 U.S. 501, 536 (1972), that "a corrupt agreement to perform legislative acts" can never be the subject of a criminal prosecution. 442 U.S. at 499.

19. 442 U.S. at 494 (emphasis added).

20. Id. at 498.

21. United States v. Brewster, 408 U.S. 501, 518 (1972).

22. See id. at 519–20; Note, "The Bribed Congressman's Immunity from Prosecution," 75 Yale L.J. 335, 349 n. 84 (1965).

23. United States v. Brewster, 408 U.S. 501, 519–20 (1972).

24. Powell v. McCormack, 395 U.S. 486, 505 (1969).

25. See §§ 10–4 to 10–6, infra. See also Buckley v. Valeo, 424 U.S. 1, 119 (1976) ("the Legislative Branch may not exercise executive authority by retaining the power to appoint those who will execute its laws"). Accord, Bowsher v. Synar, 106 S.Ct. 3181 (1986), discussed in ch. 4, supra.

confers blocked courts from considering challenges to all congressional acts unassisted by executive or judicial action.

The Supreme Court's limitation of congressional immunity to "legislative action" is perhaps best understood as an attempted accommodation of the competing constitutional commitments to judicial review and legislative autonomy. Nonlegislative action by members of Congress or their aides is entirely open to judicial scrutiny. Moreover, to the extent that legislative and nonlegislative actions are entangled in practice,[26] the privileged status of legislative action does not preclude its judicial review: without formally requiring legislators or their aides to answer personally for legislative acts, it is possible, by "questioning" the legality or constitutionality of the legislative acts' nonlegislative aspects, for courts indirectly to review the legislative action itself.[27] And frequently, such indirect review of legislative action will not defeat the objectives underlying recognition of legislative immunity, since the distinction between legislative and nonlegislative acts is often realized in the division of responsibility between members of Congress and their aides. It is usually not the legislator who, for illegal or unconstitutional actions that are not purely legislative, risks liability or waste of time in court.[28] Instead, it is ordinarily the aide who becomes the hostage of the law.[29]

26. See United States v. Brewster, 408 U.S. 501, 556 (1972) (White, J., dissenting).

27. For example, in Powell v. McCormack, 395 U.S. 486 (1969), ex-Congressman Powell brought suit to challenge his exclusion from the House of Representatives. The Supreme Court held that, under the speech or debate clause, the members of the House of Representatives who excluded Powell could not be treated as defendants. Id. at 506. The Court also held, however, that suit could be brought against the Clerk of the House, the Sergeant at Arms, and the Doorkeeper, for refusing to perform for Powell services that they performed for other members of Congress. Id. at 503–06. In order to decide whether the House employees acted properly, the Court had to decide whether the House of Representatives itself acted properly in excluding Powell from membership. Thus, judicial review of congressional action was achieved without having to bring members of Congress before the Court or even to treat them as defendants.

28. Involvement in judicial proceedings concerning the legality or constitutionality of nonlegislative acts obviously diverts the attention of members of Congress and their aides from strictly legislative acts, and thus the interests underlying the speech or debate clause may be *fully* realized only if *all* acts of members of Congress and their aides are immunized from judicial questioning. But the point of the Supreme Court's decisions is that speech or debate clause interests must be compromised to some degree in order not to block all congressional action from judicial review. Even where the Court has emphasized its concern that legislators' time not be wasted in drawn-out judicial proceedings, see, e.g., Eastland v. United States Servicemen's Fund, 421 U.S. 491, 503 (1975), it has been careful to recognize the validity of the claimed speech or debate clause immunity only after determining that the congressional activity at issue fell within "the legitimate legislative sphere.'" Id. at 503. See also "The Supreme Court, 1974 Term," 89 Harv.L.Rev. 47, 131–39 (1975).

29. In four key speech or debate clause cases, the Court has held legislative employees liable to suit but barred suit against members of Congress themselves. See Doe v. McMillan, 412 U.S. 306 (1973); Powell v. McCormack, 395 U.S. 486 (1969); Dombrowski v. Eastland, 387 U.S. 82 (1967); Kilbourn v. Thompson, 103 U.S. (13 Otto) 168 (1881).

Eastland v. United States Servicemen's Fund, 421 U.S. 491 (1975), illustrates the litigative complexity involved in the use of suits challenging nonlegislative acts of legislative aides to obtain judicial review of congressional action. USSF brought suit in 1970 against nine Senators, the Chief Counsel of a Senate subcommittee, and a bank, in order to enjoin issuance to the bank of a congressional subpoena for records of USSF, on the ground that the investigation of which the subpoena was a part had the purpose and effect of chilling exercise of USSF's first amendment rights.

§ 5–19. Congressional Investigations and the Separation of Powers: Legislative Autonomy and Judicial Review

Congressional authority to conduct investigations, and in the process to compel testimony, is not explicitly recognized by the Constitution. But the Supreme Court has quite properly held the investigatory power to be "an essential and appropriate auxiliary to the legislative function," thus making it implicit in the general article I, § 1, grant of "legislative Powers" to Congress.[1] As the histories of the Watergate and McCarthy episodes show, the investigatory power of Congress may be both greatly used and greatly abused. Judicial review of congressional investigations, although reflecting the Supreme Court's concern for congressional abuse, has traditionally been narrow in order to leave investigators the discretion their legitimate purposes require. Judicial review has also been precarious: the speech or debate clause significantly limits the circumstances in which individuals whose rights have been or will be violated by congressional investigations may seek judicial relief.[2] Ordinarily, it is only when individuals refuse to cooperate with congressional investigators, and the investigators subsequently seek to use judicial processes to punish the refusal as contempt, that

Id. at 494–95. Because jurisdiction and venue for suit against the subcommittee lay only in the District of Columbia, however, USSF ultimately could not serve process against the bank, operating in New York, and therefore the bank did not become party to the suit. Id. at 513 (Marshall, J., concurring). Since the challenged actions of the Senators and their chief counsel constituted legislative acts, see id. at 505–07, the Supreme Court held that the speech or debate clause barred the suit. Id. at 507.

At least in retrospect, it appears that USSF should have pursued either of two alternative litigative strategies. Once it became clear that suit could not be brought against both the bank and the subcommittee, USSF might have been better off choosing to sue only the bank. The gravamen of the suit would have been that the bank lacked authority to comply with the subpoena without the consent of USSF, cf. Note, "Government Access to Bank Records," 83 Yale L.J. 1439, 1466–71 (1974) (discussion in fourth amendment context). See § 15–16, infra. If the suit were successful, USSF would recover the ordinary prerogative, threatened by the third party subpoena, of refusing to consent to the bank's compliance with the subpoena and thereby inviting a contempt proceeding at which it could raise its own constitutional claims as defenses on the merits. See Eastland, 421 U.S. at 509–10 n. 16. Instead of suing the bank or the subcommittee, USSF might also have chosen to seek an injunction against U.S. Marshals who actually served the subpoena. See 421

U.S. at 494–95 n. 4. Cf. Marshall v. Gordon, 243 U.S. 521 (1917) (ordering writ of habeas corpus to release, from the custody of Sergeant at Arms of House of Representatives, an individual ordered imprisoned by House for contempt of Congress). The act of service itself in all likelihood would not be deemed legislative, and thus the Marshals could not raise the speech or debate clause as a defense. Compare Doe v. McMillan, 412 U.S. 306, 319–24 (1973).

One reason, perhaps, that USSF elected to follow neither of the litigation strategies outlined here is the uncertain status of a depositor's standing to make a direct challenge upon subpoenas of bank records: analysis of the issue from the perspective of a property theory could suggest that the depositor retains an insufficient interest to confer control over the disposal of the bank records. Cf. Fisher v. United States, 425 U.S. 391 (1976); United States v. Miller, 425 U.S. 435 (1976). But see § 15–16, infra.

§ 5–19

1. See McGrain v. Daugherty, 273 U.S. 135, 174 (1927). The Supreme Court based its conclusion in large part upon the results of a review of "the legislative practice," id. For a discussion of the history, up to the time of McGrain, of the use of legislative investigations in England and America, see Landis, "Constitutional Limitations of the Congressional Power of Investigation," 40 Harv.L.Rev. 153 (1926).

2. See, e.g., Eastland v. United States Servicemen's Fund, 421 U.S. 491 (1975), discussed in § 5–18, supra.

courts are in a position to review the validity of congressional investigatory action.[3]

Congress, of course, possesses the power to investigate and to compel testimony in connection with the exercise of its powers of self-regulation.[4] But more significantly, Congress may also investigate any matter concerning which the Constitution authorizes it to legislate. "[T]he power of inquiry . . . is as penetrating and far-reaching as the potential power to enact and appropriate [funds] under the Constitution."[5] Investigations in aid of legislation encompass "inquiries concerning the administration of existing laws as well as proposed or possibly needed statutes."[6] Congress may therefore authorize "probes into departments of the Federal Government to expose corruption, inefficiency or waste."[7] Because Congress possesses authority to legislate concerning many aspects of private conduct, investigations in aid of legislation may also inquire into the actions of private parties.

The congressional power of investigation is, however, limited by the separation of powers.[8] Congress may not usurp the functions of the courts. This certainly does not mean that Congress may not investigate matters relevant to past or future legislation that are also pertinent to litigation underway in federal or state courts. Although the Supreme Court held in *Kilbourn v. Thompson* that Congress could not

---

3. It has long been believed that each House of Congress has an inherent constitutional authority to imprison, until it adjourns, persons other than members of Congress themselves whom it finds to be in contempt of Congress. Anderson v. Dunn, 19 U.S. (6 Wheat.) 204, 231 (1821). Even if this continues to be the law, the Constitution at least limits what Congress may deem contemptuous: Congress may itself punish only those acts which would obstruct or otherwise "virtually [destroy]" congressional processes. Marshall v. Gordon, 243 U.S. 521, 545 (1917) (public statement criticizing congressional committee cannot be punished by Congress as contempt). See, e.g., Anderson v. Dunn, supra (attempted bribery of member of Congress). Although Congress has the power, without aid of the judiciary or the executive, to punish for contempt persons who refuse to comply with a subpoena issued by a congressional investigatory committee, cf. McGrain v. Daugherty, 273 U.S. 135 (1927) (upholding power of Congress to authorize its agents to arrest and bring before Congress a witness who refused to comply with a congressional subpoena), Congress ordinarily does not exercise this power, but instead requests executive officials to initiate judicial contempt proceedings under a statute such as 2 U.S.C. § 192, which punishes as a misdemeanor any refusal "to give testimony or to produce papers upon any matter under inquiry before either House. . . ." It is this congressional resort to judicial pro-

ceedings which ordinarily brings the investigations of congressional committees under constitutional scrutiny: "By thus making the federal judiciary the affirmative agency for enforcing the authority that underlies the congressional power to punish for contempt, Congress necessarily brings into play the specific provisions of the Constitution relating to the prosecution of offenses and those implied restrictions under which courts function." Watkins v. United States, 354 U.S. 178, 216 (1957) (Frankfurter, J., concurring). Accord, Eastland v. United States Servicemen's Fund, 421 U.S. 491, 509–10 n. 16 (1975) (dictum).

4. See, e.g., Barry v. United States ex rel. Cunningham, 279 U.S. 597, 616 (1929) (power of Senate to judge qualifications of its members includes power to compel the attendance of witnesses); In re Chapman, 166 U.S. 661 (1897) (senatorial power to expel members includes power to compel testimony by non-Senators concerning events which may be basis for expulsion).

5. Barenblatt v. United States, 360 U.S. 109, 111 (1959).

6. Watkins v. United States, 354 U.S. 178, 187 (1957).

7. Id.

8. For discussion of efforts by the Senate Judiciary Committee to obtain legal opinions written by a Supreme Court nominee while working at the Justice Department, see § 4–15, supra.

investigate a matter concurrently within the jurisdiction of a federal court,[9] the Court in a subsequent decision effectively confined *Kilbourn* to its facts, holding in *Sinclair v. United States* that the authority of Congress "to require pertinent disclosures in aid of its own constitutional power is not abridged because the information sought to be elicited may also be of use in [pending] suits." [10]   But Congress may not investigate private activity for the sole purpose of publicizing that activity; to do so would arguably involve assumption of the power of judgment reserved to the courts.   "[T]here is no congressional power to expose for the sake of exposure." [11]   But since courts are reluctant to inquire into legislative motive in determining the purposes of congressional investigations,[12] the impact of this restriction is highly attenuated: at least if the congressional investigation does not touch first amendment concerns,[13] a showing that the investigation is rationally related to some legitimate congressional objective is sufficient to defeat the claim of "exposure for the sake of exposure." [14]

Although only loosely restricting the *substantive* scope of congressional investigations, the Supreme Court has required Congress to adopt important *procedural* safeguards in the conduct of its investigations.   Because the Bill of Rights limits lawmaking as well as legislation,[15] congressional investigators must respect the fifth amendment privilege against self-incrimination,[16] the fourth amendment prohibition of unreasonable searches and seizures,[17] and the requirement of due process that, if government actors promulgate rules limiting their own conduct, they must comply with such rules.[18]   Perhaps more significantly, the Court has held that due process and the formally limited character of congressional investigatory power (1) require Congress, in delegating its investigatory authority to particular committees, to state clearly the scope of a given committee's authority; [19] and (2)

9.   103 U.S. (13 Otto) 168, 193–96 (1881).

10.   279 U.S. 263, 295 (1929).   Accord, Hutcheson v. United States, 369 U.S. 599, 613 (1962) (parallel state criminal proceeding).

11.   Watkins v. United States, 354 U.S. 178, 200 (1957).   Accord, Eastland v. United States Servicemen's Fund, 421 U.S. 491, 504 n. 15 (1975).

12.   Watkins, 354 U.S. at 200.

13.   See Chapter 12.

14.   Watkins, 354 U.S. at 198.

15.   Barenblatt v. United States, 360 U.S. 109, 112 (1959); Watkins v. United States, 354 U.S. 178, 188 (1957).   See generally Linde, "Due Process of Lawmaking," 55 Neb.L.Rev. 197 (1975); Chapter 17, infra.

16.   Quinn v. United States, 349 U.S. 155, 161 (1955).   Congress has generally recognized that the fifth amendment privilege may be properly asserted by witnesses called to testify by congressional investigators.   Litigation reaching the Supreme Court in connection with fifth amendment

claims has commonly involved disputes over whether the witness had in fact claimed the privilege.   See, e.g., id.; Emspak v. United States, 349 U.S. 190 (1955); cf. Hutcheson v. United States, 369 U.S. 599 (1962) (refusing to treat, as tantamount to a claim of fifth amendment privilege, an assertion that congressional questioning violated due process because, in a parallel state prosecution, even a claim before Congress of the fifth amendment privilege would be incriminating).

17.   McPhaul v. United States, 364 U.S. 372, 382–83 (1960) (holding subpoena of records not so broad as to constitute fourth amendment violation).

18.   See Gojack v. United States, 384 U.S. 702 (1966): Yellin v. United States, 374 U.S. 109 (1963); Flaxer v. United States, 358 U.S. 147 (1958).

19.   Watkins v. United States, 354 U.S. 178, 201 (1957).   Particularly exacting standards of clarity are applied whenever the congressional investigation appears to threaten first amendment rights.   See, e.g.,

require an investigating committee, if the pertinency of its inquiry is challenged by a witness, and if the subject matter of the investigation has not previously "been made to appear with indisputable clarity," "to state for the record the subject under inquiry . . . and the manner in which the propounded questions are pertinent thereto." [20]

§ 5–20. State Sovereignty as a Limit on Congressional Power: Overview

For almost four decades after 1937, the conventional wisdom was that federalism in general—and the rights of states in particular—provided no judicially-enforceable limits on congressional power. The 1968 case of *Maryland v. Wirtz,*[1] which upheld the application of minimum wage and overtime pay requirements of the Fair Labor Standards Act (FLSA) to state and municipal employees, exemplified the largely unquestioned prevailing view. Then, in 1976, the Supreme Court by a 5–4 vote in *National League of Cities v. Usery*[2] overruled *Wirtz* and struck down as inconsistent with state sovereignty a 1974 congressional amendment of the FLSA which had extended federal minimum wage and maximum hour provisions to almost all state and municipal employees. Nine years later, however, *National League of Cities* was itself overruled, again by a 5–4 vote, in *Garcia v. San Antonio Metropolitan Transit Authority.*[3] And several Justices have warned explicitly that they expect *National League of Cities* will—and should—rise again.[4] This section and sections 5–21 and 5–22 are concerned chiefly with these decisions and their implications. To understand the issues posed, however, we begin with a more general analysis.

The Constitution expressly places only a few limits on the power of Congress in the interest of state sovereignty. Article I, § 8, cl. 16, reserves "to the States respectively" the power to appoint the officers of any militia for which Congress might provide, and to train the militia according to such discipline as Congress prescribes. Article I, § 9, cl. 1, denied Congress the power to prohibit the slave trade where the states permitted it; that provision expired by its own force in 1808. Article I,

United States v. Rumely, 345 U.S. 41 (1953).

20. Watkins, 354 U.S. at 214–15. Although congressional investigations occasionally run afoul of the pertinency requirement, see, e.g., Sacher v. United States, 356 U.S. 576 (1958) (per curiam), most congressional investigators since Watkins have been able to demonstrate the pertinency of their inquiries without difficulty. See, e.g., Wilkinson v. United States, 365 U.S. 399, 413 (1961). It is not sufficient for a congressional committee simply to show pertinency at its hearings; under 2 U.S.C. § 192, if a contempt conviction is to be obtained, pertinency must also be proven at trial. See Deutch v. United States, 367 U.S. 456, 467–72 (1961); cf. Russell v. United States, 369 U.S. 749 (1962) (grand jury indictment must state

question under inquiry at time of defendant's default or refusal to answer).

§ 5–20

1. 392 U.S. 183 (1968).

2. 426 U.S. 833 (1976). Justice Rehnquist wrote for the Court, joined by Chief Justice Burger and by Justices Stewart and Powell. Justice Blackmun concurred separately. Dissenting were Justices Brennan, Marshall, White, and Stevens.

3. 469 U.S. 528 (1985). Justice Blackmun wrote for the Court, joined by the four 1976 dissenters. See note 2, supra.

4. See id. at 579 (Rehnquist, J., dissenting.); id. at 588–89 (O'Connor, J., dissenting). Also in dissent were the remaining Justices from the 1976 majority—Chief Justice Burger and Justice Powell.

§ 9, cl. 5, denies Congress the power to lay any tax or duty "on Articles exported from any State." Article I, § 9, cl. 6, prohibits Congress from discriminating among state ports in its regulation of commerce or revenue; "nor shall Vessels bound to, or from, one State, be obliged to enter, clear, or pay Duties in another." Article IV, § 3, denies Congress the power to divide or join states without their legislatures' consent. And article V, governing the amendment process, provides that "no State, without its Consent, shall be deprived of its equal Suffrage in the Senate."

This relative paucity of explicit "states' rights" limitations should not be surprising. The states existed at the time of the Constitution's drafting, and the concern of the draftsmen, both initially and over the course of history, has been chiefly with defining the scope of national powers and with identifying the individual rights that the Constitution protects from federal and state interference. The structure of state governments and their sphere of operations simply are not the subjects of the Constitution,[5] except insofar as the Constitution shifts power from the states to the national government, or protects the rights of individuals from governmental violations. There is little reason to expect, therefore, that the Constitution should contain more than a scattering of affirmative guarantees of state sovereignty: the states are simply "there."

It is clear, however, that the Constitution does presuppose the existence of the states as entities independent of the national government. This presupposition lies just below the surface of many constitutional provisions; it manifests itself most expressly in the language of the tenth amendment, which puts the states on an equal footing with "the people" as holders of the powers which the Constitution neither grants to the national government nor prohibits to the states: "The powers not delegated to the United States by the Constitution, nor prohibited by it to the States are reserved to the States respectively, or to the people."[6] Congressional action which treats the states in a manner inconsistent with their constitutionally recognized independent status, therefore, should be void, not because it violates any specific constitutional provision or transgresses the explicit boundaries of any specific grant of authority, but because it would be contrary to the structural assumptions and the tacit postulates of the Constitution as a whole.[7]

---

5. But see U.S. Const. art. IV, § 4: "The United States shall guarantee to every State . . . a Republican Form of Government, and shall protect each of them against Invasion . . . ." Luther v. Borden, 48 U.S. (7 How.) 1, 37–46 (1849), treated the guarantee clause as posing a non-justiciable political question, but Baker v. Carr, 369 U.S. 186 (1962), came close to overturning that decision by treating issues of legislative apportionment as justiciable under the fourteenth amendment. See Chapter 3, supra, and Chapter 13, infra.

6. "The [Tenth] Amendment expressly declares the constitutional policy that Congress may not exercise power in a fashion that impairs the States' integrity, or their ability to function effectively in a federal system . . . ." Fry v. United States, 421 U.S. 542, 547 n. 7 (1975).

7. See Texas v. White, 74 U.S. (7 Wall.) 700, 725 (1869) ("The Constitution, in all its provisions, looks to an indestructible Union, composed of indestructible states"); Nevada v. Hall, 440 U.S. 410, 433 (1979) (Rehnquist, J., joined by Burger, C.J., dissenting) ("[W]hen the Constitution is am-

The question, though, is what Congress must do in order to treat the states in a manner inconsistent with their independent status. In answering that question, at least the core content of state sovereignty seems fairly clear. In *Coyle v. Smith*, the Supreme Court held that Congress cannot tell a state where to locate its capitol.[8] Language in *Helvering v. Gerhardt* suggests that a state may claim an immunity from federal taxation if the federal tax clearly imposes an "actual and substantial, not conjectural" burden upon peculiarly governmental activities—publishing enacted laws, for instance—that are "indispensable to the maintenance of a state government."[9] *Murdock v. Memphis*, although on its face a decision construing a federal jurisdictional statute,[10] has been thought to have a constitutional resonance:[11] even if the commerce clause, for example, would otherwise justify it, Congress may not have the power to authorize the Supreme Court to supplant state courts as the authoritative declarers of law within their jurisdictions by functioning as a court of last resort with respect to questions of state common law and state statutory law.[12] Dicta in *Griffin v. Breckenridge*[13] appear to go even further: Congress may not have the power to use its commerce clause or thirteenth and fourteenth amendment authority wholly to federalize such traditional areas of common law as the law of torts or of contracts.[14] Similarly, it seems clear that Congress could not, under its power to regulate commerce or to protect individual rights, insist that a state alter its basic governmental structure—that it replace a bicameral with a unicameral legislature, for example, or shift from city managers to elected mayors. In sum, Congress cannot deny the states *some* symbolic corollaries of independent status, *some* revenue with which to operate, *some* sphere of

biguous or silent on a particular issue, this Court has often relied on notions of a constitutional plan—the implicit ordering of relationships within the federal system necessary to make the Constitution a workable governing charter[.]"); The Federalist No. 46 at 330 (J. Madison) (B. Wright ed. 1951).

8. 221 U.S. 559, 565 (1911).

9. 304 U.S. 405, 421, 419 (1938).

10. 87 U.S. (20 Wall.) 590, 633 (1874) (Supreme Court's appellate jurisdiction does not extend to a state court decision incorrectly adjudicating a federal question if the state court's judgment rests on an adequate and independent determination of state law). Contrast diversity cases, e.g., Loan Ass'n v. Topeka, 87 U.S. (20 Wall.) 655 (1875) (applying "general principles" of law to overturn a state taxing provision without invoking any federal constitutional violation). Justice Miller authored both Murdock and Loan.

11. See Hart, "The Relations Between State and Federal Law," 54 Col.L.Rev. 489, 503 (1954).

12. To the extent that it rests on constitutional premises, therefore, Murdock appears to be an even more fundamental

decision than Erie R. Co. v. Tompkins, 304 U.S. 64 (1938), with which it is often linked. Erie's holding that federal district courts cannot constitutionally apply a judge-made federal common law in diversity cases can be explained entirely in separation of power terms; "[t]hat Congress may have constitutional power to make federal law displacing state substantive law does *not* imply an equal range of power for federal judges." Mishkin, "Some Further Last Words on Erie—The Thread," 87 Harv.L.Rev. 1682, 1683 (1974). See also Friendly, "In Praise of Erie—And of the New Federal Common Law," 39 N.Y.U.L. Rev. 383, 397 n. 66 (1964). Erie thus says nothing about congressional power either to legislate a federal law of torts, for example, or to authorize a federal common law; Murdock, by contrast, suggests that there is a limit on the power of Congress in this respect. Cf. §§ 3–23, 3–24, supra.

13. 403 U.S. 88, 102, 104 (1971).

14. See § 5–13, supra. See also Perez v. United States, 402 U.S. 146, 158 (1971) (Stewart, J., dissenting) ("The definition and prosecution of local, intrastate crimes are reserved to the states under the Ninth and Tenth Amendments").

autonomous lawmaking competence, and *some* measure of choice in selecting a political structure.

Of course, no one expects Congress to obliterate the states, at least in one fell swoop. If there is any danger, it lies in the tyranny of small decisions—in the prospect that Congress will nibble away at state sovereignty, bit by bit, until someday essentially nothing is left but a gutted shell. The real question, therefore, is this: short of its prohibition of Armageddon, does the Constitution grant the states any judicially enforceable protection from Congress?

The full body of the Constitution—not only its tenth amendment and other explicit provisions, but also, in Justice Rehnquist's felicitous phrase, its "tacit postulates" [15]—suggests that the states should find their protection in doctrines which place a combination of internal and external limits on the power that the Constitution grants Congress. Such limits should indirectly guarantee that there *are* in fact "powers not delegated to the United States" which are as "reserved to the States" as to "the People," or ways in which powers that *are* "delegated to the United States" may not be exercised so as to destroy the essence of a state's semi-autonomous character as a polity in its own right. For some time, the Supreme Court enforced such doctrines with a narrow view of the national legislative power, finding that congressional action simultaneously exceeded constitutionally granted authority and infringed the reserved powers of the states.[16] Eventually, however, the analytical categories upon which the Court relied came to be seen as too problematic and manipulable, and the Court lost any legitimate basis for denying effect to reasonable legislative judgments.[17] Limitations on congressional power do, however, remain—including political checks, which the states exercise with considerable success on the

---

15. Nevada v. Hall, 440 U.S. 410, 433 (1979) (Rehnquist, J., joined by Burger, C.J., dissenting).

16. The Supreme Court stated the axiom of this jurisprudence in Ableman v. Booth, 62 U.S. (21 How.) 506, 516 (1859): "[T]he powers of the General Government, and of the State, although both exist and are exercised within the same territorial limits, are yet separate and distinct sovereignties, acting separately and independently of each other, within their respective spheres." Under this theory of dual sovereignty, the Supreme Court could take either of two approaches when asked to decide whether congressional legislation infringed state sovereignty. On the one hand, the Court could identify implied limits directly: it could look to the language of a particular constitutional grant of power and determine whether congressional action fell within the scope of that grant; if it did not, it necessarily infringed state sovereignty. See, e.g., Child Labor Tax Case, 259 U.S. 20 (1922) (taxing power exceeded); Hammer v. Dagenhart, 247 U.S. 251 (1918) (commerce power exceeded); United States v. Fox, 95 U.S. 670 (1878)

(bankruptcy power exceeded). On the other hand, the Court could determine whether congressional legislation infringed essential elements of state sovereignty; if it did, Congress again had exceeded its powers. See, e.g., Ashton v. Cameron County Water Improvement Dist., 298 U.S. 513 (1936) (statute providing for bankruptcy of state political subdivision infringes state control of fiscal affairs); Hopkins Federal Savings & Loan Assoc. v. Cleary, 296 U.S. 315 (1935) (statute providing for conversion of state-chartered savings and loan associations into federally-chartered entities infringes state power to regulate corporations of its own creation); Keller v. United States, 213 U.S. 138 (1909) (statute punishing keeping of houses of prostitution in which alien women reside infringes state police power); United States v. Dewitt, 76 U.S. (9 Wall.) 41 (1870) (statute regulating sale of illuminating oils infringes state police power). Both of these approaches were employed during the period from the 1870's to the mid-1930's—roughly the era of Model II. See Chapters 7 and 8, infra.

17. See § 5–4, supra, and §§ 8–5, 8–6 infra.

national level; the Bill of Rights, which limits all governmental action; and the "tacit postulates" of the Constitution, which protect the political structure of the states against federal incursion.[18]

18. The decline of dual sovereignty is summarized in Justice Stone's epigrammatic dismissal of the tenth amendment as a limit on congressional power: "The amendment states but a truism that all is retained which has not been surrendered." United States v. Darby, 312 U.S. 100, 124 (1941).

Given dual sovereignty, however, state immunity from federal taxation seemed to follow as a matter of course: "Such being the separate and independent condition of the States in our complex system, . . ., it would seem to follow, as a reasonable, if not a necessary consequence, that the means and instrumentalities employed for carrying on the operations of their governments, for preserving their existence, and fulfilling the high and responsible duties assigned to them in the Constitution, should be left free and unimpaired, should not be liable to be crippled, much less defeated by the taxing power of another government. . . ." Collector v. Day, 78 U.S. (11 Wall.) 113, 125 (1871). Collector v. Day held that Congress could not tax the salary of a state judge. Ultimately, the doctrine which Day announced extended to the point, for example, that a manufacturer of motorcycles could claim an immunity from a federal sales tax insofar as the manufacturer had sold its motorcycles to a city police department. See Indian Motorcycle Co. v. United States, 283 U.S. 570 (1931). The Supreme Court reversed direction, however, in Helvering v. Gerhardt, 304 U.S. 405 (1938). There, the Court held that the federal government could tax the salaries of employees of the Port of New York Authority; more importantly, Justice Stone's majority opinion repudiated the premise of dual sovereignty. The salient characteristic of a state immunity from federal taxation, Justice Stone observed, is not its preservation of state sovereignty, but is diminution of federal sovereignty. Id. at 416. State sovereignty is adequately protected by the political process regardless of the existence of any judge-created immunity: ". . . as was pointed out by Chief Justice Marshall in *McCulloch v. Maryland*, . . . the people of all the states have created the national government and are represented in Congress. Through that representation they exercise the national taxing power. The very fact that when they are exercising it they are taxing themselves, serves to guard against its abuse through the possibility of resort to the usual processes of political action which provides a readier and more adaptable means than any which courts can af-

ford, for securing accommodation of the competing demands for national revenue, on the one hand, and for reasonable scope for the independence of state action, on the other." Id. Subsequently, in Graves v. New York ex rel. O'Keefe, 306 U.S. 466 (1939), the Court recognized that Gerhardt had effectively overruled Collector v. Day. See id. at 486. Accordingly, in recent years federal taxation, since it has not involved the collection of a tax which falls only on the states, see New York v. United States, 326 U.S. 572 (1946), has not been limited by state tax immunities. See, e.g., Massachusetts v. United States, 435 U.S. 444 (1978) (upholding annual federal registration tax on all civil aircraft, as applied to state-owned police helicopter); Sims v. United States, 359 U.S. 108 (1959) (Congress can require state auditor to withhold from salaries of state employees money owed the federal government for income tax deficiencies); Wilmette Park Dist. v. Campbell, 338 U.S. 411 (1949) (state instrumentality operating a non-profit public beach not exempt from obligation to collect federal admission tax from its customers).

The history of congressional regulation of state government activities, at least until recently, reveals a somewhat similar pattern. The Supreme Court did not consider the question until after the heyday of dual sovereignty had already passed—most traditional tenth amendment cases concerned the question of whether Congress could displace the states in regulating private activity. But cf. Ashton v. Cameron County Water Improvement Dist., 298 U.S. 513 (1936), discussed in note 16, supra. As a result, until recently, the cases eschewed distinctions like that between the governmental (protected) and proprietary (not protected) powers of a state, distinctions associated with the dual sovereignty jurisprudence, see, e.g., South Carolina v. United States, 199 U.S. 437, 463 (1905), and have uniformly upheld federal regulation. See, e.g., Fry v. United States, 421 U.S. 542 (1975) (Congress may temporarily control wages of state employees); California v. Taylor, 353 U.S. 553 (1957) (Railway Labor Act grants National Railroad Adjustment Board jurisdiction over collective bargaining agreement negotiated between state-owned railroad and its employees); Case v. Bowles, 327 U.S. 92 (1946) (Emergency Price Control Act validly applies to state sale of timber); United States v. California, 297 U.S. 175 (1936) (Federal Safety Appliance Act validly applies to state-run railroad). In the area of conflict between federal and state regulation, the Court has

The states, then, are not without meaningful constitutional protection. As earlier discussion indicated, the political safeguards of federalism consist chiefly of the pluralist character of the political process, the interstitial nature of federal lawmaking, and the formal representation of the states in Congress.[19] Supreme Court decisions suggest that the Court has used, or can use, a number of devices to reinforce these political safeguards.

The first of these, discussed earlier,[20] is the *clear statement rule.* By refusing to construe ambiguous legislation expansively, the Court can act to prevent Congress from avoiding hard questions of federal-state relations, and can thus increase the likelihood that Congress will give full attention to the interests of the states and of those groups whose interests parallel the states'. In form, the clear statement rule is merely a rule of statutory construction. The remaining devices, less well-grounded in the case law, are necessarily constitutional in nature.

The protection of federalism most clearly visible in the Supreme Court's post-1937 decisions is probably the *anti-discrimination rule.* In *New York v. United States,*[21] a majority of the Supreme Court, although not joining in a single opinion, indicated that Congress could not levy a tax which fell only upon the states.[22] Such discriminatory taxation (although the Justices did not develop this rationale) would deprive the states of their natural allies in the legislative process, and thus arguably weaken the political check upon Congress to the point that judicial intervention could be justified.[23] But this anti-discrimination rule, even if it appears to be relatively non-controversial, affords the states only limited protection. Plainly, the Supreme Court could apply it in cases concerning congressional taxes or regulations of commerce;

clearly rejected dual sovereignty: "This is not a controversy between equals." *Sanitary District v. United States,* 266 U.S. 405, 425 (1925). But see § 5–22, infra.

19. See § 5–7, supra.

20. See § 5–8, supra.

21. 326 U.S. 572 (1946).

22. See id. at 579–80 (1946) (Frankfurter, J., plurality opinion); id. at 586 (Stone, C.J., concurring); id. at 591 (Douglas, J., dissenting). The case itself concerned a nondiscriminatory tax on bottled mineral waters, which the Court upheld.

Justice Frankfurter did not fully elaborate his nondiscrimination approach to defining the scope of the state tax immunity, holding only that there is "no restriction upon Congress to include the States in levying a tax exacted equally from private persons upon the same subject matter." Frankfurter's point, however, seems to be that the nondiscrimination rule adequately protects state interests because the essential characteristics of state governments "inherently constitute a class by themselves. Only a State can own a Statehouse; only a State can get income by taxing. These could not be included for

purposes of federal taxation in any abstract category of taxpayers without taxing the State as a State." Note that Justice Rutledge, who joined Justice Frankfurter's opinion, understood Frankfurter's point differently: "state functions may not be singled out for taxation when others performing them are not taxed or for special burdens when they are." Id. at 584–85 (Rutledge, J., concurring). Chief Justice Stone did not dispute the validity of Justice Frankfurter's nondiscrimination principle, see id. at 586; he disputed only its scope. But Stone did reject Frankfurter's basic cosmology, concluding that state functions Frankfurter thought "unique" could in fact be reached by nondiscriminatory taxes: "a general non-discriminatory real estate tax . . ., or income tax laid upon citizens and States alike could be . . . applied [although not constitutionally in Stone's view] to the State's capitol, its State-house, its public school houses, public parks, or its revenues from taxes or school lands. . . ." Id. at 587–88.

23. Compare *Railway Express Agency v. New York,* 336 U.S. 106, 112–13 (1949) (Jackson, J., concurring).

equally plainly, however, the Court could not justify applying the rule in cases involving conditioned grants of money which Congress has extended to the states in the exercise of its spending power, or involving regulations enacted under the fourteenth or fifteenth amendments: the relevant grants of power in these last three contexts, by their terms or by long-accepted practice, plainly authorize Congress to deal separately with the states, or to protect individuals from only "state action."

The anti-discrimination rule should be distinguished from the *equality rule* repudiated by the Supreme Court in *South Carolina v. Katzenbach*.[24] This latter restriction would prevent Congress from enacting otherwise proper legislation which singles out only *some*, and not *all* states for regulation. It is this rule which was the topic of discussion in *Coyle v. Smith*: there, the Supreme Court held that Congress cannot impose conditions upon a state's admission to the union which would place the state "upon a plane of inequality with its sister States in the Union. . . ."[25] An equality rule might be justified as a response to a breakdown in the political processes ordinarily protecting the states: by singling out one or a few states, Congress again reduces the likelihood that any coalition will arise which is in a position meaningfully to defend state interests. The equality rule, of course, could limit congressional exercises of the power to condition financial grants and to enforce constitutional rights to protection from state action. In *South Carolina v. Katzenbach*, however, the Supreme Court confined *Coyle v. Smith* to its facts, declaring that the equality rule limits Congress only with respect to the admission of states.[26] Arguably, that declaration was dictum: the Voting Rights Act of 1965 applied to *all* states; any apparent inequality of treatment derived from the fact that only a few states were in violation of the Act. If the equality rule were automatically satisfied whenever Congress enacted a formally general law, however, the rule would grant the states no real protection. Even if it should survive its express repudiation in *South Carolina v. Katzenbach*, therefore, the equality rule is not likely to yield a significant restraint on congressional power.

A final approach would look for *structural evidence* of the operation of political safeguards in legislation significantly burdening state government activities. Such legislation would be valid only if it (1) delegated responsibility for framing burdensome rules to administrative processes in which the states would be adequately represented, or at least (2) survived a relatively exacting "less drastic means" scrutiny; either (1) or (2) would furnish evidence that the legislation could have been the product of a congressional process in which state interests were fully heard and reasonably weighed.[27] This test finds support by analogy in decisions of the Supreme Court protecting individual rights in a number of areas.[28] It has the defect, however, of assuming the

---

24. 383 U.S. 301 (1966), discussed in § 5–14, supra.

25. 221 U.S. 559, 565 (1911).

26. See 383 U.S. at 329. See also United States v. Ptasynski, 462 U.S. 74 (1983), discussed in § 5–9, supra.

27. See Note, "Municipal Bankruptcy, the Tenth Amendment and the New Federalism," 89 Harv.L.Rev. 1871, 1884–91 (1976).

28. See, e.g., § 16–32, infra.

answer to the most difficult question: the issue is not so much *how* the Supreme Court should scrutinize legislation, but *when*; "significant burden" is less a criterion than a conclusion.

§ 5–21. State Sovereignty and the Jurisprudence of Rights: Using Individual Rights to Define State Roles

To at least a limited degree, we have seen how the Supreme Court can reinforce the political and structural safeguards of state sovereignty.[1] Can the Court, however, move beyond this limited role and substitute itself for Congress as chief protector of state sovereignty in much the same way that the Court has substituted itself for Congress as chief protector of individual rights? An affirmative answer to this question presumes that the Supreme Court can give content to the concept of state sovereignty beyond the "core" notions explored in § 5–20. One way for the Court to proceed might be to treat states' rights largely as mirror images of individual rights; in so doing, the Court would be able to set aside the clumsy and sometimes misleading vocabulary of state sovereignty as such, and restate the problem in terms more familiar to contemporary constitutional jurisprudence. It is worth noting in this regard that a focus on individual rights is hardly inconsistent with a concern for federalism. Since "[t]he federal and State governments are in fact but different agents and trustees of the people, constituted with different power, and designed for different purposes," "most of a state's rights" must ultimately be derived from the rights of its citizens.[2] And that the language of "states' rights" should be used to protect individual rights against federal encroachment is certainly understandable when the federal government, in accord with national tradition, has left to the states the responsibility of vindicating the rights in question.

Professor Richard Stewart has suggested how claims of state sovereignty might be grounded in individual rights. He identifies four features of a decentralized federal structure which can be stated as values an individual would wish to further: the *greater accuracy* with which a local decisionmaker can operate as a utilitarian calculator of costs and benefits; the *greater protection of liberty* which the state's decentralized decisionmaking affords by making it harder for any one group to seize total national power; the *greater degree of community* fostered by the opportunity for political participation that decentralization makes possible; and the *greater diversity* which decentralization fosters.[3]

Identification of such values as liberty or community, however, is only a first step. Rights—whether of individuals, or communities, or

---

§ 5–21

1. See §§ 5–8, 5–20, supra.

2. The Federalist No. 46, at 330 (J. Madison) (B. Wright ed. 1951). But, as Coyle v. Smith, 221 U.S. 559 (1911), demonstrates, some of a state's rights are derived simply from its character as a state within the federal system. See § 5–20, supra.

3. See Stewart, "Pyramids of Sacrifice? Problems of Federalism in Mandating State Implementation of National Environmental Policy," 86 Yale L.J. 1196, 1210–11 (1977).

states—*reflect* values; they are not the values themselves. To be sure, rights structure the process and substance of government so that government operates *as though* it shared certain values. But to argue for recognizing rights of a given sort, it is necessary to identify both how government would be likely to act unencumbered by such rights and how government action is likely to be affected by right-encumbering. Only when the alternative results are assessed can one identify which of an array of values are actually implicated, and then decide whether the values served warrant the encumbrance suffered. The next section will undertake to analyze the Supreme Court's major federalism decision of the post-1937 era in these terms.

§ 5–22. From National League of Cities to Garcia: The Unsteady Course of the New States' Rights

Before the mid-1970s, "states' rights" were more rhetoric than reality. In the years after 1937, the Supreme Court essentially offered the Congress *carte blanche* to regulate the economic and social life of the nation, its actions subject only to the requirements of the Bill of Rights.[1] Individual rights alone operated as trump cards over those exercises of congressional power affirmatively authorized by the Constitution. States' rights, in contrast, were not an override; they were a residue.

But in *National League of Cities v. Usery*,[2] the Supreme Court for the first time in our history created an outright override—a veto on otherwise authorized congressional legislation.[3] In *National League of Cities*, the Court invalidated the 1974 amendments to the Fair Labor Standards Act (FLSA) which had extended the federal minimum wage and maximum hour provisions to virtually every state and municipal employee.[4] In reaching its conclusion, the Court sharply distinguished federal regulation of private persons and businesses "necessarily subject to the dual sovereignty of the government of the Nation and of the State in which they reside"[5] from similar regulation "directed not to private citizens, but to the States as States."[6] Although the Court conceded that the regulations at issue were "undoubtedly within the scope of the Commerce Clause,"[7] it found that wage and hour determinations with respect to "functions . . . which [state and local] governments are created to provide [involving] services . . . which the States have traditionally afforded their citizens,"[8] were matters "essential to

---

§ 5–22

1. See §§ 5–4 to 5–7, supra.

2. 426 U.S. 833 (1976).

3. The most recent rejections of Acts of Congress as intrusions on state sovereignty had been Carter v. Carter Coal Co., 298 U.S. 238 (1936). See also Ashton v. Cameron County Water Imp. Dist., 298 U.S. 513 (1936) (bankruptcy power); Oregon v. Mitchell, 400 U.S. 112 (1970) (election regulation). But in neither case had the Court

deemed the challenged legislation to fall within Congress' affirmatively delegated powers.

4. Pub.L. No. 93–259, § 6(a)(1), (5), (6), 88 Stat. 58 (1974) (codified at 29 U.S.C. § 203(d), (s), (x)).

5. 426 U.S. at 845.

6. Id.

7. Id. at 841.

8. Id. at 851.

[the] separate and independent existence"[9] of the states and hence beyond the reach of congressional power under the commerce clause.[10]

Although the decision in *National League of Cities* startled some, its rhetoric of state sovereignty and local autonomy might well seem a natural extension of the concern for the rights of states in the federal system that the Court had recently emphasized. The Court's opinions had sounded such a note for several years,[11] and past the mid-1970's the signals had become both louder and more frequent.[12] The national mood, moreover, had increasingly become one of disenchantment with centralized power and a desire for local autonomy.[13] Perhaps the surprise came not so much from the *fact* that the Court chose to cut

9. Id. at 845 (quoting Lane County v. Oregon, 74 U.S. (7 Wall.) 71, 76 (1869).

10. The Court went on expressly to overrule that aspect of Maryland v. Wirtz, 392 U.S. 183 (1968), which had upheld the extension of the Fair Labor Standards Act to employees of state hospitals, institutions, and schools. 426 U.S. at 840. In reaching its conclusions in National League of Cities, the Court was unclear as to the source of the state sovereignty limitation on congressional power under the commerce clause. The Court cited Fry v. United States, 421 U.S. 542, 547 n. 7 (1975), to the effect that "The Tenth Amendment . . . expressly declares the constitutional policy that Congress may not exercise power in a fashion that impairs the States' integrity or their ability to function effectively in a federal system." 426 U.S. at 842–43. But the language of the tenth amendment—providing that "[t]he powers not delegated to the United States by the Constitution, nor prohibited by it to the States, are reserved to the States respectively, or to the people"—appears to reserve precisely the same sphere of autonomy "to the States respectively" and "to the people," and appears to reserve to *neither* of these the "powers . . . delegated to the United States." As a result, it is at best difficult to see in the amendment a basis for distinguishing federal commerce regulation of private employers from similar regulation of public employers, see 428 U.S. at 861–63 (Brennan, J., dissenting), and the majority opinion—which did not in fact even quote the language of the tenth amendment—may better be seen as resting on the "essential role of the States in our federal system of government," id., at 844.

11. See, e.g., Maryland v. Wirtz, 392 U.S. 183, 201 (1968) (Douglas, J., joined by Stewart, J., dissenting); Fry v. United States, 421 U.S. 542, 547 n. 7 (1975); O'Shea v. Littleton, 414 U.S. 488 (1974) (no equitable relief against state criminal magistrate and judge for alleged practice of discriminatory bond setting and sentencing); Edelman v. Jordan, 415 U.S. 651 (1974) (eleventh amendment bars liability

for damages payable out of state treasury); Younger v. Harris, 401 U.S. 37 (1971) (absent bad faith or extraordinary circumstances, federal court is precluded by considerations of equity, comity and federalism from enjoining pending state criminal prosecution); see generally § 3–30, supra.

12. See, e.g., Rizzo v. Goode, 423 U.S. 362 (1976) (federal court may not order structural changes in police department as remedy for police invasion of constitutional rights absent showing of high-level official encouragement of police misconduct); Paul v. Davis, 424 U.S. 693 (1976) (restricting range of liberty and property interests protected by fourteenth amendment).

13. It would be wrong, however, to treat the Court's references in National League of Cities to the value of local autonomy as a renewal of the theme seemingly implicit in decisions such as Village of Belle Terre v. Boraas, 416 U.S. 1 (1974), which allowed individual rights to be subordinated to community rights of self-definition analogous to individual first amendment rights. See §§ 15–17 to 15–20, infra. For in League of Cities the Court did not distinguish between the intrusion of the challenged amendments on *state* autonomy and their intrusion on *local* decisionmaking; on the contrary, it found that the provision of "integral governmental services" by local government units was due the *same* protection from federal commerce power as was the provision of such services by the states, since such local units "derive their authority and power from their respective states," and are therefore "subordinate arms of a state government," 426 U.S. at 855 n. 20. Contrast Mt. Healthy City School Dist. v. Doyle, 429 U.S. 274 (1977); Lincoln County v. Luning, 133 U.S. 529 (1890) (eleventh amendment immunity does not extend to counties). Whatever values of expression or of privacy may be possessed by decisionmaking at the level of communities like Belle Terre, it cannot plausibly be argued that decisionmaking at the state level possesses such values.

back on congressional authority, but from the *manner* in which it did so. The last great battleground over congressional power had been the commerce clause, and the legislature's victory had been total. The "stream" of commerce had been broadened to the point where Congress could regulate almost any business transaction in the nation, no matter how inconsequential or isolated; it seemed natural, then, that the Court might endeavor to read some limits into the commerce clause. But rather than narrowing the stream of commerce, the Court instead chose to create islands *in* that stream—islands where the states alone could regulate, islands off-limits to the once seemingly omnipresent federal government.

State sovereignty as a restraint on federal power is hardly the creation of the Burger Court. The Constitution and the federal system, as we saw in § 5–20, are premised on the existence of the states as independent entities. While Congress is generally the most appropriate body to determine the relative allocation of powers between the national and state governments,[14] recognition in the states of a constitutional right to survive necessarily implies certain limits on the powers of Congress. But the limits recognized in decisions like *Coyle v. Smith*[15] encompass little beyond the continued formal existence of separate and independent states.[16] If states are to have any real meaning, Congress must also be prevented from acting in ways that would leave a state formally intact but functionally a gutted shell.

The concerns that underlay *National League of Cities*, then, were real ones. The political safeguards of federalism cannot always be counted on to prevent abuses of federal legislative power. The fact that Congress is made up of (and represents) individuals does not guarantee that that body will always act in accordance with individual rights; so too the fact the Congress is made up of representatives of states does not assure that the legislature will always give adequate respect to the rights of states.[17] But to say that *National League of Cities* struck responsive chords in history and doctrine is not to say that the reasoning underlying the decision is easily understood or the result readily accepted. Even granting that the political safeguards of federalism cannot always be counted on to protect the states, fear that Congress might eviscerate a state's government cannot support the holding in *National League of Cities*; for in that case no claim could plausibly have been made that the imposition of wage and hour regulations on the states would threaten their meaningful existence.[18] Indeed, Justice

---

14. See generally Wechsler, "The Political Safeguards of Federalism: The Role of the States in the Composition and Selection of the National Government," 54 Colum.L.Rev. 543, 558–60 (1954). The fullest recent development of this theme is J. Choper, Judicial Review and the National Political Process (1980) (arguing that neither federalism nor separation-of-powers need be judicially enforced where individual rights as such are not jeopardized).

15. 221 U.S. 559 (1911) (State admission to union cannot be conditioned on federal control over location of state capitol).

16. See § 5–20, supra.

17. See Garcia v. San Antonio Metropolitan Transit Authority, 469 U.S. 528, 565 n. 8 (1985) (Powell, J. dissenting).

18. Justice Stevens in his dissent in National League of Cities, while "agree[ing] that it is unwise for the Federal Government to exercise its power in the ways described in the Court's opinion," found

Rehnquist, while pointing to cutbacks in government services that could result from application of the FLSA, was careful to avoid resting his opinion for the Court on any factual conclusions about the actual impact of the regulations.[19]

Yet it is quite clear, as the Court recognized, that *some* constitutional right, or at least a constitutionally protected interest of rather special force, must have been at stake to justify a decision invalidating an otherwise legitimate exercise of congressional power. Accordingly, *National League of Cities* may be taken as an attempt to establish new "rights" of states as against the national government—rights beyond those derived simply from the constitutional requirement of a meaningful existence for states as separate entities. But such an interpretation, while certainly consistent with the broad rhetoric of the opinion, cannot be squared with the distinctions drawn by the Court in the process of reaching its conclusion.

The problems with the decision may be illustrated by describing the fate of what came to be called the *National League of Cities* test: a three-part examination of a federal regulation which the Court said would determine whether state sovereignty had been infringed. In order to succeed, a claim that commerce power legislation was invalid under *League of Cities* had to establish that the challenged law regulated the "States as States," addressed matters that are "indisputably 'attribute[s] of state sovereignty,' " and directly impaired the ability of states "to structure integral operations in areas of traditional governmental functions." [20] The test also had a caveat, sometimes referred to as a fourth part: "Demonstrating that these three requirements are met does not . . . guarantee that a Tenth Amendment challenge to congressional commerce power action will succeed. There are situations in which the nature of the federal interest advanced may be such that it justifies state submission." [21] As the first cases interpreting *National League of Cities* reached the Supreme Court, the difficulties with the "test"—both in theory and [in] practice—became all too apparent. In *Hodel v. Virginia Surface Mining & Reclamation Assn.*,[22] the Supreme Court voted unanimously [23] to uphold against a tenth amendment challenge the Surface Mining Control and Reclamation Act of 1977.[24] The Act offered the states the option of either formulating their own programs in conformity with minimum federal standards or defaulting to a program of regulation to be financed and administered

himself "unable to identify a limitation on . . . federal power that would not also invalidate federal regulation of state activities that I consider unquestionably permissible." 426 U.S. at 881.

19. See id. at 851.

20. Hodel v. Virginia Surface Mining & Reclamation Assn., Inc., 452 U.S. 264, 287–88 (1981) (citations omitted).

21. Id. at 288 n. 29.

22. 452 U.S. 264 (1981).

23. The Chief Justice filed a concurring statement. Justice Powell filed a concur-

ring opinion, and Justice Rehnquist, the author of National League of Cities, filed an opinion concurring in the judgment.

24. Although Justice Marshall spoke of the three-part test as a derivation of the tenth amendment, it should be recalled that the majority in National League of Cities did not rely upon that amendment in formulating any of its broad states' rights language. See 426 U.S. at 845, 846, 852, 854.

by the Department of the Interior. Justice Marshall's straightforward opinion reached only the first part of the three-part test. The challenged provisions of the Surface Mining Act governed only the activities of coal mine operators who are private individuals and businesses,[25] and thereby failed to satisfy the first prong of the test. Since the states were still free to promulgate whatever regulations they wished so long as they were not inconsistent with minimum federal guidelines, *Hodel* was nothing more than a preemption case. The Court declared that the tenth amendment in no way "limits congressional power to preempt or displace state regulation of private activities affecting interstate commerce."[26] The only limitation is that the means selected be "reasonably related" to the regulatory purpose.[27]

When the Court encountered the next case in the wake of *National League of Cities*, it was forced to examine perhaps the most perplexing issue arising out of its three-part test: the question of *which* state and local government functions are so "traditional" that Congress may not under the commerce clause impinge on their performance by the states.[28] In *United Transportation Union v. Long Island R.R. Co.*,[29] the State of New York sought to avoid application of the Railway Labor Act to a dispute between the state-owned Long Island Railroad and its unions. The case thus presented a classic *National League of Cities* question: given that the commerce clause undeniably empowers Congress to regulate the labor relations of the nation's railroad companies, does the application of such legislation to an interstate railway owned and operated by a state violate state sovereignty? Chief Justice Burger's opinion for the unanimous Court focused exclusively on the third part of the test, the requirement that the "States' compliance with federal law would directly impair their ability 'to structure integral operations in areas of traditional governmental functions' " if the law is not struck down.[30] The long history of federal regulation of railroads— and an explicit exemption in *National League of Cities* of several cases involving state-run railways [31]—made the Court's task a simple one in upholding the federal regulation in *Long Island R.R. Co.* The Chief Justice went on, however, to articulate a view of the third part of the test that further mystified the scope of exclusive state control. The Court claimed that the "traditional function" test was not meant to give history a hammerlock on protected state activity but merely stated a requirement that a reviewing court inquire into whether federal regulation "would hamper the state government's ability to fulfill its role in the Union and endanger its separate and independent existence."[32] On the one hand, the Chief Justice's language seemed to allow commerce clause regulation of all but the most fundamental state functions. On the other, any special status that attached to a function

25. 452 U.S. at 288.

26. Id. at 289–90.

27. Id. 291.

28. Justice Rehnquist for the majority in National League of Cities gave as examples "fire prevention, police protection, sanitation, public health, and parks and recreation." 426 U.S. at 851. But he not- ed that his list was not meant to be exhaustive. Id. at n. 16.

29. 455 U.S. 678 (1982).

30. 455 U.S. at 684, quoting National League of Cities, supra, at 426 U.S. at 852.

31. See 426 U.S. at 854–55 & n. 18

32. 455 U.S. at 687.

by virtue of a state's decision to perform it would seem to attach as clearly, if not more so, in the case of discretionary, proprietary functions as in the case of essential, classic public services. Certainly any special respect that may be due to a state's decision to take up a novel task as its contribution to the experimental spirit of federalism [33] is enhanced, not diminished, by the fact that the task is usually left to private entrepreneurs.

The Court's unhappiness with the three-part *National League of Cities* test—and, indeed, with the decision itself—was evident in the next major states' rights case. *Federal Energy Regulatory Commission v. Mississippi* [34] involved a challenge by the State of Mississippi to certain provisions of the Public Utility Regulatory Policies Act of 1978 (PURPA). [35] The Court divided sharply over whether the statute could require the state public utility commissions, as a condition of their further regulatory activity in this area, to "consider" a set of FERC proposals. The statute described in great detail exactly how the state authorities were to "consider" those proposals, but did not compel the state to adopt them. Justice Blackmun—whose tentative concurrence had created the majority in *National League of Cities* [36] and who played Hamlet in the drama of that case's undoing—joined the four dissenters in that case in upholding the PURPA requirements. In *FERC*, the Court's discomfort with *National League of Cities* was palpable. Gone was the rigorous adherence to the three-part test applied faithfully in *Hodel* and *Long Island R.R. Co.*; the "test" merited only a bare mention in a footnote in *FERC*. [37] Instead, Justice Blackmun's opinion noted that "the ability of a state . . . administrative body—which makes decisions and sets policy for the state as a whole—to consider and promulgate regulations of its choosing must be central to a State's

33. See New State Ice Co. v. Liebmann, 285 U.S. 262, 311 (1932) (Brandeis, J., dissenting): "To stay experimentation in things social and economic is a grave responsibility. Denial of the right to experiment may be fraught with serious consequences to the Nation. It is one of the happy incidents of the federal system that a single courageous State may, if its citizens choose serve as a laboratory; and try novel social and economic experiments without risk to the rest of the country." See also F. Frankfurter, The Public and its Government 49–51 (1930).

34. 456 U.S. 742 (1982).

35. All nine Justices agreed that the part of PURPA requiring the FERC to prepare and promulgate, in consultation with state public utility commissions, a series of rules exempting certain electrical generating facilities from state laws was a straightforward example of preemption and therefore no problem. 456 U.S. at 758 (majority opinion); id. at 775 n. 1 (O'Connor, J., dissenting). Similarly, there was agreement that requiring the state public utility commissions to "implement" these federal regulations was constitution-

al. Id. at 759–61 (majority opinion); id. at 775 n. 1 (O'Connor, J., dissenting).

36. See 426 U.S. at 856.

37. See 456 U.S. at 763 n. 28. Justice O'Connor's dissent, in contrast, applied the test faithfully and concluded that the regulation failed under each count. First, the law directed its commands solely to the states, telling their utility commissions which proposed standards to consider and in what manner. 456 U.S. at 776–77. Second, the federal regulations "address attribute[s] of state sovereignty" by commandeering the agenda of a state agency and telling it how to structure its policy-making process. Id. at 780–81. Finally, the dissent argued that by taxing the limited resource of state agencies purportedly concerned with utility regulation, a traditional state function, PURPA directly impaired the ability of the states to "structure integral operations in areas of traditional governmental functions." Id. at 781–82. The majority agreed by implication with the first two parts of Justice O'Connor's analysis but disagreed on the third. Id. at 763 n. 28.

role in the federal system," [38] but still upheld the federal law.   The Court in *FERC* presumably felt justified in sweeping aside its concern for the states for the simple reason that PURPA required states to consider federal proposals, not to compel their adoption.   That approach, however, was plainly inconsistent with *Hodel*, where the Court unanimously upheld the strip-mining regulations because the states were "not compelled to enforce the steep-slope standards, or to expend any state funds, or *to participate in the federal regulatory program in any manner whatsoever.*" [39]   In short, *FERC* seemed to threaten the very holding of *National League of Cities*: that even if an activity was inside the stream of commerce—and thus subject to preemption—the Constitution still forbade congressional regulation which impinged on state sovereignty.

The rejection of *National League of Cities* was even more obvious in *Equal Employment Opportunity Commission v. Wyoming.*[40]   In 1974 Congress extended the Age Discrimination in Employment Act (ADEA) to state and local governments.   The issue was nearly identical to that in *National League of Cities*: did the postulates of federalism bar this congressional interference with the state's right to regulate its relations with its employees?   Justice Brennan's opinion, joined by the three other dissenters in *National League of Cities* and, once again, by Justice Blackmun, applied the resurrected three-part test, but held that the ADEA was constitutional.

The Court agreed that the ADEA did regulate the "States as States," and did not reach the question whether the ADEA addressed indisputable attributes of state sovereignty.[41]   The Court held, however, that the ADEA did not "directly impair the State's ability to structure integral operations in areas of traditional governmental functions." [42]   The critical point, according to the majority, was that Wyoming—like Mississippi in *FERC*—was free to pursue its goals so long as it observed a few federal procedural requirements along the way.   The state could fulfill the goal of assuring the physical fitness of its employees by conducting individualized fitness examinations or by demonstrating that the ages set out in its mandatory retirement policy constituted bona fide occupational qualifications for particular positions.[43]   The Court did not even make an effort to explain why allowing a state to

---

38.   456 U.S. at 761.

39.   452 U.S. at 288 (emphasis added). The majority in *FERC* seemed to assume that, so long as the *end* defined by complete federal preemption is constitutionally permissible, it matters not which *means* Congress uses to approach the limits of federal power.   Yet surely Justice O'Connor was correct that "[t]he Constitution permits Congress to govern only through certain channels.   If the Tenth Amendment principles articulated in *National League of Cities* . . . and *Hodel* . . . foreclose PURPA's approach, it is no answer to argue that Congress could have reached the same destination by another route."   456 U.S. at 786.   (O'Connor, J.,

dissenting).   In his dissent Justice Powell agreed, arguing that since "the Commerce Clause and the Tenth Amendment embody distinct limitations on federal power," the fact "[t]hat Congress has satisfied one demonstrates nothing as to whether Congress has satisfied the other."   Id. at 773.   See also id. at 774–75 (quoting first edition of this treatise on threat of federal actions leaving states "formally intact but functionally . . . gutted shell[s]").

40.   460 U.S. 226 (1983).

41.   See id. at 237–38 & n. 11.

42.   Id. at 239 (citations omitted).

43.   Id. at 239–40.

retire its employees whenever it wishes only so long as it meets a "reasonable federal standard" [44] is less intrusive than allowing a state to pay its employees whatever it wishes only so long as it meets a reasonable federal minimum wage. The latter, of course, is what was found impermissible in *National League of Cities*.

Indeed, the majority's reasoning in *FERC* and *Wyoming* could easily have been transposed onto the Fair Labor Standards Act context. Because the areas subject to FLSA were preemptible, Congress had the authority to dictate wages and work conditions to the states as a condition of their continued employment of personnel to provide traditional services with respect to the areas at issue: in effect, the states could continue to patrol the public highways and clean up the public hospitals (rather than have these tasks federally preempted) only on the condition that they pay public employees in these areas according to a federal schedule. Yet that is exactly what *National League of Cities* held Congress could *not* require. The tension, in short, between *National League of Cities* and its progeny had simply become untenable.

The *coup de grace* was administered in *Garcia v. San Antonio Metropolitan Transit Authority*,[45] when Justice Blackmun—his conversion complete—joined the original *National League of Cities* dissenters in an emphatic reversal of that nine-year-old case. The Court recognized that "municipal ownership and operation of a mass-transit system is a traditional governmental function," but went on to state, "[o]ur examination of this 'function' standard applied in [this] and other cases over the last eight years now persuades us that the attempt to draw the boundaries of state regulatory immunity in terms of 'traditional governmental function' is not only unworkable but is inconsistent with established principles of federalism and, indeed, with those very federalism principles on which *National League of Cities* purported to rest. That case, accordingly, is overruled." [46] After noting that the Court "has made little headway in defining the scope" of traditional government functions,[47] Justice Blackmun noted a "more fundamental problem[,] that neither the governmental/proprietary distinction nor any other that purports to separate out important governmental functions can be faithful to the role of federalism in a democratic society. The essence of our federal system is that within the realm of authority left open to them under the Constitution, the States must be equally free to engage in any activity that their citizens choose for the common weal, no matter how unorthodox or unnecessary anyone else—including the judiciary—deems state involvement to be." [48] The Court thus "reject[ed], as unsound in principle and unworkable in practice, a rule of state immunity from federal regulation that turns on a judicial appraisal of whether a particular governmental function is 'integral' or 'traditional.' " [49]

44. Id. at 240.

45. 469 U.S. 528 (1985).

46. Id. at 531.

47. Id. at 539.

48. Id. at 545–46.

49. Id. at 546–47.

The Court then went on strongly to reaffirm a broad view of federal power. Noting that the "States do retain a significant measure of sovereign authority," Justice Blackmun stated that "[t]hey do so, however, only to the extent that the Constitution has not divested them of their original powers and transferred those powers to the Federal Government." [50] The Court held that it must tread lightly when seeking to limit Congress' well-established and wide-ranging powers under the commerce clause. "In short," Justice Blackmun wrote, "we have no license to employ freestanding conceptions of state sovereignty when measuring congressional authority under the Commerce Clause." [51] The "interests of the States," the Court went on, were protected by the "structure" of the government as a whole. [52] The electoral college system for presidential elections and the election of senators by state legislators (prior to the seventeenth amendment) were cited by the majority for the proposition that "State sovereign interests, then, are more properly protected by procedural safeguards inherent in the structure of the federal system than by judicially created limitations on federal power." [53] From such a conclusion, it was a short step to hold that "we perceive nothing in the overtime and minimum wage requirements of the FLSA, as applied to SAMTA, that is destructive of state sovereignty or violative of any constitutional provision." [54]

50. Id. at 549. The majority offered only cryptic hints about the future of tenth amendment jurisprudence: "Of course, we continue to recognize that the States occupy a special and specific position in our constitutional system and that the scope of Congress' authority under the Commerce Clause must reflect that position. . . . These cases do not require us to identify or define what affirmative limits the constitutional structure might impose on federal action affecting the States under the Commerce Clause." Id. at 556. See § 5–23, infra.

51. Id. Professor Van Alstyne was especially troubled by this portion of the opinion. He saw in the Court's words the implication that "federalism questions in general (and not merely in *Garcia*-type cases) are not for the court, but fundamentally for *Congress* to determine." See Van Alstyne, "The Second Death of Federalism," 83 Mich.L.Rev. 1709, 1721 (1985). Such a result, in his view, "is fundamentally pernicious to the integrity and morale of American constitutional law [because it may lead to] the piecemeal repeal of judicial review." Id. at 1722, 1724.

52. 469 U.S. at 551.

53. Id. For a powerful defense of the Court's trust in the political system to protect the states, see Field, "Garcia v. San Antonio Metropolitan Transit Authority: The Demise of a Misguided Doctrine," 99 Harv.L.Rev. 84 (1985).

54. Id. at 554. Justice Powell's dissenting opinion, which was joined by Chief Justice Burger and Justices Rehnquist and O'Connor, was devoted primarily to a defense of the concept of "traditional governmental functions," see 469 U.S. at 561–64, and a refutation of the majority's sanguine views about the ability of the states to protect themselves against the federal government. Id. at 564–79. Justice O'Connor's dissent, joined by Justices Powell and Rehnquist, focused on the need, unmet in her opinion by the Court's ruling, "to enforce affirmative limits on federal regulation of the States to complement the judicially crafted expansion of the interstate commerce power." Id. at 587.

The most extraordinary dissent was by Justice Rehnquist. His four-sentence opinion indicated general agreement with the dissenting views of Justices Powell and O'Connor, then concluded: "But under any one of these approaches the judgment in this case should be affirmed, and I do not think it incumbent on those of us in dissent to spell out further the fine points of a principle that will, I am confident, in time again command the support of a majority of this Court." Id. at 580. See also id. at 1038 (O'Connor, J., dissenting) ("I share Justice Rehnquist's belief that this Court will in time again assume its constitutional responsibility").

Put in its most favorable light, *National League of Cities* can be seen as an attempt to identify those functions most essential to the continued significance of states as separate governmental entities and then to provide enhanced protection in those areas. The assumption behind such an attempt, presumably, was that only if these essential functions were sealed off from federal interference could the states preserve the sovereignty which the tenth amendment, and the Constitution's tacit postulates, guarantee them. But if this was the point of the decision, it is difficult to justify the Court's willingness to protect the state in its role as an employer and provider of services and not in its role as a lawmaker and regulator of private conduct.[55] To be sure, the provision of basic services is an important function of states and municipalities. But surely no less essential is the function of defining the scope of permissible conduct within a state's or a municipality's borders through regulations aimed at private parties.[56] As the decisions following *National League of Cities* made clear, the Court simply could neither justify this distinction by reference to the Constitution nor elaborate it by reference to any workable principles of federalism. The notion that the Supreme Court has the obligation to protect against federal incursions on states' rights seems unassailable; but the rickety structure which the Court put in place to protect those rights turned out to do no such thing.

Indeed, it may well be suggested that *National League of Cities* actually *detracted* from the states' ability to protect their sovereignty from federal interference. For example, in *Community Communications Co. v. Boulder*,[57] the Court faced the question of whether the state action exemption from Sherman Act liability announced in *Parker v. Brown*[58] applies to municipalities which exercise self-government under a home-rule provision of a state constitution. The Colorado Constitution "vests" in "the people" of every town with a population of two thousand or more the "full right of self-government in both local and municipal matters."[59] With respect to those matters, the City Charter

---

55. While Younger v. Harris and its progeny, see § 3–30, supra, might be said to establish such protection, these cases should be seen not as restrictions on the power of Congress but rather as restraints on the federal judiciary where state judicial proceedings are pending.

56. One view of National League of Cities propounded shortly after the decision held that the case might be read to suggest the existence of protected expectations—of rights—to basic government services. The argument, still not completely foreclosed by the demise of National League of Cities itself, was that policy-based legislation by Congress that endangers the provision of certain vital services, unlike similar legislation directed only at private parties or at government services usually provided only privately, is constitutionally problematic not because it strikes an unacceptable bal-

ance between national and state interests as such, but because it hinders and may even foreclose attempts by states or localities to meet their citizens' legitimate expectations of basic government services. See generally Tribe, "Unraveling National League of Cities: The New Federalism and Affirmative Rights to Essential Government Services," 90 Harv.L.Rev. 1065 (1977). For another analysis similarly stressing the relevance of National League of Cities to a public right to certain government services, see Michelman, "States' Rights and States' Roles: The Permutations of 'Sovereignty' in National League of Cities v. Usery," 86 Yale L.J., 1165 (1977).

57. 455 U.S. 40 (1982).

58. 317 U.S. 341 (1943), discussed in § 6–26, infra.

59. Colo. Const., Art. XX, Sec. 6.

and ordinances made pursuant thereto "supercede" the laws of the state.[60]

The City Council of Boulder—afraid that the then-dominant cable television operator was going to achieve an unbreakable monopoly—enacted an ordinance prohibiting the established company from expanding operations for three months.[61] When the cable operator sought an injunction against the ordinance on Sherman Act grounds, Boulder claimed that its statutes were exempt from antitrust scrutiny under *Parker v. Brown*. Justice Brennan, writing for the five-member majority,[62] concluded that even assuming the moratorium was within the power delegated to Boulder by the Home Rule Amendment, "[it could not] be exempt from antitrust scrutiny unless it constitute[d] the action of the State of Colorado itself in its sovereign capacity, or unless it constitute[d] municipal action in furtherance or implementation of clearly articulated and affirmatively expressed state policy."[63] The state legislature, the Court observed, was without power to legislate regarding home-rule municipalities in areas preempted by local enactments, so Boulder's ordinance could not "affirmatively express" a *state* policy.[64] The Court held, in effect, that states could delegate their powers but not their sovereign immunity from the commerce clause, thus forcing the states to bear the burden of regulating for their municipalities and preventing them from allowing local governments to experiment and profit from their different experiences.

National League of Cities was not cited, let alone questioned, by any of the opinions in *Boulder*, despite what seems an assault on principles of state autonomy. The majority ruled that principles of federalism prevent the Sherman Act, absent a clear contrary choice by Congress, from preempting state policy which supplants competition with regulation, but that the laws of the state's *subdivisions* are not similarly protected. *National League of Cities* had explicitly held that, if principles of federalism place a *state* beyond the reach of a particular exercise of commerce clause authority, then the state's *political subdivisions* are equally immunized.[65] Certainly the text of the tenth amendment itself provides no basis for the distinction between state and local governments made in *Boulder*: that provision reserves the same sphere of residual powers to the "States respectively, or to the people." And the Colorado Home Rule Amendment explicitly "vests" the "power of self-government" in those same "people."

The irony, then, is that the Court's idyll into Talmudic parsing of traditional and non-traditional state functions may have diverted it from doing the real business of preserving federalism: protecting the structure of state government from federal intrusion. Just as the

---

60. Id.

61. 455 U.S. at 45–46.

62. He was joined by Justices Marshall, Blackmun, Powell and Stevens. Justice Rehnquist, joined by the Chief Justice and Justice O'Connor, dissented. Justice White did not participate.

63. Id. at 52 (citations omitted).

64. Id. at 52–56.

65. 426 U.S. at 855–56 n. 20. Indeed, most of the services that the Court gave as examples of traditional government functions—fire prevention, police protection, sanitation, id. at 851, hospital services and education, id. at 855—are provided by local, not state, government.

Court forbade the federal government from telling a state where to locate its capitol,[66] it is strongly arguable that the Court in *Boulder* should have limited how much and in what way the federal government may control the delegation of power from a state to its subdivisions. When we return to Justice Rehnquist's "tacit postulates"—the core assumptions about the structure of constitutional government, assumptions that surely include the meaningful existence of the states—we recognize that *National League of Cities* may have been the wrong battle fought with the wrong tactics, but in a campaign whose concerns were far from trivial and indeed had solid constitutional grounding. As the Court returns to the question of states' rights, as it no doubt will some day, the task will be to ground the development of "tacit postulates" of state sovereignty in a new, more productive, and more comprehensible doctrine.

§ 5-23. The "Republican Form of Government" Clause as a Possible Touchstone for Future States' Rights Jurisprudence

The most fundamental threats to state sovereignty—those that genuinely portend reduction of the states into "field offices of the national bureaucracy" or "bureaucratic puppets of the Federal Government"[1]—would seem to arise less from federal laws that impose *substantive* constraints on state and private actors alike (such as the wage and hour provisions at issue in *National League of Cities v. Usery*[2]) than from federal laws that *restructure* the basic institutional design of the system a state's people choose for governing themselves. If there is any form of congressional assault that might truly " 'nibble away at state sovereignty, bit by bit, until someday essentially nothing is left but a gutted shell,' "[3] it is an assault on those "democratic processes through [which] . . . citizens . . . retain the power to govern . . . their local problems."[4]

In this sense, both *Federal Energy Regulatory Commission v. Mississippi*,[5] involving a federal attempt to alter a state's structures and processes for administering its economic regulations, and *Community Communications Co. v. Boulder*,[6] construing federal law so as to restrict a state's options for allocating power between local government and the state legislature, might well have been better candidates for the elaboration and enforcement of principles of state sovereignty than *National League of Cities* proved to be.

Although the "tacit postulates" of the constitutional plan may well be as sound a basis for doctrine as any express provision of the

66. See Coyle v. Smith, 221 U.S. 559 (1911).

§ 5-23

1. Federal Energy Regulatory Commission v. Mississippi, 456 U.S. 742, 777, 783 (1982) (O'Connor, J., joined by Burger, C.J., and Rehnquist, J., concurring in the judgment in part and dissenting in part).

2. 426 U.S. 833 (1976).

3. Federal Energy Regulatory Commission, 456 U.S. at 775 (Powell, J., concurring in part and dissenting in part) (quoting the first edition of this treatise).

4. Id. at 790 (O'Connor, J.).

5. 456 U.S. 742 (1982), discussed in § 5-22, supra.

6. 455 U.S. 40 (1982), discussed in § 5-22, supra.

Constitution can be,[7] there *is* an express provision that might plausibly be invoked in support of the proposition that the Constitution recognizes in the National Government a duty, running directly "to every State in this Union" rather than to individuals, to respect the state's most fundamental structural choices as to how its people are to participate in their own governance: article IV, § 4, expressly provides that the "United States shall guarantee to every State in this Union a Republican Form of Government." When Justice O'Connor observed, in her powerful dissent in *Federal Energy Regulatory Commission v. Mississippi*, that "federalism enhances the opportunity of all citizens to participate in representative government," [8]—and when she quoted Alexis de Tocqueville's remarks that " 'the love and the habits of *republican government* in the United States were engendered in the townships and in the provincial assemblies,' " and that " 'this same republican spirit [is] engendered and nurtured in the different States' " [9]—she may have hit upon an important link between the tacit postulate of state sovereignty and the textual guarantee of republican government.

No doubt both Congress and the federal judiciary are empowered under the Civil War Amendments to assure that a state's choices of governmental structure respect basic norms of equal protection.[10] And no doubt many options exist, consistent with those basic norms, for implementing the ideals of representative democracy through the requirement of "republican" form. But the authority to *choose* among those options—the authority to decide, consistent with equal protection of the laws, *how* one's people will represent themselves and participate in their own governance—seems the very essence of *all* self-government.

To be sure, the Supreme Court has denied that the guaranty clause of article IV, § 4, confers judicially cognizable rights upon *individuals*.[11] But it has not avoided all judicial involvement in this sphere; rather, the Court has invoked the equal protection clause of the fourteenth amendment to protect each individual's right to participate in state and local government on an equal footing.[12] And it need not follow from the unavailability of the guaranty clause as a textual source of protection for *individuals* that the clause confers no judicially enforceable rights upon *states as states*. It is, after all, the states to which the clause extends its explicit guarantee. If courts are once again to take up the task of preserving for states their constitutionally essential role as self-governing polities, the guaranty clause might well provide the most felicitous textual home for that enterprise.

7. Nevada v. Hall, 440 U.S. 410, 433 (1979) (Rehnquist, J., joined by Burger, C.J., dissenting).

8. 456 U.S. at 789.

9. Id., at 789–90, quoting 1 A. de Tocqueville, Democracy in America 181 (H.Reeve trans. 1961).

10. See §§ 5–12 through 5–14, supra, and Chapters 13 and 16, infra.

11. See § 3–13, supra.

12. See Chapters 13 and 16, infra. Indeed, the Burger Court, in one of the last decisions rendered during Chief Justice Burger's tenure, see Davis v. Bandemer, 106 S.Ct. 2797 (1986), launched the federal judiciary upon the even more ambitious mission of policing political gerrymandering.

§ 5–24. Reflections on the Rebirth of Federalism: Policy vs. Principle

Professor Martha Field is correct that a court is without authority to redraw the Constitution's structural boundaries in order to fit the document to its sense of what the times demand,[1] just as it is without power to invent entirely new rights to meet its sense of what an ideal constitution would require in contemporary circumstances. Creating states' rights out of whole cloth in order to redress a perceived shift in power to central government is an arrogation of authority as illegitimate as conjuring rights of privacy or minimum income out of thin air[2] or transforming the Constitution into a source of inviolable protections for contract and property regardless of public need.[3]

It does not follow, however, that rights of states, or of individuals, are limited to those that are indisputably manifest on the surface of the document.[4] Even those Justices least inclined to perceive implicit rights reject the "simplistic view that constitutional interpretation can be limited to the 'plain meaning' of the Constitution's text or to the subjective intention of the Framers. The Constitution is not a deed setting forth the precise metes and bounds of its subject matter; rather, it is a document announcing fundamental principles in value-laden terms that leave ample scope for the exercise of normative judgments by those charged with interpreting and applying it."[5] A process of structural inference, aimed at discerning the tacit premises of the Constitution's language and architecture in light of its historic purposes, is an indispensable part of the interpretive task—as the preceding sections have sought to show.

But such a process must be sharply distinguished from an attempt to treat the Constitution as a mirror either for some favored view of the interpreter or for the interpreter's perception of the public mood. It is therefore no answer, for example, to the case for recognizing at least some rights for states—see §§ 5–20 through 5–23, supra—that "hardly anyone, from President Reagan to the ordinary citizen, really cares about federalism as a principle" and that, "like Tinker Bell, [federalism] must be close to expiring because no one believes in it anymore."[6] It is manifestly irrelevant whether either the Chief Executive or the

---

§ 5–24

1. Field, "Garcia v. San Antonio Metro. Transit Auth.: The Demise of a Misguided Doctrine," 99 Harv.L.Rev. 84, 102 (1985).

2. For proper approaches to rights of privacy and autonomy in particular, see Chapter 15, infra.

3. See generally R. Epstein, Takings: Private Property and the Power of Eminent Domain (1985), discussed in § 9–6, infra.

4. See Tribe, "Contrasting Constitutional Visions: Of Real and Unreal Differences," 22 Harv.Civ.Rts.-Civ.Lib.L.Rev. 95 (1987).

5. Thornburgh v. American College of Obstetricians, 106 S.Ct. 2169, 2193–94 (1986) (White, J., joined by Rehnquist, J., dissenting).

6. "The Third Death of Federalism," 3 Const'l. Commentary 293, 294 (1986) (D. Bryden & D. Farber, eds.). In any event, some people still believe very strongly indeed in federalism, as evidenced by The Status of Federalism In America (November 1986), a report of the Reagan Administration's Domestic Policy Council Working Group on Federalism. The report makes a highly exaggerated—but, at least, a legal—argument for the view that the Constitution's vision of federalism has been perverted to subordinate the states impermissibly ever since the tenure of Chief Justice Marshall. Because of this departure from the true path of federalism, the Reagan

man in the street currently "believes" in federalism or in any other constitutional principle. The chronicle of constitutionalism as a cultural phenomenon over the past two centuries reveals that popular American understanding of the Constitution is often the stuff of either tragedy or comedy, depending upon one's literary preferences.[7] The issue is not whether federalism is a popular notion, or whether its proponents are in step with the *zeitgeist*, but whether principles of federalism are implicit in our national charter. If tacit postulates of federalism are indeed ingrained in the Constitution, courts are not free to dismiss them out of hand as ghosts or spirits in which no one any longer believes.[8]

Justice Department declared, our "once robust scheme of popular government has been allowed to decline into something approaching a tyranny of clerks and accountants." Letter of G. McDowell, Assoc.Dir. of the Justice Dept. Office of Public Affairs, in The New York Times, December 4, 1986 at A34. That counter-revolutionary approach to centralized government is hard to square with the sweeping view of federal power espoused by President Ronald Reagan himself in a 1986 press conference: "If our Constitution means anything it means that we, the Federal Government, are entrusted with preserving life, liberty and the pursuit of happiness." The New York Times, June 12, 1986, at A20 cols. 2–3 (late ed.).

7. See generally M. Kammen, A Machine That Would Go Of Itself: The Constitution in American Culture (1986).

8. Cf. J. Ely, Democracy and Distrust 39 (1980).

Chapter 6

FEDERALISM–BASED LIMITS ON STATE AND LOCAL POWER: REGULATION AND TAXATION OF COMMERCE, FEDERAL SUPREMACY, AND PROBLEMS OF INTERSTATE DISCRIMINATION

§ 6-1. The Judicial Role in Confining Economic Localism

Even judges and commentators ordinarily hesitant about federal judicial intervention into legislative choice tend to support a relatively active role for the federal judiciary "when the centrifugal, isolating or hostile forces of localism are manifested in state legislation." [1] This is particularly true when state or local law is challenged under the supremacy clause or the commerce clause or some combination of the two, since in such cases federal judges are called upon to make what they deem a proper allocation of power in a manner that is "tentative and subject to reallocation by Congress." [2] Had such intervention been limited, as some have advocated,[3] to the judicial invalidation of state and local action that conflicts with existing federal legislation, we would surely have experienced "frictions and strains which we have been spared." [4]

Unlike those constitutional provisions that establish the relationship of the citizen to governmental power in general, the commerce clause, and the privileges and immunities clause of article IV, centrally define the relationship of the states to one another and delineate the treatment that one state must accord the citizens of another. And the supremacy clause defines the hierarchy of federalism. Without these provisions, the Union as we know it would be unthinkable. For the very reason that these clauses are constitutionally indispensable, judicial review of state and local actions alleged to violate them is necessarily robust. As Ernest Brown observed in what remains one of the most thoughtful analyses of this area, the "mechanisms of our government . . . give to Congress [no] opportunity or duty of reviewing, to test for compatibility with the federal system, state statutes even in their skeletal form as enacted, much less as fleshed by application, interpre-

---

§ 6-1

1. Brown, "The Open Economy: Mr. Justice Frankfurter and the Position of the Judiciary," 67 Yale L.J. 219, 220 (1957).

2. Id. at 221. See §§ 6-25 to 6-33, infra.

3. See Livingston v. Van Ingen, 9 Johns. 507, 572–80 (N.Y. 1812) (Chancellor Kent); 2 Thayer, Cases on Constitutional Law 2190 (1895). No Justice since Chief Justice Taney has consistently espoused such a view, and even he concurred in the rather different position formulated in Cooley v. Board of Port Wardens of Port of Philadelphia, 53 U.S. (12 How.) 299, 318 (1851).

4. Brown, supra note 1, at 222.

tation and administration. Nor has Congress been so idle that such matters could be assured a place on its agenda without competition from other business which might often be deemed more pressing; in Justice Jackson's phrase, the inertia of government would be heavily on the side of the centrifugal forces of localism." [5]

The central thrust of the Supreme Court's work in federal-state relations has been to put the inertia on the other side—on the side of the centralizing forces of nationhood and union. But that thrust has been at times deflected, in part perhaps for lack of clear judicial vision but in larger part, surely, because of intersecting forces and considerations that it would have been folly for judges to ignore. This chapter seeks to trace both the major theme and its minor variations, starting with a textual and historical point of departure but moving rather quickly to contemporary perspectives and problems. Issues of state regulation of interstate commerce are canvassed in §§ 6–1 to 6–14; state taxation of interstate commerce in §§ 6–15 to 6–20; state regulation and taxation of foreign commerce in §§ 6–21 to 6–23; the impact of the twenty-first amendment in § 6–24; and the effect of federal legislation in §§ 6–25 to 6–33, with problems of federal immunity from state taxation and regulation receiving special attention in §§ 6–30 to 6–32 and issues of congressional ratification receiving particular attention in § 6–33. Finally, §§ 6–34 to 6–35 explore constitutional claims to non-discriminatory treatment in an area that builds a bridge from the topic of federal-state relations to the subject of rights against government generally: the privileges and immunities clause of article IV, section 2. As will become evident, there is much more than a formal link between the federalism-based idea of shielding persons from the parochial forces of localism and the broader notion of protecting individuals against unfair and oppressive action by the state.[6]

---

5. Id. (footnote omitted).

6. Other commentators have other general approaches to this area. See, e.g., Maltz, "How Much Regulation is Too Much—An Examination of Commerce Clause Jurisprudence", 50 Geo.Wash.L. Rev. 47 (1981) (commerce clause creates a "free location principle": state boundaries should not be barriers to movement of goods); Eule, "Laying the Dormant Commerce Clause to Rest", 91 Yale L.J. 425 (1982) (basing evaluation of state regulations discriminating against or unduly interfering with interstate commerce in the privileges and immunities clause of article IV); Monaghan, "Foreword: Constitutional Common Law", 89 Harv.L.Rev. 1, 15–17 (1975) (the dormant commerce clause is a development of constitutional common law based on a national free trade philosophy embedded in the commerce clause); Sedler, "The Negative Commerce Clause as a Restriction on State Regulation and Taxation: An Analysis in Terms of Constitutional Structure", 31 Wayne L.Rev. 885 (1985) (the commerce clause should be held to invalidate all discriminatory state regulation and taxation but not regulation and taxation that unduly burden interstate commerce); Varat, "State 'Citizenship' and Interstate Equality", 48 U.Chi.L.Rev. 487 (1981) (offering a general theory of state citizenship to separate those benefits which belong peculiarly to state residents and those to which nonresidents must be accorded equal access); Regan, "The Supreme Court and State Protectionism: Making Sense of the Dormant Commerce Clause", 84 Mich.L.Rev. 1091 (1986) (the Court's primary project in dormant commerce clause cases has been and should be to prevent states from engaging in purposeful economic protectionism); Tushnet, "Rethinking the Dormant Commerce Clause", 1979 Wisc.L.Rev. 125 (the Court should inquire whether the political process underlying the regulation of interstate commerce was distorted; and the Court should apply a standard of "efficiency" to invalidate state regulations that create large price increases in other states).

§ 6–2. Judicial Review of State Regulation of Interstate Commerce: Historical Origins and Fundamental Considerations

Article I, section 8, is phrased as an affirmative grant of power to Congress: "The Congress shall have Power . . . . To regulate Commerce with foreign Nations, and among the several States, and with the Indian Tribes . . ." Although the Constitution contains language explicitly limiting state interference with foreign commerce,[1] nowhere does it explicitly limit state interference with interstate commerce. All of the doctrine in this area is thus traceable to the Constitution's *negative implications;* it is by interpreting "these great silences of the Constitution"[2] that the Supreme Court has limited the scope of what the states might do.

Occasionally, the Framers' failure to employ explicit words of exclusion has seemed somewhat puzzling. They may have regarded the privileges and immunities clause of article IV as sufficient limitation upon state parochialism.[3] Or possibly they felt themselves unable to fathom the implications of the commerce power with sufficient certainty to justify completely proscribing a sharing of that power by the states.[4] Whether the affirmative grant of commercial power to Congress should be construed to circumscribe state action in some or all cases has posed no small problem of construction.[5] The controversy has ultimately been framed by asking whether, as a general rule or in selected instances, the nature of the power vested in Congress requires its exclusive exercise by that body.[6]

The fact that the constitutional limitations upon state interference with interstate commerce are implied rather than expressed entails one crucial doctrinal corollary. Given their origin as negative judicial inferences from a constitutional grant of power to Congress, the Supreme Court's doctrinal limitations on state interference are always

§ 6–2

1. See § 6–23, *infra.*

2. H. P. Hood & Sons, Inc. v. Du Mond, 336 U.S. 525, 535 (1949) (Jackson, J.).

3. See §§ 6–34 to 6–35, *infra.* It should be noted in this regard, however, that the typical beneficiary of the commerce clause's negative implications is a *corporate* entity and as such cannot claim the protection of article IV's privileges and immunities clause. Bank of Augusta v. Earle, 38 U.S. (13 Pet.) 519, 586 (1839). See also Paul v. Virginia, 75 U.S. (8 Wall.) 168, 181 (1869). See § 6–14, *infra.*

4. Alternatively, the failure to delimit state actions explicitly may have been activated by the Framers' recognition that state controls might subsequently be barred by the scope of the power conferred upon Congress, if such a limit should prove compatible with the lessons of history and the dictates of economic pragmatism. See F. Ribble, State and National Power Over Commerce 30–31 (1937); Sholley, "The Negative Implications of the Commerce Clause," 3 U.Chi.L.Rev. 556, 561–62 (1936).

5. Compare Helson v. Commonwealth of Kentucky, 279 U.S. 245, 248 (1929) ("Regulation of interstate and foreign commerce is a matter committed exclusively to the control of Congress") with St. Louis-S.F. Ry. v. Public S.C. of Missouri, 261 U.S. 369, 371 (1923) (". . . although interstate commerce is outside of regulation by a state, there may be instances in which a state, in the exercise of a necessary power, may affect that commerce").

6. Cf. Sturges v. Crowninshield, 17 U.S. (4 Wheat.) 122, 193 (1819), where Chief Justice Marshall, in passing upon the legitimacy of a New York statute regulating bankruptcy, observed: "Whenever the terms in which a power is granted to Congress, or the nature of the power, require that it should be exercised exclusively by Congress, the subject is as completely taken from the state legislatures as if they had been expressly forbidden to act on it."

subject to congressional revision.[7] Judicial intervention in this sphere is therefore less problematic than in other constitutional realms, and the proper blend of judicial and legislative activity in this area is akin to that in other fields in which subsequent legislative enactments may overrule the decisions of the courts. Thus the argument for judicial activism on behalf of the commerce clause is largely a reference to the durable attractiveness of the common law.[8]

§ 6–3. Early Interpretations of the Commerce Clause

Important not only for their historical significance but also as sources of themes that recur to the present day are two conflicting strands in the earliest interpretations of the commerce clause. The Madisonian interpretation was premised on the widely-held belief that the Articles of Confederation had failed in large part because the states had waged destructive trade wars against one another. A common diagnosis was that the state governments had been too responsive to local economic interests, with the result that interstate economic competition was conducted more through political processes than through the marketplace.[1] Discriminatory, self-protective, and retaliatory state actions were explained by the biased accountability of state governments—their inevitable tendency to pursue their separate interests at the expense of one another. Madison's prescription for economic matters affecting more than one state was to shift legislative authority over such matters to Congress, a national body in which competing economic factions would neutralize one another and thereby free commerce from stifling regulation.[2] Under the Madisonian interpretation of the commerce clause, therefore, Congress would be expected to do very little in the field of commercial regulation, and the states would be powerless to regulate interstate commerce even when Congress did nothing at all.[3]

Madison's conception of the commerce clause was elaborated by Chief Justice Marshall, an advocate and architect of a strong central government; it was a conception that powerfully informed Marshall's early pronouncements on the construction of that clause.[4] The Madisonian position, at least as embraced by Marshall, insisted that the commerce power was exclusively federal but did not maintain that every exercise of state power that somehow impacted upon interstate commerce was constitutionally repugnant. Marshall distinguished the

7. See Prudential Ins. Co. v. Benjamin, 328 U.S. 408 (1946), discussed in § 6–33, infra.

8. See Levmore, "Interstate Exploitation and Judicial Intervention," 69 Va.L. Rev. 563, 568–570 (1983). Cf. Monaghan, "Foreword: Constitutional Common Law," 89 Harv.L.Rev. 1, 15–17 (1975).

§ 6–3

1. See Ribble, in § 6–2, supra, note 4, at 1; G. Reynolds, The Distribution of Power to Regulate Carriers Between the Nation and the States 32–35 (1928); Sholley, in § 6–2, supra, note 4, at 559–60. See generally Baldwin v. G.A.F. Seelig, Inc., 294 U.S.

511, 522–23 (1935); H. P. Hood & Sons v. Du Mond, 336 U.S. 525, 533–34 (1949).

2. See generally The Federalist Nos. 41, 42. See also 3 M. Farrand, Records of the Federal Convention of 1787, at 547.

3. See Gibbons v. Ogden, 22 U.S. (9 Wheat.) 1, 209 (1824) (Marshall, C.J.) (dictum). See also Missouri Pacific R. Co. v. Stroud, 267 U.S. 404, 408 (1925) (". . . there can be no divided authority over interstate commerce").

4. See, e.g., Gibbons v. Ogden, supra. See generally B. Gavitt, Commerce Clause of the United States Constitution 10 (1932).

commerce *power* from the *subject matter* upon which that power *operated*: while a state could not regulate "commerce" for its own sake, it might, in the pursuit of other legitimate state goals, take actions which impinged, to some extent, upon the commercial intercourse among the states.[5]

Opposing so severe a limitation on state power, Roger Taney, Marshall's successor as Chief Justice, advanced the view that the commerce clause left states free to regulate as they wished so long as their actions did not conflict with validly enacted federal legislation.[6] Under this view, the only negative implications of the commerce clause were those derivable from the power of Congress to preempt state action conflicting with the actual exercise of its lawful authority.[7]

Each of these views has left a distinct and enduring mark on commerce clause jurisprudence. Even after it was no longer accepted in its pure version, the Madisonian view left its legacy in the form of a pervasive suspicion of any state action seriously burdening individuals or enterprises outside the state and hence unable to influence its policies, as well as any state action threatening to revive interstate economic rivalries of the sort that had undermined the Articles of Confederation. And even after Taney's anti-Madisonian view had been rejected as doctrine, it too persisted in the form of a reluctance to treat subjects as exclusively within the regulatory authority of Congress unless those subjects were of such national concern as to make federal regulation likely; this reluctance has been defended as necessary to avoid a regulatory vacuum in which states *cannot* regulate and Congress *will not* regulate. Flying in the face of Madison's conclusion that the commerce clause *should* cause precisely such a vacuum, this view has surfaced repeatedly throughout the history of commerce clause adjudication.[8]

Another important strand of early commerce clause jurisprudence was the distinction drawn between "commerce" and "police" regulations. Chief Justice Marshall was apparently the first to employ the rubric "police power" to describe the residual prerogatives of sovereignty which the states had not surrendered to the federal government.[9] In

---

5. See the discussion of the "police power" in notes 9–10, infra. See also Ribble in § 6–2, supra, note 4, at 37–38.

6. See The License Cases, 46 U.S. (5 How.) 504, 573 (1847) (separate opinion of Chief Justice Taney). These cases sustained the constitutionality, in the absence of a conflicting act of Congress, of state statutes which required the licensing of anyone selling intoxicating beverages brought into the state from without. Taney opined that the challenged state action did regulate interstate commerce, but that such regulation was proper given the abstention of Congress. While the Court unanimously upheld the statutes, several of the Justices based their conclusions on other grounds. See, e.g., id. at 631 (Grier, J., concurring on the ground that the state was properly exercising its police power);

id. at 618 (Woodbury, J., concurring on the ground that interstate commerce was not implicated by the licensing requirement because the interstate character of the transaction expired prior to regulation).

7. See § 6–1, supra.

8. See, e.g., Parker v. Brown, 317 U.S. 341, 362–63 (1943) (Stone, C.J.) (". . . the matter is one which . . . because of its local character, and the practical difficulties involved, may never be adequately dealt with by Congress"), discussed in §§ 6–8, 6–26, infra.

9. See R. Roettinger, The Supreme Court and the State Police Power 10 (1957). It was this "police power" that Marshall had in mind when he referred to "[t]he acknowledged power of a State to regulate its police, its domestic trade, and to govern

Brown v. Maryland, while holding that the commerce clause prevented Maryland from requiring a foreign importer to be licensed by the state prior to selling imported goods, Marshall proclaimed: "The power to direct the removal of gunpowder is a branch of the police power, which unquestionably remains, and ought to remain, with the States." [10]

In the years between *Gibbons v. Ogden* and the middle of the nineteenth century, the tension between the Madisonian and anti-Madisonian interpretations was most frequently resolved by reference to Marshall's talisman: state regulations were either deemed invalid because of their character as "regulations of interstate commerce" or valid because of their character as "police power regulations." [11] To the modern observer, these labels appear to have been largely conclusory; whatever their internal coherence or their predictive value for those who used them, they reveal little of the analysis underlying the decisions in which they played a role. [12]

§ 6–4. The Cooley Doctrine: Bridge to the Modern Cases

In *Cooley v. Board of Wardens of the Port of Philadelphia*, [1] the Supreme Court attempted to reconcile all that had gone before in a formulation that laid the groundwork for all that has come since. Upholding the power of Pennsylvania to require ships in interstate and foreign commerce to engage local pilots when entering or leaving the port of Philadelphia, [2] the Court revoked a congressional statute pur-

---

its own citizens." Gibbons v. Ogden, 22 U.S. (9 Wheat.) 1, 208 (1824).

10. 25 U.S. (12 Wheat.) 419, 443 (1827). The police power was always a flexible notion. See, e.g., Day-Brite Lighting, Inc. v. Missouri, 342 U.S. 421, 424 (1952) ("the police power is not confined to a narrow category; it extends . . . to all great public needs"); The License Cases, 46 U.S. (5 How.) 504, 584 (1847) (Taney, C.J.) (". . . the police powers of a state are nothing more or less than the powers of government inherent in every sovereignty to the extent of its dominions").

11. See, e.g., Willson v. Black-Bird Creek Marsh Co., 27 U.S. (2 Pet.) 245 (1829), where the Supreme Court held, per Marshall, C.J., that Delaware could safeguard the health of its citizens by draining a marshy creek which was technically an interstate waterway, even though such action blocked federally licensed boating. In Mayor of the City of New York v. Miln, 36 U.S. (11 Pet.) 102 (1837), the Court later sustained a New York statute requiring the master of any vessel arriving in the port of New York from any out-of-state point to report the names and residences of its passengers, deeming the act "not a regulation of commerce, but of police." Dissenting, Justice Story announced that the late Chief Justice Marshall had planned to concur with his view of the law's unconstitutionality.

12. See generally F. Frankfurter, The Commerce Clause Under Marshall, Taney and Waite (1937).

§ 6–4

1. 53 U.S. (12 How.) 299 (1851).

2. The Court quite clearly thought that the statute regulated commerce. See id. at 316. No note was taken of such subtleties as whether or not a statute which affects commerce but is motivated by a goal anterior to commercial regulation should be deemed to regulate commerce. *Cooley* was foreshadowed by a line of cases which focused on the nature of the regulated subject matter rather than on the considerations that motivated the regulation. See, e.g., The License Cases, 46 U.S. (5 How.) 504 (1847); The Passenger Cases, 48 U.S. (7 How.) 283, 559 (1849) (invalidating a New York statute imposing on the masters of ships coming from any out-of-state port a tax for each passenger to defray the costs of examining passengers for contagious diseases and of hospitalizing those found to be diseased, and a similar Massachusetts statute applicable to aliens and adding a requirement that masters should post a $1,000 bond for each alien likely to become a public charge); accord, Henderson v. Mayor of New York, 92 U.S. (2 Otto) 259 (1875). The Passenger Cases, decided in 1849, were the first to hold a state's action violative of the commerce clause in the absence of a relevant federal statute.

porting to authorize such state regulation to bolster its own conclusion that the subject being regulated was "local" rather than "national."[3]

The *Cooley* doctrine was that states are free to regulate those aspects of interstate and foreign commerce so *local* in character as to demand diverse treatment, while Congress alone can regulate those aspects of interstate and foreign commerce so *national* in character that a single, uniform rule is necessary.[4] Although the attempt to test state regulation by classifying its subject matter as local or national has been largely abandoned,[5] the enduring legacy of *Cooley* has been this basic theme: The validity of state action affecting interstate commerce must be judged in light of the desirability of permitting diverse responses to local needs and the undesirability of permitting local interference with such uniformity as the unimpeded flow of interstate commerce may require.

During the decades following *Cooley*, the Court often employed the subject matter analysis used in the *Cooley* decision itself. The most important such case of the post-*Cooley* era was *Wabash, St. Louis & Pacific Ry. Co. v. Illinois*.[6] There the Supreme Court struck down an Illinois attempt to regulate intrastate railway rates charged Illinois customers for goods brought from other states or destined to points in other states, despite the absence of conflicting federal legislation.[7] The Court reasoned that the cumulative burdens[8] which would be imposed on the railroads if all states attempted similar rate regulation would be so great, and so disruptive of commerce, that this was an area best left to Congress alone. The following year, Congress responded by creating the Interstate Commerce Commission.[9]

3. An Act of Congress of August 7, 1789, 1 Stat. 54, permitted the states to regulate pilotage. The role of this statute in the Court's decision is both pivotal and murky. The Court may have treated Congress' action as authoritatively establishing that the subject matter involved was local; in contrast, the Court may have taken note of the congressional act simply as a legally significant expression of Congress' position in the course of the Court's own independent, authoritative, judicial disposition of this issue. The distinction is crucial, because in the first formulation Congress is the ultimate arbiter of the local or national character of subject matter, while in the second formulation that role is reserved to the Court. The weight of historical authority supports the second formulation. See Ribble, in § 6–2, supra, note 4, at 76; Sholley, in § 6–2, supra, note 4, at 577. This construction does seem to comport best with the language of the Cooley Court. See 53 U.S. at 318. But the contemporary view has tended to follow the first formulation. See § 6–33, infra.

4. The impact of the *Cooley* doctrine on state regulation of foreign commerce is discussed in § 6–21, infra.

5. But cf. Goldstein v. California, 412 U.S. 546 (1973), discussed in § 6–29, infra.

6. 118 U.S. 557 (1886), overruling Peik v. Chicago & Nw. Ry. Co., 94 U.S. (4 Otto) 164 (1877). For other applications of the Cooley paradigm, see Gilman v. Philadelphia, 70 U.S. (3 Wall.) 713 (1866); Ex parte McNeil, 80 U.S. (13 Wall.) 236 (1872).

7. The Illinois regulation had forbidden long-haul, short-haul rate discrimination.

8. See § 6–18, infra.

9. See 24 Stat. 379 (1887). The states nonetheless retained the power to regulate railway rates for the carriage of persons and property picked up and delivered within their borders, but subject to the ICC-enforced rule that such rates must not discriminate against interstate commerce. Wisconsin R.R. Comm. v. Chicago, B. & Q.R. Co., 257 U.S. 563 (1922).

One distinguished observer has noted that, in reviewing state encroachments, the judiciary "acts only as an intermediate agency between the state and Congress," and has gone so far as to suggest that a federal agency with expertise in commerce and a legislative mandate from Congress— and, hence, a better sense of congressional

By the time of the *Wabash* decision, it had already become clear that the classification of regulatory subject matter as "national" or "local," like the earlier dichotomy between "police" and "commerce" regulations, was more conclusory than explanatory. Whether a given subject matter should be judged appropriate for state regulation often depended upon how the state proposed to regulate it in the particular case. *What the states did*, and not *what subject they did it to*, came to be seen as the crucial question in deciding whether state action was compatible with the commerce clause. Therefore, in the years following *Cooley*, Supreme Court decisions have focused increasingly on the precise method and context of challenged regulation, attempting in this way to ascertain the extent to which state action impedes interstate commerce, and the justifications with which it does so. Such analysis was at first conducted (some would now say "masked") by classifying the impact of state regulation on interstate commerce as either "direct" or "indirect." State regulations affecting interstate commerce were permitted by the Supreme Court in the pre-1938 period if the regulatory impact was felt by interstate commerce "only indirectly, incidentally, and remotely." [10] Conversely, state regulations affecting interstate commerce were struck down by the Court if the regulatory impact upon interstate commerce was deemed so substantial as to be a "direct" burden.[11]

§ 6–5. Judicial Review of State Regulation of Interstate Commerce: Contemporary Doctrine and the Theme of Political Representation

Since the mid-1930s, the Supreme Court has sought to clarify the process by which it determines whether state regulation is prohibited by the commerce clause. The distinction between "direct" and "indirect" burdens has been rejected as overly conclusory and misleadingly precise. In its place, the Court has substituted the following, more openly indeterminate, principle: State regulation affecting interstate commerce will be upheld if (a) the regulation is rationally related to a legitimate state end, and (b) the regulatory burden imposed on interstate commerce, and any discrimination against it, are outweighed by the state interest in enforcing the regulation.[1]

wishes—might be established to act in the judiciary's stead. See Choper, "The Scope of National Power Vis-a-vis the States: The Dispensability of Judicial Review," 86 Yale L.J. 1552, 1585, 1587 n. 194 (1977).

10. Smith v. Alabama, 124 U.S. 465, 482 (1888) (upholding a state law requiring that all locomotive engineers within the state be licensed by a state board of examiners). Accord, Erb v. Morasch, 177 U.S. 584 (1900) (municipality may restrict train speed within city limits); Chicago, R.I. & Pac. Ry. Co. v. Arkansas, 219 U.S. 453 (1911) (state may require three brakemen on freight trains of over 25 cars); Atchison T. & S.F. Ry. Co. v. Railroad Comm., 283 U.S. 380 (1931) (state may require electric headlights of specified minimum capacity).

11. See, e.g., Seaboard Air Line Ry. v. Blackwell, 244 U.S. 310 (1917) (striking down state law requiring railroad trains to check their speed before coming to any public crossing; under the requirement, an interstate train would have been obliged to come almost to a complete stop as many as 124 times within 123 miles, increasing the time required to get from Atlanta to South Carolina by more than six hours). Cf. Southern Railway Co. v. King, 217 U.S. 524 (1910) (burden on interstate commerce not unduly heavy where fewer crossings were involved).

§ 6–5

1. See, e.g., Southern Pacific Co. v. Arizona, 325 U.S. 761, 770–71 (1945); Cities

The first part of the test would be inadequate by itself because of the recognition implicit in the commerce clause that state and local lawmakers are especially susceptible to pressures which may lead them to make decisions harmful to the commercial interests of those who are not constituents of their political subdivisions. That recognition reflects not a cynical view of the failings of statesmanship at a sub-federal level, but only an understanding that the proper structural role of state lawmakers *is* to protect and promote the interests of their own constituents. That role is one that they will inevitably try to fulfill even at the expense of citizens of other states.

In this context, the rhetoric of judicial deference to the democratically fashioned judgments of legislatures is often inapposite. The checks on which we rely to curb the abuse of legislative power—election and recall—are simply unavailable to those who have no effective voice or vote in the jurisdiction which harms them. This problem is most acute when a state enacts commercial laws that regulate extraterritorial trade, so that unrepresented outsiders are affected even if they do not cross the state's borders.[2] Whatever may be the general merit of a system of judicial review which sanctions intervention by the counter-democratic courts only when the normal processes of democracy have broken down,[3] that model is of little use if mechanically applied in the context of interstate commerce, where problems often arise precisely because the individual states' democratic processes have worked *well*.

Because regulation unduly burdening or discriminating against interstate commerce or out-of-state enterprise has been thought to result from the inherently limited constituency to which each state or local legislature is accountable, the Supreme Court has viewed with suspicion any state action which imposes special or distinct burdens on

Service Gas Co. v. Peerless Oil & Gas Co., 340 U.S. 179, 186–87 (1950). The origin of the Court's balancing test approach to the dormant commerce clause is usually attributed to Dowling, "Interstate Commerce and State Power", 27 Virg.L.Rev. 1 (1940). For a general attack on the balancing approach see Maltz, "How Much Regulation is Too Much—An Examination of Commerce Clause Jurisprudence", 50 Geo. Wash.L.Rev. 47 (1981) (no basis in constitution for valuing some state interests more than others, a process of evaluation required for applying the balancing test); Regan, "The Supreme Court and State Protectionism: Making Sense of the Dormant Commerce Clause", 84 Mich.L.Rev. 1091 (1986).

2. In Brown-Forman Distillers v. New York Liquor Authority, 106 S.Ct. 2080 (1986), the Court struck down a New York Law requiring liquor producers, when setting prices for in-state wholesalers, to affirm that no lower price would be charged in other states during the same month. Since distillers had to have permission from New York before they could lower their prices in other states below their New York prices, the law effectively gave the New York Liquor Authority power to control prices beyond the state's borders. Id. at 2086. In Edgar v. MITE Corp., 457 U.S. 624 (1982), the Court invalidated an Illinois statute that imposed various requirements beyond those of federal law on tender offerors attempting to take over corporations that, although national or multinational in nature, were either chartered in Illinois or had some capital in the state. The Court accepted Illinois' interest in protecting its citizens from the ravages of takeover battles, but, in denouncing the law's "sweeping extraterritorial effect," id. at 642, the majority held that a "state has no legitimate interest in protecting nonresident shareholders," id. at 644. See § 6–33, infra. See also Southern Pacific Co. v. Arizona, 325 U.S. 761, 775 (1945) (striking down law where the "practical effect of such regulation is to control [conduct] beyond the boundaries of the state).

3. See generally J. Ely, Democracy and Distrust (1980).

out-of-state interests unrepresented in the state's political process.[4] For example, in *Public Utilities Commission of Rhode Island v. Attleboro Steam & Electric Co.*,[5] the Supreme Court struck down a Rhode Island regulatory agency's attempt to raise the price at which a Rhode Island company sold electricity to a Massachusetts company supplying a Massachusetts town. The Court reasoned that, if Rhode Island were allowed to protect its own citizens' economic interests by ordering an *increase* in the price paid for electricity by Massachusetts citizens, then Massachusetts could likewise protect *its* citizens' economic interests by ordering the Rhode Island electric company to *decrease* the price. The Court concluded that this conflict could be avoided only by holding that *neither* state could control the price charged.[6]

To be sure, even regulations significantly burdening interstate commerce have been tolerated when the interests adversely affected have been adequately represented in the regulating state's own political process. For example, in *South Carolina State Highway Dept. v. Barnwell Bros.*,[7] the Court upheld a state regulation which barred from state highways all trucks wider than 90 inches or heavier than 10 tons. At that time, all but ten to fifteen percent of the trucks used in interstate transportation exceeded these limits. Nonetheless, in weighing the state interest in safe highways against the burden on interstate commerce, the Court was able to tip the scales in favor of the state by stressing the fact that the South Carolina action did not discriminate against interstate commerce: "The fact that [the regulations] affect alike shippers in interstate and intrastate commerce in large numbers within as well as without the state is a safeguard against their abuse." [8]

Conversely, where a restrictive regulation affects only those from other states, the interests of presumably well-represented in-state businesses have been effectively divorced from their out-of-state counterparts. In such circumstances, the Court has properly declined to indulge the presumption that "a State's own political processes will

---

4. See, e.g., Southern Pacific Co. v. Arizona, 325 U.S. 761, 767–68 n. 2 (1945) (Stone, C.J.) ("The Court has often recognized that to the extent . . . the burden of state regulation falls on interests outside the state, it is unlikely to be alleviated by the operation of those political restraints normally exerted when interests within the state are affected"). See also South Carolina State Highway Dept. v. Barnwell Bros., 303 U.S. 177, 184 n. 2 (1938); Cooley v. Board of Port Wardens, 53 U.S. (12 How.) 299, 315 (1851); Gilman v. Philadelphia, 70 U.S. (3 Wall.) 713, 731 (1866). Cf. McGoldrick v. Berwind-White Coal Mining Co., 309 U.S. 33, 36 n. 2 (1940), discussed in § 6–15, infra. The fear that unrepresented commercial interests will be unduly burdened by provincial state action has important doctrinal analogues elsewhere; much the same political concern is at the root of one branch of the "suspect classification" doctrine in equal protection analysis. See Chapter 16, infra.

5. 273 U.S. 83 (1927).

6. The opinion was couched in terms of the now discredited direct-indirect dichotomy: "Being the imposition of a direct burden upon interstate commerce . . . it must necessarily fall, regardless of its purpose." Id. at 89. And in Arkansas Electric Cooperative Corp. v. Arkansas Public Service Commission, 461 U.S. 375 (1983), the Court retired Attleboro Steam's excessively formal distinction between retail sales of electricity, which the states could regulate, and wholesale interstate transmission of electricity, which they could not. See 461 U.S. at 390–93. Employing a balancing test, the Court in Arkansas Electric upheld state jurisdiction over wholesale rates charged by a rural power cooperative.

7. 303 U.S. 177 (1938).

8. 303 U.S. at 187. See also id. at 184 n. 2. Cf. Southern Pacific Co. v. Arizona, 325 U.S. 761, 783 (1945).

serve as a check against unduly burdensome regulations." [9] Thus, in *Kassel v. Consolidated Freightways Corp.*,[10] and *Raymond Motor Transportation, Inc. v. Rice*,[11] the Court invalidated state safety regulations banning 65-foot double tractor-trailers from their highways, because exemptions enacted with the restrictions reduced their impact on domestic truckers.

Since this approach to judicial review rests on the premises that unaccountable power is to be carefully scrutinized and that legislators are accountable only to those who have the power to vote them out of office, it is inevitable that this approach counsels frequent and probing judicial intervention under the commerce clause. It is, after all, in the nature of state lawmaking bodies to commit the sort of transgression forbidden by that clause: economic localism cannot be characterized as a symptom of breakdown in a local democratic process. Because this defect is routine rather than exceptional, this model of review serves not as a brake on judicial scrutiny of state laws, but as a directive to the courts to review and invalidate a wide range of quite ordinary legislative measures.

It is perhaps because of the speed with which the traditional democracy-reenforcing model of judicial review descends from judicial deference to judicial activism in the sphere of interstate commerce that the Court has on occasion committed itself to a vigorous search for some in-state economic surrogate for the interests of disenfranchised outsiders. In *Minnesota v. Clover Leaf Creamery Co.*,[12] the Court refused to permit a Minnesota state court to strike down a Minnesota statute that banned the sale of milk products in plastic, non-returnable containers. The statute was a boon to the state's powerful pulp-wood industry, whose containers would fill the void left by the excluded plastic containers, all of which were made from resins produced outside of Minnesota. Although the Minnesota Supreme Court had invalidated the statute under the commerce clause,[13] the United States Supreme Court reversed on the ground that the burden imposed by the statute on the interstate movement of goods was "relatively minor" [14] and because the ban on plastic containers served the substantial state interests in conserving resources and reducing solid waste.[15] Minnesota's highest court had found that the asserted state interests were negligible and not even promoted by the ban, but the Supreme Court deferred to the judgment of the Minnesota legislature because the interests of out-of-state plastic container manufacturers were adequately represented by the few Minnesota firms that were in any way adversely affected by the ban. These overlapping interests provided a "powerful safeguard against legislative abuse." [16] Thus, the presence of

9. Kassel v. Consolidated Freightways Corp., 450 U.S. 662, 676–76 (1981) (plurality opinion).

10. 450 U.S. 662 (1981), discussed in § 6–7, infra.

11. 434 U.S. 429 (1978), discussed in § 6–7, infra.

12. 449 U.S. 456 (1981).

13. The state court also held that the law failed to meet even the requirement of minimum rationality under the federal equal protection clause. This holding was likewise overruled by the Supreme Court.

14. 449 U.S. at 472.

15. Id. at 473.

16. Id. at 473 n. 17.

an in-state surrogate who may assert the claims of burdened out-of-state interests serves to lower the level of commerce clause scrutiny.

The concept of surrogate representation should be deployed with restraint, since its logic cannot easily be contained. Beyond the commercial interests that may be offended by statutes and regulations limiting the availability of goods and services provided by out-of-state concerns, the Court could as easily rely on the political voice of in-state consumers to challenge such regulations before they are enacted. Because such economic restrictions limit competition and tend to drive up prices or to reduce availability of goods and services,[17] a consumer check on abusive state legislation ought to be triggered almost automatically by commerce clause violations. Indeed, the decision in *Exxon Corp. v. Governor of Maryland*,[18] upholding a state law barring producers or refiners of petroleum products from owning or operating retail gasoline service stations within the state, may rest in part on an implicit notion of surrogate representation by consumers. Justice Stevens' majority opinion stressed that the commerce clause "protects the interstate market, not particular interstate firms, from prohibitive or burdensome regulation." [19] The Court found no impermissible advantage bestowed on in-state interests because the Maryland statute left in-state and out-of-state independent gasoline dealers on the same competitive footing.[20] The only possible remaining discrimination would have been against out-of-state goods, but the Maryland statute did not demonstrably alter the flow of interstate oil, only the identity of those who could sell it as gasoline at retail.[21]

Justice Blackmun argued in dissent that the Court's opinion glossed over the fact that the statute disadvantaged producers and refiners of oil, all of whom were out-of-state, while benefitting independent dealers in gasoline, a group overwhelmingly composed of local businesses.[22] No doubt aware of this relative disadvantage, the Court might have concluded that the protection provided by in-state groups whose interests overlapped with those out-of-state producers constituted a sufficient safeguard. One consequence of the Court's decision to root commerce clause concern in the market itself, rather than in the rights of particular commercial enterprises,[23] is the possibility that in-state consumers may be a surrogate for non-resident commercial interests. Undue burdens on interstate trade, after all, may provoke the political ire of resident consumers who depend on the market's efficient operation to keep the flow of goods smooth and the level of prices down.

17. See, e.g., Hunt v. Washington State Apple Advertising Comm'n, 432 U.S. 333, 351–52 (1977) (state law forbidding out-of-state apple growers to ship apples into state in crates marked with state-of-origin's grading system reduces availability of product and denies local consumers a competitive market and product information); Tushnet, "Rethinking the Dormant Commerce Clause," 1979 U.Wisc.L.Rev. 125, 138–39.

18. 437 U.S. 117 (1978), discussed further in § 6–6, infra.

19. Id. at 127–28.

20. Id. at 126.

21. Id. at 126 n. 16.

22. Id. at 137–38 (Blackmun, J., dissenting).

23. 437 U.S. at 127–28.

Hence commerce clause scrutiny need not be automatically triggered by rules that disadvantage out-of-state firms.[24]

Of course, a political check in the form of consumer pressure is theoretically present in *every* case to prevent discrimination against the interstate market. For this very reason, the Court is unlikely to embrace consumers as an indirect surrogate for out-of-state commercial interests. Frequent reliance on this sort of indirect representation would come close to turning traditional commerce clause analysis on its head: for if a state can demonstrate that the challenged enactment in fact results in a reduction in the interstate flow of goods and services, an increase in prices, or a reduction in the information available to consumers—precisely the effects that the commerce clause has been understood to counteract—then the statute will be insulated from judicial scrutiny because significant local consumer interests will have been injured by the statute and these interests will then be relied upon, as surrogates for out-of-state interests, to check state legislators who would enact such laws. Nor could litigants escape this logic by arguing that only particular out-of-state businesses had been injured while there was no real impact on the market. For if the commerce clause truly protects only the interstate market, as the *Exxon* Court held, then proof that there are no in-state surrogates (consumers or others) for interstate interests comes very close to being proof that there has been no violation at all.

It should be noted that state regulations are rarely struck down for the explicit reason that they are the product of unrepresentative political processes. Rather, this political defect should be seen as underlying the forms of economic discrimination which the Supreme Court has treated as invalidating certain state actions with respect to interstate commerce.[25]

§ 6–6. Restrictions on Access to Local Markets by Out-of-State Sellers and Suppliers

The validity of state regulations limiting the extent to which out-of-state sellers and suppliers have access to state markets has depended heavily upon the reasons for which the regulations were imposed. State efforts to protect local economic interests through measures limiting access to local markets by out-of-state sellers or suppliers have

---

24. Even the dissent in *Exxon v. Maryland* endorsed a version of the surrogate-representation approach, suggesting that the Court's decision might be correct if production or refining of oil took place in Maryland, because the industry would then have had a "fair opportunity to influence their local legislators and thereby to prevent the enactment of economically disruptive legislation." 437 U.S. at 151 (Blackmun, J., dissenting).

25. A similar political defect may also underlie the Supreme Court's refusal, in some instances, to give national preemptive effect to federal regulations adopted by essentially local processes. See Florida Lime & Avocado Growers, Inc. v. Paul, 373 U.S. 132 (1963), discussed in § 6–25, infra. Although it is no easy task for judges to frame criteria adequate to the task of assessing political unrepresentativeness directly, it is by no means clear that the use of surrogate criteria like "discrimination" is a wholly satisfactory alternative. For an insightful critique of "non-discrimination" as an independently crucial touchstone of commerce clause analysis, see Brown, in § 6–2, supra, note 1, at 225–28. Discrimination is necessarily a central issue, however, in privileges and immunities litigation under article IV. See §§ 6–34 to 6–35, infra.

repeatedly been struck down as inconsistent with the principles underlying the commerce clause. The leading case is *Baldwin v. G.A.F.
Seelig, Inc.*[1] There, New York had sought to protect its dairy farmers
by fixing the minimum price at which their milk could be sold in local
markets;[2] in order to keep this fixed price from being undercut by out-
of-state suppliers in the competition generated by New York's raising of
the in-state price level, New York barred the resale within its borders
of any milk purchased at prices below the New York minimum.[3] In a
seminal opinion by Justice Cardozo, the Supreme Court unanimously
struck down the New York regulations insofar as they applied to milk
purchased outside the state: "If New York, in order to promote the
economic welfare of her farmers, may guard them against competition
with the cheaper prices of Vermont, the door has been opened to
rivalries and reprisals that were meant to be averted by subjecting
commerce between the states to the power of the nation. The Constitution was framed under the dominion of a political philosophy less
parochial in range. It was framed upon the theory that the peoples of
the several states must sink or swim together, and that in the long run
prosperity and salvation are in union and not division."[4]

The Supreme Court has reacted more favorably, however, to nondiscriminatory regulations protecting local residents from the deceptive
or socially intrusive trade practices of local and out-of-state sellers
alike. For example, in *California v. Thompson*,[5] the Court upheld a
state measure which sought to limit fraud in the local sale of intrastate

§ 6-6

1. 294 U.S. 511 (1935) (striking down
New York State's refusal of a milk-selling
license to a dealer who had procured his
milk in Vermont at a price below the floor
set by New York for in-state purchases).

2. The intrastate aspects of New York's
regulatory scheme had been upheld in
Nebbia v. New York, 291 U.S. 502 (1934)
and Hegeman Farms Corp. v. Baldwin, 293
U.S. 163 (1934).

3. It has been suggested that the regulation might have been upheld if it had
merely required payment to the state of
the difference between the minimum price
and the price actually paid the suppliers
for their milk, whether produced within or
without the state. See Note, "Commerce
Clause Decisions: 1936–1942," 42 Colum.L.
Rev. 1333, 1336 n. 31 (1942); cf. Henneford
v. Silas Mason Co., 300 U.S. 577, 585–86
(1937), discussed in § 6–17, infra.

4. Baldwin v. G.A.F. Seelig, Inc., 294
U.S. 511, 522–23 (1935). See also id. at
527; Polar Ice Cream & Creamery Co. v.
Andrews, 375 U.S. 361 (1964) (Florida may
not regulate the business of local milk distributors in a way that deprives out-of-
state milk suppliers of a share in the local
market by compelling local distributors to
accept their total supply from designated
local suppliers); Minnesota v. Barber, 136
U.S. 313 (1890) (invalidating state law

which effectively decreed that only meat
processed in Minnesota could be sold
there). But cf. Henneford v. Silas Mason
Co., 300 U.S. 577 (1937), discussed in § 6–
17, infra. The theme of Baldwin v. Seelig
is close to that of article IV's privileges and
immunities clause. See §§ 6–34 to 6–35,
infra. See also Great Atl. & Pac. Tea Co.,
Inc. v. Cottrell, 424 U.S. 366, 375 (1976)
(holding that Mississippi cannot condition
the right to sell milk produced or processed
in another state on that state's reciprocal
acceptance of milk produced or processed
in Mississippi; contention that the reciprocity provision serves Mississippi's
health interest "borders on the frivolous").
The Court has also held that a state cannot
prevent out-of-state sellers from marking
the containers in which they ship their
products into the state with designations
indicating the state of origin and that
state's classification of the products in
question; an open economy entails a right
to appeal to positive consumer attitudes
toward the state of a product's origin and
to take advantage of that state's superior
classification scheme. Hunt v. Washington State Apple Advertising Commission,
432 U.S. 333 (1977) (crates of Washington
State apples cannot be prevented by North
Carolina from bearing Washington State
grade).

5. 313 U.S. 109 (1941).

and interstate automobile tours by requiring that all ticket agents be licensed by the state. Similarly, in *Breard v. Alexandria*,[6] the Supreme Court approved a municipal privacy ordinance which banned unconsented door-to-door solicitation by both out-of-state and local salesmen.[7]

Health and environmental regulations which incidentally limit access to local markets by out-of-state sellers have likewise been upheld with some regularity. For example, in *Mintz v. Baldwin*,[8] the Court upheld a New York law requiring all cattle imported into the state for dairy or breeding purposes to be certified as coming from herds free of Bang's disease. The Court's arguably unfortunate willingness to sustain that law notwithstanding its possibly unwarranted discrimination against suppliers of out-of-state cattle [9] serves to underscore the high judicial tolerance for measures that appear reasonably calculated to advance local interests distinct from the economic. Especially when such measures do not discriminate on their face between in-state and out-of-state enterprises, not even a heavy burden on out-of-state enterprises is likely to result in their invalidation when the interests they serve "are . . . not divisible by the same units of measurement as [the] economic loss to [outside] industry," [10] so that the process of weighing burdens against benefits seems inescapably political. In such cases, the tendency is to leave to state legislatures the task of striking the balance, subject only to the power of Congress to override their choices.[11]

Even when a challenged rule discriminates against interstate commerce on its face, the Court remains solicitous of legitimate—that is, non-protectionist—local concerns. In *Maine v. Taylor*,[12] the Court upheld a law prohibiting the importation of live baitfish after requiring Maine to show that its statute served a legitimate local purpose that could not be served as well by nondiscriminatory means.[13] The Court

6. 341 U.S. 622 (1951).

7. Cf. Head v. New Mexico Board of Examiners in Optometry, 374 U.S. 424 (1963) ("The statute [regulating the sale of eyeglasses] thus falls within the most traditional concept of . . . the police power . . . . A state law may not be struck down on the mere showing that its administration affects interstate commerce in some way").

8. 289 U.S. 346 (1933).

9. It should be noted that in Mintz, the Supreme Court failed to inquire into whether the state regulation was discriminatory—that is, whether New York imposed similar restrictions on local settlers. If, as appears, no similar restriction was locally imposed, New York should have been required to show that the condition feared was peculiar to out-of-state herds. Contrast the decision in Hannibal & St. Joseph R. v. Husen, 95 U.S. 465 (1877) (invalidating Missouri statute prohibiting bringing certain cattle into the state for designated three-fourths of year; such interference with interstate commerce not

shown to be "absolutely necessary" to protect health).

10. American Can Co. v. Oregon Liquor Control Comm'n, 15 Or.App. 618, 517 P.2d 691, 697 (1973) (upholding against commerce clause attack the Oregon Bottle Bill, which required all soft drinks and beer sold in Oregon to be packaged in returnable containers). Accord, Brotherhood of Locomotive Firemen and Enginemen v. Chicago, R.I. & P.R. Co., 393 U.S. 129 (1968) (state full-crew laws upheld where balancing safety against adverse economic impact deemed a "legislative judgment").

11. See also § 6–7, infra.

12. 106 S.Ct. 2440 (1986).

13. Id. at 2449–2450. See Hughes v. Oklahoma, 441 U.S. 322, 336 (1979), discussed in § 6–10, infra. A number of commentators have argued that this standard, as applied, was so strict that it could never be met. See, e.g., Sedler, "The Negative Commerce Clause as a Restriction on State Regulation and Taxation: An Analysis in Terms of Constitutional Structure," 31 Wayne L.Rev. 885, 897 (1985). Taylor be-

accepted the district court's findings that (1) Maine's fisheries are unique and fragile; (2) parasites and non-native sea animals in baitfish shipments would import disease and upset the aquatic ecology of these fisheries; and (3) there exists no satisfactory way to inspect baitfish shipments to screen out such problems.[14] *Taylor* demonstrates that even overt discrimination against nonresidents or nonresident interests may be upheld under the commerce clause, as under the privileges and immunities clause of article IV, if it can be shown that the out-of-state interests "constitute a particular source of the evil at which the statute is aimed." [15]

Even if a statute's direct aims clearly include revamping an interstate market, the Court may yet be inclined to uphold the challenged law if it is facially neutral and is not structured so as to impose a manifestly discriminatory or transparently excessive burden on interstate commerce. Thus, in *Exxon Corporation v. Governor of Maryland*,[16] the Court upheld a statute that required vertically-integrated oil companies, whether in-state or out-of-state, to divest themselves of their retail operations. Although the statute's burden fell overwhelmingly on out-of-state firms,[17] the Court was untroubled by this differential impact. Justice Stevens' opinion for the majority asserted that the commerce clause "protects the interstate market, not particular interstate firms, from prohibitive or burdensome regulation." [18]

This aspect of the *Exxon* holding was expressly distinguished in *Lewis v. BT Investment Managers, Inc.*,[19] where the Court unanimously struck down a Florida law that prohibited out-of-state banking institutions from controlling in-state investment advisory firms. The facial neutrality of the Maryland statute upheld in *Exxon*, which operated to the detriment of all vertically-integrated oil companies, was markedly absent from Florida's law, which discriminated among affected business entities according to the extent of their contacts with the local economy.[20] The law ran afoul of the commerce clause because it protected domestic financial conglomerates from competition by their out-of-state counterparts. In *Exxon*, by contrast, in-state firms were given no advantage over competing out-of-state concerns, and since there was no evidence that the regulation had adversely affected the flow of interstate goods and service as such, the statute was within the limits imposed by the dormant commerce clause.[21]

lies this view, although it is an exceptional case: the state succeeded in making a difficult factual showing that few litigants will be able to match.

14. 106 S.Ct. at 2450, 2452–53.

15. Toomer v. Witsell, 334 U.S. 385, 398 (1948). See Taylor, 106 S.Ct. at 2453 n. 19; United Building & Trades Union v. Camden, 465 U.S. 208, 222 (1984). See §§ 6–34 and 6–35, infra.

16. 437 U.S. 117 (1978).

17. Of the 199 service stations affected by the law, all but two were run by out-of-

state companies. Of the remaining 3,581 stations unaffected by the law, all but 34 were run by local retail dealers. 437 U.S. at 137–38 (Blackmun, J., concurring in part and dissenting in part).

18. 437 U.S. at 127–28.

19. 447 U.S. 27 (1980), discussed further in § 6–33, infra.

20. Id. at 41–43.

21. Id. at 125–26. See also Minnesota v. Clover Leaf Creamery Co., 449 U.S. 456 (1981), discussed in § 6–5, supra.

Behind the Court's analysis in *Exxon* stands an important doctrinal theme: the negative implications of the commerce clause derive principally from a *political* theory of union, not from an *economic* theory of free trade. The function of the clause is to ensure national solidarity, not economic efficiency.[22] Although the Court's commerce clause opinions have often employed the language of economics, the decisions have not interpreted the Constitution as establishing the inviolability of the free market. More particularly, the constitutional vice of economic protectionism is not implicated by a regulation which makes impossible the economies of scale that a fully open market permits. As Justice Stevens stressed for the *Exxon* Court, the commerce clause does not protect "the particular structures or methods of operation in a retail market."[23]

§ 6–7. Restrictions on Access to Local Transportation Facilities by Out-of-State Users

While a state may not restrict access to its transportation facilities in order to regulate economic competition,[1] it has long been accepted as a general proposition that a state may regulate the use of its railroad tracks and highways in the interest of public safety.[2] The Court originally responded to the potential for conflict between the dictates of the dormant commerce clause and state pursuit of public safety by establishing a unitary approach to transportation regulations in *Cooley v. Board of Wardens*,[3] where the Court reviewed a Pennsylvania law requiring vessels in the port of Philadephia to employ local harbor pilots. The Court upheld the regulation and announced a general principle of allowing states great leeway in such matters, while saying that it would not allow state restrictions on the freedom of interstate movement where the subjects of the regulation were "in their nature national, or admit of only one uniform system" because these subjects "may justly be said to be of such a nature as to require exclusive regulation by Congress."[4]

Federal judicial tolerance for state autonomy has particularly been the rule when a federal court has been asked not to review a general

---

22. See, e.g., Baldwin v. G.A.F. Seelig, Inc., 294 U.S. 511, 522–23 (1935).

23. 437 U.S. at 127. Nonetheless, the Court may be faulted for neglecting to respond more explicitly to Justice Blackmun's cogent argument that the statute constituted an unconstitutional discrimination against out-of-state oil companies while protecting a group of retailers overwhelmingly composed of local businessmen. Id. at 140–141 (Blackmun, J., dissenting). Justice Blackmun's conclusion was bolstered by the state's failure to show that its legitimate goals—preserving retail competition and preventing unfair trade practices such as predatory pricing—were actually threatened by the participation of vertically integrated oil companies in Maryland's retail gasoline market, or that those interests could not be served by nar-

rowly drawn measures prohibiting the feared abuses. Id. at 141–45.

§ 6–7

1. See Buck v. Kuykendall, 267 U.S. 307 (1925) (Washington's refusal to license a common carrier to operate between Seattle, Washington, and Portland, Oregon on the ground that the route was already "adequately served" was held impermissible, given Oregon's prior certification of the carrier to operate that route as evidence of *its* view that the route was *not* yet served to capacity).

2. See, e.g., Smith v. Alabama, 124 U.S. 465 (1888).

3. 53 U.S. (12 How.) 299 (1851), discussed in § 6–4, supra.

4. Id. at 319.

safety rule but to reverse a specific and apparently reasonable adjudication of transportation privileges. For example, in *Bradley v. Public Utilities Commission of Ohio*,[5] the Supreme Court upheld Ohio's refusal to license an interstate common carrier over a particular route because of the traffic congestion on that route, noting that the carrier received a full hearing on the issue and failed to choose another available route. And such tolerance has predictably prevailed when states have sought to condition use of their highways by interstate travelers upon compliance with regulations reasonably calculated to facilitate enforcement of independently valid criminal laws. In *Duckworth v. Arkansas*,[6] the Court rejected a commerce clause challenge to a state requirement that interstate transporters of alcohol obtain a permit before traveling through the state: the object of the rule was to give local officials advance notice so that they could take steps to prevent unlawful diversion of liquor into the state.[7]

In applying the *Cooley* test, the Court settled for a time upon a bifurcated approach in which the degree of permitted state regulation of transportation effectively depended on whether goods crossed state lines by highway or rail. In *South Carolina State Highway Department v. Barnwell Brothers*,[8] the Court upheld a South Carolina statute that, unlike regulations in nearly every other state, barred from the state's highways trucks greater than 90 inches in width or ten tons in loaded weight. The Court left to the state the task of deciding the need for such safety measures, arguing that "the judicial function, under the commerce clause as well as the fourteenth amendment, stops with the inquiry . . . whether the means of regulation chosen are reasonably adapted to the end sought."[9] Under this minimal level of scrutiny, myriad road safety regulations have received the Court's imprimatur.[10]

However, in *Southern Pacific Co. v. Arizona*,[11] Justice Stone, who had authored the unanimous *Barnwell* opinion, wrote a decision for the Court striking down a statute outlawing trains more than 14 passenger cars or 70 freight cars in length from operating within Arizona. Between 93 and 95% of the rail traffic affected by the regulation was interstate; such train limit laws were enforced only in Arizona and Oklahoma. Trains crossing the border either had to be broken up into shorter segments and reformed upon leaving the state, or had to conform to the limit from the beginning to the end of their journeys.

---

5. 289 U.S. 92 (1933).

6. 314 U.S. 390 (1941).

7. For a discussion of the effect of the twenty-first amendment on the commerce clause, see § 6–24, infra.

8. 303 U.S. 177 (1938).

9. Id. at 190.

10. See, e.g., Hendrick v. Maryland, 235 U.S. 610 (1915) (non-residents may be compelled to obtain driver's licences); Morris v. Duby, 274 U.S. 135 (1927) (speed and size of trucks may be regulated). See generally McCormick, "The Regulation of Motor Transportation," 22 Calif.L.Rev. 24 (1933);

Powell, "Current Conflicts Between the Commerce Clause and State Police Power," 12 Minn.L.Rev. 321, 470, 607 (1928). Not all highway safety regulations have been sanctioned, especially in more recent decades. In Bibb v. Navajo Freight Lines, Inc., 359 U.S. 520, 529 (1959), the Court struck down an Illinois mudguard law, observing: "This is one those cases—few in number—where local safety measures that are nondiscriminatory place an unconstitutional burden on interstate commerce." See § 6–12, infra.

11. 325 U.S. 761 (1945).

Either alternative entailed enormous costs, and there was evidence that the incremental increase in safety garnered through shorter trains was completely offset by the incremental hazards of operating a larger number of trains.[12] The same Justice who had opined in *Barnwell* that "courts do not sit as legislatures," [13] now declared that the " 'convenient apologetics of the police power' " do not relieve the Court of the responsibility of weighing the safety evidence for itself.[14] Because the states could not provide uniform regulation of railroad transportation, allowing diverse state regulation of this mode of transportation would subject interstate carriers to a "crazy-quilt of state laws." [15]

The same analysis was apparently not thought to apply with equal force to interstate truck traffic in the late 1930s, before the ambitious federal highway building program forever changed the American landscape. The *Southern Pacific* Court distinguished *Barnwell* on the ground that the state had constructed the highways (whereas railroads were privately built) and was therefore entitled to control the conditions under which they may be used in order to promote safety.[16]

Several developments suggest that the *Barnwell* exception to the *Cooley* doctrine has narrowed considerably. First, the intervening decades have witnessed an explosion in interstate truck traffic and the relative decline of the role of the iron horse; it is no longer safe to assume, if it ever was, that traffic on state highways is predominantly local. Second, the collapse of the traditional "right/privilege" distinction has undercut the foundation of the notion that a state has the right, free of independent constitutional norms such as the commerce clause, to condition the use of those "gratuities" such as highways that it chooses to provide.[17] Third, the Court's recent transportation cases suggest that the screws of judicial review are tightening on state highway safety laws, to the point that Justice Rehnquist has been heard to lament that "the only state truck-length limit 'that is valid is one which this Court has not been able to get its hands on.' " [18]

Thus, in *Raymond Motor Transportation, Inc. v. Rice*,[19] while reciting that the states are primarily responsible for the construction and maintenance of highways and that highway conditions vary from state to state,[20] and while paying lip service to the superiority of legislatures over courts in making policy judgments and weighing evidence,[21] the Court had no difficulty striking down a Wisconsin law banning from state highways trucks longer than 55 feet. The Court largely discounted the state's safety claims because Wisconsin made no effort to rebut a massive array of evidence showing that the regulation made no real contribution to highway safety. Nor did the state contradict the

12. 325 U.S. at 775–76.

13. 303 U.S. at 190.

14. 325 U.S. at 780.

15. Morgan v. Virginia, 328 U.S. 373, 388 (1946) (Frankfurter, J., concurring).

16. 325 U.S. at 783.

17. See § 10–8, infra.

18. Kassel v. Consolidated Freightways Corp., 450 U.S. 662, 687 (1981) (Rehnquist, J., dissenting).

19. 434 U.S. 429 (1978).

20. Id. at 444 n.18.

21. Id. at 449 (Blackmun, J., concurring).

trucking company's showing that the regulation imposed a substantial burden of delay and expense on the interstate movement of goods.

Perhaps most significant, the Court noted the numerous administrative exceptions the state had made to permit the use of oversized vehicles by in-state manufacturers and important Wisconsin industries.[22] But it is not the resulting discriminatory impact on non-residents that distinguishes *Raymond* from the Court's previous transportation cases, so much as the Court's willingness to look for and recognize the implication of such an impact. For example, in *Brotherhood of Locomotive Firemen & Enginemen v. Chicago, R.I. & P.R. Co.*,[23] the Court upheld an Arkansas law requiring trains traveling more than a specified distance within the state to be operated by a designated minimum crew, despite the Court's awareness that the particular distance threshhold chosen by the state legislature had the effect of exempting all of Arkansas' intrastate railroads from the regulation. All but one of the Justices [24] found that narrowing the law's application to interstate train traffic was rationally related to the legitimate state goal of averting an adverse economic impact on local railroads![25] In contrast, Justice Powell argued for the *Raymond* Court that exemptions of this type weaken the presumption in favor of safety regulations by undermining the political pressure that local interests may bring to bear on state lawmakers who frame burdensome regulations.[26]

While all the Justices were persuaded that the Wisconsin statute in *Raymond* violated the commerce clause, the Court divided over the right approach to review of safety regulations. Wisconsin pointed out that the Court had previously refused to balance safety considerations against burdens on interstate commerce,[27] relying on language in *Barnwell* suggesting that highway safety measures were subject to a "rational relation" test rather than a balancing test.[28] Justice Powell's opinion for the Court [29] rejected that contention, stating that "the inquiry necessarily involves a sensitive consideration of the weight and nature of the state regulatory concern in light of the extent of the burden imposed on interstate commerce."[30] Justice Blackmun's concurring opinion [31] also rejected Wisconsin's contention, but only insofar as the cases show the court weighing "slight or problematical" safety interests against the national interest in uninhibited commerce: "[I]f safety justifications are not illusory, the Court will not second-guess legislative judgment about their importance in comparison with related burdens on interstate commerce."[32]

Raymond should be read as a warning to state legislatures and to lower courts that they cannot refuse to balance the local and national

---

22. 434 U.S. at 447; id. at 450–51 (Blackmun, J., concurring).

23. 393 U.S. 129 (1968).

24. Justice Douglas dissented on the separate ground that Congress had preempted the field. Id. at 144.

25. Id. at 142.

26. Id. at 444 n.18, 446.

27. 434 U.S. at 442–43.

28. For a discussion of rationality tests, see Chapter 16, infra.

29. This opinion was joined by every Justice except Justice Stevens, who took no part in the consideration of the case.

30. 434 U.S. at 441.

31. Joined by Chief Justice Burger and Justices Brennan and Rehnquist.

32. 434 U.S. at 449.

interests promoted and impaired by a state law. Contrary to some suggestions, courts sometimes *must* attempt to "weigh" non-comparables.[33] The point is not that such concerns as local health and safety on the one hand and increased cost to outside industry on the other be reduced to some common unit of measurement, but that the state's accommodation between such concerns must be critically assessed. The presumption of validity for traffic regulations and other judicial rules of thumb cannot be applied mechanically. As the Court unanimously observed in *Raymond*, "experience teaches that no single conceptual approach identifies all of the factors that may bear on a particular case." [34] In every case, the judiciary is called upon to make a "delicate adjustment of the conflicting state and federal claims." [35]

One of the quirks of the *Raymond* litigation—that the state made no visible effort to defend the effectiveness of its regulation—might have cast doubt on the force of the Court's insistence that state interests be weighed against the constitutional concern with unimpeded commerce. After all, how hard could it be to compare the apples of safety with the oranges of commerce when the state all but admits by default that its apples are full of worms? But the decision in *Kassel v. Consolidated Freightways Corp.*[36] makes clear that courts must weigh the state's asserted interests in safety even where they are substantiated by more than the hollow claims made for them in *Raymond*.

Kassel invalidated under the commerce clause an Iowa law banning the use of 65-foot double tractor trailers on its highways. A plurality of the Court [37] found that the rule substantially burdened interstate commerce because loads carried by 65-foot doubles had to be routed around Iowa or reloaded onto smaller trucks for shipment through the state. The truck company adduced substantial evidence that the bigger trucks were at least as safe as the smaller ones, and that any reduction in accidents achieved by decreased truck footage would be offset by the heightened accident opportunities created by increased truck mileage, as more small truck-miles were logged to carry the same loads previously managed by the 65-foot doubles. And, once again, the Justices noted a maze of exemptions which allowed many Iowans the benefits of the larger trucks.

Justices Brennan and Marshall concurred in the opinion, choosing to analyze the state's motives for the adoption of the rule rather than to debate the relative safety merits of large and small trucks. The legislative history of the rule, the Iowa Governor's veto message, and the state's defense of the rule in the lower courts revealed that the state's real motive was to reduce interstate traffic on its roads. The concurring Justices found this motive to be "*protectionist* in nature" and therefore impermissible.[38]

---

33. See § 6–6, supra.

34. 434 U.S. at 441.

35. H. P. Hood & Sons, Inc. v. Du Mond, 336 U.S. 525, 553 (1949) (Black, J., dissenting).

36. 450 U.S. 662 (1981).

37. Justice Powell wrote for himself and for Justices White, Blackmun and Stevens.

38. 450 U.S. at 685.

The doctrinal divide that separates the plurality from the concurrence in *Kassel* may be far narrower than it seems, and a closer examination of that divide may shed light on the bond between the commerce clause and the privileges and immunities clause of article IV. The motivation analysis undertaken by Justice Brennan concludes, contrary to the factual inquiry of the plurality, that the Iowa statute would in fact produce the safety advantages claimed for it by the state. Although more accidents might well occur after the law's implementation, either because more truck miles would be traveled by smaller trucks or because the allegedly more dangerous double-trucks would have to travel as far or farther in order to bypass Iowa, the important point for Iowa legislators was that this increase in truck traffic and accidents would take place *outside* Iowa. The plurality's emphasis on the mere statistical incidence of trucking accidents was therefore misplaced, because Iowa's concern was with the place, not the frequency, of highway deaths. Those who would die because of Iowa's rule might be citizens of Illinois, Wisconsin or Missouri, but they and their kin would never vote in Iowa elections even if they managed to survive the stampede of giant killer trucks.

Kassel thus stands for the rule that under the commerce clause a state may not reduce the risks posed to its own citizens by the stream of commerce by diverting that stream out-of-state, thereby increasing the hazards to non-residents, any more than a state may "isolate itself from the [problems of poverty] common to all states by restraining the transportation of [indigent] persons . . . across its borders." [39] The privileges and immunities clause of article IV likewise requires that the states show the same regard for the citizens of other states that they would for their own when a state's rules affect outsiders.[40] *Kassel* shows how commonly, in an interdependent economy, a state's rules may burden out-of-staters even when they remain out-of-state—and how cavalierly non-residents' lives may be jeopardized when they do not have the power to vote against those who would thrust risks upon them.

§ 6–8. **Restrictions on Access by Out-of-State Buyers to Scarce Local Resources or Commodities: Price, Production, and Use Controls**

American agricultural production routinely tends to outrun demand, depressing food prices below the level which American farmers think necessary for their profitable survival. Agricultural interests have persistently pressured both the state and federal governments to take some action to alleviate the conditions brought about by this endemic oversupply. State governments have generally responded in two ways: (a) *by fixing prices* at levels above those that could be obtained in the open market; and (b) *by regulating agricultural produc-*

---

39. Edwards v. California, 314 U.S. 160, 173–74 (1941) (striking down a Depression-era law making it a misdemeanor knowingly to bring a non-resident indigent into the state), discussed in § 16–34, infra.

40. But see Edgar v. MITE Corp., 457 U.S. 624 (1982) (denying that states have any legitimate interest in protecting non-resident shareholders), discussed in § 6–12, infra.

tion and allocation in ways that control the supply made available for sale in the market. Both forms of regulation have also been used to conserve scarce local resources and are vulnerable to commerce clause challenge to the degree that they adversely affect out-of-state buyers.

States may control the price which local sellers charge out-of-state buyers only to the extent that such regulation of the interstate market is an incidental consequence of regulation of the local market. For example, in *Milk Control Board v. Eisenberg Farm Products*,[1] the Supreme Court held that Pennsylvania could fix the price charged by local dealers selling to a Pennsylvania-based processing company that subsequently shipped the milk it purchased to New York. The Court noted: (a) that the regulated transaction took place entirely within Pennsylvania; (b) that the state could not effectively control the price paid for milk eventually consumed in Pennsylvania if it were not permitted incidentally to fix the price of milk purchased in Pennsylvania but later shipped out-of-state; and (c) that "[only] a small fraction of the milk produced . . . in Pennsylvania is shipped out of the Commonwealth."[2] In earlier cases, this last factor had been absent. Thus, for example, in *Lemke v. Farmers Grain Co.*,[3] a North Dakota attempt to fix the price paid by interstate dealers for local grain was found by the Supreme Court to be unconstitutional, given the absence of any significant local market for the regulated commodity.[4]

In *Cities Service Gas Co. v. Peerless Oil and Gas Co.*,[5] the substantial state interest in natural gas conservation substituted for the incidental character of the interstate agricultural price regulations affirmed in *Eisenberg*, as the Supreme Court approved an Oklahoma program attempting to reduce economic waste by fixing the price paid by a pipeline monopoly for natural gas produced by local suppliers, even though the gas was destined almost exclusively for out-of-state users.[6] The decision in *Cities Service* seems dubious in light of the major concern of the commerce clause with avoiding any state's exploitation of its geographical or resource position "to the disadvantage and displeasure of [its] less strategically situated neighbors."[7]

Like price controls that incidentally but significantly affect consumers of a state's exports, even production controls which substantially affect interstate commerce are not unconstitutional *per se* under the commerce clause. In *Parker v. Brown*,[8] for example, the Supreme Court upheld a complex California plan for regulating the supply of

---

§ 6-8

1. 306 U.S. 346 (1939).

2. Id. at 353. Justice Roberts, writing for the Court, invoked language reminiscent of *Cooley*: "But in matters requiring diversity of treatment according to the special requirements of local conditions, the States remain free to act within their respective jurisdictions until Congress sees fit to act." Id. at 351.

3. 258 U.S. 50 (1922).

4. See also Shafer v. Farmers Grain Co., 268 U.S. 189 (1925).

5. 340 U.S. 179 (1950).

6. "That a legitimate local interest is at stake in this case is clear. A state is justifiably concerned with preventing rapid and uneconomic disruption of one of its chief natural resources." 340 U.S. at 187. This case is discussed from another doctrinal perspective in § 6–13, infra.

7. Brown, in § 6–1, supra, note 1, at 228. See also id. at 233 n. 72.

8. 317 U.S. 341 (1943).

raisins made available on the market even though 95% of the raisins sold in California eventually found their way into interstate commerce. The Court noted the substantial state interest in production control and found no contrary federal interest, given the way in which the state program filled a gap in the larger federal statutory scheme of agricultural production regulation.[9]

Production controls are forbidden, however, if they discriminate against or expressly exclude interstate commerce. Thus, in *H. P. Hood & Sons, Inc. v. Du Mond*,[10] the Supreme Court held that New York could not maintain a constant supply of milk for its local markets by preventing a milk processor serving Massachusetts markets from establishing an additional receiving plant in New York.[11]

Similarly, in rationing scarce natural resources previously made unconditionally available to out-of-state users, a state may not allocate the available supply in a way that favors local users at the expense of out-of-state consumers.[12] For example, in *Philadelphia v. New Jersey*,[13] the Court struck down a New Jersey law barring the importation of solid or liquid waste destined for disposal in the state's rapidly-filling sanitary landfills. New Jersey sought to extend the life of its existing landfill sites and to minimize the need for new ones that would force the loss of scarce open lands by stemming the flow of out-of-state waste.[14] The Court accepted the state's environmental and health goals, but reminded New Jersey that "the evil of protectionism can reside in legislative means as well as legislative ends." [15]

The Court assumed that New Jersey could accomplish its goals by slowing the flow of all waste into the scarce landfills, even though interstate commerce would incidentally be affected.[16] But the state

9. The Court also seized upon the fact that the regulations involved purportedly took their effect before interstate commerce commenced. 317 U.S. at 361. The observation, however, seems functionally irrelevant: the fact that the regulations take their toll before interstate shipment hardly divests the transaction of its interstate character or the regulations of their out-of-state impact; the spectre of commercial rivalry that actuated the Framers is certainly not dispelled by this particular chronology. Further aspects of this case are discussed in § 6–26, infra.

10. 336 U.S. 525 (1949).

11. The Court proceeded formulaically—submitting that states could not burden interstate commerce—and obscured the balancing process that was actually taking place. In a similar case, United States v. Rock Royal Cooperative, Inc., 307 U.S. 533 (1939), the Court rejected the argument that the regulatory scheme did not implicate the commerce clause because the sales in question were consummated before interstate commerce began. It held that, where commodities are bought for out-of-state use, the sale is "part of interstate commerce." Id. at 568–69. See also Lem-

ke v. Farmers Grain Co., 258 U.S. 50 (1922); Currin v. Wallace, 306 U.S. 1 (1939).

12. See Pennsylvania v. West Virginia, 262 U.S. 553 (1923) (holding unconstitutional a West Virginia statute requiring West Virginia natural gas producers to give first preference to their local customers). Presumably, Congress could prohibit interstate shipments of a product until local demands were satisfied, or authorize the states to do the same. See H. P. Hood & Sons v. Du Mond, 336 U.S. 525, 542 (1949) (dictum).

13. 437 U.S. 617 (1978).

14. The law also, of course, had the effect of reducing the price residents would have to pay for waste disposal by eliminating out-of-state competition for limited space and by delaying the day when New Jersey's cities would have to transport their refuse to more distant and more expensive locations.

15. 437 U.S. at 626.

16. See, e.g., Minnesota v. Clover Leaf Creamery, 449 U.S. 456 (1981) (upholding power of state to ban sale of milk in non-biodegradable, non-refillable plastic con-

could not accomplish its objectives, however worthy, by means which discriminated against "articles of commerce coming from outside the state unless there is some reason, apart from their origin, to treat them differently." [17]   There was neither argument nor evidence that out-of-state garbage was more noxious than the domestic variety, and thus New Jersey's law was treated as typical protectionist legislation, subject to "a virtually per se rule of invalidity." [18]

To the extent that some early livestock quarantine cases might be understood as inconsistent with the Court's reasoning in *Philadelphia v. New Jersey*,[19] the critical distinction lies in the sort of burden that the policy of exclusion imposed on the excluded states and their citizens. The cattle quarantine cases at most put the home state to the task of disposing of some diseased cows or contaminated meat.[20]   In our advanced industrial society, the burden that a waste exclusion law imposes is obviously of a different magnitude: even if New Jersey could think of no better solution to the mounting waste disposal problem, neither could its neighbors count on finding more suitable disposal sites.   The states may no more solve their waste problems by rerouting the market's allocation of that waste than they may solve their highway safety problems by routing the market's private participants, and all their attendant hazards, through neighboring states.[21] *Philadelphia v. New Jersey* thus lays the foundation for a unified approach to state and local attempts to fence out national problems.   When the inscription on the base of the Statue of Liberty invites the world's "wretched refuse" to these shores, it extends an invitation to join a union of states that are not free to halt the flow of supposed undesirables—whether human [22] or inanimate—at their respective borders.   For the commerce clause can have no tolerance for politically expedient decisions "by one State to isolate itself in the stream of interstate commerce from a

tainers, regardless of where the containers and milk originated).

17.   437 U.S. at 627.   The Court rejected the argument that the dormant commerce clause did not apply because garbage is not a legitimate subject of commerce, apparently satisfied that anything someone pays to move across state lines comes within the stream of interstate commerce.   See 437 U.S. at 622; see also Sporhase v. Nebraska ex rel. Douglas, 458 U.S. 941 (1982) (submitting to commerce clause scrutiny interstate transfers of ground water, even where, under state law, only a usufructuary right was recognized in ground water, which could not be reduced to possession). Of course, in Philadelphia v. New Jersey, the commerce in question was not trade in sewage or trash itself, but a service (waste disposal) or a resource (empty landfill space) of a different color.

18.   437 U.S. at 624; see id. at 627.   If New Jersey itself entered the garbage-disposal market—e.g., by investing substantial public resources in developing facilities to dispose of wastes (nuclear or convention-

al)—it could invoke the "market participant" exception to justify preferring instate wastes.   See § 6–11, infra.

19.   See 437 U.S. at 629–33 (Rehnquist, J., dissenting).

20.   See, e.g., Reid v. Colorado, 187 U.S. 137 (1902) (upholding law requiring inspection of livestock coming from other states with purpose of excluding diseased animals, on record in which nothing indicated that affected cattlemen could not reasonably comply).   Blatantly protectionist or otherwise unreasonable statutes were routinely struck down.   See, e.g., Hannibal & St. J. Railroad Co. v. Husen, 95 U.S. (5 Otto) 465 (1877) (statute prohibiting importation of cattle into Missouri during eight months of year, whether particular cattle were diseased or not, held not to be a legitimate quarantine law).

21.   See Kassel v. Consolidated Freightways Corp., 450 U.S. 662 (1981), discussed in § 6–7, supra.

22.   See Edwards v. California, 314 U.S. 160 (1941).

problem shared by all." [23] To put a gloss on Justice Cardozo's memorable summation, "the peoples of the several states must sink or swim together," [24] even in their collective garbage. [25]

§ 6–9. Restrictions Which Put Pressure on Out-of-State Businesses to Relocate Within the Regulating State

The Supreme Court "has viewed with particular suspicion state statutes requiring business operations to be performed in the home State that could more efficiently be performed elsewhere." [1] The seminal case is *Pike v. Bruce Church, Inc.*,[2] where the Court held that Arizona could not compel a company growing cantaloupes there to pack the fruit locally, instead of shipping it to California for crating. Cantaloupe crates are labeled with the name of the state in which the fruit is packed, but not with the name of the state in which the fruit was grown. Because Bruce Church fruit was of exceptionally high quality, Arizona had an interest in taking credit for its production. The Court, however, held that this interest was insufficient to justify forcing Bruce Church to move its crating facilities 31 miles, at a cost to the company of some $200,000. "Even where the state is pursuing a clearly legitimate local interest, this particular burden on commerce has been declared to be virtually *per se* illegal." [3]

Such "local grab" regulations have generally taken one of two forms:

(a) regulations which induce business relocations by *prohibiting imports* of out-of-state products unless certain processes have occurred locally; or

(b) regulations which induce business relocations by *prohibiting exports* of local resources unless certain processes have occurred locally.

As to import controls, the Supreme Court has held that even the state or municipal interest in insuring the health of local residents may not be substantial enough to justify regulations which force business relocations by prohibiting imports which have not been subjected to local processing. For example, in *Dean Milk Co. v. City of Madison*,[4] the Court struck down a municipal ordinance forbidding the local sale of milk that had not been pasteurized and bottled at an approved plant within five miles of the center of the city; "reasonable and adequate

---

23. 437 U.S. at 629.

24. Baldwin v. G.A.F. Seelig, Inc., 294 U.S. 511, 523 (1935).

25. Individual states nonetheless retain the freedom to base their internal economic decisions—such as the decision about how heavily to rely on, say, nuclear power plants within their borders to meet their energy needs—upon their assessments of whether the nation as a whole will discover adequate means of disposing of the resulting refuse (e.g., long-term radioactive

waste) in time to prevent plant shutdowns. See Pacific Gas & Electric Co. v. California State Energy Resources Conservation & Development Comm'n, 461 U.S. 190 (1983), discussed in § 6–26, *infra*.

§ 6–9

1. Pike v. Bruce Church, Inc., 397 U.S. 137, 145 (1970).

2. 397 U.S. 137 (1970).

3. Id. at 145.

4. 340 U.S. 349 (1951).

alternatives" could have been found by the city to serve the interest in health.[5]

Neither the state interest in conserving local resources, nor the related state interest in preserving or enhancing the reputation of local products or their processors, justifies state requirements that items must be processed locally before they may be exported. For example, in *Foster-Fountain Packing Co. v. Haydel*,[6] the Supreme Court held that Louisiana could not forbid the exportation of locally-caught shrimp from which the heads and shells had not been removed. The Court found that the state's minimal interest in conserving shrimp heads and shells for local use as chicken feed[7] was clearly outweighed by the adverse impact of the regulation upon interstate commerce. Ninety-five percent of Louisiana shrimp were processed in Mississippi. If the regulation had been upheld, all shrimp canneries located there would have been forced to move to Louisiana. Similarly, in *Toomer v. Witsell*,[8] the Court held that South Carolina could not require that shrimp caught off its coast be unloaded, packed, and stamped at a South Carolina port prior to being taken out-of-state.[9] And in *South-Central Timber Development, Inc. v. Wunnicke*,[10] the Court struck down Alaska's attempt to contractually require that timber felled on state lands be processed within Alaska prior to export.[11]

§ 6–10. State "Ownership" of Natural Resources

Foster-Fountain Packing Co. v. Haydel[1] and *Toomer v. Witsell*[2] did not purport to disturb the rule laid down by several earlier cases that a

5. See also Minnesota v. Barber, 136 U.S. 313 (1890) (state may not prohibit the local sale of meat derived from animals that had not been inspected by local officials within twenty-four hours of the time of slaughter). In Dean Milk, the Court explained that the regulation, which "plainly discriminates against interstate commerce," was impermissible given that it was "not essential for the protection of local health." 340 U.S. at 355–56. If the Court believed the regulation truly essential to the city's well-being, it would no doubt have sustained the action, its discrimination against out-of-staters notwithstanding. The "less restrictive alternative" aspect of this case is discussed in § 6–13, infra. See also Great Atl. & Pac. Tea Co., Inc. v. Cottrell, 424 U.S. 366, 376–78 (1976) (even if insisting on reciprocal acceptance by Louisiana of Mississippi milk as condition of Mississippi's acceptance of Louisiana milk could serve to assure Mississippi that Louisiana's health standards are substantially equivalent to its own, Mississippi must pursue less burdensome alternatives such as applying its own inspection standards to Louisiana milk).

6. 278 U.S. 1 (1928).

7. "They have no market value, cannot be sold or given away, and often constitute

a nuisance." Id. at 9. The Court rendered transparent the claim that the statute was designed to conserve a local resource: "the purpose [of the statute] is not to retain the shrimp for the use of the people of Louisiana; it is to favor the canning of the meat and the manufacture of bran in Louisiana . . . ." Id. at 13.

8. 334 U.S. 385 (1948).

9. The Court expressed concern that "the necessary tendency of the statute is to impose an artificial rigidity on the economic pattern of the industry." Id. at 403–04. Other aspects of this case are discussed in §§ 6–34 to 6–35, infra.

10. 467 U.S. 82 (1984).

11. A parallel federal policy requiring timber taken from federal lands in Alaska to be processed in-state was held insufficient to authorize Alaska's contract policy, since it did not amount to express congressional approval. 467 U.S. at 88–90 (White, J., joined by Brennan, Blackmun and Stevens, JJ.); id. at 101 (Powell, J., joined by Burger, C.J., concurring in part and concurring in the judgment).

§ 6–10

1. 278 U.S. 1 (1928).

2. 334 U.S. 385 (1948).

state may confine the consumption of natural resources like fish, game and streams—resources which have not yet been reduced to private possession and ownership—to consumption occurring wholly within the state's borders.[3] For example, in *Geer v. Connecticut*,[4] the Supreme Court held that a state may forbid the killing of woodcock, ruffled grouse, and quail for purposes of interstate shipment, and may forbid such interstate shipment itself.[5] The Court had long held to the fiction that the state in which wild game was found could forbid the harvest of those animals for export because the state "owned" the wild animals within its borders, and although the commerce clause forbade the states to interfere with the stream of commerce channeled and traveled by the nation's citizens, nothing in the Constitution required the states to put their own possessions up for sale. The *Geer* rule thus pressed upon the Court an artificial ownership distinction, in which lurked all the byzantine niceties of property law,[6] and saddled the Court with the uncomfortable sense that the more a state's game laws burdened commerce, the more likely they were to survive commerce clause scrutiny, since total embargoes were permitted in cases where conditional limitations were not.[7]

In *Hughes v. Oklahoma*,[8] the Court explicitly abandoned *Geer* and invalidated an Oklahoma law barring the export of minnows taken from Oklahoma waters.[9] Even in cases involving state control over natural resources, the balancing test developed in *Pike v. Bruce Church, Inc.*[10] applies, "thus bring[ing the] analytical framework into conformity with practical realities."[11] The Court noted, however, that "the legitimate state concerns for conservation and protection of wild animals underlying the 19th century legal fiction of state ownership" are still among the factors that can be weighed in the balance.[12] Thus the idea of state as trustee for its citizens in ownership of natural resources is

---

3. However, *Foster-Fountain* and *Toomer v. Witsell* do stand for the proposition that, *if* a state allows any out-of-state use of particular local resources, then it cannot allocate or control the use of those resources in a way that needlessly discriminates against dealers, buyers, or ultimate consumers solely because of their out-of-state status. These cases are considered from the perspective of the privileges and immunities clause of article IV in §§ 6–34 to 6–35, infra.

4. 161 U.S. 519 (1896).

5. See also Hudson County Water Co. v. McCarter, 209 U.S. 349 (1908) (New Jersey may prohibit the transport of water from the Passaic River to New York City); Clason v. Indiana, 306 U.S. 439 (1939) (Indiana may prohibit the transportation of dead horses to Illinois); Lee v. New Jersey, 207 U.S. 67 (1907) (New Jersey may regulate the oyster industry carried on under tidal waters within that state); but cf. West v. Kansas Natural Gas Co., 221 U.S. 229 (1911) (natural gas distinguished since, "when reduced to possession, [it] is a commodity").

6. "A state does not stand in the same position as the owner of a private game preserve and it is pure fantasy to talk of 'owning' wild fish, birds or animals. . . . The 'ownership' language was no more than a 19th century legal fiction. . . ." Douglas v. Seacoast Products, Inc., 431 U.S. 265, 284 (1977).

7. See Hughes v. Oklahoma, 441 U.S. 322, 335–36 (1979).

8. 441 U.S. 322 (1979).

9. For an argument that the regulation in Hughes should have been upheld as congressionally authorized, see Hellerstein, "Hughes v. Oklahoma: The Court, the Commerce Clause, and State Control of Natural Resources," 1979 S.Ct.Rev. 51, 54–55 & n. 20.

10. 397 U.S. 137, 142 (1970), discussed in § 6–9, supra.

11. Hughes v. Oklahoma, 441 U.S. at 335.

12. 441 U.S. at 336.

now mediated by the idea prevalent in the rest of the Court's recent commerce clause jurisprudence: a state may not put the burden of achieving in-state environmental goals exclusively on citizens of other states.[13]

If public ownership with respect to wildlife is a dead letter under contemporary commerce clause analysis,[14] the extent to which a state may claim ownership of its inanimate natural resources is also in doubt. In response to the alarming decline of the Ogallala Aquifer, Nebraska enacted legislation requiring that the withdrawal of groundwater for interstate transfer be "reasonable," conducive to "conservation," and "not otherwise detrimental to the public welfare," and further imposed a flat ban on exports to states that did not permit their groundwater to be withdrawn for use in Nebraska.[15] In *Sporhase v. Nebraska ex rel. Douglas*,[16] the Supreme Court upheld the reasonableness requirements but struck down the reciprocity rule.[17] The Court conceded that Nebraska's claim to public ownership of its groundwater was significant,[18] and concluded that, because the state's conservation program contributed to the continuing availability of groundwater, "the natural resource has some indicia of a good publicly produced and owned in which a state may favor its own citizens in times of a shortage."[19] Yet despite the Court's consistent holding in its original jurisdiction cases that a state has a "quasi-sovereign" interest in the subterranean flow of water within its borders,[20] and despite the fact that Nebraska law recognized only a usufructuary right in groundwater and did not allow its "possession" even by Nebraska citizens,[21] the majority in *Sporhase* relied on *Hughes v. Oklahoma* in dubbing the state ownership argument a "legal fiction."[22]

13. See id. at 338–39. See also Philadelphia v. New Jersey, 437 U.S. 617 (1978), discussed in § 6–8, supra. See Wells & Hellerstein, "The Governmental-Proprietary Distinction in Constitutional Law," 66 Va.L.Rev. 1073 (1980) (discussing the market participant exception, see § 6–11, infra, in the context of the Court's treatment of the governmental-proprietary distinction in other doctrinal areas); Comment, "A Proposed Model of the Sovereign/Proprietary Distinction," 133 U.Pa.L.Rev. 661 (1985) (same).

14. The Court has not completely forsaken the "ownership" approach to cases brought under the privileges and immunities clause of article IV. A state may still claim a superior—if not an exclusive—right of exploitation of natural resources such as wildlife on behalf of its citizens to the extent that it has contributed to the resource by maintaining the species or its habitat. See Baldwin v. Fish & Game Comm. of Montana, 436 U.S. 371, 386 (1978) (state may charge non-residents more for a hunting license), discussed in § 6–35, infra.

15. Sporhase v. Nebraska ex rel. Douglas, 458 U.S. 941, 944 (1982).

16. 458 U.S. 941 (1982).

17. The ban on exports to non-reciprocating states was invalidated only as a per se rule; the Court left open the possibility that on some set of facts even this total barrier to interstate commerce might be permissible. Id. at 958.

18. Id. at 956–57.

19. Id. at 957, citing Reeves, Inc., v. Stake, 447 U.S. 429 (1980), discussed in § 6–11, infra.

20. Id. at 962–63 (Rehnquist, J., dissenting).

21. Justice Rehnquist, consistent with his affinity for legal positivism, argued that Nebraska groundwater did not even rise to the level of an article of commerce: " 'Commerce' cannot exist in a natural resource that cannot be sold, rented, traded or transferred, but only *used*." Id. at 963 (Rehnquist, J., dissenting) (original emphasis).

22. Id. at 951. The Court further held that routine congressional approval of interstate water compacts and a pattern of deference to the states revealed in 37 separate pieces of federal water legislation did not mean that the field had been expressly

§ 6–11. State Participation in the Market

On June 24, 1976, in the year of the nation's bicentennial, the commerce clause—the Constitution's primary epoxy of national cohesion—gave way to the claims of state autonomy. In two decisions announced that day, *National League of Cities v. Usery*[1] and *Hughes v. Alexandria Scrap Corp.*,[2] the Supreme Court inaugurated the era of the New Federalism. *National League of Cities*, at the time the more apparently important of the two cases, held that the tenth amendment embodies a preserve of state sovereignty which can operate as a constitutional trump to circumscribe congressional authority under the commerce clause. *Alexandria Scrap*, little noted at the time, established that "[n]othing in the purposes animating the commerce clause prohibits a state, in the absence of congressional action, from participating in the market and exercising the right to favor its own citizens over others."[3] Although the principles set forth in *National League of Cities* were never again deployed to limit congressional power over commerce, and the case has in fact been overruled,[4] the market participant doctrine announced in *Alexandria Scrap* has enjoyed vigorous expansion.

Alexandria Scrap involved a challenge to a Maryland statutory scheme whereby the state purchased crushed automobile hulks from in-state scrap processors at a premium price in order to help rid the state of derelict cars. Virginia scrap processors asserted a commerce clause violation because of Maryland's refusal to buy scrap cars from out-of-state processors. The Court held that the statute was not subject to commerce clause scrutiny at all inasmuch as Maryland was not interfering with the natural functioning of an interstate market but was merely participating in the market as a purchaser which chose to give its business exclusively to in-state sellers.[5]

Since the commerce clause was directed, as an historical matter, only at regulatory and taxing actions taken by states in their sovereign capacity, the Court reasoned that the clause simply does not apply, as a source of negative implication, to state decisions to "distribute government largesse"[6] on a basis that favors state residents.[7] Moreover, the

---

abandoned to the states. Id. at 959–60. This seems sound enough. See § 6–33, infra. But in refusing to accept Nebraska's ownership argument (and thus its reciprocity rule) for fear of compromising Congress' unexercised authority to deal with the national problem of groundwater overdraft, the Court seems to have forgotten that if Congress were to find that such overdraft affected interstate commerce—in agriculture, for example—it could regulate the area *regardless* of whether that groundwater itself constituted an article of commerce, and that contrary laws such as Nebraska's would then be pre-empted. See 458 U.S. at 961–62 (Rehnquist, J., dissenting).

§ 6–11

1. 426 U.S. 833 (1976).

2. 426 U.S. 794 (1976).

3. 426 U.S. at 810.

4. Garcia v. San Antonio Metropolitan Transit Authority, 469 U.S. 528 (1985). See § 5–22, supra.

5. It is noteworthy in this regard that the state's bounty program neither increased costs to out-of-state firms, cf. Baldwin v. G.A.F. Seelig, Inc., 294 U.S. 511 (1935), nor forced them to leave the market, cf. Great Atlantic & Pacific Tea Co., Inc. v. Cottrell, 424 U.S. 366 (1976). See the helpful discussion in Note, 90 Harv.L. Rev. 58, 61–62 (1976).

6. Reeves, Inc. v. Stake, 447 U.S. 429, 441 (1980).

7. It has never been suggested that the commerce clause is inapplicable as a source of *affirmative* congressional authority to regulate state decisions of this sort.

commerce affected by Maryland's policy was commerce itself created by that statutory scheme—commerce that would not exist if the state had not entered the market.[8]

Any suspicions that *Alexandria Scrap* was an aberration, perhaps attributable to judicial indulgence for Maryland's environmental concerns, were dispelled by *Reeves, Inc. v. Stake*,[9] where the Court confirmed its holding that the distinction between "States as market participants and States as regulators makes good sense and good law." [10] A narrow majority of the Court [11] upheld a policy of preferential sales to state residents during periods of shortage by a cement plant owned and operated by South Dakota. Noting that " 'the commerce clause was directed, as an historical matter, only at regulatory and taxing actions taken by states in their sovereign capacity,' " [12] the Court relied on the absence of any "indication of a constitutional plan to limit the ability of the States themselves to operate freely in the free market." [13] The state's role as " 'guardian and trustee for its people' " [14] was also stressed: a state "may fairly claim some measure of a sovereign interest in retaining freedom to decide how, with whom, and for whose benefit to deal." [15] It is only fair to accord state proprietary activities the long-recognized right of private traders to exercise their independent judgment in such matters, the Court reasoned, since state-owned businesses would be "burdened with the same restrictions imposed on private market participants." [16] Finally, applying the com-

On the contrary, the Court has been *more* willing to extend Congress' regulations of commerce to state proprietary activity than to state regulatory activity. See, e.g., United Transp. Union v. Long Island R.R. Co., 455 U.S. 678 (1982) (upholding regulation of state-run railroad over tenth amendment challenge); Jefferson County Pharmaceutical Assoc., Inc. v. Abbott Labs., 460 U.S. 150 (1983) (no antitrust immunity when the state acts as a market participant). In Wisconsin Dept. of Industry v. Gould, Inc., 106 S.Ct. 1057 (1986), Wisconsin had barred repeated violators of the National Labor Relations Act (NLRA) from doing business with the State. The Court, in a unanimous decision, refused to apply the market participant exception to insulate Wisconsin's actions from NLRA preemption. The Court described Wisconsin's debarment as being "tantamount to regulation." Id. at 1063. The Court also emphasized the limited scope of the exception: "[It] reflects the particular concerns underlying the commerce clause, not any general notion regarding the necessary extent of state power where Congress has acted." Id.

The notion that the government should be subject to different legal standards when it is operating in other than its sovereign capacity has arisen within a number of constitutional settings. See, e.g., Board of Education v. Pico, 457 U.S. 853, 908–09 (1982) (Rehnquist J., dissenting) (arguing that first amendment scrutiny

should be more lenient when the government is not acting in sovereign capacity); Connick v. Myers, 461 U.S. 138 (1983) (first amendment does not protect government employee from being fired for speech related to mere employee grievances, rather than to matters of public concern); cf. Polk County v. Dodson, 454 U.S. 312 (1981) (allegedly inadequate legal representation by state-paid public defender does not constitute state action).

8. Alexandria Scrap, 426 U.S. at 809 n. 18; id. at 815–16 (Stevens, J., concurring).

9. 447 U.S. 429 (1980).

10. 447 U.S. at 436. The Court expressly refused to distinguish the earlier case on environmental grounds, labeling such a reading of Alexandria Scrap an "oversimplification." Id. at 442 n. 16.

11. The decision was 5–4, with Justices Powell, Brennan, White and Stevens dissenting.

12. 447 U.S. at 437 (quoting from the first edition of this treatise).

13. 447 U.S. at 437.

14. 447 U.S. at 438, quoting Heim v. McCall, 239 U.S. 175, 191 (1915).

15. 447 U.S. at 438 n. 10.

16. 447 U.S. at 438–39. And, as subsequent decisions have revealed, the Court has a very narrow view of non-proprietary, "traditional governmental functions." See, e.g., United Transportation Union v.

merce clause to such phenomena as South Dakota's innovative solution to the state's chronic cement shortage would diminish the value of the states as social and economic laboratories.[17]

The Court's reasoning in these cases is in some respects problematic.[18] The historical argument about the purpose of the commerce clause proves less than it claims, for although the framers may have been primarily concerned with preventing states from interfering with private interstate trade, there is no evidence that they even considered the problem of state proprietary activity. And there are obvious tensions between the image of the state as just another economic actor, responding to the same pressures as private enterprises, and the image of the state intervening in the market, propelled by the power to tax, in order to promote the interests of its citizens. These are in fact inconsistent alternative defenses.[19]

This tension has not been resolved by subsequent cases. Indeed, the line between market participation and market regulation, which was less than pellucid even in *Alexandria Scrap*,[20] has been further obscured. In *White v. Massachusetts Council of Construction Employers, Inc.* ("MCCE"),[21] the Court rejected a commerce clause challenge to an order by the Mayor of Boston requiring all construction projects funded in whole or in part by funds administered by the city to be performed by a work force composed of at least 50% bona fide Boston residents.[22]

The Court deemed it irrelevant whether the city directly hired workers and constructed buildings itself or instead chose to impose a resident quota on the private contractors with whom it dealt: "Everyone affected by the order is, in a substantial if informal sense, 'working for the city.'"[23] Although the majority agreed with the dissent that "there are some limits on a state or local government's ability to

Long Island Railroad, 455 U.S. 678 (1982), discussed in § 5–22, supra.

17. 447 U.S. at 441. The Court quoted Justice Brandeis' famous dissenting dictum in New State Ice Co. v. Liebmann, 285 U.S. 262, 311 (1932). In an echo of the language used by the ephemeral majority opinion in National League of Cities v. Usery, 426 U.S. 833, 852 (1976), the Reeves Court also noted that application of the commerce clause would hamper the state's "ability to structure relations exclusively with its own citizens." 447 U.S. at 441.

18. Many commentators have criticized the entire market participant exception. See, e.g., Note, "The Market Participant Test in Dormant Commerce Clause Analysis—Protecting Protectionism?", 1985 Duke L.J. 697; Varat, "State 'Citizenship' and Interstate Equality," 48 U.Chi.L.Rev. 487, 503–08 (1981); Note, "The Commerce Clause and Federalism: Implications for State Control of Natural Resources," 50 Geo.Wash.L.Rev. 601 (1982).

19. See L. Tribe, Constitutional Choices 144–46 (1985).

20. Maryland's bounty for in-state scrap hulks was, as Justice Brennan noted in dissent, 426 U.S. at 824, 828–29, an integral part of the state's regulatory effort to affect the trade in hulks so as to rid the state's roadsides of abandoned automobiles.

21. 460 U.S. 204 (1983). The author was counsel for Mayor White and the City of Boston in this case before the Supreme Court.

22. Justice Rehnquist wrote the opinion of the Court, joined by Chief Justice Burger and Justices Brennan, Marshall, Powell, Stevens and O'Connor. The Court had no occasion to consider the order's validity under the privileges and immunities clause of article IV. 460 U.S. at 214 n. 12; id. at 215–16 n. 1 (Blackmun, J., dissenting in part).

23. Id. at 211 n. 7. The Court stated that, so long as Boston was a participant in rather than a regulator of the construction market, it mattered not whether the local-hire rule had any adverse impact on outsiders. 460 U.S. at 209–10. Yet the Court took the trouble to point out, as it had in

impose restrictions that reach beyond the immediate parties with whom the government transacts business," it declined to specify those limits, saying only that the commerce clause "does not require the city to stop at the boundary of formal privity of contract." [24]   Thus, whether state action is deemed market *participation* or market *regulation* may well depend on which facts are emphasized and how particular transactions or trading choices are characterized: Mayor White's executive order could be seen as a proprietary choice by the city that it would deal only with contractors willing to reserve 50% of their jobs for locals; or it might be recast as a regulatory device designed to shape the construction market so as to promote local employment.

A plurality [25] of the Court attempted in *South-Central Timber Development, Inc. v. Wunnicke* [26] to distinguish participation from regulation—and thereby to cabin the market participant exception—by limiting the definition of the relevant market. The plurality concluded that Alaska's policy of requiring that timber taken from state forests be processed in-state prior to export did not fall within the exception.[27] "The State may not impose conditions, whether by statute, regulation, or contract, that have a substantial regulatory effect outside of that particular market. Unless the 'market' is relatively narrowly defined, the [market-participant exception] has the potential of swallowing up the rule." [28]

This approach, with its intolerance of "downstream restrictions" on the market,[29] is consistent with that taken by the Court in *White* itself, where the majority distinguished the "Alaska hire" statute struck down under article IV's privileges and immunities clause in *Hicklin v. Orbeck*.[30] In contrast to Boston's relatively modest demand that its own building projects employ at least as many local as non-local workers, Alaska had attempted to require that state residents be given preference in *all* work even remotely connected with Alaskan oil and gas leases—a far more sweeping effort to dictate the employment practices of virtually all the businesses benefitting from the economic ripple effect of commercial exploitation of the state's natural mineral wealth.

Moreover, *White, Reeves*, and *Alexandria Scrap* all involved government expenditures of public revenues to create commerce which generated benefits that those governments wished to keep within their communities.[31] The state legislation struck down in *Wunnicke* did not

Reeves, 447 U.S. at 444 n. 17, that there was no basis in the record for concluding that non-residents would be significantly disadvantaged. 460 U.S. at 209–10 n. 6.

24. 460 U.S. at 211 n. 7; id. at 222 (Blackmun, J., dissenting).

25. Justices White, Brennan, Blackmun and Stevens.

26. 467 U.S. 82 (1984).

27. The Court's reluctance to extend the market participant exception in Wunnicke is also consistent with the Court's long-standing aversion to regulations that put pressure on out-of-state businesses to relocate within the state by prohibiting

exports of local products unless certain processes have occurred locally. See § 6–9, supra.

28. 467 U.S. at 97–98. Justice Rehnquist argued in dissent that the plurality's mechanism for distinguishing market regulation from participation depends on judgments more intuitive and conclusory than objective and reasoned. Id. at 102.

29. 467 U.S. at 99.

30. 437 U.S. 518 (1978), discussed in § 6–35, infra.

31. In White, Boston also applied its local-hire requirement to federal building funds administered by the city—a restric-

expend community tax revenues to create new commerce; rather, like Alaska's previously invalidated local-hire statute, the law sought to exploit existing commerce in natural resources that happened to be situated on state lands. As early as *Reeves v. Stake*, the Court drew a line between government actions limiting access to "the end product of a complex process whereby a costly physical plant and human labor act on raw materials," and efforts to control access to the raw materials themselves.[32] That distinction, in turn, resonates with the Court's unwillingness to treat a state's undeveloped natural resources as government "property" that the state may control as it wishes.[33]

The Court's interest in defining some limits to the market participant exception is well placed. For a doctrine that purports to be merely a limited exemption from the commerce clause—while roping in such diverse state endeavors as industrial production for the private market and contractual conditions on public works projects, and while twining together such varied commodities as cement, abandoned cars, and construction jobs—is a doctrine with the potential to knot up the remainder of the commerce clause, or to come unravelled altogether.

Yet from another perspective, *Alexandria Scrap* and its progeny can be seen as ushering in a new day for federalism, one that allows state and local governments the freedom to experiment with different packages of benefits for their citizens without fear that they will have to share the contents with everyone else. Central heating is a marvelous thing, but it makes little sense in a house without walls. The market participant exception to the commerce clause, as an aspect of the new federalism, encourages states and cities to improve the lives of their citizens by allowing the benefits they generate to be contained within their borders.

§ 6–12. State Regulations Which Discourage Multi-State Business Structures

Just as activities which appear to be entirely local when viewed in isolation can become so nationally significant in the aggregate that they may be regulated by Congress under the commerce clause,[1] so too regulations that individually seem only local in impact can collectively burden multi-state enterprises to such a degree that all will be barred by the negative implications of the commerce clause. Even if nondiscriminatory and nonprotective when perceived in isolation, regulatory measures applied by several states to the same multi-state business may in the aggregate so operate against interstate commerce that, when viewed in combination, they exert a potent localizing bias by making commercial activities which are confined to a single state far less difficult and more profitable than more national enterprises. State

tion unanimously upheld by the Court on federal statutory grounds.

32. 447 U.S. at 444.

33. See § 6–10, supra. Under the privileges and immunities clause of article IV, the Court still recognizes that a state and its residents may have a superior claim to natural resources developed and maintained by the state. See Baldwin v. Fish & Game Commn. of Montana, 436 U.S. 371 (1978), discussed in § 6–35, infra.

§ 6–12

1. See Wickard v. Filburn, 317 U.S. 111 (1942), discussed in § 5–5, supra.

regulations may discourage national enterprises in this way either by being *contradictory* or by imposing weighty *cumulative burdens* upon multi-state business concerns.

The localizing bias inherent in regulations capable of multiple application is most apparent when a multi-state enterprise is required to comply with contradictory state regulations—a circumstance that could never befall the purely local operator. Although the Supreme Court has at times invalidated a state regulation simply because of the *possibility* that it might conflict with another state's regulation, in more recent cases the Court has required a demonstration of *actual conflict*.

Cases involving the application to multi-state businesses of state laws requiring racial integration or state laws requiring racial segregation provide the most prominent illustrations of Supreme Court decisions striking down state regulatory measures that potentially conflict with the actions of other states. In *Hall v. De Cuir*,[2] the Court held that a Louisiana law prohibiting racial segregation could not be applied to steamboat operations on the Mississippi River because of the burden that could be imposed upon the steamboat operators if other states along the river enacted laws requiring segregation. A Virginia law requiring racial segregation was struck down for similar reasons in *Morgan v. Virginia*.[3]

However, commerce clause barriers to the enforcement against multi-state businesses of laws prohibiting racial discrimination were removed by the Supreme Court with its decision in *Colorado Anti-Discrimination Commission v. Continental Airlines, Inc.*[4] The Court there held that a multi-state airline could not justify its failure to comply with a state anti-discrimination law on the ground that a contradictory requirement might be imposed by another state in which the airline operated; because decisions subsequent to *Hall* and *Morgan* had made clear that any federal or state law requiring racial discrimination would be unconstitutional,[5] no conflict could in fact arise.

In recent cases the Supreme Court has refused to invalidate otherwise nondiscriminatory and nonexclusionary local regulations absent a showing of *actual conflict* among the rules of different states; in cases of actual conflict, however, the Court has been extremely severe in its scrutiny of state action.

For example, in *Bibb v. Navajo Freight Lines, Inc.*,[6] the Supreme Court decided that an interstate trucker certified by the ICC could not constitutionally be required to comply with an Illinois regulation which required trucks operating in that state to be equipped with contour rear-fender mudguards. This particular kind of mudguard was not unequivocally safer than other kinds that were permitted in at least 45 other states; and in one state, Arkansas, such contour mudguards were

2. 95 U.S. 485 (1878).

3. 328 U.S. 373 (1946).

4. 372 U.S. 714 (1963). See also Bob-Lo Excursion Co. v. Michigan, 333 U.S. 28 (1948) (upholding application of Michigan anti-discrimination law to boat line that operated in international waters).

5. See § 16–15, infra.

6. 359 U.S. 520 (1959).

illegal.[7] Contrasting *Bibb* with *Huron Portland Cement Co. v. City of Detroit* [8] casts the differing doctrinal import of actual and potential conflict in high relief. In *Huron*, the Supreme Court rejected a commerce clause challenge to the enforcement of a municipal pollution ordinance against ships operating in interstate commerce; the challenge failed because those questioning the validity of the law were unable to cite "any . . . competing or conflicting local regulations" to back up their claim that the ordinance unduly burdened multi-state businesses.[9]

In some cases, the Supreme Court has suggested that the aggregate cost of complying with multiple regulations, a burden uniquely placed on interstate businesses, must be taken into account in determining the validity of individual state regulations—even if the difference among the various states' rules is not so dramatic as to render them contradictory, and indeed even if the rules are all identical. For example, in *Southern Pacific Co. v. Arizona*,[10] Chief Justice Stone not only stressed the burden placed on multi-state railroad operators by the need to adjust to the differing train length limits imposed by different states, but also contended that the alternative available to the railroads—national compliance with the rule of the most restrictive state—was equally improper under the commerce clause because requiring such compliance would in effect extend the authority of that one state beyond its borders.[11]

§ 6–13. A Doctrinal Underview: Economic vs. Other Concerns, Local Needs, and Less Restrictive Alternatives

In addition to isolating, as has been done above, the factors which the Supreme Court takes into account when it balances the importance of a state regulatory interest against the adverse effect of the regulation on interstate commerce, it is possible to note a number of more general elements often present in decisions dealing with the constitutional validity of state regulations affecting interstate commerce: the

7. "This is one of those cases—few in number—where local safety measures that are non-discriminatory place an unconstitutional burden on interstate commerce." 359 U.S. at 529. But see Kassel v. Consolidated Freightways Corp., 450 U.S. 662 (1981); Raymond Motor Transportation, Inc. v. Rice, 434 U.S. 429 (1978), discussed in § 6–7, supra.

8. 362 U.S. 440 (1960).

9. Id. at 442–43.

10. 325 U.S. 761 (1945).

11. In Brown-Forman Distillers v. New York Liquor Authority, 106 S.Ct. 2080 (1986), the Court struck down a New York Law requiring liquor producers, when setting prices for in-state wholesalers, to affirm that no lower price would be charged in other states during the same month. Since distillers had to have permission from New York before they could lower

their prices in other states below their New York prices, the law effectively gave the New York Liquor Authority power to control prices beyond the state's borders. The twenty-first amendment aspects of the case are discussed in § 6–24, infra.

In Edgar v. MITE Corp., 457 U.S. 624 (1982), the Court similarly invalidated an Illinois statute that imposed various requirements beyond those of federal law on tender offerors attempting to take over corporations that, although national or multinational in nature, were either chartered in Illinois or had some capital in the state. The Court accepted Illinois' interest in protecting its citizens from the ravages of takeover battles, but, in denouncing the law's extraterritorial effect, the majority held—strangely—that a "state has no legitimate interest in protecting non-resident shareholders." Id. at 2642. See § 6–35, infra. But see § 6–7, supra.

recurring distinction between economic and social regulation, the stress on local concerns, and the focus on the availability of less restrictive alternatives.

Although the distinction between "police regulation" and "regulation of interstate commerce" has long since been rejected as too wooden to be of much help in the actual decision of particular cases, it survives as a generally accurate retrospective determinant of the relative weights imputed by the Supreme Court to the interests asserted to justify state regulations. State regulations seemingly aimed at furthering public health or safety, or at restraining fraudulent or otherwise unfair trade practices, are less likely to be perceived as "undue burdens on interstate commerce" than are state regulations evidently seeking to maximize the profits of local businesses. Indeed, where the Supreme Court has held that the national interest in the free flow of commerce supercedes a state interest in public safety, it has generally seemed that the challenged statute contributed only marginally if at all to the public safety.[1] In contrast, economically based state regulations have almost invariably been struck down.[2] In applying this dichotomy, one would have to say that regulations seemingly focused on preserving local *employment* as such rather than on maintaining local *profits* have sometimes received treatment almost as favorable as regulations concerned with health or other non-financial aspects of well-being.[3]

In addition, decisions continue to be influenced by whether a particular regulatory subject matter can be classified as "local" or "national." Even though this distinction is no longer regarded as usefully separating permitted state action from that which is forbidden, it is plain that those state regulations provoked by purely local aspects of interstate commerce are accorded a deference not granted to state actions stimulated by problems of more obviously national dimension.

For example, in *Milk Control Board v. Eisenberg Farm Products*,[4] the Supreme Court upheld nondiscriminatory state regulations aimed at improving the economic status of depression-struck farmers (obviously a national as well as state concern) but only after noting that just 10% of the milk regulated was destined for interstate commerce. However, in *Cities Service Gas Co. v. Peerless Oil and Gas Co.*,[5] the

§ 6–13

1. See, e.g., Kassel v. Consolidated Freightways Corp., 450 U.S. 662 (1981); Raymond Motor Transportation, Inc. v. Rice, 434 U.S. 429 (1978); Bibb v. Navajo Freight Lines, Inc., 359 U.S. 520 (1959), discussed in §§ 6–7, 6–12, supra.

2. See, e.g., Baldwin v. Seelig, 294 U.S. 511 (1935); Foster-Fountain Packing Co. v. Haydel, 278 U.S. 1 (1928).

3. See, e.g., White v. Massachusetts Council of Construction Employers, Inc., 460 U.S. 204 (1983) (upholding against commerce clause challenge a city policy that 50% of workforce on municipally controlled construction projects must be city residents); Brotherhood of Locomotive Firemen v. Chicago, R.I. & P.R. Co., 393 U.S. 129 (1968) (trains travelling more than a given distance in state must have a designated minimum crew). See § 6–7, supra. Cf. United Building & Construction v. Mayor of Camden, 465 U.S. 208, (1984) (holding city's local-hire policy to be subject to article IV privileges and immunities clause); Hicklin v. Orbeck, 437 U.S. 518 (1978) (unanimously invalidating under article IV Alaska's imposition on oil and gas industry of a sweeping local-hire law).

4. 306 U.S. 346 (1939), discussed in § 6–8, supra.

5. 340 U.S. 179 (1950), discussed in § 6–8, supra.

Court approved an almost identical regulation sparked by a state interest in the conservation of a local resource (a resource not yet of similar national concern at that time) without hesitating over the fact that almost all of the natural gas there regulated was ultimately bound for out-of-state markets.

More explicit in their emphasis on the importance of the "local" quality of the state regulation at issue are those cases in which the Supreme Court has found a state safety interest so compelling that it has explicitly required only that the regulation be rationally related to the state's interest. In these cases, it is clear that there is an implicit balancing of the state's interest against the sometimes substantial burden on interstate commerce; but the balancing is conducted under the guise of "classifying" the state interest as "local" rather than being conducted more openly.[6]

In other cases, the *Cooley* legacy manifests itself in the determined search by the Supreme Court for some local incident to which it might attach a plainly not-very-burdensome state regulation of interstate commerce. For example, in *Eli Lilly & Co. v. Sav-On-Drugs, Inc.*,[7] the Court emphasized the local business activities carried out by Eli Lilly in holding that New Jersey could properly require this multistate drug company to obtain a certificate prior to doing local business there, and that Eli Lilly—having failed to obtain such a certificate—could be barred from suing for breach of contract in New Jersey courts.[8]

Finally, the significance attached by the Supreme Court to a state's or municipality's interest in its challenged regulation has been affected not only by the weight the Court gives to the *ends* the state seeks to further but also, on occasion, by *the necessity of the means* which the state has used to achieve its ends. Thus, in *Dean Milk Co. v. City of Madison*,[9] the Supreme Court struck down local regulations restricting the importation of milk because the local health interests there asserted could have been adequately served if the city had dispatched its inspectors to the out-of-state pasterurization plants to make their quality checks, or if the city had relied on available federal inspection services for the needed data: "in . . . erecting an economic barrier protecting a major local industry against competition from without the State, Madison plainly discriminates against interstate commerce. This it cannot do, even in the exercise of its unquestioned power to protect the health and safety of its people, *if reasonable nondiscriminatory alternatives, adequate to conserve legitimate local interests, are available.*" [10]

6. See Brotherhood of Locomotive Firemen, supra note 3. Justice Black, provoked by the strong local interest in railroad safety and by the traditional, if less overt, local concern for full employment, applied the "rational relationship" test twice: once to uphold the state regulation of interstate railroads, and then again to uphold the state's exception of local railroads from its safety rule. See also South Carolina State Highway Dept. v. Barnwell Bros., Inc., 303 U.S. 177 (1938).

7. 366 U.S. 276 (1961).

8. See also the discussion of this case in § 6–14, infra.

9. 340 U.S. 349 (1951), discussed in § 6–9, supra.

10. Id. at 354. Cf. Maine v. Taylor, 106 S.Ct. 2440 (1986) (finding inspection of possibly contaminated baitfish shipments to be an inadequate substitute for outright ban on imports), discussed in § 6–6, supra. Compare the use of "less restrictive alter-

§ 6–14. The Case for Doctrinal Disarray: State Treatment of Out-of-State Corporations

The Supreme Court's approach to commerce clause issues, despite such structuring devices as the emphasis on less restrictive or discriminatory alternatives, often appears to turn more on *ad hoc* reactions to particular cases than on any consistent application of coherent principles. That such disarray may at times be worth preserving is suggested by an examination of one particularly troublesome area—state treatment of out-of-state corporations.

Chief Justice Taney's 1839 opinion for the Supreme Court in *Bank of Augusta v. Earle* [1] established that a corporation organized in one state seeking to do business in another may be required by the latter to qualify under its laws as a "foreign corporation" before doing business there. Such qualification or licensing, required of domestic and foreign corporations alike,[2] typically involves the payment of a fee and the filing of certain information, and triggers submission to the state's taxing jurisdiction as well as to in-state service of process. Qualification requirements are sometimes enforced by denying access to state judicial and other facilities to corporations not "qualified" as required by state law.[3] But (1) a license or qualification to do business in the state may *not* constitutionally be required of a corporation that seeks to enter a state solely to engage in exclusively interstate commerce there; [4] and (2) an independently "unconstitutional condition"—such as a waiver of the right to sue in *federal* court—may not be extracted even as a condition of permitting a foreign corporation to engage in intrastate business within the licensing state.[5]

In applying the first of these two exceptions to the *Bank of Augusta* doctrine, the Supreme Court has strained to uphold seemingly unburdensome regulatory or taxing schemes both by (a) permitting states to demand of exclusively interstate enterprises that they obtain and pay for a license to engage in the "local" activity of doing business "in corporate form" (as opposed to the "interstate" activity of doing busi-

---

native" analysis in privileges and immunities cases, § 6–35, infra, and in first amendment cases, § 12–23, infra.

§ 6–14

1. 38 U.S. (13 Pet.) 519 (1839).

2. Cf. Southern Ry. Co. v. Greene, 216 U.S. 400 (1910) (Alabama law which imposed on foreign corporations already admitted to do business a tax beyond that levied on domestic corporations denied the foreign corporations equal protection of the laws).

3. See, e.g., Union Brokerage Co. v. Jensen, 322 U.S. 202 (1944); Paul v. Virginia, 75 U.S. (8 Wall.) 168, 181 (1869); Comment, "Foreign Corporations—State Boundaries for National Business," 59 Yale L.J. 737, 742–46 (1950); Note, "Sanctions for Failure to Comply With Corporate Qualifications

Statutes: An Evaluation," 63 Colum.L.Rev. 117, 122–26 (1963).

4. Leloup v. Mobile, 127 U.S. 640, 645 (1888); Crutcher v. Kentucky, 141 U.S. 47, 56, 57 (1891). See also International Text-Book Co. v. Pigg, 217 U.S. 91 (1910); Bucks Stove Co. v. Vickers, 226 U.S. 205 (1912); Dahnke-Walker Milling Co. v. Bondurant, 257 U.S. 282 (1921). Cf. Shafer v. Farmers' Grain Co., 268 U.S. 189 (1925) (invalidating pervasive state regulation of purchase of wheat for interstate shipment).

5. See, e.g., Insurance Co. v. Morse, 87 U.S. (20 Wall.) 445 (1874); Barron v. Burnside, 121 U.S. 186 (1887); Herndon v. Chicago, R.I. & P. Ry. Co., 218 U.S. 135 (1910). The modern "unconstitutional conditions" doctrine, see § 10–8, infra, traces to these early decisions.

ness at all),[6] and also by (b) allowing states to demand licenses for the privilege of engaging in business in the state where the foreign corporation maintains local facilities for separable intrastate transactions.[7] But merely purchasing commodities locally and storing them in local warehouses for sorting, classification, or other processing pending ultimate delivery to out-of-state destinations has been held not to constitute the sort of "separable intrastate transaction" that would permit a state to insist on licensing the purchasing corporation to do business locally and denying use of its courts for failure to obtain a license,[8] even if the locally stored commodities might be subject to state taxation while there,[9] and even if at least some state regulations might constitutionally be enforced against those commodities.[10]

The plainly manipulable and at times anachronistically metaphysical character of these doctrines and the dubious consistency of their complex exceptions suggest that the Supreme Court has preserved them with an eye to their discretionary application in order to prevent what appear to be instances of intolerable local or state interference with interstate markets. It seems likely, for example, that the result in *Allenberg Cotton* [11] was strongly influenced by the fact that the state in that case seemed to be interfering with the operation of the national futures market in cotton by preventing interstate purchasers who had failed to qualify as "foreign corporations" under local law from effectively protecting themselves against unexpected price increases.[12] There is much to be said, of course, for overthrowing formalities altogether and looking wholly to economic impact in this area just as

6. See Colonial Pipeline Co. v. Traigle, 421 U.S. 100 (1975). But see § 6–15, infra.

7. See Eli Lilly & Co. v. Sav-On-Drugs, Inc., 366 U.S. 276, 279–81 (1961) (drugs sold intrastate through local office with 18 salaried employees, as well as interstate), discussed in § 6–13, supra. See also Union Brokerage Co. v. Jensen, 322 U.S. 202, 210 (1944).

8. See Allenberg Cotton Co., Inc. v. Pittman, 419 U.S. 20 (1974) (purchaser maintained no office in the state, neither owned nor operated a warehouse there, and had no employees soliciting business there or otherwise operating there on a regular basis; state attempted to prevent purchaser from suing in its courts for breach of a contract to grow and deliver cotton). See also Coons v. American Honda Motor Co., Inc., 94 N.J. 307, 309, 463 A.2d 921, 922 (1983) (New Jersey law that tolls statute of limitations for actions against out-of-state corporations until those corporations appoint representative in state for service of process violates commerce clause), on rehearing 96 N.J. 419, 476 A.2d 763 (1984), cert. denied 469 U.S. 1123 (1985). Cf. Haskell v. Kansas Natural Gas Co., 224 U.S. 217 (1912) (state cannot deny foreign corporation the right to lay pipe lines across highways for purposes of transporting natural gas in interstate commerce).

9. See Kosydar v. National Cash Register Co., 417 U.S. 62 (1974), relied on by Justice Rehnquist to support his view that the cotton stored in Mississippi in the Allenberg case could indeed be taxed there, 419 U.S. at 40 n. 6 (dissenting opinion), cf. id. at 33–34 (majority opinion by Justice Douglas, leaving tax question open). Cf. Complete Auto Transit Inc. v. Brady, 430 U.S. 274 (1977), discussed in § 6–15, infra.

10. See Parker v. Brown, 317 U.S. 341, 361 (1943), discussed in § 6–8, supra, and § 6–24, infra. But see Shafer v. Farmers' Grain Co., 268 U.S. 189 (1925), in note 4, supra.

11. See note 8, supra.

12. See 419 U.S. at 25–26. In dissent, Justice Rehnquist acknowledged this drastic result but insisted that "the burden imposed on interstate commerce by such [qualification] statutes is to be judged with reference to the measures required to comply with such legislation, and not to the sanctions imposed for violation of it." 419 U.S. at 42 (dissenting opinion). Perhaps the majority's unspoken concern was with the administrative burden of qualifying in numerous states. Cf. National Bellas Hess v. Department of Revenue, 386 U.S. 753 (1967), discussed in § 6–18, infra.

the Court has begun to do with respect to state taxation,[13] but short of that solution it seems unlikely that the cause of economic realism would be greatly advanced by attempting to bring order to the rules governing these cases. Indeed, if it is true that the occasions peculiarly warranting a judicial rather than congressional "negative against state legislation" under the commerce clause demand "an appraisal more carefully particularized than legislation could afford," [14] then the chief virtue of the "hit-and-miss method of deciding single . . . controversies" [15] in this field, as compared with the legislative creation of integrated national rules, may be precisely its sensitivity to factual nuance, a sensitivity far more compatible with doctrinal disarray than proponents of functional coherence and consistent principle might always wish to concede.

§ 6–15. State Taxation of Interstate Commerce: Structuring the Constitutional Analysis

Like its authority to limit state regulation of interstate commerce, the Supreme Court's power to review state taxation of interstate commerce springs from the negative implications of the commerce clause. The Court's state taxation doctrines are thus always subject to congressional revision. In addition, to a greater degree than in the regulation cases, judicial willingness to consider the impact of state taxes upon interstate commerce has been controlled by the burden of proof: "The general rule . . . is that a taxpayer claiming immunity from a tax has the burden of establishing his exemption." [1]

Although decisions concerning the constitutional validity of state taxes affecting interstate commerce can be assessed in terms of an interest-balancing process similar to that employed in the judicial evaluation of state regulation, the Supreme Court has not usually organized its analysis in terms of such balancing. This is partly a consequence of the fact that the state's ultimate interest is the same in all tax cases—namely, raising revenue. The Court's distinctive approach in state tax cases also results from an overlap between the tests used to determine the significance of the state's link with the taxpayer and those employed to measure the extent to which the tax burdens interstate commerce. Judicial inspection of state taxation therefore focuses almost exclusively upon the adverse consequences of a tax for interstate commerce.

In analyzing such adverse consequences, courts have begun to abandon their previous formalistic approach in favor of a more realistic functional calculus. In *Complete Auto Transit Inc. v. Brady*,[2] the Supreme Court overruled a series of cases which had held that any state tax on "the privilege of doing business" imposed on a multi-state

---

13. See § 6–15, infra.

14. Brown in § 6–1, supra, note 1, at 222.

15. McCarroll v. Dixie Greyhound Lines, Inc. 309 U.S. 176, 188–89 (1940) (Black, J., joined by Frankfurter and Douglas, JJ., dissenting).

§ 6–15

1. Norton Co. v. Department of Revenue of Illinois, 340 U.S. 534, 537 (1951) (emphasis added) ("showing a fair difference of opinion" is not sufficient to meet the burden required of the taxpayer).

2. 430 U.S. 274 (1977).

business was *per se* unconstitutional. Rather than focusing on the language or labelling of a statute, the Court proclaimed, commerce clause analysis should concentrate on the real effects of a tax upon interstate commerce.[3] Thus, a state tax does not offend the commerce clause if it (1) is applied to an activity with a substantial nexus with the taxing state, (2) is fairly apportioned, (3) does not discriminate against interstate commerce, and (4) is fairly related to services provided by the state.

The Court's efforts to adhere to this more realistic commerce clause jurisprudence have been both welcome and, by and large, successful.[4] Yet on occasion the new realism seems to have been tempered by an extra dose of judicial sympathy for state taxing power. In *Commonwealth Edison Company v. Montana*,[5] the Court permitted Montana, which has more than half of the nation's low-sulfur coal reserves,[6] to exploit its strategic position by imposing a 30% severance tax on coal.

There was no doubt that the Montana tax satisfied the first two prongs of the *Complete Auto Transit* test: the only possible nexus of the physical severance of the coal was in Montana, and there were no apportionment or multiple taxation problems, since the severance could occur and be taxed only in that state.[7] The out-of-state utility companies challenging the tax argued that it discriminated against interstate commerce because 90% of Montana coal is shipped to other states, whose citizens consequently bear the bulk of the severance tax burden.[8] Yet the tax was computed at the same 30% rate regardless of the coal's ultimate destination, and it would be ironic indeed to invalidate the tax

---

3. Spector Motor Service v. O'Connor, 340 U.S. 602 (1951), holding that such a tax could not be imposed, was expressly overruled.

The formal doctrine which the Court overruled had been defended on the ground that it prevented imposition of a tax "on the privilege of engaging in interstate commerce." See, e.g., Nelson v. Kentucky, 279 U.S. 245 (1929). The rule usually meant, however, that the language of a tax statute rather than its effect was determinative; by changing an improper label, a state could often avoid invalidation. Compare Railway Express Agency, Inc. v. Virginia (I), 347 U.S. 359 (1954) (invalidating application of tax levied for "the privilege of doing business in this state" with Railway Express Agency, Inc. v. Virginia (II), 358 U.S. 434 (1959) (upholding tax with same economic effect where denominated as "franchise tax"). Especially after Complete Auto Transit, it would be possible and in many respects illuminating to combine consideration of state taxation and state regulation by focusing entirely on the way in which a particular state or local action is thought likely to disrupt an open national market. Thus, restrictions of access to local consumers, for example, would provide a unifying theme for discussing both regulatory barriers like those condemned in Baldwin v. Seelig, 294 U.S. 511 (1935), see § 6–6, supra, and tax barriers like those struck down in Robbins v. Shelby County Taxing District, 120 U.S. 489 (1887), see § 6–17, infra. But the Supreme Court's historically more formalistic approach to tax problems has led to the evolution of a distinct body of doctrines and principles that still merit examination in their own terms. Thus, although overarching themes of the sort noted above will be indicated at the appropriate points, this chapter treats taxation issues separately from issues of regulatory power.

4. See, e.g., Mobil Oil Corp. v. Commissioner of Taxes, 445 U.S. 425, 443 (1980); Moorman Mfg. Co. v. Bair, 437 U.S. 267, 276–81 (1978); Washington Revenue Dept. v. Association of Wash. Stevedoring Cos., 435 U.S. 734 (1978).

5. 453 U.S. 609 (1981).

6. Id. at 638 (Blackmun, J., dissenting).

7. 453 U.S. at 617.

8. The plaintiffs also argued that the tax was preempted by federal energy policy because it discouraged the use of low-sulfur coal, but the Court found that Congress had intended to permit the use of such severance taxes. 453 U.S. at 635–36.

solely because most of the coal on which it was levied was transported across the very state borders which are ordinarily considered "essentially irrelevant" to commerce clause analysis.[9] Unlike Louisiana's first-use tax on natural gas piped through the state from the federally-controlled outer continental shelf ("OCS"), which "unquestionably discriminate[d] against interstate commerce in favor of local interests as the necessary result of [an intricate scheme of] tax credits and [exemptions]," [10] Montana's severance tax fell at an equal rate on native son and non-resident alike.

The Court read the fourth and final prong of the *Complete Auto Transit* test, the requirement that the tax be fairly related to the beneficial services provided by the state, as requiring only that the measure of the tax be reasonably related to the extent of contact with the taxing state.[11] Thus the fair relation test became little more than a gloss on the nexus requirement. Since coal companies had to enter Montana in order to excavate Montana coal from Montana soil, it cannot be doubted that both the subject of the tax and those who pay it had significant contacts with the state that levied it.

The requirements of nexus and fair apportionment for state taxes on interstate commerce are rooted in the need to check the parochial pressures to which state governments, because of their limited political constituencies, are subject.[12] If the Court's supposed new realism is taken to heart, Montana's tax arguably presents just such a case of taxation without representation: 90% of the tax, after all, falls on citizens of other states, thereby enabling Montana to export most of the burden of its state budget.[13] Yet because no argument could be made that Montana could not impose *any* severance tax on coal mined within its territory—since interstate commerce must bear its share of the state tax burden—the plaintiffs were reduced to asking the Supreme Court to declare the *rate* of the tax excessive.

The Court saw no need for a factual inquiry into the relationship between the revenues generated by the tax and the value of the benefits and services conferred on the coal companies—as measured by the costs incurred by Montana on account of the taxed activity—because the severance tax was not a user fee but a general revenue tax. The rate of such taxation, the Court declared, is essentially a legislative, not a judicial matter.[14]

9. Id. at 618–19. See West v. Kansas Natural Gas Co., 221 U.S. 229, 255 (1911) ("in matters of foreign and interstate commerce, there are no state lines"); McLeod v. J. E. Dilworth Co., 322 U.S. 327, 330 (1944) ("very purpose of the commerce clause was to create an area of free trade among the several states").

10. Maryland v. Louisiana, 451 U.S. 725, 756 (1981).

11. 453 U.S. at 626.

12. See § 6–16, infra.

13. The Court's nonchalant acceptance of Montana's imposition of its fiscal needs on out-of-staters is at odds with the aversion, expressed in Kassel v. Consolidated Freightways Corp., 450 U.S. 662, 685 (1981), to state efforts to alleviate burdens on their citizens by transfering them out-of-state. But it is consistent with the Court's dictum in Edgar v. MITE Corp., 457 U.S. 624 (1982), that, far from having an obligation to consider the impact on those in other states, a state can have "no legitimate interest in protecting non-residents." See § 6–12, supra.

14. 453 U.S. at 626–27.

The Court's refusal to look beneath the surface of Montana's severance tax simply because the legislature had denominated it a general revenue measure rather than a use tax seems more consistent with the rubric-ridden formalism of the past than with the new realism supposedly ushered in by *Complete Auto Transit*. The first-use tax on federal OCS natural gas, struck down the very same year in *Maryland v. Louisiana*,[15] seems to have succumbed because it was not a general revenue tax but a measure analogous to Louisiana's severance tax on local gas production. The Court there conceded that Louisiana "has an interest in protecting its natural resources" and could therefore impose a severance tax on the privilege of taking gas from its land, but struck down the parallel first-use tax because "Louisiana has no sovereign interest in being compensated for the severance of resources from the *federally* owned OCS land." [16] Yet most of the severance tax collected by Montana was levied on coal taken from fields likewise owned by the federal government.[17] So long as state lawmakers have the foresight to affix the label "general revenue" to their tax measures, it seems that it is not for a federal court to tell them how much their natural resources are worth, whether the tax be 30% or 1000%.[18]

Commonwealth Edison gives fresh insight into what Chief Justice Marshall meant in *McCulloch v. Maryland* when he wrote that "the power to tax is the power to destroy." [19] The Chief Justice reasoned that since it would be so hard for the courts, having once given a green light to taxation, to begin turning it amber and then red when tax rates became excessive, the only way to protect the federal government from potentially destructive state taxation, short of requiring Congress to consider each case, was to promulgate a rule against *any* state tax on a federal instrumentality without prior congressional consent.[20] We may safely allow the states to take a nibble only if we are ultimately willing to let them gobble up the whole thing. In the state vs. state context where no per se rule prohibits taxes on interstate commerce, the Supreme Court has now essentially accepted the converse of that insight: if a tax is of the *kind* the states may impose, there is no occasion for federal judges to worry about *how steep* the tax rate is— even if the tax enables a state to use its propitious natural resource position to exploit the citizens and businesses of sister states.

The Court thus seems content to leave questions of actual tax rates to the state legislatures—and to Congress, since Congress retains ultimate power to rein in excesses by self-aggrandizing states.[21] Until Congress chooses to do so, however, the citizens of the Union have no right to inexpensive access to Montana's mineral wealth.[22] The Consti-

---

15. 451 U.S. 725 (1981).

16. Id. at 725 (emphasis added).

17. Commonwealth Edison, 453 U.S. at 637 (White, J., concurring).

18. See 453 U.S. at 645 (Blackmun, J., dissenting).

19. 17 U.S. (4 Wheat.) 316, 431 (1819).

20. See § 6–30, infra.

21. Indeed, Justice White was troubled by the Montana tax but concurred in the Court's decision on the ground that Congress had so far seen fit to let the matter rest. 453 U.S. at 637–38.

22. See Commonwealth Edison, 453 U.S. at 619.

tution may demand that the fifty states sink or swim together, but it does not deny Montana the right to sell life-jackets at a premium.

It thus appears that the Court's historically formalistic approach to state taxes on interstate commerce is likely to continue to make itself felt. Indeed, the "new realism" may often appear to be a one-way ratchet that the Court employs only when formalism would erode state taxing power. The following sections will therefore address the intersection of the commerce clause with state taxing power in the elaborate doctrinal framework that the Court has constructed.

§ 6–16. No Taxation Without Representation: The Basic Requirements of Nexus and Fair Apportionment

A state's generalized need for revenue, while a rationale for taxing, is not by itself an argument for the imposition of any particular tax.[1] This revenue interest must therefore be further specified in order to link taxation with the specific activity taxed.

Of course, a tax might be explained in terms of its regulatory impact, as license taxes sometimes are. Taxes thus justified raise the same issues as do state regulations and are therefore judged by the standards articulated above.[2] The more common argument, however, is that the tax is a bill presented to interstate commerce for services rendered by the taxing state. The Supreme Court has recognized that the states have a legitimate interest in compensatory taxation of interstate commerce: "It was not the purpose of the commerce clause to relieve those engaged in interstate commerce from their just share of state tax burden even though it increases the cost of doing the business. *'Even interstate business must pay its way.'* "[3] It does not follow from the "compensatory taxation" argument, however, that taxes collected from interstate commerce are valid only to the extent that the resulting revenues are ultimately *used* in a way that can be related to local activities of the multistate enterprise taxed.[4]

§ 6–16

1. See Freeman v. Hewitt, 329 U.S. 249, 253 (1946) ("revenue serves as well no matter what its source"). Compare the discussion of poll taxes and court access fees in Chapter 16, infra.

2. See §§ 6–5 to 6–12, supra. The Court has at times employed the label "regulatory" in a conclusory way to explain its invalidation of a state tax rather than simply to initiate analysis. Taxes have at times been branded regulatory or compensatory depending upon how directly they bore upon interstate commerce. See, e.g., Galveston, H. & S.A.R. Co. v. Texas, 210 U.S. 217 (1908).

3. Western Live Stock v. Bureau of Revenue, 303 U.S. 250, 254 (1938) (emphasis added). See also Freeman v. Hewit, 329 U.S. 249, 253 (1946) ("State taxation falling on interstate commerce . . . can only be justified as designed to make such commerce bear a fair share of the cost of the local government whose protection it enjoys"); Hendrick v. Maryland, 235 U.S. 610 (1915); Evansville-Vanderburgh Airport Authority District v. Delta Airlines, Inc., 405 U.S. 707 (1972); Colonial Pipeline Co. v. Traigle, 421 U.S. 100, 108, 114 (1975).

4. See, e.g., Aero Mayflower Transit Co. v. Board of Railroad Commissioners, 332 U.S. 495, 502–06 (1947) (fixed fee taxes on road use held valid even though revenues from the taxes are not specifically earmarked for state services related to road use). See also Clark v. Poor, 274 U.S. 554, 557 (1927); Morf v. Bingaman, Comm'r. of Rev. for New Mexico, 298 U.S. 407, 412 (1936). The holding in Aero Mayflower that flat highway use taxes do not violate the commerce clause was expressly overruled in American Trucking Assn. Inc. v. Scheiner, 107 S.Ct. 2829 (1987), but the earlier case is still valid in "its recognition that the commerce clause does not require the states to avoid flat

To assess the significance of a state's compensatory interest in the application of its tax to a particular taxpayer, one must determine the degree to which the taxpayer's activities in interstate commerce benefit from state government services. And, as a rough but constitutionally adequate measure of benefits conferred, one must look to the ways in which the taxed activities can be "connected" with the taxing state. The degree of "connection," "contact," or "nexus" between the taxing state and the interstate commerce taxed is also the fundamental measure of whether or not a state tax violates the commerce and due process clauses. Therefore, to the extent that a state can point to a substantial connection with a particular aspect of interstate commerce, it can also demonstrate that its program is consistent with the commerce and due process clauses.

The Supreme Court has held that the commerce clause prevents a state from taxing aspects of interstate commerce plainly unconnected with activities taking place within the taxing state, rooting this restriction in the need to check the perverse pressures to which state governments, because of their narrow accountability, would otherwise be subject: "Lying back of these decisions is the recognized danger that, to the extent that the burden falls on economic interests without the state, it is not likely to be alleviated by those political restraints which are normally exerted on legislation where it affects adversely interests within the state." [5]

The commerce clause "requires 'some definite link, some minimum connection, between a state and the person, property or transaction it seeks to tax'," [6] in part as a prophylactic device designed to protect "the free flow of trade between the States." [7] Because failure to meet the requirement often manifests itself in visibly discriminatory or cumulatively burdensome taxation, it is not always necessary for the Supreme Court explicitly to reach the "minimum contacts" question even though it is this jurisdictional requirement which lies at the heart of most commerce clause tax litigation.

The "minimum contacts" rule can be aptly illustrated by judicial treatment of sales and use taxes. A state *sales tax* is most often measured by a percentage of the gross receipts collected from sales made within the taxing state. The fact that a product has travelled or will travel in interstate commerce does not preclude a tax being levied at the time of its sale.[8] A state *use tax* is usually measured by a

taxes when they are the only practicable means of collecting revenue from users and the use of a more finely gradated user fee schedule would pose genuine administrative burdens." Id. at 2847.

5. McGoldrick v. Berwind-White Coal Mining Co., 309 U.S. 33, 45–46 n. 2 (1940). See also Robbins v. Shelby Taxing District, 120 U.S. 489, 499 (1887), discussed in § 6–17, infra. Compare § 6–5, supra.

6. National Bellas Hess, Inc. v. Department of Revenue of the State of Illinois, 386 U.S. 753, 756 (1967), quoting Miller Bros. Co. v. Maryland, 347 U.S. 340, 44–45

(1954). See also American Oil Co. v. Neill, 380 U.S. 451, 458 (1965).

7. Freeman v. Hewitt, 329 U.S. 249, 252 (1946).

8. See Woodruff v. Parham, 75 U.S. (8 Wall.) 123 (1869) (Alabama may impose nondiscriminatory tax on sales in the original package of merchandise brought into the state from another state). But see Robbins v. Shelby County Taxing District, 120 U.S. 489, 497 (1887) (dictum). To proscribe such taxation would severely disadvantage local merchants. See Lockhart, "The Sales Tax in Interstate Commerce,"

percentage of the gross receipts from sales made outside of the taxing state, but is imposed on the consumption or use of the purchased goods within the taxing state.[9] A use tax is not repugnant to the Constitution merely because it is imposed on goods imported from other states.[10] Use taxes are often levied in tandem with sales taxes in order to prevent buyers from abandoning the purchase of locally available goods which have been made more expensive than similar out-of-state goods by the institution of a local sales tax.[11]

So long as the taxes are otherwise nondiscriminatory, therefore, the constitutionality of sales and use taxes depends on the outcome of a jurisdictional analysis.[12] Commerce clause questions have been raised in two kinds of cases: (a) where the burden of collecting and subsequently remitting a state sales tax falls on local sellers who have made sales to out-of-state customers; and (b) where the burden of collecting and subsequently remitting state sales or use taxes falls on out-of-state sellers who have made sales to local customers.

A state may require a local seller to collect and remit a tax on receipts from sales made to out-of-state customers only if the sale itself can be sufficiently connected with the taxing state. *Delivery within the taxing state* can establish such a nexus. For example, in *International Harvester Co. v. Department of Treasury*, the Supreme Court indicated that an Indiana manufacturer could be required to pay an Indiana tax on sales of Indiana goods to an out-of-state buyer who came to Indiana, took delivery there, and subsequently transported the goods to another state: "The consummation of the transaction was an event within the borders of Indiana which gave it authority to levy the tax on gross receipts from the sales." [13]

52 Harv.L.Rev. 617, 624 (1939). See Eastern Air Transport, Inc. v. South Carolina Commission, 285 U.S. 147 (1932) (sales tax valid as applied to the sale of gasoline to an interstate air line).

9. Sales and use taxes are ultimately paid by buyers whenever sellers are able to pass on the burden of such taxes by charging higher prices. But sellers may nonetheless find themselves unable to escape the obligation to serve as tax collectors, an obligation the taxing state typically seeks to impose with respect to sales and use taxes alike inasmuch as direct collection by the state from a widely dispersed group of buyers and/or users would constitute an administrative nightmare.

10. See Henneford v. Silas Mason Co., 300 U.S. 577 (1937), discussed in § 6–17, infra. The Court reasoned that a use tax was much like a property tax which, according to well settled commerce clause doctrine, could be applied to any property that had come to rest within the state. Id. at 582. See also Felt & T. Mfg. Co. v. Gallagher, 306 U.S. 62 (1939); Monamotor Oil Co. v. Johnson, 292 U.S. 86 (1934). Nor is a use tax unconstitutional as applied to particular property merely because sales or use taxes were paid on that property in other jurisdictions. See Southern Pacific Co. v. Gallagher, 306 U.S. 167 (1939). See generally Powell, "Sales and Use Taxes: Collection from Absentee Vendors," 57 Harv.L.Rev. 1086 (1944).

11. The relationship between sales and use taxes is also discussed from the perspective of limits on state discrimination in § 6–17, infra.

12. See J. D. Adams Mfg. Co. v. Storen, 304 U.S. 307, 311 (1938) (Indiana may not require a local corporation to pay a tax on gross receipts from the interstate sale of goods manufactured in Indiana but delivered out-of-state, because no attempt was made to link the tax with any local incident of the multistate activity taxed).

13. 322 U.S. 340, 348 (1944). See also State Tax Comm. of Utah v. Pacific States Cast Iron Pipe Co., 372 U.S. 605 (1963) (per curiam). The tax involved in International Harvester was a gross receipts tax levied directly upon the in-state seller, not a sales or use tax levied upon the out-of-state buyer which the seller was simply obligated to collect. In the present context, this distinction may be more semantic than real;

Where delivery is effected *outside* the taxing state, a sufficient nexus is less likely to be found. In *American Oil Co. v. Neill,* for example, Idaho was not permitted to tax a sale made by a multi-state petroleum dealer licensed to do business in Idaho because the sale in question had been negotiated in Washington and the oil had been delivered by the seller to the buyer's receiving plant in Utah prior to the buyer's eventual transportation of the oil into Idaho. The Court argued: "There is no reason to suppose . . . that Utah Oil's activities in Idaho contributed in any way to the procurement or performance of the contract." [14]

Similarly, a state may require an *out-of-state seller* to collect and remit a tax on receipts from sales made to local customers only if the sale itself can be sufficiently connected with the taxing state. Once again, delivery within the taxing state can help justify the imposition of a tax. Thus, in *McGoldrick v. Berwind-White Coal Mining Co.,*[15] the Supreme Court held constitutional the collection of a New York City sales tax from a Pennsylvania coal dealer who maintained a sales office in New York City, who had there negotiated a contract for the sale of coal to a New York City customer, and who had then delivered the coal from Pennsylvania to the customer in New York City. The Court found a sufficient local connection in the *"transfer of possession to the purchaser within the state,* which is the taxable event regardless of the time and place of passing title." [16]

Berwind-White was given a narrow reading by the Supreme Court in *McLeod v. J. E. Dilworth Co.*[17] There, Arkansas was held unable to tax sales made by Tennessee corporations soliciting business in Arkansas through the use of traveling salesmen, direct mail advertising, and telephone inquiries, because (a) orders were not accepted until approved by the Tennessee headquarters, and (b) the goods were shipped from Tennessee to Arkansas customers by common carrier, with title passing to the customers upon delivery of the goods to the carrier in Tennessee and before arrival in Arkansas. In distinguishing *Berwind-White,* Justice Frankfurter's opinion for the Court emphasized *all* of the New York activities of the Pennsylvania coal dealer taxed by New York in the latter case, while noting that *all* the critical elements of the sales Arkansas sought to tax in *Dilworth* took place in Tennessee. In particular, the two cases were found to differ with regard to the point at which the seller ceased to take responsibility for the goods sold: "In *Berwind-White* the Pennsylvania seller completed his sales in New

---

the Court recognized the economic equivalence of the two taxes posited and observed that a mere difference in label should not warrant a difference in the applicable legal standard. 322 U.S. at 346. See also Lockhart, "Gross Receipt Taxes on Interstate Transportation and Communication." 57 Harv.L.Rev. 40, 87 (1944); Powell, "New Light on Gross Receipts Taxes," 53 Harv.L. Rev. 909, 911 (1940).

14. 380 U.S. 451, 458–59 (1965). This case was decided under the due process clause, but the standards are equivalent.

15. 309 U.S. 33 (1940).

16. Id. at 49 (emphasis added). See also McGoldrick v. Felt & Tarrant Mfg. Co., 309 U.S. 70, 77 (1940). The Berwind-White Court saw no grounds for distinguishing the sales tax from the property tax which, it was well established, could be applied to goods when their interstate journey terminated. 309 U.S. at 52, 55.

17. 322 U.S. 327 (1944).

York; in this case the Tennessee seller was through selling in Tennessee." [18]

In the sales tax cases, commerce clause jurisdictional analysis has thus required that a taxing state show sufficient contacts with an out-of-state seller or buyer to justify a conclusion that significant aspects of the taxed sale occurred within its boundaries; and the standards applied have been framed so as to limit to a single state the jurisdictions capable of making such a showing. In the use tax cases, the emphasis is again on the local activities of an out-of-state seller, not because a sale must be shown to be local, but because the out-of-state seller must be shown to have established sufficient sale-connected contacts with the taxing state to make it reasonable for the taxing state to require the out-of-state seller to collect its use tax. [19]

In more recent use tax cases, the existence of some relationship between the out-of-state sale and the seller's local activities has been apparent. The critical question has instead been whether the local contacts were sufficiently "substantial" to warrant the imposition of a collection duty. Central to this inquiry has been the distinction, thought significant by the Supreme Court, between local, face-to-face solicitation of sales by salesmen, and local solicitation of sales by direct mail, telephone, or other interstate advertising media.

An out-of-state seller has sufficient contact with a taxing state to justify the imposition of a use tax collection duty if the seller employs salesmen (or uses independent contractors) in order systematically to exploit the local market—even if sales are not final unless approved at an out-of-state office, deliveries are made to out-of-state warehouses, and payment is made directly to the out-of-state headquarters. [20] However, a systematic program of direct mail advertising is *not* sufficient to

---

18. Id. at 330. The Court concluded: "For Arkansas to impose a tax on such transactions would be to project its powers beyond its boundaries and to tax an interstate transaction." Id. It should be noted that while transfer of possession had been declared more significant than the passage of title in Berwind-White, Dilworth equated the two events, perhaps because they occurred at the same time and place and because other contacts with the taxing state were lacking. The effect of the Court's equation is to render unclear the relative import of the two events when they do not coincide; probably, the key event should be the passage of *economic risk* from seller to buyer.

19. See, e.g., Nelson v. Sears, Roebuck & Co., 312 U.S. 359 (1941) (Iowa may require Sears to collect the Iowa use tax from its Iowa mail order customers because Sears operates retail stores in Iowa: although those stores are not directly involved with the interstate mail order business, it is not unreasonable to assume that there is some connection, however indirect, between the mail order transactions and Sears' local presence). Cf. Norton Co. v.

Department of Revenue of Illinois, 340 U.S. 534 (1951).

20. See Scripto, Inc. v. Carson, 362 U.S. 207 (1960) (Florida may require Georgia-based Scripto agents to collect a use tax from its Florida customers because Scripto employed, on a commission basis, "10 wholesalers, jobbers, or 'salesmen' conducting continuous local solicitation in Florida"). The Scripto Court expressly deemed constitutionally insignificant the fact that the "salesmen" were not employees of Scripto. Id. at 211. See also General Trading Co. v. State Tax Commission of the State of Iowa, 322 U.S. 335 (1944) (allowing a collection duty to be imposed by Iowa where "[the] property on which the use tax was laid was sent to Iowa as a result of orders solicited by traveling salesmen sent into Iowa from their Minnesota headquarters"). In General Trading, the company maintained no place of business or property within the taxing state; the personal solicitation by salesmen within the borders of the taxing state was held sufficient to support the tax. Similarly, companies maintaining retail sales outlets within the state have been required to col-

justify a use tax collection requirement if that is the only contact between the out-of-state seller and the taxing state.[21] Similarly, sporadic direct mail advertising, occasional local deliveries, and systematic advertising on out-of-state radio stations and in out-of-state newspapers known to reach local residents, have been held insufficient to justify imposition of a use tax collection requirement.[22]

The distinction between employment of local salesmen and other, less physical, forms of local soliciting has not invariably been deemed crucial by the Court in other circumstances.[23] Underlying the resort to this distinction in the tax-collection context has been a manifest concern with the administrative burden that a use tax collection requirement imposes on some out-of-state sellers. In *National Bellas Hess v. Department of Revenue of the State of Illinois*,[24] the Court recognized the administrative difficulties that mail order houses would face in keeping track of the different use tax requirements of the different states in which they did business.[25] And in *Miller Brothers v. Maryland*,[26] the Court was plainly concerned with the difficulty that the department store involved in that case would face if it tried to identify those of its customers who were from Maryland. Whether or not the employment of local salesmen facilitates such record-keeping, it is clear that the administrative burden of use tax collection in particular cases can be substantial enough to require more than minimal contacts between the out-of-state seller and the taxing state.

lect use taxes. See, e.g., Nelson v. Montgomery Ward & Co., 312 U.S. 373 (1941); Nelson v. Sears, Roebuck & Co., 312 U.S. 359 (1941); National Geographic Society v. Calif. Bd. of Equalization, 430 U.S. 551 (1977) (irrelevant that taxpayer's in-state advertising offices have no relation to taxpayer's in-state mail order sales).

21. National Bellas Hess, Inc. v. Department of Revenue of the State of Illinois, 386 U.S. 753 (1967) (mail order business in which (1) orders were solicited by a program of direct-mail advertising which sent catalogues twice a year to over 5,000,000 people, and supplementary mailings to an even larger number, and (2) deliveries were made by mail or by common carrier). Justice Stewart observed for the Court: ". . . the Court has never held that a State may impose the duty of use tax collection and payment upon a seller whose only connection with customers in the State is by common carrier or the United States mail. Indeed, in the *Sears, Roebuck* case the Court sharply differentiated such a situation from one where the seller had local retail outlets, pointing out that 'those other concerns . . . are not receiving benefits from Iowa for which it has the power to exact a price.'" Id. at 758. It should be noted that National Bellas Hess does *not* require the same amount of "nexus" for a use tax as the Court has required for sales taxes; sales agents appear to constitute sufficient nexus for use taxes, though not for sales taxes. The reasons for the difference remain unexplained.

22. See Miller Bros. Co. v. Maryland, 347 U.S. 340 (1954), holding that there was too weak a nexus between the taxing state and the seller despite the fact that the company regularly dispatched its trucks to the taxing state to deliver orders. The Court emphasized that this was the *only* physical link between the seller and the taxing state. Id. at 345.

23. See, e.g., Breard v. Alexandria, 341 U.S. 622 (1951) (upholding a local ordinance banning door-to-door selling without the prior consent of potential customers in part because other "usual methods of solicitation—radio, periodicals, mail, local agencies—are open").

24. 386 U.S. 753 (1967), discussed in note 21, supra.

25. Justice Fortas, dissenting, thought the majority had seriously underestimated the potentialities of modern computers as record-keeping devices for this purpose. 386 U.S. at 766.

26. 347 U.S. 340, 343 (1954), discussed in note 22, supra. See generally Dane, "A Solution to the Problem of State Taxation of Interstate Commerce." 12 Vill.L.Rev. 507, 524 (1967).

The sales and use tax cases make clear that the inversely related requirements that interstate commerce "pay its way" and that states not seek to extend their tax powers beyond their respective borders can be summarized in the principle that a state may require multi-state businesses to pay only those taxes which can be rationally related to local activities substantial enough to warrant compensation to the state. The manner in which the elements of this principle determine the extent of constitutionally permitted taxation is especially apparent in those decisions which focus on tax apportionment as a means of localizing the tax burden, and on the fourteenth amendment due process clause as a supplementary source of standards for ascertaining the degree of local connection which must be demonstrated to justify taxation.

In particular, a tax on an aspect of commerce otherwise wholly interstate in character may be linked with local business activities through the use of an apportionment formula. For example, in *Northwestern States Portland Cement Co. v. Minnesota*,[27] the Court held that Minnesota could collect its fairly apportioned net income tax from an Iowa cement manufacturer who employed salesmen to solicit business in Minnesota but otherwise dealt with Minnesota customers only through the Iowa headquarters. In order to determine what proportion of the Iowa corporation's net income could be attributed to its Minnesota activities, the Minnesota tax used a formula incorporating three ratios: "The first is [the ratio] of the taxpayer's sales assignable to Minnesota during the year to its total sales during that period everywhere; the second, [the ratio] of the taxpayer's total tangible property in Minnesota for the year to its total tangible property used in the business that year wherever situated. The third is [the ratio of] the taxpayer's total payroll in Minnesota for the year to its total payroll for its entire business in the like period."[28] The Court found the critical question the same one as that raised in *Central Greyhound Lines, Inc. v. Mealey*: "whether what the State is exacting is a constitutionally fair demand by the State for that aspect of the interstate commerce to which the State bears a special relation."[29] The Court concluded that "[the] apportioned tax is designed to meet this very requirement".[30]

Not all tax apportionment schemes, however, can survive judicial scrutiny; if it is not "to 'project the taxing power of the state plainly beyond its borders'," any tax apportionment formula that is used "must bear a rational relationship, both on its face and in its application, to

27. 358 U.S. 450 (1959). See also § 6–17, infra.

28. Id. at 453–54.

29. 334 U.S. 653, 661 (1948). The Portland Cement Court quoted this language with approval. See 358 U.S. at 462.

30. Id. See also Butler Brothers v. McColgan, 315 U.S. 501 (1942) (sustaining net income tax apportioned on the basis of property, payroll, and sales ratios); Canton Ry. Co. v. Rogan, 340 U.S. 511 (1951) (up-

holding an apportioned gross receipts tax as applied to a railroad engaged exclusively in handling interstate commerce at an in-state port). For a critique of the Court's approach to these cases, see Brown in § 6–1, supra, note 1, at 228–33, arguing that taxes like those sustained in Canton Ry. Co. v. Rogan were in reality transportation tariffs falling primarily on outsiders. It is unclear whether the Court's approach will survive the new realism of Complete Auto Transit, discussed in § 6–15, supra.

. . . values connected with the taxing State." [31] But the taxpayer has the burden of proving an apportionment formula irrational.

Even in cases where the state tax is rationally related to local business activities through the use of a reasonable apportionment formula, however, one must address the threshold question whether the local activities are sufficiently substantial to warrant *any* tax under the fourteenth amendment due process clause.[32] Although the due process standard of review is similar to that of the commerce clause in this regard,[33] reformulation of the rule in terms of the due process requirement of "situs" helps to highlight the jurisdictional nature of the question.[34]

Perhaps because of its family resemblance to the weaker "rational relationship" standard used in due process scrutiny of the constitutionality of *all* legislative action,[35] employment of the due process "situs" test has occasionally led courts to approve state taxes which might have been struck down if viewed from the perspective of the policies underlying the commerce clause. *Northwestern States Portland Cement Co. v. Minnesota* [36] is perhaps the most prominent recent example of this tendency. In that 1959 case, the Court found that an apportioned net income tax could be collected from an out-of-state corporation whose only local activity, solicitation of business through the use of salesmen, was held to be a connection sufficient to satisfy the due process situs requirement.

Within seven months of this decision, Congress enacted a statute [37] specifying that "mere solicitation" in a state does not constitute a local connection substantial enough by itself to justify a state "net income tax on the income derived within such State by any person from interstate commerce. . . ." As the Supreme Court has subsequently recognized, Congress acted because "*Northwestern States Portland Cement* did not adequately specify what local activities were enough to create a 'sufficient nexus' for the exercise of the State's power to tax." [38]

---

31. Norfolk & Western Ry. Co. v. Missouri State Tax Commission, 390 U.S. 317, 325 (1968) (striking down the application of a Missouri property tax to an interstate railroad because the apportionment formula's reliance on railroad track mileage was demonstrated by the railroad to have inaccurately inflated the tax base by a factor of 260–300%). See also Union Tank Line Co. v. Wright, 249 U.S. 275 (1919).

32. See, e.g., Northwestern States Portland Cement Co. v. Minnesota, 358 U.S. 450, 464 (1959) ("Nor will the argument that the exactions contravene the Due Process Clause bear scrutiny. . . . These activities form a sufficient nexus between such a tax and transactions within a state for which the tax is an exaction").

33. See National Bellas Hess, Inc. v. Department of Revenue, 386 U.S. 753, 756 (1967).

34. Cf. International Shoe Co. v. Washington, 326 U.S. 310, 316 (1945) ("due pro-

cess requires only that in order to subject a defendant to a judgment *in personam*, if he be not present within the territory of the forum, he have certain minimum contacts with it such that the maintenance of the suit does not offend 'traditional notions of fair play and substantial justice' "). See also Shaffer v. Heitner, 433 U.S. 186 (1977), extending the International Shoe standard to cases of *in rem* jurisdiction and *quasi-in rem* jurisdiction.

35. See, e.g., § 5–3, supra; § 16–2, infra.

36. 358 U.S. 450 (1959), discussed in § 6–17, infra.

37. 73 Stat. 555, 15 U.S.C. §§ 381–384.

38. Heublein, Inc. v. South Carolina Tax Commission, 409 U.S. 275, 280 (1972). Although the Court has generally shown greater concern subsequent to the passage of this statute for the character and degree of the local activities claimed by states to

Recent cases confirm that the due process clause can be a significant restraint on a state's power to tax wealth created beyond its borders. In *Asarco Inc. v. Idaho State Tax Commission* [39] and *F. W. Woolworth v. Taxation & Revenue Department*,[40] the Court invalidated efforts to tax dividend income derived by resident corporations from out-of-state subsidiaries that had no other contact with the taxing state. The Court found that the subsidiaries were operated as discrete enterprises, rather than as part of a unitary business; the parent companies did not actively control the subsidiaries, but engaged only in the occasional oversight that any corporation gives to an investment.[41] Even if a corporation has the potential to control subsidiaries, there is no basis for taxation of dividend income unless there is functional integration, centralization of management, or achievement of other economies of scale.[42] The Court expressly rejected the infinitely expandable theory that dividend income should be taxable as part of a "unitary business" if the intangible property is merely acquired or managed for purposes relating to the taxpayer's business.[43]

"[B]eyond the presence of a sufficient connection in a due process or 'jurisdictional' sense, whether or not a 'local incident' related to or affecting commerce may be made the subject of state taxation depends upon other considerations of constitutional policy having reference to the *substantial effects* . . . of the particular tax in suppressing or burdening unduly the commerce." [44] In defining the negative implications of the commerce clause for state taxation, the Supreme Court has emphasized two related but distinct consequences of state taxes either of which renders a particular tax unconstitutional: (a) *discrimination against out-of-state commerce* in favor of local competitors; and (b) *cumulative burdening of interstate commerce* by several states' collection of similar taxes.

§ 6–17. Forbidden Discriminatory Taxes

The Supreme Court has traditionally recognized that a large part of the rationale for granting Congress control over interstate commerce "was to insure . . . against discriminating State legislation." [1] Therefore, the Court has consistently struck down those state taxes which it concludes unjustifiably benefit local commerce at the expense of out-of-

justify taxation of multistate businesses, the statute itself has been quite narrowly construed.

Compare Scripto, Inc. v. Carson, 362 U.S. 207 (1960), with National Bellas Hess, Inc. v. Department of Revenue, 386 U.S. 753 (1967), discussed in notes 20–21, supra, see Heublein, Inc. v. South Carolina Tax Commission, 409 U.S. 275 (1972) (as part of its program of alcoholic beverage control, a state may require a multi-state distributor to deliver its liquor products to a local employee who then distributes the liquor to local retailers—even though this requirement prevents the distributor from taking advantage of 15 U.S.C. § 381, and thus makes possible state net income taxa-

tion). The Court did not rely on the twenty-first amendment, discussed in § 6–24, infra.

39. 458 U.S. 307 (1982).

40. 458 U.S. 354 (1982).

41. Asarco, 458 U.S. at 322–24; Woolworth, 458 U.S. at 369.

42. Woolworth, 458 U.S. at 364–67.

43. Asarco, 458 U.S. at 326.

44. Nippert v. Richmond, 327 U.S. 416, 423–24 (1946) (emphasis added).

§ 6–17

1. Welton v. Missouri, 91 U.S. (1 Otto) 275, 280 (1875).

state commerce. In contrast, state taxes which favor out-of-state commerce at the expense of local commerce are not similarly suspect.[2]

A state tax which burdens interstate enterprises more than it burdens exclusively local business operations is not always deemed unconstitutionally discriminatory. However, the taxing state must adequately justify the differential—by specifically demonstrating, for example, (a) that the state conferred benefits on the interstate enterprises which it did not grant local businesses; or (b) that the state incurred additional administrative costs in taxing businesses located outside the state; or (c) that the local activities of interstate enterprises created regulatory problems capable of solution by the increased taxation which were not raised by the otherwise similar actions of local businesses.

The Supreme Court has found invalid as plainly discriminatory those state taxes which, without sufficient justification, explicitly exempt local activities from the obligations imposed on comparable interstate enterprises. For example, in *Hale v. Bimco Trading, Inc.*, the Court held unconstitutional a Florida statute which imposed an inspection fee 60 times the actual cost of inspection upon cement imported into the state for sale or use, because that statute exempted locally produced cement from all inspection and inspection fee requirements: "[It] would not be easy to imagine a statute more clearly designed than the present to circumvent what the Commerce Clause forbids." [3] Recently the Court has applied the ban against explicitly discriminatory tax legislation to schemes which discriminate *among* interstate transactions in order to benefit in-state commerce. In *Boston Stock Exchange v. State Tax Comm'n*,[4] the Court invalidated a New York statute which imposed a greater tax burden on interstate stock transactions having significant in-state elements but consummated outside of the state than on those in which the sale itself took place within the state, holding that the state could not thus encourage business operations to be performed within its borders.[5] And in *Westinghouse Electric Corpora-*

2. See, e.g., Allied Stores of Ohio, Inc. v. Bowers, 358 U.S. 522, 528 (1959) (consistent with the fourteenth amendment equal protection clause, a state may explicitly exempt nonresidents storing property in local warehouses from the property tax liability incurred by residents, since the discriminatory application of the tax can be rationally related to the legitimate state goal of attracting out-of-state warehouse business). But cf. Foster-Fountain Packing Co. v. Haydel, 278 U.S. 1 (1928), discussed in § 6–10, supra. Compare the discussion of "benign discrimination" in §§ 16–22, 16–27, infra.

3. 306 U.S. 375, 380–81 (1939). See also Tyler Pipe Industries, Inc. v. Washington Dept. of Revenue, 107 S.Ct. 2810 (1987) (invalidating business and occupation tax falling on local manufacturers who sell to out-of-state customers but exempting local manufacturers who sell to local customers; this overrules General Motors Corp. v.

Washington, 377 U.S. 436 (1964)); Armco, Inc. v. Hardesty, 467 U.S. 638 (1984) (invalidating gross receipts tax falling on businesses selling tangible property wholesale but exempting local manufacturers who were subject to a higher manufacturing tax; tax cannot be justified as compensatory since manufacturing and wholesaling are not substantially equivalent). Accord, Welton v. Missouri, 91 U.S. 275 (1876) (declaring unconstitutional a license fee imposed for the privilege of peddling but exempting peddlers of instate goods); Morrill v. Wisconsin, 154 U.S. 626 (1877); Guy v. Baltimore, 100 U.S. 434 (1880); Tiernan v. Rinker, 102 U.S. 123 (1880); Webber v. Virginia, 103 U.S. 344 (1881); cf. Voight v. Wright, 141 U.S. 62 (1891).

4. 429 U.S. 318 (1977).

5. The Court analyzed New York's discriminatory taxing scheme as it would have assessed regulatory legislation requir-

tion v. Tully,[6] the Court unanimously condemned a New York law that gave franchise tax credits to domestic international sales corporations in proportion to the percentage of their shipping activities conducted from within the state. The fact that it was a franchise tax credit rather than an added transaction tax did not make the scheme constitutional.[7]

The Supreme Court has also found unconstitutionally discriminatory those state taxes nondiscriminatory on their face which, without sufficient justification, impose economic burdens on interstate enterprises which are not in fact imposed on local competitors. Judicial concern with the discriminatory consequences of ostensibly neutral taxing statutes has been most apparent in cases dealing with the constitutionality of fixed-fee license taxes collected from all local and out-of-state practitioners of the art of "drumming," i.e., the solicitation of orders for goods which are to be delivered to the customer at some future time, such as door-to-door solicitation of magazine subscriptions.

The seminal case is *Robbins v. Shelby County Taxing District*.[8] There, the Supreme Court struck down, as applied to drummers soliciting sales on behalf of out-of-state firms, a Tennessee statute which required all drummers operating in the city of Memphis to pay a fixed license fee for the privilege of doing business there. Most of the Court's opinion was devoted to demonstrating that, in this context, soliciting orders was a local activity inextricably linked with wholly interstate commerce.[9] However, at the close of his majority opinion, Justice Bradley also argued that the tax discriminated against out-of-state merchants and manufacturers: "They can only sell their goods in Memphis by the employment of drummers and by means of samples; whilst the merchants and manufacturers of Memphis, having regular licensed houses of business there, have no occasion for such agents, and, if they had, they are not subject to any tax therefor. They are taxed for their licensed houses, it is true; but so, it is presumable, are the merchants and manufacturers of other states in the places where they reside; and the tax on drummers operates greatly to their disadvantage in comparison with the merchants and manufacturers of Memphis." [10]

Robbins was expressly reaffirmed in *Nippert v. City of Richmond*.[11] There, the Supreme Court found that the potential discriminatory and indeed exclusionary effects of a municipal license tax imposed on all soliciting, which took the form of both a fixed fee and a percentage of gross receipts, rendered the tax unconstitutional: "Provincial interests

ing interstate business operations to be performed within the regulating state in cases such as Pike v. Bruce Church, Inc., 397 U.S. 137 (1970). See § 6–9, supra.

6. 466 U.S. 388 (1984).

7. Id. at 404–05.

8. 120 U.S. 489 (1887).

9. That this factor may soon be deemed irrelevant is suggested by the "new realism" in tax cases. See § 6–15, supra.

10. 120 U.S. at 498. See also Best & Company, Inc. v. Maxwell, 311 U.S. 454 (1940) (striking down, as applied to a nonresident merchant, a North Carolina statute levying a fixed fee of $250 on *all* retail merchants displaying samples in hotel rooms for the purpose of securing retail orders; the relevant competitors were thought to be North Carolina retail merchants permanently doing business in the state who paid only a one dollar privilege-of-doing-business tax); Memphis Steam Laundry Cleaner, Inc. v. Stone, 342 U.S. 389 (1952).

11. 327 U.S. 416 (1946).

and local political power are at their maximum weight in bringing about acceptance of this type of legislation. With the forces behind it, this is the very kind of barrier the commerce clause was put in the fundamental law to guard against." [12]

The logic of *Robbins* and *Nippert* not only extends to drumming but embraces as well any activity which is essential for an out-of-state enterprise but not essential for a local business. Thus, in *West Point Wholesale Grocery Co. v. City of Opelika*,[13] the Court read the "drummer" cases as prohibiting the collection of an annual fixed fee license tax of $250, imposed on the *delivery* into Opelika of wholesale groceries from warehouses located outside the municipality, from a Georgia firm soliciting and delivering wholesale orders in the Alabama city, when the city exacted no comparable flat-sum tax from local merchants.[14]

Different reasoning surfaces in decisions concerning state taxes on "peddlers," sales personnel who travel "from place to place within the State selling goods that are carried about with the seller for the purpose". [15] Such taxes are constitutional under the commerce clause "where no discrimination against interstate commerce appears either upon the face of the tax laws or in their practical operation." [16] In practice, "peddler" taxes are usually upheld unless they are facially discriminatory. The differing treatment given "peddler" and "drummer" taxes is best explained by the interaction of two factors: (a) the Court has found peddling to be a local activity distinct from any interstate movement which preceded it, and a nondiscriminatory license tax on peddlers is therefore "a valid exercise of the power of the State over persons and business within it borders;" [17] and (b) while drummers have been assumed to compete with local retail merchants operating from fixed locations,[18] the Court has concluded [19] that peddlers ordinarily compete with other peddlers, so that a tax structure

12. Id. at 434. The Court reasoned that the burden of the municipal tax involved in Nippert was heavier upon small out-of-state solicitors than upon local sellers because the former solicit intermittently throughout the state and could thus be subjected to several such levies—a kind of intrastate multiple burden. Id. at 429–31. Cf. § 6–18, infra. See also Real Silk Hosiery Mills v. Portland, 268 U.S. 325 (1925); Corson v. Maryland, 120 U.S. 502 (1887). Cf. McLeod v. J. E. Dilworth Co., 322 U.S. 327 (1944), discussed in § 6–16, supra. But see Brennan v. Titusville, 153 U.S. 289 (1894) (implying that the police power might justify such a tax in the proper circumstances).

13. 354 U.S. 390 (1957).

14. See also Memphis Steam Laundry Cleaner, Inc. v. Stone, 342 U.S. 389 (1952) (if a Mississippi tax upon "the privilege of soliciting interstate business for a laundry not licensed in that State" is read so as to tax solicitation, then the tax is void under the "drummer" cases because it burdens a

local activity inextricably linked with wholly interstate commerce). One might well question the plausibility of the Court's assumptions about competitive structure, see note 10, supra, as applied to solicitations for *services* rather than for *sales*.

15. Wagner v. Covington, 251 U.S. 95, 101 (1919).

16. See Memphis Steam Laundry Cleaner, Inc. v. Stone, 342 U.S. 389 (1952) (even if a Mississippi tax on the privilege of soliciting business for a laundry not licensed in that State is read to tax the local activity of picking up and delivering laundry, the tax is not supported by the peddler decisions because local laundries pay a lower tax). The alternate holding is discussed in note 14, supra.

17. Emert v. Missouri, 156 U.S. 296, 322 (1895). See also Wagner v. Covington, 251 U.S. 95, 103 (1919).

18. See, e.g., Best & Co., Inc. v. Maxwell, 311 U.S. 454 (1940), in note 10, supra.

19. With little or no evidence.

not discriminating among peddlers may be assumed not to discriminate at all.[20]

Critical to the distinction between the "drummer" and "peddler" cases are the different factual conclusions the Supreme Court has drawn in those two series of decisions concerning the identity of the local competition facing the out-of-state sellers. Because institutional factors have been thought to limit the extent to which the Court can make such factual analyses,[21] the connection between judicial decisions and judicial perception of economic facts is in many cases less explicit. In general, claims of discriminatory taxation are judged primarily on the basis of the facial characteristics of the taxing statutes; the only economic conclusions reached are those which plainly derive from the structure of the industry taxed.[22] But *Complete Auto Transit* may presage increased judicial willingness to examine specific factual circumstances.[23]

The Supreme Court's treatment of discrimination claims in cases involving state use taxes is indicative of the kind of judicial analysis that has most commonly been undertaken when economic facts are not self-evident. It should be noted that, unlike the previous discussion of use taxes,[24] where the claim of unconstitutionality was brought by out-of-state *sellers* required to *collect* the tax, the discussion that follows focuses on claims made by in-state *consumers* required to *pay* the tax.

In *Henneford v. Silas Mason Co., Inc.*[25] the Supreme Court upheld a state use tax which applied only to goods purchased outside the taxing

---

20. See, e.g., Caskey Baking Co., Inc. v. Virginia, 313 U.S. 117, 119–20 (1941) (Virginia may collect its "peddling" tax from a West Virginia baker who sells bread door-to-door in Virginia, even though the tax exempts local bakers supplying fixed retail outlets, because "peddlers resident in Virginia who buy their goods within the State, or buy or procure them from extrastate sources, are alike subject to the Act"). But cf. Dunbar-Stanley Studios, Inc. v. Alabama, 393 U.S. 537, 542 (1969), (holding constitutional a state tax on traveling photographers because the tax applied to both out-of-state and local traveling photographers, and because "[i]n none of the cities . . . would the transient tax imposed . . . have exceeded that which a fixed-location photographer would have had to pay to operate in the city"). See generally Hartman, "Sales Taxation of Interstate Commerce," 9 Vand.L.Rev. 138, 142–43 (1956). It seems likely that much of the difference in treatment accorded drummers and peddlers stems from the historical accident that the drummer cases first arose in the sympathetic context of criminal prosecutions whereas the peddler cases first arose in the setting of suits seeking refund of license fees.

21. See Northwestern States Portland Cement Co. v. Minnesota, 358 U.S. 450, 476 (1959) (Frankfurter, J., dissenting).

22. Cf. Alaska v. Arctic Maid, 366 U.S. 199 (1961) (4% license tax collected from out-of-state freezer ships operating in the salmon banks off the Alaska coast held to be nondiscriminatory even though local land-based freezer plants paid only a 1% tax: the freezer ships supplied out-of-state canneries, and therefore did not compete with local freezers who serviced the fresh-frozen retail market, but with local canneries, which were taxed at a 6% rate).

23. Then again, it may not. Compare Complete Auto Transit, Inc. v. Brady, 430 U.S. 274 (1977), with Commonwealth Edison Company v. Montana, 453 U.S. 609 (1981), discussed in § 6–15, supra. But see American Trucking Assn., Inc. v. Scheiner, 107 S.Ct. 2829 (1987), where the Court looked beyond Pennsylvania's "registration fees" and "axle taxes" to conclude that the entire statutory tax regime amounted to a flat highway use tax that charged all trucks the same, even though the "privilege" of using Pennsylvania's highways was far more valuable to in-state trucking firms than to out-of-state firms. Charging the same fee therefore discriminated in practical economic terms against out-of-staters, although not on the face of the relevant statute.

24. See § 6–16, supra.

25. 300 U.S. 577 (1937).

state and subsequently imported for in-state use. Justice Cardozo's opinion for the Court looked to the taxing statute as a whole and found that the use tax imposed a burden exactly equivalent to that imposed on locally purchased goods by the state sales tax: "Equality is the theme that runs through all the sections of the statute.. . . . When the account is made up, the stranger from afar is subject to no greater burdens as a consequence of ownership than the dweller within the gates. The one pays upon one activity or incident, and the other upon another, but the sum is the same when the reckoning is closed." [26]

The decision in *Henneford* is commonly contrasted with Justice Cardozo's earlier ruling in *Baldwin v. G.A.F. Seelig, Inc.*[27] In both cases, the state acted to affect the prices at which local residents could purchase out-of-state goods (in *Baldwin* by price regulation; in *Henneford* by use taxes collected for the state by the seller), in order to eliminate the competitively disadvantageous situation in which local business had been placed by another action of the same state (in *Baldwin*, setting a price floor; in *Henneford*, imposing a sales tax collection duty). However, in *Baldwin* the state action affecting out-of-state commerce was struck down, while in *Henneford* it was upheld. The cases are usually distinguished on the grounds (a) that in *Baldwin* all price differentials were eliminated whereas in *Henneford* only that price differential attributable to other state action was neutralized,[28] and (b) that the state revenue interest advanced in *Henneford* was more "local" and hence more acceptable than the more "national" state interest in economic regulation asserted in *Baldwin*.[29] However, the difference in the decisions can also be ascribed in part to the Supreme Court's unwillingness in *Henneford* to look beyond the statutory framework of the tax and beyond the shibboleth of "equality" so as to confront directly the economic consequences of the state's action.[30]

26. Id. at 583–84. The fact of equivalence between sales and use taxes stems from the basic purpose of a compensating use tax. In Henneford, the state tax not only exempted local purchases that were subject to the local sales tax but also granted a similar credit for imported goods subjected to another state's sales tax. The Court refused to decide whether this second exemption was required. 300 U.S. at 587. Although the Court subsequently approved on other grounds a state use tax which did not allow the out-of-state sales tax credit, in Southern Pacific Co. v. Gallagher, 306 U.S. 167 (1939), it has not yet ruled on the claim that a state use tax which fails to take into account out-of-state sales taxation discriminates impermissibly against interstate commerce.

27. 294 U.S. 511 (1935), discussed in § 6–6, supra.

28. See Henneford v. Silas Mason Co., Inc., 300 U.S. at 585–86.

29. See § 6–6, supra.

30. See generally T. R. Powell, "Vagaries and Varieties in Constitutional Interpretation" 190 (1956); Brown, in § 6–1, supra, note 1, at 234–36. It is not clear whether the formal distinction between cases such as Baldwin and Henneford will survive the new realism of Complete Auto Transit, supra note 23. The Court has recently explained the result in Henneford, however, as based on the "equal treatment of interstate commerce" involved in the Washington scheme. See Boston Stock Exchange v. State Tax Comm., 429 U.S. 318, 331–32 (1977). It should be noted that a use tax which is collected only for the local consumption of goods purchased *outside* the taxing state is unconstitutionally discriminatory in the absence of "adequate justification" if no complementary sales tax is imposed on equivalent locally sold goods. Halliburton Oil Well Cement Co. v. Reily, 373 U.S. 64, 71–72 (1963) (the discrepancy in this case was "explained" by the state as an "accident of statutory drafting").

§ 6–18. State Taxes Which Cumulatively Burden Interstate Commerce

Taxes which do not exclude or discriminate against interstate commerce when viewed in isolation are nonetheless prohibited by the commerce clause if they place on multistate business "burdens of such a nature as to be capable . . . of being imposed . . . or added to . . . with equal right by every state which the commerce touches, ... so that without the protection of the commerce clause it would bear cumulative burdens not imposed on local commerce."[1] Not all multiple taxation, however, contravenes the Constitution: interstate enterprises which are required to pay taxes in more than one state are not thereby subjected to constitutionally prohibited cumulative burdens so long as every tax collected "is one that is essentially local and is not repeated in each taxing unit."[2]

At one time the Court maintained that the mere theoretical possibility of multiple taxation was insufficient to establish a commerce clause violation—a taxpayer was required to prove that particular interstate transactions were actually cumulatively burdened.[3] That requirement has since been categorically rejected because it displaced the focus of judicial inquiry from the challenged state tax measure to the unchallenged tax laws of other states: " 'The immunities implicit in the Commerce Clause and the potential taxing power of a State can hardly be made to depend, in the world of practical affairs, on the shifting incidence of the varying tax laws of the various States at a particular moment.' "[4]

The distinction between allowable taxes imposed by different states on different aspects of interstate commerce and forbidden taxes im-

§ 6–18

1. Western Live Stock v. Bureau of Revenue, 303 U.S. 250, 255 (1938); Gwin, White and Prince, Inc. v. Henneford, 305 U.S. 434 (1939). Justice Stone, writing for the Court in Western Live Stock, continued: "The multiplication of state taxes measured by the gross receipts from interstate transactions would spell the destruction of interstate commerce and renew the barriers to interstate trade which it was the object of the commerce clause to remove." 303 U.S. at 256. Justice Stone envisioned the multiple burden rule as a functional test that would supplant the overly mechanistic direct-indirect dichotomy he had so long vociferously opposed. See DiSanto v. Pennsylvania, 273 U.S. 34, 44 (1927) (Stone, J., dissenting). Although not explicitly relied upon as a basis for decision, the multiple burden rhetoric can be traced to some earlier cases. See, e.g., Case of the State Freight Tax, 82 U.S. (15 Wall.) 232, 280 (1872). The cumulative burden theory was most vital in opinions between 1938 and 1946 and has not been relied upon extensively in more recent cases, which often treat multiple taxation

as a matter of discrimination against interstate commerce, rather than as a cumulative burden thereon. See, e.g., Tyler Pipe Industries, Inc. v. Washington Dept. of Revenue, 107 S.Ct. 2810, 2815 (1987). Nevertheless, it should be recognized as the substantive foundation of some of the more technical doctrinal formulations of the modern decisions.

2. Joseph v. Carter & Weekes Stevedoring Co., 330 U.S. 422, 429 (1947).

3. See, e.g., General Motors Corp. v. Washington, 377 U.S. 436, 449 (1964); Standard Pressed Steel Co. v. Washington Dept. of Revenue, 419 U.S. 560, 563 (1975).

4. Armco, Inc. v. Hardesty, 467 U.S. 638, 645 n.8 (1984) (quoting Freeman v. Hewit, 329 U.S. 249, 256 (1946)). See also Tyler Pipe Industries, Inc. v. Washington Dept. of Revenue, 107 S.Ct. 2810, 2817 (1987) ("The facial unconstitutionality of Washington's gross receipts tax cannot be alleviated by examining the effect of legislation enacted by its sister States."); Moorman Manufacturing Co. v. Blair, 437 U.S. 267, 276–78 (1978).

posed by different states on the same aspect of interstate commerce makes evident the link between cumulative burdens and the jurisdictional analysis discussed above. Cumulative burdens are possible only when states do not link the taxes they impose on interstate commerce with sufficiently local, and therefore unique, aspects of that commerce. It is thus not surprising that the Supreme Court has employed for the solution of the problem of cumulative burdens analytical devices which it also uses to resolve jurisdictional questions.

The jurisdictional requirement that states tax only local aspects of interstate commerce has as a corollary the proposition that taxes which can be related to no sufficiently local activities of multi-state businesses, and are therefore realistically capable of multiple application, can be constitutionally imposed by no states, but only by Congress. To the extent that commerce clause jurisdictional requirements nationalize taxation of interstate commerce, they therefore prevent cumulative burdens.

For example, in *National Bellas Hess, Inc. v. Department of Revenue*,[5] the Supreme Court rejected on commerce clause jurisdictional grounds an Illinois requirement that a Missouri-based corporation collect and remit to Illinois a use tax upon Illinois users who engaged in purely mail order transactions with the company. The Court observed that "if Illinois can impose such burdens, so can every other State, and so, indeed, can . . . every other political subdivision throughout the Nation with power to impose sales and use taxes". "The very purpose of the Commerce Clause was to ensure a national economy free from such unjustifiable local entanglements. Under the Constitution, this is a domain where Congress alone has the power of regulation and control".[6] Congress can, of course, cede this power back to the states.[7]

For the most part, however, the judicial approach to the problem of cumulative burdens has not been to nationalize the subject matter of a tax as in *National Bellas Hess*. Instead, analysis has focused primarily on two potential solutions: localizing the subject matter of a tax, and apportioning the measure of a tax.

§ 6–19. Localizing the Subject Matter of a Tax as a Solution to the Problem of Cumulative Burdens

State taxes which meet the jurisdictional requirements of the commerce clause because related to sufficiently local activities of multi-state business are by that very fact uniquely defined, and thus not capable of multiple application. For example, in *Western Live Stock v. Bureau of Revenue*, the Supreme Court upheld the collection of an

---

5. 386 U.S. 753 (1967), discussed in § 6–16, supra.

6. Id. at 759–60. If delivery in the mail-order transactions occurred in Illinois, then Missouri would be as powerless to tax the sales as Illinois was to require collection and remission of the tax on use.

7. See, e.g., Western & Southern Life Insurance Co. v. State Bd. of Equalization, 451 U.S. 648 (1981) (Congress so completely abdicated authority to the states in passing the McCarran Act that California may now impose discriminatory, retaliatory taxes on out-of-state insurance companies in order to induce their home states to tax California insurers at rates equal to those California itself imposes). See § 6–33, infra.

unapportioned gross receipts tax, laid on the privilege of selling magazine advertising, from a magazine having an interstate circulation: "The tax is not one which in form or substance can be repeated by other states. . . . [R]eceipts from subscriptions are not included in the measure of the tax. It is not measured by the extent of the circulation of the magazine interstate. All the events upon which the tax is conditioned—the preparation, printing and publication of the advertising matter, and the receipt of the sums paid for it—occur in New Mexico and not elsewhere." [1]

An illustration of the distinction between permissible and impermissible taxes in this context is provided by judicial treatment of property in transit. The Supreme Court has concluded that taxes imposed on goods while in transit through the taxing state are in effect potentially repeatable taxes on interstate commerce itself and thus barred by the commerce clause.[2] But nondiscriminatory taxes imposed on goods prior to their movement into interstate transit, or subsequent to the completion of such transit, are taxes incapable of multiple application and are thus sufficiently local to survive jurisdictional scrutiny.[3] This distinction is expressed in the decision of particular cases through rules defining what does and does not constitute interstate transportation.

The mere fact that goods will someday be shipped in interstate commerce does not immunize them from state taxation; "goods do not cease to be part of the general mass of property in the State, subject, as such, to its jurisdiction, and to taxation in the usual way, until they have been shipped, or entered with a common carrier for transportation to another State, or have started upon such transportation in a continuous route or journey." [4] The Supreme Court thus upheld the constitutionality of a license tax imposed upon a compress operator whose cotton was eventually to be traded in interstate commerce,[5] reasoning that the "privilege taxed is exercised before interstate commerce begins." [6]

§ 6–19

1. 303 U.S. 250, 260 (1938).

2. See Champlain Realty Co. v. Town of Brattleboro, 260 U.S. 366 (1922); Kelley v. Rhoads, 188 U.S. 1 (1903).

3. See Brown v. Houston, 114 U.S. 622, 632–33 (1885) (coal from Pittsburgh had "come to rest" in New Orleans and could thus be taxed under the state's general *ad valorem* property tax; the Court added in dictum that a tax triggered by the very fact of *entry* into the state would be void).

4. Coe v. Errol, 116 U.S. 517, 527–28 (1886) (logs stored on the bank of a river prior to being floated out-of-state may be validly subjected to a local property tax). See also Bacon v. People of Illinois, 227 U.S. 504 (1913). Cf. Kosydar v. National Cash Register Co., 417 U.S. 62 (1974), discussed in § 6–23, infra. The Court emphasized in Coe that even goods being brought to a depot for out-of-state shipment are subject to tax prior to their actual commitment to the common carrier; prior to such commitment, the owner can still decide not to export the goods. 116 U.S. at 526. By selling the goods within the state he could thus entirely avoid paying his just tax. The Court was also concerned with the economic plight of the Western States, the bulk of whose produce was intended for export. A holding that the mere intent to export goods immunized them from tax would leave those states fiscally crippled. Id. at 527–28.

5. See Federal Compress & Warehouse Co. v. McLean, 291 U.S. 17 (1934).

6. Id. at 22. The Court thus branded the burden on interstate commerce "too indirect and remote to transgress constitutional limitations." Although the compress operator's contract with the common carrier designated the operator as the carrier's agent and the operator's plant as the

A state in which an interstate shipment temporarily halts, however, may not impose a property tax on the shipment if the interruption of interstate transportation is "only to promote . . . safe or convenient transit," even though "the property . . . is under the complete control of the owner" during the interruption.[7] In such cases, the property is said to be in "continuity of transit" and hence immune to state tax. But in the absence of a showing that continuity has been interrupted only ancillary to shipment for reasons of safety or convenience, goods may be taxed by the state within whose boundaries they repose. For example, in *Minnesota v. Blasius*,[8] the Supreme Court held that cattle, shipped from out-of-state and sold to a buyer who kept the cattle in a stockyard at his expense pending resale, may be subjected to a local property tax even though eventual resale was to an out-of-state buyer.[9] In addition, although a product has been shipped in interstate commerce, it becomes subject to the taxing power of the state to which it has been sent once it mingles with the general mass of property of that state.[10] The tax immunity conferred by the commerce clause on goods shipped interstate ends when the goods reach their destination unless further acts by the vendor are necessary after the arrival of the goods in order to make delivery effective.[11]

A further illustration is provided by state taxes related to local aspects of interstate transportation. A state may tax such local aspects providing they can be sufficiently distinguished from the process of transit itself. For example, in *United Air Lines, Inc. v. Mahin*,[12] the Court held that the acts of *storing* and then *withdrawing* aviation fuel

carrier's depot, the Court rejected this contractual attempt "to convert a local business into an interstate commerce business protected by the interstate commerce clause." Id.

7. Champlain Realty Co. v. Brattleboro, 260 U.S. 366, 376 (1922) (logs detained in a river pending the recession of high waters may not be subjected to a local property tax); Carson Petroleum Co. v. Vial, 279 U.S. 95 (1929) (oil held within a state pending the accumulation of sufficient oil to load a ship is immune from local property taxation); Kelley v. Rhoads, 188 U.S. 1 (1903) (grazing of sheep is a necessary incident of transport); Hughes Brothers Timber Co. v. Minnesota, 272 U.S. 469, 476 (1926). See generally Hartman, "Sales Taxation in Interstate Commerce," 9 Vand. L.Rev. 138, 162 (1956).

8. 290 U.S. 1 (1933).

9. Id. at 10. See also Independent Warehouses, Inc. v. Scheele, 331 U.S. 70, 83 (1947), (license tax on the storage of coal held not a forbidden tax on the privilege of interstate commerce even though the coal is received from out-of-state and almost all of it subsequently shipped out-of-state; the interruption in transit brought about by the storage is "for reasons primarily concerned with the owner's business inter-

est"); Bacon v. Illinois, 227 U.S. 504 (1913) (no commerce clause tax immunity for grain subjected to a local property tax after its transportation had been halted to allow for inspection, grinding and sorting); Susquehanna Coal Co. v. South Amboy, 228 U.S. 665 (1913). But cf. Eureka Pipe Line Co. v. Hallanan, 257 U.S. 265, 272 (1921) (West Virginia may not tax all oil stored by a pipeline company for local suppliers even though the pipeline company shipped oil at the suppliers' direction to either local or out-of-state customers; the local suppliers' oil was mixed by the pipeline firm with oil from out-of-state suppliers, and thus "the pipe line company not the producer was the master of the destination of *any specific oil*") (emphasis added).

10. See Brown v. Houston, 114 U.S. 622 (1885).

11. Compare York Mfg. Co. v. Colley, 247 U.S. 21 (1918) (assembly of ice making plant under the supervision of an expert employed by the seller constitutes part of the process of interstate transit protected by the commerce clause), with Browning v. Waycross, 233 U.S. 16, 23 (1914) (municipality may tax the installation of a lightning rod made by an out-of-state seller).

12. 410 U.S. 623 (1973).

from storage for loading into aircraft flying interstate routes were sufficiently local aspects of the interstate transportation process to justify use taxation by Illinois.[13] Likewise, in *Washington Revenue Department v. Stevedoring Association*,[14] the Court upheld a tax on stevedoring since such a tax does not relate to the value of the goods themselves and simply compensates the state for local services offered to businesses.[15] And in *Evansville-Vanderburgh Airport Authority District v. Delta Airlines, Inc.*,[16] the Court responded to an argument that fixed-fee service taxes levied on emplaning passengers of interstate airlines using state airport facilities were capable of multiple application and therefore cumulatively burdensome, by emphasizing the jurisdictional validity of the taxes in question.

A final illustration is that of unapportioned gross receipt taxes: It was said in a case whose formalism no longer represents the law in this area [17] that a state may not levy a tax "*on*" the gross receipts from interstate commerce.[18] However, a state may use gross receipts from

13. Ever since 1963, Illinois revenue authorities insisted on applying their use tax to all the fuel loaded, rather than limiting it to the fuel actually burned over Illinois. See also Edelman v. Boeing Air Transport Inc., 289 U.S. 249 (1933); Nashville, Chattanooga & St. Louis B. Co. v. Wallace, 288 U.S. 249 (1933). The Mahin Court argued that "[d]ouble taxation is minimized because the fuel cannot be taxed by States through which it is transported," 410 U.S. at 630, see Michigan-Wisconsin Pipe Line Co. v. Calvert, 347 U.S. 157 (1954), "nor by the State in which it is merely consumed . . ." See Helson v. Kentucky, 279 U.S. 245 (1929) (a state may not impose a use tax on gasoline purchased and loaded in a ferry boat outside the taxing state but consumed within the taxing state). The Mahin Court also observed that this distinction between storing the fuel and consuming it provides the tax revenues to the most appropriate state: "a state in which pre-loading storage facilities are maintained is likely to provide substantial services to those facilities, including police protection and the maintenance of public access roads." 410 U.S. at 630. Compare Michigan-Wisconsin Pipe Line Co. v. Calvert, 347 U.S. 157 (1954) (invalidating a severance tax on the transfer of gas from a refinery pipeline to an interstate pipeline).

14. 435 U.S. 734 (1978).

15. The Court held that application of the test promulgated in Complete Auto Transit, Inc. v. Brady, 430 U.S. 274 (1977), required the overruling of Puget Sound Stevedoring Company v. State Tax Commission, 302 U.S. 90 (1937) and Joseph v. Carter & Weekes Stevedoring Company, 330 U.S. 422 (1947), which had held that state taxes on stevedoring constituted impermissible taxation of the privilege of conducting interstate business.

16. 405 U.S. 707, 722 (1972). The Court distinguished Crandall v. Nevada, 73 U.S. (6 Wall.) 35 (1867), invalidating a statute exacting a fee of one dollar from any passenger leaving the state by interstate carrier. The tax in Crandall, the Court submitted, was not compensatory; it was not designed merely to impose upon the interstate traveler his fair share of the cost of government. 405 U.S. at 712. In dissent, Justice Douglas argued that the "fair share" argument was inapposite because the tax burdened the constitutionally guaranteed right to travel. Analogizing the right to travel to first amendment rights, he wrote that, "though a local resident can be made to pay taxes to support the community, he cannot be required to pay a fee for making a speech . . ." Id. at 726. Justice Douglas' argument seems misconceived. The majority did not suggest that travelling itself was taxable. The tax was justified because the particular *medium* of travel employed was one that imposed special costs upon the state. The proper first amendment analogy, then, would be the city's exacting a fee for leasing sound equipment or a meeting hall to a private speaker.

17. See § 6–15, supra.

18. Freeman v. Hewit, 329 U.S. 249 (1946). In State Tax on Ry. Gross Receipts, 82 U.S. (15 Wall.) 284 (1873), the Court sustained an unapportioned gross receipts tax on the proceeds of transportation through the state, arguing that the tax, which applied several months after the receipts were realized, was imposed on the receipts only after they had co-mingled with the general mass of property of the taxing state. This distinction was clearly untenable, see Note, "The Multiple Burden Theory in Interstate Commerce Taxation," 40 Col.L.Rev. 653, 654 n. 4 (1940), and was

such commerce as the *measure* of an otherwise constitutionally palatable tax.[19] These rules can be capsulized in a formulation that better highlights their interface with the cumulative burden doctrine: a state may collect an otherwise unapportioned tax so long as it is imposed only on those receipts from interstate transactions which can be ascribed to activities taking place wholly within the jurisdiction of the taxing state. By tying the use of a gross receipts tax to the isolation of some local incident, the Court has attempted to avoid taxation of the same revenue by more than one state.[20]

For example, in *General Motors Corp. v. Washington*, the Supreme Court upheld a state tax on the privilege of doing business within the state, where the tax was measured by the gross receipts on sales of goods delivered within the state.[21] The Court found that the various General Motors divisions either maintained branch offices or warehouses within the state or otherwise retained "district managers, service representatives, and other employees who were residents of the State and who performed substantial services in relation to General Motors' functions therein, particularly with relation to . . . sales, upon which the tax was measured."[22] The Court articulated the governing standard: "The validity of the tax rests upon whether the

repudiated in Philadelphia & Southern Steamship Co. v. Pennsylvania, 122 U.S. 326 (1887). The Court has tended to be more solicitous of taxes levied upon *net* income. See, e.g., United States Glue Co. v. Oak Creek, 247 U.S. 321 (1918); Peck & Co. v. Lowe, 247 U.S. 165 (1918). The difference in treatment accorded these two levies is not difficult to fathom: By definition, a gross receipts tax applies to the very fruits of commerce once realized and imposes a burden even if there are no profits; in contrast, a net income tax applies only to those receipts, if any, left after the costs of conducting business have been deducted. But *either* form of tax may be objectionable, *even if fairly apportioned to in-state activity*, as an exploitation by the tolltaker on a strategic trade route, cf. Condliffe, The Commerce of Nations Chs. I–V (1950), and thus the very sort of provincialism the commerce clause was meant to end. See Brown, § 6–1, supra, note 1, at 228–32. See also Lockhart, "Gross Receipts Taxes on Interstate Transportation and Communication," 57 Harv.L.Rev. 40, 65, 66 (1943).

19. Courts and commentators have sometimes bifurcated this principle and argued that there are two exceptions to the ban on gross receipts taxation. First, gross receipts may be used to measure the value of a taxed local activity. Second, a tax may be levied "on" gross receipts "in lieu" of exacting the normal property tax. See United States Express Co. v. Minnesota, 223 U.S. 335 (1912); Cudahy Packing Co. v. Minnesota, 246 U.S. 450 (1918). There is

no sound reason for not treating the maintenance of property within the state as the taxable activity and thus subsuming both classes of cases within the same exception.

20. The Court has also been quick to strike down cumulative taxation *within* a state. Compare Cudahy Packing Co. v. Minnesota, 246 U.S. 450 (1918) (sustaining a gross receipts tax levied in lieu of a property tax), with Meyer v. Wells, Fargo & Co., 223 U.S. 298, 299 (1912) (invalidating a gross receipts tax levied *in addition* to the property tax). If more than one state finds a local "incident", however, the cumulative taxation problem remains. It is essential, therefore, that each state seek to reach only that portion of the company's receipts that fairly reflects the value of the activities carried on within its boundaries. See Gwin, White & Prince, Inc. v. Henneford, 305 U.S. 434 (1939).

21. 377 U.S. 436 (1964). Accord, Ficklen v. Shelby County Taxing District, 145 U.S. 1 (1892) (tax on gross commissions of solicitors for out-of-state seller upheld, distinguishing the "drummer" cases). The reasoning of the General Motors decision with respect to discrimination against interstate commerce was overruled in Tyler Pipe Industries, Inc. v. Washington Dept. of Revenue, 107 S.Ct. 2810, 2817 (1987), but the Tyler Court had no occasion to question the earlier case's conclusions with respect to nexus and fair apportionment. Id. at 2820 n.16.

22. 377 U.S. at 447.

State is exacting a constitutionally fair demand for that aspect of interstate commerce to which it bears a special relation." [23]

While a state may collect an unapportioned gross receipts tax from the *local* sales of an *out-of-state* corporation, it may not lay a similar tax on receipts from *out-of-state* sales made by *local* companies.[24] In *J. D. Adams Mfg. Co. v. Storen*, the Court held unconstitutional Indiana's attempt to tax the gross receipts of a local corporation's out-of-state sales of locally manufactured road machinery to out-of-state customers: "the exaction is of such a character that if lawful it may in substance by laid to the fullest extent by States in which the goods are sold as well as those in which they are manufactured." [25]

§ 6–20. Apportioning the Measure of a Tax as a Solution to the Problem of Cumulative Burdens

Consistent with the jurisdictional requirements of the due process and commerce clauses, a state may levy a nondiscriminatory tax on an aspect of a multi-state transaction otherwise wholly immune from taxation because interstate in character (such as gross receipts from an out-of-state sale made by a local corporation), if the method by which the tax is measured *apportions* the tax burden in conformity with a formula that rationally relates the amount of the tax to the fraction of interstate activity taking place within the taxing state.[1] Because they seek to derive uniquely local bases for state taxation from otherwise interstate aspects of taxed transactions, apportionment formulas in theory prevent interstate commerce from being cumulatively burdened by repeated taxation of the same incident.[2] However, where states taxing the same aspect of an interstate transaction use different apportionment formulas, there may arise overlapping tax liabilities and thus cumulative burdens.

23. Id. at 440. See also Wisconsin v. J. C. Penney Co., 311 U.S. 435, 444 (1940); Standard Pressed Steel Co. v. Washington Dept. of Revenue, 419 U.S. 560 (1975) (Washington may levy a tax on the unapportioned gross receipts of an aerospace manufacturing company resulting from the latter's sales to a Washington customer, Boeing, where the company maintained a full-time agent in Washington to advise the customer on its anticipated needs).

24. See Evco v. Jones, 409 U.S. 91 (1972) (per curiam) (invalidating unapportioned gross receipts tax levied on out-of-state sales of locally produced educational materials, where state refused to re-label the tax as a levy on local services and thus deliberately failed to invoke rule allowing such a levy). But see § 6–15, supra.

25. 304 U.S. 307, 311 (1938). Justice Roberts' opinion was replete with the verbiage of the direct-indirect distinction. The decision turned, in large part, upon his finding the tax to be levied "upon" gross receipts from commerce after an examination of the text and title of the act. As the quoted language makes manifest, Justice Roberts assumed that the state of origin and the state of market must be treated equally: either both could tax or neither could. It is not clear, however, that such parallel treatment is constitutionally mandated. See International Harvester Co. v. Wisconsin Dept. of Taxation, 322 U.S. 340, 361 (1944) (Rutledge, J., concurring) (arguing that the state of sale, but not the state of origin, should be allowed to tax receipts from an interstate transaction).

§ 6–20

1. See e.g., General Motors Corp. v. Washington, 377 U.S. 436, 440 (1964), discussed in § 6–19, supra; Illinois Cent. R. Co. v. Minnesota, 309 U.S. 157 (1940). Cf. Meyer v. Wells Fargo & Co., 223 U.S. 298 (1912) (tax not fairly apportioned). Note that apportionment may not be a sufficient cure to the special problem of strategic exploitation. See § 6–19, supra, note 18.

2. See Northwestern States Portland Cement Co. v. Minnesota, 358 U.S. 450 (1959).

For example, in *General Motors Corp. v. District of Columbia*,[3] the Court construed a District of Columbia net income tax statute to require use of a widely-adopted three factor apportionment formula rather than a single-factor method. The Court argued that its statutory interpretation conformed with constitutional policy: "The use of an apportionment formula based wholly on the sales factor, in the context of general use of the three-factor approach [giving equal weight to the geographical distribution of plant, payroll, and sales], will ordinarily result in multiple taxation of corporate net income; for the States in which the property and payroll of the corporation are located will allocate to themselves 67% of the corporation's income, whereas the jurisdictions in which the sales are made will allocate 100% of the income to themselves." [4] The Court further suggested in dictum that apportionment formulas significantly varying from those usually employed would be subjected to closer jurisdictional scrutiny than usual.

Yet in *Moorman Manufacturing Company v. Bair*,[5] the Court upheld Iowa's single-factor sales formula. The Court reiterated that such a formula is presumptively valid, and the record did not reveal either arbitrary results or duplicative taxation. Absolute uniformity in apportioning methods may, of course, be required by Congress, but it is not mandated by the Constitution.[6]

Related to the problem of *how* to apportion the income of a multistate company is the question of *what* income to apportion: is sales or dividend income from the company's subsidiaries to be included on the theory of a unitary business enterprise? The burden of showing that out-of-state corporate departments or subsidiaries are discrete enterprises rather than parts of a unitary business rests on the company seeking to avoid the tax. In *Exxon Corporation v. Wisconsin Department of Revenue*,[7] a unanimous Court concluded that Exxon had not carried this burden, and therefore upheld Wisconsin's application of its apportionment formula to Exxon's total income, even though only one of the company's three functional departments was located in the state. A company's internal accounting methods, the Court declared, are not binding on a state's tax policy.[8] The commerce clause can indulge an administrative presumption that affiliated or subsidiary corporations engaged in the same line of business are unitary enterprises.[9]

The prerequisite to a constitutionally acceptable finding of unitary business need not be a flow of goods; a flow of value, such as improved financing opportunities or technical, personnel, or logistical assistance may suffice.[10] "One must look principally at the underlying activity [of the out-of-state business], not at the form of investment [by the in-state

3. 380 U.S. 553 (1965).

4. Id. at 559–60.

5. 437 U.S. 267 (1978).

6. Id. at 280.

7. 447 U.S. 207 (1980).

8. Id. at 221.

9. Container Corporation of America v. Franchise Tax Board, 463 U.S. 159, 178 (1983).

10. See id. at 179–80. Evidence of centralized management and functional integration may also be sufficient. See Mobil Oil Company v. Commissioner of Taxes, 445 U.S. 425, 438 (1980).

company], to determine the propriety of apportionability." [11]   The reasons for allocation to a single situs that often dictate the result in cases of property taxation carry little force in the context of income taxation,[12] where the Court has been indulgent toward unitary business apportionment in the absence of evidence of actual multiple taxation of foreign source income.[13]

Although the Court does not usually inquire into the effects of the interaction of different states' apportioned taxes, the Court has developed three rules defining the effect of *apportioned* taxes on the validity of other states' *unapportioned* taxes in a series of cases dealing with state taxes imposed on instrumentalities (interstate carriers and their equipment—trains, airplanes, ships,[14] and the like) of interstate commerce.

First, any state may levy an adequately apportioned property tax on those interstate instrumentalities with which it has sufficient contacts.   In *Braniff Airways, Inc. v. Nebraska State Board of Equalization and Assessment*, the Supreme Court sustained a contested tax, observing that eighteen stops per day by Braniff's aircraft was sufficiently "regular contact".[15]   In *Braniff*, the apportionment method was based on a three-factor formula; but the Supreme Court has also approved single-factor formulas which determined the tax base from a proportion given by a *mileage ratio*,[16] or from a calculation of *the value of the average number of instrumentalities* within the taxing state at any time.[17]

Second, any state in which a corporation is domiciled may tax at full value that corporation's interstate instrumentalities, but only so long as no showing is made that any of the taxed instrumentalities

11.   Mobil Oil, 445 U.S. at 440.

12.   Mobil Oil, 445 U.S. at 445; Exxon, 447 U.S. at 229.

13.   The due process clause, however, imposes some limits on state power to tax dividend income derived from out-of-state subsidiaries.   See Asarco, Inc. v. Idaho State Tax Commission, 458 U.S. 307 (1982), and F. W. Woolworth v. Taxation & Revenue Department, 458 U.S. 354 (1982), discussed in § 6–17, supra.

14.   In the area of maritime transportation, the Supreme Court had traditionally dealt with the problem of cumulatively burdensome taxation through the application of the "home port" doctrine, which prohibited any state except the state of domicile (the "home port") from taxing ships involved in interstate or foreign navigation.   See, e.g., Hays v. The Pacific Mail Steamship Co., 58 U.S. (17 How.) 596 (1855).   However, the Court has more recently limited the reach of the "home port" doctrine to ships involved in *oceanic* navigation, permitting nondomiciliary states to levy apportioned taxes on ships plying inland waterways, in effect bringing the cases involving vessels on inland water

routes into line with cases involving carriers by rail and air.   See Ott v. Mississippi Valley Barge Line Co., 336 U.S. 169 (1949); Standard Oil Co. v. Peck, 342 U.S. 382 (1952).

15.   347 U.S. 590, 600–01 (1954).

16.   See Pullman's Palace-Car Co. v. Pennsylvania, 141 U.S. 18 (1891) (tax on railroad rolling stock calculated by reference to the ratio of the number of miles of railroad track over which Pullman's cars ran within the taxing state to the total number of miles of track traveled throughout the country).   But cf. Norfolk & Western Ry. Co. v. Missouri State Tax Commission, 390 U.S. 317, 325 (1968) (mileage ratio shown to be arbitrary as applied to taxpayer).

17.   See Johnson Oil Refining Co. v. Oklahoma, 290 U.S. 158 (1933) (dictum) (railroad rolling stock).   A state may collect an apportioned *ad valorem* property tax on the intangible *and* tangible property of interstate transporters.   See, e.g., Nashville, Chattanooga & St. Louis Ry. v. Browning, 310 U.S. 362 (1940); Treichler v. Wisconsin, 338 U.S. 251 (1949).

have an established tax situs in any other state. Thus, the Supreme Court held in *Northwest Airlines v. Minnesota* that Minnesota could constitutionally collect a full value property tax on the entire fleet of airplanes operated interstate and internationally by a Minnesota corporation with its principal business headquarters in that state: "It is not shown here that a defined part of the domiciliary corpus has acquired . . . a taxing situs, elsewhere." [18]

Third, if a showing is made that any of the taxed instrumentalities have an established tax situs in any other state, the domiciliary state may validly tax those instrumentalities only on an apportioned basis. For example, in *Central Greyhound Lines, Inc. v. Mealey,*[19] the Court ruled that New York could not levy an unapportioned gross receipts tax on receipts collected by a New York corporation operating a bus line which had its points of departure and arrival within New York: nearly 43% of the mileage traveled between the points of departure and arrival lay in New Jersey and Pennsylvania, and Pennsylvania collected an apportioned gross receipts tax from the bus company for operating part of the route within that state.[20]

§ 6-21. State Regulation of Foreign Commerce

Article I, § 8, grants Congress the authority "to regulate Commerce with foreign Nations." This clause has been construed as all but exclusive: "It is an essential attribute of the power that it is . . . plenary . . . [and that] its exercise may not be limited, qualified or impeded to any extent by state action." [1] "Foreign commerce" has been defined broadly: it concludes "intercourse, navigation, and not traffic alone." [2] Thus, congressional authority embraces not only trade with foreign nations, but also the regulation of shipments on the high seas, even where the ports of embarkation and destination are in the same American state.

As was the case with federal control of *interstate* commerce, the Supreme Court, in the face of congressional silence, has allowed only such state action as seems consistent with the nationalizing policies perceived to underlie the congressional power delegated in the commerce clause itself. Thus, in *Cooley v. Board of Wardens of the Port of Philadelphia,*[3] the Court allowed state regulation even of some aspects of in-port piloting and navigation of ships "in" foreign commerce. In

---

18. 322 U.S. 292, 295 (1944). See Powell, "Northwest Airlines v. Minnesota: State Taxation of Airplanes—Herein Also of Ships and Sealing Wax and Railroad Cars," 57 Harv.L.Rev. 1097 (1944).

19. 334 U.S. 653 (1948).

20. For an argument that Pennsylvania and New Jersey should not have been allowed thus to exploit their strategic location and that New York should therefore have been permitted to levy its tax without apportionment, see Brown in § 6-1, supra, note 1, at 231-32. See also Central Railroad Co. v. Pennsylvania, 370 U.S. 607 (1962) (taxpayer must show not merely

that some determinable number of its taxed railroad cars were absent from the taxing state for part of the year, but that another state has actually acquired a tax situs over the cars).

§ 6-21

1. Board of Trustees of the University of Illinois v. United States, 289 U.S. 48, 56 (1933).

2. Lord v. Steamship Co., 102 U.S. (12 Otto) 541, 544 (1881).

3. 53 U.S. (12 How.) 299 (1851), discussed in § 6-4, supra.

cases involving foreign commerce, however, the judicial interest-balancing which lies behind a determination under *Cooley* is strongly affected by the inherently national character of most regulation of external affairs. If state action touching foreign commerce is to be allowed, it must be shown not to affect national concerns to any significant degree, a far more difficult task than in the case of interstate commerce. For example, in *Bob-Lo Excursion Co. v. Michigan*,[4] the Court approved the application of a state civil rights law [5] to excursion boat traffic between Detroit and a Canadian island, but only after concluding that the location and population of the island caused the excursion business to be insulated "from all the commercial or social intercourse or traffic with the people of another country usually characteristic of foreign commerce," so that "no detraction whatever from [Canada's] sovereignty [and hence no interference with United States foreign policy] is implied by saying that the business itself is economically and socially an island of local Detroit business, although so largely carried on in Canadian waters." [6]

A distinction must be drawn between state regulation of foreign commerce, and state participation in foreign commerce. The former activity is tightly proscribed by the negative implications of what might be called the foreign commerce clause. Thus, a state or local government that opposed the regime of apartheid in the Union of South Africa could not, absent congressional authorization, enact a measure denying South African companies the privilege of doing business within its jurisdiction; nor could a state or locality forbid its citizens and resident corporations from investing in or trading with multinational corporations which have affiliates or subsidiaries in South Africa.[7] But under the Supreme Court's market participant exception to the commerce clause,[8] a state would be free to pass laws forbidding investment of the state's pension funds in companies that do business with South Africa, or rules requiring that purchases of goods and services by and for the state government be made only from companies that have divested themselves of South African commercial involvement.[9]

§ 6–22. State Taxation of Foreign Commerce

Limits on state authority to tax foreign commerce are implicit in the commerce clause's grant of congressional power to regulate foreign commerce.[1] State taxation is also limited explicitly by article I, § 10,

4. 333 U.S. 28 (1948).

5. The Michigan law prohibited racial discrimination; no statute or treaty of either the United States or Canada conflicted with it.

6. 333 U.S. at 36.

7. See Zschernig v. Miller, 389 U.S. 429 (1968) (striking down an Oregon law which barred probate courts from awarding property to citizens of communist countries), discussed in § 4–5, supra.

8. See, e.g., Hughes v. Alexandria Scrap Corp., 426 U.S. 794 (1976); Reeves, Inc. v.

Stake, 447 U.S. 429 (1980); White v. Massachusetts Council of Construction Employers, Inc., 460 U.S. 204 (1983), discussed in § 6–11, supra.

9. Such state or local enactments would not be preempted by the Anti-Apartheid Act of 1986, Pub.L. No. 99–440, 100 Stat. 1086. See § 6–25, infra.

§ 6–22

1. Article I, § 8.

which prohibits the states from imposing "any duty of tonnage" without congressional consent. This proscription embraces any exaction, however measured, "for the privilege of arriving and departing from a port of the United States." [2] But the clause does not bar state or local exactions, even at a profit, for services actually provided for an embarking or arriving vessel, including charges for pilotage, towing, stevedoring, wharfage, or stowing.[3]

A different analysis obtains under the commerce clause when a state seeks to tax the instrumentalities of foreign commerce. In considering the application of a California *ad valorem* tax to an international shipping company's cargo containers in *Japan Line, Ltd. v. County of Los Angeles*, the Court noted that there is no authoritative tribunal to adjudicate international multiple taxation claims, and that foreign states may be prompted by such duplicative taxes to retaliate against American commerce.[4] Therefore, two factors beyond those relevant to interstate commerce must be evaluated: (1) the enhanced risk of multiple taxation by foreign sovereigns, and (2) the possible impairment of federal uniformity in this sensitive area so intimately connected with foreign relations.[5] The application of the California tax to Japan Line's containers realized both fears: the containers were in fact taxed in Japan and California's levy therefore constituted double taxation; and the California tax appeared to undermine the uniform national policy established by the Customs Convention on Containers, which both Japan and the United States had signed.[6]

The analysis is less clear-cut when the issue is not a tax on services or property associated with foreign trade, but taxation of foreign income.[7] Even the Supreme Court's heightened concern for international commerce can sometimes give way to the Court's sympathy for state taxing authority. Thus, in *Container Corporation of America v. Franchise Tax Board*,[8] the commerce clause proved to be no barrier to California's application of the unitary business principle to tax the income of a domestic corporation's foreign subsidiaries. Container Corporation's subsidiaries were each taxed on all their income by the foreign jurisdictions in which they were located, under the internationally-accepted "arm's length" formula, which assumes that corporations deal with their foreign affiliates and subsidiaries as independent entities. California thus subjected the plaintiff to double taxation by attributing a portion of the subsidiaries' income to the domestic corporation within its jurisdiction. And the Court conceded that "our own Federal Government, to the degree it has spoken, seems to prefer the

2. Cannon v. City of New Orleans, 87 U.S. (20 Wall.) 577 (1874).

3. See, e.g., Washington Revenue Department v. Stevedoring Association, 435 U.S. 734 (1978); Cooley v. Port Wardens, 53 U.S. (12 How.) 299 (1851).

4. 441 U.S. 434, 453–54 (1979).

5. Id. at 446–48.

6. Id. at 452–53.

7. The correct situs for taxation of income, as opposed to property, is less than obvious. See. e.g., Container Corporation of America v. Franchise Tax Board, 463 U.S. 159, 187–88 (1983); Mobil Oil Corp. v. Commissioner of Taxes, 445 U.S. 425, 445 (1980).

8. 463 U.S. 159 (1983).

taxing method adopted by the international community to the taxing method adopted by California." [9]

Yet the California tax was upheld. The Court dispensed with the multiple taxation problem by observing that adoption of an arm's length formula would not completely eliminate multiple taxation, since each jurisdiction's formula would still differ in many details.[10] As to the possibility that the tax would prevent the United States from "speaking with one voice" on international trade,[11] the majority noted that "the Executive Branch has decided not to file an *amicus curiae* brief in opposition to the state tax" and, in contrast to *Japan Line*, there was no international treaty or other specific indication of a federal policy mandating identical treatment of foreign income by the states.[12] The Court dismissed the possibility of foreign retaliation as unlikely because California's tax did not create an automatic assymetry: it was levied on domestic corporations, and the same *amount* of tax could have been levied under another formula by simply increasing the corporate tax rate.[13]

Thus, the Court's modern foreign commerce clause cases suggest that judicial wariness of double taxation will remain an important consideration in those cases where the state could be required simply to refrain from taxing the entity in question, such as the *ad valorem* property tax invalidated in *Japan Line*. But with respect to income taxes, so long as there is the potential for double taxation under seemingly legitimate alternatives to the taxing scheme in question, the existence of double taxation under that challenged scheme will not be sufficient to invalidate it, despite "serious divergence" with prevailing international and federal tax practice. Until international accounting practice becomes refined to the point of uniformity in each detail, the logic of *Container Corporation* will in most cases diminish the *bête noire* of multiple taxation to the status of something that goes bump in the night.

§ 6–23. Tax Immunity Under the Import-Export Clause

State power to tax foreign commerce is also limited by article I, § 10, which declares that "[n]o State shall, without the Consent of the Congress, lay any Imposts or Duties on Imports or Exports, except what may be absolutely necessary for executing its inspection Laws." The clause has been construed as an absolute proscription: once an object or activity is shown to fall within its compass, taxes on that object or

---

9. Id. at 187.

10. Id. at 192. But, as the dissent argued, the vice of double taxation inheres in the difference between arm's length and unitary apportionment, and the unitary system will always favor, as it did in this case, the jurisdiction where wages, property values, and sales prices are higher. For example, under the arm's length method over 27% of the plaintiff's income was earned in Latin America, but the relatively depressed economic conditions in that region (which constituted attractive business

economies) made the corresponding apportionment under the California method a mere 13%. Id. at 199–200 (Powell, J., dissenting).

11. 463 U.S. at 193.

12. Id. at 195.

13. The Court further noted that, since Container Corporation was an American company, foreign jurisdictions would have less interest in whether its subsidiaries were subject to double taxation. Id. at 195.

activity are barred without resort to the type of interest-balancing or functional analysis that characterizes commerce clause litigation generally.[1] The import-export clause does not apply to interstate commerce,[2] but does protect all overseas commerce even if not with a sovereign foreign nation.[3]

Until recently, the duration of the tax immunity for imports was determined by the so-called "original package" doctrine. Under this rule, all state taxes, however nondiscriminatory, were void if imposed on foreign imports before the package in which the goods arrived was broken or before actual sale or use, whichever occurred first.[4] It is frequently debatable whether an import has remained in its original form or package,[5] and the results produced by the doctrine often seemed confusing and contradictory. In *Michelin Tire Corp. v. Wages*,[6] however, the Supreme Court finally abandoned the formality of the package doctrine and held that a nondiscriminatory *ad valorem* state property tax could be applied to imported tires stored in a warehouse in their original packages.[7] The import-export clause, the Court reasoned, prohibits only state or local taxes imposed on imports while they are still in transit; otherwise, so long as they are not singled out for special tax burdens because of their foreign origin, imports may be taxed on the same basis as other property.[8]

With respect to exports, the doctrinal analogue of the "original package" doctrine is the "final journey" rule. Goods sold to foreign buyers become exports when they become irrevocably committed for exportation in the most literal sense: "It is the entrance of the articles into the export stream that marks the start of the process of exporta-

---

§ 6–23

1. Compare §§ 6–4 to 6–20, supra.

2. Woodruff v. Parham, 75 U.S. (8 Wall.) 123 (1868). See also Brown v. Houston, 114 U.S. 622 (1885); 3 M. Farrand, The Records of the Federal Convention of 1787, at 328 (1911).

3. Hooven & Allison Co. v. Evatt, 324 U.S. 652 (1945) (trade with the Philippines, then a colonial possession of the U.S., held within the import tax immunity).

4. See, e.g., Brown v. Maryland, 25 U.S. (12 Wheat.) 419, 441–42 (1827); Hooven & Allison Co. v. Evatt, 324 U.S. 652 (1945), overruled, Limbach v. Hooven & Allison Co., 466 U.S. 353 (1984).

5. Compare Low v. Austin, 80 U.S. (13 Wall.) 29 (1871) (imported wine stored in original case on display pending sale retained tax-exempt import status), with Youngstown Sheet & Tube Co. v. Bowers, 358 U.S. 534 (1959) (iron ores stored in original package outside steel manufacturers' factory to be fed daily into furnaces lost tax-exempt import status).

6. 423 U.S. 276 (1976).

7. In Limbach v. Hooven & Allison Co., 466 U.S. 353 (1984), a unanimous Court relied on Michelin to uphold Ohio's imposition of an *ad valorem* property tax on imported fibers in their original packages. The Court expressly overruled Hooven & Allison Co. v. Evatt, 324 U.S. 652 (1945), which, 40 years earlier, had involved the same parties, the same tax, and the same product. Of course, *ad valorem* property taxes on imports being stored for subsequent export, while not forbidden as import duties, might be preempted by Congress. See Xerox Corp. v. Harris, 459 U.S. 145 (1982). Cf. R. J. Reynolds Tobacco Co. v. Durham County, 107 S.Ct. 499 (1986) (no preemption where imported goods are stored for subsequent *domestic* use). See § 6–26, infra.

8. Michelin, 423 U.S. at 283–86, 293–94. Presumably the Court will employ a similar definition to decide when goods are "in transit" in foreign commerce cases as in interstate commerce litigation. Cf. id. at 290 n. 11. See § 6–19, supra. The Court had long ago disparaged the "unbroken-package doctrine as applied to *interstate* commerce . . . as more artificial than sound." Whitfield v. Ohio, 297 U.S. 431, 440 (1936) (emphasis added).

tion. Then there is certainty that the goods are headed for their foreign destination and will not be diverted to domestic use. Nothing less will suffice." [9] Such entry into the stream of exports must be marked at least by delivery to a common carrier for shipment.[10] In *Empresa Siderurgica v. County of Merced*,[11] the Court made clear that mere intent to export—or even a fully worked out and partially implemented plan of exportation complete with passage of title—is inadequate to invoke the import-export clause's protection. There, the Court sustained the application of a personal property tax to that portion of a dismantled cement plant in California that had yet to be delivered to a common carrier, despite the fact that title to the plant had passed to the foreign buyer and the rest of the plant had already been shipped overseas to Colombia pursuant to a contract which called for the shipment of the entire plant.[12] Although the Supreme Court will undoubtedly be invited to abandon this "final journey" rule in light of the Justices' specific rejection of the original-package doctrine and their more general abandonment of formalism in state taxation cases,[13] it was not so long ago that the Court extolled the simplicity and predictability of the final journey formula,[14] and it seems defensible to resist doctrinal formalism when it operates to *erode* state taxing power,[15] leaving to Congress the more politically sensitive task of overturning those mechanical rules that work to *expand* state taxing authority.[16]

The export tax immunity embraces not only the goods themselves but also the proceeds derived from their sale,[17] although the import tax immunity does not apply to the first sale of an already imported item and hence does not extend to a tax on the proceeds of such sale.[18] But both immunities extend to documents and activities inextricably linked to the processes of importation or exportation. Thus, in *Thames & Mersey Marine Ins. Co. v. United States*,[19] the Supreme Court overturned a stamp tax applied to policies insuring exports.[20]

9. Empresa Siderurgica v. Merced, 337 U.S. 154, 156–57 (1949).

10. The same definition of "export" applies to the article I, § 9, provision that "No Tax or Duty shall be laid [by Congress] on Articles exported from any State." See, e.g., Turpin v. Burgess, 117 U.S. 504, 507 (1886); Spalding & Bros. v. Edwards, 262 U.S. 66, 68 (1923).

11. 337 U.S. 154 (1949).

12. Accord, Kosydar v. National Cash Register Co., 417 U.S. 62 (1974) (sustaining application of state *ad valorem* personal property tax to machines built to foreign buyer's specifications and virtually certain of eventual exportation, because there had not yet been a "physical entry into the stream of exportation"). Compare Richfield Oil Corp. v. State Board of Equalization, 329 U.S. 69 (1946) (immunity from non-discriminatory state sales tax triggered by completed pumping of oil from seller's dockside tanks into hold of foreign navy ship).

13. See Complete Auto Transit v. Brady, 430 U.S. 274 (1977), discussed in § 6–15, supra.

14. See Kosydar, 417 U.S. at 71.

15. Both the original-package doctrine rejected in Michelin Tire Corp. v. Wages, 423 U.S. 276 (1976), and the privilege-tax doctrine rejected in Complete Auto Transit, supra note 13, had that effect.

16. Compare § 6–32, infra.

17. Selliger v. Kentucky, 213 U.S. 200 (1909) (property tax levied on warehouse receipts for whiskey exported to Germany held unconstitutional as a tax on exports).

18. Burke v. Wells, 208 U.S. 14 (1908). See also Waring v. Mobile, 75 U.S. (8 Wall.) 110, 122 (1868).

19. 237 U.S. 19 (1915). This was a federal tax, but the same rule would apply in a state case. See note 10, supra.

20. But an act requiring the stamping of all packages of tobacco intended for ex-

The import-export clause also works to immunize from both direct and indirect state taxation the privilege of importing or exporting itself. This is so whether the state attempts to tax that privilege by imposing a fixed-fee license tax upon an exporter or importer [21] or seeks instead to levy a tax upon the gross receipts from exportation.[22] However, in *William E. Peck & Co., Inc. v. Lowe,*[23] the Supreme Court upheld the validity of the federal net income tax on profits derived from exporting despite the article I, § 9 requirement that "[n]o Tax or Duty shall be laid [by Congress] on Articles exported from any State." [24] In so holding, the Court distinguished such a tax from a levy on exporting: "The tax is levied after exportation is completed, after all expenses are paid and losses adjusted, and after the recipient of the income is free to use it as he chooses. Thus what is taxed—the net income—is as far removed from exportation as are articles intended for export before the exportation begins." [25] In that regard, the ban on taxes levied on the act of importing or exporting does not extend to prior preparatory actions. Thus, a state may impose a franchise tax on a railroad, not engaged exclusively in foreign commerce, measured by properly apportioned gross receipts for its services in handling imports and exports at its marine terminal: "For if the handling of the goods at the port were part of the export process, so would hauling them to and from distant points or perhaps mining them or manufacturing them." [26] Similarily, a state may exact taxes on the capital a company maintains within its boundaries—despite the fact that the capital is used in part to conduct an import or export business.[27] However, such a tax has been held impermissible if the company's *only* business within the state is importing or exporting.[28]

Finally, the import-export clause by its terms does not extend to those state-imposed fees that "may be absolutely necessary for executing [the state's] inspection Laws." Inspection charges that are unreasonable violate the clause,[29] but because article I, § 10 also declares that "all such Laws shall be subject to the Revision and Controul of the Congress," it has been held that the reasonableness of facially nondiscriminatory state inspection fees must be left to Congress, and not to

port in order to prevent fraud was upheld in Pace v. Burgess, 92 U.S. 372 (1876).

21. Brown v. Maryland, 25 U.S. (12 Wheat.) 419, 447 (1827).

22. Crew Levick Co. v. Pennsylvania, 245 U.S. 292 (1917). See also note 17, supra.

23. 247 U.S. 165 (1918).

24. See note 10, supra.

25. 247 U.S. at 175. Compare the differential treatment accorded net income taxes and gross receipts taxes in the context of interstate commerce. See § 6–19, note 18, supra.

26. Canton Railroad Co. v. Rogan, 340 U.S. 511, 515 (1951). See also Washington Revenue Department v. Stevedoring Association, 435 U.S. 734 (1978) (upholding tax

on stevedoring as legitimate compensation to state for services offered to interstate commerce conducted within the state).

27. See New York v. Roberts, 171 U.S. 658 (1898).

28. See Anglo-Chilean Nitrate Sales Corp. v. Alabama, 288 U.S. 218 (1933). But see Complete Auto Transit v. Brady, supra note 13.

29. Cf. Brimmer v. Redman, 138 U.S. 78 (1891) (voiding state statute prohibiting sale of meat killed 100 miles or more from place of sale unless inspected in state). Inspection schemes discriminating financially or otherwise against out-of-state products have uniformly been held invalid. See, e.g., Voight v. Wright, 141 U.S. 62 (1891); Hale v. Bimco Trading Co., 306 U.S. 375 (1939).

the courts, for decision.[30]　This does not mean, however, that the magnitude of what purports to be an inspection fee is of no concern to the courts.　In determining whether an exaction was "in fact" an inspection fee, the Supreme Court has looked to the size of the fee to see "whether . . . the charge was so excessive as to deprive the act of its character as an inspection law . . ."[31]　The impact of such judicial scrutiny, however, has been limited: even if it is shown that the exaction exceeds the real cost of inspection, "the presumption is that in the orderly conduct of the public business of the State the necessary correction will be made to cause the act to conform to the authority possessed which is to impose a fee solely to recompense the State for the expenses properly incurred in enforcing the authorized inspection."[32]

§ 6–24.　The Effect of the Twenty-First Amendment on the Operation of the Commerce Clause

The balance of constitutional policy and state interest which ordinarily characterizes commerce clause litigation is altered by the twenty-first amendment in cases dealing with state alcoholic beverage regulation and taxation.　That amendment, as part of its repeal of eighteenth amendment prohibition, declares in § 2 that "[t]he transportation or importation into any State, Territory, or possession of the United States for delivery or use therein of intoxicating liquors, in violation of the laws thereof, is hereby prohibited."　Thus, there has been a constitutional adjustment in the allocation of authority between the federal and state governments in matters touching on alcoholic beverage control: "The Twenty-First Amendment has placed liquor in a category different from that of other articles of commerce.　Though the precise amount of power it has left in Congress to regulate liquor under the Commerce Clause has not been marked out by decisions, this much is settled: local, not national, regulation of the liquor traffic is now the general Constitutional policy."[1]

---

30. See Neilson v. Garza, 17 F.Cas. 1302, 1303 (C.C.E.D.Tex.1876) (No. 10,091) (Bradley, J., sitting as Circuit Justice) ("If the law is really an inspection law, the duty must stand until congress shall see fit to alter it").　See the discussion of the political question doctrine, § 3–16, supra.

31. Patapsco Guano Co. v. North Carolina Board of Agriculture, 171 U.S. 345, 351 (1898) (dictum).　The Court thus struck down what purported to be inspection fees even in the context of *interstate commerce.* See, e.g., id.; Phipps v. Cleveland Rfg. Co., 261 U.S. 449 (1923) (petroleum inspection fees invalidated).

32. Red "C" Oil Mfg. Co. v. Board of Agriculture of North Carolina, 222 U.S. 380, 393–94 (1912).　The import-export clause also has been held to limit the application of the twenty-first amendment: states cannot tax foreign liquor until it becomes a part of local commerce.　Department of Revenue v. James Beam Distilling Co., 377 U.S. 341 (1964).

§ 6–24

1. Carter v. Virginia, 321 U.S. 131, 138 (1944) (Black, J., concurring).　Federal antitrust prosecution of producers and distributors charged with conspiring to fix liquor prices in Colorado was nonetheless held consistent with the twenty-first amendment in United States v. Frankfort Distilleries, Inc., 324 U.S. 293, 297–99 (1945).　And nothing in that amendment tempers congressional authority under the spending power to induce the states to comply with a nationwide minimum drinking age by threatening to withhold federal highway funds.　South Dakota v. Dole, 107 S.Ct. 2793 (1987), discussed in § 5–10, supra.　Congress can thus achieve by way of its spending power much of what the twenty-first amendment may deny it the ability to achieve through its commerce power.

The twenty-first amendment does not render the commerce clause completely inapplicable to state restrictions on interstate trade in alcoholic beverages. Earlier judicial statements had seemed to suggest that the commerce clause was entirely irrelevant in situations where the amendment is directly in point.[2] But in *Craig v. Boren*,[3] the Supreme Court noted that, while the primary effect of the amendment is to create an exception to the normal operation of the commerce clause, it does not "*pro tanto* repeal the Commerce Clause, but merely requires that each provision 'be considered in the light of the other, and in the context of the issues at stake in any concrete case.'"[4] For example, state power over alcoholic beverages in transit through the regulating state is quite limited, since the twenty-first amendment is limited by its very terms to importation of liquor into a state "for delivery or use therein." While a state may regulate such transit to the extent demonstrably essential to prevent any unlawful diversion of liquor into the state, it may not regulate the shipment in a manner more restrictive of interstate commerce than avoidance of in-state diversion requires.[5] In *United States v. State Tax Comm. of Mississippi*,[6] even the strong possibility of in-state diversion at the point of retail sale was held insufficient to justify a Mississippi attempt, in furtherance of its plan to monopolize wholesaling of liquors within the state, to prevent United States military bases located in the state from buying cheaper out-of-state liquor.

State power over alcoholic beverages in foreign commerce is similarly limited. A state may regulate the transportation of foreign-bound liquor in order to prevent in-state diversion, but it may not bar such transit entirely.[7] Similarly, a state may not tax imported liquor until it becomes a part of domestic commerce.[8]

On the other hand, considerable power to control importation is reserved to the states by the twenty-first amendment. The amendment sanctions state action which taxes, regulates, or completely bars the importation of liquor for actual use within the state itself, even where

2. Hostetter v. Idlewild Bon Voyage Liquor Corp., 377 U.S. 324, 330 (1964); Finch v. McKittrick, 305 U.S. 395, 398 (1939).

3. 429 U.S. 190 (1976) (invalidating Oklahoma law discriminating between men and women as to minimum age for purchasing 3.2% beer). See also note 15, infra.

4. Id. at 206, citing Hostetter v. Idlewild Bon Voyage Liquor Corp., 377 U.S. 324, 332 (1964).

5. Carter v. Virginia, 321 U.S. 131, 135 (1944). The Court in Carter nonetheless upheld the challenged State regulation of liquor transport under the commerce clause. See also Duckworth v. Arkansas, 314 U.S. 390 (1941), discussed in § 6–7, supra.

6. 412 U.S. 363 (1973). See also Collins v. Yosemite Park & Curry Co., 304 U.S. 518 (1938) (state may not prohibit the importa-tion of intoxicating liquor into National Park territory over which it has ceded exclusive jurisdiction to the United States). The Mississippi case was remanded for further proceedings and ultimately led to a holding that the state mark-up fee on out-of-state liquor sold to the military bases was an invalid tax on a federal instrumentality. 421 U.S. 599, (1975), discussed in § 6–31, infra.

7. See Hostetter v. Idlewild Bon Voyage Liquor Corp., 377 U.S. 324 (1964) (airport dealer immune from state control with respect to liquor acquired for resale exclusively to airline passengers, with delivery deferred until they arrive at foreign destinations).

8. See Department of Revenue v. James Beam Distillers, 377 U.S. 341, 345–46 (1964).

such action would be forbidden as to any other commodity.[9] It was long unclear whether the amendment empowered states to regulate importation beyond the degree reasonably necessary to control the level of liquor consumption within the state's boundaries. Some early cases suggested that the state's power extends well beyond such control, even authorizing political trade wars among the states.[10] Indeed, the amendment has been held to immunize state regulation of liquor *exportation* from commerce clause attack, although it speaks only of "importation." [11] As now interpreted by the Supreme Court, however, the amendment does not give blanket power to the states even to regulate or tax importation as such, when the interest implicated by the regulation is something other than controlling liquor consumption as such. In *Bacchus Imports, Ltd. v. Dias*,[12] the Supreme Court held that Hawaii's twenty percent excise tax on wholesale liquor sales, which exempted certain locally-produced liquors, violated the commerce clause—despite the twenty-first amendment. "State laws that constitute mere economic protectionism are . . . not entitled to the same deference as laws enacted to combat the perceived evils of an unrestricted traffic in liquor." [13] Thus, a purpose requirement was im-

9. See State Board of Equalization v. Young's Market Co., 299 U.S. 59, 62 (1936). See generally Note, "State Control of Alcoholic Beverages in Interstate Commerce," 27 N.Y.U.L.Rev. 127 (1952).

10. See Indianapolis Brewing Co. v. Liquor Control Comm., 305 U.S. 391 (1939) (upholding Michigan prohibition of resident beer dealers' selling beer manufactured in Indiana because Indiana laws discriminated against Michigan beer). See also Mahoney v. Joseph Triner Corp., 304 U.S. 401 (1938) (upholding statute barring importation of all non-patented liquors with specified alcoholic contents). See generally Crabb, "State Power Over Liquor Under the Twenty-First Amendment," 12 U.Det.L.J. 11, 28 (1948).

11. Ziffrin, Inc. v. Reeves, 308 U.S. 132 (1939) (upholding Kentucky ban on transportation of liquor by Indiana corporation into Illinois, where Indiana corporation had been denied Kentucky transportation license).

12. 468 U.S. 263 (1984). Justice White wrote for the Court, in an opinion joined by Chief Justice Burger and Justices Marshall, Blackmun, and Powell. Justice Stevens dissented, joined by Justices Rehnquist and O'Connor. Justice Brennan took no part.

13. Id. at 276. In his dissent, Justice Stevens refused to constrict the textually explicit scope of the amendment by adding such a purpose requirement: "This is a totally novel approach to the Twenty-first Amendment. The question is not one of 'deference,' nor one of 'central purposes,' the question is whether the provision . . . is an exercise of a power expressly con-

ferred upon the States by the Constitution." Id. at 287 (footnote omitted). In finding Hawaii's statute to be an exercise of expressly conferred power, Justice Stevens first noted that "Hawaii may surely prohibit the importation of all intoxicating liquors." Id. at 286. Without elaboration, he then concluded that "clear[ly] . . . it may do so without prohibiting the local sale of liquors produced within the state," id. at 286, and that, if Hawaii could impose so severe a discrimination on liquor originating out-of-state, "it may also engage in a less extreme form of discrimination . . . in the form of . . . a tax exemption, for locally produced alcoholic beverages." Id. at 286.

The dissenters found the case "clearly cover[ed]" by Young's Market, supra note 9. 468 U.S. at 282. In that 1936 case, Justice Brandeis, writing for a unanimous Court, opined that any rule requiring states to "let imported liquors compete with the domestic on equal terms" would "involve not a construction of the [Twenty-first] Amendment, but a rewriting of it." 299 U.S. at 62. Despite this statement's venerable source, it should now be rejected as a gratuitous extension of the twenty-first amendment's reach. The majority in Bacchus dismissed it as needlessly "broad language . . . written shortly after enactment of the Amendment," 468 U.S. at 274 (footnote omitted). Particularly since Justice Brandeis found it necessary to add that "exaction of a high license fee for [liquor] importation may . . . serve as an aid for policing the liquor traffic," 299 U.S. at 63, it would make sense today to confine the Young's Market holding to those cases in which the less favorable treatment ac-

ported into the amendment: state power over liquor is reduced, and
may be subordinated to federal commerce power, when the objective of
a state regulation does not comport with the central purpose of the
twenty-first amendment—namely, controlling liquor consumption.[14]
Any broader interpretation of the twenty-first amendment would revive
the spectre of balkanized commerce which haunted the framers and
motivated the commerce clause itself.[15]

corded imported liquor by a state is shown
to be reasonably necessary to policing liquor traffic, the end Brandeis posited. Accord, Comment, 13 Hastings Const.L.Q. 361
(1986) (arguing that § 2 of the twenty-first
amendment was meant not to grant plenary power over liquor to the states but to
protect the ability of dry states to enforce
statewide prohibition).

14. Thus, in California Liquor Dealers
v. Midcal Aluminum, Inc., 445 U.S. 97
(1980), a California statute which instituted a system of resale price maintenance for
wine was invalidated under the Sherman
Act. The state's objectives were "to promote temperance and orderly market conditions." Id. at 113. Although promoting
temperance is a core twenty-first amendment state power, both the state's highest
court and the Supreme Court "found little
correlation between resale price maintenance and temperance." Id. at 114. The
remaining state purpose, that of promoting
orderly market conditions, was outside the
twenty-first amendment core and was simply "not of the same stature as the goals of
the Sherman Act." Id. at 115. Accord,
324 Liquor Corp. v. Duffy, 107 S.Ct. 720
(1987) (Sherman Act invalidates New York
liquor pricing statute requiring retailers to
charge at least 112% of "posted" wholesale
price filed with state).

When in conflict with the commerce
clause, powers reserved by the twenty-first
amendment appear to be at their weakest
not only when the state's regulatory *purpose* is other than to control liquor consumption, but also when the regulated *subject-matter* is something other than the
importation or distribution of liquor as
such. See California Liquor Dealers v.
Midcal Aluminum, 445 U.S. at 110. In
Capital Cities Cable, Inc. v. Crisp, 467 U.S.
691 (1984), for example, the Court struck
down an Oklahoma regulation that required cable television operators to delete
all advertisements for alcoholic beverages
contained in the out-of-state signals that
they retransmitted within Oklahoma. The
state's decision to regulate *not* "the conditions under which liquor may be imported
or sold within the state" but *only* "the
importation of [certain liquor advertising]

signals by cable television operators" was
held, in a unanimous opinion, to "engage[ ]
only indirectly" the state's core twenty-
first amendment power. Id. at 715. Such
indirect invocation of that power, the
Court held, could not prevail when in direct conflict with important federal policies
regarding retransmissions. Id. at 715–16.
The preemption holding of Capital Cities
Cable is discussed in § 6–28, infra, note 7.

15. The Court has similarly resisted
readings of the twenty-first amendment so
broad as to override equal protection limits
on state power, see Craig v. Boren, 429 U.S.
190, 204–09 (1976), supra note 3; procedural due process limits, see Wisconsin v.
Constantineau, 400 U.S. 433, 436 (1971); or
establishment clause limits, see Larkin v.
Grendel's Den, Inc., 459 U.S. 116, 122 n. 5
(1982). The one glaring exception to the
Court's reluctance to permit a state's twenty-first amendment power to override independent constitutional constraints has
been the doctrine that seemingly liberates
states and localities from first amendment
principles when they act to separate sex
from alcohol, as through banning nude
dancing in bars that serve liquor. See City
of Newport v. Iacobucci, 107 S.Ct. 383
(1986); New York State Liquor Authority
v. Bellanca, 452 U.S. 714 (1981); California
v. LaRue, 409 U.S. 109 (1972). This line of
decisions has led Justice Stevens to remark
that the twenty-first amendment now "is
toothless except when freedom of speech is
involved." City of Newport, supra, 107
S.Ct. at 387 (dissenting opinion). No doubt
the Court would heed Justice Stevens'
warning and invalidate a state statute or
local ordinance banning political argument
or religious discussion in bars—and even a
law purporting to outlaw raucus jokes or
heated controversies wherever liquor is
served. The cases from Larue through
City of Newport should probably be understood as standing not for the proposition
that the twenty-first amendment overrides
the first but for the more modest notion
that twenty-first amendment power over
alcohol consumption is broad enough to
embrace state power to zone strong sexual
stimuli away from places where liquor is
served.

§ 6–25. The Effect of Federal Legislation on State Action: Preemption

So long as Congress acts within an area delegated to it, the preemption of conflicting state or local action—and the validation of congressionally authorized state or local action [1]—flow directly from the substantive source of power of the congressional action coupled with the supremacy clause of article VI; such cases may pose complex questions of statutory construction but raise no controversial issues of power. Those issues are raised, however, when state power is said to be ousted not because of specific conflict with what Congress has *done* but because of negative implications thought to flow from what Congress *might* have done. Such ouster of state authority because of "dormant" congressional power of course lies at the heart of most commerce clause litigation. There is a third category of preemption, a hybrid of the other two, within which states are deemed powerless to act because of a vacuum deliberately, even if not expressly, created by federal legislation. In such cases, *any* state or local action, however consistent in detail with relevant federal statutes, is held invalid—not because of a "dormant" federal power thought to be constitutionally exclusive but rather because the federal legislative scheme announces, or is best understood as implying, a congressional purpose to "occupy the field." [2]

In *Gibbons v. Ogden*,[3] Chief Justice Marshall recognized the statutory hierarchy of the federal system. He observed that as "to such acts of the State Legislatures as do not transcend their powers, but . . . interfere with, or are contrary to the law of Congress, made in pursuance of the constitution, . . . [i]n every such case, the act of Congress . . . is supreme; and the law of the State, though enacted in the exercise of powers not controverted, must yield to it." [4] Because the commerce power, "like all others vested in Congress, is complete in itself, may be exercised to its utmost extent, and acknowledges no limitations, other than are prescribed in the constitution," [5] Congress has complete authority to define the distribution of federal and state regulatory power over what is conceded to be interstate commerce.[6] Courts assess the validity of state regulation in independent constitutional terms only when Congress has not chosen to act.

The question whether federal law preempts state action, cannot be reduced to general formulas, but there does appear to be an overriding reluctance to infer preemption in ambiguous cases.[7] Such reluctance seems particularly appropriate in light of the Supreme Court's repeated

---

§ 6–25

1. See § 6–33, infra.

2. See generally Note, "Pre-emption as a Preferential Ground: A New Canon of Construction," 12 Stan.L.Rev. 208 (1959).

3. 22 U.S. (9 Wheat.) 1 (1824).

4. Id. at 209.

5. Id. at 195.

6. Subject, however, to the tenth amendment doctrine of National League of Cities v. Usery, 426 U.S. 833 (1976), discussed in § 5–22, supra.

7. The Supreme Court has referred to this reluctance as a presumption that "Congress did not intend to displace state law." Maryland v. Louisiana, 451 U.S. 725, 746 (1981).

emphasis on the central role of Congress in protecting the sovereignty of the states.[8] In *Garcia v. San Antonio Metropolitan Transit Authority*,[9] which ended the decade-long reign of *National League of Cities v. Usery*,[10] a closely-divided Supreme Court held that state sovereignty is "more properly protected by procedural safeguards inherent in the structure of the federal system than by judicially created limitations on federal power."[11] By declining to infer preemption in the face of congressional ambiguity, the Court is not interposing a judicial barrier to Congress's will in order to protect state sovereignty—an interposition that would violate *Garcia*—but is instead furthering the spirit of *Garcia* by requiring that decisions restricting state sovereignty be made in a deliberate manner by Congress, through the explicit exercise of its lawmaking power to that end. The Court evidently envisions that the constitutional procedure for lawmaking will result in a sound balance between state sovereignty and national interests. But to give the state-displacing weight of federal law to mere congressional *ambiguity* would evade the very procedure for lawmaking on which *Garcia* relied to protect states' interests.[12]

Although the Supreme Court is therefore properly reluctant to find preemption when Congress has been ambiguous, the question whether federal law in fact preempts state action in any given case necessarily remains largely a matter of statutory construction. In evaluating patterns of statutory interaction, the Supreme Court has declared

---

8. See §§ 5–7, 5–8, 5–20 through 5–23, supra.

9. 469 U.S. 528 (1985), discussed in § 5–22, supra.

10. 426 U.S. 833 (1976) (holding that state sovereignty constitutes a judicially enforceable limit on Congress' commerce power).

11. Garcia, 469 U.S. at 552.

12. Compare Immigration and Naturalization Service v. Chadha, 462 U.S. 919 (1983), discussed in § 4–3, supra. Recently, after the Senate and House passed the Anti-Apartheid Act of 1986, Pub. L. No. 99–440, 100 Stat. 1086, but before it was vetoed by the President—a veto subsequently overridden by Congress—the question arose whether the Act might preempt efforts by states and localities to limit their own economic ties to the South Africa regime, either by divesting public pension funds or by refusing to use, as state or municipal contractors or suppliers, companies doing business in South Africa. It seems clear that, since the Act itself establishes a national prohibition on certain imports, exports, and business relationships with the South African government and with private companies in South Africa, but indicates no congressional intent to affect state or local decisions to further sever their own ties with the South Africa regime, no preemption exists. See also § 6–20, supra, at note 9. Although one Senator had expressed a different view of the matter, he "should not be able to deter states from deciding how to invest or spend their funds. If a few legislators could insert calculated snippets of legislative history and thereby instruct the courts to regulate the finances of states and cities, they could circumvent the need to articulate that scheme of regulation through the usual legislative process"—the single, exhaustively-considered procedure set forth in the Constitution for making laws. Tribe, "Memorandum on the Nonpreemptive Effect of the Comprehensive Anti-Apartheid Act of 1986 Upon State and Local Measures," Cong. Rec. S. 12535 (Sept. 15, 1986). Moreover, a holding that the Act preempted some sphere of state and local governmental investment decisions, in a situation where Congress has provided no replacement mechanism, would leave federal judges in the difficult and perhaps constitutionally untenable role of having to review portfolios to decide precisely which investment strategies are preempted, thus "employ[ing] their own notions of state sovereignty in delineating the boundaries of the preemption." Id. at 12536. Thus, a finding of preemption would not only circumvent lawmaking procedures, but would also place the federal judiciary in the role of delineator of the boundaries of state sovereignty—a role the Supreme Court in Garcia held is properly reserved to Congress.

generally that whether challenged state action has been preempted turns on whether or not it "stands as an obstacle to the accomplishment and execution of the full purposes and objectives of Congress." [13] Since congressional purposes can be either substantive or jurisdictional, a state action may be struck down as an invalid interference with the federal design either because it is in actual conflict with the substantive operation of a federal program, or because, whatever its substantive impact, it intrudes upon a field that Congress has validly reserved to the federal sphere.[14]

§ 6–26. Actual Conflict Between Federal and State Law

State action must give way to federal legislation where a valid "act of Congress fairly interpreted is in actual conflict with the law of the State." [1] Regulations duly promulgated by a federal agency, pursuant to congressional delegation, have the same preemptive effect.[2] Such "actual conflict" is most clearly manifest when the federal and state enactments are directly contradictory on their face. Federal regulation obviously supersedes state regulation where compliance with both is a literal impossibility. For example, it was held in *McDermott v. Wisconsin* [3] that Wisconsin could not prosecute retail merchants who sold syrup obtained from other states and labeled in a manner that complied with regulations promulgated under the Federal Food and Drugs Act of 1906, where any compliance with the federal law would have caused the syrup to be mislabeled under the Wisconsin statute.[4] Federal law was also given effect over directly conflicting state law in *Free v. Bland*,[5] where the Supreme Court held that, despite the Texas community property law, United States savings bonds held in co-ownership

---

13. Hines v. Davidowitz, 312 U.S. 52, 67 (1941) (invalidating state alien registration law in light of federal statute governing same conduct). See Powell, "Current Conflicts Between the Commerce Clause and State Police Power, 1922–27," 12 Minn.L. Rev. 321, 327 (1928); Savage v. Jones, 225 U.S. 501, 533 (1912).

14. The Supreme Court typically divides preemption analysis into the three categories of "express preemption," where Congress has in express terms declared its intention to preclude state regulation in a given area; "implied preemption," where Congress, through the structure or objectives of federal law, has impliedly precluded state regulation in the area; and "conflict preemption," where Congress did not necessarily intend preemption of state regulation in a given area, but where the particular state law conflicts directly with federal law, or stands as an obstacle to the accomplishment of federal objectives. See, e.g., Pacific Gas & Electric Co. v. State Energy Resources Conservation & Development Comm'n, 461 U.S. 190, 203–04 (1983). These three categorties of preemption are anything but analytically air-tight. For example, even when Congress declares its preemptive intent in express language, de-

ciding exactly what it meant to preempt often resembles an exercise in implied preemption analysis. So too, implied preemption analysis is inescapably tied to the presumption that Congress did not intend to allow state obstructions of federal policy, a central inquiry in conflict preemption analysis.

§ 6–26

1. Savage v. Jones, 225 U.S. 501, 533 (1912) (dictum); McDermott v. Wisconsin, 228 U.S. 115, 132 (1913); Florida Lime & Avocado Growers, Inc. v. Paul, 373 U.S. 132, 142–43 (1963) (dictum).

2. "We have held repeatedly that state laws can be pre-empted by federal regulations as well as by federal statutes." Hillsborough County, Fla. v. Automated Med. Labs, 471 U.S. 707, 713 (1985). See also § 6–28, infra. And see Fidelity Federal Savings & Loan Ass'n v. de la Cuesta, 458 U.S. 141 (1982).

3. 228 U.S. 115 (1913).

4. The Court also held it irrelevant that the goods in question had been removed from the "original packages" in which they had been shipped into the state.

5. 369 U.S. 663 (1962).

form should, upon the death of one co-owner, pass to the surviving co-owner in accord with applicable Federal Treasury regulations. So too, in *Southland Corp. v. Keating*,[6] the Supreme Court held that a California statute that nullified certain arbitration clauses in contracts and instead submitted disputes to judicial review was preempted by the Federal Arbitration Act, which withdrew the power of the states to require a judicial forum for the resolution of claims which the contracting parties agreed to resolve by arbitration.[7]

But state and federal laws need not be contradictory on their face for the latter to supersede the former: there are more subtle forms of actual conflict. Even if state action does not go so far as to prohibit the very acts which the federal government requires (or vice versa), it may nonetheless be struck down if it is in "actual conflict" with narrow objectives that underlie federal enactments.[8] Thus, state action must

---

6. 465 U.S. 1 (1984).

7. An apparent facial conflict may at times disappear upon closer examination of the federal law. For example, in Midlantic Nat'l Bank v. New Jersey Dept. of Env. Protection, 474 U.S. 494 (1986), a state's environmental laws forbade abandonment of land on which toxic wastes had been dumped, without first decontaminating the site. Section 554 of the federal bankruptcy code, in contrast, expressly permits a trustee to abandon property if the property is either "burdensome to the estate, or . . . of inconsequential . . . benefit to the estate." Despite the apparent facial conflict between the federal and state statutes, a closely divided Supreme Court looked behind the plain words of the federal statute and found, by examining its legislative history, no congressional intent to preempt important state environmental laws. Justice Powell's opinion for the majority, joined by Justices Blackmun, Brennan, Marshall, and Stevens, offered no persuasive response to the dissent's attack on the majority's stretching of the legislative history. See id. at 763 (Rehnquist, J., joined by Burger, C.J., and White and O'Connor, JJ., dissenting). Yet, since it seems unlikely that Congress meant to use its bankruptcy power to alter substantive state law rights and responsibilities as deeply as the Bankrupt's trustee proposed, the majority's result seems defensible. See Ohio v. Kovacs, 469 U.S. 274 (1985). Indeed, as a purely linguistic matter, see Midlantic, 106 S.Ct. at 759–62, the federal law may be read as setting only the *minimum* conditions for circumstances in which a trustee may abandon property, subject to a variety of generally applicable background rules having nothing to do with bankruptcy as such. Cf. California Federal Savings & Loan Assn. v. Guerra, 107 S.Ct. 683 (1987), discussed in note 8, infra. Had the Court adopted this reading, a somewhat broader holding would have followed—one not limited to state environmental laws. That Congress could have, but did not, make this reading explicit, see id. at 766 (Rehnquist, J. dissenting), was properly treated as irrelevant by the majority.

Of course, when the governing federal law simply *cannot* be read to leave room for a challenged state measure to operate, inquiry into Congress' purposes cannot properly avoid a conclusion of preemption. Thus, in Aloha Airlines, Inc. v. Director of Taxation of Hawaii, 464 U.S. 7 (1983), the Supreme Court unanimously invalidated Hawaii's imposition of a gross income tax on airlines operating within the state, because the federal Airport and Airway Development Act expressly preempted gross receipts taxes. Although Hawaii's highest court "sought to avoid this direct conflict by looking beyond the language of [the Act] to Congress's purpose in enacting the statute," and concluded that Congress's preemptive intent applied only to per-passenger taxes and not to taxes, such as Hawaii's, imposed on air carriers rather than on air travellers, the Supreme Court correctly refused to rewrite the unambiguous preemption clause that Congress had enacted into law. The reluctance to infer preemption cannot be stretched into "a [judicial] license to rewrite [statutory] language." United States v. Albertini, 472 U.S. 675 (1985).

8. The governing federal statute may, however, restrict its own preemptive effect—by providing, for example, that it preempts only those laws which purport to require or permit conduct which would be a violation of the federal statute. When this is the case, it seems quite improper for a court even to *ask* whether a challenged state law which clearly purports to require or permit no such thing nonetheless "conflicts" in some more nebulous sense with the federal statute or its objectives. To engage in such a broader inquiry is to

ordinarily be invalidated if its effect is to discourage conduct that federal action specifically seeks to encourage. It was on this basis that the Supreme Court, in *Nash v. Florida Industrial Commission*, invali-

forget that preemption is ultimately a matter of *construing* a federal statute; when the statute contains its own preemption or anti-preemption provision, a court that fails to give that provision dispositive effect and instead applies its own preemption criteria is illegitimately disregarding the source of its authority and, regardless of where its preemption inquiry leads it, is pursuing a fundamentally lawless path.

Unfortunately, however, only Justice Scalia appears to have followed this basic precept in California Federal Savings & Loan Ass'n v. Guerra, 107 S.Ct. 683 (1987), in which the Court reached what seems to be the correct result by a route that the approach of this footnote would condemn as incorrect. At issue in that case was a California law requiring employers to provide leave and reinstatement to employees disabled by pregnancy. Title VII of the 1964 Civil Rights Act, as amended by the Pregnancy Discrimination Act of 1978, bars sex discrimination by covered employers, specifies that sex discrimination includes discrimination on the basis of pregnancy, and provides that "women affected by pregnancy, childbirth, or related medical conditions shall be treated the same for all employment-related purposes, including receipt of benefits under fringe benefit programs, as other persons not so affected but similar in their ability or inability to work." The Court, in an opinion by Justice Marshall joined in all respects by Justices Brennan, Blackmun, and O'Connor, and in all but one limited respect by Justice Stevens, concluded that Congress intended the Pregnancy Discrimination Act to be a floor beneath which pregnancy disability benefits may not drop and not a ceiling above which they may not rise. Because California's pregnancy disability leave statute and Title VII as amended share the common goal of promoting equal employment opportunity for women, the Court held, the federal law does not preempt the state law at issue.

As Justice Scalia observed in a separate opinion concurring in the Court's judgment, most of the Court's analysis was beside the point if one took seriously the quite strict anti-preemption provision of Title VII, 42 U.S.C. § 2000e–7, which specified that Title VII preempts *only* laws which "purport[ ] to require or permit the doing of any act which would be an unlawful employment practice" under the title. As Justice Scalia rightly said, California's requirement that employers provide certain benefits to employees disabled by pregnancy "does not remotely purport to require or permit any refusal to accord federally mandated equal treatment to others similarly situated. No more is needed to decide this case." 107 S.Ct. at 697. An employer who provides leave and reinstatement for employees disabled by pregnancy in compliance with the challenged California law, but then chooses *not* to provide similar protection for, let us say, men suffering somewhat similar disabilities, cannot plausibly point to the California law at issue as "authority" for this latter, internally-motivated choice. Such an employer might or might not be subject to suit under Title VII for discriminating against men. If such a suit could succeed, then California's requirement, *combined* with the federal law, could well have the effect of *forcing* covered employers in California to provide disability benefits to persons other than pregnant women—something that neither the federal law *alone* nor the state law *alone* would have done. That possibility struck the dissenters (Justice White, joined by Chief Justice Rehnquist and Justice Powell) as bizarre. Id. at 702. And so it may have been. Perhaps it follows that the hypothesized employer should not be deemed in violation of federal *or* state law. But it does not follow that the employer's decision to deny men and non-pregnant women the same treatment that the state law mandates for pregnant women whenever the disabilities are similar is a decision either mandated or authorized by the state law in question.

To be sure, the Court's central rationale for upholding the California law—that pregnant women *need* special benefits in the employment context to assure meaningful equality—appears to undercut this very reading of the California law by attributing to the state a policy of encouraging employers *not* to treat pregnant workers "the same" way they treat others similarly situated. (See also Justice Stevens' concurring opinion, id. at 695–97, drawing an analogy to race-based affirmative action.) Perhaps the dissenters were reacting more to this rationale than to the mandate of the state law at issue. In any event, it seems wrong to dismiss the difference between the Court's rationale and that of Justice Scalia as resting on an optional "choice between two grounds of statutory construction." Id. at 696 n. 1 (Stevens, J., concurring). It rests, rather, on a choice between approaching the issue as a genuine one of statutory construction and approaching it as essentially one of policy.

dated a state unemployment compensation law insofar as it denied benefits to otherwise eligible applicants solely because they had filed an unfair labor practice charge with the NLRB.[9] Similarly, in *Xerox Corp. v. County of Harris*,[10] the Court held that a state tax could not be imposed on goods manufactured in Mexico, shipped to the United States, and held under bond in a customs warehouse awating shipment abroad. For Congress, in enacting a series of laws with a long history, had clearly intended to create duty-free enclaves for such imported goods stored in customs bonded warehouses pending export to foreign markets, so as to encourage merchants to use American ports. Although a state tax on such goods was not expressly prohibited, its imposition was preempted because it would manifestly discourage and indeed would financially penalize the very acts the federal law was meant to foster.[11]

So too, in the context of federal pension plans, when Congress strikes a delicate balance among budgetary constraints, the interest in supporting retired employees, and the interest in encouraging employees to retire, state action directly diminishing the benefits received by a retiree frustrates Congress' objectives, and is preempted. Thus, in *Hisquierdo v. Hisquierdo*,[12] while acknowledging that family law is normally a matter for state control, that state action in family matters is preempted only if "positively required by direct [congressional] enactment," [13] and that state law "must do 'major damage' to 'clear and substantial' federal interests" [14] to be preempted, the Court nonetheless held state community property laws preempted when they require dividing up the interest in railroad retirement income upon divorce of a future beneficiary: the federal statute creating the retirement benefits explicitly stated that the benefits would not be subject to legal attachment.[15]

9. 389 U.S. 235, 239 (1967). The state law disqualified for benefits any person unemployed as a result of a labor dispute; in the Nash case itself, the unemployed person's discharge had been occasioned by her filing of an unfair labor practice charge against her employer with the National Labor Relations Board. Contrast Ohio Bureau of Employment Services v. Hodory, 431 U.S. 471 (1977) (state may choose to maintain neutrality by withholding unemployment compensation from all persons unemployed as a result of a labor dispute).

10. 459 U.S. 145 (1982).

11. Cf. R.G. Reynolds Tobacco Co. v. Durham County, N.C., 107 S.Ct. 499 (1986) (preemption holding of Xerox Corp. inapplicable to imported goods destined for domestic use only).

12. 439 U.S. 572 (1979). Justice Blackmun wrote the majority opinion. Justice Stewart dissented, joined by Justice Rehnquist.

13. Id. at 581.

14. Id.

15. The majority did not fully answer the argument of the dissent that community property laws, which deal with ownership during marriage and not merely with rules for attachment upon divorce, are unlike state laws purporting to allow creditors to attach retirement benefits as such, and that, by prohibiting creditor attachment of railroad benefits, Congress did not evince an intent to withdraw such benefits from the reach of community property law. In accord with Hisquierdo was McCarty v. McCarty, 453 U.S. 210 (1981), holding that, because Congress clearly intended that military retirement pay actually reach the beneficiary, any state law dividing up pension rights upon divorce frustrates that federal objective and to that degree is preempted. Justice Rehnquist, in a dissent joined by Justices Brennan and Stewart, criticized the McCarty majority for not abiding by the strict test of Hisquierdo, which decreed preemption of state family law only if Congress "positively required [it] by direct enactment," quoting 439 U.S. at 581. Instead, in the dissenters' view, the majority used only "vague implications

In *Hisquierdo*, it was not the delicate congressional balance alone that preempted California's laws, but Congress' explicit enactment that the benefits not be subject to attachment. *Hisquierdo* was thus unlike *Edgar v. MITE Corp.*[16], where the Court considered a challenge to the Illinois Business Takeover Act—a state law which regulated interstate tender offers, favoring incumbent management in various ways. It was claimed that Congress, by enacting the Williams Act to protect public investors and by striking a delicate balance favoring neither entrenched management nor takeover bidders—a balance not as favorable to management as the Illinois act—had preempted any state regulation upsetting that balance. While the state statute was struck down on commerce clause grounds, the preemption argument attracted only three votes.[17] Lacking was hard evidence of congressional intent to preclude state regulation of tender offers; that the state statute upset a congressional balance was not by itself enough.

State action may also be preempted as interfering with federal regulation if it encourages conduct whose absence would aid in the effectuation of the federal scheme as interpreted and applied. In *City of Burbank v. Lockheed Air Terminal Inc.*,[18] a city ordinance making it unlawful for jet aircraft to take off from the privately owned city airport between 11 p.m. and 7 a.m. was found to conflict with the purpose of the Federal-Aeronautics Act "to insure the safety of aircraft and the efficient utilization of . . . airspace." The Court concluded that "control of the timing of takeoffs and landings would severely limit the flexibility of the FAA in controlling air traffic flow. The difficulties of scheduling flights to avoid congestion and the concomitant decrease in safety would be compounded." [19] So, too, in *Jones v. Rath Packing Co.*,[20] the Court invalidated a California regulation of the labeling of packaged flour sold in the state, after speculating that national flour manufacturers seeking to meet the California standard would probably

from tangentially related enactments or Congress' *failure* to act." 453 U.S. at 237 (emphasis in original).

16. 457 U.S. 624 (1982).

17. Justices White and Blackmun and Chief Justice Burger found preemption. Justices Powell and Stevens thought the Williams Act left open the possibility of state regulation of tender offers. The other members of the Court did not reach the preemption issue. In CTS Corp. v. Dynamics Corp., 107 S.Ct. 1637 (1987), a majority of the Court reached a similar preemption issue and distinguished the conclusion of the MITE plurality in the course of upholding an Indiana takeover regulation as consistent with the Williams Act. Joined by Chief Justice Rehnquist and Justices Brennan, Marshall and O'Connor, Justice Powell summarized "the overriding concern of the MITE plurality [as being] . . . that the Illinois statute considered in that case operated to favor management against offerors, to the detriment of shareholders. By contrast, the statute now before the

Court protects the independent shareholder against both of these contending parties. Thus, the act furthers a basic purpose of the Williams Act, 'plac[ing] investors on an equal footing with the takeover bidder.'" Id. at 1645–46 (citation omitted). The CTS majority's concern was that a broader reading of the Williams Act and the commerce clause would cast doubt on a wide range of state corporation law. In a statement joined by Justice Scalia as well, the CTS majority observed that "[n]o principle of corporation law and practice is more firmly established than a state's authority to regulate domestic corporations, including the authority to define the voting rights of shareholders." Id. at 1649. Edgar v. MITE is discussed from a dormant commerce clause perspective in § 6–12, supra.

18. 411 U.S. 624 (1973).

19. Id. at 639.

20. 430 U.S. 519 (1977).

overpack in order to ensure that moisture loss during distribution would not bring the weight of distributed flour packages below the weight stated on their labels, while local manufacturers, who could adjust their packing practices to the region's humidity conditions, and manufacturers distributing only in states following the federal standard (which permitted reasonable weight variations resulting from loss of moisture during distribution), would probably not be inclined to overpack. The result would be to frustrate a major purpose of the federal Fair Packaging and Labeling Act, the facilitation of value comparisons among similar products, since "consumers throughout the country who attempted to compare the value of identically labeled packages of flour would not be comparing packages which contained identical amounts of flour solids." [21]

A similar sort of conflict with federal objectives may occur when state action undermines a congressional decision in favor of national uniformity of standards—a situation similar in practical effect to that of federal occupation of a field.[22] In *Ray v. Atlantic Richfield Co.*,[23] a Washington state law required all tankers in Puget Sound either to have certain safety design features more stringent than federal requirements, or to have a tug escort. The Supreme Court found that, by enacting the Ports and Waterways Safety Act of 1972, "Congress intended [to establish] uniform national standards for design and construction" of tanker vessels, thus preempting more stringent state design requirements.[24] Had the state statute required *only* the safety designs, it would have been preempted. But, since the statute required *either* the safety designs *or* a tug escort, preemption was avoided.[25] In reaching this conclusion, the Court first found that the escort requirement, if enacted alone, would have been allowable: such an escort was not a design requirement; it was a local matter—at least until a tug-escort rule is promulgated by a federal authority.[26] Furthermore, since the state could require *all* ships to have a tug escort, it could also

21. Id. at 543. The Court offered no persuasive response to the dissenters' observations (1) that the majority's entire line of argument rested on factual suppositions not fully supported by the record, and (2) that overpacking of flour is hard to regard as unduly threatening to the federal scheme once the Court has been told that, "should a manufacturer deliberately overpack, for *whatever* reason, there will be no federal action taken against him even though value comparisons might then 'be misleading.'" Id. at 546 (Rehnquist, J., joined by Stewart, J., dissenting in part). The Court was unanimous, however, in its holding that the state's labeling requirement for packaged bacon, unlike that for flour, was expressly preempted by federal statute.

22. See § 6–27, infra.

23. 435 U.S. 151 (1978). Justice White's plurality opinion was joined in full only by Chief Justice Burger and by Justices Stewart and Blackmun.

24. Id. at 163. The Court distinguished its holding in Huron Portland Cement Co. v. City of Detroit, 362 U.S. 440 (1960), discussed in § 6–26, infra, in which the federal safety objectives were entirely independent of the municipalities' health and environmental goals, and in which no federal purpose was frustrated by coexisting regimes of regulation. Also, compare Hillsborough County, Fla. v. Automated Labs, Inc., 471 U.S. 707 (1985), where federal safety regulations governing blood donations were held to be merely *minimum* standards, and where the Court found no federal objective to establish *uniform* standards as such. See also Shaw v. Delta Air Lines, Inc., 463 U.S. 85, 99 n. 20 (1983).

25. 435 U.S. at 172–73.

26. The Ports and Waterways Safety Act authorized, but did not require, federal regulation in this area. No federal regulation had yet been promulgated either requiring tug escorts for tankers in Puget Sound, or stating that tug escorts are un-

require such an escort of a lesser category of ships—namely, those ships that did not meet certain design standards.[27]   Although the Court noted that its decision might be different if the tug escort requirement were shown to exert pressure on tanker operators to comply with the state's design requirements,[28] the basic teaching of the *Atlantic Richfield* decision is that state pressure to act in derogation of a federal statutory scheme is not to be inferred lightly.

So too, even when there is no doubt as to the direction in which state law pushes behavior, no such direction is to be lightly condemned as inconsistent with federal policy. Thus, while state action is preempted if it specifically frustrates fairly narrow and concrete objectives that underlie federal enactments,[29] no such conclusion follows where the most that can be said is that the direction in which state law pushes someone's actions is in general tension with broad or abstract goals that may be attributed to various federal laws or programs. In *Commonwealth Edison Co. v. Montana*,[30] for example, Montana coal producers challenged the state's coal severance tax, asserting that the state tax,

necessary. In dictum, the plurality implied that, if the Secretary of Transportation so regulates, the state escort requirement would then be preempted. 435 U.S. at 171–72.

27. Justice Stevens, dissenting in part, joined by Justice Powell, agreed that the federal objective of uniformity preempted state design requirements. But they disagreed with the plurality's holding that the disjunctive nature of Washington's statute should save it. In their view, the tug requirement was merely a special penalty for non-compliance with the state design requirements: "Since . . . the tug escort requirement is an inseparable appendage to the invalid design requirement, the invalidity of one necessarily infects the other." Id. at 190.

Justice Marshall, dissenting in part, joined by Justices Brennan and Rehnquist, found the tug escort requirement allowable, but saw no reason speculatively to invalidate the state's design requirements, especially since all tanker operators had thus far selected the tug alternative rather than attempting to comply with the expensive safety design requirements. Id. at 181. Justice Marshall did not expressly disagree with the plurality's finding that there was a federal goal of uniformity of design, or that the goal was sufficiently narrow and explicit to preempt state design requirements. Rather, he found that the issue was not before the Court: the state rule " 'may be viewed as simply a tug-escort requirement since it does not have the effect of forcing compliance with the design specifications.' " Id. at 181 (quoting the plurality opinion at 179).

28. Id. at 173 n. 25 (plurality opinion). The Court also held that the tug escort

requirement did not violate the commerce clause. Its cost was thought to be slight and, like "a local pilotage requirement, a requirement that a vessel take on a tug escort is not the type of regulation that demands a uniform national rule." Id. at 179, citing Cooley v. Board of Wardens, 53 U.S. (12 How.) 299 (1851), discussed in § 6–4, supra. But see 435 U.S. at 189 (Stevens, J., joined by Powell, J., dissenting in part).

29. An example of a state statute frustrating such a narrow and concrete congressional objective is presented by Philko Aviation, Inc. v. Shacket, 462 U.S. 406 (1983). An Illinois law had been construed and applied to recognize transfers of airplane title even for sales not recorded with the Federal Aviation Administration. Id. at 408. Because Congress had intended, by enacting the Federal Aviation Act, to make the FAA the "central clearing house for recordation of title," id. at 411, the Court held that any state law permitting unrecorded aircraft transfers stood in "direct conflict" with that federal objective and was therefore preempted. Id. at 410. The congressional objective—to entrust FAA with this central clearing house function—was quite concrete. See also Chicago North Western Transportation Co. v. Kalo Brick & Tile Co., 450 U.S. 311, 324 (1981) (unanimously holding that state-law actions for failure to provide adequate rail service may not be asserted against a regulated carrier when the ICC has approved the decision to abandon the line in question); Arkansas Louisiana Gas Co. v. Hall, 453 U.S. 571, 584 (1981).

30. 453 U.S. 609 (1981).

by making coal production more costly, "substantially frustrated national energy policies, reflected in several federal statutes, encouraging the production and use of coal." [31] The Supreme Court acknowledged the broadly-declared congressional purpose of encouraging the use of coal,[32] but made it clear that state laws that merely push against the grain of "general expressions of 'national policy'" in federal statutes will not, for that reason alone, be deemed to be preempted.[33]

Similarly, in *Pacific Gas & Electric Co. v. State Energy Resources Conservation & Development Comm'n*,[34] after California had instituted a moratorium on construction of new nuclear power plants until a satisfactory technology was found for disposal of radioactive waste, the Supreme Court unanimously rejected the claim that the state's moratorium "frustrates the Atomic Energy Act's purpose to develop the commercial use of nuclear power." [35] The Court concluded that Congress had not intended to accomplish the promotion of nuclear power "at all costs," [36] and held that "Congress has left sufficient authority in the states to allow the development of nuclear power to be slowed or even stopped for economic reasons." [37] No preemptive effect was given

31. Id. at 633.

32. Id.

33. Id. at 634. The Court noted, see id. at 633, that it had rejected a similar argument, addressed to the "national policy favoring free competition," in Exxon Corp. v. Governor of Maryland, 437 U.S. 117, 133 (1978).

34. 461 U.S. 190 (1983). The author of this treatise was counsel for California in the Supreme Court.

35. Id. at 220.

36. Id. at 222.

37. Id. While declining to give preemptive effect to Congress's general purpose of promoting nuclear power, the majority found that any state nuclear *safety* regulation would be preempted, regardless of whether it conflicted with federal objectives. "[T]he Federal Government has occupied the entire field of nuclear safety concerns, except the limited powers expressly ceded to the States." Id. at 212. See § 6-25, infra. Justice Blackmun, in a concurrence joined by Justice Stevens, would have limited the preemptive effect of the Atomic Energy Act even further—to the narrow area, within nuclear safety concerns, of "how a nuclear plant should be constructed and operated to protect against radiation hazards." Id. at 224 (footnote omitted). Compare Hillsborough County, Fla. v. Automated Labs, 471 U.S. 707 (1985), holding that, in spite of "the federal goal of maintaining an adequate supply of plasma," federal safety regulations governing blood donations were "merely minimum safety standards," not preemptive of stricter local ordinances. Id. at 721.

In *Pacific Gas & Electric*, in deciding whether the California moratorium on construction of nuclear plants was an economic regulation (not preempted) or a safety regulation (preempted), the Court largely relied on California's own characterization of its enactment as economic, not safety-related. The Court did not attempt to ascertain California's "true" motives—partly because that inquiry is often unsatisfactory, but also partly because, regardless of California's motive, it was undisputed that the state *could have* halted construction of new nuclear plants on economic grounds, in individual proceedings. Id. at 216. This was not a case in which California sought to defend, as motivated by nonsafety concerns, any regulation of the mode of construction or operation *as such*. By refusing to be skeptical, the Court showed itself distinctly inhospitable to claims of actual conflict when the allegedly preempting federal objective is as broadly-framed as it was in this case.

See also New York Telephone Co. v. New York State Labor Dept., 440 U.S. 519 (1979), holding that a state strike insurance program that paid unemployment compensation to striking workers (among others) and that made "the struck, rather than all, employers primarily responsible for financing [such] striker benefits," id. at 535, was not preempted by the National Labor Relations Act even though the state program unquestionably "affects the relative strengths of the antagonists in a bargaining dispute," id. at 546, because New York *purported* not "to regulate the collective bargaining relationships" between employees and employers, in which case the program would have been preempted, "but

to an unmistakeable, but general and abstractly-framed, federal purpose—the promotion of nuclear power—where Congress itself had failed to prohibit (and indeed had in other contexts affirmatively authorized) state actions that could undercut the federal objective by retarding the use of nuclear power.

Finally, in the context of the preemptive reach of the Sherman Act against state action, the Supreme Court has been even more reluctant to base preemption solely on a supposed conflict of state law with broadly-framed federal objectives. Thus, the Court has given no weight at all to the pro-competition objective of federal antitrust law except to the extent that Congress manifested that objective in the actual requirements and prohibitions of its antitrust enactments. In *Rice v. Norman Williams Co.*[38] and *Fisher v. Berkeley*,[39] the Court held that, although the Sherman Act broadly seeks to encourage price competition, "a state statute [or local ordinance] is not pre-empted by the federal antitrust laws simply because it might have an anti-competitive effect." [40] Instead, a state or local measure "should be struck down on pre-emption grounds 'only if it mandates or authorizes conduct that necessarily constitutes a *violation* of the antitrust laws in all cases.' " [41]

As a corollary of the rule that state action will not lightly be found to be inconsistent with federal policy, not only are broad and abstract federal goals given scant preemptive effect, but even congressional goals that are tightly-stated will be interpreted narrowly when testing traditional forms of state action for conflict with those goals. In *Silkwood v. Kerr-McGee Corp.*,[42] traditional state law provided for the possibility of compensatory and punitive damages for tort victims, including victims of radiation injuries from nuclear power plants. When a jury awarded such damages to the victim of radiation injuries at a plant whose safety features were in compliance with federal regulations, the Supreme Court rejected a preemption challenge, even though the Court had shortly before found, in *Pacific Gas & Electric Co. v. State Energy Resources Conservation & Development Comm'n*,[43] that "the Federal Government has occupied the entire field of nuclear safety concerns," [44] implying that no state could impose its own more stringent safety regulations on nuclear power plants.[45] As Justice Blackmun

instead to provide an efficient means of insuring employment security in the State." Id. at 533.

38. 458 U.S. 654 (1982).

39. 106 S.Ct. 1045 (1986). The author of this treatise was counsel for Berkeley in the Supreme Court.

40. Rice, 458 U.S. at 659; Fisher, 106 S.Ct. at 1048.

41. Fisher, 106 S.Ct. at 1048 (quoting Rice, 458 U.S. at 661) (emphasis added). Thus, although a private rent-fixing cartel would violate the Sherman Act, as would a state or local law authorizing such a cartel or enforcing its decisions, a local government's action to control rents or rent increases at levels fixed by local government itself did not *violate* the Act (despite the unavailability of the Parker v. Brown, 317 U.S. 341 (1943), exception) and hence was not preempted. Fisher, 106 S.Ct. at 1051. A thoughtful assessment of how Fisher fits into the evolving Parker v. Brown jurisprudence appears in Garland, "Antitrust and State Action: Economic Efficiency and the Political Process," 96 Yale L.J. 486, 499–507 (1987).

42. 464 U.S. 238 (1984).

43. 461 U.S. 190 (1983). See the text at notes 34–37, supra.

44. Id. at 212.

45. "[T]he statute does not seek to regulate the *construction* or operation of a nuclear powerplant. It would clearly be impermissible for California to attempt to do so, [see Northern States Power v. Minneso-

explained in *Silkwood*, "[w]hatever compensation standard a state imposes . . . a [nuclear] licensee remains free to continue operating under federal standards and to pay for the injury that results." [46]

In *Ferebee v. Chevron Chemical Co.*,[47] an analogous case close on the heels of *Silkwood*, an agricultural worker alleged that Chevron, notwithstanding its compliance with Federal labeling laws, had failed to give adequate warning of dangers posed by the insecticide paraquat, which it produced—a failure that would soon lead to the death of the worker. The court of appeals found that Maryland's "cause of action in strict products liability for failure to warn adequately of a product's inherently dangerous condition" [48] was not preempted by the Federal Insecticide, Fungicide, and Rodenticide Act (FIFRA) and ensuing EPA labelling regulations, which provide that no state shall "impose or continue in effect any requirements for labeling . . . in addition to or different from those required under this subchapter." [49] The court, reading narrowly, found that Congress preempted only state labelling *requirements* more stringent than the federal. Maryland did not *require* more stringent warnings; it merely said that, if more stringent warnings were not used, the defendant may have to *pay* for the resulting damages.[50] This result seems eminently defensible. FIFRA aims at ensuring that the health costs to society from the use of a particular pesticide, with its EPA-approved label, do not exceed "the benefit to society at large from use of the chemical;" [51] it is not meant as "an affirmative subsidization of the pesticide industry," [52] preventing states from providing for victim compensation. *Ferebee* was not followed by the Third Circuit in the very similar case of *Cipollone v. Liggett Group, Inc.*,[53] holding that state tort law was preempted to the extent it allowed the estate of a lifetime smoker to sue tobacco companies on the theory of inadequate warning. As in *Ferebee*, Congress expressly preempted any state labelling requirement more stringent than the federal requirement. But, unlike the court in *Ferebee*, the Third Circuit found that state law allowing such a lawsuit was in actual conflict with the objectives behind federal cigarette warning requirements. The Third Circuit, in reading Congress' preemption language expansively, apparently found that Congress meant to exempt the tobacco industry from the choice, faced by manufacturers in virtually every other industry, among increasing product safety, increasing warnings, or paying damages to injured consumers. That holding

ta, 447 F.2d 1143 (8th Cir. 1971), aff'd mem., 405 U.S. 1035 (1972),] for such regulation, even if enacted out of nonsafety concerns, would nevertheless directly conflict with the NRC's exclusive authority over plant construction and operation." 461 U.S. at 212.

46. 464 U.S. at 264 (Blackmun, J., joined by Marshall, J., dissenting as to punitive damages only).

47. 736 F.2d 1529 (D.C. Cir. 1984), cert. denied 469 U.S. 1062 (1984).

48. Id. at 1533.

49. Id. at 1540.

50. Id. at 1541. In this sense, the Maryland law resembles the disjunctive Washington law *not* preempted in Ray v. Atlantic Richfield Co., 435 U.S. 151 (1978), which required that tanker operators *either* comply with safety requirements more stringent than the federal, *or* use a tug escort in Puget Sound. See the text at notes 23–28, supra.

51. 736 F.2d at 1540.

52. Id. at 1542–43.

53. 789 F.2d 181 (3d Cir. 1986), cert. denied 107 S.Ct. 907 (1987).

seems hard to square with *Silkwood* and with the Supreme Court's admonition that there is an overriding presumption that "Congress did not intend to displace state law." [54]

It was once thought that, when the federal government regulated a given subject, any state law which purported to govern the same area was invalid. It mattered not whether there was an inescapable conflict between the letter or the spirit of the enactments or whether the state law simply duplicated, or went further than, the federal law.[55] In *Charleston W.C. Ry. v. Varnville Furniture Co.*, the Supreme Court spoke in unequivocal terms: "When Congress has taken the particular subject matter in hand, coincidence is as ineffective as opposition, and a state law is not to be declared a help because it attempts to go farther than Congress has seen fit to go." [56] Over time, however, the Court tempered its undifferentiated hostility to state regulation of matters already regulated by the federal government. Generally speaking, the Court has come to sanction state regulations that supplement federal efforts so long as compliance with the letter or effectuation of the purpose of the federal enactment is not likely to be significantly impeded by the state law.[57]

Among the most troublesome illustrations of this relatively tolerant posture toward "supplementary" state regulation is *Parker v. Brown*,[58] a 1943 decision in which the Supreme Court unanimously upheld a complex California plan for marketing that state's crop of raisins, all but five to ten percent of which were destined for shipment in interstate or foreign commerce. The state program had the undenied purpose and effect of eliminating competition in the terms of sale of the raisin crop, including price.[59] By upholding that program, the Court permitted California, through a scheme in which local raisin producers played a dominant role,[60] to control the terms on which "almost all the raisins consumed in the United States, and nearly one-half of the world crop," [61] could be purchased. The Court's rejection of the basic commerce clause attack on the California program [62] relied

54. Maryland v. Louisiana, 451 U.S. 725, 746 (1981). In contrast, see Allis-Chalmers Corp. v. Lueck, 471 U.S. 202 (1985), holding that the Wisconsin tort of bad-faith handling of an insurance claim is preempted, to the extent that the state would apply it to insurance plans included in a collective bargaining agreement, because federal labor laws classify such a claim as a grievance, and explicitly require resolution under the grievance procedures specified in the contract—in this case, by arbitration.

55. This was the thrust of Daniel Webster's argument in Gibbons v. Ogden, 22 U.S. (9 Wheat.) 1, 8–18 (1824).

56. 237 U.S. 597, 604 (1915). See also Missouri Pacific R. v. Porter, 273 U.S. 341, 346 (1927).

57. See California v. Zook, 336 U.S. 725, 730 (1949) (upholding state prohibition of transportation not licensed by ICC); Colorado Anti-Discrimination Commission v.

Continental Air Lines, Inc., 372 U.S. 714, 722–24 (1963) (state statute barring discriminatory hiring upheld); California Federal Sav. & Loan Assn. v. Guerra, 107 S.Ct. 683 (1987) (state statute requiring pregnancy disability reinstatement upheld); Fort Halifax Packing Co., Inc. v. Coyne, 107 S.Ct. 2211 (1987) (upholding state law requiring a lump sum severance pay benefit to employees thrown out of work by a plant closing; the Federal Employment Retirement Income Security Act regulates only benefit *plans*, and therefore preempts *only* state regulation of *plans*, not state requirement of one-time-only *benefits*).

58. 317 U.S. 341 (1943).

59. Id. at 359.

60. Id. at 347, 352.

61. Id. at 345.

62. See § 6–8, supra.

heavily on the Court's twin perceptions *first* that the economic distress of the less powerful California raisin producers was too local a problem to be a likely subject of direct congressional solution,[63] and *second* that Congress had in fact pursued the indirect course of authorizing the Secretary of Agriculture either to establish locally-based agricultural stabilization programs under federal authority (something the Secretary had done for some 20 commodities other than raisins)[64] or to cooperate in formulating and funding the operation of similar stabilization programs under state authority (something the Secretary had chosen to do with respect to raisins).[65] But for these strong indications that the California program's effect on interstate commerce was "one which it [had] been the policy of Congress to aid and encourage,"[66] the Court would almost surely have found the state's action to be in conflict with the commerce clause.[67]

The same reasoning also explains the Court's conclusion that the California program was not rendered invalid by the Agricultural Marketing Act of 1937:[68] a stabilization program adopted under that Act would of course supersede the state's program,[69] but the Secretary had chosen to order no federal program in the case of raisins, and the legislative history of the Act coupled with the Secretary's other actions made clear that the Act's policies could be effectuated by a state program of the type California had adopted.[70]

More complex and controversial[71] was the further holding of *Parker* that the California program was not invalidated by the Sherman Act,[72] since Congress had never intended by that Act to restrain or regulate "state action or official action directed by a state."[73] Although this holding might be understood as reflecting a requirement of congressional "clear statement" before federal legislation is construed to reach state programs as well as private conduct,[74] the central role played by private producers in both triggering and approving the

---

63. 317 U.S. at 362–63. See §§ 6–3, 6–12, supra.

64. 317 U.S. at 367–68 n. 18.

65. Id. at 357–58, 365–68.

66. Id. at 368. Cf. § 6–33, infra.

67. Indeed, the Court as much as conceded the weakness of its attempt to distinguish Parker, viewed purely as a commerce clause case, from Shafer v. Farmers Grain Co., 268 U.S. 189 (1925). See 317 U.S. at 362–63. Particularly since Parker was first argued the day after Wickard v. Filburn, 317 U.S. 111 (1942), see § 5–5, supra, and was reargued on the same day as Wickard, it seems soundest to construe the case in an atmosphere of substantial deference to congressional agricultural policy.

68. That federal statute, which broadly restricted agricultural competition, had itself only recently been upheld in United States v. Rock Royal Co-Operative, Inc., 307 U.S. 533 (1939).

69. See 317 U.S. at 353.

70. Id. at 354–58. The Court noted the possibility of a federal-state conflict if the state program "were to raise [raisin] prices beyond the parity price prescribed by the federal act," but found that this had not occurred. Id. at 355.

71. Compare, e.g., Posner, "The Proper Relationship Between State Regulation and the Federal Antitrust Laws," 49 N.Y. U.L.Rev. 693 (1974), with Note, "Of Raisins and Mushrooms: Applying the Parker Antitrust Exemption," 58 Va.L.Rev. 1511 (1972). See also Note, 24 Hast.L.J. 287 (1972); Note, 50 Tex.L.Rev. 474 (1972); Note, 19 Wayne L.Rev. 1245 (1973).

72. 15 U.S.C. §§ 1–7.

73. 317 U.S. at 351. See also Continental Ore Co. v. Union Carbide Corp., 370 U.S. 690, 706–707 (1962).

74. See 317 U.S. at 350.

organization of a marketing scheme under the California program[75] makes it difficult to distinguish the case from one in which the state has merely attempted to authorize private conduct violative of the Sherman Act, something a state clearly cannot do.[76] More plausible as an account of *Parker* is the theory that, at least where Congress has arguably implied an anti-trust exemption by establishing a federal policy with similar effects,[77] the purposes of the Sherman Act do not require its extension to situations in which (1) the premises of a competitive market fail to hold,[78] and (2) the state has carefully re-

75. See id. at 346–47.

76. The Parker Court conceded as much, id. at 351, citing Northern Securities Co. v. United States, 193 U.S. 197, 332, 344–47 (1904), but stressed that it is the State of California, "acting through the Commission, which adopts the program and which enforces it with penal sanctions, in the execution of a governmental policy." 317 U.S. at 352. Some lower courts had extended Parker to actions by regulated utilities where state regulatory commissions had merely *passively acquiesced* in the challenged practices, see, e.g., Washington Gas Light Co. v. Virginia Electric & Power Co., 438 F.2d 248 (4th Cir. 1971), criticized in Kintner & Kaufman, "The State Action Anti-trust Immunity Defense," 23 Am.U.L.Rev. 527, 530–33 (1974). But the Supreme Court then held that the Parker defense could apply only where anticompetitive action is *required* by direction of the State: "It is not enough that . . . anticompetitive conduct is 'prompted' by state action; rather, anticompetitive activities must be *compelled* by direction of the state acting as a sovereign." Goldfarb v. Virginia State Bar, 421 U.S. 773, 791 (1975) (emphasis added) (holding violative of the Sherman Act a minimum fee schedule for lawyers published by the Fairfax County Bar Association and enforced by the Virginia State Bar). Contrast Bates v. State Bar of Arizona, 433 U.S. 350, 360–63 & nn. 11–12 (1977) (state supreme court's ban on price advertising by lawyers held not subject to Sherman Act attack, because the ban "reflect[ed] a clear articulation of the State's policy" and was "subject to pointed re-examination by the policymaker . . . in enforcement proceedings"), discussed in § 12–15, infra. Cf. Cantor v. Detroit Edison Co., 428 U.S. 579 (1976); New Motor Vehicle Board of Cal. v. Orrin W. Fox Co., 439 U.S. 96 (1978).

Based on those cases, the Court in Cal. Retail Liquor Dealers Ass'n v. Midcal Aluminum, 445 U.S. 97 (1980), see § 6–24, note 14, supra, enunciated "two standards for antitrust immunity under *Parker v. Brown*. First, the challenged restraint must by 'one clearly articulated and affirmatively expressed as state policy'; second, the policy must be 'actively supervised' by the

State itself." Id. at 105 (citation omitted). The California statute at issue in Midcal established a state wine-pricing scheme which, unless immune, constituted a violation of the Sherman Act. The wine-pricing scheme satisfied the first of the two tests for immunity: the state clearly established it. But it failed the second test: the state "simply . . . enforces the prices established by private parties," without reviewing the reasonableness of the prices. Id. at 105. Neither does the state "monitor market conditions or engage in any 'pointed reexamination' of the program." Id. at 106. Since the scheme did not meet the standards for Parker v. Brown immunity, the statute enacting the scheme was preempted by the Sherman Act. Accord, 324 Liquor Corp. v. Duffy, 107 S.Ct. 720 (1987).

More recently, the Court made clear that, while state compulsion of anticompetitive behavior "often is the best evidence that the State has a clearly articulated and affirmatively expressed policy to displace competition," Southern Motor Carriers Rate Conference, Inc. v. United States, 471 U.S. 48, 62 (1985), the first prong of the Midcal test, requiring the existence of such a policy, may be satisfied *absent* compulsion "when other evidence conclusively shows that a State intends to adopt a permissive policy" toward anticompetitive private conduct. Id. The Court found such evidence in Southern Motor Carriers, where the state had clearly delegated substantial power to "rate bureaus"—composed of state-regulated private competitors—to propose and effectively fix prices for common carriers. Id. at 50–52. Because state regulatory commissions "actively supervise the collective ratemaking activities" at issue, id. at 62, Midcal's second prong was satisfied as well.

77. See P. Areeda, Antitrust Analysis 57 (2d ed. 1974).

78. This seems the case, e.g., in the area of public utility regulation. For a rare defense of Washington Gas Light Co., supra note 76, in these terms, see Verkuil, "State Action, Due Process and Anti-trust: Reflections on Parker v. Brown," 75 Colum.L.Rev. 328, 337–39 (1975).

placed market forces with a regulatory scheme that is procedurally fair both in its openness to all significantly affected interests,[79] and in its supervision by a relatively disinterested and adequately accountable public agency.[80] Just as the procedural fairness of SEC regulation was thought sufficient to warrant a measure of anti-trust exemption for security exchanges in *Silver v. New York Stock Exchange*,[81] so too federal deference to a procedurally fair and adequately enforced system of state controls could arguably point to a like result.[82]

79. This Parker Court argued, perhaps implausibly, that the "prerequisite approval of the [raisin proration] program upon referendum by a prescribed number of producers is not the imposition by them of their will upon the minority . . ." 317 U.S. at 352. Cf. Eubank v. Richmond, 226 U.S. 137 (1912).

80. The Parker Court stressed that "[t]he state itself exercises its legislative authority in making the regulation and in prescribing the conditions of its application." 317 U.S. at 352. But to say that this satisfies the demands of fairness, see also Verkuil, supra note 78, at 345, is to reduce those demands unjustifiably. If a licensing board composed of self-employed optometrists cannot constitutionally discipline salaried optometrists, Gibson v. Berryhill, 411 U.S. 564 (1973), it is unclear why a program designed by producers without consumer participation can constitutionally circumvent market forces to raise the prices consumers must pay.

81. 373 U.S. 341, 364 (1963). See also Gordon v. New York Stock Exchange, Inc., 422 U.S. 659 (1975).

82. See Verkuil, supra note 78, at 347–49. There has been considerably less deference to *municipalities* that instituted anticompetitive programs, even if procedurally fair and adequately supervised by the municipality. In Lafayette v. Louisiana Power & Light Co., 435 U.S. 389 (1978), the Supreme Court rejected an interpretation of Parker v. Brown as a general antitrust immunity for all governmental entities, but limited the immunity to " 'official action directed by the state.' " Id. at 412, quoting Parker v. Brown, 317 U.S. at 351. This result was further elucidated in Community Communications Co. v. Boulder, 455 U.S. 40 (1982), in which the City of Boulder argued that its anticompetitive action should be exempt not because of an inherent municipal exemption (rejected in Lafayette), but because of a derived exemption, since the state had empowered the city to act—Colorado had granted Boulder extensive powers of self-government as a home-rule municipality; that is, it was "acting as the State in local matters." Id. at 53. The Court rejected this argument, holding that the first prong of the Midcal test for *Parker v. Brown* immunity, requir-

ing that a state clearly articulate and affirmatively express its anticompetitive policy, is not satisfied by a delegation of power which is neutral respecting the municipal action challenged as anticompetitive. On the other hand, the Court deems the first prong met even when the state legislature neither *compels*, nor *explicitly states* that it expects, its municipalities to "engage in conduct that would have anticompetitive effect," Town of Hallie v. City of Eau Claire, 471 U.S. 34, 42 (1985), so long as "[s]uch conduct is a foreseeable result of empowering" municipalities with "broad authority to regulate" in a particular field. Id. The Court thus found the first Midcal prong satisfied where the state "specifically authorized [its] cities to provide sewage services and . . . delegated to the cities the express authority to take action that foreseeably will result in anticompetitive effects." Id. at 43.

In Town of Hallie, the Court went on to hold Midcal's second prong entirely inapplicable to municipalities, reasoning that "the active state supervision requirement should not be imposed in [such] cases," id. at 46, since it is appropriate to "presume, absent a showing to the contrary, that the municipality acts in the public interest . . . [whereas] [a] private party . . . may be presumed to be acting primarily on his or its own behalf." Id. at 45. Cf. Southern Motor Carriers Rate Conference, Inc. v. United States, 471 U.S. 48 (1985) (second prong of Midcal test is applicable where price-setting actor is a private combination, id. at 57 n.20, but not where actor is a municipality, Town of Hallie, 471 U.S. at 46). The upshot of Town of Hallie was to extend Parker v. Brown immunity to a case in which, but for that immunity, a plausible antitrust claim might have been made against the city's use of its monopoly power over sewage treatment services to gain monopolies in sewage collection and transportation. See 471 U.S. at 37.

The Court subsequently made clear that, absent an *actual violation* of the antitrust laws by the municipality involved, the issue of Parker v. Brown immunity need not be reached at all: without a violation, there is no preemption in this area. Fisher v. Berkeley, 475 U.S. 260 (1986) (holding that a municipal rent control ordinance

In part because it nicely fits a vision of the Sherman Act as a broad charter of personal economic liberty,[83] this reading of the *Parker* doctrine has undoubted appeal. But a major difficulty with applying the doctrine as thus reconstructed to the facts of *Parker* itself is the vast power that the decision delegated to local raisin producers over unrepresented consumers. Consumers in California, at least, could exert influence over the marketing program through the state's own political processes even if they had no direct voice on the relevant agricultural boards; but all but five to ten percent of the raisins were to be consumed elsewhere, and one may at least question whether the willingness of Congress and the Secretary of Agriculture to tolerate such local control over outsiders adequately accommodates their interests.[84]

The Supreme Court has evidently begun to doubt the adequacy of this sort of accommodation. Ironically, those doubts were signaled by a decision which, like *Parker v. Brown*, rejected federal preemption and again upheld a California agricultural regulation: *Florida Lime & Avocado Growers v. Paul*.[85] In that 1963 decision, a bare majority of the Court upheld a California law which regulated the marketing of avocados sold in California on the basis of oil content in order to protect consumers from being disappointed by edible but unsavory avocados. Federal regulation of Florida avocado production determined marketability on the basis of size, weight and picking date, with the same general objective. About six of every one hundred Florida avocados meeting the federal marketing standards were excluded from California's markets by that state regulation.[86]

under which a local public agency imposes ceilings on rent increases involves neither a conspiracy between the city and private parties to fix prices nor a municipal authorization or encouragement of private price-fixing, and therefore entails no violation of, or conflict with, the Sherman Act). See P. Areeda, *Antitrust Analysis* 395 (3d ed. 1981). See also Gifford, "The Antitrust State-Action Doctrine After *Fisher v. Berkeley*," 39 Vand.L.Rev. 1257 (1986). The author of this treatise argued Berkeley's position against antitrust preemption in the Supreme Court.

Town of Hallie and Fisher leave some (limited) room to make antitrust arguments against particular municipalities or their officials. See, e.g., Affiliated Capital Corp. v. City of Houston, 735 F.2d 1555, 1557–59 (5th Cir. 1984) (en banc) (mayor abdicates decision over cable TV franchise to four firms for reasons unrelated to the merits, allows the four to divide up the city, and requires them to make room for a fifth firm controlled by the mayor's personal attorney), cert. denied 106 S.Ct. 788 (1986). But the Local Government Antitrust Act of 1984, 15 U.S.C. § 35(a), eliminates antitrust *damage* liability for actions

taken "in an official capacity" by any "local government, or official or employee thereof." The principal avenues of relief remaining against local officials are thus declaratory and injunctive.

83. Id. at 333, 357–58. See also United States v. Topco Associates, Inc., 405 U.S. 596, 610 (1972).

84. See § 6–5, supra.

85. 373 U.S. 132 (1963).

86. An avocado which appears satisfactory at the time of purchase may fail to ripen properly because it was prematurely picked. The disappointed avocado buyer, whose avocado has "decay[ed] or shrivel[ed] and become rubbery and unpalatable," 373 U.S. at 137, then turns to other fruits next time he is at the market. The oil-content test is evidently a more accurate gauge of maturity at picking as applied to California-grown avocados, most of which are of Mexican ancestry, than as applied to avocados shipped to California from South Florida, most of which are of Guatemalan or hybrid origin and many of which may become mature before their oil content is as high as 8%. See 373 U.S. at 140.

Despite the apparent history of avocado warfare between California and Florida,[87] and despite evidence that an oil content standard which satisfactorily measures the ripeness of California avocados cannot simultaneously measure with equal accuracy the different kinds of avocados grown in Florida,[88] the Court upheld California's regulation as consistent with the commerce clause and the supremacy clause, overtly resting decision on the lack of any necessary conflict between the state and federal rules.[89]

Given the difficulty of perceiving the California regulation as anything but an obstacle to full enforcement of the federal scheme,[90] the result in *Florida Lime & Avocado Growers* should probably be understood as deriving from concerns that the Court noted but did not expressly deem dispositive: The Federal marketing rules for Florida avocados had not been drafted "by impartial experts in Washington or even in Florida, but rather by the South Florida Avocado Administrative Committee," [91] a self-interested committee of Florida growers and handlers who sought to promote orderly marketing and competition among the South Florida growers in the exercise of their federally delegated authority.[92] In the face of what thus appeared to be a delegation of federal power to a local cartel, rather like the delegation to raisin growers the Court had unanimously upheld in 1943,[93] a majority of the Supreme Court could not conclude—despite the lawfulness of the delegation according to current constitutional doctrine [94]—that California's law interfered with any truly *national* program of federal regulation. Thus, although there would probably have been no comparable way to limit the territorial impact of the raisin marketing scheme upheld in

---

87. Id. at 153–54 n. 19.

88. See note 86, supra.

89. 373 U.S. at 141. There was no demonstrated impossibility of dual compliance since "the Florida growers might have avoided [the California] rejection by leaving the fruit on the trees beyond the earliest picking date permitted by the federal regulations . . ." Id. at 143. Nor was there reason to assume federal occupation of the field, see § 6–26, infra, absent such a direct conflict: "The maturity of avocados seems to be an inherently unlikely candidate for exclusive federal regulation." Id. at 143. However comprehensive the federal regulation of picking and processing in Florida, "Congressional regulation at one end of the stream of commerce does not, *ipso facto*, oust all state regulation at the other end." Id. at 145.

90. As the dissent pointed out, id. at 167–69, the regulations at both ends of the "stream of commerce" in avocados were concerned with precisely the same economic interest: that of sellers in not disappointing buyers. Once the Secretary of Agriculture specifically rejected chemical tests (such as California's) as inadequate to protect the good will of the avocado industry, id. at 139 n. 8, sustaining California's power to impose

such tests to the disadvantage of Florida competitors became an extraordinary step for the Supreme Court to take, see id. at 171, 175 (White, J., dissenting).

91. 373 U.S. at 150–51.

92. The Court noted that the Secretary of Agriculture had "invariably adopted the Committee's recommendations for maturity dates, sizes, and weights." Id. at 151. Thus the majority perceived the federal program as "essentially local in nature" and as "chiefly . . . . a 'self-help' program, . . ." Id. at 151 n. 17.

93. Parker v. Brown, 317 U.S. 341 (1943).

94. See § 5–17, supra. Responding to the majority's emphasis upon the self-interested character of the federal avocado regulations for Florida, the dissenters pointed to cases like Parker v. Brown, 317 U.S. 341 (1943), in insisting that "the delegation to the regulatees of the power to propose regulations in the first instance" violates no constitutional requirement. However that may be, it need not follow that self-interested regulation should have the same preemptive effect as might regulation that is more broadly based.

Parker v. Brown,[95] the *Florida Lime & Avocados* Court was able to treat the federal regulatory scheme for avocados as though it were merely the law of Florida, giving it no binding effect upon consumers or producers who had no opportunity to affect the law's content. It would be difficult, to say the least, to convert the *Florida Lime & Avocados* concern about adequacy of participation into coherent preemption doctrine;[96] perhaps the best reading of the case is one that views it as eroding the premises of *Parker v. Brown* by suggesting a new level of judicial sensitivity to the fairness of schemes that delegate economic power over others.

§ 6–27. Federal Occupation of the Field

Even where state regulation is found not to conflict in its actual operation with the substantive policies underlying federal legislation, it must still be established, if the state regulation is to survive judicial scrutiny, that Congress did not exercise its jurisdictional veto. For if Congress has validly decided to "occupy the field" for the federal government, state regulations will be invalidated no matter how well they comport with substantive federal policies. But federal occupation of a field will not be lightly inferred: "The principle to be derived from [the Supreme Court's] decisions is that federal regulation of a field of commerce should not be deemed preemptive of state regulatory power in the absence of persuasive reasons—either that the nature of the regulated subject matter permits no other conclusion, or that the Congress has unmistakably so ordained."[1] Where such "persuasive reasons" have been found, however, state action has been held to be preempted even prior to the effective date of the federal legislation; even nascent federal occupation of a field suffices to oust the states.[2]

The less comprehensive is a federal regulatory scheme, the more likely it is that a holding ousting state jurisdiction would create a substantial legal vacuum—and hence,[3] the less likely is such a holding.[4] For example, in *Pacific Gas & Electric Co. v. State Energy Resources Conservation & Development Comm'n*,[5] it was largely this "anti-vacuum" principle that led the Supreme Court to hold California's nuclear power plant moratorium not preempted by the Atomic Energy Act. In that case, the Court noted that both safety-related and economic problems are associated with disposal of wastes from nuclear power plants: first, the nuclear wastes themselves might endanger human health;

---

95. 317 U.S. 341 (1943).

96. Numerous federal laws delegate initiating or ratifying authority to local groups; to treat all such laws as lacking "supremacy" status under article VI would obviously be unacceptable, and to draw principled distinctions among them would not be an easy task.

§ 6–27

1. Florida Lime & Avocado Growers v. Paul, 373 U.S. 132, 142 (1963). See also Allen-Bradley Local No. 1111 v. Wisconsin Employment Relations Board, 315 U.S. 740, 749 (1942); Rice v. Santa Fe Elevator Corp., 331 U.S. 218, 230 (1947). The reluc-

tance to find complete federal preemption comports with the basic conception of federal law as interstitial in nature. See §§ 5–7, 5–8, supra.

2. Erie Railroad v. New York, 233 U.S. 671 (1914).

3. See the discussion of the anti-Madisonian interpretation in § 6–3, supra.

4. See, e.g., Askew v. American Waterways Operators, Inc., 411 U.S. 325, 336–37 (1973).

5. 461 U.S. 190 (1983), also discussed in § 6–24, supra. The author was counsel for California in this case.

second, insufficiency of storage space for the spent fuel might lead to service shutdowns, "rendering nuclear energy an unpredictable and uneconomical adventure." [6] After finding that Congress, in passing the Atomic Energy Act, "intended that the [Nuclear Regulatory Commission] should regulate the radiological safety aspects involved in the construction and operation of a nuclear plant," [7] but that "[t]he Commission . . . was not given authority over . . . the economic question whether a particular plant should be built," [8] the Court concluded that "[i]t is almost inconceivable that Congress would have left a regulatory vacuum; the only reasonable inference is that Congress intended the States to continue to make" judgments about need, reliability, economic consequences of service shutdowns due to waste disposal problems, and other economic matters.[9] Thus, absent a more explicit congressional mandate than was present in *Pacific Gas & Electric*, Congress' decision *not* to regulate *nationally* the economic concerns of power generation was not to be equated with a congressional determination that the states may not *themselves* enact *local* regulations addressing those same concerns; such an inference does not follow logically, and would result in an undesirable regulatory vacuum.[10]

Conversely, where a multiplicity of federal statutes or regulations [11] govern a given field, the pervasiveness of such federal laws will help to sustain a conclusion that Congress intended to exercise exclusive control over the subject matter.[12]

6. Id. at 196–97 (footnotes omitted).

7. Id. at 205.

8. Id. at 207.

9. Id. at 207–08. In deciding how to classify California's moratorium on construction of nuclear power plants, the Court held that, inasmuch as the state was not directly regulating how a plant was constructed or how the radioactive effluent of the plant or of its fuel were to be controlled, the state's *purpose* in enacting its regulation was the touchstone: if the state's purpose were economic, the regulation would not be preempted. Id. at 216. The Court distinguished its prior holding in Perez v. Cambell, 402 U.S. 637, 651 (1971) ("that state law may not frustrate the operation of federal law simply because the state legislature in passing its law had some purpose in mind other than one of frustration"), see 461 U.S. at 216 n. 28, by noting that "[i]n *Perez*, unlike this case, there was an actual conflict between state and federal law." Id. The Court went on to explain that the *Perez* principle is apposite *only* in cases of actual conflict, implying that the principle is *inapposite* where the claimed preemption is said to flow from federal occupation of the field. For a discussion of how the Court determined the state's purpose, see § 6–26, supra, note 37.

10. Congress may in other situations have *desired* to leave a regulatory gap, in which case "an authoritative federal determination that the area is best left *unregu*lated . . . would have as much pre-emptive force as a decision *to* regulate." Arkansas Electric Cooperative Corp. v. Arkansas Public Serv. Comm'n, 461 U.S. 375, 384 (1983) (finding no such congressional desire) (emphasis in original).

11. The Supreme Court has been "more reluctant to infer pre-emption from the comprehensiveness of regulations than from the comprehensiveness of statutes. [Since] . . . agencies normally deal with problems in far more detail than does Congress[,] [t]o infer pre-emption whenever an agency deals with a problem comprehensively . . . [would be] virtually tantamount to saying that whenever a federal agency decides to step into a field, its regulations will be exclusive." Hillsborough County, Fla. v. Automated Medical Laboratories, Inc., 471 U.S. 707, 717 (1985). See also § 6–28, infra, note 1.

12. See, e.g., Amalgamated Association of Street, Electric Railway & Motor Coach Employees of America v. Lockridge, 403 U.S. 274, 296 (1971) (state wrongful discharge actions requiring interpretation of labor contract's union security clause precluded by pervasiveness of federal regulation in the area); Castle v. Hayes Freight Lines, Inc., 348 U.S. 61 (1954).

However, where Congress legislates "in a field which the States have traditionally occupied . . . we start with the assumption that the historic police powers of the States [are] not to be [ousted] by the Federal Act unless that was the clear and manifest purpose of Congress." [13] Because this test looks to the nature of the subject regulated rather than the character of the federal regulatory scheme, the standards upon which it relies closely parallel those that would be applied if the state regulation or taxation were challenged under the commerce clause. If, under the *Cooley* doctrine,[14] the activity or interest affected by a challenged state action is regarded as "local," and if the state action contravenes no other commerce clause requirement, then total federal preemption will not be inferred in the absence of an obvious congressional intent to bar state action over the same subject matter.[15] On this basis, the Court ruled in *Huron Portland Cement Co. v. City of Detroit* [16] that a municipality may enforce its smoke abatement ordinance against a federally licensed steamship engaged in interstate commerce, even though structural modification of the vessel was required to bring it into compliance with the anti-pollution statute.[17] Similarly, while federal occupation of the field defined by direct regula-

---

13. Rice v. Santa Fe Elevator Corp., 331 U.S. 218, 230 (1947). See also Arkansas Electric Cooperative Corp. v. Arkansas Public Serv. Comm'n, 461 U.S. 375, 377 (1983), in which the Court held that a state public service commission could assert rate-setting jurisdiction over a rural electric cooperative even though two federal agencies were peripherally involved in supervising such rates. See § 6–28, infra. The Court reached its conclusion after balancing state regulation of utilities—"one of the most important of the functions traditionally associated with the police power of the States," id.—against the "patent[ ] interfer[ence] with broader national interests" that may result from uncontrolled regulation by the states. And see Hillsborough County, Fla. v. Automated Medical Laboratories, Inc., 471 U.S. 707 (1985), holding that, in spite of numerous federal regulations governing collection of blood plasma, "the regulation of health and safety matters is primarily, and historically, a matter of local concern," id. at 719. In Pacific Gas & Electric v. State Energy Resources Conservation & Development Comm'n, 461 U.S. 190 (1983), the Court likewise found the field of economic regulation of electric utilities to be one "'which the States have traditionally occupied.'" 461 U.S. at 206, quoting Rice, 331 U.S. at 230. Accordingly, the Court found it appropriate to use the Rice presumption against preemption. This presumption is not, however, an absolute bar to preemption. For example, in Hisquierdo v. Hisquierdo, 439 U.S. 572, 581 (1979), even after the Court acknowledged a *strong* presumption against preemption in the field of family law, normally a matter for

state control, the Court nonetheless held state community property laws preempted by the federal law at issue in that case. See § 6–26, supra, text at notes 12 to 15. See also McCarty v. McCarty, 453 U.S. 210 (1981), discussed in § 6–26, supra, note 15; Ridgway v. Ridgway, 454 U.S. 46, 54 (1981).

14. See § 6–4, supra.

15. It should be noted, however, that in San Diego Bldg. Trades Council v. Garmon, 359 U.S. 236, 245 (1959), discussed in § 6–28, infra, the Supreme Court established a more lenient standard of preemption with regard to state intrusion into activities "arguably subject" to §§ 7 or 8 of the National Labor Relations Act.

16. 362 U.S. 440 (1960).

17. See the discussion of the implications of federal licensing in § 6–26, infra. Cf. Askew v. American Waterways Operators, Inc., 411 U.S. 325, 343 (1973) (Florida may create tort liability for damages from oil spills in its territorial waters despite a similar congressional grant of federal maritime and admiralty jurisdiction: regulation of "sea-to-shore pollution—historically within the reach of the police power of the state—is not silently taken away from the States by the Admiralty Extension Act, which does not purport to supply the exclusive remedy"). The Court was aided in Huron Portland Cement by a congressional declaration that local responsibility should continue. 362 U.S. at 445–46. For a discussion of preemption in the environmental field generally, see Note, "State Environmental Protection and the Commerce Clause," 87 Harv.L.Rev. 1762, 1769–72 (1974).

tion of safety designs for nuclear power plants had been made clear in *Pacific Gas & Electric Co.*,[18] the Court in *Silkwood v. Kerr-McGee Corp.*[19] held that state law providing for compensatory and punitive damages for tort victims, including victims of radiation injuries, was *outside* the occupied field and therefore not preempted. In reaching this conclusion, the Court was clearly influenced by the long tradition of state concern with the compensation of victims of negligently, recklessly, or intentionally inflicted injury.[20]

On the other hand, if the field is one that is traditionally deemed "national," the Court is more vigilant in striking down state incursions into subjects that Congress may have reserved to itself. It was not surprising, therefore, that the Court invalidated the state alien registration law in *Hines v. Davidowitz*;[21] the Court was extremely solicitous of the paramount federal interest in matters germane to foreign affairs.[22]

Of course, an unambiguous declaration by Congress that it intends to occupy a particular field must be treated as dispositive regardless of the nature of the subject; state action in such a case is invariably preempted, providing Congress has acted constitutionally.[23] Rare is the

---

18.   461 U.S. 190 (1983). See also Northern States Power Co. v. Minnesota, 447 F.2d 1143 (8th Cir. 1971), aff'd mem. 405 U.S. 1035 (1972) (state law regulating nuclear waste effluents of power plant held preempted).

19.   464 U.S. 238 (1984). See § 6–26, supra, text at notes 42 to 54.

20.   464 U.S. at 251, 253–55.

21.   312 U.S. 52 (1941).

22.   Other examples of peculiarly national concerns, where one seeking to establish preemption faces a lighter burden, have included migratory bird protection, see North Dakota v. United States, 460 U.S. 300, 309 (1983) ("protection of migratory birds has long been recognized as 'a national interest of very nearly the first magnitude'") (citation omitted); regulation of Indian tribal affairs, see Ramah Navajo School Board, Inc. v. Bureau of Revenue, 458 U.S. 832, 839 (1982) (construction and financing of Indian educational institutions is "a sphere . . . heavily regulated by the Federal Government"); control of immigration, see Toll v. Moreno, 458 U.S. 1, 10 (1982) ("recogniz[ing] the preeminent role of the Federal Government with respect to the regulation of aliens within our borders"); and regulation of labor-management relations, see Sears, Roebuck & Co. v. Carpenters, 436 U.S. 180, 193 (1978); San Diego Building Trades Council v. Garmon, 359 U.S. 236 (1959).

23.   See Rice v. Santa Fe Elevator Corp., 331 U.S. 218, 247, 255 (1947). Accord, Jones v. Rath Packing Co., 430 U.S. 519, 536–37 (1977) (state labeling requirement with respect to packaged bacon held ex-

pressly preempted by congressional provision forbidding imposition of "labeling, packaging, or ingredient requirements in addition to, or different than, those made under" the federal statutes); Capital Cities Cable, Inc. v. Crisp, 467 U.S. 691 (1984) (discussed in § 6–26, infra, note 7). In Shaw v. Delta Air Lines, Inc., 463 U.S. 85, 96 (1983), federal law expressly preempted "any and all state laws insofar as they may now or hereafter relate to any employee benefit plan" covered by ERISA, id. at 91 n. 6. The issue was whether the New York Human Rights Law "relate[d] to" employee benefit plans within meaning of the federal statute. The Court held that it did. See also Alessi v. Raybestos-Manhattan, Inc., 451 U.S. 504, 522–25 (1981); cf. Metropolitan Life Ins. Co. v. Massachusetts, 471 U.S. 724, (1985) (state law related to employee benefit plans, and thus fell within the sphere of the preemption clause of ERISA, but was not preempted because it also fell within a statutory exception to that preemption clause); Fort Halifax Packing Co., Inc. v. Coyne, 107 S.Ct. 2211 (1987) (state law mandating one-time, lump-sum severance payment to workers unemployed by plant closing is not preempted by ERISA, because that statute regulates only benefit *plans*, not any and all *benefits*); Fidelity Federal Savings & Loan Assoc. v. de la Cuesta, 458 U.S. 141, 147 (1982) (state law restricting operation of due-on-sale clauses in mortgages held preempted by federal regulation that explicitly empowered federal savings and loan associations to include and enforce such clauses, and that stated that such clauses must be governed "exclusively by Federal law").

case, however, where Congress makes the judicial task so simple. A "clearly expressed" congressional purpose will normally be divined only through close analysis of the statute in question as applied in the particular case. For example, in *Campbell v. Hussey*,[24] the Supreme Court held that "Congress, in legislating concerning the types of tobacco sold at auction, preempted the field and left no room for any supplementary state regulation concerning those same types." But the Court reached this conclusion only on the basis of a detailed examination of the statutory language and history.[25]

§ 6–28.　The Effect of the Presence of Relevant Federal Regulatory Agencies or of Federal Licensing on Preemption Decisions

The fact that Congress created a regulatory agency, or delegated regulatory authority to the Executive, in order to carry out its statutory program, is not by itself determinative of the preemption inquiry. But understanding the implications of the presence of a relevant federal regulatory agency is a prerequisite to the correct application, in particular cases, of the principles set forth above. An analysis of the reasons why Congress created a particular regulatory agency, or of the policies pursued by that agency, may reveal that restriction of remedial access to a particular range of agency procedures was substantively motivated, and that the very existence of overlapping state action may therefore frustrate federal policy.[1]

---

24. 368 U.S. 297, 301 (1961).

25. See, e.g., id. at 301.

§ 6–28

1. But see Farber, "State Regulation and the Dormant Commerce Clause," Constitutional Commentary 395 (1986), for the view that, where Congress has empowered a federal agency to prohibit certain state actions, and where that agency has not done so, there should be a strong presumption against a judicial finding of implied preemption. Farber argues that the practical impediments of inadvertence, lack of expertise, insufficient time, or inability to agree, that prevent Congress from including explicit language in each enactment detailing its preemptive intent, do not warrant a similar approach to *agency* silence on the subject of preemption. On the contrary, an agency charged with formulating and implementing national policy in a particular domain could easily promulgate regulations explicitly barring state actions perceived to threaten that national policy. Thus, an agency's failure *explicitly* to bar such state action should be taken as a strong sign that the state action does not threaten national policy and is not *impliedly* preempted. The Court seemed to have adopted an analysis of this sort in Hillsborough County v. Automated Medical Laboratories, Inc., 471 U.S. 707, 721 (1985): "The FDA possesses the authority to promulgate regulations pre-empting local legislation . . . and can do so with relative ease. Moreover, the agency can be expected to monitor . . . the effects on the federal program of local requirements. Thus, since the agency has not suggested that the county ordinances interfere with federal goals, we are reluctant in the absence of strong evidence to find a threat to the federal goal." See Farber at 409. See also City of Milwaukee v. Illinois, 451 U.S. 304, 312–13 (1981); Ray v. ARCO, 435 U.S. 151, 171–73 (1978). It should be noted that, although this theme was present in the unanimous Hillsborough opinion, it was but one of several alternative grounds for decision. More prominent in the Court's opinion were (1) the FDA's own explicit statement "that it did not intend its regulations to be exclusive," 471 U.S. at 714, a statement that the Court deemed "dispositive on the question of implicit intent to pre-empt unless either the agency's position is inconsistent with . . . congressional intent, or subsequent developments reveal a change in that position," id., and (2) "the presumption that state or local regulation of matters related to *health and safety*," such as the local regulations at issue in the case, are not preempted. Id. at 715. See also California Coastal Comm'n v. Granite Rock Co., 107 S.Ct. 1419 (1987) ("[i]f . . . it is the federal intent that Granite Rock conduct its mining un-

As to labor-management relations, for example, the Supreme Court has recognized that one of the reasons underlying the creation of the National Labor Relations Board (NLRB) was the need "to provide an informed and coherent basis for . . . delicately structuring the balance of power among competing forces so as to further the common good." [2] Accordingly, the Court held in *Teamsters Local 20 v. Morton* [3] that a state could not prevent strikers from asking their employer's customers to refrain from doing business with him, since that practice was permitted by Congress and the NLRB. So too, in *Golden State Transit Corp. v. Los Angeles,* [4] the Court held that the National Labor Relations Act (NLRA) preempts a city's action that conditioned renewal of a taxi franchise on settlement by a certain date of a labor dispute between the drivers and owners: Congress intended to leave the resolution of strikes "to be controlled by the free play of economic forces." [5]

Similarly, as to communications regulation, in *Farmers Union v. WDAY, Inc.,* [6] the Supreme Court refused to allow state libel actions against broadcasters for statements made over the air by political candidates, in light of the policy of Congress and the FCC to prevent the radio and television operators from censoring such statements; to allow the libel suits "would either frustrate the underlying purposes for which [the FCC rule] was enacted, or alternatively impose unreasonable burdens on the parties governed by that legislation." [7]

hindered by any state environmental regulation, one would expect to find the expression of this intent in the[ ] Forest service regulations").

Farber urges that a strong presumption against implied preemption when an agency could have, but failed to, expressly preempt state action makes good *structural* sense: federal agencies, rather than federal courts, should be charged with the decision whether to preempt state action because agencies have superior expertise and information-gathering capabilities, are politically accountable, and have an express mandate from Congress to make policy. Farber at 408. See, e.g., Chevron, U.S.A., Inc. v. NRDC, Inc., 467 U.S. 837, 865–66 (1984) (in which the Court recognized the appropriateness of having agencies make policy choices which Congress either inadvertently did not resolve, or intentionally left to be resolved by an agency). However, as a matter of political reality, agencies may occasionally *thwart* the will of Congress rather than *advance* it. It thus seems appropriate that the Court, rather than any agency, be entrusted with the basic authority to decide how far Congress meant to displace state action. For the judiciary to impose a flat presumption that there should (or should not) be preemption whenever an agency enters a field, without first examining the circumstances of the congressional delegation, would undesirably alter the federal-state balance. Cf. § 6–25, supra, note 11.

2. Amalgamated Association of Street Employees v. Lockridge, 403 U.S. 274, 286 (1971).

3. 377 U.S. 252 (1964).

4. 106 S.Ct. 1395 (1986).

5. Id. at 1398, quoting Machinists v. Wisconsin Employment Relations Comm'n, 427 U.S. 132, 140 (1976). Compare Baker v. General Motors Corp., 106 S.Ct. 3129 (1986) (NLRA does not preempt state statute that denied state unemployment benefits to workers whose union required them to pay strike fund dues, in addition to regular union dues, and who thereby financed a strike causing their own unemployment, even though the NLRA protects employees' right to authorize a strike).

6. 360 U.S. 525, 535 (1959).

7. Id. at 535. It is unnecessary to analyze either the reasons Congress created an agency, or the policies pursued by that agency, if there are more direct ways of determining whether a state law is preempted. Thus, in Capital Cities Cable, Inc. v. Crisp, 467 U.S. 691 (1984), the Court held that Oklahoma's ban on advertising alcoholic beverages was preempted to the extent that it prohibits cable television systems within the state from retransmitting out-of-state signals that contain such ads, for two reasons: (1) the FCC, acting within its congressionally delegated authority, "unambiguously expressed its intent to pre-empt any state . . . regulation of this entire array of signals carried by cable

The very existence of a federal regulatory agency may signify a congressional determination that some jurisdictionally-definable aspect of the regulated subject matter demands uniform national supervision, and that the judicial grant to the states of jurisdiction to act is, to that degree, legislatively withdrawn. Thus, in *San Diego Building Trades Council v. Garmon*,[8] the Supreme Court ruled that a tort action would not lie under state law for damages reputedly occasioned by a union's organizational picketing. The Court perceived the unifying theme of its labor decisions as an emphasis on "the fact that Congress has entrusted administration of [national] labor policy . . . to a centralized administrative agency."[9] In light of that choice, the Court concluded that "to allow the States to control conduct which is the subject of national regulation would create potential frustration of national purpose," and therefore held that, "[w]hen activity is arguably subject to section 7[10] or section 8[11] of the [National Labor Relations] Act, the States as well as the federal courts must defer to the exclusive competence of the National Labor Relations Board if the danger of state interference with national policy is to be averted."[12] Similarly, in *Maryland v. Louisiana*,[13] the Court held that Louisiana's tax on the

television systems," id. at 701; (2) furthermore, apart from the FCC's general preemption of state regulation in this field, the state's advertising ban was in actual conflict with specific federal regulations that required carriers to retransmit signals *in full* from nearby out-of-state stations, and that authorized and encouraged carriers to retransmit signals, but only *in full*, from distant out-of-state stations.

8. 359 U.S. 236 (1959).

9. Id. at 242. See also Wisconsin Dept. of Industry v. Gould Inc., 475 U.S. 282, (1986), in which the Court, citing Garmon, held that the NLRA preempts a state statute that prohibited firms that violated the NLRA three times within a five-year period from doing business within the state; the state statute stood as a supplemental sanction to the already-comprehensive scheme of regulation imposed by the NLRB.

10. Section 7 protects "concerted activities." 29 U.S.C. § 157 (1970).

11. Section 8 proscribes "unfair labor practices." Id. § 158 (Supp. V 1975).

12. 359 U.S. at 245. The Garmon test controversially extended federal preemption even to those situations where it was uncertain "whether the particular activity regulated by the States was governed by Sec. 7 or Sec. 8 or was, perhaps, outside both these sections": "It is essential to the administration of the Act that those determinations be left in the first instance to the National Labor Relations Board." Id. See also Garner v. Teamster Local 776, 346 U.S. 485, 490–91 (1953). See generally, Cox, "Labor Law Preemption Revisited,"

85 Harv.L.Rev. 1337 (1972). And see International Longshoremen's Ass'n, AFL–CIO v. Davis, 106 S.Ct. 1904 (1986). In that case, after a state court awarded a verdict against a union, the union raised a claim that the state court lacked jurisdiction because the suit should have been decided by the NLRB. The state's highest court held that, according to the state's procedural rules, this preemption defense was waived, since the union did not affirmatively plead it. The Supreme Court reversed, holding that the state's procedural rules themselves were preempted, to the extent they purported to relieve the state court from deciding on the merits whether its own jurisdiction was preempted in favor of the NLRB. The Court then went on to examine the merits, and held that a party asserting preemption in this context "must make an *affirmative* showing that the activity is arguably subject to the [NLRA]," id. at 1916, and therefore subject to the exclusive jurisdiction of the NLRB, rather than relying on the *absence* of an NLRB ruling to the contrary. The Court found that the union had made no such showing, thus determining "on the merits" that the union was subject to state jurisdiction.

13. 451 U.S. 725 (1981). Compare Transcontinental Gas Pipeline Corp. v. State Oil & Gas Board of Mississippi, 474 U.S. 409 (1986) (state rule that interstate pipeline operator take natural gas ratably from various producers that used common pool of gas, was preempted by Congress' detemination, in enacting the Natural Gas Policy Act, that market forces should determine the supply, demand, and price of such gas; when Congress stripped FERC of

"first use" of any natural gas brought into that state that was not previously subject to taxation—namely, gas brought in from offshore wells—was preempted by a congressional delegation to FERC, under the Natural Gas Act, of authority to determine the proper allocation of costs associated with the sale of natural gas to consumers. The Court also found the tax to be discriminatory against interstate commerce, since in-state users of the gas received credit against other Louisiana taxes, substantially insulating them from the impact of the tax, whereas gas that subsequently moved out of the state bore the full burden of the tax.

Yet the presence of a federal regulatory agency is not itself determinative of the questions of actual conflict or federal occupation of the field; state action not otherwise violative of the commerce clause may be shown in a particular case to concern itself with matters so local as to be inherently unlikely candidates for federal preemption, despite the apparent comprehensiveness of the federal regulatory scheme as enforced by an administrative agency. As to communications regulation, for example, in *Head v. New Mexico Board of Examiners in Optometry,*[14] the Supreme Court held that, despite the relatively comprehensive program of federal regulation under the Federal Communications Act, New Mexico could enjoin a radio station located in that state from broadcasting the price quotations of a Texas optometrist, pursuant to a state statute banning all such advertising.[15] Similarly, as to labor-management regulation, in *Linn v. United Plant Guard Workers Local 114,* the Supreme Court held that a defamation action arising out of a union-organizing campaign could be brought in state court, given " 'an overriding state interest' in protecting its residents from malicious libel." [16] Likewise, the Court held in *Farmer v. United Brotherhood of Carpenters and Joiners* that the National Labor Relations Act does not preempt a state court action for intentional infliction of emotional distress.[17]

Whereas regulation of interstate utilities, particularly for rate-setting purposes, is an important national concern, regulation of the

its jurisdiction to directly set the price of such gas, it did so not to allow states to regulate the price, but to leave it unregulated).

14. 374 U.S. 424 (1963).

15. The Court noted that the FCC had viewed state advertising regulations "as complementing its regulatory function." Id. at 432. Such a ban would today be of doubtful validity under the first amendment. See § 12–15, infra.

16. 383 U.S. 53, 61 (1966). See also Allen-Bradley Local No. 1111 v. Wisconsin Employment Relations Board, 315 U.S. 740 (1942) (picketing and personal threats may be regulated by the state). But cf. Amalgamated Association of Street Employees v. Lockridge, 403 U.S. 274 (1971) (applying the Garmon doctrine to hold that a state court cannot take jurisdiction of a suit

sounding in contract brought by a former union member against a union that had dropped him from membership for failure to pay dues).

17. 430 U.S. 290 (1977). The Court reasoned that the federal interest in labor regulation and the state interest in allowing tort recovery were sufficiently discrete that the potential for interference with the federal scheme by the state cause of action was insufficient to counterbalance the state's legitimate and substantial interest, since the state tort action could be resolved without reference to any of the special federally protected interests (in this case, in the context of activities at a union hiring hall). Id. at 1064–66. Compare Baker v. General Motors Corp., 106 S.Ct. 3129 (1986), discussed supra, note 5.

intrastate activities of a utility is primarily a local matter; the Court will not lightly infer that a congressional delegation to a federal agency precludes state power to regulate intrastate utility rates. It was on this basis that the Court, in *Arkansas Electric Cooperative Corp. v. Arkansas Public Serv. Comm'n*,[18] held that Arkansas' Public Service Commission could assert jurisdiction over the rates charged by a rural electric cooperative to its local member cooperatives, even though two federal agencies, the Federal Power Commission and the Rural Electrification Administration, each regulated rates charged by such electric utilities. The FPC had no authority to regulate wholesale rates charged by cooperatives under the supervision of the REA, and the REA supervised rates only to the extent necessary to make its loans secure, but neither agency had determined as a matter of policy that the wholesale cooperatives should *not* be subject "to the type of pervasive rate regulation almost universally associated with electric utilities in this country."[19] So too, in *Louisiana Public Service Comm'n v. FCC*,[20] the Court held that state regulation of methods of depreciating telephone equipment, for intrastate ratemaking purposes, was not preempted where Congress established a system that gave jurisdiction to the FCC to regulate depreciation of such equipment used in *inter*state communication, but left jurisdiction with the states, and in fact forbade the FCC to exercise jurisdiction, over charges, classifications, and practices in connection with *intra*state communication, and where, in practice, a single piece of telephone equipment may be used both in *inter-* and *intra*state communication. The Court thus rejected an earlier FCC ruling that, to avoid frustrating the *objectives* of Congress, state regulation of depreciation of dual-jurisdiction equipment is preempted.

As to transportation regulation, despite the fact that the Motor Carrier Act of 1935 permitted the Interstate Commerce Commission to establish minimum qualifications for taxi drivers engaged in interstate or foreign commerce, a closely divided Supreme Court, in *Buck v. California*,[21] held that San Diego County could impose additional qualifications. Similarly, in *California v. Zook*,[22] the Court by a bare majority upheld a state statute that was almost identical to the federal Motor Carrier Act of 1935. And, in *Wardair Canada, Inc. v. Florida Dept. of Revenue*,[23] the Court held that a state tax imposed uniformly on airline fuel sold within the state—regardless of whether the fuel was subsequently used to fly within the state, without the state, or even in foreign commerce—was not preempted, in spite of the fact that "agencies charged by Congress with regulatory responsibility over foreign air travel exercise power . . . over licensing, route services, rates and fares, tariffs, safety, and other aspects of air travel".[24] The Court found no indication that Congress wished to preclude state sales taxation of fuel, and even found some evidence that Congress intended to invite such taxation.

18. 461 U.S. 375 (1983).

19. Id. at 382.

20. 106 S.Ct. 1890 (1986).

21. 343 U.S. 99, 102 (1952).

22. 336 U.S. 725 (1949).

23. 106 S.Ct. 2369 (1986).

24. Id. at 2372.

Like the circumstance that a relevant federal regulatory agency is present, the fact that interstate commerce is federally licensed does not by itself determine that state regulation is preempted.[25] In *Gibbons v. Ogden*, Chief Justice Marshall made what would today be characterized as an "actual conflict" argument to hold that a federal statute licensing steamboats in interstate commerce prevented New York from protecting its steamboat monopoly by enjoining a federally licensed competitor from operating a parallel New York-to-New Jersey route: the New York restriction interfered with a provision of the federal statute which granted to steamboats the same privileges as those enjoyed by sailing ships.[26] Accordingly, the Supreme Court has held that a Federal Power Commission determination that a given power project be approved precludes any state attempt to proscribe the project.[27] Similarly, in *Castle v. Hayes Freight Lines, Inc.*, the Supreme Court held that Illinois could not bar an ICC-licensed interstate truck operator from its roads for repeated violations of state highway regulations governing weight and load, because the congressional aim in designing the licensing statute—"to provide stability for operating rights of carriers"—required a uniform national mechanism (the ICC) for enforcing highway regulations of the sort there involved.[28] So too, in *Ray v. Atlantic Richfield Co.*,[29] the Court reasoned that state efforts to impose design requirements on oil tankers operating in Puget Sound would be preempted by a federal statute requiring Coast Guard inspection and licensing of all tankers, since Congress' goal was uniformity of design requirements.[30]

Whether federal licensing operates to preempt state regulation will ordinarily depend on the respective aims of the state and federal

25. But "[t]hat no state may *completely exclude* federally licensed commerce is indisputable." Florida Lime & Avocado Growers v. Paul, 373 U.S. 132, 142 (1963) (dictum) (emphasis added). In California Coastal Comm'n v. Granite Rock Co., 107 S.Ct. 1419 (1987), the Court upheld a California statute that required a mining company to apply for a state permit, even though the company was operating on national forest land pursuant to a National Forest Service permit. Although the Court hinted that an attempt by California to *prohibit* federally-authorized mining would conflict with federal law, the Court was not willing to assume that was the state's intent. Instead, by a 5–4 margin, it held that environmental regulation, as opposed to land use regulation, would not be preempted. The Court's holding that the state requirement was not facially invalid seems to imply that California, under certain circumstances, could deny the mining company's permit application—perhaps for failure to comply with environmental regulations—and thus prohibit federally-authorized mining.

26. 22 U.S. (9 Wheat.) 1 (1824). Accord, Douglas v. Seacoast Products, Inc., 431 U.S.

265 (1977) (state cannot exclude federally licensed vessel from fishing off state coast; even if Gibbons was a misinterpretation of Congress' original intent in licensing vessels, its construction has been congressionally ratified).

27. See First Iowa Hydro-Electric Coop. v. Federal Power Commission, 328 U.S. 152 (1946). Cf. Illinois Natural Gas Co. v. Central Illinois Public Service Comm., 314 U.S. 498 (1942) (a state cannot mandate that a utility, in contravention of an FPC order, extend its facilities).

28. 348 U.S. 61 (1954). The Court based its conclusion largely upon the statutory language which provided that a certificate of convenience and necessity "shall remain in effect until suspended or terminated as provided [by the Motor Carrier Act of 1935]." Id. at 64.

29. 435 U.S. 151 (1978). See also § 6–26, and § 6–25, supra.

30. However, state efforts to impose tug-escort requirements on such tankers were not preempted, even though Congress had authorized, but did not require, the Secretary of Transportation to regulate in this area. See § 6–26, supra, note 26.

schemes. In *Huron Portland Cement Co. v. City of Detroit,*[31] for example, the Court upheld Detroit's regulation of smoke emitted while a
ship's boilers were being cleaned, despite extensive federal licensing of
such ships in interstate and foreign commerce. The Court submitted
"that there is no overlap between a municipal pollution control ordinance and the scope of the federal ship inspection laws" that set the
standards for federal safety licensing of sea-going vessels.[32] And, in
*Pacific Gas & Electric Co. v. State Energy Resources Conservation &
Development Comm'n,*[33] the Court upheld a state's action in suspending
future construction of federally-licensed nuclear power plants within
the state. The state's concern that insufficient capacity for storage of
radioactive wastes might ultimately lead to federally-required service
shutdowns—and that nuclear plants would thus be an undependable
and economically risky source of energy for the state's people—was
deemed an appropriate predicate for such a moratorium despite the
required licensing of such plants by the NRC and despite the NRC's
responsibility to find a place to store long-term nuclear wastes by the
time the storage space would be needed,[34] since the NRC was empow-

31. 362 U.S. 440 (1960), discussed in § 6-12, *supra.*

32. 362 U.S. at 446. See also Union Brokerage Co. v. Jensen, 322 U.S. 202 (1944); Ziffrin v. Reeves, 308 U.S. 132 (1939). In Ray v. Atlantic Richfield Co., 435 U.S. 151 (1978), the Court indicated—arguably in dictum—that the State of Washington could not impose, on tankers operating in Puget Sound, safety design requirements more stringent than the federal requirements. The Court distinguished its prior holding in Huron Portland Cement, noting that "the sole aim of the Detroit ordinance [was] the elimination of air pollution to protect . . . the local community," 435 U.S. at 164, whereas the purpose of the federal design requirements was "to insure the seagoing safety of vessels." Id. Thus, while the Detroit ordinance affected the same *subject-matter* as federal law—namely, design of ships—Congress had intended that the federal government occupy only the field of *safety* standards for ship design. The federal regulations do "not prevent a State or city from enforcing local laws *having other purposes*, such as a local smoke abatement law." Id. (emphasis added). By contrast, in Atlantic Richfield, the state imposed its stringent requirements "on the ground that [certain ships'] design characteristics constitute an undue hazard," id.—a concern held by the Court to fall squarely within the field occupied by the federal government. The Court's distinction between Atlantic Richfield and Huron Portland Cement illustrates the difficulty of searching for the relevant state purpose, since it would seem that the State of Washington, by regulating only *oil tankers* rather than ships generally, was concerned not with "the seagoing safety of vessels," id., the federally occupied field, but with the effects of oil spills on the shores and communities of Puget Sound, in a manner closely analogous to Detroit's non-preempted objective in Huron Portland Cement. In any event, after an extensive discussion of why Washington's safety requirements would be preempted, the Court did not strike them down, since the state's law actually required *either* the stringent design requirements, *or* a tug escort: "[N]o tanker then afloat had all of the design features required by the [state's] Tanker Law," 435 U.S. at 173 n.24. Thus the Court viewed the law as merely a tug escort requirement with certain potential exemptions, a local matter not preempted by federal law. See § 6-26, *supra.*

33. 461 U.S. 190 (1983). See § 6-26, *supra,* text at note 34.

34. The Court, in assessing Congress' preemptive intent, had before it the telling rejection by Congress of an amendment to pending legislation, proposed by Senator McClure, that would have essentially overturned California's moratorium. The moratorium was imposed by California law only until the federal government approved a technology and facilities for nuclear waste disposal, and Senator McClure's proposed amendment would have declared that the pending federal legislation satisfied any such state requirements for the existence of technology and facilities. Thus California's moratorium would have ended if the McClure Amendment had been enacted. See 128 Cong.Rec. § 4310 (daily ed. Apr. 29, 1982); id. at § 6404 (daily ed. May 27, 1982) (remarks of Sen. Hart). This language was *deleted* from the pending legis-

ered to consider only the *safety* aspects of waste disposal when licensing a plant, not the *economic* consequences of subsequent failure to find or develop the necessary storage capacity.

§ 6–29. Uses of Preemption Analysis Outside the Commerce Clause Context

Most problems pertaining to federal preemption have arisen in close connection with the commerce clause; the relevant federal legislation was enacted pursuant to that clause, and the challenged state or local action was vulnerable to commerce clause attack as well as to preemption arguments. But the principles developed in the preceding sections are not limited to this context; essentially the same techniques are used to determine the consequences for state action of *any* exercise of a plenary federal authority.[1] Several areas in which preemption has previously been at issue will serve to illustrate the application of these techniques.

In *Pennsylvania v. Nelson*,[2] the Supreme Court held that a state could not proscribe sedition against the United States because Congress, in passing the Smith Act, had enacted a sufficiently comprehensive regulatory scheme to evidence an intent to occupy the field, and because the nature of the subject matter was such as to lead to a presumption of national, rather than local, regulation. The Court adverted also to the conflict that might arise between federal and state officials if the regulatory schemes were allowed to coexist.[3] The Court has read *Nelson* narrowly. In *Uphaus v. Wyman*,[4] it upheld a conviction traceable to a New Hampshire subversive activities statute, distinguishing *Nelson* on the ground that the prior decision related merely to state statutes governing sedition *against the United States*; the federal government had evidenced no intent to preempt laws proscribing sedition against the states themselves.[5]

Another example is provided by state laws penalizing debtors who initiate federal bankruptcy proceedings. In *Perez v. Campbell*,[6] the Court stressed the conflict between federal and state law in holding that Arizona, by withholding driving privileges from automobile acci-

---

lation, the House was told, precisely "to insure that there be no preemption." Id. at H8797 (Dec. 2, 1982) (remarks of Rep. Ottinger). In assessing this history, the Court stated that, "[w]hile we are correctly reluctant to draw inferences from the failure of Congress to act, it would, in this case, appear improper for us to give a reading to the [Atomic Energy Act] that Congress considered and rejected." 461 U.S. at 220.

§ 6–29

1. See, e.g., California Coastal Comm'n v. Granite Rock, Co., 107 S.Ct. 1419 (1987), discussed in § 6–28, supra, note 25. In that case, the Supreme Court regarded federal laws pertaining to mining on national forest lands as exercises of Congress' power under the Property Clause of Art. IV, rath-

er than under the Commerce Clause. Yet, against the urging of Justice Powell's dissent, joined by Justice Stevens, id. at 1432, the Court used its standard preemption test: "[E]ven within the sphere of the Property Clause, state law is preempted only when it conflicts with the operation or objectives of federal law, or when Congress 'evidences an intent to occupy a given field.'" Id. at 1431–32 (citation omitted).

2. 350 U.S. 497 (1956).

3. Id. at 507.

4. 360 U.S. 72 (1959).

5. Id. at 76.

6. 402 U.S. 637 (1971), overruling Kesler v. Dept. of Public Safety, 369 U.S. 153 (1962).

dent judgment debtors who discharged their judgments in bankruptcy, interfered with the federal Bankruptcy Act policy of giving debtors a fresh start.[7]

Patent and copyright laws provide a third example. As a general rule, when an article is unprotected by a federal patent or copyright, state law may not forbid others to copy it. The Supreme Court expounded the logic underlying this rule in *Sears, Roebuck & Co. v. Stiffel Co.*: "To allow a state by use of its law of unfair competition to prevent the copying of an article which represents too slight an advance to be patented would be to permit the state to block off from the public something which federal law has said belongs to the public."[8] But otherwise constitutional state action has been upheld in the absence of evidence that congressional withholding of federal copyright protection was meant to implement a policy of "free access." In *Goldstein v. California*,[9] the Court upheld a California law which made the commercial reproduction of recordings produced by others a misdemeanor. The absence of a federal "free access" policy was perceived in a congressional act granting limited federal copyright protection to future recordings and by the administrative difficulties that would have been entailed in 1909, the date of the relevant copyright law, by any federal attempt to regulate the reproduction of recordings: "Congress has drawn no balance; rather it has left the area unattended, and no reason exists why the State should not be free to act."[10]

Conflicts between Indian tribes and state authorities provide a final example. In the context of Congress' power to regulate commerce with the Indian tribes—power derived from the so-called Indian commerce clause—the Supreme Court has consistently "rejected the narrow focus on congressional intent to pre-empt state law as the sole touchstone . . . [as well as] the proposition that pre-emption requires . . . an

---

7. But cf. Reitz v. Mealey, 314 U.S. 33, 37 (1941) (state suspension of driver's licenses of persons negligently involved in automobile accidents and unable to pay compensation held not inconsistent with federal bankruptcy law despite lack of state exemption for bankrupts, since the law's emphasis was on preventing irresponsible driving rather than on assuring payment of judgments).

8. 376 U.S. 225, 231–32 (1964). See also Compco Corp. v. Day-Brite Lighting Co., 376 U.S. 234, 237 (1964) ("To forbid copying would interfere with the federal policy, found in Article I, Section 8, Clause 8, of the Constitution and in the implementing federal statutes, of allowing free access to copy whatever the federal patent and copyright laws leave in the public domain"). Cf. Teamsters Local 20 v. Morton, 377 U.S. 252 (1964), discussed in § 6–28, supra.

9. 412 U.S. 546 (1973).

10. Id. at 570. Cf. Kewanee Oil Co. v. Bicron Corp., 416 U.S. 470 (1974) (holding that federal patent law does not preempt state trade secret protection since trade secret law, which affords weaker protection than the patent laws, does not deter patent applications by inventors of clearly patentable subject matter, and since the elimination of trade secret protection in cases of doubtfully patentable subject matter would increase resort to self-help of a type which could balkanize and fragment research and marketing efforts). A powerfully critical examination of the Goldstein decision and an illuminating comparison with the Kewanee case is contained in Brown, "Publication and Preemption in Copyright Law: Elegiac Reflections on Goldstein v. California," 22 U.C.L.A.L. Rev. 1022 (1975). Compare also Aronson v. Quick Point Pencil Co., 440 U.S. 257 (1979) (federal patent law does not preempt state law that would make enforceable a contract between inventor and licensee calling for payment of royalties even if invention proved to be unpatentable, since contract, which enabled licensee to be first in the market with a new idea, did not *withdraw* any idea from the public domain, and such contracts would not discourage anyone from seeking a patent).

express congressional statement to that effect."[11] Instead, the Court rests its preemption analysis on a consideration of the nature of the state, federal, and tribal interests at stake.[12] In *New Mexico v. Mescalero Apache Tribe*,[13] a tribe challenged New Mexico's assertion that, should the tribe choose to permit hunting and fishing on its reservation by non-members, such hunting and fishing would be subject to generally applicable state-imposed rules. The tribe, with federal assistance, had undertaken substantial development of its fish and game resources, both for its own use and to provide income for the tribe from sale to non-members of tribal hunting and fishing licenses and related services. The tribe had established its own bag limits, seasons, and licensing requirements, which conflicted seriously with state regulations.[14] The Court found that the tribal and federal interest at stake was the promotion of tribal self-sufficiency and economic development.[15] The state, on the other hand, "cannot point to any off-reservation effects that warrant state intervention," except for its loss of revenues from sale of state licenses to non-members who hunt or fish on the reservation.[16] The Court concluded that, because of the "strong federal interests favoring exclusive tribal jurisdiction" and the absence of strong state interests, the state's laws, as applied, were preempted.[17] Thus, the Court's analysis is reminiscent of typical preemption analysis where there is a claim of actual conflict with a federal objective. It differs in that under the Indian commerce clause, but not under the interstate commerce clause, the Court will give preemptive effect to a broadly-framed or abstract federal objective. However, almost as a quid pro quo, the Court will consider the magnitude of the state's interest, which is irrelevant in typical preemption analysis.[18]

Above all, perhaps the most fundamental point to remember is that preemption analysis is, or should be, a matter of statutory construction rather than free-form judicial policymaking. The fact that Congress may override a preemption holding (as opposed to a constitutional interpretation) should not be taken to liberate courts in general, or the Supreme Court in particular, from a sense of fidelity to law, and to the judicial task of interpretation. To be sure, there are specialized areas in which Congress may be presumed to have acted against the backdrop of a well-known set of judicial assumptions and approaches; the regula-

---

11. New Mexico v. Mescalero Apache Tribe, 462 U.S. 324, 334 (1983) (Marshall, J., for a unanimous Court). See also, e.g., White Mountain Apache Tribe v. Bracker, 448 U.S. 136, 143–144 (1980); Ramah Navajo School Bd., Inc. v. Bureau of Revenue of New Mexico, 458 U.S. 832, 838 (1982); Three Affiliated Tribes of the Fort Berthold Reservation v. Wold Engineering, 106 S.Ct. 2305, 2310 (1986).

12. Mescalero Apache Tribe, 462 U.S. at 333–34.

13. 462 U.S. 324 (1983).

14. For instance, "[t]he Tribe permits a hunter to kill both a buck and a doe; the State permits only buck to be killed." Id. at 329. Moreover, the tribe specified that

state hunting and fishing licenses were not required on the reservation.

15. Id. at 335.

16. Id. at 342.

17. Id. at 344.

18. It is unclear whether the state law would have been preempted if the state's interest were *strong* (for instance, if the state were able to show that on-reservation game normally commingled with off-reservation game, and that tribal hunting policies were adversely affecting strengths of herds off the reservation) and the federal or tribal interest were broadly-framed or weak.

tion of Indian affairs, described above, may be an example. But it is one thing to pursue a specialized approach unless and until Congress says something to overturn it, and something else again to approach preemption issues generally as though one were doing something other than reading an applicable federal statute. Thus, where the relevant federal law itself speaks in a seemingly definitive way on the preemption issue—either by broadening or by narrowing the preemptive effect the law would otherwise have been thought to possess—a court should deem itself bound by what Congress has said on the subject. In the pregnancy disability decision, *California Federal Savings & Loan Ass'n v. Guerra*,[19] for example, it appears that only Justice Scalia took with sufficient seriousness Congress' explicit mandate that the federal law at issue preempts *only* state laws that purport to compel or authorize employers to act in violation of the relevant federal law—*not* all state laws that might be in some more nebulous sort of tension with the federal mandate of equal treatment. Although the outcome of the case did not turn on the difference between Justice Scalia's approach and that of the others in the majority, the legitimacy of the Court's decision as a matter of statutory interpretation rather than as an exercise in open-ended policymaking may well have been undercut by the failure of the rest of the Court to follow Justice Scalia's lead. In matters of statutory interpretation no less than in matters of constitutional construction, the Court's task is an interpretive one; that the task entails choices cannot be taken to make it indistinguishable from lawmaking pure and simple.

§ 6–30. The Special Role of Federal Supremacy in Direct Intergovernmental Confrontation: Immunizing Federal Institutions, Agents, and Contractors

In all the areas thus far examined in this chapter, the federal-state interaction has been indirect: the question has been how to allocate constitutional power as between the two levels of government when each seeks to deal with the same area of private conduct. This section turns to a different sort of interaction, although one that is best understood as posing an issue essentially of federal preemption: The subject is that of state attempts to regulate or tax entities with some special link to the federal government.[1]

In those rare cases where Congress has expressly granted or withheld regulatory or tax immunity to certain of its instrumentalities, agents, or contractors, the validity or invalidity of state action is definitively settled by such federal legislation.[2] When Congress has not

19. 107 S.Ct. 683 (1987), discussed in § 6–26, supra.

§ 6–30

1. On the converse topic of federal regulation and taxation of state activities or property, see §§ 5–20 to 5–22, supra. On the related but even more specialized topic of the immunity of Indians and Indian property on reservations, see, e.g., McClanahan v. Arizona State Tax Comm., 411 U.S.

164 (1973) (income derived from reservation sources immune to state taxation); Mescalero Apache Tribe v. Jones, 411 U.S. 145 (1973) (upholding state gross receipts tax on revenue from ski resort operated by reservation Indians on off-reservation land leased from the federal government).

2. See, e.g., Carson v. Roane-Anderson Co., 342 U.S. 232, 234, 236 (1952) (sales tax held unenforceable as to sales of commodi-

spoken, or has spoken but not clearly, the remaining question is the degree of so-called "constitutional immunity"—the immunity to be inferred, subject to congressional revision, from the plan of the Constitution.

The law in this area traces to *McCulloch v. Maryland*,[3] where Chief Justice Marshall wrote for a unanimous Court holding that the supremacy clause prevented Maryland from levying a stamp tax on bank notes issued by the Baltimore branch of the Bank of the United States, a corporation chartered by Congress. Applying to the federal structure the principle that a government may not tax or control those whom it does not represent, the Chief Justice concluded that the states could not tax or control a federal instrumentality.[4] Operation of a federal instrumentality necessarily affects the interests of all since it is for the benefit of all; the national power must therefore remain unfettered if control and representation are to be coincident:[5] "In the legislature of the Union alone, are all represented. The legislature of the Union alone, therefore, can be trusted by the people with the power of controlling measures which concern all, in the confidence that it will not be abused." In addition, Chief Justice Marshall doubted the ability of the federal courts to review the reasonableness of taxes imposed upon federal instrumentalities if a state's power to tax were to be recognized in principle.[6] *McCulloch* thus announced the prophylactic per se rule that has been followed ever since. If Congress does not authorize state taxation or regulation of federal instrumentalities, the possibility of interference with substantive federal policy is sufficient to raise a presumption of immunity.[7]

ties to contractor employed by Atomic Energy Commission, immunity having been expressly conferred by federal statute); City of Cleveland v. United States, 323 U.S. 329, 333 (1945) (power of Congress to confer exemptions and immunities as deemed necessary is settled "by such an array of authority that citation would seem unnecessary"). Congress must make clear its intent to subject federal installations or instrumentalities to state control. See, e.g., EPA v. State Water Resources Control Board, 426 U.S. 200 (1976); Hancock v. Train, 426 U.S. 167 (1976) (federal installations and instrumentalities not subject to state permit requirements for air and water pollution).

3. 17 U.S. (4 Wheat.) 316 (1819), discussed in § 5–3, supra. See also Weston v. Charleston, 27 U.S. (2 Pet.) 449 (1829) (city tax on stock issued by United States held void under article VI), codified in a modified version by Congress in 12 Stat. 709, 710, § 1 (1863), 31 U.S.C. § 742. The current codification of the federal obligations immunity is 31 U.S.C. § 3124(a), which essentially restates the constitutional rule. See Rockford Life Ins. Co. v. Illinois Dept. of Revenue, 107 S.Ct. 2312 (1987) (federal corporation's role as guarantor of "Ginnie Mae" mortgage investment instruments is

too indirect, contingent and unliquidated to transform Ginnie Maes into federal obligations immune from state taxation) (unanimous opinion).

4. 17 U.S. at 428–31.

5. Id. at 435–36. See also Gibbons v. Ogden, 22 U.S. (9 Wheat.) 1, 197 (1824); Helvering v. Gerhardt, 304 U.S. 405, 412, 416 (1938).

6. 17 U.S. (4 Wheat.) at 429–30, 436. Hence, "the power to tax involves the power to destroy." Id. at 431.

7. See Osborn v. United States Bank, 22 U.S. (9 Wheat.) 738, 865 (1824) (rejecting Ohio's argument that the presumption, when Congress is silent, should be against immunity). See also First National Bank v. Anderson, 269 U.S. 341, 347 (1926): Instrumentalities or "agencies of the United States created under its laws to promote its . . . policies . . . cannot be taxed under state authority except as Congress consents and then only in conformity with the restrictions attached to its consent." Note that federally-chartered corporations engaged in private business are not federal instrumentalities for purposes of this rule. See McCulloch v. Maryland, 17 U.S. (4 Wheat.) 316, 426 (1819) (dictum); Thomson v. Pacific Railroad, 76 U.S. (9 Wall.) 579,

But immunity from "interference" obviously cannot include "a general immunity from state law" for all federal agents acting within the scope of their agency;[8] given the interstitial character of federal law, any contrary principle would require Congress to undertake the overwhelming burden of having to provide a comprehensive body of rules to govern *all* of the rights and obligations of all those who act on its behalf, including "the mode of turning at the corners of streets."[9] Thus, even in military bases or other federal enclaves, where such enclaves are ceded by a state without reserving a right of continuing regulation, the general body of state law extant at the time the enclave is acquired continues to govern primary activity[10] unless such state law actually conflicts with a federal law, program, or policy.[11] A similar principle emerges from cases involving immunity of federal instrumentalities from state regulation. State law is presumptively applicable, but absent explicit congressional consent no state may command federal officials, instrumentalities, or agents to take action in derogation of their validly delegated federal responsibilities.[12]

588 (1869). Compare Dept. of Employment v. United States, 385 U.S. 355, 359–60 (1966) (holding that the American Red Cross, chartered by Congress in 1905, is a federal instrumentality immune from state taxation until Congress declares otherwise: "time and time again, both the President and Congress have recognized and acted in reliance upon the Red Cross' status virtually as an arm of the Government").

8. Johnson v. Maryland, 254 U.S. 51, 56 (1920) (Holmes, J.) (dictum). The rule was recognized as early as First National Bank v. Commonwealth, 76 U.S. (9 Wall.) 353, 362 (1870).

9. Johnson, 254 U.S. at 56.

10. See Pacific Coast Dairy v. Dept. of Agriculture, 318 U.S. 285, 294 (1943) (California cannot penalize milk dealer for selling milk to War Department below state minimum price where sales and deliveries occurred entirely within federal territory).

11. Congressional jurisdiction over federal enclaves is exclusive only if exercised. State law enacted prior to federal acquisition continues to govern within the enclave if the state law is "not inconsistent with federal policy" and if it is not "altered by national legislation." Id. "This assures that no area however small will be left without a developed legal system for private rights." James Stewart & Co. v. Sadrakula, 309 U.S. 94, 100 (1940). Absent congressional action, the state law applied within federal enclaves is static. Id. Congress, however, may validly legislate a policy of dynamic conformity under which all state laws enacted subsequent to creation of a federal enclave will apply within the enclave unless they directly conflict with federal legislation. See e.g., United States v. Sharpnack, 355 U.S. 286 (1958). Con-

duct occurring outside the enclave, but affecting the enclave, is subject to general state regulation, see, e.g., Penn Dairies, Inc. v. Milk Control Comm'n, 318 U.S. 261 (1943) (state can refuse to renew license of milk dealer who sold milk at below state minimum price to United States agents for consumption by troops where sales occurred outside federal jurisdiction), so long as it does not actually conflict with federal law. See, e.g., Public Util. Comm'n of Calif. v. United States, 355 U.S. 534, 544, 547–58 (1958) (essentially same facts as Penn Dairies, but federal law had been altered, giving procurement officers exclusive responsibility for negotiating price without regard to state law); Paul v. United States, 371 U.S. 245 (1963); United States v. Georgia Pub. Serv. Comm'n, 371 U.S. 285 (1963).

12. See e.g., Sperry v. Florida, 373 U.S. 379, 385 (1963) (state is prohibited from enjoining, as unauthorized practice of law, the giving of advice by patent agents licensed by U.S. Patent Office to give such advice); Leslie Miller, Inc. v. Arkansas, 352 U.S. 187 (1956) (per curiam) (private contractor cannot be required to submit to state licensing procedures as precondition of bidding for federal contract where governing federal procurement statute provides standards for judging responsibility of competitive bidders); Arizona v. California, 283 U.S. 423, 451–52 (1931) (Arizona cannot enjoin construction of congressionally authorized Boulder Dam, despite failure of United States to comply with state approval procedures); Johnson v. Maryland, 254 U.S. 51, 56–57 (1920) (U.S. Post Office employee, directed by United States to deliver mail by truck and hence presumably found competent for that task by Federal authorities, cannot be convicted and

Mayo v. United States [13] illustrates the reach of this principle. The Soil Conservation and Domestic Allotment Act of 1936 empowered the Secretary of Agriculture to purchase and distribute fertilizer as part of the national soil conservation program, while state regulations required each bag of fertilizer to be stamped as evidence of payment of an inspection fee.[14] After the Florida Commissioner of Agriculture issued a "stop sale" notice, a precondition to seizure, the United States obtained an injunction against enforcement of the state law. In upholding this injunction, the Supreme Court noted that the state law authorizing seizure and sale by the sheriff of unstamped fertilizer could jeopardize administration of the federal program. Any such dramatic confrontation, in which the supremacy clause of article VI would plainly require that federal law prevail, was averted by holding the state regulation wholly unenforceable as applied to federally distributed fertilizer. Despite the Court's extravagant assertion that "the activities of the Federal Government are free from regulation by any state," [15] the decision in *Mayo*, properly understood, establishes only a far more modest principle: a state statute contravening the hegemony of federal law and backed by threatened seizure of federal property for noncompliance cannot be enforced against the United States.

§ 6–31. The Scope of Federal Tax Immunity

Although immunity from state taxation was initially accorded on a far broader basis to persons dealing with the federal government,[1] it is the narrow principle at the heart of *Mayo* [2] rather than its sweeping pronouncement that has defined federal tax immunities absent congressional consent in the great majority of the cases decided since 1937. This principle can provide a doctrinal basis for the sometimes bewilderingly complex array of judicial decisions in this area: The supremacy clause implies that, absent congressional consent, no state may (1) impose upon the United States or its instrumentalities [3] an obligation to pay any tax; [4] or (2) make any property interest owned by the United States or its instrumentalities subject to seizure or forced sale in order

fined under state law for driving without a state license). The rule of these cases emerged as early as In re Neagle, 135 U.S. 1, 75 (1890).

13. 319 U.S. 441 (1943).

14. Id. at 442.

15. Id. at 445.

§ 6–31

1. See, e.g., Osborn v. Bank of the United States, 22 U.S. (9 Wheat.) 738, 867 (1824) (dictum): Panhandle Oil Co. v. Knox, 277 U.S. 218 (1928) (vendor to federal government immune to state sales tax), overruled in Alabama v. King & Boozer, 314 U.S. 1, 9 (1941), discussed below. The early cases which recognized broad *state* immunity from *federal* taxation as well as the converse are canvassed in Powell, "An Imaginary Judicial Opinion," 44 Harv.L. Rev. 889 (1931).

2. Mayo v. United States, 319 U.S. 441 (1943), in § 6–30, supra.

3. "Instrumentalities" do not include independent contractors, employees, or others dealing for their own purposes with the federal government but only those entities "so assimilated by the Government as to become one of its constituent parts." United States v. Township of Muskegon, 355 U.S. 484, 486 (1958).

4. The critical issue is whether the state purports to require collection from the United States or any of its instrumentalities; the legal incidence of the tax must be on an immune entity for this bar to apply. Legal incidence, in turn, depends not only on the party *from whom* the state seeks to *collect* its tax but also on the party *to whom* the state requires that the tax be *passed*. In particular, "where a state requires that its sales tax be passed on to the

to satisfy a state tax liability.[5] This rule of legal incidence seems defensible despite its apparent woodenness: either of the direct affronts to federal sovereignty noted above would offend the most basic notions of national supremacy, unless explicitly authorized by Congress.[6] Moreover, to extend this doctrinal formulation so as to make congressional authorization a prerequisite to state taxation of federal employees or contractors on their income, receipts, property or activities—simply because of their contractual connection with the United States, or because the executive branch voluntarily assumes the economic burden imposed on them by state taxes—would be to create unwarranted inroads upon the revenue bases of the states.[7]

purchaser and be collected by the vendor from him, this establishes as a matter of [federal] law that the legal incidence of the tax falls upon the purchaser." United States v. State Tax Comm. of Mississippi, 421 U.S. 599, 608 (1975); First Agricultural National Bank v. Tax Commission, 392 U.S. 339, 347–48 (1968). For a somewhat novel application of this settled rule, see Gurley v. Rhoden, 421 U.S. 200, 203, 210 (1975).

5. The key is whether the state purports to subject to potential seizure, at the time its tax is levied, a property interest held by the federal government at that time. Thus a state cannot tax federally owned land under a threat of seizure for nonpayment, and a state cannot sell for taxes lands the United States owned at the time such taxes were levied even if the United States has no interest in such lands at the time of sale. See Van Brocklin v. Tennessee, 117 U.S. 151, 179–80 (1886). Where the United States retains only legal title to land as security for payment of the purchase price, application of the same principle correctly indicates that a state may impose a tax on the land measured by its full value so long as the tax is enforceable under state law only by a levy on the equity interest that has already passed to the purchaser at the time the tax is imposed. S.R.A., Inc. v. Minnesota, 327 U.S. 558, 565–66 (1946). That the United States may indirectly be hurt in its ability to sell the land is constitutionally irrelevant, id. at 570, since the test turns entirely on whether the interest which the state asserts a right to seize is an interest belonging to the United States or its instrumentalities. The Court in S.R.A., Inc. v. Minnesota dismissed as "too mechanical" any rule that would make tax immunity last until the full purchase price had been paid and legal title had passed to the purchaser. Id. at 569. Since the locus of economic injury is deemed irrelevant, id. at 570, the Court must be understood as objecting not to the idea of a formal test of immunity but simply to a test that would confer immunity even where the state has

claimed no right to proceed against something belonging to the federal government. Accord, United States v. Detroit, 355 U.S. 466, 469 (1958) (denying tax immunity to private lessee of federal property where state law did not make owner liable and did not subject the property to a lien in the event of nonpayment); City of Detroit v. Murray Corp., 355 U.S. 489, 492 (1958) (same result even where tax is denominated a "personal property tax"). The rules governing tax and regulatory immunity are, of course, subject to the overriding requirement that a state not discriminate against the federal government or those with whom it deals. See United States v. Detroit, 355 U.S. 466, 473 (1958).

6. That the allocation of tax immunity should ultimately be decided by Congress does not necessarily provide any reason for judicial invalidation of state legislation taxing federal instrumentalities; if Congress objects to such interference, it can always pass a law denying immunity, which federal courts would then enforce against the states. However, an opposite rule follows from considerations that have led courts to adopt a prophylactic, prohibitory approach. If the harm a state may inflict on a federal instrumentality can be so great as to support injunctive relief, see Osborn v. Bank of the United States, 22 U.S. (9 Wheat.) 738 (1824); Mayo v. United States, 319 U.S. 441 (1943), and if courts are not in a good position to assess what a reasonable infringement of federal interests might be, then a judicial rule protecting the status quo while Congress decides whether to claim immunity would seem justified.

7. See, e.g., Union Pac. R.R. v. Peniston, 85 U.S. (18 Wall.) 5, 33, 36 (1873) (immunity for persons who deal with the federal government from time to time from all state taxes on property used in their federal dealings and on the fruits of their work would exempt a "very large proportion of the property within the states" and leave them "paralyzed"). Any result potentially so drastic should at least require a clear

The legal incidence rule was developed in a series of cases that considered tax immunity claims arising from contracts between the federal executive and private parties. In the 1937 case of *James v. Dravo Contracting Co.*[8] a contractor sought immunity from a state gross receipts tax imposed on amounts received under a contract to construct locks and dams for the federal government. Before *Dravo*, immunity was almost always implied when the state tax would otherwise have increased the cost of the government's operations.[9] *Dravo*, however, broke new ground by announcing that even if "the gross receipts tax may increase the cost to the Government, that fact would not invalidate the tax."[10] Instead, the Court sought to apply a "practical criterion" and held that "where no direct burden is laid upon" the federal government,[11] a nondiscriminatory tax collected from its contractors did not violate the *McCulloch* principle.[12] The force of *Dravo's* conclusion must, however, be qualified by the fact that the United States agreed in the Supreme Court that the tax was valid in the absence of congressionally conferred statutory immunity, perhaps because the federal government did not in fact reimburse the contractor for the state taxes in question.[13]

Dravo's legal incidence test was followed in the 1941 case of *Alabama v. King & Boozer*.[14] There, King and Boozer sold lumber to contractors that had cost-plus contracts with the federal government. Alabama sought to collect a sales tax from King and Boozer, although by state law, King and Boozer was merely a collector and the obligation to pay the tax fell on the contractors.[15] The economic impact of the tax reached the United States because, under the terms of its contract, it had agreed to reimburse the contractors for all taxes paid.[16] The Court held that economic impact was not enough,[17] that the United States was not a "purchaser" within the contemplation of Alabama law and therefore was not legally obligated to pay the tax,[18] and that the contractors were not mere agents of the federal government so as to make the tax on them in effect one on the government.[19] Again, extraneous circumstances make *King & Boozer's* use of the legal inci-

---

statement of purpose by Congress. See §§ 3–37, 5–8, 5–22, supra.

8. 302 U.S. 134 (1937).

9. See, e.g., Dobbins v. Erie County, 41 U.S. (16 Pet.) 435 (1842) (salary of federal officer); Panhandle Oil Co. v. Mississippi ex rel. Knox, 277 U.S. 218 (1928) (sales made to federal government); Gillespie v. Oklahoma, 257 U.S. 501 (1922) (income of lessee of federal lands). But see note 18, infra.

10. 302 U.S. at 160; accord, Graves v. New York ex rel. O'Keefe, 306 U.S. 466 (1939) (applying legal incidence test in upholding state taxes on income of federal officers).

11. 302 U.S. at 150, 152.

12. 302 U.S. at 160–61.

13. See id. at 149, 159–60. The Court's much-cited declaration that a voluntary

pass-through makes no difference, id. at 160, was thus pure dictum.

14. 314 U.S. 1 (1941).

15. Id. at 9–10.

16. Id. at 10.

17. Id. at 8–9.

18. Where state law requires that the vendor collect the tax from the purchaser, then it follows as a matter of federal law that the legal incidence of the tax is on the purchaser, id. at 9–10, 13–14, even if title to the items purchased vests in the United States rather than in its contractor at the time of the contractor's purchase.

19. 314 U.S. at 12–14. The Court thus overruled Panhandle Oil Co. v. Mississippi ex rel. Knox, 277 U.S. 218 (1928), supra note 9.

dence test less than a fully compelling precedent—the Senate had earlier refused to grant cost-plus contractors tax immunity, and the Court might have been persuaded by this deliberate omission not to imply such immunity from the Constitution.[20]

Dravo and *King & Boozer* establish that a federal contractor cannot escape payment of nondiscriminatory gross receipts or sales taxes where state law makes the contractor, but not the United States, liable for payment of the tax. The rule applies even if the ultimate financial burden of the tax is passed through to the United States pursuant to the contract, and even if title to the property whose sale is being taxed passes to the United States before the state tax is levied.[21] Drawing on the United States' concession that an economic burden rule would be "illusory and incapable of consistent application," [22] the Court has claimed the government's "full support" [23] for a legal incidence rule. The dispositive inquiry in tax immunity cases has become the search for the legal incidence of a state tax. If the state imposes no legal obligation on the United States or its instrumentalities but only on persons contracting with them, no immunity will be implied simply because a voluntary pass-through has been engineered.[24]

Where state or local taxes are assessed against the user of federal property, the cases find no implied immunity unless state law purports to hold the United States or its instrumentalities liable for the tax, or attempts to make federal property subject to a lien in the event of nonpayment.[25] This is so whether the tax is denominated by the state as one on the privilege of using the property [26] or as one on the property itself; [27] even if the tax is measured by the value of the federal property; [28] and even if the government has agreed to reimburse the

20 See 314 U.S. at 8 & n. 1.

21. See note 5, supra.

22. See United States v. Detroit, 355 U.S. 466, 473 n. 4 (1958) (quoting from the Government's King & Boozer brief).

23. Id. at 472–73.

24. Just as a voluntary pass-through to the United States or one of its instrumentalities does not confer immunity absent an applicable act of Congress, so too a refusal to assume the tax does not withdraw immunity. Rohr Aircraft Corp. v. San Diego, 362 U.S. 628 (1960) (property owned by Reconstruction Finance Corporation could not be subject to taxes assessed against the federal instrumentality notwithstanding a private lessee's agreement to pay all such taxes).

25. See United States v. County of Fresno, 429 U.S. 452 (1977) (upholding county tax on the possessory interest of U.S. Forest Service employees in housing located in National Forests supplied to the employees as part of their compensation, pursuant to state statutes authorizing counties to impose annual use or property tax on possessory interest in improvements on tax-exempt land). The Court also upheld the tax

against a claim that it discriminated against Forest Service employees, although Justice Stevens dissented on that issue. Id. at 707–11.

26. See Esso Standard Oil Co. v. Evans, 345 U.S. 495 (1953) (state tax of $.06 per gallon for privilege of storing gas may be collected from federal contractor who stores high-octane aviation fuel owned by United States in tanks owned or privately leased by the contractor).

27. Although the Court in Esso Standard Oil Co., 345 U.S. at 499 (1953) relied on such a distinction, it was abandoned as overly formalistic in City of Detroit v. Murray Corp. of America, 355 U.S. 489, 492, 493, 495 (1958) (upholding a state "personal property tax" imposed on a private corporation with "no effort to hold the United States or its property accountable"); see note 5, supra.

28. City of Detroit v. Murray Corp. of America, 355 U.S. 489, 491–92 (1958); United States v. Detroit, 355 U.S. 466, 468 (1958); S.R.A., Inc. v. Minnesota, 327 U.S. 558, 570 (1946). These decisions can only be understood as abandoning United States v. Allegheny County, 322 U.S. 174, 185

user for paying the tax.[29] In all these cases, unless the state deliberately precipitates a federal-state confrontation by insisting that the United States or its instrumentalities be answerable for the tax, the underlying theory must be that only affirmative congressional action should be sufficient to strip the state of power to collect nondiscriminatory taxes from third parties. Understanding and defending that theory requires that its central paradox be confronted.

§ 6–32. Formalism, Realism, and the Role of Congress in Intergovernmental Immunity Cases

Because of the tensions between the rigidly formal yet admirably precise legal incidence rule and the palpably realistic but impracticably indeterminate economic burden test, the field of federal tax immunity "has been marked from the beginning by inconsistent decisions and excessively delicate distinctions." [1] The Court reached its nadir in this regard in *Kern-Limerick, Inc. v. Scurlock*.[2] The case presented a three-party situation identical to that in *Alabama v. King & Boozer*: [3] the tax was collected by the state from a vendor who supplied the federal government's contractor. No immunity was found in the earlier case, but the Court prohibited collection of the tax from the vendor-taxpayer in *Kern-Limerick* because the contract between the United States and the vendee-contractor (1) described the latter's purchases as being made "by the Government," (2) provided that the "Government shall be obligated to the Vendor for the purchase price," and (3) identified the contractor as a federal "purchasing agent" despite state law designating the contractor as the "purchaser" from whom the vendor was to collect the tax.[4]

The first edition of this treatise criticized *Kern-Limerick* and argued that it should be overruled. The decision's vice is that the tax immunity it recognized resulted, without action by Congress, from an obligation gratuitously assumed by the executive branch—one costing nothing, since the obligation of the tax evaporated due to federal immunity as soon as the executive agreed to absorb it. The Supreme Court admitted that its holding meant that "the form of [federal] contracts may determine [tax immunity]" where Congress has not

---

(1944) (state cannot impose real estate tax on bailee of machinery owned by United States where the value of the machinery is added to the assessment of the real estate in measuring the tax). After the 1946 and 1958 decisions, Allegheny County must be regarded either as overruled altogether or as limited to the special situation in which the threat of a tax lien against the underlying non-federal property amounts to an assertion of state power to enforce its tax by putting the federal government to a choice between allowing sale of its property (the machinery) and physically moving that property as the land is sold "out from under [it]" so as to defeat the government's "purpose . . . in owning and leasing it." Id. at 187.

29. United States v. Detroit, 355 U.S. 466, 468, 472 (1958).

§ 6–32

1. United States v. New Mexico, 455 U.S. 720, 730 (1982).

2. 347 U.S. 110 (1954).

3. 314 U.S. 1 (1941).

4. 347 U.S. at 119. The lawyers who drafted the contract had read the U.S. Reports very carefully indeed: dicta in *King & Boozer* suggested that even if state law locates the onus of the tax as falling on a contractor, the contractor might be immunized if the contract was written to make the contractor a federal purchasing agent. 314 U.S. at 13.

chosen to confer it,[5] but failed to explain why a federal contracting official's choice of language should thus be allowed to amputate the reach of a state's revenue power. Certainly the executive must have the power to decide for its own internal purposes who is the "purchaser" of materials under a construction contract; but that administrative necessity cannot justify permitting the executive to escalate its intramural definition into a confrontation between state and federal authority where a state disclaims any intention to impose a tax obligation on the United States or to compel collection from it.

Faced with an opportunity to correct the aberration of *Kern-Limerick* in a recent tax immunity case, *United States v. New Mexico*,[6] the Supreme Court unanimously concluded "that the confusing nature of our precedents counsels a return to the underlying constitutional principle."[7] The Department of Energy (DOE) had brought suit against New Mexico seeking a declaratory judgment that several private management contractors were constitutionally immune from state taxation. The government conceded that the legal incidence of the tax fell on the contractors, but argued that the contractors were essentially federal agents, who in fact drew checks directly on the United States Treasury by means of an "advanced funding" procedure.[8]

The Court rejected DOE's arguments by adopting the reasoning of the dissenting opinion in *Kern-Limerick*: "We cannot believe that an immunity of constitutional stature rests on such technical considerations, for that approach allows 'any government functionary to draw a constitutional line by changing a few words in a contract.' "[9] Although it did not expressly overrule *Kern-Limerick*, the *New Mexico* Court virtually read it out of existence. All that is left to distinguish *Kern-Limerick* are the facts that the contract language there designated the contractor a "purchasing agent," that the purchase orders declared the purchase was made by the government, and that the contractor had to obtain advance government approval for each transaction.[10] Given the Court's refusal to allow its constitutional doctrine to be manipulated by a civil servant's pen, such distinctions are surely meaningless.

The Court continued its "recent tendency to be sympathetic with States in their urgent quest for new taxes"[11] in *Washington v. United States*,[12] where the Court's tax immunity doctrine became even more pragmatic. Washington's principal source of revenue was a sales and use tax imposed on all consumers of tangible personal property. With regard to construction materials, the legal incidence of the tax fell on the landowner who purchased construction work from the contractor, and who therefore paid the tax on the full price of the project. However, since such a tax would fall directly on the federal government

---

5. 347 U.S. at 122–23.

6. 455 U.S. 720 (1982).

7. Id. at 733.

8. Id. at 737.

9. Id. (quoting Kern-Limerick, 347 U.S. at 126 (dissenting opinion)).

10. New Mexico, 455 U.S. at 738–42 & n. 17.

11. Washington v. United States, 460 U.S. 536, 547 (1983) (Blackmun, J., dissenting).

12. 460 U.S. 536 (1983).

in the case of federal building projects, in such instances the state imposed the sales tax on the contractor's purchase of the materials.[13]

The federal government charged that the State of Washington was trying to circumvent federal tax immunity by selectively taxing federal contractors. The Supreme Court disagreed, noting that an identical tax rate is imposed on every construction transaction in the state: [14] "The only deviation from equality between the Federal Government and federal contractors on the one hand, and every other taxpayer on the other, is that the former are taxed on a smaller portion of the value of the project than the latter. Thus the Federal Government and federal contractors are both better off than other taxpayers because they pay less tax than anyone else in the state." [15] Washington thus did not discriminate against federal contractors but merely shifted the legal incidence of the sales tax in order to "accommodate" the Constitution.[16] This in itself does not offend the supremacy clause, and as the Court stated in *United States v. New Mexico*, "[i]f the immunity of federal contractors is to be expanded beyond its narrow constitutional limits, it is Congress that must take responsibility for the decision." [17]

The unanimous decision in *United States v. New Mexico* signals a return to the principal purpose of the immunity doctrine: "forestalling 'clashing sovereignty' by preventing the States from laying demands directly on the Federal Government." [18] To resist a state's revenue power, "a private taxpayer must actually 'stand in the Government's shoes.'" [19] Such a narrow approach to intergovernmental tax immunity serves two ends. First, it comports with federalism by "giving full range to each sovereign's taxing authority." [20] Second, it reserves to Congress the authority to adjust the competing symbolic and fiscal claims of federal autonomy and state revenue needs. The Court has thus recognized and returned to the wisdom which the first edition of this treatise argued was implicit in the Court's own bewildering and apparently inconsistent precedents (except for *Kern-Limerick*): the nature of the line between permissible and impermissible taxation depends most of all upon who is assigned the task of drawing it. Congress is best suited to reconcile competing state and national claims in this sphere because it alone represents both state *and* national interests. Therefore, when Congress speaks, full effect should be given to its determinations. And when Congress is silent, a decision to make immunity turn on the legal incidence of a tax under a state's own laws

---

13. 460 U.S. at 539–40.

14. The case is therefore unlike Memphis Bank & Trust Co. v. Garner, 459 U.S. 392 (1983), where the Court struck down a Tennessee law that taxed the income from federal bonds but not comparable state bonds.

15. 460 U.S. at 541.

16. Id. at 546. See also Minneapolis Star & Tribune Co. v. Minnesota Commissioner of Revenue, 460 U.S. 575, 589 n. 12 (1983) ("The special rule prohibiting direct taxation of the Federal Government but permitting the imposition of an equivalent economic burden on the Government may not only justify the State's use of different methods of taxation, but may also force us, within limits, to compare the burdens of two different taxes").

17. 455 U.S. at 737–38.

18. Id. at 735.

19. Id. at 736.

20. Id.

avoids both the hazards inherent in ad hoc determinations, and unnecessary collisions between state law and federal instrumentalities.[21]

§ 6–33. Congressional Authorization and Ratification and Their Limits

Although Congress cannot authorize a state to violate a constitutional command designed to protect private rights against government action (such as the commands of the fourteenth amendment), and cannot authorize a state to disregard an explicit constitutional prohibition (such as the article I, § 10 provision that no state may enter into any "Treaty, Alliance, or Confederation," coin money, issue bills of credit, or take certain other designated steps), congressional consent or ratification may suffice to validate otherwise unconstitutional state action in three different settings: *first*, where the Constitution expressly makes congressional consent a prerequisite of state action, as in the provisions of article I, § 10, with respect to import and export duties, interstate compacts, and certain other topics; *second*, where the existence of a constitutional ban on state action is inferred entirely from a grant of legislative power to Congress, as in the case of the commerce clause; and *third*, where the constitutional prohibition against state intrusion is thought to follow from concerns of federalism that may properly be entrusted to Congress, as in the case of federal immunity from state taxation. Judicial analysis in three contexts—interstate compacts, commerce regulation, and taxation of federal instrumentalities—serves to illustrate the relevant principles.

Article I, § 10 declares that "[n]o State shall, without the Consent of Congress, . . . enter into any Agreement or Compact with another State . . ." The Court revealed its inclination to read that language narrowly as early as 1893, when it suggested that congressional consent is required only of compacts and agreements that affect "the political power or influence" of particular states or "encroach . . . upon the full and free exercise of federal authority."[1] That view was fully embraced by the Court in the leading modern case on compacts, *United States Steel Corp. v. Multistate Tax Commission*.[2]

In *Multistate Tax Commission*, some 21 states had adopted legislation establishing a "Multistate Tax Compact" to coordinate the taxation of businesses that generate income in several states. The legislation created a commission composed of the member states' tax administrators, and empowered it to study state tax systems, develop proposals for uniform state tax laws, adopt advisory uniform administrative regula-

---

21. In United States v. New Mexico, supra, the Court noted a final irony that reveals how attentive the Court is to congressional will in this area. In Carson v. Roane-Anderson Company, 342 U.S. 232 (1952), the Court held that Atomic Energy Commission management contracts essentially identical to the DOE contracts at issue in the New Mexico case were statutorily exempt from state taxation because of a sentence in the Atomic Energy Act that prohibited state or local taxation of AEC "activities." Congress promptly repealed that sentence. The DOE in 1982 was thus asking the Supreme Court to establish a *constitutional* immunity where Congress had expressly *eliminated* a *statutory* immunity. See 455 U.S. at 743–44.

§ 6–33

1. Virginia v. Tennessee, 148 U.S. 503, 520 (1893).

2. 434 U.S. 452 (1978).

tions, and conduct audits on behalf of member states. In rejecting a compact clause challenge, the Court concluded that the legislation, its creation of a multistate authority notwithstanding, did not enhance the political power of the compacting states in a manner that encroached upon or otherwise interfered with the just supremacy of the federal government. Although the compact clearly increased the bargaining power of member states vis-a-vis multistate corporations, the Court ruled that the relevant test was "whether the compact enhance[d] state power *quoad* the national government."[3] The Court noted that historically it had "upheld a variety of interstate agreements effected through reciprocal legislation without congressional consent,"[4] and held that the Multistate Tax Compact went little beyond such reciprocal arrangements: each member state retained complete freedom to adopt or reject the Commission's recommendations and was free to withdraw at any time; moreover, the Commission possessed no powers that the member states did not themselves possess independently.[5]

After *Multistate Tax Commission*, the Court had little trouble in unanimously upholding reciprocal, unilaterally revocable, regional bank acquisition statutes in *Northeast Bancorp, Inc. v. Bd. of Governors of the Federal Reserve System.*[6] The Massachusetts and Connecticut laws challenged there as an unauthorized compact allowed bank holding companies from other New England states to acquire banks within the two states, provided that the acquiror's home state extended reciprocal acquisition privileges. No multistate commission or other third level of authority was injected into the federal structure, no change in the political relationship of the states was effected, and no challenge was mounted to federal authority, for the Federal Reserve Board continued to regulate mergers and other aspects of the banking business.[7]

---

3. Id. at 473.

4. Id. at 469. See, e.g., Bode v. Barrett, 344 U.S. 583 (1953) (reciprocal exemptions of non-resident motorists from highway use tax require no consent); St. Louis & San Francisco Ry. Co. v. James, 161 U.S. 545 (1896) (reciprocal permission for out-of-state corporations to operate within state).

5. 434 U.S. at 473.

6. 472 U.S. 159 (1985).

7. The Court went on to assume arguendo that the reciprocal legislation constituted a compact, and still found the compact clause inapplicable. Having previously found that Congress, in passing the Douglas Amendment to the Bank Holding Company Act, intended to authorize the type of actions taken by Massachusetts and Connecticut, the Court stated that the compact clause did not come into play because the "challenged state statutes *which comply with that Act* cannot possibly infringe federal supremacy." 472 U.S. at 176 (emphasis added). Thus, the import of congressional consent was not that the compact clause had not been violated, but that the clause was wholly inapplicable. Although the Court did not emphasize this point, there is obviously an incentive for supporters of a state agreement to conclude that the compact clause is inapplicable, since the consequence of finding that there is no violation (due to congressional consent) is that the states' agreement becomes federal law. This subtle aspect of the Northeast Bancorp opinion may be a harbinger of future efforts to cut back on the notion that prior congressional consent necessarily transforms reciprocal state legislation into federal law. Justice Rehnquist, the author of the unanimous opinion in Northeast Bancorp, had warned in his earlier dissent in Cuyler v. Adams, 449 U.S. 433, 454 (1980), discussed infra, that "the Court's opinion threatens to become a judicial Midas meandering through the state statute books, turning everything it touches into federal law."

If *Multistate Tax Commission* limited the range of interstate agreements that Congress *must* authorize, *Cuyler v. Adams* [8] expanded the range of agreements that Congress *may* authorize. *Cuyler* involved the procedures accorded a Pennsylvania state prisoner transferred to New Jersey pursuant to the Interstate Agreement on Detainers, reciprocal legislation adopted by both states. In ruling on the prisoner's challenge, the Court first had to determine whether the Detainer Agreement was a formal "compact" within the meaning of the clause—hence federal law requiring federal judicial interpretation [9]—or mere reciprocal legislation to which Congress may have given its consent in advance, albeit unnecessarily.

The Court ruled that the *Multistate Tax Commission* test did not apply: "where Congress has authorized the states to enter into a cooperative agreement, and where the subject matter is an appropriate subject for congressional legislation, the consent of Congress transforms the states' agreement into federal law under the compact clause." [10] Because crime control was an appropriate subject for federal legislation, it was sufficient for the Court that, 22 years before, Congress had given blanket approval to all interstate crime prevention agreements in the Crime Control Act of 1934.

Cuyler underscores the Court's belief that federal supremacy is the core of the compact clause. The reason for the requirement that compacts be approved by Congress—rather than solely by the states involved—is, in Justice Story's words, "to check any infringement on the rights of the national government." [11] There can be little concern that those rights have been infringed if Congress has already given its blessing to an interstate compact. Therefore, the probability that the Detainer Agreement fell well below the threshold of impact on the federal system set forth in *Multistate Tax Commission* simply did not interest the *Cuyler* majority. Since the "requirement that Congress approve a compact is to obtain its political judgment," [12] the Court concluded that the Detainer Agreement was to be treated as a compact pursuant to the compact clause because Congress wished it, whether or not the Constitution demanded it. *Cuyler* thus stands for the proposition that, if Congress enacts some kind of consent legislation, the Court will defer to Congress' political judgment that the compact is good for the nation and simply ignore the *Multistate Tax Commission* test. But if Congress has been silent or has actively disapproved, the Court will then examine the challenged agreement on its own terms, in accord with the Court's own precedents, to determine whether the compact clause (or perhaps the commerce clause) makes the absence of congressional authorization or approval fatal.

Congressional consent, when required, may be inferred from a statute or pattern of enactments,[13] may take the form of prior authori-

---

8. 449 U.S. 433 (1981).

9. 449 U.S. at 438 & n. 7.

10. Id. at 440.

11. J. Story, Commentaries on the Constitution ¶1403 (1833). See *Multistate Tax Commission*, 434 U.S. at 473 (the "test is whether [a compact] enhances state power *quoad* the national government").

12. 449 U.S. at 441 n. 8.

13. See, e.g., Virginia v. Tennessee, 148 U.S. 503, 521 (1893); Green v. Biddle, 21 U.S. (8 Wheat.) 1, 85–86 (1823).

zation as well as that of subsequent approval,[14] and may be conditioned on state acceptance of congressionally mandated modifications.[15] Whether or not the United States chooses to become one of the compacting parties,[16] a valid compact is binding on the citizens of the signatory states,[17] may be enforced by federal statute,[18] and itself operates as federal law in the sense that construction of its terms is a federal question for purposes of Supreme Court review of a state court decision [19] and in the further sense that signatory states cannot plead state law, even state constitutional law, as a defense to compliance with the compact's terms as construed by the Supreme Court.[20] But a multistate commission established by an authorized compact should not necessarily be considered a federal agency for the purposes of such constitutional provisions as the appointments clause.[21]

A second example is congressional ratification of state commerce regulation. Although the seminal decision in *Cooley v. Board of Port Wardens* [22] is most accurately read as having implied that Congress lacks power to legitimate what would otherwise be an invalid state intrusion upon interstate commerce, that position was abandoned in dictum in *Leisy v. Hardin* [23] and in any event could hardly have been reconciled with the prevalent theory that state intrusions upon commerce can be judicially invalidated only *because* of Congress' paramount and plenary authority over the activities the state is said to have improperly affected.[24] By 1945, the Supreme Court was thus able to describe as "undoubted" the power of Congress "to redefine the distribution of power over interstate commerce" so as to "permit the states

---

14. See, e.g., Cuyler v. Adams, 449 U.S. 433 (1981).

15. See, e.g., Petty v. Tennessee-Missouri Bridge Comm., 359 U.S. 275 (1959).

16. See Grad, "Federal-State Compact: A New Experiment in Co-operative Federalism," 63 Colum.L.Rev. 825 (1963).

17. See Poole v. Fleeger's Lessee, 36 U.S. (11 Pet.) 185, 209 (1837); Hinderlider v. La Plata Co., 304 U.S. 92, 104, 106 (1938).

18. See Virginia v. West Virginia, 246 U.S. 565, 601 (1918).

19. See Delaware River Joint Toll Bridge Commission v. Colburn, 310 U.S. 419 (1940).

20. See West Virginia ex. rel. Dyer v. Sims, 341 U.S. 22 (1951). Insofar as Justice Frankfurter's majority opinion suggests federal power to revise the state court's interpretation of its own constitution, cf. id. at 33–34 (Reed, J., concurring), it seems plainly wrong; the outcome of the decision, binding West Virginia to its compact, is amply supported by the supremacy clause of article VI.

21. See Seattle Master Builders Ass'n v. Pacific Northwest Power Planning Council, 786 F.2d 1359 (9th Cir.1986) (officers of interstate council may be appointed by state governors, rather than pursuant to article II, § 2, cl. 2, because a compact agency's officers are not "officers of the United States"). Cf. Melcher v. Federal Open Market Comm., 644 F.Supp. 510 (D.D.C.1986) (private persons appointed by directors of federal reserve banks, rather than pursuant to art. II, § 2, cl. 2, may serve on a Federal Reserve committee and may engage in open market trading of government securities as element of national monetary policy).

22. 53 U.S. 299 (1851). See § 6–4, supra.

23. 135 U.S. 100, 108, 109–10 (1890). Congress responded to Leisy's invitation by passing a statute authorizing precisely the state liquor regulations Leisy had held unconstitutional, and the Court promptly upheld the statute. In re Rahrer, 140 U.S. 545 (1891). Accord, Whitfield v. Ohio, 297 U.S. 431 (1936).

24. To the extent that state intrusion is deemed offensive because of a constitutionally mandated allocation of responsibility independent of Congress' wishes, however, congressional ratification would amount to an impermissible delegation of federal authority. See § 5–17, supra.

to regulate the commerce in a manner which would not otherwise be permissible. . . ."[25]

Shortly after the Supreme Court had held in 1944 that the Sherman Anti-Trust Act of 1890 applied to interstate insurance business as a form of "commerce," [26] Congress passed the McCarran Act, which not only deferred and limited the applicability of federal antitrust laws to the insurance business but also provided that "silence on the part of Congress shall not be construed to impose any barrier to the regulation or taxation of such business by the several States." In *Prudential Insurance Co. v. Benjamin*,[27] the McCarran Act was held to have congressionally ratified a South Carolina tax on out-of-state insurance companies doing business within that state, even though the tax was not matched by any comparable tax on local insurance companies and therefore discriminated against interstate commerce in a manner that would not have survived judicial scrutiny in the absence of such congressional action.[28]

The principle of *Prudential v. Benjamin* applies only to the commerce clause, and cannot properly be extended to a conclusion that Congress has limitless power to authorize state discrimination against out-of-state citizens. The equal protection clause still imposes limits on state action, and nothing in the fourteenth amendment suggests that Congress has authority to deprive people of constitutional protection against discrimination by state government.[29] Properly understood, the privileges and immunities clause of article IV, § 2, likewise confers a personal right against state action unjustifiably discriminating against out-of-staters, whether or not such discrimination has purportedly been sanctioned by Congress.[30]

Congressional authorization of state regulation otherwise impermissible under the commerce clause comes in different degrees, and the Court will examine the federal legislation carefully before upholding challenged state laws. The McCarran Act has been read as tantamount to congressional abdication to the states of the field of insurance regulation.[31] Therefore, in *Western & Southern Life Insurance Co. v.*

---

25. Southern Pacific Co. v. Arizona, 325 U.S. 761, 769 (1945) (dictum).

26. United States v. South-Eastern Underwriters Association, 322 U.S. 533 (1944).

27. 328 U.S. 408 (1946).

28. See, e.g., Welton v. Missouri, 91 U.S. 275 (1876), discussed in § 6–17, supra.

29. Section 5 of the fourteenth amendment "grants Congress no power to restrict, abrogate, or dilute these guarantees." Katzenbach v. Morgan, 384 U.S. 641, 651 n. 10 (1966). And while the Supreme Court "give[s] deference to congressional decisions and classifications, neither Congress nor a State can validate a law that denies the rights guaranteed by the fourteenth amendment." Mississippi University for Women v. Hogan, 458 U.S. 718, 732–33 (1982).

30. See §§ 6–34 and 6–35, infra. But see White v. Mass. Council of Constr. Employers, 460 U.S. 204, 215 n. 1 (1983) (Blackmun, J., concurring in part and dissenting in part) (indicating that the question is still open whether Congress can authorize what would otherwise be a violation of the privileges and immunities clause); Shapiro v. Thompson, 394 U.S. 618, 666 (1969) (Harlan, J., dissenting) (arguing that it "appears settled" that the privileges and immunities clause does not limit federal power).

31. The Court will not infer such sweeping abdication. In Sporhase v. Nebraska, 458 U.S. 941 (1982), the Court reviewed groundwater legislation enacted by Nebraska that barred groundwater exports unless the state receiving the water had reciprocal laws authorizing the export of

State Board of Equalization,[32] the Court had little difficulty in upholding a California law that inflicted a retaliatory tax on foreign insurance companies whose home states imposed higher taxes on California insurers. That is, if Ohio imposed a 3% premium tax on all insurance policies issued in Ohio, including those issued by companies incorporated in California, while California charged only a 2% premium tax, California would hit all policies issued by Ohio companies with a 1% premium surtax in order to induce those insurers to persuade the Ohio legislature to lower its tax rate, at least as applied to California insurance companies.[33] The Court upheld the resulting interstate tariff war over both commerce clause and equal protection challenges, declaring that there "can be no doubt that the promotion of domestic industry by deterring barriers to interstate business is a legitimate state purpose." [34]

Not all congressional authorizations of state regulation are as sweeping as the McCarran Act. In *Northeast Bancorp, Inc. v. Bd. of Governors*,[35] the Court unanimously upheld state bank acquisition statutes enacted by several New England states that discriminated against bank holding companies from outside a six-state region.[36] The Justices

water to Nebraska. It was clear that Congress had not specifically approved this arrangement, nor had it previously authorized states to erect such barriers to trade with non-reciprocating states. Therefore, Nebraska's only hope was to convince the Court that Congress had abdicated control over water rights to the states. But the Court held that routine congressional approval of interstate water compacts and a pattern of deference to the states evidenced by 37 separate pieces of federal water legislation did not mean that the field had been expressly abandoned to the states. Id. at 959–60. The case is discussed further in § 6–10, supra.

32. 451 U.S. 648 (1981).

33. Id. at 650–51. His rhetoric carried aloft by the drama of the contemporaneous Iran hostage crisis, see Dames & Moore v. Regan, 453 U.S. 654 (1981), discussed in § 9–7, infra, Justice Stevens characterized the California law as yet another deplorable example of the practice of "holding economic hostages to coerce another sovereign to change its policies." 451 U.S. at 674 (Stevens, J., dissenting).

34. Id. at 671. In Metropolitan Life Insurance Co. v. Ward, 470 U.S. 869 (1985), the Court ruled 5–4 that a state law imposing a higher gross premiums tax on out-of-state insurers than on in-state insurance companies would violate the equal protection clause if it were not related to a legitimate state interest, and remanded for development of the record. Although the Court had upheld California's promotion of domestic insurance companies by levying a tax that discriminated against non-resident

competitors, see Western & Southern, the narrow majority in Metropolitan Life opined that the "promotion of domestic business within a state, by discriminating against foreign corporations that wish to compete by doing business there, is not a legitimate state purpose." 470 U.S. at 880. See Chapter 16, infra. A few weeks later, the Court unanimously upheld state legislation that discriminated against bank holding companies on the basis of their state residence; the Court deemed promotion of smaller, responsive, locally-oriented banks to be a legitimate state goal. Northeast Bancorp, Inc. v. Bd. of Governors, 472 U.S. 159, 172–73 (1985).

Metropolitan Life, which is criticized in Cohen, "Federalism in Equality Clothing: A Comment on Metropolitan Life Ins. Co. v. Ward," 38 Stan.L.Rev. 1 (1985), is best seen as an aberration. Once Congress has given the states free reign to regulate a particular field unconstrained by commerce clause objections, there would seem to be little merit in applying the equal protection clause to re-impose the very same policies against economic protectionism that Congress swept aside when it legislatively suspended the dormant commerce clause. See Metropolitan Life, 470 U.S. at 898–900, 105 S.Ct. at 1693 (O'Connor, J., dissenting); Northeast Bancorp, 472 U.S. at 179–80 (O'Connor, J., concurring).

35. 472 U.S. 159 (1985).

36. The author argued in the Supreme Court on behalf of the New England banks, defending the state statutes.

read the Bank Holding Company Act of 1956 as itself balkanizing banking along state lines, while authorizing the individual states to lift the general federal barrier to interstate bank acquisitions to the extent that they saw fit. The power to exclude out-of-state holding companies altogether was understood in *Northeast Bancorp* to encompass the power to admit only holding companies from reciprocating New England states, thereby providing the congressional authorization without which the state statutes would have violated the commerce clause.[37] Yet in *Lewis v. BT Investment Managers, Inc.*,[38] the Court had deployed the commerce clause to strike down a Florida law that prohibited out-of-state banking institutions from owning or controlling a Florida investment advisory business. The statute was overtly parochial, in that it prevented foreign enterprises from competing in local markets, and hence implicated the dormant commerce clause. The Court unanimously opined that the freedom granted to the states by the Bank Holding Company Act to allow interstate acquisitions in whole or in part did not include the freedom to discriminate between local and foreign holding companies with respect to *other* areas of bank regulation, or the freedom to use that power as a lever to induce out-of-state holding companies, as a condition to entry to the Florida market, to accept extraneous regulation by the state.[39]

Finally, as §§ 6–30 and 6–31 indicated, Congress may ratify what would otherwise be struck down as an invalid state tax on the United States, its instrumentalities, or its property. To suppose that this is so simply because Congress has the power of the purse and could directly shift federal resources to the states if it wished would be a mistake, since it is not the fiscal burden of a state tax but its legal incidence that triggers immunity in the absence of congressional consent.[40] Thus the power of Congress to consent to an otherwise invalid state action in this area and others like it must be understood as reflecting a judgment that, although the underlying limit on state action rests on deeper values and concerns than a mere negative inference from a grant of congressional power, Congress can safely be assumed to have given those values and concerns adequate weight in deciding to override the underlying limit.[41]

But that judgment of confidence in Congress must itself be tempered by three kinds of reservations: First, Congress must not have the final word in every instance on the degree to which national responsibilities may be delegated to the states.[42] Second, the courts rather than Congress must be the arbiters of whether a particular ratification

---

37. Although not the compact clause. See note 7, supra.

38. 447 U.S. 27 (1980).

39. For an anticipatory defense of the Northeast Bancorp decision in the face of BT Investment Managers, by analogy to the "market participant" theory discussed in § 6–11, supra, see L. Tribe, Constitutional Choices 138–48 (1985).

40. See § 6–31, supra.

41. See § 6–32, supra.

42. Just as article I, § 10 distinguishes between state actions (such as import levies) that require congressional consent and state actions (such as entering into foreign alliances) that are absolutely forbidden, so too it seems clear that Congress could not ratify a state's intrusion into foreign affairs, for example. Cf. Zschernig v. Miller, 389 U.S. 429, 443 (1968) (Stewart, J., concurring). Limits on congressional delegation are considered in § 5–17, supra.

impermissibly intrudes upon the constitutional responsibilities of the Executive Branch.[43] And third, insofar as federalism-based limits on state action also affirm underlying personal rights against government generally, Congress should be no more able to authorize state invasion of such rights than either Congress or a state is able independently to invade them.[44]

§ 6–34. The Privileges and Immunities of State Citizenship: The Classic Doctrine

Article IV, § 2 builds a bridge between federalism and personal rights by providing that "[the] Citizens of each State shall be entitled to all the Privileges and Immunities of Citizens in the several States." [1] The modern understanding of this interstate privileges and immunities clause, an understanding that sets the clause on a course closely parallel to that of the commerce clause, was announced by the Supreme Court in *Toomer v. Witsell*: [2] "The primary purpose of this clause . . . was to help fuse into one nation a collection of independent, sovereign states. It was designed to insure to a citizen of State A who ventures into State B the same privileges which the citizens of State B enjoy." There has been little debate about this basic purpose. Courts and commentators from the beginning have agreed that the clause facilitates national unification by promising some measure of federal protection for citizens who venture beyond the borders of their own state.[3] "Indeed, without some provision of this kind removing from the citizens of each state the disabilities of alienage in the other States . . . the Republic would have constituted little more than a league of States." [4]

---

43. Cf. Myers v. United States, 272 U.S. 52 (1926), discussed in § 4–10, supra. In making that judgment, however, courts must be mindful of the constitutional (if not political) dominance ordinarily accorded congressional power when it clashes with that of the executive.

44. See, e.g., Shapiro v. Thompson, 394 U.S. 618, 629–31, 641–42 (1969) (one-year waiting period for new residents seeking welfare infringes personal right to travel interstate and can be saved neither by congressional authorization nor, in the case of the District of Columbia, by direct congressional enactment); Crandall v. Nevada, 73 U.S. (6 Wall.) 35, 43–44 (1868) (state tax on privilege of leaving state violates rights of national government and "correlative rights" of citizens in a national polity).

§ 6–34

1. The "privileges or immunities" of *national* citizenship are discussed in Chapter 7, infra. Article IV, § 2, limits only *state* power. On the relationship between state deprivation of privileges secured by article IV, § 2, and congressional authorization, see § 6–33, supra, notes 29–30.

2. 334 U.S. 385, 395 (1948).

3. Article IV, § 2, is a shortened version of the privileges and immunities clause of article IV of the Articles of Confederation. Persuaded that article IV, § 2 of the proposed constitution was "formed exactly upon the principles of the 4th article of the present Confederation . . .", 3 M. Farrand, Records of the Federal Convention of 1787 at 112 (1911), the Constitutional Convention adopted the privileges and immunities clause with little discussion. 2 id., at 173, 187, 443. Alexander Hamilton later asserted that the policy expressed in the privileges and immunities clause was "the basis of the Union." The Federalist No. 80 at 575 (Modern Lib. Ed., 1937).

4. Paul v. Virginia, 75 U.S. (8 Wall.) 168, 180 (1869). The commerce clause, of course, could have served as a unifying and centralizing force of a comparable sort— and indeed has served something like that function. See, e.g., Baldwin v. Seelig, 294 U.S. 511, 522–23 (1935), discussed in § 6–6, supra. But it would have been more difficult for the commerce clause to serve as a charter of personal rights secure against *all* governmental action.

But as to the specific content of national protection, no consensus was forged until the post-Civil War years.

In *Corfield v. Coryell*,[5] the first major case decided under article IV, § 2, Justice Bushrod Washington concluded that the privileges and immunities clause encompassed those privileges "which are in their very nature, fundamental; which belong, of right, to the citizens of all free governments." Among these fundamental rights he included "the right of a citizen of one state to pass through or reside in any other state, for purposes of trade . . . or otherwise; to claim the benefit of the writ of habeas corpus; to institute and maintain actions of any kind in the courts of the state; to take, hold, and dispose of property; and an exemption from higher taxes or impositions than are paid by the other citizens of the state." [6]

Justice Washington chose to frame only one right in terms of unequal treatment. The remainder he took to be absolute rights, "the enjoyment of [which] by the citizens of each state, in every other state, was manifestly calculated. . . ." [7] The natural rights of state citizens were clothed, in his view, with national protection against the desires of the foreign states through which they passed. Behind the 1823 *Corfield* opinion lay the nineteenth century controversy over the status of "natural rights" in constitutional litigation. Some judges had supposed an inherent limitation on state and federal legislation that compelled courts to strike down any law "contrary to the first great principles of the social compact." [8] They were the proponents of the natural rights doctrine which, without specific constitutional moorings, posited "certain vital principles in our free republican governments, which will determine and overrule an apparent abuse of legislative powers." [9]

Corfield can be understood as an attempt to import the natural rights doctrine into the Constitution by way of the privileges and immunities clause of article IV. By attaching the fundamental rights of state citizenship to the privileges and immunities clause, Justice Washington would have created federal judicial protection against state encroachment upon the "natural rights" of citizens. On its face, his decision held only that states must accord the fundamental, "natural" rights of state citizenship to non-residents. But broader implications were irresistible: for a state to withhold from its own citizens the personal and property rights that it extended, whether under constitutional compulsion or otherwise, to citizens of other states would have been anomalous in the extreme. Furthermore, the courts need only take a small step beyond *Corfield* to require similar treatment of *all* state citizens in every state, establishing in effect a body of uniform national rights protected from state intrusion by the Federal Government.

5. 6 Fed.Cas. 546, 551–52 (No. 3230) (C.C.E.D.Pa.1823) (on circuit) (non-citizens have no right to gather shellfish in New Jersey waters).

6. Id. at 552.

7. Id.

8. Calder v. Bull, 3 U.S. (3 Dall.) 386, 388 (1798) (Chase, J.), discussed further in § 8–1, infra.

9. 3 U.S. at 388.

But the Supreme Court never acceded to the natural rights doctrine that informed *Corfield*.[10] And in a series of cases beginning with *Paul v. Virginia* [11] and *Downham v. Alexandria*,[12] the Court rejected the natural rights theory of the privileges and immunities clause entirely, concluding in the *Slaughter-House Cases* [13] that article IV "did not create those rights, which it called privileges and immunities of citizens of the States. It threw around them in that clause . . . no security for the citizen of the State in which they were claimed." [14] In other words, the privileges and immunities clause of article IV was not a source of substantive federal protection for natural rights. Rather, the object of the clause was found to be solely that of "relieving state citizens of the disabilities of alienage in other States and of inhibiting discriminatory legislation against them by other States." [15] To serve this more limited objective, the Court need not define a set of fundamental rights that states must grant to citizens of other states; it need only declare that "whatever . . . rights [each state] grants . . . to [its] own citizens . . . shall be the measure of the rights of citizens of other states within [that state's] jurisdiction." [16] Thus a state might withhold what might be deemed fundamental rights from citizens of other states so long as it withheld the same rights from its own citizens; and nonfundamental rights might be extended to a state's own citizens without parity of treatment for outsiders. State laws that failed both tests were struck down: only they transgressed the right to nondiscriminatory treatment of fundamental rights of state citizenship.

Although this interpretation of the privileges and immunities clause necessitated a determination of which rights were fundamental to state citizenship and which were not, the Supreme Court refused to offer a general definition, believing it "safer, and more in accordance with the duty of a judicial tribunal, to leave [the matter] to be determined, in each case, upon a view of the particular rights asserted and denied therein." [17] So the lower federal courts were left to hammer out the categories of protected and unprotected rights over the course of litigation. In performing that function, they relied heavily on the illustrations in *Corfield v. Coryell*. As a result, the natural rights doctrine continued to play a part, albeit indirect, in article IV adjudication.[18]

---

10. A number of individual Supreme Court Justices did embrace the natural rights theory of the privileges and immunities clause in dissenting opinions, however. See, e.g., Justice Curtis, dissenting in Dred Scott v. Sandford, 60 U.S. (19 How.) 393, 580 (1857), and Justice Bradley, dissenting in the Slaughter-House Cases, 83 U.S. (16 Wall.) 36, 117, 118 (1873).

11. 75 U.S. (8 Wall.) 168 (1869).

12. 77 U.S. (10 Wall.) 173 (1870).

13. 83 U.S. (16 Wall.) 36 (1873), discussed in §§ 7–2, 8–1, infra.

14. 83 U.S. at 77.

15. Paul v. Virginia, 75 U.S. (8 Wall.) 168, 180 (1869).

16. Slaughter-House Cases, 83 U.S. (16 Wall.) 36, 77 (1873).

17. Conner v. Elliot, 59 U.S. (18 How.) 591, 593 (1856). For a discussion of what were and were not fundamental rights of state citizenship under the traditional interpretation of privileges and immunities, see Meyers, "The Privileges and Immunities of Citizens in the Several States", 1 Mich.L.Rev. 286, 364 (1902).

18. Compare the closely analogous role played by "fundamental rights" in triggering equal protection strict scrutiny. See §§ 16–7 to 16–12, infra.

The natural rights theory of *Corfield* had been abandoned by the mid-1870's but its holding lived on in *McCready v. Virginia*.[19] In that case, a Virginia law effectively prohibited citizens of other states from oyster farming in the Ware River. Writing for the Court, Chief Justice Waite upheld the discrimination: "[T]he right which the people of the State . . . acquire [in common property] comes not from citizenship alone but from citizenship and property combined. . . .   The right thus granted is not a privilege or immunity of general but of special citizenship; it does not belong of right to the citizens of all free governments. . . ."[20] Because farming oysters was not a fundamental right that attached to state citizenship, the privileges and immunities clause did not guarantee its equal availability.

The rigid application of the standards outlined here would have struck down all discriminatory state legislation that touched fundamental rights of state citizenship. But sensitive to the special problems that non-residents presented for state policies, the Supreme Court, in the late nineteenth and early twentieth centuries, carved out exceptions for discriminations that "could not reasonably be characterized as hostile to the rights of citizens of other states."[21] The clearest cases presented procedural "discriminations" against nonresidents, in the form of rules requiring them to appoint state officials as agents for service of process before being permitted to drive[22] or conduct business[23] in the state. In each case, the Supreme Court held that the discrimination was more apparent than real since the statutes simply tended to put non-residents "on the same footing as residents" in amenability to process for actions arising within the state.

But the criteria for judging reasonableness remained vague. Laws forbidding non-residents from selling insurance[24] and restricting their access to state courts[25] passed as reasonable regulations on the tenuous ground that they discriminated against non-residents rather than against citizens of other states.[26] The reasonableness exception thus

---

19. 94 U.S. (4 Otto) 391 (1876).

20. Id. at 396. The common property doctrine subsequently spread to commerce clause litigation. See, e.g., Geer v. Connecticut, 161 U.S. 519 (1896); Hudson County Water Co. v. McCarter, 209 U.S. 349 (1908), discussed in § 6–9, supra.

21. Blake v. McClung, 172 U.S. 239, 256 (1898).

22. Kane v. New Jersey, 242 U.S. 160 (1916); Hess v. Pawloski, 274 U.S. 352 (1927).

23. Doherty & Co. v. Goodman, 294 U.S. 623 (1935).

24. La Tourette v. McMaster, 248 U.S. 465 (1919).

25. Douglas v. New Haven R.R., 279 U.S. 377 (1929).

26. The Court had seen through this guise in other cases. Blake v. McClung,

172 U.S. 239 (1898); Travis v. Yale & Towne Mfg. Co., 252 U.S. 60 (1920). A different justification for upholding a state statute that restricted the rights of non-residents to sue in the state's courts was provided in Canadian Northern Ry. v. Eggen, 252 U.S. 553 (1920). The statute in question barred by lapse of a designated period of time actions arising outside of the state unless the plaintiff was a citizen of the state. The Court simply ignored the discrimination and held that "a man cannot be said to be denied . . . . the privilege of resorting to courts to enforce his rights when he is given free access to them for a length of time *reasonably sufficient* to enable an ordinarily diligent man to institute proceedings for their protection." Id. at 562 (emphasis added). Compare the shift from equal to minimal protection in poverty cases in §§ 16–51 to 16–59, infra.

tempered the otherwise rigid impact of the privileges and immunities clause but did so in an unpredictable and seemingly arbitrary manner.[27]

§ 6-35. Privileges and Immunities of State Citizenship: The Modern Interpretation

The equal right to fish reached the Supreme Court for the third time in *Toomer v. Witsell*.[1] A South Carolina law limited commercial access to migratory shrimp in the three-mile maritime belt off the state's coast by imposing a license fee of $25 for each shrimp boat owned by a resident, but $2500 for each such boat owned by a nonresident. South Carolina attempted to justify the discrimination as reasonable, claiming that it furthered the state's interest in conserving its supply of shrimp and paid for the additional conservation expenses attributable to non-taxpaying shrimpers. The state also pleaded the common property doctrine of *McCready v. Virginia*.[2] From the collision of a discriminatory state tax, the common property doctrine, and the reasonableness exception emerged the modern interpretation of the privileges and immunities clause of article IV, § 2. Chief Justice Vinson, speaking for the Court, rejected the "well-settled"[3] rule of *McCready*. The Court initially distinguished the *McCready* case on two grounds: shrimp swimming past a state's shore could not easily be called state property;[4] and while a state may regulate activity off its shore, a recent Supreme Court decision had held that no state actually *owned* off-shore waters.[5] More importantly, the *Toomer* Court proclaimed "the whole ownership theory [to be] but a fiction expressive . . . of the importance [of recognizing each state's] power to preserve and regulate the exploitation of an important resource."[6] Thus South Carolina would be allowed to discriminate against non-residents only so far as necessary to execute the state's responsibility to safeguard important natural resources. That holding, in turn, subsumed the whole common property doctrine under a second exception to the rule of nondiscrimination. In place of the traditional interpretation of the privileges and immunities clause of article IV, the *Toomer* Court enunciated the substantial reason test:[7] "Like many other Constitutional provisions, the Privileges and Immunities Clause is not absolute . . . [I]t does not preclude disparity of treatment in the many situations where there are perfectly valid independent reasons for it . . . [But] it does bar discrimination against citizens of other States

27. For a discussion of other doctrinal excuses for allowing "reasonable" discriminations, see Note, "The Equal Privileges and Immunities Clause of the Federal Constitution," 28 Colum.L.Rev. 347 (1928).

§ 6-35

1. 334 U.S. 385 (1948). Another aspect of Toomer is discussed in § 6-9, supra.

2. 94 U.S. (4 Otto) 391 (1876), discussed in § 6-34, supra.

3. Described as such in Note, "The Equal Privileges and Immunities Clause of the Federal Constitution," 28 Colum.L.Rev. 347 n. 9 (1928).

4. The Court relied on Justice Holmes' statement in Missouri v. Holland, 252 U.S. 416, 434 (1920): "To put the claim of the State upon title is to lean upon a slender reed. Wild birds are not in the possession of anyone; and possession is the beginning of ownership."

5. United States v. California, 332 U.S. 19 (1947).

6. 334 U.S. at 402.

7. Id. at 396.

where there is *no substantial reason for the discrimination beyond the mere fact that they are citizens of other States.*"

In the first application of the substantial reason test, the Supreme Court struck down the South Carolina licensing act. The state's interests in conserving shrimp and paying the costs of doing so were insufficient because the state failed to establish (1) a sufficiently *unique* link between the interests served and the discrimination practiced;[8] (2) a sufficiently *demonstrated* link between the legitimate interests served and the discrimination practiced;[9] and (3) the actual impracticality of apparent and *less restrictive alternatives.*[10] Later doctrine, both under the commerce clause and under the equal protection clause, was to be much influenced by this 1948 formulation. Its "substantial reason" test permits disparate treatment of non-residents, but only where the very fact of their non-residence demonstrably creates problems for legitimate state objectives that cannot be remedied in less discriminatory ways.

Toomer v. Witsell dramatically shifted the focus of review under the privileges and immunities clause from categorizing fundamental rights of state citizenship to analyzing state justifications for maintaining the challenged discriminatory burdens. A flexible approach that seeks to allow discrimination but only where necessary was substituted for the rigidity inherent in a test that cast down any discrimination once found to diminish a fundamental right of state citizenship. In addition, the *Toomer* standard explicity isolated the factors involved in a privileges and immunities clause judgment of reasonableness, factors previously vague and ad hoc.

In spite of this shift in focus, the fundamental rights approach has not been purged from privileges and immunities clause analysis. In *Toomer* itself the Court took time to point out that the right in question, pursuing a business on equal terms with state residents, was fundamental.[11] In *Doe v. Bolton,*[12] which struck down Georgia's residency requirement for those seeking abortions in-state, the Court appeared to be adding to the panoply of protected privileges when it relied on *Toomer* to hold that, if article IV, § 2 "protects persons who enter other States to ply their trade, so must it protect persons who enter Georgia seeking the medical services that are available there."[13] And

8. "[T]he purpose of the clause . . . is to outlaw classifications based on . . . non-citizenship unless there is something to indicate that non-citizens constitute a peculiar source of the evil at which the statute is aimed." Id. at 398.

9. "Nothing in the record indicates that non-residents use larger boats or different fishing methods than residents, or that any substantial amount of the State's general funds is devoted to shrimp conservation." Id.

10. "The State is not without power . . . to restrict the type of equipment used . . . to graduate license fees according to the size of the boat, or even to

charge non-residents a different fee which would merely compensate the State for any added enforcement burden . . . or for any conservation expenditure which only residents pay." Id. at 398–99. It should be noted that neither in Toomer nor in any subsequent case has the Court treated requirements of bona fide residency as burdens on interstate travel: only *durational* residency requirements have been so treated. See §§ 7–4, 16–8, infra.

11. 334 U.S. at 394.

12. 410 U.S. 179 (1973).

13. Id. at 200.

Corfield v. Coryell [14] was invoked in *Austin v. New Hampshire* [15] to invalidate a state commuter income tax which fell on the New Hampshire-derived income of non-residents while exempting the income residents earned within the state: among the "fundamental" privileges is an "exemption from higher taxes or impositions than are paid by the other citizens of the state." [16] Finally, *Baldwin v. Montana Fish and Game Commission* [17] upheld the practice of charging non-residents more than residents for an elk-hunting license on the ground that the privileges and immunities clause protects only "basic and essential activities." [18] The Court declined to apply the substantial reason test to Montana's blatantly discriminatory policy because big-game hunting is mere recreation: out-of-state sportsmen therefore have no "fundamental" right to shoot Montana elk. [19]

These invocations of "fundamental" rights are in reality echoes, rather than true incarnations, of the 19th-century natural rights notions that animated Justice Washington's opinion in *Corfield*. The *Toomer* Court may have used the term "fundamental," but it was the smallest of rhetorical tails on a body of new and refreshingly practical privileges and immunities analysis: the substantial reason test. Nor does the offhand way in which *Bolton* added "medical services"—*not* just abortion—to the list of protected privileges, without any use of the label "fundamental," suggest that such characterizations were much on the Court's mind. A closer reading of *Austin* and *Baldwin* indicates that their reliance on Justice Washington's opinion in *Corfield* was more a matter of convenience than of adherence to outdated doctrine. The privilege vindicated by *Austin*—the outsider's privilege against paying taxes higher than those required of locals—is the only right that *Corfield* framed in terms of *discriminatory* treatment. *Austin's* result is perfectly compatible with the modern approach inaugurated by *Toomer v. Witsell. Baldwin* is a more difficult case, but it, too, must be seen to some extent as a product of the fact, often noted by the Court, [20] that the relative dearth of precedents on the privileges and immunities clause leaves the Justices with fewer references when they sit down to draft their opinions. *Baldwin's* facts—a state acting as guardian for its citizens in preserving the wildlife that sovereigns were once thought to "own"—provided a setting in which it was particularly easy to slip back into 19th-century rubrics and rationales. [21]

Although the dissent in *Baldwin* may have overstated the degree of retrograde motion represented by the majority's resort to the vestigal

14. 6 Fed.Cas. 546 (No. 3230) (C.C.E.D. Pa.1823).

15. 420 U.S. 656 (1975).

16. 420 U.S. at 661, citing 6 Fed.Cas. at 552.

17. 436 U.S. 371 (1978).

18. Id. at 387.

19. Id. at 388.

20. See, e.g., Baldwin, 436 U.S. at 379 (Blackmun, J., for the Court) (the "Clause is not one the contours of which have been precisely shaped by the process and wear of constant litigation and judicial interpretation"); id. at 395 (Brennan, J., dissenting) ("the Clause has not often been the subject of litigation before this Court").

21. The majority in Baldwin conceded that "title" to wild animals was " 'no more than a 19th-century legal fiction,' " 436 U.S. at 386, but reviewed the old cases nevertheless and said that state stewardship of natural resources remains an important consideration. Id. at 384–86. See § 6–10, supra.

rhetoric of fundamental rights,[22] there can be little doubt that the dissent's misgivings about the majority's unfortunate choice of language were justified. For while the Court had never expressly repudiated the fundamental rights limitation on privileges and immunities analysis, that view played no substantial part in any of the Court's opinions from *Toomer v. Witsell* onward. By restoring it to a place of prominence, the Court payed homage to a doctrinal anachronism.[23]

What is most curious about the *Baldwin* decision is that the Court created for itself much the same problem that it sought to avoid in equal protection jurisprudence in *San Antonio Independent School District v. Rodriguez*:[24] the creation of autonomous catalogues of fundamental rights. This is not to say that the list of fundamental privileges and immunities under article IV is co-extensive with the very limited list of fundamental interests recognized by equal protection doctrine. Indeed, if it took a fundamental equal protection interest to trigger article IV, § 2, the privileges and immunities clause would be superfluous. As the *Baldwin* Court itself recognized, the equal protection clause guards the interests of the class of non-residents in any given state; the presence of a fundamental equal protection interest would therefore activate strict scrutiny independent of the privileges and immunities clause.[25] On the other hand, the catalogue of fundamental privileges includes interests—such as the opportunity to work [26]—which are not considered fundamental in equal protection doctrine.[27] The prospect that true resurrection of the *Corfield* approach would require the Court to define a wholly separate category of fundamental rights makes *Baldwin* all the more puzzling.

An understanding of what may really have been going on in *Baldwin* can be obtained by comparison with the Court's application of the privileges and immunities clause one month later in *Hicklin v. Orbeck*.[28] There, the Court unanimously struck down the Alaska Hire statute, which required that qualified residents be given preference in all employment "resulting from" oil and gas leases or pipeline projects to which the State of Alaska was a party.[29] Alaska was openly exploiting its propitious natural resource position, and doing so in a manner that could not be entirely explained as a way of helping local

---

22. See 436 U.S. at 394–402 (Brennan, J., joined by White and Marshall, JJ.) (quoting the first edition of this treatise for the proposition that Corfield was tainted by 19th-century "natural rights" notions).

23. This is not to say that the natural rights theory lacks merit in and of itself, only that it has no place in the article IV privileges and immunities clause, which is best understood as embodying the anti-discrimination principle that the framers deemed to be the basic cement of the union. In contrast, the development of a vigorous natural rights jurisprudence might make eminent sense with regard to the fourteenth amendment's privileges or immunities clause, which suffered an unfortunate and unnecessary demise soon after its birth. See § 7–4, infra.

24. 411 U.S. 1 (1973), discussed in § 16–9, infra.

25. The right to vote is, of course, the exception, since it is a fundamental interest for equal protection purposes but does not implicate article IV, § 2. See § 13–12, infra.

26. See, e.g., Hicklin v. Orbeck, 437 U.S. 518 (1978).

27. See, e.g., Massachusetts Bd. of Retirement v. Murgia, 427 U.S. 307 (1976) (per curiam); New Orleans v. Dukes, 427 U.S. 297 (1976).

28. 437 U.S. 518 (1978).

29. Id. at 520.

unemployables.[30]   Moreover, even if the state could have proven that non-residents were a "peculiar source of evil," as *Toomer v. Witsell* requires,[31] the Alaska Hire statute's grant of an across-the-tundra job preference to all Alaskans clearly swept too broadly.[32]

Hicklin itself was unsurprising.   What was surprising was *Hicklin*'s failure to distinguish *Baldwin*: one learns from the two decisions that working on pipelines is "basic to the maintenance or well-being of the Union" [33] while hunting elk is not.[34]   Where this kind of distinction comes from is less than clear.   *Why* it should be made is even more obscure: one would suppose that *neither* elk-hunting nor pipeline employment "bear[s] upon the vitality of the Nation as a single entity," [35] but that the avoidance of unjustified interstate contests with respect to either does.

One possible explanation for the Court's differing approaches in *Hicklin* and *Baldwin* is suggested by the familiar theory that the privileges and immunities clause was historically designed to safeguard "all the privileges of trade and commerce." [36]   Such a design suggests that the occupations of life must be protected while sideshows such as the recreational slaughter of elk need not be.[37]   This distinction serves to explain why discriminatory commercial fishing license fees were invalidated in *Toomer* while the disparities in resident and non-resident recreational hunting license fees in *Baldwin* were upheld without even being subjected to privileges and immunities clause scrutiny.   This explanation draws substance from the historically close relationship between the privileges and immunities clause and the commerce clause. Both originated in the fourth or so-called states' relations article of the Articles of Confederation.[38]   The *Hicklin* Court explicitly linked the two clauses on the basis of their "shared vision of federalism" and relied on commerce clause decisions.[39]

30.   The record indicated that the newly arrived workers were generally more skilled than unemployed residents, and their ability to command jobs was therefore a symptom of, rather than the cause of, conditions resulting in high unemployment rates among Native Alaskans and other residents.   Id. at 526–37.

31.   334 U.S. at 398.

32.   437 U.S. at 527–28;   see Toomer v. Witsell, 334 U.S. at 398–99.

33.   Baldwin, 436 U.S. at 388.

34.   The key to this distinction—and to the Court's failure to reconcile the holdings in Baldwin and Hicklin—may simply lie in the authorship of the opinions.   Justice Brennan, who wrote for the Court in Hicklin, had no use for the fundamental rights analysis employed by Justice Blackmun in Baldwin, see 436 U.S. at 402 (Brennan, J., dissenting), and may simply have been loath to legitimate it by distinguishing Baldwin on that basis.   Justice Brennan's opinion for the unanimous Court in Hicklin is strikingly similar to, and even relies upon, the dissent he wrote for himself and Justices White and Marshall in Baldwin. See, e.g., 437 U.S. at 526.   Both opinions rely heavily on Toomer v. Witsell.

35.   Baldwin, 436 U.S. at 383.

36.   See Austin v. New Hampshire, 420 U.S. 656, 660–61 & n. 6 (1975).

37.   See Baldwin, 436 U.S. at 388 ("Elk hunting by non-residents in Montana is a recreation and a sport . . .   It is not a means to the non-resident's livelihood").

38.   "The better to secure and perpetuate mutual friendship and intercourse among the people of the different States in this Union, the free inhabitants of each of these States, paupers, vagabonds and fugitives from justice excepted, shall be entitled to all privileges and immunities of free citizens in the several States; and the people of each State shall have free ingress and regress to and from any other State and shall enjoy therein all the privileges of trade and commerce, subject to the same duties, impositions and restrictions as the inhabitants thereof respectively. . . . ."

39.   See 437 U.S. at 531–34.

But the history of the privileges and immunities clause also indicates that it was designed to bind the citizens of the several states socially and politically as well as commercially. The explicit purpose of the states' relations article was to "secure and perpetuate mutual friendship and intercourse among the people of the different States." [40] If the *Baldwin* Court meant to say that "mutual friendship" among the states is not threatened when blatant state discrimination affects only a non-resident's recreational activities, it made a rather dubious assumption about human nature,[41] and one not shared by earlier Courts. *Corfield v. Coryell* held that states may not interfere with "the right of a citizen to pass through, or to reside in any other state, for purposes of trade, agriculture, professional pursuits, *or otherwise;*" [42] Justice Washington included in his catalog of "fundamental" privileges and immunities "the enjoyment of life" and the right "to pursue and obtain happiness." [43] Similarly, Justice Field declared for the unanimous Court in *Paul v. Virginia* that the clause "insures to [non-residents] in other States the same freedom possessed by the citizens of those States in the . . . pursuit of happiness." [44] Thus those who would urge the difference between vocational and avocational pursuits to rationalize the holdings in *Hicklin* and *Baldwin* cannot easily locate the distinction even in the older case law.

Nor is there authority in other areas of constitutional jurisprudence for considering play less fundamental than work when the issue is one of discrimination.[45] Indeed, in the equal protection area, the Court has abjured the temptation to rank activities or benefits on a scale of "relative societal significance." [46] Moreover, even if a narrowly historicist view of the purposes of the privileges and immunities clause did justify a subcategory of interests with respect to which national uniformity is deemed especially important, the underlying *vision* of the framers—that the states not war with one another by discriminating against one another's citizens without good reason—should nonetheless be regarded as giving rise to the dominant meaning of the clause even if the framers themselves may have had a more limited set of *examples* in mind. This, of course, is precisely the virtue of the Court's flexible approach in *Toomer v. Witsell*: looking first to the state's justification for discrimination, rather than to whether the privilege in question is on some short list, allows for consideration of a fuller range of unequal

40. See n. 38, supra.

41. It is not difficult to imagine the outrage of a non-resident who is told that she may not travel on Vermont's state roads if she seeks only the pleasure of viewing the autumn foliage, or the hostility of a vacationing tourist who is charged ten times as much as a resident for the privilege of soaking up sunshine on a southern California state beach. See Varat, "State 'Citizenship' and Interstate Equality," 48 U.Chi.L.Rev. 487, 515–16 (1981) (criticizing Baldwin).

42. 6 Fed.Cas. 546, 552 (No. 3230) (C.C. E.D.Pa.1823) (emphasis added).

43. Id.

44. 75 U.S. (8 Wall.) 168, 180 (1869).

45. See Varat, "State 'Citizenship' and Interstate Equality," 48 U.Chi.L.Rev. 487, 515–16 (1981) ("the fundamentality doctrine reaffirmed in Baldwin reflects neither an appreciation of the instances in which interstate divisiveness is likely to result from residence classifications, nor the fundamental interest or suspect classification approaches to equal protection, nor any other discernible concept that can be tied to the purposes of the privileges and immunities clause").

46. See San Antonio Independent School District v. Rodriguez, 411 U.S. 1, 33 (1973).

treatment of outsiders that may well transgress the Constitution's "norm of comity"[47] without good cause.

If neither the history of the clause's interpretation by the Court nor the broader aims of the clause justify restricting the privileges and immunities of state citizenship to a list of "fundamentals," the explanation for *Baldwin* may lie in a desire on the part of the majority to uphold Montana's license scheme, coupled with a belief that this desired result could not be reached within the terms of the Court's current jurisprudence. Montana could constitutionally charge nonresidents more for elk hunting privileges to the extent that their presence imposed added costs on the state or to the extent that residents, through taxes other than license fees, contributed more to the state's wildlife management program.[48] But uncontroverted testimony had estimated that the increased costs to the state, both direct and indirect, could justify a non-resident fee no more than $2\frac{1}{2}$ times the resident fee.[49] With a $9 elk hunting fee for natives and a $225 fee for outsiders,[50] the non-resident elk hunter was charged a fee 25 times greater. This degree of disparity was clearly too great to permit the Court to treat the discrimination as substantially related to the state's interest in recouping expenditures on behalf of out-of-state hunters.[51] Yet the discrimination could pass muster if scrutinized only for minimum rationality. By holding that elk-hunting was not a fundamental privilege and therefore that the interest of non-resident sportsmen was beyond the purview of the privileges and immunities clause, the *Baldwin* Court could apply its least exacting standard of review under the equal protection clause.[52]

It is not readily apparent why the Court wished to uphold a licensing regime that shifted a grossly disproportionate share of the state's conservation costs onto the shoulders of non-residents. But the majority's frequent reference to the necessity of attentive and expensive management of the elk herds and their environment, and to Montana's commitment to conservation of this unique natural resource,[53] reveals that the Court deemed elk to be something Montana

47. Austin v. New Hampshire, 420 U.S. at 660.

48. 436 U.S. at 390–91; id. at 404 (Brennan, J., dissenting).

49. Montana Outfitters Action Group v. Fish and Game Commission, 417 F.Supp. 1005, 1008 (D.Mont.1976).

50. A non-resident wishing to hunt only elk still had to buy a combination hunting license for elk and other species at a price of $225. The resident combination license cost $30, which would render a fee discrimination ratio of 7.5 to 1, but a resident could buy an elk-only license for a mere $9. 436 U.S. at 373–74.

51. The discriminatory license structure invalidated in Toomer v. Witsell required non-residents to pay a fee 100 times greater than that paid by residents for commercial shrimp fishing; the fishing license fee regime struck down in Mullaney v. Anderson, 342 U.S. 415 (1952), required non-residents to pay 10 times as much as residents.

52. See 436 U.S. at 388–89.

53. See 436 U.S. at 375, 377, 388–90. The dissent pointed out that Montana had not asserted its interest in conservation as a justification for the fee differential, nor was there anything in the record to show that the influx of non-resident hunters created a special danger to Montana's elk. 436 U.S. at 403 (Brennan, J., dissenting). For a discussion of the limits on the use of justification by afterthought, see § 16–32, infra.

"held in trust for [its] own people"—something the state was "not obliged to share." [54]

The Court appears to have been groping for a principle that would immunize from privileges and immunities review a sphere of rights and opportunities that a people may preserve for themselves. The intuitive notion lurking beneath *Baldwin's* surface is a strong one. No one would deny that "[s]ome distinctions between residents and non-residents merely reflect the fact that this is a nation composed of individual states." [55] Indeed, "without certain residency requirements the state 'would cease to be the separate political communit[y] that history and the constitutional text make plain w[as] contemplated.'" [56] So it is that a polity is entitled to reserve to its citizens the right to vote [57] and to hold elective office. [58]

There also appear to be some goods and services that a state's citizens, having created or preserved for themselves, are entitled to keep for themselves. Thus Montana's carefully-tended elk herds are akin to public libraries, public schools, [59] state universities, [60] state-supported hospitals, [61] and public welfare programs [62]—things that the Court has suggested a state may reserve for the use or enjoyment of its citizens. The Court implied in *Baldwin* that it would approve even a total exclusion of non-resident hunters upon a showing by the state that any additional hunting opportunities beyond those Montana chose to reserve to its citizens would endanger the elk population to the point of extinction. [63] If a state like Montana were forced to act evenhandedly

54. Baldwin, 436 U.S. at 384.

55. Id. at 383.

56. Supreme Court of New Hampshire v. Piper, 470 U.S. 274, 282 n. 13 (1985), quoting Simson, "Discrimination Against Non-residents and the Privileges and Immunities Clause of Article IV," 128 U.Pa.L. Rev. 379, 387 (1979).

57. See Dunn v. Blumstein, 405 U.S. 330 (1972).

58. See Kanapaux v. Ellisor, 419 U.S. 891 (1974). A city or state may also be entitled to require residency as a condition of direct employment by the polity. Compare McCarthy v. Philadelphia Civil Service Comm'n, 424 U.S. 645 (1976) (per curiam) (rejecting an equal protection challenge to municipal residency requirement for municipal workers), with United Building & Construction Trades Council v. Mayor of Camden, 465 U.S. 208 (1984) (requirement that contractors on city-funded public works projects give hiring preference to local residents is not immune from scrutiny under privileges and immunities clause).

59. See Martinez v. Bynum, 461 U.S. 321 (1983) (upholding residence requirement for tuition-free public education).

60. See Starns v. Malkerson, 401 U.S. 985 (1971), summarily aff'g 326 F.Supp.

234 (D.Minn.1970) (upholding one-year residency requirement for reduced, in-state tuition rate). Cf. Vlandis v. Kline, 412 U.S. 441 (1973) (state may not use irrebutable presumption of non-residence to deny in-state tuition rate).

61. See Doe v. Bolton, 410 U.S. 179, 200 (1973) (residency requirement for medical services invalidated because "not based on any policy of preserving state-supported facilities for Georgia residents [and because there was] no intimation that . . . Georgia facilities are utilized to capacity in caring for Georgia residents"). Cf. Memorial Hospital v. Maricopa County, 415 U.S. 250 (1974) (striking down a one-year residency requirement for non-emergency county medical care).

62. See Shapiro v. Thompson, 394 U.S. 618 (1969) (state may not impose one-year residency requirement for welfare payments). The Shapiro Court objected not to the requirement of residency per se, but to the unjustified duration of the residency requirement. Cf. Memorial Hospital v. Maricopa County, 415 U.S. 250 (1974).

63. 436 U.S. at 387, citing State v. Kemp, 44 N.W.2d 214 (1950) (upholding total exclusion of non-resident recreational waterfowl hunters), dismissed for want of a substantial federal question, 340 U.S. 923 (1951).

in distributing its state-created "goodies," perhaps it would simply give up the effort to conserve or create them.

With respect to goods and opportunities that exist within a given state but that are not attributable to state programs or revenues, the privileges and immunities clause by and large forbids a regime of unequal access for outlanders. If the state is not thus involved, there is no concern that requiring equal access for resident and non-resident alike will curtail state innovation and experimentation.[64] The Alaska Hire statute succumbed in *Hicklin* because oil, unlike elk, is a nonrenewable resource that cannot be regarded as created by the state;[65] and while Alaska may own the oil that lies beneath state land, it certainly does not "own" the jobs created within the state by the economic ripple effect that flows from the private sector's exploitation of that mineral wealth.[66] Likewise, a state may not restrict non-resident use of in-state private medical facilities and services.[67] And the respect for a polity's self-definition and self-governance implicit in allowing states to restrict their elective offices to their own citizens cannot justify a requirement that all members of the state bar reside within the state, since lawyers in private practice, even though "officers of the court," are not state officers who wield public power.[68]

The interests of national cohesion may also forbid discrimination against those from out-of-state even when state programs or revenues play a significant role in creating or sustaining the privilege, opportunity, or other good in question. Police and fire departments are quintessentially creatures of the state, supported by state or local revenue and operated for the good of the local citizenry, yet it is inconceivable that a state would be permitted to deny police and fire protection to tourists or short-term visitors, or to charge a premium to those just passing through for the service of extinguishing a blaze or apprehending a hit-and-run perpetrator.[69] Discrimination against non-residents with re-

---

64. See *Varat*, supra n. 45, 48 U.Chi.L. Rev. at 556.

65. The Court took a different approach from this, arguing that "[r]ather than placing a statute completely beyond the clause, a state's ownership of the property with which the statute is concerned is a factor—although often the crucial factor—to be considered in evaluating whether" the statute violates the clause. Hicklin, 437 U.S. at 529. Yet the Court's conclusion that, regardless of Alaska's purported "ownership" of the oil, its claim of employment-policy hegemony over nearly the entire state economy constituted outrageous overreaching, id. at 531, is not so different from the explanation offered here: that Alaska had not done enough to warrant its claim to control.

66. Alaska may exploit its geological good fortune by imposing a severance tax on that oil at almost any rate it chooses, see Commonwealth Edison Co. v. Montana, 453 U.S. 609 (1981), discussed in § 6–15, supra, but the state may not hoard its

mineral wealth to the detriment of its sister states. See West v. Kansas Natural Gas Co., 221 U.S. 229 (1911).

67. In striking down Georgia's residency requirement for abortions in Doe v. Bolton, the Court noted that the law could not have been based "on any policy of preserving state-supported facilities for Georgia residents, for the bar also applie[d] to private hospitals and to privately retained physicians." 410 U.S. 179, 200 (1973).

68. Supreme Court of New Hampshire v. Piper, 470 U.S. 274 (1985). Cf. Frazier v. Heebe, 107 S.Ct. 2607 (1987) (invoking its inherent supervisory power over the lower federal courts, the Court struck down a rule promulgated by a Louisiana district court denying admission to its bar to those members of the Louisiana bar who did not live in-state or maintain an office in-state).

69. Similarly, a state could not restrict visitors' access to the services of volunteer fire departments, both because they would be creations of the private sector rather

spect to such basic advantages of civilization would surely undermine national cohesion and deter intercourse among the states.[70]

Even in less critical areas, a state's attempt to deny non-residents equal access to benefits generated by its own expenditures may run afoul of the privileges and immunities clause. In *United Building & Construction Trades Council v. Mayor of Camden*,[71] the Court held that a city could not require private contractors on city-funded public works projects to give hiring preference to city residents without implicating the privileges and immunities clause.[72] The opportunity to seek a job with such private sector employers is " 'sufficiently basic to the livelihood of the nation' as to fall within the purview" of the clause.[73] Yet the Court cautioned that "states should have considerable leeway in analyzing local evils and in prescribing appropriate cures," particularly when the government "is merely setting conditions on the expenditure of funds it controls," as the Camden ordinance did, rather than trying to bias employment opportunities throughout the state economy, as Alaska had attempted to do in the law struck down in *Hicklin v. Orbeck*.[74] Thus, state creation of a resource or other good might not always immunize disparate treatment of outsiders from scrutiny under article IV, § 2, but it would remain a powerful argument for justifying such discrimination.[75] The fact that Camden was "expending its own

than the state, and because of the adverse impact such discrimination would have on national unity.

70. Justice Washington included "[p]rotection by the government" among the "fundamental" privileges of citizenship. Corfield v. Coryell, 6 Fed.Cas. at 551–52.

71. 465 U.S. 208 (1984).

72. The Court rejected the contention that the clause was not implicated by municipal residency classifications that discriminate against some state residents as well as all non-residents. 465 U.S. at 216–18. New Jersey residents had no claim under the privileges and immunities clause against the Camden ordinance, but they were represented in the state legislature that had enacted the legislation pursuant to which Camden's ordinance was adopted. Id. at 217 & n. 9. Since New Jersey residents living outside Camden were free to enact their own local-preference schemes, the Court rejected Justice Blackmun's dissenting argument that non-Camden New Jersey residents burdened by the ordinance would protect the interests of jobseekers from out-of-state. Id.; see id. at 227, 231–32 (Blackmun, J., dissenting). Although the Camden majority was certainly correct to be worried that a blanket exemption for all residency classifications that are less than state-wide would make it easy for states to evade the strictures of the clause, by simply denying the relevant privilege or immunity to some geographic

segment of the state, id. at 217–18 n. 9, its cavalier rejection of an analogy to the surrogate representation analysis so central to commerce clause jurisprudence required more explanation. See, e.g., South Carolina Highway Dept. v. Barnwell Bros., Inc., 303 U.S. 177, 187 (1938) ("The fact that [regulations] affect alike shippers in interstate and intrastate commerce in large numbers within as well as without the state is a safeguard against their abuse"). See § 6–5, supra.

73. Id. at 221–22, quoting Baldwin v. Montana Fish and Game Comm'n.

74. 465 U.S. at 223.

75. The Court distinguished White v. Massachusetts Council of Construction Employers, 460 U.S. 204 (1983), in which it had rejected a commerce clause challenge to a nearly identical local-hire requirement by invoking the market participant exception. The Camden Court explained that such an exception completely immunized government action from commerce clause scrutiny because the dormant elements of that clause restrain only government regulation. In contrast, the privileges and immunities clause is implicated by all state discrimination against outsiders, without regard to the mechanism by which it is achieved. See 465 U.S. at 220. In White the Court had noted that it did not pass on the import of the privileges and immunities clause. 460 U.S. at 214–15 n. 12. White is discussed in § 6–11, supra.

funds or funds it administers in accordance with the terms of a grant is . . . perhaps the crucial factor . . . to be considered." [76]

Zobel v. Williams[77] illustrates how even restrictions on state-created goods that undeniably *can* be limited to residents may nevertheless implicate the principles underlying the privileges and immunities clause. In *Zobel*, a nearly unanimous Court [78] struck down Alaska's [79] statutory program for distributing its surplus oil-boom wealth to state residents in the form of dividends in direct proportion to the recipient's length of post-statehood residence—in evident recognition of the early settlers' longer and larger sacrifices in the state's behalf. The effect of the dividend statute, wrote the Court, was to create "fixed, permanent distinctions between an ever increasing number of perpetual classes of concededly *bona fide* residents. . . ." [80]

Although the law was invalidated on equal protection grounds,[81] a far more compelling rationale for the decision can be found in the concurring opinions of Justices Brennan and O'Connor. Justice O'Connor argued that Alaska's dividend scheme impermissibly burdened the freedom to travel, which she located squarely in the text of article IV, § 2.[82] Justice Brennan agreed that the statute ran afoul of the right to travel and of norms of national cohesion: "For if each state were free to reward its citizens incrementally for their years of residence, so that a citizen leaving one state would thereby forfeit his accrued seniority, only to have to begin building such seniority again in his new state of residence, then the mobility so essential to the economic progress of our nation, and so commonly accepted as a fundamental aspect of our social order, would not long survive." [83]

---

76. 465 U.S. at 221. The Court remanded the case for full development of a record that would permit evaluation of Camden's claim that the influx of outsiders who lived off Camden without living in the city, thereby exacerbating local unemployment problems, necessitated restrictions on the hiring of non-residents. Id. at 222–23.

77. 457 U.S. 55 (1982).

78. Justice Rehnquist was the sole dissenter.

79. Alaska has generated a disproportionate number of privileges and immunities precedents. In addition to Zobel v. Williams and Hicklin v. Orbeck, Alaska has also given us Mullaney v. Anderson, 342 U.S. 415 (1952) (discriminatory fishing license fees invalidated), a case decided when our 49th state was still a territory. When one recalls that Alaska is the second-youngest member of the union, is physically removed from the continental United States, and constitutes what might be called our sole remaining "frontier" state, its prominence in Article IV, § 2 jurisprudence breathes real life into the Court's rhetoric about "constitut[ing] the citizens of the United States [as] one people." Paul v. Virginia, 75 U.S. (8 Wall.) 168, 180 (1869).

80. 457 U.S. at 59.

81. 457 U.S. at 65. Cf. Plyler v. Doe, 457 U.S. 202 (1982) (invoking equal protection clause to invalidate a law denying free public education to children of illegal immigrants, observing that such a law would create a permanent underclass of illiterates). See § 16–23, infra.

82. 457 U.S. at 73–74 (O'Connor, J., concurring in the judgment).

83. 457 U.S. at 68, (Brennan, J., joined by Marshall, Blackmun and Powell, JJ., concurring). Justice Brennan noted that he did not find it necessary to assign the right to travel to a particular textual source in the Constitution, id. at 66–67, and his use of the term "fundamental" therefore carries no particular doctrinal significance.

Justice Brennan's primary objection to the law was that it would establish "degrees of citizenship based on length of residence," in direct contravention of the Constitution's norm of equality of citizenship under law. Id. at 69; see id. at 69 n. 3 (citing the title of nobility clause of article I, § 9).

Alaska was clearly entitled to limit distribution of largesse from its treasury to *bona fide* residents. And, by holding out the promise of dividend payments of some size to all new Alaskans, the scheme actually constituted an incentive to outsiders to emigrate to Alaska. Yet by classifying many citizens on the basis of their former status as non-residents, the statute imposed a deferred "disability of alienage" [84] in the form of a relative burden on those who moved to Alaska more recently. Such a burden on former non-residents, and such a penalty on recent arrivals, must fall because it interferes with the capacity to vote with one's feet.[85] In Justice O'Connor's words: "Just as our federal system permits the states to experiment with different social and economic programs, it allows the individual to settle in the state offering those programs best tailored to his or her tastes." [86]

Barely a week after its decision in *Zobel v. Williams*, a majority of the Court in *Edgar v. MITE Corp.* struck down an Illinois corporate takeover law—one having impact well beyond the state—with the remarkable assertion that a "state has no legitimate interest in protecting non-resident shareholders." [87] Yet the national cohesion argument underlying *Zobel* and most privilege and immunities precedents surely suggests that a state not only may but *must* be interested in the well-being of non-residents who may ultimately be affected by its policies. The notion that state legislators should be assumed to have thought only of the welfare of their own citizens when passing laws has been persuasively debunked in the conflict-of-laws literature.[88] If those same legislators are forbidden by the Constitution from concerning themselves substantively with the welfare of non-residents, then it ought to suffice for one state to accord to another state's citizens only those privileges and immunities which the non-residents enjoy at home. This cannot be. The anti-discrimination principle has been understood as the core of the privileges and immunities clause at least since *Paul v.*

84. Paul v. Virginia, 75 U.S. (8 Wall.) 168, 180 (1869).

85. In this respect Zobel is in line with those decisions in which the Court has invalidated durational residency requirements, albeit on equal protection grounds. See, e.g., Shapiro v. Thompson, 394 U.S. 618 (1969) (one-year residency requirement for welfare payments); Memorial Hospital v. Maricopa County, 415 U.S. 250 (1974) (non-emergency state medical services), discussed in § 16–8, infra.

86. 457 U.S. at 77.

87. Edgar v. MITE Corp., 457 U.S. 624, 644 (1982). Justice White's opinion for the Court on this point was joined by Chief Justice Burger and Justices Powell, Stevens and O'Connor. In CTS Corp. v. Dynamics Corp., 107 S.Ct. 1637 (1987), the Court clarified its thinking on this point in the course of upholding an Indiana takeover regulation as consistent with the Williams Act. Justice Powell was joined by Chief Justice Rehnquist and Justices Bren-

nan, Marshall and O'Connor in stating for the Court "that Indiana has no interest in protecting nonresident shareholders *of nonresident corporations*. But this act applies only to corporations incorporated in Indiana. We reject the contention that Indiana has no interest in providing for the shareholders of its corporations the voting autonomy granted by the Act. Indiana has a substantial interest in preventing the corporate form from becoming a shield for unfair business dealing." Id. at 1651–52 (emphasis in original).

88. See Brilmayer, "Interest Analysis and the Myth of Legislative Intent," 78 Mich.L.Rev. 392 (1980). Thus it is arguable—and has been argued by no less formidable a scholar than John Hart Ely—that interest analysis, the dominant contemporary choice-of-law theory, is unconstitutional. See Ely, "Choice of Law and the State's Interest in Protecting Its Own," 23 Wm. & Mary L.Rev. 173, 185–91 (1981).

Virginia,[89] and the Court made clear in *Austin v. New Hampshire* [90] that the content of a challenger's home-state law is irrelevant.

The Court's contrary statement in *Edgar v. MITE* notwithstanding, a state must consider the impact of its laws on out-of-staters, particularly if the law would deter them from travelling into or establishing residence in the state, or would otherwise make their treatment and status within the state turn on their current or prior non-residence. The only shortcoming of the Court's substantial reason analysis, as set forth in *Toomer v. Witsell*, is that it did not explicitly require consideration of a state's legitimate interest in discriminating against outsiders in order to preserve goods and opportunities to which the citizens and government of that state have devoted their labor and their public fisc. The unresolved issue of contemporary privileges and immunities jurisprudence is how to honor the state's interest in keeping some things for itself. One way is to restrict the clause to a list of "fundamental" privileges—as the Court did in *Baldwin*. The alternative is to recognize, as the Court did in *Camden*, that even if the clause is implicated by a challenged residence classification, the state may be able to justify its discrimination by adverting to its role in creating and nurturing the good or opportunity in question and to its character as a politically cohesive entity. The latter appears to be the wiser course.

The standard of review employed in *Toomer, Bolton, Piper* and *Camden*—characterized by a shift in the burden of proof to the discriminating state and by an insistence on a fairly precise fit between remedy and classification—is almost as demanding as that elaborated by the Warren Court in equal protection and first amendment strict scrutiny.[91] If the privileges and immunities clause as currently construed does not precisely duplicate the equal protection clause of the fourteenth amendment, the major reasons are that the former does not protect aliens and corporations,[92] and that non-residence and out-of-state citizenship have *not* in fact been deemed suspect classifications for equal protection purposes.[93] Indeed, equal protection challenges to durational residency

---

89. 75 U.S. (8 Wall.) 168, 180 (1869) ("It was undoubtedly the object of the clause in question to place the citizens of each state upon the same footing with citizens of other states, so far as the advantages resulting from citizenship in those states are concerned").

90. 420 U.S. 656 (1975).

91. After creating a mode of review that would subsequently be used in a revolutionary addition to equal protection analysis, the Toomer Court declined to pass on the equal protection challenge to the statute. 334 U.S. at 403. One rationale for the privileges and immunities clause is the protection it affords non-residents, who are not represented in the discriminating state's legislature. This rationale is similar to that most frequently offered to explain judicial protection of discrete and insular minorities. See §§ 16-5, 16-6. One conspicuous difference between article

IV review and strict scrutiny under the equal protection clause remains: truly suspect classifications must be justified as *necessary* to serve a *compelling* state interest in order to meet equal protection requirements. The Toomer Court spoke only in terms of *substantial connection* to *valid state objectives*. 334 U.S. at 398. Cf. §§ 16-32, 16-33, infra (intermediate scrutiny).

92. Corporations and aliens are not "citizens" within the meaning of article IV, § 2. Paul v. Virginia, 75 U.S. (8 Wall.) 168 (1869).

93. The protections of the article IV privileges and immunities clause do significantly overlap those of the commerce clause, however. The Toomer holding, for example, could probably have been reached under the principles of that clause, although invoking commerce clause principles to uphold the abortion rights of non-

requirements have found objection in the length of time affixed rather than in the ordinarily valid requirement of state or local residency as such. Were they subject to equal protection scrutiny alone, the non-durational residency requirements struck down in cases like *Bolton* would be assessed solely for minimal rationality and in all likelihood upheld.

The equal protection clause of course concerns a vastly broader range of discriminations than those against nonresidents closely scrutinized under article IV. Perhaps the deepest significance of the overlap that does exist is the fact that the *core* concerns of equal protection, article IV, and the commerce clause, are remarkably similar: all address the problems that occur when governments inflict injury upon outsiders—whether *geographical* outsiders, as in the case of burdens imposed on persons from other states; or *political* outsiders, as in the case of disadvantages visited upon minorities insulated from other groups within the state itself; or *psychological* outsiders, as in the case of actions adverse to persons whom those in power regard as different or inferior.[94]

residents in the Bolton case would have required some stretching.

94. This theme, which was expressed in these same words in the first edition of this treatise, see L. Tribe, American Constitutional Law 412 (1978 ed.), has since been advanced as a unifying principle that might serve not only to *justify* selective judicial activism but also to *limit* active judicial review to cases where fair political representation has broken down. See J. Ely, Democracy and Distrust (1980). For doubts as to the wisdom and coherence of any such purported "limitation," see Tribe, "The Puzzling Persistence of Process-Based Constitutional Theories," 89 Yale.L.J. 1063 (1980).

Chapter 7

DIRECT PROTECTION OF INDIVIDUALS AND GROUPS: MODELS BEYOND THE SEPARATION AND DIVISION OF POWER

§ 7-1. The Limited Nature of Direct Federal Protection in the Pre-Civil War Era

The first century of government under the Constitution was understandably characterized by a preoccupation with structural issues. Charting a course for a federal republic demanded attention above all else to the respective roles of the national and state governments and to the tripartite separation of powers at the national level. But although Model I—the Model of Separated and Divided Powers—therefore occupied center stage,[1] it would be a serious mistake to underestimate the significance of three additional themes, all struck early in American constitutional history, pointing directly to federal protection of individuals and groups against governmental overreaching.

First, as Chapter 6 demonstrated, both the commerce clause and the interstate privileges and immunities clause of article IV provided a setting for federal judicial intervention to control state and local impositions upon the citizens and residents of other states, not only in the service of nationhood but also in the interest of the adversely affected citizens and residents themselves.[2]

Second, as Chapters 3 and 4 suggested, separation-of-powers doctrines, particularly those limiting the Executive Branch, have been invoked from the very beginning—indeed, from the Court's decision in *Marbury v. Madison*[3] itself—to articulate the relationship between the rule of law and a regime of individual rights. Congress created Marbury's position by statute; it provided a procedure whereby the Executive Branch was to make appointments. The procedure having been employed, and Marbury having been duly appointed, he had a vested right to his post that the Executive was not free to disregard. To be sure, the Court said it all in dictum—perhaps the most famous dictum in all of American constitutional law—but the theme was struck and has never been abandoned: In protecting expectations created by law, and in assuring governmental regularity, we defend a part of what liberty must ultimately mean.[4] In Chapters 9 and 10 those notions are

§ 7-1

1. See Chapters 2–6, supra.

2. See particularly §§ 6–34, 6–35, supra.

3. 5 U.S. (1 Cranch.) 137 (1803), discussed in Chapter 3, supra.

4. "The very essence of civil liberty . . . consists in the right of every individual to claim the protection of the laws, whenever he receives an injury. One of the first duties of government is to afford that protection. . . . The government of the United States has been emphatically

developed in some detail; suffice it at this point to observe that the core idea has its roots in Model I.

Third, growing partly out of separation-of-powers doctrine but grounded also in a set of explicit constitutional prohibitions, a particularly feared trio of legislative excesses—ex post facto laws, bills of attainder, and impairments of contract—was singled out for explicit federal judicial invalidation. Although ex post facto laws and bills of attainder were condemned only in dicta prior to the Civil War (both are taken up in Chapter 10), impairments of contract (considered in Chapter 9, together with the just compensation requirement) were not only identified by the Supreme Court as forbidden, but were invalidated in landmark holdings as early as 1810,[5] making the contract clause the most formidable early restraint upon the dealings of states with their own residents.[6]

Of these three themes, all moving beyond government structure to a direct concern with persons, the first is in many respects the most significant for the remainder of this book. Its central idea is that, even while they look primarily to matters of structure and procedure, federal courts have a special mission in defending substantive personal interests from governmental action that overreaches because of its unduly limited constituency—action that oppresses people because they are outsiders. Once the premises of that idea are understood, the stage is set for its extension to substantive controversies between the states and their own citizens whenever the appeal to local politics seems an insufficient source of protection.

The contract clause, to be sure, represented a potential source of general substantive protection for persons burdened by their own states. And one should not understate the importance of the role that the clause played.[7] Still, as we shall see in Chapter 9, its dramatic limitation in a seminal 1834 decision [8] prevented the clause from having as broad a reach as it might, and left a vast realm of state-citizen controversy beyond the cognizance of the federal judiciary and indeed of the federal Constitution.

The Civil War, and the three constitutional amendments that were its fairly immediate legacy, [9] changed all that. We will be tracing the changes, and their many implications, in the remaining chapters of this book. Six models of constitutionalism remain to be examined. One elusive thread will help us wind our way through the story: it is the

termed a government of laws, and not of men. It will certainly cease to deserve this high appellation, if the laws furnish no remedy for the violation of a vested legal right." Id. at 163.

5. See Fletcher v. Peck, 10 U.S. (6 Cranch.) 87 (1810), discussed in Chapter 9, infra.

6. For example, almost half the pre-1889 decisions in which the Supreme Court invalidated state legislation were based on the contract clause. B. Wright, The Contract Clause of the Constitution 95 (1938).

7. Many have overestimated it as well. See, e.g., Sir Henry Maine's paean to the clause as "the bulwark of American individualism against democratic impatience and socialistic fantasy." Popular Government 247–48 (1886).

8. Ogden v. Saunders, 25 U.S. (12 Wheat.) 213 (1827) (upholding non-retroactive insolvency laws), discussed in Chapter 9, infra.

9. The thirteenth, fourteenth, and fifteenth.

thread of fourteenth amendment privileges or immunities. As we will see in the remainder of Chapter 7, that thread has yet to sew together a single enduring doctrine. But it links the privileges and immunities clause of article IV, and with it the entire topic of federalism, to the general subject of personal rights; its meandering through the cases, even when it proves not at all decisive, reveals strands of thought that might otherwise have been obscure; and it suggests lines of doctrinal development still unexplored.

§ 7–2. Fourteenth Amendment Privileges or Immunities: Historical Background and Early Interpretation

Section 1 of the fourteenth amendment declares: "All persons born or naturalized in the United States and subject to the jurisdiction thereof, are citizens of the United States and of the State wherein they reside. No State shall make or enforce any law which shall abridge the privileges or immunities of citizens of the United States. . . ." The words "privileges" and "immunities" first appear in the Constitution in article IV, § 2,[1] and their recurrence in the fourteenth amendment naturally inspires comparison. State citizenship carries with it, by virtue of article IV, the right to non-discriminatory treatment within each state of the fundamental rights of citizens of all the states. The protection is broad, in the sense that numerous rights have been held to be fundamental rights of state citizenship, but weak, because only relative equality of rights is conferred: each state retains discretion over what rights are granted to its citizens as long as citizens of other states are accorded the same rights.[2]

The constitutional guardianship of the privileges of national citizenship, on the other hand, is more rigid: "[T]he Fourteenth Amendment prohibits any State from abridging the privileges or immunities of citizens of the United States, whether its own citizens or any others. It not merely requires equality of privileges; but it demands that the privileges or immunities of all citizens shall be absolutely unimpaired."[3] But this rigidity does not imply breadth of protection; the Supreme Court has greatly narrowed the rights that attach to national citizenship so that "instances of valid 'privileges or immunities' must be but few."[4] Thus in at least one respect the fourteenth amendment privileges or immunities clause and its ancestor in article IV are much alike: courts rarely rely upon either to protect the privileges of citizens, state or federal.

§ 7–2

1. "The Citizens of each State shall be entitled to all Privileges and Immunities of Citizens in the several States." For a discussion of article IV, § 2, see §§ 6–34 to 6–35, supra.

2. And even if they are not, the state's only duty is to show the difference in treatment reasonably necessary. See § 6–35, supra.

3. Colgate v. Harvey, 296 U.S. 404, 428 (1935).

4. Edwards v. California, 314 U.S. 160, 183 (1941) (Jackson, J., concurring). The emasculation has been so thorough that Justice Stone was prompted to call it "the almost forgotten . . . clause." Colgate v. Harvey, supra note 3 at 443 (dissenting opinion). Indeed, commentators have often treated the clause as essentially dormant. See, e.g., Howard, "The Privileges and Immunities of Federal Citizenship and Colgate v. Harvey." 87 U.Pa.L.Rev. 262, 267 (1939).

The Civil War settled at least two issues, the existence of slavery and the supremacy of the national government. The decisions of the battlefield were given constitutional expression in the Reconstruction Amendments. The thirteenth and fifteenth straightforwardly abolished slavery and prescribed equal voting rights for the freedmen. The fourteenth amendment, in § 1, approached unification under a supreme national government more subtly: it made state citizenship derivative of national citizenship and transferred to the federal government a portion of each state's control over civil and political rights. Before the Civil War, the status of national citizenship remained at best vague. The Constitution mentioned it [5] without defining what it was. Interest in the question quickened when slavery (and its champion, states' rights) divided lawmakers. Calhoun thought that national citizenship must be a function of state citizenship and that, as a result, there could be no citizenship in the United States without state permission, a theory that meshed well with his notion of state supremacy.[6] No congressional action ensued on the matter, but in 1857 the Supreme Court lept into the fray with its infamous decision in *Dred Scott v. Sandford*.[7]

Dred Scott is often recalled for its politically disastrous dictum, the wholly gratuitous announcement by Chief Justice Taney that the Missouri Compromise was unconstitutional. But the decision's greatest constitutional significance lay in its holding: whether enslaved or free, "persons who are descendants of Africans . . . imported into this country, and sold as slaves," cannot bring suit in federal courts, even if their state citizenship is unquestioned. Access to federal courts presumed national citizenship, a status distinct from state citizenship and denied to such persons as Scott by the Constitution. The *Dred Scott* Court construed the Constitution to grant citizenship only to the residents of states that formed the Union and to the descendants of those initial arrivals, unless Congress legislated otherwise.

The fourteenth amendment rejected Calhoun's theory and squarely overruled *Dred Scott*. The citizenship clause perfected the distinction between state and national citizenship, but defined national citizenship so as to nullify *Dred Scott*'s conclusion: "All persons born or naturalized in the United States . . . are citizens of the United States. . . ."[8] Section 1 also fixed a definition of state citizenship, and did so in a way that made it depend on national citizenship: "All persons born or naturalized in the United States . . . are citizens . . . . of the State wherein they reside." National supremacy was thus highlighted by "causing citizenship of the United States to be paramount and dominant instead of being subordinate and derivative."[9]

---

5. Article I, § 2 (qualification for Representatives); id., § 3 (qualification for Senator); art. II, § 1 (qualification for President); cf., art. I, § 8 (power of Congress to regulate naturalization).

6. See Slaughter-House Cases, 83 U.S. (16 Wall.) 36, 51, 52 (1873) (abstract of the argument against monopolies); Morris, "What Are the Privileges and Immunities of Citizens of the United States?," 28 W.Va.L.Q. 38 (1921).

7. 60 U.S. (19 How.) 393 (1857).

8. Amend. XIV, § 1. The power of Congress to grant or revoke national citizenship is discussed in Chapter 5, supra.

9. Selective Draft Law Cases (Arver v. United States), 245 U.S. 366, 389 (1918).

Lest the symbolism of citizenship be lost on the states' rightists, the framers of the fourteenth amendment, in its very next clause, hoped to place the power of the federal government between state legislatures and the privileges or immunities of national citizens. For one thing, the Congress was persuaded that "notwithstanding the formal recognition by those states of the abolition of slavery, the condition of the slave race would, without further protection of the Federal government, be almost as bad as it was before." [10] The privileges or immunities clause, along with the due process and equal protection clauses, promised the additional protection Congress thought necessary.

But beyond that, the proponents of the amendment perceived the need to assert a federal role in state affairs. "The mischief to be remedied was not merely slavery and its . . . consequences; but that spirit of insubordination and disloyalty to the National government which had troubled the country for so many years in some of the states." [11] Civil rights seemed the obvious place to intervene: "The Amendment was an attempt to give voice to the strong National yearning for that time . . . . in which American citizenship should be a sure guaranty of safety, and in which every citizen of the United States might stand erect on every portion of its soil, in the full enjoyment of every right and privilege belonging to a freeman. . . . ." [12]

The choice of language to accomplish federal intervention was not difficult. Representative Bingham, the Congressman who framed the privileges or immunities clause of the fourteenth amendment, pointed to the privileges and immunities clause of article IV as his model.[13] The article IV clause had been interpreted by Justice Washington in 1823 to protect against state action the privileges "which are, in their very nature, fundamental; which belong, of right, to the citizens of all free governments." [14] The framers wished to protect those very fundamental rights from state encroachment, and there was every reason to believe that the new clause would be similarly interpreted.[15]

Whatever goals the framers set for the fourteenth amendment, the Supreme Court quickly dismantled them. In the *Slaughter-House Cases*,[16] the Court's first decision interpreting the amendment, it was held that laws enacted by the Louisiana legislature establishing a slaughterhouse monopoly did not violate the fourteenth amendment's privileges or immunities clause. The right to carry on a lawful trade was squarely among the fundamental rights of citizens enumerated by

10. Slaughter-House Cases, 83 U.S. (16 Wall.) at 70.

11. Id. at 123 (Bradley, J., dissenting).

12. Id.

13. Cong. Globe, 39th Cong., 1st Sess., part 2, pp. 1033–34 (1866).

14. Corfield v. Coryell, 6 Fed.Cas. 546, 551 (No. 3230) (C.C.E.D.Pa.1825), discussed in § 6–34, supra.

15. Senator Howard, for example, quoted from Corfield during the Congressional discussion of the fourteenth amendment, and added: "Such is the character of the privileges and immunities spoken of in the second section of the fourth Article of the Constitution. To these privileges and immunities . . . should be added the personal rights guarantied and secured by the first eight Amendments of the Constitution." Cong. Globe, 39th Cong., 1st Sess., part 3, p. 2765 (1866). For a different view of the circumstances surrounding the adoption of the fourteenth amendment, see Fairman, "Does the Fourteenth Amendment Incorporate the Bill of Rights?," 2 Stan.L.Rev. 5 (1949).

16. 83 U.S. (16 Wall.) 36 (1873).

Justice Washington,[17] but that made little difference to the majority in *Slaughter-House*, for in their view the state and federal roles in securing civil rights had not been altered at all by the fourteenth amendment.[18] First, the primary purpose of the amendment, as Justice Miller saw it in his opinion for the majority, was to protect the rights of newly emancipated slaves.[19] The Court conceded that persons other than newly freed slaves could claim the guarantees of the amendment, but noted that the argument of such persons for protection would depend on the amendment's language and not its history.[20]

The framers selected the "privileges or immunities" language for the fourteenth amendment in anticipation of a judicial construction identical to that given the privileges and immunities of state citizenship in article IV, and so the plaintiffs argued.[21] But that was history, not language, and in the language of the amendment, interpreted as a whole, the plaintiffs' argument faltered before the majority.[22] Specifically, the Court turned to the words of the citizenship clause, words which emphatically distinguished state from national citizenship. "We think this distinction and its explicit recognition in the amendment of great weight . . . because the next paragraph . . . speaks only of privileges and immunities of citizens of the United States, and does not speak of those of citizens of the several States. . . . It is a little remarkable, if this clause was intended as a protection to the citizen of a state against the legislative power of his own state, that the word citizen of the State should be left out when it is so carefully used . . . in contradistinction to citizens of the United States in the very sentence which precedes it."[23]

The majority then proceeded to turn the supposed identity of the fourteenth amendment privileges or immunities clause and the article IV privileges and immunities clause on its head. Justice Miller noted that recent interpretations of article IV had restricted that article's force to the equalizing of rights, rather than the protection of any rights as such, so that discretion over civil rights remained in the state

---

17. Nor did the Court express doubt that the right of a butcher to ply his trade was among those civil rights of state citizens that could not lawfully be infringed. But, as the Court saw it, a legislative monopoly over slaughtering was a classic exercise of the state police power and not an interference with the right to be a butcher.

18. Thus it was up to the courts of Louisiana, or a federal Circuit Court (as the federal trial courts were then called) sitting in a diversity case, to protect the right to slaughter if and when it should be jeopardized—something the Court said had not occurred here.

19. "[O]n the most casual examination of the language of [the 13th, 14th, and 15th Amendments], no one can fail to be impressed with the one pervading purpose found in them all, lying at the foundation of each, and without which none of them

would have been even suggested; we mean the freedom of the slave race, and the security and firm establishment of that freedom, and the protection of the newly-made freeman and citizen from the oppressions of those who had formerly exercised unlimited dominion over him." 83 U.S. (16 Wall.) at 71.

20. Id. at 72.

21. Id. at 74.

22. The Supreme Court, in a later case, offered the following explanation for ignoring the framers' statements and other legislative discussion: "what is said in Congress upon such an occasion may or may not express the views of the majority of those who favor the adoption of the measure. . . ." Maxwell v. Dow, 176 U.S. 581, 601 (1900).

23. 83 U.S. (16 Wall.) at 74.

governments.[24] That meant that "the entire domain of the privileges and immunities of citizens of the states, [as defined by Justice Washington], lay within the constitutional and legislative power of the states, and without that of the Federal government."[25] The fourteenth amendment retained the distinction between the privileges of state citizenship and those of national citizenship; therefore, the Court reasoned, the fourteenth amendment left responsibility over the fundamental rights of state citizenship where it had always rested, in the state governments. Since the privilege claimed by the *Slaughter-House* plaintiffs numbered among the rights of state citizenship, they were told to look to Louisiana for redress: the privileges or immunities clause provided federal protection only for the rights of *national* citizenship.[26]

Competing attitudes toward federal-state relations played a large part in the *Slaughter-House* dispute. The nineteenth century legal mind grasped the concept of federalism by visualizing two coextensive spheres, one defining the power of the federal government, the other that of the states.[27] Each citizen was subject to two governments, "but there need be no conflict between the two. The powers which one possesses, the other does not. . . . The citizen . . . owes allegiance to the two departments, so to speak, and *within their respective spheres* must pay the penalties which each exacts for disobedience to its laws. In return, he can demand protection from each *within its own jurisdiction*."[28]

The Civil War conclusively established that "Within the scope of its powers . . . [the federal government] is supreme and above the States."[29] But the effect of the Union victory on the states' sphere was less clear: the victors were states as well, and whatever powers they took from the vanquished they lost for themselves. Historically, a large part of the states' sphere consisted in the power and duty to guard the "rights and privileges of the citizen, which form a part of his political inheritance derived from the mother country."[30] The federal government initially had no responsibility for safeguarding these rights. The proponents of the privileges or immunities clause sought to delegate to the federal government the power to restrain state interfer-

24. Paul v. Virginia, 75 U.S. (8 Wall.) 168 (1869), discussed in § 6–34, supra.

25. 83 U.S. (16 Wall.) at 77.

26. Justice Miller never related the narrow interpretation of the privileges or immunities clause to his understanding of the function of the fourteenth amendment, the protection of the newly freed slaves. One commentator has argued that "[i]t would have been little aid to [the negro] to have the privileges and immunities created by national laws protected against state impairment while all the fundamental rights 'which belong to him as a free man and a free citizen'—those rights which affected his whole manner of living—were left to the unfettered discretion of the local governments." Lomen, "Privileges and Immunities under the Fourteenth Amendment," 18 Wash.L.R. 120, 124 (1943).

27. I am greatly indebted to my colleague Duncan Kennedy, whose illuminating work on pre-classical and classical legal consciousness has powerfully influenced my thinking here and in § 7–3. See his "Toward an Historical Understanding of Legal Consciousness: The Case of Classical Legal Thought in America, 1850–1940," 3 Research in Law & Sociology 3–24 (1980).

28. United States v. Cruikshank, 92 U.S. 542, 550–51 (1876) (emphasis added).

29. Id. at 550.

30. Logan v. United States, 144 U.S. 263, 288 (1892).

ence with the fundamental personal rights of United States citizens. On its face, the clause left discretion in the state legislatures to determine the scope of these rights subject only to limitations enforced by the national government as authorized by the fourteenth amendment. But within the universe of the spheres, the judicial minds of the *Slaughter-House* Court were not at home with the idea of coterminous jurisdictions. What the Constitution placed in the federal sphere, it necessarily took from the states' sphere. The Justices could perceive only one authoritative jurisdiction over civil rights, and the interpretation of the privileges or immunities clause envisioned by its proponents would have made that jurisdiction federal.

Despite the radical changes that vision forebode in federal-state relations, the four dissenters in *Slaughter-House* embraced the intent of the framers: "It is objected that the power conferred is novel and large. The answer is that the novelty was known and the measure deliberately adopted. . . . Where could it be more appropriately lodged than in the hands to which it is confided?"[31] But the majority rebelled against the implications of the minority's position. They resisted the vast capacities that would be created in the Supreme Court itself should the national government become the dispenser of civil rights: "such a construction . . . would constitute this court a perpetual censor upon all legislation of the states . . . with the authority to nullify such as it did not approve."[32] Even more troublesome to the majority, Congress would acquire the power to legislate affirmatively where the Court could only strike down. "Congress . . . may also pass laws in advance, limiting and restricting the exercise of legislative power by the states, in their most ordinary and useful functions."[33] The necessary consequences of a general federal duty to safeguard civil rights settled the issue for the majority: "when . . . these consequences are so . . . great a departure from the structure and spirit of our institutions; when the effect is to fetter and degrade the state governments by subjecting them to the control of Congress, in the exercise of powers heretofore universally conceded to them of the most ordinary and fundamental character . . . the argument [from consequences] has a force that is irresistible, in the absence of language . . . [too clear] to admit of doubt."[34]

§ 7-3. The Inversion of the Slaughter-House Logic: Glimpse at a Boomerang

Less than thirty years after Justice Miller penned his *Slaughter-House* opinion, the Supreme Court appeared to have undertaken just the course that Miller most feared; during the period from 1890 to 1937, the Court tested hundreds of state laws against a broad vision of the Constitution's guarantee that no state shall deprive any person of life, liberty, or property without due process of law.[1]

31. 83 U.S. (16 Wall.) at 129 (Swayne, J., dissenting). The dissents are discussed in the context of substantive due process doctrine in Chapter 8, infra.

32. Id. at 78.

33. Id.

34. Id.

§ 7-3

1. See generally Chapter 8.

Ironically, the *Slaughter-House Cases'* reaffirmation of the spheres helped pave the way for the substantive due process doctrine of this post-1890s era. Justice Miller had reasoned that federal intrusion into civil rights under the aegis of the privileges or immunities clause was unnecessary because a well-defined body of general law, enforcible in state courts and in diversity cases, would assure that common-law rights remained intact,[2] and that such intrusion must not have been intended because broadened federal responsibility would have dangerously evaporated the content of state sovereignty. To avoid that result, Justice Miller affirmed the duty of the Supreme Court to safeguard the autonomy of the federal and state governments within their respective spheres of power over the same geographical territory. But the Justices of the 1890–1937 era, likewise imbued with Miller's sense of the state and federal spheres and persuaded of the need to protect their sanctity, discerned yet a third sphere—that of the citizen, whose autonomy both required federal protection and could be defended without federal suffocation of the states.

The discovery of a sphere of citizen autonomy judicially protectible as a matter of federal law without threat to state autonomy began in a series of commerce clause cases in which the Supreme Court held that, because Congress possessed sole power over interstate commerce, the states could not regulate the activities of persons participating in commerce between the states;[3] indeed, citizens had a *right* to engage in interstate commerce—a right to make interstate contracts free from state restraints. From the notion that negative limitations on state action in matters of interstate commerce created corresponding affirmative rights of contract in citizens, there emerged a more general concept whereby the line drawn around state power within the federal system could be extended to trace the boundary of a citizen sphere within a larger system, a sphere which no state law could legitimately pierce.[4] The due process clause set that boundary at life, liberty, and property.

In defining the boundary of the state sphere, the Supreme Court drew upon the common law doctrine of implied powers, which prescribed three areas of authority suitable for state action—the police, taxing, and eminent domain powers—and which provided general standards for judging what laws came within these zones.[5] Miller himself had proclaimed the existence and trenchancy of those standards by confidently asserting that they sufficed to protect the common law liberties of Louisiana's butchers—liberties that he asserted were not invaded by the state's slaughterhouse monopoly.[6] The Court thus came to perceive a perfect complementarity between the citizens' right to "life, liberty, and property" and the state's authority to preserve such life, liberty, and property through the exercise of its implied powers within settled common law standards. This complementarity permit-

2. See § 7–2 notes 17–18, supra. The point is more fully developed in Chapter 8.

3. See § 6–3, supra.

4. See Allgeyer v. Louisiana, 165 U.S. 578 (1897).

5. See Chapter 8, infra.

6. See § 7–2 note 17, supra.

ted the turn-of-the-century Court to believe that the federal judiciary could protect citizen autonomy without intruding upon the state's sphere—because any state action that *invaded* the liberty or property of its citizens was, by definition, *beyond* the state's sphere.

Justice Miller had feared that federal intervention into civil rights would destroy state sovereignty because it would puncture a well-defined area of state authority. The substantive due process doctrine answered this objection to the satisfaction of many of that period's jurists by building upon Miller's own reaffirmation of the spheres: *the concept of rigidly defined and mutually exclusive spheres of federal, state, and citizen autonomy created the possibility that the federal judiciary could delimit state authority without destroying it*; if the boundaries were as clear as he himself had claimed, the Court could simply enforce them. But for a belief in that possibility, the fear of crushing state sovereignty in the name of the fourteenth amendment might have powerfully deterred the development of substantive due process.

§ 7–4. The Penumbral Career of National Privileges or Immunities: Phantom or Phoenix?

In his opinion in *Slaughter-House*, Justice Miller may thus have unwittingly taken a first step toward the recognition of substantive due process. But the *Slaughter-House* holding had the opposite effect on the privileges or immunities clause, since it removed from the purview of that clause every civil right traditionally associated with state protection. There remained the question of what rights "national" citizenship conferred; Miller responded that the only such rights were those "which owe their existence to the Federal government, its National character, its Constitution, or its laws" [1]—in other words, rights, such as habeas corpus, independently secured by the federal Constitution.

In two subsequent cases,[2] the Supreme Court unfortunately suggested an even narrower definition of the rights of national citizenship. Rather than any right created by the Constitution or laws of the United States, only those rights which "arise out of the nature or essential character of the National Government" were said to be protected.[3] In *Twining v. New Jersey*,[4] however, the Court in dictum finally settled on the *Slaughter-House* definition as correct. No case has ever attempted to identify the totality of implied federal rights guaranteed by the privileges or immunities clause, but the *Twining* opinion did provide a list of the privileges or immunities which had by then been judicially recognized:[5] (1) the right to pass freely from state to state; (2) the right to petition Congress for redress of grievances; (3) the right to vote for national officers; (4) the right to enter the public lands; (5) the right to be protected against violence while in the lawful custody of a United States Marshal; and (6) the right to inform United States authorities of

§ 7–4

1. 83 U.S. (16 Wall.) 36, 79 (1873).

2. Bradwell v. State, 83 U.S. (16 Wall.) 130 (1872); Maxwell v. Dow, 176 U.S. 581 (1900).

3. Maxwell v. Dow, 176 U.S. 581, 594 (1900).

4. 211 U.S. 78 (1908).

5. Id. at 97.

violations of its laws. The *Twining* Court neglected to mention *Crutcher v. Kentucky*,[6] which had included (7) the right to carry on interstate commerce. And one right has since been added to the *Twining* group, that in *Oyama v. California* [7]—(8) the statutory right to take and hold real property.[8]

The *Slaughter-House* definition of national rights renders the fourteenth amendment's privileges or immunities clause technically superfluous; rights preexisting in "the Federal government, its National character, its Constitution, or its laws", were by definition already shielded from state infringement by the principle of federal supremacy articulated in the supremacy clause of article VI, or by more general principles of constitutional structure and relationship.[9] A mere look at the *Twining* list evidences the redundancy. For each privilege there listed, the opinion cites the case that initially held the right to be one protected from state interference. None of those cases relied on the privileges or immunities clause for its holding; other constitutional devices had achieved the desired result whenever they were necessary.[10]

The issue of federal versus state power over civil rights surfaced in a new context in *Colgate v. Harvey* [11], where Justice Sutherland, speaking for a majority of the Court, invalidated a state income tax levied against in-state residents exclusively upon dividends and interest earned outside the state: "The right of a citizen of the United States to engage in business, to transact any lawful business, or to make a lawful loan of money in any state other than that in which the citizen resides is a privilege . . . attributable to his national citizenship." [12] The majority reasoned that the power to tax was the power to destroy interstate loans and corporate ownership; Justice Stone vigorously dissented.

6. 141 U.S. 47 (1891).

7. 332 U.S. 633 (1948).

8. The statute is 42 U.S.C. § 1982: "All citizens of the United States shall have the same right, in every State and Territory, as is enjoyed by white citizens thereof to inherit, purchase, lease, sell, hold, and convey real and personal property."

9. See C. Black, Structure and Relationship in Constitutional Law (1969). Justice Field, dissenting in the Slaughterhouse Cases, pointed to the redundancy and added that, under the majority's interpretation, the privileges or immunities clause "was a vain and idle enactment, which accomplished nothing, and most unnecessarily excited Congress and the people on its passage." 83 U.S. (16 Wall.) at 96.

10. An illustration is Crandall v. Nevada, 73 U.S. (6 Wall.) 35 (1868), which Twining cited as the first case to recognize the right to pass freely from state to state. In Crandall the Court struck down a Nevada statute that levied a head tax of one dollar on every person leaving the State by any vehicle for hire. The majority held that

the tax interfered with the right to pass freely from state to state, a right implied in the Constitution from the needs of the federal government to transport its troops across state lines, to call to the capital any of its citizens to aid in its service as members of Congress, the judiciary, or the executive departments, and to have access to its seaports, revenue offices, and land offices within the states. Citing McCulloch v. Maryland, 17 U.S. (4 Wheat.) 316 (1819), the majority stated that "the right of the States in this mode to impede . . . the constitutional operation of [the Federal] government, or the rights *which its citizens hold under it*, has been uniformly denied." Id. at 45 (emphasis added). Citizens were protected because "if the government has these rights on her own account, the citizen also has correlative rights." Id. at 44. Note that the case was decided several months before the fourteenth amendment was even ratified.

11. 296 U.S. 404 (1935).

12. Id. at 430.

The arguments for each side resembled those in the *Slaughter-House Cases*, but the sides had been switched. In the intervening years, the Supreme Court had accomplished essentially the intervention that Justice Miller and his colleagues had resisted, using the fourteenth amendment due process clause as their constitutional vehicle in place of the diminished privileges or immunities clause. But the substantive due process doctrine did not clearly reach the statute attacked in *Colgate*, and the Court's still conservative majority seized the opportunity to reawaken the privileges or immunities clause, thus providing an additional means for the federal judiciary to review state laws governing property rights.

The dissent repeated the arguments of Justice Miller's opinion but from a different perspective. The substantive due process doctrine had been used since the 1890's to strike down state laws that attempted to redress the unequal bargaining power of employers and employees. Justice Stone feared that the privileges or immunities clause, as interpreted by the majority, would permit similar treatment of other laws controlling the power of wealth, perhaps even after the substantive due process doctrine itself had passed. Thus all the outrage that attached to the employment decisions appropriately accompanied the *Colgate* holding.[13] Four years later, and shortly after the passing of the substantive due process era, *Madden v. Kentucky*[14] overruled *Colgate*, reclaiming the lost taxing power for state governments and setting aside the only case in which a majority of the Supreme Court has ever held a state provision violative of the privileges or immunities clause.

Non-economic rights were less carefully guarded by the substantive due process Court. The Court twice refused, over stinging dissents, to place the Bill of Rights among the privileges of national citizenship.[15] But in *Hague v. CIO*,[16] a majority prohibited city officials from interfering with assemblies and speeches organized by the CIO for the purpose of disseminating information about the NLRA. Three Justices—Black, Hughes, and Roberts—agreed that the right to assemble and discuss national issues was a privilege of national citizenship, being part of the right to petition Congress for a redress of grievances. Two other Justices—Stone and Reed—rested their concurrence on a long line of decisions that secured first amendment freedoms of speech and assembly to all persons through the due process clause of the fourteenth amendment. Justice Stone argued that the rights of national citizenship should be restricted to those growing out of the national government and its relations to its citizens. There is little doubt that the *Colgate* decision and the danger it created for state regulation of business inspired Justice Stone's narrow interpretation of the privileges or immunities clause even where political liberties were at stake.

---

13. An example of such outrage can be found in Howard, "The Privileges and Immunities of Federal Citizenship and Colgate v. Harvey," 87 U.Pa.L.R. 262 (1939).

14. 309 U.S. 83 (1940).

15. See Maxwell v. Dow, 176 U.S. 581 (1900); Twining v. New Jersey, 211 U.S. 78 (1908). The dissents were by Justice Harlan, who argued that if any rights could be characterized as rights of national citizens, it would be those the federal government itself is forbidden to transgress.

16. 307 U.S. 496 (1939).

Whatever the merits, Justice Stone's approach outlasted the holding in *Hague*. In subsequent decisions in similar cases, the Supreme Court has not invoked the privileges or immunities theory where a first amendment-due process analysis was available.[17]

Finally, in *Edwards v. California*,[18] four Justices relied on the privileges or immunities clause as a vehicle for protecting the right of interstate travel against infringement by a California law which criminally punished persons who knowingly assisted "in bringing into the State any indigent person who is not a resident of the State. . . ." The majority reached the same result under the commerce clause. And, in more recent decisions, the Court has protected the right of interstate travel under the rubric of equal protection.[19]

In sum, the privileges or immunities clause appears technically redundant—so far. Its applications have been unstable. It has been historically eclipsed by the equal protection and due process clauses as agents of federal intervention in the civil rights duties of the states. But a fair assessment shows the record to be more complex than that. For example, even though the Supreme Court has eschewed reliance on the clause to safeguard the right to migrate from state to state, it is entirely possible that the privileges or immunities clause contributed significantly to the equal protection analysis that reached this result. Justice Brennan's majority opinion in *Shapiro v. Thompson*,[20] the case that first enunciated equal protection safeguards for the right to travel, at least cited the concurring opinions in *Edwards* in support of the recognition of that constitutional right.[21]

Future Supreme Court cases might draw upon similar interpretations of the privileges or immunities clause to suggest still other protections for personal rights. Perhaps the modern significance of the clause is simply the impetus it has furnished and may continue to furnish for the judicial articulation of rights which might otherwise have gone unprotected—as a source of inspiration if not of authority.

But one should not rule out the possibility that courts and lawyers, growing weary of the heavily encumbered and often sputtering vehicles of due process and equal protection, might yet turn to the still shadowy privileges or immunities clause not only for a rhetorical lift or for a reminder of such peculiarly "national" interests as interstate travel, but for a fresh source of distinctly personal rights. Attracted by its crisp, non-balancing cadence;[22] drawing solace from its availability only to natural persons;[23] and deeming appropriate for an era of affirmative

---

17. See generally Chapter 12, infra.

18. 314 U.S. 160, 171 (1941).

19. See Chapter 16, infra.

20. 394 U.S. 618 (1969).

21. Id. at 630. The Court had "no occasion to ascribe the source of this right to travel interstate to a particular constitutional provision." Id.

22. See, e.g., Gertz v. Welch, 418 U.S. 323, 359–60 (1974) (Douglas, J., dissenting).

23. See, e.g., Benoit, "The Privileges or Immunities Clause of the Fourteenth Amendment: Can There Be Life After Death?" 11 Suffolk L.Rev. 61, 109 (1976). That the clause excludes aliens need pose no problem given the equal protection clause as a supplement, see id. at n. 235, and that it does not apply to the federal government should present no difficulty in light of the well-known absorptive capacity of the fifth amendment's due process

government its aggressively positive rather than negative cast,[24] students of the Constitution and advocates of constitutional progress may find themselves in good company if they treat the clause as alive and potentially robust.[25]

clause. See Bolling v. Sharpe, 347 U.S. 497 (1954).

24. See, e.g., Kurland, "The Privileges or Immunities Clause: 'Its Hour Come Round At Last'?" 1972 Wash.U.L.Q. 405, 419 (urging use of the clause for claims to adequate educational opportunity, welfare and health services, police protection, and sexual equality, as well as the right to be let alone).

25. Its history and structure, too, provide considerable support for using the clause as the basis for imposing substantive limits (such as those of the Bill of Rights) upon the states. See J. Ely, Democracy and Distrust (1980).

Chapter 8

MODEL II—THE MODEL OF IMPLIED LIMITATIONS ON GOVERNMENT: THE RISE AND FALL OF CONTRACTUAL LIBERTY

§ 8–1. Evolution and Federalization of the Theory of Implied Limitations

The notion that governmental authority has implied limits which preserve private autonomy predates the establishment of the American republic.[1] During the 17th and 18th centuries, there evolved an American tradition of "natural law," postulating that "certain principles of right and justice . . . are entitled to prevail of their own intrinsic excellence."[2] It was widely believed that these principles effectively reconciled governmental power with individual liberty by identifying their respective roles in society. In particular, each level and branch of government was thought to be confined to a sphere of authority defined by the nature and function of that level or branch and by the inherent rights of citizens. Just as each of the three branches of the federal government was bound to remain within its proper jurisdiction, so the state or federal government as a whole had no power to act outside its rightful jurisdiction to intrude upon the "natural rights" reserved to the people within the private domain or to trench upon the prerogatives of other governmental departments. Rights belonging to citizens by virtue of their very citizenship, including personal security, personal liberty, and private property, would thus be preserved[3] not only by decentralization of power and mutually checking forces, as in Model I, but by rules enforceable in the proper tribunals at the behest of threatened citizens.

§ 8–1

1. For a discussion of this notion's evolution in pre-Revolutionary America and of its role in the Revolution itself, see B. Bailyn, The Ideological Origins of the American Revolution 55–93, 175–98 (1967). See also G. Wood, Creation of the American Republic (1969).

2. Corwin, "The 'Higher Law' Background of American Constitutional Law," 42 Harvard Law Rev. 149, 365 (1928–29).

3. See Wood, supra note 1, at 260–65; Bailyn, supra note 1 at 76–79. Blackstone's "Commentaries" and Montesquieu's "The Spirit of the Laws" played important roles in influencing the development of such theories in America. See Corwin, supra note 2, at 400–409; Kennedy, "The Structure of Blackstone's Commentaries," 28 Buff.L.Rev. 205 (1979); P. Spurlin, Montesquieu in America 1760–1801 (1940). See also Wood, supra note 1 at 152–160, 260–64; Bailyn, supra note 1, at 26–31. See generally E. Corwin, Liberty Against Government (1948); B. Wright, American Interpretations of Natural Law (1931); Corwin, "The Basic Doctrine of American Constitutional Law," 12 Mich.L.Rev. 247 (1914); Grey, "Do We Have An Unwritten Constitution?" 27 Stan.L.Rev. 703 (1975).

At least to some, it mattered little whether a written constitution expressed these rights and the precise governmental limits they reflected; they were to be preserved because they comprised the central tenets of the unwritten constitution or social compact among the citizenry upon which government itself was based. Common law and written constitutions expressed and elaborated these notions, but did not create them; even "Magna Carta itself" was thought "but a constrained declaration" of "original, inherent, indefeasible natural rights." [4]

Perhaps the most notable early example of these perceived limits on governmental power is to be found in Justice Chase's opinion in *Calder v. Bull* in 1798.[5] In that case, potential heirs challenged as an *ex post facto* law a Connecticut statute which invalidated a probate court decree which had failed to approve a will, resulting in a second hearing at which the will was approved, to the heirs' detriment. While the Supreme Court held that the Constitution's *ex post facto* clause applied only to criminal laws and thus rejected the heirs' claim, Chase expressed his willingness in a proper case to prevent a legislature from intruding upon private contract or property rights, even if not "expressly restrained by the Constitution . . . ."[6] A law that "takes property from A. and gives it to B.,"[7] according to Chase, would exceed the proper authority of government and would thus be invalid.

It should be noted that Chase's conception of inherent limits on legislative power did not rest on notions of immutable natural rights alone. In his opinion, Chase maintained that the limits he expounded were *implied by the creation and character of the legislature itself*—that is, by the specific purposes for which legislatures were created in the American states and by the means through which it was supposed that such legislatures might accomplish their objectives. Thus "the nature, and ends of legislative power will limit the exercise of it." [8] The attempt to take from A to give to B was void not simply because it violated A's natural rights in some ill-defined sense but because legislatures were never established—and, according to Chase, never would be—with such a function in mind. Objections, such as Justice Iredell's in dissent, to vague and romantic notions of natural rights as an insufficient basis for hardheaded judicial review, were to this degree wide of the mark; [9] Chase's natural rights were defined in large part reflexively: they were the residue marked out by the limits on government implied by its very reasons for being.

---

4. Bailyn, supra note 1, at 78 (quoting address by John Dickinson in 1766). See, e.g., Vanhorne's Lessee v. Dorrance, 2 U.S. (2 Dall.) 304, 310 (1795) (preservation of property is "a primary object of the social compact"). For a useful discussion of the influential social contract theories of Locke, Hume, and Rousseau, see E. Barker (ed.), Social Contract (1962). See also Wood, supra note 1, at 260–65, 282–91.

5. 3 U.S. (3 Dall.) 386 (1798).

6. Id. at 386 (1798) (Chase, J., seriatim opinion).

7. Id. at 388. Chase concluded that, since the probate court's initial decree had not conferred vested property rights upon the heirs under Connecticut law, the Connecticut legislature had not exceeded its authority. Id. at 391–94.

8. Id. at 388.

9. See Justice Iredell's seriatim opinion in Calder attacking Chase at 398–400.

An example perhaps more vulnerable to objections like Iredell's is provided by *Fletcher v. Peck*,[10] where the Supreme Court invalidated a Georgia statute attempting to revoke a series of state land grants. Concurring, Justice Johnson opined that the revocation violated general principles of justice which would "impose laws even on the Deity." [11] Writing for the Court, Chief Justice Marshall straddled the fence between pure natural law, implied limitations, and formal interpretation of explicit constitutional commands, suggesting simply that the Georgia statute was rendered invalid "either by general principles which are common to our free institutions, *or* by the particular provisions of the Constitution," noting that the "nature of society and government [may limit the] legislative power." [12] Similarly, in *Terrett v. Taylor* [13] the Supreme Court struck down Virginia's attempt to divest the Episcopal Church of its property. Justice Story's majority opinion declared that the statute violated "principles of natural justice" and "fundamental laws of every free government," as well as the "spirit and letter" of the Constitution.[14] Parallel invocations of natural law ideas continued to emerge well before the adoption of the fourteenth amendment.[15]

Yet in the period immediately following the Civil War Amendments, some of the same judges who endorsed natural law methods or at least methods looking to implied limitations refused to employ the fourteenth amendment itself in order to scrutinize state legislation allegedly interfering with natural rights or common-law rights. Perhaps the most notable example was Justice Miller's majority opinion in the *Slaughter-House Cases*,[16] in which the Supreme Court upheld Louisiana's law granting to a private corporation a 25-year monopoly to maintain slaughterhouses and stockyards in and around New Orleans. As we saw above in § 7-2, Justice Miller and a majority of his brethren

---

10. 10 U.S. (6 Cranch.) 87 (1810).

11. Id. at 143 (Johnson, J., concurring).

12. Id. at 139, 135 (emphasis added). Marshall's equivocation as to whether the Constitution or natural law was the basis for his decision could suggest either that many judges joined Iredell in insisting that only explicit constitutional limits on the legislature could be policed by the judiciary, see A. Mason and W. Beaney, The Supreme Court in a Free Society 198–199 (1968), or that Marshall was uncertain about applying the contract clause to state land grants. See § 9–8, supra.

13. 13 U.S. (9 Cranch.) 43 (1815).

14. Id. at 52.

15. See, e.g., Wilkinson v. Leland, 27 U.S. (2 Pet.) 627, 657 (1829) (upholding Rhode Island statute confirming otherwise void land title: ". . . fundamental maxims of a free government seem to require that the rights of personal liberty and private property should be held sacred"); Wynehamer v. People, 13 N.Y. 378 (1856) (invalidating state liquor prohibition statute). See generally Corwin, "The Doctrine

of Due Process of Law Before the Civil War," 24 Harv.L.Rev. 366 (1911); Graham, "Procedure to Substance—Extra-Judicial Rise of Due Process 1830–60," 40 Cal.L. Rev. 483 (1952). But cf. Mason and Beaney, supra note 12, at 215, discussing treatment of fifth amendment's due process clause in Murray v. Hoboken, 59 U.S. (18 How.) 272 (1856). One strong advocate of judicial review of state legislation infringing upon "natural law" rights such as those of contract and property was Thomas M. Cooley, whose famous treatise was influential in these developments. T. Cooley, A Treatise on Constitutional Limitations which Rest upon the Legislative Power of the States of the American Union (1868); see C. Jacobs, Law Writers and the Courts: The Influence of Thomas M. Cooley, Christopher G. Tiedeman, and John F. Dillon upon American Constitutional Law 27–32 (1954).

16. 83 U.S. (16 Wall.) 36 (1873), discussed in Chapter 7, supra. See also C. Fairman, History of the Supreme Court of the United States: Reconstruction and Reunion 1864–1888, Part 1, 1320–74 (1971).

interpreted the fourteenth amendment narrowly, so as not to forbid the state legislation at issue. The privileges or immunities clause guaranteed only the rights of national citizenship, which did not include the right to be free from a state-created monopoly.[17] The equal protection clause was of doubtful application where discrimination against blacks was not involved.[18] The due process claim had "not been much pressed," and could not succeed in any event since no previous or "admissible" construction of that provision had suggested that the Louisiana statute fell within its scope.[19]

Justices Field and Bradley disagreed vehemently, both arguing that no government could deprive its citizens of their inherent rights, and both relying on the natural law tradition.[20] While the federal courts may previously have possessed no power to prevent a state from infringing upon the rights of its own residents, both contended, the fourteenth amendment placed these basic rights "under the protection of the national government." [21] The monopoly created by Louisiana, they wrote, violated butchers' fundamental rights under the fourteenth amendment to pursue their occupation.[22]

While the Court was strictly limiting the application of the fourteenth amendment, however, it continued to employ a natural law-cum-implied limits approach to strike down state legislation in other settings. In the 1864 case of *Gelpcke v. Dubuque*,[23] the Supreme Court upheld the validity of Iowa municipal bonds issued in aid of railroads, despite a state supreme court decision which had recently held the bonds invalid under the state's constitution. Writing for the majority, Justice Swayne refused to adhere to the doctrine of following the latest state supreme court construction of a state's own constitution, declaring that "the plainest principles of justice" prevented the state from nullifying a municipal bond obligation which was valid when made.[24] Justice Miller dissented, emphasizing the importance of respecting the sovereignty of the states and the autonomy of their courts.[25]

Yet Justice Miller himself employed a strikingly similar approach ten years later in *Loan Association v. Topeka*,[26] invalidating a municipal ordinance which had authorized taxation to support the issuance of municipal bonds to assist private industry. Miller elaborated upon the idea of definable spheres of governmental and private power: "There

17. 83 U.S. (16 Wall.) at 75–80; Fairman, supra note 16, at 1352–54; Mason and Beaney, supra note 12, at 218.

18. 83 U.S. (16 Wall.) at 81; Fairman, supra note 16, at 1355. This interpretation of the equal protection clause, unlike Miller's construction of the privileges or immunities clause, has not survived. See Chapter 16, infra.

19. 83 U.S. (16 Wall.) at 80; Fairman, supra note 16, at 1354–55.

20. See 83 U.S. (16 Wall.) at 95–96 (Field); 114–16 (Bradley).

21. Id. at 93 (Field); 119–21 (Bradley).

22. Id. at 97–98 (Field); 120–22 (Bradley). Swayne, who wrote his own brief dissent, and Chase, who did not, agreed. Charles Fairman has argued that Field's suggested interpretation of the fourteenth amendment was too broad, while Bradley's was more workable. See Fairman, supra note 16, at 1358–60, 1387–88.

23. 68 U.S. (1 Wall.) 175 (1864); Fairman, supra note 16, at 935–44; 3 C. Warren, The Supreme Court in United States History 251–54 (1922).

24. 68 U.S. (1 Wall.) at 206–07.

25. Id. at 207–20.

26. 87 U.S. (20 Wall.) 655 (1874).

are rights in every free government beyond the control of the State," he wrote, along with "limitations on such [governmental] power which grow out of the essential nature of all free governments." [27] The most fundamental of these limits, according to Miller, was that the state must use its powers to enhance the general public welfare, rather than to redistribute resources from one citizen to another. The ordinance, by levying a tax in order to benefit a private industry, violated this principle and was thus void.[28]

The results in cases like *Loan* and *Slaughter-House*, only two years apart, may at first seem difficult to reconcile. Surely they cannot be explained entirely by a desire to protect or aid moneyed corporations; the decision in *Loan*, for example, invalidated a scheme that would have redistributed income to private industry through taxation. Similarily, an unyielding commitment to *laissez-faire* did not appear to motivate the decisions, as witnessed by the Court's approval of government regulation in *Slaughter-House*.[29]

To jurists like Miller, the principles behind cases like *Loan* and *Slaughter-House* were clear: Government regulation of economic affairs was not impermissible *per se*; it was invalid only where the state moved beyond the sphere of its inherently limited authority by using its powers to help some citizens at the expense of others, rather than to promote genuinely public purposes to benefit the citizenry as a whole.[30] But just as there was thus a clear boundary between governmental and private prerogative, so too a bright line divided federal from state authority.[31]   Cases like *Loan*, as well as such earlier decisions as *Calder*, *Fletcher*, and *Terrett*, did not gravely threaten legitimate state prerogatives because federal jurisdiction in those cases was based on diversity of citizenship. The underlying rationale of the diversity jurisdiction, parallel to that of the privileges and immunities clause of article IV, § 2,[32] was to protect residents of one state from potentially hostile treatment as "outsiders" by the courts of another. Thus in diversity cases, the federal courts were free to apply the "general common law" without infringing on legitimate state authority.[33] But in litigation pitting a state against its own citizens, Miller believed that the Court should not invalidate state legislation even if such legislation might violate "some of these principles of general constitutional law of which we could take jurisdiction if we were sitting in review of a Circuit Court of the United States, as we were in *Loan Association v. Topeka*." [34]

27. Id. at 662–63.

28. Id. at 663–65; Fairman, supra note 16, at 1101–12.

29. For the large volume of contemporary criticism of the cases, see Fairman, supra note 16, at 1369–74; Miller, supra note 27, at 261–70, 291–300.

30. See Fairman, supra note 16, at 1111.

31. Cf. United States v. DeWitt, 76 U.S. (9 Wall.) 41, 45 (1870) (holding unconstitutional a congressional prohibition of sale of

illuminating oil mixture as a "police regulation relating . . . to internal trade of the states.").

32. See Chapters 3 and 6, supra.

33. Swift v. Tyson, 41 U.S. (16 Pet.) 1 (1842); see Fairman, supra note 16, at 936–40.

34. Davidson v. New Orleans, 96 U.S. 97, 105 (1877). Another key difference between the two sources of power lay in the threat of congressional enforcement, something the Court feared if it grounded its

The federal-state boundary insisted upon by Miller could not long survive the Civil War and the constitutional amendments that followed. Increasingly, judges and critics agreed with Field and Bradley that the post-war amendments were intended to bring state actions against their own citizens within the reach of federal court scrutiny.[35] Even diversity jurisdiction sometimes aided residents against their own states; in *Loan* itself, the out-of-state loan association which had sued to recover interest on the bonds at issue lost in the Supreme Court, thus protecting the rights of Topeka resident-taxpayers from usurpation by their own government.

As the need for federal judicial review to protect the rights of citizens against their own states came to seem increasingly important, there emerged an apparent solution to Miller's fear of the seemingly limitless scope of the fourteenth amendment. *Increasingly, judges came to believe that substantive due process review could be confined by boundaries derived from common law categories*—the crucial idea leading to Model II. Just as inherent limitations on government guided natural law scrutiny of legislative action, so could they guide federal judicial review under the fourteenth amendment. Miller's very recognition of definable spheres of governmental and private authority first in *Slaughter-House* and later in *Loan*—the spheres that had enabled him to opine in the first case that the butchers' rights were not in fact violated and to opine in the second that the taxpayers' rights were— thus paved the way to the destruction of his attempted limitation of the fourteenth amendment in the *Slaughter-House Cases*.[36]

Accordingly, the years following *Loan* and *Slaughter-House* witnessed rapid movement toward substantive review of state legislation under the due process clause of the fourteenth amendment.[37] Miller himself recognized the demand for such review in 1877, grudgingly admitting that meaning could be given to the due process clause through "the gradual process of judicial inclusion and exclusion," while adhering to his view that the Court's discretion was broader in diversity cases.[38] In the same year, however, the Court warned in *Munn v. Illinois* [39] that, as to matters in which the public has no legitimate interest, "what is reasonable must be ascertained judicially," and insisted in dictum that the fourteenth amendment "prevents the states from doing that which will operate" as a violation of common law principles.

decisions on the fourteenth amendment but not if it pronounced them as general law in diversity cases.

35. See note 29, supra. Miller himself recognized the demand for stronger federal government due to the decreased confidence reposed in the states as a result of the Civil War in Slaughter-House. See 83 U.S. (16 Wall.) at 67–69, 81–82.

36. Early twentieth-century commentary recognizing this relationship between Loan and Slaughter-House is contained in Miller, supra note 23, at 291–92.

37. Some believed that such review was actually consistent with Slaughter-House, in which the due process contention was not "clearly stressed," and that it was more limited than review under the privileges and immunities clause. See Miller, supra note 23, at 268–71, 289–91.

38. Davidson v. New Orleans, 96 U.S. 97, 103–05 (1877) (upholding tax assessment as furthering public purposes).

39. 94 U.S. 113, 134, 125–26 (1877) (upholding Illinois' regulation of grain elevator charges).

Less than a decade later, the Court specifically considered the relationship between the fourteenth amendment and the police power of the states. It upheld a San Francisco ordinance prohibiting the operation of laundries at night in *Barbier v. Connolly*,[40] but warned that the due process clause protected the freedom to contract and prevented arbitrary deprivations of common-law liberty—deprivations which *by definition* could not amount to exercises of the police power, whose mission was the *protection* of common-law rights. In 1886, the Court claimed that a regulation which amounts to confiscation of property, such as one requiring a railroad to carry passengers or freight "without reward," would extend beyond state authority.[41] The next year, the Court upheld a Kansas statute prohibiting the manufacture and sale of alcoholic beverages, but declared in unmistakable terms that it would scrutinize the substantive reasonableness of state legislation pursuant to the due process clause, and would invalidate a law supposedly enacted pursuant to the police power if in fact it had "no real or substantial relation" to the public health, morals, or safety, and was "a palpable invasion of rights secured by the fundamental law." [42]

By the 1890's the Supreme Court was clearly on the verge of embarking upon the full-scale substantive due process review that formed what I have called Model II. Why those who sat on the Court were ready at that precise time remains unclear. William Nelson has attributed the change to the jurisprudential impact of the antislavery movement, which recognized the transcendent importance of liberty and gave legitimacy to arguments from moral absolutes. According to Nelson, judges influenced by the antislavery movement had gained control of the federal bench by the 1890's.[43] Other legal historians have identified other, perhaps more influential, causes. Some have argued that conservative economic philosophies and economic and social pressures influenced the judiciary.[44] Still others have pointed to

---

40. 113 U.S. 27, 31 (1885).

41. Railroad Commission Cases, 116 U.S. 307, 331 (1886). Judicial scrutiny of rate regulation rapidly advanced through a series of cases, culminating in Smyth v. Ames, 169 U.S. 466 (1898), which established the ground rules for scrutiny of the reasonableness of such regulation. For a discussion of the evolution of Smyth and its eventual repudiation, see FPC v. Hope Natural Gas Co., 320 U.S. 591 (1944), discussed in Chapter 9, infra.

42. Mugler v. Kansas, 123 U.S. 623, 661 (1887). See also Hurtado v. California, 110 U.S. 516, 532 (1884) (upholding state law substituting prosecutor's information for grand jury indictment but stating that due process guarantees "the very substance" of individual rights to life, liberty, and property). By this time, several state courts had begun to invalidate state laws which thus "exceeded" the limits of the police

power. See, e.g., In the Matter of Jacobs, 98 N.Y. 98 (1885) (invalidating state law restricting cigar manufacture); Godcharles v. Wigeman, 113 Pa. 431, 6 A. 354 (1886) (invalidating state regulation of wage payment methods); Millett v. People, 117 Ill. 294, 7 N.E. 631 (1886). See generally Mendelson, "A Missing Link in the Evolution of Due Process," 10 Vand.L.Rev. 125 (1956) (discussion of state court decisions prior to the Civil War); Nelson, "The Impact of the Antislavery Movement upon Styles of Judicial Reasoning in Nineteenth Century America," 87 Harv.L.Rev. 513, 521–532 (1974).

43. Nelson, supra note 42, at 547–66.

44. E.g., A. Paul, The Conservative Crisis and the Rule of Law (1969); B. Twiss, Lawyers and the Constitution: How Laissez-Faire Came to the Supreme Court (1942).

the effects of pressure from the organized bar [45] and hostility to labor regulations.[46]

Whatever the precise cause, the line of dicta beginning in the 1870's ripened into a landmark holding before the turn of the century. In *Allgeyer v. Louisiana*,[47] the Supreme Court invalidated a Louisiana statute prohibiting any act in the state to effect a contract for marine insurance on Louisiana property with a company not licensed to do business in Louisiana. The Court held that the statute exceeded the state's police power and violated the due process clause of the fourteenth amendment, in that it infringed upon the liberty to contract for insurance. The floodgates of substantive due process review had been opened as implied limitations analysis moved from the realm of sporadic invocation as "general law" in diversity cases and treatises to the realm of routine enforcement as part of specifically *federal* law in the name of the fourteenth amendment. Model II, the Model of Implied Limitations whose conceptual elements had been at hand for decades, came into its own as federal constitutional law.

§ 8–2. The Lochner Era: Model II Triumphant

Model II reigned in the period beginning around the turn of the century with *Allgeyer* and ending by the middle of the 1930's with *West Coast Hotel v. Parrish*.[1] That period is ordinarily described as "the *Lochner* era," but it should be so characterized only with great caution—and with a recognition that "*Lochnerizing*" has become so much an epithet that the very use of the label may obscure attempts at understanding. While the Supreme Court invalidated much state and federal legislation between 1897 and 1937, more statutes in fact withstood due process attack in this period than succumbed to it.[2] Moreover, the Court also interpreted other constitutional provisions, such as

45. Mason and Beaney, supra note 12, at 227–36.

46. L. Beth, The Development of the American Constitution 1877–1917, 138–66 (1971).

47. 165 U.S. 578 (1897). The Court also suggested that the statute unlawfully interfered with interstate commerce, an area within federal control, since the contract was made outside Louisiana.

§ 8–2

1. 300 U.S. 379 (1937), discussed in § 8–7, infra.

2. It has been estimated that the Supreme Court invalidated state or federal regulations pursuant to the due process clause, usually coupled with another provision such as the equal protection clause, in 197 cases between 1899 and 1937, while an even larger number of regulations survived scrutiny. See B. Wright, The Growth of American Constitutional Law 154, 176 (1942); G. Gunther, Constitutional Law: Cases and Materials 565 (9th ed. 1975); Warren, § 8–1 supra note 23, at 463–65

(369 state laws enacted under the police power upheld between 1889 and 1918). Several discussions of this period of constitutional history suggest that in the years surrounding World War I, the Court's composition, its concern with the integrity of wartime legislation, and the influence of the Progressive movement, temporarily produced greater tolerance on the federal bench of social and economic legislation. See E. Lewis, History of American Political Thought from the Civil War to the World War 101–07 (1937); P. Murphy, The Constitution in Crisis Times 1918–1969, 18–37 (1972); Mason & Beaney, § 8–1, supra, note 12, at 238–42. Compare Warren, § 8–1, supra, note 23 at 463–65 (53 state police power statutes held unconstitutional between 1889 and 1918) with Murphy at 63 (almost 140 laws held unconstitutional between 1920 and 1930). For a comprehensive summary of the Court's decisions between 1897 and 1937, see N. Small (ed.), The Constitution of the United States, 1392–99, 1427–87 (1964 ed.).

grants of congressional power in article I and the contract clause, so as to restrain progressive and redistributive social and economic legislation throughout the early twentieth century.[3] Nevertheless, it would be accurate to conclude that during this period the Supreme Court was quite willing—certainly more willing than it has otherwise ever been— to scrutinize and invalidate economic regulations pursuant to the due process clause.

Many observers have contended that the Supreme Court's decisions during the *Lochner* era were motivated by the majority's conservative economic ideology and by its hostility toward labor regulation.[4] Whatever the validity of these suggestions, it is clear that more than a few Americans shared the conservative beliefs held by some members of the Court. Many legislatures and courts resisted the Progressive movement, and it is clear that the Supreme Court's views echoed a powerful strand in the thought and politics of the early twentieth century.[5] For example, Charles Warren has noted that the number of contemporary commentators who approved the decision in *Lochner v. New York* [6] at least equalled the number who attacked it.[7] The Court's inclinations in the *Lochner* era of Model II were hardly in the vanguard of social and economic thought, but at least until the 1930's they were far from aberrant or peculiarly retrogressive.[8]

§ 8–3. Model II's Scrutiny of Means-Ends Relationships

In reviewing state and federal economic regulation, the Supreme Court closely scrutinized both the ends sought and the means employed in challenged legislation. In its analysis of legislative means, the Court required a "real and substantial" relationship between a statute and its objectives.[1] By itself, such a standard might have produced few if any alarming consequences; indeed, in several cases the Court yielded to factual demonstrations of the claimed relationship between legislative

3. See Chapters 5 (art. I) and 9 (contract clause). The due process cases accounted for less than half of the decisions in which the Court invalidated federal or state laws on constitutional grounds. See 3 C. Warren, The Supreme Court in United States History 108, 154, 178 (1922).

4. See § 8–1, notes 44 and 46, supra.

5. See R. Billington, American History After 1865, 86–98, 161–78 (1965 ed.); G. Kolko, The Triumph of Conservatism (1963); Murphy, supra note 2, at 141 (lower federal courts); L. Beth, The Development of the American Constitution 216–48 (1971) (state courts). For example, as of 1932, less than 20 states had enacted minimum wage laws, 22 states had not enacted "progressive" legislation regulating the employment of women, and only one state required seating accommodations for male and female workers. See E. Nichols and J. Baccus (eds.), Minimum Wages and Maximum Hours 27–28, 297–98, 311–12 (1936).

6. 198 U.S. 45 (1905) (invalidating state law setting 10-hour daily maximum and 60-hour weekly maximum for employment by bakers).

7. See 3 C. Warren, The Supreme Court in United States History 435–36 n. 1 (1922). See also Murphy, supra note 2, at 67–68 (business, government, and organized bar support for Supreme Court decisions in the 1920's); Ransom, "The Profession of Law," 2 Vital Speeches 628 (1936) (address by President of American Bar Association defending Supreme Court).

8. See Ackerman, "The Storrs Lectures: Discovering the Constitution," 93 Yale L.J. 1013, 1051–57 (1984).

§ 8–3

1. See Lochner v. New York, 198 U.S. 45, 56, 64 (1905); Jacobson v. Massachusetts, 197 U.S. 11, 31 (1905); Liggett Co. v. Baldridge, 278 U.S. 105, 111 (1928).

means and ends. The famous "Brandeis briefs" in such cases as *Muller v. Oregon* [2] helped save a number of statutes from invalidation.

Decisions such as *Muller*, however, appeared as exceptions to the rule. The more typical decisions of the era expressed profound skepticism about academic or other experts as witnesses and especially about legislators as factfinders.[3] Such "facts" were regarded as manipulable and thus unreliable.[4] Instead, the Court interpreted its requirement of a substantial means-ends relationship so as to invalidate statutes which interfered with private economic transactions unless evolving common law concepts demonstrated a proper fit between the legislation and its asserted objectives.

Lochner itself provides the best example of such strict and skeptical means-ends analysis. There, the Court rejected New York's claim that its 60-hour limit on a bakery employee's work week was significantly and directly related to the promotion of employee health. Yet considerable evidence, discussed at length by Justice Harlan in dissent, suggested that limiting the work week as New York had decided to do would enhance the health of bakers, whose working conditions appeared to pose significant threats to their health and welfare.[5] Justice Harlan found the majority's decision particularly objectionable in light of *Holden v. Hardy*,[6] which seven years earlier had upheld a similar limit on the working hours of underground miners.

The majority, however, thought the cases clearly distinguishable. Detailed empirical demonstrations had not justified the result in *Holden*; instead, the decision appeared to rest heavily on the characterization of mining as an activity which the courts had traditionally recognized as unusually dangerous or ultrahazardous.[7] Just as reputation evidence is often preferred over more pointed, but potentially also more slanted, opinion testimony in the law of evidence, so the Court was

---

2. 208 U.S. 412 (1908) (upholding maximum working hours provisions for women). See also, e.g., McLean v. Arkansas, 211 U.S. 539 (1909) (upholding state regulation of wage payment to miners); Simpson v. O'Hara, 243 U.S. 629 (1917) (upholding, by an equally divided Court, state minimum wage requirement for women factory employees); Bunting v. Oregon, 243 U.S. 426 (1917) (upholding state law establishing ten-hour work day for manufacturing employees). For more general discussion of the technique, see P. Freund, On Understanding the Supreme Court 86–91 (1949); Bikle, "Judicial Determination of Questions of Fact Affecting the Constitutional Validity of Legislative Action," 38 Harv.L. Rev. 6 (1924); Karst, "Legislative Facts in Constitutional Litigation," 1960 Sup.Ct. Rev. 75.

3. For example, when Chief Justice White was confronted with a Brandeis brief in Adams v. Tanner, 244 U.S. 590 (1917), he reportedly responded: "I could compile a brief twice as thick to prove that the legal profession ought to be abolished."

L. Pfeffer, This Honorable Court 259 (1965).

4. Id. See also Adkins v. Children's Hosp., 261 U.S. 525, 559–60 (1923) (such facts found "interesting but only mildly persuasive"); A. Mason and W. Beaney, The Supreme Court in a Free Society 242–246 (1968). In Lochner itself, for example, Justice Peckham, author of the majority opinion, refused even to reply to Justice Harlan's reliance in dissent on factual reports and treatises on industrial diseases. 198 U.S. at 58–63, 70–71.

5. Lochner v. New York, 198 U.S. 45, 68–72 (1905) (Harlan, J., dissenting).

6. 169 U.S. 366 (1898).

7. Id. at 391. See Lochner v. New York, 198 U.S. 45, 54–55 (1905). For a discussion of the English and American common law of ultrahazardous activities, see W. Prosser, Law of Torts 78 (4th ed., 1971). Even ordinary coal mining had been regarded as ultrahazarous by many American courts. Id. at 511.

plainly more willing to trust the gradually evolving categories of the common law than the readily tailored findings of "experts," committees, or even legislative majorities.

Moreover, the majority in *Lochner* reasoned that other state regulations could promote employees' health without infringing so fundamentally on their freedom to contract; limits needlessly restrictive would therefore exceed the boundaries of the police power.[8] Indeed, the fact that the New York law invaded contractual autonomy beyond the level warranted by its asserted goal of protecting employee health suggested to the Court that health was not really the statute's objective at all, so that the legislation could not be justified as a means of accomplishing its alleged aims.[9]

This strict scrutiny of means-ends relationships continued to surface in later decisions. Thus the Court invalidated a Nebraska law requiring standardized weights for loaves of bread, finding the statute "not necessary for the protection of purchasers against . . . fraud by short weights," since that problem "readily could have been dealt with" without such restrictive regulation.[10] In striking down minimum wage laws for women in *Adkins v. Children's Hospital*,[11] Justice Sutherland noted for the majority that governmental wage regulation was needed only within limited categories of activity. And in a 1928 decision which invalidated Pennsylvania restrictions on corporate ownership of pharmacies, the Court pointed to other specified types of regulatory statutes as permissible methods of promoting public health in that area.[12] Stringent analysis of the relationship between a challenged law and its alleged objectives thus formed an important part of judicial activism in the *Lochner* period.

§ 8–4. Model II's Scrutiny of Legislative Ends

Perhaps more striking than such close scrutiny of means-ends relationships during the *Lochner* era was the strict judicial assessment of legislative ends. In this respect, judges drew heavily on earlier natural law and implied limitation notions;[1] partly on the economic and social theories of Herbert Spencer advocating social Darwinism;[2] and to a degree also on the conservative legal theories of Roscoe Pound,[3] Thomas Cooley,[4] and Christopher Tiedeman,[5] advocating pro-

---

8. Lochner v. New York, 198 U.S. 45, 61–62 (1905).

9. See id. at 64 (claiming that laws like New York's are often "in reality passed for other motives").

10. Jay Burns Baking Co. v. Bryan, 264 U.S. 504, 517 (1924). Justice Brandeis' dissent predictably discussed factual proof of the need for the regulation.

11. 261 U.S. 525, 546–48 (1923).

12. Liggett Co. v. Baldridge, 278 U.S. 105 (1928). See also, e.g., Weaver v. Palmer Bros., 270 U.S. 402 (1926) (invalidating state prohibition of "shoddy" in the manufacture of bedding materials where other means of protecting health and preventing deception

were available); Adams v. Tanner, 244 U.S. 590 (1917) (total prohibition of fee collection from workers by employment agencies held not justified by potential abuses). Liggett was expressly overruled in North Dakota Bd. of Pharmacy v. Snyder's Drug Stores, 414 U.S. 156 (1973).

§ 8–4

1. See § 8–1, supra.

2. H. Spencer, Social Statics (1872). See R. Hofstadter, Social Darwinism in American Thought 1860–1915 (1945).

3. See, e.g., Pound, "Liberty of Contract," 18 Yale L.J. 454 (1909).

4.–5. See notes 4 and 5 on page 571.

tection for individual freedom of contract and property through limitations on the reach of the police power.

In broad outline, the underlying philosophy held that the only legitimate goal of government in general, and of the police power in particular, was to protect individual rights and otherwise enhance the *total* public good;[6] if they were to be upheld, governmental regulations thus had to promote "the general welfare" and not be "purely for the promotion of private interests."[7] As a corollary, it followed that any statute which was imposed upon individuals or corporations in order to redistribute resources and thus benefit some persons at the expense of others (for that is how redistribution was then conceived) would extend beyond the implicit boundaries of legislative authority. Such a law would thus violate natural rights of property and contract, rights lying at the very core of the private domain.[8]

Moreover, laws aimed at redistributing resources would by their very nature fall outside the legislative function. Governmental actions which sought to benefit some persons at the expense of others were perceived as dangerous and exceptional. If such activities were not based on notions of corrective justice between parties, they were merely disguised forms of robbery. If, on the other hand, corrective justice *was* involved, then it was solely the function of the courts to act. As Cooley wrote, even if the Constitution did not itself limit legislative deprivations of property, a statute transferring resources "would nevertheless be void" as an act "judicial in its nature," if permissible at all.[9]

At the same time it was believed that legislatures could properly enact statutes which protected the interests of certain discrete groups, such as children and women, both treated by the dominant legal ideology as unable to protect themselves. Such laws, it was thought by many, simply recognized "distinctions that exist in the nature of things."[10] But equalization or redistribution of economic or social

4. T. Cooley, A Treatise on the Constitutional Limitations which Rest upon the Legislative Power of the States of the American Union (8th ed., 1927). Cooley's treatise was originally published in 1868. The great influence of Cooley and Tiedeman is demonstrated persuasively in C. Jacobs, Law Writers and the Courts: The Influence of Thomas M. Cooley, Christopher G. Tiedeman, and John F. Dillon Upon American Constitutional Law (1954).

5. See C. Tiedeman, A Treatise on the Limitations of the Police Power in the United States (1886). Tiedeman explicitly acknowledged that his treatise was designed in part to stem what he perceived as the rising tide of governmental interference in private affairs and to promote a "return" to laissez-faire.

6. Conceived as an amalgam of (1) the aggregate welfare of individuals, and (2) conventional morality.

7. Cooley, supra note 4, at 1227–28 n. 2.

8. See, e.g., Spann v. Dallas, 111 Tex. 350, 235 S.W. 513 (1921); Cooley, supra note 4, at 1229–30, 1348.

9. Cooley, supra note 4, at 357. Even the courts, according to Cooley, could not dispense distributive justice; their function was only to do commutative justice as between parties (i.e., to transfer property from A to B in order to restore what properly belongs to B at common law according to the law of contracts, property, or torts), not to proceed "without reasons" through "mere arbitrary fiat." Id. The very idea of distributive justice was thus ruled out; but one correct "distribution" could exist— that generated by the inexorable interaction of private wills under the ground-rules of the common law.

10. Cooley, supra note 4, at 1341–42.

power, which "takes property from A. and gives it to B.," [11] was an impermissible end of legislation.

Again, *Lochner* itself usefully illustrates the application of this judicial philosophy. The Court there summarily rejected any suggestion that New York's limitation of working hours could stand as a "labor law" intended to benefit bakers at their employers' potential loss, while interfering with the formal contractual freedom of both. "The interest of the public," wrote Justice Peckham, would not be "in the slightest degree affected." [12] Nor did the bakers fall within a recognized category of persons warranting special governmental protection: "There is no contention that bakers as a class are not equal in intelligence and capacity to men in other trades or manual occupations, or that they are not able to assert their rights and care for themselves without the protecting arm of the State, interfering with their independence of judgment and of action. They are in no sense wards of the State." [13] Thus the New York law could not be justified as an attempt to help bakers, whether by enhancing their bargaining power in the contractual regime or by circumventing that regime in order directly to assure bakers of decent working conditions.

Perhaps the clearest and fullest statement of the era's dominant philosophy appeared in *Coppage v. Kansas*,[14] where the Supreme Court struck down a state law prohibiting "yellow dog" contracts—contracts which required workers to refrain from union membership as a condition of employment. Writing for the majority, Justice Pitney discussed the Court's theory of due process review at length. Restriction of freedom to contract for personal employment, he explained, was a "substantial impairment of liberty" which was "as essential to the laborer as to the capitalist, to the poor as to the rich," since only by bartering their employment could poor laborers begin to acquire property.[15] The right to join a union was a right that a worker should be able to bargain away if it was to his or her advantage.[16] Liberty of contract could be incidentally impaired by statutes in aid of the general public welfare (for "liberty" did not include the right to injure the public), but not to redress so-called inequalities of bargaining power, which were "but the normal and inevitable result" of the exercise of the right to contract itself.[17]

In contrast to *Lochner* and *Coppage*, protection of the "particular class" of coal miners was justified on the theory that their contracts were unilaterally imposed by their employers.[18] Similarly, the Court

11. Calder v. Bull, 3 U.S. (3 Dall.) 386, 388 (1798) (Chase, J.). See § 8–1, supra.

12. Lochner v. New York, 198 U.S. 45, 57 (1905).

13. Id.

14. 236 U.S. 1 (1915). Coppage reaffirmed and extended Adair v. United States, 208 U.S. 161 (1908), in which the Court invalidated a federal "yellow dog" contract restriction.

15. 236 U.S. at 14.

16. Id. at 19–21.

17. Id. at 17–18.

18. Holden v. Hardy, 169 U.S. 366, 393, 397 (1898). The Court in Lochner did not specifically explain why such "constraints" as employee fear of being fired in Holden did not apply to the bakers in Lochner; apparently the Court felt that coal miners as a class constituted a captive labor force while bakers did not. Cf. Marsh v. Alabama, 326 U.S. 501 (1946) (holding that operation of "company town" was a public function for first amendment purposes).

upheld a working hours limit for women in *Muller v. Oregon* [19] in order to protect a class which it perceived as dependent; in the Court's frame of reference, the social and biological role of women might not be compromised by limited amounts of non-domestic work, but would be jeopardized by labors so excessive as to threaten the essential reproductive functions of the female.[20]   Even where women were involved, however, the Supreme Court disallowed minimum wage laws, which could not so readily be assimilated to sexist assumptions about the nature and role of women [21] and which would have struck at the heart of private control over property and contract; even for women, minimum wages thus constituted a "naked, arbitrary exercise" of asserted legislative authority.[22]

Similar attempts to bring legislative goals into alignment with these substantive views surfaced throughout the *Lochner* era, as the Court invalidated federal and state statutes regulating labor-management relations,[23] prices and wages,[24] and entry into business.[25]   It thus

19.   208 U.S. 412 (1908).

20.   Id. at 420–22 (e.g., references to the "dependence" of women upon men and the social need for "healthy mothers"). From a modern and less sexist perspective, the Court's concern with the proper role of women can be understood partly as an attempt to freeze women within the role of wives and mothers, and partly as reflecting the then-popular conception that the genetic composition of humanity would be adversely affected should women become too involved in the labor force. The rationale for treating women differently had rested largely on claims of divine intention in the 1830's and 1840's. Although that approach was reflected in some judicial opinions even into the 1870's (see, e.g., Bradwell v. State, 83 U.S. (16 Wall.) 130, 141 (1873) (Bradley, J., concurring) (state allowed to deny women the right to practice law since the "paramount destiny and mission of women" under the "law of the Creator" is "to fulfill the noble and benign offices of wife and mother"), the dominant defense of "protective" laws and practices by the late 19th and early 20th centuries was cast along physiological lines. A popular tract in the last quarter of the 19th century, Clarke, Sex in Education, or a Fair Chance for Girls (1873), claimed that excessive non-domestic work or rigorous academic study could seriously damage a woman's reproductive system. Needless to say, Clarke's conclusions, and those of other physicians who took the same view, did not rest on reliable data; in fact, the major source of the empirical information invoked seems to have been isolated instances of menstrual difficulty among middle-class adolescents. See Trecker, "Sex, Science and Education," 26 Am.Q. 352 (1974). The physiological rationale for special treatment of women, however thin its

evidentiary base, fit well for several decades with sterilization laws and similar state attempts to shape the population's genetic future. Although feminists countered the view of people like Clarke with data about the healthy children of women who had gone to college, reformists like Jane Addams and Josephine Shaw Lowell found the older stereotypes more useful in their battle for improved conditions for working-class women. See generally E. Flexner, Century of Struggle (1973).

21.   Substandard wages did not appear to risk the same biological damage to a woman's "physical structure and the performance of maternal functions," 208 U.S. at 420, that overly strenuous or unduly prolonged periods of work were thought to entail.

22.   Adkins v. Children's Hosp., 261 U.S. 525, 559 (1923). See also Morehead v. New York ex rel. Tipaldo, 298 U.S. 587 (1936) (New York minimum wage law for women).   The Court's treatment of wage and hour legislation would tend to support the theories discussed at note 20, supra. That is, limitation of women's working hours would be justified by a perceived need to limit the participation of women in the labor force, whereas minimum wage legislation would not.

23.   E.g., Coppage v. Kansas, 236 U.S. 1 (1915) (state law prohibiting "yellow dog" contracts); Adair v. United States, 208 U.S. 161 (1908) (federal "yellow dog" restriction); Truax v. Corrigan, 257 U.S. 312 (1921) (state law restricting the use of injunctions in labor disputes); Wolff Pkg. Co. v. Court of Indust. Reltns., 262 U.S. 522 (1923) (compulsory arbitration); Railroad

24.–25.   See notes 24–25 on page 574.

became clear, especially in the late 1920's and early 1930's, that much economic and social legislation could not withstand substantive due process scrutiny by the Supreme Court.

§ 8–5. The Decline of Lochner: Internal Erosion

However firm the Court's adherence to the conception of contractual liberty and to the logic through which such liberty was "derived" from the implied limits on government power, the reign of *Lochner* came to an end in the late 1930's. Both erosion within the internal structure of the relevant doctrines and external attacks on their underlying philosophical and factual premises contributed to the era's demise and thus to the collapse of Model II.

Exceptions to the regime of governmental non-interference in contractual liberty, recognized as proper even by *Lochner's* advocates, suggested that the seeds of self-contradiction lay close to the philosophy's surface. For example, the Court's decisions in *Holden v. Hardy* [1] and *Muller v. Oregon* [2] indicated that, insofar as such groups as coal miners and women were concerned, states could attempt to assist the protected group [3] even at the expense of others, because of its supposedly vulnerable and dependent position. These recognized exceptions were cast in terms that rendered the entire theory potentially vulnerable to an argument that, as social and economic patterns change or as existing patterns are reassessed, other groups—ultimately, industrial laborers in general—may become unable, or may come to be *regarded* as unable, to protect their own interests effectively, so that governmental intervention on their behalf becomes justifiable in terms of an already available theory. Cases such as *Bunting v. Oregon* [4] may indeed reflect an early recognition of that potential, and made it more difficult for observers and critics of the doctrine's later applications to accept its persistence as mandatory.

Revealing examples of internal disarray also surface in the Supreme Court's treatment of tax legislation. The Court had ruled the income tax unconstitutional in *Pollock v. Farmers Loan and Trust Co.*,[5] reversing its earlier approval.[6] But the Court in turn saw its decision reversed by the sixteenth amendment in 1913, authorizing an unappor-

Retirement Bd. v. Alton R. Co., 295 U.S. 330 (1935) (federal railroad pension plan).

24. E.g., Connally v. General Const. Co., 269 U.S. 385 (1926) (construction workers' wages); Tyson and Bro. v. Banton, 273 U.S. 418 (1927) (theater ticket resale prices); Ribnik v. McBride, 277 U.S. 350 (1928) (employment agency fees); Williams v. Standard Oil Co., 278 U.S. 235 (1929) (gasoline prices). Olsen v. Nebraska, 313 U.S. 236 (1941), explicitly overruled Ribnik, and Tyson was overruled in Gold v. DiCarlo, 380 U.S. 520 (1965) (per curiam).

25. E.g., Adams v. Tanner, 244 U.S. 590 (1917) (collection of fees from workers by employment agencies); New State Ice Co. v. Liebmann, 285 U.S. 262 (1932) (ice manufacturing).

§ 8–5

1. 169 U.S. 366 (1898), discussed in § 8–4, supra.

2. 208 U.S. 412 (1908), discussed in § 8–4, supra.

3. Or, as in Muller, help freeze its social role.

4. 243 U.S. 426 (1917) (upholding state law establishing 10-hour work day for manufacturing employees), discussed in § 8–3, supra. See the discussion of Bunting in Adkins v. Children's Hospital, 261 U.S. 525, 550–51 (1923).

5. 157 U.S. 429 (1895).

6. Springer v. United States, 102 U.S. 586 (1881). See A. Paul, Conservative Crisis and the Rule of Law 159–200 (1969).

tioned taxing mechanism [7] and implicitly accepting the income redistribution which such a tax produced.[8] Both before and after the sixteenth amendment, however, the Court itself had approved a number of taxing schemes which appeared to belie its insistence that the government not rearrange the workings of the property and contract system ordained by the common law or interfere in private affairs. It upheld taxes on inheritance [9] and on corporate income,[10] despite arguable similarities to the tax in *Pollock*. It sustained a North Dakota plan in which tax revenues were used to operate a state-run mill and home building project.[11] On several occasions, it exhibited a hands-off policy towards taxes used to regulate private uses of property,[12] although it struck down other instances of regulatory taxation.[13] Although the Court was basing its tax decisions not on any overt assessment of the degree to which any given tax redistributed property or interfered with contract but on various article I doctrines, it would be difficult (perhaps impossible) to demonstrate that the key to how the Court acted in these cases was not in fact related to the degree of redistribution or interference.[14] What seems significant for our purposes is that a fully coherent *Lochner* model would have consistently addressed taxing schemes from such a perspective; instead, the Court's tax decisions suggest at least some ambiguity with respect to the extent to which government may properly interfere with "private" economic life.[15]

The Court's decisions during this period concerning the taking of private property also illustrate the growing internal tensions within the *Lochner* model.[16] Under the classical nineteenth century approach, eminent domain power could be employed to appropriate private land for clearly public uses, such as the construction of public roads; in

---

7. The Pollock case had ruled that a federal tax on income from state and local bonds was a "direct tax" within the meaning of art. I, §§ 2 and 9, and thus was invalid unless apportioned among the states in accord with the population of each. See Chapter 5, supra.

8. For a discussion of the evolution of the 16th Amendment in response to Pollock and the decline of the Court's restrictive policy in general, see Mason & Beaney, § 8–1, supra note 12, at 127–150; S. Surrey, W. Warren, P. McDaniel, & H. Ault, Federal Income Taxation: Cases and Materials 4–11, 284–85 (1972). The opinions in Pollock itself suggest that the redistributive consequences of an income tax were recognized early. See 158 U.S. 607 (Field, J., concurring) (claiming the tax was an "assault on capital" which would produce "a war of the poor against the rich"); id. at 695 (Brown, J., dissenting) (noting that "even the spectre of socialism" was used as an argument against the tax). See also L. Beth, The Development of the American Constitution 1877–1917, 157–60 (1971).

9. Knowlton v. Moore, 178 U.S. 41 (1900).

10. Flint v. Stone Tracy Co., 220 U.S. 107, 150, 162 (1911).

11. Green v. Frazier, 253 U.S. 233 (1920).

12. E.g., McCray v. United States, 195 U.S. 27 (1904) (oleomargarine); United States v. Doremus, 249 U.S. 86 (1919) (narcotics).

13. Bailey v. Drexel Furn. Co., 259 U.S. 20 (1922) (federal excise tax on net profits of certain employers of child labor); United States v. Butler, 297 U.S. 1 (1936) (Agricultural Adjustment Act).

14. For a discussion of the seemingly contradictory holdings, see A. Mason & W. Beaney, The Supreme Court in a Free Society 137–50 (1968).

15. For an early discussion reflecting the acceptance of progressive taxation (and thus of implicit income redistribution), see Hackett, "The Constitutionality of the Graduated Income Tax Law," 25 Yale L.J. 427 (1916). See 3 C. Warren, The Supreme Court in United States History 422 nn. 1–2, (1922), for additional early commentary.

16. These decisions are analyzed in detail from the perspective of the just compensation requirement in Chapter 9, infra.

contrast, any attempt to take private resources for the benefit of other private parties, whether by direct seizure or through regulation, would be invalid either as an attempted exercise of eminent domain or as a purported use of the police power.[17] By the 1920's, however, courts had begun to employ a novel form of eminent domain analysis in considering regulations increasingly perceived as falling into a gray area between those deemed clearly valid as promoting the public welfare, and those deemed clearly void as redistributive.

In *Pennsylvania Coal Co. v. Mahon*,[18] for example, a homeowner sought an injunction against underground coal mining which would have damaged his property on the surface, pursuant to a recently enacted Pennsylvania statute which forbade such mining. The Supreme Court recognized that a deed executed prior to the statute's enactment by the homeowner's predecessor in title had granted the coal company the right to engage in such mining, so that the law's application would "destroy previously existing rights of property and contract," [19] effectively rewriting the pre-existing deed to transfer more than the homeowner had paid or bargained for. But the Court did *not* hold that the statute violated due process of law as a taking from the coal company for the private benefit of the homeowner. Instead, the majority found for the coal company solely because it had not been compensated for the "taking" of its property (its subsurface mining rights) for public benefit by the mining restriction statute.

Yet the public nature of the benefit wrought by the Pennsylvania statute was ambiguous at best as applied to cases where damage was threatened only to a surface owner who had bought property from a mining company for a price plainly reduced to reflect the well understood surface risks of continued mining operations. One of the statute's primary functions was to protect individual private houses from subsurface mining, a goal in which the Court detected potential elements of public interest but which, as applied here, related primarily to "ordinary private affairs." [20] The statute as a whole, at least when retroactively applied as in this case, could easily have been viewed as upsetting the results of the private bargain between homeowner and mining company and of others similarly situated, just as the New York statute in *Lochner* was viewed as interfering with employer-employee bargaining. Eminent domain in *Mahon* thus became a kind of procedural substitute for substantive guarantees of contractual autonomy; rather than invalidating statutes in which the public character of the benefit was unclear while the private harm was both evident and focused, the Court in effect forced the public to internalize private costs in ambiguous cases by requiring government to compensate private parties for

17. See §§ 8–4, supra, and 9–2, infra.

18. 260 U.S. 393 (1922).

19. Id. at 413.

20. Id. The Court noted specifically that the public interest in safety was limited since the statute did not apply at all where the surface and subsurface rights were owned by the same person, and since other methods (e.g., signs warning the public) could have been used to protect the interest in safety. Nor had any claim been made that the statute was concerned with avoiding depletion of the housing stock, clearly a matter of public interest in some periods. Contrast Keystone Bituminous Coal Ass'n v. DeBenedictis, 107 S.Ct. 1232 (1987), discussed in § 9–2, infra, note 9.

what they were being forced to lose.[21] This approach obviously infringes on *Lochner*-recognized private property and contract rights and blurs the distinction between private and public purposes which lies at the heart of the *Lochner* philosophy.

This private-public distinction was blurred still further six years later in *Miller v. Schoene*.[22] There, property owners whose land contained red cedar trees infected (but not ruined) with a fungoid carrier of rust disease were ordered, pursuant to a Virginia statutory scheme to control the disease, to cut down their trees lest the contagion spread to a nearby apple orchard, where it would destroy the orchard's commercial value. Pointing to the great importance of apple orchards to the state economy, the Supreme Court upheld the statute without requiring compensation. Yet it is clear that, in terms of the conceptual scheme of *Lochner*, the state's statute and the Court's decision sustaining it infringed on the property "rights" of the cedar owners in order to benefit the apple tree owners. The orchard owners themselves could presumably have accomplished by private contract the same level of apple preservation that the statute achieved by fiat, with the apple owners rather than the cedar owners bearing the attendant expense. The Court upheld the statute as promoting an overriding *public* interest in protecting the apple orchards, even though the benefit produced fell within the *private* economy of the state and favored one party over another. The private and the public interests were thus recognized as virtually identical; the distinction between private and public benefit had plainly begun to collapse.[23]

Miller not only indicates that redistribution of property between private parties may be justified in the public interest. The decision also suggests that the state inevitably has a positive role to play, a role whose exercise in *either* direction will benefit some private actors while hurting others. For the Court opined that, if the state had done nothing and permitted disaster to strike the apple orchards, "it would have been none the less a choice." [24] If the *Lochner* philosophy had been strictly applied, common law categories would have guided the Court to the conclusion that the state was powerless to intervene unless the cedar trees constituted a public nuisance. But the majority rejected the common law of nuisance as a baseline in favor of a more generalized idea of the public interest.[25] The notion of the common law universe defining a "natural" state of affairs without governmental interference was fading. It is important, however, to note that not even *Miller* or *Mahon* contradicted the proposition that it was illegitimate for a legislature to transfer resources from one citizen to another for the very purpose of making the social or economic *distribution* more just. Nevertheless, these decisions cast serious doubt on the continuing

21. Cf. Vincent v. Lake Erie Transportation Co., 109 Minn. 456, 124 N.W. 221 (1910) (shipowner who moors his vessel to a dock during a storm is guilty of no wrong—but only if he compensates the dock owner for the injury inflicted).

22. 276 U.S. 272 (1928).

23. See, e.g., id. at 279 (". . . preponderant public concern in the preservation of the one interest over the other").

24. Id.

25. Id. at 280.

hold of the Model II philosophy on the members of the *Lochner* majority.

§ 8–6. The Decline of Lochner: External Assault

Even more important in triggering *Lochner's* demise than its internal tensions were the external pressures to which the doctrine was increasingly subject. Legal criticism of the prevailing view had of course been present from the beginning, as evidenced by the dissents of Justices Harlan and Holmes in *Lochner* itself, with Harlan questioning the Court's interference with legislative fact-finding and Holmes challenging the Court's intrusion into the legislature's choice of values. But it was by no means Justice Holmes alone who attacked the *Lochner* approach by arguing that the fourteenth amendment "does not enact Mr. Herbert Spencer's Social Statics." [1] Many members of the bench and bar roundly criticized the economic, social, and judicial philosophy expressed by the *Lochner* majority.[2] Indeed, by 1936 the composition and philosophy of the Supreme Court had changed so significantly that at least four Justices—Hughes, Brandeis, Cardozo, and Stone—were clearly prepared to abandon the *Lochner* approach.[3]

In large measure, however, it was the economic realities of the Depression that graphically undermined *Lochner's* premises. No longer could it be argued with great conviction that the invisible hand of economics was functioning simultaneously to protect individual rights and produce a social optimum. The legal "freedom" of contract and property came increasingly to be seen as an illusion, subject as it was to impersonal economic forces.[4] Positive government intervention came to be more widely accepted as essential to economic survival, and legal doctrines would henceforth have to operate from that premise.

In fact, the economic crisis provided substantial impetus to evolving legal doctrines which directly contradicted the *Lochner* thesis and constituted a frontal attack on the structure of Model II. A growing number of legal scholars, including most prominently the advocates of legal realism, came to reject the notion that the common law represented a "natural" state of affairs, and instead saw common law doctrines and decisions as expressions of positive governmental intervention to achieve identifiable, though not always laudable, human purposes. In the private law of contract and property, as well as in the public law of criminal and constitutional adjudication, the perspective shifted to one that saw the whole fabric of law and legal decision as more *chosen* than *given*.[5] Thus the basic justification for judicial intervention under

---

§ 8–6

1. Lochner v. New York, 198 U.S. 45, 90 (1905) (Holmes, J., dissenting).

2. A useful summary and discussion of such criticism appears in P. Murphy, The Constitution in Crisis Times 70–82, 99–110 (1972). See, e.g., Powell, "The Judiciality of Minimum Wage Legislation," 37 Harv.L. Rev. 572 (1924).

3. See A. Sutherland, Constitutionalism in America 498–99 (1965).

4. A typical example of contemporary criticism of this type is found in Amidon, "Due Process," 25 Survey-Graphic 412 (July 1936). See M. Weber, Law in Economy and Society 188–91 (1954 ed.).

5. See generally White, "From Sociological Jurisprudence to Realism: Jurisprudence and Social Change in Twentieth-century American Law," 58 Va.L.Rev. 999 (1972); Kennedy, "Form and Substance in Private Law Adjudication," 89 Harv.L.Rev. 1685, 1731–2, 1745–51 (1976); G. Gilmore,

Lochner—that the courts were restoring the natural order which had been upset by the legislature—was increasingly perceived as fundamentally flawed. There *was* no "natural" economic order to upset or restore, and legislative or judicial decision in any direction could neither be restrained nor justified on any such basis.[6] The legitimacy of the Court's way of identifying implied limits on legislative authority was thus subject to increasing question. Just as the *Swift v. Tyson* doctrine that federal judges should apply the "general common law" in diversity cases could not survive the belief that there just *was* no transcendent body of binding general common law,[7] so too that belief ultimately devastated *Lochner's* due process doctrine that legislatures may not upset the "natural" conditions of contract and property enshrined in common law categories and in their logical entailments.

Parallel developments in economic, political, and social thought similarly eroded the premises of the *Lochner* approach. The suffering of the underprivileged, including the misery of underpaid, overburdened, or unemployed workers, came to be seen not as an inescapable corollary of personal freedom or an inevitable result of forces beyond human control, but instead as a product of conscious governmental decisions to take *some* steps affecting the affairs of economic life—punishing some people as thieves, awarding damages to others as the victims of trespass or breach of contract, immunizing still others from liability through concepts of corporate law—while *not* taking *other* steps that might rescue people from conditions of intolerable deprivation.[8] Indeed, it became possible to see such preventable harm as a kind of violence—different in form and source from more conventional types of human violence, perhaps, but violence none the less.[9] In any

The Death of Contract (1974); N. Rumble, American Legal Realism (1968).

6. Examples of the development of these theories during the Lochner era include Cohen, "The Basis of Contract", 46 Harv.L.Rev. 553 (1933); Llewellyn, "The Constitution as an Institution," 34 Colum. L.Rev. 1 (1934); T. Arnold, the Symbols of Government (1935); J. Frank, Law and the Modern Mind (1930). A discussion of such developments, including their effect on such pivotal figures as Hughes and Roberts, is provided in Murphy, supra note 2, at 72–82, 99–115. See also the discussion of Miller v. Schoene, 276 U.S. 272 (1928), in § 8–5, supra.

7. See Erie R.R. Co. v. Tompkins, 304 U.S. 64, 78–80 (1938), overruling Swift v. Tyson, 41 U.S. 1 (1842). See Ely, "The Irrepressible Myth of Erie," 87 Harv.L.Rev. 693, 700–04 (1974). For a more focused analysis of the shift from Swift to Erie, see § 3–23, supra.

8. See Kennedy, supra note 5, at 1745–51; R. Wolff, The Poverty of Liberalism 89–93 (1968). Early examples of such analysis include H. Croly, The Promise of American Life (1909); J. Commons, Legal Foundations of Capitalism (1924); T. Veblen, The Theory of the Leisure Class (1899).

9. Marxists in particular, as one scholar observes in a powerful article, have been making the elementary but shattering point "that much of the harm that has been thought to be part of the natural hazards of life is not at all natural. . . . [but] is in fact attributable to the machinations of men. Far from being the result of the operation of gratuitous and impersonal forces, much harm must be seen as the work of assignable agents . . . [It is often objected that the infliction of such harm should not be regarded as a form of "violence," but] [to] define with any sort of clarity the concept of violence upon which the anti-Marxists rely is no easy matter. Clearly they have in mind the . . . sudden forceful, and perhaps unexpected, infliction of painful physical injury upon an unwilling victim . . . If a man is stabbed to death, we do not doubt that he has been the victim of a violent assault. Would we have to alter our judgment if we later learn that the stiletto slid between his ribs as easily as you please? This stiletto point is the thin edge of the wedge. For if we are interested in the question of the preva-

case, critics of the 1930's increasingly saw progressive legislation as a necessary and proper responsibility of government and argued that the Supreme Court, by frustrating such legislation, was partly responsible for the human suffering that resulted.[10]

Such criticisms were reflected in a rising tide of attacks on the Court by various social and economic groups in the press and elsewhere in the 1920's and 1930's. Labor unions claimed that the Court was usurping the powers of Congress and proposed constitutional amendments as a response.[11] The liberal press and organizations such as the ACLU vigorously criticized decision after decision.[12] Even the conservative press was often jolted; it was reported, for example, that 79% of all commenting newspapers criticized the Court's decision to strike down New York's minimum wage law in 1936.[13]

Political pressures mounted as well.[14] Franklin Roosevelt had ascended to the Presidency with a promise of a New Deal and he proceeded to enact programs involving extensive federal involvement in economic affairs. Such legislation, while attracting great popular support, was certain to come into conflict with the constitutional model that had animated the Court since the late 1890's.[15] As the conflict materialized, the pressure on the Court mounted, culminating in the widely condemned Presidential court-packing plan.[16] The influence of

lence of violence in human affairs, . . . it would be absurd to ignore or exclude methods men find of killing or injuring their fellows that do not happen to involve vigorous direct actions . . . Where muggings and violent demonstrations are the fear and the theorists speak for the fearful, vigorous direct actions will seem the most important features of violence. Where the streets are quiet, but people who could be saved are left to die of neglect or cold or hunger, or are crippled or killed by their living or working conditions, a different group of people may suffer, and other theorists may see their suffering as attributable to human agency, and so class it as part of man's violence to man." Harris, "The Marxist Conception of Violence," 3 Phil. & Pub.Aff. 192, 212, 215–16, 219 (1974).

10. E.g., Amidon, supra, note 4; Lauck, "Require a Two-thirds Vote," 50 Survey 260 (May 15, 1923).

11. E.g., Gompers, "Usurped Power", 50 Survey 221 (May 15, 1923); Smith, "The Supreme Court and Minimum Wage Legislation," 33 Amer. Federationist 197 (Feb. 1926). See generally Murphy, supra note 2, at 68–72; I. Bernstein, The Lean Years: A History of the American Worker 1920–33 (1960).

12. See, e.g., "The Legal Right to Starve," 34 New Republic 254 (May 2, 1953); "A Conspiracy of Lawyers," 141 Nation 369 (Oct. 2, 1935); "A Deplorable Decision," 24 Commonweal 199 (June 19, 1936). See generally Murphy, supra note 2, at 68–

72; D. Johnson, The Challenge to American Freedoms: World War I and The Rise of the American Civil Liberties Union (1963); L. Filler, Crusaders for American Liberalism (1939) (discussing "muckrakers").

13. "Wage Law Decision as Viewed by the Press," 4 U.S. News 12 (June 8, 1936). See also "Chiseling is Constitutional," Philadelphia Record (June 3, 1936) at 8. See generally Murphy, supra note 2, at 150–151. The decision at issue was Morehead v. New York ex rel. Tipaldo, 298 U.S. 587 (1936). For a selected bibliography of commentary between 1920 and 1936, see E. Nichols & J. Baccus (eds.), Minimum Wages and Maximum Hours 439–458 (1936).

14. For examples of political criticism in the 1920's, see Murphy, supra note 2, at 71–72; 50 Survey 217–19 (May 15, 1923) (comments by seven state governors).

15. Murphy, supra note 2, at 128–157. See generally W. Leuchtenberg, Franklin D. Roosevelt and the New Deal (1963). The legislation interfered with the two core concerns of Model II: liberty of contract and state autonomy; thus, although its invalidation might have been avoided, the task would have been difficult indeed. See also Chapter 5, supra.

16. See, e.g., A. Sutherland, Constitutionalism in America 481–501 (1965); L. Pfeffer, This Honorable Court 295–320 (1965).

these political forces should not be exaggerated; there is evidence, for example, that Justice Roberts' famous 1936–1937 switch in favor of minimum wage legislation—the "switch in time that saved nine" [17]— was not motivated solely by the threat of court-packing.[18] Moreover, Roosevelt's power of appointment would eventually have produced the result he desired anyway; by 1941, *only* Justice Roberts remained among the pre-Roosevelt Justices. Nevertheless, political pressures no doubt played some role in the timing of *Lochner's* decline, as was perhaps to be expected with a doctrine cutting against the grain of so deep a shift in economic and social perception.

§ 8–7. Judicial Abdication After the Collapse of Lochner

Whatever its precise cause, *Lochner's* decline proceeded even more rapidly than had its late-nineteenth century ascent. Presaged by its approval in 1934 of Minnesota's mortgage moratorium law [1] and of New York's milk price control regulations,[2] the Supreme Court dramatically reversed itself and upheld minimum wage legislation in 1937 in *West Coast Hotel v. Parrish*.[3] Judicial approval of crucial New Deal legislation, such as the Fair Labor Standards Act,[4] the National Labor Relations Act,[5] and the new Agricultural Adjustment Act,[6] quickly followed as World War II approached. Thus, as the sphere of private contractual autonomy shrank, that of federal power over subjects formerly deemed exclusively the province of states and localities expanded.[7] By 1939, the Court was moved to note that the economic theories of Adam Smith and John Maynard Keynes were equally acceptable.[8] By 1949, no headlines were made when the Court unanimously and explicitly repudiated the "*Allgeyer-Lochner-Adair-Coppage* constitutional doctrine." [9]

17. See B. Wright, The Growth of American Constitutional Law 202 (1942); Pfeffer, supra note 16, at 317.

18. Private correspondence later suggested that the switch occurred at the exact moment it did because Roberts, whose views were less firm than those of the four solid conservatives on the Court and whose attitude had evolved more over time, felt that the issues had not been properly raised in Morehead v. New York ex rel. Tipaldo, 298 U.S. 587 (1936) (invalidating minimum wage law), as opposed to West Coast Hotel v. Parrish, 300 U.S. 379 (1937) (upholding minimum wage law). See Sutherland, supra note 16, at 496–97. It should be noted that Roberts wrote the essentially anti-Lochner majority opinion two years prior to Morehead in Nebbia v. New York, 291 U.S. 502 (1934) (upholding milk price control law). For further discussion of Roberts' switch see 2 M. Pusey, Charles Evans Hughes 701 (1951); Chambers, The Big Switch: Justice Roberts and the Minimum Wage Cases, 10 Labor History 44 (Winter, 1969).

§ 8–7

1. Home Building and Loan Ass'n v. Blaisdell, 290 U.S. 398 (1934), discussed in § 9–9, infra.

2. Nebbia v. New York, 291 U.S. 502 (1934).

3. 300 U.S. 379 (1937). The legislation was not materially distinguishable from that invalidated the previous year in Morehead v. New York ex rel. Tipaldo, 298 U.S. 587 (1936).

4. United States v. Darby, 312 U.S. 100 (1941).

5. NLRB v. Jones & Laughlin Steel Co., 301 U.S. 1 (1937).

6. Wickard v. Filburn, 317 U.S. 111 (1942).

7. See Chapter 5, supra.

8. Osborn v. Ozlin, 310 U.S. 53, 62 (1940). Lochner-era precedents were often explicitly reversed. See, e.g., Phelps Dodge v. NLRB, 313 U.S. 177 (1941) (overturning Adair and Coppage).

9. Lincoln Federal Labor Union v. Northwestern Iron and Metal Co., 335 U.S. 525, 535 (1949).

In abandoning *Lochner*, however, the Court eventually moved well beyond the elder Justice Harlan's earlier suggestion that legislatures need only demonstrate a real or substantial relation between laws and their objectives. In *United States v. Carolene Products Co.*,[10] the case in which Justice Stone's famous footnote 4 would later support increased judicial intervention in non-economic affairs,[11] the Court declared that it would sustain regulation in the socioeconomic sphere if any state of facts either known or reasonably inferrable afforded support for the legislative judgment. Even this limited scrutiny soon gave way to virtually complete judicial abdication. The Court became willing to resort to purely hypothetical facts and reasons to uphold legislation [12] or, as in *Ferguson v. Skrupa*,[13] to uphold it for virtually no substantive reason at all. Indeed, in sustaining Kansas' law limiting the practice of debt-adjusting to licensed attorneys in *Ferguson*, the Court almost appeared to treat pure political interest-balancing and log-rolling compromise as normatively acceptable; writing for the majority, Justice Black stated that the legislature was "free to decide for itself" absent a violation of a specific federal law or of specific constitutional provisions, and suggested that arguments demonstrating the social utility of debt adjusting "are properly addressed to the legislature, not to us." [14] *Lochner's* discrediting of judicial review thus lent credence to the notion that the legislative process should be completely willful and self-controlled, with absolutely no judicial interference except where constitutional provisions much more explicit than due process were in jeopardy.

Yet it is significant that the Court never wholly abandoned the position that legislatures, at least in their regulatory capacity, must always act in furtherance of public goals transcending the shifting summation of private interests through the political process. The pluralist thesis that there *exists* no public interest beyond that summation [15] never became judicial dogma in economic life any more than in other sectors of human concern. Thus, even when deferring to legislative actions, the Court continually pointed to reasons that could justify such actions in terms of the general public interest,[16] and explained

---

10. 304 U.S. 144 (1938).

11. See Chapters 11–13, 15, and 16, infra.

12. See, e.g., Williamson v. Lee Optical Co., 348 U.S. 483 (1955) (upholding law restricting optometry on the supposition that legislature decided that eyeglass prescriptions were necessary to promote health). See also § 16–3, infra, on the use of the "conceivable basis" test in equal protection challenges to economic regulation.

13. 372 U.S. 726 (1963).

14. Id. at 730–1, 732.

15. See the critical discussion of that thesis in Wright, "Politics and the Constitution: Is Money Speech?", 85 Yale L.J. 1001, 1013–16 (1976). See generally, R. Dahl, A Preface to Democratic Theory

(1956); R. Dahl, Who Governs? (1961); E. Herring, Group Representation Before Congress (1929). See generally Sunstein, "Interest Groups in American Public Law," 38 Stan.L.Rev. 29 (1985), for an unusually lucid explication of how Madisonian ideals provide a critique of interest-group pluralism.

16. See, e.g., Day-Brite Lighting, Inc. v. Missouri, 342 U.S. 421 (1952) (upholding law permitting employees to leave work on election day at employers' expense as a means of safeguarding the right of suffrage); Williamson v. Lee Optical Co., 348 U.S. 483 (1955) (discussed at note 12, supra); City of New Orleans v. Dukes, 427 U.S. 297 (1976) (upholding ordinance permitting established vendors to continue operations in French Quarter while forbidding new businesses as a means of

why the legislation under review could be viewed as "an exercise of judgment" rather than "a display of arbitrary power." [17]

The political, intellectual, and economic pressures of the 1930's undoubtedly made the demise of *Lochner* inevitable. But judicial retreat from the *Lochner* doctrine need not have followed the path chosen by the Supreme Court. At least three alternatives were available: *first*, acceptance of the pluralist philosophy that no public interest exists beyond the log-rolling result of the legislative process, so that one could not scrutinize legislative choices according to any ascertainable standard of the public good beyond knowing that the political bargaining process was in working order; *second*, an institutional argument that, even if the public good or social justice could be defined apart from the aggregation of political interests, and even if particular legislative restraints on liberty were profoundly unjust according to some cognizable standard or principle, legislative choices among conflicting values were beyond judicial competence to criticize and hence beyond judicial authority to strike down; or *third*, a substantive acceptance of certain regulatory laws as supportive of human freedom, rightly understood, and *therefore* not violative of due process.

Supreme Court decisions since the 1930's demonstrate that the Court has wisely resisted the first, or pluralist, approach,[18] one that has been criticized as giving undeserved weight to highly organized, wealthy interest groups, and as tending to "drain politics of its moral and intellectual content." [19] In its neglect of substantive values and in its treatment of politics as nothing more than the clash of conflicting forces, pluralism appears hardly less parochial than *Lochner* itself.[20] But, having soundly rejected the first approach, the Court took the more dubious step of preferring the second to the third: it ultimately invoked institutional rather than substantive arguments for upholding social and economic legislation. The precise reasons for this choice remain unclear. The Justices may have believed, as Holmes and others long ago insisted, that courts possess neither the ability nor the authority to scrutinize social goals, and should facilitate legislative innovation by permitting social and economic experimentation to continue without judicial interference.[21] But such a belief would hardly justify wholesale abdication to the political process, since there exists no type of legisla-

---

gradually enhancing the area's "tourist-oriented charm" to promote city economy), discussed in § 16–2, *infra*. Even in Ferguson, the Court suggested that the limitation of debt adjusting to attorneys could be justified as a means to ensure that proper legal advice was provided to debtors. See 372 U.S. at 732.

17. Mathews v. deCastro, 429 U.S. 181, 185 (1976) (upholding provision of Social Security Act according "wife's insurance benefits" to wives living with husbands, but not to divorced wives), quoting Helvering v. Davis, 301 U.S. 619, 640 (1937) (upholding old-age benefits scheme of Social Security Act against tenth amendment attack).

18. See note 16, supra.

19. B. Wright, The Growth of American Constitutional Law 1018–19 (1942). See also T. Lowi, The End of Liberalism 46–54, 281–91 (1969).

20. Id. See generally H. Kariel, The Decline of American Pluralism (1961); R. Wolff, The Poverty of Liberalism 140–61 (1968).

21. See Holmes' dissent in Truax v. Corrigan, 257 U.S. 312, 342 (1921); cf. Olsen v. Nebraska, 313 U.S. 236 (1941) (discussing Holmes' arguments).

tion that can be guaranteed in advance to leave important constitutional principles unimpaired, and there is simply no way for courts to review legislation in terms of the Constitution without repeatedly making difficult substantive choices among competing values, and indeed among inevitably controverted political, social, and moral conceptions. Nor can it suffice to dismiss constitutional review of socioeconomic regulation as uniquely "political"; all significant constitutional judgments—from those of the nation-building Marshall Court [22] to those of the Burger Court's federalism [23]—are inescapably political. The notion of mechanically laying statutes beside the constitutional text to see if they "fit" was properly discredited long ago. And the alternative of consciously deferring to the legislature, especially if such deference is selective (as it will inevitably be), is itself no less "political" than the alternative of seriously reviewing legislation's substantive validity. The fact that judges and lawyers, most of whom knew better, often couched their anti-Lochner conclusions in institutional terms may have reflected tactical considerations as much as any genuine conviction; the extremism of *Lochner* may have fatally discredited, at least temporarily, the whole concept of judicial review of social and economic legislation.[24] Whatever the reasons, the Court's tendency to invoke institutional arguments for its retreat from Model II has structured most constitutional analysis since *Lochner*. From Justice Stone's footnote 4 to modern arguments about economic as against political liberties, the search for ways to make judicial review legitimate, given the rejection of *Lochner* for reasons of institutional competence and authority, has preoccupied (one could say obsessed) constitutional scholarship for the last forty years.[25]

This preoccupation has forestalled extensive analysis of the third possible path of retreat from *Lochner*. If one accepted fully the central notion which contributed to *Lochner's* decline—that even judicial enforcement of common-law rules of contract and property represents a governmental choice with discernable consequences for the social distribution of suffering, pleasure, and power—then it would be hard to avoid the realization that a judicial choice between invalidating and upholding legislation altering the ground rules of contract and property is nonetheless a positive *choice*, one guided by constitutional language and history but almost never wholly determined by it. Having come to that recognition, one would understand that *Lochner v. New York* [26] and *Morehead v. New York ex rel. Tipaldo*,[27] striking down maximum-hour

---

22. See, e.g., McCulloch v. Maryland, 17 U.S. (4 Wheat.) 316 (1819).

23. See, e.g., National League of Cities v. Usery, 426 U.S. 833 (1976), discussed in § 5–22, supra.

24. See Gunther, "Foreword: In Search of Evolving Doctrine on a Changing Court: A Model for a Newer Equal Protection," 86 Harv.L.Rev. 1, 43 (1972); McCloskey, "Economic Due Process and the Supreme Court: An Exhumation and Reburial," 1962 Sup. Ct.Rev. 34. But see the attempted resurrection of Lochner-style economic due pro-

cess in R. Epstein, Takings (1985), discussed in § 9–6, infra, and in B. Siegan, Economic Liberties and the Constitution (1980).

25. See, e.g., Ely, "The Wages of Crying Wolf: A Comment on Roe v. Wade," 82 Yale L.J. 920 (1973); Bork, "The Constitution, Original Intent, and Economic Rights," 23 San Diego L.Rev. 823 (1986).

26. 198 U.S. 45 (1905).

27. 298 U.S. 587 (1936).

and minimum-wage laws, and *West Coast Hotel v. Parrish*,[28] sustaining such laws, *all* involved substantive choices, so that if the latter decision was right and the former decisions wrong, the reason can *only* be that, in twentieth century America, minimum wage laws, as a substantive matter, are *not* intrusions upon human freedom in any constitutionally meaningful sense, but are instead entirely reasonable and just ways of attempting to combat economic subjugation and human domination.[29] Thus, when the Court said in *West Coast Hotel* that minimum wage laws, in light of "recent economic experience," prevented the "exploitation of a class of workers . . . [in ways] detrimental to their health and well being," [30] it might have gone on to conclude not simply that the "legislature was *entitled* to adopt measures to reduce the evils of . . . exploiting workers at wages [too] low . . . to meet the bare cost of living," [31] but also that the legislature was *right* to adopt such measures, although other ways of filling the gaps left by the state's fabric of private and public law were of course conceivable—and have indeed been employed.[32]

Taking any such position would certainly have seemed more difficult than merely deferring to legislative wisdom; it always looks more legitimate, at first, to defer to others—and sometimes it is. But in fact the Court's landmark decision in *West Coast Hotel* spoke more about the justice of minimum wages than about the right to enact them without judicial interference; [33] the emphasis on deference for institutional reasons was more prevalent in the Holmes dissents of thirty years earlier [34] and in the majority opinions of the 1950's and 1960's.[35] And even deferring to others, as we have seen, may entail an assumption of power,[36] especially when the decision-maker exercises discretion in deciding when to defer and when to intervene, as the Court obviously has done throughout its history. As long as judges do not fully and irrevocably repudiate the mission of *occasionally* rejecting majoritarian political choices, there is no honest way for them to escape the burdens of substantive judgment *in every case.*

Now of course the *right* substantive judgment cannot be insensitive to matters of institutional competence and democratic legitimacy. *Part*

28. 300 U.S. 379 (1937).

29. See Kennedy, "Form and Substance in Private Law Adjudication," 89 Harv.L. Rev. 1685, 1756–58 (1976); Harris, "The Marxist Conception of Violence," 3 Phil. & Pub.Aff. 192 (1974).

30. 300 U.S. at 399.

31. Id. at 398–99 (emphasis added).

32. See § 15–9, infra, for an analysis of a possible affirmative duty of government to fill such gaps somehow.

33. The Court spent many pages explaining why the minimum wage was a wholly reasonable regulation of liberty, see 300 U.S. at 394–95, 396–400, and several pages recalling other regulations that had similarly been upheld as reasonable, id. at 392–93, 395, 397; only a few sentences in

fact talk of the legislature's "right" to act independent of judicial veto, and not even those sentences are cast in terms of the impropriety or illegitimacy of substantive judicial review in the economic area. Thus, although West Coast Hotel has been largely recast by history as having rested on institutional grounds, it would be entirely possible, and indeed truer to its language, to invoke it as precedent not for judicial timidity but for the substantive justice of minimum wage laws.

34. See, e.g., Lochner v. New York, 198 U.S. 45, 90 (1905).

35. See notes 13 and 16, supra.

36. Cf. Marbury v. Madison, 5 U.S. (1 Cranch.) 137 (1803), discussed in Chapter 3, supra.

of what was wrong with *Lochner* was the Court's overconfidence, both in its own factual notions about working conditions and perhaps also in its own normative convictions about the meaning of liberty; at least by the 1920's, if not yet in 1905, the Court should have paid more heed to the mounting agreement, if not the consensus, that the economic "freedom" it was protecting was more myth than reality. But it would be wrong to make too much of the point; surely there can be no general duty on the part of a deliberately countermajoritarian body like a court, and especially on the part of the Supreme Court, simply to follow the election returns. At most, there is a duty not to be pigheaded, *too* certain of all of one's premises, and a solemn duty to connect one's decisions to an intelligible view of the Constitution.[37] Beyond that, one can offer no advice calculated to take judges off the hook; nor should one try—for that is where, sometimes for better and sometimes for worse, our constitutional system has put them.

37. See generally §§ 11–2 to 11–4, infra. The Justices of the Lochner majority may have violated the injunction against overconfidence, but they were guilty of no breach of this second duty; theirs was a fully understandable, and theoretically highly defensible, picture of the Constitution's words "liberty," "property," "contract," and "due process of law." It was, moreover, a picture probably more faithful to the assumptions of the Framers than can be said of many rulings we are accustomed to applaud—with respect, for example, to free speech, race, or reapportionment. What was wrong was simply that, as a picture of freedom in industrial society, the one painted by the Justices badly distorted the character and needs of the human condition and the reality of the economic situation. We may believe that judges will often get such things wrong. But so will other people, including legislators. To be sure, legislators are elected—but they cannot avoid distance from the people much more readily than judges can. And in any event, as long as judges are in the business of deciding cases—even garden-variety contract and property cases—they will be shaping the society even when they claim they are "only" deferring to others. In short, *there is no escape* from the difficult task of painting a better—a morally and economically truer—picture; to leave the canvas blank from time to time just hands the brushes over to other artists. The picture's frame, and the artist's tools, must be drawn from the Constitution's text, structure, and history; but there can be no escape from the need to supply at least some measure of one's own vision.

Chapter 9

MODEL III—THE MODEL OF SETTLED EXPECTATIONS: UNCOMPENSATED TAKINGS AND CONTRACT IMPAIRMENTS

§ 9–1. The Background of Model III

With the demise of the *Lochner* era of Model II,[1] there began a search for alternative methods of protecting individuals from majoritarian oppression. The major fruits of this post-*Lochner* search form the subject matter of Chapters 11 to 17. But two sets of restraints on governmental power both antedated and informed the *Lochner* era and survived that era's eclipse, retaining a measure of vitality even today. One such model, expressed primarily through the ex post facto clauses, the bill of attainder clauses, and the procedural due process requirement, demands *regularity* in the application of governmental power to particular persons; that model of regularity is explored in Chapter 10. The present chapter discusses a norm perhaps as basic as that of regularity: the norm of *repose*. We deal here with the idea that government must respect "vested rights" in property and contract—that certain settled expectations of a focused and crystallized sort should be secure against governmental disruption, at least without appropriate compensation.

As early as Chief Justice Marshall's great decision in *Marbury v. Madison*,[2] the American judiciary defended certain vested claims from destruction by governmental whim—even when those claims are abstract in character and have their roots in positive enactments rather than in natural law or in customary personal dominion over physical resources. It was, after all, Marshall's declaration that legal rights had "vested" in William Marbury by virtue of Congress' creation of his office and the President's signing of his seal, which provided the occasion for the Court's earliest proclamation, even if only in dictum, that the rule of law, entailing fidelity to vested rights, binds even the Chief Executive.[3] Within the next two decades, such dicta had ripened into several landmark holdings, protecting both interests in land[4] and more abstract interests such as those in a corporate charter,[5] from what the Court treated as lawless legislative action.

§ 9–1

1. See Lochner v. New York, 198 U.S. 45 (1905), discussed in Chapter 8, supra.

2. 5 U.S. (1 Cranch) 137 (1803).

3. Id. at 162.

4. See Fletcher v. Peck, 10 U.S. (6 Cranch) 87 (1810); Terrett v. Taylor, 13 U.S. (9 Cranch) 43 (1815), both discussed in § 8–1, supra.

5. See Dartmouth College v. Woodward, 17 U.S. (4 Wheat.) 518 (1819), discussed in § 9–8, infra.

In these early nineteenth century cases, the Supreme Court was less concerned to locate the protection of vested economic rights in any particular clause of the Constitution than to define such rights and to defend them in the general name of the Fundamental Law; later generations could worry about textual details.[6] Despite such nonchalance, the contract clause of article I, § 10, was soon located as the centerpiece of the Constitution's protective armor,[7] with the fifth amendment's ban on uncompensated takings of property serving as an important backstop.[8] Together those two provisions exemplified, although they did not exhaust, the sanctity of settled economic expectations under American law. Although the legal autonomy of the states left the substantive freedom of contract largely to the protection of state tribunals (and of federal tribunals sitting as common law courts under their diversity jurisdiction) until the last decade of the nineteenth century,[9] the prohibitions against uncompensated takings and contract impairments provided a foundation of federally enforceable rights upon which Model II could and did build. The primary question of interest in this chapter is what remained of that foundation after the edifice so elaborately built upon it had collapsed.[10]

§ 9–2. The Shift From Direct to Indirect Enforcement of the Ban on Takings for a Private Purpose

As early as 1798, Justice Chase, in his memorable dictum in *Calder v. Bull*, had expressed constitutional law's undisputed condemnation of any law attempting to "take property from A. and give it to B."[1] General principles of law, enforceable in a proper forum, had settled that no form of legislative authority could be employed to serve private ends: taking, taxing, and regulation were all inherently linked to the public good and depended for their legitimacy upon the preservation of that link.[2] Throughout our history, distinctive strands of thought have

---

6. See, e.g., Fletcher, 10 U.S. at 135, 139; Terrett, 13 U.S. at 52.

7. See § 9–8, infra.

8. See §§ 9–2 to 9–6, infra.

9. See § 8–1, supra.

10. This chapter considers just compensation and contract impairment law not from the perspective of a comprehensive survey but rather as sources of insights and illustrations bearing on the basic problems of protecting "settled expectations" through constitutional law. The topics of just compensations and eminent domain in particular are too large, and too specialized, to warrant more than a general analysis here. For a much more detailed review, see P. Nichols, The Law of Eminent Domain (3d ed. 1986). The most important theoretical analyses of the taking issue are B. A. Ackerman, Private Property and the Constitution (1977); Michelman, "Property, Utility, and Fairness: Comments on the Ethical Foundations of 'Just Compensation' Law," 80 Harv.L.Rev. 1165 (1967);

Sax, "Takings and the Police Power," 74 Yale L.J. 36 (1964); Sax, "Takings, Private Property and Public Rights," 81 Yale L.J. 149 (1971). Considerably more idiosyncratic, but likely to prove influential in some circles, is R. Epstein, Takings: Private Property and the Power of Eminent Domain (1985), discussed in § 9–6, infra.

§ 9–2

1. 3 U.S. (3 Dall.) 386, 388 (1798) (seriatim opinion).

2. The power to take property by eminent domain is among the powers "reserved to the States" by the tenth amendment. Despite early doubts about the eminent domain powers of the United States, see P. Nichols, 1 Eminent Domain § 1.24 (rev.ed. 1974), since 1875 the right of the United States to exercise that power when reasonably related to its other powers has been undisputed. See Kohl v. United States, 91 U.S. (1 Otto) 367 (1875); P. Nichols, supra, at § 1.24[4].

put forward very different views of what might be meant by "the public good," but that government power must serve such an end if that power is to count as "law" has never been denied. When the Court began enforcing this principle as a matter of fourteenth amendment due process,[3] the real innovation was jurisdictional, not substantive, since takings for a private purpose had widely if not uniformly been regarded as illegal long before the Court held such takings violative of the fourteenth amendment.[4] Nonetheless, it was the latter holding that opened the way to the rounded development of Model II.

We saw in Chapter 8, however, that the disintegration of Model II was foreshadowed by the gradual erosion of the distinction between public and private purposes in the law of takings.[5] Originally, the requirement of just compensation, expressed against the federal government in the fifth amendment and implied against the states through the due process clause of the fourteenth,[6] attached only after it was clear that a particular taking of property was in fact for a public purpose.[7] If such a public purpose was absent, no compensation could suffice; the taking would have to be set aside as void. But by the time of *Pennsylvania Coal v. Mahon*,[8] in 1922, the compensation requirement had begun to serve the distinct function of assuring, in sufficiently ambiguous cases, that particular actions did indeed redound to the public benefit. The public's willingness to pay, expressed through the legislative process, would serve as proof that the public had in fact been the beneficiary of what otherwise appeared to be a forbidden transfer of property from one owner or class of owners to another.[9]

3. The first Supreme Court decision to hold that a governmental taking of property violates fourteenth amendment due process if it is for a private purpose was Missouri Pac. Ry. v. Nebraska, 164 U.S. 403 (1896) (compensation cannot cure unconstitutionality of such a taking).

4. See §§ 7–3, 8–1, 8–2, supra.

5. See § 8–5, supra.

6. See Chicago, Burlington & Quincy Ry. v. Chicago, 166 U.S. 226 (1897). The constitutions of nearly every state require compensation when property is taken; and the constitutions of some 23 states require compensation when property is taken *or damaged*. See Note, "Inverse Condemnation: its Availability in Challenging the Validity of a Zoning Ordinance," 26 Stan. L.Rev. 1439, 1440 n. 3 (1974).

7. The prohibition against taking private property for public use without just compensation forbids uncompensated confiscation by the judicial and executive branches as well as by the legislature. See Hughes v. Washington, 389 U.S. 290, 298 (1967) (Stewart, J., concurring).

8. 260 U.S. 393 (1922) (uncompensated taking occurred when state sought to enforce ban on coal-mining threatening surface structure against mining company that had sold surface rights, but retained right to cause damage to surface, in deed executed prior to enactment of mining ban).

9. See § 8–5, supra. The Supreme Court's decision in Keystone Bituminous Coal Assn. v. DeBenedictis, 107 S.Ct. 1232 (1987) (upholding a more recent Pennsylvania enactment limiting coal mining), distinguished Pennsylvania Coal as containing "the indicia of a statute enacted solely for the benefit of private parties," id. at 1242, and stressed the particular public purposes of conservation, safety and preservation of property value for taxation purposes. In so doing, Keystone reinforces the extent to which the compensation requirement now seems to play the additional role of guaranteeing in ambiguous cases that a public purpose is genuinely being served. See 107 S.Ct. at 1241–45. Tellingly, Chief Justice Rehnquist's dissent, joined by Justices Powell, O'Connor, and Scalia, took issue with the majority's characterization of the act invalidated in Pennsylvania Coal as problematically private in its origins and its effects. The dissent, by contrast, described the Kohler Act invalidated in Pennsylvania Coal as aimed at "public 'evils and abuses,' " id. at 1255, and argued that in Keystone, as in Pennsylvania Coal, "the mere existence of a public purpose [is]

In the modern period, the requirement of compensation continues to serve this role of surrogate assurance of public purpose.[10] That its function is not exhausted by this role is clear enough; otherwise, if the public's *willingness* to pay had been established, or if the public gain from a particular appropriation of property was independently settled, no further end would be served by actually requiring compensation to be paid. Yet nothing could be clearer, even today, than that a sufficiently unambiguous governmental seizure of private property for public use—a sufficiently clear laying-on of official hands followed by a transfer of possession and title to the general public—is unconstitutional unless followed by payment to the former owner of the fair market value of what was taken.[11] What would have been quite unthinkable in

insufficient to release the government from the compensation requirement." Id.

10. Although federal courts retain theoretical power to invalidate a taking as insufficiently public in purpose even if compensation is provided, the practice since the first third of this century has been to treat as a legislative function the decision of "what type of taking is for a public use. . . ." United States ex rel. T.V.A. v. Welch, 327 U.S. 546, 551 (1946). The Court has recently characterized the concepts of "public use" and "public purpose" as broad enough to be "coterminous with the scope of a sovereign's police powers." Hawaii Housing Authority v. Midkiff, 467 U.S. 229, 240 (1984) (Hawaii Land Reform Act's use of eminent domain power to enable homeowners with long-term land leases to purchase the lots on which they live upheld as serving a valid "public use"). See also Ruckelshaus v. Monsanto Co., 467 U.S. 986 (1984) (provisions of federal act that authorized Environmental Protection Agency to disclose corporate trade secrets to competing license applicants in return for compensation upheld as advancing valid public use or purpose); accord, Berman v. Parker, 348 U.S. 26, 32 (1954) (upholding statute authorizing government to take private property and sell it to private management to be redeveloped for improved private use). But see Thompson v. Consolidated Gas Utilities Corp., 300 U.S. 55 (1937) (Brandeis, J.) (gas proration order held an unconstitutional taking for benefit of certain private producers).

The state enjoys wide latitude in redirecting the stream of economic wealth: "legislation readjusting rights and burdens is not unlawful solely because it upsets otherwise settled expectations . . . . This is true even though the effect of legislation is to impose a new duty or liability based on past acts." Usery v. Turner Elkhorn Mining Co., 428 U.S. 1, 15–16 (1976) (sustaining a federal statute requiring coal mine operators to compensate former employees disabled by black lung disease, even though the operators had never contracted for such

liability and the employees had long since terminated their connection with the industry). Consequently, in Connolly v. Pension Benefit Guaranty Corp., 106 S.Ct. 1018 (1986), the Court unanimously upheld federal legislation requiring an employer withdrawing from a multiemployer pension plan to pay a fixed and certain debt to the plan amounting to the employer's proportionate share of the plan's unfunded vested benefits, even though that debt exceeded the employer's obligation to the pension plan under the governing collective bargaining agreements. Id. at 1019. The Court reasoned that "such interference with the property rights of an employer arises from a public program that adjusts the benefits and burdens of economic life and, under our cases, does not constitute a taking." Id. at 1026. It was sufficient for all nine Justices that the federal government had "taken nothing for its own use," id., and had merely imposed an additional contractual obligation in a field within its regulatory purview: "We are far from persuaded that fairness and justice require the public, rather than the withdrawing employers and other parties to pension plan agreements, to shoulder the responsibility for rescuing plans that are in financial trouble." Id. at 1027.

11. The owner is entitled to the fair value to the owner (not the worth to the government) at the time of the taking. See Almota Farmers Elevator & Warehouse Co. v. United States, 409 U.S. 470, 473–74 (1973); United States v. Reynolds, 397 U.S. 14, 16 (1970); Monongahela Navigation Co. v. United States, 148 U.S. 312, 326, 343 (1893). See P. Nichols, 3 Eminent Domain § 8.62 et seq. (3d ed. 1974). The body of rules determining which expectations constitute compensable property interests and which do not, see, e.g., Flemming v. Nestor, 363 U.S. 603 (1960) (social security expectations not property subject to compensation under taking law); United States v. Petty Motor Co., 327 U.S. 372, 379–80 (1946) (leasehold renewal expectation not property), plainly requires recon-

the nineteenth century is that the constitutional obligation to provide just compensation could serve the additional ends to which Justice Holmes turned that obligation in *Pennsylvania Coal*.[12]

Even in *Pennsylvania Coal*, however, compensation was not held to be required in all cases where private loss attended a governmental measure. It was only when regulation went "too far" that it would have to be treated as a taking [13] and deemed invalid unless compensation was provided. What constituted going "too far" remained a problem to be addressed case by case, since none of the general guidelines extracted from the precedents could yield a truly definitive test of when the government had crossed the line.[14] Of course, not even

sideration in light of the broader definition of property interests now employed in the law of procedural due process. See Logan v. Zimmerman Brush Co., 455 U.S. 422 (1982) (right to use state's fair employment practice held a protected property interest under due process clause; see § 10–9, infra). But see Bowen v. Gilliard, 107 S.Ct. 3008 (1987) (child receiving court-ordered support payments has "no vested protectable expectation that his or her parent will continue to receive identical support payments on the child's behalf," so Congress may require that families receiving welfare payments assign child support income to the government in exchange for increased welfare payments not designated for the particular child).

There seems no good reason why the broader definition, incorporating wholly intangible forms of property, should not be extended to the takings context. Indeed, some of the Supreme Court's recent decisions suggest it is inching toward just such a broadened conception of "property" in takings analysis. See, e.g., Ruckelshaus v. Monsanto Co., 467 U.S. 986, 1001–03 (1984) ("commercial data" in the form of trade secrets released to the public pursuant to a federal statute held a compensable property interest under takings clause); Armstrong v. United States, 364 U.S. 40, 44, 46 (1960) (materialman's lien provided for under Maine law held protected by takings clause); cf. PruneYard Shopping Center v. Robins, 447 U.S. 74, 82 (1980) (stating that the right to exclude others is also "one of the essential sticks in the bundle of property rights"). As the focus of the takings clause shifts from land and personal goods to labor, credit, information, and the like— and as property comes to be conceived less in terms of simple and undivided dominion than in terms of complex bundles of rights and interests—care must be taken to avoid "transferring to each stick in the property bundle the powerful connotations that traditionally attach to full ownership," and equating all broad restrictions on unfettered control with "large number partial takings." Grey, "The Malthusian Consti-

tution," 41 U. Miami L.Rev. 21, 31 (1986) (showing how these two "rhetorical trick[s]" do much of the work in R. Epstein, Takings (1985)).

12. In addition to this use of the compensation requirement as a surrogate for a judicially enforceable "public use" test, note the use of judicial techniques of avoidance such as that in United States v. Security Industrial Bank, 459 U.S. 70 (1982) (rejecting an interpretation of a bankruptcy law that would destroy pre-existing property rights and hence raise a "takings" issue).

A caveat: the mere fact that a legislative action satisfies the "public purpose" requirement and provides adequate compensation to injured parties will not shelter it from challenges based on other constitutional provisions. A graphic (if unlikely) hypothetical illustrates this point. Suppose that a state legislature were to require all citizens with a rare blood type to donate a fixed amount of their blood to hospitals every month, in return for which these donors would be generously compensated. The public purpose (saving lives) and the adequacy of compensation might be beyond dispute. Yet except in the most dire of emergencies, it is hard to imagine that such a scheme would pass constitutional muster under the due process clause, see Chapter 15, infra.

13. 260 U.S. at 413.

14. Indeed, in Keystone Bituminous Coal Assn. v. DeBenedictis, 107 S.Ct. 1232 (1987), also involving a Pennsylvania statute setting stringent limits on coal mining, the Court pointedly distinguished Pennsylvania Coal as a rare takings case in which, as a result of a legislative enactment, it was impossible for parties to engage in their business profitably. In Keystone, by contrast, as Justice Stevens' opinion for the Court's majority observed, the claimants "have not even pointed to a single mine that can no longer be mined for profit." Id. at 1248; see also id. at 1246–51. The Court also distinguished the statute challenged in Keystone on the

a case-by-case inquiry is meaningful unless one specifies what the inquiry is about and why it is being conducted. Such a specification is attempted in § 9–6; but its point will be more transparent if we first set out the traditional tests courts have articulated for identifying those government actions that constitute compensable takings of property. Section 9–3 describes those tests.

§ 9–3. The Traditional Tests for Compensable Takings: Physical Takeover, Destruction of Value, and Innocent Use

Most people know a taking when they see one, or at least think they do. Before the taking, an object or a piece of land belonged to X, who could use it in a large number of ways and who enjoyed legal protection in preventing others from doing things to it without X's permission. After the taking, X's relationship to the object or the land was fundamentally transformed; he could no longer use it at all, and other people could invoke legal arguments and mechanisms to keep him away from it exactly as he had been able to invoke such arguments and mechanisms before the taking had occurred. As Professor Bruce Ackerman has shown in a thoughtful analysis of the taking problem,[1] much of the constitutional law of takings is built upon this ordinary, lay view of what a "taking" is all about.

Thus a clear case is one that intuitively seems like a taking in the layman's sense of that term: a physical takeover of a distinct entity,[2] with an accompanying transfer of the legal powers of enjoyment and

grounds that it—unlike the application of the Kohler Act at issue in Pennsylvania Coal—had indisputably valid public purposes: these included conservation, safety, preservation of land values for taxation, and the preservation of surface water drainage potential. Id. at 1242–46.

§ 9–3

1. B. A. Ackerman, *Private Property and the Constitution* 88–167 (1977).

2. See § 9–5, infra. For examples of such "physical invasions," see, e.g., Loretto v. Teleprompter Manhattan CATV Corp., 458 U.S. 419 (1982) (compensable taking occurred when city required landlords to permit installation of television cables for a $1 fee, even though landlords bore no installation costs or risks); Portsmouth Harbor Land & Hotel Co. v. United States, 260 U.S. 327 (1922) (compensable taking of servitude may be created by government's regular firing of cannon over petitioner's land); Batten v. United States, 306 F.2d 580 (10th Cir. 1962), cert. denied 371 U.S. 955 (1963) (denying compensation to landowners near, but not under, flight path); Griggs v. Allegheny County, 369 U.S. 84 (1962) (compensable taking of an easement by government's use of a flight path less than a hundred feet over respondent's land); United States v. Causby, 328 U.S. 256, 261–62 (1946) (same); Pumpelly v. Green Bay & Mississippi Canal Co., 80 U.S.

166, 177–78 (1871) (compensable taking occurred when land was destroyed by government-caused flooding). In Richards v. Washington Terminal Co., 233 U.S. 546 (1914), the Court had denied compensation to landowners adjacent to a railroad for injuries caused by unavoidable smoke, soot, and sparks. The Richards Court was concerned about the demands of progress, id. at 555, and Justice Black, dissenting in Causby v. United States, 328 U.S. at 274–75, echoed a similar refrain. Writing for the Causby majority, id. at 263, Justice Douglas distinguished Richards by pointing to the direct overflight invasions. The costs involved in finding and compensating all of the people injured by airport noise would probably have been extraordinarily high in 1946, just as they would have been for all injuries from railroad smoke in 1914. The Causby Court was able to contain such costs by compensating the limited number of readily ascertainable people immediately under approach paths, just as the Richards Court had limited costs by awarding damages only for the "direct and peculiar and substantial" injury caused by the forced funneling of smoke from a tunnel onto one plaintiff's land. To the extent that technological advances have made it possible to limit recovery costs by less artificial rules, one might expect to see compensation extended accordingly.

exclusion that are typically associated with rights of property. Moreover, forcing someone to stop doing things with his property—telling him "you can keep it, but you can't use it"—is at times indistinguishable, in ordinary terms, from grabbing it and handing it over to someone else. Thus a "taking" occurs in this ordinary sense when government controls a person's use of property so tightly that, although some uses remain to the owner, the property's value has been virtually destroyed.[3] Again in accord with ordinary intuition, government need not pay even for complete takeover or destruction if the latter is justified by the owner's insistence on using his property to injure other people or their property. In such cases of noxious use, or nuisance, the offending user may be required to stop,[4] and if he refuses his property may be seized as a means of enforcing civility.

It is this "non-noxious" or innocent use qualification that came to cause the greatest difficulty as the law of takings and of just compensa-

3. Pennsylvania Coal Co. v. Mahon, 260 U.S. 393, 413–14 (1922). For a more detailed discussion of such "regulatory takings," see § 9–4, infra. The Court's standards for making out a regulatory taking have often been most demanding. Uncompensated losses in excess of 75% of a property's value caused by regulation have been sustained both before Pennsylvania Coal, see Hadacheck v. Sebastian, 239 U.S. 394, 405 (1915) (88%), and after Pennsylvania Coal, see Village of Euclid v. Ambler Realty Co., 272 U.S. 365, 384 (1926) (75%). In Goldblatt v. Hempstead, 369 U.S. 590 (1962), a town which had expanded around a sand-and-gravel mining operation amended its zoning laws "to prohibit any excavating below the water table and to impose an affirmative duty to refill any excavation presently below that level." Id. at 592. Although the owner had argued that the ordinance totally destroyed the economic value of his property, and although the New York Court of Appeals had found that the ordinance was amended as part of "a systematic attempt to force [the owner] out of business . . . under the guise of regulation," 9 N.Y.2d 101, 172 N.E.2d 562 (1961), the Supreme Court found "no evidence in the . . . record which even remotely suggests that prohibition of further mining will reduce the value of the lot in question;" thus the Court saw no need to decide how "far regulation may go before it becomes a taking. . . ." 369 U.S. at 594. Moreover, although the New York Court of Appeals had found that it would cost over one million dollars to refill the excavation, the Supreme Court withheld decision on the validity of the mandatory-refill provision since its specific enforcement had not been sought. Id. at 597–98. Five months later, the Court considered an appeal from an extraordinary zoning case that squarely posed the question "whether zoning ordi-

nances which altogether destroy the worth of valuable land by prohibiting the only economic use of which it is capable [i.e., rock and gravel excavation] effect a taking of real property without compensation," Brief for Appellant, Jurisdictional Statement, p. 5, Consolidated Rock Products Co. v. Los Angeles, 57 Cal.2d 515, 20 Cal.Rptr. 638, 370 P.2d 342, appeal dismissed 371 U.S. 36 (1962). In an action that cast doubt on the diminution of value test, the Court dismissed for want of a substantial federal question. Id. In a similar vein, the Court's early holding in the area of rate regulation that a public utility is entitled to a fair return on the fair value of its investment, Smyth v. Ames, 169 U.S. 466 (1898), gave way by the 1940's to the far more deferential inquiry whether "the total effect of the rate order [is] unjust and unreasonable," Federal Power Commission v. Hope Natural Gas Co., 320 U.S. 591, 602 (1944), a standard that only the most egregiously confiscatory rate structure would have difficulty meeting; see also Andrus v. Allard, 444 U.S. 51 (1979) (prohibition on *sale* of lawfully acquired feathers of protected bird species held not a taking because other "strands" in the bundle of property rights remain).

4. See, e.g., Northwestern Fertilizing Co. v. Hyde Park, 97 U.S. 659 (1878) (banning animal rendering plant from residential area); Mugler v. Kansas, 123 U.S. 623 (1887) (destroying beer business by enforcing state prohibition on sale of alcohol); Sligh v. Kirkwood, 237 U.S. 52 (1915) (prohibiting exportation of unripe oranges); Northwestern Laundry v. Des Moines, 239 U.S. 486 (1916) (prohibiting dense smoke as a nuisance); Arcara v. Cloud Books, Inc., 106 S.Ct. 3172 (1986) (closing for one year a place of business—as it happened, an adult bookstore—on whose premises solicitation of prostitution was occurring).

tion developed. In one of the more extreme cases, *Hadachek v. Sebastian*,[5] the Supreme Court held that a brickyard originally located far beyond the city limits of Los Angeles could be ordered to cease its operations, without compensation for the decline in property value from $800,000 to around $60,000, when "progress" and the city's boundaries finally caught up with it. The Court also denied compensation when a village effectively closed down a fertilizing company that had moved, pursuant to a governmental agreement, from Chicago to what had then been an uninhabited swamp. "If population, where there was none before, approaches a nuisance, it is the duty of those liable at once to put an end to it."[6] Or, as Justice Sutherland colorfully put it when the Court upheld a local zoning ordinance in *Village of Euclid v. Ambler Realty Co.*,[7] "a nuisance may be merely a right thing in the wrong place, like a pig in a parlor instead of the barnyard"—even if the parlor has come to the pig rather than the other way round.

But why must the owner of the parlor not pay to remove the pig? That was the question, and even though it might have answered itself in an earlier time when "nuisance" seemed a self-defining and fixed concept, loss of faith that certain "causes" were objectively responsible for certain "harms," coupled with rapid social and economic change and a growing role for government in mediating such change, left a large question mark where once none had been perceived. If cedar trees spawned a pest that would destroy nearby apple orchards, the Court could suggest that governmental destruction of the cedars to save the apples was like abatement of a nuisance at common law,[8] but nobody could blame the cedar owners for believing that it was the apple trees which, by their proximity and their susceptibility to the cedar pest, constituted a nuisance to the cedars. The case, as one astute observer remarked, was "not essentially different from one in which the apple pest spent its whole life in the apple trees but could be exterminated only by some arcane component of cedar ash, to furnish which the [cedars] were condemned without compensation."[9] Increasingly, deciding who had harmed whom seemed too open a choice to provide any determinate solution to the question of compensation.[10]

5. 239 U.S. 394, 410 (1915). The Court relied heavily on Reinman v. Little Rock, 237 U.S. 171 (1915), which had upheld the banishment of a well-established livery stable from one section of a city. See also Laurel Hill Cemetery v. San Francisco, 216 U.S. 358 (1910), where a cemetery, originally located outside the city limits, had been overtaken and then ordered to cease operations.

6. Northwestern Fertilizing Co. v. Hyde Park, 97 U.S. 659, 669 (1878); cf. Pierce Oil Co. v. Hope, 248 U.S. 498 (1919). But see Dobbins v. Los Angeles, 195 U.S. 223 (1904).

7. 272 U.S. 365, 368 (1926). But cf. Nectow v. Cambridge, 277 U.S. 183 (1928).

8. Miller v. Schoene, 276 U.S. 272, 279–80 (1928) (deeming irrelevant the question whether the infected cedars would technically constitute a nuisance at common law but stressing government's traditional power to take reasonable measures to terminate uses of land harmful to neighboring property), discussed in § 8–5, supra.

9. Michelman, "Property, Utility, and Fairness: Comments on the Ethical Foundations of 'Just Compensation' Law," 80 Harv.L.Rev. 1165, 1198–99 (1967).

10. For a bold, if unpersuasive, argument that this sort of question, and indeed every question bearing on when government must provide compensation, has a unique constitutional answer determinable by reference to, of all things, "general economic theory," see R. Epstein, Takings 200–01 (1985), discussed in § 9–6, infra.

A final source of perplexity was the changing notion of harm itself. Difficult as it might be to fix blame in a situation like that of the cedars and the apples, at least that case left little doubt that the pest-destroyed apple orchards, and the government-felled cedar trees, constituted "harms" to the owners of the apples and the cedars, respectively. But is harm done when wildlife belonging to no "owner" is threatened by a practice? When a wilderness area is flooded? When a company is forced to stop soiling a river with its effluents? Or suppose government determines that cedar owners are too wealthy and apple owners too poor, and compels a partial redistribution of land from the former to the latter: does that inflict a harm, or had the former distribution caused a harm that the government's choice simply corrected?

The wider the range of permissible definitions of public harm and legitimate governmental purpose, the more difficult it becomes to mesh ordinary conceptions of taking and compensation with contemporary notions of what government is for, and the more urgent it becomes to ask more systematically, as we attempt to do in § 9–6, why compensation should ever be required. Initially, however, it is important to examine in some detail how the Supreme Court has responded to two broad types of government actions that can interfere with settled expectations: so-called "regulatory takings," and "physical invasions" of property. A look at these areas—regulatory takings in § 9–4, and physical invasions in § 9–5—will in turn help to fill out our sense of what the Court regards as the aims of the compensation requirement (§ 9–6) and what the Court deems "property" for the purpose of takings analysis (§ 9–7).

§ 9–4. Regulatory Takings

In 1922, Justice Holmes set an agenda for generations of lawyers with his famous epigram, "while property may be regulated to a certain extent, if regulation goes too far it will be recognized as a taking." [1] The difficulty of determining, in cases involving nothing like a physical invasion or trespass, just how far is "too far" has predictably plagued the Court for over six decades,[2] and the attempt to differentiate "regu-

§ 9–4

1. Pennsylvania Coal Co. v. Mahon, 260 U.S. 393, 415 (1922). It seems settled that regulation goes "too far" and thus constitutes a compensable taking if it deprives the property owner of such an essential attribute of property ownership as the right to exclude trespassers, see Kaiser Aetna v. United States, 444 U.S. 164 (1979) (discussed in § 9–5, infra); or the right to collect interest, see Webb's Fabulous Pharmacies, Inc. v. Beckwith, 449 U.S. 155 (1980) (discussed in § 9–7, infra); or the right to transmit the property to one's heirs by descent or devise, see Hodel v. Irving, 107 S.Ct. 2076 (1987) (invalidating, as an uncompensated taking, a 1983 congressional enactment abolishing descent or devise of undivided fractional interests in certain Indian lands, where the abolition

extended to situations in which the governmental purpose to be advanced—consolidation of ownership of Indian lands—would not conflict with the further descent of the property; fact that the property retained value during life, and could be conveyed by *inter vivos* transfer, held immaterial to claim that regulation amounted to a taking).

2. See, e.g., Keystone Bituminous Coal Assn. v. DeBenedictis, 107 S.Ct. 1232, 1237 (1987) (repeatedly emphasizing that takings decisions can be reached only after examination of "the particular facts"); United States v. Riverside Bayview Homes, Inc., 474 U.S. 121 (1985) ("[w]e have never precisely determined those circumstances where land-use regulations amount to takings"); Penn Central Transportation Co. v. New York City, 438 U.S. 104 (1978) (tak-

lation" from "taking" has become "the most haunting jurisprudential problem in the field of contemporary land-use law . . . one that may be the lawyer's equivalent of the physicist's hunt for the quark." [3]

In 1978, the Supreme Court reaffirmed its practice of engaging in "essentially ad hoc, factual inquiries" into regulatory takings in *Penn Central Transportation Co. v. New York City*.[4] The Court allowed New York City to prevent the construction of a 53-story building atop Grand Central Station, as part of a comprehensive plan to preserve the station's (and the city's) historic and aesthetic value.[5] The government's regulatory action would result in long-term economic gain for the city as a whole, thus significantly benefitting those "expropriated" as well: landmarks attract people to New York and create business for, among others, Penn Central.[6] The company could not complain of being the only [7] or an especially frequent victim of this kind of action, nor even of suffering very greatly in this particular instance: the diminution of property value was limited by the facts that (1) the law did not in any way interfere with Penn Central's primary use of the land as a railroad terminal containing office space and concessions, (2) not all development of the air space above Grand Central was categorically prohibited, and (3) New York City gave the company valuable "transferable developmental rights" which could be used on its other parcels of land nearby.[8] Whatever injury Penn Central could be said to have suffered after these circumstances were taken into account, the Court was willing to allow to go uncompensated. Governmental regulation—by definition—involves the adjustment of private rights for public benefit. To require compensation whenever the law curtailed the

---

ings analysis involves "essentially ad hoc, factual inquiries"); Goldblatt v. Hempstead, 369 U.S. 590, 594 (1962) ("no set formula to determine where regulation ends and taking begins"); United States v. Central Eureka Mining Co., 357 U.S. 155, 168 (1958) ("question properly turning upon the particular circumstances of each case"). The overwhelmingly fact-specific nature of takings inquiries led the Court in several recent cases involving alleged temporary inverse condemnations to defer judgment on takings claims until the legislative or administrative action in question has assumed final form. See, e.g., MacDonald, Sommer & Frates v. Yolo County, 106 S.Ct. 2561 (1986) ("A court cannot determine whether a regulation has gone 'too far' unless it knows just how far the regulation goes"); Williamson County Regional Planning Comm'n v. Hamilton Bank of Johnson City, 473 U.S. 172, 199 (1985) ("[t]he difficult problem [is] how to define 'too far,' that is, how to distinguish the point at which regulation becomes so onerous that it has the same effect as an appropriation of the property through eminent domain or physical possession. . . . [The effect of the application of the zoning ordinance at issue] cannot be measured until a final decision is made as to how the regulations will be applied to respondent's property"). Although the Court held in First English Evangelical Lutheran Church v. Los Angeles, 107 S.Ct. 2378 (1987), that temporary takings require just compensation, see note 13, infra, it had no occasion to determine whether the regulation at issue went so far as to constitute a taking. Id. at 2384–85.

3. C. Haar, Land-Use Planning 766 (3d ed. 1976). See generally Michelman, "Property, Utility and Fairness: Comments on the Ethical Foundations of 'Just Compensation' Law," 80 Harv.L.Rev. 1165 (1967).

4. 438 U.S. 104 (1978).

5. If the city had allowed entities other than Penn Central, the owner of the station, to build atop the terminal without the owner's permission, a case more like those analyzed in § 9–5, infra, would have been posed.

6. 438 U.S. at 134–35.

7. The New York Landmarks Preservation Law applies to all the buildings in 31 historical districts and to over 400 individual landmark structures. 438 U.S. at 134.

8. 438 U.S. at 136–37.

potential for economic exploitation "would effectively compel the government to regulate by *purchase*."[9] It has long been recognized that such a regime would be unworkable.[10]

The upshot of *Penn Central* is that, when faced with a regulation which not only (1) advances some public interest, but also (2) falls short of destroying any classically recognized element of the bundle of property rights, (3) leaves much of the commercial value of the property untouched, and (4) includes at least some reciprocity of benefit, the Supreme Court is unlikely to find a taking. For example, *Agins v. Tiburon*[11] involved open-land zoning which significantly limited the economic value of some residential acquisitions, but was enacted in the interest of coherent land development and environmental policy. The zoning plan was unanimously held *not* to be a compensable taking. No classical element was wholly destroyed, much of the value was left, and the owners could expect in the long run[12] to gain as much as they would lose.[13] Had *Agins* involved not zoning restrictions, but a more

9. Andrus v. Allard, 444 U.S. 51, 65 (1979) (no taking where federal wildlife law prohibits trade in feathers of endangered species but allows other remunerative uses) (emphasis in original).

10. See, e.g., Pennsylvania Coal Co. v. Mahon, 260 U.S. 393, 413 (1922); Penn Central, 438 U.S. at 124.

11. 447 U.S. 255 (1980).

12. This of course might mean the *very* long run which John Maynard Keynes had in mind when he said, "In the long run, we are all dead."

13. 447 U.S. at 262-63. One issue in Agins was left unresolved. The California Supreme Court had held that "inverse condemnation"—a claim by the regulated owner that there has been a *de facto* confiscation for which payment must be made—is inappropriate where only unconstitutional regulation is alleged. Compensation, the state court reasoned, is called for only when the state is literally exercising its power of eminent domain, not the police power. 24 Cal.3d 266, 272, 157 Cal. Rptr. 372, 375, 598 P.2d 25, 28 (1979). If a zoning ordinance is so intrusive as to deprive someone of property without just compensation, his remedy lies solely in an action for mandamus or declaratory relief to invalidate the regulation prospectively; no money will be paid for interim harm done. The question whether a state may thus say that the exercise of the police power can never constitute a compensable taking could have been resolved in San Diego Gas & Electric Co. v. San Diego, 450 U.S. 621 (1981), but a majority of the Court dismissed the appeal in that case for lack of a final judgment since, as it believed, the California court had yet to determine if there had in fact been a taking. 450 U.S. at 633. (Justice Blackmun's opinion for the Court was joined by Chief Justice Burger and Justices White, Rehnquist and Stevens. Justices Brennan, Stewart, Marshall and Powell dissented and reached the merits.) Justice Brennan, writing for the dissenters, argued that the majority misunderstood the lower court's ruling: there was no final judgment that there had been a taking only because the California appellate court, following the California Supreme Court in Agins, had held that it was legally impossible for San Diego to have "taken" property since a zoning ordinance—an exercise of the police power—can *never* constitute a "taking," no matter how arbitrary or excessive it may be. 450 U.S. at 639-40 (Brennan, J., dissenting).

The utility company in Agins had bought land for the purpose of constructing a nuclear power plant, only to have some of its parcels rezoned by San Diego as "open space" in anticipation of the city's buying the land for use as a public park. When a bond issue to pay for the purchase of the land was defeated, the utility company was left with $6 million of land on which it could not build a generating facility. Id. at 625-26. It sued San Diego to force the city to condemn the land formally and to buy it at fair market value. The dissenters are certainly correct that nothing in the just compensation clause empowers a court to compel the government to exercise its power of eminent domain *for the future* where the regulatory "taking" is temporary and reversible and the government would rather *end* the "taking" than buy the land. Id. at 658 (Brennan, J., dissenting): "Just as the government may cancel condemnation proceedings before passage of title, see 6 J. Sackman, Nichols' Law of Eminent Domain § 24.113, p. 21-24 (rev. 3d ed. 1980), or abandon property it has temporarily occupied or invaded, see United States v.

direct form of governmental incursion, these mitigating factors might not have saved the regulation in question.

For example, *Nollan v. California Coastal Comm'n* [14] involved an attempt by the state to condition issuance of a permit to rebuild an ocean-front residence on the property owners' willingness to grant the public a permanent easement across their beach. In an opinion by Justice Scalia,[15] the Court first deemed it "obvious" that a direct state appropriation of such an easement would constitute a taking of a classic property interest—the right to exclude others [16]—rather than "a mere restriction on its use." [17] The majority then turned to whether the state could constitutionally achieve its end by requiring conveyance of an easement as a condition for a land use permit. Assuming *arguendo* that the Coastal Commission could have altogether denied the Nollans a permit to build on their property if it concluded that such development would undermine the state's legitimate goals of reducing beach congestion and of overcoming the psychological barrier to beach use created by an over-developed shoreline, the Court agreed that the Commission could impose a permit condition *so long as it served those same ends*.[18] No such nexus could be found, for the condition in question could not by any stretch of the imagination serve the state's purported interests: the easement the state sought would not have

Dow, 357 U.S. 17, 26 (1958), it must have the same power to rescind a regulatory 'taking.'" Justice Rehnquist, in his concurrence, noted his essential agreement with the dissenters' views on the merits. 450 U.S. at 633.

It is equally plain, though, that the government must compensate the property owner for whatever "taking" occurred during the time between enactment and repeal of the offending regulation. First English Evangelical Lutheran Church v. Los Angeles, 107 S.Ct. 2378, 2389 (1987). Writing for himself and Justices Brennan, White, Marshall, Powell and Scalia, Chief Justice Rehnquist declared that "'temporary' takings which . . . deny a landowner all use of his property are not different in kind from permanent takings, for which the Constitution clearly requires compensation." Id. at 2388. The just compensation requirement is "not precatory: once there is a 'taking,' compensation must be awarded." San Diego Gas & Electric, 450 U.S. at 654. See United States v. Clarke, 445 U.S. 253, 257 (1980) (compensation clause is "self-executing"); First Evangelical Lutheran Church, 107 S.Ct. at 2386 n. 9 (squarely rejecting the Solicitor General's argument that "'the Constitution does not, of its own force, furnish a basis for a court to award money damages against the government.'"). Although this remedial question was thus finally resolved, the posture of the case gave the Court no occasion to decide whether the land-use ordinance in issue actually denied the plaintiff all use of his property, or "whether the county might

avoid the conclusion that a compensable taking had occurred by establishing that the denial of all use was insulated as a part of the State's authority to enact safety regulations." Id. at 2384–85.

14. 107 S.Ct. 3141 (1987).

15. He was joined by Chief Justice Rehnquist and Justices White, Powell and O'Connor. Justices Brennan, Marshall, Blackmun and Stevens dissented.

16. Id. at 3145.

17. Id. at 3154 n.3 (Brennan, J., joined by Marshall, J., dissenting).

18. Id. at 3147–48. Justice Scalia reasoned that a nexus between the state's legitimate purpose and the condition it would impose was mandated by a variation on the doctrine of unconstitutional conditions: "When that essential nexus is eliminated, the situation becomes the same as if California law forbade shouting fire in a crowded theater, but granted dispensations to those willing to contribute $100 to the state treasury. While a ban on shouting fire can be a core exercise of the State's police power to protect the public safety, and can thus meet even our stringent standards for regulation of speech, adding the unrelated condition alters the purpose to one which, while it may be legitimate, is inadequate to sustain the ban. Therefore, even though, in a sense, requiring a $100 tax contribution in order to shout fire is a lesser restriction on speech than an outright ban, it would not pass constitutional muster." Id. at 3148.

allowed the public access to the beach across the Nollans' property from the public street, but merely have allowed those people already on the public beach on one side of the Nollans' property to cross the private strip of sand to the public beach on the other side.[19] The Court concluded that, "unless the permit condition serves the same governmental purpose as the development ban, the building restriction is not a valid regulation of land use but 'an out-and-out plan of extortion.' "[20] If California wanted an easement across the Nollans' beach, it would have to pay for it. Such physical invasions—the governmental actions most vulnerable to takings challenges—are the subject of the next section.

§ 9–5. Physical Invasions

In a number of recent decisions, the Supreme Court has dealt with state laws which allow third parties to trespass physically upon private property. In two such cases, the Court applied its usual ad hoc approach, recognizing that, while factors developed in other cases may be helpful, "the resolution of each case . . . ultimately calls as much for the exercise of judgment as for the application of logic."[1] In a third case, however, the Court abandoned this approach in favor of what appears to be a per se repudiation of all permanent, physical invasions of even the most trivial variety.

PruneYard Shopping Center v. Robins[2] involved the right of a privately owned shopping center to resist the use of its property as a public forum. The PruneYard consisted of 21 acres, 10 restaurants and more than 65 shops which were visited by 25,000 people every day.[3] To resist use of the area by students seeking signatures on a petition, no plausible privacy claim could be made, nor a claim of protecting any right of intimate association. However, the owner of the shopping center had a general rule, neutral as to subject matter, prohibiting public expression other than the business-related variety. Unlike the ancient Greek *agora*, the PruneYard saw itself solely as a marketplace of goods, not a marketplace of ideas. Thus when some high school students tried to set up a booth to solicit signatures for a petition opposing a United Nations resolution, they were summarily ordered off the premises.

---

19. Id. at 3149.

20. Id. at 3148 (citation omitted). The Court did not specify just how tight this nexus requirement was, finding that even the Commission's proposed test—that the condition be "reasonably related to the public need or burden" that the Nollans' proposed development would create—could not be satisfied by the facts of the case before it. Id. There are, however, indications that a tight nexus would not necessarily be required where the state's condition on a land use permit involved something less than coercive abdication of a core property interest: "our cases describe the condition for abridgement of property rights through the police power as a '*substantial* advanc[ing]' of a legiti-

mate state interest. We are inclined to be particularly careful about the adjective where the actual conveyance of property is made a condition to the lifting of a land use restriction, since in that context there is a heightened risk that the [real] purpose is avoidance of the compensation requirement" Id. at 3150 (original emphasis). Outside of this concededly sensitive context, a more relaxed standard for reviewing exercise of the police power may prevail. But see id. at 3147 n. 3.

§ 9–5

1. Andrus v. Allard, 444 U.S. 51, 65 (1979).

2. 447 U.S. 74 (1980).

3. Id. at 77–78.

The California Supreme Court, however, interpreted the state constitution's free speech clause as entitling the students to set up their booth in the PruneYard—perhaps subject to reasonable time, place and manner regulations—despite the fact that the shopping center was private property.[4] The PruneYard argued that California, by inviting third persons onto its property to conduct their petition drive, was taking its property without just compensation.

In a unanimous opinion by Justice Rehnquist, the Supreme Court disagreed. The Court conceded that the right to exclude others from one's property has long been held to be a fundamental element of one's bundle of property rights.[5] But the owner did *not* exclude people from the PruneYard—indeed, its purpose was to attract people there to spend money—and the Court could find no indication in the record that permitting free expression would significantly impair the value of the PruneYard *as* a shopping center, especially since the owner could impose reasonable time, place and manner restrictions to limit any disruption of commercial activity. In these circumstances, the Court refused to view the fact that the appellant's property had been "physically invaded" as determinative.[6]

A huge shopping center open to the general public understandably did not appear to the Court to be the kind of *traditional* "property" from which one has a federal constitutional right not only to exclude the public but also to extend invitations conditional upon what one's visitors have to say while on the premises. As a consequence, the positivist argument that California possesses a "residual authority that enables it to define 'property' in the first instance"[7] carried more weight in *PruneYard* than it did in *Webb's Fabulous Pharmacies*, where the Court held, just as unanimously, that interest follows the principal no matter what the state's law may say to the contrary.[8]

4. As much as it may have wished to, the California Supreme Court could not rest its decision on the first amendment to the federal Constitution, for the latter had been read as *not* giving people a right, over and above the right of the property owner, of free access to shopping centers for expressive purposes. Hudgens v. NLRB, 424 U.S. 507 (1976); Lloyd Corp. v. Tanner, 407 U.S. 551 (1972). See §§ 12–25, 18–5, infra. And the Court has held that a state supreme court may not give the first amendment more bite than the Supreme Court would. See, e.g., Zacchini v. Scripps-Howard Broadcasting Co., 433 U.S. 562 (1977).

5. 447 U.S. at 82. See Kaiser Aetna v. United States, 444 U.S. 164, 179–80 (1979); International News Serv. v. Assoc. Press, 248 U.S. 215, 250 (1918) (Brandeis, J., dissenting).

6. 447 U.S. at 83–84.

7. 447 U.S. at 84.

8. Webb's Fabulous Pharmacies, Inc. v. Beckwith, 449 U.S. 155, 161, 164 (1980). See § 9–7, infra. The case of Pacific Gas & Electric Company v. Public Utilities Commission of California, 106 S.Ct. 903 (1986), provides a useful post-PruneYard reminder that redefinitions of property by legislatures and agencies are, of course, limited by other provisions of the federal Constitution. For 62 years, Pacific Gas, a California utility, had enclosed a newsletter in its monthly billing envelopes containing political editorials as well as more mundane items. 106 S.Ct. at 905. In 1980, after a public interest group during ratemaking proceedings called for a ban on the inclusion of these politicized enclosures, California's Public Utilities Commission (PUC) ordered the utility to allot the "extra space" in its envelopes to the public interest group to allow it to voice its point of view on ratemaking issues. Id. at 906–907. The Court, in a plurality opinion by Justice Powell, invalidated the envelope-sharing order on first amendment grounds, reasoning primarily that the forced inclusion would effectively violate the utility's right under Wooley v. Maynard, 430 U.S. 705 (1977), *not* to speak or be forced to reply. See § 12–4, infra. Both Justice Powell, id. at 909–10, and Justice Marshall in his con-

A second physical invasion case held a government regulation which invited third parties to trespass on private property to be a compensable taking. *Kaiser Aetna v. United States* [9] arose in the late Pleistocene Period—near the end of the ice age, when a lagoon was formed on what *much* later became known as Oahu, Hawaii. This lagoon, the 523 acres known as Kuapa Pond, was passed down through the ages until eventually, as an *ahupuaa* allotted by King Kamehameha III during the Great Mahele, it ended up in the hands of one Bernice Bishop, whose estate ultimately granted a long-term lease to the Kaiser Aetna Company. Kaiser Aetna decided to make the Kuapa Pond into a considerably more valuable piece of property by developing it into a residential community. To do so, the company spent millions of dollars in 1961—after receiving approval for its plans from the U.S. Corps of Engineers—to convert a land-locked, two-foot-deep fish pond into a navigable body of water connected to the Pacific Ocean by an eight-foot-deep channel.[10] A private marina-style community of some 22,000 residents surrounded Kuapa Pond, of whom about 1,700 paid fees for the maintenance of the marina.

In 1972, a dispute arose between Kaiser Aetna and the Corps of Engineers over public access to the pond—which was by then a "navigable waterway" in fact even if still "fast land" under Hawaiian law. Did the government effect a compensable taking by saying to the general public, "Come on in, the water's fine"? True, there had been no expropriation as such. But the government was regulating the property by imposing a navigational servitude which effectively invited actual physical invasion by third parties.[11] Unlike the PruneYard, Kuapa Pond was the sort of private property for which excluding the public was a critical stick in the bundle.[12] Each resident of the Kuapa Pond marina community paid a $72 annual fee to maintain the pond which the government-invited gatecrashers would get to use for free.[13] The Court, speaking again through Justice Rehnquist,[14] repeatedly stressed that Kaiser Aetna had spent millions of dollars developing a marina community on the assumption that it would stay private and not become a public aquatic park.[15] The majority held that, while the

currence, id. at 914–17, pointedly distinguished PruneYard. In particular, they contended, the access permitted in Pacific Gas would impinge on the utility's right to speak more than did what Justice Marshall termed "the slight incursion" permitted in PruneYard. Id. at 917. While states are generally free to create state-based rights, Justice Marshall noted, they may not do so in such a way as to burden federal constitutional rights. Thus the utilities commission, Marshall wrote, "has crossed the boundary between constitutionally permissible and impermissible redefinitions of private property." Id. at 917.

9. 444 U.S. 164 (1979).

10. Id. at 166–67.

11. Id. at 180. The unconstitutional result would have been the same had the

state sought to ensure public access to the marina by, for example, conditioning issuance to a marina resident of a permit to build a sundeck on the resident's granting to the general public of a right of access to the marina. See Nollan v. California Coastal Comm'n, 107 S.Ct. 3141 (1987), discussed in § 9–4, supra.

12. 444 U.S. at 176; cf. PruneYard, 447 U.S. at 84.

13. Justice Rehnquist stressed this point in the penultimate line of his opinion for the Court. 444 U.S. at 180.

14. But not unanimously: Justices Blackmun, Brennan and Marshall dissented. Id. at 180.

15. Id. at 169, 175, 176, 180.

consent of the Corps of Engineers in Kaiser Aetna's development plans could not estop the United States from now placing the pond under a navigational servitude, it *could* engender investment-backed expectations rising to the status of property rights for which the government must pay when it effectively nationalizes them.[16]

The legal-positivist argument that the state must be free to take away with one hand what it gave with the other [17] was especially leaky in the Kuapa Pond case because *two* sovereigns were involved: Justice Rehnquist noted several times that the law of *Hawaii* led the plaintiffs to believe their pond was private property,[18] until the *federal* government, in the form of the Corps of Engineers, sailed in to say, "No, it's not." The "bitter-sweet" argument—that one who relies on a state's law to claim property is not free to ignore restrictions or qualifications built into the same law but must instead take the "bitter" with the "sweet" [19]—thus posed little difficulty to a majority bent on protecting from government-invited gatecrashers what it saw as plainly private property.

The final, and in some ways the most curious, in this instructive trio of physical invasion cases is *Loretto v. Teleprompter Manhattan CATV Corp.*[20] Prior to 1973, cable television (CATV) companies like Teleprompter had given landlords 5% of their gross revenues from users living in the landlord's property in exchange for the landlord's authorization of the necessary CATV installations. In order to facilitate tenant access to the important educational and community benefits of CATV, New York passed a law requiring all landlords to allow installation of CATV cables in exchange for a $1 fee.[21] The landlord was not to bear the costs of installation, however, and could not only demand that installation conform to reasonable conditions necessary to protect the appearance and safety of the premises, but was entitled to indemnification by the CATV company for any damage resulting from installation, operation or removal of the CATV facilities.[22] When a disgruntled landlord seeking a bigger piece of the action sued Teleprompter for trespass, the Supreme Court abandoned its now-familiar ad hoc approach in favor of a per se rule: a permanent physical occupation authorized by government is a compensable taking, however significant the public interests it may serve.[23] The majority opinion contains several pages of hyperbolic rhetoric in which a few feet of ½ inch cable and a couple of small silver boxes—the totality of the offending installation—are described as having effectively destroyed the

---

16. Id. at 179–80. See A. Brownstein, "The Takings Clause and the Iranian Claims Settlement," 29 U.C.L.A.L.Rev. 984, 1064–66 (1982).

17. See § 10–12, infra.

18. 444 U.S. at 166, 167, 179.

19. Cf. Arnett v. Kennedy, 416 U.S. 134, 153–54 (1974) (Rehnquist, J.) (stating in due process context that, where state creates a right, the recipient "must take the

bitter with the sweet"). See § 10–12, infra.

20. 458 U.S. 419 (1982).

21. Id. at 423–24.

22. Id. at 423 n. 3.

23. Id. at 426. Justice Marshall delivered the opinion of the Court. Justice Blackmun, joined by Justices Brennan and White, dissented.

landlord's use of his roof space.[24] We are told that to allow a *"stranger"* to "invade" and "exercise complete dominion" over the landlord's property is "literally to add insult to injury." [25] The majority even takes the dissent to task for underestimating the size of the CATV installation, which actually displaced more than 1½ cubic feet! [26]

This obsession with permanent physical invasions of even the most de minimus variety borders on fetishism.[27] The majority apparently finds merely *temporary* limitations on the right to exclude, such as those in *PruneYard, Kaiser Aetna*, and the intermittent flooding cases,[28] to be less constitutionally offensive even though the economic deprivation of those incursions far exceeds that worked by CATV installations.[29] New York can force Penn Central not to build a multi-million dollar, 53-story office building above Grand Central Station, but it cannot force Jean Loretto to abide a couple of 1½-foot high boxes and some ½ inch cable above her apartment building. Would the result have been different if the boxes were to be removed periodically? Or if Teleprompter had simply been given a state-created right of periodic access to Ms. Loretto's rooftop, much as utility companies' meter-readers must enter an apartment building? It is hard to believe that the outcome in such cases should turn on distinctions of this sort.

The final oddity of the *Teleprompter* decision is that the majority concedes that its analysis turns upon the fact that the CATV company, rather than the landlord, *owns* the offending installation. The Court claims that its holding does not affect the state's power to require landlords to provide such things as mailboxes, smoke alarms, and utility connections. The reason is that, although the expense in those situations is imposed directly on the landlord, and her dominion over her property is certainly impaired, *she owns* the installation, albeit unwittingly.[30] This distinction is of critical importance to the majority because ownership would permit the landlord, not the CATV company, to decide how the cables were to be stapled to the roof and hence to control the aesthetic impact of the installation. But even this meager distinction collapses since the majority admits that New York's statute gives the landlord authority to prescribe reasonable conditions to protect the appearance of the premises, and the right to demand indemnification for any damage. The *only* burden remaining on the landlord is the inconvenience of initiating minor repairs. Although the majority is correct that such a burden is "cognizable," [31] it hardly amounts to cleaning out the Augean stables, and is in any event a lame excuse for abandoning the search for workable balancing tests in favor of a talisman–like "permanent physical invasions." [32]

24. Id. at 427.

25. Id. at 436.

26. Id. at 438 n. 16. The majority adds that the size of the physical invasion is not germane to the question of the existence of a taking, only to the amount of compensation.

27. See L. Tribe, Constitutional Choices 174–79 (1985).

28. See, e.g., Pumpelly v. Green Bay & Mississippi Co., 80 U.S. 166 (1871).

29. 458 U.S. at 435 n. 12.

30. Id. at 440 & n. 19.

31. Id. at 440.

32. The Court's flirtation in Teleprompter with a per se rule regarding physical invasions has appropriately generated criticism from commentators. See,

A comparison of *Teleprompter* and *Penn Central* at least suggests that the Supreme Court's takings cases harbor no consistent capitalist agenda: in *Penn Central*, an expensive real estate development project by a corporate giant lost out to the cause of historic preservation; in *Teleprompter*, the needs of important, new information technology gave way to the formal property rights of small urban landlords. Evidently the Court sees itself, or at least wishes to depict itself, as neutrally protecting property as the *Constitution*, not capitalism, dictates. Yet the Court's "Constitution" is anything but inevitable: it is the Constitution as *Lochner*-style common law. The roof-top space invaded by the law struck down in *Teleprompter* certainly looks more like *traditional* property than does the volume of air above Grand Central Station which was protected by the law upheld in *Penn Central*. One suspects that there would be a closer fit between the Court's sense of property and the demands of fairness and efficiency in post-industrial society were the Court's imagination less captivated by common law legacies resembling those the Court rigidly enforced from the 1890s to 1937. By saying, "We know a taking of property when we see it, and this physical occupation by third parties, however insignificant, is it," the Court perpetuates the myth that the just compensation clause is a template which judges may simply lay atop the facts of nature so as to detect a taking if any rough edges are seen to protrude beyond the template. Critical analysis would be fostered by a more candid concession of the choices the Court necessarily makes in filling out the "takings" concept when it follows common law habits as though it were merely doing arithmetic.[33]

e.g., DiGiovanni, "Eminent Domain—Loretto v. Teleprompter Manhattan CATV Corp.: Permanent Physical Occupation as a Taking," 62 N.C.L.Rev. 153 (1983) (criticizing Court's abandonment of a unified factual approach for a "two-track" bifurcation of takings questions into those involving physical invasions and those in which such incursions are absent); Baker, "Property and Its Relation to Constitutionally Protected Liberty," 134 U.Pa.L.Rev. 741, 766 & n. 56 (1986) (noting that, while a per se rule against physical invasions could in theory be defended as a prophylactic measure to prevent the arbitrary imposition of burdens on particular landowners, such a danger was absent in the broad regulation at issue in Teleprompter).

Perhaps because of such criticism, the Court, in Federal Communications Commission v. Florida Power Corp., 107 S.Ct. 1107 (1987), appeared to seek to narrow the scope of the per se rule suggested by Teleprompter. The Court in Florida Power upheld against a takings challenge the federal Pole Attachments Act, which empowered the FCC to set the rates that utility companies may charge cable television systems for using utility poles as the physical medium for stringing television cable. Justice Marshall's opinion for a unanimous Court noted the central difference between Teleprompter and the Florida Power statute: while the Teleprompter statute "specifically *required* landlords to permit permanent occupation of their property by cable companies, nothing in the Pole Attachments Act as interpreted by the FCC gives cable companies any right to occupy space on utility poles, or prohibits utility companies from refusing to enter into attachment agreements with cable operators." Id. Justice Marshall's reiteration in Florida Power that the Teleprompter holding was "very narrow," id., may portend a restriction of the per se ban on physical invasions to those cases involving what he termed "required acquiescence" by landowners. Id.

33. An important premise underlying all three of the foregoing cases— *PruneYard, Kaiser Aetna,* and *Teleprompter*—is that uncompensated physical invasions by third parties acting under the express authorization of government are just as unconstitutional as are takings in which the government itself is the trespasser. See Teleprompter, 458 U.S. at 432–33 n. 9 ("Permanent physical occupation authorized by state law is a taking without regard to whether the State, or instead a party authorized by the State, is

§ 9–6. The Compensation Requirement as an Attempt to Limit Arbitrary Sacrifice of the Few to the Many

As we will see even more clearly in our consideration of the first amendment in Chapter 12, seeking a systematic explanation of any constitutional requirement is a treacherous business, in part because the very notion that a "systematic" explanation exists or would be desirable may entail some doubtful assumptions.[1] The modern tendency to treat each constitutional provision as a means to some other end, or at least as a manifestation of a set of values whose internal structure may be coherently elucidated, may at times falsify the meaning of a constitutional command as a reflection of a rather concrete intuition about a particular set of problems. But having said this much, it is difficult not to indulge the modern tendency by asking what more general ends the just compensation requirement might serve or what more general norms it might reflect, particularly since the intuitive picture of the requirement seems to generate so few answers in the hard cases addressed in § 9–3.

Whether traced to a principle that society simply should not exploit individuals in order to achieve its goals,[2] or to an idea that such exploitation causes too much dissatisfaction from a strictly utilitarian point of view unless it is brought under control,[3] the just compensation requirement appears to express a limit on government's power to isolate particular individuals for sacrifice to the general good. Such a limit is relevant, although in different ways, to each of the three identifiably legitimate reasons government might have for taking an action with adverse impact on someone's property. First, government might act with the deliberate aim of redistributing wealth.[4] Second, it might act so as to reallocate property, leaving the distribution of wealth intact but seeking, through a different arrangement of objects or resources, to generate more of some uniformly desired good or less of some uniformly disliked bad. And third, it might act out of a conviction that a formerly tolerated use of property should now be deemed immoral or otherwise unacceptable.

the occupant"). This premise buttresses the understanding of modern state action doctrine that a private citizen who violates the rights of others pursuant to state authorization may be as much a state actor as is a policeman or an attorney general. See Chapter 18, infra. A taking is a taking regardless of whether the invasion of property is committed by the government or by a private party acting at government's invitation. Conversely, so long as the taking is for a public purpose and the government is willing to provide compensation, the taking is legitimate. The next section, § 9–6, examines the rationales undergirding the compensation requirement.

§ 9–6

1. See § 12–1, infra.

2. See I. Kant, Groundwork of the Metaphysic of Morals 66–67 (H. J. Paton, tr.;

2d ed. 1964); Michelman, "Property, Utility, and Fairness: Comments on the Ethical Foundations of 'Just Compensation' Law," 80 Harv.L.Rev. 1165, 1218–24 (1967).

3. Id. at 1211, citing Bentham, Theory of Legislation, chs. 7–10 (6th ed. 1890).

4. The idea that redistribution *per se* violates the constitutional duty of the state to be "neutral" among social and economic interests and classes has a venerable past but fails to capture both a major part of our 18th and 19th century heritage and a crucial dimension of the post-Depression consensus. See generally M. Horwitz, Keynote Address to American Society of Legal Historians, 16th Annual Meeting (Toronto, Oct. 25, 1986).

The first two sorts of government action typically leave unaltered the notion of what is "good," with the first seeking to carve up the collection of good things in a different way and with the second seeking to rearrange the already carved up pieces; the third sort of government action entails a shift in the very definition of the good. Only the second type of action is designed to generate an economic surplus out of which those who are left worse off could presumably be compensated. But all three types present a choice not unlike that central to the law of torts—a choice between (1) leaving the harm where the government action initially imposed it, and (2) taking steps to spread the harm more widely or at least differently. All three types of government action thus pose the same question from the perspective of the individual harmed: Why me?[5]

In the first and third categories of cases, a substantive reply may be available. Government may argue in the first situation that the injury should remain uncompensated because the person "injured" had more than his or her rightful share in the first place, an imbalance that the injury simply redressed—much as one would recapture a thief's booty.[6] Or government may argue in the third situation that the

---

5. The same question arises in some so-called "affirmative action" plans. See § 16–22, infra.

6. Naked redistributions of wealth are obviously rendered problematic, if not indeed pointless, by the just compensation requirement. For that requirement effectively mandates that government restore the *status quo ante* by compensating victims of takings, presumably out of government tax revenues. The effect of this requirement is, of course, to make the redistributive potential of government regulation, of outright redistribution followed by payment in accord with the takings clause, coextensive with, but no greater than, that of the taxing power.

Nevertheless, some foes of New Deal and Great Society legislation mistake the practical pointlessness of explicit wealth redistribution under the just compensation clause—and the respect the Constitution accords private property—for a broader and far more radical theory: that the Constitution forbids *any* measures that would alter the basic, common-law status of property holders. The leading expositor of this view is University of Chicago Professor Richard Epstein, who has argued that in including the fifth amendment's eminent domain provision, the framers of the Constitution meant to endorse and freeze for all time a singularly static view of property. In his 1985 book, Takings, Epstein interprets the takings clause as embodying a broad anti-confiscation sentiment that "forecloses virtually all public transfer and welfare programs, however designed and executed." R. Epstein, Takings 30–31, 324 (1985). "The basic rules of private proper-

ty are inconsistent with any form of welfare benefits," Epstein argues. Accordingly, he calls upon the judiciary to strike down the progressive income tax, minimum wage laws, and the National Labor Relations Act, along with many other interventionist measures of the 20th century. Id. at 303, 327–28.

While the aversion to economic and social legislation undergirding Epstein's Takings may strike a responsive chord in some circles, as a work of constitutional explication Epstein's argument is wide of the mark. The gaps, flawed assumptions and argumentative ellisions in Epstein's reactionary interpretation of the fifth amendment, while too numerous to address fairly here, are effectively—and elegantly—exposed by Professor Thomas Grey in his review of Epstein's work. See Grey, "The Malthusian Constitution," 41 U. Miami L.Rev. 21 (1986). Grey concludes that Epstein's endorsement of "nothing less than the constitutional rollback of the welfare state" is a "travesty of constitutional scholarship," id. at 22, 24. While Grey challenges Epstein's work on numerous fronts, his rejoinder rightly focuses on the fact that Epstein, sub silentio, imputes to the founding fathers a hotly contested and exceedingly dubious economically-oriented view of the Constitution. "When the verbiage about rigor and natural rights is stripped away, Epstein's core position is that 'private property' means that set of rules governing resource distribution and allocation that will produce the greatest good for the greatest number." Id. at 45. It is because the effective ban on interventionist legislation that Epstein endorses lit-

"injury" involved nothing more than being forced to cease a practice that the individual should have realized was unacceptable.[7] In the second category, however, the argument against compensation is less substantive than procedural: the losses should remain uncompensated because it would cost more to administer a compensation system for cases like yours than it would be worth, even for you, in the long run.[8]

Given the nature of the harm inflicted, the identity of the individuals harmed, and the character of the governmental body and process through which the decision to inflict harm was taken, a court may have good reason to suspect the adequacy of each reply to the "why me" question. A reply in terms of intentional redistribution is least acceptable when others still more fortunate have been spared.[9] A reply in terms of prior notice is least persuasive when no history of accumulating disapproval suggests that the individual really should have seen the handwriting on the wall.[10] And a reply in terms of long-run gain to all is most suspect when made to someone in a situation of frequent disadvantage or exploitation,[11] or when made by an agency with a programmatic goal of its own that is furthered by the injury inflicted.[12]

§ 9–7. The Problematic Nature of Property

While the just compensation clause, as § 9–4, § 9–5, and § 9–6 noted, appears to represent a substantial check on government power, it is possible for government to take a very different tack in defense of its actions. It might say simply: "You can't complain of *any injury at all*, since you *never had* what you claim we have taken away. From the very beginning, your property was subject to the *condition* that, if and when we thought it wise to do so, we could restrict it as we have or transfer it as we have."[1] Lest such a claim be dismissed as altogether preposterous, it should be recalled that, in the late 18th century, the

erally requires "government [to] leave the weak and helpless to their fate," id. at 47, that Grey terms Epstein's vision the "Malthusian Constitution." Epstein's optimistically titled rejoinder to the critiques by Grey and others, "A Last Word on Eminent Domain," 41 U. Miami L.Rev. 253 (1986), argues that his critics merely chip away at his vision of the eminent domain clause, which he contends remains the only "complete theory" of the clause. Id. at 275.

7. See, e.g., New York Central R.R. Co. v. White, 243 U.S. 188 (1917) (upholding against due process and equal protection challenges workmen's compensation laws imposing liability on employers without fault).

8. See generally Michelman, supra note 2, at 1214–15, 1223–25.

9. On "the equal protection dimensions of compensation law," see Sax, "Takings and the Police Power," 74 Yale L.J. 36, 64–45 (1964); Sax, "Takings, Private Property and Public Rights," 81 Yale L.J. 149, 169–71 (1971).

10. Cf. Michelman, supra note 2, at 1235–45.

11. See United States v. Carolene Products Co., 304 U.S. 144, 152 n. 4 (1938).

12. See Sax, 74 Yale L.J. at 61–67 (suggesting closer scrutiny of losses inflicted by government in its "enterprise" than in its "arbitral" capacity); accord, Pittsburgh v. Alco Parking Corp., 417 U.S. 369 (1974) (upholding, but more closely scrutinizing, a city tax on parking receipts of competitors of city-owned parking lots); id. at 379 (Powell, J., concurring); compare §§ 9–10 and 9–11, infra (closer scrutiny of government breach of public contracts than of government impairment of private contracts). But see Sax, 81 Yale L.J. at 150 n. 5.

§ 9–7

1. See, e.g., HFH, Ltd. v. Superior Court, 15 Cal.3d 508, 521, 125 Cal.Rptr. 365, 368, 542 P.2d 237, 247 (1975), cert. denied 425 U.S. 904 (1976) (arguing that every land investor must know that environmental controls might be imposed at any time); Dames & Moore v. Regan, 453

feudal common-law view that all property ultimately belonged to the king still had wide currency and was reflected in republican-communitarian notions of property; nothing less could explain the absence of just compensation clauses from most post-revolutionary state constitutions, or the absence from the 1787 Constitution of a just compensation clause limiting state action: even though the Constitution contained a clause barring state *contract* impairments and one barring *federal* takings without just compensation, it contained none barring uncompensated *state takings*.[2]

But a very different "liberal" tradition, one traceable through Madison's 10th Federalist,[3] co-existed with that republican heritage,[4] was ascendant in the *Lochner* era, and remains present, if not intact, in the post-1937 period. To the degree that private property is to be respected in the face of republican and positivist visions, it becomes necessary to resist even an explicit government proclamation that all property acquired in the jurisdiction is held subject to government's limitless power to do with it what government wishes. Indeed, government must be denied the power to give binding force to so sweeping an announcement, whether explicit or implicit, if we are to give content to the just compensation clause as a real constraint on federal power and, through the fourteenth amendment, on state and local power. But this shows that the expectations protected by the clause must have their source outside positive law. Grounded in custom or necessity, these expectations achieve protected status not because the state has deigned to accord them protection, but because constitutional norms entitle them to protection.[5]

These norms, however, cannot be expressed entirely within the language of expectations; that path is a circular one inasmuch as expectations are themselves subject to governmental manipulation. Instead, the norms must reflect a mix of several concerns—including *regularity*, which we consider in Chapter 10; *autonomy*, which we consider in Chapters 11 through 15; and *equality*, which we consider in Chapter 16.[6] Without appeal to such concerns, we are defenseless

U.S. 654, 674 n. 4 (1981) (holding no taking existed when U.S. nullified attachments of Iranian assets because petitioner's attachments were "revocable" and "contingent").

2. See Treanor, "The Origins and Original Significance of the Just Compensation Clause of the Fifth Amendment," 94 Yale L.J. 694, 695–701 (1985). The absence of such clauses in large part reflected a strong faith that legislatures would govern wisely and not abuse their discretion. See id. at 701: " 'All property,' Thomas Paine asserted, 'is safe under their [the people's] protection.' "

3. See id. at 708–13. While Madison "did not believe property was a natural right," he did contend that "its protection was of critical importance" because "[t]he diversity of interests that possession of property occasioned prevented tyranny, and the acquisition of property was a nec-

essary by-product of the freedom of action he deemed an essential part of liberty." Id. at 710.

4. See M. Horwitz, Keynote Address to American Society of Legal Historians, 16th Annual Meeting (Toronto, Oct. 25, 1986), at 9 (describing tension between "the liberal ideal of a neutral, night-watchman state of Madison's Tenth Federalist" and more republican visions of government).

5. For a discussion of the need for limits to legal positivism, particularly as manifested in the apparently short-lived "entitlement doctrine," see generally Flax, "Liberty, Property, and the Burger Court: The Entitlement Doctrine in Transition," 60 Tulane L.Rev. 889 (1986).

6. See generally Radin, "Property and 'Personhood,' " 34 Stan.L.Rev. 957 (1982); Michelman, "Property as a Constitutional

against the alluring but fatal argument that, since it is government that gives, government is free to take as well.[7]

The Court's conception of property in its takings analysis, however, has often rested too heavily on whether a given stick in a bundle of property rights resembles the Justices' collective hunch as to what "traditional" property is all about. Supreme Court Justices apparently believe they know a taking when they see one.[8] They seem at times to find the constitutional test transparent, and their duty simple: "to lay the article of the Constitution which is invoked beside the statute which is challenged and to decide whether the latter squares with the former." [9] What this mechanical notion of judicial review obscures is the fact that the Constitution does not in truth provide us with a template for property, and the Court's decisions in recent years suggest that it is once again sanctifying the common law as constitutional principle in the guise of drawing on common sense.

The Court's deference to common-law conceptions of property was well illustrated by the 1980 case of *Webb's Fabulous Pharmacies, Inc. v. Beckwith*,[10] in which the Court unanimously struck down a state's attempt to define as public property the interest earned on a private fund which had been deposited with a state court in the course of an interpleader proceeding. Webb's was in dire financial straits, and another pharmacy chain, Eckerd's, agreed to buy its assets. In compliance with Florida law, Eckerd's tendered the purchase price to a state court and interpleaded Webb's and some 200 of its creditors. The clerk of the court deposited the purchase fund in an interest-bearing account and deducted a statutorily determined sum as a fee for services rendered.[11] The fund was ultimately paid to a court-appointed receiver, but the clerk retained nearly $100,000 in interest on the authority of § 28.33 of the Florida Laws, which declared that "[i]nterest accruing from moneys deposited shall be deemed income of the office of the clerk." [12]

In a unanimous opinion, the Supreme Court disagreed, declaring that the "usual and general rule" is that the interest follows the principal.[13] The interest was not retained as a fee, for a statutory fee had already been deducted. The interest therefore belonged to Webb's creditors as an "incident of ownership" of the principal.[14] The Florida Supreme Court had held that, because there was no requirement that funds deposited in the court's registry be invested, and because the very statute which directed investment also declared that the interest

---

Right," 38 Wash. & L.L.Rev. 1097 (1981); Reich, "The New Property," 73 Yale L.J. 733 (1964).

7. The effort to ground a defense in what Professor Thomas Grey aptly calls "The Malthusian Constitution," see 41 U. Miami L.Rev. 21 (1986) (reviewing R. Epstein, Takings (1985)), does not merit close attention here in light of the overwhelming flaws exposed by Grey. See § 9–6, note 6, supra.

8. See B. A. Ackerman, Private Property and the Constitution 88–167 (1977); L.

Tribe, Constitutional Choices 169, 171–74 (1985).

9. United States v. Butler, 297 U.S. 1, 62 (1936).

10. 449 U.S. 155 (1980).

11. Id. at 157.

12. Id. at 156 n. 1.

13. Id. at 162 (citations omitted).

14. Id. at 164.

earned thereby was public property, the state took only what it had itself created.[15] The Supreme Court conceded that, since the Constitution itself creates no property rights, property is essentially what the state says it is,[16] yet rejected Florida's "bitter-sweet" argument nonetheless.[17] The Court unanimously rejected the only applicable positive law in favor of its own neo-Lockean notion of property, and declared that "a State, by *ipse dixit*, may not transform private property into public property without compensation." [18]

Justice Blackmun, writing for the Court, tried to restrict the holding by saying that the same result would not necessarily obtain if the expropriated interest were the only service charge levied by the state.[19] Yet he simultaneously pointed out that such a "charge" would give the state a dangerous incentive to retain the interpleader fund for as long a time as possible.[20] Despite the Court's precatory reservations, it seems doubtful that the mere act of calling the confiscation of interest a service charge would enable the state to oust the traditional notion of property to which the Justices subscribe. The state may not carve up property interests in such a way as to purloin sticks from the property owner's Hohfeldian bundle. Just as the ownership of a chicken farm includes the right to a tranquil sky overhead,[21] and the property interest in a sofa includes the right to a hearing before prejudgment replevin by the creditor,[22] so the bundle of property rights in a fund temporarily deposited with a court evidently includes the right to the interest which it earns, no matter how the state legislature may characterize the principal.

However, not every stick in a bundle of property rights is entitled to the unwavering judicial protection accorded the accrued interest in *Webb's*. Some sticks are problematic. If a particular property interest is highly speculative or evanescent, it is harder for a court to judge whether what one is given in exchange for its expropriation is sufficient compensation. The less traditional the property, the less likely the Court has been to find that there has been an uncompensated taking.

In *Duke Power Co. v. Carolina Environmental Study Group*,[23] the property alleged to have been taken was so intangible as to be all but invisible—and was untraditional. The respondents there challenged the federal Price-Anderson Act, which limited to $560 million the right to recover for injuries from an accident at a nuclear power plant. The

---

15. Id. at 163.

16. Id. at 161. The Court quoted Board of Regents v. Roth, 408 U.S. 564, 577 (1972).

17. See § 9–5, supra, at note 19; § 10–12, infra.

18. 449 U.S. at 164.

19. Id. at 164–65.

20. Id. at 162.

21. See United States v. Causby, 328 U.S. 256 (1946), cited by the Court in Webb's, 449 U.S. at 165.

22. See Fuentes v. Shevin, 407 U.S. 67 (1972) (notice and hearing required before prejudgment replevin by creditor of household goods sold to debtor on conditional sales contract, despite pre-existence of state law allowing for ex parte prejudgment replevin). See also North Georgia Finishing, Inc., v. Di-Chem, Inc., 419 U.S. 601 (1975) (probable cause hearing required before garnishment of corporate bank account, despite contract between creditor and garnishee corporation that, if construed in light of pre-existing state law, conditioned corporation's property interest in the bank account upon relinquishment of any right to demand such a hearing).

23. 438 U.S. 59 (1978).

case presented interesting questions of standing and ripeness[24] which the Court resolved in favor of respondents, in all likelihood because it seemed important to reach the merits.[25] On the merits, the Court found no taking where respondents lost a right to an uncertain recovery, in the "exceedingly remote" event of a nuclear accident, from utility companies with private insurers, and gained instead a guarantee of compensation which, although limited, would be given on a strict liability basis and would be distributed equally among the claimants, without a "race to the courthouse."[26]

The Court also rejected the respondents' claim to a right under the due process clause to be free of nuclear power or to "take advantage of the state of uncertainty which inhibited the private development of nuclear power."[27] The argument was that private insurance companies would not have insured nuclear power plants for any amount approaching the estimated liability for a major nuclear mishap, and without such insurance private utility companies would probably not have built the reactors. The Price-Anderson Act was therefore alleged to be a deliberate decision to expose some people to the risk of nuclear meltdowns and other catastrophes because Congress thought nuclear power development was in the public interest. For government to deny full compensation to the potential victims would surely sacrifice the few to the many or even, if one thinks the primary beneficiaries of nuclear power plants are the utility companies which lobbied for the Price-Anderson Act,[28] to a different, more influential, few.

An apparently minor point in the majority opinion would now seem to be crucial. The Court repeatedly placed emphasis on the fact that Congress had expressly committed itself to take whatever further emergency action would be necessary to aid victims of a nuclear accident should the insurance fund prove insufficient.[29] Yet the constitutionality of the Price-Anderson Act cannot possibly turn on a congressional promise to "make everything all right" in the event of a nuclear disaster, for such a pledge would not be binding on a subsequent Congress. Citizens have no more of a vested property interest in statutorily promised government benefits[30] than they do in any rule of the common law,[31] and the congressional pledge of *future* legislative appropriations in the Price-Anderson Act is obviously even less dependable than are the more traditional entitlement programs. No future victim could possibly enforce that pledge in court.

Thus *Duke Power* can only be understood as a judgment by the Court that the "property" of which plaintiffs claimed to have been deprived simply did not look like anything the Court was prepared to *call* property; it was far too problematic. The China Syndrome and

---

24. See §§ 3–10, 3–19, supra.

25. 438 U.S. at 103 (Stevens, J., concurring).

26. Id. at 85–86.

27. Id. at 88 n. 33.

28. Id. at 64.

29. Id. at 86–87 n. 39, 90–91, 93.

30. See Railroad Retirement Bd. v. Fritz, 449 U.S. 166 (1980), discussed in Chapter 16, infra.

31. Duke Power, 438 U.S. at 88 n. 32; see also Second Employers' Liability Cases, 223 U.S. 1, 50 (1912).

other nuclear accidents were considered unlikely in the extreme. Full recovery in the event of disaster would be highly uncertain given state tort law and the limited financial resources of the utilities and their insurers. And, even if full recovery for an accident were achieved, the worst-case, Nagasaki scenarios were so horrific as to make *any* damage award inadequate. In exchange for this extremely contingent and evanescent "property" interest, the plaintiffs received strict-liability recovery out of an established fund as well as the benefits of nuclear power which Congress found so compelling. The Supreme Court decided that the deal was fair enough; there was no taking.

The Court came to a similar conclusion in the Iranian claims case, *Dames & Moore v. Regan*.[32] In response to the seizure of the American embassy and the taking of hostages in Iran, President Carter, pursuant to his authority under the International Emergency Economic Powers Act (IEEPA), froze all Iranian assets within the jurisdiction of the United States. Prejudgment attachments against such assets were conditionally authorized, but the President barred entry of any final decree. As part of the agreement which ended the hostage crisis, the President revoked the conditional licenses to attach, nullified the attachments, and ordered that all Iranian assets be transferred to the Federal Reserve Bank of New York for return to Iran. Creditors with enforceable contract rights lost the ability to satisfy their claims against Iran out of the previously frozen assets. Their only recourse was to arbitration in a special international claims tribunal which possessed a limited capacity to satisfy the enormous claims of creditors, because it held only $1 billion and a pledge—of dubious value—of future payments by Iran. Thus the settlement sacrificed the financial interests of a narrow class of American creditors and forced them to bear the entire burden of obtaining the release of the hostages.

The Supreme Court took a narrow view of the takings issue and answered only the formal question of whether the government destroyed the creditors' property interest (liens) by nullifying the attachments of Iranian assets obtained pursuant to the President's conditional licenses.[33] The Court, in an opinion by Justice Rehnquist, held that because the "petitioner's attachments [were] 'revocable,' 'contingent,' and 'in every sense subordinate to the President's power under the IEEPA,' . . . . petitioner did not acquire any 'property' interest in its attachments of the sort that would support a constitutional claim for compensation."[34] The IEEPA made it clear that businesses conducting trade with foreign countries should not rely on the availability of foreign-owned assets in the United States, because in times of trouble those assets would become bargaining chips in a game of diplomatic poker.[35] And without access to unconditional attachments, creditors had unenforceable and essentially worthless claims. The settlement, then, deprived creditors only of the right to sue the Ayatollah, who was unlikely—to put it mildly—to pay his debts to the financial minions of

32. 453 U.S. 654 (1981).

33. See A. Brownstein, "The Takings Clause and the Iranian Claims Settlement," 29 U.C.L.A.Rev. 984, 991–92 (1982).

34. 453 U.S. at 674 n. 6.

35. See Brownstein, supra, at 1069.

"The Great Satan." Balanced against the loss of this problematic right of action was the provision of a crack at the $1 billion fund held by the international claims tribunal, and the opportunity to sue the federal government under the Tucker Act on the ground that the suspension of claims against Iran may constitute a taking.[36] Given the uncertainties of foreign policy and the evanescent character of foreign assets, Iran's creditors got about what they should have expected.

The Court's holding in *Dames & Moore*—that there was no taking— seems consistent with the broad contours of doctrine under the takings clause: unless the clause is to become a mandate for shackling government to the model of a minimal, night-watchman state, only a highly restricted set of fairly traditional, focused expectations will be protected by the just compensation requirement.

§ 9–8. Early Applications of the Contract Impairment Clause

Article I, § 10 commands that "No State shall . . . pass any . . . Law impairing the Obligation of Contracts. . . ."[1] Responding to state debtor relief laws enacted to combat the economic depression that preceded the adoption of the Constitution,[2] the clause was included primarily to protect private contracts from improvident majoritarian impairment.[3] Its first application nonetheless came in the somewhat surprising context of public land grants: In *Fletcher v. Peck*,[4] the

36. The majority concluded that, unlike the attachment issue, the question whether the suspension of claims against Iran constituted a taking was not ripe for review, but opined that the Court of Claims would have jurisdiction to consider such a suit. 453 U.S. at 688–89 n. 14. See § 4–8, supra.

§ 9–8

1. The clause applies to legislative acts (including referenda and constitutional amendments) but, unlike the just compensation clause, *not* to judgments of courts. See Tidal Oil Co. v. Flanagan, 263 U.S. 444 (1924). Although no explicit constitutional language similarly protects the sanctity of contract against federal legislation, the fifth amendment's due process clause was once thought to have essentially the same effect. See Lynch v. United States, 292 U.S. 571 (1934) (invalidating congressional attempt to cancel government war risk life insurance). But see Pension Benefit Guaranty Corp. v. R. A. Gray & Co., 467 U.S. 717, 733 (1984) (upholding against due process challenge Congress' retroactive imposition of "withdrawal liability" on private company for withdrawing from multi-company pension plan, and stating that the "standards imposed on economic legislation by the Due Process Clauses" are "less searching" than those imposed on states by the contract clause). Perry v. United States, 294 U.S. 330, 353–54 (1935), held that a congressional statute purporting to abrogate a clause in government bonds calling for payment in gold coin contra-

vened the provision of art. I, § 8, cl. 2, giving Congress "Power . . . To borrow money on the credit of the United States," although the creditor was denied any remedy absent a showing of actual damages. But cf. Lichter v. United States, 334 U.S. 742 (1948) (upholding War Contracts Renegotiation Act, which provided for recapture by government of "excess profits" on contracts made before Act's passage). Once Congress—by treaty, agreement, or statute—has guaranteed an Indian tribe a permanent right of use and occupancy in a given tract of land, Congress may not subsequently "give [such] lands to others or . . . appropriate them to its own purposes, without rendering, or assuming an obligation to render, just compensation. . . . For that would not be an exercise of guardianship, but an act of confiscation." Shoshone Tribe of Indians v. United States, 299 U.S. 476, 497 (1937); see Tee-Hit-Ton Indians v. United States, 348 U.S. 272, 277–78 (1955).

2. See B. Wright, The Contract Clause of the Constitution 4–6, 15–16, 32–33 (1938).

3. See, e.g., Sir Henry Maine's remarkable suggestion that the clause "is the bulwark of American individualism against democratic impatience and socialistic fantasy." Popular Government 247–48 (1885).

4. 10 U.S. (6 Cranch.) 87 (1810). Accord, New Jersey v. Wilson, 11 U.S. (7 Cranch.) 164 (1812) (invalidating a New

Supreme Court, in an opinion by Chief Justice Marshall, held that the contract clause prevented the Georgia legislature from annulling land titles that had previously vested in good faith purchasers from the state's original grantees.[5]

Probably the most famous decision under the clause was *Dartmouth College v. Woodward*,[6] where the Marshall Court held that New Hampshire could not pack the Dartmouth College board of trustees and alter its faculty so as to change the college into a public institution in violation if its 1769 charter from George III. That protecting contracts with the state was not the inspiration for the impairment clause made no difference; such contracts came within its purview and were thus entitled to its protection.[7]

Within weeks of its *Dartmouth College* decision, the Court applied the contract clause to the sort of law the Framers quite clearly did have in mind: New York's insolvency law, discharging debtors of their obligations upon surrender of their property. In *Sturges v. Crowninshield*,[8] the Court held the law unconstitutional. But eight years later the Court divided 4–3 in *Ogden v. Saunders*, holding that such insolvency laws can be applied without constitutional objection to debts incurred after the laws were enacted.[9] Over the bitter dissent of Chief

---

Jersey statute of 1804 repealing a tax exemption granted certain lands in 1758 by the colonial legislature).

5. Fletcher v. Peck grew out of a famous scandal in Georgia politics: the legislature attempted to annul land grants on the ground that the legislators who made the grants had been bribed. See generally Magrath, Yazoo: Law and Politics in the New Republic (1966). The land Georgia originally conveyed to defendant Peck's predecessor in interest was held and occupied by several Indian tribes at the time of that conveyance. See 10 U.S. at 88, 142–43. Plaintiff Fletcher argued that a 1763 Proclamation by the King of England had confirmed full title to the subject land in these tribes, thereby rendering Georgia incapable of transferring any interest in it. See id. at 102, 117, 141–42. The Court held for defendant on this issue, id. at 142, but that ruling did not dispose of the distinct question whether the tribe's acknowledged aboriginal rights in the land, id. at 142–43, might without more bar Georgia from conveying an interest in it. On that question, Marshall's opinion for the Court enunciated a compromise position: "The majority . . . is of opinion that the nature of the Indian title which is certainly to be respected by all courts, until it be legitimately extinguished, is not such as to be absolutely repugnant to seisin in fee on the part of the state." Id. at 142–43. This resolution set the course of Marshall's later opinions more fully treating issues arising from United States-Indian relations. See Worcester v. Georgia, 31 U.S. (6 Pet.)

515, 544, 556–57, 560 (1832); Cherokee Nation v. Georgia, 30 U.S. (5 Pet.) 1, 17 (1831); Johnson v. McIntosh, 21 U.S. (8 Wheat.) 543 (1823). On contemporary legal questions involving the aboriginal land rights of American Indians, and the allocation of state-federal-tribal rights and powers in respect to that land, see Oneida Cty., New York v. Oneida Indian Nation, 470 U.S. 226 (1985); Wilson v. Omaha Indian Tribe, 442 U.S. 653 (1979); Oneida Indian Nation v. County of Oneida, 414 U.S. 661 (1974); Tee-Hit-Ton Indians v. United States, 348 U.S. 272 (1955); Joint Tribal Council of Passamaquoddy Tribes v. Morton, 388 F.Supp. 649 (D.Me.1975), aff'd 528 F.2d 370 (1st Cir. 1975). See § 16–14, infra.

6. 17 U.S. (4 Wheat.) 518 (1819). See Baxter, Daniel Webster and The Supreme Court (1966).

7. See M. Horwitz, The Transformation of American Law 255 (1977) ("By forging constitutional doctrines under the Contracts Clause barring retroactive laws and giving constitutional status to 'vested rights,' this line of intellectual development sought basically to limit the ability of the legal system—more specifically, of the legislature—to bring about redistributions of wealth").

8. 17 U.S. (4 Wheat.) 122 (1819). See also Green v. Biddle, 21 U.S. (8 Wheat.) 1 (1821) (invalidating Kentucky law designed to make it more difficult for landowners to eject good faith squatters).

9. 25 U.S. (12 Wheat.) 213 (1827).

Justice Marshall, the majority reasoned that state laws in existence at the time a debt or other contractual obligation was incurred became part of the contract; the subsequent enforcement of such laws thus could not constitute an impairment of the contract's obligation.[10] Rejecting Marshall's theory that a contractual obligation derives not from the positive law of the place where it is made but from natural law prior to the social compact itself,[11] the majority in *Ogden* paved the way for the potential unravelling of the contract clause in the circularity to which all arguments based entirely upon legislatively grounded expectation are doomed.[12]

§ 9–9. Invoking the Contract Clause to Protect Private Agreements

From the beginning, the Court had announced a distinction between laws impairing a contract's *obligation* and those merely modifying the *remedies* provided for its enforcement.[1] But by the 1840's, the validity of remedial changes was already being assessed in terms of their "reasonableness" rather than in terms of any sharp substance-remedy dichotomy.[2] Justice Cardozo was putting the matter mildly some ninety years later when he described as "at times obscure" the resulting "dividing line" between remedy and obligation.[3] More basic still, it is crucial to recall that the Court had already held in 1827 that a contract incorporates in its terms the positive law of the time and place where it is made.[4] Once that is conceded, contract clause doctrine teeters atop the most slippery of slopes. For if a loan is extended in contemplation of the then current rules of insolvency, pursuant to which a debtor may one day claim relief, why is the loan not also extended in contemplation of the "master rule" that the rules themselves may one day change, substantively as well as remedially, in the debtor's interest? If a contract must be deemed to include, as a term made operative by law, the state's provision for excusing one of the parties, why not also the state's provision for changing such provisions pursuant to future legislation? Why, in short, did *Ogden* not in effect overrule *Sturges*?

This line of thought found its way into the leading modern case on contract impairment, *Home Building & Loan Ass'n v. Blaisdell*,[5] where the Supreme Court upheld the Minnesota Mortgage Moratorium Law of 1933. Enacted during the depression, that law authorized state courts, for the duration of the economic emergency declared to exist by the state legislature, to extend the period of redemption from mortgage foreclosure sales "for such additional time as the [appropriate county]

10. Justices Story and Duvall joined the Chief Justice in dissent. It was Marshall's only recorded failure, in thirty-four years as Chief Justice, to command a majority for his constitutional views.

11. See 25 U.S. at 332, 337, 342–48.

12. See § 9–6, *supra*.

§ 9–9

1. See *Sturges v. Crowninshield*, 17 U.S. (4 Wheat.) 122, 199–207 (1819).

2. See, e.g., *Bronson v. Kinzie*, 42 U.S. (1 How.) 311 (1843) (invalidating state law limiting mortgagee's rights on foreclosure).

3. *Worthen Co. v. Kavanaugh*, 295 U.S. 56, 60 (1935).

4. See *Ogden v. Saunders*, 25 U.S. (12 Wheat.) 213, 257–62 (1827), discussed in § 9–8, *supra*.

5. 290 U.S. 398 (1934).

court may deem just and equitable," but not beyond May 1, 1935. Each extension was to be made only upon an order requiring the mortgagor to "pay all or a reasonable part" of the property's income or rental value. Although the Court stressed the remedial and limited character of the measure and the urgency of the crisis it was designed to meet, the crux of its opinion in defense of a retroactive mortgage moratorium came in this passage: "Not only are existing laws read into contracts in order to fix obligations as between the parties, but the reservation of essential attributes of sovereign power is also read into contracts as a postulate of the legal order. . . ."[6] In other words, one of the "rules" that may be read into every contract at its inception is the rule that all *other* rules are subject to change if and when the legislature reasonably concludes that such change is needed.

But because the contract clause was successfully invoked several times in the decade after *Blaisdell*,[7] with the Court finding even some purely remedial changes too "oppressive and unnecessary" to pass muster,[8] it follows that one cannot take literally the basic postulate set forth in *Ogden v. Saunders*[9] and applied in *Home Building & Loan Ass'n v. Blaisdell*[10]—the postulate that every private contract is fully subject to the positive law that predates its formation. Indeed, such contemporary cases as *Fuentes v. Shevin*,[11] although not ordinarily analyzed in these terms, are flatly inconsistent with any such positivist notion. Without articulating the precise sources or contours of the protection it is providing, the Court has thus found in the Constitution a defense for contract-related interests going well beyond the enforcement of the state's enacted law.[12]

To the extent that Model III, the model of settled expectations, is cast exclusively in terms of the expectations that persons in fact entertain in reliance upon legal commitments expressly made by the sovereign, it is within the sovereign's power to hedge those commit-

---

6. Id. at 435.

7. See, e.g., Wood v. Lovett, 313 U.S. 362 (1941) (invalidating 1937 state legislative repeal of 1935 law protecting buyers at state tax sales from state attempts to rescind for various irregularities); Worthen Co. v. Kavanaugh, 295 U.S. 56 (1935) (striking down retroactive change in procedure for enforcing payment of benefit assessments pledged as security for municipal bonds; the destruction of "nearly all the incidents" making collateral security valuable was "oppressive and unnecessary"); Worthen Co. v. Thomas, 292 U.S. 426 (1934) (invalidating state law that exempted life insurance benefits from garnishment; despite conceded emergency, law went too far because it had no time limit and did not confine the exemption to the needs of the particular case); see also Treigle v. ACME Homestead Ass'n, 297 U.S. 189 (1936).

8. Worthen Co., 295 U.S. at 62.

9. 25 U.S. (12 Wheat.) 213 (1827).

10. 290 U.S. 398 (1934).

11. 407 U.S. 67 (1972). See also North Georgia Finishing, Inc. v. Di-Chem, Inc., 419 U.S. 601 (1975). Both cases are described in § 9–7, supra, in note 22, and in Chapter 10, infra.

12. In El Paso v. Simmons, 379 U.S. 497 (1965), although the Court upheld state legislation placing a five-year time limit on the right of land purchasers to reinstate claims to public lands after forfeiture for nonpayment of interest, it did so by stressing the non-central character of the reinstatement right, and the reasonableness of the law as a means of restoring confidence in state land titles, rather than by reminding the purchasers that state law at the time of their initial purchase had included a tacit power to alter the purchaser's rights after the fact if and when the legislature deemed it wise to do so. El Paso is discussed in § 9–10, infra.

ments in order to cut the expectations down to any desired size.[13] It must be the case, therefore, that the expectations protected by Model III in the years after *Blaisdell* are of a quite different sort. At stake must be not only what people *in fact expect* upon examining the body of positive law, but also what they are *entitled* to expect, positive law to the contrary notwithstanding. One might expect the content of this normative entitlement in the area of private contracts to be essentially coextensive with the reach of substantive due process[14] and equal protection,[15] for the contract-protection norm draws centrally on the core principle that respect for each person's equal worth limits sacrifices, for the greater good, of anyone's reliance on another's promise.[16] Nevertheless, in the 1984 case of *Pension Benefit Guaranty Corp. v. R. A. Gray & Co.*,[17] the Court seems unanimously to have rejected this view, characterizing the limitations imposed upon Congress by the due process clause as "less searching" than those imposed upon states by the contract clause—but offering little guidance as to the supposedly distinct contours of the latter constitutional provision.[18]

13. This power is subject, of course, to the requirement that substantive entitlements not be procedurally undermined. See Cleveland Board of Education v. Loudermill, 470 U.S. 532 (1985), discussed in § 10–12, infra.

14. See Chapter 8, supra, and Chapter 15, infra.

15. See Chapter 16, infra.

16. Compare § 9–6, supra. On the proposition that the contract clause is thus superfluous, see Hale, "The Supreme Court and the Contract Clause," 57 Harv.L.Rev. 852, 890 (1944). But see § 9–10, infra.

17. 467 U.S. 717 (1984).

18. 467 U.S. at 733. At issue in Gray & Co. was a congressional enactment that had the effect of imposing liability on companies for actions they had taken months before the bill was passed. In 1974, Congress was concerned about the possibility that private pension plans could terminate without sufficient funds and thereby leave workers and their beneficiaries without sufficient retirement income. Accordingly, it passed the Employee Retirement Income Security Act (ERISA), which, among other things, created a government corporation known as the Pension Benefit Guaranty Corporation (PBGC) to insure covered pension plans against termination and thereby protect participating employees from being suddenly stripped of pension protection. Id. at 720–21. Six years later, Congress amended ERISA: the Multi-Employer Pension Plan Amendments Act of 1980 required employers withdrawing from a multi-employer pension plan to pay a fixed debt to the plan. Under the 1980 amendments, this "withdrawal liability" provision applied to actions taken as long as five months before the amendments were

passed. Id. at 724–25. Accordingly, the PBGC sought to collect about $200,000 from R. A. Gray & Co., a building and construction firm that had withdrawn from its multi-employer pension plan several months before adoption of the 1980 ERISA amendments. Id. at 725.

The Supreme Court, in a unanimous opinion written by Justice Brennan, upheld the retroactive imposition of such liability. It held that only a showing that a legislature had acted in "an arbitrary and irrational way" could imperil otherwise valid economic legislation under the due process clause. In this case, Justice Brennan wrote, "it was eminently rational for Congress to conclude that the purposes of the [1980 amendments] could be more fully effectuated if its withdrawal liability provisions were applied retroactively," id. at 730, particularly because Congress had been concerned by the possibility of a spate of withdrawals prompted by employer concerns that Congress would, in fact, adopt (as it did) the more onerous burdens it was considering. "Withdrawal occurring during the legislative process not only would have required that remaining employers increase their contributions to existing pension plans, but also could have ultimately affected the stability of the plans themselves." Id. at 731.

Justice Brennan also dismissed Gray's contract clause challenge to the imposition of retroactive liability, writing: "We have never held . . . that the principles embodied in the Fifth Amendment's Due Process Clause are coextensive with prohibitions existing against state impairments of pre-existing contracts (citation omitted). Indeed, to the extent that recent decisions of the Court have addressed the issue, we have contrasted the limitations imposed on

§ 9–10. Invoking the Contract Clause to Protect Public Commitments

Particularly since the clause was not intended primarily to protect public contracts, it is not surprising that it originally provided only a mild limit on government's power to retract public agreements. Although the Marshall Court appeared willing to read such agreements with generosity toward their private beneficiaries in the *Dartmouth College* case,[1] little more than a decade had passed before the Court adopted a distinctly more cramped reading.[2] Moreover, even when no plausible reading of a public grant or contract could comport with a state's later decision to exercise its police or eminent domain powers against a corporation or individual, the Court ruled these powers inalienable so that the state could not be bound by any promise to give them up.[3] Finally, as Justice Story's concurring opinion in *Dartmouth College* had warned,[4] the states remained free to reserve in their contracts and even in their constitutions the power to change their

states by the Contract Clause with the less searching standards imposed on economic legislation by the Due Process Clauses." Id. at 733. The same withdrawal liability provisions were unanimously held not to be an uncompensated "taking" in Connolly v. Pension Benefit Guaranty Corp., 106 S.Ct. 1018 (1986). See § 9–2, supra, note 10.

In the Term following Gray & Co. the Supreme Court spelled out in somewhat more detail its test for evaluating whether federal economic legislation unconstitutionally impairs a private contractual right. In National Railroad Passenger Corp. v. Atchison, Topeka & Santa Fe Railway Co., 470 U.S. 451 (1985), the Court stated that a party complaining of unconstitutionality has the burden, first, of demonstrating that the statute alters contractual rights or obligations. "If an impairment is found, the reviewing court next determines whether the impairment is of constitutional dimension. If the alteration of contractual obligations is minimal, the inquiry may end at this stage; if the impairment is substantial, a court must look more closely at the legislation. When the contract is a private one, and when the impairing statute is a federal one, this next inquiry is especially limited, and the judicial scrutiny quite minimal. The party asserting a Fifth Amendment due process violation must overcome a presumption of constitutionality and 'establish that the legislature has acted in an arbitrary and irrational way.'" Id. at 472 (citations omitted).

§ 9–10

1. Trustees of Dartmouth College v. Woodward, 17 U.S. (4 Wheat.) 518 (1819). Dartmouth's royal charter could quite easily have been read to include no implied

promise that the trustees' rights were inviolate. The fifth amendment's due process clause was once believed to bind the federal government to its agreements to the same degree that the contract clause binds the states. However, in Pension Benefit Guaranty Corp. v. R. A. Gray & Co., 467 U.S. 717 (1984), the Court asserted—without explanation—that federal contracts are subject to "less searching" scrutiny under the due process clause than are state contracts under the contract clause. See § 9–9, supra.

2. See Providence Bank v. Billings, 29 U.S. (4 Pet.) 514 (1830) (refusing to read into a bank's ambiguous charter an implied immunity from taxation). Accord, Charles River Bridge v. Warren Bridge, 36 U.S. (11 Pet.) 420 (1837) (refusing to read into Charles River Bridge Company's charter to operate a toll bridge an implied promise by the state not to authorize construction of the competing free Warren Bridge): "[A]ny ambiguity in the terms of the contract, must operate against the adventurers, and in favour of the public."

3. Cases holding that a state cannot bind itself never to take a parcel of property even upon payment of just compensation include West River Bridge Co. v. Dix, 47 U.S. (6 How.) 507 (1848) and Pennsylvania Hosp. v. City of Phila., 245 U.S. 20 (1917). To the same effect with respect to promises to refrain from future exercises of the police power to restrict use of property is Stone v. Mississippi, 101 U.S. 814 (1880). But a state can bind itself in perpetuity to exempt a person or organization from taxation. See the discussion in Georgia Railway Co. v. Redwine, 342 U.S. 299 (1952).

4. See 17 U.S. (4 Wheat.) 518, 692 (1819).

minds. Legislatures were therefore liberated to be as openly unreliable as they pleased in their dealings with the people.

The catch is that, for a variety of reasons, legislatures may not "please" to be all that openly unreliable; they often prefer to decline the invitation extended in 1819 by Justice Story—the invitation to warn all who would deal with them that their word may well prove worthless. For its own purposes, a government may find it convenient, sometimes indeed imperative, to signal its trustworthiness and thus to induce the sort of reliance that it could instead have spurned. When government makes that choice, a powerful argument may be advanced that the most basic purposes of the impairment clause, as well as notions of fairness that transcend the clause itself,[5] point to a simple constitutional principle: *government must keep its word*.[6] What this has come to mean since the late 1970s is the subject of the following section.

§ 9–11. The Resurrection of the Contract Clause

The contract clause had remained largely dormant during the *Lochner* era—the due process clause and other constitutional provisions did much of the needed work—and was nearly interred altogether in *Home Building & Loan Ass'n v. Blaisdell*.[1] In the ensuing years, the Court backed away somewhat from its parsimonious reading of the clause, as litigants successfully invoked the clause several times, with the Court finding even some purely remedial changes too "oppressive and unnecessary" to pass constitutional muster.[2] The degree to which contracts were impaired was an important factor in evaluating challenged statutes. Yet while the courts continued to recognize the rule first announced in *Pennsylvania Coal Co. v. Mahon*[3] that the just compensation clause put a limit on government regulation of property, the parallel shield of the contract clause gradually fell into disuse. The Supreme Court seemed to adopt the view that contract rights had no special constitutional status, and that statutes impairing contractual obligations would generally be upheld on a rationality test if they arguably promoted the economic welfare of the general public.[4]

The protective shield of the contract clause lay practically forgotten[5] for three decades until the Court dusted it off and put it to use in

5. See, e.g., Raley v. Ohio, 360 U.S. 423 (1959) (state cannot convict citizen for exercising an option that its agents clearly told him he could lawfully exercise).

6. See, e.g., Indiana ex rel. Anderson v. Brand, 303 U.S. 95 (1938) (state law of 1933 repealing tenure rights of certain teachers under a 1927 law impaired obligation of contracts).

§ 9–11

1. 290 U.S. 398 (1934); see § 9–9, supra.

2. See, e.g., Wood v. Lovett, 313 U.S. 362 (1941) (invalidating 1937 state legislative repeal of 1935 law protecting buyers at state tax sales from state attempts to rescind for irregularities); Worthen Co. v. Kavanaugh, 295 U.S. 56 (1935) (striking down retroactive change in procedure for enforcing payment of benefit assessments pledged as security for municipal bonds: the destruction of "nearly all the incidents" making collateral security valuable was "oppressive and unnecessary").

3. 260 U.S. 393 (1922). The case is discussed in § 9–4, supra.

4. See, e.g., East New York Sav. Bank v. Hahn, 326 U.S. 230, 232 (1945); Veix v. Sixth Ward Bldg. & Loan Ass'n, 310 U.S. 32, 38 (1940).

5. Justice Black, the sole dissenter in El Paso v. Simmons, 379 U.S. 497 (1965), where the Court allowed Texas to limit to

United States Trust Co. of New York v. New Jersey in 1977.[6] In a 4–3 decision,[7] the Supreme Court held that the contract clause rendered void the retroactive 1974 repeal of a 1962 bi-state statutory covenant which limited the ability of the Port Authority of New York and New Jersey to subsidize rail passenger transportation from revenues and reserves pledged as security for consolidated bonds issued by the port authority. The 1962 covenant had been adopted "with full knowledge" of the concerns that ultimately led to its repudiation; any subsequent changes were found to be "of degree and not of kind."[8] Moreover, the "purpose of the covenant was to invoke the constitutional protection of the Contract Clause as security against repeal."[9] If New York and New Jersey could do what they tried to do in 1974, "the Contract Clause would provide no protection at all."[10]

It seems insufficient to reply, as did the dissenters in *United States Trust Company*, that states will be adequately restrained by political and economic pressures, fearing a loss of credibility from too fast and loose a disregard of their own contract obligations.[11] The very existence of the contract clause suggests the obvious rejoinder: when the gains from repudiation appear to exceed the losses in credibility, self-interest may tempt breach instead of fidelity to obligation. Despite the Framers' evident inattention to the danger that states might be even more tempted to break their own promises than to help private debtors break theirs,[12] the Court seems correct in stressing the heightened need for judicial oversight when "the State's self-interest is at stake,"[13] and hence in adopting "a dual standard of review,"[14] with stricter scrutiny of state (or federal) abrogations of governmental obligations than of legislative interference in the contracts of private parties.

The major modern expansion of the contract clause came the following year in *Allied Structural Steel v. Spannaus*.[15] The Court there struck down a Minnesota statute designed to protect certain workers' expectations of receiving pensions. The law provided that

a five-year period the reinstatement rights of purchasers who bought land from the state and then defaulted on interest payments, lamented that the Court had completely "balanced away" the limitation on state action imposed by the contract clause. Id. at 517.

6. 431 U.S. 1 (1977).

7. Justice Blackmun wrote for the Court, joined by Chief Justice Burger and Justices Rehnquist and Stevens. Justice Brennan, joined by Justices White and Marshall, dissented. Justices Stewart and Powell took no part.

8. 431 U.S. at 32.

9. Id. at 18.

10. Id. at 26. Had New York and New Jersey paid the bondholders fair value, however, the states' actions would apparently have passed constitutional muster. As Justice Blackmun noted, "Contract rights are a form of property and as such may be taken for a public purpose provided just compensation is paid," id. at 19 n. 16, and thus "the States remain free to exercise their powers of eminent domain to abrogate such contractual rights, upon payment of just compensation." Id. at 29 n. 27. It is uncertain, however, whether the proper measure of just compensation in the case of the abrogation of a public contract is the same as the traditional "fair value" test for eminent domain, or whether contractual principles of expectancy also inform the meaning of just compensation in such circumstances.

11. Id. at 61–62 (Brennan, J., joined by White and Marshall, JJ., dissenting).

12. See id. at 45 n. 13 (dissenting opinion).

13. Id. at 26.

14. Id. n. 25. See the parallel suggestion with respect to just compensation doctrine in § 9–6, supra, at note 8.

15. 438 U.S. 234 (1978).

when a company employing at least one hundred workers—of whom at least one was a Minnesota resident—terminated a pension plan or closed a facility in Minnesota, "pension rights" would vest for all employees who had been with the company for ten years or longer, whatever their contracts or any applicable pension plan might provide.

Allied Steel had a pension plan whereby an employee's rights vested at a time determined by one of several formulae, depending on age at retirement, but generally after much longer than ten years of working for the company. Allied expressly reserved the unilateral right to terminate the plan at any time, and then to distribute among its employees whatever assets were in the pension fund.[16] Although the company's contributions to the pension fund were irrevocable once made, the pension plan did not obligate the company to make specific contributions or impose any sanctions on it if it failed to fund the plan adequately. The employee had a right to a pension only if he or she met the various criteria and "if the company remained in business *and elected* to continue the pension plan in essentially its existing form."[17]

Justice Stewart, writing for the majority,[18] found that the law worked "a severe, permanent and immediate change"[19] in the expectations of the parties by "nullif[ying] express terms of the company's contractual obligations and impos[ing] a completely unexpected liability in potentially disabling amounts."[20] In a literal sense, the statute did not "impair" Allied Steel's obligations, as the dissent pointed out,[21] but increased them.[22] But to argue that the contract clause was therefore not implicated at all seems too wooden: after all, the same argument could be made of a law retroactively doubling the rents tenants had agreed to pay landlords for residential dwellings.

The Court, while avoiding the words "strict scrutiny," seems to have applied just such an exacting standard of review to the Minnesota law by invoking the "compelling state interest" and "necessary means" tests.[23] The Court also stressed that the legislation in question was retroactive, and in an area not previously regulated by the state, so that the company would not have expected the rules on pension plans to change.[24] Thus a decision by Allied Steel to close a plant or terminate a pension plan would have consequences that decision would not have had prior to the law's enactment: the company would be required to meet obligations it had not foreseen.

The first problem with this reasoning is that, although Minnesota had not previously regulated pension plans, it had long regulated workers' compensation, of which pension benefits are but a subset.[25]

16. Id. at 237.

17. Id. at 238 (emphasis added).

18. Justice Brennan dissented, joined by Justices White and Marshall. Justice Blackmun took no part.

19. 438 U.S. at 250.

20. Id. at 247.

21. Id. at 255, 257–58.

22. Compare 438 U.S. at 244 n. 16 with id. at 257 n. 5.

23. See, e.g., 438 U.S. at 242, 247 ("Yet there is no showing . . . that this [Act] was *necessary* to meet an *important* general social problem") (emphasis added).

24. Cf. § 9–9, supra. But see 438 U.S. at 246, 249–50, 261 n. 8 (Brennan, J., dissenting).

25. See 438 U.S. at 261 n. 8 (Brennan, J., dissenting).

Second, the statute added obligations to employment contracts only if a pension plan was terminated or a plant was closed *after* the effective date of the law.[26] This sort of retroactivity—where obligations are added to pre-existing contracts by virtue of post-enactment conduct—is not readily distinguishable from applying minimum wage, maximum hours, and health and safety regulations to a company which previously bought, for instance, a bakery in reliance on there being no such laws. In both cases, the company's long-settled business plans may be significantly upset even by the prospective application of these unforeseen laws. Yet, in the latter case, such laws are quite routinely upheld. In *Usery v. Turner Elkhorn Mining Co.*,[27] for instance, mine operators never expected to be held financially liable for employee disabilities resulting from black lung disease, especially since the mine workers may have contracted the ailment before its cause was understood and prophylactic measures were known.[28] Nevertheless, the Supreme Court upheld a statute imposing such onerous responsibility after only minimal review.[29]

The *Allied Steel* decision could eventually be seen as an early signal of a back-door return to the jurisprudence of *Lochner*, especially given the Court's exacting economic scrutiny, using "tests" that could easily be turned into engines of destruction for many economic regulations. As Justice Brennan noted in dissent, "[t]he necessary consequence of the extreme malleability of these rather vague criteria is to vest judges with broad subjective discretion to protect property interests that happen to appeal to them." [30] More likely, the *Allied Steel* decision will be confined in the future to a narrow class of cases. One possible limiting principle could be that states must not regulate economic affairs that are properly the concern of Congress.[31] The Minnesota statute was passed knowing that the Employee Retirement Insurance and Security Act (ERISA) would soon be passed by Congress, and was in effect for only a few months before being explicitly preempted by the latter.[32] The Court may even have seen Minnesota's action as an improper burden on interstate commerce, penalizing companies that chose to leave the state.[33] If this is the case, Allied Steel could signal merely a narrow departure from past tendencies to allow state legislation preserving local employment at some cost to interstate commerce.[34]

---

26. 438 U.S. at 248; id. at 254 (Brennan, J., dissenting).

27. 428 U.S. 1 (1976).

28. Id. at 15–16.

29. Id. at 18–19.

30. 438 U.S. at 261. See id. at 261 n. 8: "The only explanation for the Court's decision is that it subjectively values the interests of employers in pension plans more highly than it does the legitimate expectation interest of employees."

31. But the Court denied any such principle at roughly the same time in Exxon Corp. v. Governor of Maryland, 437 U.S. 117 (1978). And in Malone v. White Motor

Corp., 435 U.S. 497 (1978) (sustaining $19 million assessment against employer terminating its pension plan pursuant to state law imposing funding charges on such employers in order to guarantee to employees with more than ten years' service full payment of their accrued pension benefits), the Court had held that the Minnesota Pension Act was not preempted by any federal law prior to the enactment of ERISA.

32. Allied Structural Steel, 438 U.S. at 248–49 n. 21.

33. Cf. § 6–9, supra.

34. See § 6–12, supra.

Indeed, despite the sweeping language of *Allied Steel*, the Court has made it clear that its manipulable, born-again contract clause analysis will not be deployed to uphold many claims alleging unconstitutional impairment of contracts. In *Energy Reserves Group (ERG) v. Kansas Power & Light Co. (KPL)*,[35] the Court unanimously rejected a contract-impairment challenge to a state natural gas regulation.[36] ERG and KPL had contracted for the sale of natural gas, and had included within their agreements provisions for redetermining the purchase price in accord with any change in the comprehensive laws which might set a new price ceiling. In the wake of the deregulation of natural gas by the federal government, Congress empowered the state legislatures to engage in further regulation of the intrastate natural gas market. In response to that invitation, Kansas promptly imposed price controls on intrastate gas.[37] When ERG sought to redetermine the purchase price in accord with the governmental escalator clause of its contract with KPL, the utility refused on the ground that the new Kansas gas legislation prohibited the activation of such price redetermination clauses.[38]

The Court applied the analysis it had used in *United States Trust Co.* and *Allied Steel* but held that there was no violation of the contract clause. The Kansas gas regulations were not special interest legislation of the kind struck down in *Allied Steel* because they affected the entire natural gas industry, and were not aimed at merely one or two firms.[39] Moreover, the Kansas law was an attempt to deal with the "important social problem" of protecting consumers from rapidly rising gas prices due to federal deregulation, while the pension legislation in *Allied Steel* was tailored to affect the retirement benefits of only a small fraction of industrial workers.[40] The Court was willing to defer to the legislative determinations of the public interest in *Energy Reserves Group* since, unlike the situation in *United States Trust Co.*, the state itself was not a party to any of the contracts affected by its new laws.[41]

The Court further distinguished *Allied Steel* on the ground that the businesses there could not have foreseen disruption of their pension agreements since the state had never directly regulated pension plans, whereas Kansas had regulated sales of natural gas for 75 years.[42] All contracts for the purchase of natural gas in Kansas were explicitly geared to extensive state and federal regulation, and depriving ERG of windfall profits on its gas could not be said to disrupt its expectations since no one in the industry could have anticipated federal deregulation.[43]

35. 459 U.S. 400 (1983).

36. Justice Blackmun delivered the opinion of the Court. Justice Powell, joined by Chief Justice Burger and Justice Rehnquist, concurred on the ground that no contract had in fact been impaired; they thus had no occasion to decide whether Kansas had a legitimate state purpose. Id. at 421.

37. 459 U.S. at 407.

38. Id. at 408.

39. Id. at 412 n. 13.

40. Id. at 417–18 n. 25.

41. Id. at 412 n. 14.

42. Id. at 414 & n. 18.

43. Id. at 415.

A final sign that *Allied Steel* may not prove the progenitor of a new *Lochner* era—an era resting this time on the contract (or perhaps the takings) clause, rather than the due process clause—was the 1983 case of *Exxon Corp. v. Eagerton.*[44] Handed down two years after the resignation of Justice Stewart, the author of *Allied Steel, Exxon* upheld against a contract clause challenge an Alabama law imposing an oil and gas severance tax. The law in question in *Exxon* was striking in that it imposed harsh and inescapable new burdens on oil producers: it specified that producers had to bear the tax burden themselves and flatly forbade them from passing on their new tax burdens directly or indirectly to consumers.[45] A unanimous Court, speaking through Justice Marshall, held that the severance tax law passed muster because it stated "a generally applicable rule of conduct" not limited to contractual obligations or remedies.[46] In other words, the law covered all producers of oil and gas, whether or not they already were parties to sales contracts containing provisions allowing them to pass along tax increases to consumers. The Court characterized the impact on these pre-existing contracts as purely incidental.[47]

Exxon seems hard to square with *Allied Steel*, particularly when one recognizes that the Alabama law upheld in *Exxon* dealt exclusively with contracts for the sale of oil and gas while the Minnesota law struck down in *Allied Steel* announced a rule of conduct applicable to firms regardless of whether or not they had pension plans in place. If *Allied Steel* were followed faithfully, the Alabama law, like the Minnesota statute at issue in *Allied Steel*, should have been invalidated—as applied to those pre-existing contractual provisions that the new Alabama law superceded. The Court's reluctance to strike down the Alabama law may suggest that the narrow construction of the contract clause represented by *Energy Reserves*, not the broader reading put forth in *Allied Steel*, is winning the battle for the mind of the Supreme Court.[48]

---

44. 462 U.S. 176 (1983).

45. Id. at 178–79.

46. Id. at 191, quoting Allied Steel, 438 U.S. at 249.

47. Id. at 192.

48. For an illuminating analysis of the Court's recent contract clause jurisprudence, see Baker, "Has the Contract Clause Counter-Revolution Halted? Rhetoric, Rights, and Markets in Constitutional Analysis," 12 Hastings L.Q. 71, 103–04 (1984) (contrasting "the perfect market and private rights vision" of Allied with the "imperfect market and public interest vision" of Energy Reserves, and suggesting that one of these visions "will dominate the constitutional structure on economic regulation for the next generation, and so determine the agenda of American economic life"). The recent case of Keystone Bituminous Coal Ass'n. v. DeBenedictis, 107 S.Ct. 1232 (1987), further suggests that the Court is swinging back towards a nar-

rower construction of the contract clause limitation than that espoused in Allied Steel. In Keystone, the Court, in an opinion written for a 5–4 majority by Justice Stevens, rejected takings and contract clause challenges to the Subsidence Act, a Pennsylvania statute limiting coal mining. See § 9–2, supra. The majority conceded that the act "operates as a 'substantial impairment of a contractual relationship,'" id. at 1252 (citations omitted), particularly because it removed the contractual obligations of surface owners of land to waive damages caused them by underground mining operators. Id. Nevertheless, the Court held that "the impairment of petitioners' right to enforce the damage waiver is amply justified by the public purposes served by the Subsidence Act." Id. at 1253. The Court's almost casual willingness in Keystone to let Pennsylvania's mere pronouncement of a legitimate public purpose vitiate the state's obligations under the contract clause would seem to send

But the picture is incomplete without *United States Railroad Retirement Board v. Fritz*,[49] which upheld Congress's ill-informed destruction of statutorily scheduled retirement benefits for a whole class of railroad employees. The Railroad Retirement Act of 1974 phased out "dual benefits"—railroad pensions *plus* social security—both prospectively and, to a degree, retroactively: it cancelled benefits to which many workers had been entitled by statute as of their retirement from the railroad. What marked the statute—superficially a garden-variety effort at cutting costs by eliminating "double-dipping" into the federal coffers—as unique was the curious pattern of deprivation which it wove. The retirees who lost money were not those with fewer years of service to their credit but those who had retired longer ago. Specifically, retirees who had left the railroad industry prior to 1974 lost their "vested" benefits unless they had worked on the railroad at least 25 years; retirees who quit in 1974 or later retained these benefits even if they had worked barely 10 years.[50] Thus those who had the bad luck of having severed their ties to the railroad business before 1974 took it in the neck, while employees with no more seniority, but who were lucky enough to have worked on the railroad for one day after January 1, 1974, smiled all the way to the bank.

By a 7–2 vote,[51] the Supreme Court held that the law did not constitute a denial of equal protection under the fifth amendment. The majority, in an opinion by Justice Rehnquist, applied minimal scrutiny and asked only for "some reasonable basis" for the legislative formula, which it then proceeded to supply by what Justice Brennan in dissent aptly called tautology.[52] The Court assumed purpose from result by concluding that, because the Act divested some retirees but not others, Congress must have intended to do just that.[53] Justice Rehnquist's circular argument comes surprisingly close to saying that Congress may "take from A to give to B" because, if it does so, it is advancing the public purpose of making B better off and A worse off. Justice Stevens concurred in the judgment but was unwilling to accept the majority's merely "conceivable" or "plausible" rationales for the unequal treatment meted out by the Railroad Retirement Act.[54] Instead, he called for the Justices to put their imaginations to work to find a principle that, even if not the one Congress had in mind, would provide a reasonable and impartial lawmaker with a basis upon which to distinguish among the classes of retirees. He concluded that since Congress's mission was to cut costly "windfall benefits," and since it arguably had a "duty . . . to eliminate no more vested benefits than necessary to achieve its fiscal purpose," the choice of currency of railroad service—as a kind of anti-seniority basis on which to distinguish among retirees—was "impartial." [55]

---

the clause back towards the desuetude to which it had grown accustomed in the pre-United States Trust era.

49. 449 U.S. 166 (1980).

50. 449 U.S. at 172–73.

51. Justices Brennan and Marshall dissented.

52. 449 U.S. at 186–87 (Brennan, J., dissenting).

53. 449 U.S. at 176–77.

54. Id. at 180.

55. Id. at 182. One can only wonder what the difference is between this rationale and the merely "plausible" explana-

Justice Brennan's reply to both the majority and concurring opinions was an admonition to consider reality. He examined the legislative history of the act and agreed with the express findings—never repudiated—of the district court that Fritz and his fellows were short-changed by a Congress which *had no idea* that it was depriving any of these retirees of an earned and promised benefit. The highly complex legislation had been drafted by "representatives of railroad management and labor, whose self-serving interest in bringing about this result destroy[ed] any basis for attaching weight to their statements." [56] The group of dispossessed retirees was not represented on the panel which wrote the law nor in the hearings on the law before Congress.[57] When the law's proponents told the congressional committee that no retirees were being frozen out, there was no one there to contradict them. Thus, there was every reason to believe that this law was a craftily engineered accident, not a deliberate legislative approximation of a dividing line, nor a calculated policy decision to gore one person's ox in order to get a little more for someone else—which some see as the name of the game in the law-making, logrolling process. In fact, this is precisely the sort of "circumstantial evidence" [58] which convinced the *Allied Steel* Court that what it had before it was impermissible special interest legislation: [59] the selective divestiture of the pension benefits of a particular class of retirees certainly had a suspiciously "narrow focus," and the desire to save the contents of the pension fund coffers for the benefit of a class of currently employed railroad workers hardly seemed to address an "important social problem." [60]

Justice Rehnquist's retort was that the real facts and real reasons behind the law were constitutionally irrelevant, and that Congress's alleged ignorance of what it was doing was no excuse: unfortunate, improvident, or even semi-conscious legislation is a fact of life, and the injured citizen is remitted to the democratic processes for relief.[61] Justice Brennan was not satisfied here with mere political protection— yet he had argued in his dissent in *United States Trust Co. v. New Jersey* that constitutional limits on the state's power to play fast and loose with bond obligations were unnecessary because government conduct would be "adequately policed by the political processes and the bond marketplace itself." [62] The difference, one may be forgiven for noticing, seems to be that the victimized bondholder whom the contract

tions employed by the majority which Justice Stevens derides.

56. Id. at 189 (Brennan, J., dissenting); see id. at 192–93 & n. 9.

57. The notion of a due process right to adequate participation in the enactment of legislation affecting one's economic interests is also reflected in the Court's decision in Florida Lime & Avocado Growers v. Paul, 373 U.S. 132 (1963), where the Court upheld a California avocado regulation against a federal preemption challenge in part because of concern that the federal regulation had not been drafted "by impartial experts in Washington or even in Florida, but rather by the South Florida Avoca-

do Administrative Committee," id. at 150–51, as "a 'self-help' program", id. at 151 n. 17, in the longstanding avocado wars between California and Florida. Id. at 153–54 n. 19. See Chapter 17, infra.

58. See Kansas Power & Light, 459 U.S. at 417–18 n. 25.

59. Allied Structural Steel, 438 U.S. at 247–48 & n. 20.

60. See Kansas Power & Light, 459 U.S. at 412 n. 13.

61. 449 U.S. at 179 & n. 12.

62. 431 U.S. 1, 61–62 (1977) (Brennan, J., dissenting, joined by White and Marshall, JJ.).

clause protected in *United States Trust Co.* was a powerful financial institution with $300 million in Port Authority holdings,[63] while the victims in *Fritz*—for whom the Constitution was not successfully invoked—were retired blue-collar workers. The voting booth and the petition are apparently sufficient protection for the interests of *hoi polloi,* but not for the interests of the coupon-clipping financial elite.[64]

One sobering aspect of the decision in *Fritz* is that all nine Justices took for granted the unavailability of any claim that Congress had *taken property* or had abrogated some contract-like expectation in violation of the fifth amendment. Fritz and his cohorts were scheduled to receive certain retirement benefits. They had spent years expecting and planning on that income. Their expectation was written into the statute—and then suddenly repealed. The Court split over the issue of whether the criterion which cut Fritz off was a rational one, but said not a word about the fact that something workers had banked on receiving was almost literally taken out of their pockets. On *that* issue, the Court, *without a single dissenting voice,* held: there was no taking of property, "since railroad benefits, like social security benefits, are not contractual and may be altered or even eliminated at any time." [65] Those who invest their money in government bonds are fully protected, but for those who invest their time and toil in exchange for statutorily promised government pension benefits, "the legislative determination provides all the process that is due." [66]

One evident effect of prevailing doctrines of property and contract is thus to tilt in favor of those with sufficient economic clout to win bilateral contract protection vis-a-vis the government, while providing less protection for those whose only power lies in concerted political action. First, what they manage to win can be *legislatively* revoked with virtually no judicial review—as Gerhard Fritz has learned; second, their gains may even be *judicially* cancelled if the laws add obligations to those which the other side assumed by contract—as the former employees of Allied Steel now know. Relaxing the level of judicial scrutiny under the contract clause would reduce this disparity to some degree, but would still leave the weakest groups in our economy least well defended by constitutional law against the kinds of schemes put in place by the railroad management and recent retirees

63. Id. at 62 n. 18.

64. The Court was, however, deferential to the political process in Kansas Power & Light, 459 U.S. at 411–13, where the legislation had the stated purpose of indirectly protecting consumers against utility price hikes. Id. at 416–17. The direct effect of Kansas Power was nonetheless to benefit one powerful economic interest (the utility companies) against another (the gas producers).

65. 449 U.S. at 174; Flemming v. Nestor, 363 U.S. 603, 608–11 (1960) (social security payments, unlike an annuity, are not "accrued property rights"). See also Bowen v. Gilliard, 107 S.Ct. 3008 (1987), discussed in § 9–2, note 11, supra. The theory seems to be that the termination of these sorts of transfer payments does not disrupt investment-backed expectations, since receipt of them is not directly related to the individual's contributions through withholding taxes. Other government-created property interests which provide the holder with exclusive rights enforceable against third parties, such as copyrights and patents, may not be legislatively revoked without just compensation. Such rights, unlike welfare or social security benefits, are not mere wagers on the government's continued sufferance.

66. See Logan v. Zimmerman Brush Co., 455 U.S. 422, 433 (1982).

in *Fritz*. Yet this should not seem too surprising. Although constitutional protections for settled expectations may on occasion help the relatively less well off, the predominant role of such protections is to defend those who have from those who want. That might not be the path of charity, or even of fairness, but these failings are not license simply to ignore the fact that, whatever their "tilt," property and contract *are* part of the Constitution we must expound and, unless it is amended, enforce.

Chapter 10

MODEL IV—THE MODEL OF GOVERNMEN-TAL REGULARITY: EX POST FACTO LAWS, BILLS OF ATTAINDER, AND PROCEDURAL DUE PROCESS

§ 10–1. The Values and Dimensions of Governmental Regularity

The ideals of governmental *reliability* and *regularity* are related but distinct. Political philosophers have occasionally sought to explain the propositions that "statutes [should] be general" and that "penal laws should not be retroactive" by invoking the need to protect reliance on "legitimate expectations," [1] but a closer analysis suggests that regularity—with its associated norms of prospectivity, generality, and impartiality—serves both to express and to implement ends quite separate from those of respecting reliance and protecting settled expectations. Although the protection of such expectations amply explains the refusal to permit punishment in the absence of fair warning,[2] it cannot account (1) for the persistent if lesser reluctance to punish under a newly-enacted statute even where the actor plainly knew that he was committing a wrong; [3] (2) for the willingness to punish even where the presumption that persons know of pre-existing laws makes no sense whatever [4]; or (3) for the insistent view that the norms of prospectivity and generality apply with unique force to criminal punishments, relegating expectations against purely civil deprivations to sharply reduced protection.[5] Moreover, despite early efforts to analogize the bans on ex post facto laws and bills of attainder to the bans on contract impairments and uncompensated takings,[6] there has long been a deep aversion to the idea that nonconstitutional immunities of some sort "vest" upon a person's commission of a wrong.[7] Values of reliance and repose

---

§ 10–1

1. J. Rawls, A Theory of Justice 238 (1971).

2. 1 W. Blackstone, Commentaries* 46; Lanzetta v. New Jersey, 306 U.S. 451 (1939); Bouie v. Columbia, 378 U.S. 347 (1964); Marks v. United States, 430 U.S. 188 (1977); Note, "The Void-for-Vagueness Doctrine in the Supreme Court," 123 U.Pa. L.Rev. 67, 73–74 (1960).

3. See, e.g., United States v. Bell, 371 F.Supp. 220 (E.D.Tex.1973) (mistaken prosecution under subsequently enacted criminal statute).

4. See, e.g., United States v. Casson, 434 F.2d 415, 422 (D.C.Cir. 1970) (applying statute increasing punishment for burglary, signed 8 hours before, but announced simultaneously with, the burglary's commission).

5. See Chapter 9, supra; Hochman, "The Supreme Court and the Constitutionality of Retroactive Legislation," 73 Harv. L.Rev. 692 (1962).

6. See J. Bishop, Criminal Procedures § 115, at 70 (2d ed. 1872); Crosskey, "The Ex-Post-Facto and the Contracts Clauses in the Federal Convention: A Note on the Editorial Ingenuity of James Madison," 31 U.Chi.L.Rev. 248 (1968); Crosskey, "The True Meaning of the Constitutional Prohibition of Ex-Post-Facto Laws," 14 U.Chi.L. Rev. 539 (1947); Field, "Ex Post Facto in the Constitution," 20 Mich.L.Rev. 315 (1922).

7. See, e.g., State v. Arlin, 39 N.H. 179, 181 (1859); Smith, "Retroactive Laws and Vested Rights," 5 Tex.L.Rev. 231 (1927); 6 Tex.L.Rev. 409 (1928).

fit comfortably the paradigm of conduct that the society wishes (or once wished) to encourage, but such values are distinctly less well suited to the paradigm of action that all admit should never have taken place.

For these reasons, understanding is advanced by attempting to disentangle the model of governmental regularity (Model IV) from the model of settled expectations (Model III), remembering their frequent overlap in constitutional history and decisional law, but seeking nonetheless to identify as clearly as possible the elements distinctive to each. Chapter 9 accordingly explored the expectations model; this Chapter will explore the model of regularity.

To isolate the virtues of regularity, it is helpful to note at the outset the pervasive and recurring equation between the irregular and the oppressive. It is probably true that "the most significant feature of small town politics is the frequency with which legal and procedural requirements are overlooked and ignored. . . . [so as] to take account of unique conditions;" such "[p]ersonalized government" even at the local level can be as offensive as it may be intimate and effective [8]—and at the more remote level of relations with federal, state, and other relatively distant bureaucracies and institutions, personalization in government, at least when not sought by the individual, most often seems the antithesis of respect for personal integrity and autonomy. Hence the emphasis upon "a government of laws, and not of men" as the "very essence of civil liberty," [9] and the persistent war, throughout the history of liberal thought, against capricious subjugation to the whim of the sovereign. "[T]he very idea that one may be compelled to hold his life, or the means of living, or any material right essential to the enjoyment of life, at the mere will of another" has been thought "intolerable in any country where freedom prevails, as being the essence of slavery itself." [10] The classic statement in the Supreme Court's jurisprudence was that in *Hurtado v. California*: [11] "Law is something more than mere will exerted as an act of power. It must not be a special rule for a particular person or a particular case, but . . . 'the general law . . . .' so that 'every citizen shall hold his life, liberty, property and immunities under the protection of the general rules which govern society,' and thus excluding, as not due process of law, acts of attainder, bills of pains and penalties, acts of confiscation . . . and other similar special, partial and arbitrary exertions of power under the forms of legislation. Arbitrary power, enforcing its edicts to the injury of the persons and property of its subjects, is not law, whether manifested as the decree of a personal monarch or an impersonal multitude."

It is to this vision that we owe the constitutional doctrines "assuring that the fundamental policy choices underlying any exercise of state power are explicitly articulated by some responsible organ of

8. Wood, Suburbia 278–80 (1958).

9. Marbury v. Madison, 5 U.S. (1 Cranch.) 137, 163 (1803).

10. Yick Wo v. Hopkins, 118 U.S. 356, 370 (1886). See J. Locke, Two Treatises of Government §§ 22–23, at 324–25 (Laslett ed. 1960).

11. 110 U.S. 516, 535–36 (1884).

government." [12]   Such articulation begins with general lawmaking processes accountable to the electorate and ends with specific law-enforcement processes answerable to the individuals on whom the law operates; the model of regularity touches both ends of this spectrum.

Now it must be stressed that this conception of governmental power and of its relation to personal autonomy, however ill-suited to life in a truly organic community where solidarity and even love have replaced formal rules and procedures, need not regard government as some sort of "neutral guardian of the social order." [13]   Although the rise of the welfare state leads in familiar ways to a disintegration of purely formal ideals of law and justice,[14] it does not follow that ancient concerns about power and its abuse can no longer be usefully advanced, at least in part, through norms of regularity. For such norms reduce the helplessness of individuals and groups by limiting their dependence on distant and inaccessible centers of implacable authority.

The model of governmental regularity has classically expressed these aspirations by requiring that the most focused deprivations of individual interests in life, liberty, or property be accompanied by a panoply of procedural safeguards, and that the most general "policy decisions . . . be made not by . . . appointed official[s] but by [bodies] immediately responsible to the people." [15]   But the proliferation and combination of government functions, in institutions increasingly difficult to characterize in terms of the three traditional branches of government, require that we seek a doctrinal formulation less dependent on how various entities are classified or how particular functions are assigned to specific institutions.

Such a formulation is available: It requires only that a normative distinction be drawn between those processes of choice which have such wide public ramifications that adversely affected individuals need not participate personally, and those choice processes which so focus upon particular persons that their personal participation must be assured.

Whenever government excludes affected persons from participating in a choice, government in effect opts for the first type of decision-making process. Whether the choice is made by a legislature, an administrative agency, or a court, it must thus be limited in its impact upon specific persons so that their interests in life, liberty, and property are neither (1) immediately affected by it (as through a decree directly subjecting those persons to incarceration or dispossession) without their personal participation, nor (2) adversely affected, without such personal participation, by a delayed impact that they are powerless to avoid by lawful means (as through a law expressly restricting the liberty of a specific set of persons to engage in a lawful occupation).

The first limitation can be accomplished only by forcing the government to adopt a trial-like decision-making process when it acts directly

12. McGautha v. California, 402 U.S. 183, 265 (1971) (Brennan, J., dissenting). See Chapter 17, infra.

13. R. Unger, Law in Modern Society 193 (1976).

14. Id. at 192–216.

15. Arizona v. California, 373 U.S. 546, 626 (1963) (Harlan, J., dissenting).

upon particular individuals—i.e., by requiring procedural safeguards ("procedural due process") ensuring personal participation by individually and immediately affected persons. The second limitation can be accomplished only by insisting that, even when government acts in less personally focused ways, it may not apply its criminal prohibitions to persons who violated those prohibitions *before* they were promulgated; and by demanding that prohibitions be directed not at fixed groups of individuals but at whoever happens to transgress a generally applicable norm.

§ 10–2. The Ban on Ex Post Facto Laws: The Safeguard of Prospectivity

Article I of the Constitution forbids enactment of ex post facto laws by Congress [1] or by any state; [2] although the ex post facto prohibition applies of its own force only to legislative acts [3] rather than to judicial decisions,[4] unforeseeable judicial enlargements of criminal statutes have been struck down as violative of due process when applied retroactively.[5] The first Supreme Court discussion of the ex post facto prohibition came in *Calder v. Bull*.[6] In his separate opinion in that case, Justice Chase opined that no people would with "reason and justice" entrust government with power to pass ex post facto laws, so Congress and the states would be powerless to do so even if not expressly forbidden by the Constitution.[7] The ex post facto clauses were added "for greater caution" [8] by the Framers, who recalled the excesses of Parliament and of the colonial governments, motivated by ambition, personal resentment, or vindictive malice.[9] Accordingly, the clauses proscribed: [10]

"1st. Every law that makes an action done before the passing of the law, and which was innocent when done, criminal; and punishes such action. 2d. Every law that aggravates a crime, or makes it greater than it was, when committed. 3d. Every law that changes the punishment, and inflicts a greater punishment, than the law annexed to the crime, when committed. 4th. Every law that alters the legal rules of evidence, and receives less, or different testimony than the law required at the time of the commission of the offence, in order to convict the offender."

§ 10–2

1. Art. I, § 9, cl. 3.

2. Art. I, § 10, cl. 1.

3. Including, of course, constitutional changes. See Kring v. Missouri, 107 U.S. 221 (1883).

4. Frank v. Magnum, 237 U.S. 309, 344 (1915); Ross v. Oregon, 227 U.S. 150, 161 (1913).

5. See Bouie v. Columbia, 378 U.S. 347, 353–54 (1964); Rabe v. Washington, 405 U.S. 313 (1972) (per curiam); Marks v. United States, 430 U.S. 188, 191–7 (1977). Cf. Splawn v. California, 431 U.S. 595, 601 (1977).

6. 3 U.S. (3 Dall.) 386 (1798).

7. Id. at 388–89. See also W. Wade, A Treatise on the Operation and Construction of Retroactive Laws § 270, at 315 (1880); cf. Art. 11 of the Universal Decl. of Human Rts., G.A. Res. 217 (III), Art. 11, 52, 3 U.N.GAOR, pt. I, at 73, U.N.Doc. A/810 (1948).

8. 3 U.S. (3 Dall.) at 390.

9. See 2 M. Farrand, The Records of the Federal Convention of 1787, at 375–76 (1937); The Federalist No. 44, at 351 (J. Hamilton ed. 1868) (J. Madison).

10. 3 U.S. (3 Dall.) at 390.

The Court concluded in *Calder v. Bull* that a resolution of the Connecticut legislature which set aside a decree of a probate court, and which granted a new hearing on the construction of a will after the right of appeal to the ordinary court had expired, was not a forbidden ex post facto law. Although Justice Chase argued that no right to property had vested in Calder and his wife by reason of the probate court decree, and thus that no vested right was disturbed by the resolution,[11] he also suggested that "[t]he restraint against making any ex post facto laws was not considered, by the framers of the constitution, as extending to prohibit the depriving a citizen even of vested rights to property; or the provision 'that private property should not be taken for public use without just compensation' was unnecessary."[12] While the opinion of Justice Chase left open the question whether the retrospective imposition by the legislature of civil disabilities might ever come within the scope of the ex post facto clauses, the separate concurring opinions of Justices Paterson and Iredell sought to dispose of this issue as well. Justice Paterson looked to the three personal guarantees of article I, § 10—the attainder ban, the ex post facto ban, and the ban on contract impairments—and suggested that the presence of the latter established "that the framers of the constitution . . . understood and used the words [ex post facto law] in their known and appropriate signification, as referring to crimes, pains and penalties, and no further."[13] Justice Iredell looked not to the structure of the constitutional restraints on legislation, but rather to the purposes, and concluded that ". . . the act or resolution of the legislature of Connecticut, cannot be regarded as an ex post facto law; for the true construction of the prohibition extends to criminal, not to civil cases. It is only in criminal cases, indeed, in which the danger to be guarded against, is greatly to be apprehended. The history of every country in Europe will furnish flagrant instances of tyranny exercised under the pretext of penal dispensations. . . .

. . . The policy, the reason and humanity of the prohibition, do not, I repeat, extend to civil cases, to cases that merely affect the private property of citizens. Some of the most necessary and important acts of legislation are, on the contrary, founded upon the principle, that private rights must yield to public exigencies."[14]

In *Calder v. Bull*, then, the Court took a fairly restricted view of the scope of the ex post facto clauses, concluding for various reasons that they did not reach the challenged deprivation of property. It soon became clear, however, that the scope of the clauses was far from settled.

The next important discussion of the matter appears in Chief Justice Marshall's opinion for the Court in *Fletcher v. Peck*,[15] involving an act of the Georgia legislature which purported to annul, as tainted by bribery, a huge land grant by the previous legislature. While the

11. Id. at 394.

12. Id.

13. Id. at 397 (concurring opinion of Paterson, J.).

14. Id. at 399–400 (concurring opinion of Iredell, J.).

15. 10 U.S. (6 Cranch.) 87 (1810).

Court concluded that the purported annulment was rendered invalid "either by general principles which are common to our free institutions, or by the particular provisions"[16] of the Constitution, Chief Justice Marshall's application of the prohibition of ex post facto laws to the case is of particular interest in light of the decision but twelve years before in *Calder v. Bull*. The Chief Justice reasoned:[17]

"An *ex post facto* law is one which renders an act punishable in a manner in which it was not punishable when it was committed. Such a law may inflict penalties on the person or may inflict pecuniary penalties which swell the public treasury. The legislature is then prohibited from passing a law by which a man's estate, or any part of it, shall be seized for a crime which was not declared, by some previous law, to render him liable to that punishment . . . .. This rescinding act would have the effect of an *ex post facto* law. It forfeits the estate of Fletcher for a crime not committed by himself, but by those from whom he purchased. This cannot be effected in the form of an *ex post facto* law, or a bill of attainder; why then is it allowable in the form of a law annulling the original grant?" Marshall's use of the ex post facto clause in analyzing the Georgia statute implicitly repudiated the suggestions of Justices Chase and Paterson in *Calder v. Bull* that the three key restraints imposed on the legislative process by article I, § 10 must serve distinct purposes, and substituted the suggestion that the restraints were complementary and could thus overlap. Moreover, Chief Justice Marshall's opinion implied that a legislative enactment could violate the ex post facto clause even though no evidence of punitive intent was attributable to the legislature; the challenged Georgia statute was not adopted to punish Fletcher or, to borrow the imagery of Justice Iredell in *Calder v. Bull*, as a flagrant instance of tyranny. It declared no action criminal, but Marshall nonetheless thought it forbidden by the ex post facto clause.

Despite Justice Marshall's opinion in *Fletcher v. Peck*, the Supreme Court had, by 1855, once again embraced the view that the ex post facto clauses reached only criminal penalties. In *Carpenter v. Pennsylvania*,[18] the Court upheld the application of a Pennsylvania statute which imposed a special tax on certain bequests left by persons who died prior to the act's passage. The Court concluded simply that "[t]he debates in the federal convention upon the Constitution show that the terms '*ex post facto laws*' were understood in a restricted sense, relating to criminal cases only, and that the description of Blackstone of such laws was referred to for their meaning."[19] Yet the Court in the post-Civil War cases of *Cummings v. Missouri*[20] and *Ex parte Garland*[21] concluded that statutes which disqualified former Confederate sympathizers from specifically enumerated occupations violated the ex post facto clauses. In *Garland*, the Court concluded simply that "exclusion from any of the professions or any of the ordinary avocations of life for past conduct can be regarded in no other light than as punishment for

16. Id. at 139.

17. Id. at 138–39.

18. 58 U.S. (17 How.) 456 (1854).

19. Id. at 462.

20. 71 U.S. (4 Wall.) 277 (1866).

21. 71 U.S. (4 Wall.) 333 (1866).

such conduct." [22]   In *Cummings*, the Court did speak in terms of "offenses" and "guilt" [23] in explaining why the provision of the Missouri Constitution requiring the expurgatory oath from those seeking to enter the ministry was an ex post facto law, but a careful reading of the two cases makes clear that the Supreme Court did not intend to restrict the scope of the ex post facto clauses to penal legislation, seeing the ban as extending to a wide class of legislation retroactively burdening otherwise lawful activities. [24]

The only hint during the early stages of ex post facto adjudication of how far the Supreme Court might go in invalidating retrospective inflictions of civil disabilities appears in *Burgess v. Salmon*, [25] where the Court concluded that a bill signed by the President on the afternoon of March 3, 1875, raising the tax on tobacco, could not be applied to a sale of tobacco which had been completed during the morning of the same day without violating the ex post facto prohibition. The Court interpreted its prior cases as holding that the ex post facto effect of a law cannot be evaded by giving a civil form to that which is essentially criminal. [26] While the *Burgess* opinion provides no direct indication of what should be considered "essentially criminal," application of the phrase to the rescission of a land grant contested in *Fletcher* and to the sales tax challenged in *Burgess* itself suggests that the Court viewed a wide range of civil disabilities indeed as encompassed by the "essentially criminal" label.

During the early years of the 20th century, the uncertainty over the scope of the ex post facto clauses which marked the early cases was replaced by a consensus in favor of the narrower view that only criminal punishment is prohibited by the ban. The main vehicle for the articulation of this new consensus was a series of Supreme Court cases dealing with the ability of Congress to control the movement and rights of aliens. [27] By the 1950's the limited view of the scope of the

---

22. Id. at 377.

23. 71 U.S. (4 Wall.) at 327–28.

24. Id. at 327. See also § 10–4, infra.

25. 97 U.S. (7 Otto) 381 (1878).

26. Id. at 385. See generally United States v. Will, 449 U.S. 200, 225 n. 29 (1980) (federal cost-saving statutes which terminated or reduced previously automatic cost-of-living increases for federal judges, and which became law after the increases had taken effect, deemed violative of the article III compensation clause) (stating that "Burgess dealt not so much with benefits and penalties as it did with constitutional limitations on the legislative authority of Congress and the Executive."); Accord, Weaver v. Graham, 450 U.S. 24, 29 n. 10 (1981).

27. In Johannessen v. United States, 225 U.S. 227 (1912), the Court implicitly embraced the interpretation of the ex post facto clauses which had been posited by Justices Paterson and Iredell in Calder v. Bull and concluded that "[i]t is . . . set-

tled that this prohibition is confined to laws respecting criminal punishments, and has no relation to retrospective legislation of any other description." 225 U.S. at 242. The law challenged in Johannessen was a federal statute which revoked the citizenship of persons who had obtained certificates of citizenship by fraud or other illegal conduct. The Court might have avoided discussion of the scope of the ban on ex post facto laws altogether by resting its decision on the ground that the statute inflicted "no new penalty upon the wrongdoer", id., and made nothing "fraudulent or unlawful that was honest and lawful when it was done," but simply deprived the individual of a privilege that was never rightfully his. Id. A series of cases dealing with the right of Congress to provide for the deportation of aliens perpetuated the conclusion of the Johannessen Court that the ex post facto clauses operate only to prohibit retrospective criminal punishment. See e.g., Mahler v. Eby, 264 U.S. 32, 39 (1924).

constitutional ban was so well established that the Court seemed reluctant to upset the pattern of statutes and decisions based on the belief that the retrospective imposition of civil disabilities was beyond the scope of the ex post facto clauses. Thus, in *Harisiades v. Shaughnessy*, Justice Jackson, writing for the Court, argued that: [28]

"It has always been considered that that which it [the Ex Post Facto Clause] forbids is penal legislation which imposes or increases criminal punishment for conduct lawful prior to its enactment. Deportation, however severe its consequences, has been consistently classified as a civil rather than a criminal procedure. *Both of these doctrines as original proposals might be debatable, but both have been considered closed for many years* and a body of statute and decisional law has been built upon them."

The opinion in *Harisiades* adopted the rhetoric of the Court in *Burgess v. Salmon*, but dismissed the earlier cases with the comment that "[t]he . . . novel disabilities there imposed upon citizens were really criminal penalties for which civil form was a disguise." [29] Yet *Burgess*, when read in its entirety, evidences an expansive judicial perception of what was "essentially criminal," encompassing not only the land grant rescission of *Fletcher* but also the tax on tobacco challenged in *Burgess* itself. When the Court in *Harisiades* read the cases to restrict the sweep of the ex post facto clauses to "novel" civil disabilities which veil criminal penalties, and to exclude even the admittedly severe penalty of deportation from the class of such "novel" civil disabilities, the Court implied—without any real explanation—that the once-broad sweep of the "essentially criminal" theory had been greatly curtailed. [30]

28. 342 U.S. 580, 594 (1952) (emphasis added). The Court upheld deportation of legally resident aliens "because of membership in the Communist Party which terminated before enactment" of the federal statute making such membership a basis for deportation. Id. at 581. Justice Douglas, joined by Justice Black, dissenting, would have forbidden Congress to "order[ ] . . . aliens deported not for what they are but for what they once were." Id. at 601.

29. Id. at 595.

30. In Galvan v. Press, 347 U.S. 522 (1954), the Court re-emphasized the confines which history placed upon its interpretation of the ex post facto clauses when dealing with the deportation cases. Writing for the majority, and sustaining the constitutionality of § 22 of the Internal Security Act of 1950 which provided for the deportation of any alien who had been a member of the Communist Party at any time following his entry into the United States, Justice Frankfurter thought that "much could be said for the view, were we writing on a clean slate, that the Due Process Clause qualifies the scope of political discretion heretofore recognized as belonging to Congress in regulating the entry and deportation of aliens . . . But the slate is not clean. [T]hat the formulation of these policies is entrusted exclusively to Congress has become about as firmly embedded in the legislative and judicial tissues of our body politic as any aspect of our government. And *whatever might have been said at an earlier date for applying the ex post facto clause, it has been the unbroken rule of this Court that it has no application to deportation*." Id. at 530–31 (emphasis added). See also Immigration and Naturalization Service v. Lopez-Mendoza, 468 U.S. 1032, 1039 (1984) (citing Galvan and holding that a deportation proceeding is a civil action in which the exclusionary rule does not apply). While Galvan v. Press maintains a narrow scope for the constitutional ban on ex post facto laws, there is at least a hint in Justice Frankfurter's opinion that this scope is not restricted solely to criminal legislation. Rather, his opinion suggests that the ban will apply to all "punitive" legislation, excluding only the narrow field of deportation from the restraint on retrospective infliction of disabilities by the legislature. Even if one assumes that the European history of "tyranny exercised under the pretext of penal

§ 10–3. Modern Ex Post Facto Doctrine: Problems of Prevention, Increased Punishment, and Altered Procedure

Although the Supreme Court has held that the ex post facto ban cannot be avoided by clothing a penal imposition in civil dress,[1] it has upheld as nonpunitive a host of limitations imposed with respect to activity antedating the enactment of such limitations, including laws disqualifying from various offices or professions persons previously convicted of felonies,[2] and laws subjecting to augmented penalties ex-convicts who commit further crimes after such laws have been enacted.[3] In quite routinely sustaining the application of such limitations, the Court has paid scant attention to the potential abuse of the governmental power to impose a retroactive restraint "as a relevant incident to a regulation of a present situation."[4] Nor has the Court focused on the danger of abuse when striking down, on a fairly routine basis, such retroactive increases in punishment[5] as rules adding solitary confinement and delegating to the warden the power to fix a secret date of execution.[6]

Perhaps because it has not been systematically attentive to the purposes of the ex post facto ban, the Court has struck down a variety of retroactive procedural changes lightening the prosecutorial burden[7]

---

dispensations," Calder v. Bull, 3 U.S. (3 Dall.) 386, 399 (1798) (Iredell, J., concurring), was central to the adoption of the ex post facto clauses, it is extremely difficult to rationalize the conclusion that "the policy, the reason and humanity of the prohibition, do not . . . extend to civil cases, to cases that merely affect the private property of citizens." Id. at 400. Certainly the early experience of England with bills of attainder and ex post facto laws had demonstrated the willingness of Parliament to mandate the forfeiture of private estates as a penalty for actions which were lawful when committed; and cases such as Cummings and Garland v. Press evidence the continued resourcefulness of legislative bodies in fashioning civil disabilities which serve "punitive" goals. Thus, if the objective of insuring that legislatures operate only prospectively when the rights of individuals might be adversely affected is to be served in any meaningful sense, the constitutional inhibition of ex post facto laws cannot be restricted to penal legislation.

§ 10–3

1. Burgess v. Salmon, 97 U.S. (7 Otto) 381, 385 (1878).

2. See, e.g., De Veau v. Braisted, 363 U.S. 144 (1960); Hawker v. New York, 170 U.S. 189 (1898). But see Schware v. Board of Bar Examiners, 353 U.S. 232 (1957), discussed in § 15–13, infra.

3. See, e.g., Gryger v. Burke, 334 U.S. 728 (1948); Graham v. West Virginia, 224 U.S. 616 (1912); McDonald v. Massachusetts, 180 U.S. 311 (1901).

4. De Veau v. Braisted, 363 U.S. 144, 160 (1960). See Flemming v. Nestor, 363 U.S. 603 (1960) (statutory provision terminating payment of old-age benefits to alien deported for Communist affiliation not ex post facto, since designed to relieve Social Security System of administrative problems of supervision and enforcement in connection with disbursement to beneficiaries abroad). See also Usery v. Turner Elkhorn Mining Co., 428 U.S. 1, 14–20, 22–31 (1976). For a critical perspective on the cases, and a cogent argument that the ex post facto ban should apply whenever it cannot be shown that "significant regulatory interests unrelated to . . . deterrence" are served, see Note, "Ex Post Facto Limitations on Legislative Power," 73 Mich.L. Rev. 1491, 1505 (1975).

5. But changes that are not "increases"—such as a shift from hanging to the supposedly more humane punishment of electrocution—are not subject to the ex post facto ban. Malloy v. South Carolina, 237 U.S. 180 (1915).

6. In re Medley, 134 U.S. 160, 172 (1890). See also Lindsey v. Washington, 301 U.S. 397 (1937) (statute making mandatory the previously maximum sentence, while also making parole available, deemed an increase in punishment violative of ex post facto clause).

7. See, e.g., Kring v. Missouri, 107 U.S. 221 (1883) (retrospective abrogation of state rule treating conviction for lesser included offense as acquittal of greater offense); Thompson v. Utah, 170 U.S. 343

while upholding others that can hardly be distinguished in any functional way from those invalidated.[8] Although attempts to invoke concepts of reliance, repose, or fair notice are conspicuously indeterminate in many procedural settings, courts need not despair of making sensible use of those concepts—as some have occasionally done in guiding the necessarily difficult line-drawing task they have confronted in this area.[9]

In addressing the recurring and particularly troublesome problems posed by alterations in the punishment applicable to past conduct, the Supreme Court has insisted that it is "deal[ing] with substance, not shadows,"[10] and has thus deemed it irrelevant whether the change at issue affects anything that "was in some technical sense part of the sentence."[11] And, in keeping with this realism, the Court has treated ameliorative provisions that are "purely discretionary, contingent on . . . the wishes of the correctional authorities [or] special behavior by the inmate",[12] as incapable of offsetting simultaneously enacted provisions that deprive prisoners of more routine opportunities—for example, by "remov[ing] . . . the possibility of a sentence of less than [the statutory maximum],"[13] or by eliminating ordinary good-time credits and thereby "reduc[ing] [the prisoner's] opportunity to shorten his time

(1898) (retrospective application of state law requiring only 8 jurors instead of 12).

ute of limitations has fully run. See Note, supra note 4, at 1512 n. 78.

8. See, e.g., Hopt v. Utah, 110 U.S. 574 (1884) (enlarging class of competent witnesses); Duncan v. Missouri, 152 U.S. 377 (1894) (reducing number of judges hearing defendant's appeal); Gibson v. Mississippi, 162 U.S. 565 (1896) (change in mode of grand jury selection); Thompson v. Missouri, 171 U.S. 380 (1898) (broadening mode of authenticating and introducing handwriting samples); Mallett v. North Carolina, 181 U.S. 589 (1901) (granting right of appeal to the state); Beazell v. Ohio, 269 U.S. 167 (1925) (limiting right of jointly indicted defendants to receive separate trials). Not surprisingly, lower courts have therefore evidenced understandable confusion "concerning the application of the Ex Post Facto Clause to changes in rules of evidence and procedure." Murphy v. Kentucky, 465 U.S. 1072, 1073 (1984) (White, J., joined by Brennan and Powell, JJ., dissenting from denial of certiorari to review state court decision, based on Hopt v. Utah, upholding retroactive application of statute repealing bar on use of uncorroborated accomplice testimony as basis for criminal conviction).

9. See, e.g., the notion that extensions of statutes of limitation are allowed, Roberts v. United States, 239 F.2d 467 (9th Cir. 1956), while revivals of expired statutes of limitation are not, State v. Sneed, 25 Tex. Supp. 66 (1860), on the theory that defendant acquires a right to rely once the stat-

10. Weaver v. Graham, 450 U.S. 24, 31 (1981), quoting from Cummings v. Missouri, 71 U.S. (4 Wall.) at 325.

11. Weaver, 450 U.S. at 32 (striking down retroactive reduction in availability of good-time credits against sentence, without regard to whether terms for earning such credits should be deemed part of the original sentence or merely ancillary thereto). See also Miller v. Florida, 107 S.Ct. 2446, 2451–52 (1987) (ex post facto clause precludes sentencing defendant under guidelines setting presumed sentence at 5½ to 7 years where sentencing guidelines at time of the offense would have resulted in presumed sentence of only 3½ to 4 years; it is irrelevant that the sentencing guidelines at all times included a "notice that [they] might be changed", and that the guidelines do not alter the statutory limits of punishment for the particular offense).

12. Id. at 35 (refusing to treat enhanced opportunities to earn good-time credits for commendable prison behavior, at discretion of prison authorities, as offsetting reduction in automatic good-time credits). See also Lindsey v. Washington, 301 U.S. 397 (1937) (refusing to treat inclusion of discretionary parole opportunity as offsetting statutory change making maximum sentence mandatory).

13. Lindsey, 301 U.S. at 401.

in prison simply through good conduct." [14]   Although the Court's approach has been to compare the old and new "statutory procedures *in toto* to determine if the new may be fairly characterized as more onerous," [15] it has thus been sensitive to the realities of the prison situation in making such comparisons. [16]

Unfortunately, this realistic focus on the prisoner's expectations has on occasion blurred the Court's vision of one of the chief concerns of the ex post facto ban—that of "ensur[ing] that the sovereign will govern impartially and that it will be perceived as doing so." [17]   Thus, in *Dobbert v. Florida*, [18] a procedural change in Florida's death penalty procedure—a change in the roles of judge and jury in sentencing—was regarded by the Court as "ameliorative"; [19] this led the Court to uphold a death sentence under a statute enacted in late 1972—months after the period during which petitioner had committed his offense (January to April, 1972).   The majority, after reciting the genuinely horrifying tale of petitioner's torture and murder of his own children noted that the death penalty statute in effect at the time of the murders had subsequently been found by Florida's highest court to be invalid under controlling Supreme Court precedent [20]; in this sense, no "valid" death penalty provision at all was in effect at the time petitioner acted. [21]   But the Court had little difficulty concluding that the superceded statute's "existence on the statute books provided fair warning" [22] to petitioner "of the penalty which Florida would seek to impose on him if he were convicted of first degree murder." [23]

If Florida's legislature had known Dobbert's identity, or could realistically have discovered it, when it enacted the revised death penalty statute, his case would have powerfully illustrated why the ex post facto ban should prevent the imposition of penalties enacted by lawmakers who know exactly which individuals they are punishing.   In such a situation, fair notice to those individuals of what the legislature had in store for them would indeed be beside the point. [24]   The objection

---

14. Weaver, 450 U.S. at 33–34.

15. Dobbert v. Florida, 432 U.S. 282, 294 (1977) (holding changed death penalty procedure more ameliorative than onerous, viewed *in toto*).

16. See especially the opinion of Justice Rehnquist, concurring in the judgment in Weaver, 450 U.S. at 37–39. But compare the less sensitive approach of Justice Blackmun, joined by Chief Justice Burger, also concurring in the judgment. Id. at 36–37 (suggesting that, if the matter were not foreclosed by precedent, the state should have been permitted to offset the cancellation of automatic good-time credits with its more generous, if discretionary, enhancement of gain-time opportunities).

17. Dobbert, 432 U.S. at 307–08 (Stevens, J., joined by Brennan and Marshall, JJ., dissenting).

18. 432 U.S. 282 (1977).

19. Id. at 294 (majority opinion of Rehnquist, J.).

20. On June 22, 1972, in Furman v. Georgia, 408 U.S. 238 (1972), the Court struck down death penalty provisions administered through unbridled jury discretion. On July 17, 1972, Florida's highest court found that state's death penalty procedure void under Furman. Donaldson v. Sack, 265 So.2d 499 (Fla. 1972).

21. The death penalty provision under which Dobbert was sentenced, enacted in late 1972, was found constitutional in Proffitt v. Florida, 428 U.S. 242 (1976). On the jurisprudence of how a Supreme Court decision retroactively invalidating a provision such as the death penalty statute of Florida should be understood to affect the status of the law in effect prior to such invalidation, see § 3–3, supra. See also note 27, infra.

22. Dobbert, 432 U.S. at 297.

23. Id. at 298.

24. Compare Kolender v. Lawson, 461 U.S. 352 (1983) (noting that statutes void

would not be that they were entitled to rely on the state of the law at the time they acted. Dobbert's reliance interest at the time he tortured two of his children and murdered another hardly deserves mention, let alone respect. The objection would be that even such individuals are entitled to something better than a legislative lynching.

The original edition of this treatise quoted with approval the *Dobbert* dissenters' condemnation of the Court's result as "an archaic gargoyle" defacing "a majestic bulwark in the framework of our Constitution."[25] But it seems sounder, on reflection, to treat the *Dobbert* Court's inattention to this theoretical risk of legislative abuse as reflecting only the absence of any actual risk of this sort in the case at hand. For, long before Dobbert's arrest in early 1973, and well before he was tried and sentenced, later that year, the new death penalty provision—enacted in late 1972—was safely in place. Those who enacted it to cure the constitutional flaws in the prior procedure might conceivably have been aware of the *crime* at issue, but there is no reason to suspect they were aware of the *criminal*.[26] And although the capital punishment law in effect when he acted had been changed by the time he was tried and sentenced, the Court seems correct in its conclusion that the change was, on the whole, an ameliorative one—making the death penalty more difficult to inflict.[27] *Dobbert* therefore should not be read to stand for the proposition that, so long as an individual is given fair warning, the legislature may deliberately design a crime—or a punishment—to fit the criminal. Not only the ex post facto clause but the bill

because of the vague and open-ended enforcement discretion they entrust to government officials are of constitutional concern more because such discretion might be abused than because fair notice is necessarily absent). Accord, Houston v. Hill, 107 S.Ct. 2502, 2511–12 & n. 15 (1987).

25. Dobbert, 432 U.S. at 311 (Stevens, J., joined by Brennan and Marshall, JJ., dissenting).

26. If the legislature had passed a statute specifically mandating the penalty of death for "whichever individual is convicted of the first degree murder of the Dobbert children," such a statute would have been unconstitutional, quite apart from its retroactivity and specificity, on the ground that mandatory death penalty provisions, which give the jury no discretion whatever, violate the fourteenth amendment. See Woodson v. North Carolina, 428 U.S. 280 (1976); Roberts v. Louisiana, 428 U.S. 325 (1976). What if the legislature had simply taken the widely publicized facts of the killing of the Dobbert children into account in drafting the list of aggravating circumstances for juries to consider in deciding whether to impose the death penalty? If one aim of the Furman holding was to encourage lawmakers to focus in a deliberate way on what criteria juries should use in selecting who should live and who

should die, see McGautha v. California, 402 U.S. 183, 265 (1971) (Brennan, J., dissenting), then it seems hard to fault the legislature in the hypothesized case for doing just that. So long as it is willing to write the statute in terms broad enough to encompass not just the particular individual who is ultimately convicted of the specific killing at issue but anyone else who meets similar criteria, the concern that the legislature may be secretly focusing on improper characteristics of the particular individual, even if not then known to the legislators, seems inapposite.

27. Suppose Furman v. Georgia, 408 U.S. 238 (1972), had been made purely prospective—applicable only to post-Furman trials. The ex post facto clause, which surely leaves that option open, would then have left Dobbert eligible for capital punishment (under the statute in effect when he committed murder) if his trial had occurred prior to Furman. To hold, with the dissenters, that the ex post facto clause commands a different result because his arrest did not occur until 1973, and because his trial was therefore necessarily delayed until after June 22, 1972, is to make the effect of the clause a function of when someone is tried rather than when the crime occurred—a novelty that the dissent does not undertake to defend.

of attainder clause, to which we now turn, should be deemed to forbid any such departure from the rule of law.

§ 10–4. The Ban on Bills of Attainder: Generality as a Supplementary Safeguard

The ban on ex post facto laws could be readily circumvented if a legislature wishing to punish people for conduct innocent when committed could simply determine for itself the class of persons it deemed guilty of such conduct and designate the members of that class, either by name or in some equivalent manner, for imposition of a punitive disability like imprisonment or expulsion from various lawful occupations. Indeed, were such punishment by direct specification an available option, a host of other constitutional safeguards would be rendered nugatory as well. Procedural protections against the use of various categories of evidence [1] would mean little if a legislature could simply decree punishment for those whose judicial conviction might prove inconvenient or impossible by virtue of such protections. And substantive protections against the use of various criteria [2] could likewise be ignored by a legislature willing to designate the individuals it regarded as meeting those criteria and prepared to direct the punishment of those individuals by name.

Most basic of all, trial by legislature—the use of the lawmaking process, or of a trial-like process in a lawmaking setting, to inflict punitive disabilities on identifiable persons—would be radically incompatible with the safeguards provided by trial before a neutral judge and an impartial jury according to ascertainable standards, promulgated in advance of the conduct said to violate them, and enacted and applied in accord with constitutionally required substantive and procedural standards. Accordingly, article I forbids passage of any bill of attainder by Congress [3] or by any state.[4]

The term "bill of attainder" originally applied to legislative enactments decreeing death for named or described persons or groups for high crimes, "attainting" the victims, and forbidding inheritance of their property.[5] Lesser penalties inflicted in the same manner were

§ 10–4

1. The exclusionary rule prohibiting the use of evidence obtained through unreasonable searches or seizures in violation of the fourth amendment and the protection provided by the fifth amendment against being required to testify against oneself in a criminal matter are two examples.

2. The protections of freedoms of speech and religion under the first and fourteenth amendments and equal protection of the laws under the fifth and fourteenth amendments all constrain the substantive content of laws by forbidding legislative use of certain criteria. For example, absent compelling justification, freedom of speech entails a prohibition on the use of viewpoint or subject matter as criteria; freedom of religion prevents the use of religious belief or affiliation as criteria; and the equal protection of the laws protects against the use of race or (in many cases) gender as criteria in legislative line-drawing. See generally Chapters 12, 14 and 16.

3. Art. I, § 9, cl. 3. The clause protects only persons, not states, and states have no standing to invoke the clause on behalf of their citizens against the federal government. South Carolina v. Katzenbach, 383 U.S. 301, 324 (1966).

4. Art. I, § 10, cl. 1.

5. 1 T. Cooley, Constitutional Limitations 536 (8th ed. 1927); 3 J. Story, Commentaries on the Constitution 209 (Da Capo Press ed. 1970).

known as "bills of pains and penalties." [6] Early in the constitutional litigation surrounding bills of attainder, the Supreme Court determined that the prohibition against attainder applied to these bills of pains and penalties as well. Thus, in *Fletcher v. Peck*, Chief Justice Marshall wrote for the Court that "a bill of attainder may affect the life of an individual, or may confiscate his property, or may do both." [7] A half century later, Justice Field was able to conclude simply that "[w]ithin the meaning of the Constitution, bills of attainder include bills of pains and penalties." [8] And, by the 1940's, the Court could hold that the prohibition against bills of attainder extends to all "legislative acts, no matter what their form, that apply either to named individuals or to easily ascertainable members of a group in such a way as to inflict punishment on them without a judicial trial . . . ." [9] And the object of such a trial must, of course, be something more than the mechanical determination of whether the accused is indeed a member of some finite list of persons that a lawmaking process has already specifically condemned without trial safeguards—whether by directly decreeing their punishment, or by ousting them from a sphere of public life, or by conditioning their access to that sphere upon the taking of an oath that they are not in fact members of the class singled out by law for such condemnation.

Perhaps the clearest example of a bill of attainder is provided by the case of *United States v. Lovett*. [10] The House Committee on Un-American Activities had made charges against three government employees, Lovett, Dodd, and Watson, and, after investigation, the House Appropriations Committee had found that the three had engaged in "subversive activity." [11] Despite the opposition of the agencies employing the three, Congress then passed a law providing that, after a certain date, no funds could be used to compensate the three—specified by name—unless prior to that date they were appointed by the President with the advice and consent of the Senate.[12] The Supreme Court struck down the law as an unconstitutional bill of attainder, pointing out that the law accomplished the same result as one which, "stating that after investigation [Congress] had found Lovett, Dodd, and Watson 'guilty' of

6. Cummings v. Missouri, 71 U.S. (4 Wall.) 277, 323 (1866); 1 T. Cooley, supra note 5, at 538; 3 J. Story, supra note 5, at 209–10.

7. 10 U.S. (6 Cranch.) 87, 132 (1810).

8. Cummings v. Missouri, 71 U.S. (4 Wall.) 277, 323 (1866).

9. United States v. Lovett, 328 U.S. 303, 315 (1946). The concept of punishment under the bill of attainder clauses has always been a fairly broad one. The Supreme Court has struck down four laws as forbidden bills of attainder: a state law which required priests to take an oath that they had never aided the Confederacy, Cummings v. Missouri, 71 U.S. (4 Wall.) 277 (1866); a congressional enactment which required a similar oath of attorneys practicing in the federal courts, Ex parte Garland, 71 U.S. (4 Wall.) 333 (1866); a

federal statute which prohibited the payment of compensation to three named government employees who had been charged with subversive activities and investigated by the House Un-American Activities Committee, United States v. Lovett, 328 U.S. 303 (1946); and an Act of Congress making it a crime for a member of the Communist Party to serve as an officer of a labor union or to be employed by such a union except in a clerical or custodial capacity, United States v. Brown, 381 U.S. 437 (1965).

10. 328 U.S. 303 (1946). An interesting account of the evolution of this case is contained in Ely, "United States v. Lovett: Litigating the Separation of Powers," 10 Harv.Civ.Rts—Civ.Lib.L.Rev. 1 (1975).

11. 328 U.S. at 308–13.

12. Id. at 305.

the crime of engaging in 'subversive activities,' defined that term for the first time, and sentenced them to perpetual exclusion from any government employment." [13]

The essence of the bill of attainder ban is that it proscribes legislative punishment of specified persons—not of whichever persons might be judicially determined to fit within properly general proscriptions duly enacted in advance. Whether the persons improperly specified are being punished for conduct lawful when engaged in, and hence in violation of ex post facto clause principles, or by reason of their religious or political beliefs, and hence in violation of first amendment principles, or as a result of legislative distaste for them as individuals, the bill of attainder prohibition is fully applicable. But its application necessarily depends on the presence of improper *specification* by the legislature of the individuals singled out for punishment. If a law merely designates a properly general characteristic, such as employment in a regulated industry, and then imposes upon all who have that characteristic a prophylactic measure reasonably calculated to achieve a nonpunitive public purpose, no attainder may be said to have resulted from the mere fact that the set of persons having the characteristic in question might in theory be enumerated in advance and that the set is in principle knowable at the time the law is passed.

Thus, the Court has upheld such measures as § 32 of the Banking Act of 1933, which prohibited partners and employees of firms engaged in underwriting securities from serving as directors or officers of national banks.[14] Although they obviously pose closer cases, laws

13. Id. at 316.

14. Board of Governors v. Agnew, 329 U.S. 441 (1947). Although no consideration was given to an attainder argument in Agnew itself, the Court defended § 32 specifically, and conflict-of-interest laws in general, against that argument in United States v. Brown, 381 U.S. 437, 453–56 (1965). Central to the Court's distinction between § 32 of the Banking Act and § 504 of the Labor-Management Reporting Act (which made it a crime for a member of the Communist Party to serve as an officer of a labor union) was the observation that "§ 32 incorporates no judgment censuring or condemning any man or group of men. In enacting it, Congress relied upon its general knowledge of human psychology, and concluded that the concurrent holding of the two designated positions would present a temptation to *any* man—not just certain men or members of a certain political party." 381 U.S. at 453–54. The conclusion of the Brown Court was that, "insofar as § 32 incorporates a condemnation, it condemns all men." Id. at 454. Section 504 of the Labor-Management Reporting Act, on the other hand, specifically stigmatized members of the Communist Party, and thus violated the prohibition against bills of attainder.

This proposed distinction between § 32 and § 504 is by no means wholly satisfactory. One could argue that § 32, by excluding other categories, specifically condemned those persons who were officers or employees of underwriting firms; or, conversely, one could argue that § 504 merely expressed the judgment that *any* person would find it impossible in good faith concurrently to hold the positions of Communist Party member and labor union official. In his dissent in Brown, Justice White argued that no meaningful distinction between the two statutory schemes could be drawn along these lines. Id. at 466 (White, joined by Harlan, Clark, and Stewart, JJ., dissenting).

Perhaps a better distinction was made by the Court when it noted that "§ 504, unlike § 32 of the Banking Act, inflicts its deprivation upon the members of a political group thought to present a threat to the national security. . . . [S]uch groups were the targets of the overwhelming majority of English and early American bills of attainder." Id. at 453. While in Agnew the Court explained that § 32 "is directed to the probability or likelihood . . . that a bank director interested in the underwriting business may use his influence" in undesirable ways, 329 U.S. at 447, the Court in Brown pointed to "the fallacy

barring convicted and unpardoned felons from the practice of medicine,[15] or excluding such individuals from employment in a waterfront labor organization,[16] might well be regarded less as instances of legislatures singling out the class of felons—a class that might in theory be enumerated as a list of names—than as properly general measures suitably tailored to legitimate and nonpunitive ends. It is not that the concept of "punishment" encompasses solely retribution— that view was properly rejected by the Supreme Court in light of the often non-retributive aims of even the criminal process itself.[17] It is simply that the concept of legislative "specification" in this context cannot be so broad as to swallow up all laws that impose some disabling limitation upon an ascertainable group.[18] Even a law requiring airline pilots to be sighted, or brain surgeons to have steady hands, would otherwise be vulnerable to attack.

Yet it is equally true that the attainder ban cannot be rendered inapplicable simply because a law designating an identifiable class of individuals for punishment might be recharacterized as a prophylactic measure enacted to serve some legitimate public end. To be sure, the availability of other constitutional provisions, such as the free speech clause and the due process and equal protection clauses, would in any event serve as a limitation of sorts on all such laws. But the application of these other constitutional provisions sometimes requires evidence of legislative purpose or motive—evidence that is not always readily available [19] and that might easily be negated by a seemingly

---

of the suggestion that membership in the Communist Party, or any other political organization, can be regarded as an alternative, but equivalent, expression for a list of undesirable characteristics." 381 U.S. at 455. See note 25 infra and accompanying text.

15. See Hawker v. New York, 170 U.S. 189 (1898) (upholding such a law over a bill of attainder challenge on the ground that the disqualification bore a reasonable relationship to the proper state purpose of insuring that all doctors were of good character). The Hawker Court adopted a standard that gave great discretion to legislatures in inflicting "regulatory" disabilities upon various groups: "When the legislature declares that whoever has violated the criminal laws of the State shall be deemed lacking in good moral character it is not laying down an arbitrary or fanciful rule—one having no relation to the subject-matter, but is only appealing to a well recognized fact of human experience . . . ." 170 U.S. at 195–96. After United States v. Brown, 381 U.S. 437 (1965), one could perhaps argue against the result reached in Hawker on the theory, among others, that convicted felons are an ostracized group with little input, especially, in light of § 13–16, infra, into majoritarian political processes. Cf. United States v. Carolene Products Co., 304 U.S. 144, 152–

53 n. 4 (1938). See also § 15–13, infra. It is true that, even in Brown, the Court said that "Congress [properly] relied upon its general knowledge of human psychology" in enacting § 32 of the Banking Act of 1933 (conflict-of-interest legislation), 381 U.S. at 454, but financial officers are hardly a closed, ostracized class resembling the ex-convicts burdened in Hawker.

16. De Veau v. Braisted, 363 U.S. 144 (1960) (upholding such a law), discussed in § 10–5, note 13, infra.

17. See United States v. Brown, 381 U.S. at 456–60.

18. The bill of attainder clause thus "does not . . . limit[ ] Congress to the choice of legislating for the universe, or legislating only benefits, or not legislating at all." Nixon v. Administrator of General Services, 433 U.S. 425, 471 (1977).

19. For equal protection cases in the race area discussing the need to show discriminatory purpose, see Washington v. Davis, 426 U.S. 229 (1976); Arlington Heights v. Metropolitan Housing Dev. Corp., 429 U.S. 252 (1977); Mobile v. Bolden, 446 U.S. 55 (1980); Rogers v. Lodge, 458 U.S. 613 (1982); Hunter v. Underwood, 471 U.S. 222 (1985), discussed in § 16–20, infra. In the gender area, see Personnel Administrator v. Feeney, 442 U.S. 256 (1979), discussed in § 16–20, infra.

plausible assertion that the legislature had not proceeded in terms of any forbidden generalization but had in fact determined, after appropriate empirical investigation, that the individuals it had decided to restrict posed a threat to the public weal. The ban on bills of attainder prevents just such an assertion.

Consider, for example, a law excluding all members of a political party—say, the Communist Party—from service as officers or managers of any labor organization. Such a law could be attacked under the first amendment,[20] but the attack might be rebuffed by a claim that, rather than proceeding upon a forbidden generalization about political beliefs and associations, the lawmaking body was in fact proceeding on the basis of what it had learned, in extensive hearings, about members of the designated political group and about the threats those members had historically posed, and seemed likely to pose in the future, to the labor movement. The bill of attainder ban provides a powerful retort to any such claim: insofar as the legislature denies that it *has* in fact acted on the basis of what might be deemed "legislative facts" or societal generalizations and insists that it has instead acted on the basis of what some have termed "adjudicative facts" about identifiable persons, it is engaged in trial by legislature—a process that cannot constitutionally result in any punitive measure.

This was indeed the Supreme Court's precise mode of analysis in the leading modern decision under the bill of attainder clauses, *United States v. Brown.*[21] Congress had made it a crime for anyone who was, or within five years had been, a member of the Communist Party to serve as an officer or manager of a labor union.[22] In the face of an argument that Congress had really enacted "a general rule to the effect that persons possessing characteristics which made them likely to incite political strikes should not hold office, and [had] simply inserted in place of a list of those characteristics an alternative, shorthand criterion—membership in the Communist Party," the Court accurately perceived an improper attempt to recharacterize the law as a prophylactic measure enacted to serve a legitimate public end, and rejected that attempt, drawing implicitly on first amendment principles: "The designation of Communists as those persons likely to cause political strikes

---

20. In American Communications Association v. Douds, 339 U.S. 382 (1950), the Court rejected a first amendment attack on a similar statute that denied the services of the National Labor Relations Board to a labor union of which some officers failed to swear that they are not presently members of the Communist Party. The Court considered that "Congress could rationally find that the Communist Party is not like other parties in its utilization of positions of union leadership as means by which to bring about strikes and other obstructions of commerce for purposes of political advantage . . . ." Id. at 391. Showing great deference to such congressional determinations, the Court found that "the public interest in the good faith exercise of the [quasi-legislative powers of union officials

as bargaining representatives] is very great," id. at 402, while the statute, rather than being aimed at, or serving as a vehicle for, the suppression of dangerous ideas, id. at 403, merely opposed the "combination of [Communist Party] affiliations or beliefs with occupancy of a position of great power over the economy of the country," id. at 403–04. The current validity of Douds may be dubious. See Ch. 12, infra.

21. 381 U.S. 437 (1965).

22. Id. at 438 & n. 1. Section 504 was enacted to replace the provision at issue in Douds, and was "designed to accomplish the same purpose . . ., but in a more direct and effective way." Id. at 439 & n. 2. See also note 20, supra.

. . . rests . . . upon an empirical investigation by Congress of the acts, characteristics, and propensities of Communist Party members. In a number of decisions, this Court has pointed out the fallacy of the suggestion that membership in the Communist Party, or any other political organization, can be regarded as an alternative, but equivalent, expression for a list of undesirable characteristics." [23] Instead, the Court found that the statute "designates in no uncertain terms the persons who possess the feared characteristics and therefore cannot hold office without incurring criminal liability—members of the Communist Party." [24] Such a law constitutes a bill of attainder. In effect, when a legislature's designation of a group cannot, for independent constitutional reasons, be defended by treating that designation as the equivalent of a list of undesirable *characteristics* but must be defended, if at all, by treating the designation as the equivalent of a list of *names*, the bill of attainder ban prevents the designation from being used as the basis of punishment.[25]

23. 381 U.S. at 455. In Garner v. Public Works of Los Angeles, 341 U.S. 716 (1951), the Court sustained an ordinance which required each city employee to take an oath disclaiming any prior affiliation with any group which advocated the violent overthrow of government; the majority was "unable to conclude that punishment is imposed by a general regulation which merely provides standards of qualification and eligibility for employment." Id. at 722. The Garner oath would today be deemed violative of the first amendment freedom of association. See § 12–26, infra.

24. 381 U.S. at 450.

25. This distinction is not always an easy one to make; one must look not only to the nature of the class defined, but also to the nature of the legitimate, non-punitive end pursued—and, in particular, to the reasonableness of the relation between the two. For example, if it is possible for members of the asserted class to leave it at any time without foregoing the exercise of any right or privilege, there would seem to be little reason to be concerned about improper specification. See the discussion of Selective Service System v. Minnesota Public Interest Research Group, 468 U.S. 841 (1984), infra. Classes defined by present occupation, in which exit is burdensome yet possible—for example, the securities underwriters affected by § 32 of the Banking Act—would seem to be less troublesome than classes defined according to some involuntary or unchangeable characteristic, such as a disease or a physical or mental disability. A law requiring that airline pilots be sighted would not seem improperly to single out the blind, while a requirement that forbade AIDS victims from becoming airline pilots would seem unfairly to target an unpopular group of individuals; on the other hand, a law

prohibiting AIDS victims from selling blood to the Red Cross reasonably pursues a legitimate, non-punitive end. See, e.g., United States v. Brown, 381 U.S. at 454 n. 29 (suggesting that the legislature could properly prohibit, from obtaining licenses to operate dangerous machinery, all persons afflicted with a certain disease which has as one of its symptoms a susceptibility to uncontrollable seizures—simply by naming the disease rather than by describing its symptoms). Of course, those unchangeable characteristics—such as race and gender—which define "suspect" classes in the equal protection area would be expected to invite particular scrutiny under bill of attainder analyses, as would classes defined by exercise of first amendment rights.

The identification of an individual by name should raise an almost conclusive presumption of constitutionally suspect specification, given that the ban on bills of attainder is designed to prevent trial by legislature. Even so, in Nixon v. Administrator of General Services, 433 U.S. 425 (1977), the majority found that, since only Mr. Nixon's papers (and not those of other Presidents) "demanded immediate attention," he constituted "a legitimate class of one," id. at 472—a finding that Justice Stevens accepted only because of the resignation and pardon that made the Nixon case truly unique, id. at 486 (concurring opinion). But it is difficult to avoid Chief Justice Burger's conclusion in that case that legislating against a named person without judicial safeguards cannot be justified by that person's apparent uniqueness—especially since Congress could have expressed, in a law motivated by the Nixon resignation but applicable to similar future cases as well as to Nixon's, whatever factors were deemed to make his case unique. Hopefully, Chief Justice Burger is correct

The earliest direct applications of the bill of attainder clause are best understood as standing for precisely this principle. In *Cummings v. Missouri*,[26] the Court struck down a provision of Missouri's state constitution [27] which prescribed an oath disavowing various past actions of disloyalty to the United States, as well as past manifestations "by act or word" of sympathy for members of the Confederacy, as a condition for pursuing several enumerated occupations. The petitioner in *Cummings* was a Roman Catholic priest who had been convicted of preaching after refusing to take the oath and sentenced to "pay a fine of $500, and to be committed to jail until the same was paid." [28] The loyalty oath demanded by the state in *Cummings* was perceived as flawed by the Court because "[i]t was required in order to reach the person, not the calling. It was exacted, not from any notion that the several acts [of loyalty to the Confederacy] indicated unfitness for the callings, but because it was thought that the several acts *deserved punishment* . . ." [29] The Court relied upon the reasoning of *Cummings* in holding a similar, federally-required expurgatory oath unconstitutional in *Ex parte Garland*,[30] despite the argument of Justice Miller that the acts brought in question by the oath were not at all irrelevant to the practice of law in the federal courts, the affected occupation.[31]

But what if the statutes at issue in *Cummings* and *Garland* had been passed during the Civil War, and had permitted those who wished to be free of the challenged disqualifications to lift those disqualifications by putting down their arms and ending their affiliation with the Confederacy? What the Supreme Court properly treated in *Cummings* and *Garland* as the forbidden specification of an identified class for a

in his suggestion that the Court's holding might *itself* eventually constitute a "class of one." Id. at 545 (dissenting opinion).

26. 71 U.S. (4 Wall.) 277 (1866).

27. The Supreme Court has never found it significant that the challenged provision was part of the state's constitution rather than a simple enactment of its legislature. It is of course true that a state cannot use a popular referendum, either as a part of its constitution or otherwise, to circumvent federal constitutional restraints. See Reitman v. Mulkey, 387 U.S. 369 (1967); Hunter v. Erickson, 393 U.S. 385 (1969); but cf. James v. Valtierra, 402 U.S. 137 (1971); Eastlake v. Forest City Enterprises, 426 U.S. 668, 678–79 (1976). But if a central concern of the ban against attainder is the separation of governmental powers, see § 10–6, infra, it becomes relevant that a constitutional amendment adopted by popular referendum does not pose quite the same threats of overly centralized governmental power which legislation entails. On the other hand, a constitutional amendment adopted by popular referendum would exacerbate the concern for not circumventing the procedural safeguards of a judicial trial or other adversary hearing—a concern which has also been central in the jurisprudence of the bill of attainder clauses. See §§ 10–5, 10–6, infra. Eastlake v. Forest City Enterprises, 426 U.S. at 680 (Powell, J., dissenting); id. at 693 (1976) (Stevens, J., joined by Brennan, J., dissenting). This concern seems sufficient to justify application of the attainder ban to state constitutional amendments or other referenda which inflict serious disabilities on particular individuals.

28. 71 U.S. (4 Wall.) at 316.

29. Id. at 320.

30. 71 U.S. (4 Wall.) 333 (1866).

31. "That fidelity to the government under which he lives, a true and loyal attachment to it, and a sincere desire for its preservation, are among essential qualifications which should be required in a lawyer, seems to me too clear for argument." Id. at 387 (dissenting opinion). However, the Court has never endorsed the position taken by Justice Miller. In later opinions, the oath struck down in Garland has been seen as unrelated to the affected occupation. See, e.g., Dent v. West Virginia, 129 U.S. 114, 128 (1889) (upholding the right of the states to prohibit the unlicensed practice of medicine).

punitive disability would then, in all likelihood, have been transformed into the allowable enactment of a prophylactic measure—an incentive to comply with valid laws against armed rebellion, enforced by withholding the enjoyment of various benefits (and even rights) until such compliance is evidenced. Thus, the Court in *Brown* did not entirely overrule its earlier decision in *American Communications Association v. Douds*,[32] since the Taft-Hartley Act provision upheld in that case expressly allowed members of the Communist Party to resign their membership and thereby gain immediate eligibility to serve as union officials, whereas the Labor-Management Reporting Act provision struck down in *Brown* contained no such option.[33]

Today, of course, the notion that government is free to condition eligibility for an occupation upon someone's abandonment of a political belief or affiliation would be hard to square with the first amendment.[34] But, at least if we focus on a class from which the legislature is free to encourage exit—such as the class of persons who have yet to comply with some lawful obligation—there emerges a basic difference between laws disadvantaging a fixed class from which persons are unable to escape, and laws encouraging departure from an open class by conditioning benefits upon such departure.[35]

The best example is that provided by *Selective Service System v. Minnesota Public Interest Research Group*,[36] in which the Supreme Court sustained over bill of attainder attack an Act of Congress denying higher education financial aid to male students who had not complied with their draft registration requirements.[37] In *Selective Service*, the

---

32. 339 U.S. 382 (1950). See note 20, supra.

33. The Douds Court distinguished the provisions before it from those condemned in Cummings, Garland, and Lovett on the ground that, while the earlier cases involved punishment for past actions, the provisions before it sought only to prevent future action—a contention supposedly demonstrated by the fact that "there is no one who may not, by a voluntary alteration of the loyalties which impel him to action, become eligible to sign the affidavit." Douds, 339 U.S. at 414. The Brown Court pointed to this distinction as a reason why Douds was not controlling precedent, 381 U.S. at 458 (also noting, however, that even an escapable burden might impose "punishment," since the meaning of punishment encompasses more than retribution). It is revealing that the replacement of the provision in Douds by the one in Brown was prompted in part by the legislature's suspicion that many Communists were taking the prescribed oath, leaving as the only sanction a perjury prosecution that presented serious difficulties of proof. See 381 U.S. at 477 (White, J. dissenting).

34. See, e.g., FCC v. League of Women Voters of California, 468 U.S. 364 (1984), discussed in § 11–5, infra.

35. The distinction may not be determinative, of course. Thus the Court noted in Brown that inescapability was not an absolute *prerequisite* to a finding of attainder. See 381 U.S. at 457 n. 32. Conversely, inescapability alone does not *suffice* to establish an attainder—since the class definition may yet be reasonable in light of a legitimate, non-punitive end. See note 25, supra.

Thus, perhaps the best explanation that can be offered for Douds is that in 1950, at the height of the Cold War, a law excluding from service as labor union officials all those belonging to an organization dedicated to capturing the leadership of the "proletariat" in order to bring about mass violent destruction of the state could have appeared as reasonable as might a law, passed in 1987, to prohibit from service as airline pilots all those belonging to "terrorist" organizations dedicated to the achievement of political goals through the hijacking of airplanes.

36. 468 U.S. 841 (1984).

37. The Act was also challenged on the ground that it violated the fifth amendment privilege against compelled self-incrimination by forcing non-registrants to acknowledge that they have failed to register in time when confronted with the need to certify to their schools that they have complied with the registration law. 468 U.S. at 856. The Court rejected this attack, stating that "a person who has not

district court had construed § 1113 of the Department of Defense Authorization Act of 1983 as leaving no late registration option open to a student who had failed to register and thereafter sought to qualify for financial aid. Accordingly, the district court found that the statute "clearly single[d] out an ascertainable group based on past conduct." [38] The Supreme Court, on the other hand, found that the statute did not single out any identifiable group because, under its reading of the statute, any student who found himself in the class of those denied financial aid could remove himself from the class by simply registering late.[39] Thus the class was not fixed: " 'Far from attaching to . . . past and ineradicable actions,' ineligibility for Title IV benefits 'is made to turn upon continuingly contemporaneous fact' which a student who wants public assistance can correct." [40]

registered is under no compulsion to seek financial aid," id., and noting that, in the case of applicants who registered late, the statement to the school does not require them to disclose whether or not their registration was timely. Id. at 857. The government "has not refused any request for immunity for their answers or otherwise threatened them with penalties for invoking the privilege. . . ." Id. at 858. The Court implied that a student would have to assert the privilege in the act of filing late and that, by doing so, a late registrant would not necessarily admit to the commission of a crime, but would "merely call attention to himself." Id.

Dissenting, Justice Marshall, joined by Justice Brennan, found that the threat of the denial of student aid is substantial economic coercion, id. at 870, and that the process of late registration, even were a student to assert the fifth amendment privilege in filling out the registration form late, "creates a 'real and appreciable' hazard of incrimination and prosecution, and that the risk is not 'so improbable that no reasonable man would suffer it to influence his conduct.' " Id. at 868, quoting Brown v. Walker, 161 U.S. 591, 599–600 (1896).

The majority also rejected an argument that the statute violates equal protection because it discriminates against the poor, explaining, in a statement reminiscent of Anatole France, that "Section 12(f) treats all nonregistrants alike, denying aid to both the poor and the wealthy." Id. at 859 n. 17. Justice Marshall, dissenting, stressed that "[t]he wealthy do not require, are not applying for, and do not receive federal education assistance, and therefore are not subject to the requirement that they make statements that they have complied with the Selective Service registration requirement, nor to the economic compulsion to provide incriminating facts to the Government in the act of late registration." Id. at 877. Justice Marshall added that the inequity of this *de facto* classification based on wealth was intensified for

him because the classification is also based on youth, a group "less able to exercise their vote because of their transience and, frequently, state laws burdening student voter registration." Id. at 878 n. 21.

The majority responded that, "even if the statute discriminated against poor nonregistrants . . . the statute must be sustained . . . . because [It] is rationally related to the legitimate Government objectives of encouraging registration and fairly allocating scarce federal resources." Id. at 859 n. 17. Justice Marshall answered that, "[w]hen the law lays an unequal hand on those who have committed precisely the same offense, the discrimination is invidious," id. at 880, and pointed out that Congress did not similarly condition such "rich persons' Government benefits and entitlements" as "oil depletion allowances, accelerated depreciation, capital gains, [and] property owners' deductions." Id. at 881. See Chapter 16, infra.

38. Doe v. Selective Service System, 557 F.Supp. 937, 942 (D. Minn. 1983). While the Supreme Court considered the district court's interpretation to be "plainly inconsistent with the structure of § 1113 and its legislative history," 468 U.S. at 849, the Supreme Court also noted that a statute should be construed, " 'if consistent with the will of Congress, so as to comport with constitutional limitations,' " id. at 850, quoting United States Civil Service Commission v. Letter Carriers, 413 U.S. 548, 571 (1973), thus suggesting its agreement that interpreting the statute to deny eligibility to late registrants might pose fatal constitutional problems.

39. Selective Service, 468 U.S. at 847 n. 3, 849.

40. Id. at 851, quoting Communist Party of United States v. Subversive Activities Control Board, 367 U.S. 1, 87 (1961). Of course, the notion of a fixed class shows similarity with other areas of the law: all retrospective legislation necessarily creates a fixed class, as does all legislation based on gender, race, national origin, or any

The conception of the fixed class—an ascertainable group whose rights are being resolved—suggests that the *making* of a rule with regard to such a group necessarily also amounts to an *application* of that rule to members of the group, although the impact on such members might be delayed. A rule conferring a benefit upon such a group, or—in circumstances where there is no evidence of punitive intent—even a rule imposing a burden on such a group, might be acceptable as a legitimate regulation. But where there is *punishment* of a fixed class—where a deprivation is imposed with punitive intent or is one not reasonably calculated to pursue some nonpunitive aim—a bill of attainder is established.

The Court evidently accepted this view when, in *Selective Service*, it agreed with the Government that a bill of attainder is "a law that legislatively determines guilt and inflicts punishment upon an identifiable individual without provision of the protections of a judicial trial," [41] and therefore has three elements: specification of the affected persons, punishment, and lack of a judicial trial.[42]

In sum, regularity demands that, before a person may be punished, the rule imposing the punishment must first pass through filters of generality and impartiality. Where a governmental body lacks the procedures to ensure impartiality—as is normally the case with the legislature itself—it must limit itself to creating general rules. Where a governmental body necessarily must act with specificity—as is normally the case with a court—it must apply rules in accord with impartial procedures. In administrative as opposed to legislative proceedings, where quasi-judicial functions often occur, it is easy to appreciate the operational significance of the requirement that *any* government body, if it is to impose burdens, may do so only by establishing rules of appropriate generality and by applying rules with judicial impartiality. Whether the bill of attainder ban in fact imposes such a broad requirement, as opposed to limiting legislatures alone, is the subject of § 10–6. What sorts of *burdens* count as sufficiently punitive to trigger the attainder ban in *any* institutional context is the subject of § 10–5.

§ 10–5. Limiting Bill of Attainder Doctrine to Punitive Measures

Legislative measures often grant or withhold benefits or burdens from precisely identified individuals and groups. A bailout for Chrysler might be seen as a burden to Ford, a subsidy to Lockheed as a competitive blow to Boeing, a private bill for a favored constituent as a severe disappointment to a neighbor, a tax break for one company as a punishment for a competitor. Yet the bill of attainder ban has, quite

---

other characteristic that an individual cannot change.

41. Selective Service, 468 U.S. at 846–47 quoting Nixon v. Administrator of General Services, 433 U.S. 425, 468 (1977).

42. Selective Service, 468 U.S. at 847. The Government argued in Selective Service, with respect to the third requirement, that the statute at issue did not dispense with a judicial trial, because a hearing was provided in the event of disagreement between the applicant and the Secretary about whether the applicant had in fact registered, and because the decision made at that hearing was subject to judicial review. Id. at 847 n. 3. The Court properly deemed that argument "meritless [since] Congress has not provided a judicial trial to those affected by the statute." Id.

properly, never been regarded as an obstacle to all such measures—a guarantee that all lawmaking activity will proceed through majestic generalities.[1] Although the Supreme Court once struck down a statute exempting American Express by name from a generally applicable economic regulation,[2] that decision was itself overruled two decades later, when the Court upheld a law permitting two identified vendors to continue hawking their wares in New Orleans' French Quarter but forbidding all of their competitors to do so.[3]

It is only laws that inflict *punishment* on legislatively specified individuals that the bill of attainder ban condemns, and the examples noted above make plain that not all burdens may be deemed punishments for this purpose even when legislative "specification" is shown. At the same time, the Supreme Court has been careful not to limit the notion of punishments to the classic instances of death, imprisonment, banishment, and punitive fines or confiscations of property. From the earliest applications of the attainder ban, the Court has applied it to "legislative bars to participation by individuals or groups in specific employments or professions," [4] even when such bars are not demonstrably retributive in aim.[5]

There can be little doubt, for example, that a law depriving Richard Nixon by name of access to future government employment would have been struck down as a forbidden bill of attainder despite references in *Nixon v. Administrator of General Services* to the odd notion that Mr. Nixon is "a legitimate class of one." [6] How, then, is one to account for the Supreme Court's holding in that case that Congress acted constitutionally when, in the Presidential Recordings and Materials Preservation Act, it provided for governmental custody of his presidential papers and his alone? Congress might, after all, have written the legislation to cover all future presidents who resign under threat of impeachment. It is true, as the Court noted, that the papers of all other former Presidents were by that time safely ensconced in various libraries,[7] but that hardly justified drawing a bright line between Richard Milhous Nixon and any equally unfortunate successor. Equal protection doctrine does not forbid legislatures to proceed one *step* at a time,[8] but the bill of attainder ban goes beyond equal protection in forbidding at least those legislative steps that

§ 10–5

1. However, some highly individualized fiscal measures have been held to violate the ban on nonuniform bankruptcy laws. See Railway Labor Executives' Assn. v. Gibbons, 455 U.S. 457 (1982), discussed in § 5–4, supra, at note 6, and in § 5–11, supra, at note 3.

2. Morey v. Doud, 354 U.S. 457 (1957) (violation of equal protection). See Ch. 16, infra.

3. New Orleans v. Dukes, 427 U.S. 297 (1976). It was an equal protection attack that the Court rebuffed in this case, but a bill of attainder challenge should have fared no better.

4. Selective Service System v. Minnesota PIRG, 468 U.S. 841, 852, (1984) (citing Brown, Lovett, Cummings, and Garland, all discussed in § 10–4, supra).

5. United States v. Brown, 381 U.S. 437, 458–61 (1965). Not all such bars to participation have been deemed to run afoul of the attainder ban, however. See, e.g., Hawker v. New York, 170 U.S. 189 (1898), discussed in § 10–4, note 15, supra, and De Veau v. Braisted, 363 U.S. 144 (1960), discussed in note 13, infra.

6. 433 U.S. 425, 472 (1977). See § 10–4, note 25, supra.

7. 433 U.S. at 472.

8. See Chapter 16, infra.

punish one *individual* at a time.[9] The Court did not, however, deem the temporary withholding of the Nixon papers to be a "punishment" at all; and, in that conclusion, the Court may have been on defensible ground. To be sure, the very specificity of the disability—its singling out of Mr. Nixon *by name*—heightened the sting, and the stigma, of what had been done in the statute. But stigma alone may not suffice to make an attainder where the deprivation is as limited in duration, and as circumscribed by provisions for compensation should private property be taken, as was the case in *Nixon*.[10]

In developing the punishment concept for attainder purposes, the Court has at times spoken as though three independent tests must be met if an arguably punitive measure is to be rescued from that categorization: the measure must not be of the sort "historically associated with punishment";[11] it must "reasonably . . . further

9. See § 10–4, note 25, supra.

10. Nixon v. Administrator of General Services, 433 U.S. 425 (1977). The Court, in an opinion by Justice Brennan, took account of the fact that the statute placed the materials under the very same agency designated by the agreement between Mr. Nixon and the Administrator as depository of the documents for a minimum three-year period; that the statute ensured Mr. Nixon access to the materials at all times, including the right to make copies; and that the statute not only expressly preserved Mr. Nixon's opportunity to assert any legally or constitutionally based right or privilege, but also preserved for Mr. Nixon all of the protections that adhere in a judicial proceeding by assuring district court jurisdiction and appellate review over all his legal claims—even to the point of providing that such claims would have first priority on the docket of such courts. Id. at 481–82. More generally, the Court emphasized (1) the statute's provision for just compensation in the event any of Mr. Nixon's economic interests are invaded, id. at 445 n. 8; (2) the statute's failure to bar Mr. Nixon from any specified employment or vocation, id. at 475; (3) the statute's enactment in the wake of a specific agreement between Mr. Nixon and the General Services Administrator expressly contemplating the destruction of certain presidential papers and tapes that Congress reasonably deemed necessary to complete the prosecutions of Watergate-related crimes, id. at 476–77, 479; and (4) the reasonable belief of Congress that appropriate public access to the Nixon materials would be of great value to the nation in coming to terms, both currently and in the future, with a unique episode in its history. Id. at 477–78.

11. Selective Service, 468 U.S. at 853. In Cummings v. Missouri, Justice Field concluded for the Court that depriving a person of the means of his livelihood was certainly punishment: "The deprivation of any rights, civil or political, previously enjoyed, may be punishment, the circumstances attending and the causes of the deprivation determining this fact. Disqualification from office may be punishment, as in cases of conviction upon impeachment. Disqualification from the pursuits of a lawful avocation, or from positions of trust, or from the privilege of appearing in the courts, or acting as an executor, administrator or guardian, may also, and often has been, imposed as punishment." 71 U.S. (4 Wall.) 277, 320 (1866). It is true that the language in Cummings discusses punishment in terms of deprivations of "rights"; but a close reading of the Cummings opinion "discloses that the word 'right' was used by the Court to encompass what other courts have called 'privileges,' and that therefore the case stands for a repudiation of any dichotomy between the two." Note, "The Bounds of Legislative Specification: A Suggested Approach to the Bill of Attainder Clause," 72 Yale L.J. 330, 358 (1962).

Nonetheless, in Flemming v. Nestor, 363 U.S. 603 (1960), the Court rejected bill of attainder attacks—among others—upon a provision of the Social Security Act which terminated old-age benefits to aliens deported for any of several specified reasons. Nestor had immigrated to the United States from Bulgaria in 1913 and became eligible for old age benefits in November 1955. In July 1956 he was deported for having been a member of the Communist Party from 1933 to 1939. Since this was one of the benefit-termination grounds specified in § 202(n) of the Social Security Act, his benefits were terminated soon thereafter. The Court stressed that this "sanction [was] the mere denial of a noncontractual governmental benefit. No affirmative disability or restraint [was] imposed, and certainly nothing approaching the 'infamous punishment' of imprison-

nonpunitive goals"; [12] and it must not have been motivated by a desire

ment." Id. at 617. The Court's adherence to the distinction between rights and privileges was also reflected in American Communications Association v. Douds, where the Court concluded that it was not "free to treat § 9(h) [of the Taft-Hartley Act] as if it merely [withdrew] a privilege gratuitously granted by the Government . . ." 339 U.S. 382, 389–90 (1950).

In the 1960s, however, the right-privilege dichotomy again began to lose its significance in the adjudication of attainder, a downfall that corresponded with the decline of that distinction in constitutional law generally. See generally Van Alstyne, "The Demise of the Right-Privilege Distinction in Constitutional Law," 81 Harv.L. Rev. 1439 (1968); O'Neill, "Unconstitutional Conditions: Welfare Benefits with Strings Attached," 54 Calif.L.Rev. 443 (1966). See §§ 10–8, 10–9, 11–5, infra. By the time of United States v. Brown, 381 U.S. 437 (1965), the Court was ready to reaffirm the principles first articulated almost a century earlier in Cummings v. Missouri. The Court quoted with evident approval the language from Cummings noted earlier, and recalled that "the Bill of Attainder Clause was not to be given a narrow historical reading, . . . but was instead to be read in light of the evil the Framers had sought to bar: *legislative punishment of any form of severity, of specifically designated persons or groups.*" Id. at 447 (emphasis added). Read in its entirety, United States v. Brown both repudiated the right-privilege dichotomy and revitalized the ban against singling out persons for special disability without the safeguards of trial.

Even so, the Supreme Court has not altogether lost interest in the right-privilege dichotomy in this context. In Selective Service System v. Minnesota PIRG, 468 U.S. 841 (1984), where the Court rejected a bill of attainder attack upon the conditioning of federal financial assistance to male students upon their certification that they had duly registered for the draft, the Court quoted the passage in Flemming referring to the "mere denial of a non-contractual governmental benefit." Id. at 853, quoting 363 U.S. at 617. Analogizing to historical precedents of denials of employment, the district court had found that the denial of federal financial aid "deprives students of the practical means to achieve the education necessary to pursue many vocations in our society." Doe v. Selective Service System, 557 F.Supp. 937, 944 (1983). The Supreme Court intimated in a footnote that Goldberg v. Kelly, 397 U.S. 254 (1970), and Mathews v. Eldridge, 424 U.S. 319 (1976), two of the cases standing for the demise of

the right-privilege dichotomy, were distinguishable as due process cases involving special dependence on a benefit, and noted that Flemming itself provided an example of a case in which the benefit at stake was considered to fall under the protection of the due process but not the bill of attainder clause. 468 U.S. at 853 n. 10. But the Court went on to stress that, however the deprivation might be characterized, applicants could avoid it "at any time by registering late and thus 'carry the keys of their prison in their own pockets.' " Id. at 853, quoting Shillitani v. United States, 384 U.S. 364, 368 (1966). Thus the invocation of the right-privilege distinction may have been a makeweight in the Court's bill of attainder analysis.

Justice Powell, concurring, appears to have found the absence of any coercive degree of dependence decisive of the "punishment" issue: "[The statute] provides a benefit at the expense of taxpayers generally for those who request and qualify for it. There is no compulsion to request the benefit." Id. at 860. Concurring in Immigration and Naturalization Service v. Chadha, 462 U.S. 919, 967 n. 9 (1983), Justice Powell had stated more broadly that, "[w]hen Congress grants particular individuals relief or benefits under its spending power, the danger of oppressive action that the separation of powers was designed to avoid is not implicated." In Chadha, however, he took the view that action by all or part of Congress vetoing an administrative suspension of a specific individual's deportation implicated the concerns of the bill of attainder ban. Id. at 963, discussed in § 4–3, supra.

12. Selective Service, 468 U.S. at 854. Even under the expansive view in Brown, legislatively inflicted disabilities will continue to escape the attainder ban unless they contain stigmatizing elements suggesting that they go beyond anything reasonably necessary for valid governmental regulation. When the Court rejected former President Nixon's bill of attainder attack upon the Act of Congress requiring the General Services Administration to take custody of his presidential papers and tape recordings, the majority opinion stressed circumstances showing that the Act rested neither upon a congressional determination of the former President's blameworthiness nor upon a desire to punish him. Nixon v. Administrator of General Services, 433 U.S. 425 (1977). But neither the Brown opinion nor the Nixon opinion adequately explained why a concern with *blameworthiness* as such, or even an inquiry into Congress' aims, should continue to be a prerequisite to classification

to impose punishment.[13]   It seems fairly clear, however, that this is a

as a bill of attainder in a system that views punishment as encompassing deterrence and prevention as well as retribution. In the Nixon opinion, the Court noted that the absence of explicit congressional concern to fix Mr. Nixon's blame or to condemn his conduct "undercuts a major concern that prompted the bill of attainder prohibition: the fear that the legislature, in seeking to pander to an inflamed popular constituency, will find it expedient openly to assume the mantle of judge—or worse still, lynch mob." Id. at 480 & n. 45. Yet Justice Stevens seemed to offer a more realistic assessment when he observed that what Congress did "implicitly condemns [Mr. Nixon] as an unreliable custodian of his papers" and subjects him to "humiliating treatment" not unlike that "typically directed [by bills of attainder] at once powerful leaders of government." Id. at 484, 485 n. 1 (concurring opinion). The danger that such public retaliation against the once-powerful will be politically motivated seems no less serious, and no less relevant to the bill of attainder ban, than the risk that it will be inspired by a desire to punish. Indeed, although the Selective Service System opinion repeated that only *punitive* measures may be classified as bills of attainder, its principal focus in that regard was on the *structure* of Congress' statute rather than on the *motives* of those who voted for it: the Court emphasized that the law at issue permitted anyone to avoid its disabilities by belated draft registration and was in *that* sense purely regulatory rather than penalizing of any particular class. 468 U.S. at 853–55.

13. Selective Service, 468 U.S. at 855. Whether one is dealing with the deprivation of a right or the denial of a privilege, however, the prohibition against bills of attainder has traditionally been thought to apply only when the challenged enactment is in *some* suitable sense classifiable as "punitive" in nature. At one time, the Supreme Court indicated that the legislatively inflicted disability had to be *intended* by the legislature as *retribution* for past acts before the bill of attainder clauses could apply. This doctrine was first expressed in United States v. Lovett, 328 U.S. 303, 308–12 (1946). In his concurring opinion, Justice Frankfurter took the position that an act could not be termed a bill of attainder unless it contained a direct expression of an intent to punish. Id. at 326. The Frankfurter view was accepted by the Court in American Communications Association v. Douds, 339 U.S. 382 (1950). Section 9(h) of the Taft-Hartley Act, which required each officer of a union utilizing the Act's opportunities to file an affidavit stating that he was not a member of the Communist Party, was there sustained against challenges that the provision both infringed freedom of speech and was a prohibited bill of attainder. The attainder attacks on the provision's requirements were rejected because of the Court's conviction that Congress, in passing § 9(h), was concerned only with likely future conduct. 339 U.S. at 413–14. See § 10–4, supra.

Two cases decided by the Supreme Court in 1960 indicate that the Court was still searching for clear signs of punitive intent before striking down a legislative scheme as a bill of attainder. In Flemming v. Nestor, 363 U.S. 603 (1960), supra note 11, Justice Harlan concluded for the Court that "only the clearest proof could suffice to establish the unconstitutionality of a statute on such a ground. Judicial inquiries into Congressional motives are at best a hazardous matter, and when that inquiry seeks to go behind objective manifestations it becomes a dubious affair indeed." Id. at 617. In De Veau v. Braisted, 363 U.S. 144 (1960), decided the same Term as Flemming v. Nestor, the Court appeared much readier to inquire into legislative motive to support its decision upholding § 8 of the New York Waterfront Commission Act of 1953, which disqualified any person who had been convicted of a felony without subsequently being pardoned or having the disability removed by the Board of Parole, from serving in any office in a waterfront labor organization. In determining that § 8 violated neither the ban on bills of attainder nor the prohibition of ex post facto laws, the Court, in an opinion by Justice Frankfurter, asked "whether the legislative aim was to punish the individual for past activity, or whether the restriction of the individual comes about as a relevant incident to a regulation of a present situation," 363 U.S. at 160, and concluded that "[n]o doubt is justified regarding the legislative purpose of § 8. The proof is overwhelming that New York sought not to punish ex-felons, but to devise what was felt to be a much-needed scheme of regulation of the waterfront, and for the effectuation of that scheme it became important whether individuals had previously been convicted of a felony." Id.

In United States v. Brown, however, in the course of invalidating § 504 of the Labor Management Reporting Act, which made it a crime for Communists to hold union office, the Court re-examined both the history of bills of attainder and the purposes of punishment and concluded that "[i]t would be archaic to limit the definition of 'punishment' to 'retribution.' Punishment serves several purposes: retributive, rehabilitative, deterrent—and

mistaken description of the process by which a measure is classified as punitive or otherwise. Even measures historically associated with punishment—such as permanent exclusion from an occupation—have been otherwise regarded when the nonpunitive aims of an apparently prophylactic measure have seemed sufficiently clear and convincing.[14] And, conversely, measures enacted not in order to punish but in order to prevent future harm have been condemned as forbidden bills of attainder when such measures have been thought to rest on a legislative determination that particular persons have shown themselves to be blameworthy or at least culpably unreliable.[15]

In *Selective Service System v. Minnesota Public Interest Research Group*, the Court found nothing punitive in Congress' determination to withhold federal aid from college and graduate school students unwilling to comply with their draft registration obligations. Although there is language in the opinion suggesting that the temporary withholding of a statutory benefit cannot qualify as punishment for bill of attainder purposes absent punitive motive by the legislature at least where a nonpunitive aim is served,[16] it would be a mistake to read those passages apart from the special context in which they appeared. For the Court had already held that the attainder attack on the statute failed the most basic test that all such challenges must meet: the statute did not, as a bill of attainder must, single out or "specify" a fixed class of persons for disadvantageous treatment. Inasmuch as the persons designated remained free to avoid disadvantage by belated compliance with the law, the law avoided the pitfall of specifying a set of persons for some burden they were unable thereafter to avoid.[17] Thus the Court's discussion of the nonpunitive character of the disability was unnecessary to its decision. Moreover, even in that discussion, the Court stressed the ability of any student to avoid the disability simply by registering for the draft—something Congress had undoubted power to require.[18]

preventative. One of the reasons society imprisons those convicted of crimes is to keep them from inflicting future harm, but that does not make imprisonment any the less punishment." 381 U.S. 437, 458 (1965). Given this analysis, no specifically *retributive* intent need be shown before an inflicted disability can be classified as punishment. "Punishment is not limited solely to retribution for past events, but may involve deprivations inflicted to deter future misconduct." Selective Service System v. Minnesota PIRG, 468 U.S. 841, 852 (1984) (dictum), citing United States v. Brown, 381 U.S. at 458–59; see also Nixon v. Administrator of General Services, 433 U.S. 425, 476 n. 40 (1977) (dictum). The Court has nonetheless reiterated its earlier insistence, see Flemming v. Nestor, 363 U.S. at 619, supra note 11, that there be "unmistakable evidence of punitive intent" before an Act of Congress may be invalidated on this basis. Selective Service, 468 U.S. at 855 n. 15. Evidently, then, a forbidden bill of attainder must seek to punish—but need not seek to do so for retributive as opposed to preventative or rehabilitative purposes. The Court in Selective Service found no punitive intent despite "several isolated statements [by congressional sponsors] expressing understandable indignation over the decision of some nonregistrants to show their defiance of the law." Id. at 855 n. 15.

14. See, e.g., Hawker v. New York, 170 U.S. 189 (1898), discussed in § 10–4, note 15, supra, and De Veau v. Braisted, 363 U.S. 144 (1960), discussed in note 13, supra.

15. See, e.g., United States v. Brown, 381 U.S. 437 (1965), discussed in § 10–4, supra.

16. 468 U.S. at 851–56. See also Powell, J., concurring, id. at 859–62.

17. Id. at 847–51. See § 10–4, supra.

18. For example, the Court concluded that "[a] statute that leaves open perpetually the possibility of qualifying for aid does not fall within the historic meaning of

If Congress were to exclude from student aid programs, from public housing, from food stamp benefits, or from some other statutory scheme of privileges, all those who could not affirmatively certify, on pain of perjury, that they had not at any time in the past committed any of several specified criminal offenses, the fact that such exclusion might well serve nonpunitive purposes—as by deterring future violations— and the fact that Congress might have acted without "punishment" in mind but solely with the thought that scarce public resources ought not to be expended on lawbreakers, should not suffice to rebuff a bill of attainder attack on the legislative exclusion. Rather, absent a provision for the individuals named to purge themselves of disability by belated compliance, the exclusion ought to be regarded as an augmentation to the existing scheme of statutory penalties, imposed without the safeguards of criminal trial. That such imposition might also occur without a finding of willfulness or the other usual indicia of criminality, far from *saving* the measure from condemnation as a bill of attainder,[19] should mark it as an even more egregious circumvention of the protections normally afforded accused persons through the process of criminal charge and trial.

§ 10–6. Applying Bill of Attainder Doctrine to Non-legislative Action: Separation of Powers Considerations

As the Supreme Court construed it in *United States v. Brown*, the "command of the Bill of Attainder Clause" is "that a legislature can provide that persons possessing certain characteristics must abstain from certain activities, but must leave to other tribunals the task of deciding who possesses those characteristics . . . ."[1] In this sense, the

forbidden legislative punishment." Id. at 853. Under the functional test, the Court noted that "one of the primary purposes of § 1113 was to encourage those required to register to do so." Id. at 854. And the Court believed that the fact that Congress allowed *all* nonregistrants, willful or not, to qualify for Title IV aid "simply by registering late" evidenced its "nonpunitive spirit." Id. at 855.

The doctrinal separation of the analysis of the ban on bills of attainder into two tests—one for "specification," discussed in § 10–4, and one for "punishment," discussed in this section—should not be allowed to obscure the overlapping concern with the *reasonableness* of the legislature's pursuit of legitimate, nonpunitive aims. Where a fixed, identifiable group—such as ex-convicts—is singled out and a burden— such as denial of some form of employment—is imposed, but there is no indication of a legislative motive to punish and there is a legislative end that is both legitimate and nonpunitive, then the ability of such a law to pass scrutiny under bill of attainder analysis will depend on the reasonableness with which it pursues the ends it serves. Given such reasonableness, it may be plausible to say either that the law

does not entail undue "specification," see the discussion in § 10–4, or that the law does not inflict "punishment," or perhaps both. Indeed, the judgment as to reasonableness may depend largely on the relationship between the nature of the singling out, the nature of the legitimate, nonpunitive end, and the nature of the burden imposed. See § 10–4, note 25, supra.

19. The majority in Selective Service viewed the denial by § 1113 of benefits to "innocent as well as willful" nonregistrants as an indication that the statute was not punitive. 468 U.S. at 855. It is entirely consistent with the presence of a punitive intent, however, that, in a rush to condemn the "guilty" without the procedural safeguards of a trial, some of the "innocent" may be swept into the corral as well. This, of course, is the basic fear underlying the bill of attainder doctrine—that some will be dealt with unjustly. If legislatures could be depended on to condemn only those truly deserving of punishment, there would be far less need for the prohibition on bills of attainder.

§ 10–6

1. 381 U.S. 437, 454 n. 29 (1965).

ban on bills of attainder, and to some degree the more limited ban on ex post facto laws,[2] serves not "as a narrow, technical (and therefore soon to be outmoded) prohibition, but rather as an implementation of the separation of powers, a general safeguard against legislative exercise of the judicial function, or more simply—trial by legislature." [3]

Viewed as an implementation of principles of separation of powers,[4] the ban on bills of attainder is important for several reasons. First, the ban reflects the judgment that "a legislative body, from its number and organization, and from the very intimate dependence of its members upon the people, which renders them liable to be peculiarly susceptible to popular clamor, is not properly constituted to try with coolness, caution, and impartiality a criminal charge, especially in those cases in which the popular feeling is strongly excited—the very class of cases most likely to be prosecuted by this mode." [5] By preventing the legislature, or any body acting in a lawmaking mode, from inflicting injury upon specific persons, the bill of attainder clauses operate to guarantee that the procedural safeguards of a judicial trial, or at least an adversary hearing before an impartial tribunal, will be available to offset the clamor of public opinion.

Second, the prohibition reflects not only the judgment of the Framers that the legislative branch of government presented the greatest potential threat to liberty,[6] but also the further conviction that *no* branch should be empowered unilaterally to inflict a serious hardship on particular individuals or groups.[7] By restricting the legislative process to the formulation of general rules, the bill of attainder clauses work to guarantee an institutional fractionalization of power.

A third concern that links the bill of attainder clauses to notions about separation of powers "is rooted in the desirability of legislative disclosure of its purposes. When one branch may both enact and apply, it may more easily veil its real motive and even its true target. . . . Thus, separating policy making from application has the additional virtue of requiring relatively clear and candid articulation of the legislative purpose. By requiring the legislature to expose its purpose for observation the political processes are given a fuller opportunity to react to it. And the judiciary is better able to judge the validity of the purpose and to assure that it violates no constitutional restrictions." [8]

2. See §§ 10–2, 10–3, *supra.*

3. 381 U.S. at 442.

4. See Chapters 1 and 2, *supra.*

5. 1 T. Cooley, Constitutional Limitations 536–537 (8th ed. 1927).

6. See The Federalist No. 48, at 383–384 (Hamilton ed. 1880) (J. Madison): ". . . [I]n a representative republic, where the executive is carefully limited, both in the extent and the duration of its power; and where the legislative power is exercised by an assembly, which is inspired by a supposed influence over the people, with an intrepid confidence in its own strength; which is sufficiently numerous to feel all the passions which actuate a multitude, yet not so numerous as to be incapable of pursuing the objects of its passions, by means which reason prescribes; it is against the enterprising ambition of this department that the people ought to indulge all their jealousy and exhaust all their precautions."

7. See also Montesquieu, The Spirit of Laws 154 (6th ed. 1792) (translated by Nugent); The Federalist No. 47, at 373–374 (Hamilton ed. 1880) (J. Madison).

8. Note, "The Bounds of Legislative Specification: A Suggested Approach to the Bill of Attainder Clause," 72 Yale L.J. 330, 346–47 (1962). This view of the importance of the institutional separation of

Although the historic core of the bill of attainder ban requires its application to any genuinely *legislative* trial regardless of the procedural safeguards provided, the concerns behind the principle of separation of powers raise the question whether the ban should also be applied, when trial-type safeguards are absent, to punitive measures inflicted by *non*-legislative bodies, whether the people at large or an executive agency supposedly accountable to the people in some way. As Justice Powell noted in *Immigration and Naturalization Service v. Chadha*, although "the traditional characterization of [a] power as legislative, executive, or judicial may provide some guidance . . ., the more helpful inquiry . . . is whether the act in question raises the dangers the Framers sought to avoid" through the separation of powers: "the exercise of unchecked power." [9] Justice Powell treated the bill of attainder clause as a specific application to the legislature of more general separation of powers principles; [10] understood in terms of its purposes, the ban on bills of attainder could be far-reaching indeed.

For example, in *Eastlake v. Forest City Enterprises*, where a divided Supreme Court upheld a city's refusal to grant a zoning variance without approval by a 55% vote in a popular referendum, [11] the enterprise seeking the variance might have done better to argue not that the referendum requirement was an "unconstitutional delegation of legislative power to the people," [12] but that the requirement operated much like a bill of attainder—particularly since it was enacted (1) while the respondent's application "for a zoning change to permit construction of a multifamily, high-rise apartment building" was pending, [13] and (2) in the face of the City Planning Commission's recommendation that the City Council approve the change. [14] To be sure, no "existing rights

government powers suggests that one of the functions of the bill of attainder clauses is to provide protection, through a direct restraint on the process of legislating, for substantive rights, and for politically weak groups, which might be subjected to veiled assaults through legislation. One further way of viewing the ban on bills of attainder is to regard it as a mirror image of the restraints placed on judicial action by Article III. See id. at 347. Just as the institutional incapacity of judicial bodies is usually thought to reach its apex when they try to formulate general rules or policies, so the incapacity of political bodies like legislatures may be at its peak when they seek to decide which specific individuals deserve to be deprived of some opportunity. See Brown, 381 U.S. at 454 n. 29.

9. 462 U.S. 919, 965 n. 7, 967 (1983) (concurring opinion).

10. Id. at 963. Justice Powell opined that, although "independent regulatory agencies and departments of the Executive Branch often exercise authority that is 'judicial in nature,'. . . . [t]his function . . . forms a part of public law and is subject to the procedural safeguards, in-

cluding judicial review, provided by the Administrative Procedure Act." Id. at 967 n. 10, quoting Buckley v. Valeo, 424 U.S. 1, 140–41 (1976). It might be that, at least for Justice Powell, safeguards like those of the Administrative Procedure Act would be constitutionally required in the operation of regulatory agencies and executive departments.

11. 426 U.S. 668 (1976).

12. Id. at 671. The Court, in an opinion by Chief Justice Burger, easily distinguished such prior cases as Washington ex rel. Seattle Title Trust Co. v. Roberge, 278 U.S. 116 (1928), and Eubank v. Richmond, 226 U.S. 137 (1912), as having condemned only delegations of lawmaking power "to a *narrow segment* of the community, not to the people at large." 426 U.S. at 677.

13. 426 U.S. at 670.

14. Id. Strangely, respondent did not appeal the lower court's rejection of the argument "that the charter amendment could not apply to its rezoning application since the application was pending at the time the amendment was adopted." Id. at 671 n. 2. Since the issue was "therefore not before [the Court]," id., the case cannot

[were] being impaired; new use rights [were] being sought from the City Council," [15] and administrative as well as other forms of relief remained available if hardship could be shown.[16] But although such alternative avenues for obtaining the benefit that respondent sought might suffice to meet a conventional due process objection even if a protected right *were* being impaired,[17] it is doubtful that either the character of the variance as a "privilege" or the availability of relief from demonstrated hardship could meet the less familiar but in some ways more basic objection that popular assemblies—and, even more clearly, the populace itself—cannot constitutionally be empowered to dispose of important interests of identified individuals without some "realistic opportunity for the affected person to be heard, even by the electorate." [18] The fact that "the popular vote is not an acceptable method of adjudicating the rights of individual litigants," [19] even if they may have no "legal *right* to the relief [they seek]," [20] should be understood as following not simply from general notions of fairness but from the more specific concerns implicit in the ban on bills of attainder. Just as the fact that Archie Brown had no "legal right" to hold a labor union office properly made no difference in *United States v. Brown*,[21] so it should not have been decisive in *Eastlake* that the respondent had no "right" to a zoning change. And just as *Brown* probably did not turn on the absence of any procedure for "hardship" dispensations,[22] so the presence of such a procedure should not have affected the outcome in *Eastlake*. Since the referendum requirement was upheld only against a delegation challenge,[23] *Eastlake* is not authority for rejecting challenges, based either on the attainder ban or on a due process principle derived therefrom, to processes of decision that bypass normal protective procedures for resolving issues adversely affecting individual interests.[24]

be taken to have rejected the argument in text.

15. 426 U.S. at 679 n. 13.

16. Id.

17. See, e.g., Ingraham v. Wright, 430 U.S. 651 (1977), discussed in § 10–14, infra. But see Moore v. East Cleveland, 431 U.S. 494, 497 n. 5 (1977); id. at 512 (Brennan, J., joined by Marshall, J., dissenting), discussed in §§ 15–17, 15–20, infra.

18. 426 U.S. at 680 (Powell, J., dissenting).

19. Id. at 693 (Stevens, J., joined by Brennan, J., dissenting). See also id. at 680 (Powell, J., dissenting).

20. Id. at 682 (Stevens, J., joined by Brennan, J., dissenting) (emphasis added).

21. 381 U.S. 437 (1965).

22. The Court in Brown did suggest that the inclusion of an "escape clause" in § 32 of the Banking Act, at issue in Board of Governors v. Agnew, 329 U.S. 441 (1947), supports the conclusion that Congress was merely using a convenient shorthand phrase to express a concern with general characteristics rather than with a specific group of individuals. 381 U.S. at 455. It seems highly unlikely, however, that the presence of such a clause, consisting in § 32 of a provision that the prescribed disqualifications should not obtain whenever the Board of Governors determined that there would not be undue influence upon the investment policies of the bank or upon the advice given by the bank to customers, is constitutionally dispositive of the issue whether a given act is a bill of attainder. There was, for example, no further intimation by the Brown Court that a similar provision in § 504, giving the NLRB authority to allow certain Communists to serve as labor union officials when there appeared to be little risk of political strikes, would have been sufficient to convert § 504 into a constitutionally acceptable shorthand phrase.

23. Eastlake, 426 U.S. at 672–77; id. at 677 n. 11.

24. One imaginable limitation on this use of either the attainder ban or the due process requirement would focus on the character of the interest affected. Every

Nor should the ban on bills of attainder be limited to actions taken by the ever-excitable popular will, directly or through representatives. For a core aspect of the separation-of-powers theory accepted by the Supreme Court in *United States v. Brown* [25] was the belief that *no* branch of government should be empowered unilaterally to impose a serious penalty or disability on identified private individuals. The development of powerful administrative agencies was of course not foreseeable in 1787,[26] and the risk that the Executive Branch would engage in rule-making activities at all, much less rule-making aimed at particular persons, probably did not occur to those framing constitutional restraints. As a result, the ban on bills of attainder was probably conceived at first as a limitation upon the legislature alone. Today, however, as executive and administrative agencies play an increasingly significant role in government, the question whether the ban applies to actions of these agencies assumes greater significance.

The Supreme Court has never directly ruled on the applicability of the attainder ban to agency actions. But the facts of *Joint Anti-Fascist Refugee Committee v. McGrath* [27] made a powerful case for the applicability of the ban to actions by the Attorney General. Pursuant to Executive Order No. 9835, the Attorney General had compiled lists of allegedly subversive organizations. The Supreme Court reversed the dismissal of complaints by three organizations challenging their inclusion on the lists. Justice Black's separate concurrence was especially noteworthy: [28] "[I]n my judgment the executive has no constitutional authority, with or without a hearing, officially to prepare and publish the lists challenged by petitioners . . . [O]fficially prepared and proclaimed governmental blacklists possess almost every quality of bills of attainder, the use of which was from the beginning forbidden to both national and state governments. U.S.Const., Art. I, §§ 9, 10. It is true that the classic bill of attainder was a condemnation by the legislature following investigations by that body, . . . while in the present case the Attorney General performed the official tasks. But I cannot believe that the authors of the Constitution, who outlawed the bill of attainder, inadvertently endowed the executive with power to engage in the same tyrannical practices that had made the bill such an odious institution."

Justice Black's argument is bolstered by the concern for institutional fractionalization of power discussed above. Montesquieu, among others, realized that it was important to keep the Judiciary separate from the Executive as well as the Legislature: [29] "Again, there is no

---

enactment thus far held to be a forbidden bill of attainder barred designated individuals or groups from taking part in specified employments or vocations. In Nixon v. Administrator of General Services, 433 U.S. 425 (1977), the former President had been denied only unfettered access to papers and tapes most of which he could not claim to own, and Congress had provided for a future award of just compensation should any of Mr. Nixon's property interests be taken. That neither "property" nor "liberty" to pursue an occupation was involved proved important in the Court's

holding that Mr. Nixon had not been subjected to a forbidden bill of attainder. See §§ 10–4, 10–5, supra.

25. 381 U.S. 437 (1965).

26. See Note, "The Bill of Attainder Clauses and Legislative and Administrative Suppression of 'Subversives,'" 67 Colum.L.Rev. 1490, 1500 (1967).

27. 341 U.S. 123 (1950).

28. Id. at 143.

29. The Spirit of the Laws 154 (6th ed. 1792) (T. Nugent, trans.).

liberty, if the judiciary power be not separated from the legislative and the executive. Were it joined with the legislative, the life and liberty of the subject would be exposed to arbitrary control; for the judge would be then the legislator. Were it joined to the executive power, the judge might behave with violence and oppression."

But there is a more fundamental reason to accept Justice Black's conclusion. Insofar as the ban on bills of attainder is understood "not to prohibit trial by a particular *body* but rather to prohibit trial by legislative *method*, that is, to assure a defendant adequate judicial safeguards regardless of what body tries him," [30] it would make no sense to view the ban as less applicable to executive officers or administrative agencies than to legislative assemblies, or to the people acting in a general referendum. And it would make no sense to view the ban as less applicable to agencies having narrow enforcement responsibilities than to agencies exercising broad rule-making functions.[31]

The generalization that "[l]egislatures cannot properly function like Courts, [while at least some] administrative agencies can," [32] should thus be taken as having no particular force when a legislature indeed undertakes to accord trial-type safeguards to affected persons in accord with constitutionally approved procedures—or conversely, when an administrative agency omits such safeguards. When the House of Representatives sits to consider a bill of impeachment or the Senate to conduct an impeachment trial, for example, the attainder ban has no application—not because Congress loses its character as a legislative assembly on such awesome occasions but because its adversary processes are expressly delineated by a more specific constitutional provision. In contrast, for Congress to "find" a sitting or past President "guilty" in the course of enacting ordinary legislation poses the attainder problem in a powerful form [33]—and, in fact, would still pose that problem even if Congress were to provide trial-type safeguards. So too, when the Attorney General, or any agency or department of government, acts to impose a focused deprivation upon an identifiable individual, its conduct should be subject to scrutiny under attainder principles—to ascertain, in particular, whether it has accorded appropriate trial-type safeguards.

Finally, one apparent difficulty with the separation-of-powers view of the bill of attainder doctrine as applied to non-legislative action should be disposed of explicitly. As Justice White said in his *Brown* dissent, "if Art. I, § 9, cl. 3, immortalizes some notion of the separation of powers at the federal level, then Art. I, § 10 necessarily does the same for the States," a conclusion he thought incompatible with the traditional view that how the states separate or combine their legisla-

---

30. Note, "The Supreme Court, 1964 Term," 79 Harv.L.Rev. 105, 121 (1965) (emphasis added).

31. On the contrary, the desire to prevent the bill of attainder ban from imposing any particular configuration of separated powers, especially upon state and local government, see Brown, 381 U.S. at 462 (White, J., joined by Harlan, Clark, and Stewart, JJ., dissenting), points strongly to a doctrine that treats the ban as barring trial by legislative *method* and not simply trial by legislative *body*.

32. Note, supra note 26, at 1502.

33. See the discussion of Nixon v. Administrator of General Services, 433 U.S. 425 (1977), in §§ 10–4 and 10–5, supra.

tive, judicial, and executive powers is for them to determine.[34] But the cases cited in support of that view, such as *Dreyer v. Illinois*,[35] suggest only that the *particular* pattern of interbranch relationship employed in the federal government need not be copied by each state, not that a state should be any freer than the federal government to inflict deprivations upon identified persons by popular vote, by the sort of log-rolling process that is characteristic of representative assemblies, or indeed by *any* process that circumvents the safeguards of adversary hearing and judicial review.[36]

On the contrary, as early as 1810, Chief Justice Marshall argued that the Framers designed the ban on state bills of attainder as part of a system of institutional protections against the excited actions of popular assemblies: [37] "Whatever respect might have been felt for the state sovereignties, it is not to be disguised that the framers of the Constitution viewed with some apprehension the violent acts which might grow out of the feelings of the moment; and that the people of the United States, in adopting the instrument have manifested a determination to shield themselves and their property from those sudden and strong passions to which men are exposed. The restrictions on the legislative power of the states are obviously founded in this sentiment; and the Constitution of the United States contains what may be deemed a bill of rights for the people of each state."

In accord with this early vision, *Brown* should be read as interpreting the bill of attainder bans not as freezing any particular separation-of-powers configuration into the Constitution, either at the state level or, for that matter, at the federal level, but as requiring that those governmental processes which are not circumscribed by the safeguards

---

34. 381 U.S. at 473.

35. 187 U.S. 71 (1902) (upholding state's Indeterminate Sentencing Act over an attack that it impermissibly delegated judicial power to the executive), cited by Justice White in 381 U.S. at 473.

36. In his dissent in Brown, Justice White cited several cases in addition to Dreyer to support the proposition that the doctrine of separation of powers does not apply to the states. 381 U.S. at 473. Reetz v. Michigan, 188 U.S. 505 (1903), upheld the power of a state to establish a board of registration for doctors and to authorize the board to refuse to certify an applicant if he had not presented sufficient proof that he had been legally registered under a prior act. But it was the board of registration rather than the legislature which performed the individualized fact-finding under the legislative program in Reetz, and adjudication by an administrative agency need not present the same institutional or procedural dangers as adjudication by the legislature itself. Carfer v. Caldwell, 200 U.S. 293 (1906), also provides no substantial support for the position of

Justice White in Brown, for Carfer held only that claiming a state legislative investigation to be beyond the legislature's jurisdiction as established in the state constitution did not present a federal question. Finally, in Sweezy v. New Hampshire, 354 U.S. 234 (1957), while the Court did say in dictum that "the concept of separation of powers embodied in the United States Constitution is not mandatory in state governments," id. at 255, the Sweezy Court held that a conviction for contempt of the legislature visited upon petitioner for refusing to answer certain questions in an investigation conducted by the state attorney general violated the due process clause of the fourteenth amendment since there was no evidence that the legislature actually desired the information inquired about and since the petitioner's constitutional rights were jeopardized by the investigation. There is thus no real support in the cases for the proposition that a state legislature can assume fully judicial powers.

37. Fletcher v. Peck, 10 U.S. (6 Cranch.) 87, 137–38 (1810).

of adversary trial limit themselves—if they are to mete out penalties—to the promulgation of general rules.[38]

It should be stressed that the principle elaborated here is not equivalent to any mechanical ban on legislative, administrative, or other nonadjudicative actions having adverse impacts on identifiable persons or institutions; rather, it is a principle that puts government to a choice of *either* avoiding such action *or* devising procedurally fair ways for adversely affected persons to participate directly in the decision-making process.[39] And it bears repeating that the initial choice in any given case is for government to make; government must decide how *prospective* and how *general* to make its actions. To the extent that they are *retrospective*, however, they may neither frustrate justified reliance without good reason nor inflict condemnation without clearly promulgated prior authority; and to the extent that they *focus on specific persons*, they may not be effected without safeguards closely akin to those of judicial trial. What this will mean as a practical matter is *not* that executives and administrators, like legislatures or the people acting through referenda, should be expected to formulate only general policies and to avoid actions having determinate adverse impacts upon the lives or liberties of particular persons; what it will mean is that the case for procedurally fair participation by such persons should be understood to rest not only on the general norms of fairness derived from the due process clauses—norms taken up in the remaining sections of this Chapter—but also on the more precise concerns of the ex post facto and bill of attainder clauses—concerns we have canvassed in §§ 10–1 through 10–6.

§ 10–7. Procedural Due Process: Intrinsic and Instrumental Aspects

The fifth amendment commands the federal government: "No person shall . . . be deprived of life, liberty, or property, without due process of law. . . ." The fourteenth amendment similarly binds the states: "nor shall any State deprive any person of life, liberty, or

---

38. To be sure, "Congress may pass legislation affecting specific persons in the form of private bills. It may also punish persons who commit contempt before it." 381 U.S. at 473 (White, J., dissenting). But these practices should be regarded either as highly specialized exceptions for purely beneficial as opposed to burdensome measures, or as subject to procedural safeguards, and not as derogations of the truly fundamental principle that trial by logrolling or by popular vote must be forbidden.

39. Thus, although the "Constitution does not require all public acts to be done in town meeting or an assembly of the whole," Bi-Metallic Investment Co. v. State Board of Equalization, 239 U.S. 441, 445 (1915); accord, O'Bannon v. Town Court Nursing Center, 447 U.S. 773 (1980); id. at 799–800 (Blackmun, J., concurring), dis-

cussed in §§ 10–7 and 10–19, infra, and Ch. 17, infra, it does not follow that specific persons adversely affected in determinate ways by a "public act" may be completely excluded from individualized interchange with the decisionmaker and relegated to generic exercise of the right of citizens generally, see Chs. 12 & 13, to speech, petition, and voting. That the number of such persons in a given case may be large should bear on the *sort* of process that is devised, cf. Stewart, "The Development of Administrative and Quasi-Constitutional Law in Judicial Review of Environmental Decisionmaking: Lessons From the Clean Air Act," 62 Iowa L.Rev. 713, 731–33 (1977) (on "paper hearing" procedures), but not on the question whether *some* process of personalized participation is constitutionally mandated. See generally §§ 10–7 to 10–19, infra.

property, without due process of law. . . . ." These procedural safeguards have their historical origins in the notion that conditions of personal freedom can be preserved only when there is some institutional check on arbitrary government action.[1] The Supreme Court has analogized due process to the Magna Carta's "guaranties against the oppressions and usurpations"[2] of the royal prerogative, in support of the basic conclusion that due process "is a restraint on the legislative as well as on the executive and judicial powers of the government, and cannot be so construed as to leave congress [or the states] free to make any process 'due process of law,' by its mere will."[3]

The element of due process analysis characterized as "procedural due process" delineates the constitutional limits on judicial, executive, and administrative *enforcement* of legislative or other governmental dictates or decisions.[4] This has traditionally involved the elaboration of procedural safeguards designed to accord to the individual "the right to be heard before being condemned to suffer grievous loss of any kind"[5] as a result of governmental choices—which can take the form of acts or, less commonly, of omissions.

However, governmental omissions that cause loss of life, liberty, or property, but are not the result of *intentional* governmental choices or policies, do not necessarily entail "*deprivations*" without due process. In both *Daniels v. Williams*[6] and *Davidson v. Cannon*,[7] Justice Rehn-

---

§ 10–7

1. See generally, Kadish, "Methodology and Criteria in Due Process Adjudication—A Survey and Criticism," 66 Yale L.J. 319, 340 (1957) (limitations required "even in the area of legitimate governmental concern").

2. Hurtado v. California, 110 U.S. 516, 531 (1884).

3. Murray's Lessee v. Hoboken Land & Improvement Co., 59 U.S. (18 How.) 272, 276 (1855). See also Twining v. New Jersey, 211 U.S. 78, 106 (1908) (due process clause prohibits procedures which abridge any "fundamental principle of liberty and justice which inheres in the very idea of free government and is the inalienable right of a citizen of such government"). Cf. Linde, "Due Process of Lawmaking," 55 Neb.L.Rev. 197 (1976).

4. The analysis of constitutional limits on the *content* of legislative action, known as substantive due process, is discussed in Chapter 8, supra, and in Chapters 11–15, infra. And constitutional limits on the *form* of such action, or structural due process, are considered in Chapter 17, infra.

5. Joint Anti-Fascist Refugee Committee v. McGrath, 341 U.S. 123, 168 (1951) (Frankfurter, J., concurring). See also Wolff v. McDonnell, 418 U.S. 539, 557–58 (1974) (some kind of hearing is required); Grannis v. Ordean, 234 U.S. 385, 394 (1914) ("The fundamental requisite of due process of law is the opportunity to be heard");

McVeigh v. United States, 78 U.S. (11 Wall.) 259, 267 (1870) (right to notice and hearing).

6. 106 S.Ct. 662 (1986) (no "deprivation", and thus no cause of action for damages under 42 U.S.C. § 1983, where deputy sheriff negligently left a pillow on a flight of prison stairs, causing injury to a prisoner who slipped and fell on the pillow). Chief Justice Burger and Justices Brennan, White, Powell, and O'Connor joined Justice Rehnquist's opinion for the Court. Justice Marshall concurred in the judgment. Justice Blackmun concurred in the judgment, referring to his dissent in Davidson v. Cannon, 106 S.Ct. 668, 671 (1986). Justice Stevens filed a separate opinion concurring in both judgments.

7. 106 S.Ct. 668 (1986) (no "deprivation," and thus no cause of action for damages under 42 U.S.C. § 1983, where prison officials negligently failed to take action to protect a prisoner who had warned those officials of imminent danger to his life and physical safety). Chief Justice Burger and Justices White, Powell, and O'Connor joined Justice Rehnquist's opinion for the Court. Justice Stevens concurred in the judgment. Justices Brennan, Marshall, and Blackmun dissented.

In his dissent in Davidson, joined by Justice Marshall, Justice Blackmun made a powerful argument that this case should have been distinguished from Daniels. Incarcerating someone in prison does not in-

quist stated for the majority that due process functions only to curb governmental abuse, unfairness, or oppression, not to compensate for injury caused by unintentional official behavior. Accordingly, it is immaterial whether or not the state provides any post-deprivation remedy, by way of a tort suit or otherwise, for such injuries.[8] "Not only does the word 'deprive' in the Due Process Clause connote more than a negligent act, but we should not 'open the federal courts to lawsuits where there has been no affirmative abuse of power.' . . . Far from an abuse of power, lack of due care suggests no more than a failure to measure up to the conduct of a reasonable person. To hold that injury caused by such conduct is a deprivation within the meaning of the Fourteenth Amendment would trivialize the centuries-old principle of due process of law."[9] Mere negligence of an official, then, does not implicate a due process violation.[10]

The extent to which one may require officials to submit to judicial or quasi-judicial review[11] of choices which disadvantage the individu-

volve depriving him of the ability to be careful going down stairs, but it does involve stripping him of the means of self-protection: "[T]he state prevented Davidson from defending himself, and therefore assumed some responsibility to protect him from the dangers to which he was exposed." Davidson, 106 S.Ct. at 671 (Blackmun, J., dissenting). In contrast to Daniels, the injury here was "peculiarly related to the government function." Id. at 674. Cf. Boddie v. Connecticut, 401 U.S. 371, 380–81 (1971) (Connecticut's requirement that a dissolution of marriage occur only through resort to its judicial system made the conditioning of such recourse on the ability to pay court fees and costs an unconstitutional denial of due process).

8. In Daniels, the negligent deputy sheriff maintained that he was "entitled to the defense of sovereign immunity in a state tort suit," 106 S.Ct. at 663, leaving the prisoner with no state remedy. In Davidson, state law expressly provided that no public entity or employer is liable for any injury caused by a prisoner to a fellow prisoner. 106 S.Ct. at 670. Concurring in both judgments, Justice Stevens expressed the view that *both* prisoners suffered "deprivations" of liberty—"a deprivation may be the consequence of a mistake or a negligent act," 106 S.Ct. at 678—but concluded that neither prisoner alleged a constitutional inadequacy in the state's "procedural response," id. at 679, inasmuch as the circuit court had rejected Daniels' assertion that sovereign immunity would have defeated his state law claim against the deputy sheriff who left the pillow on the prison stairs, id. at 680, and inasmuch as no fundamental unfairness necessarily inheres in a state policy of not exposing the public or its agents to finan-

cial liability for prisoner-inflicted injuries such as the one Davidson sustained. Id. at 680–81. For Justice Stevens, it seems that the only colorable claim of basic unfairness was one Davidson did not make: that the state's sovereign immunity statute would not have applied if the same prisoner had assaulted a *non*-prisoner. Id. at 681.

9. Daniels, 106 S.Ct. at 664–65 (quoting Parratt v. Taylor, 451 U.S. 527, 548–49 (1981)).

10. Although the Court in 1986 reserved the question of whether official recklessness or gross negligence may result in a deprivation without due process, see Daniels, 106 S.Ct. at 667 n.3, the degree of culpability and abuse suggested by this heightened level of irresponsibility ought to suffice to satisfy the Court's view of a deprivation—especially since a finding of a deprivation in such cases would not "make of the Fourteenth Amendment a font of tort law to be superimposed upon whatever systems may already be administered by the states." Id. at 666, quoting Paul v. Davis, 424 U.S. 693, 701 (1976). See also Whitley v. Albers, 475 U.S. 312 (1986) (shooting of prisoner during quelling of riot, without prior warning, does not violate either eighth amendment ban on cruel and unusual punishment or substantive due process unless there is unnecessary and wanton infliction of pain; question of whether procedural due process is implicated in light of recklessness or gross negligence of prison officials was not presented by the prisoner).

11. The theory of due process as a guarantee of meaningful access to *judicial* protection is noted in § 10–18, infra, but is canvassed more fully in Chapter 16.

al [12] depends upon the range of personal interests qualifying as protected "life," "liberty," and "property," and upon the sort of hearing which will adequately protect these interests when threatened by governmental acts or omissions. These considerations are in turn shaped by alternative conceptions of the primary purpose of procedural due process and by competing visions of how that purpose might best be achieved.

One approach begins with the proposition that there is *intrinsic* value in the due process right to be heard, since it grants to the individuals or groups against whom government decisions operate the chance to participate in the processes by which those decisions are made, an opportunity that expresses their dignity as persons.[13] From this perspective, the hearing may be considered both as a "mode of politics," [14] and as an expression of the rule of law, regarded here as the antithesis of power wielded without accountability to those on whom it focuses. Whatever its outcome, such a hearing represents a valued human interaction in which the affected person experiences at least the satisfaction of participating in the decision that vitally concerns her, and perhaps the separate satisfaction of receiving an explanation of why the decision is being made in a certain way. Both the right to be heard from, and the right to be told why, are analytically distinct from the right to secure a different outcome; these rights to interchange express the elementary idea that to be a *person*, rather than a *thing*, is at least to be *consulted* about what is done with one. Justice Frankfurter captured part of this sense of procedural justice when he wrote that the "validity and moral authority of a conclusion largely depend on the mode by which it was reached. . . . No better instrument has been devised for arriving at truth than to give a person in jeopardy of serious loss notice of the case against him and opportunity to meet it. Nor has a better way been found for generating the feeling, so important to a popular government, that justice has been done." [15] At stake here is not just the much-acclaimed *appearance* of justice but, from a perspective that treats process as intrinsically significant, the very *essence* of justice.[16]

A second, more *instrumental* approach views the requirements of due process as constitutionally identified and valued less for their intrinsic character than for their anticipated consequences as means of assuring that the society's agreed-upon rules of conduct, and its rules

12. See generally Michelman, "The Supreme Court and Litigation Access Fees: The Right to Protect One's Rights—Part II," 1974 Duke L.J. 527, 543, 552.

13. See, e.g., Goldberg v. Kelly, 397 U.S. 254, 264–65 (1970) (right of the poor to participate in public processes). See also Michelman, "Formal and Associational Aims in Procedural Due Process," XVIII Nomos 126–71 (1977) (due process vindicates values of "participation" and "revelation"); Saphire, "Specifying Due Process Values: Toward a More Responsive Approach to Procedural Protection," 127 U.Pa.L.Rev. 111, 117–25 (1978) (due process

standard should measure whether conduct in question comports with basic notions of fairness and dignity).

14. See generally Michelman, "The Supreme Court and Litigation Access Fees: The Right to Protect One's Rights—Part I," 1973 Duke L.J. 1153, 1175.

15. Joint Anti-Fascist Refugee Committee v. McGrath, 341 U.S. 123, 171–172 (1951) (Frankfurter, J., concurring).

16. See, e.g., Marshall v. Jerrico, Inc., 446 U.S. 238 (1980) (emphasizing not only the appearance but the reality of fairness).

for distributing various benefits, are in fact accurately and consistently followed. Rather than *expressing* the rule of law, procedural due process in this sense *implements* law's rules—whatever they might be. From this "instrumental" perspective, due process is such process as may be required to minimize "substantially unfair or mistaken deprivations" [17] of the entitlements conferred by law upon private individuals or groups.[18] It ensures that a challenged action accurately reflects the substantive rules applicable to such action; its point is less to assure *participation* than to *use* participation to assure *accuracy*.

On either view—the intrinsic or the instrumental—the case for due process protection grows stronger as the identity of the persons affected by a governmental choice becomes clearer; and the case becomes stronger still as the precise nature of the effect on each individual comes more determinately within the decisionmaker's purview. For when government acts in a way that singles out identifiable individuals—in a way that is likely to be premised on suppositions about specific persons—it activates the special concern about being personally *talked to* about the decision rather than simply being *dealt with*. Moreover, the danger of action motivated by personal animus or by some other substantively impermissible factor is heightened whenever a specific individual is targeted, highlighting the need for procedures to ensure that the government's act fits within the framework of applicable law.[19]

This view was endorsed by Justice Blackmun in his lucid and probing concurrence in *O'Bannon v. Town Court Nursing Center*,[20] a case involving the unwilling transfer of elderly patients from a nursing home facility decertified by the Department of Health, Education and Welfare as a facility eligible to receive Medicare and Medicaid payments. The Court held that the patients have no "interest in receiving benefits for care in a particular facility that entitles them . . . to a hearing before the Government can decertify that facility." [21] After finding no applicable entitlement, the Court went on to observe that a facility's "decertification . . . is not the same for purposes of due

---

17. Fuentes v. Shevin, 407 U.S. 67, 97 (1972).

18. See, e.g., Boddie v. Connecticut, 401 U.S. 371, 374 (1971): "Perhaps no characteristic of an organized and cohesive society is more fundamental than its erection and enforcement of a system of rules defining the various rights and duties of its members, enabling them to govern their affairs and definitively settle their differences in an orderly, predictable manner."

19. Hearings are necessary partly because "suspicion that certain others cannot count upon effective juridical access can hardly help biasing the shape of transactions, relationships, and attitudes that arise between" government and the individual. Moreover, the "legislature, when it considers what general rules or entitlements should prevail in some sector of human affairs, tends to proceed on the

comforting assumption that the courts, fully armed not only with whatever rule or entitlement the legislature may promulgate but also with the tradition and principle of common law and equity, are there if needed to prevent unanticipated injustice." Michelman, supra note 12, at 537.

20. 447 U.S. 773, 790 (1980) (Blackmun, J., concurring in the judgment). Justice Stevens wrote for the Court, joined by Chief Justice Burger and by Justices Stewart, White, Powell, and Rehnquist. Justice Marshall took no part. Only Justice Brennan dissented.

21. Id. at 784. The Court reasoned that the relevant Medicaid provisions confer only a right to stay in *qualified* facilities, not a right that the facilities of the patient's choice remain properly certified *as* qualified. Id. at 785.

process analysis as a decision to transfer a particular patient or to deny him financial benefits, based on his individual needs or financial situation." [22] The Court noted, significantly, that the government was acting "for the benefit of the patients as a whole and the home itself ha[d] a strong financial incentive to contest" the decertification.[23]

It was this observation that Justice Blackmun deemed crucial. Regarding the majority opinion as not explaining *why* decertification and transfer are relevantly different,[24] Justice Blackmun set forth his analysis—one that courts would do well to emulate—in two parts: first, the patients claimed that they had been deprived of a property interest; second, they claimed that they had been deprived of life and liberty interests. To assess the property claim, Justice Blackmun applied a four-part analysis to determine "whether the litigant holds such a legitimate 'claim of entitlement' that the Constitution, rather than the political branches, must define the procedures attending its removal." [25] First, he applied a "representational test" and found that the nursing facility, which was "intimately involved" in the "process of deciding the disqualification question," "had the opportunity and incentive to make the very arguments the patients might make" and thus that the patients' "due process interest in accurate and informed decisionmaking . . ., in large measure, was satisfied." [26] Second, he asked whether the case implicated the conceded governmental power to abolish the program or source from which an individual receives benefits—and concluded that, because "the property of a recipient of public benefits must be limited, as a general rule, by the governmental power to remove, through prescribed procedures, the underlying source of those benefits," the government could act to decertify "Town Court . . . [as] the underlying *source* of the benefit[s] [the patients] seek to retain," by allowing *it* rather than *them* to be heard.[27] Third, he adopted the view stated above that, as individuals are more specifically singled out from a more general group, due process rights become more significant.[28] Accordingly, he also endorsed the converse proposition that less procedural protection should accrue as a uniformly affected group grows in size.[29] Thus, individuals who suffer "deprivation . . . in a nondiscriminatory fashion" only as part of a larger group, such as the 180 or so elderly nursing home residents in *O'Bannon*, may lose procedural protections that they might have retained had they been dealt with on an individual basis.[30] Fourth, and finally, he stressed that the "patients' interest has [not] been jeopardized . . . because of alleged shortcomings on their [own] part," reasoning that neither the value of

---

22. Id. at 786.

23. Id. at 790 n. 22.

24. Id. at 793 (Blackmun, J., concurring in the judgment).

25. Id. at 796.

26. Id. at 797.

27. Id. at 798 (emphasis added).

28. Id. at 800–01 (quoting part of the preceding page from the first edition of this treatise).

29. Id. at 799–801.

30. Id. at 799–800 ("When governmental action affects more than a few individuals, concerns beyond economy, efficiency, and expedition tip the balance against finding that due process attaches. We may expect that as the sweep of governmental action broadens, so too does the power of the affected group to protect its interests outside rigid constitutionally imposed procedures").

heightened accuracy nor the virtue of respecting personal dignity were significantly compromised by denying hearings to the patients individually where, as in *O'Bannon*, only a *generic* determination was being made: "It may be that patients' [personal] participation in the decertification decision would vaguely heighten their and others' sense of the decision's legitimacy, even though the decision follows extensive government inspections undertaken with the very object of protecting the patients' interests. . . . [but] that interest is far less discernible in this context than when a stigmatizing determination of wrongdoing or fault supplements removal of a presently enjoyed benefit." [31]

The second phase of Justice Blackmun's sensitive two-part examination involved the determination of whether the patients' life and liberty interests were implicated. He reasoned that a constitutionally protected liberty interest may arise where government action entails a serious likelihood of added stigma or of harmful treatment, particularly where a high risk of death or of grave illness is created.[32] Quite properly, he was not "soothed by the palliative that this harm is 'indirect'," concluding instead that "where such drastic consequences attend governmental action, their foreseeability, at least generally, must suffice to require input by those who must endure them." [33] In this case, however, Justice Blackmun was unpersuaded that there existed a "substantial . . . danger" of serious "transfer trauma". [34]

Although the two perspectives, intrinsic and instrumental, both point to a strengthened case for dialogue with the affected person as the specificity of the government action increases, the perspectives may nonetheless have different consequences for the sorts of interests to be encompassed within the protected categories of life, liberty, and property, and for the procedural safeguards that the involvement of such interests triggers. If the intrinsic justification for procedural due process—with its emphasis on promoting dialogue between citizen and government—had played a large role in shaping doctrinal development, courts would, for the most part, have adopted constitutional formulas permitting the widest possible assurance of independently valued procedural rights and would presumably have specified certain procedures as valued for their own sake—although it is the *intrinsic* view, ironically, that better illuminates the Court's recently narrowed definition of "deprivation" and therefore the scope of the due process clause.[35]

31. Id. at 801–02.

32. Id. at 803.

33. Id.

34. Id. at 804. *O'Bannon* is discussed further in § 10–19, infra, and in Chapter 17, infra.

35. See Daniels v. Williams, 106 S.Ct. 662, 665 (1986); Davidson v. Cannon, 106 S.Ct. 668, 670 (1986). Justice Rehnquist, somewhat uncharacteristically, focused in both opinions on the *intrinsic* objective of promoting fairness and preventing abuse and oppression in governmental decision-making, rather than the *instrumental* goal of reducing error and conserving govern-

ment resources—although, in this instance, to narrow rather than expand procedural protections for individual interests. For Justice Stevens, the redefinition of the term "deprivation" was unnecessary and misguided: " 'Deprivation' . . . identifies, not the actor's state of mind, but the victim's infringement or loss. The harm to a prisoner is the same whether a pillow is left on a stair negligently, recklessly, or intentionally; so too, the harm resulting from an attack is the same whether his request for protection is ignored negligently, recklessly, or deliberately. In each instance, the prisoner is losing—being 'deprived' of—an aspect of liberty as the

Such an intrinsic perspective might have been perceived as leading courts to protect a wider range of interests than those specified or fairly derivable from the Bill of Rights, federal or state statutes, or those recognized at common law,[36] and to construct procedures for hearings with no very firm foundation in the Constitution's text; thus the intrinsic perspective would predictably have been criticized as involving judges in overly political matters, turning unduly upon the subjective preferences of the particular judicial decisionmaker.[37] Alexander Bickel [38] and others [39] have downplayed the ability of courts to establish sound "neutral principles" to define and enforce constitutional rights and liberties; the suggestion is routinely made that the proper role of courts in the American polity is to protect those personal rights explicitly granted in the Constitution [40] and, beyond this, to invalidate only wholly irrational actions, leaving the pluralistic political process to define and protect other "fundamental values".[41]

The premises of this line of argument have of course been challenged.[42] Among other things, it is doubtful that those most likely to be dealt with in ways that disregard the intrinsic values of dialogue have sufficient access to the political branches to justify a presumption of their consent to the majority's specification of protected interests or values. Moreover, it is entirely consistent with democratic theory—and is at all events consistent with the text and structure of our only partly "democratic" Constitution—for the majority to bind itself to a general *concept* of due process, open to judicial elaboration in accord with changing views of fundamental fairness, rather than to endorse a specific *conception* of due process.[43] Indeed, given the continual change in societal needs and relationships over time, it has been argued that only such an interpretation would be consistent with a "living" Consti-

result, in part, of a form of state action." Id. at 680 (Stevens, J., concurring in the judgments in Daniels v. Williams and Davidson v. Cannon). However, the state of mind of the official actor is of significance from the *intrinsic* viewpoint: even a dog recognizes the difference between being *kicked* and being *tripped over.* Although Justice Stevens may have denigrated such a distinction, it is the goal of individual participation in governmental decisionmaking, and the curb on governmental abuse rather than mere official accident, that illuminates the intrinsic value of procedural due process. Political and personal meaning accrue through interaction and explanation in an intentional government act that do not occur through, and perhaps make no sense in the context of, an unintentional official accident.

36. See, e.g., Memphis Community School Dist. v. Stachura, 106 S.Ct. 2537 (1986) (refusing to permit the recovery of damages under 42 U.S.C. § 1983 for the abstract "value" or "importance" of procedural due process denied by government action).

37. See, e.g., Adamson v. California, 332 U.S. 46, 89 (1947) (Black, J., dissenting).

38. See A. Bickel, The Supreme Court and the Idea of Progress 11–42 (1970).

39. See, e.g., Frank, "What Courts Do In Fact," 26 Ill.L.Rev. 645 (1932); Llewellyn, "A Realist Jurisprudence—The Next Step," 30 Col.L.Rev. 431 (1930); W. Rumble, American Legal Realism: Skepticism, Reform, and the Judicial Process (1968).

40. See, e.g., Rochin v. California, 342 U.S. 165, 176 (1952) (Black, J., concurring).

41. See, e.g., A. Bickel, supra note 38, at 35–39.

42. See generally R. Dworkin, Law's Empire (1986); Linde, "Judges, Critics and the Realist Tradition," 82 Yale L.J. 227 (1972); Wright, J., "Professor Bickel, the Scholarly Tradition, and the Supreme Court," 84 Harv.L.Rev. 769 (1971). See §§ 1–8, 3–6, supra.

43. See R. Dworkin, Taking Rights Seriously 131–49 (1977).

tution.[44] Finally, there is little reason to suppose that the leaps of faith and exercises of judgment required of courts under the instrumental approach to due process are any less political, or subjective, than those demanded by the intrinsic approach. After all, a due process right that "the rules" (whatever they are) be followed accurately—the right identified from an instrumental viewpoint—can move off dead center only if "the rules" that present themselves for this form of enforcement are understood to exclude the rules of procedure that government has chosen to follow in resolving particular cases. For otherwise whatever process government grants is, by definition, the process that is "due." But to exclude procedural rules from the corpus of law that procedural due process instrumentally secures is to draw the same problematic, and ultimately "political," lines to which the judicial passivist, who resisted the intrinsic view of procedural due process, objected in the first place.[45]

The Court, while nonetheless pursuing an almost exclusively instrumental vision in its due process jurisprudence, has at times acknowledged, that procedural due process is of *intrinsic* significance, alluding to considerations weighing in favor of giving an individual procedural protections well beyond those that might be justified solely by the need to make an accurate determination.[46] In *Carey v. Piphus*,[47] for example, the Court ruled that a student's distress at being denied the process due him in his suspension from school was *itself* compensable by nominal damages under 42 U.S.C. § 1983, indicating at least some appreciation for the intrinsic approach.[48] Compensable distress at the wrongful denial of process, however, cannot be *presumed*, the Court said, since "[w]here the deprivation of a protected interest is substantively justified but procedures are deficient in some respect, there may well be those who suffer no distress [at all] over the procedural irregularities."[49] But even if actual distress is not shown, and even if it is ultimately determined that the suspensions were substantively justified, a student denied procedural due process in the

---

44. See Tribe, "Structural Due Process," 10 Harv.Civ.Rts.-Civ.Lib.L.Rev. 269, 290–98 (1975).

45. See §§ 10–12 to 10–14, infra.

46. In Regents of the University of California v. Bakke, 438 U.S. 265 (1978), the Court struck down a numerical set-aside for disadvantaged minority applicants to a state medical school, but permitted minority status to be used as one of many factors in admitting students. Writing only for himself but delivering the Court's judgment, Justice Powell seemed to express not only an aversion to such decisions made on an overtly racial basis but also *an aversion to mass process as such*, perhaps indicating recognition of an individual right to be treated by the government as a unique being, not a fungible object. For him, "in a broader sense, an underlying assumption of the rule of law is the worthiness of a system of justice based on fairness to the

individual." Id. at 319 n. 53. Justices Brennan, White, Marshall, and Blackmun, although disagreeing with Justice Powell on the issue of whether setting aside a number of places for qualified minorities denied the white applicant individualized treatment, did not directly dispute his conclusion that the fourteenth amendment mandates individualized consideration as an aspect of fair treatment. Id. at 378–79 (Brennan, White, Marshall, & Blackmun, JJ., concurring in the judgment in part and dissenting in part). See L. Tribe, Constitutional Choices 223–28 (1985).

47. 435 U.S. 247 (1978).

48. The Court would not permit, however, the recovery of damages for the value of time missed in school, since the student might have been suspended even if due process had been observed. Id. at 252, 260.

49. Id. at 263.

manner of his or her suspension remains entitled to nominal non-punitive damages for deprivation of a constitutional right.[50]

The Court's insistence that, absent some proof of actual distress, a procedural violation alone cannot warrant an award of more than nominal damages [51]—coupled with the Court's statement that violations of free speech, voting, and other constitutional rights may in themselves warrant substantial compensation [52]—suggests that the Court's recognition of the intrinsic value of process is limited if not begrudging.[53]

Nonetheless, while the intrinsic value of due process continues not to bear on the decision of whether or not process is *due*, and does not provide for *substantial* damages when due process is denied, *Carey v. Piphus* at least attributed *nominal* significance to the intrinsic dimension of due process in deciding upon relief. The decision thus paved the way for giving this dimension greater importance in the future. For example, in *Marshall v. Jerrico, Inc.*,[54] Justice Marshall cited *Carey v. Piphus* in writing for the majority that there are "two central concerns of procedural due process, the prevention of unjustified or mistaken deprivations and the promotion of participation and dialogue by affected individuals in the decisionmaking process." [55] The Court further held that both "the appearance and reality of fairness" were involved in preserving the feeling that "no person will be deprived of his

---

50. Id. at 266–67. While recognizing that substantial damage awards have been allowed by some common-law courts for deprivation of rights, such as voting rights, without showing of actual injury, id. at 264–65 n. 22, the Court concluded without elaboration that "the elements and prerequisites for recovery . . . appropriate to . . . deprivation of one constitutional right are not necessarily appropriate to . . . another." Id. at 264–65.

51. Id. at 264 ("[A]lthough mental and emotional distress caused by the denial of procedural due process itself is compensable under § 1983, we hold that neither the likelihood of such injury nor the difficulty of proving it is so great as to justify awarding compensatory damages without proof that such injury actually was caused"). See also Memphis Community School District v. Stachura, 106 S.Ct. 2537, 2544 n. 11 (1986) ("nominal damages, and not damages based on some undefinable 'value' of infringed rights are the appropriate means of 'vindicating' rights whose deprivation has not caused actual, provable injury").

52. See Carey, 435 U.S. at 264–65 & n. 22; Memphis Community School, 106 S.Ct. at 2547 (Marshall, J., concurring).

53. In Memphis Community School, a teacher was suspended without any hearing based on unsupported accusations that he had shown sexually explicit films to his students. He brought suit under 42 U.S.C. § 1983, claiming damages for denial of due

process. Justice Powell, who had also written the majority opinion in Carey, approved of compensatory and punitive damages in the teacher's case, but refused to grant substantial damages for the abstract "value" or "importance" of the constitutional rights violated. Id. at 2544–45.

Justice Marshall, joined by Justices Brennan, Blackmun, and Stevens, concurred with the majority "that substantial damages should not be awarded where a plaintiff has been denied procedural due process but has made no further showing of compensable damage." Id. at 2547. But they wrote separately "to emphasize that the violation of a constitutional right, in proper cases, may itself constitute a compensable injury," id., where damages are "reasonably quantifiable" and not based solely on the "inherent value" of the right violated. Id. The concurring justices seem to imply a greater appreciation for the intrinsic value of certain substantive rights than they are willing to accord to procedural due process alone.

54. 446 U.S. 238 (1980) (challenging practices of the Department of Labor's Employment Standards Administration on grounds that the administrator who heard a case might be unfairly biased against the party charged with violating the child labor laws).

55. Id. at 242 (citing Carey v. Piphus, 435 U.S. 247, 259–262, 266–67 (1978)).

interests in the absence of a proceeding in which he may present his case with assurance that the arbiter is not predisposed against him." [56] The value of process, then, is at least to assure that the individual's right to be heard provides meaningful and satisfying participation in the decision that affects her—regardless of the outcome.

Despite the fact that the Court went on in *Marshall v. Jerrico* to find that the individuals involved had received the process that they were due, its language furnished precedent for at least a limited recognition that more than accurate factfinding makes procedural regularity vital in the constitutional scheme.

By persisting, despite this recognition, in centering its more customary mode of analysis around the instrumental importance of process,[57] the Court has relaxed procedural protections in two important ways. First, by focusing on the reduction of error to the exclusion of more intrinsic concerns,[58] the Court has eroded at least part of the traditional rationale for insisting that, with very few exceptions,[59] the hearing required by due process *precede* rather than *follow* the deprivation at issue. A *prior* hearing had been required by the traditional conception of procedural due process under the precept that one should be able to continue living in quiet enjoyment of liberty or property unless and until there has been a fair determination that the state is entitled to intrude upon that situation of repose. But, as the more recent conception that the predominant value of process is accuracy has become ascendant, a *post*-deprivation remedy has more often sufficed to meet due process objections. Such an after-the-fact remedy may take either the form of a hearing scheduled and conducted after a temporary deprivation,[60] or the form of a collateral legal remedy provided under the law of the jurisdiction to persons who have suffered deprivation.[61]

56. 446 U.S. at 242 (citing Joint Anti-Fascist Committee v. McGrath, 341 U.S. 123, 172 (1951) (Frankfurter, J., concurring)). See also Aetna Life Ins. Co. v. Lavoie, 106 S.Ct. 1580, 1587 (1986) ("to perform its high function in the best way, 'justice must satisfy the appearance of justice'") (citing In re Murchison, 349 U.S. 133, 136 (1955)).

57. See, e.g., Mathews v. Eldridge, 424 U.S. 319, 344–45 (1976) (value of procedural safeguards weighed primarily in terms of contribution to accuracy). See generally, Mashaw, "The Supreme Court's Calculus for Administrative Adjudication in Mathews v. Eldridge: Three Factors in Search of a Theory of Value," 44 U.Chi.L. Rev. 28 (1976).

58. See, e.g., Mathews v. Eldridge, 424 U.S. at 319.

59. See generally § 10–14, infra.

60. See, e.g., Barry v. Barchi, 443 U.S. 55, 64 (1979) (sufficiently prompt hearing after suspension of jockey's license would be adequate); Hewitt v. Helms, 459 U.S. 460, 472 (1983) (prompt post-detention hearing adequate when prisoner placed in solitary confinement for administrative reasons), discussed in § 10–14, infra.

61. Parratt v. Taylor, 451 U.S. 527 (1981) (post-deprivation tort claim is adequate remedy for prisoner whose property was lost by negligence of prison officials), overruled in part Daniels v. Williams, 106 S.Ct. 662, 663 (1986) ("[We] reconsider our statement in *Parratt* that 'the alleged loss, even though negligently caused, amounted to a deprivation.' We conclude that the Due Process Clause is simply not implicated by a *negligent* act of an official causing unintended loss of an injury to life, liberty or property"); Ingraham v. Wright, 430 U.S. 651, 675–76 (1977) (no due process violation when school child is subjected to corporal punishment without a hearing, because the child has right under common law since Blackstone to recover damages after the fact if punishment is excessive). But see Logan v. Zimmerman Brush Co., 455 U.S. 422 (1982) (subsequent remedy would be inadequate in case where employee's cause of action is automatically extinguished, as a matter of state law, by clerical error of state employee). These cases are more fully analyzed in § 10–14, infra.

Second, the Court's increasingly instrumental approach is reflected in its increased reliance on the balancing test outlined in *Mathews v. Eldridge*,[62] holding that the degree and type of procedural protection that is due can be determined by weighing: "[f]irst, the private interest that will be affected by the official action; second, the risk of an erroneous deprivation of such interest through the procedures used, and the probable value, if any, of additional or substitute procedural safeguards; and finally, the Government's interest, including the function involved and the fiscal and administrative burdens that the additional or substitute procedural requirement would entail."[63]   This approach not only overlooks the unquantifiable human interest in receiving decent treatment,[64] but also provides the Court a facile means to justify the most cursory procedures by altering the relative weights to be accorded each of the three factors.[65]

A typical illustration of the instrumental approach is *Greenholtz v. Inmates of Nebraska Penal and Cor. Complex*,[66] in which the Court upheld Nebraska's procedure for initial parole release decisions. The state's parole review procedure was divided into two parts: an initial, informal hearing and, if granted in the first hearing, a final, formal hearing. The initial hearing consisted of an examination by the board of the inmate's entire preconfinement and postconfinement record and, second, an informal hearing where the board interviewed the inmate and permitted the inmate to present any statements or letters he wished to produce, although allowing "no evidence as such [to be] introduced" by the inmate.[67] The inmate was allowed to review his record, and therefore the evidence against him, only at the parole board's discretion.[68] After this initial hearing, the board would make a decision based on the inmate's file and on the statements and letters presented at his interview; the inmate would be informed of this decision, but no written explanation citing the evidence relied upon, or the reasons for a denial of opportunity to reach the second formal hearing (and therefore the resulting denial of parole), would be given the inmate. Nonetheless, the Court held that such meager protection provided all the procedure due to inmates in parole pre-release hearings. Chief Justice Burger wrote for the Court that "[t]he function of

---

62. 424 U.S. 319 (1976). See also §§ 10–13 to 10–17, infra.

63. Id. at 335.

64. Despite Carey v. Piphus, 435 U.S. 247 (1978), the Court has not seemed particularly interested in the psychic harm done to individuals by the very fact of their exclusion from decisions affecting them, and has not adopted the formulation of "freedom from arbitrary adjudicative procedures as a substantive element of one's liberty" propounded by Professor Van Alstyne in "Cracks in 'The New Property': Adjudicative Due Process in the Administrative State," 62 Cornell L.Rev. 445, 483 (1977). See, e.g., Memphis Community School Dist. v. Stachura, 106 S.Ct. 2537 (1986) (dismissing claims for damages

based on the "abstract" value of due process).

65. See § 10–11, infra. For discussion of how balancing tests have been employed to cut back on individual rights, see "Cases that Shock the Conscience: Reflections on Criticism of the Burger Court," 15 Harv. C.R.-C.L.L.Rev. 713, 729–31 (1980).

66. 442 U.S. 1 (1979). Chief Justice Burger wrote the majority opinion, joined by Justices Stewart, White, Blackmun and Rehnquist. Justice Powell concurred in part. Justice Marshall dissented in part, joined by Justices Brennan and Stevens. See also § 10–9, infra.

67. Id. at 4.

68. Id. at 15 n. 7.

legal process, as that concept is embodied in the Constitution, and in the realm of factfinding, is to minimize the risk of erroneous decisions. . . .; the quantum and quality of the process due in a particular situation depend upon the need to serve the purpose of minimizing the risk of error." [69] Because the state's procedures adequately minimized error,[70] the Court required no more procedural protection, concluding that any further procedures "would provide at best a negligible decrease in the risk of error." [71] In addition, Chief Justice Burger commented that "the Parole Board's decision as defined by Nebraska's statute is necessarily subjective in part and predictive in part. . . . [vesting] broad discretion in the Board. No ideal, error-free way to make parole-release decisions has been developed; the whole question has been and will continue to be the subject of experimentation involving analysis of psychological factors combined with fact evaluation guided by the practical experience of the actual decisionmakers in predicting future behavior. . . . If parole determinations are encumbered by procedures that states regard as burdensome and unwarranted, they may abandon or curtail parole." [72] Chief Justice Burger's discussion of the parole board's role of reaching "essentially an experienced prediction based on a host of variables," [73] and his defense of the necessarily "subjective" [74] nature of that role, reflected sensitivity to the subjective needs of government officials in their official capacity, while giving little heed to the subjective needs of the individual.

Justice Marshall, joined by Justices Brennan and Stevens, argued forcefully for a more intrinsic appreciation of the needs of the individual over the needs of the state, maintaining in dissent [75] that "the need to assure the appearance, as well as the existence, of fairness" [76] required more extensive procedural safeguards than were provided under the Nebraska parole system. Justice Marshall invoked the Chief Justice's own language from an earlier parole case to argue that, " 'apart from avoiding the risk of actual error, this Court has stressed the importance of adopting procedures that preserve the appearance of fairness and the confidence of inmates in the decisionmaking process.' " [77] Justice Marshall, deriding Chief Justice Burger's view that

69. Id. at 13.

70. Justice Marshall disagreed even with this view, citing error in Greenholz's own record and in a variety of other similar cases. Id. at 33–34 & n. 15 (Marshall, J., dissenting in part).

71. Id. at 14.

72. Id. at 13.

73. Id. at 16.

74. Id. at 10, 13.

75. Justice Powell's separate opinion, concurring in part and dissenting in part, found fault with the majority's holding that the due process required for parole-release decisions depends upon statutory language and that the notice provisions of the Nebraska system were adequate. Id. at 18–22.

76. Id. at 35 (Marshall, J., dissenting in part).

77. Id. at 34 (Marshall, J., dissenting in part), quoting Morrissey v. Brewer, 408 U.S. 471 (1972) (parole revocation deprives parolee of a liberty interest and must be preceded by due process). See also Parham v. J.R., 442 U.S. 584, 636 n. 22 (1979) (Brennan, J., concurring in the judgment in part and dissenting in part) (post-admission hearings for children whose parents wish to have them committed to mental institutions will prove therapeutic by giving the children satisfaction in a fair hearing, helping them accept their illness and confinement, and encouraging them to cooperate with the hospital treatment staff).

the subjective nature of the parole board's decisionmaking should not be encumbered by more process, argued instead that the parole board should be required to provide to the inmate the criteria to be applied to parole-release decisions and an explanation of the reasons and supporting facts for these decisions. "For '[o]ne can imagine nothing more cruel, inhuman, and frustrating than serving a prison term without knowledge of what will be measured and the rules determining whether one is ready for release.' " [78] Not only is subjective official decisionmaking perhaps most susceptible to arbitrary results, but—at least as importantly, under the intrinsic approach—individual participation is most required in such subjective situations precisely to avoid an individual's feeling that her life and liberty have been dealt serious affliction without reason or explanation.

In his opinion for the *Greenholtz* majority, Chief Justice Burger expressed the sharply contrasting view that the *relevant* intrinsic value inhered in summary government action rather than in extensive legal process.[79] He maintained for the Court that the procedures the lower court had prescribed—a formal hearing on parole eligibility and a statement of the evidence relied on by the Parole Board when parole is denied—were not only not required by the Constitution, but were socially undesirable as well: "[I]t will not contribute to these desirable objectives [of rehabilitating convicted persons to be useful members of society] to invite or encourage a continuing state of adversary relations between society and the inmate." [80]

Greenholtz thus adopts the view that, while due process formalities are *valued* overwhelmingly for the instrumental purpose of enhancing accurate factfinding, such formalities should be *relaxed* not only to minimize cost to the state but also for reasons *intrinsic to informality*— especially the preservation of supposedly harmonious relations in society. Whatever one's assessment of such "togetherness" in other settings, it seems a dubious aim in cases involving the continued involuntary incarceration of prisoners.[81] More fundamentally, the vision of society and law reflected by this ideal stands in some tension not only with social reality but also with the theoretical underpinnings of a Constitution that assumes individuals require legal protection from the overarching power of the state.[82] Too often, the ideal of the delegalized

78. 442 U.S. at 35 (Marshall, J., dissenting in part) (quoting K. Davis, Discretionary Justice: A Preliminary Inquiry 132 (1969)).

79. See also Mackey v. Montrym, 443 U.S. 1, 18 (1979) (suggesting that requiring a hearing before a driver's license is suspended for refusing to submit to a breathalyzer test would undermine the state's interest by giving drivers an opportunity to delay law enforcement); Parham v. J.R., 442 U.S. at 605–07 (1979) (suggesting that extensive procedural requirements for the admission of children to a state mental institution for psychiatric treatment might discourage parents from committing them).

80. 442 U.S. at 13–14.

81. See also Parham v. J.R., 442 U.S. at 610 (1979) (requiring a formal hearing when parents seek commitment of their children would constitute an undesirable "intrusion into the parent-child relationship").

82. See, e.g., Lassiter v. Department of Social Services, 452 U.S. 18, 57 (1981) (Blackmun, J., dissenting) (mother's lack of a lawyer in parental termination hearing makes "virtually incredible the Court's conclusion today that her termination proceeding was fundamentally fair").

society is a mask for a society in which one of the few tools available to combat official subjugation is taken away from potential victims of such oppression.[83]

As a plausible though not inescapable corollary of the Court's emphasis on the instrumental goal of accurately enforcing whatever lines are drawn by the applicable rules, the Court in recent years has tended to adopt a positivist theory of the private interests encompassed in "life, liberty, and property," and hence protected from governmental deprivation without "due process of law." [84]   The positivist view presupposes the existence of an independent legal rule as a prerequisite to any due process protection.   To be procedurally protected an interest must be grounded in substantive legal relationships defined by explicit constitutional provisions or by specific state or federal rules of law.[85]   It should be stressed that this positivist view is not an inevitable partner of an instrumental perspective: it has not, for example, prevailed on the Court with respect to the determination of what process is due, notwithstanding the Court's instrumental orientation.   In fact, the Court has squarely rejected such a positivist view of what process will be required.[86]   While arguably abdicating a significant part of its constitutional role in determining whether a given interest deserves the protection of due process, the Court has refused similarly to relieve itself of the power to decide what kinds of process must be followed when a protected interest *is* implicated.   Thus, while government may decide freely whether or not to accord a legal entitlement in the form of a specific benefit, it has been given far less latitude to determine what interchange with the individual to conduct in conjunction with the withdrawal of that benefit.   Instead, the Court has made an independent inquiry into what form of interchange or encounter to require; since, from the Court's instrumental perspective, procedural requirements are valued almost exclusively because they minimize the risk of error in the specification and enforcement of substantive legal relationships, the constitutionally mandated procedures have varied from case to case, depending upon the character of the risks perceived and the weight the Court has accorded to the competing substantive interests that are at stake in whatever hearing might be held.[87]

---

83. See generally J. Auerbach, Justice Without Law (1983).

84. See, e.g., Meachum v. Fano, 427 U.S. 215 (1976); Bishop v. Wood, 426 U.S. 341 (1976); Paul v. Davis, 424 U.S. 693 (1976).

85. See §§ 10–10 and 10–11, infra. See generally H. L. A. Hart, The Concept of Law (1961); Kennedy, "Legal Formality," 2 J. Legal Stud. 351 (1973); Hart, "Positivism and the Separation of Law and Morals," 71 Harv.L.Rev. 593 (1958). Cf. Yarbrough, "Mr. Justice Black and Legal Positivism," 57 Va.L.Rev. 373 (1971).

86. Cleveland Bd. of Educ. v. Loudermill, 470 U.S. 532, 541 (1985) ("[T]he

'bitter with the sweet' approach misconceives the constitutional guarantee. . . . [T]he Due Process Clause provides that certain substantive rights—life, liberty, and property—cannot be deprived except pursuant to constitutionally adequate procedures.   The categories of substance and procedure are distinct.   Were the rule otherwise, the Clause would be reduced to a mere tautology.   'Property' cannot be defined by the procedures provided for its deprivation any more than can life or liberty"). See § 10–12, infra.

87. See §§ 10–13 and 10–14, infra.

§ 10–8.　The Development of Procedural Due Process Prior to 1970:　Common-Law Interests and Unconstitutional Conditions

The actual elaboration by the Supreme Court of protected interests and procedural safeguards has been an evolving process punctuated by vague generalizations and declarations of broad, overarching principles.[1]　Due process has been held to protect "those fundamental principles of liberty and justice which lie at the base of all our civil and political institutions," [2] and to guarantee those procedures which are required for the "protection of ultimate decency in a civilized society." [3] On a somewhat more mundane level, the Court established early in its consideration of this area that procedural due process was implicated whenever government action seemingly conflicted with substantive individual rights protected either by a constitutional guarantee more specific than due process [4] or by "those settled usages and modes of proceeding existing in the common and statute law of England before the emigration of our ancestors which were shown not to have been unsuited to their civil and political condition by having been acted on by them after the settlement of this country." [5]　Thus, apart from the specific declarations of the Bill of Rights—virtually all of which later came to be applied to the states through the due process clause of the fourteenth amendment [6]—there was no attempt to tie the invocation of due process protection to positive rules.　To the contrary, until very recently "fairness," [7] "necessity," [8] and "privileges long recognized at common law as essential to the orderly pursuit of happiness by free men," [9] were the mixed underpinnings of the Court's decisions on procedural safeguards.　Moreover, in assessing the dictates of "fundamental fairness," courts determined the requirements of procedural due process in a one-step process without any clear attempt to distinguish (1) the question of what specific interests are entitled to due process

---

§ 10–8

1.　See generally Kadish, "Methodology and Criteria in Due Process Adjudication—A Survey and Criticism," 66 Yale L.J. 319, 340 (1957).　See also Mashaw, "The Supreme Court's Calculus for Administrative Adjudication in Mathews v. Eldridge: Three Factors in Search of a Value," 44 U.Chi.L.Rev. 28, 47 n. 61 (1976): This process "might be characterized as a continuous search for a theory of Due Process review that combines the legitimacy of the evolutionary theory with a flexibility that permits adaptation to contemporary circumstances. Dignitary or natural rights, utilitarian, and egalitarian theories have all been incorporated to this end." Id.

2.　Hurtado v. California, 110 U.S. 516, 535 (1884).

3.　Adamson v. California, 332 U.S. 46, 61 (1947) (Frankfurter, J., concurring).

4.　See, e.g., Board of Regents v. Roth, 408 U.S. 564, 575 n. 14 (1972) ("when [gov-

ernment] would directly impinge upon interests in free speech or free press, this Court has . . . held that opportunity for a fair adversary hearing must precede the action, whether or not the speech or press interest is clearly protected under substantive First Amendment standards.").

5.　Tumey v. Ohio, 273 U.S. 510, 523 (1927).　See also Powell v. Alabama, 287 U.S. 45, 65 (1932); Ownbey v. Morgan, 256 U.S. 94 (1921); Murray's Lessee v. Hoboken Land & Improvement Co., 59 U.S. (18 How.) 272, 276–80 (1855).

6.　See § 11–2, infra.

7.　See, e.g., Joint Anti-Fascist Refugee Committee v. McGrath, 341 U.S. 123, 162 (1951) (Frankfurter, J., concurring).

8.　See, e.g., North American Cold Storage Co. v. Chicago, 211 U.S. 306, 320 (1908).

9.　Meyer v. Nebraska, 262 U.S. 390, 399 (1923), cited with approval in Board of Regents v. Roth, 408 U.S. 564, 572 (1972).

protection, from (2) the inquiry into what process is due.[10] The simplicity of this pre-1970's mode of analysis may reflect a variety of factors; one in particular seems worth noting here. Barring emergency, at least the minimum content of the process due was largely unquestioned: notice and a hearing had to be accorded prior to any grievous government deprivation.[11]

The fifth and fourteenth amendments' due process clauses as interpreted in the Supreme Court's substantive due process analyses [12] have furnished a broad definition of the "liberty" that was in turn afforded procedural protection against arbitrary deprivation. The "core" liberty interests in this expansive sense included "not merely freedom from bodily restraint but also the right of the individual to contract, to engage in any of the common occupations of life, to acquire useful knowledge, to marry, establish a home and bring up children [and] to worship God according to the dictates of . . . conscience." [13] In addition, there were protections independently required by fundamental fairness. For example, in *Joint Anti-Fascist Refugee Committee v. McGrath*,[14] the Supreme Court declared invalid the designation of certain groups as Communist by the Attorney General, purporting to act pursuant to an Executive Order, in a list furnished to the Loyalty Review Board for use in connection with determinations of disloyalty of government employees. While the opinion of the Court rested on the ground that the Attorney General's action was not authorized by the Executive Order,[15] Justice Frankfurter, in apparent agreement with Justices Jackson,[16] Black,[17] and Douglas,[18] found the Attorney General's action authorized by Executive Order but inconsistent with the requirements of procedural due process.[19] He declared that, while "no legal sanction" was directly imposed on the groups labeled "Communist" by the Attorney General, it "would be blindness . . . not to recognize that in the conditions of our time such designation drastically restricts

---

10. See, e.g., Cafeteria & Restaurant Workers Union 473 v. McElroy, 367 U.S. 886, 895 (1961) (balancing the government interests in national security against the private interest in a specific job, the Court determined there was no entitlement to procedural protections).

11. See, e.g., Twining v. New Jersey, 211 U.S. 78, 110–11 (1908): "Due process requires . . . that there shall be notice and opportunity for hearing given the parties . . . [T]hese two fundamental conditions . . . seem to be universally prescribed in all systems of law established by civilized countries." See also Baldwin v. Hale, 68 U.S. (1 Wall.) 223 (1863) ("Parties whose rights are to be affected are entitled to be heard; and in order that they may enjoy that right they must first be notified.")

12. See Chapters 8, 11–15.

13. Meyer v. Nebraska, 262 U.S. 390, 399 (1923), cited with approval in Board of

Regents v. Roth, 408 U.S. 564, 572 (1972). See also Smith v. Organization of Foster Families, 431 U.S. 816 (1977) (suggesting that foster families, despite lack of biological relationship and despite role of state in creating foster parent-foster child relationship might have a protected "liberty interest" sufficient to trigger procedural due process when state removes child from foster home, but holding state procedures adequate).

14. 341 U.S. 123 (1951).

15. Id. (plurality opinion by Burton, J.).

16. Id. at 186 (Jackson, J., concurring).

17. Id. at 143 (Black, J., concurring).

18. Id. at 178 (Douglas, J., concurring) ("The gravity of the present charge is proof enough of the need for notice and hearing before the United States officially brands these organizations as subversive.").

19. Id. at 162 (Frankfurter, J., concurring).

the organizations, if it does not proscribe them." [20] Because this disabling designation was accomplished without granting the affected groups any prior notice or opportunity to participate in a hearing on the question, Justice Frankfurter concluded that "thus to maim or decapitate . . . an organization . . . ostensibly engaged in lawful objectives is so devoid of fundamental fairness as to offend the Due Process Clause of the Fifth Amendment." [21]

At least since 1937,[22] the Constitution has not been interpreted to give direct definitions of the "property" interests that can claim procedural, and sometimes substantive, protections; with a few exceptions, there has been no precise analogue to the continuing willingness to find specific "liberty" interests in the Constitution itself.[23] But the Supreme Court has nonetheless consistently recognized that due process requirements are implicated whenever the enforcement power of government is employed to deprive an individual of an interest, derived from the common law, in peaceful possession [24] or use [25] of real or personal "property," using that term in its colloquial sense, whether such property was being taken to meet a need of government or for the benefit of another private individual. Thus, in *Ewing v. Mytinger & Casselberry, Inc.*,[26] the Court subjected to procedural due process analysis, though eventually upholding, a provision of the Federal Food, Drug and Cosmetic Act which permitted a designated government official to act at his or her discretion, free of any requirement to hold a prior hearing, in ordering seizures of misbranded articles.

In the case of public employment or other goods and services which federal and state governments provide, however, courts adhered until quite recently to a distinction, expressed most classically by Justice

---

20. Id. at 161 (Frankfurter, J., concurring).

21. Id.

22. See discussion in Chapter 8, supra.

23. See Chapters 11–15, infra. But see §§ 9–6, 9–7, 9–9, supra, and § 10–11, infra. In a few instances, the Court has raised its own intuitive notions of what constitutes ownership to a constitutional limit on positive law. In Webb's Fabulous Pharmacies, Inc. v. Beckwith, 449 U.S. 155 (1980), a unanimous Court struck down Florida's attempt to define as public property the interest earned on a private fund deposited with a state court. The Supreme Court rejected the argument that, since the very statute that directed investment of the fund by the clerk of court also declared that the interest earned thereby was public property, the state took only what it itself had created. Instead, the Court substituted for the state's positive law its own Lockean notions of property that interest is "an incident of ownership" of the principal, and held that "a State, by *ipse dixit*, may not transform private property into public property without compensation." 449 U.S.

at 164. See also Fuentes v. Shevin, 407 U.S. 67 (1972) (state could not constitutionally define chattel ownership to essentially eliminate property right to possessions obtained in conditional sales contracts). Both cases are discussed in more detail in § 9–7, supra.

24. See, e.g., Lindsey v. Normet, 405 U.S. 56 (1972) (accepting without question the property interest of tenant in suit seeking to prevent imminent state-enforced eviction); Pennoyer v. Neff, 95 U.S. (5 Otto) 714 (1877) (procedural due process question raised by action to recover possession of tract of land).

25. See, e.g., Mullane v. Central Hanover Bank & Trust Co., 339 U.S. 306 (1950) (procedural due process violated by provisions of New York statute for triennial judicial settlement of trust estate accounts because an inadequate method of giving notice to beneficiaries of pooled trusts effectively denied at least some beneficiaries an opportunity to participate in control of their property).

26. 339 U.S. 594 (1950).

Holmes,[27] between individual "rights" stemming from constitutional or common law sources and mere "privileges" bestowed by government; the latter could be withheld absolutely and "therefore" could be withheld conditionally—even if the condition, viewed independently, would have violated a settled constitutional norm like that against ideological censorship or racial discrimination.[28]

The now somewhat eroded twentieth century doctrine of "unconstitutional conditions," which holds that government may not condition the receipt of its benefits upon the nonassertion of constitutional rights even if receipt of such benefits is in all other respects a "mere privilege," [29] theoretically allowed individuals to challenge government action which indirectly inhibits or penalizes the exercise of constitutional rights.[30] But in the absence of a general plaintiff's right of access to

27. See McAuliffe v. New Bedford, 155 Mass. 216, 220, 29 N.E. 517, 518 (1892) ("The petitioner may have a constitutional right to talk politics but he has no constitutional right to be a policeman.")

28. See, e.g., Bailey v. Richardson, 182 F.2d 46 (D.C.Cir. 1950), aff'd by an equally divided Court 341 U.S. 918 (1951) (due process protections not applicable to dismissals from federal civil service employment). See generally Frug, "Does the Constitution Prevent the Discharge of Civil Service Employees?" 124 U.Pa.L.Rev. 942, 961 (1976) (Until the 1950's courts consistently refused to review challenges to executive's power to remove employees).

29. For an early statement of this doctrine, see Frost v. Railroad Comm'n, 271 U.S. 583, 593–94 (1926). See also Sherbert v. Verner, 374 U.S. 398 (1963) (state may not deny unemployment benefits to person who refuses to work on Saturdays for religious reasons); Speiser v. Randall, 357 U.S. 513 (1958) (government may not act indirectly to "produce a result which [it] could not command directly"). A few recent Supreme Court decisions have cast doubt on the continued validity of the doctrine. In Posadas de Puerto Rico Associates v. Tourism Co. of Puerto Rico, 106 S.Ct. 2968 (1986), the Court upheld a Puerto Rico law conditioning the privilege of operating gambling casinos on forbearance of the right to advertise under the first amendment's commercial speech doctrine. In its efforts to distinguish two previous decisions striking down similiar commercial speech restrictions, the Court stated, "In *Carey* and *Bigelow*, the underlying conduct that was the subject of the advertising restrictions was constitutionally protected and could not have been prohibited by the State. . . . [Here t]he greater power to completely ban casino gambling necessarily includes the lesser power to ban advertising of casino gambling. . . ." Earlier, the Court distinguished Congress' refusal to "subsidize" the exercise of a right from

conditioning one's receipt of that subsidy upon forgoing the exercise of the right. Regan v. Taxation with Representation, 461 U.S. 540 (1983) (since organization could create one affiliate to receive tax-deductible funds and another affiliate to exercise its lobbying rights, preclusion of lobbying activities by those receiving benefits did not violate the First Amendment). Cf. F.C.C. v. League of Women Voters, 468 U.S. 364 (1984) (absolute bar on editorializing by television stations receiving federal funds not saved by subsidy argument, since the station was unable to segregate its activities according to their source of funding). The trend may ultimately lead toward further revival of the rights-privileges distinction. In fact, Chief Justice (then Associate Justice) Rehnquist was able to garner the support of two other justices for the proposition that constitutional rights are sufficiently protected any time a "rational relationship" exists between the condition imposed and Congress' purpose in providing a government benefit. F.C.C. v. League of Women Voters, 468 U.S. at 407 (Rehnquist, J., joined by Burger, C.J. and White, J., dissenting). See also Wyman v. James, 400 U.S. 309 (1971) (upholding New York law which conditioned eligibility for welfare on recipient's foregoing fourth amendment privilege to deny home visits by welfare caseworkers); Van Alstyne, "The Demise of the Right-Privilege Distinction in Constitutional Law," 81 Harv.L.Rev. 1439, 1448 (1968) ("The basic flaw in the [unconstitutional conditions] doctrine is its assumption that the same evil results from attaching certain conditions to government-connected activity as from imposing such conditions on persons not connected with government.") See § 11–5, infra.

30. See, e.g., Pickering v. Board of Education, 391 U.S. 563 (1968) (constitutionally protected speech is impermissible ground for discharge); Keyishian v. Board of Regents, 385 U.S. 589 (1967).

the courts,[31] the existence of this retrospective judicial remedy remains insufficient for many individuals—ironically those most likely to be dependent on the government's benefits.[32] The lower courts have been split,[33] and the Supreme Court has not yet authoritatively determined whether procedural due process requires a government agency to grant affected persons a hearing whenever a bona fide claim is made that the withdrawal of government benefits was a response to the exercise of constitutional rights.[34]

Including particular activities within the constitutional definition of "liberty" or "property" is not, of course, the equivalent of granting those activities total immunity from government regulation or deprivation.[35] Nevertheless, such inclusion usually implies a burden of justification for every substantive curtailment of the interest in question,[36] and always implies constitutional recognition of a procedural right to be heard even when a concededly valid government rule infringing that interest is enforced.[37]

For example, notwithstanding the existence of the common law "liberty" to follow a chosen profession,[38] "[t]he power of the state to provide for the general welfare of its people authorizes it to prescribe all such regulations as, in its judgment, will . . . tend to secure them against the consequences of ignorance and incapacity as well as deception and fraud."[39] Substantively constitutional regulations—usually, those which are rationally related to legitimate governmental objectives—taking the form of mechanically applied general eligibility stan-

31. See discussion of access to judicial protection in § 10–18, infra.

32. See generally, Michelman, supra § 10–7 in note 14.

33. Compare McDowell v. Texas, 465 F.2d 1342, 1347 (5th Cir. 1971), cert. denied 410 U.S. 943 (1973) (employee must be given hearing if he claims termination for unconstitutional reasons even though he had no expectancy of re-employment) with George v. Conneaut Board of Education, 472 F.2d 132 (6th Cir. 1972) (government not obligated to grant administrative hearings on request, though unconstitutional conditions claim is cognizable in court.).

34. See Perry v. Sindermann, 408 U.S. 593, 599 n. 5 (1972) (rejecting suggestion "that the respondent might have a due process right to some kind of hearing simply if he *asserts* to college officials that their decision was based on his constitutionally protected conduct") (emphasis in original.) The Sindermann footnote can be read to leave open the possibility that a factual showing (amounting to more than a mere assertion) that government acted to penalize the exercise of constitutional rights would trigger procedural due process obligations to provide a hearing to air fully the issue of whether government had in fact acted to penalize the exercise of constitutional rights. Once the individual

succeeds in establishing, possibly with the aid of an administrative hearing, or with help from discovery mechanisms ancillary to adjudication, that constitutionally protected conduct probably "played a 'substantial part' in [a] decision not to renew [a public benefit]," the burden shifts to government to show "by a preponderance of the evidence that it would have reached the same decision even in the absence of the protected conduct." Mt. Healthy City School Dist. Bd. of Education v. Doyle, 429 U.S. 274, 285–87 (1977).

35. See, e.g., Ewing v. Mytinger & Casselberry, Inc., 339 U.S. 594 (1950) (allowing official discretion to order summary seizure of misbranded articles over procedural due process challenge).

36. See Chapters 11 and 15, infra, for discussions of substantive due process.

37. However, the right to be heard may be limited to the right to submit a written statement. See, e.g., Hewitt v. Helms, 459 U.S. 460, 472–77 (1983), discussed in § 10–15, infra.

38. See § 15–13, infra.

39. Dent v. West Virginia, 129 U.S. 114, 122 (1889) (upholding a state law forbidding the practice of medicine without a license).

dards such as those of age, educational attainments, or residency, have not ordinarily triggered any requirement that procedural due process be accorded to each affected person individually.[40] However, regulations which are structured so as to require more individualized determinations in their application—such as findings of "good character" [41]— can be validly enforced only in a manner consistent with the dictates of procedural due process.

During the decades in which these notions were being worked out, the Supreme Court took the position that the *form* of procedural due process was not fixed; rather, its "content varies according to specific factual contexts." [42] Yet, certain procedures were consistently thought to be required either by some "higher law" [43] or as a matter of "fundamental fairness." [44] In all cases, the core content of procedural due process placed upon government the duty to give notice [45] and an opportunity to be heard [46] to individuals or groups whose interests in life, liberty or property were adversely affected by government action. The assurance of a fair trial or at least a fair hearing mandated that the individual be accorded an open hearing [47] before a "neutral and

40. But see the discussion of irrebuttable presumptions in Chapter 16, infra.

41. See, e.g., Willner v. Committee on Character & Fitness, 373 U.S. 96 (1963) (New York denied individual procedural due process by refusing to admit him to the practice of law on the basis of adverse report by bar association character committee that he was given no opportunity to contest); Goldsmith v. United States Bd. of Tax Appeals, 270 U.S. 117 (1926) (certified public accountant's application to practice before Board of Tax Appeals should not be rejected on grounds of unfitness without giving him an opportunity for a hearing and an answer). Cf. In re Ruffalo, 390 U.S. 544 (1968) (Government must afford attorney notice and opportunity for hearing before previously granted permission to practice law can be validly revoked). But cf. Greene v. McElroy, 360 U.S. 474, 507 (1959) (construing a federal statute in a way that avoided the constitutional question whether, in the context of the revocation of a defense industry engineer's security clearance, "a person may be deprived of the right to follow his chosen profession without full hearings where accusers may be confronted"); Barsky v. Board of Regents, 347 U.S. 442, 451 (1954) (criminal conviction for contempt of Congress for reasons unconnected with ability to practice medicine held a sufficient ground for state to suspend physician's license since "the practice of medicine in New York [is a 'privilege' granted by the state and] is lawfully prohibited by the state except under the conditions it imposes"). Barsky is criticized in § 15–14, infra.

42. Hannah v. Larche, 363 U.S. 420, 442 (1960).

43. See, e.g., Twining v. New Jersey, 211 U.S. 78, 106 (1908) (natural law right to live free from arbitrary exercise of government power).

44. See, e.g., Solesbee v. Balkcom, 339 U.S. 9, 16 (1950) (Frankfurter, J., dissenting). See generally, Kadish, supra § 10–7 in note 1, at 321–34.

45. See, e.g., Mullane v. Central Hanover Bank & Trust Co., 339 U.S. 306, 314–15 (1950) (notice must be "reasonably calculated, under all the circumstances, to apprise interested parties of the pendency of the action and afford them an opportunity to present their objections;" where "[t]he individual interest does not stand alone but is identical with that of a class . . . notice reasonably certain to reach most of those interested in objecting is likely to safeguard the interests of all"); In re Oliver, 333 U.S. 257, 273 (1948) (petitioner deprived of due process right to notice and hearing when, immediately after testimony before a one-judge-grand-jury, he was charged and convicted of contempt and sent to jail). See also Shaffer v. Heitner, 433 U.S. 186 (1977), extending to *quasi-in rem* jurisdiction, despite Pennoyer v. Neff, 95 U.S. (5 Otto) 714 (1877), the fair notice— minimum contacts approach of International Shoe Co. v. Washington, 326 U.S. 310 (1945).

46. See, e.g., Brinkerhoff-Faris Trust & Sav. Co. v. Hill, 281 U.S. 673, 678 (1930) (enjoining collection of tax assessment because petitioner was not afforded "at any time an opportunity to be heard in its defense").

47. See, e.g., In re Oliver, 333 U.S. 257, 266–73 (1948) (due process violated where

detached magistrate" [48] who has no "direct, personal, substantial pecuniary interest in reaching a conclusion against him in his case," [49] and who is free from domination by "a mob," [50] with counsel provided for indigents in criminal cases.[51]

Life, liberty and property could not, furthermore, be taken by virtue of a statute whose terms were "so vague, indefinite and uncertain" [52] that one cannot determine their meaning. Nor could statutes employ overly attenuated presumptions "where the inference is so strained as not to have a reasonable relation to the circumstances of life." [53] Government was expected to maintain high standards of honesty in dealing with citizens. Thus it was held violative of due process to convict "a citizen for exercising a privilege which the State clearly had told him was available to him," [54] or for the State to contrive "a conviction . . . through a deliberate deception of court and jury by the presentation of testimony known to be perjured." [55] Finally, it was held that an individual is denied due process if he is deprived of liberty "on a record lacking any relevant evidence as to a crucial element of the offense charged." [56]

The Court did, however, recognize certain limits on the availability of these protections in the context of a deprivation of an otherwise

person deprived of liberty through criminal trial conducted in camera).

48. Coolidge v. New Hampshire, 403 U.S. 443, 449 (1971) (invalidating warrant executed by active participant in investigation). See also In re Murchison, 349 U.S. 133, 134 (1955) ("The due process requirement of an impartial tribunal [is violated] where the same judge presiding at the contempt hearing had also served as the 'one man grand jury' [in the secret hearings] out of which the contempt charges arose").

49. Tumey v. Ohio, 273 U.S. 510, 523 (1927) (invalidating fine for illegal possession of intoxicating liquor where mayor received a share of such fines). See also Ward v. Monroeville, 409 U.S. 57, 62 (1972) (petitioner denied right to neutral and detached judge where a major portion of town's income came from penalties imposed by the town mayor sitting as judge).

50. Moore v. Dempsey, 261 U.S. 86, 90–91 (1923) (petitioners sentenced to death under mob pressure were deprived of life without due process of law).

51. See Gideon v. Wainwright, 372 U.S. 335, 344 (1963); see also Powell v. Alabama, 287 U.S. 45, 71 (1932) (defendant in capital case must be given reasonable time and opportunity to secure counsel and must be provided with counsel if he is "incapable adequately of making his own defense").

52. Lanzetta v. New Jersey, 306 U.S. 451, 458 (1939) (reversing conviction under statute making it penal offense to be a "gangster").

53. Tot v. United States, 319 U.S. 463, 468 (1943) (reversing conviction under statute making possession of firearm or ammunition by convicted felon or fugitive from justice presumptive evidence that such firearm was shipped in violation of the act). See also Turner v. United States, 396 U.S. 398, 415–20 (1970) (allowing jury to infer, from fact of possession of heroin, that petitioner had knowledge of its illegal importation, since the overwhelming proportion of heroin consumed in United States is illegally imported; but not allowing similar inference with respect to cocaine, since more of that drug is lawfully prepared in United States than is illegally imported); Leary v. United States, 395 U.S. 6, 36 (1969) (disallowing inference, from possession of marijuana, that petitioner had knowledge of its unlawful importation in absence of proof that most possessors have such knowledge).

54. Raley v. Ohio, 360 U.S. 423, 438 (1959).

55. Mooney v. Holohan, 294 U.S. 103, 112 (1935) (noting that a valid claim had been stated, but refusing to allow petition for writ of habeas corpus due to lack of exhaustion of state remedies).

56. Vachon v. New Hampshire, 414 U.S. 478 (1974), quoting Harris v. United States, 404 U.S. 1232, 1233 (1971) (Douglas, J., concurring). See also Thompson v. Louisville, 362 U.S. 199 (1960) (invalidating conviction for loitering and disorderly conduct where there was no evidentiary support for so characterizing petitioner's conduct).

protected interest in life, liberty, or property: first, in cases of emergency,[57] and of taking by eminent domain,[58] the Court has not required that the government-enforced seizure be *preceded* by an adversary hearing. Second, procedural due process has not been held to require that the affected individuals or groups be granted a hearing before government acts in a legislative, or broadly rule-making or policy-forming, capacity.[59] Thus, while an administrative agency was required to grant specifically affected individuals or groups a hearing before a rule was particularly enforced against them, the agency was not required by due process to grant such a hearing when simply formulating the rule.[60]

All of these holdings continued to represent the law throughout the expansion of due process rights described in § 10–9, and have remained good law through the period of contraction in due process described in §§ 10–10 through 10–14; but underlying modes of analysis have changed dramatically, and harder cases than those yet canvassed would prove sensitive to such shifts in method and emphasis.

§ 10–9. Extending Procedural Due Process Beyond the Common-Law Core of Personal Interests

During the early 1970's, the circle of interests sufficient to create "liberty" or "property" for purposes of due process was significantly widened.[1] Professor Charles Reich's ground-breaking article, *The New Property*,[2] traced the ways in which rapid expansion of the public sector of the economy, together with the acceptance of a governmental obligation to aid the downtrodden, had created increasing dependence upon government as a major source of employment, contracts, or welfare benefits on the part of increasing numbers of citizens. Yet notwithstanding their growing reliance upon the state, citizens were granted virtually no constitutional protection against the arbitrary withdrawal of needed benefits, even after the supposed demise of the rights-

57. See, e.g., North American Cold Storage Co. v. Chicago, 211 U.S. 306, 320 (1908) (allowing seizure and destruction of poultry without prior hearing on grounds of "emergency . . . which would fairly appeal to the reasonable discretion of the legislature").

58. See, e.g., Crozier v. Fried, Krupp Aktiengesellschaft, 224 U.S. 290, 306 (1912) ("Indisputably the duty to make compensation does not inflexibly . . . [require] . . . that compensation should be made previous to the taking—it being sufficient . . . that adequate means be provided for a reasonably just and prompt ascertainment and payment of compensation . . .").

59. See, e.g., Bi-Metallic Invest. Co. v. State Board of Equalization, 239 U.S. 441 (1915); see §§ 10–1, 10–6, 10–7, supra.

60. See, e.g., Opp Cotton Mills, Inc. v. Administrator of Wage & Hour Div., 312 U.S. 126 (1941) (rejecting a procedural due process attack on provisions of the Fair Labor Standards Act making recommendation as to minimum wage); United States v. Illinois C.R. Co., 291 U.S. 457 (1934) (rejecting procedural due process claim for notice and hearing prior to Interstate Commerce Commission establishment of minimum rates for common carriers on inland waterways so long as opportunity for full hearing granted before order became operative).

§ 10–9

1. See, e.g., Perry v. Sindermann, 408 U.S. 593 (1972) (teacher's continued employment at state university pursuant to "implied" tenure); Morrissey v. Brewer, 408 U.S. 471 (1972) (conditional freedom following parole); Bell v. Burson, 402 U.S. 535 (1971) (driver's license); Goldberg v. Kelly, 397 U.S. 254 (1970) (welfare benefits).

2. 73 Yale L.J. 733 (1964).

privileges distinction protected such benefits from the imposition of unconstitutional conditions.[3] Perhaps responding to the alienation and affront to human dignity which such complete dependence and vulnerability might induce in circumstances where no alternative source of relief was available, the Court ultimately rejected much of what remained of the rights-privileges distinction.[4] For the first time, the Court recognized as entitlements [5] interests founded neither on constitutional nor on common law claims of right but only on a state-fostered (and hence justifiable) expectation, as opposed to a mere hope,[6] which was derived from "an independent source such as state law" [7] or from "mutually explicit understandings." [8] While these new "statutory entitlements" did not grant a constitutional right to governmental non-arbitrariness whenever benefits were being provided (since government remained free to foster *no* expectations in distributing its largesse), they did serve to surround the "core" of liberty and property interests with a periphery activated, unlike the core, only by affirmative state choices, but secure, once activated, against destruction without due process of law.

Determining the existence of these new entitlements depended on construction of the relevant statutes, and of the pertinent understandings between government and individuals, rather than on any balancing of interests; the existence of an entitlement turned not on "the weight but [on] the nature of the interest at stake." [9] The Court appears, therefore, to have placed great emphasis both on making it possible for those who deal with the government in any way to rely on any clearly announced rules,[10] and also on reducing the helplessness of persons who are in a dependent relationship to government with respect to basic needs. As to the latter in particular, the Court has

3. See § 10–8, supra.

4. See, e.g., Morrissey v. Brewer, 408 U.S. 471, 481 (1972); Graham v. Richardson, 403 U.S. 365, 374 (1971); Bell v. Burson, 402 U.S. 535, 539 (1971); Goldberg v. Kelly, 397 U.S. 254, 262 (1970); Sherbert v. Verner, 374 U.S. 398, 404 (1963). The distinction still retained vitality, however, where government carefully avoided creating *any* expectation of receipt or renewal upon the fulfillment or non-fulfillment of stated conditions. Board of Regents v. Roth, 408 U.S. 564 (1972). However, the conditions must be "substantive limitations on discretion" in the form of standards rather than a mere procedural framework, since "[t]he State may choose to require procedures for reasons other than protection against deprivation of substantive rights. . . ." Olim v. Wakinekona, 461 U.S. 238, 249–51 (1983) (holding that no state-created liberty interest arose despite prison regulations requiring a hearing prior to interstate transfer of an inmate, since "[n]o standards govern[ed]" the determination). See also Hewitt v. Helms, 459 U.S. 460, 471 (1983); Connecticut Bd. of Pardons v. Dumschat, 452 U.S. 458 (1981).

5. The Court adopted the terminology used by Reich, supra note 2. See, e.g., Goldberg v. Kelly, 397 U.S. 254, 262 n. 8 (1970).

6. Thus the Court has not defined property interests as expansively as some commentators have urged. See, e.g., Comment, "Entitlement, Enjoyment, and Due Process of Law," 1974 Duke L.J. 89, 111 (urging the Court to "regard life, liberty, and property as encompassing everything of which a person can be deprived, and [to] hold that a person has a claim within the ambit of the due process clause whenever governmental action has accrued to his detriment").

7. Board of Regents v. Roth, 408 U.S. 564, 577 (1972).

8. Perry v. Sindermann, 408 U.S. 593, 601 (1972).

9. Roth, 408 U.S. at 571. See also Goss v. Lopez, 419 U.S. 565, 575–76 (1975); Fuentes v. Shevin, 407 U.S. 67, 86 (1972).

10. See also § 9–7, supra.

evidently sought to assure that government decisions about needs are reasonably accurate and that individuals have a personal chance to be heard when vital necessities are at stake.[11] Moreover, the Court appears to have proceeded on the premise that, when a reduction in helplessness requires participation in hearings, the cost in dollars cannot be accepted as a sufficient reason to proceed by discretionary choice, since due process will always involve administrative burdens of that sort.[12]

In *Goldberg v. Kelly*, for example, the Court held that New York could not terminate "public assistance payments to a particular recipient without affording him the opportunity for an evidentiary hearing prior to termination." [13] Writing for the Court, Justice Brennan noted that "[i]t may be realistic today to regard welfare entitlements as more like property than a 'gratuity.' Much of the existing wealth in this country takes the form of rights that do not fall within traditional common law concepts of property." [14] Thus, welfare "benefits are a matter of statutory entitlement for persons qualified to receive them." [15] Similarly, in *Bell v. Burson* [16] the Court found that a clergyman involved in a car accident had an entitlement to his driver's license under state law, and thus had a federal constitutional right to a due process hearing on the question of his responsibility for the accident prior to any suspension of his license to drive. "Once licenses are issued . . . continued possession may become essential in the pursuit of a livelihood. Suspension of issued licenses thus involves state action that adjudicates important interests of the licensees." [17]

The Court also held that "a person's liberty is equally protected even when the liberty itself is a statutory creation of the state," [18] since statutory entitlements include "many of the core values of unqualified liberty." [19] Thus, although government is not constitutionally required

11. See United States Dept. of Agriculture v. Murry, 413 U.S. 508 (1973) (invalidating as violative of due process a statutory provision basing the food stamp ineligibility of an entire household upon the presence of a member who had been claimed as a dependent by an ineligible taxpayer living outside the household; such a rule of thumb is an excessively inaccurate measure of needs).

12. See § 10–13, infra, on the question of balancing costs of hearings in determining what process is due.

13. 397 U.S. 254, 255 (1970).

14. Id. at 262 n. 8.

15. Id. at 262. See also Atkins v. Parker, 472 U.S. 115, 129 (1985) (food stamp benefits are a statutory entitlement). But see note 37, infra.

16. 402 U.S. 535 (1971).

17. Id. at 539. See also Mackey v. Montrym, 443 U.S. 1, 10 n. 7 (1979) ("That the Due Process Clause applies to a state's suspension or revocation of a driver's license is clear. . . ."); Barry v. Barchi,

443 U.S. 55, 64 (1979) (horse trainer's license, not revocable at the discretion of racing officials, constituted a "clear . . . property interest"). A particular unfairness in the scheme struck down in Bell v. Burson was its delegation of unaccountable power to the other driver involved in an accident; by simply alleging damages in some astronomical amount, the other driver could put the licensee to a choice between posting an enormous bond and submitting to license suspension. Cf. § 5–17, supra.

18. Wolff v. McDonnell, 418 U.S. 539, 558 (1974).

19. Morrissey v. Brewer, 408 U.S. 471, 482 (1972). Justice Stevens has consistently adhered to the Lockean view that the state does not "create" liberty: "[N]either the Bill of Rights nor the laws of sovereign States create the liberty which the Due Process Clause protects. The relevant constitutional provisions are limitations on the power of the sovereign to infringe on the liberty of the citizen. The relevant state laws either create property rights, or

to offer prisoners early release opportunities, once such opportunities are promised on specified conditions, they may not subsequently be withdrawn unless the government complies with the requirements of procedural due process.[20] However, since an individual in this context is deprived of a conditional liberty rather than of the absolute freedom from bodily restraint enjoyed prior to criminal conviction, the procedural safeguards government must provide in revoking the conditional grant of early release are not as stringent as those it was required to observe in order to bring about the original conviction and confinement. In *Morrissey v. Brewer*, for example, the Court held that, since an individual "can be gainfully employed and is free to be with family and friends and to form the other enduring attachments of normal life" when free subject to the conditions of parole, the termination of this "liberty" by revoking parole "inflicts a 'grievous loss' on the parolees and often on others," and must therefore be preceded by "some orderly process, however informal." [21] Similarly, in *Gagnon v. Scarpelli*, the Court found "that revocation of probation where sentence has been imposed previously is constitutionally indistinguishable from . . . revocation of parole." [22] Thus the guarantee of due process also attaches to the liberty interest in conditional freedom afforded by probation. And in *Wolff v. McDonnell*,[23] the Court held that, when a state chooses to offer prisoners a shortened jail sentence by permitting the accumulation of credits for good behavior, the revocation of a prisoner's "good-time" credits as a punishment for misconduct is valid only if carried out in a manner satisfying the obligations of procedural due process.

In more recent cases, the Court has focused on specific statutory language to determine whether the state has "created" a liberty inter-

they curtail the freedom of the citizen who must live in an ordered society." Meachum v. Fano, 427 U.S. 215, 230 (1976) (Stevens, J., dissenting), quoted in Connecticut Bd. of Pardons v. Dumschat, 452 U.S. 458, 469 n. 1 (1981) (Stevens, J., dissenting).

20. The Court has also declared that state commitment proceedings, whether civil or criminal, are subject to procedural due process. Specht v. Patterson, 386 U.S. 605 (1967) (individual convicted of sex crime for which statutory punishment was ten years imprisonment was denied due process when, without full panoply of procedural safeguards, the state sentenced him to commitment in a mental institution as a sexual psychopath for an indefinite period). See also Addington v. Texas, 441 U.S. 418 (1979) (requiring a "clear and convincing" standard of proof in civil commitment proceedings); Jones v. United States, 463 U.S. 354, 361 (1983) (commitment for any purpose constitutes a deprivation of liberty requiring due process); Vitek v. Jones, 445 U.S. 480 (1980), discussed in note 26, infra. Cf. Minnesota ex rel. Pearson v. Probate Court, 309 U.S. 270 (1940) (upholding state procedures for the indefinite commitment of sexual psychopaths; procedures included rights to prior

adversary hearing, representation by counsel, medical examination by two doctors, access to compulsory process, a written record, an appeal, and release pending hearing or appeal; the Court did not indicate whether all or merely some of these rights were required by procedural due process). The Court has also required that due process must be accorded before renewal of an individual's criminal commitment beyond the expiration date of the maximum prison sentence for the crime of which he was convicted. See Humphrey v. Cady, 405 U.S. 504 (1972). Cf. McNeil v. Director, Patuxent Institution, 407 U.S. 245 (1972) (despite refusal to submit to psychiatric examination, detention of an alleged "defective delinquent" beyond the expiration date of his criminal sentence violates due process).

21. 408 U.S. 471, 482 (1972). In the Morrissey opinion, the Court for the first time undertook to analyze due process in an explicitly bifurcated manner: "Once it is determined that due process applies, the question remains what process is due." Id. at 481.

22. 411 U.S. 778, 782 n. 3 (1973).

23. 418 U.S. 539 (1974).

est. *Greenholtz v. Inmates of Nebraska Penal and Cor. Complex*[24] for example, held that while the mere existence of a parole system fails to establish a liberty interest for those seeking parole,[25] the particular statute at issue contained such "unique structure and language" that it entitled the inmate to protection.[26]

This new "statutory entitlement" doctrine was also extended beyond those property and liberty interests, such as welfare and parole, which are conferred by the government basically to meet the needs of recipients. The Court also accorded due process protection to such "property" interests as government employment, conferred for the government's own purposes rather than the recipient's. Here, as with the new entitlements generally, the property interest in government employment was protected by procedural due process only insofar as it was derived from reliance induced by the state's express agreement or implied promise. In *Perry v. Sindermann*,[27] the Supreme Court held that a cause of action was made out by a state junior college professor's contention that he had been denied procedural due process by the failure of the junior college to grant him a hearing before deciding not to renew his teaching contract. Justice Stewart's majority opinion found that, although state law did not authorize the junior college explicitly to grant its professors tenure, there was evidence indicating that "there may be an unwritten 'common law' in [the junior college] that certain employees shall have the equivalent of tenure." [28] The Court concluded that Sindermann, previously employed by the junior college for four years, might be able to show "the existence of rules and understandings, promulgated and fostered by state officials, that . . . justify his legitimate claim of entitlement to continued employment absent 'sufficient cause.' " [29] In the companion case of *Board of Regents*

---

24. 442 U.S. 1 (1979), also discussed in § 10–7, supra, and § 10–10, infra.

25. Compare Morrissey v. Brewer, 408 U.S. 471 (1972). The Court in Greenholtz spent considerable time distinguishing Morrissey, presumably because the parolee's liberty in Morrissey existed regardless of the precise language in the parole statute. See Greenholtz, 442 U.S. at 24 (Marshall, J., dissenting in part).

26. 442 U.S. at 12. The court appeared to rely on the mandatory character of the phrase "shall order his release unless. . . ." Elsewhere, the Court has recognized that "explicitly mandatory language in connection with requiring specific substantive predicates demands a conclusion that the State has created a protected liberty interest." Hewitt v. Helms, 459 U.S. 460, 472 (1983). But the absence of mandatory language does not preclude the state's creation of a liberty. Vitek v. Jones, 445 U.S. 480, 488–491 (1980) (interest created where statutory language provided that if a psychologist "finds" that an inmate "suffers from a mental disease" which could not be properly treated in the

prison, the director "may" order his transfer). And "the presence of general or broad release criteria—delegating significant discretion to the decisionmaker—[does] not deprive the prisoner of the liberty interest in parole release created by . . . [a] statute" specifying that parole must be granted "unless one of [several] designated justifications for deferral [or denial] is found." Board of Pardons v. Allen, 107 S.Ct. 2415, 2419 (1987) (relying on Greenholtz); cf. id. at 2424 (O'Connor, J., joined by Rehnquist, C.J., and Scalia, J., dissenting) (urging that "*Greenholtz* is . . . an aberration and should be reexamined and limited strictly to its facts.").

27. 408 U.S. 593 (1972). See also Connell v. Higgenbotham, 403 U.S. 207 (1971) (holding that a state could not summarily dismiss a substitute classroom teacher who had refused to sign a loyalty oath without affording the teacher a prior hearing complying with due process).

28. Perry v. Sindermann, 408 U.S. 593, 602 (1972).

29. Id. at 602–03.

v. Roth,[30] on the other hand, the Court found no basis for the claim of a nontenured assistant professor to a hearing before the state university declined to renew his contract. Justice Stewart's majority opinion reasoned that, "to have a property interest in a benefit, a person clearly must have more than an abstract need or desire for it"; property interests "are created and . . . defined by existing rules or understandings that stem from an independent source such as state law." [31] There, state law left "the decision whether to rehire a nontenured teacher for another year to the unfettered discretion of university officials," [32] and there was no other independent source such as past custom, as there was in *Perry*, on which an entitlement could be based.[33]

The Court in *Roth* also suggested that present enjoyment [34] of a statutory entitlement is an indispensable prerequisite of due process protection, when it commented that "[t]he Fourteenth Amendment's procedural protection of property is a safeguard of the security interests that a person *has already acquired* in specific benefits." [35] It might thus be argued that there exists no due process duty to afford a hearing when the state turns down an initial request (as opposed to renewal, dismissal or revocation) for welfare, a government job or parole.[36] But it would be inconsistent with any intelligible rationale underlying due process protection to deny all procedural safeguards to the new applicant where the law provides that all individuals meeting certain objective criteria are entitled to, say, welfare.[37]

In *Memphis Light, Gas, & Water Div. v. Craft*,[38] the Supreme Court held that customers of a public utility were entitled to process before their power was disconnected for non-payment of disputed bills. Although electricity is arguably required to meet the needs of most persons, the Court chose to rest its finding of a property interest on state decisional law providing that service could be terminated only "for cause." [39]

30. 408 U.S. 564 (1972).

31. Id. at 577.

32. Id. at 567.

33. Id. at 578 n. 16.

34. See Comment, "Entitlement, Enjoyment, and Due Process of Law," 1974 Duke L.J. 89.

35. 408 U.S. at 576 (emphasis added).

36. Indeed, in Greenholtz v. Inmates of Nebraska Penal and Cor. Complex, the Court distinguished initial denial from revocation of parole, stating that "[t]here is a crucial distinction between being deprived of a liberty one has, as in parole, and being denied a conditional liberty that one desires." 442 U.S. at 9. The Court described the issue as an open one in Lyng v. Payne, 106 S.Ct. 2333, 2343 (1986).

37. Although some lower courts have done just that, see, e.g., Gregory v. Pittsfield, 479 A.2d 1304 (Me. 1984), cert. denied 470 U.S. 1018 (1985), such holdings seem "a questionable reading of [Supreme] Court precedent," are "unsettling in [their] implication[s]," and are contrary to "the weight of authority among lower courts." Id. at 1380, 1381–82 (O'Connor, J., joined by Brennan, and Marshall, JJ., dissenting). If the Court were to deny any protection to interests in statutory benefits not currently enjoyed, then the fear expressed by Justice Black in his dissent in Goldberg v. Kelly, 397 U.S. 254, 279 (1970), may be borne out: a state would be tempted to delay putting a person on welfare until absolutely sure he or she was eligible, since once the individual started receiving welfare payments, the payments could not be discontinued without a hearing. The Greenholtz ruling, see note 36 supra, is not to the contrary inasmuch as the inmate's claim to entitlement in that case rested on the "unique structure and language" of the particular statute at issue. 442 U.S. at 12.

38. 436 U.S. 1 (1978).

39. Id. at 9–12.

While the extension of procedural safeguards to statutory entitlements beyond the constitutional and common law core of personal interests was the most significant change in procedural due process jurisprudence during the early 1970's, this period was also marked by the recognition of a broader set of "core" interests; there was no inconsistency, in short, between the entitlement view and the preservation of a core of substantive "liberty" and "property" rights independent of a state's laws. The Court appeared, for example, to find a liberty interest "where a person's good name, reputation, honor or integrity is at stake because of what the government is doing to him," [40] so that government had to meet due process requirements before taking action which explicitly labeled an individual in an invidious or derogatory manner. First, in *Jenkins v. McKeithen*,[41] the Supreme Court held that, given appropriate offerings of proof, a valid claim for declaratory and injunctive relief would be made out by the contention that the Louisiana Labor-Management Commission's practice of investigating and finding facts relating to violations of state and federal criminal laws in the labor-management relations field was inconsistent with the requirements of procedural due process. Justice Marshall's plurality opinion found that the Commission performed the directly accusatory function of publicly labeling individuals and groups as violators of the criminal laws. Since the public identification of "criminals" was a direct rather than collateral consequence of the Commission's activities, "the personal and economic consequences" for the branded individuals and groups triggered procedural due process obligations.[42] Second, in *Wisconsin v. Constantineau*,[43] the Court held that state officials must comply with the requirements of procedural due process before they take action to publicly label an individual as an excessive drinker by displaying in all liquor stores of a given community a public notice that sales or gifts of liquor to the named individual are forbidden for one year. The Court found that, while posting "under the Wisconsin act may to some be merely the mark of illness, to others it is a stigma, an official branding of a person" in a degrading way. "Only when the whole proceedings leading to the pinning of an unsavory label on a person are aired can oppressive results be prevented." [44]

However, action which labels an individual only implicitly does not violate any personal interest entitled to due process protection. Thus in *Board of Regents v. Roth*, the Court held that the unexplained

40. Wisconsin v. Constantineau, 400 U.S. 433, 437 (1971). See also Board of Regents v. Roth, 408 U.S. 564, 573 (1972).

41. 395 U.S. 411 (1969). See also Joint Anti-Fascist Refugee Committee v. McGrath, 341 U.S. 123, 161 (1951) (Frankfurter, J., concurring) (government action publicly labeling groups as Communist without prior notice or opportunity to participate "is so devoid of fundamental fairness as to offend the Due Process Clause of the Fifth Amendment"), discussed in § 10–8, supra. But see Hannah v. Larche, 363 U.S. 420 (1960) (U.S. Commission on Civil Rights is not subject to due process obliga-

tions in finding facts pertaining to voting discrimination because invidious consequences such as loss of jobs, subjection to public scorn and the chance of criminal prosecution would be collateral rather than direct).

42. 395 U.S. at 424.

43. 400 U.S. 433 (1971).

44. Id. at 437. The Court reached this procedural conclusion despite its recognition of sweeping state authority to impose substantive controls in the liquor field. Cf. California v. LaRue, 409 U.S. 109 (1972).

decision of a state university not to renew the contract of an untenured assistant professor did no constitutionally significant damage to the reputation of the dismissed employee: "[I]t stretches the concept too far to suggest that a person is deprived of liberty when he simply is not rehired in one job but remains as free as before to seek another." [45] But the Court noted that, had the state invoked "any regulations to bar the respondent from all other public employment in state universities . . . this . . . would be a different case". [46] *Roth* indicates that the Court is operating on the theory that, although an individual may acquire a property interest in government employment if a statute or government-induced understandings confer such an entitlement, an individual cannot be said to possess any "liberty" to choose a specific public post which government, under the applicable substantive law, may offer or withdraw without explanation.[47]

In some respects, the Court has also broadened the core of protected liberty interests by extending the "residuum of liberty" which an inmate retains upon lawful incarceration. In *Vitek v. Jones*,[48] for example, the Court held that a prisoner's transfer to a mental hospital automatically implicated due process, since "commitment to a mental hospital is not within the range of conditions of confinement to which a prison sentence subjects an individual." [49] The prisoner's retained liberty inhered in his right not to be further stigmatized and his right to be free from unjustified intrusions on personal security—intrusions implicated by compelled behavior modification programs at the mental institution.[50]

In addition to occasionally enlarging the liberty interest in reputation and in freedom from certain kinds of incarceration the Court also appears to have built a kind of "privacy" or "repose" interest onto the core "property" interest in possession by enabling people to be secure, in their houses and personal effects, against seizures by the state (or with the state's approval) without warning and a chance to resist in advance—even in cases where the deprivation was temporary and at least theoretically reversible, or where the individuals deprived of possession by the enforcement power of government lacked full title to

---

45. 408 U.S. 564, 575 (1972). Cf. Cafeteria & Restaurant Workers Union v. McElroy, 367 U.S. 886 (1961) (holding that the unexplained revocation of security clearances did no constitutionally cognizable damage to the reputation of a short-order cook privately employed on the premises of a naval installation, even though the cook lost her job at the installation as a consequence of the revocation, since her employment opportunities elsewhere were not shown to have been impeded).

46. 408 U.S. at 573–54. See also Joint Anti-Fascist Refugee Committee v. McGrath, 341 U.S. 123, 185 (1951) (Jackson, J., concurring) ("to be deprived not only of present government employment but of future opportunity for it certainly is no small injury").

47. But compare the protected "liberty" interest in at least being considered for government employment. Hampton v. Mow Sun Wong, 426 U.S. 88 (1976). See § 15–13, infra.

48. 445 U.S. 480 (1980).

49. 445 U.S. at 493.

50. See also Hughes v. Rowe, 449 U.S. 5 (1980) (disciplinary segregation of an inmate without a prior hearing may violate due process absent emergency conditions). But see Hewitt v. Helms, 459 U.S. at 468–69 (holding that administrative segregation alone does not require due process and noting that Hughes was "essentially a pleading case" not reaching the merits).

the goods.[51] In *Sniadach v. Family Finance Corp.*,[52] the Supreme Court held that, absent a provision for a prior adversary hearing, a state could not permit the institution by civil plaintiffs by prejudgment wage garnishment actions against the employers of prospective defendants in order to halt payment to defendant-employees of a substantial portion of their wages pending the outcome of litigation. In deciding that a recovery provision allowing the defendant to post security so as to regain the property was insufficient to protect defendant's constitutional interest, Justice Harlan noted that "[t]he 'property' of which petitioner has been deprived is the use of the garnished portion of her wages during the interim period between the garnishment and the culmination of the main suit." [53]

In *Fuentes v. Shevin*, the Court faced a considerably more difficult issue since the civil plaintiff seeking prejudgment replevin of household goods unquestionably had a property interest in these goods, sold to the debtor under a conditional sales contract which the debtor had not yet paid in full. In holding that the "possessory interest in the goods clearly bought and protected by contract was sufficient to invoke the protection of the due process clause" [54] notwithstanding a pre-existing state law allowing for ex parte prejudgment replevin, the Court reasoned that "the Fourteenth Amendment's protection of 'property' . . . has never been interpreted to safeguard only the rights of undisputed ownership." [55] Justice Stewart's majority opinion reasoned that "even assuming that the [debtors] had fallen behind in their installment payments and that they had no other valid defenses . . . [t]he right to be heard does not depend upon an advance showing that one will surely prevail at the hearing." [56] In an analysis similar to that undertaken in *Perry v. Sindermann*, the Court noted that, since the state has recognized an interest in property by virtue of statutory or common law or mutual understandings, the process due for deprivation of the property interest must have its roots in substantive constitutional doctrine and is not derived either from the will of the parties [57] or from provisions of

51. In other contexts the Court has also expanded this "peaceful enjoyment" addition to the property "core" to encompass the interest on a sum of money deposited with the court. Webb's Fabulous Pharmacies, Inc. v. Beckwith, 449 U.S. 155 (1980) (interest could not be defined as public property by state for purpose of "takings" clause), discussed in § 9–7, supra.

52. 395 U.S. 337 (1969).

53. Id. at 342 (Harlan, J., concurring).

54. 407 U.S. 67, 86–87 (1972).

55. Id. at 86.

56. Id. at 87. At least one case casts doubt on the universality of this principle. In Codd v. Velger, 429 U.S. 624 (1977), the Court held that no hearing was required upon termination of an untenured employee where he does not challenge the "substantial truth" of statements impugning his reputation. Hence, the existence of

due process may apparently turn upon the potential merits of the case.

57. The Court nonetheless recognized the possibility of waiver of due process rights by the parties to the contract, although it found that in Fuentes "the language of the purported waiver provisions did not waive the appellant's constitutional right to a preseizure hearing of some kind." Id. at 96. The Court also raised serious questions about whether waiver would be found where the parties were unequal in bargaining power and/or the "bargain" was both part of a printed contract and a necessary part of the sale. Cf. D. H. Overmyer Co. v. Frick Co., 405 U.S. 174, 185 (1972) (holding that each of two corporations, both advised by counsel, had made a "voluntary, knowing and [intelligent]" waiver of its right to prejudgment notice and a hearing).

positive law enacted in advance by the legislature.[58] It is up to the Court, rather than the state, to determine the balance between the competing property interests of creditors and debtors in terms of the process due to resolve the controversy between them.[59] In striking that balance, the *Fuentes* Court concluded that a state may "seize goods before a final judgment in order to protect the security interests of creditors [only] so long as those creditors have tested their claim to the goods through the process of a fair prior hearing." [60]

§ 10–10. The Narrowing of Protected Interests: Formalizing the Entitlement Concept

Since the latter half of the decade of the 1970's, the Supreme Court's treatment of the entitlement concept has indicated a considerable narrowing of the liberty and property interests protected by procedural due process. In *Meachum v. Fano*, for example, the Court held that the interest in "liberty" contemplated by the due process clause does not entitle "a state prisoner to a hearing when he is transferred to a prison the conditions of which are substantially less favorable to the prisoner, absent a state law or practice conditioning such transfers on proof of serious misconduct or other events." [1] In expressly rejecting "the notion that any grievous loss visited upon a person by the state is sufficient to invoke the procedural protections of the due process clause," the Court was wary of subjecting "to judicial review a wide spectrum of discretionary actions that traditionally have been the business of prison administrations rather than of federal courts." [2]

58. But see Ogden v. Saunders, 25 U.S. (12 Wheat.) 213 (1827) (pre-existing state bankruptcy law governs creditor's interest in contract), discussed in §§ 9–8, 9–9, supra. While it is possible to argue that Fuentes overruled Ogden sub silentio, one might seek to distinguish Ogden from Fuentes on the ground that the state rule that was "read in" to all subsequently-entered contracts in Ogden was designed not simply to assist contracting debtors but also to serve the public interest in the orderly allocation of scarce resources when the debtors' funds cannot meet all of the claims against them, as well as the public interest in giving people a fresh start. "Reading in" a summary repossession provision, on the other hand, just "helps out" sellers or lenders by relieving them of the burden and cost of actually negotiating such provisions or of proceeding without them.

This distinction seems untenable, however; the statutes in Fuentes could also be justified on the basis of the public interest in making credit more available or less expensive for poor buyers. Moreover, if property "rights" mean anything special, they connote the idea that, although government infringements can be justified to protect conflicting "rights," they cannot be defended in the name of anything as nebulous as "public interest." Hence Fuentes must have its basis in the doctrine (1) that the process due for relinquishment of "property" is determined by constitutional standards which place great weight on the rights to peaceful private possession and uninterrupted enjoyment, and (2) that any contract disregarding these rights is at least constitutionally unenforceable by the state and perhaps void altogether.

59. See Cleveland Bd. of Educ. v. Loudermill, 470 U.S. 532 (1985) (rejecting the "bitter with the sweet" approach), discussed in § 10–12, infra.

60. 407 U.S. at 96.

§ 10–10

1. 427 U.S. 215, 216 (1976). See Comment, "Two Views of a Prisoner's Right to Due Process: Meachum v. Fano," 12 Harv. Civ.Rts.—Civ.Lib.L.Rev. 405 (1977). In Olim v. Wakinekona, 461 U.S. 238, 244–248 (1983), the Court extended Meachum to hold that no process is due when an inmate is transfered to another state's prison, "even when . . . the transfer involves long distance and an ocean crossing" (Hawaii to California), effectively separating the inmate from his family and friends.

2. 427 U.S. at 224–25. See also Jago v. Van Curen, 454 U.S. 14, 19 (1981) ("We

Justice White's majority opinion concluded that "[w]hatever expectation the prisoner may have in remaining at a particular prison so long as he behaves himself, it is too ephemeral and insubstantial to trigger procedural due process protections as long as prison officials have discretion to transfer him for whatever reason or for no reason at all." [3] Similarly, in *Hewitt v. Helms*,[4] the Court refused to find that prisoners have a procedurally protected liberty interest not to be placed in solitary confinement [5] inhering in the due process clause itself. Stating that "[a]s long as the conditions or degree of confinement to which the prisoner is subjected is within the sentence imposed upon him and is not otherwise violative of the Constitution, the Due Process Clause does not in itself subject an inmate's treatment by prison authorites to judicial oversight," [6] the Court held that "the transfer of an inmate to less amenable and more restrictive quarters for non punitive reasons is well within the terms of confinement ordinarily contemplated by a prison sentence." [7]

A corresponding reluctance to look beyond positive state law as a source of rights protected by due process guarantees was evident in *Bishop v. Wood*, where a three and a half year veteran of the police force, classified as a "permanent employee" by a city ordinance which also provided that he could be dismissed if certain grounds were present, was fired for failure to discharge his duties properly, "without affording him a hearing to determine the sufficiency of the cause for his discharge." [8]   Justice Stevens, writing for a closely divided Court, reasoned that "the sufficiency of the claim of entitlement must be, decided by reference to state law," [9] which in this case was governed by *Still v. Lance*,[10] where the North Carolina Supreme Court had held

would severely restrict the necessary flexibility of prison administrators and parole authorities were we to hold that any one of their myriad decisions with respect to individual inmates may . . . give rise to protected 'liberty' interests . . .").

3.   427 U.S. at 228. Only a completely instrumental approach to procedural due process, see § 10–7, supra, can suggest that a hearing is pointless whenever discretionary power is being exercised; in such a case, the hearing obviously cannot focus on the presence or absence of previously specified facts, but it can certainly address the question of how the challenged power ought to be exercised in the circumstances.

4.   459 U.S. 460 (1983).

5.   See 459 U.S. at 479 (Stevens, J., dissenting). While the confinement was officially labelled "administrative segregation," the majority's opinion demonstrates that "solitary confinement" is an appropriate description of the conditions in which the prisoner was placed: the segregation denied the prisoner "access to vocational, educational, recreational, and rehabilitative programs," restricted his exercise, and confined him to his cell for lengthy periods of time. 459 U.S. at 463 n. 1, 467 n. 4.

6.   Id. at 468, quoting Montanye v. Haymes, 427 U.S. 236, 242 (1976). Vitek v. Jones, 445 U.S. 480 (1980), discussed in § 10–9, represents one of the rare instances where the Court has found a change in a prisoner's status (transfer to a mental hospital) "not within the range of conditions of confinement to which a prison sentence subjects an individual." Id. at 493.

7.   Id. Although the Court had previously stated that "[s]egregation of a prisoner without a prior hearing may violate due process," Hughes v. Rowe, 449 U.S. 5, 11 (1980), as Chief Justice (then Justice) Rehnquist noted in Hewitt, the Hughes opinion explicitly refused to "express any view on [the] merits." Hewitt, 459 U.S. at 469 n. 5; Hughes, 449 U.S. at 12.

8.   426 U.S. 341, 344, 342 (1976). The Court's treatment of the policeman's claim of infringement of a "liberty" interest in reputation is discussed in § 10–11, infra.

9.   426 U.S. at 344.

10.   279 N.C. 254, 182 S.E.2d 403 (1971).

"that an enforceable expectation of continued employment in that state can exist only if the employer by statute or contract has actually granted some form of guarantee." [11] Since the federal district court's finding in *Bishop* that the policeman "held his position at the pleasure of the city" [12] was a plausible interpretation of the ordinance in light of *Still v. Lance*, the Court concluded that the finding foreclosed its independent examination of the state law issue [13] "even if an examination of [that] issue without such guidance might have justified a different conclusion." [14]

This exclusively positivist analysis of entitlements undertaken in *Meachum, Helms* and *Bishop* presents a profoundly novel vision of procedural due process. The Court in *Meachum*, for example, was able successfully to distinguish the earlier decision in *Wolff v. McDonnell*,[15] where the state had "not only provided a statutory right to good time credit but also specified that it is to be forfeited only for serious misbehavior", [16] on the ground that the Massachusetts statute in *Meachum* had not conferred on prisoners the "right" to be confined in any particular prison. But when the Court, without any detailed examination of "mutually explicit understandings," [17] characterized as "too ephemeral" prisoners' claims of a justifiable expectation of remaining at a more favorable prison if good behavior was maintained, it marked an important break from prior decisions. Thus, in *Morrissey v. Brewer*, the Court had found an "implicit promise" that an individual would not have his parole revoked in the absence of the violation of any of its provisions, notwithstanding a decision by the Iowa Supreme Court interpreting the state parole statutes to leave all parole-related issues completely within the discretion of the parole board.[18] By failing to conduct "an analysis of the common practices utilized and the expectations generated by [the city], and the manner in which the local ordinance would reasonably be read" [19] by members of the police force, the Court in *Bishop* also significantly retreated from its position in

---

11. 426 U.S. at 344. But see id. at 361–62 (Blackmun, J., dissenting) (suggesting that the statute construed in Still v. Lance, unlike the one in Bishop, had no "for cause" requirement and was therefore distinguishable).

12. Bishop v. Wood, 377 F.Supp. 501, 504 (W.D.N.C.1973). But see 426 U.S. at 356 (White, J., dissenting) ("The majority purports . . . to read the District Court's opinion as construing the ordinance not to condition dismissal on cause, and, if this is what the majority means, its reading . . . is clearly erroneous.") For a discussion of Justice White's claim that the majority in Bishop was in fact adopting Justice Rehnquist's "bitter with the sweet" position in Arnett v. Kennedy, 416 U.S. 134, 154 (1974), which supposes that the State may qualify procedurally an entitlement it has accorded, see § 10–12, infra.

13. 426 U.S. at 347.

14. Id. at 346.

15. 418 U.S. 539 (1974), discussed in § 10–9, supra.

16. Meachum v. Fano, 427 U.S. 215, 226 (1976).

17. The Court has since completely rejected the notion that "mutually explicit understandings" can form the basis of a liberty interest; since the principle is derived from contract law, it is only "useful" in determining property interests. Jago v. Van Curen, 454 U.S. 14, 17–21 (1981) (no liberty interest impaired in board's recision of parole after prisoner was notified that he would be released).

18. 408 U.S. 471, 482 (1972). See Curtis v. Bennett, 256 Iowa 1164, 131 N.W.2d 1 (1964), cert. denied 380 U.S. 958 (1965).

19. 426 U.S. at 354 (Brennan, J., dissenting).

Perry v. Sindermann,[20] where its finding that a professor arguably had a property interest in his job was based on "an unwritten common law."[21] The practical impact of the Court's adoption of a positivist approach to the definition of "property" in *Bishop v. Wood* is that a public employee can count on procedural due process protection only if the law or contract defining the employee's job expressly provides that the employee can be discharged *only* for cause. In its desire to leave "ultimate control of state personnel relationships . . . with the states,"[22] *Bishop's* approach involves "a resurrection of the discredited rights-privileges distinction, for a state may now avoid all due process safeguards . . . merely by labeling them as not constituting property."[23]

The Court's retreat from its *Morrissey* and *Perry* rationales did not end with *Bishop* and *Meachum*. In *Greenholtz v. Inmates of Nebraska Penal and Cor. Complex*,[24] the Court refused to find that due process applied to initial parole decisions apart from the specific statutory language establishing the parole system. Realizing the need to distinguish *Morrissey*, the Court pointed out that the parolees in *Morrissey* were already at liberty, while the inmates in *Greenholtz* were still confined. Since "there is a . . . difference between losing what one has and not getting what one wants," when "the state holds out the possibility of parole [it] provides no more than a mere hope that the benefit will be obtained."[25] In *Connecticut Board of Pardons v. Dumschat*,[26] the Court further withdrew actual expectations from its formalized calculus of state-created interests. Dumschat applied for commutation of his life sentence and was repeatedly rejected without explanation. The Court rejected the Second Circuit's contention that despite the absence of a statutorily created interest (since the review board was given "unfettered discretion"), Dumschat acquired a protected interest from the fact that over 75% of the life inmates' sentences were commuted. Finding that Dumschat's expectation was "simply a unilateral hope," the Supreme Court ruled that "[n]o matter how frequently a particular form of clemency has been granted, the statistical probabilities standing alone generate no constitutional protections. . . . The ground for a constitutional claim, if any, must be found in statutes or other rules defining the obligations of the authority charged with exercising clemency."[27] Finally, *Jago v. Van Curen's* extraction of the "mutually explicit understandings" doctrine from liberty interest determinations[28] suggests that even the most reasonable expectations are not enough to implicate due process.[29] This view

20. 408 U.S. 593 (1972), discussed in § 10–9, supra.

21. Id. at 602.

22. 426 U.S. at 350 n. 14.

23. Id. at 354 n. 4 (Brennan, J., dissenting).

24. 442 U.S. 1 (1979).

25. See Id. at 9–11. But see the discussion of Greenholtz in § 10–9, supra.

26. 452 U.S. 458 (1981).

27. Id. at 465.

28. See note 17, supra.

29. See also Leis v. Flynt, 439 U.S. 438, 443 (1979) (denying that out-of-state counsel had either a property or liberty interest in representing an out-of-state defendant, the Court stated, "Even if . . . respondents . . . had 'reasonable expectations of professional service,' [cite omitted] they have not shown the requisite *mutual* understanding that they would be permitted

(beginning with *Bishop* and *Meachum* and continuing through *Jago*) that mere expectations, however reasonable and however demonstrably induced by government, do not amount to interests protected by due process unless they are grounded in explicit rules of state law, is founded on the same notion as the rights-privileges distinction—namely, that what a state may decline to provide at all, it can grant on any terms it chooses. That proposition, in Justice Stevens' words, "demeans the concept of liberty itself." [30]

Although the Court has maintained that it intends to adhere to the notion of statutory entitlements, it has insisted on an increasingly narrow formula for defining the circumstances in which the interest is to be maintained. Indeed, the Court has drifted closer to the flipside of the "bittersweet" doctrine [31] by holding that statutes create protected interests only if they contain "specific substantive predicates" and "explicitly mandatory language;" the existence of a "careful procedural structure" is not enough. [32] Hence, if a statute gives an official "unfettered discretion," it creates no protected interest, even if the exercise of that discretion is channelled through required procedural mechanisms. [33] This narrowly formalistic approach, relying on verbal distinctions having no relation to reasonable expectations or to public understandings, seems far too obscure to serve the purposes of protecting reliance on government, reducing helplessness, or enhancing accountability. [34]

If the Court were to focus on real expectations and the role a government job actually plays in someone's life, then it would have to move well beyond the positivist framework it first adopted in *Bishop*. Yet the dissent in *Bishop*, unlike that in *Meachum*, does not offer a practical alternative. In the *Meachum* dissent, Justice Stevens (who authored the *Bishop* majority) suggests that the interest in liberty

to represent their clients . . . in the Ohio courts.") (emphasis in original).

30. Meachum, 427 U.S. at 233 (Stevens, J., dissenting). This failure seriously to consider the existence of justifiable expectations also created a significant internal inconsistency in Justice White's opinion, since he had earlier indicated a willingness to look for a liberty interest either in "state law *or practice*." Id. at 216 (emphasis added).

31. The "bittersweet" doctrine, introduced by the plurality in Arnett v. Kennedy, 416 U.S. 134, 152–54 (1974), would hold that since statutorily-created rights are partially defined by the procedures which accompany them, one asserting the right must "take the bitter with the sweet" and is thereby limited to the procedures which the statute provides. In its explicit rejection of this theory, the Court found itself forced to take the dubious position that "substance and procedure are distinct." Cleveland Bd. of Educ. v. Loudermill, 470 U.S. 532, 541 (1985). Such a stance implies the "flipside" of the "bit-

tersweet," that mere procedural protections also cannot expand the substance to create a protected interest.

32. Hewitt v. Helms, 459 U.S. 460, 470–472 (1983). See also Olim v. Wakinekona, 461 U.S. 238, 250 (1983) (prison regulations requiring a particular kind of hearing before transferring an inmate to another state's prison did not create a liberty interest where regulations provided "no substantive limitations on official discretion").

33. See id.

34. See generally Rabin, "Job Security and Due Process: Monitoring Administrative Discretion Through a Reasons Requirement," 44 U.Chi.L.Rev. 60 (1976). See also A. Camus, "State of Siege," in Caligula and 3 Other Plays 165 (1958): "[A]ll this rigamarole . . . [is] intended to get them used to that touch of obscurity which gives all government regulations their peculiar charm and efficacy. The less these people understand, the better they'll behave. You get my point?"

protected by due process is a "cardinal inalienable right" with which "all men are endowed by their creator" [35] and not "an interest that the state has created through its own prison regulations." [36] In *Bishop*, on the other hand, the dissenters attempt to find a statutory entitlement to a job as a policeman.[37] But there is a degree of circularity to their argument that there may have been "reasonable expectations" in *Bishop* that justified a finding of a property interest: it is questionable whether a person can truly be said to "justifiably rely" on continued employment where the person's contract or statute expressly indicates either that the employment can be terminated without cause, or that cause is theoretically required but no hearing is to be allowed. This circle can be broken only by an assertion of substantive values or norms in the name of the Constitution—norms as to what an employee, for example, is *entitled* to expect *whatever* the contract or statute may say. Indeed, breaking the circle would require an acceptance of the proposition that due process is not merely a means to the end of implementing the state's own substantive rules and allocations but either a means to some very different and larger purpose, or—as in the intrinsic approach to procedural safeguards—an end in itself.

The view announced in the procedural due process cases of the early 1970's, that protection would be given to individual interests when government had invited dependence on certain benefits and reliance on some method of their distribution,[38] must be premised on just such a substantive theory of a constitutional right to a hearing whenever important personal interests are affected by government action. The case for such a hearing could be grounded either in intrinsic or in instrumental considerations. But if the latter are relied upon, the end to which due process must be a means is *not* that of carrying out the state's own positive choices, but rather that of assuring fairness and participation in the meeting of basic human needs.

Bishop, Meachum and their progeny do not necessarily presage a general retrenchment by the Court in the scope of entitlements or a complete rejection by the Court of substantive theories of why and when "process" should be due. The Court in *Meachum* and *Helms* seems to havè confined its newly limited application of the entitlement concept to prisoners for whom "the conviction has sufficiently extinguished the . . . liberty interest to empower the State to confine [them] in *any* of its prisons" [39] or anywhere within its prisons. [40] Indeed, *Vitek v. Jones*[41] indicates that the Court is still willing to find

---

35. 427 U.S. at 230 (Stevens, J., dissenting).

36. Id. at 233 (Stevens, J., dissenting). That is only partly correct; as we have seen in § 10–9, supra, liberty interests can be of either sort. However, Justice Stevens would probably assert that the State never actually "created" those liberties either, it simply reduced the scope of its earlier constitutional restriction of the "residuum of liberty". See Hewitt v. Helms, 459 U.S. at 484, 486 n. 12 (1983) (Stevens, J., dissenting); § 10–9, note 19, supra.

37. See 426 U.S. at 353, 355, 361 (Brennan, White, Blackmun, JJ., dissenting).

38. See The Supreme Court, 1975 Term, 90 Harv.L.Rev. 56, 95 (1976).

39. 427 U.S. at 224 (emphasis in original).

40. Hewitt v. Helms, 459 U.S. 460, 468 (1983).

41. 445 U.S. 480 (1980), discussed in § 10–9, supra.

liberty interests inhering in the due process clause itself where the further deprivation of liberty "is not within the range of conditions of confinement to which a prison sentence subjects an individual." [42] Nevertheless, the Court's treatment of prison cases in and since *Meachum* remains hard to reconcile fully with the view that "even the inmate retains an inalienable interest in liberty—at the very minimum the right to be treated with dignity." [43]   Moreover, perhaps paradoxically in a case involving institutions once acknowledged to have the task of reforming and rehabilitating antisocial behavior, the Court ignored one of the most important aims of procedural due process—the promotion of individual participation and dialogue in decisions affecting a person's relationship with government.   Similarly, *Bishop's* treatment of state law as determinative in establishing the policeman's lack of entitlement to his job may be applicable only where interests are conferred by government choice rather than stemming from "core" values, and where they are provided to meet the government's own needs, rather than those of the recipient.

In *Goss v. Lopez*, for example, the Court held that high school students were denied due process when "they were temporarily suspended from their high schools without a hearing either prior to suspension or within a reasonable time thereafter." [44]   Writing for the Court, Justice White observed that "[h]ere, on the basis of state law, appellees plainly had legitimate claims of entitlement to a public education," [45] notwithstanding a provision in the entitlement-conferring statute which apparently allowed student suspensions of up to ten days without a hearing; that observation, and the Court's holding, represented a marked contrast with its other narrowly formalistic decisions.   For the *Goss* Court declined to find that the statutory grant of a substantive right to education was qualified by the statute's specifically envisioned possibility of short summary suspensions; in doing so, the majority rejected Justice Powell's fear that the Court was opening "avenues for judicial intervention in the operation of our public schools that may affect adversely the quality of education." [46]   The Court, furthermore, dismissed the contention that the infringement of the entitlement to education was "too speculative, transitory, and insubstantial to justify imposition of a *constitutional* rule" [47]; for the majority, it sufficed that the "deprivation is not *de minimis*." [48]   Focusing, in a rare departure from the instrumental mainstream, on the intrinsic quality of due process in offering an opportunity for "at least an informal give-and-take between student and disciplinarian," [49] the Court concluded that "[h]aving chosen to extend the right to education to [students] general-

---

42. Id. at 493.

43. 427 U.S. at 233 (Stevens, J., dissenting).

44. 419 U.S. 565, 567 (1975).

45. Id. at 573.

46. Id. at 585 (Powell, J., dissenting).

47. Id. at 586 (Powell, J., dissenting) (emphasis in original).

48. Id. at 576.

49. Id. at 583–84. But see Board of Curators v. Horowitz, 435 U.S. 78, 90 (1978) (because they are by their nature "more subjective and evaluative" than disciplinary decisions, academic dismissals from higher educational institutions do not require any form of a hearing, even assuming a protected liberty or property interest).

ly, Ohio may not withdraw that right on grounds of misconduct, absent fundamentally fair procedures to determine whether misconduct has occurred." [50]

Moreover, to the extent that the *Meachum* and *Bishop* line of cases may be explained by concerns for preserving federalism and reducing remote intervention in state and local affairs, they do not point to a restrained view of entitlements based on reliance induced by the *federal* government. Thus, in *Mathews v. Eldridge,*[51] again dealing with government creation of interests for the benefit of the citizens receiving them and not for the benefit of those they are asked to serve, the Court declined to take advantage of the opportunity to overrule or even cast a shadow across *Goldberg v. Kelly.*[52] Although holding that the termination of federal disability benefit payments without a prior evidentiary hearing does not violate due process, the Court in *Eldridge* recognized that "it has been implicit in our prior decisions . . . that the interest of an individual in continued receipt of [Social Security disability benefit payments] is a statutorily created property interest protected by the Fifth Amendment." [53]

§ 10–11. Narrowing Turns to Erosion: Uses of the Entitlement Concept to Cut Back the Core

The notion of entitlements protected by due process but stemming from independent sources "*such as* state law" [1] was originally introduced to provide added protection to the reasonable expectations of individuals in their relations with government over and above the rights secured by the "core" concepts of liberty and property grounded in the Constitution and in common law. In *Paul v. Davis,*[2] this new concept of entitlements seems to have been turned, for the first time, in precisely the opposite direction.[3] Writing for a majority,[4] Justice Rehnquist held that no interests protected by due process were implicated when the police put an individual's name on a flyer distributed to local merchants describing him as a "known" active shoplifter despite his lack of any convictions for such a crime, even though the characterization "would seriously impair his future employment opportunities." [5] The Court first found that past cases "do not establish the proposition that reputation alone, apart from some more tangible interests such as employment, is either 'liberty' or 'property' by itself sufficient to invoke the procedural protection of the due process clause." [6] Second, the Court looked to state law to determine whether a statutory entitlement existed, but held that "Kentucky law does not extend to respondent any legal guarantee of present enjoyment of reputation which has been

50. Id. at 574.

51. 424 U.S. 319 (1976).

52. 397 U.S. 254 (1970), discussed in § 10–9, supra.

53. 424 U.S. at 334.

§ 10–11

1. Perry v. Sindermann, 408 U.S. 593, 601 (1972) (emphasis added).

2. 424 U.S. 693 (1976).

3. Compare generally the cases discussed in § 10–9, supra.

4. Joining the majority opinion were Chief Justice Burger and Justices Stewart, Powell, and Blackmun. Joining Justice Brennan's dissent were Justices White and Marshall. Justice Stevens did not take part.

5. 424 U.S. at 697.

6. Id. at 701.

altered as a result of the actions of the police, notwithstanding the protection against injury by virtue of [the state's] tort law." [7]

In thus denying relief to a person whose reputation was seriously damaged by a state officer's action, the Court appears to have held that what previously had been recognized as a "core" interest in reputation [8] would now be cognizable only when damage to reputation was alleged to accompany government's denial of some more tangible interest such as a specific job.[9] Contrary to Justice Rehnquist's contention, this requirement of "reputation-plus" [10] was a considerable departure from past precedents concerning the core interest in reputation. Justice Rehnquist, for example, interpreted *Wisconsin v. Constantineau's* [11] recognition of a liberty interest in not having one's name posted in liquor stores as a chronic drinker, as having been based on the fact that the posting "significantly altered his status as a matter of state law, and it was that alteration of legal status which, combined with the injury resulting from the defamation justified the invocation of procedural safeguards." [12] On this view, due process was accorded in order to protect the state-conferred right to buy liquor which the posting might hinder. But the Court in *Constantineau* rested its holding *only* on the fact that "a person's good name, reputation, honor, or integrity is at stake because of what the government is doing to him." [13] And both *Board of Regents v. Roth*,[14] and *Goss v. Lopez* [15] reiterated this formulation of the "core" interest in reputation. Similarly, Justice Rehnquist attempted to distinguish the holding of *Jenkins v. McKeithen*,[16] that a Commission which undertakes a directly accusatory function of publicly labeling individuals or groups as violators of the criminal laws must first grant due process protections, on the grounds that the police in *Paul* "are not by any conceivable stretch of the imagination, either separately or together, 'an agency whose sole or predominant function, without serving any other public interest, is to expose and publicize the names of persons it finds guilty of wrongdoing.'" [17] But this verbal distinction does nothing to grapple with *Jenkins'* real aim of protecting "a person's interest in his good name and reputation," and, as Justice Brennan put it: [18] "The logical and disturbing corollary of this holding is that no due process infirmities would inhere in a statute constituting a commission to conduct ex parte trials of individuals so long as the only official judgment pronounced was limited to the public condemnation and branding of a person as a Communist, a traitor, an 'active murderer,' a homosexual, or any other mark that 'merely' carries special opprobrium. The potential of today's decision is frightening to a free people."

7. Id. at 711–12.

8. See § 10–9, supra.

9. 424 U.S. at 701.

10. Id. See also The Supreme Court, 1975 Term, 90 Harv.L.Rev. 56, 88 (1976).

11. 400 U.S. 433 (1971), discussed in § 10–9, supra.

12. 424 U.S. at 708–09.

13. 400 U.S. at 437.

14. 408 U.S. 564, 573 (1972).

15. 419 U.S. 565, 574 (1975).

16. 395 U.S. 411 (1969).

17. 424 U.S. at 706 n. 4, quoting from Jenkins, 395 U.S. at 438.

18. 424 U.S. at 721 (Brennan, J., dissenting).

That the refusal to find a "liberty" interest in reputation where there was no statutory entitlement to it and no accompanying loss of a state-conferred status is more than an "aberration" [19] was made clear when it was reiterated in *Meachum v. Fano*,[20] in spite of Justice Stevens' pronouncement that "all men [are] endowed by their Creator with liberty as one of the cardinal unalienable rights" and that "the Due Process Clause protects" those rights rather "than the particular rights or privileges conferred by special laws or regulations." [21]

As disturbing as *Paul's* iconoclastic handling of precedent [22] was its refusal to give much weight to the practical impact of the "posting" on Davis.[23] To satisfy the "reputation plus tangible interest" threshold for due process protection, it was not enough that the injury to reputation affect his chances of employment and his other dealings in the private sector,[24] since the interest in such dealings was not created by statute.[25] A similarly limited concern with the consequences of state action damaging to reputation was present in *Bishop v. Wood*, where the Court found that even assuming that a policeman's "discharge was a mistake and based on incorrect information," there is no incursion on a protected liberty interest "when there is no public disclosure of the reasons for the discharge." [26] This conclusion totally ignored the fact that the policeman is engaged "in a profession in which prospective employees are invariably investigated, [and his] job prospects will be severely constricted by the government action." [27]

A parallel indifference to the right of individuals dependent on government opportunities to participate in matters affecting their relationships with government was demonstrated in *Codd v. Velger*,[28] where the Court rejected a fired policeman's claim of a "liberty" interest in a hearing prior to the placement of stigmatizing material by the Police Department in his personnel file, which he asserted was the cause of his dismissal as a policeman and his inability to find other related employment. The Court noted that the policeman had made no claim

19. Id. at 734.

20. 427 U.S. 215, 224 (1976), discussed in § 10–10, supra. See also Leis v. Flynt, 439 U.S. 438, 443 (1979).

21. 427 U.S. at 230 (Stevens, J., dissenting).

22. See generally Shapiro, "Mr. Justice Rehnquist: A Preliminary View," 90 Harv. L.Rev. 293, 324–28 (1977).

23. See generally The Supreme Court, 1975 Term, supra note 10 at 100–101.

24. See 424 U.S. at 697.

25. The extreme insensitivity of this view prompted Justice Brennan to comment: "It is inexplicable how the Court can say that a person's status is 'altered' when the State suspends him from school, revokes his driver's license, fires him from a job, or denies him the right to purchase a drink of alcohol, but is in no way 'altered' when it officially pins upon him the brand of a criminal, particularly since the Court recognizes how deleterious will be the consequences that inevitably flow from its official act." Id. at 734 (Brennan, J., dissenting). The harshness of Paul may have been somewhat mitigated by the Court's apparent willingness to overlook the absence of clear causation between the initial stigma and the alleged injury. See Owen v. Independence, 445 U.S. 622, 633–34 n. 13 (1980) (although city manager had previously told police chief that he would be fired, city counsel's accusations, coming before his actual firing, violated due process, since, "even if they did not in point of fact 'cause' petitioner's discharge, the defamatory and stigmatizing charges 'certainly' occur[red] in the course of the termination of employment").

26. 426 U.S. 341, 348 (1976), discussed in § 10–10, supra.

27. Id. at 350 (Brennan, J., dissenting).

28. 429 U.S. 624 (1977).

that the government's characterization of him was false, and since the purpose of the hearing is solely "to provide the person an opportunity to clear his name," [29] there was no need for a hearing.[30] In viewing the sole purpose of due process as ensuring accuracy in government actions, the Court ignored not only the intrinsic purposes of a hearing, but also the liberty interest in avoiding a "stigma or other disability that forecloses employment opportunities" even where the stigmatizing assertion is true.[31] Since "[t]he discharge itself is part of the deprivation of liberty against which the employee is entitled to defend," the "hearing [should] include consideration of whether the charge, if true, warrants discharge," in light of the fact that considerable injury is caused by "an official determination, based on such information, that the employee is unfit for public employment." [32]

Paul v. Davis need not, however, portend a significant cutback in all of the "core" interests protected by due process. An alternative and at least somewhat less troublesome explanation may be found in Justice Rehnquist's concern that the case presented an important "question of the relationship between the National and State Governments." [33] Since that Court could see no difference between "the infliction by state officials of a 'stigma' to one's reputation [and] . . . the infliction by the same officials of harm or injury to other interests protected by state law," [34] it feared that allowing Davis's suit for relief under § 1983 "would seem almost necessarily to result in every legally cognizable injury which may have been inflicted by a state official acting under 'color of law' establishing a violation of the Fourteenth Amendment." [35] Thus the decision may be seen as evidence of a reluctance to federalize tort law in suits against government action.[36]

Moreover, even if *Paul v. Davis* significantly narrows the range of individual interests entitled to federal due process protection and as such might be viewed as "overtly hostile to the basic constitutional safeguards of the Due Process Clause," [37] the Court has maintained other core areas, albeit with somewhat reduced protection. For example, the Court has continued to refuse to allow state legislatures to strike the balance between competing property interests of creditors and debtors where this might unduly infringe on the "core" property interests in possession and privacy. In *North Georgia Finishing, Inc. v.*

---

29. Id. at 627, quoting from Board of Regents v. Roth, 408 U.S. 564, 573 n. 12 (1972).

30. Justice Blackmun emphasized that the Court was "not presented with a question as to the limits, if any, on the disclosure of prejudicial but irrelevant, accurate information," as there was no suggestion that the information if true was not of a kind appropriately "disclosed to prospective employers." Id. at 629 (Blackmun, J., concurring).

31. Id. at 633 n. 3 (Stevens, J., dissenting) (truth of the information does not establish that it warranted dismissal, a separate matter).

32. Id. at 633 (Stevens, J., dissenting).

33. 424 U.S. at 698.

34. Id. at 699.

35. Id. at 697.

36. This view is reinforced by the Court's willingness elsewhere to uphold state deprivations of *protected interests* against procedural due process attack where post-deprivation tort remedies exist. See Ingraham v. Wright, 430 U.S. 651 (1977), Parratt v. Taylor, 451 U.S. 527 (1981), and Hudson v. Palmer, 468 U.S. 517 (1984), discussed in § 10–14, infra.

37. 426 U.S. at 351 (Brennan, J., dissenting).

Di-Chem,[38] the Court invalidated a Georgia prejudgment garnishment statute which provided neither notice nor a hearing in a case involving commercial property. Justice White's majority opinion cited with approval *Fuentes v. Shevin's*[39] holding that the fact "[t]hat the debtor was deprived of only the use and possession of the property, and perhaps only temporarily, did not put the seizure beyond scrutiny under the Due Process Clause."[40] The Court went on to hold that procedural due process applies not only to "[c]onsumers who are victims of contracts of adhesion, and who might be irreparably damaged by temporary deprivation of household necessities" but extends to "the commercial setting . . . involving parties of equal bargaining power" even where "the double bond posted . . . gives assurance to the [debtor] that it will be made whole in the event the garnishment turns out to be unjustified."[41] In noting the need for a probable cause hearing either prior to or immediately following a prejudgment garnishment, the Court made it clear that *Fuentes* had not been completely overruled by *Mitchell v. W. T. Grant Co.*,[42] where the Court upheld the Louisiana sequestration statute permitting prejudgment seizure of consumer goods without prior notice or hearing. To be sure, *Fuentes'* requirement of notice and hearing, prior to prejudgment replevin by the creditor of consumer products which had been purchased on a conditional sales contract, no longer applies with full force. Yet *Di-Chem* indicated that the absence of a requirement of a prior hearing in *Mitchell* may have reflected the presence of other special protections offered by the Louisiana statute: "That writ . . . was issuable only by a judge upon the filing of an affidavit going beyond mere conclusory allegations and clearly setting up the facts entitling the creditor to sequestration. The Louisiana law also expressly entitled the debtor to an immediate hearing after seizure and to dissolution of the writ absent proof by the creditor of the grounds on which the writ was issued."[43] Thus the Court did not adopt a narrowly positivist approach to the determination of property interests protected by due process, rejecting the proposition that such interests could be limited by statutory or contractual attempts to tie procedural conditions to their exercise.[44]

In addition, the Court continued to recognize the individual's "core" common law "liberty" interest in freedom to follow a chosen

38. 419 U.S. 601 (1975).

39. 407 U.S. 67 (1972).

40. 419 U.S. at 606. While Justice Powell continued "to doubt whether [Fuentes] strikes a proper balance, especially in cases where the creditor's interest in the property may be as significant or even greater than that of the debtor," he did not question the notion that it was the responsibility of the Court, and not of the legislature, to find the appropriate balance. Id. at 609 (Powell, J., concurring).

41. Id. at 608.

42. 416 U.S. 600 (1974). Justice Stewart noted that his earlier report in Mitchell of the demise of Fuentes had been "greatly exaggerated." 419 U.S. at 608 (Stewart, J., concurring).

43. 419 U.S. at 607. In fact, Justice Powell raised the possibility that Mitchell has been relegated to "its narrow factual setting." Id. at 609 (Powell, J., concurring).

44. See generally Tribe, "Structural Due Process," 10 Harv.Civ.Rights-Civ.Lib. L.Rev. 269, 279–80 (1975). See also Webb's Fabulous Pharmacies, Inc. v. Beckwith, 449 U.S. 155 (1980) (interest on fund deposited with court could not be defined as public property by state for purposes of "takings" clause), discussed in §§ 10–8, note 23 and 9–7 supra.

profession.[45] Acceptance of such an interest implies that at least some regulations which are substantively constitutional can be validly enforced only in an individualized manner consistent with the dictates of procedural due process. Thus in *Gibson v. Berryhill*,[46] for example, the Court held that a State Board of Optometry which was composed solely of self-employed optometrists with a pecuniary interest in excluding others from the profession, and which had filed a complaint in state court against other optometrists for alleged misconduct, "was so biased by prejudgment and pecuniary interest that it could not constitutionally conduct hearings looking toward the revocation of [those optometrists'] licenses to practice optometry." [47] However, the Court is not always so willing to require individualized determinations, especially where licensing and regulation of a particular profession has historically been left exclusively to the States. In *Leis v. Flynt*,[48] for example, the Court rejected an argument that out-of-state lawyers had a due process right to a hearing on their application to appear *pro hac vice* in Ohio courts, stating, "[T]he suggestion that the Constitution *assures* the right of a lawyer to practice in the court of every State is a novel one, not supported by any authority brought to our attention." [49] This statement implies that the procedural aspect of the due process clause protects no more than those liberties which it substantively protects. But the statement's matter-of-fact style suggests that the Court did not intend such a sweeping change from earlier precedent.[50]

§ 10–12. What Process is Due: Identifying the Source of the Protection to be Accorded

Prior to the advent of the notion of statutory entitlements, the question of "what process is due" was not considered separately from the issue of what deprivations of personal interests by the government warrant due process protections. Both constitutional questions were answered with reference either to the dictates of natural law or in terms of fundamental fairness.[1] The process due depended in essence on whether an individual had been "condemned to suffer grievous loss," [2] and on whether the interest in avoiding that loss was greater than the government's interest in summary process.[3]

When statutory entitlements were recognized, however, the Court distinguished conceptually between the identification of the interests protected, and the assessment of the process due, and isolated different factors as crucial to the two inquiries. Whether or not a legitimate entitlement existed depended upon interpreting the relevant body of positive law to see if it recognized a "liberty" or "property" interest in

---

45. See discussion in § 10–8 supra and § 15–14, infra.

46. 411 U.S. 564 (1973).

47. Id. at 578.

48. 439 U.S. 438 (1979).

49. Id. at 444 n. 5 (emphasis added).

50. For example, the Court made no mention of Gibson v. Berryhill, discussed above.

§ 10–12

1. See § 10–8, supra.

2. Joint Anti-Fascist Refugee Committee v. McGrath, 341 U.S. 123, 168 (1951) (Frankfurter, J. concurring).

3. Cafeteria & Restaurant Workers Union v. McElroy, 367 U.S. 886, 895 (1961).

the threatened benefit or opportunity.[4] But while the Court was willing to rely on non-constitutional sources of law as the basis for a judgment about the existence of a substantive entitlement, it held that constitutional rather than nonconstitutional criteria must be employed to identify the content of the procedural obligations thereby triggered. The Court thus employed traditional modes of analysis to determine the process due, while recognizing "the importance of not imposing upon the states or the Federal Government in this developing field of law any procedural requirements beyond those demanded by rudimentary due process."[5]

The notion that the Constitution is the source of the protection to be accorded when an interest in "liberty" or "property" is infringed was challenged for the first time in *Arnett v. Kennedy*, where the Court reviewed the constitutionality of a federal law (1) guaranteeing Civil Service employees that they could be dismissed only for "cause," but simultaneously (2) denying employees any right to a hearing until after they had been dismissed.[6] Justice Rehnquist, joined by Chief Justice Burger and Justice Stewart, wrote a plurality opinion to uphold the law, arguing that "the property interest which [the employee] had in his employment was itself conditioned by the procedural limitations which had accompanied the grant of the interest"[7] and concluding that, "where the grant of a substantive right is inextricably interwined with the limitations on the procedures which are to be employed in determining that right, a litigant . . . must take the bitter with the sweet."[8]

Justices Powell, Blackmun, White, Marshall, Douglas, and Brennan disagreed, suggesting that the plurality "view misconceives the origin of the right to procedural due process. That right is conferred, not by legislative grace, but by constitutional guarantee."[9] "While the State may define what is and what is not property, once having defined those rights the Constitution defines due process."[10] In effect, six Justices were prepared to hold that Congress, having created what *looked* like a property entitlement, was powerless to qualify its character by adding a caveat that the seeming entitlement could be withdrawn without a hearing. Although a majority of the Supreme Court thus rejected Justice Rehnquist's analysis, the law was upheld as applied to the case before the Court because the six members of that majority divided

---

4. See, e.g., Goldberg v. Kelly, 397 U.S. 254, 262 (1970).

5. Id. at 267.

6. 416 U.S. 134 (1974).

7. Id. at 155.

8. Id. at 153–54. The same three Justices would have applied precisely the same form of analysis to the foster parent-foster child relationship as a creation of state law in Smith v. Organization of Foster Families, 431 U.S. 816, 856–57 (1977) (Stewart, J., joined by Burger, C.J., and Rehnquist, J., concurring in judgment).

9. Arnett, 416 U.S. at 167 (Powell, J., joined by Blackmun, J., concurring).

10. Id. at 185 (White, J., concurring in part and dissenting in part). See also id. at 167 (Powell, J., concurring) ("[The] adequacy of statutory procedures for deprivation of a statutorily created property interest must be analyzed in constitutional terms"); id. at 211 (Marshall, J., joined by Douglas and Brennan, JJ., dissenting) ("[A]lthough [the employee's] property interest arose from statute, the deprivation of his claim of entitlement to continued employment would have to meet minimum standards of procedural due process regardless of the discharge procedures provided by the statute").

among themselves on the question whether the statutory procedures that were actually provided satisfied the requirements of procedural due process.[11]

In urging that "the substantive right may [not] be viewed wholly apart from the procedure provided for its enforcement," [12] Justice Rehnquist sought to apply the narrowly positivist perspective, now dominant on the Court with regard to the identification of entitlements,[13] to the analysis of what process is due. Procedural due process, on this view, serves *only* the instrumental role of assuring that people get what is "theirs" as defined by positive rules of law. Such a positivist theory is potentially destructive; once it is unleashed, it may be hard to provide analytical justification for confining its application to certain forms of statutory entitlement, and hard not to agree that "*all* property rights are granted by the sovereign and subject to any terms which it might impose. . . ." [14]

While the positivist theory, which would produce a significant contraction in protection of "liberty" and "property," contains no *internal* contradictions, it may be criticized as an unjustifiable abdication of judicial responsibility. An emphasis on limiting federal judicial intrusion in state affairs can take one only so far: the fourteenth amendment, after all, was clearly designed to place limits on state action adverse to individuals.[15] Similarly, the fifth amendment was aimed at limiting federal deprivations of personal interests without due process of law. Thus, by allowing the government not only to determine the existence of an entitlement but also to prescribe the procedures for its deprivation, the Court would fail to fulfill its important protective function.

In *Cleveland Board of Education v. Loudermill*,[16] a majority of the Court [17] explicitly rejected the *Arnett* plurality opinion, putting to rest any speculation that other members of the Court were sympathetic to Justice Rehnquist's position.[18] At issue in *Loudermill* was a challenge

---

11. See the discussion in § 10–14, infra.

12. 416 U.S. at 152.

13. See §§ 10–10, 10–11, supra.

14. Comment, "Fear of Firing: Arnett v. Kennedy and the Protection of Federal Civil Service Employees," 10 Harv.Civ. Rights—Civ.Lib.L.Rev. 472, 483 (1975) (emphasis added).

15. See Comment, "Entitlement, Enjoyment, and Due Process of Law," 1974 Duke L.J. 89, 111.

16. 470 U.S. 532 (1985).

17. Only Justice Rehnquist dissented from the majority opinion. Justice Marshall concurred, but added that a full, trial-type hearing should be constitutionally required before any decision to terminate wages is made. Id. at 548. Justice Brennan concurred in part and dissented in part, arguing that the Court should have prescribed a procedure in which the truth of the state's assertions could have been

tested by giving the complainant "a fair opportunity before discharge to produce contrary records or testimony, or even to confront an accuser in front of the decision-maker." Id. at 553. He also argued that the Court should have remanded the case to the district court for development of the claim that administrative delay in this case violated due process guarantees, an assertion rejected by the Court. See § 10–14, infra, at note 62.

18. Prior to Loudermill, several decisions echoed the plurality decision in Arnett. For instance, in Goss v. Lopez, 419 U.S. 565 (1975), Justice Powell, joined by Chief Justice Burger and by Justices Blackmun and Rehnquist, wrote in positivist terms, apparently about procedure, in his dissenting opinion, albeit without reference to Arnett: "The very legislation which 'defines' the 'dimension' of the student's entitlement while providing a right to education generally does not establish this right

to a state civil service statute providing that employees would be discharged only for cause, but entitling them only to post-discharge administrative review. Upon finding that the statute created a property interest [19] and that principles of due process required a pre-discharge opportunity to respond,[20] the Court, through Justice White, relied on two prior opinions of the Court [21] to find that Justice Rehnquist's *Arnett* opinion had already been "clearly rejected", adding that "it is settled that the 'bitter with the sweet' approach misconceives the constitutional guarantee." [22]   The Court was adamant that "[t]he categories of substance and procedure are distinct," and asserted that "[t]he point is straightforward: the Due Process Clause provides that certain substantive rights—life, liberty and property—cannot be deprived except pursuant to constitutionally adequate procedures . . . 'Property' cannot be defined by the procedures provided for its deprivation any more than can life or liberty. The right to due process 'is conferred, not by legislative grace, but by constitutional guarantee . . . .' " [23]

In *Loudermill*, the Court decisively rejected any purely positivist approach to the procedural protection of state-conferred rights, and thus eliminated the precedential uncertainty that existed, at least for a time, after the splintered decision in *Arnett*. Nevertheless, the Court

free of discipline imposed in accordance with Ohio law." Id. at 586 (dissenting opinion). And in Bishop v. Wood, 426 U.S. 341 (1976), Justices White, Marshall, Blackmun and Brennan accused the Court of relying "on the fact that the ordinance described its own procedures for determining cause," thereby "effectively adopting the analysis rejected by a majority of the Court in Arnett." Id. at 456 (White, J., dissenting). See also id. at 353–54 n. 4 (Brennan, J., dissenting). Justice Stevens, writing for the majority of five, denied this attack, claiming that the decision was based on a finding that the policeman in Bishop had no substantive "entitlement" to his job under state law, and therefore that the majority had not even reached the question of what process was due. See id. at 345 n. 8.

19. 470 U.S. at 538.

20. The Court noted, however, that the hearing affording this opportunity "need not be elaborate." 470 U.S. at 545.

21. In Loudermill, Justice White cited Vitek v. Jones, 445 U.S. 480 (1980), and Logan v. Zimmerman Brush Co., 455 U.S. 422 (1982), as decisions that had earlier rejected Arnett. In Vitek, a state prisoner challenged the procedures followed in transferring him to a mental hospital. In his opinion for the Court, Justice White, joined by Justices Brennan, Marshall, Stevens, and Powell, rejected the state-proffered procedure for determining whether transfer to such a facility was appropriate, finding that such an adjudication must be conducted in conformance with constitu-

tional standards. The Court added that "[t]hese minimum requirements being a matter of federal law, they are not diminished by the fact that the State may have specified its own procedures. . . ." id. at 490–1, noting that "[a] majority of the Justices rejected an identical position in *Arnett* . . . ." Id. at 490 n. 6.

In Logan, an employee of the defendant company filed a claim with the state fair employment commission, alleging that he was discriminatorily discharged. When the state commission attempted to initiate proceedings beyond the statutorily-mandated 120-day period requiring the commission to commence such actions, the defendant successfully moved to dismiss the claim. The state supreme court upheld the denial, reasoning that, since the state had created the entitlement, it was empowered to establish procedures to adjudicate complaints. The Court, in an opinion by Justice Blackmun, joined by Chief Justice Burger and Justices Brennan, White, Marshall, and Stevens, found that the employee possessed a statutory entitlement to avail himself of the adjudicatory process of the commission—a species of property— and rejected the state supreme court's rationale as "misunderstand[ing]" the nature of the Constitution's due process guarantee," 455 U.S. at 432, citing Vitek and referring to Justice Powell's concurrence and Justice Marshall's dissent in Arnett. See § 10–14, infra.

22. 470 U.S. at 541.

23. Id., quoting Justice Powell's concurrence in Arnett.

failed to provide a fully convincing basis for its rejection of Justice Rehnquist's position, reasserted in his *Loudermill* dissent, that the state's prerogative in defining a substantive right ought to include the ability to limit that right through state-defined procedural devices.[24] The Court merely reasserted the rationale, grounded in the separation of powers concept, of limiting the government's powers to dictate procedural protections.

There has been no suggestion on the Court that the government should be able to tie the exercise, existence, or safeguarding of "core" rights of liberty or property to government's decisions of what procedures to provide. To the contrary, in the summary repossession cases,[25] the Court developed the theme that the process due for deprivation of rights to peaceful possession and enjoyment of tangible property definitely does *not* derive either from the will of the parties or from positive rules of law enacted in advance by the legislature.[26] Thus, the Court has extended the same procedural protections to statutorily created rights as to "core" rights.

The basic position of the Court in *Loudermill*—that while full deference must be accorded the positive law in the creation of at least some property interests (those beyond the "core"), only minimal deference need be shown to statutory provisions imposing procedural limitations on the continued enjoyment of those property interests—must rest on a notion that the Constitution treats certain procedural protections as mandatory incidents in the creation of *any* relationship terminable only on stated substantive conditions. This separation of the procedural elements of an entitlement from its substantive boundaries may reflect both intrinsic and instrumental considerations. To the extent that the separation rests upon the instrumental objective of enforcing government's own positive choices about competing economic interests, however, there are serious and probably fatal problems with the distinction. First, it leaves the Court wholly at the mercy of resource allocation arguments for limits on procedural rights—arguments of the sort expressed in *Mathews v. Eldridge*.[27] Not surprisingly, therefore, the Court in recent years has drawn back from imposing costly due process requirements in what might be seen as large-scale intrusions into government programs.[28] Second, if the state is free to define and

---

24. In his dissent, Justice Rehnquist admonished the Court to "recognize the totality of the State's definition of the property right in question," and thereby to recognize the validity of the state-provided procedure, adding that, while the Court's opinion did not "impose a federal definition of property," its decision nevertheless infringed on the state's prerogative to confer substantive rights. 470 U.S. at 561 (dissenting opinion).

25. See, e.g. North Georgia Finishing, Inc. v. Di-Chem, Inc., 419 U.S. 601 (1975); Mitchell v. W. T. Grant Co., 416 U.S. 600 (1974); Fuentes v. Shevin, 407 U.S. 67 (1972); cf. Sniadach v. Family Finance Corp., 395 U.S. 337 (1969).

26. See the discussion in § 10–9, supra.

27. 424 U.S. 319 (1976), discussed in § 10–13, infra.

28. The Court has shown a willingness in recent cases, however, to perceive as not unduly burdensome the costs that required procedures would impose on the state. In Loudermill, for instance, the Court argued that the required procedures would actually serve the state's long-term interests, including its economic concerns, to a degree outweighing the short term costs of those procedures: ". . . the employer shares the employee's interest in avoiding disruption and erroneous decisions; and until the matter is settled, the employer would con-

limit underlying substantive entitlements by positive enactment, there seems no clear reason why it should not be equally free to define the procedure that goes with each entitlement. After all, if substantive restrictions on entitlements can be adopted which have the effect of limiting procedural rights—e.g., if government can create jobs overtly terminable at the public employer's will—it seems strange not to allow government to take the intermediate course of limiting public benefits and opportunities in an explicitly procedural way. Conversely, if the judiciary is to decide what process is due, it is hard to justify completely deferring to government even on a substantive level, since the basic character of decisions as to how applicants are processed, and how disputes over eligibility for government benefits and opportunities are resolved, is inevitably substantive. Moreover, the objective of accurately enforcing the state's own positive choices hardly seems sufficient to justify judicial intrusion into the essentially legislative province of deciding how those choices can best be implemented.

On the other side, it might be argued that the *Arnett* plurality's allocation of responsibility between the political and judicial branches rests on a notion of the special relevance of judicial expertise, and the comparative irrelevance of legislative competence, in making process-oriented decisions. Values of accuracy, participation and predictability are matters that judges are continually required to consider and balance; conversely, legislative ability to adjust competing economic and political interests has little to do with designing fair ways to resolve factual disputes. If the courts have any special competence at all, it is to be found in the area of fair dispute resolution. Indeed, the Court's insistence in *Loudermill* that a clear distinction exists between substantive and procedural concerns, followed by its undertaking a detailed balancing of the opposing interests of the parties, underscores the distinction between the judicial role of prescribing constitutionally-required procedure and the legislative role of conferring and substantively delimiting the interest.[29]

tinue to receive the benefit of the employee's labors. It is preferable to keep a qualified employee on than to train a new one. A governmental employer also has an interest in keeping citizens usefully employed rather than taking the possibly erroneous and counter-productive step of forcing its employees onto the welfare rolls." 470 U.S. at 544. Only where the employee is a "significant hazard" would the government have to absorb the economic loss of suspending the employee with pay pending an adjudication of the case. See also Lassiter v. Department of Social Services, 452 U.S. 18, 27 (1981) (noting that the state provision of counsel to indigents in parental status termination hearings would advance the state's concern in protecting the interests of the child by ensuring an equally-balanced adversary hearing).

29. See also Atkins v. Parker, 472 U.S. 115, 129 (1985) (rejecting a due process challenge to notice provided in the wake of a change in welfare benefits, specifically noting that Congress has "plenary power to define the scope and the duration of the entitlement," but that "[t]he procedural component of the Due Process Clause does not 'impose a constitutional limitation on the power of Congress to make substantive changes in the law of entitlement to public benefits.' ") (citation omitted); Logan v. Zimmerman Brush Co., 455 U.S. 422, 431–32 (1982), discussed in note 21, supra. The Court in Logan compared actions whereby a state "create[s] *substantive* defenses on immunities for use in adjudication—or . . . eliminate[s] its statutorily created causes of action altogether," with actions whereby a state "amend[s] or terminates its welfare or employment programs. . . . [or] adjusts benefit levels," id. at 432 (emphasis added), contrasting both with "*procedural* limitation[s] on [a] claimant's ability to assert his rights." Id.

This notion of special judicial competence in the area of procedure, as distinguished from that of substance, may derive some support from Justice Stewart's statement for the Court in *Dandridge v. Williams*: "The Constitution may impose certain procedural safeguards upon systems of welfare administration. But the Constitution does not empower this Court to second-guess state officials charged with the difficult responsibility of allocating limited public welfare funds among the myriad of potential recipients." [30]

But this justification for the Court's greater willingness to overturn legislative decisions on matters of procedure than on questions of substance rests on the premise that procedural problems can be neatly separated from substantive choices. Plainly, this premise is open to serious question. In *Lindsey v. Normet*,[31] for example, the Court upheld Oregon's streamlined eviction procedure over the attack that it unfairly gave apartment tenants insufficient protection, deferring to Oregon's legislative judgment that landlord-tenant relations were rationally distinguishable from other creditor-debtor relations. It would be quite impossible to classify that judgment as either substantive or procedural: it was both. Similarly, in *Mathews v. Eldridge*, when the Court upheld the Social Security Administration's procedures for terminating social security benefits without an evidentiary hearing, it gave "substantial weight . . . to the good faith judgment of the [agency] charged by Congress with [administering] the social welfare system." [32] The Court expressly noted the interdependence of substantive and procedural issues: "Significantly, the cost of protecting those whom the preliminary administrative process has identified as likely to be found undeserving may in the end come out of the pockets of the deserving since resources available for any particular program of social welfare are not unlimited." [33] In sum, there must be a better reason than special judicial competence if the Court is to revise procedural judgments arising out of "what [is] essentially a legislative compromise," [34] after which "Congress may no longer have room to maneuver and balance employees' rights and executive flexibility, to find some middle ground between no justification at all and an evidentiary trial prior to removal." [35]

The Court itself has offered no alternative justification for the substance-procedure distinction whereby individuals must look to statutory and contract provisions for their definition of entitlements but need not do so for the specification of what procedures will be followed when government infringes on such entitlements.[36] Ultimately, the

at 433 (emphasis added). In the former situation but not the latter, the Logan Court reasoned, "the legislative determination provides all the process that is due," *id.*, citing Bi-Metallic Investment Co. v. State Bd. of Equalization, 239 U.S. 441, 445–46 (1915), discussed in § 10–6, supra, at note 39.

30. 397 U.S. 471, 487 (1970).

31. 405 U.S. 56 (1972).

32. 424 U.S. 319, 349 (1976).

33. Id. at 348.

34. Arnett v. Kennedy, 416 U.S. 134, 154 (1974).

35. Frug, "Does the Constitution Prevent the Discharge of Civil Service Employees?" 124 U.Pa.L.Rev. 942, 986 (1976).

36. See Tribe, "Structural Due Process," 10 Harv.Civ. Rts.—Civ.Lib.L.Rev. 269, 280 (1975).

clarity of the demarcation the Court declared in *Loudermill* between the rights-conferring function and the process-prescribing function is illusory; the Court must eventually move toward more deference on matters of procedure or less deference on matters of substance. Since the former course would leave the due process clauses with little content in the modern state, where so much has come to depend on relationships with government, the latter seems preferable, certainly in relationships created to meet the needs of the individuals involved, and probably also in relationships created to meet the needs of others.

Particularly in the latter context, the attempt to link procedural protection to the "property" interest of the individual in retaining a given relationship with government—typically, a public job—is ultimately unsatisfactory. As Professor William Van Alstyne has observed in a thoughtful reconsideration of interests in governmental relationships, attempts to squeeze public office-holding into the mold of private property entitlements are "unhappily reminiscent of a much earlier period when important positions of trust were sold (by the crown) quite literally as property. . . . [so that] the status holder acted with the officiousness of an office 'owner.' There is something abrasive and offensive, something anachronistic, in the idea that public sector positions can be appropriately described as the property of the individual status holder. . . ." [37] Rather than "the ingenious fashioning of a *new property*," what is required in the public employment and public contract contexts, in contrast to the public welfare and public housing contexts, is "the more general protection of the *old liberty, i.e.*, those personal freedoms sheltered from government in *all* its protean exercises of power." [38] Accordingly, Professor Van Alstyne proposes that we "treat *freedom from arbitrary adjudicative procedures* as a substantive element of one's liberty," and suggests that "the ideas of liberty and of substantive due process may easily accommodate a view that government may not adjudicate the claims of individuals by unreliable means." [39]

With two important modifications, that view is the one that emerges from this chapter. First, the emphasis on "unreliable means" continues the unfortunate practice of treating procedural due process as merely instrumental; once the doctrine is unhinged from notions of protecting what *belongs* to the individual, it might as well be recognized that unfairness inheres in the very act of disposing of an individual's situation without allowing that individual to participate in some meaningful way—not simply because more mistakes are likely to be made thereby, but because such treatment seems incompatible with the person's claim to be treated as a human being. Indeed, the very notion of "unreliability" or "mistake" presupposes a regime that is more rule-bound than discretionary; yet the right to be heard, and to be told why an adverse action is being taken, need not arise only when there exist objective rules specifying the permissible grounds for such action.

---

37. Van Alstyne, "Cracks in 'The New Property': Adjudicative Due Process in the Administrative State," 62 Cornell L.Rev. 445, 483 (1977).

38. Id. at 487.

39. Id.

However closely the existence of such objective rules is linked to the idea of property-like entitlements, there is no necessary connection between their existence and the intrinsic virtues of regularizing the interaction between the individual and the state through requiring an interchange of views before the state does the individual grievous harm.

Second, the stress on "adjudicating" the claims of individuals might invite government to act to the focused detriment of identified persons without giving them a hearing—so long as it purports to be acting in a rulemaking rather than adjudicatory capacity. What we saw in §§ 10–3 to 10–6, however, was that the due process requirement of an adversary hearing is triggered not by a governmental decision to proceed by adjudication but by a governmental decision to single out particular persons for deprivation. Whatever form that decision takes, the Model of Regularity implicit in the ex post facto and bill of attainder clauses as well as in the due process clauses compels proceeding in a way that accords adversely affected individuals an opportunity to participate.

§ 10–13. What Process is Due: Methods of Specifying Required Protections

The still dominant "instrumental" approach to procedural due process accords value to procedural safeguards less as expressions of the individual's dignity than as means to the minimization of factual error in the application of the relevant substantive rules.[1] In part because of this approach, the Court has stressed its view that "[t]he very nature of due process negates any concept of inflexible procedures applicable to every imaginable situation." [2] The Court has continually insisted that the procedures needed to minimize error and to reduce the dangers of arbitrary action to an acceptable level vary "according to specific factual contexts," [3] since "not all situations calling for procedural safeguards call for the same kind of procedure." [4]

The earliest methods used by the Court to determine the required form of procedural due process involved reference to natural law.[5] Later, ideas of "conventional morality" or notions of what has historically seemed "fair and right and just" [6] were at the root of the selection of procedures.[7] Although "a weighing process has long been a part of

§ 10–13

1. See § 10–7, supra.

2. Cafeteria and Restaurant Workers Union, Local 473 v. McElroy, 367 U.S. 886, 895 (1961). See also Joint Anti-Fascist Refugee Committee v. McGrath, 341 U.S. 123, 162–63 (1951) (Frankfurter, J., concurring). Of course an intrinsic approach could also make the required safeguards depend on context, but such an approach would be less likely to reflect wholly ad hoc, situational assessments.

3. Hannah v. Larche, 363 U.S. 420, 442 (1960).

4. Morrissey v. Brewer, 408 U.S. 471, 481 (1972).

5. See, e.g., Twining v. New Jersey, 211 U.S. 78, 106 (1908). See generally § 10–8, supra.

6. See, e.g., Solesbee v. Balkcom, 339 U.S. 9, 16 (1950) (Frankfurter, J., dissenting): "To kill a man who has become insane while awaiting sentence offends the deepest notions of what is fair and right and just."

7. See generally Note, "Specifying the Procedures Required by Due Process: Toward Limits on the Use of Interest-Balancing," 88 Harv.L.Rev. 1510, 1537 (1974).

any determination of the form of hearing required in particular situations by procedural due process," [8] overtly utilitarian interest-balancing has come to play a predominant role only in recent years.[9]

The preoccupation with a balancing approach has led to some refinement in the factors to be considered, and in *Mathews v. Eldridge* the Court announced something akin to a general formula for the determination of what process is due: [10] "[O]ur prior decisions indicate that identification of the specific dictates of due process generally requires consideration of three distinct factors: first, the private interest that will be affected by the official action; second, the risk of an erroneous deprivation of such interest through the procedures used, and the probable value, if any, of additional or substitute procedural safeguards; and finally, the government's interest, including the function involved and the fiscal and administrative burdens that the additional or substitute procedural requirement would entail." By requiring a weighing of the personal interest infringed, discounted by the chance that alternative procedures would be more likely to safeguard it, against the added cost of such alternative procedures, the Court's manner of determining what procedural due process mandates represents the application of a crude sort of social welfare function. The utilitarian nature of the approach contrasts sharply with the Court's mode of deciding whether a procedural due process requirement is triggered at all; at that level, "as long as a property [or liberty] deprivation is not *de minimis*, its gravity is irrelevant to the question whether account must be taken of the due process clause." [11]

The difference in treatment accorded to the two questions is generally explained by the proposition that, in a world of limited resources, society cannot afford wholly to ignore interests other than those of the individual asserting a denial of "life, liberty or property"—interests which are implicated by large expenditures on the provision of hearings. Thus, although "the cost of protecting a constitutional right cannot justify its total denial," [12] considerations of cost may play a role in deciding exactly what level of protection a right should receive. In *Mathews v. Eldridge*, for example, in holding that the termination of social security benefits without a prior evidentiary hearing does not violate due process, the Court noted that "[s]ignificantly the cost of

8. Board of Regents v. Roth, 408 U.S. 564, 570 (1972).

9. Justice Rehnquist criticized this balancing approach in his dissent in Cleveland Board of Education v. Loudermill, 470 U.S. 532 (1985), arguing that its result in that case was "unobjectionable" but unprincipled: "The balance is simply an ad hoc weighing which depends to a great extent upon how the Court subjectively views the underlying interests at stake." 470 U.S. at 562 (dissenting opinion). He suggests, not surprisingly, that one way to prevent numerous cases, all requiring unique balancing, from coming to the Court is to allow government to prescribe procedure as well as substance in creating

the entitlement. See § 10–12, supra. See generally Mashaw, "The Supreme Court's Due Process Calculus For Administrative Adjudication in Mathews v. Eldridge: Three Factors in Search of A Theory of Value," 44 U.Chi.L.Rev. 28 (1976).

10. 424 U.S. 319, 334–35 (1976).

11. Goss v. Lopez, 419 U.S. 565, 576 (1975). See also Ingraham v. Wright, 430 U.S. 651, 674 (1977); Board of Regents v. Roth, 408 U.S. 564, 570–71 (1972).

12. Bounds v. Smith, 430 U.S. 817 (1977) (right of access to courts requires prison authorities to furnish inmates with adequate law libraries or adequate aid from law-trained persons).

protecting those whom the preliminary administrative process has identified as likely to be found undeserving may in the end come out of the pockets of the deserving since the resources available for any particular program of social welfare are not unlimited." [13]   In addition to its growing worry about expense,[14] the Court has been concerned not to protect statutory entitlements through procedures which might seriously impair the purpose of the statute from which the entitlements are derived—a concern both instrumental and intrinsic in character.[15]

The restriction of procedural safeguards where an individual's interest in such safeguards conflicts with the rights of others has long been a basic tenet of procedural due process jurisprudence.[16]   But in cases where the rights of other individuals would *not* be impeded by according a full hearing to an individual prior to a significant deprivation, the contemporary emphasis upon minimizing expense and avoiding sacrifice of various governmental objectives represents a considerable break with a tradition that has identified the due process clause as "designed to protect the fragile values of a vulnerable citizenry from the overbearing concern for efficiency and efficacy that may characterize praiseworthy government officials no less, and perhaps more, than

---

13.   424 U.S. 319, 348 (1976). Note that, in this formulation, the concern with cost purports to be a concern with other individuals' rights.   Compare the much looser formulation in Ingraham v. Wright, 430 U.S. 651, 680 (1977): "[E]ven if the need for advance procedural safeguards were clear, the question would remain whether the incremental benefit could justify the cost." See also Wheeler v. Montgomery, 397 U.S. 280, 284 (1970) (Burger, C.J., dissenting).

14.   But see Ake v. Oklahoma.   470 U.S. 68 (1985) (rejecting the state's argument based on cost and requiring that an indigent accused of murder be provided with access to behavioral specialists to establish his insanity defense);   see also United States Trust Co. of New York v. New Jersey, 431 U.S. 1 (1977) (refusing to permit cost-saving justification for a state's impairment of its contract obligations to bondholders).

15.   See, e.g., Goss v. Lopez, 419 U.S. 565 (1975) (requiring an informal give-and-take between student and administrator prior to suspension would not jeopardize state objective of providing education): Morrissey v. Brewer, 408 U.S. 471, 483 (1972) (allowing hearing prior to revocation of parole would not impede purpose of deterring misbehavior).

In other cases, the Court has refused challenges to procedures on similar grounds. See, e.g., Walters v. National Association of Radiation Survivors, 473 U.S. 305 (1985) (rejecting a challenge to the $10 maximum attorney's fee established by federal law to be paid to attorneys representing claimants before the Veteran's Admin-

istration, in order to preserve the congressional purposes of maintaining informal procedures and ensuring that claimants do not have to share awards with attorneys); Parham v. J.R., 442 U.S. 584 (1979) (rejecting a challenge to informal, non-adversary procedures in determining whether a child should be voluntarily committed to a mental institution by his parents, in order to preserve the state's interest in avoiding obstacles that may unnecessarily discourage the mentally ill or their parents from taking advantage of these state benefits); Greenholtz v. Inmates of Nebraska Penal and Cor. Complex, 442 U.S. 1, 13–14 (1979) (rejecting a challenge to informal procedures for parole of prisoners, partly in order to prevent "a continuing state of adversary relations between society and the inmate" from undermining the "objective of rehabilitating convicted persons"), discussed in § 10–7, supra.

16.   See, e.g., Smith v. Organization of Foster Families, 431 U.S. 816 (1977) (state procedures for removing children from foster families held adequate especially in light of conflicting interests of the biological parents); Ewing v. Mytinger & Casselberry, Inc., 339 U.S. 594 (1950) (upholding federal law authorizing multiple seizures of apparently misbranded but physically harmless drugs in advance of any adversary hearing on the merits of the seizure); North American Cold Storage Co. v. Chicago, 211 U.S. 306 (1908) (upholding ex parte seizure and destruction of allegedly diseased poultry).

mediocre ones." [17]   Indeed, the Court has had occasion to recall even recently that "procedural due process is not intended to promote efficiency" [18] and that a procedural safeguard must be afforded "if that may be done without *prohibitive* cost." [19]

The willingness to override individual protection in the interests of efficiency flows quite readily from an instrumental perspective which perceives "fair process" as serving only the wholly "neutral" or "technical" value of accurately enforcing the state's own positive choices about how competing interests are to be adjusted through rules governing behavior and through formulas allocating scarce resources.   But even accepting that instrumental perspective for the moment, there are serious problems in striking the balance called for by decisions like *Eldridge.*[20]   How, for example, can one measure in monetary terms the social and psychological "costs" to dignity and self-respect caused by loss of a government job or of welfare?   One commentator has suggested that, as "applied by the *Eldridge* Court, the utilitarian calculus tends, as cost-benefit analyses typically do, to 'dwarf soft variables' and to ignore complexities and ambiguities." [21]   Moreover, the difficulty of the Court's task is aggravated when it fails even to consider the functional utility of alternative procedures such as confrontation and cross-examination.[22]   Nor has the Court, for the most part, been prepared to identify general procedural requirements for typically recurring situations in order to further consistency in doctrine or in application.[23]   In fact, given the complexity of the problem, and given the self-imposed framework which allocates to the Court the duty of balancing essentially the same factors that a legislature or agency presumably considered in initially selecting a procedural policy, it is hardly surprising that *Eldridge* appears to create a presumption of constitutionality for procedural safeguards provided by government: "substantial weight must be given to the good-faith judgment of the individuals charged by Congress with the administration of the social welfare system that the procedures they have provided assure fair consideration of the entitlement claims of individuals." [24]

17. Stanley v. Illinois, 405 U.S. 645, 656 (1972). See generally R. Dworkin, Taking Rights Seriously 190–92 (1977).

18. Fuentes v. Shevin, 407 U.S. 67, 90 n. 22 (1972).

19. Goss v. Lopez, 419 U.S. 565, 580 (1975) (emphasis added).

20. For a detailed critique of the Court's balancing process in Mathews v. Eldridge, see Mashaw, supra note 9.

21. Mashaw, supra note 9, at 48. The point is developed in Tribe, "Policy Science: Analysis or Ideology?" 2 Phil. & Public Aff. 66, 97 (1972).

22. See generally, Note, supra note 7, at 1516.

23. See Wheeler v. Montgomery, 397 U.S. 280, 283 (1970) (Burger, C.J., dissenting); Sanders v. United States, 373 U.S. 1, 32 (1963) (Harlan, J., dissenting); Friendly,

"Some Kind of Hearing," 123 U.Pa.L.Rev. 1267, 1301–02 (1975). Cf. Mashaw, supra note 9, at 28–29 (expressing need for general criteria to provide consistency and to minimize need for judicial testing of each procedure); Note, supra note 7, at 1517–18 (noting Court's seeming confusion about whether to specify general procedures).

24. Mathews v. Eldridge, 424 U.S. 319, 349 (1976). Cf. Walters v. National Association of Radiation Survivors, 473 U.S. 305, 319 (1985) (stating that "deference to congressional judgment must be afforded even though the claim is that a statute Congress has enacted effects a denial of the procedural due process guaranteed by the Fifth Amendment"); Schweiker v. McClure, 456 U.S. 188, 200 (1982) (finding a "strong presumption in favor of the validity of congressional action"); Ingraham v. Wright, 430 U.S. 651 (1977) (presumption that state

The Court's unwillingness to consider values beyond accuracy of result in the context of a utilitarian balancing test when deciding what process is due, and the Court's grant of a strong presumption of constitutionality to statutory procedural provisions, amount to a serious abdication of traditional notions of judicial responsibility under the due process clauses.[25] Like many other provisions of the Constitution, the due process requirement represented a decision on the part of the Framers to safeguard certain rights and values, those considered fundamental in a free society and yet unusually vulnerable to the risk of denial by the majority.[26] Adequate protection of such "core" concerns cannot be afforded by "balancing" the general interests of the majority against those of the individual.[27] Here as elsewhere the Court should decline the "invitation to engage in a utilitarian comparison of public benefit and private loss."[28] And there is no reason to believe that the judiciary would be better suited to that task of utilitarian comparison than the legislature even if it were called for.[29] The proper role of courts in this context is to define and protect those substantive and procedural rights that may not receive their due respect in the political process. It is largely this additional protection, after all, that justifies the judicial review of administrative procedures in the elaboration of constitutional norms.

§ 10–14. Current Doctrine: The Relevance of Timing and the Need for More Than *Post*-Deprivation Process

The Court has long maintained its adherence to a flexible approach in deciding what process is due. The method most commonly employed at present to determine the form of required procedures is a judicial interest-balancing process whose outcome necessarily varies from case to case.[1] There has nevertheless been considerable regularity in the procedural safeguards prescribed, since the determination of what process is due has centered on an adversary model whose core constant has involved granting notice and an opportunity to be heard to those individuals or groups whose personal interests are adversely affected by government action.[2]

tort remedies for deprivation of liberty meet due process requirements).

25. Justice Rehnquist's dissent in Cleveland Board of Education v. Loudermill, 470 U.S. 532, 559 (1985), advocates what might be viewed as an even greater abdication of judicial responsibility by eventually eliminating all judicial review in cases where procedure is prescribed at the time the entitlement is created. See § 10–12, supra.

26. See § 11–4, infra. "The Due Process Clause of the Fifth Amendment, later incorporated into the Fourteenth, was intended to give Americans at least the protection against governmental power that they had enjoyed as Englishmen against the power of the Crown." Ingraham v. Wright, 430 U.S. 651, 672–73 (1977).

27. See generally Reich, "The New Property," 73 Yale L.J. 733, 776–77 (1964) (noting that, where individual interest is balanced against public interest, the latter almost always prevails).

28. United States Trust Co. of New York v. New Jersey, 431 U.S. 1 (1977) (striking down state impairment of bondholders' contract claims despite resulting gain to goals of better mass transit, energy conservation, and environmental protection).

29. See, e.g., Goldberg v. Kelly, 397 U.S. 254, 272 (1970) (Black, J., dissenting).

§ 10–14

1. See generally § 10–13, supra.

2. See generally Subrin & Dykstra, "Notice and the Right to be Heard: The

The first question generally faced in choosing procedural safeguards is that of *timing*.[3] Although "[m]any controversies have raged about the cryptic and abstract words of the Due Process Clause," the Court's largely instrumental interest-balancing has generally required "that deprivation of life, liberty, or property by adjudication be preceded by notice and an opportunity for a hearing appropriate to the nature of the case."[4] Whether procedural requirements are designed to express respect for affected individuals or "to minimize substantially unfair or mistaken deprivations," it makes obvious sense in most cases to insist that "the right to notice and a hearing . . . be granted at a time when the deprivation can still be prevented,"[5] in part because some deprivations may be truly irreversible, and in part because institutional pressures and commitments tend to militate against reversing even those deprivations that have not yet worked irreparable harm, since the governmental decision-maker may have acquired a vested interest in ratifying an action already taken.[6] In general, the right to prior hearing should prevail unless the state successfully demonstrates that "some valid government interest is at stake that justifies postponing the hearing until after the event."[7]

Where important interests would ostensibly be impaired by a prior hearing requirement, but private rights would seemingly be jeopardized in a more permanent way by the grant of only a subsequent hearing, the Court has responded by closely examining and explicitly weighing

Significance of Old Friends," 9 Harv.Civ. Rts.—Civ.Lib.L.Rev. 449 (1974).

3. See generally Rubenstein, "Procedural Due Process and the Limits of the Adversary System," 11 Harv.Civ.Rts.—Civ. Lib.L.Rev. 48 (1976); Mashaw, "The Management Side of Due Process: Some Judicial and Litigation Notes on the Assurance of Accuracy, Fairness, and Timeliness in the Adjudication of Social Welfare Claims," 59 Cornell L.J. 772 (1974).

4. Mullane v. Central Hanover Bank & Trust Co., 339 U.S. 306, 313 (1950). Language in earlier Supreme Court decisions suggested that the distinction between "liberty" and "property" played a doctrinally significant role in the Court's resolution of prior hearing questions. Phillips v. Commissioner of Internal Revenue, 283 U.S. 589, 596–97 (1931) (Brandeis, J.) ("Where only property rights are involved, mere postponement of the judicial enquiry is not a denial of due process if the opportunity given for the ultimate judicial determination of the liability is adequate."). But recently, the Court has declared that it no longer regards the distinction between "liberty" and "property" as necessarily decisive: The "dichotomy between personal liberties and property rights is a false one. Property does not have rights. People have rights . . . In fact, a fundamental interdependence exists between the personal right to liberty and the personal right in property. Neither could have meaning without the other." Lynch v. Household Finance Corp., 405 U.S. 538, 552 (1972).

5. Fuentes v. Shevin, 407 U.S. 67, 81–82 (1972).

6. The Court has found statutory procedures for post-deprivation hearings to be inadequate in numerous cases. See, e.g., Perry v. Sindermann, 408 U.S. 593 (1972) (firing from employment at state university); Morrissey v. Brewer, 408 U.S. 471, 475–76 (1972) (termination of parole); Fuentes v. Shevin, 407 U.S. 67, 75–77 (1972) (replevin of consumer goods held under conditional sales contract); Stanley v. Illinois, 405 U.S. 645, 647–49 (1972) (removing unwed father's custody over his children); Bell v. Burson, 402 U.S. 535 (1971) (suspending driver's license); Goldberg v. Kelly, 397 U.S. 254 (1970) (withholding welfare benefits); Sniadach v. Family Finance Corp., 395 U.S. 337, 339 (1969) (prejudgment wage garnishment). Contrast Dixon v. Love, 431 U.S. 105 (1977) (state system for summary suspension or revocation of driver's license based on number of prior traffic convictions upheld partly because state made special provision for hardship and for holders of commercial licenses).

7. Boddie v. Connecticut, 401 U.S. 371, 379 (1971). See, e.g., Dixon v. Love, supra note 6, at 114 (stressing important public interest in prompt removal of safety hazards).

the relevant interests found to be affected. Thus, in *Goldberg v. Kelly*, the Supreme Court held that a state could not "terminate public assistance payments to a particular recipient without affording him the opportunity for an evidentiary hearing prior to termination." [8] The Court recognized that the requirements of a prior hearing involve greater expense, and that "the benefits paid to ineligible recipients pending decision at the hearing probably cannot be recouped, since these recipients are likely to be judgment-proof." [9] On the other hand, termination "of aid pending resolution of a controversy over eligibility may deprive an eligible recipient of the very means by which to live while he waits. Since he lacks independent resources, his situation becomes immediately desperate." [10] Moreover, because the individual who is denied welfare benefits pending the outcome of a subsequent hearing must "concentrate upon finding the means for daily subsistence," he cannot take the time necessary to prepare effectively for the subsequent hearing. And this "impaired adversary position is particularly telling" in light of evidence "of the welfare bureaucracy's difficulties in reaching correct decisions on eligibility." [11] Finally, the Court held that the drain on resources could be reduced by the less restrictive alternative of "developing procedures for prompt pre-termination hearings and by skillful use of personnel and facilities." [12]

Exceptions have traditionally been made to the general rule requiring hearings prior to government deprivations only where a prior hearing would have been inconsistent with "a countervailing state interest of overriding significance," [13] either because of the delays created by the hearing process,[14] or because of the opportunity for

---

8.   397 U.S. 254, 255 (1970).

9.   Id. at 266.

10.   Id. at 264. The Court has also given weight in other cases to the situation of the party seeking a hearing prior to removal of a government benefit or opportunity. See, e.g., Morrissey v. Brewer, 408 U.S. 471, 482 (1972) (termination of parole pending hearing would inflict "a 'grievous loss' on the parolees and often on others"); Bell v. Burson, 402 U.S. 535, 539 (1971) ("continued possession of driver's license may become essential in the pursuit of a livelihood"); Sniadach v. Family Finance Corp., 395 U.S. 337, 341–42 (1969) ("A prejudgment garnishment of the Wisconsin type may as a practical matter drive a wage-earning family to the wall."); Memphis Light, Gas & Water Div. v. Craft, 436 U.S. 1, 18 (1978) ("The consumer's interest is self-evident. Utility service is a necessity of modern life; indeed, the discontinuance of water or heating for even short periods of time may threaten health and safety.").

11.   397 U.S. at 264 n. 12. The Court made a similar point in Sniadach v. Family Finance Corp., 395 U.S. 337, 341 (1969), when it observed that empirical studies indicate that wage garnishments are often secured in a fraudulent manner.

12.   397 U.S. at 266.

13.   Boddie v. Connecticut, 401 U.S. 371, 377 (1971).

14.   For example, in Barry v. Barchi, 443 U.S. 55 (1979), the Court upheld the suspension of a horse trainer's license without a prior evidentiary hearing pursuant to a New York statute providing that where a post-race urinalysis shows the presence of drugs in the horse's system, the license of the horse's trainer may be revoked or suspended if the trainer drugged the horse, negligently failed to prevent the drugging of the horse, or knew or should have known that the horse had been drugged. Justice White, for the majority, wrote that "the State is entitled to impose an interim suspension [pending a prompt post-suspension hearing] whenever it has satisfactorily established probable cause to believe that a horse has been drugged and that a trainer has been at least negligent in connection with the drugging." Id. at 64. Although the trainer has a substantial interest in avoiding suspension, "the trainer's interest is not being baselessly compromised," and thus does not outweigh "the State's interest in preserving the integrity of the sport and in protecting the public from harm." Id. at 65.

evasion presented to the target of government action by the very fact of prior notice.[15]   At the same time, these exceptions have also required that the denial of a prior hearing not severely burden the individuals affected by summary government action—either because the action could be reversed, or because the government could be required to pay compensation if the subsequent hearing revealed that the government had acted mistakenly.   Given the asymmetric impact of a prior hearing requirement where these conditions concerning governmental and private interests have prevailed, the Court has found it relatively easy to conclude that a subsequent, rather than prior, hearing better satisfied the due process standard of "just treatment" in these exceptional cases. Thus, the Supreme Court has not required a hearing prior to emergency action in wartime [16] nor has the Court compelled prior hearings where summary action has been necessary to protect public health and safety,[17] to secure effective tax collection,[18] to seize articles used in the

See also Mackey v. Montrym, 443 U.S. 1 (1979), in which the Court found that the delay which would be created by the requirement of a hearing prior to the temporary suspension of a driver's license for refusal to submit to a breathalyzer test would compromise the state's interest in public safety: "in promptly removing such [allegedly drunken] drivers from the road, the summary sanction of the statute contributes to the safety of the public highways." Id. at 18.   Cf. Hewitt v. Helms, 459 U.S. 460, 472–73 (1983).

15. See, e.g., Mackey v. Montrym, supra, upholding a Massachusetts statute providing for automatic suspension of a driver's license for 90 days for refusal to submit to a breathalyzer test.   Chief Justice Burger, writing for the majority found that "[a] presuspension hearing would substantially undermine the state interest in public safety by giving drivers significant incentive to refuse the breath-analysis test and demand a presuspension hearing as a dilatory tactic."   Mackey, 443 U.S. at 18.

16. The Supreme Court has held that Congress, in the exercise of its war powers, may validly enact emergency legislation which grants affected individuals or groups a hearing only after the fact of adverse government action.   Thus, for example, the Court upheld World War I legislation authorizing the President unilaterally to seize property held by enemy aliens; property mistakenly seized could be recovered in a subsequent hearing.   See, e.g., Stoehr v. Wallace, 255 U.S. 239 (1921); Central Union Trust Co. v. Garvan, 254 U.S. 554 (1921).   And in World War II, the Supreme Court upheld provisions of the Emergency Price Control Act of 1942 which authorized the Office of Price Administration to fix rents without first granting landlords a hearing; judicial review was permitted only "after the order had been promulgated." "Congress was dealing here with the exi-

gencies of wartime conditions and the insistent demands of inflation control . . . .   National security might not be able to afford the luxuries of litigation and the long delays which preliminary hearings traditionally have entailed."   Bowles v. Willingham, 321 U.S. 503, 521 (1944). See also Haig v. Agee, 453 U.S. 280, 302 (1981) (no hearing prior to revocation of a passport is necessary where "there is a substantial likelihood of 'serious damage' to national security or foreign policy."

17. The Court has traditionally deferred to legislative judgments that the protection of consumer interests requires the immediate seizure of defective goods, in advance of any adversary hearing on the merits of the government action.   For example, in North American Cold Storage Co. v. Chicago, 211 U.S. 306 (1908), the Court upheld the ex parte seizure and destruction of 47 barrels of poultry even though this allegedly diseased meat was being kept in cold storage at the time and therefore posed no immediate danger to the public as long as it was not sold.

See also, Ewing v. Mytinger & Casselberry, Inc., 339 U.S. 594, 600 (1950), approving provisions of a federal law authorizing multiple seizures of apparently misbranded, but physically harmless, drugs in advance of any adversary hearing on the merits of seizure on ground that "[t]here is no constitutional reason why Congress in the interests of consumer protection may not . . . conclude . . . that public damage may result even from harmless articles if they are allowed to be sold as panaceas for man's ills."

And in Mackey v. Montrym, 443 U.S. 1 (1979), discussed in notes 14 and 15, supra, the Court reasoned that "[s]tates surely

18. See note 18 on page 722.

commission of crimes,[19] to permit emergency bank management,[20] or to protect schools, prisons, or other public institutions from serious disruption.[21]

have at least as much interest in removing drunken drivers from their highways as in summarily seizing mislabeled drugs or destroying spoiled foodstuffs," and accordingly upheld a Massachusetts statute providing for the automatic suspension of a driver's license for 90 days for refusal to submit to a breathalyzer test. Id. at 17. The Court found that the summary sanction substantially promoted the state's interest in public safety by acting "as a deterrent to drunken driving," by "effectuat[ing] the Commonwealth's interest in obtaining reliable and relevant evidence for use in subsequent criminal proceedings," and by "promptly removing such drivers from the road." Id. at 18.

18. The Supreme Court has consistently held that the federal and state governments may validly resort to summary procedures in order to assure effective collection of taxes by minimizing the taxpayer's opportunity to waste assets in anticipation of a collection attempt. See, e.g., Bob Jones University v. Simon, 416 U.S. 725, 747 (1974) (rejecting, "in light of the powerful governmental interests in protecting the administration of the tax system from premature judicial interference," the claim of an organization, whose tax-exempt status was unilaterally revoked by the IRS because of the organization's racially discriminatory practices, that a congressional provision for only "post-enforcement review" of the IRS decision violated procedural due process); Phillips v. Commissioner of Internal Revenue, 283 U.S. 589 (1931) (approving provisions of the Revenue Act of 1926 authorizing the summary collection of taxes); Scottish Union & National Insurance Co. v. Bowland, 196 U.S. 611 (1905) (upholding a state's ex parte seizure of property from a delinquent taxpayer); Springer v. United States, 102 U.S. 586 (1880) (approving an ex parte seizure of property from a tax delinquent). Cf. Murray's Lessee v. Hoboken Land & Improvement Co., 59 U.S. (18 How.) 272 (1855) (upholding ex parte seizure of property from a customs collector who had failed to turn over to the United States over $1 million in collected duties and tariffs).

19. See, e.g., Calero-Toledo v. Pearson Yacht Leasing Co., 416 U.S. 663 (1974) (upholding ex parte seizure of yacht allegedly used for marijuana smuggling).

20. See, e.g., Fahey v. Mallonee, 332 U.S. 245 (1947) (approving provision of the Home Owner's Loan Act of 1933 authorizing Federal Home Loan Bank Administra-

tion to summarily assume management of any federally insured savings and loan association conducting business in unlawful, unauthorized, or unsafe manner pending outcome of subsequent full investigation, in order to protect customers from further unlawful management and to protect bank's assets from liquidation by panicking customers during federal investigation). Cf. Coffin Brothers v. Bennett, 277 U.S. 29 (1928) (upholding a Georgia law permitting state, in event of a bank failure, to execute a lien against the property of the bank's shareholders in advance of any hearing on the merits of their liability in order to protect the interests of the bank's depositors).

21. See, e.g., Goss v. Lopez, 419 U.S. 565, 582–83 (1975) (although "as a general rule notice and hearing should precede removal of a student from school," students "whose presence poses a continuing danger to persons or property or an ongoing threat of disrupting the academic process may be immediately removed from school," with notice and a hearing following "as soon as possible").

See also Hewitt v. Helms, 459 U.S. 460 (1983), where the Court held that, following a prison riot, confinement to administrative segregation of a prison inmate viewed as a security threat, pending investigation of the misconduct charges against the inmate, need not be preceded by any hearing and need be followed only by "an informal, nonadversary evidentiary review" in which the inmate receives "some notice of the charges against him and an opportunity to present his views to the prison official charged with deciding whether to transfer him to administrative segregation." Id. at 476. So long as this review occurs "within a reasonable time after confining [the inmate] to administrative segregation," the requirements of due process are satisfied. Id. at 472. Justice Rehnquist's majority opinion rested on the conclusion that the inmate's interest in remaining in the general prison population was "not one of great consequence," since the prison is itself a restricted environment, while the state's interests in the safety of the prison's guards and inmates, in the security of the institution, and in the insulation of potential witnesses to the alleged misconduct from the possibility of coercion or harm are all of great import, far outweighing the interest of the inmate in a hearing prior to action by the prison officials. Id. at 473.

In addition, the Court has balanced the interests of the affected individuals when judging the validity of rules granting private litigants access to government processes for the purpose of attaching the property of their opponents, without prior notice or hearing, pending the outcome of litigation. In this context, the Court has declared that the "basic and important public interest" in a government's civil enforcement of its laws may justify ex parte government action on behalf of private litigants attaching private property in order to secure judicial jurisdiction.[22] In the past, a litigant was also able to make a summary attachment of property to prevent an opponent from rendering himself judgment-proof in anticipation of an unfavorable outcome in litigation.[23] But more recently, even though prior notice of attachment proceedings might result in a frustration of their purpose, the Court held in *Sniadach v. Family Finance Corp.* that ex parte prejudgment wage garnishment mechanisms which permitted litigants substantially to block their opponents' receipt of wages pending the outcome of litigation, and which were not shown to be necessary to secure jurisdiction, were constitutional only if government could demonstrate a "situation requiring special protection to a . . . creditor interest."[24] Justice Douglas' majority opinion in *Sniadach* explained the Court's finding of unconstitutionality by noting first "that a prejudgment garnishment . . . may as a practical matter drive a wage-earning family to the wall"[25], since the "leverage of the creditor on the wage earner is enormous," the collection of fraudulent debts and other "grave injustices" are "made possible by prejudgment garnishment whereby the sole opportunity to be heard comes after the taking."[26] Finally, the Court countered the suggestion that the debtor might dissipate his wages by observing that the garnished wage-earner often "just quits his job and goes on relief."[27]

The Court has nevertheless relaxed the presumption in favor of a prior hearing when conflicting property rights in the same item exist. Thus, recognizing that both debtors and creditors have "property" interests in the goods involved in disputes over the terms of installment contracts, the Court held, in *North Georgia Finishing, Inc. v. Di-Chem, Inc.*,[28] that an adversary hearing was necessary either prior to *or immediately following* a prejudgment garnishment. But where ex parte prejudgment repossession proceedings are employed, they are

---

22. Fuentes v. Shevin, 407 U.S. 67, 91 n. 23 (1972) (dictum). See also Ownbey v. Morgan, 256 U.S. 94, 111 (1921) ("a property owner who absents himself from the territorial jurisdiction of a State, leaving his property within it, must be deemed ex necessitate to consent that the State may subject such property to judicial process to answer demands made against him in his absence, according to any practicable method that reasonably may be adapted"). But see Shaffer v. Heitner, 433 U.S. 186 (1977).

23. See, e.g., Coffin Brothers v. Bennett, 277 U.S. 29 (1928). See also McKay v. McInnes, 279 U.S. 820 (1929) (summarily affirming state law authorizing government to attach property solely because of a litigant's request).

24. 395 U.S. 337, 339 (1969).

25. Id. at 341–42.

26. Id. at 340.

27. Id. at 342 n. 9.

28. 419 U.S. 601 (1975).

constitutional only if they are adequately protected from abuse and error by procedural safeguards.[29]

Recently, however, even in cases where there were *no* conflicting rights in the "life, liberty, or property" for which an individual sought protection by means of a prior hearing, the Supreme Court has indicated a reduced concern about the intrinsic and instrumental benefits of a prior as opposed to a subsequent hearing. In upholding governmental procedures denying hearings prior to important deprivations, the Court has given less weight than in the past to the possibility that personal interests cannot be adequately vindicated after deprivation, and has demanded less urgency of the governmental interest involved, so long as the alternative procedures offered by the government are shown to produce substantially accurate results. In *Ingraham v. Wright*,[30] for

29. In Mitchell v. W. T. Grant Co., 416 U.S. 600 (1974), for example, the Court upheld the constitutionality of Louisiana's prejudgment sequestration procedure—but only after noting (1) that Louisiana law permitted no one but a judge to approve the creditor's application for prejudgment repossession; (2) that such approval was permitted only when the claim and the factual and legal grounds for it were clearly stated; (3) that the creditor had to furnish a bond in an amount specified by the judge; (4) that the debtor could regain possession either by furnishing a bond of his own or by demonstrating at an immediate post-repossession adversary hearing that the repossession was unjustified; and (5) that, if such a hearing was the method used to regain possession, the debtor could secure compensation for economic and reputational damages, and payment by the creditor of the debtor's attorney's fees.

By contrast, the Florida and Pennsylvania prejudgment replevin statutes struck down in Fuentes v. Shevin, 407 U.S. 67 (1972), had been held by the Court to possess several procedural defects which rendered their ex parte proceedings an inadequate substitute for prior adversary hearings. Both states' writs of replevin issued on the approval of a clerk or prothonotary, respectively, rather than a judge. Both issued "on the bare assertion" and willingness to post bond of the party seeking the writ, without requiring even a rudimentary factual showing. Moreover, neither of the state statutes provided any immediate opportunity for the debtor to regain possession except by posting bond. Finally, while Florida law allowed for the award of damages to the debtor if the creditor's suit for repossession ultimately failed at trial, the Pennsylvania law did not even oblige the creditor to file suit for permanent repossession after the issuance of the replevin writ; the burden rested with the debtor to initiate a lawsuit for return of the property.

In New Motor Vehicle Board of California v. Orrin W. Fox Co., 439 U.S. 96 (1978), the California Automobile Franchise Act required an automobile manufacturer to obtain the approval of the New Motor Vehicle Board before opening or relocating a retail dealership within the market area of an existing franchisee if the franchisee protested its entry. Pursuant to the Act, a hearing would be held subsequent to notification of the manufacturer of the protests, and the manufacturer was denied the opportunity to enter the territory pending a determination by the Board of the lack of good cause for refusing to approve the franchise permit. Distinguishing this case from Fuentes v. Shevin, supra, the Court held that this statutory scheme did not violate due process because of its failure to provide for a pre-deprivation hearing. Where neither party has a clear entitlement and there are competing interests in a property-like hearing—granting a pre-deprivation hearing to the manufacturer, and allowing entry until such a hearing had found good cause to deny it, would be the equivalent of denying a pre-deprivation hearing to the existing franchisee—the state may have broader authority to determine the timing and contours of the process it will provide.

30. 430 U.S. 651 (1977). See also Mathews v. Eldridge, 424 U.S. 319 (1976) (upholding Social Security Administration's provision for notice and an opportunity to introduce rebutting evidence, but no evidentiary hearing, prior to termination of federal disability benefits): Arnett v. Kennedy, 416 U.S. 134 (1974). In Arnett, the Court applied a balancing test before approving the statutory procedures provided by Congress for the dismissal of Civil Service employees. Of the six Justices who extensively scrutinized these procedures in light of the requirements of due process, only Justices Powell and Blackmun found that the grant of a subsequent hearing after the fact of dismissal was sufficient.

example, the Court held that a child may be deprived, without a prior hearing of any sort, of the protected liberty interest in avoiding physical restraint and preventing the infliction of "appreciable physical pain," by corporal punishment in public schools.[31] The Court reasoned that "[i]n view of the low incidence of abuse, the openness of our schools, and the common law safeguards that already exist, the risk of error that may result in violation of a school child's substantive rights can only be regarded as minimal." [32] While "[i]mposing additional administrative safeguards as a constitutional requirement might reduce that risk marginally, [it] would also entail a significant intrusion into an area of primary educational responsibility." [33] This willingness of the Court to balance risks of irreversibly violating constitutionally protected interests in property and even liberty against considerations of efficiency and cost-avoidance, and the Court's confidence in the ability of a state judicial system to provide sufficient after-the-fact remedies to deter illegal government action, may portend a general discounting of the need for hearings *prior* to the deprivation of interests in "liberty" or "property" "as long as [the individual] can later recover damages from a state official if he [was] innocent." [34]

The novel theory announced in *Ingraham v. Wright* may indeed have much broader implications for the doctrine of what process is due. The notion that a "post-deprivation state remedy may be all the process that the Fourteenth Amendment requires," as Justice Stevens suggested in his dissent, may well come to be seen in the future as the explanation for *Paul v. Davis'* denial of relief for damage to reputation,[35] since there too one could "conclude that an adequate state remedy may prevent every state inflicted injury to a person's reputa-

---

Their view was based on the belief that the legitimate government interest in the efficiency of the civil service would be jeopardized by "prolonged retention of a disruptive or otherwise unsatisfactory employee" pending a pre-termination hearing, Id. at 168 (Powell, J., concurring), and on the impression that existing procedures produced accurate results. Id. at 170 (Powell, J., concurring). Minimal significance was attached to the effect upon the dismissed employee of the interruption in income suffered pending the subsequent hearing, since a "public employee may well have independent resources to overcome any temporary hardship, and . . . may be able to secure a job in the private sector. Alternatively, he will be eligible for welfare benefits." Id. at 169 (Powell, J., concurring).

Justices White, Marshall, Douglas and Brennan all thought a prior hearing was required by due process. Unlike Justice Powell, Justice White believed that dismissal in advance of hearing was not the only alternative to "keeping a person on the scene" prior to a hearing; "suspension with pay would obviate this problem." Id.

at 194. (White, J., concurring in part and dissenting in part). And Justice Marshall charged that to downplay the financial impact of the dismissal "is to exhibit a gross insensitivity to the plight of these employees": "Many workers, particularly those at the bottom of the pay scale will suffer severe and painful economic dislocations from even a temporary loss of wages." Id. at 220–21. (Marshall, J., dissenting).

The three remaining Justices—Rehnquist, Burger, and Stewart—contended primarily that there existed in this case no "property" interest sufficient to trigger procedural due process obligations at all, and secondarily that whatever interest in reputational "liberty" was adversely affected by dismissal could be adequately protected by a subsequent hearing. See the discussion in § 10–13, supra.

31. 430 U.S. at 674.

32. Id. at 682.

33. Id.

34. Id. at 696 (White, J., dissenting).

35. 424 U.S. 693 (1976).

tion from violating 42 U.S.C. § 1983." [36] Thus, combining *Ingraham* with Justice Stevens' interpretation of *Paul*, the Court appears to have taken a dramatic turn from the view that a timely due process hearing should be held in the government agency itself for an infringement of protected "liberty" or "property." By failing to interpret the due process clause to require such hearings, the Court further discounts the intrinsic importance of due process as providing a right to dialogue between government and the individual so that each person can participate in the focused, adverse decisions of governmental bodies—a right implicit in bill of attainder notions as well as in due process.[37] Instead, the view that courts can provide a sufficient forum to correct mistakes after the fact emphasizes the instrumental elements of due process at the expense of its participatory role.

   Parratt v. Taylor [38] and *Hudson v. Palmer* [39] applied the reasoning of *Ingraham* to circumstances in which the theory is considerably easier to defend—those in which a pre-deprivation hearing is essentially "impossible." *Parratt* and *Hudson* built upon the reluctance of the Court, alluded to in *Paul v. Davis* [40] and *Ingraham*, to "federalize" the law of torts—that is, to "make of the Fourteenth Amendment a font of tort law to be superimposed upon whatever systems may already be administered by the States" [41] by "turning every alleged injury which may have been inflicted by a state official acting under 'color of law' into a violation of the Fourteenth Amendment cognizable under [42 U.S.C.] § 1983." [42]

   In *Parratt v. Taylor*,[43] the hobby materials ordered by the respondent, an inmate of a Nebraska prison, were lost by employees of the prison. Respondent brought an action in federal court under 42 U.S.C. § 1983 against the prison officials, alleging that his hobby materials had been negligently lost and that he had been deprived of his property without due process of law. Noting that "the Fourteenth Amendment protects only against deprivations 'without due process of law,' " [44] the Court held that, because the tort remedy provided by the State of Nebraska was "sufficient to satisfy the requirements of due process," [45] it follows that "the respondent has not alleged a violation of the Due Process Clause of the Fourteenth Amendment." [46]

   The *Parratt* Court reasoned that *pre*-deprivation process cannot properly be demanded where the loss "is not a result of some established state procedure" [47] but is instead the "result of a random and

---

36. 430 U.S. at 702 (Stevens, J., dissenting).

37. See § 10–6, supra.

38. 451 U.S. 527 (1981).

39. 468 U.S. 517 (1984).

40. 424 U.S. 693 (1976).

41. Paul, 424 U.S. at 701, quoted in Parratt v. Taylor, 451 U.S. at 544.

42. Parratt, 451 U.S. at 544. See also Daniels v. Williams, 106 S.Ct. 662 (1986), and Davidson v. Cannon, 106 S.Ct. 668 (1986), discussed in § 10–7, supra, holding that there is no "deprivation" within the meaning of the due process clause if the government is merely negligent.

43. 451 U.S. 527 (1981).

44. Id. at 537.

45. Id. at 544.

46. Id. at 543. In light of Daniels and Davidson, see note 42, supra, no violation would have been alleged in Parratt even if *no* tort remedy had been provided.

47. Id. at 541.

unauthorized act of a state employee" [48] beyond the state's control, making it "not only impracticable, but impossible, [for the state] to provide a meaningful hearing before the deprivation." [49] Where the state provides the opportunity for a meaningful post-deprivation hearing (in *Parratt*, the state's tort remedy), this remedy adequately satisfies the requirements of due process.

The *Parratt* rule was extended by the Court in *Hudson v. Palmer* [50] to cover intentional deprivations of property by state employees acting under color of state law. In *Hudson* a prison employee was alleged to have intentionally destroyed non-contraband personal property of a prison inmate in the course of a "shakedown" search of his cell.[51] The Court found that the destruction was "random and unauthorized" although intentional, and that the post-deprivation tort remedy provided by the State of Virginia would satisfy the requirements of due process for the same reasons as those outlined in *Parratt*. Since the wrongful deprivation was not the result of some established state procedure,[52] a pre-deprivation hearing was impossible, and the availability of a meaningful post-deprivation hearing was thus "adequate process." "For intentional, as for negligent deprivations of property by state employees, the state's action is not complete until and unless it provides or refuses to provide a suitable post-deprivation remedy." [53]

Although the *Hudson* opinion was unanimous on this issue, the magnitude of the opinion's apparent leap beyond *Parratt* seems unwarranted. It is one thing to say that no deprivation of life, liberty, or property without due process of law has occurred simply because a state agent negligently injures someone in the course of carrying out his

---

48. Id.

49. Id.

50. 468 U.S. 517 (1984).

51. Although the Court's decision in Hudson was unanimous with regard to the procedural due process issue discussed in this section, Justice Stevens dissented (joined by Justices Brennan, Marshall and Blackmun) from the holding of the Court that a prisoner "does not have a reasonable expectation of privacy enabling him to invoke the Fourth Amendment. . . ." Hudson, 468 U.S. at 530. Justice Stevens wrote that this part of the decision in Hudson "declares prisoners to be little more than chattels," according them no measure of human dignity while incarcerated, in the name of efficient jail administration. Id. at 555.

52. An instructive contrast is provided by Logan v. Zimmerman Brush Company, 455 U.S. 422 (1982). There, the appellant filed a charge with the Illinois Fair Employment Practices Commission. Pursuant to the Illinois Fair Employment Practices Act (FEPA), a fact-finding conference was to be scheduled within 120 days of the filing of the charge. The conference, however, was inadvertently scheduled five days after the limitations period had expired,

thus depriving appellant of his FEPA claim without any fault or neglect on his part. The Court held that the state's post-deprivation tort claims procedure (for the negligence of some state employee) was a constitutionally inadequate remedy. What the appellant in Logan sought was to have his state-created FEPA claim (a species of property) heard; the state's procedural rules had rendered the negligence of a state employee a source of irreparable harm to the interest in that hearing. Thus the relevant deprivation in Logan—the use of a state rule to make a public employee's negligence the basis for destroying an individual's property—was caused not by a random and unauthorized act alone but rather by an "established state procedure" that lacked adequate safeguards against error. In fact, the appellant's claim was characterized as "challenging not the Commissioner's error [as such] but the 'established state procedure' that destroys his entitlement without according him proper procedural safeguards." Logan, 455 U.S. at 422. It followed that there was no post-deprivation remedy afforded by the state that satisfied the requirements of procedural due process.

53. Hudson, 468 U.S. at 533.

official duties—as the Court was later to hold in *Daniels v. Williams* [54] and *Davidson v. Cannon.*[55] It is quite another thing to suggest that even an intentional abuse of state authority cannot inflict any constitutional injury unless and until the state has failed to provide redress. To be sure, an intentional taking of property by the state for public use, when challenged only under the just compensation clause, is not a violation at all unless just compensation is in fact subsequently denied by state authorities. But that is the case only because the right at issue in such an instance is the right not to have the government take one's property "without just compensation." Although it therefore seems correct to say that "*Parratt*'s reasoning applies . . . by analogy because of the special nature of the Just Compensation Clause," [56] the casual extension of that analogy in *Hudson* to other categories of intentional injury seems problematic in the extreme, unless carefully confined to the kind of injury to property involved on the facts of *Hudson* itself.[57]

At least some intentional abuses of a state agent's authority—such as the killing of a prisoner after arrest by a state sheriff in the landmark case of *Screws v. United States* [58]—must surely be deemed to violate procedural due process despite the availability of post-deprivation relief (e.g., a wrongful death action, or prosecution of the wrongdoer), despite the absence of any state policy encouraging or condoning the abuse (no such policy was found or even alleged in *Screws* [59]), and despite the impracticality of asking the state to guarantee pre-deprivation process for the sort of obviously unauthorized and unpredictable act that was involved in *Screws*. Nor does it seem plausible to limit *Screws* to cases in which state officials abuse their authority by inflicting the ultimate deprivation and, in effect, serving as executioners. Certainly a police officer's deliberate and unauthorized decision to inflict a severe beating on someone he has just arrested,[60] or indeed to destroy such a person's property, rather than to await the usual processes of trial and sentencing, constitutes a violation of procedural due process complete when it occurs, regardless of the avenues of redress available under state law. Dirty Harry violated the Constitution even if the state made it possible for his victims to sue him. Any

54. 106 S.Ct. 662 (1986). See § 10–7, supra, note 6.

55. 106 S.Ct. 668 (1986). See § 10–7, supra, note 7.

56. Williamson County Regional Planning Commission v. Hamilton Bank, 473 U.S. 172, 195 (1985) (claim of taking without just compensation is "premature" until the property owner "has used the [state-provided] procedure and been denied just compensation").

57. Cf. Bonner v. Coughlin, 517 F.2d 1311, 1318–1320 (7th Cir. 1975) (per Stevens, Circuit Judge), modified en banc, 545 F.2d 565 (7th Cir. 1976), cert. denied 435 U.S. 932 (1978). See also Ingraham v. Wright, 430 U.S. 651, 700–703 (1977) (Stevens, J., dissenting).

58. 325 U.S. 91, 93 (1945) (holding that such a killing deprived the prisoner of the right to trial and thus subjected the sheriff to federal criminal prosecution under 18 U.S.C. § 242).

59. Although the Court found no official state policy encouraging behavior such as this sheriff's, it is entirely possible that the Court may have imagined a skewing of the system toward implicitly condoning the violent behavior of a white sheriff toward black prisoners, with white juries excusing such behavior, in Georgia in the 1940's.

60. If imposed as part of a sentence, such punishment would violate the eighth amendment's prohibition against "cruel and unusual punishment." Jackson v. Bishop, 404 F.2d 571 (8th Cir. 1968) (per Blackmun, Circuit Judge).

contrary intimation in the needlessly broad language of *Hudson* ought to be regarded as dictum, and should be reconsidered when a suitable case presents itself.

At the end of this section, we return to the question whether *Parratt* and *Hudson* could possibly stand for the sweeping proposition that procedural due process is *never* violated provided the state's legal system as a whole provides a constitutionally acceptable set of remedies. Before addressing that broad issue, we turn first to a question raised even when it *is* clear that some sort of post-deprivation remedy is all that procedural due process demands. In such situations, it is important to recognize that the state's mere provision of *some* post-deprivation remedy leaves open the question whether the particular remedy provided is constitutionally adequate. The adequacy of post-deprivation process is most often called into question on the ground that, even if affording relief of the right *sort*, it does not do so "at a meaningful time;" [61] "[a]t some point, a delay in the post-termination hearing would [itself] become a constitutional violation." [62] In *Barry v. Barchi*,[63] a horse trainer's license was suspended without a pre-suspension hearing after a urinalysis indicated that his horse had been drugged during a race. The New York statute pursuant to which his license was suspended provided for a subsequent administrative hearing, but it "neither on its face nor as applied in this case, assured a prompt hearing and prompt disposition of the outstanding issues between [the horse trainer] and the State." [64] The Court held that, because those subject to suspension under this statute have a weighty interest in the prompt resolution of the controversy, and because there is "little or no state interest . . . in an appreciable delay in going forward with a full hearing," [65] the statute does not comport with the requirements of due process inasmuch as it provides for an indefinite delay between suspension and hearing—a delay during which the full penalty of the suspension could be irreparably and mistakenly suffered before any hearing had been held.[66]

Under less egregious circumstances, however, the length of the delay which due process deems tolerable would necessarily depend upon the facts of each particular case.[67] As a result of this fact-specific approach, the decisions of the Court offer no "rule" [68] other than a four-

---

61. Armstrong v. Manzo, 380 U.S. 545, 552 (1965).

62. Cleveland Board of Education v. Loudermill, 470 U.S. 532, 547 n. 12 (1985) (citing Barry v. Barchi, 443 U.S. 55, 66 (1979)) (recognizing as a separate claim respondent's allegation of a distinct due process violation in administrative delay).

63. 443 U.S. 55 (1979).

64. Id. at 66.

65. Id.

66. But see Mackey v. Montrym, 443 U.S. 1, 29 n. 7 (1979) (Stewart, J., dissenting).

67. See United States v. $8,850 in United States Currency, 461 U.S. 555, 565

(1983); Cleveland Board of Education v. Loudermill, 470 U.S. at 557 (Brennan, J., concurring in part and dissenting in part).

68. Cf. Arnett v. Kennedy, 416 U.S. 134, 194 (1974) (White, J., concurring in part and dissenting in part) (approval of a statutory scheme pursuant to which over 50 percent of appeals "take more than three months"); Mathews v. Eldridge, 424 U.S. 319 (1976) (10- to 11-month delay in receipt of decision on Social Security benefits implicitly approved); United States v. $8,850 in United States Currency, 461 U.S. 555 (1983) (18-month delay between seizure of currency and the filing of a civil forfeiture proceeding not excessive); Cleveland Board of Education v. Loudermill, supra (9-month

factor test for evaluating the constitutionality of the delay between the deprivation and the post-deprivation hearing: as described in *United States v. $8,850 in United States Currency*,[69] the test calls for balancing of the length of the delay, the reasons justifying it, the "claimant's assertion of the right to a judicial hearing," [70] and the prejudice to the claimant resulting from the delay.[71]

We return, then, to the broadest question posed by the entire series of decisions assessing the adequacy of post-deprivation remedies in various circumstances, including the cases holding that there are situations in which *only* a suitable post-deprivation remedy is required by due process. Should these cases be thought to establish a general principle that a state violation of procedural due process is *never* "complete unless and until [the state] provides or refuses to provide a suitable post-deprivation remedy"? [72] Presumably not. For there is a long and venerable line of precedent holding that an abuse of state power may violate the due process clause even where the state provides fully adequate procedures for review and redress. In *Ex parte Virginia*,[73] the Supreme Court held that the provisions of the fourteenth amendment are addressed not only to the states *as states*, but also to their agents: "Whoever, by virtue of public position under a State government, deprives another of property, life, or liberty, without due process of law . . . violates the constitutional inhibition [of the fourteenth amendment]; and as he acts in the name and for the State, and is clothed with the State's power, his act is that of the State." [74] This principle was reaffirmed by the Court in *Home Telephone & Telegraph Co. v. Los Angeles*,[75] when the Court noted that, where a state agent "in the exercise of the authority with which he is clothed misuses the power possessed to do a wrong forbidden by the [Fourteenth] Amendment, inquiry concerning whether the State has authorized the wrong is irrelevant." [76] Thus "the Federal judicial power is competent to afford redress for the wrong" [77] in such an instance without a declaration from the state court that the acts were authorized. More recently, in *Monroe v. Pape*,[78] the Court held that "Congress has the power to enforce provisions of the Fourteenth Amendment against those who carry a badge of authority of a State and represent it in some capacity, whether they act in accordance with their authority or misuse it." [79] The Court added that "[i]t is no answer that the State has a law which if enforced would give relief. The federal remedy is supplementary to

delay not unconstitutional where there was no other indication that the wait was prolonged and where it stemmed in part from the thoroughness of the procedure).

69. 461 U.S. 555, 564 (1983).

70. Id. at 568–569.

71. This four-factor balancing test was first set forth by the Court in Barker v. Wingo, 407 U.S. 514 (1972), to assess claimed violations of the Sixth Amendment right to a speedy trial.

72. Hudson, 468 U.S. at 533.

73. 100 U.S. 339 (1879).

74. Id. at 347.

75. 227 U.S. 278 (1973). See discussion in § 18–4, infra.

76. Id. at 287.

77. Id.

78. 365 U.S. 167 (1961).

79. Id. at 171–172.

the state remedy, and the latter need not first be sought and refused before the federal one is invoked." [80]

How, then, are we to account for the seemingly contrary view taken in *Parratt*, and for the statement by the *Hudson* Court that, until post-deprivation relief is sought and refused, "the state's action is not complete"? [81] The answer must be that there *are* rights secured by the Constitution which cannot be said to have been violated at all until relief is sought from, and denied by, the state—and that the *Parratt* and *Hudson* decisions apply *only* to such rights. Such rights include, for example, the right not to be deprived of private property for public use without just compensation, [82] and the right—when the requirement of a *pre*-deprivation hearing is obviated by impossibility, [83] impracticability, [84] or exigent circumstances [85]—not to be deprived of property without a suitable *post*-deprivation hearing. After all, when there is no right to a pre-deprivation hearing, it is hardly surprising that, absent a refusal to provide an adequate post-deprivation hearing, no right at all may have been violated. But there is nothing in the Supreme Court's decisions to support the view that *all* procedural rights are of this character. For example, the right to a fair trial before an impartial judge [86] is a right whose violation should be deemed to be complete when punishment has been meted out by a state official without any trial, [87] or when a trial has been held that did not meet basic standards of fairness. The right to a fair trial is just that—a right to a fair *trial*, and not merely a right to fairness in the state's processes of review at some point before the Supreme Court's certiorari jurisdiction is invoked. [88]

80. Id. at 183 (unreasonable search and seizure by Chicago police officers acting in violation of Illinois law).

81. Hudson, 468 U.S. at 533.

82. See, e.g., Williamson County Regional Planning Commission v. Hamilton Bank, 473 U.S. 172, 195 (1985); Hudson, 468 U.S. at 539 (O'Connor, J., concurring) (no unconstitutional taking results if just compensation is provided). Cf. Barney v. New York, 193 U.S. 430 (1904) (dismissing federal suit seeking to enjoin city's railroad construction as a deprivation of property).

83. See, e.g., Parratt v. Taylor, 451 U.S. 527 (1981).

84. See, e.g., Ingraham v. Wright, 430 U.S. 651 (1977).

85. See, e.g., North American Cold Storage v. Chicago, 211 U.S. 306 (1908), discussed in note 17, supra.

86. See, e.g., Ward v. Monroeville, 409 U.S. 57, 61–62 (1972); In re Murchison, 349 U.S. 133 (1955); Tumey v. Ohio, 273 U.S. 510 (1927), discussed in § 10–16, infra.

87. See Screws v. United States, 325 U.S. 91 (1945), supra, note 58.

88. The Fifth Circuit took a contrary position on this issue in Holloway v. Walker, 784 F.2d 1287, 1294 (5th Cir. 1986), cert. denied 107 S.Ct. 571 (1986). Because a civil judgment of a state court cannot be set aside in an original federal action, see Rooker v. Fidelity Trust Co., 263 U.S. 413 (1923); District of Columbia Court of Appeals v. Feldman, 460 U.S. 462 (1983), even a reversal of the Fifth Circuit's extension of Parratt and Hudson would, as a practical matter, leave litigants complaining of unfair state trials in civil cases with no alternative to direct review in the state's appellate courts, with ultimate review in the Supreme Court by certiorari, if such litigants are to recover anything beyond nominal damages for the deprivation of unfairness as such under Carey v. Piphus, 435 U.S. 247 (1978) (discussed in § 10–7, supra). But cf. Dennis v. Sparks, 449 U.S. 24, 25 (1980) (holding § 1983 action in federal district court available against private co-conspirators of state trial judge alleged to have corruptly issued injunction against the federal plaintiffs, where the injunction had been "dissolved by [a state] appellate court" before the § 1983 action was filed, and where the relief sought in the § 1983 action thus presumably did not entail reviewing the concededly invalid state court injunctive decree). Whether Dennis v. Sparks would be reaffirmed after Parratt and Hudson, particularly in light of Feld-

§ 10–15. Current Doctrine: Issues of Formality, Content, and Standards of Proof

Where due process continues, even after *Paul v. Davis*,[1] *Ingraham v. Wright*,[2] *Parratt v. Taylor*,[3] and *Hudson v. Palmer*[4], to mandate a hearing within the government agency involved in inflicting a deprivation, the formality of the procedures employed by the agency may vary widely with the circumstances.[5] Given the importance of the factual background in determining the procedures required to achieve the Court's instrumental objective of insuring accuracy, this necessarily general discussion can only outline the procedural issues whose specific resolution will necessarily turn on the context of particular cases.

At the core of the procedural due process right is the guarantee of an opportunity to be heard and its instrumental corollary, a promise of prior notice.[6] The constitutionality of a particular notice mechanism is

man's resurrection of Rooker, is an open question inasmuch as the only issue litigated in Dennis and expressly addressed by the Supreme Court in that case was the question whether the private individuals who conspired with the state trial judge could be deemed to have acted "under color of law."

§ 10–15

1. 424 U.S. 693 (1976), discussed in § 10–14, supra.

2. 430 U.S. 651 (1977), discussed in § 10–14, supra.

3. 451 U.S. 527 (1981).

4. 468 U.S. 517 (1984).

5. See, e.g., Hannah v. Larche, 363 U.S. 420, 442 (1960). See generally Friendly, "Some Kind of Hearing," 123 U.Pa.L.Rev. 1267 (1975).

6. Notice must include not only information that a hearing is about to *occur* but information as to what the hearing will *entail*—including both "the nature of the charges [and] also . . . the substance of the relevant supporting evidence." Brock v. Roadway Express, 107 S.Ct. 1740, 1743 (1987) (Marshall, J., announcing judgment, joined by Blackmun, Powell, and O'Connor, JJ.); accord, id. at 1751 (Brennan, J.); id. at 1744 (Stevens, J.). Nothing less permits the person threatened with deprivation to prepare sufficiently to avoid undue risk of an erroneous outcome.

Apart from such instrumental aspects of the issue of notice, the Court in several recent cases has focused on *which* affected individuals or entities are *entitled* to notice. For instance, in Securities and Exchange Commission v. Jerry T. O'Brien, Inc., 467 U.S. 735 (1984), a unanimous Court, held that the "targets" of nonpublic SEC investigations have no right to notice when third parties are issued subpoenas in the investigation so that such targets can

ensure that the subpoenas comply with the standards set forth by the Court in United States v. Powell, 379 U.S. 48 (1964) (holding that "[t]he Due Process Clause is not implicated under such circumstances because an administrative investigation adjudicates no legal rights . . ." 467 U.S. at 742, citing Hannah v. Larche, 363 U.S. 420, 440–43 (1960)). See also Texaco, Inc. v. Short, 454 U.S. 516 (1982), upholding a state statute providing that severed mineral interests not used for a 20-year period automatically lapse and revert to the surface owner unless the owner of the mineral rights, before the expiration of the 20-year period (or before the end of a two-year grace period from the time of the effective date of the act) filed in the county recorder's office to preserve his interest. The Court found no constitutional requirement that the state should have informed the mineral rights owners of the requirements of the new law, adding that the 2-year grace period was sufficient to allow those affected by the statute to become familiar with it. The Court also refused to find that notice should have been given the mineral rights owners before their rights were to lapse, noting that "the full procedural protections of the Due Process Clause" would be provided before judgment would enter in any subsequent quiet title action. Id. at 534.

The Court reached a different result in Mennonite Board of Missions v. Adams, 462 U.S. 791 (1983), where the Court held that, "[s]ince a mortgagee clearly has a legally protected property interest, he is entitled to notice reasonably calculated to apprise him of [an] impending tax sale," id. at 798. See discussion in text at note 26, infra.

In one case, the Court upheld a state statute that conditioned the right to receive notice on whether the party seeking it had satisfied statutory requirements en-

not to be judged by its actual success—whether an individual or group is in fact notified—but turns instead on whether the chosen method is "reasonably calculated, under all the circumstances, to apprise interested parties of the pendency of the action and afford them an opportunity to present their objections." [7]

In a series of cases, the Supreme Court has examined the *type* of notice to be given and has generally required that, where a significant interest is at stake, there must be greater certainty that notice will be effective.

In *Memphis Light, Gas, & Water Division v. Craft*,[8] for instance, the Court held that mailed notice from a utility company threatening to terminate service was constitutionally deficient where it failed to advise customers of the proper procedures for protesting the utility's actions. The Court held that the notice provided failed to comport with the dictates of *Mullane* because it "was not 'reasonably calculated' to inform [consumers] of the availability of 'an opportunity to present their objections' to their bills," [9] adding that "[n]otice in a case of this kind does not comport with constitutional requirements when it does not advise the customer of the availability of a procedure for protesting termination of utility service as unjustified." [10] Emphasizing the need for ensuring that due process requirements remain flexible to respond to a variety of situations,[11] the Court noted that, although the challenged notice "may well have been adequate under different circumstances," in this case it was not. Because the notice at issue "is given to thousands of customers of various levels of education, experience and resources," and since it concerns "electrical service, the uninterrupted continuity of which is essential to health and safety," it must clearly inform consumers "of the availability of an opportunity to present their complaint[s]" and tell them "where, during which hours of the day, and before whom disputed bills appropriately may be considered." [12]

titling him to such information. In Lehr v. Robertson, 463 U.S. 248 (1983), the Court denied the putative father of an illegitimate child an absolute right to notice of adoption proceedings, holding, in an opinion by Justice Stevens, that the statute which required that putative fathers not meeting other statutory criteria file in a "putative father registry" to receive such notice did not deny the putative father his right to due process. The Court noted that, where the father of a child fails to develop "a relationship with his offspring . . . the Federal Constitution will not automatically compel a State to listen to his opinion of where the child's best interests lie." Id. at 262. Chief Justice Burger and Justices Brennan, Powell, Rehnquist and O'Connor joined the Court's opinion. Justice White, joined by Justices Marshall and Blackmun, dissented.

7. Mullane v. Central Hanover Bank & Trust Co., 339 U.S. 306, 314 (1950). See also Armstrong v. Manzo, 380 U.S. 545, 550 (1965).

8. 436 U.S. 1 (1978). Justice Powell wrote the majority opinion, in which Justices Brennan, Stewart, White, Marshall and Blackmun joined. Chief Justice Burger and Justice Rehnquist joined Justice Stevens' dissent.

9. Id. at 14.

10. Id. at 14–15.

11. Id. at 15 n. 15, citing Morrissey v. Brewer, 408 U.S. 471, 481 (1972), and Mathews v. Eldridge, 424 U.S. 319, 334 (1976).

12. Id. at 15 n. 15. Contrast the Court's approach to adequacy of notice to prisoners. In Greenholtz v. Inmates of Nebraska Penal and Cor. Complex, 442 U.S. 1 (1979), for example, the circuit court held that the due process clause required that a Nebraska prison inmate eligible for parole "receive written notice of the precise time of the hearing reasonably in advance of the hearing, setting forth the factors which may be considered by the Board in reaching its decision." Id. at 6. Nebraska required only that the Board of Parole in-

The dissent attacked the decision as imposing an unnecessary and paternalistic burden on the state, arguing that, although the additional information to be included in the notice would be "helpful", it was not constitutionally required: "a homeowner surely need not be told how to complain about an error in a utility bill . . . our democratic government would cease to function if, as the Court seems to assume, our citizenry were unable to find such information on their own initiative." [13] The majority disagreed, stressing that the magnitude of the interest at stake demanded that additional steps be taken, and arguing that "[t]he dissent's restrictive view of the process due . . . would erect an artificial barrier between the notice and hearing components of the constitutional guarantee of due process." [14]

Similarly vital interests supported the Court's requirement for more adequate notice in *Greene v. Lindsey*.[15] There the Court was presented with a challenge to a state statute regulating service of process in forcible entry and detainer actions, which allowed notice to be posted on the resident's apartment door if a single attempt at personal service failed to find the defendant or a member of his family over the age of 16 on the premises. The record indicated, however, that

form the inmate of the month in which his final parole hearing would be held, posting the exact time of the proceeding on the day of the hearing. The Supreme Court reversed the circuit court, finding the state procedure constitutionally adequate since it allowed the inmate to obtain letters or statements on his own behalf and since "[t]here is no claim that either the timing of the notice or its substance seriously prejudices the inmate's ability to prepare adequately for the hearing." Id. at 14 n. 6.

Four Justices dissented on the notice issue. Justice Marshall, joined by Justices Brennan and Stevens, disputed the majority's reasoning, arguing that the inmates "plainly have contended throughout this litigation that reasonable advance notice is necessary to enable them to organize their evidence, call witnesses permitted by the Board, and notify private counsel allowed to participate in the hearing," id. at 37–8, and adding that, "[g]iven the significant private interests at stake, and the importance of reasonable notice in preserving the appearance of fairness, I see no reason to depart from this Court's longstanding recognition that adequate notice is a fundamental requirement of due process." Id. at 38. Justice Powell's dissent pointed out that, under the majority's rationale, the right of an inmate to present evidence, call witnesses and be represented by private counsel "is reduced or nullified completely by the State's refusal to give notice of the hearing more than a few hours in advance," id. at 21, and added that "the courts below correctly determined that the current notice procedure undermines the prisoner's ability to present his case ade-

quately at the final review hearing . . . [a] conclusion accord[ing] with common sense." Id.

Even when a prisoner is notified in advance of the date of a hearing, his opportunity to participate may be impaired if he is segregated from the rest of the prison population pending the proceeding. In Hughes v. Rowe, 449 U.S. 5 (1980), the Court, in a *per curiam* opinion, reversed, *inter alia*, the circuit court's dismissal of a prisoner's claim that pre-hearing segregation violated his due process rights in the absence of any showing of an emergency situation justifying the segregation. In dissent, Justice Rehnquist argued that the Court should defer to the prison officials' determination of the need to segregate the inmate, adding that their decision demonstrated no abuse of discretion. Id. at 20–21. He went on to argue that even if emergency conditions did not exist to justify the state's action, segregation of the inmate "was fully justified in order to protect the integrity of the later hearing" because "[p]ermitting inmates to return to the general prison population following a serious breach of prison discipline or violation of prison rules poses difficulties in terms of alibi construction and witness intimidation." Id. at 22.

13. Memphis, 436 U.S. at 26.

14. Id. at 14–15 n. 15.

15. 456 U.S. 444 (1982). Justice Brennan wrote for a majority that included Justices White, Marshall, Powell, Blackmun and Stevens. Justice O'Connor dissented in an opinion joined by Chief Justice Burger and Justice Rehnquist.

the posted notices were at times removed from doors by children or other tenants; the appellee tenants, evicted after default judgments were entered against them and the period of appeal had lapsed, argued that they were thus deprived of due process because they had never seen the notices.

After declining to accept the argument that posted notice in an *in rem* proceeding is "*ipso facto* constitutionally adequate," [16] the Court, opting to focus on the importance of a resident's interest in remaining at home,[17] held that posted notice was inadequate under the circumstances of the case. Although recognizing that the use of posted notice was reasonably based on the assumption that "a property owner will maintain superintendence of his property," [18] the Court nevertheless held that posting under the circumstances presented would predictably result, too often, "in a failure to provide actual notice to the tenant concerned." [19] To the Court, "the failure to effect personal service on the first visit [could] hardly [be taken to] suggest[ ] that the tenant has abandoned his interest in the apartment such that mere *pro forma* notice might be held constitutionally adequate." [20] Although stating that it was not mandating the type of notice required, the Court observed that "[n]otice by mail in the circumstances of this case would surely go a long way toward providing the constitutionally required" notice,[21] adding that "we have no hesitation in concluding that posted service *accompanied by* mail service, is constitutionally preferable to posted service alone." [22]

The dissent asserted that the majority, in effectively prescribing mailed notice,[23] ignored the fact that the law at issue was designed "for quickly determining whether or not a landlord has a right to immediate possession of leased premises and, if so, for enabling the landlord speedily to obtain the property in wrongful possession," [24] and erroneously relied upon conflicting testimony "of a few . . . process servers" [25] in determining that posted service was constitutionally ineffective.

The fact that a significant interest was imperilled by state procedures seemed to guide the Court's decision in *Mennonite Board of Missions v. Adams*,[26] even though the Court suggested that the actual risk of deprivation may have been relatively slight. At issue was a state statutory scheme governing the sale of land for non-payment of property taxes. Under state law, owners of the property were notified by certified mail of the tax sale, but mortgagees of those owners had to rely upon posted and published notice. The Supreme Court, in striking down the scheme, reasoned that, "[s]ince a mortgagee clearly has a

16. Id. at 450.

17. Id. at 450–51.

18. Id. at 451.

19. Id. at 453.

20. Id. at 454.

21. Id. at 455.

22. Id. n. 9 (emphasis in original).

23. Id. at 459 n. 2.

24. Id. at 457.

25. Id. at 458.

26. 462 U.S. 791 (1983). The majority opinion by Justice Marshall was joined by Chief Justice Burger and Justices Brennan, White, Blackmun and Stevens. Justice O'Connor wrote in dissent, joined by Justices Powell and Rehnquist.

legally protected property interest, he is entitled to notice reasonably calculated to apprise him of an impending tax sale." [27] The Court added that, "[w]hen a mortgagee is identified in a mortgage that is publicly recorded, constructive notice by publication must be supplemented by notice mailed to the mortgagee's last known address, or by personal service. But unless the mortgagee is not reasonably identifiable, constructive notice alone does not satisfy the mandate of *Mullane*." [28] Even though the Court recognized that many of the lenders affected by its ruling were "sophisticated creditors [who] have means at their disposal to discover whether property taxes have not been paid and whether tax sale proceedings are therefore likely to be initiated," [29] the majority held that mailed notice was still required; the fact that the state is required under the dictates of the due process clause to take extraordinary measures in providing notice to inexperienced or incompetent people in other contexts [30] does not concomitantly relieve the state of its duties where many of the recipients of the notice are likely to be more sophisticated: "Notice by mail or other means as certain to ensure actual notice is a minimum constitutional precondition to a proceeding which will adversely affect the liberty or property interests of *any* party, whether unlettered or well versed in commercial practice, if its name and address are reasonably ascertainable." [31]

The fundamental procedural due process right to a hearing is generally found to embrace the right to present evidence [32] and to confront and cross-examine adverse witnesses. [33] But the Supreme Court has held that, in extraordinary circumstances, due process permits the limitation, or even the total denial, of these evidentiary safeguards.

In *Wolff v. McDonnell*, for example, the Court held that cancellation of a prisoner's "good time" credits as a punishment for misconduct is valid only if carried out in a manner satisfying procedural due process, but the Court went on to rule that the prison inmate "should be allowed to call witnesses and present documentary evidence in his defense [only] when permitting him to do so will not be unduly hazardous to institutional safety or correctional goals." [34] Furthermore, a balancing of "the inmate's interest in avoiding loss of good time against the needs of the prison" resulted in a conclusion that "at the present time" the Constitution "should not be read to impose" proce-

---

27. Id. at 798.

28. Id.

29. Id. at 799.

30. Id.

31. Id. at 800 (emphasis in original). The dissent criticized the Court for prescribing a general rule "[w]ithout knowing what state and individual interests will be at stake in future cases." Id. at 802. For the dissenters, "the constitutional obligation imposed upon the State may itself be defined by the party's ability to protect its interest," id. at 803, and the Court's failure to require mortgagees to expend even "a minimum amount of effort" to stay in-

formed of their rights, id. at 808, as well as the Court's "fashioning a broad rule for 'the least sophisticated creditor' . . . ignores the well-settled principle that 'procedural due process rules are shaped by the risk of error inherent in the truthfinding process as applied to the generality of cases, not the rare exceptions.'" Id. at 803, citing Mathews, 424 U.S. at 344.

32. See, e.g., Morgan v. United States, 304 U.S. 1, 18 (1938).

33. See, e.g., Green v. McElroy, 360 U.S. 474, 497 (1959).

34. 418 U.S. 539, 563–64 (1974).

dures of confrontation and cross-examination upon prison disciplinary hearings; if these procedures "were to be allowed as a matter of course, . . . there would be considerable potential for havoc inside the prison walls." [35]

Similarly, the Court's instrumental concentration on utilitarian interest-balancing and accuracy to the exclusion of all intrinsic reasons for a hearing [36] has led it to extend the *Wolff* approach to school hearings on disciplinary matters.[37] In *Goss v. Lopez*, the due process requirement of "at least an informal give and take" left to the discretion of the decisionmaker the choice of whether to allow cross-examination or the presentation of witnesses.[38] Moreover, although the right to present evidence usually includes a right to make an oral presentation [39] the Supreme Court has suggested that, where administrative rule-application turns primarily on the evaluation of technical matters, the administering agency may validly limit evidentiary presentations to documentary submissions.[40] And Judge Henry Friendly proposed that courts go further and abandon any general presumption of a need for oral presentation of evidence, for cross-examination, or for the calling of witnesses, replacing that presumption with an ad hoc approach to assessing the need for, and merits of, any of these safeguards.[41]

35. Id. at 566–68. Accord, Hewitt v. Helms, 459 U.S. 460 (1983) (informal, nonadversarial review suffices for decision that prison inmate poses security threat and for decision to confine inmate to administrative segregation pending misconduct investigation; inmate need not be given opportunity to appear personally to present his case). See also, Ponte v. Real, 471 US 491 (1985) (where prison officials fail to call witnesses requested by an inmate in a disciplinary hearing, burden of proof is on prison officials to show that their acts were not arbitrary or capricious; at some point, prison officials must express the reasons for their actions, but that explanation need not be in writing nor exist as part of the administrative record developed at the hearing, but may be added to the record later or presented through testimony if the failure is challenged in court, and "so long as the reasons are logically related to preventing undue hazards to 'institutional safety or correctional goals,' the explanation should meet the Due Process requirements as outlined in Wolff.").

36. See, e.g., Wolff, 418 U.S. at 557 (minimum procedures are necessary "to insure the state created right is not arbitrarily abrogated"); Richardson v. Perales, 402 U.S. 389, 407 (1971) (analyzing the functional utility of cross-examination solely in terms of contribution to accuracy). See generally § 10–7, supra.

37. See, e.g., Goss v. Lopez, 419 U.S. 565, 579–80 (1975) ("The [due process] concern would be mostly academic if the disciplinary process were a totally accurate,

unerring process, never mistaken, and never unfair").

38. 419 U.S. 565, 584 (1975).

39. See, e.g., Califano v. Yamasaki, 442 U.S. 682 (1979), in which the Court held, without dissent, that where an overpayment is made to a social security recipient, an oral hearing is required as a matter of procedural due process when one is requested by the recipient before the agency determines whether recoupment (by decreasing future payments to which the claimant would otherwise be entitled) should be waived on the grounds that the overpayment was not the "fault" of the recipient and requiring recoupment would be "against equity and good conscience." Unlike the determination of whether there actually was an overpayment, a finding which "involve[s] relatively straightforward matters of computation for which written review is ordinarily an adequate means to correct prior mistakes," id. at 696, matters like "fault", "equity", or "detrimental reliance, usually require[ ] an assessment of the recipient's credibility, and written submissions are a particularly inappropriate way to distinguish a genuine hard luck story from a fabricated tall tale." Id. at 697.

40. See Mathews v. Eldridge, 424 U.S. 319 (1976) (no oral hearing required prior to termination of social security disability insurance benefits on medical grounds).

41. See Friendly, supra note 5, at 1270, 1281, 1284–85. See also United States v. Florida East Coast Ry., 410 U.S. 224 (1973)

Quite apart from whether the government may limit the *manner* in which an individual presents his or her case, "due process requires that there be an opportunity to present every available defense." [42] But government nonetheless may validly limit the issues which individuals or groups can raise at a hearing held in *advance* of a proposed governmental action adversely affecting their interests, so long as (1) there exists an opportunity for a *subsequent* hearing at which the previously ignored issues can be aired, and so long as (2) some legitimate purpose is served by the postponement. Thus, for example, the Court has held that government "may exclude all [other] claims of . . . right from possessory actions, consistently with due process of law." [43] More recently, in *Lindsey v. Normet*,[44] the Court upheld an Oregon statute which limited the defenses tenants could raise in an eviction action brought by landlords alleging nonpayment of rent, while allowing tenants to litigate their right to damages or alternative relief in their own subsequent actions.[45]

While the Supreme Court has frequently expressed the view that the "right to be heard would be, in many cases, of little avail if it did

(opportunity to submit written comments satisfies due process requirements for rulemaking under 5 U.S.C. § 553(c)). But see Subrin & Dykstra, "Notice and the Right to be Heard: The Significance of Old Friends," 9 Harv.Civ.Rts.—Civ.Lib.L.Rev. 449, 471–72 (1974) ("The likelihood of accurate fact ascertainment in the absence of testimonial evidence, cross-examination, and an impartial decisionmaker is palpably slim"); Mashaw, "The Supreme Court's Due Process Calculus for Administrative Adjudication in Mathews v. Eldridge: Three Factors in Search of a Theory of Value," 44 U.Chic.L.Rev. 28, 50 (1976) (oral presentation is fundamental prerequisite of due process hearing); Goldberg v. Kelly, 397 U.S. 254, 268–69 (1970) ("Written submissions are an unrealistic option for most [welfare] recipients, who lack the educational attainment necessary to write effectively and who cannot obtain professional assistance.").

The Court has indirectly limited the right to confrontation and cross-examination by holding that the requirements of procedural due process were not violated by the admission into evidence, as reliable hearsay, of government-introduced medical reports at an administrative hearing on the question of a claimant's eligibility for Social Security disability benefits. Richardson v. Perales, 402 U.S. 389 (1971). Justice Blackmun's majority opinion observed that, while the claimant plainly could not cross-examine the adverse medical reports themselves, "the authors of these reports were known and were subject to subpoena and to the very cross-examination that the claimant asserts he has not enjoyed." Id. at 407. The Court also argued that the "vast workings of the social

security administration system make for reliability and impartiality in the consultant reports," and that with "over 20,000 disability claim hearings annually, the cost of providing live medical testimony at those hearings, where need has not been demonstrated by a request for a subpoena, . . . would be a substantial drain on the trust fund and on the energy of physicians already in short supply." Id. at 403, 406.

Of course in the area of criminal prosecutions, the sixth amendment provides that "the accused" is guaranteed "the right . . . to be confronted with the witnesses against him" and "to have compulsory process for obtaining witnesses in his favor." These mandatory procedural requirements directly bind the federal government and indirectly bind the states through their incorporation in the fourteenth amendment due process clause. See, e.g., Washington v. Texas, 388 U.S. 14 (1967) (right to compulsory process for obtaining witnesses); Pointer v. Texas, 380 U.S. 400 (1965) (right to confrontation, and thus cross-examination).

42. American Surety Co. v. Baldwin, 287 U.S. 156, 168 (1932) (Brandeis, J.).

43. Bianchi v. Morales, 262 U.S. 170, 171 (1923) (Holmes, J.).

44. 405 U.S. 56 (1972).

45. This restriction on the issues raised in eviction proceedings is ordinarily justified not only as a way of allocating economic advantages as between landlords and tenants, cf. Dandridge v. Williams, 397 U.S. 471 (1970), but also as a way of making formal proceedings more attractive to landlords, and thereby minimizing resort to self-help against tenants.

not comprehend the right to be heard by counsel," [46] and has firmly established a right to counsel in criminal proceedings,[47] the Court has espoused a case-by-case approach in non-criminal cases.   One case illustrating this observation is *Vitek v. Jones*,[48] in which the Court held that, when the state transfers a convicted felon from state prison to a mental hospital, due process demands that he be provided assistance in preparing his case.   Four of the five Justices in the majority held that this meant that counsel would have to be appointed for indigent inmates in this situation,[49] while the other justice, Justice Powell, concluded that the required assistance could be provided by "a qualified and independent adviser who is not a lawyer." [50]   The plurality distinguished earlier cases which had "not required the automatic appointment of counsel for indigent prisoners facing other deprivations of liberty," [51] contending that "prisoners who are illiterate and uneducated have a greater need for assistance in exercising their rights.   A prisoner thought to be suffering from mental disease or defect requiring involuntary treatment probably has an even greater need for legal assistance, for such a prisoner is more likely to be unable to understand or exercise his rights.   In these circumstances, it is appropriate that counsel be provided to indigent prisoners whom the state seeks to treat as mentally ill." [52]

The Court suggested the general contours of its approach to the right to counsel in civil cases in *Lassiter v. Department of Social Services*,[53] in which a 5–4 majority held that, although there is "a presumption that an indigent litigant has a right to appointed counsel when, if he loses, he may be deprived of personal liberty," [54] no such right attaches simply because one is losing parental rights—on the theory that, "as a litigant's interest in personal liberty diminishes, so does his right to appointed counsel." [55]   This presumption can be

46. Goldberg v. Kelly, 397 U.S. 254, 268–69 (1970), quoting from Powell v. Alabama, 287 U.S. 45, 68–69 (1932).

47. In *criminal* proceedings, the right "to have the Assistance of Counsel" is mandated by the sixth and fourteenth amendments.   See, e.g., Argersinger v. Hamlin, 407 U.S. 25, 37 (1972) (absent "a knowing and intelligent waiver, no person may be imprisoned for any offense whether classified as petty, misdemeanor, or felony, unless he was represented by counsel at his trial"); Gideon v. Wainwright, 372 U.S. 335, 344 (1963) (if "any person hauled into court . . . is too poor to hire a lawyer," the government must provide free counsel).

48. 445 U.S. 480 (1980).

49. Id. at 496. These four were Justices Brennan, White, Marshall and Stevens.

50. Id. at 499.

51. Id. at 496, citing Gagnon v. Scarpelli, 411 U.S. 778, 790 (1973) (rejecting general requirement of counsel in probation revocation hearings), and Wolff v. McDonnell, 418 U.S. 539, 569–70 (1974) (rejecting requirement of counsel in proceedings involv-

ing cancellation of prisoner's good time credits, which determined when prisoner would be eligible for parole).

52. 445 U.S. at 496–97 (citations omitted).

53. 452 U.S. 18 (1981). Justice Stewart delivered the opinion of the Court, in which Chief Justice Burger and Justices White, Powell and Rehnquist joined. Chief Justice Burger also filed a concurring opinion. Justice Blackmun dissented in an opinion joined by Justices Brennan and Marshall. Justice Stevens dissented separately.

54. Id. at 26–27.

55. Id. at 26. The Court recalled that, in Gagnon v. Scarpelli, 411 U.S. 778 (1973), it had rejected any *general* right to counsel in probation revocation hearings inasmuch as the probationer possessed only a "conditional liberty" interest. Id. at 26, quoting Morrissey v. Brewer, 408 U.S. 471, 480 (1972).

So far as the parent-child relationship is concerned, the Court evidently views minors as in a state of continuing quasi-custo-

rebutted, however, where an evaluation of the *Mathews* criteria demonstrates a need for appointed counsel.[56]

In *Goldberg v. Kelly*,[57] for example, the Court held that, while government need not itself provide welfare recipients with publicly financed counsel at pre-termination hearings, government cannot deny recipients the right to secure for themselves the representation of counsel. In *Wolff v. McDonnell*, on the other hand, the Court determined that inmate participants in prison disciplinary proceedings may be validly denied the right to counsel since "[t]he insertion of counsel into the disciplinary process would inevitably give the proceedings a more adversary character and tend to reduce their utility as a means to further correctional goals."[58] Nevertheless the Court did declare in *Wolff* that, if "an illiterate inmate is involved," or if the issue is complex, the inmate participant "should be free to seek the aid of a fellow inmate or if that is forbidden, to have adequate substitute aid in the form of help from the staff or from a sufficiently competent inmate designated by the staff."[59]

The Supreme Court has also held that the *standards of proof* with which courts are to evaluate potential deprivations of substantive interests serve important practical and symbolic purposes,[60] and thus must comport with constitutional minima in civil as well as in criminal

dy, whether by their parents (or guardians) or by the state. See Schall v. Martin, 467 U.S. 253, 265 (1984) (upholding preventive pretrial detention of juveniles in part on the theory that "juveniles, unlike adults, are always in some form of custody."). Perhaps in part because of this notion, in Secretary of Public Welfare of Pennsylvania v. Institutionalized Juveniles, 442 U.S. 640, 645 (1979), the Court similarly concluded that due process does not necessarily mandate legal counsel for a child " 'during all significant stages of the commitment process.' " Chief Justice Burger wrote for the Court, joined by Justices White, Blackmun, Powell, and Rehnquist. Justice Stewart concurred in the judgment. Concurring in part and dissenting in part, Justice Brennan, joined by Justices Marshall and Stevens, agreed that no preadmission appointment of counsel was required, but argued that the state's post-admission procedures violated due process. For children under 13, the dissent argued that the state's failure to provide either representation or "reasonably prompt post-admission hearings", id. at 651, was unconstitutional under the rationale set forth in Justice Brennan's opinion concurring in part and dissenting in part in Parham v. J.R., 442 U.S. 584 (1979). For juveniles over 13, the dissenters found that the current state practice, in which these juveniles are informed of their rights to a hearing and given the phone number of an attorney within 24 hours of admission, im-

properly placed "the burden of contacting counsel and the burden of initiating proceedings" upon the child. Id. at 651. Since "[m]any of the institutionalized children are unable to read, write, comprehend the formal explanation of their rights, or use the telephone . . . [f]ew will be able to trigger procedural safeguards," id. at 651; thus, the dissent reasoned, "[i]f the children's constitutional rights to representation and to a fair hearing are to be guaranteed in substance as well as in form and if the commands of the Fourteenth Amendment are to be satisfied, then waiver of those constitutional rights cannot be inferred from mere silence or inaction . . . . Pennsylvania must assign each institutionalized child a representative obliged to contact the child and ensure that the child's constitutional rights are fully protected." Id. at 651–2.

56. 452 U.S. at 31.

57. 397 U.S. 254 (1970).

58. 418 U.S. 539, 570 (1974).

59. Id. at 570. See also Bounds v. Smith, 430 U.S. 817 (1977) (right of access to courts requires prison authorities to assist inmates in filing of meaningful legal papers by providing prisoners with adequate law libraries or adequate assistance from law-trained persons).

60. Addington v. Texas, 441 U.S. 418, 427 (1979); Santosky v. Kramer, 455 U.S. 745, 764 (1982).

cases.[61] In passing upon the appropriate standard to be used in ordinary civil cases, the Supreme Court has followed the approach established in *Mathews v. Eldridge*,[62] balancing the public and private interests at stake along with the need to minimize erroneous decisions, with special attention devoted to proper placement of the risk of that error.

In *Addington v. Texas*,[63] for example, the Court was presented with a challenge to the use of a "clear, unequivocal, and convincing" standard in an involuntary commitment case—a civil case in form, but one in which physical liberty was at stake. The appellant, ordered committed to a state mental hospital after a jury found that he was mentally ill and required hospitalization for his own welfare or for the welfare of others, argued that a "beyond a reasonable doubt" standard should have been applied. In holding that only a "clear and convincing" [64] standard is required by due process, Chief Justice Burger, writing for a unanimous Court of those justices participating,[65] held that, although the individual obviously has a strong interest in avoiding commitment—a "significant deprivation of liberty" [66] that can "engender adverse social consequences" [67]—the state's countervailing interest in "providing care to its citizens who are unable because of emotional disorders to care for themselves," [68] and in "protect[ing] the community from the dangerous tendencies of some who are mentally ill," [69] coupled with the ability to reverse a commitment decision later found to be erroneous,[70] argued for a measure of proof between the "preponderance" and "beyond a reasonable doubt" standards.[71] Distinguishing

61. As to criminal cases, the basic requirement is that of proof beyond a reasonable doubt as to every element of the criminal offense, even in a juvenile case, so long as a deprivation of liberty may be decreed as punishment for the offense. In re Winship, 397 U.S. 358 (1970). This standard has been interpreted to prohibit states from shifting to defendants the burden of proof on any element of the crime. See, e.g., Mullaney v. Wilbur, 421 U.S. 684 (1975) (state rule in murder cases conclusively assuming malice aforethought once the prosecution proved a killing to be intentional and unlawful, shifting the burden to the defendant to show that he acted in the heat of passion on sudden provocation to reduce the charge from murder to manslaughter, held an unconstitutional violation of due process, the Court rejecting the state's argument that the principles of Winship were inapplicable since the level of intent was not part of the substantive law but rather an element relevant only in determining the appropriate sentence).

62. 424 U.S. 319 (1976). See Santosky, 455 U.S. at 754, where the majority noted that "the Court's . . . decisions concerning constitutional burdens of proof have not turned on any presumption favoring any particular standard. To the contrary, the Court has engaged in a straightforward

consideration of the factors identified in *Eldridge* to determine whether a particular standard of proof in a particular proceeding satisfies due process."

63. 441 U.S. 418 (1979).

64. The actual standard utilized by the trial court was "clear, unequivocal and convincing." The Court noted that the Constitution required a standard greater than a preponderance, adding that the "determination of the precise burden equal to or greater than the 'clear and convincing' standard which we hold is required . . . is a matter of state law." Id. at 433.

65. Justice Powell did not take part.

66. Id. at 425.

67. Id. at 426.

68. Id.

69. Id.

70. Id. at 428–29.

71. The Court's justification for its choice followed a fine line. On the one hand, the Court indicated that the preponderance standard was inappropriate because it "creates the risk of increasing the number of individuals erroneously committed." Id, at 426. On the other hand, a reasonable doubt standard over-compensated for this tendency; the Court noted that,

between the punitive exercise of state power in criminal proceedings and the non-punitive goals of the state in civil commitment matters,[72] the Court refused to rely upon the reasonable doubt measure of proof, finding that the "lack of certainty and the fallibility of psychiatric diagnosis"[73] does not lend itself to such a fact-specific standard, and thus "may impose a burden the state cannot meet and thereby erect an unreasonable barrier to needed medical treatment."[74] On the other hand, a preponderance standard would not do because it improperly forces the individual "to share equally with society the risk of error when the possible injury to the individual is significantly greater than the harm to the state."[75]

Again applying the *Mathews* test, the Court in *Santosky v. Kramer*[76] held that a "clear and convincing" standard is constitutionally required in determining whether a child is to be considered "permanently neglected" by his natural parents, thus justifying the state's

"even though an erroneous confinement should be avoided in the first instance, the layers of professional review and observation of the patient's condition, and the concern of family and friends will provide continuous opportunities for an erroneous commitment to be corrected," id. at 428–29, adding that, unlike the criminal context, "[i]t cannot be said . . . that it is much better for a mentally ill person to 'go free' than for a mentally normal person to be committed." Id. at 429.

72. Id. at 428.

73. Id. at 429.

74. Id. at 432. The Court also noted that the reasonable doubt standard is a "unique" one, "regarded as a critical part of the 'moral force of the criminal law' ", and should not be applied "too broadly or casually in noncriminal cases." Id. at 428 (citation omitted).

75. Id. at 427. Addington, however, does not stand for the proposition that a clear and convincing standard applies in all cases in which civil commitment may result. In Jones v. United States, 463 U.S. 354 (1983), the Court upheld a District of Columbia statutory scheme under which a defendant in a criminal case could be acquitted if he proved, by a preponderance of the evidence, that he was insane at the time of the crime. (Indeed, the Jones Court recalled that, under Leland v. Oregon, 343 U.S. 790, 799 (1952), a defendant may be required to prove his insanity by a higher standard than a preponderance. 463 U.S. at 368 n. 17.) Upon a finding of insanity, the defendant in Jones was committed to a state mental hospital, but failed to secure his release when he was unable to show, again by a preponderance, that he was no longer mentally ill or dangerous at a mandatory hearing held within fifty days of confinement. After a year of commitment, the maximum period of in-

carceration Jones could have served in prison for his offense, he demanded unconditional release or recommitment pursuant to civil commitment proceedings which required clear and convincing proof of mental illness or dangerousness. Justice Powell, writing for a majority that included Chief Justice Burger and Justices White, Rehnquist and O'Connor, rejected Jones' argument. The Court emphasized the fact that the Court in Addington was particularly concerned with the risk of error when it erected the clear and convincing standard and the further fact that, when "the *acquitee himself* advances insanity as a defense and proves that his criminal act was a product of his mental illness, there is good reason for diminished concern as to the risk of error." Id. at 367 (original emphasis) (footnotes omitted). The Court added that the defendant's own raising of the insanity defense "diminishes the significance of the deprivation" because "[a] criminal defendant who successfully raises the insanity defense necessarily is stigmatized by the verdict itself, and thus the commitment causes little additional harm." Id. at 367 n. 16. In dissent, Justice Brennan, joined by Justices Marshall and Blackmun, argued that the procedures at issue unconstitutionally excused the government from fulfilling its proper burden under Addington, id. at 382, asserting that the majority opinion "at most support[s] deferring *Addington*'s due process protections . . . for a limited period only, not indefinitely." Id. at 386. Justice Stevens dissented separately, asserting the last point.

76. 455 U.S. 745 (1981). Justice Blackmun wrote for the Court, joined by Justices Brennan, Marshall, Powell, and Stevens. Justice Rehnquist dissented, joined by Chief Justice Burger and Justices White and O'Connor.

termination of their parental rights. The Court found the private interest of the parents [77] in maintaining custody a "commanding" one, especially considering that, "[o]nce affirmed on appeal, a New York decision terminating parental rights is *final* and irrevocable." [78] Stressing the risk of error prong of the *Mathews* test, the Court held that "numerous factors combine to magnify the risk of erroneous factfinding." [79] Moreover, since "[t]he state's ability to assemble its case almost inevitably dwarfs the parent's ability to mount a defense," [80] a significant risk of error was created when "[c]oupled with a 'fair preponderance of the evidence' standard." [81] Recognizing the state's own interest in "preserving and promoting the welfare of the child," [82] and noting that stricter standards of proof do not impose fiscal burdens of the sort entailed when hearings or court-appointed counsel are mandated, the Court held that a stricter standard of proof would serve the basic interests of all involved. [83] The dissent replied that the standard of proof should not be evaluated in isolation, arguing that "[c]ourts must examine *all* procedural protections offered by the State, and must assess the *cumulative* effects of such safeguards," [84] lest state experimentation be threatened and a stultifying "federalization of family law" be inaugurated. [85] The dissent also attacked the majority's failure to weigh the independent interests of the child in the balance. [86] In the dissent's view, adding those interests into the balance would support a conclusion that the risk of error might be evenly distributed between the parties without offending due process. [87]

Turning from the calibrations involved in setting suitable standards of proof to a more elemental aspect of procedural due process, we observe, in closing this section, that the Supreme Court has closely

---

77. The Court defined the private interest involved as that of the parents only, explaining that, although "the child and his foster parents are also deeply interested in the outcome," id. at 759, the fact that the "factfinding hearing pits the State directly against the [natural] parents" makes the natural parents the "focus" of the proceeding. Id.

78. Id. at 759. In contrast, the state may try again if it fails in severing the parent's rights. Id. at 764. Partly because "a paternity suit terminates with the entry of a final judgment that bars repeated litigation" by either party, paternity proceedings lack the "asymmetry" that could make a preponderance standard violate due process. Rivera v. Minnich, 107 S.Ct. 3001, 3006 (1987) (due process satisfied by preponderance standard in paternity proceedings).

79. The Court noted the "imprecise standards that leave determinations unusually open to the subjective values of the judge," 455 U.S. at 762; the "unusual discretion [of the court] to underweigh probative facts that might favor the parent," id. (footnote omitted); the potential of a cultural bias against the generally poor and

uneducated parents, id. at 763; and the overwhelming power of the state. Id.

80. Id. at 763.

81. Id. at 764.

82. Id. at 766.

83. Id. at 767. Again, the Court emphasized that the state's interests are served only if the factfinding hearings are accurate, thus throwing the state's interests on the higher-standard side of the scale. See § 10–12, supra. Because the real issue is not the *total number* of errors but their *distribution* (as between erroneous deprivations and erroneous decisions not to deprive), all such arguments are of dubious validity.

84. Id. at 775.

85. Id. at 773.

86. Id. at 788 n. 13

87. Id. at 790–91. Equal distribution of this risk is least tolerable when pre-existing rights are being terminated, and most tolerable when only future responsibilities (especially economic burdens) are being allocated. See Rivera v. Minnich, 107 S.Ct. at 3004–3005, discussed in note 78, supra.

connected the fundamental procedural due process guarantee of an opportunity to be heard with the requirement that government officials provide an *explanation* (ordinarily in writing) for action which adversely affects particular individuals or groups.[88] Like government's duty to grant a hearing, its duty to provide an explanation has often been valued less for its own sake than as a device for the protection of substantive rights or entitlements: "The provision for a written record helps to insure that administrators, faced with possible scrutiny by [other] officials and the public, and perhaps even the courts, where fundamental constitutional rights may have been abridged, will act fairly." [89] However, the Court has not explained this insistence in constitutional terms, relying instead on the principles of administrative law. Similarly, decisions reviewing the adequacy of particular *forms* of explanation have been couched largely in the language of administrative law doctrine. Nevertheless, the Court has included the core content of the right to an explanation in its lists of the basic requirements of due process.[90]

Among the formal procedural safeguards ordinarily held to be required by due process, perhaps the two most striking—*the right to be heard* and *the right to hear why*—are ultimately more understandable as inherent in decent treatment than as optimally designed to minimize mistakes. When God asked Adam if he had eaten of the tree of life, the Midrash explains, the point of the exchange was less to minimize the risk of divine error than to afford Adam a moment to regain his composure. And the Code of Wild Bill Hickock—the code that forbids shooting someone without first looking him in the eye—was likewise concerned with something deeper than reducing mistakes. Those procedural formalities that are implicit in treating persons with respect as members of the community should thus be required by due process for reasons more basic than any utilitarian calculus of accuracy, although accuracy of course matters as well when the procedure is ancillary to a substantive interest of great importance to the individual.

§ 10–16. Current Doctrine: Issues of Neutrality

The Supreme Court has traditionally placed enormous weight on the *neutrality* of due process hearings. In this area, indeed, the Court's approach to due process has tended to stress its *intrinsic* aspects almost

---

88. See, e.g., Burlington Truck Lines, Inc. v. United States, 371 U.S. 156 (1962) ("The agency must make findings that support its decision, and those findings must be supported by substantial evidence"). The prison context, however, presents a special case in this regard. See, e.g., Ponte v. Real, 471 U.S. 491 (1985), where the Court held that, although the due process clause requires prison officials to state their reasons for refusing to call witnesses requested to be called by an inmate at a disciplinary hearing, these reasons need not be in writing nor be incorporated in the administrative record; due process is satisfied when a limited explanation is made at the hearing, made part of the administrative record or presented as testimony in court "if the deprivation of a 'liberty' interest is challenged because of that claimed defect in the hearing." Id. at 497.

89. Wolff v. McDonnell, 418 U.S. 539, 565 (1974).

90. See, e.g., Goldberg v. Kelly, 397 U.S. 254, 271 (1970) ("the decision maker should state the reasons for his determination and indicate the evidence he relied on, . . . though his statement need not amount to a full opinion or even formal findings of fact and conclusions of law").

as much as its *instrumental* aspects, focusing on the "moral authority" of the law as well as on the accuracy of its application. Thus "the right to an impartial decision-maker is required by due process" in every case.[1] And since "the appearance of evenhanded justice . . . is at the core of due process,"[2] the Court may disqualify even decision-makers who in fact "have no actual bias" if they might reasonably *appear* to be biased.[3]

The Court's examination of the demand for impartiality has been structured by a distinction between personal and institutional conflicts of interest. In the realm of personal conflicts, the Court has consistently held that procedural due process bars ostensibly impartial decision-makers from deciding cases whose outcome directly and substantially affects their personal financial interests[4] or the financial concerns of

§ 10–16

1. Arnett v. Kennedy, 416 U.S. 134, 197 (1974) (White, J., concurring in part and dissenting in part).

2. Mayberry v. Pennsylvania, 400 U.S. 455, 469 (1971) (Harlan, J., concurring). See also Offutt v. United States, 348 U.S. 11 (1954). Cf. Dr. Bonham's Case, 8 Co. 114a, 118a (1610) (a "person cannot be judge in his own cause . . . and one cannot be judge and attorney for any of the parties").

3. See, e.g., Morrissey v. Brewer, 408 U.S. 471, 485–86 (1972) (decisionmaker bias is grounds for reversal); Goldberg v. Kelly, 397 U.S. 254, 271 (1970) (same). But see Kirp, "Proceduralism and Bureaucracy: Due Process in the School Setting," 28 Stan.L.Rev. 841, 863 (1976) ("a challenge to a decision based on impressions of the decisionmaker's unreceptiveness is hard to foresee; all that Due Process formally demands is a particular structuring of the outward forms of decisionmaking. It readily permits the routinization of the new, enabling the administrator to proceed comfortably 'by the book' without actually altering the substance of his actions").

4. The leading case is Tumey v. Ohio, 273 U.S. 510 (1927). There, Chief Justice Taft held for a unanimous Court that the fourteenth amendment due process clause prohibited a town from granting its mayor, as reimbursement for services as judge in prohibition law cases, the court costs assessed against *convicted* defendants. The Supreme Court has extended the Tumey principle to cases unconnected with the criminal law. In Gibson v. Berryhill, 411 U.S. 564 (1973), the Court held that procedural due process was violated by a decision of the Alabama State Board of Optometry revoking the licenses of "all optometrists in the State who were employed by business corporations . . ." Justice White's majority opinion accepted the conclusions of the federal district court

that: (1) the optometrists whose licenses were revoked "accounted for nearly half of all the optometrists practicing in Alabama"; (2) "the Board of Optometry was composed solely of optometrists in private practice for their own account"; and (3) "success in the Board's efforts" could thus sufficiently "redound to the personal benefit of members of the Board". "[Those] with substantial pecuniary interest in legal proceedings should not adjudicate these disputes." Id. at 578–79.

In Aetna Life Insurance Co. v. Lavoie, 106 S.Ct. 1580 (1986), the Supreme Court applied the principle of Tumey to vacate a state supreme court's *per curiam* affirmance of a civil damages award against an insurance company where an apparently decisive vote in the state's highest court had been cast by a justice who had a legally similar suit of his own pending in a lower state court. Relying on the requirement of strict neutrality imposed upon judges by Tumey and In re Murchison, 349 U.S. 133 (1955), the Supreme Court, in an opinion by Chief Justice Burger joined by Justices Brennan, Powell, Rehnquist and O'Connor, relied on language from Tumey that "it certainly violates the Fourteenth Amendment . . . to subject [an individual's] liberty or property to the judgment of a court the judge of which has a direct, personal, substantial, pecuniary interest in reaching a conclusion against him in his case." 106 S.Ct. at 1585, citing Tumey, 273 U.S. at 523. Since the state court justice's vote as an appellate judge "had the clear and immediate effect of enhancing both the legal status and the settlement value of his own case," 106 S.Ct. at 1586, his "participation in this case violated appellant's due process rights." Id. at 1587. Even if the particular judge was not "influenced," it was fatal that his situation "would offer a temptation . . . to the average [judge] . . . to lead him not to hold the balance nice, clear and true." Id. at 1587, citing Ward v. Monroeville, 409 U.S. 57, 60

organizations for which they are officially responsible.[5] Nor may a judge or other ostensibly impartial decision-maker "give vent to personal spleen or respond to a personal grievance" in reaching a decision.[6]

Identification and separation of adversarial and adjudicative functions is more difficult in contexts where procedures are more administrative than formally adjudicative in character.[7] With respect to non-

(1972). The Court did not have to decide what it would have done had the offending judge's vote been demonstrably immaterial to the outcome of the case, inasmuch as here the "disqualified judge [had] cast[ ] the deciding vote," id. at 1588, in a 5–4 affirmance of the lower court where state law provided that the decision below would not have been affirmed had the court been equally divided, instead requiring the appointment of a special justice to participate in the decision of the case. The Supreme Court thus vacated and remanded for further proceedings. In so doing, however, the Court rejected a challenge that, since one of the cases being pressed by the disqualified state supreme court justice was a class action that included all state employees insured under a group insurance plan (apparently including the justices of the state supreme court), the entire court, or at least those six justices who had not withdrawn from the class, must be disqualified as well. The Supreme Court ruled that the interests of the other justices was not sufficiently "direct, personal, substantial [and] pecuniary" to warrant disqualification, id. at 1587–88, citing Ward, 409 U.S. at 60, and cautioning that "[c]harges of disqualification should not be made lightly." Id. at 1588.

In concurrence, Justice Brennan explained that it was the *participation* of the more directly interested justice in the decision of the case, and not the fact that he cast the deciding vote, that violated due process, since "[t]he participation of a judge who has a substantial interest in the outcome of a case of which he knows at the time he participates *necessarily* imports a bias into the deliberative process." Id. (emphasis in original). Justice Blackmun's concurrence, joined by Justice Marshall, echoed Justice Brennan's view that it was the judge's participation in the case that constituted the violation, and not the fortuity of his casting the deciding vote. Justice Stevens did not participate in the consideration or decision of the case.

5. See Ward v. Monroeville, 409 U.S. 57 (1972), where the Court held procedural due process violated by an Ohio statute authorizing mayors to sit as judges in traffic offense cases. Justice Brennan's majority opinion observed that "[a] major part of village income is derived from the fines, forfeitures, costs, and fees imposed . . . in

[the] mayor's court," concluding that " 'possible temptation' may . . . exist when the mayor's executive responsibilities for village finances may make him partisan to maintain the high level of contribution from the mayor's court." Id. at 58, 60.

6. Offutt v. United States, 348 U.S. 11, 14 (1954). See also Mayberry v. Pennsylvania, 400 U.S. 455 (1971), where the Court held that, if contempt citations are handed down after a trial rather than during the proceedings, due process requires that a defendant in the subsequent contempt proceeding, who had previously "vilified" and "cruelly slandered" the trial judge, should be given a public contempt trial "before a judge other than the one reviled by the contemnor": "No one so cruelly slandered is likely to maintain that calm detachment necessary for fair adjudication." Id. at 465. Cf. Arnett v. Kennedy, 416 U.S. 134, 196 (1974) (White, J. concurring in part and dissenting in part) (arguing that otherwise valid procedures for a preliminary supervisor's review prior to dismissal of a Civil Service employee failed to provide the impartial hearing required by statute since the grounds reviewed included the employee's public attacks on the personal reputation of the supervisor; however, a majority of the Court found that this possible bias did not violate due process, given the availability of an adequately impartial subsequent hearing). In fact, the presumptive requirement of prior rather than subsequent hearings, see § 10–14, supra, has been based in part on the risk that, once an action has been taken by a government agent, the decisionmaker may be emotionally committed to the action by the time it is challenged.

7. The Court has also considered issues of neutrality in non-adversarial contexts. In Parham v. J.R., 442 U.S. 584 (1979), for example, the Court rejected the argument that an adversary hearing was required in deciding whether children may be committed by their parents to state mental hospitals, but nevertheless held that "the risk of error inherent in the parental decision to have a child institutionalized for mental health care is sufficiently great that some kind of inquiry should be made by a 'neutral factfinder' to determine whether the statutory requirements for admission are satisfied." Id. at 606. But, consistent with

criminal proceedings, the Supreme Court has required only, if a hearing is adversarial in nature, "that the hearing be conducted by some person other than one initially dealing with the case": "The officer directly involved in making recommendations cannot always have complete objectivity in evaluating them." [8]

Two recent cases illustrate the Court's tolerance of apparent institutional biases in non-adjudicatory settings. In *Marshall v. Jerrico, Inc.*,[9] the Court was faced with a due process challenge to the procedure under which fines are collected under the Fair Labor Standards Act, in which the Employment Standards Administration (ESA), the body responsible for assessing fines under the FLSA, receives those sums back as reimbursements for the costs of determining violations and assessing penalties. The sums are, in turn, distributed to the regional offices of the ESA. In unanimously rejecting the contention that this arrangement created "an impermissible risk and appearance of bias by encouraging [the assistant regional administrators of ESA who assess the fines] to make unduly numerous and large assessments of civil penalties," [10] the Supreme Court found that, since the assistant regional administrator involved could only *assess* fines against violators, and since his decision with respect to the amount assessed was appealable to an administrative law judge, his duties "resemble[d] those of a prosecutor more closely than those of a judge",[11] thus making inapplicable "the strict requirements of *Tumey* and *Ward*." [12] Moreover, the Court found that "[n]o governmental official stands to profit economically from vigorous enforcement . . . of the Act" [13] because the salary of the assistant regional administrator is fixed by law. Additionally, since the sums collected represent "substantially less than 1% of the budget of ESA," [14] and since the sums were returned to regional offices on the basis of expenses incurred and not on the basis of amounts collected,[15] there was no "realistic possibility that the [regional officer's] judgment will be distorted by the prospect of institutional gain as a result of zealous enforcement efforts."[16] Thus the "influence alleged to impose bias is exceptionally remote." [17]

the need to maintain the flexibility of due process, see § 10–15, supra, the Court found that informal hearings conducted by "a staff physician . . . [who] is free to evaluate independently the child's mental and emotional condition and need for treatment", id. at 607, were sufficient.

8. Morrissey v. Brewer, 408 U.S. 471, 485–86 (1972). See also Goldberg v. Kelly, 397 U.S. 254, 266, 271 (1970) (while welfare termination hearings "need not take the form of a judicial or quasi-judicial trial", the impartiality of the decisionmaker must be assured: "[Prior] involvement in some aspects of a case will not necessarily bar a welfare official from acting as a decision-maker. He should not, however, have participated in making the determination under review"); cf. Wolff v. McDonnell, 418 U.S. 539, 571 (1974) (holding that an "Adjustment Committee," composed of senior prison staff members, which conducts disci-

plinary hearings at the Nebraska Prison Complex, is "sufficiently impartial to satisfy the Due Process Clause" since the Committee "is not left at large with unlimited discretion", but must "operate within the principles stated in the controlling regulations").

9. 446 U.S. 238 (1980). Justice Marshall wrote for a unanimous Court.

10. Id. at 241.

11. Id. at 243.

12. Id. But see note 17, infra.

13. Id. at 250.

14. Id. at 245.

15. Id. at 246.

16. Id. at 250.

17. Id. Principles of neutrality are not wholly inapplicable to prosecutorial matters, however. Thus, in Young v. United

In *Schweiker v. McClure*,[18] the Court rejected a similar due process challenge to the system of providing federal reimbursements to insurance carriers under a provision of Medicare under which the Secretary of Health and Human Services, the official responsible for administering the payments of claims under the program, pays insurance carriers themselves to conduct review of claims as agents of the Secretary.[19] In disputed claims over $100, oral hearings are authorized when claims are rejected by the carrier and a written appeal fails; these hearings are conducted by hearing officers appointed by and serving at the pleasure of the insurance carriers themselves, with no right of appeal reserved for dissatisfied claimants. The district court found this practice unconstitutional for two reasons. First, the hearing officers had a pecuniary interest in pleasing their employer insurance carriers since "their incomes as hearing officers are entirely dependent upon the carrier's decisions regarding whether, and how often, to call upon their services."[20] The fact that those carriers themselves had twice denied the claims at issue in the hearings created "links between the carriers and their hearing officers sufficient to create a constitutionally intolerable risk of hearing officer bias against the claimants."[21] Second, providing a hearing before an administrative law judge either before or after a hearing officer's decision was warranted by the balancing test set out in *Mathews*.[22] Disagreeing, the Supreme Court began "from the presumption that the hearing officers who decide [these] claims are unbiased."[23] The Court found no reason for a blanket disqualification,[24] given "the absence of proof of financial interest on the part of the carriers . . . [upon which to ground] a derivative bias among their

States ex rel. Vuitton et Fils S.A., 107 S.Ct. 2124 (1987), in an exercise of its supervisory power, the Supreme Court held that "counsel for a party that is the beneficiary of a court order may not be appointed to undertake contempt prosecutions for alleged violations of that order." (opinion of Brennan, J., for a 5–4 Court). The case grew out of a trademark suit filed by Vuitton in which defendants agreed to pay damages and accepted a court order barring them from selling any product bearing the Vuitton trademark. One of the defendants was sentenced to 5 years in prison for violating the court order; the other defendants received shorter prison terms. A federal district court had appointed two of Vuitton's private attorneys to act as special prosecutors representing the Federal Government in the contempt proceedings. Only Justice White, dissenting from the Court's reversal of the convictions, saw no impermissible conflict of interest in use of the interested private attorneys as prosecutors; he was joined in dissent by three Justices who agreed with the majority that use of such prosecutors was impermissible but concluded that defendants had not been prejudiced.

18. 456 U.S. 188 (1982). Justice Powell wrote for a unanimous Court.

19. The relevant Medicare provision "covers a portion (typically 80%) of the cost of certain physician services, outpatient physical therapy, X-rays, laboratory tests and other medical and health care." Id. at 190.

20. Id. at 192, quoting 503 F.Supp. 409, 415 (1980).

21. Id. Although the hearing officer considering a particular claim cannot have personally participated in the case prior to the hearing, the district court nonetheless noted the fact that five out of the seven past and present hearing officers for the carrier involved in the case "are former *or current* . . . employees" of the carrier. 456 U.S. at 193. This, along with the pecuniary interests of the hearing officers in protecting their employment with the carrier and the fact that the carrier had twice denied the claims of all those petitioning for a hearing, led the lower court to the conclusion that hearing officers were unconstitutionally biased. Id. at 192–93.

22. Mathews v. Eldridge, 424 U.S. 319 (1976).

23. 456 U.S. at 195.

24. The Court noted that "[a]ppellees neither sought to disqualify their [individual] hearing officers nor presently make

hearing officers," [25] since it was the federal government, and not the carriers, that paid all claims. In so holding, the Court rejected the assertion that the actions of the Secretary of Health and Human Services—in "help[ing] carriers identify medical providers who allegedly bill more services than are medically necessary and . . . warn[ing] carriers to control overutilization of medical services" [26]—demonstrated that the Secretary himself was "biased in favor of inadequate . . . awards" [27] because "[i]t does not establish that the Secretary has sought to discourage payment of . . . claims that *do* meet [the] requirements." [28] Moreover, in making this observation, the Court implicitly rejected any argument that the Secretary's warning to carriers created an undue incentive for carriers to minimize claim awards and thus created a biasing influence on hearing officers. And the Court rejected the district court's conclusion that the *Mathews* test required additional safeguards to reduce the risk of erroneous deprivation, finding unjustified the lower court's ruling that hearing officers were untrained and unqualified to conduct the hearings, thus warranting additional measures.[29]

It is interesting to note that in *Schweiker* the Court, focusing narrowly on the factual evidence adduced to rebut the presumption that hearing officers were in fact unbiased, also rejected the argument that hearing officers, "for reasons of psychology, institutional loyalty, or carrier coercion," [30] would *appear* "reluctant to differ with carrier determinations." [31] Arguments of this sort merit closer attention if the subtler effects of perceived institutional bias are to receive due weight.

§ 10–17. Current Doctrine: Issues of Waiver

Although the Court has recognized that due process protections may be waived, it has sought to minimize the possibility of any waiver that is not knowing and voluntary by declaring that courts and other decisionmakers must "indulge every reasonable presumption against waiver." [1] The Court has presumed that the standard for waiver in noncriminal proceedings "is the same standard applicable to waivers of constitutional rights in a criminal proceeding" [2]—namely, that it "not only must be voluntary, but must be knowing, intelligent [and] done with sufficient awareness of the relevant circumstances and likely consequences." [3]

claims of *actual* bias." Id. at 195 n. 8 (emphasis in original).

25. Id. at 197.

26. Id. at 196 n. 9.

27. Id.

28. Id. (emphasis in original).

29. Id. at 198–99.

30. Id. at 196 n. 10.

31. Id.

§ 10–17

1. Aetna Insurance Co. v. Kennedy, 301 U.S. 389, 393 (1937).

2. D. H. Overmyer Co., Inc. v. Frick Co., 405 U.S. 174, 185 (1972).

3. Brady v. United States, 397 U.S. 742, 748 (1970). The Supreme Court has declared that, as a *threshold* matter, before the validity of a waiver can be evaluated, *the existence of the waiver must be clearly demonstrated*: "We need not concern ourselves with the involuntariness or unintelligence of a waiver when the contractual language relied upon does not, on its face, even amount to a waiver." Fuentes v. Shevin, 407 U.S. 67, 95 (1972) (finding that the right to notice and a hearing in advance of repossession is not waived by sign-

The Court, however, has found that waiver of rights can be constructive as well as actual. In *Insurance Corporation of Ireland v. Compagnie des Bauxites de Guinee* [4], for example, the Court held that failure to comply with discovery being conducted to establish jurisdictional facts after several of the defendants had raised the defense of lack of personal jurisdiction permitted the district court to assert personal jurisdiction over the uncooperative parties as a sanction pursuant to Federal Rule of Civil Procedure 37(b)(2)(A). Reasoning that "the requirement of personal jurisdiction represents first of all an individual right" and can thus "be waived," [5] the Court noted that "for various reasons a defendant may be estopped from raising the issue . . . [if his] actions . . . amount to a legal submission to the jurisdiction of the court, whether voluntary or not." [6] The Court held that the petitioner's refusal to produce documents in discovery thus constituted a "waiver" [7] of any challenge grounded on a lack of personal jurisdiction,[8] adding that " 'the preservation of due process was secured by the presumption that the refusal to produce evidence material to the administration of due process was but an admission of the want of merit in the asserted defense.' " [9]

ing contracts which "simply provided that upon a default the seller 'may take back,' 'may retake' or 'may repossess' merchandise": the contracts failed to indicate "how or through what process . . . the seller could take back the goods").

Contrast D. H. Overmyer Co., Inc. v. Frick Co., 405 U.S. 174, 187 (1972), where the Supreme Court held that Ohio's statutory authorization of cognovit notes was constitutional, both on its face and as applied. In this case, the cognovit note was included in a contract supported by "adequate consideration and [was] the product of negotiations carried on by corporate parties with the advice of competent counsel." Id. at 183. Justice Blackmun's majority opinion concluded that, even if the waiver of procedural rights were judged by the stringent standard of the criminal law, "Overmyer, in its execution and delivery to Frick of the . . . note containing the cognovit provision, voluntarily, intelligently, and knowingly waived the rights it otherwise possessed to prejudgment notice and hearing . . . with full awareness of the legal consequences." Id. at 187.

However, the Overmyer Court stated in dictum that, while "a cognovit provision may well serve a proper and useful purpose in the commercial world", there could nonetheless exist situations in which this form of waiver would not be recognized: "where the contract is one of adhesion, where there is great disparity in bargaining power, and where the debtor receives nothing for the cognovit provision, other legal consequences may ensue." Id. at 188. The Court also observed that, in this case, "execution of the cognovit note" did not render defenseless the party waiving procedural rights: "In Ohio the judgment court may vacate its judgment upon a showing of a valid defense . . ." Id.

4. 456 U.S. 694 (1982).

5. Id. at 703.

6. Id. at 704–05. Cf. Illinois v. Allen, 397 U.S. 337 (1970) (holding that an accused may, by obstreperous conduct, waive his right to be personally present at his criminal trial).

7. The Court compared this refusal to a failure to file a timely objection to personal jurisdiction, long deemed a waiver of the objection.

8. In concurring in the judgment, Justice Powell argued that "[b]efore today our decisions had established that 'minimum contacts' represented a constitutional prerequisite to the exercise of *in personam* jurisdiction over an unconsenting defendant . . . . [i]n the absence of a showing of minimum contacts, a finding of personal jurisdiction . . . even as a sanction, therefore would appear to transgress previously established constitutional limitations." Id. at 712–13. The Court, however, dismissed his objections, asserting that "our holding today does not alter the requirement that there be 'minimum contacts' . . . . Rather, our holding deals with how the facts needed to show those 'minimum contacts' can be established when a defendant fails to comply with court-ordered discovery." Id. at 703 n. 10.

9. Id. at 705, quoting Hammond Packing Co. v. Arkansas, 212 U.S. 322, 350–51 (1909).

In other contexts, however, it has been unclear whether a particular party intended a waiver or was aware that certain actions would be interpreted as one. Yet the Court seems simply to have examined the underlying interests at hand to determine whether the actions of the involved party should be treated as a waiver. For instance, in *United States v. Gagnon*,[10] the Court found waiver where a district judge had stated in open court that he wished to speak to one of the jurors in chambers to ascertain whether his objectivity had been compromised because he had noticed one of the defendants sketching portraits of the jurors during the trial. At the time, none of the four defendants either objected to the proposal or requested to be present at the discussion, although the lawyer for one of the defendants was present at the meeting. On appeal, the defendants contended that the *in camera* discussion violated their constitutional and statutory rights. The Supreme Court, in a *per curiam* decision representing the views of six members of the Court, rejected that argument, emphasizing that "the presence of the four respondents and their four trial counsel at the *in camera* discussion was not required to ensure fundamental fairness or a "reasonably substantial . . . opportunity to defend against the charge," [11] and that "[t]he Fifth Amendment does not require that all the parties be present when the judge inquires into such a minor occurrence." [12] On the issue of waiver, the Court held that "[t]he district court need not get an express 'on the record' waiver from the defendant for every trial conference which a defendant may have a right to attend," [13] adding that, if the defendant wished to exercise his right to attend the conference, he must affirmatively assert it.[14]

In *Lassiter v. Department of Social Services*,[15] the Court again found a form of waiver where a party failed to act affirmatively. In *Lassiter*, the Court, having held that there was no due process right to appointed counsel in every parental termination hearing,[16] went on to consider whether due process demanded appointment of counsel in the case at hand. In doing so, the Court examined the conduct of the parent whose rights were threatened in the proceeding and noted that "a court deciding whether due process requires the appointment of counsel need not ignore a parent's plain demonstration that she is not interested in attending a hearing . . . [or] even . . . speak[ing] . . . to her retained lawyer after being notified of the termination hearing." [17] As evidence of this sort of waiver, the Court observed that Ms. Lassiter had failed to appear at an earlier custody hearing and had not discussed the termination proceeding with the attorney representing her in a separate criminal proceeding, and noted that her "failure to make an effort to contest the proceedings was without cause;" [18] the Court accordingly

10. 470 U.S. 522 (1985).

11. Id. at 527.

12. Id. at 528.

13. Id.

14. Id.

15. 452 U.S. 18 (1981). Justice Stewart wrote the opinion of the Court, joined by Chief Justice Burger and Justices White, Powell and Rehnquist joined. Chief Justice Burger also filed a concurring opinion. Justice Blackmun dissented, joined by Justices Brennan and Marshall. Justice Stevens dissented separately.

16. Id. at 23–27. See § 10–15, supra.

17. Id. at 33.

18. Id.

held that it was not error for the state court not to appoint counsel.[19] Yet Ms. Lassiter's behavior might not have indicated lack of interest; hearing in the silence of an illiterate and inarticulate mother the voice of informed consent hardly comports with due process generously conceived.

Such a due process conception seems to have motivated the dissent in *Secretary of Public Welfare v. Institutionalized Juveniles*.[20] Stressing Pennsylvania's failure to provide institutionalized juveniles over the age of 13 with "a representative obliged to initiate contact with the child and ensure that the child's constitutional rights are fully protected," [21] the dissent argued that the state was creating a situation where "it is inevitable that the children's due process rights will be lost through inadvertence, inaction or incapacity." [22] Since "[m]any of the institutionalized children are unable to read, write, comprehend the formal explanation of their rights, or use the telephone . . . [f]ew will be able to trigger the procedural safeguards and hearing rights . . . provide[d]." [23]

Certainly the assertion of *other* rights that an individual has under either the Constitution or a statute should not result in the unexpected waiver of due process rights. In *United States v. $8,850 in United States Currency*,[24] the government sought to justify an 18-month delay in instituting civil forfeiture proceedings with respect to money seized from a claimant at customs by arguing that, since the claimant had filed a petition for remission of the seized money, the government had a right to wait until an administrative decision had been made. The Court properly rejected the government's contention that "a pending administrative petition should completely toll the requirement of filing a judicial proceeding," [25] holding that "[a] claimant need not waive his right to a prompt judicial hearing simply because he seeks the additional remedy of an administrative petition for mitigation." [26] Nevertheless, the Court did allow the pendency of the petition to be weighed along with other factors proffered by the government, ultimately holding that the delay did not violate the claimant's right to due process.

Perhaps more disturbingly, in *Jones v. United States* [27] the Court held that a criminal defendant who pleaded not guilty to a criminal charge by reason of insanity under a statute authorizing acquittal if insanity is established by a preponderance of the evidence essentially waived his rights under *Addington v. Texas* [28] to proof by clear and convincing evidence of mental illness and dangerousness before being

---

19. Id.

20. 442 U.S. 640 (1979). Chief Justice Burger wrote the opinion of the Court, in which Justices White, Blackmun, Powell and Rehnquist joined. Justice Stewart concurred in the judgment. Justice Brennan concurred in part and dissented in part in an opinion joined by Justices Marshall and Stevens.

21. Id. at 652 (Brennan, J.).

22. Id.

23. Id. at 651.

24. 461 U.S. 555 (1983).

25. Id. at 566.

26. Id.

27. 463 U.S. 354 (1983). Justice Powell wrote an opinion in which Chief Justice Burger and Justices White, Rehnquist and O'Connor joined. Justices Marshall and Blackmun joined Justice Brennan's dissent. Justice Stevens dissented separately.

28. 441 U.S. 418 (1979).

recommitted.[29] In rejecting the defendant's argument, the Court held that there were "important differences between the class of civil-commitment candidates and the class of insanity acquitees that justify differing standards of proof"; [30] since "the *acquitee himself* advances insanity as a defense and proves that his criminal act was a product of his mental illness, there is good reason for diminished concern as to the risk of error," [31] justifying the lower evidentiary standard.

The Court's decisions in this area do not provide a structured approach to the issue of waiver. In failing to do so, and in hearing waivers of rights even in the silence of rights holders, the Court has allowed rights as fundamental as preserving parental relationships to be lost by inadvertence. Due process ought to mean more than this.

§ 10–18. Meaningful Access to Judicial Protection as a Separate Strand of Due Process Doctrine

In § 10–14, we saw that the Supreme Court has moved toward a view, exemplified by *Ingraham v. Wright*,[1] *Parratt v. Taylor*,[2] and *Hudson v. Palmer*,[3] that prior administrative hearings are not ordinarily required by due process where the conduct of the state agent, if insufficiently justified, would constitute a crime or a common-law tort under the state's own laws, so that the injured individual could presumably be awarded relief in a subsequent judicial proceeding. The more the Court relies on the availability of state judicial relief as a basis for concluding that due process has been accorded, however, the stronger will be the argument that access to such relief is independently presupposed by the due process clause.

In specialized settings, such as those of criminal proceedings, the Supreme Court has repeatedly affirmed a right of access to courts. In *Bounds v. Smith*, for example, the Court held that "the fundamental constitutional right of access to the courts requires prison authorities to assist inmates in the preparation and filing of meaningful legal papers by providing prisoners with adequate law libraries or adequate assistance from persons trained in the law." [4] But how far beyond the setting of crime and punishment the Constitution requires "States to shoulder affirmative obligations to assure . . . meaningful access to the courts" [5] has been a much debated question, and even in the criminal context the precise extent of such affirmative obligations has been less than clear.[6]

In Chapter 16, we explore the extent to which the Supreme Court's decisions in *Boddie v. Connecticut* [7] and *NAACP v. Button* [8] reflect a general right of unimpeded access to civil courts, including a right to a waiver of court costs for plaintiffs otherwise too poor to seek judicial

29. See the discussion in § 10–15, supra.

30. 441 U.S. at 367.

31. Id.

§ 10–18

1. 430 U.S. 651 (1977).

2. 451 U.S. 527 (1981).

3. 468 U.S. 517 (1984):

4. 430 U.S. 817, 828 (1977).

5. Id. at 824.

6. See §§ 16–11, 16–38, 16–40, 16–51, 16–52, infra.

7. 401 U.S. 371 (1971).

8. 371 U.S. 415 (1963).

relief. We also consider in that chapter the degree to which decisions like *Sniadach v. Family Finance Corp.*[9] and *Fuentes v. Shevin*[10] make sense only as aspects of a right to a judicial hearing at a meaningful time. It is crucial to understand here that such a right is analytically distinct from the due process claim of an individual who says that a government official is about to discipline her, or terminate her welfare, or injure her good name, and who insists that the official must not be permitted to do so without at least hearing her side of the story. This latter claim, which we have seen grows out of a norm that only general rules may be framed without the direct participation of the individuals adversely affected,[11] cannot ordinarily be satisfied by subsequent judicial relief—notwithstanding the holdings in such cases as *Ingraham v. Wright.*

At the same time, the right to prior or substantially contemporaneous administrative hearings cannot be made secure without an ancillary right to subsequent judicial protection; without it, government is free to ignore its hearing duties with impunity, at least when it deals with individuals too poor or powerless to defend their rights without affirmative governmental assistance, whether in the form of a waiver of court costs or through some costlier form of aid. Thus the promise of *Goldberg v. Kelly*[12] that welfare would not be terminated without a prior administrative hearing meant considerably less than met the eye after the Court held, in *Ortwein v. Schwab,*[13] that an individual challenging welfare termination in violation of *Goldberg v. Kelly* could be excluded from court for failure to pay a filing fee—a failure not entirely surprising after welfare payments have been terminated.

Unless the Court is willing to say that the due process clause means more than this, our heritage of procedural safeguards will be "only a promise to the ear to be broken to the hope, a teasing illusion like a munificent bequest in a pauper's will."[14]

In fact, the Court has on occasion held unconstitutional otherwise acceptable state requirements for access to court where such limitations have been perceived to render the promise of meaningful access to court nothing more than a "teasing illusion." "[A]t least where interests of basic importance are involved, 'absent a countervailing state interest of overriding significance, persons forced to settle their claims of right and duty through the judicial process must be given a meaningful opportunity to be heard.'"[15] Thus, "having made access to the courts an entitlement or a necessity, the State may not deprive someone of that access unless the balance of state and private interests favors the government scheme."[16]

9. 395 U.S. 337 (1969).

10. 407 U.S. 67 (1972).

11. See §§ 10–1, 10–4, 10–5, 10–6, supra.

12. 397 U.S. 254 (1970).

13. 410 U.S. 656 (1973) (per curiam).

14. Edwards v. California, 314 U.S. 160, 186 (1941) (Jackson, J., concurring).

15. Logan v. Zimmerman Brush Company, 455 U.S. 422, 430 n. 5 (1982), quoting Boddie v. Connecticut, 401 U.S. 371, 377 (1971).

16. Logan, 455 U.S. at 430 n. 5. Note, however, that the right to judicial access has not been held to encompass any right to appellate review. See McKane v. Durston, 153 U.S. 684, 687 (1894); Pittsburgh, Cincinnati, Chicago & St. Louis Railway

The right of access to court cannot, of course, be equated with a right to be free of all substantive legal obstacles to particular forms of recovery: substantive defenses and immunities to a claim may be recognized by the state without a constitutional violation.[17] For example, in *Martinez v. California*,[18] a unanimous Court upheld against a due process claim a California statute granting immunity from suit to state parole officials for their actions in releasing an inmate who was sentenced to a state mental hospital after his conviction of attempted rape. Five months after the inmate was released on parole, he tortured and murdered a fifteen year old girl. Her parents' tort action against the state officials was defeated by the California immunity statute. Rejecting the appellants' claim that the girl was deprived of her life without due process of law, the Court noted that "[t]he statute neither authorized nor immunized the deliberate killing of any human being."[19] The Court then found that, although the tort action might be deemed a form of property of which the appellants were deprived by the immunity statute, there was no deprivation without due process of law.[20] "[T]he State's interest in fashioning its own rules of tort law is paramount to any discernible federal interest, except perhaps an interest in protecting the individual citizen from state action that is wholly arbitrary or irrational."[21] Given the rational relation between the state purpose and the statute's operation in limiting governmental tort liability, there was no deprivation of the appellant's property interest in the tort claim without due process of law.[22]

Co. v. Backus, 154 U.S. 421, 427 (1894); Reetz v. Michigan, 188 U.S. 505, 508 (1903); Rogers v. Peck, 199 U.S. 425, 435 (1905); Standard Oil Company of Indiana v. Missouri, 224 U.S. 270, 287 (1912); Ohio ex rel. Bryant v. Akron Metropolitan Park District, 281 U.S. 74, 80 (1930); District of Columbia v. Clawans, 300 U.S. 617, 627 (1937); Griffin v. Illinois, 351 U.S. 12, 18 (1956); Lindsey v. Normet, 405 U.S. 56, 77 (1972); Abney v. United States, 431 U.S. 651, 656 (1977) (the right of appeal in criminal cases is "purely a creature of statute"); Jones v. Barnes, 463 U.S. 745, 751 (1983). But cf. id. at 756–757 n. 1 (Brennan, J., dissenting): "The Court surprisingly announces that '[t]here is, of course, no constitutional right to an appeal.' Ante, at 751. That statement, besides being unnecessary to its decision, is quite arguably wrong." Justice Brennan added that "[i]f the question were to come before us in a proper case, I have little doubt that the passage of nearly 30 years since Griffin and some 90 years since McKane v. Durston . . . would lead us to reassess [the bases of the Court's earlier decisions]. There are few, if any, situations in our system of justice in which a single judge is given unreviewable discretion over matters concerning a person's liberty or property. . . ."

Note also that the Court has held that "[w]hen an appeal is afforded . . . . it can-

not be granted to some litigants and capriciously or arbitrarily denied to others without violating the Equal Protection Clause." Lindsey v. Normet, 405 U.S. at 77; Griffin v. Illinois, 351 U.S. 12 (1956); Smith v. Bennett, 365 U.S. 708 (1961); Lane v. Brown, 372 U.S. 477 (1963); Long v. District Court of Iowa, 385 U.S. 192 (1966); Gardner v. California, 393 U.S. 367 (1969).

17. On constitutional limits pertaining to restrictions of access to federal courts in particular, see Ch. 3, supra.

18. 444 U.S. 277 (1980).

19. Id. at 281.

20. The Court also recognized the argument that "the immunity defense, like an element of the tort claim itself, is merely one aspect of the State's definition of that property interest." 444 U.S. at 282 n. 5. "When state law creates a cause of action, the State is free to define the defenses to that claim, including the defense of immunity. . . ." Id., citing Ferri v. Ackerman, 444 U.S. 193, 198 (1979). The Court did not, however, decide Martinez on this basis.

21. Martinez, 444 U.S. at 282.

22. See also Bi-Metallic Investment Co. v. State Board of Equalization of Colorado, 239 U.S. 441 (1915) (legislative determination provides all the process that is due), discussed in § 10–6, supra, note 39.

Martinez illustrates the general proposition that ordinarily the state does not deny due process when it restricts judicial access through reasonable procedural or evidentiary requirements, such as statutes of limitations,[23] and filing fees.[24] Where the state's requirements work to deny any "meaningful opportunity to be heard," [25] however, due process has been denied.

In *Little v. Streater*,[26] for example, the Court held that the state must pay for blood-grouping tests requested by an indigent defendant where, in a paternity action under state law, the burden rests on the defendant to prove his lack of paternity "by other evidence than his own" [27] once the mother of the child has established her prima facie case. Chief Justice Burger, writing for a unanimous Court, noted that "a cost requirement, valid on its face, may offend due process because it operates to foreclose a particular party's opportunity to be heard." [28] In this case, the unavailability of evidence from blood-grouping tests because of the defendant's inability to pay for such testing would deprive the defendant of any "meaningful opportunity to be heard" since the tests would provide virtually the only possible exculpatory evidence sufficient to rebut the plaintiff's prima facie case. Without the evidence that only the blood-grouping tests could provide, the defendant's access to court in his defense would be merely illusory, and would not comport with the requirements of due process.[29]

Unrealistically brief statutes of limitations which do not further any substantial state interest have similarly been held unconstitutional. In *Mills v. Hableutzel*,[30] a unanimous Court held that a Texas statute providing a one-year limitations period in actions to prove the identity of the natural father of an illegitimate child for the purpose of obtaining parental support, where there is no similar limitations period restricting the right of a legitimate child to receive support from the father, denies illegitimate children the equal protection of the laws. While noting that "[n]ormally . . . States are free to set periods of limitations without fear of violating some provision of the Constitu-

---

23. See, e.g., Chase Securities Corp. v. Donaldson, 325 U.S. 304 (1945); International Union of Electrical Workers v. Robbins & Myers, Inc., 429 U.S. 229, 243 (1976). Cf. Logan v. Zimmerman Brush Company, 455 U.S. 422 (1982), discussed in § 10–14, supra, in which the Court distinguished the state's termination of a claim for the claimant's failure to comply with a reasonable procedural requirement, such as a limitations period, from the state's random, arbitrary destruction of a cause of action with no fault on the part of the claimant, thus denying any opportunity for a meaningful hearing at a meaningful time, and depriving the claimant of procedural due process. See also James v. United States, 459 U.S. 1044, 1046 (1982) (Brennan, J., opinion respecting denial of writ of certiorari, joined by Blackmun, J.).

24. See United States v. Kras, 409 U.S. 434 (1973); Ortwein v. Schwab, 410 U.S. 656 (1973). Cf. Boddie v. Connecticut, 401

U.S. 371 (1971), discussed in §§ 16–44, 16–51, infra.

25. Boddie, 401 U.S. at 377.

26. 452 U.S. 1 (1981).

27. Id. at 11, quoting the Connecticut Supreme Court in Mosher v. Bennett, 108 Conn. 671, 674, 144 A. 297, 298 (1929).

28. Id. at 16, quoting Boddie, 401 U.S. at 380.

29. See also Ake v. Oklahoma, 470 U.S. 68, 77 (1985) (holding that, where the defendant's sanity at the time of the criminal offense is likely to be an issue in the defendant's trial, the state must provide free access to a psychiatrist's assistance if the defendant is indigent: "We recognized long ago that mere access to the courthouse doors does not by itself assure a proper functioning of the adversary process. . . .").

30. 456 U.S. 91 (1982).

tion," [31] and recognizing the state's interest in "avoiding the litigation of stale or fraudulent claims," [32] the Court nonetheless found that the one-year limitations period was not substantially related to the further-ance of the state's interest, which in any event did not "justify a period of limitation which so restricts [the support rights of illegitimate children] as effectively to extinguish them." [33] "[I]t is clear that the support opportunity provided by the State to illegitimate children must be more than illusory. The period for asserting the right to support must be sufficiently long to permit those who normally have an interest in such children to bring an action on their behalf. . . ." [34]

A unanimous Court reasserted the reasoning of *Mills* in *Pickett v. Brown*,[35] invalidating on equal protection grounds [36] a Tennessee statute providing a two-year limitations period in actions for paternity and support.[37] The Court found that the two-year statute of limitations was not substantially related to the state's interest in avoiding the problems of proof that arise with the passage of time in a paternity action, and that "the 2-year limitations period does not provide illegitimate chil-dren with 'an adequate opportunity to obtain support.' " [38] Although on its face the statute did not deny meaningful access to the judicial system, it provided such a narrow avenue of entry that access was in effect being arbitrarily withheld.

A right to meaningful access to court may also be implicated by denials of adequate legal representation, and even by denials of the legal representation of one's choice. The Court has not, however, found any constitutional right to court-appointed counsel in civil cases.[39] In fact, there is a presumption that the right to appointed counsel "exist[s] only where the litigant may lose his physical liberty if he loses the litigation." [40] "It is against this presumption that all other elements in the due process decision must be measured." [41] Thus, in *Lassiter v. Department of Social Services*,[42] the Court held that the right to ap-pointed counsel when the state threatens termination of parental rights depends upon the circumstances of each particular case. The factors are to be weighed according to the *Mathews v. Eldridge* [43] formula, under which the process due depends upon a balancing of the private interests affected, the risk of error in the determination, and the governmental interests supporting the continued use of the challenged procedure. In *Lassiter*, the Court concluded that, on the facts before it, "the presence of counsel . . . could not have made a determinative

31. Id. at 101 n. 9.

32. Id. at 100.

33. Id. at 101.

34. Id. at 97. See also § 16–24, infra.

35. 462 U.S. 1 (1983).

36. The Court did not reach Pickett's due process challenge to the statute. Id. at 11 n. 11.

37. The two-year statute of limitations applied unless the father had acknowl-edged his paternity in writing or provided support to the child, or the child was (or was likely to become) a public charge. Where the statute of limitations did not apply, suit could be brought at any time prior to the child's eighteenth birthday.

38. 462 U.S. at 13, quoting Mills v. Hableutzel, 456 U.S. 91, 100 (1982).

39. See discussion in § 16–51, infra.

40. Lassiter v. Department of Social Services, 452 U.S. 18, 25 (1981).

41. Id. at 27.

42. 452 U.S. 18 (1981).

43. 424 U.S. 319 (1976).

difference," [44] and that "the absence of counsel's guidance . . . did not render the proceedings fundamentally unfair." [45]   The Court cautioned, however, that "[i]f, in a given case, the parents' interests were at their strongest, the State's interests were at their weakest, and the risks of error were at their peak, it could not be said that the *Eldridge* factors did not overcome the presumption against the right to appointed counsel, and that due process did not therefore require the appointment of counsel." [46]

In *Walters v. National Association of Radiation Survivors*,[47] veteran's organizations, veterans and a veteran's widow challenged the constitutionality of 38 U.S.C. § 3404(c), which limits to ten dollars the fee which may be paid to any attorney or agent representing a veteran before the Veteran's Administration (VA).   They argued that, under the due process clause, "the right to retain and compensate an attorney in VA cases is a necessary element of procedural fairness." [48]   Treating the appellees' argument that they had been "denied 'meaningful access to the courts' to present their claims" [49] as tantamount to an argument that the process prevented "a meaningful presentation," [50] the Court disagreed, stressing that the process was reasonably designed in light of Congress' desire that it operate on an informal, nonadversary basis, thereby diminishing any real *need* for legal counsel's assistance.   The fee limitation was fair because it did not prevent claimants from making a meaningful presentation *pro se*, with an attorney working on a *pro bono* basis, or with unpaid, nonlegal counsel.[51]

Viewing litigation as a form of speech or petition, the claimants in *Walters* also contended that the fee limitation violated their first amendment rights.   The district court,[52] agreeing that the "right to 'adequate legal representation' or 'meaningful access to courts' . . . was infringed by [the fee limitation]," [53] ruled for the claimants because "the First Amendment rights to petition, association and speech protect efforts by organizations and individuals to obtain effective legal representation of their constituents or themselves." [54]   But the Supreme Court took a different view, characterizing the appellees' argument as a "questionable proposition" "based on some notion that VA claimants, who are presently allowed to speak in court, and to have someone speak for them, also have a First Amendment right to pay their surrogate

44. 452 U.S. at 33.

45. Id.

46. Id. at 31. See also Santosky v. Kramer, 455 U.S. 745 (1982) (reaffirming the right of parents to a fundamentally fair procedure when the state moves to terminate their parental rights).

47. 473 U.S. 305 (1985). Justice Rehnquist wrote for the majority; Justice O'Connor filed a concurring opinion, in which Justice Blackmun joined; Justice Brennan filed a dissenting opinion which Justice Marshall joined; and Justice Stevens filed a dissenting opinion, in which Justice Brennan and Justice Marshall joined.

48. Id. at 331.

49. Id. at 335.

50. Id.

51. Id. at 319–35.

52. 589 F.Supp. 1302 (N.D.Cal.1984).

53. 473 U.S. 315–16.

54. 589 F.Supp. at 1324. In support of this proposition the district court cited United Mine Workers of America v. Illinois State Bar Assn., 389 U.S. 217 (1967), and Brotherhood of Railroad Trainmen v. Virginia ex. rel. Virginia State Bar, 377 U.S. 1 (1964), discussed in § 16–45, infra.

speaker." [55]   In the Court's view, "such a First Amendment interest would attach only in the absence of a 'meaningful alternative,' " [56] and since the VA claims process provides a meaningful opportunity for claimants to present their claims, and "significant government interests [favor] the limitation on 'speech,' " [57] no constitutional violation was shown.

The cautious and circumscribed terms in which the first amendment argument was rejected by the majority [58]—and the fervor with which it was embraced by the dissent [59]—combine to suggest that, in a case where no informal alternative to the usual adversary process is provided by statute, restrictions operating to limit a litigant's choice of competent counsel to any significant degree, and thus constraining the litigant's ability to petition the courts for redress, might yet be subjected to close first amendment scrutiny. [60]

In *Leis v. Flynt*, [61] the Court did not address the question of whether the State of Ohio, in refusing to allow the *pro hac vice* appearance of the out-of-state attorneys for Larry Flynt and Hustler Magazine, violated any right of the defendants to meaningful access to court.   Justice Stevens, however, argued in dissent that the defendants' interest in representation by nonresident counsel may indeed be entitled to constitutional protection: "[I]n instances where the federal claim or defense is unpopular, advice and assistance by an out-of-state lawyer may be the only means available for vindication." [62]

What emerges from these disparate cases and lines of thought is, quite clearly, less than a solidly grounded or coherently elaborated right of judicial access.   But it would be surprising, and ultimately indefensible, if the separate strands of doctrine noted above—including procedural due process, equal protection, and the first amendment rights of speech and petition—were not in the end woven into a fundamental right of access to a neutral and fair tribunal in which to ventilate such claims of right as one may have under the governing body of substantive law.   That no individual constitutional clause may fully secure that right of access should not be dispositive under a Constitution whose ninth amendment commands that the enumeration of certain rights "shall not be construed to deny or disparage others retained by the people."   Inasmuch as the Court has relied upon the ninth amendment to reinforce a first amendment right of access for the press and the public to observe judicial proceedings, [63] a similar argument, grounded in constitutional history and structure, should point to

55. 473 U.S. at 335.

56. Id.

57. Id.

58. Id. at 334–35.

59. Id. at 367–72.

60. But see Roa v. Lodi Medical Group, Inc., 106 S.Ct. 421 (1985) (dismissing appeal from state court decision upholding, over first amendment challenge, a state statute setting a sliding-scale ceiling on contingency fees).

61. 439 U.S. 438 (1979) (per curiam). Flynt and Hustler Magazine had been indicted for allegedly disseminating harmful materials to minors in violation of Ohio law.

62. 439 U.S. at 446 n. 2.

63. Richmond Newspapers, Inc. v. Virginia, 448 U.S. 555 (1980) (plurality opinion), discussed in § 12–20, infra.

a no less basic right to invoke those proceedings as a litigant. It would be the height of irony if the right of access to court applied solely to those who wish to watch, and not to those who need to take part.[64]

§ 10–19. The Future of Procedural Due Process

Recent cases have exhibited tendencies toward a narrowed understanding of the substantive scope of the "life, liberty, and property" entitled to due process protection, and toward a devalued assessment of the role of personal participation in the determination of what process is due. *Bishop v. Wood* [1] and *Jago v. Van Curen*,[2] for example, demonstrate that the Supreme Court is wary of basing "property" interests, and will refuse to base liberty interests, on "mutually explicit understandings" [3] between government and an individual when such understandings are not formalized in an unambiguous contract or statute. Moreover, the Court's dubious efforts completely to separate procedure from substance [4] have led to a formalized calculus of protected interests which tends to ignore expectations arising from an existing procedural framework.[5] Similarly, in several recent cases [6] the Court has accepted the view that post-deprivation tort remedies under state law may, under some circumstances, protect even "core" liberty and property interests well enough to meet due process requirements, even though there is no opportunity for the individual to interact with a government official in time to prevent (or even promptly redress) the deprivation of liberty or property in question. If this trend should continue in a time of ever-increasing individual dealings with government, the promise of a prominent role for due process doctrine in the definition of govern-

---

64. In some circumstances, a right of access to an article III court may be deemed implicit in the constitutional plan—a matter explored in some detail in § 3–5, supra. In United States v. Mendoza-Lopez, 107 S.Ct. 2148 (1987), for example, the Supreme Court ruled by a 5–4 vote that an alien re-entering the United States after being deported cannot be convicted if he is able to show that the original deportation order was invalid. The majority, speaking through Justice Marshall (joined by Justices Brennan, Blackmun, Powell, and Stevens), held that, even though there was no evidence that Congress intended to permit illegal aliens to contest the validity of their previous deportations in such prosecutions, an opportunity to do so is mandated by the "constitutional requirement of due process." Chief Justice Rehnquist, joined in dissent by Justices White and O'Connor, saw no need to reach the constitutional issue inasmuch as the deportation orders at stake had been valid. In a separate dissent, Justice Scalia wrote: "I think it clear that Congress may constitutionally make it a felony for deportees—irrespective of the legality of their deportations—to re-enter the United States illegally." The majority's rejection of Justice Scalia's position necessarily rests on the view that,

by making the validity of the underlying deportation order relevant, the Government triggers the deportee's right to judicial review. In the majority's words, "Where a determination made in an administrative proceeding is to play a critical role in the subsequent imposition of a criminal sanction, there must be some meaningful review of the administrative proceeding."

§ 10–19

1. 426 U.S. 341 (1976), discussed in § 10–10, supra.

2. 454 U.S. 14 (1981), discussed in § 10–10, supra.

3. Perry v. Sindermann, 408 U.S. 593, 601 (1972).

4. See, e.g., Cleveland Bd. of Educ. v. Loudermill, 470 U.S. 532 (1985), discussed in §§ 10–9, 10–10, and 10–12, supra.

5. See, e.g., Hewitt v. Helms, 459 U.S. 460 (1983), discussed in § 10–10, supra.

6. See Hudson v. Palmer, 468 U.S. 517 (1984), Parratt v. Taylor, 451 U.S. 527 (1981), and Ingraham v. Wright, 430 U.S. 651 (1977), discussed in § 10–14, supra; and Paul v. Davis, 424 U.S. 693 (1976), discussed in §§ 10–11 and 10–14, supra.

ment's relationships with individuals—a promise raised by the due process cases of the early 1970's—will be broken. Instead, we may confront a retreat to the situation where government defined both the substantive and the procedural aspects of its relations with individuals free of any significant responsibility to protect the reliance it induces or to treat individuals with regularity and respect.

If, on the other hand, due process doctrine is to continue to play a significant role in structuring government's relations with individuals, it will be necessary to confront more squarely the substantive values underlying due process decisions such as *Goldberg v. Kelly*,[7] *Fuentes v. Shevin*,[8] *Perry v. Sindermann*,[9] and *Vitek v. Jones*,[10] all of which rejected the notion that government should enjoy unqualified discretion in dealing with individuals so long as it does not invade some minimal concept of the personal liberty and property interests inherited from the common law. To the extent that the substantive values underlying decisions like *Goldberg, Fuentes, Perry* and *Vitek* involve the preservation of personal dignity and self-respect, specifying the safeguards of procedural due process will be a task increasingly indistinguishable from giving substantive content to the due process clauses; the right not to be singled out for hurtful treatment by the state without a chance to talk back, and to be told why, will increasingly have to be identified as a substantive aspect of personal liberty. Thus both governmental objectives and the means chosen to accomplish them will be impermissible unless they accord with rights of personal dignity and autonomy—and with values of public participation and self-government.[11] Moreover, the purpose and scope of due process hearings will have to be increasingly tailored, as in the irrebuttable presumption cases,[12] to the substantive values of individuality and interaction at stake in their dispositions.

In addition, to the extent that the substantive values underlying the due process decisions of the early 1970's include the minimization of subservience and helplessness, it will be necessary to repudiate the notion that government can escape procedural due process merely by writing its statutes or contracts so as to exclude recognition of any entitlements at all and can thereby make individuals totally dependent on its generosity. It must be recalled in this regard that the values of governmental regularity go well beyond those of protecting settled expectations.[13] And the Supreme Court has indicated a willingness to place some limits on the extent to which an individual can be made dependent on governmental determinations of need and on government's advantageous allocations of resources: where government arrangements leave no room for individual adjustment, and "where the

---

7. 397 U.S. 254 (1970), discussed in § 10–9, supra.

8. 407 U.S. 67 (1972), discussed in § 10–9, supra.

9. 408 U.S. 593 (1972), discussed in § 10–9, supra.

10. 445 U.S. 480 (1980), discussed in § 10–9, supra.

11. See Chapters 11 and 15, infra. See also Michelman, "The Supreme Court, 1985 Term—Foreword: Traces of Self-Government," 100 Harv.L.Rev. 4 (1986).

12. See § 16–32, infra.

13. See § 10–1, supra.

private interests affected are very important and the governmental interest can be promoted without much difficulty by a well-designed hearing procedure," [14] the Court has taken steps to merge procedural due process and substantive equal protection analysis. In *United States Dept. of Agriculture v. Murry*, for example, the Court invalidated a section of the Food Stamp Act of 1964 which "create[d] a conclusive presumption that [a] . . . household is not needy and has access to nutritional adequacy," whenever any member of that household under the age of 18 has been claimed as a "tax dependent" in another household not itself eligible for food stamps. [15] The Court reasoned that "the deduction taken for the benefit of the parent in the prior year is not a rational measure of the need of a different household with which the child of the tax-deducting parent lives and rests on an irrebuttable presumption often contrary to fact," and "therefore lacks critical ingredients of due process." [16] And in *United States Dept. of Agriculture v. Moreno*, the Court struck down another section of the Food Stamp Act of 1964 which "exclude[d] from participation in the food stamp program any household containing an individual who is unrelated to any other member of the household," [17] on the ground that such an exclusion "creates an irrational classification in violation of the equal protection component of the Due Process Clause of the Fifth Amendment," [18] since it is "clearly irrelevant to the stated purposes of the Act," "to alleviate hunger and malnutrition among the more needy segments of our society." [19]

Minimizing helplessness and dependence, furthermore, may require courts to go beyond remedies that individual poor people must invoke on their own. [20] Indeed, the adversary model, with its emphasis on individual initiative, may prove quite inappropriate in the context of protecting at least some rights connected with those governmental services which are provided on a mass scale. While the provision of hearings to individuals seeking to substantiate claims against the government, and the concomitant reliance on parties acting in their own self interest to present all the issues in the strongest possible way, undoubtedly has important advantages in ensuring accuracy of result, its efficacy is conditioned on the presumption that those in a dependent position with respect to government will have sufficient knowledge and resources to employ such procedures. Yet at least some thoughtful commentators have suggested that "individual claimants [often] either do not know of, or are generally fearful of exercising, the unfamiliar

14. United States Dept. of Agriculture v. Murry, 413 U.S. 508, 518 (1973) (Marshall, J., concurring), discussed in §§ 16-34 and 16-50, infra. See generally Tribe "Structural Due Process," 10 Harv.Civ. Rights Civ.Lib.L.Rev. 269, 286-88 (1975).

15. 413 U.S. at 511.

16. Id. at 514.

17. 413 U.S. 528, 529 (1973), discussed in §§ 16-34 and 16-50, infra.

18. Id. at 533.

19. Id. at 529. But see Lyng v. Castillo, 106 S.Ct. 2727 (1986) (Food Stamp Act's irrebuttable presumption that parents, children, and siblings prepare meals together—thus entitling them to fewer benefits—is rationally related to the goals of the food stamp program and hence constitutional), discussed in §§ 16-34 and 16-50, note 5, infra.

20. Cf. §§ 5-22, 8-6, 8-7, supra, and §§ 11-4, 15-9, infra.

right to a hearing." [21]   Indeed, the often complex web of hearings and judicial review may in fact create a "perseverance bounty," which rewards those willing and able to pursue claims while disadvantaging "the ignorant, the incompetent, and the demoralized," whose claims are at least as meritorious.[22]   Moreover, because the procedural norms prescribed by the Supreme Court's due process decisions may run counter to important bureaucratic routines and be viewed by agencies as a criticism and rebuke, such agencies may "circumvent the very values that procedural justice is intended to serve, either by ignoring the judicial decision or by giving it only grudging and mechanical compliance, or by resorting to a crabbed course of literal rule-mindedness divorced of the exercise of any discretion." [23]

In light of these problems, at least one commentator has argued that a system de-emphasizing, or perhaps eliminating, ordinary hearings and judicial review in favor of "bureaucratic rationality" would more effectively address the concerns inherent in an administrative state—at least for some programs.[24]   Bureaucratic rationality would utilize sophisticated techniques of organization and management [25] in order to "develop, at the least possible cost, a system for distinguishing between true and false claims" as defined by the "democratically (legislatively) approved task." [26]   The process would include several general aspects: (1) the agency's approach to deciding any individual claim would be active and investigatory—it would seek information rather than merely rely on its supply from interested parties; [27]   (2) since "there is a fundamental political presumption that the agency is responsible for the adjudicatory performance of its employees[, a] coordinating system of management [would be] instituted to ensure . . .

21. Kirp, "Proceduralism and Bureaucracy: Due Process in the School Setting," 28 Stan.L.Rev. 841, 861 (1976). See generally Rubenstein, "Procedural Due Process and the Limits of the Adversary System," 11 Harv.Civ.Rts.—Civ.Lib.L.Rev. 48, 66–70 (1976) (claiming that, in practice, the adversary system is unavailable to the vast majority of people in positions of dependency in relation to government, given ignorance of rights and lack of access to legal aid); Mashaw, "The Management Side of Due Process: Some Theoretical Litigation Notes on the Assurance of Accuracy, Fairness, and Timeliness in the Adjudication of Social Welfare Claims," 59 Cornell L.Rev. 772, 784 n. 33 (1974) (noting that only six percent of those denied welfare benefits actually seek a hearing).

22. J. Mashaw, Bureaucratic Justice 137–139 (1983). According to Mashaw, available data indicate that white, middle-aged males, who are generally financially better off, are more likely to appeal denial of their social security disability benefits. Since 50% of those appeals are granted, the unjust disparity, at least in the social security disability context, is significant.

23. Kirp, supra note 21, at 852.

24. J. Mashaw, Bureaucratic Justice (1983). While Professor Mashaw does argue that his model may apply in other contexts, he limits most of his discussion to the social security disability (SSD) program.

25. See generally id. at 145–168.

26. Id. at 25. Since few legislative mandates can precisely define the "truth" of all claims (and thus require agency flexibility), bureaucratic rationality would require decisionmakers to (1) understand the values or goals that are to be pursued; (2) determine the relevant facts; and (3) accurately predict the connection between a particular decision and the accomplishment of one or more of the goals. See id. at 49. While Mashaw recognizes that no bureaucratic system could fully attain these three objectives, he suggests that the weaknesses provide "entry points" for "alternative conceptions of justice" which may include "some mixture of justice models and decisional techniques," such as participation through "specialized representatives." Id. at 74–77, 200. See also note 44, infra.

27. Id. at 171.

that subordinate actions are . . . premised on the policies or goals of the program . . .;" [28] (3) hierarchical control would require a systemic perspective to maintain the equilibrium of forces within its "adjudicatory" system.[29] In a nutshell, "the bureaucratic model of administrative justice is an accuracy-oriented, investigatorily active, hierarchically organized, and complexly engineered system of adjudication." [30]

The model is not without its problems. As Professors Lance Liebman and Richard Stewart have persuasively argued, its usefulness probably does not extend to programs in which, unlike social security disability, the bureaucratic orientation may be incapable of "cautious benevolence" and the administration involves a regulatory scheme instead of a cash-transfer system.[31] Moreover, even within the SSD program, we may well question whether, in a nation properly suspicious of bureaucratic administration and of the very concept of scientific expertise as a source of legitimation, civil servants should be entrusted with the sole power to decide eligibility decisions—even under regimes supervised by judges with an eye to improving the technical efficiency of administration.[32] Indeed, despite its many difficulties,[33] the adversary system has deep roots in America's political and cultural heritage,[34] so that any departure from its premises is not without risks

28. Id.

29. Id.

30. Id. at 172. One possible concrete application of Mashaw's bureaucratic jurisprudence would have courts "impose on police departments various quality control and disciplinary measures calculated to maximize observance of constitutional . . . requirements" as an alternative to the exclusionary rule. See C. Edley, Judicial Governance 266 n. 548 (June 26, 1986 manuscript) (forthcoming). Cf. Amsterdam, "Perspectives on the Fourth Amendment," 58 Minn.L.Rev. 349, 409–39 (1974). Professor Amsterdam urges that "[u]nless a search or seizure is conducted pursuant to and in conformity with either legislation or police departmental rules and regulations, [courts should hold] that it is an unreasonable search and seizure prohibited by the fourth amendment." Id. at 416.

31. See Liebman & Stewart, Book Review, 96 Harv.L.Rev. 1952, 1965–67 (1983) (reviewing J. Mashaw, Bureaucratic Justice (1983)). See also the powerful critique developed by Professor Christopher Edley, Jr., in C. Edley, supra note 30, at 265–78. Professor Edley summarizes his most important criticism as follows:

　　[T]he perspective of ideal administration cannot provide a totalizing theory of administrative justice or law within bureaucracy, for reasons conceptually related to the limitations of the rule of law and interest group representation perspectives. Such monochromatic exercises develop our sensibilities in very important ways, just as studying the music

for solo violin is helpful preparation for full appreciation of a symphony. But in the very effort to focus on one element, the whole is distorted.

Id. at 267. Mashaw is unable to escape the interrelationships between the three paradigms inherent in the separation of powers ethos. See note 38, infra. Hence, policy choices and adjudicative fairness cannot be entirely extracted; rather, they are merely "displaced to a prior moment of centralized judgment," resulting in an "impoverished version of political and policy choice, because the interests and values figuring in the choice will be those of the technocracy." Id. at 274. See also id. at 78.

32. Liebman & Stewart, 96 Harv.L.Rev. at 1963.

33. A further problem which may militate against the efficacy of adversary hearings in the context of large-scale government programs is the possibility that the considerable expense involved in the provision of hearings "may in the end come out of the pockets of the deserving since resources available for any particular program of social welfare are not unlimited." Mathews v. Eldridge, 424 U.S. 319, 348 (1976).

34. See, e.g., Walker, LaTour & Moulden, "Procedural Justice as Fairness," 26 Stan.L.Rev. 1271 (1974) (study indicating people favor adversary hearing model). See also C. Edley, supra note 30, at 370 n. 733 (suggesting that agencies adopt a "rule of presumptive desirability of quasi-adversarial processes," with a concomitant "battle of experts." In addition to testing the

of its own. Yet as Justice Frankfurter noted, due process, "unlike some legal rules, is not a technical conception with a fixed content unrelated to time, places and circumstances. . . . [It] cannot be imprisoned within the treacherous limits of any formula." [35] On the contrary, "the very nature of due process negates any concept of inflexible procedures universally applicable to every imaginable situation." [36] The Court has, in fact, recently recognized this flexibility in refraining from requiring a trial-type adversary hearing prior to short suspensions from public schools. Instead, in *Goss v. Lopez*, the Court mandated no more than "an informal give and take" between student and school disciplinarian.[37]

If the Court is really as prepared as it appears to look beyond the traditional adversary model for procedures to restrain arbitrary government action and thus fulfill the ideal of governmental regularity, such a search would not be inconsistent with the underlying jurisprudence of due process. One alternative would break down the current formalized dichotomy between adjudicative and representative processes and recognize that both sets of processes are merely the ends of a single continuum of procedures by which government action might better be shaped in accord with basic principles of accountability and participation. Until now, the Court has taken an all-or-nothing approach when determining what form of participation an individual may claim in a given context: either the right to be heard as a party, or the right to be counted as a voter, but little in between.[38] Hence, it has refused to

quality of agency expertise, such a presumption would better discern the "real limits" of the expertise paradigm by identifying scientific areas of disagreement more appropriately decided on the basis of politics or fairness).

35. Joint Anti-Fascist Refugee Committee v. McGrath, 341 U.S. 123, 162 (1951) (Frankfurter, J., concurring).

36. Cafeteria & Restaurant Workers Union v. McElroy, 367 U.S. 886, 895 (1961). See generally Friendly, "Some Kind of Hearing," 123 U.Pa.L.Rev. 1267, 1269 (1975).

37. 419 U.S. 565, 584 (1975). See also Greenholtz v. Inmates of Nebraska Penal and Cor. Complex, 442 U.S. 1, 4, 12–16 (1979) (parole determination procedures satisfy due process where Board examines the inmate's written record, informally interviews him, and considers any letters or statements he wishes to present), discussed in §§ 10–12, 10–13, supra.

38. See C. Edley, note 30 supra. Professor Edley's analysis provides a possible explanation for the Court's rigid approach. In his view, a trichotomy of decisionmaking norms, attributable to a "separation of powers ethos" generated before the emergence of the administrative state, results in "rather arbitrary selection and emphasis of one or another [of the three competing] paradigm[s] in order to draw conclusions

about the scaling of judicial deference." Id. at 118. The three paradigmatic norms constituting the trichotomy are adjudicatory fairness (and its reasoned elaboration), science and technical expertise, and politics (with interest accommodation). The three, of course, correspond roughly to the three branches of our government: the judiciary, the executive, and the legislature, respectively. However, the problem with the trichotomy is not just its use in creating formal separations, but its more subtle use in determining the "applicable verbal formula for the balance of judicial deference and intervention." Id. at 22. Thus, the Court's dichotomy in this instance may merely be part of the greater trichotomy which inhibits it from adjusting judicial and administrative roles and integrating the three paradigms to serve better the needs of the administrative state. See id. at 390–95. As Professor Edley argues, the choice of which of the two categories to identify with the problem becomes dependent not upon any proof of which procedure would better advance instrumental (or, I would add, intrinsic) concerns, but a matter of custom, which "seems 'right' in a conclusory sort of way." Id. at 60. To take it a step further, I would argue that the trichotomy helps create the choice itself—between the right to be heard and the right to vote—based upon custom rather

vary the nature of the process due as the government's actions move along the spectrum toward individualization by focusing on increasingly smaller groups or on increasingly personal assessments. Instead, the Court has clung to its *Bi-Metallic*[39] rationale and denied due process protection to individuals affected by government "en masse," without questioning whether the need for some mix of the direct and representative participation models would better approximate the goals of due process given the size and nature of the affected group and the character of the government determination.

In *O'Bannon v. Town Court Nursing Center*[40], for example, a group of elderly patients from a nursing home sought an evidentiary hearing on the home's decertification and their consequent involuntary transfer. The majority opinion noted that decertification was "not the same . . . as a decision to transfer a particular patient" and that, since "the home itself ha[d] a strong financial incentive to contest" the decision, the individual patients had "no constitutional right to participate in the enforcement proceedings."[41] Thus, instead of searching for a form of process which could satisfy the patients' participational needs while limiting its adverse effects on the government program, the Court indicated that no process at all was due. Moreover, the Court failed to analyze whether the patients' interests might differ from the nursing home's in certain respects such that some form of participation should be allowed.

A more enlightened approach could untangle at least part of the bureaucratic knot. A two-axis continuum would provide the key. First, in order to emphasize the view that the need for adjudicative process becomes more important the closer the government's focus approaches the singling out of individuals,[42] the Court could adjust the mix of direct and representative participation to which the individual is entitled. Where the group is large and the individual unidentifiable, a nearly absolute reliance on pure voting representation would be warranted. Conversely, government targeting of a specific individual would demand direct participation via an individualized hearing. Between these two poles, however, courts could fashion mechanisms appropriate to the specific context which would provide more direct forms of representation.[43]

than any reasoned explanation of why such an all-or-nothing choice is necessary.

39. Bi-Metallic Invest. Co. v. State Board of Equalization, 239 U.S. 441 (1915).

40. 447 U.S. 773 (1980).

41. Id. at 786, 789 n. 22.

42. See § 10–7, supra.

43. See Thompson v. Washington, 497 F.2d 626 (D.C. Cir. 1973). Tenants in a low-rent housing project sought the right to participate in the consideration of rent increases under the National Housing Act and the due process clause. "Informed" by the due-process interests potentially at stake but avoiding decision upon constitutional grounds, the court interpreted the National Housing Act to establish a right to be heard. In distinguishing Bi-Metallic, the court stated: "[T]he determination which emerges from the governmental process under scrutiny here is not so individualized. We do not, however, regard this difference as determinative. We believe the correct approach is to ascertain whether tenants can make relevant contribution to the issues presented for decision, notwithstanding the fact that they apply to a potentially large class." Id. at 638 n. 42. Moreover, in analyzing the process due, the court observed that "because the number of tenants potentially involved is quite large, we must be careful to shape procedures to protect the tenants' interests that

The second axis would complement the first by directing attention to the continuum of representational interests in modern society. The individual is generally not alone in his battles against the state; often various ad hoc or otherwise organized groups are equally affected by the government's decisions. The Court could actively search for the proper group in its effort better to represent the individual at the appropriate level of participation.[44] And, each time, a court would question whether the representational group provided an adequate surrogate for the individual given the strength of the competing governmental and individual interests.[45] In fact, courts already make similar inquiries when testing the adequacy of representation in class action suits[46] and third-party intervention.[47] By adopting such an approach, the Court would not only give real meaning to these democratic processes, it could also advance associational rights.[48]

While these axes would establish a range of procedural mechanisms outside the current scope of due process protections, they would not have to be written in constitutional stone. Instead, the decisions might frame a constitutional common law,[49] leaving legislatures with the power to design other methods of protecting the individual's participatory interests. Thus, such a jurisprudence could effect a "remand to the legislature,"[50] prodding it to discover and develop new systems of "due process" more compatible with the needs of the administrative state.

avoid their becoming unduly burdensome." Id. at 639. While settling for hearings of the type prescribed by the Administrative Procedure Act, the court noted that additional safeguards might be required in other specific contexts. Id. at 641. But see Harlib v. Lynn, 511 F.2d 51 (7th Cir. 1975). Cf. § 17–3, infra; Tribe, "Structural Due Process," 10 Harv.C.R.-C.L.L.Rev. 268 (1975).

44. Professor Mashaw would take a similiar approach in order to shore up the weaknesses in his system of bureaucratic rationality. Thus, he suggests that "a system that provided claimants with specialized representatives . . . could instill somewhat more confidence both that informed choices were being made concerning whether to request reconsideration and that relevant evidence was not being overlooked. Representatives could also be expected to filter out frivolous claims. . . . [They] could also play a mediating role between the claimant's perceptions of distress and the program's policies." Mashaw would require the representatives to be laymen (non-lawyers) and government employees. He suggests as an example the veterans administration system of claims representatives operating through veterans organizations. J. Mashaw, Bureaucratic Justice 200–201 (1983).

45. To some extent, Justice Blackmun agreed with these views in his concurrence in O'Bannon v. Town Court Nursing Center, 447 U.S. 773, 790 (1980) (Blackmun, J., concurring), discussed in § 10–7. For example, in his analysis of whether process was due, he tested the nature and quality of representation by the nursing home, agreed that adjudicatory process rights become more important as the individual is singled out, and probed the effects of the current process on both instrumental and intrinsic grounds. Id. at 797–82. However, Justice Blackmun failed to dissolve the dichotomy between adjudicatory and representational processes and its consequent all-or-nothing approach to due process rights. Nevertheless, his cogent analysis could well provide a foundation for a better due process jurisprudence.

46. See 7A C. Wright, A. Miller & M. Kane, Federal Practice and Procedure: Civil 2d §§ 1765–1770 (2d ed. 1986); 3B J. Moore & J. Kennedy, Moore's Federal Practice ¶23.07 (2d ed. 1985).

47. See 7C C. Wright, A. Miller & M. Kane, Federal Practice and Procedure: Civil 2d § 1909 (2d ed. 1986); 3B J. Moore & J. Kennedy, Moore's Federal Practice ¶24.07 (2d ed. 1985).

48. See §§ 12–26 and 15–17, infra.

49. See generally Monahan, "The Supreme Court, 1974 Term—Foreword: Constitutional Common Law," 89 Harv.L.Rev. 1 (1975).

50. See § 17–2, infra.

Another recurring suggestion, heard so often perhaps because of its successful introduction in many European countries, is the establishment of an ombudsman appointed by a court either (1) independently to investigate the accuracy and fairness of administrative agency determinations, or (2) to assist those dependent upon government benefits and opportunities in directing their complaints and grievances.[51] In addition to an ombudsman's instrumental utility in ensuring that legislative dictates are accurately carried out when most beneficiaries have neither the knowledge nor the resources to take protective action on their own, such court-appointed investigators might preserve and indeed reinforce the intrinsic purposes of due process hearings by giving more than symbolic content to the participation of individuals in negotiation and compromise with agency decision-makers. Surely these are worthwhile alternatives to ritualistic encounters that may have less significance even as drama than the rhetoric of trial combat encourages lawyers to believe.

51. For a general discussion of the advantages of an ombudsman system, see Rubenstein, supra note 21, at 82–87; Verkuil, "The Ombudsman and the Limits of the Adversary System," 75 Colum.L.Rev. 845 (1975). See also Special Project, "Self Help: Extrajudicial Rights, Privileges and Remedies in Contemporary American Society," 37 Vand.L.Rev. 845, 1031–40 (1984) (pointing out some advantages of an ombudsman, especially in local-government settings). Cf. J. Mashaw, Bureaucratic Justice 226–27 (1983) (suggesting creation of a "superbureau" which would "supervise the drafting of administrative legislation, review the competence of agency policy analysis, audit administrative performance in the field, provide binding counsel on managerial technique, and hear in the final instance complaints of maladministration"); Verkuil, "The Emerging Concept of Administrative Procedure," 78 Colum.L.Rev. 258, 328–29 (1978) (suggesting expansion of the Administrative Conference to conduct " 'procedural audits' to evaluate agency performance in a systematic manner"); Mashaw, supra note 21, at 776 (suggesting a court-ordered "management system for assuring adjudicatory quality in claims processing"); C. Edley, supra note 30, at 374–404, 458–461 (prescribing a partnership among court, agency and legislature while emphasizing a rather discretionary judicial responsibility to determine its own level of deference by focussing on "sound governance" as a goal and utilizing a highly contextual analysis unconstrained by the traditional "separation of powers ethos").

Chapter 11

MODEL V—THE MODEL OF PREFERRED RIGHTS: LIBERTY BEYOND CONTRACT

§ 11-1. The Basic Problem of Post-1937 Constitutional Law

We saw in Chapters 1 and 8 that 1937 marked a watershed in American constitutional law; it seems fitting that the Bicentennial of the 1787 Constitution should coincide with the Semicentennial of the Constitutional Revolution of 1937. With the final collapse of Model II, the *Lochner* [1] era drew to a close, inaugurating a search for alternative conceptions of constitutional rights. Although the downfall of *Lochner* is often explained in institutional terms,[2] the persistent involvement of federal judges from 1937 to the present in reviewing the substantive validity of federal and state actions [3] makes that explanation false as a descriptive matter: the basic relation between federal judges and political bodies has continued, without real interruption, to be one in which general constitutional principles are regularly invoked to strike down governmental choices. And as we saw in Chapter 8, the institutional account of *Lochner's* demise also seems false on a normative level: the error of decisions like *Lochner v. New York* [4] lay not in judicial intervention to protect "liberty" but in a misguided understanding of what liberty actually required in the industrial age.[5] The authority and the duty of judges, as well as legislators and executive officials, to seek a better understanding and to enforce it in accord with their constitutional oaths, were undiminished by the revolution of 1937.

As Chapters 9 and 10 showed, the constitutional models most readily available to fill the vacuum created by Model II's collapse—the model of settled expectations (Model III) and the model of governmental

§ 11-1

1. Lochner v. New York, 198 U.S. 45 (1905).

2. See § 8-7, supra.

3. See, e.g., Moore v. East Cleveland, 431 U.S. 494 (1977) (state cannot prevent grandmother from including in her home grandchildren who are not siblings); Stanley v. Georgia, 394 U.S. 557 (1969) (state cannot punish private possession of obscenity for personal use); Griswold v. Connecticut, 381 U.S. 479 (1965) (state cannot punish married couple's use of contraceptives); Aptheker v. Secretary of State, 378 U.S. 500 (1964) (Congress cannot withhold passports from members of Communist Party); Robinson v. California, 370 U.S. 660 (1962) (state cannot make narcotics addiction a crime); Skinner v. Oklahoma, 316 U.S. 535 (1942) (state cannot sterilize repeated larce-

nists while imprisoning repeated embezzlers); Lanzetta v. New Jersey, 306 U.S. 451 (1939) (state cannot make being a "gangster" a crime).

4. 198 U.S. 45 (1905).

5. See §§ 8-6, 8-7, supra. See Poe v. Ullman, 367 U.S. 497, 517 (1961) (Douglas, J., dissenting); cf. Moore v. East Cleveland, 431 U.S. 494, 541 (1977) (White, J., dissenting). Since all of the decisions listed in note 3, supra, involved determinations that the government had deprived persons of liberty in substantive violation of the due process clause of either the fifth or the fourteenth amendment, Judge Craven's assertion that "[s]ubstantive due process is synonymous with Lochner v. New York," see Craven, "Personhood: The Right to be Let Alone," 1976 Duke L.J. 699, 700 n. 4, cannot be taken literally.

regularity (Model IV)—could in the end protect little beyond the entitlements government chose to confer unless their operation were infused with substantive values beyond those of assuring the fair implementation of the state's own positive decisions. The model most squarely confronting the need to elaborate such values has been Model V, the model of preferred rights. Expressed largely through doctrines involving freedom of expression and association,[6] rights of political participation,[7] rights of religious autonomy,[8] and rights of privacy and personhood,[9] this model has not attempted to define inherent limits on the power of all governmental institutions but has aimed more modestly to *exclude* governmental power from specific substantive spheres, by identifying and protecting certain "preferred rights"[10] from all but the most compellingly justified instances of governmental intrusion.[11] Broad limitations on governmental intervention once thought to be implicit in the internal structure of governmental powers as defined and delimited by common law conceptions were thus replaced by more selective limitations imposed from without.[12] Distributions of advantage through contractual transactions came to be regarded as the shifting products of the economic system as a whole, as often coerced as freely chosen, rather than the fixed contents of a sphere of volition put beyond governmental reach.[13] But particular forms of expression, action, or opportunity perceived as touching more deeply and permanently on human personality came to be regarded as the constituents of freedom rather than the coerced reflections of the economic system, and thus served to set new boundaries on majority rule through law.

Throughout the same post-1937 period, a competing Model VI, the model of equal protection, has offered alluring alternatives for constitutional argument,[14] seeking to identify those fundamental aspects of social structure which should be presumptively open to all on equal terms, and those criteria of government classification which are most suspect as likely to reflect habitual reaction and prejudice rather than reflective understanding. Again, as with Model V, it has been possible to give content to this model only through controversial substantive judgments.

6. See Chapter 12, infra.

7. See Chapter 13, infra.

8. See Chapter 14, infra.

9. See Chapter 15, infra.

10. See Murdock v. Pennsylvania, 319 U.S. 105, 115 (1943).

11. See Thomas v. Collins, 323 U.S. 516, 530 (1945).

12. The same transformation from internal to external limitations also characterized the Burger Court's ill-starred attempt to set bounds on Congress' commerce power. See National League of Cities v. Usery, 426 U.S. 833 (1976), and compare § 5–4, supra, with § 5–22, supra.

13. See, e.g., Kovacs v. Cooper, 336 U.S. 77, 95 (1949) (Frankfurter, J., concurring): "[W]ithout freedom of expression, thought becomes checked and atrophied. Therefore, in considering what interests are so fundamental as to be enshrined in the Due Process Clause, those liberties of the individual which history has attested as the indispensable conditions of an open as against a closed society come to this Court with a momentum for respect lacking when appeal is made to liberties which derive merely from shifting economic arrangements. . . ." Such a view treats particular contractual arrangements as properly controllable by government subject to only minimal judicial scrutiny but is compatible with more searching judicial review of government actions that place some individuals at the economic mercy of others.

14. See Chapter 16, infra.

The source of such substantive judgments in both models, and especially in the model of preferred rights, has itself become a major source of controversy. Part of the sea of argument has swirled about a school of red herring. The question has been debated whether the Supreme Court has the authority to "construct new rights" [15] or instead has an "obligation to trace its premises to the charter from which it derives its authority." [16] Put that way, the question answers itself; yet it merely postpones the inquiry about how the charter's broad guarantees—of due process, equal protection, and privileges or immunities of national citizenship—should be given content. Thus, to say that a principle, however durable and appealing, must not be imposed by the Supreme Court "if it lacks connection with any value the Constitution marks as special" [17] is to say nothing false—but it reveals very little of what is true. The *Lochner* error, it bears repeating, was not in invoking a value the Constitution did not mark as special; the text evinces the most explicit concern with "liberty," "contract," and "property." [18] The error lay in giving that value a perverse content. And to say, at the other extreme, that judicial protection of human rights "would be better justified by explication of contemporary moral and political ideals not drawn from the constitutional text" [19] adds little in this context, for in the end it is the *text* that invites a collaborative inquiry, involving both the Court and the country, into the contemporary contents and demands of freedom, fairness, and fraternity. The text does so through majestic generalities that plainly summon judges and lawmakers alike to a task which simply cannot be understood as the deciphering of an ancient scroll, however much the image of purely passive interpreter might suit an enterprise whose legitimacy is sometimes doubted.[20] Truthfully portrayed, the mission of giving content to the due process, equal protection, and privileges or immunities clauses entails an inescapable assumption of responsibility; neither the strategy of locating that responsibility outside the Constitution, nor the strategy of separating principles of justice "connected" with the Consti-

---

15. Bork "Neutral Principles and Some First Amendment Problems," 47 Ind.L.J. 1, 8 (1971) (arguing, unsurprisingly, that it does not but concluding, perhaps more surprisingly, that most of the rights recognized by the Supreme Court since the 1920s have no roots in the Constitution). See also Moore v. City of East Cleveland, supra note 5, at 544 (White, J., dissenting): "That the Court has ample precedent for the creation of new constitutional rights should not lead it to repeat the process at will." Justice White has reiterated this theme both in urging the overruling of the abortion decision, Roe v. Wade, 410 U.S. 113 (1973), see Thornburgh v. American College of Obstetricians, 106 S.Ct. 2169, 2192–98 (1986) (White, J., joined by Rehnquist, J., dissenting), and in writing, for a 5–4 Court, that homosexual intimacies between consenting adults in the privacy of the home are entitled to no special constitutional protection. See Bowers v. Hardwick, 106 S.Ct. 2841, 2844–46 (1986).

16. Ely, "The Wages of Crying Wolf: A Comment on Roe v. Wade," 82 Yale L.J. 920, 949 (1973) (arguing, unsurprisingly, that it does). Who could deny it?

17. Id. at 949.

18. On the latter two, see Chapter 9, supra.

19. Gray, "Do We Have an Unwritten Constitution?" 27 Stan.L.Rev. 703, 706 (1975). Cf. Corwin, "The 'Higher Law' Background of American Constitutional Law," 42 Harv.L.Rev. 149, 365 (1928).

20. See Moore v. City of East Cleveland, supra note 5, at 543 (White, J., dissenting): "Although the Court regularly proceeds on the assumption that the Due Process Clause has more than a procedural dimension, we must always bear in mind that the substantive content of the Clause is suggested neither by its language nor by preconstitutional history. . . ." Surely that is an overstatement.

tution from those lacking this link, can finally alter this reality. How to deal with it—not how to avoid it—is the post-1937 problem.

§ 11–2. Selective Incorporation of Bill of Rights Safeguards as a Partial Answer

In 1938, in *United States v. Carolene Products Co.*,[1] the Supreme Court suggested that "[t]here may be narrower scope for operation of the presumption of constitutionality when legislation appears on its face to be within a specific prohibition of the Constitution, such as those of the first ten Amendments, which are deemed equally specific when held to be embraced within the Fourteenth." Nine years later, the Court came within one vote of holding that the fourteenth amendment guaranteed that "no state could deprive its citizens of the privileges and protections of the Bill of Rights."[2] Such a holding could have taken either of two forms: most plausibly, it could have emerged as an elaboration of the privileges or immunities of national citizenship;[3] or it could have emerged as a translation of fourteenth amendment "liberty" into the freedoms secured by the Bill of Rights, with the understanding that depriving someone of such liberty "without due process of law" means doing so "where the federal government could not."[4] In neither form has the full incorporation of the Bill of Rights into the fourteenth amendment ever commanded a majority on the Court,[5] but in giving content to the due process clause "the Court has looked increasingly to the Bill of Rights for guidance [to the point where] many of the rights guaranteed by the first eight Amendments"[6] have been "selectively" absorbed into the fourteenth. Thus the due process clause has been held to protect the right to just compensation;[7] the first amendment freedoms of speech,[8] press,[9] assembly,[10] petition,[11] free exercise of religion,[12] and non-establishment of religion;[13] the fourth amendment rights to be free of unreasonable search and seizure[14] and to exclude from criminal trials evidence illegally seized;[15] the fifth amendment rights to be free of compelled self-incrimination[16]

---

§ 11–2

1. 304 U.S. 144, 152 n. 4 (1938).

2. Adamson v. California, 332 U.S. 46, 74–75 (1947) (Black, J., dissenting, joined on this issue by Douglas, Murphy, and Rutledge, JJ.).

3. See Chapter 7, supra.

4. See Black, "Unfinished Business of the Warren Court," 46 Wash.L.Rev. 3, 34 (1970).

5. Nor has the position of "total incorporation" won scholarly approval. See, e.g., Fairman, "Does the Fourteenth Amendment Incorporate the Bill of Rights? The Original Understanding," 2 Stan.L. Rev. 5 (1949).

6. Duncan v. Louisiana, 391 U.S. 145, 148 (1968).

7. See, e.g., Chicago, B. & Q.R. Co. v. Chicago, 166 U.S. 226 (1897).

8. See, e.g., Fiske v. Kansas, 274 U.S. 380 (1927).

9. See, e.g., Near v. Minnesota, 283 U.S. 697 (1931).

10. See, e.g., DeJonge v. Oregon, 299 U.S. 353 (1937).

11. See, e.g., Hague v. CIO, 307 U.S. 496 (1939).

12. See, e.g., Cantwell v. Connecticut, 310 U.S. 296 (1940).

13. See, e.g., Everson v. Board of Education, 330 U.S. 1, 15–16 (1947).

14. See Wolf v. Colorado, 338 U.S. 25 (1949).

15. See Mapp v. Ohio, 367 U.S. 643 (1961).

16. See Malloy v. Hogan, 378 U.S. 1 (1964).

and double jeopardy;[17] the sixth amendment rights to counsel,[18] to a speedy [19] and public [20] trial before a jury,[21] to an opportunity to confront opposing witnesses,[22] and to compulsory process for the purpose of obtaining favorable witnesses; [23] and the eighth amendment right to be free of cruel and unusual punishments.[24]

In deciding which Bill of Rights provisions to "incorporate," [25] the Court has said that it was searching for "principle[s] of justice so rooted in the tradition and conscience of our people as to be ranked as fundamental" and thus "implicit in the concept of ordered liberty," [26] or for those principles that were "basic in our system of jurisprudence." [27] Given the artificiality of an inquiry into whether "a civilized system *could be imagined* that would not accord the particular protection," [28] the Court began in the early 1960's to proceed "upon the valid assumption that state criminal processes are not imaginary and theoretical schemes but actual systems bearing [specific] characteristics" and to ask "whether given this kind of system a particular procedure is fundamental—whether, that is, a procedure is necessary to an Anglo-American regime of ordered liberty." [29]

The reference to "procedure" should not be allowed to obscure the fact that Supreme Court decisions drawing on the Bill of Rights to restrict state action have frequently limited the permissible *substance* of state law and not merely its procedures for applying rules to particular cases.[30] It might have been wiser to ground such substantive

---

17. See Benton v. Maryland, 395 U.S. 784 (1969).

18. See, e.g., Gideon v. Wainwright, 372 U.S. 335 (1963).

19. See, e.g., Klopfer v. North Carolina, 386 U.S. 213 (1967).

20. See In re Oliver, 333 U.S. 257 (1948).

21. See Duncan v. Louisiana, 391 U.S. 145 (1968).

22. See, e.g., Pointer v. Texas, 380 U.S. 400 (1965).

23. See Washington v. Texas, 388 U.S. 14 (1967).

24. See Robinson v. California, 370 U.S. 660 (1962).

25. The language of "incorporation" is perhaps misleading inasmuch as the Bill of Rights provisions remain points of reference only. Although the Court ordinarily applies essentially identical constitutional standards to the state and federal governments when one of the "incorporated" areas is involved, see, e.g., Ker v. California, 374 U.S. 23 (1963) (search and seizure), the congruence is not invariably perfect. See, e.g., Apodaca v. Oregon, 406 U.S. 404 (1972), and Johnson v. Louisiana, 406 U.S. 356 (1972), in which several alignments of Justices produced holdings to the effect that (a) nonunanimous juries may constitutionally return criminal convictions in

state trials; (b) the right to jury trial applies in the same way to state and federal cases; but (c) only a unanimous jury may constitutionally return a criminal conviction in a federal trial. See id. at 369–80 (separate opinion of Powell, J.). The contradiction is likely to be resolved by ultimately abandoning (b).

26. Palko v. Connecticut, 302 U.S. 319, 325 (1937) (Cardozo, J.).

27. In re Oliver, 333 U.S. 257, 273 (1948).

28. Duncan v. Louisiana, 391 U.S. 145, 149 n. 14 (1968) (emphasis added).

29. Id. at 148–49 n. 14. The Court expressly extended the Duncan approach to substantive due process in Moore v. East Cleveland, 431 U.S. 494, 503–04, & n. 12 (1977). For a powerful attack on the entire notion of "incorporating" Bill of Rights provisions, selectively or otherwise, see Duncan, 391 U.S. at 171–93 (Harlan, J., joined by Stewart, J., dissenting).

30. See, e.g., Chicago, B. & Q.R. Co. v. Chicago, 166 U.S. 226 (1897) (just compensation); Grosjean v. American Press Co., 297 U.S. 233 (1936) (freedom of press); DeJonge v. Oregon, 299 U.S. 353 (1937) (freedom of assembly); Shelton v. Tucker, 364 U.S. 479 (1960) (freedom of association); Stanley v. Georgia, 394 U.S. 557 (1969) (right to possess even obscene literature in private).

limitations in the privileges or immunities of national citizenship,[31] but even if that strategy had been pursued, much the same question would have remained: What besides the rights secured by the first eight amendments are to be counted among the "preferred" freedoms, whether operating against the states through the due process clause or through privileges or immunities? The answer, at least if due process were the vehicle, would bear also on the possible existence of substantive freedoms against federal action beyond those enumerated in the Bill of Rights.

In *Adamson v. California*, Justice Black, joined in dissent by Justice Douglas, treated the Bill of Rights not only as fully incorporated but also as setting an outer boundary on the substantive reach of the fourteenth amendment apart from the equal protection clause.[32] Justices Murphy and Rutledge, while agreeing with Justice Black on full incorporation, rejected his "reverse incorporation" view and argued that the fourteenth amendment goes beyond extending the Bill of Rights to the States.[33] The next section explores the ramifications of that position.

§ 11–3. Beyond Incorporation: The Ninth Amendment and the "Rational Continuum"

Justice Harlan's dissenting opinion in *Poe v. Ullman* stated the thesis best:[1] "[T]he full scope of the liberty guaranteed by the Due Process Clause cannot be found in or limited by the precise terms of the specific guarantees elsewhere provided in the Constitution. This 'liberty' is not a series of isolated points picked out in terms of the taking of property; the freedom of speech, press, and religion; the right to keep and bear arms; the freedom from unreasonable searches and seizures; and so on. It is a rational continuum which, broadly speaking, includes a freedom from all substantial arbitrary impositions and purposeless restraints, . . . and which also recognizes, . . . that certain interests require particularly careful scrutiny of the state needs asserted to justify their abridgement." The history of the framing and ratification of the Constitution and of the Bill of Rights leaves little doubt about the correctness of Justice Harlan's proposition. Indeed, James Madison introduced the ninth amendment in specific response to the arguments of Hamilton and others that enactment of a Bill of Rights might dangerously suggest "that those rights which were not singled out, were intended to be assigned into the hands of the General Government, and were consequently insecure."[2] The ninth amendment, which provides that "[t]he enumeration in the Constitution, of certain rights, shall not be construed to deny or disparage others retained by the people," therefore *at least* states a rule of construction pointing away from the reverse incorporation view that only the interests secured by the Bill of

---

31. See Chapter 7, supra.

32. 332 U.S. 46, 69–72, 77–78, 83–85, 89–90 (1947) (dissenting opinion). Justice Black never veered from this view; Justice Douglas did. See, e.g., Griswold v. Connecticut, 381 U.S. 479 (1965).

33. Id. at 123–25 (dissenting opinion).

§ 11–3

1. 367 U.S. 497, 543 (1961).

2. 1 Annals of Cong. 439 (Gales and Seaton ed. 1834).

Rights are encompassed within the fourteenth amendment, and *at most* provides a positive source of law for fundamental but unmentioned rights.[3] In either case, the "Bill of Rights presumes the existence of a substantial body of rights not specifically enumerated but easily perceived in the broad concept of liberty and so numerous and so obvious as to preclude listing them."[4] The line of cases protecting, as unenumerated aspects of liberty, the right to teach one's child a foreign language,[5] the right to send one's child to a private school,[6] the right to procreate,[7] the right to be free of certain bodily intrusions,[8] and the right to travel abroad,[9] had set the stage for the most important substantive due process decision of the modern period, *Griswold v. Connecticut.*[10] That case presented the question whether a married couple could be sent to jail by the State of Connecticut for using birth control.[11] Professor Charles Black wrote of *Griswold* that it was "not so much a case that the law tests as a case that tests the law."[12] He continued: "If our constitutional law could permit such a thing to happen, then we might almost as well not have any law of constitutional limitations, partly because the thing is so outrageous in itself, and partly because a constitutional law inadequate to deal with such an outrage would be too feeble, in method and doctrine, to deal with a very great amount of equally outrageous material. Virtually all the intimacies, privacies and autonomies of life would be regulable by the legislature—not necessarily by the legislature of this year or last year, but, it might be, by the legislature of a hundred years ago, or even by an administrative board in due form thereunto authorized by a recent or long-dead legislature." The Court held that Connecticut's law was unconstitutional. Justice Douglas' opinion for the Court relied on "the zone of privacy created by several fundamental constitutional guarantees," explaining that "specific guarantees in the Bill of Rights"—he was referring to the first, third, fourth, fifth, and ninth—"have penum-

3. See generally B. Patterson, The Forgotten Ninth Amendment (1955); Redlich, "Are There 'Certain Rights . . . Retained by the People'," 37 N.Y.U.L.Rev. 787 (1962). See note 14, infra.

4. 3 Story, Commentaries on the Constitution of the United States 715–16 (1833); see also 2 Story, Commentaries on the Constitution of the United States 626–27, 651 (5th ed. 1891).

5. Meyer v. Nebraska, 262 U.S. 390 (1923).

6. Pierce v. Society of Sisters, 268 U.S. 510 (1925).

7. Skinner v. Oklahoma, 316 U.S. 535 (1942).

8. Rochin v. California, 342 U.S. 165 (1952).

9. Aptheker v. Secretary of State, 378 U.S. 500 (1964).

10. 381 U.S. 479 (1965). For useful commentary in prompt reaction to Gris-

wold, see the remarks of Professors Dixon, Emerson, Kauper, McKay, and Sutherland in 64 Mich.L.Rev. 197–288 (1965).

11. Griswold, the Executive Director of the Planned Parenthood League of Connecticut, and its medical director, a licensed physician, were convicted as accessories for giving married persons information on contraception and for prescribing a contraceptive for the wife's use. A Connecticut statute made it a crime for any person to use any drug or device to prevent conception. The Court held the statute unconstitutional and concluded that appellants could not be convicted as accessories. The majority opinion focused not on appellants' rights, but on those of the married couple. See 381 U.S. at 485–86. The Griswold case is discussed further in Chapter 15, infra.

12. "The Unfinished Business of the Warren Court," 46 Wash.L.Rev. 3, 32 (1970).

bras, formed by emanations from those guarantees that help give them life and substance." [13]

Justice Goldberg, concurring in an opinion joined by Chief Justice Warren and Justice Brennan, agreed that the unmentioned right to privacy resolved the case but was more unabashed about locating the right, with the help of the ninth amendment as a rule of construction,[14] in "the concept of liberty," [15] and had no hesitation in concluding that there existed no sufficiently compelling justification for the state's drastic infringement of the right.[16] Justice Harlan concurred in the judgment but on the still broader ground that the law violated "basic values 'implicit in the concept of ordered liberty' " [17] whether or not it could be "found to violate some right assured by the letter or penumbra of the Bill of Rights." [18] Finding the " '[s]pecific' provisions of the Constitution" no more precise or determinate than "due process," [19] Justice Harlan urged replacing the illusory certitude of reliance on the "specifics" with "continual insistence upon the teachings of history, solid recognition of the basic values that underlie our society, and wise appreciation of the great roles that the doctrines of federalism and separation of powers have played in establishing and preserving American freedoms." [20] Justice White, also concurring in the judgment, agreed that the law was a substantial denial of liberty, especially for

13. 381 U.S. at 485. The thesis that Griswold constitutes an adoption by the Court of the civil law method of reasoning by analogy from statute and statute-law is imaginatively developed in Franklin, "The Ninth Amendment as Civil Law Method and Its Implications For Republican Form of Government," 40 Tul.L.Rev. 487 (1966). Justice Douglas had originally drafted an opinion relying squarely on the first amendment, arguing that the Connecticut law violated freedom of association by intruding on marriage, which "flourishes on the interchange of ideas." B. Schwartz, The Unpublished Opinions of the Warren Court 235 (1985). At conference, Justice Black had caustically replied that, for him, associational rights stem from the "right of assembly," and the married couple's right "to assemble in bed is . . . new . . . to me." Id. at 237. Justice Brennan was similarly unpersuaded that the freedom of assembly clause was of much relevance. Id. Justice Douglas was eventually persuaded to adopt a privacy rationale. Id. at 238. How any of the Justices would have reacted to an argument equating sexual intimacy and "expression" with "freedom of speech" is unclear, but there is basis for skepticism.

14. 381 U.S. at 488–93, 496. It is a common error, but an error nonetheless, to talk of "ninth amendment rights." The ninth amendment is *not* a source of rights as such; it is simply a rule about how to read the Constitution. See Tribe, "Contrasting Constitutional Visions: Of Real and Unreal Differences," 22 Harv.Civ.Rts.-Civ.Lib.L.Rev. 95, 101–08 (1987). But it is a vital rule—one without which the Bill of Rights might have been more threatening than reassuring, see note 3, supra, and one without which, therefore, the 1787 Constitution might not have lasted. For arguments that would give considerable force to the ninth amendment, see J. Ely, Democracy and Distrust 38 (1980); C. Black, Decision According to Law 44–68 (1981). For arguments that would largely empty the ninth amendment of significance, see Berger, "The Ninth Amendment," 66 Cornell L.Rev. 1 (1980); Monaghan, "Our Perfect Constitution," 56 N.Y.U.L.Rev. 353, 366–67 (1981). To the extent the ninth amendment is deemed a "repositor[y] for an external schedule of rights," an argument is available that this "list" was "closed as of 1791 or 1868." Id. at 367, 395; Dunbar, "James Madison and the Ninth Amendment," 42 Va.L.Rev. 627, 641 (1956). But if, as seems plain, the ninth amendment is not a "repository" at all but a prohibition against certain forms of argument by negative implication, then the "closed set" position loses most of its plausibility.

15. 381 U.S. at 486. Compare the majority opinion, id. at 481–82, which purported to eschew reliance on fourteenth amendment "liberty" or "due process."

16. 381 U.S. at 497–98.

17. Id. at 500.

18. Id. at 499.

19. Id. at 501.

20. Id.

the "disadvantaged citizens of Connecticut"; [21] but for him the crucial fact was that this denial could not significantly advance any of the purposes the state claimed for it.[22] Justices Black and Stewart both dissented, claiming that the majority was usurping a legislative function.[23] By 1973, however, Justice Stewart had "accepted" *Griswold* "as one in a long line of . . . cases decided under the doctrine of substantive due process," [24] and indeed all nine of the Justices as of 1973 had accepted the Court's role in giving the fourteenth amendment due process clause substantive content beyond the Bill of Rights, despite significant disagreements over exactly how the role should be performed.[25] The topic of those disagreements is the subject of the next section: Where, beyond the Bill of Rights, is the "substance" in substantive due process to come from?

§ 11–4. True and False Starts in the Search for Substantive Rights

Justice Frankfurter believed that he could identify "those liberties of the individual which history has attested as the indispensable conditions of an open as against a closed society" [1] by a "disinterested inquiry pursued in the spirit of science, on a balanced order of facts exactly and fairly stated, on the detached consideration of conflicting claims, . . ., on a judgment not *ad hoc* and episodic but duly mindful of reconciling the needs both of continuity and of change in a progressive society." [2] But after that elaborate wind-up, and despite his references to "considerations deeply rooted in reason and in the compelling traditions of the legal profession," [3] Justice Frankfurter could explain only that the stomach-pumping he deemed violative of due process in *Rochin v. California* was "conduct that shocks the conscience." [4] References to history, tradition, evolving community standards, and civilized consensus, can provide suggestive parallels and occasional insights, but it is illusion to suppose that they can yield answers, much less absolve judges of responsibility for developing and

21. Id. at 503.

22. Id. at 504–06. But compare Justice White's dissent in Moore v. East Cleveland, 431 U.S. 494, 541 (1977), discussed in § 15–17, infra.

23. 381 U.S. at 507 (Black, J., joined by Stewart, J.); id. at 527 (Stewart, J., joined by Black, J.).

24. Roe v. Wade, 410 U.S. 113, 168 (1973) (concurring opinion). But compare Justice Stewart's dissent in Moore v. East Cleveland, supra note 22, at 531 (joined by Rehnquist, J.).

25. See, e.g., Roe v. Wade, 410 U.S. at 152–54 (Blackmun, J., writing for the Court in an opinion joined by Burger, C.J., and by Douglas, Brennan, Stewart, Marshall, and Powell, JJ.); id. at 172–73 (Rehnquist, J., dissenting); id. at 221–23 (White,

J., dissenting). See also Richmond Newspapers, Inc. v. Virginia, 448 U.S. 555, 579–80 & n. 15 (1980), discussed in § 12–20, infra.

§ 11–4

1. Kovacs v. Cooper, 336 U.S. 77, 95 (1949) (concurring opinion).

2. Rochin v. California, 342 U.S. 165, 172 (1952).

3. Id. at 171.

4. Id. at 172. Compare Irvine v. California, 347 U.S. 128 (1954) (invading privacy with microphone concealed in marital bedroom not so shocking as to render the use of evidence thus obtained violative of due process); but see id. at 142–49 (Frankfurter, J., dissenting).

defending a theory of what rights are "preferred" or "fundamental" under our Constitution and why.[5]

None of the theories offered to date is wholly satisfying. That some freedoms form "the matrix, the indispensable condition" [6] of all others, helps frame the inquiry. Thus "legislation which restricts those political processes which can ordinarily be expected to bring about repeal of undesirable legislation" must be "subjected to more exacting judicial scrutiny" than most laws.[7] But even a garden-variety ban on commercial advertising turns out to restrict the fully informed operation of the political process.[8] And physical survival is certainly as "indispensable" to the enjoyment of other freedoms as are speech or voting. One must be able to express oneself to protest the violation of other rights, but to express oneself one needs at least a decent level of nourishment, shelter, clothing, medical care, and education. To have those things, one needs either employment or income support. Too easily government may purchase the silent acquiescence of the deprived in their own constitutional undoing. People who cannot buy bread cannot follow the suggestion that they eat cake; people bowed under the weight of poverty are unlikely to stand up for their constitutional rights. Yet the Constitution cannot readily be construed to make income support an affirmative duty of the state.

The effort to identify the "indispensable conditions of an open society" thus proves inseparable from the much larger enterprise of identifying the elements of being human—and deciding which of those

5. In Moore v. City of East Cleveland, 431 U.S. 494 (1977), discussed in §§ 15–17, 15–20, infra, the Supreme Court held that an extended family has a constitutional right to live in East Cleveland despite the city's ordinance strictly limiting the relatives who could live together as a "family." The plurality opinion of Justice Powell, joined by Justices Brennan, Marshall, and Blackmun, sought escape from the perils of judicial subjectivity in history and tradition: "Our decisions establish that the Constitution protects the sanctity of the family precisely because the institution of the family is deeply rooted in this Nation's history and tradition." Id. at 503. But, as Justice White said in dissent, "[w]hat the deeply rooted traditions of the country are is arguable" and "which of them deserve the protection of the Due Process Clause is even more debatable." Id. at 549. And, as Justice Stewart, joined in dissent by Justice Rehnquist, argued, the "traditional importance of the extended family in American life" need not imply that a particular city or town may not follow a less traditional pattern. Id. at 537 n. 7. Moreover, Justice Brennan, joined in his concurring opinion by Justice Marshall, stressed the special importance of extended families as *alternatives* to the "traditional" nuclear form, especially for racial and ethnic minorities. Id. at 509–10 & nn. 6–10. Tradition alone thus cannot explain the Moore decision. Indeed even the plurality opinion in Moore, despite its attempt to use history to limit the judiciary, see id. at 503 n. 12, undertook a functional rather than purely historical analysis when it reasoned that "[i]t is through the family that we inculcate and pass down many of our most cherished values, moral and cultural." Id. at 503–04. Nor would it be consistent with the rationale of Moore to withhold the status of preferred rights in Model V from those practices or institutions that "inculcate and pass down" values that the current majority might *not* deem among its "most cherished," for the plurality opinion's closing sentence insisted that "the Constitution prevents East Cleveland from standardizing its children—and its adults—by forcing all to live in certain narrowly defined family patterns." Id. at 506. Both the historical inquiry and the functional analysis, then, must proceed at a level general enough to avoid the trap of sanctifying the conventional and preventing moral and cultural change. See also §§ 15–20, 15–21, infra.

6. Palko v. Connecticut, 302 U.S. 319, 327 (1937).

7. United States v. Carolene Products Co., 304 U.S. 144, 152 n. 4 (1938).

8. See Virginia Board of Pharmacy v. Virginia Consumer Council, 425 U.S. 748, 765 (1976), discussed in § 12–15, infra.

elements are left entirely to politics to protect, and which are entrusted to protection by judicial decree. Not surprisingly, the judicially protectable may include aspects of material well-being as well as the more ethereal facets of life ordinarily associated with constitutional protections.[9] Thus the attempt to distinguish the rights protected during the *Lochner* [10] era from the preferred rights of Model V in terms of a supposed dichotomy between economic and personal rights must fail,[11] and a wider conception of what human beings require becomes unavoidable. The day may indeed come when a general doctrine under the fifth and fourteenth amendments recognizes for each individual a constitutional right to a decent level of affirmative governmental protection in meeting the basic human needs of physical survival and security, health and housing, work and schooling. The time may come when constitutional law will answer the scholar's question, "Why education and not golf?" [12] with a reply that is likely to make human sense—"Because education is more important"—and when this answer, however odd it will seem to some lawyers,[13] will seem inescapable to those who take their lessons from life itself. But despite straws in the wind and strands of doctrine pointing in this general direction,[14] that time has not yet come,[15] and constitutional lawyers must continue to struggle with less sweeping solutions and more tentative doctrinal tools.

The enterprise of discovering and defending fundamental constitutional rights in the text and structure of the Constitution contains three additional dimensions that must be noted before embarking upon the more particular inquiries of Chapters 12 through 15. The first is the dimension of justification: granted that there is a constitutional "right" to X, what sorts of considerations warrant governmental restriction of that right? In the chapters that follow,[16] this question proves central. Without attempting to answer it here, we might simply observe that the two most conventional answers—the first focusing on the supposed distinction between self-regarding conduct and conduct affecting others,[17] and the second focusing on the supposed distinction

9. See, e.g., §§ 15–9, 15–13, 16–33, infra. Thus the Court has already recognized that state actions that limit access to the *means of effectuating* a protected decision are subject to much the same strict scrutiny as are state actions that prohibit the decision entirely. Carey v. Population Services International, 431 U.S. 678, 697–99 (1977) (invalidating state ban on distribution of nonmedical contraceptives except through licensed pharmacists).

10. See Lochner v. New York, 198 U.S. 45 (1905), discussed in Chapter 8, supra.

11. See § 15–13, infra.

12. See Michelman, "The Supreme Court, 1968 Term—Foreword: On Protecting the Poor through the Fourteenth Amendment," 83 Harv.L.Rev. 7, 59 (1969).

13. Compare Woodrow Wilson's observation: "[T]he Constitution of the United States is not a mere lawyers' document; it is a vehicle of life, and its spirit is always the spirit of the age," W. Wilson, Constitutional Government in the United States 69 (1927).

14. See §§ 8–7, 9–8, 10–9, and 10–19, supra, and §§ 15–9, 16–8, 16–33, 16–35, 16–49, 16–50, 16–59, infra.

15. See, e.g., Maher v. Roe, 432 U.S. 464, 469 (1977) (upholding state refusal to fund nontherapeutic abortions): "The Constitution imposes no obligation on the States to pay the pregnancy-related medical expenses of indigent women, or indeed to pay any of the medical expenses of indigents."

16. See Chapters 12–16, infra.

17. See §§ 15–1 to 15–3, infra.

between moral and utilitarian reasons for regulating behavior [18]—both prove strikingly unhelpful in constitutional law and theory.

The second dimension to be noted at the outset is that of institutional role: granted that a particular right is fundamental, and that only considerations of a particular sort can warrant its infringement, when should that mean strict judicial scrutiny of measures that appear to infringe the right without sufficient warrant? Again, factors relevant to that question will arise throughout the chapters that follow, but one feature in particular seems worth pointing out. In *Stanley v. Illinois*, in holding that an unwed father was entitled to a hearing on his fitness as a parent before his child could be taken from him by the state, the Court observed that "the Constitution recognizes higher values than speed and efficiency. Indeed, one might fairly say of the Bill of Rights in general, and the Due Process Clause in particular, that they were designed to protect the fragile values of a vulnerable citizenry from the overbearing concern for efficiency and efficacy that may characterize praiseworthy government officials no less, and perhaps more, than mediocre ones." [19] What makes some values more "fragile" and others more "robust" is a difficult question. Political fragility—and thus the need for special judicial protection—may be present even when a value is of universally recognized importance, and even when its deprivation would be universally perceived as a misfortune. For it is less the importance of a value than the character and intensity of its involvement in a given case that determines its political resilience in that specific situation. When a value is intangible, or its involvement in a choice diffuse, the fact that the choice threatens that value may not outweigh the immediate gains that tempt government to sacrifice it. Thus values of speech, religion, and privacy exemplify concerns whose ubiquity and widely acknowledged importance have not rendered them politically invulnerable. Finally, even though other values—such as vocational freedom or adequate food and housing—are anything but intangible, the irreversible harm of their denial may warrant a degree of judicial scrutiny undiminished by the political visibility of appeals for nutrition or shelter—especially since those who are most severely deprived are likely to be "discrete and insular minorities," [20] not the politically powerful.

The third dimension is that of penalty vs. subsidy: given the conclusion that a particular activity or choice is protected as a matter of constitutional right, it follows that making the protected choice may not subject one to governmental punishment. But must the government go so far as to support the choice affirmatively—even with public funds? And, if not, how is one to distinguish selectively withholding support from imposing a penalty? That is the subject of the next section.

18. See § 15–10, infra.

19. 405 U.S. 645, 656 (1972).

20. United States v. Carolene Products Co., 304 U.S. 144, 152 n. 4 (1938).

§ 11–5. The Elusive Distinction Between Withholding a Subsidy and Imposing a Penalty

A problem pervading much of contemporary constitutional law is that of drawing a workable distinction between government's undoubtedly broad power to decide which activities to subsidize or otherwise encourage, and government's considerably narrower power to decide which activities to penalize or otherwise discourage, whether directly or by attaching conditions to various privileges or gratuities.

The notion that, whenever a privilege or benefit might be withheld altogether, it may be withheld on whatever conditions government chooses to impose, has been repeatedly repudiated since the mid-20th century.[1] Independently unconstitutional conditions—those that make enjoyment of a benefit contingent on sacrifice of an independent constitutional right—are invalid; whether a condition is unconstitutional depends on whether government may properly demand sacrifice of the alleged right in the particular context. That was the holding of *FCC v. League of Women Voters*[2] and of *Babbitt v. Planned Parenthood Federation*.[3]

§ 11–5

1. See, e.g., Sherbert v. Verner, 374 U.S. 398 (1963) (state may not deny unemployment benefits to person who refuses to work on Saturday for religious reasons).

2. 468 U.S. 364 (1984). By a 5–4 vote, the Court invalidated a provision of the Public Broadcasting Act that prohibited any noncommercial educational station receiving public funds from endorsing candidates or editorializing. The stations were thus forced to give up their right to engage in quintessential first amendment expression if they wished to receive public subsidies for any of their programming. Writing for the Court, Justice Brennan concluded that the ban suppressed protected speech without being narrowly tailored to the goal of providing a balanced presentation of issues to the public. Id. at 380, 395. Upon close inspection of the statute, the Court rejected Justice Stevens' argument, id. at 414–16 (dissenting opinion), that the law was a legitimate way to preclude the insidious tendency that public funding might have to induce stations to skew their editorials in favor of the government, or their endorsements in favor of incumbents, in order to improve their prospects for continued benefits. In dissent, Justice Rehnquist, joined by Chief Justice Burger and Justice White, protested that all Congress had done was to attach to a discretionary subsidy a requirement that the managers of educational stations not promote their private views at public expense. Id. at 405.

3. 107 S.Ct. 391 (1986), aff'g Planned Parenthood of Central & Northern Arizona v. State of Arizona, 789 F.2d 1348 (9th Cir. 1986). An Arizona bill appropriating state funds to pay for family-planning services contained a provision forbidding the channeling of any such funds "to agencies or entities which offer abortions, abortion procedures, counseling for abortion procedures or abortion referrals." Planned Parenthood sued to enjoin enforcement of this prohibition. The state sought to defend the prohibition as a prophylactic measure designed to implement the state's right, under Maher v. Roe, 432 U.S. 464 (1977), to withhold public funds from abortion-related services. The state argued that, because "it was impossible for the state to monitor use of the funds to prevent their use for abortion-related services," 789 F.2d at 1350, through a system of "earmarking . . . [,] tracing [,] [and] auditing," id. at 1351, the state's only way to prevent use of its funds for abortion-related activities was to keep organizations like Planned Parenthood from obtaining state family-planning funds for *any* purpose. The Ninth Circuit held that no such impossibility had been established and that, on the contrary, Planned Parenthood had "successfully segregated state funds from its abortion-related expenditures." Id. at 1351. The court flatly rejected any notion that such funding segregation is *inherently* illusory and that "*any* expenditure on abortion-related activities necessarily is derived from state funds" to the extent that those funds constitute a portion of the recipient's budget, id. at 1350 (emphasis in original). Although Chief Justice Rehnquist, Justice White, and Justice Scalia would have set the case for plenary briefing and argument rather than summarily affirming, it would be difficult to justify any result other than the one the Ninth Circuit reached without holding, in effect,

But the fact that government *may not penalize* exercise of a right by withholding an otherwise discretionary benefit does not imply that government *must subsidize* exercise of the right. Thus, although *Planned Parenthood* makes it clear that those who undergo, perform, or counsel abortion may not be required to cease those activities as a condition of receiving public funding for their other activities, it certainly does not follow that government must pay for abortions or abortion counseling. Indeed, the Supreme Court held in *Harris v. McRae* [4] that the government is even free to influence an indigent pregnant woman's constitutionally protected reproductive choice by refusing public health funds for abortions while fully subsidizing medical care for childbirth within its comprehensive medical benefits program.

Even when the Constitution forbids government to interfere with an individual's choice between two alternatives—such as the choice between abortion and childbirth, or that between public and private education—it does not follow that government may not put its thumb on the scale by subsidizing one alternative but not the other. Were that not the case, the subsidy of public schooling would entail a constitutional duty to subsidize the private alternatives that, under *Pierce v. Society of Sisters*,[5] the government must leave parents free to choose. "It cannot be that because government may not prohibit the use of contraceptives, or prevent parents from sending their child to a private school, government, therefore, has an affirmative obligation to ensure that all persons have the financial resources to obtain contraceptives or send their children to private schools." [6] Whatever one thinks of the validity of educational voucher plans,[7] one surely cannot argue that the Constitution compels government to institute them.

There may well be settings, however, in which the very decision to subsidize one activity entails a decision to penalize another. Thus, if government were to pay a bounty to those who agreed to vote for incumbents, it would necessarily be penalizing supporters of the opposing candidates, in clear violation of basic norms of equality inherent in the franchise.[8] Arguably, too, if government were to fund all who advocate freedom of abortion—but not those who advocate saving the fetus—it would in effect be penalizing the "pro-life" position.[9] Or if government were to permit tax-deductible contributions to be used by pro-life advocates in their lobbying efforts while refusing "pro-choice" advocates the same privilege, it might be said to have penalized the latter.

that wholly speculative difficulties of segregating and monitoring public funds give the government a lever over all recipients of such funds whereby such recipients may be forced to choose between foregoing public subsidy and abandoning private activities in which the first and fourteenth amendments entitle those recipients to engage.

4. 448 U.S. 297 (1980). The case is discussed in more detail in Chapter 15, infra.

5. 268 U.S. 510 (1925).

6. Harris v. McRae, 448 U.S. at 318 (citations omitted).

7. See Chapters 14 and 16, infra.

8. See Chapters 13 and 14, infra.

9. Cf. Arkansas Writers' Project, Inc. v. Ragland, 107 S.Ct. 1722 (1987) (invalidating state tax on general-interest magazines that exempts newspapers and religious, professional, trade, and sports journals).

This sort of argument may be made with some plausibility in any zero-sum situation, in which amplifying the vote or even the voice of one side is the same as muffling the vote or the voice of the other. But the Court has been properly reluctant to regard selective subsidies of certain voices as automatically having such a viewpoint (or even a subject-matter) bias. Note, for example, the unanimous conclusion of the Court in *Regan v. Taxation With Representation (TWR)* that a governmental decision to subsidize the political lobbying of veterans' organizations but of no other organizations, through rules permitting only the former to engage in such lobbying with tax-deductible contributions, is subject to no heightened first amendment scrutiny.[10]

Even when viewpoint bias is acknowledged, a complicating feature of the analysis arises from whatever special freedom government might be thought to enjoy when it acts less as a regulator of expression than as a participant in the marketplace of ideas.[11] When government adds its own voice to the dialogue, and perhaps also when it subsidizes the voices of its surrogates, it is not subject to the usual form or level of first amendment scrutiny.

A second complicating feature in the analysis arises because government's power to set the terms on which it offers a subsidy must be thought to include at least some power to restrict not only how that very subsidy is used but also certain other activities of the subsidized person or entity when those other activities bear a close enough relationship to use of the subsidy. Hence, for example, the power to restrict use of public campaign funds has been held, in *Buckley v. Valeo*, to include a power to cap even the private campaign expenditures of those who receive such public funds.[12] Although the Court in the same case held campaign expenditure limits invalid under the first amendment in the absence of public funding,[13] and although the Court has held that public funding does not permit imposition of a cap on independent expenditures made by others on behalf of the publicly-funded candidate,[14] it is understandable that the Court should have concluded, in *Buckley v. Valeo*, that a candidate may be forced to choose between running a campaign funded exclusively with a public grant and running a campaign funded solely with unlimited private spending.

A third complication arises whenever the government's authority to limit use of a public subsidy, and the recipient's right not to be penalized for independently protected activity, come together in the

---

10. 461 U.S. 540 (1983). Subject only to a test for minimum rationality, the selective subsidy was upheld. Although government has long rewarded veterans with such things as special opportunities in public employment, see Personnel Administrator of Massachusetts v. Feeney, 442 U.S. 256 (1979) (upholding over equal protection challenge a lifetime, absolute veterans' preference in state civil service employment), it seems problematic to reward military service not with preferred access to a privilege or with some other traditional form of benefit, but with the "currency" of a louder political voice.

11. See § 12–4, infra.

12. 424 U.S. 1, 99 (1976). Compare South Dakota v. Dole, 107 S.Ct. 2793, 2796 (1987) (upholding Congress' authority to withhold federal highway funds from states that fail to raise the drinking age to 21, on the theory that such failure relates closely enough to highway safety, and hence to proper use of the federal subsidy in question), discussed in § 5–10, note 13, supra.

13. Id. at 58–59.

14. See Federal Election Comm'n v. NCPAC, 470 U.S. 480, 493 (1985).

same case. Both features were involved in *Regan v. TWR*, inasmuch as the Court was unanimous in agreeing that government should be free not to subsidize political lobbying,[15] but it also seemed clear that government could not penalize lobbying with private funds by one who received a public subsidy for other activities.[16] The structure of the Internal Revenue Code made it possible for both principles to be respected, since the Code permitted organizations eligible for tax-deductible contributions under § 501(c)(3) to retain that status while setting up financially independent but wholly controlled § 501(c)(4) lobbying arms that would conduct lobbying directed by their § 501(c)(3) affiliates but funded without benefit of any taxpayer-assisted dollars. This statutory scheme, which the majority noted [17] and which the concurring opinion expressly deemed crucial,[18] should be regarded as indispensable to the *Regan v. TWR* holding.[19]

Finally, cases might arise in which the option of setting up a separately funded lobbying arm poses serious independent difficulties. For example, telling broadcast licensees that they may engage in political editorializing without losing their public funding (as *FCC v. League of Women Voters* holds they must be permitted to do), but insisting that all of their political editorializing be cleanly separated from the rest of the programming—that there be a sharp division between culture and politics—would entail a problematic intrusion into those broadcasters' editorial discretion.[20] Even more severe constitutional problems would be posed by telling churches that they may retain their tax-exempt status under § 501(c)(3) only if they conduct all of their lobbying efforts through separately funded affiliates rather than from the pulpit.[21]

Whenever a problematic degree of governmental entanglement would be required to police such a division, the compromise solution approved in *Regan v. TWR* might be unavailable. A choice would then have to be made—a choice between (1) denying government the ability to restrict the use private recipients may make of public subsidies (thereby freeing some individuals or groups to lobby with public funds, for example), and (2) giving government that ability by denying recipients the opportunity to receive public subsidies without sacrificing their freedom to use private funds for exercise of private rights (thereby putting some to what would otherwise seem to be an unconstitutional choice).

15. See Cammarano v. United States, 358 U.S. 498 (1959).

16. For example, food stamp recipients surely could not be told they would be cut off and left to starve if they were to use other funds to try to influence the political process.

17. 461 U.S. at 544.

18. Id. at 552–53.

19. Cf. Babbitt v. Planned Parenthood of Arizona, 107 S.Ct. 391 (1986), aff'g Planned Parenthood of Central & Northern Arizona v. Arizona, 789 F.2d 1348 (9th Cir. 1986), discussed in note 3, supra.

20. See CBS v. FCC, 453 U.S. 367 (1981), discussed in § 12–25, infra.

21. See §§ 14–11, 14–14, infra.

Chapter 12

RIGHTS OF COMMUNICATION AND EXPRESSION

§ 12–1. The System of Free Expression

To speak of the "purposes" of the first amendment's protections of speech, press, assembly, petition, and (by implication) association,[1] is to risk begging the central question posed by the Constitution's most majestic guarantee: is the freedom of speech [2] to be regarded only as a means to some further end—like successful self-government, or social stability, or (somewhat less instrumentally) the discovery and dissemination of truth—or is freedom of speech in part also an end in itself, an expression of the sort of society we wish to become and the sort of persons we wish to be? No adequate conception of so basic an element of our fundamental law, it will be argued here, can be developed in purely instrumental or "purposive" terms.[3]

No doubt the most familiar theory of free speech gives it little beyond an instrumental role. Milton had evoked the happy image of truth and falsehood grappling "in a free and open encounter," [4] and Holmes followed suit in one of the most famous of his celebrated dissents: "Persecution for the expression of opinions seems to me perfectly logical. If you have no doubt of your premises and want a certain result with all your heart you naturally express your wishes in law and sweep away all opposition. . . . But when men have realized that time has upset many fighting faiths, they may come to believe even more than they believe the very foundations of their own conduct

---

§ 12–1

1. The complete text of the first amendment reads: "Congress shall make no law respecting an establishment of religion, or prohibiting the free exercise thereof; or abridging the freedom of speech, or of the press; or the right of the people peaceably to assemble, and to petition the Government for a redress of grievances." U.S. Const., amend. I.

Freedom of association is not mentioned in the constitutional text, but it is recognized at least as a derivative safeguard of an individual's rights of speech and assembly when exercised in a group. NAACP v. Alabama ex rel. Patterson, 357 U.S. 449 (1958). See § 12–26 infra.

2. Throughout this chapter, "freedom of speech" will be employed as shorthand for the entire collection of freedoms (other than those pertaining specifically to religion) secured from government interference by the first amendment. On religion, see Chapter 14, infra.

3. Attempts to develop a first amendment jurisprudence based on historical evidence regarding the intent of the framers have proven quite manipulable. Compare L. Levy, Legacy of Suppression: Freedom of Speech and Press in Early American History (1960) (contending that the framers had no meaningful experience with freedom of expression and understood it to mean no more than freedom from prior restraint), with L. Levy, Emergence of a Free Press xi (1985) (revising earlier views; for example, "Americans respected freedom of expression far more than theoreticians and legalists acknowledged before 1798"). See generally, Anderson, Book Review: "Levy v. Levy," 84 Mich.L.Rev. 777 (1986).

4. Areopagitica, A Speech for the Liberty of Unlicensed Printing, To the Parliament of England (1644), in Prose Writings 23–38 (Everyman ed. 1927).

that the ultimate good desired is better reached by free trade in ideas—
that the best test of truth is the power of the thought to get itself
accepted in the competition of the market, and that truth is the only
ground upon which their wishes safely can be carried out. That at any
rate is the theory of our Constitution. . . . ."[5] This "marketplace of
ideas" argument for freedom of speech may at times serve liberty well,
but it relies too dangerously on metaphor for a theory that purports to
be more hard-headed than literary. How do we know that the analogy
of the market is an apt one? Especially when the wealthy have more
access to the most potent media of communication than the poor, how
sure can we be that "free trade in ideas" is likely to generate truth?[6]
And what of falsity: is not the right to differ about what *is* "the truth"
subtly endangered by a theory that perceives communication as no
more than a system of transactions for vanquishing what is false?[7]
What, finally, of speech as an expression of self? As a cry of impulse
no less than as a dispassionate contribution to intellectual dialogue?

Closely related to the "marketplace of ideas" theory but even
narrower in its reach and more preclusive in its implications has been
the view that free speech is protected by the first amendment as
essential to intelligent self-government in a democratic system. As
expounded by Alexander Meiklejohn, its most widely cited proponent,[8]
this theory would limit the special guarantees of the first amendment
to public discussion of issues of civic importance;[9] in exchange for
offering supposedly "absolute" protection[10] to a political category of
discourse, the theory would relegate to only minimal due-process protection[11] everything outside that category. When critics respond that
the "public issues" category is obviously far too narrow unless it
becomes almost infinitely expandable,[12] the theory—in the hands of all

5. Abrams v. United States, 250 U.S.
616, 630 (1919) (Holmes, J., joined by Brandeis, J., dissenting). See Rabban, "The
Emergence of Modern First Amendment
Doctrine," 50 U.Chi.L.Rev. 1205 (1983) (discussing the development of the views of
Zechariah Chafee, Oliver Wendell Holmes,
and Louis Brandeis): Holmes' original
views, expressed in Schenck v. United
States, 249 U.S. 47 (1919), were decidedly
not libertarian. Chafee, however, in
"Freedom of Speech in War Time," 32
Harv.L.Rev. 932 (1919), provided a convenient, although historically inaccurate,
framework that Holmes, and later Brandeis, ultimately adopted. See also Rogat &
O'Fallon, "Mr. Justice Holmes: A Dissenting Opinion—The Speech Cases," 36 Stan.
L.Rev. 1349 (1984).

6. For powerful critiques of the marketplace model, see Baker, "Scope of the First
Amendment Freedom of Speech," 25 U.C.
L.A.L.Rev. 964 (1978); Ingber, "The Marketplace of Ideas: A Legitimizing Myth,"
1984 Duke L.J. 1.

7. Compare New York Times v. Sullivan, 376 U.S. 254, 279 n. 19 (1964) ("Even a
false statement may be deemed to make a

valuable contribution to the public debate,
since it brings about 'the clearer perception and livelier impression of truth, produced by its collision with error,' " quoting
John Stuart Mill), with Gertz v. Robert
Welch, Inc., 418 U.S. 323, 340 (1974)
("there is no constitutional value in false
statements of fact"), discussed further in
§ 12–13, infra.

8. See A. Meiklejohn, Free Speech and
Its Relation to Self-Government (1948); A.
Meiklejohn, Political Freedom (1960). For
an early anticipation of Meiklejohn, see
Stromberg v. California, 283 U.S. 359, 369
(1931).

9. See, e.g., A. Meiklejohn 18–19, 22–27
(1948). All other "speech" would be protected only by substantive due process.

10. See Meiklejohn, "The First Amendment is an Absolute," 1961 Sup.Ct.Rev. 245
(1961).

11. That is, the same protection to
which such liberties as the freedom to contract or to go on a picnic are now entitled.

12. See, e.g., Chafee, Book Review, 62
Harv.L.Rev. 891, 900 (1949).

but its truest believers [13]—obligingly expands to encompass "novels and dramas and paintings and poems," [14] as well as even commercial information,[15] insofar as all of these may *indirectly* contribute to the sophistication and wisdom of the electorate. Yet when the theory has been thus expanded, it tells us disappointingly little. Indeed, in none of its forms does it tell us a great deal, since it takes for granted the *virtues* of the self-governance to which it argues that free speech is so necessary.

But once one asks *why* self-government and political participation are to be valued, one is apt to come to an answer that immediately suggests a broader ground for valuing freedom of speech itself, and hence a broader notion of what "speech" is to be protected. Theorists defending free speech as crucial to the polity in a representative system are inclined to respond to the "*why*" by arguing that political participation is valuable in part because it enhances personal growth and self-realization.[16] But if that is so, then do not those values themselves explain much of our commitment to freedom of speech without the intermediate step of the Meiklejohn thesis? And do they not explain it in terms broad enough to encompass the full sweep of expressional activity with far less strain? [17]

More generally, it must be said that Meiklejohn's conception of the first amendment, and Holmes', were both far too focused on intellect and rationality to accommodate the emotive role of free expression—its place in the evolution, definition, and proclamation of individual and group identity. Justice Harlan was to recognize in *Cohen v. California* [18] that expression "conveys not only ideas capable of relatively precise, detached explication, but otherwise inexpressible emotions as well." In holding constitutionally protected an act (wearing a jacket bearing the words "Fuck the Draft" into a courthouse corridor) that the dissent dismissed as "mainly conduct and little speech," [19] Justice Harlan's opinion for the majority implicitly rejected the hoary dichotomy between reason and desire that so often constricts the reach of the

---

13. See Bork, "Neutral Principles and Some First Amendment Problems," 47 Ind. L.J. 1, 20–35 (1971).

14. Meiklejohn, "The First Amendment is an Absolute," 1961 Sup.Ct.Rev. 245, 263 (1961). See also Abood v. Detroit Board of Education, 431 U.S. 209 (1977): "But our cases have never suggested that expression about philosophical, social, artistic, economic, literary, or ethical matters . . . is not entitled to full First Amendment protection." Id. at 231.

15. See Virginia Board of Pharmacy v. Virginia Consumer Council, 425 U.S. 748, 765 (1976) (information about drug prices must not be suppressed; it is vital not only to consumer choices in a market system but also "to the formation of intelligent opinions as to how that system ought to be regulated or altered").

16. See, e.g., J. S. Mill, Considerations on Representative Government 203 (1882). Cf. Muller, Issues of Freedom 50 (1960).

17. Many thinkers have grounded their defenses of free expression on notions of self-realization and self-fulfillment. See, e.g., R. Dworkin, Taking Rights Seriously (1977); M. Redish, Freedom of Expression: A Critical Analysis (1984); Baker, "Scope of the First Amendment Freedom of Speech," 25 U.C.L.A.L.Rev. 964 (1978); Redish, "The Value of Free Speech," 130 U.Pa.L.Rev. 591 (1982); Richards, "Free Speech and Obscenity Law: Toward a Moral Theory of the First Amendment," 123 U.Pa.L.Rev. 45 (1974). But critics have argued that speech is but one possible self-expressive activity—motorcycle riding might be another—and that therefore speech cannot claim a special status on that basis. See F. Schauer, Free Speech: A Philosophical Enquiry 47–72 (1982); Schauer, "Must Speech Be Special?", 78 Nw.U.L.Rev. 1284 (1983).

18. 403 U.S. 15, 26 (1971).

19. Id. at 27 (Blackmun, J., joined by Burger, C.J., and Black, J., dissenting).

first amendment. At least implicitly, the *Cohen* Court projected a more capacious image of the place occupied by free expression in our system, defending the "constitutional right of free expression" as "putting the decision as to what views shall be voiced largely into the hands of each of us, in the hope that use of such freedom will ultimately produce a more capable citizenry and more perfect polity and *in the belief that no other approach would comport with the premise of individual dignity and choice upon which our political system rests*." [20]

This broader vision was evoked nearly half a century earlier by Justice Brandeis' masterful concurrence in *Whitney v. California*: [21] "Those who won our independence believed that the final end of the State was to make men free to develop their faculties. . . . They valued liberty both as an end and as a means. They believed liberty to be the secret of happiness and courage to be the secret of liberty. . . ." Brandeis wisely went on to defend "freedom to think as you will and to speak as you think" as a "means indispensable to the discovery and spread of political truth" [22] and as essential both to "stable government" [23] and to "political change." [24] But he did not make the mistake of reducing freedom of speech to its instrumental role in the political system.

Those who defend freedom of speech as an end in itself and as a constitutive part of personal and group autonomy [25] at times err in the opposite direction, by forgetting that freedom of speech is also central to the workings of a tolerably responsive and responsible democracy and that at least some of the first amendment's most convincing implications follow directly from this perspective.[26] And even those who conceive the freedom of speech from the dual perspective of self-realization and political operation [27] occasionally err by defining "speech" itself in ways too confined and question-begging to fit comfortably the breadth of their theoretical justification for its special constitu-

20. Id. at 24 (emphasis added).

21. 274 U.S. 357, 375 (1927) (Brandeis, J., joined by Holmes, J., concurring).

22. Id.

23. Id.

24. Id. at 377.

25. See, e.g., Scanlon, "A Theory of Free Expression," 1 Phil. & Pub.Aff. 204 (1972).

26. Compare Scanlon, supra note 25, at 205–206, with Kalven, "The New York Times Case: A Note on 'The Central Meaning of the First Amendment,'" 1964 Sup. Ct.Rev. 191, 205 (1964) (deriving the Supreme Court's New York Times decision, discussed infra in § 12–12, from the core conviction "that defamation of the government is an impossible notion for a democracy"). See also Blasi, "The Checking Value in First Amendment Theory," 1977 Am. B. Found. Research J. 521, 593 (proposing that an important function of the first amendment is to restrain government;

newsgathering privileges, for example, might be justified on the theory that "the professional press [performs] a special watchdog function over public officials"). See § 12–22, infra. Cf. Schauer, "The Role of the People in First Amendment Theory," 74 Calif.L.Rev. 761, 780–82 (1986) (advocating "greater respect [in first amendment theory] for majoritarian decisions" that represent the popular will). For a broader theory linking the first amendment to the values of tolerance and diversity, see L. Bollinger, The Tolerant Society (1986) (arguing that the urge to suppress disagreeable speech is but one aspect of a more general desire to suppress all beliefs and behavior that appear to pose a threat to the established order, and that freedom of speech is important apart from any value of the speech itself, because it serves as a low-cost means of demonstrating and instilling habits of tolerance).

27. See, e.g., Emerson, The System of Freedom of Expression 6–7 (1970).

tional status, compensating for their generous notion of why speech merits protection by adopting an artificial dichotomy between (protected) speech-related conduct in which "expression" predominates and (unprotected) conduct in which "action" is dominant.[28]

No satisfactory jurisprudence of free speech can be built upon such partial or compromised notions of the bases for expressional protection or the boundaries of the conduct to be protected. However tempting it may be to resist governmental claims for restricting speech by retreating to an artificially narrowed zone and then defending it without limit, any such course is likely in the end to sacrifice too much to strategic maneuver: the claims for suppression will persist, and the defense will be no stronger for having withdrawn to arbitrarily constricted territory. Any adequate conception of freedom of speech must instead draw upon several strands of theory in order to protect a rich variety of expressional modes.[29]

§ 12–2. The Two Ways in Which Government Might "Abridge" Speech—And the Two Corresponding "Tracks" of First Amendment Analysis

Government can "abridge" speech in either of two ways. *First,* government can aim at ideas or information, in the sense of singling out actions for government control or penalty either (a) because of the specific message or viewpoint such actions express, or (b) because of the effects produced by awareness of the information or ideas such actions impart. Government punishment of publications critical of the state would illustrate (a),[1] as would government discharge of public employees found in possession of "subversive" literature.[2] Government prohibition of any act making consumers aware of the prices of over-the-counter drugs would illustrate (b),[3] as would a ban on the teaching of a foreign language[4] or a prohibition against discussing a political candidate on the last day of an election.[5] *Second,* without aiming at ideas or information in either of the above senses, government can constrict the flow of information and ideas while pursuing other goals, either (a) by limiting an activity through which information and ideas might be

28. See, e.g., Emerson, supra, note 27, at 80–89 (excluding certain expressional conduct as more dominantly "action" than "speech"), discussed in § 12–7, infra. Contrast Meiklejohn, Free Speech and its Relation to Self-Government 42–43 (1948).

29. See Shiffrin, "The First Amendment and Economic Regulation: Away From a General Theory of the First Amendment," 78 Nw.U.L.Rev. 1212 (1983).

§ 12–2

1. See, e.g., New York Times v. Sullivan, 376 U.S. 254, 276 (1964) (Sedition Act of 1798 unconstitutional) (dictum).

2. See, e.g., Keyishian v. Board of Regents, 385 U.S. 589 (1967) (invalidating statute barring teachers from employment in the schools merely on the basis of membership in "subversive" organizations).

For discussion of the free speech rights of public employees, see § 12–18, infra. Cf. Herndon v. Lowry, 301 U.S. 242 (1937) (literature taken from black organizer for Communist Party, advocating "equal rights for the Negroes and self-determination for the Black Belt" as well as unemployment compensation and social insurance, was wholly insufficient proof of attempt to incite an insurrection).

3. See, e.g., Virginia State Board of Pharmacy v. Virginia Citizens Consumer Council, Inc., 425 U.S. 748 (1976) (invalidating such a prohibition).

4. See, e.g., Meyer v. Nebraska, 262 U.S. 390 (1923) (invalidating such a ban).

5. See, e.g., Mills v. Alabama, 384 U.S. 214 (1966) (invalidating such a prohibition).

conveyed, or (b) by enforcing rules compliance with which might discourage the communication of ideas or information. Government prohibitions against loudspeakers in residential areas would illustrate (a).[6] Governmental demands for testimony before grand juries notwithstanding the desire of informants to remain anonymous would illustrate (b),[7] as would ceilings on campaign contributions.[8] The first form of abridgment may be summarized as encompassing government actions *aimed at communicative impact*; the second, as encompassing government actions *aimed at noncommunicative impact* but nonetheless having adverse effects on communicative opportunity.[9]

Any adverse government action aimed at communicative impact is presumptively at odds with the first amendment. For if the constitutional guarantee means anything, it means that, ordinarily at least, "government has no power to restrict expression because of its message, its ideas, its subject matter, or its content . . .".[10] And if the constitutional guarantee is not to be trivialized, it must mean that government cannot justify restrictions on free expression by reference to the adverse consequences of allowing certain ideas or information to enter the realm of discussion and awareness.[11] Whatever might in theory be said either way, the choice between "the dangers of suppressing information

6. See, e.g., Kovacs v. Cooper, 336 U.S. 77 (1949) (upholding such prohibitions).

7. See, e.g., Branzburg v. Hayes, 408 U.S. 665 (1972) (upholding such demands).

8. See, e.g., Buckley v. Valeo, 424 U.S. 1 (1976) (per curiam) (upholding such ceilings, but invalidating ceilings on campaign expenditures).

9. See Ely, "Flag Desecration: A Case Study in the Roles of Categorization and Balancing in First Amendment Analysis," 88 Harv.L.Rev. 1482 (1975); Scanlon, "A Theory of Freedom of Expression," 1 Phil. & Pub.Aff. 204 (1972); Nimmer, "The Meaning of Symbolic Speech Under the First Amendment," 21 U.C.L.A.L.Rev. 29 (1973).

10. Police Department of the City of Chicago v. Mosley, 408 U.S. 92, 95–96 (1972) (ordinance prohibiting picketing in the vicinity of school held invalid because, in allowing exception for labor union picketing, the state had not been content-neutral). Although the Court has sometimes declared that the first amendment almost completely prohibits governmental regulation of speech because of its content, this is ultimately an untenable position, at least descriptively—witness the Court's doctrines in the areas of defamation, see §§ 12–12, 12–13, infra, obscenity, see § 12–16, infra, and commercial speech, see § 12–15, infra. See also Finzer v. Barry, 798 F.2d 1450, 1468 (D.C. Cir. 1986) (commenting that "a total ban on content-based restrictions of any sort" would require that first amendment law be "revolutionized"),

cert. granted sub nom. Boos v. Barry, 107 S.Ct. 1282 (1987) (No. 86–803); Note, "Content Regulation and the Dimensions of Free Expression," 96 Harv.L.Rev. 1854, 1856 n. 15 (1983).

11. See Virginia State Board of Pharmacy v. Virginia Citizens Consumer Council, Inc., 425 U.S. 748 (1976) (statute which prohibited advertising of drug prices by pharmacists, ostensibly to maintain professional standards among pharmacists by suppressing price competition, held invalid because the state's goal was achieved "by keeping people in ignorance"); Central Hudson Gas & Elec. v. Public Service Comm'n., 447 U.S. 557, 581 (1980) (Stevens, J., concurring in judgment) (striking down, as violative of the first amendment, order of state utility commission which prohibited public utilities from advertising to promote the use of electricity; "[t]he justification for the regulation is nothing more than the expressed fear that the audience may find the utility's message persuasive"). But see Posadas de Puerto Rico Associates v. Tourism Co. of Puerto Rico, 106 S.Ct. 2968, 2978 (1986) (upholding Puerto Rican statute which prohibited the advertisement of gambling casinos to the population of Puerto Rico while permitting advertising aimed outside Puerto Rico; majority found that such advertising could be regulated in order to prevent local residents from engaging in lawful but "potentially harmful conduct"). Whether Posadas may be reconciled with contemporary free speech doctrine is discussed in § 12–15, infra.

and the dangers of its misuse if it is freely available" is, ultimately, a choice "that the First Amendment makes for us." [12]

A government action belonging to the second category is of a different order altogether. If it is thought intolerable for government to ban all distribution of handbills in order to combat litter,[13] for example, the objection must be that the values of free expression are more important constitutionally than those of clean streets at low cost; if a ban on noisy picketing in a hospital zone is acceptable, the reason must be that the harmful consequences of this particular form of expressive behavior, quite apart from any ideas it might convey, outweigh the good.[14] Where government aims at the noncommunicative impact of an act, the correct result in any particular case thus reflects some "balancing" of the competing interests;[15] regulatory choices aimed at harms not caused by ideas or information as such are acceptable so long as they do not *unduly* constrict the flow of information and ideas.[16] In such cases, the first amendment does not make the choice, but instead requires a "thumb" on the scale to assure that the balance struck in any particular situation properly reflects the central position of free expression in the constitutional scheme.[17]

The Supreme Court has evolved two distinct approaches to the resolution of first amendment claims; the two correspond to the two ways in which government may "abridge" speech.[18] If a government regulation is aimed at the communicative impact of an act, analysis should proceed along what we will call *track one*. On that track, a regulation is unconstitutional unless government shows that the message being suppressed poses a "clear and present danger," constitutes a

---

12. Virginia Board, 425 U.S. at 770. See § 12–15, infra.

13. See Schneider v. State, 308 U.S. 147 (1939) (purpose of keeping streets clean insufficient to justify an ordinance which prohibits all public distribution of handbills).

14. See Grayned v. Rockford, 408 U.S. 104 (1972) (upholding validity of ordinance which barred noisy demonstrations on streets abutting schools while classes were in session).

15. See Scanlon, "A Theory of Freedom of Expression," supra note 9, at 222. See also Konigsberg v. State Bar of California, 366 U.S. 36, 50–51 (1961) (Harlan, J.) ("general regulatory statutes, not intended to control the content of speech but incidentally limiting its unfettered exercise, have not been regarded as the type of law the First or Fourteenth Amendment forbade . . ., when they have been found justified by subordinating valid governmental interests, a prerequisite to constitutionality which has necessarily involved a weighing of the governmental interest involved").

16. See Cox v. New Hampshire, 312 U.S. 569, 574 (1941) (upholding ordinance requiring parade permits where official discretion

was limited exclusively to considerations of time, place, and manner): "[T]he question in a particular case is whether [a] control is exerted so as not to *deny* or *unwarrantedly* abridge the right of assembly and the opportunities for the communication of thought . . . ." (emphasis added). See also San Francisco Arts & Athletics, Inc. v. United States Olympic Committee, 107 S.Ct. 2971, 2981 (1987) (applying track-two analysis to Congress' assignment of "Olympic" trademark preventing group organizing Gay Olympics from using that term).

17. The phrase is Professor Kalven's. See "The Concept of the Public Forum: Cox v. Louisiana," 1965 Sup.Ct.Rev. 1, 28.

18. The Court has long recognized that government may "abridge" speech in distinct ways requiring distinct judicial methods. See, e.g., Konisberg v. State Bar of California, 366 U.S. 36, 49–51 (1961). Even Justice Black distinguished "direct" abridgments which the first amendment absolutely prohibited from "indirect" abridgments whose constitutionality is tested by balancing the competing interests. See Freund, "Mr. Justice Black and the Judicial Function," 14 U.C.L.A.L.Rev. 467, 471–72 (1967).

defamatory falsehood, or otherwise falls on the unprotected side of one of the lines the Court has drawn to distinguish those expressive acts privileged by the first amendment from those open to government regulation with only minimal due process scrutiny. If a government regulation is aimed at the noncommunicative impact of an act, its analysis proceeds on what we will call *track two*. On that track, a regulation is constitutional, even as applied to expressive conduct, so long as it does not unduly constrict the flow of information and ideas. On track two, the "balance" between the values of freedom of expression and the government's regulatory interests is struck on a case-by-case basis, guided by whatever unifying principles may be articulated.

A recurring debate in first amendment jurisprudence has been whether first amendment rights are "absolute" in the sense that government may not "abridge" them at all, or whether the first amendment requires the "balancing" of competing interests in the sense that free speech values and the government's competing justifications must be isolated and weighed in each case.[19] The two poles of this debate are best understood as corresponding to the two approaches, track one and track two; on the first, the absolutists essentially prevail; on the second, the balancers are by and large victorious. While the "absolutes"—"balancing" controversy may have been "unfortunate, misleading and unnecessary,"[20] it has generated several important observations. First, the "balancers" are right in concluding that it is impossible to escape the task of weighing the competing considerations. Although only the case-by-case approach of track two takes the form of an explicit evaluation of the importance of the governmental interests said to justify each challenged regulation, similar judgments underlie the categorical definitions on track one.[21] Any exclusion of a class of activities from first amendment safeguards represents an implicit conclusion that the governmental interests in regulating those activities are such as to justify whatever limitation is thereby placed on the free expression of ideas. Thus, determinations of the reach of first amend-

19. First amendment "balancing" in the manner of the second Justice Harlan is discussed by Gunther, "In Search of Judicial Quality on a Changing Court: The Case of Justice Powell," 24 Stan.L.Rev. 1001 (1972). First amendment "absolutes" in the manner of Justice Black are discussed by Kalven, "Upon Rereading Mr. Justice Black on the First Amendment," 14 U.C.L.A.L.Rev. 428 (1967). The "absolutes"—"balancing" controversy generated an extensive literature which the reader can sample in the Mendelson-Frantz debate. See Mendelson, "On the Meaning of the First Amendment: Absolutes in the Balance," 50 Calif.L.Rev. 821 (1962); Frantz, "The First Amendment in the Balance," 71 Yale L.J. 1424 (1962); Frantz, "Is the First Amendment Law?—A Reply to Professor Mendelson," 51 Calif.L.Rev. 729 (1963); Mendelson, "The First Amendment and the Judicial Process: A Reply to Mr. Frantz," 17 Vand.L.Rev. 479 (1964). See

also, Baker, "Unreasoned Reasonableness: Mandatory Parade Permits and Time, Place, and Manner Restrictions," 78 Nw. U.L.Rev. 937 (1983) (advocating an "absolutist" rather than a "reasonableness" or balancing theory).

20. Kalven, "Upon Rereading Mr. Justice Black on the First Amendment," supra note 19, at 442–44: "But the whole balancing 'war' seems to me to have been a fruitless one, generating on the one hand an unnecessary philosophic debate and obscuring on the other by its large rhetoric, a hard technical free speech issue."

21. Nimmer expresses this thought in the term "definitional" balancing. See "The Right to Speak from Time to Time," 56 Calif.L.Rev. 935, 942 (1968). See also Mendelson, "The First Amendment and the Judicial Process: A Reply to Mr. Frantz," 17 Vand.L.Rev. 479, 481–83 (1964).

ment protections on either track presuppose some form of "balancing" whether or not they appear to do so. The question is whether the "balance" should be struck for all cases in the process of framing particular categorical definitions, or whether the "balance" should be calibrated anew on a case-by-case basis.[22]

The "absolutists" may well have been right in believing that their approach was better calculated to protect freedoms of expression, especially in times of crisis.[23] If the judicial branch is to protect dissenters from a majority's tyranny, it cannot be satisfied with a process of review that requires a court to assess after each incident a myriad of facts, to guess at the risks created by expressive conduct, and to assign a specific value to the hard-to-measure worth of particular instances of free expression.[24] The results of any such process of review will be some "famous victories" for the cause of free expression, but will leave no one very sure that any particular expressive act will find a constitutional shield.[25] When the Supreme Court draws categorical lines, creating rules of privilege defined in terms of a few factors largely independent of context, judicial authority speaks directly to the legislature by means of a facial examination of laws without regard to the context in which they are applied.[26] And categorical rules, by drawing clear lines, are usually less open to manipulation because they leave less room for the prejudices of the factfinder to insinuate themselves into a decision.[27] The jury after all is a majoritarian institution,[28] and

22. For a discussion of the debate over whether the balance should be struck on an ad hoc or categorical basis, see Schauer, "Categories and the First Amendment: A Play in Three Acts," 34 Vand.L.Rev. 265 (1983); Schlag, "An Attack on Categorical Approaches to Freedom of Speech," 30 U.C. L.A.L.Rev. 671 (1983). For an "eclectic" approach that relies on several different styles of balancing, see Shiffrin, "The First Amendment and Economic Regulation: Away From a General Theory of the First Amendment," 78 Nw.U.L.Rev. 1212, 1251–53 (1983). See also § 12–18, infra.

23. See L. Bollinger, The Tolerant Society (1986) (arguing that protecting free expression can instill values of tolerance in the citizenry); Blasi, "The Pathological Perspective and the First Amendment," 85 Colum.L.Rev. 449, 449–50 (1985) (proposing that the first amendment should be equipped "to do maximum service in those historical periods when intolerance of unorthodox ideas is most prevalent and when governments are most able and most likely to stifle dissent systematically. The first amendment, in other words, should be targeted for the worst of times."); Ely, "Flag Desecration: A Case Study in the Roles of Categorization and Balancing in First Amendment Analysis," 88 Harv.L. Rev. 1482, 1500–1502 (1975).

24. See Gertz v. Robert Welch, Inc., 418 U.S. 323, 343–44 (1974) (Powell, J.): To scrutinize and weigh the competing inter-

ests in every libel case "would lead to unpredictable results and uncertain expectations, and it could render our duty to supervise the lower courts unmanageable . . . [W]e must lay down broad rules of general application."

25. See Note, "The First Amendment Overbreadth Doctrine," 83 Harv.L.Rev. 844, 865–871 (1970).

26. See Linde, " 'Clear and Present Danger' Reexamined: Dissonance in the Brandenberg Concerto," 22 Stan.L.Rev. 1163, 1174–1182 (1970) (arguing that the first amendment should be seen as directed at the legislative process of "making a law" so as to prevent legislators from writing laws directed in terms against speech).

27. See Ely, supra note 23, at 1501.

28. Because much of the present importance of the first amendment lies in protecting unpopular speech, it is doubtful that "the jury is a reliable factfinder in free speech cases. The jury may be an adequate reflector of the community's conscience, but that conscience is not and never has been very tolerant of dissent." Monaghan, "First Amendment Due Process," 83 Harv.L.Rev. 518, 529 (1970). The problem of jury insensitivity to first amendment values has repeatedly arisen in the defamation cases. See, e.g., Gertz v. Robert Welch, Inc., 418 U.S. 323, 349–50 (1974) (common law doctrines of presumed and punitive damages in defamation ac-

judges historically have been drawn from more conservative groups. Categorical rules thus tend to protect the system of free expression better because they are more likely to work in spite of the defects in the human machinery on which we must rely to preserve fundamental liberties. The balancing approach is contrastingly a slippery slope; once an issue is seen as a matter of degree, first amendment protections become especially reliant on the sympathetic administration of the law.

On track two, when government does not seek to suppress any idea or message as such, there seems little escape from this quagmire of ad hoc judgment, although a few categorical rules are possible.[29] But on track one, when the government's concern is with message content, it has proven both possible and necessary to proceed categorically.[30]

§ 12–3. Separating Content-Based Abridgments from Those Independent of Expressive Content: Getting Onto Track One

Government may be deemed to have "abridged" speech in the first sense, thus triggering track-one analysis,[1] if *on its face* a governmental action is targeted at ideas or information that government seeks to suppress,[2] or if a governmental action neutral on its face was *motivated* by (i.e., would not have occurred but for) an intent to single out constitutionally protected speech for control or penalty.[3] Of course, the target of government action will be instantly recognizable if the government openly admits that its purpose is limiting information or suppressing an idea, but government will ordinarily defend a restriction on free expression by reference to some danger beyond the speech itself— often, by invoking the permissive talisman of "time, place, or manner" regulation.[4] Any inference that government's aim is keeping people

tions impermissibly leave juries with uncontrolled discretion to award damages bearing no relation to actual injuries and thereby selectively punish expressions of unpopular views), discussed in § 12–13, infra.

29. See, e.g., § 12–23, infra.

30. See §§ 12–8 to 12–19, infra.

§ 12–3

1. See § 12–2, supra.

2. See, e.g., Virginia State Board of Pharmacy v. Virginia Citizens Consumer Council, Inc., 425 U.S. 748 (1976) (statute singling out information about drug prices); Cohen v. California, 403 U.S. 15 (1971) (statute singling out offensive conduct, applied to offensive language); Brandenburg v. Ohio, 395 U.S. 444 (1969) (statute singling out advocacy of the doctrines of criminal syndication). In each of these cases, the Court determined that the limit on speech was invalid upon finding that government could not justify the regulation by reference to "an important or substantial governmental interest [that] is unrelated to the suppression of free expression. . . ." United States v. O'Brien, 391 U.S. 367, 377 (1968). The O'Brien opinion, upholding a law against draft-card destruction, defined this test in the course of distinguishing the case from Stromberg v. California, 283 U.S. 359 (1931): "The case at bar is therefore unlike one where the alleged governmental interest in regulating conduct arises in some measure because the communication allegedly integral to the conduct is itself thought to be harmful. In Stromberg v. California . . ., for example, this Court struck down a statutory phrase which punished people who expressed their 'opposition to organized government' by displaying 'any flag, badge, banner, or device.'" 391 U.S. at 382.

3. See § 12–5, infra.

4. See, e.g., Tinker v. Des Moines School District, 393 U.S. 503 (1969), where the state sought to justify a "place" regulation (forbidding the wearing of armbands in school as a protest against the war) on the basis of the reaction which it engendered. See id. at 526 (Harlan, J., dissenting). John Ely, in "Flag Desecration: A Case Study in the Roles of Categorization and Balancing in First Amendment Analy-

ignorant of ideas or information that it considers dangerous must normally be made in the first instance from the face of the statute.

The notion that the first amendment protects the free flow of ideas and information leads to the conclusion that the amendment's guarantees, on track one at least, apply to the speech involved, and not just to the source. The central teaching of the Court's decision in *First National Bank of Boston v. Bellotti*,[5] striking down a state ban on corporate advocacy, is that the first amendment protects speech whether or not it protects the particular speaker.[6]

The Massachusetts statute invalidated in *First National Bank* represented a bold attempt to silence corporate opposition to a proposed constitutional amendment authorizing the state legislature to impose a graduated individual income tax. The law forbade certain categories of corporations [7] to expend funds to communicate their views about any referendum subject that did not materially affect the corporate business.[8] To be sure that the courts would not miss its point, the legislature further specified that a ballot question concerning the taxation of individuals was deemed not to affect materially the business of any corporation.[9] The law thus identified a particular issue and silenced a particular class of speakers with regard to it. Few restrictions could be more offensive to a norm of viewpoint-neutrality than the government "dictating the subjects about which persons may speak and the speakers who may address a public issue." [10]

The Court's analysis emphasized that the interests of the potential audience are independent of the identity of the speaker. The rights at stake were those of Massachusetts' voters to information that would enable them to evaluate the merits of the referendum issue, and the

sis," 88 Harv.L.Rev. 1482, 1498 (1975), rightly stresses that "what sort of regulation it really is" is irrelevant, as well as unintelligible. The critical inquiry is whether the state chooses to (or must) *justify* the regulation by reference to dangers that flow from an act's communicative content.

5. 435 U.S. 765 (1978). Justice Powell delivered the opinion of the Court, in which Chief Justice Burger and Justices Stewart, Blackmun, and Stevens joined. The Chief Justice also filed a concurring opinion. Justice White dissented, joined by Justices Brennan and Marshall. Justice Rehnquist filed a separate dissenting opinion.

6. See, e.g., Lamont v. Postmaster General, 381 U.S. 301 (1965) (receipt of mail protected; source was outside U.S. and hence unprotected); Stanley v. Georgia, 394 U.S. 557 (1969) (possession in home protected; source was vendor of obscene material and hence unprotected). The Court did *not* decide in First National Bank that corporations have first amendment rights; it reserved that question. 435 U.S. at 777 & n. 13. The Court decided only that otherwise protected speech does not lose its constitutional shield simply because its source is a corporation. See also Consolidated Edison Co. v. Public Serv. Comm'n. of New York, 447 U.S. 530, 533–34 (1980); Schneider, "Free Speech and Corporate Freedom: A Comment on First National Bank of Boston v. Bellotti," 59 S.Cal.L.Rev. 1227 (1986) (criticizing the decision as a product of a "new formalism" in Supreme Court jurisprudence).

7. Essentially, only banks and business corporations were covered. The law did not apply to non-profit corporations, various trusts, labor unions, or associations. 435 U.S. at 785, 793. The Massachusetts Supreme Judicial Court subsequently held that the law was also intended to ban all referendum advocacy through expenditures by municipal or other public corporations, and upheld this construction. Anderson v. Boston, 376 Mass. 178, 380 N.E.2d 628 (1978), motion to vacate stay order denied, 439 U.S. 951 (1978), appeal dismissed, 439 U.S. 1060 (1979).

8. Mass. Gen. Laws Ch. 55 § 8.

9. 435 U.S. at 769–70 n. 3.

10. Id. at 785.

"[t]he inherent worth of the speech in terms of its capacity for informing the public does not depend upon the identity of its source, whether corporation, association, union, or individual." [11] The state could infringe these rights only upon a showing—here absent—that its law was both necessary and narrowly tailored to serve a "compelling" state interest.[12] While the view that corporate speech is constitutionally protected remains controversial,[13] it is difficult to reject the principle, endorsed by *First National Bank*, that first amendment analysis must focus on the speech itself and not only on the speaker, and that speaker-based restrictions on speech may amount to impermissible censorship of the flow of ideas and information regarding the relevant set of listeners even if the speakers subject to restriction cannot complain that *their* rights as speakers have been violated.[14]

11. Id. at 777.

12. Id. at 786. The Court voiced no doubt about the legitimacy of the state's interest in preventing corporations from exerting undue influence on the outcome of the referendum, id. at 788–89, but held that the state could not simply *assume* that corporate expenditures would distort the referendum process. Id. at 789–92. In Citizens Against Rent Control v. Berkeley, 454 U.S. 290 (1981), the Court similarly struck down on first amendment grounds a law limiting to $250 the amount of contributions that any person could make to support advocacy on a ballot measure and prohibiting organizations from receiving contributions that would cause a person to exceed his $250 limit. See also Buckley v. Valeo, 424 U.S. 1 (1976) (per curiam) (concluding that limitations on campaign contributions and expenditures reduce the quantity of political speech and thus warrant exacting first amendment scrutiny; the Court upheld contribution limits but struck down regulations on expenditures), discussed in § 13–27, infra.

13. See Pacific Gas & Elec. v. Public Utility Comm'n. of California, 106 S.Ct. 903, 920–22 (1986) (Rehnquist, J., dissenting) (attacking the majority's holding that corporate entities retain first amendment rights not to serve as vehicles for speech on important matters of public policy, where state public utility commission ordered utility to place newsletter of consumer rate-payer organization in its monthly billing envelope); Central Hudson Gas & Elec. v. Public Service Comm'n., 447 U.S. 557, 584 (1980) (Rehnquist, J., dissenting) (state rule prohibited electric utility from advertising to promote the use of electricity; "I disagree with the majority's conclusion that the speech of a state-created monopoly, which is the subject of a comprehensive regulatory scheme, is entitled to protection under the First Amendment"); Brudney, "Business Corporations and Stockholders' Rights Under the First Amendment," 91

Yale L.J. 235, 236 (1981) (arguing that constitutional protection for corporate speech "could significantly reduce the regulatory power of government over an institution whose existence is uniquely a function of government authorization, whose power and wealth often far exceed those of the government that created it, and that has long been a subject of pervasive government regulation"). Professor Brudney contends that the number of shareholders who disagree with the political expenditures of management "is not trivial." Id. at 237. The power of the state to forbid the corporation from making wasteful expenditures, whether on speech or other activities, is necessary to protect the property interest of stockholders. "A's right to receive information does not require the state to permit B to steal from C the funds that will enable B to make the communication." Id. at 247. Brudney therefore recommends a government requirement of unanimous stockholder consent for noncommercial corporate speech. See also Abood v. Detroit Bd. of Education, 431 U.S. 209 (1977) (invalidating state rule which permitted collective bargaining agreements with state employees including mandatory contributions for union political speech).

14. To be sure, the Court has upheld *some* speaker-based restrictions. A state may, for example, constitutionally enjoin labor unions from engaging in picketing, strikes, and boycotts as long as it has a rational basis for doing so. See, e.g., Teamsters, Local 695 v. Vogt, Inc., 354 U.S. 284 (1957) (upholding injunction against picketing because under state law the union's strategy of coercion amounted to an "unlawful purpose"); NLRB v. Retail Store Employees Union, Local 1001 (Safeco Title Ins. Co.), 447 U.S. 607 (1980) (upholding NLRB order that prohibited union from engaging in a secondary boycott which threatened the economic viability of third parties). See also Pope, "The Three-Systems Ladder of First Amendment Values:

A series of seven hypothetical cases, six dealt with in this section and a seventh in § 12–4, may clarify the inferential process that is required in determining whether to classify a government measure as designed to suppress particular ideas or categories of information.

Compare these ordinances:

(1) A misdemeanor to affix on a government building any sign expressing opposition to former governors of Georgia, and

Two Rungs and a (Labor) Black Hole," 11 Hast.Con.L.Q. 189 (1984); Note, "Peaceful Labor Picketing and the First Amendment," 82 Colum.L.Rev. 1469 (1982). The Court has also upheld limits on speech by management in a union representation election campaign. See, e.g., NLRB v. Gissel Packing Co., 395 U.S. 575, 616 (1969) (upholding NLRB finding of an unfair labor practice where management communications were cast as a threat of retaliatory action and not as a prediction of "demonstrable economic consequences"); NLRB v. Exchange Parts Co., 375 U.S. 405, 409 (1964) (upholding NLRB decision to set aside an election where several weeks before the representation election a company had sent its employees a letter that mentioned several new benefits; "the danger inherent in well-timed increases is the suggestion of a fist inside the velvet glove"). See J. Getman, S. Goldberg & J. Herman, Union Representation Elections: Law & Reality (1976) (contending that representation campaign speech has negligible effect on the outcome of the election); Getman, "Labor Law and Free Speech: The Curious Policy of Limited Expression," 43 Md.L. Rev. 4 (1984) (criticizing restrictions on both union and employer speech); Posner, "The Constitution As Mirror: Tribe's Constitutional Choices," 84 Mich.L.Rev. 551, 564 (1986) (noting the parallel nature of restrictions on labor and management speech). Similar activities conducted by organizations other than unions or management would enjoy first amendment protection. Compare NAACP v. Claiborne Hardware Co., 458 U.S. 886 (1982) (finding economic civil rights boycott protected by the first amendment), with Int'l Longshoremen's Ass'n v. Allied Int'l, 456 U.S. 212 (1982) (political boycott by labor union is not protected expression).

In some contexts, the Court has invalidated challenged restrictions on speech without addressing the speaker-based inequalities implicit in those restrictions. See, e.g., Consolidated Edison Co. v. Public Service Comm'n, 447 U.S. 530 (1980) (striking down Commission rule that prohibited public utilities, but not other companies, from including inserts in monthly billing envelopes); Village of Schaumburg v. Citizens for a Better Environment, 444 U.S. 620 (1980) (invalidating municipal ordinance restricting solicitation by charities that did not use 75 percent of their receipts for "charitable purposes"). But the Court has upheld, after highly deferential review, arrangements that confer benefits and subsidies on selected speakers. See, e.g., Regan v. Taxation With Representation, 461 U.S. 540 (1983) (sustaining the constitutionality of federal statute which provided that contributions made to support political lobbying by tax-exempt veterans organizations were tax deductible, but which denied deductions for contributions to any other tax-exempt organization that engaged in political lobbying), discussed further in § 11–5, supra; Perry Education Association v. Perry Local Educators' Association, 460 U.S. 37, 49 (1983) (upholding exclusive access of certified teacher union to interschool mail system; characterizing the distinction as one based on "the *status* of the unions rather than their views," the majority noted that "[i]mplicit in the concept of the nonpublic forum [see § 12–24, infra] is the right to make distinctions in access on the basis of subject matter and speaker identity"). It is not always possible to distinguish government actions which confer benefits on some speakers and not on others from those which actively punish selected viewpoints. See Perry, 460 U.S. at 65 (Brennan, J., joined by Marshall, Powell, and Stevens, JJ., dissenting) (" '[t]he access policy adopted by the Perry schools, in form a speaker restriction, favors a particular viewpoint on labor relations in the Perry schools . . .: the teachers inevitably will receive from [the certified union] self-laudatory descriptions of its activities on their behalf and will be denied the critical perspective offered by [the rival union]' ") (quoting Perry Local Educators' Association v. Hohlt, 652 F.2d 1286, 1296 (7th Cir. 1981)). Indeed, in many situations, speaker identity may serve as an accurate proxy for point of view. See Stone, "Content Regulation and the First Amendment," 25 Wm. & Mary L.Rev. 189, 249 (1983) (suggesting the example of laws denying tax deductions to individuals who contribute to the Nazi Party).

(2) A misdemeanor to affix on a government building any object not readily removable.

Both ordinances might abridge speech. The difference between the two is that the first is directed at consequences that occur only when messages critical of certain former governors are communicated, while the second is directed at the impact of acts affecting government property without regard to the content of any message those acts might convey, and, indeed, without regard to whether the acts in fact convey *any* message. Because the first is aimed at the communicative impact of the conduct proscribed, it will be unconstitutional unless the government shows that the message triggering the regulation presents a "clear and present danger" or is otherwise unprotected by the first amendment. Because the second is aimed at the noncommunicative impact of conduct, it is constitutional, even as applied to an author of political graffiti, as long as attaching posters to government buildings is not thought vital—as it might be, for example, in the People's Republic of China—to the flow of information and ideas.[15]

The Court applies the "most exacting scrutiny"[16] to regulations that discriminate among instances of speech based on its content.[17]

15. Cf. City Council of the City of Los Angeles v. Taxpayers for Vincent, 466 U.S. 789 (1984) (upholding municipal rule that forbade the posting of signs on public property, where the effect was to prevent a political candidate from posting campaign signs on utility poles), discussed in § 12–24, infra; Clark v. Community for Creative Non-Violence, 468 U.S. 288 (1984) (upholding National Park Service anti-camping regulations, as applied to protesters attempting to call attention to the plight of the homeless by sleeping outside in a park across from the White House).

16. Widmar v. Vincent, 454 U.S. 263, 276 (1981) (exclusion of religious speech from public forum violates first amendment). See also Police Department of the City of Chicago v. Mosley, 408 U.S. 92 (1972) (invalidating law which exempted labor picketing from general ban on picketing near schools).

17. The Court has recently added an ill-advised dimension to the determination of whether a restriction is based on "content". In City of Renton v. Playtime Theatres, Inc., 106 S.Ct. 925 (1986), the Court upheld a zoning ordinance which prohibited adult theaters from locating within 1,000 feet of any residential zone, dwelling, church, park, or school. The Court explained that, while the ordinance on its face "treats theaters that specialize in adult films differently from other kinds of theaters," it was *aimed* not at the content *per se* of the films, "but rather at the *secondary effects* of such theatres on the surrounding community." 106 S.Ct. at 929. It was therefore "completely consistent with our definition of 'content-neutral'

speech regulations as those that 'are *justified* without reference to the content of the regulated speech.'" Id., quoting Virginia State Bd. of Pharmacy v. Virginia Citizens Consumer Council, Inc., 425 U.S. 748, 771 (1976) (emphasis added in Renton). The Court thus found that, despite the restriction's outward appearance, it was not content-*based*, because the government chose to *defend* the rule with reasons other than its impact on the minds of listeners. Carried to its logical conclusion, the doctrine could gravely erode first amendment protections. See, e.g., Finzer v. Barry, 798 F.2d 1450, 1469–70 n. 15 (D.C. Cir. 1986) (describing as content-neutral a statute that prohibited the display of signs *critical* of a foreign government within 500 feet of that government's embassy, while permitting *all* pro-government demonstrations), cert. granted sub nom. Boos v. Barry, 107 S.Ct. 1282 (1987). In dissent, Chief Judge Wald soundly warned, "If listeners' reaction to the content of speech is deemed to be a 'secondary' effect, then there is nothing left at all of the content-based distinction doctrine." 798 F.2d at 1480 n. 5 (Wald, C.J., dissenting). For a detailed critique of Barry, see 132 Cong.Rec. H 6503–06 (daily ed. Sept. 9, 1986) (remarks of Rep. Barney Frank (D. Mass.)). The guarantees of New York Times v. Sullivan, 376 U.S. 254 (1964) (heightened protection accorded to writings about "public officials"), for example, might be eliminated on the ground that libel laws are directed not at the offending speech *per se*, or even at its impact on the minds of the speaker's audience, but rather on its indirect results—on the pain or humiliation that the audience's likely

Such restrictions are valid only if "necessary to serve a compelling state interest and . . . narrowly drawn to that end." [18]

> (3) A misdemeanor to mutilate the U.S. flag that Francis Scott Key observed over Fort McHenry while composing the "Star Spangled Banner."

This statute is the least restrictive means for preserving a specific national monument; it is independent of any message conveyed by a mutilator. If the government can preserve the fort, it can preserve the flag.[19] Of course, a vandal in this case may well intend the disfigurement of the Fort McHenry flag to express contempt for government, and any audience may well perceive the act as communicative. But the Court in *United States v. O'Brien* expressly rejected an approach which would key the constitutional analysis of conduct to whether "the person engaging in the conduct intends thereby to express an idea." [20] It cannot be concluded that the first amendment is irrelevant to a vandal's expressive behavior, but only that the right to express one's point of view in a way that mutilates the Fort McHenry flag or otherwise creates a harm unrelated to the message expressed may yield, and surely would yield in this case, to the government's interest in preserving a rare historical object.

> (4) A misdemeanor to wear or hold a U.S. flag while speaking critically of the United States.

This statute aims purely at the message conveyed; unless the conduct expresses a critical view of the United States, the conduct is allowed. The statute is thus like the law invalidated in the famous red flag case, *Stromberg v. California*,[21] where the Court struck down a state's attempt to ban flying of a red flag in symbolic opposition to organized government. The statute is also like the law voided in *Schacht v. United States*,[22] in which Congress had prohibited unauthorized wearing of army uniforms in a manner calculated to discredit the armed forces.

The hypothetical statute imposes an impermissible restriction on speech depending on its viewpoint. By allowing only speech in favor of American policy, the law results in a distortion of public debate that may be greater than if the law simply prohibited discussion of Ameri-

---

reactions cause to the subject. The Renton view will likely prove to be an aberration limited to the context of sexually explicit materials. On the same day the Court handed down that opinion, it also issued its decision in Pacific Gas & Elec. Co. v. Public Utilities Comm'n., 106 S.Ct. 903 (1986), which reaffirmed the more familiar content doctrine. "For a time, place, or manner regulation to be valid, it must be neutral as to the content of the speech to be regulated." Id. at 914.

18. Perry Education Ass'n v. Perry Local Educators' Ass'n, 460 U.S. 37, 45 (1983).

19. See Spence v. Washington, 418 U.S. 405, 409 (1974): "We have no doubt that the state or national governments constitutionally may forbid anyone from mishandling in any manner a flag that is public property".

20. 391 U.S. at 376. Nor is it enough to ask whether the act involved is likely to be perceived as conveying a message. See, e.g., Cohen v. California, 403 U.S. 15, 18 (1971); Note, "Symbolic Conduct," 68 Colum.L.Rev. 1091, 1109–1117 (1968). See § 12–7, infra.

21. 283 U.S. 359 (1931).

22. 398 U.S. 58 (1970) (invalidating the prohibition).

can policy altogether.[23] Viewpoint discrimination "is censorship in its purest form" [24] and has been traditionally subjected to the highest level of scrutiny.[25] Professor Kenneth Karst has suggested that the concept of equality among views "lies at the heart of the first amendment's protections against government regulation of the content of speech." [26] This doctrine may sometimes result, perhaps ironically, in the *reduced* protection of speech, since one method of "equalizing" is not to permit more speech but rather to adopt even more suppressive content-neutral regulations.[27] Under this approach, for example, the government may often "fare better by adopting a *more* restrictive means, a judicial incentive which [then-Justice Rehnquist] had thought this Court would hesitate to afford." [28]

> (5) A misdemeanor to display a U.S. flag with any extraneous material attached, even if the material is readily removable.

In *Spence v. Washington*,[29] the Court held such a law invalid, at least as applied in a case where the "extraneous material," there a peace symbol, was intended to express a specific message. Because the

23. Prohibition of expression about an entire subject, rather than merely a particular viewpoint or item of information, has been termed a "subject-matter" restriction. See Stone, "Restrictions of Speech Because of its Content: The Peculiar Case of Subject-Matter Restrictions," 46 U.Chi.L.Rev. 81, 83 (1978). The Court's decisions in this area are not models of consistency. See Stone, "Content Regulation and the First Amendment," 25 Wm. & Mary L.Rev. 189, 238–41 (1983). One problem arises in defining the relevant "subject matter." If defined sufficiently narrowly, a subject-matter restriction can closely approximate a viewpoint regulation. See, e.g., Greer v. Spock, 424 U.S. 828 (1976) (exclusion of political candidate seeking forum for speech from military base after some civilian speakers allowed; subject matter defined as any speech of a partisan political nature); Young v. American Mini Theatres, Inc., 427 U.S. 50 (1976) (zoning ordinance requiring dispersion of adult movie theaters; subject matter defined as nonobscene but sexually explicit movies). Faced with this ambiguity, one commentator has suggested that "the most prudent course is simply to test all subject-matter restrictions by the ordinarily stringent standards of content-based analysis." Stone, 46 U.Chi.L.Rev. at 114. See Consolidated Edison Co. v. Public Service Comm'n., 447 U.S. 530, 537 (1980) (opining that "[t]he First Amendment's hostility to content-based regulation extends not only to restrictions on particular viewpoints, but also to prohibition of public discussion of an entire topic"). See also Arkansas Writers' Project, Inc. v. Ragland, 107 S.Ct. 1722, 1728 (1987) (overturning state sales tax that taxed general interest magazines but exempted specialty journals such as profes-

sional, religious, and sports magazines and newspapers in a manner that discouraged discussion of particular *subjects*, although not necessarily advocacy of particular *views*). But see id. at 1732 (Scalia, J., joined by Rehnquist, C.J., dissenting) (disputing the argument that subject-matter distinctions are invalid and pointing to U.S. Postal Service rates which grant preferential treatment to religious, educational, scientific, philanthropic, agricultural, labor, veterans', and fraternal organizations; federal subsidies for the Kennedy Center, a performing arts theater; and governmental support for the Corporation of Public Broadcasting).

24. Perry Education Ass'n v. Perry Local Educators' Ass'n, 460 U.S. 37, 62 (1983) (Brennan, J., joined by Marshall, Powell, and Stevens, JJ. dissenting). Even when upholding restrictions on speech, the Court has been careful to insist that they do not involve viewpoint discrimination. See, e.g., Young v. American Mini Theatres, Inc., 427 U.S. 50, 67–68 (1976).

25. See Stephan, "The First Amendment and Content Discrimination," 68 Va. L.Rev. 203, 233 (1982).

26. Karst, "Equality as a Central Principle in the First Amendment," 43 U.Chi.L. Rev. 20, 21 (1975).

27. See Stone, "Content Regulation and the First Amendment," 25 Wm. & Mary L.Rev. 189, 205 (1983).

28. Carey v. Brown, 447 U.S. 455, 475 (1980) (Rehnquist, J., dissenting).

29. 418 U.S. 405 (1974) (per curiam). See also Cahn v. Long Island Vietnam Moratorium Committee, 418 U.S. 906 (1974), aff'g 437 F.2d 344 (2d Cir. 1970) (invalidating a similar New York statute).

"extraneous material" was readily removable and created no risk that viewers would think the government endorsed the message expressed,[30] the only interest government had left was the interest in preventing expression of Spence's symbolic protest against the Cambodian incursion and the Kent State tragedy.

> (6) A misdemeanor to destroy or permanently mutilate any object bearing the pattern of the U.S. flag on its surface.

On its face, this law seems to ban conduct regardless of whatever message the conduct conveys: the law would apply to someone who used a flag as fuel to keep warm, or to someone who bit into a bicentennial candy bar decorated with a flag. But what is the government's interest in preventing such acts? The Court in *Spence v. Washington* speculated on a governmental interest, not implicated by Spence's act as such, in preserving the flag as a national symbol capable of mirroring the sentiments of all who view it.[31] But how is the flag's role as such a universal symbol threatened by someone's act in destroying a particular flag? To test the question, consider whether the national symbol, which the government seeks to preserve unsullied, would be corrupted or interfered with in any way by "closet" flag burnings—people drawing their own flags on flammable fabric and igniting them in the dead of night in the privacy of their homes. The

30. Spence, 418 U.S. at 413. See also Greer v. Spock, 424 U.S. 828, 839 (1976) (preserving appearance of a politically neutral military establishment held a factor in approving as constitutional the exclusion of partisan political activities from military bases); id. at 841 (Burger, C.J., concurring); id. at 845–848 (Powell, J., concurring); Lehman v. Shaker Heights, 418 U.S. 298, 304 (1974) (avoiding appearance of favoritism held a factor in permitting municipality to refuse political advertising while allowing commercial advertising in space on city-owned buses).

31. Spence, 418 U.S. at 412–415. Drawing an analogy to a law which prevents the interruption of a scheduled speaker, see Reynolds v. Tennessee, 414 U.S. 1163 (1974) (mem.) (refusing to review conviction, under statute prohibiting disturbance of religious assemblies, for chanting during President Nixon's speech at the Reverend Billy Graham's East Tennessee Crusade), Professor Ely, see note 4, supra, at 1503–1504, 1506–1508, notes that the state's interest in protecting the message conveyed *by the flag* may be ideologically neutral with respect to the message the *defendant* is conveying by destroying or defacing the flag. But Ely argues that such a statute is distinguishable from a law prohibiting the interruption of all speakers regardless of the message spoken—a law which is neutral with respect *both* to the content of the interruption *and* to the content of the message interrupted. He then proposes to require not only that government justify its regulations by reference to harms unrelated to the content of the defendant's message, but also that government refrain from singling out a specific message or set of messages for such content-neutral protection. This extension of the requirement seems unnecessary, however: on closer inspection, the flag-protecting statute *is* aimed at the message conveyed by the defendant's act of altering or destroying the flag—for the symbol is degraded only to the degree that people comprehend the act. In a law prohibiting the interruption of speakers, the harm occurs without regard to whether listeners "get" the heckler's message; any noise will do. Moreover, Ely's extension seems to rest on a doubtful premise—one barring government from singling out messages for protection. Cf. United States Civil Service Commission v. Letter Carriers, 413 U.S. 548, 565 (1973) (upholding limitations on partisan political activities by federal employees because it was necessary to insure that "the Government and its employees" not only execute the laws impartially but also *appear* to the public to be doing so); Cox. v. Louisiana (II), 379 U.S. 559, 565 (1965) (upholding a statute prohibiting picketing in vicinity of a courthouse in part to prevent "the possibility of a conclusion by the public that the judge's action was in part a product of intimidation and did not flow only from the fair and orderly working of the judicial process"). See also § 12–4, infra.

answer is quite clearly no; the symbol is degraded, if at all, only to the degree that people learn of the act.

This hypothetical case thus differs from *United States v. O'Brien*,[32] where the Supreme Court upheld the conviction of a young man who had burned his draft card on the steps of the South Boston Courthouse to protest the war in Viet-Nam. O'Brien was convicted under an amendment to the draft laws making it a felony knowingly to destroy or mutilate a draft card. The government claimed that the statute furthered its legitimate interest in the smooth and proper functioning of the draft, an interest substantially advanced by the existence of the pieces of paper called draft cards: in a time of crisis, for example, the existence of the cards would facilitate rapid identification of men fit for immediate induction into the armed forces.[33] Once this or other purposes are accepted (as the Court in fact accepted them), the government's interests are frustrated as much by closet draft-card burning as by public burning to express open revulsion toward the war in Viet-Nam. On its face, the sixth hypothetical thus differs from *O'Brien*, since the only possibly legitimate interest advanced by prohibiting destruction or mutilation of any flag is an interest that arises only when such conduct is perceived by others, and only when the conduct is interpreted in a certain way. Thus the hypothesized law should be scrutinized by reference to the demanding standards of track one.

While this analysis may appear easy to apply, it is important to see how a notion of content-based regulation can misfire badly if it is too rigid. In *Carey v. Brown*,[34] for example, the Court invalidated an Illinois statute on the ground that it "selectively proscrib[ed] peaceful picketing on the basis of the placard's message." [35] The law, as the majority described it, barred picketing of residences but exempted *labor* picketing of places of employment.[36] In fact—as Justice Rehnquist, joined in dissent by Chief Justice Burger and Justice Blackmun, noted—the statute did no such thing. Rather, it prohibited residential picketing "except when the residence or dwelling is used as a place of business," [37] and created a further exemption for a residence used to "hol[d] a meeting or assembly on premises commonly used to discuss subjects of general public interest." To make clear its intention that

---

32. 391 U.S. 367 (1968). See §§ 12–6, 12–23, infra.

33. 391 U.S. at 378–80.

34. 447 U.S. 455 (1980).

35. Id. at 459.

36. Id. at 460. The majority thus squeezed the case into the pigeonhole established by Police Department of Chicago v. Mosley, 408 U.S. 92 (1972), which struck down a law which prohibited all picketing within 150 feet of a school building, except for labor picketing. Id. at 92–93. The Court held that the statute was flawed because "it describes permissible picketing in terms of its subject matter," id. at 95, and "government may not grant the use of a forum to people whose views it finds

acceptable, but deny use to those wishing to express less favored or more controversial views." Id. at 96.

37. Ill. Rev. Stat., ch. 38, § 21.1-2 (1977), provided:

"It is unlawful to picket before or about the residence or dwelling of any person, except when the residence or dwelling is used as a place of business. However, this Article does not apply to a person peacefully picketing a place of employment involved in a labor dispute or the place of holding a meeting or assembly on premises commonly used to discuss subjects of general public interest." See Carey v. Brown, 447 U.S. at 457.

the statute not be used to muzzle labor unions, the legislature also exempted—perhaps redundantly—labor picketing of residences used as "place[s] of employment." [38] Finally, a person was allowed to picket his or her own home.[39] The regulation was thus aimed not at content, but rather at "the character of the residence sought to be picketed." [40] Residences could not be picketed unless they fell within one of the exempted categories. But, within those categories, the statute did not restrict permissible picketing. All picketing, both labor and nonlabor, was allowed at residences used as places of business or of public assembly.[41] The majority's analogy to *Mosley* was thus inexact at best.

The distinctions between types of speech restrictions, however clear in the abstract, may thus prove arbitrary and easily manipulable.[42] "Content-based" restrictions on speech may regulate speech on the basis of its general subject matter ("no discussion of the upcoming national election") or on the basis of its particular viewpoint ("no criticism of the Democratic candidate"). Audience-based and speaker-based regulations are also possible.[43] The Court has at times attempted to separate these categories,[44] but this is in practice a difficult task. Restrictions based on the "status" of a speaker,[45] although often upheld, bear a troublesome correlation with viewpoint.[46] Exclusion of "advocacy" groups from charity drives, for example, may have the effect of limiting speech to mainstream, status quo views,[47] and the requirement

38. The redundancy arises because the regulation already exempted *all* picketing of a "residence or dwelling . . . used as a place of business."

39. Id. at 473–74 (dissenting opinion).

40. Id. at 474.

41. Id. (noting that "Illinois has not 'flatly prohibited all nonlabor picketing' since it allows nonlabor picketing at residences used as public meeting places, and at an individual's own residence").

42. For a useful criticism of the Court's efforts in this area, see Stone, "Restrictions of Speech Because of its Content: The Peculiar Case of Subject-Matter Restrictions," 46 U.Chi.L.Rev. 81, 83–100 (1978).

43. For a discussion of speaker-based restrictions, see note 14, supra. For examples of audience-based restrictions upheld by the Court, see Bethel School District No. 403 v. Fraser, 106 S.Ct. 3159 (1986) (sexually suggestive but not obscene speech at high school assembly may be penalized); Posadas de Puerto Rico Associates v. Tourism Co. of Puerto Rico, 106 S.Ct. 2968 (1986) (advertising of casino gambling aimed at local audiences may be forbidden).

44. See, e.g., Perry Education Ass'n v. Perry Local Educators' Ass'n, 460 U.S. 37, 45–46 (1983) (upholding term of collective bargaining agreement that granted preferential access to intraschool mail system to labor union representing majority of teachers, and attempting to distinguish the

"content-neutrality" rule of traditional public forums from the (ostensibly less rigorous) "viewpoint-neutrality" requirement of nonpublic forums).

45. See, e.g., Cornelius v. NAACP Legal Defense and Educational Fund, 473 U.S. 788, 806 (1985) (upholding rule which limited participation in federal charity fundraising drive to those organizations which did not "attempt to influence the outcome of political elections or the determination of public policy"); Perry, 460 U.S. at 49 ("it is more accurate to characterize the access policy as based on the *status* of the respective unions rather than their views") (emphasis in opinion).

46. See Perry, 460 U.S. at 57 (Brennan, J., joined by Marshall, Powell, and Stevens, JJ., dissenting). See also First National Bank of Boston v. Bellotti, 435 U.S. 765 (1978), and note 14, supra. Cf. Larson v. Valente, 456 U.S. 228, 246 (1982) (striking down as violative of the establishment clause a state rule which imposed registration and reporting requirements on religious organizations that solicited more than 50 percent of their funds from nonmembers; the statute was in part aimed at the Unification Church of Rev. Sun Myung Moon and reflected impermissible "denominational preferences").

47. See Cornelius, 473 U.S. at 832 (Blackmun, J., joined by Brennan, J., dissenting) (attacking as viewpoint discrimination a rule that excluded from a federal

that all groups at a state fair distribute literature from fixed booth locations might discriminate against unpopular and minority views whose representatives may be shunned by the public.[48] But such effects are often hard to detect, and the Justices are far from consistent in identifying them. In *United States Postal Service v. Greenburgh Civic Associations*,[49] for example, Justice Brennan commented that the prohibition on the placement of nonstamped mailable matter in letterboxes "is content-neutral because it is not directed at the content of the message [that the civic association members] seek to convey, but applies equally to all mailable matter."[50] While in a narrow sense this is true, it ignores the risk that, by raising the costs of communicating, such a rule may predictably freeze out those with less standard views, or those who wish to speak on new and heretofore neglected subjects.[51]

§ 12–4. Distinguishing Government's Addition of its Own Voice From Government's Silencing of Others

Consider this seventh hypothetical case:

(7) A misdemeanor to remove from a government building any representation of the U.S. flag commissioned for the building and approved by the General Services Administration.

That government must regulate expressive activity with an even hand if it regulates such activity at all does not mean that government must be ideologically "neutral." To be sure, it is the teaching of *West Virginia v. Barnette*,[1] where the Court held that school children could not be required to join in a flag salute ceremony, that government cannot *compel* a show of respect for the flag—since forcing someone to express a view is as offensive as forbidding someone to express it. Likewise government cannot compel an individual to display on his person or property a message fostering public adherence to an ideological view the individual finds unacceptable,[2] and it may not force a newspaper to print a story it does not want to print.[3] In *Abood v.*

employee fundraising drive those charities that engaged in political advocacy).

48. But see Heffron v. International Society for Krishna Consciousness (ISKCON), 452 U.S. 640, 649 n. 12 (1981) (rejecting the argument that a state fair rule restricting the distribution of printed material and the solicitation of funds to certain fixed booth locations "is not content-neutral in that it prefers listener-initiated exchanges to those originating with the speaker" and thereby especially burdens unpopular or little-known speakers). See § 12–23, infra.

49. 453 U.S. 114 (1981).

50. 453 U.S. at 135 (Brennan, J., concurring in the judgment).

51. Cf. City Council of the City of Los Angeles v. Taxpayers for Vincent, 466 U.S. 789 (1984) (upholding city ordinance that prohibited the posting of signs on public property, as applied to a political candidate who sought to post signs on the cross-arms of utility poles). Clark v. Community for Creative Non-Violence, 468 U.S. 288 (1984) (upholding National Park Service regulations that prohibited sleeping outside in a park across from the White House, as applied to protesters attempting to call attention to the plight of the homeless).

§ 12–4

1. 319 U.S. 624 (1943).

2. Wooley v. Maynard, 403 U.S. 705 (1977) (requirement that motor vehicles bear license plate embossed with state motto, "Live Free or Die," held unconstitutional).

3. Miami Herald Publishing Co. v. Tornillo, 418 U.S. 241 (1974) (statute imposing on newspaper an obligation to grant political candidates a "right of reply" held unconstitutional). See also § 12–25, infra.

Detroit Board of Education,[4] the Court extended this principle to strike down a law compelling non-members to pay to a public employees' union a service fee equal in amount to union dues; the Court required the return to each non-member of the portion of such fees used by the union to subsidize political and ideological activity to which the non-member objects.[5] In *Ellis v. Railway Clerks*,[6] the Court went even further, invalidating (as a matter of statutory construction rather than constitutional command) a rebate scheme that "allowed the union to collect the full amount of a protesting employee's dues, use part of the dues for objectionable purposes, and only pay the rebate a year later." [7] The Court argued that, given the ready availability of acceptable alternatives, such as the reduction of dues in advance or the use of interest-bearing escrow accounts, "the union cannot be allowed to

4. 431 U.S. 209 (1977).

5. The decision in Abood did not uphold any right of a non-member to withhold contributions from the cost of communicative activities with which the non-member disagrees, so long as such activities are germane to the union's duties as collective bargaining representative. Concurring in the result, Justice Powell, joined by Chief Justice Burger and Justice Blackmun, would have concluded that a non-member's first amendment rights were infringed by being compelled to contribute to any union activities to which the non-member objected, whether or not related to the union's collective bargaining activities, and would also have held that the state should bear the burden of justifying its policy of requiring fees of non-members. Id. at 259–64.

Under the "agency shop" agreement at issue, an employee was not required to become a member of the union as a condition of employment, but only to pay a service fee. The decision in Abood would require the union to refund an appropriate sum to those non-members who objected to the union's ideological activities. (Presumably, membership being voluntary, members were deemed to have consented to the expenditure.) The Court has not decided whether a public employee can be forced to join a union under a union shop agreement. Id. at 218 n. 11. See also Buckley v. American Federation of Television and Radio Artists, 496 F.2d 305 (2d Cir. 1974), cert. denied 419 U.S. 1093 (1974) (the political pundit could not be compelled to join a union or submit to its discipline, but he may be required to pay dues). If union membership were required by law or on pain of job dismissal, members would of course be entitled to a partial refund under the Abood theory to the extent of union ideological activities to which they objected.

In discussing the appropriate remedy, the majority opinion of Justice Stewart rejected a system which would require objecting non-members to identify the specific expenditures to which they object, since such a system would require the employee to publicly disclose his or her beliefs to vindicate the right to withhold support. Id. at 240–42. But the same objection may be lodged against imposing on non-members the burden of affirmatively indicating their objection, even in general terms. Cf. Lamont v. Postmaster General, 381 U.S. 301 (1965) (government cannot impose the obligation upon the addressee of affirmatively requesting delivery of foreign unsealed mail detained by the Post Office as "communist political propaganda"). A better solution might well be to require ideological activities unrelated to collective bargaining to be financed from voluntary contributions in the first place. But see Mitchell, "Public Sector Union Security: The Impact of Abood," 29 Lab.L.J. 697 (1978) (criticizing Abood as weakening union ability to bargain and engage in political activities).

6. 466 U.S. 435 (1984). Justice White delivered the opinion of the Court, in which Chief Justice Burger and Justices Brennan, Marshall, Blackmun, Rehnquist, Stevens, and O'Connor joined. Justice Powell joined in part and filed a separate opinion concurring in part and dissenting in part.

7. 466 U.S. at 441. The Court reasoned that, "[b]y exacting and using full dues, then refunding months later the proportion that it was not allowed to exact in the first place, the union effectively charges the employees for activities that are outside the scope of the statutory authorization [of the Railway Labor Act]. . . . The harm would be reduced if the union were required to pay interest on the amount refunded, but . . . [e]ven then the union obtains an involuntary loan for purposes to which the employee objects." Id. at 444.

commit dissenters' funds to improper uses even temporarily." [8] *Chicago Teachers Union v. Hudson* [9] unanimously found constitutionally inadequate a union procedure for rebating dues paid by non-members, on the grounds that the procedure permitted non-member contributions to be used temporarily for ideological purposes, that it failed to provide sufficient justification for the advance deduction of dues, and that it did not afford a prompt opportunity to challenge the amount of the fee before an impartial adjudicator. The logic of *Abood* and its progeny has been applied by the lower courts in a wide variety of contexts.[10]

8. Id. Ellis also involved a challenge to types of union expenditures before the Court for the first time. The Court held that the union could not charge objecting employees for the costs of general organizing efforts and of litigation not involving the negotiation of agreements or settlement of grievances, but that it could charge dissenting employees their pro rata share for the union's quadrennial convention, union publications, and social activities. Id. at 440–41. The Court found it "unnecessary to rule on th[e] question" of whether death benefits for employees were permissible expenditures, see id. at 454–55. The Court applied the logic of earlier cases in separating those activities inherent in the collective bargaining process from those only incidental to it: "the test must be whether the challenged expenditures are necessarily or reasonably incurred for the purpose of performing the duties of an exclusive representative of the employees in dealing with the employer on labor-management issues." Id. at 448. In International Ass'n of Machinists v. Street, 367 U.S. 740 (1961), for example, the Court had held that the Railway Labor Act did not authorize a union to spend an objecting employee's money to support political causes, because the use of funds for such purposes was unrelated to Congress' desire to eliminate "free riders" and the resentment they provoke. Id. at 768–69. The Court did not express a view as to "expenditures for activities in the area between the costs which led directly to the complaint as to 'free riders,' and the expenditures to support union political activities." Id. at 769–70; see id. at 770 n. 18 (providing the example of death benefits); these were precisely the types of expenditures at issue in Ellis. The same distinction between compelled economic and ideological association was employed by Justice O'Connor in a later case: "The Court has thus ruled that a State may compel association for the commercial purposes of engaging in collective bargaining, administering labor contracts, and adjusting employment-related grievances, but it may not infringe on associational rights involving ideological or political associations. We applied this distinction in Ellis v. Railway Clerks, 466 U.S.

435 (1984), decided earlier this Term." Roberts v. United States Jaycees, 468 U.S. 609, 639 (1984) (O'Connor, J., concurring in part and concurring in the judgment) (upholding the application of a state statute which compelled an all-male organization to accept women as regular members).

9. 106 S.Ct. 1066 (1986).

10. See, e.g., Galda v. Rutgers, 772 F.2d 1060, 1070 (3d Cir. 1985) cert. denied 106 S.Ct. 1375 (1986) (holding invalid under the first and fourteenth amendments an arrangement whereby a refundable fee was extracted from each student at a state university in order to support an independent political and educational organization); Romany v. Colegio de Abogados de Puerto Rico, 742 F.2d 32, 41 (1st Cir. 1984) (vacating and remanding, on abstention grounds, decision of district court that statutes creating and compelling financial support of bar association were unconstitutional, but holding that dissenting lawyers could not be forced to pay full dues to the bar association while litigation proceeded); Int'l Ass'n of Machinists and Aerospace Workers v. Federal Election Comm'n, 678 F.2d 1092, 1117 (D.C. Cir. 1982) (en banc) aff'd mem. 459 U.S. 983 (1982) (affirming decision of FEC that amendments to Federal Election Campaign Act authorizing corporate committees to solicit executive and administrative employees did not violate those employees' first amendment rights and that amendments authorizing use of general corporate assets to establish and support corporate committees did not violate first amendment rights of dissenting shareholders). The lower courts have also applied Abood and Ellis in a variety of labor-management situations. See, e.g., Beck v. Communications Workers of America, 776 F.2d 1187, 1202 (4th Cir. 1985), appeal pending 107 S.Ct. 2480 (1987) (holding that nonunion employees subject to agency shop agreement could be charged only for those expenses reasonably incurred by the union in performing the duties of an exclusive bargaining representative and permitting union to place the funds obtained from non-union employees in an interest-bearing escrow account, subject to later reduction); Hudson v. Chicago

But none of this means that government cannot add its own voice to the many that it must tolerate, provided it does not drown out private communication.[11] The first amendment does not, for example, prevent government from promoting respect for the flag by proclaiming Flag Day or by using public property to display the flag. Those who disdain the national symbol may express that view but may not silence government's affirmation of national values, nor may they insist that government give equal circulation to their viewpoint—any more than they may insist that the flags of their choice be flown alongside the American flags that ring the Washington Monument. And if government expends public funds to subsidize flag production,[12] the fact that some people object to this expenditure of their tax money to propagate the state's patriotic message is likely to be deemed irrelevant, either in a challenge to the expenditure itself [13] or in a challenge to the payment of the full amount of tax.[14] Many forms of government speech are

Teachers Union Local No. 1, 743 F.2d 1187, 1194–95 (7th Cir. 1984) aff'd 106 S.Ct. 1066 (1986) (finding constitutionally inadequate a union system for rebating share of dues to objecting employees); Robinson v. New Jersey, 741 F.2d 598, 607 (3d Cir. 1984), cert. denied 469 U.S. 1228 (1985) (holding that lobbying activities that are pertinent to public employee unions' duties as bargaining representatives and that are not used to advance political and ideological positions could be financed with representation fees and that union demand and return system was not unconstitutional on its face).

11. See generally Emerson, The System of Freedom of Expression 697–716 (1970). But government may not endorse a religious point of view. See Chapter 14, infra.

Whether it is possible for government to "drown out" private communication is a matter of debate. Compare M. Yudof, When Government Speaks 31–32 (1983) (describing "communications overload"); Shiffrin, "Government Speech," 27 U.C. L.A.L.Rev. 565 (1980) (discussing the "drowning out" model), with Schauer, "Is Government Speech a Problem?", 35 Stan. L.Rev. 373, 380 (1983) ("this aural metaphor is ill-fitting in the context of newspapers, magazines, books, and other sources of information because each item is available to the reader regardless of the quantity of the other items.").

12. The federal government, in fact, spends over $500 million dollars per year on hundreds of films, slide shows, TV programs, and radio broadcasts and is one of the ten largest advertisers in the nation. See M. Yudof, When Government Speaks 7 (1983).

13. Federal taxpayers have been denied standing to challenge the constitutionality of expenditures except where their challenges are based on the establishment clause of the first amendment. See Flast v. Cohen, 392 U.S. 83 (1968), discussed in Chapter 3, supra.

14. There need be no standing problem in such a case, at least if the objection is to payment of an earmarked tax. On the merits, the claim would not be that government may not spend money promoting respect for the flag, but that a person may not be compelled to furnish tax contributions toward that view. But it has been assumed that the taxpayer would lose any such challenge on the merits: in Wooley v. Maynard, supra note 2, the majority silently accepted Justice Rehnquist's assertion that citizens of New Hampshire could be compelled through their taxes to pay for the cost of erecting and maintaining billboards proclaiming "Live Free or Die," even if they could not be compelled to display that proclamation on their license plates. The rule in the establishment clause cases has been different because the very expenditure has been thought to offend a right belonging to the taxpayer. See Abood v. Detroit Board of Education, supra note 4, at 234–35 n. 31. Cf. Buckley v. Valeo, 424 U.S. 1, 92–93 & n. 127 (1976) (per curiam) (analogy between establishment and free speech clauses of the first amendment patently inapplicable to constitutionality of public financing of presidential election campaigns); but see id. at 248–51 (Burger, C.J., dissenting on constitutionality of the public financing provision). But the difference thus far assumed between the establishment and the free speech clauses in this respect is rendered questionable by the holding of Abood, affirming the right to withhold dues from the dissemination of union messages unrelated to collective bargaining. The reconciliation attempted by Justice Powell in his concurring opinion is not wholly satisfying: "compelled support of a private association" is different from "compelled support

entirely unobjectionable from a constitutional perspective. An address by the President in favor of aid to rebels seeking to overthrow the Nicaraguan government does not offend the first amendment,[15] even if it is steeped in powerful political images and resonant appeals to patriotism.[16] Indeed, "all speech has a persuasive character, and . . . persuasive government rhetoric is often desirable." [17]

Thus the seventh hypothetical statute is likely to be upheld as a permissible protection for government's message rather than an unconstitutional discrimination against private messages government does not like. But if the hypothetical statute were best understood, in its context, not as an instance of government speaking but as a case of government dedicating a forum to public communication, the discrimination against unapproved representations of the flag would be an unconstitutional departure from the neutrality required of government in regulating access to that forum.[18]

---

of government" because the former represents only "one segment of the population" while the latter is "representative of the people." Abood, 431 U.S. at 259 n. 13. But since the authority of the public employees' union to compel support is derived from the legislature, the cases seem hard to distinguish on any private-public ground. It might be argued, however, that the portion of total government expenses attributable to ideological dissemination unrelated to other government functions is probably so small that the refund right Abood would otherwise imply would be too small to be measured, whereas a significant part of union expenses come within the refund rule of the Abood case. Any notion that the very relation of taxpayer to government makes the refund argument inherently inapt seems refuted by positing a hypothetical instance in which, say, half the state budget of New Hampshire goes toward broadcasting "Live Free or Die" across the countryside. In such a case, even assuming that this allocation of public resources does not itself violate the first and fourteenth amendments, the Supreme Court should probably conclude that the broadcast cannot constitutionally be financed with the involuntary contributions of persons who disagree with the message.

15. Assuming such an address does not constitute incitement to imminent lawless action. Cf. Brandenburg v. Ohio, 395 U.S. 444 (1969) (per curiam) (reversing a criminal conviction under a statute that punished "advocat[ing] . . . crime, sabotage, violence, or unlawful methods of terrorism"), discussed in § 12–9, infra. See Yudof, supra note 11, at 260 (proposing stricter controls for governmental advocacy, short of incitement, of unconstitutional or illegal behavior than for private expression of the same sort, on the ground that "[g]overnment expression is more to be

feared when it seeks to overturn the basic political structure of the nation"). Thus, the White House Director of Communications, unlike a newspaper editor, may not enjoy full constitutional protection when he exclaims, "God Bless Colonel North," thereby expressing official approval of North's alleged circumvention of the congressional ban on aid to the rebels in Nicaragua, see § 4–4, supra. See also § 12–18, note 15, infra.

16. The increased frequency of government communication, coupled with expanding use of sophisticated mass media technologies to enhance the effectiveness of government messages, makes it likely that government can affect public opinion on a wide variety of issues. See M. Yudof, When Government Speaks 31–37, 71–89 (1983). The precise magnitude and even the direction of this effect, however, are open to debate. Although the quantity of government speech is increasing, the private sector communications industry is also undergoing unprecedented expansion and growth, and "[t]here seems to be no evidence whatsoever that the proportion of government speech within the total universe of communication is increasing. In fact, it seems quite possible that it is decreasing." Schauer, "Is Government Speech a Problem?", 35 Stan.L.Rev. 373, 380 (1983). Furthermore, because of public skepticism regarding the institution of government generally, it has been questioned whether government speech enjoys an inherent advantage over private expression due solely to its source. "On the contrary, antigovernment biases may be so great, particularly with reference to the veracity of political leaders, that much government

---

17.–18. See notes 17–18 on pages 809–810.

Not all forms of government speech are permissible, however, and the most troubling instances of governmental expression are often the

speech may encounter a public strongly predisposed to disbelief." Id. at 381. These factors, as well as the statistically indeterminate impact of mass communications on behavior generally, have led even those most concerned about the possible dangers of government speech to warn that sociological evidence cannot demonstrate that "increased government expenditures and activity" are linked with "measurable improvements in outcomes." M. Yudof, supra, at 70. This cautionary note is all the more reassuring because theories that maintain that some forms of expression should be curtailed because they are unusually effective in persuading listeners, or because of the speaker's identity, are theories that run counter to important first amendment teachings. See First National Bank of Boston v. Bellotti, 435 U.S. 765, 777 (1978) ("capacity [of speech] for informing the public does not depend on the identity of its source"), discussed in § 12–3, supra; Virginia State Board of Pharmacy v. Virginia Citizens Consumer Council, 425 U.S. 748 (1976) (extending constitutional protection to commercial speech because of interests of listeners, not speakers), discussed in § 12–15, infra; Zauderer v. Office of Disciplinary Counsel, 471 U.S. 626, 651 (1985) ("the extension of First Amendment protection to commercial speech is justified principally by the value to consumers of the information such speech provides. . . ."); Central Hudson Gas & Elec. v. Public Serv. Comm'n, 447 U.S. 557, 587 (1980) (Stevens, J., joined by Brennan, J., concurring in judgment) ("The justification is nothing more than the expressed fear that the audience may find the utility's message persuasive"); Buckley v. Valeo, 424 U.S. 1, 48–49 (1976) (per curiam) ("the concept that the government may restrict the speech of some elements of our society in order to enhance the relative voice of others is wholly foreign to the first amendment"); Miami Herald Pub. Co. v. Tornillo, 418 U.S. 241, 254 (1974) (invalidating right of reply statute). See also Schauer, supra, at 381–82 ("The assumption that government speech is likely to have a highly distorting effect on the trade in ideas is an assumption that goes to the roots not . . . of government speech but . . . of the very idea of freedom of speech. . . . [A]s a long-run strategy, we are willing to place some faith in the collective judgment of the people, and, if this is the case, there seems to be no good reason to assume that such collective judgment cannot appreciate government speech for what it is, in light of its source."). Such a doctrine also could not be logically confined to government speak-

ers, but would extend to any unusually powerful or influential voice. See Shiffrin, "Book Review: Government Speech and the Falsification of Content," 96 Harv.L. Rev. 1745, 1752–54 (1983) (criticizing Yudof's public-private distinction); Tushnet, "Talking to Each Other: Reflections on Yudof's When Government Speaks," 1984 Wis.L.Rev. 129, 132 ("if one were willing to say that government speech can limit the evaluative capabilities of citizens, one is implicitly accepting a broader critique of traditional free speech theory.").

17. M. Yudof, When Government Speaks 73 (1983). Dean Yudof himself believes that two-way communications flow between government and citizenry is necessary to the process of government, see id. at 20–22 (noting that, in its ideal type, democracy is unstable—government must lead, communicate with, and respond to the people), and to the development of a "self-controlled" citizenry that can make choices as rational, autonomous agents, see id. at 32. Indeed, in many contexts government has a *duty* to speak: "it is incumbent on government to seek actively to promote citizens' autonomy, to program the citizen to program himself." Id. at 34. Yudof concedes the difficulty of separating permissible "education" and "leadership" from "propaganda" and "impermissible manipulation of opinion" and in the end proposes a very limited role for the courts in policing government expression, see id. at 259–99. He seems content with greater legislative awareness of the possible abuses of government expression, see id. at 174–75, and an *ultra vires* doctrine that would ensure that decisions to embark on a campaign of governmental speech are made by the institutionally "correct" and politically accountable actor, see id. at 301–06. Professor Shiffrin criticizes the "search for single principles or all-encompassing models yielding easy solutions" and instead proposes an eclectic, balancing approach. Shiffrin, "Government Speech," 27 U.C. L.A.L.Rev. 565, 609 (1980). He correctly notes that government speaks in too many different contexts, with too many different effects, to expect that a single, unified theory is feasible. Id. at 610. In particular, Shiffrin proposes that government speech on partisan political issues be closely circumscribed, as when government subsidies are designed to influence the outcome of elections. See id. at 622–26. Representative of these subsidies are congressional franking privileges. See id. at 632–37. In addition, the decision-making process in programs that dispense public monies to

most subtle and insidious.[19]   Under the Foreign Agents Registration
Act,[20] for example, the Department of Justice may classify a foreign
film as "political propaganda" if it determines that the film is "reasonably adapted to . . . prevail upon, indoctrinate, convert, induce, or in
any way influence a recipient or any section of the public . . . with
reference to the political or public interests, policies, or relations" of a
foreign government or political party or the foreign policy of the United
States.[21]   In *Meese v. Keene*,[22] a member of the California State Senate
who wished to exhibit three Canadian films, one concerning the environmental effects of nuclear war and the other two on the subject of
acid rain, argued that Congress violated the first amendment by using
the term "political propaganda" as the statutory name for the regulated category in which his films concededly fell.   Not at issue in *Keene*
were the constitutionality of the underlying requirement that foreign

support the arts must be structured to minimize the risk of government propaganda.
Grant awards, for example, should be determined by a diverse set of officials who
are insulated from the political process.
See id. at 645–46.

18. See Southeastern Promotions, Ltd.
v. Conrad, 420 U.S. 546 (1975), discussed in
§ 12–24, infra.   The determination of
"public forum" status for purposes of the
government speech doctrine thus takes on
a great deal of significance.   As one commentator has noted, "To treat every area
of government communication as a 'public
forum' would deprive the government of its
legitimate role in public dialogue."   Bollinger, "The Sedition of Free Speech," 81
Mich.L.Rev. 867, 870 (1983).   For example,
if the government operates a professional
journal, or a library, see Board of Education v. Pico, 457 U.S. 853 (1982) (upholding
reversal of the summary dismissal of a suit
brought by students who challenged a
school board's decision to remove certain
books from school library), must it accept
for publication or circulation every article
or book that is submitted, or perhaps select
pieces on a first-come, first-serve basis?   If
the government is permitted to exercise
content-based editorial discretion in the
case of a journal or a public library, what
distinguishes such cases from the municipal theater in Southeastern Promotions?
One proposed dividing line is that, "where
the government's mission is to communicate and the scarcity of resources and the
nature of the enterprise make editorial selectivity inevitable, the state need not tolerate or acquiesce in use of the forum that
substantially destroys the communication
and editorial processes."   M. Yudof, supra
note 11, at 241.   In other words, if the
government's *aim* in creating the forum
requires it to retain editorial discretion,
then the use of that discretion is constitutionally permissible.   The circularity of
this argument is troubling, however.

What would stop the city in Southeastern
Promotions from announcing at the outset
that its purpose in constructing the theater
was to allow the performance of only "non-
offensive" or "truly artistic" productions,
of which it would be the judge?   Cf. Cornelius v. NAACP Legal Defense and Educational Fund, 473 U.S. 788, 823 (1985)
(Blackmun, J., joined by Brennan, J., dissenting) (criticizing a government intent or
purpose test for determining public forum
status): "Under [this] reasoning, . . . the
theater in Southeastern Promotions would
not have been a limited public forum."
See Shiffrin, supra note 17, at 580–89 (analyzing possible "convincing bases" for
schemes of "limited access.").

The question of whether a public high
school newspaper is a public forum, and
hence protected from the government's editorial and censorial powers, is presented by
Kuhlmeier v. Hazelwood School District,
795 F.2d 1368 (8th Cir. 1986), review granted 107 S.Ct. 926 (1987).

19. Government speech poses especially
difficult issues because many of its features
go to the heart of democratic theory.   The
legitimacy of government depends on the
consent of the governed, but that consent
is influenced, and, indeed, sometimes
manipulated, by the government itself.
See Tushnet, "Talking to Each Other: Reflections on Yudof's When Government
Speaks," 1984 Wis.L.Rev. 129, 130.

20. 22   U.S.C.   §§ 611–621   (1982)
(FARA).

21. 22 U.S.C. § 611(j) (1982).

22. 107 S.Ct. 1862 (1987).   Justice Stevens delivered the opinion of the Court.
Justice Blackmun filed an opinion dissenting in part, in which Justices Brennan and
Marshall joined.   Justice Scalia took no
part in the consideration or decision of the
case.

films be registered or classified and the "validity of the characteristics used to define the regulated category of expressive materials." [23]   The Court in *Keene* upheld Congress's "power to define [such] terms" as "propaganda" in its chosen manner [24] and rejected the argument that the statute could be invalid not because of what it "actually says, requires, or prohibits, but rather [because of] a potential misunderstanding of its effect." [25]   But, as Justice Blackmun, joined by Justices Brennan and Marshall, noted in dissent, "[e]ven if the statutory definition [supplied by Congress] is neutral, it is the common understanding of the Government's action that determines the effect on discourse protected by the First Amendment." [26]   The word "propaganda" has long been an explosive, value-laden term with such pejorative connotations that the registration process necessarily does more than simply label the source of a film of foreign origin; rather, it almost certainly discourages audiences from viewing the film by branding it as a product of half-truths and distortions.[27]   This alone may not be dispositive, as

23. Id. at 1864. Challenges to other aspects of the regulatory scheme were possible. For example, a foreign agent which seeks to distribute such a film in the United States must "set[ ] forth full information as to the places, times, and extent of such transmittal." 22 U.S.C. § 614(a). The Justice Department implementing regulations require the foreign agent to report the name of each individual or group receiving 100 copies or more of the material and, in the case of a film, the name of each "station, organization, or theater using" the film, the dates the film was shown, and the estimated attendance, see 28 C.F.R. § 5.401(b) (1985). A scheme which forces a distributor to identify the recipients of its film arguably violates the command of Lamont v. Postmaster General, 381 U.S. 301 (1965), where the Court invalidated a statute that required the Post Office to detain and to deliver only upon the addressee's public request unsealed foreign mailings of "communist political propaganda." Justice Douglas, writing for the Court, concluded that such a system was unconstitutional "because it require[d] an official act (viz, returning the reply card) as a limitation on the unfettered exercise of the addressee's First Amendment rights." Id. at 305. This issue was distinct from merely *labeling* material as propaganda; the scheme in Lamont deterred Americans from receiving foreign literature by forcing them to make an affirmative act and identify themselves as recipients of such material: "This requirement is almost certain to have a deterrent effect, especially as respects those who have sensitive positions. Their livelihood may be dependent on a security clearance. Public officials, like schoolteachers who have no tenure, might think they would invite disaster if they read what the Federal Government says contains the seeds of treason." Id. at 307.

The Court in Lamont in dictum also intimated that a labeling scheme alone might have this same chilling effect: "any addressee is likely to feel some inhibition in sending for literature which federal officials have condemned as 'communist political propaganda.'" Id. The D.C. Circuit Court of Appeals in Block v. Meese attempted to distinguish Lamont on the ground that the Foreign Agents Registration Act contained no requirement that recipients commit an "official" or affirmative act before they could receive the film. Block v. Meese, 793 F.2d 1303, 1311 (D.C. Cir. 1986), cert. denied 106 S.Ct. 3335 (1986). But this analysis is too simple. A recipient, in order to receive the material, must acknowledge the fact that the foreign agent distributor may disclose his identity, and this creates precisely the same chilling effect as did the rule in Lamont. It matters not that in one instance, the recipient must disclose his own name, while in another the sender must disclose it for him. A better means of distinguishing the two cases would focus instead on FARA's emphasis on commercial recipients rather that private individuals. By creating an exemption for receipt of fewer than 100 copies, the regulations permit an individual to receive material for his personal use. Commercial entities, on the other hand, must surrender their anonymity, but such a requirement is hardly a burden, since theaters and bookstores presumably *want* the public to know what they have for sale.

24. 107 S.Ct. at 1873.

25. Id. at 1870.

26. Id. at 1876 (Blackmun, J., joined by Brennan and Marshall, JJ., dissenting in part).

27. See Keene v. Meese, 619 F.Supp. 1111, 1125 (E.D.Cal. 1985) (finding that

Judge (now Justice) Scalia noted for the United States Court of Appeals for the District of Columbia Circuit, since the government may express its views on a whole range of issues, even if they sometimes collide with the opinions of private actors.[28] However, first amendment analysis should be more sensitive to the potentially chilling effects of the use of such inflammatory language in an ostensibly "neutral" labelling scheme. It will not do to concede that, when government officially condemns a film or book as suspect, readers or viewers may be deterred—and then to assert that the classification of a film as "political propaganda" does "not constitute the government's expression of its own official suspicion." [29]

Public schools, similarly, can be powerful means of indoctrination.[30] The audiences of such schools are captive and immature. The schools' messages are labelled as "educational" rather than as propaganda and promotion. And these schools may dispense a panoply of rewards and punishments to reinforce their favored views. To reduce the potential for abuse, some diversity of viewpoints must be ensured, not by limiting the spectrum of views that the school system may communicate, and not by prescribing official requirements of artificially "balanced" coverage of such topics as evolution and creationism,[31] but by providing genuine opportunities for more speech—by safeguarding the academic freedom of students and teachers,[32] and by affirming the constitutionally-protected status of private schools.[33]

"Congress' use of the phrase 'political propaganda' to describe the material subject to the registration and reporting requirements constitutes a burden on speech by making such materials unavailable to all but the most courageous"), rev'd 107 S.Ct. 1862 (1987). The Supreme Court's own prior use of the term "propaganda," however, supports the view that the term unmistakably impugns the credibility of the speech to which it is applied. See Lehman v. Shaker Heights, 418 U.S. 298, 304 (1974) (refusing to grant a right of access to public transit vehicles, in part in order to avoid the "blare of political propaganda"); National Association of Letter Carriers v. Austin, 418 U.S. 264, 279 n. 14 (1974) (distinguishing "union propaganda" from "other method[s] of peaceful persuasion"). Indeed, the entire history of the Foreign Agents Registration Act demonstrates that "Congress enacted the portion of FARA at issue in order to suppress or restrict that [speech] which it found abhorrent." 619 F.Supp. at 1124; see also 107 S.Ct. at 1874–75 (Blackmun, J., joined by Brennan and Marshall, JJ., dissenting in part).

28. Block v. Meese, 793 F.2d 1303, 1312–1314 (D.C. Cir. 1986), cert. denied 106 S.Ct. 3335 (1986). Justice Scalia, quoting the first edition of this treatise, stressed that even ardent free speech advocates concede to government a broader power to voice critical views about an item of private speech than to silence such private speech. See 793 F.2d at 1314.

29. Id. at 1312.

30. See M. Yudof, supra note 11, at 213–33; Shiffrin, supra note 11, at 568.

31. See Edwards v. Aguillard, 107 S.Ct. 2573 (1987) (striking down, as violative of the establishment clause, Louisiana statute that specified that "the subject of origins" of the universe, of life, and of species need not be taught in public schools, but that if either "creation-science" or "evolution-science" were taught, balanced treatment must be given to the other and that each must be taught as a theory "rather than as proven scientific fact"), discussed in Chapter 14, infra.

32. Lower courts have protected principles of academic freedom in elementary and secondary schools. See, e.g., Cary v. Board of Education, 598 F.2d 535, 543 (10th Cir. 1979) (upholding ban by board of education of ten books out of a list of 1,285 for use in elective language arts class, because there was no showing that exclusion was designed to promote any particular type of book or thinking, but affirming the rights of teachers to "freedom of expression in the classroom"); Minarcini v. Strongville

33. See note 33 on page 813.

Finally, it is important to keep in mind that government affects public opinion as much by what it *does not* say as by what it *does* say. The Gulf of Tonkin incident, the Pentagon Papers, the Watergate break-in, and the Iran-Contra scandal are easy examples for the point that informed debate is not possible if government reveals only selected, and sometimes distorted or even falsified, bits of information.[34] The resulting need is to impose pressure on government to speak—and truthfully—through judicially recognizing and enforcing rights of access to certain governmental institutions and proceedings,[35] legislatively enacting suitably designed freedom of information statutes, and

City School District, 541 F.2d 577, 582 (6th Cir. 1976) (holding that students have a first amendment right to know which did not permit removal of books based solely on the "social or political tastes of school board members"); Keefe v. Geanakos, 418 F.2d. 359 (1st Cir. 1969) (reversing dismissal of high school teacher who assigned magazine article containing the word "motherfucker"); Parducci v. Rutland, 316 F.Supp. 352, 355 (M.D. Ala. 1970) (ordering reinstatement of high school teacher who assigned the Vonnegut short story, "Welcome to the Monkey House"; "the safeguards of the First Amendment will quickly be brought into play to protect the right of academic freedom"); Parker v. Board of Education, 237 F.Supp. 222 (D. Md. 1965) (reversing decision of school board not to renew contract of teacher who assigned "Brave New World"), aff'd 348 F.2d 464 (4th Cir. 1965), cert. denied 382 U.S. 1030 (1966). Although the Supreme Court has not explicitly identified academic freedom as an independent first amendment doctrine, it has at least implicitly recognized its importance. See, e.g., Board of Education v. Pico, 457 U.S. 853 (1982) (Brennan, J., joined by Marshall, Blackmun, and Stevens, JJ.) (plurality opinion) ("local school boards may not remove books from school library shelves simply because they dislike the ideas contained in those books and seek by their removal to 'prescribe what shall be orthodox in politics, nationalism, religion, or other matters of opinion.' ") (citation omitted); Tinker v. Des Moines Independent Community School District, 393 U.S. 503, 511 (1969) ("in our system, state-operated schools may not be the enclaves of totalitarianism," and students may not be regarded as "closed-circuit recipients of only that which the state chooses to communicate"); Keyishian v. Board of Regents, 385 U.S. 589, 603 (1967) ("Our Nation is deeply committed to safeguarding academic freedom, which is of transcendent value to all of us and not merely to the teachers concerned. That freedom is therefore a special concern of the First Amendment, which does not tolerate laws that cast a pall of orthodoxy over the classroom."); Shelton v. Tucker, 364 U.S. 479,

487 (1960); Sweezy v. New Hamphire, 354 U.S. 234, 250 (1957) (plurality opinion). See generally, Goldstein, "The Asserted Constitutional Right of Public School Teachers to Determine What They Teach," 124 U.Penn.L.Rev. 1293 (1976); Hirschoff, "Parents and the Public School Curriculum: Is There a Right to Have One's Child Excused From Objectionable Instruction?", 50 S.Cal.L.Rev. 871 (1977).

33. See Pierce v. Society of Sisters, 268 U.S. 510 (1925), discussed in Chapter 14, infra. Some commentators have gone even further. See, e.g., M. Yudof, supra note 11, at 227 (proposing that schools should be treated as limited public forums, where "outsiders should be entitled to distribute pamphlets, give speeches in the school yard, participate in assemblies, and so forth, even if we all agree that they may not push the English teacher aside in order to teach social anthropology."). Bonner-Lyons v. School Committee of Boston, 480 F.2d 442 (1st Cir. 1973), involved a school board that had sent home with all children a notice urging parents to attend an anti-busing rally. The court of appeals found that the distribution of this notice transformed the school system into a public forum for purposes of the first amendment, thereby requiring it to distribute other, opposing viewpoints on the same issue. The court's reasoning, however, may prove too powerful to limit to this narrow context. Schools teach about many controversial subjects, and "to allow a right of reply in every instance would likely disable governments from carrying on important socialization and communications functions." M. Yudof at 298. Rather, it might have been wiser to invalidate the school board's action on an *ultra vires* theory—the board lacked an explicit legislative delegation of power to engage in drumming up opposition to busing. See note 17, supra.

34. Government refusals to speak in circumstances like these have been termed "sins of omission." See M. Yudof, supra note 11, at 9–10 (noting that "government secrecy may itself be thought of as a powerful communications device").

35. See § 12–20, infra.

undertaking both legislative and executive de-classification of documents needlessly deemed secret.[36]

§ 12–5. Facially Neutral Abridgments Motivated by Content Censorship

A crucial distinction in the previous examples has been that between government action which on its face singles out particular messages for suppression and that which is facially neutral. But a court should also subject to the more demanding scrutiny of track one any governmental act, whether taken by a legislature or by an executive or judicial official, which is intended by the government actor to control or penalize the exercise of rights of expression or association.[1] If the first amendment requires an extraordinary justification of government action which is aimed at ideas or information that government does not like, the constitutional guarantee should not be avoidable by government action which seeks to attain that unconstitutional objective under some other guise.[2]

The Supreme Court and lower courts have routinely inquired into the motivation [3] underlying executive or administrative decisions in a

---

36. The first amendment itself is, of course, neither a substitute for such legislative and executive openness nor a source of judicial doctrine mandating whatever degree of openness wisdom might dictate.

§ 12–5

1. "[W]hen the regulation is based on the content of speech, governmental action must be scrutinized more carefully to ensure that communication has not been prohibited 'merely because public officials disapprove the speaker's views,'" Consolidated Edison Co. v. Public Service Comm'n, 447 U.S. 530, 536 (1980), quoting Niemotko v. Maryland, 340 U.S. 268, 282 (1951) (Frankfurter, J., concurring in result). Accord, United States Postal Service v. Council of Greenburgh Civic Ass'ns, 453 U.S. 114, 132 (1981). See generally Brest, "Palmer v. Thompson: An Approach to the Problem of Unconstitutional Legislative Motive," 1971 Sup.Ct.Rev. 95; Ely, "Legislative and Administrative Motivation in Constitutional Law," 79 Yale L.J. 1205 (1970); Alfange, "Free Speech and Symbolic Conduct: The Draft-Card Burning Case," 1968 Sup.Ct.Rev. 1; Bickel, The Least Dangerous Branch 208–221 (1962).

2. See McCulloch v. Maryland, 17 U.S. (4 Wheat.) 316, 423 (1819) (dictum) (Marshall, C. J.): "[S]hould Congress, under the pretext of executing its powers, pass laws for the accomplishment of objects not entrusted to the government . . . such an [enactment would not be] the law of the land." But the authority of Chief Justice Marshall is more often invoked for the contrary proposition. See Fletcher v. Peck, 10 U.S. (6 Cranch.) 87, 131 (1810)

(suit by bona fide purchasers of land charging the Georgia legislature with rescinding the grant because of a prior legislature's bribery). The statement of the Chief Justice, however, was only that the issue of the legislature's intent could not be raised "collaterally and incidentally" in a private action to which the state was not a party. As to whether legislative motive may ever be scrutinized, Marshall said only that it was a problem to be approached "with much circumspection." Id. at 130. See Brest, supra note 1, at 100–101. The caution expressed by Marshall in Fletcher v. Peck had hardened by the 1930's into "a wise and ancient doctrine that a Court will not inquire into the motives of a legislative body or assume them to be wrongful." United States v. Constantine, 296 U.S. 287, 298–99 (1935) (Cardozo, J., dissenting). But the cases make clear that, confronted with the right circumstances, the Court has traversed the "forbidden" path of inquiry time and again. See P. Freund, The Supreme Court of the United States 61 (1961).

3. In this discussion, the words "purpose" and "motive" will be used interchangeably. Some scholars have attempted to establish a distinction between the two. See, e.g., A. Bickel, The Least Dangerous Branch 209 (1962) (suggesting that "purpose" is "either the name given to the Court's objective assessment of the effect of a statute or a conclusory term denoting the Court's independent judgment of the constitutionally allowable end that the legislature could have had in view," and that "motive" corresponds to the legislature's actual intentions). In

variety of contexts.[4] A frequent occasion for judicial scrutiny to detect illicit purposes has been judicial review of a decision by a government authority whose actions are ordinarily all but unreviewable given the wide discretion accorded in public administration. In *Pickering v. Board of Education,*[5] the Court held that a teacher could not be dismissed from public employment for writing a letter to a newspaper, absent proof of knowingly or recklessly false statements, except upon a showing that the expression interfered with the teacher's performance of classroom duties or with the operation of the school.[6] Given the number of subjective criteria by which teachers are regularly evaluated, and considering that nontenured teachers may be discharged for no reason whatsoever,[7] the *Pickering* rule would be empty if courts did not seek to determine whether an illicit motive had entered into a decision. A teacher who makes out an arguable claim that a dismissal was motivated by the teacher's exercise of first amendment rights is

practice, however, both terms are often employed to refer to the goals that decisionmakers seek to achieve. See, e.g., Ely, note 1, supra, at 1219; Brest, note 1, supra, at 101; Note, "Legislative Purpose and Federal Constitutional Adjudication," 83 Harv.L.Rev. 1887, 1887–88 n. 1 (1970). The Supreme Court, at any rate, fails to observe a distinction. See Village of Arlington Heights v. Metropolitan Housing Development Corp., 429 U.S. 252, 265–66 (1977) ("Washington v. Davis [426 U.S. 229 (1976)] does not require a plaintiff to prove that the challenged action rested solely on racially discriminatory *purposes*. Rarely can it be said that a legislature or administrative body operating under a broad mandate made a decision *motivated* solely by a single concern. . . . When there is proof that a racially discriminatory *purpose* has been a *motivating* factor in the decision, this judicial deference is no longer justified.") (emphasis added).

4. See, e.g., Rogers v. Lodge, 458 U.S. 613, 620–21 (1982) (affirming districting plan in county with an at-large voting scheme in which no black had ever been elected to the county council); Crawford v. Los Angeles Board of Education, 458 U.S. 527, 543–44 (1982) (upholding amendment to state constitution that restricted mandatory pupil assignment and busing as school desegregation mechanisms); Washington v. Seattle School Dist. No. 1, 458 U.S. 457, 484–87 (1982) (invalidating as violative of equal protection a state initiative that "permits busing for non-racial reasons but forbids it for racial reasons"); Keyes v. School District No. 1, 413 U.S. 189 (1973) (Denver schools held unlawfully segregated because decisions by the school board on the location of new schools and on pupil assignments were motivated by racial considerations); Griffin v. Prince Edward County School Board, 377 U.S. 218 (1964) (invalidating closing of a county school sys-

tem and the payment of tuition grants to students attending private schools because motive of the closure was to preserve segregated schooling); Yick Wo v. Hopkins, 118 U.S. 356 (1886) (discriminatory intent of board administering laundry-licensing law inferred from pattern of refusing licenses to all Chinese applicants and granting licenses to nearly all Caucasian applicants). See generally §§ 16–15 to 16–20, infra.

5. 391 U.S. 563 (1968).

6. See also Givhan v. Western Line Consolidated School Dist., 439 U.S. 410 (1979) (holding that dismissal of public school teacher because of her allegations that the school's policies were racially disciminatory violates the first amendment). Cf. Connick v. Myers, 461 U.S. 138 (1983), which upheld the discharge of an assistant district attorney for circulating a questionnaire to her co-workers. The offending document asked fellow employees for their opinions on such topics as job transfer policy, office morale, and pressure to work on political campaigns. Id. at 141. The employer objected especially to two questions, including the one concerning political pressure, "which he felt would be damaging if discovered by the press." Id. Justice White, writing for the majority, concluded that a public employee's first amendment right to free expression at work is limited to "speech on matters of public concern," id. at 145, a category that did not include an "employee grievance" such as the assistant district attorney's questionnaire. Id. at 148. Hence, the state was justified in discharging the attorney, even though there was no demonstrable impairment of her ability to perform her duties. Id. at 151.

7. See, e.g., Board of Regents v. Roth, 408 U.S. 564 (1972); Brest, supra note 1, at 138 n. 210.

thus entitled to a full hearing on the reasons for the dismissal.[8] If the teacher is able to show at such a hearing that the exercise of first amendment rights was indeed a "substantial," or "motivating," factor in the decision to discharge or not to rehire, the burden shifts to the school to show by a preponderance of the evidence that the same decision as to the teacher's employment would have been reached even in the absence of the protected conduct. If the school fails to purge its decision of the "taint" of unconstitutional motivation, that decision cannot stand.[9]

In the first amendment context, the Supreme Court has been willing to inquire regarding—and to strike down executive and administrative actions on the basis of—what it determines to be improper motives or purposes.[10] In ascertaining the purpose of a legislature,

8. See, e.g., Perry v. Sindermann, 408 U.S. 593 (1972).

9. See Mt. Healthy City Board of Education v. Doyle, 429 U.S. 274 (1977). Cf. Nardone v. United States, 308 U.S. 338, 341 (1939) (confession held admissible in evidence upon showing by prosecution that the causal link between a prior illegal arrest and the confession was "attenuated").

10. See, e.g., Cornelius v. NAACP Legal Defense and Educational Fund, 473 U.S. 788 (1985) (upholding executive order which limited participation in a charity drive among federal employees to organizations that provided direct health and welfare services to individuals or their families, and excluded legal defense and political advocacy groups). The Court opined that it was not enough that the executive order appeared facially neutral (it excluded *all* political advocacy groups, not simply those with a particular message); if the regulations were *motivated* by a desire to suppress certain views or speakers, then they were impermissible: "[T]he government's posited justifications for denying [the NAACP Legal Defense and Educational Fund] access to the [Combined Federal Campaign] appear to be reasonable in light of the purpose of the CFC. The existence of reasonable grounds for limiting access to a nonpublic forum, however, will not save a regulation that is in reality a facade for viewpoint-based discrimination." Id. at 811. The Court therefore remanded the case for consideration of the issue "whether the exclusion of [the NAACP Legal Defense and Educational Fund] was impermissibly motivated by a desire to suppress a particular point of view." Id. at 812–13. Justice Stevens, in dissent, made clear the Court's willingness to examine the motivation behind the administrative rules: "Everyone on the Court agrees that the exclusion of 'advocacy' groups from the Combined Federal Campaign (CFC) is prohibited if it is motivated by a bias against the views of the

excluded groups. . . . The problem presented by this case is whether that inference [of bias] is strong enough to support the entry of summary judgment in favor of [the NAACP]." Id. at 833–34 (Stevens, J., dissenting). Justice Stevens' interpretation of impermissible motive was sufficiently broad to include even a "subconscious bias, based on nothing more than a habitual attitude of disfavor, or perhaps a willingness to assume that frequent expressions of disagreement with the achievements of advocacy groups adequately demonstrate that they are somehow inferior to 'traditional health and welfare charities.'" Id. at 835–36 n. 3. See also Perry Education Ass'n v. Perry Local Educators' Ass'n, 460 U.S. 37 (1983) (upholding provision of public school collective bargaining agreement which granted preferential access to the interschool mail system to the union currently representing the teachers). The Court scrutinized the school board's motivation in negotiating such a provision but concluded that "[t]here is . . . no indication that the School Board intended to discourage one viewpoint and advance another." Id. at 49.

Cornelius and Perry may be viewed as specific instances of the larger doctrine of selective prosecution or enforcement, a constraint on executive decisionmaking that appears to have no precise counterpart in the legislative sphere, except perhaps in the prohibition on bills of attainder. "Selectivity in the enforcement of . . . criminal law is . . . subject to constitutional constraints." United States v. Batchelder, 442 U.S. 114, 123 (1979) (footnote omitted). In particular, the decision to prosecute may not be "deliberately based upon an unjustifiable standard such as race, religion, or other arbitrary classification," Oyler v. Boles, 368 U.S. 448, 456 (1962), including the exercise of protected statutory and constitutional rights, see United States v. Goodwin, 457 U.S. 368, 372 (1982). The general bar against selec-

however, the Court has been "reluctan[t] to attribute unconstitutional motives to the state, particularly when a plausible [permissible] purpose may be discerned from the face of the statute." [11] To be sure, the Court has made clear that motive cannot be ignored altogether, even when legislatures are involved,[12] especially in cases involving the establishment clause [13] or possible racial discrimination.[14] But the Court's decisions do indicate a general tendency, when all other things are equal,[15] to grant greater deference to Congress and to state legislatures so far as the inquiry into purpose is concerned.[16]

tive prosecution, however, does not prevent law enforcement agencies from adopting strategies that have but incidental effects on expression. See Wayte v. United States, 470 U.S. 598 (1985) (upholding Selective Service "passive" enforcement system for draft registration). Because of the large number of non-registrants, the Service found it administratively infeasible to police compliance actively. Rather, the Service prosecuted only those who by their public statements and actions advertised their failure to register. The Court upheld this enforcement strategy even though it arguably discriminated against those who exercised their first amendment rights to protest the registration requirement. See generally, "Note: The Conflict of First Amendment Rights and the Motive Requirement in Selective Enforcement Cases," 39 Okla.L.Rev. 498, 514 (1986) (proposing a less stringent motive requirement in selective enforcement cases: the burden of persuasion should shift to the government after the defendant has made a prima facie showing of discriminatory intent).

11. Mueller v. Allen, 463 U.S. 388, 394–95 (1983) (upholding Minnesota statute that permitted a tax deduction for tuition, textbook, and transportation expenses to parents whose children attended parochial schools). See also Flemming v. Nestor, 363 U.S. 603, 617 (1960) (declining to inquire into Congress' motives for terminating Social Security benefits for deported members of the Communist Party); Watkins v. United States, 354 U.S. 178, 200 (1957) (refusing to examine motives of congressional investigating committee); Arizona v. California, 283 U.S. 423, 455 (1931) (refusing to examine motives underlying Hoover Dam authorization).

12. See Grosjean v. American Press Co., 297 U.S. 233 (1936) (discussing a general press freedom from taxes, but invalidating the particular tax under challenge only because it was a deliberate device to limit the circulation of newspapers critical of state government); Ely, note 1, supra, at 1208–12.

13. See Epperson v. Arkansas, 393 U.S. 97 (1968) (holding statute prohibiting the teaching of Darwin's theory of evolution in the state's public schools unconstitutional because it was motivated by the intent to "establish" a religious viewpoint); Lemon v. Kurtzman, 403 U.S. 602, 612 (1971) (identifying three tests for determining whether a statute violates the establishment clause: "First, the statute must have a secular legislative purpose."); Stone v. Graham, 449 U.S. 39 (1980) (per curiam) (holding a statute requiring the posting of the Ten Commandments in public schools violative of the establishment clause, even though the Kentucky legislature asserted that its goal was educational); Wallace v. Jaffree, 472 U.S. 38, 56 (1985) (modifying the Lemon test by opining that "a statute motivated in part by a religious purpose may satisfy the first criterion," but invalidating an Alabama school prayer and meditation statute on the ground that "the statute had *no* secular purpose" at all); Edwards v. Aguillard, 107 S.Ct. 2573 (1987) (invalidating state statute requiring equal time for "creation-science"). See generally § 14–9, infra.

14. See, e.g., Gomillion v. Lightfoot, 364 U.S. 339 (1960) (racial gerrymandering held unconstitutional; an "uncouth twenty-eight-sided figure" excluding most black voters and no white voters from a city was evidence that the legislature was motivated solely by racial considerations); Mobile v. Bolden, 446 U.S. 55, 134 (1980) (Marshall, J., dissenting) (rejecting an equal protection claim to an at-large voting system where, despite the fact that one-third of the city's voters were black, no black had ever been elected to the city commission): "[J]udicial deference to official decisionmaking has no place under the Fifteenth Amendment."

15. All other things are frequently not equal. The Court, for example, has been unwilling to inquire into the motives of legislatures or high executive officials when it fears impugning the integrity of a coordinate branch of government or intruding too deeply into legislative and executive processes. See A. Bickel, The

---

16. See note 16 on page 818.

The Court has often rested its decisions in reviewing legislation on grounds other than motive,[17] and, while Justices have on occasion

Least Dangerous Branch 208–21 (1962). The Court has accordingly recognized that a probing examination of motive at these levels can be justified only in extraordinary circumstances. See Village of Arlington Heights v. Metropolitan Housing Development Corp., 429 U.S. 252, 268 n. 18 (1977) (upholding municipal rezoning decision because complainants had not shown racially discriminatory intent). But see id. at 265–66 ("racial discrimination is not just another competing consideration. When there is proof that a discriminatory purpose has been a motivating factor, this judicial deference is no longer justified."); Baker v. Carr, 369 U.S. 186, 209–37 (1962) (refusing to find legislative apportionment a political question). In Davis v. Bandemer, 106 S.Ct. 2797 (1986), for example, the Court ultimately refused to overturn on equal protection grounds an apportionment plan enacted by Indiana's Republican-controlled legislature and signed into law by the state's Republican governor, because the challenging Democratic party members could show no "evidence of continued frustration of the will of a majority of the voters or effective denial to a minority of voters of a fair chance to influence the political process." Id. at 2811 (plurality opinion of White, J., joined by Brennan, Marshall, and Blackmun, JJ.). Nevertheless, the Court by a firm majority held that such political gerrymandering claims are justiciable. See id. at 2805 (majority opinion of White, J., joined by Brennan, Marshall, Blackmun, Powell, and Stevens, JJ.) (rejecting the arguments that the adjudication would involve the courts "in a matter more properly decided by a coequal branch of our Government" and that no "discernible and manageable standards" exist to decide claims of political gerrymandering).

16. See Wallace v. Jaffree, 472 U.S. at 74–75 (O'Connor, J., concurring in the judgment): "[T]he inquiry into the purpose of the legislature in enacting a moment of silence law should be deferential and limited. In determining whether the government intends a moment of silence statute to convey a message of endorsement or disapproval of religion, a court has no license to psychoanalyze the legislators. If a legislature expresses a plausible secular purpose for a moment of silence statute in either the text or the legislative history, or if the statute disclaims an intent to encourage prayer over alternatives during a moment of silence, then courts should generally defer to that stated intent." (citations omitted).

17. See, e.g., NAACP v. Button, 371 U.S. 415 (1963). In 1956 the Virginia legislature, at a special session called by the governor to deal with the school segregation crisis, enacted a series of laws including new regulations of legal ethics which had the effect of prohibiting the NAACP from soliciting and financing litigation for its own lawyers or interfering with lawyer-client control of litigation. Virginia advanced the justification that the law protected black clients from the conflicts of interest that could arise from free representation by NAACP lawyers. The Court did not expressly respond that Virginia, under the guise of regulating legal ethics, had illegally sought to close the courts to constitutional litigation on behalf of black persons; yet it is difficult not to conclude that the Court's invalidation of the Virginia law as unconstitutionally broad and vague was inspired substantially by a realistic assessment of the legislature's intentions. See Kalven, The Negro and the First Amendment 63–121 (1965).

It has been suggested that vagueness and overbreadth analysis (see §§ 12–27 through 12–33, infra) serve as quick and easy substitutes for the examination of improper legislative and administrative motives. "By invalidating statutes as overly vague or overly broad, courts foreclose the threat of selective enforcement based on venal motives without scrutinizing the motives themselves." Eisenberg, "Disproportionate Impact and Illicit Motive: Theories of Constitutional Adjudication," 52 N.Y.U.L. Rev. 36, 103 (1977). See Village of Schaumburg v. Citizens for a Better Environment, 444 U.S. 620 (1980) (striking down as unconstitutionally overbroad a village ordinance that prohibited door-to-door or on-street solicitation of contributions by charitable organizations that did not use at least 75 percent of their receipts for "charitable purposes"—such purposes being defined to exclude solicitation expenses, salaries, overhead, and administrative costs). The Court examined the interests purportedly advanced by the ordinance—"protecting the public from fraud, crime, and undue annoyance," id. at 636, and concluded that they were "only peripherally promoted by the 75 percent requirement and could be sufficiently served by measures less destructive of First Amendment interests." Id. Because the Village's proffered justifications were "inadequate," the Court found that "the ordinance [could not] survive scrutiny under the First Amendment." Id. Professor Nimmer argues that a similar mode of analysis should have been applied in United States v. O'Brien, 391 U.S. 367 (1968): "[An overnarrow statute] may be said to create a conclusive

warned that "a law will not pass constitutional muster if the . . . purpose articulated by the legislature is merely a 'sham,' " [18] they sometimes manipulate the definition of "purpose" to make a showing of improper purpose nearly impossible.[19]

In *United States v. O'Brien*,[20] the Court went even further to avoid the motive inquiry, upholding a conviction for burning a draft card despite strong evidence that the intent of Congress was precisely to stop those who would demonstrate their opposition to the war in Vietnam by publicly burning their draft cards. The Court asserted broadly that a law's constitutionality did not depend on the purpose or motive that led Congress to enact it.[21] The idea was that the Constitution is primarily a document which allocates and limits *power* so that, if Congress has the power to act, a bad motive should be irrelevant just as a good motive could not save an enactment that was beyond the reach of legislative power.[22] The Court's conclusion that legislative motive is

presumption that in fact the state interest which the statute serves is an anti-speech rather than a non-speech interest. If the state interest asserted in O'Brien were truly the non-speech interest of assuring availability of draft cards, why did Congress choose not to prohibit any knowing conduct which leads to unavailability, rather than limiting the scope of the statute to those instances in which the proscribed conduct carries with it a speech component hostile to governmental policy? The obvious inference to be drawn is that in fact the Congress was completely indifferent to the 'unavailability' objective, and was concerned only with an interest which the O'Brien opinion states is impermissible—an interest in the suppression of free expression." Nimmer, "The Meaning of Symbolic Speech Under the First Amendment," 21 U.C.L.A.L.Rev. 29, 41 (1973).

18. Wallace v. Jaffree, 472 U.S. 38, 64 (1985) (Powell, J., concurring).

19. See, e.g., Personnel Administrator v. Feeney, 442 U.S. 256, 279 (1979) (" 'Discriminatory purpose,' however, implies more than intent as volition or intent as awareness of consequences. It implies that the decisionmaker, in this case a state legislature, selected or reaffirmed a particular course of action at least in part 'because of,' not merely 'in spite of,' its adverse effects upon an identifiable group."). But such judicial manipulation occurs even when the purpose involved is not a legislative one. Compare Wallace v. Jaffree, 472 U.S. 38, 56 (1985) (defining illicit purpose to mean "entirely motivated" by an impermissible intent but nevertheless striking down an Alabama silent prayer and meditation statute), with Lynch v. Donnelly, 465 U.S. 668, 680 (1984) (upholding a municipality's non-legislative decision to display a Christmas creche on the ground that the display served a secular purpose):

"The Court has invalidated *legislation or governmental action* on the ground that a secular purpose was lacking, but only when it has concluded there was no question that the *statute or activity* was motivated wholly by religious considerations." (emphasis added). See also City of Renton v. Playtime Theatres, Inc., 106 S.Ct. 925, 929 (1986) (rejecting the view that "if '*a motivating factor*' in enacting the ordinance was to restrict respondents' exercise of First Amendment rights the ordinance would be invalid, apparently no matter how small a part this motivating factor may have played in the City Council's decision") (quoting 748 F.2d at 537) (emphasis in original).

20. 391 U.S. 367 (1968), also discussed in § 12–3, supra, and §§ 12–6 and 12–23, infra.

21. Id. at 383. See also Palmer v. Thompson, 403 U.S. 217, 224–25 (1971) (upholding decision by municipal authorities closing all publicly-owned swimming pools; Court refused to inquire whether the decision was racially motivated). See § 16–16, infra.

22. See Wright v. Council of City of Emporia, 407 U.S. 451, 462 (1972) (benign purpose of city in establishing a separate school system held irrelevant where the effect of the action would be to impede the process of dismantling a segregated school system): "The existence of a permissible purpose cannot sustain an action that has an impermissible effect." Cf. Minneapolis Star & Tribune v. Minnesota Comm'r of Revenue, 460 U.S. 575, 592 (1983) (invalidating a "use tax" on the cost of paper and ink products consumed in the publication of periodicals): "We need not and do not impugn the motives of the Minnesota legislature in passing the ink and paper tax. Illicit legislative intent is not the *sine qua*

therefore irrelevant failed to acknowledge, let alone account for, the many cases in which such motive has been the focus of constitutional adjudication.[23] Nor was the Court entirely faithful to its own conclusion, since it did in fact inquire into Congress' motivation in prohibiting the burning of draft cards, concluding that O'Brien had not proven the impermissible motive that he alleged.[24] But that evidentiary conclusion was clearly reached by a Court especially sensitive to the hazards of congressional "psychoanalysis." [25]

There remains, however, the larger question of what is meant by an improper "motive." Government officials, including legislators, may make decisions in order to advance their personal careers and to bring fame and fortune to themselves.[26] These purposes surely cannot be deemed to taint the laws they inspire, for such a holding would invalidate much of the United States Code. Nor can the secret aspirations of legislators count as improper motives for the laws they favor. Even if a majority in Congress enacted a general, across-the-board tax relief provision in hopes that taxpayers would use much of the extra money to increase their contributions to religious organizations—or to a particular political party—such a tax cut would not be illegal.[27] In the free speech context, the concept of illegitimately motivated laws or other government activities should be limited to those whose *social meaning* renders them abridgements of speech. The Court should accordingly treat as facially discriminatory, and thus as subject to track one scrutiny, any evident pattern of official action that a reasonably well-informed observer would interpret as suppressing a particular point of view.[28] Such a restriction on speech should not be subject to validation either by a mask of surface neutrality or by the possibility of

non of a violation of the First Amendment."

23. The Court has also recently created doctrines which *require* that it scrutinize legislative as well as administrative intent. The test for whether a government-created forum is open to all speakers on an equal basis, for example, depends on "whether [the government] *intended* to designate a place not traditionally open to assembly and debate a public forum." Cornelius v. NAACP Legal Defense and Educational Fund, 473 U.S. 788, 802 (1985) (emphasis added), discussed further in § 12–24, infra. "The government does not create a public forum by inaction or by permitting limited discourse, but only by *intentionally* opening a non-traditional forum for public discourse." Id. (emphasis added).

24. See 391 U.S. at 385–88.

25. See United States v. Constantine, 296 U.S. 287, 298–99 (1935) (Cardozo, J., dissenting).

26. See Brest, "Palmer v. Thompson: An Approach to the Problem of Unconstitutional Legislative Motive," 1971 Sup.Ct. Rev. 95, 101; Ely, "Legislative and Administrative Motivation in Constitutional Law," 79 Yale J.L. 1205, 1218 (1970).

27. See Wallace v. Jaffree, 472 U.S. 38, 69–70 (1985) (O'Connor, J., concurring in the judgment): "A statute that ostensibly promotes a secular interest often has an incidental or even a primary effect of helping or hindering a sectarian belief. Chaos would ensue if every such statute were invalid under the Establishment Clause. For example, the State could not criminalize murder for fear that it would thereby promote the Biblical command against killing."

28. This test should be equally applicable to legislative and other kinds of official actions. Compare Wallace v. Jaffree, 472 U.S. 38, 76 (1985) (O'Connor, J., concurring in the judgment) (striking down Alabama prayer and meditation statute): "The relevant issue is whether an objective observer, acquainted with the text, legislative history, and implementation of the statute, would perceive it as a state endorsement of prayer in public schools," with Lynch v. Donnelly, 465 U.S. 668, 693–94 (1984) (O'Connor, J., concurring) (upholding Pawtucket display of Christmas creche): "whether a government activity communicates endorsement of religion is not a question of simple historical fact. Although evidentiary submissions may help answer

hypothesizing permissible motives or "secret hopes." [29] So it was that
the Court invalidated segregation by law in public schools in *Brown v.
Board of Education* [30] because that system unavoidably communicated a
social message of black inferiority, regardless of the surface symmetry
of the separate-but-equal concept, and regardless of any pretexts offered
by the Topeka school administrators.[31]

The next section seeks to advance our understanding of the issue of
motive in the context of the first amendment, and how that issue was
misconstrued in the *O'Brien* draft-card-burning case.

§ 12–6. A Closer Look at the Relevance of Motive: The O'Brien Case

Three major objections have been advanced against judicial inquiry
into the motives underlying an otherwise permissible enactment: (1) a
law may be entirely proper although it was the expression of an
improper motive; [1] (2) it would be futile to strike down an otherwise
valid law which would have to be validated as soon as it was reenacted
with a "show" of purer reasons; [2] and (3) motivation is extremely
difficult to ascertain, particularly in a collective body such as a legislature.[3]

The first argument assumes that a law may be deemed constitutional without any regard to the process that led to its enactment. But
the Court often upholds a law only after finding that the legislature has

it, the question is, like the question of
whether racial or sex-based classifications
communicate an invidious message, in
large part a legal question to be answered
on the basis of judicial interpretation of
social facts." See also Personnel Admin. of
Massachusetts v. Feeney, 442 U.S. 256, 279
n. 24 (1979) (proposing a similar "objective
test").

29. See Arcara v. Cloud Books, Inc., 106
S.Ct. 3172, 3178 (1986) (O'Connor, joined by
Stevens, J., concurring) (upholding closure
of adult bookstore on the basis that solicitation of prostitution was occurring on the
premises): "If, however, a city were to use
a nuisance statute as a pretext for closing
down a book store because it sold indecent
books or because of the perceived secondary effects of having a purveyor of such
books in the neighborhood, the case would
clearly implicate First Amendment concerns and require analysis under the appropriate First Amendment standard of review."

30. 347 U.S. 483 (1954), discussed in
Chapter 16, infra.

31. See also Hunter v. Underwood, 471
U.S. 222 (1985) (unanimously striking
down provision of Alabama state constitution that disenfranchised persons convicted
of certain enumerated felonies and misdemeanors, when it was clear that the section's enactment represented an effort to
discriminate against blacks).

§ 12–6

1. See Tussman & tenBroek, "The
Equal Protection of the Laws," 37 Calif.L.
Rev. 341, 359–60 (1949); Ely, "Legislative
and Administrative Motivation in Constitutional Law," 79 Yale L.J. 1205, 1212,
1215–16 (1970).

2. See Wallace v. Jaffree, 472 U.S. 38,
108 (1985) (Rehnquist, J., dissenting) (suggesting that the test of secular purpose for
a school prayer and meditation statute is
meaningless because it "will condemn
nothing so long as the legislature utters a
secular purpose and says nothing about
aiding religion. Thus the constitutionality
of a statute may depend upon what the
legislators put into the legislative history,
and, more importantly, what they leave
out"); Palmer v. Thompson, 403 U.S. 217,
225 (1971) (municipal decision to close
swimming pools upheld although evidently
motivated by consideration of race); United States v. O'Brien, 391 U.S. 367, 384
(1968) (law banning draft card burning upheld despite evidence that it was intended
to suppress a means of expressing dissent).

3. See Palmer, 403 U.S. at 224–25;
O'Brien, 391 U.S. at 383–84. Notably,
none of these arguments even purports to
address the role of an emphasis on motive
in doctrine as addressed to the legislature
itself; all focus exclusively, and myopically, on judicial review.

properly weighed its costs and benefits: where an illicit reason has played a substantial role in the legislature's deliberations, it may reasonably be said that the decisional calculus has been impermissibly skewed.[4]

The second argument assumes that it is a futile exercise to strike down a law which may be reenacted in a process that will lead to its validation. But the mere possibility of reenactment is insufficient warrant for a conclusion of futility. The prestige of the invalidating court may be enough to dissuade the legislature; judicial review may itself powerfully recall to legislators their constitutional oaths.[5] If the lawmakers are adamant and do re-enact, so undisciplined and disparate an institution as a legislative body may not prove capable of the tight conspiracy needed to conceal its real motives from the judiciary.[6] The courts might in any event presume that the legislature continues to entertain the illicit motive until the legislature carries the burden of showing its genuinely altered purpose in repassing the law.[7] But even if lawmakers succeed in hiding illicit objectives from the judiciary, calling the resulting process a "charade"[8] would miss an essential point. At least when the illicit motive of suppressing speech is apparent to the public or stands revealed with unmistakeable clarity,[9] vali-

4. See Califano v. Goldfarb, 430 U.S. 199, 214–17 (1977) (gender discrimination struck down because legislative history revealed motive to be stereotyped thinking, not desire to offset prior discrimination). Cf. Village of Arlington Heights v. Metropolitan Housing Development Corp., 429 U.S. 252, 265 n. 11 (1977) (rezoning decision upheld where complainants had not proved racially discriminatory intent): "Legislation is frequently multipurposed: the removal of even a 'subordinate' purpose may shift altogether the consensus of legislative judgment supporting the statute." See also Stone, "Content Regulation and the First Amendment," 25 Wm. & Mary L.Rev. 189, 230 (1983) ("The improper motivation concept, however, clearly operates as a taint. That is, if an improper motivation played a substantial role in the government's decision to restrict expression, the restriction must be invalidated even if alternative, proper justifications are available."); Brest, "Palmer v. Thompson: An Approach to the Problem of Unconstitutional Legislative Motive," 1971 Sup.Ct.Rev. 95, 116–118, 127–128. See generally § 16–20 and Chapter 17, infra.

5. See Eisenberg, "Disproportionate Impact and Illicit Motive: Theories of Constitutional Adjudication," 52 N.Y.U.L.Rev. 39, 116 (1977).

6. See Wallace v. Jaffree, 472 U.S. 38, 75 (1985) (O'Connor, J., concurring in the judgment) (invalidating a school prayer and meditation statute under the establishment clause): "I have little doubt that our courts are capable of distinguishing a sham secular purpose from a sincere one, or that

the Lemon [v. Kurtzman, 403 U.S. 602 (1971)] inquiry into the effect of an enactment would help decide those close cases where the validity of an expressed secular purpose is in doubt."

7. See Mt. Healthy City School District Board of Education v. Doyle, 429 U.S. 274, 285–86 (1977) (burden is on school officials to show by a preponderance of the evidence that a teacher who had been fired for an impermissible reason would have been fired even in the absence of that reason). Facts which might be used to show that reenactment was based on legitimate motives could include a material change of circumstances, the passage of time accompanied by a change in public attitudes, or a record showing the desirability of the enactment on the merits. Such scrutiny seems an extraordinary intrusion into the legislative process, but may well be justified by the legislature's previous misbehavior. See Brest, supra note 4, at 126–127.

8. Ely, note 1, supra, at 274.

9. While a court may be less able to take note of illicit legislative motives than political observers might, given the properly demanding evidentiary requirements, see Bickel, The Least Dangerous Branch 220 (1962), courts should nonetheless seek to narrow the gap between their perceptions of legislative realities and those of the public. Courts cannot let themselves remain "blind" to what "others can see and understand." And certainly they must not deliberately blind themselves to facts which are "palpable." "[If a]ll others can see and understand [the intent of Con-

dating the law would serve to legitimate a transparent and potentially chilling abridgment of individual liberty.[10] Even when the effect of judicial inquiry into the motives of a legislature is reduced candor, the play, it must be remembered, is performed not to the Court alone, but also to the citizenry, with a salutary decline of political rhetoric antithetical to fundamental constitutional values.[11]

Among the most telling objections to judicial review of legislative motive is the difficulty of ferreting out the real purpose of a collective lawmaking body, particularly if it must be inferred from the articulated remarks of a few legislators.[12] Nonetheless courts in the course of statutory interpretation routinely look to statements of legislators, among other evidence, for guidance as to legislative purpose.[13] The inquiry into legislative motive would be rendered all but hopeless in constitutional adjudication if courts were asked to isolate an impermissible "sole" or "dominant" purpose, since the intentions of legislators will almost always be multiple and mixed.[14] But this order of difficulty can be avoided if a complainant need only prove that the legislature was motivated *in substantial part* by an illicit purpose; once this is shown, the burden should shift to the law's defenders to establish that the same law probably would have been enacted even if the impermissible purpose had not been present. Casting the motive inquiry along these lines makes the threshold question no more difficult than the conventional inquiry into motive for purposes of statutory construction.[15]

gress h]ow can we properly shut our minds to it?" Bailey v. Drexel Furniture Co. (Child Labor Case), 259 U.S. 20, 37 (1922) (Taft, C.J.) (use of taxing power intended to control conditions of child labor). See also United States v. Kahriger, 345 U.S. 22, 40 (1953) (Frankfurter, J.) (dissenting from decision upholding federal occupational tax on gamblers): "The motive of congressional legislation is not for our scrutiny, provided only that the ulterior purpose is not expressed in ways which negative what the revenue words on their face express."

10. On the legitimating function of the Court, see Charles Black, The People and the Court 34–55 (1970). See also Max Weber, On Law In Economy and Society 322–37 (M. Rheinstein ed. 1954).

11. See Wallace v. Jaffree, 472 U.S. 38, 75–76 (1985) (O'Connor, J., concurring in the judgment): "While the secular purpose requirement alone may rarely be determinative in striking down a statute, it nevertheless serves an important function. It reminds government that when it acts it should do so without endorsing a particular religious belief or practice that all citizens do not share. In this sense the secular purpose requirement is squarely based in the text of the Establishment Clause it helps to enforce." Even if the free speech clause is not precisely analogous in this respect, a similar point may be made.

12. See O'Brien, 391 U.S. at 383–84; Edwards v. Aguillard, 107 S.Ct. 2573, 2605–07 (1987) (Scalia, J., joined by Rehnquist, C.J., dissenting); Miller, "Reductionism in the Law Schools, or Why the Blather About the Motivation of Legislators?", 16 San Diego L.Rev. 891, 893 (1979) ("it is manifestly impossible for any one member of Congress to be informed about the details of the 400 public laws enacted each session. How, then, can one speak of the motivation of Congress?"). See generally Ely, note 1, supra, at 1212–14, 1275–79.

13. See Frankfurter, "Some Reflections on the Reading of Statutes," 47 Colum.L. Rev. 527, 538–39, 543 (1947). Courts have also proven capable of determining the motivations of other collective bodies, such as labor unions and corporations. See Eisenberg, "Disproportionate Impact and Illicit Motive: Theories of Constitutional Adjudication," 52 N.Y.U.L.Rev. 39, 115 (1977).

14. See Ely, note 1, supra, at 1213–14.

15. See Ely, supra note 1, at 1278. See also note 5, supra. Once the presence of an illicit motive is shown, the question remains what degree of scrutiny is thereby triggered. In his stimulating and complex essay, supra note 1, Professor Ely argues that proof of an illicit motive should trigger only a minimal burden on government to demonstrate a "legitimately defensible" reason for burdening expressive activity, so

To determine that an illicit purpose was a "motivating factor," a court must make use of such circumstantial and direct evidence of socially observable intent as may be available.[16] Some of the proper elements of an inquiry into illicit motive may be observed through a re-examination of the claim that the law banning the burning of draft cards in *United States v. O'Brien* had been enacted with the illicit intent of stifling protest against the Vietnam war.[17] The circumstances in which the law was enacted should at least have sparked the suspicion of the Court. The amendment to the Selective Service law making the knowing destruction of a draft card a federal offense was enacted by Congress only after such conduct became a notorious form of protest. To be sure, while a predictable consequence of the enactment was the elimination of a particularly dramatic vehicle for dissent, the sequence of events might seem consistent with an intent by Congress to halt draft card burnings solely because of the threat to the effective administration of the draft laws caused by the destruction of the cards themselves. One would then look for evidence in the record that the administration of the draft had in any way been endangered. The legislative history was scant, however, the bill passing both Houses of Congress and being signed by the President in less than a month. Neither House held hearings on the merits of the draft-card-burning amendment. The only statements in the Committee Reports or from the floor of either House bearing on the merits of the law made reference to the "contumacious" and "unpatriotic" conduct of those who protested the war. More important was the striking omission from the legislative history of any explanation for protecting draft cards as such. The Court's opinion listed some possible uses which draft cards might serve: initial notification of a registrant's classification, proof of an individual's registration, verification of a local board's records in the event of administrative error, a convenient compendium of draft information for the registrant, a check on forgery or other deceptive misuse of the card, and evidence of availability for induction in the event of an emergency.[18] The listing is a plausible if uncompelling explanation for singling out draft cards for protection, but only if the amendment crowns a regulatory process which in fact seriously pursued the goal

long as the law on its face does not depart from government's paramount obligation to be content neutral. But if track one's demand for an extraordinary justification is triggered when government's concern with communicative content is evident on the face of the statute, there seems insufficient reason not to trigger the same demanding scrutiny when government's aim is rendered transparent by extrinsic evidence. See Brest, supra note 4, at 142.

Other scholars have suggested methods of determining legislative purpose. Taylor, "Judicial Review of Improper Purposes and Irrelevant Considerations," 35 Cambridge L.J. 272, 283–84 (1976); Simon, "Racially Prejudiced Government Actions: A Motivation Theory of the Constitutional Ban Against Racial Discrimination," 15 San Diego L.Rev. 1041, 1097, 1101 (1978) (proposing that the motivation of collective bodies can be determined by treating them as if they were individuals); Note, "A Case Study in Equal Protection: Voting Rights Decisions and a Plea for Consistency," 70 Nw.U.L.Rev. 934, 961 (1976) (problems of proving motive can be avoided by allocation of the burden of proof and by proper application of the rules of evidence).

16. See Village of Arlington Heights, supra note 4, at 564–65.

17. 391 U.S. 367 (1968). The following discussion draws heavily on Alfange, "Free Speech and Symbolic Conduct," 1968 Sup. Ct.Rev. 1.

18. 391 U.S. at 378–80.

that each registrant have his draft card on his person. While Selective Service regulations required registrants to have their cards in their possession at all times, the requirement had not been seriously enforced. Indeed, prior to the enactment of the amendment, little attention was paid to the possession requirement. The Selective Service had been quite casual about the possession requirement and had expressed no concern for the efficiency of the draft laws. Set in a context in which any serious concern for the asserted governmental interests would have demanded a broader solution,[19] the publicly visible evidence quite clearly shows that the amendment would not have been enacted but for the purpose of suppressing dissent;[20] thus O'Brien carried the burden of showing that an illicit purpose was a "motivating factor" in Congress' passage of the ban on burning draft cards. On this view, *United States v. O'Brien* appears to have been wrongly decided since the showing of illicit motive should have triggered the more demanding requirements of track one analysis rather than the weaker demands, met in *O'Brien*, of track two. The relevant categorical test on track one would have been "clear and present danger," and no one had even alleged that burning a draft card was an incitement to draft evasion or to any other illegal conduct.

From the doctrinal point of view, the most important conclusion is that the broad statement of the Court in *O'Brien* concerning the limited relevance of legislative motive in constitutional adjudication must be strongly qualified. In *Washington v. Davis*, Justice White wrote for the majority: "To the extent that [some of our cases suggest] a generally applicable proposition that legislative purpose is irrelevant in constitutional adjudication, our prior cases . . . are to the contrary."[21] If there is persuasive proof that a purpose to penalize or control rights of expression or association significantly motivated the enactment of a law, or the taking of any other official government action, such proof should put the case on track one and trigger the demand for an extraordinary justification of the government's departure from neutrality.

§ 12–7. The Persistent But Oversimplified Distinction Between Speech and Conduct

We have yet to consider a distinction between speech and conduct with which the Court has frequently ornamented its opinions.[1] The

---

19. See Alfange, supra note 17, at 42–44. A similar argument is made in a different context by Freund, "Review and Federalism," in Cahn, Supreme Court and Supreme Law 99 (1954). Professor Freund observes that the Supreme Court would probably not have upheld a New York law that forbade the shipment of diseased cattle into the state, Mintz v. Baldwin, 289 U.S. 346 (1933), if it had known that the disease was prevalent in New York herds and that the state was doing nothing to prevent healthy cattle from other states from being mixed with infected animals.

20. See Professor Nimmer's analysis that the statute was "overnarrow," note 17, in § 12–5, supra.

21. 426 U.S. 229, 244 n. 11 (1976) (upholding the use of a test to screen recruits for the police force, despite the test's disproportionate impact on minority applicants, because there was no showing of racially discriminatory intent).

§ 12–7

1. See Ely, "Flag Desecration: A Case Study in the Roles of Categorization and Balancing in First Amendment Analysis," 88 Harv.L.Rev. 1482, 1493–1496 (1975);

distinction originates in the labor picketing cases. In *Thornhill v. Alabama*,[2] the Court declared that peaceful picketing to publicize the fact of a labor dispute was constitutionally protected free speech. In a series of cases culminating some 17 years later in *Teamsters Local 695 v. Vogt*,[3] the Court upheld state laws which banned peaceful labor picketing for illegal purposes. To distinguish these cases from *Thornhill*, Justice Frankfurter said that picketing is "speech plus" and that a state could for various reasons regulate the "plus."[4] In decisions growing out of civil rights demonstrations, the Court took up that distinction, the Court's fullest statement appearing in *Cox v. Louisiana*.[5] *Cox* involved 2,000 students demonstrating on the sidewalk opposite the Baton Rouge courthouse to protest segregation in general and to inveigh particularly against the previous arrest of several students, then being held in the courthouse jail, who had been picketing stores that maintained segregated lunchcounters. Justice Goldberg's opinion for five justices characterized the demonstration as "speech plus," and thus found it entitled to a lesser degree of protection than the first amendment affords "pure speech."[6] Justice Black took the position that the demonstration was conduct, unprotected by the first amendment, which could be regulated or prohibited.[7] In subsequent cases involving public demonstrations and nonverbal symbolic expression, the Supreme Court has occasionally employed Justice Goldberg's language, affording full protection to conduct labeled "pure speech" and something less to what the Court labeled other forms of conduct.[8]

Nimmer, "The Meaning of Symbolic Speech Under the First Amendment," 21 U.C.L.A.L.Rev. 29 (1973); Henkin, "The Supreme Court, 1967 Term—Foreword: On Drawing Lines," 82 Harv.L.Rev. 63, 76–82 (1968); Note, "Symbolic Conduct," 68 Colum.L.Rev. 1091 (1968).

2. 310 U.S. 88 (1940) (facially invalidating for overbreadth a state law which prohibited all union picketing).

3. 354 U.S. 284 (1957) (upholding state prohibition of picketing directed at achieving a "union shop" in violation of state law). The result of the cases after Thornhill upholding state bans on peaceful picketing directed at ends the state has properly forbidden is that the states are essentially as free to regulate labor picketing today as if Thornhill had not been decided. See Kalven, The Negro and the First Amendment 134 (1966); Emerson, The System of Freedom of Expression, 435–444 (1970). See § 12–3, note 14, supra.

4. Teamsters Local 695 v. Vogt, 354 U.S. at 289, 290, 292. The distinction is traceable to Justice Douglas' concurring opinion in Teamsters Local 802 v. Wohl, 315 U.S. 769, 776–777 (1942) (invalidating an injunction directed against union picketing of wholesale bakeries and retail outlets serviced by independent peddlers who had refused to join the union or work union hours). In later cases, Justices Black and Douglas cited Giboney v. Empire Storage and Ice Co., 336 U.S. 490, 498 (1949) (validating a state ban on picketing directed at enforcing a secondary boycott made illegal by state antitrust laws) for the distinction between speech and conduct. See, e.g., Street v. New York, 394 U.S. 576, 610 (1969) (Black, J., dissenting).

5. 379 U.S. 559 (Cox II) (1965).

6. Id. at 563.

7. Id. at 581 (Black, J., dissenting). Justice Black's constitutional approach read the Bill of Rights as withdrawing from government "all power to act in certain areas—whatever the scope of those areas may be." Black, "The Bill of Rights," 35 N.Y.U.L.Rev. 865, 874–75 (1960). The areas to which Justice Black applied his absolutist thesis were determined by his definition of speech. The criticism has been that, if one does not want to protect an act, one merely defines it as "nonspeech", cf. G. Orwell, 1984, the distinction between speech and conduct serving as a sub rosa tool to escape the rigidity of the absolutist position so as to produce the desired result. See Kalven, "Upon Rereading Mr. Justice Black On the First Amendment," 14 U.C.L.A.L.Rev. 428 (1967).

8. See, e.g., Adderley v. Florida, 385 U.S. 39 (1966) (demonstration on premises

The trouble with the distinction between speech and conduct is that it has less determinate content than is sometimes supposed. All communication except perhaps that of the extrasensory variety involves conduct. Moreover, if the expression involves talk, it may be noisy;[9] if written, it may become litter.[10] So too, much conduct is expressive, a fact the Court has had no trouble recognizing in a wide variety of circumstances.[11] Expression and conduct, message and medium, are thus inextricably tied together in all communicative behavior; expressive behavior is "100% action and 100% expression."[12] It is thus not surprising that the Supreme Court has never articulated a basis for its distinction; it could not do so, with the result that any particular course of conduct may be hung almost randomly on the "speech" peg or the "conduct" peg as one sees fit. The disharmony in the cases is particularly apparent when one compares Justice Goldberg's opinion in *Cox* with an earlier opinion by Justice Stewart in *Edwards v. South Carolina*,[13] where 187 demonstrators were convicted for breach of the peace after they paraded peaceably through the grounds of the State House to protest against state segregation policies. Except that the site of the demonstration was an area around a courthouse, the style of the protest in *Cox* was essentially identical with that in *Edwards*. But in *Edwards* the Court saw "an exercise of [first amendment] rights in their most pristine and classic form,"[14] while in *Cox* the majority conjured up the specter of "mob rule."[15] While the ultimate decisions in the two cases may well be reconciled, the characterization of the two courses of conduct is strikingly inconsistent, so the distinction between speech and conduct must be seen at best as announcing a conclusion of the Court, rather than as summarizing in any way the analytic processes which led the Court to that conclusion.

Meaning might be poured into the speech-conduct dichotomy by reference to a system of free expression that permits the identification of acts that should be protected by the first amendment. Government would be guilty of impermissibly abridging speech or petition within

of county jail is conduct not protected by first amendment); Brown v. Louisiana, 383 U.S. 131 (1966) (silent demonstration on premises of public library is speech protected by first amendment); United States v. O'Brien, 391 U.S. 367 (1968) (burning draft card is conduct not protected by first amendment); Spence v. Washington, 418 U.S. 405 (1974) (per curiam) (affixing peace symbol to flag is speech protected by first amendment).

9. See, e.g., Kovacs v. Cooper, 336 U.S. 77 (1949) ("loud and raucous" sound trucks).

10. See, e.g., Schneider v. Irvington, 308 U.S. 147 (1939) (ordinance barring the distribution of leaflets as means of reducing litter).

11. See, e.g., Buckley v. Valeo, 424 U.S. 1 (1976) (contributing money); Spence v. Washington, 418 U.S. 405 (1974) (displaying flag with peace symbol attached); Co-

hen v. California, 403 U.S. 15 (1971) (wearing sign on back of jacket); Schacht v. United States, 398 U.S. 58 (1970) (wearing uniform); Tinker v. Des Moines School Dist., 393 U.S. 503 (1969) (wearing black armbands); Edwards v. South Carolina, 372 U.S. 229 (1963) (demonstration); NAACP v. Button, 371 U.S. 415 (1963) (litigation); West Virginia State Board of Education v. Barnette, 319 U.S. 624 (1943) (compulsory flag salute); Thornhill v. Alabama, 310 U.S. 88 (1940) (picketing); Stromberg v. California, 283 U.S. 359 (1931) (displaying red flag).

12. Ely, supra note 1, at 1495–96.

13. 372 U.S. 229 (1963). The comparison is more fully drawn by Kalven, "The Public Forum: Cox v. Louisiana," 1965 S.Ct.Rev. 1.

14. 372 U.S. at 230–31.

15. 379 U.S. at 562.

the first amendment's meaning, quite apart from the conduct at which its regulation is directed or to which its regulation is applied, if the regulation is properly understood as suppressing a disfavored viewpoint or idea. Thus, a rule forbidding "outdoor sleeping as a means of protesting homelessness," but permitting all other outdoor sleeping, would surely be an abridgement of speech,[16] even if camping or sleeping are not generally regarded as forms of expression.[17]

The harder problem arises when the law is not directed at anything resembling speech *or* at the views expressed,[18] but when its enforcement nonetheless serves to inhibit speech. If any such effect is merely incidental, no first amendment issue should be deemed to arise. In *Arcara v. Cloud Books, Inc.*,[19] for example, the Supreme Court upheld the closure of an adult bookstore on whose premises prostitution was taking place.[20] The Court found that the object of the state's order was the illegal conduct, which "manifests absolutely no element of protected

16. Cf. Clark v. Community for Creative Non-Violence, 468 U.S. 288 (1984) (upholding formally neutral National Park Service regulations that forbade all sleeping in designated monument areas, as applied to protesters attempting to call attention to the plight of the homeless by sleeping in symbolic tents erected in Lafayette Park, across the street from the White House). The previous winter, the CCNV had set up and slept in nine tents in Lafayette Park to protest homelessness after the D.C. Circuit found that these activities did not violate the then-existing Park Service regulations. See Community for Creative Non-Violence v. Watt, 670 F.2d 1213 (D.C. Cir. 1982). The Park Service then issued a set of new rules clearly aimed at the CCNV's demonstrations, see 47 Fed.Reg. 24,299 (1982), and this second set included the formally neutral regulations at issue in Clark. See 468 U.S. at 302 n. 1 (Marshall, J., joined by Brennan, J., dissenting).

17. See Community for Creative Non-Violence v. Watt, 703 F.2d 586, 622 (D.C. Cir. 1983) (Scalia, J., joined by MacKinnon and Bork, JJ., dissenting) (denying that "sleeping is or can ever be speech for First Amendment purposes," but conceding that "[a] law *directed at* the communicative nature of conduct must, like a law directed at speech itself, be justified by the substantial showing of need that the First Amendment requires") (emphasis added).

18. The Court, for example, has been reluctant to concede that the first amendment has any relevance whatsoever to political assassinations, radical bank robberies, or other violent modes of expression. This reluctance was evident in the tenor of the oral argument in United States v. O'Brien, 391 U.S. 367 (1968), in which the Court ultimately upheld a conviction for draft-card burning. Chief Justice Warren

asked: "What if a soldier in Vietnam, in a crowd, broke his weapon? Would it be symbolic speech?" And Justice Fortas asked whether the act of throwing a rock through a window of the White House could claim first amendment protection. See Bickel, The Supreme Court and the Idea of Progress 79–80 (1970). See also United States v. Miller, 367 F.2d 72, 79 (2d Cir. 1966) (upholding conviction for draft-card burning).

Professor Edwin Baker proposes that the manner in which both speech and conduct affects others determines whether it is protected expression. Baker, "Scope of the First Amendment Freedom of Speech," 25 U.C.L.A.L.Rev. 964 (1978). Conduct, for example, is unprotected if it includes "coercion or injury to or physical interference with another or damage to physical property." Id. at 1011. Blackmail, while clearly speech, is unprotected because it is "designed to disrespect and distort the integrity of another's mental processes." Id. at 1002. For thoughtful comments on this approach, see Thomas Emerson, "First Amendment Doctrine and the Burger Court," 68 Calif.L.Rev. 422, 474–77 (1980).

19. 106 S.Ct. 3172 (1986).

20. Cf. Schad v. Borough of Mt. Ephraim, 452 U.S. 61, 66 (1981) (invalidating a borough ordinance that permitted adult theaters and bookstores, but excluded live entertainment from its commercial zone): "[N]ude dancing is not without its First Amendment protections from official regulation." But cf. Paris Adult Theatre I v. Slaton, 413 U.S. 49, 67 (1973) ("a 'live' performance of a man and woman locked in a sexual embrace at high noon in Times Square is [not] protected by the Constitution," even if "they simultaneously engage in a valid political dialogue.").

expression." [21]   The open sexual activities were thus in no sense part of the system of free expression, either in general or in the particular case. Since this was so—and since, as Justice O'Connor pointed out in her concurrence, the enforcement order was not a pretext for harassing certain bookstores because of the sorts of literature they sold [22]—no abridgement of speech was involved at all.[23]

There are certain activities that have historically been recognized as inextricably intertwined with speech or petition; regulation of these activities implicates the first amendment regardless of whether such regulation is cast in terms of message, or motivated by message. Thus, outdoor distribution of leaflets or pamphlets; [24] door-to-door political canvassing; [25] solicitation of contributions, wherever it takes place; [26]

21. 106 S.Ct. at 3176–77 ("unlike the symbolic draft card burning in O'Brien, the sexual activity carried on in this case manifests absolutely no element of protected expression").

22. 106 S.Ct. at 3178 (O'Connor, J., joined by Stevens, J., concurring).

23. Justice Blackmun, joined by Justices Brennan and Marshall, dissented on the grounds that the closure of the bookstore represented not merely an incidental but rather a "substantial infringement of First Amendment rights." Id. at 3180. And on remand, the New York Court of Appeals found that the closure violated freedom of expression as guaranteed by the state's own constitution. Arcara v. Cloud Books, 68 N.Y.2d 553, 510 N.Y.S.2d 844, 503 N.E.2d 492 (1986). Even though the state's purpose was not to interfere with legitimate bookselling activities, its enforcement order inevitably had that effect. The state's action thus had an "incidental," albeit "not direct," impact on communication. "Actions of this type are subject to lesser scrutiny than those directed at restraining free expression, but they cannot be said to have absolutely no [state] constitutional implications." Id. The New York court, while maintaining that a bookstore can claim no "exception from statutes of general operation aimed at preventing nuisances or hazards to the public health and safety," nevertheless held that it was "entitled to special protection" under the state constitution's counterpart of the first amendment by virtue of its bookselling activities. The New York court accordingly imposed the burden on the state to demonstrate that, in closing the store, it had chosen "a course no broader than necessary to accomplish its purpose." Id. The state, in other words, had to satisfy a "least restrictive means" test: it had to show the unavailability of other measures with less detrimental effect on freedom of expression, such as the arrest of the offending prostitutes.

24. United States v. Grace, 461 U.S. 171 (1983) (invalidating statute prohibiting all leafleting and picketing on sidewalk adjoining Supreme Court building); Heffron v. International Society for Krishna Consciousness (ISKCON), 452 U.S. 640 (1981) (upholding a state fair rule that prohibited the distribution of printed material or the solicitation of funds except from duly licensed booths in the fairgrounds); Schneider v. Irvington, 308 U.S. 147 (1939) (invalidating several ordinances that prohibited leafleting on public streets and other public places).

25. Compare City of Watseka v. Illinois Public Action Council, 107 S.Ct. 919 (1987) (mem.) (affirming judgment that ordinance which limited door-to-door solicitation to the hours between 9:00 am and 5:00 pm, Monday through Saturday, was unconstitutional as applied to organization that engaged in political canvassing); Martin v. Struthers, 319 U.S. 141 (1943) (striking down an ordinance that forbade knocking on the door or ringing the door of a residence in order to deliver handbills, as applied to a Jehovah's Witness distributing religious literature), with Breard v. Alexandria, 341 U.S. 622 (1951) (upholding an ordinance forbidding the practice of going door-to-door to solicit orders for the sales of goods).

26. Cornelius v. NAACP Legal Defense and Educational Fund, 473 U.S. 788 (1985) (upholding executive order that excluded organizations engaging in political advocacy from participating in charity fundraising drive aimed at federal employees); Secretary of State of Maryland v. Joseph H. Munson Co., 467 U.S. 947 (1984) (invalidating as an unconstitutional limitation on protected first amendment solicitation a Maryland statute that prohibited charitable organizations from paying expenses of more than 25 percent of amount raised); Village of Schaumburg v. Citizens for a Better Environment, 444 U.S. 620 (1980) (invalidating as unconstitutionally over-

mailbox-stuffing; [27] picketing; [28] civil rights demonstrations [29] and boy-cotts; [30] communicating with government; [31] putting up outdoor pos-ters [32] or signs [33]—all of these activities might variously be described, without special illumination, either as "speech" *or* as "conduct," but all *must* be recognized as activities of special first amendment significance. Their regulation must therefore be assessed with particular sensitivity to the possible constriction of that breathing space which freedom of speech requires in the society contemplated by the first amendment. So, too, for searches of newsrooms,[34] eavesdropping on private conversa-tions,[35] military infiltration of antiwar meetings,[36] or coerced disclosure of journalists' sources.[37] In all of these instances, even if a regulation is

broad a limitation on door-to-door or on-street solicitation to organizations that use 75 percent of their receipts for "charitable purposes"). But see Munson, 467 U.S. at 979–80 (1984) (Rehnquist, J., dissenting) (arguing that the 25 percent rule did not have a sufficiently direct impact on expres-sive activity to warrant first amendment scrutiny): "Otherwise, national forest leg-islation would be equally suspect as tend-ing to raise the price and limit the quanti-ty of paper."

27. United States Postal Service v. Council of Greenburgh Civic Ass'ns, 453 U.S. 114 (1981) (upholding postal service statute that prohibited the deposit of un-stamped "mailable matter" in letterboxes).

28. Chicago Police Dept. v. Mosley, 408 U.S. 92 (1972) (invalidating an ordinance that banned all picketing within 150 feet of a school building while school was in ses-sion and one half-hour before and after-wards, except "the peaceful picketing of any school involved in labor dispute"); Ca-rey v. Brown, 447 U.S. 455 (1980) (invali-dating a statute that prohibited the picket-ing of residences or dwellings, except when the dwelling was "used as a place of busi-ness," or was "a place of employment in-volved in a labor dispute or the place of holding a meeting [on] premises commonly used to discuss subjects of general public interest," or when a person was "picketing his own [dwelling].").

29. Grayned v. Rockford, 408 U.S. 104 (1972) (upholding anti-noise ordinance un-der which were convicted demonstrators protesting black students' grievances at a public high school); Shuttlesworth v. City of Birmingham, 394 U.S. 147 (1969) (strik-ing down ordinance governing parade per-mits because it gave police officials too much discretion to determine who could demonstrate).

30. Compare NAACP v. Claiborne Hardware Co., 458 U.S. 886 (1982) (holding that NAACP consumer boycott was pro-tected expression immune from state pro-hibition), with International Longshore-

men's Ass'n v. Allied Int'l, 456 U.S. 212 (1982) (finding that political boycott by la-bor union is not protected expression).

31. Minnesota State Board for Commu-nity Colleges v. Knight, 465 U.S. 271 (1984) (upholding exclusion of state professional employees who were members of bargain-ing unit but not members of union from "meet and confer" sessions with state edu-cation board); Perry Educational Associa-tion v. Perry Local Educators' Ass'n, 460 U.S. 37 (1983) (upholding collective bar-gaining arrangement conferring exclusive access to interschool mail system to incum-bent union).

32. Los Angeles City Council v. Taxpay-ers for Vincent, 466 U.S. 789 (1984) (up-holding city's ban on posting of all signs on public property).

33. Metromedia, Inc. v. San Diego, 453 U.S. 490 (1981) (striking down ordinance that imposed a greater restriction on politi-cal than on commercial billboards) (plurali-ty opinion).

34. Zurcher v. Stanford Daily, 436 U.S. 547 (1978) (holding that fourth amendment does not prevent the government from is-suing a warrant based on probable cause simply because owner or possessor of place to be searched, in this case a newspaper office, is not reasonably suspected of crimi-nal involvement).

35. Katz v. United States, 389 U.S. 347 (1967) (holding that electronic eavesdrop-ping upon private conversations consti-tutes a search and seizure and must meet fourth amendment requirements).

36. Laird v. Tatum, 408 U.S. 1 (1972) (dismissing for lack of standing class action that sought declaratory and injunctive re-lief against the U.S. Army because of its "alleged surveillance of lawful civilian po-litical activity").

37. Branzburg v. Hayes, 408 U.S. 665 (1972) (declining to create a first amend-ment newsman's privilege to refuse to an-swer relevant and material questions dur-ing a good faith grand jury investigation).

"Track 2" in character, a first amendment problem is posed by any arguably gratuitous or excessively severe regulation.

The very notion of speech is, of course, incomprehensible outside a cultural and social context. Thus activities ordinarily thought to be speech-related need not be so in every setting. Regulations of loud noises used not to communicate but instead to shatter glass, or pamphlets used not to express anything but to cover the ground with litter, need not trigger any first amendment scrutiny at all. But a generic regulation of pamphlet distribution, even as applied to an airdrop of pamphlets designed solely to litter the ground, might still be invalidated on first amendment principles if, in the process of enforcement, the regulation is not narrowed to deal with the non-communicative aspect of the conduct at issue.[38]

Finally, activities not ordinarily thought to have any particularly expressive dimension—such as camping or sleeping outdoors—might properly *acquire* such a dimension in a specific regulatory context where the regulation is promulgated in response to what is generally understood to be expressive use of the activities in question.[39] The fact that a regulation was so promulgated should not be equated with a viewpoint-suppressing motive of the sort that would trigger "Track 1" scrutiny:[40] so long as a law is not *aimed* at speech, the fact that it was enacted *because* of speech should not suffice to subject it to the *strictest* scrutiny.[41] But in both *Clark v. Community for Creative Non-Violence*[42] and *United States v. O'Brien*,[43] it was at least plain that the challenged rules were enacted in light of the expressive use of the activities at issue—whether camping out, or destroying draft cards—and it is this circumstance that would have made it artificial and perhaps indefensible for the Supreme Court to take the position that the first amendment had nothing at all to do with either case.

When the acts that trigger a rule's enactment and that occasion its invocation in the case at hand are both intended to express, and understood by their audience to express,[44] a particular mes-

38. Cf. Street v. New York, 394 U.S. 576 (1969) (reversing a conviction for uttering words contemptuous of the American flag while burning it, under a statute that punished both words and acts tending to "cast contempt upon [any American flag]"). The Court did not reach the issue of whether a conviction solely for acts of flag mutilation or burning could be sustained, see id. at 594, but noted instead that the statute had not been narrowed by the trial court's instructions to exclude constitutionally protected speech from its scope. See § 12–27, infra.

39. See Clark v. Community for Creative Non-Violence, 468 U.S. 288 (1984), discussed in note 16, supra.

40. See § 12–3, supra. By contrast, when regulation is triggered by the views expressed, a high standard of review is employed. Compare the doctrine of selective enforcement, as described in Wayte v. United States, 470 U.S. 598 (1985), which

upheld the "passive" enforcement strategy of the Selective Service that prosecuted those who publicly revealed their failure to register for the draft and thus may have punished those who exercised their first amendment rights. In dictum, the Court recognized that "the decision to prosecute may not be 'deliberately based' . . . on the exercise of protected statutory and constitutional rights." (citations omitted).

41. See § 12–5, supra.

42. 468 U.S. 288 (1984) (upholding ban on sleeping in certain monument areas).

43. 391 U.S. 367 (1968) (sustaining conviction for draft card burning).

44. See Note, "First Amendment Protection of Ambiguous Conduct," 84 Colum. L.Rev. 467, 493 (1984) (suggesting that courts focus on "the likelihood that the act was intended to be communicative, and will be understood to be so").

sage,[45] it is necessary to subject the rule and its enforcement to some degree of first amendment scrutiny.[46] All that follows is that the government must meet some version of the least restrictive alternative test [47]—a relaxed version, as in *O'Brien* and *CCNV*, when the Court does not deem the activities in question particularly significant to the system of free expression. When the conduct is more closely linked to expression, as in the case of pamphleteering, a tighter version of the test is appropriate.[48] Of course, if the Court is convinced not only that the first amendment should be applied, but also that the regulation was promulgated for the purpose of suppressing a disfavored viewpoint, then the case becomes one analogous to *Stromberg v. California*,[49] where the law on its face singled out conduct in terms of the anti-government message it expressed, triggering a virtually *per se* rule of invalidity.[50]

§ 12–8. The Structure of Track-One Analysis: Evaluating Content-Based Abridgments under Chaplinsky's Two-Level Theory

Once it is determined that a government regulation is aimed at the communicative impact of expressive activity, one must invalidate the regulation unless it falls within one of several narrow exceptions to the principle that government may not prescribe the form or content of individual expression. Although capped with an exception for compellingly justified restrictions (to be discussed later), all of the other exceptions take the form of categorical rules, such as the "clear and present danger" test, which differentiate between expression protected by the first amendment and expression which is regulable as long as minimal due process requirements have been met. The particular categorical rules for these *track one* cases will be examined in subsequent sections. This section briefly sets out the general contours of judicial review of government action which abridges "speech" in this content-based sense, examines the premises underlying the categorical

---

45. See Clark v. Community for Creative Non-Violence, 468 U.S. 288 (1984); United States v. O'Brien, 391 U.S. 367 (1968); Tinker v. Des Moines School District, 393 U.S. 503 (1969) (upholding right of students to wear black armbands in anti-war protest).

46. Whether this is so when the rule was enacted long before the acts acquired any expressive significance, and when all one can say is that the rule is being applied to an act that is not intrinsically or historically communicative but that happens in the case at hand to be expressive in intent and effect, is less clear. Absent proof of selective application to expressive acts alone, see note 40, supra, and § 12–5, supra, the first amendment should probably be deemed irrelevant in such a case.

47. See § 12–23, infra.

48. In City Council of Los Angeles v. Taxpayers for Vincent, 466 U.S. 789, 805–07 (1984), the Court evidently thought that putting up posters was sufficiently speech-related to trigger first amendment scrutiny, but not sufficiently central to freedom of expression to prevent the city from defining the very presence of the posters as "visual blight" and thus assuring that the "least restrictive alternative" test would be met virtually by definition.

49. 283 U.S. 359 (1931) (invalidating statute that prohibited anyone from "publicly display[ing] a red flag [or] device of any color or form whatever [as] a sign, symbol, or emblem of opposition to organized government").

50. See §§ 12–2, 12–3, supra.

rules, and briefly describes the status of the two-level theory of the first amendment, according to which each category of speech is either protected or unprotected.

In order to establish that particular expressive activities are not protected by the first amendment, the defenders of a regulation which is aimed at the communicative impact of the expression have the burden of either coming within one of the narrow categorical exceptions or showing that the regulation is necessary to further a "compelling state interest." In first amendment cases, the Supreme Court is least likely to take into account governmental interests which, although conceivable, were not actually considered by the relevant decision-maker.[1] The Court also requires an especially close nexus between ends and means. A statute must be narrowly drawn so that a challenged act of government is clearly an efficacious means to achieve permissible objectives of government and is narrowly aimed at those permissible objectives so as not unnecessarily to reach expressive conduct protected by the first amendment.[2] The test for a content-based restriction on track one is often described as requiring that "the government . . . show that the regulation is a precisely drawn means of serving a compelling state interest."[3] *Whenever the harm feared could be averted by a further exchange of ideas, governmental suppres-*

§ 12–8

1. Although some cases, see, e.g., United States v. O'Brien, 391 U.S. 367 (1968), appear to violate this prescription, the principle is firmly established both in cases involving important personal interests, see, e.g., Cleveland Board of Education v. LaFleur, 414 U.S. 632, 641 n. 9 (1974) (Stewart, J., opinion for the Court) (mandatory maternity leave rules), and in cases involving semi-suspect criteria of classification. See, e.g., Califano v. Goldfarb, 430 U.S. 199, 214–17 (1977) (gender discrimination). See generally § 16–33, infra. It would be highly anomalous for the Court to take a more casual attitude in those cases where scrutiny has traditionally been the strictest—cases arising under the first amendment. Indeed, in analyzing restrictions on freedom of expression, the Court has scrutinized the *actual* motivation of the decison-maker, see, e.g., Cornelius v. NAACP Legal Defense and Educational Fund, 473 U.S. 788, 813 (1985) (upholding executive order that excluded advocacy organizations from charity fundraising drive aimed at federal employees and remanding the case for determination of the issue of whether the order was improperly motivated by a desire to suppress particular speakers or messages), and has refused to accept hypothetical justifications for abridgements of speech if they did not in fact serve as the basis of the decision. See generally § 12–5, supra.

2. If a statute is not narrowly enough drawn to create a close nexus between its means and its legitimate ends, the Court may disregard such ends as justifications of the challenged law. See, e.g., Village of Schaumburg v. Citizens for a Better Environment, 444 U.S. 620 (1980) (striking down as unconstitutionally overbroad a village ordinance that prohibited door-to-door or on-street solicitation of contributions by charitable organizations that did not use at least 75 percent of their receipts for "charitable purposes," defined to exclude solicitation expenses, salaries, overhead, and administrative costs; the interests purportedly advanced by the ordinance were "only peripherally promoted by the 75 percent requirement and could be sufficiently served by measures less destructive of First Amendment interests."); Street v. New York, 394 U.S. 576, 592 (1969) (reversing a conviction for publicly speaking contemptuous words about the flag and dismissing the argument that the language came within the class of "fighting words" because the statute was not narrowly drawn to punish only words of that character). Alternatively, a law which is not narrowly enough drawn may be unconstitutionally overbroad. See generally § 12–27, infra.

3. Consolidated Edison Co. v. Public Service Comm'n, 447 U.S. 530, 540 (1980) (invalidating order of public service commission that prohibited utility from includ-

sion is conclusively deemed unnecessary.[4] In addition, the Court does not refrain, as it typically does in other contexts, from substituting its own factual judgments for those made by other courts, administrative agencies, or legislative bodies.[5] In short, government must come forward with sufficient proof to justify convincingly its abridgment of the constitutional right to speak,[6] in terms consistent with the basic theory of free expression. In general, that will be impossible unless government can persuasively show a harm that would be prevented by the abridgment but could not have been prevented by dialogue; whenever "more speech" could eliminate a feared injury, more speech is the constitutionally-mandated remedy.

The decision that a government regulation is aimed at the communicative impact of expressive activity almost always implies two additional conclusions: government may not justify content-based regulations by a claim either that the content of the expression has been adequately voiced by other speakers (so that advocates of different viewpoints should be given an opportunity to speak instead), or that the expression may be voiced in another place, at another time, or in another manner.[7] The first amendment does not permit government to

ing in monthly billing envelopes an insert discussing controversial issues of public policy). See also First National Bank of Boston v. Bellotti, 435 U.S. 765, 786 (1978) (striking down a Massachusetts criminal statute that prohibited business corporations from making contributions or expenditures to influence "the vote on any question submitted to the voters, other than one materially affecting any of the property, business or assets of the corporation"); Buckley v. Valeo, 424 U.S. 1, 25 (1976) (per curiam) (sustaining provisions of the Federal Election Campaign Act, that imposed a $1,000 ceiling on contributions to a candidate for federal office, but invalidating limitations on expenditures by and in support of candidates).

4. See, e.g., Linmark Associates, Inc., v. Township of Willingboro, 431 U.S. 85 (1977) (holding unconstitutional an ordinance prohibiting the posting of real estate "For Sale" and "Sold" signs). The opinion of Justice Marshall for a unanimous Court quoted with approval the language of Justice Brandeis in Whitney v. California, 274 U.S. 357, 377 (1927): "If there be time to expose through discussion the falsehood and fallacies, to avert the evil by the process of education, the remedy to be applied is more speech, not enforced silence. Only an emergency can justify repression." The Township of Willingboro had not shown panic selling to have set in, and the township was limited by the Court, in its efforts to forestall "white flight" and thereby maintain integrated housing, to the "more speech" remedy—the posting of "Not for

Sale" signs and the use of other forms of counter-publicity.

5. See, e.g., Cox v. Louisiana (I), 379 U.S. 536 (1965) (reversing convictions of civil rights demonstrators where independent review of the record showed no conduct which the state could prohibit as a breach of the peace); Fiske v. Kansas, 274 U.S. 380 (1927) (reversing conviction for criminal syndicalism because Court's independent examination of the uncontested evidence—the preamble to the Constitution of the I.W.W.—was not sufficient to show that the organization for which Fiske was recruiting advocated "unlawful acts" as a means of effectuating industrial changes or revolution). See generally P. Bator, P. Mishkin, D. Shapiro, & H. Wechsler, Hart & Wechsler's The Federal Courts and the Federal System 574–619 (2d ed. 1973).

6. See, e.g., Linmark Associates, supra note 4, where the record developed by the Township to justify the ordinance was strong enough to persuade the Court of Appeals that Willingboro was experiencing "incipient" panic selling and that "fear psychology [had] developed," but not compelling enough by the Supreme Court's standards to show that an "emergency" existed to justify suppressing otherwise protected expression.

7. See Consolidated Edison Co. v. Public Service Comm'n, 447 U.S. 530, 540 n. 10 (1980) ("we have consistently rejected the suggestion that a government may justify a content-based prohibition by showing that

moderate public discourse on the analogy of a town meeting.[8] While
the government may foster the values of free expression found in the

speakers have alternate means of expression"); Spence v. Washington, 418 U.S. 405, 411 & n. 4 (1974) (reversing conviction for taping removable peace symbol onto flag displayed in apartment window, and "summarily" rejecting the state court's argument that the inhibition on speech was "miniscule and trifling" because of "other means" that could have been used to express the same views; the availability of other means are irrelevant when government prosecutes "for the expression of an idea through activity"); Virginia State Board of Pharmacy v. Virginia Citizens Consumer Council, Inc., 425 U.S. 748, 757 n. 15 (1976) (invalidating state ban on advertising of prices of prescription drugs; held irrelevant that consumers might be able to obtain the same information in some other ways). Accord, Wooley v. Maynard, 430 U.S. 705 (1977) (invalidating compelled display of emblem bearing state's "Live Free or Die" motto on automobile license plate; majority implicitly rejects dissenting argument, id. at 1439, that the objection to the motto could be expressed by displaying a counter-motto as easily as by removing the motto); Southeastern Promotions, Ltd. v. Conrad, 420 U.S. 546, 556 (1975) (vacating municipality's denial of a permit to allow the musical "Hair" to be performed in public theater). See also Procunier v. Martinez, 416 U.S. 396, 408–09 (1974), and Kleindienst v. Mandel, 408 U.S. 753, 762–63 (1972), as explained in Virginia State Board of Pharmacy, 425 U.S. at 57–58 n. 15.

By contrast, when dealing with what it believes to be content-neutral restrictions on speech, the Court often has inquired into the availability of alternate avenues of expression. See, e.g., City of Renton v. Playtime Theatres, Inc., 475 U.S. 41, ___ (1986) ("[t]he appropriate inquiry . . . is whether the . . . ordinance is designed to serve a substantial governmental interest and allows for reasonable alternative avenues of communication"); Clark v. Community for Creative Non-Violence, 468 U.S. 288, 293 (1984) (upholding National Park Service anti-camping regulations as applied to protesters attempting to call attention to the plight of the homeless); City Council of Los Angeles v. Taxpayers for Vincent, 466 U.S. 789, 812 (1984) (upholding city ordinance that prohibited posting signs on public property as applied to political candidate who posted campaign signs on telephone poles); Heffron v. International Society for Krishan Consciousness (ISKCON), 452 U.S. 640, 648 (1981) (up-

holding rules of Minnesota state fair that prohibited the distribution of printed matter or the solicitation of funds except from a duly licensed booth on the fairgrounds, as applied to religious group); Young v. American Mini Theatres, 427 U.S. 50, 71–72 (1976) (plurality opinion) (upholding adult movie theater zoning ordinance and quoting the district court's finding that because of the availability of alternate theater locations, "[t]his burden on First Amendment rights is slight").

8. Despite the appeal of the town meeting metaphor for moral and political philosophers who have written about freedom of expression (see, e.g., Meiklejohn, Political Freedom 24–28 (1960); Rawls, A Theory of Justice 203 (1971)), the image is strikingly inapt in many settings where freedom of expression is at stake. The Supreme Court's frequent acknowledgment that speech often serves its highest function when it shocks or stirs unrest (see, e.g., Terminiello v. Chicago, 337 U.S. 1, 4 (1949) (reversing conviction for breach of the peace interpreted to include speech which "stirs the public to anger, invites dispute, brings about unrest, or creates a disturbance")), and the Court's insistence that "one man's vulgarity is another's lyric," Cohen v. California, 403 U.S. 15, 25 (1971) (Harlan, J.), bespeaks a premise more sensitive to the unruly realities of effective discourse. To preserve civility is one thing; to insist that all dialogue proceed on the model of an ordered meeting would be quite another. Indeed, even in official public meetings themselves, the first amendment imposes severe constraints both on the power of government to decide who may speak (see, e.g., City of Madison, Joint School District No. 8 v. Wisconsin Employment Relations Commission, 429 U.S. 167 (1976) (school board cannot refuse nonunion teacher the opportunity to speak on pending labor negotiations during discussion at meeting opened to the public); but cf. Minnesota State Bd. for Community Colleges v. Knight, 465 U.S. 271 (1984) (upholding "meet and confer" provisions that prohibited union non-member faculty from meeting with state governing board)), and on government's power to control what may be said. See, e.g., Brown v. Oklahoma, 408 U.S. 914 (1972) (Powell, J. concurring in result) (offensive language of speaker invited to present the Black Panther viewpoint at a political meeting could not be penalized because the audience could have anticipated the character of the invitee's language).

first amendment, it is precluded by the amendment from compelling expression or suppressing expression, even where government would justify such intrusion on personal liberty as a pursuit of first amendment values.[9] The autonomy of the individual and of the press from government's content-based restrictions is thus nearly absolute.[10]

But "nearly" absolute does not mean "absolute." The primary gap arises because government may justify a regulation aimed at the communicative impact of expressive conduct by reference to one of several narrowly drawn categorical definitions which distinguish between speech protected by the first amendment and expression which government may regulate subject only to the barest due process scrutiny, ultimately on the theory that such unprotected expression falls outside the first amendment's purposes or fails to satisfy its premises. The notion that some expression may be regulated consistent with the

See Rutzick, "Offensive Language and the Evolution of First Amendment Protection," 9 Harv.C.R.-C.L.L.Rev. 1, 18 (1974) (criticizing, as an inappropriate model of first amendment theory, the image of "a debating society, a sedate assembly of speakers who calmly discussed the issues of the day and became ultimately persuaded by the logic of one of the competing positions."). If "the offensiveness of language used in a political protest often measures the intensity of interest in the outcome of a governmental decision," then protection for the use of "offensive language [becomes] not a luxury but a necessity in a democratic society." Id. at 19. For a criticism of Cohen, see Bickel, The Morality of Consent 72 (1975) (Cohen's speech "constitutes an assault" and "may create an environment [in which] actions that were not possible before become possible"); Cox, The Role of the Supreme Court in American Government 47–48 (1976) (state has interest in "level at which public discourse is conducted"). See also FCC v. Pacifica Foundation, 438 U.S. 726 (1978) (upholding FCC declaratory order granting a complaint against radio station for broadcast of "patently offensive" language), discussed further in § 12–18, infra. The Pacifica Court distinguished Cohen on several grounds. First, the plurality maintained, "[so] far as the evidence showed no one in the courthouse was offended by [Cohen's jacket]," 438 U.S. at 747 n. 25 (plurality opinion). In addition, while in Cohen unwilling viewers could avert their gaze, in Pacifica the "uniquely pervasive" medium of radio guaranteed that at least some children and unwilling listeners would be exposed to the offensive language. Id. at 748 (opinion of the Court). Finally, the Court noted that the penalties in Pacifica were "far more moderate" than the possible

"criminal prosecution" involved in Cohen. Id. at 747 n. 25 (plurality opinion).

9. See, e.g., Pacific Gas & Electric Co. v. Public Utilities Comm'n of California, 106 S.Ct. 903 (1986) (invalidating commission order that granted a consumer ratepayer group access to the utility's monthly billing envelopes); Citizens Against Rent Control v. Berkeley, 454 U.S. 290, 295–96 (1981) (striking down $250 limit on contributions to committees supporting or opposing ballot measures); First National Bank of Boston v. Bellotti, 435 U.S. 765 (1978) (invalidating content-based restrictions on corporate spending in state referenda); Buckley v. Valeo, 424 U.S. 1, 48–49 (1976) (per curiam) (striking down limits on expenditures by and on behalf of candidates for federal office but upholding a $1,000 contribution ceiling); Miami Herald Publishing Co. v. Tornillo, 418 U.S. 241 (1974) (holding unconstitutional a state statute mandating access to a newspaper for political candidates attacked by the newspaper).

But cf. PruneYard Shopping Center v. Robbins, 447 U.S. 74 (1980) (upholding a state-created right of access for students to distribute leaflets at a private shopping center); Red Lion Broadcasting Co. v. FCC, 395 U.S. 367 (1969) (upholding constitutionality of regulations requiring broadcasters to grant a right of reply to personal attacks and political editorials). See §§ 12–23, 12–25, infra.

10. Some commentators have argued, however, that content-based regulation is not inherently more threatening than content-neutral regulation, see, e.g., Stone, "Restrictions of Speech Because of its Content: The Peculiar Case of Subject-Matter Restrictions," 46 U.Chi.L.Rev. 81, 100–107 (1978).

first amendment without meeting any separate compelling-interest test starts with the already familiar proposition that expression has special value only in the context of "dialogue": communication in which the participants seek to persuade, or are persuaded; communication which is about changing or maintaining beliefs, or taking or refusing to take action on the basis of one's beliefs. Starting with this proposition, it is reasonable to distinguish between contexts in which talk leaves room for reply and those in which talk triggers action or causes harm without the time or opportunity for response. It is not plausible to uphold the right to use words as projectiles where no exchange of views is involved. One may not be privileged to mislead a blind man into thinking that a window is a door or to extort a sum for telling him the truth. Justice Holmes was surely right that the first amendment does not protect "a man in falsely shouting fire in a theater and causing a panic." [11] And the law need not treat differently the crime of one man who sells a bomb to terrorists and that of another who publishes an instructional manual for terrorists on how to build their own bombs out of old Volkswagen parts.[12]

The premise that speech has special value only in the context of dialogue underlies the dictum of Justice Murphy in the seminal case of *Chaplinsky v. New Hampshire*,[13] in which the Court singled out certain categories of speech as not representing "speech" within the meaning of the first amendment because they are "no essential part of any exposition of ideas," and because their "very utterance inflicts injury" or "tends to incite an immediate breach of the peace." [14] In effect, the singling out of such categories concretizes the otherwise more general, but theoretically entirely parallel, track-one inquiry into a "compelling justification" for government's decision not to leave an exchange of expressive acts in the realm of dialogue. In the *Chaplinsky* case itself, the defendant had been convicted under a statute proscribing insults in a public place after he called a city marshal a "racketeer" and "a damned Fascist." [15] These were "fighting words," a class of face-to-face epithets which tend to provoke acts of violence by the persons to whom, individually, they are addressed.[16] Such provocations are not part of

---

11. Schenck v. United States, 249 U.S. 47, 52 (1919).

12. See the "H-bomb case," United States v. Progressive, Inc., 467 F.Supp. 990 (W.D. Wis. 1979) (preliminary injunction issued Mar. 28, 1979), request for writ of mandamus denied sub nom. Morland v. Sprecher, 443 U.S. 709 (1979), case dismissed as moot, Nos. 79–1428, 79–1664 (7th Cir. Oct. 1, 1979), discussed in § 12–36, infra; Scanlon, "A Theory of Freedom of Expression," 1 Phil. & Pub.Aff. 204, 211 (1972).

13. 315 U.S. 568 (1942).

14. Id. at 571–72.

15. The fact that Chaplinsky addressed an official of the Rochester City Govern-

ment undermines the argument that the speech was devoid of political content. See Rutzick, "Offensive Language and the Evolution of First Amendment Protection," 9 Harv.C.R.-C.L.L.Rev. 1 (1974) (suggesting that Chaplinsky's epithets can be viewed as "a sharply-expressed form of political protest against indifferent or biased police services in the enforcement of his right to free speech"). See Houston v. Hill, 107 S.Ct. 2502, 2509 (1987) (overturning ordinance that made it illegal to interfere in any manner with a police officer in the course of duty): "the First Amendment protects a significant amount of verbal criticism and challenge directed at police officers."

16. 315 U.S. at 571–72.

human discourse but weapons hurled in anger to inflict injury or invite retaliation.[17] This branch of the *Chaplinsky* dictum is best understood as a special application of the "clear and present danger" test, distinguishing words used as "triggers of action" from words used as "keys of persuasion." [18]

More subtle is the branch of *Chaplinsky* focusing on outbursts which by their "very utterance inflict injury." [19] To address such situations, it helps to begin by setting aside any case like that of one who yells "boo" at a cardiac patient.[20] A rule against that "speech" is not a content regulation at all and, properly understood, poses no problem for *Chaplinsky* to solve. The message is irrelevant to the regulation. The complexity of the problem is advanced but a little if one is reading Poe's "Pit and the Pendulum" to a faint-hearted aunt; again it is more medium than message that triggers government's intervention. Much more complex are utterances which injure an individual either because they falsely damage the individual's reputation or because they reveal the individual's intimate secrets. What unites both examples, and separates both from most cases of injury caused by talk, is that "more talk" is exceedingly unlikely to cure the injury: a lie once loosed is hardly quelled by self-serving denials,[21] and

---

17. State courts have permitted the victims of abusive racial slurs to bring tort actions for intentional infliction of emotional distress. See, e.g., Contreras v. Crown Zellerbach, 88 Wash.2d 735, 565 P.2d 1173 (1977) (epithets may constitute "outrageous" conduct within the meaning of Restatement (Second) of Torts (1965)); Delgado, "Words that Wound: A Tort Action for Racial Insults, Epithets, and Namecalling," 17 Harv.C.R.-C.L.L.Rev. 133 (1982); Heins, "Banning Words: A Comment on 'Words that Wound,'" 18 Harv. C.R.-C.L.L.Rev. 585 (1983), and "Professor Delgado Replies," id. at 593. The Supreme Court has not directly passed on the issue, and it is doubtful whether more severe measures such as criminal penalties are constitutionally permissible, unless the speech involved constitutes a clear and present danger of imminent violence. If the Constitution forces government to allow people to march, speak, and write in favor of peace, brotherhood, and justice, then it must also require government to allow them to advocate hatred, racism, and even genocide. See Collin v. Smith, 578 F.2d 1197 (7th Cir. 1978), cert. denied 439 U.S. 916 (1978) (striking down Village of Skokie "Racial Slur" ordinance, making it a misdemeanor to disseminate any material promoting and inciting racial or religious hatred), discussed in § 12–10, infra; Bollinger, The Tolerant Society (1986) (arguing that free speech requires a willingness to allow the most distasteful ideas to be aired, in order to cultivate the values of

self-restraint and tolerance within the citizenry). But see Arkes, "Civility and the Restriction of Speech: Rediscovering the Defamation of Groups," 1974 Sup.Ct.Rev. 281, 310–11 (arguing that "no government that would call itself a decent government would fail to intervene" to disperse a crowd taunting a young black child on the way to a previously all-white school and that "the rights of the crowd [cannot] really stand on the same plane" as those of the child on the way to school). For an argument that such individualized taunting may well be constitutionally distinguishable from advocacy of racial or religious hatred generally, see § 12–10, infra.

18. Masses Publishing Co. v. Patten, 244 Fed. 535, 540 (S.D.N.Y. 1917) (L. Hand, J.).

19. 315 U.S. at 571–72.

20. Ely, "Flag Desecration: A Case Study in the Roles of Categorization and Balancing in First Amendment Analysis," 88 Harv.L.Rev. 1482, 1501 (1975).

21. See Gertz v. Robert Welch, Inc., 418 U.S. 323, 344 n. 9 (1974).

But see Shiffrin, "Defamatory Non-Media Speech and First Amendment Methodology," 25 U.C.L.A.L.Rev. 915, 952–53 (1978) (arguing that the view that "the truth never catches up with the lie" is incompatible with the concept of the marketplace of ideas, which posits that truth will emerge from open and uninhibited discussion).

once a secret is out of the bag it cannot be put back in again. Moreover, it may be possible to penalize defamations of private individuals, invasions of privacy, and intrusions on property rights [22] without involving the government in any judgment, either of sympathy or of hostility, about the point of view being expressed by the communicator.[23] Thus, although some first amendment values might be advanced by leaving such communication alone, most of what the first amendment is concerned with is not truly at stake.

The overriding idea in *Chaplinsky* is thus the isolation of those "utterances [that] are no essential part of any exposition of ideas [and] of . . . slight social value as a step to truth." [24] This suggests that the first amendment protects information and ideas but neither all possible ways of packaging them nor all possible ways of unearthing and deploying them. The state, on this view, can require that information must be obtained ethically and expressed in undisturbing terms, thus purifying public discourse while leaving its ultimate content untouched. But any such thesis is obviously difficult to maintain, since it assumes that content and form are somehow separable. As even the Nixon tapes show, merely deleting expletives may seriously alter the meaning of a message.[25] Moreover, to "purify" discourse may exclude from the marketplace of ideas those messages from the street which are expressed and perhaps expressible only in the language of the street.[26] And, even if the first amendment can tolerate marginal losses in content for the sake of raising the quality of public discourse, there is a second objection. It is that the first amendment protects more than the cognitive element of discourse. Even if the logic of an expression could be preserved with its packaging purified, the expression's emotive

---

22. Although ideas and information per se are not copyrightable, their particular arrangement—or "expression," in the language of copyright law—is a legally cognizable property interest. See 17 U.S.C. § 102(a) (1982); Nimmer, "Does Copyright Abridge the First Amendment Guarantees of Free Speech and Press?", 17 U.C.L.A.L. Rev. 1180 (1970) (suggesting that in most cases the idea/expression dichotomy is central to resolving the clash between copyright and the first amendment). See also Harper & Row Publishers, Inc. v. Nation Enterprises, 471 U.S. 539 (1985) (upholding copyright claim by corporation that owned exclusive publication rights to the memoirs of former President Ford against magazine that published unauthorized excerpted and paraphrased version); Zacchini v. Scripps-Howard Broadcasting Co., 433 U.S. 562 (1977) (upholding copyright claim of "human cannonball" against news agency that filmed and broadcast his commercial act without prior permission). See § 12–14, infra.

23. See Young v. American Mini Theatres, Inc., 427 U.S. 50, 67–68 (1976) (plurality opinion of Stevens, J., joined by Burger, C.J., and White and Rehnquist, JJ.) (1976): "the essence of th[e] rule [against content-based regulation of speech] is the need for absolute neutrality by the government; its regulation of communication may not be affected by sympathy or hostility for the point of view being expressed by the communicator. Thus, although the content of a story must be examined to decide whether it involves a public figure or a public issue, the Court's application of the relevant rule may not depend on its favorable or unfavorable appraisal of that figure or that issue." See generally § 12–13, supra.

24. 315 U.S. at 571–72.

25. One need only look at a bowdlerized edition of Shakespeare to recognize that changes of style are changes of substance. And Bismarck knew that a slight alteration in a message could lead to war.

26. See Cohen v. California, 403 U.S. 15, 25 (1971): "[O]ne man's vulgarity is another's lyric."

charge surely depends on how it is put.[27]   That this emotive charge is indeed part of the first amendment's concern was most persuasively argued by Justice Harlan, writing for the majority in *Cohen v. California*.[28]   Cohen was convicted for disturbing the peace by entering a county courthouse wearing a jacket inscribed with the message: "Fuck the Draft." The Court reversed his conviction ". . . [M]uch linguistic expression serves a dual communicative function: it conveys not only ideas capable of relatively precise, detached explication, but otherwise inexpressible emotions as well. In fact, words are often chosen as much for their emotive as their cognitive force. We cannot sanction the view that the Constitution, while solicitous of the cognitive content of individual speech, has little or no regard for that emotive function which, practically speaking, may often be the more important element of the overall message sought to be communicated . . . ."[29]

A similar but broader observation, ultimately at odds with *Chaplinsky's* premises, can be made about the civil rights movement of the early 1960's and the peace movement of the late 1960's. It is at least incomplete to say that Americans took those causes to the streets because other channels of communication were closed to their protest. Rather, they marched, paraded, and picketed because no other medium could adequately register either the intensity of their protest or the solidarity of their movement. In a mass society, it is not enough to launch a thought like a toy boat upon the ocean of opinions. The protesters of the sixties came together in the streets to "show their numerical strength and so to diminish the moral power of the majority."[30]   In a representative system where voting is too blunt an instrument to register the diversity of a people's hopes and fears, and where actual citizen participation in the governing process is slight, the consent of the governed must be implied, and it is dissent that implies consent.[31]   "One who knows that he may dissent knows also that he somehow consents when he does not dissent."[32]   Thus the unruly protest cannot be heard as merely an especially loud voice in the national dialogue; its strength "speaks" to the moral authority of the state.

It follows that *Chaplinsky* is carried too far when it is invoked to sterilize discourse by reducing it to logic. But it may still remain possible to distinguish governmental protection of private individuals

---

27. Even apart from any communicative message involved, Chaplinsky's outburst may have served as personal catharsis, "as a means to vent his frustration at a system he deemed—whether rightly or wrongly—to be oppressive[.] Is it not a mark of individuality to be able to cry out at a society viewed as crushing the individual? Under this analysis, the so-called 'fighting words' represent a significant means of self-realization, whether or not they can be considered a means of attaining some elusive 'truth.'" Redish, "The Value of Free Speech," 130 U.Pa.L.Rev. 591, 626 (1982).

28. 403 U.S. 15 (1971).

29. Id. at 26.

30. Arendt, The Crisis of the Republic 96 (1972), quoting de Tocqueville, Democracy in America.

31. Arendt, supra, at 88–89.

32. Id. at 88.

from verbal assaults on privacy and personality—the one category where utterance itself may work injury that no further dialogue can redress.[33]

§ 12–9. Clear and Present Danger: Advocacy of Lawless Action

The "clear and present danger" doctrine is concerned with distinguishing protected advocacy from unprotected incitement of violent or illegal conduct. It was in 1919 in *Schenck v. United States* that Justice Holmes introduced the doctrine for a unanimous court.[1] Schenck and others had been convicted of conspiring to violate provisions of the Espionage Act of 1917 forbidding anyone to obstruct the draft or to cause, or attempt to cause, insubordination in the military. The defendants had mailed circulars to draftees which declared in "impassioned language" the unconstitutionality of conscription and urged the recipients to "assert their rights."[2] Congress undoubtedly had constitutional authority under its war powers to punish individuals who interfered or attempted to interfere with the war effort.[3] But in *Schenck*, the government did not argue that the defendant's speech had actually interfered with the war effort; the only question was whether the circulars alone were sufficient evidence of an illegal *attempt* to interfere. The conventional wisdom of the day was that speech was punishable as an attempt if the natural and reasonable tendency of what was said would be to bring about a forbidden effect.[4] In addition, the criminal defendant must have used the words with an intent to bring about that effect, although such specific intent could be inferred from the tendency of the words on the presumption that one intends the natural consequences of one's speech.[5] The formula announced by Justice Holmes easily fit within this framework. "The question in every case is whether the words used are used in circumstances and are of such a nature as to create a clear and present danger that they will bring about the substantive evils that Congress has a right to prevent."[6] Since the issue whether Schenck's conduct was a "clear and present danger" thus posed a factual question, the disposition of the claim was determined by the finding of the Court that the jury, having been properly charged, had not acted unreasonably in finding that the circulars could be expected to persuade draftees unlawfully to refuse induction.

33. See § 12–14, infra.

§ 12–9

1. 249 U.S. 47 (1919).

2. Compare Keegan v. United States, 325 U.S. 478 (1945), in which the Court reversed convictions for conspiring to counsel persons to evade military service. The leaders of the German-American Bund had commanded their members to refuse induction into military service in order to test the constitutionality of the draft law. Without discussing constitutional questions, the Court held that the defendants' public counsel to its members did not constitute evasion of the draft or proof of conspiracy to evade.

3. See § 5–16, supra.

4. See Gunther, "Learned Hand and the Origins of Modern First Amendment Doctrine: Some Fragments of History," 27 Stan.L.Rev. 719, 724 (1975).

5. See Chafee, Free Speech in the United States 24, 26–28, 49–51, 57–64 (1941).

6. Schenck, 249 U.S. at 52.

A week after *Schenck*, Justice Holmes delivered two more opinions for a unanimous Court upholding convictions under the Espionage Act. One involved the editor of a German-language newspaper that had carried articles on the constitutionality of the draft and the purposes of the war;[7] the other involved Eugene Debs, the Socialist leader and candidate for President in 1920, who had made an antiwar speech.[8] In each of these cases, the Court applied the *Schenck* standard, but deferred to the jury's "reasonable" determination that the "natural and intended effect" of the expression was to obstruct recruiting or to cause insubordination in the armed services. In its next Term, a divided Supreme Court upheld three more prosecutions under the Espionage Act,[9] the majority adhering to the approach outlined in *Schenck*. But in these cases Justice Holmes and Justice Brandeis dissented.

The Supreme Court in one of these three cases—*Abrams v. United States*—sustained the convictions of five Bolshevik sympathizers under a section of the 1918 amendments to the Espionage Act making it an offense to urge curtailment of military production *with intent to hinder the war with Germany*.[10] Abrams and his friends had showered English and Yiddish leaflets from a window of a manufacturing building upon the streets of lower East Side New York denouncing American intervention in the Russian revolution and calling for a general strike to prevent ordnance shipments to anti-Soviet forces. Justice Clarke's

7. Frohwerk v. United States, 249 U.S. 204 (1919). The outcome of the case was strongly influenced by the Court's placement of the burden of proof, coupled with the inadequacy of the record on appeal: Holmes could not find evidence which would make "it impossible [to say that] the circulation of the newspaper was in quarters where a little breath would be enough to kindle the flame. . . ." Id. at 209.

8. Debs v. United States, 249 U.S. 211 (1919). The conviction of Debs was "somewhat as though George McGovern had been sent to prison for his criticism of the [Vietnam] war." Kalven, "Professor Ernst Freund and Debs v. United States," 40 U.Chi.L.Rev. 235, 237 (1973). Holmes' loose restatement of the clear and present danger test in the Debs case—"natural tendency and reasonably probable effect," 249 U.S. at 216—suggests that Holmes had yet to conceive of the test as a constitutional standard protective of first amendment values. See Kalven, "Uninhibited, Robust, and Wide-Open, A Note on Free Speech and the Warren Court," 67 Mich.L.Rev. 289, 297 n. 18 (1968). This suspicion has been confirmed by the historical evidence gathered by Gunther, supra note 4.

9. Abrams v. United States, 250 U.S. 616 (1919) (discussed in text); Schaefer v. United States, 251 U.S. 466 (1920) (upholding convictions of the officers of a German-language newspaper for publishing "false statements" with intent to interfere with

military operations, when the newspaper was too impoverished to gather its own news and thus republished edited versions of other papers' articles; the falsity alleged by the government was that the articles differed from the originals from which they were copied and were given an unpatriotic tone); Pierce v. United States, 252 U.S. 239 (1920) (upholding convictions of three socialists for distributing an anti-war pamphlet containing "false statements," including the allegation that United States entry into World War I was to secure "J. P. Morgan's loans to the allies"; Justice Pitney's opinion for the majority concluded that it was common knowledge that the causes of the war were otherwise and therefore that the defendants must have known that their allegations were false).

10. The relevant 1918 amendment amounted to a genuine sedition law, forbidding the wartime publishing of "disloyal, scurrilous and abusive language about the form of government of the United States, or language intended to bring the form of government of the United States into contempt, scorn, contumely and disrepute. . . ." The Court in Abrams declined to pass on the constitutionality of the more sweeping sections of the amended Espionage Act since the convictions could be sustained on the counts charging language intended either to incite resistance to the United States in the war or to curtail military production with the intent to hinder the war effort against Germany.

opinion for the majority dismissed appellant's first amendment claims as having been settled by *Schenck*. The principal difficulty for the majority was finding the requisite intent—no small problem, since the defendants in *Abrams* had opposed the wrong war. The difficulty was surmounted by imputing to the defendants the knowledge that strikes in munitions factories would necessarily impede the war effort against Germany, as well as operations in Russia.

Justice Holmes' dissent in *Abrams* is principally remembered for its eloquent exposition of a philosophical foundation for the first amendment. His doctrinal approach was to infuse more immediacy into the *Schenck* formulation of the clear and present danger test and thereby sharply distinguish it from the loose predictions of remote consequence which had been sufficient to sustain criminal convictions in the previous cases. Applying his invigorated test to the facts of *Abrams*, Holmes made what amounted to two arguments: Because Congress "cannot forbid all effort to change the mind of the country,"[11] it cannot make criminal the expression of opinion and exhortations without proof of a specific intent of the speakers by those words to cause a harm that Congress may prevent.[12] Holmes construed the statute at issue to conform with this requirement and concluded that the only intent proved of Abrams was to help Russia and stop American intervention there—not to impede the United States in the war against Germany.[13] Second, while the publication of Abrams' words with the intent of obstructing the war effort would have the quality of an attempt,[14] the convictions still could not be sustained because in fact that danger was not clear and present. For Holmes the law was indifferent to Abrams' words alone and likewise indifferent to his intentions alone, the latter being "internal phenomena of conscience."[15] Nor did Abrams' words and intentions combined fall on the wrong side of the line marking the difference between innocent behavior and a criminal attempt, since there was no showing that the feared consequences were imminent.

Holmes' dissent in *Abrams* is marred by ambiguity[16] and by his insistence the *Schenck, Frohwerk*, and especially *Debs* had been rightly decided.[17] One cynical interpretation of Holmes' handiwork might be that speech is protected only as long as it is ineffective. One cannot

11. 250 U.S. at 628 (Holmes, J., joined by Brandeis, J., dissenting).

12. Id. at 627.

13. Id. at 629.

14. Id. at 628.

15. See Holmes, The Common Law 88 (Howe ed., 1963). The source of the "clear and present danger" test was Holmes' understanding, apparently mistaken, of the common law of criminal attempts. Holmes' view was that the criminal law was concerned not with individuals' intentions but with their actions and the harm potentially caused thereby. This emphasis, whatever its merits in criminal law generally, is clearly appropriate in the context of freedom of belief and communication. But the source of the rule accounts for its defects along with its virtues. See Rogat, "Mr. Justice Holmes: A Dissenting Opinion," 31 U.Chi.L.Rev. 213, 216–17 (1964).

16. See Gunther, supra note 4, at 743. The principal obscurity is over whether Holmes meant that specific intent to hinder the war effort and a high risk of injurious consequences were alternative bases of criminal liability, or rather that both elements had to be shown.

17. See 250 U.S. at 627 (Holmes, J., dissenting).

ignore Holmes' description of the materials he would protect—the "silly pamphlet [published] by an unknown man," the "poor and puny anonymities" too insignificant "to turn the color of legal litmus paper." [18] But a more generous reading may take its cue from Holmes' admonition to his countrymen that "[o]nly the emergency that makes it immediately dangerous to leave the correction of evil counsels to time warrants making any exception to the sweeping command [of the first amendment]." [19] If the premise of free speech is dialogue, it makes sense to distinguish between talk in contexts where reply is plausible and talk in contexts where words trigger action without any chance for response.[20] This premise emerges most clearly in the classic opinion of Justice Brandeis, joined by Justice Holmes, concurring in *Whitney v. California*: ". . . no danger flowing from speech can be deemed clear and present, unless the incidence of the evil apprehended is so imminent that it may befall before there is opportunity for full discussion. If there be time to expose the evil by the processes of education, the remedy to be applied is *more speech*, not enforced silence. Only an emergency can justify repression." [21]

The next free speech cases to reach the Court were *Gitlow v. New York* [22] and *Whitney v. California*,[23] which involved state statutes prohibiting the advocacy of criminal anarchy and criminal syndicalism. Benjamin Gitlow was convicted for publishing a didactic tract called the Left Wing Manifesto, and Anna Whitney for participating in a meeting of the Communist Labor Party Convention which, over a dissent led by Miss Whitney, adopted a platform urging revolutionary unionism. Although the Supreme Court majority assumed that the "liberty" protected by the fourteenth amendment included the freedoms of speech and press,[24] the Court sustained the statutes as legitimate exercises of the states' "police powers," reasonably related to the end of securing the safety of the state.[25] The clear and present danger test was held inapplicable; its only purpose was to fix the point at which speech crossed the line between innocuous preparation and a criminal attempt to commit an act proscribed without reference to speech. The statutes in *Gitlow* and *Whitney* made advocacy itself the crime. Since the legislature had determined the danger of the proscribed words, it followed—if that determination was not arbitrary in the context to

18. Id. at 628, 629. See also Gitlow v. New York, 268 U.S. 652, 673 (1925) (Holmes, J., dissenting) ("futile and too remote from possible consequences"); cf. Dennis v. United States, 341 U.S. 494, 589 (1951) (Douglas, J., dissenting) ("miserable merchants of unwanted ideas; their wares remain unsold").

19. Abrams, 250 U.S. at 630–31 (dissenting opinion).

20. It is important to keep this functional definition in view rather than succumbing to any mindless formula built on such familiar examples as the false cry of fire in a crowded theater. The formulas have a way of proving inapt in particular circumstances. See, e.g., T. Stoppard, Rosencrantz & Guildenstern Are Dead, Act II, at 60 (1967): ROS: "Fire!" GUIL jumps up. GUIL: "Where?" ROS: "It's all right—I'm demonstrating the misuse of free speech. To prove that it exists. (He regards the audience, that is the direction, with contempt—and other directions, then front again.) Not a move. They should burn to death in their shoes."

21. 274 U.S. 357, 377 (1927) (Brandeis, J., joined by Holmes, J., concurring) (emphasis added).

22. 268 U.S. 652 (1925).

23. 274 U.S. 357 (1927).

24. Gitlow, 268 U.S. at 666.

25. Id. at 667.

which it was being applied— [26] that a court could not consider "whether any specific utterance coming within the prohibited class [would be] likely, in and of itself, to bring about the substantive evil. . . ." [27]

The dissent of Justice Holmes in *Gitlow* reiterated the applicability of the "clear and present danger" test without replying specifically to the majority's distinction between a statute written without reference to speech and one aimed at speech as such. The reply came two years later in Justice Brandeis' eloquent concurring opinion in *Whitney*, where he employed the clear and present danger test to assess the validity of a law directly punishing the advocacy of revolutionary violence. The legislature, by enacting a law or by making a declaration, "cannot alone establish the facts which are essential to [the law's] validity." [28] It must remain open for the court and jury to decide whether, at the time and under the circumstances, the abridgment is in fact justified by reasonable fears that a "serious" and "imminent" "evil will result if free speech is protected." [29] Ironically, because of the still underdeveloped state of any "preferred rights" theory in the late 1920's, Justice Brandeis found himself invoking the *Lochner* Court's authority to reject legislative determinations of fact. [30]

The same questions returned to the Supreme Court in *Dennis v. United States*, [31] in the context of pervasive fears of an international Communist conspiracy. In 1940, Congress passed the Smith Act, which

---

26. See, e.g., Fiske v. Kansas, 274 U.S. 380 (1927) (reversing conviction under state law prohibiting advocacy of criminal syndicalism because the evidence to convict was insufficient as a matter of due process inasmuch as the documentary proof—the preamble of the I.W.W.—nowhere suggested that unlawful means were to be employed); DeJonge v. Oregon, 299 U.S. 353 (1937) (reversing conviction under statute which outlawed assisting in the conduct of a meeting sponsored by an organization which advocated illegal means to effect political change; participation in such a meeting could not be deemed criminal where no illegal advocacy had taken place at the meeting).

27. Gitlow, 268 U.S. at 670–71. Hans Linde has persuasively argued that legislative determinations of danger from revolutionary speech deserve very little deference. For example, the New York Criminal Anarchy Act sustained in Gitlow had been enacted in 1902 in reaction to an anarchist's assassination of President McKinley. If there was a danger in 1920 when Benjamin Gitlow was prosecuted under the Act, it was not the danger the legislature had in mind in 1902. And when Congress enacted the Smith Act in 1940, which was modeled on the 1902 New York statute, it could not have imagined the circumstances in which the leaders of the Communist Party were prosecuted in 1948. See Linde, " 'Clear and Present Danger' Reexamined: Dissonance in the

Brandenburg Concerto," 22 Stan.L.Rev. 1163 (1970).

28. Whitney v. California, 274 U.S. at 374 (Brandeis, J., joined by Holmes, J., concurring).

29. Id. at 378–79.

30. See Lochner v. New York, 198 U.S. 45 (1905) (invalidating a state maximum hours law for bakery workers), discussed in Chapter 8, supra. The conventional modern reply to the Gitlow and Whitney majorities would be that the Court should not defer to political determinations where legislation has undermined the reasons for deference by eroding the very processes of communication and opinion-formation on which one can ordinarily rely to cause the political branches to change course. See United States v. Carolene Products Co., 304 U.S. 144, 152–53 n. 4 (1938) (Stone, C.J.).

31. 341 U.S. 494 (1951). Chief Justice Vinson's plurality opinion was joined by Justices Reed, Burton, and Minton. Justices Frankfurter and Jackson wrote separate concurring opinions. Justices Black and Douglas wrote separate dissenting opinions. For comment see Richardson, "Freedom of Expression and the Function of the Courts," 65 Harv.L.Rev. 1 (1951); Mendelson, "Clear and Present Danger—From Schenck to Dennis," 52 Colum.L.Rev. 313 (1952); Garfunkel and Mack, "Dennis v. United States and the Clear and Present Danger Rule," 39 Calif.L.Rev. 475 (1951);

closely resembled the New York Criminal Anarchy law upheld fifteen years earlier in *Gitlow*. In 1949, members of the National Board of the Communist Party were convicted of conspiracy to teach and advocate the overthrow of the government and conspiracy to reorganize the Party after World War II to teach and advocate such overthrow. The Supreme Court affirmed the convictions. The plurality opinion of Chief Justice Vinson purported to accept the Holmes-Brandeis rationale in *Gitlow* and *Whitney* as requiring the use of the "clear and present danger" test [32] not to evaluate the Smith Act itself, but to assess its application to a particular set of facts.[33] But Vinson rejected the Holmes-Brandeis formulation of the clear and present danger test, saying that the great dissenters had not been confronted by the development of a revolutionary fifth column in the context of recurring world crises.[34] In its place Vinson accepted Judge Learned Hand's test in the decision below: "whether the gravity of the 'evil,' discounted by its improbability, justifies [the challenged] invasion of free speech as . . . necessary to avoid the danger." [35] The revised standard was supposedly satisfied by conclusions pointing to the highly disciplined organization of the Communist Party and the tinder-box of world conditions.[36] The problem was how to determine the relevant facts. Wholesale deference to the factual determination of the jury [37] or of the legislature [38] would not be consistent with the Holmes-Brandeis legacy. The plurality disposed of the issue by relying on judicial notice or, as Justice Frankfurter put it, a "judicial reading of events still in the womb of time." [39] But it is difficult to escape the force of Justice Jackson's concurrence rejecting the "clear and present danger" standard altogether: "We must appraise imponderables, including international and national phenomena which baffle the best informed foreign offices and our most experienced politicians. . . . No doctrine can be sound whose application requires us to make a prophesy of that sort in the guise of a legal decision." [40]

Dennis is generally deemed to mark the temporary eclipse of the Holmes-Brandeis formulation of the clear and present danger test.[41] A central difficulty was that it had been so easy to misperceive factual contexts in periods of national unrest. In 1919, Holmes' example was that of a man "falsely shouting fire in a theatre and causing a panic." [42]

Konefsky, The Legacy of Holmes and Brandeis (1956).

32. 341 U.S. at 507.

33. See Linde, supra note 27, at 1173.

34. 341 U.S. at 510.

35. Id., quoting from 183 F.2d 201, 212 (2d Cir. 1950). Only Justice Douglas in dissent applied the unadulterated Holmes-Brandeis test in Dennis.

36. 341 U.S. at 511.

37. The question whether the facts alleged would establish a sufficient danger was determined to be "a matter of law" to be decided by the trial court and was therefore properly not submitted to the jury. Id. at 512–15.

38. Justice Frankfurter in his concurring opinion in Dennis indicated his view that, even without Gitlow-style deference to legislative judgments, the facts were sufficient to conclude that the conspiracy before the Court was a substantial threat to national order and security. Id. at 542.

39. Id. at 551.

40. Id. at 570.

41. See Strong, "Fifty Years of 'Clear and Present Danger': From Schenck to Brandenburg—And Beyond," 1969 Sup.Ct. Rev. 41, 52–53; Kalven, "The New York Times Case: A Note on 'The Central Meaning of the First Amendment'," 1964 Sup.Ct. Rev. 191, 213–15.

42. Schenck, 249 U.S. at 52.

Later the same year, he was conjuring up "quarters where a little breath would be enough to kindle a flame." [43] In those early cases the Supreme Court deferred to individual jury determinations of danger; by the mid-1920's, it was deferring to wholesale legislative determinations covering broad categories of situations. In 1925, for example, it was said that government cannot be expected to weigh each incident on a jeweler's scale: "A single revolutionary spark may kindle a fire that, smouldering for a time, may burst into a sweeping and destructive conflagration." [44] By the 1950's, it was the "inflammable nature of world conditions" [45]—Fire Again!—that justified government's acting preventively, striking while the iron was hot, rather than waiting until the weapon was poised.

In the period after *Dennis*, the Supreme Court moved gradually toward a notion of identifiable categories of speech-related activity with respect to which legislative and executive determinations could claim only minimal deference from judges. Correspondingly, the Court tended to recast clear and present danger analysis from an exercise in assessing likely consequences along a continuum, to an exercise in characterizing an act as either "in" or "out" of a defined category of unprotected incitements. The six majority Justices in *Dennis* were linked in distinguishing a category of protected discussion from a category of unprotected advocacy of revolutionary violence. [46] In *Yates v. United States*, involving Smith Act prosecutions against lower-echelon members of the Communist Party, the Court "reinterpreted" the *Dennis* distinction as a line between protected advocacy of doctrine and unprotected advocacy of action—i.e., incitement. [47] The earliest case to focus largely on that line and the accompanying categorical approach was *Masses Publishing Co. v. Patten*, [48] where Judge Learned Hand ordered the postmaster of New York not to exclude from the mails the August, 1917, issue of Max Eastman's *The Masses*, a revolutionary journal containing articles, poems, and cartoons attacking the war against Germany. The postmaster purported to act on the authority of a section of the Espionage Act of 1917 which made nonmailable any publication which violated the Act's criminal provisions.

In his *Masses* opinion, Judge Hand spoke of words unprotected by the first amendment as "triggers of action," rather than "keys of persuasion." [49] The line between "incitement" and "persuasion," however, is by no means clear; as Holmes once commented: "[e]very idea is an incitement." [50] Hand's distinctive contribution was the use of a per se categorical definition of unprotected speech: "[words] which have no purport but to counsel the violation of law." [51] His focus was on the

43. Frohwerk, 249 U.S. at 209.

44. Gitlow, 268 U.S. at 669 (Holmes, J., dissenting).

45. Dennis, 341 U.S. at 511 (Vinson, C. J., plurality opinion).

46. Id. at 502; id. at 544–46 (Frankfurter, J., concurring); id. at 571–72 (Jackson, J., concurring).

47. 354 U.S. 298 (1957).

48. 244 Fed. 535 (S.D.N.Y. 1917), rev'd, 246 Fed. 24 (2d Cir. 1917). See Gunther, supra note 4.

49. 244 F. at 540.

50. Gitlow, 268 U.S. at 673 (dissenting opinion).

51. Masses, 244 F. at 540.

content, not the effect, of communicative activity. A speech merely critical of a law, from Hand's perspective, could not be transformed by a jury or by a legislature into a punishable act—whatever the context, and whatever the factual findings. Although "political agitation" against the war may "arouse discontent and disaffection among the people with the prosecution of the war and with the draft," government cannot justify its suppression of speech because, "by the passions it arouses or the convictions it engenders, [it] may stimulate men to mutiny or draft evasion." [52] Political agitation may not be equated with "direct incitement to violent resistance." [53] Conversely, a speech urging the audience to defy a law might be punished on this view even if harmless in its setting.[54] For Hand, punishing a few harmless inciters was a small price to pay for securing by an "objective" test the immunity of allegedly harmful persuaders.

The current doctrinal synthesis, combining the best of Hand's views with the best of Holmes' and Brandeis', is that of *Brandenburg v. Ohio*,[55] in which the Court reversed the conviction of a Ku Klux Klan leader under Ohio's criminal syndicalism statute because the statute was not properly limited to advocacy (1) "directed to inciting or producing imminent lawless action" [56] and (2) "likely to incite or produce such action."[57] The first criterion embraces Hand's insistence on treating

---

52. Id. at 539–40.

53. Id. at 540.

54. See Gunther, supra note 4, at 729.

55. 395 U.S. 444 (1969) (per curiam), overruling Whitney v. California, 274 U.S. 357 (1927). See generally Comment, "Brandenburg v. Ohio: A Speech Test For All Seasons," 43 U.Chi.L.Rev. 151 (1975).

56. 395 U.S. at 447. Laws that on their face burden speech in terms of its content but do not limit their reach to the sort of incitement noted in Brandenburg are void. See, e.g., Communist Party of Indiana v. Whitcomb, 414 U.S. 441 (1974) (voiding statutory loyalty oath, required as condition of access to state ballot, to the effect that party taking the oath does not advocate overthrow of government by force or violence, since such oath goes beyond the incitement of imminent lawlessness that may be proscribed under Brandenburg); Kingsley International Pictures Corp. v. Regents, 360 U.S. 684, 689 (1959) (state cannot deny license to film pursuant to statute mandating denial whenever film presents "acts of sexual immorality . . . as desirable" since such advocacy of ideas is protected). Moreover, however a law is *written*, it may not constitutionally be *applied* to punish speech on content-related grounds where nothing beyond abstract advocacy is shown, and where incitement is thus absent. See, e.g., Watts v. United States, 394 U.S. 705 (1969) (per curiam) (reversing conviction for threatening President's life where defendant merely used political hyperbole in saying, at a public

rally, "If they ever make me carry a rifle, the first man I want to get in my sights is LBJ"); Bond v. Floyd, 385 U.S. 116 (1966) (Georgia legislature could not exclude elected representative Julian Bond on the sole ground that his antiwar statements, which included no advocacy of lawbreaking, cast doubt on his ability to take oath). Of course, a statement may constitute an incitement in the context in which it is uttered notwithstanding the apparent neutrality of the words. Marc Antony's funeral oration was not an explicit call to avenge the assassination of Caesar, but it might as well have been. See Letter from Z. Chafee to Learned Hand, Mar. 28, 1921, quoted in Gunther, supra note 4, at 729 n. 41. Yet the moment one permits context to transform statements into incitements, at least part of the point of Learned Hand's effort to create a clean category of unprotected utterances is fatally compromised. Such contextual transformations should therefore be kept to an absolute minimum.

57. Brandenburg, 395 U.S. at 447. In Hess v. Indiana, 414 U.S. 105 (1973) (per curiam), for example, the Court reversed a conviction for disorderly conduct during a campus protest against the Cambodia invasion. The defendant had said "We'll take the fucking street later" or "We'll take the fucking street again." (The record was ambiguous.) In either event, his remarks were directed at no-one in particular, suggesting that they might not have constituted an incitement sufficient to meet Brandenburg's first test. Id. at 107. Nor was

only words of incitement as unprotected;[58] the second criterion adds Holmes' and Brandeis' focus on likely harm, but transforms that focus into an additional safeguard for the harmless inciter.[59]

§ 12–10. Clear and Present Danger: "Fighting Words," Vulgarities, and Hostile or Otherwise Special Audiences

In *Chaplinsky v. New Hampshire*,[1] the Supreme Court upheld a conviction of a Jehovah's Witness for calling a city marshal a "damned Fascist" and "God damned racketeer"[2] under a statute providing that

there evidence that the remarks were likely to produce any imminent disorder; thus *Brandenburg's* second test was not met. Id. at 108–09.

58. The Supreme Court has made plain that it will not blindly accept a lower court's determination that speech is punishable "incitement," and not protected, albeit spirited, advocacy. In National Association for the Advancement of Colored People v. Claiborne Hardware Co., 458 U.S. 886 (1982), the Court unanimously reversed a civil judgment against the NAACP and several of its members for damages arising out of a protracted boycott of white-owned businesses in Claiborne County, Mississippi. Justice Stevens' opinion acknowledged that Charles Evers, the leader of the boycott, might under certain circumstances have been held liable for the conduct of those who acted under his influence, but approached "with extreme care" the respondent's theory, which would have imposed "liability on the basis of a public address—which predominantly contained highly charged political rhetoric lying at the core of the First Amendment." Id. at 926–27. The Court conceded that Evers' speeches referred to the possibility that "necks would be broken," and the speeches "might have been understood as inviting an unlawful form of discipline or, at least, as intending to create a fear of violence whether or not improper discipline was specifically intended." Id. at 927. Still, the Court rejected any imposition of liability on Evers or the NAACP on the basis of his speeches, holding that his rhetoric "did not transcend the bounds of protected speech set forth in *Brandenburg*." Id. at 928. The Court noted that "[s]trong and effective extemporaneous rhetoric cannot be nicely channeled in purely dulcet phrases," and even acknowledged that some violence did follow Evers' speeches. Id. But the violence occurred at a sufficient remove in time from those speeches to convince the Court that allowing liability on that basis would impermissibly chill the type of speech the first amendment is designed to protect—an apt reminder that more is needed than a ritual incantation of the word "incitement" before civil or crimi-

nal damages may be assessed on the basis of speech.

59. It remains to be seen whether the test announced in Brandenburg is flexible enough to make the answers it gives depend in part on how severe a harm is threatened. We should surely be able to say that the state cannot constitutionally penalize speech which merely "incites" pedestrians to walk on the grass or jaywalk across a street. See Whitney, 274 U.S. at 377–78 (Brandeis, J., concurring). The Court's most recent characterization of the clear and present danger test, in Landmark Communications, Inc. v. Virginia, 435 U.S. 829 (1978) (dictum), does not illuminate, as much as recapitulate, the standard. Chief Justice Burger's opinion, which was joined by all the Justices except Justices Brennan and Powell, who did not participate, and Justice Rehnquist, who concurred in the judgment, stated: "the test requires a court to make its own inquiry into the imminence and magnitude of the danger said to flow from the particular utterance and then to balance the character of the evil, as well as its likelihood, against the need for free and unfettered expression." Id. at 843.

§ 12–10

1. 315 U.S. 568 (1942).

2. Id. at 569. In Lewis v. City of New Orleans (Lewis I), 408 U.S. 913 (1972), the Court remanded to the state court, for reconsideration in light of Gooding v. Wilson, 405 U.S. 518 (1972), a conviction under a statute making it unlawful "to curse or revile or to use obscene or opprobrious language toward . . . any member of the city police" where appellant addressed the police officers who were arresting her son as "G_____ d_____ m_____ f_____ police." Justice Powell, concurring suggested that "fighting words" as defined in Chaplinsky may not be punishable when addressed to a police officer trained to exercise a higher degree of restraint than the average citizen. 408 U.S. at 913. On remand the state court sustained the conviction. In Lewis v. City of New Orleans (Lewis II), 415 U.S. 130 (1974), the Court reversed again, finding the statute void on

"[no] person shall address any offensive, derisive or annoying word to any other person who is lawfully in any street or other public place. . . ." [3] The Court acted on the theory that "fighting words," those words "which by their very utterance inflict injury or tend to incite an immediate breach of the peace," are not protected by the first amendment.[4] The "fighting words" theory as originally developed focused primarily on the content of the communication without closely examining the context within which it was uttered. The Supreme Court was willing to accept the implied legislative judgment that there is a nearly certain connection between some epithets and the outbreak of violence.

More recent Supreme Court decisions, however, made clear that the "fighting words" exception to first amendment protection must be narrowly construed. Further, contemporary opinions indicate that the fundamental methodological assumption of the original "fighting words" doctrine—that a category of words could be proscribed without regard to the context within which they might be used—is no longer favored by the Court. A "fighting words" statute is unconstitutional on its face if it is not limited to words which "have a direct tendency to cause acts of violence by the person to whom, individually, the remark is addressed," [5] and constitutional enforcement of even facially valid

its face because it was not limited to words tending to cause an immediate breach of the peace. While the Court declined to decide whether police must put up with more verbal abuse than the average citizen, id. at 132 n. 2, it held that the state may not punish such words on the theory that police officers deserve greater respect than the average citizen.

3. The Supreme Court of New Hampshire construed the law to reach only words which "have a direct tendency to cause acts of violence by the persons to whom, individually, the remark is addressed." This definition was approved in the Chaplinsky opinion. See 315 U.S. at 573. Recent decisions have favored this definition over the one given by Justice Murphy in Chaplinsky, text at note 4, infra. See, e.g., Gooding v.Wilson, 405 U.S. 518, 523 (1972).

4. Chaplinsky, 315 U.S. at 572.

5. See Houston v. Hill, 107 S.Ct. 2502, 2510 (1987) (overturning an ordinance prohibiting the interruption of a police officer in the execution of his duty): "The freedom of individuals verbally to oppose or challenge police action without thereby risking arrest is one of the principal characteristics by which we distinguish a free nation from a police state." See Gooding v. Wilson, 405 U.S. 518, 523 (1972), where the appellant was convicted on two counts of using opprobrious words and abusive language in violation of Georgia law. The words spoken to police officers were: "White son of a bitch, I'll kill you," "You

son of a bitch, I'll choke you to death," and "You son of a bitch, if you ever put your hands on me again, I'll cut you all to pieces." Without considering the constitutionality of punishing Gooding's words under a narrowly drawn statute and a correspondingly narrow jury instruction, the Court found the Georgia law as construed by the state courts void on its face because it was not limited to words having a direct tendency to cause acts of violence by the person to whom, individually, they are addressed. Id. at 523. In Plummer v. City of Columbus, 414 U.S. 2 (1973) (per curiam), the conviction of a taxi driver who had abused a female passenger with "a series of absolutely vulgar, suggestive and abhorrent, sexually-oriented statements," id. at 3–4 (Powell, J., dissenting), was reversed because the ordinance prohibiting "menacing, insulting, slanderous, or profane language" was overbroad under Gooding. Subsequent to Gooding, the Court has summarily vacated and remanded to state courts for reconsideration convictions under statutes proscribing offensive language in terms broader than the definition of "fighting words" approved in Chaplinsky. See, e.g., Rosenfeld v. New Jersey, 408 U.S. 901 (1972); Lewis v. New Orleans (Lewis I), 408 U.S. 913 (1972); Brown v. Oklahoma, 408 U.S. 914 (1972); Lucas v. Arkansas, 416 U.S. 919 (1974); Kelly v. Ohio, 416 U.S. 923 (1974); Rosen v. California, 416 U.S. 924 (1974); Karlan v. City of Cincinnati, 416 U.S. 924 (1974). See also Papish v. University of Missouri Curators, 410 U.S. 667 (1973) (summary holding that student

laws applied to "fighting words" now appears to depend as much on the factual circumstances surrounding a word's utterance as on the character of the word uttered.[6]

The contemporary doctrinal approach is best illustrated by the decision in *Cohen v. California*,[7] in which the Supreme Court refused to classify the expression, "Fuck the Draft," as "fighting words" when lettered on the back of a jacket worn in the public corridors of the Los Angeles County Courthouse.[8] While the Court acknowledged that the four-letter word displayed by Cohen is commonly "employed in a personally provocative fashion, the word in this instance was not directed at some particular person."[9] It is not as though Cohen had confronted selective service personnel with his anti-draft epithet. Nor was there any evidence that "substantial numbers of citizens are standing ready to strike out physically at whoever may assault their sensibilities with execrations like that uttered by Cohen." Justice Harlan's sensitive opinion for the Court in *Cohen* rejected the proposition that "the States, acting as guardians of public morality, may properly remove [an] offensive word from the public vocabulary."[10] Offensive utterances are necessary side effects of free expression, and a power to maintain "a suitable level of discourse within the body politic" is inherently illimitable.[11] It would be difficult to prevent government from suppressing ideas in the name of bowdlerizing the vocabulary of public discourse. Except in situations where the audience is "captive,"[12] or where the offensive message intrudes into the privacy of the

editor could not be expelled for violating "conventions of decency" for publishing in student newspaper a cartoon depicting the rape of the Statue of Liberty by a policeman and a headline "M_____ F_____ Acquitted").

6. See, e.g., Eaton v. City of Tulsa, 415 U.S. 697 (1974) (per curiam) (reversing conviction for contempt of court in witness' use of expression "chickenshit," since there was no showing that the expletive, at least when not directed to the judge, posed an imminent threat to administration of justice); Hess v. Indiana, 414 U.S. 105 (1973) (per curiam) (reversing conviction for disorderly conduct where statement during antiwar demonstration—"We'll take the fucking street later [or again]"—was not directed at any person or group in particular and there was no showing that violence was imminent); Street v. New York, 394 U.S. 576 (1969) (statement that "We don't need no damn flag," made by protestor while burning a flag, was not "so inherently inflammatory" as to come within the class of "fighting words").

7. 403 U.S. 15 (1971).

8. Because Cohen was convicted under a statute applicable throughout the state,

the Court explicitly distinguished the issue of the constitutionality of a statute drafted to preserve an appropriately decorous atmosphere in courthouses or other specified places. Id. at 19.

9. Id. at 20.

10. Id. at 22–23.

11. "[W]hile the particular four-letter word being litigated here is perhaps more distasteful than most others, it is nevertheless true that one man's vulgarity is another man's lyric. Indeed, we think it is largely because governmental officials cannot make principled distinctions in this area that the Constitution leaves matters of taste and style so largely to the individual." Id. at 25. When the speech is broadcast, however, the Court has been less tolerant of vulgarity. In FCC v. Pacifica Foundation, 438 U.S. 726, 745–47 (1978), the Court upheld an FCC complaint against a New York radio station for playing a monologue by comedian George Carlin which the Court described as "vulgar, offensive, and shocking," but not obscene. See §§ 12–18, 12–19, infra.

12. See §§ 12–16 n. 43, 12–18, 12–19, 12–25, 15–19, infra.

home,[13] government may not purge public dialogue of unwelcome words or symbols, just as it may not prohibit unwelcome ideas. [14]

With the shift in emphasis from the words themselves to the context in which they are uttered, the "fighting words" doctrine has been largely assimilated to a class of problems in which the Supreme Court has had to consider whether authorities may silence a provocative speaker or instead must control the hostile audience when an expressive act seems likely to touch off a violent response.[15] One must begin with the premise that government may not justify the suppression of speech because its content or mode of expression is offensive to some members of the audience.[16] If, as Holmes observed, "every idea is an incitement," [17] the duty of the police ordinarily must be to protect the speaker's right of expression—whatever the reaction.[18] Yet it is not

13. See §§ 12–19, 15–20, infra.

14. Cohen, 403 U.S. at 25–26. Cohen is interestingly assessed in Farber, "Civilizing Public Discourse," 1980 Duke L.J. 283. The Court also employed a modified version of the captive audience theory when it upheld disciplinary action against a high school student for vulgar but not obscene speech in Bethel School Dist. No. 403 v. Fraser, 106 S.Ct. 3159 (1986). There the Court upheld, by a 7–2 vote, a three-day suspension of a high school student who addressed a school assembly using "an elaborate, graphic and explicit sexual metaphor." Id. at 3162. Chief Justice Burger's opinion applied a balancing test: "[t]he undoubted freedom to advocate unpopular and controversial views in schools and classrooms must be balanced against the society's countervailing interest in teaching students the boundaries of socially appropriate behavior." Id. at 3164. Relying, then, on the "interest in protecting minors from exposure to vulgar and offensive spoken language," id. at 3165, the Court upheld the suspension of Fraser, noting also that "the penalties imposed in this case were unrelated to any political viewpoint." Id. at 3166. Justice Blackmun concurred in the result without opinion. Justice Brennan, concurring in the judgment, noted that school officials' "authority to regulate such speech by high school students was not limitless," id. at 3168, but concluded that "in light of the discretion school officials have to teach high school students how to conduct civil and effective discourse, and to prevent disruption of school educational activities, it was not unconstitutional for school officials to conclude . . . that respondent's remarks exceeded permissible limits." Id. at 3167. Justice Marshall dissented "because . . . the school district failed to demonstrate that the remarks were indeed disruptive." Id. at 3168. Justice Stevens wrote a spirited dissent, questioning the factual conclusions of "a group of judges who are at least two generations and 3,000 miles away from the scene of the crime." Id. at 3169 (footnote omitted). Justice Stevens would not have disturbed the findings of the district court, which concluded that the student's behavior did not disrupt school activities sufficiently to "justif[y] impinging on Fraser's First Amendment right to express himself freely." Id. at 3170 (citation omitted).

15. The phrase "heckler's veto," often used as a shorthand statement of the problem, is Professor Kalven's. See The Negro and the First Amendment 140–145 (1965).

16. See, e.g., Street v. New York, 394 U.S. 576, 592 (1969), where, in reversing a conviction for words contemptuous of the American flag, Justice Harlan wrote for the Court: "It is firmly settled that under our Constitution the public expression of ideas may not be prohibited merely because the ideas are themselves offensive to some of the hearers". But the rights of the auditors whose hostility is aroused by a speaker remain relevant. The hostility of the audience might be a factor if the speech intrudes into such sensitive areas as residential neighborhoods and schools, where many of the receivers of the message may in effect be "captive." See note 12, supra.

17. Gitlow v. New York, 268 U.S. 652, 673 (1925) (Holmes, J., dissenting).

18. See Chafee, Free Speech in the United States 245 (1948) ("The sound constitutional doctrine is that the public authorities have the obligation to provide police protection against threatened disorder at lawful public meetings in all reasonable circumstances"); Emerson, The System of Free Expression 341 (1970) ("Once it is clear that the constitutional guarantee of freedom of assembly [is threatened by violence and disorder] . . . . the remedy open to the community is . . . . to invoke emergency powers of martial law").

difficult to recognize the genuine dilemma that law enforcement officers may confront when violence is incipient; although free speech would be suppressed, silencing the speaker is certainly preferable to a blood bath.[19] Still, the discretion of government authorities must be narrowly confined; they may not enforce regulations which are not narrowed so as to focus on incitement unprotected by the first amendment.

In *Terminiello v. Chicago*,[20] the Supreme Court refused even to consider the question whether a race-baiting speech that attracted an "angry and turbulent" crowd was itself constitutionally protected.[21] Instead, the Court reversed the speaker's breach of the peace conviction because the regulatory statute, which punished speech that "stirs the public to anger, [or] invites dispute," was overbroad and thus void on its face.[22] The first amendment protects speech that has precisely those effects: "[a] function of free speech under our system of government is to invite dispute. It may indeed best serve its high purpose when it induces a condition of unrest, creates dissatisfaction with conditions as they are, or even stirs people to anger." [23]

In cases where government invokes a facially valid law to suppress what would otherwise be constitutionally protected speech because of the imminence of violence, the result is necessarily sensitive to even

19. See Note, "Protecting Demonstrators from Hostile Audiences," 19 Kan.L. Rev. 524, 530 (1974). An attempt to articulate relevant standards for police response to the problem of hostile audiences is made in Note, "Hostile-Audience Confrontations: Police Conduct and First Amendment Rights," 75 Mich.L.Rev. 180 (1976).

20. 337 U.S. 1 (1949).

21. Id. The majority opinion was based on the ambiguity of the trial judge's charge to the jury, which allowed the jury to find Terminiello guilty not for the riot he may have caused but for the anger he had aroused. See Note, "Scope of Supreme Court Review: The Terminiello Case in Focus," 59 Yale L.J. 971 (1950); Note, "Constitutional Law—Freedom of Speech—All Possible Grounds for a Verdict Must Be Constitutionally Valid," 23 S.C.L.Rev. 159 (1971). See also Bachellar v. Maryland, 397 U.S. 564 (1970) (overturning a disorderly conduct conviction because the Court could not tell whether a jury's general verdict resulted from the defendant anti-war protester's alleged intentional obstruction of a public sidewalk, or rather from the jury's enforcement of statutory language, void on its face, for prohibiting speech "which offends [or] disturbs . . . a number of people gathered in the same area"); Stromberg v. California, 283 U.S. 359 (1931) (same principle).

22. A permit requirement as a prerequisite to use of the streets, parks, or other public places is void on its face if it gives public officials discretion to withhold a permit because fo generalized fears of a hostile audience. In the context of a permit application, the official decision is not based on on-the-spot observation of an emergent riot, but on the apprehension of potentially hostile officials. See Blasi, "Prior Restraints on Demonstrations," 68 Mich.L.Rev. 1482, 1510–1515 (1970). In Hague v. C.I.O., 307 U.S. 496, 516 (1939), the Court voided on its face a system providing that a "permit shall only be refused for the purpose of preventing riots, disturbances or disorderly assemblage" because "the uncontrolled official suppression of the [right to speak] cannot be made a substitute for the duty to maintain order in connection with the exercise of the right." But only three Justices subscribed to this aspect of the opinion. Cf. Tinker v. Des Moines Independent Community School District, 393 U.S. 503, 509 (1969) (school officials cannot suspend students for wearing armbands to protest the VietNam War because of undifferentiated fear of disturbance created by hostile classmates). Some lower court decisions have accordingly held that fear of a hostile audience does not constitute a permissible basis for denying a permit. See, e.g., Stacy v. Williams, 306 F.Supp. 963, 977 (N.D.Miss.1969); Hurwitt v. City of Oakland, 247 F.Supp. 995 (N.D.Cal.1965); Williams v. Wallace, 240 F.Supp. 100 (M.D.Ala.1965). See § 12–38, infra.

23. Terminiello v. Chicago, 337 U.S. 1, 4 (1949) (Douglas, J.).

slight variations in the facts of the particular case. As a consequence, no general rule of constitutional etiquette—no functional equivalent of Robert's Rules of Order—can be stated. But it is possible to observe several recurring themes in the Court's decisions. First, the speaker cannot be silenced if his or her identity is the primary factor offered to justify the conclusion that audience violence is imminent. In the 1960's, the Supreme Court on several occasions overturned breach of the peace or similar convictions incurred by black demonstrators who peacefully protested the racial segregation of public and private facilities by attempting to make use of those facilities. In each case, the Court concluded that reversal was mandated because the only justification local authorities could ultimately offer to support their belief in the imminence of white spectator violence was the assertion that the very sight of blacks attempting to make use of these facilities would stir anger. Even if true, the assertion was constitutionally irrelevant: "Such activity . . . is not evidence of any crime and cannot be considered either by the police or by the courts." [24]

Second, government authorities may not suppress otherwise protected speech if imminent spectator violence can be satisfactorily prevented or curbed with reasonable crowd control techniques.[25] In another series of cases growing out of the civil rights demonstrations of the 1960's, the Supreme Court reversed breach of peace or similar convictions after finding that there was no evidence to support local officials' claims that breaking up demonstrations was justified by the imminent prospect of white spectator violence. In each case, the Court found that "[police] protection at the scene was at all times sufficient to meet any foreseeable possibility of disorder" by spectators.[26]

24. Garner v. Louisiana, 368 U.S. 157 (1961) (upsetting convictions for breach of the peace where there was no evidence in the record that a peaceful sit-in at a segregated lunch counter carried with it the likelihood of imminent violence); accord, Taylor v. Louisiana, 370 U.S. 154 (1962) (upsetting breach of the peace conviction for sit-in in the waiting room of bus depot). In Collin v. Smith, 578 F.2d 1197 (7th Cir. 1978), cert. denied 439 U.S. 916 (1978), the Seventh Circuit struck down a Skokie, Illinois, village ordinance which would have prohibited all public demonstrations which "incite violence, hatred, abuse or hostility toward a person or group of persons by reason of reference to religious, racial, ethnic, national or regional affiliation." Id. at 1199. The ordinance was passed in response to plans of the American Nazi Party to march in the predominantly Jewish suburb of Chicago, where a substantial number of Holocaust survivors live. The Court noted that any demonstration by the Nazis "would seriously disturb, emotionally and mentally, at least some, and probably many of the Village's residents." Id. at 1206. Nevertheless, the circuit court, relying on Terminiello, stated that speech that "invites dispute . . . induces a condition

of unrest, creates dissatisfaction with conditions as they are, or even stirs people to anger [was] among the high purposes of the First Amendment." Id. Accordingly, the Court struck down the ordinance, which made "a crime . . . of a silent march, attended only by symbols and not by extrinsic conduct offensive in itself." Id.

25. See Feiner v. New York, 340 U.S. 315, 326–27 (1951) (Black, J., dissenting): "If in the name of preserving order, [the police] ever can interfere with a lawful public speaker, they first must make all reasonable efforts to protect him".

26. Edwards v. South Carolina, 372 U.S. 229, 232–33 (1963) (187 demonstrators at the State House drew a crowd of 200 to 300 evidently peaceful onlookers; police had been given ample warning and had 30 officers at the scene, with adequate reinforcements available within a short time); Cox v. Louisiana (I), 379 U.S. 536, 550 (1965) (1500 demonstrators across the street from the county courthouse and jail were separated by 75 to 80 armed policemen from a crowd of 100 to 300 "muttering" spectators). Cf. Gregory v. Chicago, 394 U.S. 111 (1969) (holding that there was constitutionally insufficient evidence to

Finally, government authorities may suppress otherwise constitutionally protected speech if imminent spectator violence cannot be satisfactorily prevented or curbed by means of reasonable crowd control techniques, and if the speech itself is the apparent cause of the impending disorder.[27] In *Feiner v. New York*,[28] the Supreme Court upheld a disorderly conduct conviction that resulted from a soap box orator's refusal to comply with a police command that he cease speaking to a racially mixed crowd, where the orator had given "the impression that he was endeavoring to arouse the Negro people against the whites, urging that they rise up in arms and fight for equal rights;" there were only two policemen on the scene confronting a crowd of about seventy-five or eighty people; and, while some of the crowd approved of the speaker's arguments, "at least one threatened violence if the police did not act." [29]

In light of the more recent civil rights demonstration cases, *Feiner* should be read narrowly. In general, the Supreme Court became less willing by the 1960's to accept police judgments and police versions of the facts in such cases. As Justice Black's dissent in *Feiner* made clear,[30] "the police did not even pretend to try to protect" the speaker from the crowd; there was evidence that the speaker did not call on blacks to "rise up *in arms*" but rather to "rise up and fight for their rights by going arm in arm . . . black and white alike," to hear another speaker; and the sole threat of violence was made by a man accompanied by his "wife and two small children. . . ."

More illustrative of the Court's approach in later decades was *Hess v. Indiana*,[31] where the Court overturned a disorderly conduct conviction of a spectator at an anti-war demonstration who was prosecuted for his conduct while being cleared from a street on a college campus. As the local sheriff passed by, Hess exclaimed, "We'll take the fucking street later," or "We'll take the fucking street again." Hess was immediately arrested. In reversing the subsequent conviction, the Court observed "that Hess did not appear to be exhorting the crowd back into the street;" "that his tone, although loud, was no louder than that of the other people in the area;" and that "[at] best . . . the statement could be taken as counsel for present moderation; at worst it amounted to nothing more than advocacy of illegal action at some

support disorderly conduct convictions for civil rights demonstrators who failed to disperse upon a police order to do so; the Court refused to consider evidence noted by Justice Black in dissent that the hostile crowd of 1,000 spectators from the neighborhood attracted by the 85 marchers was growing unmanageable in spite of the best efforts of a special detail of 100 uniformed police: the demonstrators were charged with conducting a disorderly march, not with disobeying a lawful order to disperse).

27. See, e.g., Niemotko v. Maryland, 340 U.S. 268, 289 (1951) (Frankfurter, J., concurring): "It is not a constitutional principle that, in acting to preserve order, the police must proceed against the crowd whatever its size and temper and not against the speaker."

28. 340 U.S. 315, 316–18 (1951).

29. But see Cantwell v. Connecticut, 310 U.S. 296, 311 (1940) (overturning conviction for common law breach of the peace of a Jehovah's Witness who had angered a group by playing a phonograph record containing slurs on Catholicism; the communication, although it stirred animosity, did not pose a "clear and present danger of riot, disorder, interference with traffic upon the public streets, or other immediate threat to public safety, peace, or order").

30. 340 U.S. at 326, 324 n. 5, 326.

31. 414 U.S. 105 (1973) (per curiam).

indefinite future time. This is not sufficient to permit the State to punish Hess' speech." [32]

The Court, however, has not foreclosed the possibility of imposing costs on those whose words inflict injury by their very utterance. Indeed, that notion need not be limited to words that trigger reflexive violence.[33] The Constitution may well allow punishment for speaking words that cause hurt just by their being uttered and heard. The Court of Appeals for the Seventh Circuit appropriately rejected an ordinance passed by the village of Skokie, Illinois, in order to prevent a planned march by a group of neo-Nazis.[34] Yet a more narrowly drawn statute— one that, say, allowed for an after-the-fact award of damages for the intentional infliction of psychic trauma—might well have passed constitutional muster. So, too, might a court approve a law that sought to protect the victims of rapes or other violent attacks from being assaulted with photographic reminders of the crimes they had suffered. Such statutes would be constitutionally problematic—the potential for content-specific regulation is always great—but a commitment to protect evenhandedly the expression of all sentiments should not degenerate from an abiding faith in the first amendment to an obsession with alluring abstractions or neutral principles. The first amendment need not sanctify the deliberate infliction of pain simply because the vehicle used is verbal or symbolic rather than physical. And legislatures may create remedies for the damage done with words so long as these remedies display sufficient sensitivity to freedom of expression as well.

§ 12–11. Clear and Present Danger: The Administration of Justice and Alleged Conflicts Between Free Press and Fair Trial

The Supreme Court has consistently used the "clear and present danger" standard to determine the constitutionality of contempt citations, in the absence of a prior court order, based on either in-court or out-of-court statements critical of the administration of justice in ongoing judicial proceedings.[1] The Court in this line of cases has assumed

---

32. Id. at 108.

33. See Chaplinsky v. New Hampshire, 315 U.S. 568 (1942) and § 12–10, supra.

34. See Collin v. Smith, 447 F.Supp. 676 (N.D. Ill. 1978), aff'd 578 F.2d 1197 (7th Cir.), cert. denied 439 U.S. 916 (1978); § 12–10, note 24, supra.

§ 12–11

1. See In re Little, 404 U.S. 553, 555 (1972) (per curiam) (holding that a statement by the defendant "that the court was biased and had prejudged the case and that petitioner was a political prisoner" could not be deemed contemptuous because "[t]here is no indication . . . that petitioner's statements were uttered in a boisterous tone or in any way actually disrupted the court proceeding," while indicating in dictum that the epithet "M_____ F_____" could be found a contempt of court); Eaton v. City of Tulsa, 415 U.S. 697, 698 (1974) (per curiam) (holding that a single use in court of "street vernacular" (here the phrase "chicken shit"), at least when not directed at the judge, was not punishable as contempt without a further showing that "use of the expletive" constituted " 'an imminent . . . threat to the administration of justice,' " (quoting Craig v. Harney, 331 U.S. 367, 376 (1947)). But cf. Smith v. United States, 431 U.S. 291, 318 (1977) (Stevens, J., dissenting) (stating broadly that "offensive language in a courtroom . . . may surely be regulated").

The principal case that defines when an extrajudicial statement becomes a punishable attempt to interfere with the administration of justice is Bridges v. California, 314 U.S. 252 (1941), in which the Court overturned a contempt citation based on union leader Harry Bridges' public release

that all behavior—including purely communicative behavior—that prevents the fair adjudication of a case is punishable as contempt. In *Nebraska Press Association v. Stuart*,[2] the Supreme Court confronted directly the possible conflict between a state's interest in ensuring criminal defendants a fair and impartial trial and the first amendment guarantee of freedom of the press,[3] but unlike the earlier contempt decisions, the *Nebraska Press* case arose on appeal of a prior court order prohibiting press reporting of prejudicial news, thereby bringing into play the strong presumption against the constitutionality of prior restraints.[4]

Nebraska Press involved a court order prohibiting the reporting of the existence or nature of any confessions or other information "strong-

of a telegram he had sent the Secretary of Labor "predicting" a massive strike if a California state court attempted to enforce its decision in a jurisdictional dispute over representation of West Coast dock workers. A motion for new trial was pending at the time Bridges made his telegram public. In a companion case, the Court reversed a contempt conviction where the Los Angeles Times had editorially warned a judge, while sentence was pending, against making a "serious mistake" if he granted probation to two convicted members of a Teamsters' Union "goon squad." Id. at 271–75. Justice Black wrote for the majority that, before the state could abridge freedom of expression, the danger of prejudice to the disposition of the pending adjudication must be "extremely serious and the degree of imminence extremely high." Id. at 263. Applying this test, the Court found that the release of the telegram did not present "a clear and present danger" of interference with the administration of justice. Id. at 276–78. See R. McCloskey, The Modern Supreme Court 15 (1972) (commenting that if Bridges' threat to cripple the economy of the entire West Coast did not present clear and present danger, then the lesson of the case must be that almost nothing said outside the courtroom is punishable as contempt). Cf. Nebraska Press Association v. Stuart, 427 U.S. 539, 562 (1976) (formulating a diluted version of the test: whether "the gravity of the 'evil,' discounted by its improbability, justifies such invasion of free speech as is necessary to avoid the danger"). See Schmidt, "Nebraska Press Association: An Extension of Freedom and Contraction of Theory," 29 Stan.L.Rev. 431, 459–60 (1977) (criticizing the Nebraska Press version of the clear and present danger test).

The Court has generally reversed convictions for out-of-court publications. See Wood v. Georgia, 370 U.S. 375 (1962) (sheriff's open letter to the press and grand jury criticizing the jury's investigation into charges of electoral corruption involving bloc voting by blacks); Craig v. Harney,

331 U.S. 367 (1947) (newspaper's criticism of county judge, an elected official who was not a lawyer and who exercised both judicial and administrative responsibilities, for his mishandling of a civil case involving a veteran); Pennekemp v. Florida, 328 U.S. 331 (1946) (articles critical of local judges' reliance on "legal technicalities" to turn criminals loose). But see Riegler, "Lawyers' Criticism of Judges: Is Freedom of Speech a Figure of Speech?", 2 Const. Comm. 69 (1985).

2. 427 U.S. 539 (1976).

3. While Justice Black was surely right that "free speech and fair trial are two of the most cherished policies of our civilization, and it would be a trying task to choose between them," Bridges v. California, 314 U.S. 252, 260 (1941) (overturning union leader's contempt citation) the danger of prejudicial pretrial publicity need not force such a choice. If our system of criminal justice is functioning properly, government is prohibited from trying an accused in a prejudicial atmosphere; if pretrial publicity prevents the impaneling of an impartial jury, the defendant is entitled by the sixth amendment to a dismissal of the charges against him. See Wright, "Fair Trial-Free Press," 38 F.R.D. 435 (1965). The key conflict is therefore not between a defendant's sixth amendment rights and a publisher's first amendment rights: the interests advanced to justify suppression of prejudicial news are largely the state's interests—in putting guilty criminals in jail and in maintaining confidence in the fairness of the judicial system. Because government can ordinarily vindicate these interests by alternatives less restrictive of first amendment liberty, see Nebraska Press Association, 427 U.S. at 611–13, it has rarely been put to an extraordinary choice. See also Friendly, "Order in the Court—Freedom in the Newsroom," 20 Judge's J. 14 (1981) (arguing that fair trial and free press are not inherently antithetical).

4. See §§ 12–34, 12–35, 12–36, infra.

ly implicative" of an accused murderer. The crime charged was the
brutal slaying of six members of a family in a small Nebraska town;
the autopsy contained evidence of necrophilia. The crime had immediately attracted widespread publicity which included reports of incriminating statements by the accused. The trial judge was wholly justified
in concluding that intense and pervasive pretrial publicity would continue, and that without restraining the press it would be difficult to
impanel a jury which had not been exposed to the prejudicial information.[5] Nonetheless the Supreme Court unanimously—and rightly—
struck down the order. The opinion of the Chief Justice, joined by four
other members of the Court, found that the trial court's conclusion
about the impact of the expected publicity on prospective jurors "was of
necessity speculative, dealing . . . with factors unknown and unknow-
able." [6] While the trial judge could reasonably predict that a very
large number of veniremen would be exposed to the publicity, he could
only speculate as to what he could not legally presume—namely, that
jurors exposed to such information would be unable to render an
impartial verdict.[7] In addition, the state courts had failed to find that
measures short of an order restraining all publication—a change of
venue, postponement of the trial, a searching voir dire of the jury panel
for bias, instructions to the jury to consider only the evidence presented
in court, and sequestration of jurors—would not effectively mitigate the
adverse impact of the publicity.[8] Given the inevitably speculative
nature of any "finding" that such alternatives would have failed, the
Court's admonition must mean that the alternatives must at least be
tried before a restraint on publication may issue.[9] And the Supreme
Court's apparent confidence that the alternatives would prove adequate [10] suggests that the Court has gone further and announced a

---

5. Nebraska Press Association, 427 U.S. at 562–63, 568–69.

6. Id. at 563.

7. Id. at 565, 568–69; see also id. at 599–601 (Brennan, J., concurring). A defendant who claims he was denied a fair trial because of jury bias must ordinarily
sustain that claim by reference to the voir dire testimony of the impaneled jurors.
Compare Irvin v. Dowd, 366 U.S. 717 (1961), reversing a murder conviction
where adverse publicity had permeated a small community and where ninety percent of the 370 jurors and two-thirds of those actually seated on the jury believed
the defendant guilty, with Murphy v. Flori-da, 421 U.S. 794 (1975), holding that a
defendant had not been denied a fair trial where, as a result of publicity seven
months before the trial, some jurors re-called the robbery involved in the case and
the accused's prior crimes, but where only 20 of 78 persons questioned were excused
because they indicated an opinion as to the accused's guilt and all of those actually
seated testified that they could be impar-tial. See also United States v. Haldeman,
559 F.2d 31 (D.C. Cir. 1976) (en banc), cert.

denied, 431 U.S. 933 (1977) (upholding convictions in the Watergate cover-up case in
spite of the massive pretrial publicity,
where the tone of the publicity was not
inflammatory and a probing voir dire by
the trial judge had permitted the removal
from the jury of those who harbored any
prejudice or preconception). The Supreme
Court has reversed a conviction on a presumption of prejudice only in Rideau v.
Louisiana, 373 U.S. 723 (1963), where a
film of the defendant making an in-custody
confession of robbery, kidnapping and murder was broadcast three times to the locality from which the jury was drawn.

8. See Nebraska Press Association, 427 U.S. at 563–64.

9. See Prettyman, "Nebraska Press Association v. Stuart: Have We Seen the Last
of Prior Restraints on the Reporting of
Judicial Proceedings?" 20 St. Louis L.J. 654, 658 (1976).

10. The Court itself has always found
the contrary when holding that prejudicial
publicity vitiated a fair trial. See Nebraska Press Ass'n, 427 U.S. at 564–65; id. at
601–03 and n. 30 (Brennan, J., concurring

virtual bar to prior restraints on reporting of news about crime.[11] Although the Chief Justice was unwilling to rule out the "possibility" of the Court's approving a prior restraint on reporting crime news, he stressed that the record before the Court was illustrative of the problems inherent in meeting the heavy burden of demonstrating, in advance of trial, the necessity of the restraint.[12] And five justices may have been willing to hold that prior orders restraining the publication of news prejudicial to a criminal defendant are never permissible.[13]

Because the holding in *Nebraska Press Association v. Stuart* was strongly colored by the presumptive invalidity of prior restraints, the decision left unresolved the extent of judicial power to punish as contempt, and of legislative power to proscribe, extrajudicial statements of trial participants or highly prejudicial publications by the press in the absence of a prior restraint.[14] But the Court's more recent holding in *Richmond Newspapers, Inc. v. Virginia*[15] makes clear that the public's right of access to judicial proceedings is of constitutional dimension, and therefore restricts the ability of trial judges to close their proceedings to the public, whether or not they couple closure with a ban on extrajudicial statements by participants. *Nebraska Press* found that the part of the final order prohibiting the publication of "information strongly implicative" of the accused was both too vague and too broad to survive the scrutiny required of restraints on first amendment rights.[16] It may be possible to overcome the vagueness problem by drafting rules proscribing broad categories of statements, including all statements about the accused's prior criminal record or any confessions or admissions, all of which may be presumed to be highly prejudicial to a criminal defendant. This is the approach adopted by most federal district courts following the 1969 report of a

in result); Sheppard v. Maxwell, 384 U.S. 333, 363 (1966); Rideau v. Louisiana, 373 U.S. 723, 726 (1963) (trial court improperly refused change of venue); Irvin v. Dowd, 366 U.S. 717, 722–29 (1961) (same). There is considerable disagreement in the literature as to the efficacy of the various alternative devices. See, e.g., American Bar Association Project on Standards for Criminal Justice, Standards Relating to Fair Trial and Free Press (1968); Stanga, "Judicial Protection of the Criminal Defendant Against Adverse Press Coverage," 13 Wm. and Mary L.Rev. 1 (1971).

11. See Prettyman, note 9, supra, at 659; Howard & Newman, "Fair Trial and Free Expression," Report of the Senate Comm. on the Judiciary, 94th Cong., 2d Sess. 84 (1976); Goodale, "The Press Ungagged: The Practical Effect on Gag Order Litigation of Nebraska Press Association v. Stuart," 29 Stan.L.Rev. 497, 504 (1977). But see Sack, "Principle and Nebraska Press Association v. Stuart," 29 Stan.L. Rev. 411, 411 (1977).

12. 427 U.S. at 569–70. Cf. Capital Cities Media, Inc. v. Toole, 463 U.S. 1303,

1307 (1983) (Brennan, Circuit Justice) (suggesting the need to employ less restrictive alternatives); Smith v. Phillips, 455 U.S. 209, 227 (1982) (Marshall, J., dissenting) (contending that an absolute ban on news coverage is unjustifiable, and recommending case-by-case determinations of the need for a restraint).

13. Justice Brennan, joined by Justices Stewart and Marshall, took an absolutist position: "I would hold that resort to prior restraints on the freedom of the press is a constitutionally impermissible method for enforcing" the right to a fair trial. Id. at 572. Justice Stevens, id. at 617, subscribed to most of the views of Justice Brennan. And Justice White, although joining the Chief Justice's opinion, said he had "grave doubt . . . whether orders with respect to the press such as were entered in this case would ever be justifiable." Id. at 570–571.

14. See note 1, supra.

15. 448 U.S. 555 (1980), discussed in § 12–20, infra.

16. Nebraska Press Association, 427 U.S. at 568.

committee headed by Judge Irving Kaufman.[17] But restrictions of this kind are grossly overinclusive, since the actual risk that a trial's result will be tainted by such publicity is slight. Only a small percentage of criminal cases ever reach a jury, most jury trials generate no publicity, and much crime news goes unnoticed.[18] Moreover, mere exposure to the facts of a case, including prejudicial information, does not automatically disqualify a juror from rendering an impartial verdict, particularly if the prejudicial information is later admitted as evidence at trial.[19] And for most of the small number of cases remaining, less restrictive alternatives will be available to mitigate the adverse impact of prejudicial publicity.

This overbreadth may in turn be cured by reading into the rules a requirement that no penalties may attach to extrajudicial statements without consideration of the actual danger posed in the circumstances of a particular case, with the categorical rules functioning only to create rebuttable presumptions of prejudice.[20] The obvious vice of this "solution," however, is that it reintroduces the problem of vagueness.[21] If a jury is ultimately impaneled and a fair trial held, is the presumption rebutted? Or if a fair trial can be assured only after a change of venue or continuance, is the rebuttal rejected? In pursuing answers to these and similar questions, it should become apparent that the dilemma of overbreadth vs. vagueness in the context of the fair trial problem is insoluble for reasons that the *Nebraska Press* decision identified— namely, the inherently speculative character of any prediction, whether by the publisher of the prejudicial information or by the courts, that a

17. Judicial Conference of the United States, Committee on the Operation of the Jury System, Report of the Committee on the "Free Press-Fair Trial" Issue, 45 F.R.D. 391, 406 (1969).

18. American Bar Association Project on Standards for Criminal Justice, supra note 10.

19. See Nebraska Press Association, 427 U.S. at 565, 568–69; id. at 599–601 (Brennan, J., concurring). All of the material that was suppressed in Nebraska Press was eventually admitted at the defendant's trial. See id. at 600 n. 25 (Brennan, J., concurring).

20. See Chicago Council of Lawyers v. Bauer, 522 F.2d 242 (7th Cir. 1975), cert. denied 427 U.S. 912 (1976), where the Court of Appeals held that the rules recommended by the American Bar Association and the U.S. Judicial Conference were facially invalid because no blanket proscription of areas of comment could pass the requirement that the danger be "serious and imminent." The court suggested that per se rules were needed to provide lawyers with notice of the kinds of statements which were punishable and that, with the inclusion of the "serious and imminent threat" requirement, many of the challenged rules could validly create a pre-

sumption of danger, shifting the burden of proof to the defendant. Cf. Whitney v. California, 274 U.S. 357, 379 (1927) (Brandeis, J., concurring) ("The legislative declaration, like the fact that the statute was passed . . ., creates merely a rebuttable presumption that" a clear, present and substantial danger exists). See also Columbia Broadcasting Co. v. Young, 522 F.2d 234 (6th Cir. 1975) (restrictive order against extrajudicial statements by trial participants and others in civil damage cases arising from the Kent State shootings held invalid absent a clear showing that such restraint was "required to obviate serious and imminent threats to the fairness and integrity of the trial"); Markfield v. Association of the Bar of the City of New York, 49 A.D.2d 516, 370 N.Y.S.2d 82 (1st Dept. 1975), appeal dismissed 37 N.Y.2d 794, 375 N.Y.S.2d 106, 337 N.E.2d 612 (1975) (disciplinary sanctions against defense attorney who participated in radio discussion of prison rebellion during trial arising from the riot held invalid since attorney's words did not create a "clear and present danger to the administration of justice").

21. The problem of substituting vagueness for overbreadth is discussed generally in § 12–29, infra.

particular message will prevent the fair trial of a case. To escape the dilemma, it would be necessary to reject the relevance of the clear and present danger test and look to other non-contextual rules for solutions. Succeeding sections will take up areas in which similar dilemmas have been escaped in just this way. In particular §§ 12–12 to 12–14 will address the problem of reconciling the law of defamation with first amendment rights, a problem to which the "clear and present danger" test was never thought relevant.[22] But the defamation issue differs strikingly in its focus upon redressing consummated harm rather than preventing harm from occurring; it is primarily the latter focus that has forced the fair trial cases to concentrate on highly individualized factual elements.

§ 12–12. Defamation: From Personal Assault to Seditious Libel

Although its impact is felt on reputation rather than on bodily integrity, libelous speech was long regarded as a form of personal assault, and it was accordingly assumed that government could vindicate the individual's right to enjoyment of his good name, no less than his bodily integrity, without running afoul of the Constitution. Moreover, the defamatory statement was not speech for which "more speech" was an adequate remedy: experience had shown that the truth rarely catches up with the lie. In *Chaplinsky v. New Hampshire*,[1] Justice Murphy's opinion for the Court classified libel as wholly outside the scope of first amendment protection. And in *Beauharnais v. Illinois*,[2] a closely divided Supreme Court held, in an opinion by Justice Frankfurter, that unprotected libelous statements include defamations of groups as well as those of individuals.

A wholly different perspective on the law of defamation is derived from the history of seditious libel, the common law crime committed by words or writings that do not amount to treason but are nonetheless critical of government officials or their policies.[3] The enactment of the Alien and Sedition Acts of 1798 by a group of legislators many of whom

---

22. See Kalven, The Negro and the First Amendment 29–30 (1965).

§ 12–12

1. 315 U.S. 568 (1942) (dictum). See also Near v. Minnesota, 283 U.S. 697, 715 (1931) (dictum); Pennekamp v. Florida, 328 U.S. 331, 348–49 (1946) (dictum); Roth v. United States, 354 U.S. 476, 486–87 (1957) (dictum).

2. 343 U.S. 250 (1952). Justices Reed, Black, Douglas, and Jackson dissented in four separate opinions. For a critical discussion, see Kalven, The Negro and the First Amendment, ch. 1 (1965).

The continuing validity of the Beauharnais holding is very much an open question. See, e.g., Smith v. Collin, 439 U.S. 916, 919 (1978) (Blackmun, J., dissenting from denial of certiorari) (noting that Beauharnais "has not been overruled or formally limited"). In recent years, courts have given Beauharnais a very limited

reading. In Collin v. Smith, 578 F.2d 1197, 1204 (7th Cir. 1978), cert. denied 439 U.S. 916 (1978), the Seventh Circuit stated that "[i]t may be questioned after such cases as Cohen v. California, [403 U.S. 15 (1971)], Gooding v. Wilson, [405 U.S. 518 (1972)], and Brandenburg v. Ohio, [395 U.S. 444 (1969) (per curiam)], whether the tendency to induce violence approach sanctioned implicitly in Beauharnais would pass constitutional muster today." See § 12–10 n. 24, supra. In American Booksellers Ass'n, Inc. v. Hudnut, 771 F.2d 323, 331 n. 3 (7th Cir. 1985), aff'd mem. 106 S.Ct. 1172 (1986), the Seventh Circuit stated that subsequent cases "had so washed away the foundations of Beauharnais that it could not be considered authoritative." For further discussion of Hudnut, see § 12–17, infra.

3. See Brant, "Seditious Libel: Myth and Reality," 39 N.Y.U.L.Rev. 1 (1964); Z. Chafee, Free Speech in the United States 497–516 (1941).

had sat in the First Congress suggests that the implications of free speech and free press were still obscure. Indeed it was in the very controversy over the Alien and Sedition Acts that a powerful theory of first amendment freedoms first crystallized.[4] The theory's central tenet was that a free government could not be defamed by its citizens:[5] it is now an indisputable axiom of first amendment jurisprudence that government lacks constitutional power to silence its critics. In Madison's memorable phrase, "The censorial power is in the people over the government, and not in the government over the people."[6] The Supreme Court never ruled on the constitutionality of the Sedition Act; it expired by its own terms in 1801. But in 1812 the Court did hear the appeals of Hudson and Goodwin,[7] the editors of the Federalist *Connecticut Courant* of Hartford, who had been convicted, under federal common law, for the seditious libel of President Jefferson. The Supreme Court terminated federal sedition prosecutions for over a century when it ruled that the Courts of the United States had jurisdiction to try only acts declared criminal by Congress. When *New York Times Co. v. Sullivan*[8] reached the Court, the Justices found the more compelling analogy in seditious libel, and accordingly brushed aside the view of *Chaplinsky* that libelous speech was worthy only of constitutional contempt.

New York Times Co. v. Sullivan arose from a libel judgment of $500,000 won by the police commissioner of Montgomery, Alabama, against four clergymen and The New York Times. The allegedly defamatory publication was a paid advertisement soliciting contributions for Dr. Martin Luther King and the civil rights movement in the South. The advertising copy charged police brutality and harassment during the 1960 racial disturbances in Alabama. The defendants' liability hung on two thin threads. The commissioner had not been named in the advertisement; the only link to the commissioner was his official position as supervisor of the police whose conduct had been criticized. And the advertising copy was inaccurate only in minor particulars, although under the traditionally stringent common law test, defendants were unable to carry their burden of proving truth as a

---

4. See New York Times Co. v. Sullivan, 376 U.S. 254, 273 (1964); L. Levy, Emergence of a Free Press 279–82 (1986). The relevant history is recounted in J. Smith, Freedom's Fetters 3–111 (1956); J. Miller, Crisis in Freedom: The Alien and Sedition Acts (1951).

5. See New York Times, 376 U.S. at 272–73; Kalven, "The New York Times Case: A Note on 'The Central Meaning of the First Amendment'," 1964 Sup.Ct.Rev. 191, 205.

6. 4 Annals of Cong. 934 (1794), quoted in 376 U.S. at 275.

7. United States v. Hudson & Goodwin, 11 U.S. (7 Cranch) 32 (1812). In the early years of the Court, Chief Justices Jay and Ellsworth, and Justices Cushing, Iredell, Wilson, Paterson and Washington, had variously stated their beliefs in a federal criminal jurisdiction at common law. And, except for Justices Chase and Johnson, other members of the Court, sitting in the Circuit Courts, had upheld the common law jurisdiction. Yet Justice Johnson in his opinion in the Hudson case considered the question "as having been long since settled in public opinion," id. at 32, a reference which surely pointed to the political repudiation of federal sedition prosecutions. See C. Warren, 1 The Supreme Court in United States History 433–42 (1937).

8. 376 U.S. 254 (1964). Justice Brennan wrote the Court's opinion. Justices Black and Goldberg concurred separately, with Justice Douglas joining each concurrence, concluding that the first amendment required even more protection than the Court was affording.

defense. Alabama law, like that of most states, held the publisher of a defamatory falsehood strictly liable, and the state recognized no privilege for good faith mistakes of fact. In upholding the jury's verdict against defendants and its award of damages for injury to the commissioner's reputation, the Alabama courts had not departed from familiar rules of libel law,[9] but the inescapable conclusion was that Alabama's "white establishment" had taken the opportunity to punish The New York Times for its support of civil rights activists: the South was prepared to use the law of libel to stifle black opposition to racial segregation.[10]

The Supreme Court naturally and unanimously upset the judgment, taking as its premise "the central meaning of the First Amendment" which had crystallized in the controversy over the Alien and Sedition Acts of 1798: the "profound national commitment to the principle that debate on public issues should be uninhibited, robust, and wide-open, and that it may well include vehement, caustic, and sometimes unpleasantly sharp attacks on government and public officials . . . ."[11] From this premise the Court drew three major conclusions. First, it decided that the Sedition Act of 1798 was unconstitutional more than 160 years after its expiration; shortly afterward, the Court in *Garrison v. Louisiana* voided on its face a state criminal libel statute.[12] Second, the Court held that a public official bringing a libel suit must establish that the defamatory statement was directed at the official personally, and not simply at a government unit.[13] Third, because critical discussion of government ordinarily involves attacks on individual officials as well as impersonal criticisms of government policy, all defamation claims of aggrieved public officials must be examined closely in order to close what would otherwise be a back door to official censorship.[14]

To complete his opinion for the Court, Justice Brennan needed to explain why it was necessary to formulate a general rule at all, rather than merely strike down, case by case, prosecutions for sedition masquerading as private libel actions. The explanation was the behavioral rationale that in other contexts is called the "chilling effect":[15] activities protected by the first amendment are vulnerable and must be protected from the threat of sanctions almost as much as from the actual application of sanctions.[16] For a great danger of self-censorship arises from the fear of guessing wrong—the fear that the trier of fact, proceeding by formal processes of proof and refutation, will after the

9. See Kalven, "The New York Times Case: A Note on 'The Central Meaning of the First Amendment,'" 1964 Sup.Ct.Rev. 196–97.

10. Id. at 200. For an argument that the Court should have confined its holding to the civil rights context and refrained from a major reform of libel law, see Epstein, "Was *New York Times v. Sullivan* Wrong?" 53 U.Chi.L.Rev. 782 (1986).

11. New York Times, 376 U.S. at 270.

12. 379 U.S. 64 (1964).

13. New York Times, 376 U.S. at 292. Accord, Rosenblatt v. Baer, 383 U.S. 75 (1966).

14. New York Times, 376 U.S. at 292.

15. Dombrowski v. Pfister, 380 U.S. 479, 487 (1965).

16. New York Times, 376 U.S. at 271. See § 11–4, supra.

event reject the individual's judgment of truth.[17] This fear is exacerbated by the danger that a jury will not fairly find the facts in cases involving unpopular speakers or unorthodox ideas.[18] And there is simply the cost of litigating a defamation suit, even where publishers are relatively confident that a court somewhere will ultimately vindicate their judgments.[19]

A rule that the first amendment protects the right to utter the truth clearly does not suffice, because "erroneous statement is inevitable in free debate," [20] and the only guarantee of legal safety under such a rule is silence. To remove the inhibitory effect of defamation laws, the Court in *New York Times Co. v. Sullivan* created a constitutional privilege for good faith critics of government officials. "The constitutional guarantees require . . . a federal rule that prohibits a public official from recovering damages for a defamatory falsehood relating to his official conduct unless he proves that the statement was made with 'actual malice'—that is, with knowledge that it was false or with reckless disregard of whether it was false or not." [21] Implicit in this rule is the proposition that the first amendment establishes a right to speak defamatory truth; the common law defense of truth is thus constitutionally required at least where the publication concerns a public official.[22] Assessing the evidence in *New York Times* in light of

17. New York Times, 376 U.S. at 279; Rosenbloom v. Metromedia, Inc., 403 U.S. 29, 50 (1971) (plurality opinion by Brennan, J.) Cf. Speiser v. Randall, 357 U.S. 513, 526 (1958) (program denying tax exemptions to otherwise qualified veterans who refused to subscribe to an oath that they did not advocate violent revolution held unconstitutional because it placed burden of proof on taxpayer).

18. See New York Times, 376 U.S. at 294–95 (Black and Douglas, JJ., concurring); id. at 300 (Goldberg and Douglas, JJ., concurring). See also Gertz v. Robert Welch, Inc., 418 U.S. 323, 349–50 (1974).

19. See Rosenbloom, 403 U.S. at 52–53. See also Anderson, "Libel and Press Self-Censorship," 53 U.Tex.L.Rev. 422, 424–25 (1975).

20. New York Times, 376 U.S. at 271–72.

21. Id. at 279–80. "Actual malice" as required by the Court in New York Times is distinguishable from common law malice, which meant spite or ill will. The terms were nonetheless confused by many lower courts. See, e.g., Henry v. Collins, 380 U.S. 356 (1965) (reversing libel judgments against two public officials where the jury was instructed in terms of common law malice). In Rosenbloom, 403 U.S. at 52 n. 18, Justice Brennan pointedly noted that ill will toward the plaintiff, or bad motives, were not elements of the New York Times standard and recommended that trial courts omit reference to the phrase "actual malice".

22. See Garrison v. Louisiana, 379 U.S. 64, 74 (1964). In Cox Broadcasting Corp. v. Cohn, 420 U.S. 469, 489–90 (1975), the Court said in dictum that it had left open the question whether the Constitution requires that truth be recognized as a defense in a defamation action brought by a private person as distinguished from a public official or public figure. But the better view is surely that the constitutional necessity of recognizing a defense of truth is implicit in the standard of liability in a defamation action brought by a private person—fault with respect to the statement's truth or falsity. Id. at 498–99 (Powell, J., concurring). As to who bears the burden of proof on the issue of falsity, the Court held in Philadelphia Newspapers, Inc. v. Hepps, 106 S.Ct. 1558, 1559 (1986), that "where a newspaper publishes speech of public concern, a private-figure plaintiff cannot recover damages without also showing that the statements at issue are false." Justice O'Connor's opinion for the Court, joined by Justices Brennan, Marshall, Blackmun and Powell, stated that "the common law rule on falsity—that the defendant must bear the burden of proving truth—must fall to a constitutional requirement that the plaintiff bear the burden of showing falsity, as well as fault, before recovering damages." Id. at 1563. Justice Stevens dissented, in an opinion joined by Chief Justice Burger and Justices White and Rehnquist. See generally, Eaton, "The American Law of Defamation Through Gertz v. Robert Welch, Inc. and

its new rule, the Court determined that, on a retrial, the evidence as it stood on the record would be insufficient as a matter of law to submit the case to a jury; the Times would, on this record, be entitled to a directed verdict.[23]

In the years following Justice Brennan's magisterial invocation of the "central meaning of the first amendment," the Court has returned frequently to the libel area but with results far less satisfying than in *New York Times Co. v. Sullivan*. Indeed, since that unanimous decision, the Court has become deeply fragmented about almost every respect of libel, and the doctrine has become a frustrating tangle for all concerned—a mysterious labyrinth for those seeking to clear their names and a costly and unpredictable burden for the speakers the first amendment is designed to protect. The Court's fragmentation appeared gradually, and the development of the doctrine proceeded sensibly for the first few years after *New York Times*. The Court's first task was to define three terms that assumed great importance in the application of the doctrine: "public official," "relating to official conduct," and "actual malice." But as the Court attempted to explain the special responsibilities of judges—both trial and appellate—in applying the many libel rules, the splits in the Court—and in the doctrine itself—began to overwhelm its eminently sensible foundation. Libel law now changes yearly, often in dramatic ways, so no firm predictions should be made about its future course. The Court may yet find an anchor for its libel decisions, but if past is prologue, hopes for such stability should not be high.

As the Court began filling in its definitions, the term "public official" came to include elected officeholders and candidates for elected office, appointed officials, and government employees located near the bottom of any organizational chart, reaching at least those government employees "who have, or appear to the public to have, substantial responsibility for or control over the conduct of governmental affairs."[24] Not every person working for government is a "public official" for purposes of *New York Times Co. v. Sullivan*: "The employee's

---

Beyond: An Analytical Primer," 61 Va.L. Rev. 1349, 1381–1386 (1975).

An action for defamation thus assumes the existence of a falsehood. Because "there is no such thing as a false idea," *Gertz v. Robert Welch, Inc.*, 418 U.S. 323, 339 (1974), statements of opinion, even if expressed in pejorative terms, are protected by the first amendment. In *Old Dominion Branch 496, National Association of Letter Carriers v. Austin*, 418 U.S. 264 (1974), the Court reversed a defamation award to non-union postmen who were called "scabs" in the union's newsletter, which quoted Jack London's definition of a "scab" as a "traitor to his God, his country, his family and his class," a kin of Esau, Judas, and Benedict Arnold. The Court, construing federal labor law in light of constitutional requirements, held the statements protected expressions of opinion, ep-

ithets and hyperbole which did not falsify facts. See also *Greenbelt Cooperative Publishing Ass'n v. Bresler*, 398 U.S. 6, 14 (1970) ("blackmail"); *Cafeteria Employees Local 302 v. Angelos*, 320 U.S. 293, 295 (1943) ("unfair" and "fascist"). As a result of the Gertz and Old Dominion decisions, the American Law Institute abandoned its position that mere opinion, even ridicule, unaccompanied by defamatory factual implications, was actionable. See generally, Keeton, "Defamation and Freedom of the Press", 54 Tex.L.Rev. 1221, 1240–1259 (1976). See § 12–13, infra.

23. New York Times, 376 U.S. at 285–92.

24. *Rosenblatt v. Baer*, 383 U.S. 75, 85 (1966). See § 12–13, infra, for discussion of "public figures."

position must be one which would invite public scrutiny and discussion occasioned by the particular charges in controversy." [25] This dictum, however, has never been applied by the Supreme Court, and lower courts have tended to disregard it as well, with the net effect that the term "public official" now embraces virtually all persons affiliated with the government, such as most ordinary civil servants, including public school teachers and policemen.[26]

The "relevance" of a statement to the "official conduct" of the public official has also been defined expansively, although fewer defamations are likely to be deemed relevant as one moves lower and lower in the governmental hierarchy. The principal Supreme Court cases have concerned relatively prominent officers. In *Garrison v. Louisiana,*[27] the Court held that allegations of laziness, inefficiency, and obstruction directed against local criminal court judges were relevant to the official conduct of such judges: "anything which might touch on an official's fitness for office is relevant." [28] An allegation that a candidate for the United States Senate had been a "small-time bootlegger" during prohibition was relevant,[29] as was the allegation that the mayor of a rural Florida town had been indicated for perjury by a federal grand jury.[30] "[A]s a matter of constitutional law . . . a charge of criminal conduct, no matter how remote in time or place, can never be irrelevant to an official's or a candidate's fitness for office . . . ." [31]

As to the requirement of "actual malice," the rule is that, to recover damages for allegedly defamatory criticism of his or her official conduct, a public official must establish by "clear and convincing proof" [32] that the defendant had knowledge of, or recklessly disregarded, the falsity of the defamatory statement.[33] One aspect of this

25. Id. at 86–87 n. 13 (dictum); see also Hutchinson v. Proxmire, 443 U.S. 111, 119 n. 8 (1979) (category of "public official[s] . . . cannot be thought to include all public employees.").

26. See, e.g., cases collected by Eaton, supra note 22, at 1376–78 nn. 120–21.

27. 379 U.S. 64 (1964).

28. Id. at 77.

29. Monitor Patriot Co. v. Roy, 401 U.S. 265 (1971).

30. Ocala Star-Banner Co. v. Damron, 401 U.S. 295 (1971).

31. Monitor Patriot Co., 401 U.S. at 277. The Court has nonetheless held, not surprisingly, that the petition clause of the first amendment does not provide absolute immunity for statements made to government officials about candidates for appointed federal office. In McDonald v. Smith, 472 U.S. 479 (1985), an unsuccessful candidate for United States Attorney sued an individual who wrote a letter to the President of the United States which impugned the candidate's fitness for the office. The Court held unanimously that North Carolina law—which allowed the plaintiff to recover only if he proved "actual malice" by the defendant—provided all the protection required by the first amendment. Justice Brennan, joined by Justices Marshall and Blackmun, concurred, stating their view that the first amendment required neither more nor less than an actual malice standard, "whether the expression consists of speaking to neighbors across a backyard fence, publishing an editorial in the local newspaper or sending a letter to the President of the United States." Id. at 490. Justice Powell did not participate.

32. See Rosenbloom v. Metromedia, Inc., 403 U.S. 29, 30 (1971) (plurality opinion by Brennan, J.); New York Times, 376 U.S. at 285–86: "[T]he proof presented to show actual malice lacks the convincing clarity which the constitutional standard demands."

33. The same must be established before a public employee is discharged for nondisruptive public criticism of the public employer. See Pickering v. Board of Education, 391 U.S. 563 (1968). But see Con-

apparently straightforward rule generated years of controversy as a result of dictum in Chief Justice Burger's opinion for the the Court in *Hutchinson v. Proxmire*.[34] Because the "actual malice" standard "calls a defendant's state of mind into question," the Court stated that proof of actual malice "does not readily lend itself to summary disposition." [35] Several circuit courts interpreted this statement as an invitation to hold that the clear and convincing standard for actual malice need not serve as a filter for weak cases at the summary judgment stage.[36] This interpretation exposed press defendants to genuine hardship by subjecting them to the expense of full trials even in cases in which it was fairly predictable that the plaintiffs had virtually no chance of ultimate victory. The Court did finally settle the issue satisfactorily in *Anderson v. Liberty Lobby, Inc.*,[37] holding by a 6–3 vote that "the *New York Times* requirement of clear and convincing evidence must be considered on a motion for summary judgment"—on the sensible theory that "whether a given factual dispute requires submission to a jury must be guided by the substantive evidentiary standards that apply to the case," the standard being actual malice in public figure libel cases. Justice White's opinion for the Court relied less on first amendment principles than on judicial economy concerns—an approach which drew Justice Brennan's fire in a dissenting opinion. Justice Brennan predicted that *Anderson* "will transform what is meant to provide an expedited 'summary' procedure into a full blown paper trial on the merits." [38] It remains to be seen whether Justice Brennan's warnings are justified for the summary judgment inquiry generally, but *Anderson* surely provides a valuable accommodation of interests in the libel area.

The Court's accommodation of interests in *Anderson*—and its understanding of the need for prompt resolution of libel cases—was far superior to its approach in *Herbert v. Lando*.[39] There the Court refused to contain what may be the greatest threat to press freedom in the libel area: the monetary—and journalistic—costs of extended discovery into editorial processes. Plaintiff Anthony Herbert, who had served in Vietnam and later accused his superior officers of covering up reports of atrocities, was the subject of a CBS television documentary produced by defendant Barry Lando and of an Atlantic Monthly article written by Lando; Herbert charged that the program and article falsely portrayed him as a liar. Herbert conceded that he was a "public figure," and thus was required to prove that the defendant "in fact entertained

---

nick v. Myers, 461 U.S. 138, 143 (1983) (limiting the speech rights of public employees to "matters of public concern.") Likewise, Linn v. United Plant Guard Workers Union, 383 U.S. 53 (1966), restricted state remedies for libel committed by a party to a labor dispute to cases in which demonstrable injury results from defamatory falsehoods uttered with knowledge or reckless disregard of their falsity. Accord, Old Dominion Branch 496, Nat'l Ass'n of Letter Carriers v. Austin, 418 U.S. 264 (1974).

34. 443 U.S. 111 (1979).

35. Id. at 120 & n. 9.

36. See, e.g., Liberty Lobby, Inc. v. Anderson, 746 F.2d 1563 (D.C. Cir. 1984) (Scalia, J.), rev'd 106 S.Ct. 2505 (1986).

37. 106 S.Ct. 2505, 2508, 2513 (1986).

38. Justice Rehnquist, joined by Chief Justice Burger, also dissented, believing that juries in public figure libel cases should have wide latitude to examine the credibility of witnesses. See id. at 2520.

39. 441 U.S. 153 (1979), discussed in § 12–22, infra.

serious doubts as to the truth of his publication." [40] By the time the case reached the Second Circuit, the deposition of Lando "had lasted intermittently for over a year and had filled 2,903 pages of transcript, with an additional 240 exhibits." [41] During that deposition, Lando refused to answer 84 questions relating to: his conclusions regarding people or leads to be pursued and facts imparted by interviewees; the basis of conclusions reached on the veracity of his sources; conversations between Lando and fellow defendant Mike Wallace; and Lando's reasons for including or excluding material. [42] Lando asserted that the first amendment protected against inquiry into the editorial process and into the state of mind of those who edit, produce, or publish.

Justice White, writing for a 6–3 majority, [43] rejected that assertion, holding that such an editorial privilege was neither compelled by the Court's earlier decisions providing substantial deference to editorial discretion, [44] nor an appropriate extension of *New York Times* as a matter of federal law. [45] Mitigating against an editorial privilege, Justice White argued for the Court, were the additional burdens it would place on libel plaintiffs and the difficulty of establishing its outer boundaries. [46] The Court minimized any chilling effects of discovery into the editorial process: "if the claimed inhibition flows from the fear of damage liability for publishing knowing or reckless falsehoods, those effects are precisely what *New York Times* and other cases have held to be consistent with the First Amendment." [47] The Court found it "difficult to believe" [48] that the possibility of discovery would inhibit frank discussion among reporters and editors, particularly when exposure to liability presents an incentive to take pre-publication precautions such as editor-reporter exchanges.

The Court conceded that "it would not be surprising" if the "actual malice" standard led to more discovery than in pre-*New York Times* defamation litigation, and "it would follow that the costs and other burdens of this kind of litigation would escalate and become much more troublesome for both plaintiffs and defendants." [49] However, the Court insisted that an editorial privilege would not "cure" this problem, and that high litigation costs were not peculiar to libel litigation. Thus, "unless and until there are major changes in the present Rules of Procedure, reliance must be had on what in fact and in law are ample powers of the district judge to prevent abuse." [50]

40. St. Amant v. Thompson, 390 U.S. 727, 731 (1968). See § 12–13, infra, for further discussion of the "public figure" standard.

41. Herbert v. Lando, 441 U.S. at 202 (Marshall, J., dissenting).

42. Id. at 157 n. 2.

43. Justice Powell wrote a concurring opinion. Justice Brennan dissented in part, and Justices Stewart and Marshall each wrote dissenting opinions.

44. See, e.g., Zurcher v. Stanford Daily, 436 U.S. 547 (1978). Cf. Branzburg v. Hayes, 408 U.S. 665 (1972). See § 12–22, infra.

45. States remain free under their own law, of course, to recognize such a privilege. See § 12–22, infra.

46. Herbert, 441 U.S. at 170–71.

47. Id. at 171.

48. Id. at 174.

49. Id. at 176.

50. Id. at 177. In his concurrence, Justice Powell emphasized that, even though the editorial process did not merit a constitutional evidentiary privilege, "when a discovery demand arguably impinges on First Amendment rights, a district court should measure the degree of relevance required in light of both the private needs of the

Unfortunately, the Court refused to give judges a powerful tool for controlling discovery of the editorial process—a requirement that the plaintiff make a *prima facie* showing that the publication contains a defamatory falsehood, a suggestion made by Justice Brennan in his partial dissent.[51] The majority asserted that such a requirement would either become a "mini-trial" creating "burdensome complications and intolerable delay," or "could be satisfied by affidavit or a simple verification of the pleadings." [52] Although the Court's refusal to adopt a *prima facie* showing requirement is unfortunate, it is difficult to fault the Court's basic holding in *Herbert*: that the first amendment permits giving defamation plaintiffs access to editorial thought and notes when they must prove a particular condition within the mind of the defendant in order to prevail.[53] The halting compromises of *Herbert* and *Liberty Lobby* illustrate nothing so much as the continuing uncertainty of the Court on defamation questions.

The meaning of the Court's standards is illuminated, at least in part, by the majority's refusal to accept a rule of absolute immunity for speech defaming public officials, the position advanced by Justices Black, Douglas, and Goldberg in their concurrences.[54] The rationale of

parties and the public concerns implicated." Id. at 179.

Justice Stewart asserted that the questions Lando refused to answer were simply irrelevant under a proper reading of the New York Times rule. Because the "actual malice" standard of New York Times has nothing to do with hostility or ill will, inquiry into the motivations of the reporter, editor or producer is irrelevant. Id. at 199. Although inquiry into motivation should indeed be irrelevant for a determination of actual malice, the workings of the editorial process certainly are relevant to a determination of whether the defendant *knew* a statement was false or recklessly disregarded doubts he entertained as to its veracity. In any case, Justice Stewart's disagreement with the Court's holding illustrates the deep confusion on the subject; Justice Stewart's statement that he had "come greatly to regret the use . . . of the phrase 'actual malice,' " id., is certainly most understandable.

51. Id. at 197–98 (Brennan, J., dissenting in part).

52. Id. at 174 n. 23. It is ironic that the Court chose to rely upon trial judges to prevent discovery abuse, but declined to trust those same trial judges to administer effectively a prima facie showing requirement.

53. Justices Brennan and Marshall did agree with the Court in Herbert v. Lando that the state of mind of an individual reporter need not be privileged in itself, since it seemed implausible to them that inquiry could "chill" an individual's thoughts. Id. at 192 (Brennan, J., dissent-

ing in part); id. at 207 (Marshall, J., dissenting).

54. New York Times, 376 U.S. at 293 (Black, J. joined by Douglas, J.); id. at 297 (Goldberg, J., joined by Douglas, J.).

Two highly publicized libel cases in 1985 provided vivid reminders of the force of Justice Black's view. General William Westmoreland sued CBS for $120 million in compensatory and punitive damages for the network's portrayal, in a television documentary, of the General's role in "suppressing" CIA estimates of enemy troop strength during the Vietnam War. The documentary charged that Westmoreland engaged in a "conspiracy" to suppress the estimates in order to prove to his superiors that American forces were making greater progress than they in fact were. The testimony in the case came from a wide array of Vietnam-era political and military leaders and reflected the nation's deep divisions—then as now—about the war. In the other case, Israeli General Ariel Sharon charged that Time magazine libeled him with its description of his role in a 1982 massacre of civilians in a Lebanese refugee camp. The magazine stated that Sharon discussed with Lebanese officials "the need for revenge" of the Christian extremists who perpetrated the massacre— a phrase which Sharon charged imputed responsibility for the deaths to him. The great public attention generated by both these lawsuits—which concluded with Westmoreland dropping his suit near the end of the trial and with the Sharon jury finding that the article was false and defamatory but not made with "actual malice"—demonstrated that both of these high

the qualified privilege developed by the Court was amplified in Justice Brennan's majority opinion in the *Garrison*[55] case, which explicitly invoked the authority of Justice Murphy's *Chaplinsky*[56] dictum: the calculated falsehood, "the lie, knowingly and deliberately published about a public official," is simply beyond the constitutional pale.[57] Stressing the element of calculation, the Court has been at pains to dispel any implication that recklessness in defaming a public official is measurable by reference to the conduct of a reasonably prudent person. The Court's fullest statement of the point may be found in *St. Amant v. Thompson*: "There must be sufficient evidence to permit the conclusion that the defendant in fact entertained serious doubts as to the truth of his publication."[58] The primary (and often sufficient) evidence of the absence of such doubts as would show reckless disregard for truth is "the defendant's testimony that he published the statement in good faith and unaware of its probable falsity."[59] While the finder of fact may have reason to doubt the defendant's professions of good faith, recklessness cannot be inferred from the mere combination of falsehood and the defendant's general hostility toward the plaintiff,[60] nor may recklessness be inferred from negligence.[61] Thus, recklessness could not be found in The New York Times' publishing an advertisement submitted by prominent and responsible individuals, although it may have been negligent not to have checked the accuracy of the copy against the news stories in the paper's own files.[62] Nor could recklessness be attributed to Time magazine for its summary of a U.S. Civil Rights Commission report on police brutality, in which the newsmagazine recounted as fact an incident which the report had explicitly described in terms of allegations.[63] Given the ambiguities of the Commission Report as a whole, it was not reckless of the newsmagazine to choose, from among several conceivable interpretations, one damaging the plaintiff.[64] And there is at least some authority for the view that a publisher is completely immune to a recklessness charge if the publication clearly identifies the allegedly defamatory material as

officials had wide access to the press in their efforts to clear their names. The proper "remedy" for the disputed speech in these cases was more speech—not expensive and extended trials and judicial determinations of "truth." For a thoughtful analysis of these and similar cases and an argument that "[t]he first amendment permits no libel actions against the critics of official conduct," see Lewis, "New York Times v. Sullivan Reconsidered: Time to Return to 'The Central Meaning of the First Amendment,' " 83 Colum.L.Rev. 603, 621 (1983). For a critical view of the litigants and lawyers in these cases as well as a critique of contemporary libel law, see R. Adler, Reckless Disregard (1986).

55. Garrison v. Louisiana, 379 U.S. 64 (1964).

56. Chaplinsky v. New Hampshire, 315 U.S. 568, 572 (1942).

57. Garrison, 379 U.S. at 75, shifting from the position taken in New York

Times, 376 U.S. at 279 n. 19, to the effect that even deliberate falsehoods may advance the search for truth.

58. 390 U.S. 727, 731 (1968).

59. Id. at 731–32. See Eaton, supra note 22, at 1373.

60. Greenbelt Cooperative Publishing Ass'n, Inc. v. Bresler, 398 U.S. 6, 10 (1970).

61. St. Amant, 390 U.S. at 731.

62. New York Times, 376 U.S. at 287–88.

63. Time, Inc. v. Pape, 401 U.S. 279 (1971).

64. Id. at 290. A rational interpretation of an ambiguous document will not be accorded similar protection in cases applying the "fault" standard announced in Gertz v. Robert Welch, Inc., discussed in § 12–13, infra. See Time, Inc. v. Firestone, 424 U.S. 448, 459 n. 4 (1976).

representing not the publisher's own views but those of a responsible organization—so long as the views themselves are accurately and disinterestedly reported.[65]   In sum, recklessness may not be inferred from a publisher's failure to inquire into a matter's truth or falsity, although a responsible publisher might well have inquired.   In the world of *New York Times Co. v. Sullivan*, ignorance is bliss.[66]   So, too, is mere "opinion" blissful for speakers intent on shielding themselves from liability.   In *Gertz v. Robert Welch, Inc.*,[67] discussed more fully in the next section, the Court held directly what had been implicit in its earlier libel opinions: "Under the First Amendment there is no such thing as a false idea.   However pernicious an opinion may seem, we depend for its correction not on the conscience of judges and juries but on the competition of other ideas."[68]   The lower courts have interpreted that passage as recognizing an absolute privilege for opinions, as opposed to facts.   This rule, eminently sensible in theory, has been difficult to apply in practice.

The most extensive treatment of the subject thus far has been by a sharply divided *en banc* panel of the United States Court of Appeals for the District of Columbia Circuit, in *Ollman v. Evans*.[69]   Ollman, a political scientist, had charged that a published description of him as someone "with no status within the profession, but [rather] a pure and simple activist" was libelous.   Judge Kenneth Starr's thoughtful opinion for the majority held that the statements were protected opinion. He applied a four-part test: the common usage of the statement itself, that is, "whether the statement has a precise core of meaning for which a consensus of understanding exists or, conversely, whether the statement is indefinite and ambiguous;" the degree to which the statement is verifiable; the immediate context in which the statement occurs; and the broader social context into which the statement fits.[70]   Judge Robert Bork concurred, but objected to the application of a rigid test and instead called on the court to examine "the rich variety of factors" that must go into an analysis when core first amendment values are threatened.[71]   He called for an "evolving constitutional doctrine" in which judges addressing "modern problems. . . . discern how the framers' values, defined in the context of the world they knew, apply to the world we know."[72]   Judge Bork's words drew a sharp rebuke from

65.   Edwards v. National Audubon Society, 556 F.2d 113 (2d Cir. 1977), cert. denied 434 U.S. 1002 (1977).

66.   See Eaton, supra note 22, at 1373. Although the *substantive* standard of New York Times Co. v. Sullivan is a strict one, the Supreme Court has explicitly rejected the suggestion that first amendment concerns should also create a stricter *jurisdictional* standard.   In Calder v. Jones, 465 U.S. 783, 790–91 (1984), the Court unanimously held that, when the contacts of a media defendant with a forum state would suffice to support jurisdiction under that state's long-arm statute if the case did not include free speech and press issues, such jurisdiction should be upheld regardless of the first amendment issues that may be implicated in the case.   According to the Court, introducing such concerns into the jurisdictional analysis would "needlessly complicate an already imprecise inquiry," and any potential chill on protected first amendment activity is "already taken into account in the constitutional limitations on the substantive law governing [libel and defamation] suits."   Id. at 790.

67.   418 U.S. 323 (1974).

68.   Id. at 339–40 (footnote omitted).

69.   750 F.2d 970 (D.C. Cir. 1984), cert. denied 471 U.S. 1127 (1985).

70.   See id. at 979–84.

71.   See id. at 993–94.

72.   Id. at 995.

then-Judge (now Justice) Scalia, who disparaged the notion that the press, its security "fulsomely assured" by *New York Times*, should need any "evolving" protections.[73] In his attack on the very idea of an "evolving" jurisprudence of constitutional protection, Judge Scalia displayed a fairly narrow conception of the judicial role: "It seems to me that the identification of 'modern problems' to be remedied is quintessentially legislative rather than judicial business—largely because it is such a subjective judgment; and that the remedies are to be sought through democratic change rather than through judicial pronouncement that the Constitution now prohibits what it did not prohibit before." [74]

Judge Scalia's approach seems at odds with the direction the Supreme Court took in *Bose Corp. v. Consumers Union of the United States, Inc.*[75] There the Court held that appellate court's review of a trial court's findings on actual malice were not limited to the "clearly erroneous" standard of Federal Rule of Civil Procedure 52(a). Rather, Justice Stevens wrote, "Judges, as expositors of the Constitution, must independently decide whether the evidence in the record is sufficient to cross the constitutional threshold that bars entry of any judgment that is not supported by clear and convincing proof of 'actual malice.' " [76] *Bose* illustrates that, for all the twists libel doctrine has taken over the years, a majority of the Court still takes *New York Times* seriously—not merely trusting, as it usually does, the lower courts to apply the Court's decisions faithfully, but requiring that libel decisions receive special appellate scrutiny. *Bose* recognizes that the law has indeed evolved and undoubtedly will continue to do so; but the principle underlying *New York Times*—freedom to criticize on issues of public importance—remains paramount. Perhaps it was even in recognition of how dramatically the law of libel has changed over the past two decades that the Court in *Bose* underscored its own duty and pledged its best efforts to maintain continued vigilance for first amendment values.

---

73. Id. at 1036 (Scalia, J., dissenting).

74. Id. at 1038. Judge Bork responded to this charge by stating that "[a] judge who refuses to see new threats to an established constitutional value, and hence provides a crabbed interpretation that robs a provision of its full, fair and reasonable meaning, fails in his judicial duty. That duty, I repeat, is to ensure that the powers and freedoms the framers specified are made effective in today's circumstances. The evolution of doctrine to accomplish that end contravenes no postulate of judicial restraint." Id. at 996.

75. 466 U.S. 485 (1984).

76. Id. at 511. The Court made special note of the responsibility of the Supreme Court to protect first amendment values by undertaking independent review of the evidence in libel cases: "The requirement of independent appellate review reiterated in New York Times Co. v. Sullivan is a rule of federal constitutional law. It emerged from the exigency of deciding concrete cases; it is law in its purest form under our common law heritage. It reflects a deeply held conviction that judges—and particularly Members of this Court—must exercise such review in order to preserve the precious liberties established and ordained by the Constitution." Id. at 510–11. Chief Justice Burger concurred in the judgment. Justice Rehnquist, joined substantially by Justice White and entirely by Justice O'Connor, dissented, professing himself "at a loss to see how appellate courts can even begin to make" determinations which involve the credibility of witnesses. Id. at 519. For an interesting discussion of the larger implications of the Bose decision for judicial review of constitutional decisions, see Monaghan, "Constitutional Fact Review," 85 Colum.L.Rev. 229 (1985).

§ 12–13. Defamation of Persons Other Than Public Officials

New York Times Co. v. Sullivan [1] left open the proper standard of liability in cases brought by plaintiffs who were not government officials. But the decision's theory of the first amendment—the profound national commitment to "uninhibited, robust, and wide-open" debate on public issues—impelled the Court to extend the constitutional mantle beyond the cluster of cases dealing with libels of public officials, and in the succeeding years the Court supervised an orderly extension of *New York Times Co. v. Sullivan* until the case reached all discussion and communication involving public figures or matters of public or general concern. [2]

But the Court has since retrenched. *Gertz v. Robert Welch, Inc.,* [3] in the first major limitation of *New York Times Co. v. Sullivan*, held that private individuals—as opposed to public figures—need not prove "actual malice" in order to recover damages. *Gertz* appeared to signal that the Court had established the crucial distinction in libel law; it then undertook, in a series of cases, [4] to define the differences between public figures and private figures. But eleven years after *Gertz*, the Court appeared to change direction radically. In *Dun & Bradstreet, Inc. v. Greenmoss Builders, Inc.,* [5] the Court took the bifurcated analysis of public figure-private figure and bifurcated it once more, stating that the first amendment would protect only "speech on matters of public concern." Accordingly, when the plaintiff is not a public figure and the contested statement is not about a matter of public concern, the "actual malice" standard does not apply. [6] The road from *New York Times* to *Gertz* to *Dun & Bradstreet* provides ample evidence of the Court's changing concerns but offers scarce hints of its future course.

§ 12–13

1. 376 U.S. 254 (1964).

2. See Curtis Publishing Co. v. Butts, 388 U.S. 130 (1967) (football coach charged by national magazine with fixing football game held to be "public figure", making New York Times standard applicable); Associated Press v. Walker, 388 U.S. 130 (1967), reported sub nom. Curtis Publishing Co. v. Butts (General Walker's voluntary involvement in events involving desegregation of University of Mississippi held to have made him a "public figure", making New York Times standard applicable to his defamation action against the news service); Rosenbloom v. Metromedia, Inc., 403 U.S. 29 (1971) (defamation action against radio station for its reports concerning the arrest and legal battle of a distributor of nudist magazines subject to New York Times standard).

3. 418 U.S. 323 (1974). Justice Powell wrote the principal opinion, joined by Justices Stewart, Marshall, and Rehnquist. Although Justice Blackmun sensed "some illogic", he concurred in order to create a majority for a definitive ruling. Id. at 353–54. Chief Justice Burger and Justices Douglas, Brennan, and White each wrote separate opinions. Justice Douglas adhered to his view that the Constitution prohibited the imposition of damages upon persons for discussion of public affairs, id. at 355; Justice Brennan reiterated the position of his plurality opinion in Rosenbloom. Id. at 361. The Chief Justice briefly and Justice White in a lengthy opinion objected to the majority's new rules for defamation actions brought by private persons. Id. at 354, 369.

4. See, e.g., Wolston v. Reader's Digest Ass'n, Inc., 443 U.S. 157 (1979) (holding that libel plaintiff who had failed to appear before a grand jury and subjected himself to a criminal contempt citation was not a "public figure"); Time, Inc. v. Firestone, 424 U.S. 448 (1976) (holding that libel plaintiff who had been a party in a highly publicized divorce case was not a "public figure").

5. 472 U.S. 749, 758–759 (1985).

6. The strong implication is, accordingly, that in order for the "actual malice" standard to apply, the Court must now find both that the plaintiff is a public figure and that the contested statement is a matter of public concern.

Gertz arose when American Opinion, an organ of the John Birch Society, published an account of the murder trial of a Chicago policeman who had shot a youth. The article alleged the existence of a nationwide communist conspiracy to discredit local police, and accused Elmer Gertz, a prominent liberal attorney, of being the central figure in a conspiracy which "framed" the policeman. It also charged Gertz with past membership in "Communist-front" organizations and implied he had a criminal record. But Gertz's involvement in the murder case was limited; he had been retained by the family of the victim to bring a civil action against the policeman. Most of the statements about Gertz were not true. He filed an action for defamation, but lost in the lower courts because he had been unable to prove "actual malice" as defined by *New York Times*. On appeal, the Supreme Court reversed. The Court's holding may be briefly summarized.

First, public persons, including "public officials" and "public figures" [7] may recover for defamation only upon a clear and convincing showing of the defendant's knowledge or reckless disregard of the falsity of the defamatory publication.[8]

Second, states may define their own standards of liability in defamation actions brought by private persons against the news media "so long as they do not impose liability without fault." [9] However, any standard more lenient than that of *New York Times Co. v. Sullivan* may remain impermissible where a substantial danger to reputation is not apparent on the face of the statement.[10] This will typically be the

---

7. What is meant by these terms of art will be indicated shortly.

8. To this degree, Gertz works no change in the prior law, although the definition of public figures is, as we shall see, considerably narrowed.

9. Gertz, 418 U.S. at 347. The majority opinion may imply by its repeated references to the "media" that the application of the Gertz rules is not required in defamation actions against non-media defendants. But that conclusion would appear to be wrong to the extent that it rests on a generalization that private communications as a class merit less first amendment protection than communications made in a public manner. See Hill, "Defamation and Privacy Under the First Amendment," 76 Colum.L.Rev. 1205, 1210–11, 1221–27 (1976). See also § 12–19, infra, note 5.

10. Id. at 348. The fairness of requiring at least due care by a publisher or broadcaster in a potentially defamatory situation is underscored by the warning that any publisher should derive from the face of the story being published: if the story appears on its face to be injurious to reputation, the publisher or broadcaster is on notice to check further into its truth. The element of fairness is equally strong if the publisher has extrinsic knowledge that the statement is defamatory, and almost as strong if, by the exercise of due care, the

publisher would have learned of the defamatory potential. The Gertz decision therefore appears to require a private plaintiff to prove that the publisher knew, or should have known, that the statement was defamatory as a precondition to the application of a negligence standard of liability. If the statement is defamatory on its face, its introduction into evidence would satisfy the requirement. But what is the applicable standard if defamatory potential was hidden from the publisher? Justice White assumed that the majority's qualification indicated that the strict New York Times standard applied in this context, id. at 389 n. 27 (White, J., dissenting), and the language of the Court (stressing elements of fairness) supports the conclusion that a stricter standard is contemplated. But a plausible counter-argument can be made. It is only where the publisher is on notice of a statement's defamatory potential that self-censorship is triggered. Where there is no warning, the material will be published and first amendment values will have been fully served. At this point there is no reason why the aggrieved individual should not have the benefit of the common law presumptions of malice, falsity and damages. In reply, however, it might well be urged that a publisher subject to strict liability would too often choose simply to avoid comment on specific individuals. The argument seems a close one.

case in actions brought on a theory of depiction in a "false light", where *Time Inc. v. Hill*, decided seven years before [11] *Gertz* but possibly surviving the latter, ruled the *New York Times* standard mandatory.

Third, no punitive or presumed damages may be awarded in a defamation action brought against a media defendant without showing knowledge or reckless disregard of the falsity of the defamatory publication.[12]

Gertz represents a shift in the Court's attention from the location of defamatory falsehoods within or without a sphere of constitutional protection to the determination of the precise degree of protection to be afforded in various contexts. This shift seems attributable to two influences, the first of which seems to have remained important to the Justices, while their concern for the second appears to have waned considerably. The first is the *Gertz* majority's conclusion that for many situations the *New York Times* standard was too strong, its practical effect being to defeat recovery in nearly all litigated cases in which the standard had been applied.[13] The second is the *Gertz* majority's repudiation of the plurality opinion in *Rosenbloom v. Metromedia, Inc.* and the substantial acceptance of Justice Marshall's dissent in that case.[14] In *Rosenbloom*, the Court had extended *New York Times v. Sullivan* to an action brought by a private person who had been arrested for selling allegedly obscene material. The plurality opinion reasoned that the constitutional privilege should reach "all discussion and communication involving matters of public or general concern. . . ."[15] Justice Marshall objected that "all human events" were arguably of public interest, and that courts were not competent to judge "what information is relevant to self-government."[16] The rules announced in *Gertz* incorporated these two influences. A less exacting "fault" standard was introduced for suits by private persons, and the line between those cases in which the stricter *New York Times* standard is applicable, and those cases in which "fault" is a sufficient basis for liability, was drawn without apparent reference to any subjective "public interest" test.

On the other hand, the common law's strict liability for defamation was entirely displaced, at least with respect to media defendants, by the application of *Gertz's* "fault" requirement without regard to whether

---

11. 385 U.S. 374 (1967) (holding that damages for false-light portrayal of one's personal life, in violation of state right-to-privacy statute, can be recovered only on showing of knowing or reckless falsehood). Note that, despite its right-to-privacy label, this case did not involve breach of confidentiality or invasion of an intimate sphere of personal information. The author of Gertz has called into question the continuing validity of Time, Inc. v. Hill: "The Court's abandonment of the 'matter of general or public interest' standard as the determinative factor for deciding whether to apply the New York Times malice standard to defamation litigation brought by private individuals, Gertz v. Robert Welch, Inc., 418 U.S. 323, 346 (1974) . . . calls into question the conceptual basis of Time, Inc. v. Hill." Cox Broadcasting Corp. v. Cohn, 420 U.S. 469, 498 n. 2 (1975) (Powell, J., concurring).

12. Gertz, 418 U.S. at 349–50.

13. Id. at 342–43, 346. See also Eaton, "The American Law of Defamation Through Gertz v. Robert Welch, Inc. and Beyond: An Analytical Primer," 61 Va.L. Rev. 1349, 1375 (1975).

14. See Gertz, 418 U.S. at 346, rejecting 403 U.S. 29 (1971), and expressly approving 403 U.S. at 79.

15. 403 U.S. at 43–44.

16. Id. at 79 (dissenting opinion).

the statement concerned a matter of "public interest." A residuum of cases remained in which traditional common law rules might apply (private defamation actions against non-media defendants), but *Gertz* narrowed the range of situations in which constitutional constraints left the common law tort wholly untouched.

The Court found just such a case in *Dun & Bradstreet, Inc. v. Greenmoss Builders, Inc.*[17] Dun & Bradstreet, a credit reporting agency, released a confidential report to five of its subscribers indicating that Greenmoss had filed a voluntary petition for bankruptcy. The report was mistaken. When notified of its error, Dun & Bradstreet told its subscribers that Greenmoss "continued business as usual."[18] Greenmoss nevertheless sued for defamation and was awarded $50,000 in compensatory and presumed damages and $300,000 in punitive damages. The trial court reversed the damage judgments because its jury charge had not required the jury to find "actual malice" on the part of the defendants, but the Vermont Supreme Court reversed that ruling, holding that credit reporting firms "are not the type of media worthy of First Amendment protection as contemplated by *New York Times*."[19]

The Supreme Court affirmed, but on different grounds from the Vermont Supreme Court. Justice Powell's plurality opinion, which was joined by Justices Rehnquist and O'Connor, agreed with the Vermont court that the *New York Times* protections did not apply to the speech in question; but the reason for its ruling was the nature of the *speech*, not the status of the *defendant*.[20] The plurality's opinion traced the Court's path through the libel cases and found that the protections of *Gertz* and *New York Times* extended only to "defamatory statements involv[ing] a 'matter of public or general interest.' "[21] To reach that conclusion, the Court applied a balancing test similar to the one it had used in *Gertz*—balancing "the State's interest in compensating private individuals for injury to their reputation against the First Amendment interest in protecting this type of expression."[22] Justice Powell found that the state interest was "identical to the one weighed in *Gertz*" while the "First Amendment interest . . .—[that is, in] speech on matters of

---

17. 472 U.S. 749 (1985).

18. Id. at 752.

19. Id. (citation omitted).

20. The Court has not finally settled whether the protections belonging to "media" defendants are identical to those of "non-media" defendants. As Justice Brennan's dissenting opinion in Dun & Bradstreet points out, however, there is no good reason to draw such a distinction. First, the Court has recognized in other contexts that the inherent worth of speech does not depend on the identity of its source. See, e.g., First National Bank of Boston v. Bellotti, 435 U.S. 765, 777 (1978). Second, it would be almost impossible to generate a useful rule, in a changing technological age, for distinguishing between media and non-media defendants. See Dun & Brad-

street, 472 U.S. at 759–761 & n. 6, n. 7 (Brennan, J., dissenting).

21. 472 U.S. at 755, quoting Rosenbloom v. Metromedia, Inc., 403 U.S. 29, 44 (1971) (plurality opinion of Brennan, J.). Indeed the Court in Dun & Bradstreet seemed clearly to resurrect Rosenbloom sub silentio, notwithstanding the Court's emphatic rejection of the Rosenbloom plurality opinion in Gertz. See 418 U.S. at 346. As Justice Brennan noted in dissent in Dun & Bradstreet, "[d]istrust of placing in the courts the power to decide what speech was of public concern was precisely the rationale Gertz offered for rejecting the Rosenbloom plurality approach." 472 U.S. at 785 n. 11.

22. 472 U.S. at 749.

purely private concern—. . . . is less important than the one weighed in *Gertz*." [23] Accordingly, "In light of the reduced constitutional value of speech involving no matters of public concern, we hold that the state interest adequately supports awards of presumed and punitive damages—even absent a showing of 'actual malice.' " [24] The Court then had little trouble holding that the speech at issue in this case—"this type of credit reporting"—was not of "public concern," because it was, "like advertising, . . . hardy and unlikely to be deterred by incidental state regulation." [25]

The expressed rationale in *Gertz* for creating two degrees of first amendment protection for defamatory speech was that private persons are both more vulnerable to injury and more deserving of recovery— vulnerable because the private individual more often lacks access to the media to rebut charges against him; [26] more deserving because the private individual has not voluntarily become involved in a public controversy in order to influence its outcome. [27] The approach of the *Gertz* majority and *Dun & Bradstreet* plurality was to translate these

---

23. Id. at 758.

24. Id. at 761 (footnote omitted).

25. Id. at 762. Chief Justice Burger concurred in the judgment, on the narrow ground that the Gertz protections did not apply in this case. See id. at 764. Professor Shiffrin has offered a powerful critique of the notion that the marketplace will correct all or most false statements in advertising. See Shiffrin, "The First Amendment and Economic Regulation: Away From a General Theory of the First Amendment," 78 Nw.U.L.Rev. 1212, 1261–65 (1983).

Justice White, in a thoughtful opinion also concurring in the judgment, expressed more fundamental discomfort with the entire state of libel law, reaffirming his disagreement with Gertz and announcing, for the first time, his belief that the "Court struck an improvident balance in the *New York Times* case between the public's interest in being fully informed about public officials and public affairs and the competing interest of those who have been defamed in vindicating their reputation." Id. at 767. Justice White had come to believe that the New York Times decision, which he joined, countenanced "two evils: the stream of information about public officials and public affairs is polluted and often remains polluted by false information; and second, the reputation and professional life of the defeated plaintiff may be destroyed by falsehoods that might have been avoided with a reasonable effort to investigate the facts." Id. at 769. Gertz, he stated, was "subject to similar observations, [as it] deprived the plaintiff of his common-law remedies [and made] recovery more difficult in order to provide a margin for error." Id.

Instead of maintaining the New York Times enhanced standards for liability, Justice White urged that the Court consider limitations on damages to preserve first amendment values. He suggested that limiting or even forbidding presumed and punitive damages might better accomplish the goals sought by New York Times. See id. 772–773.

Justice Brennan dissented, in an opinion joined by Justices Marshall, Blackmun and Stevens. He viewed New York Times and its progeny as "proceed[ing] from the general premise that all libel law implicates First Amendment values to the extent that it deters true speech that would otherwise be protected by the First Amendment." Id. at 778. Accordingly, "[s]peech about commercial or economic matters, even if not implicating 'the central meaning of the First Amendment,' [New York Times,] 376 U.S. at 273, is an important part of our public discourse," 472 U.S. at 787, and should receive the New York Times and Gertz protections. In any event, according to Justice Brennan, "the credit reporting of Dun & Bradstreet falls within any reasonable definition of 'public concern,' " because "an announcement of the bankruptcy of a local company is information of potentially great concern to residents of the community where the company is located." Id. at 789. For these reasons, "Greenmoss Builders should be permitted to recover for any actual damage it can show resulted from Dun & Bradstreet's negligently false credit report, but should be required to show actual malice to recover presumed or punitive damages." Id. at 796.

26. Gertz, 418 U.S. at 344.

27. Id. at 344–45.

admittedly broad normative considerations into doctrinal tests. But why should the plaintiff's vulnerability or deservingness make a difference if the freedoms of speech and press occupy a "preferred position" in the constitutional scheme? One response is to interpret *Gertz* in light of the two ways in which government may abridge speech.[28] Where government aims at the content of speech, the first amendment demands an extraordinary justification. *New York Times Co. v. Sullivan* was clearly a case of this type,[29] and the rule forged in that decision accordingly reflected the primacy of first amendment values. But where government aims at the non-communicative impact of expressive behavior, government may act so long as the flow of information and ideas is not unduly constricted.[30] And, as *Dun & Bradstreet* made clear, the Court is especially reluctant to limit the common law of defamation when the subject matter of the speech is "purely private." Where the law is closely confined to the narrow purpose of compensating private individuals for injury to their reputational interests, the law is aimed at something other than content, at least in the sense that the objective is unrelated to whether government approves or disapproves the content of the message.[31] Defamation law in this sense is ideologically neutral, and therefore is appropriately remitted to a "balancing" test.[32] Because the reputational interest of the individual is significant, and may indeed be of federal constitutional dimension,[33] the crucial question is the degree to which the law of defamation actually constrains the communication of truthful information.

In other contexts, the present majority of the Court has indicated skepticism toward the substance and reality of a "chilling" effect on the exercise of first amendment rights flowing from the mere threat of sanctions, and it must be assumed that a similar attitude in part underlies the *Gertz* and *Dun & Bradstreet* decisions.[34] And for many the real problem is the power and unaccountability of the institutional press, not its weakness or timidity.[35] But entirely different premises also serve to justify the *Gertz* formulation. The Court has been largely guessing that rules making it more difficult for defamed individuals to

---

28. See § 12-2, supra.

29. 376 U.S. 254 (1964). See § 12-3, supra.

30. See § 12-23, infra.

31. See Young v. American Mini Theatres, 427 U.S. 50, 67-68 (1976) (Stevens, J., plurality opinion) (comparing ordinance that treated sexually explicit speech unlike other types of speech with Court's defamation rules—neither depends for its application on government's taking sides on some disputed matter).

32. See § 12-23, infra.

33. See §§ 12-14, 15-16, infra.

34. See, e.g., Branzburg v. Hayes, 408 U.S. 665 (1972); Laird v. Tatum, 408 U.S. 1 (1972). Indeed, the Court specifically rejected, in Herbert v. Lando, 441 U.S. 153, 176 (1979), the "suggest[ion] that the press needs constitutional protection from . . .

the costs and other burdens of this kind of litigation." The Court there refused to recognize any chilling effect, stating simply that "mushrooming litigation costs, much of it due to pretrial discovery, are not peculiar to the libel and slander area." Id. For discussion of Herbert and Anderson v. Liberty Lobby, Inc., 106 S.Ct. 2505 (1986), see § 12-12, supra. But compare Miami Herald Publishing Co. v. Tornillo, 418 U.S. 241 (1974), discussed in § 12-25, infra.

35. See, e.g., Gertz v. Robert Welch, Inc., 418 U.S. 323, 390-91, 402-03 (1974) (White, J., dissenting); Dun & Bradstreet, Inc. v. Greenmoss Builders, Inc., 472 U.S. 749, 767-77 (1985) (White, J., concurring in the judgment); Robertson, "Defamation and the First Amendment: In Praise of Gertz v. Robert Welch, Inc.," 54 Tex.L.Rev. 199, 208 (1976).

recover damages create "breathing space" for the exercise of first amendment rights.[36] Yet a publisher's decision to print or broadcast a libelous story is only partly influenced by the probability of winning or losing a lawsuit. While the publication decision involves a complex calculus, the salient cost factors are likely to be the probability that the publisher will be sued, and the cost of defending if suit is brought. Rules affecting the publisher's ultimate liability are thus likely to be marginal considerations in the decision to publish. One commentator's analysis concludes that the *New York Times* privilege has failed to prevent self-censorship because it does little to reduce the costs of defending against libel claims.[37] If that is correct, a less stringent "fault" standard will not significantly increase the amount of self-censorship. Short of an absolute privilege to defame which would accord no weight to society's pervasive interest in preserving reputation, the most efficacious strategy to reduce self-censorship may be liberal use of summary judgment procedures in defamation actions, so as to avoid long and costly litigation.[38] There is no reason summary judgment should be less available under *Gertz* than under *New York Times*, at least after the substance of the *Gertz* "fault" standard has become apparent. Thus *Gertz* seems justifiable in broad outline as an accommodation making it easier for aggrieved individuals to obtain redress of reputational injuries without significantly affecting the level of self-censorship by the press.

Even before *Dun & Bradstreet* complicated the Court's task further, the Court had begun the attempt of defining the difference between private and public persons—between those to whom *Gertz* applies and

36. See Kalven, "The Reasonable Man and the First Amendment: Hill, Butts, and Walker," 1967 Sup.Ct.Rev. 267, 299.

37. Anderson, "Libel and Press Self-Censorship," 53 Tex.L.Rev. 422, 424–25, 435–36 (1975). Former Mobil Oil Chairman William Tavoulareas testified that he had spent $1.8 million in legal fees, before appeals, in his libel suit against the Washington Post. See Lewis, "New York Times v. Sullivan Reconsidered: Time to Return to 'The Central Meaning of the First Amendment,'" 83 Colum.L.Rev. 603, 613 (1983). The Tavoulareas case also illustrates just how high the costs of libel litigation—monetary and otherwise—can be for media defendants. In initially setting aside the district judge's grant of judgment to the defendant, the D.C. Circuit panel held in Tavoulareas v. Piro, 759 F.2d 90, 121 (D.C. Cir. 1985), that a newspaper's policy of "hard hitting investigative journalism [or] sophisticated muckracking . . . is relevant to the inquiry of whether a newspaper's employees acted in reckless disregard of whether a statement is false or not." One can scarcely imagine a formulation more at odds with the first amendment than an equation of zeal in investigative reporting with evidence of recklessness. The entire field of defama-

tion law came under first amendment scrutiny in New York Times precisely because of the Court's interest in protecting "[c]riticism of official conduct." New York Times, 376 U.S. at 273. That such criticism might make the defendant *more* likely to be liable for damages seems to contravene the spirit, if not also the letter, of New York Times and its progeny. Fortunately, the D.C. Circuit corrected both the holding and the approach of the Tavoulareas panel in its 7–1 *en banc* reversal of the panel's decision. See Tavoulareas v. Piro, Nos. 83–1604, 83–1605, slip op. (D.C. Cir. Mar. 13, 1987) (reinstating district court's grant of judgment to defendant).

38. Anderson, supra note 37 at 437–38. The principal obstacle to liberal use of summary judgment in this context has been the judicial assumption that the publisher's state of mind is peculiarly within the competence of juries to assess. Dictum in Hutchinson v. Proxmire, 443 U.S. 111, 120 & n. 9 (1979), appeared to support this view, but the Court has since returned to the more sensible position that summary judgment is not discouraged in libel cases. See Anderson v. Liberty Lobby, Inc., 106 S.Ct. 2505 (1986). For further discussion of this subject, see § 12–12, supra.

those who remain under the regime of *New York Times*. In drawing that line, two key points of reference are (1) that discussion concerning "public" persons is close to the "core" of seditious libel and political speech, and (2) that distinctions between the public and private sectors are increasingly blurred. Many individuals by virtue of their positions or their power are intimately involved in the resolution of public questions or the shaping of events, and are private analogs of public officials.[39] The *Gertz* Court was explicit in saying that the only legitimate state interest underlying the law of libel is the compensation of individuals for harm to their reputational interest,[40] and one teaching of *New York Times Co. v. Sullivan* is that reputational interests are attenuated for persons who become affiliated with government exactly because government itself, unlike individuals, *has* no legitimate reputational interest: government cannot be defamed. With these points of reference in view, the Court in *Gertz* recognized three categories of public persons. The first category includes persons who have "general fame and notoriety in the community," and are public figures for all purposes.[41] Presumably these are the individuals who can most easily induce the media to publish their replies to defamatory attacks. They are people whose fame precedes them, those of whom the jury has probably heard prior to the litigation.[42] But notoriety created by the publication of the defamatory communication itself does not suffice to make the plaintiff "public"; sustained media attention over a long period is ordinarily required to create "general fame or notoriety in the community." [43]

The second category consists of involuntary public figures.[44] The majority in *Gertz* rightly sensed that instances of such persons should be rare.[45] The category nonetheless appears to include persons who are involved in or directly affected by the actions of public officials. Thus the magazine distributor in the *Rosenbloom* case [46] arrested by the police for distributing obscene literature would be an involuntary public figure with respect to reports or comments about the arrest.[47]

Most public figures are likely to belong to the Court's third category,[48] consisting of persons who have "voluntarily injected themselves into a public controversy in order to influence the resolution of the issues involved." [49] This formulation requires a trial court to make two determinations: first, that there is a "public controversy"; and second, that the nature and extent of the person's participation in the controversy reached some critical mass at which "voluntary injection" oc-

39. See Curtis Publishing Co. v. Butts, 388 U.S. 130, 163–64 (1967) (Warren, C.J., concurring).

40. 418 U.S. at 341, 349.

41. Id. at 351–52.

42. Id. at 352.

43. See Rosenbloom v. Metromedia, Inc., 403 U.S. 29, 78, 86 (1971) (Marshall, J., dissenting) (persons "first brought to public attention by the defamation that is the subject of the lawsuit" remain private).

44. Gertz, 418 U.S. at 345.

45. Id.

46. Rosenbloom v. Metromedia, Inc., 403 U.S. 29 (1971).

47. See Time, Inc. v. Firestone, 424 U.S. 448, 476 (1976) (Brennan, J., dissenting); Rosenbloom, 403 U.S. at 62 (White, J., concurring). Cf. Anderson, supra note 37, at 450–51.

48. Gertz, 418 U.S. at 345.

49. Id.

curred. The apparent difficulty of this test is that it is vulnerable to the very objection that persuaded the Court to repudiate the test of the *Rosenbloom* plurality! Now judges are asked to determine whether a controversy is "public," [50] a determination indistinguishable to the naked eye from whether the subject matter is of public or general concern. The difficulty became apparent in *Time, Inc. v. Firestone*,[51] a libel action by Mary Alice Firestone against Time magazine for erroneously reporting that her husband had been granted a divorce on grounds of her extreme cruelty and adultery, when the technical grounds were in fact extreme cruelty and lack of "domestication." The evidence supporting the finding of non-domestication clearly indicated that what the judge had in mind was Mrs. Firestone's extramarital escapades. But Time was technically wrong in its report of the grounds for the divorce, and a jury awarded Mrs. Firestone $100,000 for her mental anguish. The Supreme Court held that Mrs. Firestone was not a public figure, and remanded the case for determination of Time's "fault" under the *Gertz* standard. Justice Rehnquist, writing for the Court, concluded without explanation that a divorce proceeding of a prominent socialite was not a matter of "public controversy." [52] His opinion substantially discounted the strong public interest in the ability of the press to report what transpires in the courts.[53] The divorce courts are different, said the Justice, because people are compelled to use the courts in order to obtain divorces.[54] A more plausible explanation is that the *Firestone* majority decided that gossip about the rich and famous is not a matter of legitimate public interest.[55]

A fairly high threshold of public activity is evidently necessary for a finding that a person has voluntarily plunged into a public controversy. Elmer Gertz was not deemed a public figure although he had voluntarily accepted employment as counsel in a lawsuit which would

50. If instead judges are asked simply to determine whether something has become a matter of controversy, perhaps the difficulty can be mitigated.

51. 424 U.S. 448 (1976).

52. Id. at 454.

53. See id. at 476–481 (Brennan, J., dissenting), comparing Cox Broadcasting Corp. v. Cohn, 420 U.S. 469 (1975) (press cannot be held liable for publishing truthful identity of rape victim where such identity was a matter of open court record).

54. Time, Inc. v. Firestone, 424 U.S. at 454.

55. See Christie, "Injury to Reputation and the Constitution: Confusion Amid Conflicting Approaches," 75 Mich.L.Rev. 43, 55 (1976).

The Court's latest struggle with the public figure-private figure distinction brought predictably inconclusive results. Having held earlier the same Term that "regular and continuing access to the media . . . is one of the accouterments of having become a public figure," Hutchinson v. Proxmire,

443 U.S. 111, 136 (1979) (holding that scientist working in a public hospital who received a federal research grant was not a public figure), eight Justices agreed in Wolston v. Reader's Digest Ass'n, Inc., 443 U.S. 157 (1979), that the plaintiff—who had been cited, sixteen years before the contested publication appeared, for refusing to testify before a grand jury investigation of espionage—was not a public figure. "To hold otherwise," the Court stated, "would create an 'open season' for all who sought to defame persons convicted of a crime." Id. at 169. Justice Blackmun, whom Justice Marshall joined, concurred in the result, disagreeing with what he called the implication in Justice Rehnquist's opinion that "a person becomes a limited-issue public figure only if he literally or figuratively 'mounts a rostrum' to advocate a particular view." Id. at 169. Justice Brennan dissented, arguing that the plaintiff "qualified as a public figure for the limited purpose of comment on his connection with, or involvement in, espionage in the 1940's and 1950's." Id. at 172 (citation omitted).

predictably attract wide media attention; he was also a prominent member of the bar and a civic activist.[56] Mrs. Firestone was not a public figure although she was a prominent member of Palm Beach Society whose activities had received constant media attention antedating her divorce trial; the trial itself had been fully reported in Miami area newspapers, and Mrs. Firestone held several press conferences during the proceedings.[57] Exactly how she might have done more to attract public attention is unclear.

As *Dun & Bradstreet* so clearly demonstrated, the *Gertz* Court hardly settled all the issues on the non-public side of libel law. The courts have scarcely begun the task of differentiating between issues of public and private concern [58]—a subject one can fairly assume will give judges at least as much difficulty as the public figure-private figure distinction. In addition, within the broad stricture that liability cannot be imposed without fault even in a non-public plaintiff's defamation suit, *Gertz* left to the states the authority to define the appropriate standard of liability in cases of alleged defamation by the media. Most states are likely to adopt some form of negligence standard, imposing at least a duty to use reasonable care with respect to the truth or falsity of the defamatory publication.[59] But it may take years to give this notion content on a case-by-case basis. And quite apart from such delay, notions of negligence tend to remain inherently vague, with accumulated precedents serving only to mark off the outer limits of liability.[60] The requirement of reasonable care in physical torts is deliberately made flexible so as to permit the judge and jury to consider the facts of each case and to balance the equities accordingly. But where first amendment rights are at stake, such jury flexibility is dangerous inasmuch as jurors are likely to represent majoritarian attitudes toward unpopular speakers and ideas. Given its heavy dependence on how jurors will react, "fault" is not a standard which promises the predictable results or creates the certain expectations without which journalists and others may too often "kill" or emasculate reports they believe to be true because of the threat of a libel action. The conclusion is not that "fault" is an inappropriate standard, but that the first amendment should be understood to require the states to develop bodies of law markedly clearer and more coherent than is customary in the

56. Gertz, 418 U.S. at 351–52.

57. Time, Inc. v. Firestone, 424 U.S. at 453–55; id. at 484–490 (Marshall, J., dissenting).

58. In attempting to define this distinction, the Court will surely encounter the difficulties that Justice Marshall envisioned in his dissenting opinion in Rosenbloom v. Metromedia, Inc., 403 U.S. 29, 79 (1971). Justice Marshall stated that "all human events" were arguably of public interest, and that courts were not competent to judge "what information is relevant to self-government;" the Gertz majority expressly supported Justice Marshall's

view. In any event, the class of "matters of public interest" will surely be broader than those cases which merely involve "public figures." The courts no doubt will—and certainly should—be reluctant to decide that certain issues are not worthy of public interest and debate. To do so would risk impermissible government regulation of speech based on its subject matter. Cf. Chicago Police Dept. v. Mosley, 408 U.S. 92 (1972). See §§ 12–3, 12–8, supra, and § 12–18, infra.

59. See Anderson, supra note 37, at 458.

60. See id. at 460–61.

common law of negligence.[61]   Especially to permit adequate utilization of summary judgment procedures, it may be thought necessary—since the Court itself has offered no guidance—to distill from the decisional law a collection of publishing "rules of the road" which, if followed, will shield prudent publishers from defamation actions.

Absent such rules, grave dangers lurk in the current standard.   In every case under the *Gertz* rule there is one sense in which a publisher is never innocent: he published a statement knowing that it could ruin a reputation.[62]   A publisher always has the fail-safe option of avoiding liability by not printing or broadcasting the defamation.   But it is this self-censorship that the Court since *New York Times* has sought to minimize, in *Gertz* by recognizing a privilege for a publisher who takes "every reasonable precaution to ensure the accuracy of its assertions." [63]   Yet what is "reasonable" may turn in part on the societal value one assigns to a particular statement.   The majority in *Time, Inc. v. Firestone* [64] was sharply split on whether Time had been negligent in erroneously reporting the grounds of Mrs. Firestone's divorce.   The evidence concerning Time's actions showed that the editors had exercised great care in checking the accuracy of their report before it appeared in the magazine.   Time's fault, if it was fault, consisted in failing either to understand the niceties of the law or to penetrate the ambiguities of the decision awarding the divorce.   On the record, Justice Rehnquist, joined by Chief Justice Burger and Justice Blackmun, could find fault; Justices Powell and Stewart, concurring, could not.   The majority therefore remanded the case for an explicit determination by the Florida courts of Time's fault.   The *Firestone* plurality evidently calculated fault in substantial part by reference to an assessment of the social value of the speech, the worth striking the plurality as so slight that almost no amount of verification of the story's accuracy by Time could ever suffice.   But one looks in vain for a principled way of assaying the value of specific communications, and *Gertz* itself was a rejection of a subjective test based on judicial notions of what speech is in the public's legitimate interest.   Fault determined by this method easily transmutes into strict liability.   More fatally, it ceases to yield a standard which accommodates the competing expressive and reputational interests, becoming instead an abdication of the balancing duty to the fact-finder under the guise of determining the publisher's negligence.[65]

Different but no less serious pitfalls await the alternative approach, in which a definition of "fault" is derived by reference to an objective standard: did the defendant use the skill and knowledge normally exercised by the profession of journalism?   Among the factors to be considered would be the medium, the size and location of the

---

61.   Id.; Robertson, "Defamation and the First Amendment: In Praise of Gertz v. Robert Welch, Inc.," 54 Tex.L.Rev. 199, 257 (1976).

62.   Gertz, 418 U.S. at 389–90 (White, J., dissenting).

63.   Id. at 346 (Powell, J., principal opinion).

64.   424 U.S. 448 (1976).

65.   See Anderson, "A Response to Professor Robertson: The Issue is Control of Press Power," 54 Tex.L.Rev. 271, 274–276 (1976).

publisher or broadcaster, its resources and technological capabilities, and deadline pressures. Professional customs would normally be proved by expert testimony. Whatever substantive standards might emerge from a duty to imitate a reasonable and careful publisher in the search for a more objective definition of "fault", the development would constitute a subtle intrusion into the editorial process and a source of pressure upon the news media to conform to professional norms. In *Miami Herald Publishing Co. v. Tornillo*,[66] the Supreme Court struck down a Florida statute granting a right of reply to political candidates attacked by newspapers because editors cannot be compelled, consistent with the first amendment, to "publish that which 'reason' tells them should not be published." But a similar intrusion could result from elevating a norm that a defamed individual should ordinarily be granted space or time to rebut charges, into a rule that a publisher who grants "equal time" in a story is not normally negligent.[67] *Gertz* may thus be profoundly significant if it compels the courts, in the process of giving meaning to "fault," to elaborate a body of law which measures responsibility in journalism. The very existence of that body of law may be a threat of further encroachments on the liberties of the press inasmuch as its rules will be adaptable to other and more comprehensive systems of press regulation. The adoption of a "fault" standard thus seems to create more problems than it solves.

A final criticism of the *Gertz* "reform"—but also a possible avenue for reform of a more genuine sort—turns on the Court's definition of recoverable damages. *Gertz* forbade the award of presumed or punitive damages to plaintiffs who do not prove a defendant's knowledge or reckless disregard of the falsity of the defamatory statement; failing such proof, a plaintiff must show actual damages. The rationale for this damage limitation is that the state's only legitimate interest is in compensating the defamed individual. Where juries have discretion to award damages far in excess of actual damages, the judgment serves as a penalty which exacerbates the problem of self-censorship. The rule that this rationale would appear to predict is required proof of tangible and quantifiable losses—but the Court expressly disclaimed this intention.[68] The "actual damages" which may be recovered include "impairment of reputation," "personal humiliation," and "mental anguish and suffering".[69] The practical operation of the Court's broad examples of actual injury was apparent in Mrs. Firestone's defamation action against Time magazine. Before trial, plaintiff withdrew her claim for

66. 418 U.S. 241, 256 (1974), discussed in § 12–25, infra. Justice Brennan, joined by Justice Rehnquist, observed in a concurring opinion, id. at 258, that the decision left open the possibility that a right-to-reply provision might be constitutional in the specific context of a remedy for defamation.

67. Similarly, if courts evaluate journalistic conduct by reference to "the standards of investigation and reporting ordinarily adhered to by responsible publishers," Curtis Publishing Co. v. Butts,

388 U.S. at 158 (Harlan, J., plurality opinion) they may find themselves enforcing a bias against unorthodox journalism. See Anderson, supra note 37, at 466.

68. Gertz, 418 U.S. at 349–50. One thoughtful district court opinion has held that public figures may not recover punitive damages unless they also prove that they are entitled to compensatory damages. See Schiavone Construction Co. v. Time, Inc., 646 F.Supp. 1511 (D.N.J. 1986).

69. Gertz, 418 U.S. at 349–50.

damages to reputation, presumably to avoid placing her reputation in issue. The only claim of injury which went to the jury was her mental anguish, which the jury valued at $100,000.[70] The point is not that intangible injuries such as humiliation and anguish are insignificant or not deserving of compensation, but rather that the rule requiring proof of damages this broadly defined does not succeed in its aim of limiting jury discretion. Limitations on damages do, however, have the support of at least one Justice,[71] and the full Court has never squarely faced the constitutional dimension of a libel punitive damage award so large as to threaten the existence of a media defendant.[72] A limit on recoverable damages in defamation cases—if not to an actual dollar amount, then certainly to actual, provable injury to reputation—would have the advantage of protecting the press in a clear, comprehensible way, without forcing judges and juries to contend with the metaphysical commands of the "actual malice" standard.[73] So, too, would allowing "victims" of the press to sue for published retractions [74] avoid the perils of massive damage awards for defendants, although such a proposal runs directly into the holding of *Miami Herald Publishing Co. v. Tornillo.*[75] Similarly, allowing declaratory judgment actions for judicial findings of falsity protects against large damage awards,[76] but also stretches the competence of courts and offers scant relief to plaintiffs who suffer actual harm.[77]

70. Id. at 475 n. 3 (Brennan, J., dissenting). That Gertz applied rather than Time, Inc. v. Hill, 385 U.S. 374 (1967), despite the proximity of the Firestone facts to a "false light" case, reflects the fact that the material was thought to be defamatory on its face, thus putting the publisher on notice. See note 10, supra.

71. See Dun & Bradstreet, Inc. v. Greenmoss Builders, Inc., 472 U.S. 749, 772–773 (1985) (White, J., concurring in the judgment). See also Anderson, "Reputation, Compensation and Proof," 25 Wm. & Mary L.Rev. 747, 749 (1984) (contending that "compensating individuals for actual harm to reputation is the only legitimate purpose of libel law today"); Note, "The Libel-Proof Plaintiff Doctrine," 98 Harv.L. Rev. 1909 (1985) (applying a compensatory framework to doctrine governing plaintiffs whose reputations are already severely damaged).

72. Should such a situation arise, the media defendant might consider the protection of the eighth amendment ban on "excessive fines." See Aetna Life Insurance Co. v. Lavoie, 106 S.Ct. 1580, 1589 (1986) (finding that a $3.5 million punitive damage award potentially raised an "important issue[ ]" under the excessive fines clause, but declining to reach that issue).

73. For an intriguing criticism of the "actual malice" standard and a careful de-

fense of a return to strict liability but with punitive damages either disallowed, or allowed only if the defendant refuses to correct or retract a statement clearly and convincingly shown to be false, see Epstein, "Was New York Times v. Sullivan Wrong?," 53 U.Chi.L.Rev. 782 (1986).

74. For such a proposal, see Franklin, "Good Name and Bad Law: A Critique of Libel Law and a Proposal," 18 U.S.F.L.Rev. 1, 40–46 (1983).

75. 418 U.S. 241 (1974) (first amendment precludes state "right of reply" statute requiring newspapers to print, on demand, replies of candidates for public office to attacks in newspapers). See § 12–4, supra, and § 15–5, infra.

76. For an interesting statutory proposal along these lines, see H.R. 2846, 99th Cong., 1st Sess. (1985). For a more conventional approach, see Schaefer, "Defamation and the First Amendment," 52 U.Colo.L. Rev. 1, 17–18 (1980).

77. As Justice Harlan wrote, " 'truth' is not a readily identifiable concept, and putting to the pre-existing prejudices of a jury the determination of what is 'true' may effectively institute a system of censorship." Time, Inc. v. Hill, 385 U.S. 374, 406 (1967) (Harlan, J., concurring in part and dissenting in part).

But because *Gertz* and *Dun & Bradstreet* have left these and many other questions open,[78] it seems apparent that the latest accommodation between the first amendment and the individual's reputational interests lacks coherence—and, in all likelihood, staying power. Whose reputation deserves more protection: Mrs. Firestone, according to the Court, is more deserving than Wally Butts, the football coach. She is a private person;[79] he is a public figure.[80] Or is sports more important than divorce? Elmer Gertz, a prominent lawyer and defender of liberal causes, is more deserving than the unknown letter carriers whose reputations were attacked by the union they refused to join.[81] And in *Paul v. Davis*[82] the Supreme Court held that a person who was stigmatized by mistaken police distribution to local merchants of a flyer bearing his name and picture and purporting to identify known shoplifters had no federal cause of action. The Court went out of its way to suggest not only that state remedies provided due process but also that the reputational interest itself was not constitutionally cognizable.[83] Surely a real concern for the private reputations *Gertz* was designed to protect would have counseled a more sympathetic approach. One can only conclude that the Court's position is unstable and that, absent a more convinced majority, the Court will leave to the lower courts the task of filling out the substance of the *Gertz* and *Dun & Bradstreet* decisions.[84]

78. For a valuable summary of the complexity—and uncertainty—of the various libel rules, see the chart in The Supreme Court, 1984 Term, 99 Harv.L.Rev. 120, 219 (1985).

79. Time, Inc. v. Firestone, 424 U.S. at 455.

80. See Curtis Publishing Co. v. Butts, 388 U.S. 130 (1967).

81. See Old Dominion Branch, 496, Nat. Ass'n of Letter Carriers v. Austin, 418 U.S. 264 (1974).

82. 424 U.S. 693 (1976).

83. Id. at 710–12. Paul is also discussed in Chapter 10, supra, and Chapters 15 and 18, infra.

84. Of particular importance in the lower courts have been the growing number of lawsuits involving apparent fiction in which individuals believe themselves to have been defamed or their privacy to have been invaded by thinly veiled accounts of their lives, depicted so as to convey a harmful and false picture that readers or viewers will be led to think is accurate. For example, a Harvard psychiatrist sued initially for $6 million in damages and settled for $150,000 claiming that she was the basis for the suicidal lesbian character in the novel and film The Bell Jar. N.Y. Times, Feb. 3, 1987, at C17, col. 1. In a similar case, a psychologist who had conducted nude therapy sessions was awarded $75,000 in damages against an author who attended these sessions and based her nov-el Touching on her experiences. Bindrim v. Mitchell, 92 Cal.App.3d 61, 155 Cal.Rptr. 29 (1979), cert. denied 444 U.S. 984 (1979) (Brennan, Stewart, and Marshall, JJ., dissenting). See also Pring v. Penthouse International, Ltd., 695 F.2d 438 (10th Cir. 1982); Geisler v. Petrocelli, 616 F.2d 636 (2d Cir. 1980); Middlebrooks v. Curtis Publishing Co., 413 F.2d 141 (4th Cir. 1969); Fetler v. Houghton Mifflin Co., 364 F.2d 650 (2d Cir. 1966); Wheeler v. Dell Publishing Co., 300 F.2d 372 (7th Cir. 1962). Such losses through settlement or litigation create pressures on authors and publishers to limit creative expression based on actual events. Thus, the standard of liability for defamation in these suits becomes of central importance.

The defamation standard for nonfiction cases as set out in New York Times Co. v. Sullivan, 376 U.S. 254 (1964), and its progeny is inapposite to defamation in fiction. If only a showing that a defendant knowingly or recklessly made a false statement "of and concerning" the plaintiff, id. at 274, creates liability, then a literary defendant has essentially no defense once an individual can find himself or herself in a story—fiction by definition involves deliberately "false" statements. Once the identification threshold is met, see, e.g., Pring, supra, 695 F.2d at 442 ("the charged portions in context could be reasonably understood as describing actual facts about the plaintiff or actual events in which she participated"); Geisler, supra, 616 F.2d at 639

§ 12–14. The Conflict Between Free Speech and Personal Control Over Information

As the *Gertz* [1] standard is fleshed out in subsequent cases, it will be important not to lose sight of the fact that constitutional rights beyond freedom of speech and press are at work in this area. Both privacy and reputation, as § 15–16 shows, involve interests of constitutional dimension; when government acts to limit the untrammeled gathering, recording, or dissemination of data or statements about an individual, of course it inhibits speech—but it also vindicates the individual's ability to control what others are told about his or her life. Such control constitutes a central part of the right to shape the "self" that any individual presents to the world. It is breached most seriously when intimate facts about one's personal identity are made public against one's will and in defiance of one's most conscientious efforts to share those facts only with close relatives or friends. It is breached, perhaps less seriously but with unmistakable force, when one's good name is deliberately and falsely besmirched, doing violence to one's public identity. Not surprisingly, therefore, defamation has long been regarded as a form of "psychic mayhem," not very different in kind, and in some ways more wounding, than physical mutilation. [2]

("reasonable reader must rationally suspect" character is plaintiff); Bindrim, supra, 92 Cal.App.3d at 78, 155 Cal.Rptr. at 39 (reasonable person "would understand that the fictional character . . . [was] the plaintiff acting as described"), damages are awarded on what amounts to a strict liability basis. Yet much fiction might be stifled by that prospect. Hemingway's The Sun Also Rises, based on his European experiences with companions who might have disliked their fictional counterparts, might never have been published without more protection than that of New York Times v. Sullivan. The same is true of the works of F. Scott Fitzgerald, whose characters—for example, the protagonist in The Great Gatsby—were thought by many to be based on real people.

This dilemma has engendered a spate of legal commentary on the subject. Some commentators advocate a new standard of liability to protect fiction, see, e.g., Garbus and Kurnit, "Libel Claims Based on Fiction Should Be Lightly Dismissed," 51 Brooklyn L.Rev. 401, 405 (1985); Franklin & Trager, "Literature and Libel," 4 Comm./Ent.L.J. 205, 223–30 (1982); Note, "Toward a New Standard of Liability for Defamation in Fiction," 92 Yale L.J. 520, 538–42 (1983), including an absolute privilege against defamation suits. Comment, "Defamation in Fiction: The Case for Absolute First Amendment Protection," 29 Am.U.L.Rev. 571, 593 (1980). Others suggest that no new constitutional protection or standard may be warranted, see, e.g., Schauer, "Liars, Novelists, and the Law of Defamation," 51 Brooklyn L.Rev. 233, 247, 258

(1985), or that fiction should receive no first amendment protection at all. Bork, "Neutral Principles and Some First Amendment Problems," 47 Ind.L.J. 1, 28 (1971).

A plausible first amendment standard would hold a fiction writer liable only where she is shown by "clear and convincing" evidence to have created an impression that a supposedly fictional character is really a true portrait. See, e.g., Schauer, supra, at 259; Franklin and Trager, supra, at 222; Note, 92 Yale L.J. at 538. No author of fiction should be held liable for negligently suggesting an actual person in fiction. But, if a defendant attempts to exploit an audience's tendency to believe that what she calls "fiction" is actually truth, it should suffice for a plaintiff defamed as a result to show, with "clear and convincing" evidence, that the defendant's disclaimer that the work is fictional (and that any resemblance to actual persons, living or dead, is purely coincidental) was offset by a calculated effort, through promotional or other material, to convey the impression that the fictional work is actually a truthful account of real persons.

§ 12–14

1. Gertz v. Robert Welch, Inc., 418 U.S. 323 (1974), discussed in § 12–13, supra.

2. See Cahn, "Jurisprudence," 30 N.Y. U.L.Rev. 150, 158 (1955). Even when the abuse of personal identity takes the form of portrayal in a falsely *favorable* rather than unfavorable light, the state has a legitimate interest in providing redress.

So too, interests in property and livelihood continue to rest on a powerful constitutional base, as we point out in § 15–14. When an actor or performer is deprived of the very source of his "ability to earn a living as an entertainer" [3] by another's appropriation of his act, for example, the first amendment does not prevent government from fashioning an appropriate remedy. Just as the right to disseminate truthful information may be restricted to prevent the pirating of copyrighted material and other discrete configurations in which individuals have specific property interests so long as no underlying idea or fact is thereby suppressed, so too the entertainer may be protected against the information predator.[4] Thus, in the Human Cannonball Case, the Court concluded that a television station was not immune from liability arising from the station's filming of a performer's entire (15-second) act over his objection and broadcasting it on a nightly news show, thereby significantly injuring the performer's ability to pursue his vocation by attracting a paying audience to watch his feat.[5]

Insofar as remedies against speech that defames, intrudes, or pirates are used to provide government with censorial devices of a kind we reject when we insist that the state has no protectable interest in its image, such remedies offend the first and fourteenth amendments. No more than that need be recognized in order to agree with *New York Times Co. v. Sullivan.* If the cumulative impact of defamation and false light remedies, remedies to protect privacy, and remedies to protect property interests in information about oneself, while not quite arming government with tools for silencing its critics, nonetheless equipped the state with mechanisms for reducing public discourse to unacceptably bland and uncontroversial levels—if robust public discussion were stilled or greatly chilled by the threat of jury censorship after

See Time, Inc. v. Hill, 385 U.S. 374 (1967), discussed in § 12–13, notes 11, 70, supra.

3. Zacchini v. Scripps-Howard Broadcasting Co., 433 U.S. 562, 576 (1977). Cf. International News Service v. Associated Press, 248 U.S. 215 (1918) (one news service may be enjoined from pirating the news gathered and reported by another news service).

4. Such concerns were clearly paramount in the Court's decision in Harper & Row, Publishers, Inc. v. Nation Enterprises, 471 U.S. 539 (1985). There a six-Justice majority upheld a finding of copyright infringement against the Nation magazine, which had published excerpts from former President Gerald Ford's memoirs before its official publication date. The Nation's "scoop" had caused Time magazine to cancel a deal with Ford to publish a portion of the book. Although Justice O'Connor's majority opinion, as well as Justice Brennan's dissent, which was joined by Justices White and Marshall, expressly avoided the constitutional issues and reached only the question of first publication rights under the copyright doctrine of fair use, the Court plainly seemed of-

fended by what it characterized as the exploitation of a "purloined manuscript." Id. at 542. Like the television station's use of Zacchini's stunt, the Nation's use of word-for-word quotations from former President Ford's memoirs tripped over the line between journalism and theft. As the Court stated, "The Nation had every right to seek to be the first to publish information. But The Nation went beyond simply reporting uncopyrightable information and actively sought to exploit the headline value of its infringement, making a 'news event' out of its unauthorized first publication of a noted figure's copyrighted expression." Id. at 561. See also San Francisco Arts & Athletics, Inc. v. U.S. Olympic Committee, 107 S.Ct. 2971 (1987) (upholding grant of exclusive use of word "Olympic" to U.S. Olympic Committee).

5. See Zacchini, supra note 3. Justice White wrote for the Court, joined by Chief Justice Burger and Justices Stewart, Blackmun and Rehnquist. Justice Powell filed a dissenting opinion, joined by Justices Brennan and Marshall. Justice Stevens also filed a dissenting opinion.

the fact—significant first amendment dangers would become relevant despite the absence of any clear risk that government will insulate itself from the critical views of its enemies. But in such cases, these first amendment dangers are offset to some degree by constitutional concerns of informational autonomy on the part of the individuals injured by such supposedly critical discourse. Within this zone, there can be no escape from continuing efforts to accommodate the value of uninhibited public discussion with the value of preserving control for individuals over what is known and said about them by and to others.[6]

Finally, there comes a point at which only this latter value plays a significant role in a case—a point at which such public discussion as occurs is wholly parasitic upon a clear invasion of an individual's right to retain control over personal information.[7] Nothing in the Court's defamation decisions, and nothing in the three decisions coming closest to addressing the conflict between speech and privacy,[8] remotely sug-

6. The Court accommodated a conflict between these values in Seattle Times Co. v. Rhinehart, 467 U.S. 20, 22 (1984), where the Court considered "whether parties to civil litigation have a First Amendment right to disseminate, in advance of trial, information gained through the pre-trial discovery process." Rhinehart, the leader of a small religious order, filed a defamation action against the Seattle Times. In the course of discovery, the trial court compelled the religious order to produce extensive membership records, but it also prohibited the newspaper from disclosing the contents of the material. The Supreme Court unanimously ruled that the trial court's action was subject to first amendment scrutiny, but nonetheless proper. The test applied was "whether the practice in question furthers an important or substantial government interest unrelated to the suppression of expression and whether the limitation of First Amendment freedoms is no greater than is necessary or essential to the protection of the particular governmental interest involved." Id. at 32 (citations omitted). Pointing out that the newspaper could publish the material if it obtained it outside the discovery process, id. at 34, Justice Powell's opinion also noted that "[t]here is an opportunity . . . for litigants to obtain—incidentally or purposefully—information that not only is irrelevant but if publicly released could be damaging to reputation and privacy. The government clearly has a substantial interest in preventing this sort of abuse of its processes." Id. at 35. Such potential for abuse "is sufficient justification for the authorization of protective orders." Id. at 36 (footnote omitted).

7. See, e.g., McMullan v. Wohlgemuth, 453 Pa. 147, 164, 308 A.2d 888, 897 (1973), appeal dismissed 415 U.S. 970 (1974) (state statutes barring disclosure of welfare recip-

ients' names, addresses, and grant amounts did not violate freedom of the press since state's "interest in protecting the privacy of those it aids through public assistance is paramount and compelling"). But see Cullen v. Grove Press, Inc., 276 F.Supp. 727, 728–29 (S.D.N.Y.1967) (noting that film depicting conditions inside Massachusetts institution for criminally insane concerned a matter "of great interest to the public generally" and refusing to enjoin its exhibition). A Massachusetts court erred by failing to appreciate the film's public value and barred its showing, except to professional groups, despite the absence of complaint by any of the institution's inmates or their families. See Commonwealth v. Wiseman, 356 Mass. 251, 249 N.E.2d 610 (1969), cert. denied 398 U.S. 960 (1970) (over dissent of Harlan, J., joined by Douglas and Brennan, JJ.).

8. Cox Broadcasting Corp. v. Cohn, 420 U.S. 469 (1975) (newspaper has right to publish rape victim's identity once it has become a matter of public record); Time, Inc. v. Hill, 385 U.S. 374 (1967) (magazine cannot be held liable for inaccurate portrayal of individual's private life unless plaintiff establishes knowing or reckless falsehood); Smith v. Daily Mail Publishing Co., 443 U.S. 97 (1979) (holding that state statute imposing criminal penalties for truthful publication of the names of juvenile offenders, without written permission of state court, violates first and fourteenth amendments). Cf. Cantrell v. Forest City Publishing Co., 419 U.S. 245 (1974) (finding verdict against publisher consistent with Time v. Hill). The limited scope of the Court's decisions in Cox and the "false light" privacy cases is stressed by Hill, "Defamation and Privacy Under the First Amendment," 76 Colum.L.Rev. 1205, 1207, 1264–68, 1272–75 (1976).

gests that, when this point is reached, government must exalt an abstract right to know,[9] here reduced to a right to gossip, above the deeper concerns of personhood. On the contrary, once this point is reached, it would deprive individuals of liberty or property without due process of law to provide no legal remedy.[10]

Both accommodating free speech values with those of informational autonomy, and defining the point at which only the latter are at stake, involve difficult judgments of degree. One helpful consideration, at least, is the extent to which the harm done by a statement is truly of a sort that "more speech" could not possibly cure. To be sure, the truth may never quite catch up with a lie, but at least in cases of injured reputation a chance to clear one's name after the fact may substantially reduce, if it cannot wholly erase, the harm. In cases involving clear breaches of privacy, however, the very idea that more talk could do anything but add insult to injury betrays a misunderstanding of the character of the harm. Once the cat is out of the bag, it cannot be put back. To this degree, a return to the concept at the heart of *Chaplinsky* [11]—the elimination of those communications "which by their very utterance inflict injury" [12]—may provide one of the few steady guides in a poorly charted sea.

§ 12–15. The Assimilation of Commercial Speech into the First Amendment

In the preceding sections, we have examined the Supreme Court's attempts to elaborate a doctrine denying protection to communications "which by their very utterance inflict injury." [1] If the state may treat murder as injurious, it follows that it may forbid solicitation to murder, or the placing of an advertisement offering a reward for the first person to kill a designated enemy. More generally, an advertisement proposing an unlawful transaction may be forbidden on the theory that the harm threatened is within government's power to prevent—and that more speech cannot be expected to avert it.[2] In *Pittsburgh Press Co. v.*

9. Cf. § 12–19, infra. See generally Hill, supra note 8; Comment, "An Accommodation of Privacy Interests and First Amendment Rights in Public Disclosure Cases," 124 U.Pa.L.Rev. 1385 (1976); Bloustein, "The First Amendment and Privacy: The Supreme Court Justice and the Philosopher," 28 Rutgers L.Rev. 41 (1974); Nimmer, "The Right To Speak from Times to Time: First Amendment Theory Applied to Libel and Misapplied to Privacy," 55 Calif.L.Rev. 935 (1968); Kalven, "Privacy in Tort Law—Were Warren and Brandeis Wrong?," 31 Law and Contemp.Prob. 326 (1966); Prosser, "Privacy," 48 Calif.L. Rev. 383 (1960); Warren & Brandeis, "The Right to Privacy," 4 Harv.L.Rev. 193 (1890).

10. In Paul v. Davis, 424 U.S. 693 (1976), the Court assumed the existence of a state remedy against official defamation of the plaintiff; thus the holding of that case, denying a federal remedy in the cir-

cumstances, is not authority against the conclusion reached in text. See § 15–16, infra. But see Zacchini, supra note 3, at 433 U.S. at 578 (dictum) (state could confer press immunity from damages for pirating, as a matter of state law).

11. Chaplinsky v. New Hampshire, 315 U.S. 568 (1942).

12. Id. at 571–72.

§ 12–15

1. Chaplinsky v. New Hampshire, 315 U.S. 568, 572 (1942). See §§ 12–10 to 12–14, supra.

2. Cf. Whitney v. California, 274 U.S. 357, 377 (1927) (Brandeis, J., concurring): "If there be time to expose through discussion the falsehood and fallacies, to avert the evil by the process of education, the remedy to be applied is more speech, not enforced silence."

Pittsburgh Commission on Human Relations,[3] for example, the Court upheld governmental power to forbid sex-designated help-wanted advertisements where the refusal to interview or hire on a gender-neutral basis would have constituted unlawful employment discrimination. Unlike an advertisement against the Equal Rights Amendment, for example, a help-wanted ad that appears under a "women need not apply" column threatens, without any further opportunity for dialogue, to cause an injury that government has power to prevent. So long as inflicting the injury is something that government has not attempted to make unlawful, however, such a rationale is unavailable. Thus decisions suggesting that government may forbid the advertising of harmful commodities while leaving people free to purchase them if they wish[4] plainly go beyond the theory suggested here.

Such decisions might be thought defensible because the advertiser seeks to earn money in a marketplace beyond that of ideas. But as the series of decisions that have come to be known as the commercial speech cases illustrate, the fact that an advertiser seeks a profit certainly cannot justify stripping the communication of all first amendment protection. Notwithstanding its suggestion to the contrary in its three-page opinion in *Valentine v. Chrestensen*,[5] the Court by the next year was suggesting that commercial speech must receive some protection where the primary motive of the individual appeared non-commercial despite the solicitation of money.[6] Within less than a decade, Justice Douglas, who had joined the unanimous *Chrestensen* opinion, admitted that the ruling in that case had been "casual, almost offhand," and that it had not "survived reflection."[7] *New York Times Co. v. Sullivan*,[8] after all, upheld the right of a newspaper to publish a paid

3. 413 U.S. 376 (1973). Justice Powell's opinion for the majority was joined by Justices Brennan, White, Marshall and Rehnquist. Chief Justice Burger and Justices Douglas, Stewart and Blackmun each filed dissenting opinions.

In a related setting, the Court had little trouble approving, over first amendment objections, an antitrust injunction against the National Society of Professional Engineers' rule prohibiting its members from submitting competitive bids. In National Soc'y of Prof. Engineers v. United States, 435 U.S. 679 (1978), the Court, by an 8–1 vote, held that the injunction "represents a reasonable method of eliminating the consequences of the illegal conduct." Id. at 698. The Court held that by lifting the organization's ban on competitive bidding, the injunction did "nothing [to] prevent[ ] NSPE and its members from attempting to influence governmental action." Id. at 698 n. 27 (citation omitted).

4. See, e.g., Posadas de Puerto Rico Associates v. Tourism Co. of Puerto Rico, 106 S.Ct. 2968, 2980 & n. 10 (1986) (holding that Puerto Rico may constitutionally ban advertising of casino gambling to residents of Puerto Rico and suggesting, in dictum, that a state could also ban all cigarette and alcohol advertising); Capital Broadcasting Co. v. Mitchell, 333 F.Supp. 582, 584 (D.D.C. 1971), aff'd without opinion sub nom. Capital Broadcasting Co. v. Acting Attorney-General, 405 U.S. 1000 (1972) (holding that "Congress has the power to prohibit the advertising of cigarettes in any medium," based on its power to regulate commerce, without special regard to its authority to regulate electronic media).

5. 316 U.S. 52 (1942) (refusing to enjoin enforcement of ordinance against distribution of commercial advertising matter in the streets, as applied to distribution of leaflet urging visitors to attend exhibition of former Navy submarine for a fee).

6. See, e.g., Murdock v. Pennsylvania, 319 U.S. 105, 112 (1943) (invalidating license tax on sales, as applied to Jehovah's Witnesses selling religious literature, emphasizing that the sales were "merely incidental and collateral" to the principal aim of disseminating religious beliefs).

7. Cammarano v. United States, 358 U.S. 498, 514 (1959) (concurring opinion).

8. 376 U.S. 254, 266 (1964), discussed in § 12–12, supra.

political advertisement. And *Joseph Burstyn, Inc. v. Wilson* [9] held that "operation for profit" does not strip film distributors of first amendment rights.

Attempting to separate dominant from subsidiary motives was bound to fail, in part because the purveyor of ideas and information is likely to want both to convince others and to earn money,[10] in part because selfish and selfless persuaders may both claim a right to first amendment protection,[11] and in part because the advertiser who believes deeply in profits has no less right "to preach [the adman's] Gospel" [12] than the Marxist has to preach his. To be sure, the demise of *Lochner v. New York* [13] had taught that many were the victims rather than the masters of the economic system of contract and property,[14] but any notion that only economic expression may be coerced or coercive would be untenable, and in any event rules wholly suppressing commercial information are hardly calculated to protect the economy's oppressed.[15]

Finally recognizing these realities,[16] in *Virginia State Board of Pharmacy v. Virginia Consumer Council* [17] the Court repudiated the *Chrestensen* dogma and invalidated a state statute declaring it unprofessional conduct for a licensed pharmacist to advertise the prices of prescription drugs. The Court stressed that "[t]hose whom the suppres-

9. 343 U.S. 495, 502 (1952).

10. The petitioner in Chrestensen had printed on the reverse side of the leaflet a political protest against the refusal of New York City to grant him wharfage at a city-owned pier to exhibit his submarine. Alone, this non-commercial message could be distributed without violating the New York City ordinance. Because the Court perceived petitioner's conduct as an obvious attempt to evade the prohibition of the ordinance, 316 U.S., at 55, it did not seriously consider whether petitioner's motives in exhibiting his submarine were mixed, or why a guided tour of a submarine is less informative because a fee is charged.

11. Even if truly selfless action were imaginable, see T. Nagel, The Possibility of Altruism (1970), it is unthinkable that first amendment protection should extend only to saints.

12. Black, "He Cannot Choose But Hear: The Plight of the Captive Audience," 53 Colum.L.Rev. 960, 968 (1953).

13. 198 U.S. 45 (1905) (invalidating maximum hour law for bakers).

14. See § 8–6, supra.

15. Thus one cannot ultimately accept the interesting suggestion in Baker, "Commercial Speech: A Problem in the Theory of Freedom," 62 Ia.L.Rev. 1 (1976), that the distinction between constitutionally-protected personal rights and unprotected property rights, which emerged after the demise of Lochner, points to the exclusion of commercial speech from the scope of first amendment protection. Insofar as the concern of commentators like Baker is that the protection of commercial speech may help to rigidify the prevailing distribution of wealth or to preserve the class structure, their charge could more plausibly be leveled at decisions like Buckley v. Valeo, 424 U.S. 1 (1976), to the degree the Court there invalidated Congress' attempt to distribute political power away from the wealthiest groups by limiting campaign expenditures. See the discussion in § 16–58, infra.

16. The basic tenet of Chrestensen that "purely commercial speech" was wholly unprotected by the first amendment had been repeatedly questioned. See Bigelow v. Virginia, 421 U.S. 809, 822 (1975) (reversing conviction of newspaper editor who had violated a Virginia statute by publishing an advertisement for an abortion referral service in New York, but stressing that the advertised activity related to the public's "constitutional interests"): Pittsburgh Press Co. v. Pittsburgh Human Relations Commission, 413 U.S. 376, 388 (1973) (declining to overrule Chrestensen because, even if the first amendment protected commercial advertisement, the advertisement in question involved illegal gender discrimination); see also id. at 398 (Douglas, J., dissenting); id. at 401 & n. 6 (Stewart, J., dissenting).

17. 425 U.S. 748 (1976).

sion of prescription drug price information hits the hardest are the poor, the sick, and particularly the aged. A disproportionate amount of their income tends to be spent on prescription drugs; yet they are the least able to learn, by shopping from pharmacist to pharmacist, where their scarce dollars are best spent." [18] Even when the victims of an anti-advertising policy are less sympathetic and the policy's objectives more compelling, the Court has insisted that commercial speech merits first amendment protection. In *Linmark Associates, Inc. v. Township of Willingboro*,[19] for example, the Court, in a unanimous opinion by Justice Marshall, struck down a township ordinance prohibiting the posting of real estate "For Sale" and "Sold" signs to stem what the township perceived as the flight of white homeowners from a racially integrated community. Like the ban on prescription drug price information held unconstitutional in *Virginia Board of Pharmacy*, this was a content-based prohibition on speech; [20] like the ban in *Virginia Board of Pharmacy*, this one was not demonstrably necessary to achieve a compelling objective attainable in no other manner; [21] and, like the ban in *Virginia Board*, this one suffered from the independently fatal flaw of seeking its objective through "restricting the free flow of truthful information." [22]

Recognizing that under a paternalistic approach, it might be believed that "the only way [a state] could enable its citizens to find their self-interest was to deny them information that is neither false nor misleading," [23] the Court noted the existence of an alternative approach: "to assume that . . . information is not in itself harmful, that people will perceive their own best interests if only they are well enough informed, and that the best means to that end is to open the channels of communication rather than to close them." [24] But the choice "among these alternative approaches," as the Court said in a powerful opinion by Justice Blackmun, "is not ours to make or the [state's]. It is precisely this kind of choice, between the dangers of suppressing information, and the dangers of its misuse if it is freely available, that the First Amendment makes for us." [25]

The Court's landmark holding in *Virginia Board of Pharmacy* rested on a combination of three notions. First, as we have just seen, the state's rationale was itself forbidden by the first and fourteenth

---

18. Id. at 763. Similarly, in Bates v. Arizona State Bar, 433 U.S. 350 (1977), the Court held that a total ban on advertising of prices by private attorneys, as enforced by an integrated state bar and the state's highest court, violates the first and fourteenth amendments. Left open were the possible validity of a ban on *in-person* solicitation, or on advertising claims relating to the *quality* of legal services. Id. at 2700.

19. 431 U.S. 85 (1977).

20. Id. at 93–94.

21. Id. at 95 ("respondents failed to establish that this ordinance is needed to assure that Willingboro remains an integrated community"); id. at 96 n. 10 ("banning signs may actually fuel public anxiety

over sales activity by increasing homeowners' dependence on rumor and surmise"). Among alternatives to the ordinance, the Court suggested that the township could post "Not for Sale" signs to calm community fears. Presumably, the township could not compel homeowners to show such signs. See Wooley v. Maynard, 430 U.S. 705 (1977), discussed in § 12–4, supra, and § 15–5, infra.

22. Linmark Associates, 431 U.S. at 95.

23. Id. at 97.

24. Virginia Board of Pharmacy, 425 U.S. at 770.

25. Id.

amendments, which preclude regulating an activity on the premise that ignorance is preferable to knowledge. Second, the values of free speech are not limited to political dialogue but extend to any exchange of ideas or information that might make individual choices better informed.[26] And third, just as commercial information "is indispensable to the proper allocation of resources in a free enterprise system, it is also indispensable to the formation of intelligent opinions as to how that system ought to be regulated or altered. Therefore, even if the First Amendment were thought to be primarily an instrument to enlighten public decisionmaking in a democracy, we could not say that the free flow of information does not serve that goal." [27]

Still, maintaining some residual distinctions between commercial and ideological expression on the ground that the former is valued only for the "facts" it conveys while the latter "is integrally related to the exposition of thought—thought that may shape our concepts of the whole universe of man," [28] may be more likely to succeed than did *Chrestensen* itself. However, the Court has repeatedly struggled with defining the differences between commercial and non-commercial speech, notwithstanding its offhand announcement that the difference between the two is based on "commonsense." [29] Certainly, though, principled reasons for some such distinction do exist. Because the advertiser ordinarily "seeks to disseminate information about a specific product or service that he himself provides and presumably knows more about than anyone else," [30] there is little "danger that governmental regulation of false or misleading price or product advertising will chill accurate and nondeceptive commercial expression" [31] and thus "little need to sanction 'some falsehood in order to protect speech that matters,'" [32] particularly since "advertising is the *sine qua non* of commercial profits." [33] The "greater objectivity" with which falsity

---

26. Id. at 763: "As to the particular consumer's interest in the free flow of commercial information, that interest may be as keen, if not keener by far, than his interest in the day's most urgent political debate." See also id. at 765: "So long as we preserve a predominantly free enterprise economy, the allocation of our resources in large measure will be made through numerous private economic decisions. It is a matter of public interest that those decisions, in the aggregate, be intelligent and well informed. To this end, the free flow of commercial information is indispensable."

27. Id. at 765. The Court in Virginia Board identified both a right of the pharmacist to advertise and a reciprocal right to receive the advertising, id. at 757; in Linmark Associates, 431 U.S. at 92, the Court noted the equal interest of the home-owner-seller and the would-be-purchaser in the free flow of commercial information. But the discussion in both cases focusing on the inadequacy of alternative sources of information implied that the Court was more concerned with protecting listeners

than with protecting speakers who have commercial messages to deliver.

28. Virginia Board of Pharmacy, 425 U.S. at 779 (Stewart, J. concurring).

29. Ohralik v. Ohio State Bar Ass'n, 436 U.S. 447, 455–56 (1978). See also Virginia Board of Pharmacy, 425 U.S. at 771 n. 24 (recognizing the "commonsense differences between speech that does no more than propose a commercial transaction, . . . and other varieties") (citations omitted). But cf. Bolger v. Youngs Drug Product Corp., 463 U.S. 60, 81 (1983) (Stevens, J., concurring in the judgment) (remarking that "the impression that 'commercial speech' is a fairly definitive category of communication . . . may not be wholly warranted.").

30. Id. at 772 n. 24.

31. Id. at 777 (Stewart, J., concurring).

32. Id. at 778 (Stewart, J., concurring), quoting Gertz v. Robert Welch, Inc., 418 U.S. 323, 341 (1974).

33. Virginia Board of Pharmacy, 425 U.S. at 772 n. 24. See also Bates v. Arizo-

may be identified in most commercial contexts,[34] and the corresponding-ly reduced danger of ideological censorship in the guise of consumer protection,[35] also support broader power to suppress false advertising than to censor false or misleading speech generally.   Furthermore, given the legitimate and often quite compelling governmental interest in protecting individuals from injury caused by deceptive practices against which they cannot effectively guard themselves, it may be "appropriate to require that a commercial message appear in such a form, or include such additional information, warnings, and disclaim-ers, as are necessary to prevent its being deceptive." [36]   Finally, inas-much as the falsity of an advertisement may be reliably ascertainable in advance of such irreparable harm as its dissemination may cause, features distinctive to commercial speech "may also make inapplicable the prohibition against prior restraints." [37]

To be sure, none of these generalizations is airtight; all of them rest upon the obviously troublesome distinction that plagued the *Chrestensen* doctrine—the distinction between talk for profit, and talk for other purposes.   But it is one thing to make *eligibility* for first amendment protection turn on a difficult line, and quite another to use the same line for the far less momentous purpose of recognizing *shades of difference* in the application of settled principles.   That there are and will remain hard cases—is the coal company's ad proclaiming its concern for environment and warning of the hazards of nuclear fuel commercial speech or political expression?—is an insufficient reason either to return to the unprincipled extreme of excluding all commer-cial speech from first amendment protection,[38] or to embrace the equally indefensible position that government cannot stop someone from selling 7-Up claiming it to be insulin.

But, for a doctrine in its infancy, the "commercial speech" doctrine has demonstrated remarkable vigor.   In recent years, the Court has regularly taken up commercial speech controversies, even if it has not settled the exact degree of protection owed to that form of expression.[39]

na State Bar, 433 U.S. 350 (1977) (rejecting applicability of overbreadth analysis to ban on price advertising by attorneys).

34. Virginia Board of Pharmacy, 425 U.S. at 772 n. 24.

35. See Note, "Freedom of Expression in a Commercial Context," 78 Harv.L.Rev. 1191, 1195 (1965).

36. Virginia Board of Pharmacy, 425 U.S. at 772 n. 24. The Court contrasted Miami Herald Publishing Co. v. Tornillo, 418 U.S. 241 (1974) (newspaper cannot be compelled to give political candidate space to reply to attack) with Banzhaf v. F.C.C., 405 F.2d 1082 (D.C.Cir. 1968), cert. denied sub nom. Tobacco Institute, Inc. v. F.C.C., 396 U.S. 842 (1969) (upholding requirement that broadcast licenses schedule counter-advertising indicating the health hazards of cigarette smoking). See also Zauderer v. Office of Disciplinary Counsel, 471 U.S. 626 (1985) (upholding right of state to disci-

pline lawyers for misleading omissions in advertising).

37. Virginia Board of Pharmacy, 425 U.S. at 772 n. 24. See § 12–36, infra.

38. See Redish, "The First Amendment in the Marketplace: Commercial Speech and the Values of Free Expression," 39 Geo.Wash.L.Rev. 429, 450 (1971). For an attempt to provide a principled defense of this extreme position, see Baker, "Commer-cial Speech: A Problem in the Theory of Freedom," 62 Iowa L.Rev. 1 (1976).

39. Focusing on the first amendment's protection of speech as opposed to speak-ers, the Court held in First Nat'l Bank of Boston v. Bellotti, 435 U.S. 765 (1978), that otherwise protected speech does not lose its constitutional shield simply because its source is a corporation. For a critical analysis, see Brudney, "Business Corpora-tions and Stockholders' Rights Under the

Indeed, the Court has sent conflicting signals on that fundamental question since its announcement of a "different degree of protection" for commercial speech in *Virginia Board of Pharmacy*.[40] The Constitution affords "commercial speech a limited measure of protection, commensurate with its subordinate position in the scale of First Amendment values," [41] but the actual application of this intermediate level of review has produced something less than a seamless web of precedent. In a powerful essay surveying the Supreme Court's handiwork in this area, Professor Shiffrin concludes that the Court's "general balancing methodology or . . . eclectic approach," characterized by a reluctance to rely on "excessively romantic generalizations," has been singularly appropriate to the commercial speech context.[42] Accepting a lesser level of first amendment protection for any distinct category of speech does provoke discomfort—as does any constitutional view based on "tensions, compromises or accommodation" rather than "Fourth of July speeches." [43] But principled accommodation of the conflicting values at stake may indeed be the most appropriate course in the commercial speech area, and the Supreme Court—albeit in a somewhat halting fashion—seems to have generally stayed that course in recent years.

As an initial matter, the Court's blithe admonition that the difference between commercial and non-commercial speech is determined by "commonsense" [44] has not provided reliable guidance for the resolution of individual cases. Indeed, one of the problems with commonsense, as opposed to analytical, distinctions is that they vary enormously with the facts of particular cases. In *Hoffman Estates v. Flipside*,[45] a "headshop" [46] challenged a village ordinance which required a business to obtain a license and keep certain detailed records if it sold any items "designed or marketed for use with illegal cannabis or drugs." [47] The shop—Flipside—charged that the ordinance constituted a forbidden abridgement of speech, because its guidelines for enforcement treated the physical proximity of drug-related literature [48] as an indication that the paraphernalia were marketed for use with drugs.[49] Justice Marshall's opinion [50] upholding the ordinance considered separately the commercial and non-commercial expression involved in the headshop's business, and held that the law did not regulate non-commercial (and

First Amendment," 91 Yale L.J. 235 (1981). See § 12–4, supra.

40. Virginia Board of Pharmacy, 425 U.S. at 772 n. 24.

41. Ohralik v. Ohio State Bar Ass'n, 436 U.S. 447, 456 (1978). See also Bolger v. Youngs Drug Products Corp., 463 U.S. 60, 64–65 (1983) (Constitution "accords less protection to commercial speech than to other constitutionally safeguarded forms of expression.")

42. Shiffrin, "The First Amendment and Economic Regulation: Away From a General Theory of the First Amendment," 78 Nw.U.L.Rev. 1212, 1251 (1983).

43. Id. at 1282–83.

44. Ohralik v. Ohio State Bar Ass'n, 436 U.S. 447, 455–56 (1978), discussed in note 66, infra.

45. 455 U.S. 489 (1982).

46. A retail establishment which sells, among other things, papers, pipes and other items intended for use with illegal drugs.

47. Id. at 494–95.

48. The titles included "A Child's Garden of Grass," "Marijuana Growers' Guide," and magazines such as Rolling Stone and High Times. Id. at 491 n. 1.

49. Id. at 496.

50. Justice White filed an opinion concurring in the judgment. Justice Stevens did not participate.

therefore more closely protected) speech at all. Because the sale of the literature was not forbidden or regulated in any way, the only first amendment interest at stake was the retailer's "attenuated" interest in marketing and displaying merchandise in his preferred manner. Hoffman Estates restricted Flipside's ability to communicate only by its regulation of the display of certain items, thereby inhibiting solely the store's commercial encouragement of drug use.[51] The government may suppress or ban that type of expression entirely, the Court held, because it is "speech proposing an illegal transaction." [52]

In *Flipside*, the Court separated commercial from non-commercial speech. In *Bolger v. Youngs Drug Products Corp.*,[53] it conflated them. Respondent, a manufacturer of condoms, successfully challenged a federal law which banned from the mails unsolicited advertisements for contraceptives.[54] In order to determine which constitutional standard to apply, the Court had to classify the speech contained in Youngs' mailings. Certain flyers contained only product names and prices and thus were easily identified as commercial speech, but the informational pamphlets on venereal disease and contraception presented a challenge. The Court added up various factors and concluded that the pamphlets, too, constituted commercial speech, "notwithstanding the fact that they contain discussions of important public issues such as venereal disease and family planning." [55] Yet a few paragraphs later, the Court apparently reversed itself and stressed that, because Youngs sought to convey truthful information about "important social issues such as family planning and the prevention of venereal disease[,] . . . the First Amendment interest served by such speech [was] *paramount*." [56]

The subtle influence of commercial and non-commercial expression on one another is perplexing. In *Flipside*, the unprotected "speech" involved the display of drug paraphernalia next to constitutionally-protected counter-culture literature. Regulation by the government was permissible even though it was triggered by establishing the proximity of certain items to other material which clearly was within the embrace of the first amendment. In *Bolger*, the condom manufacturer's information pamphlets seemed to become commercial speech by osmosis because they were mailed with traditional advertisements and mentioned specific products. In one case, then, products became subject to regulation because of the presence of constitutionally-protected non-commercial speech, and in the other, pamphlets bearing information which "implicates substantial individual and societal interests" [57]

---

51. Flipside never asserted that its placement of the items was intended to communicate anything. Rather, the items were sold at the counter, near the magazines, to hinder shoplifters. Id. at 496 n. 8.

52. Id. at 496. The Court appeared untroubled by the fact that any drugs which would be used with Flipside's merchandise would have to be obtained elsewhere, and that Flipside therefore would have no role in the actual illegal transaction in question.

53. 463 U.S. 60 (1983).

54. 39 U.S.C. § 3001(e)(2) originated in 1873 as part of Anthony Comstock's famous jihad against smut. See Bolger, 463 U.S. at 70 n. 19.

55. 463 U.S. at 67–68 (footnote omitted).

56. Id. at 69 (emphasis added).

57. Id., quoting Carey v. Population Services Int'l, 431 U.S. 678, 700–01 (1977).

were demoted to the status of commercial speech, but protected none-theless, because of the presence of promotional advertising.[58] The lesson of these cases, then, is less than clear.

However, once the Court files the speech into the appropriate commercial or non-commercial category, its analysis has begun to follow a now-familiar pattern. Two opinions by Justice Powell in companion cases in 1980 demonstrate the Court's current approach. In *Consolidated Edison Co. v. New York Public Service Commission*,[59] the Court, by a 7–2 vote, struck down a state regulation forbidding public utilities to include inserts in their electricity bills which promoted the utilities' position on controversial public policy issues.[60] Consolidated Edison had placed an insert in its monthly bills to ratepayers advocating the use of nuclear power. An environmental group asked, in effect, for equal time, requesting the Public Service Commission to compel Consolidated Edison to include inserts bearing opposing views in future

---

58. The Court's analysis of commercial and non-commercial speech was even more baffling in Metromedia, Inc. v. San Diego, 453 U.S. 490, 501 (1981), where the Court struck down a municipal regulation on outdoor advertising and stated solemnly, "[w]e deal here with the law of billboards." A San Diego ordinance banned all off-site commercial billboards and all but a very select category of non-commercial billboards. Property owners could still erect billboards to advertise their own goods and services, but no one else's. No one could post any signs anywhere to convey non-commercial messages, although there were several, content-based exceptions, for religious symbols, temporary political campaigns and government signs. Id. at 494–95.

Justice White's plurality opinion, which was joined by Justices Stewart, Marshall and Powell, upheld the law's ban on commercial billboards, but struck it down regarding non-commercial speech. Justice Brennan, joined by Justice Blackmun, concurred in the judgment. Justice Stevens concurred in part of the plurality opinion but dissented from the judgment. Chief Justice Burger and Justice Rehnquist filed dissenting opinions. On the commercial speech issue, the plurality accepted at face value the city's interest in beautifying the city and reducing motorist distractions, id. at 507–08, and overlooked the requirement that the city's action be the least restrictive means available. Id. at 511–12. So offended by San Diego's having given more protection to commercial than non-commercial speech, id. at 520–21, the Court righted one wrong by reversing the ban on most non-commercial speech. But the Court then created another wrong—by neglecting to give full consideration to the rights of the commercial speakers. For a

thoughtful review of the case, see The Supreme Court, 1980 Term, 95 Harv.L.Rev. 91, 211 (1981). For the Court's latest pronouncement on the "law of billboards," albeit in a different context, see Los Angeles City Council v. Vincent, 466 U.S. 789 (1984), discussed in § 12–24, infra.

59. 447 U.S. 530 (1980).

60. Justice Blackmun filed a dissenting opinion, joined by Justice Rehnquist, on the ground that the utility's monopoly power made "the use of the insert . . . an exaction from the utility's customers by way of forced aid for the utility's speech." 447 U.S. at 549. The dissent also accused the majority of "gloss[ing] over the difficult allocation issue underlying this controversy. It is not clear to me from the Court's opinion whether it believes that charging the shareholders with the marginal costs associated with the inserts, that is, the costs of printing and putting them into the envelope, will satisfy the state's interest, or whether the Court is suggesting some division of the fixed costs of the mailing, that is, the postage, the envelope, the creation and maintenance of the mailing list, and any other overhead expense." Id. at 554. Indeed, this uncertainty in the majority opinion was highlighted, when, on remand, the Public Service Commission ordered that, if the utilities included any bill inserts on controversial issues, the utilities' shareholders would have to pay half of the cost of the mailing. The New York Court of Appeals rejected a first amendment attack on the Commission's action, see Consolidated Edison Co. of New York, Inc. v. New York Public Service Comm'n, 66 N.Y.2d 369, 497 N.Y.S.2d 337, 488 N.E.2d 83 (1985), and the Supreme Court upheld that result. See 106 S.Ct. 1627 (1986) (dismissing appeal).

bills.[61]   Instead, the Commission chose to forbid utility action effectively coercing utility ratepayers to subsidize *anyone's* message on public issues, and to prohibit utilities from using bill inserts to "discuss political matters" or to express "their opinions or viewpoints on controversial issues of public policy." [62]   But such a ban, Justice Powell wrote, was a content-based restriction on speech which struck "at the heart of the freedom to speak." [63]

The Court had little trouble concluding that the government's designation of certain subjects as off limits to particular speakers and audiences was a form of content-based censorship and presumptively unconstitutional.[64]   The Court could find no significant governmental purpose in protecting the "privacy" of utility ratepayers since they were hardly a "captive" audience: "[t]he customer of Consolidated Edison may escape exposure to objectionable material simply by transferring the bill insert from envelope to wastebasket." [65]   The limited intrusion of the billing inserts, coupled with the emphatically content-based nature of the Public Service Commission's restriction, combined to lead the justices to think of *Consolidated Edison* more as a political speech case than a commercial speech case—and thus made the Court far more reluctant to allow any regulation.[66]

---

61. When the California Public Service Commission did just that, a sharply divided Supreme Court struck the action down on first amendment grounds in Pacific Gas & Electric Co. v. California Public Utilities Comm'n, 106 S.Ct. 903 (1986). Justice Powell's plurality opinion rejected the requirement chiefly on the grounds that the right of access might (1) deter the utility from saying things that might trigger an adverse response, and (2) induce it to respond to subjects about which it might prefer to remain silent, in violation of the rights established in Miami Herald Publishing Co. v. Tornillo, 418 U.S. 241 (1974) and Wooley v. Maynard, 430 U.S. 705 (1977). Justice Rehnquist's powerful dissent, joined by Justices White and Stevens, particularly took the plurality to task for its reading of Tornillo and Wooley. The dissenters questioned the plurality's conclusion that the "right of access . . . implicates PG & E's right not to speak or to associate with the speech of others, thereby triggering heightened scrutiny." Id. at 920. Wooley, Justice Rehnquist stated, was inapplicable to the regulation of a public utility: "Extension of the individual freedom of conscience decisions to business corporations strains the rationale of those cases to the breaking point. To ascribe such artificial entities an 'intellect' or 'mind' for freedom of conscience purposes is to confuse metaphor with reality." Id. at 921. Chief Justice Burger filed a concurring opinion, and Justice Marshall concurred in the judgment. Justice Blackmun did not participate.

62. Consolidated Edison, 447 U.S. at 532–33.

63.   447 U.S. at 535.

64. See § 12–2, supra.

65.   447 U.S. at 542 (footnote omitted).

66. A pair of 1978 companion cases also illustrates that commercial speech which involves elements of political expression will always receive more protection than "pure" commercial speech. In Ohralik v. Ohio State Bar Ass'n, 436 U.S. 447 (1978), the Court upheld a disciplinary action against an attorney who violated the state's Canon of Ethics by soliciting a client face-to-face. Justice Powell's opinion, delivered without dissent, stated that because of the state's "special responsibility for maintaining standards among members of the licensed professions," it could restrict the attorney's action. In In re Primus, 436 U.S. 412 (1978), the Court, again per Justice Powell, invalidated a disciplinary action under the same state provision against an American Civil Liberties Union attorney who sought to organize a lawsuit on behalf of mothers who had been sterilized or threatened with sterilization as a condition for the continued receipt of government assistance. The Court, with only Justice Rehnquist dissenting, held that Primus' action was exactly the kind of associational activity protected in NAACP v. Button, 371 U.S. 415 (1963), see § 12–26, infra, when Virginia sought to enforce its ban on client solicitation against the activities of the NAACP Legal Defense Fund. In Primus, the Court held that, "[w]here

The commerical nature of the speech was far more evident in the companion case, *Central Hudson Gas & Electric Corp. v. New York Public Service Commission.*[67] There the Court ruled by an 8–1 vote that New York could not completely ban utility advertising which promoted the use of electricity. Unlike the bill inserts in *Consolidated Edison*, the promotional advertising at issue here "related solely to the economic interests of the speaker and its audience."[68] It encouraged utility customers to buy more kilowatts from Central Hudson, and therefore constituted the purest form of commercial speech.[69] Justice Powell, again writing for the Court, formulated what he described as a four-part test for determining whether particular commercial speech is protected by the first amendment. As a threshhold matter, the speech must concern lawful activity and not be misleading. Turning to the nature of the regulation, the state interest advanced by the restriction must be "substantial." Next, the regulation must directly advance that state interest. Finally, the regulation must not be "more extensive than is required" to serve the governmental interest.[70]

The utility satisfied the first prong, because New York had not alleged that the utility's advertising had been deceptive, and the use of electricity is certainly legal. Second, Justice Powell accepted "without reservation the argument that [energy] conservation . . . is an imperative national goal," and agreed that the states may "take appropriate action to further this goal."[71] Third, the Court stated that the ban on advertising must have had some effect on demand for electricity, or Central Hudson would not have challenged it. Finally, though, the Court found that the Commission's ban on promotional advertising might actually suppress speech promoting some devices or services which *decrease* energy use. The rule thus could have had the effect of *increasing* the use of electricity, at least in comparison with a more narrowly tailored rule. The Court accordingly concluded that the ban was impermissibly broad.

The most interesting argument made by Justice Rehnquist, the lone dissenter, was that there was no constitutional value served by closely controlling a state regulation of this sort, while rubber-stamping, under minimum rationality review, a regulation that would force up the price of electricity or directly control its consumption.[72] To Justice Rehnquist, the "only" difference between an undoubtedly per-

political expression or association is at issue," a member of the bar "may not be disciplined unless her activity in fact involve[s] the type of misconduct" at which anti-solicitation rules are directed. 436 U.S. at 434.

67. 447 U.S. 557 (1980).

68. Id. at 561. Justices Brennan, Blackmun and Stevens filed opinions concurring in the judgment. Justice Rehnquist dissented.

69. Justices Brennan, Blackmun and Stevens disagreed with the majority's finding that the regulation reached only commercial speech. As Justice Stevens stated,

"[t]his ban encompasses a great deal more than mere proposals to engage in certain kinds of commercial transactions. It prohibits all advocacy of the immediate or future use of electricity. It curtails expression by an informed and interested group of persons of their point of view on questions relating to the production and comsumption of electrical energy—questions frequently discussed and debated by our political leaders." Id. at 580–81 (Stevens, J., concurring in the judgment).

70. Id. at 566.

71. Id. at 571.

72. Id. at 591.

missible form of economic regulation and the Commission's regulation of commercial speech is that one operates on the marketplace of goods and the other on the marketplace of ideas. A sharp distinction between those two marketplaces could not, in Justice Rehnquist's view, be long maintained. Just as the decline of the *Lochner* era signaled judicial acquiesence in a governmental role in the marketplace of goods, he suggested, so could government regulate the marketplace of ideas, especially to make sure that certain vendors do not exercise monopoly power.[73] Although not expressly endorsing this view, the Court's opinion was easier to reconcile with it than with the *Virginia Board of Pharmacy* theory that truthful advertising cannot be banned in order to discourage consumers from being convinced to respond to it.

Justice Rehnquist had the opportunity to expand on his view of the intersection between the marketplaces of commerce and ideas for a majority of the Court in *Posadas de Puerto Rico Associates v. Tourism Co. of Puerto Rico*,[74] the last opinion for the Court that he filed before his promotion to Chief Justice. There a 5–4 majority upheld, against a facial challenge by a casino operator, a Puerto Rican statute which prohibited local casinos from advertising their gambling facilities to residents of Puerto Rico, but allowed them to advertise to potential tourists in the continental United States and elsewhere.

The Court applied the four-part test of *Central Hudson* to uphold the statute. First, it stated that casino gambling was legal and assumed that any potential advertisements "would not be misleading or fraudulent, at least in the abstract." [75] Second, the Court evaluated the

---

73. Id. at 592–594. Contrast regulation of this "marketplace" to assure that those with more dollars do not exert disproportionate influence—a form of regulation Justice Rehnquist condemned in his opinion for the Court in Federal Election Comm'n v. National Conservative Political Action Comm., 470 U.S. 480 (1985). The Court has tended to view commercial speech as a shield to protect open competition, not a sword to permit collusion among competitors. Compare Virginia Board of Pharmacy, 425 U.S. at 766–80 (rejecting ban on pharmacy advertising on the ground, inter alia, of fostering open competition), with National Soc'y of Professional Engineers v. United States, 435 U.S. 679, 696–99 (1978) (holding that Sherman Act prosecution of trade association which prohibits competitive bidding does not violate first amendment). Furthermore, the Court in Zauderer v. Office of Disciplinary Counsel, 471 U.S. 626 (1985), upheld a requirement that attorneys who advertise availability on a contingency fee basis also disclose in the ad that clients pay costs if the lawsuit is unsuccessful. The Court noted that "[b]ecause the extension of First Amendment protection to commercial speech is justified principally by the value to consumers of the information such speech provides [citing Virginia Board of

Pharmacy], appellant's constitutionally protected interest in *not* providing any particular factual information in his advertising is minimal." Id. at 631.

74. 106 S.Ct. 2968 (1986). Justice Rehnquist's opinion was joined by Chief Justice Burger and Justices White, Powell and O'Connor. Justices Brennan and Stevens filed dissenting opinions, which were joined by Justices Marshall and Blackmun.

75. Id. at 2976. The Court in Friedman v. Rogers, 440 U.S. 1 (1979), citing concerns about misleading advertising, upheld a Texas ban on practicing optometry under a trade name. The Court distinguished the advertisements in Virginia Board of Pharmacy and Bates, which it said were "self-contained and self-explanatory," and held that trade name regulation concerned "a form of commercial speech that has no intrinsic meaning." Id. at 12. The Court thus tested the law by the minimum rationality standard applicable to other economic regulations. A ban on trade names was permitted because "these ill-defined associations of trade names with price and quality information can be manipulated by the[ir] users . . . [and] there is a significant possibility that trade names will be used to mislead the public." Id. at 12–13. Justice Blackmun, joined by Justice Mar-

government interest at stake—here, "the reduction of demand for casino gambling by the residents of Puerto Rico." [76] The Court had "no difficulty in concluding that the Puerto Rico Legislature's interest in the health, safety, and welfare of its citizens constitutes a 'substantial' governmental interest." [77] Third, the Court found that the challenged restriction did "directly advance" this governmental interest—on the theory that, as in *Central Hudson*, there is a direct connection between advertising for a product and demand for it.[78] Finally, the Court held that the law was not overly restrictive, deferring to the legislature's finding that it could reduce gambling more successfully by banning advertising outright rather than "promulgating additional speech designed to *discourage*" gambling.[79] Had the Court stopped there—that is, decided the case on a straightforward application of the *Central Hudson* balancing test—the decision would have been a largely unremarkable application of the commercial speech doctrine.[80]

But Justice Rehnquist's opinion added a new—and disturbing— twist to that doctrine. The Court concluded by stating that "the

shall, dissented on the trade name issue, arguing chiefly that, because trade names have no intrinsic meaning, they cannot be misleading and thus should not be prohibited by the state. See id. at 24–26. Another concern was that the majority's deference to a fanciful state legislative justification may be inappropriate where those who would benefit by the restriction wield too much influence in the legislature. Cf. Ferguson v. Skrupa, 372 U.S. 726 (1963) (upholding law limiting debt-adjustment to licensed attorneys), and Williamson v. Lee Optical Co., 348 U.S. 483 (1955) (upholding restrictions on optometrists which favor ophthalmologists), discussed in § 8–7, supra.

Friedman notwithstanding, the Court has shown some reluctance to assume that advertising is misleading, without actual *evidence* of deception. In In re R.M.J., 455 U.S. 191 (1982), the Court unanimously invalidated regulations on lawyer advertising that (1) allowed only certain subject areas to be listed as specialties; (2) forbade listings of admission to the bars of neighboring states and the United States Supreme Court; and (3) banned the mailing of announcements of office openings except to clients, former clients, friends and relatives. The Court stated, "[t]here is no finding that appellant's speech was misleading. Nor can we say that it was inherently misleading, or that restrictions short of an absolute prohibition would not have sufficed to cure any possible deception. . . . States may regulate commercial speech, [but] the First and Fourteenth Amendments require that they do so with care and in a manner no more extensive than reasonably necessary to further substantial interests." Id. at 206–07.

76. Posadas, 106 S.Ct. at 2977.

77. Id. at 2977, quoting Renton v. Playtime Theaters, Inc., 475 U.S. 41, ___ (1986).

78. 106 S.Ct. at 2977. The Court also made short work of the casino's argument that the law was underinclusive because other forms of gambling, including horseracing and cockfighting, could be advertised in Puerto Rico. The Court stated first that the law did not have to reduce demand for all games of chance to reduce demand for casino gambling, and second that the legislature could legitimately single out casino gambling as a target—and not other games, which "have been traditionally part of the Puerto Rican's roots." Id.

79. Id. at 2978 (emphasis in original).

80. Justice Brennan's dissenting opinion, which was joined by Justices Marshall and Blackmun, was devoted principally to challenging the majority's application of the Central Hudson test to what he characterized as "constitutionally protected expression." 106 S.Ct. at 2983. There was no controversy about the first factor. But, regarding the second, Justice Brennan stated that the evidence indicated that the legislature did not want to reduce casino gambling among the local populace; after all, the practice was and remains legal. Id. Third, the dissent found it unclear how an *advertising* ban "would directly advance" the objectives of reducing crime and corruption. Id. at 2984–85. Finally, Justice Brennan found the statute excessively broad to accomplish its stated objectives. Vigorous enforcement of existing criminal laws would, in his view, achieve the purpose of the law without interfering with any protected speech. Id. at 2985–86. Justice Stevens also dissented, in an opinion joined by Justices Marshall and Blackmun.

greater power to completely ban casino gambling necessarily includes the lesser power to ban advertising of casino gambling[.]" [81]   The Court observed that it would be "a strange constitutional doctrine which would concede to the legislature the authority to totally ban a product or activity, but deny to the legislature the authority to forbid the stimulation of demand for the product or activity through advertising on behalf of those who would profit from such increased demand." [82] There is only slight exaggeration in the dissenters' retort that this "strange" doctrine is called the first amendment.[83]   At the very least, the "greater power including the lesser power" form of analysis seems singularly inappropriate in the first amendment context.[84]   Chief Justice Rehnquist's misapprehensions notwithstanding,[85] the Court has long required government to regulate with a far lighter touch when regulating in the marketplace of ideas—even ideas parlayed for profit— than in the marketplace of commerce.   The entire commercial speech doctrine, after all, represents an accommodation between the right to speak and hear expression *about* goods and services and the right of government to regulate the sale *of* such goods and services.[86]   Adoption of the *Posadas* approach throughout the commercial speech area would plainly upset the Court's carefully evolved balancing test, and lead to dilution of existing protections of speech that are well-settled and seem defensible.

In any event, Justice Rehnquist's observation that a state may ban *all* advertising of an activity that it permits but could prohibit poses, as Justice Stevens put it, only "an elegant question of constitutional law." [87]   For that question was not in fact the one posed in *Posadas*. The ban there was *selective*, not universal; it was directed only at a specific target audience: residents of Puerto Rico.   An "audience-specific" regulation of speech offends first amendment values as much as a "content-specific" ban, for both involve government controlling

81. Id. at 2979.

82. Id.

83. Id. at 2984 n. 4 (Brennan J., dissenting).

84. The notion of requiring individuals to take the "bitter with the sweet" is a familiar one in Chief Justice Rehnquist's jurisprudence, albeit one that his colleagues have consistently rejected. Compare Arnett v. Kennedy, 416 U.S. 134 (1974) (plurality opinion of Rehnquist, J.) (government not obligated to provide procedural due process protections to public employee because the source of law creating the employee's entitlement simultaneously made his job terminable without a full prior hearing), with Cleveland Bd. of Educ. v. Loudermill, 470 U.S. 532, 559 (1985) (explicitly overruling "bitter with the sweet" holding of Arnett); Compare FCC v. League of Women Voters, 468 U.S. 364, 402 (1984) (Rehnquist, J., dissenting) (government subsidy of public television should entitle government to prohibit sta-

tions' expression of editorial opinions), with id. at 364 (majority opinion striking down such regulations as violative of the First Amendment); Compare Larkin v. Grendel's Den, Inc., 459 U.S. 116, 127 (1982) (Rehnquist, J., dissenting) (governmental power to forbid the granting of any liquor licenses to establishments located less than 500 feet from churches includes power to delegate that authority to the discretion of the churches themselves), with id. at 116 (majority opinion striking down governmental grant of veto power to churches as an impermissible establishment of religion).

85. See, e.g., Central Hudson, 447 U.S. at 597–99 (Rehnquist, J., dissenting).

86. See, e.g., Virginia Board of Pharmacy, 425 U.S. at 761–63. But Central Hudson had arguably jettisoned the key premise of the doctrine, at least in dictum, half a dozen years before Posadas.

87. Id. at 2986 (Stevens, J., dissenting).

who may hear what.[88] Justice Stevens' incredulity that the Court "is willing to uphold a Puerto Rico regulation that applies one standard to The New York Times and another to the San Juan Star" is well-justified.[89]

Until *Posadas*, the Court seemed to have reached a comfortable, if not always predictable, understanding in commercial speech cases. As Professor Shiffrin observed, the Court had come to balance "the impact of the challenged regulations on first amendment values against the seriousness of the evil that the state seeks to mitigate or prevent, the extent to which the regulation advances the state's interest, and the extent to which the interest might have been furthered by less intrusive means."[90] Those words, of course, are by no means self-executing—but, applied with decent respect for speakers, listeners, and legitimate governmental objectives, they provided tolerable guideposts in a confounding corner of first amendment jurisprudence. But, in the wake of the *Central Hudson* dictum that government may seek to discourage even truthful promotion for profit of a lawful product or service[91] and the *Posadas* holding that it may do so on an audience-specific basis, the Court's commercial speech doctrine seems poised on a makeshift—and unsteady—foundation for the future.[92]

§ 12–16. The Continuing Suppression of Obscenity

If it was true in 1968 that the effort to separate unprotected obscenity from other sexually oriented but constitutionally protected

88. Speaker-specific bans have expressly been equated with those that are content-based. See First Nat'l Bank of Boston v. Bellotti, 435 U.S. 765, 784–85 (1978); City of Madison Joint School District v. Wisconsin Employment Relations Comm'n, 429 U.S. 167 (1976), discussed in § 12–3, supra, and § 12–24, infra. Moreover, both speaker-specific and content-specific bans represent actions that selectively deprive consumers of information necessary to make informed choices based on paternalistic premises. As Justice Stevens stated, "Perhaps, since Puerto Rico somewhat ambivalently regards a gambling casino as a good thing for the local proprietor and an evil for the local patrons, the ban on local advertising might be viewed as a form of protection against the poison that Puerto Rico uses to attract strangers into its web. If too much speech about the poison were permitted, local residents might not only partake of it but also decide to prohibit it." 106 S.Ct. at 2987 n. 1.

89. Acceptance of the practice of "sanitizing" information for local consumption, while allowing greater access to information for outsiders, places the United States in most ill-becoming company. See N.Y. Times, June 20, 1986, § 1, at 10:1 (describing South African press restrictions as they affected domestic and international journalists).

90. Shiffrin, supra note 42, at 1252.

91. Central Hudson, 447 U.S. at 563–65.

92. Perhaps the most plausible basis for reconciling Posadas with the invalidation of Virginia's ban on prescription drug price advertising by pharmacists, see Virginia Board of Pharmacy, supra, is the proposition that, where a state has determined that an activity is intrinsically harmful and should be stopped but would be too impractical or intrusive on privacy to ban altogether, the state may choose to ban advertising that would directly encourage the activity to go on. That was Puerto Rico's position as to casino gambling by local residents, but it was *not* Virginia's position as to prescription drug use. The first amendment does not permit a state to decide, as Virginia did, that a product's use is ordinarily desirable but that potential users cannot be trusted to deal intelligently with truthful price information provided by suppliers. Put otherwise, it is not all paternalistic government actions that the first amendment forbids but only government actions predicated on the view that people will be gullible and will misuse even information that neither misleads nor urges a dangerous course of conduct.

speech had "produced a variety of views among the members of the Court unmatched in any other course of constitutional adjudication," [1] then certainly nothing in the intervening years has occurred to support a different verdict; the Supreme Court's bare majority in 1973 for yet another definition of the obscene and yet another set of rationales for its suppression has produced a formula likely to be as unstable as it is unintelligible. Although this section will summarize that formula and the doctrines surrounding it, the discussion is organized around historical and philosophical rather than doctrinal themes, reflecting a conviction that we have by no means seen the end of major development in the constitutional law of obscenity.

In the sixteenth century, ecclesiastical [2] and royal [3] censorship of expression in England was more concerned with political and religious themes than with the sexually obscene. The earliest licensing systems were primarily addressed to the vices of sedition and heresy. [4] During the seventeenth century, the influence of puritanism resulted in a sober intolerance of bawdy literature; the portrayal of sexual pleasure was strictly condemned. Shortly after the restoration, in the year 1663, Sir Charles Sedley, an intimate of the King and a notorious profligate, after a drinking spree in a tavern by Covent Garden, mounted the balcony of the tavern as a crowd gathered below. There he proceeded to disrobe, haranguing his audience with antireligious epithets as he showered them with bottles of urine. The crowd, now turned mob, stormed the tavern. Sedley's subsequent conviction [5] is widely regarded as the first reported English case on obscenity—making Sedley the first adjudicated "streaker." Because he employed force to cause a breach of the peace, Sedley's offense was clearly cognizable at common law. Yet his case was subsequently relied upon in *Dominus Rex v. Curl* [6] for the proposition that obscenity alone—that is, Sedley's nakedness—was a breach of the peace. In a third early case, *Rex v. Wilkes*, [7] the Tory government used the new common law of obscenity to send Wilkes, a Whig foe, to jail for having published a poem entitled "Essay on Woman." [8] There was little further common law development in

---

§ 12–16

1. Interstate Circuit, Inc. v. Dallas, 390 U.S. 676, 704–05 (1968) (separate opinion of Harlan, J.).

2. The church began to censor works with the Council of Trent in the mid-sixteenth century.

3. Henry VII established the first licensing system in 1538.

4. See generally Alshuler, "Origins of the Law of Obscenity," in 2 Technical Report of the Commission on Obscenity and Pornography 65 (1970). The author suggests that the Medieval mind was not unduly alarmed by a mixture of the ribald with the religions. She notes for example that The Exeter Book, an early devotional work, contained a collection of obscene riddles.

5. Sir Charles Sydlyes Case, 1 Keble 620 (K.B.1663). See 8 The Cambridge History of English Literature 158 (1912).

6. 2 Strange 788 (K.B.1727).

7. 4 Burr. 2527 (K.B.1770).

8. The prosecution of Wilkes was a typically political affair. In order to prove publication, the government bribed the printer of the essay to provide the prosecution with a thirteenth copy, since the twelve early copies were circulating privately among the members of a club to which the author belonged. On the political nature of these early cases, see Reynolds, "Our Misplaced Reliance on Early Obscenity Cases," 61 A.B.A.J. 220 (1975). It has also been argued that religious impiety was a necessary element of the common law offense. See Schroeder, "Obscene Literature at Common Law," 69 Albany L.J. 146 (1907). See Regina v. Read, 11 Mod.Rep. 142 (1708) (holding obscenity punishable only in ecclesiastical court), overruled by Rex v. Curl, 2 Strange 788 (1727).

England;[9] there was no common law development in the American colonies at all. And at the time of the Revolution, only one state[10] had any statutory law on the subject.

The first reported obscenity case in the United States occurred in 1815. In *Commonwealth v. Sharpless*[11], a Pennsylvania court decided that it was an offense at common law to exhibit for profit a picture of a nude couple. Several states, beginning with Vermont in 1821, subsequently passed obscenity statutes. The first federal statute, passed in 1842, was aimed at the French post card trade[12] and prohibited the importation of obscene pictorial matter. Until the 1870's, none of these statutes was rigidly enforced. But three years after the end of the Civil War, a New York City grocer named Anthony Comstock joined with Protestant leaders in that city in a campaign to suppress obscenity. At their urging, the New York State legislature enacted a bill to prohibit obscenity in 1868.[13] In 1873, after intense lobbying, Congress made it a criminal offense to send obscene material through the mails.[14] More state enactments followed.[15]

Few of the cases prior to the late nineteenth century attempted to define the obscene. In 1868, in *Regina v. Hicklin*, Lord Chief Justice Cockburn was called upon to provide a definition under the recently enacted Lord Campbell's Act. For him, the "test of obscenity" was "whether the tendency of the matter charged . . . is to deprave and corrupt those whose minds are open to such immoral influences, and into whose hands a publication of this sort may fall."[16]

The *Hicklin* test was widely adopted by American courts. It came to stand for the double proposition that obscenity was to be measured by its effect on the most susceptible, and that obscenity of the work as a whole was to be judged by the effect of isolated passages.[17] In the years following *Hicklin*, judges made ad hoc exceptions for "the classics," saving the likes of Rabelais and Ovid. But prosecutions under the *Hicklin* rule took a heavy toll on contemporary literature. In the same

9. Legislative prohibition in England began with the Vagrancy Act which forbade the exposure of obscene books or prints in public. 5 Geo. 4, c. 83 (1824).

10. In 1711, Massachusetts had extended its rigid censorship system to include the ". . . wicked, profane, impure, filthy and obscene . . ." Ancient Charter, Colony Laws and Province Laws of Massachusetts Bay, 1814.

11. 2 S.R. 91 (1815).

12. 5 Stat. 566 (1842).

13. 7 New York Stats. 309 (1868).

14. 17 Stat. 599 (1873).

15. At one time or another, obscenity has been made the object of criminal law in all of the fifty states. For a detailed, though dated, breakdown, see Note, "More Ado About Dirty Books," 75 Yale L.J. 1364, 1406 (1966). In recent years, four states (Iowa, Montana, South Dakota and West Virginia) have chosen to restrict their laws to the punishment of sales to minors, adopting the recommendations of the Report of the Commission on Obscenity and Pornography (1970). See Lockhart, "Escape from the Chill of Uncertainty: Explicit Sex and the First Amendment," 9 Georgia L.Rev. 533, 535 (1975).

16. L.R. 3 Q.B. 360, 368 (1868).

17. It has been suggested that Hicklin does not support a test based on "isolated passages," since fully one half of the anti-Catholic tract in that case was found to be obscene. Note, supra note 15, at 1369 n. 24. The "isolated passages" test reached something of an apotheosis in Commonwealth v. Friede, 271 Mass. 318, 171 N.E. 472 (1930), where the state's highest court upheld the refusal by a trial judge to allow defense counsel to read Theodore Dreiser's An American Tragedy to the jury in its entirety.

year, 1930, both Theodore Dreiser's *An American Tragedy*[18] and D. H. Lawrence's *Lady Chatterly's Lover*[19] were declared obscene.

The work of extra-judicial groups, such as the National Organization for Decent Literature (NODL), had an equally pernicious effect on American literature, taking up where Comstock's Protestant organization left off. Blacklists[20] of allegedly obscene literature were circulated and enforced by threats of boycott and prosecution; the NODL exercised a powerful influence on distributors and publishers alike. Other local citizen's groups joined the crusade, and official censorship boards were created in many cities.[21]

The first break in the *Hicklin* stranglehold over contemporary letters came in two opinions, in 1933 and 1934, which held that James Joyce's *Ulysses* was not obscene.[22] Both Judge Woolsey at the trial level and Judge Augustus Hand on appeal forcefully rejected the *Hicklin* rules based on the most susceptible persons and on isolated passages, and suggested instead a standard based on the effect on the average reader of the dominant theme of the work as a whole. Most courts soon adopted the new approach.

The constitutionality of legal restraints on obscenity had been widely assumed both by courts and by litigants during the period between Comstock and *Ulysses*. On several occasions the Supreme Court had dealt with convictions under anti-obscenity statutes without considering their constitutionality;[23] and dicta in other cases suggested that the Court would find no constitutional barrier should the issue arise.[24] It was not until 1948 that the Supreme Court squarely faced the contention that legal restraints on the publication of obscenity were an unconstitutional violation of the first amendment's guarantees of freedom of speech and press. In that year Doubleday & Co. was convicted under a New York law for having published an allegedly obscene work, Edmund Wilson's *Memoirs of Hecate County*. Despite the fact that Wilson was America's foremost literary critic, the conviction was upheld on appeal.[25] A divided Supreme Court affirmed the conviction in a per curiam decision without opinion.[26] The oral argument suggests, however, that the Court divided over the application to

18. Commonwealth v. Friede, 271 Mass. 318, 171 N.E. 472 (1930).

19. Commonwealth v. Delacey, 271 Mass. 327, 171 N.E. 455 (1930).

20. Authors on the NODL blacklist included, among many others, Faulkner, O'Hara, Hemingway and Flaubert.

21. See generally, Lockhart & McClure, "Literature, the Law of Obscenity, and the Constitution," 38 Minn.L.Rev. 295, 311–316 (1954).

22. United States v. One Book Called "Ulysses," 5 F.Supp. 182 (S.D.N.Y.1933), aff'd 72 F.2d 705 (2d Cir. 1934). The suggestion to drop the Hicklin standards had been made much earlier, by Learned Hand, in United States v. Kennerley, 209 Fed. 119, 121 (S.D.N.Y.1913).

23. Rosen v. United States, 161 U.S. 29 (1896); United States v. Limehouse, 285 U.S. 424 (1932).

24. Near v. Minnesota, 283 U.S. 697, 716 (1931); Chaplinsky v. New Hampshire, 315 U.S. 568, 571–72 (1942). For a comprehensive review of these early cases, see United States v. Roth, 237 F.2d 796, 803–04 (2d Cir. 1956) (Frank, J., concurring).

25. People v. Doubleday & Co., 272 App. Div. 799, 71 N.Y.S.2d 736 (1947), aff'd 297 N.Y. 687, 77 N.E.2d 6 (1947).

26. Doubleday & Co. v. New York, 335 U.S. 848 (1948). Justice Frankfurter, a personal friend of Wilson's, did not participate in the decision.

obscenity of the clear and present danger test employed in other first amendment cases.[27]

Nine years later, the Supreme Court granted certiorari in a case involving a Manhattan bookseller convicted under 18 U.S.C. § 1461 of having used the mails to transport obscene matter. The petition was granted limited to the question of the constitutionality of § 1461 on its face.[28] The issue of obscenity vel non was consequently not before the Court.[29]

Despite the probing concurring opinion by Judge Frank in the circuit court below,[30] Justice Brennan, writing for the majority in *Roth v. United States*,[31] found the issues less complex. As for the first amendment, Justice Brennan confirmed what, according to him, the Court had always assumed—namely, that "obscenity is not within the area of constitutionally protected speech or press."[32] And the Court dismissed the "fair notice" claim based on the fifth amendment requirement of due process with the statement that, while obscenity statutes may not be precise, the Constitution did not demand "impossible standards."[33] The test for obscenity, said that Court, was "whether to the average person, applying contemporary community standards, the dominant theme of the material taken as a whole appeals to prurient interest."[34] Thus the rejection by the lower courts of the *Hicklin* standards acquired constitutional significance.[35] And the focus of judicial concern shifted from the alleged "immoral influence" of the work to a judgment about its "prurient appeal."

Roth presumed obscenity to be "utterly without redeeming social importance";[36] nine years later, in *Memoirs v. Massachusetts*,[37] a three-Justice plurality treated the lack of such "redeeming social importance" not as *reason* to exclude obscenity but as part of its *definition*:

27. See Lockhart & McClure, supra note 21, at 300. One state trial judge, Judge Curtis Bok, concluded in a lengthy and probing opinion that the "clear and present danger" test should apply to literature allegedly deemed obscene. In Commonwealth v. Gordon, 66 Pa. D & C 101 (1949), aff'd sub nom. Commonwealth v. Feigenbuum, 166 Pa.Super. 120, 70 A.2d 389 (1950), Judge Bok applied that standard to find that works by Faulkner and James T. Farrell, among others, were protected by the first and fourteenth amendments. See generally §§ 12–9 to 12–11, supra.

28. Roth v. United States, 352 U.S. 964 (1957).

29. The consequences were unfortunate. It was obscenity in the flesh, so to speak, which would later elude definition and thus raise the key problem of a "chilling effect" on protected speech. The Roth majority set itself the much simpler task of contemplating obscenity in the abstract. Thus the Court could—and did—ignore the definitional issue. Ironically it is that very issue which caused Justice Brennan, the

author of Roth, to reject that opinion sixteen years later in Paris Adult Theatre I v. Slaton, 413 U.S. 49, 73 (1973) (dissenting opinion).

30. United States v. Roth, 237 F.2d 796, 801–27 (2d Cir. 1956). Judge Frank relied heavily on Judge Bok's opinion in Commonwealth v. Gordon, supra note 27.

31. 354 U.S. 476 (1957).

32. Id. at 485. Ninth and tenth amendment arguments that hinged on the first amendment claim fell with the latter. Id. at 492–93.

33. Id. at 491–92.

34. Id. at 489.

35. Butler v. Michigan, 352 U.S. 380 (1957), rejected the "most susceptible persons" test by holding unconstitutional a statute forbidding the distribution to adults of materials tending to corrupt minors.

36. Roth, 354 U.S. at 484–85.

37. 383 U.S. 413 (1966) (reversing "Fanny Hill" conviction).

utter lack of redeeming social significance became one of "three elements [that] must coalesce" in order for material to be condemned as obscene; [38] in addition, it had to be shown that "the dominant theme of the material taken as a whole appeals to a prurient interest in sex," and that "the material is patently offensive because it affronts contemporary community standards relating to the description or representation of sexual matters." [39] Because Justices Black and Douglas would have reversed essentially all obscenity convictions, that plurality opinion established a floor for subsequent obscenity prosecutions, but not until 1973 could any five Justices agree on a definition of "what constitutes obscene, pornographic material subject to regulation under the States' police power." [40] In 1973, in *Miller v. California*, a five-Justice majority converged on a modified "test": [41] "The basic guidelines for the trier of fact must be: (a) whether the 'average person, applying contemporary community standards' would find that the work, taken as a whole, appeals to the prurient interest, . . .; (b) whether the work depicts or describes, in a patently offensive way, sexual conduct specifically defined by the applicable state law; and (c) whether the work, taken as a whole, lacks serious literary, artistic, political, or scientific value."

Thus the Court had moved from a view in which the obscene was unprotected *because* utterly worthless (*Roth*), to an approach in which the obscene was unprotected *if* utterly worthless (*Memoirs*), to a conclusion in which obscenity was unprotected even if *not* "utterly" without worth (*Miller*). There is little likelihood that this development has reached a state of rest—or that it will ever do so until the Court recognizes that obscene speech *is* speech nonetheless, although it is subject—as is all speech—to regulation in the interests of unwilling viewers,[42] captive audiences,[43] young children,[44] and beleaguered neigh-

---

38. Id. at 418.

39. Id.

40. Miller v. California, 413 U.S. 15, 22 (1973).

41. Id. at 24. The Court obligingly provided illustrations of what it meant by (b). A state could, for example, proscribe "[p]atently offensive representations or descriptions of masturbation, excretory functions, and lewd exhibition of the genitals." Id. at 25. This aspect of Miller was deemed not an expansion of criminal liability and hence could be applied retroactively. Hamling v. United States, 418 U.S. 87, 116 (1974). On the other hand, the shift from "utterly without redeeming social value" to "lack[ing] serious literary, artistic, political, or scientific value" *was* an expansion and could be applied only to post-Miller conduct. Marks v. United States, 430 U.S. 188 (1977). On the limited relevance of the Miller Court's illustrations, see Ward v. Illinois, 431 U.S. 767 (1977), discussed in note 51, infra.

42. See, e.g., Erznoznik v. Jacksonville, 422 U.S. 205, 211, 215 n. 13 (1975) (invali-

dating an ordinance prohibiting drive-in movie theatres from exhibiting films containing nudity, where the screen is visible from a public street and might offend passersby, as a content-based discrimination among movies which had the effect of deterring theatres from showing nonobscene films containing nudity, but implying that a "narrowly drawn nondiscriminatory traffic regulation requiring screening of drive-in theatres from public view" would be upheld). Cf. Kovacs v. Cooper, 336 U.S. 77, 87–89 (1949) (upholding municipal ordinance forbidding the use of sound trucks which emit "loud and raucous noises": respect for "claims by citizens to comfort and convenience" through barring loud noises justifiable and not an infringement on free expression); Breard v. Alexandria, 341 U.S. 622, 641–45 (1951) (upholding municipal ordinance prohibiting door-to-door solicitation of orders for the sale of goods at private residences without prior consent of owners or occupants: no first amendment right "to force a community to admit the

43.–44. See notes 43–44 on page 910.

borhoods [45]—but *not* in the interest of a uniform vision of how human sexuality should be regarded and portrayed.[46] Until that time, the rules will presumably remain roughly those announced in 1973, with several surviving from the past and a few tacked on more recently.

Specifically, the *Miller* test would apply to words as well as pictures [47] and would require consideration of the work "as a whole." [48] States remain free to adopt communitywide, statewide, or nationwide standards of prurience and patent offensiveness—subject to continuing supervision by the Court to assure that juries do not go too far.[49] Prurient appeal may be defined in terms of the target audience, with more protective standards for children than for adults,[50] and with attention to whatever special groups a book or film might be designed to stimulate.[51] Indeed, a test for obscenity may evaluate not only

solicitors of publications to the home premises" of unwilling residents). See § 12–19, infra.

43. See, e.g., Lehman v. Shaker Heights, 418 U.S. 298, 304 (1974) (Blackmun, J., for four-member plurality), 305–08 (Douglas, J., concurring) (rejecting first amendment challenge to municipal policy of not permitting political advertising, while allowing commercial advertising, on public transit; plurality relying in part, and concurrence entirely, on the interests of the "captive audience" and the resulting "invasion of privacy through forced exposure" to petitioner's ads). See also Public Utilities Commission v. Pollak, 343 U.S. 451, 467 (1952) (Douglas, J., dissenting).

44. See, e.g., Ginsberg v. New York, 390 U.S. 629 (1968) (state may prohibit distribution of materials to minors which may not be barred from adults. Cf. Jacobellis v. Ohio, 378 U.S. 184, 195 (1964) (dictum) (states and localities "might well consider" effectuating their "exigent interest" in preventing the dissemination of materials deemed harmful to children through "preventing distribution of objectionable material to children, rather than . . . totally prohibiting its dissemination"); Federal Communications Commission v. Pacifica Foundation, 438 U.S. 726, 749 (1978) (upholding restrictions on radio broadcasts that include indecent "swear words" because such broadcasts are "uniquely accessible to children").

45. See, e.g., Young v. American Mini Theatres, Inc., 427 U.S. 50, 71–72 (1976) (upholding zoning ordinances limiting the places where movie theatres showing "adult" films may be located; "the city's interest in preserving the character of its neighborhoods" justifies the line drawn in its ordinances); City of Renton v. Playtime Theatres, 106 S.Ct. 925 (1986) (upholding zoning ordinance aimed exclusively at adult theaters and concluding that such an ordinance was content-neutral, thus warranting only minimal scrutiny). Cf. Cox v.

Louisiana, 379 U.S. 559, 562–64 (1965) (finding facially valid a state statute prohibiting picketing in or near a courthouse with the intent to disrupt justice, although reversing a conviction under the statute in the particular case); Grayned v. Rockford, 408 U.S. 104 (1972) (ban on willful noise making near school building, which disrupts the school session, upheld against facial challenge).

46. For a discussion of viewpoint discrimination as it relates to pornography, see § 12–17, infra.

47. Kaplan v. California, 413 U.S. 115 (1973). See id. at 120 (stressing special difficulty of keeping printed material from being handed on to children).

48. Miller v. California, 413 U.S. at 25 n. 7: "'A quotation from Voltaire in the flyleaf of a book will not constitutionally redeem an otherwise obscene publication'", quoting Kois v. Wisconsin, 408 U.S. 229, 231 (1972).

49. Jenkins v. Georgia, 418 U.S. 153 (1974), for example held that no jury could properly find obscene the film "Carnal Knowledge."

50. See, e.g., Ginsberg v. New York, 390 U.S. 629, 638 (1968). But cf. Pinkus v. United States, 436 U.S. 293, 297–98 (1978) (where there is no evidence that children have received the challenged materials, children should not be included as part of the relevant community); Butler v. Michigan, 352 U.S. 380 (1957) (materials may not be kept from adults solely because of their possible or supposed harmful effect on children). Thus, although risk of ultimate exposure to children is relevant in justifying state power to ban obscenity altogether, see note 47, supra, that risk does not warrant adopting for adults a relaxed standard of obscenity that would be permissible when children are directly exposed. Cf. note 44, supra.

51. Mishkin v. New York, 383 U.S. 502 (1966), upheld a conviction for distributing

whether the materials in question appeal to the prurient interest of the average person, but also whether they appeal to the prurient interest of a "deviant sexual group." [52] In close cases, it may be made decisive that "the purveyor's sole emphasis [is] on the sexually provocative aspects of his publications." [53] Neither expert testimony on community

sado-masochistic, fetishistic, and homosexual literature to groups who would find it appealing. Miller left Mishkin undisturbed. See Ward v. Illinois, 431 U.S. 767 (1977) (finding that sado-masochistic materials could be proscribed by state law even though they were not expressly included within the examples of the kinds of sexually explicit representations that Miller used to explicate the aspect of its obscenity definition dealing with patently offensive depictions of sexual conduct). Indeed, in reaffirming Mishkin's continuing approval of bans on sado-masochistic literature, Ward may have extended the scope of Miller. The Illinois statute challenged in Ward failed to define specifically the kinds of sexual conduct description or representation of which the state sought to proscribe. Id. at 770. Such specificity had been required by Miller. 413 U.S. at 24, 27. The Ward majority simply "interpreted" the Illinois statute as incorporating the Miller guidelines—and construed those guidelines to allow the prohibition of sado-masochistic materials even though Miller itself had not referred to such materials. In dissent, Justice Stevens, joined by Justices Brennan, Stewart, and Marshall, argued that the Court's decision marked a substantial departure from the specificity of state law requirement which had been integral to Miller. 431 U.S. 777–78.

Mishkin may be seen as illustrating the lack of a principled foundation for the Court's early obscenity decisions. The defendant in that case had contended that publications depicting deviant sexual practices could not satisfy the "prurient appeal" test of the then-governing Roth decision because they did not excite prurient thoughts in Roth's "average person": "instead of stimulating the erotic," he argued, "they disgust and sicken." 383 U.S. at 508. The Court rejected the argument, modifying the Roth definition to permit suppression of erotica exciting only to the deviant. The Roth average person was replaced by the deviant person in cases where material appealing to the deviant was at stake. However, in reconciling Mishkin with Roth, the Court never asked whether sexual excitement of deviants posed the same social dangers as excitement of the "average person." Dangerous conduct, in the Mishkin Court's view, was not the dominant theme of Roth; the only relevant evil would appear to be the stimu-

lation of "dirty thoughts." Appeal to prurient interest without any regard to further social consequences thus provides the only justification for the decision. But that in effect means a return to the regime of Regina v. Hicklin, L.R. 3 Q.B. 360 (1868), albeit with "new standards of taste for . . . thought control." See generally Note, "More Ado About Dirty Books," 75 Yale L.J. 1364, 1397–98 (1966). Pinkus v. United States, 436 U.S. 293 (1978), appears to have cleared up some of this doctrinal confusion by endorsing a broader formulation of jury instructions. The Court in Pinkus asserted that the determination of the prurient interest of the "average person" can take into account the prurient interests of members of a "deviant social group," among other members of the community. Id. at 302–03. This holding, permitting as it does consideration of the effects of material on *all* members of the community, eliminates the curiously exclusive focus on "dirty thoughts" that Mishkin appeared to invite.

52. Pinkus v. United States, 436 U.S. 293, 302–03 (1978).

53. Ginzburg v. United States, 383 U.S. 463, 470 (1966) (conviction for mailing obscene material upheld on "pandering" theory); Splawn v. California, 431 U.S. 595 (1977) (upholding conviction for sale of allegedly obscene films where jury was instructed it could convict even if the films were protected under Miller provided the circumstances of sale and distribution indicated that the matter was being commercially exploited by the defendants for the sake of its prurient appeal); Pinkus v. United States, 436 U.S. 293, 303–04 (1978) (pandering instruction to jury appropriate in light of evidence including merely the names, locations, and occupations of recipients). But cf. Rabe v. Washington, 405 U.S. 313, 315 (1972) ("pandering" cannot justify conviction for exhibition of nonobscene film where vague obscenity statute fails to give fair notice that pandering is proscribed; Rabe relied on Cole v. Arkansas, 333 U.S. 196, 201 (1948)).

The pandering doctrine is most troubling, not least because identifying "pandering" would appear to be particularly vague and subjective—this in an area not otherwise characterized by the existence of objectively determinate criteria. In Ginzburg, a principal factor found by the Court to support conviction was the fact that

standards [54] nor instructions on precisely what "community" to consider [55] are constitutionally required.

The one group whom the Court has permitted judges to exclude from the community considered by a jury are children, and that exclusion, endorsed in *Pinkus v. United States*, came in a case whose facts may prove readily distinguishable: there was no showing in *Pinkus* that children had actually received the material in question. [56] Thus, each jury, in each town and city, may be a law unto itself, applying what might represent not any widely-shared sense of value

mailing privileges had been sought in Intercourse and Blue Ball, Pennsylvania, and had been obtained in Middlesex, New Jersey, because of the "appeal" of the postmark. 383 U.S. at 467. But where the Court detected the "leer of the sensualist," id., other commentators saw only "the giggle of the college sophomore." Note, supra note 51, at 1387.

The pandering doctrine is made further problematic by the commercial speech doctrine. See § 12–15, supra. Truthful statements which are neither misleading nor obscene are protected to some degree by the first amendment even though made for a commercial purpose. Virginia State Board of Pharmacy v. Virginia Consumers Council, Inc., 425 U.S. 748 (1976); Linmark Associates, Inc. v. Willingboro, 431 U.S. 85 (1977). Nothing said in connection with the marketing of materials in the pandering cases was alleged to be false or misleading, and in both Ginzburg and Splawn the Court assumed that the materials in question might be found nonobscene under the governing tests. Justice Stevens, dissenting in Splawn, suggested that Ginzburg cannot survive Virginia Board of Pharmacy. 431 U.S. at 603 n. 2. Ginzburg was based on the premise that advertising the character of sexual materials may "catch the salaciously disposed," 383 U.S. at 472, and "stimulat[e] the reader to accept them as prurient." Id. at 470. Virginia Board of Pharmacy, wrote Justice Stevens for himself and Justices Stewart and Marshall, rejects " 'this highly paternalistic approach' " (quoting Justice Blackmun's majority opinion in Virginia Board of Pharmacy, 425 U.S. at 770), and assumes " 'that . . . information is not in itself harmful, that people will perceive their own best interests if only they are well enough informed, and that the best means to that end is to open the channels of communication rather than to close them.' ").

Although tainted by vagueness and based on a notion of the diminished legitimacy of commercial speech no longer followed in the adjudication of challenges to restrictions on advertising in sale and distribution of other materials, the pandering

doctrine may illuminate some of the underlying, albeit unstated, assumptions of the Court in the obscenity context. For under the pandering doctrine, "the offensive character of the defendant [is] relevant along with the noxious quality of his speech." Note, supra note 51, at 1364. The Ginzburg Court condemned not so much what the defendant sold but the way he sold it: "the purveyor's sole emphasis is on the sexually provocative aspects of his publication," 383 U.S. at 470–71, rather than on its serious literary merits. It was not the sexual practices described or depicted but Ginzburg's search for "titillation"—his gleeful glorification of the erotic—which constituted the "sordid business of pandering" that so offended the Court. As Professor Richards has suggested, it is opposition to this aspect of pornography "as the unique medium of a vision of sexuality, a 'pornotopia'—a view of sensual delight in the erotic celebration of the body," which may be at the root of obscenity regulation. Richards, "Free Speech and Obscenity Law: Toward a Moral Theory of the First Amendment," 123 U.Pa.L.Rev. 45, 81 (1974). See also note 99, infra.

54. Hamling v. United States, 418 U.S. 87, 125–27 (1974); Paris Adult Theatre I v. Slaton, 413 U.S. 49, 56 (1973).

55. Jenkins v. Georgia, 418 U.S. 153, 157 (1974).

56. 436 U.S. 293, 299–301 (1978) (upholding instructions excluding children but including "sensitive persons" in relevant community). In early 1987, however, the Court agreed to hear a case, Virginia v. American Booksellers Ass'n, 107 S.Ct. 1281 (1987), whose outcome could signal a heightened sensitivity to the effects of sexually explicit material on child viewers. The case raises the question whether states may ban stores from displaying materials obscene for juveniles under Ginsberg v. New York, 390 U.S. 629 (1968), in places where minors might be able to "examine and peruse" them. So long as the risk to children is real rather than imagined, and so long as the challenged ban is not unduly broad or vague, the constitutional case for it seems very strong.

but merely an average of local extremes.[57]   State and local anti-obscenity statutes cannot, however, go so far as to characterize as obscene that which provokes only "normal and healthy sexual desires." [58]   And redeeming social value must be assessed from the supposed perspective of the "reasonable person" rather than in terms of any particular community, whether local or regional or nationwide.[59]

Particularly in light of the possibility of both state and federal prosecution in any locale through which allegedly obscene matter might pass,[60] the pressure on a publisher or distributor to conform to the lowest common denominator of sexual acceptability of course becomes enormous, especially since the defendant need not be shown to have realized that his work was obscene.[61]   Thus, even those states that

57. Nor are states and localities that seek to restrict, ban or penalize obscene films necessarily limited by stringent burden-of-proof standards. See Cooper v. Mitchell Bros. Santa Ana Theater, 454 U.S. 90 (1981) (city, in public nuisance abatement action, is not required as a matter of constitutional law to establish the obscenity of the motion pictures at issue beyond a reasonable doubt).

58. Brockett v. Spokane Arcades, Inc., 472 U.S. 491, 505 (1985) (rejecting overbreadth challenge to Washington state's obscenity statute, but only after excising "normal sexual appetites" from the statutory term "lust").

59. See Pope v. Illinois, 107 S.Ct. 1918 (1987), holding that how the members of "any given community" would value a work cannot constitutionally determine its status as "obscene," Justice White's majority opinion was joined by Chief Justice Rehnquist and Justices Powell, O'Connor, and Scalia. In a dissent joined by Justices Brennan and Marshall, Justice Stevens complained that even the "reasonable person" test could foster "intolerable orthodoxy" and offers no guidance in cases where "reasonable" people might disagree about social value. Justice Blackmun also dissented, but on narrower grounds. In a separate concurrence, Justice Scalia called for reexamination of Miller v. California, 413 U.S. 15 (1973).

60. The need for reconsideration of the constitutional law of obscenity was sharply highlighted by Smith v. United States, 431 U.S. 291 (1977), where the Court upheld a federal criminal conviction, under 18 U.S.C. § 1461, for mailing materials, in response to a request, from one place in Iowa to another, in violation of no Iowa law and without reference to any standard of conduct or depiction recognized by Iowa law. This use of federal criminal prosecutions to vindicate no discernible policy of the place either of mailing or of receipt, and indeed no discernible policy of any involved community, is aggravated by federal power to select, as the place of prosecution and trial, any locality through which allegedly obscene matter is shipped or mailed. Article III, § 2, cl. 3, provides that the "trial of all crimes, except in Cases of Impeachment. . . . shall be held in the State where the said Crimes shall have been committed . . . ." Thus the Framers expressly rejected nationwide venue for federal prosecutions. Yet the "continuing offense" doctrine has made it possible for Congress to provide, in 18 U.S.C. § 3237(a), that "[a]ny offense involving the use of the mails, or transportation in interstate or foreign commerce, is a continuing offense and, except as otherwise expressly provided by enactment of Congress, may be inquired of and prosecuted in any district from, though, or into which such commerce or mail matter moves." In 1958, Congress amended the statute prohibiting the mailing of obscene material, 18 U.S.C. § 1461, to ensure that the continuing offense doctrine would apply to that offense. In Reed Enterprises v. Clark, 278 F.Supp. 372 (D.D.C.1967), aff'd mem. 390 U.S. 457 (1968), a three-judge district court upheld the amendments. In Hamling, Justice Rehnquist rejected the assertion that local standards would impermissibly force national distributors to learn of, and comply with, the local standards of every community through which their material might pass; the danger of state prosecution already compels as much, so no added problem is created by the federal statute. 418 U.S. at 106. But that hardly meets the objection; if anything, it argues against state prosecutions as well. Moreover, it is at least unseemly for the federal government's enormous prosecutorial resources to be deployed in a pursuit of actors and distributors designed to catch them in the most favorable district for prosecutors on the slim ground that their allegedly obscene material passed through on the mail train.

61. Hamling v. United States, 418 U.S. 87, 119–24 (1974); see also Ward v. Illinois,

grant added protection to obscene works under their state constitutions [62] offer relatively little succor to those who would peddle sexually explicit materials across state borders. Despite an ingenious proposal that distributors of sexually explicit material seek declaratory judgments of its "serious value," joining public prosecutors as a class under Federal Rule of Civil Procedure 23,[63] *Miller* and its progeny offer only relatively limited protection to depictions or descriptions of sex, even if only consenting adults are involved.[64]

The Court has offered particularly skimpy protection for sexually explicit materials in cases where such materials involved children either as participants in the events being filmed or as members of the viewing audience. At issue in the 1982 case of *New York v. Ferber* [65] was a state criminal law which prohibited persons from "knowingly promoting sexual performances by children under the age of 16 by distributing material which depicts such performances." The Court, in an opinion by Justice White, took careful note of the severity of the national problem of abuse of children in the production of pornography,[66] and of the fact that the network for marketing "kiddie porn" must be closed down if the campaign against sexual exploitation is to be successful.[67] For the first time in four decades, all nine Justices agreed that a particular kind of communicative material enjoys no first amendment protection whatsoever.[68] Despite the fact that the law proscribed speech that was neither obscene nor otherwise unprotected in itself,[69] the Court upheld the New York criminal statute over a facial

431 U.S. 767 (1977) (upholding against vagueness and overbreadth challenges Illinois statute banning sale of "sado-masochistic materials" in spite of statute's failure to state specifically the kinds of sexual conduct proscribed). But defendant must be shown to have been aware of what the work in fact contained, Smith v. California, 361 U.S. 147 (1959), and must have a personal opportunity to contest its obscenity. McKinney v. Alabama, 424 U.S. 669 (1976).

62. See, e.g., State v. Henry, 302 Or. 510, 732 P.2d 9, 11–12 (1987) (construing protection for speech under Oregon constitution as broader than that provided in the Miller test, quoting from first edition of this treatise to reject idea that obscenity is not entitled to protection as a form of expression).

63. See Note, 88 Harv.L.Rev. 1838 (1975).

64. Paris Adult Theatre I v. Slaton, 413 U.S. 49, 68 (1973) (upholding injunction against showing of hard-core films in "adult theatres").

Of course, even when the first amendment does not protect speech, the rest of the Constitution continues to limit governmental measures aimed at obscenity. Even those who traffic in obscenity are entitled to procedural protections. See, e.g., Vance v. Universal Amusement Co., Inc., 445 U.S. 308 (1980) (per curiam) (in-

validating a state public nuisance statute that permitted injunctions against future exhibition of films not yet shown to be obscene by theatres shown to have exhibited obscene films in the past); Lo-Ji Sales, Inc. v. New York, 442 U.S. 319 (1979) (invalidating use of fill-in-the-blanks "boxcar" warrant to seize obscene material from bookstore); but see Cooper v. Mitchell Bros. Santa Ana Theater, 454 U.S. 90 (1981) (refusing to require that determination of obscenity in civil proceeding be made by a jury or based on proof beyond a reasonable doubt).

65. 458 U.S. 747, 749 (1982). Justice White wrote for the Court, joined by Burger, C.J., and Powell, Rehnquist, O'Connor, JJ. Justice O'Connor also concurred separately, and Justices Brennan, Marshall, Blackmun, and Stevens concurred in the judgment.

66. Id. at 749 & n. 1, 758–59 & nn. 9, 10.

67. Id. at 760 & n. 11 (citing first edition of this treatise).

68. In 1942, the Court had unanimously held that the first amendment protected neither commercial speech, Valentine v. Chrestensen, 316 U.S. 52 (1942), but see § 12–15, nor "fighting words," Chaplinsky v. New Hampshire, 315 U.S. 568 (1942).

69. Ferber, 458 U.S. at 753, 756. Indeed, the Court conceded that the statute

challenge on the ground that preventing the sexual exploitation and abuse of children constitutes a governmental objective of "surpassing importance." [70]

Ferber seems to signal a heightened sensitivity on the Court's part to the harms that pornographic activity can inflict upon *participants* in obscene productions as well as viewers of the resulting materials. Previous opinions, as well as scholarly analyses, had tended to focus almost exclusively on the impact upon the reader or viewer of the obscene.[71] The difference between protecting children as viewers and children as participants is that between a child labor law as enforced in a newspaper shop—which is concerned not with what the paper says, but with the conditions under which children might be harnessed in its production—and a law that suppresses the newspaper because of what it says and the impact it might have on the reader.

In spite of this receptiveness to the regulation of obscenity and child pornography, the Court has insisted that "thematic obscenity" is fully protected as a form of speech, so that a state cannot, for example, ban distribution of a film on the ground that it advocates adultery or makes fornication seem like fun.[72] On this basis the Court has main-

had "arguably impermissible applications," id. at 773, "ranging from medical textbooks to pictorials in the National Geographic," id.; see also id. at 775 (O'Connor, J., concurring), but deemed facial invalidation for overbreadth improper since such applications would not "amount to more than a tiny fraction of the materials within the statute's reach," id. at 773 (opinion of Court); id. at 775 (O'Connor, J., concurring); id. at 776 (Brennan, J., joined by Marshall, J., concurring in judgment). Justice Stevens' concurrence cautioned, however, that the Court's rejection of the facial overbreadth challenge was premature and that a decision on this claim should await a case with a less pressing governmental interest—one in which only a fraction of a film in question was lewd. Id. at 779–80.

70. Id. at 757. See Schauer, "Codifying the First Amendment: New York v. Ferber," 1982 S.Ct.Rev. 285, 287–88 (1982) (arguing that Ferber, in carving out "yet another distinct category of material unprotected by the First Amendment," signals a move on the part of the Court away from applying the "same tests or analytical tools to the entire range of First Amendment problems" and towards a more complex mode of analysis).

71. Until recently, research and writing stressed, for example, the rather tenuous link to crime by the *viewer* or *reader* of the obscene. Consistently overlooked as a rationale for banning at least some types of films had been the link to crime by the *persons being filmed*. Governmental power to prevent murder, rape, and child abuse, for example, should imply power to

destroy the primary economic incentive for a distinct category of abusive acts: the desire to *film the criminal abuse itself* for the titillation of a potential audience jaded by its satiation with other sights and sounds. Although government cannot be allowed the circular argument that films of consenting adult sex should be banned in order to diminish an economic incentive for fornication that might be too private to be punishable (see §§ 15–20, 15–21, infra) but for the fact that the acts are being filmed for viewing by others, no circle is involved when the argument is applied to films of child torture and mutilation, a genre of distressing popularity, see, e.g., Anson, "The Last Porno Show," New Times, Vol. 8, No. 13, June 24, 1977, or of child exploitation, as in Ferber. See 458 U.S. at 752. Given the great practical difficulty of directly enforcing laws against the crimes being filmed (especially if faces are concealed) and given the lack of any economic incentive to commit such crimes *apart* from the market for films of their commission (contrast films of bank robberies, say), it seems insufficient to reply that government must pursue the less restrictive alternative of prosecuting the underlying crimes rather than prosecuting the filmmaker or indeed confiscating the film. It should be noted that this rationale does not apply to descriptions as opposed to actual photographs or recordings. Nor does it apply to films of simulated acts, or to films of conduct causing no harm other than that supposedly caused by the act of viewing.

72. Kingsley International Pictures Corp. v. Regents, 360 U.S. 684 (1959).

tained that the regime it is permitting "is distinct from a control of reason and the intellect." [73] It may be that hardcore pornography has little ideological content—although hedonism is surely an idea—but the first amendment has not generally been confined to the protection of high-minded discussion among savants, and in *Cohen v. California*, the Court reversed a conviction for wearing a jacket inscribed with the words "Fuck the Draft," reasoning that the Constitution protects the "emotive function" of communication no less than its "cognitive content." [74] That obscenity or pornography appeals to viewers at a subconscious level and elicits a response more visceral than cerebral hardly distinguishes it from a great deal of the most effective advertising or, for that matter, political rhetoric.

When it undertook for the first time to explain *why* society could suppress the obscene rather than merely protect the right of people to avoid it if they wished,[75] the Court essentially offered three reasons, placed here in ascending order of generality and diffuseness: (1) that "there is at least an arguable correlation between obscene material and crime;" [76] (2) that states "have the power to make a morally neutral judgment" [77] that public exhibition of obscene material, or commerce in the obscene, tends to "injure the community as a whole" by polluting

73. Paris Adult Theatre I v. Slaton, 413 U.S. 49, 67 (1973).

74. 403 U.S. 15, 26 (1971). To be sure, Cohen's message was political, but cf. Winters v. New York, 333 U.S. 507 (1948) (entertainment materials such as crime and detective stories protected from overbroad ban on obscenity); Joseph Burstyn, Inc. v. Wilson, 343 U.S. 495 (1952) (statute authorizing denial of license to films deemed sacreligious invalidated on vagueness grounds; first amendment protection of motion pictures is "not lessened by the fact that they are designed to entertain as well as to inform").

75. Compare Rowan v. Post Office Dept., 397 U.S. 728 (1970) (upholding statutory scheme whereby individuals could exclude unwelcome mail).

76. Paris Adult Theatre I v. Slaton, 413 U.S. 49, 58 (1973) (citing The Report of the Commission on Obscenity and Pornography 390–412).

77. Paris Adult Theatre I, 413 U.S. at 69. The Court's protestations about the "moral neutrality" of anti-obscenity laws may reflect a view, not shared by this book (see § 15–10, infra), that laws interfering with basic freedoms must above all be defended in amoral terms—whatever those may be. Compare Henkin, "Morals and the Constitution: The Sin of Obscenity," 63 Colum.L.Rev. 391 (1963), arguing that obscenity laws are not based on any concern for the prevention of sex offenses or other forms of crime, but rather are "rooted in this country's religious antecedents, of governmental responsibility for communal and individual decency and morality." Id. at 391, 392–95. Henkin suggests that a morally neutral consensus may be defined and legislated—an approach apparently inconsistent with established first amendment jurisprudence even if the determination of a consensus on morality were currently possible. See, e.g., West Virginia State Board of Education v. Barnette, 319 U.S. 624 (1943) ("If there is any fixed star in our constitutional constellation, it is that no official, high or petty, can prescribe what shall be orthodox in politics, nationalism, religion, or other matters of opinion . . ."); Kingsley International Pictures Corp. v. Regents, 360 U.S. 684 (1959) (first amendment protection "not confined to the expression of ideas that are conventional or shared by a majority. It protects advocacy of the opinion that adultery may sometimes be proper, no less than advocacy of socialism or the single tax."); Wooley v. Maynard, 430 U.S. 705, 714–15 (1977) (that "most individuals agree with the thrust of New Hampshire's motto is not the test; . . . [t]he First Amendment protects the right of individuals to hold a point of view different from the majority and to refuse to foster . . . an idea they find morally objectionable").

the "public environment;"[78] and (3) that "what is commonly read and seen and heard and done intrudes upon us all, want it or not." [79]

The first and third of these reasons apply not only to people watching hard-core films in "a place of public accommodation," [80] where *Paris Adult Theatre I v. Slaton* upholds state power to prosecute, but also to the same people watching the same films in "the privacy of the home," [81] where *Stanley v. Georgia* [82] denies state power to prosecute.[83] Thus those reasons, quite apart from their tenuous character,[84] do not suffice to explain current constitutional doctrine. What of the second reason—"the interest of the public in the quality of life and the total community environment, the tone of commerce in the great city centers?" [85] One may perhaps grant that, even if the marquees were sanitized and the bookstores reduced to unmarked doorways, with just enough warning to exclude those who would be offended but not so much as to accost passersby, there would still be secondary impacts on the surrounding area. But to assert, as the Court has,[86] that unmarked brown envelopes speeding through the mails to Mr. Stanley's protected home impinge on the "total community" environment is surely to claim too much.

Cutting across the Court's three arguments is a general defense of government regulation based on "unprovable assumptions about what is good for the people." [87] We demand no proof of the uplifting quality of "good books, plays, and art" and hence should be satisfied with conjecture when the state acts "on the corollary assumption that commerce in obscene books, or public exhibitions focused on obscene conduct, have a tendency to exert a corrupting and debasing impact. . . ." [88] But the parallel seems fatally flawed, for the state does not and could not compel its adult citizens, on pain of imprisonment, to read Dante, watch Shakespeare, or listen to Brahms.[89]

78. Paris Adult Theatre I, 413 U.S. at 68–69.

79. Id. at 59, quoting from Bickel, 22 The Public Interest 25–26 (Winter 1971).

80. Id. at 66.

81. Id.

82. 394 U.S. 557 (1969), discussed in § 15–20, infra.

83. See Katz, "Privacy and Pornography: Stanley v. Georgia," 1969 Sup.Ct.Rev. 203. See also Marks v. United States, 430 U.S. 188, 198 (1977) (Stevens, J., concurring in part and dissenting in part).

84. See note 27, supra, on applying "clear and present danger" standard to obscenity regulation.

85. Paris Adult Theatre I, 413 U.S. at 58. Presumably these "great city centers" include such places as New York City's Times Square and Boston's Combat Zone.

86. See, e.g., United States v. Reidel, 402 U.S. 351 (1971) (Congress may forbid mailing obscenity to a consenting adult buyer); United States v. Twelve 200-foot Reels, 413 U.S. 123 (1973) (Congress may forbid importation of obscene material for importer's private use); United States v. Orito, 413 U.S. 139 (1973) (Congress may forbid interstate transportation of obscenity for transporter's private use).

87. Paris Adult Theatre I, 413 U.S. at 62.

88. Id. at 63.

89. The Court's sensitivity to the possibility that sexually explicit materials or productions might have redeeming social, literary, artistic or political merit that saves them from condemnation as "obscene" is notably absent in one set of cases: those in which sexually explicit (or even merely nude) performances are accompanied by the sale of alcohol. The doctrinal rationale typically invoked by the Court in defense of this decisional practice is that the twenty-first amendment confers upon the states broad regulatory authority regarding intoxicating liquors. See City of Newport v. Iacobucci, 107 S.Ct. 383 (1986) (upholding Kentucky city ordinance,

To some, the obscene and the pornographic depict man reduced to the sorry sum of his basest appetites;[90] to others, obscenity eases psychosexual tensions or provides a release through fantasy, much like disaster films or soap operas, from the confines of the dreary present. To some, it represents shameless exploitation of the frustrated and the compulsive; to others, it symbolizes liberation from the compulsions of a leaden, regimented, and ultimately oppressive social order. The pride Comstock felt at having destroyed "something over fifty tons of vile books [and] 3,984,063 obscene pictures,"[91] most of which today would be likely to shock no one, should suggest a sober skepticism about any claim that the latest threat to decency has finally crossed the line of the tolerable: what was once beyond the pale rests comfortably on today's living-room end table.

The mid-1970's prosecutions of people who publish magazines like *Hustler*—a mix of eroticism, violence, and misogyny—may finally have separated the literati from the targets of government censorship. It has been thoughtfully observed that the "journey from *Ulysses* to *Hustler* involves more than a move from literature to smut, from words to images. It involves the transition from the preoccupation of an educated minority to the everyday fantasies of the bluecollar majority. . . . Once upon a time, obscenity was confined to expensive leather-bound editions available only to gentlemen. . . . One of the questions asked by the crown prosecutor [in the trial of the publisher of Lady Chatterly's Lover] . . . was: 'Would you let your servant read this book?' . . . *Hustler* is the servant's revenge."[92] Understandably anxious to avoid the embarrassing literary censorship of earlier times, the Court has retreated to a posture in which the erotic tastes of the educated and well bred emerge as part of the "grand conception of the First Amendment and its high purposes in the historic struggle for freedom," while the less fashionable eroticism of the masses becomes the mere subject of "commercial exploitation of obscene material."[93] Even if an intelligible line could be drawn between the two categories—

passed pursuant to state delegation, prohibiting nude or nearly nude dancing in local establishments licensed to sell liquor); New York State Liquor Authority v. Bellanca, 452 U.S. 714 (1981) (upholding as within state's broad powers under the twenty-first amendment a New York regulation prohibiting nude dancing in establishments licensed by the state to sell liquor, regardless of any artistic or communicative value attaching to such dancing); California v. LaRue, 409 U.S. 109 (1972) (upholding California regulations prohibiting explicitly sexual live entertainment in bars and other establishments licensed to sell liquor). But see 324 Liquor Corp. v. Duffy, 107 S.Ct. 720 (1987) (no twenty-first amendment exception in anti-trust laws), discussed in § 6–24, supra. Nevertheless, in practice one senses that the Court is primarily motivated by its perception of a detrimental (and potentially crime-inducing) synergy between sex or nudity and alcohol. It is noteworthy that the Court has looked with stern disfavor on similar bans on nude dancing in places *not* serving liquor. See Schad v. Borough of Mt. Ephraim, 452 U.S. 61 (1981) (striking down New Jersey ordinance banning live entertainment, including nude dancing, for impermissibly prohibiting a wide range of expression protected by the first amendment).

90. See, e.g., H. Clor, Obscenity and Public Morality: Censorship in a Liberal Society (1969).

91. C. G. Trumbull, Anthony Comstock, Fighter 239 (1913).

92. Neville, "Has the First Amendment Met its Match?" N.Y. Times, March 6, 1977, § 6, at p. 16.

93. Miller v. California, 413 U.S. 15, 34 (1973).

and Justice Brennan seems correct in concluding that it cannot [94]—it would remain the case that "grossly disparate treatment of similar offenders," [95] to use Justice Stevens' phrase, would inhere in the Supreme Court's own "enlightened" position of selective tolerance for the tastefully salacious coupled with contempt for the coarsely vulgar.[96]

Although it might be possible to reconcile first amendment premises as well as norms of even-handed treatment with "time, place, and manner" regulations of sexually explicit or violent materials,[97] the attempt to single out some images or ideas for complete suppression outside the protected enclave of the home seems ultimately incompatible with the first amendment premise that awareness can never be deemed harmful in itself.[98] For in the last analysis, suppression of the obscene persists because it tells us something about ourselves that some of us, at least, would prefer not to know. It threatens to explode our uneasy accommodation between sexual impulse and social custom—to destroy the carefully-spun social web holding sexuality in its place.[99] One need not "sound the alarm of repression" [100] in order to argue that the desire to preserve that web by shutting out the thoughts and impressions that challenge it cannot be squared with a constitutional commitment to openness of mind.

94. See Paris Adult Theatre I v. Slaton, 413 U.S. 49, 73 (1973) (Brennan, J., joined by Stewart and Marshall, JJ., dissenting); id. at 84 ("none of the available formulas . . . can reduce the vagueness to a tolerable level;" "[a]lthough we have assumed that obscenity does exist and that we 'know it when [we] see it,' . . ., we are manifestly unable to describe it in advance except by reference to concepts so elusive that they fail to distinguish clearly between protected and unprotected speech"). See also Marks v. United States, 430 U.S. 188, 198 (1977) (Stevens, J., concurring in part and dissenting in part) ("the present . . . standards . . . are so intolerably vague that evenhanded enforcement of the law is a virtual impossibility . . . [G]rossly disparate treatment of similar offenders is a characteristic of the criminal enforcement of obscenity law").

95. Marks v. United States, 430 U.S. at 198.

96. Even the line between Stanley v. Georgia, 394 U.S. 557 (1969), and Paris Adult Theatre I v. Slaton, 413 U.S. 49 (1973), tends to coincide with a distinction between polite society and hoi polloi; for protecting the living-room gathering around the privately-owned film projector, but not the adult theatre crowd, smacks of economic and cultural discrimination. See § 12–23, infra.

97. See, e.g., Young v. American Mini Theatres, 427 U.S. 50 (1976), discussed in §§ 12–18, 12–19, infra.

98. See Virginia State Board of Pharmacy v. Virginia Citizens Consumer Council, Inc., 425 U.S. 748 (1976) (commercial advertising protected by first amendment); Linmark Associates, Inc. v. Willingboro, 431 U.S. 85 (1977) (residential "for sale" signs protected); see § 12–15 supra. But see the discussion of New York v. Ferber, 458 U.S. 747 (1982), supra, for a more limited (though more powerful) rationale for suppressing a special category of films.

99. See, e.g., Richards, supra note 53, at 81: "In opposition to the Victorian view that narrowly defines proper sexual function in a rigid way that is analogous to ideas of excremental regularity and moderation, pornography builds a model of plastic variety and joyful excess in sexuality. In opposition to the sorrowing Catholic dismissal of sexuality as an unfortunate and spiritually superficial concomitant of propagation, pornography affords the alternative idea of the independent status of sexuality as a profound and shattering ecstasy."

100. Miller v. California, 413 U.S. 15, 34 (1973).

§ 12–17. New Approaches to the Problem of Sexually Explicit Material: Pornography and Feminism

In recent years, the predominant means of checking the spread of sexually explicit materials—time, place and manner restriction—has begun to give way in some locales to ordinances designed not to disperse or suppress erotica but to eliminate something described as "pornography." Typically such measures have operated by empowering women allegedly injured by the production or dissemination of pornography to bring civil suits against those who make or sell it, seeking damages or injunctive relief.[1] Spurred on by feminist groups and literature,[2] these measures—largely drafted by Professor Catherine MacKinnon and Andrea Dworkin—have sought to define and attack pornography as coercive of women and as establishing and reinforcing male supremacy. The one such measure challenged in the courts, an Indianapolis ordinance, was invalidated as impermissibly viewpoint-specific, and other such measures—despite their good intentions and the creativity reflected by their structure—seem likely to fall prey to other potent constitutional attacks, including overbreadth and vagueness. Nevertheless, the growing national hostility to pornography, epitomized by the late 1986 endorsement of a national anti-pornography campaign by the Attorney General's Commission on Pornography,[3] makes it likely that more and more anti-pornography measures will arise and provoke constitutional challenges.

The impetus for such new anti-pornography legislation stems largely from the distinctive gender-related harms posed by pornography, defined not as supposedly offensive erotic material but as the graphic, sexually explicit depiction of rape or other forms of male subordination of females. Such harms have been emphasized (and indeed conceptualized) only in recent years.[4] First, pornography directly harms women who are either coerced into or brutalized during the process of participating in pornographic works.[5] The resulting protective rationale for suppressing pornography resonates with the concern for child participants in pornographic films evoked by the Supreme Court in the child-pornography case of *New York v. Ferber*,[6] although the concern for children's legal incapacity and the consequent involuntariness under-

---

§ 12–17

1. As of early 1987, sweeping anti-pornography legislation had been passed in Indianapolis and proposed in Cambridge, Los Angeles and Minneapolis. The mayor of Minneapolis twice vetoed anti-pornography bills approved by the city council. See Attorney General's Comm'n on Pornography, U.S. Dep't of Justice, Final Report 392 (1986).

2. For examples of such literature, see, e.g., A. Dworkin, Pornography: Men Possessing Women (1981); MacKinnon, Address, Women and the Law Conference, Washington, D.C. (April, 1983); MacKinnon, "Not a Moral Issue," 2 Yale L. & Pol'y Rev. 321 (1984); MacKinnon, "Pornogra-

phy, Civil Rights and Speech," 20 Harv. C.R.-C.L.L.Rev. 1 (1985).

3. See supra note 1.

4. See Sunstein, "Pornography and the First Amendment," 1986 Duke L.J. 589, 594–602 (1986) (arguing that the specific rationales for regulating pornography—particularly the harms to participants, to the victims of sex crimes generated by pornography, and to society through social conditioning—differ from the vague justifications for restricting obscenity as it had previously been defined).

5. Id. at 595–97.

6. 458 U.S. 747 (1982), discussed in § 12–16, supra.

girding *Ferber* makes that case theoretically distinguishable from those involving adult women or men.[7]

Second, pornography is widely believed to encourage sexual violence against women.[8] Finally, and most indirectly, pornography is thought to condition both men and women into accepting certain gender roles and relationships as appropriate [9]—perceptions that in turn can encourage judges and jurors to blame victims of rape rather than their assailants,[10] and can fuel discrimination in hiring, education, and other walks of life. Because the Supreme Court's definition of obscenity in the *Roth-Miller* line of cases [11] does not extend so far as to permit localities to respond to many such perceived harms by banning pornographic works as unprotected obscenity, cities have increasingly considered anti-pornography measures to restrict sexually explicit books, productions and practices, defined in terms reflecting *not* the anti-erotic premises of the Court's obscenity concept but the feminist premises suggested by this gender-specific set of injuries to women.

By far the most celebrated such ordinance was that adopted by the city of Indianapolis in 1984 and ultimately struck down by the United States Court of Appeals for the Seventh Circuit in *American Booksellers Association, Inc. v. Hudnut*,[12] a decision summarily affirmed by the Supreme Court.[13] Indianapolis' ordinance was predicated upon its city council's finding that "pornography is a systematic practice of exploitation and subordination based on sex which differentially harms women." [14] Accordingly, the council prohibited a wide and disparate

---

7. See Ferber, 458 U.S. at 756–57 ("a State's interest in 'safeguarding the physical and psychological well-being of a minor' is 'compelling.'" (quoting Globe Newspaper Co. v. Superior Court for Norfolk County, 457 U.S. 596, 607 (1982)).

8. See Sunstein, supra note 4, at 597–601 (summarizing laboratory studies, victim accounts and governmental reports linking pornography and sexual violence); Attorney General's Comm'n on Pornography, supra note 1, at 852–69 (demonstrating connection between the spread of pornography and illegal activity); MacKinnon, "Pornography, Civil Rights, and Speech," 20 Harv.C.R.-C.L.Rev. 1, 12 n. 20 (1985) (citing sources demonstrating connection between pornography and violence).

9. See Sunstein, supra note 4, at 601. Cf. Beauharnais v. Illinois, 343 U.S. 250 (1952) (upholding conviction under statute prohibiting dissemination of materials promoting racial or religious hatred), a holding widely assumed not have survived New York Times Co. v. Sullivan, 376 U.S. 254 (1964) (holding, in relevant part, that public officials bringing libel suits must prove that a defamatory statement was directed at the official personally, and not simply at a unit of government). See Collin v. Smith, 578 F.2d 1197, 1205 (7th Cir. 1978) (citing cases expressing "doubt, which we

share, that *Beauharnais* remains good law after the constitutional libel cases").

10. See generally S. Estrich, Real Rape (1987).

11. The Supreme Court's evolving obscenity doctrine is discussed in § 12–16, supra.

12. 771 F.2d 323 (7th Cir. 1985).

13. Hudnut v. American Booksellers Assn., Inc., 106 S.Ct. 1172 (1986).

14. The Indianapolis City Council included the following "findings of fact" in the text of its ordinance:

"Pornography is a discriminatory practice based on sex which denies women equal opportunities in society. Pornography is central in creating and maintaining sex as a basis for discrimination. Pornography is a systematic practice of exploitation and subordination based on sex which differentially harms women. The bigotry and contempt it promotes, with the acts of aggression it fosters, harm women's opportunities for equality of rights in employment, education, access to and use of public accommodations, and acquisition of real property; promote rape, battery, child abuse, kidnapping and prostitution and inhibit just enforcement of laws against such acts; and contribute significantly to restricting women in particular from full exer-

array of practices it termed discriminatory. Among them were "trafficking" [15] in pornography and "forcing" pornography on a person in any place of employment, school, home or public place.[16] The city also sought to act against those who coerced, intimidated or tricked others into performing in a pornographic production or appearing in a pornographic work,[17] giving victims rights to enjoin such behavior through cease and desist orders and rights to collect compensatory damages. Finally, the city sought to provide victims of sexual violence with a civil cause of action against sellers of specific pornographic works that the victims alleged had directly caused an assault or physical attack on them.[18] For all these purposes, the city defined "pornography" as "the graphic sexually explicit subordination of women." [19] The ordinance provided for no enforcement by criminal proceedings, or by official condemnation proceedings of the black-listing variety,[20] or by civil forfeiture actions initiated by public authorities.[21]

Despite this absence of any criminal or quasi-criminal enforcement mechanism, the Indianapolis ordinance drew an immediate anticipatory challenge from an array of distributors of books, magazines and films, all of whom sought to enjoin the regulation. A federal district court in Indiana struck the regulation down. Because much of the speech curtailed by the city was non-obscene, the ordinance was subject to first amendment scrutiny—and because adult women generally have the ability to protect themselves from being victimized by pornography, the district court held the city's interest in checking pornography to be

cise of citizenship and participation in public life, including in neighborhoods."

American Booksellers Assn., Inc. v. Hudnut, 598 F.Supp. 1316, 1320 (S.D. Ind. 1984) (quoting § 16–1(a)(2) of the Code of Indianapolis and Marion County, Indiana) (hereinafter, "the Code").

15. Id. (quoting § 16–3–(g)(4) of the Code). The ordinance defined "trafficking" as "[t]he production, sale, exhibition, or distribution of pornography."

16. Id. (quoting § 16–3(g)(6) of the Code).

17. Id. (quoting § 16–3(g)(5) of the Code). The ordinance embodied a broad notion of coercion, specifically providing that consent was not to be inferred from a grant of permission from a spouse or other relative, from the fact that the person had previously posed for a sexually explicit picture, or even from the fact that the person knew that the purpose of the acts or events in question was to make pornography and accepted payment for engaging in such acts. Id. (quoting § 16–3(g)(6)).

18. Id. (quoting § 16–3(g)(7) of the Code). If a victim could persuade a local committee of such causation, she would be entitled to remedies including a cease and desist order, compensatory damages, and "further affirmative action as will effectuate the purposes of this chapter." Id. at

1324 (quoting § 16–24 of the Code of Indianapolis and Marion County, Indiana).

19. Id. at 1320 (quoting § 16–3(q) of the Code). In adding content to this arguably vague definition of pornography, the city limited its ordinance to situations where such works presented women as sexual objects enjoying pain or humiliation or rape; or as tied up, cut up, mutilated or penetrated by objects or animals; in scenarios of degradation, injury, abusement, or torture; or as meant for domination, conquest, violation, exploitation, possession, use or submission. Id.

20. Cf. Bantam Books, Inc. v. Sullivan, 372 U.S. 58 (1963) (invalidating as impermissible "informal censorship" a Rhode Island law empowering a commission to recommend prosecutions of distributors of those books it deemed to contain "obscene, indecent, or impure language" or "manifestly tending to the corruption of the youth").

21. The ordinance did establish a city "operating board" which was empowered, based on a complaint by any aggrieved person or by one of its own members with reasonable cause, to initiate an investigation and public hearing into the offending activity. Id. at 1321 (quoting § 16–17(a) of the Code).

insufficiently compelling to justify the curtailment of speech, even by threatened civil actions brought by alleged victims. Moreover, the court held, the ordinance's indefinite terminology—for example, its reference to literature graphically showing the "subordination of women"—was impermissibly vague and thus violated the due process clause.[22]

On appeal, the United States Court of Appeals for the Seventh Circuit affirmed.[23] Judge Frank Easterbrook's opinion for a unanimous panel agreed that Indianapolis' conception of "pornography" included much that was not encompassed within the Supreme Court's definition of unprotected "obscenity." As a result, the appeals court, invoking an array of Supreme Court decisions protecting unpopular or offensive speech,[24] held unconstitutional the city's attempt to subject all such speech to a special legal regime. It did so even while conceding that pornography does not convey a cognitive idea like those expressed in some of the cases on which the court relied. "If pornography is what pornography does," concluded Judge Easterbrook, "so is other speech" to which the Supreme Court had granted protection.[25]

The most striking aspect of Judge Easterbrook's opinion—and the one most likely to influence future courts evaluating anti-pornography measures—was his conclusion that the Indianapolis ordinance constituted impermissible discrimination on the basis of viewpoint. Defending its ordinance, Indianapolis had argued that the measure was justifiable because it restricted only "low value" speech. The Seventh Circuit responded that in no case in which low value speech was subjected to special regulation had a legislature expressly sought to differentiate between viewpoints. By contrast, emphasized Judge Easterbrook, Indianapolis, in banning all "graphic sexually explicit subordination in works great and small" in its definition for "pornography," [26] had created a constitutionally impermissible "approved point of view," which the appeals court likened to "thought control." [27] In particular, the court concluded, the city's ordinance "established an approved view of women, of how they may react to sexual encounters [and] of how the sexes may relate to each other." [28] Because the

22. American Booksellers Assn., Inc. v. Hudnut, 598 F.Supp. 1316, 1329–42 (S.D. Ind. 1984).

23. American Booksellers Assn., Inc. v. Hudnut, 771 F.2d 323 (7th Cir. 1985).

24. Id. at 328, citing Brandenburg v. Ohio, 395 U.S. 444 (1969) (protecting racist advocacy by Ku Klux Klan members), De Jonge v. Oregon, 299 U.S. 353 (1937) (protecting Communists' right to speak and seek office), and Collin v. Smith, 578 F.2d 1197 (7th Cir.), cert. denied 439 U.S. 916 (1978) (permitting Nazi Party march through substantially Jewish community).

25. 771 F.2d at 329. In this vein, the court observed, "Racial bigotry, anti-semitism, violence on television, reporters' biases—these and many more influence the culture and shape our socialization. None is directly answerable by more speech. . . . Yet all is protected as speech, however insidious. Any other answer leaves the government in control of all of the institutions of culture, the great censor and director of which thoughts are good for us." Id. at 330.

26. Id. at 331–32.

27. Id. at 328.

28. Id. See also the amicus brief filed against the ordinance by a group that called itself Feminists Against Censorship Taskforce, arguing that the ordinance constitutes forbidden gender discrimination, denying women who want them the erotic experiences they would find liberating.

definition of pornography was "defective root and branch," [29] the court concluded, the ordinance—in all its applications—was unconstitutional. By a 6–3 vote, the Supreme Court summarily affirmed.[30]

The Seventh Circuit's underlying hostility to the Indianapolis ordinance in *Hudnut* was understandable in light of the broad character of the legislation, which—unlike the Supreme Court's definition of obscenity—failed entirely to take into account whether the subordinating works in dispute had any social, literary, artistic, political or scientific value. Nevertheless, the court's anticipatory repudiation of the ordinance (which had not yet been applied) seemed at once premature and unduly sweeping. For one thing, Judge Easterbrook's opinion oddly failed to draw any distinctions between the very different categories of behavior addressed by the city's ordinance. A decision to remove from public areas posters featuring a graphic depiction of a woman proven to have been coerced into performing in a pornographic production would hardly be suspect under the first amendment. Yet, in lumping such protective steps alongside the more constitutionally questionable actions sanctioned by the ordinance—for example, the removal from bookstores of works found to have inspired some rapists—the court paid insufficient heed to the ways in which many potential applications of the ordinance could be defended as valid. Judge Easterbrook's summary condemnation of the ordinance for sweeping beyond the Supreme Court's definition of obscenity likewise overlooked the considerable overlap between the graphic depictions which Indianapolis characterized as "pornography" and those depictions defined as "obscene" under the *Roth-Miller* line of cases. It would have been more appropriate—and surely more consonant with a restrained view of federal judicial intervention—to abstain from deciding *Hudnut* until a specific civil enforcement challenge had emerged.[31]

In spite of its apparent rush to judgment, the *Hudnut* court's overarching substantive conclusion—that Indianapolis impermissibly discriminated among viewpoints by installing heavy legal artillery aimed at sexually explicit works that depict women as desiring or deserving subordination to men—seems correct, although this shortcoming need hardly have scuttled those aspects of the ordinance aimed solely at the products of coerced conduct—for example, the ordinance's *Ferber*-like provision for the victims of forced pornographic performances.[32] As the Supreme Court stated in 1959 when it struck down a

---

29. 771 F.2d at 332.

30. Hudnut v. American Booksellers Assn., Inc., 106 S.Ct. 1172 (1986). Chief Justice Burger and Justices Rehnquist and O'Connor voted to hear arguments in the case.

31. Judge Easterbrook's contention that the case was in fact ripe rested on his assertion that "[W]e gain nothing by waiting. Time would take a toll, however, on the speech of the parties subject to the act. . . . Deferred adjudication would produce tempered speech without assisting in resolution of the controversy." Id. at

327. The Seventh Circuit's opinion overlooked, however, the fact that none of the plaintiffs challenging the antipornography ordinance in Hudnut had alleged that they suffered any actual or threatened injury, much less an actual threat of prosecution or even civil suit, as a result of the ordinance. See Jurisdictional Statement of Appellees, Hudnut v. American Booksellers Assn., Inc., at 26 (1986).

32. The ordinance's effort to rectify non-beholder harms need not founder on the shoals of viewpoint-specificity. Such a measure seems functionally similar to tort-

New York law denying licenses to show movies presenting adultery in a favorable light, the first amendment's "guarantee is not confined to the expression of ideas that are conventional or shared by a majority. It protects advocacy of the opinion that adultery may sometimes be proper, no less than advocacy of socialism or the single tax." [33] Presumably, the first amendment similarly protects advocacy—however sexually explicit or graphic—of the opinion that women were meant to be dominated by men, or blacks to be dominated by whites, or Jews by Christians, and that those so subordinated not only deserve but subconsciously enjoy their humiliating treatment. That such opinions are despicable and that their dissemination works real injury does not render their suppression consistent with the first amendment.

It is an inadequate response to argue, as do some scholars, that ordinances like that enacted by Indianapolis take aim at harms, not at expression.[34] *All* viewpoint-based regulations are targeted at some supposed harm, whether it be linked to an unsettling ideology like Communism or Nazism or to socially shunned practices like adultery. Indeed, the most interesting defenses of at least some parts of the Indianapolis ordinance, while provocative, seem to rest on too narrow a conception of the ban on viewpoint-based restrictions. It has been suggested, for example, that courts would be likely to uphold a statute selectively criminalizing incitement to violent lawless action in speech aimed *against* the government, so long as the standards of *Brandenburg v. Ohio* [35] were met.[36] That prediction may well be correct, but relying on it to defend the anti-pornography ordinance elides a critical distinction between the *Brandenburg* scenario and laws suppressing speech that endorses the subordination of women. It is beyond dispute that government may choose to outlaw the incitement of various acts independently deemed crimes—including murder, rape, or, indeed, the

law remedies for defamation or invasion of privacy—constitutionally valid even when such remedies do not sweep beyond some content-based subset of the entire set of materials posing the same sort of threat to personal integrity. Judge Easterbrook's opinion attempted to distinguish application of the Indianapolis ordinance to a coerced sexual performance from a hypothetical case in which "someone forced a prominent political figure, at gunpoint, to endorse a candidate for office." 771 F.2d at 332. In such a case, the Seventh Circuit reasoned, "a state could forbid the commercial sale of the film containing that coerced endorsement." Id. The court's supposed distinction—that the Indianapolis statute, unlike the ban on the sale of the film featuring the politician, is "not neutral with respect to viewpoint," id. at 332—overlooks the fundamental objection to coerced performances: that the injury they pose, like that in Ferber, see § 12–16, supra, is not an injury to anyone who watches, and may occur even if the performances are never, in fact, viewed. Rather, the injury is felt by the person coerced into

performing or having graphic depictions of her performance displayed or distributed so that they *might* be viewed. The fact that similar harms could in theory also occur in entirely non-sexual settings neither requires the city to draft a law broad enough to reach all such harms, nor renders impermissibly viewpoint-based a law of less ambitious scope. Ferber itself necessarily establishes as much.

33. Kingsley International Pictures Corp. v. Regents of N.Y.U., 360 U.S. 684, 689 (1959).

34. See, e.g., Sunstein, "Pornography and the First Amendment," 1986 Duke L.J. 589, 612 (1986) (endorsing as constitutional anti-pornography legislation "directed at harm rather than at viewpoint [whose] purpose would be to prevent sexual violence and discrimination, not to suppress expression of a point of view").

35. 395 U.S. 444 (1969).

36. See, e.g., Sunstein, supra note 34, at 614.

violent overthrow of the government. Likewise, government may surely outlaw the direct incitement of sexual violence against women. Nor,
in so doing, need it outlaw equally the incitement of all other illegal
acts.[37] It is, however, altogether different, and far more constitutionally tenuous, for government to outlaw, or to make civilly actionable, the
incitement of violence against women *only* when such incitement is
caused by words or pictures that express a particular point of view:
that women are meant for domination.[38] The analogue would be a ban
on anti-capitalist speeches that incite robbery, leaving other equally
effective incitements to robbery unprohibited; or a ban on incitements
to violence against racial or religious minorities, applicable only when
such incitements are conveyed through expressions of racial or religious
bigotry. To be sure, one who incites arson against an NAACP headquarters in a racist speech is more reprehensible than one who incites
the very same arson to collect insurance proceeds, but to punish the
former more severely than the latter is, arguably, to penalize a reprehensible point of view *as such*.[39]

A related harm-based rationale for creating causes of action like
some of those established by Indianapolis—that pornography conditions
society to accept an abusive and hierarchical view of relationships
between men and women—would also appear to run afoul of the
Supreme Court's demanding first amendment jurisprudence. The argument in favor of the ordinance is akin to that with respect to "group
libel": those who defame an entire social group, like blacks, or women,
or Jews, should be no less accountable merely because their victims are
not individually identifiable. Decades ago, the Supreme Court showed
some receptiveness to such claims, particularly in the 1952 case of
Beauharnais v. Illinois,[40] in which the Court upheld a conviction under
an Illinois statute prohibiting the dissemination of materials promoting
racial or religious hatred. Nevertheless, subsequent cases seem to have
sapped *Beauharnais* of much of its force. In particular, the landmark
libel case of *New York Times Co. v. Sullivan*[41] seemed to some[42] to
eclipse *Beauharnais'* sensitivity to group libel or group defamation
claims—not only because *New York Times* sweepingly endorsed "a

---

37. Cf. note 32, supra. See, e.g.,
Posadas de Puerto Rico Associates v. Tourism Co. of Puerto Rico, 106 S.Ct. 2968
(1986) (upholding Puerto Rican law that
forbade advertisements inviting citizens of
Puerto Rico to gamble legally in casinos).

38. Defenders of the Indianapolis approach might argue that their law is not
precisely of this character, since the criminal laws of most states *already* criminalize
incitement to lawless violence of *all* kinds.
Even if this is so, singling out for especially
burdensome treatment those films or books
that express a particular viewpoint *and*
might later be found to have met the incitement test surely represents viewpoint-
based regulation. Particularly is this so
where, as in the Indianapolis ordinance,
films and books graphically expressing the
objectionable viewpoint are subject to civil
suits on any of several theories, some of

them completely unrelated to any assault
allegedly incited by the offending material.

39. Perhaps, however, a legislature
could properly decide that, for example,
only racist or sexist incitements posed a
serious threat of racial or sexual violence
and could, on that basis, justify making
only such incitements criminally punishable or civilly actionable. Even if that is so,
however, considerable portions of the Indianapolis ordinance would remain constitutionally infirm.

40. 343 U.S. 250 (1952). See § 12–12,
supra.

41. 376 U.S. 254 (1964).

42. See, e.g., Collin v. Smith, 578 F.2d
1197, 1205 (7th Cir. 1978) (citing cases expressing "doubt, which we share, that
Beauharnais remains good law after the
constitutional libel cases").

profound national commitment to the principle that debate on public issues should be uninhibited, robust, and wide-open," [43] but also because *New York Times* required public officials bringing libel suits to prove that a defamatory statement was directed at the official personally, and not simply at a unit of government. The arguments animating *New York Times'* suspicion of claims seeking to vindicate group reputational interests seem particularly devastating to the cause of action Indianapolis sought to give women affronted by works depicting the subordination of women. How could a group "disprove" the viewpoint, despicable though it is, that women enjoy being subordinated? [44] And what public body is qualified or entitled to decide which claims about entire social groups are true and which are false? If "under the First Amendment there is no such thing as a false idea," [45] then *no* official may be entrusted with power to resolve such matters.

Nor, finally, is the constitutional case against regulation substantially weakened by the fact—conceded by the Seventh Circuit—that pornography, unlike much overtly political speech, works primarily through the subconscious and triggers a reaction more physiological than rational. For while pornography imperfectly suits the utilitarian "marketplace of ideas" rationale for the first amendment, the Supreme Court has never hinged the first amendment protection it accords a statement on the intellectual power of the ideas contained within. [46] The fact that pornography's effect on a viewer's outlook may be subliminal thus hardly justifies granting authority to a licensing board, or to a judge, to determine which depictions qualify as subliminal subordination, or which instances of the eroticization of violence are acceptable. [47] It is also difficult to conceive of a meaningful limiting principle to a constitutional doctrine according reduced protection to speech that works on the unconscious.

The ordinance condemned in *Hudnut* derived much of its political strength from the perception that it rectified—not created—an imbalance in speech. Specifically, advocates of Indianapolis' ordinance urged, pornography has the effect of silencing women by broadly disempowering them—and thus Indianapolis' anti-pornography measure was justified as an effort, in effect, to remove the gags on women

---

43. 376 U.S. at 270.

44. See Philadelphia Newspapers, Inc. v. Hepps, 475 U.S. 767 (1986) (placing burden of proving falsity of speech—as well as fault—on the person claiming to have been defamed).

45. Gertz v. Robert Welch, Inc., 418 U.S. 323, 339 (1974).

46. Indeed, the Court in Cohen v. California, 403 U.S. 15 (1971), in reversing a conviction for wearing a jacket bearing the words "Fuck the Draft," powerfully endorsed the idea that the "emotive function" of words, as well as their impact on reason, also warrants first amendment protection. Id. at 26. Judge Easterbrook's assertions that "almost all cultural stimuli provoke unconscious responses" and that even speech triggering primarily "unthink-

ing responses" warrants protection, 771 F.2d at 330, thus properly recognize the limits to the "marketplace of ideas" metaphor as the rationale for first amendment protection. See § 12–10, supra.

47. In any event, the central feminist argument in favor of suppressing pornography itself concedes, and indeed draws much of its strength from, the idea that pornography has an ideological component, distasteful as the ideology of male dominance may be, and that pornography serves to reinforce that ideology and thus to silence women. See Sunstein, supra note 4, at 607 (citing S. Brownmiller, Against Our Will: Men, Women and Rape 394 (1975) ("Pornography is the undiluted essence of antifemale propaganda")).

imposed by pornographers. The difficulty with this proposition, appealing though it may seem, is that the Supreme Court has been strongly resistant to arguments that would justify governmental restrictions on speech as a means of equalizing power in the "marketplace of ideas." Even in the heavily regulated area of election finance law—an area where one might expect the Court to look more favorably upon ceilings imposed on moneyed speech—the Court has inveighed against restrictions on expenditures on behalf of political candidates.[48] More generally, arguments in favor of suppressing a type of speech on the ground that it has the ultimate effect of devaluing or disempowering others' speech appeal to unverifiable and deeply contested intuitions. Arguments of this sort seem in principle illimitable. Claims of a "disempowering impact" could, with some plausibility, result in the government-ordered cancellation of numerous television commercials that depict women as deferential, or in the restriction of numerous works of literature, like *Huckleberry Finn*, that appear to characterize blacks as inferior to whites.

The Supreme Court's refusal to explain its summary affirmance of the Seventh Circuit's decision in *Hudnut* leaves unsettled the viability of future anti-pornography ordinances. Nevertheless, it is likely that states and localities concerned about the proliferation of sexually explicit books and films, whether for genuinely feminist reasons or out of prudishness, will take their cue from *Hudnut* and draft more targeted legislation in the future. Those measures carefully focusing on non-beholder harms—on the outrageous treatment of participants in pornographic enterprises, for example—would seem to stand a decent chance of survival. But, barring a major drift away from the Court's long-standing if not always present suspicion of viewpoint-specific measures,[49] any legislation purporting to designate a preferred or disfavored perception of male-female relations, or of sexuality and power and the relation between the two, seems likely to meet the fate of Indianapolis' well-intended but constitutionally overambitious ordinance.

§ 12–18. The New Theory of Content-Based Abridgments on Track One: From Mandatory Content Neutrality to Permissible Content Discrimination

From the dictum in *Chaplinsky*[1] the Supreme Court had gradually derived what became known as the two-level theory of the first amendment, recognizing speech at one level as fully entitled to first amend-

---

48. See Buckley v. Valeo, 424 U.S. 1 (1976) (invalidating federal ceilings on direct expenditures on behalf of political candidates); Federal Election Commission v. National Conservative Political Action Committee, 470 U.S. 480 (1985) (invalidating federal ceilings on expenditures by political action committees in publicly financed presidential elections), discussed in Chapter 13, infra.

49. That many areas of existing first amendment doctrine—ranging from obscenity law to the law of labor-management communications—implicitly tolerate content-based, and perhaps even viewpoint-based, controls of speech, see Sunstein, supra note 34 at 613, seems an insufficient justification for inviting a new, and a particularly dramatic, departure from the overarching principle that government should not be empowered to suppress expression based on the rejection of the world view that it propounds as evil, or false, or both.

§ 12–18

1. Chaplinsky v. New Hampshire, 315 U.S. 568, 571–72 (1942), discussed in § 12–8, supra.

ment protection and relegating to a lower level speech so worthless as to be beyond the constitutional ken.[2] Fighting words, according to *Chaplinsky*, were in the latter class.[3] Libelous utterances were placed outside the circle of constitutionally protected speech in *Beauharnais v. Illinois*,[4] and obscenity in *Roth v. United States*,[5] a case which was the centerpiece of the two-level theory. While not part of the *Chaplinsky* litany, commercial advertising had been similarly removed from first amendment scrutiny.[6] But the two-level theory began to unravel in *New York Times Co. v. Sullivan*,[7] where the Court rejected the argument that libel was not constitutionally protected. "Libel," said the Court, "can claim no talismanic immunity from constitutional limitations. It must be measured by standards that satisfy the first amendment." [8] The Court's skepticism toward "mere labels" of state law inevitably called into question the whole structure of first amendment rights erected on the *Chaplinsky* foundation, and ever since, that structure has been coming apart.

The fighting words doctrine itself has been narrowly construed.[9] More fundamentally, in the place of a dual-level theory composed of

2. The label "two-level theory" is attributable to Kalven, "Metaphysics of the Law of Obscenity," 1960 Sup.Ct.Rev. 1. The "two-level theory" should not be confused with the two-track analysis elaborated in § 12–2. The "two-level theory", as explained by Professor Kalven, is descriptive of an approach of the Court to content-based abridgments of speech, and is thus a theory about the class of restraints which are on track one. The "two-level theory" is not concerned with track-two problems—abridgments which are aimed at the non-communicative impact of a communication.

3. 315 U.S. at 572–73, discussed in § 12–10, supra.

4. 343 U.S. 250 (1952), discussed in §§ 12–12 and 12–17, supra.

5. 354 U.S. 476 (1957), discussed in § 12–16, supra.

6. See Valentine v. Chrestensen, 316 U.S. 52 (1942), discussed in § 12–15, supra.

7. 376 U.S. 254 (1964), discussed in §§ 12–12, 12–13, 12–14, supra.

8. Id. at 269.

9. The Court has in effect incorporated the clear and present danger test into the fighting words doctrine. See Note, "The Fighting Words Doctrine—Is There a Clear and Present Danger to the Standard?", 84 Dick.L.Rev. 75, 76–78 (1979). This result is in accord with the original thrust of Chaplinsky, which was apparently "intended to be a very narrow opinion premised on the sole ground that the first amendment did not foreclose the states from preserving the public peace by prohibiting words thought likely to cause a brawl." Gard, "Fighting Words as Free Speech," 58 Wash.U.L.Q. 531, 534 (1980). The Court

has restricted the fighting words doctrine in several ways. First, it has struck down as overbroad statutes proscribing offensive language. See, e.g., Gooding v. Wilson, 405 U.S. 518 (1972) (invalidating a Georgia ordinance primarily because it had been previously applied to "utterances where there was no likelihood that the person addressed would make an immediate violent utterance"); Lewis v. New Orleans, 415 U.S. 130 (1974) (invalidating statute that punished "opprobrious language," deemed by the Court to embrace words that do not "by their very utterance inflict injury or tend to invite an immediate breach of the peace").

Next, the Court weakened the conceptual foundation of the fighting words doctrine in Cohen v. California, 403 U.S. 15 (1971) (reversing conviction for wearing, in a Los Angeles courthouse corridor, a jacket that bore the words "Fuck the Draft"). Cohen turned "the presumptions in Chaplinsky around: instead of presuming that profane or defamatory speech was beneath constitutional protection, [the Court in Cohen] presumed that the speech was protected and that the burden of proof lay with those who would restrict it." Arkes, "Civility and the Restriction of Speech: Rediscovering the Defamation of Groups," 1974 Sup.Ct.Rev. 281, 316. Furthermore, by opining that "one man's vulgarity is another's lyric," 403 U.S. at 25, the Court created definitional problems in the "fighting words" area, see Rutzick, "Offensive Language and the Evolution of First Amendment Protection," 9 Harv.C.R.-C.L.L.Rev. 1, 20 (1974); Greenawalt, "Speech and Crime," 1980 Am.B.Found. Res.J. 645, 770: "classifying particularly offensive expressions is difficult. Forms of expression vary so much in their contexts

two types of speech—that which enjoys full, although not absolute, constitutional protection and that which enjoys no such elevated status—the Court is beginning to construct a multi-level edifice with several intermediate categories of less-than-complete constitutional protection for certain kinds of expression. These new categories include commercial speech,[10] near-obscene [11] and offensive [12] speech, non-obscene child pornography,[13] defamation,[14] and possibly the speech of public employees.[15]

and inflections that one cannot specify particular words or phrases as always being 'fighting.' What is gross insult in one setting is crude humor in another. And what is offensive shifts over time." See § 12–10, supra.

10. Commercial speech is defined as communication that proposes a business transaction, see Zauderer v. Office of Disciplinary Counsel of Supreme Court of Ohio, 471 U.S. 626 (1985). The topic is discussed in § 12–15, supra.

11. See Young v. American Mini Theatres, Inc., 427 U.S. 50 (1976); City of Renton v. Playtime Theatres, Inc., 106 S.Ct. 925 (1986).

12. See F.C.C. v. Pacifica Foundation, 438 U.S. 726 (1978).

13. See New York v. Ferber, 458 U.S. 747 (1982). Child pornography now enjoys little, if any, first amendment protection. See id. at 763 ("Recognizing and classifying child pornography as a category of material *outside the protection of the First Amendment* is not incompatible with our earlier decisions.") (emphasis added).

14. The Court in New York Times Co. v. Sullivan, 376 U.S. 254 (1964), did not say that all defamatory and false statements of fact have constitutional value. See Gertz v. Robert Welch, Inc., 418 U.S. 323, 340 (1974). Instead, the Court in New York Times Co. v. Sullivan and its progeny may be taken as holding two things: (1) that the first amendment is an absolute bar to seditious libel, so that government cannot claim to have been defamed; and (2) that the amendment requires protection of some worthless falsehoods defamatory of individuals in order to protect speech that matters. As to the first holding, the Court's conclusion is "absolute"; seditious speech is protected unless the government can show a compelling necessity for its suppression, a standard nearly always fatal to government regulation. As to the second holding, the Court's conclusion is not that defamatory falsehoods are themselves protected but rather, as with a case on track two, see § 12–23, infra, that the regulation of such defamatory falsehoods may incidentally and unduly constrict the flow of protected speech. So long as sufficient care is taken to avoid that result, defama-

tory falsehoods may be made actionable. That very conclusion implies that some speech is less worthy than other speech and may be suppressed so long as government does not, incident to the regulation of such less worthy speech, unduly hamper the exchange of ideas and information protected by the first amendment.

15. In determining a public employee's rights of free speech, the Court attempts to strike "a balance between the interests of the [employee] as a citizen, in commenting upon matters of public concern and the interest of the State, as an employer, in promoting the efficiency of the public services it performs through its employees." Pickering v. Board of Education, 391 U.S. 563, 568 (1968) (holding impermissible under the first amendment the dismissal of a high school teacher for openly criticizing a board of education for its allocation of school funds between athletics and education and for its methods of informing taxpayers about the need for additional revenue). Only when a government employee engages in expression addressed to "matters of public concern" does the first amendment protect him from termination. "When employee expression cannot be fairly considered as relating to any matter of political, social, or other concern to the community, government officials should enjoy wide latitude in managing their offices, without intrusive oversight by the judiciary in the name of the First Amendment." Connick v. Myers, 461 U.S. 138, 146 (1983) (upholding the discharge of an assistant attorney general who circulated a questionnaire among her co-workers, asking them about office transfer policy, office morale, the need for a grievance committee, the level of confidence in supervisors, and whether employees felt pressured to work in political campaigns). The Court has not suggested that speech by public employees on matters not of public concern is "totally beyond the protection of the First Amendment," id. at 147, or that it "falls into one of the narrow and well-defined classes of expression which carries so little social value, such as obscenity, that the State can prohibit and punish such expression by all persons in its jurisdiction," id, but the Court clearly views such speech as a form of communication

Commercial speech provides an illustration of the process by which the Court has moved from the two-level theory to the approach of intermediate categories.[16]　The original view, represented by the Court's comment in *Valentine v. Chrestensen*,[17] was that "the Constitution imposes no . . . restraint on government as respects purely commercial advertising."[18]　Gradually, the "casual, almost offhand"[19] remark in *Valentine* lost favor, and the Court began to question the tenet that "purely commercial speech" was wholly unprotected by the

beneath full first amendment protection. And even when an employee's speech relates to matters of public concern, the first amendment interest must be weighed against the government's interest as an employer, see id. at 154.　This approach invites the Court to engage in standardless balancing and subjective, content-based determinations of the social importance of speech, a mode of analysis that the Court has rightly rejected in other contexts. See Gertz v. Robert Welch, Inc., 418 U.S. 323, 346 (1974) (repudiating Rosenbloom v. Metromedia, Inc., 403 U.S. 29, 43–44 (1971), which had extended constitutional privilege to defendants sued for defamatory statements that involved "matters of public or general concern"), discussed further in § 12–13, supra.

The judgment of when speech by public employees touches a "matter of public concern" is particularly difficult to make because communications about "the manner in which the government is operated or should be operated" are an essential part of comment on the process of self-governance, a major purpose of the first amendment. Mills v. Alabama, 384 U.S. 214, 218 (1966).　In the public employee sphere, it appears that "[b]ased on its own narrow conception of which matters are of public concern, the Court implicitly determines that information concerning employee morale at an important government office will not inform public debate. To the contrary, the First Amendment protects the dissemination of such information so that the people, not the courts, may evaluate its usefulness." Connick, 461 U.S. at 164–65 (Brennan, J., joined by Marshall, Blackmun, and Stevens, JJ., dissenting).

The anomalies of the public employee speech doctrine are illustrated by Rankin v. McPherson, 107 S.Ct. 2891 (1987), in which the Court, by a 5–4 vote, ordered the reinstatement of a police clerk-typist who was fired after commenting, upon hearing of the assassination attempt on President Reagan in 1981, "if they go for him again, I hope they get him."　The solicitor general had argued in his amicus brief to the Supreme Court that hoping for the assassination of the President "is not a position which should be regarded as a matter within the realm of publicly debatable proposi-

tions"—a contention that was all too reminiscent of the English Statute of Treason, which provided capital punishment for "compassing or imagining the death of the king."　Perhaps this needlessly extravagant argument led the Court to overreact. Justice Marshall, writing for the Court, found that the statement "plainly dealt with a matter of public concern" simply because it "was made in the course of a conversation addressing the policies of the President's administration."　Id. at 2897. Because there was but minimal danger that McPherson's outburst would be heard by the public or would interfere with the efficient functioning of the office, see id. at 2899, the police department's interest in discharging her was outweighed by the first amendment value served by her expression.　But as Justice Scalia, joined by Chief Justice Rehnquist and Justices White and O'Connor, persuasively argued in dissent, McPherson could certainly have been *reprimanded*—as a lesser alternative to being fired—after her remark.　See id. at 2904.　Although a warning is a less severe move than a discharge, the point supports Justice Scalia's view that McPherson was not *entitled* to make her comment.　A rule that permitted a typist within the police department to "ride with the cops and cheer for the robbers," id. at 2902, would also allow nonpolicymaking employees of the EEOC repeatedly to crack racist jokes while on the job.　Id. at 2905.

The Court has also recently narrowed the fourth amendment rights of public employees against intrusive searches, see O'Connor v. Ortega, 107 S.Ct. 1492 (1987).

16.　For a fuller discussion of the commercial speech doctrine, see § 12–15, supra.

17.　316 U.S. 52 (1942) (upholding municipal ordinance that prohibited the distribution of printed "handbills, cards and circulars" bearing commercial advertising messages and that specifically exempted "the lawful distribution of anything other than commercial and business advertising matter").

18.　Id. at 54 (emphasis added).

19.　Cammarano v. United States, 358 U.S. 498, 514 (1959) (Douglas, J., concurring).

first amendment.[20] In *Virginia State Board of Pharmacy v. Virginia Citizens Consumer Council, Inc.*,[21] the Court finally repudiated the *Valentine* doctrine and extended a modicum of first amendment protection to commercial speech. The Court rejected the notion that such expression "is wholly outside the protection of the First Amendment"[22] and was careful not to hold "that it is wholly undifferentiable from other forms" of speech.[23] The Court clearly was concerned that vigorous protection of commercial speech would require the invalidation of truth-in-advertising and anti-fraud consumer protection legislation and therefore cautioned that "[a]ttributes such as . . . the greater objectivity and hardiness of commercial speech . . . may make it less necessary to tolerate inaccurate statements for fear of silencing the speaker."[24] The Court based its holding not on any doctrine that attributed reduced constitutional value to commercial speech,[25] but rather on empirical judgments about the conditions such speech requires in order to survive. The Court accordingly concluded that the risk of reduced professionalism among pharmacists could not justify a ban on truthful commercial speech urging consumers to purchase products that are both lawful and safe when used as intended. To be sure, there are dangers that even accurate information about a safe product will be misused. But "[i]t is precisely this kind of choice, between the dangers of suppressing information, and the dangers of its misuse if it is freely available, that the First Amendment makes for us."[26]

Two years later, however, in *Ohralik v. Ohio State Bar Association*,[27] the Court qualified its endorsement of this view. The choice to accord full constitutional protection to commercial speech was no longer made by the first amendment: "we . . . have afforded commercial speech a limited measure of protection, *commensurate with its subordinate position in the scale of First Amendment values*, while allowing modes of regulation that might be impermissible in the realm

---

20. See Bigelow v. Virginia, 421 U.S. 809, 822 (1975) (reversing conviction for violation of a Virginia statute that criminalized the circulation of any publication encouraging or promoting abortions, but stressing that the advertised activity related to the public's "constitutional interests"); Pittsburgh Press Co. v. Pittsburgh Comm'n on Human Relations, 413 U.S. 376, 388 (1973) (upholding an order that forbade Pittsburgh Press from carrying sex-designated "help wanted" ads, except for certain jobs, on the theory that such a practice involved illegal gender discrimination).

21. 425 U.S. 748 (1976).

22. Id. at 761. The Court asked whether commercial speech "lacks all protection. Our answer is that it [does] not." Id. at 762.

23. Id. at 771 n. 24.

24. Id. at 771–72 n. 24.

25. Indeed, the Court emphasized repeatedly the important interests served by commercial speech. "As to the particular consumer's interest in the free flow of commercial information, that interest may be as keen, if not keener by far, than his interest in the day's most urgent political debate," id. at 763. And "society may also have a strong interest," id. at 764, in commercial speech because "the free flow of commercial information . . . is indispensable to the proper allocation of resources in a free enterprise system" and "to the formation of intelligent opinions as to how that system ought to be regulated or altered," id. at 765.

26. Id. at 770.

27. 436 U.S. 447 (1978) (upholding the authority of a state bar to discipline a lawyer for soliciting clients in person, for pecuniary gain, and under circumstances likely to pose dangers that the state may constitutionally prevent).

of noncommercial expression." [28] By the time of *Central Hudson Gas & Electric Corp. v. Public Service Commission of New York*,[29] it had become accepted wisdom [30] that "[t]he Constitution . . . affords a lesser protection to commercial speech than to other constitutionally guaranteed expression. The protection available for particular commercial expression turns on the nature of both the expression and of the governmental interests served by the regulation." [31] It is on this

28. Id. at 456 (emphasis added). The Court worried that "[t]o require a parity of constitutional protection for commercial and noncommercial speech alike could invite dilution, simply by a leveling process, of the [First] Amendment's guarantee with respect to the latter kind of speech." Id. See Shiffrin, "The First Amendment and Economic Regulation: Away From a General Theory of the First Amendment," 78 Nw.U.L.Rev. 1212, 1218, 1220–21 (1983): In Virginia State Bd. of Pharmacy v. Virginia Citizens Consumer Council, Inc., 425 U.S. 748 (1976), "the Court never admitted that commercial speech was less valuable than political speech. The 'commonsense differences' had nothing to do with value. . . . [Although] Justice Blackmun labored to defend the asserted equal relationship between commercial speech and political speech for the Virginia Pharmacy majority, Justice Powell in Ohralik was content to lead the Court to an opposite position without explanation. In so doing, Justice Powell steered the Court to accept a hierarchy of protected speech for the first time, despite his own stated opposition to creating any such hierarchy [in Young v. American Mini Theatres, Inc., 427 U.S. 50, 73 n. 1 (1976) (Powell, J., concurring)]." Shiffrin, supra, at 1220–21.

29. 447 U.S. 557 (1980) (striking down order of commission that prohibited utility from advertising to promote the consumption of electricity).

30. See Young v. American Mini Theaters, Inc., 427 U.S. 50, 69 n. 32 (1976) (Stevens, J., plurality opinion) (noting that the difference between commercial price and product advertising and ideological communication permits regulation of the former "that the First Amendment would not tolerate with respect to the latter"); Linmark Associates, Inc. v. Willingboro Tp., 431 U.S. 85, 91–92 (1977) (striking down statute that regulated posting of real estate "for sale" and "sold" signs); Friedman v. Rogers, 440 U.S. 1, 8–10 (1979) (upholding state ban on the use of tradenames by optometrists); Metromedia, Inc. v. San Diego, 453 U.S. 490, 513 (1981) (White, J., plurality opinion) (striking down ordinance that prohibited much outdoor advertising but contained an exception for onsite commercial displays): "our recent commercial speech cases have con-

sistently accorded noncommercial speech a greater degree of protection than commercial speech. San Diego effectively inverts this judgment, by affording a greater degree of protection to commercial than to noncommercial speech. . . . Insofar as the city tolerates billboards at all, it cannot choose to limit their content to commercial messages; the city may not conclude that the communication of commercial information concerning goods and services is of greater value than the communication of noncommercial messages." See also Pacific Gas & Elec. Co. v. Public Utilities Comm'n of California, 475 U.S. 1, ___ (1986) (contrasting expression that "receives the full protection of the First Amendment" with "speech that proposes a business transaction").

31. Central Hudson, 447 U.S. at 562–63. The different tests applied by the Court to restrictions of commercial and noncommercial speech illustrate the subordinate position now occupied by the former. Content-based regulations of *non*commercial speech receive vigorous review: "[w]here a government restricts the speech of a private person, the state action may be sustained only if the government can show that the regulation is a precisely drawn means of serving a compelling state interest." Consolidated Edison Co. of New York, Inc. v. Public Service Comm'n of New York, 447 U.S. 530, 540 (1980) (striking down commission rule that prohibited utility from enclosing monthly billing inserts discussing controversial issues of public policy); see also First National Bank of Boston v. Bellotti, 435 U.S. 765, 786 (1978) (invalidating a Massachusetts statute that forbade business corporations from making contributions or expenditures to influence "the vote on any question submitted to the voters, other than one materially affecting any of the property, business or assets of the corporation"); Buckley v. Valeo, 424 U.S. 1, 25 (1976) (per curiam) (striking down limits on expenditures by and on behalf of candidates for federal office while upholding campaign contribution limits). A restriction on lawful and nonmisleading *commercial* speech, on the other hand, is permissible so long as it "directly advances the [substantial] governmental interest asserted . . . and is not more extensive than is necessary to serve that interest." Central

basis that the Court in *Posadas de Puerto Rico Associates v. Tourism Co. of Puerto Rico*,[32] upheld Puerto Rico's law banning entirely truthful and non-misleading advertising, whenever aimed at the local populace, of lawful gambling in Puerto Rico's casinos. Perhaps the Court has come to view at least some advertising as less akin to *advocacy* than to *incitement*, and has decided that, if the activity being incited is sufficiently harmful in itself, the state's decision not to ban that activity outright—out of respect for privacy, or anticipated difficulties of enforcement—need not entail a first amendment duty to permit self-interested exhortation to engage in the activity.[33]

A plurality of the Court created another category of speech that enjoys less-than-full first amendment protection in *Young v. American Mini Theatres, Inc.*,[34] by upholding a zoning ordinance which restricted the locations of new theaters showing sexually explicit "adult" movies. While the decision bears on the Court's treatment of obscenity, *American Mini Theatres* is not itself an obscenity case. The ordinance defined an "adult" movie as one presenting material characterized by an emphasis on matter depicting "specified sexual activities" or "specified anatomical areas," each term being defined with some precision. The ordinance clearly included non-obscene, but sexually explicit expression, protected by the first amendment; it was not even argued that the ordinance regulated only unprotected obscenity.[35] The plurality approached the "erogenous zoning" ordinance from a perspective novel in first amendment jurisprudence. While acknowledging the strong constitutional aversion to content-based regulation of expression, the plurality gave two reasons to justify the departures from neutrality in the Detroit ordinance. First, the "paramount obligation of neutrality" was not violated, since the ordinance did not regulate speech on the basis of government approval or disapproval of the particular expression's "point of view."[36] Second, sexually-explicit expression has

Hudson Gas & Electric Corp. v. Public Service Comm'n of New York, 447 U.S. 557, 566 (1980).

32. 106 S.Ct. 2968 (1986), discussed in § 12–15, supra.

33. Such a theory would, for example, support a law prohibiting individuals from urging others to commit suicide, at least where such encouragement is motivated by self-interest (as in the case of one who would like to film another's death). This theory would also support a law prohibiting businesses from advertising cigarettes for profit, but *not* a law prohibiting the advertisement of driving or skiing or other merely risky but not intrinsically harmful activities—activities that the state cannot plausibly claim it would ban outright but for the intrusiveness or impracticality of enforcing a direct prohibition. Indeed, the Court's application of this approach to *local gambling*—the activity at issue in Posadas, supra note 32—may well be more problematic than the approach itself. As applied to a uniquely harmful but hard to

ban activity like smoking, the approach set forth here seems unthreatening to basic free speech values.

34. 427 U.S 50 (1976) (plurality opinion by Stevens, J., joined by Burger, C.J., and White and Rehnquist, JJ.). Justices Brennan, Stewart, Marshall, and Blackmun dissented.

35. Id. at 61, 62.

36. Id. at 70. See also Greer v. Spock, 424 U.S. 828, 828–29 & n. 10 (1976) (Stewart, J.) (upholding military regulations banning partisan political activities in open areas of military base). The military authorities were found not to have discriminated in any way among candidates for public office based upon the candidates' supposed political views and no candidate had ever been permitted to campaign on the base. Nor would discrimination be inferred by the Court from the decision of military authorities to invite non-political civilian speakers and entertainers to appear at the base.

"lesser" value than other protected speech, particularly political debate: "Few of us would march our sons and daughters off to war to preserve the citizen's right to see 'Specified Sexual Activities' exhibited in the theaters of our choice." [37] The plurality then applied a "balancing test" which it quickly resolved in favor of the government on the basis of a finding, which was apparently not contested by respondents, that Detroit's zoning ordinance did not greatly restrict access to sexually explicit (albeit protected) expression, since it left enough sites for "adult" theaters to accommodate all patrons.[38] The market for sexually explicit material was thus said to be "essentially unrestrained."

Although the dissenters in *American Mini Theaters* trusted that the Court's decision had been an "aberration," [39] later developments proved them wrong. In *Federal Communications Commission v. Pacifica Foundation*,[40] the Court upheld the FCC's authority to proscribe radio broadcasts which it finds "indecent but not obscene." [41] The case involved a recorded monologue by comedian George Carlin about "the swear words, the cuss words, and the words you can't say" [42] which concluded a radio talk show devoted to a discussion of society's attitudes toward language. Just before airing the piece, the program's host advised listeners that the record contained "sensitive language which might be regarded as offensive to some." [43] On the basis of a citizen's complaint, the FCC issued a "Memorandum Opinion and Order" in which the agency concluded that the "seven dirty words" that Carlin spoke "depicted sexual and excretory activities and organs

---

37. American Mini Theatres, 427 U.S. at 70. (Powell, J., joined all but this part of the plurality opinion; Burger, C.J., White, J., and Rehnquist, J., joined the entire opinion.) The dissenters, in an opinion by Justice Stewart, id. at 84, 86, properly took Justice Stevens to task for the standard implicit in his rhetoric. The Bill of Rights is needed precisely because few of us *would* make great sacrifices to preserve its principles when confronted with an immediate choice. It is because collectively we have agreed that our individual attitudes would be short-sighted that the Constitution proves so vital. See §§ 1–7, and 11–4, supra.

38. 427 U.S. at 62. The petitioners did not claim that access to the market for sexually explicit material had been restricted for the distributors of adult films or for the viewing public, but it is difficult to believe that such a case could not have been made. The decision in American Mini Theatres thus leaves open exactly how much restraint is compatible with an essentially free market in "adult" fare.

39. 427 U.S. at 87 (Stewart, J., dissenting).

40. 438 U.S. 726 (1978). Justice Stevens announced the judgment and delivered the opinion of the Court with respect to those parts of his opinion holding that the challenged broadcast was "indecent"

within the meaning of the FCC's enabling statute and that such a broadcast could be regulated because of the uniquely pervasive nature of the radio medium and its easy accessibility by children. He was joined by Chief Justice Burger and Justice Rehnquist and, except with respect to his contention that an indecent broadcast merited less first amendment protection than other forms of speech, by Justices Powell and Blackmun. Justice Powell, joined by Justice Blackmun, filed an opinion concurring in part and concurring in the judgment, in which he disagreed with Justice Stevens' conclusion that indecent speech should be relegated on the basis of its content to a low position in a constitutional hierarchy of speech. Justice Brennan filed a dissenting opinion, in which Justice Marshall joined, that addressed constitutional issues presented by the FCC's regulation, and Justice Stewart filed a dissenting opinion, in which Justices Brennan, White, and Marshall joined, that focused on the issue of the proper construction of the FCC's governing statute.

41. 438 U.S. at 729.

42. Id. at 751–55 (appendix, in which a transcript of the broadcast appears). The "seven dirty words" to which the FCC took offense were fuck, shit, piss, motherfucker, cocksucker, cunt, and tit.

43. Id. at 730.

in a manner patently offensive by contemporary community standards for the broadcast medium," [44] and were therefore prohibited by 18 U.S.C. § 1464, which forbids the use of "any obscene, indecent, or profane language by means of radio communications." [45] Expressly stating that the "indecent" speech it sought to control was "*not* subsumed by the concept of obscenity" [46] as defined by *Miller v. California,*[47] the FCC justified its broader category of restricted speech by reference to the "unique qualities" of the broadcast media.[48]

Justice Stevens' opinion for the Court seized upon these "unique qualities" to justify the FCC's censorship of the Carlin monologue. First, the Court focused on the intrusion of the broadcast medium into the home and permitted the FCC to conclude that a listener should not be put even to the minimal discomfort of enduring offensive speech for the short interval required to change the channel or turn off the set. The majority held that the avoidance of such discomfort outweighed the first amendment interests of other listeners who would have wanted to hear the Carlin monologue.[49]

Second, the Court emphasized the presence of unsupervised children in the listening audience and agreed with the Commission's finding that the language used by Carlin, although not obscene,[50] was

---

44. In re A Citizen's Complaint Against Pacifica Foundation WBAI (FM), 56 F.C.C.2d 94 (1975). Although it upheld the complaint, the Commission declined to impose formal sanctions against the station.

45. The Commission also grounded its action in 47 U.S.C. § 303(g) (1982), which requires the FCC to "encourage the larger and more effective use of radio in the public interest." Justice Stewart, in dissent, characterized the invocation of § 303(g) as an independent authority for the FCC order as a "passing reference" and added that its general language is limited by the scope of the more specific § 1464, see 438 U.S. at 778 n. 3 (Stewart, J., dissenting). Justice Stevens, writing for the Court, did not consider whether § 303(g) had independent significance since he decided that § 1464 provided ample authority to regulate the use of indecent language in broadcasting. 438 U.S. at 739 n. 13.

46. 56 F.C.C.2d at 97 (emphasis in original). The Commission argued that indecent speech lacks appeal to prurient interests and added that, when children are in the audience, such speech cannot be saved by any literary, artistic, political, or scientific value it might possess. Id. at 98.

47. 413 U.S. 15, 24 (1973), discussed in § 12–16, supra.

48. 56 F.C.C.2d at 97.

49. 438 U.S. at 748–49 (opinion of Stevens, J., for the Court).

But see Wilkinson v. Jones, 107 S.Ct. 1559 (1987), in which a 7–2 majority—Chief Justice Rehnquist and Justice

O'Connor would have set the case for plenary briefing and argument—summarily affirmed a Tenth Circuit decision, Jones v. Wilkinson, 800 F.2d 989 (10th Cir. 1986) (per curiam), invalidating a Utah statute which imposed civil financial penalties on cable television systems that showed "indecent" or "patently offensive" nudity or sexual acts regardless of whether the films at issue were obscene. See 800 F.2d at 991 n. 2 (the statute was concededly aimed at "matters that go beyond outright 'obscenity' "). The state attorney general's promise to enforce the statute only between the hours of 7 a.m. and midnight did not prevent the court of appeals from holding the law facially void for vagueness and overbreadth and pre-empted by a 1984 congressional enactment. One remarkable aspect of the case was the Tenth Circuit's willingness, see 800 F.2d at 991, to adopt the reasoning of the district court, which had thoroughly blended the first amendment and pre-emption rationales: "If state regulations are unconstitutional, they are also pre-empted under the terms of the Policy Act. The final resolution of the pre-emption question necessarily requires a ruling on the first amendment issue." Community Television of Utah, Inc. v. Wilkinson, 611 F.Supp. 1099, 1105 (D. Utah 1985). The case thus arguably requires courts to decide the constitutionality of state cable regulations before determining whether they are pre-empted by federal law.

50. Justice Stewart, in a dissent joined by Justices Brennan, White, and Marshall, would have avoided the constitutional is-

potentially degrading and harmful to children.[51] Society has an interest in the "well-being of its youth," and this permits government to
lend the support of the law to parents, who have the primary responsibility of rearing and educating children.[52] The Court went beyond
these principles in holding that government may come to the aid of
those parents who would keep their children from hearing smutty
language although other parents, perhaps a minority, might therefore
be prevented from exposing their children to the manner in which Mr.
Carlin defuses the taboo surrounding the "dirty words."[53] And the
Court also went further in holding that the convenience of some
parents may be invoked to force adults wishing to hear Mr. Carlin's
words to leave their homes to get the comedian's message.[54]

The strangest thing about the Court's decision was that no one
could reasonably suppose that children were listening to the radio
station at 2 o'clock in the afternoon. WBAI, the broadcast station
involved, is listener-supported, carries no ads, does not play "top forty"
records, and directs its programming at a distinctly adult, left-to-
radical, upper-middle-class audience.[55] In addition, studies show that
virtually no children listen to any radio station whatsoever at that time
on a weekday for the reason that most children are then in school.[56]

Nor is it probable that any significant number of adults were
offended by Carlin's monologue. Certainly WBAI's regular listeners
were unlikely to be scandalized; in any case, the station prefaced the
broadcast with warnings of the sensitive language to come. That left at
risk the radio listeners who, turning the dials, stumbled briefly onto the

sues by construing the term "indecent" as
used in § 1464 as meaning no more than
"obscene," see 438 U.S. at 778–80. The
Court had previously taken the course
urged by Justice Stewart in construing a
statute that prohibited that mailing of
"[e]very obscene, lewd, lascivious, indecent,
filthy or vile article." Hamling v. United
States, 418 U.S. 87 (1974). The majority in
Pacifica argued that differences between
the print and broadcast media required
different constructions of the term "indecent," see 438 U.S. at 741 (opinion of Stevens, J., for the Court).

51. Id. at 749–50 (Stevens, J., opinion
for the Court); id. at 758–59 (Powell, J.,
joined by Blackmun, J., concurring).

52. Cf. Ginsberg v. New York, 390 U.S.
629, 639 (1968), discussed in § 12–16, supra. Justice Stevens' opinion can also be
read as stating the broader proposition
that government may act *as* a parent, not
merely *aid* parents, and therefore may
keep young children from hearing indecent
language which the government has concluded is harmful to them. But, as Justice
Brennan pointed out, such an approach
would deprive minors of their first amendment rights altogether, see 438 U.S. at 768,
citing Erznoznik v. Jacksonville, 422 U.S.
205, 213–14 (1975) (nudity on drive-in movie screen): "Speech that is neither obscene

as to youths nor subject to some other
legitimate proscription cannot be suppressed solely to protect the young from
ideas or images that a legislative body
thinks is unsuitable for them." See also
Planned Parenthood of Central Missouri v.
Danforth, 428 U.S. 52, 74 (1976) (striking
down provision of a law that required an
unmarried woman under the age of 18 to
secure parental consent before obtaining
an abortion): "Constitutional rights do not
mature and come into being magically only
when one attains the state-defined age of
majority. Minors, as well as adults, are
protected by the Constitution and possess
constitutional rights."

53. 438 U.S. at 770 (Brennan, J., joined
by Marshall, J., dissenting).

54. Contrast Butler v. Michigan, 352
U.S. 380, 383–84 (1957) (government may
not "reduce the adult audience . . . to
reading only what is fit for children"); Pinkus v. United States, 436 U.S. 293 (1978)
(children cannot be included in "community" by whose standards obscenity is to be
judged).

55. See von Hoffman, "Nine Justices
for Seven Dirty Words," More Magazine 12
(June 1978).

56. See Amicus Brief of American
Broadcasting Companies, Inc., et al.

offensive program. The number of such accidents had to be miniscule, much smaller than the number of WBAI listeners who enjoyed Mr. Carlin's satire. Indeed, the record showed that only one person complained—an unidentified citizen who, while driving in his car with his son, tuned into WBAI, heard Carlin's monologue, and apparently chose to turn no further. Given the facts, that the Court did not hold the FCC's order unconstitutional suggests something else was afoot.

Justice Stevens, writing for a plurality that included Chief Justice Burger and Justice Rehnquist, contended that the FCC ruling would "have its primary effect on the form, rather than on the content, of serious communication . . . [because] few, if any, thoughts cannot be expressed by less offensive language." [57] Furthermore, argued Justice Stevens, indecent speech is at the "periphery of First Amendment concern," [58] and while it is "not entirely outside the protection of the First Amendment," [59] protection might vary according to context. [60] The plurality thus attempted to place offensive expression in a second tier of constitutional protection.

Although the Court has clearly embarked on the task of erecting a hierarchy of expression within the first amendment, it is important to note that no Court has yet squarely held that offensive or sexually explicit but non-obscene speech enjoys less than full first amendment protection. In *American Mini Theatres*, a plurality, including Chief Justice Burger and Justices White, Stevens, and Rehnquist, held that "it is manifest that society's interest in protecting [sexually explicit although non-obscene speech] is of a wholly different, and lesser, magnitude than the interest in untrammeled political debate." [61] This proposition, however, was not accepted by the four dissenters or by Justice Powell. [62] In *Pacifica*, [63] only Chief Justice Burger and Justice Rehnquist joined Justice Stevens' opinion in its entirety. [64] Justice Powell, joined by Justice Blackmun, refused to agree with the plurality that offensive, nonobscene speech is deserving of less protection than other kinds of speech. [65] Thus, while the pure two-level model is no longer confidently employed by the Court, it has not yet been formally repudiated. [66]

57. 438 U.S. at 743 n. 18 (plurality opinion).

58. Id. at 743 (plurality opinion).

59. Id. at 746 (plurality opinion).

60. Id. at 747 (plurality opinion).

61. Young v. American Mini Theatres, Inc., 427 U.S. 50, 70 (1976).

62. See 427 U.S. at 73 (Powell, J., concurring).

63. F.C.C. v. Pacifica Foundation, 438 U.S. 726 (1978).

64. See id. at 762–63 (Brennan, J., joined by Marshall, J, dissenting): "For the second time in two years, the Court refuses to embrace the notion, completely antithetical to basic First Amendment values, that the degree of protection the First Amendment affords protected speech varies with the social value ascribed to that speech by five Members of this Court."

65. "I do not subscribe to the view that the Justices of this Court are free generally to decide on the basis of its content which speech protected by the First Amendment is most 'valuable' and hence deserving of the most protection, and which is less 'valuable' and hence deserving of less protection." Id. at 726 (Powell, J., joined by Blackmun, J., concurring).

66. Arguably, the Court's decision in City of Renton v. Playtime Theatres, Inc., 475 U.S. 41 (1986), might constitute such repudiation. Justice Rehnquist delivered the opinion of the Court for a majority that included Chief Justice Burger and Justices White, Powell, Stevens, and O'Connor. Justice Rehnquist cited American Mini Theatres in a footnote for the proposition

The creation of intermediate categories of speech might appear to be a positive development, or at least a mixed one, because it has led the Court to extend *some* first amendment protection to forms of expression, such as commercial speech, that might not otherwise have received any at all.[67]   In *New York v. Ferber*,[68] the Court upheld a New York statute that prohibited persons from knowingly distributing material that depicted a sexual performance by a child under the age of 16, a law that admittedly went beyond the *Miller*[69] test for obscenity. After examining the social costs[70] and benefits[71] of child pornography, the Court concluded that it was "a category of material outside the protection of the First Amendment."[72]   The Court engaged in generalized balancing to assess the constitutional value of the entire category of speech, rather than weighing the merits of the particular restriction on expression in an ad hoc way.   The Court thus accepted a concededly "content-based classification of speech" because it concluded that, "within the confines of the given classification, the evil to be restricted so overwhelmingly outweighs the expressive interests, if any, at stake, that no process of case-by-case adjudication is required."[73]   The dangers of censorship were minimized because the "evil" at which the law was aimed related not to the effect of the speech on *viewers* or *listeners* but to the effect on those children used to *produce* the speech.   Justice Stevens, one of the moving forces on the Court behind the idea of intermediate categories,[74] commented in his concurrence that although "it is probably safe to assume that the category of speech that is covered by the New York statute generally is of a lower quality than

that "it is manifest that society's interest in protecting this type of [sexually explicit] expression is of a wholly different, and lesser, magnitude than the interest in untrammeled political debate." 475 U.S. at __ n. 2. But it is doubtful that Renton can fairly be read as endorsing the concept of a hierarchy of intermediate categories, because the case turned on the majority's characterization of the restriction as content-neutral, see id. at 929, and the issue of the relative importance of the speech involved was, strictly speaking, irrelevant. Justice Blackmun concurred in the result without opinion. Justice Brennan, joined in dissent by Justice Marshall, noted that "the Court's analysis is limited to cases involving 'businesses that purvey sexually explicit materials,' and thus does not affect our holdings in cases involving state regulation of other kinds of speech." Id. at 933 (Brennan, J., joined by Marshall, J., dissenting).

67. See Schauer, "Categories and the First Amendment: A Play in Three Acts," 34 Vand.L.Rev. 265, 286 (1981) (supporting reduced first amendment protection for the categories of commercial and defamatory speech but criticizing the categories of offensive and indecent speech).

68. 458 U.S. 747 (1982). Justice White delivered the opinion of the Court, in which Chief Justice Burger and Justices Powell, Rehnquist, and O'Connor joined. Justice O'Connor also wrote a concurring opinion. Justice Brennan, joined by Justice Marshall, filed an opinion concurring in the judgment. Justice Stevens also filed an opinion concurring in the judgment. Justice Blackmun concurred in the result. The case is discussed more fully in § 12–16, supra.

69. Miller v. California, 413 U.S. 15 (1973), discussed in § 12–16, supra.

70. See 458 U.S. at 756–63.

71. See id. at 762–63 (concluding that "[t]he value of permitting live performances and photographic reproductions of children engaged in lewd sexual conduct is exceedingly modest, if not *de minimis*").

72. Id. at 763.

73. Id. at 763–64.

74. See Metromedia, Inc. v. San Diego, 453 U.S. 490, 544–48 (1981) (Stevens, J., dissenting in part); Schad v. Borough of Mt. Ephraim, 452 U.S. 61, 85 (1981) (Stevens, J., concurring in judgment); F.C.C. v. Pacifica Foundation, 438 U.S. 726, 742–43 (1978) (opinion of Stevens, J.); Young v. American Mini Theatres, Inc., 427 U.S. 50, 59–61 (1976) (opinion of Stevens, J).

most other types of communication," he disagreed "with the Court's position that such speech is totally without First Amendment protection." [75]

There are, however, powerful reasons to resist departures from a narrowly confined two-level theory. A hierarchy of ever-proliferating intermediate categories requires the Court to assign relative values to different classes of expression, a task that is all but impossible to reconcile with "the basic theory of the First Amendment." [76] This does not mean that no content-based categorization is ever permissible. In a sense, the entire jurisprudence of free speech reflects a general categorization, composed of assumptions about which kinds of communicative acts are inside the first amendment and which are outside.[77] But once an expressive act is determined to be within the coverage of the first amendment, its entitlement to protection must not vary with the viewpoint expressed, and all attempts to create content-based subcategories entail at least some risk that government will in fact be discriminating against disfavored points of view. Even categories ostensibly created to address harms to participants or to bystanders rather than to beholders—as in the case of child pornography [78] and erogenous zoning [79]—might be singled out in part because of the antipathy of those in power toward the ideas implicit in, or conveyed through, the materials identified for special state supervision or outright suppression. If we are to reduce that danger, we must be most reluctant to tolerate doctrines that identify new categories of "low value" speech.

It is therefore crucial to stress that, within the sphere of protected speech, the Supreme Court has ordinarily called all expression equal, labeling no individual or class of expression as more or less valuable than any other and regarding all as deserving the same first amendment protection.[80] This presumption of the equality of ideas is a

75. 458 U.S. at 781 (Stevens, J., concurring in the judgment).

76. T. Emerson, The System of Free Expression 326 (1970); Cox, "The Supreme Court, 1979 Term—Foreword: Freedom of Expression in the Burger Court," 94 Harv. L.Rev. 1, 28 (1980) (discussing "established principle" that court should not attempt to differentiate among values of different messages). The aversion to regulations based on the content of the message is widely shared among commentators. See, e.g., Farber, "Content Regulation and the First Amendment: A Revisionist View," 68 Geo.L.J. 727 (1980); Karst, "Equality as a Central Concept in the First Amendment," 43 U.Chi.L.Rev. 20 (1975); Scanlon, "Freedom of Expression and Categories of Expression," 40 U.Pitt.L.Rev. 551 (1979).

77. See Schauer, "Categories and the First Amendment: A Play in Three Acts," 34 Vand.L.Rev. 265, 267–74 (1981).

78. See New York v. Ferber, 458 U.S. 747 (1982).

79. See Young v. American Mini Theatres, Inc., 427 U.S. 50 (1976).

80. Discrimination among ideas has been deemed tantamount to forbidden censorship. See Karst, "Equality as a Central Principle in the First Amendment," 43 U.Chi.L.Rev. 20 (1976). Although the Court has often treated differently the several media of expression, see § 12–25, infra, and has at times tolerated differential treatment of entire classes or categories of protected expression such as the political and the commercial, see, e.g., Lehman v. Shaker Heights, 418 U.S. 298 (1974) (sustaining constitutionality of municipal policy refusing political advertising but allowing commercial advertising on spaces on city transit system), distinctions based on the subject matter of expression (e.g., labor picketing as opposed to public interest picketing) have often been treated with as much suspicion as distinctions based on point of view. See Carey v. Brown, 447 U.S. 455, 462–63 & n. 7 (1980); Police Dept. of Chicago v. Mosley, 408 U.S. 92, 95, 98–99 (1972).

corollary of the basic requirement that the government may not aim at the communicative impact of expressive conduct without triggering the exacting and usually fatal scrutiny of track one analysis. The classic exemplar of this approach is *Police Department of Chicago v. Mosley*,[81] involving a man who had been picketing peacefully near a school with a sign protesting "black discrimination." A city ordinance prohibited picketing within 150 feet of a school during school hours but excepted "peaceful picketing of any school involved in a labor dispute." Advised of the ordinance, Mosley sought to enjoin its enforcement. He won, and the Supreme Court affirmed. Justice Marshall's opinion for the Court was keyed to the exception for labor picketing: "[Government] may not select which issues are worth discussing or debating in public facilities."[82] It was no defense that Chicago's ordinance did not depend on government's favorable or unfavorable appraisal of the speech that the city would exclude because of its proximity to schools. Because the government discriminated among pickets in terms of their messages, the ordinance was unconstitutional. The principle for which *Mosley* stands is that the first amendment requires that time, place and manner regulations affecting protected expression be content-neutral,[83] except in the very limited context of a captive or juvenile audience.[84] Any departure from this principle must therefore be seen as having major implications for first amendment jurisprudence.[85]

81. 408 U.S. 92 (1972).

82. Id. at 95–96. Nor may government decide which citizens or groups of citizens are worth listening to at public meetings. See City of Madison, Joint School District No. 8 v. Wisconsin Employment Relations Commission, 429 U.S. 167 (1976) (held that school board could not refuse to hear one speaker—a non-union teacher—from among the speakers at a public meeting that had been called to discuss the board's labor relations). Just as Police Department of the City of Chicago v. Mosley is limited to public facilities, 408 U.S. at 96, so City of Madison School District v. Wisconsin Employment Relations Commission, 429 U.S. at 176. It remains the law that "[t]he Constitution does not require all public acts to be done in town meeting or an assembly of the whole." Bi-Metallic Investment Co. v. State Board of Equalization, 239 U.S. 441, 445 (1915) (Holmes, J.).

83. "Content-neutral time, place, and manner restrictions are acceptable so long as they are designed to serve a substantial governmental interest and do not unreasonably limit alternative avenues of communication." City of Renton v. Playtime Theatres, Inc., 475 U.S. 41, __ (1986). See also Clark v. Community for Creative Non-Violence, 468 U.S. 288, 293 (1984); members of City Council of Los Angeles v. Taxpayers for Vincent, 466 U.S. 789, 807 (1984); Heffron v. International Society for

Krishna Consciousness (ISKCON), 452 U.S. 640, 647 (1981).

84. See, e.g., Bethel School Dist. No. 403 v. Fraser, 106 S.Ct. 3159 (1986) (rejecting civil rights claim by student who was disciplined after he delivered a sexually suggestive speech at a high school assembly); Lehman v. Shaker Heights, 418 U.S. 298 (1974) (Blackmun, J., plurality opinion) (sustaining constitutionality of limitation on use of advertising space on municipally-owned buses to innocuous and less controversial commercial advertising as minimizing imposition upon the captive audience of commuters); Rowan v. United States Post Office Department, 397 U.S. 728 (1970) (upholding law which provided that addressees who received in the mail "a pandering advertisement" which they deemed offensive could obtain the removal of their names from the advertiser's mailing list and stop all future mailings; "a mailer's right to communicate must stop at the mail box of an unreceptive addressee"); Ginsberg v. New York, 390 U.S. 629 (1968) (upholding conviction for selling to a minor magazines which were "not obscene" if shown to adults).

85. A plurality of the Court, at least, has apparently reserved the presumption of equality of ideas for speech that receives full constitutional protection. See Metromedia, Inc. v. San Diego, 453 U.S. 490 (1981), where Justice White, in a plurality opinion joined by Justices Stewart, Mar-

The Court, moreover, has not yet articulated the basis by which it creates new categories of speech. In *New York v. Ferber*,[86] the child pornography case, the Court weighed "the evil to be restricted" against the "expressive interests" at stake,[87] but it provided no indication of how it calculated those values, beyond mere intuition. As a result, *Ferber* fails to provide the "full exposition necessary to fit the [Court's first amendment] decisions into a coherent body of law," [88] and suggests a "troubling disregard of the gravity of any departure from scrupulous first amendment protection." [89]

The particular categories thus far created by the Court are objectionable in part because they appear to defy clear definition. A Court that has been unable to pin down the word "obscenity" [90] with any success will scarcely have an easier time with the "indecent." A central difficulty with the statute at issue in *Federal Communications Commission v. Pacifica Foundation*,[91] like the standard involved in *Miller v. California*,[92] was that it did not on its face clearly define the conduct prohibited. Indeed, it was this very lack of precise definition that led the Court in the first place to construe the term "indecent" in related statutes to mean no more than "obscene." [93] By accepting the FCC's broader interpretation of indecency, the *Pacifica* Court implicitly embraced a general or national standard of offensiveness.[94] Speech, however, cannot properly be valued according to the preferences of the majority.[95] "The words that the Court and the Commission find so unpalatable may be the stuff of everyday conversations in some, if not

shall, and Powell, held that, although the city could constitutionally regulate commercial billboard advertising, it could not impose what amounted to a partial ban on signs carrying noncommercial messages. "Although the city may distinguish between the relative value of different categories of commercial speech, the city does not have the same range of choice in the area of noncommercial speech to evaluate the strength of, or distinguish between, various communicative interests." Id. at 514. The plurality cited for this proposition two authorities that support the traditional view of mandatory content neutrality: Carey v. Brown, 447 U.S. 455, 462 (1980), and Police Dept. of Chicago v. Mosley, 408 U.S. 92, 96 (1972). Thus, the plurality concluded, "[b]ecause some noncommercial messages may be conveyed on billboards throughout the commercial and industrial zones, San Diego must similarly allow billboards conveying other noncommercial messages throughout these zones." 453 U.S. at 515. See also Stone, "Content Regulation and the First Amendment," 25 Wm. & Mary L.Rev. 189, 196 (1983).

86. 458 U.S. 747 (1982).

87. Id. at 763–64.

88. Cox, "The Supreme Court, 1979 Term—Foreword: Freedom of Expression

in the Burger Court," 94 Harv.L.Rev. 1, 72 (1980).

89. "The Supreme Court, 1981 Term," 96 Harv.L.Rev. 62, 145 (1982).

90. "Between 1957 and 1973, the Court decided over 30 obscenity cases; yet, over that period, a majority never agreed upon a precise definition of obscenity." "The Supreme Court, 1977 Term," 92 Harv.L. Rev. 57, 156 n. 68 (1978). See generally § 12–16, supra.

91. 438 U.S. 726 (1978).

92. 413 U.S. 15, 23–24 (1973).

93. See Note, "Filthy Words, the FCC, and the First Amendment: Regulating Broadcast Obscenity," 61 Va.L.Rev. 579 (1975).

94. Indeed, Justice Powell specifically embraced a standard defining as offensive that which offends "most people," see Pacifica, 438 U.S. at 757 (Powell, J., joined by Blackmun, J., concurring in part and concurring in the judgment).

95. Id. 438 U.S. at 766 (Brennan, J., joined by Marshall, J., dissenting): "[The Court] permits majoritarian tastes completely to preclude a protected message from entering the homes of a receptive, unoffended minority."

many, of the innumerable subcultures that compose this nation." [96] Justice Brennan correctly viewed the Court's contrary approach as reflecting "acute ethnocentri[sm]," the product of a "depressing inability to appreciate that in our land of cultural pluralism, there are many who think, act, and talk differently from the Members of [the] Court, and who do not share their fragile sensibilities." [97]

The commercial speech category, too, is fraught with potential vagueness. As early as *Virginia Board of Pharmacy*,[98] for example, the Court recognized the difficulty of distinguishing the "commercial" from the "noncommercial." After noting that "not all commercial messages contain . . . a very great public interest element," the Court suggested that "[t]here are few to which such an element, however, could not be added." [99] It continued: "Our pharmacist, for example, could cast himself as a commentator on store-to-store disparities in drug prices, giving his own and those of a competitor as proof. We see little point in requiring him to do, and little difference if he does not." [100] Professor Steven Shiffrin has proposed several examples which suggest that a sharp "distinction between commercial and political speech [is] impossible to maintain." [101]

More fundamentally, the fragmentation of the first amendment into a grab bag of rubrics under which different types of speech receive different degrees of protection exemplifies a propensity for pigeonholing as a method of deciding first amendment questions.[102] Such a method masks the political dimension of the underlying choices by pretending to cabin judicial discretion within the limits established by the categories themselves. This sort of pigeonholing endangers the pigeon: if one

96. Id. at 776 (Brennan, J., joined by Marshall, J., dissenting).

97. Id. at 775 (Brennan, J., joined by Marshall, J., dissenting).

98. Virginia State Board of Pharmacy v. Virginia Citizens Consumer Council, Inc., 425 U.S. 748 (1976), discussed in § 12–15, supra.

99. Id. at 764.

100. Id. at 764–65. In Metromedia, Inc. v. San Diego, 453 U.S. 490 (1981), the city of San Diego attempted to distinguish between commercial messages, which it permitted on the site of the business that purchased them, and noncommercial displays, which, for the most part, it outlawed. Justice Brennan, joined by Justice Blackmun, properly took the city to task for its attempt to draw the distinction:

"I would be unhappy to see city officials dealing with the following series of billboards and deciding which ones to permit: the first billboard contains the message 'Visit Joe's Ice Cream Shoppe'; the second, 'Joe's Ice Cream Shoppe uses only the highest quality dairy products'; the third, 'Because Joe thinks that dairy products are good for you, please shop at Joe's Shoppe'; and the fourth, 'Joe says to support dairy price supports: they mean lower prices for you at his Shoppe.' Or how about some San Diego Padres fans—with no connection to the team—who together rent a billboard and communicate the message, 'Support the San Diego Padres, a great baseball team.' May the city decide that a United Automobile Workers billboard with the message, 'Be a patriot—do not buy Japanese-manufactured cars' is 'commercial' and therefore forbid it? What if the same sign were placed by Chrysler?"

453 U.S. at 538–39.

101. Shiffrin, "The First Amendment and Economic Regulation: Away From a General Theory of the First Amendment," 78 Nw.L.Rev. 1212, 1229 (1983). This impossibility does not, however, support full first amendment protection for self-interested promotion of a misleading variety, or of dangerous products or services.

102. See L. Tribe, Constitutional Choices 218 (1985); Schlag, "An Attack on Categorical Approaches to Freedom of Speech," 30 U.C.L.A.L.Rev. 671, 733–53 (1983).

parses first amendment doctrine too finely, one may soon discover that little protection for expression remains.

§ 12–19. Accommodating Rights to Know, Rights Not to Know, Open Minds, and Closed Communities

The preceding section discussed the contemporary proliferation of intermediate categories of speech, categories which enjoy less than full constitutional protection. This section analyzes the forces behind this development.

One strand of emergent doctrine may be an increasingly sharp differentiation between the focused right of an individual to speak and an undifferentiated right of the public to know. Some have argued that the first amendment does not confer individual rights, but protects a systemic freedom for expressive activities.[1] This view unduly flattens the first amendment's complex role;[2] but even if the view were accepted, the language of rights would nonetheless be appropriate where the liberty guaranteed by the first amendment has as its primary focus the autonomy of individuals or of the press. A right to speak may be said to exist when the Court will not allow government to justify a restriction on expressive conduct by a claim that the ideas or information expressed are dangerous; that the speaker may exercise liberty of expression in some other place, time or manner; or that the speaker should be muffled in order that a diversity of viewpoints might be heard in the marketplace of ideas.

A right to know at times means nothing more than a mirror of such a right to speak, a listener's right that government not interfere with a willing speaker's liberty.[3] But the right to know at times means more: it may include an individual's right to acquire desired information or ideas free of governmental veto,[4] undue hindrance,[5] or unwar-

---

§ 12–19

1. See Meiklejohn, "The First Amendment is an Absolute," 1961 Sup.Ct.Rev. 245, 255, quoted in Hynes v. Mayor and Council of Borough of Oradell, 425 U.S. 610, 628 (1976) (Brennan, J., concurring in part).

2. See § 12–1, supra. See also Shiffrin, "The First Amendment and Economic Regulation: Away from a General Theory of the First Amendment," 78 Nw.L.Rev. 1212, 1252 (1983): "the Court has been unwilling to confine the first amendment to a single value or even to a few values. In recent years, the first amendment literature has exploded with commentary finding first amendment values involving liberty, self-realization, autonomy, the marketplace of ideas, equality, self-government, checking government, and more."

3. See Baker, "Commercial Speech: A Problem in the Theory of Freedom," 62 Iowa L.Rev. 1, 8 (1976) (arguing that a right to know is never more than a right to have the government not interfere with a willing speaker's liberty).

4. See, e.g., Meyer v. Nebraska, 262 U.S. 390 (1923) (reversing a conviction for teaching German in violation of a state law prohibiting the teaching of foreign languages to young children, in part because the law interfered "with the opportunities of pupils to acquire knowledge"); Stanley v. Georgia, 394 U.S. 557 (1969) (reversing a conviction for possession of pornographic material in defendant's home; such application of the statute held to interfere with the possessor's rights to know and to be free of unwarranted intrusions into privacy).

5. Such "undue hindrance" may entail deliberate interference with the acquisition of specified information; more commonly, it entails government action that is largely indifferent to information-gathering but that nonetheless operates as a deterrent to its uninhibited pursuit. Researchers—academic or journalistic—may find their attempts to acquire information inhibited by otherwise legitimate governmental demands that they reveal the identities of their confidential sources. In such cases,

ranted exposure.[6] It may even impose an affirmative obligation on government to open to the public certain of its processes such as criminal trials.[7] A right to know may entail no correlative right in any particular source to originate the communication.[8] In this latter sense,

ordinary first amendment theory should require government to demonstrate that it had no less inhibiting alternative than to demand disclosure. See § 12–23, infra. See generally Note, "The Rights of the Public and the Press to Gather Information," 87 Harv.L.Rev. 1505 (1974). When the Supreme Court declined to require such a demonstration in Branzburg v. Hayes, 408 U.S. 665 (1972) (denying even a qualified journalist's privilege to withhold source identity from good faith grand jury inquiry), it may have been assuming that the journalist's claim was tantamount to a plea of special privilege, something the Court has insisted the press does not enjoy. See, e.g., Pell v. Procunier, 417 U.S. 817, 827–28, 830 (1974) (press enjoys no greater right than general public to acquire information about prison conditions). For a discussion of the news-gathering issue, see § 12–22, infra. The dangers of recognizing a privileged status for the press are considerable; they include the risk that, just as a broadcaster's exclusive use of a given wavelength in a given market is said to justify imposition of legal duties of fair coverage, see Red Lion Broadcasting Co. v. F.C.C., 395 U.S. 367 (1969), so a newspaper's privilege might be said to justify imposition of parallel duties. Contrast Miami Herald Publishing Co. v. Tornillo, 418 U.S. 241 (1974) (newspaper cannot be forced to print reply to a personal attack published in its pages). See § 12–25, infra. Although it has been urged by no less considerable an authority than Justice Stewart, see "Or of the Press," 26 Hast.L.J. 631, 634–36 (1975), that giving the press special powers of access would have no such effect, the risk certainly exists—and there is no clear need to incur it, since it seems doubtful that reversal of such decisions as Branzburg v. Hayes, supra, would require any special press immunities. See Van Alstyne, Comment: "The Hazards to the Press of Claiming a 'Preferred Position'," 28 Hast.L.J. 761, 768 n. 15 (1977). Nor would the "freedom of the press" clause be rendered redundant of the "freedom of speech" clause if it were treated as establishing that the great power of the technology inaugurated by Guttenberg in the fifteenth century in no way strips the press of the freedom the first amendment would otherwise confer. Id. at 769 n. 16. But the matter contains more complexities than this brief note can explore. See, e.g., Anderson, "The Origins of the Press Clause," 30 U.C.L.A.L.Rev. 455 (1983); Nimmer, "Introduction—Is Freedom of the

Press a Redundancy: What Does it Add to Freedom of Speech?" 26 Hast.L.J. 639 (1975); Lange, "The Speech and Press Clauses," 23 U.C.L.A.L.Rev. 77 (1975); Nimmer, "Speech and Press: A Brief Reply," 23 U.C.L.A.L.Rev. 120 (1975). On either view—whether the press is regarded as occupying a special constitutional role or not—freedom from undue interference with the acquisition of knowledge should be deemed central to the first amendment. See §§ 12–20, 12–21, 12–22, infra. Needless to say, government's duty (if any) affirmatively to provide knowledge—as by declassifying information or opening its files—ordinarily rests on principles other than those of the first amendment. See § 12–4, supra. See, e.g., United States v. Nixon, 418 U.S. 683 (1974), discussed in Chapter 4, supra. For an argument finding such a duty in the first amendment itself, however, see Emerson, "Legal Foundations of the Right to Know," 1976 Wash. U.L.Q. 1 (arguing that the citizenry has a first amendment right to government's information).

6. See, e.g., Lamont v. Postmaster General of United States, 381 U.S. 301 (1965) (first amendment right to receive information violated by congressional requirement that persons wishing to receive mail from foreign communist organizations publicly identify their wish to do so). Lamont was, surprisingly, the first case in which the Supreme Court found that an act of Congress violated the first amendment.

7. See § 12–20, infra.

8. The mail that Lamont had a right to receive, supra note 6, originated from persons or organizations abroad whose "speech" was unprotected by the first amendment. Id. In Virginia State Board of Pharmacy v. Virginia Citizens Consumer Council, Inc., 425 U.S. 748 (1976), the right to receive information about prescription drug prices was vindicated in a lawsuit brought by consumers; no pharmacist or seller was before the Court, and it is not clear that such a party would have had a personal right to disseminate the information. In First National Bank of Boston v. Bellotti, 435 U.S. 765 (1978), the Court invalidated a state ban on most corporate contributions and expenditures in referendum and initiative proposals. The Court reserved the question whether corporations have first amendment rights, id. at 777 & n. 13, and merely found "no support in the First or Fourteenth Amendment . . . for the proposition that speech that otherwise

the right to know is the first amendment filtered through the prism of Holmes' marketplace of ideas; such a right carries the implication that government, while it may not close the market, may move to correct its defects and regulate its incidental consequences.[9] To perceive *Young v. American Mini Theatres, Inc.*[10] along these lines, it is important to note Justice Powell's observation in his concurrence that the respondent-theater owners were no more than commercial purveyors: "they do not profess to convey their own personal messages through the movies they show."[11] The theater owners may be thought to have been denied the opportunity to sell certain movie tickets because they had no expressional interest of their own, and were afforded only a lesser right derived from the generalized "right to know" of the viewing public, a right which on the facts of *American Mini Theatres* had not been infringed by the Detroit ordinance. This strand of doctrine is most pronounced in the commercial speech field, where the Court has explic-

would be within the protection of the First Amendment loses that protection simply because its source is a corporation." Id. at 784. The Court thus focused on the *speech* involved, and not exclusively on the speaker. See Baker, "Realizing Self-Realization: Corporate Political Expenditures and Redish's 'The Value of Free Speech,'" 130 U.Pa.L.Rev. 646, 652 (1982) ("If the importance of speech lies in its provision of information, analysis, or argument to the audience, . . . then the source of the speech is irrelevant."). See § 12–3, supra.

9. See Red Lion Broadcasting Co. v. F.C.C., 395 U.S. 367 (1969) (upholding the constitutionality of regulations implementing general requirement that broadcasters provide fair coverage of opposing viewpoints on controversial issues of public importance), discussed in § 12–25, infra. To be sure, the Court has ordinarily rejected the notion that the speech rights of some may be sacrificed to enhance the relative access of others, especially when dealing with expression deemed deserving of full constitutional protection, see Pacific Gas and Elec. Co. v. Public Utilities Comm'n of California, 106 S.Ct. 903 (1986) (plurality opinion) (finding violative of the first amendment an order by a utility commission that granted consumer group access to utility billing envelopes); Citizens Against Rent Control/Coalition for Fair Housing v. Berkley, Cal., 454 U.S. 290, 295–96 (1981) (striking down a $250 limit on contributions to committees supporting or opposing ballot measures); Buckley v. Valeo, 424 U.S. 1, 48–49 (1976) (per curiam) (invalidating limits on candidate expenditures but affirming contribution limits); Miami Herald Pub. Co. v. Tornillo, 418 U.S. 241, 254 (1974) (striking down newspaper right of reply statute). Some commentators urge government regulation of speech to correct market failures and ensure more egalitarian access to the channels of communica-

tions, see Chevigny, "The Paradox of Campaign Finance," 56 N.Y.U.L.Rev. 206, 220 (1981) (arguing that "there is a compelling interest in regulating campaign expenditures [in order] to prevent distortion of the democratic process by money"). Others, however, point out that such plans presuppose a "standard with which to identify a 'properly functioning marketplace.'" Baker, note 8, supra, at 651 & n. 21. For a detailed critique of the "market failure" theories of the first amendment, see Baker, "Scope of the First Amendment Freedom of Speech," 25 U.C.L.A. 964, 981–90 (1978).

10. 427 U.S. 50 (1976), discussed in § 12–18, supra.

11. Id. at 78 n. 2. In Railway Express Agency v. New York, 336 U.S. 106, 116 (1949) (validating the constitutionality of a ban on advertising on the sides of vehicles, but exempting business notices of the vehicle's owners), Justice Jackson in his concurring opinion argued that "there is a real difference between doing in self-interest and doing for hire, so that it is one thing to tolerate action from those who act on their own and it is another thing to permit the same action to be promoted for a price." But it is difficult, to say the least, to distinguish the self-interested motives underlying most speech activity from profit-motivation. Somewhat different is the distinction between the expressive activities of the publicly-owned corporation and those of individuals. See Bell v. Maryland, 378 U.S. 226, 246 (1964) (Douglas, J., joined by Goldberg, J., concurring in result) (reversing trespass convictions of demonstrators who sat-in at private restaurant; "the corporate interest is in making money, not in protecting personal prejudices"). For a fuller discussion, see Baker, "Commercial Speech: A Problem in the Theory of Freedom," 62 Iowa L.Rev. 1 (1976).

itly justified "the extension of First Amendment protection" by the "value to consumers of the information that such speech provides." [12] "Consequently, there can be no constitutional objection to the suppression of commercial messages that do not accurately inform the public about lawful activity." [13] The government, for example, may ban forms of communication more likely to deceive the public than to inform it,[14] as well as commercial speech related to illegal activity.[15]

Second, the decisions in *American Mini Theatres* and other "erogenous zoning" cases, such as *City of Renton v. Playtime Theatres, Inc.*,[16] reflect a concern by the Court to find a way for localities to protect the quality and character of community life without at the same time "making the closed mind a principal feature of the open society." [17] In *Renton*, for example, the Court accepted the city's justification for the

12. Zauderer v. Office of Disciplinary Counsel of Supreme Court of Ohio, 471 U.S. 626, 651 (1985). See also Central Hudson Gas & Elec. Corp. v. Public Serv. Comm'n of New York, 447 U.S. 557, 563 (1980) ("The First Amendment's concern for commercial speech is based on the informational function of advertising"); Virginia State Board of Pharmacy v. Virginia Citizens Consumer Council, Inc., 425 U.S. 748, 761–65 (1976) (extending constitutional protection to commercial speech because of interests of listeners, not of speakers); Jackson & Jeffries, "Commercial Speech: Economic Due Process and the First Amendment," 65 Va.L.Rev. 1, 25 (1979) ("Ordinary business advertising does not advance the goal of individual self-fulfillment through free expression, nor does it contribute to political decisionmaking in a representative democracy."). This tendency has been strong, even in cases that are not, strictly speaking, commercial speech cases at all. See Pacific Gas and Elec. Co. v. Public Utilities Comm'n of California, 106 S.Ct. 903, 921 (1986) (Rehnquist, J., dissenting) (contending that corporations do not have "negative free speech rights," that is, rights to refrain from forced speech): "[C]orporate free speech rights do not arise because corporations, like individuals, have any interest in self-expression. . . . [I]nstead . . . such rights are recognized as an instrumental means of furthering the First Amendment purpose of fostering a broad forum of information to facilitate self-government."

13. Central Hudson Gas & Elec. Corp. v. Public Serv. Comm'n of New York, 447 U.S. 557, 563 (1980). Indeed, Virginia Pharmacy had provided protection only for "truthful and legitimate commercial information." 425 U.S. at 771 n. 24. But the tenor of the opinion rejected a "highly paternalistic approach" toward commerical speech on the assumptions that "this information is not in itself harmful, that people will perceive their own best interests if only they are well enough informed, and that the best means to that end is to open the channels of communication rather than to close them." Id. at 765, 770. See also Zauderer v. Office of Disciplinary Counsel of Supreme Court of Ohio, 471 U.S. 626, 642 (1985) (striking down disciplinary rules from Ohio's Code of Professional Responsibility that forbade attorneys to use illustrations or to give advice in newspaper advertisements, on the ground that such advertisements were "conducive to reflection and the exercise of choice").

14. Friedman v. Rogers, 440 U.S. 1, 13, 15–16 (1979) (upholding a statute that prohibited optometrists from practicing under a trade name on the grounds that such activity would be deceptive); Ohralik v. Ohio State Bar Ass'n, 436 U.S. 447, 464–65 (1978) (upholding ban on in-person solicitation by attorneys). "Government remains free to purge commercial advertising of speech that is deceptive or misleading or perhaps merely unverifiable." Jackson & Jeffries, note 12, supra, at 39. See, e.g., Warner-Lambert Co. v. F.T.C., 562 F.2d 749, 758–59, 763 (D.C. Cir. 1977) (rejecting first amendment objection to FTC order requiring manufacturer of Listerine to cease and desist representations that the product cures colds and sore throats and requiring disclaimer in future advertisements). Cigarette advertising that implies the product is healthful could obviously be prohibited on this basis. See generally § 12–15, supra.

15. Pittsburgh Press Co. v. Pittsburgh Comm'n on Human Relations, 413 U.S. 376, 388 (1973).

16. 106 S.Ct. 925 (1986) (upholding municipal zoning ordinance that prohibited adult motion picture theaters from locating within 1,000 feet of any residential zone, single- or multi-family dwelling, church, park or school).

17. Kalven, The Negro and the First Amendment 159 (1965).

statute as promoting "the City of Renton's great interest in protecting and preserving the quality of its neighborhoods, commercial districts, and the quality of urban life through effective land planning." [18]   And in *Federal Communications Commission v. Pacifica Foundation*, a case which may be likened to zoning of the airwaves,[19] the plurality quoted a description of the speech at issue as "[o]bnoxious, gutteral language" that "has the effect of debasing and brutalizing human beings by reducing them to their mere bodily functions." [20]   Even in cases that do not involve obscene or near-obscene materials, the Court has been willing to grant wide latitude to a community's decision to preserve its quality of life by freeing itself from "visual clutter," although speech rights are sacrificed in the process.[21]

Outside the home, the burden is generally on the observer or listener to avert his eyes or plug his ears against the verbal assaults, lurid advertisements, tawdry books and magazines, and other "offensive" intrusions which increasingly attend urban life.[22]   The Court seems understandably troubled that the individual may be able to find refuge from such bombardments of his sensibilities only in the sanctuary of the home—a castle fortress under siege.[23]   Yet the Court has not generally allowed government to suppress speech solely to protect

18. App. to Juris. Statement 81a, quoted at 106 S.Ct. 935 (Brennan, J., joined by Marshall, J., dissenting).

19. 438 U.S. 726 (1978). Justice Stevens, in the plurality opinion, conceded that "[s]ome uses of even the most offensive words are unquestionably protected. Indeed, we may assume, *arguendo*, that this monologue would be protected in other contexts. Nonetheless, the constitutional protection accorded to a communication containing such patently offensive sexual and excretory language need not be the same in every context." Id. at 746–47 (plurality opinion) (citations omitted); see id. at 750 (likening offensive language on the radio to a " 'nuisance [which] may be merely a right thing in the wrong place—like a pig in the parlor instead of the barnyard,' " quoting Village of Euclid, Ohio v. Ambler Realty Co., 272 U.S. 365, 388 (1926) (upholding zoning ordinance that restricted industrial use of land near residential area)). Justice Stevens also sought "to emphasize the narrowness of [the plurality's] holding," id. at 750: "The [decision to forbid use of offensive language] requires consideration of a host of variables. The time of day was emphasized by the Commission. The content of the program in which the language is used will also affect the composition of the audience, and differences between radio, television, and perhaps closed circuit transmissions, may also be relevant," id. But see "The Supreme Court, 1977 Term," 92 Harv.L.Rev. 57, 158–59 (1978).

20. 438 U.S. at 746 n. 23, quoting 56 F.C.C.2d at 98.

21. See Members of City Council of City of Los Angeles v. Taxpayers for Vincent, 466 U.S. 789, 807 (1984) (upholding ordinance that prohibited the posting of signs on public property, as applied to political candidate who sought to post campaign signs on utility poles): "the visual assault on the citizens of Los Angeles presented by an accumulation of signs posted on public property [ ] constitutes a significant substantive evil within the City's power to prohibit." The Court then quoted Young v. American Mini Theatres, Inc., 427 U.S. 50 at 71 (1976) (plurality opinion) ("the city's interest in attempting to preserve [or improve] the quality of urban life is one that must be accorded high respect"). Similarly, in Metromedia, Inc. v. San Diego, 453 U.S. 490 (1981) (invalidating ordinance that restricted billboard advertising on the ground that it gave greater access to commercial than non-commercial speech), seven Justices appeared to conclude that the city's interest in avoiding "visual clutter" was sufficient to justify a prohibition of billboards, see id. at 507–08, 510 (opinion of White, J., joined by Stewart, Marshall, and Powell, JJ.); id. at 552 (Stevens, J., dissenting); id. at 559–61 (Burger, C.J., dissenting); id. at 570 (Rehnquist, J., dissenting).

22. See Cohen v. California, 403 U.S. 15, 21 (1971) (jacket bearing the slogan "Fuck the Draft"); Erznoznik v. Jacksonville, 422 U.S. 205, 211, 212 (1975) (filmed nudity visible from outside drive-in theater).

23. See, e.g., Paris Adult Theatre I v. Slaton, 413 U.S. 49 (1973) (upholding in-

unwilling listeners from "offensive" expression unless substantial privacy interests have been invaded.[24]

junction against the exhibition of obscene films in commercial adults-only theatre). The Court's opinion by Chief Justice Burger strongly affirms a legitimate interest of the public in "the style and quality of life" and "the total community environment", id. at 58–59, and draws an analogy to laws which protect the physical environment. Id. at 62. These concerns are evidently shared by a large part of the urban population. See Wilson, "The Urban Unease: Community vs. City," 12 Public Interest 25 (1968).

24. Cohen v. California, 403 U.S. 15, 21 (1971). Indeed, in Pacifica the plurality noted that "the fact that society may find speech offensive is not a sufficient reason for suppressing it. Indeed, if it is the speaker's opinion that gives offense, that consequence is a reason for according it constitutional protection." 438 U.S. at 745. The "privacy" interests of unwilling listeners are strongest in the home. See, e.g., Rowan v. United States Post Office Department, 397 U.S. 728 (1970) (upholding addressee's statutory right to compel a mailer of material which is deemed erotic at the sole discretion of the addressee to remove addressee's name from mailing list and stop all future mailings); Kovacs v. Cooper, 336 U.S. 77 (1949) (upholding ordinance proscribing the use of sound trucks in a "loud and raucous" manner, in part because the individual in his home is "practically helpless to escape" the intrusion). But each householder must be left with the right to decide what messages to receive; government cannot make this choice in gross. See, e.g., Martin v. Struthers, 319 U.S. 141 (1943) (voiding ordinance prohibiting door-to-door distribution of any advertisements, distinguishing the case of those who call at the home in defiance of a previously expressed will of the occupant not to be disturbed).

See also City of Watseka v. Illinois Public Action Council, 107 S.Ct. 919 (1987) (affirming lower court decision that struck down as applied a city ordinance which limited door-to-door canvassing to the hours of 9:00 am to 5:00 pm, Monday through Saturday). But cf. Breard v. Alexandria, La., 341 U.S. 622 (1951) (upholding ordinance prohibiting door-to-door distribution of *commercial* advertising), discussed in § 12–15, supra.

To what extent the special "privacy" claims of householders may justify bans on picketing, leafleting, and other expressive activities in residential areas remains undecided. Justice Black was surely right that "the homes of men, sometimes the last citadel of the tired, the weary, and the sick, can be protected by government from noisy, marching, tramping, threatening picketers and demonstrators. . . ." Gregory v. Chicago, 394 U.S. 111 (1969) (concurring opinion) (reversing convictions for disorderly conduct for holding a demonstration which the Court found to be peaceful and orderly; the majority did not reach the question of residential picketing, peaceful or otherwise, since that was not the crime for which defendants were charged). But if the expressive activities of the demonstrators are not intrusive, the householder should not be able to keep speakers from communicating their messages to the public comprising a person's neighbors. Cf. Organization for a Better Austin v. Keefe, 402 U.S. 415, 420 (1971) (invalidating injunction against leafleting in suburban residential area as unjustified prior restraint; Chief Justice Burger distinguished the right of privacy involved in stopping "the flow of information into [one's] household" from preventing the flow of the same information to the public). See generally, Note, "Picketers at the Doorstep," 9 Harv.Civ. Rts.-Civ.Lib.L.Rev. 95 (1974).

In public places an individual's privacy interests in avoiding offensive communications are generally thought insubstantial unless the person is deemed a member of a "captive audience", either because the person is literally not free to leave without great burden (see, e.g., Lehman v. Shaker Heights, 418 U.S. 298, 307 (1974) (Douglas J., concurring) (commuters deemed captives of advertising on municipally-owned buses); Mailloux v. Kiley, 323 F.Supp. 1387, 1392 (D.Mass.1971) (school children as a captive audience); cf. West Virginia State Board of Education v. Barnette, 319 U.S. 624 (1943) (flag salute compelled of public school students)), or because the person is in a place where there is a basic right to remain and where one cannot readily avoid exposure to the unwanted communication. On these grounds it may be possible to justify community control over architectural styles and at least some outdoor displays precisely because they are more permanent and visible. See Packer Corp. v. Utah, 285 U.S. 105, 110 (1932) (Brandeis, J.): "Other forms of advertising are ordinarily seen as a matter of choice on the part of the observer. The young as well as the adults have the message of the billboard thrust upon them. . . . In the case of newspapers and magazines, there must be some seeking by the one who is to see and read the advertisement. The radio can be turned off, but not so the billboard or street car placard." See also, although to a somewhat different end, Note, "Aes-

Ironically, a "privacy" right equally fails to secure the converse freedom to receive information that the majority says is worthless. The right of a man to view an obscene film in the privacy of his home [25] may seem somewhat trivial [26] if, as the Court has said, that man and others have no right to gather discreetly to have the same film shown to them for a fee.[27] A line which accommodates the contrarieties of rights to know and not to know—rights to receive ideas and to exclude them—cannot be satisfactorily drawn in "privacy" terms alone, for involved in both cases is the individual's right to constitute his own life. That process cannot go forward if it is conceived wholly as Zarathustra meditating on the mountain top, since each man's freedom is exercised in part through the "help and security given him by his fellow man." [28] *American Mini Theatres* and *Renton* may signal the willingness of some members of the Court to fashion rules for speech in public places which will try to accommodate the conflicting demands of individuals and communities to have government shield each from intrusion by the other.

Within this calculus, the Court has promised that it will assure the continued availability of constitutionally protected materials. In *Pacifica*, concluded Justice Powell, "the Commission's order does not prevent willing adults from purchasing Carlin's record, from attending his performances, or, indeed, from reading the transcript as reprinted as an appendix to the Court's opinion. On its face, it does not prevent respondent Pacifica Foundation from broadcasting the monologue during late evening hours when fewer children are likely to be in the audience, nor from broadcasting discussions of the contemporary use of language at any time during the day." [29] And in *Renton*, the Court concluded that the city had struck a reasonable balance between the potentially conflicting interests, by "mak[ing] some areas available for adult theaters and their patrons, while at the same time preserving the quality of life in the community at large." [30]

---

thetic Control of Land Use: A House Built Upon Sand," 59 Northwestern L.Rev. 372 (1964). But in the end it must be stressed that the concept of a "captive audience" is dangerously encompassing, and the Court has properly been reluctant to accept its implications whenever a regulation is not content-neutral. See, e.g., Erznoznik v. Jacksonville, 422 U.S. 205, 210 (1975) (ordinance banning the exhibition of movies containing nudity on drive-in screens visible from the street could not be upheld in order to protect sensibilities of involuntary passers-by): "The plain, if at times disquieting, truth is that in our pluralistic society, constantly proliferating new and ingenious forms of expression, we are inescapably captive audiences for many purposes."

25. See Stanley v. Georgia, 394 U.S. 557 (1969).

26. See Marks v. United States, 430 U.S. 188, 198 (1977) (Stevens, J., dissenting).

27. See Paris Adult Theatre I v. Slaton, 413 U.S. 49, 59, 66 (1973).

28. See Green, "Liberal Legislation and the Freedom of Contract," in Green, Works, Vol. III: Miscellanies and Memoir 371 (1888).

29. F.C.C. v. Pacifica Foundation, 438 U.S. 726, 760 (1978) (Powell, J., joined by Blackmun, J., concurring in part and concurring in the judgment).

30. City of Renton v. Playtime Theatres, Inc., 475 U.S. 41 (1986). In so finding, the Court rejected the determinations of both the district court and the court of appeals, which had concluded that there were no commercially viable adult theater sites within the 520 acres left open by the Renton ordinance. See 748 F.2d at 534 (noting that the ordinance "would result in a substantial restriction" on speech).

Weighing these interests, and determining how much access must remain in order for alternative avenues of communication to be deemed "reasonable," are difficult tasks, at which the Court has not proven particularly adept. In *Schad v. Borough of Mt. Ephraim*,[31] the Court struck down an ordinance that prohibited all forms of live entertainment, not merely those of the "adult" variety, from the borough's commercial district. The borough was unable to explain to the Court why a total ban on commercial live entertainment, including such varied diversions as concerts, plays, and nude dancing, was justified despite the fact that all of the usual parking, trash, or police protection problems resulting from it were equally likely to arise from such permitted commercial enterprises as restaurants and movie houses.[32] The Court gave short shrift to the argument that those wishing to view nude dancers could travel to nearby establishments outside the town; in the absence of any evidence to that effect in the record, the defense was unavailable.[33] But the most interesting aspect of the live-entertainment case was left open by the Court. The borough argued that, if there were county-wide rather than borough zoning, it might be constitutional to limit nude dancing to selected areas of the county and exclude it altogether from primarily residential areas such as Mt. Ephraim.[34] The Court admitted that this might be true but opined that, in the instant case, there was no scheme of zoning at the county level. The borough's suggestion was the inverse of *American Mini Theatres*: rather than *dispersing* the adult theaters in order to dilute their capacity to pollute neighborhoods, a county could *concentrate* such enterprises in one area that it was willing to sacrifice in order to preserve the rest of the community. Would a law banning sexually explicit films everywhere in Massachusetts *but* Boston be constitutional? The interplay of the holding in *American Mini Theatres* with the dictum in *Mt. Ephraim* creates some interesting scenarios.[35] A plan by the sprawling city of Los Angeles to disperse adult movie houses— which would be undeniably constitutional—might well be a more geographically significant restriction of first amendment rights than a decision by Rhode Island to ban all such entertainment from the entire state. If what the Court means to stress is reasonable access to a particular kind of expression, the doctrine in this area could soon become a tangled, rather than a seamless, web.

31. 452 U.S. 61 (1981) (opinion of the Court by White, J.). Chief Justice Burger, joined by Justice Rehnquist, dissented.

32. Id. at 73–75.

33. Id. at 76.

34. Id.

35. The Court's later cases have not provided clarification. In Renton, for example, the Court emphasized the need to permit local flexibility: "Cities may regulate adult theaters by dispersing them, as in Detroit, or by effectively concentrating them, as in Renton. 'It is not our function to appraise the wisdom of [the city's] deci-

sion to require adult theaters to be separated rather than concentrated in the same areas. . . . [T]he city must be allowed a reasonable opportunity to experiment with solutions to admittedly serious problems.' " 106 S.Ct. at 931, quoting Young v. American Mini Theatres, Inc., 427 U.S. 50 at 71 (1976). See also City of Newport, Kentucky v. Iacobucci, 107 S.Ct. 383 (1986) (per curiam) (upholding city's authority to enact an ordinance that prohibited nude or nearly nude dancing in local establishments licensed to sell liquor for on-premises consumption).

Third, the Court in *American Mini Theatres* and *Renton* signaled a growing willingness to entertain content-based restrictions on protected expression at least where the government's interest is not in protecting listeners from exposure to the speech as such but rather in protecting third-party bystanders from the "secondary effects" of the speech—the physical deterioration and crime, for example, which accompany the concentration of adult theaters in a "red light" district.[36] However, while in *American Mini Theatres* the Court did not pretend the zoning rule was content-neutral, the *Renton* Court found that "the ordinance is completely consistent with our definition of 'content-neutral' speech regulations as those that are '*justified* without reference to the content of the regulated speech.'"[37] The Court thus found that, despite the restriction's outward appearance, it was not content-*based*, because the government chose to *defend* the rule with reasons distinct from its impact on the minds of listeners. The *Renton* view should be quickly renounced. Carried to its logical conclusion, such a doctrine could gravely erode the first amendment's protections.[38] Indeed, the Court itself may see the case as an aberration: on the same day that it decided *Renton*, the Court also released its opinion in *Pacific Gas and Electric Co. v. Public Utilities Commission of New York*,[39] which reaffirmed the more familiar track-two doctrine.[40]

Fourth, although *Erznoznik v. Jacksonville*[41] plainly shows, as had *Manual Enterprises, Inc. v. Day*[42] before, it, that the Court is unwilling to equate nudity with offensiveness, nonetheless it seems likely that a

36. See American Mini Theatres, 427 U.S. at 71–72 & n. 34, n. 35. The Court accepted a similar justification in Renton even though the city council added these stated goals as amendments to the ordinance *after* litigation challenging it was commenced. See 106 S.Ct. at 935 (Brennan, J., joined by Marshall, J., dissenting). Indeed, the lower court had concluded that "[t]he record presented by Renton to support its asserted interest in enacting the zoning ordinance is very thin." 748 F.2d at 536. Justice Brennan, too, doubted the veracity of the city's post-hoc rationalizations and suggested that the legislative history of the ordinance pointed to more sinister motives: "the ordinance was designed to suppress expression, even that constitutionally protected." 106 S.Ct. at 936. By contrast, in Erznoznick v. Jacksonville, 422 U.S. 205 (1975), the Court voided on its face a statute making it a public nuisance for a drive-in movie theater to show films containing nudity if the screen is visible from a public street or place. The justifications offered by the city rested primarily on the unwanted exposure of some Jacksonville residents to "offensive" images. The only secondary effect advanced to justify the rule was its impact on traffic, an effect likely to be caused by any movie, even one without nudity. See id. at 214–15.

37. 106 S.Ct. at 929 (quoting Virginia State Board of Pharmacy v. Virginia Citizens Consumer Council, Inc., 425 U.S. 748, 771 (1976) (emphasis added in Renton)).

38. See, e.g., Finzer v. Barry, 798 F.2d 1450, 1450, 1469–70 n. 15 (D.C. Cir. 1986) (Bork, J.) (labeling as content-neutral a rule that required demonstrations critical of a foreign government to take place more than 500 feet away from that country's embassy but that imposed no restriction on pro-government demonstrations), cert. granted sub nom. Boos v. Barry, 107 S.Ct. 1282 (1987). The danger lies in the fact that most, if not all, speech may thus be subject to regulation on the basis of its "secondary effects." As Chief Judge Wald warned in dissent, "If listeners' reaction is deemed to be a 'secondary' effect, then there is nothing left at all of the content-based distinction doctrine." 798 F.2d at 1480 n. 5 (Wald, C.J., dissenting).

39. 106 S.Ct. 903 (1986).

40. "For a time, place, or manner restriction to be valid, it must be neutral as to the content of the speech to be regulated." Id. at 914.

41. 422 U.S. 205 (1975).

42. 370 U.S. 478, 489–90 (1962) (Harlan, J., announced the judgment of the Court in an opinion joined by Stewart, J.,) (magazines which portrayed nudes but did not include the model's genitals, held mailable).

distinction will persist, even after obscenity is one day assimilated into the first amendment, between sexually explicit displays and forms of speech less physiological and anatomical in their content and appeal.[43] The observer and listener are ordinarily required to turn the other way if they would avoid offense in public, but we may assume that constitutional doctrine will continue to distinguish among forms of offense in applying such a principle. In *Paris Adult Theatre I v. Slaton*, for example, the Court noted offhandedly that "a 'live' performance of a man and woman locked in a sexual embrace at high noon in Times Square" is unprotected even if they "simultaneously engage in a valid political dialogue."[44] Perhaps the most interesting aspect of that remark was not its suggestion that the dialogue cannot shield the exhibition from the police power—that amounted to no more than a repetition of the famous dictum that a quote from Voltaire on the flyleaf of an obscene book cannot save it[45]—but the assumption that the sexual embrace itself may be banned from the public arena.

The reason, presumably, is not simply that people may take offense; that could have been said of the inscription on the jacket in *Cohen v. California*[46] as well, and indeed it might be said of the political dialogue in which the Court's hypothetical couple engaged along with their other activities. Nor does it seem satisfactory to rely on the possibility that children will be injured by the sight; the Court has, after all, held that adults may not be reduced to a literary and visual environment that is safe for children,[47] and it is at least imaginable that communities where children are rarely if ever present would seek to exercise the power that *Paris Adult Theatre* presumes they possess.

We might come closer to the mark by noting the Court's observation that *Cohen v. California* was "not . . . an obscenity case" since the "Fuck the Draft" slogan on defendant's jacket was not "in some significant way, erotic."[48] Inasmuch as no "psychic stimulation" would be caused by "Cohen's crudely defaced jacket," the state could not rely on its power to protect persons from uninvited affront.[49] The special features of the "psychic stimulation" found absent in *Cohen* are plain enough: it occurs at once, so that the offended really have no time to avoid the unwanted impact—as one might avoid the unwanted impact of most political harangues simply by sampling enough to know that one wanted to hear no more, and then moving on. Moreover, and more significantly, an odd sort of privacy interest is at stake: the right of the

---

43. In Renton, for example, Justice Brennan noted that the Court's holding was limited "to cases involving 'businesses that purvey sexually explicit materials.'" 106 S.Ct. at 933 (Brennan, J., joined by Marshall, J., dissenting), quoting majority opinion, id. at 929 n. 2.

44. 413 U.S. 49, 67 (1973).

45. See Kois v. Wisconsin, 408 U.S. 229, 231 (1972) (per curiam).

46. 403 U.S. 15 (1971) (reversing conviction for wearing a jacket bearing the words

"Fuck the Draft", under ordinance which proscribed "offensive conduct").

47. See Butler v. Michigan, 352 U.S. 380, 383–84 (1957) (invalidating state statute that banned the publication, sale, or distribution of reading materials inappropriate for children).

48. Cohen, 403 U.S. at 20.

49. Id.

observer not to be "put on the spot" by having to react, openly and in public, to anything quite so powerful and intimate as overt sexual activity.[50] For the very reason that the defendant in *Stanley v. Georgia*[51] had a constitutional right to resist public efforts to expose his reading habits and to rummage through his private liberary of sexual materials, the individual who comes upon a couple locked in sexual embrace in Times Square might plausibly argue that he is entitled to resist public scrutiny of his response: Will he wince? Smirk? Look away in shame? Smile in shared satisfaction? If one believes that the state has no right to put him to such a test, then one may say that government no more than vindicates his right to privacy when it tells the couple to move indoors. Only with respect to displays of an unusually powerful sort—displays that cannot plausibly pass unnoticed—can such an argument prevail; for most forms of communication, the decisive answer will be that passersby are not in fact "put on the spot," given their ability simply to move on without making an involuntary "statement" about their innermost reactions. When such a retort is unavailable, however, government may defend its prohibition against public display by invoking the right of privacy.

Finally, a content-based regulation of protected expression cannot deny speakers access to a willing public, a requirement which accords with the primary inquiry on track two:[52] whether the regulation unduly constricts the ultimate flow of information and ideas. But, as will be seen, the word "unduly" implies for track-two analysis a "balancing" of affected interests.[53] It is not clear in *American Mini Theatres* what track the first amendment inquiry took. If the strong presumption against content-based regulation remains intact, however, it should follow that, when the plurality opinion asked whether the ordinance had "the effect of suppressing, or greatly restricting access to, lawful speech,"[54] an affirmative answer would have been decisive against the ordinance without further inquiry into government's regulatory interests. But if the Court had cast its inquiry in terms of a track-two analysis, the inquiry might not have been so swiftly terminated—even with a finding of substantial restriction on expression. Given the ordinance's reliance on content, it is the first track that accords best with the basic architectural plan from which first amendment jurisprudence has been building. That plan begins with the fundamental recognition that government may "abridge" speech in two conceptually distinct ways,[55] and that when government aims at the *communi-*

---

50. See Knowles & Poorkaj, "Attitudes and Behavior on Viewing Sexual Activities in Public Places," 58 J.Soc. & Soc. Research 130 (1973–74).

51. 394 U.S. 557 (1969).

52. Track two encompasses abridgments of speech which are not aimed at ideas or information but at a goal independent of communicative content, but with the indirect result that the flow of informa-

tion or ideas is constricted. See § 12–2, supra.

53. See § 12–23, infra.

54. American Mini Theatres, 427 U.S. at 71 & n. 35. The plurality opinion said only that the situation would be "quite different if the ordinance had the effect of suppressing, or greatly restricting access to, lawful speech."

55. See § 12–2, supra.

cative impact of conduct, the justifications which it may successfully advance in defense of its action must be truly extraordinary.[56]

§ 12–20. The First Amendment Right to Know: Proceedings Presumptively Open to the Public

Although the system of free expression established by the first amendment does not decree that government conduct all of the people's business in full view of the public, it does impose limits on the ability of government to withold certain types of information *from* the public. These limits are especially strict when the information is produced or released in a forum (such as a trial) that, by its nature or by express constitutional command, is open to the public and not wholly internal to government. This section elaborates upon that basic insight by reviewing the course of Supreme Court adjudication in a number of related areas from the early 1970's into the late 1980's.

In *Branzburg v. Hayes*[1] the Supreme Court first offered the tantalizing suggestion that "news gathering is not without its First Amendment protections."[2] Six years later, in *Houchins v. KQED*,[3] the Court directly confronted for the first time the issue of whether the press has any affirmative right of access to information controlled by the government. KQED sought access to inspect a section of the Alameda county jail where a prisoner reportedly had committed suicide and where a scant three years earlier a federal judge had found "shocking and debasing conditions."[4]

The Supreme Court, with only seven Justices participating,[5] held that the county sheriff could not be ordered to permit access to the troubled section of the jail or to permit inmate interviews.[6] All seven members of the Court adhered in some degree to two propositions. The first was that the press has no constitutional right of access to government information superior to that of the public at large.[7] The second was that the Court's institutional capacity to enforce a right of access to information still in the government's hands is limited, even assuming that such a right were protected by the Constitution. Both the plurali-

---

56. See § 12–3, supra.

§ 12–20

1. 408 U.S. 665 (1972), discussed more fully in § 12–22, infra.

2. 408 U.S. at 707.

3. 438 U.S. 1 (1978).

4. Brenneman v. Madigan, 343 F.Supp. 128, 132–33 (N.D. Cal. 1972) (Ziropoli, J.).

5. Chief Justice Burger announced the judgment of the Court and delivered an opinion joined by Justices White and Rehnquist. Justice Stewart concurred in the judgment. Justice Stevens, joined by Justices Brennan and Powell, dissented. Justices Marshall and Blackmun took no part in the case.

6. 438 U.S. at 9, 15–16; id. at 18 (Stewart, J., concurring in the judgment).

7. Id. at 11 (Burger, C.J., joined by White and Rehnquist, JJ.) (plurality opinion); id. at 16 (Stewart, J., concurring in the judgment); id. at 27–28 (Stevens, J., dissenting, joined by Brennan and Powell, JJ.). See also Pell v. Procunier, 417 U.S. 817, 834 (1974) (declaring that the media has "no constitutional right of access to prisons or their inmates beyond that afforded the general public"); Branzburg v. Hayes, 408 U.S. 665, 684 (1972) (contending that "the First Amendment does not guarantee the press a constitutional right of special access to information not available to the public generally").

ty [8] and dissenting [9] opinions stressed the difficulty of deriving constitutional standards for governing the disclosure of information. How much information to disclose was a matter of degree, involving delicate questions of policy which the Constitution reserved for the political branches.

Chief Justice Burger concluded that no constitutional guidelines exist and held that the first and fourteenth amendments require no right of access.[10] In dissent, Justice Stevens, joined by Justices Brennan and Powell, drew on a reservoir of first amendment theory to conclude that "[w]ithout some protection for the acquisition of information about the operation of public institutions . . . the process of self-governance contemplated by the Framers would be stripped of its substance." [11] Their answer to the plurality was that some cases do not involve matters of degree, and *Houchins* is one of them.[12] In the judgment of these Justices, the record demonstrated the existence of "an official policy of concealing from the public knowledge" about the conditions of the Alameda jail "by arbitrarily cutting off the flow of information at its source." [13] Although there are occasions where government may act in total secrecy,[14] no government interest exists that could justify a policy of concealing prison conditions from the public.[15] Once the illicit policy of concealment becomes evident, a court must act to remedy the consequences of the constitutional violation. A court has broad discretion in tailoring remedial action, and it may impose remedial duties that are not themselves specifically required by the Constitution.[16] Justice Stevens' reply to the plurality was that the Court need not create at the outset detailed standards governing disclosure of information. Its task can be more limited, familiar, and peculiarly judicial—to determine that a constitutional violation has occurred and to select an appropriate remedy.

8. Houchins, 438 U.S. at 14 (Burger, C.J., joined by White and Rehnquist, JJ.) (plurality opinion).

9. Id. at 34–35 (Stevens, J., dissenting, joined by Brennan and Powell, JJ.).

10. Id. at 12–13 (Burger, C.J., joined by White and Rehnquist, JJ.) (plurality opinion).

11. Id. at 32 (Stevens, J., dissenting, joined by Brennan and Powell, JJ.) (footnote omitted).

12. Id. at 34.

13. Id. at 38.

14. See, e.g., Landmark Communications, Inc. v. Virginia, 435 U.S. 829, 845 (1978) (recommending "careful internal procedures" to protect the confidentiality of proceedings of commission investigating judicial misconduct); United States v. Nixon, 418 U.S. 683, 705 (1974) (affirming the need for confidentiality for communications among high government officials).

15. 438 U.S. at 35–36 (Stevens, J., dissenting, joined by Brennan and Powell, JJ.) (distinguishing prior cases such as Saxbe v. Washington Post Co., 417 U.S. 843 (1974), and Pell v. Procunier, 417 U.S. 817 (1974), on the ground that they held only that legitimate penological interests justified restrictions on the *time* and *manner* of public access to information about prisons). Other "legitimate penological interests," such as concerns for security, may justify severe internal restrictions on inmate-to-inmate mail, although not on inmate marriages. Turner v. Safley, 107 S.Ct. 2254, 2261 (1987) (test is whether rule is "reasonably related to legitimate penological interests").

16. 438 U.S. at 40, citing Milliken v. Bradley, 433 U.S. 267, 287 (1977) (discussing a court's discretion in formulating desegregation decrees for public schools), discussed in §§ 16–19, 16–20, infra.

The first case in which a majority [17] of the Court reached agreement in this area was *Gannett Co. v. DePasquale*,[18] which held that the Constitution allows a trial court, at the request of the defendant and without objection by the prosecution, to exclude the press and public from a pretrial suppression hearing, at least with respect to the determination of the admissibility of the defendant's confession. The Court, relying exclusively on a sixth amendment rationale, concluded that the right to a public trial could be invoked only by the criminal defendant, and it reserved the issue of whether the first amendment contains a right of access to such proceedings by finding that, even if that amendment applied, its requirements had been satisfied in the instant case.[19]

The definitive answer to the question of whether the first amendment mandates open *trials* came in *Richmond Newspapers, Inc. v. Virginia*.[20] In September 1978, John Paul Stevenson was on trial on a charge of murder for the fourth time.[21] Despite the spirit of liberty which pervaded the site of the trial,[22] the presiding judge took the unprecedented step of granting the defense counsel's request that the trial be conducted in secret.[23] Ultimately, the sole reason provided by the trial court for banishing all observers (including Richmond Newspapers' two reporters) for the duration of the proceedings was that the public's presence might distract the jury [24]—an astonishing rationale strikingly incompatible with the centuries-old norm of public trials. The trial continued in secret and, for unknown reasons, the court struck the Commonwealth's evidence and declared the defendant not guilty. Such an unexplained acquittal in the midst of a secret retrial for murder portends a regime of "mystery, miracle and authority" [25]— one wholly inhospitable to first amendment values and traditions. Yet the Virginia Supreme Court denied all of Richmond Newspapers' petitions for mandamus, prohibition, and leave to appeal.[26]

17. The vote was 5–4.

18. 443 U.S. 368 (1979). Justice Stewart delivered the opinion of the Court, in which Chief Justice Burger and Justices Powell, Rehnquist, and Stevens joined. Chief Justice Burger and Justices Powell and Rehnquist also filed concurring opinions. Justice Blackmun filed an opinion concurring in part and dissenting in part, in which Justices Brennan, White, and Marshall joined.

19. Id. at 392.

20. 448 U.S. 555 (1980). The author of this treatise argued the case before the Supreme Court on behalf of the appellant newspaper.

21. His initial conviction had been reversed, and two subsequent retrials ended in mistrials. Id. at 559 (Burger, C.J., joined by White and Stevens, JJ.) (plurality opinion).

22. The place of the trial was the Hanover County Courthouse, a prototype of the American trial forum, where two centuries before Patrick Henry had gained immortal fame by delivering a stirring oration to a courtroom crowded to the rafters.

23. Va. Code § 19.2–266 (1950) provides that criminal trials may be closed, with the defendant's consent, to "any persons whose presence would impair the conduct of a fair trial."

24. See 448 U.S. at 561, 580–81 (Burger, C.J., joined by White and Stevens, JJ.) (plurality opinion).

25. F. Dostoevsky, The Brothers Karamazov 301 (D. Magarshack trans. 1958).

26. 448 U.S. at 562 (Burger, C.J., joined by White and Stevens, JJ). (plurality opinion).

In a 7–1 [27] decision which spawned seven opinions,[28] none commanding a majority, the Court reversed and ruled that the first amendment guarantees a public right of access to criminal trials.[29] Chief Justice Burger, in an opinion joined by Justices White and Stevens, traced the historical evolution of the modern criminal trial and concluded that openness was required if trials were to perform their traditional functions of educating the populace in the ways of democracy, creating a public perception of fairness, and providing an outlet for community concern, emotion, and hostility.[30] The courthouse is a "theatre of justice," [31] wherein a vital social drama is staged; if its doors are locked, the public can only wonder whether the solemn ritual of communal condemnation has been properly performed.

Justice Brennan, joined by Justice Marshall, concurred in the judgment on the ground that a right of public access to criminal trials was required by the "structural" [32] role played by the first amendment. Rather than viewing the right to observe and discuss the criminal justice system as a derivative of the general first amendment policy of protecting the intrinsic value of self-expression, Justice Brennan argued that a right of access was a necessary corollary to the constitutional purpose of ensuring government accountability.[33] Open trials, Justice Brennan concluded, advance broad constitutional objectives; they "as-

27. Justice Powell, whose separate opinion was pivotal in Gannett, see J. Choper, Y. Kamisar, and L. Tribe, 1 The Supreme Court: Trends and Developments 1978–1979, at 225–30 (1979), did not participate.

28. Chief Justice Burger wrote for a plurality consisting of himself and Justices White and Stevens. Justice Brennan concurred in the judgment and was joined by Justice Marshall. Justice Stevens joined the plurality opinion and also filed a separate concurring opinion. 448 U.S. at 582. Justice Blackmun concurred in the judgment primarily on sixth amendment grounds, relying on the argument made by the dissenters in Gannett. Id. at 601. Justice White, who had joined the Gannett dissent, expressed a similar sentiment. Id. at 581–82. Justice Stewart, long an advocate of an "adversary" model of government-press relations, see Branzburg v. Hayes, 408 U.S. 665, 726–27 (1972) (Stewart, J., dissenting); Stewart, "Or of the Press," 26 Hast.L.J. 631, 636 (1975), also concurred in the judgment, stressing that the right of access was not absolute. See 448 U.S. at 600. Justice Rehnquist was the lone dissenter.

29. Of course, that right remains subject to a court's power to regulate the speech of parties, witnesses, and observers in the interest of fair and decorous proceedings. The Court has assumed that all behavior—including purely communicative behavior—that prevents the fair adjudica-

tion of a case is punishable as contempt. See Wood v. Georgia, 370 U.S. 375, 383 (1962) ("We start with the premise that the right of the courts to conduct their business in an untrammeled way lies at the foundation of our system of government"); Pennekamp v. Florida, 328 U.S. 331, 353 (1946) (Frankfurter, J., concurring) ("Among the 'substantive evils' with which legislation may deal is the hampering of a court in a pending controversy, because the fair administration of justice is one of the chief tests of a true democracy"). See § 12–11, supra.

30. 448 U.S. at 563–73 (plurality opinion).

31. 1 J. Bentham, The Rationale of Judicial Evidence 597 et passim (J. Mill ed. 1827).

32. For an exposition of this theory, see Brennan, Address, 32 Rutgers L.Rev. 173, 176–82 (1979).

33. As James Madison wrote nearly two centuries ago:

"A popular Government, without popular information, or the means of acquiring it, is but a Prologue to a Farce or a Tragedy; or, perhaps both. Knowledge will forever govern ignorance: And a people who mean to be their own Governors, must arm themselves with the power which knowledge gives."

9 Writings of James Madison 103 (G. Hunt ed. 1910)

sure the public that procedural rights are respected, and that justice is afforded equally." [34]

As in *Gannett*, the defense counsel had requested a closed proceeding, so a sixth amendment argument was unavailable. Indeed, given that neither the defendant nor the prosecutor desired an open trial,[35] an argument could be made that the first amendment actually prohibited an open proceeding in such circumstances on the ground that it would represent the forced speech of unwilling speakers. While this objection need not prove fatal,[36] any satisfying interpretation of *Richmond Newspapers* must explain why the public has a right to receive information in spite of its supplier's desire that it not be disclosed. Similarly, the theory must define the right to know in limited terms, without presupposing anything like a constitutionally-based, all-encompassing Freedom of Information Act.

The strongest case for a first amendment right of access to criminal trials rests on the fact that such trials are public by constitutional command. The sixth amendment, which confers on the accused the right to demand a public trial,[37] implies that the government cannot claim unfettered discretion to treat criminal trials as though they involved wholly internal or confidential matters, or to view the information produced by such trials as "information generated and controlled by government." [38] The *Richmond Newspapers* plurality correctly recognized the Anglo-American tradition of open trials; this openness is a result not of historical accident but rather of explicit constitutional command.[39]

---

34. 448 U.S. at 595 (Brennan, J., concurring in judgment). For a favorable assessment of Justice Brennan's structural approach as "the only rationale for the Richmond Newspapers decision true to the purposes of the first amendment," see The Supreme Court, 1979 Term, 94 Harv.L.Rev. 149, 154–59 (1980).

35. Presumably the judge wanted a closed proceeding, see 448 U.S. at 561 (Burger, C.J., joined by White and Stevens, JJ.) (plurality opinion), and perhaps the jurors and witnesses preferred a closed trial as well.

36. It is settled, for example, that the first amendment protects the right to *receive* information as well as the right to *communicate* it. See, e.g., First National Bank of Boston v. Bellotti, 435 U.S. 765, 781–83, 791–92 (1978); Virginia State Bd. of Pharmacy v. Virginia Citizens Consumer Council, 425 U.S. 748, 756–57 (1976); Red Lion Broadcasting Co. v. FCC, 395 U.S. 367, 390 (1969). See generally § 12–19, supra. This right is protected even when the speaker is not entitled to first amendment protection. See Lamont v. Postmaster General, 381 U.S. 301, 306–07 (1965). The fact that the original source of information

now in the hands of others might have been unwilling to communicate it is also unconstitutionally irrelevant. See Smith v. Daily Mail Publishing Co., 443 U.S. 97 (1979); New York Times Co. v. United States, 403 U.S. 713 (1971). Moreover, when the source of information at issue is not a person or organization but a *proceeding*, the dichotomy between "willing" and "unwilling" speakers is unhelpful.

37. Nothing in the Constitution entitles the accused to compel a *private* trial. See Richmond Newspapers, Inc. v. Virginia, 448 U.S. 555, 580 (1980); Gannett Co. v. DePasquale, 443 U.S. 368, 382, 383–84 n. 11 (1979).

38. Houchins v. KQED, Inc., 438 U.S. 1, 16 (1978) (Stewart, J., concurring in judgment).

39. See Gannett Co. v. DePasquale, 443 U.S. 368, 368 (1979) (noting that "the Sixth Amendment . . . presumes open trials as a norm"); Houchins v. KQED, Inc., 438 U.S. 1, 36 (1978) (Stevens, J., joined by Brennan and Powell, JJ., dissenting) (contending that "[b]y express command of the Sixth Amendment the proceeding must be a 'public trial' ").

This crucial fact serves to remove criminal trials from the realm of official proceedings within government's unilateral control.[40] Unlike the "unshared power" over foreign policy data conferred by the Constitution on the Executive,[41] the power over access to a criminal trial *is* shared—at least with the accused—simply by virtue of the sixth amendment. The first amendment thus does not operate as "some sort of constitutional 'sunshine law';"[42] it does not reveal to the public information and proceedings already securely within the government's control. The first amendment instead opens a constitutional window into material and events already identified by the sixth amendment as beyond such control.

In this context, the decision as to *which* requests for closure by defendants will be honored and which will not be cannot be left solely in the hands of the trial judge, for this would in effect constitute a system of government censorship.[43] Although none of the opinions stressed this threat of censorship, it may well form the core of *Richmond Newspapers*: the central flaw of the Virginia closure statute was that it invited trial judges to act exactly as the trial court in Stevenson's case did—to exercise completely unbridled discretion, in virtually summary fashion, to close entire trials either for the trifling convenience of proceeding in secret, or for less obvious, more content-based reasons.

If discretion to decide when to close trials is exercised not by a court but by a legislature, enacting criteria to be applied by the trial judge, a system amounting to censorship may still result. In *Globe Newspaper Co. v. Superior Court*,[44] the Court, in an opinion by Justice Brennan,[45] struck down a Massachusetts law which had been construed by the state's highest court to *require* trial judges to exclude the public

---

40. Cf. Landmark Communications v. Virginia, 435 U.S. 829, 834–37, 841 (1978) (discussing confidentiality for commissions of judicial inquiry); United States v. Nixon, 418 U.S. 683, 705 (1974) (establishing confidentiality for communications among high level officials); Pell v. Procunier, 417 U.S. 817, 834 (1974) (discussing right of access to prisons); Branzburg v. Hayes, 408 U.S. 665, 684 (1972) (noting that "the press is regularly excluded from grand jury proceedings, our own conferences, the meetings of other official bodies gathered in executive session, and the meetings of private organizations"); Zemel v. Rusk, 381 U.S. 1, 16–17 (1965) (concluding that there is no "unrestrained right to gather information" that entitles one to insist on a passport to Cuba or, e.g., to demand entry to the White House).

41. See New York Times Co. v. United States, 403 U.S. 713, 729 (1971) (Stewart, J., joined by White, J., concurring).

42. Gannett, 443 U.S. at 405 (Rehnquist, J., concurring).

43. The Court has consistently struck down as unconstitutional censorship stat-

utes making the exercise of first amendment speech contingent upon the discretion of a public official. See, e.g., Staub v. Baxley, 355 U.S. 313, 322 (1958); Lovell v. Griffin, 303 U.S. 444 (1938). See also Post, "The Management of Speech: Discretion and Rights," 1984 Sup.Ct.Rev. 169, 183–87. Nor are judges trustworthy censors. See Blasi, "Towards a Theory of Prior Restraint: The Central Linkage," 66 Minn.L. Rev. 11, 52 (1981) (concluding that underlying much first amendment theory and doctrine is the perception "that judges tend to be unduly risk averse in ruling upon the claims of speakers."). But see Jeffries, "Rethinking Prior Restraint," 92 Yale L.J. 409, 426–27 (1983). See generally §§ 12–34, 12–35, 12–36, infra.

44. 457 U.S. 596 (1982).

45. Justice Brennan was joined by Justices White, Marshall, Blackmun, and Powell. Justice O'Connor concurred in the judgment. Chief Justice Burger, joined by Justice Rehnquist, dissented. Justice Stevens would have dismissed the appeal; he accused the majority of rendering an advisory opinion.

and press from the courtroom during the testimony of underage victims in cases of rape and other sexual offenses. The Court conceded the importance of shielding young victims from further trauma and embarrassment, but ruled that even such a compelling interest could not justify a *mandatory* closure rule which operated regardless of the wishes and interests of the public, the parties, and the witnesses.[46]

In the particular trial involved in *Globe*, the judge had relied on the state closure statute to close the *entire* trial of a man charged with forcibly raping three girls aged 16 and 17 at the time of trial. The majority's comment that a case-by-case closure determination by the trial judge would be constitutional [47] is therefore mere dictum. However, the majority's willingness to endorse such a view even in the abstract is ominous. Given a choice between a rule allowing closure by the judge based on an *ad hoc* review of the "victim's age, psychological maturity and understanding, the nature of the crime, the desires of the victim, and the interests of parents and relatives," [48] and a rule requiring closure whenever the underage victim so requests, the latter might well be preferable. It would obviously provide more certain protection for the complaining witness, even if it did result in greater exclusion of the press and public. Yet this may well be an instance where "less is more," for the alternative rule permitting *ad hoc* decisions by the judge might result in less closure but more hidden censorship by the government.

A third possibility would be to defer to the defendant's request rather than (or in addition to) the victim's. If the courtroom *had* to be cleared during a defendant's testimony upon his request—for example, in a rape case where the truth would exonerate but embarrass him— there would again be more closure but far less risk of government censorship.[49] A case challenging this rule would be more difficult to decide than *Gannett*, since the rule would not permit any official to decide what is fit for the public to see and hear. Such a case would also be more complex than *Globe*, since it would not involve legislative censorship,[50] and since the defendant arguably has an even greater interest in testifying in his own defense than does an underage victim in testifying against her alleged attacker.

But the Court did not explicitly decide either *Richmond Newspapers* or *Globe* on such a risk-of-censorship theory. Given the broader grounds invoked, the case for an affirmative right to gather news and information is substantially stronger after these two cases. In that sense, *Richmond* was indeed a "watershed case." [51] Yet the contours and the growth potential of the principles there established are far

---

46. Id. at 607–08.

47. Id. at 608–11 & nn. 25, 27.

48. Id. at 608.

49. The Court, however, has held that the sixth amendment right to public trials does not imply a concomitant right to private ones. See Richmond Newspapers, Inc. v. Virginia, 448 U.S. 555, 580 (1980); Gannett Co. v. DePasquale, 443 U.S. 368, 382, 383–84 n. 11 (1979); id at 416–33 (Black-

mun, J., concurring in part, dissenting in part).

50. The Massachusetts Supreme Judicial Court in Globe interpreted the closure law not only to *mandate* closure during the testimony of underage rape victims, but also to *allow* closure during other portions of the trial at the judge's discretion.

51. 448 U.S. at 582 (Stevens, J., concurring). The case and its potential for ex-

from definite, in part because of the diversity of the seven opinions. Thus far the Court has relied on its reading of the common law tradition to extend the right of public access to voir dire proceedings [52] and preliminary hearings,[53] but has refused to grant the public or press access to discovery hearings.[54] The opinions in *Richmond Newspapers* suggest that a majority of the Court stands ready to extend the right of press and public access to civil trials,[55] and such an extension would comport with the principles underlying both Chief Justice Burger's and Justice Brennan's opinions.[56]

The partial reliance, in Chief Justice Burger's *Richmond Newspapers* opinion, on the ninth amendment as the repository of the public right of access to criminal (and presumably also civil) trials [57] consti-

pansion are discussed in D. O'Brien, The Public's Right to Know: The Supreme Court and the First Amendment 136–46 (1981); Cox, "Freedom of Expression in the Burger Court," 94 Harv.L.Rev. 1, 19–26 (1980); Fenner and Koley, "Access to Judicial Proceedings: To Richmond Newspapers and Beyond," 16 Harv.C.R.-C.L.L.Rev. 415 (1981); Lewis, "A Public Right to Know About Public Institutions: The First Amendment as a Sword," 1980 Sup.Ct.Rev. 1; The Supreme Court—1979 Term, 94 Harv.L.Rev. 149, 154–59 (1980).

52. See Press-Enterprise Co. v. Superior Court of California, 464 U.S. 501, 505–10 (1984) (noting the long history of public participation in jury selection and the important role of open trials in the administration of justice).

53. See Press-Enterprise Co. v. Superior Court of California, 106 S.Ct. 2735, 2740 (1986) (stating that the test is "whether the place and process has historically been open to the press and general public").

54. See Seattle Times v. Rhinehart, 467 U.S. 20 (1984) (holding that a protective order, entered on a showing of good cause, which bars dissemination of information gained through discovery, does not offend the first amendment). Since the discovery process is established and enforced by the state, it more closely resembles proceedings wholly internal to government than it does the criminal trial, where the command of the sixth amendment denies the government unilateral control over a trial's openness. See id. at 35–36 (the state's "substantial interest in preventing . . . abuse of its processes" justified delegation of "broad discretion on the trial court to decide when a protective order is appropriate and what kind of protection is required."); id. at 32 (since litigants gain information "only by virtue of the trial court's discovery processes," the information is provided as "a matter of legislative grace" and thus "continued court control over the discovered information does not raise the same spectre of government cen-

sorship that such control might suggest in other situations."). For a fuller discussion of the protective order issue, see § 12–21, infra.

55. See 448 U.S. at 580 n. 17 (Burger, C.J., joined by White and Stevens, JJ.); id. at 590, 594–95, 596 (Brennan, J., joined by Marshall, J., concurring in the judgment). See also Gannett Co. v. DePasquale, 443 U.S. 368, 386 n. 15 (1979); id. at 420, 424 (Blackmun, J., concurring in part and dissenting in part). But see Globe Newspaper Co. v. Superior Court, 457 U.S. 596, 611 (1982) (O'Connor, J., concurring in the judgment) (arguing that the value of openness is unique to criminal trials and "interpret[ing] neither Richmond Newspapers nor the Court's decision today to carry any implications outside the context of criminal trials").

56. See Note, "Trial Secrecy and the First Amendment Right of Access to Judicial Proceedings," 91 Harv.L.Rev. 1899, 1921–23 (1978). Lower courts have tended to uphold a public right of access to civil trials. See, e.g., Westmoreland v. Columbia Broadcasting System, Inc., 752 F.2d 16, 22–23 (2d Cir. 1984) (dictum), cert. denied 472 U.S. 1017 (1985); Publicker Industries, Inc. v. Cohen, 733 F.2d 1059, 1067–71 (3d Cir. 1984); Brown & Williamson Tobacco Corp. v. FTC, 710 F.2d 1165, 1177–79 (6th Cir. 1983), cert. denied 465 U.S. 1100 (1984); see also In re Continental Illinois Securities Litig., 732 F.2d 1302, 1308–09 (7th Cir. 1984) (agreeing with the reasoning of those courts holding that there is a public right of access to civil trials although not specifically recognizing such a right). Other courts, while not explicitly joining those recognizing a right of access to civil trials in general, have recognized a right of access to certain fundamental aspects of civil proceedings. See, e.g., Wilson v. American Motors Corp., 759 F.2d 1568 (11th Cir. 1985) (presumptive right of access applied to the trial record).

57. See 448 U.S. at 579 n. 15.

tutes the first use of that text as a guarantor of fundamental rights since the Court articulated the rights of privacy [58] and freedom of travel.[59] Such an approach is likely to broaden the range of proceedings to which *Richmond Newspapers* will ultimately be held to apply. Even so, it is not likely to be so broadened so as to encompass the kinds of proceedings and places that have traditionally been closed to the public.[60]

But, regardless of the proceeding, the Court would be unlikely to uphold a rule which permitted the general public to enter a proceeding while denying access to reporters. To be sure, despite its separate protection by the first amendment,[61] the prevailing view is that the press enjoys no special status under the Constitution.[62] But the press *is* protected at least from invidious discrimination.[63] Conversely, a "press access only" rule would probably be unconstitutional as applied to exclude, for example, the victim's family.

There remains the question whether particular media—such as television—may be totally excluded from the courtroom. The Court did not settle the issue in *Chandler v. Florida*.[64] The Court there held only that the due process clause does not invariably entitle the defendant, as a matter of his right to a fair criminal trial, to compel the exclusion of television cameras from the courtroom. The Court in effect ruled that television is now so ubiquitous that its presence cannot be deemed inherently prejudicial. To be sure, *Chandler* said nothing at all about the "right" of television to be there; indeed, the Court had no occasion to question the Florida Supreme Court's statement that neither photog-

---

58. See Griswold v. Connecticut, 381 U.S. 479 (1965), discussed in Chapter 15, infra.

59. Although the Court has not explicitly invoked the ninth amendment in order to support a right of travel, its attempts to lodge that right in other constitutional texts have been so vague and various as to suggest that the Court has in effect been engaged in ninth amendment analysis. See, e.g., Zobel v. Williams, 457 U.S. 55, 78–81 (1982) (O'Connor, J., concurring) (article IV privileges and immunities clause); Shapiro v. Thompson, 394 U.S. 618, 669–70 (1969) (Harlan, J., dissenting) (fifth amendment due process); United States v. Guest, 383 U.S. 745, 757–59 (1966) ("concept of our Federal Union"); Aptheker v. Secretary of State, 378 U.S. 500, 505, 514, 517 (1964) (first and fifth amendments). See also J. Ely, Democracy and Distrust 177 (1980).

60. See, e.g., Landmark Communications v. Virginia, 435 U.S. 829 (1978) (proceedings of commission investigating judicial misconduct); Saxbe v. Washington Post Co., 417 U.S. 843 (1974) (prisons); Rehnquist, "The First Amendment: Freedom, Philosophy, and the Law," 12 Gonz.L. Rev. 1, 13–14 (1976) (Supreme Court conferences).

61. "Congress shall make no law . . . abridging freedom of speech, or of the press." U.S. Const. amend. I.

62. See Anderson, "The Origins of the Press Clause," 30 U.C.L.A.L.Rev. 455 (1983).

63. See, e.g., Minneapolis Star & Tribune Co. v. Minnesota Comm'r of Revenue, 460 U.S. 575 (1983) (invalidating "use tax" on the cost of paper and ink products consumed in the production of newspapers and periodicals under the first amendment in part because it "singles out the press"); accord, Arkansas Writers' Project, Inc. v. Ragland, 107 S.Ct. 1722 (1987); cf. Smith v. Daily Mail Publishing Co., 443 U.S. 97 (1979) (newspaper may not be punished for publishing name of alleged juvenile offender if information is legally obtained); Oklahoma Pub. Co. v. District Court, 430 U.S. 308 (1977) (per curiam) ("freedom of press" prohibits injunction against publication of name of alleged juvenile delinquent available in public record); Cox Broadcasting Corp. v. Cohn, 420 U.S. 469 (1975) (newspaper may not be punished for publishing name of rape victim once it is a matter of public record).

64. 449 U.S. 560 (1981).

raphers nor the broadcast media enjoyed either a state or a federal constitutional right of access to the state's courtrooms. Yet the right of the public and the press to attend and observe criminal trials, as recognized in *Richmond Newspapers*, cannot plausibly be limited to the few who are fortunate enough to fit physically into whatever courtroom space is made available. Unless *Richmond Newspapers* and its progeny stand only for the exceedingly limited proposition that *totally* secret trials are unconstitutional, it should follow that wholesale exclusion of the larger public—both contemporary and historic—that is unable to witness the proceedings without the aid of a TV camera cannot stand in the absence of a compelling justification in the particular case. Whether state and federal courts may continue to exclude even unobtrusive TV coverage from the courtroom therefore seems dubious—although the Supreme Court has yet to address the matter.[65]

In *Schneider v. Irvington*,[66] the Supreme Court first held that the government cannot prohibit public pamphleteering simply because it costs money to clean up the inevitable litter. The streets are a public forum, and handbills are the poor man's printing press. The public forum doctrine [67] is an important recognition that it is not enough for government to refrain from invading certain areas of liberty. The state may, even at some cost to the public fisc, have to provide at least a minimally adequate opportunity for the exercise of certain freedoms.

65. Especially after the holding in Chandler that TV cameras are not inherently prejudicial, it is less than obvious how a court could persuasively distinguish the electronic media from the press in light of the first amendment values which animated Richmond Newspapers and lurked in the background of Chandler. See Ares, "Chandler v. Florida: Television, Criminal Trials, and Due Process," 1981 Sup.Ct.Rev. 157. The author of this treatise made that argument without success in Westmoreland v. Columbia Broadcasting System, 752 F.2d 16 (2d Cir. 1984), cert. denied 472 U.S. 1017 (1985), but the Second Circuit all but conceded that it was simply unprepared to carry Richmond Newspapers to its logical conclusion. If Richmond Newspapers and its progeny protect merely the right of a few public attendees to be physically present within the courtroom itself, there could be no first amendment objection to attempts to reduce the number of observers to the few who arrive first, or even to the deliberate use of "court-packing" or the calculated choice of the smallest possible courtroom. The first amendment is trivial if, unlike the fourth, cf. Katz v. United States, 389 U.S. 347, 351 (1967) (eliminating the requirement that a "constitutionally protected area" be invaded before fourth amendment guarantees come into play), it protects *places* rather than *people*—if it protects only the paltry privilege of a few to sit amidst bench, bar,

and jury box, and not the fundamental right of the many "to listen, observe, and learn" at first-hand, Richmond Newspapers, 448 U.S. at 578 (opinion of Burger, C.J.). The first amendment's "protection . . . is [of] the communication itself," Virginia Board of Pharmacy v. Virginia Citizens Consumer Council, Inc., 425 U.S. 748, 756 (1976). This right of access is limited, of course, by the same "compelling" interests that justify the partial or total exclusion of the public itself. See KPNX Broadcasting Co. v. Arizona Superior Court, 459 U.S. 1302, 1306–08 (1982) (Rehnquist, Circuit Justice) (denying stay of trial judge's order which banned court personnel, counsel, witnesses, and jurors from speaking directly with the press and which required that all drawings of jurors shown on television be reviewed by the court being broadcast); United States v. Chagra, 701 F.2d 354 (5th Cir. 1983) (bar of press and public from pretrial bond reduction hearing held not violative of constitutional access rights when closure is necessary to protect defendant's fair trial rights). But a clear danger to these interests must be shown. See United States v. Columbia Broadcasting, Inc., 497 F.2d 102 (5th Cir. 1974) (order banning in-court sketching invalid absent showing that sketching was obtrusive or disruptive).

66. 308 U.S. 147 (1939).

67. See § 12–24, infra.

In a sense, *Richmond Newspapers* is of this ilk: it is not enough that the government refrain from positively gagging and censoring the press.[68] It must, even at some inconvenience to its courts and juries, let the press and the public enter its courtrooms to observe a kind of public drama—a public forum for *watching* and *listening*, rather than a forum for *speech*. In this respect, perhaps the most interesting and far-reaching feature of *Richmond Newspapers* has less to do with the freedoms of speech or press than with the growing realization that the Constitution is no longer simply a source of fences around private spheres, but is increasingly drawn into question when the state is asked to take affirmative steps to make liberty or equality meaningful. This new and unaccustomed role may be one that some of the Framers might have found surprising, but it is a role that the larger concepts implicit in the document they wrote and ratified may require contemporary lawyers, judges, and legislators to grapple with for much of their careers.

§ 12–21. The First Amendment Right to Know: Preventing or Penalizing Dissemination of Information "Leaked" From Proceedings or Sources *Not* "Open to the Public"

Whatever may prove to be the ultimate reach of the public and press rights of access to information that is at least partly controlled by government, the Supreme Court has left no doubt that, once someone outside government acquires official information, the government cannot, absent an extraordinary showing, penalize its publication. There may be some rough "law of the jungle" notion at work here: even if no sweeping right to know will be recognized as a limit on government's power to *try* to keep matters bottled up, an outsider who manages to obtain otherwise confidential information cannot then be prevented from disseminating it [1]—or *punished* for having done so.[2]

Thus, the Supreme Court has repeatedly ruled that disseminators of confidential information obtained from judicial proceedings are entitled to first amendment protection. In *Cox Broadcasting Corp. v. Cohn*,[3] for example, the Court held that a state cannot constitutionally punish a television station for broadcasting a 17-year-old rape-murder

---

68. See, e.g., 448 U.S. at 576 n. 11, 577–78, 581 n. 18 (plurality opinion). See also id. at 599–600 (Stewart, J., concurring in the judgment) (observing that "a trial courtroom is a public place," and relying on analogies to reasonable time, place, and manner restrictions).

§ 12–21

1. See Stewart, "Or of the Press," 32 Hastings L.J. 631, 636 (1975) ("So far as the Constitution goes, the autonomous press may publish what it knows, and may seek to learn what it can. . . . The Constitution itself is neither a Freedom of Information Act nor an Official Secrets Act."). See also A. Bickel, The Morality of Consent 79–81 (1975); Brennan, Address,

32 Rutgers L.Rev. 173, 176–77 (1979). On prior restraints generally, see §§ 12–34, 12–35, 12–36, infra.

2. The showing required to justify after-the-fact liability is considerably less than that required to justify prior restraint. See § 12–34, infra.

3. 420 U.S. 469 (1975). Justice White delivered the opinion of the Court, in which Justices Brennan, Stewart, Marshall, Blackmun, and Powell joined. Justice Powell also filed a concurring opinion. Chief Justice Burger concurred in the judgment. Justice Douglas filed an opinion concurring in the judgment. Justice Rehnquist filed a dissenting opinion.

victim's name, when obtained by the station from courthouse records that were open to public inspection. Justice White's majority opinion focused on the public importance of trial proceedings,[4] as well as the potential chilling and self-censorship effects of a rule that made public records generally available to the press but created a negligence-standard privacy tort for revelations that were "offensive to the sensibilities of the supposedly reasonable man." [5] Similarly, the Court has held that a state cannot punish the news media for the accurate publication of an alleged juvenile delinquent's name, when that information has been lawfully obtained.[6]

In *Landmark Communications v. Virginia*,[7] the Court reversed the conviction of a newspaper that had violated a Virginia statute imposing criminal sanctions on persons who breached the confidentiality of proceedings before a commission responsible for inquiries into complaints of judicial disability or misconduct. The Court did not doubt that the state had a legitimate interest in keeping such proceedings confidential, or that the state could punish a breach of confidentiality by commission members or staff or by participants in the proceedings.[8] But, once the information came into the hands of a newspaper, Virginia could penalize its publication only by demonstrating a clear and present danger to the administration of justice, a standard it had failed to meet in the instant case.[9]

---

4. See id. at 492–93. But the Court cautioned that it meant "to imply nothing about any constitutional questions which might arise from a state policy of not allowing access by the public and press to various kinds of official records, such as records of juvenile-court proceedings." Id. at 496 n. 26. This was, after all, five years before Richmond Newspapers, Inc. v. Virginia, 448 U.S. 555 (1980), discussed in § 12–20, supra.

5. 420 U.S. at 496.

6. See Smith v. Daily Mail, 443 U.S. 97 (1979); Oklahoma Publishing Co. v. District Court, 430 U.S. 308 (1977) (per curiam). In both cases the Court stressed that the information had in fact been obtained lawfully. See 443 U.S. at 100–02; 430 U.S. at 311. The same concerns for truth and self-censorship, however, arguably apply to both lawfully and unlawfully obtained materials, and the appeal to legality as a talisman may in part beg the access issue, discussed in § 12–20, supra, since the question of "what is lawful?" cannot be answered without reference to the first amendment. On the other hand, the illegal appropriation of confidential information belonging to another raises issues of private or public property rights, as in trade secrets and copyright cases. See § 12–14, supra. Moreover, according to the logic of Seattle Times v. Rhinehart, 467 U.S. 20 (1984), discussed infra, if the government is conceded the ability to deny access altogether, then it may well be that

government must also be conceded the authority to punish those who *illegally* obtain access—although perhaps not those third parties who *innocently* obtain such illegally acquired information and thereafter disseminate it.

7. 435 U.S. 829 (1978). Chief Justice Burger delivered the opinion of the Court, in which Justices White, Marshall, Blackmun, Rehnquist, and Stevens joined. Justice Stewart filed an opinion concurring in the judgment. Justices Brennan and Powell took no part in the decision.

8. Id. at 841 n. 12, 845. Justice Stewart, concurring in the judgment, stressed the importance of the governmental interest at stake and his certainty that the state may properly seek to keep such proceedings confidential, although he too believed that the law could not be extended to punish a newspaper unless the need for secrecy was "manifestly overwhelming," id. at 849 (Stewart, J. concurring in the judgment), as it might be in some national security contexts, see infra.

9. 435 U.S. at 843–44. See § 12–11, supra. The Court properly declined to defer to the finding of the Virginia legislature that the divulgence of confidential proceedings of the commission *automatically* created a clear and present danger to the orderly administration of justice. Id. at 845. On its independent evaluation of the facts, the Court found that the threat to the administration of justice posed by

In the area of national defense, as Justice Stewart expected,[10] just such an extraordinary showing may be possible. In *Snepp v. United States*,[11] the Court upheld a "secrecy agreement" required by the government as a condition of employment with the Central Intelligence Agency, under which an employee was prohibited from publishing "any information or material relating to the Agency, its activities or intelligence activities generally, either during or after the term of [his] employment . . . without specific prior approval by the agency."[12] Snepp, a vociferous critic of the CIA, sought to publish a book called *Decent Interval*, in violation of this contract. Although the government conceded that the book divulged no confidential or otherwise sensitive information,[13] the Court found that "[t]he Government has a compelling interest in protecting both the secrecy of information important to our national security and the appearance of confidentiality so essential to the effective operation of our foreign intelligence service."[14] Similarly,

the speech and publications in Bridges v. California, 314 U.S. 252 (1941), discussed in § 12–11, supra, "was, if anything, more direct and substantial than the threat posed by Landmark's article."

10. See Landmark Communications, Inc. v. Virginia, 435 U.S. 829, 849 (1978) (Stewart, J., concurring in the judgment).

11. 444 U.S. 507 (1980) (per curiam).

12. Id. at 508.

13. Id. at 511. The government's concession on this point distinguished the case from United States v. Marchetti, 466 F.2d 1309 (4th Cir. 1972), cert. denied 409 U.S. 1063 (1972). There, the government had claimed that a former CIA employee intended to violate his agreement not to publish any *classified* information, see 466 F.2d at 1313. Marchetti, therefore, did not consider the issue of the breach of an agreement to submit *all* material for prepublication review. See 444 U.S. at 510 n. 4.

14. Id. at 509 n. 3. The Court reasoned that "a former intelligence agent's publication of unreviewed material relating to intelligence activities can be detrimental to vital national interests even if the published information is unclassified," id. at 511–12. The CIA might have a "broader understanding" than an individual agent regarding the type of unclassified material that might be harmful if disclosed, id. at 512. In addition, the CIA's inability to enforce its secrecy agreements might discourage foreign sources of information from cooperating with the Agency, out of fear that their anonymity could not be guaranteed. Id. Cf. Haig v. Agee, 453 U.S. 280 (1981) (holding that "repeated disclosures of intelligence operations and names of intelligence personnel" for the "purpose of obstructing intelligence operations and the recruiting of intelligence personnel" are "clearly not protected by the

Constitution," and upholding passport revocation of one who had been guilty of such disclosures).

The Snepp Court declared that "even in the absence of an express agreement," the CIA "could have acted to protect substantial government interests by imposing reasonable restrictions on employee activities that in other contexts might be protected by the First Amendment." 444 U.S. at 509 n. 3. The Supreme Court has often deferred to military and executive branch expertise in identifying governmental interests in the area of foreign policy. See, e.g., Goldman v. Weinberger, 106 S.Ct. 1310, 1313 (1986) (rejecting a challenge under the free exercise clause to the Air Force's refusal to permit religious exemptions from its standardized dress code, based on "great deference to the professional judgment of military authorities concerning the relative importance of a particular military interest"); Brown v. Glines, 444 U.S. 348, 354–58 (1980) (upholding Air Force regulations requiring members of that service to obtain approval from their commanders before circulating petitions on Air Force bases, because of the governmental interest in discipline); Greer v. Spock, 424 U.S. 828, 840 (1976) (denying political candidate access to military base, and noting that "nothing in the Constitution . . . disables a military commander from acting to avert what he perceives to be a clear danger to the loyalty, discipline, or morale of troops on the base under his command"); New York Times Co. v. United States, 403 U.S. 713, 757 (1971) (Harlan, J., dissenting, joined by Burger, C.J., and Blackmun, J.) ("[T]he very nature of executive decisions as to foreign policy is political, not judicial. . . . They are decisions of a kind for which the judiciary has neither aptitude, facilities, nor responsibility and which has long been held to belong in the domain of political power not subject

where those outside government obtain properly classified material, they may be punished for disseminating it—and even enjoined from doing so—if the government makes a suitable showing.[15]

It is an altogether different issue whether a court may, by means of protective orders under such rules as Fed. R. Civ. P. 26(c), attempt to prevent the confidential information from leaking in the first place. Certainly, a court may punish a participant's dissemination of such information if the proceeding is one from which outside observers may properly be excluded.[16] But should dissemination by a party in an ordinary trial be considered a "leak" that a court may seek to prevent? The Court, in some circumstances, answers "yes". In *Seattle Times v. Rhinehart*,[17] a unanimous Court upheld protective orders issued in a defamation action brought against a newspaper publishing company by a religious organization, the Aquarian Foundation, and its spiritual leader, Keith Rhinehart. The defendant newspapers sought to publish the identities of the plaintiff organization's members and donors, information that the defendants had obtained through discovery. The Foundation responded that dissemination of the material—which might never be admitted in evidence and thus might remain private but for the proposed out-of-trial dissemination—would "violate the First Amendment rights of members and donors to privacy, freedom of religion, and freedom of association." [18] Justice Powell's opinion for the Court purported to apply traditional first amendment analysis in examining whether the "practice in question"—i.e., a bar on dissemination—furthers "an important or substantial governmental interest unrelated to the suppression of expression," and whether "the limitation of First Amendment freedoms [is] no greater than is necessary or essential to the protection of the particular governmental interest involved." [19] Such a test may have been unnecessary, however, because Justice

---

to judicial intrusion or inquiry"), quoting Chicago & Southern Air Lines v. Waterman Steamship Corp., 333 U.S. 103, 111 (1948). See also United States v. Stanley, 107 S.Ct. 3054, 3063 (1987) (dismissing former serviceman's suit for having been subjected to LSD, because "unique disciplinary structure" of military counsels deference); United States v. Johnson, 107 S.Ct. 2063, 2069 (1987) (denying tort recovery to survivors of service member killed because of negligence of a civilian employee). In addition, the Court has circumscribed the political participation rights of federal employees. See, e.g., CSC v. Letter Carriers, 413 U.S. 548, 565 (1973) (holding that Congress may constitutionally forbid federal employees from engaging in plainly identifiable acts of political management and campaigning, such as organizing a political party or actively participating in fund-raising activities); United Public Workers v. Mitchell, 330 U.S. 75, 100 (1947) (a federal employee may be prevented from holding a political party office, working at the polls, and acting as a paymaster for other party workers).

15. See United States v. Progressive, Inc., 467 F.Supp. 990 (W.D. Wis. 1979) (preliminary injunction issued March 28, 1979), request for mandamus den. sub nom. Morland v. Sprecher, 443 U.S. 709 (1979), case dismissed 710 F.2d 819 (7th Cir. 1979), discussed in § 12–36, infra.

16. See § 12–20, supra.

17. 467 U.S. 20 (1984). Justice Powell delivered the Court's opinion. Justice Brennan filed a concurring opinion, in which Justice Marshall joined.

18. Id. at 25. Cf. NAACP v. Alabama ex rel. Patterson, 357 U.S. 449, 462 (1958), discussed in § 12–26, infra.

19. 467 U.S. at 32, quoting Procunier v. Martinez, 416 U.S. 396, 413 (1974). Justices Brennan and Marshall applied this test and found that protecting the Foundation's religious and associational rights represented an important governmental interest that justified the restriction on free expression caused by the protective order. 467 U.S. at 38 (Brennan, J., joined by Marshall, concurring).

Powell's opinion for the Court implied that the protective order simply did not implicate first amendment interests, except perhaps in a very incidental way.[20] The opinion noted that the newspapers gained the plaintiffs' membership and donor lists "only by virtue of the trial court's discovery processes" and "as a matter of legislative grace." [21]

20. See, e.g., id. at 36 n. 23 (refusing to apply "heightened First Amendment scrutiny of each request for a protective order"). Under Justice Powell's analysis, the traditional first amendment test would presumably have been met, since he found that "Rule 26(c) furthers a substantial governmental interest unrelated to the suppression of expression," 467 U.S. at 34, by preventing abuse of the judicial discovery process and protecting personal reputation and privacy. Id. at 35. The view taken in Justice Powell's opinion for the Court permits protective orders in many more circumstances than would Justice Brennan's view, which apparently limits such restraints on publishing the results of discovery to cases implicating such constitutional values as association and the free exercise of religion, and perhaps other "compelling interests." Rule 26(c), however, includes much broader concerns among its express purposes—the protection of a "party or person from annoyance, embarrassment, oppression or undue burden or expense."

Commentators disagree on the extent to which protective orders implicate first amendment interests. Compare Marcus, "Myth and Reality in Protective Order Litigation," 69 Cornell L.Rev. 1, 5 (1983) (criticizing the first amendment "public access approach" to discovery as a "myth not only contrary to reality, but also lacking [in] legal support," and recommending a doctrine of waiver that would foreclose any later claim of a right to disclose material initially obtained under a protective order); Note, "The First Amendment Right to Disseminate Discovery Materials: In Re Halkin," 92 Harv.L.Rev. 1550, 1553, 1557 (1979) (describing full first amendment review as "illogical" and "unwarranted," and proposing instead a lower standard of scrutiny—namely, a "specific finding[ ] of a threat to a legitimate interest"), with Post, "The Management of Speech: Discretion and Rights," 1984 Sup.Ct.Rev. 169, 187–93, 201–06 (criticizing the Court for its failure to consider more fully the first amendment rights of litigants to disseminate information, but defending the result in Rhinehart as protecting the necessary discretion of trial judges to manage pretrial discovery); Comment, "Protective Orders Prohibiting Dissemination of Discovery Information: The First Amendment and Good Cause," 1980 Duke L.J. 766, 767 (arguing that first amendment analysis compels recognition of a right to disseminate information obtained through discovery and suggesting a balancing-of-interests theory); Note, "Role 26(b) Protective Orders and the First Amendment," 80 Colum.L.Rev. 1645, 1660–61 (1980) (proposing that protective orders should not be issued absent a showing that "disclosure is substantially likely to cause serious harm to the discovery system and no less intrusive alternative to prevent the harm is available").

21. 467 U.S. at 32. But this interpretation may be at odds with the Court's contemporary approach to the right-privilege distinction, see Vitek v. Jones, 445 U.S. 480 (1980) (holding violative of fourteenth amendment due process the transfer of a convicted felon to a mental hospital without adequate notice and the opportunity for a hearing): "[The right to procedural due process] is conferred, not by legislative grace, but by constitutional guarantee. While the legislature may elect not to confer a property interest in federal employment, it may not constitutionally authorize the deprivation of such an interest, once conferred, without appropriate procedural safeguards. . . . [T]he adequacy of statutory procedures for deprivation of a statutorily created property interest must be analyzed in constitutional terms." Id. at 490 n. 6, quoting Arnett v. Kennedy, 416 U.S. 134, 166–67 (1974) (Powell, J., joined by Blackmun, J., concurring in part and concurring in the result in part). See also Logan v. Zimmerman Brush Co., 455 U.S. 422, 431–32 (1982) (invalidating as violative of fourteenth amendment due process the extinguishment of a statutorily-created cause of action for employment discrimination); Goldberg v. Kelly, 397 U.S. 254, 261–63 (1970) (establishing right of AFDC recipients to evidentiary hearing prior to termination of benefits). So regarded, the Court's approach in Rhinehart may also run afoul of the doctrine of unconstitutional conditions. See § 11–5, supra. First amendment rights may not "be infringed by the denial of or placing of conditions upon a benefit or privilege." Sherbert v. Verner, 374 U.S. 398, 404 (1963). In Schlagenhauf v. Holder, 379 U.S. 104 (1964), for example, the Court extended to defendants the Fed. R. Civ. P. requirement that a party making certain allegations regarding his or her physical condition must submit to a medical examination. The Court rejected the argument that plaintiffs alone should be subject to this requirement, because by filing suit they had voluntarily

The Court concluded that "[a] litigant has no First Amendment right of access to information made available only for purposes of trying his suit," [22] and that the trial court was therefore free to impose restrictions on dissemination of that information.[23]

waived any privacy rights they might have had. "[C]onstitutional problems" result from any theory that constitutional rights are waived merely by exercising a "right of access to the federal courts." Id. at 114.

22. Rhinehart, 467 U.S. at 32.

23. The Court conceded in Rhinehart that litigants do not "surrender their First Amendment rights at the courthouse door," id. at 32 n. 18, quoting In re Halkin, 598 F.2d 176, 186 (D.C. Cir. 1979) (vacating order that prohibited extrajudicial disclosure of information obtained through discovery). It pointed to other contexts, however, in which the rights of trial participants may be restricted. The Supreme Court has, for example, affirmed the power of trial judges to restrain statements by lawyers, court officials, witnesses, and defendants. See, e.g., Sheppard v. Maxwell, 384 U.S. 333, 360, 361, 363 (1966) (dictum); Nebraska Press Ass'n v. Stuart, 427 U.S. 539, 564 (1976); id. at 601 n. 27 (Brennan, J., concurring). See also KPNX Broadcasting Co. v. Arizona Superior Court, 459 U.S. 1302, 1306–08 (1982) (Rehnquist, Circuit Justice) (denying stay of trial judge's order that banned court personnel, counsel, witnesses, and jurors from speaking directly with the press and that prohibited the broadcast of drawings of jurors without the review and approval of the court); Gulf Oil v. Bernard, 452 U.S. 89, 104 n. 21 (1981) ("In the conduct of a case, a court often finds it necessary to restrict the free expression of participants, including counsel, witnesses, and jurors.")

Restraints of this sort are evidently acceptable when aimed at government's own officers and agents. See Wood v. Georgia, 370 U.S. at 393–94 (1962) (Wood's position as sheriff provided no basis for restricting his first amendment rights but might have provided such a basis if his statements had interfered with his official duties). But nothing about a person's status as criminal defendant can explain a diminution of that person's first amendment rights. See, e.g., Chase v. Robson, 435 F.2d 1059, 1061 (7th Cir. 1970) (vacating order proscribing public statements by defendants and defense counsel in case arising out of destruction of selective service records in absence of specific findings that such conduct posed a clear and present danger). Indeed a defendant may have very strong interests in gaining media attention in order to combat the stigma of a criminal indictment, expose abuses of prosecutorial or judicial discretion, raise a defense fund, or discuss the

political significance of the trial. See Chicago Council of Lawyers v. Bauer, 522 F.2d 242 (7th Cir. 1975), cert. denied sub nom. Cunningham v. Chicago Council of Lawyers, 427 U.S. 912 (1976) (court rules restricting extrajudicial statements by attorneys are valid only if limited to statements posing a serious and imminent threat to a fair trial); Hirst, "Silence Orders—Preserving Political Expression by Defendants and their Lawyers," 6 Harv.Civ.Rts.—Civ.Lib.L.Rev. 595 (1971). To the extent that criminal defendants rely on counsel to represent their interests both in and out of court, it would be problematic to impose greater restrictions on counsel than on the accused. Nevertheless, the broadest restrictions have been imposed on defense attorneys on the theory that lawyers are "officers of the court" with a special responsibility to assure the fairness of the trial process. See, e.g., Judicial Conference of the United States, Committee on the Operation of the Jury System, Report of the Committee on the "Free Press-Fair Trial" Issue, 45 F.R.D. 391, 406 (1969). But the label "officer of the court" cannot be decisive; a private attorney cannot simply be assimilated into the category of government agents. See Cammer v. United States, 350 U.S. 399, 405 (1956) (lawyers cannot be summarily tried for contempt on authority of federal statute empowering a court to punish "misbehavior of any of its officers in their official transactions"). To be sure, a lawyer may have a "fiduciary obligation to the courts." See American Bar Association Project on Standards for Criminal Justice, Standards Relating to Fair Trial and Free Press 82 (1968). But as Congressman (later President) Buchanan argued at the impeachment trial of Judge Peck for imprisoning a lawyer on the basis of the latter's criticism of the judge, it is "the imperative duty of an attorney to protect the interests of his client out of court as well as in court." A. J. Stansbury, Report of the Trial of James H. Peck 455 (1833). Nor can restraints on the defense be justified as preserving a balance between prosecution and defense. The scales of justice are already "weighed extraordinarily heavy against an accused after his indictment. A bare denial and a possible reminder that a charged person is presumed innocent until proved guilty is often insufficient to balance the scales." Chicago Council of Lawyers v. Bauer, 522 F.2d at 250. Most fundamentally, as long as defense statements fall short of a serious and imminent threat to the fair adjudi-

§ 12–22. The First Amendment Right to Know: Protecting Confidentiality in News Gathering

Although journalists have long stressed the importance of confidentiality for effective reporting,[1] the Burger Court consistently refused to modify legal procedures to protect the privacy of reporters' sources or the editorial process. In three cases during the 1970's, the Court made its postition on reporters' confidentiality clear. Unsympathetic to Justice Stewart's argument that the first amendment grants special constitutional status to the organized press,[2] the Court was suspicious of any claim of privilege that appeared to elevate journalists above other citizens.[3] The Court invited Congress and state legislatures to provide the press with whatever level of statutory protection they deem prudent,[4] but insisted that the Constitution accords journalists no shield from legal process beyond the normal checks provided by judicial supervision.

In the first case, *Branzburg v. Hayes*,[5] the Court refused to grant reporters even a qualified immunity from good-faith grand jury questioning regarding confidential sources. Writing for the Court, Justice White acknowledged that the first amendment provided "some protection" for news gathering,[6] but he found the hindrance of reporting likely to be caused by compelling journalists to testify before grand juries too insubstantial and speculative to overcome the paramount public interest in bringing criminals to justice.[7] Although the Constitution would not allow grand juries to engage in purposeful harassment of the press, the majority trusted that judges supervising grand jury investigations would be sufficiently sensitive to first amendment concerns to minimize the danger of such abuse.[8]

cation of the case, the balance that counts—that in the courtroom—will not be disturbed. See generally Howard & Newman, "Fair Trial and Free Expression," Report of the Senate Comm. on the Judiciary, 94th Cong., 2d Sess. 18–24, 36–38, 43–44, 67–76 (1976). Cole and Spak, "Defense Counsel and the First Amendment: 'A Time to Keep Silence, and a Time to Speak'," 6 St. Mary's L.J. 347 (1974); Freedman and Starwood, "Prior Restraints on Freedom of Expression by Defendants and Defense Attorneys: Ratio Decidendi v. Obiter Dictum," 29 Stan.L.Rev. 607 (1977).

§ 12–22

1. See, e.g., Blasi, "The Newsman's Privilege: An Emprical Study," 70 Mich.L. Rev. 229, 239–53 (1971); Guest & Stanzler, "The Constitutional Argument for Newsmen Concealing Their Sources," 64 Nw. U.L.Rev. 18, 51–61 (1969).

2. See Stewart, "Or of the Press," 26 Hast.L.J. 631 (1975). Recent historical scholarship supports Justice Stewart's position. See Anderson, "The Origins of the Press Clause," 30 UCLA L.Rev. 455 (1983).

3. See Herbert v. Lando, 441 U.S. 153, 165 (1979) (evidentiary rules "are applica-

ble to the press and other defendants alike"); Branzburg v. Hayes, 408 U.S. 665, 684 (1972) (press has no "constitutional right of special access not available to the public generally"). See also, e.g., First National Bank v. Bellotti, 435 U.S. 765, 796–802 (1978) (Burger, C.J., concurring); Pell v. Procunier, 417 U.S. 817, 827–28, 830 (1974) (press enjoys no greater right than general public to acquire information about prison conditions); Anderson, supra note 2, at 457 ("no Supreme Court decision has rested squarely on the Press Clause, independent of the Speech Clause"). But cf. Minneapolis Star & Tribune Co. v. Minnesota Comm'r of Revenue, 460 U.S. 575, 583–85, 590 (1983) (suggesting special constitutional solicitude for press).

4. See Zurcher v. Stanford Daily, 436 U.S. 547, 567 (1978); Branzburg v. Hayes, 408 U.S. 665, 706 (1972).

5. 408 U.S. 665 (1972).

6. 408 U.S. at 681.

7. Id. at 695.

8. Id. at 707–08.

Despite the holding in *Branzburg* and the discouraging tone of the majority opinion, lower federal courts have consistently read the case to support some kind of qualified privilege for reporters.[9] The basis for this reading is that five justices in *Branzburg* explicitly acknowledged that the Constitution may at times protect the confidentiality of a journalists' sources. Four justices dissented from the Court's decision: Justices Brennan, Marshall and Stewart would have recognized a qualified privilege,[10] and Justice Douglas advocated absolute immunity.[11] Concurring, Justice Powell argued that the first amendment hazards of compromising a reporter's confidences should be balanced on a case-by-case basis against the public's interest in criminal investigation, and suggested that courts should grant relief from questioning that "implicates confidential source relationships without a legitimate need of law enforcement."[12]

The alignment of the Court was substantially the same in *Zurcher v. Stanford Daily*,[13] where the Court upheld, 5–3,[14] the authority of police officers acting pursuant to a warrant to search the offices of a newspaper, forcibly and without notice, for evidence of a crime. Given probable cause to believe the place to be searched—newspaper office or otherwise—contains evidence of a crime, the Court ruled that the fourth and fourteenth amendments require neither a showing that the place is owned or possessed by someone reasonably suspected of a crime,[15] nor a determination by a neutral magistrate that seeking to obtain the same evidence by a subpoena after an adversary hearing would likely trigger its destruction or removal from the jurisdiction.[16] Writing for the same majority as in *Branzburg*, Justice White reasoned that the warrant requirement, applied with particular care when the

---

9. See, e.g., Zerilli v. Smith, 656 F.2d 705 (D.C. Cir. 1981); Bruno & Stillman, Inc. v. Globe Newspaper Co., 633 F.2d 583 (1st Cir. 1980); In re Petroleum Products Antitrust Litigation, 680 F.2d 5 (2d Cir. 1982), cert. denied sub nom. Arizona v. McGraw-Hill, Inc., 459 U.S. 909 (1982); United States v. Criden, 633 F.2d 346 (3d Cir. 1980), cert. denied sub nom. Schaffer v. United States, 449 U.S. 1113 (1981); United States v. Steelhammer, 561 F.2d 539 (4th Cir. 1977); Miller v. Transamerican Press, Inc., 621 F.2d 721 (5th Cir. 1980), cert. denied 450 U.S. 1041 (1981); Cervantes v. Time, Inc., 464 F.2d 986 (8th Cir. 1972), cert. denied 409 U.S. 1125 (1973); Silkwood v. Kerr-McGee, 563 F.2d 433 (10th Cir. 1977); McArdle v. Hunter, 7 Med.L.Rptr. 2294 (E.D. Mich. 1981); Gulliver's Periodicals, Ltd. v. Chas. Levy Cir. Co., 455 F.Supp. 1197 (N.D. Ill. 1978).

10. Branzburg v. Hayes, 408 U.S. at 725 (Stewart, J., dissenting).

11. Id. at 711 (Douglas, J., dissenting).

12. Id. at 710 (Powell, J., concurring). Justice Stewart later commented that Justice Powell's opinion may have made the vote in the case four and a half to four and

a half. See Stewart, "Or of the Press," 26 Hast.L.J. 631, 635 (1975). Cf. notes 14 and 21, infra.

13. 436 U.S. 547 (1978).

14. Justice White delivered the Court's opinion, joined by Chief Justice Burger and Justices Blackmun and Rehnquist. Concurring, Justice Powell stressed that a magistrate, before issuing a warrant, should consider the values of a free press as well as the social interest in detecting and prosecuting crime. Id. at 568 (Powell, J., concurring). Justices Stevens, Stewart, and Marshall dissented. Justice Brennan took no part.

15. 436 U.S. at 553–60. Indeed, Justice White suggested for the Court that the fourth amendment interests of persons not suspected of criminal involvement are *less* weighty than the interests of those who are, and therefore that "a less stringent standard of probable cause is acceptable where the entry is not to secure evidence of crime against the possessor." Id. at 555–56.

16. Id. at 560–63.

place to be searched is a newspaper office, affords adequate protection to first amendment interests.[17]

Despite the novelty of the protections the Court was asked to fashion, it would be a mistake to minimize the degree to which constitutional values lying at the intersection of the first, fourth, and fifth amendments were jeopardized by the Court's holding. As Justice Stewart stressed in dissent, searches, unlike subpoenas, compromise the confidentiality of news gathering to an inherently uncontrollable degree: "[a] search warrant allows police officers to ransack the files of a newspaper, reading each and every document until they have found the one named in a warrant, while a subpoena would permit the newspaper itself to produce only the specific documents requested. A search, unlike a subpoena, will therefore lead to the needless exposure of confidential information completely unrelated to the purpose of the investigation." [18]

Nor can the possibilities of abuse be discounted. When a subpoena is served on a newspaper, it has the opportunity to assert constitutional and statutory rights to keep certain materials confidential. Such protection is circumvented when officials can proceed *ex parte*, by search warrant.[19] And the risk of abuse may be greatest exactly when the press plays its most vital and creative role in our political system, the role of watchdog on official corruption and abuse. Officials who find themselves the targets of newspaper or media investigations may well be tempted to conduct searches to find out precisely what various journalists have discovered, and to retaliate against reporters who have unearthed and reported official wrongdoing.[20]

In the third case, *Herbert v. Lando*,[21] the Court held that a journalist's thoughts about the information he gathers, as well as his professional conversations with his editorial colleagues, are not immune from discovery in libel actions brought by public figures. Justice White, writing for the majority once again,[22] reasoned that, since the "actual

17. Id. at 565–67.

18. 436 U.S. at 573 (Stewart, J., dissenting) (footnote omitted).

19. Disturbingly, the Court argued that the search warrant was more advantageous to law enforcement officials than the subpoena precisely *because* use of a warrant may deny potential criminal defendants a chance to assert their fifth amendment privilege against self-incrimination. Id. at 561–62 n.8 (opinion of the Court).

20. Citizens Privacy Protection Act: Hearings Before the Subcomm. of the Constitution of the Senate Comm. on the Judiciary, 95th Cong., 2d Sess. 70–93 (1978) (statement and testimony of Paul Davis, Vice President, Radio Television News Directors Association).

The dangers posed by the Zurcher decision are not confined to the press. Justice Stevens' dissent properly warned of the damage the decision could do to privacy rights generally. The *ex parte* warrant procedure enables the police to obtain access to privileged documents, including medical and legal files and other highly confidential records, that could not lawfully be examined if the holder of the documents had notice and an opportunity to object. Indeed, a search for the documents described in a warrant may well involve inspection of diaries, letters, and other highly personal papers. See 436 U.S. at 579–80 (Stevens, J., dissenting).

21. 441 U.S. 153 (1979), discussed in § 12–12, supra.

22. Chief Justice Burger and Justices Blackmun, Powell, Rehnquist and Stevens joined in the majority opinion. Justice Brennan dissented in part; Justices Marshall and Stewart each dissented. As in Branzburg and Zurcher, Justice Powell filed a concurring opinion stressing that, in their supervisory capacity, judges should keep first amendment interests in mind. Id. at 178 (Powell J., concurring).

malice" standard of *New York Times Co. v. Sullivan* [23] and *Curtis Publishing Co. v. Butts* [24] requires a libel case brought by a public figure to focus on the defendant's state of mind,[25] even a qualified privilege for editorial processes would interfere intolerably with the ability of defamed public figures to bring suit.[26] The Court found it "difficult to believe" that honoring legitimate discovery requests would significantly discourage frank editorial discussion,[27] and trusted judicial supervision to minimize abuses of the discovery rules [28]—abuses that the Court noted were not unique to libel litigation.[29]

As Justice Marshall argued in dissent, however, the problem of vindictive discovery is likely to be especially acute in libel suits, because "many self-perceived victims of defamation are animated by something more than a rational calculus of their chances of recovery. Given the circumstances under which libel actions arise, plaintiffs' pretrial maneuvers may be fashioned more with an eye to deterrence or retaliation than to unearthing germane material." [30] The subsequent history of major libel litigation—including *Herbert v. Lando* on remand—has shown just how punishing discovery requests in these cases can be.[31] The possibility of such "*in terrorem* discovery" [32] has substantially undercut the protection provided to the press in *Sullivan* and *Butts*: the "actual malice" standard is of little help to defendants if plaintiffs can exact their retribution before (or without) going to trial.[33]

Although the ultimate impact of *Herbert v. Lando* remains to be seen,[34] much of the protection the Court refused to provide in *Branzburg v. Hayes* and *Zurcher v. Stanford Daily* has since been furnished though state and federal legislation, state court decisions, and federal administrative action. Twenty-six states have enacted "shield laws" providing reporters with an absolute or qualified privilege

23. 376 U.S. 254 (1964).

24. 388 U.S. 130 (1967).

25. For a discussion of the "actual malice" standard, see §§ 12–12, 12–13, supra.

26. Herbert v. Lando, 441 U.S. at 170.

27. Id. at 174.

28. Id. at 177.

29. Id. at 176.

30. Id. at 204–05 (Marshall, J., dissenting).

31. See Lewis, "New York Times v. Sullivan Reconsidered: Time to Return to 'The Central Meaning of the First Amendment,'" 83 Colum.L.Rev. 603, 609–12 (1983) (reporting that the process of discovery in significant defamation actions is so extensive and costly that "a cynic might suspect a conspiracy of lawyers"). Discovery in Herbert v. Lando took eight years and reportedly cost the defendants between three and four million dollars. Id. at 611–12.

32. Herbert v. Lando, 441 U.S. at 153 (Marshall, J., dissenting).

33. Cf. Nixon v. Fitzgerald, 457 U.S. 731, 763 (1982) (upholding claim of absolute Presidential immunity from damages liability) (Burger, C.J., concurring): "When litigation processes are not tightly controlled—and often they are not—they can be and are used as mechanisms of extortion. Ultimate vindication on the merits does not repair the damage."

34. Discovery requests regarding the editorial process can still be blocked under Fed. R. Civ. P. 26 as irrelevant or oppressive. See 441 U.S. at 153 (majority opinion); Rosario v. New York Times Co., 84 F.R.D. 626 (S.D.N.Y. 1979) (sustaining objections to deposition questions concerning editorial judgment). In addition, at least one state shield law has been authoritatively construed to grant reporters sued for libel an absolute privilege not to disclose confidential sources and editorial processes. See Maressa v. New Jersey Monthly, 89 N.J. 176, 445 A.2d 376 (1982) (discussed in 28 Villanova L.Rev. 225 (1982)), cert. denied 459 U.S. 907 (1982).

not to divulge information they received in confidence.[35] The courts of ten other states have found such a privilege in common law or the state constitution.[36] Congress has provided strong statutory protections

35. See Ala. Code § 12–21–142 (1977); Alaska Stat. §§ 0.9.25.150–.220 (1973 & Supp. 1982); Ariz. Rev. Stat. Ann. § 12.2237 (1982); Ark. Stat. Ann. § 43–917 (1977); Cal. Evid. Code § 1070 (West Supp. 1982) (incorporated into state constitution in 1980, Cal. Const., art. 1, § 2(b)); Del. Code tit. 10, § 4320–4326 (1975); Ill. Ann. Stat. ch. 110, ¶¶8–901 to 8–909 (Smith-Hurd Supp. 1983); Ind. Code Ann. § 34–3–5–1 (Burns Supp. 1982); Ky. Rev. Stat. § 421.100 (1972); La. Rev. Stat. Ann. §§ 45:1451–45:1454 (West 1982); Md. Cts. & Jud. Proc. Code Ann. § 9–112 (1980); Mich. Comp. Laws Ann. § 767.5a (West 1982); Minn. Stat. Ann. §§ 595.021–595.025 (West Supp. 1982); Mont. Code Ann. §§ 26–1–901 to 26–1–903 (1981); Neb. Rev. Stat. §§ 20–144 to 20–147 (1977); N.J. Stat. Ann. §§ 2A:84A–21 to 2A:84A–21.8 (West Supp. 1983); N.M. Stat. Ann. § 20–1–12.1 (Supp. 1975) (invalidated under state constitution in Ammerman v. Hubbard Broadcasting Inc., 89 N.M. 250, 551 P.2d 1354 (1976)); N.Y. Civ. Rights Law § 79–h (McKinney 1976 & Supp. 1982); N.D. Cent. Code Ann. § 31–01–06.2 (1976); Ohio Rev. Code Ann. §§ 2739.04, 2739.12 (Page 1981); Okla. Stat. Ann. tit. 12, § 2506 (West 1980); Ore. Rev. Stat. §§ 44.510–44.540 (1981); Pa. Stat. Ann. tit. 42, § 5942 (Purdon 1982); R.I. Gen. Laws §§ 9–19.1–1 to 9–19.1–3 (Supp. 1982); Tenn. Code Ann. § 24–1–208 (1980).

The constitutionality of these shield laws is problematic only to the degree they are employed so as to compromise the fairness of criminal trials. This issue, as well as the conflict of first amendment interests with sixth amendment guarantees, was presented in 1978 by the refusal of New York Times reporter Myron Farber to surrender to a judge, for the latter's in camera inspection, Farber's notes of interviews with witnesses in the murder trial of Dr. Mario Jascalevich. The trial judge ordered the disclosure after certifying that the documents sought appeared sufficiently material to warrant in camera inspection, stating that after this inspection Farber could have a full hearing on whether any part of the reporter's notes should be passed on to the defense attorneys who subpoenaed them. The New Jersey courts refused to stay, and denied leave to appeal, the order of a second judge refusing to quash the subpoena. Justice White and then Justice Marshall denied Farber's application for a stay pending filing and disposition of a petition for certiorari in the Supreme Court, each noting that it was

doubtful that four members of the Court would vote to grant a petition for certiorari at this stage of the proceedings. New York Times Co. v. Jascalevich, 439 U.S. 1301 (1978) (White, J.); id. at 1304 (Marshall, J.). Although Justice White found no basis for believing that reporters enjoy any special protection from subpoenas, id. at 1302 (White, J.), Justice Marshall thought Farber's case presented "important and unresolved questions," id. at 1305 (Marshall, J.).

Subsequently the New Jersey Supreme Court took Farber's appeal, apparently unable to unravel the procedural tangle which had led to Farber being jailed for civil contempt without any court having heard his defenses. New Jersey's highest court, by a 5–2 vote, held that Farber had no first amendment protection against being compelled to turn over his notes. The court ruled that the subpoena was not overly broad, because the trial judge could not adequately deal with the question of whether Farber's notes were relevant to Jascalevich's defense without first examining them. The court also ruled that the New Jersey shield law protecting reporters against disclosure of confidential material must yield in these circumstances to the defendant's right to a fair trial. Ironically, the court held that reporters in future cases would be entitled to a hearing on their claims, but that Farber was not—because something like a hearing, although clearly not a hearing, had been afforded by the presiding judge at the murder trial. See In re Farber, 78 N.J. 259, 394 A.2d 330 (1978), cert. denied 439 U.S. 997 (1978).

36. See City Council v. Hall, 180 Conn. 243, 429 A.2d 481 (1980); Morgan v. State, 337 So.2d 95 (Fla. 1976); Winegard v. Oxberger, 258 N.W.2d 847 (Iowa 1977), cert. denied 436 U.S. 905 (1978); State v. Sandstrom, 224 Kan. 573, 581 P.2d 812 (1978), cert. denied 440 U.S. 929 (1979); Opinion of the Justices, 117 N.H. 390, 373 A.2d 644 (1977); Dallas Oil & Gas, Inc. v. Mouer, 533 S.W.2d 70 (Tex. Civ. App. 1976); State v. St. Peter, 132 Vt. 226, 315 A.2d 254 (1974); Brown v. Commonwealth, 214 Va. 755, 204 S.E.2d 429 (1974), cert. denied 419 U.S. 966 (1974); Senear v. Daily Journal American, 8 Med.L.Rptr. 1151 (Wash. 1982); Zelenka v. Wisconsin, 83 Wis.2d 601, 266 N.W.2d 279 (1978). See generally Comment, "Developments in the News Media Privilege: The Qualified Constitutional Approach Becoming Common Law," 33 Maine L.Rev. 401 (1981).

against newsroom searches,[37] and several state legislatures have done likewise.[38] Although no federal shield law has been enacted, Department of Justice guidelines recognize a qualified privilege as a matter of prosecutorial policy.[39]

As disturbing as the practical impact of *Branzburg, Zurcher* and *Herbert* is what these decisions reveal about the Burger Court's approach to freedom of expression. Mesmerized by its insistence that the press not be given a privileged status, the Court exhibited considerable insensitivity to the special first and fourth amendment concerns raised by indirect burdens on communication. Legal procedures that threaten the confidentiality of reporters' sources or disrupt the editorial process clearly implicate constitutional concerns not present when ordinary businesses are searched or most professionals questioned about their work—regardless of whether the first amendment gives the organized press unique institutional protection. In particular, qualified privileges of the sort rejected by the Court in *Branzburg* and *Herbert* are arguably required by the first amendment's implicit guarantee against undue interference with the acquisition of knowledge. That guarantee, and its special importance for reporters functioning as "surrogates for the public," was recognized by the Court in *Richmond Newspapers, Inc. v. Virginia.*[40] Given the problems that required disclosure of confidences creates for effective information gathering, traditional first amendment theory should prohibit government compulsion of such disclosure—from reporters or other researchers—absent a demonstration that the legal system lacks a less inhibiting alternative.[41]

Similarly, to acknowledge the need for special safeguards against unnecessary searches of newsrooms, one need not agree that the press as an institution deserves extraordinary constitutional protection; one need only recognize that the fourth amendment acquires special force when first amendment values are also implicated. Throughout the 1960's and into the 1970's, the Court stressed the close historical ties between government surveillance and suppression of dissent,[42] and required search and seizure procedures to meet heightened standards of exactitude when used in ways that burdened constitutionally protected

---

37. Privacy Protection Act of 1980, 42 U.S.C. §§ 2000aa to 2000aa–12 (Supp. V 1981). The act limits searches on both the federal and state levels. Id. § 2000aa.

38. See, e.g., Ill. Ann. Stat. ch. 38, ¶108–3(b) (Smith-Hurd 1980); N.J. Stat. Ann. §§ 2A:84A–21.9 to 2A:84A–21.13 (West Supp. 1983); Neb. Rev. Stat. § 29–813(b) (1979); Ore. Rev. Stat. § 44.520(2) (1981).

39. 28 C.F.R. § 50.10 (1986). The guidelines have been held binding on the Justice Department, see United States v. Blanton, 534 F.Supp. 295, 297 (S.D. Fla. 1982), and on the National Labor Relations Board, see Maurice v. NLRB, 7 Med.L. Rptr. 2221 (S.D.W.Va. 1981), rev'd on other grounds 691 F.2d 182 (4th Cir. 1982). See also Ollman v. Evans, 750 F.2d 970, 1039 (D.C. Cir. 1984) (Scalia, J., joined by Wald and Edwards, JJ., dissenting in part)

(describing 28 C.F.R. § 50.10 as "approach[ing] the issue in a much more calibrated fashion than judicial prohibition could achieve").

40. 448 U.S. 555, 573 (1980). The Richmond Newspapers decision is discussed in § 12–20, supra. For an argument that the decision confirms and strengthens the reporter's constitutional privilege, see Goodale, Rutan & Smeall, "An Outline of Reporter's Privilege Cases," in 2 Communications Law 1982, at 561, 578–79 (Practicing Law Institute, 1982).

41. See § 12–23, infra.

42. The classic judicial account of the intertwined histories of free expression and freedom from unreasonable search and seizure appears in Marcus v. Search Warrants, 367 U.S. 717, 724–729 (1961).

expression.[43] Starting with *Zurcher*, however, the Court became less sensitive to the interplay between the first and fourth amendments.

In the Term following that in which *Zurcher* was decided, the Court ruled in *Smith v. Maryland* that no warrant was required before the telephone company, at the behest of law enforcement officials, electronically monitored the numbers dialed from a private telephone.[44] Because the numbers were transmitted to a third party—the phone company—the Court reasoned that the dialer could have no "reasonable expectation of privacy" in the information,[45] and therefore held that the monitoring was not a fourth amendment "search" under the test set forth in *Katz v. United States*.[46] The communicative function of the telephone apparently played no part in the Court's analysis. If, however, "reasonable expectation of privacy" is to have any normative content—and the Court expressly acknowledged that it must[47]—then whether an individual can reasonably expect a particular kind of privacy should depend in part on the importance of such privacy for related constitutional concerns, including freedom of expression. Indeed, in ruling that the fourth amendment covers electronic surveillance of calls made from pay telephones, the *Katz* Court emphasized "the vital role that the public telephone has come to play in private communication."[48] By simply ignoring the hazards of telephonic surveillance for vital first amendment interests, the Burger Court made plain that the narrow approach it took to the fourth amendment in *Zurcher* was unfortunately not an aberration.

§ 12–23. Government Abridgments of Speech Independent of Expressive Content: Track-Two Analysis and Less Restrictive Alternatives

We saw in § 12–2 that government may abridge speech in two ways, leading to two distinct forms of first amendment analysis. Sections 12–3 through 12–21 focused on the first type of abridgment—abridgment on track one, in which government action is targeted at ideas or information that it wished to suppress. Section 12–22, this section, and the succeeding two sections, focus on the second type of abridgment—abridgment on track two, in which government does not

---

43. See United States v. United States District Court, 407 U.S. 297, 313 (1972) (imposing warrant requirement for presidential wiretaps); Stanford v. Texas, 379 U.S. 476, 482, 485 (1965) (invalidating seizure of books); A Quantity of Copies of Books v. Kansas, 378 U.S. 205 (1964) (same); Marcus v. Search Warrants, 367 U.S. 717, 729 (1961) (same).

44. Smith v. Maryland, 442 U.S. 735 (1979). Justice Blackmun wrote the majority opinion. Justices Brennan, Marshall and Stewart dissented. Unsurprisingly, the Court hinted strongly during the same Term that the confidentiality of calls made by reporters warranted no greater constitutional protection. See Reporters Committee for Freedom of the Press v. Ameri-

can Tel. & Tel. Co., 440 U.S. 949 (1979), denying cert. to 593 F.2d 1030 (D.C. Cir. 1978) (ruling that telephone company may turn over journalist's long distance billing records to law enforcement officials without judicial supervision or prior notice to journalist). Justices Brennan, Marshall and Stewart voted to hear the case.

45. 442 U.S. at 744.

46. 389 U.S. 347 (1967).

47. Smith v. Maryland, 442 U.S. at 740 n. 5.

48. Katz v. United States, 389 U.S. at 352. For a discussion of the interplay between technology and free expression, see § 12–25, infra.

aim at ideas or information but seeks a goal independent of communicative content or impact, with the *indirect* result that the flow of information or ideas is in some significant measure constricted.

One could imagine a constitutional system in which such governmental behavior would automatically be upheld, however devastating its consequences for freedom of expression. In such a system, government's only duty would be to avoid gratuitous and deliberate suppression of ideas; so long as government's aims were ideologically neutral, speakers would have to take what they could get. That is not our system; at least since 1939,[1] it has been established that even a wholly neutral government regulation or policy, aimed entirely at harms unconnected with the *content* of any communication, may be invalid if it leaves too little breathing space for communicative activity, or leaves people with too little access to channels of communication, whether as would-be speakers or as would-be listeners.[2] The problem is to decide

§ 12–23

1. The seminal case was Schneider v. State, 308 U.S. 147 (1939) (invalidating restrictions on door-to-door distribution of circulars, and bans on street distribution of circulars, where valid governmental purposes could be at least approximately achieved by less restrictive alternatives). Accord, Teamsters Union v. Vogt, 354 U.S. 284, 295 (1957); Kunz v. New York, 340 U.S. 290, 293 (1951); Niemotko v. Maryland, 340 U.S. 268, 276–77 (1951) (Frankfurter, J., concurring); Follett v. McCormick, 321 U.S. 573 (1944); Martin v. Struthers, 319 U.S. 141 (1943); Cantwell v. Connecticut, 310 U.S. 296, 308 (1940); Hague v. CIO, 307 U.S. 496, 515–16 (1939) (Roberts, J.).

2. See Ely, "Legislative and Administrative Motivation in Constitutional Law," 79 Yale L.J. 1205, 1335–36 (1970). It would, however, be wrong to conclude that some form of first amendment scrutiny is triggered whenever government does anything that happens to reduce the flow of information or ideas. Otherwise, someone who is arrested for running a red light would be entitled to first amendment consideration if he happened to be a news anchor on his way to the TV studio—or a law professor on her way to a lecture. Such an individual can no more demand a showing that the government proceeded in the least restrictive manner possible than can any other person or business. See, e.g., Arcara v. Cloud Books, Inc., 106 S.Ct. 3172, 3178 (1986) (upholding state action closing down a bookstore for a year, pursuant to a generally applicable state statute providing for such closure whenever any place of business is used for "lewdness, assignation, or prostitution," and refusing to submit such one-year closure to special first amendment scrutiny; the legislation providing the closure sanction "was direct-

ed at unlawful conduct having nothing to do with books or other expressive activity"). As Chief Justice Burger wrote for the Arcara majority, "If the city imposed closure penalties for demonstrated Fire Code violations or health hazards from inadequate sewage treatment, the First Amendment would not aid the owner of premises who had knowingly allowed such violations to persist." Id. at 3177. Justice O'Connor, joined by Justice Stevens in a concurring opinion, correctly noted that "[a]ny other conclusion would lead to the absurd result that any government action that had some conceivable speech-inhibiting consequences, such as the arrest of a newscaster for a traffic violation, would require analysis under the First Amendment. If, however, a city were to use a nuisance statute as a pretext for closing down a book store because it sold indecent books or because of the perceived secondary effects of having a purveyor of such books in the neighborhood, the case would clearly implicate First Amendment concerns and require analysis under the appropriate First Amendment standard of review." Id. at 3178. Had the law at issue been directed at bookstores, or at activities likely to have a significant expressive component, the dissenting views expressed by Justice Blackmun, joined by Justices Brennan and Marshall, see id. at 3178–81, would have had greater force. Moreover, even a law not directed at communicative activities might properly be subjected to first amendment scrutiny as applied to a particular expressive act that triggered the law's enforcement, see United States v. O'Brien, 391 U.S. 367 (1968), distinguished in Arcara, 106 S.Ct. at 3175. But when *neither* the law, *nor* the act triggering its enforcement, has any significant first amendment dimension, the fact that the law *incidentally* operates to restrict first

when a measure leaves "too little" space or access. To that end, courts have employed what is typically called a "balancing" approach—the sort of approach it is easier to eschew while on track one.[3]

To be weighed in the balance are, on the one hand, the extent to which communicative activity is in fact inhibited; and, on the other hand, the values, interests, or rights served by enforcing the inhibition. Two variables have been important in structuring the balancing process, and in deciding how heavy a burden of justification—and how large a sacrifice of other goals—to impose on government. The first has been the degree to which any given inhibition on communicative activity falls unevenly upon various groups in the society. Like the proverbial ban on sleeping under the bridges of Paris, a ban on using loudspeakers or distributing handbills obviously falls with greater force upon the poor than upon those who can afford access to other methods of communication;[4] thus the Court has in the past scrutinized such bans with special care.[5] However neutral their intention with respect

amendment activity, and that some alternative state measure might offer a less restrictive means of pursuing the state's legitimate objectives, should not serve to condemn what the state has done as unconstitutional. On remand in Arcara, the New York Court of Appeals found that the closure of the bookstore violated freedom of expression as guaranteed by the state constitution. See Arcara v. Cloud Books, Inc., 68 N.Y.2d 553, 510 N.Y.S.2d 844, 503 N.E.2d 492 (1986).

3. See generally Note, "Less Drastic Means and the First Amendment," 78 Yale L.J. 464 (1969).

4. See, e.g., Martin v. Struthers, 319 U.S. 141, 146 (1943): "Door to door distribution of circulars is essential to the poorly financed causes of little people." Cf. Kovacs v. Cooper, 336 U.S. 77, 102 (1949) (Black, J., dissenting): "There are many people who have ideas that they wish to disseminate but who do not have enough money to own or control publishing plants, newspapers, radios, moving picture studios, or chains of show places." See also Kalven, "The Concept of the Public Forum: Cox v. Louisiana," 1965 Sup.Ct.Rev. 1, 30: "We would do well to avoid . . . new epigrams about the majestic equality of the law prohibiting the rich man, too, from distributing leaflets or picketing."

5. Although narrow limits on time, place, and manner—like the limit on using loud sound trucks on public streets in Kovacs, supra note 4—have been upheld, see, e.g., Grayned v. Rockford, 408 U.S. 104, 116 (1972), many broader prohibitions, see note 1, supra, have been struck down. Of late, however, the Court has been less willing to apply heightened scrutiny to facially content-neutral regulations on speech that have a disproportionately severe impact on underprivileged socio-economic groups. In

Clark v. Community for Creative Non-Violence, 468 U.S. 288 (1984), for example, the Court upheld facially neutral National Park Service anti-camping regulations as applied to forbid protesters who wished to call attention to the plight of the homeless from sleeping in symbolic tents erected in Lafayette Park, across the street from the White House. Justice Marshall, joined in his dissent by Justice Brennan, warned that the seemingly "neutral" principles of the majority predictably discriminated in practice against the poor and others who—lacking access to the mass media and lacking decent housing—naturally focused on such demonstrations to express their ideas: "[T]his case . . . lends credence to the charge that judicial administration of the First Amendment, in conjunction with a social order marked by large disparities of wealth and other sources of power, tends systematically to discriminate against efforts by the relatively disadvantaged to convey their political ideas." Id. at 313–14 n. 14. See also City Council of Los Angeles v. Taxpayers for Vincent, 466 U.S. 789, 812–13 n. 30 (1984) (upholding a municipal regulation which prohibited the posting of signs on public property, such as telephone poles, and observing that the "special solicitude" previously "shown [by the Court] for [inexpensive] forms of expression that . . . may be important to large segments of the citizenry . . . has practical boundaries"); United States Postal Service v. Greenburgh Civic Associations, 453 U.S. 114 (1981) (sustaining a ban on the placement of unstamped "mailable matter" in mailboxes used to receive U.S. mail). This growing insensitivity to how background disparities in wealth and power operate to distort the impact of facially neutral rules is by no means limited to strictly first amendment cases. In Selective Service System v. Minnesota Public Interest Re-

to speakers and messages, their impact is anything but neutral, and government must therefore go a substantial distance to justify enforcing them.[6] Similarly, a ban on anonymous pamphleteering falls with much greater force upon individuals and groups who fear majoritarian disapproval and reprisal—upon dissidents and upon the unpopular— than upon those with widely approved messages to deliver; thus the Court has again demanded more than minimal justification for bans of this type.[7]

At the same time, when deciding whether a particular ban or a specific regulation of time, place, or manner does indeed have a disproportionate impact on expression by the unpopular, the dispossessed, or the little-known, the Court has demanded more than speculative argument that such an impact might exist. In *Heffron v. International Society for Krishna Consciousness (ISKCON)*,[8] the Court upheld a rule of the Minnesota State Fair which required all persons who wished to sell, exhibit, or distribute written material on the fairgrounds to do so from fixed, rented booths. ISKCON, a religious organization, challenged the rule on the ground that it discriminated in favor of well-known or well-liked groups that fair-goers were willing, without embarrassment, to seek out affirmatively.[9] ISKCON argued that the rule was

search Group, 468 U.S. 841 (1984), a case challenging the constitutionality of a statute which denied financial aid to male students who failed to register for the draft, Chief Justice Burger, writing for the Court, casually dismissed—in terms reminiscent of Anatole France—the argument that the law discriminated against economically deprived students. The law, asserted the Chief Justice, "treats all nonregistrants alike, denying aid to both the poor and the wealthy." Id. at 859 n. 17. See § 10–4, supra.

It is noteworthy that, even when the Court protects first amendment interests, its decisions—whether or not justifiable— often work to enlarge the advantages of monied groups by facilitating their efforts to exploit their favored positions. See, e.g., Secretary of State of Maryland v. Joseph H. Munson Co., 467 U.S. 947 (1984) (striking down statute which limited expenses of charitable fundraisers); FCC v. League of Women Voters, 468 U.S. 364 (1984) (upholding the right of publicly-subsidized television stations to broadcast political editorials); Citizens Against Rent Control v. Berkeley, 454 U.S. 290 (1981) (invalidating $250 ceiling on individual contributions to referendum campaign organizations); Buckley v. Valeo, 424 U.S. 1 (1976) (striking down Congressionally-imposed ceilings on expenditures by, or in support of, candidates for public office). For a fuller discussion of these issues, see L. Tribe, Constitutional Choices 192–98 (1985).

6. It is not a sufficient justification that the only alternatives available to government would be "less efficient and convenient." Schneider v. State, 308 U.S. 147, 164 (1939).

7. See, e.g., Talley v. California, 362 U.S. 60 (1960) (invalidating ordinance which prohibited distribution of any handbill not bearing name and address of person who prepared, distributed, or sponsored it; defense that ordinance could help identify those responsible for fraud, false advertising, or libel rejected since ordinance went further than necessary to achieve those goals). Although Buckley v. Valeo, 424 U.S. 1, 60–84 (1976), upheld disclosure requirements of federal campaign regulations as essential to intelligent use of franchise and necessary to control corruption and enforce valid contribution limits, the Court in Brown v. Socialist Workers Party, 459 U.S. 87 (1982), struck down various facially valid disclosure requirements in a state campaign regulation as applied to the Socialist Workers Party. See § 13–31, infra.

8. 452 U.S. 640 (1981). Justice White delivered the opinion of the Court, in which Chief Justice Burger and Justices Stewart, Powell, and Rehnquist joined. Justice Brennan filed an opinion concurring in part and dissenting in part, in which Justices Marshall and Stevens joined. Justice Blackmun filed an opinion concurring in part and dissenting in part. The author of this treatise represented ISKCON in the Supreme Court.

9. Not at issue in Heffron was the question whether Minnesota could constitutionally charge fees for its required state fair booths, even if those fees were so high that

therefore not content-neutral, because it contained a built-in bias against minority and unpopular political and religious groups. Although prior decisions had made clear that government may not limit door-to-door speech to that which homeowners take positive steps to seek out,[10] limiting face-to-face speech to that which fair-goers invite by entering fixed booths is not predictably calculated to filter out unpopular speakers. Accordingly, the Court dismissed ISKCON's contention in a footnote: "the argument is interesting but has little force." [11]

The second variable has been the degree to which the inhibition on communicative activity operates to shut down places that have traditionally been associated with the public exchange of views, or places that have been specifically opened by government to such exchange. As we will see in § 12–24, such "public forums" represent areas within which tolerance for inhibitions on speech, petition, and assembly is at a minimum, and government's burden of justification at its highest. Indeed, as we shall see in the next section, a governmental action that excludes a communication from such a public forum cannot be defended by pointing to the availability of alternative ways to transmit the same message; like a governmental abridgment based upon the content of an expression,[12] an abridgment in this special realm is not deemed insignif-

they effectively priced less affluent groups out of the marketplace. Nor did ISKCON raise a free exercise claim to enjoy rights above and beyond those that political speakers could enjoy.

10. Compare Martin v. Struthers, 319 U.S. 141, 143–44, 146 (1943) (invalidating municipal ordinance that forbade door-to-door distribution of handbills as applied to a Jehovah's Witness attempting to distribute religious literature; noting that such a method of delivery is "essential to the poorly financed causes of little people," the Court opined that "[t]he ordinance does not control anything but the distribution of literature, and in that respect it substitutes the judgment of the community for the judgment of the individual householder"); City of Watseka v. Illinois Public Action Council, 107 S.Ct. 919 (1987) (affirming without opinion a Seventh Circuit decision that invalidated a municipal ordinance limiting door-to-door solicitation to the hours between 9:00 a.m. and 5:00 p.m., Monday through Saturday), with Breard v. Alexandria, 341 U.S. 622, 644 (1951) (upholding ordinance that forbade the commercial door-to-door solicitation of magazine subscriptions; "[s]ubscriptions may be made by anyone interested in receiving the magazines without the annoyance of house-to-house canvassing").

11. 452 U.S. at 649 n. 12. Even for one who served as ISKCON's advocate in the Supreme Court, it seems hard not to concede in hindsight that the Court's conclusion was a sensible one. The dangers of requiring listeners to initiate communication are likely to be peculiarly insubstan-

tial in the free-wheeling environment of a state fair. Visitors may well be in an adventurous mood, and the crowds and commotion should be expected to provide an anonymity that minimizes any fear of social stigma. At least without proof to the contrary, this expectation probably suffices to support the ISKCON result.

Board of Airport Commissioners of City of Los Angeles v. Jews for Jesus, Inc., 107 S.Ct. 2568 (1987), suggests the question whether a public airport may go further and limit the use of its interior facilities to purposes directly related to air travel. If an airport permits newstands to continue to operate but excludes in-person leafleteers and solicitors, then that policy arguably discriminates in favor of wealthier, more mainstream organizations which already publish established journals—and against smaller, less popular groups which lack the resources and readership to compete in this market. Whether this argument, too, may be dismissed as more "interesting" than forceful is unclear. But the Court did not need to reach it, because the airport's regulation was fatally overbroad: it proscribed all "First Amendment activities," including "even talking and reading, or the wearing of campaign buttons or symbolic clothing." Id. at 2572. See § 12–27, infra.

12. See Virginia Board of Pharmacy v. Virginia Consumer Council, 425 U.S. 748, 757 n. 15 (1976) (invalidating state ban on pharmacist's advertising of prices of prescription drugs; held irrelevant that consumers might be able to obtain same information in other ways); Spence v.

icant simply because alternative channels are available to the speaker or to the listener.[13]

Unless a track two inhibition occurs in a public forum, however, government's burden of justification is minimal unless the inhibition on communication is shown to be substantial. That is, with the exception noted above for public forums, the availability of alternative channels for the speaker to reach the same audience with the same message, or of alternative sources for the listener to receive the message, is a necessary part of the constitutional analysis when government abridges speech without regard to its expressive content. Unless the inhibition resulting from such a content-neutral abridgment is significant, government need show no more than a rational justification for its choice; and if equally effective alternatives are readily available to the speaker or listener, the inhibition is not deemed significant.[14]

One of the best illustrations of the latter point is provided by *United States v. O'Brien*,[15] the draft-card burning case. As we saw in § 12–6, a plausible argument exists that the government's decision to make the destruction of one's draft card a crime should have been treated by the *O'Brien* Court as an abridgment of speech based upon the ideas expressed; as such, the case arguably belonged on track one and should probably have received the strictest scrutiny, with government's action being invalidated unless compellingly justified by considerations that could not be satisfied with "more speech". Instead, as we saw, the Court regarded the abridgment as content-neutral and thus treated the case as belonging on track two. Assuming for the sake of analysis that this threshold determination was correct, what the Court did next was unobjectionable: it subjected the government's prohibition

Washington, 418 U.S. 405, 411 n. 4 (1974) (reversing conviction for taping removable peace symbol onto flag displayed in apartment window, and "summarily" rejecting the state court's argument that the inhibition on speech was "miniscule and trifling" because of "other means" that could have been used to express the same views; availability of other means held irrelevant when government prosecutes "for the expression of an idea through activity"). Accord, Wooley v. Maynard, 430 U.S. 705 (1977) (invalidating compelled display of emblem bearing state's "Live Free or Die" motto on automobile license plate; majority implicitly rejects dissenting argument, id. at 722, that objections to the motto could be expressed by displaying a counter-motto as well as by removing the state's motto). See also Procunier v. Martinez, 416 U.S. 396, 408–09 (1974), Kleindienst v. Mandel, 408 U.S. 753, 762–63 (1972), and Lamont v. Postmaster General, 381 U.S. 301 (1965), as explained in Virginia Board of Pharmacy, 425 U.S. at 57–58 n. 15.

13. See Schneider v. State, 308 U.S. 147, 163 (1939).

14. See Lloyd Corp., Ltd. v. Tanner, 407 U.S. 551, 566–67 & n. 12 (1972) (rejecting

alleged first amendment right to distribute antiwar handbills in privately-owned shopping center, partly on the basis that surrounding public roads and sidewalks gave handbillers adequate alternative public forums for disseminating their message). See also Greer v. Spock, 424 U.S. 828, 839 (1976) (rejecting alleged first amendment right to have political candidates speak at Fort Dix military reservation, partly on the basis that members of Armed Forces stationed at Fort Dix are free to attend political rallies off base); Pell v. Procunier, 417 U.S. 817, 827–28, 830 (1974) (rejecting alleged first amendment right of press and other media to interview specified inmates, since inmates retain alternative channels of communication with outside world and since the press and general public are both "accorded full opportunities to observe prison conditions through such means as interviews of random inmates"); Saxbe v. Washington Post Co., 417 U.S. 843, 846–47 (1974) (same).

15. 391 U.S. 367 (1968), discussed in §§ 12–3, 12–5, 12–6, supra.

to relaxed scrutiny, upholding it as the least restrictive way of achieving the legitimate purpose of protecting draft cards.

But understanding *why* this next step was appropriate requires further analysis.[16] For the Court's generous definition of a governmental purpose—preserving every last draft card in perfect shape—*guaranteed* that the law under review would indeed be the "least restrictive means" to the end being pursued.[17] Had the Court defined the relevant purpose more generically—by looking, say, to the effective functioning of the selective service system—or had it insisted that government consider less restrictive alternatives that were *almost* as effective,[18] then government could not have shown that its ban on draft-card destruction was the least restrictive possible means of achieving the goal. Yet on the record in *O'Brien*, assuming that the case belonged on track two at all, the Court was right to define the relevant purpose as generously as it did. For, as Justice Harlan observed in his concurring opinion,[19] O'Brien made no showing that alternative, equally effective, ways of expressing his message were unavailable. He could, after all have burned a *copy* of his draft card in front of the very same audience as a means of making precisely the same point. If that alternative is to be dismissed as less effective and hence constitutionally insufficient, the only reason must be the special drama of burning a *real* draft card. But why was that particularly dramatic? The only plausible reason, it seems, is that the act was illegal. But surely O'Brien could not be permitted to rely on the act's illegality to establish its unique effectiveness in the course of claiming that the act really was *not* illegal because the law in question violated the Constitution.[20] One is reminded of the young man who kills his parents and then pleads for mercy as an orphan. Assuming that the case belonged on track two, it was therefore quite clear that no special burden was imposed upon the ability to

---

16. The following defense of relaxed scrutiny on the Court's premises should be distinguished from the suggestion that the Court applied only minimal scrutiny in O'Brien because draft-card burning constituted an unorthodox mode of communication. See Ely, "Flag Desecration: A Case Study in the Roles of Categorizing and Balancing in First Amendment Analysis," 88 Harv.L.Rev. 1482, 1488 (1975). If only orthodox modes of expression were protected, "the old saw that familiarity breeds contempt," id. at 1489, might mean that truly *effective* communication would be left undefended by the first amendment. Moreover, just as "[l]aws which hamper the free use of some instruments of communication thereby favor competing channels," Kovacs v. Cooper, 336 U.S. 77, 102 (1949) (Black, J., dissenting), so laws which leave unorthodox media defenseless in effect favor orthodox messages, a flaw that in itself should compel the strict scrutiny of track one. See §§ 12–2, 12–3, supra.

17. A law requiring continued possession of one's draft card, see T. Emerson, The System of Freedom of Expression 84–

85 (1970), would neither fully serve the government's purpose—since one person might destroy another's card—nor be unambiguously less restrictive—since the law's reach would be broader, and since a person compelled to carry a draft card might regard that requirement as akin to a compelled flag salute, see West Virginia State Board of Education v. Barnette, 319 U.S. 624 (1943). But see Wooley v. Maynard, 430 U.S. 705, 717 n. 15 (1977) (dictum suggesting that the bearer of currency inscribed with the National Motto, "In God We Trust," is not required to advertise the motto publicly and may thus be in a situation distinguishable from that of the person forced to display "Live Free or Die" on his or her license plate). Cf. Lynch v. Donnelly, 465 U.S. 668, 693 (1984) (O'Connor, J., concurring) (suggesting that "In God We Trust" serves a purely secular purpose).

18. See Ely, supra note 2, at 1340.

19. 391 U.S. at 388–89.

20. See Ely, supra note 12, at 1489 & n. 29.

communicate the same message in other ways to the same audience—and that any rational explanation for the law should thus have sufficed. Had the Court been willing to treat the law as aimed at O'Brien's message, it would have been the government rather than O'Brien that would have been estopped to discuss alternative ways of getting the message across. Given the way the Court did treat the law, however, its subsequent analysis seems entirely appropriate.

But it plainly does not follow that, in all instances of track-two analysis, the appropriate level of scrutiny is equally minimal. On the contrary, whenever it can be demonstrated that the result of the government's rule or policy is to limit in some significant degree the ease or effectiveness with which a speaker or category of speakers can reach a specific audience with a particular message, the government should lose the case unless it can establish that an important public objective unrelated to the message would be sacrificed by any less restrictive alternative.[21] In *Schneider v. State*,[22] for example, anti-handbill ordinances were invalidated as applied to distributors of labor, political, and religious circulars despite the state's plainly legitimate purposes of minimizing litter, noise, and traffic congestion and protecting people from fraud and invasion of privacy.[23] Had the Court been willing to define the state's purposes with an eye to upholding the ordinances at all costs, it could easily have said that the aims were to spare the state the cost of controlling traffic or cleaning up such handbills as might be left behind by distributors; even the cost of picking up a single stray handbill was a cost the state might wish to be spared, and no less restrictive alternative could fully achieve that purpose.[24] Instead, the Court recognized the state's only sufficiently

---

21. In Federal Election Commission v. Massachusetts Citizens for Life, Inc. (MCFL), 107 S.Ct. 616 (1986), for example, the Court invalidated sections of the Federal Election Campaign Act (FECA) as applied to a nonprofit corporation that published "pro-life" literature. The FECA prohibits corporations from using treasury funds (i.e., general resources of the corporation) to make an expenditure "in connection with any election to any public office," and requires that any expenditure for such a purpose must be financed by voluntary contributions to a separate segregated fund. Although the Court has often endorsed the "legislative judgment that the special characteristics of the corporate structure require particularly careful regulation," FEC v. National Right to Work Committee, 459 U.S. 197, 209–10 (1982) (upholding restrictions on organization and solicitation), in Massachusetts Citizens for Life the Court recognized that the particular situation of the group involved made the FECA requirements especially onerous and, because of the obviously political nature of the organization, unnecessary. Contributors were well aware that their money was being used to support pro-life candidates—indeed, they would have been

surprised if it was *not* used for that purpose. "Some corporations have features more akin to voluntary political associations than business firms, and therefore should not have to bear burdens on independent spending solely because of their incorporated status." 107 S.Ct. at 631. The Court thus found that the FECA rules, while content-neutral, intruded too deeply into MCFL's publishing and advocacy activities. See § 13–29, infra.

22. 308 U.S. 147 (1939).

23. See id. at 158, 160, 164.

24. No argument was advanced in Schneider that each handbill distributed constituted an aesthetic nuisance *in itself*; when such an argument may be advanced—as with billboards, see Metromedia, Inc. v. San Diego, 453 U.S. 490, 510 (1981) (plurality opinion), or with posted signs, see City Council of Los Angeles v. Taxpayers for Vincent, 466 U.S. 789, 808–09 (1984)—a "least restrictive alternative" test imposes no real obstacle to a government determined to avoid "visual clutter." Id. at 816. In such situations, whether the regulated activity is "label[ed] . . . a discrete medium of expression," id. at 815 n. 32, and whether the property being used

important objectives to be such more general ones as maintaining reasonably clean streets at non-prohibitive cost—and such objectives could be achieved tolerably well by measures less draconian than a total ban.[25] Thus the state was required to incur affirmative costs in order to facilitate communicative activity [26]—a requirement characteristic of track two, but only where the adverse impact on such activity is substantial or is skewed against one type of group or, as in the *Schneider* case itself, is both substantial *and* skewed, and occurs in a public forum at that.

Two further points should be noted here. The first is that "less restrictive alternative" analysis in this context is not simply a label for the conclusion that government has acted in an impermissibly broad manner, unacceptably sweeping protected conduct under its prohibitory rules. As we will see in §§ 12–27 to 12–33, the reference to less restrictive alternatives in the context of facial overbreadth challenges, particularly where government has acted in terms of expressive content and is thus subjected to track-one scrutiny, is essentially conclusory; there, to say that less restrictive alternatives exist is really to insist that government had better *find* such alternatives. In contrast, the discussion of less restrictive alternatives in track-two cases is a genuine part of the analysis itself; the availability of such alternatives is relevant to deciding whether government has in fact left too little opportunity for communicative activity, whether for speakers or for listeners.[27]

Second, the principle that government must incur affirmative costs in order to facilitate communicative activity is not lightly extended to cases in which private individuals are asked to be the cost-bearers—and especially cases in which private individuals are compelled to serve as message-bearers. Thus, although a legislature may require private individuals to make various economic sacrifices in the interest of facilitating political or communicative activity, as in *Day-Brite v. Mis*

by the speaker "should be deemed a public forum," id., may not furnish "workable analytical tool[s]" and should "not [be] dispositive." Id.

25. Schneider, 308 U.S. at 162: "There are obvious methods of preventing littering. Amongst these is the punishment of those who actually throw papers on the streets." See also id. at 164: "Frauds may be . . . punished by law. Trespasses may similarly be forbidden."

26. Id. at 164: "If it is said that these means are less efficient and convenient than [more sweeping abridgment], the answer is that considerations of this sort do not empower a municipality to abridge freedom of speech and press." See Ely, supra note 2, at 1335, 1340. See also Martin v. Struthers, 319 U.S. 141, 148 (1943) (invalidating ordinance against knocking on doors to distribute circulars, as applied to distribution of religious literature, in

light of the less drastic alternative of protecting privacy by punishing "those who call at a home in defiance of the previously expressed will of the occupant"). Contrast Breard v. Alexandria, 341 U.S. 622 (1951) (upholding a similar ordinance as applied to door-to-door solicitation of orders to sell out-of-state goods). Justice Black, writing for the majority in Martin, assumed that the less drastic means would be so plainly equivalent that the state's choice made sense only as a gratuitous suppression of speech. 319 U.S. at 147. For a critical view of this account, see Note, "Less Drastic Means and the First Amendment," 78 Yale L.J. 464, 469–70 n. 27 (1969).

27. See, e.g., Nixon v. Administrator of General Services, 433 U.S. 425 (1977) (archival screening of ex-President's papers upheld as least restrictive means of securing vital public needs for access to information).

souri,[28] courts have at times been reluctant to construe the Constitution itself as imposing a requirement of such sacrifice. As we will see in § 12–25, that proposition helps to explain some of the cases dealing with private as opposed to public forums, although, for reasons to be explored in that section, courts have occasionally been more reluctant than they should.

§ 12–24. Public and Semi-Public Forums: From Streets and Parks to Special-Purpose Public Places and Institutions

Its safe delivery aided by a seminal 1965 essay by Professor Harry Kalven,[1] the concept of "public forums" was spawned in a series of decisions in the 1930's and 1940's,[2] went through a troubled period of gestation in several decisions in the 1960's,[3] and emerged as a fully viable creation as a group of decisions in the 1970's.[4] In the 1980's, the

---

28. 342 U.S. 421 (1952) (upholding law requiring employers to give employees paid time off in order to vote). But cf. Thornton v. Caldor, Inc., 472 U.S. 703 (1985) (striking down as violative of the establishment clause a state law providing that "those who observe a Sabbath any day of the week as a matter of religious conviction must be relieved of the duty to work on that day, no matter what burden or inconvenience this imposes on the employer or fellow workers"), discussed in Chapter 14, infra.

§ 12–24

1. "The Concept of the Public Forum: Cox v. Louisiana," 1965 Sup.Ct.Rev. 1.

2. See Saia v. New York City, 334 U.S. 558 (1948); Martin v. Struthers, 319 U.S. 141 (1943); Jamison v. Texas, 318 U.S. 413 (1943); Cox v. New Hampshire, 312 U.S. 569 (1941); Schneider v. State, 308 U.S. 147 (1939); Hague v. C.I.O., 307 U.S. 496 (1939). These cases established that leafleting, parading, and other speech-related uses of streets, sidewalks, and parks could be neither banned nor subjected to discretionary licensing. The Jamison decision expressly rejected the older theory of Davis v. Massachusetts, 167 U.S. 43, 47–48 (1897) (affirming 162 Mass. 510, 511 (1895)) that a state legislature has an owner's absolute control over public speaking and assembly in streets and parks belonging to the state. See 318 U.S. at 415–16.

3. See Cox v. Louisiana, 379 U.S. 536, 555 (1965) (reversing conviction for obstructing public passageway by assembling near courthouse but raising possibility that nondiscriminatory closing of all "streets and other public facilities" to parades and meetings might be permissible); Edwards v. South Carolina, 372 U.S. 229 (1963) (reversing breach of peace conviction for orderly carrying of anti-segregation placards on state capitol grounds). By the late

1960's, the hesitant approach of Cox was replaced by the more confident approach of Edwards. See Shuttlesworth v. Birmingham, 394 U.S. 147, 152 (1969), citing approvingly (and relying on) the dictum of Justice Roberts, writing for the plurality in Hague v. C.I.O., 307 U.S. 496, 515–16 (1939) (invalidating ordinance forbidding all public meetings in streets and other public places without a permit): "Wherever the title of streets and parks may rest, they have immemorially been held in trust for the use of the public and, time out of mind, have been used for purposes of assembly, communicating thought between citizens, and discussing public questions. Such use of the streets and public places has, from ancient times, been a part of the privileges, immunities, rights, and liberties of citizens. The privilege of a citizen of the United States to use the streets and parks for communication of views on national questions may be regulated in the interest of all; it is not absolute, but relative, and must be exercised in subordination to the general comfort and convenience, and in consonance with peace and good order; but it must not, in the guise of regulation, be abridged or denied."

4. See Southeastern Promotions, Ltd. v. Conrad, 420 U.S. 546, 555 (1976) (municipal theater and privately owned theater leased to city "were public forums designed for and dedicated to expressive activities" and thus could not be made unavailable for showing of "Hair"; refusal to permit showing constituted forbidden prior restraint); Police Department of City of Chicago v. Mosley, 408 U.S. 92, 98–99 (1972) (city cannot enforce ordinance prohibiting all non-labor picketing within 150 feet of a school): "[J]ustifications for selective exclusions from a public forum must be carefully scrutinized." See also Grayned v. Rockford, 408 U.S. 104, 115–19 (1972).

Court described and reformulated public forum doctrine in ways that have proven to be quite manipulable and problematic. In its principal attempt at a comprehensive doctrinal synthesis,[5] the Court set out three categories of forums: (1) traditional, "quintessential public forums"—"places which by long tradition or by government fiat have been devoted to assembly and debate," such as "streets and parks";[6] (2) "limited purpose" or state-created semi-public forums opened "for use by the public as a place for expressive activity," such as university meeting facilities or school board meetings;[7] and, finally, (3) public property "which is not by tradition or designation for public communication" at all.[8]

The "public forum" doctrine holds that restrictions on speech should be subject to higher scrutiny when, all other things being equal, that speech occurs in areas playing a vital role in communication—such as in those places historically associated with first amendment activities, such as streets, sidewalks, and parks [9]—especially because of how indispensable communication in these places is to people who lack access to more elaborate (and more costly) channels.[10] Public forum analysis adds a frequently significant location-specific dimension—or at least a location-specific *label*—to the threshold inquiry of whether the values of free expression are involved in a given case.[11] In some places, some activities are said to be entitled to greater first amendment protection than the same activities might claim in other places.[12] The designation "public forum" thus serves as shorthand for the recognition that a particular context represents an important channel of communication in the system of free expression.[13]

Yet many recent cases illustrate the blurriness, the occasional artificiality, and the frequent irrelevance, of the categories within the public forum classification. When the government clearly takes aim at a disfavored message, as on track one, for example, it makes no difference where that speech occurs or even what means, verbal or nonverbal, the speaker uses to communicate it. In cases such as these,

---

5. See Perry Education Association v. Perry Local Educators' Association, 460 U.S. 37 (1983).

6. Id. at 45–46.

7. Id.

8. Id. at 46.

9. See Hague v. C.I.O., supra note 3.

10. See Martin v. Struthers, 319 U.S. 141, 146 (1943). But see City Council of the City of Los Angeles v. Taxpayers for Vincent, 466 U.S. 789, 813–15 (1984) (finding that utility poles upon which political signs are posted are not public forums).

11. The prior, threshold issue of whether a particular activity possesses any first amendment significance is discussed in §§ 12–7, 12–23, supra.

12. This, for example, is the Court's rationale for distinguishing Cornelius v. NAACP Legal Defense and Educational

Fund, 473 U.S. 788 (1985), from other charitable solicitation cases, and Lehman v. Shaker Heights, 418 U.S. 298 (1974), from City Council of the City of Los Angeles v. Taxpayers for Vincent, 466 U.S. 789, 813–15 (1984), and Metromedia, Inc. v. San Diego, 453 U.S. 490 (1981). See notes 18 & 20, infra.

13. See Cornelius, 473 U.S. at 820 (Blackmun, J., joined by Brennan, J., dissenting) ("the public forum, limited public forum, and nonpublic categories are but analytical shorthand for the principles that have guided the Court's decisions regarding claims to access to public property for expressive activity. The interests served by the expressive activity must be balanced against the interests served by the uses for which the property was intended and the interests of all citizens to enjoy the property").

public forum classifications are unnecessary and unhelpful.[14] It is only when the law does not regulate the content of messages as such, and when there is no evidence of a governmental motive to discriminate in favor of or against a particular viewpoint,[15] that the Court properly inquires into such factors as the place of the speech, the character of the particular activity being regulated, and the nature of the restriction imposed.

Activities such as leafleting [16] and solicitation [17] are by tradition and function so closely linked with free expression that the Court has properly scrutinized restrictions upon those activities with special care, without pausing to establish at the outset that the restrictions operate in a public forum. Instead, the approach has been to presume a need for strict scrutiny unless a peculiarly *non*-public forum is involved. Restrictions on charities engaging in fundraising drives, for example, have been upheld only when the forum for such solicitation is entirely state-created, and when government has evinced no intent to create

14. At times, however, the Supreme Court has suggested that rules deemed sufficiently content-neutral in other settings might be too content-based to pass muster in a public forum. See, e.g., Perry Education Association v. Perry Local Educators' Association, 460 U.S. 37, 45–46, 48–50 (1983); Police Department of Chicago v. Mosley, 408 U.S. 92, 96–99 (1972).

15. See, e.g., Consolidated Edison Co. v. Public Service Comm'n., 447 U.S. 530, 535 & 536 (1980) (striking down order of state utility commission which prohibited the inclusion by privately-owned public utilities of monthly billing inserts discussing controversial issues of public policy; the majority, while conceding that time, place, and manner restrictions are permissible if they serve "significant government interest[s]" and leave open "ample alternative channels for communication," found that "when regulation is based on the content of speech, government action must be scrutinized more carefully to ensure that communication has not been prohibited 'merely because public officials disapprove the speaker's views'", quoting Niemotko v. Maryland, 340 U.S. 268, 282 (1951) (Frankfurter, J., concurring); Perry Education Association v. Perry Local Educators' Association, 460 U.S. 37, 61, 62 (1983) (Brennan, J., dissenting) (upholding township rule which granted preferential access to internal public school mail system to bargaining agent of teachers; the Court has "never held that government may allow discussion of a subject and then discriminate among viewpoints on that particular topic. . . . Viewpoint discrimination is censorship in its purest form"). See generally, Stephan, "The First Amendment and Content Discrimination," 68 Va.L.Rev. 203, 233 (1982).

16. See, e.g., Schneider v. State, 308 U.S. 147 (1939). Cf. Heffron v. Int'l Soc.

for Krishna Consciousness (ISKCON), 452 U.S. 640 (1981), which upheld, as applied to religious solicitation, a state rule confining the distribution of printed material at a state fair to certain fixed booth locations. The Court found that the state's interest in crowd control was "substantial," id. at 650, and held that the regulation, because it afforded many alternative speech opportunities, was a valid time, place, and manner restriction. Id. at 654–55. The Court also opined that the rule did not really operate in a discriminatory fashion at all, because the booths provided to ISKCON were "not secreted away in some nonaccessible location," but rather "located within the area of the fairgrounds where visitors are expected, and indeed encouraged to pass." Id. at 655 n. 13. On this characterization of the restriction, it did not seem unreasonable. See § 12–23, supra.

17. See, e.g., Secretary of State of Maryland v. Joseph H. Munson Co., 467 U.S. 947 (1984) (invalidating state statute which prohibited charitable organizations engaged in fundraising activities from expending on solicitation more than 25% of the total amount raised); Larson v. Valente, 456 U.S. 228, 254–55 (1982) (striking down a state law which required all religious organizations receiving more than 50% of their total contributions from nonmembers to file highly detailed financial disclosure statements, a rule which appeared targeted specifically at such smaller or newer religions as the Unification Church); Village of Schaumburg v. Citizens for a Better Environment, 444 U.S. 620 (1980) (invalidating a municipal rule which barred door-to-door or on-street solicitation by charitable organizations using more than 25% of their receipts for non-charitable purposes, such as administrative costs and overhead).

that forum as one meant "for expressive activity." [18]   And, even in such cases, the Court has been sensitive to the possibility that impermissible motives may underlie the restrictions on solicitation.[19]

Similarly, regulations on the act of posting signs—even outside a public forum—clearly implicate first amendment values.[20] Open sexual activity and prostitution, on the other hand, are for the most part unrelated to free expression; hence, restrictions on these activities are not subject to first amendment scrutiny—whether or not they occur in a public forum.[21]   At the same time, if it could be shown that such restrictions were motivated by a purpose inimical to free speech—if a city used "a nuisance statute as a pretext for closing down a book store

18. See Cornelius v. NAACP Legal Defense and Educational Fund, 473 U.S. 788 (1985), which upheld an executive order that excluded organizations engaging in legal defense or political advocacy from participating in a charity fund-raising drive aimed at federal employees. The Court opined that inclusion of these groups would make the Combined Federal Campaign "administratively unmanageable," id. at 809, and would also jeopardize the continued success of the Campaign, since many contributors had expressed concern about the participation of such "political advocacy" organizations. Id. at 810–11. "The First Amendment does not forbid a viewpoint-neutral exclusion of speakers who would disrupt a nonpublic forum and hinder its effectivenss for its intended purpose." Id. at 811. The government may draw the advocacy-nonadvocacy distinction in other contexts as well. That a city may, for example, require that sanitation workers be allowed on a homeowner's property in order to collect his garbage certainly does not imply that any speaker on the issue of garbage collection must automatically be granted access.

19. See id. at 811 (noting that "reasonable grounds for limiting access to a nonpublic forum . . . will not save a regulation that is in reality a facade for viewpoint-based discrimination," and remanding the case for a determination of the viewpoint-neutrality issue).

20. See, e.g., City Council of the City of Los Angeles v. Taxpayers for Vincent, 466 U.S. 789, 813–14 & nn. 31 & 32 (1984) (upholding, after first amendment analysis, a provision of a municipal code which prohibited the posting of signs on public property, with the effect that a political candidate could not post campaign signs on utility poles; majority denied that the poles were a public forum, but did not make the analysis turn on that conclusion); Metromedia, Inc. v. San Diego, 453 U.S. 490, 501 (1981) (invalidating municipal restrictions on noncommercial billboard advertising but upholding restrictions on off-

site commercial billboards; plurality, citing other public forum cases, noted that " '[t]he outdoor sign or symbol is a venerable medium for expressing political, social, and commercial ideas' "). But see Greer v. Spock, 424 U.S. 828, 833 n. 10 (1976) (denying the public forum status of a military base and hence rejecting the right of a political candidate to make a speech there, even though a variety of civilian speakers, including a lecturer on drug abuse, a visiting preacher, and a rock music band, had been granted access previously; "the decision of the military authorities" to allow *some* civilian speakers "surely did not leave the authorities powerless thereafter to prevent any civilian from entering [the base] to speak on any subject whatever"); Lehman v. Shaker Heights, 418 U.S. 298, 304 (1974) (upholding a city's refusal to deny space to political candidates for advertising on municipal transit vehicles, even though the city sold commercial and service-centered advertising; the plurality declared that "[n]o First Amendment forum is here to be found," because the audience was essentially captive and because the city was acting in a merely "proprietary capacity" as the owner and operator of the transit system). The Metromedia plurality distinguished Lehman and Greer on the basis that they "turned on unique fact situations involving *government-created* forums and have no application here." 453 U.S. at 514 n. 19 (emphasis added). The same distinction appears to explain the Cornelius decision in the charitable solicitation area, see note 12, supra.

21. Compare Arcara v. Cloud Books, Inc., 106 S.Ct. 3172 (1986) (upholding the closure of a business that happened to sell sexually explicit books where that closure was triggered by the presence of a pattern of prostitution), with Paris Adult Theatre I v. Slaton, 413 U.S. 49, 67 (1973) ("sexual embrace at high noon in Times Square" is constitutionally unprotected, even if the participants "simultaneously engage in a valid political dialogue").

because it sold indecent books," [22] or if the particular act triggering the law's enforcement was of first amendment significance [23]—then more exacting first amendment scrutiny would be required even if no public forum were involved. The presence or absence of a public forum may thus prove immaterial in a wide variety of cases.

A close look at the Court's attempts to refine the public forum categories illustrates the important role of another variable: the concrete character of the particular regulation at issue. The Court, for example, scrutinized only loosely—and readily upheld—a federal law prohibiting the deposit of unstamped "mailable matter" in letter boxes in the face of a challenge that such a ban discriminated against those groups unable or unwilling to send their literature through the mails. [24] While mailboxes undoubtedly serve as an important channel of communication, and while the alleged discrimination was surely present, the undeniable availability of other equally effective methods of distributing handbills, such as placing them under doors, hanging them on doorknobs, leaving them on the windshields of parked cars, or delivering them person-to-person in public areas, made the Postal Service's rule seem too unthreatening to warrant strict scrutiny. [25] The Court signaled this conclusion by denying that the mailboxes were public forums—but that denial may have done more to obscure than to illuminate the Court's underlying analysis. [26] The real issue was wheth-

---

22. Arcara, 106 S.Ct. at 3178 (O'Connor, J., joined by Stevens, J., concurring).

23. See, e.g., United States v. O'Brien, 391 U.S. 367 (1968) (upholding the conviction of draft card burner after applying first amendment analysis). It is not that the destruction of government property always communicates a message; rather, the point is that in this particular instance, O'Brien's behavior was both intended and understood as an expressive act, and the law used to prosecute him—even if not motivated by a desire to suppress dissent against the war—was indisputably enacted in response to draft-card burnings universally understood as expressive acts. See § 12–6, supra. See also Clark v. Community for Creative Non-Violence, 468 U.S. 288 (1984) (upholding the National Park Service's "anti-camping" regulations as applied to a homeless advocacy organization that sought, as part of a political protest, to sleep overnight in national monument areas). In June 1982, the Park Service revised the relevant regulations, see National Capitol Park Regulations: Camping, 47 Fed.Reg. 24, 299–306 (1982), largely in response to a similar CCNV demonstration. See Community for Creative Non-Violence v. Watt, 670 F.2d 1213 (D.C. Cir. 1982); Clark, 468 U.S. at 302 n. 1 (Marshall, J., joined by Brennan, J., dissenting). On the issue of symbolic speech and the speech-conduct distinction, see generally § 12–7, supra.

24. United States Postal Service v. Council of Greenburgh Civic Ass'ns, 453 U.S. 114 (1981).

25. But cf. Southeastern Promotions, Ltd. v. Conrad, 420 U.S. 546, 556 (1975) (striking down as a forbidden prior restraint a municipal theater's refusal to allow a performance of the musical "Hair"; "'one is not to have the exercise of his liberty of expression in appropriate places abridged on the plea that it may be exercised in some other place'"), quoting Schneider v. State, 308 U.S. 147, 163 (1939).

26. Thus, the majority ostensibly disposed of the case by finding that the letterbox is not a public forum. 453 U.S. at 131. Although it noted the easy availability of alternative means of distribution, id. at 119, the majority said that it did not need to reach this issue. Id. at 132. Justice Brennan, in contrast, would have upheld the statute as a reasonable time, place, and manner restriction, by stressing the availability of alternative channels. Id. at 135 (Brennan, J., concurring in the judgment). Justice Brennan's analysis seems sounder. Without it, there appears to be no answer to Justice Stevens' dissenting objection, id. at 152, that the mailbox is in fact the homeowner's property.

The individual provides and maintains the mailbox, which typically sits on private property. In order to receive mail, however, the individual must comply with federal postal law. The majority thus charac-

er the restriction on nonstamped mailable matter so inhibited the free communication of ideas as to violate the first amendment; the "public forum" status of mailboxes was only superficially relevant to the outcome of the decision.[27]

Similarly, when the Court rejected the right of a nonunion community college faculty member to participate in "meet and confer" sessions conducted by the state community college board with the union which served as the faculty's exclusive bargaining representative,[28] it made no attempt to deny that the right to communicate with the government—to "petition," in the first amendment's terms—is an important value. Rather, the Court noted the confluence of two key factors: (1) the "meet and confer" sessions were "neither by long tradition nor by government designation open for general public participation," [29] a feature which meant that they were not public forums; and (2) the nonunion faculty members retained access to both union and government officials through alternative channels of communication.[30] It is hard not to regard the first factor as largely a makeweight and the second factor as more influential. The Court's decision seemed to hinge not at all on any formal notion of "public forum"; rather, as the exchange between Justices Marshall and Stevens indicates, the crux of the matter was the practical effect of the Minnesota statute, and whether nonunion teachers retained access to the governing board.[31]

terized the mailbox as part of the national postal system, the use of which the government could freely restrict in order to further the system's purposes. 453 U.S. at 123, 128–29. Justice Stevens, on the other hand, saw the mailbox as private property, to which the owner had an independent right to grant access, a right penalized by the government's refusal to deliver mail to individuals who allowed unstamped mailable matter to be deposited in their mailboxes. Id. at 152 (Stevens, J., dissenting). The dispute was not over statutory entitlements but over description: the majority and Justice Stevens agreed on the specific rights and privileges vested in the individual and in the Postal Service, but disagreed about who should be deemed the "true" owner of the box for purposes of the first amendment.

27. See Farber and Nowak, "The Misleading Nature of Public Forum Analysis: Content and Context in First Amendment Adjudication," 70 Va.L.Rev. 1219, 1223 (1984). For a fuller discussion of this issue in Greenburgh, see L. Tribe, Constitutional Choices 194–98 (1985).

28. Minnesota State Bd. for Community Colleges v. Knight, 465 U.S. 271 (1984). Justice O'Connor delivered the opinion of the Court, in which Chief Justice Burger and Justices White, Blackmun, and Rehnquist joined. Justice Marshall filed an opinion concurring in the judgment. Justice Brennan wrote a dissenting opinion.

Justice Stevens also filed a dissenting opinion, in which Justices Brennan and Powell joined in part.

29. Id. at 280.

30. See id. at 288 ("[t]he State has in no way restrained [the nonunion teachers'] freedom to speak on any education-related issue").

31. Justice Stevens charged that "[t]he statute prohibits [the nonunion teachers] from expressing 'any view' on issues affecting their colleges to the administration, and as a practical matter it 'blocks effectively meaningful expression' [by them] on the public policy issues facing the state agencies that employ them." 465 U.S. at 310–11 (Stevens, J., dissenting) (citation omitted). As such, the statute amounted to a restriction based on viewpoint. Id. at 320. Justice Marshall, relying on the finding of the majority that "[the statute] in no way impairs the ability of individual employees to express their views to their employer outside that formal context [of 'meet and confer' sessions], and [the absence of any] suggestion in these cases that . . . any such communication of views has ever been restrained," 465 U.S. at 277 n. 4, found that the restriction on speech was not severe. Id. at 295 (Marshall, J., concurring in the judgment). Justice Marshall also pointed to the fact that the restriction had been imposed by the university itself, and not by the state legis-

In a case in which these two factors were largely absent,[32] the Court upheld the right of a nonunion teacher to speak out against a mandatory union dues proposal during a public and open meeting of a municipal board of education.[33] In contrast, the Court affirmed a collective bargaining agreement entered into by an Indiana township which granted preferential access to the internal mail system of public schools to the union currently representing the teachers, against the wishes of rival union.[34] Again, the two variables stressed in the Court's analysis were the nonpublic-forum status of the mail system [35] and the allegedly neutral nature of the restriction.[36] Justice Stevens, in a later description of the decision, emphasized that the preferential access was justified by the union's duties as the exclusive representative of the teachers within the collective bargaining process.[37] He thus limited the case to the narrow labor relations context.

As this overview of the cases strongly suggests, whether or not a given place is deemed a "public forum" is ordinarily less significant than the nature of the speech restriction—despite the Court's rhetoric. Indeed, even the rhetoric at times reveals as much. Thus, the Court has said that speech within public forums may not ordinarily be abridged unless the regulation is content-neutral, serves a significant governmental interest, and leaves open adequate alternative channels for communication.[38] But even where property does *not* constitute a public forum, the Court has said that government regulation must ordinarily be content-neutral, and must still be reasonable as to time,

lature, prompting him to "defer to the judgment of college administrators," whose decisions he found less "suspicious" than those of the legislature. Id. at 294. These facts relate to the nature of the restriction, not the forum. See § 17–3, infra.

32. Madison School District v. Wisconsin Employment Relations Comm'n, 429 U.S. 167 (1976).

33. The school board meetings at issue were "opened [as] a forum for direct citizen involvement," 429 U.S. at 175, and "public participation [was] permitted," id. at 169.

34. Perry Education Association v. Perry Local Educators' Association, 460 U.S. 37 (1983).

35. The majority found that the mail system was a nonpublic forum to which the rival union could expect no access, id. at 47, in spite of the fact that there was evidence that outside organizations such as the YMCA, Cub Scouts, and various church groups had been permitted to use the facilities, id.

36. The majority characterized the restriction as "based on the *status* of the respective unions rather than on their views." Id. at 49.

37. See Minnesota Bd. for Community Colleges v. Knight, 465 U.S. 271, 320–21 (1984) (Stevens, J., dissenting, joined in part by Brennan, J., and Powell, J.) (distin-

guishing Perry); see also Perry, 460 U.S. at 52 (noting that "exclusion of a rival union may reasonably be considered a way of insuring labor peace within the schools. The policy 'serves to prevent the District's schools from becoming a battlefield for inter-union squabbles'.") The Court thus situated Perry in a long line of labor law cases upholding exclusive representation arrangements in the private sector, see, e.g., Emporium Capwell Co. v. Western Addition Community Organization, 420 U.S. 50 (1975); J.I. Case Co. v. NLRB, 321 U.S. 332 (1944), and restricting the ability of outside organizers to distribute union literature on company property during working hours, see NLRB v. Babcock and Wilcox Co., 351 U.S. 105 (1956).

38. See, e.g., Consolidated Edison Co. v. Public Service Comm'n., 447 U.S. 530, 535–36 (1980) (striking down a state regulation of utility bill inserts), discussed in note 15, supra; Grayned v. Rockford, 408 U.S. 104, 121 (1972) (upholding antinoise statute because it "represents a considered and specific legislative judgment that some kinds of expressive activity should be restricted at a particular time and place, in order to protect the schools") (citation omitted). Cf. United States Postal Service v. Council of Greenburgh Civic Ass'ns, 453 U.S. 114, 132 (1981) (stating the test but finding no public forum).

place, and manner.[39] To be sure, what the Court views as content-neutral, and what it sees as reasonable, could in theory depend on whether it regards a particular forum as public, or at least semi-public. But since the cases provide scant support for that supposition, and instead suggest that the Court uses "public forum" talk to signal conclusions it has reached on other grounds, it might be considerably more helpful if the Court were to focus more directly and explicitly on the degree to which the regulation at issue impinges on the first amendment interest in the free flow of information; translating this inquiry into public forum language may simply "confuse[ ] the development of first amendment principles."[40]

Beyond confusing the issues, an excessive focus on the public character of some forums, coupled with inadequate attention to the precise details of the restrictions on expression, can leave speech inadequately protected in some cases,[41] while unduly hampering state and local authorities in others.[42] In *Southeastern Promotions, Inc. v. Conrad*,[43] for example, the Court found that the refusal of the directors of two municipal theaters in Chattanooga, Tennessee—one owned, the

39. Greenburgh, 453 U.S. at 140 (Brennan, J., concurring in the judgment). See also Linmark Associates, Inc. v. Willingboro, 431 U.S. 85, 92–93 (1977) (striking down municipal ordinance prohibiting the posting of real estate "for sale" and "sold" signs in order to stem the flight of white homeowners from racially integrated community; majority found alternative modes of expression, such as newspaper advertisements, less effective); Young v. American Mini-Theatres, Inc., 427 U.S. 50, 63 n. 18 (1976) (upholding city zoning ordinance as applied to adult movie theaters; majority found that the rules limited only the location of theaters and hence were a valid time, place, and manner restriction); Virginia Board of Pharmacy v. Virginia Citizens Consumer Council, Inc., 425 U.S. 748, 771 (1976) (invalidating state ban on advertising of prescription drug prices; the Court noted that such a complete prohibition on price advertising could not be characterized as a mere time, place, or manner restriction); Pell v. Procunier, 417 U.S. 817, 826 (1974) (upholding state corrections regulation which denied prison inmates access to face-to-face press interviews; the Court pointed out that prisoners retained the right to receive at least some visitors, correspond by mail, and communicate indirectly with the press and public through their visitors).

40. Farber and Nowak, "The Misleading Nature of Public Forum Analysis: Content and Context in First Amendment Adjudication," 70 Va.L.Rev. 1219, 1223 (1984).

41. See, e.g., Cornelius v. NAACP Legal Defense and Educational Fund, Inc., 473 U.S. 788 (1985) (upholding an executive order excluding political "advocacy" groups from a charity fundraising drive aimed at federal employees, on the theory that the drive is a nonpublic forum and that the government may restrict access to such a forum by means of any "reasonable" regulation). As Justice Stevens noted in dissent, "I do not find the precise characterization of the forum particularly helpful in reaching a decision." Id. at 833 (Stevens, J., dissenting). See also City of Cleburne, Texas v. Cleburne Living Center, 473 U.S. 432, 451–54 (1985) (Stevens, J., joined by Burger, C.J., concurring) (voicing a similar view with respect to equal protection analysis), discussed in § 16–32, infra. "Everyone on the Court agree[d]" that if the exclusion of advocacy groups from the charity drive constituted viewpoint discrimination, then their exclusion was invalid, regardless of how the forum was characterized. Cornelius, 473 U.S. at 833 (Stevens, J., dissenting). See also Perry Education Ass'n. v. Perry Local Educators' Ass'n., 460 U.S. 37, 57 (1983) (Brennan, J., joined by Marshall, Powell, and Stevens, JJ., dissenting) ("This case does not involve an 'absolute access' claim. It involves an 'equal access' claim. As such, it does not turn on whether the internal school mail system is a 'public forum.' In focusing on the public forum issue, the Court disregards the First Amendment's central proscription against censorship, in the form of viewpoint discrimination, in any forum, public or nonpublic."). Often, the central issue is thus the nature of the restriction, not the forum.

42. See, e.g., the discussion of Carey v. Brown, 447 U.S. 455 (1980), in § 12–3, supra.

43. 420 U.S. 546 (1975).

other leased by the city—to permit the performance of the musical "Hair" amounted to a prior restraint in violation of the first amendment. The majority opinion, written by Justice Blackmun, noted that the theaters "were public forums designed for and dedicated to expressive activities." [44] Having opened them ostensibly as "common meeting place[s] . . . for . . . entertainment," [45] Chattanooga was not free selectively to deny permission to use the theaters on the basis of a production's content.[46] But the Court's call for "precise and clear standards" [47] to regulate the discretion of municipal authorities left unanswered many of the questions raised in Justice Rehnquist's dissent: "May an opera house limit its productions to operas, or must it show rock musicals? May a municipal theater devote an entire season to Shakespeare, or is it required to book any potential producer on a first come, first served basis?" [48] The majority's quick emphasis on the theaters' public forum status perhaps contributed to its relative inattention to the hard issues of appropriate standards for show selection and theater management.[49]

In addition, the Court's approach invites manipulation in the definition of "public forum." At times, for example, the Court appears to have circumscribed the category of "traditional" public forums by focusing on appearance rather than function—on whether the place *looks* like a forum for expressive activity rather than on whether it does in fact serve as a significant medium of communication.[50] The inherent limitations of this approach are suggested by *United States v. Grace*.[51] The appellees had been ejected from the sidewalks surrounding the Supreme Court building for violating a federal statute that prohibited a wide range of expressive activity in the vicinity of the building.[52] Mary Grace had been carrying a sign displaying, aptly

44. 420 U.S. at 555.

45. 420 U.S. at 549 n. 4.

46. But see Perry Education Ass'n. v. Perry Local Educators' Ass'n., 460 U.S. 37, 46 n. 7 (1983) (suggesting that "[a] public forum may be created for a limited purpose such as use by certain groups" or "for the discussion of certain subjects").

47. 420 U.S. at 553.

48. 420 U.S. at 572–73 (Rehnquist, J., dissenting).

49. See Karst, "Public Enterprise and the Public Forum: A Comment on Southeastern Promotions, Ltd. v. Conrad," 37 Ohio St.L.J. 247 (1976) (criticizing the Court's decisions in Columbia Broadcasting Sys., Inc. v. Democratic Nat'l. Comm., 412 U.S. 94 (1973), Lehman v. Shaker Heights, 418 U.S. 298 (1974), and Southeastern Promotions, Ltd. v. Conrad, 420 U.S. 546 (1975), for focusing on an "on/off," all-or-nothing public forum analysis rather than on the nature of the restriction at issue).

50. Cf. Grayned v. Rockford, 408 U.S. 104, 120–21 (1972) (proposing instead an "incompatibility" of function test which would ask whether expressive activity "in-

terfer[es] with" or "obstruct[s]" a forum's intended purpose or operation). Whether the Court in Grayned actually applied such a standard, or merely articulated one, is open to debate. See 408 U.S. at 121–24 (Douglas, J., dissenting in part).

51. 461 U.S. 171 (1983). Justice White delivered the opinion of the Court, in which Chief Justice Burger and Justices Brennan, Blackmun, Powell, Rehnquist, and O'Connor joined. Justices Marshall and Stevens both filed opinions concurring in part and dissenting in part.

52. The challenged statute made it unlawful "to parade, stand, or move in processions or assemblages in the Supreme Court Buildings or grounds" or "to display therein any flag, banner, or device designed or adapted to bring into public notice any party, organization, or movement." Id. at 175, quoting 40 U.S.C. § 13k (1976). See also Finzer v. Barry, 798 F.2d 1450, 1476 (D.C. Cir. 1986) (Bork, J.) (upholding statute which prohibited the display of signs bringing a foreign government into "public odium" or "public disrepute" within 500 feet of that country's embassy; the majority dismissed concerns

enough, the text of the first amendment; a second appellee had been peacefully distributing political literature. The Supreme Court declared the statute unconstitutional as applied to expressive activity on the sidewalks surrounding the Court, but declined to invalidate the statute as applied to the interior of the Supreme Court building itself.[53]

Significantly, the Court's argument for striking down the prohibition on sidewalk expression relied more on imagery than on the functional importance of the Supreme Court sidewalks as a public forum. Conspicuously absent from the Court's opinion was any recognition that, for many issues, the sidewalks around the Supreme Court building are indeed a uniquely appropriate forum. The Court stressed instead that the sidewalks around its building *look* like other sidewalks in the area and that there is no physical barrier or separation to indicate to the passerby that the Supreme Court sidewalks are in any way special, or that access to them is in any way restricted.[54] The Court thus suggested that whether a place qualifies as a traditional public forum might depend more on whether it resembles such a forum, than on its functional significance as a channel of communication.[55] Needless to say, appearances are well within the government's control; a doctrine that even suggests that posting "no public speakers" signs could alter the outcome in a case like *Grace* hardly offers secure protection to first amendment concerns.

The public forum doctrine is susceptible to manipulation in other ways as well. In *City Council of the City of Los Angeles v. Taxpayers for Vincent*,[56] the Court held that utility poles and lampposts upon

about discrimination based on the views of the speaker as "entirely theoretical" and "academic" because "there is not and never has been political debate about the merits of foreign governments and their policies within 500 feet of their embassies"), cert. granted sub nom. Boos v. Barry, 107 S.Ct. 1282 (1987) (No. 86–803). For a trenchant criticism of the analysis and result in Finzer, see 132 Cong.Rec. H 6503–06 (daily ed. Sept. 9, 1986) (remarks of Rep. Barney Frank (D. Mass.)).

53. 461 U.S. at 180.

54. Id. at 179–80. A different image, one of pandemonium in the Supreme Court building, may lie behind the majority's refusal to invalidate the statute in toto. The Court of Appeals had held the statute unconstitutional on its face as a total prohibition on expressive activity in a public place, see Grace v. Burger, 665 F.2d 1193 (D.C. Cir. 1981), and Justice Marshall would have done the same, see 461 U.S. at 184 (Marshall, J., concurring in part and dissenting in part). The Court had earlier signaled its concern that the first amendment not be interpreted in a manner that would threaten the decorum of the Supreme Court building. During the oral argument in Heffron v. International Society for Krishna Consciousness, Inc., 452 U.S. 640 (1981), the Court asked counsel for

respondents (the author of this treatise) whether a ruling in their favor would permit the public to walk about the courtroom, and followed up with a similar question about the building's hallways and museums. See Transcript of Oral Argument at 30–31 (1981).

55. Imagery may also have helped to shape the Court's earlier thinking about expressive activity on private property. Stressing the physical indistinguishability of a company-owned town from any other American town of comparable size, the Court treated the sidewalks of a company town's shopping district as a kind of public forum. See Marsh v. Alabama, 326 U.S. 501, 502–03 (1946). In contrast, the Court, pointing out the novel layout of modern shopping malls, refused to extend to them the rules of public forums. See Lloyd Corp. v. Tanner, 407 U.S. 551, 553 (1972); accord, Hudgens v. NLRB, 424 U.S. 507 (1976). See generally, Chapter 18, infra (discussing Marsh, Lloyd, and Hudgens). Compare B. Ackerman, Private Property and the Constitution (1977) (demonstrating the central importance of imagery in the law of takings).

56. 466 U.S. 789 (1984). Justice Stevens delivered the opinion of the Court, in which Chief Justice Burger and Justices White, Powell, Rehnquist, and O'Connor

which various organizations affixed their respective signs were not public forums.[57] In a cloud of logic that threatened quickly to evaporate in circles of tautology, the Court argued that these signposts were not public forums because the Constitution didn't say they were: "the mere fact that government property can be used as a vehicle for communication does not mean that the Constitution requires such uses to be permitted." [58] True enough. But the point sheds little light on the central issue of the case: how strictly should courts scrutinize the challenged restriction on the use of this property for posting political signs? In addressing that issue, the Court paid scant attention to the historical dimension of the public forum doctrine as it had evolved from the 1930's into the 1970's. If telephone poles in Los Angeles were in fact commonly and consistently used as means of communication, then, by the logic of that earlier doctrine, they should have qualified as "traditional" public forums. That classification would not have been decisive,[59] but it would have set the stage for an analysis more sensitive to first amendment values.

In recent years the Court has also restricted the protection offered to speech under the public forum doctrine by greatly expanding the third category listed in *Perry*—that of nonpublic forums. In *Cornelius v. NAACP Legal Defense and Educational Fund*,[60] for example, the Court divided 4–3 to uphold the constitutionality of an Executive Order that excluded organizations engaging in legal defense or political advocacy from participating in a charity fund-raising drive aimed at federal employees. Justice O'Connor, writing for the majority, argued that the government does not create even a "limited purpose" public forum unless it intends, when it opens a non-traditional forum for public discourse, to permit a wide range of expressive activity.[61] This reasoning was correctly assailed by Justice Blackmun, who noted in dissent that it stood for the proposition that the charity drive was "not a limited public forum because the Government intended to limit the forum to a particular class of speakers." [62] This effectively turned the public forum doctrine on its head: carried to its logical conclusion, it would make nearly all restrictions on speech self-justifying, since the very fact that the government had denied the plaintiff access could be invoked to prove that the government never intended to create a public forum.[63]

The Court manipulated the public forum definition by a similar process in *United States v. Albertini*,[64] which reversed a decision by the

---

joined. Justice Brennan filed a dissenting opinion, in which Justices Marshall and Blackmun joined.

57. See 466 U.S. 813–14.

58. Id. at 814.

59. See § 12–23, supra.

60. 473 U.S. 788 (1985). Justice O'Connor's majority opinion was joined by Chief Justice Burger and Justices White and Rehnquist. Justice Blackmun dissented, in an opinion joined by Justice Brennan. Justice Stevens also filed a dissent-

ing opinion. Justices Marshall and Powell took no part in the decision of the case.

61. Id. at 804–05.

62. Id. at 813–14 (Blackmun, J., dissenting).

63. Id. at 825.

64. 472 U.S. 675 (1985). Justice O'Connor wrote the opinion for the Court, in which Chief Justice Burger and Justices White, Blackmun, Powell, and Rehnquist joined. Justice Stevens filed a dissenting

Ninth Circuit Court of Appeals that a peace activist, who had been barred from a military base nine years earlier for trespassing and destroying official Air Force documents, had a first amendment right to attend an "open house" at that same base. The circuit court found that portions of the military base constituted at least a temporary public forum, because the military had opened those areas to the public for purposes related to expression.[65] The Supreme Court disagreed, arguing that the "military [had not] so completely abandoned control of the base" that it became a public forum.[66] This mode of reasoning, which allows the government itself to set the terms by which the public will be allowed to speak on the property, carries the same danger as *Cornelius*: where so much discretion is vested in the government, the forum itself can be defined in terms of viewpoint.[67] The open house at the base featured displays of military aircraft, parachute jumps by Marines, Navy helicopter displays, and a Coast Guard rescue simulation. Against this backdrop of militarism, Albertini and his companions sought to convey a different message: they gathered in front of a B–52 bomber display, unfurled a banner reading "Carnival of Death," and passed out leaflets criticizing the nuclear arms race.[68] Although the base commander may not in fact have acted out of a desire to suppress the content of Albertini's speech, the Court's analysis seems strikingly insensitive to this possibility. This again suggests that the cloud of doctrine to which the public forum debate has led needs to be cleared away, the better to expose what is actually at stake in the restrictions and regulations at issue.

opinion, in which Justices Brennan and Marshall joined.

65. See 710 F.2d 1410, 1417 (9th Cir. 1983). Albertini also alleged that the advertisements inviting the public onto the base provided him written permission to enter, satisfying the terms of his bar letter, and that enforcement of a 9-year-old letter violated due process. Id. at 1413. The Court of Appeals rejected the first contention and found it unnecessary to consider the due process argument. Id. at 1413, 1417.

66. 472 U.S. at 686.

67. Two closely-related images from a bygone era, the right-privilege distinction and the notion of government as a proprietor or property-owner, pervade the Court's recent treatment of the nonpublic forum issue. The Court has justified the wide latitude it affords the government in limiting access by characterizing the use of such forums as a kind of government subsidy that may be restricted in order to further state interests. See, e.g., Davis v. Massachusetts, 167 U.S. 43, 47 (1897) ("For the legislature absolutely or conditionally to forbid public speaking in a highway or public park is no more an infringement of the rights of a member of the public than for the owner of a private house to forbid it in his house"). The Court's opinions in Greenburgh, Perry, Grace, and Vincent, for example, all quoted Adderley v. Florida, 385 U.S. 39, 47 (1966) (prison grounds not public forum), for the proposition that the government, "no less than a private owner of property, has the power to preserve the property under its control for the use to which it is lawfully dedicated." See Vincent, 466 U.S. at 814 n. 31; Grace, 461 U.S. at 178; Perry, 460 U.S. at 46; Greenburgh, 453 U.S. at 129–30. For a fuller discussion of the influence of the notion of government as a proprietor, and the concomitant right-privilege distinction, see § 11–5, supra, and L. Tribe, Constitutional Choices 203–10 (1985).

68. 472 U.S. at 678. Albertini himself merely took photographs of the displays, and the government stipulated that he did not disrupt the activities of the open house. Id.

§ 12–25. Private Forums: From Shopping Centers to the Media

In 1941 Professor Chafee identified what was to become among the most significant first amendment issues of the modern period: the need for affirmative governmental action to facilitate expression.[1] Whether by allocating more public resources to cleaning up litter so that the poor may distribute their leaflets unimpeded, or by mandating that the mass media provide direct access to various speakers—clearly a more powerful remedy—a government committed to "the widest possible dissemination of information" [2] may find it essential to impose burdens on some in order that others might hear or be heard. For if no one will rent an unpopular speaker a hall or print the speaker's views, it may be of little use that government has not gone out if its way to muzzle the speech. Supreme Court decisions as early as 1939 [3] had established the existence of a governmental duty to do more than merely refrain from censorship,[4] and by 1945 the Court was saying that "[f]reedom of the press from governmental interference under the first amendment does not sanction repression of that freedom by private interests," [5] with the clear suggestion that government may, and perhaps must, act positively to reduce such repression.

At the same time, the "private interests" to which the Court referred have rights as well—both defensive rights, as illustrated by situations where attempts to protect privacy or reputation are challenged as abridging the freedoms of speech or press; [6] and aggressive rights, as illustrated by situations where the owner of a building or a broadcast facility wishes to convey a message different from the messages that the building's invitees, the broadcaster's audience, or others, might wish to convey or to receive.

In §§ 12–12 through 12–14, we examined the accommodation of these rights in conflict in the setting of damage actions for defamation or breach of privacy. Among the lessons to be drawn from that analysis is the simple but easily forgotten proposition that even ordinary legal rules, whether of defamation or of trespass, entail at least

§ 12–25

1. Z. Chafee, Free Speech in the United States 559 (1941).

2. Associated Press v. United States, 326 U.S. 1, 20 (1945).

3. See Schneider v. State, 308 U.S. 147 (1939), discussed in § 12–24, supra.

4. See § 12–23, supra. Particularly with respect to the press, the Court has been careful to scrutinize government actions that, while facially noncensorial, might in application prove unduly burdensome on publishers. See Minneapolis Star v. Minnesota Comm'r of Revenue, 460 U.S. 575 (1983) (invalidating "use tax" on the cost of paper and ink products consumed in newspaper publication); Murdock v. Pennsylvania, 319 U.S. 105 (1943) (invalidating potentially prohibitive fees for distributing literature). In addition, the Court has viewed with suspicion "selective taxation of the press—either singling out the press as a whole or targeting individual members of the press"—because it "poses a particular danger of abuse by the State." Arkansas Writers' Project, Inc. v. Ragland, 107 S.Ct. 1722, 1727 (1987) (invalidating as violative of the press clause a state sales tax scheme that taxed general interest magazines but exempted newspapers and religious, professional, trade, and sports journals); see also Grosjean v. American Press Co., 297 U.S. 233, 250–51 (1936) (invalidating state tax on receipts of advertising in newspapers with weekly circulation exceeding 20,000 copies; the tax seriously burdened news distribution and appeared to be aimed solely at opponents of Huey Long's state administration).

5. Associated Press, 326 U.S. at 20.

6. See §§ 12–12 through 12–14, supra.

implicit—and sometimes explicit—governmental choices as to how the competing claims of owners, speakers, listeners, and others are to be resolved.[7] Those choices are no less attributable to government when embodied in common law than when expressed in statute or regulation.[8] Thus, if the state's rules of property and trespass are employed to permit a private corporation to prevent an individual, because of her religious or political views, from distributing literature to any of the inhabitants of a self-contained area in which they live and work, those rules violate the first and fourteenth amendments as clearly as if a government official had chosen to exclude the individual from a municipality on the same forbidden basis.[9]

When a homeowner is permitted, under the state's property rules, to exclude individuals on ideological grounds, the rules are again subject to first and fourteenth amendment scrutiny but are valid because, as a substantive matter, the Constitution tolerates[10] (and may even compel[11]) placing the homeowner's right to exclude unwanted views above the speaker's desire to intrude them.

Intermediate cases like those of privately owned shopping centers or, more clearly, migrant labor camps,[12] require a similar form of analysis: in light of the degree to which the exchange of ideas or information is in fact inhibited by a particular allocation of exclusionary power under state law, and in light of the burdens on private individuals that would be entailed by a less inhibiting allocation (a less restrictive alternative), can first amendment principles tolerate the allocation that the state has chosen to enforce? Having initially approached that question with close attention to the inhibitions and burdens actually involved in specific cases,[13] the Supreme Court later succumbed to the temptations of a mechanical jurisprudence, pronounc-

---

7. See Chapter 18, infra.

8. See, e.g., New York Times v. Sullivan, 376 U.S. 254, 265 (1964) (tort law of recovery for defamation is state action subject to first and fourteenth amendments); Shelley v. Kraemer, 334 U.S. 1 (1948) (rules for enforcing contracts restricting land sale constitute state action subject to fourteenth amendment).

9. See Marsh v. Alabama, 326 U.S. 501 (1946) (when state law allows private owner of "company town" to prevent distribution of literature, first and fourteenth amendment rights of the distributors are violated).

10. See, e.g., Rowan v. Post Office Department, 397 U.S. 728 (1970) (homeowner may be authorized to exclude unwanted mail).

11. See § 15–19, infra.

12. See, e.g., Illinois Migrant Council v. Campbell Soup Co., 519 F.2d 391 (7th Cir. 1975); Petersen v. Talisman Sugar Corp., 478 F.2d 73, 82–83 (5th Cir. 1973): "[T]here are no effective alternatives open to the

plaintiffs for communicating with the [workers] other than through access to the living area of the labor camp." See generally Note, "First Amendment and the Problems of Access to Migrant Labor Camps After Lloyd Corporation v. Tanner," 61 Cornell L.Rev. 560 (1976).

13. Compare Lloyd Corp. v. Tanner, 407 U.S. 551, 566–67 & n. 12 (1972) (emphasizing that the war protesters who sought entry to the shopping center could easily have conveyed their message to their intended audience by distributing their handbills from public sidewalks and streets surrounding the privately owned shopping center) and Central Hardware Co. v. NLRB, 407 U.S. 539 (1972) (refusing to equate small parking lots adjacent to freestanding private stores with entire shopping centers), with Food Employees Local 590 v. Logan Valley Plaza, Inc., 391 U.S. 308, 322–23 (1968) (upholding right of labor picketers to enter privately owned shopping center where there was no other safe and effective way to communicate with patrons of the store they sought to unionize).

ing a rule akin to its often wooden approach in the public forum area.[14] In *Hudgens v. NLRB*,[15] a decision whose result may be more defensible than its rationale,[16] the Court overruled *Food Employees Union Local 590 v. Logan Valley Plaza, Inc.*,[17] and rejected the right of individuals, including laborers with a dispute related to a shopping center's operation, to enter a privately owned center against its owner's wishes in order to lodge a peaceful protest.

Part of what might be said for the *Hudgens* outcome is that the "private property" interest that stood against the first amendment interest of the picketers was itself linked to a first amendment concern, for the choice of "placing one's property at the service of some ideologies and not others"[18] arguably lies near the core of the "marketplace of ideas." Indeed, when the Supreme Court in *Wooley v. Maynard*[19] struck down New Hampshire's requirement that all drivers display the state motto "Live Free or Die" on their license plates, the Court observed that the state had compelled its citizens to "*use their private property* as . . . 'mobile billboard[s]' for the State's ideological message."[20] It was not decisive that New Hampshire compelled no actual affirmation of belief,[21] apparently permitting dissenting citizens to accompany the display of the motto with their own public disclaimers.[22]

14. See Greer v. Spock, 424 U.S. 828, 858–60 (1976) (Brennan, J., dissenting) (urging more flexible approach to issues of who may use a forum for what purposes, discussed in § 12–24, supra.

15. 424 U.S. 507 (1976), overruling Logan Valley Plaza, supra note 13, in a case factually closer to Lloyd v. Tanner, supra note 13. The Court in Hudgens concluded that Logan Valley Plaza and Lloyd were constitutionally irreconcilable, 424 U.S. at 518–20, and that the Court's "institutional duty" was (for some unexplained reason) to follow the more recent case. Id. at 518. The Court's further argument (1) that a shopping center either is or is not the "functional equivalent of a municipality," (2) that if it is *not* the functional equivalent then the first amendment is irrelevant, and (3) that if it *is* the functional equivalent then the first amendment forbids different treatment of war protesters (as in Logan Valley Plaza) and labor picketers (as in Lloyd v. Tanner), see id. at 520, seems mistaken. The first and fourteenth amendments should apply to test the state's allocation of exclusionary power through its rules of property and trespass, *whether or not* the shopping center is "functionally equivalent" to a municipality; the different treatment of the two protesting groups reflects not discrimination based on the content of their expression but discrimination based on the availability of alternative opportunities to reach the relevant audience: that the protesters in Lloyd had a war-related message and not a labor message to convey bears on the degree to which excluding them from the privately owned areas of the shopping center would in fact inhibit their communicative opportunities.

16. It is not clear what impact exclusion from the shopping center had on the picketers' access to the audience they needed or wished to reach in the Hudgens case; as Justice White pointed out, for example, the picketers' dispute was with the operation of a warehouse not located at the center, although their picketing was aimed at one of the warehouses' retail outlets which was located at the center. 424 U.S. at 524–25 (concurring in result). Indeed, in none of the shopping center cases is the record wholly satisfactory on this issue, in part because the Court appears to have invited analysis more in terms of analogy to Marsh v. Alabama, supra note 9, than in terms of the constitutional validity of state property rules as applied to specific factual circumstances.

17. 391 U.S. 308 (1968).

18. Schauer, "Hudgens v. NLRB and the Problem of State Action in First Amendment Adjudication," 61 Minn.L.Rev. 433, 449 (1977).

19. 430 U.S. v. 705 (1977).

20. Id. at 715 (emphasis added).

21. Compare West Virginia State Board of Education v. Barnette, 319 U.S. 624 (1943) (invalidating compulsory flag salute and compulsory recital of pledge of allegiance), with 430 U.S. at 720 (Rehnquist, J., joined by Blackmun, J., dissenting).

22. See 430 U.S. at 722 (Rehnquist, J., joined by Blackmun, J., dissenting).

Being forced to devote one's property to a display one finds offensive was enough to make out a first amendment violation.

Shopping center owners who refuse to tolerate pickets with whose message they disagree are unable to make a similar claim. The Court held unanimously in *PruneYard Shopping Center v. Robins*[23] that a state may constitutionally force the owner of a private shopping center to permit individuals to exercise free speech on the shopping center's property. As early as *Hudgens*, the Court had held that the NLRB could compel a shopping center owner to let picketers in,[24] a position incompatible with the view that the owner's refusal rests on a first amendment base. But several factors distinguish the shopping center from the automobile. First, when shopping center owners exclude picketers, the ability of such picketers to communicate their message to the audience they hope to affect may be greatly restricted; the state's ability to display its motto is hardly impaired by selective refusals to serve as the motto's vehicles.[25] Furthermore, when the state itself does not dictate the content of the message that will be displayed, there is much less danger of governmental discrimination for or against particular views.[26] Next, a shopping center is, in a sense, inherently public; customers come and go as they please, by the very design of the owner. The views expressed by demonstrators are unlikely to be associated with those of the specific proprietor, and he or she is always able to post disclaimers.[27]

Given the historic function of newspapers and broadcasters as speakers in their own right as well as conveyers of the messages of others, the analogy to *Wooley v. Maynard*[28] is considerably less strained when one turns to attempts to subordinate the editorial rights of the print or electronic media to the first amendment rights of those with messages they wish to convey or of those with messages they wish to receive. In fact, the Court in *Wooley* relied in part on *Miami Herald*

---

23. 447 U.S. 74 (1980). See generally Comment, "PruneYard Progeny: State-Created Free Speech Access to Quasi-Public Property," 1984 Ann.Surv.Am.L. 121 (1985).

24. See 424 U.S. at 521. Indeed, on remand the NLRB did just that as a matter of federal labor law. See Hudgens, 230 NLRB No. 73, 95 L.R.R.M. (BNA) 1351 (1977).

25. But this factor alone cannot be decisive. The Court has held, in a wide variety of contexts, that access guarantees are unconstitutional even if, without them, the targeted speakers have no effective alternative by which to air their views. See, e.g., Pacific Gas & Elec. v. Pub. Util. Comm'n. of Cal., 106 S.Ct. 903 (1986) (denying ratepayer organization access to utility billing envelope); Miami Herald Publishing Co. v. Tornillo, 418 U.S. 241 (1974) (invalidating right-of-reply statute).

26. See PruneYard, 447 U.S. at 87. For a general discussion of the dangers in-

volved when government voices a particular view in the marketplace, see § 12–4, supra.

27. See PruneYard, 447 U.S. at 87. But see id. at 99 (Powell, J., concurring in part and in the judgment) (arguing that the owner's "right to refrain from speaking at all" is thereby infringed); Pacific Gas & Elec. v. Pub. Util. Comm'n. of Cal., 106 S.Ct. 903, 909 (1986) ("the State is not free . . . . to force appellant to respond to views that others may hold"). When the right of access is granted outright, however, rather than predicated on the owner's behavior, the possible chilling effect seems slight. See Pacific Gas & Elec., 106 S.Ct. at 917–20 (Rehnquist, J., joined by White and Stevens, dissenting) ("PG & E cannot prevent the access by remaining silent or avoiding discussion of controversial subjects").

28. 430 U.S. 705 (1977).

Publishing Co. v. Tornillo,[29] a decision which had unanimously upheld editorial rights over rights of access by invalidating a Florida statute that compelled newspapers to publish the replies of political candidates whom they had attacked.[30] The Court reasoned both in *Miami Herald v. Tornillo* and in *Wooley v. Maynard* that the power to compel speech comes too close to the power to censor speech: both must be forbidden.[31] Indeed, entrusting government with power to assure media access entails at least three dangers:[32] the danger of deterring those items of coverage that will trigger duties of affording access at the media's expense; the danger of inviting manipulation of the media by whichever bureaucrats are entrusted to assure access; and the danger of escalating from access regulation to much more dubious exercises of governmental control.

At the same time, *not* entrusting government with access-regulating power entails its own counter-dangers, especially when a few powerful individuals or corporations control a central channel of communication, or when access to a communication channel is so structured that only the wealthy can afford to exploit it.[33] Stressing these counter-dangers, and omitting any reference to the tradition of unfettered editorial discretion for the print media, the Supreme Court in *Red Lion Broadcasting Co. v. FCC*[34] unanimously upheld the validity of FCC rules embodying two aspects of the fairness doctrine, the first requiring broadcasters to afford an opportunty to reply to personal attacks that they broadcast and the second requiring them to afford an opportunity to reply to their political editorials. Although the *Red Lion* decision did not imply FCC power to mandate or encourage broadcasters throughout the nation to pursue programming policies substantively satisfactory to government,[35] and although *Red Lion* did not disturb the

---

29. 418 U.S. 241 (1974). See 430 U.S. at 714.

30. See generally B. Schmidt, Freedom of the Press v. Public Access 217–54 (1976); Abrams, "In Defense of Tornillo," 86 Yale L.J. 361 (1976). Ironically, the Court decided Gertz v. Robert Welch, Inc., 418 U.S. 323 (1974), discussed in § 12–13, supra, on the same day as Miami Herald. The negligence standard of liability in private figure defamation cases established by Gertz arguably poses almost as great a threat to editorial autonomy as would guaranteed access statutes. See generally Baker, "Press Rights and Government Power to Structure the Press," 34 U. Miami L.Rev. 819 (1980).

31. See 2 Z. Chafee, Government and Mass Communications 709–10 (1947): "If officials can tell newspapers what to put into their editorial pages, . . . it is only a step to tell them what to leave out."

32. See generally the excellent analysis in Bollinger, "Freedom of the Press and Public Access: Toward a Theory of Partial Regulation of the Mass Media," 75 Mich.L. Rev. 1, 29–31 (1976).

33. See, e.g., Barron, "Access to the Press—A New First Amendment Right," 80 Harv.L.Rev. 1641 (1967); Nimmer, "Is Freedom of the Press a Redundancy? What Does It Add to Freedom of Expression?", 26 Hast.L.J. 639, 644–46 (1975), suggesting that free speech and press can conflict: "[T]he issue cannot be resolved merely by noting, as did [Miami Herald], that a right of reply statute 'constitutes the [state] exercise of editorial control and judgment.' This is but one half of the equation. [Miami Herald] ignored the strong conflicting claim of 'speech.' " Id. at 657. But see Lewis, "A Preferred Position for Journalism?", 7 Hof.L.Rev. 595, 603 (1979) (contending that the issue in Miami Herald was compelled speech, not a possible conflict between the values of speech and press). For a compendious review of the early literature, see Lange, "The Role of the Access Doctrine in the Regulation of the Mass Media," 52 N.Car. L.Rev. 1, 2 n. 5 (1973).

34. 395 U.S. 367 (1969).

35. But see B. Schmidt, Freedom of the Press v. Public Access 166 (1976) (Red Lion "left broadcaster autonomy almost entirely

Court's 1943 holding that radio licensees must exercise discretion independent of the national networks,[36] the decision in *Red Lion* nonetheless amounted to a chain-breaking departure from the constitutional approach to newspapers and magazines.[37] Still more striking indeed than *Red Lion's* failure even to mention the newspaper analogy was the absence of so much as a passing reference to *Red Lion* when the Court, in another unanimous opinion delivered five years later, invalidated Florida's personal attack rule in *Miami Herald Publishing Co. v. Tornillo*.[38]

The development of the law in this area is simpler to summarize than to comprehend. One must bear in mind Justice Holmes' famous observation that "a page of history is worth a volume of logic." [39] The advent of radio and television initially *did* require federal regulation to avert a cacophony of speakers on the airwaves, and the Court's sensitivity to first amendment values, combined with its layman's attitude to technology, has led it to treat each medium of communication as "a law unto itself." [40] Gutenberg, Marconi, and Bell gave us three distinct communications technologies, and the law has responded with a trifurcated communications system: print, broadcasting, and common carriage.[41] The first amendment guarantee of freedom from government intrusion reigns most confidently in the realm of the print media, since newspapers and pamphlets were the most significant modes of mass communication in the world of the Framers.[42] In the domain of the telegraph, telephone, computer, and postal network, the prevailing legal policy has been one of fair and universal access to the facilities of

at the mercy of the FCC"). From the beginning, the federal government—by its licensing practices and by rules directed at the substantive content of broadcasting—has strongly influenced what broadcasters have had to say. But the most comprehensive censorship is achieved without resort to formal mechanisms. It consists of elaborate systems of "self-regulation" which the broadcast industry imposes on itself, see Brenner, "The Limits of Broadcast Self-Regulation Under the First Amendment," 28 Fed.Com.B.J. 1 (1975), and which the FCC encourages. See Writers Guild of America v. FCC, 423 F.Supp. 1064 (C.D. Cal. 1976) (holding that first amendment was violated when FCC, national networks, and national professional associations jointly pressured local TV stations to set aside a "family hour" during which only programs suitable for children would be shown), vacated on other grounds, 609 F.2d 355 (9th Cir. 1979), cert denied 449 U.S. 824 (1980). Those systems are largely self-enforcing because the government has dedicated the airwaves predominantly to commercial use, see E. Barnouw, The Sponsor: Notes on a Modern Potentate (1978), and commercial broadcasters are loathe to offend any significant segment of listeners, since advertising revenues are closely linked to Nielsen ratings. See The Report of the Comm. on Obscentity and Pornography 278–85 (1970).

36. National Broadcasting Co. v. United States, 319 U.S. 190, 204–06 (1943).

37. While the Court's move was important doctrinally, the practical effects of the fairness doctrine have been disputed. See M. Yudof, When Government Speaks 294 (1983) (describing the doctrine's supporters as "hopelessly optimistic"); Van Alstyne, "The Möbius Strip of the First Amendment," 29 S.C.L.Rev. 539, 571 (1978) ("the technique of the fairness doctrine in particular may represent a very trivial egalitarian gain and a major first amendment loss").

38. 418 U.S. 241 (1974).

39. New York Trust Co. v. Eisner, 256 U.S. 345, 349 (1921).

40. See, e.g., Metromedia, Inc. v. San Diego, 453 U.S. 490, 501 (1981) ("We deal here with the law of billboards"), discussed supra in §§ 12–23, 12–24.

41. I. de Sola Pool, Technologies of Freedom 2 (1983).

42. The same can be said of traditional forums such as pulpits, soap boxes, and public meetings. Id.

the "common carriers." [43]   The Constitution's promise of free speech
has eroded under this technological pressure: while the Framers fought
a war precipitated in part by the Stamp Act,[44] today's telephone bills
are subject to a special federal tax.

The first amendment's sweeping guarantees have been most compromised in the realm of the most modern medium: electronic broadcasting.

From the time of the Supreme Court's 1943 decision that the FCC
can constitutionally forbid radio licensees to sell time to the networks
without retaining discretion over their own programming and can
constitutionally select licensees in terms of their projected "service to
the community," [45] broadcast regulation has proceeded on the premise
that, since government must somehow carve up the electromagnetic
spectrum so as to prevent interference among broadcast frequencies,
those who are permitted to use the public airwaves may be selected on
criteria, and subjected to controls, that would be unacceptable in the
case of the print media. In effect, the lucky few who are allowed to
speak over the radio or television medium may be compelled to share
their good fortune with others; it is "the right of the viewers and
listeners, not the right of the broadcasters, which is paramount." [46]
Since government "could surely have decreed that each frequency
should be shared among all or some of those who wish to use it, each
being assigned a portion of the broadcast day or . . . week," [47] there
could be no constitutional objection to compelling stations to set aside
time for reply to personal attacks and political editorials. Without
such compulsion, "station owners and a few networks would have
unfettered power to make time available only to the highest bidders, to
communicate only their own views . . . ., and to permit on the air only
those with whom they agreed." [48]

Perhaps Congress could constitutionally require radio and television broadcasters to sell time for editorial advertising to the "highest
bidders," but it is unsurprising, given the sentiment quoted above from
Red Lion, that the Court was unwilling, four years later in *Columbia
Broadcasting System, Inc. v. Democratic National Committee*,[49] to compel such a broadcast practice, or to hold the FCC's refusal to compel it
violative either of the Communications Act of 1934 or of the first
amendment. With three Justices acting on the ground that the policy
of not selling time for editorials was insufficiently attributable to

43. Id.

44. See Minneapolis Star and Tribune
Co. v. Minnesota Comm'r. of Revenue, 460
U.S. 575 (1983) (striking down special tax
on newspaper and ink as violative of free
press clause); Grosjean v. American Press
Co., 297 U.S. 233, 250 (1936) (tax on newspapers of large circulation invalid as "calculated device in the guise of a tax" to
punish critics of Huey Long). This historical reference is offered not as a dispositive
argument, but as an illustration of how
times and technologies have changed. Justice O'Connor's dictum in Minneapolis

Star, 460 U.S. at 583–4 n. 6 ("when [the
Court has] evidence that a particular law
would have offended the Framers, [it has]
not hesitated to invalidate it on that
ground alone"), is plainly overstated.

45. National Broadcasting Co. v. United
States, 319 U.S. 190, 216 (1943).

46. Red Lion, 395 U.S. at 390. See also
§ 12–19, supra.

47. Id. (dictum).

48. Id. at 391–92.

49. 412 U.S. 94 (1973).

government for the first amendment to apply,[50] and three on the ground that the policy, even if attributable to government, satisfied the first amendment,[51] the Court rejected the suggestion[52] that it supplement the fairness doctrine upheld in *Red Lion* with a constitutional requirement that the electronic media sell at least some of their time for unedited discussion of public issues.

Columbia Broadcasting System took a step away from *Red Lion* by its treatment of broadcasters as part of the "press" with an important editorial function to perform rather than as analogous to the postal or telephone systems,[53] but *CBS* was firmly in the *Red Lion* tradition when it refused to consider the possibility that either the technologically scarce radio and television channels, or the finite time available on such channels, might be allocated much as economically scarce newspaper opportunities are allocated: by a combination of market mechanisms and chance rather than by government design coupled with broadcaster autonomy.[54] The clear failure of the "technological scarcity" argument as applied to cable television[55] amounts to an invitation to reconsider the tension between the Supreme Court's radically divergent approaches to the print and electronic media.[56] Indeed, since the

50. Id. at 114–21 (Burger, C.J., joined on this point by Stewart and Rehnquist, JJ.).

51. Id. at 146–47 (White, J., concurring); id. at 147–48 (Blackmun, J., joined by Powell, J., concurring). Justice Stewart disagreed, insisting that, if broadcaster action were equivalent to governmental action, broadcasters would "inevitably [be] drawn to the position of common carriers." Id. at 140 (concurring opinion). He found this a grave peril to first amendment values, id. at 133, 140–41, 144–46, and was able to avoid the peril only by joining Chief Justice Burger's conclusion that the challenged policy was not governmental and hence was not subject to first amendment scrutiny. Justice Stewart appears to have been mistaken: to say that government is responsible for a particular action need not entail disregarding the private character and constitutional rights of the actor. See, e.g., Glennon & Nowak, "A Functional Analysis of the Fourteenth Amendment 'State Action' Requirement," 1976 Sup.Ct. Rev. 221, 256–57. See generally Chapter 18, infra.

52. See 412 U.S. at 182–201 (Brennan, J., joined by Marshall, J., dissenting). But the Court has *permitted* the FCC, on the basis of a congressional mandate, to enforce a right of "reasonable access" for political candidates, see CBS, Inc. v. FCC, 453 U.S. 367 (1981).

53. Id. at 124–25 (Burger, C.J., joined by White, Blackmun, Powell, Rehnquist, JJ., assimilating broadcast editors to the paradigm of newspaper editors).

54. See, e.g., Kalven, "Broadcasting, Public Policy and the First Amendment,"

10 J. Law & Econ. 15, 30–32 (1967); Coase, "Evaluation of Public Policy Relating to Radio and Television Broadcasting," 41 J. Land & P.U.Econ. 161 (1965).

55. See, e.g., Home Box Office, Inc. v. FCC, 567 F.2d 9, 43–47 (D.C. Cir. 1977), cert. denied 434 U.S. 829 (1977) (rejecting content regulation of cable TV, noting that the "essential precondition" of broadcast regulation, physical interference and scarcity, is absent here). See also Wilkinson v. Jones, 107 S.Ct. 1559, summarily aff'g 800 F.2d 989 (10th Cir.1986) (per curiam) (invalidating cable television indecency statute), see § 12–18, supra.

56. The Court, in City of Los Angeles v. Preferred Communications, Inc., 106 S.Ct. 2034 (1986), explicitly left open the question whether cable television should be regulated like newspapers or like television. The Court was faced only with the issue of whether cable television regulations *might* implicate first amendment interests; a lower court, by granting a Fed. R. Civ. P. 12(b)(6) motion, had answered in the negative. Justice Blackmun summarized the task facing the Court in the future: "In assessing First Amendment claims concerning cable access, the Court must determine whether the characteristics of cable television make it sufficiently analogous to another medium to warrant application of an already existing standard or whether those characteristics require a new analysis." Id. at 2038 (Blackmun, J., joined by Marshall and O'Connor, concurring). The Court had earlier limited the FCC's statutory authority to impose common carrier-style regulations on the cable industry.

scarcity argument made little sense as a basis for distinguishing news-papers from television even in the late 1960's and early 1970's,[57] such reconsideration seems long overdue.[58] The Court in recent years, while conceding that "[t]he prevailing rationale for broadcast regulation based on spectrum scarcity has come under increasing criticism," [59] has not abandoned the fairness doctrine.[60] In 1984, the Court announced:

See FCC v. Midwest Video Corp., 440 U.S. 689 (1979) (invalidating, as outside statutory authority, FCC rules requiring certain cable operators to develop 20-channel capacity; to make available certain channels for access by public, educational, local government, and leased-access users; and to furnish equipment and facilities for access purposes): "The Commission may not regulate cable systems as common carriers, just as it may not impose such obligations on television broadcasters." Id. at 708–09. For an attempt at a functional first amendment classification of cable operators, see Berkshire Cablevision of Rhode Island v. Burke, 571 F.Supp. 976 (D.R.I. 1983) (upholding mandatory access rules), judgment vacated on other grounds, 773 F.2d 382 (1st Cir. 1985). See generally Mininberg, "Circumstances Within Our Control: Promoting Freedom of Expression Through Cable Television," 11 Hastings Const.L.Q. 551 (1984).

57. See Bollinger, "Freedom of the Press and Public Access: Toward a Theory of Partial Regulation of the Mass Media," 75 Mich.L.Rev. 1, 10–11, 15 (1976). See also Fowler and Brenner, "A Marketplace Approach to Broadcast Regulation," 60 Tex.L.Rev. 207, 221–26 (1982) (with the advent of cable and satellite television technology, communities now have access to such a wide variety of stations that the scarcity doctrine is obsolete); The Supreme Court, 1980 Term, 95 Harv.L.Rev. 93, 228 & n. 39 (1981) (noting that "the economic realities of today's newspaper industry make the supply of significant sources of information in the print media even more limited [than in the broadcast media]"). For a detailed critique of the scarcity rationale, see M. Spitzer, Seven Dirty Words and Six Other Stories 7–42 (1986) (concluding that the content of broadcast material should not be more strictly regulated than that of print).

58. See, e.g., Karst, "Equality as a Central Principle in the First Amendment," 43 U.Chi.L.Rev. 20, 49–61 (1975), arguing that Red Lion is a "shaky" precedent. The Court has been unwilling to extend this "limited spectrum" idea as a justification for a forced right of access. In Consolidated Edison Co. v. Public Service Comm'n, 447 U.S. 530 (1980), for example, the Court rejected the argument that, because the limited space in a utility billing envelope is like the finite electromagnetic spectrum, a

state may regulate the use of that scarce resource to keep a monopoly from bombarding the public exclusively with its point of view. See id. at 542–43.

59. FCC v. League of Women Voters, 468 U.S. 364, 376 n. 11 (1984) (invalidating statute that prohibited political editorializing by federally-funded public broadcasting stations). The Court made clear that the government's interest in ensuring balanced coverage of matters of public interest was not unlimited. "[B]roadcasters are engaged in a vital and independent form of communicative activity. As a result, the First Amendment must inform and give shape to the manner in which Congress exercises its regulatory power in this area." Id. at 377. See CBS, Inc. v. FCC, 453 U.S. 367, 395 (1981) (upholding FCC administration of a statutory provision guaranteeing "reasonable" access to the airwaves for federal election candidates): "[B]roadcasters are entitled under the First Amendment to exercise the 'widest journalistic freedom consistent with their public [duties].'" For the view that the Court in CBS v. FCC gave short shrift to this sweeping language, see Polsby, "Candidate Access to the Air: The Uncertain Future of Broadcaster Discretion," 1981 Sup.Ct. Rev. 223.

60. Neither has the Court limited the FCC's power to regulate broadcasts containing indecent language. See FCC v. Pacifica Foundation, 438 U.S. 726 (1978), discussed in §§ 12–18, 12–19, supra. There, the Court focused on certain physical characteristics of broadcasting—specifically, its uniquely pervasive presence, which prevents listeners who may be offended by indecent language from receiving any prior warning, and the ease with which children may gain access to the medium, creating a risk that they may be exposed to offensive expression without parental supervision. See id. at 748–49. The FCC has extended its definition of indecent language to include any material "that depicts or describes, in terms patently offensive as measured by contemporary community standards for the broadcast medium, sexual or excretory activities or organs," whether or not such material includes the "seven dirty words" of Pacifica. See "FCC Takes Actions on Regulation of Indecency and Obscenity," FCC News, April 16, 1987, at 1 (quoting 56 F.C.C.2d 94, 98 (1975), quoted with approval in FCC v. Pacifica

"We are not prepared, however, to reconsider our longstanding approach without some signal from Congress or the FCC that technological developments have advanced so far that some revision of the system of broadcast regulation may be required." [61]

The twentieth century technological revolution has fundamentally altered the map of our trifurcated communications system. The printing press has been replaced by the picture tube. The influence of the nation's 1,730 daily newspapers is dwarfed by that of nearly 10,000 commercial and educational radio stations,[62] not to mention the gargantuan television networks with their myriad affiliates. The typical family is tuned into its TV for more than a third of its waking hours, and television has become the primary source of news for a majority of the population.[63] By 1977, broadcasting had grown to the point where the average American consumed four times as many words through the airwaves as through newsprint, and the disparity is increasing.[64]

The trouble lies in the fact that, although these powerful new media have acquired the functions of the press, they have not yet obtained the rights of the press. The rate of technological change has outstripped the ability of the law, lurching from one precedent to another, to address new realities. Novel communications are pressed into service while still in their infancy, and the legal system's initial encounters with these newborns have a lasting influence. As one astute observer has explained, "[t]echnical laymen, such as judges, perceive the new technology in that early, clumsy form, which then becomes their image of its nature, possibilities, and use. This perception is an incubus on later understanding." [65]

Foundation, 438 U.S. 726, 732 (1978)). On this basis, the Commission in the spring of 1987 threatened enforcement actions—ranging from fines of $2,000 per day to revocation of a broadcaster's license to operate—against one amateur broadcaster and three commercial radio stations, including WYSP-FM in Philadelphia for its airing of the Howard Stern show. See "FCC Takes Actions," supra. In addition, the FCC warned that "airing indecent matter after 10:00 p.m. does not necessarily render the broadcast permissible" because "recent evidence indicates that, at least on weekends, there is still a reasonable risk that children are in the listening audience at that hour." Id. at 2.

61. FCC v. League of Women Voters, 468 U.S. at 376 n. 11. The FCC recently abolished the fairness doctrine, see The New York Times, Aug. 5, 1987, at 1, col. 6. The Commission had long been moving in that direction. See Notice of Proposed Rulemaking In re Repeal or Modification of the Personal Attack and Political Editorial Rules, 48 Fed.Reg. 28298, 28301 (1983); FCC, [General] Fairness Doctrine Obligations of Broadcast Licensees, 102 F.C.C.2d 143 (1985) (concluding, after a 15-month administrative hearing, "we no longer believe that the fairness doctrine, as a matter

of policy, serves the public interest," and inviting Congress to repeal it). In Meredith Corp. v. FCC, 809 F.2d 863 (D.C. Cir. 1987), the D.C. Circuit held that the FCC, in light of this 1985 conclusion, must explicitly consider an individual broadcaster's claim, asserted in defense to an FCC enforcement proceeding, that application of the fairness doctrine to it violates the first amendment. In the 100th Congress, Senator Packwood introduced S. 827, a bill to repeal the fairness doctrine, see 133 Cong.Rec. S3741 (daily ed. Mar. 24, 1987). But in the Senate at least, the doctrine enjoys substantial support. By a vote of 59–31, the Senate approved the Fairness in Broadcasting Act, a measure co-sponsored by Senators Hollings and Danforth that codifies the fairness doctrine. See 133 Cong.Rec. S5218–S5232 (daily ed. April 21, 1987). The bill was later vetoed by President Reagan.

62. See Kaufman, "Reassessing the Fairness Doctrine," N.Y. Times Magazine 17, 18 (June 19, 1983).

63. Id. at 17.

64. I. de Sola Pool, Technologies of Freedom 21 (1983).

65. Id. at 7.

The response to cable TV is an example of how unreflective adherence to arguably outmoded doctrines can threaten the expansion of first amendment freedoms made possible by new technologies.[66] In *Loretto v. Teleprompter Manhattan CATV Corp.*,[67] the Court struck down a New York law which granted cable companies easy access to apartment-dwelling customers as an unconstitutional taking of the landlord's property.[68] The law was passed by the New York legislature in the face of fee-gouging by landlords in order to ensure tenants access to an important new medium of receiving—and perhaps sending—messages.[69] The state court held that the law was a legitimate exercise of the police power, since it served the public purpose of "rapid development of and maximum penetration by a means of communication which has important educational and community aspects," [70] and the *Teleprompter* majority conceded that it had no reason to question that judgment. But the Court nonetheless held that, regardless of the public interests at stake, government authorization of a "permanent, physical occupation"—even of the most trivial kind [71]—amounts to an unconstitutional taking. Apparently, CBS can be compelled to allow a political candidate to use its broadcast facilities to reach viewers, but Jean Loretto cannot be ordered to permit cable TV companies to reach her tenants. Yet the rights of the audience in each case seem indistinguishable.[72]

In dissent, Justice Blackmun accused the majority of slavish adherence to a "constitutional rule that is uniquely unsuited to the modern urban age." [73] "The 19th-century precedents relied on by the Court," he continued, "lack any vitality outside the agrarian context in which they were decided." [74] The most significant feature of the *Teleprompter* decision is that the Court thought only in terms of the law of takings—the majority opinion never even mentioned the first amendment.

A Court wedded to the inapposite doctrines of an irrelevant context is bound to be in for a jolt when it confronts still other problems presented by the explosion in communications technology. The pace of change may soon render our trifurcated communications structure—

---

66. This is not to say that new technologies pose no dangers. Ample warnings to the contrary have been sounded. See P. Goodman, Growing Up Absurd (1960); T. Roszak, The Making of a Counter Culture (1969); P. Goldstene, The Collapse of Liberal Empire (1977). The risks of a loss of community and of identification with mediating institutions make the Court's response to the technological explosion all the more important.

67. 458 U.S. 419 (1982).

68. This aspect of the case is discussed in Chapter 9, supra. The implications of Teleprompter were narrowed by FCC v. Florida Power Corp., 107 S.Ct. 1107 (1987).

69. Id. at 444 n. 3 (Blackmun, J., joined by White and Brennan, JJ., dissenting). The legislature determined that "[i]n the electronic age, the landlord should not be able to preclude a tenant from obtaining CATV service (or to exact a surcharge for

allowing the service) any more than he could preclude a tenant from receiving mail or telegrams directed to him." 53 N.Y.2d 124, 141, 440 N.Y.S.2d 843, 851, 423 N.E.2d 320, 328 (1981) (citing Regulation of Cable TV by the State of New York, Report to the New York Public Service Comm'n. by Commissioner William K. Jones 207 (1981)).

70. 458 U.S. at 425 (citation omitted).

71. The total amount of space occupied by the CATV installation amounted to 1½ cubic feet on the unused roof of the landlord's building. See id. at 437–38 n. 16.

72. The Court noted that the CATV company, not the tenants, had been given an enforceable right of access to the landlord's property. See 458 U.S. at 439.

73. Id. at 447 (Blackmun, J., dissenting).

74. Id. at 446.

print media, common carriers, broadcast media—obsolete.[75] As computer terminals become ubiquitous and electronic publishing expands, the once obvious boundaries between newspapers and television, telephones and printing presses, become blurred.[76] With all media using electronic forms of communications, the Court must face the fact that "[t]elecommunications policy is becoming communications policy." [77] If the *Teleprompter* decision is any indication, the legalistic myopia which afflicted the Court's decision could degenerate into acute astigmatism when the Court is forced to confront the convergence of three once distinct models of communications regulation.[78]

Professor Lee Bollinger has argued in a perceptive essay [79] that "the very similarity of the two major branches of the mass media provides a rationale for treating them differently," [80] and that Congress' decision to vindicate rights of access with respect to the electronic media but not the print media may be seen as simultaneously realizing two competing constitutional values: "access in a highly concentrated press and minimal governmental intervention." [81] By regulating access in the electronic media exclusively, one achieves significant assurance that information not disseminated by the regulated (electronic) sector will be published by the unregulated (print) sector; and the competition provided by such publication should in turn help to offset any indirect tendency of access regulation to induce narrow or timid coverage within the regulated (electronic) sector.[82]

75. See I. de Sola Pool, Technologies of Freedom 232–34 (1983).

76. The distinction between "public" and "private" speech formulated in Dun & Bradstreet, Inc. v. Greenmoss Builders, Inc., 472 U.S. 749 (1985), for example, is undermined by continuous online services which make credit information readily available to thousands of subscribers.

77. I. de Sola Pool, Technologies of Freedom, at 233.

78. This does not mean that the new technologies should, or constitutionally *must*, be deregulated. Indeed, we cannot depend upon those who own and control the new media to resolve the critical issues of access and availability in a publicly-responsible manner. "Newspapermen come from a tradition of political combativeness and First Amendment principle; cablecasters come from the tradition of show business." I. de Sola Pool, Technologies of Freedom 239 (1983). If new pathways of communication are controlled by mammoth communications conglomerates, we will hear not a diversity of tongues but only a few loud voices droning on with one common message. See Kaufman, "Reassessing the Fairness Doctrine," N.Y. Times Magazine 17, 19 (June 19, 1983) (noting that "[n]ew technology alone . . . cannot guarantee a diversity of opinion if each communications outlet is flooded by pre-existing corporate communicators"). In this regard, FCC v. National Citizens

Comm. for Broadcasting, 436 U.S. 775 (1978) (upholding FCC ban on joint ownership of radio or TV station and daily newspaper in same town), may represent an encouraging trend. Cf. Quincy Cable TV, Inc. v. FCC, 768 F.2d 1434 (D.C. Cir. 1985) (invalidating rules which required cable TV operators to transmit to their subscribers every over-the-air television broadcast that was "significantly viewed in the community"). For a discussion of the access issue, see generally Kreiss, "Deregulation of Cable Television and the Problem of Access Under the First Amendment," 54 S.Cal.L.Rev. 1001 (1981); Lee, "Cable Franchising and the First Amendment," 36 Vand.L.Rev. 867 (1983); Note, "Access to Cable Television: A Critique of the Affirmative Duty Theory of the First Amendment," 70 Calif.L.Rev. 1393 (1982).

79. 75 Mich.L.Rev. 1 (1976). See also Bollinger, "On the Legal Relationship Between Old and New Technologies," 26 German Yearbook of International Law 269 (1983).

80. 75 Mich.L.Rev. at 36.

81. Id.

82. Id. at 32–33. Indeed, Bollinger maintains that Congress, even today, should be allowed to reverse its field and regulate newspapers, at least to some extent, if it stops regulating broadcasters. Id. at 37.

It is conceivable that this argument could have been run in the opposite direction if Congress had chosen to leave the electronic media largely unregulated while legislating access to the print media instead. But the situations need not be quite symmetrical. Since each new medium tends to be widely perceived as "a law unto itself," [83] the danger of escalating from a tolerable to an intolerable level of regulation may be minimized by initially focusing regulatory efforts on new technologies. If it is correct that "[a]ccess regulation in the print media would have immediately signified a pronounced break with traditional first amendment theory," [84] with an attendant transformation in the boundaries of the legally thinkable and a corresponding increase in pressure to regulate still more deeply, then perhaps the initial selection of the electronic media as the regulated sector illustrates a way of exploiting new technology to permit regulatory experimentation while maintaining vital links with constitutional tradition.[85]

Even if first amendment concerns will eventually require a more candid equation between the new media and the old, with a consequent increase in broadcaster rights and a parallel diminution of newspaper rights, the juxtaposition of *Red Lion* and *Tornillo* may well represent an instructive if inadvertent paradigm for constitutional approaches to new technologies generally.

§ 12–26.   The First Amendment Freedom of Association

Critics of the American Constitution as an unacceptably individualistic document, one insufficiently sensitive to the social dimension of humanity and the communal dimension of society, will find at least a limited answer in the "freedom of association" that the Supreme Court has repeatedly described as among the preferred rights derived by implication from the first amendment's guarantees of speech, press, petition, and assembly.[1] For association in its communal sense— activity understandable only as it exists in the context of group experience, as in a family or a commune, for example [2]—has recently begun to find a place in first amendment doctrine. Such association had been protected previously, if at all, only as an aspect of the less well

---

83. Kovacs v. Cooper, 336 U.S. 77, 97 (1949) (Jackson, J., concurring). See, e.g., Mutual Film Corp. v. Industrial Comm'n, 236 U.S. 230, 244 (1915) (film exhibition not entitled to first amendment protection). Even after that view was retracted, see, e.g., Joseph Burstyn, Inc. v. Wilson, 343 U.S. 495 (1952), the Court continued to uphold schemes for licensing films that would undoubtedly be struck down in the case of books. Compare Freedman v. Maryland, 380 U.S. 51 (1965), and Times Film Corp. v. Chicago, 365 U.S. 43 (1961), with Kingsley Books, Inc. v. Brown, 354 U.S. 436, 441 (1957). See § 12–36, infra.

84. Bollinger, supra note 57, at 21.

85. Id. at 25, 33–34. But see M. Spitzer, Seven Dirty Words and Six Other Stories 46–47 (1986) (criticizing Bollinger's analy-

sis). Print and broadcast, for example, are not fungible media. Millions cannot read, and many others strongly prefer broadcast for other reasons.

§ 12–26

1. See, e.g., NAACP v. Claiborne Hardware Co., 458 U.S. 886 (1928); Buckley v. Valeo, 424 U.S. 1 (1976); United Mine Workers v. Illinois State Bar Ass'n, 389 U.S. 217 (1967); NAACP v. Button, 371 U.S. 415 (1963); NAACP v. Alabama ex rel. Patterson, 357 U.S. 449 (1958).

2. See, e.g., United States Dep't of Agriculture v. Moreno, 413 U.S. 528 (1973); New Jersey Welfare Rights Organization v. Cahill, 411 U.S. 619 (1973); Griswold v. Connecticut, 381 U.S. 479 (1965).

pedigreed rights of privacy and personhood considered in Chapter 15. But, as we shall see, more recent developments portend an independent concern with association as such.

If these developments continue, then believers in the richness and diversity of a pluralist society, where a variety of voluntary private associations and groups operate simultaneously to maximize opportunities for self-realization and minimize the strength of centralized power,[3] may begin to find comfort in the freedom of association.

More than a hundred years ago, Alexis de Tocqueville observed that the "most natural privilege of man, next to the right of acting for himself, is that of combining his exertions with those of his fellow creatures and of acting in common with them." [4] It was for this reason that he thought the "right of association . . . almost as inalienable in its nature as the right of personal liberty." [5] But the doctrine to which such a perception points—that "whatever action a person can [lawfully] pursue as an individual, freedom of association must ensure he can pursue with others" [6]—has only recently emerged in our constitutional law. Before *Citizens Against Rent Control v. Berkeley*,[7] the Supreme Court had quite consistently regarded arguments about freedom of association as reducible not to the question of whether those who act in concert are seeking together a goal they would be privileged to seek separately, but to the narrower question of whether the actors are seeking a goal independently protected by the first amendment—the Court's focus being not on the *right of association within the group* but solely on the *ends* the group sought to attain.[8] Nowhere is the point clearer than in the contrast between the Court's careful scrutiny and frequent invalidation of state interference with group legal practice,[9]

3. See, e.g., A. Bentley, The Process of Government (1908); R. Dahl, A Preface to Democratic Theory (1956); H. Lasky, Foundations of Sovereignty 238–43 (1921); C. Lindblom, The Intelligence of Democracy (1965); D. Truman, The Governmental Process (2d ed. 1971). See also The Federalist No. 10, at 57 (J. Cooke ed. 1961). From the pluralist viewpoint, political parties, professional associations, social clubs, families, labor unions, religious organizations, and other private collectivities are thought entitled "to lead their own free lives and exercise within the area of their competence an authority so effective as to justify labeling it . . . sovereign." Howe, "Foreword: Political Theory and the Nature of Liberty," 67 Harv.L.Rev. 91 (1953). Much of the political thought of the West has been an oscillation between this view and the view that intermediate associations simultaneously weaken public authority and threaten to overpower the individuals left in their grip. See R. Nisbet, The Quest For Community (1969). For critical commentary on the pluralist viewpoint, see H. Kariel, The Decline of American Pluralism (1961); T. Lowi, The End of Liberalism (1969).

4. 1 A. de Tocqueville, Democracy in America, 196 (P. Bradley, ed. 1945).

5. Id.

6. Raggi, "An Independent Right to Freedom of Association," 12 Harv.Civ.Rts.-Civ.Lib.L.Rev. 1, 15 (1977).

7. 454 U.S. 290 (1981).

8. For example, in Runyon v. McCrary, 427 U.S. 160, 175–76 (1976), the Court quite correctly rejected a freedom of association argument on behalf of racially segregated private academies and the parents who send their children to such academies, not on the plausible ground that individuals and institutions have no right to do in concert that which is unlawful when done individually, but on the strikingly narrow ground that ending discriminatory admission practices need not inhibit the teaching of any idea or dogma. See Raggi, supra note 6, at 26.

9. See United Transportation Union v. Michigan, 401 U.S. 576 (1971); United Mine Workers v. Illinois State Bar Association, 389 U.S. 217 (1967); Brotherhood of Railroad Trainmen v. Virginia ex rel. Virginia State Bar, 377 U.S. 1 (1964); NAACP v. Button, 371 U.S. 415 (1963).

and the Court's summary affirmance of a decision barely scrutinizing, and thus upholding, state interference with group medical practice.[10] In both areas, the associational undertaking seemed indispensable to reasonably adequate service at a non-prohibitive cost; the only difference was that health maintenance, and indeed survival, seemed to enjoy no special link to speech or petition, while litigation and lawyering were obvious species of both.[11]

Not until *Citizens Against Rent Control v. Berkeley* [12] did the Court suggest that individuals acting in concert have an associational right to be as free to pursue lawful aims as they would if the same individuals pursued the same aims acting separately.[13] In *Citizens Against Rent Control*, the city imposed a limit of $250 on individual contributions to *committees* formed to support or oppose referendum decisions; no such limitation on expenditures of an individual acting alone was imposed.[14] Stating that such a limit *could not* validly have been imposed on solitary expenditures,[15] the Court held this dichotomous situation unconstitutional: "There are, of course, some activities, legal if engaged in by one, yet illegal if performed in concert with others, but political expression is not one of them. To place a Spartan limit—or indeed any limit—on individuals wishing to band together to advance their views on a ballot measure, *while placing none on individuals acting alone*, is

10. In Garcia v. Texas State Board of Medical Examiners, 421 U.S. 995 (1975), aff'g mem. 384 F.Supp. 434 (W.D.Tex.1974), the Court summarily affirmed a lower court decision upholding statutes which barred the operation of health maintenance organizations except where all decisions, non-medical as well as medical, were left with doctors. The plaintiffs were low-income residents of San Antonio who had formed a consumer-controlled health maintenance organization which planned by pooling its members' resources to hire doctors on a salaried basis and thereby to lower the cost of medical care to its members. Because all doctor-controlled organizations existing in Texas delivered health care on a fee-for-service basis, the plaintiffs argued that only if consumers controlled non-medical decisions in such an organization would a non-fee-for-service plan be adopted.

11. See, e.g., NAACP v. Button, 371 U.S. 415, 430–31 (1963) (Harlan, J. dissenting): "Freedom of expression embraces more than the right of the individual to speak his mind. It includes also his right to advocate and his right to join with his fellows in an effort to make that advocacy effective . . . And just as it includes the right jointly to petition the legislature for redress of grievances . . . so it must include the right to join together for purposes of obtaining judicial redress."

12. 454 U.S. 290 (1981).

13. See also Roberts v. United States Jaycees, 468 U.S. 609, 623 (1984) ("An indi-

vidual's freedom to speak, worship, and to petition the Government for the redress of grievances could not be vigorously protected from interference by the State unless a correlative freedom to engage in group effort toward those ends were not also guaranteed"). But both the Jaycees decision and the 7–0 ruling in Board of Directors of Rotary International v. Rotary Club of Duarte, 107 S.Ct. 1940 (1987), in upholding state laws against all-male business establishments (including clubs), made clear that associational rights provide no shield against otherwise valid anti-discrimination rules.

14. 454 U.S. at 296.

15. The Court endorsed its previous holding in Buckley v. Valeo, 424 U.S. 1 (1976), which struck down ceilings on political expenditures by individuals, even though the rationale of that holding, and its ability to endure, have been seriously questioned. See §§ 13–28, 13–29, infra. In Citizens Against Rent Control, the Court reaffirmed that "contributors cannot be protected from the possibility that others will make larger contributions." 454 U.S. 290, 295 (1981). As to political contributions under the circumstances of this case, the Court stated that Buckley permitted "limits on contributions to *candidates* and their committees" (emphasis added) but not "limitations on contributions to committees formed to favor or oppose *ballot measures*." Id. at 297 (emphasis the Court's).

clearly a restraint on the right of association. [The Berkeley ordinance] does not seek to mute the voice of one individual, and it cannot be allowed to hobble the collective expressions of a group." [16] In *Citizens Against Rent Control*, the Court for the first time recognized constitutional protection of associational conduct not solely on the ground that the conduct was independently protected as speech or religion, but rather on the ground (at least in part) that the state had not sought to limit the conduct *except* when engaged in by persons banding together. What is nonetheless unclear is whether the principle of that decision would in fact be extended to cases in which the conduct concededly *could* have been banned outright when engaged in by individuals. For example, the Court has upheld limitations on direct contributions to political candidates and their committees.[17] Might it nevertheless strike down a statutory scheme that chooses not to restrict *individual* contributions to candidates, but *does* restrict *group* contributions to candidates? Part of the Court's language in *Citizens Against Rent Control*—"[t]o place . . . any limit . . . on individuals wishing to band together to advance their views on a ballot measure, while placing none on individuals acting alone, is clearly a restraint on the right of association" [18]—implies that the Court might well invalidate such a statutory scheme. However, the opinion could be read more narrowly since much of it focuses on the fact that limitations on contributions with respect to ballot measures are simply unconstitutional.[19] On this view, Berkeley's ordinance was struck down as unconstitutional whether applied to individuals *or* to groups— *not* solely because it restricted groups (as opposed to individuals) in a manner that penalized association as such. And, on this view, the hypothesized restriction on group contributions to candidates might be upheld.

What the Court before *Citizens Against Rent Control* had recognized as implicit in the first amendment, and therefore in the liberty secured by the fourteenth, is *a right to join with others to pursue goals independently protected by the first amendment*—such as political advocacy,[20] litigation (regarded as a form of advocacy),[21] or religious wor-

---

16. Id. (emphasis added). In this case, the Court did not find an overriding government interest that would justify infringement on the group's expressive associational rights. Rather, the goal that the City of Berkeley was allegedly seeking to accomplish—"to make known the identity of supporters and opponents of ballot measures . . . [to prevent] individuals or corporations [who] speak through committees [from adopting] seductive names that may tend to conceal the true identity of the source"—was adequately achieved by another part of the ordinance that "requires publication of lists of contributors in advance of the voting." Id. at 298.

17. See Buckley v. Valeo, 424 U.S. 1, 26–27 (1976); Citizens Against Rent Control v. Berkeley, 454 U.S. 290, 296–97 (1981).

18. Citizens Against Rent Control v. Berkeley, 454 U.S. 290, 296 (1981).

19. Id. at 297–99. The Court endorsed the view of the "Federal Courts of Appeals . . . that *Buckley* does not support limitations on contributions to committees formed to favor or oppose *ballot measures.*" Id. at 297 (emphasis the Court's).

20. See, e.g., Cousins v. Wigoda, 419 U.S. 477 (1975) (autonomy of political party); Tashjian v. Republican Party of Connecticut, 107 S.Ct. 544 (1986) (right of political party to have *non*-members vote in its primary).

21. See, e.g., NAACP v. Button, 371 U.S. 415 (1963) (autonomy of group legal practice); In re Primus, 436 U.S. 412 (1978) (South Carolina's application of its disciplinary rules to an attorney's solicitation by letter on behalf of the ACLU interferes

ship.[22] Along with this *positive* right, the Court has also recognized its *negative* counterpart: the right *not* to join with others in their pursuit of such first amendment objectives.[23] In striking down a state law that would have compelled the Democratic Party, at its National Convention, to seat delegates chosen at a state primary that was open to *non*-Democrats, the Supreme Court, quoting the first edition of this treatise, stressed that " '[f]reedom of association would prove an empty guarantee if associations could not limit control over their decisions to those who share the interests and persuasions that underlie the association's being.' " [24] But it would be a mistake to suppose that, unless *Citizens Against Rent Control* were extended to conduct altogether unprotected by the first amendment, "freedom of association" would add nothing whatever to rights otherwise protected. For one can at least imagine a legal system in which only the solitary pursuit of certain ends would be protected from majoritarian control by law—a system in which the very existence of group activity was thought sufficient to transform otherwise preferred rights into legally cognizable threats to the society as a whole. If the jurisprudence of freedom of association developed by the Supreme Court over the past four decades were to be summarized in a single sentence, it would be this: Ours is not such a system.[25] To be sure, it is unclear how far the Court will carry its recently taken move in the opposite direction—toward a system in which concerted effort *itself* is seen as entitled to independent constitutional protection.[26] But, however limited is our Constitution's protection for the concerted

with the freedom of political association granted by the first amendment).

22. See, e.g., Serbian Eastern Orthodox Diocese v. Milivojevich, 426 U.S. 696 (1976) (autonomy of religious hierarchy); Kedroff v. St. Nicholas Cathedral, 344 U.S. 94 (1952) (same).

23. See also Chicago Teachers Union v. Hudson, 475 U.S. 292, 106 S.Ct. 1066, 1077 (1986) (holding constitutionally insufficient a union's procedure to minimize risk that nonunion employees' union dues might be temporarily used for support of political parties or political views); Roberts v. United States Jaycees, 468 U.S. 609, 623 (1984) (dictum) ("Freedom of association . . . plainly presupposes a freedom not to associate"); Branti v. Finkel, 445 U.S. 507, 517 (1980) (discharging county public defenders solely on the basis of their lack of membership in the chief public defender's party violated the subordinate public defenders associational rights); Abood v. Detroit Board of Education, 431 U.S. 209, 255 (1977) (requiring nonunion employees to support their collective bargaining agent in communication of ideas interferes with first amendment associational rights); Elrod v. Burns, 427 U.S. 347 (1976) (holding violative of the first amendment the patronage practice in which a county sheriff, on assuming office, would automatically replace non-civil-service employees with members of his own party).

24. Democratic Party of United States v. Wisconsin, 450 U.S. 107, 122 n. 22 (1981) (citation omitted).

25. That such a system was at least thinkable seems fairly clear. One thoughtful scholar has surmised that the Framers "had been so thoroughly educated by Rousseau that they were fearful that the recognition of rights in associations would threaten not only the authority of government but the liberty of individuals." Howe, supra note 3, at 92. Compare the initial treatment of labor unions in American law. See A. Blum, A History of the American Labor Movement (1972).

26. See, e.g., Citizens Against Rent Control v. Berkeley, 454 U.S. 290, 294 (1981) ("[T]he practice of persons sharing common views banding together to achieve a common end is deeply embedded in the American political process. The 18th-century Committees of Correspondence and the pamphleteers were early examples of this phenomena (sic) and the Federalist Papers were perhaps the most significant and lasting example. The tradition of volunteer committees for collective action has manifested itself in myriad community and public activities; in the political process it can focus on a candidate or on a ballot measure. Its value is that by collective effort individuals can make their view known, when, individually, their voices would be faint or lost").

pursuit of lawful but not especially "preferred" ends, at least it protects the concerted pursuit of those ends that would represent fundamental rights in the context of purely individual activity.

Even if *Citizens Against Rent Control* were limited to situations in which the conduct at issue could not be banned when pursued individually, an "abridgment of the first amendment freedom of association" could be defined as any insufficiently justified governmental rule, practice, or policy that interferes with or discourages a group's pursuit of ends having special first amendment significance—such as literary expression, or political change, or religious worship. Government can abridge this implied first amendment freedom, and therefore be guilty of violating due process unless a showing of compelling necessity is made, in any of four ways: (1) directly punishing the fact cf membership in a group or association or the fact of attendance at a meeting of such a group or association; (2) intruding upon the internal organization, or integral activities, of an association or group, including its decisions of whom to include as members and its decisions as to which non-members to invite to take part in its processes; (3) withholding a privilege or benefit from the members of a group or association; and (4) compelling disclosure of a group's membership or of an individual's associational affiliations, either through a focused investigation or as part of a general disclosure rule, in circumstances where anonymity is likely to prove important to the continued viability of various associational ties.

The most obvious cases are those in which government seeks to outlaw an association or to punish the bare fact of affiliation with it. In these cases, the governing constitutional principle is twofold. First, an association or organization cannot be made illegal, whether on a conspiracy theory or otherwise, in the absence of a clear showing that the group is actively engaged in lawless conduct, or in such incitement to lawless action as would itself be punishable as a clear and present danger of harm that more speech could not avoid.[27] And second, an individual cannot be punished for joining, associating with, or attending meetings of, an association or organization unless the association meets the first requirement and the individual is shown to have affiliated with it (a) with knowledge of its illegality, and (b) with the specific intent of furthering its illegal aims by such affiliation.[28] Although each of these requirements took time to evolve,[29] all are now firmly fixed as elements of first amendment jurisprudence.[30]

---

27. In Noto v. United States, 367 U.S. 290, 297–98 (1961), the Court reversed a conviction for membership in the Communist Party because the evidence did not suffice to establish that the Party had engaged in unlawful advocacy. See § 12–9, supra.

28. See Elfbrandt v. Russell, 384 U.S. 11 (1966).

29. Compare, e.g., American Communications Ass'n v. Douds, 339 U.S. 382 (1950)

(upholding federal statute requiring union officers, as condition of access to NLRB, to file affidavits of non-membership in organizations believing in violent overthrow), effectively overruled by United States v. Brown, 381 U.S. 437 (1965), discussed in §§ 10–4 to 10–6, supra.

30. See § 12–9, supra.

Somewhat more difficult are those cases in which government makes no attempt to brand an association, or affiliation with it, as unlawful, but nonetheless interferes significantly either (a) with its internal structure or organization—for example, by attempting to control delegate seating procedures to a political convention,[31] or by attempting to control defrocking procedures in a religious organization [32]—or (b) with an activity integral to the association in the sense that the association's protected purposes would be significantly frustrated were the activity disallowed—as in the case of attempts to deny a campus organization the opportunity to use state college facilities to disseminate its views,[33] or attempts to prevent labor unions from referring their members to union attorneys for assistance in litigation,[34] or attempts to impose tort damages against boycotters who may cause injury to discriminatory businesses,[35] or attempts to prevent a political party from seeking to broaden its appeal by including non-members in its primary election.[36] In all such cases, the governmental interference violates the first and fourteenth amendments if it is justified only by marginal administrative concerns [37] or by the existence of an associational link to a group with a history of illegal or disruptive behavior.[38] Such governmental interference also violates the first and fourteenth amendments even if it is justified by a legitimate objective, such as the avoidance of conflicts of interest in attorney-client relationships, unless government shows that a serious impairment of the objective would

31. Cousins v. Wigoda, 419 U.S. 477 (1975), invalidated such attempted control by a state of the procedures of a national political convention, and Democratic Party of United States v. Wisconsin, 450 U.S. 107 (1981), held that a state cannot compel a national party to seat a delegation chosen in a manner that violates the party's rules. See § 13–22, infra. See also FEC v. National Conservative Political Action Committee, 470 U.S. 480 (1985) (invalidating federal statutory limitations on expenditures by political action committees), discussed in § 13–29, infra. But see Federal Election Comm'n v. National Right to Work Committee, 459 U.S. 197 (1982) (upholding constitutionality of federal statute restricting solicitation of contributions, by a corporation without capital stock, to members of that corporation), discussed in § 13–29, infra; Marchioro v. Chaney, 442 U.S. 191, 197, 199 (1979) (upholding a state's requirement that each major political party have a state committee consisting of two persons from each county, in order to perform various functions such as electing delegates to the party's national convention and filling any vacancies on the party ticket, but imposing no requirements on the committee with respect to its, or the party's, purely internal activities; the case differed from Democratic Party v. Wisconsin in that only the internal activities performed by the state committee, and not the election of delegates and other external

functions, were challenged), discussed in § 13–22, infra.

32. Serbian Eastern Orthodox Diocese v. Milivojevich, 426 U.S. 696 (1976), invalidated such attempted control by a state of the procedures of the Serbian Orthodox Church. See §§ 14–11, 14–14, 14–16, infra.

33. Healy v. James, 408 U.S. 169 (1972), invalidated such attempts by Central Connecticut State College, which had sought to prevent a local chapter of Students for a Democratic Society (SDS) from holding meetings or otherwise organizing on campus.

34. Brotherhood of Railroad Trainmen v. Virginia ex rel. Virginia State Bar, 377 U.S. 1 (1964), invalidated such attempts by a state which had sought to prevent a union from recommending lawyers of its choice to prosecute members' personal injury claims.

35. NAACP v. Claiborne Hardware Co., 458 U.S. 886 (1982).

36. Tashjian v. Republican Party of Connecticut, 107 S.Ct. 544 (1986), discussed in § 13–22, infra.

37. See id.

38. See Healy v. James, 408 U.S. 169 (1972) (stressing that the local SDS chapter had been guilty of no misconduct but was being branded solely because of its affiliation with the national organization).

clearly occur in the absence of the challenged interference, and that no less intrusive regulation could prevent such impairment.[39]

The third set of cases, those in which associational ties are made the basis for denial of a governmental benefit or privilege, seemed to pose no problem as long as a sharp line could be drawn between rights and privileges.[40] With the demise of that line,[41] there arose the constitutional problem of governmental attempts to make nonmembership in disfavored associations a condition of various opportunities, or to condition such opportunities upon oaths of disaffiliation with such associations or their programs, or upon other sacrifices that could not be required, at least on pain of criminal punishment, of the populace generally. Shortly after the Civil War, in a pair of cases involving occupational restrictions upon former Confederate sympathizers,[42] the Supreme Court began a line of doctrinal development that was to be interrupted for more than three-quarters of a century. Although the Court relied on the ex post facto and bill of attainder clauses to strike the restrictions down as punitive measures insufficiently related to occupational qualification,[43] it was effectively holding that neither an individual's beliefs nor an individual's associations, without more, may be regarded as automatically disqualifying with respect to positions of significant public trust.

In recent decades, the Court has fulfilled the promise of those early decisions by holding that mere membership in the Communist Party could not suffice to justify denial of an opportunity to practice law,[44] to work in the merchant marine,[45] to receive a security clearance,[46] to travel abroad with the protection of a United States passport,[47] to serve

39. See, e.g., United Mine Workers v. Illinois Bar Ass'n, 389 U.S. 217, 223–25 (1967).

40. See, e.g., McAuliffe v. Mayor of New Bedford, 155 Mass. 216, 220, 29 N.E. 517 (1892) (Holmes, J.) ("The petitioner may have a constitutional right to talk politics, but he has no constitutional right to be a policeman"); Waugh v. Mississippi University, 237 U.S. 589, 596 (1915) (state may prevent students in public educational institutions from affiliating with fraternities since "the right to attend" public universities is not "absolute," but "conditional").

41. Van Alstyne, "The Demise of the Right-Privilege Distinction in Constitutional Law," 81 Harv.L.Rev. 1439 (1968). See § 11–5, supra.

42. Ex parte Garland, 71 U.S. (4 Wall.) 333 (1866) (invalidating denial of right to practice in federal courts for persons refusing or unable to swear absence of former Confederate sympathy); Cummings v. Missouri, 71 U.S. (4 Wall.) 277 (1866) (invalidating denial of right to preach for persons refusing or unable to swear absence of former Confederate sympathy).

43. See §§ 10–2, 10–4, supra.

44. See Schware v. Board of Bar Examiners, 353 U.S. 232 (1957), discussed in § 15–13, infra.

45. Schneider v. Smith, 390 U.S. 17 (1968) (construing a federal statute narrowly so as not to support any congressional delegation to executive officials of the authority to condition employment on American merchant vessels upon non-membership in the Communist Party).

46. Greene v. McElroy, 360 U.S. 474 (1959) (to avoid a constitutional question, the Court construed a federal statute as authorizing the Secretary of Defense to revoke security clearances—and thus indirectly deprive individuals of their jobs with defense contractors—only after adversary hearings in which the affected individuals were "afforded the safeguards of confrontation and cross-examination" as a protection against false charges of subversive association).

47. Aptheker v. Secretary of State, 378 U.S. 500 (1964), discussed in § 15–14, infra.

as an officer or employee of a labor union,[48] or to work in a defense facility.[49] And of course membership in, or affiliation with, such other national organizations as Students for a Democratic Society cannot suffice to justify denial of similar opportunities.[50]

On the other hand, even membership in an otherwise protected association, or adherence to an otherwise protected belief, can in certain very limited settings justify denial of a governmental benefit. It is clear, for example, that persons who hate children and speak ill of them—something the first amendment protects even if without great enthusiasm—have no right to work for a public day care center.[51] Just so, Democrats have no right to consideration on equal terms with Republicans when the newly elected Republican governor of a state is choosing a speechwriter or a high-level special assistant. Although there is no similar justification for making party membership decisive in filling the ranks of lower government posts,[52] the argument for allowing ideological criteria at levels of high policy significance seems sufficiently compelling to withstand first amendment attack.[53] More generally, those associational activities that are demonstrably incompatible with the mission of a given public agency or calling may be forbidden—not on a theory that public servants lose their constitutional rights when they assume government duty, but on a theory that such rights cannot be defined independent of the contexts in which they are asserted. Thus the Court has held that "[p]artisan political activities by federal employees must be limited if the Government is to operate effectively and fairly, elections are to play their proper part in representative government and employees themselves are to be sufficiently free from improper influences." [54]

48. United States v. Brown, 381 U.S. 437 (1965), discussed in §§ 10–4, 10–5, supra.

49. United States v. Robel, 389 U.S. 258 (1967), discussed in § 12–33, infra.

50. Healy v. James, 408 U.S. 169 (1972) (denial of opportunity to use local campus facilities). See also § 15–17, infra.

51. Cf. Rankin v. McPherson, 107 S.Ct. 2891, 2904–05 (1987) (Scalia, J., joined by Rehnquist, C.J., and White and O'Connor, JJ., dissenting), discussed in § 12–18, supra; Hollon v. Pierce, 257 Cal.App.2d 468, 64 Cal.Rptr. 808 (3d Dist. 1967) (city may discharge school bus driver who believes in the religious sacrifice of children).

52. See Elrod v. Burns, 427 U.S. 347 (1976) (holding violative of the first amendment the patronage practice in which the Sheriff of Cook County, Illinois, on assuming office from a Sheriff of a different political party, would automatically replace non-civil-service employees with members of his own party); and Branti v. Finkel, 445 U.S. 507 (1980) (holding unconstitutional the firing of Assistant Public Defenders solely on the basis that they were affiliated with a different political party than the newly appointed Public Defender of Rockland County, New York).

53. Elrod, 427 U.S. at 367–368 (dictum). In Pickering v. Board of Education, 391 U.S. 563 (1968), the Court held that a teacher could not be dismissed for criticizing the Board of Education. The Court noted, however, that the relationship between the teacher and the Board did not involve "the kind of close working relationship for which it can persuasively be claimed that personal loyalty and confidence are necessary to their proper functioning." Id. at 570.

54. United States Civil Service Commission v. National Association of Letter Carriers, 413 U.S. 548 (1973) (upholding a prohibition of federal employees' taking an "active part in political management or in political campaigns"); Broadrick v. Oklahoma, 413 U.S. 601 (1973) (upholding state regulation of political activities by state employees more stringent than the federal law). See also United Public Workers of America v. Mitchell, 330 U.S. 75 (1947) (upholding constitutionality of Hatch Act limitations on federal employees' political activities).

The fourth set of cases, in some respects the easiest and in others the most difficult, are those in which government purports to be outlawing no organization, interfering in no association's internal structure or activities, and withholding no benefit because of belief or association, but simply inquiring of an organization who its members are, or of an individual what organizations he or she has joined.[55] The cases are easy from one perspective: anonymity has long been recognized as absolutely essential for the survival of dissident movements; the glare of public disclosure, so healthy in other settings, may operate in the context of protected but unpopular groups or beliefs as a clarion call to ostracism or worse.[56] Thus the Court has had little difficulty recognizing, in such classic cases as *Talley v. California*,[57] *NAACP v. Alabama ex rel. Patterson*,[58] and *Shelton v. Tucker*,[59] that "compelled disclosure . . . may constitute a restraint on freedom of association."[60] Recently the Court has taken even further steps toward protecting dissident political groups by holding unconstitutional as applied to the Socialist Workers Party a statute that required disclosure of campaign contributors and recipients of campaign disbursements and that would be perfectly constitutional as applied to more traditional political parties.[61] But from another perspective the cases are hard: knowledge is highly valued in our society, and secrecy often seems the shield of dangerous and irresponsible designs. Perhaps because the tension between these two perspectives has been so constant, the decisions in this fourth area have not produced a body of doctrine as cogent as in the first three. Early cases, never quite

55. Since involvement in partisan politics is close to the first amendment's core, and since compelled disclosure of political affiliations or contributions "in itself can seriously infringe on privacy and belief guaranteed by the First Amendment," Buckley v. Valeo, 424 U.S. 1, 64 (1976), the Court has upheld such compelled disclosure only when nothing less intrusive could serve compelling national needs, and particularly the integrity of political processes themselves. See id. at 66 (disclosure of campaign contributions), discussed in § 13–31, infra; Nixon v. Administrator of General Services, 433 U.S. 425, 467 (1977) (archival screening of former President's papers).

56. Talley v. California, 362 U.S. 60, 64–65 (1960).

57. Id. (upsetting convictions based on ordinance which banned the distribution of handbills which did not carry the name and address of the author, printer, and sponsor).

58. 357 U.S. 449, 463–65 (1958) (reversing civil contempt judgment against NAACP for refusing to disclose its membership list; likely adverse effect on NAACP's ability to survive in Alabama after disclosure held not sufficiently justified by state's alleged need for the list, given lack of substantial relevance of such list to the inquiry allegedly making the list important—i.e., whether NAACP was doing business in state in violation of foreign corporation registration statute), discussed in § 15–17, infra. See also Bates v. Little Rock, 361 U.S. 516 (1960) (amendment to ordinance involving occupational license tax requiring membership lists of all organizations held invalid where the state could claim no need for information based on state interest in matters of taxation); Louisiana ex rel. Gremillion v. NAACP, 366 U.S. 293 (1961) (upholding temporary injunction restraining enforcement of statute requiring certain not-for-profit organizations to file membership lists).

59. 364 U.S. 479 (1960) (invalidating as overbroad an Arkansas statute which required each teacher in a state-supported school, as a condition of employment, to file annually a list of every organization to which the teacher belonged or made a contribution in the preceding five years). See § 12–31, infra.

60. NAACP v. Alabama ex rel. Patterson, 357 U.S. 449, 462 (1958).

61. Brown v. Socialist Workers Party, 459 U.S. 87, 95 (1982), discussed in § 13–31, infra. See Stone & Marshall, "Brown v. Socialist Workers: Inequality as a Command of the First Amendment," 1983 S.Ct. Rev. 583.

repudiated, upheld state power to ascertain the membership of the Ku Klux Klan [62] and the Communist Party.[63] Later cases, now clearly representing settled law, refused to permit suspicion of connection with the Communist Party to justify compelled disclosure of the membership of the NAACP.[64] In a parallel vein, early cases upheld contempt convictions for refusing to answer legislative questions about past or present Communist Party membership,[65] while later cases held such questions impermissible at least when the membership was other than extremely recent.[66]

Finally, in what might best be viewed as an intersection of this fourth area with that of conditioned government benefits, a complex and confused set of precedents permits denial of bar membership, and of the opportunity to practice law, on the basis of refusal to discuss Communist Party membership;[67] but only where it is clear that such refusal represents unwillingness to cooperate with a proper inquiry [68]

62. New York ex rel. Bryant v. Zimmerman, 278 U.S. 63 (1928) (upholding compulsory disclosure of the membership list of the Ku Klux Klan on the theory that the requirement would deter illegal activities which the organization was tempted to undertake).

63. Communist Party of the United States v. SACB, 367 U.S. 1 (1961) (upholding a requirement that the Communist Party reveal its membership because the Board could and did rationally conclude that the Communist Party was part of "a world-wide integrated movement which employs every combination of possible means, peaceful and violent, domestic and foreign, overt and clandestine, to destroy the government itself").

64. Gibson v. Florida Legislative Investigation Committee, 372 U.S. 539 (1963) (holding that the president of the NAACP's Miami branch could not be required to provide a legislative committee with a list of members and contributors because the committee investigating alleged Communist infiltration of the NAACP had no "adequate foundation" of evidence showing "a nexus between the NAACP and subversive activities" to justify the inquiry). See Kalven, The Negro and the First Amendment 105–120 (1966).

65. See Braden v. United States, 365 U.S. 431 (1961) (sustaining contempt conviction for failing to reveal Communist Party membership to HUAC subcommittee investigating Communist infiltration of basic industries in the South); Wilkinson v. United States, 365 U.S. 399 (1961) (same); Barenblatt v. United States, 360 U.S. 109 (1959) (sustaining contempt conviction for refusing to answer questions concerning alleged Communist infiltration into education). Cf. Uphaus v. Wyman, 360 U.S. 72 (1959) (upholding contempt conviction for refusing to produce list of guests attending

summer camp and discussion sponsored by World Fellowship, Inc., at behest of New Hampshire attorney general, acting on behalf of state legislature as one-man investigating committee). The unease with which the Court even in 1957 approached these cases is evidenced by the readiness with which it reached results contrary to these on highly attenuated procedural theories. See, e.g., Sweezy v. New Hampshire, 354 U.S. 234 (1957) (reversing contempt conviction for refusing to answer questions put by state attorney general since it could not be stated with sufficient certainty that the state legislature had asked the attorney general to gather the kinds of facts about which he had inquired); Watkins v. United States, 354 U.S. 178 (1957) (reversing conviction for contempt of Congress since the defendant had not been accorded an adequate opportunity to determine whether the questions were within the scope of the committee's authority).

66. See, e.g., DeGregory v. Attorney General, 383 U.S. 825, 829–30 (1966) (reversing a contempt conviction for refusal to answer questions put in 1963 about Communist Party membership prior to 1957: "There is no showing whatsoever of present danger of sedition against the State itself, the only area to which the authority of the State extends").

67. Law Students Civil Rights Research Council, Inc. v. Wadmond, 401 U.S. 154 (1971) (bar examiners could require an answer to a two-part inquiry into whether an applicant was knowingly a member of an organization advocating the overthrow of the government by force or violence, and also specifically intended to further the group's illegal goals).

68. See In re Anastaplo, 366 U.S. 82, 88 (1961) (holding that an Illinois applicant could be denied bar admission on account of his refusal to answer questions dealing

rather than a simple assertion of a right not to be disadvantaged solely because of party affiliation.[69]

A final complication is introduced by the fifth amendment privilege against compulsory self-incrimination, whose interaction with first amendment rights of association and belief has not always been clearly enough understood. So long as an individual's answers to official questions might be employed by the questioning jurisdiction as evidence, or as leads to evidence, in a future criminal prosecution of that individual, the fifth amendment, applicable to the states through the fourteenth,[70] confers a privilege to be silent.[71] Exercise of such a privilege can neither be equated with guilt [72] nor be treated as a forbidden failure to cooperate with a proper inquiry [73] and used by government as the basis for adverse treatment, including denial of a

with Communist Party membership): "An applicant will not be admitted to the practice of law . . . so long as, by refusing to answer material questions, he obstructs a bar examining committee in its proper functions of interrogating and cross-examining him upon his qualifications".

69. Baird v. State Bar of Arizona, 401 U.S. 1 (1971); In re Stolar, 401 U.S. 23 (1971). The theory appears to be that inquiry into party membership as an end in itself would be forbidden, but that such inquiry is permissible as a first step toward determining whether the individual had joined an illegal organization with the requisite knowledge and intent; the individual who frustrates even this first step as a means of preventing the permissible determination may thus be penalized.

70. Malloy v. Hogan, 378 U.S. 1 (1964); Murphy v. Waterfront Commission of New York, 378 U.S. 52 (1964).

71. See Lefkowitz v. Cunningham, 431 U.S. 801 (1977) (state cannot deny right to hold political party office solely because of refusal to testify or waive immunity); Spevack v. Klein, 385 U.S. 511 (1967) (lawyer may not be disbarred for professional misconduct when the only charge is that the lawyer claimed the fifth amendment privilege rather than produce financial records conceded to be unrelated to professional conduct); Albertson v. SACB, 382 U.S. 70 (1965) (order directing named members of Communist Party held to violate privilege against self-incrimination where admission of Party membership would be evidence to prosecute the registrant for illegal membership). One who is forced by government to speak under the threat of discharge or some other disability may invoke the fifth amendment privilege to exclude the testimony and its fruits at any future criminal trial, Garrity v. New Jersey, 385 U.S. 493 (1967) (evidence so secured must be deemed coerced and hence is constitutionally inadmissible in a crimi-

nal trial). Nor may one be convicted for failure to register as a gambler, Marchetti v. United States, 390 U.S. 39 (1968), to register a firearm. Haynes v. United States, 390 U.S. 85 (1968), or to pay the transfer tax on marijuana, Leary v. United States, 395 U.S. 6 (1969), where the information received by compliance with the requirement could be used in a federal or state prosecution.

72. See Slochower v. Board of Education, 350 U.S. 551 (1956) (finding unconstitutional a city college professor's dismissal following the professor's valid assertion of the fifth amendment privilege to block a congressional inquiry into his past Communist Party activities).

73. Earlier decisions suggesting that assertion of the fifth amendment privilege may be the basis for adverse treatment on an insubordination theory, see Lerner v. Casey, 357 U.S. 468 (1958) (approving the dismissal as a "security risk" of a fifth amendment-invoking subway operator who had refused to answer his employer's questions concerning Communist Party membership); accord, Nelson v. Los Angeles, 362 U.S. 1 (1960); Beilan v. Board of Education, 357 U.S. 399 (1958), plainly cannot survive the rationale of Gardner v. Broderick, 392 U.S. 273 (1968) (holding unconstitutional the dismissal of a policeman because of his failure to sign a "waiver of immunity" from prosecution after being called before a grand jury investigating police misconduct in connection with illegal gambling), and Lefkowitz v. Turley, 414 U.S. 70 (1973) (holding unconstitutional law providing for cancellation of public contracts for contractors refusing to waive immunity when called to testify concerning their contracts). For a powerful (but rejected) argument that these latter decisions should not control the case of a high policymaking official, see Lefkowitz v. Cunningham, 431 U.S. 801, 810 (1977) (Stevens, J., dissenting).

public benefit.[74] But once the individual has been promised immunity from future prosecutorial use of compelled answers or their fruit, refusal to answer questions closely linked to a legitimate interest of government may be punished, both criminally and civilly.[75] This principle in no way entitles government, however, to insist on information probing with unjustifiable breadth into beliefs or associations; the protections of the first amendment are in no way reduced by the grant of an immunity sufficient to eliminate claims otherwise available under the fifth.[76]

§ 12–27. Overbreadth: Facial Invalidation as the Response to Deterrent Effect

A law is void on its face if it "does not aim specifically at evils within the allowable area of [government] control, but . . . sweeps within its ambit other activities that constitute an exercise" of protected expressive or associational rights.[1] Such overbreadth analysis ordinarily compares the *statutory* line defining burdened and unburdened conduct with the *judicial* line specifying activities protected and unprotected by the first amendment; if the statutory line includes conduct which the judicial line protects, the statute is overbroad and becomes eligible for invalidation on that ground. Of course, almost every law, such as the ordinary trespass ordinance reviewed in *Marsh v. Alabama*,[2] is potentially applicable to constitutionally protected acts; that danger does not invalidate the law as such but merely invalidates its enforcement against protected activity. A plausible challenge to a law as *void for overbreadth* can be made only when (1) the protected activity is a significant part of the law's target, and (2) there exists no satisfactory way of severing the law's constitutional from its unconstitutional applications so as to excise the latter clearly in a single step from the law's reach.

74. See, e.g., Spevack v. Klein, 385 U.S. 511 (1967) (opportunity to practice law); Lefkowitz v. Turley, 414 U.S. 70 (1973) (opportunity to serve as public contractor).

75. See Gardner v. Broderick, 392 U.S. 273, 278 (1968) (dictum): A public employee may be compelled to answer questions "specifically, directly, and narrowly relating to the performance of his official duties," if his answers or the fruits thereof cannot be used in a subsequent criminal prosecution. See also Uniformed Sanitation Men Ass'n v. Comm'r of Sanitation, 392 U.S. 280 (1968).

76. The first amendment rights asserted in Shelton v. Tucker, 364 U.S. 479 (1960), and NAACP v. Alabama ex rel. Patterson, 357 U.S. 449 (1958), for example, did not depend in any way on a risk of criminal prosecution.

§ 12–27

1. Thornhill v. Alabama, 310 U.S. 88, 97 (1940) (statute prohibiting all picketing void on its face since it bans peaceful pick-

eting protected by the first amendment). See Board of Airport Commissioners of Los Angeles v. Jews for Jesus, Inc., 107 S.Ct. 2568 (1987) (unanimously invalidating rule which proscribed *all* "First Amendment activities" in airport terminal). See generally Monaghan, "Overbreadth," 1981 S.Ct. Rev. 1; Note, "The First Amendment Overbreadth Doctrine," 83 Harv.L.Rev. 844 (1970).

2. 326 U.S. 501 (1946) (trespass statute held not enforceable against distribution of religious literature on streets of company town). See also Eastern R.R. Presidents Conference v. Noerr Motor Freight, Inc., 365 U.S. 127 (1961) (Sherman Act held not applicable to concerted lobbying activities of businessmen); NAACP v. Button, 371 U.S. 415 (1963) (state barratry law held not enforceable against NAACP activities sponsoring litigation directed against segregation); United States v. Spock, 416 F.2d 165 (1st Cir. 1969) (conspiracy law held not enforceable against protected advocacy of opposition to Vietnam War).

In laws having these two characteristics, the usual approach of constitutional adjudication—gradually cutting away the unconstitutional aspects of a statute by invalidating its improper applications case by case—does not respond sufficiently to the peculiarly vulnerable character of activities protected by the first amendment. For an "overbroad" law of the sort described here "hangs over [people's] heads like a Sword of Damocles." [3] That judges will ultimately rescue those whose conduct in retrospect is held protected is not enough, "for the value of a sword of Damocles is that it hangs—not that it drops." [4] The resulting deterrent to protected speech is not effectively removed if "the contours of regulation would have to be hammered out case-by-case—and tested only by those hardy enough to risk criminal prosecution [or other sanctions] to determine the proper scope of regulation." [5] The only solution, then, is to strike down such an overbroad law altogether until it is rewritten or until an appropriate court authoritatively narrows it.

The overbreadth doctrine has often been understood as an exception to the rule that individuals generally may not litigate the rights of third parties. [6] As the Supreme Court recently described the doctrine, "an individual whose own speech or expressive conduct may validly be prohibited or sanctioned is permitted to challenge a statute on its face because it also threatens others not before the court—those who desire to engage in legally protected expression but who may refrain from doing so rather than risk prosecution or undertake to have the law declared partially invalid." [7] But, at least outside the context of purely

3. Arnett v. Kennedy, 416 U.S. 134, 231 (1974) (Marshall, J., dissenting) (federal statute authorizing dismissal of tenured government employees for "such cause as will promote the efficiency of the service" should have been held an overbroad restriction on civil servants' free expression rights).

4. Id.

5. Dombrowski v. Pfister, 380 U.S. 479, 487 (1965) (Brennan, J.), discussed in § 3–30, supra. But the Court is prepared to assume that persons advertising goods or services for a profit—i.e., commercial speakers—will indeed be hardy enough. Bates v. State Bar of Arizona, 433 U.S. 350, 379–81 (1977) (holding advertisement of lawyers' fees protected but refusing to strike down ban on its face; overbreadth doctrine held inapplicable to commercial speech); San Francisco Arts & Athletics, Inc. v. United States Olympic Committee, 107 S.Ct. 2971, 2981 n. 15 (1987) (upholding exclusive grant to U.S. Olympic Committee of the word "Olympic" and noting that "the application of the overbreadth doctrine [to commercial speech] is highly questionable.") See § 12–15, supra.

6. See e.g., Barrows v. Jackson, 346 U.S. 249, 255 (1953); United States v. Raines, 362 U.S. 17, 21–22 (1960); Note, "Standing to Assert Constitutional Jus

Tertii," 88 Harv.L.Rev. 423 (1974), discussed in § 3–19, supra.

7. Brockett v. Spokane Arcades, Inc., 472 U.S. 491, 503 (1985). For other anticipatory relief cases, see Secretary of State of Maryland v. Joseph H. Munson Co., 467 U.S. 947, 954–59 (1984) (granting declaratory and injunctive relief to professional fundraising organization which challenged, on overbreadth grounds, a state statute prohibiting charitable organizations from spending no more than 25% of their funds raised on administrative expenses); NAACP v. Button, 371 U.S. 415, 432–33 (1963) (enforcement of barratry statute may be invalid if it prohibits privileged exercise of first amendment rights "whether or not . . . the petitioner has engaged in privileged conduct"); cf. Aptheker v. Secretary of State, 378 U.S. 500, 515–17 (1964) (communist party members successfully challenging statute denying them opportunity to obtain passports as an overbroad infringement on the freedom to travel secured by fifth amendment due process clause need not prove that Congress could not have enacted a narrower statute constitutionally prohibiting their travel abroad). Indeed, the Court recently implied that the overbreadth doctrine may be employed *only* if the contested regulation violates the rights of those not before the Court. In City Council of Los Angeles v.

anticipatory challenges, overbreadth doctrine does not in fact possess a distinctive standing component. Rather, the doctrine recognizes that, even "under 'conventional' standing principles, a litigant has always had the right to be judged in accordance with a constitutionally valid rule of law."[8] When an act, or course of conduct, contains elements that would permit it to be penalized under a properly drawn rule, a conviction for that act or course of conduct, returned under a statute and a jury charge creating a substantial risk that the defendant has instead been punished on a forbidden basis, must be set aside. When an appellate court takes this step in a ruling that focuses on the forbidden breadth of the law under which the conviction was obtained, it may *appear* to be vindicating the rights of third parties,[9] but is in fact doing no more than judging the party before it by a permissible standard.

§ 12–28. Requiring Substantial Overbreadth: The Diminishing Concern with Deterrence

Implicit in overbreadth analysis is the notion that a law should not be voided on its face unless its deterrence of protected activities is substantial. Thus the Court has not struck down on their face trespass, breach of the peace, or other ordinary criminal laws in which the number of instances in which these laws may be applied to protected

Taxpayers for Vincent, 466 U.S. 789 (1984), the Court refused to entertain an overbreadth challenge to a city ordinance which prohibited the posting of signs on public property. The Court held that the overbreadth doctrine was not applicable because the record did not indicate that the ordinance would have any greater impact on any third parties' interests in free speech than it had on the first amendment interests of the parties themselves. The Court stated that those "challenging the ordinance have simply failed to demonstrate a realistic danger that the ordinance will significantly compromise recognized First Amendment protections of individuals not before the Court. It would therefore be inappropriate in this case to entertain an overbreadth challenge to the ordinance." Id. at 802. In short, the Court did not need—and thus did not employ—the overbreadth doctrine in Vincent, a point elaborated upon in dicta from Brockett: Courts need not entertain an overbreadth challenge "where the parties challenging the statute are those who desire to engage in protected speech that the overbroad statute purports to punish, or who seek to publish both protected and unprotected material. There is then no want of a proper party to challenge the statute, no concern that the attack on the statute will be unduly delayed or protected speech discouraged. The statute may forthwith be declared invalid to the extent that it reaches too far, but otherwise left intact." Brockett, 472 U.S. at 504. For further discussion of standing requirements and the overbreadth doctrine, see § 12–32, infra.

8. Monaghan, supra note 1, at 3.

9. For examples of overbreadth cases that involve parties seeking only to be judged in accordance with constitutionally valid rules of law, see Schad v. Mount Ephraim, 452 U.S. 61 (1981) (reversing conviction of adult bookstore owner for violation of statute that banned all live entertainment); Gooding v. Wilson, 405 U.S. 518 (1972) (reversing conviction under statute that penalized use of "opprobrious words or abusive language"); Thornhill v. Alabama, 310 U.S. 88, 97–98 (1940) (one prosecuted under an overbroad anti-picketing statute "does not have to sustain the burden of demonstrating" that he could not have been convicted under a more narrowly drawn, constitutional statute covering his activities). Cf. Brandenberg v. Ohio, 395 U.S. 444, 448–49 (1969) (per curiam) (convictions under state statute which forbade "advocat[ing] . . . the duty, necessity or propriety of crime, sabotage, violence or unlawful methods of terrorism" must be reversed because trial judge's instructions to jury did not "refine[ ] the statute's bald definition of the crime in terms of mere advocacy not distinguished from incitement to imminent lawless action.")

expression is small in comparison to the number of instances of unprotected behavior which are the law's legitimate targets. A statute drafted narrowly to reflect a close nexus between the means chosen by the legislature and the permissible ends of government is thus not vulnerable on its face simply because occasional applications that go beyond constitutional bounds can be imagined.[1]

In *Broadrick v. Oklahoma*,[2] the Supreme Court made a strong version of the substantiality requirement explicit and extended it beyond the area of criminal laws barely touching on protected expression: when a statute regulates "conduct" as opposed to "pure speech," its "overbreadth. . . . must not only be real, but substantial as well, judged in relation to the statute's plainly legitimate sweep."[3] State employees in *Broadrick* had challenged Oklahoma statutory provisions forbidding all civil service employees to engage in political fund-raising, belong to any political party committee, be an officer or member of any partisan political club, run for any paid public office, or take part in the management or affairs of any political party or campaign "except to exercise [the] right [as citizens] privately to express . . . opinion[s] and vote."[4] Adopting a view that had been expressed in two dissents in 1971[5] and 1972,[6] the *Broadrick* majority conceded that the language of the state's law seemed to reach such protected acts as wearing campaign buttons and displaying bumper stickers but held that such applications, although substantial in absolute number, were insubstantial *when compared with the law's legitimate applications*.[7] For this reason the Court rejected the employees' facial challenge. Recognizing that a "censorial statute, directed at particular groups or viewpoints"[8] and in that sense regulating "pure speech"[9] could not be saved from overbreadth invalidation by this process of offsetting valid applications against a substantial number of invalid ones, the *Broadrick* majority in effect treated the state's regulation of political activity the way an ordinary trespass or theft statute might be treated. In those settings, however, a doctrine of "comparative substantiality" seems both unavoidable and unlikely to chill or deter much protected speech; to apply that approach to a law dealing with a sensitive area—one bristling with first amendment dangers—is to reject the very premise of overbreadth analysis, by allowing the "sword of Damocles" to hang over a significant range of protected, and yet easily deterred, choices.[10]

§ 12–28

1. See, e.g., Cox v. Louisiana, 379 U.S. 559 (1965) (Cox II) (statute prohibiting picketing "near" courthouse upheld against overbreadth challenge and found to be a "precise, narrowly drawn" regulation, but prosecution held unconstitutional as applied to demonstration which police officials had indicated was permissible).

2. 413 U.S. 601 (1973).

3. Id. at 615.

4. Id. at 602–07 & n. 1.

5. Coates v. Cincinnati, 402 U.S. 611, 617–21 (1971) (White, J., joined by Burger, C.J. and Blackmun, J.).

6. Gooding v. Wilson, 405 U.S. 518, 528–30 (1972) (Burger, C.J.).

7. Broadrick, 413 U.S. at 609–18.

8. Id. at 616.

9. See §§ 12–2, 12–7, supra. The Court has since made clear that the requirement of substantial overbreadth also applies to statutes involving "pure speech." See New York v. Ferber, 458 U.S. 747, 770–71 (1982) (rejecting overbreadth challenge to state statute which prohibited distribution of depictions of sexual performances by children under the age of 16).

10. See Arnett v. Kennedy, 416 U.S. 134, 231 (1974) (Marshall, J., dissenting).

Underlying this shift in approach has been the skepticism of the Nixon appointees to the Supreme Court, joined by Justice White, toward the reality and significance of the deterrence caused by an overbroad law.[11] This skepticism has been nurtured and reinforced by an institutional concern expressed by as ardent a believer in first amendment values as Justice Black. Writing for the majority in *Younger v. Harris*,[12] where the Court required federal judges to abstain from resolving first amendment issues while state prosecutions were pending,[13] Justice Black opined that testing the constitutionality of a statute on its face is to some degree "fundamentally at odds with the function of the federal courts" to resolve concrete cases and controversies.[14] But such a claim hardly supports the Court's obviously troublesome distinction between "pure speech" regulations and "conduct" regulations,[15] and the plain effect of the Burger Court's reluctance to assume the existence of a significant chilling of protected speech is to lift from government the traditionally heavy burden of proving that first amendment rights are not being infringed. Despite a facial appearance of infringement, the upshot is a mounting burden on the *individual* to show that the apparent inhibition of protected expression is in fact highly probable and socially significant.[16]

Recent cases demonstrate, however, that the Court has not abandoned as much as refined the overbreadth doctrine. The key development has been the Court's greater reluctance to strike a law down altogether because of its potential to deter protected expression, and its greater willingness to allow state courts to narrow statutes in the application process.[17] For example, in *New York v. Ferber*[18], the Court upheld without dissent a criminal conviction under a state statute which prohibited the distribution of depictions of sexual performances by children under the age of 16. The Court acknowledged that books and films which depicted child pornography were "pure speech," but still found that the overbreadth would have to be "substantial" in order to invalidate the law—even in the context of a retrospective challenge by someone convicted under it.[19] The Court found no such overbreadth in *Ferber*, even though it acknowledged that "some protected expres-

---

11. See, e.g., Branzburg v. Hayes, 408 U.S. 665 (1972); Laird v. Tatum, 408 U.S. 1 (1972).

12. 401 U.S. 37 (1971).

13. Id. at 43–54. See § 3–30, supra.

14. 401 U.S. at 52.

15. See § 12–7, supra, and note 9, supra.

16. Contrast Speiser v. Randall, 357 U.S. 513 (1958) (invalidating state procedure because it placed burden on individual to show that infringement on free speech was unjustified).

17. Monaghan, supra note 1, at 21–22.

18. 458 U.S. 747 (1982). Justice White's opinion was joined by Chief Justice Burger and Justices Powell, Rehnquist and O'Connor. Justice O'Connor filed a concurring opinion. Justice Brennan, joined by Justice Marshall, filed an opinion concurring in the judgment. Justice Blackmun concurred in the result. Justice Stevens also filed an opinion concurring in the judgment.

19. Id. at 770–71; see § 12–27, note 9, supra. Similarly, in the commercial speech realm, the Court has eliminated anticipatory overbreadth challenges by those whose conduct may permissibly be restricted even if the statute in question might also prohibit some protected activities by others. See, e.g., Friedman v. Rogers, 440 U.S. 1, 10–11 & n. 9 (1979) (upholding state law prohibiting the practice of optometry under a trade name); Ohralik v. Ohio State Bar Ass'n, 436 U.S. 447, 462–63 & n. 20 (1978) (holding that state may discipline a lawyer for in-person solicitation of clients). See also § 12–15, supra.

sion, ranging from medical textbooks to pictorials in the National Geographic," could fall prey to the statute.[20]   Because the Court doubted that these "arguably impermissible applications of the statute amount to more than a tiny fraction of the materials within the statute's reach," [21] neither the conviction nor the statute were disturbed.

In the same spirit, the Court has been increasingly willing to perform reconstructive surgery on overbroad statutes rather than eliminate entire laws, and it has trusted the states to rehabilitate their laws without violating the Constitution.   In *Brockett v. Spokane Arcades, Inc.*[22], Justice White, writing for a 6 to 2 majority, reviewed a lower court decision which, in an anticipatory challenge brought for declaratory and injunctive relief, had invalidated in its entirety a Washington statute aimed at preventing and punishing the publication of obscene material.   The statute declared to be a "moral nuisance" any place "where lewd films are publicly exhibited as a regular course of business" and any place of business "in which lewd publications constitute a principal part of the stock in trade." [23]   The statute defined "lewd," in part, as that which "appeals to the prurient interest."   The word "prurient," in turn, was defined as "that which incites lasciviousness or lust." [24]   Shortly after the law went into effect, several sellers of sexually oriented books and movies sought a declaratory judgment that the statute was "overbroad" and an injunction preventing any prosecutions under it.   The Court of Appeals for the Ninth Circuit held that, "by including 'lust' in its definition of 'prurient,' the Washington state legislature had intended the statute to reach material that merely stimulated normal sexual responses, material that it considered to be constitutionally protected.   Because in its view the statute did not lend itself to a saving construction by a state court and any application of the statute would depend on a determination of obscenity by reference" to an overbroad standard, the Ninth Circuit declared the statute as a whole null and void.[25]

The Supreme Court reversed.   The Court agreed that the law's use of the word "lust" was unacceptably broad and that only "material whose predominant appeal is to a shameful or morbid interest in nudity, sex, or excretion" could permissibly be restricted.[26]   But the Court found the ban on materials that excite only "normal" lust to be

---

20.   458 U.S. at 773.   There was no risk in the case at bar that the defendant might have been convicted for distributing any protected materials.   The case was thus distinguishable from those cited in § 12–27, note 9, supra.   Similarly, in Regan v. Time, Inc., 468 U.S. 641 (1984), the Court, in upholding a law which prohibited most photographic reproductions of U.S. currency against a challenge seeking declaratory and injunctive relief, refused to allow the publisher to raise an overbreadth argument because the record in that case indicated that "the legitimate reach of [the law] 'dwarfs its arguably impermissible applications'." Id. at 651–52, quoting New York v. Ferber, 458 U.S. at 773.

21.   458 U.S. at 773.

22.   472 U.S. 491 (1985).   Justice O'Connor, joined by Chief Justice Burger and Justice Rehnquist, filed a concurring opinion.   Justice Brennan, joined by Justice Marshall, filed a brief dissenting opinion.   Justice Powell did not participate.

23.   Id. at 493.

24.   Id. at 494.

25.   Id.   See J-R Distributors, Inc. v. Eikenberry, 725 F.2d 482 (9th Cir. 1984).

26.   472 U.S. at 498, quoting A.L.I. Model Penal Code, § 207.10(2) (Tent. Draft No. 6, 1957).   See § 12–16, supra.

severable from the ban insofar as it reached genuinely obscene matter. Citing the well-established rule that "a federal court should not extend its invalidation of a statute further than necessary to dispose of the case before it," [27] the Court was "unconvinced that the identified overbreadth is incurable and would taint all possible applications of the statute." [28] *Brockett* presented the Court with a persuasive array of factors in favor of only partial invalidation of the statute: the law contained a plainly constitutional definition of obscenity in addition to the contested phrasing; it included a severability clause; and the state courts had not yet had the opportunity to construe the statute.[29] Thus the Court's decision to avoid the extreme remedy of total invalidation was eminently understandable.[30]

This is not to say, however, that the Court has removed facial invalidation of entire statutes from its arsenal whenever it can imagine some constitutional applications of the contested law. In *Village of Schaumburg v. Citizens for a Better Environment,*[31] the Court by an 8 to 1 vote struck down in its entirety a municipal ordinance which prohibited the solicitation of contributions by charitable organizations that did not use at least 75 percent of their receipts for "charitable"—i.e., non-administrative—purposes. Noting first the settled principle that charitable appeals for funds are within the protection of the first amendment,[32] Justice White's opinion for the Court held that the "75-percent limitation is a direct and substantial limitation on protected activity that cannot be sustained unless it serves a sufficiently strong, subordinating interest that the Village is entitled to protect." [33] The Court rejected the sole argument the Village offered in support of its ordinance: that any organization which uses more than 25-percent of its receipts for fundraising, salaries and overhead is actually a for-profit enterprise. The Court stated simply that "this cannot be true of those organizations that are primarily engaged in research, advocacy, or public education and that use their own paid staff to carry out these functions as well as to solicit public support." [34] Finding no other rationale to support the ordinance and no logical point of severability, the Court had no choice but to strike the law down in full.

27. 472 U.S. at 501, citing, inter alia, Cantwell v. Connecticut, 310 U.S. 296 (1940), and Marsh v. Alabama, 326 U.S. 501 (1946).

28. 472 U.S. at 503.

29. Id. at 506 n. 14; id. at 491–510 (O'Connor, J., concurring). Though not proceeding in overbreadth terms, the United States Court of Appeals for the Seventh Circuit, when rejecting in its entirety the Indianapolis "pornography" statute, raised but then rejected the possibility that part of the ordinance might stand. See American Booksellers Ass'n, Inc. v. Hudnut, 771 F.2d 323 (7th Cir. 1985), aff'd mem. 106 S.Ct. 1172 (1986). Despite the law's "strong severability clause . . . [n]o construction or excision of particular terms could save it [because] the [law's] definition

of 'pornography' is unconstitutional." 771 F.2d at 332. See also § 12–17, supra.

30. However, if a conviction had been obtained under the law in its broad form, under instructions permitting the jury to find obscenity *without* finding any appeal to abnormal lust, then the conviction would have to be reversed whether or not such a finding *could* have been made on the facts at hand. See § 12–27, supra.

31. 444 U.S. 620 (1980). Justice Rehnquist dissented.

32. Id. at 628–32, citing, inter alia, Schneider v. State, 308 U.S. 147 (1939), and Cantwell v. Connecticut, 310 U.S. 296 (1940).

33. 444 U.S. at 636.

34. Id. at 636–37.

The Court went even further four years later in answering a question left open in *Schaumburg*: whether the "constitutional deficiencies in a percentage limitation on funds expended in solicitation are remedied by the possibility of an administrative waiver of the limitation for a charity that can demonstrate financial necessity."[35] Again, the Court found the restriction on charities unacceptably overbroad and invalidated it in full. Justice Blackmun's opinion for the five-Justice majority in *Secretary of State of Maryland v. Joseph H. Munson Co.* found that the law was unlikely to prevent most forms of fraud and stated that "[i]t is equally likely that the statute will restrict First Amendment activity that results in high costs but is itself a part of the charity's goal or that is simply attributable to the fact that the charity's cause proves to be unpopular."[36]

The Court's overbreadth analysis was both a testament to the doctrine's vigor and an excellent study in its current application. The Court sought but could not find a "core of easily identifiable and constitutionally proscribable conduct that the statute prohibits."[37] Thus the flaw in the statute was "not simply that it includes within its sweep some impermissible applications, but that in all its applications it operates on a fundamentally mistaken premise that high solicitation costs are an accurate measure of fraud."[38] Unlike the "lust" definition attached to the state's otherwise clearly permissible obscenity ban in *Brockett*,[39] the statute in *Munson* could not be trimmed of unconstitutional branches: it was rotten at its very root.

---

35. Secretary of State of Maryland v. Joseph H. Munson Co., 467 U.S. 947, 962 (1984), citing Schaumburg, 444 U.S. at 635 n. 9. See § 12–24, supra.

36. 467 U.S. at 967. Justice Stevens filed a concurring opinion. Justice Rehnquist wrote a scathing dissent, which was joined by Chief Justice Burger and Justices Powell and O'Connor. Justice Rehnquist not only found the statute an unexceptionable attempt by Maryland to control "the external, economic relations between charities and professional fundraisers," id. at 979, but also took particular exception to the majority's decision to declare the entire statute unconstitutional rather than invalidating it merely as applied to the parties in this case. Id. at 975–77.

37. Id. at 965–66. See also Houston v. Hill, 107 S.Ct. 2502, 2513 (1987) (invalidating ordinance that forbade interrupting a police officer in the course of duty; "[t]he enforceable portion of this ordinance is a general prohibition of speech that 'simply has no core' of constitutionally unprotected expression to which it might be limited," quoting Smith v. Goguen, 415 U.S. at 578). Similarly, the Court reversed the conviction of an adult bookstore owner for showing live nude dancing in Schad v. Mount Ephraim, 452 U.S. 61 (1981), because the statute, which banned all live entertainment, was overbroad. Because the ordinance prohibited "a wide range of expression that has long been held to be within the protections of the First and Fourteenth Amendments," id. at 65, the defendants could not be convicted under it—even if, under another more narrowly drawn statute, their own actions could permissibly be proscribed. In New York v. Ferber, 458 U.S. 747, 773 (1982), the Court later upheld a conviction for distribution of pornographic depictions of children, even though it acknowledged that "some protected expression . . . would fall prey to the statute." Although the Court did not refer to Schad in Ferber, the two decisions may be harmonized by noting that the Court affords the type of speech at issue in Schad—live entertainment of all kinds—more generous protection than that at issue in Ferber—child pornography. See Ferber, 458 U.S. at 781 (Stevens, J., concurring in the judgment).

38. Munson, 467 U.S. at 966 (footnote omitted).

39. Brockett v. Spokane Arcades, Inc., 472 U.S. 491, 503 (1985).

§ 12–29. The Limited Possibility of Judicial Reconstruction as an Alternative to Facial Invalidation: Trading Overbreadth for Vagueness Where First Amendment Privileges Cannot be Categorically Defined

When a court recognizes situations in which a law could be applied unconstitutionally, why does the court not simply promulgate a saving interpretation under its usual "duty to adopt that construction which will save the statute from constitutional infirmity"?[1] The answer is that a court can adopt an adequate saving construction only if the surviving portion of the statute clearly and unambiguously restricts conduct that is not privileged by the first amendment—and only such conduct. By pruning a statute of its overbroad sections, courts run the risk of leaving the remainder impermissibly vague.

Consider first an example of permissible reconstruction of a statute or of a common-law rule: the Supreme Court's use of the *New York Times Co. v. Sullivan*[2] rule in lawsuits involving defamatory speech perfectly exemplifies the use of a categorical definition to distinguish expressive acts privileged by the first amendment (statements that are not deliberate or reckless falsehoods) from those open to government regulation;[3] rather than holding any state's overbroad rule of liability for defamatory speech void on its face, the Court applies its categorical definition to excise the invalid applications of the state's rule in a single step. Thus, in *Time, Inc. v. Hill*,[4] after holding that a judgment imposing civil liability on a publisher under a state's "right to privacy" statute was rendered impermissible by the first amendment constraints of *New York Times Co. v. Sullivan*, the Court rejected an argument that "the statute should be declared unconstitutional on its face if construed by the New York courts to impose liability without proof of knowing or reckless falsity."[5] While abiding by the general policy of refusing to substitute a Supreme Court interpretation of a state statute for that of the state's own courts,[6] Justice Brennan's majority opinion indirectly achieved the same result—statutory reconstruction—by resting the

---

§ 12–29

1. United States v. Delaware & Hudson Co., 213 U.S. 366, 407 (1909). See also Crowell v. Benson, 285 U.S. 22, 62 (1932); Ashwander v. TVA, 297 U.S. 288, 348 (1936) (Brandeis, J., concurring).

2. 376 U.S. 254 (1964) (first amendment prohibits a public official from recovering damages, under state libel law, for a defamatory falsehood relating to his official conduct unless he proves "actual malice"; that the statement was made with knowledge of its falsity or with reckless disregard of whether it was true or false), discussed in § 12–12, supra.

3. A categorical approach to distinguish privileged from unprivileged expression had also been taken in the commercial speech context, see, e.g., Valentine v. Chrestensen, 316 U.S. 52 (1942) ("purely commercial advertising" not protected by the first amendment). But see Bigelow v. Virginia, 421 U.S. 809 (1975) (newspaper advertisement of out-of-state abortion service held privileged); Virginia State Board of Pharmacy v. Virginia Citizens Consumer Council, Inc., 425 U.S. 748 (1976) (state prohibition of advertisement of drug prices invalid; "commercial speech" not wholly outside the scope of the first amendment privilege). See § 12–15, supra.

4. 385 U.S. 374 (1967).

5. Id. at 397.

6. See, e.g., Smiley v. Kansas, 196 U.S. 447, 455 (1905) ("the interpretation placed by the highest court of the State upon its statutes is conclusive" for the Supreme Court); cf. Railroad Commission of Texas v. Pullman Co., 312 U.S. 496, 499–500 (1941) (federal court abstention appropriate so that state courts may interpret unclear state statute; "the last word" on the meaning of a state statute belongs to the state supreme court). See §§ 3–32, 3–40, supra.

Court's refusal to invalidate the law as a whole upon the express expectation "that the New York courts will apply the statute consistently with the constitutional command." [7]

The risk of introducing vagueness when attempting to reconstruct statutes reveals a structural relationship of general importance in the interplay of overbreadth and vagueness. This relationship is most sharply focused in a hypothetical statute: *"It shall be a crime to say anything in public unless the speech is protected by the first and fourteenth amendments."* This statute is guaranteed not to be overbroad since, by its terms, it literally forbids nothing that the Constitution protects. The statute is nonetheless patently vague, although it is identical with the gloss Chief Justice Rehnquist would apparently put on every law in order to "save" it from an overbreadth challenge. In *Arnett v. Kennedy*,[8] he proposed to solve overbreadth problems by "construing" any challenged statute as excluding all constitutionally protected speech. The problem with that solution is that it simply exchanges overbreadth for vagueness.[9] Indeed, the premise underlying *any* instance of facial invalidation for overbreadth must be that *the Constitution does not, in and of itself, provide a bright enough line to guide primary conduct*, and that a law whose reach into protected spheres is limited *only* by the background assurance that unconstitutional applications will eventually be set aside is a law that will deter too much that is in fact protected.

The discussion of the risk of exchanging overbreadth for vagueness is not meant to show that these doctrines are somehow anomalous in first amendment jurisprudence. As Professor Monaghan has observed, "[i]n reviewing any case involving free expression, the Court invariably accepts the gloss the highest state court has placed on a state statute. To be sure, the statute, however narrowed in the state system, may still be constitutionally infirm; but any such defect is the product of substantive First Amendment principles rather than a special nonseparability restriction imposed on the state courts by the First Amendment." [10] The point is that courts must recognize that litigants are

---

7. Time, Inc. v. Hill, 385 U.S. at 397. See also Brockett v. Spokane Arcades, Inc., 472 U.S. 491, 507 (1985) (striking down only the impermissibly broad portion of a state statute regulating obscenity and finding that "the remainder of the statute retains its effectiveness as a regulation of obscenity"). Cf. New York v. Ferber, 458 U.S. 747, 773 (1982) (in upholding a state prohibition on child pornography, the Court "will not assume that the New York courts will widen the possibly invalid reach of the statute").

8. 416 U.S. 134, 158–63 (1974) (plurality opinion of Rehnquist, J., joined by Burger, C.J., and Stewart, J.).

9. An overbroad statute can be given a saving construction only if it is possible to define a precise category of conduct privileged by the first amendment which can be clearly stated to fall outside the reach of the restructured statute. Otherwise, the overbroad statute remains vague. See, e.g., Aptheker v. Secretary of State, 378 U.S. 500, 515–17 (1964) (" 'constru[ing]' " overbroad statute in order to find its "core of constitutionality" would inevitably inject an element of vagueness into its scope and application; "the plain words would thus become uncertain in meaning . . . if courts proceeded on a case-by-case basis to separate out constitutional from unconstitutional areas of coverage").

10. Monaghan, "Overbreadth," 1981 Sup.Ct.Rev. 1, 21–22. See also Winters v. New York, 333 U.S. 507, 519–20 (1948) (even accepting state court's narrowing interpretation of statute, the Court finds law impermissibly vague).

entitled to be judged according to permissible standards—both before and after courts decide to trim any provisions in a statute.

§ 12–30. Further Limits on the Use of Saving Constructions: Federalism and Separation-of-Powers Considerations

Although a saving construction is possible in any area where the Court may draw on a precise categorical definition of first amendment privilege,[1] considerations of the federal judicial role may prevent the Court from rehabilitating an unconstitutionally overbroad or vague statute. In dealing with state laws, the Court cannot simply substitute a saving reinterpretation of a statute for that authoritatively given the statute by the state's highest court,[2] although in such cases the Supreme Court may of course decline to hold the statute facially void upon the expectation that the state's courts will themselves give it the narrowing construction that the Court has said would save it.[3]

In cases involving federal laws, the Court is mindful that the lawmaking power lies with Congress, and that there is a difference between adopting a saving construction and rewriting legislation altogether.[4] This difference was recognized most dramatically in *Marchetti v. United States*,[5] where the Court effectively barred the enforcement of the federal wagering tax statutes by holding that the fifth amendment was a complete defense to prosecution for noncompliance with the statutory registration requirements because compliance created substantial risks of conviction for violating federal and state gambling laws. The Court declined to save the tax statutes by imposing a restriction, suggested by the government, on prosecutorial use of information obtained as a result of compliance with the registration requirements. Such a use restriction could save the tax, but it might also impede the efforts of federal and state law enforcement authorities by requiring them to establish in each case that their evidence had not

---

§ 12–30

1. See § 12–29, supra.

2. See § 12–29, supra, at note 6. Compare Freedman v. Maryland, 380 U.S. 51, (1965) (invalidating state scheme of prior censorship of obscene films for want of stringent procedural safeguards), with United States v. Thirty Seven Photographs, 402 U.S. 363 (1971) (upholding federal statute prohibiting the importation of obscene materials and providing for seizure by customs officials despite statute's lack of explicit procedural safeguards; Court supplied such safeguards itself).

3. See, e.g., Time, Inc. v. Hill, 385 U.S. 374, 397 (1967), discussed in § 12–29, supra, text at note 4. Justice O'Connor suggested in Brockett v. Spokane Arcades, Inc., that "a federal court should await a definitive construction by a state court rather than precipitously indulging a facial challenge to the constitutional validity of a state statute." 472 U.S. 491, 507 (1985) (O'Connor, J., concurring). Furthermore,

"[s]peculation by a federal court about the meaning of a state statute in the absence of a prior state court adjudication is particularly gratuitous when . . . the state courts stand willing to address questions of state law on certification from a federal court." Id. at 472 U.S. 509, 2805 (citation omitted).

4. See, e.g., United States v. Reese, 92 U.S. 214, 221 (1875) (for the Court to "introduce words of limitation" into overbroad criminal statute in order to make it constitutional "would, to some extent, substitute the judicial for the legislative department. . . . To limit this statute . . . would be to make a new law, not to enforce an old one. This is no part of our duty."); Scales v. United States, 367 U.S. 203, 211 (1961) ("[a]lthough this Court will often strain to construe legislation so as to save it against constitutional attack, it must not . . . carry this to the point of perverting the purpose of a statute.").

5. 390 U.S. 39 (1968).

been discovered on the basis of information derived from the tax and registration schemes.[6] Whether Congress would think those impediments worth enduring to uphold the tax could not be divined by the Court, turning as it would on nonconstitutional policy choices. Accordingly, the Court left the task of rehabilitation to the Congress.

§ 12–31. Relations Between Vagueness and Overbreadth—The Void for Vagueness Doctrine

Vagueness is a constitutional vice conceptually distinct from overbreadth in that an overbroad law need lack neither clarity nor precision,[1] and a vague law need not reach activity protected by the first amendment.[2] As a matter of due process, a law is void on its face if it is so vague that persons "of common intelligence must necessarily guess at its meaning and differ as to its application." [3] Such vagueness occurs when a legislature states its proscriptions in terms so indefinite that the line between innocent and condemned conduct becomes a matter of guesswork. This indefiniteness runs afoul of due process concepts which require that persons be given fair notice of what to avoid,[4] and that the discretion of law enforcement officials, with the attendant dangers of arbitrary and discriminatory enforcement, be limited by explicit legislative standards.[5]

But vagueness is not calculable with precision; in any particular area, the legislature confronts a dilemma: to draft with narrow particularity is to risk nullification by easy evasion of the legislative purpose; to draft with great generality is to risk ensnarement of the innocent in a net designed for others.[6] Because that dilemma can rarely be

6. Id. at 58–60.

§ 12–31

1. See, e.g., Shelton v. Tucker, 364 U.S. 479 (1960) (invalidating as an overbroad restriction on freedom of association an Arkansas statute clearly requiring each state teacher to file annually an affidavit listing without limitation every organization to which he or she belonged or regularly contributed).

2. See, e.g., Lanzetta v. New Jersey, 306 U.S. 451 (1939) (voiding statute making it criminal to be a member of a "gang").

3. Connally v. General Construction Co., 269 U.S. 385, 391 (1926). See generally Note, "The Void-for-Vagueness Doctrine in the Supreme Court," 109 U.Pa.L.Rev. 67 (1960). The Court applies an objective test for determining whether a statute is vague. In upholding a local ordinance requiring licensing for the sale of products "designed or marketed for use" with illegal drugs, the Court found that the law's meaning would be clear to a "business person of ordinary intelligence" and thus held that the law was not impermissibly vague. Village of Hoffman Estates v. Flipside, Hoffman Estates, Inc., 455 U.S. 489, 501 (1982). But, in applying the vagueness doctrine,

courts may scrutinize laws which criminalize omissions more closely than those which penalize affirmative acts. See, e.g., Kolender v. Lawson, 461 U.S. 352 (1983) (invalidating, on vagueness grounds, law which required persons to produce, on police demand, "credible and reliable" identification); Lambert v. California, 355 U.S. 225, 229 (1957) (reversing conviction of individual who violated law which required all persons convicted of felonies to "register" with the police on grounds that the law failed to require "actual knowledge of the duty to register or proof of the probability of such knowledge and subsequent failure to comply").

4. See, e.g., Papachristou v. Jacksonville, 405 U.S. 156, 162 (1972) (holding unconstitutional a vagrancy ordinance drafted in the terms of the archaic English poor laws), and cases collected in Grayned v. Rockford, 408 U.S. 104, 108 n. 3 (1972).

5. See, e.g., Papachristou, 405 U.S. at 162, and cases collected in Grayned, 408 U.S. at 108–09 n. 4.

6. See, e.g., Winters v. New York, 333 U.S. 507, 525 (1948) (Frankfurter, J., dissenting). See also Colten v. Kentucky, 407 U.S. 104, 107 (1972).

resolved satisfactorily, the Supreme Court will not ordinarily invalidate a statute because some marginal offenses may remain within the scope of a statute's language.[7] The conclusion that a statute is too vague and therefore void as a matter of due process is thus unlikely to be triggered without two findings: that the individual challenging the statute is indeed one of the entrapped innocent,[8] and that it would have been practical for the legislature to draft more precisely.[9]

Discussions of vagueness in first amendment cases often borrow "fair notice" concepts from vagueness challenges of other sorts. But in the first amendment area, the objectionable aspects of vagueness need not depend upon the absence of fair notice, for the first amendment's demand for specificity is also a product of the concern for a statute's chilling effect. "Those . . . sensitive to the perils posed by . . . indefinite language, avoid the risk . . . only by restricting their conduct to that which is unquestionably safe. Free speech may not be so inhibited." [10] The fear, in short, is that the "notice" may be *too* effective.[11] As a consequence, the Supreme Court requires more specificity of a statute potentially applicable to expression sheltered by the first amendment than in other contexts,[12] although no doctrinal formulation of the required increment in specificity has seemed possible.

7. See, e.g., Boyce Motor Lines, Inc., v. United States, 342 U.S. 337 (1952) (regulation requiring carriers to "avoid, so far as practicable" "congested" routes held not void for vagueness); United States v. National Dairy Products Corp., 372 U.S. 29 (1963) (provision of Robinson-Patman Act making it unlawful to sell goods at "unreasonably low prices" with the intent of hurting competitors held not unconstitutionally vague as applied to sales below cost where specific intent to destroy competition shown). Compare Palmer v. Euclid, 402 U.S. 544 (1971) ("suspicious person ordinance" making it unlawful to wander about the streets or be out at late or unusual hours held vague, although only "as applied" to appellant who discharged a female passenger from a car late at night and then used a two-way car radio while parked on the street).

8. See Note, supra note 3, at 87.

9. See United States v. Petrillo, 332 U.S. 1, 7–8 (1947). The Court will generally strike down an ordinance for vagueness only if the actual activity proscribed is vaguely defined; if a statute merely uses a vague formulation to subject certain individuals to investigation but the prohibition itself is not unduly vague, the law may stand. See City of Mesquite v. Aladdin's Castle, Inc., 455 U.S. 283, 288–90 (1982) (upholding local ordinance which directs chief of police to consider whether applicants to operate coin-operated amusement establishments have "connections with criminal elements").

10. Baggett v. Bullitt, 377 U.S. 360, 372 (1964) (invalidating loyalty oath for state teachers which required the affiant to swear that he or she will "by precept and example promote respect for the flag" and American institutions and promote "undivided allegiance" to the United States Government.

11. Justice O'Connor's opinion for the Court in Kolender v. Lawson, 461 U.S. 352 (1983), questioned the primacy of lack of notice among the evils associated with vague statutes: "the more important aspect of the vagueness doctrine 'is not actual notice, but the other principal element of the doctrine—the requirement that a legislature establish minimal guidelines to govern law enforcement.' Where the legislature fails to provide such minimal guidelines, a criminal statute may permit 'a standardless sweep [that] allows policemen, prosecutors and juries to pursue their personal predilections.'" Id. at 358, quoting Smith v. Goguen, 415 U.S. 566, 574–75 (1974). See § 12–38, infra. For critical analyses of the Court's approach to the vagueness doctrine, see generally Jeffries, "Legality, Vagueness and the Construction of Statutes," 71 Va.L.Rev. 189, 201–19 (1985), and Dan-Cohen, "Decision Rules and Conduct Rules: On Acoustic Separation in Criminal Law," 97 Harv.L.Rev. 625 (1984).

12. See, e.g., Smith v. Goguen, 415 U.S. 566, 573 (1974) (flag desecration statute that subjects to criminal liability anyone who "treats contemptuously" the United

Because vagueness closely parallels overbreadth in its deterrence of protected expression, the analysis of excessive vagueness in the first amendment area closely parallels that of overbreadth: The expression deterred by a vague statute must be both real and substantial.[13] And a precise and narrow judicial reconstruction must be unavailable.[14] But there is one difference. Overbreadth analysis is often perceived as an exception to the rule that an individual is not ordinarily permitted to litigate the rights of third parties; vagueness is not perceived as such an exception. The next section addresses that apparent anomaly.

§ 12–32. Third Party Standing in First Amendment Litigation: Differences Between Vagueness and Overbreadth

Why should a litigant whose own conduct is not protected by the first amendment, and who could thus be penalized under a narrower or more precise statute, be given a prize—in the form of a ruling invalidating the statute in advance and in its entirety—for bringing to judicial attention a statute's potential unconstitutional applications to third parties?[1] The answer is that there is not likely to be a better party. Those whose expression is "chilled" by the existence of an overbroad or unduly vague statute cannot be expected to adjudicate their own rights, lacking by definition the willingness to disobey the law.[2] In addition, such deterred persons may not have standing to obtain affirmative relief, since the hypothetical "chilling effect" of the mere existence of an overbroad or vague law does not by itself constitute the sort of "injury-in-fact" which confers standing.[3]

States flag is void for vagueness; void for vagueness doctrine "demands a greater degree of specificity" in first amendment as opposed to other contexts). In addition, a precise statute in an area involving first amendment interests reflects a specific legislative judgment which "has focused on the first amendment interests and determined that other governmental policies compel regulation." Grayned v. Rockford, 408 U.S. at 104 n. 5. Cf. Kolender v. Lawson, 461 U.S. 352, 358–59 n. 7 (1983) (striking down, on vagueness grounds, a law requiring persons who walk on city streets to provide "credible and reliable" identification to police and making criminal their failure to do so on the grounds that, inter alia, "when a statute imposes criminal penalties, the standard of certainty is higher").

13. See, e.g., Young v. American Mini Theatres, Inc., 427 U.S. 50 (1976) (zoning ordinance regulating the locations of motion picture theaters featuring "adult" movies "characterized by an emphasis" on sexual matters upheld against vagueness challenge; ordinance considered unlikely to have "significant deterrent effect" on exhibition of films protected by the first amendment). But see Hynes v. Mayor and Council of Borough of Oradell, 425 U.S. 610 (1976) (local ordinance imposing an "identi-

fication" requirement on door-to-door canvassers held invalid solely on vagueness grounds).

14. See, e.g., Screws v. United States, 325 U.S. 91, 98 (1945) (Douglas, J.) (plurality opinion) (interpretation of vague legislation which supports its constitutionality preferred; criminal and conspiracy provisions of federal law punishing "knowing" and "willful" deprivation of constitutionally protected civil rights interpreted to require proof of specific intent in order to avoid question of statute's constitutionality).

§ 12–32

1. See generally Note, "Standing to Assert Constitutional Jus Tertii," 88 Harv.L. Rev. 423 (1974).

2. See, e.g., Gooding v. Wilson, 405 U.S. 518, 521 (1972) (dictum).

3. See, e.g., Laird v. Tatum, 408 U.S. 1, 13–16 (1972) (unlike a claim of "present objective harm," such as threat of imprisonment or unemployment, the allegation of a subjective "chilling effect" produced by the "mere existence, without more" of the Army's domestic surveillance system did not state a claim of injury in fact; federal courts thus lacked jurisdiction to determine whether Army's program was

While this rationale of "chilling effect" thus justifies relaxation of the rule against third-party claims, some nexus is nevertheless required, even in first amendment cases, between the vice of the statute and the conduct of the litigant. Where the vice is vagueness, the litigant asserting the vagueness defense must demonstrate that the statute in question is vague either in all possible applications or at least as applied to the litigant's conduct, and not simply as applied to some others.[4] One may in turn posit two circumstances. A *"perfectly vague"* statute is one which provides no "ascertainable standard for inclusion or exclusion" and is thus vague in all its applications.[5] The ordinance in *Coates v. Cincinnati*[6] made it illegal for "three or more persons to assemble [on] any sidewalk [and] there conduct themselves in a manner annoying to persons passing by."[7] The "annoying" criterion is not vague merely in the sense that it is an imprecise but comprehensible normative standard; it specifies *no standard at all*, because one may *never* know in advance what "annoys some people [but] does not annoy others."[8] Being "perfectly" vague, the ordinance in *Coates* is vague in all its applications and does not present a problem of third-party standing.

Alternatively, a statute may apply without question to a "hard-core" of conduct and apply only uncertainly to other activities. One to whose conduct a statute clearly applies may not challenge it on the basis that it is "vague as applied" to others. In *Parker v. Levy*,[9] the Supreme Court sustained Captain Levy's court-martial for public statements counseling enlisted men under his command to defy orders to go to Vietnam. The Captain was not permitted to argue the vagueness of the articles of the Uniform Code of Military Justice under which he was convicted because the broad scope of the articles (proscribing "conduct unbecoming an officer and gentleman" and "disorders and neglects to the prejudice of good order and discipline") had been narrowed at least partially by authoritative military constructions, and Levy's conduct was clearly within those somewhat more precise proscriptions. He therefore had fair notice that his conduct was punishable.[10]

When the Supreme Court declares a statute void on its face for overbreadth, such a holding implies two conclusions: first, that a saving construction is unavailable, usually because there is no precise

---

overbroad) (dictum inasmuch as litigants asserted no personal chill whatever, see id. at 13–14 n. 7). See § 3–16, supra.

4. See, e.g., Parker v. Levy, 417 U.S. 733, 753–58 (1974).

5. See, e.g., Coates v. Cincinnati, 402 U.S. 611, 614 (1971); Smith v. Goguen, 415 U.S. 566, 578 (1974).

6. 402 U.S. 611 (1971).

7. Id. at 611–12.

8. Id. at 614. So, too, one could never know what "credible and reliable" identification was to be shown to the police in Kolender v. Lawson, 461 U.S. 352, 357–58 (1983).

9. 417 U.S. 733 (1974).

10. In Parker, the Court distinguished Smith v. Goguen, 415 U.S. 566, 573 (1974), and the principle that greater clarity and precision are required of statutes regulating expression than in other contexts, see § 12–31, supra, by emphasizing that the regulations in question were articles of the Uniform Code of Military Justice and that the proscribed conduct in effect occurred in a military enclave. "Because of the factors differentiating military society from civilian society," the less stringent standard of vagueness analysis applicable to criminal statutes regulating economic affairs, see, e.g., United States v. National Dairy Products Corp., 372 U.S. 29, 32–33 (1963), was held to be appropriate; less precision was thus required. 417 U.S. at 757–58.

category of protected conduct which can be clearly enough stated to fall outside the reach of the statute; and second, that to attempt a limiting construction of a statute without such a determinate rule of first amendment privilege would turn an overbroad law into a vague one. Thus an overbroad law, even as enforced against unprotected conduct, is "perfectly vague", since the law could be "saved" only by introducing a serious element of vagueness that would leave *every* person who is subject to the law uncertain whether the law can be *enforced at all* or will instead be held void for vagueness. One might therefore say that the "nexus" provided by a litigant challenging an overbroad law is the facial inseparability of protected expression and the unprotected expression of the litigant. In this sense, the third-party exception is not truly needed in overbreadth cases where a saving construction is unavailable, just as the exception is not available in vagueness cases.

§ 12–33. Facial Invalidation and Substantive Values in First Amendment Jurisprudence: Less Restrictive Alternatives or Hidden Balancing?

The conclusion that a statute is fatally overbroad or impermissibly vague is often accompanied by an assumption that legislatures possess the ingenuity needed to develop statutory schemes essentially as effective as, but less sweeping or ambiguous than, the law judged void. This presumption is often stated in the language of "less restrictive alternatives." [1] In practice, the Court rarely rests a finding of overbreadth or vagueness upon its discovery of a genuinely "less restrictive alternative," [2] although an affirmative showing that any alternative to the statute would be seriously ineffectual might negate the overbreadth or vagueness conclusion. [3] Subject to this possibility, the Court's approach has taken these two first amendment vices as decisive: because a statute is substantially overbroad or impermissibly vague, government *must* make use of less drastic means if it would regulate at all— *whatever* substantive reduction in efficacy a less drastic means might entail. [4]

§ 12–33

1. See, e.g., Shelton v. Tucker, 364 U.S. 479, 488 (1960); see generally Note, "Less Drastic Means and the First Amendment," 78 Yale L.J. 464 (1969).

2. In United States v. Robel, 389 U.S. 258, 267–68 (1967), the Supreme Court expressly refused to inquire into the existence of any practical "less restrictive alternatives." But see Martin v. Struthers, 319 U.S. 141, 147–48 (1943) (holding ordinance banning door-to-door solicitation overbroad where intrusions on householders and dangers of fraud could "so easily be controlled by traditional legal methods").

3. The burden is on government to show that there are no less restrictive alternatives to statutory overbreadth. See Talley v. California, 362 U.S. 60, 66–67 (1960) (Harlan, J., concurring) (striking down ordinance banning all distribution of

anonymous handbills; government had made no showing as to its actual experience with alternative means of preventing fraud, false advertising and libel). See also Thornhill v. Alabama, 310 U.S. 88, 98 (1940). But the refusal of the Court in United States v. Robel, 389 U.S. at 267–68, to enter upon an evaluation of legislative alternatives would seem to imply that only the gravest peril could persuade the Court to accept a representation that it is impossible for government to proceed by narrower means. See Note, "The First Amendment Overbreadth Doctrine," 83 Harv.L. Rev. 844, 917–18 (1970).

4. Contrast the Court's requirement that the restriction on free expression caused by a governmental regulation not aimed at an act's communicative impact be the least restrictive alternative furthering

At the same time, because the Court talks as though its invalidation of an overbroad or vague law leaves open other, essentially as
effective, means of furthering the law's permissible ends, the Court
usually avoids making any overt comparision between the gravity of
the regulatory need and the burden upon activities privileged by the
first amendment but chilled by the law's vagueness or overbreadth.
Implicit in any such holding, of course, is a judgment that the reduced
effectiveness entailed by a less restrictive alternative is outweighed by
the increment in first amendment protection gained by demanding such
an alternative. In *United States v. Robel*,[5] for example, the Court held
that Congress could not prevent every member of the Communist Party
from working in any defense facility; less drastic means would have to
be employed. The implicit judgment was that a rule of thumb which
presumed all Communists to be security risks involved a sacrifice of
associational rights not justified by the possibility that a more individualized screening process might not efficiently weed out all dangerous
party members from sensitive defense jobs.[6]

While *Robel* clearly entailed a decision that the costs of more
individualized screening could not justify the legislature's wholesale
invasion of associational rights, Chief Justice Warren pointedly denied
in his opinion for the Court that the decision turned on any balancing
of interests.[7] Although that denial has been criticized as unpersuasive,[8] it seems more defensible if one recognizes that the "balance"
struck in *Robel* reflects not the Court's analysis of the competing
interests demonstrably present in the particular case, but rather a
general principle of first amendment jurisprudence: government must
sacrifice its marginal regulatory interests in a "buffer zone" where the
statutory scheme, while advancing valid but not compelling purposes
conceivably attainable in no less restrictive way, nonetheless threatens
significant inhibition of protected expression or association.[9] In formulating its rules of privilege in the area of defamation, for example, the
Court has stated that, if "the freedoms of expression are to survive,"
they must have "breathing space that can be purchased only by
allowing some constitutionally unprotected defamatory falsehoods to go
unpunished." [10] The doctrines of overbreadth and vagueness serve
precisely the same function in areas where the Court has not been able
to formulate a determinate rule of first amendment privilege and has
thus been forced to swallow laws whole or invalidate them in their
entirety.

the government's interest. See § 12–23,
supra.

5. 389 U.S. 258 (1967).

6. Cf. United States v. Brown, 381 U.S.
437 (1965) (federal law making it a crime
for a member of the communist party to
serve as an officer or an employee of a
labor union held a bill of attainder), discussed in § 10–4, supra.

7. 389 U.S. at 268 n. 20.

8. See Gunther, "Reflections on Robel:
It's Not What the Court Did But the Way
It Did It," 20 Stan.L.Rev. 1140, 1148 (1968).
Cf. Shelton v. Tucker, 364 U.S. 479, 493
(1960) (Frankfurter, J., dissenting).

9. See Note, "The Void-For-Vagueness
Doctrine in the Supreme Court," 109 U.Pa.
L.Rev. 67, 75–85 (1960).

10. New York Times Co. v. Sullivan,
376 U.S. 254, 271–72 (1964).

In effect, when the Court's choices have thus been limited to two extremes, it has selected a two-tiered mode of accommodation, one that implicitly "balances" *against* government wherever the latter's interest seems dubious or marginal, but reserves the possibility of balancing *for* government whenever its interest is clearly compelling. Reduced to such a two-leveled or bivalent balancing process, little would be gained from more overt talk of balancing as such—talk that, even at its best, is only mildly illuminating. Indeed, far from representing the conclusory and dissembling devices some have seen in them, the doctrines of overbreadth and vagueness capture the essence of a demand that, *in close cases, government must leave speech ample room to breathe.* How best to do that is properly left to the majoritarian branches; when it must be done is a judgment properly enforced by the judiciary.

§ 12–34. Constitutional Limits on the Use of Prior Restraints: Two Meanings of "Prior"

When the first amendment was approved by the First Congress, it was undoubtedly intended to prevent government's imposition of any system of prior restraints similar to the English licensing system under which nothing could be printed without the approval of the state or church authorities.[1] This intention was first invoked by the Supreme Court in the always-cited case of *Near v. Minnesota*[2] to strike down the state's procedure for abating scandalous and defamatory newspapers as public nuisances.[3] The view that prior restraints are especially burdensome on free speech helps explain the Supreme Court's nearly absolute rejection of prior judicial restraints in the Pentagon Papers Case, *New York Times Co. v. United States*,[4] and the Fair Trial Gag Order Case, *Nebraska Press Association v. Stuart.*[5] The prior retraint doctrine has also been applied to void procedurally inadequate schemes of governmental censorship of films,[6] books,[7] and plays;[8] to strike down over-

§ 12–34

1. See Near v. Minnesota, 283 U.S. 697, 713 (1931). Indeed, a common view had been that the first amendment was designed to forbid nothing *but* such restraints. See generally Emerson, "The Doctrine of Prior Restraint," 20 Law & Contemp. Probs. 648 (1955); Mayton, "Toward a Theory of First Amendment Process: Injunctions of Speech, Subsequent Punishment, and the Costs of the Prior Restraint Doctrine," 67 Cornell L.Rev. 245, 247–49 (1982).

2. 283 U.S. 697 (1931).

3. See also Organization for a Better Austin v. Keefe, 402 U.S. 415 (1971) (voiding injunction against distribution of leaflets in residential neighborhood issued to protect appellee's privacy). For a discussion of Near, see Blasi, "Toward a Theory of Prior Restraint: The Central Linkage," 66 Minn.L.Rev. 11, 15–19 (1981).

4. 403 U.S. 713 (1971) (per curiam).

5. 427 U.S. 539 (1976), discussed in § 12–11, supra.

6. See, e.g., Vance v. Universal Amusement Co., 445 U.S. 308 (1980) (per curiam) (striking down obscenity-nuisance statute); Freedman v. Maryland, 380 U.S. 51 (1965); Joseph Burstyn, Inc. v. Wilson, 343 U.S. 495 (1952).

7. See, e.g., Bantam Books, Inc. v. Sullivan, 372 U.S. 58 (1963).

8. See, e.g., Southeastern Promotions, Ltd. v. Conrad, 420 U.S. 546 (1975).

broad permit requirements [9]; and to invalidate discriminatory taxes on the press.[10]

Indeed, the doctrine has been used to invalidate such a variety of restrictions on speech, under such a wide range of conditions, that some scholars have questioned the conceptual clarity of the term.[11] There is much to this criticism, for the Court has often used the cry of "prior restraint" not as an independent analytical framework but rather to signal conclusions that it has reached on other grounds. Only rarely has the Court acknowledged the central feature of prior restraints: the doctrine imposes a special bar on attempts to suppress speech prior to publication, a bar that is distinct from the scope of constitutional protection accorded the material *after* publication.[12] In order to test the extent and strength of the prior restraint doctrine, therefore, one must examine expression that is at least arguably outside the ambit of substantive first amendment protection, yet inside the ban on prior restraints.[13] A frequent pitfall of both courts and commentators is to

9. See, e.g., National Socialist Party v. Skokie, 432 U.S. 43 (1977) (per curiam) (requiring procedural safeguards for state rule that barred Nazis from displaying swastika); Shuttlesworth v. Birmingham, 394 U.S. 147 (1969) (parade permit); Staub v. Baxley, 355 U.S. 313 (1958) (permit to solicit membership in dues-paying organization); Kunz v. New York, 340 U.S. 290 (1951) (permit for religious meeting); Saia v. New York, 334 U.S. 558 (1948) (permit to operate sound amplifiers); Cantwell v. Connecticut, 310 U.S. 296 (1940) (permit to solicit for charitable causes); Lovell v. Griffin, 303 U.S. 444 (1938) (permit to distribute literature). Cf. Carroll v. Princess Anne, 393 U.S. 175 (1968) (injunction against public meeting).

10. See, e.g., Grosjean v. American Press Co., 297 U.S. 233, 250 (1936) (tax on gross receipts of newspapers with circulation over 20,000 copies per week invalid because it was a "deliberate and calculated device in the guise of a tax" to punish critics of Huey Long). The same Court dismissed, for want of a substantial federal question, an appeal of a state judgment upholding the application to newspapers of a nondiscriminatory tax on the gross income of businesses. See Giragi v. Moore, 301 U.S. 670 (1937), dismissing appeal from 49 Ariz. 74, 64 P.2d 819 (1937).

In Murdock v. Pennsylvania, 319 U.S. 105 (1943), and Follett v. McCormick, 321 U.S. 573 (1944), a closely divided Court invalidated, as unconstitutional prior restraints, general and nondiscriminatory occupational license taxes applied to Jehovah's Witnesses selling religious literature. See § 14–13, infra. The decisions distinguished direct taxes on the exercise of first amendment rights from indirect taxes on income, property or sales attributable to protected expression. But cf. City of Corona v. Corona Daily Independent, 115 Cal. App.2d 382, 252 P.2d 56 (1953), cert. denied 346 U.S. 833 (1953) (lower court upheld a license tax on the privilege of doing business as applied to newspapers; Justices Black and Douglas dissented on the authority of Murdock and Follett, 346 U.S. at 834). The alternate, and more persuasive, ground for the decisions in Murdock and Follett is that a tax on non-commercial solicitation falls unevenly, unduly burdening the exercise of expressive rights by those unable to afford more expensive means of communication. See § 12–23, supra; Emerson, The System of Freedom of Expression 421 (1970).

11. See, e.g., Jeffries, "Rethinking Prior Restraint," 92 Yale L.J. 409, 437 (1982): "I suggest that . . . the conventional doctrine of prior restraint be laid to one side. In my judgment, that doctrine is so far removed from its historic function, so variously and discrepantly applied, and so often deflective of sound understanding, that it no longer warrants use as an independent category of First Amendment analysis."

12. See Jeffries, supra note 11, at 410.

13. Activities with no first amendment significance can of course be restricted without regard to the prior restraint doctrine, see Arcara v. Cloud Books, Inc., 106 S.Ct. 3172 (1986) (prostitution), discussed in § 12–36, infra. Cf. S.E.C. v. Lowe, 556 F.Supp. 1359, 1366 (E.D.N.Y. 1983): "Pre-publication restraints are ordinarily justifiable only when the nonprotected character

employ the doctrine in cases involving expression clearly within the first amendment guarantees, in ignorance of the fact that "[w]here the speech in question is in all events guaranteed by the First Amendment, attributing that guarantee to the circumstance of prior restraint is at best irrelevant and often misleading." [14]

Although the first amendment is not an absolute bar to prior restraints, the Supreme Court has repeatedly said that any "system of prior restraints comes to this Court bearing a heavy presumption against its constitutional validity." [15] Apart from the historic stigma attached to the use of prior restraints, what is it that concerns the Court? Plainly, it is not the mere existence of "restraint," since an individual ordinarily assumes a risk of subsequent punishment for conduct eventually found to be constitutionally unprotected.[16] The trouble is evidently that the restraint is "prior," but prior to what? The Court has given two answers: [17] prior to a communication's dissem-

of the content is ascertainable with 'relative certainty' prior to dissemination" (citing first edition of this treatise).

14. Jeffries, supra note 11, at 411. See also Nebraska Press Ass'n v. Stuart, 427 U.S. 539, 598 (1976) (Brennan, J., concurring in judgment) ("any immunity from punishment subsequent to publication of given material applies *a fortiori* to immunity from suppression of that material before publication"). For example, in Secretary of State of Maryland v. Joseph H. Munson Co., 467 U.S. 947 (1984), the Court invalidated a Maryland statute that prohibited charities engaged in fundraising from paying in administrative expenses any more than 25% of the amount raised. As an enforcement mechanism, the rule empowered the Maryland Secretary of State to deny registration to fundraisers not in compliance with the 25% limit, which gave rise to the charge of "prior restraint." Id. at 969. The Court determined that the law, by prohibiting solicitation where the charity was not in compliance with the percentage limitation, "impose[d] a direct restriction on protected First Amendment activity." Id at 967. Having reached that substantive result, the Court correctly noted that the procedural prior restraint issue was irrelevant: "whether the statute regulates before- or after-the-fact makes little difference in this case." Id. at 969. Since the state was aiming at an unconstitutional substantive result, the Court viewed the prior restraint issue as at best redundant—not independently determinative. Some scholars have levelled a similar criticism at the conventional interpretation of Near v. Minnesota, 283 U.S. 697 (1931). See Jeffries, supra note 11, at 416: "The real defect [in the statute at issue in Near] was the substan-

tive standard for authorizing suppression"—since the statute authorized judicial abatement of any newspaper or other periodical deemed "malicious, scandalous, and defamatory." 283 U.S. at 701.

15. Bantam Books, Inc. v. Sullivan, 372 U.S. 58, 70 (1963); New York Times Co. v. United States (Pentagon Papers Case), 403 U.S. 713, 714 (1971) (per curiam); Nebraska Press Ass'n. v. Stuart, 427 U.S. 539, 556–59 (1976). See A. Bickel, The Morality of Consent 61 (1975).

16. Indeed, in some instances the chilling effect on the press of subsequent punishment may far outweigh that of prior restraint. Consider, for example, the editor of a small newspaper contemplating whether to publish a possibly defamatory article. If sued after the fact, the newspaper could be ruined financially. If subjected to a prior restraint, the editor's only loss may be the sunk costs of writing the article. In such a situation, a system of exclusively prior restraints may well produce more "vehement, caustic, and sometimes unpleasantly sharp" debate, New York Times Co. v. Sullivan, 376 U.S. 254, 270 (1964), than a scheme of ex post punishments. See Mayton, supra note 1, at 246: "the preference for subsequent punishment over injunctive relief diminishes the exercise of free speech." But see Hunter, "Toward a Better Understanding of the Prior Restraint Doctrine: A Reply to Professor Mayton," 67 Cornell L.Rev. 283 (1982).

17. The case law reflects greater confusion than the text suggests. "Despite an ancient and celebrated history, the doctrine of prior restraints remains today curiously confused and unformed." Emerson, supra note 1, at 649.

ination,[18] or prior to "an adequate determination that [the expression] is not protected by the First Amendment." [19]

While both meanings may describe a particular case, separately considered they suggest two distinct concerns. In some cases the primary concern is that any restraint before dissemination, however temporary, allows the government to destroy the immediacy of the intended speech, overriding the individual's choice of a persuasive moment or an editor's decision of what is newsworthy; dissemination delayed may prove tantamount to dissemination denied.[20] In other cases the primary concern is that any system of censorship insufficiently constrained by the safeguards of the judicial process is apt to overreach; censors uncontrolled by courts tend to deny publication to material protected by the first amendment. In §§ 12–35 and 12–36, we consider pre-publication restraints; §§ 12–37 to 12–39 discuss restraints prior to an adequate judicial determination of first amendment issues.

§ 12–35. Pre-Publication Restraints: Their Procedural Significance

The extraordinary power of a prior restraint to foreclose timely expression is derived primarily from the body of procedural rules which form a backdrop to the doctrines in this field.[1] An individual who speaks, or a newspaper that publishes, is ordinarily free in a subsequent criminal prosecution to assert the claim that the speech or publication was protected by the first amendment. But when a court has issued an injunction, anyone who ignores it may forfeit the right to assert that constitutional defense in a subsequent prosecution.[2] The so-

---

18. See, e.g., Southeastern Promotions, Ltd. v. Conrad, 420 U.S. 546, 559 (1975): "[A] free society prefers to punish the few who abuse rights of speech *after* they break the law than to throttle them and all others beforehand. It is always difficult to know in advance what an individual will say, and the line between legitimate and illegitimate speech is often so finely drawn that the risks of freewheeling censorship are formidable."

19. Pittsburgh Press Co. v. Pittsburgh Commission on Human Relations, 413 U.S. 376, 390 (1973) (order requiring newspaper to cease placing help wanted advertisements in sex-designated columns, stayed during pendency of judicial proceedings, held not a prior restraint once court had authoritatively ruled that the practice was unprotected speech).

20. See Carroll v. Princess Anne, 393 U.S. 175, 182 (1968); Wood v. Georgia, 370 U.S. 375, 392 (1962); Pennekamp v. Florida, 328 U.S. 331, 346–47 (1946); Bridges v. California, 314 U.S. 252, 268–69 (1941).

§ 12–35

1. The heightened fear of prior restraints also derives from the fact that they are issued without any of the elaborate safeguards that normally attend a criminal prosecution. See Bantam Books, Inc. v. Sullivan, 372 U.S. 58, 69–70 (1963); Monaghan, "First Amendment 'Due Process,'" 83 Harv.L.Rev. 518, 543–44 (1970).

2. Even if the procedural rules assuring this result were relaxed or abandoned as some propose, see Redish, "The Proper Role of the Prior Restraint Doctrine in First Amendment Theory," 70 Va.L.Rev. 53, 97 (1984) (proposing that the collateral bar rule should apply only where an injunction is issued "after a full and fair hearing by a competent judicial tribunal"); Note, "Defiance of Unlawful Authority," 83 Harv.L.Rev. 626, 639–47 (1970), it might well remain the case that prepublication restraints, especially those affirmatively singling out the would-be disseminator, would deter far more protected conduct than criminal statutes ordinarily would. The latter is essentially a mute, impersonal threat; being told personally not to publish is apt to cause more second thoughts—no matter what defenses are ultimately available. See Blasi, "Toward a Theory of Prior Restraint: The Central Linkage," 66 Minn.L.Rev. 11, 35–38 & 85–88 (1981) (arguing that self-censorship would still occur even without the collateral bar rule because of the personalized nature of injunc-

called "collateral bar rule" insists that "a court order must be obeyed until it is set aside, and that persons subject to the order who disobey it may not defend against the ensuing charge of criminal contempt on the ground that the order was erroneous or even unconstitutional." [3] The continued vitality of the collateral bar rule is in doubt; the Supreme Court has sometimes declined to follow it, [4] and lower courts have curtailed its reach. [5] But it is still frequently invoked, and whether the constitutional defense is lost depends on the source of the regulation.

If a statute or regulation is *void on its face* because it is unconstitutionally overbroad or impermissibly vague or both, an individual may refuse to comply with the law's requirements and still raise the law's facial invalidity as a defense in a subsequent prosecution under it. [6] This rule was applied and elaborated in *Shuttlesworth v. Birmingham*, [7] in which the Supreme Court overturned a conviction for engaging in a civil rights march in violation of a local ordinance which required a parade permit but which, as written, was overbroad and therefore facially void. In reviewing Shuttlesworth's conviction, the Alabama Supreme Court construed the language of the ordinance so as to bring it within constitutionally permissible limits. It was argued before the Supreme Court that the statute, so construed, was not void on its face, and that Shuttlesworth could no longer challenge its constitutionality. [8] Justice Stewart's majority opinion disagreed, contending that, at the time the permit was refused, it "would have taken extraordinary

tions and more aggressive, "expeditious enforcement" by prosecutors).

3. Barnett, "The Puzzle of Prior Restraint," 29 Stan.L.Rev. 539, 552 (1977). At least one writer has concluded that the collateral bar rule provides the only cogent explanation why "injunctions plausibly can be claimed to have a First Amendment impact significantly greater than the threat of subsequent punishment." Jeffries, "Rethinking Prior Restraint," 92 Yale L.J. 409, 431 (1983). Some lower courts have held that certain judicial orders prohibiting publication are not prior restraints precisely because they are not subject to the collateral bar rule. See, e.g., Chicago Council of Lawyers v. Bauer, 522 F.2d 242, 248–49 (7th Cir. 1975), cert. denied 427 U.S. 912 (1976); Waldo v. Lakeshore Estates, Inc., 433 F.Supp. 782, 788 (E.D. La. 1977), appeal dismissed 579 F.2d 642 (5th Cir.1978).

4. See, e.g., Maness v. Meyers, 419 U.S. 449 (1975) (allowing privilege against self-incrimination to be invoked at contempt hearing for failure to produce evidence); Branzburg v. Hayes, 408 U.S. 665 (1972) (permitting first amendment newsgathering defense to be raised in contempt proceedings for failure to testify).

5. See, e.g., In re Timmons, 607 F.2d 120 (5th Cir. 1979); In re Halkin, 598 F.2d 176 (D.C. Cir. 1979); Goldblum v. NBC, 584 F.2d 904 (9th Cir. 1978); Glen v. Hongisto, 438 F.Supp. 10 (N.D. Cal. 1977); Cooper v. Rockford Newspapers, Inc., 50 Ill.App.3d 250, 8 Ill.Dec. 508, 365 N.E.2d 746 (1977). Some states have refused to adopt the collateral bar rule as a matter of state equity law. See, e.g., State v. Sperry, 79 Wash.2d 69, 483 P.2d 608 (1971); In re Berry, 68 Cal.2d 137, 65 Cal.Rptr. 273, 436 P.2d 273 (1968).

6. See, e.g., Staub v. Baxley, 355 U.S. 313 (1968) (holding that a labor organizer prosecuted for soliciting membership in her union without a permit could raise in her defense the facial unconstitutionality of the law); Lovell v. Griffin, 303 U.S. 444, 452–53 (1938) ("As the ordinance is void on its face, it was not necessary for appellant to seek a permit under it. She was entitled to contest its validity in answer to the charge against her").

7. 394 U.S. 147 (1969).

8. See Cox v. New Hampshire, 312 U.S. 569, 576 (1941) (upholding convictions for violation of a state statute prohibiting a "parade or procession" upon a public street without a license where subsequently the New Hampshire Supreme Court had narrowly construed the statute to limit the discretion of the licensing authority to considerations of time, place, and manner exclusively).

clairvoyance" for anyone to predict the subsequent narrowing construction.[9]

In contrast, a licensing statute *valid on its face* may not be ignored even if it has been invalidly applied. In *Poulos v. New Hampshire*,[10] the Supreme Court held that, because the relevant licensing law was constitutional *on its face*, an applicant who had been improperly refused a permit to hold religious services in a public park should have sought available judicial relief, even at the cost of some delay, rather than holding the services and attempting to defend against the subsequent criminal prosecution by pointing to the permit's unlawful refusal. However, the obligation to obey a facially valid licensing requirement is dissolved if the applicant could not obtain prompt judicial review of the administrative decision refusing the applicant's request for the license.[11]

It is much more difficult in practice to ignore an injunction and then raise the defense of its unconstitutionality against a subsequent contempt charge. In *Walker v. Birmingham*,[12] a state court issued an injunction prohibiting parades without a permit. The language of the injunction tracked the language of the city ordinance which the Supreme Court later found void on its face in *Shuttlesworth*. The Court nonetheless upheld a contempt conviction for violating the injunction, on the ground that the demonstrators, not having challenged the injunction in court before marching, could not assert the unconstitutionality of the injunction in the contempt proceedings.[13] The Court indicated in dictum that an individual could defend a conceded violation of an injunction only by showing (1) that the court was without in personam or subject matter jurisdiction to issue the injunction,[14] or (2)

9. Shuttlesworth, 394 U.S. at 153. The Court did not decide whether, when expeditious judicial relief is available, rejected permit applicants must seek a narrowing construction of an apparently void law as a precondition to a facial challenge.

10. 345 U.S. 395 (1953).

11. A narrower reading of Poulos would emphasize that there was a long interval (seven weeks) between the refusal of the permit and the date of the scheduled service, during which the defendant could have obtained judicial review. Id. at 420 (Frankfurter, J., concurring). This interpretation of Poulos was approved by the Court in Shuttlesworth, 394 U.S. at 155 n. 4. See also § 12–39, infra.

12. 388 U.S. 307 (1967).

13. Id. Justice Stewart, writing for a bare majority, stressed the complete failure of the defendants to seek dissolution of the injunction before disobeying it and concluded that "respect for judicial process is a small price to pay for the civilizing hand of law." Id. at 321. The four dissenters found the ordinance invalid on its face and thought that its power to command respect gained nothing from its restatement in a

court order. Id. at 328 (Warren, C.J., joined by Brennan and Fortas, JJ., dissenting; id. at 345–46 (Brennan, J., joined by Warren, C.J., Douglas and Fortas, JJ., dissenting). For critical commentary, see Rodgers, "The Elusive Search for the Void Injunction: Res Judicata Principles in Criminal Contempt Proceedings," 49 B.U.L.Rev. 251, 270–84 (1969); Selig, "Regulation of Street Demonstrations by Injunction: Constitutional Limitations on the Collateral Bar Rule in Prosecutions for Contempt," 4 Harv.Civ.Rts.-Civ.Lib.L.Rev. 135 (1968).

14. Walker, 388 U.S. at 315. A court has jurisdiction to issue a temporary restraining order, at least where necessary to preserve the status quo, until the court has the opportunity to decide whether it has jurisdiction over the case itself. See United States v. United Mine Workers, 330 U.S. 258, 293 (1947) (upholding criminal contempt conviction of union for violation of restraining order although Norris-La Guardia Act presumably denied the issuing court jurisdiction). See generally Cox, "The Void Order and the Duty to Obey," 16 U.Chi.L.Rev. 86 (1948).

that the injunction was not only an unconstitutional prior restraint, but that its challengers had sought judicial review before disobeying it "and had met with delay or frustration of their constitutional claims," thus threatening the timely exercise of first amendment rights,[15] or (3) that the injunction was "transparently invalid." [16]   But this last argument is plagued by a curious paradox: if a court recognizes a broad "transparent invalidity" exception, it may undermine the prior restraint doctrine by virtually eliminating the collateral bar rule. When a person can violate an injunction and then argue as a defense that it was an unconstitutional prior restraint, the injunction is no different in practice from a statute.[17]

Given the rules ordinarily requiring appellate challenge rather than open defiance of prior restraints, it becomes crucial to consider the standard by which such restraints will be judged in the appellate process—the topic of § 12–36.

§ 12–36. Constitutionally Permissible Prior Restraints

The Supreme Court has spoken of constitutionally permissible prior restraints as "exceptional cases." [1]   This impression has been reinforced by the Court's decisions refusing to perceive threats to

15. Walker, 388 U.S. at 318. That the validity of an order may be challenged in a contempt proceeding if there was no opportunity for effective review of the order prior to its violation is clear from United States v. Ryan, 402 U.S. 530 (1971) (since an order denying a motion to quash a grand jury subpoena duces tecum is not appealable, it may be disobeyed and the validity of the order raised on appeal from the contempt proceedings). See generally Wright, 3 Federal Practice and Procedure: Criminal § 702 (1982). But the mere opportunity for review is not alone decisive. Where time does not allow an adequate remedy, the order may be violated without losing the constitutional defense. See, e.g., Thomas v. Collins, 323 U.S. 516 (1945) (reversing contempt conviction of union organizer served six hours before his scheduled speech with a temporary restraining order which enjoined him from soliciting union members without first obtaining an organizer's card as required by Texas statute; although defendant had disobeyed the order, the Court heard and sustained his contention that the order and the statute were unconstitutional prior restraints).

16. See Walker, 388 U.S. at 315; United States v. Dickinson, 465 F.2d 496, 509–10 (5th Cir. 1972). See also In re Providence Journal Co., 809 F.2d 63 (1st Cir. 1986) (reversing criminal contempt sanction applied to newspaper that published, in violation of a temporary restraining order, private materials obtained from illegal FBI surveillance program). The First Circuit limited its holding to "transparently

void" orders and maintained that the collateral bar rule still applied to "arguably proper orders," id. at 68, while admitting that the dividing line between the two is "not always distinct." Id. at 69. The court's reasoning, however, seemed to imply that *all* prior restraints "upon the right of the press to communicate news" that involve "pure speech"—as opposed to conduct—would be "transparently invalid" because they faced a "presumption of unconstitutionality" that was "virtually insurmountable." Id. Despite its protestations to the contrary, the court of appeals may thus have erected in effect a categorical prohibition on prior press restraints.

17. See Nat'l L.J., Jan. 26, 1987, at 39, col. 2 (quoting Prof. Stephen Barnett). Cf. Vance v. Universal Amusement Co., 445 U.S. 308, 324 (1980) (White, J., joined by Rehnquist, J., dissenting) (arguing that a particular injunction should be upheld because it "does not impose a traditional prior restraint" and is "functionally indistinguishable from a criminal obscenity statute").

§ 12–36

1. Near v. Minnesota, 283 U.S. 697, 716 (1931). In dictum, Chief Justice Hughes gave three illustrations of such "exceptional cases": (1) restraints during wartime to prevent the disclosure of military deployments or obstruction of the military effort, (2) enforcement of obscenity laws, and (3) enforcement of laws against incitement to acts of violence or revolution. See id. at 716.

national security,[2] to the sixth amendment rights of criminal defendants,[3] to the psychological health of Holocaust survivors,[4] or to a homeowner's privacy [5] as sufficiently exceptional to justify prior restraints. But prior restraints have been approved in the seemingly less momentous areas of film censorship,[6] commercial advertising,[7] and permit requirements to use public places for expressive activities.[8] The *relative importance* of the government's interests therefore cannot explain the cases.

Nor does it help to distinguish situations in which the "speech" involved does not merit first amendment protection from those in which it does merit such protection, the latter alone deserving the benefit of the full-blown presumption against prior restraints.[9] A

2. See New York Times Co. v. United States, 403 U.S. 713 (1971).

3. See Nebraska Press Association v. Stuart, 427 U.S. 539 (1976). But see KPNX Broadcasting Co. v. Arizona Superior Court, 459 U.S. 1302 (1982) (Rehnquist, Circuit Justice) (denying stay of state trial court order that directed that all sketches of jurors be reviewed by the court before being broadcast on television).

4. See National Socialist Party v. Skokie, 432 U.S. 43 (1977) (per curiam) (holding that if a state wished to impose a prior restraint such as a prohibition on displays of the swastika during a Nazi rally, the state's courts must either provide "immediate appellate review" or allow a stay of the restraint pending review). See also Collin v. Smith, 447 F.Supp. 676 (N.D. Ill. 1978), affirmed 578 F.2d 1197 (7th Cir. 1978), cert. denied 439 U.S. 916 (1978), which overturned several town ordinances aimed at barring the proposed march by a group of neo-Nazis in Skokie, Illinois, through an area populated by Jews, many of whom were concentration camp survivors. The Seventh Circuit rejected Skokie's justifications for the ordinances, holding that speech which inflicts such "psychic trauma" is "indistinguishable in principle from speech that 'invite[s] dispute . . . [or] induces a condition of unrest, . . . or even stirs people to anger.'" 578 F.2d at 1206, quoting Terminiello v. Chicago, 337 U.S. 1 (1949) (reversing conviction for making race-baiting statements under statute banning speech that "stirs public to anger"). The court concluded that the shock effect of the words could only be "attributed to the content of ideas expressed," 578 F.2d at 1206, quoting Street v. New York, 394 U.S. 576, 592 (1969) (holding that the statement "we don't need no damn flag," made while burning an American flag, was not so "inherently inflammatory" as to come within the class of "fighting words"), and maintained that, under the first amendment, the state could no more restrict a Nazi rally in Skokie than it could prohibit a

civil rights march in Birmingham. For a discussion of Skokie as an exercise in the application of neutral principles, see L. Tribe, Constitutional Choices 219–20 (1985).

5. See Organization for a Better Austin v. Keefe, 402 U.S. 415 (1971).

6. See Times Film Corp. v. Chicago, 365 U.S. 43 (1961); Fehlhaber v. North Carolina, 675 F.2d 1365 (4th Cir. 1982) (obscenity nuisance statute).

7. See, e.g., Posadas de Puerto Rico Associates v. Tourism Co. of Puerto Rico, 106 S.Ct. 2968 (1986); Donaldson v. Read Magazine, 333 U.S. 178, 189–191 (1948); FTC v. Standard Education Society, 302 U.S. 112 (1937); E. F. Drew & Co. v. FTC, 235 F.2d 735, 739–740 (2d Cir. 1956), cert. denied 352 U.S. 969 (1957), cited in Virginia State Board of Pharmacy v. Virginia Citizen's Consumer Council, 425 U.S. 748, 771–72 n. 24 (1976). See also note 8, infra.

8. See, e.g., Cox v. New Hampshire, 312 U.S. 569 (1941) (upholding narrowly drawn parade permit law).

9. See Nebraska Press Association, 427 U.S. at 590–91 (Brennan, J., joined by Stewart and Marshall, JJ., concurring in judgment). In Lowe v. Securities and Exchange Comm'n, 472 U.S. 181 (1985), for example, the Court was faced with a challenge to the Investment Advisors Act of 1940 by the publisher of a semimonthly newsletter containing investment advice and commentary. Lowe was convicted of several securities-related offenses: misappropriating funds from an investment client; engaging in the business of investment advice without filing the required registration application with the regulatory authority; tampering with evidence to cover up the fraud of an investment client; and stealing from a bank. Id. at 183. The Securities and Exchange Commission (SEC) revoked Lowe's registration under the Act and sought an injunction to prevent him from publishing or distributing investment advice newsletters in the future. Lowe

particular communication cannot authoritatively be called protected or unprotected at a point when, by definition, no court has yet determined the constitutional question. A licensing requirement for all films entangles non-obscene films along with those that would ultimately be held obscene. And speech in war-time which reveals military deployments to the enemy is not "protected" speech if the Court will not protect it. A more satisfactory resolution may be reached by abstracting the general characteristics of constitutionally permissible prior restraints from the list of exceptions the Court has approved officially or in dictum. The generalization which emerges from this analysis is a narrow set of circumstances in which the presumption against prior restraints may be overcome—where the expected loss from impeding speech in advance is minimized by the unusual clarity of the prepublication showing of harm.

In *New York Times Co. v. United States*,[10] the government sought to prevent the publication by the New York Times and the Washington Post of the Pentagon Papers, classified documents dealing with United States activities in the Vietnam war prior to 1968. The government's claim was that publication of the documents would prolong the war by providing the enemy with helpful information and would embarrass the United States in the conduct of its diplomacy. The government sought to fit its case within the military security exception to the prohibition against prior restraints suggested by Chief Justice Hughes in dictum in

contended in part that the SEC's injunction was an invalid prior restraint. A district court denied for the most part the SEC's injunctive relief, determining that Lowe's publications were protected by the first amendment and that the Act must be construed to permit a publisher who is willing to comply with the Act's reporting requirements to register for the limited purpose of publishing such material. See S.E.C. v. Lowe, 556 F.Supp. 1359, 1366 (E.D.N.Y. 1983). The circuit court of appeals reversed, holding that Lowe's history of criminal conduct justified the characterization of his publications as "potentially deceptive commercial speech." 725 F.2d 892, 901 (2d. Cir. 1984). The Supreme Court overturned the injunction on the ground that Lowe was exempted from the Act's coverage by virtue of section 202(a) (11)(D), which excludes from the Act's definition of "investment advisor" any person who is "the publisher of any bona fide newspaper, news magazine, or business or financial publication of general or regular circulation." 472 U.S. at 187. The Court thus avoided "the constitutional issue [that it had] granted certiorari to decide." Id. at 211. Regardless of the *substantive* constitutional protection accorded to Lowe's speech, the SEC's injunction would have been *procedurally* invalid unless it had issued subsequent to a proper judicial determination that the speech in question was unprotected. As Thomas Emerson has

pointed out, "the doctrine deals with limitations of form rather than substance." Emerson, "The Doctrine of Prior Restraint," 20 Law & Contemp. Probs. 648 (1955). Product and service—especially professional service—advertisements present hard cases, because they involve a strong potential for consumer deception and confusion. See, e.g., Zauderer v. Office of Disciplinary Counsel, 471 U.S. 626, 676 (1985) (O'Connor, J., joined by Burger, C.J., and Rehnquist, J., concurring in part, concurring in the judgment in part, and dissenting in part) (suggesting that "state regulation of professional advice in advertisements is qualitatively different from regulation of claims concerning commercial goods and merchandise, and is entitled to greater deference"). Nevertheless, the Court has adhered to the principle that restrictions upon such advertising may be "no broader than reasonably necessary to prevent the deception." In re R.M.J., 455 U.S. 191, 203 (1982). And the remedy against potentially misleading advertising "in the first instance is not necessarily a prohibition but preferably a requirement of disclaimers or explanation," id., citing Bates v. State Bar of Arizona, 433 U.S. 350, 375 (1977). The topic of commercial speech is discussed in § 12–15, supra.

10. 403 U.S. 713 (1971) (per curiam).

Near v. Minnesota.[11] The Court held that the government had not met the heavy burden of justifying a prior restraint.[12] While a majority of the Justices was prepared to believe that the publication of the documents would probably be harmful to the Nation,[13] they were not persuaded that the publication of the Papers would *surely* cause the harm alleged by the government.[14] Unlike the situation hypothesized by Chief Justice Hughes—the publication of "the sailing dates of transports or the number and location of troops" [15]—the causal allegations in the Pentagon Papers Case plainly could not be established as a matter of substantial certainty rather than speculation.[16] Only the actual publication of the documents could determine the issue.

By way of contrast, relative certainty can ordinarily be obtained in the context of prepublication restraints on the publication of obscene material or commercial advertisements. The existence of obscenity and the falsity of an advertiser's factual representations need not depend on contextual elements which take shape only after the material's dissemination. Obscenity, as defined by the Court, exists in the eye of the legal finder of fact as surrogate for the "community;" [17] the falsity of an advertiser's claims may be tested by reference to the information which the advertiser may be expected to have at hand to support its factual representations.[18] A court's determination that material is obscene or an advertisement false is thus as plausible before as after the communication's publication.

This argument applies to an injunction that prohibits the dissemination of those specific materials determined obscene in a judicial proceeding. It cannot account, however, for the increasingly common use of the blanket or "standards" injunction, which bars the distribution of unnamed "obscene" materials and leaves the individual to interpret the term for himself.[19] The standards injunction is frequently authorized by state obscenity-nuisance statutes, which define a "nui-

11. Near, 283 U.S. at 716.

12. New York Times Co. v. United States, 403 U.S. 713 (1971) (per curiam). See Henkin, "The Right to Know and the Duty to Withhold: The Case of the Pentagon Papers," 120 U.Pa.L.Rev. 271 (1971); "Developments in the Law—The National Security Interest and Civil Liberties," 85 Harv.L.Rev. 1130, 1189–1244 (1972).

13. Cf. Nebraska Press Association, 427 U.S. at 591–92 (Brennan, J., concurring in the judgment).

14. See New York Times Co., 403 U.S. at 726–27 (Brennan, J., concurring) (government must show that disclosure "must inevitably, directly, and immediately cause the occurrence of an event kindred to imperiling the safety of a transport already at sea. . . ."); id. at 730 (Stewart, J., joined by White, J., concurring) (government must show that disclosure "will surely result in direct, immediate, and irreparable damage to our Nation or its people").

15. Near, 283 U.S. at 716.

16. Cf. Nebraska Press Association, 427 U.S. at 563 (Burger, C.J., opinion for the Court) (trial court's determination that prejudicial publicity *could* impinge on defendant's fair trial right does not justify a prior restraint on publication; the conclusion as to the impact of publicity was "speculative"). See discussion in § 12–11, supra.

17. Of course the point holds only as to facially obscene material, not as to matter whose obscenity depends on pandering or on exploiting a special audience. See § 12–16, supra.

18. See Virginia State Board of Pharmacy, 425 U.S. at 777 (Stewart, J., concurring).

19. The phrase "standards injunction" was coined by Professor Rendleman. See Rendleman, "Civilizing Pornography: The Case for an Exclusive Obscenity Nuisance Statute," 44 U.Chi.L.Rev. 509, 555 (1977).

sance" to include obscene materials and incorporate the definition of "obscene" announced by the Supreme Court in *Miller v. California.*[20] Since the standards injunction operates against materials that have not yet been determined to be obscene, it appears to violate the prior restraint doctrine.[21] But this argument is too simple: a criminal statute that barred exhibition of obscene films and imposed subsequent punishment on violators—concededly constitutional—would trigger, at first blush at least, the same self-censorship behavior among theater owners called upon to define for themselves the term "obscenity."[22] The Supreme Court, in *Vance v. Universal Amusement Co.*,[23] invalidated on different grounds a Texas public nuisance statute that authorized state judges to enjoin, on the basis of a showing that a theater had exhibited obscene films in the past, the future exhibition of movies not yet found to be obscene. The majority argued that the statute restrained speech to a much greater extent than a comparable criminal rule that punished exhibitions after they occurred. The Court accepted a lower court's interpretation of the statute, which maintained that "a short-lived temporary restraining order could be issued on the basis of an ex parte showing" of obscenity and that "a temporary injunction of indefinite duration could be obtained on the basis of a showing of probable success on the merits."[24] The Court thus invalidated the Texas statute because of "the absence of any special safeguards governing the entry and review of orders restraining the exhibition of named or unnamed motion pictures."[25] Whether or not the Court in fact interpreted the Texas law correctly,[26] the Court's decision in *Vance* not to ground its opinion on the inherent characteristics of the standards injunction paved the way for states to insulate nuisance statutes from constitutional attack—by incorporating into them the necessary

---

20. 413 U.S. 15 (1973), discussed in § 12–16, supra. At least nine states and "an indeterminable number of municipalities" have passed nuisance statutes specifically targeted at obscenity. Note, "Enjoining Obscenity As a Public Nuisance and the Prior Restraint Doctrine," 84 Colum.L.Rev. 1616, 1617 (1984).

21. See id. at 1619–20.

22. See Vance v. Universal Amusement Co., 445 U.S. 308, 320 (1980) (per curiam) (White J., joined by Rehnquist, J., dissenting).

23. 445 U.S. 308 (1980) (per curiam). Chief Justice Burger, joined by Justice Powell, dissented on the ground that the appeal presented no real and substantial controversy. Justice White, joined by Justice Rehnquist, dissented on the view that the standards injunction was valid and "functionally indistinguishable from a criminal obscenity statute." Id. at 324 (White, J., joined by Rehnquist, J., dissenting).

24. 445 U.S. at 316 n. 14.

25. Id. at 317. For a discussion of the procedural issues in nuisance-obscenity statutes, see Comment, "The Constitutionality of North Carolina's Nuisance Abatement Statute: A Prior Restraint on Nonobscene Speech," 61 N.C.L.Rev. 685 (1983); Comment, "Regulation of Obscenity Through Nuisance Statutes and Injunctive Remedies—The Prior Restraint Dilemma," 19 Wake Forest L.Rev. 7 (1983).

26. Chief Justice Burger, joined by Justice Powell, argued that the majority misconstrued the Texas statute. "[T]here is a serious question as to whether the Texas statute even authorizes an injunction against a *named* film," and, if it does, it is doubtful "that it can be obtained on a showing of probable success." Id. at 319 (Burger, C.J., joined by Powell, J., dissenting). See also id. at 322–23 (White, J., joined by Rehnquist, J., dissenting) (explaining that at a criminal contempt proceeding, "the State would bear the burden of proving beyond a reasonable doubt that the film which allegedly violated the injunction was obscene") (footnote omitted).

procedural safeguards, such as guarantees of prompt judicial review.[27] The Court instead might have focused on the effect and operation of the statute in *Vance* to generate a broader criticism of the standards injunction. It has been suggested, for example, that the chilling effect of an injunction is greater than that of a criminal prohibition because the injunction is a direct "personalized" command backed by the awe-invoking prestige and mystique of the judiciary.[28] The nuisance statute may also influence prosecutorial decisions in a manner antithetical to first amendment interests: prosecutors may be more likely to bring actions against distributors of allegedly obscene materials when a standards injunction has already been issued.[29] In *Vance*, an undue emphasis on the procedural shortcomings of the injunction statute blinded the Court to its more substantive flaws.

A second difference between the classes of permissible and impermissible prior restraints is found in the quality of the competing interests at stake. Little harm will ordinarily result from a brief postponement in publication of the protected communications which will be caught up in regulatory schemes directed at the prevention of unprotected commercially distributed messages. Delay is tolerable because the class of expression, both protected and unprotected, generally lacks topical content.[30] But restraints "of even a day or two" may be intolerable when applied to " 'political' speech in which the element of timeliness may be important".[31] In the latter cases, the government could justify a prior restraint only upon showing that the injury which

27. After Vance, standards injunctions were upheld by several state appellate courts, see, e.g., State ex rel. Kidwell v. U.S. Mktg., Inc., 102 Idaho 451, 631 P.2d 622 (1981), appeal dismissed, 455 U.S. 1009 (1982); Chateau X. Inc. v. State ex rel. Andrews, 302 N.C. 321, 275 S.E.2d 443 (1981), and the Court of Appeals for the Fourth Circuit, see Fehlhaber v. North Carolina, 675 F.2d 1365 (4th Cir. 1982). But see Spokane Arcades, Inc. v. Brockett, 631 F.2d 135, 138 (9th Cir. 1980) (invalidating nuisance statute as an impermissible prior restraint, citing Vance); Cosgrove v. Cloud Books, Inc., 83 A.D.2d 789, 443 N.Y.S.2d 450 (App. Div. 1981). The Supreme Court has declined opportunities since Vance to pass on obscenity nuisance statutes, see, e.g., Brockett v. Spokane Arcades, Inc., 472 U.S. 491 (1985) (partially invalidating statute on overbreadth grounds), see § 12–28, supra; Avenue Book Store v. Tallmadge, 459 U.S. 997 (1982) (White, J., joined by Brennan and Marshall, JJ., dissenting from denial of certiorari).

28. See Blasi, "Toward a Theory of Prior Restraint: The Central Linkage," 66 Minn.L.Rev. 11, 41 (1981): "injunctions appear to have in the minds of many citizens a mystique that engenders compliance. Potential speakers who would think nothing of violating criminal laws in order to test their constitutionality or even as exer-

cises in civil disobedience are reluctant to disobey injunctions. The personalized nature of the law's command seems to cast a spell."

29. See Comment, "Enjoining Obscenity as a Public Nuisance and the Prior Restraint Doctrine," 84 Colum.L.Rev. 1616, 1624–25 (1984).

30. See A Quantity of Books v. Kansas, 378 U.S. 205, 224 (1964) (Harlan, J.) ("sex is of constant but rarely particularly topical interest").

31. Carroll v. Commissioner of Princess Anne, 393 U.S. 175, 182 (1968). In KPNX Broadcasting Co. v. Arizona Superior Court, 459 U.S. 1302 (1982) (Rehnquist, Circuit Justice), Justice Rehnquist engaged in ad hoc balancing and refused to stay a judicial order that barred the broadcasting of courtroom sketches of jurors in a criminal trial. While conceding that the order amounted to a prior restraint, id. at 1307–08, he argued that "of all conceivable reportorial messages that could be conveyed by reporters or artists watching such trials, one of the least necessary to appreciate the significance of the trial would be individual juror sketches." Id. at 1308. This type of content-based analysis departs from the more limited scrutiny of time sensitivity and is at odds with basic assumptions of the first amendment, see § 12–18, supra.

it seeks to prevent is "irreparable." The disclosure of government's secrets, like the disclosure of an individual's intimacies,[32] would fall into this class—speech for which "more speech" [33] cannot be an alternative remedy. Likewise licensing or permit systems which are administered pursuant to narrowly drawn, reasonable and definite standards are government's only practical means of managing competing uses of public facilities (including traffic control), arranging the orderly assignment of limited space to competing expressive uses,[34] and assigning police to protect the rights of demonstrators.[35] Taken together, the requirements that government prove the unprotected character of the particular speech with certainty and show the irreparable nature of the harm that would occur if a prepublication restraint were not imposed, at least where timing is an important factor, sharply delimit the areas in which prepublication restraints can ever be justified.[36]

The Supreme Court has proven more willing to accept conjectural evidence as justification for a prior restraint when the form of the regulation appears less restrictive: when it can be characterized as an incidental restraint on speech rather than a gag order.[37]   In *Haig v.*

32. See, e.g., Commonwealth v. Wiseman, 356 Mass. 251, 249 N.E.2d 610 (1969), cert. denied 398 U.S. 960 (1969) (enjoining the commercial distribution of a film portraying inhumane conditions in mental hospital as invasion of patients' rights of privacy; first amendment interests held to be served sufficiently by allowing the showing of the film to professional groups). But see Cullen v. Grove Press, Inc., 276 F.Supp. 727 (S.D.N.Y.1967) (refusing to enjoin same film). Organization for a Better Austin v. Keefe, 402 U.S. 415 (1971), is distinguishable in that the privacy right claimed by a homeowner against the distribution of literature in a residential neighborhood has generally been thought to turn on the degree of intrusion into the home itself, a factual question which cannot confidently be resolved in advance of the expressive acts sought to be enjoined.

33. Whitney v. California, 274 U.S. 357, 377 (1927) (Brandeis, J., joined by Holmes, J., concurring).

34. See §§ 12–23 to 12–25, supra.

35. See Blasi, "Prior Restraints on Demonstrations," 68 Mich.L.Rev. 1481, 1485–86 (1970).

36. One may wonder, if preventing virtually certain death of a dozen troops would justify a prior restraint, why preventing a 50% chance of the death of two dozen would not justify the same restraint—i.e., why the Court should look to the certainty of the predicted harm without regard to its extent. The reason may relate to the same factors that lead society to invest more resources in saving a single trapped miner than in reducing the loss of "statistical lives" through mining safety. See Schelling, "The Life You Save May Be

Your Own," in Problems in Public Expenditure Analysis 127, 142–62 (S.B. Chase ed. 1968). Cf. Tribe, "Trial by Mathematics: Precision and Ritual in the Legal Process," 84 Harv.L.Rev. 1329, 1373 n. 140 (1971).

37. The Court frequently finds that regulations with only indirect or minor effects on speech are not really prior restraints at all. The Court has held, for example, that a restriction cannot be a prior restraint unless it is directed at expressive activities and substantially eliminates opportunities for such expression. In Arcara v. Cloud Books, Inc., 106 S.Ct. 3172 (1986), the Supreme Court rejected the reasoning of the New York Court of Appeals that the closure of an adult bookstore constituted a prior restraint. The bookstore had been ordered to close pursuant to a public health nuisance statute on the ground that solicitation of prostitution was occurring on the premises, but the state court found that "[p]rior restraints or other restrictions on First Amendment rights may be present not only where a statute directly prohibits expression but also where the impact of the statute curtails the exercise of these rights." People ex. rel. Arcara v. Cloud Books, Inc., 65 N.Y.2d 324, 335, 491 N.Y.S.2d 307, 315, 480 N.E.2d 1089, 1097 (1985). The New York court relied on cases analogizing an order closing a bookstore or movie theatre based on previous distribution of obscene materials to an impermissible prior restraint. See, e.g., Gayety Theatres, Inc. v. Miami, 719 F.2d 1550 (11th Cir. 1983); General Corp. v. State ex rel. Sweeton, 294 Ala. 657, 320 So.2d 668 (1975), cert. denied 425 U.S. 904 (1976); People ex. rel. Busch v. Projection Room Theater, 17 Cal.3d 42, 130 Cal.Rptr. 328, 550 P.2d 600 (1976), cert. denied sub nom.

Agee,[38] for example, the Court upheld the power of the Secretary of State to revoke a former CIA agent's passport on the ground that his disclosures of sensitive information threatened national security. The Court found it unnecessary to balance Agee's first amendment rights against the government's foreign policy interests: it simply stated that revoking Agee's privilege to travel abroad inhibited only his *action*, not his *speech*.[39] The Court seemed to rely heavily on Agee's "declared purpose" of directly disrupting American foreign intelligence operations [40] and hinted that his disclosures were more akin to bullets than words and therefore were not protected by the Constitution.[41] Even when the extreme sort of danger alleged in *Agee* is not involved, the government retains the power to limit the speech of certain former employees on the basis of secrecy agreements signed as a condition of employment.[42] The *Agee* Court noted that the respondent had agreed

Van de Kamp v. Projection Room Theater, 429 U.S. 922 (1976). The U.S. Supreme Court distinguished Arcara from this line of argument, holding that the closure of the bookstore did not constitute a prior restraint. The Court maintained that "the order would impose no restraint at all on the dissemination of particular materials, since respondent is free to carry on his bookselling business at another location, even if such locations are difficult to find." 106 S.Ct. at 3177 n. 2. Next, the Court upheld the closure because the order was "not imposed on the basis of an advance determination that the distribution of particular materials is prohibited—indeed, the imposition of the closure order has nothing to do with any expressive conduct at all." Id. On remand, the New York Court of Appeals found that the closure violated freedom of expression as guaranteed in the *state* constitution. See Arcara v. Cloud Books, Inc., 68 N.Y.2d 553, 510 N.Y.S.2d 844, 503 N.E.2d 492 (1986).

Similarly, in Seattle Times Co. v. Rhinehart, 467 U.S. 20, 33 (1984), the Court upheld a protective order issued under Federal Rule of Civil Procedure 26(c)(3), finding that "an order prohibiting dissemination of discovered material before trial is not the kind of classic prior restraint that requires exacting First Amendment scrutiny." The Court noted that a party was free to distribute the same information governed by a protective order, so long as "the information is gained through means independent of the court's processes." Id. at 34.

38. 453 U.S. 280 (1981). Chief Justice Burger delivered the opinion of the Court, in which Justices Stewart, White, Blackmun, Powell, Rehnquist, and Stevens joined. Justice Blackmun also filed a concurring opinion. Justice Brennan, joined by Justice Marshall, dissented.

39. Compare id. at 309, with id. at 320–21 n. 10 (Brennan, J., dissenting) (arguing

that majority's rationale was tantamount to holding that imprisoning those who criticize government policy only inhibits action, since prisoners retain the right to criticize government from their jail cells). Cf. Arcara v. Cloud Books, Inc., 106 S.Ct. 3172, 3177 (1986), discussed in note 37, supra: "every civil and criminal remedy imposes some conceivable burden on First Amendment protected activities. One liable for a civil damages award has less money to spend on paid political announcements or to contribute to political causes, yet no one would suggest that such liability gives rise to a valid First Amendment claim." In Arcara, there was no suggestion that the closure order was directed at expressive conduct such as bookselling, see id. at 3177. It was instead triggered by a desire to curtail prostitution, an activity with no first amendment significance, at least in this context.

40. 453 U.S. at 283–85, 308–09. Agee had called a press conference in 1974 to announce his campaign against the CIA, id. at 283–84 n. 2, and had been deported by several Western democracies on the express ground that his activities harmed their national security, see id. at 283 n. 1, 308 n. 59.

41. Id. at 285–86 n. 7, 308–09. There was undisputed evidence in the record that Agee's campaign against the CIA and its operatives had enjoyed some grisly success: after his disclosures of the names and activities of alleged CIA agents operating abroad, several of the named individuals were murdered. See id. at 285 n. 7. Agee's counsel stipulated to the State Department's allegations of harm, id. at 287 n. 11—obviously in an effort to compel consideration of the case as a facial rather than as an applied challenge to the law, see id. at 321 n. 10 (Brennan, J., dissenting).

42. See United States v. Marchetti, 466 F.2d 1309 (4th Cir. 1972), cert. denied 409

not to make any public statements about CIA matters, either during or after his employment by the Agency, without specific governmental approval.[43]

A suit for an injunction against unauthorized publication is not the government's only recourse. In *Snepp v. United States*,[44] the Court awarded the government an unprecedented form of relief: a constructive trust under which all the profits from a former CIA agent's unauthorized book went into the public treasury. The government thus enforced the secrecy agreement through a *post*-publication civil action for monetary recovery.

The Supreme Court's disdain for conjectural harms is justified by the fact that a requirement of ad hoc scrutiny of regulations on speech may *itself* constitute a de facto prior restraint.[45] In the *Pentagon Papers* case,[46] Justice Brennan remarked that "every restraint issued in this case [has] violated the First Amendment—and not less so because that restraint was justified as necessary in order to afford the courts an opportunity to examine the claim more thoroughly." [47] The Court once tolerated systems for previewing publication and exhibition of materials only when those systems "assured an almost immediate judicial determination of the validity of the restraint." [48] Yet when *The Progressive* magazine attempted to publish an article on the manufacture of the hydrogen bomb, the Supreme Court—in a silent echo of the outraged dissenters in the *Pentagon Papers* case [49]—declined to order an expedited appeal, and *The Progressive* languished under prior restraint for almost seven months.

The Progressive sought to publish a piece entitled, "The H-Bomb Secret; How We Got It, Why We're Telling It," in order to "provide the people with needed information to make informed decisions on an urgent issue of public concern." [50] The government conceded that

U.S. 1063 (1972) (granting injunction against publication, without government approval, of ex-CIA agent's book about the Agency).

43. 453 U.S. at 309.

44. 444 U.S. 507 (1980) (per curiam). Justice Stevens dissented, joined by Justices Brennan and Marshall.

45. See Emerson, "First Amendment Doctrine and the Burger Court," 68 Calif.L. Rev. 422, 457–58 (1980).

46. New York Times Co. v. United States, 403 U.S. 713 (1971) (per curiam).

47. Id. at 727 (Brennan, J., concurring). See also Capital Cities Media, Inc. v. Toole, 463 U.S. 1303, 1304 (1983) (Brennan, Circuit Justice) ("even a short-lived 'gag' order in a case of widespread concern to the community constitutes a substantial prior restraint and causes irreparable injury to First Amendment interests as long as it remains in effect"); Redish, "The Proper Role of Prior Restraint Doctrine in First Amendment Theory," 70 Va.L.Rev. 53, 57 (1984) ("interim prior restraints are espe-

cially disfavored because they authorize abridgement of expression prior to a full and fair determination of the constitutionally protected nature of the expression by an independent judicial forum").

48. Bantam Books, Inc. v. Sullivan, 372 U.S. 58, 70 (1963) (striking down practice of state morality commission that in effect suppressed disfavored literature). See, e.g., M.I.C., Ltd. v. Bedford Township, 463 U.S. 1341, 1342 (1983) (Brennan, J., Circuit Justice) (granting stay of injunction against showing of allegedly obscene films because of projected six month delay in prosecuting appeal in state court).

49. 403 U.S. 713, 753 (1971) (Harlan, J., joined by Burger, C.J., and Blackmun, J., dissenting) (criticizing the "almost irresponsibly feverish" pace of the expedited appeal).

50. United States v. Progressive, Inc., 467 F.Supp. 990, 994 (W.D. Wis. 1979) (preliminary injunction issued Mar. 28, 1979), request for writ of mandamus denied sub nom. Morland v. Sprecher, 443 U.S. 709

much of the information in the article had been either declassified or gathered from the public domain,[51] yet it advanced the novel thesis that "national security" empowered it to censor information originating in the public domain "if[,] when drawn together, synthesized, and collated," such information presents "immediate, direct, and irreparable harm to the interests of the United States."[52] Unlike Snepp and Agee, the authors of *The Progressive* piece had signed no secrecy pledges. While admitting that the issuance of an injunction in the case represented a radical departure from nearly two centuries of legal tradition, the district court enjoined publication on the ground that, if the alleged spectre of nuclear proliferation materialized, the right to life, as well as the right to free speech, would be mooted along with the case.[53]

The government's dire predictions and the district court's rhetoric would have been more plausible and more appropriate if the information that *The Progressive* sought to publish had been classified. The government's success in censoring the article because of the way in which the material was "synthesized" amounts to nothing less than suppression of the creative talent of journalists in perceiving the significance of freely available information. The government objected not to the disclosure of the information per se but rather to what the article's authors *had done with it*. The court ignored the fact that "drawing together" knowledge and ideas and attributing meaning to them is the essence of expression.

Few would deny the danger of nuclear weapons proliferation or the unthinkable horrors which even a "limited" nuclear war would entail. Yet in the case of *The Progressive* article, this argues as much for publication as suppression. The piece served to inform the public debate, by demonstrating how easy it is to construct a nuclear bomb and how the government's weapons security system is plagued with shortcomings. If there was risk involved in publishing the article, there was also risk involved in *not* publishing it. The world may be more likely to face a nuclear apocalypse if its leaders are not compelled to answer to an educated, and worried, public.

§ 12–37. First Amendment Due Process [1]: Judicial Primacy in the Resolution of First Amendment Claims

Once specific expressional acts are properly determined to be unprotected by the first amendment, there can be no objection to their

(1979), case dismissed as moot, Nos. 79–1428, 79–1664 (7th Cir. Oct. 1, 1979).

51. 467 F.Supp. at 993. The court noted, however, that it did find "concepts within the article that it does not find in the public realm—concepts that are vital to the operation of the hydrogen bomb." Id. Even the way public material was interpreted conveyed some information: "The right questions had to be asked or the correct educated guesses made." Id. The result, according to the court, was that "the article could possibly provide sufficient information to allow a medium size

nation to move faster in developing a hydrogen weapon." Id.

52. Id. at 991.

53. Id. at 995–96. The case was actually mooted when another magazine published the same material. At least as of this writing, the world has not ended.

§ 12–37

1. The phrase is from Monaghan, "First Amendment 'Due Process,'" 83 Harv.L. Rev. 518 (1970), where it is used to summarize two basic principles the author distills from the case law: that a judicial body,

subsequent suppression or prosecution. But who can authoritatively and finally determine what speech is protected? The Supreme Court's answer has been that no forum except a court can be permitted to impose a valid final restraint on expressional activities, and that this allocation of authority is demanded by the first amendment.[2] The allocation of such primacy to the judiciary rests on concern that an administrative censor is unlikely to be sensitive to the values of freedom of expression.[3] Censorship both tends to develop its own institutional momentum and also lacks the procedural safeguards characteristic of the judicial process. The objection is not to *any* system of censorship or to the delegation of any decisional authority to an executive officer where first amendment interests may be affected. The objection is to any system which allows administrative determinations either directly or indirectly to determine *finally* the scope or application of first amendment privileges. In order to guarantee judicial primacy in first amendment jurisprudence, the Supreme Court has reached a number of specific conclusions about the structural and procedural characteristics of constitutional regulatory schemes which affect the exercise of speech rights; we consider those conclusions in §§ 12–38 and 12–39.

§ 12–38. The Problem of Overbroad Delegation

The earliest major uses of overbreadth analysis came in the context of the Supreme Court's facial invalidation of statutes which delegated dangerously discretionary power to lay juries [1] and executive licensors.[2]

following an adversary hearing, must decide on the protected character of the speech; and that the judicial determination must precede or immediately follow any governmental action which restricts speech.

2. See, e.g., Freedman v. Maryland, 380 U.S. 51, 58 (1965). Cf. Lo-Ji Sales, Inc. v. New York, 442 U.S. 319, 325–26 (1979) (holding that an official seizure of presumptively protected materials is not "reasonable" within the fourth amendment unless a detached and neutral magistrate has issued a warrant particularly describing the items to be seized); Maryland v. Macon, 472 U.S. 463, 476 (1985) (Brennan, J., joined by Marshall, J., dissenting) (arguing for reversal of "obscenity convictions based on arrests unsupported by any prior judicial determination of probable cause").

3. See Emerson, "The Doctrine of Prior Restraint," 20 Law & Contemp.Probs. 648, 658 & n. 34 (1955). On the proposition that "[c]ourts alone are institutionally able consistently to discern, and to apply, the values embodied in the constitutional guarantee of freedom of speech," see Monaghan, supra note 1, at 522–24.

In Seattle Times Co. v. Rhinehart, 467 U.S. 20, 36 (1984), the Court declined to apply heightened first amendment scrutiny to the procedures by which Washington

state courts issue discovery protective orders. The Court upheld the wide range of discretion afforded to trial judges on the theory that "[t]he trial court is in the best position to weigh fairly the competing needs and interests of parties affected by discovery." Id.

But see Vance v. Universal Amusement Co., 445 U.S. 308, 317 (1980) (per curiam) (invalidating obscenity-nuisance statute): "Nor does the fact that the temporary prior restraint is entered by a state trial judge rather than an administrative censor sufficiently distinguish this case from Freedman v. Maryland [380 U.S. 51 (1965)]. . . . That a state trial judge might be thought more likely than an administrative censor to determine accurately that a work is obscene does not change the unconstitutional character of the restraint if erroneously enacted."

§ 12–38

1. See, e.g., Herndon v. Lowry, 301 U.S. 242, 261–63 (1937) (invalidating a state subversive advocacy control statute which did not "furnish a sufficiently ascertainable standard of guilt" and thereby "license[d] the jury to create its own standard in each case").

2. See, e.g., Lovell v. Griffin, 303 U.S. 444, 450–53 (1938) (invalidating an ordi-

Out of these cases emerged the general rule that, while legislatures "ordinarily may delegate power under broad standards . . ., [the] area of permissible indefiniteness narrows . . . when the regulation . . . potentially affects fundamental rights," [3] like those protected by the first amendment. And where a law authorizes a system of prior licensing, the Supreme Court has consistently required the statutory delegation to provide "narrowly drawn, reasonable and definite standards for the [administering] officials to follow." [4]

Statutes which open-endedly delegate to administering officials the power to decide how and when sanctions are applied or licenses issued are overbroad because they grant such officials the power to discriminate—to achieve indirectly through selective enforcement a censorship of communicative content that is clearly unconstitutional when achieved directly.[5] This covert censorship cannot be checked adequate-

nance forbidding the distribution of literature without the written permission of the city manager); Cantwell v. Connecticut, 310 U.S. 296, 305–07 (1940) (invalidating a state statute prohibiting solicitation of money for religious causes without prior approval of local officials, who are required to determine whether the cause is that of a "recognized" religion and to deny certification if it is not).

3. United States v. Robel, 389 U.S. 258, 274–75 (1967) (Brennan, J., concurring).

4. Niemotko v. Maryland, 340 U.S. 268, 271 (1951) (reversing disorderly conduct conviction for holding meeting in city park without a permit, where permit administration had been based only on custom). The constitutional administration of a facially valid permit requirement is discussed in Blasi, "Prior Restraints on Demonstrations," 68 Mich.L.Rev. 1481 (1970). See also § 12–10, supra.

5. See, e.g., Secretary of State of Maryland v. Joseph H. Munson Co., 467 U.S. 947, 964 n. 12 (1984) (state official's discretion to waive a requirement that charities spend no more than 25% of their proceeds on administrative expenses does not save statute from being overbroad because "a statute that requires . . . a license for the dissemination of ideas is inherently suspect. By placing discretion in the hands of an official to deny or grant a license, such a statute creates a threat of censorship that by its very existence chills free speech."); Cox v. Louisiana, 379 U.S. 536, 557–58 (1965) (Cox I) (where Louisiana statute prohibited all obstructions of "public passages", discretionary enforcement to permit certain parades and street meetings but to disallow others held invalid). Cf. Marcus v. Search Warrant, 367 U.S. 717, 731–33 (1961) (state procedure giving law enforcement officials broad discretion to seize allegedly obscene publications found

to lack adequate safeguards to assure the protection of nonobscene materials).

The Court has similarly shown aversion to criminal statutes that amount to "standardless sweep[s] allow[ing] policemen, prosecutors, and juries to pursue their personal predilections." Smith v. Goguen, 415 U.S. 566 (1974). In Kolender v. Lawson, 461 U.S. 352 (1983), for example, the Court struck down a California statute that required persons who loiter or wander on the streets to identify themselves and to account for their presence when requested by a police officer. The Court found that "the statute vests virtually complete discretion in the hands of the police to determine whether the suspect has satisfied that statute and must be permitted to go on his way in the absence of probable cause to arrest." Id. at 358. Just as the scheme in Bantam Books, Inc. v. Sulivan, 372 U.S. 58 (1963), discussed in § 12–39, infra, chilled expression, the Court feared that the law at issue in Kolender implicated "the constitutional right to freedom of movement," id., and had the "potential for arbitrarily suppressing First Amendment liberties." Id., quoting Shuttlesworth v. Birmingham, 382 U.S. 87, 91 (1965). See also Board of Airport Commissioners of Los Angeles v. Jews for Jesus, Inc., 107 S.Ct. 2568, 2573 (1987) (invalidating overbroad rule that, on its face, banned all "First Amendment activities" in airport, and rejecting limiting construction that would give airport "official alone the power to decide in the first instance whether a given activity" is permissible); Houston v. Hill, 107 S.Ct. 2502, 2511 (1987) (overturning overbroad rule that banned interruption of police officers, in part because it gave them "unfettered discretion to arrest individuals for words or conduct that annoy or offend them").

ly by judicial review of the scheme as applied in particular cases.[6] For first amendment protection often depends on balancing free speech rights and governmental interests in particular situations, which depends in turn on a close, after-the-fact scrutiny of the factual circumstances by the reviewing court. Except in those rare instances in which bad faith is manifest,[7] the abuse of administrative discretion is likely to find shelter behind a record of contradictory testimony and retrospective rationalization.[8] A court may seek to make its own characterization of the expressive activity, but its perception of the facts is inherently subjective. When was a demonstration too obstructive of traffic? A noise too loud? Violence imminent? The tendency is to be satisfied that the evidence is sufficient if the record is not "totally devoid of evidentiary support," the minimal due process standard.[9] Factual review is therefore an unreliable cure for an overbroad delegation, and thus the Supreme Court has consistently chosen facial invalidation of statutes containing essentially standardless delegations in areas affecting first amendment rights.[10]

6. See United States v. Reese, 92 U.S. 214, 221 (1875); Note, "The First Amendment Overbreadth Doctrine," 83 Harv.L. Rev. 844, 876–82 (1970).

7. Id. at 870.

8. Id. at 868. And even where states do not act in bad faith, a licensing scheme "is inherently suspect. By placing discretion in the hands of an official to grant or deny a license, such a statute creates a threat of censorship that by its very existence chills free speech." Secretary of State of Maryland v. Joseph H. Munson Co., 467 U.S. 947, 964 n. 12 (1984).

9. See Thompson v. Louisville, 362 U.S. 199 (1960).

10. In Posadas de Puerto Rico Associates v. Tourism Co. of Puerto Rico, 106 S.Ct. 2968 (1986), however, the Court failed to invalidate a system of administrative licensing established by a statute and regulations that restricted advertisements of casino gambling aimed at citizens of Puerto Rico. The licensing scheme was created by a narrowing construction adopted by the Superior Court of Puerto Rico, which authorized "the publicity of the casinos in newspapers, magazines, radio, television or any other publicity media, of our games of chance in the exterior *with the previous approval of the Tourism Company* regarding the text of said ad, which must be submitted in draft to the Company." App. to Juris. Statement 38b, quoted in 106 S.Ct. at 2987 (emphasis added) (Stevens, J., joined by Marshall and Blackmun, JJ., dissenting). As Justice Stevens commented, "A more obvious form of prior restraint is difficult to imagine." Id. The majority expressed no view on the prior restraint argument, on the ground that it had not been raised by the casino operators challenging the statute, either in the lower court or in the Supreme Court, see 106 S.Ct. at 2980 n. 11. Had the Court faced the issue directly, it might have held that because of the lesser constitutional value accorded to commercial speech, see §§ 12–15 and 12–18, supra, a state may require "a system of previewing advertising campaigns to insure that they will not defeat" state restrictions. Central Hudson Gas & Electric Corp. v. Public Service Comm'n, 447 U.S. 557, 571 n. 13 (1980); see also Zauderer v. Office of Disciplinary Counsel, 471 U.S. 626, 668 n. 13 (1985) (Brennan, J., joined by Marshall, J., concurring in part, and dissenting in part) (explaining that "traditional prior restraint principles do not apply to commercial speech"). One difficulty with this approach is that it permits nonjudicial determinations of what is "commercial speech." As § 12–18 makes apparent, the dividing line between the "commercial" and the "political" is hazy at best, and licensing schemes for advertising therefore run a great risk of impermissibly chilling expression that enjoys full constitutional expression. Moreover, a system which permitted regulation of speech prior to a judicial determination of its constitutional status cannot be justified on the basis that the speech in question is unprotected, for that decision cannot be made until after judicial review. The Posadas scheme thus violated the procedural safeguards required by the prior restraint doctrine.

§ 12–39. Procedural Overbreadth

Overbreadth reasoning has also been used to invalidate schemes which failed to assure adequate judicial review of administrative acts affecting expressional activitives. An extreme illustration is *Bantam Books, Inc. v. Sullivan*,[1] in which the Supreme Court declared unconstitutional the system of informal censorship practiced by the Rhode Island Commission to Encourage Morality in Youth. The Commission was authorized by legislative resolution "to educate the public" concerning obscene material "manifestly tending to the corruption of the youth" and "to investigate and recommend the prosecution of all violations" of the state's obscenity laws. The Commission carried out its mandate by notifying distributors about material the Commission found obscene, by notifying the police of its findings, and by informing the distributors that it had notified the police. The Court held "the vice of the system" to be the use of "these black lists . . . as instruments of regulation independent of the law against obscenity. In . . . obviating the need to employ criminal sanctions, the State has at the same time eliminated the safeguards of the criminal process. . . . The Commission's practice . . . provides no safeguards whatever against the suppression of nonobscene, and therefore constitutionally protected, matter."[2]

Bantam Books is an extreme illustration because the "black-listing" there was entirely informal, and thus entirely free of any opportunity for judicial supervision short of facial invalidation.[3] Almost all

§ 12–39

1. 372 U.S. 58 (1963).

2. Id. at 69–70.

3. The Court in Bantam Books entertained a facial challenge to a regulatory system by four publishers who had yet to suffer any criminal penalties at the hands of the Rhode Island authorities. Justice Harlan, in dissent, castigated the majority for countenancing such a "broadside attack" on the state procedures. 372 U.S. at 82 (Harlan, J., dissenting). "Any affected distributor or publisher wishing to stand his ground on a particular publication may test the Commission's views by way of a declaratory judgment action or suit for injunctive relief or by simply refusing to accept the Commission's opinion and awaiting criminal prosecution in respect of the questioned work." Id. at 78–79 (Harlan, J., dissenting). In Times Film Corp. v. Chicago, 365 U.S. 43 (1961), for example, the Court rejected a facial attack on a city ordinance that required all motion pictures to be examined and licensed by a city official prior to exhibition and remitted the petitioners to a challenge of the application of the ordinance to specific films, id. at 46. Similarly, in Laird v. Tatum, 408 U.S. 1 (1972), the Court rejected the claims of peace activists and others who sought declaratory and injunctive relief that their rights were being in-

vaded by the Army's alleged surveillance of public disorders and lawful civilian political activities. The claimants could point to no specific Army activities directed against them but contended instead that the mere existence of the surveillance program inhibited the exercise of their first amendment rights. The Court disagreed, holding that "[a]llegations of a subjective 'chill' are not an adequate substitute for a claim of specific present objective harm or a threat of specific future harm." Id. at 13–14.

The announcements of the commission in Bantam Books met this test—they were essentially warning shots in a closely-targeted enforcement program. Cf. Playboy Enterprises, Inc. v. Meese, 639 F.Supp. 581 (D.D.C.1986) (enjoining Attorney General's Commission on Pornography from sending letters to distributors of Playboy and other publications informing them that they might be listed as distributors of pornography in the commission's final report). In other contexts, however, courts have entertained anticipatory facial challenges when specific threats have appeared less concrete and less imminent. In American Booksellers, Inc. v. Hudnut, 771 F.2d 323 (7th Cir. 1985), summarily aff'd. 106 S.Ct. 1172 (1986), for example, the court of appeals invalidated an Indianapolis anti-pornography statute on the ground that its

regulatory systems make formal use of the legal process in one way or another; few operate without generating any occasion for the use of ad hoc judicial safeguards. However, because *all* regulatory systems permit *some* administrative discretion, the vice in *Bantam Books* is to some extent an endemic problem, one most consistently dealt with by demanding strict procedural safeguards as a precondition for any valid prior restraint of activities linked with the first amendment.[4]

The procedures which the Supreme Court has found required by the first amendment may be briefly summarized: (1) The burden of proof must rest on government to justify any restraint on free expression prior to its judicial review [5] and on government to demonstrate the particular facts necessary to sustain a limitation on expressive behavior; [6] (2) The administrator of a censorship or licensing scheme regulating speech activities must act within a specified brief period of time; [7] (3) The administrator of a censorship or licensing scheme must be required, by statute or authoritative judicial construction, either to issue a license or to go to court to restrain unlicensed expressive acts; mere denial of the license cannot create an enforceable legal bar to

definition of "pornography" was unconstitutional, see id. at 332. The court rejected the suggestion that it should wait until the city had had an opportunity to administer the statute and develop a permissible interpretation of the term: "We gain nothing by waiting. Time would take a toll, however, on the speech of the parties subject to the act. They must take special care not to release material that might be deemed pornographic, for that material could lead to awards of damages." Id. at 327. See § 12–17, supra; see also Pierce v. Society of Sisters, 268 U.S. 510 (1925) (invalidating statute that did not become effective until two years after challenge was brought); Jones v. Wilkinson, 800 F.2d 989 (10th Cir. 1986) (per curiam), summarily aff'd 107 S.Ct. 1559 (1987) (striking down cable television indecency statute that had never been enforced in a concrete factual situation).

4. "[P]rocedural safeguards often have a special bite in the First Amendment context." G. Gunther, Cases and Materials on Constitutional Law 1373 (10th ed. 1980). Special procedural safeguards have been erected in such areas as obscenity, see § 12–16, supra; Monaghan, "First Amendment 'Due Process'," 83 Harv.L.Rev. 518, 520–24 (1970); vagueness, see Gunther, supra, at 1185–95 & 1373 n. 2; public forum permits, see Blasi, "Prior Restraints on Demonstrations," 68 Mich.L.Rev. 1481, 1534–72 (1970); and rebates of union dues to nonmembers, see § 12–4; Ellis v. Railway Clerks, 466 U.S. 435, 443 (1984). "The purpose of these safeguards is to insure that the government treads with sensitivity in areas freighted with First Amend-

ment concerns." Chicago Teachers Union v. Hudson, 475 U.S. 292, ___ n. 12 (1986) (invalidating union dues rebate scheme, in part because it failed to afford a reasonably prompt opportunity for dissenters to challenge the amount of the fee before an impartial arbiter).

5. See Freedman v. Maryland, 380 U.S. 51, 58 (1965) (striking down, for lack of procedural safeguards, motion picture censorship statute which required exhibitors to submit films to an administrative board prior to their showing).

6. See Speiser v. Randall, 357 U.S. 513, 526 (1958) (invalidating statute which allowed tax assessor to deny tax exemptions to veterans and placed on claimant the burden of proving that he did not advocate the violent overthrow of the government). Cf. Smith v. California, 361 U.S. 147 (1959) (striking down statute which held booksellers criminally liable for possession of obscene books without the necessity of government proving the bookseller's knowledge of the contents of the books).

7. See Freedman, 380 U.S. at 59. See, e.g., Teitel Film Corp. v. Cusack, 390 U.S. 139 (1968) (50 to 57 days too long); Interstate Circuit, Inc. v. Dallas, 390 U.S. 676 (1968) (12 days, or earlier if practicable, held a permissible period). In United States v. Thirty-Seven Photographs, 402 U.S. 363 (1971), the Court construed the statute authorizing customs seizures and forfeitures of obscene materials to allow no more than 14 days from the seizure of the goods to the institution of judicial proceedings.

expressive activities;[8] (4) No ex parte court order is valid if an adversary hearing on the question of interim relief is practicable;[9] (5) "Any restraint imposed in advance of a final judicial determination on the merits must be . . . limited to preservation of the status quo for the shortest fixed period compatible with sound judicial resolution;"[10]

8. Freedman, 380 U.S. at 59. See, e.g., Blount v. Rizzi, 400 U.S. 410 (1971) (holding unconstitutional a federal statute which enabled the post office to block the delivery of mail administratively determined to be obscene; the postmaster's order became effective without judicial review, and the burden of obtaining judicial relief was placed on the individual).

9. See Carroll v. President and Commissioners of Princess Anne, 393 U.S. 175, 181–183 (1968) (invalidating a 10-day ex parte order, issued without notice, restraining a white supremacist group from holding public rallies or meetings).

10. Freedman, 380 U.S. at 59. In Kingsley Books, Inc. v. Brown, 354 U.S. 436 (1957), the Court upheld a statute permitting issuance ex parte of temporary orders against the distribution of obscene material. Justice Frankfurter's opinion for the Court stressed the brevity of the restraint. In Freedman, 380 U.S. at 60, the Court understood the procedure in Kingsley to have postponed any restraint against sale until after a judicial decision following an adversary hearing.

The issue often arises in the context of the application for a warrant authorizing the seizure under obscenity statutes of materials presumptively protected by the first amendment. In A Quantity of Books v. Kansas, 378 U.S. 205 (1964), and Marcus v. Search Warrants, 367 U.S. 717 (1961), the Court invalidated the large-scale seizures of obscene material in circumstances where they effectively would constitute prior restraints and held that such seizures must be preceded by an adversary hearing. In Lee Art Theatre, Inc. v. Virginia, 392 U.S. 636 (1968) (per curiam), the Court held that a warrant authorizing the seizure of materials presumptively protected by the first amendment may not issue on the conclusory testimony of a police officer but must instead be based on affidavits setting forth specific facts in order that the magistrate may "focus searchingly on the question of obscenity," id. at 637, quoting Marcus, 367 U.S. at 732. And in Roaden v. Kentucky, 413 U.S. 496 (1973), the Court determined that police may not rely on the "exigency" exception to the fourth amendment's warrant requirement in seizing allegedly obscene materials. But the Court has also upheld seizures of allegedly obscene materials by narrowing the meanings of "seizure" and "prior restraint." In Maryland v. Macon, 472 U.S.

463 (1985), a plainclothed detective entered an adult bookstore, browsed through it, and ultimately purchased two magazines, which the state later offered into evidence at the trial of the bookstore's owner for distribution of obscene materials. The Court held that a sale in the ordinary course of business did not constitute a "search" within the meaning of the fourth amendment, id. at 468–69, and noted that the purchase by the police "of a few of a large number of magazines and other materials offered for sale" did not raise the specter of a "prior restraint, which is the underlying basis for the special Fourth Amendment protections accorded searches for and seizures of First Amendment materials." Id. at 470. In Heller v. New York, 413 U.S. 483 (1973), the Court upheld the seizure of a single copy of a film and its detention as evidence where there was "no showing or pretrial claim that the seizure of the copy prevented continuing exhibition of the film." Id. at 492. Even though the seizure did not amount to a prior restraint, the Court still required that it be made pursuant to a warrant and that there be an opportunity for a prompt post-seizure judicial determination of obscenity, see id. at 493.

The Court has also ruled that no standard higher than mere probable cause is required by the first amendment for issuance of a warrant to seize allegedly obscene materials. See New York v. P.J. Video, Inc., 475 U.S. 868 (1986). Such a warrant must therefore be evaluated under the same probable-cause standard used to review warrant applications generally— that there be a "fair probability" that evidence of a crime will be found in the particular place to be searched. See id. at 1615–16. A persuasive case can be made, however, that allegedly obscene materials should be treated differently. The Supreme Court itself has been incapable of articulating a precise definition of "obscenity," see § 12–16, supra. It is difficult to believe that a magistrate, armed only with the bare affidavit of an investigator and a sketchy decription of the work at issue, will be able to do any better. "A mere listing of sex acts depicted in a film, or a description of excerpted scenes, says little about the predominant effect of the film considered as a whole[,] . . . whether the film, considered as a whole, has any artistic value[,] . . . [and] how the film should be regarded in light of contemporary com-

(6) A scheme of censorship or licensing must assure a "prompt final judicial decision" reviewing any "interim and possibly erroneous denial of a license;" [11] (7) If a prior restraint is ordered by a court, the state must either stay the order pending its appeal or provide immediate appellate review.[12] The Court's commitment to these procedural safeguards, as well as to the substantive values that underlie the first amendment, remains powerful. As the Constitution stands poised to enter its third century, its majestic guarantees of free expression deserve no less.

munity standards." 475 U.S. at ___ (Marshall, J., joined by Brennan and Stevens, JJ., dissenting). This problem is compounded by the fact that many affidavits do not contain descriptions of every scene (or even most of the scenes) of the film in question. Id. There is therefore a grave danger in such situations that the authority to define "obscenity," rests not with the judiciary but rather with the police.

11. Freedman, 380 U.S. at 59. See also Vance v. Universal Amusement Co., Inc., 445 U.S. 308, 316–17 (1980) (striking down state nuisance statute which authorized injunctions against future exhibition of unnamed films not yet found obscene). The requirement of a deadline for a final judicial decision applies to the trial stage. Interstate Circuit, Inc. v. Dallas, 390 U.S. at 690 n. 22. It is clear that it is the decision, and not merely the hearing, which must be prompt. See, e.g., Teitel Film Corp. v. Cu-

sack, 390 U.S. at 142; Southeastern Promotions, Ltd. v. Conrad, 420 U.S. 546, 562 (1975).

12. See National Socialist Party of America v. Skokie, 432 U.S. 43 (1977) (per curiam) (where state court enjoined a demonstration by the Nazi Party and Illinois Supreme Court refused a petition for expedited appeal of the injunction order, the state was required to allow a stay of the injunction). M.I.C., Ltd. v. Bedford Township, 463 U.S. 1341, 1342–43 (1983) (Brennan, Circuit Justice) (granting stay of preliminary injunction which prohibited applicants from showing allegedly obscene films because state appellate review would not be forthcoming for up to six months). On the difficulties of obtaining timely review, see Rendleman, "Free Press-Fair Trial: Review of Silence Orders," 52 N.C.L. Rev. 127 (1973).

Chapter 13

RIGHTS OF POLITICAL
PARTICIPATION

§ 13–1. Political Participation: Rights Poised Between Procedural Due Process and the Freedoms of Expression and Association

Voting rights subsume such distinct concerns as the citizen's opportunity to cast a vote, the community's chance to be represented within a larger polity in proportion to its population, the racial group's ability to prevent the purposeful dilution of its voting power, the candidate's capacity to gain a place on the ballot, and the constituent's chance to contribute to a chosen candidate. These distinct interests, however, spring from a common root. They share a concern with the election process that is both a source and a product of our federal scheme of representative government. At their core, all voting-related rights are rights to participate in this process, and the import of the process for our system of government freights them with their indisputable moment.[1] Given their essential character as parts of the election process, rights relating to the franchise stand poised between procedural due process, with its guarantee that an individual may participate in the application of general rules to that individual's particular situation,[2] and the first amendment, with its guarantee that an individual be allowed to participate in the most general communicative processes that determine the contours of our social and political thought.[3] At the same time, election-related rights display the special feature that the *equality* with which they are made available, rather than the *fact* of their availability or absence, ordinarily proves decisive. Although most of the law in this area is thus part of equal protection doctrine,[4] its unique significance—and its close relationship to both due process and free speech—justifies its separate analysis at this point under the general heading of "preferred rights," before the general Model of Equal Protection is itself set forth.[5]

§ 13–1

1. In Wesberry v. Sanders, 376 U.S. 1, 17 (1964), the Court testified to the fundamental character of the right to vote: "No right is more precious in a free country than that of having a choice in the election of those who make the laws under which, as good citizens, they must live. Other rights, even the most basic, are illusory if the right to vote is undermined."

2. See Chapter 10, supra.

3. See Chapter 12, supra. Rights to vote on referenda or other direct popular measures, to campaign for such measures, or to win the opportunity to present them to the public, are of course closely allied with rights pertaining to the choice of governmental representatives. Such "plebiscite rights" will be separately discussed in § 13–17 of this chapter.

4. See Chapter 16, infra.

5. Id.

§ 13–2. Apportionment

While a discussion of the complete abnegation of an identifiable group's right to vote may seem logically antecedent to a discussion of the dilution of the franchise through malapportionment, the latter subject will be addressed first. Historically, it was the reapportionment issue that first compelled the courts to assay the scope and content of the right to vote. Moreover, the reapportionment cases draw to the surface many of the theoretical conundrums that underlie other aspects of the right to vote.

When the long-standing judicial reluctance to interfere in the political task of apportionment finally yielded to the manifest need to rectify gross malapportionment, the Court envisioned no great difficulty in resolving the substantive issues that the Court had just brought within its purview: "Judicial standards under the Equal Protection Clause are well developed and familiar. . . ."[1] History has proved the Court more hopeful than clairvoyant. Courts and commentators have divided sharply on the criteria that should govern apportionment.[2] Even where a particular rule is universally embraced, its philosophical premises seldom command a clear consensus—a situation that presages controversy when a more subtle problem arises whose solution is sensitive to the premises accepted. The general precepts of apportionment doctrine are, nonetheless, easy to articulate. There is a guarantee of some form of mathematical equality: every individual has the right to have her district represented in proportion to its population. There is, as well, a more elusive guarantee of fair representation: certain mathematically palatable apportionment schemes will be overturned because they systematically circumscribe the voting impact of specific population groups. The following sections seek to define these principles more sharply.

§ 13–3. The Quantitative Dimension: One Person, One Vote

The Court's first substantive venture into the "political thicket"[1] came in *Gray v. Sanders*,[2] where the plaintiffs challenged Georgia's county-unit method of tallying votes in Democratic party primary elections for state-wide offices. The method closely paralleled the electoral college system used to elect the President: Georgia candidates

§ 13–2

1. Baker v. Carr, 369 U.S. 186, 226 (1962).

2. See, e.g., the contrasting views espoused by the contributors to Reapportionment in the 1970s (N. Polsby ed. 1971). The uncertainty about the proper standard of review for apportionment schemes was manifest in Baker itself. Writing for the majority, Justice Brennan held the apportionment issue justiciable because "it has been open to courts since the enactment of the Fourteenth Amendment to determine . . . that a discrimination reflects *no* policy, but simply arbitrary and capricious action." Id. at 226. The language points toward the rational relation standard of equal protection review. See §§ 16–2 to 16–3, infra. But the rational relation standard of review would support only the most limited judicial intervention in matters of legislative apportionment—a result seemingly at odds with the aggressive tone of Baker. See Casper, "Apportionment and the Right to Vote: Standards of Judicial Scrutiny," 1973 Sup.Ct.Rev. 1, 7.

§ 13–3

1. The less-than-neutral phrase was coined by Justice Frankfurter in Colegrove v. Green, 328 U.S. 549, 556 (1946).

2. 372 U.S. 368 (1963).

for positions such as Governor and United States Senator were nominated by a vote of the state's counties, in which each county was allocated a number of votes and all the votes allocated to a given county were imputed to the candidate who had received a plurality of that county's popular vote. The Supreme Court held that a unit-vote system in elections for a single office in a single constituency contravened the equal protection clause.[3] Justice Douglas, writing for the Court, emphasized the citizens' votes that were "wasted" when small popular vote margins were translated into a sweep of all of the county's votes.[4] Although he carefully delimited the decision so as to exclude issues of legislative apportionment,[5] the logical implications of the decision proved hard to confine. In brief, the opinion implied that there existed a personal right to cast a vote that was the mathematical equivalent of the vote cast by any other member of the same constituency. Justice Stewart put the proposition succinctly in a concurring opinion: "Within a given constituency, there can be room for but a single constitutional rule—one voter, one vote." [6]

Problems concerning congressional apportionment were squarely posed by *Wesberry v. Sanders*,[7] another Georgia case. The plaintiffs, residents of an allegedly underrepresented Atlanta congressional district, objected to the fact that the district contained almost 20 percent of the state's population but elected only 10 percent of the state's representatives in Congress. Relying upon article I, § 2, which provides that Representatives shall be chosen "by the People," the Court struck down Georgia's districting system.[8] Justice Black, writing for the majority, rooted his conclusion in an historical argument: Article I, § 2, was said to have been intended to govern intrastate congressional apportionment, so as to eliminate population disparities among districts. Although the Court's historical scholarship may have been suspect,[9] the Court made clear its independent conviction that there

3. Id. at 379.

4. One spectre that plainly troubled the Court was that of the winner of the popular vote losing the election. It is commonly suggested, in reference to the electoral college, that such mere possibilities are not relevant; rather, the focus should be upon the patterns of results that the challenged arrangements actually entail. See generally Auerbach, "The Reapportionment Cases: One Person, One Vote—One Vote, One Value," 1964 Sup.Ct.Rev. 1, 32–34.

5. 372 U.S. at 378

6. Id. at 382. See also id. at 381 ("one person, one vote"). In subsequent cases and commentaries, the equal population rule was generally capsulized as "one *man*, one vote." Later, in apparent recognition of the fact that the franchise does extend to both sexes, the Court fortunately returned to the more universal "one person, one vote" formula. See Mahan v. Howell, 410 U.S. 315, 319 (1973).

7. 376 U.S. 1 (1964).

8. "[C]onstrued in its historical context, the command of Art. I, § 2, that Representatives be chosen 'by the People of the several States' means that as nearly as is practicable one man's vote in a congressional election is to be worth as much as another's." Id. at 7–8.

9. The majority's attempt to show that Article I, § 2, was concerned with intrastate population disparities seems unconvincing in light of the evidence adduced by Justice Harlan in dissent. See id. at 30–32. See also Kelly, "Clio and the Court: An Illicit Love Affair," 1965 Sup.Ct.Rev. 119. Justice Harlan conceded that the Framers expected Congress to use its powers under §§ 4 and 5 of Article I to ensure that there were no substantial intrastate population disparities. He contended, however, that Congressional action was to be the exclusive remedy for malapportionment. 376 U.S. at 23, 30 n.13, 33–39. Significantly, he did not comment on the probability that legislators who had achieved their positions through malappor-

existed a basic right to have one's legislative representatives apportioned according to population. The decision was based upon a straightforward notion: "[O]ne man's vote . . . is to be worth as much as another's." [10]

The reapportionment revolution reached full strength in *Reynolds v. Sims* [11] and its companion cases.[12] Unlike *Wesberry*, *Reynolds* and its companions dealt with state legislative apportionment rather than congressional apportionment; consequently, the cases were cast in equal protection terms rather than in terms of article I, § 2. While the source of the doctrine varied, its content was largely the same: the Court insisted that equal numbers of voters should elect equal numbers of representatives. *Reynolds*, the case the Court chose to bear the principal opinion, dealt with the gross malapportionment of the Alabama state legislature. Ratios between constituency populations ranged as high as 46 to 1 in the state senate and 16 to 1 in the lower house. A majority of each house of the legislature could be elected from districts comprising about 25 percent of the state's population. Not surprisingly, the Court invalidated this apportionment scheme. In doing so, it ascribed broad constitutional status to the premise that informed the *Gray* and *Wesberry* opinions: "[A]n individual's right to vote for State legislators is unconstitutionally impaired when its weight is in a substantial fashion diluted when compared with votes of citizens living in other parts of the State." [13] The conclusion: again, one person one vote. More specifically, representation in a state legislature must be closely based upon population unless a legitimate state objective demands otherwise.[14]

The *Reynolds* opinion did little to illuminate the specific scope and content of the one person, one vote rule. Left unclear were the types of legislatures which would be covered by the rule, the degree of mathematical equality among districts required, and the types of state policy which could justify extraordinary deviations from mathematical equality. These issues were left to a process of ongoing judicial resolution, which will be assayed in the following sections.

Reynolds and its companions did, however, resolve several pivotal problems. Specifically, in *Maryland Committee for Fair Representation v. Tawes*,[15] the Court held that the equal population rule applied to both houses of a bicameral state legislature.[16] In *Lucas v. Forty-Fourth*

tionment would be unlikely to remedy such electoral schemes.

10. 376 U.S. at 8.

11. 377 U.S. 533 (1964).

12. Several reapportionment cases before the Court at the same time as Reynolds received full dress opinions. See Lucas v. Forty-Fourth Colorado General Assembly, 377 U.S. 713 (1964); Roman v. Sincock, 377 U.S. 695 (1964); Davis v. Mann, 377 U.S. 678 (1964); Maryland Committee for Fair Representation v. Tawes, 377 U.S. 656 (1964); WMCA, Inc. v. Lomenzo, 377 U.S. 633 (1964). Several other apportionment cases before the Court at

that time were disposed of by per curiam orders.

13. 377 U.S. at 568.

14. See id. at 579.

15. 377 U.S. 656 (1964).

16. The Court rejected the validity of Maryland's "federal plan" in which the lower house was apportioned on the basis of population and the upper house apportioned so as to give each county one vote regardless of its population. The Court, adopting the view that the relevant concern was the "combined total representation" of the state legislature, invalidated both houses of the legislature. Id. at 672,

Colorado General Assembly,[17] the Court dispelled any notion that an otherwise impermissible apportionment could be saved by its adoption through popular referendum,[18] and in *Reynolds* it ruled that an apportionment would not be saved by its origin in the state constitution.[19] Finally, *Lucas* imposed upon the state the burden of justifying deviations from the equal population standard. The imposition of this burden was of singular practical importance, given the difficulty of proof and argument in matters so elusive as proper representation.

§ 13–4. The Scope of the Guarantee

The equal population rule has been held to extend to a variety of election situations. *Reynolds v. Sims*[1] and its companions brought state legislative districting within the compass of the one person, one vote mandate. The rule, as we have seen, applied to both houses of a bicameral state legislature. And the Court's earlier pronouncement in *Gray v. Sanders*[2] had brought statewide executive offices within the proposition's reach.

The relevance of the rule of mathematical equality to local governments confounded the Court for a time. Early decisions tended to except local apportionment from the *Reynolds* rule, but the distinctions on which this exception was based were eroded over time. The Court's first pronouncements on the subject of local apportionment came in *Sailors v. Board of Education*[3] and *Dusch v. Davis*.[4] *Sailors* involved the school consolidation plan of Kent County, Michigan. The county school board was selected by representatives of local school boards, each such board casting one vote regardless of the population it represented. The Court unanimously held the one person, one vote rule inapposite on these facts—first, because the county board was basically appointive rather than elective,[5] and second, because the board was administrative rather than legislative.[6]

674. See also Reynolds v. Sims, 377 U.S. at 568. Some were dismayed that the Court would hold unconstitutional the very accommodation of majoritarianism and territoriality that the Framers had settled upon for the federal government. See, e.g., Lucas v. Forty-Fourth Colorado General Assembly, 377 U.S. 713, 756–57 (1964) (Stewart, J., dissenting on the ground that the federal plan ensured some representation of small localities). The Reynolds Court, however, thought the analogy to the federal legislature ill-founded: states are sovereignties and as such are provided representation in the Senate; but "[p]olitical subdivisions . . . counties, cities, or whatever—never and never have been considered as sovereign entities." 377 U.S. at 575.

17. 377 U.S. 713 (1964).

18. In a one person, one vote referendum, Colorado voters had opted for a federal plan, rather than one that apportioned

each house on the basis of population. The Court invalidated the popularly endorsed federal plan, explaining that "[a]n individual's constitutionally protected right to cast an equally weighted vote cannot be denied even by a vote of a majority of a State's electorate." Id. at 736.

19. 377 U.S. at 584.

§ 13–4

1. 377 U.S. 533 (1964).

2. 372 U.S. 368 (1963).

3. 387 U.S. 105 (1967).

4. 387 U.S. 112 (1967). See also Dallas County v. Reese, 421 U.S. 477 (1975) (per curiam).

5. Sailors, 387 U.S. at 109.

6. Id. at 109–10. The Court left open the question whether there were lawmaking offices that *must* be elective rather than appointive. See § 16–10, note 1.

In *Dusch v. Davis*[7] the Court upheld the election system for Virginia Beach's consolidated city council, even though the at-large election system imposed the requirement that at least one council member reside in each of the city's seven boroughs, which varied greatly in population. The Court reasoned that the plan did not violate the one person, one vote principle because the council members who were required to reside in particular boroughs were, nonetheless, representatives of the entire city population rather than of the borough in which they resided. Thus each council member represented the same number of people.

In *Avery v. Midland County*[8] the Court explicitly extended the rule of *Reynolds v. Sims* to local governmental units with "general responsibility." Overturning the selection process for the Commissioner's Court of Midland County, the Court declared that the Equal Protection Clause extended to any body that possessed "general governmental powers over an entire geographic area."[9] For such subdivisions, the Court expressly rejected the propriety of non-population apportionment criteria such as the number of qualified voters, land area, miles of county road, and taxable values.[10]

The Court handed down its next edict on the scope of the one person, one vote rule in *Hadley v. Junior College District*.[11] This case involved a challenge to a Missouri statute allowing the creation of a junior college district only half of whose trustees were elected by member districts accounting for almost 60 percent of its population. The Court, in disapproving this electoral scheme, held that "as a general rule, whenever a state or local government decides to select persons by a popular election to perform governmental functions, the equal protection clause of the fourteenth amendment requires that each qualified voter must be given an equal opportunity to participate in that election, and when members of an elected body are chosen from separate districts, each district must be established on a basis that will insure, so far as practicable, that equal numbers of voters can vote for proportionately equal numbers of officials.[12] Although this holding appeared to abandon *Avery's* limitation of the *Reynolds* rule to bodies with "general governmental powers," the Court fell short of extending the one person, one vote standard to all local elections. *Hadley* declined to apply that standard to "case[s] in which a state [opts to elect] certain functionaries whose duties are . . . far removed from normal governmental activities and . . . disproportionately affect different groups."[13] *Hadley* held that the election of school board trustees did not fall within this excepted category because such officials performed

---

7. 387 U.S. 112 (1967).

8. 390 U.S. 474 (1968).

9. Id. at 484–86.

10. Id. at 478. But see § 13–25, infra, note 10.

11. 397 U.S. 50 (1970).

12. Id. at 56. The language is noteworthy because it says that "so far as practica-

ble" there must be equality. Ostensibly the Court applied the more stringent test of mathematical equality to this matter of local apportionment. Elsewhere, however, the Court stressed that "mathematical exactitude is not required." Id. at 58.

13. Id. at 56.

traditionally important governmental functions, which did not disproportionately affect specific groups.[14]

Since *Hadley*, however, the Court has twice declined to apply the
one person, one vote principle to specialized local bodies. *Salyer Land
Co. v. Tulare Lake Basin Water Storage District*[15] held the *Reynolds*
rule inapplicable to the election of members of a water district whose
primary purpose was to provide for the acquisition, storage, and distribution of water for farming in the surrounding river basin.[16] *Ball v.
James*[17] reached the same conclusion in the context of a much larger
water district, which not only stored and delivered water but also
generated and supplied electricity for many of the residents of the
State.[18] In *Ball*, the Court held that the district's purpose was "sufficiently specialized and narrow" and that its activities affected landowners "so disproportionately" as to release it from the demands of the
Reynolds rule.[19] Whether the Court will extend *Salyer* and *Ball* to
special purpose local bodies that are not primarily concerned with
supplying water and power remains unclear.[20] Taken together, *Hadley,
Salyer*, and *Ball* give the Court much room for maneuver in deciding
whether a particular local unit with specialized responsibilities is
subject to the requirements of the *Reynolds* rule.

§ 13–5. One Person, One Vote: The Requisite Approximation of Equality

Even where the one person, one vote principle governs, a recurring
question is how far from precise mathematical equality an apportionment scheme may stray before it violates the Constitution. In *Reynolds*, the Court emphasized that it was not requiring precise numerical
equality of the state legislative districts: "[W]e mean that the Equal

---

14. Id. at 53–54, 56.

15. 410 U.S. 719 (1973).

16. Indeed, the Court went so far as to
find that certain voters who did not have
property interests in the basin had no right
to vote at all. See §§ 13–11, 16–50, infra.

17. 451 U.S. 355 (1981). Justice Stewart wrote for the majority, joined by Chief
Justice Burger and Justices Powell, Rehnquist, and Stevens. Justice White, joined
by Justices Brennan, Marshall, and Blackmun dissented. See also § 13–11, infra.

18. As in Salyer, the Court not only
held that the one person, one vote standard
was inapplicable, but also held that residents of the district who did not own land
had no right to vote at all. See §§ 13–11,
16–56, infra.

19. 451 U.S. at 362. The Court's conclusion that the district's activities disproportionately affected landowners seems
doubtful. Unlike the district in Salyer, the
district in Ball provided electricity to hundreds of thousand of state residents—landowners and nonlandowners alike. See id.
at 365.

20. In a dissent to the majority opinion
in Ball, Justice White suggested that the
Court's holding was based on the premise
that the provision of power and water is an
essentially proprietary activity. See id. at
386. Thus, the Court may refuse to apply
the reasoning in Salyer and Ball to special
purpose units that perform more "traditional" governmental functions. However,
Justice Powell's decisive fifth vote reflected
the view that, so long as those excluded by
the specialized local body can appeal to a
properly apportioned statewide legislature
in which they are fairly represented, federal courts should defer to the electoral
scheme that the state legislature chose to
permit the local body to employ. 451 U.S.
at 373–74 (concurring opinion). Justice
Powell conceded that this theory had been
rejected by Kramer v. Union Free School
District No. 15, 395 U.S. 621 (1969), discussed in § 13–11, infra, but noted that
"some of the [Kramer] reasoning . . . has
been questioned." 451 U.S. at 373 n.2.

Protection Clause requires that a State make an honest and good faith effort to construct districts . . . *as nearly of equal population as is practicable.*" [1] Taken literally, this formulation is troublesome. If no non-population constraints are imposed and if a jurisdiction proceeds diligently, virtually exact equality of legislative districts *is* practicable.[2] Unless the Court's practicability language is to be deemed superfluous, one or both of the following propositions must be true: first, there are permissible non-population constraints; second, states need not expend the effort to reduce interdistrict inequality below a certain threshold. The first of these propositions will be dealt with in the following section; the second will be addressed here.

The facts of the 1964 reapportionment decisions were such that the cases shed scant light on the degree of mathematical equality the Court would exact from the states. In all of the cases, the malapportionment was gross and indisputable; [3] hence Court disapproval of the schemes was not inconsistent with the proposition that some modicum of mathematical deviation would be tolerated. And as we have seen, the "practicability" language of *Reynolds* does little to clarify matters. The failure of the 1964 decisions to clarify the requisite degree of equality probably traces to the Court's inability to fashion a theory which accommodated the need for exact equality that flowed so imperatively from the logic undergirding one person, one vote, with the judicial reluctance to intrude upon what was primarily a legislative domain when the error to be corrected was rather small.[4] While the Court seemed to resolve this tension in favor of the latter consideration, it never made explicit its process of resolution.

By the time the Court next considered the reapportionment problem, the pendulum had swung in favor of demanding almost exact mathematical equality—again, without explicit explanation. In *Swann v. Adams*,[5] invalidating a Florida apportionment plan purportedly constructed so as to comply with the *Reynolds* mandate, the Court declared that no deviations from strict equality would be sanctioned unless they were *de minimis* [6] or justified by "a satisfactory explanation grounded on acceptable state policy." [7] Though the Court failed to define the

1. 377 U.S. at 577 (emphasis added). See also 377 U.S. at 579 ("substantial equality of population among the various districts").

2. See R. Dixon, Representative Government (1968). But the Court was firm upon the impracticality of effecting exact equality: "We realize that it is a practical impossibility to arrange legislative districts so that each one has an identical number of residents, or citizens, or voters. Mathematical exactness or precision is hardly a workable constitutional requirement." 377 U.S. at 577. See also Roman v. Sincock, 377 U.S. 695, 710 (1964).

3. Every legislative house that was deemed constitutionally repugnant had a maximum population variance ratio of 2.4

to 1 or more. In every case, districts comprising 45.1 percent of the population or less could elect a majority of the house's members. In most cases the disparities were substantially more pronounced than these outer limits suggest. See generally Auerbach, "The Reapportionment Cases: One Person, One Vote—One Vote, One Value," 1964 Sup.Ct.Rev. 1, 16–17.

4. See Reynolds v. Sims, 377 U.S. 533, 586 (1964); Davis v. Mann, 377 U.S. 678, 693 (1964); Ely v. Klahr, 403 U.S. 108, 114 (1971); White v. Weiser, 412 U.S. 783, 795 (1973).

5. 385 U.S. 440 (1967).

6. Id. at 444.

7. Id.

range of deviations that would be deemed *de minimis*, it was evident
that *Swann* imposed a significantly stricter standard than had *Reynolds*.

The Supreme Court tightened the reins still further in *Kirkpatrick
v. Preisler*, a decision that overturned a Missouri apportionment plan
allowing only minuscule deviations from numerical equality.[8] The
Court held that even slight deviations were permissible only if they
were unavoidable despite good faith efforts to achieve absolute equality.[9] The Court, in other words, rejected the *de minimis* defense of
population deviations and instead embraced an unwavering practicality
standard: in its congressional districting plans a state was required to
approximate precise mathematical equality as closely as possible.
Kirkpatrick failed to announce whether the standard of strict equality
applied to all apportionment schemes or pertained only to the apportionment of congressional districts. In *Mahan v. Howell*,[10] however, the
Court chose the latter course, upholding the apportionment of Virginia's House of Delegates despite substantial interdistrict population
deviations. The *Mahan* court held that the rigid standards enunciated
in *Kirkpatrick* were inapplicable to problems concerning state legislative apportionment.[11]

The distinction articulated in *Mahan* has been honored in subsequent cases. The Court reaffirmed the applicability of *Kirkpatrick's*
strict equality standard to Texas congressional districting in *White v.
Weiser*,[12] yet on the same day announced two state legislative apportionment decisions in which it employed the more lax standard of equality.[13] In one of these decisions, *Gaffney v. Cummings*,[14] the Court held
that population deviations ranging up to 7.83 percent in Connecticut
legislative districts did not establish a prima facie case of invidious
discrimination. A decade later, the Court once again affirmed the
Mahan distinction in a pair of cases decided on the same day. In
Karcher v. Daggett[15] the Court rejected an argument that a congressional districting plan is per se valid if the maximum population
deviation among districts is smaller than the statistical imprecision of

---

8. 394 U.S. 526 (1969). The population
variance ratio involved in Kirkpatrick was
approximately 1.06 to 1, and no district
deviated from the ideal by more than
3.13%.

9. 394 U.S. at 531. See also Wells v.
Rockefeller, 394 U.S. 542 (1969). Kirkpatrick left no room for doubt about the strin-
gency of the test it espoused: "the State
must justify each variance, no matter how
small." 394 U.S. at 531. The record in
the case showed that the Missouri legislature had before it an alternative plan with
smaller deviations from the mathematical
ideal. 394 U.S. at 532.

10. 410 U.S. 315 (1973).

11. The Mahan distinction had been
hinted at in earlier decisions reaching all
the way back to Reynolds v. Sims, in which
the Court had opined that "[s]omewhat
more flexibility may . . . be constitution-

ally permissible with respect to state legislative apportionment than in congressional
districting." 377 U.S. 533, 578 (1964). The
Court almost certainly overstated the case,
however, when it insisted that the "dichotomy between the two lines of cases has
consistently been maintained." 410 U.S.
at 322.

Justices Brennan, Marshall and Douglas
dissented from the Court's opinion in Mahan, contending that the absolute equality
rule should govern all apportionments. Id.
at 349.

12. 412 U.S. 783 (1973).

13. Gaffney v. Cummings, 412 U.S. 735
(1973); White v. Regester, 412 U.S. 755
(1973).

14. 412 U.S. 735 (1973).

15. 462 U.S. 725 (1983).

available census data.[16] The Court reiterated the *Kirkpatrick* holding
that no population deviation that could practically be avoided was
permissible in congressional districting plans.[17] In *Brown v. Thomson* [18], however, the Court wrote that in state legislative districts,
population disparities ranging up to 10% were *de minimis* and did not
require justification by the state. As in prior cases, the Court made
little effort to justify this distinction between congressional and state
legislative apportionment schemes.[19] While there may be some justification for distinguishing between congressional and state legislative
apportionment when considering how far a state may stray from exact
equality in pursuit of a legitimate objective, no such rationale supports
a distinction concerning the appropriateness or extent of the de
minimis defense. An appropriately formulated standard of interdistrict equality, allowing minor deviations, could well be applied to both
types of cases.[20]

§ 13–6. One Person, One Vote: Deviations Justified by a Legiti-
mate State Goal

Apart from those deviations from the one person, one vote standard
that have been tolerated as *de minimis*, avoidable deviations have been
sanctioned where designed to effectuate a substantive state policy
deemed legitimate by the Court. Here, as was the case with the *de
minimis* defense, different standards obtain with respect to state and
local apportionment on the one hand and congressional districting on
the other. With respect to state legislative apportionment, the Court
was quick to sound a permissive note. While espousing the one person,
one vote principle, *Reynolds* acknowledged that its application was
limited by relevant state goals: "So long as the divergences from a
strict population standard are based on legitimate considerations incident to the effectuation of a rational state policy, some deviations from
the equal-population principle are constitutionally permissible . . . ".[1]

16. The maximum population deviation
in the case was approximately .7%; the
state presented evidence that the predictable undercount in census data was at
least 1%. See id. at 728, 735.

17. Id. at 731–34.

18. 462 U.S. 835 (1983).

19. In Gaffney v. Cummings, 412 U.S.
735 (1973), the Court averred that "there
are fundamental differences between congressional districting under Article I . . .
and . . . state legislative reapportion-
ments governed by the Fourteenth Amendment." Id. at 741–42. The Court, however, failed to explain why the difference in
the constitutional source of the rights
should bear the consequence that the
Court has given it.

20. While there is, perhaps, no non-ar-
bitrary way to choose a cutoff point separating minimal from substantial inequality
for purposes of such a standard, it is not
clear why the choice of an arbitrary level

is repugnant, as suggested by Kirkpatrick
v. Preisler, 394 U.S. 526 (1969). If the
cutoff level were determined by the deviations that would be expected from strict
equality due to shifts in population and the
administrative difficulty of drawing district lines precisely, an acceptable standard
could be formulated. Moreover, a state
that attempted to aim precisely for the
cutoff level rather than for strict equality
would court the danger that the "natural"
deviations mentioned would push the total
amount of inequality outside of the acceptable range.

§ 13–6

1. 377 U.S. at 579. Reynolds indicated
that the burden of proof rested upon the
state to justify the deviations. The normal
presumption of legislative rationality commands minimal support in the apportionment context. That presumption derives
from the fact that the legislature acts in
the community's interest, a fact of uncer-

Reynolds identified some conceivably justifiable state policies: "A State may legitimately desire to maintain the integrity of various political subdivisions, insofar as possible, and provide for compact districts of contiguous territory in designing a legislative apportionment scheme." [2] But the Court was quick to limit the range of acceptable justifications for deviations from the equal population rule: "[N]either history alone, nor economic or other sorts of group interests, are permissible factors in attempting to justify disparities from population-based representation." [3] It also rejected keeping districts a manageable size,[4] balancing urban and rural interests in the state legislature [5] and discriminating against areas because of their disproportionate number of military personnel,[6] as justifications for deviations from the equal population rule. On a more general level, the Court insisted that the proffered state justifications could only modify, not "submerge," the equal population principle.[7]

When the Court assumed its more stringent posture on deviations from mathematical equality in *Swann v. Adams*,[8] it preserved the exception as formulated in *Reynolds.* Deviations from mathematical equality would be sanctioned if justified by "a satisfactory explanation grounded on acceptable state policy." [9] The Court reaffirmed that sentiment in *Brown v. Thomson* when it held that a substantial population variance in an apportionment scheme for the Wyoming legislature was justifiable in light of the state's longstanding and neutrally-applied policy of using counties as the basic units of representation.[10]

tain validity when the very complaint in the case is that the legislature does not accurately reflect the community. See R. Dixon, Representative Government (1968); Washington, "Does the Constitution Guarantee Fair and Effective Representation to all Interest Groups Making up the Electorate," 17 How.L.J. 19 (1971). Cf. Kramer v. Union Free School District No. 15, 395 U.S. 621, 628 (1969).

2. 377 U.S. at 578. Of the justifications advanced for deviations from the equal population rule, the desire to preserve local political boundaries is the most commonly voiced and most frequently accepted. Reynolds acknowledged that ignoring extant political lines would invite partisan gerrymandering. See 377 U.S. at 578–79. See also Wells v. Rockefeller, 394 U.S. at 550–51 (Harlan, J., dissenting); id. at 547 (White, J., dissenting). Reynolds also rooted the political subdivision exception in the fact that "[l]ocal government entities are frequently charged with responsibilities incident to the operation of state government," 377 U.S. at 580, and that much state legislative activity is "directed to the concerns of particular political subdivisions." Id. at 580–81.

3. 377 U.S. at 579–80.

4. Id. at 580.

5. Davis v. Mann, 377 U.S. 678, 692 (1964).

6. Id. at 691.

7. Reynolds, 377 U.S. at 578.

8. 385 U.S. 440, 444 (1967).

9. Id. at 444. In Mahan v. Howell, 410 U.S. 315, 328 (1973), the Court testified to the continuing vitality of the rule by sustaining the apportionment of the Virginia legislature notwithstanding a variance of 16.4% among house districts. The variance had been produced by the legislature's efforts to respect political subdivision lines when constructing legislative's districts. Two years later, in Chapman v. Meier, 420 U.S. 1 (1975), the Court held that a population variance of 20% in a court-ordered reapportionment plan for the North Dakota legislature was "constitutionally impermissible *in the absence of* significant state policies or other acceptable considerations that require adoption of a plan with so great a variance." Id. at 24 (emphasis added). In general, court-ordered plans for state and local apportionment are tested more strictly than legislatively-ordered plans. Id. at 26–27; Connor v. Finch, 431 U.S. 407, 414 (1977).

10. 462 U.S. 835, 847–48 (1983). In Brown, in an opinion by Justice Powell joined by Chief Justice Burger and Justices Rehnquist, Stevens, and O'Connor, the Court dealt with a strange set of facts. The Wyoming apportionment plan resulted in a maximum deviation of 89% from pop-

Local government apportionment proposals have been judged by standards essentially identical to those applied to states. If anything, the Court has been more receptive to justifications for deviation from mathematical equality in the context of local government apportionment. As we have already observed, the Court explicitly recognized the need for experimentation at the local level and the consequent imprudence of applying a strict version of the one person, one vote concept to the apportionment of local governing bodies. In *Abate v. Mundt*,[11] this inclination to accede to the decisions of the local governing units led the Court to approve the apportionment of a county legislature which deviated from strict mathematical equality by a maximum range of 11.9 percent. The deviation was justified by the need to respect the boundaries of the towns that comprised the county. The Court recognized the legitimacy of this concern.[12]

Although it is settled that certain state policies can justify deviations from a strict one person, one vote standard, several aspects of the rule are unsettled. First, the scope of permissible justifications remains unclear. While compactness, contiguity, and the preservation of political subdivisions are concededly legitimate goals, possibilities such as protecting incumbents and ensuring political fairness beget more uncertainty. Second, the Court appears to waver concerning the applicable equal protection standard. At times its language suggests that state justifications for deviations from one person, one vote must survive the strict scrutiny usually reserved for cases dealing with suspect classifications or implicating fundamental rights.[13] At other times, it appears to apply the rational relation test.[14] Third, the Court has yet to decide whether a balancing test, in which the magnitude of the state's deviation from equality is weighed against the value of the policy affected by the deviation, is the appropriate standard.

The Court has been much less solicitous of justifications advanced in the context of congressional apportionment. In *Kirkpatrick v. Preis-*

ulation equality. But the League of Women Voters, which brought the suit, challenged not the state apportionment plan as a whole, but only the legislature's decision to grant a representative to the state's least populous county. The issue for the Court, then, was not whether Wyoming's policy justified a statewide legislative plan with an 89% maximum deviation, but only whether the state's policy justified the *incremental* deviation from equality resulting from the provision of representation to the county. In a separate concurrence, Justice O'Connor, joined by Justice Stevens, underscored this fact. She stated that the interest in preserving county boundaries would almost certainly not justify a statewide legislative plan with an 89% maximum deviation. Writing that "there is clearly some outer limit to the magnitude of the deviation that is constitutionally permissible even in the face of the strongest justifications," Justice O'Connor

pointed to the 16.4% maximum deviation in Mahon as approaching constitutional limits. Id. at 849–50. Justice Brennan, joined by Justices White, Marshall, and Blackmun, dissented.

11. 403 U.S. 182 (1971).

12. Id. at 187.

13. Reynolds, for example, made clear that not all state justifications would be deemed legitimate. This inquiry into the urgency of the state's goal smacks of strict scrutiny. See also Mahan v. Howell, 410 U.S. 315, 340–41 (1973) (Brennan, J., dissenting).

14. Beyond the fact that it indicated that not all state objectives would be acceptable, Reynolds gave no hint that anything other than the rational relation test would apply. See Casper, "Apportionment and the Right to Vote: Standards of Judicial Scrutiny," 1973 Sup.Ct.Rev. 1, 15.

ler [15] the Court acknowledged the possibility of justifying deviations from the equal population standard: "Art. I, § 2 . . . permits only the limited population variances . . . for which justification is shown." The Court proceeded to reject the justifications Missouri had offered for the deviations in that case. Of particular note was the Court's unwillingness to accept the need to keep political subdivisions intact—a position very much at odds with its attitude toward preserving political boundaries in the context of state and local apportionment.[16] Since *Kirkpatrick*, the Court has appeared somewhat more willing to recognize potentially valid justifications for minor deviations from political equality. In *White v. Weiser*, the Court treated as an open question whether preserving the constituencies of incumbents could justify some population variance.[17] And in *Karcher v. Daggett*, the Court listed a variety of policies that might support some variance; it included in this list the policy rejected in *Kirkpatrick* of respecting municipal boundaries.[18] But in both these cases the Court held that the states had not shown that the population variances were in fact necessary to promote the policies in question.[19] The Court's relatively non-deferential approach in these cases breeds the suspicion that, as far as congressional apportionment is concerned, the possibility of justifying deviations from exact equality is more theoretical than real.

§ 13–7. The Qualitative Dimension: Fair and Effective Representation

When Chief Justice Warren proclaimed one person, one vote an essential component of our constitutional regime, he paid some heed to the non-quantitative components of that regime as well: "achieving . . . fair and effective representation for all citizens is . . . the basic aim of legislative apportionment." [1] The key word is "representation." Ostensibly it imports more than the mere right to cast a vote that will be weighed as heavily as the other votes cast in the election. But how much more? The 1964 reapportionment case did nothing to illuminate this problem.[2] In the years since *Reynolds*, however, the qualitative

---

15. 394 U.S. 526, 531 (1969).

16. 394 U.S. at 533–34. See also White v. Weiser, 412 U.S. 783, 790–91 (1973). The Court in similar fashion rejected the compactness goal: "A State's preference for pleasingly shaped districts can hardly justify population variances." 394 U.S. at 536. The Court emphasized the difference in the standards applicable to state and congressional apportionment plans when, in Mahan v. Howell, 410 U.S. 315, 321 (1973), it suggested that since there were generally more state legislative seats than congressional seats in a given state, political subdivisions could probably be given more recognition in electing state representatives than in electing members of Congress. See generally Martin, "The Supreme Court and State Legislative Apportionment: The Retreat from Absolutism," 9 Val.U.L.Rev. 31, 39 (1974).

17. 412 U.S. 783, 791 (1973).

18. 462 U.S. 725, 740 (1983). The other policies listed as potentially justifying some variance were making districts compact, preserving the cores of prior districts, avoiding contests between incumbent representatives, and preserving the voting strength of minority groups.

19. Karcher v. Daggett, 462 U.S. 725, 742–44 (1983); White v. Weiser, 412 U.S. 783, 791–92 (1973).

§ 13–7

1. Reynolds v. Sims, 377 U.S. 533, 565–66 (1964).

2. Some commentators have accused the Reynolds Court of taking a unidimensional approach to the apportionment problem and of equating equal representation and equal population. See, e.g., R. Dixon,

dimensions of the apportionment puzzle have been thrust upon the Court with increasing frequency.

Claims concerning the qualitative aspect of the right to fair representation have arisen from two distinct apportionment practices. First, apportionment plans sometimes provide that the residents of certain districts are to elect more than one representative. Assuming that such plans allocate representatives to districts in direct proportion to district population, the plans will comply with the equal population rule. Yet multimember district plans may work to submerge particular minority groups.[3] The "winner-take-all" character of the typical election scheme creates the possibility that a specific majority will elect all of the representatives from a multimember district whereas the outvoted minority might have been able to elect some representatives if the multimember district had been broken down into several single member districts. The decision to use multimember districts, then, may serve to eradicate the voice that a minority would otherwise have had in the election halls.[4] Second, apportionment plans often rely on gerrymandering—the drawing of district lines so as to delimit the voting power of cognizable groups of voters.[5] A majority might attempt to abridge or dilute the voting power of a minority by grouping minority voters disproportionately in one or a few districts. While minority voters might thus be assured of a controlling influence in those few districts, they would have no impact on the choice of representatives outside of those districts. Because any vote in excess of a majority (or a plurality) is in a sense wasted, such a plan would render essentially irrelevant the ballots of many of the minority voters. Conversely, the majority might draw district lines so as to spread minority

Representative Government 17, 267–71, 582–83 (1968). These commentators have denied the validity of this equation and stressed the import of the qualitative dimension of apportionment. See, e.g., id. at 582–83; A. Degrazia, Apportionment and Representative Government 53–63 (1963); Sickels, "Dragons, Bacon Strips and Dumnnells—Who's Afraid of Reapportionment?," 75 Yale L.J. 1300 (1966).

3. Multimember districts have also been criticized on other grounds. First, residents of multimember districts allegedly enjoy greater voting power than residents of single member districts or smaller multimember districts. The argument is that while voting power—defined as the ability to cast votes that change election outcomes—declines as the size of the district increases, it declines less than proportionally. As a result, residents of large districts that are represented in proportion to their population are actually overcompensated for the fact that each of them has less impact upon the election of each particular representative than their neighbors have in smaller districts. See Banzhaf, "Multi-member Electoral Districts—Do They Violate the 'One Man, One Vote' Principle?," 75 Yale L.J. 1309 (1966). Sec-

ond, multimember districts allegedly offend the Constitution for logistical reasons. Representatives of such districts are said to command undue significance in the legislature because of the prospects that several members of the same district will vote in a bloc.

4. A minority, even in a fair apportionment scheme, would probably lack the power to ensure that the policies it favors are adopted by the legislature. It is, after all, a minority. But it would have a *voice* in the formulation of policy, and this voice has value independent of its ability to cast a deciding ballot, first because minority spokesmen might persuade the majority on any given occasion and second, because such spokesmen might alter the long-run character of political thought by their participation in legislative deliberations.

5. Gerrymandering is sometimes defined more broadly as apportioning so as to delimit the voting power of a group. So defined, it embraces the use of multimember districts as well as the unscrupulous crafting of district lines. For the sake of clarity, we will use gerrymandering in its narrower sense.

voters out among a number of districts, thereby guaranteeing that they comprise a minority in every district and that they can elect no representative.[6]

In confronting these two apportionment practices, the Court has often proceeded in an uncertain and confusing manner. This lack of clarity was perhaps predictable, because the qualitative aspects of fair apportionment can be assayed only by addressing issues far more subtle than those involved in the one person, one vote context.[7] In recent years, however, a set of articulable standards has begun to emerge for determining when an apportionment plan accords a population group less voting power than is its due. These standards vary according to whether the population group is defined by its race or by its political and ideological views; we shall survey each of these emerging standards in turn.

§ 13–8. Vote Dilution and Racial Groups

The Court first confronted an attempt to cancel out the voting power of a racial minority in *Gomillion v. Lightfoot*,[1] a case which antedated the reapportionment revolution by several years. The Alabama law contested in *Gomillion* had redrawn the boundaries of the City of Tuskegee so as to exclude almost all of the city's black population from the city limits.[2] Justice Frankfurter, writing for the Court, declared the law unconstitutional: "When a legislature thus singles out

---

6. Although the spectre of multimember districts and gerrymanders is conjured most often when dealing with the abridgment of minority rights, the possibility exists that these two techniques might be employed to confine the political power of the electoral majority. Judicious use of multimember districting and gerrymandering might relegate a majority to a much smaller portion of a state's elected representatives than would be the case under an apportionment plan that used all single member disticts and randomly drew district lines. The resulting scheme could condemn a popular majority to representation by a minuscule portion of the elected legislators. For example, if a jurisdiction consisting of 540 Republicans and 460 Democrats were subdivided randomly into 10 districts, Republicans would probably be elected in six or more districts. However, if malevolent Democrats could draw district lines with precision, they might be able to isolate 100 Republicans in one district and win all the other district elections by a margin of one or two votes, thus capturing 90% of the state legislature while commanding only 46% of the popular vote. Although the risk of such outcomes is minimized by the fact that power over districting is likely to be lodged in the group that constitutes the electoral majority, this will not always be the case.

7. In his dissent in Baker v. Carr, Justice Frankfurter admonished: "What is ac-

tually asked of this Court in this case is to choose among competing bases of representation—ultimately, really, among competing theories of political philosophy—in order to establish an appropriate frame of government . . . for all of the States of the Union." 369 U.S. 186, 300 (1962). Cases dealing with the qualitative aspects of the right to fair representation may seem to vindicate Frankfurter's prediction. It does not follow, however, that judicial abstinence is always in order. Some theories of representation are surely constitutionally unacceptable. For example, the Court should feel free to reject a theory of representation that would completely deny votes to members of certain religions. The problem troubling Justice Frankfurter was how the Court was to choose among competing theories of which none was obviously unconstitutional. The Court can minimize the need to make such choices by forcing the states to make and articulate them, but *no* strategy can avoid the necessity for at least some hard substantive decisions of political theory by the federal judiciary.

§ 13–8

1. 364 U.S. 339 (1960).

2. The Court observed: "The result of the act is to deprive the Negro petitioners discriminatorily of the benefits of residence in Tuskegee, including, *inter alia*, the right to vote in Municipal elections." Id.

a readily isolated segment of a racial minority for special discriminatory treatment, it violates the Fifteenth Amendment." [3] The exact import of this holding, however, remained unclear. In *Gomillion*, the Court had struck down an overt and purposeful scheme to deprive a minority racial group of all of its voting power. The question remained whether other devices that diluted or minimized a racial minority's voting power would violate constitutional standards.

The Court began to address this question in *Whitcomb v. Chavis*,[4] in which the plaintiffs urged the Court to overturn the multimember district for Marion County, Indiana because it operated to minimize the voting strength of blacks living in a ghetto within the county. Although declining to rule the multimember district illegal,[5] the Court did make clear that on an adequate record other multimember districts could be overturned for this vice.[6] The plaintiffs had contended that if Marion County were subdivided into single member districts, the ghetto area would elect three members of the House and one Senator, whereas the extant scheme afforded them "almost no political force or control." [7] For the Court, the mere fact that the ghetto did not have a number of elected representatives proportionate to its population did not adequately establish that ghetto residents had less opportunity than did other residents of the county to "participate in the political processes and to elect legislators of their choice." [8] The Court concluded that the challengers had failed to discharge their burden of proving that the use of multimember districts operated "to minimize or cancel out the voting strength of racial or political elements of the voting population" [9] or that it was motivated by an intent to discriminate against the allegedly disadvantaged groups.[10]

---

3. Id. at 346.

4. 403 U.S. 124 (1971). Some years earlier, in Wright v. Rockefeller, 376 U.S. 52 (1964), the Court had upheld with little discussion another districting plan challenged by members of a racial minority. The plaintiffs in Wright had assailed the districting of Manhattan County in which a disproportionate number of the county's blacks and Puerto Ricans were confined in one of the county's four districts. The effect of the plan was that there almost inevitably would be one minority candidate and three non-minority candidates chosen in any election. There was no reason to believe that minorities would elect a smaller total number of representatives under the plan than under a racially neutral scheme, so its impact was not racially disproportionate. Since the Court also rejected the contention that the boundaries were drawn with the intent of fencing minorities in, nothing remained of plaintiffs' claims under the fourteenth and fifteenth amendments.

5. 403 U.S. at 159–60.

6. Id. at 143. Indeed, the Court left open the possibility not only that a particular multimember district might be shown to be unconstitutional, but also that multimember districts might eventually be declared illegal per se if persuasive evidence could establish that such districts generally cancelled out the voting power of minority groups.

7. Id. at 129.

8. Id. at 149.

9. Id. at 143.

10. Id. at 149. The Court also held that the plaintiffs had failed to discharge their burden of showing that the use of multimember districts was unconstitutional for other reasons. Plaintiffs had argued that residents of multimember districts were unduly advantaged because of the possibility that their representatives would vote as a bloc. The Court, however, remained agnostic: "The theory that plural representation itself unduly enhances a district's power and the influence of its voters remains to be demonstrated in practice and in the day-to-day operation of the legislature. Neither the findings of the trial court nor the record before us sustains it, even where bloc voting is posited." Id. at 147. Nor was the Court willing to overturn the multimember district because of alleged math-

The Supreme Court first held a multimember district unconstitutional in *White v. Regester*.[11] Reiterating *Whitcomb's* learning that "plaintiffs' burden is to produce evidence to support findings that the political processes leading to nomination and election were not equally open to participation by the group in question," [12] the Court found the requisite showing in an amalgam of historical and contemporary evidence. The record supported the district court's findings that blacks and Mexican-Americans had been historically discriminated against in the election processes of Dallas and Bexar counties; that they had in fact elected only a few representatives since Reconstruction days; that, in the most recent election, the white-dominated organization that effectively controlled candidate selection in Dallas had relied upon racial campaign tactics in white precincts to ensure the defeat of candidates supported by the black community; and that cultural barriers combined with the most restrictive voter registration procedures in the nation operated effectively to exclude Mexican-Americans from the political processes of Texas even longer than blacks were formally excluded by the white primary.[13]

White v. Regester and *Whitcomb v. Chavis* appeared to suggest that plaintiffs could make out a claim of vote dilution without proving discriminatory intent, but each opinion was ultimately ambiguous on this point. In *Mobile v. Bolden*,[14] the Court resolved this ambiguity in favor of requiring plaintiffs to show discriminatory intent; according to a majority of the Justices, neither the fourteenth nor the fifteenth amendment could invalidate an innocently motivated apportionment scheme.[15] The Court was notably unclear in explaining what kind of proof was necessary to satisfy the intent requirement it had estab-

ematical overrepresentation of its residents. While not disputing the mathematical basis of the plaintiffs' argument, the Court observed that the mathematical model relied upon did not take into account any "political or other factors which might affect the actual voting power of the residents, which might include party affiliation, race, previous voting characteristics or . . . other factors which go into the entire political voting situation." Id. at 146. The Court thus concluded that "the real-life impact of multi-member districts on individual voting power has not been sufficiently demonstrated . . . to warrant departure from prior cases." Id.

11. 412 U.S. 755 (1973). The Court had once before struck down a multimember districting plan, but did so on non-constitutional grounds. In Connor v. Johnson, 402 U.S. 690 (1971), the Court addressed a judicially-created apportionment scheme that provided for some multimember districts in both houses of the state legislature. Invoking its supervisory powers over the federal judicial system, the Court directed the district court, "absent insurmountable diffi-

culties," to devise a plan that did not employ multimember districts. Id. at 692. There was no hint in Connor that the districting scheme did not pass constitutional muster; the Court struck it down on prudential grounds, creating a virtually per se rule against court-ordered multimember district plans in the absence of exigent circumstances. See also Chapman v. Meier, 420 U.S. 1 (1975).

12. Id. at 766.

13. Id. at 766–68.

14. 446 U.S. 55 (1980).

15. A plurality opinion, written by Justice Stewart and joined by Chief Justice Burger, Justice Powell, and Justice Rehnquist, set forth the intent requirement. Id. at 62, 66. Justice White, in a dissenting opinion, explicitly adopted this standard. Id. at 94. Justice Blackmun, concurring in the result, assumed arguendo that intent had to be shown, opined that it was shown, but found the relief afforded by the district court to be excessive. Justice Stevens concurred in the judgment. Justices Brennan, Marshall, and White dissented.

lished.[16] But the Justices left no room for doubt that lower courts had
to find such intent; a mere finding that a districting scheme effectively
excluded a racial minority from a community's political life was insufficient to establish a constitutional violation.

Congress responded to the Court's opinion in *Bolden* by amending
section 2 of the Voting Rights Act to restore the effects standard used
by many lower courts prior to *Bolden*. The amendment made clear
that a violation of the Act could be proved by showing discriminatory
effect alone and established as the relevant legal standard the test
enunciated by the Court in *Whitcomb* and *White v. Regester*.[17] According to the Senate Report which accompanied the amendment, the
intent test established by *Bolden* "ask[ed] the wrong question." [18] The
"right" question, the Report stated repeatedly, was whether "as a result
of the challenged practice or structure plaintiffs do not have an equal
opportunity to participate in the political processes and to elect candidates of their choice." [19]

In *Thornburg v. Gingles*,[20] the Supreme Court reviewed a district
court's determination that a North Carolina redistricting plan violated
the amended section 2 and, in the process, the Court set forth a detailed

16. The plurality opinion in Bolden
found that evidence of the electoral
scheme's discriminatory impact, combined
with proof of past and present discrimination on the part of government officials,
was insufficient to show improper intent in
the case. Id. at 73–74. The opinion, however, gave little indication of what kind of
proof would satisfy the intent requirement.
Two years later, in Rogers v. Lodge, 458
U.S. 613 (1982), a 6–3 majority of the Court
upheld a finding of purposeful discrimination that was based on proof nearly identical to that offered in Mobile. Id at 623–27.
Taken together the opinions gave courts
little or no guidance regarding what kind
of proof was necessary to establish intentional discrimination. Justice Marshall
powerfully argued in his dissent in Bolden
that inquiry into motive should be avoided
when the claim is that a constitutionally
protected right has been abridged and not
simply that something to which the citizen
has *no* independent right or entitlement
has been distributed in a discriminatory
manner.

17. At the time Bolden was decided,
section 2 of the Voting Rights Act provided
that "no voting qualification or prerequisite to voting or standard practice, or procedure shall be imposed or applied by any
State or political subdivision *to deny or
abridge* the right of any citizen of the United States to vote on account of race or
color." (emphasis added). Bolden interpreted section 2 as "intended to have an
effect no different from that of the Fifteenth Amendment itself." 446 U.S. at 61.
In 1982, Congress substituted the words
"in a manner which results in a denial or
abridgment of" for the words in section 2
italicized above. Congress also enacted a
new subsection which stated that "a violation . . . is established if, based on the
totality of the circumstances, it is shown
that the political processes leading to nomination or election in the State or political
subdivision are not equally open to participation by members of a [protected] class of
citizens . . . in that its members have less
opportunity than other members of the
electorate to participate in the political
process and to elect representatives of
their choice. The extent to which members of a protected class have been elected
to office in the State or political subdivision is one circumstance which may be
considered: Provided, That nothing in this
section establishes a right to have members of a protected class elected in numbers
equal to their proportion in the population." 42 U.S.C. § 1973.

18. S. Rep. No. 97–417 at 36 (1982).

19. Id. at 28. See also id. at 2, 27, 29,
36. The Senate Report also charged the
intent standard with being "unnecessarily
divisive" and with placing an "inordinately
difficult" burden of proof on plaintiffs. Id.
at 36.

20. 106 S.Ct. 2752 (1986). Justice Brennan wrote for the Court in an opinion
joined in part by Justices White, Marshall,
Blackmun, and Stevens. Justice O'Connor
concurred in the judgment, in an opinion
joined by Chief Justice Burger and Justices
Powell and Rehnquist. Justice Stevens,
joined by Justices Marshall and Blackmun,
concurred in part and dissented in part.

legal standard for adjudicating section 2 claims.[21]   The Court started
from the premise that minority voters challenging an apportionment
scheme must prove that the use of that scheme "operates to minimize
or cancel out their ability to elect their preferred candidates."[22]   Plaintiffs would be deemed to have established this claim when they had
shown that a "bloc voting majority [was] usually . . . able to defeat
candidates supported by a politically cohesive, geographically insular
minority group."[23]   Under this standard, the Supreme Court stated,
two factors became of primary importance.   First, a court must determine whether minority group members had in fact experienced "substantial difficulty electing representatives of their choice."[24]   Second, a
court must determine whether "significant" racial bloc voting existed.[25]
When these two factors appeared in conjunction, the Court concluded,
plaintiffs should be held to have established their section 2 claim.[26]

Justice O'Connor, joined by Chief Justice Burger and Justices
Powell and Rehnquist, argued that the Court had applied incorrectly
the test enunciated in *Whitcomb* and *White v. Regester* and had failed
to respect congressional intent.   She argued that the Court's standard
resulted in the "creation of a right to a form of proportional representation in favor of all geographically and politically cohesive minority
groups" and that neither Congress nor the Court had ever contemplated going so far.[27]   Yet, as Justice O'Connor herself noted, any theory of
vote dilution will result in the incorporation of some elements of
proportional representation into the electoral system.[28]   When those
bringing such claims are members of minority races, not only the
Voting Rights Act, but also our history and Constitution suggest that
this cost is well worth bearing.

§ 13–9. Vote Dilution and Political Groups

While the Supreme Court grappled with the many claims of vote
dilution brought by plaintiffs representing racial groups, it rarely
confronted vote dilution claims brought by members of political or
ideological groups.   The first Supreme Court case presenting such a

21. The Court held that under the standard articulated, the lower court had ruled
correctly as to four of the North Carolina
districts and incorrectly as to one.

22. 106 S.Ct. at 2765.

23. Id. at 2766 (emphasis omitted).

24. Id. at 2766 n.15.

25. Id.

26. The Court stressed that plaintiffs
could establish a section 2 claim even
though in one or a few elections racial bloc
voting was absent and/or a minority candidate won.   The key questions were whether racial bloc voting usually occurred and
whether minority candidates usually lost.
Id. at 2770.

27. Id. at 2785 (O'Connor, J., concurring
in judgment).   Justice O'Connor here noted

the clause in the amended section 2 that
"nothing in this section establishes a right
to have members of a protected class elected in numbers equal to their proportion in
the population."   42 U.S.C. § 1973.   See
106 S.Ct. at 2784.

28. "[A]ny theory of vote dilution must
necessarily rely to some extent on a measure of minority voting strength that
makes some reference to the proportion
between the minority group and the electorate at large."   Id.   Cf. Note, "The Constitutional Imperative of Proportional Representation," 94 Yale L.J. 163 (1984) (arguing
that proportional representation in an at-
large electoral system is constitutionally
required, because it is the only system that
fully achieves minority representation and
majority rule).

claim was *Gaffney v. Cummings*,[1] in which the Court upheld a Connecticut reapportionment plan drawn with careful attention to party voting habits. There was no factual dispute: "The record abounds with evidence, and it is frankly admitted by those who prepared the plan, that virtually every Senate and House district line was drawn with the conscious intent to create a districting plan that would achieve a rough approximation of the statewide political strengths of the Democratic and Republican parties, the only two parties in the State large enough to elect legislators from discernible geographic areas."[2] The Court thought it idle "to contend that any political consideration taken into account in fashioning a reapportionment plan is sufficient to invalidate it,"[3] and then inveighed against the futility of the "politically mindless approach" of demanding "that those who redistrict and reapportion should work with census, not political, data."[4] After making this pronouncement, the Court fell silent for more than a decade regarding voter apportionment plans designed to affect the voting strength of political and ideological groups.

In *Davis v. Bandemer*,[5] the Court returned to this question and inserted itself foursquare into political apportionment schemes. The plaintiffs in *Bandemer* were Indiana Democrats who challenged a partisan reapportionment accomplished by the Republican-dominated legislature. The plaintiffs complained that the legislature had intentionally drawn district lines and established multimember districts so as to deprive the state's Democrats of their rightful share of voting power. Six members of the Court declared that claims involving political apportionment were justiciable under the Equal Protection Clause. Relying in part on *Gaffney's* implicit finding of justiciability,[6] the Court also argued that the issue in the case presented none of the identifying characteristics of a nonjusticiable political question.[7] The six Justices, however, failed to agree on the standard that courts should use in deciding political apportionment claims. Justice White, in his plurality opinion on the merits, began by asserting that the plaintiffs were required to prove both intentional discrimination against a politi-

---

§ 13–9

1. 412 U.S. 735 (1973).

2. Id. at 752.

3. Id.

4. Id. at 753. The Court's holding appeared to conflict with dictum in Wright v. Rockefeller, 376 U.S. 52 (1964), in which the Court addressed a vote dilution claim brought by members of a racial group. In Wright, as in Gaffney, plaintiffs attacked a districting plan on the ground that it intentionally minimized the voting power of a population group in specific districts while maintaining its power in the jurisdiction as a whole. The Wright Court found no such intention and rejected the plaintiffs' challenge to the scheme. The Court assumed, however, that if a showing of intent had been made, the plan would have been invalidated in spite of its overall neutral impact. The conflict between this dictum and the Gaffney holding no doubt reflects the Court's greater sensitivity to racial discrimination than to discrimination along other lines.

5. 106 S.Ct. 2797 (1986). Justice White wrote for the Court, joined by Justices Brennan, Marshall, Blackmun, and, as to justiciability, by Justices Powell and Stevens as well.

6. Id. at 2803–04.

7. "Disposition of this question does not involve us in a matter more properly decided by a coequal branch of our Government. There is no risk of foreign or domestic disturbance, and in light of our cases since *Baker* we are not persuaded that there are no judicially discernible and manageable standards by which political gerrymander cases are to be decided." Id. at 2805. See also § 3–13, supra.

cal group and a discriminatory effect on that group.[8] The plaintiffs, Justice White stated for the plurality, had easily met the intent requirement;[9] the opinion thus focused on whether the plaintiffs had shown the requisite effects. The proper standard involved what he called a "threshold": "unconstitutional discrimination occurs only when the electoral system is arranged in a manner that will consistently degrade a voter's or a group of voters' influence on the political process as a whole."[10] The mere disadvantaging of a political party in one or two elections, the plurality stated, would not suffice: "equal protection violations may be found only where a history (actual or projected) of disproportionate results appears."[11] Because the plaintiffs had not shown such a history of voter degradation, they had not established a violation of the equal protection clause.

Justice Powell, joined by Justice Stevens, dissented from all but the part of Justice White's opinion that asserted justiciability. Justices Powell and Stevens articulated a different standard for deciding political apportionment challenges, under which they concluded that the plaintiffs had proved their case. Charging that the plurality opinion established no clear guidelines for either legislatures or courts,[12] the two Justices recommended a multi-faceted approach. According to Justices Powell and Stevens, courts should look into "the shapes of voting districts and adherence to established political subdivision boundaries, . . . the nature of the legislative procedures by which the apportionment law was adopted, . . . legislative history reflecting contemporaneous legislative goals, . . . evidence concerning population disparities and statistics tending to show vote dilution."[13] The evidence that the plaintiffs had presented regarding these factors, these two Justices concluded, entitled them to a finding that an equal protection violation had occurred.

In a strongly argued opinion joined by Chief Justice Burger and Justice Rehnquist, Justice O'Connor concurred in the judgment, but attacked the majority's holding that claims of partisan apportionment were justiciable. Justice O'Connor argued for these three Justices that the equal protection clause could not supply judicially manageable standards for resolving political apportionment claims and that the inevitable result of holding such claims justiciable would be to move towards a requirement of roughly proportional representation for every

---

8. Id. at 2808 (White, J., joined by Brennan, Marshall, and Blackmun, JJ., as to the merits).

9. Justice White strongly suggested that the intent requirement in this context was quite minimal. "[Q]uite aside from the anecdotal evidence, the shape of the House and Senate Districts, and the alleged disregard for political boundaries [in this case], we think it most likely that whenever a legislature redistricts, those responsible for the legislation will know the likely political composition of the new districts. . . . As long as redistricting is done by a legislature, it should not be very difficult to prove that the likely political consequences of the reapportionment were intended." Id. at 2808, 2809 (footnote omitted).

10. Id. at 2810. The effects test articulated by Justice White in Bandemer is clearly more difficult to meet than the effects standard the Court has used in determining racial apportionment claims. See § 13–8, supra.

11. Id. at 2814.

12. Id. at 2831 (Powell, J., concurring and dissenting).

13. Id. at 2832 (footnote omitted).

cohesive political group.[14]   Claims of racial gerrymandering, these three Justices noted, presented a different question: they were justiciable because of the greater warrant the equal protection clause gave the Court to intervene in matters affecting race and because of the greater need to protect members of minority races against violations of their voting rights.[15]   Indeed, Justice O'Connor wrote, evidence suggested that political—as opposed to racial—gerrymandering was a "self-limiting enterprise" which could not go beyond narrow bounds.[16]   In these circumstances, the costs of intervention far outweighed any possible advantages that could derive from it.

Justice White's opinion for the Court on the justiciability issue failed adequately to deal with Justice O'Connor's concerns. He equated the Court's decision to intervene in the case with the Court's determination in *Baker v. Carr* to hear claims relating to the disparate size of election districts.[17]   Yet the two kinds of intervention are surely distinct. Although the *Baker* Court did not itself announce the one person, one vote rule, that rule was looming on the near horizon; the *Baker* Court had little reason to fear that no judicially manageable standard could be found. The Court in *Bandemer* had every reason to fear such an eventuality. Neither Justice White's nor Justice Powell's approach to the question of partisan apportionment gives any real guidance to lower courts forced to adjudicate this issue; thus, Justice O'Connor's apprehension that courts will resort to a standard of rough proportional representation appears well-founded.[18]   Further, intervention in *Baker* was necessary in a way in which intervention in *Bandemer* was not. The political system boasted no mechanism that would keep inequalities in district size within an acceptable range. In contrast, as Justice O'Connor noted, the political system itself may be able to keep partisan gerrymandering within narrow bounds. Of

---

14. Id. at 2817 (O'Connor, concurring in the judgment). See Lowenstein & Steinberg, "The Quest for Legislative Districting in the Public Interest: Elusive or Illusory?", 33 UCLA L.Rev. 1 (1985) (arguing that there are no politically neutral criteria for districting—e.g., that the standards of compactness and keeping political subdivisions intact favor Republicans). Cf. Levinson, "Gerrymandering and the Brooding Omnipresence of Proportional Representation: Why Won't It Go Away", 33 UCLA L.Rev. 257 (1985) (arguing that proportional representation is the inevitable result of focusing on individual voting rights rather than giving some "right" or priority to political structures). See also Cain, "Simple vs. Complex Criteria for Partisan Gerrymandering", 33 UCLA L.Rev. 213, 226 (1985) ("Partisan gerrymandering is more like pornography than [it is like] racial discrimination: It occurs between consenting parties (each will do it to the other if given the chance), what is offered is a matter of taste, and any attempt to ban it would lead to more harm than good").

15. Id. at 2820.

16. Id. "In order to gerrymander, the legislative majority must weaken some of its safe seats, thus exposing its own incumbents to greater risks of defeat—risks they may refuse to accept after a certain point. Similarly, an overambitious gerrymander can lead to disaster for the legislative majority: because it has created more seats in which it hopes to win relatively narrow victories, the same swing in overall voting strength will tend to cost the legislative majority more and more seats as the gerrymander becomes more ambitious." Id. at 2820–21 (citations omitted).

17. Id. at 2804–05 (majority opinion). See Baker v. Carr, 369 U.S. 186 (1962), discussed in § 13–2, supra.

18. It is interesting to note that Justice White and Justice Powell each accused the other of articulating a standard that would lead to a system of court-ordered proportional representation. See 106 S.Ct. at 2814–15; id. at 2832 n.13 (Powell, J., concurring and dissenting). Each appears correct in his evaluation of the other's approach, even if incorrect as to his own.

course, the results that *Bandemer* will spawn remain uncertain, but the Court may well come to regret involving the judiciary so deeply in this delicate political sphere.

§ 13–10. Restrictions on the Franchise

Every state, as well as the federal government, imposes some restrictions on the franchise. Although free and open participation in the electoral process lies at the core of democratic institutions, the need to confer the franchise on all who aspire to it is tempered by the recognition that completely unlimited voting could subvert the ideal of popular rule which democracy so ardently embraces. Moreover, in deciding who may and who may not vote in its elections, a community takes a crucial step in defining its identity. If nothing else, even though anyone in the world might have some interest in any given election's outcome, a community should be empowered to exclude from its elections persons with no real nexus to the community as such. Few cases, however, are so clearly defined. This section attempts to identify the doctrinal structure within which the constitutionality of franchise restrictions is appraised.

The Constitution endows the states with the power to determine qualifications for voting even in federal elections, subject to the power of the Congress to override the qualifications states create. Article I, § 2, provides that Members of the House of Representatives are to be elected by the people and that the voters should have the qualifications requisite to vote for members of the state assembly.[1] The Constitution originally conferred the power to elect Senators upon the state legislatures, but the seventeenth amendment provided for the popular election of Senators by voters with the same qualifications required of voters for members of the House of Representatives.

Article I, § 4, conditions this state power to prescribe voting qualifications on congressional acquiescence: "The Times, Places and Manner of holding Elections for Senators and Representatives, shall be prescribed in each State by the Legislature thereof; but the Congress may at any time by Law make or alter such Regulations, except as to the Places of chusing Senators." [2] The Court has explicitly ruled that article I, § 4, invests Congress with broad power to regulate the entire

---

§ 13–10

1. Article I, § 2, instructs that voters for Representatives should have "the Qualifications requisite for electors of the most numerous Branch of the State Legislature." Similarly, § 1 of the seventeenth amendment provides that voters for United States Senators "shall have the qualifications requisite for electors of the most numerous branch of the State legislatures." These qualifications clauses had the basic purpose of "prevent[ing] the mischief that would arise if state voters found themselves disqualified from participation in federal elections." Tashjian v. Republican Party of Connecticut, 107 S.Ct. 544,

556 (1986). Thus, although the qualifications clauses apply to party primaries for House and Senate seats, id., a party rule that would *permit* voting in primaries for these federal offices by non-party members who could *not* vote in primaries for State legislative office does not offend the clauses. Id. See the discussion of Tashjian in § 13–22, infra.

2. On several occasions, the Supreme Court has also bottomed the power of Congress to override state-fashioned voting qualifications on the necessary and proper clause. See United States v. Classic, 313 U.S. 299 (1941); Wiley v. Sinkler, 179 U.S. 58 (1900).

spectrum of voting qualifications in congressional elections.[3] Although the Constitution does not explicitly concede Congress dominion over the qualifications of voters in presidential and vice-presidential elections, the Court has nonetheless ruled that Congress possesses the same power over such elections that it enjoys with respect to congressional elections.[4]

Since the Constitution does not confer upon Congress any general authority to regulate the qualifications for voters in state elections, those qualifications are the exclusive province of the state governments except insofar as they contravene the Constitution or a statute validly enacted by Congress pursuant to some other constitutional authorization. In *Oregon v. Mitchell*,[5] the Court considered the constitutionality of the Voting Rights Acts Amendments of 1970 whereby Congress, purportedly acting under the authority conferred by the enforcement clauses of the fourteenth and fifteenth amendments, lowered the minimum voting age in state elections to 18 years and barred the use of literacy tests in state elections. In a sharply divided opinion, the Court upheld the proscription of literacy tests as a proper means of enforcing the fourteenth and fifteenth amendments in light of the historical evidence demonstrating that such tests had been a vehicle of racial discrimination.[6] In contrast, the Court struck down the 18-year-old vote provisions of the Act because "Congress [had] made no legislative findings that the 21-year-old vote requirement was used by the States to disenfranchise voters on account of race,"[7] and there was probably no evidence to support such a finding. *Mitchell* thus establishes that Congress may not justify a general regulation of state voting qualification requirements by reference to the Civil War Amendments.[8]

Whether enacted by the states or by the federal government, restrictions on the franchise must not abrogate constitutionally guaranteed rights: the fifteenth amendment bars racial restrictions; the nineteenth bars gender restrictions; the twenty-fourth bars poll taxes in federal elections; and the twenty-sixth bars minimum voting ages in excess of 18 years. The most formidable constitutional obstacle for most franchise restrictions, however, is the equal protection clause of the fourteenth amendment. That clause requires, at the least, that a franchise restriction be based upon a principled distinction between the enfranchised and disenfranchised groups; ordinarily it requires that a franchise restriction be shown necessary to serve a compelling state interest.

3. See Smiley v. Holm, 285 U.S. 355, 366 (1932).

4. Oregon v. Mitchell, 400 U.S. 112, 124 (1970); Burroughs v. United States, 290 U.S. 534 (1934).

5. 400 U.S. 112 (1970), discussed in § 5–14, supra.

6. 400 U.S. at 132–33.

7. Id. at 130.

8. The Court's holding that Congress could lower the voting age to 18 in federal but not state elections triggered enough chaos to ensure passage of the twenty-sixth amendment, lowering the voting age to 18 for all elections.

§ 13–11. Restricting the Franchise to "Primarily Interested" Persons

At times, states have limited the right to vote in particular elections to persons who have a special interest or stake in their outcome.[1] Such limitations on the franchise spring, ostensibly, from the perception that voters with an "interest" in the election would cast more fully considered ballots and that such voters should thus be accorded a greater voice in determining the election's outcome. Although the Supreme Court has accepted this argument in one context, the Court has generally proved unwilling to allow such restrictions on the franchise to survive.

Kramer v. Union Free School District No. 15[2] constituted the Court's first vigorous sally into this legal realm. In *Kramer*, a childless bachelor who neither owned nor leased real property challenged a New York statute that limited the vote in certain school district elections to owners or lessees of taxable property, their spouses, and the parents or guardians of children who attended district schools. The state attempted to justify the law by invoking the need to confine the franchise to the group that was " 'primarily interested' in school affairs." The Court declined to pass upon the legitimacy of the asserted state interest but, applying vigorous equal protection scrutiny, found the statute unconstitutional because it was not carefully and precisely tailored to effect that interest.[3] The Court explicitly assumed that the state was concerned not with subjective interest, but rather with an objective stake in the outcome of the election.[4] Having so construed the state interest, the Court held the franchise restriction ill equipped to serve it with the precision demanded by the strict standard of review. The Court found the restriction both underinclusive and overinclusive: "The classifications . . . permit inclusion of many persons who have, at best, a remote and indirect interest in school affairs and, on the other hand, exclude others who have a distinct and direct interest in the school meeting decisions."[5]

The most salient aspect of the Court's opinion in *Kramer* was its endorsement of strict scrutiny for interest-based restrictions on the franchise. The Court bottomed the need to subject restrictions on the franchise to exacting scrutiny on the fundamental character of the right to vote,[6] suggesting that right-to-vote cases challenge the very presumption upon which the minimal scrutiny standard is based— namely, that the elected officials who enacted the statute fairly represent the community.[7]

§ 13–11

1. See also § 13–17, infra.

2. 395 U.S. 621 (1969).

3. Id. at 631.

4. Id.

5. Id. at 632.

6. Id. at 626–27. The Court added that the need for exacting scrutiny is not diminished because, "under a different statutory scheme, the offices subject to election might have been filled through appointment." Id. at 628–29. See also Harper v. Virginia Board of Elections, 383 U.S. 663, 665 (1966).

7. 395 U.S. at 628–29. As applied to a case like Kramer, this point seems uncompelling. There was no suggestion that the New York State Legislature was not fairly elected by all deserving voters, and it was the Legislature that created the voting restrictions for school district elections.

In *Cipriano v. City of Houma*,[8] a companion case to *Kramer*, the plaintiff challenged a Louisiana statute which permitted only property taxpayers to vote in elections called to approve the issuance of public utility revenue bonds. The state asserted that property taxpayers had a special pecuniary interest in the election because the efficiency of the utility system directly affected property values. The Court reserved the question whether the state "might, in some circumstances, constitutionally limit the franchise to qualified voters who are also 'specially interested'," [9] and held simply that the restriction did not serve this interest with the requisite precision since "the benefits and the burdens of the bond issue fall indiscriminately on property owner and non-property owner alike." [10]   In *Phoenix v. Kolodziejski*,[11] the Court extended the *Cipriano* rule to elections called to approve the issuance of general obligation bonds.[12]   Under Arizona law, only otherwise qualified voters who were also real property taxpayers were permitted to vote on such bond issues. The state sought to justify this restriction by observing that, under Arizona law, property taxes had to be levied in amounts sufficient to service the general obligation bonds, which in turn were secured only by the taxing power of the issuing municipality and not by the revenues of particular facilities as was the case with revenue bonds. Rejecting the state's conclusion that property taxpayers' special stake in the outcome of the election warranted the restriction of the franchise to them, the Court noted that all residents have a substantial interest in public facilities; that non-property tax revenues were available to service the bonds; and that the ultimate incidence of the property tax might lie not upon the property owner but upon those who would eventually pay the higher prices or rents charged by the owner to cover the tax. The Court thus found that "there is no basis for concluding that non-property owners are substantially less interested in the issuance of these securities than are property owners." [13]

Although *Kramer, Cipriano*, and *Kolodziejski* each invalidated attempts to confine the franchise to persons with a special interest in the election in question, they all reserved the question whether, in proper circumstances, such a restriction of the franchise would be permissible. In *Salyer Land Co. v. Tulare Lake Basin Water Storage District*,[14] the Court addressed that question and answered it affirmatively. The Court ruled that a statute restricting the vote for directors of a water storage district to landowners in that district, and weighting votes by value of lands held, need only be subjected to minimal scrutiny, because the water district was endowed with few general governmental powers and because its limited purpose of regulating the district's water supply involved an activity disproportionately affecting landowners; since the state's restriction entrusted the franchise to those who bore the prima-

8. 395 U.S. 701 (1969).

9. Id. at 704.

10. Id. at 705.

11. 399 U.S. 204 (1970).

12. The Court, recognizing the extent to which persons might have relied on the

assumption that franchise restrictions in general bond elections were constitutional, applied its holding prospectively only. Id. at 213–15.

13. 399 U.S. at 212.

14. 410 U.S. 719 (1973).

ry burdens and reaped most of the benefits of the district's special activities, the statute was upheld as rational.[15]

In *Ball v. James*,[16] the Court extended the *Salyer* holding when it approved yet another scheme restricting the vote for directors of a water district to landowners in the district. The water district in *Ball*, unlike that in *Salyer*, supplied not only water but also electricity to residents of the state; indeed, 98% of the district's revenues came from sales of electricity whereas only 2% derived from charges assessed for water deliveries.[17] The five-member majority nonetheless held that the district's purpose was so specialized and narrow and that its activities affected landowners so disproportionately as to subject the franchise restriction to only minimal review.[18] The Court found this standard easily satisfied, again asserting that landowners bore most of the burdens and reaped most of the benefits of the district's operations.[19] Justice White, in a spirited dissent, challenged each of the Court's findings. He argued that the district, in supplying both water and electricity, "exercise[d] broad governmental power" and that consumers of electricity, rather than landowners, shouldered the primary burdens of the district's activities.[20] Justice White's assertions appear clearly correct; the Court in *Ball* had treated as controlling a precedent which had only superficial application. The Court seems unlikely, however, to follow *Salyer* and *Ball* in cases that do not involve specialized and apparently proprietary local bodies.[21] *Salyer* and *Ball* rest on the most problematic of foundations [22] and should be treated as a limited exception to the powerful general principle that interest based restrictions are constitutionally disfavored.

§ 13–12. Residency, Durational Residency Requirements, and Voting

Perhaps the most striking exception to the constitutional presumption against interest-based restrictions on the franchise is a rule so well established that it is rarely conceived as an "exception" at all: the rule that a state or municipality may restrict the franchise to its bona fide

---

15. The Court made no attempt to reconcile its holding with its pronouncement in Kramer v. Union Free School District No. 15, 395 U.S. 621, 629 (1969), that the school district's lack of general governmental powers did not diminish the need for strict scrutiny.

16. 451 U.S. 355 (1981). See also § 13–4, supra, text at notes 17–20, and note 20.

17. Id. at 381–82.

18. Once again, the Court did not even attempt to reconcile its holding with its statement in Kramer v. Union Free School District No. 15, 395 U.S. 621 (1969), that the absence of general governmental powers had no bearing on the level of review. Neither did the Court attempt to distinguish Cipriano v. Houma, 395 U.S. 701

(1969), which had necessarily held that the provision of electrical and gas utility services was a sufficiently important governmental function to require application of strict scrutiny.

19. 451 U.S. at 371.

20. Id. at 379, 383–85.

21. The "proprietary" nature of the water district appeared of great significance to the Ball majority. It stressed that the district "cannot enact any laws governing the conduct of citizens, nor does it administer such normal functions of government as the maintenance of streets, the operation of schools, or sanitation, health, or welfare services." Id. at 366.

22. See § 16–56, infra.

residents.¹ The rule recognizes that nonresidents may be affected by and interested in what a state or municipality does, but nonetheless accepts *territory* as the best available means of drawing a boundary for purposes of the franchise. The rule ordinarily applies even to cases in which a municipality or other state subdivision exercises direct extra-territorial powers over individuals residing beyond the subdivision's geographic confines. In *Holt Civic Club v. Tuscaloosa*,² the Court reviewed a variety of Alabama statutes which extended Tuscaloosa's police, sanitary, and business-licensing powers to individuals residing within three miles of the city's corporate boundaries. The majority applied minimal scrutiny and found the rational relationship test fully satisfied.³ Although a footnote in the opinion suggests that the Court might rule differently when a municipality can exercise all of its powers beyond its corporate limits,⁴ the decision clearly indicates that most schemes permitting a subdivision to exercise extraterritorial powers will meet constitutional muster.

The Court, however, has struck down various efforts by the states artificially to circumscribe the concept of residency. In *Dunn v. Blumstein*, for example, the Court held unconstitutional one method that some states had adopted to assess the bona fides of a prospective voter's purported residency.⁵ The Court there ruled that durational residency requirements—requirements that a prospective voter must have been a resident for some specified period of time—are subject to strict scrutiny and, when assayed by that stringent standard, prove constitutionally deficient at least if they set a period as long as several months as a precondition for voting.⁶

The plaintiff in *Dunn* challenged a Tennessee law that required residence in a state for a year and in the county for three months before a citizen became eligible to vote. The state did not deny that the

§ 13–12

1. See Dunn v. Blumstein, 405 U.S. 330, 343 (1972); Pope v. Williams, 193 U.S. 621 (1904).

2. 439 U.S. 60 (1978). Justice Rehnquist wrote for the Court, joined by Chief Justice Burger and Justices Stewart, Blackmun, Powell, and Stevens.

3. The Court stated that "a government unit may legitimately restrict the right to participate in its political processes to those who reside within its borders," id. at 68, and questioned whether any distinction could be drawn between those subject to a municipality's direct extraterritorial powers and those burdened by "the indirect extraterritorial effects of . . . purely internal municipal actions," id. at 69.

4. See id. at 73 n.7. See also id. at 76 (Stevens, J., concurring). The Court noted that Tuscaloosa had no authority to levy ad valorem taxes, invoke the power of eminent domain, or zone property within the police jurisdiction. In dissent, Justice Brennan, joined by Justices White and

Marshall, chided the Court for "ceding to geography a talismanic significance," Id. at 81, and observed that the Court does not "provide any standards for determining when those subjected to extraterritorial municipal legislation will have been 'governed enough' to trigger the protections of the Equal Protection Clause." Id. at 86.

5. 405 U.S. 330 (1972). See also Evans v. Cornman, 398 U.S. 419 (1970) (declaring unconstitutional a Maryland statute that denied the franchise to persons living on the grounds of the National Institutes of Health, a federal enclave carved out of Maryland property); Carrington v. Rash, 380 U.S. 89 (1965) (declaring unconstitutional a Texas statute that denied the franchise to certain residents because they belonged to the armed forces). See § 13–14, infra.

6. The Court thus overruled its earlier pronouncement in Drueding v. Devlin, 380 U.S. 125 (1965) (per curiam), upholding Maryland's durational residency requirements.

plaintiff was in fact a resident (in the usual sense of someone intending to remain), but it denied him the right to vote because he had recently arrived in the state. The Court proffered two reasons for subjecting the franchise restriction to strict scrutiny. First, relying principally on *Kramer v. Union Free School District No. 15*[7] and *Reynolds v. Sims*,[8] it concluded that an "exacting test" is required for statutes that burden the right to vote.[9] Second, it ruled that strict scrutiny was warranted because the durational residency requirement penalized those persons who moved from one jurisdiction to another and thereby burdened the fundamental right to travel.[10] Having thus resolved that the franchise restriction was unconstitutional unless it was "*necessary* to promote a *compelling* state interest," [11] the Court examined the interests articulated by the state and found them inadequate to sustain the voting restriction. The Court acknowledged the urgency of preventing voting by non-residents but insisted that this goal could be realized by some less restrictive means than the durational residency requirement, in an era of sophisticated communications. The Court also questioned the ability of the durational residency requirements to prevent voter fraud, particularly since the record did not reveal that the state attempted to verify the statements of prospective voters that they had indeed been in residence for the requisite period. If a prospective voter were willing to swear falsely that he was a resident, he would presumably be willing to swear falsely about the duration of his alleged residency; the only effect of the requirement, therefore, would be to deny the vote to some persons who were in fact residents.[12] The second interest advanced in support of the durational residency requirement—ensuring "knowledgeable voters"—devolved into three distinct claims, all of which the Court found wanting. First, it rejected the contention that the requirement was needed to ensure that the voter had become part of the community, insisting that a simple residency requirement would serve this end as well. Second, the Court deemed illegitimate the asserted state interest in ensuring that the community has had ample time to impress its views on the voter; states have no right, the Court concluded, to so insulate themselves from novel ideas.[13] Third, the Court found the durational residency requirement too crude a device to effect the state interest in limiting the franchise to voters familiar with local issues; undoubtedly, some new residents were well versed in local issues and some long-time residents were uninformed about them.

---

7. 395 U.S. 621 (1969).

8. 377 U.S. 533 (1964).

9. 405 U.S. at 336–37.

10. 405 U.S. at 338–42. See § 16–8, infra.

11. 405 U.S. at 342.

12. The Court also observed that the one-year residency requirement for living within the state could not possibly be necessary to detect voting fraud if, as the statute apparently contemplated, county officials required only three months to ascertain the bona fides of a prospective voter's alleged residency. Id. at 347.

13. "Tennessee's hopes for voters with a 'common interest in all matters pertaining to [the community's] government' is impermissible. To paraphrase what we said elsewhere, 'All too often, lack of a [common interest] might mean no more than a different interest.' Evans v. Cornman, 398 U.S. at 423. 'Differences of opinion' may not be the basis for excluding any group or person from the franchise. Cipriano v. Houma, 395 U.S. at 705–706." 405 U.S. at 355. See also Carrington v. Rash, 380 U.S. 89, 94 (1965).

Despite the force of these arguments, the Court in 1973 upheld 50-day voter residency requirements as "necessary" to serve the states' "important interest in accurate voter lists." [14]   The dissenters,[15] while insisting that 30 days would give the states ample time to achieve their aims, did not question the permissibility of at least minimal durational rules.

§ 13–13.   Implications of Voter Residency Requirements for Exclusionary Zoning

If territorially-based franchise restrictions (i.e., residency requirements as prerequisites for voting) are to be squared with the basic principle that voting eligibility rules must not be used to fence out persons of any distinct group or persuasion,[1] it follows that zoning and other regulations must not be employed to ensure that only persons belonging to the same racial, ethnic, ideological, or socioeconomic group live (and vote) in a given state, municipality, or other political subdivision.   Although countervailing associational rights of the community itself justify some limitations designed to preserve a community's character,[2] the casualness with which the Court has upheld restrictions frankly intended to preserve "property values" by excluding persons unable to afford large-lot single-family dwellings [3] is understandable only if one recognizes both that this argument linking exclusionary zoning to the franchise has received little attention in the past and that its implications are perhaps too far-reaching to fit comfortably in a judicial approach that stresses deference to state and local autonomy.

§ 13–14.   Voting by Military Personnel or Others Initially Moving to a Community for a Limited Purpose

In *Carrington v. Rash,*[1] the Supreme Court ruled that a state could not deny the franchise to a bona fide resident simply because he was a member of the armed forces.   At issue was a Texas constitutional provision that barred from voting any member of the military who moved his home to Texas during his tour of duty.   Texas sought to justify the franchise restriction on two grounds.   First, it argued that the restriction was necessary to avert "concentrated balloting of military personnel, whose collective voice may overwhelm a small local

---

14. Marston v. Lewis, 410 U.S. 679 (1973) (per curiam); Burns v. Fortson, 410 U.S. 686 (1973) (per curiam).

15. Justices Douglas, Brennan, and Marshall.

§ 13–13

1. Note Dunn v. Blumstein's holding that voting requirements cannot be used to exclude persons of differing perspective or type, § 13–12, supra, note 13; the holding of Carrington v. Rash, 380 U.S. 89, 94 (1965), that " 'fencing out' . . . . a sector of the population because of the way they may vote is constitutionally impermissible," in § 13–14, infra; and the principle that apportionment and districting plans

may not be employed to the end of fencing cognizable groups in or out of particular voter districts.   See §§ 13–8 and 13–9, supra.   See also § 13–15, infra.

2. See the discussion of Village of Belle Terre v. Boraas, 416 U.S. 1 (1974) in § 15–17, infra.

3. See Village of Arlington Heights v. Metropolitan Housing Development Corp., 429 U.S. 252 (1977); James v. Valtierra, 402 U.S. 137 (1971), discussed in § 16–58, infra.   Contrast the poll-tax cases discussed in § 13–15, infra.

§ 13–14

1. 380 U.S. 89 (1965).

civilian community." [2] The Court stressed that Texas might properly deny the vote to military personnel stationed in the state who were not bona fide residents, but it held that the state had no legitimate interest in distinguishing among bona fide residents on the basis of their military status: " 'Fencing out' from the franchise a sector of the population because of the way they may vote is constitutionally impermissible." [3] Second, the state contended that the restriction was justified because of the transient nature of military personnel. The Court again stressed that the state was free to fashion tests of residency that would exclude transients; it could not, however, deny the ballot to prospective voters who passed those tests on the ground that they were members of the military. [4] Employing language that presaged the conclusive presumption cases, [5] the Court held that because the right to vote is so fundamental, military personnel must be permitted to demonstrate that their ties with the state are sufficiently close to entitle them to ballots.

The Court's logic would seem to apply with equal vigor to laws denying the franchise to students or indeed to any other group whose original decision to enter a community might have been unrelated to any wish to remain but who might in the interim have developed deeper ties: as long as the members of such a group can satisfy the traditional tests of residency to which a state subjects all other prospective voters, there is no constitutionally sufficient warrant for excluding them from the franchise.

§ 13–15. Poll Taxes and Literacy Tests

The twenty-fourth amendment forbids conditioning the right to vote in federal elections on the payment of a poll tax, but the Constitution does not explicitly address itself to poll taxes in state elections. In *Breedlove v. Suttles* [1] and *Butler v. Thompson*, [2] the Supreme Court upheld the right of states to make payment of a poll tax a prerequisite to participating in state elections. But in *Harper v. Virginia Board of Elections*, [3] the Court dramatically reversed ground and declared unconstitutional the Virginia poll tax it had upheld 15 years earlier in *Butler*. The Court could divine no state interest that would enable the poll tax to withstand strict scrutiny since "[v]oter qualifications have no relation to wealth nor to paying or not paying this or any other tax." [4]

Prior to *Harper*, the Court had found a legitimate state interest in some literacy tests. In *Lassiter v. Northampton Election Board*, [5] the Court upheld the constitutionality of a North Carolina provision re-

---

2. Id. at 93–94.

3. Id. at 94.

4. "But if they are in fact residents, with the intention of making Texas their home indefinitely, they, as all other qualified residents, have a right to an equal opportunity for political representation." Id.

5. "[T]he presumption here created is . . . definitely conclusive—incapable of being overcome by proof of the most posi-

tive character." Id. at 96. See § 16–32, infra.

§ 13–15

1. 302 U.S. 277 (1937).

2. 341 U.S. 937 (1951) (per curiam).

3. 383 U.S. 663 (1966), discussed more fully in §§ 16–10, 16–47, infra.

4. Id. at 666.

5. 360 U.S. 45 (1959).

stricting the franchise to persons who passed a literacy test.[6] The
Court acknowledged that states could not exercise their power over the
franchise in a capricious manner, but it held that the literacy test had
"some relation to standards designed to promote intelligent use of the
ballot."[7] *Lassiter*, however, antedated the era of exacting scrutiny of
restrictions on the franchise. Although it seems unlikely that the
Court would invalidate all literacy tests, it is not clear how they could
survive the properly herculean demands of strict equal protection
review. Even assuming that a state may properly limit the franchise to
"informed" voters, a literacy test is both underinclusive and overinclusive since some literate persons are completely uninformed on public
issues and, especially in an age of electronic communications,[8] some
illiterate persons are knowledgeable on many public matters. Although literate persons as a group are undoubtedly better informed
than the illiterate, the Court has discredited such group analysis when
rights as fundamental as the franchise are implicated.[9]

While *Lassiter* upheld the North Carolina literacy test, it underscored two scenarios in which a literacy test might be unconstitutional
because it was invidiously discriminatory. First, a literacy test may be
unconstitutional on its face because it gives a state official unfettered
power to make literacy determinations, power the official could exercise
in an invidious manner.[10] Second, even a literacy test fair on its face is
unconstitutional insofar as it is in fact applied in a discriminatory
manner.[11] Finally, the Court has upheld the power of Congress to
suspend literacy tests and to provide other extraordinary remedies in

6. By the time Lassiter was decided, the
Supreme Court had already determined
that literacy requirements could not be
used in conjunction with "grandfather
clauses" to flout the prohibitions of the
fifteenth amendment by imposing a restriction on voting which was in fact based on
race. In Guinn v. United States, 238 U.S.
347 (1915), the Court invalidated the
"grandfather clause" of Oklahoma's constitution under which all voters were required to be able to read and write except
that an inability to read and write would
not disqualify voters, and descendants of
voters, who were "on January 1, 1866, or
at any time prior thereto, entitled to vote
under any form of government, or who at
that time resided in some foreign nation. . . ." The Court found the clause
violated the fifteenth amendment since its
obvious effect was to impose the literacy
test upon former slaves and their descendants. See also Lane v. Wilson, 307 U.S.
268, 275 (1939) (state statute allowing only
12 days for registration for those who had
been disenfranchised by unconstitutional
"grandfather clause" held unconstitutional
because the fifteenth amendment "nullifies
sophisticated as well as simpleminded
modes of discrimination"). See § 5–14, supra.

7. 360 U.S. at 51.

8. Even if the Court could plausibly say
in 1959 that a state might reasonably
equate illiteracy with political ignorance
"in our society where newspapers, periodicals, books, and other printed matter can-
vass and debate campaign issues," 360 U.S.
at 52, such a view in the television-saturat-
ed 1980's would be much harder to maintain.

9. See §§ 13–11, 13–14 supra.

10. For this proposition, the Lassiter
Court cited Davis v. Schnell, 81 F.Supp.
872 (S.D. Ala. 1949), affirmed 336 U.S. 933
(1949). In Davis, the test was the citizen's
ability to "understand and explain" an article of the Federal Constitution; the legislative background of that pliable literacy
test rendered transparent its nature as a
vehicle for racial discrimination. See also
Louisiana v. United States, 380 U.S. 145,
152 (1965) (holding unconstitutional Louisiana statute requiring applicant for registration to give a reasonable interpretation
of any section of the state or federal constitution read to him by the registrar; statute
provided no check on the registrars and
the requirement was used "with phenome-
nal success to keep Negroes from voting. . . .")

11. 360 U.S. at 53. See § 16–17, infra.

states and municipalities where the use of such tests has coincided with low voter participation, a linkage Congress reasonably found to be indicative of past discriminatory practices.[12]

§ 13–16. Disenfranchising Persons Convicted of Crime or Awaiting Trial

In *Richardson v. Ramirez*,[1] the Supreme Court held that, because § 2 of the fourteenth amendment apparently contemplates the disenfranchisement of convicted criminals,[2] the equal protection clause of the fourteenth amendment does not invalidate state laws which deny the ballot to ex-felons.[3] The Court opined that the drafters of the fourteenth amendment "could not have intended to prohibit outright in § 1 . . . [the disenfranchisement of criminals] which was expressly exempted from the lesser sanction . . . imposed by § 2."[4]

The Court's attempt to read these sections of the fourteenth amendment *in pari materia* appears fundamentally misconceived. Although the Court argues fairly persuasively that § 2 of the fourteenth amendment establishes that the framers accepted the disenfranchisement of those convicted of crimes, that section provides no warrant for circumscribing the reach of the equal protection clause which, as the Court had previously emphasized,[5] is not bound to the political theories of a particular era but draws much of its substance from changing social norms and evolving conceptions of equality. If measured against such conceptions in a manner consistent with general equal protection analysis, denial of the franchise to convicted criminals would appear unconstitutional. Because the restriction infringes upon the right to vote, it would be sustained only if it were necessary to secure a compelling state interest. But it is not needed to prevent voter fraud since registration provisions and criminal sanctions constitute less oppressive means of realizing that end even if convicted criminals are unusually prone to indulge in such fraud. Nor can the state's interest in an informed electorate sustain the restriction, since some convicted criminals are, no doubt, even more informed and discerning than their law-abiding fellows. The state interest in deterring crime and punishing criminals is surely compelling, but attempts to justify franchise restriction as an additional penal sanction would founder in the face of alternative criminal sanctions that do not encumber the right to vote.[6]

---

12. South Carolina v. Katzenbach, 383 U.S. 301 (1966); Katzenbach v. Morgan, 384 U.S. 641 (1966); § 5–14, supra.

§ 13–16

1. 418 U.S. 24 (1974).

2. Section 2 provides: "Representatives shall be apportioned among the several States according to their respective numbers . . . But when the right to vote at any election . . . is denied to any of the male inhabitants of such State, being twenty-one years of age, and citizens of the United States, or in any way abridged, *except for participation in rebellion, or other crime*, the basis of representation there-

in shall be reduced . . . .". (Emphasis added.)

3. Davis v. Beason, 133 U.S. 333 (1890), had upheld a law denying the franchise to bigamists, but the only constitutional issue raised in that case concerned the free exercise clause of the first amendment.

4. 418 U.S. at 43.

5. Harper v. Virginia Bd. of Elections, 383 U.S. 663, 669 (1966).

6. This argument highlights a subliminal tension in constitutional doctrine. Because the denial of the vote is not a uniquely needed sanction, it fails to survive strict scrutiny; on the other hand, the imposi-

Even if the holding of *Richardson v. Ramirez*[7] is accepted, however, its rationale plainly does not extend to persons incarcerated awaiting trial but not yet finally convicted. Although the Court has thus far had occasion to vindicate the right of such detainees to vote by absentee ballot only where the state would allow them to do so if incarcerated outside the counties of their residence,[8] and although no right to cast an absentee ballot need exist if alternative means of voting are adequately provided,[9] it should be clear that absolutely foreclosing or significantly burdening an unconvicted detainee's opportunity to vote would be unconstitutional.[10]

§ 13–17. The Power to Recognize Distinctive Voter Interests in Direct Referendum Elections

The principles "applicable in gauging the fairness of an election involving the choice of legislative representatives" have been deemed "of limited relevance . . . in analyzing the propriety of recognizing distinctive voter interests in a 'single-shot' referendum" where voter will is expressed directly rather than through elected representatives, and where the existence of a single, discrete issue makes it far easier "to determine whether its adoption or rejection will have a disproportionate impact on an identifiable group of voters."[1]

For example, when a proposed county reorganization contains provisions that could significantly shift power and responsibility from towns within the county either to cities located in the same county or to the more distant county government itself, it is appropriate for the state to recognize the separate and potentially conflicting interests of town and city dwellers by requiring that the reorganization be separately approved by a majority of each.[2] There is, after all, no absolute constitutional requirement that a change be instituted by a political unit whenever a majority of the people in the unit favor it; from the Constitution itself to a wide array of intermediate devices such as the

---

tion of a prison sentence on a convicted criminal is assumed to comport with the equal protection clause despite the fact that there are probably alternative sanctions and that neither society nor the criminal can conclusively be shown to be benefited by imprisonment for some crimes.

7. 418 U.S. 24 (1974).

8. See O'Brien v. Skinner, 414 U.S. 524 (1974) (holding wholly irrational a state's decision to permit detainees to vote by absentee ballot along with others physically incapacitated if detained outside home county but not if detained near home).

9. McDonald v. Board of Election Comm'rs, 394 U.S. 802, 808 (1969).

10. Cf. Goosby v. Osser, 409 U.S. 512 (1973) (holding the issue to be left open by McDonald and thus proper for a three-judge court).

§ 13–17

1. Town of Lockport v. Citizens for Community Action, 430 U.S. 259, 266 (1977) (upholding provision of New York Constitution whereby county charter can be adopted only if approved by a majority of the city dwellers voting in the county and by a majority of the voting noncity dwellers; citizens favoring a proposed charter for Niagara County are not deprived of any constitutional right when its adoption fails for want of a majority approval by noncity voters, notwithstanding a favorable vote by a majority of those voting in the entire county).

2. Id. The Court noted the absence of any indication that this state requirement tended in general to "favor city to town voter, or town to city voter," id. at 272 n. 18. Had such an inherent tendency been demonstrable, the requirement would clearly have denied equal protection to the category disfavored.

very institution of representative government, our political system has hedged the power of popular majorities to work their will.[3] To give one group a veto over the larger community's wishes even when all have "substantially identical interests" would violate equal protection,[4] but one-shot proposals differently affecting several political communities may be subject to voter approval or veto in each.[5]

Such provisions for what might be called "advice and consent" by each of several distinctly affected geographically or functionally defined constituencies might be analogized to systems for policy-making by centrally appointed officials whose power is checked and partially decentralized by requirements of consultation and consent by each of the groups on whom the power is exercised. So long as the result is not the systemic favoring of one group or interest over another,[6] or the delegation of unaccountable power to groups not acting as politically responsible units,[7] no constitutional right is violated by the procedure.

Acceptance of this argument merely formalizes the pervasive practice of giving separate and distinct weight, when making specific political decisions, to each of several differently affected groups. But that practice should be sharply distinguished from state systems of weighted or otherwise skewed legislative *representation*. It is one thing to pay more attention to, say, landowners or environmentalists on a particular policy issue with special impact on them; it is something else again for the state to translate this supposedly greater interest of a

3. In Gordon v. Lance, 403 U.S. 1 (1971), the Court upheld a state law requiring 60% approval in a referendum as a prerequisite to a political subdivision's incurring of bonded indebtedness. Although such supermajority requirements might appear to violate the "one person, one vote" principle, the Court distinguished them from malapportioned representation schemes by noting that there is "no independently identifiable group or category that favors bonded indebtedness over other forms of financing. Consequently no sector of the population may be said to be 'fenced out' from the franchise because of the way they will vote." 403 U.S. at 5.

Because a law requiring 60% approval is mathematically equivalent to a law requiring only majority approval but weighting "no" votes 1.5 times as heavily as "yes" votes, the ruling in Gordon v. Lance serves to underscore the sense in which voting is distinct from expressing an opinion. For there is no doubt that a law allocating 1.5 times as much access to a public forum to speakers who oppose bonded indebtedness as to speakers who favor it would violate first amendment principles. See § 12–24, supra. In the voting context, a supermajority rule operates not to skew the *expression* of views but to tilt against their direct *translation* into certain kinds of political outcomes—something a jurisdiction must be able to do with respect to

those things that it deems fundamental. Otherwise, states could not, for example, create state constitutional "rights" more generous than those secured by the federal Constitution and resistant to change by ordinary majorities. Because supermajority rules do have this deliberate effect, they can presumably be put in place only by the more rigorous processes jurisdictions adopt for constitution-making or constitution-amending. Otherwise, the mere majority of the moment could freeze its views into law in a way that only a much larger majority could thereafter undo—a possibility that would seem hard to square with the premises of a "republican form of government," art. IV, § 4, discussed in §§ 3–13 and 5–23, supra.

4. Town of Lockport, supra note 1 at 269 (dictum).

5. For example, "a proposal that several school districts join to form a consolidated unit could surely be subject to voter approval in each constituent school district." Id. at 271 (dictum).

6. See note 2, supra.

7. See Eubank v. Richmond, 226 U.S. 137 (1912); Cusack Co. v. Chicago, 242 U.S. 526 (1917); Washington ex rel. Seattle Title Trust Co. v. Roberge, 278 U.S. 116 (1928); cf. City of Eastlake v. Forest City Enterprises, Inc., 426 U.S. 668 (1976).

group into a disproportionate number of representatives for the group in a decision-making body exercising continuing power over a whole class of issues. Now that the Supreme Court has clearly expressed its approval of recognizing distinctive voter interests in the one-shot case, there is even less need than might previously have been thought to accept the far more drastic step of recognizing distinctive voter interests in the context of representation.[8]

§ 13–18. Regulation of Candidates, Campaigns, Conventions, and Elections

Democracy envisions rule by successive temporary majorities. The capacity to displace incumbents in favor of the representatives of a recently coalesced majority is, therefore, an essential attribute of the election system in a democratic republic. Consequently, both citizens and courts should be chary of efforts by government officials to control the very electoral system which is the primary check on their power. Few prospects are so antithetical to the notion of rule by the people as that of a temporary majority entrenching itself by cleverly manipulating the system through which the voters, in theory, can register their dissatisfaction by choosing new leadership.

But in the political marketplace, much as in its economic analogue, laissez faire is not always a satisfactory alternative. Without at least some government regulation of elections, election day—if such a "day" could itself be chosen without collective measures—would yield only the cacophony of an atomized body politic, not the orchestrated voice of an electorate. Although this electoral chaos might not be susceptible to control by prevailing government officials, neither would it permit the orderly selection of their successors. And so the government comes to regulate certain aspects of the electoral process: the eligibility of candidates and voters; ballot access by independent candidates and political parties; conduct during election campaigns; and the financing of such campaigns.

Constitutional review of election and campaign regulation amounts, in large part, to accommodating the fear of a temporary majority entrenching itself with the necessity of making the election a readable barometer of the electorate's preferences. It is not surprising, therefore, that the vigor of judicial review of election laws has been roughly proportioned to their potential for immunizing the current leadership from successful attack. Thus, courts have reviewed rather summarily laws that specify eligibility requirements for particular candidates,[1] but have more carefully appraised the fairness and openness of laws that determine which political groups can place *any* candidate of their choice on the ballot.[2]

---

8. See § 13–11, supra.

§ 13–18

1. There will ordinarily be some eligible candidate to represent any given political persuasion, and there may be no great virtue in having multiple candidates support a given view.

2. That courts should proceed in precisely this manner is the conclusion of Anderson v. Celebrezze, 460 U.S. 780, 793 n.15 (1983) (quoting the preceding language from this treatise's first edition), discussed in § 13–20, infra.

Similarly, laws regulating eligibility to vote are carefully scrutinized by the courts.

§ 13–19. Candidate Eligibility Requirements

The states demand a variety of qualifications from potential political candidates.[1] Since these state-enacted eligibility requirements bar certain persons from holding political office, they must satisfy the requisites of the equal protection clause. The threshold question is whether, as a rule, these eligibility requirements are evaluated by the lower tier equal protection test or whether they demand more exacting judicial scrutiny. Because candidate eligibility requirements do not, as a class, infringe upon constitutionally fundamental rights or draw suspect classifications, they are generally assessed only under the lower tier test discussed in § 16–2, and are sustained so long as they rationally relate to a legitimate state interest.

In *Clements v. Fashing*,[2] the Court upheld two provisions of the Texas Constitution restricting a public official's ability to become a candidate for another public office—a "serve-your-term" provision that prohibited officeholders from cutting short their current terms in order to serve in the state legislature,[3] and a "resign-to-run" rule providing that the holders of certain offices automatically resign their positions if they become candidates of any other elected office.[4] A plurality of the Justices, refusing to characterize candidacy as a fundamental right, found that "the existence of barriers to a candidate's access to the ballot does not itself compel close scrutiny."[5] Heightened scrutiny would be required only if the restriction "unfairly or unneccessarily

See §§ 13–10, 13–11, supra. This is appropriate in part because controlling who is eligible to vote obviously has a profound impact on who can be elected. One eligible candidate may adequately reflect the perspective of those who might have voted for a candidate who has been excluded, but the fact that some voters might represent the viewpoints of a disenfranchised person or group is hardly relevant, since votes, unlike candidates, are additive.

§ 13–19

1. See also § 13–21, infra, on candidate filing fees.

2. 457 U.S. 957 (1982).

3. Article III, § 19, of the Texas Constitution, required officeholders to serve out their current terms of office before they may be eligible to serve in the legislature:

"No judge of any court, Secretary of State, Attorney General, clerk of any court of record, or any person holding a lucrative office under the United States, or this State, or any foreign government shall during the term for which he is elected or appointed, be eligible to the Legislature."

4. Article XVI, § 65, of the Texas Constitution provided, in relevant part:

"[I]f any of the officers named herein [i.e., District Clerks, County Judges, District Attorneys, County Commissioners, Justices of the Peace, and Sheriffs] shall

announce their candidacy, or shall in fact become a candidate, in any General, Special or Primary Election, for any office . . . other than the office then held, at any time when the unexpired term of the office then held shall exceed one (1) year, such announcement or such candidacy shall constitute an automatic resignation of the office then held."

5. 457 U.S. at 963. This holding, announced by Justice Rehnquist, was joined only by Chief Justice Burger, Justice Powell and Justice O'Connor. The holding nonetheless seems entirely defensible. For although groups of voters have a first amendment-based right to associate so as to advance a candidate to represent their views, these associational rights do not seem to require that any *particular* individual serve as that candidate. See "Developments in the Law: Elections," 88 Harv.L.Rev. 1117, 1135 n.81 (1975). Moreover, there is something more than faintly odd, even in a country boasting that anyone can become President, about a society's describing as a "fundamental right" an activity bound to be unthinkable for a vast majority of its members. Thus the efforts to cull a right to candidacy from loose language in Turner v. Fouche, 396 U.S. 346, 362 (1970) (see Note, 45 S.Cal.L.Rev. 996, 1009 n.71 (1972); Note, 40 U.Chi.L. Rev. 357, 367 (1973)) should probably be rejected.

burdens the availability of political opportunity."[6] The plurality observed that, as applied to the only appellee who alleged that he would run for the state legislature, the "serve-your-term" provision operated simply to require that he complete his four-year term as Justice of the Peace before becoming eligible for the legislature; since "legislative elections are held every two years," the only effect was to impose a "maximum 'waiting period' of two years for candidacy by a Justice of the Peace for the legislature," which the plurality deemed a *"de minimis* burden on the political aspirations of a *current* officeholder."[7] That burden was permissible, in the plurality's view, because it helped preserve the integrity of the office of Justice of the Peace by insuring that those serving in that role are not diverted from their duties by election campaigns, and by removing one incentive for such public officials to resign their positions.[8]

The *Clements* plurality rejected the lower court's holding that the "resign-to-run" rule violated the equal protection clause because it applied only to some elected officials and not others.[9] Noting that its

6. 457 U.S. at 964. The plurality recognized that in the ballot access context, the Court has departed from traditional equal protection analysis in cases involving "classifications based on wealth," Bullock v. Carter, 405 U.S. 134 (1972), and "classification schemes that impose burdens on new or small political parties or independent candidates." 457 U.S. at 962. See, e.g., Illinois State Board of Elections v. Socialist Workers Party, 440 U.S. 173 (1979), discussed in § 13–20, infra. However, these exceptions were held inapplicable to the challenged Texas regulations. See also § 13–20, infra. A majority of the Court agreed that the Texas Constitution's restrictions on political candidacy easily survive first amendment analysis in light of restrictions on partisan political activity previously upheld even as to civil servants. Id. at 971–72 (opinion of Rehnquist, J., joined by Burger, C.J., and Powell, Stevens, and O'Connor, JJ.).

7. 457 U.S. at 967. The plurality's arithmetic seems curious. As applied to anyone who has just begun a four-year term, the serve-your-term rule may force a wait of up to six years—the four years left in the officeholder's term plus another two years until another legislative election is held.

8. Id. at 968. Justice Brennan, in a dissent joined by Justices Marshall and Blackmun and, in relevant part, by Justice White, argued forcefully that the plurality was misguided in its attempt to find a legitimate rationale for the law as applied to Justices of the Peace, in particular, rather than focusing on the *classifications* upon which the law was based: "[O]ur equal protection cases have always assessed the legislative purpose in light of the class as the legislature has drawn it, rather than

on the basis of some judicially drawn subclass for which it is possible to posit some legitimate purpose for discriminatory treatment." Id. at 980. The dissent argued that the classifications written into the challenged Texas law were so substantially over- and under-inclusive with respect to the state's goals that the law could not survive even "minimal equal protection scrutiny." Id. at 984 (footnote omitted). The dissent found it "beyond dispute" that the "serve-your-term" provision was over-inclusive when "viewed in light of the asserted purposes of discouraging abuse of office." Id. Likewise, the under-inclusiveness of the "serve-your-term" rule was clear to the dissenters: "The distracting and corrupting effects of campaigning are obviously present in *all* campaigns, not only those for the legislature." Id. The under-inclusiveness was equally apparent because the "resign-to-run" provision only applied to "persons holding any of approximately 16 enumerated offices." Id. "Neither appellants nor the plurality offer any explanation why the State has a greater interest in having the undivided attention of a 'Public Weigher' than of a state criminal court judge, or any reason why the State has a greater interest in preventing the abuse of office by an 'Inspector of Hides and Animals,' than by a justice of the Texas Supreme Court. Yet in each instance [the 'resign-to-run' provision] . . . applies to the former office and not to the latter." Id. at 983–84.

9. "The District Court found § 65 deficient . . . not because of the nature or extent of the provision's restriction on candidacy, but because of the manner in which the offices are classified. According to the District Court, the classification system cannot survive equal protection scruti-

burdens were even less substantial than those imposed by the "serve-your-term" provision,[10] the plurality reasoned that the resignation rule "may be upheld consistent with the 'one step at a time' approach that this Court has undertaken with regard to state regulation not subject to more vigorous scrutiny than that sanctioned by the traditional principles." [11] The fifth vote for the plurality's conclusion was qualified by an insistence that the "one step at a time" approach be limited to distinctions among public offices.[12]

The approach taken by the plurality in *Clements*, and perhaps that of a Court majority, thus seems to support the view that candidate eligibility requirements are not to be evaluated according to the strict scrutiny suitable for abridgments of fundamental rights unless they effectively deny a cognizable group a meaningful right to representation.[13] In *Turner v. Fouche*,[14] the Supreme Court invalidated a provision of the Georgia constitution that required appointees to county school boards to own real property in that state. It reasoned that the property ownership requirement could not possibly serve any state interest since the requirement was satisfied by the ownership of even one square inch of real property.[15] Although *Turner* did not exclude "the possibility that other circumstances might present themselves in which a property qualification for office-holding could survive constitutional scrutiny," it is difficult to conceive of such circumstances. The Court should subject a property ownership requirement to heightened scrutiny,[16] and it bears an exceedingly attenuated relation, at best, to any legitimate state goal.[17]

ny because Texas has failed to explain sufficiently why some elected public officials are subject to § 65 and why others are not." Id. at 970.

10. Id. at 970.

11. Id.

12. Justice Stevens, while concurring in the judgment, opined that the plurality's "one step at a time" analysis was "simply another way of stating that there need be no justification at all for treating two classes differently during the interval between the first step and the second step—an interval that, of course, may well last forever." Id. at 976. He found "such an approach . . . unobjectionable in a case involving the differences between different public offices," but "could not subscribe to [it] in evaluating state legislation that treats different classes of persons differently." Id. at 976 (footnote omitted). The four dissenters also rejected the plurality's approach, adopting Justice Stevens' critique. Id. at 981.

13. Qualification requirements that implicitly exclude controverted political positions are therefore the most suspect. Candidate loyalty oath requirements, for

example, might well deny eligibility to all proponents of a political philosophy that sanctioned the overthrow of the government under certain circumstances. Similarly, property ownership requirements might render ineligible for office all advocates of a political theory that opposed the private ownership of property, or all whose personal circumstances would tend to assure their effective identification with an impecunious constituency. It thus seems crucial to inquire whether there exists any political group upon which a given eligibility requirement is likely to bear in a particularly burdensome way.

14. 396 U.S. 346 (1970). Accord, Chappelle v. Greater Baton Rouge Airport District, 431 U.S. 159 (1977) (per curiam).

15. Turner, 396 U.S. at 363.

16. See Bullock v. Carter, 405 U.S. 134, 144 (1972), discussed in §§ 13–21, 16–48, 16–55, infra.

17. Although reluctance to indulge in wasteful spending may be a fair indicator of responsibility, the ownership of real property—which is simply one species of investment good—is plainly much too ill-fitting a criterion to use in assessing thrift.

The Supreme Court has upheld residency requirements for candidates,[18] and has summarily affirmed judgments of lower federal courts upholding durational requirements as well.[19] Arguably, however, the burden that durational residency requirements impose upon the right to travel in order to change one's state of residence requires stricter scrutiny than such requirements have hitherto received.[20]

Minimum age requirements for candidates for public office should probably be upheld since they rationally relate to the legitimate state interest in ensuring maturity and experience in state office-holders. Since there is no convincing reason to subject these requirements to strict scrutiny,[21] this loose correlation between the statutory classification and the state interest that underlies it should prove sufficient.[22]

Although states often require candidates for political office to take loyalty oaths, many of these requirements appear unconstitutional in light of *Communist Party v. Whitcomb*,[23] where the Court invalidated an Indiana statute which required parties and individuals seeking elective office to file affidavits disavowing advocacy of the violent overthrow of national, state, or local government. Applying the doctrine enunciated in *Brandenburg v. Ohio*,[24] the Court ruled that this oath requirement contravened the first and fourteenth amendments because it embraced the advocacy of political doctrine, and not just the incitement of imminent lawless action. But a candidate may, of course, be required to swear to uphold the federal and state constitutions.

§ 13–20. Party Organization and Political Support

States ordinarily demand minority parties or independent candidates seeking a place on the ballot to demonstrate some degree of political support within the state.[1] In addition, many states deny ballot access to political parties that fail to satisfy certain organizational requirements. Although these barriers to the ballot are not unconstitutional *per se*, they become unconstitutional when too restrictive. De-

18. See, e.g., McCarthy v. Philadelphia Civil Service Comm'n, 424 U.S. 645 (1976) (per curiam) (city employees may be required to reside in city).

19. See Sununu v. Stark, 383 F.Supp. 1287 (D.N.H.1974) (three-judge court), aff'd mem 420 U.S. 958 (1975) (upholding seven year residency requirement for state senatorial candidates); Chimento v. Stark, 353 F.Supp. 1211 (D.N.H.1973) (3 judge court), aff'd mem 414 U.S. 802 (1973) (upholding seven-year residency requirement for gubernatorial candidates). See also Kanapaux v. Ellisor, 419 U.S. 891 (1974).

20. See § 13–12, supra, and § 16–8, infra.

21. But see § 16–31, infra, on the argument for intermediate scrutiny.

22. The fear of ill-informed or immature youth argues more persuasively for a minimum age for voters than for candidates, however. If a youth casts a ballot

imprudently, there can be no check upon it; the electoral process will suffer for immaturity's folly. On the other hand, if a young candidate appears imprudent, the electorate can take that into account and no substantial harm will be done. These possibilities highlight the fact that candidate eligibility requirements, unlike voting eligibility requirements, are designed largely to protect the electorate from its own shortsightedness. A perfectly informed and rational electorate unconstrained by time would need no candidate eligibility requirements, since it could presumably make intelligent individualized determinations of the merits of each candidate.

23. 414 U.S. 441 (1974).

24. 395 U.S. 444 (1969) (per curiam). See § 12–9, supra.

§ 13–20

1. See also § 13–24, infra.

spite several Supreme Court pronouncements on this issue, the border between permissible and impermissible ballot access requirements remains ill-defined. The Court's initial forays into the realm of access requirements were oblique and not wholly consistent. In *Williams v. Rhodes* [2] the Court, with little elucidation, invalidated Ohio's ballot access requirements. In *Jenness v. Fortson* [3] the Court, while professing allegiance to *Williams*, upheld Georgia's access requirements almost summarily. As thesis and antithesis, *Williams* and *Jenness* frame the relevant issues and reveal the doctrinal enigmas that bedevil the law of ballot access.

In *Williams*, the American Independent Party challenged Ohio statutes that would have denied its candidate, George Wallace, access to the 1968 presidential ballot. Ohio required any political party that failed to receive ten percent of the vote in the previous gubernatorial election to file a nominating petition signed by a number of registered voters at least equal to fifteen percent of the number of votes cast in that gubernatorial election; the petitions had to be filed nine months before the presidential election in which ballot access was sought. In addition, parties were required to comply with extensive organizational requirements and to conduct primary elections and national nominating conventions. No independent candidates or write-in votes were permitted. On those facts, the Court held that Ohio's ballot access requirements denied minority parties the equal protection of the laws,[4] and it directed Ohio to place Wallace's name on the presidential ballot.[5] It found that the access requirements trenched on two constitutionally protected rights—"the right of individuals to associate for the advancement of political beliefs, and the right of qualified voters, regardless of their political persuasion, to cast their votes effectively" [6]—and it therefore subjected those requirements to strict scrutiny. The Court acknowledged that the access requirements served legitimate state interests but found none of those interests sufficiently compelling to justify so severe an encroachment upon constitutionally protected rights.

In many respects, *Williams* was an easy case. Ohio's election laws were peculiarly unfavorable to minority parties.[7] As the Court reflected at the outset of the opinion: "The State of Ohio . . . has made

---

2. 393 U.S. 23 (1968).

3. 403 U.S. 431 (1971).

4. The Court easily rebuffed Ohio's argument that its system for selecting presidential electors was immune to equal protection challenge because article 2, § 1, of the Constitution granted every state plenary power to "appoint, in such Manner as the Legislature thereof may direct, a Number of Electors" to choose a President and Vice President. See 393 U.S. at 29.

5. The Court granted declaratory relief to the Socialist Labor Party, the other plaintiff, but determined that it would be impractical to require Ohio to place the Labor Party's candidate on the ballot at the last minute. The position of the two

plaintiff parties differed only in that the Independent Party sought relief from Justice Stewart, sitting as Circuit Justice, several days earlier than the Socialist Labor Party did; Justice Stewart had granted interim relief to the Independent Party, but denied such relief to the Socialist Party because of the pendency of the election. When the case was before the Court, therefore, Ohio had already taken steps to include the former party on the ballot, but had taken no such steps with respect to the latter. Id. at 27–28.

6. 393 U.S. at 30.

7. For a comparison of petition requirements of the several states, see 393 U.S. at 47 n.10 (Harlan J., concurring in result).

it virtually impossible for a new political party, even though it has hundreds of thousands of members . . . to be placed on the state ballot. . . ."[8] The severity of Ohio's laws permitted the Court to treat cavalierly the constitutional basis of its decision, a temptation no doubt augmented by the need for a hasty resolution in light of the fast-approaching election.[9] As a result, both the nature of the constitutional rights implicated and the propriety and urgency of the state interests articulated remained shrouded beneath a veneer of doctrinal generalizations. Since subsequent opinions have professed their fidelity to the paradigm supposedly enunciated in *Williams*, it proves instructive to analyze in some detail the issues there addressed.

The Court strictly scrutinized Ohio's election laws because they infringed upon the right to associate politically and the right to vote, but it did little to illuminate the precise nature of these rights. In its entirety, the Court's treatment of this crucial constitutional issue reads: "The right to form a party for the advancement of political goals means little if a party can be kept off the election ballot and thus denied an equal opportunity to win votes. So also, the right to vote is heavily burdened if that vote may be cast only for one of two parties at a time when other parties are clamoring for a place on the ballot."[10] The right to vote invoked here differs radically from the right to vote that underlay the reapportionment and franchise cases,[11] which involved the right of every citizen to cast a vote as weighty as that of every other. Because there was no claim in *Williams* that any voters were denied the franchise or conferred a diluted vote, the right implicated in *Williams* must have dealt with the right of voters to cast their ballots for particular candidates.[12] In its most extreme form, such a right would lend constitutional foundation to the right to ballot access of any candidate supported by a single voter. And while the right might be more circumscribed, *Williams* shed no light upon its proper boundaries.[13]

The right to associate is more familiar, but it poses similar questions. The right to associate politically commands the protection of the first amendment, and the Court has invalidated statutes that preclude

8. 393 U.S. at 24.

9. Chief Justice Warren, in dissent, reflected that "[a]ppellants' belated requests for extraordinary relief have compelled all members of this Court to decide cases of this magnitude without the unhurried deliberation which is essential to the formulation of sound constitutional principles." 393 U.S. at 63.

10. 393 U.S. at 31.

11. Compare §§ 13–2, 13–10, supra.

12. Because Ohio did not permit any write-in candidates, it is impossible to discern from the Court's opinion whether the rights of voters are satisfied by the ability to write in the candidate of their choice or whether voters must have their chosen candidate placed on the printed ballot. If the core of the voting rights with which the Court was concerned is the ability to declare one's true political preference, write-in votes might be adequate; in contrast, if the voting rights in question deal with the prerogative of each voter to cast a vote that has some real chance of affecting the election outcome, then the poor record of write-in candidates suggests that a place on the printed ballot is essential. In Anderson v. Celebrezze, 460 U.S. 780, 799 n.26 (1983), discussed later in this section, the Court adopted the latter conception of the right to vote. See also Lubin v. Panish, 415 U.S. 709, 719 n.5 (1974), discussed in § 13–21, infra.

13. The Court eventually construed Williams in a rather modest fashion with respect to the nature of the implicated voting rights. See Lubin v. Panish, 415 U.S. 709, 716 (1974).

effective association.[14] *Williams* acknowledged that a statutory regime denying a group the fruits of their association—political impact—runs afoul of the first amendment no less than one that precludes association itself. As Justice Harlan observed in his concurrence, barriers to ballot access deprive minority parties and independent candidates of "much of the substance, if not the form, of their protected rights." [15] That Ohio's election laws, which effectively sterilized all political activity by anyone other than the established political parties, impermissibly burdened the right to associate was clear. But the Court failed to indicate whether a statute that encumbered the ballot access only of those groups that enjoyed no widespread support must also be regarded as so burdening association as to compel strict scrutiny.[16]

Williams' treatment of Ohio's interests in the election laws was also somewhat cryptic. Ohio advanced four interests. First, and perhaps most fundamentally, Ohio asserted an interest in promoting the two-party system in order to "encourage compromise and political stability." [17] The Court did not appraise the legitimacy of the state interest in the two-party system; [18] rather, it concluded that Ohio's election laws were fatally flawed because they protected two *particular* parties, not the two-party system in general. Ohio fashioned such obstacles to ballot access, the Court reasoned, that its election laws effectively required all candidates to affiliate themselves with the Democratic or Republican Parties, a requirement wholly incompatible with the first amendment.[19] The Court underscored the significance of minority parties in our political system and squarely proclaimed the illegitimacy of any state interest in preserving the political status quo.[20]

Second, Ohio professed an interest in ensuring that election winners are the choice of a majority of the electorate. It correctly observed that a simple ballot with more than two candidates ran the risk that the majority of the state's voters might prefer the runner up to the plurality winner. The Court conceded the legitimacy of the state interest in majoritarian rule, but deemed it insufficiently compelling to warrant the suppression of minority interests that Ohio's laws effected.[21] And, of course, several alternative methods of guaranteeing that

---

14. See § 12–26, supra.

15. 393 U.S. at 41 (Harlan, J., concurring in result).

16. The Court did acknowledge that "the number of voters in favor of a party, along with other circumstances, is relevant in considering whether state laws violate the Equal Protection Clause." 393 U.S. at 34. This does not necessarily imply, however, that access barriers disadvantaging groups that lack popular support will not be strictly scrutinized; it may mean only that a less compelling interest will prove adequate when the degree to which political participation is stifled is substantially less than it was in Williams.

17. 393 U.S. at 31–32.

18. It is doubtful that avoiding political extremism is a legitimate state interest;

but if a two-party system only channeled extreme political views into the major parties and did not stifle them altogether, then the posited interest might not run afoul of the first amendment. See generally Barton, "More Nominees or More Representative Nominees?", 22 Stan.L.Rev. 165 (1970).

19. But compare § 13–24, infra.

20. "Competition in ideas and governmental policies is at the core of our electoral process and of the First Amendment freedoms. New parties struggling for their place must have the time and opportunity to organize in order to meet reasonable requirements for ballot position. . . ." 393 U.S. at 32.

21. "But to grant the State power to keep all political parties off the ballot until

the election winner is a majority choice are wholly compatible with a multiparty system.

Third, Ohio claimed that the requirements of party structure and organized primaries ensured that those disaffected with the two major parties would have a choice of leaders and platforms. The Court opined that this goal might be desirable, but that Ohio's election statutes could not achieve it. It postulated that the policies of the major parties did not crystalize until shortly before the election, and that disaffected groups would lack cohesion until that time. Thus Ohio's requirements, rather than affording disaffected groups a choice of candidates and positions, denied them the chance to choose any representative at all.

Finally, Ohio contended that open access to the ballot would lead to lengthy ballots that would confuse the voters and thereby undermine the efficacy of the entire election system. The Court quickly dismissed this justification by observing that forty-two states had petition requirements of one percent or less yet gave no evidence of unduly long ballots or voter confusion; as a practical matter, very few political parties would satisfy even minimal petition requirements. Thus the legitimate state interest in a manageable ballot failed to support restrictions as severe as Ohio's.

In its next major ballot access decision, the Court dramatically reversed field.[22] In *Jenness v. Fortson*,[23] the Court rejected a challenge to Georgia's regulations which denied ballot access to independent candidates unless they paid a filing fee [24] and filed a petition signed by at least five percent of the number of voters registered in the previous election. The Court made only a cursory mention of voting and associational rights, and held simply that "Georgia in no way freezes the status quo, but implicitly recognizes the potential fluidity of American political life." [25] Although it did not explicitly indicate what standard of review it employed, it appeared that the Court subjected the Georgia laws to only minimal scrutiny.[26]

they have enough members to win would stifle the growth of all new parties working to increase their strength from year to year. Considering these Ohio laws in their totality, this interest cannot justify the very severe restrictions on voting and associational rights which Ohio has imposed." 393 U.S. at 32.

22. In the interim, the Court handed down its decision in Moore v. Ogilvie, 394 U.S. 814 (1969), which invalidated an Illinois requirement that independent candidates secure at least 200 signatures in 50 of the state's 102 counties. Moore's scope is uncertain because the Court emphasized that the state's population was unevenly distributed among its counties so that a prospective candidate supported by a large majority of the electorate might be kept off the ballot. 394 U.S. at 816. But a require-

ment that petition signatures be gathered in a specified geographical pattern may be unconstitutional even where county populations are equal, since such an access barrier discriminates against candidates who reflect geographically concentrated interests.

23. 403 U.S. 431 (1971).

24. The validity of the fee requirement was not at issue. Cf. § 13–21, infra.

25. 403 U.S. at 439.

26. In particular, the Court did not inquire whether a petition requirement lower than 5 percent would have satisfied the state's interests; such inquiry into the existence of less restrictive alternatives has always been deemed an essential aspect of strict scrutiny.

The difference in outcome in the two seminal ballot access cases was not that surprising; the Georgia laws upheld in *Jenness* were substantially less oppressive than the Ohio laws overturned in *Williams*.[27] The doctrinal divergence between the cases, however, was striking. *Williams* invoked two ill-defined constitutional rights to justify the most exacting brand of constitutional scrutiny; *Jenness*, in contrast, shunned discussion of the standard of review, contented itself with emphasizing that the laws being reviewed were less suffocating than those in *Williams*, and found the state interests quite sufficient to satisfy whatever standard it did apply.[28] While *Williams* and *Jenness* are counterpoised, if not contradictory, subsequent cases attempted the synthesis. The lesson of these ballot access cases appears to be that *Williams* and *Jenness* marked the end points of a continuum in the responsiveness of an election system to political flux; election schemes more closely approximating *Williams* are unconstitutional, while those bearing a closer resemblance to *Jenness* are acceptable. From the viewpoint of political theory this result may be tolerable; as a pronouncement of doctrine under the equal protection clause, it is positively delphic.

In *American Party v. White*,[29] the plaintiffs challenged a Texas statute that denied ballot position to any political party that neither secured two percent of the vote in the previous general election nor filed petitions signed by registered voters numbering at least one percent of the votes cast in that prior election.[30] The Court acknowledged that the access requirements burdened associational rights, but upheld them because they served two compelling state interests: preserving the integrity of the electoral process and avoiding voter confusion. It emphasized that the qualification requirements did not freeze the political status quo; indeed, two of the plaintiffs had previously satisfied them and qualified for a place on the ballot. *Storer v. Brown*[31] sounded a similar note. The challenged California qualification scheme imposed a five-percent petition requirement for independent candidates and restricted the pool of eligible signers to those who had not participated in another party's primary election.[32] The Court deemed the

27. Unlike Ohio, Georgia freely provided for write-in votes, did not require every candidate to be the nominee of a political party, did not fix an unreasonably early filing deadline for candidates not endorsed by established parties, and did not impose upon a small party or a new party the requirement of establishing elaborate primary election machinery. Thus "Georgia's election laws, unlike Ohio's, [did] not operate to freeze the political status quo." 403 U.S. at 438.

28. See id. at 442.

29. 415 U.S. 767 (1974).

30. They also challenged the Texas statutes to the extent that they required smaller parties to choose their candidates by conventions rather than by primaries as in the case of established parties. The Court was "wholly unpersuaded . . . that

the convention process is invidiously more burdensome than the primary election. . . ." 415 U.S. at 781.

31. 415 U.S. 724 (1974).

32. California also required that an independent candidate not have voted in a party's immediately preceding primary election or have been a registered member of any party within the preceding twelve months. The Court sustained this disaffiliation requirement since it furthered "the State's interest in the stability of its political system," an interest the Court considered "not only permissible, but compelling. . . ." 415 U.S. at 736. The Court indicated that the state interest in political stability was related to preserving the "integrity" of the electoral process and curbing "unrestrained factionalism." The Court's analysis of the disaffiliation re-

record inadequate to determine whether the access requirements were "unconstitutionally severe," and thus remanded the case to the district court to ascertain whether a "reasonably diligent" candidate could be expected to satisfy them.[33]

The most baffling aspect of *American Party* and *Storer* was the standard of review being applied. Although both decisions purported to subject the access requirements to strict scrutiny,[34] each actually assayed the requirements by a far less demanding standard. In particular, the Court in several instances did not inquire whether a less restrictive alternative would adequately protect the state's interests;[35] in other cases the Court placed the burden on those challenging the statutes to establish that a less restrictive alternative existed.[36] On the other hand, the Court did insist that the state interests be not merely legitimate, but compelling.[37] The standard of review actually applied, therefore, seems to have been a mix of strict and minimal scrutiny.

In *Illinois State Board of Elections v. Socialist Workers Party*,[38] the Court, relying on the equal protection clause, struck down an Illinois law requiring new political parties and independent candidates for offices of a political subdivision to file petitions with 5% as many signatures as the number of votes cast in the previous election in that subdivision. In 1977, this provision meant that political parties in Chicago had to obtain 35,947 signatures to appear on the local ballot. Yet, to be placed on the ballot for state-wide offices, new parties and independent candidates had to acquire only 25,000 signatures.[39]

Consistent with its previous ballot access decisions, the Court applied strict scrutiny in *Socialist Workers Party* because the restrictions burdened the "right of individuals to associate for the advancement of political beliefs, and the right of qualified voters, regardless of their political persuasion, to cast their votes effectively." [40] However, unlike *American Party* and *Storer*, the *Socialist Workers Party* Court employed *traditional* strict scrutiny, requiring that the state "establish that its classification is necessary to serve a compelling interest," [41] and

---

quirement was based substantially on Rosario v. Rockefeller, 410 U.S. 752 (1973), in which it had upheld an eleven month disaffiliation requirement for voters. See note 59, infra, and § 13–24, infra.

33. The Court's reference to a "reasonably diligent candidate" is misleading: it seems to imply that access barriers are unconstitutional if any diligent candidate cannot surmount them. The rest of the Storer opinion, however, leaves no doubt that the Court is referring to a reasonably diligent candidate who has a fair amount of popular support.

34. American Party, 415 U.S. at 780; Storer, 415 U.S. at 736.

35. The Court did not inquire whether a more modest petition requirement would adequately serve.

36. Justice Brennan inveighed in dissent against this deviation from traditional strict scrutiny burdens. 415 U.S. at 761. See "The Supreme Court, 1973 Term," 88 Harv.L.Rev. 41, 95–97 (1974).

37. The two-tier equal protection standard has been the object of substantial criticism. See § 16–32, infra.

38. 440 U.S. 173 (1979). Justice Marshall wrote for the Court, joined by Justices Brennan, Stewart, White, Blackmun, and Powell. Chief Justice Burger and Justices Stevens and Rehnquist concurred in the judgment.

39. Id. at 175–77.

40. Id. at 184 (footnote omitted).

41. Id.

that it "adopt the least drastic means to achieve [its] ends." [42]　Because the state's interest was adequately served by 25,000 signatures for state-wide offices, the requirement that a candidate running for office in Chicago receive more than 35,000 signatures was "plainly not the least restrictive means of protecting the State's objectives." [43]　Although it is unlikely that ballot access cases will always be subject to strict scrutiny, the Court's approach in *Socialist Workers Party* may be significant, since the Court could easily have achieved the same result under a form of scrutiny considerably less rigid. [44]

Uncertainty over just how strict the level of scrutiny should be was perpetuated by the Court's decision in *Anderson v. Celebrezze*, [45] which struck down an Ohio statute that, as applied, required John Anderson, an independent candidate for President in 1980, to file signatures of 5,000 voters by March 20 in order to have his name appear on the November ballot. [46]　In *Anderson*, the Court seemingly abandoned the two-tiered equal protection analysis for a more open-ended balancing approach. [47]　Thus, the Court said that it "must first consider the character and magnitude of the asserted injury to the rights protected by the First and Fourteenth Amendments that the plaintiff seeks to vindicate.　It then must identify and evaluate the precise interests put forward by the State as justifications for the burden imposed by its rule.　In passing judgement, the Court must not only determine the legitimacy and strength of each of those interests, it also must consider the extent to which those interests make it necessary to burden the

---

42. Id. at 185.　Although requirements of a "compelling state interest" and the "least restrictive alternative" are traditionally part of heightened equal protection analysis, Justice Blackmun, in a separate concurrence, questioned the usefulness of these terms: "I add these comments to record purposefully, and perhaps somewhat belatedly, my unrelieved discomfort with what seems to be a continuing tendency in this Court to use as tests such easy phrases as 'compelling [state] interest' and 'least drastic [or restrictive] means.'　I have never been able fully to appreciate just what a 'compelling state interest' is. . . .　And, for me, 'least drastic means' is a slippery slope and also a signal of the result the Court has chosen to reach." Id. at 188.

43. Id. at 186.

44. "[A]ppellant has advanced no reason, much less a compelling one, why the State needs a more stringent requirement for Chicago." Id.　Also, as Justice Rehnquist pointed out in his concurrence, the Court's opinion "employs an elaborate analysis where a very simple one would suffice.　The disparity between the state and city signature requirements does not make sense, and this Court is intimately familiar with the reasons why. . . .　The courts having knocked out key panels in an otherwise symmetrical mosaic, it is not

surprising that little sense can be made of what is left." Id. at 190–91.　See Moore v. Ogilvie, 394 U.S. 814 (1969) (holding Illinois law requiring minimum of 200 signatures *in each county* violative of equal protection because different counties had different populations).

45. 460 U.S. 780 (1983).　Justice Stevens wrote for the Court, joined by Chief Justice Burger and Justices Brennan, Marshall, and Blackmun.　Justice Rehnquist dissented, joined by Justices White, Powell, and O'Connor, stressing that "Art. II, § 1, cl. 2, . . . grants an express plenary power to the States" for deciding how Presidential electors shall be appointed. Id. at 806.

46. Id. at 782–83.

47. The Court based its "conclusions directly on the First and Fourteenth Amendments and [did] not engage in a separate Equal Protection analysis." Id. at 786–87 n.7.　However, the Court claimed that it relied on "the analysis in a number of our prior election cases resting on the Equal Protection Clause of the Fourteenth Amendment." Id.　In spite of this professed reliance on its traditional analysis, nowhere in its opinion did the Court even mention the need for "strict scrutiny," a "compelling state interest," or a "least restrictive alternative."

plaintiff's rights. Only after weighing all these factors is the reviewing court in a position to decide whether the challenged provision is unconstitutional." [48]

Of crucial significance to the Court's use of this balancing test in *Anderson* was the fact that the March filing deadline placed a distinctive burden on the rights of an indentifiable class of independent-minded voters because "a late emerging Presidential candidate outside the major parties, whose position on the issues could command widespread community support, is excluded from the Ohio general election ballot." [49] The Court quoted from the first edition of this treatise [50] in explicating its conclusion that "it is especially difficult for the State to justify a restriction that limits political participation by an identifiable political group whose members share a particular viewpoint, associational preference, or economic status." [51] The Court also opined that, in the context of a Presidential election, "state-imposed restrictions implicate a uniquely important national interest." [52]

Ohio attempted to justify its early filing deadline based on the state interest in providing ample time to educate the voters about the candidates,[53] in treating all candidates alike,[54] and in political stability.[55] The Court rejected Ohio's asserted need for seven months to educate the voters, arguing that "[i]n the modern world it is somewhat unrealistic to suggest that it takes seven months to inform the electorate about a particular candidate simply because he lacks a partisan label." [56] The state's equal treatment argument was also found to be without merit. "The name of the nominees of the Democratic and Republican Parties will appear on the Ohio ballot in November even if they did not decide to run until after Ohio's March deadline had passed, but the independent is simply denied a position on the ballot if he waits too long." [57] Finally, the Court rejected Ohio's political stability justification: "Ohio's asserted interest in political stability amounts to a [forbidden] desire to protect existing political parties from competition—competition for campaign workers, voter support, and other campaign resources generated by independent candidates who have previously been affiliated with a party." [58] While the Court's conclusion in *Anderson* seems entirely appropriate, its labored attempt to distinguish Ohio's early filing deadline from the California law it found acceptable in *Storer* [59] is unpersuasive.[60]

48. Id. at 789.

49. Id. at 792.

50. The language quoted appears in this edition in § 13–18, supra, at p. 1097 & note 2.

51. Id. at 792–93.

52. Id. at 794–95.

53. Id. at 796.

54. Id. at 799.

55. Id. at 801.

56. Id. at 797.

57. Id. at 799.

58. Id. at 801.

59. In Storer v. Brown, 415 U.S. 724 (1974), the Court upheld a California statute requiring that an independent candidate not have been affiliated with a political party for the 12 months preceding the primary election. The Court reasoned that the disaffiliation statute "protects the direct primary process by refusing to recognize independent candidates who do not make early plans to leave a party and take the alternative course to the ballot. It works against independent candidacies prompted by short-range political goals, pique, or personal quarrel. It is also a sub-

60. See note 60 on page 1110.

Such doctrinal inconsistency pervades the ballot access cases, and the Court's most recent decision, *Munro v. Socialist Workers Party*,[61] did little to decrease the ambiguity. In *Munro*, the Court upheld a Washington statute requiring that a minor political party's candidate receive over 1% of all votes cast for the office sought in the primary, to be eligible for the general election ballot. In spite of the fact that only one of 12 minor party candidates who sought access to the ballot had qualified since the law's enactment,[62] the Court found that the magnitude of the access restrictions on constitutional rights was "slight when compared to the restrictions we upheld in *Jennes* and *American Party*."[63] The Court opined that the Washington statute was less burdensome because it afforded the Socialist party easy access to a statewide ballot—the primary ballot.[64] Thus, the Court essentially concluded that a statute that allowed reasonable access to a statewide primary would not significantly burden first amendment rights, even if the chance of subsequent access to the general election ballot was remote.[65]

It is still too early to predict whether these cases portend a general retreat from the rigid, two-tiered standard of equal protection review, or whether election cases are for some reason sui generis. Whatever its doctrinal roots, there is a principle to be distilled from the Court's approach in the ballot access cases: in order to keep ballots manageable and protect the integrity of the electoral process, states may condition

---

stantial barrier to a party fielding an 'independent' candidate to capture and bleed off votes in the general election that might well go to another party. . . . It appears obvious to us that the one-year disaffiliation provision furthers the State's interest in the stability of its political system. We also consider that interest as not only permissible, but compelling and as outweighing the interest the candidate and his supporters may have in making a late rather than early decision to seek independent ballot status." 415 U.S. at 735–36. See note 32, supra.

60. Justice Rehnquist, joined by Justices White, Powell and O'Connor, pointed out in dissent that "[t]he similarities between the effect of the Ohio filing deadline and the California disaffiliation statute are obvious. . . . What the Ohio filing deadline prevents is a candidate such as Anderson from seeking a party nomination and then, finding that he is rejected by the party, bolting from the party to form an independent candidacy. This is precisely the same behavior that California sought to prevent by the disaffiliation statute this Court upheld in Storer." Anderson, 460 U.S. at 814.

61. 107 S.Ct. 533 (1986). Justice White's opinion for the Court was joined by Chief Justice Rehnquist and Justices Blackmun, Powell, Stevens, O'Connor, and Scalia.

62. Id. at 538.

63. Id. at 539. The Court also rejected the Party's argument that Washington should be required to prove actual voter confusion, ballot overcrowding, or the presence of frivolous candidates—the justifications the State had offered for the requirement. "Legislatures . . . should be permitted to respond to potential deficiencies in the electoral process with foresight rather than reactively, provided that the response is reasonable and does not significantly impinge on constitutionally-protected rights."

64. Id.

65. However, the Court's treatment of primary elections seems misguided. As Justice Marshall, joined by Justice Brennan, noted in dissent, "to conclude that access to a primary ballot is adequate ballot access presumes that minor party candidates seek only to get elected. But . . . minor party participation in electoral politics serves to expand and affect political debate. Minor parties thus seek "[t]o 'influence, if not always electoral success. Their contribution to diversity and competition in the marketplace of ideas,' does not inevitably implicate their ability to *win* elections. That contribution cannot be realized if they are unable to participate meaningfully in the phase of the electoral process in which policy choices are most seriously considered." Id. at 541 (citations omitted).

access to the ballot upon the demonstration of a "significant, measurable quantum of community support," [66] but cannot require so large or so early a demonstration of support that minority parties or independent candidates [67] have no real chance of obtaining ballot positions. Petition requirements as high as five percent are not unconstitutional per se, but requirements substantially in excess of five percent probably are.[68] In addition, even lower petition requirements might be excessively burdensome if the state substantially restricts the pool of eligible signers,[69] requires the signatures to be collected in an unreasonably short time, or imposes additional burdens on prospective candidates through party organization requirements. In appraising the collective burden imposed by access requirements, one must place substantial weight on empirical evidence demonstrating how often minority parties and independent candidates have actually been able to satisfy them.[70]

§ 13–21. Candidate Filing Fees

In *Lubin v. Panish*,[1] a decision handed down on the same day as *American Party* and *Storer*, the Court sustained the challenge of an indigent candidate to a California statute that required candidates for the office of county supervisor to pay a filing fee in order to secure a ballot position for the primary election. The Court explained: "[I]n the absence of reasonable alternative means of ballot access, a State may not, consistent with constitutional standards, require from an indigent candidate filing fees he cannot pay." [2] In some respects the analysis in *Lubin* paralleled that of *American Party* and *Storer*; the Court applied a standard of review more critical than minimal scrutiny because of the burden on associational and voting rights, and it acknowledged that the state interests in maintaining a manageable ballot and barring frivolous candidacies are compelling. On the other hand, *Lubin*, unlike the other cases, insisted that the state demonstrate that no less restrictive alternatives could promote its interests.[3] Moreover, it spoke of the voting rights at stake in a way that seemed to emphasize the right of the candidate to run for office rather than the right of voters to cast their ballots for a candidate of their choice. *Lubin* thus compounded

---

66. American Party, 415 U.S. at 782.

67. The Court indicated that access to the ballot must be available for both independent candidates and minority parties: "But the political party and the independent candidate approaches to political activity are entirely different and neither is a satisfactory substitute for the other." Storer, 415 U.S. at 745.

68. Id. at 738, 740.

69. A state may regulate the right to sign a candidate's nominating petition, Storer, 415 U.S. at 740–41; American Party, 415 U.S. at 785. As the state restricts the pool of eligible signers, however, the effective signature requirement becomes a higher percent of the real voter pool than is apparent from the face of the statute.

70. American Party, 415 U.S. at 783–84; Storer, 415 U.S. at 742; Williams v. Rhodes, 393 U.S. 23, 33 (1968).

§ 13–21

1. 415 U.S. 709 (1974). See § 16–55, infra.

2. Id. at 718. The Court thus took quite a different doctrinal route than it had in Bullock v. Carter, 405 U.S. 134 (1972), an earlier filing fee case which strictly scrutinized a Texas filing fee provision because it had heavily burdened voting rights in a manner that amounted to a wealth discrimination. See § 16–48, infra.

3. The Court observed that petition requirements would be a less restrictive way of promoting the state interests articulated. 415 U.S. at 718–19. See § 13–20, supra.

the constitutional confusion surrounding the Supreme Court's review of limitations on ballot access.

§ 13–22. Party Autonomy versus Governmental Regulation

Every state has enacted laws that circumscribe, to some extent, the freedom of political parties.[1] While in most cases the parties have yielded to the state's demands, in recent years a number of state laws, especially regulations governing eligibility of delegates to national nominating conventions, have been challenged. Any state law that circumscribes the discretion of a political party infringes associational interests. The critical question here is which such restraints pass constitutional muster.

Before examining the substantive propriety of state regulation of political parties, it is worth addressing the justiciability of party-state disputes. The argument that these disputes are not justiciable is bottomed most frequently upon the political question doctrine. But the mere fact that the suit seeks protection of a political right and is laden with political implications does not mean it presents a political question. In *O'Brien v. Brown*,[2] the Supreme Court nonetheless intimated that the political nature of state-party disputes might put them beyond the reach of the federal courts. In *O'Brien*, the credentials committee of the 1972 Democratic convention had recommended that some of Senator McGovern's California delegates, elected pursuant to that state's winner-take-all primary, be unseated and replaced by delegates favoring Senator Humphrey so that the California delegation would better reflect the distribution of votes in the California primary. The United States Court of Appeals for the District of Columbia granted the relief requested by the unseated McGovern delegates. The Supreme Court reversed because, *inter alia*, it "entertain[ed] grave doubts as to the action taken by the Court of Appeals."[3] These doubts traced, the Court explained, to its realization that courts have traditionally been loath to intervene in delegate disputes and that the convention itself has historically been deemed the proper forum for resolving such controversies; therefore the case raised "[h]ighly important questions . . . concerning justiciability."[4]

Although *O'Brien* thus hinted that credentials disputes might pose non-justiciable political questions, it did not expressly hold as much; rather, the possibility that the case might be non-justiciable was just one of the three reasons advanced by the Court for refusing to consider the merits of the controversy.[5] Our primary recourse must therefore be to the general principles governing the political question doctrine.[6] In terms of those principles credentials disputes and other state-party

1. In particular, most states regulate the processes whereby political parties nominate candidates for state office and select delegates to national nominating conventions.

2. 409 U.S. 1 (1972) (per curiam).

3. Id. at 5.

4. Id. at 4.

5. The other bases for the Court's refusal were the limited time available to resolve the case prior to the opening of the convention, and the possibility that the full convention would provide the plaintiffs with the relief they had requested.

6. See § 3–13, supra.

confrontations seem well within the purview of the federal courts.[7]
Thus the Court's hint in *O'Brien* that such cases are nonjusticiable
seems in error. The Court apparently recognized that its comments in
O'Brien were questionable: in *Cousins v. Wigoda*,[8] the second credentials dispute to reach it, the Court addressed the substantive issue
rather than dismissing the case as nonjusticiable. If the Court had
thought that the issue it confronted was indeed a political question, it
would probably have resolved the case on that ground rather than
examining the plaintiffs' substantive claim and finding it wanting.[9]
Indeed, since *Cousins*, the Court has continued to decide the merits of
state-party confrontations without even mentioning the justiciability
issue.[10]

There is some appeal to the argument that courts should refrain
from entering the state-party fray, since disputes in this area almost
inevitably arise immediately before a convention or election, rarely
leaving courts with enough time to decide them intelligently. But
courts are not without means of devising procedures that can give them
adequate time to consider the cases more fully. Some issues are
litigable well before the convention or election, in other cases a court
can grant relief between the convention and the election; finally, a
court can make its opinion operative only for the future.[11]

Once one reaches the merits, the analytic paradigm employed in
determining the constitutionality of state impingements upon party
autonomy is a familiar one: mild restrictions on political parties must
relate rationally to some legitimate state interest; if a state rule
substantially erodes the freedom of association of party members,
however, the rule will be upheld only if it is shown necessary to serve a
compelling state interest. The only aspect of this paradigm that is at
all peculiar to disputes surrounding political parties concerns the
determination of what state interests are legitimate or compelling, an
issue first broached in *Cousins v. Wigoda*,[12] where the Supreme Court
reviewed a ruling by an Illinois appellate court upholding an order
preventing the 1972 Democratic convention from replacing certain
delegates elected in conformity with Illinois law but in violation of a
party rule.[13] The Supreme Court reversed, reasoning that the injunc-

7. See "Developments in the Law—Elections," 88 Harv.L.Rev. 1111, 1203–04 (1975); Comment, "The Supreme Court and the Credentials Challenge Cases: Ask a Political Question, You Get a Political Answer," 62 Calif.L.Rev. 1344, 1346–47 (1974). But see Kester, "Constitutional Restrictions on Political Parties," 60 Va.L. Rev. 735, 780–81 (1974).

8. 419 U.S. 477 (1975).

9. On some occasions, courts have passed over threshold questions pertaining to justiciability and have resolved cases on more straightforward substantive grounds. See, e.g., Ripon Society, Inc. v. National Rep. Party, 525 F.2d 567 (D.C.Cir. 1975) (en banc), cert. denied, 424 U.S. 933 (1976). This is indeed what the Court in Cousins

purported to do. But the growing inclination of the Court to dispose of thorny issues on threshold grounds strongly suggests that its disclaimer should not be taken too seriously.

10. See, e.g., Democratic Party of United States v. Wisconsin, 450 U.S. 107 (1981); Marchioro v. Chaney, 442 U.S. 191 (1979).

11. Cf. Moore v. Ogilvie, 394 U.S. 814, 816 (1969) (declining to overturn election at behest of unconstitutionally excluded candidate).

12. 419 U.S. 477 (1975).

13. The delegates had been elected in violation of the Democratic Party rule forbidding slate-making. They were excluded

tion served no compelling state interest and that the state therefore lacked sufficient warrant to intrude so severely into the associational rights of the party members.[14] The gravamen of *Cousins* was that the states have a meager interest in preserving the integrity of a *national* nominating convention. Since the national convention is designed to select nominees for the presidency and the vice-presidency, and since "the States themselves have no constitutionally mandated role" in selecting candidates for those offices,[15] the Court concluded that the national convention should be the ultimate arbiter of credentials disputes.

The Court reached a similar result in *Democratic Party of United States v. Wisconsin*,[16] reversing a Wisconsin Supreme Court decision that ordered the National Democratic Party to seat delegates chosen, in compliance with Wisconsin law, by a process that required them to vote in accordance with the results of the state's binding "open" primary.[17] The Democratic Party had refused to seat the delegates because the Wisconsin system violated the party's rule against seating delegates selected in conjunction with binding "open" primaries.[18] Holding that the *Cousins* analysis controlled,[19] the Court found that "[a] political party's choice among the various ways of determining the makeup of a State's delegation to the party's national convention is protected by the Constitution."[20] The Court also found no compelling state interest to

first by the party credentials committee and later by the entire convention.

14. See § 12–26, supra.

15. 419 U.S. at 489–90. But see 419 U.S. at 495–96 (Rehnquist, J., concurring) (arguing that article II, § 1, confers some role on the states in the election of national candidates and that in any event the states possess "residual authority" in that regard).

16. 450 U.S. 107 (1981). Justice Stewart wrote for the Court, joined by Chief Justice Burger and Justices Brennan, White, Marshall, and Stevens. Justice Powell dissented, joined by Justice Blackmun and Rehnquist.

17. "The election laws of Wisconsin allow non-Democrats—including members of other parties and independents—to vote in the Democratic primary without regard to party affiliation and without requiring a public declaration of party preference. The voters in Wisconsin's 'open' primary express their choice among Presidential candidates for the Democratic Party's nomination; they do not vote for delegates to the National Convention. Delegates to the National Convention are chosen separately, after the primary, at caucuses of persons who have stated their affiliation with the Party. But these delegates, under Wisconsin law, are bound to vote at the National Convention in accord with the results of the open primary election." Id. at 110–12.

18. Rule 2A of the Democratic Selection Rules for the 1980 National Convention stated: "Participation in the delegate selection process in primaries or caucuses shall be restricted to Democratic voters only who publicly declare their party preference and have that preference publicly recorded." Id. at 109. Although technically the primary process is not involved in selecting the delegates to the convention, National Party rules stated that the delegate selection process includes any procedure by which delegates to the Convention are bound to vote for the nomination of particular candidates. Id. at 110.

19. Id. at 121: "The issue is whether the State may compel the National Party to seat a delegation chosen in a way that violates the rules of the Party. And this issue was resolved, we believe, in *Cousins v. Wigoda*."

20. Id. at 124. The Court explained that, in its view, freedom to associate to advance political beliefs "necessarily presupposes the freedom to identify the people who constitute the association, and to limit the association to those people only," id. at 122, and quoted this language from the first edition of this treatise: " 'Freedom of association would prove an empty guarantee if associations could not limit control over their decisions to those who share the interests and persuasions that underlie the association's being,' " id. at 122 n.22, quoting what now appears in § 12–26, supra, at p. 1014. Although the state party used

justify the law's burden on associational rights: "The State asserts a compelling interest in preserving the overall integrity of the electoral process, providing secrecy of the ballot, increasing voter participation in primaries, and preventing harassment of voters. But all those interests go to the conduct of the Presidential preference primary—not to the imposition of voting requirements upon those who, in a separate process, are eventually selected as delegates." [21]

While the result in *Democratic Party* may have been correct, the Court paid little or no attention to the public power being wielded by such "private" groups as the National Democratic Party. The Court's indifference to the public influence of the political parties is regrettable. Because the nomination processes of the major parties have become so inextricably bound up with the outcome of the general election, it seems unrealistic to argue that states have no legitimate interest in regulating the electoral system until the major parties have chosen their candidates. Moreover, failure to recognize that these state interests may justify some regulation of the political parties in effect gives those parties the power to *make the law* governing statewide primary elections. Indeed, the Massachusetts Supreme Judicial Court relied on *Democratic Party* in holding that the freedom of association secured by the first amendment in effect compelled Massachusetts to conform its election laws to the state Democratic Party's rule permitting an individual's name to be placed on the primary ballot prescribed by law only if he or she receives 15% of the votes at the state party's convention.[22] Although the Massachusetts court expressedly relied on *Democratic Party*,[23] it is hard to believe that the Supreme Court contemplated giving political parties such lawmaking authority. Yet the Court, over the dissents of Justices Rehnquist, Stevens and O'Connor, refused to hear the state's appeal.[24]

empirical evidence to attack the rationality of the National Party's preclusion of delegates selected in "open primaries," the Court was unpersuaded. "[A]s is true of all expressions of First Amendment freedoms, the courts may not interfere on the ground that they view a particular expression as unwise or irrational." Id. at 124.

21. Id. at 124–25. Justice Powell, in a dissent joined by Justices Blackmun and Rehnquist, disputed the majority's analysis of Wisconsin's interests: "The Court does not dispute that the State serves important interests by its open primary plan. Instead the Court argues that these interests are irrelevant because they do not support a requirement that the outcome of the primary be binding on delegates chosen for the convention. This argument, however, is premised on the unstated assumption that a non-binding primary would be an adequate mechanism for pursuing the state interests involved. This assumption is unsupportable because the very purpose of a Presidential primary . . . [is] to give control over the nomination process to individual voters. Wisconsin cannot do this, and

still pursue the interests underlying an open primary, without making the open primary binding." Id. at 134. While the majority's rationale for refusing to characterize Wisconsin's interests as "compelling" indeed seems flawed, the Court could have easily repeated its reasoning in Cousins—that an individual state has an insufficient interest in the selection of candidates in national elections.

22. Langone v. Secretary of Commonwealth, 388 Mass. 185, 446 N.E.2d 43 (1983), appeal dismissed and cert. denied sub nom. Bellotti v. Connolly, 460 U.S. 1057 (1983).

23. Id. at 194, 446 N.E.2d at 47.

24. Bellotti v. Connolly, 460 U.S. 1057 (1983). Justice Stevens, speaking for the dissenters, argued that "[t]hese appeals present substantial, unresolved questions regarding the accommodation of competing First Amendment values: the interests of would-be candidates and voters in eligibility for the ballot, and the interests of party members in political association without undue governmental intrusion." Id. Fur-

In *Tashjian v. Republican Party of Connecticut*,[25] the Court again sided with a political party in a state-party dispute, striking down a Connecticut statute prohibiting independent voters from participating in the Republican Party's primary. The Party, which had adopted a rule permitting independent voters to vote in Republican primaries for federal and state-wide offices, successfully argued that the statute violated its "first amendment right to enter into political association with individuals of its own choosing."[26] Justice Marshall's opinion for the Court[27] reasoned that the Party's associational rights were significantly burdened although the disenfranchised voters were not even party members: "The statute here places limits upon the group of voters whom the party may invite to participate in the 'basic function' of selecting the Party's candidate. The State thus limits the Party's associational opportunities at the crucial juncture at which the appeal to common principles may be translated into concerted action, and hence to political power in the community."[28] The Court then rejected as "insubstantial"[29] in this case Connecticut's asserted interests in "ensuring the administrability of the primary system, preventing raiding, avoiding voter confusion, and protecting the responsibility of party government."[30]

The Court's conclusion that the statute significantly implicated associational rights is problematic because the disenfranchised voters in this case never sought to join the Republican Party. As Justice Scalia argued in dissent, "[t]he Connecticut voter who, while steadfastly refusing to register as a Republican, casts a vote in the Republican primary, forms no more meaningful an 'association' with the Party than does the independent or the registered Democrat who responds to questions by a Republican Party pollster. If the concept of freedom of association is extended to such casual contacts, it ceases to be of any analytical use."[31]

---

thermore, the dissent rejected the Massachusetts court's reliance on Democratic Party, saying that "Wisconsin's requirement constituted a more significant intrusion on the associational rights of party members than the interpretation of the Massachusetts statute rejected by the Supreme Judicial Court under the perceived compulsion of our Democratic Party decision. Wisconsin required convention delegates to cast their votes for candidates who might have drawn their support from nonparty members. . . . Here, if [the Massachusetts election laws] nullified the 15% rule, Massachusetts would require only that enrolled party members be given a chance to vote for candidates whose nominating papers were signed by some nonparty members and who have drawn less than 15% of the votes at the party convention." Id. at 1062–63. The dissent also distinguished Democratic Party on another ground, saying that, "unlike Wisconsin's attempt to control delegates in a nationwide party contest, the Massachusetts rule

applies to campaigns for statewide office." Id.

25. 107 S.Ct. 544 (1986).

26. Id. at 546. The result of the Court's holding was to create a state-federal disparity arguably violative of the qualification clauses. See note 31 infra. But see § 13–10, supra, note 1, explaining the Court's rejection of this argument.

27. Justice Marshall was joined by Justices Brennan, White, Blackmun, and Powell.

28. Id. at 549–50 (citations omitted).

29. Id. at 554.

30. Id. at 550.

31. Id. at 559–60. But See Note, "Primary Elections and the Collective Right of Freedom of Association", 94 Yale L.J. 117 (1984) (arguing that the closed primary prohibited individuals with whom the party members wish to affiliate from participating in establishing the group's shared ideals). Justice Scalia, who was joined by

The Court, however, has not deferred to political parties in all state-party disputes. In *Marchioro v. Chaney*,[32] a unanimous Court upheld a Washington law requiring each major political party to have a state committee consisting of two persons from each county. The statute in question, enacted in 1927, gave the state committee "the power to call conventions, to provide for the election of delegates to national conventions and for the nomination of Presidential electors, and to fill vacancies on the party ticket."[33] The state committee also received authority from the Washington Democratic Party Charter to "act as the party's governing body when the Convention is in adjournment."[34] In 1976, the party adopted a charter amendment "directing that the State Committee include members other than those specified by state statute."[35] When a question was raised as to the legality of such a change, members of the party brought suit, alleging that "the statutory restriction on the composition of the Democratic State Committee violated their rights to freedom of association."[36] While the party members raised no objection to the statute's regulation of the state-conferred operations of the state committee, they claimed that the statute unconstitutionally regulated the committee's other, purely internal, activities.[37] Hearing the case on appeal, the Court had little trouble dismissing the party's claim. The Court acknowledged that the committee played a significant role in internal party affairs, but noted that "none of these activities . . . [was] required by statute to be performed by the Committee."[38] Therefore, the answer to the party's claim of a substantial burden on first amendment rights was simple: "There can be no complaint that the party's right to govern itself has been substantially burdened by statute when the source of the complaint is the party's own decision to confer critical authority on the State Committee."[39]

The Court in *Marchioro*, unlike *Democratic Party*, seemed to recognize the legitimate state interests in controlling party influence by regulating both primary and general elections: "The requirement that political parties form central or county committees composed of specified representatives from each district is common in the laws of the States. These laws are part of broader election regulations that recog-

Chief Justice Rehnquist and Justice O'Connor, rejected the Court's argument that independents' input into the candidate selection process was necessary to enable the Republicans to nominate "electable" candidates: "The Party is entirely free to put forward, if it wishes, that candidate who has the highest degree of support among Party members and independents combined. The State is under no obligation, however, to let its party primary be used, instead of a party-funded opinion poll, as the means by which the party identifies the relative popularity of its potential candidates among independents." Id. at 560. Cf. Marchioro v. Chaney, 442 U.S. 191 (1979), discussed infra. Justice Stevens, joined by Justice Scalia, dissented on the basis of the qualification clauses of

article I, § 2, and the seventeenth amendment, since the Republican Party's rule, unless overriden by the state statute, would require lesser qualifications for voting in primaries for the House and Senate than for voting in elections of state legislators. See § 13–10, supra, note 1.

32. 442 U.S. 191 (1979).

33. Id. at 193.

34. Id.

35. Id. at 194.

36. Id.

37. Id. at 197.

38. Id. at 198.

39. Id. at 199.

nize the critical role played by political parties in the process of selecting and electing candidates for state and national office. The State's interest in ensuring that this process is conducted in a fair and orderly fashion is unquestionably legitimate." [40] While these observations are undoubtedly correct, it remains unclear, in the context of state party disputes, which state interests should be deemed important enough to justify significant burdens on party autonomy.

§ 13–23. State Action Problems in Political Party Activity

The first, fourteenth, and fifteenth amendments do not regulate private conduct; they govern only the behavior of government.[1] Prior to determining whether various actions taken by or on behalf of political parties comport substantially with the requirements of these amendments, therefore, one must ascertain whether those actions are the state's responsibility.[2] Political parties exhibit many of the attributes of ordinary voluntary associations and yet seem imbued with a quasi-governmental character. While this hybrid aspect of political parties has left uncertain the extent to which constitutional strictures bind their conduct, it is clear that to the extent the law delegates to political parties roles that fit significantly into official electoral or other governmental processes, their claims to private autonomy necessarily begin to give way not only to governmental regulatory power,[3] but also to direct application of federal constitutional norms.[4]

The White Primary Cases, in which the Supreme Court invalidated successive attempts to prevent blacks from participating in Democratic Party politics in the state of Texas, established that the actions of political parties can, under certain circumstances, constitute state action. The cases left unclear, however, exactly what circumstances would justify such a finding. In *Nixon v. Herndon*,[5] the Court had struck down a Texas statute that barred blacks from voting in primary elections. Texas then enacted a law that permitted party executive committees to establish requirements for primary voters; the State

40. Id. at 195–96.

§ 13–23

1. See Chapter 18, infra.

2. Conceptually, the state action question must be addressed at the threshold. As a practical matter, however, courts sometimes address the substantive issue prior to considering the state action question if they think that the substantive issue lacks merit. They can thus dispose of the case without having to resolve the less tractable threshold issue. See, e.g., Cousins v. Wigoda, 419 U.S. 477 (1975); Ripon Society v. National Rep. Party, 525 F.2d 567 (D.C.Cir. 1975) (en banc), cert. denied 424 U.S. 933 (1976).

3. See, e.g., Marchioro v. Chaney, 442 U.S. 191 (1979) (upholding Washington statute requiring major political parties to have state committee authorized to call conventions, provide for election of delegates to the national convention and nomi-

nation of Presidential electors, and fill vacancies on party ticket), discussed in § 13–22, supra.

4. Certainly the direction in which the Court, in Bellotti v. Connolly, 460 U.S. 1057 (1983), allowed the Massachusetts' Supreme Judicial Court to carry a precedent like Democratic Party v. Wisconsin, 450 U.S. 107 (1981), discussed in § 13–22, supra, pushes toward the application of constitutional norms directly upon political parties. For instance, if the Massachusetts Democratic Party may enforce its 15% rule to keep people off the ballot despite their compliance with the state's signature and other requirements, then surely the Constitution imposes some limits on how the party may limit entry to the statewide convention at which the 15% rule is enforced. See also § 18–5, infra.

5. 273 U.S. 536 (1927).

Democratic Executive Committee seized that opportunity and disqualified all blacks from the party primary. In *Nixon v. Condon*,[6] the Court held the executive committee regulation violative of the fourteenth amendment, finding the required state action in the fact that the executive committee had been invested by the state with the power to proclaim voting qualifications. In *Smith v. Allwright*,[7] the Court overruled an earlier decision [8] and held that a resolution by the Democratic Party's state convention excluding blacks from primary elections violated the fifteenth amendment. The Court reasoned that, by guaranteeing ballot access to the winner of the party primary, the state had endorsed the party's disenfranchisement of black members. Finally, in *Terry v. Adams*,[9] the Court ruled that the exclusion of blacks from the pre-primary election of the Jaybird Democratic Association, a group whose candidate almost always secured the nomination of the Democratic Party, contravened the fifteenth amendment.[10]

Read in the context of other state action cases,[11] the White Primary Cases seem to support the proposition that all activities of political parties that are closely related to the nomination of a candidate who will receive some preferential state treatment as the nominee of a political party are deemed the state's responsibility; other activities of political parties constitute private action. Although this reading of the cases commands the support of most commentators [12] and has been endorsed by many lower courts,[13] it has yet to receive the explicit imprimatur of the Supreme Court.[14] The Court of Appeals for the District of Columbia Circuit, moreover, has expressed doubt about

6. 286 U.S. 73 (1932).

7. 321 U.S. 649 (1944).

8. Grovey v. Townsend, 295 U.S. 45 (1935).

9. 345 U.S. 461 (1953).

10. The eight-member majority of the Terry Court reached no consensus on the basis for the finding of state action. Compare 345 U.S. at 475–77 (Frankfurter, J.) (the state had acquiesced in the Jaybird's exclusion of blacks), with id. at 484 (Clark, J.) (the Jaybird election in fact effectively determined the winner of the general election).

11. It has been suggested that the White Primary Cases should be limited to instances of invidious racial discrimination. The Supreme Court lent mild support to this theory in O'Brien v. Brown, 409 U.S. 1, 4 n.1 (1972), by citing the White Primary Cases in a footnote intended to distinguish overt racial discrimination from other less invidious species of discrimination.

12. See, e.g., Rauh, Bode & Fishback, "National Convention Apportionment: The Politics and the Law," 23 Am.U.L.Rev. 1, 3–11 (1973).

13. See, e.g., Redfearn v. Delaware Rep. State Comm., 502 F.2d 1123 (3d Cir. 1974),

vacated and remanded in light of intervening legislation 429 U.S. 809 (1976); Bode v. National Dem. Party, 452 F.2d 1302 (D.C. Cir. 1971), cert. denied 404 U.S. 1019 (1972); Georgia v. National Dem. Party, 447 F.2d 1271 (D.C.Cir. 1971), cert. denied 404 U.S. 858 (1971).

14. However, in Marchioro v. Chaney, 442 U.S. 191, 197–98 (1979), discussed in § 13–22, supra, the Court seemed to recognize the distinction between "external" party activities in which the state has a legitimate interest, and purely "internal" party affairs: "That interest [in the integrity of elections] is served by a state statute requiring that a representative central committee be established, and entrusting that committee with authority to perform limited functions, such as filling vacancies on the party ticket, providing for the nomination of Presidential electors and delegates to national conventions, and calling statewide conventions. Such functions are directly related to the orderly participation of the political party in the electoral process. Appellants have raised no objection to the Committee's performance of these tasks. Rather, it is the Committee's other activities—those involving 'purely internal party decisions,'—that concern appellants." 442 U.S. at 196–97 (footnote omitted).

whether the actions of a political party relating to the selection of candidates do involve state action.[15]

At least three different theories have been advanced in support of the position that various activities of political parties are reviewable as actions of the state. First, it has been argued that political parties discharge a "public function" when they select their candidate.[16] It is not evident, however, why *nominating* a political candidate is a public function.[17] Arguably, the public function doctrine [18] can explain the White Primary Cases because Texas was a one-party state; selection as the candidate of the Democratic Party was tantamount to success in the general election. In a state where nomination by a particular party far from ensured success in the general election, a "public function" determination would have to be bottomed on the fact that state nominating procedures have become so bound up in the state's election process that they have become an "integral part" [19] of the process. Such a statement, however, seems too conclusory to identify which attributes of the nominating process transform otherwise private action into action of the state.[20]

Second, state action has been predicated upon the government's regulation of the party's nominating processes. In the White Primary Cases the Court emphasized that Texas had statutorily required primary elections and had subjected them to some governmental control. This state involvement in and regulation of the political party nominating process helped the Court conclude that the actions of the Democratic Party were state actions.[21] More recent state action decisions, however, shed substantial doubt upon this formulation.[22]

15. Ripon Society v. National Rep. Party, 525 F.2d 567 (1975) (en banc), cert. denied 424 U.S. 933 (1976) (not explicitly resolving the state action issue but intimating that intervening Supreme Court decisions had cast doubt on its earlier determinations that there was state action in the conduct of political parties).

16. See, e.g., Rotunda, "Constitutional and Statutory Restrictions on Political Parties in the Wake of Cousins v. Wigoda," 53 Tex.L.Rev. 935, 952 (1975).

17. See "Developments in the Law—Elections," 88 Harv.L.Rev. 1111, 1160 n.52 (1975).

18. See § 18–5, infra.

19. United States v. Classic, 313 U.S. 299, 314 (1941). Classic reversed the dismissal of an indictment against a state official for miscounting ballots in a primary election. In dictum, the Court indicated that a suit could be instituted against a party official who committed such acts. Id. at 315. Some commentators have predicated the existence of state action in the behavior of political parties on this dictum in Classic. See, e.g., Comment, "Judicial Intervention in Political Party Disputes: The Political Thicket Reconsidered," 22 U.C.L.A.L.Rev. 622, 627 (1975). This reli-

ance on Classic seems misplaced. Classic intimated that party officials would be liable only because their actions would violate the right to vote in congressional elections founded on article I of the Constitution, a right protected, and congressionally protectable, against state and private infringements alike. See id.; "Developments in the Law—Elections," 88 Harv.L.Rev. 1111, 1158–59 (1975); Ripon Society v. National Rep. Party, 525 F.2d 567, 599 (Tamm, J., concurring in result), cert. denied 424 U.S. 933 (1976). Basing state action on the relation between general elections and political party nominating procedures also finds support in a dictum in Gray v. Sanders, 372 U.S. 368 (1963), suggesting that "the action of [the] party in the conduct of its primary constitutes state action," id. at 374. But that statement was not controlling since the party nominating procedure challenged in Gray was in fact dictated by a state statute.

20. See generally "Developments in the Law—Elections," 88 Harv.L.Rev. 1111, 1158–59 (1975).

21. See Nixon v. Condon, 286 U.S. 73, 85 (1932); Smith v. Allwright, 321 U.S. 649, 662–64 (1944).

22. See § 18–7, infra.

The third, and most persuasive, basis for finding state action in the behavior of political parties is that the state incorporates that behavior into its political structure by granting preferential ballot access to the nominees of political parties, thereby making party nomination a kind of "feeder" into the state's official political system. Every state grants access to the general election ballot to the nominees of political parties that satisfy certain conditions, conditions that typically differ from those that independent candidates must satisfy. In effect, therefore, the state delegates to the political party the decidedly governmental function of determining who may gain a place on the ballot.[23] Notwithstanding the failure of the Supreme Court to formulate the governing principle, it thus seems clear that those actions of a political party integrally involved in the selection of a candidate for public office should be treated as state action when the state incorporates the party's choice by conferring some political benefit, such as preferential ballot access, upon that candidate.

§ 13–24. Party Affiliation Requirements

Since the selection of a candidate by a political party will often constitute state action,[1] parties may not arbitrarily restrict the right to vote or to be a candidate in a party primary. The most commonly erected barrier to the franchise or to candidacy is the affiliation requirement:[2] prospective voters or candidates are required to assert or establish their affiliation with the political party either at the time of the primary or convention or for a specified period of time prior thereto.

Voter affiliation requirements are normally designed to safeguard political parties from the perversion wrought by the votes of those who do not share a party's political beliefs or its hopes for electoral success.[3] There can be no doubt that the political party has a legitimate—indeed,

23. See "Developments in the Law," supra note 17, at 1159–63; Kester, "Constitutional Restrictions on Political Parties," 60 Va.L.Rev. 735, 766–67 (1974). This theory finds strong support in the Court's opinions, see Nixon v. Condon, 286 U.S. at 85; Smith v. Allwright, 321 U.S. at 664, and differs radically from the state regulation view; indeed, on this theory it is the *absence* of certain state regulations that effectively ensures the delegation of key questions to the political parties. Cf. Rotunda, supra note 16, at 953–54. This theory is noteworthy for its implication that political parties can divest themselves of state character, and thus broaden the scope of their decision making, if they disavow any special benefits that the state stands prepared to allow them.

§ 13–24

1. See § 13–23, supra.

2. Parties sometimes posit candidate qualification requirements similar to those state-created requirements discussed in §§ 13–19 to 13–20, supra. These requirements should be evaluated by the same test applied to the state-created requirements once the requisite state-action finding has been made; but the fact that a party's legitimate interests obviously differ from a state's gives the test a distinct cast in this setting. A party can demand a pledge of support of the party's nominee, for example, whereas a state can insist only on more neutral forms of loyalty.

3. See, "Developments in the Law—Elections," 88 Harv.L.Rev. 1111, 1164 (1975). Problems of a very different sort are posed by voter affiliation requirements challenged *by political parties* seeking to have *un*affiliated voters participate in their electoral processes. See, e.g., Tashjian v. Republican Party of Connecticut, 107 S.Ct. 544 (1986), discussed in § 13–22, supra. The issues discussed in this section all deal with cases in which the party and the state are aligned in seeking to require affiliation of the would-be voter.

compelling—interest in ensuring that its selection process accurately reflects the collective voice of those who, in some meaningful sense, are affiliated with it. Freedom of association would prove an empty guarantee if associations could not limit control over their decisions to those who share the interests and persuasions that underlie the association's being.[4]

Although a political party's interest in preserving the integrity of its selection system is thus substantial, the constitutionality of some state-imposed affiliation requirements is open to challenge by excluded would-be voters. The Supreme Court has twice examined durational affiliation requirements for voting in party primaries; in one instance the requirement passed constitutional muster, but in the other it was deemed fatally defective. In *Rosario v. Rockefeller*, the Court upheld a New York statute that required those who wished to vote in the primary of a political party to declare their affiliation with that political party eight months prior to the primary in a presidential election and eleven months prior to the primary in a non-presidential election.[5] The plaintiffs urged the Court to scrutinize the affiliation requirement strictly because it purportedly abridged their freedom to associate and their right to vote. The Court declined the invitation, reasoning that the plaintiffs were denied the right to vote in the primary of their party not by the edict of the state, but by their "own failure to take timely steps to effect their enrollment." [6] The Court thus found the state interest in preventing "raiding"—the participation of voters sympathetic to one party in the primary of another for the purpose of selecting a weak representative of that other party as the candidate in the general election—sufficient to justify the affiliation requirement.

In *Kusper v. Pontikes*,[7] however, the Court held unconstitutional an Illinois statute that barred from voting in the primary election of any political party anyone who had voted in the primary of another party within the preceding twenty-three months.[8] The Court deemed the interest in preventing raiding insufficient to warrant locking a voter, for a period of almost two years, into the party in whose primary she had once voted. The Court thought *Rosario* distinguishable: "Unlike the petitioners in *Rosario*, whose disenfranchisement was caused by their own failure to take timely measures to enroll, there was no action that Mrs. Pontikes could have taken to make herself eligible to vote in

---

4. Compare § 15–17, infra.

5. 410 U.S. 752 (1973). The statute created some exceptions. For example, those who only recently reached voting age and those who only recently satisfied the residency requirements for voting were permitted to make a belated profession of their party affiliation.

6. 410 U.S. at 758, 762.

7. 414 U.S. 51 (1973).

8. The Court has subsequently interpreted Kusper to be a vindication of a right of a political party, as well as of its members, to associate free of unreasonable governmental interference: "[T]he freedom to associate for the 'common advancement of political beliefs,' necessarily presupposes the freedom to identify the people who constitute the association and to limit the association to those people only. 'Any interference with the freedom of a party is simultaneously an interference with the freedom of its adherents.' " Democratic Party of United States v. Wisconsin, 450 U.S. 107, 121–22 (1981) (footnotes omitted), discussed in § 13–22, supra.

the 1972 Democratic primary." [9]   Indeed, the Court deemed the scheme approved in *Rosario* a less restrictive means of effecting the articulated state interest in preventing raiding.[10]

A principled reconciliation of the two cases is not as simple as *Kusper* indicated. It it clear, first of all, that the divergent holdings cannot be attributed entirely to the longer affiliation period required in *Kusper*.[11] Although the Court was plainly and properly disturbed by the twenty-three month affiliation period, its language suggested that the crucial distinction was that in *Kusper* the state prevented the plaintiff from voting in a particular primary while in *Rosario* the plaintiffs prevented themselves from voting in the primary by failing to enroll on time. But unless certain purifying factual assumptions are made in *Rosario*, this distinction is untenable. In both *Rosario* and *Kusper*, the plaintiffs pursued a pattern of behavior that, by operation of state law, barred them from voting in a primary election of their party. In *Rosario*, the plaintiffs failed to enroll eight months before the election; in *Kusper*, the plaintiff failed to abstain from voting in the primary election of another political party. It is thus incorrect to conclude that in *Rosario* it was the plaintiffs and in *Kusper* the state that erected the barrier to voting; in both cases it was the conjunction of public and private action that caused the denial of the franchise.

A principled distinction between the two cases is possible, however, if we assume that eight months prior to the primary election the plaintiffs in *Rosario* knew or ought to have realized that they would want to vote in the primary election of that political party.[12] In that event, the Court's emphasis on the self-inflicted character of the disenfranchisement becomes more reasonable. For if the plaintiffs did intend to vote in a particular party's primary election, it was truly their tardiness, rather than the operation of state law, that should be blamed for their inability to cast a ballot. In contrast, it seems unreasonable to insist that the plaintiff in *Kusper* should have thought of the still distant primary election when she cast her ballot in the preceding primary. It is thus probable that, from the moment she decided to switch to the Democratic party, there was nothing she could do to ensure her vote in its next primary—even though it may have been almost two years away. If this is the critical distinction between the cases, then the New York statute approved in *Rosario* might still be deemed unconstitutional as applied to voters who decided to change their affiliation within the eight month or eleven month periods.[13]

9. Id. at 60.

10. It is unclear that the New York statute was actually less restrictive in all situations. As far as new voters and those voters who did not cast ballots in recent primary elections were concerned, the Illinois statute seemed less restrictive since they were under no obligation to declare their affiliation in advance of the election.

11. This is not to say, however, that an otherwise acceptable affiliation requirement could not be rendered unconstitutional because the affiliation period was unreasonably long.

12. Although the Rosario Court did not explicitly make this assumption, it did observe that the plaintiffs failed to explain their failure to enroll as party members within the required time.

13. Admittedly, once any but the narrowest exceptions are crafted for those who change their political stance shortly before an election, the ability of the durational affiliation requirements to preserve the in-

When the Supreme Court next addresses the constitutionality of durational voter affiliation requirements, it should regard them with a most critical eye. For if the disenfranchisement is, in some real sense, ordered by the state rather than chosen by the voter, then the requirement clearly abridges fundamental associational rights.[14] Although preserving the integrity of the primary election is a compelling state interest, the link between durational affiliation requirements and the integrity of the primary is attenuated by its dependence on two key assumptions: first, that voters will attempt to "raid" in sufficient numbers to jeopardize the primary's integrity; and second, that the durational affiliation is a necessary and sufficient way of preventing this evil.

Contemporaneous affiliation requirements are far less troubling, when imposed by a political party, or by state law at the party's behest. There can be little objection to a requirement sought by a party that those wishing to vote in its primary profess that, as of that time, they are affiliated with that party. Absent a willingness to profess such affiliation, it would be tenuous to assert that a would-be voter's substantial associational rights were being abridged; without a commonality of interest, there is little association to abridge.[15] Although the ability of contemporaneous affiliation requirements to effect the proffered state interests is questionable—a dishonest person may simply lie and profess affiliation where none exists—the possibility that these requirements will immunize primary elections from at least some voters who do not identify with the party is plausible enough to render these requirements constitutional.

Both contemporaneous and durational affiliation requirements for candidates (as opposed to voters) are likely to be upheld even if they require quite long affiliation periods. Since denying an individual the

---

tegrity of the primary election is diluted inasmuch as any raider could assert that he or she was a recent convert to the party, and might even be able to adduce convincing evidence of a genuine change of political belief. It may be, therefore, that the counterpoised interests cannot be simultaneously secured in their entirety, and that an acceptable accommodation of those interests would be a rigid affiliation period that was not excessively long, viewed as a conclusive presumption that any changes-of-heart within that period were not genuinely motivated. See generally Rosario, 410 U.S. at 771 (Powell, J., dissenting) (suggesting 30 or 60 day affiliation period); cf. Weinberger v. Salfi, 422 U.S. 749 (1975), discussed in § 16–34, infra.

14. If a voter simply chose not to comply with an affiliation requirement, that voter could be said to have waived his associational rights. It is difficult to claim that there has been any waiver, however, if the voter was unaware of the affiliation requirement, since constitutional rights must generally be knowingly and intelli-

gently relinquished. A prospective voter might also predicate on the right to vote a claim that a durational affiliation requirement should be strictly scrutinized. But the Court has yet to declare constitutionally fundamental the right to vote in a primary election.

15. To be sure, a political party is deemed to have an associational interest, even absent such commonality, in inducing non-members to participate in the party's primary, see Tashjian v. Republican Party of Connecticut, 107 S.Ct. 544 (1986), discussed in § 13–22, supra. But the non-member's associational claim to take part over such a party's *objection* is much more attenuated.

Special cases in which a public profession of party affiliation could deter persons from joining locally unpopular groups may of course require protecting the anonymity of such persons. See, e.g., NAACP v. Alabama, 357 U.S. 449 (1958); § 12–26, supra. But such protection obviously runs against the *public* rather than against the *party*.

right to be a candidate probably implicates no constitutionally fundamental right,[16] the affiliation requirement need bear only a rational relation to a legitimate state goal. The interest in preventing adherents of one political party from running in the primary of another party—either to win the nomination or to induce destructive factionalism [17]—is sufficient warrant for these laws. The fact that this raiding by candidates can prove destructive as soon as a single individual engages in the practice makes the case for the constitutionality of these requirements even stronger.[18]

The party affiliation issue arose in a different context in *Rodriguez v. Popular Democratic Party*,[19] where the Court unanimously upheld a Puerto Rico statute allowing a vacating legislator's political party to appoint his or her successor.[20] Appellants, potential candidates for the vacant seat who were not affiliated with the previous incumbent's political party, challenged the law, arguing that "qualified voters have a federal constitutional right to elect their representatives to the Puerto Rico Legislature, and that vacancies in legislative offices therefore must be filled by a special election open to all qualified electors, not by interim appointment of any kind." [21] The Court quickly dismissed this argument, reasoning that "the right to vote, *per se*, is not a constitutionally protected right," [22] and that the Constitution does not compel a "fixed method of choosing state or local officers or representatives." [23] The Court also rejected the appellants' alternate argument that the party appointment mechanism impermissibly infringed upon their right of association and denied them equal protection of the laws, finding that the statute did not "restrict access to the electoral process or afford unequal treatment to different classes of voters or political parties. All qualified voters have an equal opportunity to select a district representative in the general election; and the interim appointment provision applies uniformly to all legislative vacancies, whenever they arise." [24] Although the Court recognized that the Commonwealth's scheme "may have some effect on the right of its citizens to

---

16. See § 13–19, supra.

17. Cf. Storer v. Brown, 415 U.S. 724 (1974) and Anderson v. Celebrezze, 460 U.S. 780 (1983), discussed in § 13–20, supra.

18. See "Developments in the Law," supra note 3, at 1178. In Lippitt v. Cipollone, 404 U.S. 1032 (1972), the Supreme Court summarily affirmed, by a 5–4 vote, a lower federal court decision, 337 F.Supp. 1405 (N.D.Ohio 1971), upholding an Ohio law forbidding a person to run in a party primary "if he voted as a member of a different political party at any primary election within the next preceding four calendar years."

19. 457 U.S. 1 (1982).

20. Id. at 4–5.

21. Id. at 7.

22. Id. at 9. Of course, if Puerto Rico had "provided that its representatives be elected, 'a citizen has a constitutionally protected right to participate in elections on an equal basis with other citizens in the jurisdiction.' " Id. at 10.

23. Id. The Court referred to Valenti v. Rockefeller, 393 U.S. 405 (1969), where it had sustained the authority of the Governor of New York to fill the vacancy in the United States Senate after Robert F. Kennedy's assasination. "[T]he fact that the Seventeenth Amendment permits a state, if it chooses, to forgo a special election in favor of a temporary appointment to the United States Senate suggests that a state is not constitutionally prohibited from exercising similar latitude with regard to vacancies in its own legislature." Id. at 11.

24. Id. at 10.

elect the members of the Puerto Rico Legislature," [25] the statute's effect was considered minimal, and was justified by the fact that "the interim appointment system plainly serves the legitimate purpose of ensuring that vacancies are filled promptly, without the necessity of the expense and inconvenience of a special election." [26]

§ 13-25. Equal Representation in the Party Nominating Process

Political parties employ two major means of selecting their candidates for state and federal office: the primary election and the convention. Because the selection of candidates by political parties will ordinarily be deemed state action,[1] rules governing access to a party's primary election or convention must conform to the requirements of the equal protection clause. In a general election, the central imperative of equal protection is equal representation or, in the parlance of the reapportionment cases, "one person, one vote." We consider here the extent to which the one person-one vote rule, or any analogue to it, operates in the context of a primary election or a political convention.

In *Gray v. Sanders*,[2] the Supreme Court overturned a Georgia law under which votes in a primary election for a state office were not allocated on a one person-one vote basis. Although the rule that *Gray* invalidated was created by the state rather than by a political party, the tenor of the opinion suggests that even a rule formulated by a political party that caused votes in its primary election to be allocated on anything other than a one person-one vote basis would run afoul of the equal protection clause.[3] In any national primary, a party would presumably also be obliged to ensure intra-state equality of voting power. *Gray* expressly declined, however, to pass on the applicability of an equal representation standard to political nominating conventions. In the case of national nominating conventions, there are two distinct levels at which the equal representation standard is arguably applicable: first, the allocation of national delegates among the states; and second, the distribution of those delegates within each state. It would prove imprudent to mimic blindly the rules governing general elections when dealing with the nominating convention of a political party since the distinctions in goals and character between states and political parties demand a careful reconsideration of the implications of equal protection principles.

25. Id. at 12.

26. Id. The Court also accepted as legitimate the Commonwealth's conclusion that "appointment by the previous incumbent's political party would more fairly reflect the will of the voters than appointment by the Governor or some elected official," id., and the goal of protecting "the political mandate of the previous election and [preserving] the 'legislative balance' until the next general election." Id. at 13. In essence, the Court held that, "[a]bsent [a clearer] constitutional limitation, Puerto Rico is free to structure its political system to meet its 'special concerns and political

circumstances.'" Id. at 13-14 (citation omitted).

§ 13-25

1. See § 13-23, supra.

2. 372 U.S. 368 (1963).

3. But see Ripon Society, Inc. v. National Rep. Party, 525 F.2d 567 (D.C.Cir.1975) (en banc), cert. denied 424 U.S. 933 (1976) (arguing that Gray turned on the fact that it involved a state rule and that Georgia was a one-party state in which the Democratic Party primary was the effective equivalent of the general election).

The Court recognized in *Gray* that "[t]he concept of political equality in the voting booth . . . extends to all phases of state elections. . . ."[4] It thus squarely repudiated any notion that the concept of equal representation was limited to general elections. The reapportionment cases then established that, when members of an elected body are chosen from separate districts, the districts must be drawn so "that equal numbers of voters can vote for proportionately equal numbers of officials. . . ."[5] Since the concept of equal protection governs primary elections, and since the possession of equally weighted votes is essential to equal protection of the laws, it should follow that some conception of equal representation governs the operation of all state nominating procedures, including political conventions.[6]

It is obvious, however, that political parties differ from states in that they do not elect public officials; rather, they select candidates whom they believe are electable as public officials. And, the argument continues, if a political party believes that an allocation system bearing no relation to any concept of equal representation best effects its purpose of selecting a good and electable candidate, then it is perfectly free to adopt such an allocation system. The argument carries some force. Political parties do not exist for the purpose of holding a shadow election; they are concerned primarily with identifying their chosen candidate. And it seems plausible that some alternative to equal representation could prove a fair and effective way of achieving that end.[7]

The argument, however, ignores one crucial point: the state incorporation of the party's decision that renders that decision state action also subjects it to standards that are ordinarily inapplicable to private organizations.[8] So long as political parties avail themselves of automatic or preferred ballot access, the state is in effect endorsing the result of the political convention by placing the convention nominee's name on the ballot.[9] And even if some alternative to equal representation is the

---

4. 372 U.S. at 380.

5. Hadley v. Junior College Dist., 397 U.S. 50, 56 (1970).

6. A contrary conclusion would be enigmatic since a state could presumably make each party member a delegate to the nominating convention. It would surely be anomalous if the party members could be given differently weighted votes at the convention despite *Gray*'s insistence that they have equal votes when cloistered in the election booth. Despite the obviously different dynamic of delegate interaction, there is no discernible reason why branding the voters "delegates" and directing them to cast their ballots in public should strip them of their right to equal representation. The equal representation mandated by *Gray* derives not from the mystique of the election booth, but from the sanctity of the election process.

7. For example, apportioning delegates among the states on the basis of their

electoral votes would provide a more accurate barometer of the appeal of candidates in the states most critical to victory in a national election. Alternatively, a party might maximize its prospects in the general election by allocating no delegates to those states in which it has little or no chance of ultimate victory; the party's nominee would thus be the choice of those states that are of potential value to the party in the final election.

8. See, e.g., § 13–23, note 4, supra.

9. The Court of Appeals thus sidestepped the relevant inquiry in Ripon Society, Inc. v. National Rep. Party, 525 F.2d 567 (D.C.Cir. 1975) (en banc), cert. denied 424 U.S. 933 (1976), when it observed that presidential nominating conventions have never been conceived as having "the function of providing a strict one person, one vote representation to a definable national constituency." Id. at 581. Although the conventions may not be conceived as hav-

wisest way of selecting a candidate, our system is premised on the fact that the *state* will not forsake the principle of equal representation. Although equal representation in national political conventions is thus the required goal, we must still decide who or what must be equally represented. In a general election, the answer is generally self-evident: people. Since the obligation of most elected officials is to represent people, it follows easily that each representative should ordinarily represent an equal number of people. It is this concept of equal constituencies that gives rise to the prescription of one person-one vote.

Ascertaining the constituency of a political convention delegate, however, is more problematic. It seems inaccurate to describe the delegate's constituency as the entire population of some geographic area;[10] a delegate's concern, after all, is with the interests of those who share the same party affiliation. Although it seems that one party affiliate-one vote should thus be the basic equal protection prescription for national nominating conventions, trouble arises when an attempt is made to define or measure "affiliate."[11] It is not constitutionally imperative, however, that a uniquely "correct" conception of affiliation be articulated and applied by every political party. Respect for the autonomy of these quasi-private organizations counsels that the courts sanction any reasonable definition and measurement of party affiliates.[12]

Even when affiliation is broadly and variably conceived, the one affiliate-one vote rule should not be a straight-jacket. Just as states are permitted to deviate somewhat from the strict one person-one vote rule in order to effect legitimate state interests, so too deviation from the one affiliate-one vote rule should be permitted where necessary to serve legitimate party interests. But just as the reapportionment cases established that the deviations could not submerge population as the central allocating factor, neither may deviations in the case of political

---

ing that task, the states may not properly incorporate their result unless they accede to that requirement. A political party, of course, may choose to give up automatic ballot access and seek to place its nominee on the ballot as an independent. In that case there would be no state action in the conduct of a nominating convention, and there could be no equal protection challenge to the allocation system employed.

10. But see Bode v. National Dem. Party, 452 F.2d 1302 (D.C.Cir. 1971), cert. denied 404 U.S. 1019 (1972). The reapportionment cases themselves indicated that population need not always be the central apportionment criterion; in rare cases, an alternative indicator better served the goal of equal representation. Thus, in Burns v. Richardson, 384 U.S. 73 (1966), the Court upheld Hawaii's reapportionment scheme based on the number of registered voters in a district rather than on the district's population. Hawaii had stressed that the large number of servicemen and other transient residents in certain districts would cause them to be grossly overrepresented if actual population were used as the apportionment criterion.

11. The alternative conceptions of "affiliates" include: long-term party adherents; those who voted in the preceding party primary; those who voted for the party's candidate in the preceding general election; those who are active in party activities; those who share the party's fundamental political aspirations; and those who intend to vote in the upcoming party primary.

12. Cf. Democratic Party of United States v. Wisconsin, 450 U.S. 107 (1981), discussed in § 13-22, supra. There may be greater reason to defer to judgments of a political party than those of a state since there is intense inter-party competition for voters that knows no close analogue at the state level.

conventions submerge equal representation of party affiliates as the transcendent allocating criterion.

Although apportioning delegates to a national convention wholly on the basis of population would not be acceptable, it would probably be proper to accord population some weight in a delegate allocation formula. The population of a state gives an approximate estimate of the state's significance in a national election—a closer estimate, certainly, than could be obtained by perusing data on party affiliates. In a sense, moreover, population constitutes a measure of potential party affiliates and thus of the outer limit of actual party affiliates in the upcoming election.

A second possible deviation from the one affiliate-one vote rule is the allocation of delegates among the states on the basis of the number of votes each state commands in the electoral college. Just as population was relevant because it approximated the importance of a state in a national election, the number of electoral votes a state controls is relevant because it yields the same information even more precisely. Lower courts have thus held that a political party may properly allocate some of its delegates on the basis of electoral votes.[13] It is doubtful, however, that a political party may properly accord as much weight to electoral votes as the two major parties currently do.[14] By according dominant weight to electoral votes, the major parties effectively submerge the one affiliate-one vote rule as the basic prescription for allocating delegates.

The third commonly suggested deviation from equal representation concerns bonus votes—that is, the allocation of additional delegates to those states in which the party was successful in recent elections. The principal justification for this deviation from the equal representation norm is that parties have to give greater weight to the candidate preferences of states in which they are strong because it is these states that are the key to the parties' electoral success.[15]

§ 13–26. Regulation of Campaign Speech

The fear that a prevailing government might some day wield its power over political campaigns so as to perpetuate its rule generates a commendable reluctance to invest government with broad control over the conduct of political campaigns. Nonetheless, the countervailing concern that completely unregulated political campaigns would degenerate in such a way that the electorate would be divested of *its* power to

---

13. See Ripon Society, Inc. v. National Rep. Party, 525 F.2d 567 (D.C.Cir. 1975) (en banc), cert. denied 424 U.S. 933 (1976); Bode v. National Dem. Party, 452 F.2d 1302 (D.C.Cir.1971), cert. denied 404 U.S. 1019 (1972).

14. The allocation scheme upheld in Ripon Society allocated 72% of the delegates on the basis of electoral votes. The formula upheld in Bode allocated 54% of the delegates on the basis of electoral votes.

15. See Ripon Society, Inc., 525 F.2d at 587, A less persuasive warrant for bonus votes is that they will encourage state parties to work harder in order to secure additional votes at the succeeding convention. It seems unlikely that these bonus votes would provide much incentive for a strong party organization beyond that supplied by the desire to have an organization that will secure state offices. But see Branti v. Finkel, 445 U.S. 507 (1980); Elrod v. Burns, 427 U.S. 347 (1976).

make a reasoned choice among the candidates has persuaded state legislatures to enact and courts to uphold some restrictions on campaign practices.

In one of the few cases addressing the constitutionality of campaign speech statutes, the Supreme Court, in *Brown v. Hartlage*,[1] struck down a Kentucky anti-corruption statute as applied to require rescission of Brown's election to a seat on the County Commission because he had impermissibly pledged to reduce his salary if elected.[2] While acknowledging that "the States have a legitimate interest in preserving the integrity of their electoral process,"[3] the Court ruled that, "[w]hen a State seeks to restrict the offer of ideas by a candidate to the voters, the First Amendment surely requires that the restriction be demonstrably supported by not only a legitimate state interest, but a compelling one, and that the restriction operate without unnecessarily circumscribing protected expression."[4] The Court found none of Kentucky's asserted interests sufficiently compelling to survive strict scrutiny. While "a State may surely prohibit a candidate from buying votes,"[5] the Court seemed to recognize that accepting the state's decision equating a promise to reduce the salary of a public official with practices such as buying votes would start the Court down a slippery slope where all campaign promises would be vulnerable to such restrictions: "Like a promise to lower taxes, to increase efficiency in government, or indeed to increase taxes in order to provide some group with a desired public benefit or public service, Brown's promise to reduce his salary cannot be deemed beyond the reach of the First Amendment, or considered as inviting the kind of corruption which a State may have a compelling interest in avoiding."[6] The Court also rejected Kentucky's argument that allowing candidates to promise to serve in public office without

---

§ 13–26

1. 456 U.S. 45 (1982). Justice Brennan delivered the opinion of the Court, in which Justices White, Marshall, Blackmun, Powell, Stevens, and O'Connor joined. Chief Justice Burger and Justice Rehnquist each concurred separately.

2. Kentucky's highest court had justified the application of the state's Corrupt Practices Act to Brown, reasoning that "when a candidate offers to discharge the duties of an elective office for less than the salary fixed by law, a salary which must be paid by taxation, he offers to reduce pro tanto the amount of taxes each individual taxpayer must pay, and thus makes an offer to the voter of pecuniary gain. It appears to us [that this promise] . . . is so vicious in its tendency as to constitute a violation of the Corrupt Practices Act." Id. at 50–51 (footnotes omitted).

3. Id. at 52.

4. Id. at 53–54.

5. Id. at 54.

6. Id. at 58. The Court also noted that "Brown's commitment to serve at a re-

duced salary was made openly, subject to the comment and criticism of his political opponent and the scrutiny of the voters. We think the fact that the statement was made in full view of the electorate offers a strong indication that the statement contained nothing fundamentally at odds with our shared political ethic." Id. at 57. Furthermore, the Court reasoned that just because "some voters may find their self-interest reflected in a candidate's commitment does not place that commitment beyond the reach of the First Amendment. . . . So long as the hoped for personal benefit is to be achieved through the normal processes of government, and not through some private arrangement, it has always been, and remains, a reputable basis upon which to cast one's ballot." Id. at 56. Cf. *Fisher v. Berkeley*, 106 S.Ct. 1045 (1986) (refusing to equate rent control imposed by local government upon landlords with a private rent-fixing cartel, despite landlords' argument that those who voted for rent control were self-interestedly joining a conspiracy with the city).

pay would "make gratuitous service the *sine qua non* of plausible candidacy."[7] While recognizing the legitimacy of the State's interest in preventing such an outcome, the Court held the statute in question an impermissible means of addressing Kentucky's concern. "It is simply not the function of government to 'select which issues are worth discussing or debating' in the course of a political campaign."[8] Finally, the Court found that because, under Kentucky law, Brown's victory would have to be nullified even if his pledge had been made in good faith and was promptly repudiated, "[t]he chilling effect of such absolute accountability for factual misstatements in the course of political debate is incompatible with the atmosphere of free discussion contemplated by the First Amendment in the context of political campaigns."[9]

Similar constitutional issues arise when states supplement their defamation laws with statutes specifically proscribing deceptive campaign speech. Like other laws that govern the content of speech, laws against campaign deception demand exacting judicial scrutiny.[10] There is little doubt that a state's interest in purging political campaigns of deceptive content far outweighs any marginal interest in disseminating false or misleading information; the assessment becomes more difficult, however, when the possible chilling effect of such laws on non-deceptive campaign speech is taken into account. In *Monitor Patriot Co. v. Roy*[11] and *Ocala Star-Banner Co. v. Damron*,[12] the Supreme Court invoked the rule of *New York Times Co. v. Sullivan*[13] and held that a political candidate could not recover from a newspaper for defamation without clearly establishing that the newspaper had printed the defamatory statement with knowledge or reckless disregard of its falsity. In *Gertz v. Robert Welch, Inc.*,[14] however, the Court refused to apply the *New York Times* standard where a magazine had defamed a private person in an article on a matter of public interest. The state's interest in conducting elections that permit the electorate to choose among candidates on the basis of accurate information outweighs even its considerable interest in protecting the reputations of its citizens. Yet the consequences of chilling free expression by attempting to purge speech of false charges are peculiarly pronounced in the context of political

7. 456 U.S. at 59.

8. Id. at 60 (footnote omitted).

9. Id. at 61.

10. The Court in Brown v. Hartlage, supra, implied that controls over deceptive campaign speech would undergo the same strict scrutiny that the Court applied to Kentucky's anti-corruption statute: "Although the state interest in protecting the political process from distortions caused by untrue and inaccurate speech is somewhat different from the state interest in protecting individuals from defamatory falsehoods, the principles underlying the First Amendment remain paramount. Whenever compatible with the underlying interests at stake, under the regime of that Amendment 'we depend for . . . correction not on the conscience of judges and

juries but on the competition of other ideas.'" Id. See generally Chapter 12, supra.

However, Justice Rehnquist, concurring in Brown, questioned the Court's analogy to the defamation cases because he would, on different facts, "give more weight to the State's interest in preventing corruption in elections," id. at 62, than he would to its interest in preventing even defamatory campaign falsehoods.

11. 401 U.S. 265 (1971).

12. 401 U.S. 295 (1971).

13. 376 U.S. 254 (1964), discussed in § 12–12, supra.

14. 418 U.S. 323 (1974), discussed in § 12–13, supra.

elections, which are absolutely dependent upon the free exchange of ideas that lies at the core of the first amendment. Although courts have yet to choose between these competing interests, it seems quite clear that a law imposing punitive or even merely compensatory sanctions on defamatory campaign speech that was neither intentionally nor recklessly false would run afoul of the first amendment.[15] Perhaps the most salient factor in striking this balance is the peculiar access to the media that political candidates enjoy. Since a candidate is virtually guaranteed a forum in which to respond to defamatory charges by an opponent, the extent to which false statements can impair the electoral process is limited.[16] In contrast, a law that punished all negligently false statements would often inhibit accurate campaign speech simply because a candidate was less than completely certain of its accuracy.

Most states impose some requirement that the author or sponsor of campaign literature be identified. These disclosure laws are obviously troublesome in that some authors might be unwilling to disseminate their views if required to identify themselves in the process.[17] But the risk that free expression will be chilled must be offset by the two major interests that such laws advance: deterring the defamation of candidates (and the possible further harm of discouraging candidacy), and enabling voters to assess campaign literature more accurately. The interest in preventing candidate defamation is certainly significant, but it seems achievable by the less restrictive alternative of enforcing campaign falsity statutes. The interest in providing voters with information that will permit them better to assess campaign literature, on the other hand, is not so readily protected by other means. As a general proposition, therefore, carefully drafted campaign literature disclosure laws should probably be deemed constitutionally permissible.[18]

§ 13–27. Campaign Finance: General Considerations

In the aftermath of the election abuses unearthed during the Watergate investigations, Congress undertook to insulate the electoral

---

15. Corrective remedies, however, might pass constitutional muster, since a requirement that a candidate who negligently made false statements about an opponent issue a public retraction would be less likely to chill political expression. But see "Developments in the Law—Elections," 88 Harv.L.Rev. 1111, 1283 (1975).

16. A candidate might nonetheless find it impossible to correct publicly a false statement issued by an opponent in the closing hours of the campaign. Punitive or compensatory damages might, therefore, be constitutionally permissible redress for negligent falsehoods uttered, say, in the twenty-four hours immediately before the polls open. Compare Mills v. Alabama, 384 U.S. 214 (1966) (holding unconstitutional a law completely proscribing all campaign-related speech on election day).

The constitutionality of such a law draws further support from the minor degree to which it would inhibit speech motivated by anything other than a deliberate wish to deceive without benefit of dialogue; a candidate could ordinarily take care to make factually controversial statements about an opponent further in advance of the election.

17. In Talley v. California, 362 U.S. 60 (1960), the Court overturned a law forbidding the distribution of all anonymous circulars on the ground that it might impermissibly chill protected expression. Talley, of course, is not dispositive of the constitutionality of a law restricted solely to campaign literature.

18. Cf. § 13–31, infra.

process from some of the more disturbing results of heavily financed election campaigns. There was a clear need to dispel both the reality and the appearance of corruption deriving from the influence that large contributors to political campaigns wielded over those public officials to whom they directed their bounty. Congress thus enacted the 1974 amendments to the Federal Election Campaign Act of 1971, regulating the financing of federal election campaigns in four primary respects: first, Congress limited the amount that an individual, a group, or a political committee could contribute in all elections in any given year or to a particular candidate in any given election; second, it limited the aggregate expenditures by any candidate, the expenditures by individuals on the candidate's behalf, and the candidate's expenditures from his or her personal or family resources; third, it required the reporting and disclosure of political contributions; and fourth, it provided for federal subsidies to candidates in presidential election campaigns.

The Campaign Finance Act as amended (hereinafter, the "Act") was immediately subjected to a vigorous constitutional challenge. A coterie of plaintiffs representing the full breadth of the political spectrum objected to the Act on the grounds, among others, that it inhibited freedom of speech and association in violation of the first amendment and drew classifications in violation of the equal protection principle implicit in the due process clause of the fifth amendment. An expedited judicial battle [1] culminated in the landmark Supreme Court's decision in *Buckley v. Valeo*, upholding most of the provisions of the Act but invalidating, among other things, its expenditure limitations.[2]

Whether assayed by its impact on first amendment doctrine generally or by its implications for the Act, the most pivotal issue the Court addressed in *Buckley* was the extent to which regulation of campaign expenditures amounted to regulation of campaign speech. Limitations on campaign contributions and expenditures restrict, at the least, the quantity of speech in conjunction with election campaigns. On the other hand, such restrictions seem entirely content-neutral; they do not pass judgment on or inhibit any particular political message or even any identifiable *kind* of message. Yet the *Buckley* Court concluded that the contribution limitations—and, even more plainly, the expenditure limitations—impinged heavily upon first amendment rights, grounding this conclusion on the indisputable fact that large sums of money are indispensible for the mass media communication that characterizes contemporary political campaigns. After correctly observing

---

§ 13-27

1. The district court certified questions to the United States Court of Appeals for the District of Columbia Circuit, which upheld the Act in large part in Buckley v. Valeo, 519 F.2d 821 (D.C.Cir. 1975) (en banc). One consequence of this expedited review was that the Supreme Court, working in a factual vacuum, was forced to indulge in more than a little empirical speculation about such issues as the circumvention of expenditure limits and the impact of those limits on campaign speech.

2. 424 U.S. 1 (1976) (per curiam). In addition to striking down the expenditure limitations, the Court held the Act's composition of the Federal Election Commission unconstitutional in light of the appointments clause of article II, § 2, except with respect to the commission's investigative and informative powers. For a discussion of this aspect of the case, see § 4-9, supra.

that the first amendment assumes particular importance in the context of political speech, the Court opined that because the contribution and expenditure limitations would reduce the quantity of political speech, they could be upheld only if they withstood exacting constitutional scrutiny.

A critique of *Buckley's* first amendment analysis should begin with the Court's attempt to distinguish *United States v. O'Brien*,[3] which had affirmed the conviction of a war protestor under a statute that proscribed the burning of draft cards. In *O'Brien*, the Court expressly rejected the contention that draft card burning was tantamount to "pure speech" in that it expressed the dissident's opposition to the Vietnam War; since the statute banning draft card burning was directed at a harm unrelated to the message that a card-burner might seek to convey, its incidental effect upon speech was justified as the least restrictive way of securing the governmental interest in avoiding that harm: preserving draft cards. *O'Brien* had thus recognized a dichotomy between regulation of pure speech—which would be upheld, if at all, only upon a showing of dire necessity—and regulation of non-speech harms arising from speech-related conduct, which was subject to considerably less exacting scrutiny. The Court in *Buckley* distinguished *O'Brien* on two grounds. First, the Court observed that the presence of a non-speech element—the expenditure of money—did not strip political speech of its first amendment protection.[4] But the obvious proposition that an otherwise invalid restriction on speech could not be salvaged by its incidental impact on something other than ideas hardly shows that a restriction ostensibly aimed at evils independent of message—whether draft-card unavailability, or the undue influence of money on politics—should be subjected to the most painstaking first amendment review because it incidentally limits communicative action.[5] Second, the Court noted that, in *O'Brien*, the government had not sought to justify its statute in terms of any interests predicated on "suppressing communication" whereas the Act was designed, among other things, to restrict the political voice of the affluent and to curb excessive campaign spending for the very purpose of restricting campaign speech.[6] But the assumption that the situation prior to the Act's

---

3. 391 U.S. 367 (1968), discussed in §§ 12–2, 12–5, 12–6, supra.

4. 424 U.S. at 16. See also § 12–15, supra.

5. See generally Wright, "Politics and the Constitution: Is Money Speech?," 85 Yale L.J. 1001, 1007–08 (1976). See also §§ 12–2, 12–3, 12–23, supra.

6. The Court attempted to distinguish prior cases upholding limits on the "volume" of communicative conduct by arguing that, unlike contribution and expenditure limitations, they did not restrict the quantity of political speech. 424 U.S. at 18. In Kovacs v. Cooper, 336 U.S. 77 (1949), for example, the Court had upheld limits upon the volume at which a soundtruck could broadcast its political message,

limits that clearly controlled the quantity of communication. Buckley unpersuasively attempted to argue that the decibel limit upheld in Kovacs regulated only the manner, not the extent, of communication by the soundtruck. 424 U.S. at 18 n.17. Later decisions have preserved this tenuous Kovacs/Buckley distinction. Thus, in Baldwin v. Redwood City, 540 F.2d 1360 (9th Cir. 1976), the Court of Appeals for the Ninth Circuit held unconstitutional a municipal limitation on the aggregate area of all posters supporting a single candidate or issue in a political campaign. The Court of Appeals drew a parallel between this restriction and the FECA limitations on campaign expenditures struck down in Buckley. Id. at 1369. However, the Baldwin court upheld a municipal limitation on the

intervention was more conducive to freedom of speech than the situation the Act sought to create was itself in controversy. Congress believed that money, by shaping public officers to the viewpoints of their benefactors,[7] fettered speech even if it increased its quantity.[8] Whether or not one regards government as responsible for the distribution of wealth underlying this distortion,[9] it is hardly self-evident that the contribution and expenditure limitations do not redress that distortion in a manner that enhances freedom of speech.[10] If the net effect of the legislation is to do so, then the exacting review reserved for abridgments of free speech may be inapposite.

On the other hand, such legislation is not concerned with harms that would arise even if giving and spending money had no communicative impact at all; however content-neutral, the legislation is plainly designed to regulate money that talks precisely because of how loudly it may make itself heard.[11] Although it ought not to follow that the legislation requires the strictest possible scrutiny,[12] it would be prob-

---

size of any individual sign, comparing this restriction to the decibel limitation on sound trucks upheld in Kovacs. Id.

7. There are many forms of political bondage that might derive from large campaign contributions. At the most corrupt end of the spectrum stands the contributor who expressly conditions a contribution upon a politician's advocating clearly prescribed policies; less culpable, but perhaps equally inconsistent with democratic ideals, is the large contributor who seeks and receives only the good wishes and attentive ear of the candidate, but thereby finds an opportunity to persuade the candidate proportional to the contributors' largesse. See generally Nicholson, "Campaign Financing and Equal Protection," 26 Stan.L.Rev. 815 (1974) (characterizing the problem of large campaign contributions as according the wealthy "multiple representation").

8. The assumption that increased campaign expenditures translate into increased speech or communication is not self-evident. Arguably, even the marketplace of political ideas—or the forums for political expression—can become saturated. Whether increased speaking actually translates into increased communication in the din of an election campaign is a question whose answer turns upon formidable empirical problems and troubling conceptual questions about what constitutes real communication. Congress should not be given excessive latitude in resolving these conceptual and empirical difficulties lest it employ a subterfuge to stifle disfavored expression, but to perceive in the Act any real risk of such subterfuge would require the liveliest imagination coupled with no small measure of political naiveté. Who could have had the political clout to smuggle into Congress' campaign restrictions a design to assure that the views of the rich

would not be heard? But see note 10, infra.

9. It has become characteristic of the post-Depression period to acknowledge that the distribution of wealth is in large measure a result of the legal system's rules of contract, property, corporate structure, and the like, coupled with government's overt resource-allocation decisions. See §§ 8–6 to 8–7, supra. Fully understanding Buckley v. Valeo requires putting it in the context of other Supreme Court decisions of the 1970's attempting to secure for the wealthy the advantages of their position, even when legislatures move in a more egalitarian direction. See § 16–58, infra.

10. Cf. Red Lion Broadcasting Co. v. FCC, 395 U.S. 367 (1969) (upholding fairness doctrine for television coverage). It is nonetheless possible that the limitations so protect incumbents that they should for that reason be suspiciously regarded.

11. See BeVier, "Money and Politics: A Perspective on the First Amendment and Campaign Finance Reform," 73 Cal.L.Rev. 1045, 1058 (1985).

12. But see id. See Federal Election Commission v. National Conservative Political Action Committee, 470 U.S. 480, 508 (1985) (White, J., dissenting): "I agree with the majority that the expenditures in this case 'produce' core First Amendment speech. . . . But that is precisely the point: they produce such speech; they are not speech itself. At least in these circumstances, I cannot accept the identification of speech with its antecedents. Such a house-that-Jack-built approach could equally be used to find a First Amendment right to a job or to a minimum wage to 'produce' the money to 'produce' speech." But, of course, laws restricting Jack's income *in order to limit the volume of his*

lematic for a court to adopt a highly deferential form of review on the *premise* that laws of this type do not potentially abridge rights of free expression. The level of scrutiny must therefore be searching enough to explore how particular regulations of communicative spending, whether in the form of contributions or in the form of direct expenditures, actually affect the workings of the system of free expression.[13]

Freedom of speech was not the only first amendment right that *Buckley* found implicated by the campaign finance restrictions. The Court observed that the first amendment "protects political association as well as political expression." [14] It concluded that making a political contribution "affiliate[s] a person with a candidate" and that expending resources on behalf of a candidate enables associations to "effectively [amplify] the voice of their adherents." [15] The Court thus invoked the right of association to buttress its conclusion that the first amendment dictated careful scrutiny of the campaign finance regulations.[16]

Before looking at *Buckley* and its often confusing progeny in closer detail, it may be helpful to keep in mind two recurring and problematic themes that run through these cases. First, in *Buckley*, the Court distinguished between limits on campaign *expenditures*, considered to be at the core of the first amendment, and restrictions on campaign *contributions*, which the Court found to involve little direct restraint on speech. In spite of subsequent cases which have cast doubt on the utility and coherence of this distinction, a majority of the Court continues to subscribe to it. The second prevalent theme in these cases has dealt with the sufficiency of the asserted state interest in enacting the restrictions. While the Court has consistently recognized the state's interest in preventing actual or perceived corruption *of elected officials* arising from their indebtedness to large campaign donors, it has never accepted as legitimate any asserted interest in preventing actual or perceived corruption *of the electoral system itself* caused by large disparities in the amount of money spent on behalf of various candidates or positions.

§ 13–28. Contribution Limits

Buckley v. Valeo represented the Supreme Court's first attempt to determine the constitutionality of limitations on contributions to political campaigns.[1] The legislation at issue contained three contribution

speech would pose a distinct issue—arguably, the very issue in the campaign expenditure cases.

13. See BeVier, supra note 11, at 1071 (criticizing the first edition of this treatise for too readily assuming that such regulations in fact have the salutary consequences for freedom of speech that Congress attributes to them).

14. 424 U.S. at 15.

15. Id. at 22.

16. Id. at 15. See § 12–23, supra.

§ 13–28

1. 424 U.S. 1 (1976) (per curiam). The Court had upheld restrictions on campaign activity by civil servants in United States Civil Serv. Comm'n v. National Ass'n of Letter Carriers, 413 U.S. 548 (1973), and Broadrick v. Oklahoma, 413 U.S. 601 (1973), discussed in § 12–25, supra. These restrictions, however, affected a much narrower group than the general public, and they were explained by a desire to insulate public servants from political pressures, rather than by a need to regulate elections as such. Thus the relevant considerations were very different from those involved in

limitations: first, individuals, groups, and authorized campaign committees were permitted to contribute no more than $1,000 to any candidate for federal office;[2] second, political action committees were permitted to contribute no more than $5,000 to any such candidate; and third, individuals were permitted to contribute a total of no more than $25,000 to candidates for federal office in a given calendar year. In appraising the constitutionality of these provisions, the Court tempered its application of rigorous first amendment scrutiny by recognizing that "a limitation upon the amount that any one person or group may contribute to a candidate or political committee entails only a marginal restriction upon the contributor's ability to engage in free communication."[3] It observed that contributions do not reveal the underlying basis of the contributor's support and that, in any event, any communicative value of the contribution is not proportional to its size.[4] Thus the state interest in preventing the appearance and reality of corruption stemming from the real or imagined pressure imposed on political candidates by those who contribute heavily to their campaigns was sufficiently weighty to sustain the $1000 limitation on contributions by individuals or groups to a particular candidate despite its marginal curtailment of expressional and associational freedoms: since money had become "an ever more essential ingredient of an effective candidacy" in the era of mass media communication, the Court observed that "[t]o the extent that large contributions are given to secure political *quid pro quo's* from current and potential office holders, the integrity of our system of representative democracy is undermined,"[5] and dispelling the *appearance* of such illicit impact on candidates from their large contributors is of "almost equal concern."[6] The Court specifically rejected the contention that less restrictive means could serve these state interests. Although bribery laws undoubtedly deter some attempts to exact political favors, such laws deal only with the most blatant cases of illegal pressure upon political candidates. Similarly, the disclosure provisions of the Act, while a positive step toward curbing untoward political pressure, were not necessarily sufficient to obviate the entire problem.[7]

The Court also sustained the contribution limitations against two other constitutional challenges. First, the Court concluded that the limitations did not unfairly favor incumbents. On their face the limitations applied equally to all candidates for political office; moreover, no empirical evidence established that the contribution limitations would bear more heavily upon challengers than upon incumbents. Indeed, the Court suggested that the contribution limitations may

an across-the-board imposition of contribution limits.

2. The value of volunteer services contributed to a candidate was exempted from the contribution ceiling, as was the first $500 expended by volunteers for designated campaign-related activities.

3. 424 U.S. at 20–21. The Court noted that it was not greatly troubled by the restrictive effect that contribution limitations might have on the *candidate's*

speech, because the limitations were not so severe that they would greatly curtail the resources available to candidates. Id.

4. 424 U.S. at 21.

5. Id. at 26–27.

6. Id. at 27.

7. Id. at 28. The Court treated the less restrictive alternative argument somewhat more casually than it usually does in first amendment cases. Cf. § 12–23, supra.

actually favor challengers because incumbents ordinarily have access to larger contributors and are therefore more constrained by the Act's contribution ceilings.[8] Second, the Court found the possibility that the contribution limitations might disproportionately burden minor parties and independent candidates not sufficient to render the limitations unconstitutional on their face. The possible inhibitory effect these limitations might have on such minor parties or independent candidates was "more troubling" than their impact upon candidates generally, but the Court noted that the record was barren of evidence that the limitations would circumscribe the ability of such candidates to compete effectively for political office.

In addition to upholding the $1000 limit on contributions to particular candidates, the Court upheld the $25,000 limitation on the aggregate contributions that an individual could make annually to all political campaigns. The Court reasoned: "[T]his quite modest restraint upon protected political activity serves to prevent evasion of the $1000 contribution limitation by a person who might otherwise contribute massive amounts of money to a particular candidate through the use of unearmarked contributions to political committees likely to contribute to that candidate, or huge contributions to the candidate's political party. The limited, additional restriction on associational freedom imposed by the overall ceiling is thus no more than a corollary of the basic individual contribution limitation that we have found to be constitutionally valid." [9]

Since *Buckley*, the Court has twice examined the constitutionality of campaign contribution limitations. In *California Medical Association v. Federal Election Commission* [10] (hereinafter, *CMA*), the Court upheld provisions of the Federal Election Campaign Act of 1971, which prohibited "individuals and unincorporated associations such as CMA from contributing more than $5,000 per calender year to any multi-candidate political committee such as CALPAC." [11] While acknowledging that campaign contributions are worthy of some first amendment protection, the Court held that "the 'speech by proxy' that CMA seeks to achieve through its contributions to CALPAC is not the sort of political advocacy that [the] Court in *Buckley* found entitled to full First Amendment protection." [12] The Court reasoned that, because the Act limited only contributions *to* committees as opposed to expenditures *by* committees, its impact on first amendment rights was no greater than that upheld in *Buckley*: "If the First Amendment rights of a contributor are not infringed by limitations on the amount he may contribute to

---

8. Id. at 31–33. This line of analysis seems quite dubious.

9. Id. at 38.

10. 453 U.S. 182 (1981). Justice Marshall delivered the opinion of the Court, in which only Justices Brennan, White, and Stevens joined on the first amendment issue. Justice Blackmun agreed with the Court's conclusion that the Act did not violate the first amendment, but disagreed with the plurality's analysis. It is unclear whether the four dissenters (Justice Stewart, joined by Chief Justice Burger and Justice Powell and Rehnquist) would have accepted Justice Marshall's first amendment analysis because they contended that the Court did not have jurisdiction over the appeal, and thus never addressed the merits of the case.

11. Id. at 185. CALPAC was a registered political action committee formed in 1976 by the California Medical Association.

12. Id. at 196.

a campaign organization which advocates the views and candidacy of a particular candidate, the rights of a contributor are similarly not impaired by limits on the amount he may give to a multicandidate political committee, such as CALPAC, which advocates the views and candidacies of a number of candidates."[13] The Court accordingly subjected the Act's restrictions to less than strict scrutiny and found them valid because they furthered the legitimate government interest in preventing actual or perceived corruption. While the restrictions did not further that goal directly, they were deemed necessary to protect the integrity of the contribution restrictions upheld in *Buckley*.[14]

But less than six months after *CMA* the Court, in *Citizens Against Rent Control v. Berkeley*,[15] struck down as unconstitutional a $250 limitation on individual contributions to committees formed to support or oppose ballot measures.[16] The Court initially focused on the law's impact on associational rights: "To place a Spartan limit—or indeed any limit—on individuals wishing to band together to advance their views on a ballot measure, while placing none on individuals acting alone, is clearly a restraint on the right of association."[17] But the Court also found that "[p]lacing limits on contributions which in turn limit expenditures plainly impairs freedom of expression,"[18] concluding that this abridgement of free speech is "virtually inseparable . . . in this context" from "the impermissible restraint on freedom of association,"[19] and opining that, in the case at hand, "[t]he two rights overlap and blend."[20] Nor could the Court discern any state interest sufficient

---

13. Id. at 197. The Court noted that nothing in the statute limited the amount CMA could expend to further its political beliefs, but only how much it could contribute to groups like CALPAC. Id. at 195.

14. Id. at 197–98. "Congress enacted [these provisions] in part to prevent circumvention of the very limitations on contributions that this Court upheld in *Buckley*. . . . If appellants' position—that Congress cannot prohibit individuals and unincorporated associations from making unlimited contributions to multicandidate political committees—is accepted, then [the limitations upheld in *Buckley*] could be easily evaded." Id. A similar line of argument might well be used to support the need for limitations on independent committee expenditures, because unlimited expenditures by independent committees could well have the same corrupting effect on politicians as do unlimited campaign contributions. As Professor Archibald Cox cogently argues: "Wherever gratitude for the past or fear that the money may not be forthcoming in the future is enough to influence official action, little will turn upon whether the financial help takes the form of a contribution or a so-called independent expenditure in a campaign where contributions are prohibited." Cox, "Constitutional Issues in the Regulation of the

Financing of Election Campaigns," 31 Clev. St.L.Rev. 395, 410 (1982). See also discussion in § 13–29, infra.

15. 454 U.S. 290 (1981). While only Justice White dissented from Chief Justice Burger's majority opinion, the Court was divided on the proper first amendment analysis, as shown by separate concurrences from Justices Rehnquist, Marshall, and Blackmun (joined by Justice O'Connor).

16. The ordinance in question provided that "[n]o person shall make, and no campaign treasurer shall solicit or accept, any contribution which will cause the total amount contributed by such person with respect to a single election in support of or in opposition to a measure to exceed two hundred and fifty dollars." Id. at 292. Acting alone, an individual could "spend without limit . . . on a ballot measure." Id. at 296.

17. Id. See § 12–23, for analysis of the associational aspect of the Court's holding.

18. Id. at 299.

19. Id.

20. Id. at 300. "As we have noted, an individual may make expenditures without limit under [the ordinance] on a ballot measure but may not contribute beyond

to justify the law's impact on associational and expressional rights, distinguishing *Buckley* on the ground that it applied only to the "perception of undue influence of large contributors to a *candidate*" and not to "limitations on contributions to committees formed to favor or oppose *ballot measures*." [21]

The Court's reasoning in *Citizens Against Rent Control* is problematic in part because it seems to have elevated the first amendment's protection for contributions to a status nearly equivalent to that of expenditures, without ever repudiating the Court's earlier reliance, in *Buckley* and *CMA*, on a supposedly significant difference between the two.[22]   Nor was this confusion necessary.   After all, the contribution limitations upheld in *Buckley* and *CMA* were deemed legitimate because they attempted to prevent corruption of elected officials, whereas the Berkeley ordinance obviously did not further this interest.   The Court noted as much [23] but did not make as much of the point as it might have—especially since the only other interest urged by Berkeley was that of "making known the identity of supporters and opponents of ballot measures," [24] an interest already amply served by the city's unchallenged disclosure requirements.[25]

the $250 limit when joining with others to advocate common views. The contribution limit thus automatically affects expenditures, and limits on expenditures operate as a direct restraint on freedom of expression of a group or committee desiring to engage in political dialogue concerning a ballot measure." Id. at 299.

21. Id. at 297 (emphasis in original). Justice Rehnquist concurred because the Berkeley ordinance, unlike the law he would have upheld in First National Bank of Boston, see 435 U.S. at 822 (dissenting opinion), "was not aimed only at corporations . . . as opposed to individuals." 454 U.S. at 300.

22. As Justice White pointed out in dissent, "[i]n *Buckley* the Court found that contribution limitations 'entai[l] only a marginal restriction upon the contributor's ability to engage in free communication.' As with contributions to candidates, ballot measure contributions 'involv[e] speech by someone other than the contributor' and a limitation on such donations 'does not in any way infringe the contributor's freedom to discuss candidates and issues.' Id. at 21. Indeed what today has become 'a very significant form of political expression' was held just last Term to involve only 'some limited element of speech.'" Id. at 305 (contrasting CMA v. Federal Election Commission, 453 U.S. 182 (1981)). Justice Marshall, concurring in the judgment, was also concerned about the Court's apparent disregard of the contribution/expenditure

distinction, but concluded that "[b]ecause the Court's opinion is silent on the standard of review it is applying to this contributions limitation, I must assume that the Court is following our consistent position that this type of governmental action is subjected to less rigorous scrutiny than a direct restriction on expenditures." Id. at 301. See § 13–29, infra, for discussion of the Court's subsequent treatment of this distinction.

23. In support of its holding, see 454 U.S. at 298, the Court cited First National Bank of Boston v. Bellotti, 435 U.S. 765 (1978), discussed in § 13–29, infra, quoting its statement in the latter case that "[r]eferenda are held on issues, not candidates for public office. The risk of corruption perceived in cases involving candidate elections [citations omitted] simply is not present in popular vote on a public issue." 435 U.S. at 790.

24. 454 U.S. at 298.

25. Id. Justice White's dissent suggested that large corporate expenditures had "skyrocketed" to a degree arguably threatening to drown out less well-funded voices in the democratic process. Id. at 306–08, 310–11. The majority, like Justice Rehnquist (see note 21, supra), replied by treating the case as readily distinguishable from one involving a limit on corporate contributions and thus charged the dissent with "argu[ing] a case not before the Court." Id. at 299 n.6.

§ 13–29. Expenditure Limitations

The Campaign Finance Act challenged in *Buckley v. Valeo* contained three restrictions on expenditures: first, a $1,000 limit on expenditures with respect to a specifically designated candidate; second, a $25,000 limitation on expenditures by a candidate from his or her personal or family funds; and third, a limit on the total amount of expenditures by any candidate in an election campaign. Unlike contribution limitations, the Court concluded, limitations on expenditures "impose direct and substantial restraints on the quantity of political speech." [1] Accordingly, it tested the expenditure ceilings by the strictest of constitutional standards, and found that the interests proffered for the expenditure limitations did not withstand rigorous constitutional scrutiny.

With respect to the $1,000 limitation on expenditures by individuals on behalf of a clearly identified candidate, the Court construed the provision to relate only to expenditures that expressly advocated the election or defeat of such a candidate and found the expenditure limitation, thus interpreted, unwarranted by the two interests advanced by the government. First, the Court concluded that the expenditure limitation was ill-equipped to obviate perceived and actual political corruption, because persons wishing to purchase political leverage could spend money on behalf of a candidate without expressly advocating his election. In defense of Congress, however, the value of expenditures that expressly advocate the election of a named candidate is undoubtedly greater than that of general pronouncements in favor of the candidate's positions or oblique references to the candidate; one would be much more likely to curry the favor of those who offer a specific endorsement. The Court attempted to buttress its argument by observing that uncontrolled expenditures by individuals might even be counterproductive to a candidate's efforts. Even accepting the Court's assumption, the fact remains that, in those cases where expenditures did seem to benefit a candidate, the appearance or reality of corruption would ensue.

Second, and most fundamentally, the Court rejected the legitimacy of the goal of "equalizing the relative ability of individuals and groups to influence the outcome of elections." [2] It explained: "[T]he concept

---

§ 13–29

1. Buckley v. Valeo, 424 U.S. 1, 39 (1976) (per curiam).

2. Id. at 48. See § 13–28, supra, for discussion of subsequent cases also rejecting this asserted interest. The Court's assertion cannot be accepted uncritically. It is one thing to say that government cannot silence some in order to amplify the views of others in the open marketplace of *ideas*, and quite another to insist that, in the arguably zero-sum "marketplace" of *electoral* influence, where amplifying the reach and impact of some voices necessarily reduces that of their opponents, government cannot reduce the clout of some in order to advance the goal of equalizing influences of election outcomes. As Professor Forrester put it, "[t]hat Congress cannot seek equality in *political* power is an ipse dixit of unusual superficiality, especially in the face of the historic decisions since Baker v. Carr, 369 U.S. 186 (1962), which imposed political equality in reapportionment. The Court ignores the strong analogy between one person, one vote and one person one buck." Forrester, "The New Constitutional Right to Buy Elections," 69 A.B.A.J. 1078, 1080 (Aug. 1983) (emphasis added) (urging the overruling of Buckley). But see BeVier, "Money and Politics: A Perspective on the First Amendment and Campaign Finance Reform," 73 Cal.L.Rev. 1045, 1066–74 (1985).

that the government may restrict the speech of some elements of our society in order to enhance the relative voice of others is wholly foreign to the First Amendment, which was designed "to secure the widest possible dissemination of information from diverse and antagonistic sources,'" and "'to assure unfettered interchange of ideas for the bringing about of political and social changes desired by the people.'" [3] The Court cited its prior decisions in *Mills v. Alabama* [4] and *Miami Herald Publishing Co. v. Tornillo* [5] in support of its conclusion. In *Mills* the Court held unconstitutional a law proscribing the publication on election day of editorials urging people to vote in a certain way. The statute overturned in *Mills*, however, was an outright restriction on speech that was in no sense intended to equalize the input into the electoral process of persons with differing economic means. In *Miami Herald*, the Court held unconstitutional a Florida statute that required a newspaper to make space available to political candidates who wished to respond to criticism that the newspaper had leveled at them. Unlike the expenditure limitations involved in *Buckley*, the law overturned in *Tornillo* actually required those supporting a given candidate to subsidize speech by the opposing candidate. The Court's conclusion that equalizing the political or at least electoral role of differing economic groups was an impermissible objective, therefore, was obviously not grounded on prior constitutional authority, but reflected instead a distinctly non-egalitarian vision of the role of government and the role of elections in creating governments. [6]

3. Id. at 48–49. The Court held that a restriction on the total expenditures of a candidate could, however, be imposed as a condition of the candidate's receiving federal subsidies. 424 U.S. at 57 n.65. At first glance this holding appears to resurrect the discarded right-privilege distinction. On reflection, however, the intimate connection between the expenditure limitation and the purpose of the government subsidies suggests a different and more defensible distinction. The government is making the decision that its funds will be used to swell the coffers only of those candidates who have not already received and expended private monies above a certain level. This decision closely parallels a decision to grant welfare stipends only to those with incomes and expenditures *below* a certain level. In both cases, the condition is in the nature of a criterion for allotment—necessary to fulfilling the purpose of the government outlays, and only incidentally affecting the behavior of those who may wish to receive the outlays. Conditions imposed for reasons unrelated to the purpose of granting the governmental benefit to which the conditions are attached stand on an entirely different and weaker footing. See § 11–5, supra.

4. 384 U.S. 214 (1966).

5. 418 U.S. 241 (1974).

6. See generally L. Tribe, Constitutional Choices 192–98 (1985); Cox, "Constitutional Issues in the Regulation of the Financing of Election Campaigns," 31 Clev. St.L.Rev. 395 (1982); Wright, J., "Politics and the Constitution: Is Money Speech?," 85 Yale L.J. 1001 (1976). See also Buckley v. Valeo, 424 U.S. 1, 287–88 (1976) (Marshall, J., concurring in part and dissenting in part) (citing the ballot access cases for the legitimacy of the goal of assuring equal access to the political arena). The Buckley Court deemed the ballot access cases irrelevant on the ground that they did not involve restrictions on free expression. 424 U.S. at 49 n.55. But the cases cannot be dismissed so easily. Although they did not involve first amendment issues, they established the constitutional stature of the right to political participation, and of equal access to the ballot as part of that right. If Congress concluded that the enormous sums of money available to some candidates essentially foreclosed meaningful access to the political arena for others, any impingement of free speech entailed by expenditure limitations would have to be considered in light of the other constitutional right at stake: equal access. See § 16–58, infra, for a possible explanation of the Court's premises in Buckley.

The Court also overturned the $25,000 limitation on expenditures by a candidate from personal or family funds on behalf of his or her own candidacy. It observed that the provision implicated the same first amendment interests as did the restriction on expenditures by other individuals. Additionally, it noted that the state interest in curbing the appearance and reality of political corruption assumed minimal importance with respect to expenditures from the candidate's own funds, since she could hardly be suspected of bribing herself. Although the Court's reasoning in this respect seems sound, its rejection of the ancillary goal of muting the relative voice of the rich in elections is much more dubious. First, the Court observed that the expenditure limitation might not effectuate that state interest since rich candidates might still conduct more expensive campaigns by soliciting more contributions than their poorer opponents. The Court conceived of the relevant governmental interest too broadly. Whether or not Congress decided that all campaigns should be funded equally, it could rationally decide to limit those disparities that derive directly and immediately from candidates' differing economic status, thereby committing to the electorate the relative funding of candidates' campaigns.[7] Second, the Court concluded, without any real analysis, that the limitation was unconstitutional because "the First Amendment simply cannot tolerate [the] restriction upon the freedom of a candidate to speak without legislative limit on behalf of his own candidacy."[8]

Finally, the Court could find no governmental interest sufficient to justify the limitation on aggregate campaign expenditures. It found the interest in reducing dependence on large contributors insufficient because the contribution limitations adequately eradicated that dependence. The Court again expressly rejected the legitimacy of the interest in equalizing the voices of candidates—much as it had, during the 1890–1937 period discussed in Chapter 8, rejected the legitimacy of any interest in equalizing *economic* power. Finally, the Court held that the interest in curbing the skyrocketing cost of election campaigns could not support an infringement of first amendment rights.

Relying in large part on the principles enunciated in *Buckley*, the Court, in *Federal Election Commission v. National Conservative Political Action Committee*[9] (hereinafter, *NCPAC*), struck down, on their face, provisions of the Presidential Election Campaign Fund Act (hereinafter, Fund Act) which made it a criminal offense for an independent political committee to expend more than $1,000 to further a presidential candidate's election if the candidate had opted for public financing.[10] NCPAC, an independent committee that sought to raise and

---

7. To the extent that the wealthy might have been able to put together better fundraising efforts simply by virtue of having wealthy friends, the contribution ceilings sustained by the Court would tend to offset the distortion, leaving only spending from the candidate's own resources as a major link between candidate wealth and campaign affluence.

8. 424 U.S. at 54.

9. 470 U.S. 480 (1985). Justice Rehnquist wrote for the Court. While the Court was fragmented on the statutory interpretation of the Fund Act, only Justices White and Marshall dissented from the Court's first amendment analysis. See Note, 99 Harv.L.Rev. 223–33 (1985).

10. Buckley had upheld congressional power to limit private campaign spending by publicly funded candidates and by their

spend money in excess of $1,000 for the reelection of President Ronald Reagan, claimed that the Fund Act violated its first amendment rights. The Court agreed, basing its holding on the *contributors'* right to band together, and to use NCPAC as a vehicle for their expression, rather than on the spending rights, as such, of NCPAC itself.[11] Yet the Court rejected the FEC's assertion that this was merely the "speech by proxy" that the Court in *California Medical Association v. Federal Election Commission*[12] had found entitled only to partial first amendment protection, because "the present cases involve limitations on expenditures by PACs, not on the contributions they receive."[13] After concluding that NCPAC's expenditures were thus entitled to full first amendment protection, the Court examined the government's asserted interests in the challenged provisions and found those interests insufficient to justify burdening first amendment rights. Relying on *Buckley*, the Court rejected the alleged connection between independent expenditures on behalf of a candidate and the actual or perceived corruption that would be entailed if the same sums were contributed to the candidate's own campaign.[14] And even if the asserted interest in

own campaign organizations. See note 3, supra. The restriction on private spending by "independent" committees in support of these same publicly funded campaigns was part of a congressional scheme to limit the total amount of money spent on Presidential elections by offering federal financing to candidates who would agree to keep all spending in their support within certain limits. Believing that this scheme would be meaningless if so-called "independent" groups could spend unlimited amounts on the candidate's behalf, Congress provided that: "[I]t shall be unlawful for any political committee which is not an authorized committee with respect to the eligible candidates of a political party for President and Vice President in a presidential election knowingly and willfully to incur expenditures to further the election of such candidates, which would constitute qualified campaign expenses if incurred by an authorized committee of such candidates, in an aggregate amount exceeding $1,000." Id. at 491.

11. "The First Amendment is squarely implicated in this case. NCPAC and FCM [Fund for a Conservative Majority] are mechanisms by which large numbers of individuals of modest means can join together in organizations which serve to 'amplif[y] the voice of their adherents.'" Id. at 494.

12. 453 U.S. 182 (1981), discussed in § 13–27, supra.

13. 470 U.S. at 495. The Court seemed to imply that contributors have a fully protected first amendment right to contribute as effectively as possible up to the point where their individual contributions could be corrupting. In other words, the NCPAC supporters have a right to have their small, and independently insignificant, contributions pooled and used effectively. The Court found it noteworthy that in "1979–1980 approximately 101,000 people contributed an average of $75 each to NCPAC." Id. at 494. Treating this fact as crucial ignores the widely held view that it is a political action committee's *leaders*, and not the individual *contributors* to the committee, who present the greatest potential threat of corruption. Moreover, Justice White, noted in dissent that "[t]he growth of independent PAC spending has been a direct and openly acknowledged response to the contribution limits in the FECA. . . . That the PAC's expenditures are not formally 'coordinated' is too slender a reed on which to distinguish them from actual contributions to the campaign. The candidate cannot help but know of the extensive efforts 'independently' undertaken on his behalf." Id. at 510.

14. Id. at 497. The Court could hardly avoid noting the risk that independent expenditures may be valued by the candidate and thus be corrupting, but held that, on the record before it, "such an exchange of political favors for uncoordinated expenditures remains a hypothetical possibility and nothing more." Id. at 498. But, as Justice White pointed out, the Court "need not evaluate the accuracy . . . of the perception that large-scale independent PAC expenditures mean 'the return of the big spenders whose money talks and whose gifts are not forgotten'. . . . It is enough to note that there is ample support for the congressional determination that the corrosive effects of large campaign contributions—not least among these a public

preventing corruption had been meritorious, the Court deemed the Fund Act a "fatally overbroad response to that evil. It is not limited to multimillion dollar war chests; its terms apply equally to informal discussion groups that solicit neighborhood contributions to publicize their views about a particular Presidential candidate." [15]

By couching its analysis in terms of the law's character as a limit on spending while focusing on the law's "overbroad" impact on small contributors' rights of expressive association, the *NCPAC* Court seems to have invited Congress to enact spending limits carefully confined to large expenditures, or expenditures by large entities; in doing so, the Court also strained even further *Buckley's* distinction between controls on campaign contributions and limits on campaign expenditures. While this distinction has always seemed problematic, it should by now have become clear that it is ripe for complete reassessment by the Court.[16] Dissenting in *NCPAC*, Justice Marshall urged the distinction's complete rejection [17] and concluded that "the limitations on independent expenditures challenged in [*Buckley*] and here are justified by the congressional interests in promoting 'the reality and appearance of equal access to the political arena,' and in eliminating political corruption and the appearance of such corruption." [18]

A sub-theme in the campaign finance cases concerns the different levels of protection that the first amendment provides to individuals and corporations. In *First National Bank of Boston v. Bellotti,*[19] the

perception of business as usual—are not eliminated solely because the 'contribution' takes the form of an 'independent expenditure.' " Id. at 511. Also, Professor Cox has argued quite persuasively that the Court should give greater deference to Congress' factual conclusions about the social and political tendencies that give rise to corruption: "While the extreme deference required by the normal presumption of constitutionality should be withheld in strict scrutiny cases in order to prevent the dilution of fundamental rights, the Court should ask no more than whether there is solid support for any debatable conclusions concerning conditions and tendencies upon which the justification for the legislation rests." Cox, "Constitutional Issues in the Regulation of the Financing of Election Campaigns," 31 Clev.St.L.Rev. 395, 414 (1982).

15. 470 U.S. at 498. See generally §§ 12–27 to 12–32, supra.

16. See Forrester, "The New Constitutional Right to Buy Elections," 69 A.B.A.J. 1078, 1080 (Aug. 1983), arguing that "the critical distinction the Court makes [in Buckley] between corrupting aspects of contributions compared with the corrupting aspects of independent and personal spending is so obviously thin and debatable that the issue might more properly have been resolved by respecting the findings of Congress that it is necessary and

proper to regulate non-contribution spending as a means to render effective the regulation of contributions."

17. 470 U.S. at 519–20. "Although I joined the portion of the Buckley *per curiam* that distinguished contributions from independent expenditures for First Amendment purposes, I now believe that the distinction has no constitutional significance. . . . First, the underlying rights at issue—freedom of speech and freedom of association—are both core First Amendment rights. Second, in both cases the regulation is of the same form: It concerns the amount of money that can be spent for political activity. Thus, I do not see how one interest can be deemed more compelling than the other." Justice Marshall noted that, at the time of the Buckley decision, Chief Justice Burger, Justice White, and Justice Blackmun also rejected the contribution/expense distinction. See id., note * at 520. While Justice White continued in NCPAC to disavow this distinction, the impact of Justice Marshall's assertion is limited by the fact that Chief Justice Burger and Justice Blackmun joined the Court's NCPAC opinion.

18. Id. at 521.

19. 435 U.S. 765 (1978), discussed in §§ 12–3, 12–19, supra. Justice Powell delivered the opinion of the Court, in which Chief Justice Burger and Justices Stewart,

Court held unconstitutional a Massachusetts statute forbidding certain business corporations from making contributions or expenditures to influence the outcome of any ballot referendum "other than one materially affecting any of the property, business or assets of the corporation." [20]   The Court rejected the notion that "speech that otherwise would be within the protection of the First Amendment loses that protection simply because its source is a corporation," [21] and found that "the speech proposed by the [bank was] at the heart of the First Amendment's protection." [22]   In holding that the statute was not sufficiently justified by important state interests,[23] the Court noted that "[r]eferenda are held on issues, not candidates for public office. The risk of corruption perceived in cases involving candidate elections simply is not present in a popular vote on a public issue." [24]   But the Court left open the possibility that, if this had been an election for public office, a legislature could reasonably conclude that corporate speech corrupts or appears to corrupt candidates, and could thus constitutionally place restrictions on corporate speech that would be impermissible if applied to speech by individuals.

In *Federal Election Commission v. National Right to Work Committee* [25] (hereinafter, *NRWC*), the Court, speaking through Justice Rehnquist, unanimously upheld provisions of the Federal Election Campaign Act of 1971 making it unlawful for a corporation's PAC to solicit funds from non-members of the corporation for use in federal elections. The Court concluded that "the associational rights asserted by [NRWC] may be and are overborne by the interests Congress has sought to protect in enacting [the provisions]." [26]   First, the state has a legitimate interest in preventing the "substantial aggregations of wealth amassed by the special advantages which go with the corporate form of organization" from being converted into " 'political warchests' which could be used to incur political debts from legislators who are aided by the contribu-

---

Blackmun, and Stevens joined. The Chief Justice also concurred separately. Justice White dissented, joined by Justices Brennan and Marshall. Justice Rehnquist filed a separate dissent.

20. Id. at 768. The statute made clear that the referendum in question proposing an individual graduated income tax did not involve an issue in which the corporation could become involved: "No question submitted to the voters solely concerning the taxation of the income . . . of individuals shall be deemed materially to affect the property, business or assets of the corporation." Id.

21. Id. at 784.

22. Id. at 776.

23. The Court found that the interest in preventing candidate corruption is inapplicable to referenda. Id. at 788–89. But, while again rejecting the state's interest in trying to equalize relative abilities to speak effectively, the Court offered this glimmer of hope: "According to appellee, corpora-

tions are wealthy and powerful and their views may drown out other points of view. If appellee's arguments were supported by record or legislative findings that corporate advocacy threatened imminently to undermine democratic processes, thereby denigrating rather than serving First Amendment interests, these arguments would merit our consideration." Id. at 789. See notes 14 and 25, supra. But see Justice White's dissent in Citizens Against Rent Control, 454 U.S. at 303, discussed in § 13–28, supra.

24. 435 U.S. at 791. "To be sure, corporate advertising may influence the outcome of the vote; this would be its purpose. But the fact that advocacy may persuade the electorate is hardly a reason to supress it." Just what might be meant by the "drowning out" notion (see note 23, supra) in light of this recognition is not entirely clear.

25. 459 U.S. 197 (1982).

26. Id. at 207.

tions." [27]   Second, the provisions "protect individuals who have paid money into a corporation or union for purposes other than the support of candidates to whom they may be opposed." [28]   Finally, the Court examined the long history of regulation of corporate and union involvement in political campaigns and opined that "there is no reason why" the government's legitimate interest in preventing actual or perceived corruption may not "be accomplished by treating unions, corporations, and similar organizations differently from individuals." [29]

However, in *Federal Election Commission v. Massachusetts Citizens For Life* [30] (hereinafter, *MCFL*), the Court struck down, as applied, a provision of the Federal Election Campaign Act which prohibited a corporation from using treasury funds to make expenditures "in connection with any election to any public office," rather than financing such expenditures with voluntary contributions to a separate segregated fund.[31]   MCFL, a nonprofit corporation dedicated to advancing pro-life legislation, violated the Act by distributing a "Special Election Edition" of its newsletter which gave the abortion voting records of various candidates for office and urged readers to "VOTE PRO-LIFE." [32]

Justice Brennan, speaking for a divided Court,[33] found that because the Act required corporations to establish segregated funds for political activity, it forced some groups, like MCFL, to employ a much more complex and formalized organization than they could reasonably handle, in order to exercise their constitutional rights.   "[W]hile [the Act] does not remove all opportunities for independent spending by organizations such as MCFL, the avenue it leaves open is more burdensome than the one it forecloses.   The fact that the statute's practical effect may be to discourage protected speech is sufficient to characterize [it] as an infringement of First Amendment activities." [34]

Although reaffirming that "special characteristics of the corporate structure require particularly careful regulation," [35] the Court found this general rule inapplicable to MCFL.   "Regulation of corporate political activity . . . has reflected concern not about use of the

---

27. Id.

28. Id. at 208. This is, however, virtually the same interest that Massachusetts forwarded in defense of its statute in First National Bank v. Bellotti, 435 U.S. 765 (1978), and that the Court there rejected as overinclusive, stressing that it would "prohibit a corporation from supporting or opposing a referendum even if its shareholders unanimously authorized the contribution or expenditure." Id. at 794.

29. 459 U.S. at 210–11.

30. 107 S.Ct. 616 (1986).

31. Id. at 619.

32. Id. at 620.

33. While the Court unanimously agreed that MCFL violated the Act, on the constitutional issue Justice Brennan was joined in full only by Justices Marshall, Powell, and Scalia, with Justice O'Connor concurring in part and concurring in the judgment. Chief Justice Rehnquist, joined by Justices White, Blackmun, and Stevens, dissented on the constitutional issue.

34. Id. at 626. While a majority of the Court agreed that the Act burdened MCFL's first amendment rights, Justice O'Connor wrote separately to stress her view that "the significant burden on MCFL in this case comes not from the disclosure requirements that it must satisfy, but from the additional organizational restraints imposed upon it by the Act." Id. at 632. See also § 12–23, supra.

35. Id. at 627. The Court had previously recognized the legitimacy of the state's interest in regulating corporate speech in NRWC, supra, 459 U.S. at 209–10.

corporate form *per se*, but about the potential for unfair deployment of wealth for political purposes. Groups such as MCFL, however, do not pose that danger of corruption. MCFL was formed to disseminate political ideas, not to amass capital. The resources it has available are not a function of its success in the economic marketplace, but its popularity in the political marketplace." [36]

While increased protection of such "political" corporations seems defensible, it is hard to square with the Court's decision in *NRWC*. Justice Brennan unpersuasively distinguished the two cases by arguing that *NRWC* involved restrictions on contributions, which "require less compelling justification than restrictions on independent spending." [37] However, the Court later undermined its own reasoning by arguing that "[i]t is not the case . . . that MCFL merely poses less of a threat of the danger that has prompted regulation. Rather, it does not pose such a threat at all." [38] Therefore, if NRWC, like MCFL, was a "political" corporation,[39] the assertion that contribution restrictions require a less compelling governmental interest would be irrelevant, because the NRWC posed *no* threat of the danger justifying regulation.

Taken together, the corporate campaign speech cases seem to stand for the proposition that no corporation may be excluded (at least on a speaker-specific or content-specific basis) from speaking about ballot measures, but "business" corporations may be excluded from involvement in campaigns to elect candidates when the legislature determines that corporate influence may cause or appear to cause corruption of public officials.

§ 13–30. Subsidies to Candidates

The Campaign Finance Act challenged in *Buckley v. Valeo* [1] endeavored to equalize the financial resources available to political candidates not only by limiting contributions to and expenditures by candidates, but by providing federal subsidies that would increase the resources available to political candidates who might otherwise have poorly financed campaigns. Under the subsidy provisions of the Act, major political parties—defined as those that had secured over 25% of the vote in the preceding presidential election—qualified for reimbursement for up to two million dollars of expenses incurred in connection with their nominating campaigns and for subsidies of up to 20 million

36. MCFL, 107 S.Ct. at 628. The Court laid down three conditions necessary to immunize a corporation from restrictions on its political spending:

1. It must be formed for the "express purpose of promoting political ideas, and cannot engage in business activities;"

2. It must have "no shareholders or other persons affiliated so as to have a claim on its assets or earnings;" and,

3. It may not be "established by a business corporation or a labor union," and its policy must be not to "accept contributions from such entities." Id. at 631.

37. Id. at 629.

38. Id. at 630.

39. NRWC would probably also meet the three-part test enunciated in MCFL. See note 36, supra. As Chief Justice Rehnquist argued in dissent, "I would have thought the distinctions drawn by the Court today largely foreclosed by our decision in NRWC. . . . The corporation [NRWC] whose fund was at issue was not unlike MCFL—a nonprofit corporation without capital stock, formed to educate the public on an issue of perceived public significance." Id. at 4075.

§ 13–30

1. 424 U.S. 1 (1976) (per curiam).

dollars for their candidate's presidential campaigns. Minor parties—defined as those that secured between 5% and 25% of the vote in the preceding presidential election—qualified for convention reimbursements and campaign subsidies proportional to their share of the vote in the preceding election, with the possibility of additional post-election payments if they increased their share of the vote. Other political parties or candidates qualified for no pre-election payments and qualified for post-election support only if they obtained over five percent of the vote in the current election. Major party candidates could qualify for federal funds only if they forswore private contributions; other parties and candidates were permitted to supplement their federal payments with private contributions so long as their total campaign expenditures did not exceed twenty million dollars.

The plaintiffs in *Buckley*, by drawing an analogy to the clause proscribing the establishment of religion, argued that the provision of subsidies to political candidates impermissibly entangled the government in political campaigns and thus contravened the first amendment.[2] As the Court observed, however, the portion of the first amendment that deals with freedom of speech contains no establishment clause; the amendment forbids only government abridgment of speech, not enhancement of speech.[3] Accordingly, the Court refused to find that the subsidy provisions on their face violated the first amendment. It left open the possibility, however, that the subsidy provisions could be unconstitutional as applied if they entailed excessive governmental intermeddling in the internal affairs of political campaigns.[4]

Buckley also sustained the subsidy provisions of the Act against the claim that they denied non-major-party candidates equal protection in violation of the fifth amendment's due process clause. The plaintiffs urged that the subsidy and reimbursements provisions of the Act should be strictly scrutinized since they denied certain candidates effective access to the political process and infringed the right to vote of supporters of those candidates. The Court, however, found the ballot access cases upon which the plaintiffs relied [5] unpersuasive authority in the context of the Campaign Finance Act. The Court observed that the Act "does not prevent any candidate from getting on the ballot or any voter from casting a vote for the candidate of his choice," so that the inability of any candidate to wage an effective campaign would derive

---

2. Compare §§ 14–11, 14–14, infra.

3. The Court thought it obvious that the subsidies augmented, rather than restricted, free expression: "Subtitle H is a congressional effort, not to abridge, restrict, or censor speech, but rather to use public money to facilitate and enlarge public discussion and participation in the electoral process, goals vital to a self-governing people." 424 U.S. at 92–93. Although the Court's conclusion is probably accurate, the issue is not as straightforward as the Court intimates. If the Act, by lavishing federal funds on candidates already relatively well off, enabled them to monopsonize certain limited communication resources (such as particularly valuable television time), its effect would be to reduce the effective freedom of speech of the poorer candidates who might otherwise have purchased at least part of that resource. Admittedly, however, the record was barren of such evidence.

4. 424 U.S. at 93 n.126. See § 13–22, supra.

5. See §§ 13–19 to 13–21, supra.

from that candidate's inability to raise private contributions, not from any invidious line drawn by the legislation.[6]

In many respects, the Court's paradigm was oversimplified. Candidates who could not qualify for federal payments under the Act might have had little chance of success in any event, but their prospects of victory are surely diluted still further to the extent that the Act increases the funds available to their already richer rivals. The effect of the Act is thus somewhat similar to that of statutes that deny ballot access to certain candidates but permit write-in votes for such candidates;[7] like such statutes, the payment provisions of the Act raise the possibility of effectively subverting a candidacy. On the other hand, it is possible that the Act will actually reduce the financial disparity between major-party candidates and other candidates. If a minor party or new party candidate secured 5% of the vote in the prior election and secures 5% of the vote in the current election, the candidate qualifies for a subsidy.[8] In contrast, major party candidates must forsake private contributions in order to qualify for federal payments. On balance, therefore, it is difficult to ascertain whether the effect of the Act is to increase or decrease the relative chances of minor party and new party candidates, and the Court's conclusion that the Act need not be scrutinized in this respect with the strictness accorded direct restraints on ballot access appears tenable.[9]

The Court, moreover, found the differential treatment of candidates under the payment provisions of the Act to be supported by weighty governmental interests. In particular, the Court deemed it appropriate to deny aid to candidates with marginal public support in order that the Act not "foster frivolous candidacies, create a system of splintered parties, and encourage unrestrained factionalism."[10] The Court thus endorsed the theme it had sounded in the ballot access cases wherein it had sanctioned the state interest in promoting the two party system and condemned only those schemes that effectively insulated two particular political parties from all challenges by other candidates.[11]

6. 424 U.S. at 94–95.

7. See § 16–53, infra.

8. One pragmatic difficulty with this provision is that the candidate needs the funds before, not after, the election. There are probably candidates who would be able to secure 5% of the vote if only they were given prior to the election the funds that they would be entitled to after the election if they did secure 5% of the vote; because they lack these resources during the campaign, however, the likelihood of their reaching the 5% threshold becomes slim. The Court's suggestion that such candidates could secure loans before the election, 424 U.S. at 102, may be overly optimistic; there is, in any event, something troubling about committing the fate of a candidate to the receptivity of the financial community—a community that may well be hostile to the candidate's views.

9. On the other hand, the possibility that present legislators drafted the Act so as to enhance the electoral chances of candidates of the major parties that they represent counsels against subjecting the payment provisions of the Act to minimal equal protection scrutiny; such a possibility of a government seeking to perpetuate itself by discriminatory means argues for subjecting the Act to fairly careful review.

10. 424 U.S. at 101.

11. See § 13–20, supra. Although Buckley comports fully with the ballot access cases in this regard, it is difficult to accept the Court's indication that suppression of minority parties may itself be a compelling state interest.

§ 13–31. Disclosure Provisions

The legislation reviewed in *Buckley v. Valeo* [1] contained two primary disclosure provisions: first, candidates were required to divulge the source of all contributions in excess of ten dollars; and second, individuals who contributed or independently spent in excess of one hundred dollars for political candidates in any year were required to itemize such actions. The plaintiffs in *Buckley* did not contend that these disclosure provisions were unconstitutional *per se*; [2] rather, they contended that the disclosure provisions were unconstitutional as applied to minority parties and to small contributions and contributors. The Court concluded that the disclosure provisions should be carefully scrutinized because they limited freedom of association, but found that the provisions served sufficiently compelling state interests to survive that exacting scrutiny.

The Court, relying on a series of civil rights cases, [3] started from the premise that "compelled disclosure, in itself, can seriously infringe on privacy of association and belief guaranteed by the First Amendment." [4] The Court correctly dismissed any argument that the prior cases were distinguishable because they involved disclosure of the members of an organization rather than of contributors to an organization. If exposing the names of an association's adherents runs the risk of deterring potential members from joining, exposing the names of contributors surely imperils the financial health of the association and thereby jeopardizes its ability to represent the views of its members.

The Court found that the disclosure provisions nonetheless advanced three compelling interests. First, they informed the electorate of a candidate's supporters and thereby enhanced the electorate's ability to evaluate the candidate. Second, the provisions deterred actual corruption and the appearance of corruption "by exposing large contributions and expenditures to the light of publicity." [5] Third, the disclosure provisions augmented the state's ability to detect violations of the contribution limitations. Although the Court purported to scrutinize the disclosure provisions strictly, it did not inquire whether means that less seriously impaired first amendment values could serve the proffered public interests as adequately. [6]

§ 13–31

1. 424 U.S. 1 (1976) (per curiam).

2. Indeed, plaintiffs affirmatively relied on the constitutionality of the disclosure provisions by arguing that they obviated the need for limitations on contributions and expenditures. See §§ 13–28, 13–29, supra.

3. See § 12–26, supra.

4. 424 U.S. at 64.

5. Id. at 67. The Court cited Justice Brandeis's sage advice: "Publicity is justly commended as a remedy for social and industrial diseases. Sunlight is said to be the best of disinfectants; electric light the most efficient policeman." L. Brandeis, Other People's Money 62 (1933). A simi-

lar, but distinct, rationale underlay the opinion in Burroughs v. United States, 290 U.S. 534 (1934), the leading Supreme Court decision on disclosure prior to Buckley. Burroughs upheld provisions of the Federal Corrupt Practices Act of 1925 requiring periodic disclosure of contributions to, and expenditures by, interstate campaign committees for congressional candidates.

6. Several less intrusive means in fact commend themselves. Arguably, disclosure provisions that did not require public dissemination of information, or disclosure limited to post-election statements by victorious candidates, could have served the government's interests fairly well. See "The Supreme Court, 1975 Term," 90 Harv.L.Rev. 56, 182 (1976).

The Court in *Buckley* rejected the argument that the decision in *NAACP v. Alabama* [7] required invalidation of the disclosure provisions insofar as they applied to minor political parties and independent candidates. Although acknowledging that disclosure provisions at times inhibit the success of such candidates, and that the warrant for disclosing contributions was less pronounced with respect to minor parties since they were seldom victorious,[8] the Court reasoned that compulsory disclosure was constitutional unless the evidence showed a "reasonable probability that the compelled disclosure of a party's contributors' names will subject them to threats, harassment, or reprisals from either Government officials or private parties." [9] Since the record was found to be barren of any evidence that the plaintiffs in *Buckley* had met this test,[10] the Court held that the provisions were constitutional as applied. Finally, the Court rejected the argument that the disclosure provisions were overbroad in that they extended to very low monetary thresholds. Although the Court conceded that the "$10 and $100 thresholds are indeed low," [11] it properly ruled that the drawing of the appropriate line was an issue on which it should not upset a defensible congressional judgment.

In *Brown v. Socialist Workers '74 Campaign Committee*,[12] the Court struck down, as applied to the Socialist Workers Party (SWP), provisions of an Ohio statute that required every political party to report the names and addresses of campaign contributors and recipients of campaign disbursements. Repeating its warning that compelled disclosures "can seriously infringe on privacy of association and belief guaranteed by the First Amendment," [13] the Court held that *Buckley*'s "reasonable probability of harassment" test was met here because the evidence supported the three-judge district court's finding of "both governmental and private hostility toward and harassment of SWP members and supporters." [14] The Court found no reason to treat disclosure of campaign expenditures differently from disclosure of campaign contributions.[15] While Ohio had a concededly strong interest in monitoring

---

7. 357 U.S. 449 (1958), discussed in § 12–26, *supra*.

8. 424 U.S. at 70. As the Court acknowledged, however, nonvictorious candidates can play a large role in some elections because even "when a minor-party candidate has little or no chance of winning, he may be encouraged by major party interests in order to divert votes from other major-party contenders." Id.

9. Id. at 74.

10. Id. at 69–72.

11. Id. at 83.

12. 459 U.S. 87 (1982). Justice Marshall wrote for the Court, joined in whole by Chief Justice Burger and Justices Brennan, White, and Powell, and in part by Justice Blackmun, who also concurred separately.

13. Id. at 91, quoting Buckley, 424 U.S. at 64.

14. Id. at 98–99.

15. Justice O'Connor, joined by Justices Rehnquist and Stevens, dissented in part, arguing that, while the Buckley test should apply equally to disclosure of contributions and expenditures, the SWP had "failed to carry its burden of showing that there is a reasonable probability that disclosure of recipients of expenditures will subject the recipients themselves or the SWP to threats, harassment, or reprisals." Id. at 107. Justice O'Connor correctly noted that, although the state interest in preventing corruption of the process may be less for minor candidates who seldom win, a minor party "whose short-term goal is merely recognition, may be as tempted to resort to impermissible methods as are major parties, and the resulting deflection of votes can determine the outcome of the election of other candidates." Id. at 110. Moreover, on the other side of the equa-

campaign expenditures to prevent misuse of funds, this interest had "less force in the context of minor parties." [16] More importantly, the Court found that compelled disclosure of disbursements seriously burdened the SWP because "expenditures by a political party often consist of reimbursements, advances, or wages paid to . . . supporters whose activities lie at the very core of the First Amendment. Disbursements may also go to persons who choose to express their support for an unpopular cause by providing services rendered scarce by public hostility and suspicion. Should their involvement be publicized, these persons would be as vulnerable to threats, harassment, and reprisals as are contributors whose connection with the party is solely financial." [17]

tion, the partial dissent considered the burden of expenditure disclosure insignificant. "Many expenditures of the minority party will be for quite mundane purposes to persons not intimately connected with the organization. . . . Unlike silent contributors, whom disclosure would reveal to the public as supporters of the party's ideological positions, persons providing business services to a minor party are not generally perceived by the public as supporting the party's ideology, and thus are unlikely to be harassed if their names are disclosed." Id. at 111.

16. Id. at 95.

17. Id. at 97. However, as the partial dissent pointed out, "once an individual has openly shown his close ties to the organization by campaigning for it, disclosure of receipt of expenditures is unlikely to increase the degree of harassment so sig-

nificantly as to deter the individual from campaigning for the party." Id. at 111–12. See also Stone & Marshall, "Brown v. Socialist Workers: Inequality as a Command of the First Amendment," 1984 Sup.Ct.Rev. 583, 626 ("Against the backdrop of a constitutional jurisprudence committed to content neutrality, it is surprising to find a decision that holds that a content-based distinction is constitutionally compelled. Although the Court in Brown failed adequately to explain this seeming anomaly, the decision is in fact consistent with the fundamental principles that have shaped First Amendment jurisprudence. The simple lesson of Brown is that when the commitment to neutrality conflicts with the commitment to preservation of ideas in the political marketplace, the latter will prevail.").

Chapter 14

RIGHTS OF RELIGIOUS AUTONOMY

§ 14-1. The Relation of Religious Autonomy to Other Constitutional Concerns

The role of reason—particularly its role in public life—has been central in the model of preferred rights (Model V) elaborated in Chapters 12 and 13.[1] But the concept of preferred rights plainly extends beyond these dimensions, as this chapter and the next will illustrate. In this chapter we discuss religion, a realm in which faculties beyond reason, and experience often removed from the public sphere, prove central to most conceptions of the values at stake.[2]

The constitutional concepts of religious autonomy were first articulated in the religion clauses of the first amendment, assuring both free exercise and nonestablishment.[3] Those guarantees were originally forged in a context where both the idea of the state and the concept of religion were fairly well defined and quite narrowly limited,[4] and where it was thought that the core ideal of religious autonomy could be secured by placing matters of religion beyond the competence of the national government. The application of the religion clauses to the states through the due process clause of the fourteenth amendment, the movement from a government of closely limited powers to the affirmative state, and the gradual expansion of our understanding of the nature of religion, have combined to work a fundamental transformation in the question of how religious groups and interests should be treated. In this context, the religion clauses, which for the Framers represented relatively clear statements of highly compatible goals, have taken on new and varied meanings that frequently appear to conflict. The tensions thus created between the two clauses represent a major theme throughout this chapter.

The chapter will begin by briefly examining the historical context in which the religion clauses were written.[5] It will then consider the tensions between the clauses, and several formulations and approaches designed to alleviate the tensions.[6] After considering the courts' ap-

---

§ 14-1

1. Despite occasional cases such as Cohen v. California, 403 U.S. 15, 26 (1971) (recognizing the emotive role of expression), first amendment jurisprudence has focused on the cognitive place of speech, and especially its cognitive place in public life.

2. See, e.g., R. Otto, The Idea of the Holy (1929); P. Tillich, The Dynamics of Faith (1957); Garvey, "Free Exercise and the Values of Religious Liberty," 18 Conn. L.Rev. 779, 798–801 (1986). See also § 14–6, note 28, infra.

3. U.S.Const., amend. I: "Congress shall make no law respecting an establishment of religion, or prohibiting the free exercise thereof. . . ." See also U.S. Const., art. VI: "[N]o religious Test shall ever be required as a Qualification to any Office or public Trust under the United States."

4. See, e.g., M. Howe, The Garden and the Wilderness (1965); A. P. Stokes and L. Pfeffer, Church and State in the United States (1964).

5. §§ 14–2, 14–3, infra.

6. §§ 14–4 through 14–8, infra.

proaches to laws challenged under the establishment clause [7] and the free exercise clause,[8] as well as the courts' abstinence from certain forms of inherently religious inquiries,[9] the chapter will turn to two particularly important examples of the tension between the clauses: the involvement of religious people and organizations in politics,[10] and government's official acknowledgment and endorsement of religious values.[11]

Any attempt to constitutionalize the relationship of the state to religion must address the fact that much of religious life is inherently associational,[12] interposing the religious community or organization between the state and the individual believer. Especially in the area of religion, courts in this country have been reluctant to interfere with the internal affairs of private groups.[13] The doctrine of judicial deference to a religion's internal decision-making organs, for example, has deep historical roots.[14] Such deference to intermediate groups entails potential domination by the group over the individual member, especially the dissident; the resulting tension between the religious rights of the group and those of the individual will be explored in § 14–16, bringing this chapter to a close.

§ 14–2. Constitutional Text and History: The Religion Clauses

The Constitution's most important guarantees with respect to religion [1] are set forth in the first amendment's opening words: "Congress shall make no law respecting an establishment of religion, or prohibiting the free exercise thereof. . . ." The difficulty that has historically plagued courts in implementing these provisions stems in part from the fact that their purpose "was to state an objective, not to write a statute." [2] Thus, the judiciary has necessarily been left with the task of

7. §§ 14–9, 14–10, 14–11, infra.

8. §§ 14–12, 14–13, infra.

9. § 14–11, infra.

10. § 14–14, infra.

11. § 14–15, infra.

12. See M. Eliade, Sacred and Profane 20–24 (1959).

13. See Chafee, "The Internal Affairs of Associations Not for Profit," 43 Harv.L. Rev. 993, 1027–29 (1930); "Developments in the Law: Judicial Control of Actions of Private Associations," 76 Harv.L.Rev. 983, 986–91 (1963). See also, e.g., Healy v. James, 408 U.S. 169 (1972). See generally § 12–26, supra, and §§ 15–17, 15–20, infra.

14. See § 14–11, infra.

§ 14–2

1. The only language outside the Bill of Rights bearing directly on religion is the religion test clause of article VI, which provides that "no religious Test shall ever be required as a Qualification to any Office or public Trust under the United States." The clause applies only to the federal government, although state religious tests for public office have been held to run afoul of both the establishment clause and the free exercise clause. Torcaso v. Watkins, 367 U.S. 488 (1961) (invalidating an oath of belief in God required of a notary public). As a practical matter, the latter two clauses are dispositive in cases challenging alleged "religious tests"; hence the religious test clause is now of little independent significance. See, e.g., id. at 489 n.1; American Communications Ass'n v. Douds, 339 U.S. 382, 414–15 (1950); Anderson v. Laird, 316 F.Supp. 1081, 1093 (D.D.C. 1970), rev'd on other grounds 466 F.2d 283 (D.C.Cir. 1972) cert. denied 409 U.S. 1076 (1972).

2. Walz v. Tax Commission, 397 U.S. 664, 668 (1970) (stressing that tax exemptions for religious groups are not aimed at establishing, sponsoring, or supporting religion, and that they entail less entanglement than would taxation, particularly since the history of freedom from taxation has not led to an established church but, on the contrary, has helped guarantee the free exercise of all forms of religious belief).

developing rules and principles to realize the goal of the religion clauses without freezing them into an overly rigid mold. Both clauses apply to state as well as federal action through the incorporation of their principles into the fourteenth amendment due process clause.[3] The free exercise clause was first applied to the states in 1940 in *Cantwell v. Connecticut*;[4] the establishment clause was first so applied seven years later, despite difficulties of syntax and history, in *Everson v. Board of Education*.[5]

To the Framers, the religion clauses were at least compatible and at best mutually supportive. A harmonious relationship occasionally obtains even today. Allocating religious choices to the unfettered

3. One of the best discussions of the history of this incorporation appears in Justice Brennan's concurring opinion in Abington School Dist. v. Schempp, 374 U.S. 203, 253–58 (1963), discussed in notes 4–5, infra. See also P. Kauper, Religion and the Constitution 53–57 (1964).

4. 310 U.S. 296 (1940) (reversing conviction of persons disseminating religious messages). Justice Brennan, in his concurring opinion in Abington School Dist. v. Schempp, 374 U.S. 203, 253–54 n.18 (1963), noted that the Court's decision in Cantwell actually marked the completion of a long process of absorption of the free exercise clause into the due process clause of the fourteenth amendment, a process that had begun nearly two decades earlier when, in 1923, the Court said that the protections of the fourteenth amendment included at least a person's freedom "to worship God according to the dictates of his own conscience. . . ." Meyer v. Nebraska, 262 U.S. 390, 399 (1923) (dictum). At least one state court before Meyer had assumed that claims of abridgment of free exercise in the public schools must be tested under the guarantees of the first amendment as well as those of the state constitution. See Hardwick v. Board of School Trustees, 54 Cal.App. 696, 704–05, 205 P. 49, 52 (1921). And, even before the fourteenth amendment, New York had enacted a general common school law in 1844 which provided that no religious instruction should be given that could be construed to violate the rights of conscience "as secured by the constitution of this state and the United States". N.Y. Laws, 1844, c. 320, § 12. Thus, despite the decades intervening between the adoption of the fourteenth amendment in 1868 and the free exercise clause's absorption in Cantwell in 1940, the idea that the religious liberty secured by the free exercise clause would eventually be regarded as a fundamental right protected by the due process clause has been seen as "easily understandable," with a development that can be "easily charted." P. Kauper, Religion and the Constitution 53 (1964); Abington School Dist. v. Schempp, 374 U.S. 203, 254 (1963) (Brennan, J., concurring).

5. 330 U.S. 1 (1947) (upholding publicly financed transportation for parochial school children as part of program for all school-age children). Justice Brennan noted and responded to the special problems of incorporating the establishment clause in his concurring opinion in Abington School Dist. v. Schempp, 374 U.S. 203, 254–58 (1963). First, some objected—with historical support—that the absorption of the first amendment's ban against establishment was conceptually troublesome inasmuch as the Framers intended the establishment clause to block Congress from disestablishing existing official state churches. But, Justice Brennan responded, this argument had become irrelevant since the last formal state establishment had been dissolved more than thirty years before the fourteenth amendment was ratified. Second, some had suggested that the "liberty" guaranteed by the fourteenth amendment could not be held to encompass the establishment clause because that clause did not protect a "freedom" of the individual. For Justice Brennan, the fallacy in this contention lay in its underestimation of the role that the establishment clause plays as co-guarantor with the free exercise clause of religious liberty: the Framers did not trust either clause to stand alone in protecting the individual's freedom. Finally, it was argued that, if the fourteenth amendment had made the establishment clause binding upon the states, the abortive Blaine Amendment, 4 Cong.Rec. 5580 (1876)—which, several years after the adoption of the fourteenth amendment, proposed prohibiting state religious establishments (see § 14–3, note 27, infra),—would have been superfluous. This argument too, Justice Brennan maintained, was unconvincing, since the fourteenth amendment's protection of free exercise was not being questioned even though the Blaine Amendment would have added an explicit protection against state laws abridging that liberty as well.

consciences of individuals under the free exercise clause remains, in part, a means of assuring that church and state do not unite to create the many dangers and divisions often implicit in such an established union.[6] Similarly, forbidding the excessive identification of church and state through the establishment clause remains, in part, a means of assuring that government does not excessively intrude upon religious liberty.[7] Thus the Supreme Court has frequently recognized that "the two clauses may overlap."[8] For example, the Sunday closing laws presented both a free exercise issue in their economic pressure on persons whose religions compelled refraining from work on Saturday,[9] and an establishment issue in their selection of Sunday as a universal day of rest.[10] Although a secular purpose sufficiently compelling to satisfy the first amendment was perceived by a majority of the Justices,[11] it is noteworthy that the religion clauses in that context did overlap. And to the extent that the two clauses are understood as reinforcing one another, doctrines developed under one are relevant to the other as well.

Despite this harmony, serious tension has often surfaced between the two clauses. For example, spending federal funds to employ chaplains for the armed forces might be said to violate the establishment clause; "[y]et a lonely soldier stationed at some faraway outpost could surely complain that a government which did *not* provide him the opportunity for pastoral guidance was affirmatively prohibiting the free exercise of his religion."[12] A pervasive difficulty in the constitutional jurisprudence of the religion clauses has accordingly been the struggle "to find a neutral course between the two Religion Clauses, both of which are cast in absolute terms, and either of which, if expanded to a logical extreme, would tend to clash with the other."[13]

6. It has been said that such a union may tend "to destroy government and to degrade religion." Engel v. Vitale, 370 U.S. 421, 431 (1962) (New York Board of Regents prepared a "nondenominational" prayer which a local school board directed to be recited in class every day; held, a violation of the establishment clause). See Sutherland, "Establishment According to Engel," 76 Harv.L.Rev. 25 (1962).

7. This is a response to the historical perception "that cruel persecutions were the inevitable result of government established religions." Everson v. Board of Education, 330 U.S. 1, 12 (1947). See §§ 14-11, 14-15, infra.

8. Abington School Dist. v. Schempp, 374 U.S. 203, 222 (1963) (a Pennsylvania law required at least ten verses from the Holy Bible to be read without comment each day with children excused upon written request of their parents; held, a violation of the establishment clause).

9. For the Court's rejection of the free exercise attack, see Braunfeld v. Brown, 366 U.S. 599 (1961); Gallagher v. Crown Kosher Supermarket, 366 U.S. 617 (1961).

10. For the Court's rejection of the establishment attack, see McGowan v. Maryland, 366 U.S. 420 (1961); Two Guys from Harrison-Allentown, Inc. v. McGinley, 366 U.S. 582 (1961).

11. In light of Sherbert v. Verner, 374 U.S. 398 (1963) (state must modify its unemployment compensation requirement of willingness to work on Mondays through Saturdays in order to accommodate the needs of those religiously opposed to working on Saturdays but willing to work on Sundays instead), it is arguable that Braunfeld and Crown Kosher should now be overturned, especially if a limited exemption is urged. See § 14-13, infra.

12. See Abington School Dist. v. Schempp, 374 U.S. 203, 309 (1963) (Stewart, J., dissenting) (emphasis in original).

13. Walz v. Tax Commission, 397 U.S. 664, 668-69 (1970).

§ 14–3. Framers' Intent, Pre-Adoption History, and Post-Adoption History as Aids to Understanding

Both the Court[1] and various commentators[2] have explored the historical background of the first amendment in order to guide interpretation of the two religion clauses, but here as elsewhere, "too literal [a] quest for the advice of the Founding Fathers" is often futile.[3] The historical record is ambiguous,[4] and many of today's problems were of course never envisioned by any of the Framers.[5] Under these circumstances, one must consult the values and purposes underlying the religion clauses to decide what doctrinal framework might best realize those ends today.

Such an examination reveals at least three distinct schools of thought which influenced the drafters of the Bill of Rights: first, the evangelical view (associated primarily with Roger Williams) that "worldly corruptions . . . might consume the churches if sturdy fences against the wilderness were not maintained";[6] second, the Jeffersonian view that the church should be walled off from the state in order to safeguard secular interests (public and private) "against ecclesiastical

---

§ 14–3

1. See, e.g., Everson v. Board of Education, 330 U.S. 1, 8–16 (1947) (majority opinion of Black, J.); id. at 31–43 (Rutledge, J., dissenting); Illinois ex rel. McCollum v. Board of Education, 333 U.S. 203, 244–48 (1948) (Reed, J., dissenting); Engel v. Vitale, 370 U.S. 421, 425–36 (1962) (Black, J., dissenting); Walz v. Tax Commission, 397 U.S. 664, 681–87 (1970) (Brennan, J., concurring); Larson v. Valente, 456 U.S. 228, 244–246 (1982) (majority opinion of Brennan, J.); Marsh v. Chambers, 463 U.S. 783, 787–792 (1983) (majority opinion of Burger, C.J.); Lynch v. Donnelly, 465 U.S. 668, 673–674 (1984) (majority opinion of Burger, C.J.); Wallace v. Jaffree, 472 U.S. 38, 67 (1985) (O'Connor, J., concurring in judgment); id. at 91 (Rehnquist, J., dissenting).

2. For a discussion of the varying interpretations, see, e.g., T. Curry, The First Freedoms: Church and State in America to the Passage of the First Amendment (1986); L. Levy, The Establishment Clause: Religion and the First Amendment (1986); R. Cord, Separation of Church and State: Historical Fact and Current Fiction (1982); M. Malbin, Religion and Politics: The Intentions of the Authors of the First Amendment (1981); S. Cobb, The Rise of Religious Liberty in America (1902); Eckenrode, Separation of Church and State in Virginia (1910); Hunt, "James Madison and Religious Liberty," 1 Am.Hist.Ass'n. Rep. 165 (1961); M. Howe, The Garden and the Wilderness (1965).

3. Abington School Dist. v. Schempp, 374 U.S. 203, 237 (1963) (Brennan, J., concurring).

4. See Summers, "The Sources and Limits of Religious Freedom," 41 Ill.L.Rev. 53, 55–58 (1946). On the question of Jefferson's views, for example, compare Everson v. Board of Education, 330 U.S. 1, 11–13 (1947) (Black, J.), with Illinois ex rel. McCollum v. Board of Education, 333 U.S. 203, 244–48 (1948) (Reed, J., dissenting).

5. See Wallace v. Jaffree, 472 U.S. 38, 67 (1985) (O'Connor, J., concurring in judgment); Lynch v. Donnelly, 465 U.S. 668, 720–723 (1984) (Brennan, J., dissenting); Thomas v. Review Bd., 450 U.S. 707, 721 (1981) (Rehnquist, J., dissenting); Abington School Dist. v. Schempp, 374 U.S. 203, 237–38 (1963) (Brennan, J., concurring). Surely the Framers did not dream of a society as pervasively regulated by the state as is ours. To ignore this fact and rigidly adhere to views characteristic of the Framers could gravely imperil the freedoms sought by the two religion clauses. One commentator has posed a hypothetical collectivist society in which the state makes its resources—such as land, electricity, and water—available to all kinds of voluntary associations without any charge. In such a society, to prohibit the state from extending to religious associations the same kind of direct aid afforded others, while perhaps historically appropriate under the establishment clause, would emasculate the free exercise clause. See Giannella, "Religious Liberty, Non-Establishment, and Doctrinal Development: Part II, The Non-Establishment Principle," 81 Harv.L. Rev. 513, 516–26 (1968).

6. See M. Howe, The Garden and the Wilderness 6 (1965); P. Miller, Roger Williams: His Contributions to the American Revolution 89, 98 (1953).

depredations and incursions";[7] and, third, the Madisonian view that religious and secular interests alike would be advanced best by diffusing and decentralizing power so as to assure competition among sects rather than dominance by any one.[8]

Roger Williams saw separation largely as a vehicle for protecting churches against the state. To the extent that it was possible to accept state aid without state control, he urged cooperation; indeed, he argued that the state must "countenance, encourage and supply" those in religious service. Thus, his view has been called one of positive toleration, imposing on the state the burden of fostering a climate conducive to all religion.[9]

Thomas Jefferson, in contrast, saw separation as a means of protecting the state from the church. As early as 1779, he presented a bill to the Virginia Legislature to disestablish the tax-supported Anglican church. He also urged that the clergy be barred from public office.[10] That view would today strike most people as clearly violative of free exercise, but it was Jefferson's conviction that only the complete separation of religion from politics would eliminate the formal influence of religious institutions and provide for a free choice among political views; he therefore urged a "wall of separation between Church and State."[11]

James Madison believed that both religion and government could best achieve their high purposes if each were left free from the other within its respective sphere; he thus urged that the "tendency to a usurption on one side or the other, or to a corrupting coalition or alliance between them, will be best guarded against by an entire abstinance [sic] of the Government from interference in any way whatever, beyond the necessity of preserving public order, & protecting each sect against trespass on its legal rights by others."[12]

These three views are in some respects complementary, and in others conflicting. In choosing among them, the Supreme Court has occasionally assumed the role of constitutional historian to seek guidance in the origins and original meanings of the religion clauses.[13] For nearly thirty years Justices Black and Rutledge served as the chief chroniclers of these investigations.[14] Although, as in *Everson v. Board*

---

7. M. Howe, supra note 6, at 2.

8. See R. Alley, James Madison on Religious Liberty (1985); Hunt, "James Madison and Religious Liberty," 1 Am.Hist. Ass'n.Rep. 165, 170 (1961); Cassad, "The Establishment Clause and the Ecumenical Movement," 62 Mich.L.Rev. 419, 421 (1964).

9. Whitson, "American Pluralism," Thought 402 (Winter, 1962).

10. This Jeffersonian position is by no means dead. See McDaniel v. Paty, 435 U.S. 618, 621–622 (1978) (striking down state statute drawn along these lines), discussed in §§ 14–8, 14–14, infra.

11. Everson v. Board of Education, 330 U.S. 1, 16 (1947).

12. IX The Writings of James Madison 487 (G. Hunt ed. 1910).

13. For a useful general discussion of the Court's uses of history, see C. Miller, The Supreme Court and the Uses of History (1969).

14. See Everson v. Board of Education, 330 U.S. 1 (1974) (Black, J.); id. at 28 (Rutledge, J. dissenting); See also the majority opinions of Justice Black in Illinois ex rel. McCollum v. Board of Education, 333 U.S. 203 (1948); Torcaso v. Watkins, 367 U.S. 488 (1961); Engel v. Vitale, 370 U.S. 421 (1962), for development of the discussion.

of Education,[15] Justice Black (who wrote the opinion for the Court) and Justice Rutledge (who wrote in dissent) sometimes reached different results, their histories share three essential elements: first, they seek the meaning of the clauses in the background of the period in which they were adopted; second, they view the ideas of Jefferson and Madison as the direct antecedents of the first amendment and as particularly relevant to its interpretation; and, third, they accept the postulate that a union between church and state leads to persecution and civil strife.[16] Whether the Black-Rutledge version is accurate history has been disputed vigorously off the Court, as we shall momentarily see; what is indisputable is that, with remarkable consensus, later Courts accepted the perspective of these Justices as historical truth.[17] What emerges from the Court's examination of history is a pair of fundamental principles, seen in the Court's religion discussions as animating the first amendment: voluntarism and separatism.

Of the two principles, voluntarism seems the more fundamental.[18] The free exercise clause was at the very least designed to guarantee freedom of conscience [19] by preventing any degree of compulsion in matters of belief.[20] It prohibited not only direct compulsion but also any indirect coercion which might result from subtle discrimination; hence it was offended by any burden based specifically on one's religion.[21] So viewed, the free exercise clause is a mandate of religious voluntarism. The establishment clause, at least when interpreted broadly and applied to the states, can be understood as designed in part to assure that the advancement of a church would come only from the voluntary support of its followers and not from the political support of the state.[22] Religious groups, it was believed, should prosper or perish

---

15. 330 U.S. 1 (1947).

16. Id. at 1–18 (Black, J.); id. at 28–74 (Rutledge, J., dissenting).

17. See, e.g., Larson v. Valente, 456 U.S. 228, 246 (1982); Committee for Public Education v. Nyquist, 413 U.S. 756, 770 & n.28 (1973); Flast v. Cohen, 392 U.S. 83, 103–04 (1968); Abington School Dist. v. Schempp, 374 U.S. 203, 214 (1963); McGowan v. Maryland, 366 U.S. 420, 430 & n. 7, 437–43 (1961). But see Wallace v. Jaffree, 472 U.S. 38, 90 (1985) (White, J., dissenting); id. at 91–92 (Rehnquist, J., dissenting).

18. See Walz v. Tax Commission, 397 U.S. 664, 694 (1970) (Harlan, J., concurring in result); Freund, "Public Aid to Parochial Schools," 82 Harv.L.Rev. 1680 (1969); Giannella, "Religious Liberty, Non-Establishment, and Doctrinal Development: Part II, the Non-Establishment Principle," 81 Harv.L.Rev. 513, 517 (1968).

19. "[W]e hold it for a fundamental and undeniable truth, 'that Religion or the duty which we owe to our Creator and the Manner of discharging it, can be directed only by reason and conviction, not by force or violence.'" J. Madison, "Memorial and Remonstrance Against Religious Assess-

ments," quoted in Walz v. Tax Commission, 397 U.S. 664, 719 (1970) (Douglas, J., dissenting).

20. " '[T]he rights of conscience are, in their nature, of peculiar delicacy, and will little bear the gentlest touch of the governmental hand . . .,'" Abington School Dist. v. Schempp, 374 U.S. 203, 231 (1963) (Brennan, J., concurring), quoting Rep. Daniel Carroll of Maryland during the debate on proposed Bill of Rights in the First Congress.

21. J. Madison, "Memorial and Remonstrance Against Religious Assessments," quoted in Walz v. Tax Commission, 397 U.S. 664, 719 (1970) (Douglas, J., dissenting). See also Engel v. Vitale, 370 U.S. 421, 431 (1962) (Black, J.). The nondiscrimination theme inherent in the concept of voluntarism was of particular importance to Justice Harlan, who enunciated the view in Walz that the requirement of "neutrality" compelled an equal protection mode of analysis. See 397 U.S. at 696 (concurring in result); see also § 14–7, infra.

22. See Giannella, "Religious Liberty, Non-Establishment, and Doctrinal Development: Part II, The Non-Establishment

on the intrinsic merit of their beliefs and practices. The establishment clause, then, might also be seen as an expression of religious voluntarism.

Separatism, sometimes called the "noninvolvement" or "nonentanglement" principle, expresses the second major concept underlying the two clauses and reflects Madison's view that both religion and government function best if each remains independent of the other. This ideal calls for much more than the institutional separation of church and state; it means that the state should not become involved in religious affairs or derive its claim to authority from religious sources, that religious bodies should not be granted governmental powers, and—perhaps—that sectarian differences should not be allowed unduly to fragment the body politic.[23] Implicit in this ideal of mutual abstinence was the principle that under no circumstance should religion be financially supported by public taxation: "for the men who wrote the Religion Clauses . . . the 'establishment' of a religion connoted sponsorship, financial support, and active involvement of the sovereign in religious activity."[24]

It has become popular to see both the free exercise clause and the establishment clause as expressions of voluntarism and separatism in the Black-Rutledge sense just described. But the actual history of the establishment clause may belie this interpretation. A growing body of evidence suggests that the Framers principally intended the establishment clause to perform two functions: to protect state religious establishments from national displacement, and to prevent the national government from aiding some but not all religions.[25] Although the Court in 1947 "incorporated" the establishment clause against the states through the fourteenth amendment,[26] additional evidence suggests that the amendment's authors did not intend to extend the religion clauses to the states.[27] "By superficial and purposive interpre-

Principle," 81 Harv.L.Rev. 513, 516–18 (1968).

23. See §§ 14–14, 14–15, infra.

24. Walz v. Tax Commission, 397 U.S. 664, 668 (1970).

25. The leading recent studies are R. Cord, Separation of Church and State: Historical Fact and Current Fiction (1982); and M. Malbin, Religion and Politics: The Intentions of the Authors of the First Amendment (1981). See also M. Howe, The Garden and Wilderness 23–27 (1965); W. Katz, Religion and American Constitutions 9 (1964); A. Sutherland, The Church Shall Be Free 20 (1965); Snee, "Religious Disestablishment and the Fourteenth Amendment," 1954 Wash.U.L.Q. 371. Practice in the states seems to support this view. Until 1844, New Jersey limited full civil rights to Protestants. Pennsylvania and Maryland required belief in God of public office holders, Maryland until 1961. Connecticut taxed for the support of the Congregational establishment until 1818.

The Massachusetts Constitution, until 1833, authorized towns to maintain ministers where voluntary contributions were inadequate; New Hampshire did so into the twentieth century. R. Morgan, The Supreme Court and Religion 30–31 (1972).

26. See § 14–2, note 5, supra.

27. Seven years after the states ratified the fourteenth amendment, Congress debated a constitutional amendment that would have expressly subjected the states to the religion clauses:

"No State shall make any law respecting an establishment of religion or prohibiting the free exercise thereof; and no money raised by taxation in any State for the support of public schools or derived from any public fund therefor, nor any public lands devoted thereto, shall ever be under the control of any religious sect or denomination; nor shall any money so raised or lands so devoted be divided between religious sects and denominations."

tations of the past," one distinguished commentator accused, "the Court has dishonored the arts of the historian and degraded the talents of the lawyer." [28] Counterrevisionists have disputed both bodies of evidence,[29] and a clearcut resolution seems unlikely.

The debate reached the Supreme Court in *Wallace v. Jaffree* in 1985.[30] Three Alabama statutes permitting silent prayer or meditation in schools, with varying references to religion, had been upheld by a district court. That court, relying on recent scholarship, had audaciously concluded that "no doubt" existed that the first and fourteenth amendments "were not intended to forbid religious prayers in the schools," and that Supreme Court precedents to the contrary were based on a misreading of history.[31] The court of appeals reversed, and the Supreme Court affirmed the reversal. The Court's opinion, by Justice Stevens, responded to the district court by citing the precedents it had attacked, rather than entering the debate over history directly.[32] In separate opinions, two Justices did consider the question of Framers' intent. Justice O'Connor, concurring in the result, concluded that history left open the relevant questions about public schools, which barely existed at the time of the Framing—either of the first amendment or of the fourteenth.[33] Justice Rehnquist, dissenting, followed the district court's emphasis, writing that "[t]he true meaning of the Establishment Clause can only be seen in its history." [34] Unlike the district court, however, the Justice accepted without discussion the clause's "incorporation" through the fourteenth amendment against the states.[35] After reviewing what he considered the relevant history, Justice Rehnquist concluded that "nothing in the Establishment Clause requires government to be strictly neutral between religion and irreligion, nor does that Clause prohibit Congress or the States from pursuing legitimate secular ends through nondiscriminatory sectarian means." [36]

The *Jaffree* opinions, especially those of Justices O'Connor and Rehnquist, touch on four questions concerning Framers' intent. First, how broad a spectrum of history ought the Court examine? That is, where should the Court look in order to find Framers' intent? Justice Rehnquist applied an unusually narrow approach to pre-adoption history. He dismissed Thomas Jefferson's contributions to first amendment

4 Cong.Rec. 5580 (1876). The debates indicate that neither proponents nor opponents of the measure, including two of the drafters of the fourteenth amendment, believed that the latter had already applied the religion clauses to the states. See A. Meyer, "The Blaine Amendment and the Bill of Rights," 64 Harv.L.Rev. 939 (1951).

28. M. Howe, The Garden and the Wilderness 4 (1965).

29. See T. Curry, The First Freedoms: Church and State in America to the Passage of the First Amendment (1986); L. Levy, The Establishment Clause: Religion and the First Amendment (1986).

30. 472 U.S. 38. Justice Stevens wrote for the Court. Justice Powell filed a con-

curring opinion, id. at 62. Justice O'Connor filed an opinion concurring in the judgment, id. at 67. Dissenting opinions were filed by Chief Justice Burger, id. at 84, Justice White, id. at 90, and Justice Rehnquist, id. at 91.

31. Jaffree v. Board of School Comm'rs of Mobile County, 554 F.Supp. 1104, 1128 (S.D. Ala. 1983).

32. 472 U.S. at 48–56.

33. 472 U.S. at 80.

34. 472 U.S. at 113.

35. Id.

36. Id.

principles by noting that "Jefferson was of course in France" when the Bill of Rights was written and ratified.[37]   Justice Rehnquist likewise focused on James Madison's politically motivated support for a bill of rights, rather than his well-established views on religious freedom.[38] The Justice went on to recount in some detail the debates in the First Congress over what would become the first amendment.[39]   He then took a broad approach to post-adoption history, citing the Northwest Ordinance, early presidents' Thanksgiving proclamations,[40] federal aid to the religious education of American Indians, and constitutional treatises written a half-century after the first amendment's adoption.[41]

Justice Rehnquist's emphasis on post-adoption practice, an emphasis that the Court had previously applied in two other cases,[42] seems a helpful counterbalance to the Black-Rutledge focus on pre-adoption history.   But such post-adoption history must be used cautiously as a guide to Framers' intent, particularly where, as in *Jaffree*, the issues are far from identical.[43]   As Justice O'Connor responded in *Jaffree*: "The primary issue raised by Justice Rehnquist's dissent is whether the historical fact that our Presidents have long called for public prayers of Thanks should be dispositive on the constitutionality of prayer in public schools.   I think not." [44]

That raises the second question considered in *Jaffree*: How should judges apply history to questions, like the permissibility of various practices in public schools, that the Framers could not have contemplated? [45]   As late as the 1890s the British ambassador to the United States, Lord Bryce, could compare the American national government to a commercial company formed for a specific business purpose; it would be unnatural, Bryce wrote, for such an entity to concern itself with its shareholders' religion.[46]   The twentieth century, with labor law regulations, the social security system, and widespread public education, has created circumstances (and problems) the Framers could not have envisioned.   As Justice Rehnquist wrote in another case: "Because those who drafted and adopted the First Amendment could not have

37. 472 U.S. at 92.

38. 472 U.S. at 94, 97. Consistent with Justice Rehnquist's approach, one commentator has suggested that Madison's activities and statements about religious disestablishment in Virginia should not be applied to the first amendment, because of Madison's belief that factions (including religious ones) were a particular danger in states, but less so in the nation as a whole. M. McConnell, "Accommodation of Religion," 1985 S.Ct.Rev. 1, 20 n.71.

39. 472 U.S. at 95–98.

40. A still broader study of post-adoption history would, however, have included notes that Madison wrote sometime after his presidency, in which he argued that Thanksgiving proclamations improperly mingle government and religion. E. Fleet, ed., "Madison's 'Detached Memoranda'," 3 Wm. & Mary Q. 534, 560–562 (3d series 1946).

41. 472 U.S. at 100–106.

42. Lynch v. Donnelly, 465 U.S. 668, 674–678 (1984); Marsh v. Chambers, 463 U.S. 783, 790–792 (1983).   The Court in Marsh also emphasized practices concurrent with the first amendment's framing—namely, the appointments of chaplains by the First Congress. 463 U.S. at 787–789. But cf. Edwards v. Aguillard, 107 S.Ct. 2573, 2584 n. 19 (1987) ("The Court has previously found the postenactment elucidation of the meaning of a *statute* to be of little relevance in determining the intent of the legislature contemporaneous to the passage of the statute.") (emphasis added).

43. See notes 47, 48, infra.

44. 472 U.S. at 81 (concurring opinion).

45. See note 5, supra.

46. 2 J. Bryce, The American Commonwealth 701 (3d ed. 1895).

foreseen either the growth of social welfare legislation or the incorporation of the First Amendment into the Fourteenth Amendment, we simply do not know how they would view the scope of the two clauses." [47] In light of such changes, analogies offered by specific practices, such as Presidential Thanksgiving proclamations, are helpful only to the degree that they shed light on the broad principles underlying the religion clauses.[48] The relevant inquiry demands a careful examination of the context in which the constitutional language was written.

The third question raised by *Jaffree* is a narrower one: Where precedents seem to be based on misreading of history, how should judges balance the new, apparently correct historical account with the demands of *stare decisis*? "[T]he ultimate touchstone of constitutionality is the Constitution itself and not what we have said about it." [49] But, as is illustrated by the recent revisionist and counterrevisionist views of the Framers' intent concerning the religion clauses,[50] our understanding of history is not static. Certainly courts should take note of new studies that help illuminate Framers' intent. But they should be wary of enshrining into constitutional law what may prove to be an aberrant trend in historiography.

The fourth *Jaffree* question is broader: When Framers' intent on a specific issue is clear, should it be dispositive? Rhetoric and practice, pre- and post-adoption, make the Framers' deep-rooted opposition to granting government powers to religious bodies too clear and too central to ignore in construing the religion clauses in the modern era.[51] Similarly, legislative prayers were so widespread that the Framers' general silence on the subject must be taken to represent, if not active support, at the very least tolerance.[52]

Where the original intent *not* to outlaw a practice is clear, a judge ought to view the history as evidence that the practice does not violate the Constitution.[53] The showing should not, however, settle the ques-

---

47. Thomas v. Review Bd., 450 U.S. 707, 722 (1981) (Rehnquist, J., dissenting). See also W. Rehnquist, "The Notion of a Living Constitution," 54 Tex.L.Rev. 693, 694 (1976).

48. See Wallace v. Jaffree, 472 U.S. at 81 (O'Connor, J., concurring in judgment) ("When the intent of the Framers is unclear, I believe we must employ both history and reason in our analysis. . . . At the very least, Presidential [Thanksgiving] proclamations are distinguishable from school prayer in that they are received in a non-coercive setting and are primarily directed at adults. . . ."); Lynch v. Donnelly, 465 U.S. 668, 718 (1984) (Brennan, J., dissenting) ("Simply enumerating the various ways in which the Federal Government has recognized the vital role religion plays in our society does nothing to help decide the question presented in *this* case.") (emphasis in original). See generally R. Dworkin, Taking Rights Seriously

134–136 (1978) (distinguishing general concepts from specific conceptions).

49. Graves v. New York ex rel. O'Keefe, 306 U.S. 466, 491–492 (1939) (Frankfurter, J., concurring). See also Wallace v. Jaffree, 472 U.S. at 99 (Rehnquist, J., dissenting) ("[S]tare decisis may bind courts as to matters of law, but it cannot bind them as to matters of history.").

50. See notes 25 and 29, supra.

51. See Larkin v. Grendel's Den, Inc., 459 U.S. 116, 126–127 (1982); § 14–11, infra.

52. See Marsh v. Chambers, 463 U.S. 783, 786–90 (1983). But see E. Fleet, ed., "Madison's 'Detached Memoranda'," 3 Wm. & Mary Q. 554, 558 (3d series 1946) ("Does not this [law appointing legislative chaplains] involve the principle of a national establishment [of religion] . . .?").

53. See Wallace v. Jaffree, 472 U.S. at 79 (O'Connor, J., concurring in judgment)

tion entirely—particularly if the context has changed, as it surely had with public schools.[54] Instead, such a showing should simply shift the burden of persuasion to the opponent. To prevail, the opponent ought to demonstrate that, history notwithstanding, the practice offends the fundamental concepts—as described, for example, by Williams, Jefferson, or Madison—that underlie the constitutional language.[55]

Perhaps the Framers themselves, if confronted with the contradiction, would have altered the practice, especially if—as with the evolution of social institutions and practices like public schooling, or with the rise in numbers and forms of religions [56]—the context had changed, but conceivably *even if it had not.*[57] Those of the Framers who strongly

(" '[F]idelity to the notion of *constitutional*—as opposed to purely judicial—limits on governmental action requires us to impose a heavy burden on those who claim that practices accepted when [the provision] was adopted are now constitutionally impermissible.' ") (quoting Tennessee v. Garner, 471 U.S. 1, 25 (1985) (O'Connor, J., dissenting) (emphasis in original)).

54. See Lynch v. Donnelly, 465 U.S. 668, 718–719 (1984) (Brennan, J., dissenting) ("[H]istorical acceptance of a particular practice alone is never sufficient to justify a challenged government al action. . . . Attention to details of history should not blind us to the cardinal purposes of the Establishment Clause. . . ."); McDaniel v. Paty, 435 U.S. 618, 637 (1978) (Brennan, J., concurring in judgment) ("The fact that responsible statesmen of the day, including some of the United States Constitution's Framers, were attracted by the concept of clergy disqualification . . . does not provide historical support for concluding that those provisions are harmonious with the Establishment Clause."); Abington School Dist. v. Schempp, 374 U.S. 203, 236 (1963) (Brennan, J., concurring) ("[Framers' view concerning religious exercises in public schools], even if perfectly clear one way or the other, would [not] supply a dispositive answer to the question presented by these cases. A more fruitful inquiry . . . is whether the practices here challenged threaten those consequences which the Framers deeply feared; whether, in short, they tend to promote that type of interdependence between religion and state which the First Amendment was designed to prevent.") (footnote omitted); Brown v. Board of Educ., 347 U.S. 483, 492 (1954) ("[W]e cannot turn the clock back to 1868 when the Amendment was adopted. . . . We must consider public education in light of its full development and its present place in American life. . . ."); West Virginia State Bd. of Educ. v. Barnette, 319 U.S. 624, 639–40 (1943) ("These principles [in the Bill of Rights] grew in soil which also produced a philosophy that the individual was the center of society, that his liberty was attainable through mere absence of governmental restraints, and that government should be entrusted with few controls and only the mildest supervision over men's affairs. We must transplant these rights to a soil in which the *laissez-faire* concept or principle of non-interference has withered at least as to economic affairs, and social advancements are increasingly sought through closer integration of society and through expanded and strengthened governmental controls."). But see Minneapolis Star & Tribune Co. v. Minnesota Comm'r of Revenue, 460 U.S. 575, 584 n.6 (1983) ("[W]hen we do have evidence that a particular law would have *offended* the Framers, we have not hesitated to invalidate it on that ground alone.") (emphasis added).

55. Even proponents of "original intent" as the exclusive guide to legitimate interpretation are hard-pressed to urge a narrower focus. See, e.g., E. Meese, "Toward a Jurisprudence of Original Intention," 2 Benchmark 1, 8 ("[T]he principles which informed the writing of our Constitution were not conceived in an afternoon in Philadelphia. Those principles were the product of several centuries of experience.") (revised version of address to American Bar Assn., July 9, 1985).

56. See § 14–6, infra.

57. See Marsh v. Chambers, 463 U.S. 783, 814–815 (1983) (Brennan, J., dissenting) ("[T]he Court assumes that the Framers of the Establishment Clause would not have themselves authorized a practice [legislative prayers] that they thought violated the guarantees contained in the clause. . . . This assumption, however, is questionable. Legislators, influenced by the passions and exigencies of the moment, the pressures of constituents and colleagues, and the press of business, do not always pass sober constitutional judgment on every piece of legislation they enact, and this must be assumed to be as true of the members of the First Congress as any others."). Cf. Madison's post-presidency re-

favored clergy disqualification from legislative office in the 1780s and 1790s, for example, would in all likelihood agree with the result of *McDaniel v. Paty*, holding such disqualification to be inconsistent with the free exercise clause in the 1970s and 1980s.[58] The majority opinion in *Jaffree* suggested a relevant growth in the very concept of "religion" when it noted Justice Story's assertion that the religion clauses were intended to prevent rivalry among Christian religions, and not "to countenance, much less to advance," Mahomedanism, Judaism, or infidelity.[59] "But," the *Jaffree* Court continued, "when the *underlying principle* has been examined in the crucible of litigation, the Court has unambiguously concluded that the individual freedom of conscience protected by the First Amendment embraces the right to select any religious faith or none at all."[60] It is to that underlying set of principles that judges ought to turn in order to decide concrete cases.

§ 14–4. Attempts to Reconcile the Two Clauses: Forbidden, Permissible, and Required Accommodation

Perhaps the earliest of the attempts to reconcile the two religion clauses was the "strict separation theory," an interpretation suggested by the Jeffersonian image of a "wall of separation between Church and State." Both the majority and the dissenters in *Everson v. Board of Education*,[1] upholding publicly funded transportation for parochial school pupils along with others, accepted this approach, but the very fact that Justices who agreed on the governing principle could divide so sharply on the result suggests that the principle evoked by the image of a wall furnishes less guidance than metaphor.

Separation is usually said to mean at least that the state can do nothing to "aid" religion. The "no-aid" formulation, however, remains indeterminate because of the obvious difficulty of specifying precisely what constitutes "aid." Justice Reed, dissenting in *Illinois ex rel. McCollum v. Board of Education*,[2] where the Court struck down a program of released-time for prayer on public school premises, argued that "aid" referred only to "purposeful assistance directly to the church itself or to some religious group . . . performing ecclesiastical functions,"[3] but the majority viewed "aid" as any government action

---

thinking of several church-state issues. E. Fleet, ed., "Madison's 'Detached Memoranda'," 3 Wm. & Mary Q. 554 (3d series 1946).

58. 435 U.S. 618 (1978). See id. at 629 (plurality opinion) ("The essence of the Tennessee restriction on ministers is that if elected to public office they will necessarily exercise their powers and influence to promote the interests of one sect or thwart the interests of another. . . . However widely that view may have been held in the 18th century by many, including enlightened statesmen of that day, the American experience provides no persuasive support for the fear that clergymen in public office will be less careful of anti-establishment interests or less faithful to their oaths of civil office than their

unordained counterparts.") (citation and footnote omitted) (case discussed in § 14–14, infra).

59. 472 U.S. at 52 n.36 (quoting J. Story, Commentaries on the Constitution of the United States § 1877 (1851)).

60. 472 U.S. at 52 (emphasis added).

§ 14–4

1. 330 U.S. 1, 8–18 (1947) (Black, J.); id. at 26–28 (Jackson, J., dissenting); id. at 29, 31–33, 40 (Rutledge, J., joined by Frankfurter, Jackson, and Burton, JJ., dissenting).

2. 333 U.S. 203 (1948).

3. Id. at 248.

designed to promote religion as such.[4] Justice Stevens, dissenting in *Committee for Public Education v. Regan*,[5] urged the Court to adopt a strict no-aid approach in cases concerning religious schools.[6] An even broader definition of "aid" was advanced in *Everson* by Justice Rutledge in dissent; he urged that any governmental expenditure of tax funds that helps support or sustain religious training, teaching or observance is a violation of the principle of separation.[7]

Since neither the strict separation nor the no-aid theory offers much guidance in determining what manner or degree of economic benefit constitutes impermissible "aid" to religion, the Supreme Court has increasingly sought refuge in the elusive and variable notion of "neutrality."[8] The Court has never adopted the so-called "strict neutrality theory," which would prohibit government from using religious classifications either to confer benefits or to impose burdens.[9] In several cases,[10] the Court has held that religious classifications not only

4. Id. at 210–11 (Black, J.).

5. 444 U.S. 646 (1980) (statute appropriating public funds to reimburse nonpublic schools for state-mandated objective testing and other such services does not violate establishment clause).

6. Id. at 671 ("Rather than continuing with the sisyphean task of trying to patch together the 'blurred, indistinct, and variable barrier' described in Lemon v. Kurtzman, 403 U.S. 602, 614, I would resurrect the 'high and impregnable' wall between church and state constructed by the Framers of the First Amendment.").

7. Everson, 330 U.S. at 52. Clearly, the concept of "aid" is itself ambiguous. One commentator has noted that, taken to its logical conclusion the "no-aid" theory would require "children attending churches preaching personal study of the Bible [to] be barred from the public schools so as not to relieve these churches of the heavy financial burden of teaching their members to read." Giannella, "Religious Liberty, Non-Establishment, and Doctrinal Development: Part II, The Non-Establishment Principle," 81 Harv.L.Rev. 513, 568 (1968). Moreover, the ideal of separation is itself said to be an aid to religion: "The First Amendment rests upon the premise that both religion and government can best work to achieve their lofty aims if each is left free from the other within its respective sphere." Illinois ex rel. McCollum v. Board of Education, 333 U.S. 203, 212 (1948) (Black, J.). Similarly, as Justice Douglas noted in his concurrence in Engel v. Vitale, 370 U.S. 421, 443 (1962), "[t]he First Amendment teaches that a government neutral in the field of religion better serves all religious interests." Thus only some kinds of governmental "aid" are forbidden, and the task remains one of defining which. Unfortunately, other areas of constitutional law do not offer much help.

The Court has made it clear, for example, that assistance carefully limited so as to avoid the prohibition of the establishment clause may still amount to state action for purposes of the fourteenth amendment, thus requiring such assistance to be withheld from schools which practice racial discrimination. See Norwood v. Harrison, 413 U.S. 455 (1973), discussed in Chapters 16 and 18, infra. The controversial statutory holding of Bob Jones University v. United States, 461 U.S. 574 (1983)—construing the Internal Revenue Code as denying tax benefits under § 501(c)(3) to racially discriminatory private religious schools—might have been better founded on the equal protection component of the fifth amendment. See Chapter 16, infra.

8. For a discussion of various formulations of neutrality, see § 14–7, infra.

9. See P. Kurland, Religion and the Law (1962); Weiss, "Privilege, Posture, and Protection: 'Religion' in the Law," 73 Yale L.J. 593 (1964). See generally P. Kauper, Religion and the Constitution 64–67 (1964); Giannella, "Religious Liberty, Non-Establishment, and Doctrinal Development: Part II, The Non-Establishment Principle," 81 Harv.L.Rev. 513 (1968); § 14–7, infra.

10. Hobbie v. Unemployment Appeals Comm'n, 107 S.Ct. 1046 (1987); Thomas v. Review Board, 450 U.S. 707 (1981) (state must modify its unemployment compensation requirement of "good cause" in order to accommodate Jehovah's Witness who refused, for religious reasons, to work in weapons production); Wisconsin v. Yoder, 406 U.S. 205 (1972) (state must modify its compulsory education requirements in order to accommodate the tenets—and, perhaps more importantly, to permit the survival—of the Old Order Amish religion); Sherbert v. Verner, 374 U.S. 398 (1963) (state must modify its unemployment compensation requirement of willingness to

are *permitted* in some instances but at times are even *required* by the free exercise clause. These exceptions to "strict neutrality" reflect a more pragmatic, less formalistic approach to the two religion clauses. This *zone of required accommodation* recognizes that government's actions impinge on different persons in dramatically different ways, so that truly even-handed treatment at times compels exempting those whose religious beliefs are exceptionally burdened by a challenged state action.[11]

In attempting to distinguish between situations where accommodation [12] of programs to religious needs has been held excessive and those where it has been held permissible or even mandatory, it is helpful to posit a dichotomy between governmental actions arguably (even if not beyond doubt) compelled by the free exercise clause, and governmental actions supportive of religion in ways clearly not mandated by free exercise. Actions "arguably compelled" by free exercise are not forbidden by the establishment clause.[13] Thus, for example, although it is at least arguable that the free exercise clause requires some accommodation in public schools to the views of persons religiously opposed to teaching or learning about the theory of evolution,[14] no plausible

work Mondays through Saturdays in order to accommodate the needs of those religiously opposed to working on Saturdays but willing to work on Sundays instead). See also Bowen v. Roy, 106 S.Ct. 2147 (1986), where a majority of the Justices indicated that they would create an exemption from the requirement that applicants for welfare benefits must provide their social security numbers, where the applicants objected on religious grounds to using social security numbers (case discussed in § 14–13, infra).

11. Legislatures as well as courts may be free to make such accommodations. See Corporation of the Presiding Bishop of the Church of Jesus Christ of Latter-Day Saints v. Amos, 107 S.Ct. 2862, 2869 (1987) (precedents teach "that there is ample room for [legislative] accommodation of religion under the Establishment Clause"); Wallace v. Jaffree, 472 U.S. 38, 83 (1985) (O'Connor, J., concurring in judgment) (where legislation, challenged under the establishment clause, lifts a government-imposed burden on free exercise, a court should focus on whether that legislation "conveys the message of endorsement of religion or a particular religious belief" to an objective observer "acquainted with the Free Exercise clause and the values it promotes"); §§ 14–7, 14–15, infra.

12. The term "accommodation" is here used to describe practices or policies whereby government steps aside or creates an exemption in order to produce free exercise neutrality. See, e.g., Zorach v. Clauson, 343 U.S. 306, 312–314 (1952) (Douglas, J.) (upholding program of released time for prayer off public school premises). The

term does not include practices whereby government affirmatively supports or endorses a particular religion. See § 14–15, infra.

13. See Wallace v. Jaffree, 472 U.S. 38, 83 (1985) (O'Connor, J., concurring in judgment) (recommending that establishment clause challenges to statutes that lift government-imposed burdens on free exercise should be assessed differently from other establishment clause challenges).

14. Cf. Mozert v. Hawkins County Public Schools, 647 F.Supp. 1194 (E.Tenn. 1986) (requiring schools to exempt students from readings and discussions that offend their religious beliefs). Mozert was subsequently overturned by the Sixth Circuit, N.Y. Times, August 25, 1987, at p. 1, col. 2, but further appeal was contemplated as this book went to press. Another example of the kind of accommodation that is arguably required by the free exercise clause and thus not violative of the establishment clause is found in Wilder v. Sugarman, 385 F.Supp. 1013 (S.D.N.Y. 1974), which upheld New York State's constitutional and statutory provisions regarding religious matching for publicly-funded foster care of children. The court noted that "[t]he issue posed by the present case arises out of the fact that the state must wear two hats, one as a surrogate parent obligated to enforce the biological parent's individual rights to provide religious direction and the other as a government obligated to refrain from use of its powers to further or inhibit religion." Id. at 1026. See Comment, "A Reconsideration of the Religious Element in Adoption," 56 Cornell L.Rev. 780 (1971); Casenote, 3 Fordham U.L.J. 703 (1975).

argument could be advanced to the effect that the clause mandates the total exclusion of that theory from the public school curriculum; such exclusion therefore goes too far.[15]

While any distinction based on what is "arguable" is inherently indefinite, the concept at least serves to highlight the way in which the two religion clauses intersect: cases within the area of intersection are difficult precisely because different results are arguably mandated by the two religion clauses. The theory suggested here recognizes this source of difficulty and uses it to help identify the zone in which the free exercise clause dominates the intersection, permitting the accommodation of religious interests. This carved-out area might be characterized as the *zone of permissible accommodation.*

§ 14–5. A Case Study of Forbidden, Permissible, and Required Accommodation: Religious Exercises and Public Schools

The preceding section proposed that governmental actions arguably compelled by free exercise lie in the zone of permissible accommodation, and that actions reducing those burdens that stem from conflict between religious beliefs and governmental requirements may lie in the zone of required accommodation. Those two zones—along with the third, which is the core of the establishment prohibition, the zone of forbidden accommodation—are well illustrated by cases dealing with religion in the public schools: prayer as an official part of the school day, released time for students to attend religious exercises, and students' use of classrooms for religious meetings during nonschool hours. The analysis here focuses on three related but distinct questions, each of which will be discussed at greater length in a subsequent section: (1) Does the program at issue lend the powers and privileges of government to religion?[1] (2) Does it lend the aura and authority of religion to government?[2] (3) Does it violate the concept of denominational neutrality by suggesting an official endorsement of a particular religion?[3]

Prayer as an established part of the official school day is always forbidden.[4] It violates one of the establishment clause's most funda-

---

15. See Epperson v. Arkansas, 393 U.S. 97 (1968) (holding that the state cannot forbid teaching evolution in public schools where the sole explanation for the prohibition is that a particular religious group considers the evolution theory to conflict with the Biblical account of the origins of man). Cf. Edwards v. Aguillard, 107 S.Ct. 2573 (1987) (striking down state statute that required schools to provide equal classroom treatment to evolution and "creation-science"). The holdings in Epperson and Aguillard were based on a finding of nonsecular purpose, which will be discussed in § 14–9, infra.

§ 14–5

1. See § 14–11, infra.

2. See § 14–15, infra.

3. See §§ 14–7, 14–15, infra.

4. One exception is conceivable in theory, although almost impossible to envision in practice: Prayer and other officially instituted but purely optional religious exercises might be permissible on a high school campus during an activity period if religion were only one of many available alternatives. The number and breadth of the options might mitigate the establishment clause concerns. But because (in contrast to equal access programs) leaving campus would probably not be an option, an additional factor would enter the analysis: the relative attractiveness of the nonreligion choices. If those choices all seemed undesirable, then the deck would be stacked in religion's favor—making the establishment clause problems insuperable. See Abington School Dist. v. Schempp, 374 U.S. 203, 318 (1963) (Stewart, J., dissenting) (if offi-

mental tenets: Government power cannot be turned over to religion or religious bodies.[5] When schools conduct official religious exercises, an audience gathered by state power is lent, however briefly, to a religious cause. Even where dissenting students are entirely free to leave the room, state power remains at issue. The choice presented to students— either to take part in a particular religious exercise or to wait passively elsewhere—implies that the exercise is a valid element of a legally required education; the norm is religion and dissenters must opt out.[6] In addition, the combination of official ceremony and peer pressure is likely to make any such religious session inherently coercive.[7]

Such programs not only turn state power over to religion; they also turn fundamentally religious power over to the state. This clearly takes place when the government writes students' prayers. "[T]he constitutional prohibition against laws respecting an establishment of religion must at least mean that . . . it is no part of the business of government to compose official prayers for any group of the American people to recite as a part of a religious program carried on by government." [8] The state also takes on religious power whenever it selects, from the range of religious practices, which ones will enter the classroom.[9] In that sense, moreover, any form of official school prayer

cially sanctioned religious exercises were "merely one among a number of *desirable* alternatives, it could hardly be contended that the exercises did anything more than to provide an opportunity for the voluntary expression of religious belief") (emphasis added) (footnote omitted). Another determining factor would be whether students were indirectly coerced, despite the lack of official compulsion, to take part in the religious exercises rather than the other theoretically available activities. Any significant risk of coercion would render the program unconstitutional.

5. See Larkin v. Grendel's Den, 459 U.S. 116, 123 (1982) (wall between church and state is "substantially breached by vesting discretionary governmental powers in religious bodies"); § 14–11, infra.

6. Justice Brennan has suggested that an excusal option may in effect "require a student to profess publicly his disbelief as the prerequisite to the exercise of his constitutional right of abstention." Abington School Dist. v. Schempp, 374 U.S. 203, 289 (1963) (concurring opinion). Cf. Wooley v. Maynard, 430 U.S. 705, 714 (1977) (first amendment protects "both the right to speak freely and the right to refrain from speaking at all") (case discussed in § 12–4). But note that the opt-out solution was deemed sufficient in West Virginia St. Bd. of Educ. v. Barnette, 319 U.S. 624 (1943) (compulsory secular flag salute violates first amendment).

7. See Engel v. Vitale, 370 U.S. 421, 431 (1962) ("When the power, prestige and financial support of government is placed

behind a particular religious belief, the indirect coercive pressure upon religious minorities to conform to the prevailing officially approved religion is plain."); Illinois ex rel. McCollum v. Board of Educ., 333 U.S. 203, 227 (1948) (Frankfurter, J., joined by Jackson, Rutledge, Burton, JJ., concurring in part and dissenting in part) (noting "obvious pressure upon children to attend" religious exercises).

8. Engel v. Vitale, 370 U.S. 421, 425 (1962).

9. See, e.g., Wallace v. Jaffree, 472 U.S. 38, 62–67 (1985) (Powell, J., concurring) (although statute setting aside time for "meditation or silent prayer" is unconstitutional, a moment of silence statute with no mention of prayer would be constitutional); id. at 67–79 (O'Connor, J., concurring) (same); Stone v. Graham, 449 U.S. 39 (1980) (striking down Kentucky statute requiring copy of Ten Commandments, purchased with private funds, to be posted in each public classroom); Abington School Dist. v. Schempp, 374 U.S. 203 (1963) (striking down statutes and public school policies requiring reading of Bible or reciting of Lord's Prayer). Cf. Engel v. Vitale, 370 U.S. 421, 429 (1962) (Americans at time of Framing knew that "one of the greatest dangers to the freedom of the individual to worship in his own way lay in the Government's placing its official stamp of approval upon one particular kind of prayer or one particular form of religious service"); Marsh v. Chambers, 463 U.S. 783, 808 (1983) (Brennan, J., dissenting) (legislative prayer "requires the State to commit itself

violates principles of neutrality.[10] Even if different days were given over to different religions' prayers, government would be endorsing religion over nonreligion,[11] endorsing religions that include prayers over those that do not,[12] and endorsing religions that favor public prayer over those that believe prayer must be private.[13]

In addition, the inclusion of prayer as part of the official school program may borrow the aura of religious authority to shore up the power and prestige of a coercive government program—compulsory education. Such an alliance presents several potential problems. It may compromise the religion itself as political figures, many of whom enjoy greater visibility than the religion's leaders, reshape the religion's beliefs for their own purposes. The alliance may also link the religion's fortunes with the fortunes of political leaders. As the playwright Arthur Miller has written, "Public skepticism toward politicians when they fail, as ours are bound to do from time to time, can extend out toward the religion that seeks to sanctify them quite as easily as it once shielded them." [14] The alliance may also undermine free political discourse: The more political leaders wrap themselves in the mantle of religion, the more readily those who oppose them may be accused of opposing God.[15] That, in turn, may polarize citizens and leaders around a religious axis, creating the sort of divisiveness that the first amendment was partly intended to minimize. True, official school prayer did not create these situations during the decades prior to the early 1960s. Most people apparently viewed school prayer as an aspect of the American civil religion, whose tenets, including the existence of God and the special destiny of the United States, were very widely accepted.[16] But school prayer retained the potential to convey the message that religion and the state were one. That potential grew more worrisome as the number of non-believers increased; what the

on fundamental theological issues"). But cf. Marsh, id. at 783 (upholding legislative prayers).

10. See § 14–7, infra.

11. See Torcaso v. Watkins, 367 U.S. 488, 495 (1961) (neither state nor federal government may "pass laws or impose requirements which aid all religions as against nonbelievers"); Everson v. Board of Educ., 330 U.S. 1, 15 (1947) (neither state nor federal government may "pass laws which . . . aid all religions").

12. Theravada Buddhism, for instance, does not include prayer. See Marsh v. Chambers, 463 U.S. 783, 819 n.40 (1983) (Brennan, J., dissenting) (citing H. Smith, The Religions of Man 138 (Perennial Library ed. 1965)).

13. See Abington School Dist. v. Schempp, 374 U.S. 203, 283–284 (1963) (Brennan, J., concurring) (some people's "reverence for the Holy Scriptures demands private study or reflection," and to them "public reading or recitation is sacrilegious").

14. A. Miller, "School Prayer: A Political Dirigible," N.Y. Times, March 12, 1984, at A17, col. 1. In part for this reason, Roger Williams argued that the "garden" of the church should remain separate from the "wilderness" of the state. See § 14–3, supra. See generally Churches on the Wrong Road (S. Atkins & T. McConnell eds. 1986).

15. See Miller, supra note 14, at A17 ("A Khomeini in our day is impossible to controvert, let alone dislodge, because he has achieved a total identification of religion with his political regime, so that to oppose him is to oppose God."). See also § 14–15, infra.

16. Robert Bellah has argued that "there actually exists alongside of and rather clearly differentiated from the churches an elaborate and well-institutionalized civil religion in America." R. Bellah, "Civil Religion in America," 96 Daedalus 1 (1967). See also R. Bellah & P. Hammond, Varieties of Civil Religion (1980). See the further discussion in § 14–15, notes 80 and 85.

majority saw as a relatively inconsequential expression of civil religion, the minority was likely to see as an improper, highly significant linkage between church and state.[17] In addition, the circumstances of school prayer—that it took place before a young, impressionable, and captive audience, in a state-controlled and -identified institution— differed significantly from those of other expressions of civil religion.[18] Thus, even if most *voters* gave little or no thought to school prayer, the *students* who confronted it daily may have perceived it as signaling an alliance between religion and government.

Finally, no plausible free exercise argument supports an official school prayer program. Students may have a reasonable claim to use an empty classroom for prayer before the school day begins, and perhaps even during recess or an activity period, but their free exercise rights cannot warrant imposing their religion on others—or putting others to a choice between officially sanctioned religious observance and visibly opting out. If the free exercise clause were to extend that far, the Amish could force public high schools to shut down because secondary education offends their religious beliefs.[19] In fact, though, " '[t]he First Amendment . . . gives no one the right to insist that in pursuit of their own interests others must conform their conduct to his own religious necessities.' " [20]

Although the state may not make religion an official part of the school day, it may release individual students from school to attend religious exercises. Letting students observe their religious obligations during school hours is arguably compelled by the free exercise clause. Thus, under the theory outlined above, the basic concept of released time lies in the zone of permissible accommodation.[21] As the case law illustrates, though, released time may in practice extend beyond what is arguably compelled by free exercise, and may accordingly raise establishment clause problems.

Where the state permits the religious exercises to take place on campus during the school day, for instance, it makes religious observance a part of the curriculum, and thereby lends government power to

---

17. See §§ 14–6, 14–15, infra.

18. The Supreme Court has cited the age of participants as a relevant factor in several cases. See note 53, infra.

19. Cf. Wisconsin v. Yoder, 406 U.S. 205 (1972) (Amish exempt from compulsory education after eighth grade). See also note 44, infra.

20. Estate of Thornton v. Caldor, 472 U.S. 703, 710 (1985) (quoting Otten v. Baltimore & Ohio R. Co., 205 F.2d 58, 61 (2d Cir. 1953) (L. Hand, J.)). See also Bowen v. Roy, 106 S.Ct. 2147, 2152 (1986) ("The Free Exercise Clause affords an individual protection from certain forms of governmental compulsion; it does not afford an individual a right to dictate the conduct of the Government's internal procedures."). A free exercise argument *against* the school prayer program is, however, entirely plau-

sible, given the likely pressure to participate from peers and teachers. See note 7, supra. The program will push some students to engage in practices contrary to their consciences, and thereby violate their free exercise rights. Cf. West Virginia St. Bd. of Educ. v. Barnette, 319 U.S. 624, 642 (1943) ("[N]o official . . . can prescribe what shall be orthodox in politics, nationalism, religion, or other matters of opinion. . . .").

21. See § 14–4, supra. Justice Stewart advanced the free exercise argument, dissenting in Abington School District v. Schempp: "[A] compulsory state educational system so structures a child's life that if religious exercises are held to be an impermissible activity in schools, religion is placed at an artificial and state-created disadvantage." 374 U.S. 203, 313 (1963).

religion. The Court emphasized this factor in *Zorach v. Clauson*,[22] upholding a program that let students leave campus during a specified period each day for off-campus religious instruction. The Court distinguished *Illinois ex rel. McCollum v. Board of Education*,[23] which had struck down a released time program, on the basis that the religious exercises in *McCollum* had been conducted on the public school's campus. "In the *McCollum* case," Justice Douglas wrote for the Court in *Zorach*, "the force of the public school was used to promote [religious] instruction. Here . . . the public schools do no more than accommodate their schedules to a program of outside religious instruction."[24]

Justice Jackson, one of three dissenters in *Zorach*, found the distinction "trivial, almost to the point of cynicism."[25] The two released time programs did share a number of attributes. Both seemingly had a potential for coercion, although there was no evidence of actual coercion.[26] Both also seemingly had a potential for discrimination, in that not all religions chose to take part in the programs.[27] In both programs, school officials apparently held the power to determine which religions were appropriate for inclusion and which were not.[28] It appears that neither program offered any active alternative for nonbelievers.[29]

Most importantly, both programs apparently employed the machinery of the state to gather an audience for religion.[30] The result in both

22. 343 U.S. 306 (1952).

23. 333 U.S. 203 (1948).

24. 343 U.S. at 315.

25. 343 U.S. at 325. Justices Black and Frankfurter also dissented.

26. In McCollum the Court did not consider appellant's argument that "subtle pressures were brought to bear on the students to force them to participate." 333 U.S. at 207 n.1. The four Justices who wrote separately were willing to infer coercion from the circumstances. See 333 U.S. at 227 (Frankfurter, J., joined by Jackson, Rutledge, and Burton, JJ., concurring in part and dissenting in part). In Zorach the Court found "no evidence in the record" of coercion, but added: "If in fact coercion were used, if in fact it were established that any one or more teachers were using their office to persuade or force students to take the religious instruction, a wholly different case would be presented." 343 U.S. at 311. Justice Frankfurter, dissenting, would have inferred coercion based on the pleadings. Id. at 322. Subsequently the Court has been more willing to infer coercion in putatively voluntary school programs. See, e.g., Engel v. Vitale, 370 U.S. 421, 431 (1962).

27. The four Justices who wrote separately in McCollum found this particularly troubling: "The children belonging to these nonparticipating sects will thus have inculcated in them a feeling of separatism when the school should be the training

ground for habits of community, or they will have religious instruction in a faith which is not that of their parents." 333 U.S. at 227–228 (Frankfurter, J., joined by Jackson, Rutledge, and Burton, JJ., concurring in part and dissenting in part). Presumably some religions also did not participate in the Zorach program.

28. The school superintendent, according to the four Justices in McCollum, would determine "whether or not it is practical" for a particular religious group to teach in the schools, which would seem to open the way for discrimination. 333 U.S. at 226–227 (Frankfurter, J., joined by Jackson, Rutledge, and Burton, JJ., concurring in part and dissenting in part). School officials in Zorach apparently had discretion to determine what constituted a legitimate religious activity that entitled the student to leave campus. See 343 U.S. at 325 (Jackson, J., dissenting) (accusing program of "conced[ing] to the State power and wisdom to single out 'duly constituted religious' bodies as exclusive alternatives for compulsory secular instruction").

29. This aspect prompted Justice Black, dissenting in Zorach, to accuse the majority of "drawing invidious distinctions between those who believe in no religion and those who do believe." 343 U.S. at 320.

30. As the Court put it in McCollum: "Here not only are the State's tax-supported public school buildings used for the dissemination of religious doctrines. The

programs, it could be argued, was a norm of religion, virtually indistinguishable from the norm created by official school prayer. In a class of nine Baptists and one atheist, the atheist would end up standing alone in the hallway during school prayer, or sitting alone in a study hall during released time. True, the released time program would require the Baptists to bring notes from their parents, and thus formally to opt in, whereas the prayer program would require the atheist to opt out. Nonetheless, both programs present a choice between religion and, in essence, nothing—dead time in a hallway or a study hall.[31] The result, under this argument, is "a message to nonadherents that they are outsiders, not full members of the political community, and an accompanying message to adherents that they are insiders, favored members of the political community." [32]

Because both released time programs created a norm of religion that affected believers and nonbelievers alike, it appears that both programs—and any other program that offered a religion-or-nothing choice—would fail the "arguably compelled" test. In contrast, a school is at least "arguably compelled" to permit individual students to be absent for religious reasons. A school would also be free, although by no argument compelled, to close down entirely on a religious holiday.[33]

Although the above factors might point to a different result in *Zorach* today, the factor that the majority emphasized—that the religious activities were held off campus—is nonetheless vitally important. On-campus, school-time exercises are particularly offensive to the establishment clause because of public schools' special place in American life. School is the forum through which basic norms are transmitted to our young, as well as "a most vital civic institution for the preservation of a democratic system of government." [34] When government permits a religion to take over part of a public school's facilities during the school

State also affords sectarian groups an invaluable aid in that it helps to provide pupils for their religious classes through the use of the State's compulsory public school machinery." 333 U.S. at 212. The Zorach majority noted that the churches reported which students in the program failed to attend the religious classes, but the majority added that the evidence did not indicate "that the public schools enforce attendance at religious schools by punishing absentees from the released time programs for truancy." 343 U.S. at 308, 311 n.6. It seems likely, however, that the church attendance reports had some purpose. The dissenters inferred that the school had put its coercive force behind the program. See id. at 318 (Black, J., dissenting) ("New York is manipulating its compulsory education laws to help religious sects get pupils. This is not separation but combination of Church and State."); id. at 323 (Frankfurter, J., dissenting) ("The unwillingness of the promoters of this movement to dispense with such use of the public schools betrays a surprising want of confidence in the inherent

power of the various faiths to draw children to outside sectarian classes—an attitude that hardly reflects the faith of the greatest religious spirits."); id. at 324 (Jackson, J., dissenting) (school "serves as a temporary jail for a pupil who will not go to Church").

31. See Zorach, 343 U.S. at 324 (Jackson, J., dissenting) ("[S]chooling is more or less suspended during the 'released time' so the nonreligious attendants will not forge ahead of the churchgoing absentees.").

32. Lynch v. Donnelly, 465 U.S. 668, 688 (1984) (O'Connor, J., concurring) (finding no such message, however, in an official nativity display during Christmas).

33. See Zorach, 343 U.S. at 320 (Frankfurter, J., dissenting) ("There is all the difference in the world between letting the children out of school and letting some of them out of school into religious classes.").

34. Abington School Dist. v. Schempp, 374 U.S. 203, 230 (1963) (Brennan, J., concurring).

day, it strongly implies official endorsement of the particular religion. The central difference between *Zorach* and *McCollum*, Justice Brennan later wrote, was not the use of school premises per se; rather, it was that "the *McCollum* program placed the religious instructor in the public school classroom in precisely the position of authority held by the regular teachers of secular subjects, while the *Zorach* program did not. The *McCollum* program, in lending to the support of sectarian instruction all the authority of the governmentally operated public school system, brought government and religion into that proximity which the Establishment Clause forbids." [35] It is not surprising, therefore, that the Court has not permitted any major religious activity, however voluntary, organized by school authorities to take place on campus during school hours. From this perspective, the telling conclusion in *McCollum* was that "[r]eligious education so conducted on school time and property is patently woven into the working scheme of the school." [36] The outcome is dictated not so much by the "theoretical accounting" [37] perspective as by the symbolic support for religious instruction.

A different analysis, however, applies to classroom use during *non-school* hours by privately organized and privately led groups of students (or others). The building is, in a sense, surplus land. Religious instructors will no longer stand in "the position of authority held by the regular teachers," because the activities lie outside the mandatory school day. Although coercion is conceivable, it is not inherent, as it probably is with official school prayer; students who do not want to take part in the religious activities may take part in other activities or leave the campus.[38] No symbolic mingling of church and state functions takes place, so long as access to the campus is entirely independent of the religious or other content of the meetings. Thus, the state neither lends power to religion, nor borrows legitimacy from religion. Permitting a religious group to use school facilities during non-school hours, accordingly, conveys no message of endorsement.

A message of *exclusion*, however, is conveyed where the state refuses to let religious groups use facilities that are open to other groups. Any meaningful formulation of neutrality will dictate that,

35. Id. at 262–263. See also Grand Rapids School Dist. v. Ball, 473 U.S. 373, 391 (1985) ("The symbolic connection of church and state in the *McCollum* program presented the students with a graphic symbol of the 'concert or union or dependency' of church and state. This very symbolic union was conspicuously absent in the *Zorach* program.") (citation and footnote omitted) (quoting Zorach, 343 U.S. at 312).

36. 333 U.S. at 227 (Frankfurter, J., joined by Jackson, Rutledge, Burton, JJ., concurring in part and dissenting in part). Several cases have taken a similar approach in striking down certain forms of state aid to religious schools. See, e.g., Aguilar v. Felton, 473 U.S. 402 (1985) (striking down program that sent public school teachers into parochial schools to conduct classes for educationally deprived students); Grand Rapids School Dist. v. Ball, 473 U.S. 373 (1985) (striking down program that sent public teachers into parochial schools to teach supplementary classes, and program that paid parochial teachers for teaching after-school classes in parochial schools); Meek v. Pittenger, 421 U.S. 349 (1975) (permitting textbook loans to parochial school students, but striking down loans of instructional equipment and materials to parochial schools). The cases are discussed in § 14–10, infra.

37. McCollum, 333 U.S. at 238–239 n.2 (Reed, J., dissenting).

38. On the breadth of a program's aid as a mitigating factor in establishment clause challenges, see § 14–10, infra.

when the state makes a facility available to *non*religious groups, it must give religious groups no less opportunity.[39]   To do otherwise would demonstrate not neutrality but hostility toward religion.   "[T]he Establishment Clause does not license government to treat religion and those who teach or practice it, simply by virtue of their status as such, as subversive of American ideals and therefore subject to unique disabilities." [40]

True, an equal access policy does employ public school classrooms to aid religion, a factor that *McCollum* and *Zorach* emphasized.[41]   But the existence of aid has not been dispositive in assessing policies that benefit religion and nonreligion alike,[42] as an equal access policy does, particularly not in cases where contrary policies would discriminate *against* religion.[43]   Moreover, the strongest argument against letting religion use school property is that a message of official endorsement will result; but that message is counteracted where a number of different groups, religious and nonreligious, are equally free to use the facilities and in fact do so:[44]

39. See § 14–7, infra.

40. McDaniel v. Paty, 435 U.S. 618, 641 (1978) (Brennan, J., concurring in judgment) (striking down state law disqualifying clergy from legislative office).

41. McCollum, 333 U.S. at 212; Zorach, 343 U.S. at 315.

42. See, e.g., Mueller v. Allen, 463 U.S. 388 (1983) (tax deductions for children's education); Everson v. Board of Educ., 330 U.S. 1 (1947) (state payment of bus fares).

43. See Widmar v. Vincent, 454 U.S. 263, 274–275 (1981) ("If the Establishment Clause barred the extension of general benefits to religious groups, 'a church could not be protected by the police and fire departments, or have its public sidewalk kept in repair.'") (quoting Roemer v. Maryland Public Works Bd., 426 U.S. 736, 747 (1976) (plurality opinion)); McDaniel v. Paty, 435 U.S. 618, 641 (1978) (Brennan, J., concurring in judgment) (establishment clause "may not be used as a sword to justify repression of religion or its adherents from any aspect of public life") (citing first edition of this treatise).

44. The equal access question can be recast as an inquiry into whether government may dispense benefits discriminatorily, denying them to religious groups.   However, even a formally nondiscriminatory approach may violate the free exercise clause, when the burden falls much more heavily on members of a particular religion. See §§ 14–4, supra, 14–7, infra.   In Wisconsin v. Yoder, 406 U.S. 205 (1972), for example, the Court required Wisconsin to exempt the Amish from compulsory school attendance requirements beyond the eighth grade, because those requirements directly conflicted with the Amish's fundamental religious belief in "life aloof from

the world and its values."   406 U.S. at 210. Somewhat analogous arguments have been raised by parents who allege that their own or their children's fundamental religious beliefs are denied or offended by specific school curricular materials.   See Grove v. Mead School Dist., 753 F.2d 1528 (9th Cir. 1985) (rejecting free exercise argument where students were permitted to avoid reading and discussing books that offended their beliefs), cert. denied 106 S.Ct. 85 (1985); Mozert v. Hawkins County Public Schools, 647 F.Supp. 1194 (E.Tenn. 1986) (requiring schools to exempt students from readings and discussions that offended their beliefs).   Mozert was subsequently overturned by the Sixth Circuit, N.Y. Times, August 25, 1987, at p. 1, col. 2, but further appeal was contemplated as this book went to press.   Such cases are distinguishable from Yoder, however, in that the plaintiffs seek to reshape the public school curriculum to conform with their beliefs, or to opt out of some but not all elements of the curriculum, rather than to opt out of education entirely.   See G. Will, "Tailored Textbooks," Washington Post, Nov. 9, 1986 at H7 ("In the cases the Supreme Court has decided, the religious persons only sought access to a state benefit [or relief from a state burden].   In Tennessee, the plaintiffs insisted that the benefit (education) be tailored to their tastes.").   It does not follow that the district court in Mozert was wrong—only that its ruling went beyond Yoder, at least in its potential administrative complexity.   See § 14–13, infra. Cf. Parents' Ass'n of P.S. 16 v. Quinones, 803 F.2d 1235 (2d Cir. 1986) (striking down, under establishment clause, program that used public funds, public employees, and public school facilities to teach remedial courses to Hasidic Jewish girls, where, con-

Widmar v. Vincent,[45] although it concerned a college, suggests that public secondary schools are constitutionally required to open their facilities equally to religious and nonreligious groups. In *Widmar*, officials of the University of Missouri at Kansas City told a religious student group that, unlike other student groups on campus, it could no longer use university facilities for its meetings; otherwise, the officials believed, the university would violate the establishment clause. The Supreme Court agreed that incidental benefits would probably accrue to the religious groups that used the facilities. But, the Court held, such benefits are not significant enough to constitute an establishment of religion.[46] First, the Court said, a university's forum does not "confer any imprimatur of state approval on religious sects or practices."[47] Second, the facilities are open to nonreligious as well as religious speakers—a breadth of benefit which is "an important index of secular effect."[48] In *Bender v. Williamsport Area School District*,[49] the four Justices who reached the merits of the case would have applied the *Widmar* holding to a public secondary school.[50]

In 1984 Congress enacted the equal access approach into law. The Equal Access Act requires a public secondary school with a "limited open forum"—that is, a school that permits one or more noncurriculum-related student groups to meet on campus before or after classes—to permit all groups of students to enjoy the same privileges, notwithstanding the "religious, political, philosophical, or other content of the speech at such meetings."[51]

One additional factor may, however, prohibit otherwise permissible released time and equal access programs in some settings: the age of the students. Young students are likely to be vulnerable to coercion and intimidation. Although student-initiated coercion is not state action, the state nonetheless must anticipate it and respond to it where the coercion results directly and foreseeably from a state program. No less important is the risk that younger children may see endorsement in the school's otherwise-permissible accommodation. At least concerning public schools, the endorsement question ought to be asked from two perspectives: that of an objective observer sympathetic to free exercise concerns,[52] and that of the students involved. The objective observer test alone misses the mark when the *actual* observers who will

sistent with their religious beliefs, the Hasidic students were taught only by women, were taught in Yiddish, and were permitted to use a wing of the school separate from other students).

45. 454 U.S. 263 (1981).

46. 454 U.S. at 273–4.

47. Id. at 274.

48. Id. at 275. The Court went on to hold that the university's rule discriminated among speakers on the basis of content, and thereby violated freedom of speech.

49. 106 S.Ct. 1326 (1986).

50. See id. at 1337–1338 (Burger, C.J., joined by White and Rehnquist, JJ., dissenting); id. at 1339–1340 (Powell, J., dissenting). The majority remanded with instructions to dismiss for lack of standing. Id. at 1330–35.

51. 20 U.S.C. § 4071 et seq. See Religious Speech Protection Act: Hearing on H.R. 4996 Before the Subcomm. on Elementary, Secondary, and Vocational Education of the House Comm. on Education & Labor, 98th Cong., 2d Sess. 45 (1984) (statement of L. Tribe).

52. See Wallace v. Jaffree, 472 U.S. 38, 82 (O'Connor, J., concurring in judgment) (suggesting that "purpose" and "effects" tests in establishment clause challenges be measured from the perspective of an objective observer acquainted with free exercise values).

be most affected are, by reason of age, barely capable of objectivity.[53] If only religious groups in fact took advantage of a school's equal access program, for instance, young children might perceive, however wrongly, the imprimatur of state approval.[54] A program's facial neutrality alone

53. Age has been given weight in Grand Rapids School Dist. v. Ball, 473 U.S. 373, 385 (1985) (program using public funds to pay for teaching state-required subjects at parochial schools "may provide a crucial symbolic link between government and religion, thereby enlisting—at least in the eyes of impressionable youngsters—the powers of government to the support of the religious denomination operating the school"); id. at 390 ("The symbolism of a union between church and state is most likely to influence children of tender years, whose experience is limited and whose beliefs consequently are the function of environment as much as of free and voluntary choice."); Wallace v. Jaffree, 472 U.S. 38, 81 (1985) (O'Connor, J., concurring in judgment) ("At the very least, Presidential proclamations are distinguishable from school prayer in that they are received in a non-coercive setting and are primarily directed at adults, who presumably are not readily susceptible to unwilling religious indoctrination."); Marsh v. Chambers, 463 U.S. 783, 792 (1983) ("Here, the individual claiming injury by the [legislative chaplain] practice is an adult, presumably not readily susceptible to 'religious indoctrination' or peer pressure.") (citations omitted); Widmar v. Vincent, 454 U.S. 263, 274 n.14 (1981) ("University students are, of course, young adults. They are less impressionable than younger students and should be able to appreciate that the University's policy is one of neutrality toward religion."); Abington School Dist. v. Schempp, 374 U.S. 203, 298–299 (1963) (Brennan, J., concurring) (finding "of special significance" the fact that military chaplains generally deal with adults, "not with impressionable children"); Illinois ex rel. McCollum v. Board of Educ., 333 U.S. 203, 227 (1948) (Frankfurter, J., joined by Jackson, Rutledge, Burton, JJ., concurring in part and dissenting in part) ("The law of imitation operates, and nonconformity is not an outstanding characteristic of children."). But cf. Bender v. Williamsport Area School Dist., 106 S.Ct. 1326, 1339 (1986) (Powell, J., dissenting) ("I do not believe—particularly in this age of massive media information—that the few years difference in age between high school and college students justifies departing from *Widmar*."); Engel v. Vitale, 370 U.S. 421, 442 (1962) (Douglas, J., concurring) (implying that coercive element of official prayer is no different for school children than for legislators or Justices; "[e]very such audience is in a sense a 'captive' audience").

54. Widmar left open the possibility that a de facto religious takeover of the college public forum, even if it resulted from the free choices of individuals, might constitute an establishment clause violation: "At least in the absence of empirical evidence that religious groups will dominate [the university's] open forum, we agree . . . that the advancement of religion would not be the forum's 'primary effect.'" Widmar v. Vincent, 454 U.S. 263, 275 (1981). But cf. Mueller v. Allen, 463 U.S. 388, 400–401 (1983) (facially neutral tax deduction cannot be challenged merely because its financial benefits accrue principally to families of parochial school children). The problem of students' potential misperceptions arose sharply in Cooper v. Eugene School Dist. No. 4J, 301 Or. 358, 723 P.2d 298 (1986), appeal dismissed 107 S.Ct. 1597 (1987). The Oregon Supreme Court there upheld a statute that prohibited public schoolteachers from wearing religious clothing in the classroom; thus, the law sought to prevent students from wrongly perceiving religious endorsements, although at the cost of some constriction on schoolteachers' free exercise. The court held that, although teachers could wear religious clothing on special holidays, the statute as thus limited was constitutional. Id. at 313 (statute does not violate state or federal constitution). The court recognized the central importance of religious garb to some denominations. Id. at 307. However, the court agreed with the legislature that religious clothing might "giv[e] children or their parents the impression that the school, through its teacher, approves and shares the religious commitment of one group and perhaps finds that of others less worthy." Id. at 308. The plaintiff, a Sikh who wished to wear a religious turban while teaching, contended that such principles might hold weight concerning the dominant religion, which the state might credibly seek to endorse, but not concerning fringe religions like hers; the court responded by asserting, but without supporting analysis, that "religious freedom . . . can[not] depend on calculations [of] which faiths are more likely than others to snatch a young soul from a rival creed." Id. at 311. Although the court seemed to undervalue the teacher's free exercise rights, the problem is a difficult one. Clearly, teachers occupy a special place of influence in young students' lives. The state has the duty to prevent teachers from proselytizing in the classrooms; the court's conclusion, that a teacher's reli

is insufficient where impressionable children are concerned—certainly in the public schools, and perhaps in other spheres as well.

Audience perceptions and misperceptions are particularly thorny concerning schoolchildren, but they arise—and influence the outcomes of cases—concerning adults as well. This essential flexibility in the definition of "religion" in the first amendment is the subject of the next section.

§ 14–6. Defining "Religion" in the First Amendment

At least through the nineteenth century, courts defined "religion" narrowly, in terms of theistic notions respecting divinity, morality, and worship.[1] In order to be considered legitimate, religions had to be viewed as "civilized" by Western standards.[2] Courts, moreover, were considered competent forums for making such determinations.[3] Finally, this view of religion combined easily with a belief-action distinction so as to limit religious liberty to immunity for beliefs and traditional forms of worship, leaving unprotected religiously motivated actions of a less conventional sort.[4]

But even before the turn of the century, dramatic changes were surfacing in American religion and in theological reflection upon its many variations. Religion in America, always pluralistic, has become radically so in the latter part of the twentieth century. In colonial times there were dozens of major religious groups;[5] today there are well over 250 recognized, major churches,[6] and this number does not include hundreds of smaller, "fringe" groups. Even within a single religion—Christianity—tremendous diversity has appeared, with some

gious clothing may exert the same sort of effect as proselytizing, is not utterly implausible. Probably, however, that conclusion, should have been applied only to identifiably hierarchical religious garb—such as a priest's collar or a nun's habit—that the average viewer would see as signaling not only religious *affiliation* but religious *authority*. The Supreme Court dismissed the teacher's appeal for want of a substantial federal question. 107 S.Ct. 1597 (1987). Justices Brennan, Marshall, and O'Connor would have heard argument.

§ 14–6

1. See, e.g., Reynolds v. United States, 98 U.S. (8 Otto) 145, 164–66 (1878) (holding that the Mormons' practice of polygamy was not protected by the religion clauses of the first amendment); Davis v. Beason, 133 U.S. 333, 342–44 (1890) (holding that Mormon appellant's opinions respecting polygamy were not, according to "the common sense of mankind," religious tenets at all, and stating that not only the practice but also the teaching or counseling of polygamy constituted criminal actions); Late Corporation of the Church of Jesus Christ of Latter-Day Saints v. United States, 136 U.S. 1, 49–50 (1890) (Charter of Mormon

Church repealed because it was not a religious or charitable corporation since one of its supposed religious tenets, polygamy, was a "pretense" according to "the enlightened sentiments of mankind").

2. See Davis, 133 U.S. at 341–42; Late Corporation of the Church of Jesus Christ of Latter-Day Saints, 136 U.S. at 49–50.

3. See the cases cited in note 1, supra. But cf. Watson v. Jones, 80 U.S. (13 Wall.) 679 (1872) (leaving to religious tribunal the decision as to which of two competing groups represented "true" church; although the holding was based on federal common law rather than the Constitution, the case was later cited in first amendment context).

4. See Galanter, "Religious Freedom in the United States: A Turning Point?", 1966 Wis.L.Rev. 217, 255–58; Giannella, "Religious Liberty, Non-Establishment, and Doctrinal Development: Part I, The Religious Liberty Guarantee," 80 Harv.L. Rev. 1381, 1386–88 (1967).

5. See Whitson, "American Pluralism," Thought 493–503 (Winter, 1962).

6. See L. Rosten, Religions in America 221 (1963).

Christian groups formally accepting members who regard the concept of "God" as irrelevant or even harmful.[7] This growing diversity in religious belief and practice has been mirrored, and even magnified, by developments in theology. There are, of course, many traditionally theistic American theologians, but for many others there has been a shift in religious thought from a theocentric, transcendental perspective to forms of religious consciousness that stress the immanence of meaning in the natural order.[8] Thus, the British biologist Sir Julian Huxley spoke for many contemporary American religious thinkers when he said that "God is beginning to resemble not a ruler but the last fading smile of a cosmic Cheshire Cat."[9]

These changed circumstances made it all but inevitable that the Supreme Court would modify the narrow understanding of "religion" that had characterized the early development of the law. The idea of religious liberty—combined with the special place of religion in the constitutional order[10]—demands a definition of "religion" that goes beyond the closely bounded limits of theism, and accounts for the multiplying forms of recognizably legitimate religious exercise.[11]

Although the Court has abandoned its narrow, theistic view of religion in free exercise analysis, it has not escaped the necessity of drawing some boundary around religion. Indeed, avoiding the task would violate the principles underlying the clause. As the Court has noted, "the Free Exercise Clause, . . . by its terms, gives special protection to the exercise of religion."[12] One commentator's point

---

7. See, e.g., Unitarian Universalist Association, Report of the Committee on Goals 24 (1967).

8. This phenomenon, though by no means limited to Christianity, is perhaps most striking within a tradition so readily assumed to be theistic and transcendent. The theme "God is dead" was popularized by such "Christian atheists" as Altizer and Hamilton in the 1960's. Certainly more widely followed, however, would be Paul Tillich: "The name of this infinite and inexhaustable depth and ground of all being is *God*. That depth is what the word *God* means. And if that word has not much meaning for you, translate it, and speak of the depths of your life, of the source of your being, of your ultimate concern, of what you take seriously without any reservation. Perhaps, in order to do so, you must forget everything traditional that you have learned about God, perhaps even the word itself. For if you know that God means depth, you know much about him. You cannot then call yourself an atheist or unbeliever. For you cannot think or say: Life has no depth! Life is shallow. Being itself is surface only. If you could say this in complete seriousness, you would be an atheist; but otherwise you are not. He who knows about depth knows about God." P. Tillich, The Shaking of the Foundations 63 (1962).

9. J. Huxley, Religion Without Revelation 58 (rev. ed. 1957).

10. See generally M. Smith, "The Special Place of Religion in the Constitution," 1983 Sup.Ct.Rev. 83.

11. It has been urged that, if the free exercise clause—which in many ways was an outgrowth of Protestant dissent and humanistic rationalism—is to realize its historic purpose, its concept of religion must be expanded to accommodate changes in religious consciousness. See, e.g., Stahmer, "Defining Religion: Federal Aid and Academic Freedom," 1963 Religion and Public Order 116, 122–28. Others argue that the religious liberty claims of non-theistic groups are more appropriately considered in the context of free speech, press, and assembly or of substantive due process. See, e.g., M. Howe, The Garden and the Wilderness 156 (1963); W. Gorman, "Problems of Church and State in the United States: A Catholic View," in The Wall Between Church and State 41, 47 (D. Oakes ed. 1963). For a general discussion of the issue, see Giannella, supra note 4, at 1423–31; see also Weiss, "Privilege, Posture and Protection: 'Religion' in the Law," 73 Yale L.J. 593 (1964).

12. Thomas v. Review Bd., 450 U.S. 707, 713 (1981). See also Marsh v. Chambers, 463 U.S. 783, 812 (1983) (Brennan, J., dissenting) ("in one important respect, the

about a spiritual-based definition applies more broadly: "If this definition excludes some philosophies, that, it may be said, is exactly what the Constitution intended." [13]

Still, in order to realize the goals of religious liberty, "religion" must be defined broadly enough to recognize the increasing number and diversity of faiths. Furthermore, "religion" must be defined from the believer's perspective. Excessive judicial inquiry into religious beliefs may, in and of itself, constrain religious liberty.[14] Thus, the Court held in *Thomas v. Review Board*,[15] beliefs are adequately religious even if they are not "acceptable, logical, consistent, or comprehensible"; [16] even if the religious adherent's beliefs are, although sincerely held, not fully developed; [17] and even if other believers construe and apply the religious tenets differently from the claimant.[18] In other cases too, the Court has emphasized the believer's own perspective.[19]

The most common approach to defining religion is to draw analogies to generally accepted religions. When such analogies focus on the externalities of a belief system or organization, they unduly constrain the concept of religion. As the theologian Harvey Cox has written: "[A] man-in-the-street approach would surely have ruled out early Christianity, which seemed both subversive and atheistic to the religious Romans of the day. The truth is that one man's 'bizarre cult' is another's true path to salvation. . . ." [20] Externalities upon which courts cannot properly rely include the belief system's age, its apparent social value,[21] its political elements,[22] the number of its adherents,[23] the

Constitution is *not* neutral on the subject of religion: Under the Free Exercise Clause, religiously motivated claims of conscience may give rise to constitutional rights that other strongly held beliefs do not") (emphasis in original).

13. J. Mansfield, "The Religion Clauses of the First Amendment and the Philosophy of the Constitution," 72 Cal.L.Rev. 847, 851 (1984).

14. See United States v. Ballard, 322 U.S. 78 (1944) (courts may inquire into the sincerity of putatively religious beliefs, but not their accuracy or truthfulness). Cf. Jones v. Wolf, 443 U.S. 595 (1979) (limiting judicial inquiry into religious doctrine in church property cases). See §§ 14–11, 14–12, infra.

15. 450 U.S. 707 (1981) (state must exempt from unemployment benefit regulations a Jehovah's Witness who quit his job in a weapons foundry because of sincerely held religious beliefs).

16. Id. at 714.

17. Id. at 715 ("Courts should not undertake to dissect religious beliefs because the believer admits that he is 'struggling' with his position. . . .").

18. Id. ("Intrafaith differences . . . are not uncommon among followers of a particular creed, and the judicial process is singularly ill equipped to resolve such dif-

ferences in relation to the Religion Clauses.").

19. See Hobbie v. Unemployment Appeals Comm'n, 107 S.Ct. 1046 (1987) (the fact that the claimant is a recent convert to a faith does not alter her eligibility for an otherwise-available free exercise exemption from unemployment benefit regulations); Wisconsin v. Yoder, 406 U.S. 205 (1972) (exempting Amish from mandatory school attendance beyond eighth grade, based on the importance of social separation to the Amish); United States v. Ballard, 322 U.S. 78 (1944) (holding that courts may not inquire into the truthfulness or accuracy of religious beliefs).

20. N.Y. Times, Feb. 16, 1977, at p. 25, col. 1.

21. Although the discussion did not concern the question of whether Amish was a religion, Chief Justice Burger's recital of the Amish's history and uprightness in Yoder was irrelevant and potentially misleading. See, e.g., 406 U.S. at 224 (noting "Amish qualities of reliability, self-reliance, and dedication to work"); id. at 225–226 ("[T]he Amish communities singularly parallel and reflect many of the virtues of Jefferson's ideal of the 'sturdy yeoman' who would form the basis of what he considered as the ideal of a democratic socie-

22.–23. See notes 22–23 on page 1182.

sorts of demands it places on those adherents,[24] the consistency of practice among different adherents,[25] and the system's outward trappings—e.g., prayers, holy writings, and hierarchical organizational structures.[26] To be sure, courts should be wary of sudden births of religions that entitle practitioners to special rights or exemptions. But the proper place for that inquiry is in the assessment of the believer's sincerity, not in any evaluation of the belief's externalities.[27]

More promising are functional analogies, which define "religion" in terms of the role a belief plays in the individual's or group's life.[28] But such approaches raise problems of their own. A generous functional

---

ty."). As Justice Douglas responded: "A religion is a religion irrespective of what the misdemeanor or felony records of its members might be." 406 U.S. at 246 (Douglas, J., concurring in part and dissenting in part).

22. The Third Circuit ruled that a belief system, MOVE, was not religious, partly because the claimant had at one point referred to MOVE as a "revolutionary" organization "opposed to all that is wrong." Africa v. Pennsylvania, 662 F.2d 1025, 1033–34 (3d Cir. 1981), cert. denied 456 U.S. 908 (1982). Another court held that "Eclatarian," a faith founded by a federal prisoner, was not a legitimate religion in part because one follower testified that the "ministry is basically to destroy . . . the repressive rulers and the powercrats of the system." Theriault v. Carlson, 495 F.2d 390, 394 (5th Cir. 1974), cert. denied 419 U.S. 1003 (1974). Using political activism and beliefs to invalidate a religion suggests that religions may not participate in politics, contrary to the Supreme Court's holding in McDaniel v. Paty, 435 U.S. 618 (1978) (state may not prohibit clergy from holding political office). Cf. Holy Spirit Ass'n for the Unification of World Christianity v. Tax Comm'n of New York, 55 N.Y.2d 512, 450 N.Y.S.2d 292, 435 N.E.2d 662 (1982) (where recognized religion espouses political views and engages in political activities, court must accept religious body's characterization that such views are part of its faith and that the resulting activities are religiously required). See generally § 14–14, infra.

23. See Larson v. Valente, 456 U.S. 228 (1982) (striking down state rules particularly burdensome to newer and smaller faiths unable to raise most of the funds they need from their own membership).

24. See United States v. Kauten, 133 F.2d 703, 708 (2d Cir. 1943) (religion by definition "categorically requires the believer to disregard elementary self-interest and to accept martyrdom in preference to transgressing its tenets"); Jacques v. Hilton, 569 F.Supp. 730, 734 (D.N.J. 1983) (rejecting as religion a philosophy that, in the court's view, amounted to nothing

more than "[l]et your conscience be your guide"), aff'd 738 F.2d 422 (3d Cir. 1984).

25. See Thomas v. Review Bd., 450 U.S. 707, 715 (1981).

26. See, e.g., Africa v. Pennsylvania, 662 F.2d at 1035 (holding MOVE was not religion in part because it lacked " 'formal services, ceremonial functions, the existence of clergy, structure and organization, efforts at propagation, observances of holidays and other similar manifestations associated with the traditional religions' ") (quoting Malnak v. Yogi, 592 F.2d 197, 209 (3d Cir. 1979) (Adams, J., concurring in result); Church of the Chosen People v. United States, 548 F.Supp. 1247, 1251 (D.Minn. 1982) (holding Demigod Socko Pantheon was not a religion, in part because it "possesses no outward characteristics that are analogous to other religions").

27. See § 14–12, infra.

28. See, e.g., United States v. Sun Myung Moon, 718 F.2d 1210, 1227 (2d Cir. 1983) (defining "religion" as " 'the feelings, acts, and experiences of individual men in their solitude, so far as they apprehend themselves to stand in relation to whatever they may consider the divine' "; and defining "divine" to encompass "any object that is godlike, whether it is or is not a specific deity") (quoting W. James, The Varieties of Religious Experience 31 (1910)), cert. denied 466 U.S. 971 (1984); Africa v. Pennsylvania, 662 F.2d 1025, 1032 (3d Cir. 1981) (requiring would-be religion to show that it addresses fundamental, ultimate concerns, and does so comprehensively), cert. denied 456 U.S. 908 (1982); Founding Church of Scientology v. United States, 409 F.2d 1146, 1160 (D.C. Cir. 1969) (central to religions are "underlying theories of man's nature or his place in the Universe"), cert. denied 396 U.S. 963 (1969). See generally K. Greenawalt, "Religion as a Concept in Constitutional Law," 72 Cal.L.Rev. 753 (1984); Note, "Toward a Constitutional Definition of Religion," 91 Harv.L.Rev. 1056, 1072–83 (1978). Several cases and commentators have urged a standard that combines functional and content-based elements, and asks whether a particular belief system rests on faculties beyond reason

definition would seem to classify any deep-rooted philosophy as religion, Marxism as well as Methodism.[29]   Although such a broad definition is arguably consistent with the Court's statutory interpretation in the conscientious objector cases,[30] it clashes directly with the Court's constitutional holding in *Wisconsin v. Yoder*.[31]   There the Court specifically distinguished religious from philosophical beliefs.   The Court wrote: "[I]f the Amish asserted their claims because of their subjective evaluation and rejection of the contemporary secular values accepted by the majority, much as Thoreau rejected the social values of his time and isolated himself at Walden Pond, their claims would not rest on a religious basis." [32]   Thus, too broad a functional definition may prove unacceptable to many.

Once "religion" is defined—and however it is defined—what of "free exercise" and "establishment"?   The Court has often indicated that "free exercise" protects religious beliefs absolutely, but religious actions only qualifiedly.[33]   The Court first expounded the distinction in *Reynolds v. United States*,[34] which upheld a statutory ban on polygamy as applied to a person whose religious beliefs required him to take more than one wife: "Laws are made for the government of actions and while they cannot interfere with mere religious belief and opinions, they may with practices." [35]

or incentives beyond normal experience. E.g., United States v. Kauten, 133 F.2d 703 (2d Cir. 1943) ("Religious belief arises from a sense of the inadequacy of reason as a means of relating the individual to his fellow-men and to his universe. . . ."); J. Choper, "Defining 'Religion' in the First Amendment," 1982 U.Ill.L.Rev. 579, 597–604 (urging that "religion" be defined in terms of "extratemporal consequences"); J. Garvey, "Free Exercise and the Values of Religious Liberty," 18 Conn.L.Rev. 779, 798–801 (1986) (making the not very flattering but nonetheless potentially useful suggestion that religion can be viewed as analogous to insanity, in terms of defects in practical reasoning and of inabilities to abide by applicable legal norms). Cf. K. Greenawalt, "The Concept of Religion in State Constitutions," 8 Campbell L.Rev. 437 (1986).

29. See, e.g., Choper, supra note 28, at 596–597 n.104; Greenawalt, "Religion as a Concept in Constitutional Law," supra note 28, at 769.

30. Welsh v. United States, 398 U.S. 333, 344 (1970) (statute providing military exemptions for people religiously opposed to war held to cover "all those whose consciences, spurred by deeply held moral, ethical, or religious beliefs, would give them no rest or peace if they allowed themselves to become a part of an instrument of war"); United States v. Seeger, 380 U.S. 163, 166 (1965) (statutory requirement of "belief in relation to a Supreme Being" held to embrace any sincere belief that

occupied "a place in the life of its possessor parallel to that filled by the orthodox belief in God of one who clearly qualifies for the exemption"). Several lower courts have applied a similarly broad definition of religion in construing statutes that provide tax exemptions for religious institutions. See, e.g., Washington Ethical Soc'y v. District of Columbia, 249 F.2d 127 (D.C.Cir. 1957); Fellowship of Humanity v. Alameda County, 153 Cal.App.2d 673, 315 P.2d 394 (1st Dist. 1957).

31. 406 U.S. 205 (1972).

32. Id. at 216.

33. See, e.g., Bowen v. Roy, 106 S.Ct. 2147, 2152 (1986); Sherbert v. Verner, 374 U.S. 398, 402–03 (1963); Cantwell v. Connecticut, 310 U.S. 296, 303–04 (1940). Early cases indicated that the free exercise clause protected *only* religious belief, and not "conduct." See generally Cushman, Civil Liberties in the United States: A Guide to Current Problems and Experience (1956). It is somewhat peculiar that the distinction between belief and action would persist in the free exercise context, for the guarantee refers explicitly to the *exercise* of religion, and thus seems to extend by its own terms beyond thought and talk. Cf. Widmar v. Vincent, 454 U.S. 263, 282–86 (1981) (White, J., dissenting) (arguing that only the religion clauses protect religious worship, and that the speech clause is inapplicable).

34. 98 U.S. (8 Otto) 145 (1878).

35. Id. at 166.

This belief-action dichotomy, much like the speech-conduct dichotomy, is at best an oversimplification.[36] Short of government-mandated or state-immunized brainwashing—whether called "deprogramming" [37] or given some other name—the state does not directly attack citizens' religious beliefs.[38] Rather, the state rewards or punishes beliefs indirectly, by encouraging or discouraging actions that are based on those beliefs. Occasionally, the state may act in advance to prevent especially dangerous forms of action based on religious beliefs; although the state may in such cases seem to be punishing belief, it is actually trying to forestall action. A school district, for example, could permissibly fire a bus driver whose religious beliefs appeared to support child sacrifice; the district would not be required to wait until he acted on those beliefs.[39] At the same time, though, the district could not imprison or brainwash the driver; consistent with free exercise principles, it could pursue only a minimally restrictive alternative that would achieve the secular interest in the children's safety.[40] But such cases are exceptional. More typically, the Court is asked to recognize a free exercise exemption in order to protect action (or inaction), grounded in religious beliefs, from state interference either through criminal prosecution [41] or through the denial of benefits.[42]

A dichotomy more analytically useful than belief-action was suggested by Justice Brennan in *McDaniel v. Paty*.[43] It distinguishes government measures that make religious classifications from those that burden religious activity only in a manner ancillary to an undeniably secular choice.[44] In the former set of cases, the state imposes burdens or denies benefits on the basis of specifically religious lines— whether profession of faith or the lack of it, or pursuit of a religious vocation, or undertaking a religiously motivated act (such as proselytiz-

36. See § 12–7, supra.

37. See Colombrito v. Kelly, 764 F.2d 122, 130 (2d Cir. 1985) (listing civil rights cases brought against religious deprogrammers); § 14–16, note 30, infra.

38. Some have argued that public education sometimes does just that. Parents, however, have the right to educate their children privately. Pierce v. Society of Sisters, 268 U.S. 510 (1925). In addition, it has been suggested that parents have a right to have their children excused from classes that deeply and directly offend their sincerely held religious beliefs. See Mozert v. Hawkins County Public Schools, 647 F.Supp. 1194 (E.Tenn. 1986) (requiring that school excuse offended students from classroom discussions). Mozert was subsequently overturned by the Sixth Circuit, N.Y. Times, August 25, 1987, at p. 1, col. 2, but further appeal was contemplated as this book went to press. See also Grove v. Mead School Dist. No. 354, 753 F.2d 1528, 1542 (9th Cir. 1985) (Canby, J., concurring) (if school had not permitted excusal during classroom discussions, students would have had colorable free exercise claim), cert. denied 106 S.Ct. 85 (1985).

39. See Hollon v. Pierce, 257 Cal.App. 2d 468, 64 Cal.Rptr. 808 (1967).

40. See § 14–13, infra.

41. E.g., Wisconsin v. Yoder, 406 U.S. 205 (1972).

42. E.g., Thomas v. Review Bd., 450 U.S. 707 (1981); Sherbert v. Verner, 374 U.S. 398 (1963).

43. 435 U.S. 618, 634–35 (1978) (Brennan, J., concurring in judgment).

44. On permissible and impermissible religious classifications, see §§ 14–7, 14–13, infra. Note that cases like Sherbert v. Verner (state may not deny unemployment benefits to person who refuses for religious reasons to work on Saturdays), and those listed in McDaniel, 435 U.S. at 628 (plurality opinion), involve laws that aim at a secular dimension of the subject matter that is being regulated or supported; thus, they are properly tested by balancing the legitimate claims to the free exercise of religion against the importance of the state interests at stake. See § 14–13, infra.

ing or delivering a sermon).[45] In the latter set of cases, religiously neutral government actions, neither cast in terms of faith nor triggered by religiously motivated choices as such, have only the incidental effect of burdening such choices. Just as the first amendment's free speech clause is not even implicated in the arrest of a newscaster for speeding, or in the closure of a bookstore for violation of a health regulation,[46] so the free exercise clause is not implicated in the imprisonment of a member of the clergy for embezzlement, or in the closure of a church as a fire hazard.[47] Such actions should not occasion any heightened constitutional concern, unless they are shown to be mere pretexts for government interference with religion as such,[48] or unless the burdens that they impose on religious activity are far more serious than the burdens they impose on comparable nonreligious activity.[49] Only in those exceptional cases is the free exercise of religion meaningfully affected.[50]

The task of defining "establishment" in the first amendment raises a different sort of concern. While the forms and concepts of religion have grown, the reach of the state has also grown. As a consequence, church concerns often overlap substantially with state concerns. Religious tenets, for example, may compel believers and churches to undertake the same kind of humane programs that the welfare state also undertakes. Indeed, the state's programs may be based, directly or indirectly, on the religious values of citizens, and occasionally on political pressures exerted by religious organizations. As a result, "legislation whose purpose or effect is to advance human dignity, equality, national destiny, freedom, enlightenment, and morality"[51] may seem to have effects and aims falling within the broad definition of "religion," and thus may seem to run afoul of the establishment clause. This point seems particularly striking where the free exercise clause requires the state to accommodate religion, and thus forces the state directly to recognize that a given practice is religious. If, for example, a religious group could advance a colorable free exercise claim in favor of transcendental meditation, it might seem to follow that the state could not teach TM in the public schools.[52]

45. See, e.g., McDaniel v. Paty (invalidating state provision prohibiting members of clergy from serving in various state offices); Torcaso v. Watkins, 367 U.S. 488 (1961) (invalidating state constitutional requirement that public officeholders must declare belief in God).

46. See Arcara v. Cloud Books, Inc., 106 S.Ct. 3172 (1986), discussed in § 12–23, supra.

47. Cf. Heffron v. International Soc'y for Krishna Consciousness, 452 U.S. 640 (1981) (rejecting, on free speech grounds, religious group's request to be permitted to wander among crowd to distribute religious literature and solicit donations at state fair, where fair rules permitted such activities to occur only at licensed booths).

48. See Arcara v. Cloud Books, 106 S.Ct. at 3178 (O'Connor, J., concurring).

49. Cf. Wisconsin v. Yoder, 406 U.S. 205, 210–12 (1972), where the Court noted that imposition of the school attendance requirement on the Amish would potentially undermine their entire way of life. See also § 14–11, infra, discussing the doctrine of "regulatory entanglement," under which religious groups may be exempted from government regulations that threaten to produce excessive church-state entanglement.

50. The Court's specific approach to free exercise cases is discussed in §§ 14–12 and 14–13, infra.

51. Galanter, "Religious Freedom in the United States: A Turning Point?", 1966 Wis.L.Rev. 217, 266.

52. Cf. Malnak v. Yogi, 592 F.2d 197 (3d Cir. 1979) (per curiam) (finding establishment of religion in TM class, based in part

One solution to the apparent conflict is to craft dual definitions. Under this approach, "religion" in the free exercise clause is defined more broadly than "religion" in the establishment clause, in order to prevent the two concepts from colliding.[53] But such an approach presents a number of problems, most importantly the first amendment's text. The language of the amendment, as Justice Rutledge wrote, shows that the single word "religion" "governs two prohibitions and governs them alike. It does not have two meanings, one narrow to forbid 'an establishment' and another, much broader, for securing 'the free exercise thereof.' 'Thereof' brings down 'religion' with its entire and exact content, no more and no less, from the first into the second guaranty. . . ."[54]

The dual-definition approach thus constitutes a dubious solution to a problem that, on closer inspection, may not exist at all. The first amendment does not, after all, prohibit or mandate religion; it prohibits *establishment*[55] and mandates tolerance of *free exercise*. Thus, the Supreme Court may create a free exercise exemption for people who religiously oppose war,[56] Congress may require that the land worshipped by Native Americans be left unspoiled,[57] and a city may

on apparently religious initiation ceremony in which students knelt while the teacher chanted the names of Hindu deities).

53. The first edition of this treatise, in § 14–6, proposed that solution. The approach was followed in United States v. Allen, 760 F.2d 447, 450–51 (2d Cir. 1985); Grove v. Mead School Dist., 753 F.2d 1528, 1537 (9th Cir. 1985) (Canby, J., concurring), cert. denied 106 S.Ct. 85 (1985). See also Sheldon v. Fannin, 221 F.Supp. 766, 775 (D.Ariz. 1963) ("religion" in establishment clause "looks to the majority's concept," whereas "religion" in the free exercise clause looks to the minority's).

54. Everson v. Board to Educ., 330 U.S. 1, 32 (1947) (Rutledge, J., joined by Frankfurter, Jackson, and Burton, JJ., dissenting). See also Malnak v. Yogi, 592 F.2d 197, 211 (3d Cir. 1979) (Adams, J., concurring in result) ("It is difficult to justify a reading of the first amendment so as to support a dual definition of religion, nor has our attention been drawn to any support for such a view in the conventional sources that have been thought to review the intentions of the framers."). For other critiques of the dual-definition approach, see J. Choper, "Defining 'Religion' in the First Amendment," 1982 U.Ill.L.Rev. 579, 605–06; K. Greenawalt, "Religion as a Concept in Constitutional Law," 72 Cal.L. Rev. 753, 813–815 (1984); P. Johnson, "Concepts and Compromise in First Amendment Religious Doctrine," 72 Cal.L. Rev. 817, 834–835 (1984).

55. The full phrase is "respecting an establishment." For the Framers, the word "respecting" apparently fulfilled two functions. First, and most obviously, it broadened the clause's reach; in this sense "respecting" is synonymous with "tending toward." Second, use of the word "respecting" was also intended to prevent Congress from interfering with the existing state establishments. See M. Malbin, Religion and Politics: The Intentions of the Authors of the First Amendment 15–16 (1978). Most discussions have focused only on the former point. E.g., Lemon v. Kurtzman, 403 U.S. 602, 612 (1971); L. Levy, The Establishment Clause: Religion and the First Amendment 95 (1986).

56. See Thomas v. Review Bd., 450 U.S. 707 (1981) (Jehovah's Witness who, for religious reasons, quit job in weapons plant must be granted unemployment benefits). Compare the cases concerning the conscientious objector statutes, where the Court construed accommodations created by Congress. See note 30, supra.

57. 42 U.S.C. § 1996. Moreover, where Native Americans seek protection of such lands under the free exercise clause, their claim should not be rejected on the ground that accommodation is inevitably establishment. Such issues arose in Badoni v. Higginson, 638 F.2d 172 (10th Cir. 1980), cert. denied 452 U.S. 954 (1981). For more than a century, Navajos had worshiped a mountain and a sandstone arch, located in a Utah Indian reservation. The arch in particular was viewed as a god; some holy ceremonies were performed only at that location. In the 1960s, a dam flooded some of the prayer sites. Then, beginning in the 1970s, the National Park Service began promoting tourism in the area, installing a floating dock at the arch and licensing tour boats. Tourists created noise, left behind

prohibit bars within a certain distance of churches [58]—without creating official establishments of the benefited religions. Government violates the establishment clause only if its actions are born of a religious intent, or if they exert primarily religious effects, or if they create excessive church-state entanglement.[59] Not surprisingly, therefore, courts have largely avoided defining "religion" under the establishment clause, focusing instead on the more important concept of "establishment." [60]

Whether a given practice constitutes a forbidden establishment may ultimately depend on whether most people would view it as religiously significant. This is well illustrated by *Wallace v. Jaffree*,[61] where the Supreme Court struck down a moment-of-silence statute that included the word "prayer." The Court indicated that the statute's predecessor, which had contained the word "meditation," raised no establishment clause problems, despite the fact that, as the Court noted, meditation is for some people a form of worship.[62] "Prayer" holds religious significance for most people, and thus cannot be officially endorsed; "meditation" holds religious significance for relatively few people, and thus may be officially endorsed. In the same way, no plausible establishment clause challenge could be made against the use of the eagle as an official symbol, despite its religious significance to some people; but a decisive challenge could be launched against use of a cross, whose religious significance is clear to nearly all.[63]

The religious significance of a given practice may, of course, increase or decrease over time; establishment clause holdings concerning particular practices thus cannot be considered immutable. Such flux is entirely consistent with the demands of religious freedom. As the religious composition of the United States has changed, the free exercise clause has had to change in order to accomplish the Framers' goals.[64] The free exercise clause alone, however, cannot sufficiently safeguard religious liberty; the establishment clause also plays a central role in guaranteeing such freedom, by forbidding official actions that signify official endorsement or exclusion based on an individual's

litter, and defaced the arch. The Navajos sought some form of free exercise accommodation from the state, such as lowering the level of the lake, relocating the floating dock, prohibiting alcohol at the site, limiting the numbers of tourists, or closing the area during religious ceremonies. The Tenth Circuit rejected the claim, holding that any such accommodation would violate the establishment clause and create "a government-managed religious shrine." Id. at 179. That decision seems indefensible.

58. See *Larkin v. Grendel's Den, Inc.*, 459 U.S. 116, 121 (1982) ("There can be little doubt about the power of a state to regulate the environment in the vicinity of schools, churches, hospitals, and the like by exercise of reasonable zoning laws.").

59. *Lemon v. Kurtzman*, 403 U.S. 602 (1971). See §§ 14–9, 14–10, 14–11, infra.

60. See, e.g., *United States v. Allen*, 760 F.2d 447, 451–452 (2d Cir. 1985) (even assuming that "nuclearism"—the national worship of nuclear weapons—is a religion, the punishment of people who damaged a B–52 bomber did not violate the establishment clause).

61. 472 U.S. 38 (1985).

62. Id. at 2491 n.47.

63. See *Friedman v. Board of County Comm'rs of Bernalillo County*, 781 F.2d 777 (10th Cir. 1985) (establishment clause is violated by county seal with Latin cross and Spanish motto that translates into the phrase "With This We Conquer"), cert. denied 106 S.Ct. 2890 (1986).

64. See §§ 14–14, 14–15, infra.

religious beliefs.[65] Given the unique power of such official messages, it is appropriate that applications of the establishment clause, like those of the free exercise clause, adapt to reflect changing public conceptions and attitudes, so long as its central meaning remains fixed.

§ 14–7. Neutrality

The Supreme Court has referred to "the established principle that the Government must pursue a course of complete neutrality toward religion." [1] In application, the principle of neutrality displays several distinct facets. Neutrality sometimes permits, sometimes requires, and sometimes forbids religious classifications.[2] This section will consider the major formulations of neutrality: strict neutrality, political neutrality, denominational neutrality, and free exercise neutrality.

The most straightforward and comprehensive form, *strict neutrality*, would resolve the problem of religious classifications by forbidding them entirely.[3] Under a strict neutrality view, government would be forbidden to "utilize religion as a standard for action or inaction because [the religion clauses] prohibit classification in terms of religion either to confer a benefit or impose a burden." [4] So long as no religious classifications were employed, however, governmental programs—including direct subsidies—which benefited religion would be permitted [5]; indeed, restrictions based on a recipient's religious character would be forbidden as non-neutral. So too, legislatures could regulate behavior to achieve an otherwise proper objective without ever worrying about a free exercise challenge to the failure to grant religious exemptions; indeed, exemptions based on the religious nature of an act or of the actor's motives or beliefs would be banned as violative of strict neutrality.

---

65. See Lynch v. Donnelly, 465 U.S. 668, 687–88 (1984) (O'Connor, J., concurring).

§ 14–7

1. Wallace v. Jaffree, 472 U.S. 38, 60 (1985) (footnote omitted). See also Committee for Public Educ. v. Nyquist, 413 U.S. 756, 792–93 (1973) ("A proper respect for both the Free Exercise and the Establishment Clauses compels the State to pursue a course of 'neutrality' toward religion."); Walz v. Tax Comm'n, 397 U.S. 664, 669 (1970) ("[T]here is room for play in the joints productive of a benevolent neutrality which will permit religious exercise to exist without sponsorship and without interference."); Abington School Dist. v. Schempp, 374 U.S. 203, 226 (1963) ("In the relationship between man and religion, the State is firmly committed to a position of neutrality.").

2. See McDaniel v. Paty, 435 U.S. 618, 639 (1978) (Brennan, J., concurring in judgment) ("[G]overnment [may] take religion into account when necessary to further sec-

ular purposes unrelated to the advancement of religion, and to exempt, when possible, from generally applicable governmental regulation individuals whose religious beliefs and practices would otherwise thereby be infringed, or to create without state involvement an atmosphere in which voluntary religious exercise may flourish. Beyond these limited situations . . . government may not use religion as a basis of classification. . . .") (footnotes omitted) (citing first edition of this treatise, § 14–4).

3. See P. Kurland, Religion and the Law (1962); P. Kurland, "Of Church and State and the Supreme Court," 29 U.Chic. L.Rev. 1, 96 (1961); Weiss, "Privilege, Posture, and Protection: 'Religion' in the Law," 73 Yale L.J. 593 (1964). See generally P. Kauper, Religion and the Constitution 64–67 (1964).

4. P. Kurland, Religion and the Law 18 (1962).

5. Id. at 80–85.

To most observers, however, strict neutrality has seemed incompatible with the very idea of a free exercise clause. The Framers, whatever specific applications they may have intended, clearly envisioned religion as something special; they enacted that vision into law by guaranteeing the free exercise of *religion* but not, say, of philosophy or science. The strict neutrality approach all but erases this distinction. Thus it is not surprising that the Supreme Court has rejected strict neutrality, permitting and sometimes mandating religious classifications.[6]

Political neutrality requires that religious organizations enjoy, on the same basis as nonreligious organizations, the general benefits of the political community, such as the ability to own property and make contracts.[7] "[M]aking religious voluntarism a reality requires that religious associations be treated with political equality and accorded civil opportunities for self-development on a par with other voluntary associations."[8] Political neutrality embraces both *voluntarism*, in forbidding actions that would create artificial disincentives for forming religious organizations, and *pluralism*, in placing religious organizations on the same plane as their nonreligious counterparts.

Unlike strict neutrality, political neutrality permits some religious classifications, based on two principles. First, the state may make classifications based on a "secularly relevant factor."[9] For example, zoning regulations may keep churches separate from incompatible property uses, such as bars. Second, the state may use religious classifications to deny benefits to a religious organization that abuses those benefits in a manner that distorts the principle of religious

---

6. See Wallace v. Jaffree, 472 U.S. 38, 82 (1985) (O'Connor, J., concurring in judgment) ("It is difficult to square any notion of 'complete neutrality' with the mandate of the Free Exercise Clause that government must sometimes exempt a religious observer from an otherwise generally applicable obligation."); McDaniel v. Paty, 435 U.S. 618, 638–39 (1978) (Brennan, J., concurring in judgment) (Supreme Court has rejected "[s]uch rigid conceptions of neutrality" as strict neutrality). Some individual justices have, however, voiced theories that approach strict neutrality. See, e.g., United States v. Lee, 455 U.S. 252, 263 n.2 (1982) (Stevens, J., concurring in judgment) (A strong presumption against free exercise claims is appropriate in light of "the overriding interest in keeping the government—whether it be the legislature or the courts—out of the business of evaluating the relative merits of differing religious claims. The risk that governmental approval of some and disapproval of others will be perceived as favoring one religion over another is an important risk the Establishment Clause was designed to preclude."); Welsh v. United States, 398 U.S. 333, 356 (1970) (Harlan, J., concurring in result) ("[H]aving chosen to exempt, [Congress] cannot draw the line between theis-

tic or nontheistic religious beliefs on the one hand and secular beliefs on the other. Any such distinctions are not, in my view, compatible with the Establishment Clause of the First Amendment.").

7. See Giannella, "Religious Liberty, Non-Establishment, and Doctrinal Development: Part II, The Non-Establishment Principle," 81 Harv.L.Rev. 513 (1968). For other discussions of the special issues concerning religious organizations, see Esbeck, "Tort Claims Against Churches and Ecclesiastical Officers: The First Amendment Considerations," 89 W.Va.L.Rev. 1 (1986); Laycock, "Towards a General Theory of the Religion Clauses: The Case of Church Labor Relations and the Right to Church Autonomy," 81 Colum.L.Rev. 1373 (1981); Lupu, "Keeping the Faith: Religion, Equality, and Speech in the U.S. Constitution," 18 Conn.L.Rev. 739 (1986); S. Bates, "Institutions of Freedom: Church, Press, and Democracy" (unpublished paper on file at Harvard Law Library).

8. Id. at 520. See Cushman, "Public Support of Religious Education in American Constitutional Law," 45 Ill.L.Rev. 333, 348 (1950).

9. Giannella, supra note 7, at 528.

voluntarism. If, for example, a publicly aided hospital is used to proselytize patients, a "disqualifying religious function" exists.[10]

Although the Supreme Court has never adopted the political neutrality theory as such, many establishment clause holdings are consistent with it.[11] Among them are the cases in which the Court has emphasized the breadth of the aided class, upholding programs that benefited nonreligious as well as religious organizations.[12] Thus the Court has permitted the state to let religious organizations share in the benefits of the community. But the principles of political neutrality only partially explain church-state relations. In particular, the theory does not explain those situations where religious organizations may or must be treated differently even in the absence of a secularly relevant factor or disqualifying religious function. For example, in construing deeds or wills, courts have consistently refused to interpret and apply religious terms; the fear has been that the judicial inquiry traditional as to non-religious terms would cut too deeply into the autonomy of religious institutions.[13] The state may similarly exempt all religious organizations [14] from recordkeeping or reporting requirements imposed on nonreligious organizations; in some circumstances, indeed, such exemptions may be required.[15] These cases suggest that a third limiting principle must be applied to political neutrality: Religious classifications are permitted in order to maintain the autonomy of religious institutions. Once that principle is added, political neutrality explains a substantial area of establishment clause jurisprudence.

Denominational neutrality has a more limited ambit than either strict or political neutrality: it prevents the state from drawing lines between religions, when such lines are not supported by any free exercise argument. In *Larson v. Valente*,[16] the Court considered a Minnesota statute that imposed registration and reporting requirements only on religious organizations that solicited more than fifty per cent of their funds from nonmembers.[17] Writing for the majority, Justice Brennan argued that the two religion clauses mandated equal treatment of different denominations.[18] However, the Court did not

---

10. Id.

11. The theory was initially advanced to complement free exercise neutrality. Id. at 521.

12. See § 14–10, infra.

13. See, e.g., Jones v. Wolf, 443 U.S. 595 (1979); Presbyterian Church in the United States v. Mary Elizabeth Blue Hull Memorial Presbyterian Church, 393 U.S. 440 (1969); § 14–11, infra.

14. But not just large ones. See Larson v. Valente, 456 U.S. 228 (1982).

15. In Tony and Susan Alamo Found. v. Secretary of Labor, 471 U.S. 290, 305 (1985), the petitioners argued that a labor regulation, as applied to their religious organization, would exert primarily anti-religious effects and create excessive church-state entanglement. The Court disagreed, but only after carefully considering the

statute's effects and the dangers of regulatory entanglement. See § 14–11, infra.

16. 456 U.S. 228 (1982).

17. As originally enacted, the statute exempted religious organizations entirely. A 1978 amendment limited the exemption to religious organizations that received more than half their total contributions from members or from affiliated organizations. Id. at 231–32.

18. See id. at 244 ("The clearest command of the Establishment Clause is that one religious denomination cannot be officially preferred over another."); id. at 245 ("Free exercise . . . can be guaranteed only when legislators—and voters—are required to accord to their own religions the very same treatment given to small, new, or unpopular denominations."). Justice Brennan's opinion was joined by Justices Marshall, Blackmun, Powell, and Stevens.

apply its traditional establishment clause or free exercise clause tests to the statute. Instead, it enunciated a new test: strict scrutiny, which would henceforth be applied to laws that "grant[ ] a denominational preference." [19] The Court assumed that the state's interest—there, the interest in protecting citizens from fraud—was compelling. But, the Court held, the state had failed to show that the fifty per cent rule was closely tailored to that interest. The Court added that the traditional establishment clause test of *Lemon v. Kurtzman* [20] did not apply to statutes that discriminate among religions. [21] However, the Court continued, the Minnesota statute would fail the *Lemon* test anyway. [22]

The *Larson* principle of neutrality among denominations is unremarkable; at least two other major holdings reinforce it. [23] But two

Justice Stevens concurred, id. at 256. Justice White, joined by Justice Rehnquist, dissented on the basis of standing and on the merits, id. at 258. Justice Rehnquist, joined by Chief Justice Burger and Justices White and O'Connor, dissented on the basis of standing, id. at 264.

19. Id. at 246–47. The Court's analysis asked one establishment clause question—whether the statute had a secular purpose—and two questions that traditionally arise under the free exercise clause—whether the statute pursued a "compelling governmental interest," and whether the means applied were "closely fitted to further that interest." Id. at 248–51. The Court did not explicitly consider the other elements of the free exercise test: whether the statute significantly burdened the affected religions (although the conclusion that it did is implicit in the opinion), and whether soliciting from nonmembers was based on a sincerely held religious belief. See §§ 14–12, 14–13, infra. Thus it appears that a religious adherent may face no hurdles (beyond standing) in challenging a statute that overtly discriminates among religions; an adherent who challenges a statute that is not overtly discriminatory, in contrast, must demonstrate his or her own sincerity.

20. 403 U.S. 602, 612–13 (1971) (requiring state to show that challenged statute or action has a secular purpose, has a secular primary effect, and does not create excessive church-state entanglement). See generally §§ 14–9, 14–10, 14–11, infra.

21. 456 U.S. at 252 ("[T]he *Lemon v. Kurtzman* 'tests' are intended to apply to laws affording a uniform benefit to *all* religions, and not to provisions, like [the Minnesota statute], that discriminate *among* religions.") (emphasis in original) (footnote omitted).

22. Id. ("Although application of the *Lemon* tests is not necessary to the disposition of the case before us, those tests do reflect the same concerns that warranted the application of strict scrutiny. . . .").

Although the record did not show a specific nonsecular purpose, the legislative history did demonstrate a purpose to impose the requirements on certain churches and not others, id. at 250 n.25, 254–255; the Eighth Circuit construed this to indicate a nonsecular intent. Valente v. Larson, 637 F.2d 562, 568 (8th Cir. 1981). The Supreme Court, however, focused its attention elsewhere—on the statute's nonsecular effects, 456 U.S. at 253–54; on the risk that it would create political divisiveness, id. at 252–53; and—curiously—on the excessive church-state entanglement that resulted, apparently from the legislature's line-drawing in crafting the statute, id. at 252, 255.

23. In Sherbert v. Verner, 374 U.S. 398 (1963), the Court required South Carolina to waive its Saturday work requirement for Seventh-Day Adventists. The Court noted: "Significantly South Carolina expressly saves the Sunday worshipper from having to make the kind of choice which we here hold infringes the Sabbatarian's religious liberty," because another South Carolina statute provided that no one could be fired for refusing, because of religious beliefs, to work on Sundays. Id. at 406. "The unconstitutionality of the disqualification of the Sabbatarian is thus compounded by the religious discrimination which South Carolina's general statutory scheme necessarily effects." Id. And in Estate of Thornton v. Caldor, 472 U.S. 703 (1985), the Court struck down a Connecticut statute that required employers to permit employees without any penalty to abstain from work on their weekly Sabbaths. Although the majority did not focus on the issue, the statute obviously benefited those individuals whose religion commanded a Sabbath over those whose religion did not, and thus discriminated among religions. See id. at 711 (O'Connor, J., concurring) ("All employees, regardless of their religious orientation, would value the benefit which the statute bestows on Sabbath observers. . . ."). See also Hobbie v. Unemployment Appeals Comm'n, 107 S.Ct. 1046,

aspects of the opinion are worth special note. The first is the application of the neutrality principle to strike down a statute that distinguished among religions not in terms of their theology or even their religious practices as such, but in terms of a seemingly secular factor—there, the ratio of the funds they raised from members to the funds they raised in toto. An earlier case, *Gillette v. United States*,[24] concerned Congress's denial of conscientious objector status to individuals who religiously opposed not war in general, but only certain ("unjust") wars. The Court upheld the congressional distinction, in part because it was not on its face discriminatory among denominations—even though the *effect* of the *Gillette* distinction was to deny conscientious objector status to Catholics, whose religion required them to take part in just wars and to refuse to participate in unjust wars.[25] Presumably the *Larson* approach would replace the *Gillette* approach today, even though the *Gillette* result would, in light of the Court's traditional deference to military needs, probably remain the same.[26]

Larson's second major feature is its unique analytic approach to statutes that discriminate among religions. Nearly any law challenged under either clause will discriminate in effect, and sometimes intentionally.[27] The *Larson* Court failed to explain when the new strict scrutiny approach applies.[28] Perhaps the *Lemon* test applies to laws that alter the status quo in a way that benefits some religions, as is most frequently the case in establishment clause cases, while *Larson*

1051 n.11 (1987) (suggesting that the statute in Thornton "ha[d] the effect of implicitly endorsing a *particular* religious belief") (emphasis added).

24. 401 U.S. 437 (1971).

25. See id. at 470–75 (Douglas, J., dissenting). The Larson Court distinguished Gillette on the basis that the Gillette statute involved individuals who might or might not follow the tenets of the religion to which they belonged, whereas the Larson statute "focuses precisely and solely upon religious organizations." 456 U.S. at 228 n.23. Unless religious organizations are to receive greater protection than individual adherents, it is difficult to understand the relevance of the difference. Another difference between the two statutes—that Larson concerned imposition of a burden and Gillette concerned withdrawal of a benefit—is generally not decisive under modern free exercise doctrine. See Sherbert v. Verner, 374 U.S. 398, 404 (1963); § 14–13, infra. Indeed, one could argue that, whether cast as a benefit withdrawn or a burden imposed, the Gillette line was more denominationally discriminatory than the Larson line. The Unification Church in Larson could, at least in theory, attract more than half of its contributions from members, and thus escape from the Minnesota regulatory scheme, without violating any tenet of its faith. But for the believers in Gillette to

achieve conscientious objector status, they would have to alter, or act in conflict with, a fundamental religious belief.

26. See, e.g., Goldman v. Weinberger, 106 S.Ct. 1310 (1986); § 14–13, infra.

27. A religious adherent raising a free exercise clause challenge must demonstrate that the statute imposes a significant burden on his or her religious beliefs. See § 14–12, infra. Implicit, almost invariably, is the notion that the statute imposes a greater burden on this adherent than on the majority of affected persons, and thus that religion-blind application leads to unequal results. Most establishment clause challenges similarly raise issues of nonneutrality. Aid to religious schools, for example, benefits religions that fund their own schools, and not other religions. More striking are the challenges to various forms of religious exercise in the public schools. The Bible, the Ten Commandments, and other such documents are basic to some religions and irrelevant, or even offensive, to others. See § 14–5, supra.

28. Justice Brennan, who wrote the Larson opinion, later suggested that Larson's strict scrutiny "might well" apply where a state legislature had appointed a single chaplain for a sixteen-year period. Marsh v. Chambers, 463 U.S. 783, 801 n.11 (1983) (Brennan, J., dissenting).

applies to laws that alter the status quo in a way that burdens some religions. Or perhaps *Lemon* applies where the constitutionality of the benefit or burden is itself the focus of the litigation, while *Larson* applies where the benefit or burden, if applied uniformly to all religions, would apparently be constitutional.[29] But such distinctions are somewhat formalistic and, at least for now, largely speculative.

One can say with greater confidence that *Larson*'s neutrality principle does not extend to cases where the state's denominational line is based on free exercise values. For where a burden falls with special weight on some religions, religious classifications are called for; religion blindness would produce only an illusory and hostile neutrality. Under *free exercise neutrality*, accordingly, "the government may (and sometimes must) accommodate religious practices." [30]

In several cases, the Supreme Court has required that personal choices born of religious motivations be exempted from otherwise valid and formally neutral state requirements. In *Sherbert v. Verner*,[31] the Court required the state to make unemployment benefits available to a Seventh-Day Adventist who for religious reasons refused to work on Saturdays. *Thomas v. Review Board* [32] reaffirmed and extended *Sherbert*. The *Thomas* Court required the state to make unemployment benefits available to a Jehovah's Witness who had for religious reasons quit his job in a weapons plant. *Hobbie v. Unemployment Appeals Commission* [33] reaffirmed *Sherbert* yet again, applying it to a recent convert to the Seventh-Day Adventist Church. The Court rejected the government's argument that the claimant was not entitled to an exemption because, as the "agent of change," she was herself responsible for creating the clash between religious and employment duties; "[t]he timing of Hobbie's conversion is immaterial." [34] In *Wisconsin v. Yoder*,[35] the Court, for the first and only time, mandated a free exercise exemption in a criminal law. *Yoder* exempted the Amish from Wisconsin's law requiring school attendance, because the law would have gravely jeopardized the religion's very survival.[36]

29. Note, however, that neither of these formulations would seem to cover the legislative chaplain case, which Justice Brennan suggested considering under the Larson approach. See note 28, supra.

30. Hobbie v. Unemployment Appeals Comm'n, 107 S.Ct. 1046, 1051 (1987).

31. 374 U.S. 398 (1963).

32. 450 U.S. 707 (1981).

33. 107 S.Ct. 1046 (1987). Justice Brennan wrote for the Court, joined by Justices White, Marshall, Blackmun, O'Connor, and Scalia. Justices Powell, id. at 1052, and Stevens, id. at 1053, concurred in the judgment. Only Chief Justice Rehnquist dissented, id. at 1052.

34. Id. at 1051.

35. 406 U.S. 205 (1972).

36. See also Bowen v. Roy, 106 S.Ct. 2147 (1986), where a majority of the Justices indicated that they would have required a religious exemption from the requirement that welfare applicants submit their social security numbers in order to receive benefits. See id. at 2160 (Blackmun, J., concurring in part); id. at 2166–69 (O'Connor, J., joined by Brennan and Marshall, JJ., concurring in part and dissenting in part); id. at 2169 (White, J., dissenting). Justice Stevens would have required exemption if, as appeared to be the case, individuals with linguistic and other handicaps were routinely aided in filling out required benefit forms; "it would seem that a religious inability should be given no less deference." Id. at 2163 (Stevens, J., concurring in part and concurring in result). Chief Justice Burger and Justices Powell and Rehnquist would have denied any exemption. See id. at 2153–58.

One reason the Court has granted only a few free exercise exemptions may be the fear that, once easy accommodations are granted, neutrality will demand that more difficult accommodations be granted as well. This concern was voiced in *United States v. Lee*,[37] where the Court unanimously refused to exempt Amish employers from paying social security taxes; one basis for the decision was that recognizing such an exemption might require future courts to exempt religious groups which oppose the state's use of tax monies from paying generally applicable revenue taxes.[38] In *Goldman v. Weinberger*,[39] several Justices debated whether, if the Court were to permit Orthodox Jews in the military to wear yarmulkes, it would (or should) also permit Sikhs to wear turbans.[40]

In practice, the Court has placed significant hurdles in the way of free exercise claimants.[41] However, the Court has extended the principle of free exercise neutrality to *permit* Congress and the states to carve out necessary exemptions. These accommodations arise in situations where, although free exercise values may be at stake, the free exercise clause does not *mandate* special treatment—resulting in a zone of permissible accommodation.[42] As Justice Brennan has written, "[E]ven

37. 455 U.S. 252 (1982).

38. Id. at 260. Justice Stevens considered the Amish's claim to be "readily distinguishable from the typical claim to an exemption from general tax obligations on the ground that the taxpayer objects to the government's use of his money," id. at 262 n.1 (concurring in the judgment), because the Amish had demonstrated their ability to care for their own without accepting social security benefits, and because a claimant seeking a religious exemption from general taxes could not "supply the government with an equivalent substitute" as the Amish had done through their self-help, id. at 262. However, Justice Stevens concurred in the judgment on grounds approaching strict neutrality: "The risk that governmental approval of some [religious claims for exemptions] and disapproval of others will be perceived as favoring one religion over another is an important risk and Establishment Clause was designed to preclude." Id. at 263 n.2.

39. 106 S.Ct. 1310 (1986).

40. Justice Brennan wrote that, although yarmulkes ought to be permitted, the military might still permissibly forbid more visible forms of religious wear, based on concerns of "functional utility, health and safety considerations, and the goal of a polished, professional appearance." Id. at 1319 (Brennan, J., joined by Marshall, J., dissenting). Four other Justices concluded that such distinctions would improperly discriminate against unconventional religions. Id. at 1316 (Stevens, J., joined by White and Powell, JJ., concurring); id. at 1323 (Blackmun, J., dissenting). Justice Rehnquist's opinion for the Court did not

address the question. The case is discussed further in § 14–13, infra.

41. Formally, the Court's requirements have strongly favored free exercise claimants; in application, however, they have not. Although most plaintiffs have successfully made their required showings of sincerity and religious burden, states have usually overcome those showings by demonstrating a strong need for uniform enforcement of the statute. Indeed, the Court has often accepted the state's asserted interest in uniform enforcement without substantial scrutiny, and has thus resisted claims for free exercise exemptions. See §§ 14–12, 14–13, infra.

42. See Corporation of the Presiding Bishop of the Church of Jesus Christ of Latter-Day Saints v. Amos, 107 S.Ct. 2862 (1987) (Congress may permissibly exempt religious organizations' secular, nonprofit activities from Title VII's prohibition on religious discrimination in employment, even though the free exercise clause would not mandate the exemption). In several other cases, the Court has in passing noted, either approvingly or at least without disapproval, voluntary legislative accommodations of religion. See, e.g., Ansonia Bd. of Educ. v. Philbrook, 107 S.Ct. 367 (1986) (concluding on basis of text and legislative history that § 701(j) of Title VII requires only that an employer offer a reasonable accommodation to an employee's religious practices, and not that an employer must accept the employee's proposed accommodation unless doing so would create undue hardship); United States v. Lee, 455 U.S. 252, 255 n.4, 260–61 (1982) (noting without disapproval that self-employed Amish are

when the government is not compelled to do so by the Free Exercise Clause, it may to some extent act to facilitate the opportunities of individuals to practice their own religion." [43]

Leaving room for legislatures to craft religious accommodations recognizes that they may be in a better position than courts to decide when the advantages of strict neutrality are overstated.[44] But unbounded tolerance of governmental accommodation in the name of free exercise neutrality could eviscerate the establishment clause.

congressionally exempt from social security taxes); Braunfeld v. Brown, 366 U.S. 599, 608 (1961) (plurality opinion) (noting with no hint of disapproval that some states had chosen to exempt from Sunday closing laws people whose religion required them not to work on days other than Sunday; "this may well be the wiser solution to the problem"). See also Everson v. Board of Education, 330 U.S. 1, 16 (1947) (Black, J.) ("While we do not mean to intimate that a state could not provide transportation only to children attending public schools, we must be careful, in protecting the citizens of New Jersey against state-established churches, to be sure we do not inadvertently prohibit New Jersey from extending its general state law benefits to all its citizens without regard to their religious belief"); Abington School Dist. v. Schempp, 374 U.S. 203, 299 (1963) (Brennan, J., concurring) (". . . hostility, not neutrality, would characterize the refusal to provide chaplains and places of worship for prisoners and soldiers cut off by the State from all civilian opportunities for public communion, the withholding of draft exemptions for ministers and conscientious objectors, or the denial of the temporary use of an empty public building to a congregation whose place of worship has been destroyed by fire or flood. I do not say that government *must* provide chaplains or draft exemptions, or that the courts should intercede if it fails to do so"); Welsh v. United States, 398 U.S. 333, 371–74 (1970) (White, J., dissenting); Meek v. Pittinger, 421 U.S. 349, 386–87 (1975) (Burger, C.J., concurring in part and dissenting in part); id. at 395–96 (Rehnquist, J., joined by White, J., dissenting). Cf. Walz v. Tax Comm'n, 397 U.S. 664, 674–75 (1970), where the Court held that states could choose to exempt churches from property taxes, in part because the exemption created fewer church-state entanglements than collecting the taxes would create. Chief Justice Rehnquist would transfer most cases that currently fall in the sphere of required accommodation to the sphere of permissible accommodation. See Thomas v. Review Bd., 450 U.S. 707, 723 (1981) (Rehnquist, J., dissenting) ("although a State could choose to grant ex-

emptions to religious persons from state unemployment regulations, a State is not constitutionally compelled to do so") (footnote omitted).

In Wallace v. Jaffree, 472 U.S. 38 (1985), however, the Court seemingly implied for the first time that perhaps no zone of permissible accommodation exists after all, and that the state may accommodate religion only where the free exercise clause requires it to do so. Id. at 57 n.45 ("there was no governmental practice impeding students from silently praying for one minute at the beginning of each school day; thus, there was no need to 'accommodate' or to exempt individuals from any general governmental requirement because of the dictates of our cases interpreting the Free Exercise Clause"). This seems to misstate precedent as well as practice. Perhaps all the Court meant was that, as a defense to a government action transparently endorsing a practice as religious as prayer, see § 14–15, infra, the excuse that government was merely lifting a perceived impediment to individual participation in the practice could not be accepted where there was no proof that any impediment had really been perceived. In any event, the Court reaffirmed the existence of a zone of permissible accommodation in Hobbie v. Unemployment Appeals Commission, 107 S.Ct. 1046, 1051 (1987) ("This Court has long recognized that the government may (and sometimes must) accommodate religious practices and that it may do so without violating the Establishment Clause.") (footnote omitted), and in Amos, 107 S.Ct. at 2869 ("there is ample room for accommodation of religion under the Establishment Clause").

43. Marsh v. Chambers, 463 U.S. 783, 812 (1983) (Brennan, J., dissenting).

44. See M. McConnell, "Accommodation of Religion," 1985 Sup.Ct.Rev. 1, 31 ("The most important reason not to confine accommodation to instances compelled by the Free Exercise Clause is that the government is in a better position than the courts to evaluate the strength of its own interest in governing without religious exemptions.").

In *Estate of Thornton v. Caldor*,[45] the Court considered the extent to which a state could force *private* accommodation of religious beliefs. The case concerned a Connecticut statute that required employers to give employees an absolute right not to work on their religion's weekly Sabbath: "No person who states that a particular day of the week is observed as his Sabbath may be required by his employer to work on such day. An employee's refusal to work on his Sabbath shall not constitute grounds for his dismissal." [46] The Court held that the statute violated the establishment clause. Chief Justice Burger's majority opinion emphasized the "absolute and unqualified" nature of the accommodation mandated by the state,[47] and concluded that the statute "contravenes a fundamental principle of the Religion Clauses . . . .: 'The First Amendment . . . gives no one the right to insist that in pursuit of their own interests others must conform their conduct to his own religious necessities.' " [48] The opinion's language suggests that the statute might have survived if it had balanced the employee's religious needs with the employer's reasonable needs, as is the case with the Title VII of the Civil Rights Act.[49]

In a concurring opinion, Justice O'Connor expressly distinguished Title VII from the Connecticut statute. First, according to Justice O'Connor, Title VII prohibits various forms of religious and nonreligious discrimination, and thus exhibits breadth of protected class, whereas the Connecticut statute covered only religious beliefs.[50] Second, as the majority opinion also emphasized, Title VII requires only reasonable accommodation, not the absolute accommodation required by the Connecticut law.[51] Third, Title VII's benefits extend to all religions, and not merely to the religions benefited by the Connecticut statute—those with a weekly Sabbath.[52]

The Court returned to the question of accommodation—this time directly concerning Title VII—in *Corporation of the Presiding Bishop of the Church of Jesus Christ of Latter-Day Saints v. Amos.*[53] Although

---

45. 472 U.S. 703 (1985).

46. Conn.Gen.Stat. § 53–303e(b) (Supp. 1962–1984), quoted in Thornton, 472 U.S. at 706.

47. 472 U.S. at 709. Justice O'Connor, joined by Justice Marshall, concurred, id. at 711. Only Justice Rehnquist dissented, id.; he did not file an opinion.

48. Id. at 710 (quoting Otten v. Baltimore & Ohio R. Co., 205 F.2d 58, 61 (2d Cir. 1953) (L. Hand, J.)).

49. 42 U.S.C. § 2000e(j) imposes on employers a duty to "reasonably accommodate . . . an employee's . . . religious observance or practice without undue hardship on the conduct of the employer's business."

50. 472 U.S. at 711 (O'Connor, J., joined by Marshall, J., concurring). The Court has often relied on the breadth of the beneficiary class in concluding that a program did not generate primarily religious effects.

See § 14–10, infra. The application of that notion here, however, is dubious. Although Title VII does prohibit religious and nonreligious discrimination, it imposes a "reasonably accommodate" duty only concerning religious observance and practice.

51. 472 U.S. at 712. Under the Connecticut statute, the employee's Sabbath request had to be met without any resulting loss of status or benefit to the employee regardless of the burden to the employer and to fellow employees.

52. Id. Cf. Edwards v. Aguillard, 107 S.Ct. 2573, 2596 (1987) (Scalia, J., dissenting) ("few would contend that Title VII . . . violates the Establishment Clause, even though its 'purpose' is, of course, to advance religion, and even though it is almost certainly not required by the Free Exercise Clause"). See note 75, infra.

53. 107 S.Ct. 2862 (1987).

Title VII prohibits religious discrimination in employment, section 702 of the statute exempts religious organizations from the prohibition.[54] The question in *Amos* was whether that exemption could permissibly apply to a religious organization's dismissal of an employee involved in its *secular* activities—specifically, an employee's dismissal, on religious grounds, from his job as a building engineer with a nonprofit gymnasium operated by the Mormon Church—or whether such an application would unconstitutionally aid religion. The Court unanimously ruled that the exemption did not violate the establishment clause, at least as applied to nonprofit secular activities. But the Justices divided on the reasoning.

Writing for the majority, Justice White suggested that establishment clause questions simply do not arise where government benefits religion only indirectly: "A law is not unconstitutional simply because it *allows* churches to advance religion. . . .   For a law to have forbidden 'effects' under *Lemon*, it must be fair to say that the *government itself* has advanced religion through its own activities and influence." [55]   That factor, the majority continued, makes *Amos* "a very different case" from *Thornton*: In *Thornton*, the state "had given the force of law to the employee's designation of a Sabbath day," whereas in *Amos*, the dismissed employee "was not legally obligated to take the steps necessary to [meet the employer's religious requirements], and his discharge was not required by statute." [56]   This distinction, which formed the crux of the majority's opinion, seems insubstantial at best— as four Justices pointed out.[57] Both statutes presented the beneficiaries with legal *alternatives*—for the employee in *Thornton* to designate a Sabbath, for the employer in *Amos* to set religious standards for employees—but not with legal *obligations*. The factor emphasized by the *Thornton* majority also cannot distinguish the two statutes: Both statutes apparently required "absolute" rather than "reasonable" religious accommodation.[58]

The two statutes are not easily distinguished. Both of them gave the force of law to one party's designation of a religion-related norm, and required the other party either to respect that norm or to pay a price. Nonetheless, some lines can be drawn between the statutes on

---

54. 42 U.S.C. § 2000e–1 provides in part that Title VII "shall not apply . . . to a religious corporation, association, educational institution, or society with respect to the employment of individuals of a particular religion to perform work connected with the carrying on by such corporation, association, educational institution, or society of its activities."

55. 107 S.Ct. at 2868–69 (emphasis in original).

56. Id. at 2869 n. 15.

57. See id. at 2870 n. 1 (Brennan, J., joined by Marshall, J., concurring in the judgment) ("The fact that a religious organization is permitted, rather than required,

to impose this burden is irrelevant; what is significant is that the burden is the effect of the exemption."); id. at 2873 (Blackmun, J., concurring in the judgment) ("I fully agree that the distinction drawn by the Court seems 'to obscure far more than to enlighten'. . . ."); id. at 2874 (O'Connor, J., concurring in the judgment) ("Almost any government benefit to religion could be recharacterized as simply 'allowing' a religion to better advance itself, unless perhaps it involved actual proselytization by government agents."). See, e.g., Larkin v. Grendel's Den, Inc., 459 U.S. 116 (1982), discussed in § 14–11, infra.

58. 472 U.S. at 709.

the basis of three factors, which together define some—but not all—of the boundaries of permissible legislative accommodation.

The first factor is an evenhandedness requirement. The Court has suggested that the *Thornton* statute was flawed at least partly because it made a benefit available only to members of Sabbatarian faiths.[59] The Title VII exemption in *Amos,* in contrast, was available to all religious organizations with employees. Although this factor can explain the cases' different results, it cannot suffice to limit the zone of permissible accommodation: The Court would not, for example, uphold a statute that gave members of *all* religions the power to designate a weekly day off from work, even though such a statute would be evenhanded.

A second, more comprehensive limitation on legislative accommodation focuses on whether the accommodation reduces regulatory entanglement between church and state. The *Amos* majority noted that "it is a significant burden on a religious organization to require it, on pain of substantial liability, to predict which of its activities a secular court will consider religious."[60] In that respect, as Justice O'Connor noted, government is lifting two separate burdens from religion: the burden of Title VII's requirements, and the burden of having to demonstrate that a given activity is religious.[61] Whereas the *Amos* statute sought to reduce the entanglement between a religious community and the government, by minimizing the occasions for government scrutiny of the community's activities, the *Thornton* statute could claim no such justification. But this principle also must be limited. Although church-state entanglement would be minimized by exempting *all* operations of religious organizations from Title VII, four Justices in *Amos* emphasized that only *nonprofit* operations should be accorded a *per se* exemption.[62]

A third limitation on accommodation derives from the source of the burden on religion that government seeks to lift. Perhaps government

---

59. Hobbie v. Unemployment Appeals Comm'n of Florida, 107 S.Ct. 1046, 1051 n. 11 (1987) (suggesting that the Thornton statute "ha[d] the effect of implicitly endorsing a particular religious belief"). Note, though, that the Court in Thornton did not apply its test for laws that discriminate among religions, enunciated in Larson v. Valente, 456 U.S. 228 (1982).

60. 107 S.Ct. at 2868. In his separate opinion in Amos, Justice Brennan elaborated on the point. A religious community, he wrote, partly defines itself by determining what activities advance the organization's religious mission, and by limiting participation in those activities to individuals who share a religious faith. 107 S.Ct. at 2871 (Brennan, J., concurring in the judgment). "This rationale suggests that, ideally, religious organizations should be able to discriminate on the basis of religion *only* with respect to religious activities, so that a determination should be made in each case whether an activity is religious

or secular." Id. at 2872 (emphasis in original). However, such a determination invariably creates "considerable ongoing government entanglement in religious affairs," a constitutional concern in itself. Id. The religious community's desire to avoid such entanglement may in turn chill its free exercise activity, because "the community's process of self-definition would be shaped in part by the prospects of litigation." Id. See § 14–16, infra.

61. Id. at 2875 (O'Connor, J., concurring in the judgment).

62. See id. at 2873 n. 6 (Brennan, J., joined by Marshall, J., concurring in the judgment); id. at 2873 (Blackmun, J., concurring in the judgment); id. at 2874 (O'Connor, J., concurring in the judgment). The majority opinion repeatedly noted that the activities at issue were nonprofit, but it did not directly limit its approach to nonprofit activities. See id. at 2865, 2869, 2870 (majority opinion).

may permissibly lift government-imposed burdens but not burdens that are privately imposed.[63]   Along these lines, Justice O'Connor has recommended applying a modified establishment clause test to those accommodations that lift government-imposed burdens.[64]   The modified test would uphold a statute if an objective observer would construe it to be a mere accommodation of religious exercise, rather than an official endorsement of religion.   Such a statute would be permissible, in Justice O'Connor's view, even though mere accommodation "*does* have the effect of advancing religion." [65]   However, she would continue to apply the *Lemon* test to government actions that aim to lift privately imposed burdens on religion.[66]   Under that test, a statute with an "effect of advancing religion" is impermissible.   This distinction could explain the results in *Thornton* and *Amos*: The Court struck down the statute that lifted a burden imposed by a private employer, and upheld the statute that lifted a burden imposed by government.

It is obvious that some limits on accommodation of religion by government are necessary, but it is less than obvious that Justice O'Connor's dichotomy between lifting privately imposed burdens and lifting government imposed burdens points to the proper division between forbidden and allowable accommodations.   The problem of denominationally discriminatory accommodation may be posed as readily when government selectively lifts some (but not all) of the burdens on religion it has imposed, as when it selectively mandates some private accommodations.   Nor is it the case that burdens on private individuals are imposed only when private accommodations to religion are called for by a challenged state action; even when the state "merely" lifts, in the name of religion, a state-imposed burden, costs are often imposed on innocent private individuals.   Property taxes must be higher whenever taxing authorities choose to exempt land owned by religious organizations.[67]   Unemployment insurance programs cost somewhat more because benefits are extended to otherwise-ineligible people.[68]   More people must be drafted because Congress decides to exempt conscientious objectors from combat duty.[69]   Victims of religious fraud who seek to recover their losses face hurdles that victims of nonreligious fraud do not face.[70]   Each of these rules—whether reflecting a constitutionally

---

63. The burden in Amos was regulatory entanglement, and so the second and third factors collapse into each other. But government may impose burdens other than entanglement.

64. See Amos, 107 S.Ct. at 2874–75 (O'Connor, J., concurring in the judgment); Wallace v. Jaffree, 472 U.S. 38, 84 (1985) (O'Connor, J., concurring in the judgment).

65. Amos, 107 S.Ct. at 2874–75 (emphasis in original). The "objective observer," who must be "acquainted with the text, legislative history, and implementation of the statute," id. at 2874, would see no *endorsement* of religion in such an accommodation. See § 14–15, infra.

66. See Thornton, 472 U.S. at 712 (O'Connor, J., concurring) (refusing to ex-

tend modified approach to a statute that lifts a burden imposed by private employers).

67. See Walz v. Tax Comm'n, 397 U.S. 664 (1970).

68. See Hobbie v. Unemployment Appeals Commission, 107 S.Ct. 1046 (1987); Thomas v. Review Board, 450 U.S. 707 (1981); Wisconsin v. Yoder, 406 U.S. 205 (1972); Sherbert v. Verner, 374 U.S. 398 (1963).

69. See Welsh v. United States, 398 U.S. 333 (1970); United States v. Seeger, 380 U.S. 163 (1965).

70. See United States v. Ballard, 322 U.S. 78 (1944).

mandated exemption or a voluntary choice—is backed by principles of religious liberty, and the private burdens that result can be viewed as secondary consequences of those fundamental principles. The point is that respecting religious liberty often imposes costs on innocent bystanders independent of the source of the burden being lifted.

Nonetheless, the *nature* of such costs varies with the source of the burden, as Justice O'Connor's dichotomy recognizes. When the state lifts a burden of its own, it remedies a problem that it itself created, and the resulting costs are likely to be widely distributed.[71] When the state lifts a private burden, in contrast, its intervention seems more intrusive and confrontational, and the costs are likely to fall more directly on individuals who cannot avoid recognizing them.[72] Where government in the former case seems to be *lifting* a burden, government in the latter case seems merely to be *shifting* a burden. Such perceptions may not be entirely accurate; but, as we have seen, they occupy a place of central importance in the law of religious freedom.[73]

Selectivity is also a problem. Although a legislature might discriminate among religions in lifting government-imposed burdens, the realm of legitimate accommodation is narrow enough that such opportunities are limited.[74] If a legislature were equally free to lift privately imposed burdens, however, the opportunities for discrimination among benefited religions—and among burdened sectors of society—would be vast; courts might believe the tasks of divining legislative intent and separating proper from improper accommodations would be both burdensome and difficult to discharge with accuracy.[75] By limiting permissible legislative accommodation to the lifting of government-imposed burdens, courts might provide a bright—and neutral—line. No such line is available once states may permissibly lift private burdens as well. Whatever else it may require, neutrality clearly requires that government not select among religions, on the basis of content or denomination, in lifting burdens. Courts that restrict permissible

---

71. Exceptions do exist. The costs of accommodation in Amos fell, sharply and directly, on the relatively few individuals who were fired because of their religious beliefs, and who would have a legal remedy against a nonreligious employer.

72. Requiring only *reasonable* accommodation, as is the case with Title VII, mitigates this impact considerably. The Court's emphasis in Thornton on the *absolute* nature of the accommodation required under the Connecticut statute may be best understood in terms of the public perception of the requirements.

73. See § 14–5, supra; § 14–15, infra.

74. But not nonexistent. Even if accommodation frequently (perhaps usually) benefits non-dominant religions—see, e.g., 26 U.S.C. § 1402(g)(1) (exempting from social security taxes self-employed persons who, for religious reasons, oppose acceptance of social security benefits); 42 U.S.C.

§ 1996 (enunciating federal policy to accommodate traditional Native American religious practices)—the dangers implicit in all selective accommodation seem great.

75. Some of the complexity stems from the wide range of religious accommodations that are possible. Cf. Day-Brite Lighting v. Missouri, 342 U.S. 421 (1952), where the Court upheld a statute that permitted employees to take up to four hours off from work in order to vote, without loss of pay. See § 12–23, supra. Such a statute accommodates the needs of nearly all voters—and, the Court found, only voters had been exposed to the particular evil that the statute addressed, id. at 425. It is virtually impossible to imagine a statute that could similarly accommodate the needs of nearly all religious adherents. Certainly the statute in Thornton did not do so.

accommodation to the relief of government-imposed burdens reduce the potential for selectivity.

Finally, it may be that, as Justice O'Connor has suggested, the free exercise clause simply does not contemplate the lifting of privately imposed burdens.[76] If that is the case, then the establishment clause might be deemed to forbid all such accommodations.[77]

Before leaving the issues of neutrality, it must be noted that the Court has twice upheld state practices that could not be justified under any meaningful neutrality theory. In *Marsh v. Chambers*,[78] the Court upheld legislative prayers, based largely on their long-standing history. The majority did not respond to the point, raised by Justice Stevens in dissent, that in practice minority and fringe religions were not being invited to participate, resulting in a violation of denominational neutrality.[79] In *Lynch v. Donnelly*,[80] the Court held that a Christmas crèche scene on public property did not violate the establishment clause, in part because it merely acknowledged the religious views of the majority of Americans—a concept that, by definition, goes beyond the dictates of neutrality. Both cases will be considered below.[81]

§ 14–8. The Free Exercise Principle as Dominant in Cases of Conflict

The preceding three sections have pointed to the conclusion that the free exercise principle should be dominant when it conflicts with the anti-establishment principle. Such dominance is the natural result of tolerating religion as broadly as possible rather than thwarting at all costs even the faintest appearance of establishment. In contrast, Jefferson initially believed that religion—and of course the clergy—should be excluded completely from the political realm.[1]

---

76. Thornton, 472 U.S. at 712 (O'Connor, J., concurring) (lifting private burdens "is not the sort of accommodation . . . specifically contemplated by the Free Exercise Clause").

77. But see M. McConnell, "Accommodation of Religion," 1985 Sup.Ct.Rev. 1, 32 (while "most occasions for religious accommodation will involve state action, . . . there is no reason in the logic of accommodation or of the Establishment Clause to limit the principle in this way").

78. 463 U.S. 783 (1983).

79. See id. at 823 (Stevens, J., dissenting) ("In a democratically elected legislature, the religious beliefs of the chaplain tend to reflect the faith of the majority of the lawmakers' constituents. Prayers may be said by a Catholic priest in the Massachusetts Legislature and by a Presbyterian minister in the Nebraska legislature, but I would not expect to find a Jehovah's Witness or a disciple of Mary Baker Eddy or the Reverend Moon serving as the official chaplain in any state legislature. Regardless of the motivation of the majority that exercises the power to appoint the chaplain, it seems plain to me that the designation of a member of one religious faith to serve as the sole official chaplain of a state legislature for a period of 16 years constitutes the preference of one faith over another in violation of the Establishment Clause.") (footnote omitted).

80. 465 U.S. 668 (1984).

81. See § 14–15, infra.

§ 14–8

1. Jefferson's 1783 draft constitution for Virginia would have prohibited clergy from serving in public offices. However, by 1800 Jefferson had concluded that such measures were no longer necessary. "The clergy here," he wrote, "seem to have relinquished all pretensions to privilege, and to stand on a footing with lawyers, physicians, &c. They ought therefore to possess the same rights." 9 Works of Jefferson 143 (P. Ford ed. 1905), quoted in McDaniel v. Paty, 435 U.S. 618, 623–24 n.4 (1978) (plurality opinion).

In *McDaniel v. Paty*,[2] the Supreme Court flatly rejected the Jeffersonian idea of a wall between religion and politics.[3] The Court unanimously struck down a provision of the Tennessee constitution[4] which prohibited any member of the clergy from serving in the state legislature.[5] Although the Justices agreed on the result, they differed on the underlying rationale. None of the four opinions attracted a majority of the Court.

Justice Brennan's concurring opinion, which Justice Marshall joined,[6] accorded the fullest measure of protection to the appellant's free exercise claim. That opinion characterized the Tennessee law as establishing a religious classification which burdened those whose religious beliefs were so intense as to impel them to join the ministry, and did not burden those who felt free to eschew the ministry—Tennessee imposed a religious test for office on the former but not on the latter.[7] Because government may not constitutionally use religion as the basis for burdensome classifications, the law could not stand. At the same time, Justice Brennan avoided conflict with the establishment clause by arguing that, far from justifying the infringement of the free exercise rights at stake, establishment clause principles likewise pointed to an infirmity in Tennessee's law: "As construed, the exclusion manifests patent hostility toward, not neutrality in respect of, religion . . . and [it] has a primary effect which inhibits religion."[8] Tennessee, by excluding religionists, favored the political participation of those with less intense religious beliefs. "The mere fact that a purpose of the Establishment Clause is to reduce or eliminate religious divisiveness or strife, does not place religious discussion, association, or political participation in a status less preferred than rights of discussion, association, and political participation generally."[9]

Chief Justice Burger's plurality opinion[10] agreed that Tennessee had encroached on the clergy's rights to the free exercise of religion,

2. 435 U.S. 618 (1978). Chief Justice Burger wrote for the plurality, joined by Justices Powell, Rehnquist, and Stevens. Opinions concurring in the judgment were filed by Justices Brennan and Marshall, id. at 629; Justice Stewart, id. at 642; and Justice White, id. at 643. Justice Blackmun took no part in the decision.

3. See also § 14–14, infra.

4. Tenn. Const., Art. IX, § 1 (1796) ("Whereas Ministers of the Gospel are by their profession, dedicated to God and the care of Souls, and ought not to be diverted from the great duties of their functions; therefore, no Minister of the Gospel, or Priest of any denomination whatever, shall be eligible for election to a seat in either House of the Legislature.").

5. The appellant had been elected to the state's constitutional convention, not the legislature. However, state law provided that only people who met the eligibility requirements for the legislature were eligible to seek election to the convention. 435 U.S. at 621.

6. Id. at 629 (concurring in judgment).

7. Justice Brennan argued that Torcaso v. Watkins, 367 U.S. 488 (1961) (holding unconstitutional a law requiring a declaration of belief in God as a condition of becoming a notary public) supported the conclusion that the Tennessee statute violated the free exercise clause. Id. at 632–33 (concurring in judgment). Justice Stewart, also concurring, went further, finding that Torcaso wholly controlled the outcome in McDaniel. Id. at 642–43 (concurring in judgment).

8. Id. at 636. See also §§ 14–7, supra; 14–10, infra.

9. 435 U.S. at 640. It will be argued below that, although religious divisiveness may result from an establishment clause violation, divisiveness is neither necessary nor sufficient to demonstrate that a violation has occurred. See §§ 14–11, 14–14, infra.

10. 435 U.S. at 620 (Burger, C.J., joined by Powell, Rehnquist, and Stevens, JJ.).

but left more room than Justice Brennan would for the states to justify restraints on religious liberty. The free exercise clause, the plurality wrote, gives absolute protection only to the "freedom of religious belief." [11] The Tennessee disqualification, however, operated against appellant not by reason of his "religious beliefs" but only by reason of his ministerial status defined in terms of "conduct and activity." [12] Although not absolutely forbidden, this infringement on appellant's religiously motivated activities could be justified by the state only by reference to interests of the highest order. Given Tennessee's failure to demonstrate the reality of the alleged dangers of clergy participation in the political process, [13] its infringement could not stand.

The belief-action dichotomy applied by the plurality is at best an oversimplification. [14] Moreover, the *McDaniel* plurality's application of that dichotomy is questionable. The plurality concluded that *Torcaso v. Watkins* [15] had concerned beliefs rather than actions, and thus that *Torcaso* was not relevant to *McDaniel*. [16] In *Torcaso*, the Court had struck down Maryland's requirement of an oath of belief in God as a condition of service as a notary public. Although pronouncing a single oath may be distinguishable from joining the clergy, the distinction seems to be one between types of acts rather than one between belief and action. The plurality's attempt to distinguish *Torcaso* thus fails to convince.

Far more persuasive is Justice Brennan's dichotomy between government measures that make expressly religious classifications and those that burden religious activity only incidentally, in a manner ancillary to an undeniably secular choice. [17] Such analysis offers a

---

11. Id. at 626. Justice White took the jesuitical position that, because McDaniel had not in fact been forced to abandon the ministry or disavow his religious beliefs, his free exercise rights had not been infringed at all. Instead of resting the decision on free exercise, Justice White concluded that the Tennessee statute unjustifiably infringed McDaniel's right to seek elective office. Id. at 643–46 (White, J., concurring in judgment).

12. Id. at 627 (plurality opinion).

13. Id. at 628–29. Compare First Nat'l Bank of Boston v. Bellotti, 435 U.S. 765 (1978), in which the majority was also unpersuaded of the factual bases for the state's concern that the political process would be distorted—there, by corporate participation. Even if Tennessee had successfully demonstrated that elected clergy would inevitably pursue sectarian goals, its anti-establishment rationale would still have been subject to challenge. First, the state must prove that it is pursuing interests of the highest order. The McDaniel plurality never reached the question whether preventing elected officials from pursuing a church's agenda is an interest of that magnitude, or indeed is a legitimate interest at all. 435 U.S. at 628. See

§§ 14–13, 14–14, infra. Second, and more fundamentally, any nonsecular consequence of permitting clergy to hold elective office results not from any government action but from the choices of individual voters. Cf. Mueller v. Allen, 463 U.S. 388, 399 (1983) ("Where, as here, aid to parochial schools is available only as a result of decisions of individual parents no 'imprimatur of State approval' can be deemed to have been conferred on any particular religion, or on religion generally.") (citation omitted) (quoting Widmar v. Vincent, 454 U.S. 263, 274 (1981)). This sort of justification, of course, insulates from establishment clause challenge only benefits conferred through individual citizen choices, such as votes for candidates or educational vouchers. It does not apply to choices made by the state, even at the behest of direct voter allocation through initiative or referendum.

14. See § 14–6, supra.

15. 367 U.S. 488 (1961).

16. 435 U.S. at 626–27. Justices Brennan, Marshall, and Stewart believed that Torcaso was relevant. See note 7, supra.

17. See also § 14–13, infra.

tolerable resolution of the dispute between those who claim the first amendment is "absolute" in its protection, and those who claim it always requires case-by-case "balancing" of competing interests of government.[18]

Whenever both religion clauses are potentially relevant, as in *McDaniel*, the dominance of the free exercise clause follows from the principles underlying both clauses. For both clauses embody a broad concept of the relationship between religion and the state, which must be modified to adapt to changing conceptions both of religion and of government. If individuals and groups are to enjoy meaningful religious freedom, the protection afforded by the free exercise clause must vary with the extent of governmental regulation and subsidy in society generally. The opinions of the Framers offer general guidance, expressed in such core values as voluntarism and separatism. In the context of these general values, we must consider whether a nation committed to religious pluralism must, in the age of the affirmative state, make active provision for maximum diversity; we must ask whether, in the present age, religious tolerance must cease to be simply a negative principle and must become a positive commitment that encourages the flourishing of conscience. Whenever tension is perceived between free exercise and non-establishment, ". . . a value judgment [is required] as to which is to become dominant . . .—the one premised on a vital civil right, or the one premised on . . . eighteenth century political theory. The resolution [is] preordained—to pose the conflict is to resolve it." [19] Even if one takes a more charitable view of the political theory underlying the opposed position, it seems doubtful that sacrificing religious freedom on the altar of anti-establishment would do justice to the hopes of the Framers—or to a coherent vision of religious autonomy in the affirmative state.

We have traced the roots of the religion clauses, and studied how the clauses interrelate. We turn now to the doctrinal tests that arise in litigation. We begin with the establishment clause's requirements: secular purpose, secular effect, and no excessive entanglement.

§ 14–9. The Requirement of Secular Purpose

A fundamental requirement in the law of the religion clauses is that governmental actions must be justifiable in secular terms, broadly defined. Where the purpose of a government action is " 'to endorse or disapprove of religion,' " [1] the action will typically violate the establish-

---

18. See § 12–7, supra.

19. Giannella, "Religious Liberty, Non-Establishment, and Doctrinal Development: Part I, the Religious Liberty Guarantee," 80 Harv.L.Rev. 1381, 1389 (1967). To the degree that Giannella deems the "political theory" underlying anti-establishment to be "outmoded," id., his views go further than seems defensible in matters of constitutional interpretation. Cf. § 5–24, supra. But one need not dismiss the establishment clause and its underlying vision as outdated in order to affirm the necessity for construing that clause in a manner that advances the larger purposes of the two religion clauses taken together.

§ 14–9

1. Wallace v. Jaffree, 472 U.S. 38, 56 (1985) (quoting Lynch v. Donnelly, 465 U.S. 668, 690 (1984) (O'Connor, J., concurring).

ment clause; to the extent that it limits freedom to act upon one's religious beliefs, it may violate the free exercise clause as well.

The requirement of secular purpose received its clearest enunciation in cases dealing with the establishment clause, where it became one of the three characteristics deemed necessary to justify state action against an establishment clause attack: secular purpose, primary secular effect, and absence of excessive entanglement.[2] Despite these origins, however, the requirement of secular purpose has perhaps its most basic application in the context of governmental control of activities which some persons wish to undertake for religious reasons. Such control plainly cannot be sustained on the ground that the government disagrees with the religion in question; the government must instead point to a secular purpose to justify its regulation.[3] In the requirement of secular purpose we find, therefore, a central test which originated in establishment clause litigation, but which has obvious application in the free exercise area as well.

The definition of "secular" here must be a generous one. If a purpose were to be classified as non-secular simply because the resulting state practice coincided with the beliefs of a religion, or because it originated in a religion, then virtually nothing that government does would be acceptable.[4] Laws against murder, for example, would be forbidden because they overlap the fifth commandment of the Mosaic Decalogue. In Justice O'Connor's helpful formulation, something should be deemed sufficiently secular in aim if a fully informed, independent observer would judge it to have a predominantly secular purpose at the time it is challenged.[5]

The Court itself has interpreted the secular purpose requirement in much this way. For example, the fact that Sunday closing laws had their origins in religious considerations, and that Sunday remains a day of special religious significance for many, has not led the Court to conclude that such laws fail to meet the requirement of secular purpose. On the contrary, the Court said in *McGowan v. Maryland*: "The present . . . effect of most of [these laws] is to provide a uniform day of rest for all citizens; the fact that this day is Sunday, a day of

2. Lemon v. Kurtzman, 403 U.S. 602, 612–13 (1971). The Court has applied the Lemon framework in all but one establishment clause case. The exception was Marsh v. Chambers, 463 U.S. 783 (1983) (upholding legislative chaplains because of long history of practice) (case discussed in § 14–15, infra). See also Larson v. Valente, 456 U.S. 228, 252–55 (1982) (noting that Lemon test need not be reached where laws discriminate among different religions, but reviewing Lemon factors anyway) (case discussed in § 14–7, supra).

3. See also § 14–13, infra.

4. See Wallace v. Jaffree, 472 U.S. 38, 69–70 (1985) (O'Connor, J., concurring in judgment) ("[I]t is inevitable that the secular interests of Government and the religious interests of various sects and their adherents will frequently intersect, conflict, and combine. A statute that ostensibly promotes a secular interest often has an incidental or even a primary effect of helping or hindering a sectarian belief. Chaos would ensue if every such statute were invalid under the Establishment Clause.").

5. See id. at 76 ("The relevant issue is whether an objective observer, acquainted with the text, legislative history, and implementation of the statute, would perceive it as a state endorsement. . . ."). This low threshold might be an inadequate protection if a secular purpose were the only requirement a government action had to meet in order to be acceptable. Other requirements, however, also apply. See §§ 14–10, 14–11, infra.

particular significance for the dominant Christian sects, does not bar the State from achieving its secular goals." [6] Indeed, even in the school prayer cases some Justices were convinced that a secular purpose was at least arguably present.[7] Appropriately, the Court will usually find in the statutory language or elsewhere a secular purpose for a challenged law, and will then move on to consideration of the remaining two establishment clause criteria.[8]

The secular purpose requirement has proven decisive, however, in four cases. In *Epperson v. Arkansas,*[9] the Court considered an Arkansas statute, adopted in 1928, that prohibited the teaching of evolution in public schools and universities. The statute was an adaptation of the Tennessee statute under which John Thomas Scopes had been convicted for teaching evolution.[10] The Court found in the record no "suggestion . . . the Arkansas' law [could] be justified by considerations of state policy other than [a desire to support] the religious views of some of its citizens" [11] and therefore concluded that *the absence of any secular purpose whatever* for the state's excision rendered it violative of the establishment clause: "The overriding fact is that Arkansas' law selects from the body of knowledge a particular segment which it proscribes *for the sole reason* that it is deemed to conflict with a particular religious doctrine; that is, with a particular interpretation of the Book of Genesis by a particular religious group." [12]

6. 366 U.S. 420, 445 (1961) (Warren, C.J.). The Court in McGowan held that Sunday closing laws were constitutional because, in spite of their origin, they conferred only a remote and incidental benefit to religious institutions and because choosing another day would manifest not neutrality but hostility toward religion.

7. See Engel v. Vitale, 370 U.S. 421, 449–50 (1962) (Stewart, J., dissenting); Abington School Dist. v. Schempp, 374 U.S. 203, 212–14, 223, 225 (1963) (opinion of Clark, J.).

8. See, e.g., Lemon v. Kurtzman, 403 U.S. 602, 613 (1971) ("the statutes themselves clearly state that they are intended to enhance the quality of the secular education in all schools covered by the compulsory attendance laws. There is no reason to believe the legislatures meant anything else"); Gillette v. United States, 401 U.S. 437 (1971) (rejecting, *inter alia*, an establishment clause challenge to Congress' statutory limitation of conscientious objector status to those who object to participation in war in any form, and Congress' concomitant denial of such status to those individuals—typically Catholics—objecting only to participation in "unjust" wars, as a means of achieving two secular goals: maintaining the credibility and morale of the armed services, and avoiding otherwise undetectable fraud). See Hochstadt, "The Right to Exemption from Military Service of a Conscientious Objector to a Particular War," 3 Harv.Civ.Rts.—Civ.Lib.L.Rev. 1

(1967); MacGill, "Selective Conscientious Objection: Divine Will and Legislative Grace," 54 Va.L.Rev. 1355 (1968).

9. 393 U.S. 97 (1968).

10. See Scopes v. State, 154 Tenn. 105, 289 S.W. 363 (1927) (conviction reversed on nonfederal ground that the trial judge had levied a $100 fine against Scopes, which the jury had failed to assess in accordance with state law). The successor to the Scopes statute was struck down in Daniel v. Waters, 515 F.2d 485 (6th Cir. 1975). As in Epperson, the Daniels court found an impermissible religious purpose.

11. Epperson, 393 U.S. at 107.

12. Id. at 103 (emphasis added). Justice Black, concurring on other grounds, found this analysis unpersuasive. The Court, it seemed to him, had simply chosen to see a non-secular purpose when the statute could as easily have been perceived as an exercise of the state's power "to withdraw from its curriculum any subject deemed too emotional and controversial for its public schools." Id. at 113. Nonetheless, in Epperson the Court recognized that the "anti-evolution" statute was "a product of the upsurge of 'fundamentalist' religious fervor of the twenties." 393 U.S. at 98. Given that context, and given the fact that the legislature did not choose "to excise from the curricula of its schools and universities all discussion of the origin of man," or for that matter all emotional and controversial topics, the Court refused to

In *Stone v. Graham*,[13] the Court struck down a Kentucky statute that required public schools to post in each classroom a copy of the Ten Commandments, which was paid for by private contributions. Each copy was to include a secular disclaimer in fine print at the bottom: "The secular application of the Ten Commandments is clearly seen in its adoption as the fundamental legal code of Western Civilization and the Common Law of the United States."[14] In a summary reversal of state courts' decisions upholding the statute, the Court rejected this avowed purpose and found that the principal purpose was "plainly religious," given the Decalogue's status as a sacred text and the fact that its edicts go beyond the arguably secular (e.g., proscribing murder) to embrace the indisputably religious (e.g., not using the Lord's name in vain).[15] The Court suggested that a secular purpose might be present if the Decalogue were "integrated into the school curriculum," but not if it was simply posted on classroom walls.[16]

The Court in *Wallace v. Jaffree* struck down an Alabama law mandating a period of silence in public schools "'for meditation or voluntary prayer,'"[17] concluding that "the statute had *no* secular purpose."[18] As in *Epperson*, the statute unmistakably echoed a directly religious law: in *Epperson*, Tennessee's famous anti-evolution statute; in *Jaffree*, a statute that authorized teachers to lead students in reciting a specific prayer.[19] In addition, the Alabama statute's principal sponsor said that the bill's only purpose had been religious,[20] and no evidence to the contrary was introduced.[21] Most significantly, Alabama law already mandated a moment of silence "for meditation." The only conceivable purpose of the new statute, the Court held, was to convey an endorsement of religion.[22] "The addition of 'or voluntary prayer'

select a legitimate purpose from a range of conceivable ones and relied on what appeared to have been the actual legislative motive. Id. at 109.

13. 449 U.S. 39 (1980) (per curiam).

14. Id. at 41 (quoting Ky. Rev. Stat. § 158.178 (1980)).

15. Id. at 41–42.

16. Id. at 42. Four Justices dissented. Chief Justice Burger and Justice Blackmun would have given the case plenary consideration. Id. at 43. Justice Stewart dissented because the Kentucky courts, "so far as it appears, applied wholly correct constitutional criteria in reaching their decisions [upholding the statute]." Id. Justice Rehnquist, the only dissenter to file a full opinion, would have accepted the avowed secular purpose. Id. at 43–47.

17. 472 U.S. 38, 40 n.2 (1985) (quoting Alabama Code § 16–1–20.1 (Supp. 1984)).

18. Id. at 56 (emphasis in original).

19. See id. at 40 n.3 (quoting Alabama Code § 16–1–20.2 (Supp. 1984)). See also id. at 62 (Powell, J., concurring) ("My concurrence is prompted by Alabama's persistence in attempting to institute state-spon-

sored prayer in the public schools by enacting three successive statutes.").

20. Id. at 43, 56–57.

21. Id. at 58.

22. Id. The statute that the Court struck down differed from the earlier statute in two other respects. One difference was that the challenged statute applied to all grades, whereas the earlier one applied only to the first through sixth grades. See id. The Court considered that difference irrelevant to the litigation, in that the plaintiff's children were affected under either statute. The fact that the children were covered by both statutes, however, does not make the two statutes identical; extending the coverage of the moment-of-silence program could have been an independent, secular purpose for the second statute. See M. McConnell, "Accommodation of Religion," 1985 Sup.Ct.Rev. 1, 45–46 ("That Mr. Jaffree's children were not among those affected does not make the legislature's action meaningless or irrational; there are other children in Alabama."). In light of the other factors that pointed toward an impermissible purpose,

indicates that the State intended to characterize prayer as a favored practice." [23]

In *Edwards v. Aguillard*,[24] the Court struck down a Louisiana statute that mandated equal treatment for evolution and "creation science" in public classrooms. Under the statute, the teaching of neither theory was required, but once a teacher presented one theory, he or she was required to devote equal attention to the other theory. In finding an impermissible purpose underlying the statute, the Court looked particularly at three elements. First, the state had failed to identify a "clear secular purpose" for its law.[25] Second, as in *Epperson*, the Court took note of the "historic and contemporaneous link between the teachings of certain religious denominations and the teaching of evolution." [26] Third, some aspects of the legislative history pointed clearly to an impermissible primary purpose, "to change the science curriculum of public schools in order to provide persuasive advantage to a particular religious

however, the result would almost certainly have been the same.

23. Id. at 60. The majority opinion did not discuss whether any statute including the word "prayer" would, for that reason, fail the purpose inquiry. Justices O'Connor and White and Chief Justice Burger argued that it need not. Id. at 73 (O'Connor, J., concurring in judgment) ("Even if a statute specifies that a student may choose to pray silently during a quiet moment, the State has not thereby encouraged prayer over other specified alternatives."); id. at 91 (White, J., dissenting) ("[I]f a student asked whether he could pray during that moment, it is difficult to believe that the teacher could not answer in the affirmative. If that is the case, I would not invalidate a statute that at the outset provided the legislative answer to the question 'May I pray?' "); id. at 85 (Burger, C.J., dissenting) ("To suggest that a moment-of-silence statute that includes the word 'prayer' unconstitutionally endorses religion, while one that simply provides for a moment of silence does not, manifests not neutrality but hostility toward religion."). But see W. Dellinger, "The Sound of Silence: An Epistle on Prayer and the Constitution," 95 Yale L.J. 1631, 1636 (1986) ("Imagine a state statute providing that a moment of silence be conducted at the beginning of each school day for 'meditation or erotic fantasy.' Could one plausibly say in that case that the state is being wholly 'neutral' with regard to 'erotic fantasy,' that the statute merely reflects the fact that students can (and some no doubt will) use any period of silence for that purpose?").

Chief Justice Burger also suggested that adding "prayer" to a moment-of-silence statute might simply be intended to clarify the fact that prayer is permitted under the statute. Id. at 88. See also McConnell, supra note 22, at 46 ("Given the common misperception that the Supreme Court has forbidden children to pray in the schools, the legislators might have thought a clarification useful.") (footnote omitted). The argument might be plausible if the state could demonstrate that teachers had misconstrued the law and had told students that they could meditate but not pray, but absolutely no such evidence was presented.

24. 107 S.Ct. 2573 (1987). Justice Brennan wrote for the Court. Justice Powell filed a concurring opinion, joined by Justice O'Connor. Id. at 2584. Justice White concurred in the judgment. Id. at 2590. Justice Scalia, joined by Chief Justice Rehnquist, dissented. Id. at 2591.

25. Id. at 2578. The state had named a secular purpose, to promote academic freedom, but the Court concluded that " '[a]cademic freedom,' at least as it is commonly understood [to refer to the freedom of teachers and scholars], is not a relevant concept in this context." Id. at 2578 n. 6. Justice Scalia responded that the legislators intended "academic freedom" to mean (and the statute to promote) "students' freedom from indoctrination." Id. at 2601 (Scalia, J., dissenting) (emphasis omitted).

26. Id. at 2580–81.

doctrine that rejects the factual basis of evolution in its entirety." [27] The Court did *not* examine the scientific validity of creation science.[28]

As applied in establishment clause litigation, the secular purpose test remains only hazily defined.[29] Although the Court has never required an *exclusively* secular purpose,[30] for example, at some point it is plain that a law's religious purposes overshadow its secular aims. *Stone* demonstrates that such a point exists, but does not define it. *Epperson* and *Jaffree* both insist that no secular purpose whatever lay behind the statutes at issue. The state's proffered secular purpose in *Aguillard*, to promote academic freedom, was ruled irrelevant to the statute.[31] In addition, the question of where the Court ought to look for evidence of legislative purpose remains unresolved. In *Epperson*, the Court looked partly to the times—"the upsurge of 'fundamentalist' religious fervor of the twenties" in general,[32] and the Tennessee Scopes statute in particular.[33] In *Aguillard*, the Court looked partly to the antagonism that some fundamentalists have voiced toward evolution.[34]

27. Id. at 2582. In his concurring opinion, Justice Powell highlighted two particularly enlightening elements of the legislative history: the bill as originally introduced referred to the belief that the universe was "created ex nihilo and fixed by God"; and part of the pending bill, which listed the unmistakably biblical tenets of creation science, was dropped one day after a court challenge to a creation science statute in Arkansas focused on the parallels between a similar listing and the Genesis account of creation. Id. at 2586 (Powell, J., concurring). In his Aguillard dissent, Justice Scalia emphasized that the question was not the legislators' "*wisdom* in believing that [secular] purpose [to promote academic freedom] would be achieved by the bill, but their *sincerity* in believing it would be." Id. at 2598 (Scalia, J., dissenting) (emphasis in original). The evidence mustered by Justice Powell fatally undermines the presumption of sincerity.

28. The majority suggested that schools could legitimately teach "a variety of scientific theories about the origins of humankind" if the decision to do so were based on "the clear secular intent of enhancing the effectiveness of science instruction." Id. at 2583. Justice Powell more bluntly wrote that "there is no need" to consider whether valid scientific evidence underlies creation science: "Whatever the academic merit of particular subjects or theories, the Establishment Clause limits the discretion of state officials to pick and choose among them for the purpose of promoting a particular religious belief." Id. at 2588 (Powell, J., concurring). In dissent, Justice Scalia agreed that "[o]ur task is not to judge the debate about teaching the origins of life, but to ascertain what the members of the

Louisiana Legislature believed." Id. at 2598 (Scalia, J., dissenting). But see G. Will, "Good Grief, Scalia!", Washington Post, June 25, 1987, at A17 (criticizing the Court for failing to question the scientific pretensions of the creation theory, and critizing Justice Scalia for failing to acknowledge that "Louisiana's legislators . . . were legislating a religious assertion disguised as a scientific inquiry"). Nothing in Aguillard suggests that public schools may not teach *about* "creationism" in courses about speculative or religious philosophies; it was the mandated teaching of religious views *as* "science" that the Court found troublesome.

29. See Edwards v. Aguillard, 107 S.Ct. 2573, 2607 (1987) (Scalia, J., dissenting) (the secular purpose test "exacerbates the tension between the Free Exercise and Establishment Clauses, has no basis in the language or history of the amendment, and . . . has wonderfully flexible consequences"); Wallace v. Jaffree, 472 U.S. at 108 (Rehnquist, J., dissenting) ("The secular purpose prong has proven mercurial in application because it has never been fully defined, and we have never fully stated how the test is to operate.").

30. See Wallace v. Jaffree, 472 U.S. at 56 (noting that "a statute that is motivated in part by a religious purpose may satisfy the first criterion").

31. 107 S.Ct. at 2578 n. 6.

32. 393 U.S. at 98.

33. Id. at 98, 108–09.

34. 107 S.Ct. at 2580–81. In his concurring opinion, Justice Powell went still farther afield and examined the forthrightly religious nature of the principal creation-

In *Jaffree*, the Court relied partly on the post-enactment statements of one legislator,[35] but in *Aguillard* the Court discounted the value of such evidence.[36] Justice O'Connor has suggested that the Court limit itself to a statute's text, its official legislative history, and its interpretation by the responsible administrative agency.[37]

The cases also raise several questions about the burden of persuasion. Must the state present evidence of a secular purpose? If so, how much evidence? How "clear" must a statute's stated purpose be?[38] What sort of evidence will be construed as proof of a non-secular purpose—if, for example, the bill's sponsor alone has a religious motive, is the legislation invalid, "on a theory, perhaps, that even though everyone else's intent was pure, what they produced was the fruit of a forbidden tree?"[39] Absent specific evidence, when will the Court impute a secular or a non-secular purpose? Is the goal of the inquiry to determine legislators' actual, subjective motives, or is it to determine how a reasonable outsider would read their motives?[40] How much scrutiny will the Court give to the state's assertion of secular motivation? In the cases where religious purpose has been held dispositive, relatively little scrutiny has been necessary: *Stone* dealt with an inextricably religious text; *Jaffree* dealt with an inextricably religious practice; and the laws in *Epperson*, *Jaffree*, and—to some extent— *Aguillard* seemed to fit into a pattern with other, candidly religious laws. Where the question has been closer, the Court has proceeded to other inquiries.[41] Justice O'Connor has advocated a highly deferential

science organizations. Id. at 2587 (Powell, J., concurring). Absent evidence to the contrary, Justice Powell then implied, those organizations' religious purpose must be imputed to the Louisiana legislature: "[T]he statements and purpose of the sources of creation-science in the United States make clear that their purpose is to promote a religious belief. I find no persuasive evidence in the legislative history that the legislature's purpose was any different." Id. at 2588.

35. See 472 U.S. at 43, 56. Justice O'Connor argued against considering such post-enactment statements, at least where the legislative record demonstrates a satisfactory, secular aim. Id. at 75, 76 (O'Connor, J., concurring in judgment). See also id. at 87 (Burger, C.J., dissenting) ("No case in the 195-year history of this Court supports the disconcerting idea that post-enactment statements by individual legislators are relevant in determining the constitutionality of legislation.").

36. 107 S.Ct. at 2584 n. 19 ("The Court has previously found the postenactment elucidation of the meaning of a statute to be of little relevance in determining the intent of the legislature contemporaneous to the passage of a statute."). Such a limi-

tation seems worthwhile. Otherwise, it is conceivable that a legislator could exercise a de facto veto power by voting for a bill and afterward voicing a religious purpose for having done so.

37. Jaffree, 472 U.S. at 74–75 (O'Connor, J., concurring in the judgment).

38. See Aguillard, 107 S.Ct. at 2578 ("the petitioners have identified no clear secular purpose").

39. Id. at 2606 (Scalia, J., dissenting).

40. This issue touches on a tension in Justice Scalia's Aguillard dissent. The opinion emphasized that the Court must search for legislators' actual motives, and not consider the reasonableness of those motives. Id. at 2593 (Scalia, J., dissenting). However, in a later section of the opinion, Justice Scalia wrote that "discerning the subjective motivation of those enacting the statute is, to be honest, almost always an impossible task." Id. at 2605.

41. See note 6, supra. Cf. Marsh v. Chambers, 463 U.S. 783, 793–94 (1983) (legislature's reappointment of same chaplain for sixteen years indicates satisfaction with chaplain's performance, rather than preference for his religious views) (case not applying Lemon test).

approach: "Even if the text and official history of a statute express no secular purpose, the statute should be held to have an improper purpose only if it is beyond purview that endorsement of religion or a religious belief 'was and is the law's reason for existence.' "[42]

The secular purpose requirement, partly because of its sketchy parameters, could raise two particularly important conceptual problems in application. First, it might be used to strike down laws whose effects are utterly secular.[43] A legislature might, for example, vote to increase welfare benefits because individual legislators feel religiously compelled to do so. So too, when a legislature passes a neutral moment-of-silence statute, many legislators may hope that students will use the time for prayer. However improper these purposes may be, it is hard to see a meaningful establishment clause problem so long as the statute's effects are completely secular.[44] A visible religious purpose may independently convey a message of endorsement or exclusion, but such a message, standing alone, should rarely if ever suffice to transform a secular action into an establishment clause violation.[45] A religious message may be conveyed by the legislative debates concerning a bill, but the same result is possible from debates that lead to no legislation; it can hardly be said that the debates themselves establish a religion.

The second major problem with the secular purpose requirement is, as Justice O'Connor has noted, that it might invalidate any legislative act intended to equalize religious burdens or otherwise to advance free exercise values.[46] Title VII of the Civil Rights Act of 1964, for example, requires that employers make "reasonable accommodations" to the

---

42. Wallace v. Jaffree, 472 U.S. at 75 (O'Connor, J., concurring in judgment) (quoting Epperson v. Arkansas, 393 U.S. at 108).

43. See also § 14–14, infra.

44. Aguillard, 107 S.Ct. at 2594 (Scalia, J., dissenting) ("We surely would not strike down a law providing money to feed the hungry or shelter the homeless if it could be demonstrated that, but for the religious beliefs of the legislators, the funds would not have been approved."); id. at 2604 ("If a history teacher falsely told her students that the bones of Jesus Christ had been discovered, or a physics teacher that the Shroud of Turin had been conclusively established to be inexplicable on the basis of natural causes, I cannot believe . . . that legislators or school board members would be constitutionally prohibited from taking corrective action, simply because that action was prompted by concern for the religious beliefs of the misinstructed students."); see Dellinger, supra note 23, at 1639 ("The fact that some legislators may hope . . . that children will use an undesignated moment of reflective silence for prayer should not in itself be sufficient to

invalidate such a statute. It is often the case that one who helps create an open, 'neutral' forum has some hope or expectation about how that forum will be used. . . . The key factor, for neutrality analysis, is the dispositive role of private citizen choice.").

45. See § 14–14, infra. But see Wallace v. Jaffree, 472 U.S. at 75 (O'Connor, J., concurring in judgment) (secular purpose requirement "serves an important function" of "remind[ing] government that when it acts it should do so without endorsing a particular religious belief or practice that all citizens do not share").

46. Concurring in Wallace v. Jaffree, Justice O'Connor wrote: "[A] rigid application of the Lemon test would invalidate legislation exempting religious observers from generally applicable government obligations. By definition, such legislation has a religious purpose and effect in promoting the free exercise of religion." 472 U.S. at 82. Her solution was to eliminate the purpose inquiry concerning statutes that remove government-imposed burdens on free exercise. Id. See § 14–7, supra.

"religious observances and practices" of employees and potential employees—clearly demonstrating a non-secular purpose.[47] In *Corporation of the Presiding Bishop of the Church of Jesus Christ of Latter-Day Saints v. Amos,*[48] the Supreme Court suggested that the purpose inquiry does not demand "that the law's purpose must be unrelated to religion"; instead, the requirement "aims at preventing the relevant governmental decisionmaker . . . from abandoning neutrality and acting with the intent of promoting a particular point of view in religious matters."[49] That limitation on the purpose test seems to go too far. It would permit not only legislation that pursues free exercise values, but also seemingly legislation that "aid[s] all religions as against nonbelievers," which the Court has correctly held to be impermissible.[50]

A more satisfactory solution is suggested by Justice O'Connor's "objective observer" approach.[51] Such an observer, fully informed about the values underlying the religion clauses, would not strike down religiously motivated laws if they even-handedly lift a government-imposed burden on free exercise.[52] The objective observer would also permit religiously motivated laws whose effects are purely secular, such as welfare and neutral moment-of-silence laws.[53] Where a law partly advances religion, however, the observer would view a non-secular

---

47. 42 U.S.C. §§ 2000e(j), 2000e(a)(1). Justice O'Connor, joined by Justice Marshall, has argued that Title VII is constitutional because it is based on a secular purpose—that of "assuring employment opportunity to all groups in our pluralistic society." Estate of Thornton v. Caldor, Inc., 472 U.S. 703, 712 (1985) (O'Connor, J., joined by Marshall, J., concurring). It has been persuasively argued, however, that the legislative history of Title VII reveals at least a partial non-secular purpose—that of accommodating Saturday Sabbatarians. See M. McConnell, "Accommodation of Religion," 1985 Sup.Ct.Rev. 1, 33. Title VII is also discussed in § 14–7, supra.

48. 107 S.Ct. 2862 (1987).

49. Id. at 2868.

50. Torcaso v. Watkins, 367 U.S. 488, 495 (1961).

51. See Wallace v. Jaffree, 472 U.S. at 76, 83 (O'Connor, J., concurring in judgment); Lynch v. Donnelly, 465 U.S. 668, 687 (1984) (O'Connor, J., concurring). Although the approach developed here borrows Justice O'Connor's framework, it differs from hers significantly. See notes 52, 53, infra.

52. Cf. Amos, 107 S.Ct. at 2874–75 (O'Connor, J., concurring in the judgment); Wallace v. Jaffree, 472 U.S. at 83 (O'Connor, J., concurring in judgment). In Estate of Thornton v. Caldor, Inc., 472 U.S. 703 (1985), the Court considered a statute designed to lift *privately* imposed free exercise burdens by requiring private employers to permit employees not to work on their Sabbaths. Without explaining why, the Court did not consider the statute's purpose—even though the statute was passed in order to accommodate religious observers after the state had repealed its Sunday closing laws. See id. at 705 n.2, 706 n.3 (case discussed in § 14–7, supra).

53. But cf. Wallace v. Jaffree, 472 U.S. at 75 (O'Connor, J., concurring in judgment) (purpose inquiry "require[s] that the legislature manifest a secular purpose and omit all sectarian endorsements from its laws"). Her objective observer might correctly strike down religiously motivated laws that have no concrete effect whatever. Such laws might be viewed as a form of government speech whose sole function is to convey messages of endorsement or exclusion. A state constitutional amendment that announced, "This is a Christian state," without any mechanism for enforcement or plans to create one, would send such a message, and should be struck down. The holding in Epperson, striking down a forty-year-old statute that had apparently never been enforced, supports this approach, although there are limits, under Article III, to how far a federal court may go in weeding old, unenforced statutes out of a state's law.

legislative motivation as additional, helpful evidence of an establishment clause violation. Under this approach, the purpose inquiry would no longer stand as an independent test, capable of striking down legislation on its own. Rather, it would be an additional, subordinate index of unconstitutionality. This modification of the purpose test seems consistent with the Court's holdings in *Epperson, Stone, Jaffree,* and *Aguillard*. To a degree, it is also consistent with the approach of the Court's opinions: in each of the cases, the Court seemed to take into account the law's likely non-secular *effect* as well as its non-secular purpose.[54]

Several factors support this attenuated use of the secular purpose inquiry. Merging the purpose and effect tests reduces the likelihood and the consequences of an erroneous conclusion about legislative motive. This approach also eliminates the danger that a rigidly applied purpose test might strike down laws whose effects are purely secular or whose effects advance free exercise values. At the same time, the modified approach recognizes that purpose will be relevant in many cases. A constitutionally suspect motivation, just as in equal protection jurisprudence,[55] tends to show that constitutionally suspect effects are not accidental or incidental. When a statute is based on a publicly broadcast religious purpose, those who are charged with enforcing it may infer that religious effects in application are permitted, encouraged, or even mandated. In addition, when a religious motivation combines with religious effects, the result is to put the voice and the power of government behind religion in a way that religious

---

54. In Epperson, the Court found "overriding" the fact that the law "selects from the body of knowledge a particular segment which it proscribes for the sole reason that it is deemed to conflict with a particular religious doctrine." 393 U.S. at 103. Indeed, the possibility that the law lacked any concrete effect, because it had apparently never been enforced, led Justice Black to question whether a justiciable case or controversy existed. 393 U.S. at 109 (Black, J., concurring). In Stone v. Graham, the Court wrote: "If the posted copies of the Ten Commandments are to have any effect at all, it will be to induce the schoolchildren to read, meditate upon, perhaps to venerate and obey, the Commandments." 449 U.S. at 42. In Wallace v. Jaffree, the Court noted, although it did not discuss, Jaffree's allegations that teachers were leading students in vocal prayer. 472 U.S. at 42. The Court also devoted a lengthy footnote to the dangers of religious indoctrination, particularly of schoolchildren, through government actions that endorse a particular religion. Id. at 60 n.51. In Aguillard, the Court concluded that "the term 'creation science,' as contemplated by the legislature that

adopted this Act, embodies the religious belief that a supernatural creator was responsible for the creation of humankind." 107 S.Ct. at 2582. That finding relates not only to the legislature's purpose, but also to the likely effect of teaching creation science in the public schools.

A different approach, which would have reached the same results in the four cases, would have been to focus on the statutes' non-neutrality among religions. The Epperson, Stone, and Aguillard statutes were plainly non-neutral, and the Jaffree statute, in recognizing prayer, was arguably so. None of the statutes lifted any government-imposed burden on free exercise. The Court thus might have struck them down as violating the denominational neutrality requirement, and avoided the Lemon test entirely. See Larson v. Valente, 456 U.S. 228, 252 (1982) ("[T]he Lemon v. Kurtzman 'tests' are intended to apply to laws affording a uniform benefit to *all* religions, and not to provisions . . . that discriminate *among* religions.") (footnote omitted) (emphasis in original). See § 14-7, supra.

55. See § 16-20, infra.

motivation alone does not. One consequence is to convey signals of endorsement and exclusion to citizens, depending on their religious beliefs. Another consequence may be to cloak government actions in religious authority.[56]

§ 14–10. The Requirement of Secular Effect

A second fundamental requirement in the law of the religion clauses is the requirement of secular effect. Although the requirement has some relevance for the free exercise clause, it arises principally in establishment clause litigation.[1] Even if it cannot be shown that a governmental policy was *aimed* at a religious aspect of behavior, the policy should generally [2] be struck down as a violation of the establishment clause if the essential *effect* of the action is to influence, either positively or negatively,[3] the pursuit of a religious tradition or the expression of a religious belief.

The religion clauses absolutely prohibit three sorts of effects, discussed elsewhere in this chapter: the state's discriminating among different denominations, except as a consequence of lifting a government-imposed burden on free exercise [4]; the state's lending its powers to religious bodies [5]; and the state's borrowing the aura of legitimacy from religion.[6] This section will discuss the range of cases where no

---

56. See §§ 14–14, 14–15, infra.

§ 14–10

1. In order to prevail against a free exercise claimant, the state must show that the challenged policy pursues an unusually important end, and that creating an exemption would undercut the policy. See § 14–13, infra. "Unusually important" almost certainly implies secular, but obviously not all secular ends will qualify as unusually important. At this point, the clauses diverge further. If, under the free exercise clause, the state succeeds in making that showing, then its policy may continue to operate without religious exemptions, even though it imposes a burden on some people's religious practices—a primary religious effect, at least to the people burdened. Under the establishment clause, in contrast, any primary religious effect constitutes a per se violation.

2. The only exceptions are statutes that raise government-imposed burdens on free exercise. Such statutes will invariably have a primary religious effect, but such an effect should not cause courts to strike them down. See § 14–7, supra.

3. Although most establishment clause cases concern benefits to religion, the clause also forbids burdens whose primary impact is on religion. See Tony and Susan Alamo Found. v. Secretary of Labor, 471 U.S. 290, 305–06 (1985) (considering and rejecting, on the facts, argument that labor regulations created anti-religious primary effect as applied to religious organization).

See also Larson v. Valente, 456 U.S. 228, 244 (1982) (establishment clause prohibits burdens that fall on some but not all religions) (case applying strict scrutiny analysis, rather than traditional establishment clause tests), see § 14–7, supra; Lemon v. Kurtzman, 403 U.S. 602, 612 (1971) (in order to pass "effects" test, a statute's "principal or primary effect must be one that neither advances *nor inhibits* religion") (emphasis added). Thus it is plausible that religious adherents or organizations may be able to use the establishment clause, as well as the free exercise clause, in opposing statutes whose primary effects are anti-religious. Compare Esbeck, "Establishment Clause Limits on Governmental Interference With Religious Organizations," 41 Wash. & Lee L.Rev. 347 (1984) (establishment clause should be construed to protect religious organizations), with Marshall & Blomgren, "Regulating Religious Organizations Under the Establishment Clause," 47 Ohio St. L.J. (1986) (establishment clause should not be construed in such a way). Cf. § 14–11, infra (discussing the doctrine of "regulatory entanglement," under which religious organizations use the third establishment clause inquiry, impermissible church-state entanglement, to seek exemptions from burdensome state regulatory schemes).

4. See § 14–7, supra.

5. See § 14–14, infra.

6. See § 14–15, infra.

such categorical imperatives apply, such that the courts must weigh secular against non-secular effects in order to determine which are "primary."

As the secular effect requirement has developed, the premise of governmental neutrality in religious matters has generally been held to imply that, while no law may be passed whose primary effect is to aid a particular religion or even religion in general, a law may not be struck down simply because the secular effects government seeks to produce (for example, fire and police protection) happen to be realized in a religious context (for example, preventing arson of a church or robbery of a priest).[7] To strike down a public choice on the sole ground that it incidentally makes religious actions easier or less costly would clearly be to single out religious groups for hostile treatment, contrary to the mandate of the first amendment's free exercise clause: "That Amendment requires the state to be a neutral in its relations with groups of religious believers and non-believers; it does not require the state to be their adversary. State power is no more to be used so as to handicap religions than it is to favor them."[8]

When a governmental policy has both secular and religious effects, as in the case of aid to parochial schools, the Supreme Court has increasingly sought to avoid any attempt to determine which of the effects is "primary" and which "secondary." Denying that "such metaphysical judgments are either possible or necessary,"[9] the Court has substituted an almost equally metaphysical distinction between direct and immediate effects on the one hand and effects deemed indirect and incidental on the other: "Our cases simply do not support the notion that a law found to have a 'primary' effect to promote some legitimate and under the State's police power is immune from further examination to ascertain whether it also has the direct and immediate effect of advancing religion."[10] The constitutional requirement of "primary secular effect" has thus become a misnomer; while retaining the earlier label, the Court has transformed it into a *requirement that any non-secular effect be remote, indirect and incidental.* This shift is

---

7. One commentator calls this principle "political neutrality" as opposed to "free exercise neutrality." The latter may justify exempting a person from legal requirements on religious grounds, while the former forbids depriving persons or groups of "those benefits that are generally available as a by-product of organized society." Giannella, "Religious Liberty, Non-Establishment, and Doctrinal Development: Part II, The Non-Establishment Principle," 81 Harv.L.Rev. 513, 521 (1968). See § 14–7, infra.

8. Everson v. Board of Education, 330 U.S. 1, 18 (1947). But see Grand Rapids School Dist. v. Ball, 473 U.S. 373, 393–94 & n.12 (1985) ("indirect subsidy" may still create impermissible effects) (discussed below).

9. Committee for Public Education v. Nyquist, 413 U.S. 756, 783–84 n.39 (1973).

10. Id. The Court introduced yet another metaphysical distinction in Corporation of the Presiding Bishop of the Church of Jesus Christ of Latter-Day Saints v. Amos, 107 S.Ct. 2862 (1987): "A law is not unconstitutional simply because it *allows* churches to advance religion, which is their very purpose. For a law to have forbidden 'effects' under *Lemon*, it must be fair to say that the *government itself* has advanced religion through its own activities and influence." Id. at 2868–69 (emphasis in original). As Justice O'Connor responded, the distinction seems "to obscure far more than to enlighten," id. at 2874 (O'Connor, J., concurring in the judgment). Taken literally, the majority's distinction would render the effects test virtually meaningless, but it seems unlikely that the Court will apply it in such a stark fashion. Amos is discussed in § 14–7, supra.

analytically significant, for the remote-indirect-and-incidental standard plainly compels a more searching inquiry, and comes closer to the absolutist no-aid approach to the establishment clause than the primary effect test did. In practice, however, the formulation has not always resulted in a particularly searching inquiry, and a number of forms of aid have survived.[11]

In deciding whether a program or regulation has a sufficiently secular effect, the Court has asked whether the secular impact is sufficiently *separable* from the religious, and whether the class benefited is sufficiently *broad*. Thus, even when plainly motivated by secular purposes, government may not ordinarily act so as to support practices or rituals whose religious aspects are inseparable from the secular benefits government seeks. The establishment clause has accordingly been held to forbid even nominally voluntary religious exercises in public schools where such exercises take the form not of merely historical Bible study but rather of religious indoctrination,[12] of government-composed prayers,[13] or of non-sectarian readings from the Bible.[14] In each instance, although there might be a secular purpose, the direct sponsorship of indisputably religious activities in public schools has been held to violate the primary effect standard.[15]

An important element of separability is whether the aid to religion results from the direct, private choices of individuals. A group of people might, for example, announce that they plan to sign over their tax refund checks to their churches. For the Treasury Department to issue the checks will clearly advance religion, but it will do so through individuals' decisions rather than through state action. *Witters v. Washington Department of Services for the Blind* [16] illustrates this principle. Witters's application for vocational rehabilitation training had been denied because his course of study, at a Christian college, was preparing him for a religious career. Permitting such aid, in the state court's view, would have the primary effect of advancing religion.[17]

11. In many cases, a denominational neutrality approach would have led to the same result as the effects inquiry. Classroom Bible readings, for example, favor Christians over non-Christians. See § 14–7, supra.

12. Illinois ex rel. McCollum v. Board of Education, 333 U.S. 203 (1948).

13. Engel v. Vitale, 370 U.S. 421 (1962).

14. Abington School Dist. v. Schempp, 374 U.S. 203 (1963).

15. Given these principal cases, it is interesting to note that the Supreme Court has frequently expressed the view that the establishment clause is *not* offended by opening prayers in Congress, by the inclusion of such mottos as "In God We Trust" on United States coins, or by the persistence of the ceremony opening the Supreme Court's sessions with a phrase "which invokes the grace of God." Abington School Dist., 374 U.S. at 213. See also Lynch v. Donnelly, 465 U.S. 668 (1984)

(upholding inclusion of crèche in city-sponsored Christmas display); Marsh v. Chambers, 463 U.S. 783 (1983) (upholding legislative prayers); Engel v. Vitale, 370 U.S. 421, 435 n.21 (1962) (students singing anthems that refer to God, and other such "patriotic or ceremonial occasions, bear no true resemblance to the unquestioned religious exercise that the State of New York has sponsored in this instance"). This may reflect the judgment that, because of their central and delicate role in American life, public schools must be thoroughly insulated from religious ceremony under the aegis of the establishment clause. See also § 14–15, infra.

16. 106 S.Ct. 748 (1986).

17. The state supreme court's decision stemmed from its wrongly narrow focus. In measuring the non-secular effect, it looked solely at the effect on the petitioner, which was indisputably religious. Id. at 750 (citing Witters v. Washington Dep't of

The Supreme Court unanimously reversed the decision, finding that "[a]ny aid provided under Washington's program that ultimately flows to religious institutions does so only as a result of the genuinely independent and private choices of aid recipients." [18]

If the result truly does flow from private choices, then the amount or proportion of aid to religion ought to be irrelevant. In our hypothetical, the Treasury Department would not be able to withhold tax refunds even if every citizen announced an intention to donate the money to religion. The Court adopted this view in *Mueller v. Allen*, writing: "We would be loath to adopt a rule grounding the constitutionality of a facially neutral law on annual reports reciting the extent to which various classes of private citizens claimed benefits under the law." [19] Elsewhere, however, the Court has indicated that large-scale aid to religious institutions, even if mediated through individual choices, may create an impermissible effect.[20] The *Mueller* view seems wiser, at least so long as the statute, and the choices it presents, can reasonably be called neutral.[21] In determining whether a program is neutral, the separability and the breadth inquiries both apply.[22] A program that offered free communion wine and wafers to any individual or organization, for example, would be impermissible. In order to help establish the program's non-neutrality, it would be relevant that

Services for the Blind, 102 Wn.2d 624, 689 P.2d 53, 56 (1984)). "In effect, the court analyzed the case as if the Washington legislature had passed a private bill that awarded respondent free tuition to pursue his religious studies." Id. at 754 (Powell, J., concurring). Instead, the court should have examined the overall effect of the aid program, which was predominantly non-religious.

18. Id. at 752. See also Mueller v. Allen, 463 U.S. 388, 399 (1983) (non-secular effects requirement not violated where benefit to religion stems from "numerous, private choices of individual parents"); Widmar v. Vincent, 454 U.S. 263, 274 (1981) (requirement not violated by college's permitting religious groups to use public forum, because no "imprimatur of state approval" as conveyed and because the forum is open to a broad class of groups); Reuben Quick Bear v. Leupp, 210 U.S. 50 (1908) (treaty money, held in trust by federal government for Indians, could at Indians' designation be given to private religious schools to pay for education).

19. 463 U.S. at 401. See also Witters, 106 S.Ct. at 754 n.3 (Powell, J., concurring) (conclusion that program does not have impermissible non-secular effects "does not depend on the fact that respondent appears to be the only handicapped student who has sought to use his assistance to pursue religious training").

20. See Witters, 106 S.Ct. at 752 ("importantly, nothing in the record indicates that, if petitioner succeeds, any significant portion of the aid expended under the Washington program as a whole will end up flowing to religious education"); Widmar v. Vincent, 454 U.S. at 275 ("At least in the absence of empirical evidence that religious groups will dominate [the university's] open forum, we agree . . . that the advancement of religion would not be the forum's 'primary effect.' "). Cf. Mueller v. Allen, 463 U.S. at 409–10 & n.4 (Marshall, J., dissenting) (discussing parochial school cases where Court had taken into account the fact that most of the aid went to religious schools). The Witters majority opinion omitted Mueller from its discussion, prompting criticism from five of the Justices. See 106 S.Ct. at 753 (White, J., concurring); id at 753–54 (Powell, J., joined by Burger, C.J., and Rehnquist, J., concurring); id. at 755 (O'Connor, J., concurring).

21. See Mueller, 463 U.S. at 401 ("[T]he fact that private persons fail in a particular year to claim the tax relief to which they are entitled—under a facially neutral statute—should be of little importance in determining the constitutionality of the statute permitting such relief.").

22. Mueller suggests that breadth, although irrelevant in considering who claims benefits from the tuition deduction, *is* relevant in viewing the deduction in context, as part of the overall tax scheme. The Court considered the fact that the tuition deduction was "only one among many deductions" to be "an essential feature" of the program. 463 U.S. at 396.

the benefit, although theoretically available to everyone, would predictably be claimed principally by members of particular religions.

The Court's inquiry into separability has extended into cases dealing with facilitative programs, either in cash or in services, that might be seen as subsidies of religion. The paradigmatic case of this type is that of aid to schools. Two Supreme Court holdings summarize much of the law in this area. In *Roemer v. Board of Public Works of Maryland*,[23] the Court examined a Maryland statute which authorized the payment of state funds to any private institution of higher learning within the state which met certain minimum criteria and which awarded more than just seminarian or theological degrees. The aid took the form of an annual subsidy to qualifying colleges and universities, based upon the number of students excluding those in seminarian or theological academic programs. The grants were non-categorical but could not, under a provision added in 1972, be utilized by the institutions for sectarian purposes. At the end of each fiscal year, the recipient institution was required to make a report separately identifying the aided non-sectarian expenditures, subject to a state board's verification if necessary. The Court found that, despite their formal affiliation with the Roman Catholic Church, the aided colleges were not "pervasively sectarian." [24] The Court also found that aid was in fact extended to the secular side and did not have the primary effect of advancing religion.[25] The colleges, as the Court found, performed "essentially secular educational functions," and the state could identify and subsidize such separate, secular functions without on-site inspections.[26]

In *Wolman v. Walter*,[27] decided the following year, the Court took a different approach in considering an Ohio statute which provided several forms of aid to nonpublic schools and their pupils. The Court upheld the state's textbook loan program and its programs for providing standardized testing and scoring as well as diagnostic services on parochial school premises, in addition to its program for providing therapeutic, guidance, and remedial services off parochial school premises. But the Court invalidated the state's program for lending instructional materials and equipment to pupils at nonpublic schools as well as its program to pay for field trips by pupils at such schools. Although prior decisions had permitted the states to supply bus transportation [28]

23. 426 U.S. 736 (1976).

24. Id. at 755 (plurality opinion). The Court indicated that a pervasively sectarian school was one in which "secular activities cannot be separated from sectarian ones." Id. The colleges in question were not of that sort: none of the colleges received funds from, or reported to, the church; attendance at religious functions was not mandatory; though theology courses were required, they only supplemented a broad liberal arts curriculum; apart from theology departments, faculty hiring decisions were not based on religion;

and students were not chosen on the basis of their religion. Id. at 755–59 (plurality).

25. Id. at 745–47, 755–59 (plurality).

26. Id. at 761–67 (plurality). See also Tilton v. Richardson, 403 U.S. 672 (1971), and Hunt v. McNair, 413 U.S. 734 (1973), upholding federal and state financial aid to church-related colleges for the construction of buildings to be used for secular purposes only.

27. 433 U.S. 229 (1977).

28. Everson v. Board of Education, 330 U.S. 1 (1947).

and secular textbooks [29] on an equal basis to children attending public and private (including parochial) schools and had disallowed attempts to provide certain instructional materials and auxiliary services to nonpublic schools,[30] *Roemer, Wolman,* and subsequent cases have settled a number of previously open questions. Although the results in these parochial school cases sometimes seem arbitrary,[31] the decisions indicate five factors that are often relevant and sometimes dispositive.

First, if equipment or materials are to be supplied or lent at public expense, they must be supplied only to pupils or their parents and not to parochial schools themselves. Insofar as textbooks are truly used by individual schoolchildren, they may be provided even if they are at times stored on parochial school premises.[32] But such equipment as projectors, tape recorders, maps and globes, science kits, blackboards, and the like are too integral a part of the school itself to be supplied at public expense, even if the equipment is formally loaned to pupils or to parents and is simply "used" at school.[33]

Second, if services are to be supplied at public expense, they must be supplied by personnel not subject to parochial school control,[34] and their content cannot be subject to specification by parochial school teachers or administrators. Thus church-sponsored schools cannot be reimbursed for the costs of teacher-prepared testing,[35] and public funds cannot be used to pay for field trips whose destinations are controlled by parochial school teachers and on which such teachers accompany the pupils.[36] But state funds may permissibly reimburse schools for essentially ministerial tasks carried out by parochial school teachers.[37]

Third, publicly funded services cannot be provided to schoolchildren on parochial school premises if such services afford opportunity for anything beyond the most impersonal and limited contact with the

29. Board of Education v. Allen, 392 U.S. 236 (1968); Meek v. Pittenger, 421 U.S. 349 (1975).

30. Meek v. Pittenger, 421 U.S. 349.

31. Then Justice Rehnquist summarized the case law (as of 1985) as follows: "[A] State may lend to parochial school children geography textbooks that contain maps of the United States, but the State may not lend maps of the United States for use in geography class. A State may lend textbooks on American colonial history, but it may not lend a film on George Washington, or a film projector to show it in history class. A State may lend classroom workbooks, but may not lend workbooks in which the parochial school children write, thus rendering them nonreusable. A State may pay for bus transportation to religious schools but may not pay for bus transportation from the parochial school to the public zoo or natural history museum for a field trip. A State may pay for diagnostic services conducted in the parochial school but therapeutic services must be given in a different building; speech and hearing 'services' conducted by the State inside the sectarian school are forbidden, but the State may conduct speech and hearing diagnostic testing inside the sectarian school. Exceptional parochial school students may receive counseling, but it must take place outside of the parochial school, such as in a trailer parked down the street. A State may give cash to a parochial school to pay for the administration of state-written tests and state-ordered reporting services, but it may not provide funds for teacher-prepared tests on secular subjects." Wallace v. Jaffree, 472 U.S. 38, 110–11 (1985) (Rehnquist, J., dissenting) (footnotes and citations omitted).

32. See id. at 379 (Brennan, J., dissenting in part).

33. Wolman, 433 U.S. at 248–49.

34. See Lemon v. Kurtzman, 403 U.S. 602 (1971).

35. Levitt v. Committee for Public Education, 413 U.S. 472 (1973).

36. Wolman, 433 U.S. at 252–53.

37. Committee for Public Educ. v. Regan, 444 U.S. 646 (1980).

child. " 'The State must be certain, given the Religion Clauses, that subsidized teachers do not inculcate religion.' " [38] The Court has discerned two dangers in more extensive contacts between state-paid service-providers and parochial school students: that the students may perceive a symbolic link between government and religion, and that the religious setting may cause the service-providers to transmit sectarian views to the students.[39] Thus therapeutic, guidance, and remedial services, as well as enrichment and supplementary classes, must be provided off the parochial school premises, "at truly religiously neutral locations." [40] However, standardized testing and scoring, as well as speech, hearing, and psychological diagnostic services, may be provided on parochial school premises.[41] Also, the more personal contacts between student and service-provider, which may not take place on the parochial school's campus, *may* permissibly take place close by, even if the result is that a particular location serves only parochial school pupils.[42] This is permissible because, in the Court's eyes, the dangers arise from the parochial school as an institution, rather than from the students as individuals.

Fourth, the *form* in which aid is given may be decisive. As noted above, aid that results from individual choices, and only indirectly through government action, is generally permissible. At the other extreme, the Court has repeatedly struck down programs that directly paid government funds to religious schools.[43] The Court has sometimes found aid more palatable when it flows directly to students or parents rather than to schools.[44]

Finally, as *Roemer* illustrates, the Court has been more willing to find a secular purpose in programs benefiting religious colleges than in those benefiting religious grade schools and secondary schools. In part the distinction is based on different assumptions about the institutions. The Court has frequently asserted that parochial schools are "pervasively sectarian," but it has not applied the same conclusion to colleges.[45] The different treatment is also based on the age of the students

---

38. Grand Rapids School Dist. v. Ball, 473 U.S. 373, 385 (1985) (quoting Lemon v. Kurtzman, 403 U.S. 602, 619 (1971)).

39. See Grand Rapids, 473 U.S. at 386–87, 389, 397. The Court has applied the latter requirement to parochial school employees paid with state funds and, more dubiously, to public schoolteachers brought into parochial schools to teach special classes.

40. Wolman, 433 U.S. at 247. See also Grand Rapids, 473 U.S. at 384–98; Meek v. Pittenger, 421 U.S. 349 (1975).

41. Wolman, 433 U.S. at 238–44. As in every case of permissible service-provision, the Court required that the service be identical to that provided in public schools.

42. Wolman, 433 U.S. at 247.

43. The one exception is Committee for Public Education v. Regan, 444 U.S. 646 (1980) (upholding state payments to non-

public schools for costs of complying with state-mandated testing and other requirements). See Grand Rapids, 473 U.S. at 393 (listing cases).

44. See Board of Education v. Allen, 392 U.S. 236, 243–44 (1968) (in program that lent books to students, "no funds or books are furnished to parochial schools, and the financial benefit is to parents and children, not to schools"). But see Grand Rapids, 473 U.S. at 396 ("Where, as here, no meaningful distinction can be made between aid to the student and aid to the school, 'the concept of a loan to individuals is a transparent fiction.' ") (quoting Wolman, 433 U.S. at 264 (Powell, J., concurring in part and dissenting in part)).

45. This is not to say that any form of aid to a religious college is permissible. In Tilton v. Richardson, 403 U.S. 672 (1971), the Court sustained most aspects of a federal aid program concerning church-affili-

involved: Young students are thought to be likely to misinterpret state aid, seeing it as signaling an alliance between government and religion.[46]

Another reason that religious colleges are treated differently from parochial schools is the *public's* view of the aid programs. Aid for secular programs in all colleges, including those with church affiliation, is generally perceived as assistance to non-religious activities. But the moment aid is sent to a parochial school as such, it is widely seen as aid to religion. The number of dollars released for religious purposes may be identical; the symbolism is not. The public perception is probably based partly on the fact that, whereas most nonpublic primary and secondary schools are religious, most nonpublic colleges are non-religious. Here we reach the second major element of secular effect: breadth.

In defining secular effect, inquiry into the *breadth of the class benefited* has augmented the concern with separability; however separable from religion the benefited aspect of an enterprise might be, the government's policy is frequently unconstitutional unless religious enterprises are benefited no more than, and only as part of, some much broader category.[47] Thus generalized government activities or exemptions not aimed specifically at religious groups or institutions, but assisting them only as part of a far wider group, have been deemed to benefit religion indirectly enough to meet the "primary secular effect" requirement.[48] Again, what turns on the breadth of the benefited class

ated colleges, but it struck down the portion that permitted the colleges ultimately to assume total control over the use of buildings constructed partly with federal funds. Id. at 683. Thus, although church-related colleges are generally not considered pervasively religious, the state still may not underwrite the institutions' non-secular activities.

46. Compare Grand Rapids School Dist. v. Ball, 473 U.S. at 390 ("The symbolism of a union between church and state is most likely to influence children of tender years, whose experience is limited and whose beliefs consequently are the function of environment as much as of free and voluntary choice."), with Widmar v. Vincent, 454 U.S. at 274 n.14 ("University students are, of course, young adults. They are less impressionable than younger students and should be able to appreciate that the University's policy is one of neutrality toward religion."). See § 14–5, n.53, supra.

47. But not invariably. See Corporation of the Presiding Bishop of the Church of Jesus Christ of Latter-Day Saints v. Amos, 107 S.Ct. 2862, 2869 (1987) ("Although the Court has given weight to this consideration in its past decisions . . . it has never indicated that statutes that give special consideration to religious groups are *per se* invalid. . . . Where, as here, government acts with the proper purpose

of lifting a regulation that burdens the exercise of religion, we see no reason to require that the exemption comes packaged with benefits to secular entities."). Amos is discussed in § 14–7, supra. When it does apply, the breadth inquiry looks at the program as a whole, and not just at its impact on the party before the Court. That is, a program is permissible even if its sole impact on an individual is to facilitate religious exercises, so long as its overall effect is acceptably secular. See Witters, 106 S.Ct. at 754 (Powell, J., concurring). Cf. Lynch v. Donnelly, 465 U.S. 668, 680 (1984) ("The District Court plainly erred by focusing almost exclusively on the crèche.").

48. One commentator has suggested that the breadth of the benefiting class may determine whether aid is forbidden by the establishment clause, or required by the free exercise clause, or left to state discretion. Mansfield, "The Religion Clauses of the First Amendment and the Philosophy of the Constitution," 72 Cal.L. Rev. 847, 878 (1984) ("In Walz [v. Tax Comm'n, 397 U.S. 664 (1970)], property used for religious purposes was exempted along with property used for a variety of other activities. . . . [H]ad the list of exempt activities been shorter, it might have been impermissible to exempt reli-

is not dollars—the amount of aid plainly does not depend on how many others also receive it—but symbols: the broader the class benefited, the less likely it is that the program will be perceived as aid to religion, and the less likely it is that the program will be invoked first as precedent for more religious aid, then for strings attached to aid dollars, and eventually for pervasive government involvement in matters of the spirit.

Thus the narrowness of the benefited class was a key factor in *Committee for Public Education v. Nyquist*,[49] which struck down a tax relief program for the parents of New York's nonpublic school children: parochial school children composed over 80% of the benefited class. As discussed above, *Mueller* indicates that the breadth inquiry is inapplicable where aid flows through genuinely free, private decisions based on a neutral statute. Although both cases concerned tax benefits, the *Nyquist* Court concluded that the benefits at issue there actually amounted to tuition grants, and that they were available only to parents of private school children.[50] These factors cast doubt on whether the *Mueller* approach would change *Nyquist*'s outcome, if the latter case arose today. It is at least arguable that the choices were neither private, given the tuition-grant nature of the program, nor free, given the limited availability of the benefits. In contrast, the *Mueller* benefits looked more like traditional tax deductions, and they were available to all parents. As the Court wrote in *Widmar v. Vincent*, "The provision of benefits to so broad a spectrum . . . is an important index of secular effect."[51]

This aspect of the breadth element helps clarify the controversial issue of educational vouchers. In *Nyquist*, the Court distinguished two precedents[52] on the ground that the class benefited in those cases "included *all* school children, those in public as well as those in private schools."[53] Similarly, the Court has struck down a program to provide auxiliary services to non-public school students only,[54] and it has summarily affirmed a lower court's invalidation of a program which lent books to public school children, but which reimbursed parents of private school children for the purchase of secular, non-ideological books.[55]

---

gion, and had the list been longer, it might have been required.").

49. 413 U.S. 756, 768 (1973).

50. The Court in Nyquist construed the benefits as falling outside the tax system, and it expressly reserved the question of the constitutionality of a "genuine tax deduction." 413 U.S. at 790 n.49.

51. 454 U.S. 263, 274 (1981) (striking down, on free speech grounds, university's rule that religious groups could not enjoy benefits accorded to non-religious groups; and rejecting university's claim that the content discrimination was necessary in order to comply with the establishment clause).

52. Board of Education v. Allen, 392 U.S. 236 (1968) (permitting textbook loans to parochial school children); Everson v. Board of Education, 330 U.S. 1 (1947) (permitting busing of parochial school children to and from school).

53. Nyquist, 413 U.S. at 782 n.38 (emphasis in original).

54. Meek v. Pittenger, 421 U.S. 349 (1975).

55. Public Funds for Public Schools v. Marburger, 358 F.Supp. 29 (D.N.J. 1973), aff'd mem. 417 U.S. 961 (1974). It is also noteworthy that the majority opinion in Everson v. Board of Education, 330 U.S. 1 (1947), might have gained additional support (it was a 5–4 decision) if the program had appeared to apply to all students. Two dissenting Justices believed that the program extended only to public and Cath-

Where aid has been available to public and non-public students alike, as would be the case under some voucher programs, the Court has been more favorable. This element is central to the Court's holding in *Mueller*—even though the public school students who paid tuition (and thus who would benefit from the deduction), those who attended a school outside their district, constituted a small proportion of total beneficiaries. *Witters*, although dealing with higher education, is also relevant, particularly because five Justices agreed that individuals' private choices eliminate any impermissible effects.[56] These decisions suggest that the Court would uphold an educational voucher scheme that would permit parents to decide which schools, public or private, their children should attend.[57] The establishment clause probably would not stand as an obstacle to a purely neutral program, at least one with a broad enough class of beneficiary schools and one that channeled aid through parents and children rather than directly to schools.[58]

The breadth of the class benefited has also been a consideration in areas beyond school aid. As part of a more general program of tax relief to all educational and charitable non-profit institutions, for example, a state may exempt non-profit church property from taxation.[59] In so holding, the Supreme Court in *Walz v. Tax Commission* stressed that the state, far from singling out "one particular church . . . or even churches as such," had "granted exemption to all houses of religious worship within a broad class of property owned by non-profit quasi-public corporations which include hospitals, libraries, playgrounds, scientific, professional, historical and patriotic groups." [60] Yet when a tax exemption is granted to a religious organization, especially if the exemption extends to commercial activities conducted by that organization, the situation bears an unsettling resemblance to a forbidden cash grant to a religion. It may nonetheless be sound to draw the line of acceptability so as to permit such exemptions because of the church-state entanglement that could be encountered in any attempt to tax religion, including religiously owned commercial enterprises.[61]

olic parochial school students, and not to *all* public and private school students. Id. at 18 (Jackson, J., dissenting, joined by Frankfurter, J.).

56. See 106 S.Ct. at 754 (Powell, J., joined by Burger, C.J., and Rehnquist, J., concurring) ("state programs that are wholly neutral in offering educational assistance to a class defined without reference to religion do not violate the second part of the *Lemon v. Kurtzman* test, because any aid to religion results from the private choices of individual beneficiaries") (footnote omitted); id. at 753 (White, J., concurring) (agreeing with Powell opinion); id. at 755 (O'Connor, J., concurring in judgment and concurring in part) (same).

57. The one probable exception is racially discriminatory private schools. See Norwood v. Harrison, 413 U.S. 455 (1973) (holding book lending program violative of

equal protection insofar as it aided racially discriminatory private schools).

58. But see Grand Rapids, 473 U.S. at 397 (noting as "cardinal principle" that "the State may not in effect become the prime supporter of the religious school system").

59. Walz v. Tax Commission, 397 U.S. 664 (1970).

60. Id. at 673. See note 48, supra.

61. See § 14–11, infra. If the society decides that all enterprises whose dominant purpose is charitable (but which nonetheless own profit-generating ventures which support their charitable activities) should be granted an exemption for all their activities, there seems no strong reason to withhold such beneficial treatment from charitable institutions which are religious in character. This may give the ex-

Justice O'Connor has suggested that the effects test be considered through the framework of endorsement. "Endorsement sends a message to nonadherents that they are outsiders, not full members of the political community, and an accompanying message to adherents that they are insiders, favored members of the political community." [62] Endorsement, in turn, is measured from the perspective of an objective observer, familiar with free exercise values.[63] An endorsement perspective comprises both separability and breadth. From one perspective, separability's most important aspect is the subjective understanding of the individuals affected, particularly school children, as to endorsement; and breadth's most important aspect is the objective understanding of the community as to endorsement.

The endorsement approach, which the Court has noted approvingly,[64] helps explain cases like *Bradfield v. Roberts*,[65] where the Court sustained federal financial support of a hospital owned and operated by an order of Catholic nuns. Even more clearly than in the case of a college, a hospital that serves all without regard to religion may be assisted without any affront to the public commitment to non-establishment, despite the fact that dollars, as always, are released for potential religious uses.

History is often an important element of such perceptions.[66] Thus the endorsement approach helps explain cases where the Court has upheld long-established state practices that began in religion, such as Sunday closing laws,[67] and practices that acknowledge religion, such as legislative prayers [68] and state-owned crèches.[69] Such holdings may be viewed as reflecting in part the Court's sense that such policies simply do not seem religious in the public consciousness.[70] But the public

empted commercial aspects a comparative advantage over commercial competition not linked to any charitable body, and some may perceive this to be a symbolic support of religion, but the entanglement dangers of taxing religion are probably great enough to overcome this concern.

62. Lynch v. Donnelly, 465 U.S. 668, 688 (1984) (O'Connor, J., concurring). See also Wallace v. Jaffree, 472 U.S. 38, 69 (1985) (O'Connor, J., concurring in judgment). See § 14–15, infra.

63. Wallace v. Jaffree, 472 U.S. at 83 (O'Connor, J., concurring in judgment).

64. See, e.g., Witters v. Washington Dep't of Services for the Blind, 474 U.S. 481, (1986) (petitioner's decision to use neutrally available state aid for a religious education does not convey a message of endorsement); Grand Rapids School Dist. v. Ball, 473 U.S. 373, 389 (1985) (when government conveys a message of endorsement or disapproval of religion, "a core purpose of the Establishment Clause is violated"). Several earlier cases adopted a similar perspective, asking whether a government practice provided a symbolic benefit or sign of approval to religion. See, e.g., Larkin v. Grendel's Den, Inc., 459 U.S.

116, 125–26 (1982) ("the mere appearance of a joint exercise of legislative authority by Church and State provides a significant symbolic benefit to religion in the minds of some"); Widmar v. Vincent, 454 U.S. 263, 274 (1981) ("an open forum in a public university does not confer any imprimatur of state approval on religious sects or practices").

65. 175 U.S. 291 (1899).

66. Compare Walz v. Tax Comm'n, 397 U.S. 664, 678 (1970) (noting that, if tax exemptions for church property were a "first step" toward the evils of religious establishment, "the second step has been long in coming"), with Committee for Public Education v. Nyquist, 413 U.S. 756, 792 (1973) (noting that Court was unaware of any "historical precedent for New York's recently promulgated tax relief program").

67. McGowan v. Maryland, 366 U.S. 420 (1961).

68. Marsh v. Chambers, 463 U.S. 783 (1983).

69. Lynch v. Donnelly, 465 U.S. 668 (1984).

70. See § 14–15, infra.

consciousness certainly should not be allowed to supplant the first amendment's principles. It is here that the perspective of an objective observer, able to step back from the conventional understanding of the majority and to comprehend the viewpoint of the minority, is particularly important.[71]

Of course, neither separability nor breadth can alter the reality that aid to religious organizations, however indirect and limited, benefits the organizations' sectarian aspects, if only by easing their total budgetary burden. The Court has almost invariably recognized that such benefits are inevitable and permissible. "The Court 'has not accepted the recurrent argument that all aid is forbidden because aid to one aspect of an institution frees it to spend its other resources on religious ends.' "[72] In one recent case, however, the Court suggested that such "indirect subsidies" may generate impermissible effects in one subset of cases, those concerning pervasively religious institutions.[73] In *Grand Rapids School District v. Ball*, the Court feared that, if the state were permitted to take over part of the non-secular teaching requirements at parochial schools, "no principled basis" would exist for preventing the state from taking on all such requirements. "To let the genie out of the bottle in this case would be to permit ever larger segments of the religious school curriculum to be turned over [to] the public school system, thus violating the cardinal principle that the State may not in effect become the prime supporter of the religious school system."[74]

If taken literally, this "cardinal principle" might strike down even purely neutral voucher plans. The principle, however, seems dubious. Imagine, for example, that a parochial school decides to operate only as a released-time facility, to which students will come for religious

71. It can be argued that Justice O'Connor's Lynch opinion asked the right question but produced the wrong answer. See Lynch, 465 U.S. at 701 (Brennan, J., dissenting) ("The effect [of a city-sponsored crèche] on minority religious groups, as well as on those who may reject all religion, is to convey the message that their views are not similarly worthy of public recognition nor entitled to public support."). See also § 14–15, infra.

72. Committee for Public Educ. v. Regan, 444 U.S. 646, 658 (1980) (quoting Hunt v. McNair, 413 U.S. 734, 743 (1973)). See also Corporation of the Presiding Bishop of the Church of Jesus Christ of Latter-Day Saints v. Amos, 107 S.Ct. 2862, 2868 (1987) ("religious groups have been better able to advance their purposes on account of many laws that have passed constitutional muster"); Widmar v. Vincent, 454 U.S. 263, 275 n.15 (1981) (also quoting Hunt v. McNair); Roemer, 426 U.S. at 747 ("The Court has not been blind to the fact that in aiding a religious institution to perform a secular task, the State frees the institution's resources to be put to sectarian ends."); Board of Educ. v. Allen, 392 U.S.

236, 244 (1968) ("Perhaps free books make it more likely that some children choose to attend a sectarian school, but that . . . does not alone demonstrate an unconstitutional degree of support for a religious institution.").

73. See Grand Rapids School Dist. v. Ball, 473 U.S. 373, 394 n.12 (1985) ("This 'indirect subsidy' effect only evokes Establishment Clause concerns when the public funds flow to 'an institution in which religion is so pervasive that a substantial portion of its functions are subsumed in the religious mission. . . .' ") (quoting Hunt v. McNair, 413 U.S. 734, 743 (1973)).

74. Grand Rapids, 473 U.S. at 397 (citation omitted). See also Aguilar v. Felton, 473 U.S. 402, 417 (1985) (Powell, J., concurring) ("[B]y directly assuming part of the parochial schools' education function, the effect of the Title I aid is 'inevitably . . . to subsidize and advance the religious mission of [the] sectarian schools,' even though the program provides that only secular subjects will be taught.") (citation omitted) (quoting Committee for Public Educ. v. Nyquist, 413 U.S. 756, 779–80 (1973)).

training each day after they have studied the required, secular subjects in public school.[75] The effect—the state's take-over of secular requirements, thereby aiding religion—is no different from what was feared in *Grand Rapids*. The same is true where public employees teach classes off the parochial school's campus. Also, parochial school officials might plausibly argue that the state at present is a significant *hindrance* to the religious school system, in imposing curricular, attendance, record-keeping, and other requirements. Thus state aid partly lifts a burden that the state itself has imposed. If the state may permissibly pay the costs of administrative and testing requirements, as the Court has held,[76] then why may it not undertake to perform curricular requirements itself? The distinction seems hollow. Thus it seems unlikely that the Court will follow the extreme path charted in *Grand Rapids*.

Another tension illustrated by *Grand Rapids*, however, is likely to remain a part of establishment clause jurisprudence. Where state aid, by its nature, might be used either for secular or for non-secular purposes, the Court requires mechanisms to ensure that the aid is used for secular purposes alone. In *Grand Rapids*, for instance, the Court struck down two state teaching programs, conducted on the parochial school campus, because the classes were "not specifically monitored for religious content."[77] But in *Aguilar v. Felton*,[78] the Court struck down a parochial school aid program *because* of its monitoring mechanism. The reason, the entanglement inquiry, is the topic of the next section.

§ 14–11. The Requirement of No Excessive Entanglement

The doctrines that prohibit excessive church-state entanglement reflect the Madisonian concern that secular and religious authorities must not interfere with each other's respective spheres of choice and influence. This "jurisdictional" principle [1] stems from the fears that church-state entanglement might strain the political system,[2] compromise liberty of conscience for both adherents and nonadherents,[3] and, ultimately, "destroy government and degrade religion."[4]

Entanglement forms the basis of five first amendment doctrines: (1) In challenges to government action under the establishment clause, the action is unconstitutional if it creates excessive administrative entanglement between church and state. (2) Under the establishment clause, the action is also unconstitutional if it turns over traditionally governmental powers to religious institutions. (3) In establishment clause challenges, the challenged action is subjected to stricter scrutiny if it breeds religiously based political divisiveness. (4) In seeking a

75. See § 14–5, supra.

76. Committee for Public Educ. v. Regan, 444 U.S. 646 (1980).

77. 473 U.S. at 387.

78. 473 U.S. 402 (1985).

§ 14–11

1. See Illinois ex rel. McCollum v. Board of Educ., 333 U.S. 203, 212 (1948) ("[T]he First Amendment rests upon the premise that both religion and government

can best work to achieve their lofty aims if each is left free from the other within its respective sphere.").

2. See Walz v. Tax Comm'n, 397 U.S. 664, 694 (1970) (Harlan, J., concurring in result).

3. See Aguilar v. Felton, 473 U.S. 402, 410 (1985).

4. Engel v. Vitale, 370 U.S. 421, 431 (1962).

religiously based exemption from a law or regulation, a party *may* be able to prevail under the establishment clause by showing that enforcement would create excessive administrative entanglement. (5) Courts and other agencies of government may not inquire into pervasively religious issues.

The first doctrine, administrative entanglement, reflects Roger Williams' fear that government, unless carefully controlled, might trespass into the spiritual realm.[5] Under the Court's three-part test for establishment clause violations,[6] a finding of excessive administrative entanglement invalidates a statute. Improper entanglement sometimes arises when religious and public employees must work closely together in order to carry out the legislative plan,[7] or—apparently—when the legislature, in crafting regulations for religious bodies, scrutinizes religious content.[8]

Most commonly, administrative entanglement arises when government aid is followed by government investigators, who must make on-site inspections to ensure, as the establishment clause itself requires, that aid moneys are expended only for secular purposes.[9] The Court has singled out several factors, some of which also appear in the secular effects test.[10] One-time grants, as opposed to continuing aid, reduce the danger of entanglement.[11] "Pervasively sectarian" recipient organizations are more entangling than partly sectarian ones.[12] Parochial school aid in the form of teaching, either through subsidies that help pay the religious school's employees or through public employees who teach secular subjects, is more entangling[13] than mechanical forms of aid, such as textbooks and public health services.[14] When the aid takes the form of student testing, tests prepared by parochial school teachers are more entangling[15] than tests prepared by the state.[16]

---

5. See § 14–3, supra.

6. See Lemon v. Kurtzman, 403 U.S. 602 (1971).

7. See Aguilar v. Felton, 473 U.S. 402, 414 (1985) (program to aid parochial schools threatened to produce "'a kind of continuing day-to-day relationship which the policy of neutrality seeks to minimize'") (quoting Walz v. Tax Comm'n, 397 U.S. 664, 674 (1970).

8. See Larson v. Valente, 456 U.S. 228, 255 (1982) (finding that line that discriminated among denominations amounted to "'[the] kind of state inspection and evaluation of the religious content of a religious organization [that] is fraught with the sort of entanglement that the Constitution forbids'") (quoting Lemon v. Kurtzman, 403 U.S. 602, 620 (1971)). The relevance of the point is unclear, in that the Court struck down the statute based on strict scrutiny, rather than the Lemon tests; thus, the result would have been the same even if the legislature had undertaken no such inspection. See § 14–7, supra.

9. See Aguilar v. Felton, 473 U.S. at 412; Roemer v. Maryland Public Works Board, 426 U.S. 736, 765 (1976) (plurality opinion).

10. See § 14–10, supra.

11. See Aguilar v. Felton, 473 U.S. at 411 (citing Tilton v. Richardson, 403 U.S. 672 (1971)).

12. See Aguilar v. Felton, 473 U.S. at 411; Roemer v. Public Works Board, 426 U.S. at 758–59 (plurality opinion).

13. See Aguilar v. Felton, 473 U.S. at 412; Lemon v. Kurtzman, 403 U.S. 602, 619 (1971).

14. See Wolman v. Walter, 433 U.S. 229, 236–38, 241–44 (1977).

15. See Levitt v. Committee for Public Educ., 413 U.S. 472 (1973).

16. See Committee for Public Educ. v. Regan, 444 U.S. 646 (1980); Wolman v. Walter, 433 U.S. at 238–40.

Several members of the Court, particularly Chief Justice Rehnquist and Justice O'Connor, have criticized the administrative entanglement inquiry. Chief Justice Rehnquist has argued that the inquiry creates a " 'Catch-22' paradox," [17] under which state aid must be both supervised, in order to avoid religious effects, and unsupervised, in order to avoid excessive entanglement. He has also noted that the state permissibly regulates churches and church schools in a number of ways. "[I]f the entanglement prong were applied to all state and church relations in the automatic manner in which it has been applied to school aid cases, the State could hardly require anything of church-related institutions as a condition for receipt of financial assistance." [18] Justice O'Connor has agreed with this critique, and has added that "the anomalous results" in the Court's establishment clause cases stem largely from the entanglement inquiry.[19] Whereas Chief Justice Rehnquist would eliminate the entanglement inquiry (along with the rest of the *Lemon* approach),[20] Justice O'Connor would fold the entanglement inquiry in with the effects test.[21]

The second entanglement doctrine prohibits the state from vesting government powers in religious bodies; "vesting entanglement" reflects Thomas Jefferson's fear that religion might take over the political machinery of government.[22] In *Larkin v. Grendel's Den, Inc.*,[23] the Court considered a Massachusetts statute that permitted schools and churches to veto liquor license applications within a 500-foot radius of the organization's grounds. The Court struck down the statute as applied to churches, in large part because of improper church-state entanglement.[24] The Court concluded that "few entanglements could be more offensive to the spirit of the Constitution" than one that "enmeshes churches in the processes of government." [25]

17. Aguilar v. Felton, 473 U.S. at 420 (Rehnquist, J., dissenting). See also Wallace v. Jaffree, 472 U.S. 38, 109 (1985) (Rehnquist, J., dissenting).

18. Wallace v. Jaffree, 472 U.S. at 110 (Rehnquist, J., dissenting).

19. Aguilar v. Felton, 473 U.S. at 430 (O'Connor, J., joined by Rehnquist, J., dissenting) (citing Choper, "The Religion Clauses of the First Amendment: Reconciling the Conflict," 41 U.Pitt.L.Rev. 673, 681 (1980)).

20. See Wallace v. Jaffree, 472 U.S. at 110 (Rehnquist, J., dissenting).

21. See Aguilar v. Felton, 473 U.S. at 430 (O'Connor, J., joined by Rehnquist, J., dissenting). For another critique, see Roemer v. Board of Public Works, 426 U.S. 736, 769 (1976) (White, J., concurring) (entanglement test merely restates effect test); Lemon v. Kurtzman, 403 U.S. 602, 664–71 (1971) (White, J., concurring in part and dissenting in part) (same).

22. See § 14–3, supra.

23. 459 U.S. 116 (1982). The author of this treatise argued the case for Grendel's Den in the Supreme Court.

24. The Court also held that the statute's primary effects advanced religion. First, churches might use the veto power selectively and discriminatorily, for example by giving licenses only to fellow believers or contributors. Second, "the mere appearance of a joint exercise of legislative authority by Church and State provides a significant symbolic benefit to religion in the minds of some by reason of the power conferred." Id. at 125–26.

25. Id. at 127. In dissent, Justice Rehnquist agreed with the principle but disagreed with its applicability to the case: "Surely we do not need a three-part test to decide whether the grant of actual legislative power to churches is within the proscription of the Establishment Clause. . . . The question in this case is not whether such a statute would be unconstitutional, but whether [the Massachusetts law] is such a statute." Id. at 129 (Rehnquist, J., dissenting).

Several points are noteworthy about vesting entanglement. First, the principle is deeply rooted in American history. As the *Grendel's Den* Court noted: "At the time of the Revolution, Americans feared not only a denial of religious freedom, but also the danger of political oppression through a union of civil and ecclesiastical control." [26] In this sphere, history's lessons are so basic that the Court saw no need to ask whether they still apply, in contrast to the Court's approach to Tennessee's clergy disqualification rule.[27]

Second, vesting entanglement seems to be an independent test of constitutionality. Even if a state ceded power to a church in a way that avoided any on-going administrative entanglement, the action would be unconstitutional. And, although legislation that creates vesting entanglement will usually violate the effects inquiry as well, the vesting inquiry goes farther. Under the effects test, the breadth of the benefited class often cleanses an otherwise-impermissible statute [28]; under the vesting entanglement test, breadth is irrelevant so long as the power remains a traditionally governmental one. Effects are measured in relative terms; vesting is measured absolutely. Thus, *any* degree of vesting entanglement—not merely "excessive" entanglement—is prohibited.

Finally, vesting entanglement does not apply where the state simply uses its powers to accommodate religion—as by taking the views of a religious organization into account.[29] It applies only where the state lends discretionary powers to a religious body. States may flatly refuse to grant liquor licenses near churches [30]; but states may not let churches make the decisions. In this regard, vesting entanglement embodies a procedural or structural prohibition, rather than a substantive one.

The third doctrine, political divisiveness, also reflects the Jeffersonian concern that religion might pollute politics. The doctrine will be considered more fully in § 14–14; here it is sufficient to note that the doctrine's boundaries and operation remain only hazily defined. The Court has suggested, although with some ambiguities, that the political divisiveness inquiry applies only to a subset of establishment clause challenges, those concerning direct money grants to religious institutions.[31] Where the inquiry does apply, it is not entirely clear how it

26. Id. at 127 n.10 (citing B. Bailyn, Ideological Origins of the American Revolution 98–99 n.3 (1967)).

27. See McDaniel v. Paty, 435 U.S. 618, 628–29 (1978) ("However widely that view may have been held in the 18th century by many, including enlightened statesmen of that day, the American experience provides no persuasive support for the fear that clergymen in public office will be less careful of anti-establishment interests or less faithful to their oaths of office than their unordained counterparts.") (citation and footnote omitted) (case discussed in § 14–14, infra).

28. See § 14–10, supra.

29. See Grendel's Den, Inc., 459 U.S. at 123–24 (the statute's "valid secular objectives" could be accomplished "by ensuring a hearing for the views of affected institutions at licensing proceedings where, without question, such views would be entitled to substantial weight").

30. See id. at 121 ("[T]here can be little doubt about the power of a state to regulate the environment in the vicinity of schools, churches, hospitals, and the like by exercise of reasonable zoning laws.").

31. See Lynch v. Donnelly, 465 U.S. 668, 684 (1984) ("This case does not involve a direct subsidy to church-sponsored schools or colleges, or other religious insti-

applies.   The Court has never held that political divisiveness alone
suffices to show a violation of the establishment clause,[32] but it has also
never specifically held that the inquiry occupies a particular role
subordinate to the three *Lemon* factors.[33]

The fourth type of entanglement could be called "regulatory entanglement."   Its list of entangling relationships is identical to the list
under administrative entanglement.   The difference is that administrative entanglement arises in suits to strike down government benefits to
religion;   regulatory entanglement arises in suits to create religiously
based exemptions to government burdens.   Potentially, the regulatory
entanglement doctrine permits religious bodies to use the *establishment
clause*, like the free exercise clause, as a shield from government
intrusion.[34]   Although the Supreme Court has not yet based any holding on regulatory entanglement, it has implicitly recognized the doctrine.[35]   And several lower courts have carved out regulatory entangle-

---

tutions, and hence no inquiry into potential political divisiveness is even called
for.") (citation omitted); Mueller v. Allen,
463 U.S. 388, 403 n.11 (1983) ("rather elusive inquiry" of political divisiveness is
"confined to cases where direct financial
subsidies are paid to parochial schools or to
teachers in parochial schools").   But see
Aguilar v. Felton, 473 U.S. 402, 414 (1985)
(implying that political divisiveness may
result from administrative entanglement,
at least where the entanglement includes
state-made decisions about matters of religious significance); Lynch v. Donnelly, 465
U.S. at 703 n.9 (Brennan, J., dissenting)
(Court's suggestion that "inquiry into potential political divisiveness is unnecessary
absent direct subsidies to church-sponsored
schools or colleges, derives from a distorted
reading of our prior cases"); Larkin v.
Grendel's Den, Inc., 459 U.S. 116, 127
(1982) (referring to danger of political divisiveness concerning statute that lent state
power to religious body).

32.   See Lynch v. Donnelly, 465 U.S.
668, 684 (1984) ("The Court of Appeals
correctly observed that this Court has not
held that political divisiveness alone can
serve to invalidate otherwise permissible
conduct.   And we decline to so hold today.").   See also Corporation of the Presiding Bishop of the Church of Jesus Christ of
Latter-Day Saints v. Amos, 107 S.Ct. 2862,
2870 n. 17 (1987) (quoting and following
Lynch).

33.   The Court came closest in Committee for Public Educ. v. Nyquist, 413 U.S.
756, 797–98 (1973): "[W]hile the prospect
of such divisiveness *may not* alone warrant
the invalidation of state laws that otherwise survive the careful scrutiny required
by the decisions of this Court, it is certainly a 'warning signal' not to be ignored"
(emphasis added) (quoting Lemon v. Kurtz-

man, 403 U.S. 602, 625 (1971) (Douglas, J.,
concurring).

34.   The doctrine might, for example,
require a special threshold showing before
the state could place an informant in a
religious organization, such as a sanctuary
church.   See § 14–13, infra.   Note that the
effects test may operate as a similar tool,
where a state action's primary effect is to
burden religion.   See § 14–10, note 3, supra.

35.   In Tony and Susan Alamo Foundation v. Secretary of Labor, 105 S.Ct. 1953,
1964 (1985), petitioners argued that the
Fair Labor Standards Act would, if applied
to them, exert primarily anti-religious effects and create excessive church-state entanglement.   The Court rejected the argument, but only after weighing the statute's
effects and regulatory entanglement dangers.   See also Widmar v. Vincent, 454
U.S. 263, 272, n.11 (1981) ("We agree with
the Court of Appeals that the University
would risk greater 'entanglement' by attempting to enforce its exclusion of 'religious worship' and 'religious speech' [than
by opening its forum to religious as well as
nonreligious speakers].");   NLRB v. Catholic Bishop of Chicago, 440 U.S. 490, 504
(1979) (NLRB jurisdiction over teachers in
religious schools would raise "serious First
Amendment questions").   Cf. Corporation
of the Presiding Bishop of the Church of
Jesus Christ of Latter-Day Saints v. Amos,
107 S.Ct. 2862, 2868 (1987) ("Under the
Lemon analysis, it is a permissible legislative purpose to alleviate significant governmental interference with the ability of religious organizations to define and carry out
their religious missions.");   Walz v. Tax
Comm'n, 397 U.S. 664, 674 (1970) ("Either
course, taxation of churches or exemption,
occasions some degree of involvement with
religion.   Elimination of exemption would

ment exemptions for religious organizations, especially in employment laws.[36]

The final type of prohibited entanglement is doctrinal entanglement in religious issues. Doctrinal entanglement would subvert fundamental first amendment values: Whereas the other forms of entanglement involve government in the *apparatus* of religion, doctrinal entanglement involves government in religion's very *spirit*, in its decisions on core matters of belief and ritual. The Supreme Court recognized long ago that it "would lead to the total subversion of . . . religious bodies, if any one aggrieved by one of their decisions could appeal to the secular courts and have them reversed." [37] Thus, American courts—both state and federal—have uniformly held that "[c]ourts are not arbiters of scriptural interpretation." [38]

The doctrinal entanglement rule only partly reflects a desire to preserve the autonomy and self-government of religious organizations.[39] More deeply, it reflects the conviction that government—including the judicial as well as the legislative and executive branches—must never take sides on religious matters, a conviction "requiring on the part of all organs of government a strict neutrality toward theological questions." [40] At the very heart of first amendment theory is the proposition that "[t]he law knows no heresy, and is committed to the support of no dogma, the establishment of no sect." [41] Delivering one of its most ringing defenses of liberty, the Supreme Court, in upholding the right of children of Jehovah's Witnesses to refuse to salute the American flag, concluded: "If there is any fixed star in our constitutional constellation, it is that no official, high or petty, can prescribe what shall be orthodox in politics, nationalism, religion, or other matters of opinion or force citizens to confess by word or act their faith therein." [42] The Constitution thus leaves religion to succeed or fail "according to the

tend to expand the involvement of government by giving rise to tax valuation of church property, tax liens, tax foreclosures, and the direct confrontations and conflicts that follow in the train of those legal processes."). See generally Esbeck, "Establishment Clause Limits on Governmental Interference with Religious Organizations," 41 Wash. & Lee L.Rev. 347 (1984).

36. See, e.g., McClure v. Salvation Army, 460 F.2d 553 (5th Cir. 1972) (religious organizations are exempt from some sex discrimination suits under Title VII), cert. denied 409 U.S. 896 (1972); Madsen v. Erwin, 395 Mass. 715, 481 N.E.2d 1160 (1985) (Christian Science Monitor, as a religious organization, is immune from some employment discrimination suits). See generally Laycock, "Towards a General Theory of the Religion Clauses: The Case of Church Labor Relations and the Right to Church Autonomy," 81 Colum.L.Rev. 1373 (1981).

37. Watson v. Jones, 80 U.S. (13 Wall.) 679, 729 (1871).

38. Thomas v. Review Bd., 450 U.S. 707, 716 (1981). See also Wehmer v. Fokenga, 57 Neb. 510, 518–19, 78 N.W. 28, 36–37 (1899) (religious freedom "would not long survive" if church members unsatisfied about "some matter of religious faith or church polity, could successfully appeal to the secular courts for redress"); Watson v. Garvin, 54 Mo. 353, 378 (1873) ("in matters purely religious or ecclesiastical, the civil courts have no jurisdiction").

39. Indeed, under the "neutral principles" approach, discussed below, courts will sometimes ignore the decision of an ecclesiastical body and impose a contrary outcome dictated by state policy.

40. Abington School Dist. v. Schempp, 374 U.S. 203, 243 (1963) (Brennan, J., concurring). See § 14–7, supra, on the neutrality idea.

41. Watson v. Jones, 80 U.S. (13 Wall.) at 728.

42. West Virginia State Board of Educ. v. Barnette, 319 U.S. 624, 642 (1943).

zeal of its adherents and the appeal of its dogma," [43] and not according to its access to the levers of civil power. It follows that the most clearly forbidden church-state entanglement occurs when institutions of civil government use the legal process in order to discover religious error or to promulgate religious truth.

In his brilliant "Memorial and Remonstrance Against Religious Assessments," [44] James Madison labeled the suggestion that "the Civil Magistrate is a competent Judge of Religious truth" an "arrogant pretension falsified by the contradictory opinion of Rulers in all ages, and throughout the world." It was in this great tradition that the Supreme Court took its stand when it ruled in 1944 that, under constitutional principles of church-state separation, no judge or jury had the power or competence to determine whether the religious experiences claimed by the defendants in a mail fraud prosecution had in fact occurred. [45]

In short, law in a nontheocratic state cannot measure religious truth. [46] The converse proposition—that "only in a theocratic state . . . [can] ecclesiastical doctrines measure legal right or wrong" [47]—is equally valid. Insofar as religion exists in society rather than in the abstract, and insofar as religious organizations act in ways that affect the physical life, civil liberty, or tangible property of individuals, it is inevitable that at least some disputes affecting religion or touching the interests of religious institutions will be brought before the civil courts or other secular agencies. That such courts or agencies may at times be proper forums for resolving such disputes is clear. But it is now settled that the resolution of religious questions can play no role in the civil adjudication of such disputes—that ecclesiastical doctrines cannot be used to measure right or wrong under civil law. In order to understand the leading case on the subject, *Presbyterian Church in the United States v. Mary Elizabeth Blue Hull Memorial Presbyterian Church*, [48] it is necessary briefly to survey the background of doctrine against which that case was decided.

Judges in late eighteenth and early nineteenth century England did not hesitate to pass on the most arcane questions of religious doctrine and theology when those questions happened to arise in disputes over contract obligations, property rights, tort claims, or the

---

43. Zorach v. Clauson, 343 U.S. 306, 313 (1952).

44. II The Writings of James Madison 183–91 (G. Hunt ed. 1901).

45. United States v. Ballard, 322 U.S. 78, 86–87 (1944), discussed in § 14–12, infra. Cf. Holy Spirit Ass'n v. Tax Comm'n, 55 N.Y.2d 512, 450 N.Y.S.2d 292, 435 N.E.2d 662 (1982) (a court must accept an organization's good-faith characterization that it operates solely for religious purposes, and thus that it qualifies for tax exemption, and may not reject its purposes as non-religious because of the seemingly worldly or secular nature of the matters on which the religion's doctrine takes a stand).

46. "[H]aving identified belief as religious, a court is not competent to pass on its truthfulness or validity. Not only is religious truth by its nature not subject to a test of validity determined by rational thought and empiric knowledge, but a principal purpose underlying religious liberty is to remove the question of what is true religion from the domain of secular authority." P. Kauper, Religion and the Constitution 26 (1964).

47. West Virginia State Board of Education v. Barnette, 319 U.S. 624, 654 (1943) (Frankfurter, J., dissenting).

48. 393 U.S. 440 (1969).

application of criminal laws designed to protect the public from fraud or other secular injury. In particular, the English courts had held— ever since Lord Eldon's opinion in *Attorney General v. Pearson* [49]—that property contributed to a religious body by its members is impressed with an implied trust in favor of the fundamental doctrines and practices of the religious body at the time the contribution was made, and that civil courts in disputes concerning such contributed property are to award control of the property to the group most faithful to the trust. Although this rule required civil courts to determine ecclesiastical matters, its application in England was consistent with a legal system that included an established church under parliamentary control.

Despite the rule's rather more alien character when transplanted to American soil, it took root for a time and proved surprisingly difficult to dislodge. Even in England, the abstruse character of the theological issues presented to civil courts for resolution under the implied trust doctrine—and the correspondingly limited capacity of judges to deal intelligently with such issues—soon became evident.[50] In the United States, even more than in England, this institutional incompetence of civil authorities in religious matters became but an aspect of their inability effectively to settle, to the satisfaction of the parties affected and of the wider public, the controversies they undertook to resolve.[51] And this problem was in turn aggravated (1) by the growing perception that both doctrinal evolution and the autonomy of religious organizations were being stifled by judicial insistence that original doctrine be retained without fundamental departure,[52] and (2) by the mounting conviction that the political and personal leanings of judges were given too much sway over legal rights when courts were invited to make legal results turn on their reading of religious truth.[53]

In 1872, at a time when federal courts in cases of diverse citizenship were still applying general common law rather than state law, the Supreme Court attempted to reduce judicial reliance on the implied trust doctrine with all its attendant difficulties by holding, in the seminal case of *Watson v. Jones,*[54] that civil courts should decide disputes over church property in accordance with the terms of any express trust applicable to the property and, where no express trust has been created, should defer to the decision of the majority in a "congregational" church or of the highest applicable authority in a "hierarchical" church. Since *Watson v. Jones* had been announced by the Court as a matter of common law rather than constitutional law, states remained free to disregard it—and quite a few did.[55] In 1952, however,

49. 3 Mer. 353, 36 Eng.Rep. 135 (Ch. 1817).

50. See, e.g., Craigdallie v. Aikman, 2 Bligh 529, 543–44, 4 Eng.Rep. 435, 440–41 (H.L.1820) (Scot.) ("[A]fter racking my mind again and again upon the subject, I really do not know what more to make of it").

51. See L. Pfeffer, Church, State, and Freedom 301 (1967 ed.).

52. See C. Zollman, American Church Law § 251 at 238–39.

53. See L. Pfeffer, supra note 51 at 301; Note, "Judicial Intervention in Disputes Over the Use of Church Property," 75 Harv.L.Rev. 1142, 1156 (1962).

54. 80 U.S. (13 Wall.) 679 (1871).

55. See Note, 75 Harv.L.Rev., at 1158.

in *Kedroff v. Saint Nicholas Cathedral*,[56] the Supreme Court reaffirmed the *Watson* rule and implied that it was required by the free exercise and establishment clauses of the first amendment, which had been held binding on the states in *Cantwell v. Connecticut*[57] and *Everson v. Board of Education*,[58] respectively.[59] Even then, since *Kedroff* had not actually involved a claim of implied trust or of departure from doctrine, some state courts continued to scrutinize such departure and continued to award church property to those adhering most closely to the faith.[60]

The Georgia Supreme Court was among those that had retained a departure-from-doctrine rule. Holding that the Presbyterian Church-U.S.A. had substantially departed from established Presbyterian doctrine (by such actions as the ordination of women ministers, the making of pronouncements on civil matters, the support of steps to end Bible reading in the schools, and the teaching of neo-orthodoxy alien to the Confession of Faith and Catechism as originally adopted by the general church), the state court decreed that the implied trust of the local congregational property in favor of the national body had terminated. Accordingly, the state court awarded custody of the property to the local members and ministers who withdrew from the general church.

The Supreme Court reversed in *Presbyterian Church*, holding that the free exercise and establishment clauses of the first amendment forbid any application of a departure-from-doctrine test by a civil court resolving a dispute over property. Although recognizing the state's legitimate interest in resolving such disputes in civil courts, the Supreme Court said:[61] "[T]he First Amendment severely circumscribes the role that civil courts may play in resolving church property disputes. . . . First Amendment values are plainly jeopardized when church property litigation is made to turn on the resolution by civil courts of controversies over religious doctrine and practice. If civil courts undertake to resolve such controversies in order to adjudicate the property dispute, the hazards are ever present of inhibiting the free development of religious doctrine and of implicating secular interests in matters of purely ecclesiastical concern . . . . [T]he Amendment therefore commands civil courts to decide church property disputes without resolving underlying controversies over religious doctrine." The Court stressed that the departure-from-doctrine rule "can play *no* role in any future judicial proceedings."[62] Secular authorities may not resolve civil disputes that engage them "in the forbidden process of interpreting and weighing church doctrine."[63]

56. 344 U.S. 94 (1952).

57. 310 U.S. 296 (1940) (free exercise).

58. 330 U.S. 1 (1947) (establishment).

59. Kedroff invalidated a New York statute that sought to wrest control of a cathedral from the church hierarchy; in Kreshik v. St. Nicholas Cathedral, 363 U.S. 190 (1960), the Supreme Court unhesitatingly applied the Kedroff principle to a parallel attempt by New York courts.

60. See, e.g., Vogler v. Salem Primitive Baptist Church, 415 S.W.2d 72 (Ky.1967);

Cantrell v. Anderson, 390 S.W.2d 176 (Ky. 1965); Huber v. Thorn, 189 Kan. 631, 371 P.2d 143 (1962); Davis v. Scher, 356 Mich. 291, 97 N.W.2d 137 (1959).

61. Presbyterian Church in the United States v. Mary Elizabeth Blue Hull Memorial Presbyterian Church, 393 U.S. 440, 449 (1969).

62. Id. at 450 (emphasis in original).

63. Id. at 451. It is noteworthy that Epperson v. Arkansas, 393 U.S. 97 (1968), was decided in the same Term of Court

Once it is conceded that first amendment values are unacceptably compromised when civil courts undertake to settle religious issues, it becomes clear that allowing a legal determination about property or some other secular matter to turn on a court's answer to a religious question represents a path fraught with peril: the path is one along which unsatisfied former believers could drag the civil courts into the theological thicket by the simple expedient of suing for a refund of their prior donations to a religious organization. The Court of Appeals for the District of Columbia, in rejecting an attempt by the Food and Drug Administration to destroy various electrical instruments and accompanying pamphlets as falsely and misleadingly labeled, stressed this very danger—that "a disgruntled former adherent could [otherwise] sue a church for fraud and deceit because it had collected money from him on the basis of allegedly 'false' doctrines concerning salvation, heaven and hell—or for that matter on the basis of doctrines, such as those of Christian Scientists, concerning the cause and cure of disease." [64]

Even when the right to use St. Nicholas Cathedral in New York City was at stake in a lawsuit, Justice Frankfurter pierced the veil of property to detect the essence of religious controversy. "St. Nicholas Cathedral is not just a piece of real estate. . . . What is at stake here," he said, "is the power to exert religious authority." [65] The same is true when a church contributor seeks return of a donation on the ground that the religious beliefs inducing the contribution were false; once we assume that the underlying dispute is properly characterized as religious, the suit for a refund becomes a transparent vehicle for invoking governmental assistance to benefit one side in a religious conflict at the expense of the other, something the establishment clause plainly forbids. [66]

The existence of dissidents is a pervasive fact of religious life; their role within religious organizations can be the healthy one of spurring continuing introspection and re-examination of doctrine. But it is not hard to imagine what would occur if each potential dissenter were told: contributing to a religious organization—your own or indeed that of a group you reject—will give you a judicial platform from which to air your religious differences with others and potentially win a favorable verdict; all you need do in order to overcome the normal bar to civil adjudication of ecclesiastical matters is sue for a refund! Not only would such an invitation declare open season on churches and their followers; it could at the same time make at least some religious groups resist the very attempt to solicit donations, while inducing others—

(1968–69) as Presbyterian Church; just as Presbyterian Church prevents governmental dispute-resolution from turning on religious determinations, so Epperson prevents governmental service offerings from being determined by religious beliefs.

64. Founding Church of Scientology v. United States, 133 U.S.App.D.C. 229, 409 F.2d 1146, 1156 n.32 (1969). The Court of Appeals reasoned that such a result would "present the gravest constitutional difficulties," 409 F.2d at 1157, in light of the

Supreme Court's holding, in United States v. Ballard, 322 U.S. 78 (1944), that the first amendment prohibits trial of the truth or falsity of religious beliefs in a fraud prosecution.

65. Kedroff v. St. Nicholas Cathedral, 344 U.S. 94, 121, 123 (1952) (Frankfurter, J., concurring).

66. Fowler v. Rhode Island, 345 U.S. 67, 69–70 (1953). See also Torcaso v. Watkins, 367 U.S. 488, 495 n.11 (1961).

those too desperate for resources to refrain from financial appeals—to rigidify their doctrines and freeze or at least conceal their own evolution for fear that doctrinal change, ordinarily immune from censorship, could trigger refund-seeking litigation. It is in part for reasons such as these that the first amendment has been construed to mean that religious questions remain non-justiciable even when they do not reach civil courts independently but instead form preliminary or ancillary issues in an otherwise justiciable dispute.[67]

It is not only the sanctity of religious conscience in the abstract which has been of concern in these cases; it has also been the integrity of religious associations viewed as organic units. Recognition of the principle that associations have rights different from those of the persons constituting them has been somewhat grudging in American constitutional law.[68] But one sphere in which such recognition has been clear is that of religious organizations and their autonomy. As the Supreme Court expressed the matter in *Kedroff v. St. Nicholas Cathedral*,[69] governmental transfer of control over property from the church's Russian authorities to an American Diocese violated the religion clauses not so much because any individual's religious liberty was demonstrably infringed by the transfer, but because the governmentally compelled shift in authority "directly prohibit[ed] the free exercise of an ecclesiastical right, . . . the Church's choice of its hierarchy."[70] Thus, the Supreme Court has recognized for nearly a quarter-century that, whatever may be true of other private associations, religious organizations as spiritual bodies have rights which require distinct constitutional protection. When John Figgis wrote his *Churches in the Modern State*,[71] he was expressing his agreement with Maitland that "the dead hand" of the law "fell with a resounding slap upon the living body" of the Church when the House of Lords denied effective powers of self-government to the Free Church of Scotland.[72] In *Kedroff*, the United States Supreme Court read the first amendment as extending to all religions a corporate liberty which the House of Lords had denied.

---

67. American judicial decisions have tended to treat anything even *resembling* inquiry into doctrinal departure or deviance as part of the forbidden religious realm. In Sustar v. Williams, 263 So.2d 537, 543 (Miss.1972), for instance, the Supreme Court of Mississippi held that a nonjusticiable religious question was posed by the need to determine whether "there exists a deep-seated and irreconcilable hostility or tension" between two groups of religious trustees. See also Molko v. Holy Spirit Ass'n, 179 Cal.App.3d 450, 224 Cal. Rptr. 817, 829 (trial court could conclude that "the psychological techniques of the [Unification] Church deprived [the plaintiffs] of the ability to reason critically and make independent judgments" only by "questioning the authenticity and the force of the Unification Church's religious teachings and permitting a jury to do likewise, which is constitutionally forbidden") (em-

phasis and citations omitted), review granted 721 P.2d 40, 228 Cal.Rptr. 159 (1986); Katz v. Superior Court, 73 Cal.App.3d 952, 987, 141 Cal.Rptr. 234, 255 (1977) ("When the court is asked to determine whether [the proposed conservatees' change in life style] was induced by faith or by coercive persuasion is it not in turn investigating and questioning the validity of that faith?").

68. See generally § 12–26, supra, and §§ 14–16, 15–17, 15–20, infra.

69. 344 U.S. 94, 119 (1952).

70. Id. at 116.

71. (2d ed. 1914).

72. See "Moral Personality and Legal Personality," in 3 Collected Papers of Frederic William Maitland 304, 319 (Fisher ed. 1911).

Quite apart from its grounding in general notions of associational freedom and autonomy—and apart from its status as a particularly well-established instance of such associational liberty—the doctrine of judicial deference to a religion's internal decision-making organs has deep roots in history; far from representing a delegation of political power to religious bodies, the doctrine represents a recognition of their necessary separation from governmental entanglement, a separation designed as much to protect the state as to defend the church. The New Testament provided early precedent for civil deference to religious authority on ecclesiastical questions.[73] And throughout most of the Middle Ages, the notion of autonomous civil and religious jurisdictions—of dividing God's dispute-resolving realm from Caesar's—commanded wide respect.[74] Such breaches as occurred could be traced to the occasional union of church and state authority in the same heads in parts of the Continent, in England, and in some of the American colonies. Most colonies, however, deliberately separated civil and church authorities in parallel judicial systems. Like many accused wrongdoers, Anne Hutchison was tried twice for her alleged blasphemy, once by the church and once by the colonial government.[75] Indeed, John Adams once attributed the settlement of America to "a hatred, a dread, a horror, of the infernal confederacy" between civil and ecclesiastical law.[76]

This section has already summarized the development of a broad rule of civil deference, beginning in a major way with *Watson v. Jones*[77] in 1871 and culminating in the final rejection of any departure-from-doctrine test in *Presbyterian Church in the United States v. Mary Elizabeth Blue Hull Memorial Presbyterian Church*[78] in 1969. In rejecting that test, the Supreme Court struck a blow for the principle of judicial deference to religious authority, since it effectively ruled out the implied-trust approach through which civil courts had attempted to hold religions in line during the nineteenth century and even in the twentieth. But the Court also gave notice that even judicial deference to religious authority is limited by the overriding need to extract all ecclesiastical questions from civil adjudication; when deference to religious authority would pose problems of religious interpretation or evaluation, such deference must give way to "neutral principles of law, developed for use in all property disputes."[79]

---

73. See Acts 18:12–16, describing Gallio's refusal, as proconsul of Achaia, to judge a claim that Paul "persuadeth men to worship God contrary to the law." Because it was a matter of "words and names, and of your law," Gallio told Paul's accusers, " 'look ye to it; for I will be no judge of such matters.' And he drave them from the judgment seat."

74. See O'Brien & O'Brien, "Separation of Church and State in Restatement of Inter-Church-and-State Common Law," 7 Jurist 259, 267–68 (1947); cf. Pound, "A Comparison of Ideals of Law," 47 Harv.L.

Rev. 1, 6 (1933). See also 24 Henry 8, c. 12 (1532): "Causes spiritual must be judged by judges of the spiritual and causes temporal by temporal judges."

75. See G. Haskins, Law and Authority in Early Massachusetts 89 (1960).

76. "A Dissertation on the Feudal and Canon Law," in 3 Works 451 (1851).

77. 80 U.S. (13 Wall.) 679 (1871).

78. 393 U.S. 440 (1969).

79. Id. at 449.

In *Jones v. Wolf*,[80] the Court explained when and how such "neutral principles" may apply in disputes over church property. The key inquiry is whether church documents—such as the property deed, the local church's charter, or the general church's constitution—contain express, secular language indicating "what is to happen to church property in the event of a particular contingency, or what religious body will determine the ownership in the event of a schism or doctrinal controversy."[81] If the documents contain both secular and nonsecular language on such subjects, the court apparently must separate the secular language if possible.[82] If the documents do contain express, secular language, separable from nonsecular language, then that language dictates the outcome. If the documents do not contain such language, then the state's neutral rule, in favor of either general churches or local churches, determines the outcome.[83] If the documents are silent and the state has no rule, then the court apparently must defer to the decision of the authoritative ecclesiastical body.[84]

The neutral-principles approach is best understood as a way to reduce the entanglement that may result from judicial fact-finding, and not as an attempt to reduce conflicts between church bodies and state courts.[85] Under the approach, a court may overturn the decision of the authoritative church body where relevant documents are written in religious terms—and, as the *Jones v. Wolf* dissenters noted of church constitutions, all such documents "tend to be drawn in terms of religious precepts."[86] Even though future donors, duly warned, may be

80. 443 U.S. 595 (1979).

81. Id. at 603.

82. See id. at 604 (court must "take special care to scrutinize the document in purely secular terms").

83. If the rule favors local churches, the state may, in addition, create a presumption that local churches operate by majority rule. The presumption could be rebutted by language in the local church's corporate charter or in the general church's constitution. Id. at 607–08. Note, though, that here as elsewhere, the court may consider only secular language in the documents.

84. Although the Court never stated it directly, this conclusion seems to follow from what the Court did say: that states are "constitutionally entitled," rather than required, to adopt a neutral rule; and that where religious doctrine cannot be avoided in interpreting a document, a court must defer to the ecclesiastical body's resolution of the doctrinal issue. Id. at 604.

85. The majority and the dissenting opinions in Jones v. Wolf spoke of the approach in consistent terms. The majority said the rule "promises to free civil courts completely from entanglement in questions of religious doctrine, polity, and practice." Id. at 603 (Blackmun, J., writing for the Court, joined by Rehnquist,

Stevens, Brennan, and Marshall, JJ.). The dissenters responded: "The First Amendment's Religion Clauses are meant to protect churches and their members from civil law interference, not to protect the courts from having to decide difficult evidentiary questions." Id. at 613–14 n.2 (Powell, J., joined by Burger, C.J., and Stewart and White, JJ., dissenting).

86. Id. at 612. A donor's intent may be overridden not only where documents are so permeated with religion that the court must ignore them, but also where documents contain some religious and some nonreligious language, which the court must disentangle. Trying to read such documents in purely secular terms may, as the dissent noted, "[be] more likely to promote confusion than understanding." Id. See also Mansfield, "The Religion Clauses of the First Amendment and the Philosophy of the Constitution," 72 Cal.L.Rev. 847, 863 (1984) ("This right of the general church [to prevail where relevant documents contain express, secular language to that effect] is founded not on the intention of the donors, but on a governmental, indeed a constitutional, policy. If the intention of the donors were consulted—which would require reference to all the evidence pertinent to that intention, not just to particular language in the documents, which evidence might present a religious ques-

able to express their wishes in secular terms,[87] several problems may block the realization of donors' intent. First, some concepts cannot survive translation from religious language to secular language.[88] Second, churches may not be free to rewrite documents relating to previous gifts.[89] Third, although the general church might be able to realize a past donor's intent by amending its constitution, it may refuse to do so for reasons of history, theology, or, conceivably, self-interest.[90]

The four dissenting Justices in *Jones v. Wolf* advocated a rule designed to reduce church-state conflicts, at the cost of requiring some judicial scrutiny of church doctrine: civil court enforcement of the decisions of authoritative church bodies.[91] However, the principle of doctrinal noninterference is so deeply rooted that some form of neutral state rules may be unavoidable. Although the noninterference principle, like the establishment clause, on occasion will create problems for religion, the alternative—judicial scrutiny of religious doctrines and processes—might create more fundamental and long-term problems. If civil judges resolved religious issues, the Court noted in *Presbyterian Church*, "the hazards are ever present of inhibiting the free development of religious doctrine and of implicating secular interests in matters of purely ecclesiastical concern." [92]

Outside of church property cases, the *Jones v. Wolf* dissenters' position—that courts must enforce the decisions of responsible religious bodies—is in some circumstances a mandatory mode of civil adjudication. In *Serbian Orthodox Diocese v. Milivojevich*,[93] the Supreme Court found that the Illinois Supreme Court had improperly interfered with the highest authorities of a hierarchical church in violation of the first and fourteenth amendments when the Illinois Court set aside a bishop's defrockment and invalidated a related religious reorganization. In a 7–

---

tion—it might be found that the local church should control.").

87. See 443 U.S. at 604 (majority opinion) (problems in applying neutral-principles approach "should be gradually eliminated as recognition is given to the obligation of 'States, religious organizations, and individuals [to] structure relationships involving church property so as not to require the civil courts to resolve ecclesiastical questions' ") (quoting Presbyterian Church of the United States v. Mary Elizabeth Blue Hull Memorial Presbyterian Church, 393 U.S. 440, 449 (1969)).

88. As Professor Mansfield has pointed out, it is problematic for a donation to hinge on a description like "Roman Catholic." Even such a description as "the person determined by the Pope to be the Roman Catholic Archbishop of Chicago" may create problems: "[W]ho is the Pope is itself a religious question under the *Hull* rule. There was a time when three persons claimed to be the Pope." 72 Cal.L. Rev., supra note 86, at 866–67. Instead, donors must turn to nonreligious substitutes, such as whether the recipient church

continues to recite a particular religious text.

89. "Although the redrafting of documents to eliminate religious questions may be authorized by some trusts, it surely is not authorized by many." Mansfield, supra note 86 at 866.

90. The Jones v. Wolf majority implied that churches could make necessary modifications, 443 U.S. at 606. However, even where the donor intended that the local church own the property, it may be that only the general church has the power to make the necessary modification. The general church may choose not to surrender its state-granted property right. Even if it wishes to do so, the general church may fear that raising the issue will precipitate property disputes. See id. at 614 n.2 (Powell, J., dissenting).

91. Id. at 616–17.

92. Presbyterian Church in the United States v. Mary Elizabeth Blue Hull Memorial Presbyterian Church, 393 U.S. 440, 449 (1969).

93. 426 U.S. 696 (1976).

2 decision, the Supreme Court concluded that the state court's judgment had rested "upon an impermissible rejection of the decisions
of the highest ecclesiastical tribunals of this hierarchical
church. . . ." [94]

As to the state court's view that the defrockment was "arbitrary" [95]
because not in accord with the church's own rules, the Supreme Court
held that no such determination can ever be made by a civil court once
it is conceded that the challenged action was taken by the highest
ecclesiastical tribunal of a hierarchical church. Any analysis of such
an action's consistency with church laws and regulations would entail
inquiry into the procedures that canon or ecclesiastical law require the
church to follow, or into the substantive criteria by which church action
is to be judged. "But this," said the Court, "is exactly the inquiry that
the First Amendment prohibits." [96] Since "it is the essence of religious
faith that ecclesiastical decisions are reached and are to be accepted as
matters of faith whether or not rational or measurable by objective
criteria," [97] secular concepts of arbitrariness or fair process have absolutely no relevance, and "a civil court must accept the ecclesiastical
decisions of church tribunals as it finds them." [98]

As to the state court's view that the Mother Church's reorganization of the American-Canadian Diocese into three dioceses was invalid
because "in clear and palpable excess" of the Mother Church's "own
jurisdiction," the Supreme Court held that a civil court has no more
power to make such a determination than it has to find an ecclesiastical action "arbitrary" because inconsistent with church rules. Again,
once a hierarchical church's highest ecclesiastical tribunal has interpreted its own constitution and that of its subordinate diocese to permit
a particular reorganization, such an interpretation is binding on all
civil courts. [99] Issues of church organization, no less than questions of
church procedure or substantive theology, are regarded as doctrinal
matters beyond civil authority. As the Court had said in *Kedroff v. St.
Nicholas Cathedral*, [100] religious freedom encompasses the "power [of
religious bodies] to decide for themselves, free from state interference,
matters of church government as well as those of faith and doctrine."

The *Serbian Orthodox Diocese* decision thus reaffirmed the constitutional prohibition against civil resolution of religious disputes, and
severely limited any possible exception for church decisions challenged
as arbitrary, inconsistent with church rules, or beyond church jurisdiction. All nine of the Justices, including the two dissenters, agreed
"that the government may not displace the free religious choices of its
citizens by placing its weight behind a particular religious belief, tenet,
or sect." [101] Whatever the object in dispute, this is an absolute prohibition, and one commanding unanimous assent from the Supreme Court.

---

94. Id. at 708.

95. See Gonzales v. Archbishop, 280
U.S. 1 (1929) (suggesting that there is an
arbitrariness or a fraud exception to the
rules against interfering with a religious
body).

96. 426 U.S. at 713.

97. Id. at 714–15.

98. Id. at 713.

99. Id. at 717–18.

100. 344 U.S. 94, 116 (1952).

101. 426 U.S. at 733 (Rehnquist, J.,
joined by Stevens, J., dissenting).

Of even greater significance may be a distinction stressed by the *Serbian Orthodox Diocese* majority. Writing for himself and five other members of the Court, Justice Brennan distinguished between (1) disputes over church property as such, and (2) religious disputes that only "incidentally" affect church property or other secular matters.[102] As to the first category—property disputes "as such"—civil courts have a duty to adjudicate them in neutral terms if at all, without resolving underlying religious issues. As the Supreme Court subsequently made clear in *Jones v. Wolf*,[103] this duty does not necessarily require deference to church tribunals, and in some circumstances prohibits it. But as to the second category—disputes over religious doctrine, administration, or organization—a civil court can discharge its duty in only one way: by accepting the decisions of the proper church authorities "as it finds them," [104] whatever might be the "incidental effect" on property or other secular matters.[105] In other words, *Serbian Orthodox Diocese* settled a question left open by the Court's prior decisions: whatever room the first amendment might leave for independent civil resolution of secular but church-related disputes through neutral principles of law, it leaves no room whatever for independent civil adjudication of "questions . . . at the core of ecclesiastical concern." [106]

It is noteworthy that the Court in *Serbian Orthodox Diocese* included, in its enumeration of questions so quintessentially religious as to oust civil jurisdiction altogether, not only matters of religious doctrine and hierarchical composition but also "questions of church discipline." [107] Thus, the Supreme Court has said that it would be unconstitutional for state tribunals to question a church's suspension or expulsion of a member for defying the church's hierarchy and challenging the church's authority through civil litigation.[108]

Justice Rehnquist, joined by Justice Stevens, argued in dissent in *Serbian Orthodox Diocese* that even the Court's holding would necessarily require proof as to what the authoritative religious tribunal *is*,[109]

102. Id. at 709, 720–23 (Brennan, J., joined by Stewart, White, Marshall, Blackmun, and Powell). Chief Justice Burger concurred in the judgment.

103. 443 U.S. 595 (1979).

104. 426 U.S. at 713.

105. Id. at 720.

106. Id. at 717.

107. Id.

108. Id. at 718.

109. This decision is often dispositive of the outcome of such cases, and the outcome of such cases can affect the survival of a religious tradition. For example, in Baker v. Fales, 16 Mass. 488 (1820), the Supreme Judicial Court of Massachusetts was asked to determine what actually constituted the voting unit (and hence membership) of the Congregational Church in Dedham, Massachusetts. One group consisted of the church-going Congregationalists: the other, more liberal, consisted of the voters of the "parish" (a town). At stake was control of the church property. It was agreed that Congregational Church polity dictated a decision by the majority, but a majority of what? The Supreme Judicial Court's decision that the broader, more liberal group constituted the proper unit was one of the most important factors in stimulating the "separation" of liberals from the Congregationalist Churches (taking the property with them) during the Unitarian Controversy. Dozens of such "separations" occurred, providing the basis for the establishment of the American Unitarian Association shortly after the Dedham case. Cf. E. Wilburn, A History of Unitarianism in England and America (1955). See also Jones v. Wolf, 443 U.S. 595 (1979), where one issue was which group constituted the local church: the majority, which had separated from the general church, or the minority, which remained loyal to the general church.

and as to what that religious tribunal in fact *decided*. If civil courts may do this much—that is, resolve disputes over *who* decides and *what* was decided—the dissenters ask why civil courts may not do what the Illinois court did in *Serbian Orthodox Diocese*.[110] The difference between forbidden and permissible governmental intrusion into a religious organization to protect individual members from fraud and oppression must ultimately be a difference of degree—but the difference of degree between the examples Justice Rehnquist offered in dissent and the facts of the *Serbian Orthodox* case seem wide enough to constitute differences in kind. Right or wrong on the facts of the case before them, Justices Rehnquist and Stevens did well to highlight in their dissent the inescapable conflict between, on the one hand, the religious community which is furthered by governmental disentanglement from decisions of a religious organization, and, on the other hand, the religious autonomy which may be compromised if such disentanglement subjects individuals to unbounded domination by oppressive religious authorities.[111]

§ 14–12. The Requirement that Free Exercise Claimants Show Sincerity and Religious Burden

Under the free exercise clause, a claimant may seek exemption from a government requirement—either a free-standing requirement, such as a criminal statute, or a requirement linked to a benefit program, such as a rule that recipients of unemployment insurance must be willing to work on Saturdays. In order to gain the exemption, the claimant must show (1) a sincerely held religious belief, which (2) conflicts with, and thus is burdened by, the state requirement. Once the claimant has made that showing, the burden shifts to the state. The state can prevail only by demonstrating both that (3) the requirement pursues an unusually important governmental goal,[1] and that (4) an exemption would substantially hinder the fulfillment of the goal.[2] This section will examine the first two showings, those that the religious claimant must make.

At the outset, it is appropriate to note three limitations on the reach of the free exercise clause. First, the Court has often oversimplified the issues by asserting that the free exercise clause accords

---

110. "Suppose the Holy Assembly in this case had a membership of 100; its rules provided that a bishop could be defrocked by a majority vote of any session at which a quorum was present, and also provided that a quorum was not to be less than 40. Would a decision of the Holy Assembly attended by 30 members, 16 of whom voted to defrock Bishop Dionisije, be binding on civil courts in a dispute such as this? The hypothetical example is a clearer case than the one involved here, but the principle is the same. If the civil courts are to be bound by any sheet of parchment bearing the ecclesiastical seal and purporting to be a decree of a church court, they can easily be converted into handmaidens of arbitrary lawlessness." 426 U.S. at 727

(Rehnquist, J., joined by Stevens, J., dissenting).

111. See generally § 14–16.

§ 14–12

1. Justice O'Connor used the phrase "unusually important" in her dissenting opinion in Goldman v. Weinberger, 106 S.Ct. 1310, 1325 (1986); the Court has employed several different formulations to describe the requirement. See § 14–13, infra.

2. This requirement has also been described variously, and the different formulations seem to reflect substantive differences. See § 14–13, infra.

absolute protection to religious belief, but lesser protection to religion-based actions. More useful is a distinction between government measures that make religious classifications, and those that burden religious activity only in a manner ancillary to an undeniably secular choice.[3]

Second, the clause applies only when government interacts, or refuses to interact, with believers. "The Free Exercise Clause affords an individual protection from certain forms of governmental compulsion; it does not afford an individual a right to dictate the conduct of the Government's internal procedures." [4]

Third, the free exercise clause protects only religious beliefs and actions. As § 14–6 showed, the courts have yet to settle on a single approach to defining "religion." The Supreme Court has excluded purely secular philosophies from its definition of "religion." [5] Beyond that limitation, the Court has made relatively few demands of people who claim religious motivations. In *Thomas v. Review Board*, the claimant was admittedly struggling with his beliefs; other members of his religion disagreed with his views as to what actions the beliefs forbade; and his translation of beliefs into actions seemed inconsistent.[6] Nonetheless, the free exercise clause applied: "[R]eligious beliefs need not be acceptable, logical, consistent, or comprehensible to others in order to merit First Amendment protection." [7] In *Hobbie v. Unemployment Appeals Commission*,[8] the Court held that newly adopted religious beliefs are fully protected.[9] Although the Court has stipulated that some beliefs may be "so bizarre, so clearly nonreligious in motivation, as not to be entitled to protection under the Free Exercise Clause," [10] the threshold appears to be a low one. In *Bowen v. Roy*, for example, the Court accepted, without any discussion, the claimants' assertion that their belief was religious, where the belief—that the government's use of a social security number in their daughter's name would injure her spirit—was apparently not held by any organized religious group.[11]

Even though the courts apply an expansive approach to defining "religion" in free exercise cases, as *Thomas* and *Bowen* illustrate, claimants cannot have unlimited recourse to free exercise exemptions;

3. See §§ 14–6, supra; 14–13, infra.

4. Bowen v. Roy, 106 S.Ct. 2147, 2152 (1986) (holding that no free exercise claim was presented where religious adherents believed that, if government used their child's social security number, the child's spirit would be endangered).

5. See Wisconsin v. Yoder, 406 U.S. 205, 216 (1972) ("if the Amish asserted their claims because of their subjective evaluation and rejection of the contemporary secular values accepted by the majority, much as Thoreau rejected the social values of his time and isolated himself at Walden Pond, their claims would not rest on a religious basis").

6. 450 U.S. 707, 711 n.3, 715–16 (1981).

7. Id. at 714.

8. 107 S.Ct. 1046 (1987).

9. Id. at 1051 ("In effect, the Appeals Commission asks us to single out the religious convert for different, less favorable treatment than that given an individual whose adherence to his or her faith precedes employment. We decline to do so. . . . The timing of Hobbie's conversion is immaterial to our determination that her free exercise rights have been burdened. . . ."). The claimant's sincerity was not challenged, id. at 1048 n.2. The newness of a belief may be relevant as a factor in demonstrating that the belief is not sincerely held.

10. Thomas, 450 U.S. at 715.

11. See 106 S.Ct. 2147, 2150 & n.3 (1986).

if they did, the concept of required accommodation [12] could become a limitless excuse for people to avoid all unwanted legal obligations. At the same time, however, an intrusive government inquiry into the nature of a claimant's beliefs would in itself threaten the values of religious liberty.

In *United States v. Ballard*,[13] the Supreme Court struck a balance: A jury could determine whether religious beliefs were sincerely held, but not whether they were true. In *Ballard*, a mail fraud prosecution, the defendants had solicited money by representing themselves as divine messengers. Writing for the Court, Justice Douglas carefully delimited the permissible judicial inquiry, in a strong defense of religious liberty. No judge or jury, he wrote, had the power *or* competence to determine whether the religious experiences claimed by the defendants had in fact occurred. "Freedom of thought, which includes freedom of religious belief, is basic in a society of free men. . . . It embraces the right to maintain theories of life and of death and of the hereafter which are rank heresy to orthodox faiths. Heresy trials are foreign to our Constitution. Men may believe what they cannot prove. They may not be put to the proof of their religious doctrines or beliefs. Religious experiences which are as real as life to some may be incomprehensible to others. Yet the fact that they may be beyond the ken of mortals does not mean that they can be made suspect before the law. Many take their gospel from the New Testament. But it would hardly be supposed that they could be tried before a jury charged with the duty of determining whether those teachings contained false representations. The miracles of the New Testament, the Divinity of Christ, life after death, the power of prayer are deep in the religious convictions of many. If one could be sent to jail because a jury in a hostile environment found those teachings false, little indeed would be left of religious freedom. The Fathers of the Constitution were not unaware of the varied and extreme views of religious sects, of the violence of disagreement among them and of the lack of any one religious creed on which all men would agree. They fashioned a charter of government which envisaged the widest possible toleration of conflicting views. . . . The religious views espoused by respondents might seem incredible, if not preposterous, to most people. But if those doctrines are subject to trial before a jury charged with finding their truth or falsity, then the same can be done with the religious beliefs of any sect. When the triers of fact undertake that task, they enter a forbidden domain. The First Amendment does not select any one group or any one type of religion for preferred treatment. It puts them all in that position. . . ." [14]

Chief Justice Stone, joined by Justices Roberts and Frankfurter in dissent, thought that "[t]he state of one's mind is a fact as capable of fraudulent misrepresentation as one's physical condition or the state of his bodily health." [15] But in his dissent, Justice Jackson found it

---

12. See § 14–4, supra.

13. 322 U.S. 78 (1944).

14. Id. at 86–87.

15. Id. at 90 (Stone, C.J., joined by Roberts and Frankfurter, JJ., dissenting on the ground that "freedom of religion [does not afford] . . . immunity from criminal pros-

impossible to separate the question of religious verity, which the *Ballard* Court held was beyond the power of courts or jurors to consider, from the question of religious sincerity: "I do not see how we can separate what is believed from considerations as to what is believable. The most convincing proof that one believes his statements is to show that they have been true in his experience." [16] More importantly, "any inquiry into intellectual honesty in religion raises profound psychological problems," [17] for "[t]he appeal in such matters is to a very different plane of credulity than is invoked by representations of secular fact in commerce." [18] In such matters, it is hard "to say how literally one is bound to believe the doctrine he teaches and even more difficult to say how far it is reliance upon a teacher's literal belief which induces followers to give him money." [19]

Justice Jackson's arguments against even a judicial inquiry into sincerity are most convincing when government seeks to protect gullible citizens from fraudulent religious claims, since protection from the "wrong" of mental and spiritual poison is precisely what the Constitution put beyond the prosecutor's reach. On this view, to allow the government in a situation like *Ballard* to restrict false prophets in order to protect their potential flock is fundamentally at odds with the special protection afforded the dissemination of religious ideas. However, Justice Jackson's arguments are less persuasive when individuals seek special treatment from the state, because the whole community, not just the believer's flock, suffers from the dilution of a governmental program.[20]

But perhaps the ground yielded to Justice Jackson by this assessment is insufficient. True, courts since *Ballard* have inquired into the sincerity of religious objectors,[21] and perhaps this is a necessity unless a strict neutrality approach to the free exercise clause is adopted.[22] Nonetheless, any such inquiry can be extraordinarily dangerous. The perception of the claimant's sincerity inevitably reflects the factfinder's view of the reasonableness of the claimant's beliefs. Especially given the widening understanding of what constitutes religion in our socie-

---

ecution for the fraudulent procurement of money by false statements as to one's religious experience," id. at 88).

16. Id. at 92 (Jackson, J., dissenting on the ground that sincerity should also be off-limits for the jury).

17. Id. at 93.

18. Id. at 94.

19. Id.

20. See Giannella, "Religious Liberty, Non-Establishment, and Doctrinal Development: Part I, The Religious Liberty Guarantee," 80 Harv.L.Rev. 1381, 1418 (1967).

21. For example, the Court's extensive review of Amish culture in Wisconsin v. Yoder, 406 U.S. 205, 222–29, 235–36 (1972), was undertaken partially to indicate that

the Amish objections to education beyond the eighth grade were rooted in sincere religious beliefs. See also In re Grady, 61 Cal.2d 887, 39 Cal.Rptr. 912, 394 P.2d 728 (1964) (determining that petitioner, a self-styled "peyote preacher," was not an honest and bona fide user of peyote for religious purposes); Teterud v. Burns, 522 F.2d 357 (8th Cir. 1975) (holding that an Indian inmate of a state penitentiary could wear long braided hair in accordance with his religious beliefs, since those beliefs were sincerely held and the state's interests could be served by less restrictive means).

22. See, e.g., Giannella, supra note 20, at 1417–18; R. Morgan, The Supreme Court and Religion 150–51 (1972); § 14–7, supra.

ty,[23] the very rights ostensibly protected by the free exercise clause might well be jeopardized by any but the most minimal inquiry into sincerity.

What indicia of sincerity should this minimal inquiry entail? Clearly a belief should not be dismissed because it has little historical pedigree or fails to resemble the factfinder's own idea of what a religion should resemble. But, equally clearly, a person's word cannot automatically be accepted if a religious exemption is at issue. Where extrinsic evidence exists to establish that "religion" is being used as a completely fraudulent cloak, such evidence must be considered.[24] In *Ballard*, for example, the prosecutor stressed that the defendants had composed form-letter testimonials from non-existent persons claiming to have been healed [25] and noted that the defendants had failed even to call their system a "religion" until they were placed on trial.[26] Full protection of the values underlying the first amendment suggests that any test of sincerity as a prerequisite of exemption must be strictly limited to inquiries of this relatively "neutral" sort, so that agents of government cannot readily bend the test to their religious prejudices.[27] The animating spirit of these inquiries should be that proclaimed by the Supreme Court in upholding the right of children of Jehovah's Witnesses to refuse to salute the American flag.[28] "If there is any fixed star in our constitutional constellation, it is that no official, high or petty, can prescribe what shall be orthodox in politics, nationalism, religion, or other matters of opinion or force citizens to confess by word or act their faith therein. If there are any circumstances which permit an exception, they do not now occur to us."

Closely related to the question of sincerity is the element of how substantially the prohibition or requirement burdens the religion. Clearly a conflict that threatens the very survival of the religion or the core values of a faith poses more serious free exercise problems than does a conflict that merely inconveniences the faithful. In *Wisconsin v. Yoder*,[29] the Court's extensive examination of Amish life and culture may be seen in part as an attempt to evaluate the degree to which Amish religious beliefs and practices would be burdened by applying the state's compulsory education law to their adolescent children be-

23. See § 14–6, supra. Our society is truly one in which one person's seemingly bizarre cult, easily dismissed by an outsider as insincerely held, is another's true religion. And, to the extent that we achieve the goal of religious pluralism, the problem becomes still more complex. See H. Cox, N.Y. Times, Feb. 16, 1977, at p. 25, col. 1.

24. See United States v. Kuch, 288 F.Supp. 439, 445 (D.D.C.1968) (denying a religious exemption from federal drug regulations where extrinsic evidence made it transparent that only a tactical pretense of religion was involved: members of the Neo-American Church were known as Boo Hoos, the seal of the church was a three-eyed toad, and the church motto was "Victory over Horseshit"). See also Dobkin v.

District of Columbia, 194 A.2d 657 (D.C. App.1963) (denying a merchant who regularly conducted business on Saturday an exemption from appearing in court on that day because of his claim that he was a Sabbatarian).

25. Record, 322 U.S., Vol. 4, at 1519–20, 1542.

26. Id. at 1496.

27. See, e.g., Founding Church of Scientology v. United States, 409 F.2d 1146 (D.C.Cir.1969), cert. denied 396 U.S. 963 (1969), discussed in § 14–16, infra.

28. West Virginia State Board of Education v. Barnette, 319 U.S. 624, 642 (1943).

29. 406 U.S. 205, 222–29, 235–36 (1972).

yond the eighth grade. Similarly, Justice Brennan's opinion for the majority in *Sherbert v. Verner* rested in part on the undisputed fact that the person seeking an exemption from the Saturday work requirement considered the religious injunction against Saturday work "a cardinal principle of her religious faith. . . ." [30]

In the wake of *Sherbert*, the California Supreme Court found the factor of religious burden decisive in *People v. Woody*, when holding unconstitutional the application of state criminal statutes to Native Americans using peyote in an obviously bona fide religious ceremony.[31] Assuming peyote to be an hallucinogenic substance the use of which is within the state's police power to proscribe,[32] the court found that the religious use of peyote had a long history among various Indian tribes and that the sacramental use of peyote was indeed the cornerstone of the Navaho appellants' religion; the court could find no sufficiently compelling reason for prohibiting a practice so central to the religion. In reaching this conclusion, the court relied upon the magnitude of the burden to distinguish *Reynolds v. United States*: [33] "Polygamy, although a basic tenet in the theology of Mormonism, is not essential to the practice of the religion; peyote, on the other hand, is the *sine qua non* of defendants' faith." [34] The statute's application to the Navaho thus tore out "the theological heart of Peyotism." [35]

The magnitude of the religious burdens is often stated in terms of the centrality of the tenet to the believer's faith; however, "centrality" only partially describes the courts' inquiry. True, centrality does help explain some holdings,[36] and the Supreme Court in *Sherbert* and especially in *Yoder* emphasized the centrality of the burdened beliefs. However, the Court has never specifically required free exercise claimants to demonstrate that the state requirement burdens a central tenet of their beliefs.

Conceptually, the requirement that claimants show an actual burden on their beliefs usually reflects the centrality of the belief, but it does not invariably do so. Centrality looks to the importance of a belief to the believer; burden looks to the degree that the government's requirement will, directly or indirectly, make the believer's religious duties more difficult or more costly.[37] Although substantial burdens on

30.   374 U.S. 398, 406 (1963).

31.   61 Cal.2d 716, 40 Cal.Rptr. 69, 394 P.2d 813 (1964); accord, Arizona v. Whittingham, 19 Ariz.App. 27, 504 P.2d 950 (1973), cert. denied 417 U.S. 946 (1974). See § 14–13, note 102, infra.

32.   But see § 15–7, infra, for an analysis questioning this assumption.

33.   98 U.S. (8 Otto) 145 (1878).

34.   Woody, 61 Cal.2d at 725, 40 Cal. Rptr. at 76, 394 P.2d at 820.

35.   61 Cal.2d at 722, 40 Cal.Rptr. at 74, 394 P.2d at 818.

36.   The cases dealing with the right to disseminate religious ideas reflect the notion that such activity lies at the core of

religious practice, second only to worship itself. See § 14–13, infra. More broadly, the belief-action distinction may be seen in part as affirming that "belief, prayer, and worship" lie at the "central and essential core of religion." Galanter, "Religious Freedom in the United States: A Turning Point?", 1966 Wis.L.Rev. 217, 274.

37.   Where the requirement is inherently incompatible with the adherent's religious duty, the case for an exemption is stronger than where the requirement simply makes following the religious duty more costly. Although the Court has not expressly adopted this distinction, its holdings seem to reflect it. See note 42, infra, and § 14–13, infra.

the claimant will, almost by definition, impinge on central aspects of the claimant's belief, the opposite is not necessarily true: A burden might be minimal, and thus outside the protection of the free exercise clause, even though it relates to the central aspect of a religion.

In *Tony and Susan Alamo Foundation v. Secretary of Labor*,[38] for example, a nonprofit religious organization claimed that an important tenet of its workers' religious beliefs would be burdened if the organization were required to abide by minimum wage requirements. The workers, mostly rehabilitated drug addicts or former criminals, worked for the organization's commercial enterprises in exchange for food, clothing, and shelter.[39] Several of them testified that the concept of wages was anathema to their religious tenets; the testimony indicated that the tenets were central ones.[40] Although the Supreme Court did not dispute the sincerity or the centrality of the claimants' beliefs, the Court unanimously rejected their free exercise claim. The Court concluded that the state requirements did not significantly burden the workers' beliefs, because the law would apparently allow the organization to continue compensating the workers with lodging and other in-kind benefits; and, even if the law did require cash wages, the workers could simply return the money to the organization.[41] *Alamo Foundation* thus illustrates that sincerity and centrality do not always suffice to meet a claimant's required showing; the claimant must also demonstrate a significant burden.[42]

Whether a court looks to the centrality of the tenet or to the burden that the state requirement places on the religion, it is clear that some such inquiry is essential. But, as with the sincerity inquiry, any more than minimal scrutiny might impinge upon free exercise values. A searching investigation could create troubling entanglement between the judiciary and the believer.[43] In addition, judges might impose their own views of the seriousness of the burden—views inevitably based partly on their own religious beliefs—rather than accepting the claimant's explanation of the burden.[44]

---

38. 471 U.S. 290 (1985).

39. See id. at 292.

40. See id. at 303 n.27.

41. See id. at 304. Cf. Marchioro v. Chaney, 442 U.S. 191 (1979) (case discussed in § 13–22, supra).

42. Consistent with this thesis are passages in several Supreme Court opinions, noting that the burden that the requirement imposed on the religion, although significant, would not be fatal to the religion. See Bob Jones University v. United States, 461 U.S. 574, 603–04 (1983) ("Denial of tax benefits will inevitably have a substantial impact on the operation of private religious schools, but will not prevent those schools from observing their religious tenets."); Braunfeld v. Brown, 366 U.S. 599, 605 (1961) ("The statute at bar does not make unlawful any religious practices of appellants; the Sunday [closing] law simply regulates a secular activity

and, as applied to appellants, operates so as to make the practice of their religious beliefs more expensive."). Such passages indicate that the burden must be significant; however, the free exercise clause has never required that burdens be fatal. A more analytically useful distinction is between laws that are directly incompatible with a religion and laws that, as an incidental effect, place a burden on the religion. See § 14–13, infra. From a somewhat different perspective, the Supreme Court has suggested that free exercise exemptions may be available only where "important [state] benefits" are concerned. See Thomas v. Review Bd., 450 U.S. 707, 717–18 (1981). Perhaps the denial of unimportant state benefits does not create a recognizable burden.

43. See § 14–11, supra.

44. Cf. Thomas v. Review Bd., 450 U.S. at 714 ("religious beliefs need not be ac-

In providing a mechanism to reduce these dangers, *Sherbert v. Verner* [45] and its progeny [46] are especially significant in departing from any purportedly "objective" judicial notion of what constitutes the core of a religion, and in moving toward the view that the core of any religion must always be defined from the perspective of the religion itself.[47] This shift undoubtedly comports with the purposes of the free exercise clause, but it poses new problems as courts in each case must identify appropriate sources of authority to assist in determining the weight of the government burden on the religion in question.[48] When a claimant avers that a prohibition or requirement conflicts with his or her own faith, the appropriate inquiry may begin but cannot end by looking to the dogma of a religious tract or organization; the ultimate inquiry must look to the claimant's sincerity in stating that the conflict is indeed burdensome *for that individual*.[49] Again, if values central to the first amendment are to be respected, this ultimate inquiry must not degenerate into an inquisition.

No standards of sincerity and burden will completely eliminate the tension between generously accommodating religious liberty and assuring that religion is not invoked as a cheap excuse for every conceivable form of self-indulgence. This tension, however carefully reduced, remains a threat to freedom for individuals and communities alike, as well as a threat to the separation of church and state, whenever people are forced to rely on free exercise claims in order to resist governmental invasions of their privacy and personality. It therefore becomes crucial to minimize that tension whenever possible, by recognizing rights independent of what one's private reasons for resisting an

ceptable, logical, consistent, or comprehensible to others in order to merit First Amendment protection"); id. at 715 ("it is not for us to say that the line [petitioner] drew [between religiously acceptable and unacceptable work] was an unreasonable one"); § 14–15, infra (discussing danger that judges will be insensitive to claims that public acknowledgments of the majority religion offend nonadherents of that religion).

45. 374 U.S. 398 (1963).

46. See Hobbie v. Unemployment Appeals Comm'n, 107 S.Ct. 1046 (1987) (requiring state to pay unemployment benefits to Seventh-Day Adventist who was fired because of her refusal, on religious grounds, to work Saturdays); Thomas v. Review Bd., 450 U.S. 707 (1981) (requiring state to pay unemployment benefits to claimant who, when transferred into weapons production, had quit his job for religious reasons); In re Jenison, 375 U.S. 14 (1963) (vacating for reconsideration in light of Sherbert a Minnesota judgment finding a woman in contempt of court for refusing jury duty on religious grounds) (the Minnesota Supreme Court then reversed the conviction, 267 Minn. 136, 125 N.W.2d 588 (1963) (per curiam)); People v. Woody, 61

Cal.2d 716, 40 Cal.Rptr. 69, 394 P.2d 813, (1964), supra note 31.

47. This shift parallels, of course, the shift in the free exercise context away from an "objective" to a "subjective" definition of religion. See § 14–6, supra.

48. There are other problems as well, for the very concepts of "centrality" and "religious burden" may be tied to particular religious traditions. Various forms of Christianity, for example, have clear divisions between secular and religious spheres, while other Christian sects, and other religions, perceive themselves as consisting of an integrated way of life. See generally Galanter, supra note 36, at 274–78. Cf. Bowen v. Roy, 106 S.Ct. 2147, 2152 n.6 (1986) ("Roy's religious views may not accept this distinction between individual and governmental conduct. . . . It is clear, however, that the Free Exercise Clause, and the Constitution generally, recognize such a distinction; for the adjudication of a constitutional claim, the Constitution, rather than an individual's religion, must supply the frame of reference.").

49. Thomas v. Review Bd., 450 U.S. 707, 714–16 (1981) (discussed above); § 14–6, supra.

intrusion might be. In Chapter 15, such rights are explored in detail. Here, we consider just two examples.

In *West Virginia State Board of Education v. Barnette*,[50] where a group of Jehovah's Witnesses challenged school regulations requiring students to salute the American flag, Justice Jackson, writing for the majority, focused not on freedom of religion, but on freedom of expression: the issue was whether any person could be compelled to salute the flag in violation of personal conviction. He wrote: "Nor does the issue as we see it turn on one's possession of particular religious views or the sincerity with which they are held. While religion supplies appellees' motive for enduring the discomforts of making the issue in this case, many citizens who do not share these religious views hold such a compulsory rite to infringe constitutional liberty of the individual. It is not necessary to inquire whether non-conformist beliefs will exempt from the duty to salute unless we first find power to make the salute a legal duty."[51]

So too in *Wooley v. Maynard*,[52] upholding the right of individuals to resist New Hampshire's requirement that they display the state's motto, "Live Free or Die," on their passenger car license plates, the Court avoided ruling on the individuals' argument that their religious freedom was infringed by the requirement. Instead the Court rested on the broader ground that compelling persons to serve as vehicles for views they find abhorrent invades a protected sphere of intellect and spirit.[53] *Why* the views were abhorrent—whether the reasons were religious or otherwise—became irrelevant; thus the Court avoided the dangers of inquiring into the genuineness and centrality of such religious views as were advanced.[54]

But the sphere of personal freedom recognized without regard to religion cannot cover every case that the free exercise clause should protect. For example, government has no duty to exempt bookstores [55] or newspapers [56] from enforcement of generally applicable regulations, even if the enforcement may burden free expression. But in some circumstances government does have a duty to carve exemptions for religious believers and organizations, where enforcement would unduly burden religious freedom.[57] In cases that remain unavoidably linked to

---

50. 319 U.S. 624 (1943).

51. Id. at 634–35.

52. 430 U.S. 705 (1977).

53. Id. at 714–15.

54. This case is discussed further, as is Barnette, in § 15–5, infra.

55. See Arcara v. Cloud Books, 106 S.Ct. 3172 (1986).

56. See Zurcher v. Stanford Daily, 436 U.S. 547 (1978).

57. See Hobbie v. Unemployment Appeals Comm'n, 107 S.Ct. 1046 (1987); Thomas v. Review Board, 450 U.S. 707 (1981); Wisconsin v. Yoder, 406 U.S. 205 (1972); Sherbert v. Verner, 374 U.S. 398 (1963). Even in cases refusing to recognize

such an exemption, the Court's willingness to entertain the possibility is nonetheless significant. See, e.g., Bowen v. Roy, 106 S.Ct. 2147 (1986) (claimants sought to bar government from using their daughter's social security number); United States v. Lee, 455 U.S. 252 (1982) (claimant sought exemption from paying social security taxes). Indeed, in Roy, it appears that a majority of the Justices were of the view that government could not require applicants for food stamps and other such benefits "to cooperate actively with the Government by themselves providing [a] social security number on benefit applications" over their religious objection. 106 S.Ct. at 2159 (Blackmun, J., concurring in part) (deeming this position at least tenable); id. at

the free exercise clause, the dangers of undue government involvement in matters of personal faith cannot be wholly eliminated. However generous a test of sincerity and centrality is adopted, however hard courts try not to impose any uniform orthodoxy, and however genuinely they attempt to limit evidence in such cases to extrinsic indications of fraud, they are already engaged in a treacherous business indeed when they try to assess the place that religion occupies in a person's life or the sincerity with which religious views are held.

§ 14–13. The Requirement that the State Show that Only Uniform Enforcement Can Achieve an Unusually Important End

The state's required showing in a free exercise case—that an unusually important goal can be achieved only through uniform enforcement of the regulation in question—strikes a balance between individuals' free exercise rights and government's functional needs.[1] This required showing arises after a religious claimant has proven, as set forth in § 14–12, the existence of a sincere religious belief that is burdened by the government regulation. At that point the state must overcome the claimant's showing by demonstrating, first, that the regulation pursues a particularly important governmental goal, and, second, that an exemption would substantially hinder the fulfillment of that goal. The precise nature and extent of the state's required showings are not clear: The Supreme Court has recently altered its formulation of the elements in a way that appears to reduce the state's burden of persuasion.

In order to understand the evolution of the doctrine, we must begin in the late 1930s and early 1940s, when the Supreme Court began to formulate the requirement that government pursue the least drastic means to a compelling secular end — although the decisions were not perceived in those terms at the time they were handed down. The earliest such decision was *Schneider v. New Jersey*,[2] where the Court reversed a conviction of a Jehovah's Witness for distributing religious circulars and soliciting contributions door-to-door without first obtaining a police permit as required by a municipal ordinance. The town had not embarked upon a policy of suppressing religion, and the

2163 (Stevens, J., concurring in part and dissenting in part) (accepting this position at least where exceptions are made by government for *non*-religious "inability" to "'provide' required information"); id. at 2166–67 (O'Connor, J., joined by Brennan and Marshall, JJ., concurring in part and dissenting in part) (exemption must be granted to the claimant "and to the handful of others who can be expected to make a similar religious objection"); id. at 2169 (White, J., dissenting) (government must exempt religious objectors not only from having to *provide* their social security numbers but also, it seems, from having those numbers *used internally* by government in processing their claims). The Roy case is discussed in § 14–13, infra.

§ 14–13

1. For a proposed doctrine that would require government to justify policies creating a significant risk of entanglement with religion by invoking a compelling secular justification, see Tribe, "Foreword: Toward a Model of Roles in the Due Process of Life and Law," 87 Harv.L.Rev. 1, 22–26 (1973). More conventionally, notions of compelling justification have been employed only in free exercise cases; government actions have been deemed either violative of the anti-establishment principle or not—the balancing process in that setting has been incorporated into the definitions of the terms themselves.

2. 308 U.S. 147 (1939).

Court recognized that the town's permit requirement might simply be a way of preventing "fraudulent appeals . . . in the name of charity and religion," [3] but it noted that less restrictive means were available (though the Court did not label them that)—namely, prosecuting frauds and trespassers. If "these means are less efficient and convenient than bestowal of power on police authorities to decide when information may be disseminated from house to house, and who may impart the information, the answer is that considerations of this sort do not empower a municipality to abridge freedom of speech and press." [4]

Although the Court noted the religious character of petitioner's canvassing activities,[5] no mention was made of the free exercise clause. In three companion cases, the Court reversed convictions for distributing political and labor handbills in the streets in violation of ordinances prohibiting all such distribution. The element of prior censorship was absent in those cases, as was the religious dimension; again the Court reasoned that the purposes of the ordinances—minimizing street litter and reducing the costs of street cleaning—could be served adequately by less drastic means.[6]

It remained only to connect the less restrictive alternative requirement with explicit concern for religious freedom. In *Cantwell v. Connecticut*,[7] that step was taken. The Court there reversed the convictions of Jehovah's Witnesses Newton Cantwell and his sons Jesse and Russell for soliciting religious contributions without a state certificate and for committing a breach of the peace, both offenses stemming from the Cantwells' going from house to house and playing an anti-Catholic record to anyone who would listen. The Court held that the "free exercise . . . of religion" is embraced by the "fundamental concept of liberty embodied in [the Fourteenth] Amendment;" [8] that to condition religious solicitation "upon a license, the grant of which rests in . . . determination by state authority as to what is a religious cause, is to lay a forbidden burden upon the exercise of liberty protected by the Constitution" [9] inasmuch as the state has less drastic means of preventing fraud and preserving peace, safety, and order; [10] and that the conduct of the Cantwell family was not so threatening to privacy or tranquility as to be punishable as a common law breach of the peace, particularly since the state had made no "legislative judgment that . . . the playing of a phonograph on the streets should in the interest of comfort or privacy be limited or prevented." [11] Thus the *Cantwell* Court was requiring not only the choice of a less drastic means but also the use of "a statute narrowly drawn to define and punish specific conduct as a clear and present danger to the State," [12] so that the

---

3. Id. at 164.

4. Id. See also § 12–23, supra.

5. 308 U.S. at 158. The Court also contrasted "commercial soliciting and canvassing." Id. at 165.

6. Id. at 162. The Court suggested "punishment of those who actually throw papers on the streets." Id. The "public forum" aspect of these cases is discussed in § 12–24, supra.

7. 310 U.S. 296 (1940).

8. Id. at 303.

9. Id. at 307.

10. Id. at 306–07.

11. Id. at 307.

12. Id. at 311.

suggestion of a compelling secular purpose must appear as a considered judgment before the fact, and not simply as a convenient post-hoc rationalization.[13]

Three years after *Cantwell*, in *Murdock v. Pennsylvania*,[14] the Court reversed a conviction for distributing religious pamphlets and soliciting donations without first obtaining a license that cost $1.50 per day (or $7.00 per week). No discretionary prior censorship of the sort involved in *Schneider* and *Cantwell* could be charged. As in those cases, there was no suggestion that the government's ends were themselves illegitimate or that its means could serve no valid purpose. Just as it was permissible to combat fraud as well as litter in *Schneider* and to control noise in *Cantwell*, so it was permissible to seek revenue from those who take advantage of the pubic thoroughfares to make profits in a case like *Murdock*, and the Court could not "say that religious groups . . . are free from all financial burdens of government."[15] But "[s]preading religious beliefs in [an] ancient and honorable manner"[16] by "moving throughout a state or from state to state" could be "crushed and closed out by the sheer weight of the toll or tribute which is exacted town by town, village by village."[17] Because "freedom of religion [is] in a preferred position,"[18] the most the Constitution might tolerate is a "nominal [fee] imposed as a regulatory measure and calculated to defray the expense of protecting those on the streets and at home against the abuse of solicitors."[19] Even such a fee might be suspect, however: "Freedom of speech, freedom of the press, freedom of religion are available to all, not merely to those who can pay their own way."[20] Although *Murdock* relied on a formalistic notion that states may not "exact a license tax for the privilege of carrying on interstate commerce . . . [or] activities guaranteed by the First Amendment,"[21] the demise of such formalism in the commerce clause area[22] need not threaten the continued validity of the *Murdock* holding, for the notion at the core of *Murdock* was plainly that the state could reasonably meet its legitimate needs for regulation and revenue without imposing potentially crushing burdens on religious activity.

So viewed, *Murdock* combines with *Schneider* and *Cantwell* to establish a basic principle: The government's secular purpose must be tightly linked to the burden the government imposes on religion; if the government can approximately attain its goal without burdening religion then it must follow that path, regardless of how compelling the goal may be.[23]

13. Compare § 16–32, infra.

14. 319 U.S. 105 (1943).

15. Id. at 112.

16. Id.

17. Id. at 115.

18. Id.

19. Id. at 116.

20. Id. at 111.

21. Id. at 113.

22. See Complete Auto Transit, Inc. v. Brady, 430 U.S. 274 (1977), discussed in § 6–15, supra.

23. The holdings in these three cases could, however, be given a relatively limited reading. First, all were concerned with activities protected as ancillary not only to religion but also to speech; indeed, Schneider was decided before the free exercise clause had been "incorporated" into the fourteenth amendment by Cantwell. And the Court in Murdock noted that the tax on solicitation presented on its face a "re-

Braunfeld v. Brown[24] showed that not all disabilities on religion amounted to constitutionally significant burdens. The four-justice plurality found that Sunday closing laws, without exemptions, were the least burdensome way that the state could pursue its goal of providing "a weekly respite from all labor."[25] The plurality opinion made two somewhat conflicting points. First, the Justices emphasized that the statute only *indirectly* burdened the claimants—Orthodox Jews whose faith forbade working on Saturdays, and whose state was forbidding them to work on Sundays—because it did "not make unlawful any religious practices," but "simply . . . operates so as to make the practice of their religious beliefs more expensive."[26] The Justices implied that many such statutes, creating indirect burdens, were constitutionally "unassailable."[27]

The plurality's second point, however, contradicted that implication, and instead reaffirmed the principle laid down by *Murdock, Schneider,* and *Cantwell*: Even indirect burdens are constitutionally

striction of the free exercise of these freedoms which are protected by the First Amendment." 319 U.S. at 114. "A license tax certainly does not acquire constitutional validity because it classifies the privileges protected by the First Amendment along with wares and merchandise of hucksters and peddlers and treats them all alike. Such equality of treatment does not save the ordinance. Freedom of press, freedom of speech, and freedom of religion are in a preferred position." Id. at 115. Arguably, only the simultaneous involvement of all three of these freedoms triggered the severe scrutiny the Court gave to the laws in Schneider, Cantwell and Murdock.

Moreover, viewing the cases as involving religion alone, the Court saw the laws in question as striking at the very essence of the religious enterprise: "We only hold that spreading one's religious beliefs or preaching the Gospel through distribution of religious literature and through personal visitations is an age-old type of evangelism with as high a claim to constitutional protection as the more orthodox types." Murdock, 319 U.S. at 110. Indeed, the Court thought that the very existence of the religion in question might be at stake: "Itinerant evangelists moving throughout a state or from state to state would feel immediately the cumulative effect of such ordinances as they became fashionable. The way of the religious dissenter has long been hard. But if the formula of this type of ordinance is approved, a new device for the suppression of religious minorities will have been found. . . . The spread of religious ideas through personal visitations by the literature ministry of numerous religious groups would be stopped." Id. at 115. Many American religions have itinerant evangelism as their very essence.

See § 15–14, infra, for a parallel concern with respect to vagrancy statutes.

Finally, the Court noted an equal protection dimension in Murdock: "Freedom of speech, freedom of the press, freedom of religion are available to all, not merely to those who can pay their own way." 319 U.S. at 111. In these early cases and certainly in Murdock, then, the Court seemed concerned primarily with pamphleteering as the printing press of the poor.

But even this confined a reading of the cases shows that Sherbert v. Verner, 374 U.S. 398 (1963), to be discussed shortly, could not be regarded as the pure "aberration" that Professor Ely deemed it to be, see Ely, "Legislative and Administrative Motivation in Constitutional Law," 79 Yale L.J. 1205, 1322 (1970), for it was not Sherbert but the early cases canvassed here that established the principle that even "a regulation's unintended adverse impact upon persons of a particular faith can invalidate it" as applied to them. Id. at 1319.

24. 366 U.S. 599 (1961).

25. Id. at 607 (Warren, C.J., joined by Black, Clark, and Whittaker, JJ.).

26. Id. at 605.

27. "Of course, to hold unassailable all legislation regulating conduct which imposes solely an indirect burden on the observance of religion would be a gross oversimplification. If the purpose or effect of a law is to impede the observance of one or all religions or is to discriminate invidiously between religions, that law is constitutionally invalid even though the burden may be characterized as being only indirect." Id. at 607. The Justices said nothing more about those forbidden categories; the silence implied that the Sunday closing law did not fall into any of them.

forbidden if "the State may accomplish its purposes by means which do not impose such a burden." [28]   Given the nature of the state's interests in Sunday closing laws, however, the Justices concluded that no such burdenless alternative was available.   Exemptions might fail to "bring[ ] about a general day of rest," undercut the goal of "eliminat[ing] the atmosphere of commercial noise and activity," give exempted people an unfair competitive advantage, encourage fraudulent religious claims, and require more costly enforcement.[29]

In his classic dissent in *Braunfeld*, Justice Stewart put the matter plainly: "Pennsylvania has passed a law which compels an Orthodox Jew to choose between his religious faith and his economic survival. That is a cruel choice.   It is a choice which I think no State can constitutionally demand.   For me this is not something that can be swept under the rug and forgotten in the interest of enforced Sunday togetherness.   I think the impact of this law upon these appellants grossly violates their constitutional right to the free exercise of their religion." [30]

Two years after *Braunfeld*, the Supreme Court took a major step beyond these precedents, extending and solidifying the principles latent in its previous holdings.   *Sherbert v. Verner* [31] concerned a member of the Seventh-Day Adventist Church, who was discharged by her South Carolina employer because she would not work on Saturday, the Sabbath of her faith.   Unable to obtain other employment because she refused to work on Saturday, she filed a claim for unemployment compensation benefits under the South Carolina Unemployment Compensation Act, which provided that a claimant was ineligible for benefits if she failed, without good cause, to accept suitable work that had been offered.   The Unemployment Commission denied her claim on the ground that she would not accept suitable work, but the Supreme Court held that this denial abridged Mrs. Sherbert's right to the free exercise of her religion.

Sherbert went well beyond the precedents in two important ways, the combination of which made the free exercise clause a vastly more powerful instrument for generating government accommodations of religion.

First, *Sherbert* rejected *Braunfeld*'s distinction between direct and indirect burdens,[32] and held that free exercise protection applied not

---

28.   Id.   As a result, the indirect nature of the burden seemed irrelevant to the decision.   The direct-indirect dichotomy has not survived in subsequent case law. However, as will be discussed below, a similar distinction helps to explain the Court's treatment of free exercise claims.

29.   Id. at 608–09.

30.   366 U.S. at 616 (Stewart, J., concurring in part and dissenting in part).

31.   374 U.S. 398 (1963).

32.   For that and other reasons, Braunfeld itself may no longer represent the law. Justice Stewart, concurring in Sherbert, urged that "the *Braunfeld* case was wrong-

ly decided and should be overruled."   374 U.S. at 418 (Stewart, J., concurring in result).   Justice Brennan, who wrote the majority opinion in Sherbert, later wrote: "Candor compels the acknowledgment that to the extent that *Braunfeld* conflicts with *Sherbert* in this regard [that the free exercise clause applies only where government directly prohibits religious activity], it was overruled."   McDaniel v. Paty, 435 U.S. 618, 633 n.6 (1978) (Brennan, J., concurring in judgment).   Moreover, Thomas v. Review Board, 450 U.S. 707 (1981), reaffirmed the Sherbert principle and, significantly, did not even cite Braunfeld (although Braunfeld has been cited in cases since

only where government imposed a direct cost, but also where government withheld an economic benefit.[33] The emergence of an increasingly pervasive, affirmative state had blurred the distinction between benefits and burdens too thoroughly to make it a tolerable dividing line in constitutional adjudication: "In a sense the consequences of such a disqualification to religious principles and practices may be only an indirect result of welfare legislation within the State's general competence to enact; it is true that no criminal sanctions directly compel appellant to work a six-day week. But this is only the beginning, not the end, of our inquiry. . . . Here not only is it apparent that appellant's declared ineligibility for benefits derives solely from the practice of her religion, but the pressure upon her to forego that practice is unmistakable. The ruling forces her to choose between following precepts of her religion and forfeiting benefits, on the one hand, and abandoning one of the precepts of her religion to accept work, on the other hand. Governmental imposition of such a choice puts the same kind of burden upon the free exercise of religion as would a fine imposed against appellant for her Saturday worship."[34]

Significantly, the Court added: "Nor may the . . . construction of the statute be saved from constitutional infirmity on the ground that unemployment compensation benefits are not appellant's 'right' but merely a 'privilege.' It is too late in the day to doubt that the liberties of religion and expression may be infringed by the denial of or placing of conditions upon a benefit or privilege."[35]

Sherbert's second important doctrinal advance was in formally adopting the least restrictive alternative-compelling state interest mode of analysis in a free exercise context.[36] Schneider, Cantwell, and Murdock had pointed toward those two requirements. Braunfeld had applied the least restrictive alternative requirement but not the compelling state interest one, and the plurality's focus on the direct burden-indirect burden dichotomy had muddied the issue.

By these two doctrinal advances, Sherbert showed that government could not adopt a position of "religion-blindness." There would, of course, be no cases of impermissible failure to accommodate religion if government's refusal to do so could automatically be justified simply by invoking the desirability, given the establishment clause, of complete governmental inattention to religious circumstances. Some commenta-

Thomas). Finally, Braunfeld rested partly on McGowan v. Maryland, 366 U.S. 420 (1961), where the Court had upheld Sunday closing laws against an establishment clause challenge. However, to pass the establishment clause inquiry in McGowan, the Sunday closing laws had only to be secular; to pass the Sherbert free exercise inquiry, a statute must pursue a compelling governmental interest. Braunfeld did not hold that Sunday closing laws meet that burden. It is at least debatable whether the state's interest in a *mandated, uniform* "day of rest, repose, recreation and tranquillity" could qualify as compelling. Braunfeld, 366 U.S. at 607 (plurality opinion). But a dichotomy similar to di-

rect-indirect seems to lie behind the Court's reasoning in free exercise cases: the distinction between laws that address religiously mandated or prohibited practices, and laws that simply make religious practices more difficult or expensive. The distinction will be considered below.

33. See generally § 11–5, supra.

34. 374 U.S. at 403–04.

35. Id. at 404.

36. Such analysis had previously been made explicit in free speech cases. See, e.g., NAACP v. Button, 371 U.S. 415, 438 (1963); Shelton v. Tucker, 364 U.S. 479, 487–90 (1960). See Chapter 12, supra.

tors [37] have urged such a view upon the Court, but without success: the Court has viewed governments' failure to accommodate religion, when the government could substantially achieve its legitimate goals while granting religious exemptions, as hostility toward religion.[38] In *Sherbert*, the state did not demonstrate that there could be no less restrictive ways of preventing fraudulent claims by persons using Sabbatarian beliefs as a front for laziness.[39] Thus, the only significant interest the state could argue on behalf of its refusal to make an exception for religious objectors to Saturday work was the interest in treating religious objectors the same way as anyone else,[40] an interest the Court was unwilling to regard as consistent with the free exercise clause where the consequences of remaining studiously religion-blind were as drastic as they were to the Seventh-Day Adventist in *Sherbert*.[41]

The Court reaffirmed this principle in *Wisconsin v. Yoder*,[42] where the consequences of religion-blindness appeared even more drastic than in *Sherbert*. The state could not, the Court held, enforce its criminal statute against Amish families who refused to send their children to

37. See the discussion of strict neutrality in § 14–7, supra.

38. The supposed interest in avoiding a *preference* for the religious, so that they could no more be excused from Saturday work than could those who, for example, preferred to work on Sundays because their favorite babysitter was never available on Saturdays, is hard to square with the fact that the free exercise of religion clause is not followed in the Constitution by *other* "free exercise" clauses for *other* activities; there is, after all, no "free choice of babysitter" clause. Moreover, the interest seems belied by the state's decision to save "the Sunday worshipper from having to make the [same] kind of choice. . . ." 374 U.S. at 406.

39. See 374 U.S. at 407.

40. The possible interest in minimizing the drain on unemployment compensation funds by insisting on availability for work throughout the six days on which the largest number of private employers have work to offer represents the sort of dollar-and-cents concern that the Court has long treated as insufficient to warrant imposition of a significant burden on a preferred right. Moreover, that interest involves some rather uncomfortable bootstrapping on the continued validity of the Sunday closing laws—without which more work would presumably be available on Sundays. Refusal to grant an exemption either to the statute in Sherbert or to the Sunday closing laws is double punishment of the Sabbatarian: in effect, the Sabbatarian is told that there is not enough Sunday work—because the state has helped establish Sunday as a common day of rest—and that, although this state action was contrary to the Sabbatarian's interest, she will be held accountable for its effects

when it comes to distributing resources for unemployment insurance. Finally, whatever the case in Braunfeld, there is surely no interest in "enforced Sunday togetherness" among the unemployed. Cf. Stewart, J., dissenting in Braunfeld at 616. See also Comment, "Religious Accommodation under Sherbert v. Verner: The Common Sense of the Matter," 10 Vill.L.Rev. 337 (1965).

Contrast Trans World Airlines, Inc. v. Hardison, 432 U.S. 63 (1977), holding that a congressional enactment requiring employers to make "reasonable accommodations," not incurring "undue hardship," to facilitate their employees' religious choices, does not compel an employer to arrange Saturdays off for employees celebrating Sabbath on Saturdays where doing so would force the employer either to incur more than minimal costs (such as overtime pay for replacements) or to assign substitute employees in violation of their seniority privileges; and Thornton v. Caldor, 472 U.S. 703 (1985), striking down, on establishment clause grounds, a Connecticut statute that gave employees an absolute right not to work on their religion's Sabbath. Just as forcing employers to take such steps might well cause unequal treatment of employees on the basis of religion, so it seems crucial to the analysis in Sherbert that no significant sacrifice would have been required of the state or its citizens had it complied with requests like Mrs. Sherbert's.

41. Compare Johnson v. Robison, 415 U.S. 361 (1974) (denying special veterans benefits to conscientious objector who did alternative service is not an added burden on religion but is simply a way of equalizing burdens).

42. 406 U.S. 205 (1972).

school beyond the eighth grade. The Court concluded that the interests served by Wisconsin's compulsory education law—those of preparing citizens for effective, intelligent and self-reliant political and social participation—were ably served by the contested actions of the Old Order Amish, who withdrew their children from public schools after the first eight grades in order to train them informally for rural community life, in keeping with the tenets of their religious faith. The Court thought that the state's "interest in universal education, however highly" ranked, could not be "totally free from a balancing process when it impinges on [other] fundamental rights and interests, such as those specifically protected by the Free Exercise Clause of the First Amendment, and the traditional interest of parents with respect to the religious upbringing of their children. . . ." [43] Stressing that it was dealing not "with a way of life and mode of education by a group claiming to have recently discovered some 'progressive' or more enlightened process for rearing children for modern life" but rather with a long-established and "deep religious conviction, shared by an organized group, and intimately related to daily living," the Court thought it decisive "that enforcement of the State's requirement of compulsory formal education after the eighth grade would gravely endanger if not destroy the free exercise of respondents' [the parents'] religious beliefs." [44] Having accepted as the only legitimate goal of educating the respondents' children their "preparation . . . for life in the separated agrarian community that is the keystone of the Amish faith," the Court concluded that "compulsory education for a year or two beyond the eighth grade" was hardly "necessary" in the context of this case. Accordingly, the Court held the Amish parents immune to criminal punishment for violating the compulsory education law.

The children in *Yoder*, it might have been argued, were harmed by the deprivation of post-elementary education; instead, the Court signaled its refusal to permit the state to define as harmful anything it might deem undesirable. Certain widely recognized harms—such as physical injury—can be prevented even at the cost of infringing religious freedom, but the state cannot impose its ideal of the "best possible life" as a way of justifying intrusion upon the religious autonomy of a citizen. [45] The diffuse harm of depriving someone of more advanced education and the best life the governing majority can imagine is not enough to justify impinging upon the autonomy of a religious community. But in a case like *Yoder*, it is at least arguable that the community's autonomy—or the rights of the parents—must yield if the rights of the children are to be defended. [46]

Some language in both *Sherbert* and *Yoder* implied that the holdings did not necessarily create a broad principle of free exercise exemptions. The *Sherbert* holding rested partly on non-neutrality.

---

43. Id. at 214. Cf. Pierce v. Society of Sisters, 268 U.S. 510 (1925) (invalidating a state ban on all private school education).

44. Yoder, 406 U.S. at 216.

45. Cf. O'Connor v. Donaldson, 422 U.S. 563, 575 (1975) (holding, among other things, that the state cannot "confine the mentally ill merely to assure them a living standard superior to that they enjoy in the private community").

46. For a discussion of the tension in *Yoder* between the individual and the intermediate group, see § 14–16, infra.

During periods when the state permitted its textile mills to operate seven days a week, it prohibited employers from discriminating against employees who, for religious reasons, refused to work on Sundays. "The unconstitutionality of the disqualification of the Sabbatarian is thus compounded by the religious discrimination which South Carolina's general statutory scheme necessarily effects." [47] The Court made clear that non-neutrality was not the statute's only infirmity, or even its primary one; but some question remained as to whether multiple infirmities were required in order to justify a free exercise exemption. *Yoder* left open a different sort of question, whether the nature and history of the religious group determined its eligibility for an exemption. The Court's lengthy recital of Amish virtues was consistent with the conclusion that a less praiseworthy sect, or even one with a shorter history, might not be eligible for an exemption. [48]

These doubts about the uniqueness of *Sherbert* and *Yoder* were partly laid to rest by *Thomas v. Review Board*. [49] Thomas, a Jehovah's Witness, worked in a steel mill. When the mill closed, its owners transferred Thomas to a foundry that made military tank turrets. Thomas quit for what he said were religious reasons, but the unemployment board found that his reasons fell short of the statutorily required "good cause." [50] The Supreme Court, following *Sherbert*, held that the state could not deny unemployment benefits to Thomas. "Here, as in *Sherbert*, the employee was put to a choice between fidelity to religious belief or cessation of work; the coercive impact on Thomas is indistinguishable from *Sherbert*. . . ." [51] The facts mirrored *Sherbert* to a considerable degree; for present purposes,[52] the *Thomas* holding is important principally in reaffirming *Sherbert*, including *Sherbert's* holding that indirect infringements on religious liberty could support free exercise claims, under circumstances where non-neutrality was not an issue. [53]

The Court again reaffirmed *Sherbert* in *Hobbie v. Unemployment Appeals Commission*. [54] Hobbie converted to the Seventh-Day Adventist faith and told her employer that she could no longer work on Saturdays. She was fired. The state refused her application for unemploy-

---

47. 374 U.S. at 406.

48. The Court detailed the "Amish qualities of reliability, self-reliance, and dedication to work," 406 U.S. at 224, and suggested that "the Amish communities singularly parallel and reflect many of the virtues of Jefferson's ideal of the 'sturdy yeoman' who would form the basis of what he considered as the ideal of a democratic society," id. at 225–26. Justice Douglas responded: "A religion is a religion irrespective of what the misdemeanor or felony records of its members might be." 406 U.S. at 246 (Douglas, J., concurring in part and dissenting in part).

49. 450 U.S. 707 (1981).

50. Id. at 709–12.

51. Id. at 717.

52. Thomas also clarified several issues about what sorts of religious beliefs qualify

for free exercise exemptions. See §§ 14–6, 14–12, supra.

53. But see Bowen v. Roy, 106 S.Ct. 2147, 2156 (1986) (opinion of Burger, C.J., joined by Powell and Rehnquist, JJ.) (limiting Sherbert and Thomas to circumstances where statutes provide mechanisms for individualized exemptions); id. at 2163–64 n. 17 (Stevens, J., concurring in part and concurring in result) (religious exemptions in Thomas and Sherbert were "necessary to prevent the treatment of religious claims less favorably than other claims").

54. 107 S.Ct. 1046 (1987). Justice Brennan delivered the opinion of the Court, joined by Justices White, Marshall, Blackmun, O'Connor, and Scalia. Justices Powell and Stevens filed opinions concurring in the judgment, id. at 1052, 1053. Only Chief Justice Rehnquist dissented, id. at 1052.

ment benefits, finding that she was dismissed for "misconduct." [55] In the Supreme Court, the state emphasized Hobbie's religious conversion, arguing that she was the " 'agent of change' . . . responsible for the consequences of the conflict between her job and her religious beliefs." [56] The Court rejected the argument, writing: "The timing of Hobbie's conversion is immaterial to our determination that her free exercise rights have been burdened; the salient inquiry under the Free Exercise Clause is the burden involved." [57]

Between *Thomas* and *Hobbie*, however, the Supreme Court rejected several free exercise claims.[58] The results seemed to stem partly from the Court's unconfessed readjustment of the free exercise test. The test's required showings by a religious claimant—a burden, direct or indirect, on a sincere religious belief—seem to remain the same. However, the showing that the state must make to overcome the claimant's showing has apparently changed.

The doctrinal change appeared in *United States v. Lee*, where the Court rejected the Amish's claim for exemption from social security taxes.[59] The Court emphasized the importance of the social security program in general, as well as the apparent necessity of uniform participation in particular, and found that the government's interest was "very high." [60] The Court then determined that exempting the Amish would "unduly interfere with fulfillment of the governmental interest." [61] The feared interference seemed to be based largely on the concern that exempting the Amish from social security taxes would require future exemptions for other groups from general revenue taxes. "If, for example, a religious adherent believes war is a sin, and if a certain percentage of the federal budget can be identified as devoted to war-related activities, such individuals would have a similarly valid claim to be exempt from paying that percentage of the income tax. The tax system could not function. . . ." [62]

---

55. Id. at 1048.

56. Id. at 1050. There was no allegation that Hobbie's belief was not sincerely held. Id. at 1048 n.2.

57. Id. at 1051.

58. Bowen v. Roy, 106 S.Ct. 2147 (1986) (rejecting Native Americans' religion-based claim that the government not make internal use of their daughter's social security number); Goldman v. Weinberger, 475 U.S. 503 (1986) (rejecting Orthodox Jew's claim to wear yarmulke while on military duty); Tony & Susan Alamo Found. v. Secretary of Labor, 471 U.S. 290 (1985) (rejecting religious organization's claim for exemption from minimum wage and other labor laws); Bob Jones Univ. v. United States, 461 U.S. 574 (1983) (rejecting religious university's claim for tax-exempt and tax-deductible status despite racially discriminatory admissions policies, where policies are religiously compelled); United States v. Lee, 455 U.S. 252 (1982) (rejecting Amish employer's claim for exemption from social security taxes).

59. 455 U.S. 252 (1982). Self-employed Amish were exempt from paying social security taxes under 26 U.S.C. § 1402(g); Lee concerned an Amish employer.

60. 455 U.S. at 259.

61. Id.

62. Id. at 260. Justice Stevens, concurring in the judgment, found this risk "overstate[d]." First, the Amish's partial exemption from social security taxes showed that the administrative problems would not be insuperable. Id. at 262. Second, the Amish are a small community who had successfully "demonstrated their capacity to care for their own." Id. Finally, Justice Stevens wrote, the exemption would not stand as the dangerous precedent that the majority feared, because the Amish would, through self-help, achieve the government's goals; where a taxpayer objects to the way in which the government uses his or her tax money, in contrast, "the taxpayer is not in any position to supply the government with an equivalent substitute. . . ." Id. at 262 n.1. But Justice

Although *Lee*'s facts are unusual, its modifications of the free exercise test appear to be generally applicable. *Lee* seems to weaken both aspects of the required state showing: that the program pursue a compelling state interest, and that the state's means of pursuing that interest present the lowest possible burden on the claimant's religion.

As for the first aspect, the state interest had previously been defined narrowly.[63] The Court's opinions made clear that the only constitutionally relevant factor was the state's interest in denying the claimant's exemption, *not* the state's usually much greater interest in maintaining the underlying rule or program for unexceptional cases. *Lee*, in contrast, discussed both interests—the social security program as a whole, and the importance of uniform participation in it.[64] To the degree that the state's interest is defined to include the program as a whole, the state will find it easier to present a compelling interest, and thereby to pass its first hurdle.[65]

As for the second aspect, prior cases had required the state to apply the least restrictive means to achieve its goal, and thus to accommodate the religious claimant as far as possible. Under *Lee*, the state apparently must accommodate the claimant only if doing so will not "unduly interfere with fulfillment of the governmental interest."[66] However the Court ultimately defines "unduly interfere," it seems likely that it will be a looser standard than "least restrictive means."

In sum, previous cases required the state to show that it was pursuing a compelling interest, *narrowly* defined, and that an exemption would *defeat* that interest; *Lee* seems to require the state to show only that it is pursuing a compelling interest, *broadly* defined, and that

Stevens concluded that the free exercise doctrine ought to be altered such that the claimant would "shoulder the burden of demonstrating that there is a unique reason for allowing him a special exemption from a valid law of general applicability." Id. at 262.

63. See Thomas v. Review Bd., 450 U.S. at 719 (although interests proffered by state are important, "[w]hen the focus of the inquiry is properly narrowed," the interests do not justify the burden on Thomas's religion).

64. 455 U.S. at 258–60. The Court in Lee also went beyond the social security system, and discussed "the broad public interest in maintaining a sound tax system." Id. at 260.

65. The Court has subsequently followed Lee's general approach. In Bob Jones University v. United States, 461 U.S. 574, 604 (1983), the Court focused on the state interest in "eradicating racial discrimination in education" generally, and did not discuss the degree to which exempting institutions like Bob Jones University would frustrate that interest. Cf. Tony & Susan Alamo Found. v. Secretary of Labor, 471 U.S. 290, 304 n.29 (1985), where the petitioners claimed that government had no compelling interest in enforcing minimum wage requirements against their religious organization, because the employees would simply return the money to the organization; the Court relegated the point to a footnote and, rather than responding to it, used it to illustrate that the minimum wage requirements would not create a significant burden on the religious organization.

66. 455 U.S. at 259. Although Bob Jones University v. United States used the term "less restrictive means," it did not discuss the alternative means available to the state, and its analysis seemed consistent with the Lee approach: "That governmental interest [in eliminating racial discrimination in education] substantially outweighs whatever burden denial of tax benefits places on petitioners' exercise of their religious beliefs. The interests asserted by petitioners cannot be accommodated with that compelling governmental interest, and no 'less restrictive means' are available to achieve the governmental interest." 461 U.S. at 604 (citations and footnote omitted).

an exemption would "unduly interfere" with the interest.[67] Moreover, some Justices have indicated that they would go farther in reducing the scope of the free exercise clause.[68]

Despite uncertainty about the precise content of the free exercise test, it is possible to make several general points. Even when the Court's formulation has remained constant, its free exercise holdings seem to reflect a recurring polarity: one set of government rules has been subjected to strict scrutiny; another, to more cursory review. Although such specific factors as deference to military decisions have often been important (such factors will be examined below), a more general dichotomy appears to be operating. Yet, as we have seen, the Court has abandoned the "direct-indirect" approach applied in *Braunfeld*, and the "belief-action" dichotomy is not generally helpful in illuminating the cases.[69]

A more plausible dichotomy may be that between those government measures (1) that put an individual to a choice between adherence to religious duties and enjoyment of government benefits (or, as in *Yoder*, avoidance of a government burden like criminal prosecution), and (2) those government measures that are not triggered by the religious choice in question but burden religious activity only in a manner ancillary to an undeniably secular choice. Rules in the first category are subject to higher scrutiny. Such rules may facially discriminate against religious adherents, as in the case of a rule prohibiting members of the clergy from serving in various state of-

67. The Court has sometimes used phrases other than "compelling state interest," the phrase employed in Sherbert, 374 U.S. at 406, although the substantive significance, if any, is unclear. Yoder limited state goals to "only those interests of the highest order," 406 U.S. at 215, whereas Lee used the phrase "overriding governmental interest," 455 U.S. at 257–58. But see Hobbie v. Unemployment Appeals Comm'n, 107 S.Ct. 1046, 1049 (1987) ("compelling state interest"); Larson v. Valente, 456 U.S. 228, 247 (1982) ("compelling governmental interest") (case applying strict scrutiny analysis; see § 14–7, supra).

68. In Bowen v. Roy, three Justices wrote: "Absent proof of an intent to discriminate against particular religious beliefs or against religion in general, the Government meets its burden when it demonstrates that a challenged requirement for governmental benefits, neutral and uniform in its application, is a reasonable means of promoting a legitimate public interest." 106 S.Ct. 2147, 2156 (1986) (opinion of Burger, C.J., joined by Powell and Rehnquist, JJ.). These Justices relied on Bob Jones University v. United States, 461 U.S. 574, 604 (1983), for the proposition that denial of benefits is constitutionally less serious than an imposition of direct

burdens, and they said that the courts ought to measure indirect burdens differently from direct burdens. 106 S.Ct. at 2155–56. The Justices limited the Sherbert and Thomas holdings to statutes that provide for individualized exemptions, as the unemployment statutes in those cases did; "[i]f a state creates such a mechanism, its refusal to extend an exemption to an instance of religious hardship suggests a discriminatory intent." Id. at 2156. This attenuation of the test was necessary, the Justices added, because nearly any government requirement is likely to offend someone's religious beliefs, and the stricter test would require the government to demonstrate a compelling interest in order to proceed. "While libertarians and anarchists [would] no doubt applaud this result, it is hard to imagine that this is what the Framers intended." Id. at 2156 n.17. Subsequently, however, the Court flatly rejected this approach. Hobbie v. Unemployment Appeals Comm'n, 107 S.Ct. 1046, 1049 (1987). Justice Stevens has also advocated an attenuated free exercise test, in order to prevent the appearance of official favoritism toward particular religions. See note 124, infra.

69. See § 14–6, supra.

fices,[70] or a rule making vocational rehabilitation benefits available for any form of education except religious training.[71] More often, such rules impose burdens indirectly: a rule requiring recipients of state unemployment benefits to be available for Saturday work, which conflicts with the religious duties of Sabbatarians;[72] a rule requiring children to attend school through age 16, which conflicts with the religious duties of the Old Order Amish;[73] a rule prohibiting members of the military from wearing unauthorized headgear, which conflicts with the religious duties of Orthodox Jews;[74] a rule requiring recipients of welfare benefits to submit their social security numbers, which conflicts with the religious beliefs of some Native Americans.[75]

In contrast, rules in the second category, although they do have an incidental effect of burdening religiously motivated choices, are neither cast in terms of religious faith nor triggered by religiously motivated choices. An example is a Sunday closing law. Such a law makes the practice of Sabbatarian faiths more burdensome; in order to meet civic and religious duties, adherents must close their businesses on two days a week, whereas members of other faiths must close only one day a week. However, Sabbatarian faiths do not *require* members to work on Sundays. Rather, Sabbatarian claims for exemption are based on the fact that the state rule makes the practice that their faith *does* require—closing on Saturdays—more costly to them.[76] In this second category, there is more room for courts to balance the state's interests against the religious adherents' interests without imposing on the state a burden of proving that granting exemptions would sacrifice a crucial state policy.

70. See McDaniel v. Paty, 435 U.S. 618 (1978) (striking down such a provision as a violation of the free exercise clause).

71. Cf. Witters v. Washington Dep't of Services for the Blind, 474 U.S. 481 (1986) (finding that such a rule was not required by the establishment clause; not reaching the issue of whether the rule was forbidden by the free exercise clause).

72. See Hobbie v. Unemployment Appeals Comm'n, 107 S.Ct. 1046 (1987); Sherbert v. Verner, 374 U.S. 398 (1963).

73. See Wisconsin v. Yoder, 406 U.S. 205 (1972).

74. See Goldman v. Weinberger, 475 U.S. 503 (1986) (holding that no exemption is required, because of high deference accorded military decisions) (case discussed below).

75. Five, possibly six, Justices in Bowen v. Roy, 106 S.Ct. 2147 (1986), would have required a religious exemption to the recipient's duty to submit the social security number. See id. at 2160 (Blackmun, J., concurring in part); id. at 2166–69 (O'Connor, J., joined by Brennan and Marshall, JJ., concurring in part and dissenting in part); id. at 2169 (White, J., dissent-ing). Justice Stevens would have required exemption if, as appeared to be the case, individuals with linguistic and other handicaps were routinely aided in filling out required benefit forms; "it would seem that a religious inability should be given no less deference." Id. at 2163 (Stevens, J., concurring in part and concurring in result). Chief Justice Burger and Justices Powell and Rehnquist would have denied any exemption. See id. at 2153–58.

76. See Braunfeld v. Brown, 366 U.S. 599, 605–06 (1961) (plurality opinion) (denying exemption to Sunday closing law because the law did not prohibit any religious practices, but only made them more expensive; "[f]ully recognizing that the alternatives open to appellants and others similarly situated—retaining their present occupations and incurring economic disadvantage or engaging in some other commercial activity which does not call for either Saturday or Sunday labor—may well result in some financial sacrifice in order to observe their religious beliefs, still the option is wholly different than when the legislation attempts to make a religious practice itself unlawful").

Assigning a state rule to one or the other category only begins the analysis. Rules in the first category may prove constitutional, where they pursue unusually important state interests and where consistent enforcement is necessary to achieve their goals.[77] By the same token, rules in the second category may prove unconstitutional, where the state's interest in upholding the rule turns out to be minimal or, as might be the case with some Sunday closing laws, religiously motivated. Using this categorization does not itself answer the constitutional questions, but it helps point the way toward the proper approach. And it is consistent with the Court's language: " 'Where the state conditions receipt of an important benefit upon conduct *proscribed by a religious faith,* or where it denies such a benefit because of conduct *mandated by religious belief,* thereby putting substantial pressure on an adherent to modify his behavior and to violate his beliefs, a burden upon religion exists.' "[78]

Several points are also worth making about the way courts have evaluated some of the particular interests that states have proffered. Although it seems impossible to divine a coherent set of principles to explain the judicial evaluations, the relevant state interests can be described on three levels: most broadly, the systemic interests in judicial deference to legislative or other, non-judicial decisions; more narrowly, the state's interests in various programmatic goals; and, most narrowly, the state's interests in enforcing its regulations consistently, without exemptions.

At the broad level of deference, in some cases the Court has deferred almost completely to state legislatures and Congress. In *Braunfeld,* the plurality posited various undesirable consequences that might have motivated the state to refuse religious exemptions to Sunday closing laws.[79] In a curious linguistic inversion of the concept of strict scrutiny, the Justices also voiced general concern for maintaining the sphere of legislative discretion: "To strike down, without the most careful scrutiny, legislation which imposes only an indirect burden on the exercise of religion . . . would radically restrict the operating latitude of the legislature."[80] In *Lee,* the Court emphasized the need for consistent application of the social security laws, but then noted Congress' decision to provide religious exemptions to self-employed individuals, and finally concluded that the decisions should remain with Congress: "The tax imposed on employers to support the

77. See, e.g., Bob Jones University v. United States, 461 U.S. 574 (1983) (accepting school's racially discriminatory policies as religiously motivated, but denying exemption because the government's compelling interest in eradicating racial discrimination in education could not be achieved through less restrictive means). Such rules may also be found constitutional where special circumstances are thought to demand unusual judicial deference, as with military regulations. See Goldman v. Weinberger, 475 U.S. 503 (1986).

78. Hobbie v. Unemployment Appeals Comm'n, 107 S.Ct. 1046, 1049 (1987) (some emphasis added, some omitted) (quoting Thomas v. Review Bd., 450 U.S. 707, 717–18 (1981)).

79. 366 U.S. at 608–09 (plurality opinion).

80. Id. at 606 (plurality).

social security system must be uniformly applicable to all, except as Congress provides explicitly otherwise." [81]

More striking still is the Court's traditional deference to the military.[82] In *Goldman v. Weinberger*,[83] the Court ruled 5–4 that the free exercise clause did not mandate a religious exemption from Air Force dress regulations in order to permit an Orthodox Jew to wear a yarmulke while on active duty as a military psychologist. The Court noted that "[o]ur review of military regulations challenged on First Amendment grounds is far more deferential than constitutional review of similar laws or regulations designed for civilian society." [84] Accordingly, one might have expected the Court to give special weight to the asserted state interest in uniform appearance and resultant morale as it applied its free exercise analysis. However, the Court went farther: Without explanation beyond the need for deference, it jettisoned its usual analysis entirely. The Court conceded that refusing to grant the exemption might make military service "more objectionable" for Goldman,[85] but concluded that the requirement was reasonable and evenhanded, and therefore that no free exercise exemption was necessary.[86]

The deference is also illustrated in the setting of military manpower procurement. There, the issue should be whether the more modest

---

81. 455 U.S. at 261 (footnote omitted).

82. Such deference exists beyond the free exercise sphere. See, e.g., Rostker v. Goldberg, 453 U.S. 57 (1981) (deferring concerning gender); Greer v. Spock, 424 U.S. 828 (1976) (deferring concerning free speech); Katcoff v. Marsh, 755 F.2d 223, 235 (2d Cir. 1985) (deferring concerning alleged establishment of religion).

83. 106 S.Ct. 1310 (1986). Justice Rehnquist wrote the opinion for the Court, joined by Chief Justice Burger and Justices White, Powell, and Stevens. Justice Stevens wrote a concurring opinion, joined by Justices White and Powell. Id. at 1314. Dissenting opinions were filed by Justice Brennan, joined by Justice Marshall, id. at 1316; Justice Blackmun, id. at 1322; and Justice O'Connor, joined by Justice Marshall, id. at 1324.

84. Id. at 1313 (majority opinion).

85. Id. at 1314. In dissent, Justice Brennan responded that the requirement "does not simply render military life for observant Orthodox Jews 'objectionable'. . . . It sets up an almost absolute bar to the fulfillment of a religious duty." Id. at 1317.

86. "The Air Force has drawn the line essentially between religious apparel which is visible and that which is not, and we hold that those portions of the regulations challenged here reasonably and evenhandedly regulate dress in the interest of the military's perceived need for uniformity. The First Amendment therefore does not prohibit them from being applied to

petitioner even though their effect is to restrict the wearing of the headgear required by his religious beliefs." Id. at 1314 (majority opinion). Justice O'Connor, dissenting, responded: "The Court rejects Captain Goldman's claim without even the slightest attempt to weigh his asserted right to the free exercise of his religion against the interest of the Air Force in uniformity of dress within the military hospital. No test for Free Exercise claims in the military context is even articulated, much less applied. It is entirely sufficient for the Court if the military perceives a need for uniformity." Id. at 1325. After reviewing the Court's usual approach to free exercise cases, she added: "There is no reason why these general principles should not apply in the military, as well as the civilian, context. . . . [T]he test that one can glean from this Court's decisions in the civilian context is sufficiently flexible to take into account the special importance of defending our Nation without abandoning completely the freedoms that make it worth defending." Id. Applying the test, she found that the government's interest was sufficiently important, in light of the special needs and conditions of the military; but, she concluded, granting an exemption would not substantially undermine pursuit of the interest. Id. at 1325–26. See Michelman, "Foreword: Traces of Self-Government," 100 Harv.L.Rev. 4, 35 (1986) (contrasting Justice O'Connor's focus on "the social conflict of religion and regulation" with the majority opinion's focus on separation of powers).

interest in conscripting everyone—including conscientious objectors—is sufficient to override free exercise. The Supreme Court has held that those whose religions forbid them to take part in "unjust wars" but allow them to participate in other conflicts can constitutionally be denied conscientious-objector exemption from military conscription, since the admittedly hard choice to which they are put by such a denial—violating their religious beliefs or going to jail—is justified in this instance by "the government's interest in procuring the manpower necessary for military purposes pursuant to the . . . grant of power to Congress to raise and support armies . . .," [87] coupled with the deleterious effects on morale and confidence that such selective exemption would entail.[88] Indeed, the mesmerizing force of the interest in national security has led the Court to say in dictum that Congress need not grant an exemption for *any* conscientious objectors.[89] The interest in fairly and efficiently procuring military manpower is, however, the sort of diffuse societal goal that may deserve more scrutiny than these cases suggest. In light of the relative ease with which the conscientious-objector exemption has been administered throughout our history without placing a noticeable burden on the country's military manpower needs, a court might well require a concrete showing of threat to such needs in order to justify abolition of the exemption. The use of conscientious objectors—even selective conscientious objectors—in paramedical or other non-military roles could meet both the personnel argument and the morale argument well enough to constitute a required alternative under *Sherbert*.[90]

The decisions of prison administrators, like those of the military, are accorded substantial deference by the Court. In *O'Lone v. Estate of Shabazz*,[91] the Court ruled 5–4 that a prison need not alter the uniform enforcement of its work regulations, where the regulations prevented Muslim prisoners from attending a weekly religious service important to their faith. The Court applied a "reasonableness" test, refusing to substitute its own judgment "for the determinations of those charged with the formidable task of running a prison." [92] The regulation passed this reasonableness test, the Court concluded, based on three factors: the regulation was logically connected to a legitimate governmental interest; prison officials had accommodated Muslim worship and dietary requirements in other respects; and prison officials believed that the accommodation requested was not feasible.[93]

---

87. Gillette v. United States, 401 U.S. 437, 462 (1971).

88. Id. at 460.

89. See Jacobson v. Massachusetts, 197 U.S. 11, 29 (1905); cf. Welsh v. United States, 398 U.S. 333, 359 (1970) (Harlan, J., concurring in result).

90. Affirming a constitutional right of conscientious objection would be especially appropriate since such a right was only mysteriously left out of the Bill of Rights. The Committee of the Whole defeated an attempt to strike from the Bill of Rights a clause exempting religious conscientious objectors from service. Inexplicably, the clause was not included in the Bill of Rights finally approved. 1 Annals of Cong. 749–51 (1789). See Giannella, "Religious Liberty, Non-establishment, and Doctrinal Development: Part I, The Religious Liberty Guarantee," 80 Harv.L.Rev. 1381, 1412 n.89 (1967).

91. 107 S.Ct. 2400 (1987).

92. Id. at 2407.

93. Id. at 2405–2407.

At the narrower level of programmatic goals, courts have considered a variety of interests. The state's interest in minimizing expenditures, the Supreme Court has implied, may be a compelling goal, but in cases to date states have failed to demonstrate that the exemptions requested would hinder that goal's achievement.[94]

Courts have been more sympathetic to the state's interest in looking after minor children. Thus, in *Prince v. Massachusetts*,[95] the government's purpose—protecting children from burdensome and exploitative labor—could not be achieved if adults were permitted to enlist the young as street proselytizers for their faith. To be sure, Justice Murphy argued in dissent that the child in question was not demonstrably injured,[96] but the Court permitted government to deal with focused, serious harms in categorical ways, protecting classes of victims from such harms without fully individualized findings that each person within the protected class would in fact become a victim if such protection were withheld in order to facilitate someone's religiously motivated activity.[97]

Having held that the state may protect children from physical harm at the hands of their religiously motivated parents or guardians, the Court found it easy to decide summarily that a parent could not, even on religious grounds, withhold a blood transfusion that was necessary to save a child's life,[98] and lower courts have likewise had little difficulty in concluding that parents cannot prevent their children, on religious grounds or otherwise, from receiving medical treatment without which the children's health would be seriously jeopard-

---

94. See Bowen v. Roy, 106 S.Ct. at 2167 (O'Connor, J., joined by Brennan and Marshall, JJ., dissenting in part) (only a "handful" of people will likely take advantage of a religious exemption to the requirement that welfare benefit recipients provide their social security numbers); Thomas v. Review Bd., 450 U.S. at 719 ("There is no evidence . . . that the number of people who find themselves in the predicament of choosing between benefits and religious beliefs is large enough to create 'widespread unemployment,' or even to seriously affect unemployment. . . ."); Sherbert v. Verner, 374 U.S. at 407 ("even if the possibility of spurious claims did threaten to dilute the fund and disrupt the scheduling of work, it would plainly be incumbent upon the appellees to demonstrate that no alternative forms of regulation would combat such abuses without infringing First Amendment rights") (footnote omitted). See also note 40, supra.

95. 321 U.S. 158 (1944).

96. Id. at 174. See § 16–31, infra.

97. The Court had hypothesized a still more clearcut case in dictum in Reynolds v. United States, 98 U.S. (8 Otto) 145, 166 (1878): "Suppose one believed that human sacrifices were a necessary part of religious worship, would it be seriously contended that the civil government under which he lived could not interfere to prevent a sacrifice?"

The California courts faced an equally stark case in deciding that a school transportation supervisor whose religious expression took the form of virulent attacks on society and named public officials, statements of violence and hatred, and threats of widespread death and destruction, should not be employed by the school system. In a religious tract published by petitioner, he stated that while it might be "a sin" for a person to gun down a school house full of children, there is hardly a clergyman in the world today who does not commit a worse sin every day. Hollon v. Pierce, 257 Cal.App.2d 468, 470–71, 64 Cal. Rptr. 808, 810–11 (1967).

98. Jehovah's Witnesses v. King County Hospital, 390 U.S. 598 (1968) (per curiam), aff'g 278 F.Supp. 488 (W.D.Wash.1967) (three judge court). The New Jersey courts likewise concluded that a woman who was thirty-two weeks pregnant could be forced, over religious objection, to submit to a blood transfusion. Raleigh Fitkin-Paul Morgan Memorial Hospital v. Anderson, 42 N.J. 421, 201 A.2d 537 (1964), cert. denied 377 U.S. 985 (1964).

ized.[99] In fact, some courts have held that parents with minor children who remain dependent upon them are not even free to risk their *own* lives in a religious cause [100]—not out of paternalistic concern for the parents but out of concern for the welfare of the children.[101]

However, courts have found the state's interest in overseeing autonomous, adult citizens to be weaker. Where the *only* immediately affected person is the one whose religious scruples the state seeks to override, free exercise principles point to a wide berth for religious freedom. For example, compulsory vaccinations have been sustained against free exercise clause challenges in light of the state's compelling interest in protecting the health and safety of members of the community.[102] As the Court noted in *Prince v. Massachusetts*, "[t]he right to practice religion freely does not include liberty to expose the community . . . to communicable disease. . . ." [103] Yet compulsory vaccination of the adult religious objector may not be *necessary* to prevent an epidemic.[104] Presumably an exemption for religiously objecting adults would expose only those who chose exposure on religious grounds. Thus the only state interest in denying the exemption would be to protect the believer from the consequences of his or her own faith. It is easy enough to evoke the image of the contagious disease carrier; but if

---

99. See, e.g., In re Green, 448 Pa. 338, 292 A.2d 387 (1972) (remanding for a hearing to ascertain whether or not the 16-year-old son of a Jehovah's Witness wished to accept, over his mother's religious objection, medical treatment for curvature of the spine); In re Sampson, 65 Misc.2d 658, 317 N.Y.S.2d 641 (Fam.Ct.1970) (ordering non-essential surgery, over mother's religious objections, to remedy a 15-year-old child's facial disfigurement); In re Seiferth, 309 N.Y. 80, 127 N.E.2d 820 (1955) (ordering non-essential corrective surgery for a 14-year-old boy with a harelip and cleft palate despite the non-critical nature of the operation and over father's desire to leave the change to the powers of "mental healing").

100. See Application of the President & Directors of Georgetown College, Inc., 331 F.2d 1000, 1010 (D.C.Cir.1964), cert. denied sub nom. Jones v. President & Directors of Georgetown College, Inc. 377 U.S. 978 (1964) (where the mother of minor children was both critically ill and incompetent and her husband would not approve a blood transfusion for her, the court may order one); Powell v. Columbian Presbyterian Medical Center, 49 Misc.2d 215, 267 N.Y.S. 2d 450 (1965) (where critically ill mother of six minor children, including a new-born infant, did not object to receiving blood transfusions but refused on religious grounds to give prior written authorization, the court may order the hospital to administer such transfusions as in the attending physicians' opinions were neces-

sary to save the patient's life); United States v. George, 239 F.Supp. 752 (D.Conn. 1965) (court may order blood transfusions for a critically ill father of four minor children while he is in extremis). See also In re Brook's Estate, 32 Ill.2d 361, 205 N.E.2d 435 (1965) (in the case of a critically ill mother of *adult* children, court does not have the same right to order lifesaving measures against her religious beliefs as it would if minor children were involved).

101. Cf. United States v. Lee, 455 U.S. 252, 261 (1982) (the exemption requested by the employer would "operate[ ] to impose the employer's religious faith on the employees"); Wisconsin v. Yoder, 406 U.S. 205, 242 (1972) (Douglas, J., dissenting in part) (exemption from mandatory schooling forces parents' religion on children).

102. See, e.g., Jacobson v. Massachusetts, 197 U.S. 11 (1905) (compulsory vaccination upheld); Wright v. Dewitt School Dist., 238 Ark. 906, 385 S.W.2d 644 (1965) (same). See also Hill v. State, 38 Ala.App. 404, 88 So.2d 880 (1956), cert. denied 264 Ala. 697, 88 So.2d 887 (1956) (prohibition against snake handling sustained); Lewellyn v. State, 489 P.2d 511 (Okl.1971) (statute prohibiting drug use constitutionally applied to religious users).

103. 321 U.S. 158, 166 (1943).

104. See Marcus, "The Forum of Conscience: Applying Standards Under the Free Exercise Clause," 1973 Duke L.J. 1217, 1255 (1973); Giannella, supra note 90, at 1390–96.

everyone else is inoculated, the government's only purpose must be the protection of the individual against himself.

If the harm is grave enough, the issue raised is the power of the state to mandate life and forbid risk-taking, matters considered in §§ 15–11, and 15–12, below. If the harm is ill-defined or plainly not serious, the case seems clearer than *Yoder*: an exemption must be granted. *People v. Woody*,[105] where the California Supreme Court found unconstitutional the conviction of American Indians for the religious use of peyote, is one such case. Insofar as the government advanced arguments beyond harm to self—controlling overall drug traffic, for example—less restrictive alternatives for dealing with the problem were clearly available. The one argument which could not be so easily met was the contention that drug use is harmful to the user—that a hallucinogenic experience, for example, is bad in itself.[106] But at this point, the state is telling the individual that it knows what is best for his body and mind. Surely the individual may respond, "I know what is best for my soul." [107] To allow the government thus to impose the

---

105. 61 Cal.2d 716, 40 Cal.Rptr. 69, 394 P.2d 813 (1964); accord, Arizona v. Whittingham, 19 Ariz.App. 27, 504 P.2d 950 (1973), cert. denied 417 U.S. 946 (1974). Montana's statute exempting sale and use of peyote for religious purposes from its prohibition of peyote was upheld in State ex rel. Offerdahl v. District Ct., 156 Mont. 432, 481 P.2d 338 (1971); but see Kennedy v. Bureau of Narcotics, 459 F.2d 415 (9th Cir. 1972), cert. denied 409 U.S. 1115 (1973) (holding that "Church of the Awakening" could not be granted the same exemption for peyote use in bona fide religious ceremonies as enjoyed by members of the Native American Church, not because "Church of the Awakening" members were not Indians or because peyote was not as central to their religion as to Peyotism— although both were true—but because an amended regulation exempting petitioners would still fail to exempt other churches using peyote in bona fide religious ceremonies); Native American Church of Navajoland, Inc. v. Arizona Corporation Commissioner, 329 F.Supp. 907 (D.Ariz.1971), aff'd 405 U.S. 901 (1972) (upholding refusal to grant incorporation to peyote-using church); see also Golden Eagle v. Johnson, 493 F.2d 1179 (9th Cir. 1974), cert. denied 419 U.S. 1105 (1975) (holding that special procedural safeguards, such as those applicable to the seizure of allegedly obscene material, did not apply to the seizure of peyote from a member of the Native American Church).

Cases rejecting free exercise claims in use of marijuana or LSD include United States v. Kuch, 288 F.Supp. 439 (D.D.C.1968); Gaskin v. Tennessee, 490 S.W.2d 521 (Tenn.1973); Leary v. United States, 383 F.2d 851 (5th Cir. 1967), rev'd on other grounds 395 U.S. 6 (1969); People v. Crawford, 69 Misc.2d 500, 328 N.Y.S.2d 747 (Dist.Ct.1972), aff'd mem. 72 Misc.2d 1021, 340 N.Y.S.2d 848 (1973).

106. See, e.g., State v. Bullard, 267 N.C. 599, 148 S.E.2d 565 (1966), cert. denied 386 U.S. 917 (1967) (holding that defendant's free exercise rights were not violated by forbidding him to possess a drug which would produce "symptoms similar to those produced in cases of schizophrenia, dementia praecox or paranoia").

107. In Woody, the California Attorney General had argued "that since 'peyote could be regarded as a symbol, one that obstructs enlightenment and shackles the Indian to primitive conditions,' the responsibility rests with the state to eliminate its use." 61 Cal.2d at 723, 40 Cal.Rptr. at 74, 394 P.2d at 818. Justice Tobriner replied for the California Supreme Court: "We know of no doctrine that the state, in its asserted omniscience, should undertake to deny to defendants the observance of their religion in order to free them from the suppositious 'shackles' of their 'unenlightened' and 'primitive condition.'" Id.

Alternatively, the individual might reject the evidence presented by the state as to what the likely outcomes of various courses of action will be, choosing instead to affirm an outcome predicted not through science but through faith. Under United States v. Ballard, 322 U.S. 78 (1944), the state is not free to inquire into the accuracy of that faith. For example, Professor Robley Whitson reports in "American Pluralism," Thought 524 (Winter, 1962), that Amish religious doctrines of absolute trust in the Providence of God have led the Amish to believe that they are forbidden to enter into any type of insurance contract—hence their claim, ultimate-

World of the Flesh upon the World of the Spirit seems an overwhelming abridgment of religious freedom.[108]

Beyond such paternalistic laws, and the occasional law (like the one in *Yoder*) that threatens the very existence of a religious order, exemptions from criminal laws will be rare. However, the free exercise clause may require religion-based exemptions to criminal *procedures*. For example, if worshipers suspected that their clergyman was actually a policeman in disguise, their religious exercises would be greatly chilled. Although the issue has not been litigated extensively, the problem has arisen. Agents of the Federal Bureau of Investigation have impersonated clergy in order to gather information, according to a congressional report.[109] The Immigration and Naturalization Service has placed informants in sanctuary churches. In the most publicized case, an INS informant spent ten months in a Phoenix church, secretly recording 91 services and meetings. The trial judge admitted the taped evidence, terming the infiltration "unacceptable but not outrageous,"[110] and eight sanctuary workers were convicted. After the informant's activities became known, the church's mostly Hispanic congregation immediately dispersed, and other sanctuary churches began to suspect that some of their members might be government agents.[111] The issue is not the propriety of government's prosecuting sanctuary workers, but rather the means by which government gathers its evidence. Although flatly prohibiting police from infiltrating churches would probably go too far, the free exercise clause ought at least to require police to obtain search warrants in advance of such infiltrations.[112]

States often pursue—and the Court has often accepted as compelling—what might be termed diffuse societal interests. Many such goals, which seemed proper and fundamental in a religiously homogeneous society, now seem more dubious—particularly when the goal is defined to forbid any exemptions. Probably, as the *Braunfeld* Court held, enforced Sunday togetherness is a legitimate state goal. However, it is clear that the state's interest in *absolute* Sunday togetherness,

---

ly unsuccessful, to be exempted from social security taxes in United States v. Lee, 455 U.S. 252 (1982).

108. In addition to the religious grounds of objection, see §§ 15–6 (freedom of inquiry), 15–7 (sources of consciousness), 15–8 (right to resist coerced conditioning), 15–11 (right to die), and 15–12 (right to live a risky life).

109. House Committee on the Judiciary, Subcommittee on Civil and Constitutional Rights, FBI Undercover Operations, 98th Cong., 2d Sess. 6 (1984).

110. Judge Earl H. Carroll, quoted in Nute, "Free Exercise of Religion in Phoenix," 102 Christian Century 727, 728, August 14, 1985.

111. See generally Brown, "Paid Informers, Deception and Lies," 102 Christian Century 1027, 1028, November 13, 1985; Hentoff, "Snoops in the Pews," The Progressive, Aug. 1985, at 25; Renner,

" 'Black Bags' Are Back," 103 Christian Century 229–231, March 5, 1986; "Sanctuary: Church Workers Face Trial," 71 A.B. A.J. 19, April 1985.

112. The Supreme Court has refused to view informant placements as searches under the fourth amendment. See, e.g., United States v. White, 401 U.S. 745 (1971); Hoffa v. United States, 385 U.S. 293 (1966). Conceivably, the introduction of first amendment, free exercise values would shift the balance. Cf. United States v. Henry, 447 U.S. 264 (1980) (sixth amendment right to counsel violated where police put informant in jail cell to talk with prisoner). But cf. Zurcher v. Stanford Daily, 436 U.S. 547 (1978) (rejecting first amendment claim for higher threshold showing before police may search newspaper office); Laird v. Tatum, 408 U.S. 1 (1972) (rejecting action for injunction against Army surveillance of political movements, where alleged chilling effect was indirect).

without exemptions for Sabbatarians, cannot meet the modern free exercise test, especially given that the Sunday closing laws themselves provide for numerous exemptions.

Similar problems are presented by *Reynolds v. United States*,[113] in which the Court affirmed a polygamy conviction over the Mormon defendant's religious objection. The *Reynolds* Court perceived a sufficient secular purpose in preserving monogamous marriage and preventing exploitation of women. Few decisions better illustrate how amorphous goals may serve to mask religious persecution. The early history of the Mormons in this country is in large part a chronicle of such persecution. Soon after the Morman religion was formed in April 1830, its adherents fled West, literally driven by mobs. One Presbyterian minister dubbed them "the common enemies of mankind [who] ought to be destroyed." [114] In October 1838, the Governor of Missouri called out the state militia, writing: "The Mormons must be treated as enemies, and must be exterminated. . . ." [115] After the Mormons had settled in Utah, they were subjected to harassment by the federal government, culminating in 1887 with the Edmunds-Tucker Act, which purported to disenfranchise Mormon voters, remove corporate status from the Mormon church, and confiscate all church property.[116] It has been estimated that some 1,300 Mormons were imprisoned or fined for violations of the Act; many avoided penalties only by fleeing to Mexico or Canada.[117] The anti-polygamy statutes are best understood as parts of the same stained fabric. Born in the same era and of the same fears,[118] they should have been strictly scrutinized.

Little is demonstrated by the fact that the law's defenders could invoke a goal as attenuated as the "preservation of monogamous marriage"; that might also be said of a law compelling priests and nuns to marry.[119] The Court's acceptance of that goal in turn amounted to a recognition that the preservation of an "aspirational aspect of morality" [120] may be essential to society. We may accept that proposition, but it does not follow that government should be able to use such an amorphous purpose to force its views upon those who do not share them—particularly those who, for religious reasons, find it offensive to

113. 98 U.S. (8 Otto) 145 (1878), also discussed in § 14–6, supra.

114. Reverend Finis Ewing, quoted in Whitson, "American Pluralism," Thought 492, 518 (Winter, 1962).

115. Quoting Governor Lilburn Boggs of Missouri, id. at 519.

116. Id. at 521.

117. Id. at 522.

118. After the Civil War, and the successful elimination of slavery, the leaders of the Eastern Establishment turned their attention to the "treason" and "immorality" of the Mormons. The Anti-Bigamy Act was passed in 1862; it was followed by several other similar acts and the imposition of so-called "carpetbagger" regimes in Utah much like those in the South. Id. at 521. See generally A. Reichley, Religion in American Public Life 121 (1985) ("Polygamy proved extraordinarily offensive to members of competing evangelical Protestant denominations, who regarded the monogamous family as not only divinely established but also as an institutional check against egoistic chaos in the unstable social atmosphere of the American frontier.").

119. The goal of protecting women from male exploitation in plural marriage is, however, more focused. Cf. Bob Jones University v. United States, 461 U.S. 574 (1983) (goal of protecting racial minorities from exclusion and stigmatization).

120. Giannella, "Religious Liberty, Non-Establishment, and Doctrinal Development: Part I, The Religious Liberty Guarantees," 80 Harv.L.Rev. 1381, 1403 (1967).

act as the government insists. Indeed, refusing religious exemptions from governmental prohibitions or requirements of this sort may pose establishment clause difficulties, if the moral value underlying the prohibition or requirement is closely linked to a competing religious tradition.[121] At the very least, the question, after *Sherbert*, must be whether the monogamy-promotion goal is sufficiently compelling, and the refusal to exempt Mormons sufficiently crucial to the goal's attainment, to warrant the resulting burden on religious conscience.

The third category of relevant state interests centers upon the desirability of avoiding lines that exempt religious practitioners. One such interest is that of avoiding administrative complexities.[122] Another is avoiding a situation in which religious practitioners would gain an advantage over others,[123] which would go beyond free exercise principles and possibly violate the establishment clause. Still another is avoiding the appearance of favoring one religion over another—a factor that several Justices, particularly Justice Stevens, have emphasized.[124]

121. It is true that a state cannot be "extricated from its history and culture" and "then somehow programmed anew to create a society in which property and social relationships are arranged with justice but without deep inquiry into basic religiously-based human values." Giannella, supra note 120, at 1404. Nonetheless, at least in cases where the full moral censure of society is not involved, the underlying values of the first amendment might require religious exemptions.

122. The Court accepted this interest in Braunfeld, 366 U.S. at 608 ("Although not dispositive of the issue, enforcement problems would be more difficult since there would be two or more days to police rather than one and it would be more difficult to observe whether violations were occurring."); see Sherbert, 374 U.S. at 408–09 ("Requiring exemptions for Sabbatarians [in Braunfeld], while theoretically possible, appeared to present an administrative problem of such magnitude, or to afford the exempted class so great a competitive advantage, that such a requirement would have rendered the entire statutory scheme unworkable."). See also Mozert v. Hawkins County Public Schools, 647 F.Supp. 1194 (E.D. Tenn. 1986) (school must permit religiously objecting students to opt out of reading class and study at home; but school need not provide alternative texts and classes at school, partly to avoid establishment clause violations and partly to "relieve the school system of any burden that would have been caused by providing alternative teaching arrangements"). Mozert was subsequently overturned by the Sixth Circuit, N.Y. Times, August 25, 1987, at p. 1, col. 2, but further appeal was contemplated as this book went to press.

123. See Braunfeld, 366 U.S. at 608–09 ("To allow only people who rest on a day

other than Sunday to keep their businesses open on that day might well provide these people with an economic advantage over their competitors who must remain closed on that day; this might cause the Sunday-observers to complain that their religions are being discriminated against.") (footnote omitted); Gillette v. United States, 401 U.S. 437, 454 (1971) ("A claimant, seeking judicial protection for his own conscientious beliefs, would be hard put to argue that § 6(j) encourages membership in putatively 'favored' religious organizations. . . .").

124. See Bowen v. Roy, 106 S.Ct. 2147, 2163–64 n.17 (1986) (Stevens, J., concurring in part and concurring in result) (exemptions in Thomas and Sherbert were "necessary to prevent the treatment of religious claims less favorably than other claims"); Goldman v. Weinberger, 106 S.Ct. at 1316 (Stevens, J., joined by White and Powell, JJ., concurring) (emphasizing "interest in uniform treatment for the members of all religious faiths," and noting that exemptions granted for yarmulkes but not for other, more visible forms of religious apparel would inevitably be based on "the decisionmaker's evaluation of the character and the sincerity of the requestor's faith—as well as the probable reaction of the majority to the favored treatment of a member of that faith"; "The Air Force has no business drawing distinctions between such persons when it is enforcing commands of universal application."); United States v. Lee, 455 U.S. 252, 263 n.2 (1982) (Stevens, J., concurring in judgment) ("the principal reason for adopting a strong presumption" against free exercise claims is "the overriding interest in keeping the government—whether it be the legislature or the courts—out of the business of evaluating the relative merits of differing religious

Avoiding fraud, whatever the incentive, is an important state interest.[125] As with the problem of administrative complexity, one factor in fraud is the likelihood that many people will seek an exemption.[126] In addition to the direct problem of fraud, states also often seek to avoid a related problem, the necessity of conducting entangling inquiries into religious sincerity, which may be necessary in order to prevent abuse.[127]

The likelihood of fraud is related to the magnitude of the petitioner's request. For example, if Sherbert had said that her religion forbade her to hold *any* employment, the state's interest in denying her unemployment benefits would have been much stronger.[128] Another factor, as Justice Stevens has pointed out, is whether the religious exemption benefits only a disadvantaged group of people, or whether, in contrast, it provides general benefits to any religious claimant.[129] The former, like the *Sherbert* and *Thomas* exemptions for people already

claims. The risk that governmental approval of some and disapproval of others will be perceived as favoring one religion over another is an important risk the Establishment Clause was designed to preclude."). See also Bowen v. Roy, 106 S.Ct. at 2156 (opinion of Burger, C.J., joined by Powell and Rehnquist, JJ.) ("legitimate interests are implicated in the need to avoid any appearance of favoring religious over nonreligious applicants"). Appearances are particularly important in public education, see § 14–5, supra, but they are also important elsewhere, see § 14–15, infra. The best way to assess such appearances may be from the perspective of an independent observer, familiar with free exercise values. See Wallace v. Jaffree, 472 U.S. 38, 82 (1985) (O'Connor, J., concurring in judgment).

125. See Sherbert, 374 U.S. at 407 (implying that an exemption would not be required if the state proved that fraud was likely and that the fraud could not be eliminated consistent with the free exercise exemption, although finding it "highly doubtful" that the state could make such a showing).

126. See Bowen v. Roy, 106 S.Ct. at 2167–68 (O'Connor, J., concurring in part and dissenting in part) (in light of evidence that few people would seek religious exemption, "the unanchored anxieties of the welfare bureaucracy" concerning possibility of fraud did not constitute an overriding state interest).

127. The Court accepted this interest in Braunfeld and in Thomas, though it found facts to support the interest only in the former case. See Braunfeld, 366 U.S. at 609 (some people might, for competitive reasons, falsely claim that their religion compels them to rest on a day other than Sunday; "This might make necessary a state-conducted inquiry into the sincerity

of the individual's religious beliefs, a practice which a State might believe would itself run afoul of the spirit of constitutionally protected religious guarantees.") (footnote omitted); Thomas, 450 U.S. at 719 ("although detailed inquiry by employers into applicants' religious beliefs is undesirable, there is no evidence in the record to indicate that such inquiries will occur"). See also Bowen v. Roy, 106 S.Ct. at 2156 (opinion of Burger, C.J., and Powell and Rehnquist, JJ.) ("Although in some situations a mechanism for individual consideration will be created, a policy decision by a government that it wishes to treat all applicants alike and that it does not wish to become involved in case-by-case inquiries into the genuineness of each religious objection to such condition or restrictions is entitled to substantial deference."). Cf. Bob Jones Univ. v. United States, 461 U.S. 574, 604–05 n.30 (1983) (" 'the uniform application of the rule to all religiously operated schools *avoids* the necessity for a potentially entangling inquiry into whether a racially restrictive practice is the result of sincere religious belief' ") (quoting United States v. Bob Jones Univ., 639 F.2d 147, 155 (4th Cir. 1980) (emphasis in original)); § 14–11 (discussing "regulatory entanglement" between church and state).

128. See Sherbert v. Verner, 374 U.S. at 409–10 ("Nor do we, by our decision today, declare the existence of a constitutional right to unemployment benefits on the part of all persons whose religious convictions are the cause of their unemployment. This is not a case in which an employee's religious convictions serve to make him a nonproductive member of society.").

129. United States v. Lee, 455 U.S. 252, 263–64 n.3 (1982) (Stevens, J., concurring in judgment).

unemployed for reasons beyond their control, probably will not create an incentive for fraud. However, "[a] tax exemption entails no cost to the claimant; if tax exemptions were dispensed on religious grounds, every citizen would have an economic motivation to join the favored sects." [130]

Whereas the evaluation of these state interests has created problems in deciding specific cases, two broad tensions have created conceptual problems in free exercise jurisprudence generally. The first is the fuzzy line between state distinctions that impermissibly mirror religious beliefs, and state distinctions that permissibly do so. The state may not exclude people, "because of their faith, or lack of it, from receiving the benefits of public welfare legislation." [131] So, under *Sherbert* and its progeny, the state may not deny unemployment benefits to people who, for religious reasons, cannot fulfill some of the eligibility requirements.[132] However, the state may sometimes exclude people from benefit programs based on some extrinsic factor, even where the factor in part reflects religious beliefs. The Supreme Court has permitted the government to deny veterans' benefits to people who, for religious reasons, cannot fulfill the active duty requirement—conscientious objectors.[133] Presumably the government could provide subsidized loans to beef producers without facing a colorable free exercise claim brought by people whose religion requires them to raise and eat only vegetables; or provide tax benefits to medical or military professionals without facing a claim brought by people whose religious tenets forbid such work. But the principles underlying such distinctions resist ready definition.

The second tension is that between the free exercise clause and the establishment clause. *Sherbert*, *Thomas*, and *Hobbie*, as well as cases outside the religion sphere, indicate that the state may not condition public benefits on a claimant's surrender of constitutional liberties.[134] However, the establishment clause has been construed to limit the sorts of benefits that may be provided to religious organizations. As Chief Justice (then Justice) Rehnquist has described the tension: "[I]f the State in *Sherbert* could not deny compensation to one refusing work for religious reasons, it might be argued that a State may not deny reimbursement to students who choose for religious reasons to attend

---

130. Id. at 264 n.3. See M. McConnell, "Accommodation of Religion," 1985 Sup.Ct. Rev. 1, 35 ("An accommodation must facilitate the exercise of beliefs and practices independently adopted rather than inducing or coercing beliefs or practices acceptable to the government.") (emphasis omitted).

131. Everson v. Board of Educ., 330 U.S. 1, 16 (1947) (emphasis deleted).

132. See Hobbie v. Unemployment Appeals Comm'n, 107 S.Ct. 1046 (1987) (claims examiner and Unemployment Appeals Commission found that reason petitioner was fired from her job—for refusing, based on religious beliefs, to work on Saturdays—constituted work-related miscon-

duct, and thus that she was not eligible for benefits; Supreme Court reversed); Thomas v. Review Bd., 450 U.S. 707 (1981) (hearing board found that petitioner's reason for quitting job—that work in weapons factory conflicted with his religious beliefs—did not meet statute's "good cause" requirement; Supreme Court reversed); Sherbert v. Verner, 374 U.S. 398 (1963) (board found that petitioner's reason for refusing to work—that work on Saturdays conflicted with her religious beliefs—did not meet "good cause" requirement; Supreme Court reversed).

133. See Johnson v. Robison, 415 U.S. 361 (1974).

134. See also § 11–5, supra.

parochial schools. The argument would be that although a State need not allocate any funds to education, once it has done so, it may not require any person to sacrifice his religious beliefs in order to obtain an equal education. . . . There can be little doubt that to the extent secular education provides answers to important moral questions without reference to religion or teaches that there are no answers, a person in one sense sacrifices his religious belief by attending secular schools." [135] If the free exercise principle applies to public education—and *Yoder* suggests that it does—then it may require some sort of accommodation, but it need not go as far as the Chief Justice suggested. In religion, as in other spheres, government has no general duty to subsidize the exercise of constitutional rights; [136] and in religion, unlike other spheres, the Constitution often prohibits subsidies. But accommodation short of subsidy is possible. In public school cases, some courts have required the schools to excuse students from assignments or discussions that would conflict with their religious beliefs.[137] Congress might also attempt to address the problem by providing a neutral voucher system, under which the government would finance religious as well as nonreligious education.[138] Although the tension between the establishment and free exercise clauses is not to be minimized, both the courts and the legislatures have space in which to pursue the values underlying both clauses.

§ 14–14. The Entanglement Concept Disentangled: Distinguishing the Mandated Separation of Religious and Governmental Power From the Forbidden Separation of Religion and Politics

As the Supreme Court has noted, Jefferson's metaphor of a wall between church and state is "not a wholly accurate description of the

---

135. Thomas v. Review Bd., 450 U.S. 707, 724 n.2 (1981) (Rehnquist, J., dissenting).

136. See Harris v. McRae, 448 U.S. 297 (1980) (constitutional right to abortion does not require government to fund abortions, or to abstain from funding alternatives to abortion); § 11–5, supra.

137. See Mozert v. Hawkins County Public Schools, 647 F.Supp. 1194 (E.Tenn. 1986) (requiring school system to permit students to opt out of reading class, spending the class time in a study hall and studying reading at night with their parents, where the school's assigned readings conflicted with students' religious beliefs). Mozert was subsequently overturned by the Sixth Circuit, on the arguably problematic ground that the plaintiffs had failed to prove that "any plaintiff student was ever called upon to say or do anything that required the student to affirm or deny a religious belief or to engage or refrain from engaging in any act either required or forbidden by the students' religious convictions." N.Y. Times, August 25, 1987, at p.

1, col. 2. Further appeal was contemplated as this book went to press. Cf. Grove v. Mead School District No. 354, 753 F.2d 1528, 1533 (9th Cir. 1985) (rejecting free exercise claim where school had already instituted alternative readings for students offended by the assigned book), cert. denied 106 S.Ct. 85 (1985); id. at 1542 (Canby, J., concurring) (students would probably have raised a free exercise claim absent excusal option). But see G. Will, "Tailored Textbooks," Washington Post, Nov. 9, 1986, at H7 ("The free exercise clause protects a broad sphere of conduct. However, it is not a guarantee of intellectual spiritual serenity or a commitment to protect parents and children from influences that might complicate the transmission of sectarian beliefs.").

138. Such a system is neither mandated by the free exercise clause nor automatically forbidden by the establishment clause; rather, it probably lies in the zone of permissible accommodation. See § 14–5, supra.

practical aspects of the relationship that in fact exists. . . ." [1] The first amendment does not require—indeed, it does not permit—government to be totally oblivious to religion. Government may sometimes accommodate religion; in some circumstances, it must do so.[2] Thus the question is not *whether* government and religion will interact, but *how*. Other sections discuss several prohibited interactions: Government may not enforce certain laws and regulations against believers, where the believers will be forced to choose between civic duty and religious duty;[3] it may not intervene in matters of theology, either by asking intrusive religious questions[4] or by providing state-written religious answers;[5] government may not discriminate among religions in allocating benefits or burdens;[6] government may not lend innately state power to religion;[7] and government may not symbolically endorse religion.[8] At least in these senses, "both religion and government can best work to achieve their lofty aims if each is left free from the other within its respective sphere." [9]

But when the wall between church and state prevents religion from entering politics, it proves too formidable a barrier. Although the distinction between politics and government may in some circumstances seem unduly formalistic, it is nonetheless essential to reconciling the establishment clause with the free exercise clause and with other freedoms. For example, government may listen with special attentiveness to religious views, and may at times act on the basis of those views; however, government may not delegate its decision-making power to churches.[10] The result may be much the same, but the process is crucially different.

In properly distancing religion from government power and resources, the Supreme Court has sometimes made the troubling suggestion that religion may be kept away from politics as well. In *McDaniel*

§ 14–14

1. Lynch v. Donnelly, 465 U.S. 668, 673 (1984).

2. See §§ 14–4, 14–5, supra.

3. See Hobbie v. Unemployment Appeals Comm'n, 107 S.Ct. 1046 (1987) (requiring exemption from unemployment regulations); Thomas v. Review Bd., 450 U.S. 707 (1981) (same); Wisconsin v. Yoder, 406 U.S. 205 (1972) (requiring exemption from mandatory schooling); Sherbert v. Verner, 374 U.S. 398 (1963) (requiring exemption from unemployment regulations); §§ 14–4, 14–5, supra.

4. See Jones v. Wolf, 443 U.S. 595 (1979) (courts must defer to ecclesiastical bodies' resolution of inherently religious questions); Presbyterian Church in the United States v. Mary Elizabeth Blue Hull Memorial Presbyterian Church, 393 U.S. 440 (1969) (same); United States v. Ballard, 322 U.S. 78 (1944) (courts may not inquire into correctness of individuals' religious beliefs, only sincerity); §§ 14–11, 14–12, supra.

5. See Engel v. Vitale, 370 U.S. 421 (1962) (state may not write prayers to be recited in public schools); §§ 14–5, supra, 14–15, infra.

6. See Larson v. Valente, 456 U.S. 228 (1982) (state may not impose reporting regulations on some but not all religions); § 14–7, supra.

7. See Larkin v. Grendel's Den, Inc., 459 U.S. 116 (1982) (striking down statute under which churches could veto liquor license applications); § 14–11, supra.

8. See Lynch v. Donnelly, 465 U.S. 668, 690–94 (1984) (O'Connor, J., concurring) (suggesting endorsement standard); § 14–15, infra.

9. Illinois ex rel. McCollum v. Board of Educ., 333 U.S. 203, 212 (1948).

10. See Larkin v. Grendel's Den, Inc., 459 U.S. 116 (1982).

v. Paty,[11] for example, where the Court held that a state may not bar clergy from public office, the plurality opinion implied that different evidence might have produced a different result.[12]   The problem, according to the plurality, was that Tennessee had "failed to demonstrate that its views of the dangers of clergy participation in the political process have not lost whatever validity they may once have enjoyed." [13] The plurality chose not to rule on whether a state could legitimately act to reduce such dangers.[14]   Thus, in the case that most directly presented the issue of religious involvement in the political process, four Justices hedged their bets.

Two aspects of establishment clause doctrine are consistent with the *McDaniel* plurality's equivocating position.   These are the two doctrines suggesting that, when religious believers arrive at political debates, they must check their beliefs at the door or risk losing their efficacy.

Consider first the *Lemon* test's secular purpose requirement.[15]   As noted above,[16] the requirement could in theory strike down laws whose application will be entirely secular.   Legislators might increase aid to the poor because of religious convictions, or fund a public forum because they hope that it will be used mainly for religious events, or reduce taxes because they hope that most citizens will donate the money to churches.   Although courts would not strike such statutes down, current doctrine could be construed to require them to do so.   As a consequence, some legislators may feel that they cannot voice whatever religious beliefs form the grounds for their political positions, lest they poison the relevant legislation.   Constitutional doctrine should not be permitted to generate such a religious chill.[17]

11.   435 U.S. 618 (1978).   Chief Justice Burger wrote for a plurality comprising himself and Justices Powell, Rehnquist, and Stevens.   Opinions concurring in the judgment were filed by Justice Brennan, joined by Justice Marshall, id. at 629; Justice Stewart, id. at 642; and Justice White, id. at 643.

12.   Prohibiting clergy from holding certain offices, the plurality believed, related not to the clergy's beliefs, but rather to their conduct; thus, "the Free Exercise Clause's absolute prohibition of infringements on the 'freedom to believe' is inapposite here."   435 U.S. at 627 (footnote omitted).   Two concurring Justices argued that "freedom of belief protected by the Free Exercise Clause embraces freedom to profess or practice that belief, even including doing so to earn a livelihood."   435 U.S. at 631 (Brennan, J., joined by Marshall, J., concurring in judgment) (footnote omitted). See also § 14–8, supra.

13.   435 U.S. at 628.

14.   Id. ("There is no occasion to inquire whether promoting such an interest is a permissible legislative goal. . . .").

Even aside from the special issues raised by religious activism in politics, it could be argued that pursuit of such an interest is impermissible, because the harm addressed comes about through individuals' private choices—a factor that the Court has found relevant in other settings.   See § 14–8, note 13, supra.

15.   Under the three-part test first set out in Lemon v. Kurtzman, 403 U.S. 602 (1971), a government action violates the establishment clause if it has a nonsecular purpose, or if it exerts nonsecular primary effects, or if it creates excessive church-state entanglement.

16.   See § 14–9, supra.

17.   "The secular purpose requirement . . . means that if enough people take religion seriously, they cannot enact their program, but if they favor the same program for other reasons, they can enact it. It seems fair to say that this rule does not accept the view that religion should play an important part in public life." Tushnet, "The Constitution of Religion," 18 Conn.L.Rev. 701, 725 (1986).

Consider second the *Lemon* test's political divisiveness inquiry. Under that inquiry, a statute is more likely to be found unconstitutional if it generates religion-based political division. As noted previously,[18] the Court has not yet delineated this inquiry's independent power. In a number of cases, the Court has emphasized divisiveness as a factor in striking down various programs, particularly aid to parochial schools.[19] On the other hand, the Court has specifically declined to hold that the threat of divisiveness is alone sufficient to strike a program down.[20] The Court has suggested that the inquiry applies only in a limited set of cases.[21] And the Court has noted the legitimacy of religious activists' participating in politics.[22]

The Court most fully explained the alleged dangers of political divisiveness in *Lemon v. Kurtzman*.[23] The analysis began with original intent: "[P]olitical division along religious lines was one of the principal evils against which the First Amendment was intended to protect."[24] The Court then advanced the somewhat paternalistic argument that debate over religious issues would "tend to confuse and

---

18. See § 14–11.

19. The Court has suggested that state aid to parochial schools possesses a uniquely divisive potential. See, e.g., Grand Rapids School Dist. v. Ball, 473 U.S. 373, 383 (1985) ("[T]he occasional rivalry of parallel public and private school systems offers an all-too-ready opportunity for divisive rifts along religious lines in the body politic.") (citations omitted); Lemon v. Kurtzman, 403 U.S. 602, 623 (1971) (potential divisiveness concerning parochial schools is especially significant because of "the need for continuing annual appropriations and the likelihood of larger and larger demands as costs and population grow"); Aguilar v. Felton, 473 U.S. 402, 416–17 (1985) (Powell, J., concurring) ("[A]ny proposal to extend direct governmental aid to parochial schools alone is likely to spark political disagreement from taxpayers who support the public schools, as well as from non-recipient sectarian groups, who may fear that needed funds are being diverted from them."). See also Meek v. Pittenger, 421 U.S. 349 (1975); Committee for Public Educ. v. Nyquist, 413 U.S. 756, 794–98 (1973).

20. See Lynch v. Donnelly, 465 U.S. 668, 684 (1984) ("The Court of Appeals correctly observed that this Court has not held that political divisiveness alone can serve to invalidate otherwise permissible conduct. And we decline to so hold today."); Corporation of the Presiding Bishop of the Church of Jesus Christ of Latter-Day Saints v. Amos, 107 S.Ct. 2862, 2870 n. 17 (1987) (quoting and following Lynch).

21. See id. ("This case does not involve a direct subsidy to church-sponsored schools or colleges, or other religious insti-

tutions, and hence no inquiry into potential political divisiveness is even called for.") (citation omitted); Mueller v. Allen, 463 U.S. 388, 403 n.11 (1983) ("rather elusive inquiry" of political divisiveness is "confined to cases where direct financial subsidies are paid to parochial schools or to teachers in parochial schools"). But see Aguilar v. Felton, 473 U.S. 402, 414 (1985) (implying that political divisiveness may result from administrative entanglement, at least where the entanglement includes state-made decisions about matters of religious significance); Larkin v. Grendel's Den, Inc., 459 U.S. 116, 127 (1982) (referring to danger of political divisiveness concerning statute that lent state power to religious body); Lynch v. Donnelly, 465 U.S. at 703, n.9 (Brennan, J., joined by Marshall, Blackmun, and Stevens, JJ., dissenting) (Court's suggestion that "inquiry into potential political divisiveness is unnecessary absent direct subsidies to church-sponsored schools or colleges, derives from a distorted reading of our prior cases").

22. See Walz v. Tax Comm'n, 397 U.S. 664, 670 (1970) ("Adherents of particular faiths and individual churches frequently take strong positions on public issues. . . . Of course, churches as much as secular bodies and private citizens have that right."); McDaniel v. Paty, 435 U.S. 618, 641 (1978) (Brennan, J., concurring in judgment) ("Religionists no less than members of any other group enjoy the full measure of protection afforded speech, association, and political activity generally.").

23. 403 U.S. 602 (1971).

24. Id. at 622.

obscure other issues of great urgency." [25]   The Court went on to hint that religion's entry into politics could lead to government's entry into religion: "The highways of church and state relationships are not likely to be one-way streets, and the Constitution's authors sought to protect religious worship from the pervasive power of government." [26]   The Court closed by returning to the past, noting that "[t]he history of many countries attests to the hazards of religion's intruding into the political arena. . . ." [27]

The divisiveness inquiry begins with two valid precepts. First, it correctly focuses on outsiders' reactions as importantly measuring establishment clause violations. In this way the inquiry parallels, more closely than the other traditional inquiries of the *Lemon* test, Justice O'Connor's symbolic endorsement approach: that the establishment clause forbids practices that "make religion relevant, in reality or public perception, to status in the political community." [28]   Second, the divisiveness inquiry correctly notes that religious cleavages could fragment politics, and that the first amendment in part reduces that danger.[29]   The political scientist Robert Dahl has suggested that religious divisions in a state that did not recognize the autonomy of religious groups could make consensus impossible on such issues as education, welfare programs, and social security.[30]   In Dahl's view, consensus could be restored by giving religious groups substantial autonomy.

But it does not follow that the first amendment requires, or even permits, whatever steps might be needed to reduce religion-based political divisiveness.[31]   The divisiveness inquiry directly discourages at least some constitutionally protected religious involvements in politics; and the secular purpose test, if construed to rule out even secular actions that are in fact religiously motivated, does so indirectly. For at least six reasons, both are misguided.

First, democracy is ill-protected by steps that reduce political participation, even steps taken in the name of consensus. The Court has spoken of a "profound national commitment to the principle that debate on public issues should be uninhibited, robust, and wide-open." [32]   Carving out an exception for any form of rhetoric, including religious

---

25. Id. at 622–23.

26. Id. at 623.

27. Id.

28. Lynch v. Donnelly, 465 U.S. 668, 692 (1984) (O'Connor, J., concurring). See § 14–15, infra.

29. It has been argued, however, that the potential of religious divisions in politics has diminished considerably. See Smith, "The Special Place of Religion in the Constitution," 1983 Sup.Ct.Rev. 3, 97–98.

30. R. Dahl, Dilemmas of Pluralist Democracy 89 (1982).

31. Several Justices have criticized the divisiveness inquiry. See Aguilar v. Felton, 473 U.S. at 429 (O'Connor, J., joined by Rehnquist, J., dissenting) (political divisiveness inquiry should be eliminated); Lynch v. Donnelly, 465 U.S. at 689 (O'Connor, J., concurring) ("In my view, political divisiveness along religious lines should not be an independent test of constitutionality."). Cf. Lynch v. Donnelly, 465 U.S. at 703 n.9 (Brennan, J., dissenting) ("I agree . . . with Justice O'Connor's helpful suggestion that while political divisiveness is 'an evil addressed by the Establishment Clause,' the ultimate inquiry must always focus on 'the character of the government activity that might cause such divisiveness.' ").

32. New York Times Co. v. Sullivan, 376 U.S. 254, 270 (1964).

rhetoric, would undercut that principle. As Justice Brennan wrote in *McDaniel*, "[t]hat public debate of religious ideas, like any other, may arouse emotion, may incite, may foment religious divisiveness and strife does not rob it of constitutional protection. The mere fact that a purpose of the Establishment Clause is to reduce or eliminate religious divisiveness or strife, does not place religious discussion, association, or political participation in a status less preferred than rights of discussion, association, and political participation generally." [33]

Second, actions that discourage religious involvement in politics raise free exercise concerns, by imposing a disability on the basis of religious conduct and, perhaps, belief. The disability remains problematic even if it requires believers who participate in politics to do no more than omit religious references, with the sanction that failing to do so may doom the legislation that they favor. Marxists, Republicans, ecologists, and members of other groups may voice their deep-seated beliefs during political debates without self-censorship; religious believers deserve no less. Indeed, under the free exercise clause they may deserve more, when religious doctrine itself requires active political involvement. [34]

Third, both the secular purpose requirement and the political divisiveness inquiry are unusually difficult to administer. Legislative motivation is difficult to discern under the best of circumstances, and legislators may try to mask their true motives when those would be fatal to a statute. A plethora of familiar problems arise when courts try to psychoanalyze legislators. [35] Those problems are complicated by the fact that many legislative motivations will be partly religious, and that few if any will be wholly so.

Divisiveness is even thornier. Cases have not made clear whether the focus ought to be on the community actually affected, or on some hypothetical community of average or unusual religious diversity. [36] Focusing on the actual community would create a variety of standards across the country, depending on each community's religious homogeneity; but focusing on a hypothetical community requires courts to define

---

33. 435 U.S. at 640 (Brennan, J., joined by Marshall, J., concurring in judgment) (citations and footnote omitted).

34. Different religions, and different members of the same religion, disagree on how politically active religionists must be. Compare R. Neuhaus, The Naked Public Square: Religion and Democracy in America (1984) (Lutheran clergyman urging greater infusion of religion into political processes); with S. Atkins and T. McConnell, Churches on the Wrong Road (1986) (Episcopal clergymen urging religion to avoid political involvement). See also note 48, infra.

35. Cf. Wallace v. Jaffree, 472 U.S. 38, 74 (1985) (O'Connor, J., concurring in judgment) ("[A] court has no license to psychoanalyze the legislators."). See generally J. Ely, "Legislative and Administrative Moti-

vation in Constitutional Law," 79 Yale L.J. 1205 (1970).

36. Compare Lynch v. Donnelly, 465 U.S. at 684 (focusing on actual community), and Lemon v. Kurtzman, 403 U.S. 602, 622 (1971) (focusing on "communit[ies] where such a large number of pupils are served by church-related schools"), with Lynch, 465 U.S. at 703–04 (Brennan, J., dissenting) ("[T]he Court should not blind itself to the fact that because communities differ in religious composition, the controversy over whether local governments may adopt religious symbols will continue to fester. In many communities, non-Christian groups can be expected to combat practices similar to Pawtucket's; this will be so especially in areas where there are substantial non-Christian minorities.") (footnote omitted).

a standard. Case law is also somewhat ambiguous on whether the test measures potential or actual divisiveness.[37] Potential divisiveness is obviously difficult to gauge. But if divisiveness is measured after the fact, then opponents will be encouraged to create political friction in order to invalidate the law—giving them a form of veto power and, perversely, increasing the likelihood of fragmentation.

Fourth, it is dubious whether the divisiveness inquiry can significantly reduce religious polarization. Some degree of division is inevitable, however politically quiescent churches and their members might be. Such divisiveness will surround not only aid to religious organizations, but also such social issues as welfare and abortion. Moreover, divisiveness is equally likely whether religious bodies are seeking to protect the status quo or to overturn it. Thus it seems likely, for example, that any legal approach to abortion will generate religious fragmentation; it cannot follow that all possible approaches violate the establishment clause.[38] In addition, walling religious organizations off from politics could alienate religious believers, creating entirely new "political ruptures." [39] And the Court's own opinions on church-state issues sometimes create divisiveness.[40]

Fifth, although the divisiveness inquiry correctly focuses on public perceptions, it gauges those perceptions inadequately. When a government action concerning religion produces no visible opposition, the silence may stem from community satisfaction—but it may also stem from the opponents' "sense of futility in opposing the majority." [41] People who do not adhere to the majority religion may, despite their discomfort over a government action respecting religion, choose to avoid confrontation, preferring to suffer in silence rather than to risk creating a backlash against themselves and their beliefs.[42] It is wise to ask whether a government action "sends a message to nonadherents that they are outsiders, not full members of the political community"; [43] but it is unwise to require that the nonadherents prove it by public opposition.

37. See Aguilar v. Felton, 473 U.S. 402, 429 (O'Connor, J., joined by Rehnquist, J., dissenting) (1985) ("The Court's reliance on the potential for political divisiveness as evidence of undue entanglement is also unpersuasive. There is little record support for the proposition that New York's admirable Title I program has ignited any controversy other than this litigation."). The Court has generally focused on potential divisiveness. See, e.g., Aguilar v. Felton, 473 U.S. 402, 414 (1985); Meek v. Pittenger, 421 U.S. 349, 372 (1975); Committee for Public Educ. v. Nyquist, 413 U.S. 756, 795–96 (1973); Lemon v. Kurtzman, 403 U.S. 602, 622 (1971). But see Lynch, 465 U.S. at 684 (focusing on lack of actual divisiveness).

38. See § 15–10, infra.

39. 77 Harv.L.Rev. 1353, 1357 (1964).

40. See Meek v. Pittenger, 421 U.S. 349, 382 (1975) (Burger, C.J., concurring in judgment in part and dissenting in part) ("I see at least as much potential for divisive political debate in opposition to the crabbed attitude the Court shows in this case."). See generally A. Reichley, Religion in American Public Life 146–51 (1985) (discussing public reaction to Court's decisions forbidding official school prayers).

41. Lynch v. Donnelly, 465 U.S. at 703 (Brennan, J., dissenting).

42. See, e.g., Donnelly v. Lynch, 525 F.Supp. 1150, 1180 (D.R.I. 1981) (noting "anger, hostility, name calling, and political maneuvering" triggered by plaintiffs' suit), aff'd 691 F.2d 1029 (1st Cir. 1982), rev'd 465 U.S. 668 (1984).

43. Lynch v. Donnelly, 465 U.S. at 688 (O'Connor, J., concurring).

Finally, the purpose and divisiveness inquiries fail to recognize religion's long history of positive contributions to public debate: " 'church and religious groups in the United States have long exerted powerful political pressures on state and national legislatures, on subjects as diverse as slavery, war, gambling, drinking, prostitution, marriage, and education.' " [44] As one commentator has asked: "Should all laws that the churches have played an essential role in passing, like the civil rights laws of the 1960s, be declared unconstitutional?" [45] Many observers have viewed such activism as natural and desirable aids to democracy. Tocqueville considered religion to be Americans' first political institution;[46] one need not go that far in order to recognize religion's contribution to the American political system.[47] Although other systems of belief and their attendant organizations could also serve such functions, none has yet developed the audience, influence, and resources of religion.

For these reasons, legislation should not be struck down merely because its supporters had religious motives, or because the legislation may exacerbate religious divisions in the polity.[48] Instead, courts should view nonsecular motive or purpose, and political divisiveness along religious lines, as warning signals,[49] suggesting stricter judicial scrutiny but not serving to condemn what government has done. The significance of such warning signals should not be underestimated. We saw in § 14–10 that the very symbolism of conspicuous governmental aid to an identifiably religious enterprise is regarded as an independent evil. Indeed, we saw that nothing short of a concern with such

---

44. McDaniel v. Paty, 435 U.S. 618, 641 n.25 (1978) (Brennan, J., concurring in judgment) (quoting first edition of this treatise (footnotes omitted)). See generally M. Howe, The Garden and the Wilderness 62 (1965); P. Kauper, Religion and the Constitution 83–85 (1964); A. Reichley, supra note 40; Carroll, "The Constitution, the Supreme Court, and Religion," 61 Am. Pol.Sci.Rev. 657, 662 (1967).

45. A. Reichley, supra note 40, at 167.

46. A. de Tocqueville, Democracy in America 292 (G. Lawrence transl. J. Mayer ed. 1969).

47. See generally R. Bellah, R. Madsen, W. Sullivan, A. Swidler, & S. Tipton, Habits of the Heart: Individualism and Commitment in American Life (1985); H. Berman, The Interaction of Law and Religion (1974); C. Mooney, Public Virtue: Law and the Social Character of Religion (1986); R. Neuhaus, The Naked Public Square: Religion and Democracy in America (1984); S. Bates, "Institutions of Freedom: Church, Press, and Democracy" (unpublished paper on file at Harvard Law Library).

48. By the same token, courts should look more closely at statutes or regulations that deny government benefits, such as tax exemptions, to religious bodies that engage

in political debate. Compare Christian Echoes Nat'l Ministry v. United States, 470 F.2d 849 (10th Cir. 1972) (upholding IRS revocation of radio evangelist Billy James Hargis's tax exempt status because of political activities), cert. denied 414 U.S. 864 (1973), with Girard Trust Co. v. Commissioner, 122 F.2d 108 (3d Cir. 1941) (contribution to Methodist temperance organization held deductible because church regarded organization's activism as religiously compelled). See also Holy Spirit Ass'n v. Tax Comm'n, 55 N.Y.2d 512, 450 N.Y.S.2d 292, 435 N.E.2d 662 (1982) (a court must accept an organization's goodfaith characterization that it operates solely for religious purposes, so that it qualifies for tax exemption, and may not reject purposes as non-religious because of the seemingly worldly or secular nature of the matters on which the religion's doctrine takes a stand).

49. See Committee for Public Educ. v. Nyquist, 413 U.S. 756, 797–98 (1973) ("[W]hile the prospect of such divisiveness may not alone warrant the invalidation of state laws that otherwise survive the careful scrutiny required by the decisions of this Court, it is certainly a 'warning signal' not to be ignored.") (quoting Lemon v. Kurtzman, 403 U.S. 602, 625 (1971) (Douglas, J., concurring)).

symbolism could distinguish those cases of aid to the religious enterprise which the Court has deemed impermissible from those which the Court has readily tolerated.   Apart from the significance of symbols in establishing precedents for more dangerous incursion, the fact of symbolic governmental identification with a religious activity must be understood to constitute a separate evil in a system that regards matters of religious concern as ultimately delegated to individual and community conscience.   When Madison objected to the coerced contribution to religion by an individual taxpayer,[50] it was surely not out of concern for the taxpayer's pocket; and when the Supreme Court in *Flast v. Cohen*[51] held that taxpayers have standing to challenge religious expenditures despite the ordinary rule against taxpayer standing, it was not out of a judgment that taxpayers' economic interests were truly at stake: there was no required showing that any money saved by eliminating a challenged religious expense would be returned to the taxpayer.   The only way to understand Madison's concern, or to make sense of the Court's conclusion in *Flast v. Cohen*, is to recognize in the religion clauses a fundamental personal right not to be a part of a community whose official organs endorse religious views that might be fundamentally inimical to one's deepest beliefs.[52]   Just as the Supreme Court held in *Wooley v. Maynard*[53] that individuals cannot be made the involuntary vehicles of views with which they disagree, so the experience of living in a political community which endorses or affirmatively supports religious positions with which one disagrees may be regarded as a peculiar offense to freedom of conscience.

Indeed, that concern may be the best way to understand the Court's attention to political divisiveness.   When government improperly aids religion, divisiveness is likely to follow and, because religion constitutes for many people the most fundamental set of beliefs, such divisiveness is uniquely offensive.   But divisiveness is only a symptom of the constitutional problem; it should not be deemed a constitutional problem in itself.[54]   As Justice Brennan wrote in *McDaniel v. Paty*: "The antidote which the Constitution provides against zealots who would inject sectarianism into the political process is to subject their ideas to refutation in the marketplace of ideas and their platforms to rejection at the polls.   With these safeguards, it is unlikely that they will succeed in inducing government to act along religiously divisive lines, and, with judicial enforcement of the Establishment Clause, any measure of success they achieve must be short-lived, at best."[55]

50. II Writings of James Madison 183 (G. Hunt ed. 1901).   See also Everson v. Board of Educ., 330 U.S. 1, 11–12 (1947); § 14–3, supra.

51. 392 U.S. 83 (1968), discussed in Chapter 3, supra.

52. See § 14–15, infra.   See also § 12–4, supra.

53. 430 U.S. 705 (1977).   In the free speech context, however, mere spending of one's tax dollars on a message one rejects is not deemed equivalent to being forced to identify with such a message.

54. That is not, however, to suggest that certain forms of rhetoric do not raise problems.   Legislators, other officials, and political candidates should be aware of the dangers raised by certain types of religious statements, particularly those that depict their opponents as enemies of God.   Such statements threaten the civil peace and the always-delicate accommodation of religion.   But this concern is more a political than a constitutional one.

55. McDaniel v. Paty, 435 U.S. at 642 (Brennan, J., joined by Marshall, J., concurring in judgment).

This section has accordingly suggested that the wall between church and state should not bar religion from politics—either directly or indirectly. The wall should, however, prohibit government from symbolically endorsing religion. That is the subject of the next section.

§ 14–15. Official Acknowledgment and Endorsement of Religious Values

"[A] core purpose of the Establishment Clause is violated," the Supreme Court has held, where a government action "conveys a message of government endorsement or disapproval of religion." [1]   An endorsement approach usefully focuses the constitutional inquiry, but it neither covers all issues [2] nor eliminates the need to balance competing values.[3]   In one area, however, an endorsement approach precisely fits the constitutional problem at hand.   The religion clauses' values and a number of the Supreme Court's precedents [4] support the principle that, when government uses religious means where nonreligious ones would suffice, it moves from accommodating religion to participating in religion by endorsing it as a preferred path to a desired end.

It is clear that government may sometimes accommodate religious observances and beliefs, through purely secular means that lift government-imposed burdens. Government may, for example, declare Christmas a national holiday for federal employees, exempt conscientious objectors from combat duty, and require employers to grant reasonable accommodations to employees' religious needs. Those means, in and of themselves, raise no insuperable establishment clause obstacle. The obstacle arises in the way the secular means chosen interact with religious institutions (the entanglement test), or in the ends sought (the purpose test) or achieved (the effects test). To be sure, government "acknowledges" a religion whenever it accommodates that religion

---

§ 14–15

1. Grand Rapids School Dist. v. Ball, 473 U.S. 373, 389 (1985) (citing Lynch v. Donnelly, 465 U.S. 668, 688 (1984) (O'Connor, J., concurring)). See also Wallace v. Jaffree, 472 U.S. 38, 56 (1985) ("In applying the purpose test, it is appropriate to ask 'whether government's actual purpose is to endorse or disapprove of religion.' ") (footnote omitted) (quoting Lynch, 465 U.S. at 690 (O'Connor, J., concurring)).

2. An aid program that excessively entangles government and religion may violate the establishment clause even though the program conveys no message of endorsement. See Lynch v. Donnelly, 465 U.S. 668, 687–88 (1984) (O'Connor, J., concurring) (distinguishing entanglement inquiry from endorsement inquiry).

3. A strictly applied endorsement approach might strike down even those government accommodations to religion that are based on the free exercise clause and its underlying values. Cf. Wallace v. Jaffree, 472 U.S. at 83 (O'Connor, J., concurring in judgment) (where a statute seeks to

advance free exercise values, endorsement is measured from the perspective of an objective observer who is familiar with, and seemingly sympathetic to, those values).

4. See, e.g., Abington School Dist. v. Schempp, 374 U.S. 203, 281 (1963) (Brennan, J., concurring) ("it seems to me that the State acts unconstitutionally if it either sets about to attain even indirectly religious ends by religious means, or if it uses religious means to serve secular ends where secular means would suffice"). But see Wallace v. Jaffree, 472 U.S. at 113 (Rehnquist, J., dissenting) ("nothing in the Establishment Clause . . . prohibit[s] Congress or the States from pursuing legitimate secular ends through nondiscriminatory sectarian means"); Lynch v. Donnelly, 465 U.S. 668 (1984) (display of city-owned and maintained crèche does not violate establishment clause); Marsh v. Chambers, 463 U.S. 783 (1983) (state-paid legislative chaplain does not violate establishment clause).

through such secular means without accommodating similar, non-religious beliefs and believers. But such acknowledgment is not a forbidden endorsement in and of itself: its validity turns on purpose and effect in the particular case.

The situation becomes dramatically different when government uses religious tools where secular ones would do.[5] The issue is not whether the religious tools chosen will help achieve secular goals. Of course they will. Bible readings in public schools, for example, might instill desirable moral values, simplify the task of disciplining children, and create a more hospitable learning environment.[6] Rather, the problem is that, when government needlessly uses means that are inherently religious, a message of endorsement is virtually unavoidable. By adopting the language and precepts of a religion as its own, government implies that non-adherents are outsiders. In a sense, the religious medium becomes the state's message. Indeed, one prominent commentator has written that the establishment clause is "the only substantive constitutional restraint on what governments may say."[7] When a government gratuitously adopts religious tools, it violates this restraint.

Secular tools will almost always suffice to pursue government's interests. Occasionally, however, religious tools may be essential to promote free exercise values.[8] For example, government can facilitate

5. This distinction was recognized in a law review discussion of Lynch v. Donnelly, 465 U.S. 668 (1984): "[T]he citizens of Pawtucket sought not accommodation of their religious beliefs; rather, they sought the city's active participation in celebrating Christmas. . . ." "The Supreme Court, 1983 Term," 98 Harv.L.Rev. 87, 180 (1984).

6. See Abington School Dist. v. Schempp, 374 U.S. at 223 (rejecting state defense that Bible readings would not advance religion, but would simply "promot[e] . . . moral values, . . . contradict[ ] . . . the materialistic trends of our times, . . . perpetuat[e] . . . our institutions and . . . teach[ ] . . . literature"). Cf. American Civil Liberties Union v. Rabun County Chamber of Commerce, 698 F.2d 1098, 1109–11 (11th Cir. 1983) (rejecting argument that purpose behind cross mounted on hilltop was to promote tourism); Hall v. Bradshaw, 630 F.2d 1018, 1019–20 (4th Cir. 1980) (rejecting argument that purpose behind printing "Motorist's Prayer" on official state road maps was to promote highway safety), cert. denied 450 U.S. 965 (1981).

7. M. Yudof, When Government Speaks: Politics, Law, and Government Expression in America 214 (1983).

8. Several Justices have even suggested that religious acknowledgments may at times be the only means by which government can pursue non-free exercise goals,

such as "solemnizing public occasions." Lynch v. Donnelly, 465 U.S. at 693 (O'Connor, J., concurring); id. at 717 (Brennan, J., joined by Marshall, Blackmun, and Stevens, JJ., dissenting). Although religious language may effectively serve such ends, it seems implausible that *only* religious language could do so. Justice Brennan, responding to the argument that Bible reading in school pursues valid secular goals, made the point well: "It has not been shown that readings from the speeches and messages of great Americans, for example, or from the documents of our heritage of liberty, daily recitation of the Pledge of Allegiance, or even the observance of a moment of reverent silence at the opening of class, may not adequately serve the solely secular purposes of the devotional activities without jeopardizing either the religious liberties of any members of the community or the proper degree of separation between the spheres of religion and government. Such substitutes would, I think, be unsatisfactory or inadequate only to the extent that the present activities do in fact serve religious goals." Abington School Dist. v. Schempp, 374 U.S. 203, 281 (1963) (Brennan, J., concurring). See also Marsh v. Chambers, 463 U.S. 783, 797–78 (1983) (Brennan, J., dissenting) ("whatever secular functions legislative prayer might play—formally opening the legislative session, getting the members of the body to quiet down, and imbuing them with a sense of seriousness and high pur-

soldiers' free exercise only by hiring military chaplains and, through them, engaging in religious speech and observances; no non-religious alternative is plausible.[9] But such exceptions are exceedingly rare.[10] Legislators, for example, have opportunities for religious observances that are not available to soldiers; thus, legislative chaplains [11] and state house prayer rooms [12] stand on a different footing.

When government employs religious tools unnecessarily, at least seven dangers may arise. First, government must select a particular approach from among different religions, and different doctrines of particular religions; the state thus makes essentially religious decisions, decisions which the Constitution leaves to religious organizations and individuals.[13] Second, in making such decisions, government will almost invariably violate denominational neutrality.[14] Third, if government does try to achieve neutrality—by using tools borrowed from different religious and non-religious philosophies—administrative entanglement is likely to result.[15] Fourth, government's use of religious

pose—could so plainly be performed in a purely nonreligious fashion that to claim a secular purpose for the prayer is an insult to the perfectly honorable individuals who instituted and continue the practice"); Y. Mirsky, "Civil Religion and the Establishment Clause," 95 Yale L.J. 1237, 1256 (1986) (reading Declaration of Independence aloud would perform same function as legislative prayer).

9. See Abington School Dist. v. Schempp, 374 U.S. 203, 226, n.10 (1963) ("We are not of course presented with and therefore do not pass upon a situation such as military service, where the Government regulates the temporal and geographic environment of individuals to a point that, unless it permits voluntary religious services to be conducted with the use of government facilities, military personnel would be unable to engage in the practice of their faiths."); Katcoff v. Marsh, 755 F.2d 223, 234 (2d Cir. 1985) (upholding military chaplaincy program as applied to active soldiers not located in urban U.S., in part because Congress must "make religion available to soldiers who have been moved by the Army to areas of the world where religion of their own denominations is not available to them").

10. Katcoff v. Marsh, supra, is illustrative. In an establishment clause challenge to the military chaplaincy system, the Second Circuit there concluded that the system permissibly facilitated the free exercise rights of soldiers stationed far from ministers of their faith. But the court remanded to the district court to determine whether the system also provided chaplains (a) in urban centers, where local clergy would suffice, and (b) to retired military personnel, who could freely move to a place where local private clergy would serve their needs. Id. at 237–38.

11. In upholding the constitutionality of legislative chaplains, the Supreme Court relied principally on history, and did not advance a free exercise justification. Marsh v. Chambers, 463 U.S. 783 (1983).

12. See Van Zandt v. Thompson, 649 F.Supp. 583 (N.D. Ill. 1986) (enjoining state from converting legislative hearing room to prayer room).

13. See Engel v. Vitale, 370 U.S. 421, 435 (1962) ("It is neither sacrilegious nor antireligious to say that each separate government in this country should stay out of the business of writing or sanctioning official prayers and leave that purely religious function to the people themselves and to those the people choose to look to for religious guidance.") (footnote omitted).

14. See Marsh v. Chambers, 463 U.S. at 823 (Stevens, J., dissenting) ("Prayers may be said by a Catholic priest in the Massachusetts Legislature and by a Presbyterian minister in the Nebraska Legislature, but I would not expect to find a Jehovah's Witness or a disciple of Mary Baker Eddy or the Reverend Moon serving as the official chaplain in any state legislature."); § 14–7, supra.

15. See Marsh v. Chambers, 463 U.S. at 799 (Brennan, J., dissenting) ("the process of choosing a 'reasonable' chaplain . . . and insuring that the chaplain limits himself or herself to 'suitable' prayers, involves precisely the sort of supervision that agencies of government should if at all possible avoid") (footnote omitted); cf. Lynch v. Donnelly, 465 U.S. at 702 (Brennan, J., dissenting) ("Jews and other non-Christian groups . . . can be expected to press government for inclusion of their symbols, and faced with such requests, government will have to become involved in accommodating the various demands.").

means entails government's lending a religious organization an inherently state power: the power of official endorsement through government speech.[16] Fifth, when government uses the tools of religion, the religion itself may become secularized, recalling Roger Williams' fear that, if church and state mingle, the "wilderness" of the state might pollute the "garden" of the church.[17]

The sixth possible danger is that government may, by using religious means, put itself on a religious pedestal. The borrowed aura of such legitimacy may be extremely powerful, given the fundamental importance that religion holds for many people. Fervent nationalism is troubling in ways that fervent religious faith is not; such nationalism may be particularly distressing when it is borrowed rather than earned. In that regard, the temptation may be great for government to identify itself with religion; religion, as one leading commentator has written, can become "an irresistibly useful instrument of state policy." [18] But the costs may be high. As the distinguished playwright Arthur Miller has written. "A Khomeini in our day is impossible to controvert, let alone dislodge, because he has achieved a total identification of religion with his political regime, so that to oppose him is to oppose God." [19] It may seem a bit farfetched to compare the budding tyrant who denounces his enemies as devils with the school board that wishes to shore up the waning authority of schoolteachers by including a brief prayer at the start of the schoolday, or with the legislature that wishes to reassure a skeptical populace by opening its sessions with God's blessing. But the path toward the tyrannical marriage of cross and sword may lie along a steeper slope than some suppose.[20]

16. Cf. Larkin v. Grendel's Den, Inc., 459 U.S. 116 (1982). In Grendel's Den, religious bodies benefited; here, religion in general benefits. The principle, however, is much the same. See § 14-11, supra.

17. See Grand Rapids School Dist. v. Ball, 473 U.S. 373, 385 (1985) (government-sponsored indoctrination into religious beliefs would "taint[ ] the resulting religious beliefs with a corrosive secularism"); Engel v. Vitale, 370 U.S. 421, 431-32 (1962) ("The Establishment Clause . . . stands as an expression of principle on the part of the Founders of our Constitution that religion is too personal, too sacred, too holy, to permit its 'unhallowed perversion' by a civil magistrate."); § 14-3, supra.

18. Van Alstyne, "Trends in the Supreme Court: Mr. Jefferson's Crumbling Wall—A Comment on Lynch v. Donnelly," 1984 Duke L.J. 770, 786. In a useful warning, Professor Van Alstyne goes on to depict a government that cynically exploits religion: "In . . . marginal, gradual, ordinary ways, . . . virtually from the beginning the nation has drifted, reidentified itself, and become, like so many others, accustomed to the political appropriation of religion for its own official uses. In exchange, it now purchases religious support. Late arrivals to America may suppose they can take the government's religiosity or leave it, but they are stuck with the reality that clashes so clearly with the first amendment: Ours is basically a Christian-pretending government where they will be made to feel ungrateful should they complain. The gradual but increasingly pervasive installment of compromised religious ritual within government itself thus draws that which was formerly outside to the inside; the prevailing monotheism has been made a commonplace exhibition in state practice, and put to service and supported by the state when felt useful. Additional appropriations from sectarianism may then become logically fitted as part of this 'secular' but sectarian state." Id. at 787.

19. A. Miller, "School Prayer: A Political Dirigible," N.Y. Times, March 12, 1984, at A17, col. 1.

20. Cf. Engel v. Vitale, 370 U.S. 421, 436 (1962) ("[T]he governmental endorsement of that prayer seems relatively insignificant when compared to the governmental encroachments which were commonplace 200 years ago. To those who may subscribe to the view that . . . there can be no danger to religious freedom in [the prayer's] governmental establishment, however, it may be appropriate to say in

Finally, and perhaps most importantly, government's gratuitous use of a religious means is likely to convey a message of exclusion to all those who do not adhere to the favored religion. When such people learn that government has gone out of its way to adopt the religion's tools, they may believe that government must have adopted its tenets as well; they may quite reasonably feel as if they are "not full members of the political community." [21] When government is pursuing a free exercise goal, some such feelings may be unavoidable; the endorsement question in such cases ought to be asked from the perspective of an "objective observer" who is "acquainted with the Free Exercise Clause and the values it promotes." [22] Such a perspective will validate many government efforts that facilitate free exercise, but not those efforts that needlessly rely on religious tools; this far, free exercise values do not extend.

Because of these many dangers to principles embedded in the religion clauses, government should be required to use secular tools unless only religious tools will suffice to pursue a relevant free exercise value.[23] It may also be necessary to require that government take steps to ensure that private acknowledgments of religion are not erroneously attributed to government.[24]

The Supreme Court's approach is partly consistent with the analysis advanced here. In a number of cases, the Court has struck down programs that used religious tools to pursue supposedly secular ends.[25] Although the cases dealt with public school-children, the Court's language implied that the principle held true for other settings and other

the words of James Madison . . . .: '[I]t is proper to take alarm at the first experiment on our liberties. . . . ' ").

21. Lynch v. Donnelly, 465 U.S. at 688 (O'Connor, J., concurring). See also Friedman v. Board of County Comm'rs of Bernalillo County, 781 F.2d 777, 782 (10th Cir. 1985) ("A person approached by officers leaving a patrol car emblazoned with this [official county] seal [containing prominent cross and Spanish motto translating as 'With This We Conquer'] could reasonably assume that the officers were Christian police, and that the organization they represented identified itself with the Christian God. A follower of any non-Christian religion might well question the officers' ability to provide even-handed treatment."), cert. denied 106 S.Ct. 2890 (1986).

22. See Wallace v. Jaffree, 472 U.S. at 83 (O'Connor, J., concurring in judgment) (from the vantage point of such an observer, "individual perceptions, or resentments that a religious observer is exempted from a particular government requirement, would be entitled to little weight if the Free Exercise Clause strongly supported the exemption").

23. See Abington School Dist. v. Schempp, 374 U.S. 203, 294 (1963) (Bren-

nan, J., concurring) ("[T]he States may not employ religious means to reach a secular goal unless secular means are wholly unavailing.").

24. See McCreary v. Stone, 739 F.2d 716, 728 (2d Cir. 1984) (requiring disclaimer message on privately owned crèche displayed in government-owned park), aff'd by an equally divided court sub nom. Board of Trustees of Scarsdale v. McCreary, 471 U.S. 83 (1985); Allen v. Morton, 495 F.2d 65, 67–68 (D.C. Cir. 1973) (per curiam) (if government terminates its relationship with Christmas pageant organization, but organization continues to display crèche on government property, then disclaimer plaques are necessary).

25. E.g., Wallace v. Jaffree, 472 U.S. 38 (1985) (striking down silent prayer or meditation statute where legislative history and language demonstrated that statute meant to endorse prayer as a preferred activity); Stone v. Graham, 449 U.S. 39 (1980) (per curiam) (striking down statute requiring copy of Ten Commandments, purchased with private contributions, to be posted in each public classroom); Engel v. Vitale, 370 U.S. 421 (1962) (striking down program under which state-written prayer was recited in public school classrooms).

audiences as well.[26] But in two seemingly anomalous cases decided in the early 1980s, the Court indicated that government may sometimes use religious tools when free exercise claims are nonexistent, and that even purely religious government speech does not necessarily violate the establishment clause.

Marsh v. Chambers [27] concerned a challenge to a state-paid legislative chaplain. The Eighth Circuit had concluded that the practice violated all three prongs of the *Lemon* test,[28] and thus was prohibited by the establishment clause.[29] The Supreme Court reversed, in an opinion that quietly—and, it later developed, only temporarily—jettisoned the *Lemon* test. Instead of applying *Lemon*'s three inquiries, the *Marsh* Court turned to history.[30] The Court found that legislative prayers were both widespread [31] and venerable.[32] The Court noted evidence that the first amendment's Framers had believed that the practice did not violate the establishment clause, particularly the fact that the First Congress had selected chaplains for both houses; this, the Court said, demonstrated that "the men who wrote the First Amendment Religion Clause did not view paid legislative chaplains and opening prayers as a violation of that Amendment. . . ." [33] The Court concluded that legislative prayers are "simply a tolerable acknowledgment of beliefs widely held among the people of this country." [34]

---

26. See, e.g., Wallace v. Jaffree, 472 U.S. at 60 ("The importance of that principle [requiring government neutrality toward religion] does not permit us to treat [a religious motivation underlying a moment of silence statute] as an inconsequential case involving nothing more than a few words of symbolic speech on behalf of the political majority. For whenever the State itself speaks on a religious subject, one of the questions that we must ask is 'whether the Government intends to convey a message of endorsement or disapproval of religion.' ") (footnotes omitted) (quoting Lynch v. Donnelly, 465 U.S. at 691 (O'Connor, J., concurring)).

27. 463 U.S. 783 (1983). Chief Justice Burger wrote the Court's opinion. Dissents were filed by Justice Brennan, joined by Justice Marshall, id. at 795; and by Justice Stevens, id. at 822.

28. Under Lemon v. Kurtzman, 403 U.S. 602 (1971), government violates the establishment clause if it acts with a nonsecular motive, or if its action produces non-secular primary effects, or if its action will produce excessive church-state entanglement.

29. Chambers v. Marsh, 675 F.2d 228, 234–35 (8th Cir. 1982).

30. The Court did not explain its departure from the usual tests. In dissent, Justice Brennan wrote: "In sum, I have no doubt that, if any group of law students

were asked to apply the principles of *Lemon* to the question of legislative prayer, they would nearly unanimously find the practice to be unconstitutional." 463 U.S. at 800–01 (Brennan, J., joined by Marshall, J., dissenting) (footnote omitted).

31. See id. at 789 n.11 (listing states).

32. See id. at 786 ("From colonial times through the founding of the Republic and ever since, the practice of legislative prayer has coexisted with the principles of disestablishment and religious freedom."); id. at 790 (referring to "Nebraska's practice of over a century, consistent with two centuries of national practice").

33. Id. at 788. The fact that some Framers opposed the practice, the Court added, only "demonstrat[es] that the subject was considered carefully and the action not taken thoughtlessly. . . ." Id. at 791.

34. Id. at 792. The Court also rejected the contention that the Nebraska's chaplain's 16-year tenure constituted an impermissible religious preference. "[T]he evidence indicates that [the chaplain] was reappointed because his performance and personal qualities were acceptable to the body appointing him. . . . Absent proof that [his] reappointment stemmed from an impermissible motive, we conclude that his long tenure does not in itself conflict with the Establishment Clause." Id. at 793–94 (footnotes omitted).

While *Marsh* relied principally on history, *Lynch v. Donnelly* [35] combined several approaches to uphold, by a 5–4 vote, a city's official display of a nativity scene alongside other Christmas decorations. [36] In *Lynch* the Court formally returned to its traditional *Lemon* test, albeit with the slightly petulant remark that "we have repeatedly emphasized our unwillingness to be confined to any single test or criterion in this sensitive area." [37] Even though the crèche was undeniably religious, the Court found that the city's purpose was secular, [38] at least when the crèche was viewed in the context of the holiday season; the district court, which had struck down the city's display of the crèche, "plainly erred by focusing almost exclusively on the crèche." [39] The Court found that the crèche's primary effects were no more religious than had been the case in other programs the Court had previously permitted. [40] The Court dismissed as "irrelevant" the argument that the city's goals might have been served by a crèche-less Christmas display. [41] Also in apparent reference to effects, the Court relied on the history, not of nativity scenes as such, but rather of "official acknowledgment . . . of the role of religion in American life. . . ." [42] It repeatedly dwelt on several such acknowledgments, particularly official recognitions of the Christmas holiday, [43] and museum displays of religious paintings and artifacts. [44] Finally, the Court found that the crèche created no admin-

35. 465 U.S. 668 (1984). Chief Justice Burger wrote for the Court. Justice O'Connor concurred, id. at 687. Justice Brennan, joined by Justices Marshall, Blackmun, and Stevens, dissented. Id. at 694.

36. Although the Court did not rest its conclusion or any of its arguments on the fact, the display of the city-owned and maintained crèche did not take place on municipally owned property. See id. at 671.

37. Id. at 679.

38. Indeed, both the majority and the concurring opinions specifically suggest that government may permissibly join in religious celebrations. See 465 U.S. at 681 ("The display is sponsored by the City to celebrate the Holiday and to depict the origins of that Holiday. These are legitimate secular purposes.") (footnote omitted); id. at 692 (O'Connor, J., concurring) ("The display celebrates a public holiday. . . . Government celebration of the holiday, which is extremely common, generally is not understood to endorse the religious content of the holiday. . . .").

39. Id. at 680.

40. Id. at 681–82.

41. Id. at 681 n.7.

42. Id. at 674.

43. See id. at 676, 680, 681, 683, 685, 686. Justice Brennan responded: "To say that government may recognize the holiday's traditional, secular elements of giftgiving, public festivities and community

spirit, does not mean that government may indiscriminately embrace the distinctively sectarian aspects of the holiday." Id. at 709–10 (dissenting). It would surely be unacceptable for the fact that Christmas is a national holiday to serve as the basis for a holding that a city may display a Christian nativity scene but not, say, a Jewish menorah.

44. Id. at 676–77, 683. Justice Brennan responded that a museum setting would provide "objective guarantees that the crèche could not suggest that a particular faith had been singled out for public favor and recognition." Id. at 713 (dissenting). See also "The Supreme Court, 1983 Term," 98 Harv.L.Rev. 87, 181 (1984) ("At a museum or in a classroom, observers expect to be exposed to a variety of works of art and literature, including those influenced by religion; thus, inclusion of such works carries no message about the display organizers' view or endorsement of religion. Further, the educational and expositive nature of such displays distances the organizer, in the mind of the public, from the materials presented. In contrast, the public perceives a governmental display celebrating Christmas as a promotion, rather than an exposition, of the holiday."). Cf. Marsh v. Chambers, 463 U.S. at 811 (Brennan, J., dissenting) ("members of the clergy who offer invocations at legislative sessions are not museum pieces, put on display once a day for the edification of the legislature. Rather, they are engaged by the legislature to lead it—as a body—in an act of religious worship.").

istrative entanglement.[45]   The Court held that the entanglement inquiry's political divisiveness subtest was inapplicable and added that, in any event, no divisiveness was evident.[46]

Both the *Marsh* and the *Lynch* approaches are deeply problematic. In *Marsh*, the Court glossed over serious ambiguities in the historical record.[47] More importantly, the Court failed to explain how and when a history suggesting early acceptance of a practice trumps the Framers' apparent adoption of a principle inconsistent with that practice.[48] "Standing alone," the Court wrote, "historical patterns cannot justify contemporary violations of constitutional guarantees, but there is far more here than simply historical patterns"—namely, the First Congress' concrete understanding of the limits of the religion clauses.[49] But if constitutionality could be conferred by such a concrete understanding, then *Brown v. Board of Education*[50] would have followed the rule of *Plessy v. Ferguson*[51] and upheld public school segregation.[52] And if one assumes that Framers' intent as to specific practices ought always to prevail over competing values, then the consistent solution, faithful to that principle, would be to recast the establishment clause test itself in order to match original intention.[53] Surely the Court should not feel free to carve exceptions in the test when a majority of the Justices prefer to follow the Framers' more concrete views.

Lynch is even more perplexing. To begin with, it is unclear just what features of the Pawtucket crèche led the Court to uphold it. The Court insisted that the crèche be considered "in context," but the majority never explained whether "context" referred to (a) other forms of official recognition of Christmas, or (b) the Santa Claus, talking wishing well, and other secular symbols surrounding Pawtucket's crèche.[54] The ambiguity has led to confusion in lower courts.[55]

45. 465 U.S. at 683–84 (adopting conclusion of district court).

46. Id. at 684. The district court had held that, although the crèche had not previously created divisiveness, the litigation challenging it had done so. The Supreme Court responded: "A litigant cannot, by the very act of commencing a lawsuit, . . . create the appearance of divisiveness and then exploit it as evidence of entanglement." Id. at 684–85.

47. See Marsh v. Chambers, 463 U.S. at 800 & n.10 (Brennan, J., dissenting) (reviewing early controversies over legislative prayers).

48. See also § 14–3, supra.

49. 463 U.S. at 790.

50. 347 U.S. 483 (1954).

51. 163 U.S. 537 (1896).

52. See § 16–15, infra.

53. See Wallace v. Jaffree, 472 U.S. at 110 (Rehnquist, J., dissenting) ("[T]he *Lemon* test has no more grounding in the history of the First Amendment than does the wall theory upon which it rests.").

54. The Court's language "crèche in the context of the Christmas season" suggests the former possibility. 465 U.S. at 679. But the sentences that immediately follow concern the integration of religious texts, like the Bible and the Ten Commandments, into a secular school curriculum as objects of study; that discussion, by relating more to physical context, suggests the latter possibility.

55. Compare McCreary v. Stone, 739 F.2d 716 (2d Cir. 1984) ("The Supreme Court did not decide the Pawtucket case based upon the physical context within which the display of the crèche was situated; rather, the court consistently referred to 'the crèche in the context of the Christmas season' . . .") (citing Lynch v. Donnelly, 465 U.S. at 679), aff'd by an equally divided court sub nom. Board of Trustees of Scarsdale v. McCreary, 471 U.S. 83 (1985), with American Civil Liberties Union v. Birmingham, 791 F.2d 1561 (6th Cir. 1986) ("When surrounded by a multitude of secular symbols of Christmas, a nativity scene may do no more than remind an observer that the holiday has a religious origin. But when the nonreli-

The Court's formal analysis is equally confusing. The crux of the *Lynch* holding was what one commentator has called an "any-more-than" test,[56] which the Court had briefly mentioned in *Marsh*.[57] Because the crèche was not any more a religious endorsement than other programs the Court had permitted, it was constitutional.[58] But the precedents on which the Court relied were not truly analogous to *Lynch*.[59] Moreover, the approach has no greater intrinsic validity than "a no-less-than" test, which, by citing different precedents, would have reached the opposite result. Furthermore, the "any-more-than" approach could, by selectively citing precedents, move establishment clause doctrine toward ever-larger official endorsements as, in future applications, programs are compared to *Lynch*.[60] Thus might the well-known tyranny of small decisions eventually eclipse a core purpose of the establishment clause.

Most troubling was *Lynch*'s conclusion, without analysis, that the crèche would not be perceived as a symbol of government endorsement.[61] The very existence of the underlying litigation cast that conclusion into at least some doubt.[62] Justice O'Connor's concurring

gious trappings . . . are stripped away, there remains only the universally recognized symbol for the central affirmation of a single religion—Christianity."), cert. denied 107 S.Ct. 421 (1986). The dissenting judge in the Birmingham case termed the latter approach "a 'St. Nicholas too' test— a city can get by with displaying a crèche if it throws in a sleigh full of toys and a Santa Claus, too." 791 F.2d at 1569 (Nelson, J., dissenting).

56. Van Alstyne, "Trends in the Supreme Court: Mr. Jefferson's Crumbling Wall—A Comment on *Lynch v. Donnelly*," 1984 Duke L.J. 770, 783.

57. See Marsh v. Chambers, 463 U.S. at 791 ("We conclude that legislative prayer presents no more potential for establishment than the provision of school transportation, beneficial grants for higher education, or tax exemptions for religious organizations.") (citations omitted).

58. In dictum, the Lynch Court also applied the "any-more-than" test to other government actions, and suggested that striking down the Pawtucket crèche would have widespread implications: "If the presence of the crèche in this display violates the Establishment Clause, a host of other forms of taking official note of Christmas, and of our religious heritage, are equally offensive to the Costitution." 465 U.S. at 686.

59. "The Court was apparently unconcerned that these examples involved situations in which the government had extended a clearly secular benefit to a wide range of similarly situated nonreligious and religious beneficiaries. The appropriate question in those cases was indeed whether the

benefit to religion was sufficiently incidental. In contrast, the cases more appropriate for comparison to *Lynch* would have been those in which the government had used and was identified with a religious symbol." "The Supreme Court, 1983 Term," 98 Harv.L.Rev. 87, 176 (1984). Of the cases mustered in Lynch, only Marsh concerned religious speech by government.

60. See Grand Rapids School Dist. v. Ball, 473 U.S. 373, 401 (1985) (Rehnquist, J., dissenting) ("One wonders how the teaching of [various high school subjects], which is struck down today, creates a greater 'symbolic link' than the municipal crèche upheld in Lynch v. Donnelly, or the legislative chaplain upheld in Marsh v. Chambers.") (citations omitted).

61. See 465 U.S. at 683 ("The dissent asserts some observers may perceive that the City has aligned itself with the Christian faith by including a Christian symbol in its display and that this serves to advance religion. . . . Here, whatever benefit to one faith or religion or to all religions, is indirect, remote and incidental; display of the crèche is no more an advancement or endorsement of religion than the Congressional and Executive recognition of the origins of the Holiday itself as 'Christ's Mass,' or the exhibition of literally hundreds of religious paintings in governmentally supported museums.").

62. Such use of the lawsuit itself to cast doubt on the Court's premise as to the perceptions triggering the suit should be distinguished from use of a lawsuit to show the existence of divisiveness triggered *by* the suit. See note 46, supra.

opinion at least asked the right question, by focusing more intently on whether the crèche would "send[ ] a message to nonadherents that they are outsiders. . . ."[63] But her analysis seemed to proceed from the perspective of an adherent. One could, without disrespect but with some dismay, term this the view of the "reasonable Christian."[64]

Justice O'Connor partly recognized that people receive messages differently, by noting that some listeners will have evidence of the speaker's actual intent, and others will not.[65] But the point is a larger one: When deciding whether a state practice makes someone feel like an outsider, the result often turns on whether one adopts the perspective of an outsider or that of an insider.[66] Judges must recognize the range of possible responses and cannot avoid selecting among them. For many adherents of the majority's religion—as the majority and the concurring opinions in *Lynch* demonstrate—the endorsement threshold is quite high.[67] But the opposite extreme also presents problems. For some especially sensitive non-adherents, the threshold may be unacceptably low and may cast doubt on free exercise accommodations and on practices that have outgrown their religious roots.

It seems clear that, in deciding whether a government practice would impermissibly convey a message of endorsement, one should adopt the perspective of a non-adherent; actions that reasonably offend non-adherents may seem so natural and proper to adherents as to blur into the background noise of society.[68] But this does not answer the question of how to define a suitable non-adherent vantage point. Presumably judges will posit some form of "reasonable non-adherent" perspective, based on the judges' notion of what is reasonable and what is hypersensitive. Some such hypothetical norm is probably unavoidable, but it requires considerable empathy on the part of judges, particularly those who themselves adhere to the majority religion.[69] Although he was speaking of the military rather than of the judiciary, Justice Brennan sounded the right warning: "[I]n pluralistic societies such as ours, institutions dominated by a majority are inevitably, if inadver-

---

63. 465 U.S. at 688 (O'Connor, J., concurring).

64. Dorsen & Sims, "The Nativity Scene Case: An Error of Judgment," 1985 U.Ill.L.Rev. 837, 860.

65. Lynch, 465 U.S. at 690.

66. Compare id. at 685 (majority opinion) ("The [Christmas] display engenders a friendly community spirit of good will in keeping with the season."), with N. Redlich, "Nativity Ruling Insults Jews," N.Y. Times, March 26, 1984 ("When I see a government-supported crèche, I suddenly feel as if I have become a stranger in my own home, to be tolerated only as long as I accept the dominant religious values.").

67. In Marsh, the Court also seemed to adopt the majority perspective: "We do not doubt the sincerity of those, who like respondent, believe that to have prayer in

this context risks the beginning of the establishment the Founding Fathers feared. But this concern is not well founded. . . ." 463 U.S. at 795.

68. See Dorsen & Sims, supra note 64, at 859 ("In determining whether litigants who seek establishment clause protection have been harmed by government's display of religious symbols, the Court must decide whether there has been a religious endorsement not from the viewpoint of the majority, or of a hypothetical reasonable man, but rather from the viewpoint of those who reasonably claim to have been harmed.").

69. Cf. Lynch, 465 U.S. at 696 (Brennan, J., dissenting) ("this case appears hard not because the principles of decision are obscure, but because the Christmas holiday seems so familiar and agreeable").

tently, insensitive to the needs and values of minorities when these needs and values differ from those of the majority." [70]

Positing a proper analytical perspective is only one unavoidable difficulty that arises when government uses seemingly religious tools. Another is the resolution of conflicts between establishment clause prohibitions and government officials' rights to free exercise and free speech. As we saw above, the principle that church and state should remain separate goes too far when it separates religion from politics.[71] Legislators and political activists ought to be free to express the religious roots of their beliefs, without tainting any resultant legislation. But at some point political speech becomes governmental speech; when that line is crossed, religious messages take on a constitutionally problematic character that is absent when the voice heard is not that of the state itself but only that of individuals who work for the state.[72] For example, Presidents' inaugural addresses seem more political than governmental, and religious references in such messages are common and venerable.[73] But, although religious references there are also frequent and longstanding,[74] presidential proclamations fall closer to the line.

A final difficulty is in many ways the most serious. There is a legitimate and necessary exception to the rule against government's using religious tools: the religious quality of some messages is neutralized by context. Like many exceptions, however, this one has the potential to undercut the rule completely.

As the Court has noted, physical contexts may serve a neutralizing function. This occurs when religion enters a setting where observers expect to *study* it, rather than to *take part* in it—to "observe" in the passive rather than the active sense: museums [75] and classrooms [76] furnish possible illustrations. Similarly, when religious messages emanate from private actors, even on public property, no message of official endorsement need result.[77]

History itself may sometimes serve as a context capable of neutralizing religion. Clearly, practices can outgrow their religious roots, in

---

70. Goldman v. Weinberger, 106 S.Ct. 1310, 1321 (1986) (Brennan, J., dissenting).

71. See § 14–14, supra.

72. This distinction has no precise counterpart in the "state action" area. See Chapter 18, infra.

73. See Bellah, "Civil Religion in America," 96 Daedalus 1, 19, n.3 (1967) ("God is mentioned or referred to in all inaugural addresses but Washington's second, which is a very brief (two paragraphs) and perfunctory acknowledgment.").

74. See Wallace v. Jaffree, 472 U.S. 38, 113 (1985) (Rehnquist, J., dissenting) (noting that President Washington, at the request of the First Congress, proclaimed a day of "public thanksgiving and prayer"). See generally A. Menendez, Religion and the U.S. Presidency (1986), and sources cited therein.

75. See Lynch, 465 U.S. at 676–77; id. at 713 (Brennan, J., dissenting).

76. See Stone v. Graham, 449 U.S. 39, 42 (1980) (per curiam) (Bible may be used in schools for studying "history, civilization, ethics, comparative religion, or the like") (citing Abington School Dist. v. Schempp, 374 U.S. 203, 225 (1963)).

77. See Widmar v. Vincent, 454 U.S. 263 (1981) (student prayers on public college campus); McCreary v. Stone, 739 F.2d 716 (2d Cir. 1984) (private groups' nativity scene in public park), aff'd by equally divided Court sub nom. Board of Trustees of Village of Scarsdale v. McCreary, 471 U.S. 83 (1985). Where viewers might mistakenly attribute the private action to the state, a disclaimer may be necessary. See note 24, supra.

the common understanding of non-adherents as well as adherents. The Court held, with at least some plausibility, that history had removed the religious significance from Sunday closing laws.[78] A lower court correctly reached the same conclusion concerning government's use of "A.D.," the abbreviation for the Latin phrase meaning "the year of our Lord." [79] History has also neutralized religion-based place names, like Corpus Christi, St. Louis, and San Francisco, as well as such religion-rooted practices as Christmas trees, which were once associated with the Tree of Life in the Garden of Eden.[80]

In both *Lynch* and *Marsh*, the Court implied that history had similarly neutralized the religious effects of the practices challenged in those cases. In *Marsh*, the Court found that the Framers viewed legislative prayers as " 'conduct whose . . . effect . . . harmonize[d] with the tenets of some or all religions,' " [81] and noted that a state does not violate the establishment clause merely by actions that " 'harmonize[ ] with religious canons.' " [82] In *Lynch* the Court adopted as its own the conclusion that *Marsh* had attributed to the Framers: "What was said about the legislative prayers . . . and implied about the Sunday Closing Laws . . . is true of the City's inclusion of the crèche: its 'reason or effect merely happens to coincide or harmonize with the tenets of some . . . religions.' " [83]

Such harmony is obviously not a mere accident.[84] Given the undeniable religious roots of legislative prayers and crèches, the Court must have meant that those practices, although born of religion, had with time lost their religious nature. In the end, that seems to be the strongest argument one can make in support of the *Marsh* and *Lynch* programs, as well as other religion-based practices that persist in American public life, such as the legend "In God We Trust" on currency, the words "one nation, under God" in the Pledge of Allegiance, and the courtroom proclamation "God save the United States and this Honorable Court." [85] People will differ on whether history has erased religion from such practices. If the endorsement question is

78. McGowan v. Maryland, 366 U.S. 420 (1961).

79. benMiriam v. Office of Personnel Management, 647 F.Supp. 84 (M.D.N.C. 1986).

80. See American Civil Liberties Union v. St. Charles, 794 F.2d 265, 271 (7th Cir. 1986) (citing Crippen, Christmas and Christmas Lore 153 (1923); II Encyclopaedia Britannica: Micropaedia 904 (15th ed. 1975)), cert. denied 107 S.Ct. 458 (1986).

81. 463 U.S. at 792 (quoting McGowan v. Maryland, 366 U.S. 420, 442 (1961)).

82. Id. (quoting McGowan v. Maryland, 366 U.S. at 462 (Frankfurter, J., concurring)).

83. 465 U.S. at 682 (citing McGowan v. Maryland, 366 U.S. at 442).

84. See Marsh v. Chambers, 463 U.S. at 810 (Brennan, J., dissenting) ("prayer is fundamentally and necessarily religious").

85. Justice Brennan has, somewhat tentatively, suggested that history has removed the religious element from such practices. See Lynch v. Donnelly, 465 U.S. at 716 (Brennan, J., dissenting) ("While I remain uncertain about these questions, I would suggest that such practices . . . can best be understood . . . as a form of 'ceremonial deism,' protected from Establishment Clause scrutiny chiefly because they have lost through rote repetition any significant religious content.") (footnote omitted); Marsh v. Chambers, 463 U.S. at 818 (Brennan, J., dissenting) ("I frankly do not know what should be the proper disposition of [such] features. . . . I might well adhere to the view expressed in *Schempp* that such mottos are consistent with the Establishment Clause, not because their import is *de minimis*, but because they have lost any true religious significance."); Abington Township School Dist. v. Schempp, 374 U.S. 203, 303 (1963)

asked from the perspective of a "reasonable non-adherent," as urged above, then some of those practices will be found impermissibly religious. But even from the minority perspective, some such practices should be deemed to have outgrown their religious births.

Yet time may restore what it has removed. A community's number of non-adherents may grow, or the non-adherents may become more sensitive. To non-adherents, "In God We Trust" and similar recognitions may return to their religious, and exclusionary, roots. Increased religious diversity has already influenced the law. As Justice Brennan has written, "practices which may have been objectionable to no one in the time of Jefferson and Madison may today be highly offensive to many persons, the deeply devout and the nonbelievers alike." [86] In the same way, the Supreme Court's flat assertion, "[T]his is a Christian nation," [87] which may have seemed unremarkable in 1892, would strike nearly any court as outrageous today. As the religious composition and attitudes of the American population change, future courts may react with similar incredulity to the suggestion that crèches merely happen to coincide with religion.

When government adopts religious tools, the religious autonomy of non-adherents conflicts with the shared beliefs of the political commu-

(Brennan, J., concurring) ("we have simply interwoven the motto ['In God We Trust'] so deeply into the fabric of our civil polity that its present use may well not present that type of involvement which the First Amendment prohibits"). The Fourth Circuit put the point more confidently: "In a very real sense [such references to God] may be treated as 'grandfathered' exceptions to the general prohibition against officially composed theological statements. Present at the very foundations, few in number, fixed and invariable in form, confined in display and utterance to a limited set of official occasions and objects, they can safely occupy their own small, unexpandable niche in Establishment Clause doctrine." Hall v. Bradshaw, 630 F.2d 1018, 1023 n.2 (4th Cir. 1980), cert. denied 450 U.S. 965 (1981). See also Aronow v. United States, 432 F.2d 242 (9th Cir. 1970) ("In God We Trust" on currency does not violate establishment clause); O'Hair v. Blumenthal, 462 F.Supp. 19 (D.C.Tex. 1978) (same), aff'd per curiam sub nom. O'Hair v. Murray, 588 F.2d 1144 (5th Cir. 1979), cert. denied sub nom. O'Hair v. Blumenthal, 442 U.S. 930 (1979).

A different resolution, also based on history, is suggested by the concept of "civil religion." See Mirsky, "Civil Religion and the Establishment Clause," 95 Yale L.J. 1237 (1986). As Robert Bellah has described it, American civil religion includes God but rarely Christ. See "Civil Religion in America," 96 Daedalus 1, 7 (1967). If traditional civil religion defines the boundaries of government's permissible religious

speech, then "In God We Trust" and the other occupants of the "unexpandable niche," Hall, 630 F.2d at 1023 n.2, would be constitutional, but crèches, crosses, and references to Christ would not be. Cf. American Civil Liberties Union v. St. Charles, 794 F.2d 265 (7th Cir. 1986) (distinguishing traditional invocations of God from display of cross, because of the latter's sectarian nature in Christ story), cert. denied 107 S.Ct. 458 (1986). But it is important to note that Bellah's description is based on tradition and practice, rather than on any independent normative vision. See, e.g., 96 Daedalus at 7 ("The words and acts of the founding fathers, especially the first few presidents, shaped the form and tone of the civil religion as it has been maintained ever since."). As certain elements of the civil religion grow increasingly offensive and alienating to some people, political rhetoric is likely to change; when that change has occurred on a large enough scale, the civil religion itself will have changed. Until then, those who are offended would probably have no recourse. Thus, an approach focusing on civil religion would apparently ask the endorsement question from the perspective of the majority, not from the perspective of the non-adhering minority.

86. Abington School Dist. v. Schempp, 374 U.S. 203, 241 (1963) (Brennan, J., concurring).

87. Rector, etc. of Church of the Holy Trinity v. United States, 143 U.S. 457, 471 (1892).

nity's majority. Religious autonomy and community also conflict in more general ways, as the next section will show.

§ 14–16. Tensions Between Religious Autonomy and Religious Community

Alexis de Tocqueville observed in 1835 that no other country has relied more broadly or successfully on "the principle of association" [1]— a principle in which political parties, professional associations, social clubs, families, labor unions, religious organizations, and other private collectivities are thought entitled "to lead their own free lives and exercise within the area of their competence an authority so effective as to justify labeling it . . . sovereign." [2] Much of the political thought of the West has been an oscillation between this view—that a plurality of associations interposed between the individual and the state is vital both as an expression of the need to congregate and as a buffer against all-powerful central authority—and the opposite view—that intermediate associations simultaneously weaken public authority and threaten to overpower the individuals left in their grip.[3]

Although neither pole of this dichotomy has entirely eclipsed the other in American law, there has been significant reluctance by courts in this country to interfere with the internal affairs of private groups—in part out of a pluralistic desire to preserve their autonomy and diversity;[4] in part because of the sheer complexity and weight of the burden involved in judicial forays into the uncharted terrain of organizational rules;[5] and in part because of the resentment such intrusion can produce and its sharply limited prospects for success.[6]

For reasons of this sort, and because of its obviously pivotal role in a system relying on the freedoms of expression and assembly, the right to associate—especially for purposes related to the first amendment—has long been regarded as a fundamental liberty secured by the Constitution.[7] The Supreme Court has been particularly respectful of the autonomy of religious associations. As Justice Brennan has written: "For many individuals, religious activity derives meaning in large measure from participation in a larger religious community. Such a community represents an ongoing tradition of shared beliefs, an organic

---

§ 14–16

1. 1 A. de Tocqueville, Democracy in America 242 (2d ed. 1863).

2. Howe, "Foreword: Political Theory and the Nature of Liberty," 67 Harv.L.Rev. 91 (1953). See also A. Schlesinger, Paths to the Present 23 (1949). But see §§ 15–17, 15–20, infra.

3. See R. Nisbet, The Quest for Community (1969).

4. See H. Laski, Foundations of Sovereignty 238–43 (1921); Chafee, "The Internal Affairs of Associations Not For Profit," 43 Harv.L.Rev. 993, 1027–29 (1930); "Developments in the Law: Judicial Control of Actions of Private Associations," 76 Harv. L.Rev. 983, 986–91 (1963); C. Rice, Free-

dom of Association 54 (1962); R. Horn, Groups and the Constitution 13–18 (1968).

5. See Chafee, supra note 4, at 1023–26; Developments, supra note 4, at 991–92.

6. See Chafee, supra note 4, at 1026–27.

7. See, e.g., Healy v. James, 408 U.S. 169 (1972); Brotherhood of R.R. Trainmen v. Virginia ex rel. Virginia State Bar, 377 U.S. 1, 5–6 (1964); NAACP v. Alabama ex rel. Patterson, 357 U.S. 449, 460–61 (1958). See also Emerson, "Freedom of Association and Freedom of Expression," 74 Yale L.J. 1, 2–3 (1964); D. Fellman, The Constitutional Right of Association 1–2 (1963); M. Abernathy, The Right of Assembly and Association 235–39 (1961). See generally § 12–26, supra.

entity not reducible to a mere aggregation of individuals." [8] Yet the freedom and autonomy thus recognized have been circumscribed by governmental (including judicial) interventions calculated to protect both external public interests and internal private rights.

While the majority in *Serbian Eastern Orthodox Diocese v. Milivojevich* [9] amply demonstrated the dangers inherent in governmental intrusion into religious organizations to prevent overreaching, it left unanswered the question of when civil courts should intervene to ensure that religious disputes are not, as Justices Rehnquist and Stevens worried, resolved by brute force or other plainly improper means. [10] To make ecclesiastical decisions wholly unassailable in civil courts could deprive members of churches of one of the fundamental legal protections enjoyed by members of other voluntary associations.

The Court suggested a partial solution in *Jones v. Wolf* [11]: Religious groups must structure their processes so that, when disputes arise, civil courts can resolve them by reference to documents drafted in unambiguously secular terms. If the groups fail to do so, or if their concepts cannot survive such translation into secular terms, civil courts may be forced either (a) to enforce the decisions of what they find to be the highest church judicatory, however fraudulent, collusive, or arbitrary those decisions may be, or (b) to apply the state's "neutral principles of law" to determine the outcome. Neither alternative offers members of religious organizations the same full-scrutiny judicial protection available to members of other organizations, but that distinction is acceptable so long as religious disputes remain completely internal to the religious community.

But the *Jones v. Wolf* approaches become untenable once the stakes spill over into the civil realm. For example, courts have allowed former members of religious groups to sue those groups in tort for "mind control," if the groups employed force or the threat of force, intentional outrageous conduct, or fraud concerning purely secular matters. [12] When important secular interests are implicated in such a way, the best that constitutional doctrine can achieve is to constrain the *grounds* on which courts act, instructing them above all to avoid resolving issues of religious faith or doctrine. [13]

---

8. Corporation of the Presiding Bishop of the Church of Jesus Christ of Latter-Day Saints v. Amos, 107 S.Ct. 2862, 2871 (1987) (Brennan, J., concurring in the judgment).

9. 426 U.S. 696 (1976), discussed in § 14–12, supra.

10. 426 U.S. at 724–25 (dissenting opinion).

11. 443 U.S. 595 (1979), discussed in § 14–11, supra.

12. See Esbeck, "Tort Claims Against Churches and Ecclesiastical Officers: The First Amendment Considerations," 89 W.Va.L.Rev. 2, 110 (1986).

13. See United States v. Ballard, 322 U.S. 78 (1944) (in fraud action against religious group, civil court may not determine the truth of religious claims, but only whether the beliefs were sincerely held); Molko v. Holy Spirit Ass'n, 179 Cal.App.3d 450, 224 Cal.Rptr. 817, 829 (1986) ("It would be entirely possible for a trial court to accept the view of [the expert witnesses] that [the plaintiffs] did not willingly submit to the religious teachings of the Unification Church because the psychological techniques of the Church deprived them of the ability to reason critically and make independent judgments . . . but it would not be possible for a trial court to reach this result without questioning the authenticity and the force of the Unification Church's religious teachings and permitting a jury to do likewise, which is constitutionally forbidden. The idea that reli-

Even in this sphere, where the religious community clashes with the civil realm, religious interests may still demand special substantive as well as procedural consideration. This seems particularly so where clearcut religious interests collide with more diffuse civil interests. Thus, for example, although historic preservation regulations may validly be applied to prevent churches, no less than other bodies, from destroying landmarks in order to generate cash, it seems clear that religious interests must dominate where religious doctrine—such as Vatican II's command that priests move church altars forward in order to face the congregation [14]—mandates an action that conflicts with state or local regulations of marginal secular significance.

The tension between autonomy and community which has thus become evident in the cases involving church disputes may be aggravated by an intersecting tension between autonomy and community within the structure of the family. In affirming family autonomy in *Pierce v. Society of Sisters*,[15] the Supreme Court showed insufficient sensitivity to the dangers involved. Denying that the child is "the mere creature of the State," [16] the Court in that case conspicuously passed over "the right of the child to influence the parents' choice of a school," [17] which the Society of Sisters had pressed as one ground of relief from a state prohibition of private school education, and seemingly opined that the child is entirely the creature of "those who nurture him and direct his destiny" and who therefore "have the right, coupled with the high duty, to . . . prepare him for additional obligations." [18] And the Court's approach in *Wisconsin v. Yoder*,[19] nearly half a century later, was of a piece with that in *Pierce*. For in upholding the right of Amish parents under the first amendment's free exercise clause to keep their children out of public schools after the eighth grade, the majority was plainly more concerned about the parents' ability to prevent their adolescent children from being exposed to "attitudes, goals, and values contrary to [parental] beliefs," [20] than with the opportunity of children themselves to develop independent life styles and to pursue options potentially at odds with the views and aspirations of their families and religious mentors. As Justice Douglas observed in dissent, allowing the Amish parents a religious exemption operated "to impose the parents' notions

---

gious doctrine can be . . . manipulatively employed to subvert reason . . . is one we may entertain as individuals but which the First Amendment forbids us to consider as judges.") (emphasis and citations omitted), review granted 228 Cal.Rptr. 159, 721 P.2d 40 (1986); Katz v. Superior Court, 73 Cal. App.3d 952, 987, 141 Cal.Rptr. 234, 255 (1977) ("When the court is asked to determine whether [the proposed conservatees' change in life style] was induced by faith or by coercive persuasion is it not in turn investigating and questioning the validity of that faith?"). See also Esbeck, supra note 12, at 82–83 (noting that first amendment would be implicated if, in claim for "clergy malpractice," a court tried to determine the prevailing standards of clergy counseling).

14. See generally Note, "Applying Historic Preservation Ordinances to Church Property," 63 N.C.L.Rev. 404 (1985); Note, "Land Use Regulation and the Free Exercise Clause," 84 Colum.L.Rev. 1562 (1984).

15. 268 U.S. 510 (1925). See §§ 15–6, 15–20, infra.

16. 268 U.S. at 535.

17. Id. at 532.

18. Id. at 535. See also Rowan v. United States Post Office Dept., 397 U.S. 728 (1970); Ginsberg v. New York, 390 U.S. 629 (1968).

19. 406 U.S. 205 (1972).

20. Id. at 218.

of religious duty upon their children." [21]   And although the Justice would have protected the child's rights to the extent of allowing the state to prosecute those parents whose children's views had not been canvassed, even he stopped short of vindicating the possibly independent perspective of the child in the lawsuit who had merely indicated in the most general and inconclusive way "that her own religious views are opposed to high-school education." [22]

The solution, however, cannot be for the state to intervene routinely or casually between parent and child, just as it must not intervene casually between believer and church. In the seminal case of *Meyer v. Nebraska*,[23] which the Supreme Court in *Prince v. Massachusetts*,[24] some two decades later, significantly described as having guarded "*children's* rights to receive teaching in languages other than the nation's common tongue," [25] the Court recalled that children in Plato's *Republic* were to be raised outside of any family structure so that "no parent [would] know his own child, nor any child his own parent," [26] and that Sparta, "[i]n order to submerge the individual and develop ideal citizens, . . . assembled the males at seven into barracks and intrusted their subsequent education and training to official guardians." [27]   The point, of course, is that some form of "family" as a focal point for human feeling and solidarity has been perceived in virtually every society as a latent counterweight to central authority. Thus, in denying to the state "any general power . . . to standardize its children," [28] the *Pierce* Court, like the Court in the earlier *Meyer* case and the Court in the more recent *Yoder* case, quite naturally looked to the family as a constitutional buffer between the individual and the state. In historical periods when families may be relied upon to protect the autonomy of children, this general approach has much to commend it. But it is obviously no easy matter to characterize the place of "family" in our own time and culture, a characterization without which no confident assertion can be offered as to the direction in which judicial intervention should tilt.[29]

The triangular tension among the religious rights of parents, those of children, and those of religious communities is exacerbated when the child has reached majority. In 1977, a California Superior Court granted a conservatorship to the parents of five members (aged 21 to 26) of the Unification Church (popularly known as "Moonies") so that the children could be "deprogrammed." Remarking that "the child is the child even though a parent may be 90 and the child 60," the judge stretched the umbilical cord to the grave and elevated the rights of one intermediate group (the family unit as represented by the parents) over those of another (the church) and, more important, over the rights of

---

21. Id. at 242 (concurring in part and dissenting in part).

22. Id. at 243. See generally § 16–31, infra.

23. 262 U.S. 390 (1923).

24. 321 U.S. 158 (1944).

25. Id. at 166 (emphasis added).

26. 262 U.S. at 401–02.

27. Id. at 402.

28. 268 U.S. at 535.

29. See generally R. Nisbet, The Quest for Community (1969). See also § 15–20, infra.

the individual adherents.[30]   In a similar case, a New York grand jury granted the request of a parent that the leaders of the Hare Krishna sect be tried for "unlawfully imprisoning" her 24-year-old daughter, a Hare Krishna nun.[31]   In an age of growing religious diversity, we may expect this type of clash to become more frequent. Harvey Cox notes: "Some psychiatrists contend that young people who join Oriental religious movements or Jesus communes have obviously been 'brainwashed' since they now share their money and have lost interest in becoming successful executives. That someone could freely choose a path of mystical devotion, self-sacrifice and the sharing of worldly goods seems self-evidently impossible to them. They forget that . . . according to the Gospel of Mark, Jesus was a candidate for 'deprogramming,' since his own family thought he was berserk and his religious leaders said he was possessed by the devil." [32]

If the state is to be prevented from intruding too deeply into either individual conscience or the autonomy of intimate religious communities and associations, one pattern for constitutional doctrine is greater deference to the claims of religion. But where a policy of deference proves indeterminate because of internal conflict among individuals and groups (to whom shall one defer?), and even where the pattern of deference seems unambiguous but is fraught with the perils of religious inquisition to ascertain sincerity, at least some of the doctrinal difficulties may be more readily resolved from the broader perspective provided by the rights to which religious autonomy contributes but which it does not exhaust—the rights of privacy and personhood that are the subject of Chapter 15.

---

30. N.Y. Times, March 25, 1977, at p. 1, col. 9. The ruling was properly reversed, Katz v. Superior Court, 73 Cal.App.3d 952, 141 Cal.Rptr. 234 (1977). Where "deprogrammers" act without adequate legal authorization, courts are increasingly willing to hold them liable for false imprisonment and other torts, as well as for civil rights claims. See, e.g., Taylor v. Gilmartin, 686 F.2d 1346 (10th Cir. 1982) (reversing trial court's dismissal of several claims), cert. denied sub nom. Taylor v. Howard, 459 U.S. 1147 (1983); Ward v. Connor, 657 F.2d 45 (4th Cir. 1981) (reversing trial court's dismissal of a civil rights action brought by a member of Unification Church against his parents and others for deprogramming activities, where the complaint alleged that the defendants' actions were based in part on their animosity toward members of the church), cert. denied sub nom. Mandelkorn v. Ward, 455 U.S. 907 (1982). See also Colombrito v. Kelly, 764 F.2d 122, 130 (2d Cir. 1985) (listing civil rights cases brought against religious deprogrammers).

31. Time Magazine, March 28, 1977, at p. 82. The New York State Supreme Court dismissed this case on grounds of religious liberty.

32. N.Y. Times, Feb. 16, 1977, at p. 25, col. 1.

Chapter 15

RIGHTS OF PRIVACY AND PERSONHOOD

§ 15–1. Attempts to Classify the Kinds of Interests That Count as Privacy

Justice Louis Brandeis defined the constitutional right of privacy as "the right to be let alone—the most comprehensive of rights and the right most valued by civilized men."[1]   That eloquent formulation reveals the animating paradox of the right of privacy: it is revered by those who live within civil society as a means of repudiating the claims that civil society would make of them. It is a right that has meaning only within the social environment from which it would provide some degree of escape. Homo sapiens is first and foremost a social animal, yet "the concept of privacy embodies the 'moral fact that a person belongs to himself and not others nor to society as a whole.' "[2]   Looking inward toward the individual from the widest perimeter of social organization, privacy is nothing less than society's limiting principle.

Much judicial and scholarly ink has been spilt in the task of expounding this paradoxical right. Justice Stevens stated for a unanimous Court in *Whalen v. Roe*[3] that the right embraces both a general "individual interest in avoiding disclosure of personal matters" and a similarly general, but nonetheless distinct, "interest in independence in making certain kinds of important decisions."[4] These concerns are not unrelated; physical privacy is as necessary to "relations of the most fundamental sort . . . respect, love, friendship and trust" as "oxygen is for combustion."[5]

Less authoritative if more exhaustive taxonomies of the aspects of privacy have been suggested, often centered around values of repose, sanctuary, and intimate decision. In one commentator's lexicon, repose refers to freedom from unwanted stimuli; sanctuary, to protection against intrusive observation; and intimate decision, to autonomy with respect to the most personal of life choices.[6] Another effort of the same genre, more ambitiously seeking to identify the single core common to all of what passes under the privacy label, attempts to build a conceptual wall around the idea of autonomy with respect to the intimate aspects of identity.[7]

§ 15–1

1. Olmstead v. United States, 277 U.S. 438, 478 (1928) (dissenting opinion).

2. Thornburgh v. American College of Obstetricians & Gynecologists, 106 S.Ct. 2169, 2187 n.5 (1986) (Stevens, J., concurring) (quoting Fried, Correspondence, 6 Phil. & Pub. Affairs 288–89 (1977)).

3. 429 U.S. 589 (1977).

4. Id. at 599–600.

5. Fried, "Privacy," 77 Yale L.J. 475, 477–78 (1968).

6. See, e.g., Comment, "A Taxonomy of Privacy: Repose, Sanctuary, and Intimate Decision," 64 Cal.L.Rev. 1447 (1976).

7. Gerety, "Redefining Privacy," 12 Harv.Civ.Rts.-Civ.Lib.L.Rev. 233, 236, 268 (1977). For Gerety, all three elements—

Whatever the outcome of the philosophical debate between those who regard privacy as but a name for a grab-bag of unrelated goodies [8] and those who think it a unitary concept,[9] these kinds of definitional attempts share two important limitations. First, however helpful taxonomies might be, they usually leave essentially unspecified the substance of what is being protected, telling us neither the character of the choices or the information we are to classify as special, nor the contexts of decision in which such classification is to be employed. The taxonomists themselves, to be sure, are willing to offer opinions on these matters, but the taxonomies they provide operate on a level of abstraction that fails to be suggestive with respect to substance.

Second, by focusing on the inward-looking face of privacy, the taxonomies slight those equally central outward-looking aspects of self that are expressed less through demanding secrecy, sanctuary, or seclusion than through seeking to project one identity rather than another upon the public world. Indeed, one reason that rights of privacy cannot be confined to John Stuart Mill's category of activities having impact only on the actor [10] is that freedom to have impact on others—to make the "statement" implicit in a public identity—is central to any adequate conception of the self. To confine fundamental rights to activities having no effects on others, or to acts of consenting persons having no effects beyond their circle, is to eviscerate such rights—first, because virtually any action has non-trivial consequences beyond any perimeter defined in advance;[11] and second, because the generation of such consequences is essential to personhood as virtually everyone experiences it. Thus, such seemingly disparate matters as the protection of one's good name,[12] the selection of one's appearance or apparel,[13] the choice of symbols one publicly endorses,[14] and the choice of one's companions [15]—many of which have received widespread judicial protection from too easy a habit of governmental interference—are all reflections of this outward-looking dimension of personality and yet seem artificially severed from the more introspective side of the "right to be let alone" in the categorizations attempted to date. Other matters, such as the determination of one's vocation [16] and the bearing and raising of one's children,[17] which combine significant elements of

autonomy, intimacy, and identity—are essential.

8. See, e.g., Thomson, "The Right to Privacy," 4 Phil. & Pub. Affairs 295 (1975). See also Note, "The Right to Privacy in Nineteenth Century America," 94 Harv.L. Rev. 1892 (1981). Cf. Note, "Toward a Constitutional Theory of Individuality: The Privacy Opinions of Justice Douglas," 87 Yale L.J. 1579 (1978) (for the Justice, the right of privacy was just one manifestation of the principle of individuality including rights to self-fulfillment, nonconformity, and dignified treatment by the government).

9. See, e.g., Reiman, "Privacy, Intimacy and Personhood," 6 Phil. & Pub. Affairs 26 (1976); Gavison, "Privacy and the Limits of Law," 89 Yale L.J. 421 (1980).

10. J. S. Mill, On Liberty (Bobbs-Merrill ed. 1956). See generally Note, "Limiting the State's Police Power: Judicial Reaction to John Stuart Mill," 37 U.Chi.L.Rev. 605 (1970).

11. See Ely, "Democracy and the Right to Be Different," 56 N.Y.U.L.Rev. 397 (1981).

12. See § 15–16, infra.

13. See § 15–15, infra.

14. See § 15–5, infra.

15. See §§ 15–17, 15–21, infra.

16. See § 15–13, infra.

17. See § 15–10, infra.

both an inward-directed *and* a social dimension, seem to deserve inclusion in any enumeration of essential aspects of personhood.

To be sure, the categorizers advert to these instances of outward self in their analyses.[18] But the categories they employ incline them to stress, as the very word "privacy" suggests, the inward aspects of the choices they analyze. So Justice Stevens understandably focused in *Whalen v. Roe*[19] not upon the general right to control the personal information an individual projects on the society but upon the more narrowly formulated right to *withhold* information that one does not want to share with others.[20] On either formulation, the result in *Whalen v. Roe*—sustaining a statutory scheme for maintaining computerized records of dangerous prescription drugs and the patients who receive them[21]—is the same. But the first formulation artificially distinguishes between a person's desire *not* to be known as a user of drug X and that person's desire to *be* known as someone who does *not* use the drug. Both desires are aspects of the same aspiration: to be master of the identity one creates in the world. No conception of personal rights that protects one of these aspects alone can prove sufficient.

Yet the urge to confine "privacy" to the inward dimension is certainly understandable. A concept in danger of embracing everything is a concept in danger of conveying nothing.[22] The question is whether privacy can be protected from such explosion only by the artificial exclusion of all social dimensions of the self. Believing such exclusion to be neither feasible nor necessary, we will employ an alternative conceptualization, one taking a different slice through the problem by attempting to identify substantive dimensions, social as well as solitary, of the values and activities courts have thought worthy of protection under a wide variety of names but with a single aim: preservation of "those attributes of an individual which are irreducible in his selfhood."[23]

§ 15–2. The Significance and Substance of Rights of Personhood

Words like "personhood," "autonomy," "intimacy," "identity," and "dignity" have been thrust into a social and political vacuum to define some reliable limits upon the state's power to shape the behavior of individuals and groups, whether by controlling the experiences available to them or by regulating the experiences with which their choices confront others. It is worth pausing to note at the outset just why there exists a vaccum within which an operative definition of privacy and personhood struggles to be born.

Three reasons can be identified. First, the seamless web of common-law and constitutional definitions that characterized the *Lochner*

18. See, e.g., Comment, 64 Cal.L.Rev. 1447, 1469, 1470, 1475 (1976).

19. 429 U.S. 589 (1977).

20. Id. at 600.

21. The case is discussed in § 15–16, infra.

22. Cf. Gerety, "Redefining Privacy," 12 Harv.Civ.Rights—Civ.Lib. Law Rev. 233, 234 (1977).

23. Freund, 52nd ALI Ann.Mtg. 42–43 (1975).

era's model of implied limitations was ruptured beyond repair in the 1930's;[1] thus any attempt to define the essentials of personal freedom through that model cannot succeed. Second, and for reasons related to the downfall of the *Lochner* model, we have come to recognize that freedom cannot be defined wholly in the negative language of containing the wayward state. Whatever its precise contents, meaningful freedom cannot be protected simply by placing identified realms of thought or spheres of action beyond the reach of government, any more than it can be defended entirely by establishing minimum levels of specific services for government to provide. Ultimately, the affirmative duties of government cannot be severed from its obligations to refrain from certain forms of control; both must respond to a substantive vision of the needs of human personality.[2]

Third and finally, as already noted, the tight interdependence of persons in advanced industrial and post-industrial societies precludes any attempt to define the protected sphere in terms of conduct that is wholly self-regarding or needs that are wholly personal. Particularly as the acceptance of affirmative governmental responsibilities grows, and as the idea of such responsibilities comes to embrace increasing attention to the health and welfare of individuals, even self-endangering conduct that might otherwise be dismissed as affecting others only emotionally begins to have a potentially coercive dimension. It is not only another's heart-strings but also his pocketbook at which the self-mutilator tugs in a world where costs are externalized through private and public insurance schemes. Thus the account of liberty generally associated with John Stuart Mill has become decreasingly useful for the definition of constitutional constraints and obligations in the modern state.[3]

There is a related point that deserves explicit mention. The very idea of articulating constitutional constraints and obligations is threatened with incoherence by the same interdependence that has made liberal individualism of Mill's variety inadequate to the contemporary task of building doctrine. For it is arguable that the more human activity and human personality are shaped by the forces and pressures of homogenization spawned by mass industry and the mass media—the forces that define the culture and constitute the economy—the less sense it makes to spin out special limits and duties for *government* in its dealings with individual persons and groups. In the end, little beyond a profession of faith can be offered in response to such a perception. The very idea of a fundamental right of personhood rests on the conviction that, even though one's identity is constantly and profoundly shaped by the rewards and penalties, the exhortations and scarcities and constraints of one's social environment, the "personhood" resulting from this process is sufficiently "one's own" to be deemed fundamental

§ 15-2

1. See § 8-5 and § 8-6, supra.

2. See R. Unger, Knowledge and Politics (1975).

3. The answer to Professor Paul Brest's question, "If the Constitution does not en-

act Herbert Spencer's *Social Statics*, does it enact John Stuart Mill's *On Liberty?*", Processes of Constitutional Decisionmaking 798 (1975), must therefore be: No.

in confrontation with the one entity that retains a monopoly over legitimate violence—the government. Thus active coercion by government to alter a person's being, or deliberate neglect by government which permits a being to suffer, are conceived as qualitatively different from the passive, incremental coercion that shapes all of life and for which no one bears precise responsibility.[4]

Although relevant factors can be identified, neither the artistry nor the archaeology of constitutional doctrine can determine finally the extent to which such a right of personhood, and of enough privacy to develop and function as an individual and to share intimacies with others,[5] can be asserted against governmental control or deliberate governmental indifference. To make sense for constitutional law out of the smorgasbord of philosophy, sociology, religion and history upon which our understanding of humanity subsists, we must turn from absolute propositions and dichotomies so as to place each allegedly protected act, and each allegedly illegitimate intrusion, in a social context related to the Constitution's text and structure. The inquiry must examine likely results. It must seek out submerged classifications or differential impacts. In an epidemic the state assuredly has the power to require testing, vaccination, and quarantine, but those intrusions must be measured for their necessity and efficacy, and if the intrusions are extreme alternatives must be considered.[6] In each case, it will be necessary to ask: Who is being hurt? Who benefits? By what process is the rule imposed? For what reasons? With what likely effect as precedent?

Those questions might be taken to suggest an alternative to substantive analysis of the rights and values at stake. Nothing could be further from the truth. Despite its venerable origins,[7] the requirement that legislation be rationally related to a legitimate governmental purpose[8] or a recognizable community value[9] can serve as little more than a source of pressure on government to articulate purposes that fit a challenged law,[10] unless substantive principles are put forth to exclude from consideration (1) purposes manufactured with the benefit of hindsight but not in fact motivating a challenged provision;[11] and, even more important, (2) purposes deemed illegitimate or inadequate[12] in the context of the provision being challenged.

---

4. This does not imply that focused governmental omissions may be overlooked in a definition of government's duties to persons. See § 15–9, infra. On the idea of "state action" as a limit to constitutional norms generally, see Chapter 18, infra.

5. See generally C. Fried, An Anatomy of Values (1970). For a critique of Fried's notion that the essence of privacy is its role in providing a context for selecting some persons as recipients of intimate information that one withholds from others, see Reiman, "Privacy, Intimacy and Personhood," 6 Phil. & Pub. Affairs 26 (1976). For a reply by Fried, see Correspondence, 6 Phil. & Pub. Affairs 288 (1977).

6. See § 15–16, infra.

7. See Thayer, "The Origin and Scope of the American Doctrine of Constitutional Law," 7 Harv.L.Rev. 129, 143–44 (1893).

8. See, e.g., Craven, "Personhood: The Right to Be Let Alone," 1976 Duke L.J. 699, 711, 720.

9. See, e.g., Ratner, "The Function of the Due Process Clause," 116 U.Pa.L.Rev. 1048, 1070 (1968).

10. On the values of pressuring government to provide such articulation, see § 16–30, infra. See also Chapter 17.

11. See, e.g., Califano v. Goldfarb, 430 U.S. 199 (1977).

12. Ratner, supra note 9 at 1079, rightly suggests that an "unenforceable regula-

The central problem, then, is to decide what makes a purpose illegitimate or insufficient. That in turn depends on the nature of the right being asserted and the way in which it is brought into play; it is at this point that context becomes crucial—to inform substantive judgment. Thus a purpose adequate to justify regulating the quality of brake linings might not serve to justify requiring the wearing of seat belts. And one sufficient to justify such a requirement might in turn be thought insufficient to sustain a requirement targeted at a more insular group—motorcyclists, for example, instead of automobile drivers.[13] But, after all is said and done, there is no escape, if the essence of personality is to be protected, from the attempt to define, for a given time and place, wherein that essence lies.[14]

Thus a court must decide, in this society and at this time, whether a person's choice to act or think in a certain way should be fundamentally protected against coercion by law, recognizing that the alternative in some situations may be coercion by economic or peer pressure and, in others, more meaningfully undominated choice. And to add to the difficulty of the task: neither judges nor legislators nor citizens should permit decisions of this kind, focused as each must be upon its precise context, to be taken without attention to the drift of their cumulative result. Those charged with the responsibility of choice must avoid too myopic an adherence to the matter at hand, recognizing that the ultimate results of incremental change might be wholly alien, and perhaps profoundly objectionable, to those who acquiesce step by step.[15] And yet they must be equally sensitive not to misuse the power which comes with the authority to identify some governmental impositions, but not others, as harbingers of disastrous change; they must be scrupulous to distinguish the slip which leads inexorably down the slope from the one which does not.

tion does not implement its purpose;" see also id. at 1105–06. Cf. White, J., concurring in Griswold v. Connecticut, 381 U.S. 479, 506 (1965) (stressing the "total nonenforcement . . . and apparent nonenforceability" of the ban on contraception invalidated in that case).

13. That it should be at least relevant to inquire into what the actual purposes of an alleged invasion of personhood were, cf. Ely, "Legislative and Administrative Motivation in Constitutional Law," 79 Yale L.J. 1205 (1970), should be clear enough. Knowing why government chose to enact a particular requirement, and why it is being enforced on a given occasion, bears on the way in which the requirement is likely to be perceived and hence the degree of affront it is likely to carry; it bears on the extent to which government's action is likely to chill protected choices in adjacent areas by persons who will inevitably understand not only what government has demanded but the principle on which government appears to have acted; it illuminates the degree to which invalidation of

the requirement would serve to educate government itself with respect to the sorts of designs those in power should resist; and it assists courts in the inevitably difficult task of deciding how much weight to give to an alleged concern, recognizing that the history of how an argument found its way into a case—whether by hindsight or more genuinely—sheds at least some light on how doubts regarding the argument's validity ought to be resolved.

14. In defining "limits [that] leave the individual a significant private sphere to live his life," the standards one evolves, rather than being "fixed and neutral," must draw on "the changing political and economic arrangements of the subject society. . . . It is a serious mistake to be disturbed by this." Fried, "Is Liberty Possible?", III The Tanner Lectures on Human Values 100, 109 (1982).

15. See Kahn, "The Tyranny of Small Decisions," Kyklos: Int'l. Rev. for Soc. Sci. 19, 23 (1966).

Society alters, some say evolves. Values change. Majorities grow more complacent; factions rigidify. Locked into frozen configurations, legislators may either ignore sound opportunities for progress, or opt for novelty without adequate thought of consequences. An unchecked spiral of change ultimately entails the same danger threatened by the most stubborn opposition to change. Either possibility can impart a teleology to positivist lawgiving which may equal legislated perpetual conformity.

It is to resist such dangers that rights of personhood are elaborated, serving both as reminders of values to be preserved and as hints of values not yet realized. Yet there is hubris and fragility and, paradoxically, a bleak conservatism, in designing and defending any absolute right.[16] Any fundamental rights of personhood and privacy too precisely or inflexibly defined defy the seasons and are likely to be bypassed by the spring floods. The best we can hope for is to encourage wise reflection—through strict scrutiny of any government action or deliberate omission that appears to transgress what it means to be human at a given time and place. Nothing less will yield a language and structure for creating a future continuous with and contiguous to the most humane designs of the past.

§ 15-3. Sources of Protected Rights of Personhood

Human beings are of course the intended beneficiaries of our constitutional scheme. The Constitution was consecrated to the blessings of liberty for ourselves and our posterity—yet it contains no discussion of the right to be a *human* being; no definition of a person; and, indeed, no express provisions guaranteeing to persons the right to carry on their lives protected from the "vicissitudes of the political process"[1] by a zone of privacy or a right of personhood. Nor, apart from the obviously incomplete listing in the Bill of Rights,[2] does the document enumerate those aspects of self which must be preserved and allowed to flourish if we are to promote the fullest development of human faculties and ensure the greatest breadth to personal liberty and community life. But the Constitution's is not a totalitarian design, depending for its success upon the homogenization or depersonalization of humanity. The judiciary has thus reached into the Constitution's spirit and structure, and has elaborated from the spare text an idea of the "human" and a conception of "being" not merely contemplated but required.

The resulting rights have been located in the "liberty" protected by the due process clauses of the fifth and fourteenth amendments.[3] They have been cut from the cloth of the ninth amendment[4]—conceived as a

---

16. See G. W. F. Hegel, The Phenomenology of Mind 78–79 (Harper Torchbook ed. 1967).

§ 15–3

1. West Virginia State Bd. of Educ. v. Barnette, 319 U.S. 624, 638 (1943), discussed in § 15–5, infra.

2. See Chapter 11, supra.

3. See Roe v. Wade, 410 U.S. 113, 153 (1973). See also Stevens, "The Third Branch of Liberty," 41 U. Miami L.Rev. 277, 286–93 (1986).

4. See Tribe, "Contrasting Visions: Of Real and Unreal Differences," 22 Harv.Civ. Rts.-Civ.Lib.L.Rev. 95, 101–09 (1987); Redlich, "Are There Certain Rights . . . Retained by the People?", 37 N.Y.U.L.Rev.

rule against cramped construction [5]—or from the privileges and immunities clauses of article IV [6] and of the fourteenth amendment.[7] Encompassing rights to shape one's inner life and rights to control the face one presents to the world, they have materialized from the "emanations" and "penumbras"—most recently dubbed simply the "shadows" [8]—of the first, third, fourth, and fifth amendments. They elaborate the "blessings of liberty" promised in the Preamble,[9] and have been held implicit in the eighth amendment's prohibition against cruel and unusual punishments.[10] Wherever located, they have inspired among the most moving appeals to be found in the judicial lexicon. Justice Brandeis, apparently embarrassed at employing the *Allgeyer-Lochner* version of substantive due process [11] to support his activist position, yet proud of the values he was affirming, cast the beliefs of the framers in memorable words: [12] "The makers of our Constitution undertook to secure conditions favorable to the pursuit of happiness. They recognized the significance of man's spiritual nature, of his feelings and of his intellect. They knew that only a part of the pain, pleasure, and satisfaction of life are to be found in material things. They sought to protect Americans in their beliefs, their thoughts, their emotions and their sensations. They conferred, as against the government, the right to be let alone—the most comprehensive of rights and the right most valued by civilized men."

"Natural law," the common law, and statutory enactments, provide three possible sources of content and meaning for this "most comprehensive of rights." But separately or together, those sources prove inadequate to serve as either the fount or the guardian of privacy or personhood in the modern era.

Natural law philosophy, current at the time the Constitution was written,[13] included, among other things, those "inalienable rights" affirmed in the Declaration of Independence as beyond the scope of governmental power to control or the free human being to surrender. James Madison, the principal sponsor of the Bill of Rights, distinguished natural rights, such as life and liberty, from rights that are part of the compact between citizen and government, such as the right

787 (1962); Patterson, The Forgotten Ninth Amendment (1955). But see Berger, "The Ninth Amendment," 66 Cornell L.Rev. 1 (1980). See generally § 11–3, supra.

5. See Griswold v. Connecticut, 381 U.S. 479, 486–99 (1965) (Goldberg, J., concurring).

6. See Doe v. Bolton, 410 U.S. 179, 200 (1973); see also § 6–35, supra.

7. See Chapter 7, supra.

8. Whalen v. Roe, 429 U.S. 589, 598 n. 23 (1977).

9. See Doe v. Bolton, 410 U.S. 179, 210 (1973) (Douglas, J., concurring).

10. See Robinson v. California, 370 U.S. 660 (1962) (cruel to punish a disease as

criminal). See also Coker v. Georgia, 433 U.S. 584 (1977) (death penalty is disproportionately cruel and unusual punishment for crime of rape).

11. See Chapter 8, supra. In 1928, little else was yet available.

12. Olmstead v. United States, 277 U.S. 438, 478 (1928) (dissenting opinion).

13. See, e.g., Corwin, "The 'Higher Law' Background of American Constitutional Law," 42 Harv.L.Rev. 149 (1928–29). See also Cohen, "Jus Naturale Redivivus," 25 Phil.Rev. 761 (1916); Pollock, "The History of the Law of Nature," Essays in the Law 31–79 (1922); W. Berns, Taking the Constitution Seriously (1987).

to jury trial.[14] Some courts and commentators have insisted that an intense and widely shared adherence to natural rights ideas by the Constitution's framers led them to neglect more specific mention of rights deemed too obvious to require elaboration.[15] This notion helps in penetrating the frame of mind in which the Constitution's authors acted, and thus in reconstructing a frame of reference through which their work might best be understood. Although natural rights have been rendered something of an historical curiosity by the succeeding course of constitutional debate, they have been invoked by more than one Justice of the Supreme Court in modern times as a suggested framework for delineating the reach of the liberty clause of the fourteenth amendment.[16]

Seeking grounding in something less ephemeral, the Justices of the late 19th and early 20th centuries looked, as we saw in Chapter 8, to the common law for definitions both of protected liberty and of implied limits on governmental power. And indeed the common law includes a potpourri of writs and actions of varying vintage which bear on aspects of privacy and personhood as currently conceived. Defamation, assault and battery, and the invasion of privacy action itself, all contribute to a common law construct of what legally redressable rights an individual enjoys against private parties, and what privileges or immunities the individual maintains against government. But these actions are largely of recent pedigree and questionable origin as sources of a constitutional guarantee. More importantly, they are widely understood to be subject to legislative modification or even extinction.[17] The common

---

14. Remarks of James Madison, introducing the Bill of Rights in the House of Representatives, June 8, 1789, in 2 Schwartz, The Bill of Rights: A Documentary History 1029 (1971). Indeed, what may well be the very first draft of the Bill of Rights, the July, 1789 handwritten draft of Representative Robert Sherman, would have expressly incorporated natural rights into the Constitution. Sherman, the only Framer to sign all three original founding documents—the Declaration, the Articles of Confederation and the Constitution— was a member of the select committee appointed by the House to consider amendments to the Constitution. The most intriguing aspect of his draft, written the month after Madison first addressed the Congress on the subject of amendments guaranteeing basic rights, is that it included, among the "natural rights which are retained by [the people] when they enter into Society," the "rights . . . of pursuing happiness & Safety . . . ." See The New York Times, July 29, 1987 at A1, col. 4.

15. See Richards v. Thurston, 424 F.2d 1281, 1285 (1st Cir. 1970); Craven, "Personhood: The Right to Be Let Alone," 1976 Duke L.J. 699, 701 n.12, 704–06.

16. See Meachum v. Fano, 427 U.S. 215, 230 (1976) (Stevens, J., dissenting); Stevens, "The Third Branch of Liberty," 41 U.

Miami L.Rev. 277, 286–93 (1986); Smith v. Organization of Foster Families, 431 U.S. 816 (1977) (Brennan, J., for the Court); Poe v. Ullman, 367 U.S. 497, 541–42 (1961) (Harlan, J., dissenting) (citing Corfield v. Coryell, 6 Fed.Cas. 546 (C.C.E.D.Pa. 1823)). Although the " 'natural rights' theory that underlay Corfield was discarded long ago, th[e 'fundamental'] privileges . . . list[ed there] would still be protected by the [privileges and immunities] clause." Supreme Court of New Hampshire v. Piper, 470 U.S. 274, 281 n.10 (1985). Cf. Chase Securities Corp. v. Donaldson, 325 U.S. 304, 314 (1945) ("what now is called a 'fundamental' right . . . used to be called a 'natural' right of the individual"). See Barnett, "Are Enumerated Constitutional Rights the Only Rights We Have?: The Case of Associational Freedom," 10 Harv.J. Law & Pub. Policy 101, 102–04 (1987) (arguing that a proper historical interpretation of the Constitution requires assuming that natural rights exist, since the document was the product of eighteenth century Lockean, natural rights philosophy). See also note 13, supra.

17. For example, one might observe how ringing pronouncements asserting common law limits on the power of federal courts to order a civil plaintiff to submit to a medical examination, Union Pacific Ry.

law has nonetheless served as a valuable tool in elucidating the meaning of liberty, and its insights should be preserved as suggestive if not authoritative for constitutional analysis.

Finally, statutes provide evidence of majoritarian sentiment regarding the legitimacy and importance of particular facets of the rights of personhood and privacy. Statutes creating actions for invasion of privacy,[18] misappropriation of identity,[19] or preservation of the confidentiality or secrecy of information collected or employed by the government [20] or by the press,[21] have been enacted by Congress or by various state legislatures. Congress, indeed, has gone so far as to "find" that a constitutional right of privacy exists.[22] But such "legislative rights" are creatures of the majority, theirs to give, and theirs to take away. The ultimate authority of such rights must yield more readily to other asserted interests of government than would rights ascribed to the Constitution itself.[23]

More generally, attempts to ground constitutional rights of privacy or personhood in conventional morality,[24] or in broadly if not yet universally shared ideas of public welfare,[25] are helpful but have inherently limited power. For we are talking, necessarily, about rights of individuals or groups *against* the larger community, and against the majority—even an overwhelming majority—of the society as a whole. Subject to all of the perils of antimajoritarian judgment,[26] courts—and all who take seriously their constitutional oaths—must ultimately define and defend rights against government in terms independent of consensus or majority will.

Although he was dissenting, Justice Stevens' recent affirmation of the constitutional grounding of basic liberty was cast in terms that the

Co. v. Botsford, 141 U.S. 250, 251 (1891), dissolved in the face of the subsequent enactment of Rules 35 and 37 of the Federal Rules of Civil Procedure, upheld with respect to plaintiffs in Sibbach v. Wilson, 312 U.S. 1 (1941), and with respect to any party in Schlagenhauf v. Holder, 379 U.S. 104 (1964).

18. See, e.g., Mass.G.L.A. c. 214 § 1B ("A person shall have a right against unreasonable, substantial, or serious interference with his privacy.")

19. See, e.g., Mass.G.L.A. c. 214 § 3A (action for unauthorized use of name, portrait, or picture for purposes of advertising or trade).

20. See, e.g., the New York state statutory scheme for protecting the confidentiality of drug prescription information upheld in Whalen v. Roe, 429 U.S. 589 (1977).

21. Such statutes were in effect invited by the Court in Branzburg v. Hayes, 408 U.S. 665 (1972) (rejecting first amendment journalists' privilege), and in Zurcher v. Stanford Daily, 436 U.S. 547 (1978) (upholding search warrants directed at press offices and newsrooms in quests for evidence of criminal activity by third parties whose acts may been the subject of those news organizations). Two years after Zurcher, Congress overwhelmingly enacted the Privacy Protection Act of 1980, Pub.L. No.96–440. See § 12–22, note 37, supra.

22. Privacy Act of 1974, P.L. 93–579, 5 U.S.C. § 552a: "The Congress finds that . . . the right of privacy is a personal and fundamental right protected by the Constitution of the United States."

23. At least one state has amended its constitution to guarantee a right of privacy to its citizens. See Alaska Const. Art. I, § 22: "The right of the people to privacy is recognized and shall not be infringed. The legislature shall implement this section."

24. See, e.g., Wellington, "Common Law Rules and Constitutional Double Standards: Some Notes on Adjudication," 83 Yale L.J. 221 (1973).

25. See, e.g., Perry, "Abortion, the Public Morals, and the Police Power: The Ethical Function of Substantive Due Process," 23 U.C.L.A.L.Rev. 689 (1976).

26. See Chapter 1, supra.

majority could not, and did not, deny: [27] "If a man were a creature of the State, the majority's analysis would be correct. But neither the Bill of Rights nor the laws of sovereign States create the liberty which the Due Process Clause protects. The relevant constitutional provisions are limitations on the power of the sovereign to infringe on the liberty of the citizen. The relevant state laws either create property rights, or they curtail the freedom of the citizen who must live in an ordered society. Of course, law is essential to the exercise and enjoyment of individual liberty in a complex society. But it is not the source of liberty, and surely not the exclusive source.

"I had thought it self-evident that all men were endowed by their Creator with liberty as one of the cardinal unalienable rights. It is that basic freedom which the Due Process Clause protects, rather than the particular rights or privileges conferred by specific laws or regulations."

§ 15–4. Points of Intersection Between Personhood and Law

The task of defining substantive rights is eased, though obviously not emptied of its gravity or difficulty, if it can be located within a specific regulatory setting. Thus the remainder of this chapter will be organized in terms of various possible points of intersection between personhood and law. In each instance, the focus will be not simply on the aspect of self thought to be at stake but on the way in which government appears to be usurping it. Often, it will be the *avowed purpose* of a government action that enables courts to characterize it as impermissibly invasive of human personality; occasionally it will be the *likely impact* of governmental choice that suggests such a characterization; and at times it will be a *blend* of avowed and hidden purpose and projected effect.[1]

The plan of this chapter is to look first at perhaps the starkest form of governmental invasion of personality—the naked attempt to determine the contents and processes of the mind. Sections 15–5 through 15–8 will examine such efforts from the most blatant to the most benign and will offer generalizations about the constitutional limits to which these efforts are subject. Next we will take up governmental invasion of personality through bodily intrusion or control—by physical invasion, public command, or deliberate omission. Sections 15–9 through 15–11 will accordingly explore questions of bodily integrity, first in contexts where bodily inviolability itself is the central issue, and then in contexts involving the body but more centrally concerned with the allocation of decision-making power over who should be brought into the world and who should be permitted to leave it.

Our attention to decisions about death and dying in § 15–11 will be followed by a third form of governmental invasion of personality— efforts by government to dictate choices of life plan, pattern, or style.

---

27. Meachum v. Fano, 427 U.S. 215, 230 (1976), discussed in Chapter 10, supra, and quoted with approval by the majority in Smith v. Organization of Foster Families, supra note 16.

§ 15–4

1. See § 15–2, text at note 13, supra.

We will explore governmental interference with risk-taking in § 15–12; with choice of vocation in § 15–13; with travel in § 15–14; and with appearance and apparel in § 15–15. In all of these areas, the central objection is that government has undertaken to dictate the kinds of lives people may lead, and our task will be to sort out the principles by which such an arrogation of decision-making power is to be assessed.

Section 15–16 will turn explicitly to a dimension of personal choice often submerged in discussions of personhood despite its centrality to the most classic notions of privacy: [2] controlling a life's informational traces—the impressions and images that a person leaves with others and through which a person's public identity is defined. The concern in this section will be with reputation and records, as both exemplify the social side of self. The presentation of self is in turn inescapably linked to rights of association—not only because freedom to associate often requires control over who learns about such association,[3] but also because a government with the power to shape what the community thinks of an individual is a government with the power to assure that individual's ostracism by others.[4] Thus § 15–16 leads naturally to a consideration of associational issues, and these in turn lead to a discussion, in § 15–17, of the dual character of associational rights— their character as sources of a power to exclude unwanted persons and behaviors while including in one's circle those with whom affinity is felt. This duality silhouettes the deepest problem in the elaboration of rights of privacy and personhood: the tension between the rights of individuals to be the sorts of persons they wish to be, and the rights of those among whom they live to create and maintain the sort of community in which they wish to settle. Recapitulated here is an ancient dilemma of liberalism: to destroy the authority of intermediate communities and groups in the name of freeing their members from domination destroys the only buffer between the individual and the state;[5] but submerging persons in the intermediate communities and groups that seek dominion over their lives creates the risk that individuals will remain at the mercy of hierarchical and subjugating social structures.[6]

Sections 15–18 through 15–20 examine ways in which constitutional doctrine has sought to escape this dilemma. Section 15–18 focuses on a category of harms that might animate the exercise of government

---

2. Cf. A. Westin, Privacy and Freedom (1967) (defining privacy as control over information about the person).

3. See NAACP v. Alabama, 357 U.S. 449 (1958) (state-required disclosure of membership lists held an impermissible burden on constitutional right to associate); Shelton v. Tucker, 364 U.S. 479 (1960) (statute requiring school teachers to list every organization joined or contributed to during previous five-year period unjustifiably interferes with associational freedom). See § 12–23, supra.

4. See Paul v. Davis, 424 U.S. 693 (1976) (denying federal cause of action for police circulation of photos of person arrested for shoplifting to local shopkeepers); Wisconsin v. Constantineau, 400 U.S. 433 (1971) (granting cause of action to challenge "posting" of names of excessive drinkers).

5. See Cover, "Foreword: Nomos and Narrative," 97 Harv.L.Rev. 4 (1983) (communities should be encouraged to elaborate legal norms opposed to those adopted by the state).

6. See generally R. Nisbet, The Quest for Community (1968 ed.).

power, but that exist only in the eye or mind of the beholder. The section suggests limits on government's reliance upon such harms to justify what would otherwise be deemed invasions of personhood.[7] Recognizing, however, that such limits can never be complete—that government must indeed retain the authority to regulate at least some conduct whose only harm lies in its psychic impact on those who become aware of it—the penultimate sections, § 15–19 and § 15–20, explore additional ways the Constitution constrains the community's power over persons—first, by recognizing territorial sanctuaries wherein conduct inappropriate in public or offensive enough to community sensibilities to warrant prohibition acquires constitutionally immune status (§ 15–19); and second, by recognizing a power to form special associational relationships within which behavior otherwise threatening enough to community values to justify condemnation achieves constitutionally secure footing (§ 15–20).

Finally, § 15–21 collects these themes and determines how they were implicated—and how they should have been addressed—in resolving a case, *Bowers v. Hardwick,*[8] which offers both a perspective on the deficiencies of the Supreme Court's contemporary privacy jurisprudence, and a glimpse of what it could become.

§ 15–5. Governmental Shaping of the Mind: Mandatory Incantation and Liberty of Conscience

The operations of the mind are continuous and inchoate, extending well beyond an individual's conscious control. Although the ongoing experiences of thought and feeling may theoretically be fragmented into discrete processes, constitutional no less than common sense quickly reveals the difficulty and disingenuousness of ignoring their inevitable interdependence. Attempts to differentiate thought into categories such as ideational or intellectual as against emotional or passionate

---

7. To say that government may not, in certain contexts, foist beholders' moral views or aesthetic tastes onto others—that attempts to do so must be evaluated with special solicitude for the impact of such attempts on the dignity and autonomy of those whose behavior, appearance, or personality is thought to give offense—is not at all to suggest that communities are without power to control their members for "moral" as opposed to "instrumental" or "utilitarian" purposes, see § 15–10, infra, at notes 90–92 and accompanying text. Nor does limiting government's ability to rely on beholder harms require drawing a line between (1) government controls justified by considerations of what is moral as opposed to immoral, just as opposed to unjust, or ideal as opposed to lamentable; and (2) government controls justified by a wish to favor the preferences of some people or groups over the preferences of other people or groups. Professor Ronald Dworkin's celebrated effort to elaborate just such a line, and to suggest that only justifications of the first of these two types are constitutionally acceptable (see R. Dworkin, Taking Rights Seriously 232–278, 357–58 (rev.ed. 1978); Dworkin, "The Forum of Principle," 56 N.Y.U.L.Rev. 469, 513–14 (1981); Dworkin, "Commentary," 56 N.Y. U.L.Rev. 525, 544 (1981)), has been subjected to trenchant critique, see Ely, "Professor Dworkin's External/Personal Preference Distinction," 1983 Duke L.J. 959, and is not to be confused with the approach taken in this Chapter. The fact that it may be impossible to distinguish a law predicated on the view that homosexual acts are immoral from a law predicated on the view that homosexuals' preferences count for less than the preferences of straight people, see Ely, supra, at 968–972, does not mean that government's power to extend a beholder's aversion to homosexual conduct into every private bedroom is as great as its power to rely on such aversion to patrol public places. See §§ 15–18 through 15–21, infra.

8. 106 S.Ct. 2841 (1986).

have either been abandoned [1] or at least subjected to intense controversy without satisfying resolution.[2]

Not surprisingly, the Court has insisted that the activities actually going on within the head are absolutely beyond the power of government to control.[3] But courts have at times taken a rather insular view of this protected sphere, choosing to approve regulations constricting mental intake or output, or invading the zones in which the values and convictions that define each individual are formed. In a society whose "whole constitutional heritage rebels at the thought of giving government the power to control men's minds," [4] the governing institutions, and especially the courts, must not only reject direct attempts to exercise forbidden domination over mental processes; they must strictly examine as well oblique intrusions likely to produce, or designed to produce, the same result.

The Constitution has enumerated specific categories of thought and conscience for special treatment: religion [5] and speech.[6] Courts have at times properly generalized from these protections, together with the guarantees of liberty in the due process clauses of the fifth and fourteenth amendments, to derive a capacious realm of individual conscience, and to define a "sphere of intellect and spirit" [7] constitutionally secure from the machinations and manipulations of government.

The invasion of this protected sphere produced by compelling an individual to express beliefs and convictions, whether actually held or only vacantly mouthed, represents a particularly insidious regulation, in order to shape the mind itself, of the expressive end of that spectrum which runs from private perception to public participation. In an especially outspoken and characteristically eloquent opinion by Justice Jackson, the Supreme Court, during the throes of the Second World War, denied the West Virginia State Board of Education the right to condition public education upon a compulsory flag salute and the recitation of the pledge of allegiance.[8] The state asserted as its justification for coercing participation in this public ceremony the intention that the ritual instill feelings of patriotism in the individual participants and thus promote "national unity".[9] Alluding to historical and

---

§ 15–5

1. See, e.g., Cohen v. California, 403 U.S. 15, 25–26 (1971) (rejecting the distinction between "cognitive" and "emotive" dimensions of expression).

2. See Miller v. California, 413 U.S. 15 (1973) (5–4) (upholding state power to ban obscenity); Marks v. United States, 430 U.S. 188 (1977) (reaffirming Miller but holding it nonretroactive); id. at 198 (Stevens, J., dissenting in part).

3. See Stanley v. Georgia, 394 U.S. 557, 565, 566 (1969), discussed in § 15–7, infra; Paris Adult Theatre I v. Slaton, 413 U.S. 49, 67 (1973) ("The fantasies of a drug addict are his own and beyond the reach of government . . ."). See also Abood v. Detroit Bd. of Educ., 431 U.S. 209, 235 (1977): "[I]n a free society one's beliefs should be shaped by his mind and his conscience rather than coerced by the State."

4. Stanley v. Georgia, 394 U.S. 557, 565 (1969).

5. See Chapter 14, supra.

6. See Chapter 12, supra.

7. West Virginia State Bd. of Educ. v. Barnette, 319 U.S. 624, 642 (1943), overruling Minersville School Dist. v. Gobitis, 310 U.S. 586 (1940).

8. Barnette, 319 U.S. at 642.

9. Id. at 631–32 n.12.

contemporary struggles against totalitarianism,[10] Justice Jackson emphasized that the method chosen by the state was an impermissible short cut to what was otherwise a legitimate state interest. The flaw in the chosen means—forcing young children to utter professions of their loyalty—was that the wrong sort of person would ultimately be produced; and such "officially disciplined uniformity" and "compulsory unification of opinion"[11] could only lead to "a disappointing and disastrous end":[12] "the unanimity of the graveyard."[13]

Although the original plaintiffs, members of the Jehovah's Witnesses, had brought the action chiefly on religious grounds, the Court ignored the free exercise claim altogether, resting decision on a broad reading of the first amendment's rights of free speech and expression. The Bill of Rights was hailed as the source of the "freedom to be intellectually and spiritually diverse or even contrary":[14] "Freedom to differ is not limited to things that do not matter much. That would be a mere shadow of freedom. The test of its substance is the right to differ as to things that touch the heart of the existing order.

"If there is any fixed star in our constitutional constellation, it is that no official, high or petty, can prescribe what shall be orthodox in politics, nationalism, religion, or other matters of opinion or force citizens to confess by word or act their faith therein."[15]

In *Wooley v. Maynard*,[16] the Court applied this reasoning to conclude that a state may not "constitutionally require an individual to participate in the dissemination of an ideological message by displaying it on his private property in a manner and for the express purpose that it be observed and read by the public."[17] New Hampshire license plates are embossed with the state motto, "Live Free or Die," and two Jehovah's Witnesses who objected to that message on moral, religious, and political grounds were repeatedly fined for covering up the offending words on their plates. Unlike the flag salute and pledge in *Barnette*, there was no issue in *Wooley* of a state attempt to reshape the individual's own views through compulsory incantation. Instead, the state was attempting to use its citizens as vehicles, as it were, for views not their own; the Court described the state law as expropriating the Maynards' car "as a 'mobile billboard' for the state's ideological message."[18]

---

10. Id. at 627, 628 n.3 (noting resemblance of flag salute to Nazi salute); id. at 641: "Ultimate futility of such attempts to compel adherence is the lesson of every such effort from the Roman drive to stamp out Christianity as a disturber of its pagan unity, the Inquisition as a means to religious and dynastic unity, the Siberian exiles as a means to Russian unity, down to the fast failing efforts of our present totalitarian enemies." See also R. Clark, Einstein, The Life and Times 14 (1971): ". . . most of his teachers did little more—in Einstein's later opinion—than encourage an academic kadaverighorsamkeit (the obedience of the corpse). . . ."

11. Barnette, 319 U.S. at 637, 641.

12. Id. at 637: To enforce the Bill of Rights today "is only to adhere as a means of strength to individual freedom of mind in preference to officially disciplined uniformity for which history indicates a disappointing and disastrous end."

13. Id. at 641.

14. Id.

15. Id. at 642.

16. 430 U.S. 705 (1977).

17. Id. at 713.

18. Id. at 715.

But *Wooley* cannot be satisfactorily understood purely in terms of a constitutional aversion to coerced speech. It is hard to take seriously the notion that those who saw the license plate on the Maynards' car—or the plate on any other car registered in New Hampshire—actually thought that the driver of the vehicle endorsed the state's motto. A license plate, after all, is not a bumper sticker; one has no choice about displaying the state plate on one's car. The Court may well have grasped this point, for while it adverted to the "right to speak and the right to refrain from speaking," it deemed those rights to be "components of the broader concept of 'individual freedom of mind.' " [19] The real problem with criminal penalties for defacing or covering up the motto on one's license plate, therefore, is not that it compels car owners to take a stand or forces them to support a position to which they may object,[20] but that, in a more existential way, it "invades the sphere of intellect and spirit." [21] Whether or not anyone else ever noticed the motto embossed on the Maynards' license plate or gave it a second thought, the Maynards saw it there every day and it offended *them*.

In *Barnette*, official prescription of belief was especially odious because it occurred within an institution dedicated in part to inculcating and nurturing values in young people.[22] Each public school represents an association thrust upon children by a combination of statutory obligation and economic circumstance, yielding a classic "captive audience." [23] Such a context requires "scrupulous protection of Constitutional freedoms of the individual." [24] As the Court reaffirmed in the midst of a far more divisive war a quarter-century later, in striking down a high school prohibition on anti-Vietnam-War arm bands: [25] "In our system, state-operated schools may not be enclaves of totalitarianism. . . . [Students] may not be regarded as closed-circuit recipients of only that which the State chooses to communicate. They may not be confined to the expression of those sentiments that are officially approved."

19. Id. at 714.

20. See Abood v. Detroit Bd. of Education, 431 U.S. 209 (1977) (public employees' union cannot spend dues, coerced from objecting employees by law or by threatened loss of public employment, on ideological causes not germane to union's duties as collective bargaining agent), discussed in § 12–4, supra.

21. Wooley, 430 U.S. at 715 (citation omitted). Indeed, if forcing car owners to take a stand were really the focus of the Court's first amendment concern, its own decision actually aggravated the constitutional problem. When the New Hampshire plate law was in effect, everyone knew better than to think that the presence of the motto actually meant that the driver was willing to die for his freedom. But once the Court declared that folks were free to cover up the words if they found them offensive, *everyone* in New Hampshire was in effect *forced* to take a public stance on the state's credo: if they

left their plates unaltered, others knew they were pugnacious freedom lovers; if they taped them up, it was clear they were pacifists or Jehovah's Witnesses. They no longer had the freedom simply to remain silent and keep their views to themselves.

22. Barnette, 319 U.S. at 637. ("That [Boards of Education] are educating the young for citizenship is reason for scrupulous protection of Constitutional freedoms of the individual, if we are not to strangle the free mind at its source and teach youth to discount important principles of our government as mere platitudes."). See also id. at 635 n.15.

23. Cf. Public Utilities Comm'n v. Pollak, 343 U.S. 451, 467–69 (1952) (Douglas, J., dissenting) (subjecting passengers on public buses to radio programming violated rights of privacy).

24. 319 U.S. at 637.

25. Tinker v. Des Moines School Dist., 393 U.S. 503, 511 (1969).

But since schools are expressly permitted, indeed even created, to promote the very same lessons in the classroom which they are prohibited from dispensing by shibboleth and coerced ceremony, the allocation of power and control in the educational system has been the object of frequent struggles among groups and individuals within the community, each advancing a meaning of "liberty" adequate to sustain its own authority and generally conflicting with that of others.

§ 15–6. Governmental Shaping of the Mind: Compulsory Education and Freedom of Inquiry

Free public education operated as the principal instrument of "Americanization" during the era when large and diverse groups of immigrants were being assimilated into the United States. The public schools have served, and continue to serve, as conduits through which national pride, community morality, "useful knowledge," and socially acceptable patterns of behavior have been impressed upon and inculcated in the nation's youth. The authority to determine and regulate the structure and content of the educational system has been coveted to a greater or lesser degree by state legislatures, educators, parents, and students themselves. The Supreme Court has recognized the tendency and capacity of educational institutions to coerce uniformity by controlling a child's fund of knowledge, and has imposed upon the governing entities a duty not to preempt choices better left within the less centralized decision-making processes of children, their families, and occasionally their teachers.

At the height of the *Lochner* era,[1] this limitation on state power was found to derive from the "liberty" guaranteed by the due process clause of the fourteenth amendment, with particular emphasis upon the teacher's liberty to pursue a vocation and the liberty of parents and the school of their choice to conclude a contract for the education of their children. The obvious tension between individual liberty and majoritarian aspirations toward homogeneity in the educational context was directly presented to the Supreme Court in controversies disputing the validity of state laws that forbade the teaching of foreign languages before the eighth grade,[2] and that required all students to attend public schools.[3] In both cases, the statutes were invalidated.

Both *Meyer v. Nebraska*[4] and *Pierce v. Society of Sisters*,[5] nearly always cited in tandem, have remained durable and fertile sources of constitutional doctrine concerning the nature of liberty, the respective

---

§ 15–6

1. See § 8–2, supra.

2. Meyer v. Nebraska, 262 U.S. 390 (1923). The law was invalidated as applied to non-public schools; the Court purported to leave undisturbed "the State's power to prescribe a curriculum for institutions which it supports." Id. at 402. See Goldstein, "The Asserted Constitutional Rights of Public School Teachers to Determine What They Teach," 124 U.Penn.L.Rev. 1293, 1305–09 (1976) (arguing that Meyer is not authority for a public school teach-

er's right to teach a subject not included in the public school curriculum).

3. Pierce v. Society of Sisters, 268 U.S. 510 (1925). The companion case, disposed of in the same opinion, was Pierce v. Hill Military Academy, 268 U.S. 510 (1925), making it clear that Pierce was not merely a free exercise holding in secular clothing or simply a disguised equal protection decision.

4. 262 U.S. 390 (1923).

5. 268 U.S. 510 (1925).

rights of social institutions, and the limits of governmental power to homogenize the beliefs and attitudes of the populace. The cardinal principle animating the Court's decisions, despite the expected bow to liberty of contract, was that the state had no power to "standardize its children" [6] or "foster a homogeneous people" [7] by completely foreclosing the opportunity of individuals and groups to heed the music of different drummers. The child was not to be deemed "the mere creature of the State." [8] Using the tools of his time, Justice McReynolds, author of the majority opinions in both cases, recognized that such laws violated the traditional conception of liberty. "Without doubt," he wrote, liberty "denotes not merely freedom from bodily restraint but also the right of the individual to contract, to engage in any of the common occupations of life, to acquire useful knowledge, to marry, establish a home and bring up children, to worship God according to the dictates of his own conscience, and generally to enjoy those privileges long recognized at common law as essential to the orderly pursuit of happiness by free men." [9]

The decisions held that the teachers' right to practice their professions,[10] and the parents' right to "direct the upbringing and education of children under their control," [11] were decisive. The concern that appeared to underlie the Court's conviction that power over these matters should not reside in legislative majorities was revealed in a disparaging review of ancient practices: [12] "For the welfare of his Ideal Commonwealth, Plato suggested a law which should provide: 'That the wives of our guardians are to be common, and their children are to be common, and no parent is to know his own child, nor any child his parent . . . The proper officers will take the offspring of the good parents to the pen or fold, and there they will deposit them with certain nurses who dwell in a separate quarter; but the offspring of the inferior, or of the better when they chance to be deformed, will be put away in some mysterious, unknown place, as they should be.' In order to submerge the individual and develop ideal citizens, Sparta assembled the males at seven into barracks and entrusted their subsequent education and training to official guardians. Although such measures have been deliberately approved by men of great genius, their ideas touching the relation of the individual and the state were wholly different from those upon which our institutions rest; and it hardly will be affirmed that any legislature could impose such restrictions upon the people of a state without doing violence to both letter and spirit of the Constitution."

Later interpretations of *Meyer* and *Pierce* have enlarged the precedential effect of these cases and assured their continued vitality in constitutional decisionmaking. One subsequent explanation of their

---

6. Pierce, 268 U.S. at 535.

7. Meyer, 262 U.S. at 402.

8. Pierce, 268 U.S. at 535.

9. Meyer, 262 U.S. at 399. But see Justice Holmes' dissent, appearing in the companion case of Bartels v. Iowa, 262 U.S. 404, 412 (1923), appealing to the value of judicial restraint and the importance of allowing the legislature to experiment with economic regulation.

10. But see note 2, supra.

11. Pierce, 268 U.S. at 534–35.

12. Meyer, 262 U.S. at 401–02.

joint import has been that they demonstrated judicial solicitude for the Catholics in Oregon and the Germans in Nebraska against whom the invalidated statutes had evidently been directed because of the inability of those groups adequately to safeguard their interests through the political processes of their states.[13] That notion is worth stressing as illustrative of a general technique—that of assessing alleged invasions of personhood in their historical and social context. The character and extent of the personal affront, and indeed even the degree to which government is in fact usurping judgments crucial to personal definition and development, are powerfully shaped by the circumstance that the government has targeted an insular group for its requirement.[14] A rule that might be sustained as a proper expression of community interest were it to affect the population as a whole might thus be invalidated as a violation of personality when it operates to single out, if not to submerge, a distinct group in the society.[15]

More recently, the principle of the *Pierce* and *Meyer* cases was reinterpreted, in the reflected light of the first amendment, to prevent the state from "contract[ing] the spectrum of available knowledge." [16] For example, in *Board of Education v. Pico*,[17] a plurality [18] of the Court took exception to a school board's decision to remove from high school libraries a list of books it deemed to be "anti-American." [19] The Justices acknowledged the school board's broad discretion to promote certain values and ideas through curriculum design and through decisions about which books to *add* to the library, but stressed the Constitution's ban on the "official suppression of *ideas*": [20] "we hold that local school boards may not remove books from school library shelves simply because they dislike the ideas contained in those books and seek by their removal to 'prescribe what shall be orthodox in politics, nationalism, religion, or other matters of opinion.' " [21]

References to the virtues of inquiry should not be thought to confer an absolute immunity on activities that generate knowledge while causing harms having no connection with the knowledge itself. When regulation is directed at such harms, it must be tested by the relatively

---

13. See United States v. Carolene Prods. Co., 304 U.S. 144, 152–153 n.4. (1938). But see note 3, supra. Foreshadowing future equal protection analysis, the Court in Meyer declared that "the individual has certain fundamental rights which must be respected. The protection of the Constitution extends to all, to those who speak other languages, as well as to those born with English on the tongue." 262 U.S. at 401.

14. See Chapter 16, infra.

15. Of course, even a rule of very general application might so invade personality as to be struck down at the behest of the singular objector; the point is simply that invalidation should come more easily when the target group is an historic subject of prejudice.

16. Griswold v. Connecticut, 381 U.S. 479, 482 (1965). The Court in Meyer stat-

ed: "The American people have always regarded education and acquisition of knowledge as matters of supreme importance which should be diligently promoted. The Ordinance of 1787 declares, 'Religion, morality, and knowledge being necessary to good government and the happiness of mankinds, schools and the means of education shall forever be encouraged'." 262 U.S. at 400.

17. 457 U.S. 853 (1982).

18. Justices Brennan, Marshall, Stevens and Blackmun.

19. One book was denounced because it mentioned that George Washington was a slaveholder. 457 U.S. at 873 n.25.

20. Id. at 871 (original emphasis).

21. Id. at 872 (quoting Barnette). Justice White concurred solely in the result, remanding the case for trial.

relaxed standards appropriate for laws that incidentally restrict the flow of information but only in the pursuit of ends wholly unconnected to the information itself.[22]   Yet if an avenue of research is restricted not because of hazards implicit in the research methods being pursued but because of harms thought likely to follow from what the research will uncover about the nature of reality or about the means of achieving some specific goal, it becomes relevant to note that the Supreme Court has flatly rejected governmental measures whose justification "rests . . . on the advantages of [people] being kept in ignorance." [23] The choice "between the dangers of suppressing information, and the dangers of its misuse if freely available," the Court has said, is one "that the first amendment makes for us." [24]   In effect, the Court has embraced the view of Justice Cardozo that we "are free only if we know. . . .   There is no freedom without choice, and there is no choice without knowledge—or none that is not illusory.   Implicit, therefore, in the very notion of liberty is the liberty of the mind to absorb and to beget." [25]   For this reason, any governmental decision to halt a form of biomedical research, for example, because of the fear that its results might dangerously alter popular ways of viewing human nature and might thus erode respect for individual rights and personal dignity, is immediately suspect as a usurpation of the sort of choice that ought to be made at more decentralized, personal levels.[26]   Yet, the more one can link profound and irreversible shifts in basic conceptions or ideals to a specific area of research, and the less one can accept as realistic the vision of truly decentralized choice on the questions at stake, the stronger becomes the argument for a collective, society-wide decision (one that would indeed have to be world-wide in order to be effective) to suspend, or even to phase out altogether, an avenue of inquiry.[27]

§ 15–7. Governmental Shaping of the Mind: Screening the Sources of Consciousness

Whatever the combination of paths the mind's contents might have traveled to their destination in a particular individual's consciousness,

---

22. See § 12–23, supra.

23. Virginia Bd. of Pharmacy v. Virginia Citizens' Consumer Council, 425 U.S. 748, 769 (1976) (ban on drug price advertising struck down because justified only as a means of avoiding "the reactions it is assumed people will have to the free flow of drug price information").   In Diamond v. Chakrabarty, 447 U.S. 303 (1980), the Court, which received briefs presenting "a gruesome parade of horribles," id. at 316, ruled 5–4 that a living, man-made organism may be patented.   Chief Justice Burger wrote for the Court that judges interpreting a statute "are without competence to entertain . . . arguments [predicting disaster]—either to brush them aside as fantasies generated by fear of the unknown, or to act on them." Id. at 317. But cf. id. at 322 (Brennan, J., joined by White, Marshall, and Powell, JJ.) (in con-

struing the patent laws, it is "especially" significant that "the composition sought to be patented uniquely implicates matters of public concern.").

24. Virginia Bd. of Pharmacy, 425 U.S. at 770. See § 12–15, supra, for a full discussion of this theory as applied to price advertising of the sort at issue in Virginia Bd.

25. Selected Writings of Benjamin Cardozo 317–318 (1947).

26. See generally Lederberg, "The Freedoms and the Controls of Science: Notes from the Ivory Tower," 45 So.Cal.L.Rev. 596 (1972); L. Tribe, Channeling Technology Through Law 60, 178, 185, 323 (1973).

27. See L. Tribe, "Technology Assessment and the Fourth Discontinuity: The Limits of Instrumental Rationality," 46 S.Cal.L.Rev. 617, 648–49 (1973).

it is beyond dispute that those inner thoughts and feelings cannot themselves subject a person to any governmental deprivation of rights or privileges. "The fantasies of a drug addict are his own, and beyond the reach of the state." [1]

Among the many less drastic possible courses of action government may undertake with the purpose or effect of limiting freedom of thought, some will be relatively easy to identify and to bring within a principled prohibition. Attempts to restrict the thinkable by shaping or screening sensory inputs—the sources of consciousness—are taken up in this section; attempts to restructure a person's thought or feeling by coercive conditioning are taken up in § 15–8.

Whether by threats one cannot resist or by offers one cannot refuse, government might initially try to regulate the perceptions available to persons in the formation of their attitudes and beliefs. *Stanley v. Georgia* [2] stands as the Supreme Court's most significant limitation to date on governmental attempts of this sort. There, government agents searching Stanley's home for evidence of bookmaking activities discovered three reels of film which they viewed on Stanley's projector and there determined to be obscene. Stanley was convicted under a Georgia law for "knowingly hav[ing] possession of . . . obscene matter." [3] In reversing that conviction, the Supreme Court held that mere private possession of such matter could not be made a crime even if the matter itself was unprotected by the first and fourteenth amendments and thus could not be imported, mailed, or sold to a willing buyer without subjecting the importer or seller to a criminal prosecution and exposing him to a conviction that the courts would routinely uphold.

The Court held it "wholly inconsistent with the philosophy of the first amendment" for government to exercise "the power to control men's minds" or "the right to control the moral content of a person's thoughts." [4] The guarantee of free expression is inextricably linked to the protection and preservation of open and unfettered mental activity; no state interest articulated or plausibly conceivable was found sufficient, on *Stanley's* facts, to override that guarantee, even if the materials which formed the subject of the prosecution would in other settings have been unprotected as "inimical to the public morality." [5] Neither protecting minors nor facilitating enforcement of the laws against distribution of obscenity required application of the law to mere private enjoyment. [6] As for the danger that Stanley himself might be induced by such enjoyment to commit anti-social acts, the Court thought that risk no greater, and no more acceptable a basis for prosecution, than the risk that Stanley might build a bomb after reading a chemistry text. [7]

§ 15–7

1. Paris Adult Theatre I v. Slaton, 413 U.S. 49, 67 (1973).

2. 394 U.S. 557 (1969).

3. Id.

4. Id. at 565–66.

5. Id. at 566.

6. Id. at 567–68.

7. Id. at 567. Cf. United States v. Progressive, Inc., 467 F.Supp. 990 (W.D.Wis. 1979) (issuing preliminary injunction against publication by political magazine

Yet it is partly on the basis of just such an assumption (that obscenity might trigger antisocial conduct) that government's special power to ban its commercial distribution rests.[8] One is entitled to ask, then, why such power did not extend to the authority asserted by Georgia over Stanley's personal reading and viewing habits.[9] That he indulged those habits only in the privacy of his home was, of course, significant to the Court; the independent importance of that factor is examined in § 15–19, below. But it seems unlikely that the location of the activity was by itself decisive in the *Stanley* case. Perhaps even more crucial was the focus of the government's search upon his books, papers, and films.[10]

The risk of exposure of a person's innermost thoughts and intimate fantasies through the threatened confiscation or public examination of the *lawful* items through which government must rummage if it is to weed out the obscene or otherwise illegal—the person's papers, letters, personal effects, even diaries—in no way depends on the precise place in which the person chooses to secrete such documentary traces of his or her inner life.[11] So too a governmental effort to question all of someone's friends or associates to determine his beliefs and aspirations,[12] or a governmental demand that the individual identify publicly the materials he or she wishes to receive in the mail,[13] can cause

of an article entitled "The H-Bomb Secret" containing information, allegedly compiled exclusively from declassified sources, on how to build a bomb), dismissed, 610 F.2d 819 (7th Cir.) (sum.), request for mandamus denied sub nom. Morland v. Sprecher, 443 U.S. 709 (1979), reconsideration denied, 486 F.Supp. 5 (W.D.Wis. 1979). See §§ 12–34 to 12–36, supra.

8. See Paris Adult Theatre I v. Slaton, 413 U.S. 49, 63 (1973) (upholding ban on commercial showing of hard-core film to consenting adults on the ground, *inter alia*, that a legislature could act on the debatable "assumption that . . . public exhibitions focused on obscene conduct, have a tendency to exert a corrupting and debasing impact leading to antisocial behavior"), discussed in § 12–16, supra.

9. See, e.g., Marks v. United States, 430 U.S. 188, 198 (1977) (Stevens, J., concurring in part and dissenting in part), characterizing as "somewhat illogical" the "premise that a person may be prosecuted . . . for providing another with material he has a constitutional right to possess").

10. 394 U.S. at 565 ("[Stanley] is asserting the right to be free from state inquiry into the contents of his library . . .").

11. Because government cannot support an argument that the existence or possession of such personal items in itself increases the risk of illegal activity, and because their use as evidence in a trial can only result from a person's assumption that such effects would be immunized from seizure and evidentiary use by a right of

privacy, government can hardly claim any loss to legitimate law enforcement if the items are indeed held to be as immune as those who would otherwise have disposed of them (and thus made them unavailable as evidence) assumed them to be. Cf. Raley v. Ohio, 360 U.S. 423, 440 (1959) ("Conviction of citizen for exercising a privilege which the State clearly had told him was available to him" violates due process). For this reason, a rule forbidding the evidentiary use of a person's private letters, diaries, or other intimate papers against that person in a criminal trial would implement fourth and fifth amendment values without any loss to law enforcement of which government could properly complain. For an argument advocating such a rule, see Note, "Formalism, Legal Realism, and Constitutionally Protected Privacy under the Fourth and Fifth Amendments," 90 Harv.L.Rev. 945 (1977).

12. Cf. Shelton v. Tucker, 364 U.S. 479 (1960) (statute requiring school teachers to list every organization joined or contributed to during previous five-year period unjustifiably interferes with associational freedom); NAACP v. Alabama, 357 U.S. 449 (1958) (state-required disclosure of membership lists excessively burdens constitutional right of association).

13. Lamont v. Postmaster General, 381 U.S. 301 (1965) (invalidating a federal statute requiring addressees of "communist political propaganda" from foreign countries to identify themselves in writing before being allowed to receive such mail).

exactly the same apprehensions and inhibitions, and chill personal choices in precisely the same way, as was the case in *Stanley* itself.

Governmental pressure on the choice of what expressive materials to create, obtain, or retain, or on the choice of what attitudes to reveal to associates, in some ways parallels the sort of coercion invalidated in *West Virginia v. Barnette*,[14] for it induces some people to express themselves falsely—in a case like *Stanley*, to express themselves as blandly as possible—and leads either to a flattening or to a repression of the inner self.[15]

Governmental efforts to achieve such ends can take quite a different form. Instead of seeking to prevent persons from experiencing certain sensations by threatening to expose their private fantasies to public view and even threatening to punish them for possessing certain literary materials, government might attempt to regulate the ways in which the mind processes the sensory data it receives from the world. Put in those terms, the notion that the state might attempt any such thing may sound a bit preposterous. Yet courts that affirm the power of government to ban the use of such psychoactive substances as marijuana appear to be saying something very much like that.

Although several courts have held that the use of specific psychoactive substances is protected in connection with genuine religious ceremonies to which the substances are essential,[16] such holdings have been limited to cultural settings readily distinguishable from the more widely publicized uses of the substances in question.[17] When dealing with such uses, some courts have struck down as violative of equal protection the treatment of mild drugs like marijuana as harshly as that of more dangerous substances like heroin,[18] but few have reached the conclusion that the basic assertion of governmental power over the individual psyche in this area is illegitimate as a matter of due process.[19] Typical was a North Carolina court's assertion that it is "not

---

14. 319 U.S. 624 (1943), discussed in § 15–5, supra.

15. See also § 15–16, infra.

16. See, e.g., People v. Woody, 61 Cal.2d 716, 40 Cal.Rptr. 69, 394 P.2d 813 (1964) (use of peyote in religious rituals upheld under free exercise clause as central to the spiritual practices of the Native American Church); State v. Whittingham, 19 Ariz. App. 27, 504 P.2d 950 (1973), cert. denied 417 U.S. 946 (1974) (upholding peyote use in wedding ceremony of Native American Church).

17. See, e.g., Leary v. United States, 383 F.2d 851, 861 (5th Cir. 1967) (denying individual's claim of right to possess marijuana for religious reasons; restricting *Woody* to situations where the use of the proscribed substance "played a central role in the ceremony and practice of the Native American Church, a religious organization of Indians"), rev'd on other grounds 395 U.S. 6 (1969); State v. Bullard, 267 N.C. 599, 148 S.E.2d 565, 568–69 (1966) (crimi-

nal conviction for possession of marijuana in Chapel Hill upheld as valid exercise of police power despite defendant's free exercise claim as a member of the Neo-American Church), cert. denied 386 U.S. 917 (1967). Accord, In re Grady, 61 Cal.2d 887, 39 Cal.Rptr. 912, 394 P.2d 728 (1964).

18. See People v. McCabe, 49 Ill.2d 338, 275 N.E.2d 407 (1971) (holding that the classification of marijuana with hard drugs is arbitrary and deprives criminal defendant of equal protection of law); People v. Sinclair, 387 Mich. 91, 104–15, 123–31, 194 N.W.2d 878, 881–87, 891–95 (1972) (reversing criminal conviction for possession of marijuana, two judges holding the classification of marijuana with hard narcotics violative of state and federal equal protection clauses).

19. Compare Ravin v. State, 537 P.2d 494 (Alaska 1975) (state constitutional right of privacy protects the use of marijuana in the home) and People v. Sinclair, supra note 18, at 896 (Kavanagh, J., con-

a violation of [an individual's] constitutional rights to forbid him . . . to possess a drug which will produce hallucinatory symptoms similar to those produced in cases of schizophrenia, dementia praecox, or paranoia. . . ." [20]

If in fact the state were to prohibit the use of all substances posing a given level of threat to the user, including, say, alcohol, caffeine, and nicotine—all of which appear to entail significantly greater threats than marijuana [21]—then the issue posed would be the one taken up in § 15–12, below: to what degree can government veto the individual's choice to find expression through an activity entailing more than the customary degree of physical risk to the user? But in fact the state enforces no such uniform prohibition, and tolerates widespread use of substances which are almost certain to cause more extensive harms than those associated with some of the substances the state chooses to ban. One court at least has justified this dissimilarity in treatment by stressing how much is known about the effects of alcohol and how comparatively little about the effects of marijuana,[22] but the distinction seems strained when the total impact of the greater knowledge about alcohol works to support a rather confident judgment that it is indeed substantially more likely to be harmful, and not only to the user but to others as well.

The reason for the disparity of treatment might be difficult to prove, but is not difficult to discern. Substances that have long appealed to the great majority, whose use might reasonably be thought to reinforce the existing order by inducing mental states of acceptance, lubricating social interaction, and ameliorating the tensions of contemporary life, understandably tend to become integrated into lawful

curring) (the Michigan statute criminalizing possession of marijuana "violates the Federal and State constitutions in that it is an impermissible intrusion on the fundamental rights to liberty and the pursuit of happiness, and is an unwarranted interference with the right to possess and use private property. . . . 'Big Brother' cannot, in the name of *public* health, dictate to anyone what he can eat or drink or smoke in the *privacy* of his own home") (emphasis in original), with Commonwealth v. Leis, 355 Mass. 189, 243 N.E.2d 898 (1969) (no right to smoke marijuana exists under federal or state constitution); Borras v. State, 229 So.2d 244 (1969) (use of marijuana in home not protected by first amendment or right of privacy), cert. denied 400 U.S. 808 (1970); People v. Aguiar, 257 Cal.App.2d 597, 603, 65 Cal.Rptr. 171, 175 (1968) ("no constitutionally protected right to indulge in the use of euphoric drugs"). Cf. State v. Kantner, 53 Hawaii 327, 493 P.2d 306 (1972) (conviction for possession of marijuana upheld, with two dissenting justices who would have found the criminalization of private possession of marijuana violative of due process, and one concurring justice indicating that he would have joined that

position if the issue had not been conceded at trial), cert. denied 409 U.S. 948 (1972). See also Scott v. United States, 129 U.S. App.D.C. 396, 395 F.2d 619 (1968) (suggesting that laws regulating personal use of marijuana would bear close scrutiny for due process violation on a more complete record), cert. denied 393 U.S. 986 (1968); Louisiana Affiliate of NORML v. Guste, 380 F.Supp. 404 (E.D.La.1974) (claim of constitutional protection for use and possession of marijuana on privacy grounds does not present a substantial federal question requiring convocation of three-judge court).

20. State v. Bullard, 267 N.C. 599, 148 S.E.2d 565, 569 (1966), cert. denied 386 U.S. 917 (1967).

21. See People v. Sinclair, 387 Mich. 91, 104–08, 113–15, 194 N.W.2d 878, 881–84, 886–87 (1972) (indicating that the evidence establishes that alcohol is more harmful than marijuana); J. Kaplan, Marijuana—The New Prohibition (1970).

22. State v. Kantner, 53 Hawaii 327, 331–32, 493 P.2d 306, 309 (1972), cert. denied 409 U.S. 948 (1972).

practice. Thus smoking cigarettes, sipping coffee, and drinking alcohol, are all activities validated by law and custom. On the other hand, substances that have tended to appeal to less conventional groups—and particularly to groups whose life styles have challenged the conventional morality—are a source of anxiety to the majority and have been natural targets for criminalization, despite the enormous difficulty of enforcing the resulting laws evenhandedly without an inordinate and indeed quite unthinkable commitment of resources.

It is not surprising that the partial relaxation of efforts to make criminals of marijuana smokers has accompanied the spread of marijuana's use beyond the more obviously alienated groups with whom it was originally associated. But that very fact seems to underscore the striking selectivity characterizing the official approach to personal use of consciousness-altering chemical substances. If the Stanleys of the world could obtain from a new drug called "obscenamine" the sensation that Stanley in fact obtained from the obscene film whose possession Georgia unsuccessfully sought to make a crime, one might expect a legislative attempt to make possession or use of obscenamine a criminal offense. The precedents appear, on the whole, to affirm the state's power to take such a step. Yet it does seem bizarre to draw the distinction implicit in such an outcome. To be sure, at stake in *Stanley* was the value of preventing government from rummaging through someone's library to discover evidence of his mental and emotional tastes. Yet is it so much less offensive for government to rummage through someone's medicine chest, kitchen, and wine cellar to put together a picture of his oral and chemical predilections? In either case, the offense is governmental invasion and usurpation of the choices that together constitute an individual's psyche.

§ 15–8. Governmental Shaping of the Mind: Coercive Conditioning

Governmental attempts to shape the minds of the populace may, as we have seen in § 15–7, take the form of screening out, or withholding, various stimuli. At least as troublesome from a constitutional perspective is the converse: governmental efforts to coerce mental conformity by requiring affirmative participation in behaviorial, or electrochemical, "therapies" of varying forms.[1] As Judge Frankel aptly observed in *Sobell v. Reed*,[2] the notion of "rehabilitation," on the record to date, has little or no content: "Totalitarian ideologies we profess to hate have styled as 'rehabilitation' the process of molding the unorthodox mind to the shape of prevailing dogma."[3] Although some experimenters have

---

§ 15–8

1. See generally, "Symposium: Behavior Control in Prisons," Hastings Center Report, vol. 5 (Feb. 1975).

2. 327 F.Supp. 1294 (S.D.N.Y.1971) (holding that parole board's selective denials of travel requests which included plans to lecture and demonstrate violated parolee's first amendment rights).

3. Id. at 1305. For such a view of one such "therapy", see Breggin, "Psychosurgery for Political Purposes," 13 Duq.L.Rev. 841 (1975) (recounting political statements of prominent advocates of psychosurgery and discussing its potential as mechanism of social control). Cf. J. Cohen, The Criminal Process in the People's Republic of China 256 (1968). See also A. Burgess, A Clockwork Orange (1962).

confessed ambitions of broader scope,[4] the major governmental efforts thus far have taken the form either of (1) purely symbolic requirements applicable to the population as a whole or at least to a broad segment of the population, as in the compulsory flag salute considered in § 15–5; or of (2) more focused and intrusive requirements applicable only to persons already involuntarily incarcerated for their antisocial behavior or for their supposed mental illness.[5] This section will briefly address the latter cases; intermediate situations, such as those of mandatory drug therapies for hyperactive school children, pose closely analogous issues and will not be separately canvassed here.[6]

Two sorts of issues are presented. The most straightforward concerns the constitutionality of the overtly coercive use of behavior modification techniques, typically but not necessarily accompanied by the use of chemical and/or electronic methods designed to bypass the subject's unaided, conscious will. Since confinement itself may be regarded as a crude form of behavior modification, it seems clear that there can be no general prohibition against a governmental decision to subject persons who have caused harm to at least some such techniques.

The rules vary depending on the purpose of confinement. With respect to the mentally retarded, state institutions "may not restrain residents except when and to the extent professional judgment deems this necessary to assure . . . safety or to provide needed training."[7] Indeed, the fourteenth amendment obliges the state to provide an institutionalized retarded citizen with "such training as an appropriate professional would consider reasonable to ensure his safety and to facilitate his ability to function free from bodily restraints."[8]

Though it may seem paradoxical from the perspective of those complaining of our penal system's inability to rehabilitate effectively, there is little doubt that constitutional objections to coercive therapy rise in direct proportion to the therapy's power to produce changes against the will of the person subjected to it, and to the irreversibility of any such results. At a minimum, it is clear that a prisoner or a patient[9] threatened with aversive conditioning,[10] treatment with

4. See, e.g., B. F. Skinner, Beyond Freedom and Dignity (1971); J. Delgado, Physical Control of the Mind—Towards a Psychocivilized Society (1969).

5. See O'Connor v. Donaldson, 422 U.S. 563 (1975), discussed in § 15–18, infra.

6. For a useful treatment of the area as a whole, see Shapiro, "Legislating the Control of Behavior Control: Autonomy and the Coercive Use of Organic Therapies," 47 S.Cal.L.Rev. 237 (1974).

7. Youngberg v. Romeo, 457 U.S. 307, 324 (1982).

8. Id. "Respondent thus enjoys constitutionally protected interests in conditions of reasonable care and safety, reasonably nonrestrictive confinement conditions, and such training as may be required by these interests." Id.

9. These two obviously distinct categories of confinees are discussed together for the sake of convenience with respect to this issue, since one's interest in avoiding coercive alteration of one's psyche remains much the same regardless of *why* the government would impose alteration. The state obviously owes different duties to those who are confined for the purpose of punishment, and those who are confined for the purpose of treatment, even if, sad to say, it is often difficult in practice to distinguish the two. Cf. Jones v. United States, 463 U.S. 354, 370 (1983) (holding that an acquittal by reason of insanity on a single charge of shoplifting—which carries a maximum sentence of one year—provides all the process due for indefinite confinement in a mental institution); id. at 381–

10. See note 10 on page 1328.

psychotropic drugs,[11] or any other technique designed to produce results without regard to the individual's freely chosen preferences, confronts a deprivation of liberty sufficiently distinct from incarceration itself to warrant the full range of procedural protections.[12] In *Youngberg v. Romeo*,[13] the Supreme Court held that, when courts determine whether a state mental institution has met its obligation to provide sufficient treatment and training to enable a retarded patient to function free from bodily restraints, the "decisions made by the appropriate professional are entitled to a presumption of correctness."[14] In the wake of *Romeo*, the lower courts have developed various standards for the administration of drug therapy.[15] One district court has held that there is no "absolute right on the part of the competent involuntarily committed patient to refuse administration of psychotropic medications."[16] One court of appeals has held that an involuntarily committed mentally ill patient has a constitutional right to refuse antipsychotic drugs unless, in the exercise of professional judgment, such treatment is deemed necessary to prevent the patient from endangering himself or others.[17] And the Supreme Judicial Court of Massachusetts has held that, "[i]n a non-emergency situation, no state interest is

85 (Brennan, J., dissenting) (objecting that government should have to meet the due process standards for regular civil commitment, and that extended institutionalization may effectively make it impossible for an individual to prove that he is no longer ill or dangerous; in the instant case, the government justified continued confinement by relying in part on testimony that Jones was "not a very active participant in the informal activities on the ward," even though his medication—1,000 milligrams of Thorazine daily, plus a tranquilizer— "made it unlikely he could be an active participant in anything"); United States v. Salerno, 107 S.Ct. 2095, 2101 (1987) (pretrial preventative detention for "dangerous" defendants is "regulatory, not penal").

10. See Note, "Aversion Therapy: Punishment as Treatment and Treatment as Cruel and Unusual Punishment," 49 S.Cal. L.Rev. 880 (1976).

11. See Mills v. Rogers, 457 U.S. 291, 293 n.1 (1982) ("It is not disputed that [antipsychotic] drugs are 'mind-altering.' Their effectiveness resides in their capacity to achieve such effects.").

12. See Clonce v. Richardson, 379 F.Supp. 338, 348 (W.D.Mo.1974) (prisoner's transfer to involuntary behavior modification program required hearing). Cf. Mackey v. Procunier, 477 F.2d 877 (9th Cir. 1973). See generally Vitek v. Jones, 445 U.S. 480 (1980) (prisoner's transfer to mental hospital necessarily implicates due process), discussed in 10–9, supra.

13. 457 U.S. 307 (1982).

14. Id. at 324.

15. Romeo was decided under the due process clause of the fourteenth amendment. The Third Circuit Court of Appeals had held that the eighth amendment, prohibiting cruel and unusual punishment of criminals, was not an appropriate source for determining the rights of the involuntarily committed. See 457 U.S. at 312. That ruling was not appealed to the Supreme Court. Id. at 315 n.16. Cf. Knecht v. Gillman, 488 F.2d 1136 (8th Cir.1973) (summary administration of apomorphine, a drug inducing sustained and painful vomiting, for infractions of a mental institution's rules constitutes cruel and unusual punishment); Scott v. Plante, 532 F.2d 939 (3d Cir.1976) (suggesting that first amendment, as well as the eighth, might be violated by involuntary administration of psychotropic drugs to inmates of a state institution).

16. R.A.J. v. Miller, 590 F.Supp. 1319, 1322 (N.D.Tex.1984) (approving, under Romeo, a proposed medical review panel rule that (1) lists appropriate circumstances, to be weighed in professional judgment, for the use of such drugs; (2) provides for two tiers of medical review of such treatment decisions; and (3) for committed mental patients who have been adjudged mentally competent by the reviewing medical director, permits review of such treatment decisions by an independent consultant psychiatrist).

17. Rennie v. Klein, 720 F.2d 266, 269 (3d Cir.1983), after remand for reconsideration in light of Youngberg v. Romeo.

sufficiently compelling to overcome a patient's decision to refuse treatment with antipsychotic drugs." [18]

It is conceivable that the coercive use of painless therapies which have a demonstrated capacity to produce highly specific improvements in violent behavior could be upheld as no violation of the inmate's basic rights of personhood.[19] But the experimental use of a new therapy or technique may in turn pose a further issue for consideration here.[20] Assuming that the experiment involves a method too untried to warrant any confident assessment that it will benefit the experimental subject himself, the question may arise whether the subject's alleged consent to that experiment is sufficient to validate the institution's decision to proceed. In *Kaimowitz v. Department of Mental Health*,[21] a county court held that an involuntarily confined patient cannot give informed consent to an experiment designed to compare the effects of psychosurgery (specifically, an experimental operation on the amygdaloid portion of the brain) with the effects of the drug cyproterone acetate on the male hormone flow. The point of the comparison was to determine which procedure, if either, could successfully control aggression in institutionalized males, reducing their torment and enhancing the safety of those with whom they come in contact. Given the experimental character of psychosurgery and its power to work little-understood but profound and almost certainly irreversible changes,[22] the court held that state administration of the technique to generate new knowledge violates the individual's right "to be free from interference with his mental processes," and that the conditions of confinement preclude the sort of informed consent without which such interference offends the right of privacy protected by the fourteenth amendment.[23]

§ 15–9. Governmental Intrusion on the Body: From Physical Invasion to Gross Neglect

One astute student of privacy argues convincingly that any "plausible definition" of the term, "whatever the sources of its normative

18. Rogers v. Commissioner of Dept. of Mental Health, 390 Mass. 489, 458 N.E.2d 308, 323 (1983). In Mills v. Rogers, 457 U.S. 291 (1982), the Supreme Court had granted certiorari "to determine whether involuntarily committed mental patients have a constitutional right to refuse treatment with antipsychotic drugs," id. at 293, but intervening state law decisions led a unanimous Court to remand the case. Id. at 306. The Massachusetts court subsequently handed down its decision in Rogers, and the state procedures approved therein were thereafter adjudged to "equal or exceed the rights provided in the federal Constitution." Rogers v. Okin, 738 F.2d 1, 9 (1st Cir.1984).

19. Coupled with a recognition of "the uncertainties of psychiatric diagnosis," Addington v. Texas, 441 U.S. 418, 432 (1979), a healthy skepticism should greet any claim that benign coercive therapies

have been discovered and perfected. To the extent that such therapies become available, an involuntarily committed person might well have a right to insist on their use in lieu of continued confinement. Cf. Delgado, "Organically Induced Behavioral Change in Correctional Institutions," 50 S.Cal.L.Rev. 215, 239 (1977).

20. See generally, J. Katz, Experimentation With Human Beings (1972).

21. Civ. No. 73–19434–AW (Mich.Cir. Ct., Wayne Cty., July 10, 1973), 42 U.S. L.W. 2063 (July 10, 1973).

22. See generally, Symposium, "Psychosurgery," 54 B.U.L.Rev. 215 (1974).

23. For a critical perspective on Kaimowitz, see Shapiro, "Therapeutic Justifications for Intervention into Mentation and Behavior," 13 Duq.L.Rev. 673, 739 (1975).

commitments, must take the body as its first and most basic reference for control over personal identity." [1] But this notion in turn makes sense only if we think of bodily integrity as the sphere of personality encapsulated in, and expressed by, the individual's physical being rather than focusing on every detail of that physical being itself. Although it is undeniable that the body constitutes the major locus of separation between the individual and the world and is in that sense the first object of each person's freedom, not all forms of bodily compulsion, and not even all actions that entail an unwanted touching or intrusion into the body, can plausibly be regarded as violations of the self or usurpations of personality.

Thus, it is important to have a way of talking about these matters in which the intrusion caused by the police officer who gently shoves a person back to clear the way for an ambulance, for example, does not count even potentially as an invasion of privacy or personhood. To be sure, every such interference with liberty calls for some sort of justification. But it would demean the very concept of preferred rights to call upon government for a compelling showing of necessity, or indeed for anything more than a plausible account, in cases such as these.

Yet it seems dangerous to move to the opposite extreme and insist that, unless a particular bodily intrusion "offends the intimacy of . . . personal identity" in some widely or almost universally acknowledged sense, no special justification is required of the state.[2] For part of what bodily integrity signifies is the right *not* to be governed by the majority in setting the physical perimeters of one's personality. There is no way to escape the necessity for making a threshold judgment about whether a governmental intrusion reaches a level of significance sufficient to invoke strict scrutiny as an invasion of personhood, but that task can be discharged with sensitivity to the eccentric, the unusually sensitive, or the otherwise unorthodox individual only if the interest intruded upon is scrupulously defined at a level of generality sufficient to protect persons who deviate from the norm. Thus, although an appeal to shared experiences and national traditions is inescapable in defining general categories of importance [3]—such as bodily integrity, appearance, or freedom to take risks—it is vital to abandon reliance on notions of the average or the norm in deciding whether a particular instance within a recognized category rises to a serious constitutional level. Even if the Constitution was framed and should be understood in terms of the paradigm "man of the new republic," whose general categories of importance would at least fit within an identifiable mainstream, our conclusion must be that the protections of personhood span the spectrum from the most hardy to the most tender.

§ 15–9

1. Gerety, "Redefining Privacy," 12 Harv.Civ.Rts.—Civ.Lib.L.Rev. 233, 266 & n. 119 (1977).

2. Gerety, supra note 1, at 274–75 n. 153, which goes on to deny that military conscription or compulsory vaccination or mandatory blood tests involve invasions of privacy.

3. See Chapter 11, supra.

Although compulsory vaccinations,[4] compelled blood tests,[5] extractions of contraband narcotics from the rectal cavity,[6] and even surgical removal of a bullet,[7] have sometimes been upheld on a showing of clear necessity,[8] procedural regularity,[9] and minimal pain,[10] in each case the matter has been taken with enough seriousness [11] to warrant a conclu-

---

4. E.g., Jacobson v. Massachusetts, 197 U.S. 11 (1905) (compulsory vaccinations for smallpox upheld over religious objections). See also Dowell v. City of Tulsa, 273 P.2d 859, 43 A.L.R.2d 445 (Okl.1954), cert. denied 348 U.S. 912 (1955), rejecting an attack by a citizen taxpayer group on an ordinance authorizing the addition of fluorides to a public water supply to reduce tooth decay; the superintendent of health testified, without contradiction, that unsupervised individual fluoridation might be dangerous and that the treatment is effective only if all water consumed over an extended period of time has been treated.

5. E.g., Schmerber v. California, 384 U.S. 757 (1966) (blood test of auto accident victim for alcoholic content conducted in hospital held a reasonable search under fourth amendment).

6. Compare Rivas v. United States, 368 F.2d 703 (9th Cir. 1966), cert. denied 386 U.S. 945 (1967) (border search of male rectum upheld); Blefare v. United States, 362 F.2d 870 (9th Cir. 1966) (border searches of male rectum and stomach upheld); Blackford v. United States, 247 F.2d 745 (9th Cir. 1957) (border search of anal cavity over violent objection of suspect, conducted in hospital by doctor, according to scientific procedures, held reasonable search and seizure) with Huguez v. United States, 406 F.2d 366 (9th Cir. 1968) (initiation of forced border search of rectum under non-medical conditions violated fourth amendment; the search itself violated fifth amendment guarantee of humane treatment); Henderson v. United States, 390 F.2d 805 (9th Cir. 1967) (border search of vagina invalidated for lack of "clear indication" that evidence would be found). See generally United States v. Montoya de Hernandez, 473 U.S. 531 (1985) (upholding detention of traveler, on basis of reasonable suspicion that she was an alimentary canal smuggler, until she had a bowel movement allowing Customs agents to search her feces for balloons containing narcotics; she was initially detained for sixteen hours and eventually excreted approximately 80 drug-filled balloons).

7. See United States v. Crowder, 543 F.2d 312 (D.C.Cir.1976) (en banc) (surgical removal of bullet from the arm, under hospital conditions with full procedural safeguards, is not an unreasonable intrusion into the body), cert. denied 429 U.S. 1062 (1977). Accord, Creamer v. State, 229 Ga.

511, 192 S.E.2d 350 (1972) (bullet in side of chest just under skin), cert. dismissed, 410 U.S. 975 (1973). But see Winston v. Lee, 470 U.S. 753, 764 (1985) (unanimous) (because surgery under general anesthesia "involves a virtually total divestment of [one's] ordinary control over surgical probing beneath [one's] skin," compulsory surgery violates the fourth amendment where the state already possesses independent and "substantial evidence of the origin of the bullet"); Adams v. Indiana, 260 Ind. 663, 668, 299 N.E.2d 834, 837 (1973) (removal of bullet even superficially lodged in hips or buttocks "would be an intrusion of the most serious magnitude"), cert. denied 415 U.S. 935 (1974); People v. Smith, 80 Misc.2d 210, 362 N.Y.S.2d 909 (1974) (application to remove bullet sought as evidence in murder investigation denied).

8. Necessity can refer either to the importance of acting quickly to preserve ephemeral evidence—e.g., the blood alcohol content in Schmerber v. California, 384 U.S. 757, 770–71 (1966)—or to the indispensability of the evidence to the prosecution's case, see Winston v. Lee, 470 U.S. 753, 764 (1985) (no such necessity for surgery because the state already possessed independent and "substantial evidence of the origin of the bullet").

9. For an example of a court upholding the admission of evidence obtained by compelled surgery largely because it was dazzled by a model of procedural regularity, see United States v. Crowder, supra note 7.

10. See Schmerber v. California, 384 U.S. 757, 771 (1966) (". . . for most people the [blood test] procedure involves virtually no risk, trauma, or pain").

11. One indicium of judicial concern is the explicit limitation of each decision permitting bodily intrusion to the specific facts before the Court. Thus the Court in Schmerber, id. at 772, admonished that "[i]t bears repeating . . . that we reach this judgment only on the facts of the present record. The integrity of the individual's person is a cherished value of our society. That we hold today that the Constitution does not forbid the States minor intrusions into an individual's body under stringently limited conditions in no way indicates that it permits more substantial intrusions, or intrusions under other conditions."

sion that an aspect of personhood was at stake, and that government's burden was to provide more than minimal justification for its action.[12]

Because "[o]ne's body simply cannot be equated with his car, his clothing, or even his home as a repository of evidence," [13] this heavier burden must attach long before the governmental invasion reaches the outrageous proportions present in *Rochin v. California*,[14] where the Supreme Court held the forcible pumping of a suspect's stomach a flagrant violation of fourteenth amendment due process because it "shocks the conscience," [15] notwithstanding the impossibility of otherwise obtaining the criminal evidence that the police sought. In order to be "brutal and . . . offensive to human dignity," [16] a bodily intrusion need not leave the civilized jurist reeling; it should suffice (1) that the imposition was deficient in procedural regularity, or (2) that it was needlessly severe, or (3) that it was too novel, or (4) that it was lacking in a fair measure of reciprocity.

A note of warning is in order with respect to the initial criterion of procedural regularity: even the most awful tortures, it must be remembered, can be cloaked with such clockwork logic that many become persuaded of their perverse justice.[17] Turning square corners, then, must never become a substitute for respecting the humanity of each individual. It should be even clearer that, when an individual's bodily integrity is at stake, a determination that the state has indeed accorded procedurally adequate protection should not be made lightly. Since bodily invasions cannot be as readily remedied after the fact (through damage awards) as can at least some deprivations of property,[18] it ought to follow, in particular, that the state, absent a clear emergency, must *precede* any deliberate invasion by an adversary hearing, even if only an informal one. "The infliction of physical pain is final and irrepara-

---

12. A drug screening program requiring Customs agents seeking transfer to sensitive positions involving use of firearms, access to classified information, or duty on drug interdiction force to undergo urinalysis was upheld in National Treasury Employees Union v. Von Raab, 816 F.2d 170 (5th Cir. 1987). The court noted that the program applied only in transfer situations, which were themselves initiated by the agents, and concluded that exacting consent for a pre-scheduled urinalysis as a condition of transfer to a limited number of sensitive assignments was not unreasonable. The court also stressed that the program was for administrative rather than law enforcement purposes, and that reasonable steps were taken to protect the dignity of the test subjects: an observer hands the subject a specimen bottle as the subject enters a restroom stall; the observer remains in the bathroom to "listen for the normal sounds of urination but does not visually observe the act of urination." See also Bostic v. McClendon, 650 F.Supp. 245 (N.D.Ga.1986) (urine sample may be required from police department employee for chemical analysis only on reasonable suspicion that urinalysis will produce evidence of illegal drug use by that particular employee).

13. United States v. Crowder, 543 F.2d 312, 322 (D.C.Cir. 1976) (en banc) (Robinson, J., dissenting), cert. denied 429 U.S. 1062 (1977).

14. 342 U.S. 165 (1952).

15. Id. at 172.

16. Id. at 174.

17. See F. Kafka, "The Penal Colony" in Penal Colony: Stories & Short Pieces (Schocken ed. 1948) (convicts strapped to elaborate machine that exquisitely tattooed their bodies with the letters spelling out their crimes).

18. Cf. Parratt v. Taylor, 451 U.S. 527 (1981) (state law remedy provides due process where no immunity bars tort suit for prison mail clerk's negligent loss of prisoner's mail-order hobby kit); Hudson v. Palmer, 468 U.S. 517 (1984) (state remedy likewise provides due process for unpredictable acts of prison guard in destroying prisoner's legal materials and personal correspondence).

ble; it cannot be undone in a subsequent proceeding." [19]   Yet a closely divided Supreme Court concluded in *Ingraham v. Wright* that, although a schoolchild's interest in avoiding the physical pain and degradation of corporal punishment by school authorities is substantively protected as a fourteenth amendment liberty,[20] a system of state remedies that provided nothing beyond the prospect of subsequent liability for excessive punishment supplied the only "process" to which the child was entitled.   Although the four dissenting Justices appear to have made the more convincing argument,[21] the majority showed at least some sensitivity to the likely impact of the prior procedural safeguards for which the child argued.   The Court majority theorized that "interposing prior procedural safeguards may well . . . make the punishment more severe by increasing the anxiety of the child." [22]   Although that rationale pushes uncomfortably close to that of the Queen in Alice's Wonderland, who extolled the virtues of punishing the King's Messenger before trial, and holding the trial before the crime,[23] it is nonetheless possible to understand how the Court might regard the school environment as unique.[24]   Even if that approach is misguided, it is surely preferable to one that extends the theory of shooting first and asking questions later—with fancy remedies to boot—to the full range of possible deprivations directed against citizens generally.[25]

In applying the criterion of needless severity, the crucial factors to be considered are the presence of physical pain, the creation of anxiety and apprehension of medical or other damage, the permanence of any disfigurement or any ensuing complication, the risk of irreversible injury to health, and the danger to life itself.   Most courts would be properly reluctant to validate an intrusion that fared ill along any of those dimensions.   Moreover, an intrusion otherwise sufficiently minimal to pass the severity test should be deemed an intolerable offense if

19. Ingraham v. Wright, 430 U.S. 651, 695 (1977) (White, J., joined by Brennan, Marshall, and Stevens, JJ., dissenting).

20. Id. at 674 & n.43 (majority opinion by Powell, J.) (this liberty interest is protected notwithstanding absence of any state-created entitlement to enjoy it); see also id. at 659 & n.12 (grant of certiorari had been limited so as to exclude question whether substantive due process was violated by the corporal punishment inflicted in this case); id. at 671 (ban on cruel and unusual punishments held inapplicable to school discipline).

21. See id. at 683–700.

22. Id. at 681 n.51.

23. See L. Carroll, Through the Looking Glass 88 (Harper & Bros. ed. 1902).

24. Note the Court's idyllic description: "The schoolchild has little need for the protection of the [ban on cruel and unusual punishments]. Though attendance may not always be voluntary, the public school remains an open institution. Except perhaps when very young, the child is not physically restrained from leaving school during school hours; and at the end of the school day, the child is invariably free to return home.   Even while at school, the child brings with him the support of family and friends and is rarely apart from teachers and other pupils who may witness and protest any instances of mistreatment." 430 U.S. at 670.

25. See, e.g., City of Los Angeles v. Lyons, 461 U.S. 95, 111 (1983) ("The legality of the violence [a police chokehold] to which Lyons claims he was once subjected is at issue in his suit for damages and can be determined there.") Cf. id. at 137 (Marshall, J., joined by Brennan, Blackmun, and Stevens, JJ., dissenting) ("under the view expressed by the majority today, if the police adopt a policy of 'shoot to kill,' or a policy of shooting one out of ten suspects, the federal courts will be powerless to enjoin its continuation."). See also Tennessee v. Garner, 471 U.S. 1 (1985) (invalidating on due process grounds a statute authorizing the police to use deadly force against *any* felon fleeing arrest).

less severe means might be devised to achieve the state's evidentiary or other purposes with approximately the same effectiveness. Thus, the Supreme Court has unanimously held that compelling a suspect to submit to the surgical removal under general anesthesia of a bullet that authorities believe will link him to a crime violates the fourth amendment where the state already possesses substantial, independent evidence of the origin of the bullet.[26]

As a further criterion of offense, the element of novelty provides useful guidance, for lack of routine use in a broad range of situations deprives us of confidence that a technique represents no great affront to human dignity.[27] Both because frequency of use furnishes evidence of wide acceptability, and because the very fact of regular use diminishes the insult, the value of this factor should not be underestimated. The framers recognized as much when they banned "cruel and *unusual* punishments;" we incorporate no more than their insight here.

Finally, if a nontrivial bodily intrusion is to be upheld, the situation should be characterized by some degree of reciprocity.[28] That element might have been invoked to justify the Supreme Court's validation of the federal rule [29] requiring parties to submit to medical examination when tendering claims making their physical condition relevant; [30] the simple fairness of not letting a party both claim a fact and conceal the only evidence that could verify or disprove it made it impossible to say that the party was being forced to yield a right in return for no personal benefit.[31] So too, when the Court upheld a compulsory blood test for a person stopped for intoxicated driving, it could have stressed not only that the person received in return a quick way to dispel suspicion [32] but also that the administration of such tests protects all who are subjected to them from the great bodily injury that they might suffer if their drunk driving, and that of others similarly inebriated, could not be effectively prevented.

A requirement of reciprocity serves to minimize the danger that a bodily invasion will be justified solely on the basis that the greater good of the society is served thereby; that one person's two good eyes, distributed to two blind neighbors, might yield a net increase in happiness on the theory that one blind person will experience less misery than two, cannot justify a governmental decision to compel the exchange.[33] Even if one does not believe that human sacrifice is *never*

---

26. Winston v. Lee, 470 U.S. 753, 764 (1985).

27. See Breithaupt v. Abram, 352 U.S. 432, 436 (1957); Schmerber v. California, 384 U.S. 757, 771 (1966).

28. Cf. Fletcher, "Fairness and Utility in Tort Theory," 85 Harv.L.Rev. 537, 543–56 (1972).

29. F.R.Civ.P. 35, 37.

30. Sibbach v. Wilson, 312 U.S. 1 (1941); Schlagenhauf v. Holder, 379 U.S. 104 (1964).

31. Cf. National Treasury Employees Union v. Von Raab, 816 F.2d 170 (5th Cir.

1987) (upholding a Customs Service drug testing program requiring agents to undergo pre-scheduled urinalysis if they wish to be transferred to sensitive positions involving use of firearms, access to classified information, or duty on drug interdiction force).

32. See Breithaupt, 352 U.S. at 439.

33. Cf. Strunk v. Strunk, 445 S.W.2d 145 (Ky.1969) (mother's petition to permit operation to remove kidney from legally incompetent son in order to save the life of mentally normal son approved, but only because the handicapped son emotionally depended on his brother's companionship).

justifiable, courts have long recognized the wisdom of acting *as though* persons could never be used as means to the ends of others, knowing that any clear departure from that ideal could spell the beginning of a disastrous slide.

Thus far, we have spoken exclusively of active invasion of the body. But physical violation need not be of the "rape, murder, fire and sword" variety characterized by the "sudden forceful, and perhaps unexpected, infliction of painful physical injury upon an unwilling victim." [34] "Where muggings and violent demonstrations are the fear and the theorists speak for the fearful, vigorous direct actions will seem the most important features of violence. Where the streets are quiet, but people who could be saved are left to die of neglect or cold or hunger, or are crippled or killed by their living or working conditions, a different group of people may suffer, and other theorists may see their suffering as attributable to human agency, and so class it as part of man's violence to man." [35] Surely Justice Stevens was right to insist in *Estelle v. Gamble*, for example, that "[w]hether the conditions in Andersonville were the product of design, negligence, or mere poverty, they were cruel and inhuman," [36] and to conclude that governmental indifference to a prisoner's medical needs violates the eighth and fourteenth amendments.[37] Similarly, the Court was plainly correct in concluding in *Youngberg v. Romeo* that the state has an affirmative duty under the fourteenth amendment not only to "provide adequate food, shelter, clothing, and medical care" to those confined in its mental institutions, but also to provide a mentally retarded resident with "training . . . to ensure his safety and to facilitate his ability to function free from bodily restraints." [38]

Now it plainly requires a further step to conclude that governmental indifference to extreme human suffering and deprivation *in any context* violates the Constitution,[39] but we have already seen that the demise of the *Lochner* [40] era reflected the view that "much of the harm [once] thought to be part of the natural hazards of life is . . . in fact

---

34. Harris, "The Marxist Conception of Violence," 3 Phil. & Pub.Aff. 192, 215 (1974).

35. Id. at 219.

36. 429 U.S. 97, 116–17 (1976) (dissenting opinion).

37. The majority held only that the inmate's complaint was insufficient to suggest such indifference by prison personnel to the inmate's medical condition as to constitute cruel and unusual punishment. Although the majority indicated that "deliberate indifference to serious medical needs of prisoners," id. at 106, would violate the eighth amendment, and expressed no view on the constitutional status of inattention that could not be characterized as "deliberate," Justice Stevens disagreed both with the majority's cramped reading of the complaint and with the majority's apparent concern with "the subjective motivation of the defendant as a criterion for determining whether cruel and unusual punishment has been inflicted." Id. at 116. See also Whitley v. Albers, 475 U.S. 312 (1986), discussed in § 10–7, note 10, supra.

38. 457 U.S. 307, 324 (1982).

39. Such a step would not be inconsistent with the governing premise of this chapter—that active governmental imposition *or* conscious governmental neglect differs qualitatively from the passive coercion that shapes life generally. See § 15–2, supra, at note 4. It should be noted that relief against unjust indifference need not always take the form of active assistance by government; at times such relief may require only that government relax its otherwise reasonable regulations to accommodate acute instances of need.

40. Lochner v. New York, 198 U.S. 45 (1905), discussed in Chapter 8, supra.

attributable to the machinations of men," [41] and that the system of governmental decisions—some statutory and some made by common-law judges—bore an active responsibility for the plight of those who could not earn a decent living. Emerging notions that government has an affirmative obligation somehow to provide at least a minimally decent subsistence with respect to the most basic human needs,[42] subject to all of the familiar difficulties with judicial enforcement of affirmative duties, thus fit quite naturally into a conception of bodily integrity in which a governmental omission can be as deadly as the most pointed of governmental acts.[43]

It should be stressed that this perspective does *not* entail a judicially cognizable remedy against government for every instance of substandard wages or unmet needs. The problems of proving causation alone, not to mention the institutional difficulties of framing appropriate relief, would plainly defeat any doctrine so sweeping. We have not yet come to the point where government is thought to be responsible for every personal misfortune; far from it, our notions of personal responsibility and autonomy—indeed, of personhood—rebel at the suggestion that persons are not at least sometimes accountable for their plight. The point of *Lochner's* downfall was not the rejection of human freedom as an idea, but the recognition that there was less of such freedom, in the ordinary workings of the economy, than sometimes met the eye. If it follows that, at least sometimes, the person who is forced to work too hard for too little, or can find no work at all, must be regarded as the victim of the system of contract and property rights rather than the author of his own plight, still it does not follow that this is always so, and plainly it does not follow that we will always, or even often, be able to discern in the individual case whether it is so or not.

These observations imply that the affirmative governmental duty to meet basic human needs cannot always be enforced directly—apart from such special situations as that of the prisoner in *Estelle v. Gamble*,[44] as to whom it was easy to fix blame on the government for the deprivation experienced. Instead, it will usually be necessary to reflect affirmative duties less directly—through governmental obligations to provide various procedural safeguards when the deprivation of welfare,[45] wages,[46] or household goods [47] is involved; governmental

---

41. Harris, supra note 34, at 212.

42. The seminal work suggesting a constitutional theory of such obligation is Michelman, "The Supreme Court, 1968 Term—Foreword: On Protecting the Poor Through the Fourteenth Amendment," 83 Harv.L.Rev. 7 (1969). See also Michelman, "Welfare Rights in a Constitutional Democracy," 1979 Wash.U.L.Q. 659, 674–80 (relying on J. Ely, Democracy and Distrust (1980), to support welfare rights as an aspect of facilitating political representation).

43. Cf. Tribe, "The Abortion Funding Conundrum: Inalienable Rights, Affirmative Duties, and the Dilemma of Dependence," 99 Harv.L.Rev. 330, 340–43 (1985).

But see Bork, "The Impossibility of Finding Welfare Rights in the Constitution," 1979 Wash.U.L.Q. 695.

44. 429 U.S. 97 (1976). See also Bounds v. Smith, 430 U.S. 817 (1977) (prison authorities have affirmative duty to facilitate access to courts by providing adequate law libraries or assistance from persons trained in the law).

45. E.g., Goldberg v. Kelly, 397 U.S. 254 (1970).

46. E.g., Sniadach v. Family Finance Corp., 395 U.S. 337 (1969).

47. E.g., Fuentes v. Shevin, 407 U.S. 67 (1972). The preceding three cases are dis-

responsibilities to determine eligibility for welfare and other basic services in terms of need rather than through such unrelated criteria as duration of residence [48] or composition of family; [49] and governmental duties to determine need with substantial accuracy.[50]

All of these doctrines depend for their efficacy upon some initial choices by government; if the state and federal governments were to wash their hands altogether of the sick, hungry, and poor, none of the interstitial doctrines sketched here could provide a remedy. But that is simply a reminder of the basic point suggested as long ago as 1827 by Chief Justice Marshall [51]—that a government which wholly failed to discharge its duty to protect its citizens would be answerable primarily in the streets and at the polling booth, and only secondarily if at all in the courts. To say this is not to deny that government has affirmative duties to its citizens arising out of the basic necessities of bodily survival, but only to deny that all such duties are perfectly enforceable in the courts of law.[52]

§ 15–10. Governmental Control Over the Body: Decisions About Birth and Babies

In all of the situations examined in § 15–9, the individual's bodily integrity was the primary interest implicated; government action or neglect was challenged because of its failure to respect the elements of personhood inherent in someone's physical being. In this and the succeeding section, bodily integrity will again be implicated, but in a way that is linked to an analytically distinct and additional concern: the allocation of decision-making power over birth and death. Of all decisions a person makes about his or her body, the most profound and intimate relate to two sets of ultimate questions: first, whether, when,

cussed more fully in Chapter 10, supra, and Chapter 16, infra.

48. E.g., Shapiro v. Thompson, 394 U.S. 618 (1969) (welfare benefits); Memorial Hosp. v. Maricopa County, 415 U.S. 250 (1974) (non-emergency medical care).

49. E.g., New Jersey Welfare Rights Organization v. Cahill, 411 U.S. 619 (1973) (unconstitutional to withhold welfare benefits from families with only illegitimate children); United States Dep't of Agriculture v. Moreno, 413 U.S. 528 (1973) (unconstitutional to withhold food stamps from households containing unrelated persons).

50. E.g., United States Dep't of Agriculture v. Murry, 413 U.S. 508 (1973) (unconstitutional to withhold food stamps from households containing at least one individual over 18 claimed as dependent by a taxpayer ineligible for food stamps).

Professor Michelman has advanced a powerful argument for minimal entitlements or insurance rights to the fulfillment of basic wants by all citizens, and has likewise suggested that difficulties of definition and remedy may limit courts to the elimination of gaps in, or withdrawals of,

such basic services or programs of assistance as the legislative branch has already undertaken. See Michelman, "In Pursuit of Constitutional Welfare Rights: One View of Rawls' Theory of Justice," 121 U.Pa.L.Rev. 962, 997–1003, 1005–07, 1010–11, 1013–15 (1973).

51. See Ogden v. Saunders, 25 U.S. (12 Wheat.) 213, 350–51 (dissenting opinion), discussed in § 9–8, supra.

52. See, e.g., Maher v. Roe, 432 U.S. 464, 480 (1977) (stressing resort to politics as exclusive remedy for governmental refusal to fund nontherapeutic abortions), discussed in § 15–10, infra. See also Tribe, "Unravelling National League of Cities: The New Federalism and Affirmative Rights to Essential Government Services," 90 Harv.L.Rev. 1065, 1088–89 (1977) (the obviously great institutional difficulties of framing appropriate relief may sometimes entail a conclusion that a judicially cognizable remedy simply is not available); Sager, "Fair Measure: The Legal Status of Underenforced Constitutional Norms," 91 Harv.L.Rev. 1212 (1978).

and how one's body is to become the vehicle for another human being's creation; second, when and how—this time there is no question of "whether"—one's body is to terminate its organic life. The first of these sets of questions is the subject of this section; the next is the subject of § 15–11.

In *Griswold v. Connecticut*,[1] the Supreme Court held that the state cannot make the use of contraceptives by married persons a crime, and so cannot punish someone who provides married persons with contraceptives, and with information concerning their use, for the crime of aiding and abetting such use.[2] The state's regulation was condemned as invading "the area of protected freedoms" which included "the zone of privacy created by several fundamental constitutional guarantees"[3] and extended at least to those intimacies of married life that involved decisions about whether or not to bear a child. Although the separately concurring Justices offered differing rationales[4], the majority opinion by Justice Douglas was plainly influenced by a sense of outrage at the only imaginable means of directly enforcing the law. "Would we," the Justice asked, "allow the police to search the sacred precincts of marital bedrooms for tell-tale signs of the use of contraceptives?"[5] The answer, of course, would be *yes*—if contraceptives had no relationship to intimate personal choices. Although, as we shall see in § 15–19, the community's power to control behavior *is* limited by its occurrence within the home, *Griswold* is surely not one of those cases in which the precise physical sanctuary wherein the conduct occurs proves decisive.[6]

§ 15–10

1. 381 U.S. 479 (1965).

2. But compare Stanley v. Georgia, 394 U.S. 557 (1969) (recognizing constitutional right of individual to possess and view obscenity in the home), with subsequent cases reaffirming government power to forbid sale of obscenity even to consenting adults, discussed in § 12–16, supra. In this area, unlike that of obscenity, undue restrictions on sale have been struck down. See Carey v. Population Services International, 431 U.S. 678 (1977) (sale of contraceptives cannot be limited to sales by licensed pharmacists or to sales to persons over 16).

3. 381 U.S. at 485.

4. Justice Goldberg, joining in the opinion and judgment with Chief Justice Warren and Justice Brennan, concurred to "emphasize the relevance of [the ninth] amendment . . .," id. at 487, which "lends strong support" to the view that the first eight amendments do not exhaust the list of rights protected by the fourteenth amendment. Id. at 493. Justice Harlan believed that the statute violated basic values protected by the due process clause of the fourteenth amendment, which, he declared, "stands on its own bottom." Id. at 499–500. Justice White concurred, finding

the statute repugnant to due process guarantees of liberty, id. at 502, and suggesting that the statute would have a disproportionate impact on the "disadvantaged." Id. at 503. Justices Stewart and Black dissented, lamenting this "uncommonly silly" law, id. at 527, but unable to find the constitutional mandate which would permit them to substitute their judgment for that of the legislature.

5. 381 U.S. at 485–86. Note the shift in rationale by the time the Court decided Carey, 431 U.S. at 688: "[A] prohibition against all sales, since more easily and less offensively enforced, might have an even more devastating effect upon the freedom to choose contraception."

6. ". . . [T]he constitutionally protected privacy of family, marriage, motherhood, procreation, and child-rearing is not just concerned with a particular place, but with a protected intimate relationship. Such protected privacy extends to the doctor's office, the hospital, the hotel room or as otherwise required to safeguard the right to intimacy involved. Cf. Roe v. Wade, 410 U.S. 113, 152–154, . . . Griswold v. Connecticut, 381 U.S. 479, 485–486 . . . .", Paris Adult Theatre I v. Slaton, 413 U.S. 49, 66 n.13 (1973).

Writing for the majority in *Eisenstadt v. Baird*,[7] Justice Brennan identified what was plainly at stake in the contraception cases when he observed that, if "the right of privacy means anything, it is the right of the *individual*, married or single, to be free from unwanted governmental intrusions into matters so fundamentally affecting a person as the decision whether to bear or beget a child." [8] In §§ 15–20 and 15–21 we will examine the extent to which this pronouncement, and the holding underlying it, signal an extension of *Griswold's* protection to relationships outside the traditional core of heterosexual marriage. For purposes of this section, however, it is sufficient to note that the effect of *Eisenstadt v. Baird* [9] was to single out as decisive in *Griswold* the element of reproductive autonomy, something the Court made clear in 1977, when it extended *Griswold* and *Baird* to invalidate a state ban on commercial distribution of nonmedical contraceptives in *Carey v. Population Services International*.[10]

The fundamental character of the reproductive decision was recognized in a watershed 1942 decision, *Skinner v. Oklahoma*,[11] where the Court invalidated a state statute providing for the sterilization of persons convicted two or more times of "felonies involving moral turpitude." The Court characterized the right to reproduce as "one of the basic civil rights of man" [12] and observed that the "power to sterlize, if exercised . . . [i]n evil or reckless hands . . . can cause races or types which are inimical to the dominant group to wither and disappear." [13] Justice Jackson, concurring, spoke of limits on "the extent to which a legislatively represented majority may conduct biological experiments at the expense of the dignity and personality and natural powers of a minority—even those who are guilty of what the majority define as crimes." [14] These observations, as we will see more fully in § 16–12, indicate that the Court in *Skinner* was moved to recognize the fundamental personal character of a right to reproductive autonomy in part because of fear about the invidious and potentially genocidal way in which governmental control over reproductive matters might be exercised if the choice of whether or when to beget a child were to be transferred from the individual to the state.

Although the Court had earlier upheld the state's power to sterilize an individual against her objection in order to prevent the birth of what Justice Holmes callously characterized as "imbeciles," [15] and although

7. 405 U.S. 438 (1972) (invalidating regulation, viewed as health measure, which made contraceptives less available to the unmarried than to married couples).

8. Id. at 453 (emphasis in original).

9. Id.

10. 431 U.S. 678 (1977).

11. 316 U.S. 535 (1942).

12. Id. at 541.

13. Id.

14. Id. at 546.

15. Buck v. Bell, 274 U.S. 200, 207 (1927). Although the involuntary steriliza-

tion performed by the State of Virginia on Carrie Buck, and its subsequent, undisclosed sterilization of her sister Doris— neither of whom "would be considered mentally deficient by today's standards," S. J. Gould, The Mismeasure of Man 336 (Norton paperback ed. 1981)—were enormous tragedies in themselves, the law upheld in Buck v. Bell continued to be implemented for almost fifty years. All told, over 7,500 involuntary sterilizations were performed by Virginia between 1924 and 1972. See id. at 335.

that earlier holding continues to be cited without obvious disapproval from time to time,[16] it is hard to square the basic philosophy of *Skinner v. Oklahoma* [17] with the proposition that the state may usurp the individual's procreative choices in an irreversible way—whether by sterilization or by compulsory breeding.[18] Taken together with *Griswold*,[19] which recognized as equally protected the individual's decision *not* to bear a child, the meaning of *Skinner* is that *whether one person's body shall be the source of another life must be left to that person and that person alone to decide.*[20] That principle seems to collide in the abortion cases with a command that is no less fundamental: *an innocent life may not be taken except to save the life of another.* Few decisions prove more difficult than those in which these two absolutes stand opposed.

If a man is the involuntary source of a child—if he is forbidden, for example, to practice contraception—the violation of his personality is profound; the decision that one wants to engage in sexual intercourse but does not want to parent another human being may reflect the deepest of personal impulses and convictions. But if a woman is forced to bear a child—not simply to provide an ovum but to carry the child to term—the invasion is incalculably greater. Quite apart from the physical experience of pregnancy itself, an experience which of course has no analogue for the male, there is the attachment the experience creates, partly physiological and partly psychological, between mother and child. Thus it is difficult to imagine a clearer case of bodily intrusion, even if the original conception was in some sense voluntary.[21] Responding more to these concerns and their obvious significance for women's liberation than to the claims pressed on behalf of the unborn,

16. See, e.g., Roe v. Wade, 410 U.S. 113, 154 (1973); Doe v. Bolton, 410 U.S. 179, 215 (1973) (Douglas, J., concurring). But see Regents of the Univ. of California v. Bakke, 438 U.S. 265, 326 (1978) (Brennan, White, Marshall, and Blackmun, JJ., concurring in the judgment and dissenting in part).

17. 316 U.S. 535, 542 (1942).

18. Nine years prior to Buck, a New York court deemed it "inhuman" to sterilize someone in order to "save the State . . . the expense of the care of the feebleminded." In re Thompson, 103 Misc. 23, 169 N.Y.S. 638 (1918), aff'd 185 App.Div. 902, 171 N.Y.S. 1094 (1918). More recently, in In re Cavitt, 182 Neb. 712, 157 N.W.2d 171 (1968), appeal dismissed 396 U.S. 996 (1970), the Nebraska Supreme Court voted 4–3 to hold violative of due process a statute requiring sterilization of "mentally deficient" persons as a prerequisite to release from a mental institution; the law was saved by the state's rule requiring a 5–2 vote to invalidate a statute.

19. 381 U.S. 479 (1965).

20. It may be noteworthy, however, that Skinner was not decided in a period of

concern with overpopulation. Government policies narrowly and nondiscriminatorily tailored to limit population growth need not be invalidated by Skinner.

21. To suppose that contraception by itself, or abortion immediately following conception, adequately preserves the right to avoid childbearing, see Louisell & Noonan, "Constitutional Balance," in The Morality of Abortion: Legal and Historical Perspectives 220, 234–35 (J. Noonan ed. 1970); cf. Stone, "Abortion and the Supreme Court: What Now?," in Modern Medicine, Apr. 30, 1973, at 36, assumes that contraception efforts never fail and overlooks the potential relevance of such changed family circumstances as separation, illness, and economic collapse during pregnancy. Further, to suppose that giving up a child for adoption can save a woman from unwanted parenthood ignores the emotional pressures that make it difficult to abandon one's offspring as well as the legal constraints society imposes upon such a choice. Thus, to say that a veto over the abortion choice would not affect the capacity for self-definition overlooks the realities both before pregnancy begins and after it ends.

the Supreme Court in 1973 took the dramatic step of extending *Gris-wold*[22] and *Baird*[23] to the case of abortion, holding in *Roe v. Wade*[24] and *Doe v. Bolton*[25] that the right of privacy recognized in prior cases was "broad enough to encompass a woman's decision whether or not to terminate her pregnancy."[26]

Specifically, the Court held that, because the woman's right to decide whether or not to end a pregnancy is fundamental, only a compelling interest can justify state regulation impinging in any way upon that right.[27] During the first trimester of pregnancy, when abortion is less hazardous in terms of the woman's life than carrying the child to term would be, the state may require only that the abortion be performed by a licensed physician;[28] no further regulations peculiar to abortion as such[29] are compellingly justified in that period.

After the first trimester, the compelling state interest in the mother's health permits it to adopt reasonable regulations in order to promote safe abortions[30]—but requiring abortions to be performed in hospitals,[31] or only after approval of another doctor[32] or committee[33] in

22. 381 U.S. 479 (1965).

23. 405 U.S. 438 (1972).

24. 410 U.S. 113 (1973).

25. 410 U.S. 179 (1973).

26. Wade, 410 U.S. at 153.

27. Id. at 155–56. The Court divided 7–2, with Justice Blackmun writing the majority opinion and Justices Douglas and Stewart and Chief Justice Burger writing separate concurring opinions. Although Justice Rehnquist dissented, he agreed that the "liberty" protected by fourteenth amendment due process "embraces more than the rights found in the Bill of Rights." Id. at 172–73. And, if "the Texas statute were to prohibit an abortion even where the mother's life is in jeopardy," he would have had "little doubt that [the law] . . . would lack a rational relation to a valid state objective. . . ." Id. at 173. Since Justice White left open the possibility that he would find abortions constitutionally protected whenever required to avoid "substantial hazards to either life or health," Bolton, 410 U.S. at 223 (dissenting opinion); cf. Eisenstadt v. Baird, 405 U.S. 438, 464 (1972) (White, J., concurring), the Court was evidently unanimous in accepting a fairly sweeping concept of substantive due process, although various Justices continued to resist that characterization. See also Griswold v. Connecticut, 381 U.S. 479 (1965); although the Court there invalidated a state ban on the use of contraceptives, it insisted that it was "declin[ing] the invitation" to be guided by Lochner v. New York, 198 U.S. 45 (1905), see 381 U.S. at 482, and seemed to deny that its judgment rested on fourteenth amendment due process, although of course no other constitutional provision

was applicable. In Wade, Justice Stewart recognized, however, that Griswold "stands as one in a long line of [pre-1963] cases decided under the doctrine of substantive due process," and he proceeded to "accept it as such." 410 U.S. at 168 (concurring opinion). See generally Chapter 11, supra.

28. Wade, 410 U.S. at 163, 165.

29. Apart from reporting and record-keeping requirements carefully safeguarding confidentiality, which are discussed infra.

30. Roe v. Wade, 410 U.S. at 163.

31. Doe v. Bolton, 410 U.S. at 194–95. Six Justices confirmed the unconstitutionality of second-trimester hospitalization requirements in Akron v. Akron Center for Reproductive Health, 462 U.S. 416, 431–39 (1983) (Powell, J., joined by Burger, C.J., and Brennan, Marshall, Blackmun, and Stevens, JJ.); Planned Parenthood of Kansas City v. Ashcroft, 462 U.S. 476, 481–82 (1983) (same). In Simopoulos v. Virginia, 462 U.S. 506 (1983), the Court upheld a hospitalization requirement by reading the statutory definition of "hospital" as sufficiently broad to include licensed outpatient clinics. Justice Powell wrote for the Court, joined by Chief Justice Burger and Justices Brennan, Marshall, and Blackmun. Justices White, Rehnquist, and O'Connor concurred. Justice Stevens, who had joined the Court in striking down hospitalization requirements in the companion cases, dissented on the basis of his doubts that the Virginia statute would in fact be read broadly.

32. Doe v. Bolton, 410 U.S. at 198–200.

33. Id. at 195–98.

addition to the woman's physician, is impermissible, as is requiring that the abortion procedure employ a technique that, however preferable from a medical perspective, is not widely available.[34]

Once the fetus is viable, in the sense that it is capable of survival outside the uterus with artificial aid,[35] the state interest in preserving the fetus becomes compelling. The state may therefore proscribe abortion during the third trimester except when necessary to preserve the mother's life or health.[36] Although a physician may be required to exercise due care to preserve the life of a viable fetus, the Court has held that requiring such care is unconstitutional if it poses any additional risk to maternal health.[37] Thus, a statute that imposes a higher standard of care when the fetus "*may be* viable" impermissibly suggests that the physician may be forced to "make a 'trade-off' between the woman's health and additional percentage points of fetal survival."[38] When the fetus *is* viable, however, a state may require that a second doctor be present to provide additional protection for the life of the fetus,[39] so long as the requirement contains a medical emergency exception to ensure that attention to the fetus is not bought at expense of increased risk to the mother's health.[40]

State requirements that doctors keep records and file reports regarding abortions are permissible only to the extent that they are reasonably tailored to the preservation of maternal health and ensure the confidentiality of information about the patient.[41] Thus the Court

---

34. Planned Parenthood v. Danforth, 428 U.S. 52, 75–79 (1976), invalidated a state ban on the use of saline amniocentesis as a means of abortion after the first trimester; the Court, virtually constituting itself "the country's . . . *ex officio* medical board," id. at 99 (White, J., concurring in part and dissenting in part), determined that the alternative method—prostaglandin—was insufficiently available in Missouri to warrant the state's choice.

35. Roe v. Wade, 410 U.S. at 160, 163. Viability "is usually placed at about seven months (28 weeks) but may occur earlier, even at 24 weeks." Id. at 150. The Court upheld in Danforth, as consistent with Roe v. Wade, Missouri's statutory definition of viability as "that stage of fetal development when the life of the unborn child may be continued indefinitely outside the womb by natural or artificial life-supportive systems." 428 U.S. at 52. Although the Court noted in Roe v. Wade such advances in biomedical technology as fetal transplants and artificial wombs, 410 U.S. at 161, it did not explore the implications that such devices would have for its holding as to the first trimester if they should become widely available in very early pregnancy. Nor did the Court indicate *how much* artificial aid would be necessary before a fetus could be deemed non-viable in fact despite its viability in theory.

36. Roe v. Wade, 410 U.S. at 163–64.

37. Thornburgh v. American College of Obstetricians & Gynecologists, 106 S.Ct. 2169, 2182–83 (1986) (Blackmun, J., for the Court, joined by Brennan, Marshall, Powell, and Stevens, JJ.) (invalidating law that excused the doctor from maximizing the chances of fetal survival only if the technique "would present a *significantly* greater risk to the life or health of the pregnant woman") (emphasis added). Justice White, joined by Justice Rehnquist, dissented, attacking the basic premise that a woman has a fundamental right to choose abortion over childbirth. Chief Justice Burger also dissented, agreeing with much of Justice White's opinion and concurring in the conclusion that it was time to reexamine Roe v. Wade. Justice O'Connor dissented as well, arguing that the Court should not have reached the merits because the case had proceeded only to the preliminary injunction stage.

38. Colautti v. Franklin, 439 U.S. 379, 397–401 (1979) (striking down a statute that "does not clearly specify that the woman's life and health must always prevail over the fetus' life and health when they conflict").

39. Planned Parenthood of Kansas City v. Ashcroft, 462 U.S. 476, 482–86 (1983).

40. See id. at 485 n.8; Thornburgh, 106 S.Ct. at 2183–84.

41. See Danforth, 428 U.S. at 79–81. Record-keeping and reporting require-

has shown no tolerance for "extreme" reporting requirements that would make available to the public detailed information about the woman, the physician, and the circumstances of the abortion, perceiving in such requirements a design to facilitate public exposure and harassment of women seeking to exercise their constitutional right to control their reproductive destiny.[42]

The Supreme Court has reviewed a range of legislative measures regarding the information given to and the consent required of women seeking abortions. States may insist that a woman certify in writing prior to an abortion "that her consent is informed and freely given and is not the result of coercion." [43] Legislative attempts to specify the information to be provided, however, have been struck down as designed "to influence the woman's informed choice between abortion or childbirth." [44] The Court has thus invalidated laws requiring that women seeking abortions be given detailed descriptions of fetal development,[45] informed of particular physical and psychological risks associated with abortion,[46] and reminded of the availability of assistance from the father [47] or from social service agencies [48] should the woman decide to give birth. Moreover, states cannot require that a woman wait for a

ments are permissible even during the first trimester provided they are not "utilized in such a way as to accomplish, through the sheer burden of record-keeping detail, what [the Court has] held to be an otherwise unconstitutional restriction." Id. at 81. To promote the compilation of medical data on maternal health, a state may also require that tissue removed in an abortion be examined by a pathologist for signs of "abnormalities . . . [that] may warn of serious, possibly fatal disorders." Ashcroft, 462 U.S. at 487 (plurality opinion).

42. Thornburgh, 106 S.Ct. at 2180–82. The Thornburgh opinion implicitly acknowledged the powerful, albeit nongovernmental, coercion by private anti-abortion groups. See id. at 2183. See generally People v. Krizka, 92 Ill.App.3d 288, 48 Ill.Dec. 141, 416 N.E.2d 36 (1980) (finding 12 defendants guilty of trespassing at a medical center in order to interfere with patients' exercise of abortion rights).

43. Danforth, 428 U.S. at 65. The consent requirement was deemed constitutional because it "insures that the pregnant woman retains control over the discretion of her consulting physician." Id. at 66.

44. Akron v. Akron Center for Reproductive Health, 462 U.S. 416, 443–44 (1983). According to the Court, "much of the information required is designed not to inform the woman's consent, but to persuade her to withhold it altogether." Id. at 444. Equally important to the Court's holding was the fact that categorical information requirements impermissibly infringe upon the decision of the physician to exercise her best medical judgment under

individual circumstances. See id. at 443–45. The Court has also concluded that a doctor must retain discretion not to relate gratuitous or inappropriate information that could be "cruel, as well as destructive of the physician-patient relationship." Thornburgh, 106 S.Ct. at 2180 (referring to requirement that a pregnant rape victim be informed that her rapist is liable for child support should she choose to carry her unborn child to term).

45. See Akron, 462 U.S. at 444; Thornburgh, 106 S.Ct. at 2178–79.

46. See Akron, 462 U.S. at 444–45 (stating that the statutory section describing "numerous possible physical and psychological complications of abortion is a 'parade of horribles' intended to suggest that abortion is a particularly dangerous procedure"). In fact, the risk of death or serious complication is at least seven times greater in childbirth than in first trimester abortion. Cates, Smith, Rochat & Grimes, "Mortality From Abortion and Childbirth: Are the Statistics Biased?," 248 J.A.M.A. 192 (1982); LeBolt, Grimes & Cates, "Mortality from Abortion and Childbirth: Are the Populations Comparable?," 248 J.A.M.A. 188 (1982). The health risks of pregnancy and childbirth are greatly exacerbated when a pregnancy is unwanted. Cates, "Legal Abortion: The Public Health Record," 215 Sci. 1586, 1587 (1982).

47. See Thornburgh, 106 S.Ct. at 2179–80.

48. See id. at 2178–80; Akron, 462 U.S. at 442.

statutorily fixed period after signing a consent form before the abortion procedure may be performed.[49]   To the extent that informed consent may constitutionally be required, a state may not mandate that the attending physician obtain it; any qualified person may counsel a patient and obtain her valid consent.[50]

Blanket requirements of third-party consent to a woman's decision to have an abortion are unconstitutional even as applied only to non-therapeutic procedures, regardless of the woman's age. The Court has been unwilling to allow states to give either the pregnant woman's husband or her parents an absolute veto over an abortion that the states themselves would be powerless to forbid.[51]   Minors' constitutional rights warrant no less respect than those of adults,[52] but the state's interest in protecting immature minors is sufficient to uphold at least the facial validity of certain requirements of parental involvement in minors' decision making.[53]   Requirements of parental consent must provide for an alternative form of approval—a judicial "bypass"—for a minor who is sufficiently mature to make the decision herself, or who can demonstrate that an abortion would be in her best interests.[54]   In

49. See Akron, 462 U.S. at 449–51 (invalidating 24-hour waiting period as lacking medical basis, imposing added financial burdens of extra travel, and increasing medical risks associated with delay caused by scheduling difficulties).

50. See id. at 446–49.

51. Danforth, 428 U.S. at 67–75. The Court pointed out that a statutory spousal consent requirement would be relevant only when the spouses disagreed—actually, only when the husband wished to veto an abortion sought by his wife. The Court agreed that, ideally, both spouses would concur in the abortion decision; but since only one party could prevail in such a situation, the woman's interests in the consequences of her pregnancy outweighed those of the father of the fetus. See id. at 71.

52. See id.; Bellotti v. Baird, 443 U.S. 622, 633 (1979) (Powell, J., for the plurality, joined by Burger, C.J., and Stewart and Rehnquist, JJ.). Justices Brennan, Marshall, Blackmun and Stevens concurred in the judgment in Bellotti v. Baird. Justice White dissented.

53. At least one district court extensively reviewed actual practice under a parental notification statute that is facially valid under Bellotti v. Baird and found the law to be unconstitutional "in actual operation." Minnesota's law required women under 18 either to notify both parents or to obtain judicial approval before having an abortion. Although the state courts approved virtually all such requests, the law nevertheless took a terrible toll in the form of emotional trauma on young women faced with the choice between having the most intimate aspects of their lives dragged into court and notifying not one but both parents, even in cases involving broken families or parents "likely to react with psychological, sexual or physical violence." After a five week trial, the court found no factual basis for holding that the Minnesota law "on the whole furthers in any meaningful way the state's interest in protecting pregnant minors or assuring family integrity." Hodgson v. Minnesota, 648 F.Supp. 756 (D.Minn. 1986) (Alsop, J.). The Eighth Circuit affirmed that ruling on August 27, 1987. See The New York Times, Aug. 28, 1987, at A1, col. 1. See also Dembitz, "The Supreme Court and a Minor's Abortion Decision," 80 Colum.L. Rev. 1251 (1980) (mandating parental involvement serves primarily to obstruct minors' access to abortions: minors do not need a statutory command to consult with parents in times of personal crisis, and parental opposition to a daughter's efforts to secure abortions rarely relates to and is often contrary to the daughter's well-being).

54. See Akron, 462 U.S. at 439–40; Ashcroft, 462 U.S. at 490–91; Bellotti, 443 U.S. at 643–44, 647–48. State rules requiring parental involvement, whether they mandate actual parental consent or mere notification, are subject to the same constitutional requirements of waivability, confidentiality, and expedition. In H.L. v. Matheson, 450 U.S. 398, 400 (1981), Chief Justice Burger, joined by Justices Stewart, White, Powell, and Rehnquist, upheld a Utah statute requiring the doctor to "notify, if possible," the parents or guardian of a minor seeking an abortion. Justice Stevens concurred in the judgment. The Court did not consider the statute's lack of a judicial bypass mechanism for mature

addition, the Court will not sustain a parental involvement rule unless it is accompanied by procedures ensuring that the judicial bypass will be accomplished confidentially and expeditiously.[55]

Despite the Court's sensitivity to practical obstacles to the exercise of abortion rights—including its intolerance of regulations that would significantly drive up the cost of an abortion [56]—it has held that government may refuse to pay for abortions,[57] even if they are medically necessary to preserve the mother's life or health.[58] Even if the state pays for all other medical treatments, and in particular funds all health care incident to childbirth, the state need not pay for the far less expensive abortion procedure. Although the state's interest in encouraging childbirth is not compelling until after viability, the Court has held that it is nonetheless "a significant state interest existing throughout the course of the woman's pregnancy." [59] The state can therefore make "a value judgment favoring childbirth over abortion, and . . . implement that judgment by the allocation of public funds." [60]

minors and those whose interests would best be served by waiver of notice because the plaintiff had made no showing sufficient to give her standing to challenge the law on those grounds.

55. See Thornburgh, 106 S.Ct. at 2177 n.9. Upholding a consent requirement without an effective judicial bypass would allow the parents to wield a de facto veto over their minor daughter's decision to have an abortion. See Bellotti, 443 U.S. at 643.

56. See, e.g., Akron, 462 U.S. at 434 (invalidating second-trimester hospitalization requirement, a "primary burden" of which was its "additional cost to the woman"); Ashcroft, 462 U.S. at 489 (upholding a pathology reporting requirement because the costs it imposed were "comparatively small" and "would not significantly burden" the abortion choice).

57. See Maher v. Roe, 432 U.S. 464 (1977); Beal v. Doe, 432 U.S. 438 (1977). Justice Powell wrote the opinion of the Court in both cases, joined by Chief Justice Burger and Justices Stewart, White, Rehnquist, and Stevens. Justices Brennan, Marshall, and Blackmun dissented.

58. See Harris v. McRae, 448 U.S. 297 (1980); Williams v. Zbaraz, 448 U.S. 358 (1980). Justice Stewart wrote for the Court in both cases, joined by Chief Justice Burger and Justices White, Powell, and Rehnquist. Justices Brennan, Marshall, and Blackmun dissented. Justice Stevens, who voted to uphold government refusals to fund *non*therapeutic abortions, see note 57, supra, dissented in Zbaraz and McRae on equal protection grounds. 448 U.S. at 349. He argued that, under its comprehensive health program, the state must fund all medically necessary services—including abortion—on equal terms. To do

otherwise would be to deny health care to eligible women "solely because they must exercise the constitutional right to have an abortion in order to obtain the medical care they need." Id.

Justice Brennan had previously argued in Beal v. Doe, 432 U.S. at 449, that there is no meaningful distinction between "elective" and "medically necessary" abortions: because "pregnancy is unquestionably a condition requiring medical services," even an "elective" abortion must be deemed a form of health care, since it is one of the medically necessary alternative treatments for that condition. Even if a woman has additional reasons for not wanting to carry a pregnancy to term, it would be irresponsible to ignore the fact that, as previously noted, the risk of death or serious complication is at least seven times greater in childbirth than in first trimester abortion. See note 46, supra.

59. Beal v. Doe, 432 U.S. 438, 446 (1977).

60. Maher v. Roe, 432 U.S. 464, 474 (1977). See also Poelker v. Doe, 432 U.S. 519 (1977) (per curiam), where the Court held that city-owned hospitals need not provide nontherapeutic abortion services, even in communities where the public hospital is the only health facility and the unavailability of abortion services may therefore create an insurmountable obstacle for women seeking abortions, without direct regard to their ability to pay. See id. at 524 (Marshall, J., joined by Brennan and Blackmun, JJ., dissenting). Cf. Akron, 462 U.S. at 49–51 (invalidating a 24-hour waiting period because of unconstitutional burden of potential scheduling delays and health risks due to extra travel by pregnant woman).

In reaching these holdings in *Maher v. Roe* [61] and *Harris v. Mc-Rae*,[62] a majority of the Court drew a distinction between direct state interference with a woman's freedom to choose, and whatever deterrence of the abortion choice results from a state's decision to pay for health care related to childbirth but to provide no analogous support for the same woman if she chooses to have an abortion.[63] Justice Stewart opined for the *McRae* majority that the funding restrictions "placed no obstacles—absolute or otherwise—in the pregnant woman's path to an abortion." [64] The barrier to an indigent woman's exercise of her right to choose was the price the medical market placed on the abortion procedure; and her inability to pay—whether attributable to sloth, misfortune, or the harsh realities of the marketplace—was certainly not attributable to the state. In this context, the state's decision to subsidize childbirth "may have made childbirth a more attractive alternative, thereby influencing the woman's decision, but it has imposed no restriction on abortions that was not already there." [65] The Court has thus allowed the state to influence with money the same decision that it is prohibited from influencing with information. There is a certain logic in all this: if the abortion choice is constitutionally private, why should the state be prevented from declining to make it a matter for public funding?

But this logic is far from inexorable. The government obviously has the constitutional *authority* to make abortion, like childbirth, available at no charge to the woman, either in a public facility or by public subsidy. The government's *affirmative* choice *not* to do so can fairly be characterized as a decision to enforce alienation of the woman's right to end her pregnancy, whether that alienation—or "waiver"—was brought about voluntarily (by the woman's failure to save money for an abortion), or involuntarily (by economic circumstances beyond her control).[66] After all, the unavailability of abortion to such a woman follows from her lack of funds only by virtue of the government's quite conscious decision to treat that medical procedure in particular as a purely private commodity available only to those who can pay the market price. The constitutionality of that decision is rendered dubious by the government's simultaneous decision to take *childbirth* procedures for the same poor women *off* the private market: the result, as Justice Stevens put it, is a government program that self-consciously "require[s] the expenditure of millions and millions of dollars in order to thwart the exercise of a constitutional right. . . ." [67] The state's position with respect to reproductive

61. 432 U.S. 464 (1977).

62. 448 U.S. 297 (1980).

63. See McRae, 448 U.S. at 314 (citing Maher, 432 U.S. at 475–76). At no point has the Court suggested, however, that unrelated public benefits—food stamps, say, or public housing or blood transfusions—could be withheld from a woman simply because she had elected an abortion. See § 11–5, supra.

64. Id.

65. Id.

66. See Tribe, "The Abortion Funding Conundrum: Inalienable Rights, Affirmative Duties, and the Dilemma of Dependence," 99 Harv.L.Rev. 330, 334–36 (1985).

67. McRae, 448 U.S. at 356 (Stevens, J., dissenting).

rights—rights it is bound to respect—is therefore neither as neutral nor as passive as a majority of the Court supposed in *Maher* and *McRae*.

The current state of constitutional law on abortion, as described above, is obviously not the product of merely one or two perhaps aberrational Supreme Court decisions. It is instead a sophisticated albeit controversial body of doctrine generated by fifteen years of decisions defending the rule announced in *Roe v. Wade*. In 1983, in *Akron v. Akron Center for Reproductive Health*,[68] the Court made a point of enumerating the "especially compelling reasons for adhering to *stare decisis* in applying the principles of *Roe v. Wade*":

> That case was considered with special care. It was first argued during the 1971 Term, and reargued—with extensive briefing—the following Term. The decision was joined by the Chief Justice and six other Justices. Since *Roe* was decided in January 1973, the Court repeatedly and consistently has accepted and applied the basic principle that a woman has a fundamental right to make the highly personal choice whether or not to terminate her pregnancy.

It would be a mistake, however, to assume that this commitment to procreative freedom has secured an unassailable niche in our constitutional order. The margin by which the Justices endorse the principles of *Roe v. Wade* has gradually shrunk from the original 7 to 2 to a more precarious 5 to 4.[69] And the arguments advanced in dissent often concern not disagreement with the fine-tuning of abortion regulations,[70] but diametrical opposition to the central premise of reproductive autonomy.[71] That position, in turn, cannot readily be distinguished from a

---

68. 462 U.S. 416, 420 n.1 (1983).

69. Justice Stewart, who had dissented in Griswold v. Connecticut, 381 U.S. 479 (1965), concurred in Roe v. Wade, accepting the majority opinion as part of a "rational continuum" of cases in which the Court strictly scrutinized infringements of fundamental liberties guaranteed by the fourteenth amendment. 410 U.S. at 169–70. Although he wrote the opinion of the Court upholding state refusals to fund even therapeutic abortions, Harris v. McRae, 448 U.S. 297 (1980), Justice Stewart otherwise consistently voted to uphold a woman's freedom to choose. Justice Stewart's seat on the Court was taken in 1981 by Justice O'Connor, who dissented on the merits in Akron v. Akron Center for Reproductive Health, 462 U.S. 416 (1983), and its sister cases. This reduced the margin to 6 to 3. (Justice O'Connor also dissented in Thornburgh on the ground that the posture of the case precluded consideration of the merits of the challenged regulations.)

Chief Justice Burger, who concurred in Roe v. Wade, 410 U.S. at 208, continued to join the majority until the decision in Thornburgh v. American College of Obstetricians & Gynecologists, 106 S.Ct. 2169 (1986), from which he dissented on the ground that the Court had simply gone too far toward accepting a claim of abortion on demand. Id. at 2190. See Roe v. Wade, 410 U.S. at 208 (Burger, C.J., concurring) ("Plainly, the Court today rejects any claim that the Constitution requires abortion on demand."). This made the vote in Thornburgh 5 to 4. When Justice Rehnquist was elevated to the Chief Justice's chair in 1986, his own seat was taken by Justice Scalia, who was expected to be unsympathetic to "non-textual" claims of fundamental rights.

70. Compare the dissenting opinions of Chief Justice Burger and Justice O'Connor, discussed in note 69, supra.

71. Justices White and Rehnquist, the dissenters in Roe v. Wade, dissented in Thornburgh as well, renewing their attack on the premise that the right to choose abortion is a "fundamental liberty." 106 S.Ct. at 2194. Justice White wrote that the state's interest in protecting fetal life should not be limited to that period when the fetus could survive outside the womb, because fetal survival is contingent on the state of medical technology, which is itself "morally and constitutionally irrelevant." Id. at 2197. He asserted that the abortion decision involves the termination of a life, and therefore should not be accorded the same constitutional protection as other de-

frontal assault on the Supreme Court's half-century old privacy jurisprudence.[72]

Critics of the Court's abortion decisions occasionally express some misgivings even about *Griswold v. Connecticut*[73] but more commonly approve that holding and seek to draw the line there,[74] believing that the government's "general obligation to protect life"[75] can reasonably be thought to extend to the human fetus "from the moment of conception."[76] Even if drawing such a line is problematic from a biological perspective,[77] it must be conceded that it reflects an entirely intelligible moral impulse. We began, after all, from a perspective that attached special significance to child-bearing autonomy—a perspective that treated the decision whether to bear a child as vastly more fundamentally personal and significant to the individual than the decision whether, say, to undergo plastic surgery or get a haircut. Given that starting point, it is disingenuous to think of the fetus, at *any* stage of its development, as "simply a group of specialized cells" differing in no material way from any other part of the woman's anatomy.[78] And it demeans the value and dignity of all human life, fetal or adult, to refer to a fetus—to that which would become a human being—as "the products of conception." Nor can one get anywhere on this issue by debating whether "fetal life" is "human life": what other form or

cisions about family and procreation. Id. at 2195–97.

72. A few weeks after he filed his dissent in Thornburgh, Justice White delivered the opinion of the Court in Bowers v. Hardwick, 106 S.Ct. 2841 (1986), where a five-member majority held that the Constitution allows states to invade private bedrooms to criminalize consensual, adult sexual intimacies whenever a majority of a state's legislature decrees that those private acts offend public morality. The centerpiece of Justice White's opinion was the proposition that the Court must "[s]trive[ ] to assure itself and the public that announcing rights not readily identifiable in the Constitution's text involves much more than the imposition of the Justices' own choice of values. . . ." Id. at 2844. See § 5–21, infra.

73. 381 U.S. 479 (1965). See, e.g., Ely, "The Wages of Crying Wolf: A Comment on Roe v. Wade," 82 Yale L.J. 920, 928–29 (1973). The most extreme view is that of Judge Robert Bork, to the effect that the entire line of cases from Meyer v. Nebraska, 262 U.S. 390 (1923), through Griswold and all of its progeny, is constitutionally unprincipled and illegitimate. Bork, "Neutral Principles and Some First Amendment Problems," 47 Ind.L.J. 1, 7–12 (1971).

74. See, e.g., Wellington, "Common Law Rules and Constitutional Double Standards: Some Notes on Adjudication," 83 Yale L.J. 221, 285–311 (1973).

75. Wade, 410 U.S. at 150.

76. Id. at 131. For an interesting but problematic argument that, even if the fetus were to be deemed a full human being throughout pregnancy, the woman would have a moral right to abort, see Thomson, "A Defense of Abortion," 1 Phil. & Pub.Aff. 47 (1971).

77. "Substantial problems for precise definition . . . are posed . . . by new embryological data that purport to indicate that conception is a 'process' over time, rather than an event, and by new medical techniques such as menstrual extraction, the 'morning-after' pill, implantation of embryos, artificial insemination, and even artificial wombs." Roe v. Wade, 410 U.S. at 161. Deeming the "moment of conception" to be the time that the sperm penetrates and fertilizes the egg, for example, would, in conjunction with a requirement to protect embryonic life from that moment on, effectively outlaw such common contraceptive devices as the IUD, which is believed to operate by interfering with implantation of a fertilized egg in the uterine lining. Contraceptive advances subsequent to Roe v. Wade raise additional problems for the purported distinction between contraception and abortion. See, e.g., Kaye, "Are you For RU–486?," The New Republic, Jan 27, 1986, at 13 (oral drug that induces miscarriage several days after conception).

78. Guttmacher, Symposium, "Law, Morality, and Abortion," 22 Rutgers L.Rev. 415, 436 (1968).

species of life could it be? There is simply no intellectually honest way of getting around the fact that the interest in preserving the life of a fetus is significant.[79] Therefore, holding that the woman's right to decide whether to give birth is a fundamental aspect of her liberty does not preclude the possibility that the state's interest in saving the fetus might override the woman's claim.[80]

Although the Court in *Roe v. Wade* spoke at length about the profound divisions in society on the question of what significance to attach to the interest in fetal life and when to attach it,[81] and made much of the fact that the challenged laws were for the most part enacted less out of concern with the fetus than out of a no-longer warranted concern with the woman's health,[82] nothing in the Supreme Court's opinion provides a satisfactory explanation of why the fetal interest should not be deemed overriding prior to viability,[83] particularly when a legislative majority chooses to regard the fetus as a human being from the moment of conception [84] and perhaps even when it does not.[85]

Suggestions have been advanced that the interest in fetal life is intrinsically religious,[86] or at least that the inescapable involvement of

79. One otherwise plausible defense of the Court's decision, see Heymann & Barzelay, "The Forest and the Trees: Roe v. Wade and its Critics," 53 B.U.L.Rev. 765 (1973), asserts that—but does not explain why—the Court was "surely . . . right," id. at 776, to hold that the interest in the fetus is "not . . . overriding" until well into pregnancy. Critics, on the other hand, who experience difficulty even at the threshold level of finding a fundamental right on the woman's part—"[t]he Constitution has little to say about contract [and] less about abortion," Ely, supra note 73, at 939—and who therefore think that the state need discharge no special burden of justifying coercive intervention in the woman's bodily and reproductive liberty, id. at 926, must be adopting a vastly more limited concept of "liberty" than any Supreme Court majority has embraced at least since the 1890's. To be sure, the state can "prohibit killing [dogs even] in the exercise of the First Amendment right of political protest." Id. But the obvious difference is that a fundamental liberty of protest *need not* entail killing anything; a woman's fundamental liberty of reproductive autonomy and bodily integrity *necessarily* collides with fetal survival prior to viability: that is what the dispute is all about.

80. In 1975, the Federal Constitutional Court of the Federal Republic of Germany noted that a woman's right to self-determination was guaranteed by article 2 of the German Constitution, which protects "the free development of her personality," but that the "human dignity" clause of article 1 and the "right to life" clause of article 2

combined to require that fetal life take precedence over the rights of the pregnant woman. Judgment of Feb. 25, 1975, 39 BVerfG 1, 42–43. See note 99, infra.

81. 410 U.S. at 156–62.

82. Id. at 148–49, 151–52, 163.

83. All the Court says on that subject is that "the 'compelling' point is at viability . . . because the fetus then presumably has the capability of meaningful life outside the womb." Wade, 410 U.S. at 163. As John Ely aptly put it, this "seems to mistake a definition for a syllogism." Ely, supra note 73, at 924.

84. See, e.g., Rhode Island Senate Bill 73–S287 Substitute A, March 13, 1973, declaring that "Human life commences at the instant of conception. . . ."

85. Given the Court's essential endorsement of the view that restrictive abortion statutes were by and large enacted out of an "interest in protecting the woman's health rather than protecting the embryo and fetus," Wade, 410 U.S. at 151, it would have been possible for the Court to hold, as it did in the context of gender discrimination in Califano v. Goldfarb, 430 U.S. 199 (1977), discussed in Chapter 16, infra, that an otherwise impermissible violation of fourteenth amendment rights cannot be rescued with a justification supplied purely as an afterthought. Yet such a holding in this context would plainly have seemed hypertechnical to anyone convinced that the unborn have rights.

86. Chief Justice Weintraub of New Jersey wrote in his dissent in Gleitman v. Cosgrove, 49 N.J. 22, 59, 227 A.2d 689, 709

religious groups in the debate over abortion rendered the subject inappropriate for political resolution and hence proper only for decision by the woman herself.[87] But, on reflection, that view appears to give too little weight to the value of allowing religious groups freely to express their convictions in the political process,[88] underestimates the power of moral convictions unattached to religious beliefs on this issue, and makes the unrealistic assumption that a constitutional ruling could somehow disentangle religion from future public debate on the question.[89]

It has also been proposed that restrictions on the woman's decision to terminate a pregnancy are unconstitutional when they reflect "merely" a moral, as opposed to an instrumental or utilitarian, justification.[90] But *all* normative judgments are rooted in moral premises; surely the judgment that it is wrong to kill a two-week old infant is no less "moral" in inspiration than the judgment, less frequently made but no less strongly felt by many of those who make it, that it is wrong to kill a two-day old fetus.[91] Archibald Cox seems correct, therefore, when he concludes that *Roe v. Wade* must be wrong if it rests on the premise that a state can never interfere with individual decisions relating to sex or procreation "with only moral justification." [92] But it is clear that

(1967) ("wrongful life" action), that "[c]ontraception and abortion have this in common, that . . . here there is evil or none at all depending wholly upon a spiritual supposition, for while men agree it is wrong to take life, yet knowing nothing about the void before or after their earthly presence, they cannot agree upon the point at which a living thing should be thought to be human in its being." And the only American court that appears to have squarely confronted the argument that anti-abortion laws in effect "establish" religion accepted the argument with remarkable ease. People v. Robb (Orange Cty.Mun. Ct., Central Orange Cty.Jud.Dist., Calif., 1970) (Mast, J.) For a general analysis of such arguments, see § 14–12, supra.

87. See L. Tribe, "The Supreme Court, 1972 Term—Foreword: Toward a Model of Roles in the Due Process of Life and Law," 87 Harv.L.Rev. 1, 21–25 (1973).

88. See Chapter 14, infra. This 1973–1978 shift in the author's thinking has been both criticized, see Law, "Rethinking Sex and the Constitution," 132 U.Pa.L.Rev. 955, 1025–26 & n.249 (1984), and supported, see McDaniel v. Paty, 435 U.S. 618, 641–42 n.25 (1978) (Brennan, J., concurring in the judgment) (quoting the first edition of this treatise).

89. Witness, for example, the frequent injection of the abortion issue into the 1976 and 1984 presidential campaigns. Yet there may be some value in channeling public debate into the merits of a constitutional amendment, as the holdings in the abortion cases have to some extent.

90. See, e.g., Henkin, "Privacy and Autonomy," 74 Colum.L.Rev. 1410, 1432 (1974); see also Henkin, "Morals and the Constitution: The Sin of Obscenity," 63 Colum.L.Rev. 391 (1963).

91. The distinction between utilitarian or "preference counting" justifications on the one hand, and moral or "ideal" justifications on the other, is not as clear as one might think. Compare R. Dworkin, Taking Rights Seriously 232–278, 357–58 (rev.ed. 1978); Dworkin, "The Forum of Principle," 56 N.Y.U.L.Rev. 469, 513–14 (1981), with Ely, "Professor Dworkin's External/Personal Preference Distinction," 1983 Duke L.J. 959. See § 15–4, supra, note 7. In either case, whether arguments for protecting fetal life are predicated on government power to create a just society, or on government power to favor the external preferences of right-to-life advocates (and, perhaps, the imputed internal preferences of the unborn) over the preferences of those (pregnant and otherwise) who would favor women's autonomy, it remains the case that powerful values are aligned on *both* sides of the abortion debate. And that debate cannot be resolved in an illuminating manner by engaging philosophical machinery that discounts one set of values or the other. There is simply no way to avoid the tragic decisions that must be made.

92. A. Cox, The Role of the Supreme Court in American Government 113 (1976).

Roe v. Wade rests on no such premise. Although the matter is by far the most troublesome in modern constitutional law, the result in the abortion decision seems defensible on other grounds.

Initially, it is important to put in perspective the often-heard argument that the Court should have deferred to the political process.[93] "Tossing the problem back to the states . . . would do nothing more than delegate the fate of mothers and unborn children alike to shifting majorities in 50 legislatures. The rights of women would be trampled in some states; the rights of the unborn sacrificed in others. Regardless of whether one sides with the woman or the fetus—or denounces any approach to the abortion problem that pits pregnant women against their unborn children—treating the issue as one properly resolved by a legislative vote is the least legitimate alternative." [94] It is worth recalling Abraham Lincoln's warning, voiced on a previous occasion when the nation was deeply divided over a different issue of fundamental liberty, that the Union could not long endure "half slave and half free." [95]

The fatal flaw of this "legislative solution" argument is that it presumes that fundamental rights can properly be reduced to political interests. That may well be the case under a parliamentary government where the legislative will is supreme,[96] but it ignores the choice of a fundamentally different form of government that was made for our nation two centuries ago: "The very purpose of a Bill of Rights was to withdraw certain subjects from the vicissitudes of political controversy. . . . [F]undamental rights may not be submitted to vote; they depend on the outcome of no elections. . . ." [97] As in the case of racial segregation, it is often when public sentiment is most sharply divided that the independent judiciary plays its most vital national role in expounding and protecting constitutional rights.[98]

Even if judicial resolution of the issue were not mandated by our form of constitutional government, the political resolution argument fails on its own terms to decide the *substantive* issue: it says nothing at all about how a legislator *within* the political process, who is also bound

93. This position was advanced by the Solicitor General in his role as amicus curiae in Thornburgh v. American College of Obstetricians & Gynecologists, 106 S.Ct. 2169 (1986), and embraced by Justices White and Rehnquist in dissent in that case. The author of this treatise filed a brief amicus curiae on behalf of 81 members of Congress who disagreed with the Solicitor General's argument. See also H.J.Res. 527, which would have amended the Constitution to provide that nothing therein shall bar any state "from allowing, regulating, or prohibiting the practice of abortion."

94. Koukoutchos, "A No-Win Proposal on Abortion Rights," N.Y.Times, July 25, 1985, at A23, col. 1.

95. Speech in Springfield, Illinois (June 16, 1858).

96. See P. Norton, The Constitution in Flux 253 (1982) ("The primary argument against a Bill of Rights [for Great Britain] is that it would . . . remove from Parliament a decision-making capacity which rightly belongs to Parliament. Disputes as to encroachments on fundamental rights are essentially political disputes and must be resolved politically, not judicially.").

97. West Virginia Bd. of Education v. Barnette, 319 U.S. 624, 638 (1943).

98. As Chief Justice Warren wrote in Brown v. Board of Education (Brown II), 349 U.S. 294, 300 (1955), "[t]he vitality of . . . constitutional principles cannot be allowed to yield simply because of disagreement with them."

to observe the Constitution, should have acted. Nor does it say anything about whether the Supreme Court should have answered the
abortion question as it did rather than as the Federal Constitutional
Court of West Germany did when it struck down the abortion laws of
that nation as insufficiently protective of unborn life.[99]

The constitutional quandary presented by abortion involves two
central questions. First, what precisely is the right that is at stake for
the pregnant woman? Second, how is that right to be balanced against
the interest in preserving unborn life? *Roe v. Wade* answered the first
question in terms of the woman's right to privacy, a fundamental right
recognized in a half century of prior cases. This is something of a
misnomer: what is truly implicated in the decision whether to abort or
to give birth is not privacy, but autonomy.[100] And the issue of individual autonomy—of control over one's body and reproductive destiny—is in
turn a question of power, pure and simple. *Roe v. Wade* was less a
judgment about the relative importance of maternal liberty and fetal
life, than it was a decision about *who* should make judgments of that
sort.[101] As in the original reproductive rights case, *Skinner v. Oklahoma*,[102] the Court affirmed the value of individual autonomy over the
virtue of collective choice and the prerogative of majoritarian coercion.

The plaintiff in *Roe v. Wade* also asserted an individual's right to
care for her own health and a physician's freedom to prescribe treatment without arbitrary interference by the government;[103] the decision
consequently seemed to cast the abortion issue in terms of the doctor-
patient relationship.[104] Since the Court has repeatedly reaffirmed that

99. On the petition of 193 members of
the German Federal Parliament (those
whc had been outvoted in 1974 when a
statute legalizing all first-trimester abortions was adopted in West Germany), the
West German Constitutional Court ruled,
by a vote of 6–2 (Feb. 25, 1975, 39BVerfGE
p. 1), that the State has an affirmative
duty to protect the unborn from abortion
by any person, at all stages of pregnancy,
at least from the 14th day after conception.
The Court then took the extraordinary
step of promulgating an interim penal
code, effective until the legislature should
enact valid provisions of its own, making
abortion a crime after the 14th day except
when continuation of the pregnancy would
gravely imperil the woman's life or health.
An English translation of the German
Court's decision, including the dissent, appears in 9 J.Mar.J. of Prac. & Proc. 605–84
(1976). See Annual Review of Population
Law, 1974, at 59 (Fletcher School of Law &
Diplomacy). Of the six major courts that
ruled on abortion statutes in 1973–75
(those of Austria, Canada, France, Italy,
West Germany, and the United States),
only the West German Court ruled that its
legislature had not gone far enough to protect unborn life; and only the American
Court ruled that abortion well beyond the
first trimester had to be left to personal

choice. For a summary of developments in
West German abortion law since 1975, see
Eser, "Reform of German Abortion Law:
First Experiences," 34 Am.J.Comp.L. 369,
374–80 (1986).

100. Justice Rehnquist's dissenting argument that no "right of 'privacy'" was
involved because a "transaction resulting
in an operation such as this is not 'private'
in the ordinary usage of that word," 410
U.S. at 172, is therefore nothing more than
a rhetorical joust. Justice Rehnquist went
on to argue that, if the Court instead
meant that a woman's "liberty" was impaired by the abortion ban, the appropriate
standard of judicial review was that traditionally applied to state economic regulations. Id. at 172–73.

101. See Tribe, "Foreword: Toward a
Model of Roles in the Due Process of Life
and Law," 87 Harv.L.Rev. 1, 11 (1973).

102. 316 U.S. 535 (1942).

103. See 410 U.S. at 120–22. Likewise,
the plaintiffs in Doe v. Bolton argued, inter
alia, that Georgia's abortion law infringed
the physician's right to practice medicine.

104. The Court held that leaving the
abortion issue to the physician's judgment
is tolerable, whereas officially empowering
hospital review committees to veto the

the decision belongs to the pregnant woman,[105] this choice of rhetoric should not be taken to mean too much. The nineteenth century laws struck down in *Roe v. Wade* had outlawed abortion in part because the procedure was at one time a serious threat to the life of the woman as well as the fetus,[106] and, since the case thus came before the Court in a medical context, the Court unsurprisingly employed the vocabulary characteristic to that field.[107]

The Court's apparent intuition that abortion rights are somehow grounded in *relational* concerns [108] is nonetheless correct—but the relevant relationships are not those between doctors and patients, but those between women and men, and between pregnant women and the fetuses they carry. The failure of both plaintiffs and courts to frame the abortion controversy in terms of sexual equality [109] has profoundly affected the law in this area. Having won abortion rights in *Roe v. Wade* in the name of abstract personal privacy, women were poorly situated in *Harris v. McRae* [110] to demand public funds for the exercise of such rights. Abortion has not been perceived by the Court as involving the intensely public question of the subordination of women to men through the exploitation of pregnancy.[111] The salient feature of government choices like the one struck down in *Roe v. Wade* and the

physician's choice is unconstitutionally intrusive. See Roe v. Wade, 410 U.S. at 164, 166; Doe v. Bolton, 410 U.S. at 197–99.

105. See, e.g., Planned Parenthood v. Danforth, 428 U.S. 52, 66 (1976) (requirement of informed consent was deemed constitutional because it "insures that the pregnant woman retains control over the discretions of her consulting physician.").

106. See 410 U.S. at 148–50. But see text at notes 125 & 126, infra.

107. Justice Blackmun, author of the opinion of the Court in Roe v. Wade, may have been predisposed to the medical approach to the issue by the fact that he spent a significant part of his private legal career as counsel to the Mayo Clinic. In general, courts have often displayed a distressing tendency to view issues of patients' rights in terms of the prerogatives of the medical profession, as if the latter were the sacrosanct privileges of a technological priesthood. For example, courts usually weigh a terminally ill patient's right to die against the state's countervailing interest in, among other things, maintaining the high purpose and ethical integrity of the medical profession. See § 15–11, infra at note 14.

108. See Tribe, "The Abortion Funding Conundrum: Inalienable Rights, Affirmative Duties, and the Dilemma of Dependence," 99 Harv.L.Rev. 330, 333–38 (1985).

109. The plaintiffs in Roe v. Wade and Doe v. Bolton did not challenge the abortion restrictions as a form of sex discrimination, and the Supreme Court did not rely upon the sex-specific impact of abortion

laws. Although hundreds of legal challenges to abortion laws have been brought since 1973, see generally Legal Docket, ACLU Reproductive Freedom Project, claims of gender equality have been raised only in a handful of lower courts, usually on the basis of equal rights amendments to state constitutions. See Law, "Rethinking Sex and the Constitution," 132 U.Pa.L.Rev. 955, 985–86 & n.115 (1984). The national ACLU's Reproductive Freedom Project has long pursued a policy of discouraging sex discrimination claims in abortion cases. But see Thornburgh, 106 S.Ct. at 2184–85: "Our cases have long recognized that the Constitution embodies a promise that a certain private sphere of individual liberty will be kept largely beyond the reach of government. That promise extends to women as well as men. Few decisions are more personal and intimate, more properly private, or more basic to individual dignity and autonomy, than a woman's decision . . . whether to end her pregnancy. A woman's right to make that choice freely is fundamental. Any other result, in our view, would protect inadequately a central part of the sphere of liberty that our law guarantees equally to all."

110. 448 U.S. 297 (1980).

111. See L. Tribe, Constitutional Choices 243–44 (1985). Nor has it been seen as implicating the equally public question of the subordination of the poor to the rich through the instrument of coerced childbirth for those unable to afford the medical procedures placed by the state on an ability-to-pay basis. Id.

one upheld in *McRae*—choices that leave some women with no alternative to continuing an unwanted pregnancy—is that they require those women to make affirmative use of their bodies for childbearing purposes. Such governmental choices require women to sacrifice their liberty in order to enable others to survive and grow in circumstances likely to create lifelong attachments and burdens.[112] A woman forced by law to submit to the pain and anxiety of carrying, delivering, and nurturing a child she does not wish to have is entitled to believe that more than a play on words links her forced labor with the concept of involuntary servitude.[113] To give society—especially a male-dominated society—the power to sentence women to childbearing against their will is to delegate to some a sweeping and unaccountable authority over the lives of others. Any such allocation of power operates to the serious detriment of women as a class, given the myriad ways in which unwanted pregnancy and unwanted children burden the participation of women as equals in society. Even a woman who is not pregnant is inevitably affected by her knowledge of the power relationships thereby created.

Even if we view pre-viable fetuses as full human beings, the intimate and personal sacrifice that a ban on abortion would impose by requiring pregnant women to nurture unborn life is one that our legal system almost never demands. The common law contains a deeply rooted principle that people are not required to aid others in distress, particularly when aid can be provided only at significant cost or risk to the rescuer.[114] And the law nowhere forces *men* to devote their bodies and restructure their lives even in those tragic situations (such as organ transplants) where nothing less will permit their children to survive. Yet those who would outlaw abortion (or who would refuse to fund it) would rely upon economic and physiological circumstances—the supposed dictates of nature [115]—to conscript women as involuntary incubators and thereby to usurp a control over sex and its consequences that men take for granted. A right to terminate one's pregnancy might therefore be seen more plausibly as a matter of resisting sexual and economic domination than as a matter of shielding "private" transactions between patients and physicians from public control. If this were seen to be the nature of the right at issue, then even the state's use of selective funding to "encourage" the birth of unwanted children might more closely resemble a program to foster involuntary servitude than an exercise of the state's prerogative to promote preferred values.

112. Although two-thirds of births to unmarried teenagers are unintended, 96% of unmarried teenage mothers keep their children. Alan Guttmacher Institute, Teenage Pregnancy: The Problem That Hasn't Gone Away (1981).

113. The thirteenth amendment's relevance is underscored by the historical parallel between the subjugation of women and the institution of slavery. See, e.g., Frontiero v. Richardson, 411 U.S. 677, 685 (1973) (Brennan, J., joined by Douglas, White, and Marshall, JJ.) ("throughout much of the nineteenth century the position of women in our society was in many respects comparable to that of blacks under the pre-Civil War slave codes.").

114. See Regan, "Rewriting Roe v. Wade," 77 Mich.L.Rev. 1569 (1979). See also Thompson, "A Defense of Abortion," 1 Phil. & Pub.Aff. 47 (1971).

115. See § 16–29, infra, for a discussion of the way courts confuse "nature" and "biology" with their legally and socially determined consequences.

Women are uniquely vulnerable to imposition of this burden of self-sacrifice on behalf of the unborn because women must call on others for assistance if they would choose not to make such a sacrifice. It is not as though, after engaging in sexual intercourse and conceiving a child, a woman could simply and safely decline, on her own, to put her life and liberty at risk in order to come to her fetus' rescue, the way a man could, for example, refuse to donate blood or a needed organ to save the life of a fetus he had voluntarily fathered. Since women and men are differently situated with respect to reproduction, it begs the question to say that a ban on abortion does not compel either gender to take any *affirmative* act to save a fetus, but at most compels one gender to *refrain* from extinguishing fetal life. If one recognizes, as the Supreme Court itself sometimes has, that "the grossest discrimination can lie in treating things that are different as though they were exactly alike," [116] then one may discern a constitutionally problematic subjugation of women in the law's *indifference* to the biological reality that sometimes requires women, but never men, to resort to abortion if they are to avoid pregnancy and retain control of their own bodies. [117] What are we to say when the state exploits this special vulnerability of women in a way that reinforces their subordination to men, and thus their lack of fully autonomous and equal roles in social, economic, and political life? [118] When this is the thrust of a regime of public law, all of the constitutional norms precluding legally reinforced subjugation come into play, leaving government with a duty to justify the resulting derogation of women's rights. [119]

That burden of justification would be particularly hard to meet with respect to the dozens of abortion laws rendered invalid by *Roe v. Wade*, because those laws were enacted in the late nineteenth century largely to keep women in their place. The first recorded convention on women's rights was held in 1848, and the following two decades were the most active period in the struggle for women's rights until modern times. [120] The Victorian reaction to the women's movement was a major motivation in the enactment of criminal restrictions on abortion. [121] In the final decades of the last century, abortions were no longer merely a solution to illegitimate or adulterous pregnancies; they were sought by "respectable" women as a means of limiting family size [122]—an obvious rebellion against the homemaker role industrial society sought to impose upon them. Demographic concerns also spurred the criminalization of abortion, as medical journals expressed alarm that birthrates were declining among white, Yankee Protestants—" 'our most intelli-

116. Jenness v. Fortson, 403 U.S. 431, 442 (1971).

117. See § 16–29, infra.

118. See Ginsburg, "Some Thoughts on Autonomy and Equality in Relation to Roe v. Wade," 63 N.C.L.Rev. 375, 383 & n.61 (1985) (stressing a woman's right to "autonomous charge of her full life's course" vis-a-vis man and society).

119. See §§ 16–27 to 16–29, infra.

120. See 1 E. Stanton, S. Anthony & M. Gage, History of Woman Suffrage 70–71 (1881).

121. L. Gordon, Women's Body, Women's Right: A Social History of Birth Control in America 414–18 (1976); J. Mohr, Abortion in America: The Origins and Evolution of National Policy 1800–1900, 168 (1978).

122. See L. Gordon, supra note 121, at 51–60; J. Mohr, supra note 121, at 46–50, 86–102.

gent communities' "—relative to the burgeoning ethnic, Catholic, and non-white populations.[123] Finally, the medical profession took the lead in lobbying to outlaw abortion, but apparently not primarily because the procedure was dangerous.[124] In fact, abortion was not criminalized until the advent of antisepsis made it possible for abortion and other surgical procedures to do the patient more good than harm.[125] The major motivation of Victorian physicians seems to have been the desire to suppress competition by midwives and the other irregular practitioners who performed most abortions and who were predominantly female.[126]

Even if undue legal restrictions on abortion are deemed to violate the Constitution by subordinating women to men, there remains the question of whether such subordination must be demanded as the price of avoiding the arguably greater constitutional offense of sacrificing the lives of unborn children. But even regarding the fetus as a person does not necessarily mean that abortion is murder. First, as previously discussed, the law generally does not require us to put ourselves at risk in order to save others—including our own children—even if most of us would denounce such a refusal. Second, terminating an unwanted pregnancy can plausibly be seen not as aggression against the fetus but as a defensive reaction. For, "[h]owever gratifying pregnancy may be to a woman who desires it, for the unwilling it is literally an invasion— the closest analogy is the difference between love-making and rape. . . .   [A]bortion is by normal standards an act of self-defense." [127]

The virtue of these perspectives is that they unabashedly confront the full power of arguments in favor of protecting fetal life. But the ways in which they justify abortion are extraordinarily disturbing. In the first instance a fetus is depicted as a child trapped within a burning building and abortion is defended as a parent's entirely legal refusal to risk the harms entailed in coming to the child's aid. In the second, the fetus is likened to a marauding Hun and abortion is portrayed as a sort of defensive preemptive strike; it does not help matters any that this "invader" whose death we would justify is in fact an innocent party who does not threaten the mother's life or liberty out of choice.

The underlying problem with both approaches is that they seek to fit the relationship between a pregnant woman and the fetus she carries into the pigeonholes framed to deal with other problems in the law. We do not get much farther by comparing abortion to a nonculpable omission or a justifiable homicide than we would by analogies to property law that might try to place a fetus within a

123. L. Gordon, supra note 121, at 138; see also J. Mohr, supra note 121, at 166–67.

124. But cf. Roe v. Wade, 410 U.S. at 148–50 (abortion outlawed in part to protect pregnant women from medical procedures that "placed her life in serious jeopardy").

125. Compare P. Starr, The Social Transformation of American Medicine 156–57 (1982) (improvements in surgery and antiseptic technique) with J. Mohr, supra note 121, at 200–25 (criminalization of abortion).

126. See J. Mohr, supra note 121, at 147–70; L. Gordon, supra note 121, at 59– 60.

127. Willis, "Abortion: Is a Woman a Person?," in Powers of Desire: The Politics of Sexuality 473 (A. Snitow, C. Stansell & S. Thompson ed. 1983).

framework of uterine invitees, licensees, and trespassors. The relationship of woman and fetus is unique; it requires a unique legal analysis. As Professor Sylvia Law has written:

> Fetal life is starkly different from all other forms of human life in that the fetus is completely dependent upon the body of the woman who conceived it. It cannot survive without her. Although all human infants, and many adults, are dependent upon others for survival, that support can be provided by many people. The fetus by contrast is dependent upon a particular woman.[128]

This unique characteristic of fetal life justifies the line that the Supreme Court has drawn between a woman's freedom to abort and the state's authority to protect a fetus.[129]   Until the fetus is viable, *only* the pregnant woman can respond to and support her fetus' "right" to life; during this period, the state cannot abridge the woman's autonomy. But once the fetus "has the capability of meaningful life outside the mother's womb" [130]—that is, once the responsibility for the nurture that is essential to life can be assumed by others with the aid of medical technology—the state may limit abortions so long as it poses no danger to the woman's life or health.

Justice White is thus surely mistaken when he argues that fetal viability and the state of medical technology are "morally and constitutionally irrelevant." [131]   It is the lack of viability that makes the fetus a unique human phenomenon justifying a unique rule of law; viability constitutes nothing less than the operative fact that makes a fetus like other human beings, and that therefore requires that a fetus be accorded state protection similar to that accorded the rest of humanity. Likewise, Justice O'Connor is wide of the mark when she deems it an egregious flaw that the "*Roe* framework . . . is clearly on a collision course with itself. . . .   As medical science becomes better able to provide for the separate existence of the fetus, the point of viability is moved further back toward conception." [132]   That is precisely the point: as technology enhances the ability to relieve the pregnant woman of

---

128. Law, "Rethinking Sex and the Constitution," 132 U.Pa.L.Rev. 955, 1023 (1984).

129. Roe v. Wade, 410 U.S. at 163.

130. Id.

131. Thornburgh v. American College of Obstetricians & Gynecologists, 106 S.Ct. 2169, 2197 (1986) (dissenting opinion). Elsewhere in his dissent, Justice White makes much of the fact that, because a fetal life is at stake, the abortion "decision must be recognized as *sui generis*, different in kind from the others the Court has protected under the rubric of personal or family privacy and autonomy." Id. at 2195. That is certainly true enough, although it does not dictate the balance that must still be struck between fetal life and maternal health and liberty. But it is noteworthy that Justice White fails to see how fetal life itself is also *sui generis*, since

its continued existence requires an enormous sacrifice by another—and only *one* other—human being.

132. Akron v. Akron Center for Reproductive Health, 462 U.S. 416, 458 (1983) (dissenting opinion). Justice O'Connor further opined that collision was imminent, since "fetal viability in the first trimester of pregnancy may be possible in the not too distant future." Id. In fact, the evidence offered by the Justice does not support her claim, and the experts on whose articles she relied have emphatically disavowed her conclusions. See Law, supra note 128, at 1023–24 n.245. In any event, the Court has always understood that its analysis is contingent on the state of the medical arts. See, e.g. Colautti v. Franklin, 439 U.S. 379, 387 (1979) (Roe v. Wade left viability "flexible for anticipated advancements in medical skill").

the burden of her pregnancy and transfer nurture of the fetus to other hands, the state's power to protect fetal life expands—*as it should*. A viability rule thus allows society to optimize the protection of women *and* their unborn children by choosing how much to invest in the technologies pushing viability toward conception.[133]

Underlying the result in *Roe v. Wade* is a conviction that the safety and liberty of a life in being are of greater constitutional value than the protection of nonviable fetal life. Fetal claims to society's compassion and sustenance—like the claims of infants, indigents, and the infirm— are powerful both morally and legally. But, unlike the others who lay claim to society's resources, "the sustenance the [nonviable] fetus needs is not society's to give. It can only be provided by a particular pregnant woman."[134] Compelling *her* to nurture the dependent fetus forecloses her freedom to decide whether that is a relationship she can and will sustain, and imposes enormous costs on her life, health, and autonomy. Respect for the fetus may not be bought by denying the value of the woman.[135]

The fact that this resolution of competing rights is less than perfectly satisfying—that it requires the subordination of some claims to others—does not mean that it is wrong. To assume that even the most fundamental conflicts of moral and legal principles can be resolved under the Constitution without any compromise and without any pain, remorse or regret is to indulge an insufficiently tragic view of both life and law. Nor does the fact that the argument in favor of the result in *Roe v. Wade* cannot be concluded with a brisk Q.E.D. show that the result is wrong or that any alternative resolution would have been more principled or more just. One cannot establish the constitutional legitimacy of protecting fetal life at the expense of women's lives and liberty simply by demonstrating that the compromise wrought in *Roe v. Wade* is an uneasy one. And one certainly cannot justify relegating the controversy to legislative tie-breakers in fifty statehouses by the utterly jejune observation that the issue is destined to be difficult and divisive. This sort of democratic default is wholly inappropriate in this context because "[a]bortion is not merely a policy choice; it lies at the intersection of powerful conflicting rights. [And] [f]undamental rights, unlike liquor regulations or traffic laws, should not vary from state to state."[136]

Those who criticize the importance the Supreme Court places on fetal viability are nonetheless correct in their recognition that improvements and innovations in medical technology may pose problems for the Court's theory of abortion rights. Questions that require no answer in current

---

133. See Tribe, "Structural Due Process," 10 Harv.C.R.-C.L.L.Rev. 269, 297–98 (1975). The state also retains many options for minimizing the conflict between maternal and fetal rights, whether by averting the tragic choice by providing better sex education and making contraception universally available, or by making unplanned pregnancies easier for women to want or to bear by providing improved prenatal care and increasing funding for programs that support women and their children. See Tribe, "The Abortion Funding Conundrum: Inalienable Rights, Affirmative Duties, and the Dilemma of Dependence," 99 Harv.L.Rev. 330, 341 (1985).

134. Law, supra note 128, at 1027.

135. Id.

136. Koukoutchos, "A No-Win Proposal on Abortion Rights," N.Y.Times, July 25, 1985, at A23, col. 1.

circumstances will become ripe for resolution if and when fetal viability is pushed into the early months of pregnancy. For example, current doctrine tends to blur the distinction between a woman's right to control her own body and a woman's right to control her reproductive destiny. Under the current state of both law and medicine, both rights may be furthered by the woman in the same way: deciding between childbirth and abortion. And both rights must be respected by the state in the same way: the decision whether to abort or to give birth must be left up to the pregnant woman. But what of the day when even the youngest fetus can safely be removed to another woman's womb or to some artificial incubator by a procedure no more threatening to the pregnant woman's well-being than that used to accomplish an abortion? In that instance, the woman's right to terminate her pregnancy and the fetus' right to life may be vindicated simultaneously. But the woman would no longer have complete control over her reproductive destiny, since her body would be the source of a new life she may not have wished to come into being. In order to vindicate *that* right, may a pregnant woman insist not only that the unwanted fetus be removed from her body, but also that it be killed? Apart from the problematic character of any claim in behalf of such a right,[137] its recognition and enforcement would be indistinguishable from licensing infanticide.[138]

Recognition of a true right to decide whether one's body shall be the source of another life would also be problematic on equal protection grounds, since such a right cannot be recognized in a man without empowering him to compel the abortion of any fetus conceived with his sperm—something forbidden under the Court's current doctrine.

Not all of these problems need to be puzzled out now. Indeed, one criticism of *Roe v. Wade* is that the Court went too far too fast in answering questions unnecessary to resolution of the case before it, which implicated plaintiff Roe's claim—retracted in 1987—that she had been impregnated during a gang-rape;[139] the Court could therefore have found principled reasons for striking down application of Texas' flat ban on abortion in those circumstances without reaching beyond the facts of the case to rank the rights of the mother categorically over those of the fetus and to delineate a framework for review of all abortion regulations. The Court might thereby have achieved more in the long run with less injury both to itself and to the sensibilities of those whose perspectives it appeared to ignore.[140]

---

137. See Tribe, "Foreword: Toward a Model of Roles in the Due Process of Life and Law," 87 Harv.L.Rev. 1, 4 & n.24 (1973).

138. See id. at 27–28. This quandary already exists to whatever extent abortion procedures used after viability present the same risks to the woman whether the removed fetus is saved or destroyed. The Court appears, perhaps inadvertently, to have recognized this, since the Court has upheld a requirement that a second physician be present during post-viability abortions to provide additional protection for the life of the fetus, so long as there is a medical emergency exception to ensure that attention to the fetus is not bought at the price of increased risk to the mother's health. Planned Parenthood of Kansas City v. Ashcroft, 462 U.S. 476, 485 n.8 (1983).

139. See L. Tribe, God Save This Honorable Court 16 (1985).

140. See Freund, "Storms Over the Supreme Court," 69 A.B.A.J. 1474, 1480 (1983).

Yet some of the questions raised by new reproductive technologies not only loom on the horizon, they are already in our midst. May a state impose responsibility for a child conceived by artificial insemination on the man who made the donation to a sperm bank? If such a child develops an hereditary disease, does it violate the donor's privacy if the state requires the sperm bank to reveal his identity to the parents and physicians of the child? Must a surrogate mother assume responsibility for her baby if those who contracted for the child decide not to accept it? If a surrogate mother refuses to give up her baby as promised, are her maternal rights violated if the state steps in to snatch the infant from her embrace? And, in the latter two cases, does it matter whether the child is genetically half hers or was gestated from an ovum and sperm taken from other parties?

The heavily publicized case of Baby "M" [141] illustrates the difficulty of the questions posed and the indeterminacy (and inadequacy) of current doctrine. Is there a constitutional right to procreate when reproduction can be achieved only by use of the genetic material or body of a third party? The Baby "M" court held that, since "a woman with her husband has the right to procreate and rear a family," the "means to do so can be withheld from them only on the showing of a compelling state interest." [142] The court perceived authority for this proposition in *Roe v. Wade*'s defense of abortion rights, on the opaque reasoning that, "[i]f the law of our land sanctions a means to end life, then that same law may be used to create and celebrate life." [143] But *Roe v. Wade* does not require any showing of a compelling justification for a state decision to withhold from would-be parents the *financial* means necessary for in vitro fertilization or artificial insemination, at least not in the wake of *Harris v. McRae*.[144] Nor do the holdings in the abortion and contraception cases automatically entitle infertile couples (or individual men and women, fertile or infertile) [145] to buy genetic material from others or to contract for gestation "services." [146] The Baby "M" court nevertheless endorsed just such a freedom of contract on the basis of a single citation to *Lochner v. New York*! [147]

---

141. In the Matter of Baby "M," 217 N.J.Super. 313, 525 A.2d 1128 (1987).

142. 525 A.2d at 1165. See also Note, "Redefining Mother: A Legal Matrix for New Reproductive Technologies," 96 Yale L.J. 187, 199 (1986) (state regulations that effectively prohibit procreation by surrogate motherhood should be subject to strict scrutiny).

143. 525 A.2d at 1164.

144. 448 U.S. 297 (1980). Even if McRae is wrong, Roe v. Wade hardly supports a right to have the state help one to produce genetic offspring.

145. See Note, "Reproductive Technology and the Procreative Rights of the Unmarried," 98 Harv.L.Rev. 669 (1985).

146. See Doe v. Kelley, 106 Mich.App. 169, 307 N.W.2d 438, 441 (1981) (state may forbid the exchange of money for a promise

to change the adoptive legal status of a child, because the fundamental right to bear and beget does not extend to contract and compensation in surrogate motherhood), cert. denied 459 U.S. 1183 (1983). Only Justice Brennan would have granted the writ.

147. 198 U.S. 45 (1905), discussed in Chapter 8, supra. See In the Matter of Baby "M", 217 N.J.Super. 313, 525 A.2d 1128, 1165 (1987). The court also asserted that, because sperm donation "is legally recognized in all states," a "woman must equally be allowed" to "offer the means for procreation," id.— that is, to sell her ova or rent her uterus. On the basis of this incredibly shallow and cursory analysis, the court concluded that a refusal to sanction and enforce womb-for-rent contracts would somehow "den[y] equal protection of the law to the childless couple, the surro-

If we are to make our way in this brave new world of reproductive technology, the courts must provide far better guidance than this. For in the context of test tube babies and other marvels of modern medicine, Justice Brandeis' oft-quoted statement about the virtues of the states as "laborator[ies]" engaged in "novel . . . experiments" [148] takes on a sobering and decidedly *non*-metaphorical significance.[149] Yet even the most basic issues have failed to receive adequate judicial attention. The sale of sperm or ova is not unlike the sale of blood or body parts, things the state is free to elevate above the status of commodities. Nor is the payment of money to a woman for gestating and handing over a child—whether or not the child is linked to her by chromosomes as well as an umbilical cord—totally unlike baby-selling, another practice the state is free to forbid.[150] Indeed, the states might well be *compelled* by the thirteenth amendment to outlaw any exchange of a human being for money. And the opportunities for exploitation of women created by legal concubinage are obvious. The fact that a surrogate mother might wish to provide her services to a childless couple does not necessarily require the state to sanction the arrangement: many prostitutes are no doubt willing, too. Nor does the possibility that surrogacy deals may genuinely enhance the lives of both surrogates and infertile couples automatically require the state to include such deals within the realm of protected privacy: the sale of "spare" kidneys or other transplantable organs might also optimize utility in many instances. And there is the imponderable impact on the child of knowing that she or he was conceived to be sold.

The foregoing discussion reveals that much of what is at stake with new methods of reproduction is not new at all: the possibility of abuse and exploitation, especially of women, and perhaps of babies. As one observer has pointed out, "a maternity contract is not a scientific development; it is a piece of paper. Physically . . . it involves merely artificial insemination, a centuries-old technique which requires a device no more complicated than a turkey baster. And artificial insemination itself is a social contrivance, the purpose of which is to avert not infertility but infidelity. What is new about contract motherhood lies

gate whether male or female, and the unborn child." Id.

148. New State Ice Co. v. Liebmann, 285 U.S. 262, 311 (1932) (dissenting opinion).

149. See Attanasio, "The Constitutionality of Regulating Human Genetic Engineering: Where Procreative Liberty and Equal Opportunity Collide," 53 U.Chi.L. Rev. 1274 (1986).

150. The Baby "M" court stated that the money paid to the surrogate mother was compensation not for the surrender of the child, but solely for "her willingness to be impregnated and carry [the] child to term." In the Matter of Baby "M", 217 N.J.Super. 313, 525 A.2d 1128, 1157 (1987). It was said that since the child was the contracting man's biological daughter as

much as she was the surrogate mother's, the father "cannot purchase what is already his." Id. This exclusive focus on the father is misleading, to say the least. The surrogacy contract clearly required the complete renunciation by the natural mother of her parental rights, just as adoption agreements do. Since the payment of money in exchange for that renunciation is outlawed in the context of adoption, it is not clear why it should be permitted in the context of a surrogacy arrangement. The court's assertion that statutes concerning adoption and the termination of parental rights were not enacted with surrogacy arrangements in mind, id. at 1157–58, is hardly a sufficient explanation for its failure to consider the relevance of the principles underlying the statutory ban on paying to obtain a child.

in the realm of law and social custom." [151]　The law, as shaped by both courts and legislatures, must determine how new phenomena and the new (as well as old) problems they create are to be woven into the fabric of public and private life.　At the most elementary level, we will need a new nomenclature that better describes the genetic and biological links between one generation and the next while also reflecting, as faithfully as possible, the emotional and psychological ties that truly bind "mom" and "dad" to their "sons" and "daughters."　For example, if a woman who gestates for another couple has herself contributed an egg to the child that grows in her womb—and perhaps even if she has not—it seems more than passing strange to refer to her as a "surrogate mother," since the child she carries is very much hers.　As medical science compels—or does it merely tempt?—us to redefine parenthood,[152] the challenge confronting the law is to avoid the degradation of personhood and the debasement of birth by treating it as a matter of contract and technology rather than as a celebration of life and continuity.[153]

§ 15–11.　Governmental Control Over the Body:　Decisions About Death and Dying

The interest in "death with dignity" and in the idea of the "living will" is perhaps best understood as resting on a belief analogous to, but even more fundamental than, the conviction of a couple that the birth of their child should not be debased by its treatment as a medical episode.[1]　In the context of birth, the state can at least attempt to interpose a countervailing concern for the health of the newborn child; if evidence can in fact be adduced to show that the child is at significantly greater risk outside the hospital environment, the state's power to protect children from abuse at the hands of their parents [2] might well suffice to overcome the parental claim.　But in the context

---

151.　Pollitt, "The Strange Case of Baby M," The Nation, May 23, 1987, at 683.

152.　See generally Note, "Redefining Mother: A Legal Matrix for New Reproductive Technologies," 96 Yale L.J. 187 (1986).

153.　In Fitzgerald v. Porter Memorial Hospital, 523 F.2d 716 (7th Cir.1975), then Judge Stevens authored a decision rejecting a married couple's challenge to a public hospital's rule against the presence of husbands in delivery rooms.　The couple had prepared for childbirth by the LaMaze method, which requires the participation of the man during delivery.　In holding that the couple stated no claim for relief, Judge Stevens stressed the couple's acknowledgement that their asserted right was "subordinate to the dictates of sound medical practice" inasmuch as they agreed that, absent the "consent of the attending physician," they had no right to proceed with the husband present.　Id. at 721.　Having reduced their claim to one about *whose* medical judgment should be decisive—that

of the doctor or that of the hospital staff— the couple plainly took themselves beyond the reach of any plausible rule grounded in a personal right to make intimate choices about how to bring one's child into the world.　A different case—perhaps involving a claim of right to give birth at home rather than in a hospital—would squarely present the question whether the state's insistence on medical precautions should be allowed to override the belief that the birth of a human being is demeaned when treated primarily as a matter of medicine.

§ 15–11

1.　See § 15–10, supra, at note 153.　For a useful overview of the issues, the secondary literature and the cases in the "right to die" area, see N. Cantor, Legal Frontiers of Death and Dying (1987).

2.　See Prince v. Massachusetts, 321 U.S. 158 (1944) (upholding child labor law as applied to guardian who permitted distribution of religious literature by 9-year old child).

of a claim to die in a dignified home environment rather than in the demeaning tangle of technology that has become death's least human face, the state would be hard pressed to advance a sufficient rationale for insisting on the medical model.

Somewhat more difficult for the individual is an argument claiming not simply a right to die with dignity when death is conceded to be imminent, but a right to die sooner rather than later when ways to significantly prolong life appear available. Parents have of course been denied the right to sacrifice their children's lives, or even to risk grave injury to their children's health, even when motivated by religious conviction.[3] And individuals have been denied the right to refuse life-saving treatment for themselves in circumstances strongly suggesting that they lacked the time or the capacity for reflection on the matter, so that the course least likely to do irreversible harm was an insistence on proceeding with treatment.[4]

Nonetheless, courts have become increasingly receptive to arguments that competent adults have a right to refuse any kind of medical treatment, even if that treatment would significantly prolong the patient's life.[5]

3. See, e.g., Jehovah's Witnesses v. King County Hosp., 390 U.S. 598 (1968) (per curiam) (upholding statute permitting children to be declared wards of court where parents opposed blood transfusions for them); In re Sampson, 29 N.Y.2d 900, 328 N.Y.S.2d 686, 278 N.E.2d 918 (1972) (operation to correct adolescent child's severe facial deformity ordered over parent's religious objection to blood transfusion that would be needed to perform the operation). See also Raleigh Fitkin-Paul Morgan Memorial Hosp. v. Anderson, 42 N.J. 421, 201 A.2d 537 (1964), cert. denied 377 U.S. 985 (1964) (authorizing blood transfusions to pregnant woman over her religious objection); Crouse Irving Memorial Hosp., Inc. v. Paddock, 127 Misc.2d 101, 485 N.Y.S.2d 443 (1985) (hospital entitled to give blood transfusion to mother and child during delivery in order to save baby's life and health despite parents' objections based on their religious beliefs).

4. See, e.g., Application of President and Directors of Georgetown College, Inc., 331 F.2d 1000 (D.C.Cir. 1964) rehearing en banc denied 331 F.2d 1010 (1964), cert. denied 377 U.S. 978 (1964); Osgood v. District of Columbia, 567 F.Supp. 1026 (D. D.C. 1983) (summary judgment precluded because factual questions remain at issue, including whether refusal of treatment was based on religious beliefs or was a product of "paranoid schizophrenia").

5. See, e.g., Brophy v. New England Sinai Hospital, 398 Mass. 417, 497 N.E.2d 626 (1986) (permitting removal of a feeding tube from a patient in a chronic vegetative state who had previously expressed a desire not to be sustained by medical inter-

vention); Rasmussen v. Fleming, ___ Ariz. ___, 741 P.2d 674 (1987) (permitting removal of feeding tube from patient in a chronic vegetative state, who had never expressed her medical treatment desires, upon agreement by physicians, family, and court-appointed guardian that best interests of patient counsel removal); Bouvia v. Superior Court, 179 Cal.App.3d 1127, 225 Cal.Rptr. 297 (1986) (affirming a patient's right to have her feeding tube removed even though she was not terminally ill); Matter of Conroy, 98 N.J. 321, 486 A.2d 1209 (1985) (stating in dictum that a competent adult may generally refuse any kind of medical care, no matter what the prognosis); Bartling v. Superior Court, 163 Cal. App.3d 186, 209 Cal.Rptr. 220 (1984) (granting a non-terminally ill, competent patient a right to have his respirator disconnected); Matter of Storar, 52 N.Y.2d 363, 438 N.Y.S.2d 266, 420 N.E.2d 64 (1981) (suggesting in dictum that right of competent patient to refuse medical treatment is broad, even if failure to treat will inexorably lead to death); Satz v. Perlmutter, 379 So.2d 359 (Fla. 1980) (recognizing the right of a competent adult with no minor dependents to refuse extraordinary medical care); Lane v. Candura, 6 Mass.App.Ct. 377, 376 N.E.2d 1232 (1978) (upholding right of competent individual to refuse amputation of gangrenous leg, even though procedure would have saved patient's life and patient was otherwise in good health). In a recent series of cases, the New Jersey Supreme Court broadened and elaborated the rights of both competent and incompetent patients to discontinue life-sustaining medical treatment. In the Matter of Far-

This broad right to refuse treatment has evolved incrementally. Initially, some courts bounded what appeared to be a drift towards a dangerously expansive right to self-determination by drawing a distinction between "ordinary" life-sustaining and "extraordinary" life-prolonging medical treatment.[6] While a patient had the right to decline "extraordinary" care, these courts held that a patient's rights were outweighed by countervailing state interests in the case of so-called "ordinary" care. The courts took up this distinction because it appeared to offer the kind of objective, scientific standard that would dictate a circumscribed right to self-determination. The right to refuse treatment had to be contained for fear that it might eventually be construed to sanction euthanasia[7] or even suicide. Yet, the distinction between ordinary and extraordinary treatment, current in the literature of medical ethicists at a time when courts were asked to recognize a patient's right to resist involuntary treatment, was subsequently criticized by both medical ethicists[8] and the courts. If there had ever been a consensus in the medical community about how to draw the distinction, it no longer existed by the mid-1980s; medical experts regularly disagree whether a form of treatment is ordinary or extraordinary. In light of this controversy in medical circles, it is no surprise that the always somewhat artificial distinction has also fallen into general disfavor in the courts.

Recent court decisions have rejected many of the distinctions commentators had proposed in earlier discussions about the right to die: not only the distinction between ordinary and extraordinary (or proportionate and disproportionate)[9] treatment, but also the distinctions between actively hastening death by terminating treatment and passively allowing a person to die of a disease, between withholding and withdrawing life-sustaining treatment, and between the termination of

rell, 108 N.J. 335, 529 A.2d 404 (1987), discussed at 56 U.S.L.W. 2019, upheld a competent person's right to choose to have her life-supporting treatment discontinued. In the Matter of Peter, 108 N.J. 365, 529 A.2d 419 (1987), discussed at 56 U.S.L.W. 2020, allowed the discontinuation of treatment for a patient in a persistent vegetative state when there was clear and convincing evidence that she would have wanted the treatment ended, regardless of the life expentancy of the patient if treatment was continued. Peter modified the Court's earlier decision in Conroy, supra, in which the Court implied that treatment could be discontinued only if the patient had a life expentancy of one year or less. In the Matter of Jobes, 108 N.J. 394, 529 A.2d 434 (1987), discussed at 56 U.S.L.W. 2021, allowed a close relative or close friend of a patient in a persistent vegetative state to decide in the name of the patient to discontinue medical treatment. Following the ruling, Nancy Ellen Jobes' feeding tube, which had sustained her body for seven years, was removed at the direc-

tion of her husband. She died six weeks later. See The New York Times, Aug. 8, 1987 at A30, col. 1.

6. See, e.g., Superintendent of Belchertown v. Saikewicz, 373 Mass. 728, 370 N.E.2d 417, 424 (1977); Matter of Quinlan, 70 N.J. 10, 355 A.2d 647, 668 (1976).

7. Cf. In re P.V.W., 424 So.2d 1015, 1022 (La. 1982) (statute recognizing right of permanently comatose child to have her parents and physician discontinue medical treatment on life-support systems does not violate state constitutional provision that "no law shall subject any person to euthanasia").

8. See President's Commission for the Study of Ethical Problems in Medicine and Biomedical and Behavioral Research, Deciding to Forego Life-Sustaining Treatment 82–90 (1983).

9. See Barber v. Superior Court, 147 Cal.App.3d 1006, 195 Cal.Rptr. 484, 491 (1983).

artificial feedings and the termination of other forms of life-sustaining treatment.[10]

Paralleling the decline of distinctions based on the nature of the treatment is a shift in the doctrinal rubrics which courts tend to use to analyze these cases. In the past, courts located the right to refuse medical treatment in constitutional principle.[11] Although some courts still cite both a constitutional right to privacy and a common law right to refuse medical treatment,[12] several courts which formerly relied on both, or on constitutional principle alone, now exclusively emphasize common law doctrine.[13]

That the doctrinal emphases have changed simultaneously with the limiting principles which courts have applied in these cases may be more than coincidence. As long as the extraordinary/ordinary distinction seemed meaningful, courts were comfortable applying a federal constitutional standard. Analysis proceeding from the patient's constitutional privacy rights focused courts on a balance between the invasiveness of the medical treatment and the primary countervailing state interest, preservation of life.[14] Distinctions based on the nature of the treatment not only served as medical judgments that would inform the judicial analysis, but became the very point on which the constitutional analysis pivoted: while a patient generally had a right to refuse invasive extraordinary care, courts suggested that the constitutional balance would come out differently if the treatment were ordinary.

The erosion of distinctions based on treatment complicated the constitutional analysis since there was no other readily apparent standard which courts could use to calibrate the burden on an individual's privacy rights inflicted by particular kinds of involuntary treatment. This indeterminacy encouraged a shift from a constitutional to a

---

10. See Matter of Conroy, 486 A.2d at 1233–1237; see also Brophy v. New England Sinai Hosp., Inc., 398 Mass. 417, 497 N.E.2d 626, 637–638 (1986); Corbett v. D'Alessandro, 487 So.2d 368, 371 (Fla.App. 1986); Matter of Hier, 18 Mass.App.Ct. 200, 464 N.E.2d 959, 964 (1984).

11. See Matter of Quinlan, 355 A.2d at 662–663; Superintendent of Belchertown v. Saikewicz, 370 N.E.2d at 424–425.

12. See, e.g., Matter of Conservatorship of Torres, 357 N.W.2d 332 (Minn. 1984); Foody v. Manchester Memorial Hosp., 40 Conn.Sup. 127, 482 A.2d 713 (1984); Matter of Welfare of Colyer, 99 Wn.2d 114, 660 P.2d 738 (1983).

13. The New Jersey Supreme Court acknowledged that, although it had previously spoken in terms of a constitutional right in its seminal decision in Matter of Quinlan, supra note 6, its decision in Matter of Conroy, supra note 5, rested entirely on the common law right of refusing medical treatment. Similarly, while a state appellate court cited the federal Constitution in explicating the scope of a patient's right to refuse medical treatment in Eichner v. Dillon, 73 A.D.2d 431, 426 N.Y.S.2d 517 (1980), the state's highest court subsequently avoided a constitutional holding and relied instead solely on common law rights. See Matter of Storar, supra note 5.

14. See, e.g., Matter of Quinlan, 355 A.2d at 664 ("the State's interest contra weakens and the individual's right to privacy grows as the degree of bodily invasion increases and the prognosis dims").

In the right-to-die litigation, the courts have usually followed Superintendent of Belchertown v. Saikewicz, 370 N.E.2d at 425, in listing four possible countervailing state interests: (1) the preservation of life, (2) maintaining the ethical integrity of the medical profession, (3) the prevention of suicide, and (4) the protection of the interests of innocent third parties. However, most courts have concluded that in cases involving patients who could not be restored to full health all but the last interest must fall away in the face of the individual common law or constitutional right to refuse medical treatment. See, e.g., Matter of Conroy, 486 A.2d at 1223–1226.

common law doctrinal framework.[15] While courts undertaking a constitutional analysis considered the invasiveness of medical procedures in order to calculate the burden on privacy rights, within the common law framework courts were able to treat the patient's right as a constant unaffected by the nature of the treatment.[16]

While courts have spoken broadly of patients' rights to refuse or discontinue medical treatment, and have generally devalued countervailing state interests, courts have often narrowed their holdings to the facts of the cases before them: situations where death was imminent, the patient was comatose or the patient's condition was terminal.[17] This situation is conducive to a rhetorical justification of the cases— authorizing the patient's choice is merely allowing an inexorable dying process to continue.[18] While this distinction is rhetorically convenient, it is not easily justifiable by principle: where the patient's right to refuse medical treatment is a constant, the patient's condition and prognosis would no longer seem to be relevant.

At least one court may have taken the common law standard to its logical conclusion by extending to a competent adult the right to refuse any kind of medical treatment no matter what the patient's prognosis.[19] Yet despite a trend toward more extensive patient rights, some courts have resisted the full logic of a standard which would essentially fix an individual's rights to refuse any and all medical treatment. For example, although in *Brophy v. New England Sinai Hospital* the Massachusetts Supreme Judicial Court acknowledged the difficulty of drawing meaningful distinctions among particular medical treatments and thus seemed poised to announce a clear-cut right to refuse medical treatment altogether, the court made clear that a patient's rights might sometimes be subordinated to competing state interests.[20] Perhaps the court hesitated to embrace an unqualified right to refuse medical treatment because it perceived prospects for the most extreme exercises of such a right. For instance, an unbounded right would seem to empower a person who, animated entirely by a desire to die, refuses the most minor treatment and subsequently succumbs to a disease that

---

15. A common law basis for determining rights for refusing treatment also has the advantage of leaving the issue open for the legislature to establish different standards and procedures for dealing with these difficult problems. See Jobes, supra note 5, slip op. at 6 n. 3 (Handler, J., concurring).

16. "The New Jersey Supreme Court did not consider the fact that a nasogastric tube is less invasive than hemodialysis or a respirator. The court concluded that the individual's interest in bodily integrity, which is weighed against competing State interests, is a constant value to be considered." Brophy v. New England Sinai Hospital, 497 N.E.2d at 636.

17. Compare Matter of Storar, supra note 5 (allowing discontinuation of treatment for elderly patient in chronic vegeta-

tive state in accordance with his earlier expressed wishes) with Delio on Behalf of Delio v. Westchester Cty., 134 Misc.2d 206, 510 N.Y.S.2d 415 (1986) (refusing to apply Storar to patient in chronic vegetative state because he was not terminally ill and because he was only 33 years old), rev'd 129 A.D.2d 1, 516 N.Y.S.2d 677 (1987).

18. See, e.g., In re L.H.R., 253 Ga. 439, 321 S.E.2d 716, 722 (1984) ("the life support system was prolonging her death rather than her life"); Leach v. Akron General Medical Center, 68 Ohio Misc. 1, 426 N.E.2d 809, 812 (Com.Pl. 1980) ("She is on the threshold of death, and man has, through a new medical technology devised a way or holding her on that threshold").

19. See Farrell, supra note 5.

20. 497 N.E.2d at 635.

would have been completely arrested if treated.[21]   Under these circumstances, when the person is not threatened with imminent death or with a life of enduring pain, and when the medical procedure is routine and minimally invasive by any standard, the state's acquiescence in the person's choice to refuse treatment appears not substantially different from state sanction of suicide.

Although the Massachusetts court's standard might be attributable to a belief that an unchanneled right to refuse treatment might occasionally furnish a pretext for suicide, the court's qualification of the right creates deeper problems than it can possibly solve.   At the same time that the court said that the invasiveness or type of treatment would no longer weigh heavily in the balance, the court insisted that the interests of state and individual continue to be balanced.[22]   But since the right of the individual will often be considered a constant in light of the indeterminacy of judgments about the invasiveness of treatment, the outcome of the balancing process would seem to turn primarily on the other side of the equation, the countervailing state interests in preserving life.   If asked to weigh those interests, courts may be inclined to evaluate the quality and quantity of life that remains to be preserved.[23]   Yet, having courts focus on a patient's prognosis when determining whether a patient's desire to refuse treatment should be effectuated raises the specter of the worst kind of state

21. Cf. Lane v. Candura, supra note 5 (allowing a patient to refuse an amputation operation needed to save her life, even though, with the operation, she would have been in good health); Matter of Quackenbush, 156 N.J.Super. 282, 383 A.2d 785 (1978) (same). This question has also been presented in the strange context of cases where hunger-striking prisoners have sought to enjoin prison officials from force-feeding them. See Zant v. Prevatte, 248 Ga. 832, 286 S.E.2d 715 (1982) (upholding the prisoner's right to refuse medical intrusions); but see In re Caulk, 125 N.H. 226, 480 A.2d 93 (1984) (rejecting the prisoner's claim, largely on the ground of institutional interests of the prison); State ex rel. White v. Narick, 292 S.E.2d 54 (1982) (same).

Courts have recently authorized the refusal of relatively minor medical treatment even though the refusal would be life-threatening, when the patient's refusal was based on religious scruples. The courts have held that the right to refuse treatment, when so bolstered, outweighs the countervailing state interests. See In re Milton, 29 Ohio.St.3d 20, 505 N.E.2d 255 (1987); Wons v. Public Health Trust of Dade County, 500 So.2d 679 (Fla.App. 1987); In re Brown, 478 So.2d 1033 (Miss. 1985); Mercy Hosp. v. Jackson, 62 Md.App. 409, 489 A.2d 1130 (1985); vacated as moot 306 Md. 556, 510 A.2d 562 (1986). In recent cases of this type, the State's inter-

ests, see supra note 15, in particular the interest in protecting innocent third parties, have been held to outweigh the patient's right only if the patient's death would lead to "abandonment" of the patient's children. See St. Mary's Hosp. v. Ramsey, 465 So.2d 666, 668–669 (Fla.App. 1985); Wons v. Public Health Trust of Dade County, 500 So.2d at 688; Mercy Hosp. v. Jackson, 489 A.2d at 1134.

22. Brophy v. New England Sinai Hospital, 497 N.E.2d at 635.

23. See Matter of Welfare of Colyer, 660 P.2d at 743. Courts that focus on the quantity of the patient's life often seem not to emphasize the life's quality. Compare Delio on Behalf of Delio v. Westchester Cty., 510 N.Y.S.2d at 418–420 (refusing to authorize discontinuation of treatment, noting that the patient could be maintained in his chronic vegetative state indefinitely), rev'd 129 A.D.2d 1, 516 N.Y.S.2d 677 (1987), with Bouvia v. Superior Court, 225 Cal.Rptr. at 305 ("Who shall say what the minimum amount of available life must be? Does it matter if it be 15 to 20 years, or 15 to 20 months, or 15 to 20 days, if such life has been physically destroyed and its quality, dignity and purpose gone? As in all matters lines must be drawn at some point, somewhere, but that decision must ultimately belong to the one whose life is in issue").

paternalism: having the state regularly make judgments about the value of a life.[24]

Even if a court would grant a patient's request to forego medical treatment were the patient able to express that wish, a further complication arises if the patient is unable to express that desire because incompetent. Most courts have extended to incompetent patients whatever rights competent patients have through the doctrine of substituted judgment.[25] There are basically three approaches courts have taken to decisionmaking in treatment decisions for incompetent patients. First, if the patient had when competent stated what decision she would have wanted made in this situation, those wishes tend to be deemed decisive.[26] Second, where there is no direct evidence of the patient's preferences, if there is a relative or a friend who was close enough to the patient to be able to surmise how she would have decided, this relative or friend may be allowed to choose in the name of the patient.[27] Third, if there is no basis for deciding what the patient would have decided, a decision is made according to what would be in the patient's

---

24. In Brophy, the Massachusetts Supreme Judicial Court maintained that subjective judgments about a person's quality of life should not enter into a court's calculus of the state interest in preservation of that life. 497 N.E.2d at 635. At the same time the court said, somewhat contradictorily, that the state interest in preserving life is strongest when human life can be saved through treatment and "wanes when the underlying affliction is incurable" and the patient faces death in any event. Id. The tension between these two pronouncements might be reconcilable if one supposed that the Massachusetts court meant to endorse a single, sharp distinction between terminally ill (where the state interest is low) and non-terminally ill (state interest high) patients, and to discourage courts from any more particular consideration of prognosis. Yet the court's favorable citation to Lane v. Candura, supra note 5—an appellate decision allowing a non-terminally ill patient to refuse lifesaving treatment—implies that the balance between state interests and individual right will not necessarily turn cleanly on the distinction between terminal and nonterminal prognosis. Furthermore, since the court admitted that the invasiveness of particular medical procedures will often defy precise valuation, it is not clear how a balance between state interests and individual right can be struck. If the "weight" of the right to refuse care cannot be ranked according to the nature of the prescribed treatment, courts told to "balance" interests may resort to subjective judgments about the "worth" of the patient's life in order to discriminate among cases.

25. See, e.g., Superintendent of Belchertown v. Saikewicz, 370 N.E.2d at

427 ("The recognition of that right must extend to the case of an incompetent, as well as a competent, patient because the value of human dignity extends to both"); Rasmussen v. Fleming, __ Ariz. __, 741 P.2d 674 (1987) (allowing physicians, family, and court-appointed guardian to exercise right to terminate treatment on behalf of comatose patient whose views on the issue were unknown).

Given the fact that these patients are irreversibly comatose or in a chronic vegetative state, attributing "rights" to these patients at all is somewhat problematic. Of course a sleeping person has rights, as does someone who has temporarily lost consciousness. On the other hand, someone who has died cannot be said to have "rights" in the usual sense; although a person may have a right to determine how her body is dealt with after her death, even that is a troublesome concept. Consider, for example, an individual who opposes a decision to cremate her brother in accord with his will, claiming that she would suffer severe anguish if the will were carried out. Whose rights are involved? Might it depend on the religious beliefs of the deceased? To be sure, these patients are not "dead" in most of the increasingly multiple senses of the term, but the task of giving content to the notion that they have rights, in the face of the recognition that they could make no decisions about how to exercise any such rights, remains a difficult one.

26. See Matter of Conroy, 486 A.2d at 1229; Matter of Storar, 420 N.E.2d at 70–72.

27. See Matter of Welfare of Colyer, 660 P.2d at 748.

"best interests", as defined by the court,[28] by the patient's family,[29] or by a court-appointed guardian.[30]

All three forms of "substituted judgment" are at best imperfect ways to effectuate the patient's right of self-determination. No matter how much evidence there is of subjective intent, how well the guardian knew the patient, and how well-intentioned the patient's guardian, family, and physician may be, there will always be some residual doubt that the decision made in fact expresses what the patient would have wanted done.[31] Sometimes the fiction that the person deciding for the incompetent patient is effectuating the patient's subjective wishes reaches almost Alice in Wonderland proportions: "the decision in cases such as this should be that which would be made by the incompetent person, if that person were competent, but taking into account the present and future incompetency of the individual as one of the factors which would necessarily enter into the decision-making process of the competent person."[32] In fact, in that case and in many others, the decisionmaker must keep in mind not only the patient's present and future incompetency, but also the fact that the patient had never been legally competent.[33] In contrast with the other forms of substituted judgment, the "best interests" approach does not even claim to effectuate the patient's right of self-determination. The problem with *any* "objective" or "best interests" standard is that there is no consensus in our society about how the value of a life is affected by the loss of higher brain function, severe physical deterioration, or unrelievable extreme pain.[34] A best interests approach for making a treatment decision imposes highly contested societal values paternalistically on the individual. However, for many incompetent patients, a subjective approach is unavailable.[35] Given that a decision must be made, and that continuing treatment for a patient who would have wanted treatment stopped may be as unfortunate as discontinuing treatment for a patient who would have wanted treatment continued,[36] courts may have no choice but to formulate "objective" criteria for these treatment deci-

28. See Matter of Conroy, 486 A.2d at 1231–1233.

29. See In re Guardianship of Barry, 445 So.2d 365, 371 (Fla.App. 1984).

30. See Matter of Guardianship of Hamlin, 102 Wn.2d 810, 689 P.2d 1372, 1378 (1984).

31. See Jobes, supra note 5 (Handler, J., concurring); Minow, "Beyond State Intervention in the Family: For Baby Jane Doe", 18 U.Mich.J.L.Ref. 933, 972–74 (1985).

32. Superintendent of Belchertown v. Saikewicz, 370 N.E.2d at 431.

33. See In re L.H.R., supra note 18 (treatment decision for infant in chronic vegetative state); Superintendent of Belchertown v. Saikewicz, supra note 6 (treatment decision for terminally ill adult severely retarded since birth).

34. See Minow, supra note 31, at 973–74; Matter of Conroy, 486 A.2d at 1246–1250 (Handler, J., concurring in part and dissenting in part). Many people also have a strong visceral reaction against the idea that death can ever be in someone's best interests. See, e.g., Becker v. Schwartz, 46 N.Y.2d 401, 413 N.Y.S.2d 895, 386 N.E.2d 807, 812 (1978) (refusing to recognize a claim for "wrongful life"); Berman v. Allan, 80 N.J. 421, 404 A.2d 8, 12 (1979) (same).

35. See Minow, supra note 31, at 973: "[W]hatever the success of efforts by family and friends to imagine the past wants of a now comatose eighty-year old, substituted judgment makes little sense for a newborn who has no history nor prior expression of wants."

36. See Matter of Conroy, 486 A.2d at 1220.

sions.[37] Even recognizing the conceptual difficulties that are raised by various forms of substituted judgment, courts continue to subscribe to it. This judicial inclination to expand the rights of patients, even incompetent patients, accords with legislative trends. A number of states have passed "living will" legislation which gives patients who may subsequently become unconscious or otherwise incompetent an opportunity formally to record their desire not to be sustained by medical intervention.[38] Although courts have looked to these legislative efforts for guidance, this legislation has not supplanted judicial initiative. In light of the generally restrictive criteria of these statutes,[39] several courts have refused to give such legislation preemptive effect. Even if the patient's medical condition or the manner in which she expressed her desire not to be sustained by medical intervention does not fit the statutory criteria, courts may still choose to authorize the discontinuation of treatment.[40]

Despite the continuing lead of the state courts in expanding the scope of a patient's right to determine the course of his or her medical treatment, the shift in doctrinal emphasis from constitutional to common law principle in some of these courts suggests that these courts may be approaching a limit to the right to die. The right of a patient to accelerate death as such—rather than merely to have medical procedures held in abeyance so that disease processes can work their natural course—depends on a broader conception of individual rights than any contained in common law principles. A right to determine when and how to die would have to rest on constitutional principles of privacy and personhood or on broad, perhaps paradoxical, conceptions of self-determination.

Although these notions have not taken hold in the courts, the judiciary's silence regarding such constitutional principles probably reflects a concern that, once recognized, rights to die might be uncontainable and might prove susceptible to grave abuse, more than it suggests that courts cannot be persuaded that self-determination and personhood may include a right to dictate the circumstances under which life is to be ended. In any event, whatever the reason for the absence in the courts of expansive notions about self-determination, the resulting deference to legislatures may prove wise in light of the complex character of the rights at stake and the significant potential that, without careful statutory guidelines and gradually evolved proce-

---

37. See N. Cantor, supra note 1, at 63–82, 177–182.

38. See, e.g., California Natural Death Act, California Health & Safety Code §§ 7185, et seq.; Annotated Code of Maryland, Health-General §§ 5–601 et seq.; Florida Statutes Annotated §§ 765.01 et seq.; Revised Code of Washington §§ 70.122 et seq.

39. See, e.g., California Health & Safety Code § 7191(c) (physician not compelled to follow the directive of the living will if the directive was executed before patient was diagnosed as terminally ill).

40. See Barber v. Superior Court, 195 Cal.Rptr. at 489, where the court said that the procedural requirements of the legislation were so cumbersome that only a small number of "highly educated and motivated" patients would be able to effectuate their desires. The court concluded that practical utility as well as statutory directive justified its holding that the statute would not be "the exclusive means by which such decisions can be made." Id. See also Matter of Guardianship of Hamlin, 689 P.2d at 1376; Matter of Welfare of Colyer, 660 P.2d at 740–741; Corbett v. D'Alessandro, 487 So.2d at 372.

dural controls, legalizing euthanasia, rather than respecting people, may endanger personhood.[41]

§ 15–12. Governmental Interference With Choice of Life Plan, Pattern, or Style: Risk-Taking

As an element of personhood, a right to die is paradoxical, for personhood derives its claim from the irreducible perception that life and the organic base on which it subsists are somehow sacred; it is, as Edward Shils has observed, "the primordial experience of being alive, of experiencing the elemental sensation of vitality and of fearing its extinction"[1] that generates the sense of sanctity that attaches to the living human being. Yet the courts have come to recognize that, when vitality gives way to morbidity—when the prospect of continued existence is fraught with more fear and suffering than the prospect of extinction—the individual will that animates a human life must be allowed some room to determine its fate. If there is a limited right to die, it is tempting to suppose that there must be a less restricted right to live dangerously—to define one's self by courting (or even savoring) avoidable risks. Surely the latter right is less paradoxical: after all, one who opts for the fate of Achilles—the short life of glory—is not *choosing* death or mutilation, even though he is willing to accept it.

This sense of a right to place oneself in peril has long been the basis for opposition to mundane safety regulations mandating the wearing of seat belts or compelling the use of motorcycle helmets. At one time some courts held such rules impermissibly paternalistic, insisting that the cyclist's crushed skull was nobody's business but his own.[2] The notion that the state may not intervene where it seeks only to save one from oneself has considerable intuitive, as well as philosophical,[3] appeal. That intuition fueled a referendum campaign in Massachusetts in 1986 that repealed the Commonwealth's seat belt law just a few short months after it was enacted. A notion of individual autonomy that is so widely and deeply felt—and that can claim such a distinguished intellectual pedigree—cannot be dismissed as flaky.

But the popular argument against seat belt and helmet laws overlooks the externalities that exclude an activity from John Stuart Mill's realm of unfettered freedom.[4] In a society unwilling to abandon

---

41. See § 16–31, infra, for a discussion of how an expansive right to die might offer a pretext for discrimination against the disabled that would endanger personhood.

§ 15–12

1. Shils, "The Sanctity of Life," Encounter, Jan. 1967, at 39.

2. See, e.g., People v. Fries, 42 Ill.2d 446, 250 N.E.2d 149 (1969), overruled People v. Kohrig, 113 Ill.2d 384, 101 Ill.Dec. 650, 498 N.E.2d 1158 (1986) (per curiam), cert. denied 107 S.Ct. 1264 (1987); American Motorcycle Ass'n v. Davids, 11 Mich. App. 351, 158 N.W.2d 72 (1968), overruled People of the City of Adrian v. Poucher, 67

Mich.App. 133, 240 N.W.2d 298 (1976) (per curiam).

3. The classic formulation is of course that of John Stuart Mill: "the only purpose for which power can be rightfully exercised over any member of a civilized community, against his will, is to prevent harm to others. . . . Over himself, over his own body and mind, the individual is sovereign." On Liberty 68–69 (Penguin ed. 1984) (1st ed. London 1859).

4. See Mill, supra note 3, at 141 ("As soon as any part of a person's conduct affects prejudicially the interests of others, society has jurisdiction over it").

bleeding bodies on the highway, the motorcyclist or driver who endangers himself plainly imposes costs on others.[5] His choice to risk a range of possible injuries, instead of certain death, in one respect strengthens society's case for regulating him; the social and economic cost of caring for the motorist who suffers an accident is likely to be considerably greater than the cost of burying the terminally ill patient who refuses extraordinary measures to prolong his life.

Few of us would relish a government mandate that we all endure lives of safe timidity dictated by the most risk-averse common denominator—no mountain climbing, no skiing, no sunbathing, no coffee, no ice cream. And so long as there are democratic elections and referenda, we are unlikely to face that prospect. But those political constraints must be our mainstay, for there are few constitutional checks on the government's power to protect us from ourselves, whether by requiring the wearing of crash helmets and seat belts, or by banning the smoking of tobacco, the snorting of cocaine, or the recreational use of all-terrain vehicles.[6] The intuition that one's safety is wholly one's

---

5. See, e.g., People v. Kohrig, 113 Ill.2d 384, 101 Ill.Dec. 650, 498 N.E.2d 1158 (1986) (per curiam) (upholding seat belt law over state and federal due process challenges; rejecting notion that the right of privacy includes the right to "do one's thing" on an expressway; and accepting legislative rationale that law would (1) protect others by helping drivers to maintain control of their vehicles, and (2) reduce the public and private costs associated with accident injuries), cert. denied 107 S.Ct. 1264 (1987). See also State v. Odegaard, 165 N.W.2d 677 (N.D.1969); State v. Albertson, 93 Idaho 640, 470 P.2d 300 (1970).

6. There remain factors that argue for more searching scrutiny of some safety measures. First, particular risky behavior may have significant expressive character—for example, riding a motorcycle bareheaded. If a state required cyclists to wear helmets but did not require drivers to wear seat belts, there would be a legitimate suspicion that the legislature's singling out of motorcycle riders for forced protection results not from a careful calculation of the relative medical drain they impose on society, but from the preponderance among legislators of the view that riding without a helmet is not to be admired as a celebration of the life of the open road, but to be suppressed as a glorification of the cult of defiant bravado. At least one rationale government might convincingly offer for a helmet law—that it precludes the displays of courage that some cyclists might demand of their peers in the absence of a law, cf. Schelling, "Hockey Helmets, Concealed Weapons, and Daylight Saving," 17 J.Confl.Res. 381 (1973)—presupposes the communicative nature of the choice to forego a helmet. If conduct posing similar risks for the actor and others (e.g., un-

belted driving) but communicating nothing in particular to legislators is exempt from state control, the selective prohibition of *this* conduct might plausibly be characterized as a governmental choice to take aim at the life style unhelmeted cyclists *suggest* rather than the life style they *pursue*.

Second, safety requirements that directly impinge on the body are more problematic than those that do not. Forcing someone to buckle a belt about her waist or to strap on a helmet on her head intrudes on her inner sensations and outward "statement" in a way that installing a guardrail on her favorite highway or banning a possibly carcinogenic sweetener from her favorite diet soda does not.

A third element, reinforcing the second, is the special imposition of requiring an individual to lower his level of risk by his own affirmative act. A state prohibition (no sky-diving) may force a person to alter his plans, and a state modification of the environment (mandatory fire escapes in residential buildings, airbags and seatbelts in automobiles) may exact an additional and undesired expense from his wallet, but only a mandatory act of self-protection forces him to curtail his freedom by lifting his own hand. The result may be the same, but the decision of the Framers to draw a similar line in the fifth amendment—between being incriminated with one's active participation and being convicted by independent evidence—suggests that the distinction is not without significance. Indeed, two years after it struck down the state's helmet law in People v. Fries, 42 Ill.2d 446, 250 N.E.2d 149 (1969), the Illinois Supreme Court upheld the state's requirement that boats carry life preservers. People v. Roe, 48 Ill.2d 380,

own business is simply too far out of phase with the reality of our interdependent society to find any plausible expression in our constitutional order.

§ 15–13. Life Plan or Style: Vocation

In giving satisfactory content to the idea of personhood, it will not do to draw a bright line between "economic" and "civil" liberties, or between "property" rights and "personal" rights. As Justice Stewart observed in *Lynch v. Household Finance Corp.*,[1] "The dichotomy between personal liberties and property rights is a false one. Property does not have rights. People have rights. . . . In fact, a fundamental interdependence exists between the personal right to liberty and the personal right in property. Neither could have meaning without the other. That rights in property are basic civil rights has long been recognized . . ."

Robert McCloskey wrote in a classic article that a "major difficulty with [the] formulation [that treats free choice in the intellectual and spiritual realms as more deserving of protection than economic liberty] is that there is the smell of the lamp about it: it may reflect the tastes of the judges and dons who advance it, rather than the real preferences of the commonality of mortals. Judges and professors are talkers both by profession and avocation. It is not surprising that they would view freedom of expression as primary to the free play of their personalities. But most men would probably feel that an economic right, such as freedom of occupation, was at least as vital to them as the right to speak their minds. Mark Twain would surely have felt constrained in the most fundamental sense, if his youthful aspiration to be a river-boat pilot had been frustrated by a State-ordained system of nepotism."[2] As

270 N.E.2d 27 (1971). The court emphasized that the latter statute did not require anyone to *wear* a life preserver: the law left any boater accidentally catapulted into the water "free to choose whether or not to accept the life-saving benefits of such a device." 48 Ill.2d at 381, 270 N.E.2d at 28. The holding in Fries was subsequently overruled. See note 2, supra.

§ 15–13

1. 405 U.S. 538, 552 (1972). At this point, Justice Stewart cited none other than Locke and Blackstone. For those to whom this might have seemed an unsettling sign of a return to the era of Lochner v. New York, 198 U.S. 45 (1905), it bears repeating that the Court's error in the Lochner period was not in according significance to property and contract but in misreading the necessary preconditions of human freedom in the industrial state. See §§ 8–6, 8–7, supra.

It is worth remembering that the idea of state protection of property rights had solid intellectual and political currency long before the Lochner era. Many of the Framers believed that preservation of economic rights was the *central* purpose of civil government. See, e.g., Federalist No. 10 (J. Madison); 1 Records of the Federal Convention 533 (Farrand ed. 1911) (statement of Gouverneur Morris). This purpose was written into the Constitution in various places, most obviously in the takings and contract clauses. See Chapter 9, supra.

2. McCloskey, "Economic Due Process and the Supreme Court: An Exhumation and Reburial," 1962 Sup.Ct.Rev. 34, 46. The footnote at this point in the McCloskey argument singled out Kotch v. Pilot Commissioners, 330 U.S. 552 (1947), discussed in § 16–3, infra. Cf. Easterbrook, "Implicit and Explicit Rights of Association," 10 Harv.J.L.Pub. Policy 91, 98 (1987) (suggesting that associational rights receive more protection than economic liberties because "free association is especially important to the intellectual and economic groups from which judges are drawn. Intellectuals feel free to regulate the economic lives of others but resist the regulation of the most important elements of their own lives.").

McCloskey rightly concluded, it works "no disparagement of freedom of expression" or of "its inarguable importance to the human spirit" to give economic rights their due as well.[3]

Apart from its analytic weakness, the distinction between economic and non-economic rights overlooks the importance of property and contract in protecting the dispossessed no less than the established; [4] it forgets the political impotence of the isolated job-seeker who has been fenced out of an occupation; [5] and in no event could it justify more than a modest difference in degree between the judicial roles in the two areas.[6]

It is particularly crucial to recognize, as we saw in § 15–9, that *Lochner's* downfall did not represent a denigration of economic liberties but a recognition that such liberties were not meaningfully protected by the "free" market, at least for those who were more its victims than its masters.[7] Although the tendency has been to equate the rejection of *Lochner* with a policy of judicial deference in economic matters, we have seen in Chapter 8 why that is a misguided characterization. Moreover, the procedural protections accorded to economic interests (see Chapter 10) plainly belie any equation of modernism with a total abdication of concern with economic justice.

3. McCloskey, supra note 2, at 46. In what remains perhaps the most persuasive defense in print of a measured return to judicial scrutiny of the justifications for particular economic restrictions, McCloskey went on to argue that "it is not entirely clear why liberty of economic choice is less indispensable to the 'openness' of a society than freedom of expression," id. at 48, and that, although there are "economic subjects so recondite that judicial surveillance of them would be anomalous," id. at 51, any consistent attempt "to identify the issues that present difficulties and then to discard them as improper subjects for judicial review. . . . would be to abandon judicial review in most of the fields where it is now exercised." Id. at 52.

See also Easterbrook, supra note 2, at 98: "For most people economic rights—where to work, at what price to buy milk or rent apartments—are more important than whether the Jaycees admit women or whether a political party must seat the delegates selected in a primary rather than a caucus. Economic rights are entitlements over resources, and through things one's surroundings and comfort; they are personal liberties to the same extent as other forms of freedom. People who cannot control inanimate objects, either at all or against competing claims by others . . . are not in control of their destinies." See also Radin, "Property and Personhood," 34 Stan.L.Rev. 957 (1982) (individual self-development requires some control over resources, and those property interests that are personal should be pro-

tected against invasion by government and against cancellation by the conflicting claims of others).

4. See Reich, "The New Property," 73 Yale L.J. 733, 771–74 (1964). See also the decisions providing procedural protection for welfare, wages, and household goods, discussed in § 10–9, supra, and §§ 16–43, 16–53, 16–56, infra.

5. McCloskey rightly argued that the thrust of concern for discrete and insular minorities or isolated individuals should not be "restricted to ethnic and religious minorities. Perhaps it is true that a prosperous corporation can effectively plead its case at the bar of legislative judgment by resort to publicity and direct lobbying. Economic power may be an adequate surrogate for numerical power; no tears need be shed for helpless General Electric. But the scattered individuals who are denied access to an occupation by State-enforced barriers are about as impotent a minority as can be imagined." McCloskey, supra note 2, at 50.

6. Id. at 51.

7. To the extent that economic conservatives advocate resurrection of Lochner, see § 8–7, supra, at note 24, they tend to persist in focusing on the economic rights of the owners of capital over the economic rights of those who labor. Such a distinction or disparate emphasis is not supported by the Constitution's text, structure, or history. See also § 9–11, supra, for a similarly lopsided reinvigoration of the contract clause.

Although we have argued in § 15–9 that among the rights to bodily integrity are rights to at least minimal subsistence and that such rights give rise to affirmative governmental duties, we could not deduce from such duties a judicially cognizable remedy for every instance of unmet needs; as we saw, government's affirmative duties must ordinarily be translated into doctrine somewhat more obliquely—through a variety of procedural, structural, and other protections designed, in their cumulative effect, to minimize the risk that someone will in fact suffer extreme deprivation. Among those protections has been a revitalized concern to prevent at least procedurally unfair exclusions from the occupation or vocation of one's choice.

In *Gibson v. Berryhill*, for example, the Court held that Arizona's self-employed optometrists could not lawfully deprive other optometrists, their own competitors, of licenses to practice.[8] To be sure, *Williamson v. Lee Optical*[9] has not been overruled; it remains the law that a state may, if it wishes, require a prescription from an optometrist or an ophthalmologist before an optician can even fit old lenses into a new frame.[10] The distinction appears to be that legislatures are free to enact rules to favor those with money and legislative influence over their competitors while administrative bodies may not deprive individuals of statutory benefits in a similarly biased manner, at least not if the administrators benefit personally from such decisions. But institutional bias has been recognized as relevant to procedural due process[11] and to the fourth amendment.[12] Moreover, even if only personal bias were fatal, it is easy to criticize a decision like *Ferguson v. Skrupa*,[13] in which a state legislature, most of its members no doubt lawyers, was allowed to forbid anyone to engage in debt-adjusting unless he works through a lawyer.

Schware v. Board of Bar Examiners of New Mexico[14] held that the state deprived Schware of liberty without due process of law when it denied him admission to the bar on a record which could not rationally justify a finding of unfitness to practice law. Although first amendment problems were mixed with the right-to-work issue,[15] the Court's

8. 411 U.S. 564 (1973). Alabama's Board of Optometry "was composed solely of optometrists in private practice for their own account;" in the challenged proceedings, "the aim of the Board was to revoke the licenses of all optometrists in the State who were employed by business corporations such as Lee Optical;" "success in the Board's efforts would possibly redound to the personal benefit of members of the Board. . . ." Id. at 578. Because "those with substantial pecuniary interest in legal proceedings should not adjudicate these disputes," id. at 579, the delicensing effort by the Board violated due process. Id. at 579.

9. 348 U.S. 483 (1955).

10. See § 8–7, supra, and § 16–3, infra.

11. Ward v. Monroeville, 409 U.S. 57 (1972) (due process forbids requiring person to stand trial for traffic offenses before mayor who was responsible for village finances and whose court through fines and forfeitures yielded a substantial portion of village funds). See § 10–15, supra.

12. Coolidge v. New Hampshire, 403 U.S. 443, 449–53 (1971) (search warrant fails to meet fourth amendment standards when issued by prosecutor in his capacity as magistrate).

13. 372 U.S. 726 (1963), discussed in § 8–7, supra.

14. 353 U.S. 232 (1957).

15. Schware had been a Communist from 1932 to 1940, and it was that prior association that constituted the centerpiece of the case for his alleged unfitness. Id. at 243–47.

theory suggested a rejection of all discriminations that would prevent someone from practicing a chosen vocation or profession for wholly arbitrary reasons. State-imposed qualifications, the Court held in an opinion by Justice Black, "must have a rational connection with the applicant's fitness or capacity" to practice the occupation.[16] Here is a decision, plainly, that could "go far to bring economic rights back under the shelter of the Constitution" [17] by requiring fair licensing in the trades and professions generally. But even if *Schware* is ultimately limited to cases in which an invidious or independently offensive criterion appears to have animated someone's exclusion from a chosen vocation, it would be extraordinarily hard to square that case with total abdication from judicial review of the fairness of occupational exclusions.

Several years before *Schware*, in the case of *Barsky v. Board of Regents*,[18] the Court upheld the suspension of a physician's license for being convicted of a crime—namely, failure to produce papers subpoenaed by the House Un-American Activities Committee. The majority accorded extreme deference to the license-revoking authority—far greater deference than would be appropriate today in light of *Schware*. Justices Black, Douglas, and Frankfurter dissented, in opinions that would now represent the sounder view. Although first amendment considerations were again mingled with economic justice, one passage in particular from the dissent of Justice Douglas bears full quotation: [19] "The right to work I had assumed, was the most precious liberty that man possesses. Man has indeed as much right to work as he has to live, to be free, to own property. The American ideal was stated by Emerson in his essay on *Politics*, 'A man has a right to be employed, to be trusted, to be loved, to be revered.' It does many men little good to stay alive and free and propertied, if they cannot work. To work means to eat. It also means to live. For many it would be better to work in jail, than to sit idle on the curb. The great values of freedom are in the opportunities afforded man to press to new horizons, to pit his strength against the forces of nature, to match skills with his fellow man."

That account would be hard to fault as a statement of a widely shared and deeply felt belief about the meaning of liberty.[20] Any suggestion that this belief finds no reflection in current constitutional doctrine was dramatically refuted by *Hampton v. Mow Sun Wong*,[21] the first majority opinion authored by Justice Stevens. In explaining its more than minimal scrutiny of a Civil Service Commission rule barring all noncitizens from employment in the federal competitive civil service, the Court observed that the rule, which operated to the disadvantage of a "class of persons . . . already subject to disadvantages not

16. Id. at 239. See, e.g., Regents of Univ. of Michigan v. Ewing, 106 S.Ct. 507, 509 (1985) (upholding the university's decision to dismiss a medical student with an "unfortunate academic history").

17. McCloskey, supra note 2, at 58.

18. 347 U.S. 442 (1954).

19. Id. at 472.

20. Were the statement written today rather than in the 1950's, one hopes it would have spoken not of the liberties of "man" but of the liberties of both men and women.

21. 426 U.S. 88 (1976).

shared by the remainder of the community," worked to create a further disadvantage—"ineligibility for employment in a major sector of the economy"—which the Court thought to be "of sufficient significance to be characterized as a deprivation of an interest in liberty." [22]   In a footnote at that point, the Court quoted with approval the language of *Truax v. Raich*: [23] "It requires no argument to show that the right to work for a living in the common occupations of the community is of the very essence of the personal freedom and opportunity that it was the purpose of the [Fourteenth] Amendment to secure." [24]   Finding the Civil Service Commission's ban on alien employment insufficiently justified, the Court held it violative of the due process clause of the fifth amendment.

The mode of analysis employed by the Court in *Hampton v. Mow Sun Wong* may provide a model for future cases involving governmental infringements of personal freedom to pursue a vocation. The Court considered (1) the breadth of the infringement, (2) the character of the group upon which it was imposed, (3) the nature and responsibilities of the body that imposed it, (4) the availability of less restrictive alternatives, (5) the reasons actually canvassed in the process of adopting the challenged rule, and (6) the arguments made in defense of the rule's enforcement. Arguments not corresponding to considerations that actually led to the rule's adoption were disregarded; claims about the rule's hypothetical advantages were rejected where not supported by the record; and defenses of the rule cast in terms of interests beyond the delegated responsibilities of the body promulgating it were deemed irrelevant.

At least one commentator has urged a similar mode of scrutiny for economic regulation generally,[25] but the likelihood that federal courts will risk skating that close to the *Lochner* hole in the already thin ice of substantive due process is slim indeed. Nor is it at all clear that judicial scrutiny as active as that of *Hampton v. Mow Sun Wong* would be appropriate in dealing with regulations restricting economic options but not intruding in any significant way on concerns close to an individual's sense of self.[26] To be sure, government actions that do not

22. Id. at 102.

23. 239 U.S. 33, 41 (1915).

24. 426 U.S. at 102 n.23. The Hampton decision is discussed further in §§ 16–23, 16–32, and Chapter 17, infra.

25. See Struve, "The Less-Restrictive-Alternative Principle and Economic Due Process," 80 Harv.L.Rev. 1463 (1967).

26. Perhaps McCloskey was right when he said that "no tears need be shed for helpless General Electric." See note 5, supra. See also note 7, supra. One possible way to facilitate a doctrinal limitation along these lines might be to rely on the fourteenth amendment's guarantee of the privileges or immunities of national citizenship, since that clause does not protect corporations. See Chapter 7, supra.

Indeed, the privileges and immunities clause of article IV has long been a bulwark against state attempts to preserve vocational opportunities for their own citizens by denying them to outsiders. See, e.g., Supreme Court of New Hampshire v. Piper, 470 U.S. 274, 282 (1985) (state may not dictate that only residents may be members of the state bar); United Building & Construction Trades Council v. Mayor of Camden, 465 U.S. 208 (1984) (a city may not require private contractors on city-funded public works projects to give hiring preference to city residents without implicating the privileges and immunities clause); Hicklin v. Orbeck, 437 U.S. 518, 520 (1978) (unanimously striking down the Alaska Hire statute, which required that qualified residents be given preference in all employment "resulting from" oil and

even arguably intrude upon anyone's dignity or self-respect might form part of a fabric of laws and policies that in the aggregate leave unmet the basic economic needs of an individual or group. But just as we have seen that a claim of unmet needs does not automatically give rise to a judicially cognizable basis for insisting that government step in with specific services, so it must be the case that, even with respect to employment, not every frustrated wish creates a constitutional cause of action against the state. As Justice Douglas said in his *Barsky* dissent,[27] "[c]ertainly a man has no affirmative right to any particular job or skill or occupation. The Bill of Rights does not say who shall be doctors or lawyers or policemen. But it does say that certain rights are protected, that certain things shall not be done. And so the question here is not what government must give, but rather what it may not take away." What it may not take away without clear and focused justification is a fair opportunity for an individual to realize her identity in a chosen vocation.

§ 15–14. Life Plan or Style: Travel

Concurring in *Shapiro v. Thompson*, Justice Stewart described the right to travel as "not a mere conditional liberty subject to regulation and control under conventional due process or equal protection standards . . ." but "a virtually unconditional personal right."[1] It might be suggested that the decisions recognizing a liberty interest in either interstate[2] or international[3] travel represent only a recognition that Congress, not the states or the Executive Branch, has the ultimate authority over travel across state or national borders. But so limited a view of the cases is flatly refuted by the Court's holding in *Aptheker* that the congressional denial of passports to members of the Communist Party "too broadly and indiscriminately restricts the right to travel and thereby abridges the liberty guaranteed [against Congress] by the Fifth Amendment."[4] It is refuted as well by the Court's holding that Congress can neither authorize states to penalize persons for exercising the right to travel[5] nor impose such a penalty itself.[6] One finds the

gas leases or pipeline projects to which the State of Alaska was a party). See § 6–35, supra.

27. 347 U.S. 442, 472–73 (1954).

§ 15–14

1. 394 U.S. 618, 642–43 (1969).

2. See, e.g., Shapiro v. Thompson, 394 U.S. 618 (1969) (durational residency requirements for welfare unjustifiably burden right of interstate travel); Memorial Hospital v. Maricopa Cty., 415 U.S. 250 (1974) (durational residency requirements for free medical care excessively burden right to travel). See also Chapter 7, supra. The difficulty with treating these as "true" right-to-travel cases is explored in § 16–8, infra.

3. See, e.g., Aptheker v. Secretary of State, 378 U.S. 500, 507–08, 514 (1964) (invalidating federal statute prohibiting mem-

bers of Communist-action organizations registered under Internal Security Act from obtaining passports, as putting individuals to an unconstitutional choice between exercising their right of international travel or their right of association). Cf. Kent v. Dulles, 357 U.S. 116 (1958). But see Haig v. Agee, 453 U.S. 280 (1981) (upholding executive power to revoke passport on ground that holder's activities are seriously damaging national security); Regan v. Wald, 468 U.S. 222 (1984) (upholding executive power to restrict travel to Cuba as part of economic boycott of that nation).

4. 378 U.S. at 505.

5. Shapiro v. Thompson, 394 U.S. 618, 641 (1969).

6. Id. at 641–42 (invalidating congressionally-enacted waiting period for welfare

"unmistakable essense" of a "principle of free interstate migration" in the very existence of a "document that transformed a loose confederation of states into one nation." [7]   Although the modern cases speak primarily of this right of interstate travel,[8] and though the right is often linked to notions of federalism,[9] it is clear that the right in question relates as much to the importance of lifting all artificial barriers to personal mobility as to the virtues of an integrated national economy and society.[10]

receipt by new residents of Washington, D.C.).

7. Zobel v. Williams, 457 U.S. 55, 67 (1982) (Brennan, J., joined by Marshall, Blackmun, and Powell, JJ., concurring).

8. See, e.g., id.; United States v. Guest, 383 U.S. 745 (1966) (holding criminally punishable under 18 U.S.C. § 242 a conspiracy to interfere with a citizen's right to travel, deeming such a right to be one secured by the Constitution within the meaning of § 242). The modern Court has consistently and firmly separated the right of interstate travel—which is "virtually unqualified"—from the "right" of international travel—"considered to be no more than an aspect of the 'liberty' protected by the due process clause of the fifth amendment . . . [which] can be regulated within the bounds of due process." Califano v. Aznavorian, 439 U.S. 170, 176 (1978); Haig v. Agee, 453 U.S. 280, 307 (1981).

9. See Zobel, supra note 7. See generally Chapters 6 and 7, supra. Both article IV's privileges and immunities clause—often taken as the source of a right to travel—and the commerce clause, originated in the fourth or so-called states' relations article of the Articles of Confederation: "The better to secure and perpetuate mutual friendship and intercourse among the people of the different States in this Union, the free inhabitants of each of these States, paupers, vagabonds and fugitives from justice excepted, shall be entitled to all privileges and immunities of free citizens in the several States; and the people of each State shall have free ingress and regress to and from any other State and shall enjoy therein all the privileges of trade and commerce, subject to the same duties, impositions and restrictions as the inhabitants thereof respectively. . . ."

10. As Chief Justice Fuller remarked at the turn of the century, "Undoubtedly the right of locomotion, the right to remove from one place to another according to inclination, is an attribute of personal liberty. . . ." Williams v. Fears, 179 U.S. 270, 274 (1900) (dictum). In Edwards v. California, 314 U.S. 160 (1941), a California law made it a crime to bring indigents into the state or to assist in their entry. Plainly enacted to stem the tide of poor people

who hoped to find a better life in the West, the law was invalidated as a forbidden interference with interstate commerce. But in a concurring opinion expressing no view on the soundness of the commerce clause rationale, Justice Douglas, joined by Justices Black and Murphy, relied on the theory that the right of interstate travel is an essential "incident of national citizenship protected by the privileges and immunities clause of the Fourteenth Amendment . . . ." Id. at 178 (emphasis omitted). See Chapter 7, supra. He argued: "[T]he right of persons to move freely from State to State occupies a more protected position in our constitutional system than does the movement of cattle, fruit, steel, and coal across state lines." Id. at 177. Justice Jackson concurred in the majority's opinion but also concluded that interstate migration was a privilege of national citizenship that could not be denied on the basis of "indigence." Id. at 184–86. The concurring opinions expressed the view that unimpeded travel represented not only an aspect of national unity but " 'an attribute of personal liberty,' " 314 U.S. at 179 (Douglas, J., quoting from Williams v. Fears, 179 U.S. 270, 274 (1900)); they realized that "[t]o hold that the measure of . . . rights [to travel] is the commerce clause is likely to result eventually either in distorting the commercial law or in denaturing human rights." Id. at 182 (Jackson, J., concurring). They saw freedom of travel as part of the "power of citizenship as a shield against oppression," id., and not simply as part of the binding force of nationhood. Indeed, explicit protections of freedom of movement predate our nationhood. See Zobel v. Williams, 457 U.S. at 79 n.9 (O'Connor, J., concurring in the judgment).

Perhaps the most peculiar invocation of the right to travel can be found in B. Siegan, The Supreme Court's Constitution 106 (1987), which argues that the decision in Brown v. Board of Education, 347 U.S. 483 (1954), can be defended *only* on the ground that segregation by law—including forced travel by children to achieve segregated schools—violates "the right to travel, a right long secured by the federal courts," both "interstate and intrastate," as an element of due process "liberty." Perhaps

When the Supreme Court gave a narrow construction to the Secretary of State's passport denial power in order to avoid a constitutional question in *Kent v. Dulles*, it opined that "[t]ravel abroad, like travel within the country, may be necessary for a livelihood. It may be as close to the heart of the individual as the choice of what he eats, or wears, or reads." [11] And in *Shapiro v. Thompson*, the Court concluded that "our constitutional concepts of personal liberty . . . require that all citizens be free to travel throughout the length and breadth of our land uninhibited by statutes, rules, or regulations which unreasonably burden or restrict this movement." [12] Although a federalism-based interpretation of such freedom of travel would deny special protection to intrastate and international travel,[13] predicating freedom of travel on the mobility required for full personhood precludes any such construction of the right.

The Supreme Court in *Memorial Hospital v. Maricopa County* left open the question whether to "draw a constitutional distinction between interstate and intrastate travel," [14] but lower courts have uniformly treated intrastate travel as entitled to no less protection than travel across state lines. The Court of Appeals for the Second Circuit, in one of the major opinions on the subject, concluded that "the use of the term 'interstate travel' in Shapiro" was nothing "more than a reflection of the state-wide enactment involved in that case." The Second Circuit reasoned that it "would be meaningless to describe the right to travel between states as a fundamental precept of personal liberty and not to acknowledge a correlative constitutional right to travel within a state." [15]

Restrictions on the right to travel may be of several types. The first involves rules that impermissibly seek or operate to lock people into a jurisdiction by restricting emigration either directly or by making re-entry inordinately difficult.[16] The second involves rules that

Professor Siegan has confused the Jim Crow regime that once pervaded the American south with the distinct geographic "homelands" into which the Union of South Africa has herded many of its blacks. Curiously, the General Secretary of the Soviet Communist Party, Mikhail Gorbachev, seems to have labored under a similar misunderstanding when he suggested in 1987 that America address its "black problem" by establishing apartheid "homelands."

11. 357 U.S. 116, 126 (1958).

12. 394 U.S. 618, 629 (1969).

13. Protection for travel would then be limited to constraints imposed upon grounds that were independently forbidden or suspect. Note that Aptheker and Kent could have been decided the same way even if travel were of no constitutional magnitude, since *no* interest may be burdened or denied solely on the basis of political belief or association.

14. 415 U.S. 250, 255 (1974).

15. King v. New Rochelle Municipal Housing Auth., 442 F.2d 646, 648 (2d Cir. 1971), cert. denied 404 U.S. 863 (1971). See also Krzewinski v. Kugler, 338 F.Supp. 492 (D.N.J.1972); Eggert v. Seattle, 81 Wn.2d 840, 505 P.2d 801 (1973); McCay v. South Dakota, 366 F.Supp. 1244 (D.S.D.1973), vacated as moot 420 U.S. 904 (1975).)

16. Even when, as in Aptheker v. Secretary of State, 378 U.S. 500, 514 (1964), a restraint on leaving a jurisdiction does not turn on the individual's "purposes in and places for travel," it might of course operate to deter emigration by those who are uncertain of their ultimate intentions. See also In re King, 3 Cal.3d 226, 90 Cal.Rptr. 15, 474 P.2d 983 (1970) (striking down state statute making nonsupport a misdemeanor for a father within the state but a felony for one who remains outside the state for more than 30 days), cert. denied 403 U.S. 931 (1971); cf. Bigelow v. Virginia, 421 U.S. 809, 824 (1975), indicating, inter alia, that "Virginia [could not] prevent its residents from traveling to New York to obtain

restrict entry either (a) by discriminating against new residents with respect to various public services or benefits [17] or (b) by imposing quantitative controls on in-migration; [18] both (a) and (b) are void unless compellingly justified. The power of the federal government to limit immigration [19] thus has no parallel at the state or local level. In this second type of case, it is important to note that any state or local law restricting the sort of conduct that may occur within the jurisdiction may incidentally discourage in-migration by persons who would rather live in a place not having such a restriction. It does not follow, however, that an otherwise constitutional state or local law is rendered suspect, much less invalid, simply because of this inevitable effect. Qualitative as opposed to quantitative restraints on how a jurisdiction's land many be developed or used should thus be immune to challenge on right-to-travel grounds so long as they do not discriminate against new residents.[20]

Third, rules that neither lock people in nor fence them out, and indeed may have no effect whatever on personal decisions about where to reside, might impermissibly inhibit travel either (a) by making movement itself unjustifiably difficult or hazardous; [21] or (b) by attach-

[abortion services legal in New York but illegal at that time in Virginia] or . . . prosecute them for going there." But cf. note 28, infra.

17. See, e.g., Zobel v. Williams, 457 U.S. 55 (1982) (striking down Alaska's statutory formula for dividing shares of its surplus oil-boom wealth to state residents in direct proportion to the recipient's length of post-statehood residence); Memorial Hospital v. Maricopa County, 415 U.S. 250 (1974) (striking down a one-year residency requirement for non-emergency county medical care); Shapiro v. Thompson, 394 U.S. 618 (1969) (striking down one-year residency requirement for welfare payments; Constitution's objection is not to the requirement of residency per se, but to the unjustified duration of the residency requirement). But cf. Starns v. Malkerson, 401 U.S. 985 (1971), summarily aff'g 326 F.Supp. 234 (D.Minn.1970) (upholding one-year residency requirement for reduced, in-state tuition rate). See § 6–35, supra, and note 22, infra.

18. In Construction Industry Ass'n v. City of Petaluma, 375 F.Supp. 574, 581 (N.D.Cal.1974), rev'd for lack of standing to raise the travel issue, 522 F.2d 897 (9th Cir. 1975), cert. denied 424 U.S. 934 (1976), a local zoning ordinance designed to limit growth by excluding "substantial numbers of people who would otherwise have elected to immigrate into the city . . ." was held to violate "the people's right to travel." The court deemed "the question of where a person should live" to be "one within the exclusive realm of the individual's prerogative, not within the decision-making power of any governmental unit."

See also Appeal of Girsh, 437 Pa. 237, 263 A.2d 395 (1970); Appeal of Kit-Mar Builders, 439 Pa. 466, 268 A.2d 765 (1970). See generally Ellickson, "Suburban Growth Controls: An Economic and Legal Analysis," 86 Yale L.J. 385 (1977).

19. See § 5–16, supra.

20. The Court was thus entirely correct to reject the right-to-travel challenge in Village of Belle Terre v. Boraas, 416 U.S. 1 (1974) (upholding zoning ordinance that limited to two the number of unrelated persons who could live in any household), discussed in §§ 15–17 to 15–20, infra. The validity of such a law should be tested against its impact upon the rights of all persons subject to it, rather than against any incidental tendency to inhibit certain outsiders from moving in. However, it is conceivable that the local laws making towns and municipalities homogeneous enclaves might cumulatively lead to a society in which migration from one jurisdiction to another, as a practical matter, becomes extremely difficult. If a showing is made that persons must in effect choose between changing their ways of life and staying put, a right-to-travel challenge should succeed. Cf. Aptheker v. Secretary of State, 378 U.S. at 507 (individual cannot constitutionally be put to a choice between travel and "membership in a given association").

21. Such rules may in turn take two forms. The first and perhaps most pernicious makes moving, walking, or wandering about a crime. The second makes travel a crime if undertaken with a specified purpose. As to the first, the Court struck a major blow for freedom of movement in

ing adverse consequences, without reasonable justification, to the fact of nonresidence.[22]

A final distinction may be worth making between travel as an aspect of expression or education,[23] and travel as a means of changing

Papachristou v. Jacksonville, 405 U.S. 156 (1972), holding violative of due process a municipal vagrancy ordinance which targeted for criminal penalties a wide variety of individuals including "dissolute persons who go about begging, . . . common night walkers, . . . persons wandering or strolling around from place to place without any lawful purpose or object, habitual loafers, disorderly persons, persons neglecting all lawful business and habitually spending their time by frequenting houses of ill fame," id. at 156–57 n.1, and a host of others. Noting that persons "wandering or strolling" from place to place "have been extolled by Walt Whitman and Vachel Lindsay," id. at 164, the Court said boldly that "these activities are historically part of the amenities of life as we have known them." Although "not mentioned in the Constitution or in the Bill of Rights," these "unwritten amenities have been in part responsible for giving our people the feeling of independence and self-confidence, the feeling of creativity." They "have dignified the right of dissent and have honored the right to be nonconformists and the right to defy submissiveness. They have encouraged lives of high spirits rather than hushed, suffocating silence." Id. Thus the Court recognized a protected right to move about. See also Kolender v. Lawson, 461 U.S. 352 (1983) (invalidating, as unconstitutionally vague, a California statute making it a misdemeanor to "loiter[ ] or wander[ ] upon the streets or from place to place without apparent reason or business and [to] refuse[ ] to identify [oneself] and to account for [one's] presence when requested by any police officer so to do, if the surrounding circumstances are such as to indicate to a reasonable man that the public safety demands such identification"). Cf. United States v. Chalk, 441 F.2d 1277 (4th Cir. 1971), cert. denied 404 U.S. 943 (1971) (finding a citywide nighttime curfew imposed after civil disorders a "reasonable" limitation on the right to travel).

As to the second form, the most important opinion may be United States v. Dellinger, 472 F.2d 340, 358, 362 (7th Cir. 1972), cert. denied 410 U.S. 970 (1973), upholding the federal Anti-Riot Act against a right-to-travel claim; existence of a "relation to action which can be made illegal . . . narrow[ed] the imposition on travel to instances adequately involving a purpose which the government may counter," but there "would be the most serious doubt

whether an individual's travel with intent to do something inimical to the interests of the community, but without taking any step other than the individual travel being taken to effect the intent, could be made an offense."

22. A polity is entitled to reserve to its citizens certain aspects of self-government, such as the franchise, see Dunn v. Blumstein, 405 U.S. 330 (1972), and the right to hold elective office, see Kanapaux v. Ellisor, 419 U.S. 891 (1974). There also appear to be some goods and services that a state's residents, having created or preserved for themselves, are entitled to keep for themselves. See, e.g., Martinez v. Bynum, 461 U.S. 321 (1983) (public schools); Doe v. Bolton, 410 U.S. 179, 200 (1973) (medical services—residency requirement invalidated because "not based on any policy of preserving state-supported facilities for Georgia residents"); Baldwin v. Montana Fish and Game Commission, 436 U.S. 371 (1978) (state maintained elk herds—upholding higher hunting license fees for non-residents). But with respect to goods and opportunities that exist within a given state but that are not attributable to state programs or revenues, the privileges and immunities clause by and large forbids a regime of unequal access for outlanders. See, e.g., Hicklin v. Orbeck, 437 U.S. 518 (1978) (unanimously striking down the Alaska Hire statute, which required that residents be given preference for most jobs in the state's booming oil industry). The interests of national cohesion may also forbid discrimination against those from out-of-state even when state programs or revenues play a significant role in creating or sustaining the other good in question. Police and fire departments are quintessentially creatures of the state, supported by state or local revenue and operated for the good of the local citizenry, yet it is inconceivable that a state would be permitted to deny police and fire protection to tourists or short-term visitors. See § 6–35, supra. For a discussion of travel as a fundamental right under equal protection analysis, see § 16–8, infra.

23. "This freedom of movement is the very essence of our free society, setting us apart. Like the right of assembly and the right of association, it often makes all other rights meaningful—knowing, studying arguing, exploring, conversing, observing and even thinking. Once the right to travel is curtailed, all other rights suffer, just

one's place of residence and beginning life anew. Both dimensions of personal mobility are important in fleshing out the notion of personhood, and the close surveillance and control of travel in both its senses has always been a central technique of the totalitarian state,[24] but centuries of experience should suffice to mark as especially suspect any government measure designed to prevent the emigration of those dissatisfied with the existing order,[25] or the immigration of those who

as when curfew or home detention is placed on a person." Aptheker v. Secretary of State, 378 U.S. 500, 520 (1964) (Douglas, J., concurring). In Zemel v. Rusk, 381 U.S. 1 (1965), however, the Court upheld the Secretary of State's refusal to validate American passports for travel to Cuba. Recognizing that such refusal "renders less than wholly free the flow of information concerning that country," id. at 16, the Court trivialized the challenge to the restraint by observing that "the prohibition of unauthorized entry into the White House" likewise "diminishes the citizen's opportunities to gather information he might find relevant to his opinion of the way the country is being run . . ." Id. at 17. To be sure, the "right to speak and publish does not carry with it the *unrestrained* right to gather information," id. (emphasis added), but the question remains whether a given restraint, not even mandated but merely authorized by Congress, is sufficiently justified in light of the significance of the inhibition it entails. The "only . . . danger present [in the Zemel case] is the Communist regime in Cuba. The world, however, is filled with Communist thought; and Communist regimes are on more than one continent. They are part of the world spectrum; and if we are to know them and understand them, we must mingle with them, as Pope John said [in Pacem in Terris]. Keeping alive intellectual intercourse between opposing groups has always been important and perhaps was never more important than now." Id. at 25 (Douglas, J., dissenting). Although Justice Douglas might have been overstating the case in light of "the Cuban missile crisis of October, 1962," which "preceded the filing of appellant's complaint by less than two months," id. at 16 (majority opinion of Warren, C.J.), his was a useful reminder that the power approved in Zemel must be limited to the most extraordinary situations. It is a reminder the Court has not recently heeded. See, e.g., Regan v. Wald, 468 U.S. 222 (1984) (upholding executive power to restrict travel to Cuba as part of economic boycott of that nation; Court effectively equates presidential power to restrict trade in cigars with power to ban movement of people). Cf. Edwards v. California, discussed in note 10, supra.

In Haig v. Agee, 453 U.S. 280 (1981), the Court upheld the State Department's power to revoke a passport on a finding that the holder's foreign activities constituted a serious threat to national security or foreign policy. Agee, a former CIA official, had been traveling around the world exposing hundreds of CIA employees, resulting in the assassination of agents and the disruption of operations. See id. at 283–85 & n.7. The majority found that, "[t]o the extent the revocation of his passport operates to inhibit Agee, 'it is an inhibition of *action*,' rather than of speech." Id. at 309 (emphasis supplied by the Court) (citation omitted). The precise nature of Agee's attack on the CIA, regardless of whether one deems it speech or action, obviously had a major impact on the Court, which noted that, " '[w]hile the Constitution protects against invasions of individual rights, it is not a suicide pact.' " Id. at 309–10 (citation omitted).

24. "Free movement by the citizen is of course as dangerous to a tyrant as free expression of ideas or the right of assembly and it is therefore controlled in most countries in the interests of security. That is why riding boxcars carries extreme penalties in Communist lands. That is why the ticketing of people and the use of identification papers are routine matters under totalitarian regimes, yet abhorrent in the United States." Aptheker v. Secretary of State, 378 U.S. 500, 520 (1964) (Douglas, J., concurring). See also Kolender v. Lawson, 461 U.S. 352 (1983), where the Court struck down a California statute making it a crime to "loiter[ ] or wander[ ] upon the streets or from place to place without apparent reason or business and [to] refuse[ ] to identify [oneself] and to account for [one's] presence when requested by any police officer so to do, if the surrounding circumstances are such as to indicate to a reasonable man that the public safety demands such identification." The Court determined that the law was unconstitutionally vague and therefore, by leaving too much discretion in the hands of individual police officers, created great opportunity for abuse and oppression.

25. See, e.g., The Bible, Exodus 5 (King James version): "And afterward Moses and Aaron went in, and told Pharaoh, Thus

might alter the status quo.[26] Just as government should be forbidden to expel the citizen who has become a source of unrest,[27] so it cannot be permitted to imprison the citizen who seeks freedom in another land.[28]

§ 15–15. Life Plan or Style: Appearance and Apparel

In 1958, the Supreme Court invoked the existence of a right to control personal appearance as support for its recognition of the right to travel canvassed in § 15–15. "The right to travel," the Court reasoned in *Kent v. Dulles*, "may be as close to the heart of the individual as the choice of what he eats, *or wears*, or reads." [1] In nearly

saith the LORD GOD of Israel, Let My people go. . . ."

26. Kleindienst v. Mandel, 408 U.S. 753 (1972), is not authority to the contrary. There the Court reversed a federal district court decision ordering the Attorney General to grant a temporary nonimmigrant visa to a Belgian journalist and Marxist theoretician whom various Americans had invited to take part in academic conferences and discussions in this country. Mandel was ineligible for admission under statutory provisions that excluded aliens who advocate "the . . . doctrines of world communism," id. at 755, and the Attorney General had declined to exercise his statutory power to waive Mandel's ineligibility on the ground that "previous abuses by Mandel," involving unscheduled activities on a previous visit to the United States, "made it inappropriate to grant a waiver again." Id. at 769. The Court held that this "facially legitimate and bona fide reason" for refusing a waiver made irrelevant the first amendment interests of those wishing to communicate with Mandel. Id. at 770. Having conceded "that Congress could enact a blanket prohibition against entry of all aliens" who, like Mandel, were advocates of international communism, id. at 767, the appellees were in the difficult posture of having to claim a right to a waiver from a ban whose legitimacy they accepted. Moreover, although the Court wisely rejected any suggestion that appellees' "free access to Mandel's ideas through his books and speeches [or even through] tapes or telephone hook-ups" could fully substitute for "sustained, face-to-face debate, discussion and questioning," id. at 765, the availability of such partial replacements for Mandel's "physical presence," id., plainly precludes invocation of this case as precedent for any general exclusion of a group of persons for the purpose, or with the effect, of preventing their ideas from challenging governmental policy or prevailing ideology. The fact that Congress may have done just that in the statutory provisions from which Mandel sought a waiver does not alter this conclusion inasmuch as the validity of those pro-

visions was conceded by counsel in the case and thus was not an issue before the Court. See Brief for Appellees at 16.

27. Cf. Trop v. Dulles, 356 U.S. 86 (1958) (holding it a cruel and unusual punishment violative of the eighth amendment to strip person of citizenship upon court martial conviction and dishonorable discharge for deserting armed services in time of war).

28. See generally A. O. Hirschmann, Exit, Voice & Loyalty: Responses to Decline in Firms, Organizations, and States (1970). This does not mean that the government must facilitate a citizen's crusade against the government by granting him a passport, see Haig v. Agee, 453 U.S. 280 (1981), discussed in note 23, supra, nor that the government is forbidden to make travel an independent or aggravating element of a crime. See Jones v. Helms, 452 U.S. 412, 422–23 (1981) (upholding a Georgia law that transforms willful child abandonment from a misdemeanor into a felony when accompanied by departure from the state: "although a simple penalty for leaving a state is plainly impermissible, if departure aggravates the consequences of conduct that is otherwise punishable, the state may treat the entire sequence of events . . . as more serious than its separate components"). A contrary result in Jones might have cast doubt on the validity of myriad federal laws criminalizing interstate travel when, for example, it involves flight to avoid prosecution or transportation of stolen goods.

§ 15–15

1. 357 U.S. 116, 125–26 (1958) (emphasis added). Some courts have cited the distinction drawn in Tinker v. Des Moines Independent School District, 393 U.S. 503, 507–08 (1969), between a prohibition of armbands worn in protest against the Vietnam War and the "regulation of the length of skirts or the type of clothing, [or] hair style, or deportment," as minimizing the rights affected by the latter regulations. See, e.g., King v. Saddleback Junior College District, 445 F.2d 932, 937 & n.9 (9th Cir. 1971), cert. denied 404 U.S. 979 (1971).

two hundred reported cases in the past two decades, individuals have challenged regulations seeking to control dress or grooming. The prolific efforts of the states to regulate personal appearance are reflected in the range of plaintiffs—high school [2] and college [3] students, teachers,[4] national guardsmen,[5] active military personnel,[6] reservists,[7] prisoners,[8] probation officers,[9] policemen,[10] firemen,[11] even attorneys.[12] Perhaps it is "understandable [that] some judges find students' 'long hair' claims constitutionally insubstantial" if "[m]easured against today's great constitutional issues [of] capital punishment, abortion, [and] school segregation," [13] but "[n]othing is more indicative of the importance currently being attached to hair growth by the general populace than the barrage of cases reaching the courts evidencing the attempt by one segment of society to control the plumage of another." [14] The fact is that while "[i]ndividual rights never seem important to those who tolerate their infringement," [15] the constitutional guarantee of "liberty" is "an incomplete protection if it encompasses only the right to do momentous acts, leaving the state free to interfere with those personal aspects of our lives which have no direct bearing on the ability of others to enjoy their liberty." [16]

However, the statement in Tinker need imply no more than that the state must meet an even stricter burden of justification when political speech is at stake.

2. See note 14, infra.

3. See, e.g., King v. Saddleback Junior College District, 425 F.2d 426 (9th Cir. 1970), on remand 318 F.Supp. 89 (C.D.Cal. 1970), rev'd 445 F.2d 932 (9th Cir.), cert. denied 404 U.S. 979 (1971) (Douglas & White, JJ., dissenting); Lansdale v. Tyler Junior College, 318 F.Supp. 529 (E.D.Tex. 1970), aff'd 470 F.2d 659 (5th Cir. 1972) (en banc), cert. denied 411 U.S. 986 (1973) (Douglas, J., dissenting).

4. See, e.g., Miller v. School District No. 167, 495 F.2d 658 (7th Cir. 1974), reh'g denied 500 F.2d 711 (1974); Jeffries v. Turkey Run Consolidated School Dist., 492 F.2d 1 (7th Cir. 1974).

5. See, e.g., Friedman v. Froehlke, 470 F.2d 1351 (1st Cir. 1972); Anderson v. Laird, 437 F.2d 912 (7th Cir.), cert. denied 404 U.S. 865 (1971).

6. See, e.g., Doyle v. Koelbl, 434 F.2d 1014 (5th Cir. 1970), cert. denied 402 U.S. 908 (1971).

7. See note 28, infra.

8. See, e.g., Hill v. Estelle, 537 F.2d 214 (5th Cir. 1976); Burgin v. Henderson, 536 F.2d 501 (2d Cir. 1976).

9. See, e.g., Forstner v. San Francisco, 243 Cal.App.2d 625, 52 Cal.Rptr. 621 (1966); Burlingame v. Milone, 62 Misc.2d 853, 310 N.Y.S.2d 407 (1970).

10. See, e.g., Ashley v. Macon, 505 F.2d 868 (5th Cir. 1975); Stradley v. Andersen, 478 F.2d 188 (8th Cir. 1973).

11. See, e.g., Kamerling v. O'Hagan, 512 F.2d 443 (2d Cir. 1975), cert. denied 425 U.S. 942 (1976); Michini v. Rizzo, 379 F.Supp. 837 (E.D.Pa.1974), aff'd 511 F.2d 1394 (3d Cir. 1975).

12. See, e.g., Sandstrom v. State, 309 So.2d 17 (Fla.App.1975) (criminal contempt conviction for failure to wear tie), aff'd 311 So.2d 804 (Fla.Dist.Ct.App.1975), cert. discharged 336 So.2d 572 (Fla.Sup.Ct.1976).

13. Arnold v. Carpenter, 459 F.2d 939, 941 n.5 (7th Cir. 1972) (invalidating school hair code despite preparation by teacher/ student/parent committee and provision for deviation with parental consent).

14. Ham v. South Carolina, 409 U.S. 524, 529–30 (1973) (Douglas, J., dissenting from the Court's refusal to require trial judge, in criminal prosecution for illegal drug possession, to permit bearded defendant to inquire of jurors' possible bias against beards; majority relied on trial judge's willingness to permit defense inquiry into bias in general and stressed "the traditionally broad discretion accorded the trial judge in conducting *voir dire*," id. at 528.). The past two decades have seen at least 120 reported cases concerning grooming regulations in secondary schools alone.

15. Karr v. Schmidt, 460 F.2d 609, 619 (5th Cir. 1972) (en banc) (dissenting opinion of Wisdom, J., joined by Brown, C.J., and Thornberry, Goldberg, and Simpson, JJ.), cert. denied 409 U.S. 989 (1972).

16. Richards v. Thurston, 424 F.2d 1281, 1284–85 (1st Cir. 1970) (invalidating school suspension of 17-year-old boy for refusing to cut his shoulder-length hair).

Although many courts have recognized that a person's appearance and apparel, and particularly hair growth, may well represent "an affirmative declaration of an individual's commitment to a change in social values," [17] most have rejected "the notion that . . . hair length is of a sufficiently communicative character to warrant the full protection of the First Amendment," [18] even while finding particular governmental interferences with hair to be unwarranted intrusions into personal liberty. The motivations of most high school students for resisting hair-length rules were probably typified by the refreshingly candid statements of the plaintiffs in *Freeman v. Flake*—"they 'wanted' to have longer hair, they 'liked' it and they thought it was their 'right.'" [19] But one need not regard a person's hair length as fully equivalent to speech in order to perceive that governmental compulsion in this realm invades an important aspect of personality.

The assumption that such an invasion would be unconstitutional is reflected in the 1789 debates in Congress over which guarantees needed explicit articulation in the Bill of Rights.[20] "[W]hile [the Founders] may have regarded the right as a trifle as long as it was honored, they clearly would not have so regarded it if it were infringed." [21] History abounds with examples of governments asserting virtually boundless authority over the details of personal appearance and manners. Rome's Oppian Law in 215 B.C. banned colorful dresses; Charles V forbade the wearing of pointed shoes; Peter the Great issued an edict in 1698 regulating the wearing of beards throughout Russia.[22] When American school boards promulgated rules in the 1960's telling their

17. Ham v. South Carolina, 409 U.S. 524, 529–30 (1973) (Douglas, J., dissenting).

18. Richards, supra note 16, at 1283.

19. 320 F.Supp. 531, 537 (D.Utah 1970), aff'd 448 F.2d 258 (10th Cir. 1971), cert. denied 405 U.S. 1032 (1972). However, in some cases, square first amendment claims were much more weighty. For example, in New Rider v. Board of Education, 480 F.2d 693 (10th Cir. 1973), cert. denied 414 U.S. 1097 (1973), three Pawnee Indian junior high school students sought a right to wear long braided hair, claiming religious heritage and tradition and adducing some expert testimony to that effect. The state's experts spoke of school spirit, discipline, pride, maturity, and the relation between hair length and scholarly attainments as well as between hair length and troublemaking. The court found no fundamental right or suspect classification, upholding the hair rule as advancing the rational state goal of "instilling pride and initiative among the students" and advancing "scholarship attainment and high school spirit and morale." See also Hatch v. Goerke, 502 F.2d 1189 (10th Cir. 1974); cf. School District No. 11–J v. Howell, 33 Colo.App. 57, 517 P.2d 422 (1973). Justice Douglas's dissent from the Court's denial of certiorari in the New Rider case noted the history of forced assimilation in Indian

education, and argued that the desire of the Indian children to wear braids was sufficiently "akin to pure speech" to bring the case "within the ambit of Tinker." 414 U.S. at 1099.

20. See I. Brant, The Bill of Rights 53–67 (1965).

21. Kelley v. Johnson, 425 U.S. 238, 252 (1976) (Marshall, J., dissenting). Dissenting from one of the Court's many refusals to take up student hair length controversies, Justice Douglas surmised "that a nation bent on turning out robots might insist that every male have a crew cut and every female wear pigtails," but supposed "that it would be an invidious discrimination to withhold [basic government services such as health protection or education] merely because a person was an offbeat nonconformist when it came to hairdo and dress as well as diet, race, religion, or his views on Vietnam". Ferrell v. Dallas Independent School District, 393 U.S. 856 (1968). See also Justice Douglas's dissent from the denial of certiorari in Olff v. East Side Union High School District, 404 U.S. 1042 (1972).

22. See W. & A. Durant, The Age of Louis XIV 386–410 (1963); J. Robinson, Readings in European History (1906).

students how to dress and how to wear their hair, they were asserting a similarly sweeping power over personality and its presentation: "Hair . . . for centuries has been one aspect of the manner in which we hold ourselves out to the rest of the world. . . . A person shorn of the freedom to vary the length and style of his hair is forced against his will to hold himself out symbolically as a person holding ideas contrary, perhaps, to ideas he holds most dear. Forced dress, including forced hair style, humiliates the unwilling complier, forces him to submerge his individuality in the 'undistracting' mass, and in general, smacks of the exaltation of organization over member, unit over component, and state over individual." [23]

In *Kelley v. Johnson*, the Supreme Court nonetheless upheld a police department regulation of officers' hair styles, rationalizing the rule in terms of "the deference due [the county's] choice of an organizational structure for its police force," [24] and the county's possible "desire to make police officers readily recognizable to the members of the public, or a desire for the esprit de corps which such similarity is felt to inculcate within the police force itself." [25] The majority required only that the regulation not be "so irrational that it may be branded 'arbitrary.' " [26]

It remains uncertain how widely the *de minimis* standard of review of *Kelley v. Johnson* will be applied.[27] The Court emphasized that there was no need to decide "whether the citizenry at large had some sort of 'liberty' interest within the Fourteenth Amendment in matters of personal appearance," since its analysis was dictated by the fact that the plaintiff brought suit "not as a member of the citizenry at large,"

---

23. Karr v. Schmidt, 460 F.2d 609, 621 (5th Cir. 1972) (en banc) (Wisdom, J., dissenting from the announcement of an essentially per se rule upholding all school hair regulations), cert. denied 409 U.S. 989 (1972).

24. 425 U.S. 238, 246 (1976).

25. Id. at 248. Justice Powell, in a concurring opinion, wrote that imposition of a grooming code in many contexts would constitute "an impermissible intrusion upon liberty," and that even judicial review of police grooming rules required a "weighing of the degree of infringement of the individual's liberty interest against the need for the regulation." Id. at 249.

26. Id. The majority did not feel compelled to offer any reply to Justice Marshall's dissenting observation that simply requiring a policeman to wear an appropriate wig while on duty would serve all of the interests articulated by the county. Id. at 255 n.7. If pressed, the county would have to respond that it is entitled to limit its police force to the kinds of people who would find no offense in being told how to wear their hair. Although government cannot limit its ordinary employees to

those whose political affiliations accord with the majority's, see Elrod v. Burns, 427 U.S. 347 (1976) (patronage firings held unconstitutional for non-policy making employees), perhaps the state can at least limit membership in its military or its police to individuals of a more conformist and authoritarian leaning. Cf. Lewis v. Hyland, 554 F.2d 93 (3d Cir. 1977) (class of "long-haired highway travelers" established that they were subjected to illegal stops and searches by New Jersey State Police solely because of their "highly individualized personal appearance;" injunctive relief denied solely because of the institutional concerns articulated in Rizzo v. Goode, 423 U.S. 362 (1976)), cert. denied 434 U.S. 931 (1977).

27. Compare Jacobs v. Kunes, 541 F.2d 222, 224 (9th Cir. 1976) (standard applies to all public employees), with Syrek v. Pennsylvania Air National Guard, 537 F.2d 66, 67 (3d Cir. 1976) (reversing trial court's dismissal, for failure to state a claim, of suit concerning hair length regulation brought by civilian employees of National Guard, and remanding to trial court to determine relevance of Kelley).

but "as an employee of the county and, more particularly, a police-man." [28]

The most prolific area of hair litigation has concerned rules applied in the public schools.[29] Students attend school neither at their own voluntary discretion nor under the same compulsion and disabilities as prisoners.[30] Yet many courts have been reluctant to interfere with the discretionary authority of school officials, which has been recognized as to other aspects of school affairs.[31] Some of the lower courts have responded by subjecting school hair rules to little or no scrutiny, but most have analyzed such rules more strictly, requiring that school officials at least demonstrate an actual relationship to important school objectives, and a few have invalidated such rules where a still more substantial relationship could not be proven.[32]

Despite occasional dicta to the effect that the rights of children to control their appearance are dependent upon parental consent,[33] there is no sound reason to reject in this context the basic proposition that children are persons with enforceable rights of their own. The freedom

---

28. 425 U.S. at 244, 245. The Court's later per curiam dismissal of a writ of certiorari, see Quinn v. Muscare, 425 U.S. 560 (1976), did suggest that the same level of scrutiny would be applied to fire departments' grooming rules, although some lower courts had drawn distinctions between the two uniformed forces. See, e.g., Black v. Rizzo, 360 F.Supp. 648 (E.D.Pa. 1973). Lower courts have split as to whether military reservists may be compelled to comply with hair regulations by cutting their hair compelled to comply with hair regulations by cutting their hair rather than by wearing wigs. See Ayen v. McLucas, 401 F.Supp. 1001, 1004 (D.Nev.1975) (collecting cases).

29. Schools have not stopped at regulating hair. See, e.g., Wallace v. Ford, 346 F.Supp. 156 (E.D.Ark.1972), one interesting decision approving some aspects of a high school dress code (e.g., a ban on short dresses), and disapproving others (e.g., a ban on long dresses). See also Bannister v. Paradis, 316 F.Supp. 185 (D.N.H.1970) (striking prohibition of dungarees); Hernandez v. School District No. 1, 315 F.Supp. 289 (D.Colo.1970) (upholding prohibition of berets); Johnson v. Joint School District No. 60, 95 Idaho 317, 508 P.2d 547 (1973) (striking requirement that girls wear dresses).

30. Cf. Brooks v. Wainwright, 428 F.2d 652 (5th Cir. 1970) (upholding grooming regulation for prisoners and distinguishing school regulations).

31. See, e.g., Ingraham v. Wright, 430 U.S. 651 (1977) (corporal punishment); Epperson v. Arkansas, 393 U.S. 97, 104, 105 (1968) (dicta on curriculum control).

32. The circuits have actually fallen into four rough categories: (1) The Fourth, Seventh and Eighth Circuits have explicitly required something greater than "reasonableness" of grooming rules; (2) The First, Second, Third, Sixth and Ninth Circuits have all purported to apply "reasonableness" tests, but the actual degree of scrutiny underlying that formula has varied from quite strict (First and Second Circuits) to highly deferential (Third, Sixth and Ninth Circuits); (3) The Fifth Circuit has erected a per se rule against district courts' entertaining high school hair claims, apparently leaving the door open only to allegations of an especially "arbitrary effect"; on the other hand, a general rule *against* grooming regulation has been imposed at the college level; (4) Finally, the Tenth and District of Columbia Circuits have held that there is not a sufficient constitutional interest at stake even to raise a substantial federal question. See generally Freeman v. Flake, 405 U.S. 1032 (1972) (Douglas, J., dissenting from denial of certiorari) (collecting cases).

Although over 15 years have passed since the dissenters in Karr v. Schmidt, 460 F.2d 609, 619 (5th Cir. 1972), cert. denied 409 U.S. 989 (1972), thought it "hard to believe that the [Supreme] Court will close its eyes eternally to the disparate recognition now being given the constitutional rights of students who quite fortuitously inhabit different judicial circuits," the Court has continued to deny certiorari in such cases.

33. Arnold v. Carpenter, 459 F.2d 939, 944 (7th Cir. 1972) (Stevens, J., dissenting from invalidation of hair regulation where parents of student upheld son's claim but simply refused to sign consent form).

to shape one's personality through appearance is at least as important during the psychologically formative years of youth and adolescence as during adulthood. Indeed, it could be argued that such freedom is even more fundamental for the young: after all, they will have ample opportunity to experience the joys of conformity—and to reap its rewards—after they come of age.

§ 15–16. Controlling a Life's Informational Traces: Reputation and Records

Among the rights of personality that must be of central concern are those that relate to the presentation of self—not simply in the sense of shaping one's appearance and selecting one's apparel, but in the more general sense of controlling the mass of information by which the world defines one's identity. Of concern here are not solely those techniques of information-gathering that independently offend such constitutional guarantees as those of the first and fourth amendments, as in unlawful search and seizure,[1] nor solely those activities that entail independently unconstitutional uses of information already in government's possession,[2] nor even those informational probes thought to be objectionable solely because they unduly chill the exercise of otherwise protected rights of personal choice with respect to expression or association[3] or some other specially protected sphere of action,[4] but something at once more general and more elusive.

Of concern in this section is any system of governmental information-gathering, information-preservation, and/or information-dissemination that threatens to leave individuals with insufficient control over who knows what about their lives. Such control must be understood as a basic part of the right to shape the "self" that one presents to the

---

§ 15–16

1. See, e.g., United States v. United States District Court, 407 U.S. 297 (1972) (warrantless domestic security wiretapping violates fourth amendment and implicates policies of first amendment). But cf. Anderson v. Sills, 56 N.J. 210, 265 A.2d 678 (1970) (holding extensive system of dossiers consistent with Constitution).

2. Some uses of information by government are unconstitutional because they were obtained through an unlawful search and seizure, Mapp v. Ohio, 367 U.S. 643 (1961), or through coercion, Garrity v. New Jersey, 385 U.S. 493 (1967) (fifth amendment), or in some other unlawful manner; other uses of information are forbidden, regardless of how obtained, because they involve impermissible ways of acting on particular kinds of facts—whether facts about race, Brown v. Board of Education, 347 U.S. 483 (1954), or facts about political party, Elrod v. Burns, 427 U.S. 347 (1976), or about some other facet of a person's life.

3. See, e.g., Shelton v. Tucker, 364 U.S. 479 (1960) (overbroad inquiry into teacher's past associations); Talley v. California, 362

U.S. 60 (1960) (forbidden breach of leafleteers' anonymity); NAACP v. Alabama, 357 U.S. 449 (1958) (anonymity of organization's membership lists).

4. Compare, e.g., Thornburgh v. American College of Obstetricians & Gynecologists, 106 S.Ct. 2169, 2180–82 (1986) (striking down abortion reporting requirements that would have made available to the public detailed information about the woman, the doctor and the circumstances of the abortion), with Planned Parenthood v. Danforth, 428 U.S. 52, 79–81 (1976) (upholding abortion recordkeeping and reporting requirements "perhaps approaching permissible limits" but reasonably directed to preservation of maternal health and properly respecting patient's confidentiality and privacy); also compare Roberts v. Superior Court, 9 Cal.3d 330, 107 Cal.Rptr. 309, 508 P.2d 309 (1973) (blocking discovery of psychotherapist's records where plaintiff's mental condition was not at issue), with In re Lifschutz, 2 Cal.3d 415, 85 Cal. Rptr. 829, 467 P.2d 557 (1970) (requiring psychotherapist to answer questions directly relevant to subject of suit).

world, and on the basis of which the world in turn shapes one's existence. "Am I not what I am, to some degree in virtue of what others think and feel me to be?"[5]

The fourth amendment more than any other explicit constitutional provision reflects the existence of such a right, particularly since the Supreme Court recognized, in *Katz v. United States*,[6] the fundamental principle that the fourth amendment "protects people, not places." Yet, despite the elimination in *Katz* of the requirement that one show an invasion of a "constitutionally protected area,"[7] the Court has continued to hold that such practices as governmental encouragement and exploitation of misplaced personal confidences do not even *implicate* the fourth amendment. For example, in *United States v. Miller*,[8] the Court concluded that an individual has no fourth amendment expectation of privacy with respect to checks and deposit slips that he voluntarily conveys to a bank and thereby exposes to its employees in the ordinary course of business: "The depositor takes the risk, in revealing his affairs to another, that the information will be conveyed by that person to the government."[9] In *Smith v. Maryland*,[10] the Court again retreated by finding *Katz* to be irrelevant even in the context of telephone privacy unless actual interception of the phone conversation itself is at stake. The Court there held that no search occurs, and therefore no warrant is needed, when police, with the assistance of the phone company, make use of a pen register—a mechanical device placed on someone's phone line that records all numbers dialed from the phone and the times various numbers were dialed. The majority found that there is no legitimate expectation of privacy in the numbers dialed because the digits one dials are routinely recorded by the phone company for billing purposes. But, as Justice Stewart—the author of *Katz*—aptly pointed out, "that observation no more than describes the basic nature of telephone calls."[11] Come to think of it, the phone company, in its normal course of business, also electronically duplicates and transmits the *actual conversations* we have on our telephones; yet we are nonetheless entitled to assume that the words we utter "will not be broadcast to the world."[12] It should follow that "[w]hat the telephone company does or might do with those numbers is no more relevant to this inquiry than it would be in a case involving the conversation itself. It is simply not enough to say, after *Katz*, that there is no legitimate expectation of privacy in the numbers dialed

---

5. I. Berlin, Four Essays on Liberty 155 (1969).

6. 389 U.S. 347, 351 (1967).

7. Id.

8. 425 U.S. 435 (1976).

9. Id. at 443. Justices Brennan and Marshall dissented. In apparent agreement with the thrust of their dissent, Congress enacted the Right to Financial Privacy Act of 1978, Pub.L.No.95–630, which requires that bank customers be served with a copy of any federal subpoena or summons in court prior to its execution absent a protective order issued upon a showing that such notice would seriously jeopardize the investigation.

10. 442 U.S. 735 (1979). The first amendment aspects of Smith and Katz are discussed in §§ 12–22, supra.

11. Id. at 746 (dissenting opinion).

12. Katz, 389 U.S. at 352.

because the caller assumes the risk that the telephone company will disclose them to the police." [13]

The "assumption of risk"—more aptly, "assumption of broadcast"—notion underlying the holdings in *Smith* and *Miller* reveals alarming tendencies in the Supreme Court's understanding of what privacy means and ought to mean. The Court treats privacy almost as if it were "a discrete commodity, possessed absolutely or not at all." [14] Yet what could be more commonplace than the idea that it is up to the *individual* to *measure out information* about herself *selectively*—to whomever she chooses? Otherwise, we would not shield our account balances, income figures, and personal telephone and address books from the public eye, but might instead go about with this information written on our foreheads or our bumperstickers. Those "who disclose certain facts to a bank or phone company for a limited business purpose need not assume that this information will be released to persons for other purposes." [15] A majority of the Justices apparently confuse privacy with secrecy; yet even their notion of secrecy is a strange one, for a secret remains a secret even when shared with those whom one selects for one's confidences.

The Court's counter-intuitive understanding of "assumed risks" generates a terribly crabbed sense of the contemporary possibilities for privacy. Since "checks are not confidential communications but negotiable instruments," [16] we have no privacy interest protected by the federal Constitution in limiting public or government access to knowledge of our financial transactions unless we make all our deals in cash. Yet the world can learn a vast amount about us by knowing how and with whom we spend our money. And since we must dial numbers into the phone company's computers if we wish to talk on the phone, we have no federally protected privacy interest in the timing or duration of our conversations—or in the location or identity of those with whom we converse—unless we speak to people only face to face. Yet, as Justice Stewart put it, the "numbers dialed from a private telephone—although certainly more prosaic than the conversation itself—are not without 'content.' I doubt there are any [telephone users] who would be happy to have broadcast to the world a list of the local or long distance numbers they have called. This is not because such a list might in some sense be incriminating, but because it easily could reveal the identities of the persons and places called, and thus reveal the most intimate details of a person's life." [17] The mail that one receives from others, including the postmarks and return addresses on letters, can likewise reveal an enormous amount about an individual, yet a lower federal court has held that the police may freely ask postal authorities to record all such information contained on mail delivered to a given address. [18] Once one engages in correspondence, apparently, neither

---

13. Smith v. Maryland, 442 U.S. at 747 (Stewart, J., dissenting).

14. Id. at 749 (Marshall, J., dissenting).

15. Id.

16. Miller, 425 U.S. at 442.

17. Smith, 442 U.S. at 748 (dissenting opinion).

18. United States v. Choate, 576 F.2d 165 (9th Cir.1978) ("While the Supreme Court has not expressly passed on the mail cover device, recent analogous opinions

snow, nor rain, nor gloom of night, nor legitimate expectation of privacy can stay government from the swift and secret violation of one's privacy.[19]

Yet one can hardly be said to have assumed a risk of surveillance in a context where, as a practical matter, one had no choice. Only the most committed—and perhaps civilly commitable—hermit can live without a telephone, without a bank account, without mail. To say that one must take the bitter with the sweet when one licks a stamp is to exact a high constitutional price indeed for living in contemporary society.[20] Under so reductive and coercive a concept of assumed surveillance, to be modern is to be exposed.

In the words of Professor Yale Kamisar, "It is beginning to look as if the only way someone living in our society can avoid 'assuming the risk' that various intermediary institutions will reveal information to the police is by engaging in drastic discipline, the kind of discipline characteristic of life under totalitarian regimes."[21] The background rule is no longer that citizens are to be secure against unreasonable government searches, but that the Constitution's protections are waived whenever a person apprises another of facts that are of a sort the state might sometime find valuable—and not only in a criminal investigation. For the Court in these cases was not merely tinkering with the nuances of the exclusionary rule;[22] it was forthrightly declaring that government surveillance in these forms does not implicate the fourth amendment in any way. Hence not even civil remedies are available to prevent or redress such invasions of privacy, even where the target is not suspected of any wrongdoing.

At bottom, the Court's assumption of risk edges too close to a presumption of exposure: "whether privacy expectations are legitimate within the meaning of *Katz* [ought to] depend[ ] not on the risks an individual can be presumed to accept when imparting information to third parties, but on the risks he should be forced to assume in a free and open society."[23] As Justice Harlan—who formulated the standard the Court purported to apply in *Smith* and *Miller*—himself recognized, "[s]ince it is the task of the law to form and project, as well as mirror

lead us to conclude that it would not hold mail covers unconstitutional even though neither the addressee nor the sender is aware that the exterior data is being used for purposes other than the proper routing of the mail.").

19. Cf. Inscription on the New York City Post Office; Herodotus, Histories bk. VIII, ch. 98 (5th Cent. B.C.).

20. Cf. United States Postal Service v. Council of Greenburgh Civic Ass'ns, 453 U.S. 114 (1981) (Rehnquist, J., for the Court) (when one puts up a mailbox and receives deliveries from the U.S. Postal Service, one agrees to all Postal Service regulations, including rules barring the deposit in said mailbox of unstamped "mailable matter").

21. J. Choper, Y. Kamisar & L. Tribe, 1 The Supreme Court: Trends and Developments 143–44 (1979).

22. Perhaps one hidden cost of the exclusionary rule has been the incentive it creates, for a Court bent on strengthening the hand of the prosecution in criminal trials, to cut back on the substantive reach of the fourth amendment itself. Inasmuch as the amendment protects individuals entirely outside the context of criminal investigation and prosecution, this represents a particularly overbroad solution to whatever imbalance the exclusionary rule might be thought to have created.

23. Smith, 442 U.S. at 750 (Marshall, J., dissenting).

and reflect, we should not . . . merely recite . . . risks without examining the desirability of saddling them upon society." [24]

As unfortunate as these holdings are, cases like *Smith* and *Miller* do not end all discussion of control over life's informational traces; there remains the more general guarantee that liberty will not be infringed without due process of law. Government should be recognized to have a duty to provide reasonable assurance (1) that it is not needlessly, or in breach of the terms on which information was gathered, (a) maintaining or (b) releasing (or encouraging maintenance or release of) information [25] about people, however accurate; and (2) that such information as government either maintains or releases (or encourages others to maintain or release) is indeed as accurate as it can reasonably be made.

The duty to provide such assurance arises only when information is gathered, stored, or disseminated in ways that make likely its association with particular individuals; we are not talking here of any broad limit on governmental acquisition, processing, or release of data not linked with, or readily attached to, specific persons. Thus *United States v. Little*,[26] for example, upheld the practice of asking census questions involving personal and family characteristics, on pain of criminal punishment for refusing to reply, since the answers could be used only statistically and would never be disclosed so as to identify any individual.

At the same time, the very existence of stored information in which various facts are linked with identifying characteristics of particular persons entails potential threats to informational privacy and autonomy. As one commentator has observed,[27] "[r]ecords are mechanical memories not subject to the erosions of forgetfulness and the promise of eventual obliteration. The threat of misuse becomes as permanent as the records themselves. The risks to autonomy multiply not simply because of the heightened possibilities of unconsented reproduction and distribution at any given time, but also because those possibilities, however reduced by regulation, now extend indefinitely through time. Such a chronic and enduring risk must count as itself an injury."

Whether that injury should be cognizable as a matter of due process will invariably depend upon the need for retaining the records in question and the safeguards surrounding access to such records. Among the most suggestive modern cases bearing on this area is *California Bankers Ass'n v. Shultz*.[28] Following extensive hearings on the unavailability of foreign and domestic bank records of customers believed to be engaged in conduct entailing civil or criminal liability, Congress enacted the Bank Secrecy Act of 1970, which required financial institutions to maintain records of their customers' identities, to make microfilm copies of certain checks, to maintain records of various

---

24. United States v. White, 401 U.S. 745, 786 (1971) (dissenting opinion).

25. The term "information" is used here in its broadest sense, to include perceptions or assessments, whether conveyed verbally or pictorially.

26. 321 F.Supp. 388 (D.Del.1971).

27. Gerety, "Redefining Privacy," 12 Harv.Civ.Rts.-Civ.Lib.L.Rev. 233, 288 (1977).

28. 416 U.S. 21 (1974).

transactions, and to report currency transactions in excess of $10,000. The Court upheld the Act without reaching the plaintiffs' first, fourth, and fifth amendment claims.[29] Yet five Justices [30] perceived "substantial and difficult constitutional questions" in any governmental information-gathering or dissemination policies that would extend the challenged regulations' reporting requirements into a wider range of "transactions [that could] reveal much about a person's activities, associations, and beliefs," particularly as long as access to the reported information continued to be permitted "without invocation of the judicial process." [31]

Lower courts, at least, have widely recognized protected rights both to expunge potentially derogatory but inaccurate records and to prevent needless dissemination of records, however accurate, obtained for one purpose but employed for another, rights which of course entail an underlying right of reasonable access to all government files in which one's identity figures. In *Menard v. Saxbe*, for example, the District of Columbia Circuit recognized a statutory right to the expungement of FBI arrest records where probable cause for arrest had been absent.[32] The district court decision which *Menard* modified, likewise relying on statutory grounds chosen to avoid constitutional problems, had ruled that there is a right to prevent dissemination of arrest records, however accurate, for employment, licensing, or other non-law-enforcement purposes.[33]

Acquired Immune Deficiency Syndrome (AIDS) has created the most controversial context in which the right of record privacy arises today. Obviously, the compilation of accurate information about the incidence and transmission of this fatal condition is essential for the development of an effective public health response. It is equally obvious that such information must be handled with extreme discretion. Dissemination of the fact that someone has contracted AIDS, or even tested positive for antibodies to the virus that causes the disease, can cause that person to lose his employment, housing, insurance coverage, visitation rights with his children, and other privileges, rights and opportunities.[34] In particular, since gay men constituted the major risk group in the initial phases of the AIDS epidemic in the United States, a diagnosis of AIDS or a positive antigen test was tantamount to

---

29. Id. at 69–70, 73–76.

30. See id. at 78 (concurring opinion of Powell, J., joined by Blackmun, J.); id. at 79 (Douglas, J., dissenting); id. at 91 (Brennan, J., dissenting); id. at 93 (Marshall, J., dissenting).

31. Id. at 78–79 (Powell, J., concurring). Cf. Note, "Electronic Funds Transfer Systems: A Need for New Law?" 12 N.Eng.L. Rev. 111, 120 n.26 (1976).

32. 498 F.2d 1017 (D.C.Cir. 1974) (construing statute to avoid constitutional difficulties). See also Sullivan v. Murphy, 478 F.2d 938 (D.C.Cir. 1973), cert. denied 414 U.S. 880 (1974) ("Mayday" mass arrests); Hughes v. Rizzo, 282 F.Supp. 881 (E.D.Pa. 1968) (arrests harassing "hippies").

33. Menard v. Mitchell, 328 F.Supp. 718 (D.D.C.1971) (Gesell, J.). See also Eddy v. Moore, 5 Wn.App. 334, 487 P.2d 211 (1971) (ordering local authorities to return fingerprints and photographs taken at time of plaintiff's arrest since charges had been dismissed at trial and no compelling showing was made of need to retain prints or photos): Davidson v. Dill, 180 Colo. 123, 503 P.2d 157 (1972); Annotation, 46 A.L.R.3d 900 (1972).

34. See Closen, Connor, Kaufman & Wojcik, "AIDS: Testing Democracy—Irrational Responses to the Public Health Crisis and the Need for Privacy in Serologic Testing," 19 J.Marsh.L.Rev. 835, 903–16 (1986).

identification as a homosexual—itself a grievous stigma and the source of much discrimination and harassment in contemporary America.[35] Indeed, the harms of exposure as a current or potential AIDS victim are so great that concern about the confidentiality of medical records itself jeopardizes medical research and public health measures.[36] As AIDS antibody testing becomes more extensive and as state- and even nation-wide computer registries are established to centralize data about the disease and those whom it has touched, the need for tight regulation of access to such records can only become more dramatic. By 1986, several states had acted to codify the right of privacy with respect to AIDS antibody testing.[37]

Implicit in one major Supreme Court decision is a parallel principle about needless governmental dissemination of defamatory information. In *Doe v. McMillan*, parents were prevented by the speech and debate clause from successfully suing congressional committee members and their staffs for releasing the names of students about whom the committee had learned in its investigation of the District of Columbia public schools, but they were permitted, notwithstanding congressional authorization of the release of names, to proceed against the printer and superintendent of documents for disseminating the students' names.[38] The majority did not reach the question whether such dissemination served legitimate legislative functions and was thus immune to suit (the case was remanded on that question), but a concurring opinion by Justice Douglas, joined by Justices Brennan and Marshall, opined that exposure for its own sake had been demonstrated and that such exposure, especially in an age of computerized data banks that magnify

35. See § 15–21, infra. In California, a man was fired after his medical records were leaked to his employer. Although he did not have AIDS, rumors spread that he did. He received abusive phone calls and his house was set on fire. See Comment, "AIDS: A Legal Epidemic?" 17 Akron L.Rev. 717, 735 (1984).

36. See Curran, Morgan, Hardy, Jaffe, Darrow & Dowdle, "The Epidemiology of AIDS: Current Status and Future Prospects," 229 Sci. 1352, 1357 (1985). In Farnsworth v. Proctor & Gamble Co., 758 F.2d 1545 (11th Cir. 1985), the court noted the threat that lack of confidentiality posed to the study of Toxic Shock Syndrome by the Center for Disease Control: "the Center's purpose is the protection of the public's health. Central to this purpose is the ability to conduct probing scientific and social research supported by a population willing to submit to in-depth questioning. Undisputed testimony in the record indicates that disclosure of the names and addresses of these research participants could seriously damage this voluntary reporting." Id. at 1547. This observation applies with far greater force to the AIDS context, since being exposed as an AIDS carrier or victim constitutes a harm several orders of magnitude above

the embarrassment of having aspects of genital hygiene, including one's use of tampons, revealed to the public.

37. California, 1985 Cal.Legis.Serv. ch. 1519 § 199.35–38; Wisconsin, 1985 Wis. Laws 73 § 103.15, § 146.025; Florida, 1985 Fla. Laws ch. 85–52 § 381.606. The District of Columbia enacted a 5-year moratorium to prohibit insurance companies from denying coverage, setting rates, or altering benefits on the basis of a positive AIDS test or a refusal to be tested. The act also bars insurance company decisions based on age, marital status, area of residence, occupation, gender, or sexual orientation. D.C. Act 6–170 (1986). San Francisco, among other California cities, adopted an ordinance barring anyone from requiring another to undergo any medical procedure designed to reveal whether that person has AIDS, with an exception for employers who can show that the absence of AIDS is a bona fide occupational qualification. San Francisco Munic.Code § 3809 (1986).

38. 412 U.S. 306, 324 (1973). See also Eastland v. United States Servicemen's Fund, 421 U.S. 491 (1975). See the further discussion of the speech and debate clause in Chapter 5, supra.

the potential for abuse, violates the Constitution.[39] Crucially, the Court appeared to be unanimous on the proposition that exposure without sufficient justification would be unconstitutional even if the information in question was neither intimate nor inaccurate; the only issue dividing the majority from their concurring brethren was the need to remand to determine whether the exposure was warranted on the facts of this case.

Of course, where exposure of potentially derogatory information about an individual serves a significant governmental purpose, such exposure is not automatically unconstitutional. The key point to note is that a valid and sufficient governmental purpose may not be presumed lightly, since the individual's right to the protection of his or her good name "reflects no more than our basic concept of the essential dignity and worth of every human being—a concept at the root of any decent system of ordered liberty. The protection of private personality, like the protection of life itself, is left primarily to the individual states under the Ninth and Tenth Amendments. But this does not mean that the right is entitled to any less recognition by this Court as a basic of our constitutional system." [40] Nothing less could account for the fact that reputation, when protected by state law, "is sufficient to overcome the specific protections of the First Amendment." [41] Thus the Supreme Court had unmistakably held, in a long series of cases, that even an individual with no other basis to demand the protections of procedural due process could do so if government was acting in such a way as to threaten the individual's "good name, reputation, honor or integrity." [42]

In *Paul v. Davis*, however, the Supreme Court held that a person cannot obtain relief under 42 U.S.C. § 1983 against a police chief who, in the course of his duty but without official state judicial approval, inaccurately circulates the person's photograph to local merchants as

39. 412 U.S. at 329–30. See also Whalen v. Roe, 429 U.S. 589, 607 (1977) (Brennan, J., concurring) ("[t]he central storage and easy accessibility of computerized data vastly increase the potential for abuse of . . . information, and I am not prepared to say that future developments will not demonstrate the necessity of some curb on such technology").

40. Rosenblatt v. Baer, 383 U.S. 75, 92 (1966) (Stewart, J., concurring), quoted in Gertz v. Robert Welch, Inc., 418 U.S. 323, 341 (1974).

41. Paul v. Davis, 424 U.S. 693, 723 n. 11 (1976) (Brennan, J., dissenting). See R. Dworkin, Taking Rights Seriously 190–92 (1977) (when a fundamental right exists, government may override it "when necessary to protect the rights of others, or to prevent a catastrophe," but not, so long as the right is truly fundamental, simply "to obtain a clear and major public benefit").

42. Board of Regents v. Roth, 408 U.S. 564, 573 (1972) (failure to renew employment of nontenured public employee, in a manner injurious to employee's reputation,
would constitute deprivation of liberty and would thus require procedural due process); Joint Anti-Fascist Refugee Committee v. McGrath, 341 U.S. 123 (1951) (invalidating designation of certain groups as Communist by Attorney General); id. at 143, 162, 178, 186 (concurring opinions of Black, J., Frankfurter, J., Douglas, J., and Jackson, J.); Jenkins v. McKeithen, 395 U.S. 411, 424–25, 427–28 (1969) (holding that commission which undertakes accusatory function of publicly labeling persons violators of criminal laws must first grant such persons due process protections); Wisconsin v. Constantineau, 400 U.S. 433, 436–37 (1971) (invalidating state statute authorizing government officials to "post" in retail liquor establishments the names of excessive drinkers, without according named individuals procedural due process); cf. Goss v. Lopez, 419 U.S. 565, 574–76 (1975) (holding that student suspended from public school in a manner injurious to reputation has suffered injury to liberty interest separate from whatever property interest student may have in education).

that of someone "known" to be an "active shoplifter" without any hearing, prior or subsequent, to clear the person's name—even if it is assumed that this police action "would inhibit [plaintiff] from entering business establishments for fear of being suspected of shoplifting and possibly apprehended, and would seriously impair his future employment opportunities." [43]   The Court insisted that no "right or status previously recognized by state law was distinctly altered or extinguished" by the official defamation; the basis for its decision appears to have been that the state's law of defamation, while not conferring a "legal guarantee of present enjoyment" sufficient to create a separately protected entitlement,[44] made the plaintiff's claim the sort that would be "actionable in the courts of virtually every State." [45]   Although it flew in the face of some venerable precedents to give such significance to the hypothetical availability of state judicial relief,[46] the Court evidently believed that any contrary result would have the unthinkable consequence of federalizing the entire state law of torts whenever government officers are the wrongdoers.[47]

Given the clear resonance between this reading of the case—treating it essentially as a matter of exhaustion, permitting the state to take first crack at disciplining its own officers—and the *Younger v. Harris* [48] line of cases discussed in Chapter 3, and given also the absence of a subsequent general retreat from constitutional privacy protection employing *Paul v. Davis*, it seems a mistake to attach enduring significance to the Court's statement that no liberty or privacy right is violated, as a matter of substantive fourteenth amendment law, when the state needlessly or inaccurately (or both) publicizes a record of an official act such as an arrest.[49]

It is particularly ironic that the majority opinion by Justice Rehnquist should have gone out of its way to stress that the Court's prior privacy decisions had related not to such matters as arrest records but rather to marriage, procreation, contraception, family relations, child rearing, or education.[50]   That was the very fact Justice Rehnquist had

---

43.   424 U.S. 693, 697 (1976).

44.   Id. at 711. The inadequacy of this fact in itself to distinguish the case from Roth, Constantineau, and Goss, see note 42, supra, is discussed in § 10–11, supra. See also Tushnet, "The Constitutional Right to One's Good Name: An Examination of the Scholarship of Mr. Justice Rehnquist," 64 Ky.L.J. 753 (1977).

45.   424 U.S. at 697.

46.   Monroe v. Pape, 365 U.S. 167, 183 (1961); Home Tel. & Tel. Co. v. Los Angeles, 227 U.S. 278 (1913). See § 10–14, supra, and § 18–4, infra.

47.   424 U.S. at 699. See also Griffin v. Breckenridge, 403 U.S. 88, 102 (1971) ("The Constitutional shoals that would lie in the path of interpreting § 1985(3) as a general federal tort law can be avoided by . . . requiring, as an element of the cause of action, [an] invidiously discriminatory motivation. . . .").

48.   401 U.S. 37 (1971) (federal court must ordinarily abstain when state judicial proceedings are pending). See § 3–30, supra.

49.   The suggestion in Justice White's concurring opinion in Monitor Patriot Co. v. Roy, 401 U.S. 265, 301 (1971), that a publisher should be privileged to circulate information of an official act such as an arrest, cf. Cox Broadcasting Corp. v. Cohn, 420 U.S. 469 (1975), of course raises a wholly separate point: the issue in Paul v. Davis should have been not the ability of a private individual to suppress, or recover damages for, publication of a report of an official act, but the right of such an individual to a reasonably timely hearing to prevent the mistaken impression the individual alleges will be conveyed by circulation of the report.

50.   424 U.S. at 713; see id. at 735–36 n. 18 (Brennan, J., dissenting).

previously criticized as indicative of how far the Court had strayed from the fourth amendment search-and-seizure core of the privacy concept.[51]

If the Court's denial that *Paul v. Davis* involved any substantively protected interest had been truly authoritative, the Court's careful canvassing of the procedural safeguards provided by New York to the patients whose drug prescriptions were retained for five years in computer banks would have been quite unnecessary in *Whalen v. Roe*,[52] and there would have been no need, in a decision handed down on the same day as *Whalen*, for the Court to stress the fact that a nontenured public employee, who sought damages for his former employer's dissemination of the derogatory information leading to his dismissal, had failed to challenge the truth of the information in question.[53] Assuming, therefore, that *Paul v. Davis* must be understood as a case about federalism-based limits on the remedial powers of a federal court acting under § 1983 rather than as a repudiation of deep substantive principles under the fourteenth amendment,[54] constitutional review of information-gathering and information-dissemination practices remains very much a possibility in subsequent cases.

The legality of the government's program for gathering and storing data in the first place will of course affect the success of any challenge to subsequent dissemination, although dissemination might indepen-

---

51. See, e.g., Roe v. Wade, 410 U.S. 113, 172 (1973) (Rehnquist, J., dissenting).

52. 429 U.S. 589 (1977), discussed in § 15–1, supra.

53. Codd v. Velger, 429 U.S. 624 (1977).

54. Reading Paul v. Davis to hold that "an adequate state remedy may prevent every state inflicted injury to a person's reputation [or other significant liberty interests] from violating 42 U.S.C. § 1983," Ingraham v. Wright, 430 U.S. 651, 702 (1977) (Stevens, J., dissenting) (see § 10–14, supra), would do far less damage to the fabric of constitutional law and theory than reading it to hold that an interest as close to "the essential dignity and worth of every human being," Rosenblatt v. Baer, 383 U.S. 75, 92 (1966) (Stewart, J., concurring) as a person's good name is substantively excised from the fourteenth amendment's concept of liberty. Supporting such a view of Paul v. Davis is the more recent approach of the Court in Ingraham v. Wright, supra, where the Court's denial of relief against corporal punishment in public schools proceeded by acknowledging the existence of a protected liberty interest in the child but explaining why the state's panoply of common-law remedies for invasion of that interest proved sufficient, in the Court's view, to "constitute due process of law." 430 U.S. at 675. Although dissenting from the Court's holding of sufficiency, Justice Stevens saw the majority opinion as suggesting that the Court might "one day agree with Mr. Justice Brennan's appraisal of the importance of the constitu-

tional interest at stake in [Paul v. Davis]" without returning to a regime in which every deprivation by a state agent of an interest protected by the fourteenth amendment is federally actionable without regard to the legal system provided by the state to protect the interest in question. Id. at 701–02. (dissenting opinion). Whether viewed as an exhaustion requirement or as a rule holding a state responsible only for the consequences of its scheme of rules, rights, and remedies, doctrines like those of Paul v. Davis and Ingraham v. Wright, enunciated out of evident concern for values of federalism, understandably appear to a public unschooled in the finer points of § 1983 jurisprudence as Supreme Court denigrations of the substantive rights at stake. Whether such appearances are encouraged by the Court's own pronouncements, as in Paul v. Davis, or simply by the predictable focus of press attention upon the substantive issues in the cases, as in Ingraham v. Wright, their pernicious consequences should make courts reluctant to employ vague notions of federalism in the construction of such statutory provisions as § 1983. Unless core values of state sovereignty are truly threatened, or individual rights indirectly jeopardized, the rhetoric of federalism should be used more sparingly than has become the habit, and the invocation of federalism to defend results like those of Paul and Ingraham should at least be offset by sensitivity to the likely substantive effects of such purportedly procedural rulings.

dently violate a constitutional norm such as that of procedural due process even where no objection exists to the way in which the information was obtained or retained by government.[55]   In any case, it is crucial to see that, although cases like *Paul v. Davis* present the issue in a "one-shot" form, its more common and significant shape will be in the form of a systemic challenge to the government's safeguards for processing information about individuals.   Such individuals should be able to challenge the overall sufficiency of the safeguards provided.[56]

Because this is an area of increasing legislative interest and activity [57] much can be achieved simply by judicial attention of the form that generated the majority's discussion in *Whalen v. Roe* [58] and the separate opinions in *California Bankers Ass'n v. Shultz.*[59]   But in a situation where government has constructed a plainly insufficient system of controls, nothing less than outright judicial invalidation will suffice.[60]

This argument should be clearly distinguished from any claim that sufficiently personal or testimonial records ought to be extended fifth amendment immunity from seizure and evidentiary use regardless of the hands through which such records have passed.[61]   The argument advanced here is wholly independent of the personal or intimate

55. See, e.g., Wisconsin v. Constantineau, 400 U.S. 433 (1971) ("posting" name of excessive drinker).

56. See, e.g., Whalen v. Roe, 429 U.S. 589 (1977). Care must of course be taken to assure that those challenging the information-processing system include persons directly affected by the features identified as deficient or objectionable. See California Bankers Ass'n v. Shultz, 416 U.S. 21 (1974); Laird v. Tatum, 408 U.S. 1 (1972).

57. For example, Congress enacted the Right to Financial Privacy Act of 1978, Pub.L.No.95–630, in response to the Supreme Court's decision in United States v. Miller, 425 U.S. 435 (1976). See note 9, supra. And when the Court held, in Zurcher v. Stanford Daily, 436 U.S. 547 (1978), that search warrants could be directed at press offices and newsrooms in quests for evidence of criminal activity by third parties whose acts may have been the subject of those news organizations, Congress overwhelmingly passed the Privacy Protection Act of 1980, Pub.L.No.96–440. See § 12–22, note 37 supra. Whatever the limits on congressional power to protect informational privacy under the enforcement section of the fourteenth amendment, see § 5–14, supra, Congress possesses ample authority under the commerce clause to regulate the intermediate institutions—banks, telephone companies, and the like—that are almost always involved in these cases. For a review of earlier privacy legislation, see generally the massive compendium of federal and state regulations and statutes in Project, "Govern-

ment Information and the Rights of Citizens," 73 Mich.L.Rev. 971–1340 (1975). See also Hanus & Relyea, "A Policy Assessment of the Privacy Act of 1974," 25 Am. U.L.Rev. 555 (1976).

58. 429 U.S. 589 (1977).

59. 416 U.S. 21, 78–79 (1974) (Powell, J., joined by Blackmun, J., concurring); id. at 82–91 (Douglas, J., dissenting); id. at 91 (Brennan, J., dissenting); id. at 93 (Marshall, J., dissenting).

60. For a similar focus on judicial review of the efficacy of a bureaucratic system as a whole rather than merely of its performance in particular cases, see Amsterdam, "Perspectives on the Fourth Amendment," 58 Minn.L.Rev. 349 (1974). Suggestions for the design of a system to preserve informational privacy and access may be found in A. Westin & M. Baker, Databanks in a Free Society 341–404 (1972).

61. Compare Fisher v. United States, 425 U.S. 391, 415 (1976) (Brennan, J., concurring in the Court's holding that taxpayers have no fifth amendment privilege to withhold certain business records but suggesting that majority should have stressed the fact that the records in question were not private papers or effects). See also the suggestion that sufficiently personal papers should be wholly immune to search or seizure, in Note, "Formalism, Legal Realism, and Constitutionally Protected Privacy Under the Fourth and Fifth Amendments," 90 Harv.L.Rev. 945 (1977).

character of the records themselves [62] and would apply to any information ceded by the individual for one purpose but sought or employed by government for another without the individual's consent. In an information-dense technological era, when living inevitably entails leaving not just informational footprints but parts of one's self in myriad directories, files, records and computers, to hold that the fourteenth amendment does not reserve to individuals some power to say when and how and by whom that information and those confidences are to be used would be to denigrate the central role that informational autonomy must play in any developed concept of the self.[63]

§ 15–17. The Dual Character of Associational Rights

An individual whose public self is at the mercy of government— who can be slandered at will without redress—suffers wrongs at many levels, but surely one of the most serious is the infringement of the freedom to form associations of one's choosing. Thus the citizen whose face became a mug shot without justification or opportunity for timely challenge in *Paul v. Davis* [1] was plainly confronted with a diminished range of opportunities to associate, whether as customer or employee or friend, with others in the community. Governmental intrusion upon a life's informational traces, considered in § 15–16, thus entails invasion of associational autonomy. So too governmental intervention in matters of appearance and apparel, considered in § 15–15, invades associational freedom. As then Judge Stevens recognized in a 1973 decision, what a person wears and how a person looks is a signal of welcome to some and avoidance to others.[2] Indeed, virtually every invasion of personhood is also an interference with association, just as virtually every intrusion upon association works a displacement of human personality.

Justice Brennan's opinion for the Court in *Roberts v. United States Jaycees*,[3] after recognizing that "the Bill of Rights . . . must afford the formation and preservation of certain kinds of highly personal relationships a substantial measure of sanctuary from unjustified interference by the State," [4] described the intrinsic value of these relationships and,

---

62. Cf. York v. Story, 324 F.2d 450 (9th Cir. 1963) (awarding relief for federal civil rights violation where policeman fraudulently obtained young woman's consent to photograph her in the nude after she came to stationhouse to report a crime; the photographs were later circulated among other officers at the station house), cert. denied 376 U.S. 939 (1964).

63. On the proposition that the technological capacity to collect, maintain and retrieve information has outstripped the law's ability to protect privacy, see Shattuck, "In the Shadow of 1984: National Identification Systems, Computer-Matching, and Privacy in the United States," 35 Hastings L.J. 991 (1984). On the first amendment aspects of legal remedies for breach of informational autonomy, see §§ 12–12 to 12–14, supra.

§ 15–17

1. 424 U.S. 693 (1976), discussed in § 15–17, supra.

2. Miller v. School Dist. No. 167, 495 F.2d 658, 665 n.29 (7th Cir. 1974) ("those who choose not to conform to tradition in matters of appearance must anticipate, as a consequence, that a number of other people may elect not to associate with them"), discussed in § 15–16, supra.

3. 468 U.S. 609 (1984). Chief Justice Burger and Justices Blackmun, Powell, Stevens, and White joined in the majority. Justice O'Connor concurred in part and concurred in the judgment. Justice Rehnquist concurred in the judgment.

4. Id. at 615.

in the course of denying special associational protection to "private" clubs that affect economic life, essayed the Court's first major attempt to define their contours: "Without precisely identifying every consideration that may underlie this type of constitutional protection, we have noted that certain kinds of personal bonds have played a critical role in the culture and traditions of the Nation by cultivating and transmitting shared ideals and beliefs; they thereby foster diversity and act as buffers between the individual and the power of the State. . . . Moreover, the constitutional shelter afforded such relationships reflects the realization that individuals draw much of their emotional enrichment from close ties with others . . . [and also promotes the] ability to define [their] identity that is central to any concept of liberty." [5]

The vital role that such freedom of intimate association plays in our cultural and social history must receive protection *by* as well as *from* the state. For rights to associate with X are necessarily rights to dissociate from Y. And doing so may require governmental help. There is little meaning in a right to associate at home with family or with friends if one is unable to invoke police assistance in expelling intruders, be they neighbors or FBI agents. Yet the right of one person or group to exclude others is *inevitably* a limitation upon the freedom— including the associational freedom—of those others. For example, if a group of men wish to associate in a certain social context with men only, the women excluded necessarily suffer associational deprivation in that same social context.[6] Such exclusion of differing individuals by a group of women, of blacks, or of Mormons would also deprive those differing individuals of associational freedom. This dual character of associational rights impinges in complex ways upon doctrines of privacy and personhood and is the subject of this section.

In seeking to define and delimit the fundamental rights of persons who wish to enter an association or community against the majority's will, or to conduct themselves while there in a way objectionable to the majority, our starting point must be the rejection of two extreme views, the first giving the majority intolerably great authority and the second leaving it with intolerably little.

The first view would confine the rights of individuals or minorities to conduct that has no impact beyond the actor or the circle of consenting actors; as we have seen,[7] that category constitutes a virtually empty set in any complex society. So limiting fundamental rights to such a category would leave the community with nearly total authority over the lives of its present members and over the composition of its

---

5. Id. See also Board of Directors of Rotary Int'l v. Rotary Club of Duarte, 107 S.Ct. 1940 (1987); Karst, "The Freedom of Intimate Association," 89 Yale L.J. 624, 630–37 (1980) (identifying four values that freedom of intimate association promotes and enlivens: society, "the opportunity to enjoy the society of certain other people;" caring and commitment, "to love . . . and to be loved;" intimacy, what "is kept secret from all but a few" and what those people who are close friends or lovers share; and self-identification, what helps us be seen and see ourselves "as a whole person rather than as an aggregate of social roles" and has "powerful influences over the development of our personalities").

6. See Roberts v. United States Jaycees, 468 U.S. 609 (1984); Board of Directors of Rotary International v. Rotary Club of Duarte, 107 S.Ct. 1940 (1987).

7. In § 15–1, supra.

membership through time. The second view would confine the authority of the group or community to the enactment and enforcement of rules predicated on something other than "moral" notions; as we have seen,[8] that category too constitutes an empty set. So limiting governmental authority to that category would leave the community incapable of structuring its life and regulating the conduct of its members in any enforceable way. Between these two extremes, the question remains: what concerns *may* a community invoke to identify the presence of certain persons or the occurrence of certain actions as sufficiently "harmful" to justify governmental action burdening the personhood of others?

The most obvious concern that qualifies for this purpose is protecting the rights of persons in the community, defined in terms of their claims to bodily integrity and the other recognized elements of personhood. Among such rights are those of association. Perhaps the best example is suggested by *Village of Belle Terre v. Boraas*,[9] in which some two hundred families living on a square mile of Long Island's north shore sought to preserve the character of their town by excluding shops, stores, even home mail deliveries—and groups of three or more persons unrelated by blood or marriage sharing the same household. Although the ordinance limiting land use to single-family dwellings defined families to include unmarried couples, the ordinance in effect excluded communes, groups of several students living together, and others living in arrangements less consistent with Belle Terre's self-image than the traditional family (or the by-now almost traditional unwed couple). The Court upheld the ordinance after applying merely minimal scrutiny, since the majority concluded, in an opinion by Justice Douglas, that the "ordinance places no ban on . . . association [or any other fundamental rights], for a 'family' may, so far as the ordinance is concerned, entertain whomever it likes."[10] The argument appears to be: nonconforming groups can always visit.

Yet other claims of associational freedom in the Supreme Court have not been so lightly treated: the NAACP in Alabama was not told it could just as well organize in Georgia;[11] the SDS members at Central Connecticut State College were not told they could just as well form a chapter at Yale;[12] the women seeking full membership in the Jaycees[13] or partnership in a law firm[14] were not told to seek civic involvement or employment elsewhere. Why then could the students of the State University of New York at Stony Brook be told to find someplace else to live together? To be sure, theirs was not a political association, but then neither were the households containing unrelated persons that the Court held could not be denied food stamps in *United*

---

8. In § 15–10, supra, at notes 90–92. See also § 15–4, supra, at note 7.

9. 416 U.S. 1 (1974).

10. Id. at 9.

11. NAACP v. Alabama ex rel. Patterson, 357 U.S. 449 (1958) (invalidating state attempt to compel NAACP to produce membership lists), discussed in § 12–23, supra.

12. Healy v. James, 408 U.S. 169 (1972) (invalidating state college refusal to permit students to form local SDS chapter, and to use college facilities for meetings), discussed in § 12–26, supra.

13. Roberts v. United States Jaycees, 468 U.S. 609 (1984).

14. Hishon v. King & Spalding, 467 U.S. 69 (1984).

States Department of Agriculture v. Moreno,[15] or the households containing illegitimate children that the Court held could not be denied welfare in *New Jersey Welfare Rights Organization v. Cahill*.[16]

The town might have argued that, although its action limited the associational freedom of the students, the impact was too marginal to warrant strict scrutiny; being told to live elsewhere is far less serious than being denied food stamps or welfare. But the town had not discharged the burden of showing that the impact was in fact trivial; where else the students might have lived, and at what sacrifice, remains conjectural.[17] Moreover, it seems odd to suggest that the impact is minimal because the students could have lived in a community that found them more congenial; any such argument would devalue the most political aspect of the students' claim—that they might wish not just to live in a certain way but to live that way in a place that they hope to change by their example.

It may be possible to limit *Village of Belle Terre* to zoning ordinances that seek community stability by preventing *transiency*. As Chief Judge Breitel suggested in *City of White Plains v. Ferraioli*, one might expect that "[e]very year or so, different college students would come to take the place of those before them."[18] Arguably, therefore, *Belle Terre* involved *neither* a rejection of the associational right to choose one's more permanent living companions, *nor* an affirmation of government's power to concern itself with the "identity, as opposed to the number, of persons who may comprise a household [beyond assuring that] such households . . . remain nontransient, single-housekeeping units."[19] Yet in *Moore v. City of East Cleveland*, when the Supreme Court invalidated East Cleveland's attempt to enforce a single-family zoning ordinance that defined "family" so narrowly as to prevent a grandmother from living in the same residence with her son and two grandsons who were first cousins rather than brothers,[20] only

15. 413 U.S. 528 (1973). The claimants in Moreno included a middle-aged diabetic living with a friend and the latter's children, as well as two women sharing living expenses in a single apartment so that the child of one could attend a school for the deaf located nearby. Moreno's force as a precedent might be limited in light of the Court's condemnation of the federal food stamp provision as irrationally excluding "*only* those . . . so desperately in need of aid that they cannot even afford to alter their living arrangements so as to retain their eligibility." Id. at 538.

16. 411 U.S. 619 (1973).

17. In Moore v. East Cleveland, 431 U.S. 494 (1977), neither the plurality opinion nor the concurring opinions, id. at 506 and 513, even bothered to reply to the dissenting argument that the appellant grandmother had been "denie[d] . . . the opportunity to live with all her grandchildren . . . only in East Cleveland, an area with a radius of three miles and a population of 40,000." 550 (White, J., dissenting).

Belle Terre might have been distinguishable, however, in light of subsidized housing the state made available to the students in that case. The village's brief argued that "not everyone . . . enjoys publicly subsidized housing within walking distance of their work," Brief for Appellants at 21, and that the students should be pleased to live together either in dormitory housing or in "[l]arger communities, such as the Town of Brookhaven . . ." Id. at 23.

18. 34 N.Y.2d 300, 304–05, 357 N.Y.S.2d 449, 451, 313 N.E.2d 756, 758 (1974) (distinguishing the case of a "group home").

19. Moore v. East Cleveland, 431 U.S. 494, 520–21 (1977) (Stevens, J., concurring in judgment holding that city cannot prevent grandmother from having her two grandchildren live with her).

20. Id. at 520. The city ordinance defined "family" to include, in addition to the spouse of the "nominal head of the household," the couple's childless unwed children, but at most one dependent child (wed

Justice Stevens, concurring in the result, distinguished *Belle Terre* on this basis; [21] the plurality opinion of Justice Powell, joined by Justices Brennan, Marshall, and Blackmun, treated *Belle Terre* as distinguishable simply because "[t]he ordinance there affected only *unrelated* individuals," whereas East Cleveland had "chosen to regulate the occupancy of its housing by slicing deeply into the family itself." [22] Given the close division of the Court even on the facts of *Moore*,[23] it seems unlikely that *Belle Terre* can be properly understood as limited to transient groups. Treating the decision as at least highly relevant (if not fully dispositive) to more enduring associations of living companions, we must therefore regard the village as having asserted a general power to dictate the intimate composition of domestic associations.

From this perspective, the adverse impact on association should not have been deemed negligible; the Court should thus have demanded at least a substantial justification for the ordinance in Belle Terre. Perhaps the most plausible candidate for such a justification would be *the associational rights of the villagers themselves*.[24] Two claims of association are at stake—that of the students, wishing to live with one another in their preferred way in the village, and that of the great majority of the village's inhabitants, wishing to preserve the integrity of their preferred associational form as a community of traditional families.[25] It is noteworthy that such an argument would not have been available to Alabama in the NAACP case, to Connecticut in the SDS case, to New Jersey in the welfare case, or to the United States in the food stamp case. Thus the argument might help to explain the result in *Belle Terre* without conferring any general governmental right to discriminate against persons choosing unconventional forms of association or uncommon patterns of domestic living.

or unwed) with dependent children, and at most one parent of the nominal head of the household or of his or her spouse. The appellant grandmother was charged with violating the ordinance because one 10-year old grandson (who had moved in when his mother died) was living in the home with his grandmother, her son, and her other grandson (the 10-year old's cousin). Thus "extended families" were forbidden in all but the most limited sense. The case is also discussed in § 15–20, infra.

21. Id. at 519 n.15. Although Justice Stevens phrased his concurring opinion in terms of the grandmother's "right to use her own property as she sees fit," id. at 513, Justice Stewart seems correct in concluding that her right to choose her living companions is independent of her status as a property owner. Id. at 540 n.10 (dissenting opinion).

22. Id. at 498. See also id. at 507 (Brennan, J., joined by Marshall, J., concurring).

23. Chief Justice Burger dissented on the ground that federal courts are too busy to decide such cases given the grandmoth-

er's failure to seek an administrative variance on hardship grounds. Id. at 522. Justice Stewart, joined in dissent by Justice Rehnquist, would limit associational rights to situations involving first amendment guarantees, id. at 535–36, cf. § 12–26 supra, and would limit substantive due process to rights involving family life choices about marriage, childbearing, and childraising. Id. at 537. Justice White, dissenting separately, could see nothing of fundamental importance in the appellant's "interest in residing with more than one set of grandchildren." Id. at 549.

24. The Court did not refer to such rights explicitly, but it came close when it spoke of Belle Terre as "a sanctuary for people." 416 U.S. at 9.

25. The exclusion of unmarried couples from the ban, rather than rescuing the ordinance as it seemed to for Justice Douglas, 416 U.S. at 8 & n.6, might be thought to spoil the argument for Belle Terre—but a political body should not fare worse in litigation because it mitigates the rigors of its laws to deal with special cases.

The first factor that might be thought to militate against this form of defense for the ordinance is the fact that Belle Terre is, after all, not simply a private association but an official political subdivision of the state. Yet that can hardly be thought decisive; even a "privately owned" village—a company town functioning in every other way like a municipality—would have to meet the requirements of the first and fourteenth amendments,[26] so we might just as well assume that Belle Terre was owned by a development corporation and proceed to identify the arguments that would remain.

The second factor that could be thought to argue against the town, closely related to the first but nonetheless distinct, is that the town's exclusionary policy is embodied in an *ordinance* rather than in a restrictive *covenant*. But judicial enforcement of an anti-commune covenant would probably have to meet the same constitutional tests as those applicable to an ordinance.[27] In either case, constitutional norms come into play most clearly when someone dissents and the others invoke governmental coercion to bring the dissident into line with the majority. But that suggests a factor more basic than the ordinance/contract distinction:

This third factor is that, whatever consensus might once have united the villagers behind their exclusionary regulation, the consensus was broken when one of the village families decided to rent to a group of unrelated students. Perhaps we should endorse a principle that community must be consensual and cannot rely on coercive enforcement. Although such a principle would have some appeal, it is hard to see why a commune or other cohesive group should be forbidden to buy up a square mile of land and expel members who insist on inviting outsiders whom the majority see as compromising the group's character—CIA agents, perhaps, or unreconstructed capitalists.[28] When the shoe is on the other foot, and the champions of capital and of traditional family life perceive an equal challenge to the integrity of their community from the influx of persons with a different pattern of life,[29] why should the power to expel not be as great? And, once the power to expel is recognized, surely its peaceful exercise by owners who prefer police action to self-help cannot alter the result.

The fourth possible factor cutting against the village is that it has opened itself to the public; as Justice Douglas noted in his majority opinion, anyone could visit. The case was thus unlike *Kotch v. Pilot Commissioners*, where the Court upheld exclusionary nepotism with the

26. See Marsh v. Alabama, 326 U.S. 501 (1946), discussed in Chapter 18, infra.

27. See Shelley v. Kraemer, 334 U.S. 1 (1948), discussed in Chapter 18, infra.

28. Although it has of course been argued that an individual owner's right to exclude is uniquely entitled to legal protection so long as the ownership arose under just rules of property acquisition and transfer, see J. Locke, Second Treatise of Government; R. Nozick, Anarchy, State and Utopia (1974), the demise of Model II,

see Chapter 8, supra, precludes any ready translation of so Lockean a notion into constitutional doctrine. Cf. note 21, supra.

29. See Hadden & Barton, "An Image That Will Not Die: Thoughts on the History of Anti-Urban Ideology," in The Urbanization of the Suburbs 79 (L. Masotti & J. Hadden eds. 1973); Wood, Suburbia 153–67 (1958). Cf. Moore v. East Cleveland, 431 U.S. 494, 537, n.7 (1977) (Stewart, J., joined by Rehnquist, J., dissenting).

supposed purpose of maintaining the close-knit character of a traditionally closed community.[30] The case was also unlike *Jaycees*, where the Court, in upholding a Minnesota anti-discrimination statute [31] as applied to the Jaycees, placed great weight on the fact that the Jaycees were not selective in choosing new members and on the fact that the Jaycees did not prevent the excluded group from nonetheless taking part in most of Jaycee activities. The Court found it significant that "a local officer [of one of the two chapters involved in this case] testified that he could recall *no instance* in which an applicant had been denied membership on any basis other than *age or sex*." [32] The Court placed particular emphasis on the fact that women, while being denied *full* membership, were permitted *partial* membership and were allowed to partake in almost all of the Jaycees activities except voting, holding office, and receiving certain awards.[33] Ironic as it may seem, the Jaycees were thus disadvantaged in their litigation against women seeking full membership partly because they had not been *even more exclusionary*. It thus seems curious that this same lack of selectivity as to new inhabitants, so long as they were grouped in traditional families, did not weigh against Belle Terre in its argument before the Court. For, although it may seem odd to reward exclusivity and penalize outreach, when the rationale for constitutional protection of a group's interest in limiting its membership is the group's allegedly cohesive character as an intimate community, what could otherwise be praised as openness becomes evidence of hypocrisy.

All four of the factors thus far canvassed—the legal status of the village, the source of its exclusionary rule, the non-consensual character of the situation, and the village's openness to the public—thus fail to defeat the attempt of the village to counter the students' associational rights with associational rights of its own. But a fifth factor may prove more telling: Belle Terre may not be a real "community" or "association" at all but simply a collection of persons—not because it opens its streets to the public (so do many obviously genuine communities) but because it has no organic life as a center of communal perceptions and common activities. The accident of overlapping location at some point in space and time should not suffice to invoke the preferred freedom of association, a freedom recognized out of respect for the autonomy and integrity of groups whose shared experiences provide centers of value formation and value expression that can perpetuate some of society's traditions while challenging others and can thus provide sources of social and cultural evolution. Rather like the audience huddled together but apart in the darkness of the Paris Adult Theatre,[34] or the commuters on the 6:45 returning from offices in New

---

30. 330 U.S. 552 (1974).

31. The Minnesota Human Rights Act states: "It is an unfair discriminatory practice: To deny any person the full and equal enjoyment of the goods, services, facilities, privileges, advantages, and accommodations of a place of public accommodation because of race, color, creed, religion, disability, national origin or sex." Minn. Stat. § 363.03, subd. 3 (West Supp. 1987).

32. Roberts v. United States Jaycees, 468 U.S. 609, 621 (1984) (emphasis added).

33. Id.

34. Paris Adult Theatre I v. Slaton, 413 U.S. 49 (1973) (upholding power to enjoin showing of "hard-core" film at adult theatre). "Mobs, crowds, and audiences are not publics, because they lack presumptive continuity, internal organization, common

York, those who inhabit a bedroom-suburb, with homes for sale to the highest bidder subject only to the very criterion under challenge, may not be able to assert a positive associational right of their own.[35]

In a case that would confirm this view, *Roberts v. United States Jaycees*,[36] the Court was more willing to scrutinize the interrelationships of the particular group in question to determine if they were of such a nature as to permit exclusion of others from their "community" or "association" under the guise of constitutional protection.[37] Justice Brennan proposed analysis along a spectrum in which one pole would be exemplified by, "the selection of one's spouse"—something that obviously implicated intimate assocational rights; and in which the opposite pole would be exemplified by "the choice of one's fellow employees"—something that obviously did not implicate intimate association.[38] To evaluate where on the spectrum less obvious cases would fall, Justice Brennan proposed focusing on "size, purpose, policies, selectivity, congeniality, and other characteristics that in a particular case may be pertinent."[39]   Under this analysis, Justice Brennan concluded that "the local chapters are neither small nor selective.   Moreover, much of the activity central to the formation and maintenance of the association involves the participation of strangers to that relationship.   Accordingly, we conclude that the Jaycees chapters lack the distinctive characteristics that might afford constitutional protection to the decision of its members to exclude women."[40]   Thus, the Court identified a form of association that does not qualify for constitutional protection.

Assuming that the record in *Belle Terre* supported a similar conclusion,[41] the Court's failure to articulate it may nonetheless be understandable; it is plainly so value-laden as to embarrass an institution that derives part of its authority from an asserted neutrality.   However, in *Jaycees* the Court was more willing to make that decision.   Yet *either* resolution of this sort of conflict—protecting the claims of Belle Terre over those of the students or protecting the claims of the students over those of Belle Terre—represents a value choice.   As soon as the

affairs, procedures, and autonomy." M. G. Smith, "A Structural Approach to Comparative Politics," in Varieties of Political Theory 115–16 (D. Easton ed. 1966).

35. Compare Runyon v. McCrary, 427 U.S. 160, 172 & n.10, 175–79 (1976) (no associational or privacy right to exclude non-white children from private schools that advertised in telephone directory "yellow pages" and by mass mailings). See generally Bloustein, "Group Privacy: The Right to Huddle," 8 Rutgers-Camden L.J. 219 (1977).

36. 468 U.S. 609 (1984).

37. Jaycees, 468 U.S. at 621. Compare Zablocki v. Redhail, 434 U.S. 374, 386–87 (1978) (holding unconstitutional a state prohibition of marriage without a court order by any resident having minor children not in his custody and which he is under obligation to support by court order)

with Hishon v. King & Spalding, 467 U.S. 69 (1984) (denying associational protection to law firms who exclude female associate attorneys from firm partnership on the basis of sex).

38. Id.

39. Jaycees, 468 U.S. at 621.

40. Id.

41. In fact, the record is exceedingly thin both on the character of Belle Terre as a community and on the nature of the "community" that the students wished to form. In assessing evidence bearing on such matters, one must be wary of the almost desperate desire to perceive institutions, places, and groups as "communities" whether or not they can realistically be so described. See G. Suttles, The Social Construction of Communities 264–70 (1972).

town puts forth a claim to associational freedom, that choice seems inescapable.

In *Jaycees*, the Court avoided making this choice overtly, instead seeking to base its decision on the less controversial ground that the Jaycees lack the *type* of relationship to which associational rights apply. The same approach was employed in *Rotary International v. Rotary Club of Duarte*,[42] where a local Rotary Club had its charter revoked for violating the International's constitution and bylaws by deciding to admit women to its membership. When the club and its female members sued the International under a California antidiscrimination statute, the International sought to escape the force of *Jaycees* by arguing that Rotary's selective membership set it apart. The Supreme Court was not persuaded. In a unanimous decision, Justice Powell declared for the Court [43] that, although "we have not held that constitutional protection is restricted to relationships among family members . . . the relationship among Rotary Club members is not the kind of intimate or private relation that warrants constitutional protection." [44] Justice Powell noted that many central Rotary activities "are carried on in the presence of strangers," [45] that the Club's program is "to keep their 'windows and doors open to the whole world,' " [46] and that Rotary's avowed purpose " 'is to produce an inclusive, not exclusive, membership, making possible the recognition of all useful local occupations, and enabling the club to be a true cross section of the business and professional life of the community.' " [47]

But suppose the village of Belle Terre makes no such claim to associational protection, or puts it forth and loses on the issue. We are still left with a political subdivision claiming that it perceives harm in the influx of nontraditional groups. Since we have rejected any notion that only "instrumental," "utilitarian," or otherwise "non-moral" appeals may be advanced in support of restraints on fundamental freedoms,[48] we may yet be persuaded that the harm the village's majority

---

42. 107 S.Ct. 1940 (1987).

43. Justice Powell's opinion for the Court was joined by all except Justice Scalia, who concurred in the judgment. Justices Blackmun and O'Connor took no part in the case.

44. Id. at 1946.

45. Id.

46. Id. at 1947 (citing Rotary Club documents).

47. Id. at 1946 (citing Rotary Club documents). The Court also found that no rights of expressive association were implicated, since Rotary Clubs are not formed for expressive purposes and as a matter of policy do not take positions on " 'public questions.' " Id. at 1947. Nor could the Court discern how the admission of women would hinder, rather than enhance, expressive activity. Id. Finally, any "slight infringement on Rotary members' right of expressive association [is] justified because it serves the state's compelling interest in eliminating discrimination against women." Id.

48. See § 15–10, supra, at notes 90–92. See also § 15–4, supra, at note 7. In his Belle Terre dissent, Justice Marshall responded only to such appeals, arguing that less restrictive alternatives could be found to control population density, prevent noise, limit traffic, preserve the rent structure, and so on. 416 U.S. at 18–20. The town itself had cast its arguments largely in that form, see Brief for Appellants at 15, but had added that "a social preference in favor of promoting and supporting family organization through residential proximity is in itself a proper object of state police power," id. at 25, even if it "rests . . . on imponderables that are intuitively perceived rather than empirically demonstrated . . ." Id. at 27.

sees in the presence of the students should suffice to permit that majority to force them to seek housing elsewhere.

But if there are no principled limits on what may count as a "harm," and on what "harms" may suffice to override claims of personhood, we will have succeeded only in tempting government simply to *define* as harmful the very thing it seeks to ban or to exclude. Since dislike for a group is not enough to warrant its exclusion,[49] we must ascertain what *is* enough; that is the purpose of the succeeding four sections.

§ 15-18. Bounding the Community's Power Over Persons: Harms Existing Only in the Mind of the Beholder

Any acceptable set of allowable definitions of harm would seem to rule out, as an ordinarily inadmissible reason to restrict fundamental rights, the "harm" of finding a person or act unpleasant to behold or to contemplate.[1] If simply finding another's appearance or habits offensive to hear, see, or think about were enough to justify exclusionary regulation, rights of personhood and indeed of expression would be at an end.

With respect to first amendment rights, at least, this principle is well established. The expression of ideas or emotions cannot be shut off to protect unwilling viewers or hearers without "a showing that substantial privacy interests are being invaded in an essentially intolerable manner," [2] since any "broader view . . . would effectively empower a majority to silence dissidents simply as a matter of personal predilections." [3] So long as "the special plight of the captive auditor" [4] is not involved,[5] the Constitution thus requires those who are offended to "avoid further bombardment of their sensibilities simply by averting their eyes." [6]

So too where freedom of assembly or association are involved, "mere public intolerance or animosity cannot be the basis for abridgment." [7] Thus, the right to "gather in public places" for "social" as well as political purposes cannot be "subject to . . . suspension" even "through the good-faith enforcement of a prohibition against annoying

---

49. United States Dept. of Agriculture v. Moreno, 413 U.S. 528, 534 (1973) (holding that bare desire to harm "hippie communes" as unpopular groups would be constitutionally illegitimate).

§ 15-18

1. But such unpleasantness should suffice to justify restrictions of non-fundamental rights. See generally Note, "Architecture, Aesthetic Zoning, and the First Amendment," 28 Stan.L.Rev. 179 (1975).

2. Cohen v. California, 403 U.S. 15, 21 (1971). Cf. Rowan v. Post Office Dept., 397 U.S. 728 (1970). See § 12-19, supra.

3. Cohen, 403 U.S. at 21.

4. Id. at 22.

5. See generally Public Utilities Commission v. Pollak, 343 U.S. 451, 469 (1952) (Douglas, J., dissenting) (discussing captive audiences for streetcar radio broadcasts); cf. Lehman v. Shaker Heights, 418 U.S. 298, 305 (1974) (Douglas, J., concurring).

6. Cohen, 403 U.S. at 21. The Court has been readier to sustain restrictions based upon "secondary effect"—such as the criminalization and deterioration of an area—than upon offensiveness as such. See, e.g., Young v. American Mini Theatres, 427 U.S. 50, 71 & n.34 (1976). Cf. Erznoznik v. Jacksonville, 422 U.S. 205, 210-15 (1975).

7. Coates v. Cincinnati, 402 U.S. 611, 615 (1971).

conduct." [8] In this context, government cannot limit the freedom of those whose "ideas, . . . lifestyle, or . . . physical appearance is resented by the majority of their fellow citizens." [9]

Thus, in dealing with activities in the core of the first amendment, government is constrained by the principle that harms existing only in the eye or mind of the voluntary beholder cannot justify restricting otherwise protected behavior. It is worth noting that this is so not because the beholder wrongs the actor in the very process of learning of the offensive activity,[10] for the actor in most of these cases wishes to be beheld; rather, harms of the identified type are deemed insufficient to warrant restriction because any contrary rule would leave first amendment values in shambles.

The same rationale applies to aspects of personhood not closely connected to the freedoms of expression, assembly, or association. In a decision ordinarily studied from other perspectives, a unanimous Supreme Court in 1975 unequivocally extended the principle of the first amendment cases analyzed here to an area quite clearly beyond the first amendment's perimeter. *O'Connor v. Donaldson* held, as a matter of substantive due process, that the state cannot confine someone involuntarily if the individual endangers neither himself nor others and is receiving no medical treatment for whatever "mental illness" is thought to justify his detention.[11]

Remaining to be defined, however, is the meaning of "danger" to self or others; if we know that involuntary confinement may be justified only by such danger, we must still decide when a state or community may say that such danger exists. On that issue, the *Donaldson* case is especially instructive. The Court there held that the state cannot "confine the mentally ill merely to ensure them a living standard superior to that they enjoy in the private community," opined that "the mere presence of mental illness does not disqualify a person from preferring his home to the comforts of an institution," and, most important, explained that the state may not "fence in the harmless mentally ill solely to save its citizens from exposure to those whose ways are different." [12] "One might as well ask," the Court remarked, "if the State, to avoid public unease, could incarcerate all who are physically unattractive or socially eccentric. Mere public intolerance or animosity cannot constitutionally justify the deprivation of a person's physical liberty." [13]

Interestingly, the Court cited as precedents for the inadmissibility of harm existing only in the beholder's consciousness the first amendment cases noted earlier. What seems most significant about *Donald-*

---

8. Id.

9. Id. at 612.

10. See Gerety, "Redefining Privacy," 12 Harv.Civ.Rts.-Civ.Lib.L.Rev. 233, 279 (1977).

11. 422 U.S. 563 (1975). The decision left open the permissibility of involuntary confinement for the purpose of *treating* a condition that poses no significant risk of dangerous behavior. On that issue, the Supreme Court of West Virginia, in a thoughtful opinion, has held involuntary confinement in the patient's own "best interest" unconstitutional. State ex rel. Hawks v. Lazaro, 157 W.Va. 417, 202 S.E.2d 109 (1974).

12. O'Connor, 422 U.S. at 575.

13. Id.

son for our purposes was its extension of those precedents to a setting not involving first amendment freedoms. Even without establishing that apparel, appearance, or life style touches upon these freedoms, therefore, one can argue strongly that "the Constitution leaves matters of taste and style . . . largely to the individual," [14] so that, outside such special contexts as that of intrusion into privacy or imposition upon a captive audience, government may not dictate how a person or group chooses to appear or to interact solely on the ground that others may find the display distasteful. This is as it must be if rights of personhood are to retain significance. *For the necessary premise of all such rights is that being forced by the sovereign to conform is more intrusive than being forced by the unusual to avert one's gaze.* [15] Neither the majority, nor the idiosyncratic individual abnormally offended by another's rampant personhood, can be accommodated by extinguishing the offense, without leaving personhood a hollow shell.

But this principle in turn has limits. At some point the sum total of looking away, staying away, and putting up, *does* become an undeniably profound invasion, and a departure from that pluralist harmony— the diversity of identities with minimal abrasion and the possibility of community—that may have been contemplated as "implicit in ordered liberty." [16] Moreover, the persons or groups seeking to be different make a less compelling case if the state threatens not incarceration, or denial of a basic benefit, but simply a requirement of moving elsewhere if they wish to be themselves. That observation brings us back to *Village of Belle Terre v. Boraas,* [17] and to the government's claim that the burden on the students who sought exemption from the ban on unrelated groups living together was not, after all, as severe as the burden on a community asked to endure an influx of people whose ways of life the majority would find alien.

The government, moreover, may insist that the harms it fears are not solely harms existing in the minds of those who observe what the students do and how they live—harms one could avoid simply by looking the other way. On the contrary, the very presence of significant numbers of student or other non-family groups (if one such group has a right to move in, why not two? twenty?) will gradually alter the character of life in the community, not simply because of everyone's knowledge about what sorts of people live behind the drawn shades but because the entire fabric of cultural, economic, and social existence inevitably responds to the tastes and preferences of those who make up any given population. Thus one might, for example, expect a change in the character of the entertainments shown at a neighborhood theatre after the composition of the neighborhood has changed; such collective changes cannot be avoided simply by looking the other way. Nor can they be reduced to any compendium of discrete harms avoidable, one by

---

14. Cohen v. California, 403 U.S. 15, 25 (1971).

15. This is the case even if the sovereign's coercion takes the form not of physical incarceration but of deprivation of vital public benefits.

16. Palko v. Connecticut, 302 U.S. 319, 325 (1937).

17. 416 U.S. 1 (1974).

one, through less restrictive alternatives than zoning out identified types of persons.

§ 15–19. Bounding the Community's Power Over Persons: Conduct Occurring Within Protected Sanctuaries

We may begin by focusing on the possible *limits* of our first principle, developed in § 15–18, that harms existing only in the mind of the beholder do not suffice. Among such limits, perhaps the most basic is that, when the affront seems offensive enough in relation to the importance of the choice to the person making it, the community may require at least that the choice be made in some less obtrusive way—at home, perhaps, or in a nudist camp, but not on the main street at high noon. The person who likes chartreuse walls may have to settle for painting the inside of his house his favorite color when the community says it will not put up with a chartreuse exterior.[1] Conversely, the community may be able to say "no" to public nudism (even though the harm is wholly in the eye of the beholder) but must stop short of commanding full dress in the privacy of one's living room.[2] The underlying idea is that even the eccentric individualist, or the peculiarly sensitive "victim" who finds it terribly painful to avert his gaze, should have some right to sanctuary, but no license to bend others to his preferences in the public arena.

As Chief Justice Burger stated for the Court in *United States v. Orito*, the "Constitution extends special safeguards to the privacy of the home, just as it protects other special privacy rights such as those of marriage, procreation, motherhood, child rearing and education."[3] Indeed, privacy of the home has the longest constitutional pedigree of the lot, "for the sanctity of the home . . . has been embedded in our traditions since the origins of the Republic."[4] These traditions, given concrete form in the fourth and fourteenth amendments, have "drawn a firm line at the entrance of the house."[5] When we retreat across that threshold, the government must provide escalating justification if it wishes to follow, monitor, or control us there.

More than just the procedural protections of the fourth amendment are heightened when one goes home and shuts the door. Property

§ 15–19

1. See generally Note, "Architecture, Aesthetic Zoning, and the First Amendment," 28 Stan.L.Rev. 179 (1975).

2. See South Florida Free Beaches, Inc. v. Miami, 734 F.2d 608, 610 (11th Cir. 1984) (no constitutional right to sunbathe or associate in the nude), aff'g in part 548 F.Supp. 53 (S.D.Fla. 1982); Williams v. Kleppe, 539 F.2d 803 (1st Cir. 1976) (upholding National Park Service regulation banning nude bathing in Cape Cod National Seashore, even in remote areas, in light of uncontrollable increase in beach usage—and hence environmental burden—caused by sunbathing); DeWeese v. Palm Beach, 616 F.Supp. 971, 978 (S.D.Fla. 1985) (upholding ordinance against jogging without a shirt: "It is a matter so well known that judicial notice can be taken of the uniqueness of Palm Beach; among small cities, it is truly one of a kind").

3. 413 U.S. 139, 142 (1973).

4. Payton v. New York, 445 U.S. 573, 601 (1980).

5. Id. at 590. As Justice Stevens wrote for the Court in Payton, "[i]n no [setting] is the zone of privacy more clearly defined than when bounded by the unambiguous physical dimensions of an individual's home—a zone that finds its roots in clear and specific constitutional terms. 'The right of the people to be secure in their . . . houses . . . shall not be violated.'" Id. at 589 (quoting fourth amendment).

rights in themselves "reflect society's explicit recognition of a person's authority to act as he wishes in certain areas." [6] The home not only protects us from government surveillance, but also "provide[s] the setting for those intimate activities that the fourth amendment is intended to shelter from governmental interference." [7] It thus may make all the difference *where* the state seeks to regulate personal conduct: "[i]t is hardly necessary to catalog the myriad activities that may be lawfully conducted within the privacy and confines of the home, but may be prohibited in public." [8] As the Court noted in *Paris Adult Theater I v. Slaton*,[9] for example, a married couple's right to engage in sexual relations in their bedroom affords no protection to a sexual embrace at high noon in Times Square. Conversely, government power to zone live "adult" entertainment restrictively [10] or to dictate that nude dancing shall not accompany the serving of alcohol in restaurants or bars [11] hardly implies similar authority to tell citizens how to dress when entertaining guests or serving drinks in their own homes. And the Supreme Court held in *Stanley v. Georgia* [12] that, however free the state may be to ban the *public* dissemination of constitutionally unprotected obscene materials, the state cannot criminalize the purely *private* possession of such materials at home. Even though the first amendment did not protect the material involved as such, the Court observed that "[i]f the first amendment means anything, it means that a state has no business telling a man, sitting alone in his own house, what books he may read or what films he may watch." [13]

Even when the harm feared has existence independent of the beholder's awareness of the offending conduct, as in the supposed danger of antisocial behavior induced by Stanley's reading or viewing of obscenity, the power to translate belief about such danger into a rule reaching into people's homes is limited by substantive rights of personhood. The Alaska Supreme Court has gone so far as to hold that, under the state's constitution, the possession of marijuana could not be made a crime at home even if the same possession in other settings could be punished.[14]

6. Rakas v. Illinois, 439 U.S. 128, 153 (1978) (Powell, J., concurring). See also R. Epstein, Takings: Private Property and the Power of Eminent Domain 109 n.4 (1985) ("the notion of private property is designed to exclude [moral] judgments about the conduct of others," particularly judgments by moral consensus that certain "activities . . . are unworthy in themselves even if they cause no harm to others").

7. Oliver v. United States, 466 U.S. 170, 179 (1984). As Justice Harlan wrote in dissent in Poe v. Ullman, 367 U.S. 497, 551 (1961), "if the physical curtilage of the home is protected, it is surely as a result of solicitude to protect the privacies of the life within." By contrast, areas lying beyond the curtilage lack constitutional protection from government incursion because they "are unlikely to provide the setting for activities whose privacy is sought to be protected by the fourth amendment." Oliver, 466 U.S. at 179 n.10.

8. United States v. Orito, 413 U.S. at 142.

9. 413 U.S. 49, 65 (1973).

10. See Schad v. Mt. Ephraim, 452 U.S. 61, 71–72, 76 (1981).

11. See California v. LaRue, 409 U.S. 109 (1972).

12. 394 U.S. 557, 559 (1969).

13. Id. at 565. The Stanley case is discussed in § 15–7, supra.

14. Ravin v. State, 537 P.2d 494, 504, 510–12 (Alaska 1975), discussed in § 15–7, supra. Whether state power to control the use of dangerous substances ought in fact to vary with the location where such use occurs is not entirely clear. Insofar as the privacy of the home, expressly recognized in the third amendment as well as in the

Thus, whatever the threshold of harm the state must otherwise establish to justify intruding upon an aspect of personhood in the public realm, the required threshold is significantly higher when the conduct occurs in a place, or under circumstances, that the individuals involved justifiably regard as private.

Of course that hardly settles the dispute in a case like *Village of Belle Terre v. Boraas*,[15] where no attempt was made to ban specific acts by the six unrelated students in the privacy of the home they sought to rent; on the contrary, the effort was to prevent them from living in the community—whatever they might do, or fail to do, behind closed doors. The theory must have been that their continuing presence in the town, and their regular participation in its public life, would alter the character of the community to the regret of those who got there first. But their presence would have that effect only because of the nature of their relationship. At this point, then, it becomes necessary to move to a final consideration: to what extent does the fact that a proposed choice is integral to a *personal relationship* alter the argument on behalf of personhood when the larger society challenges that choice in the name of the law?

§ 15–20. Bounding the Community's Power Over Persons: Choices Implicit in Special Personal Relationships— Families and Other Intimate Communities

A point "as important as it is easy to overlook" is that "the family unit does not simply co-exist with our constitutional system" but "is an integral part of it," for our "political system is superimposed on and presupposes a social system of family units, not just of isolated individuals. No assumption more deeply underlies our society. . . ."[1] To the extent that this description suggests a constitutional infirmity in any governmental decision to assume the basic functions of deciding who will form a family with whom and determining what values and beliefs will be inculcated in the children that families raise, it is plainly correct. This much, at least, is implicit in the Supreme Court's invalidation of state laws telling parents what language their children shall learn to speak[2] and what kinds of schools their children shall attend.[3] It is implicit too in the Court's invalidation of statutes purporting to

fourth, reflects a concern for personal autonomy with respect to a characteristic set of activities, it is plain that this set of activities ought to include choices bearing on personal appearance and intimate association as well as on such matters as reading material. It is less plain that the activities with respect to which privacy of the home has special significance ought to include choices bearing on physiological risk. Surely the state's power to ban suicide, for example—see §§ 15–11, 15–12, supra—is not diminished by the would-be suicide's retreat into the solitude of the home. That the third amendment bans the peacetime quartering of government regiments in the home may well imply that government cannot regiment every detail of how one

dresses at home, with whom one associates there, how long one chooses to sleep there, and the like—but need not imply that government's power to act paternalistically stops or even diminishes drastically at one's doorstep.

15.   416 U.S. 1 (1974).

§ 15–20

1. Heymann & Barzelay, "The Forest and the Trees: Roe v. Wade and its Critics," 53 B.U.L.Rev. 765, 772–73 (1973). See Moore v. East Cleveland, 431 U.S. 494 (1977) (invalidating ordinance excluding certain extended families from residence in city), discussed in § 15–17, supra.

2.–3. See notes 2–3 on page 1415.

arrogate to government the decision of who should be permitted to bear children [4] and of laws interfering with particular decisions either to have children [5] or not to have them.[6] Finally, that the line of relevant decisions goes beyond questions of childbirth and childrearing becomes clear when one adds decisions holding that freedom to marry the person of one's choice is "one of the vital personal rights essential to the orderly pursuit of happiness," [7] decisions holding that marriage and divorce are so fundamental that indigents cannot be charged a fee for the right to go to court to dissolve a marital relationship [8] or confronted with state-created financial barriers to remarriage,[9] and decisions holding that the community's undoubted zoning power stops short of any authority to confine local residence to nuclear families and certain limited categories of extended families.[10]

But, although the Court has spoken of decisions such as these as recognizing a "private realm of family life which the state cannot

2. Meyer v. Nebraska, 262 U.S. 390 (1923).

3. Pierce v. Society of Sisters, 268 U.S. 510 (1925).

4. Skinner v. Oklahoma, 316 U.S. 535 (1942), discussed in § 15–10, supra.

5. Cleveland Bd. of Educ. v. LaFleur, 414 U.S. 632 (1974).

6. Griswold v. Connecticut, 381 U.S. 479 (1965); Roe v. Wade, 410 U.S. 113 (1973). See § 15–10, supra.

7. Loving v. Virginia, 388 U.S. 1, 12 (1967) (invalidating law against racial intermarriage). But see Reynolds v. United States, 98 U.S. 145 (1878) (upholding federal law against polygamy); Cleveland v. United States, 329 U.S. 14 (1946) (same); Rappaport v. Katz, 380 F.Supp. 808 (S.D. N.Y.1974) (upholding city guidelines requiring certain forms of attire to be worn at marriage ceremonies performed by city clerk); cf. § 15–15, supra.

8. Boddie v. Connecticut, 401 U.S. 371 (1971), discussed in § 16–11, infra, from the perspective of the right to equal litigation opportunity. Unlike total deprivations of divorce opportunities, waiting periods have been subjected to only minimal scrutiny. See Sosna v. Iowa, 419 U.S. 393 (1975), discussed in § 16–8, infra.

9. Zablocki v. Redhail, 434 U.S. 374 (1978) (squarely establishing a constitutional right to marry in the course of striking down a Wisconsin law allowing parents with court-imposed child-support obligations to remarry only if said obligations were met and only if the children were "not likely thereafter to become public charges"). The Court observed that a parent who was unemployed or had a low income could not keep his child off welfare even if he met his support obligations;

with respect to such parents, the law was an absolute barrier to remarriage. Justice Marshall's opinion for the Court, joined by Chief Justice Burger and Justices Brennan, White, and Blackmun, was based on a denial of equal protection. Justice Stewart concurred, labeling the freedom to marry another "liberty" protected by the due process clause. Id. at 391. Justice Powell concurred on the ground that the law failed under an intermediate standard of review, but declined to call marriage a fundamental right for fear that many state regulations of marriage would be undermined. Id. at 397. Justice Stevens agreed with this reading and concurred on grounds of wealth discrimination. Id. at 404. In Turner v. Safley, 107 S.Ct. 2254 (1987), the Court unanimously extended the fundamental right recognized in Zablocki to prison inmates, striking down a virtually flat ban on marriage, whether to other inmates or to civilians, while leaving open the possibility that legitimate security concerns might justify prohibiting a particular union if the warden were to find that it would present a threat to public safety or prison order. Id. at 2266 (citing the rule for federal prisons). In reviewing the importance of marriage to those behind bars, the Court noted (1) that inmate marriages, like all others, "are expressions of emotional support and public commitment," (2) that such unions may have "spiritual significance," (3) that most such marriages are formed in the "expectation that they ultimately will be fully consummated," and (4) that "marital status is often a precondition to the receipt of government benefits, . . . property rights, . . . and other, less tangible benefits." Id at 2265.

10. Moore v. East Cleveland, 431 U.S. 494 (1977).

enter" without compelling justification,[11] the very decision in which that phrase appeared denied a guardian the right to direct her ward, a 9-year old niece, to distribute religious literature in violation of a state law forbidding child labor. More recently, in upholding the power of Congress, acting under the thirteenth amendment, to outlaw segregated private academies, the Court thought no privacy right was at stake since the schools appealed to a public constituency,[12] and saw no threat to any right of the family as a unit, or of the parents directing it, so long as those parents "remain . . . free to inculcate whatever values and standards they deem desirable."[13] Moreover, earlier the same Term, the Court in *Baker v. Owen*[14] "held in a summary affirmance that parental approval of corporal punishment [in school] is not constitutionally required."[15]

If decisions like *Runyon v. McCrary* and *Baker v. Owen* move in the direction of reduced parental control in controversies pitting the child *against* outside institutions, it is also noteworthy that decisions like *Planned Parenthood v. Danforth*,[16] rejecting an absolute parental veto over a minor's abortion, move in the parallel direction of reduced parental control in situations where the child seeks aid *from* outside institutions. If one adds the holding in *Danforth* that a *spouse* cannot veto an abortion either, what at first may appear to be "family rights" emerge as rights of individuals only.[17]

Now add the decisions holding that government cannot use the threat of withholding subsistence benefits in order to reinforce the traditional family,[18] and the decisions holding that government cannot treat the parent-child relationship as automatically less significant simply because the parents are unwed;[19] if one brings all of these decisions together, one cannot avoid the conclusion that the stereotypical "family unit" that is so much a part of our constitutional rhetoric is

---

11. Prince v. Massachusetts, 321 U.S. 158, 166 (1944).

12. Runyon v. McCrary, 427 U.S. 160, 172 & n.10, 178 & n.14 (1976). Cf. Bob Jones University v. United States, 461 U.S. 574, 592–96, 604 & n.29 (1983) ("the government has a fundamental, overriding interest in eradicating racial discrimination in education"); id. at 607 (Powell, J., concurring in part and concurring in the judgment) ("if any national policy is sufficiently fundamental to constitute . . . an overriding limitation on the availability of tax-exempt status, it is the policy against racial discrimination in education").

13. Runyon v. McCrary, 427 U.S. at 177–78. See also Wisconsin v. Yoder, 406 U.S. 205, 239 (1972); Norwood v. Harrison, 413 U.S. 455, 461–62, 469 (1973).

14. 423 U.S. 907 (1976) (mem.), affirming 395 F.Supp. 294 (M.D.N.C.1975).

15. Ingraham v. Wright, 430 U.S. 651, 662 n. 22 (1977), discussed in § 15–9, supra.

16. 428 U.S. 52, 72–75 (1976). See also Bellotti v. Baird, 443 U.S. 622, 633 (1979)

(law requiring parental notification and consent before minor child has abortion is facially valid so long as it allows minor to pursue alternate route of obtaining judicial consent for abortion in instances where minor is sufficiently mature to make decision for herself or where she can show abortion is in her best interests).

17. See generally § 15–17, supra.

18. United States Dept. of Agriculture v. Moreno, 413 U.S. 528 (1973); New Jersey Welfare Rights Organization v. Cahill, 411 U.S. 619 (1973), discussed in § 15–17, supra.

19. See Stanley v. Illinois, 405 U.S. 645 (1972) (unwed fathers cannot automatically be presumed unfit); Levy v. Louisiana, 391 U.S. 68 (1968) (illegitimate child cannot be disqualified from wrongful death recovery for death of mother); Glona v. American Guarantee Co., 391 U.S. 73 (1968) (mother of illegitimate child cannot be disqualified from wrongful death recovery for death of child); see also § 16–23, infra.

becoming decreasingly central to our constitutional reality.[20] Such "exercises of familial rights and responsibilities"[21] as remain prove to be *individual* powers to resist governmental determination of who shall be born, with whom one shall live, and what values shall be transmitted.

Another illuminating approach to the Supreme Court's family jurisprudence has been offered by Professor Robert Burt, who contends that, "[n]otwithstanding an occasional rhetorical flourish from spokesmen for both blocs, principled legitimacy for parental authority as such in preference to other sources of social power commands no adherents yet among liberal or conservative Justices of this generation."[22] Thus, purportedly "pro-family" cases such as *Wisconsin v. Yoder*,[23] where the Court upheld the right of Amish parents to keep their children out of school after the eighth grade, can be reconciled with apparently interventionist cases such as *Planned Parenthood v. Danforth*, where the Court rejected parental power to veto a child's abortion, by observing *which* child-rearing strategies have won the Justices' respect: "parental authority must be honored only when parents succeed (as the Court found that 'the Amish succeed') in bringing obedient social conformance from their children"; no respect is due to parents whose utter failure to socialize their children has been demonstrated by the very fact of premarital pregnancy.[24] The more conservative members of the Court[25] have not consistently deferred to family authority as such because they are more concerned with protecting social order, a value only occasionally served by according special prerogatives to "mom and dad."[26] In contrast, Burt suggests, the Court's more liberal Justices have rejected this deference because they deem parent-child conflict—like all other conflict—to be inevitable and best resolved by state mechanisms. They would therefore require parents—like any other repository of authority in our society—to give reasoned justifications for major decisions regarding their children.[27] Hence the decision in

20. Even the Supreme Court decision containing the most pronounced praise in recent years for family values was in fact a defense of the *extended* family more common among ethnic and racial minorities than in the modern American mainstream. Moore v. East Cleveland, 431 U.S. 494 (1977); id. at 509–10 & nn.6–10 (Brennan, J., joined by Marshall, J., concurring).

21. Runyon, 427 U.S. at 178.

22. Burt, "The Constitution of the Family," 1979 Sup.Ct.Rev. 329, 351.

23. 406 U.S. 205 (1972). See Chapter 14, supra.

24. Burt, supra note 22, at 339–40. In Yoder itself, the Court indicated that this special solicitude for the prerogatives of traditional Amish communities would not be extended to progressive or utopian communities, religious or secular. See 406 U.S. at 216. Sometimes the interest in promoting social order can be vindicated by favoring some familial ties over others.

This perspective may help to explain the result in Quilloin v. Walcott, 434 U.S. 246 (1978), where the Court unanimously rejected a due process challenge to Georgia's adoption laws brought by a man who wished to block the adoption of his illegitimate son by the child's stepfather. The Court explained the desirability of preserving family units already in existence, and allowed the value of what might be called a "complete," if artificially created, family unit to trump the value of the biological father's relationship with his child.

25. When he wrote his article, Burt included under this admittedly inadequate rubric Chief Justice Burger and Justices Blackmun, Powell, and Rehnquist. He deemed Justices Brennan and Marshall to be the counterbalancing "liberals" on family issues. 1979 Sup.Ct.Rev. at 332 n.18.

26. Id. at 351–52.

27. Id. at 352.

Bellotti v. Baird,[28] where the Court upheld a law requiring parental notification and consent before a minor may obtain an abortion because the law contained a judicial bypass mechanism whereby the rational judgment of a court could be substituted for the judgment of the parents. This proclivity for mediating intra-family conflict by state intervention reflects the recurring puzzle of liberal individualism: [29] once the state, whether acting through its courts or otherwise, has "liberated" the child—and the adult—from the shackles of such intermediate groups as the family, what is to defend the individual against the combined tyranny of the state and her own alienation?

Certainly the whole answer cannot lie in the municipalities and other political subdivisions that are euphemistically portrayed as tight-knit, cohesive communities in various Supreme Court decisions of the 1970's.[30] Whatever the elusive ideal of community might require,[31] one is entitled at least to be skeptical that it can be found in America's governmental units, even those that are relatively responsive to their citizens. The polis of ancient Greece simply is not ours to re-create.[32] Nor is a rebirth of religious community a realistic prospect for more than a handful of moderns. However much power we delegate to church hierarchies or congregations under doctrines precluding judicial interference in ecclesiastical disputes,[33] it seems exceedingly unlikely that the social and cultural cohesion that family provided in our national mythology will be supplied by worship or sacrament.

What all of this has to do with constitutional law should be clear enough. The dilemma of contemporary individuals—isolated and made vulnerable to the state's distant majorities at the very moment that they are liberated from domination by those closes to them—cannot be ignored by those seeking to give meaning to the terms "life" and "liberty," or to the "privileges" or "immunities" of citizenship. If there is any answer, it is to be found in facilitating the emergence of relationships that meet the human need for closeness, trust, and love in ways that may jar some conventional sensibilities but without which there can be no hope of solving the persistent problem of autonomy and community.

Although Justice Brandeis was of course thinking about states rather than smaller units of human association when he made his famous statement about the virtues of federalism, his thought is worth recalling in our quite different context. "To stay experimentation in

---

28. 443 U.S. 622, 633 (1979). See § 15–10, supra.

29. See generally R. Nisbet, The Quest for Community 212–79 (1969 ed.).

30. See, e.g., Paris Adult Theatre I v. Slaton, 413 U.S. 49 (1973); San Antonio Independent School Dist. v. Rodriguez, 411 U.S. 1 (1973); G. Suttles, The Social Construction of Communities 264–70 (1972). But cf. Dahl, "The City in the Future of Democracy," 61 Am.Pol.Sci.Rev. 953, 968 (1967).

31. See, e.g., R. Unger, Knowledge and Politics (1974); R. J. Wilson, In Quest of Community (1968).

32. See generally H. Arendt, The Human Condition (1958). But see Frug, "The City As a Legal Concept," 93 Harv.L. Rev. 1057, 1120–49 (1980). This of course assumes that we would *want* to return to that supposedly halcyon time, when most of the residents of Athens were slaves and when social critics such as Socrates were democratically executed at the bidding of demagogues.

33. See Chapter 14, supra.

things social and economic is a grave responsibility," he said; "[i]t is one of the happy incidents of the federal system that a single courageous State"—we might substitute the word "community"—"may serve as a laboratory; and try novel social and economic experiments without risk to the rest of the country." [34]

In a time of social transformation, we must not forget that a small community genuinely seeking to preserve—or, more accurately, to restore—what it perceives to be traditional forms, even by limiting residence to nuclear and extended families,[35] might be regarded as hardly less courageous, and even experimental, than the commune or the group attempting to share some other less widely understood pattern of life. For example, one gains a more sympathetic understanding of the "nuclear family" ordinance struck down in *Moore v. East Cleveland* when one learns that it was enacted by an upwardly mobile, middle-class, predominantly black community with a largely black government to exclude families deemed to be characteristic of the lower-class ghetto life that many of the community's residents had labored long to leave.[36] As Professor Burt has observed, "the very oddity of the East Cleveland ordinance suggests that Mrs. Moore is not alone in her opposition to it, that the city residents are more the vulnerable, isolated dissenters than she in the broader society, that they more than she deserve special judicial solicitude as a 'discrete and insular minority.' The Court in *Moore* myopically saw the case as a dispute between 'a family' and 'the state' rather than as a dispute among citizens about the meaning of 'family.' "[37] Of course, to the extent that one group of citizens had captured the machinery of the state and was wielding state power to impose its notion of family on other citizens, forcing them either to conform or to leave, the Court's concern with unduly intrusive social engineering was warranted.[38] The power to reinforce one type of relationship must not extend to an

---

34. New State Ice Co. v. Liebmann, 285 U.S. 262, 311 (1932) (dissenting opinion).

35. Cf. Moore v. East Cleveland, 431 U.S. 494 (1977).

36. See Burt, supra note 22, at 389–90; see also 431 U.S. at 537 n.7 (Stewart, J., dissenting).

37. Burt, supra note 22, at 391.

38. Cf. Village of Belle Terre v. Boraas, 416 U.S. 1 (1974), discussed in § 15–17, supra, where the Court upheld a residential community's power to exclude households comprising unmarried and unrelated individuals. There is obviously some tension between Belle Terre, where a white, suburban, bedroom community was allowed to define itself by excluding student households and other non-family groups, and Moore, where a black, middle-class, residential community was denied the power to define itself by excluding households characteristic of the urban ghetto. Those who would condemn the East Cleveland ordinance as race- or class-based conformism underrate the value—both to society at large and to individual communities—of promoting family structures deemed to be both healthy and healthful. As one astute commentator has observed, "The defenders of the matrifocal family, posing as critics of cultural parochialism, have unthinkingly absorbed the rising middle-class dissatisfaction with the isolated, 'privatized' suburban family, a dissatisfaction that has become especially pervasive in the very suburbs in which the 'sentimental model of the family' is said to originate. Claiming to have liberated themselves from the assumptions of their own class, these writers share the fashionable concern with 'alternatives to the nuclear family' and project the search for alternative life-styles onto the ghetto. They idealize the matrifocal family, exaggerate the degree to which it is embedded in a rich network of kinship relations, and ignore evidence which plainly shows that blacks themselves prefer a family in which the male earns the money and the mother rears the young." C. Lasch, Haven in a Heartless World 162–63 (1977).

authority to stamp out another altogether; to defend an anti-commune ordinance, one must show that no such result actually occurs.

If, however, it can be demonstrated that a community's efforts to preserve its character do not operate to freeze out alternatives indefinitely or to exclude them from an area wider than a few square miles, such efforts should be regarded as entitled to at least some constitutional protection from the imposed uniformity of state or federal law. Of course the larger society—in our system, the state or the nation—must still enforce norms reflecting widely shared ideals about human rights. Thus it would certainly be wrong to treat as protected a decision to injure children simply because such a decision happened to be shared by adults in a group purporting to be experimenting with an alternative style of life. But the embedding of a choice within a close human relationship or network of relationships should always be regarded as significantly increasing the burden of justification for those who would make the choice illegal or visit it with some deprivation. In *Moore v. City of East Cleveland*, where the Court treated as fundamental the right to live in an extended as opposed to a nuclear family, the plurality opinion's emphasis upon the blood relationship of the parties [39] should not, therefore, be treated as decisive. If a city or town may require that every home be occupied by a single "family," consisting entirely of persons related by blood or marriage, it would be difficult to respond to the argument that the same city or town may also decide what a "family" is: If longtime friends can be excluded by ordinance, why not second cousins? And if second cousins, why not certain grandchildren? [40] The functions of shaping and transmitting values, which the *Moore* plurality identified as justifying protection for the extended family, [41] inhere in a wide variety of enduring relationships; governmental interference with *any* such relationship should be invalidated unless compellingly justified. [42] For although the Supreme Court's solicitude for intimate associations has most often been expressed in terms of marriage and family, the Court has on occasion gone out of its way to remind us that it has "not held that constitutional protection is restricted to relationships among family members." [43]

39. See § 15–17, supra.

40. In Moore, this argument was in fact advanced by Justice Stewart, joined in dissent by Justice Rehnquist, 431 U.S. at 531. See also Smith v. Organization of Foster Families, 431 U.S. 816, 843–44 nn.49–50 (1977) (protection of "family" not limited to blood relationships) (dictum).

41. Moore, 431 U.S. at 503–04 & n.13. See also Smith, 431 U.S. at 844 (identifying family's importance, to individuals and to society, in "the emotional attachments that derive from the intimacy of daily association").

42. Although it was argued in § 15–17 that Village of Belle Terre v. Boraas, 416 U.S. 1 (1974), cannot properly be read as involving an ordinance limited to transient groups, it remains the case that the students involved in Belle Terre did not claim to have an enduring relationship; the decision thus cannot be said to foreclose the position taken here about groups alleging such a relationship.

43. Rotary International v. Rotary Club of Duarte, 107 S.Ct. 1940 (1987), discussed in § 15–17, supra.

§ 15–21. The Future of Privacy and Personhood: Sex and Sexual Orientation

The Supreme Court has frequently recognized the fundamental importance—and the constitutional stature—of the freedom to enter into and carry on intimate associations. Although, as we saw in the preceding section, the initial focus of this awareness was, understandably, the traditional nuclear family, the Justices "have not held that constitutional protection is restricted to relationships among family members. We have emphasized that the first amendment protects those relationships . . . that presuppose deep attachments and commitments to the necessarily few other individuals with whom one shares not only a special community of thoughts, experiences, and beliefs but also distinctly personal aspects of one's life." [1] Prominent among those personal aspects is sexual intimacy: "a sensitive, key relationship of human existence, central to family life, community welfare, and the development of human personality." [2] "The fact that individuals define themselves in a significant way through their intimate sexual relationships with others suggests, in a nation as diverse as ours, that there may be many 'right' ways of conducting those relationships, and that much of the richness of a relationship will come from the freedom to *choose* the form and nature of these intensely personal bonds." [3]

Unfortunately, the reality of the Court's privacy jurisprudence does not always parallel the caliber of its rhetoric. The preceding quotations are drawn from three different cases where the Court found that there was no intimate association worthy of the Constitution's special protection. With respect to the first two cases, this result in no way undermines the credibility of the Court's commitment to privacy. The first passage is quoted from *Rotary International v. Rotary Club of Duarte*,[4] where the Court found that a men's business club aiming to be "a true cross section of the business and professional life of the community" and avowedly dedicated to keeping its "windows and doors open to the whole world" [5] was not the sort of intimate association that could escape a state ban on discrimination against women. The second quotation comes from *Paris Adult Theatre I v. Slaton*,[6] where the Court upheld a community's power to enjoin commercial exhibition of hardcore pornographic films: the patrons had not purchased tickets in order to come together and share something in the darkened theater, but merely to huddle before the screen, strangers in the isolation of their seats. It is hard to quarrel, from an associational perspective, with the outcome in either case.

§ 15–21

1. Rotary International v. Rotary Club of Duarte, 107 S.Ct. 1940, 1946 (1987) (citation omitted).

2. Paris Adult Theatre I v. Slaton, 413 U.S. 49, 63 (1973).

3. Bowers v. Hardwick, 106 S.Ct. 2841, 2851 (1986) (Blackmun, J., dissenting).

4. 107 S.Ct. 1940, 1946 (1987), discussed in § 15–17, supra.

5. 107 S.Ct. at 1947, (quoting Rotary Club documents).

6. 413 U.S. 49, 63 (1973).

But the third excerpt is from Justice Blackmun's stirring dissent in *Bowers v. Hardwick*,[7] where a five-member majority [8] held that it is "facetious" even to suggest that two adult homosexuals engaging in consensual sex in the privacy of their home are carrying on an intimate association entitled to constitutional protection.[9] The author of this treatise argued the case for Michael Hardwick in the Supreme Court.

The Atlanta police arrested Hardwick in his bedroom and charged him with the crime of "sodomy" [10] for engaging in oral sex with another consenting adult in that very room. In rejecting Hardwick's challenge to the Georgia sodomy statute, the Supreme Court stated the issue as "whether the federal Constitution confers a fundamental right upon homosexuals to engage in sodomy. . . ." [11] Six decades of privacy precedents, from *Meyer v. Nebraska* [12] and *Skinner v. Oklahoma* [13] to *Griswold v. Connecticut* [14] and *Roe v. Wade*,[15] were dismissed in two brisk paragraphs as having no relevance to this issue, since those cases involved rights related to "family, marriage, or procreation." [16] The dissenters replied that this case "is no more about 'a fundamental right to engage in homosexual sodomy' . . . than *Stanley v. Georgia* was about a fundamental right to watch obscene movies, or *Katz v. United States* was about a fundamental right to place interstate bets from a telephone booth. Rather, this case is about 'the most comprehensive of rights and the right most valued by civilized men,' namely, 'the right to be let alone.' " [17]

The *Hardwick* majority's decision to cut off constitutional protection "at the first convenient, if arbitrary boundary" [18] drawn by prior cases is not only antithetical to the evolutionary genius of the common law,[19] it also ignored the warning in *Moore v. East Cleveland* against "clos[ing] our eyes to the basic reasons *why* certain rights . . . have been accorded shelter under the fourteenth amendment's due process clause." [20] As the dissenters pointed out, "we protect the decision

---

7. 106 S.Ct. 2841 (1986). Justice Blackmun was joined by Justices Brennan, Marshall, and Stevens.

8. Justice White wrote for the Court, joined by Chief Justice Burger and Justices Powell, Rehnquist, and O'Connor.

9. Id. at 2846 (opinion of the Court).

10. This crime, punishable by imprisonment for up to twenty years, is defined by Georgia law as "any sexual act involving the sex organs of one person and the mouth or anus of another." Official Code of Georgia § 16–6–2.

11. 106 S.Ct. at 2843. See id. at 2844.

12. 262 U.S. 390 (1923).

13. 316 U.S. 535 (1942).

14. 381 U.S. 479 (1965).

15. 410 U.S. 113 (1973).

16. Id. at 2844. Three weeks earlier, Justice White, author of the Hardwick opinion, had characterized these very same cases as protecting "personal or family privacy and autonomy." Thornburgh v. American College of Obstetricians & Gynecologists, 106 S.Ct. 2169, 2194 (1986) (White, J., dissenting).

17. Id. at 2848 (Blackmun, J., dissenting, joined by Brennan, Marshall, and Stevens, JJ.) (quoting Olmstead v. United States, 277 U.S. 438, 478 (1928) (Brandeis, J., dissenting)) (citations omitted).

18. Moore v. East Cleveland, 431 U.S. 494, 502 (1977) (plurality opinion).

19. The tradition of liberty under the due process clause has never "been reduced to any formula" nor "determined by reference to any code," Poe v. Ullman, 367 U.S. 497, 542 (1961) (Harlan, J., dissenting), but rather has been "a living thing," id. at 542. "Great concepts like . . . 'liberty' . . . were purposely left to gather meaning from experience[,] [f]or . . . only a stagnant society remains unchanged." Nat'l Mutual Ins. Co. v. Tidewater Transfer Co., 337 U.S. 582, 646 (1949) (Frankfurter, J., dissenting).

20. Id. at 501 (emphasis added).

whether to marry precisely because marriage 'is an association that promotes a way of life, not causes; a harmony in living, not political faiths; a bilateral loyalty, not commercial or social projects.' . . . And we protect the family because it contributes so powerfully to the happiness of individuals, not because of a preference for stereotypical households." [21]   The underlying value in those contexts, as in the *Hardwick* case, is protection for intimate human associations.

Special constitutional solicitude for marriage and the family cannot by itself explain the protection the Court gave to the activities involved in the various birth control cases. After all, the right to control the size of one's family can be vindicated, without any resort to contraceptives, by simply refraining from sexual intercourse—"just saying 'No.' " No law of any of the states involved in *Griswold v. Connecticut, Eisenstadt v. Baird,*[22] or *Carey v. Population Services Int'l*[23] prohibited celibacy or abstinence as methods of avoiding childbirth. Rather, those states' laws were challenged and struck down because, by barring access to contraceptives, they imposed the onerous risks of disease and unwanted pregnancy on the very sexual relations that people otherwise wished to enjoy.[24]   And neither the right of access to contraceptive technology affirmed in *Eisenstadt* and *Carey,* nor the right to abortion upheld in *Roe v. Wade,*[25] was limited to married couples. Indeed, in *Eisenstadt* the Court declared that just such a distinction between married and single persons was unconstitutional. The plaintiff in *Roe v. Wade* was likewise unmarried. These decisions, therefore, can hardly be said to have revolved around "marriage" or "the family."

As the Court itself stressed in *Carey,* the constitutional principle of "individual autonomy" affirmed in these cases protected not procreation, but the individual's "right of *decision*" about procreation.[26]   In each case, the Court protected the decision to engage in sex *without* bearing or begetting a child. These holdings thus mandated heightened scrutiny not of state restrictions on procreative sex, but of restrictions on recreational or expressional sex—sex solely as a facet of associational intimacy—whether between spouses or between unmarried lovers. The *Hardwick* majority nevertheless treated prior decisions upholding access to contraceptives as if they involved the right to buy and use a particular pharmaceutical product, rather than the right to engage in sexual intimacy as such. Yet decision-making about contraceptive use occupies a zone of presumptive protection from the state not just because it touches upon child-bearing, but also because it arises solely in the context of "a field that by definition concerns the most intimate of human activities and relationships" [27]—namely, *sexual* activities and relationships. And those activities and relationships do not lose that intimate status when engaged in for reasons other than

21. 106 S.Ct. at 2851 (quoting Griswold v. Connecticut, 381 U.S. at 486).

22. 405 U.S. 438 (1972).

23. 431 U.S. 678 (1977).

24. See, e.g., Eisenstadt, 405 U.S. at 448; Carey, 431 U.S. at 694–95 (plurality opinion); id. at 714–15 (Stevens, J., concur-ring in part and concurring in the judgment).

25. 410 U.S. 113 (1973).

26. 431 U.S. at 687–89 (original emphasis).

27. Carey, 431 U.S. at 685.

procreation.[28] As Justice Blackmun put it, the Constitution's protection of decisions about childbearing has nothing to do with "demographic considerations or the Bible's command to be fruitful and multiply." [29]

It should come as no surprise that respect for individual autonomy and reverence for human relations are so tightly intertwined in the sexual privacy cases. For the "'ability independently to define one's identity that is central to any concept of liberty' cannot truly be exercised in a vacuum; we all depend on the 'emotional enrichment of close ties with others.'" [30] The right to choose the people with whom we make such ties is the very essence of freedom of association. And a "necessary corollary of giving individuals freedom to choose how to conduct their lives"—and with whom—"is acceptance of the fact that different individuals will make different choices." [31]

The behavior for which Michael Hardwick was arrested and temporarily jailed [32] took place in his home, a sanctuary to which, as we have

28. Professor Thomas Grey has argued that these cases are "dedicated to the cause of social stability and have nothing to do with the sexual liberation of the individual. The contraception and abortion cases are simply family planning cases. They represent two standard conservative views: that social stability is threatened by excessive population growth; and that family stability is threatened by unwanted pregnancies, with their accompanying fragile marriages, single-parent families, irresponsible youthful parents, and abandoned or neglected children." Grey, "Eros, Civilization and the Burger Court," 43 Law & Contemp.Prob. 83, 88 (1980). Precisely because the Court deems sex to be "a great and mysterious motive force in human life," Roth v. United States, 354 U.S. 476, 487 (1957), the Court harbors traditional Freudian fears of anti-social consequences unless sex is repressed by society. Grey, supra, at 91.

29. Hardwick, 106 S.Ct. at 2851 (dissenting opinion).

30. Id. (quoting Roberts v. United States Jaycees, 468 U.S. 609, 619 (1984)). Professor Kenneth Karst suggests the following catalog of values inherent in intimate association: the opportunity to enjoy the society of certain other people; the opportunity for caring, commitment, and love; the opportunity to know another human being as a whole person rather than as the occupant of a particular role; and the opportunity to be seen—and to see oneself—as a whole person rather than as an aggregate of social roles. Karst, "The Freedom of Intimate Association," 89 Yale L.J. 624, 630–36 (1980).

31. Hardwick, 106 S.Ct. at 2852 (Blackmun, J., dissenting). As the Court observed in holding that state control over public education must give way to a competing claim by the Amish that extended formal schooling threatened their traditional way of life, "There can be no assumption that today's majority is 'right' and the Amish and others like them are 'wrong.' A way of life that is odd or even erratic but interferes with no rights or interests of others is not to be condemned because it is different." Wisconsin v. Yoder, 406 U.S. 205, 223–24 (1972).

32. Justice Powell filed a concurring opinion, in which he stated that there would be a serious eighth amendment issue if anyone were actually to be given a prison sentence, especially a long one, for an act of consensual, adult sodomy in "the private setting of a home." 106 S.Ct. at 2847. But he believed that the issue was not before the Court, since the plaintiff had yet to be tried, let alone convicted and sentenced. Id. at 2848. But surely consideration of whether criminalizing homosexual conduct constitutes cruel and unusual punishment cannot be thought to require actual imprisonment. For it is the very criminalization of an involuntary condition, not the terms of any specific sentence imposed, that violates the Constitution. The eighth amendment "imposes substantive limits on what can be made criminal." Ingraham v. Wright, 430 U.S. 651, 667 (1977). Just as "[e]ven one day in prison would be a cruel and usual punishment for the 'crime' of having a common cold," Robinson v. California, 370 U.S. 660, 667 (1962), so even a day in jail for engaging in sexual intimacies inherent in a homosexual orientation might violate the eighth and fourteenth amendments. Cf. Powell v. Texas, 392 U.S. 514, 548 (1968) (White, J.,

seen,[33] the fourth amendment accords special protection.[34] This outrage was compounded by the fact that Hardwick was watched, seized and handcuffed by police in his own bedroom—the arresting officer refused even to leave the room or turn his back while Hardwick and his companion dressed.[35] Thus this was not a case where a purportedly intimate association could be deemed unprotected because it was "carried on in the presence of strangers" or because the participants decided "to keep their 'windows and doors open to the whole world.' "[36] Justice White, on behalf of the *Hardwick* majority, brushed aside the plaintiff's claim to sanctuary in his home with the astounding remark that the "right pressed upon us here has no . . . support in the text of the Constitution."[37] Justice Blackmun reminded the majority that " '[t]he right of the people to be secure in their . . . houses,' expressly guaranteed by the fourth amendment, is perhaps the most 'textual' of the various constitutional provisions that inform our understanding of the right of privacy."[38] The Court conceded that *Stanley v. Georgia*[39] "protect[ed] conduct that would not have been protected outside the

concurring in the result) (under Robinson it cannot be a crime "to yield" to "an irresistible compulsion").

Moreover, Michael Hardwick actually spent that day in jail following his arrest by the Atlanta police. He was incarcerated despite the fact that a bondsman was present at the processing desk almost immediately upon his arrival at the jail. While putting him behind bars—for the "crime" of defining and expressing his personality through private acts of love—the jail officers made it clear to the other inmates that Hardwick was gay and had been charged with sodomy, saying, "Wait until we put [him] into the bullpen. Well, fags shouldn't mind—after all, that's why they are here." To defer resolution of the eighth amendment issue until after such harassment is followed by a jail sentence—something that may never occur hereafter—is to give state officials a license to inflict cruelty without legal accountability, since the laws criminalizing consensual adult intimacies are most typically used "only" to stigmatize, to justify discriminatory treatment, and to victimize individuals in the very way Michael Hardwick was victimized—without trial or sentence. Cf. Carey v. Population Services Int'l, 431 U.S. 678, 716 (1977) (Stevens, J., concurring). Thus jailers and prosecutors could forever insulate statutes such as Georgia's from judicial review by the simple expedient of arresting and temporarily jailing offenders but declining to complete prosecution. In a strange inversion of the civil contempt context, where prisoners hold the keys to their own jail cells, jailers in Atlanta and elsewhere would hold the keys to the federal courthouse.

33. See § 15–19, supra.

34. The dissenters in Hardwick described the relevant privacy interests as those relating to "certain *decisions* that are properly for the individual to make," and to "certain *places* without regard for the particular activities in which the individuals who occupy them are engaged." 106 S.Ct. at 2851. Sex between consenting adults in the privacy of the home has been described by commentators as implicating two intertwined strands of the privacy right: "autonomy" and "seclusion." See Wilkinson & White, "Constitutional Protection for Personal Lifestyles," 62 Cornell L.Rev. 563 (1977).

35. Cf. Payton v. New York, 445 U.S. 573, 617 (1980) (White, J., dissenting) (police procedures must at a minimum "protect individuals against the fear, humiliation and embarrassment of being roused from their beds in states of partial or complete undress").

36. Rotary International v. Rotary Club of Duarte, 107 S.Ct. 1940, 1947 (1987) (citation omitted). Cf. Smayda v. United States, 352 F.2d 251 (9th Cir.1965) (toilet stall in public park used for homosexual acts held not to be protected area under fourth amendment), cert. denied 382 U.S. 981 (1966); Britt v. Superior Court, 58 Cal. 2d 469, 24 Cal.Rptr. 849, 374 P.2d 817 (1962) (right to privacy requires dismissal of charge in consensual act between two men spied through hole in ceiling of department store toilet stall).

37. 106 S.Ct. at 2846.

38. Id. at 2853 (dissenting opinion).

39. 394 U.S. 557 (1969).

home" by overturning a conviction for possession of constitutionally unprotected obscene material in the home, but deemed *Stanley* to be exclusively a first amendment case without relevance to the issue at hand. It would be more than passing strange if government were constitutionally barred, whatever its justification, from entering a man's home to stop him from obtaining sexual gratification by viewing an obscene film, but were free, without any burden of special justification, to enter the same dwelling to interrupt his sexual acts with a willing adult partner. Surely the home protects more than our fantasies alone. In any event, Justice White's reading of *Stanley* ignores the opinion itself, which expressly anchored its holding in respect for the "privacy of [a person's] own home," [40] and it flies in the face of the Court's prior treatment of *Stanley* as having been decided on substantive grounds derived largely from the fourth amendment.[41]

The fourth amendment's solicitude for privacy is not limited to requiring procedural safeguards such as search warrants. In the words of the second Justice Harlan, "[i]t would surely be an extreme instance of sacrificing substance to form were it to be held that the constitutional principle of privacy against arbitrary official intrusion comprehends only physical invasions by the police." [42] Indeed, "the essence of a fourth amendment violation is 'not the breaking of [a person's] doors, and the rummaging of his drawers,' but rather is 'the invasion of his indefeasible right of personal security, personal liberty, and private property.' " [43] A citizen must therefore be entitled to demand not only a warrant of the police officer who enters his bedroom, but also a justification of the legislature when it declares criminal the consensual intimacies he chooses to engage in there.

The only justification offered to, or considered by, the *Hardwick* majority was that a majority of the Georgia legislature had decreed that private acts of oral and anal sex offend public morality. The Court deemed this sufficient, since "[p]roscriptions against that conduct have ancient roots." [44] In a concurring opinion, Chief Justice Burger applauded this deference to "millenia of moral teaching" and endorsed a characterization of sodomy "as an offense of 'deeper malignity' than rape, an heinous act 'the very mention of which is a disgrace to human nature. . . .' " [45] The majority concluded that, "[a]gainst this back-

---

40. Id. at 565.

41. See, e.g., Paris Adult Theatre I v. Slaton, 413 U.S. 49, 66 (1973). In his dissenting opinion in Thornburgh v. American College of Obstetricians & Gynecologists, 106 S.Ct. 2169 (1986), Justice White relied on Stanley for the proposition that there are circumstances where "the evil of [an act] does not justify the evil of forbidding it." Id. at 2198. It is obvious that the only evil involved in stamping out Stanley's possession of constitutionally unprotected obscene material was the necessity of invading his house and ransacking his private library in order to do so. That concern unmistakeably sounds in the fourth amendment.

42. Poe v. Ullman, 367 U.S. 497, 551 (1961) (dissenting opinion).

43. California v. Ciraolo, 106 S.Ct. 1809, 1819 (1986) (Powell, J., dissenting) (quoting Boyd v. United States, 116 U.S. 616, 630 (1886)).

44. 106 S.Ct. at 2844.

45. Id. at 2847 (quoting Blackstone's Commentaries *215).

ground, to claim that a right to engage in such conduct is 'deeply rooted in this nation's history and tradition' or 'implicit in the concept of ordered liberty' is, at best, facetious." [46]

The Court's lengthy recitation of instances where homosexuality has been disapproved in western history [47] is beside the point. As the Court acknowledged the previous Term, even the "pure[st]" of "common law pedigree[s]" cannot ensure the continuing constitutional validity of long-practiced invasions of body or home.[48] In Justice Blackmun's words, neither "the length of time a majority has held its convictions [n]or the passions with which it defends them can withdraw legislation from th[e] Court's scrutiny." [49] Like Justice Holmes, the dissenters found it "revolting to have no better reason for a rule of law than that so it was laid down in the time of Henry IV. It is still more revolting if the grounds on which it was laid down have vanished long since, and the rule simply persists from blind imitation of the past." [50]

The Court's error in *Hardwick* was that it used the wrong level of generality to conceptualize the plaintiff's claim of liberty and to test its pedigree. Obviously, the history of homosexuality has been largely a history of opprobrium; [51] indeed, it would not be implausible to find on this basis that homosexuals constitute a discrete and insular minority entitled to heightened protection under the equal protection clause.[52]

---

46. Id. at 2846.

47. Justice White devoted far more space in his opinion to reviewing the history of state sodomy laws, see id. at 2844–45 & nn.5–7, than to examining their impact on privacy.

48. Tennessee v. Garner, 471 U.S. 1, 14 (1985) (holding unconstitutional the time-honored rule that police may use deadly force to stop any fleeing felon).

49. Hardwick, 106 S.Ct. at 2854 (dissenting opinion).

50. Holmes, "The Path of the Law," 10 Harv.L.Rev. 457, 469 (1897), quoted in Hardwick, 106 S.Ct. at 2848 (Blackmun, J., dissenting). Lest this deployment of Holmesian rhetoric appear a bit hyperbolic, it should be noted that Chief Justice Burger relied in his concurring opinion on the first English statute criminalizing sodomy, which was enacted during the reign of Henry VIII. Id. at 2847.

51. The range of discrimination against gays and lesbians is canvassed in E. Bogan, M. Haft, C. Lister, J. Rupp & T. Stoddard, The Rights of Gay People: The Basic ACLU Guide to a Gay Person's Rights (rev.ed. 1983). The AIDS epidemic, which in its initial stages in this country primarily afflicted gay men, has predictably created new rationales and new opportunities for abridging the rights of homosexuals. See § 15–16, supra.

52. See Note, "The Constitutional Status of Sexual Orientation: Homosexuality as a Suspect Classification," 98 Harv.L. Rev. 1285 (1985). This issue is discussed in § 16–31, infra. Sodomy laws remain on the books in some states precisely because of popular aversion to homosexuals. For example, when the Texas penal code was amended to legalize adultery, fornication and heterosexual sodomy, the legislature deliberately singled out " 'the private homosexual acts of consenting adults' " for continued criminalization out of " 'fear[ ] [of] a backlash against the entire Penal Code [revision] should such acts be decriminalized.' " Baker v. Wade, 553 F.Supp. 1121, 1151 (N.D.Tex.1982) (quoting Von Beigel, "The Criminalization of Private Homosexual Acts: A Jurisprudential Case Study of a Decision by the Texas Bar Penal Code Revision Committee," 6 Human Rights 23 (1977)), aff'd on other grounds 743 F.2d 236 (5th Cir. 1984), rev'd 769 F.2d 289 (5th Cir.1985) (en banc); rehearing en banc denied, 774 F.2d 1285 (5th Cir.1985); cert. denied 106 S.Ct. 3337 (1986). The government defendants in Baker ultimately defended the Texas statute and the distinction it draws between heterosexual sodomy and homosexual sodomy as justified by a " 'phobic response' " to homosexuality. 553 F.Supp. at 1145. In reversing the district court, the Fifth Circuit declared that popular antipathy tied the court's hands: the court warned

Yet when the Court uses the history of violent disapproval of the behavior that forms part of the very definition of homosexuality as the basis for denying homosexuals' claim to protection, it effectively inverts the equal protection axiom of heightened judicial solicitude for despised groups and their characteristic activities and uses that inverted principle to bootstrap antipathy toward homosexuality into a tautological rationale for continuing to criminalize homosexuality. Therefore, in asking whether an alleged right forms part of a traditional liberty, it is crucial to define the liberty at a high enough level of generality to permit unconventional variants to claim protection along with mainstream versions of protected conduct. The proper question, as the dissent in *Hardwick* recognized, is not whether oral sex as such has long enjoyed a special place in the pantheon of constitutional rights, but whether private, consensual, adult sexual acts partake of traditionally revered liberties of intimate association and individual autonomy.

Once the inquiry is shifted from the particular proscribed acts— and the group of people who engage in them [53]—to the claim of liberty that must be balanced against the state's assertion of power, it becomes clear that a proscription on private acts of sodomy should not survive. It is beyond cavil that protection of the public realm is a legitimate state interest. But the Court in *Hardwick* "fail[ed] to see the difference between laws that protect public sensibilities and those that enforce private morality." [54] The law at issue there bans all sexual contacts of a specified kind—even if conducted out of public view behind closed bedroom doors, even if engaged in by married couples or other consenting adults, and even if engaged in for love and not for money. It thus intrudes the grasp of the criminal law deep into an area that implicates no state interest in protecting public decency, nor in protecting vulnerable persons such as minors from coercion, nor in restricting potentially coercive commercial trade in activities offensive to public morality. It should come as no surprise that, in the kind of society contemplated by our Constitution, government must offer greater justification to police the bedroom than it must to police the streets. Therefore, the relevant question is not what Michael Hardwick was doing in the privacy of his own bedroom, but what the State of Georgia was doing there.

Because Georgia's sodomy law slices deeply into the sanctity of the home and the autonomy of private sexual choices, it cannot be defended, as a zoning ordinance or other regulation of the public sphere might be, by "the mere assertion that the action of the state finds justification

---

that, were it to affirm the invalidation of the Texas sodomy law, the "feelings of [those who disapprove of homosexuality] . . . could be elevated . . . and their frustrations might be vented upon [homosexuals] to a degree that increased the burdens of the latter beyond the consequences endured under the invalidated statute." 774 F.2d at 1287.

53. Indeed, *only* this effort to lift the inquiry to a higher level of generality can assure that the state is not simply masking

forbidden antipathy to a *group* in the form of a moral aversion to what the group *does*. See Dworkin, "The Forum of Principle," 56 N.Y.U.L.Rev. 469, 513–14 (1981); see also Dworkin, "Is There a Right to Pornography?," 1 Oxford J.Leg.Stud. 177, 194–209 (1981); R. Dworkin, Taking Rights Seriously 273 (rev.ed.1978). See § 15–4, supra, note 7.

54. 106 S.Ct. at 2855 (Blackmun, J., dissenting).

in the controversial realm of morals." [55]   Granted, there are those who will take great offense at the prospect that many homes and hotel rooms are populated by people who are pursuing sexual intimacy in ways that would scandalize others; H. L. Mencken once defined puritanism as the haunting fear that someone, somewhere, may be having a good time.[56] But "the mere knowledge that other individuals do not adhere to one's value system cannot be a legally cognizable interest, let alone an interest that can justify invading the houses, hearts, and minds of citizens who choose to live their lives differently." [57]

There is a "good news/bad news" approach to *Bowers v. Hardwick* that throws light on the decision's implications for the Supreme Court's entire privacy jurisprudence.   The "bad news" is that, if the case is seen as having been decided on principled grounds, it portends the possibility that decades of privacy decisions may eventually be overruled. *Meyer v. Nebraska,*[58] *Skinner v. Oklahoma,*[59] *Griswold v. Connecticut,*[60] *Roe v. Wade,*[61] and *Moore v. East Cleveland,*[62] all protect rights unmentioned in the Constitution's text—rights whose judicial recognition is nonetheless legitimated in significant part by the rule of constitutional construction contained in the ninth amendment.   That rule signifies that, even if a particular right is unenumerated, the Constitution's textual guarantee of liberty limits the power of government at least to the extent of requiring an articulated rationale by government for an intrusion on the person and the home as pervasive as Georgia's sodomy law.   As Justice Blackmun wrote in his dissent in *Bowers v. Hardwick*, "[i]f that right means anything, it means that, before Georgia can prosecute its citizens for making choices about the most intimate aspects of their lives, it must do more than assert that the choice they have made is an 'abominable crime not fit to be named among Christians.' " [63]   Yet this principle of limited government is precisely what the Court refused to reaffirm in *Bowers v. Hardwick*.[64]

Claims to constitutional protection against government invasions of privacy "must be considered against a background of constitutional purposes, as they have been rationally perceived and historically developed. . . .   [E]ach new decision must take its place in relation to

---

55. Poe v. Ullman, 367 U.S. at 545 (Harlan, J., dissenting).

56. See H. L. Mencken, A Book of Burlesques (1920).

57. Hardwick, 106 S.Ct. at 2865 (Blackmun, J., dissenting).

58. 262 U.S. 390 (1923) (right to teach one's child a foreign language).

59. 316 U.S. 535 (1942) (right to procreate).

60. 381 U.S. 479 (1965) (right to use contraceptives).

61. 410 U.S. 113 (1973) (right to abort a pregnancy).

62. 431 U.S. 494, 502 (1977) (right to choose which relatives to live with).

63. 106 S.Ct. at 2848 (quoting Herring v. State, 119 Ga. 709, 46 S.E. 876, 882 (1904)).

64. Justice White, writing for the Hardwick majority, stated in a footnote that the ninth amendment was not implicated because the plaintiff did not invoke that amendment in defending his privacy claim. 106 S.Ct. at 2846 n.8.   But, as Justice Blackmun pointed out, id. at 2849 (dissenting opinion), plaintiff Hardwick expressly relied on the ninth amendment in his Complaint.   Moreover, the amendment was invoked by plaintiff during oral argument in answer to Justice White's own questions as to "what provision of the Constitution [plaintiff would] rely on or [the Court] should rely on to strike down this statute." Tr. of Oral Arg. 33–34.

what went before and further [cut] a channel for what is to come." [65]
But, as demonstrated above, the principles of private liberty endorsed
by the Court since the 1920s can be limited to the three contexts of
marriage, family, and procreation only by the most arbitrary judicial
fiat.[66] Because the *Hardwick* decision provides no principle which can
distinguish the Constitution's protection of privacy along these three
branches, it prepares the way for replowing that constitutional soil and
repudiating the entire privacy line, both root and branch. Surely if the
Constitution does not support a judgment that criminalization of
Michael Hardwick's consensual, noncommercial sexual conduct—in the
isolation of his home and involving no harm to another—requires
special government justification, it can be argued that the Constitution
offers no protection to a woman's access to abortion—since, as the
author of the *Hardwick* opinion wrote that very same Term, " '[t]he
pregnant woman cannot be isolated in her privacy' [and] the termination of a pregnancy typically involves the destruction of another entity:
the fetus." [67] Bereft of unifying principles of intimacy, privacy, or
autonomy, the Court's cases protecting family, marriage, and procreative choice may be in danger of becoming not enduring monuments to
the rule of limited government, but merely ephemeral opinions of
transient judicial majorities.

The "good news" about the Court's decision in *Bowers v. Hardwick*
is, paradoxically, that it probably was *not* decided on principled
grounds. The case may therefore pose less of a threat to other privacy
precedents than would otherwise be the case. Indications that
prejudice rather than legal principle was responsible for the outcome
can be found in what the four dissenting Justices called the majority's

---

65. Poe v. Ullman, 367 U.S. at 544
(Harlan, J., dissenting) (citation omitted).

66. Even such conservative commentators as George Will deemed the Court's
distinction between the sexual privacy at
issue in Hardwick and that involved in
prior privacy rulings unprincipled. See,
e.g., Will, "What 'Right' To Be Let
Alone?," The Washington Post, July 3,
1986 at A23, col. 1. Others concluded that,
given the vastly different countervailing
state interests in the abortion and sodomy
cases, the Court got the results backward.
See, e.g., Easterbrook, "Implicit and Explicit Rights of Association," 10 Harv.J.L. &
Pub. Policy 91, 92 (1987).

67. Thornburgh v. American College of
Obstetricians & Gynecologists, 106 S.Ct. at
2195 (White, J., joined by Rehnquist, J.,
dissenting) (citations omitted). The centerpiece of Justice White's dissent in Thornburgh was the proposition that, "when the
Court . . . defines as 'fundamental' liberties that are nowhere mentioned in the
Constitution (or that are present only in
the so-called 'penumbras' of specifically

enumerated rights), it must . . . act with
more caution, lest it open itself to the
accusation that . . . the Court has done
nothing more than impose its own controversial choices of value upon the people."
Id. at 2194. Justice White would leave
resolution of such "hotly contested moral
and political issue[s]" to the state legislatures. Id. at 2197. This approach tracks
perfectly the position Justice White took
three weeks later in his opinion for the
Court in Hardwick: "the Court must
"[s]trive[ ] to assure itself and the public
that announcing rights not readily identifiable in the Constitution's text involves
much more than the imposition of the Justices' own choice of values. . . ." Id. at
2844.

Solicitor General Charles Fried applauded the majority opinion in Hardwick
because it employed the " 'exact constitutional methodology' " he had advanced in
his unsuccessful effort to persuade the
Court in the Thornburgh case to overrule
Roe v. Wade. The Boston Globe, July 13,
1986, Sec. I, p. 9, col. 4.

"almost obsessive focus on homosexual activity." [68] The Court repeatedly characterized the issue presented as involving an alleged "fundamental right to engage in homosexual sodomy," [69] even though the Georgia statute—which was challenged on its face [70]—criminalizes *all* oral and anal sexual contact, whether homosexual or heterosexual, married [71] or unmarried; and even though the gravamen of Hardwick's offense was the physical act he performed, not the gender of the person with whom he performed it, [72] since the statute defines the crime of sodomy solely by reference to which parts of the anatomy may not come into contact.

The majority's interest in "distort[ing]" the case [73] in order to uphold the sodomy statute only as applied to homosexuals was confirmed a few months after the decision in *Hardwick* by the disposition of *Post v. State*. [74] The Supreme Court denied certiorari, even though a state appellate court, prior to *Hardwick*, had overturned a heterosexual sodomy conviction on the ground that the federal constitutional right of privacy had been extended by the Supreme Court "to matters of sexual gratification," at least with respect to heterosexuals. [75]

There are thus some reasons to suppose that, despite its sweeping language and logic, *Hardwick* does not necessarily doom any and all sexual privacy claims relating to unorthodox or nonmarital sex between consenting adults. Conversely, had *Hardwick* come out the other way, there would remain a variety of state regulations or pro-

68. Hardwick, 106 S.Ct. at 2849 (Blackmun, J., joined by Brennan, Marshall, and Stevens, JJ., dissenting).

69. Id. at 2844, 2843 (opinion of the Court).

70. As Justice Rehnquist recognized during oral argument, the only sense in which Hardwick's challenge to the law could be deemed "as applied" rather than "facial" was that Hardwick attacked the law "only as applied in the home." Tr. of Oral Arg. 31. Since the case was before the Court on appeal from a motion to dismiss prior to discovery, the complaint constituted the entirety of the record, and there was absolutely nothing in the complaint to indicate whether Hardwick was arrested for engaging in oral sex with a man or a woman. The allegations in the complaint as to Hardwick's sexual orientation, as a question from the Court made plain at oral argument, Tr. of Oral Arg. 9, bore solely on the danger of continued and future prosecution which gave Hardwick standing to sue. See 106 S.Ct. at 2849 (Blackmun, J., dissenting).

71. The Georgia Attorney General conceded that the sodomy law would be unconstitutional as applied to a married couple. See Tr. of Oral Arg. 8; 106 S.Ct. at 2858 n. 10 (Stevens, J., dissenting). The state's avowed interest in prosecuting only homosexuals despite the statute's neutral terms raises serious issues of selective enforcement violative of the equal protection clause. See 106 S.Ct. at 2850 (Blackmun, J., dissenting); id. at 2858–59 (Stevens, J., dissenting). The Hardwick majority's notation that no equal protection issue was before the Court should not be taken to mean that the Justices would have been interested in resolving it if it had been. For the Court denied certiorari that same term in Baker v. Wade, 769 F.2d 289 (5th Cir.1985) (en banc), rehearing en banc denied 774 F.2d 1285 (5th Cir.1985), cert. denied 106 S.Ct. 3337 (1986), which involved a Texas law, Tex.Penal Code § 21.06, that targeted only homosexual acts.

72. See 106 S.Ct. at 2856 (Stevens, J., joined by Brennan and Marshall, JJ., dissenting).

73. Id. at 2848 (Blackmun, J., dissenting).

74. 715 P.2d 1105 (Okl.Cr.1986), rehearing denied 717 P.2d 1151 (1986), cert. denied 107 S.Ct. 290 (1986).

75. 715 P.2d at 1109. See also 717 P.2d at 1152.

scriptions of sexual activity that would be beyond constitutional reproach. To begin with, protected conduct must be consensual—neither accompanied by force [76] nor engaged in with people [77] legally incapable of consent.[78] Rape laws thus rest on the firm foundation that their curtailment of the violator's sexual liberty is directly in the interest of *sustaining* the importance of free choice in sexual matters as a cornerstone of the victim's autonomy and dignity. Prohibitions of pedophilia and child molestation clearly fall within the ambit of the consent requirement, as does the prohibition of most forms of incest.[79] Some consent issues are less obvious. For example, a plausible argument could perhaps be advanced in favor of outlawing prostitution because of the risks of coercion inherent when money and sex are overtly mingled,[80] not to mention the obvious coercion involved in the pimping hierarchy. As to particular sexual behavior, a state could make at least a colorable argument that such practices as sado-masochism and bondage and dominance also involve an irreducible risk of coercion, along with violence and physical injury.

A strong presumption of sexual liberty would by no means necessarily entail any closer scrutiny of criminal laws against adultery [81] or polygamy (or polyandry). For unlike statutes that define a crime in terms of particular physical acts, these laws protect the estate of monogamous marriage. Marriage, unlike other manifestations of intimate association, is a contract controlled by the state—and, like "any other institution"—it is "subject to the control of the legislature." [82] Adultery is often not a "victimless" crime, although it may be when a marriage lives only in law. When there is truly a victimized spouse or child,[83] it is not clear that the state should be forbidden to use the

---

76. See, e.g., Cotner v. Henry, 394 F.2d 873 (7th Cir. 1968), cert. denied 393 U.S. 847 (1968). See generally S. Estrich, Real Rape (1986). See also Note, "To Have and to Hold: The Marital Rape Exemption and the Fourteenth Amendment," 99 Harv.L. Rev. 1255 (1986).

77. As to regulation of bestiality, it seems less helpful to think in terms of the animal lacking the ability to give meaningful consent, than in terms of analogies to laws against cruelty to animals, or bans on bear-baiting, cock-fighting and pit bull contests. A less powerful state interest would suffice to justify prohibiting bestiality rather than exclusively human sexual practices, since there could not be a plausible countervailing invocation of a right of intimate association; the notion of a faithful dog as man's best friend, after all, must have some limits.

78. See, e.g., Polk v. Ellington, 309 F.Supp. 1349 (W.D.Tenn.1970); Allan v. State, 91 Nev. 650, 541 P.2d 656 (1975).

79. The majority in Bowers v. Hardwick confessed ignorance as to how freedom to engage in oral and anal sex could be prevented from sliding down a slippery slope into freedom to commit incest. 106

S.Ct. at 2846. As the dissenters pointed out, and as plaintiff Hardwick had argued, courts might well agree that, even with respect to adults, "the nature of familial relationships renders true consent to incestuous activity sufficiently problematical that a blanket prohibition of such activity is warranted." Id. at 2854 (Blackmun, J., dissenting). And at some point, the state might well be able to make a strong argument for banning at least successive incestuous relationships among blood relatives on eugenic grounds.

80. But see generally Richards, "Commercial Sex and the Rights of the Person: A Moral Argument for the Decriminalization of Prostitution," 127 U.Pa.L.Rev. 1195 (1979) (arguing not on intimate association rationale but on a right of sexual autonomy or a woman's right to self-determination).

81. This was the other "sex crime," in addition to incest, about which the Court in Hardwick expressed concern.

82. Maynard v. Hill, 125 U.S. 190, 205 (1888).

83. See Hardwick, 106 S.Ct. at 2854 n.4 (Blackmun, J., dissenting).

sanctions of criminal law to punish the wrong to the marriage partner—and the marriage—inflicted by adultery. It is less certain whether the social interest in protecting and strengthening marriages generally—through deterrence, or through a symbolic expression of social
condemnation which may enter into the solemnity with which people
view marriage as an institution—can sustain a per se criminal prohibition on extramarital sexual contacts.[84] Such an outcome seems to
assign too much weight to sex itself as a cause of marital disintegration,
and to accord too little weight to the importance of other intimacies in
close relationships between human beings.

It is even less likely that these state interests are strong enough to
justify laws against fornication or cohabitation, on a theory that all
non-marital heterosexual activity somehow undermines marriage, or
laws against extra-marital sexual activity of any description on a
theory that tolerating any sexuality except heterosexual conduct between spouses likewise subverts marriage.[85]

Close scrutiny of criminal prohibitions on consensual intimacies
would also not compel the same tough examination of noncriminal
laws that might favor certain sexual unions over others.[86] As Justice
Harlan once wrote, the standard of judicial scrutiny when the state
seeks to codify public morality may vary with the state's "*choice of
means*." [87] The wisdom of refusing to provide civil legitimacy for long-
term intimate associations other than monogamous heterosexual marriage is, of course, a different matter.[88] Once it is recognized that social

---

84. A prohibition on polygamy, however, seems more secure if only as a matter
of precedent. See Cleveland v. United
States, 329 U.S. 14 (1946); Reynolds v.
United States, 98 U.S. 145 (1878).

85. New Jersey invalidated its fornication statute on grounds of sexual privacy.
See State v. Saunders, 75 N.J. 200, 381
A.2d 333 (1977). But cf. Shawgo v. Spradlin, 701 F.2d 470 (5th Cir. 1983), cert.
denied sub nom. Whisenhunt v. Spradlin,
464 U.S. 965 (1983) (upholding suspension
of unmarried police officers disciplined for
fornication with one another (Brennan,
Marshall, and Blackmun, JJ., dissented
from the denial of certiorari). See generally Note, "Fornication, Cohabitation, and
the Constitution," 77 Mich.L.Rev. 252
(1978).

86. Compare Briggs v. City of North
Muskegon, 563 F.Supp. 585 (W.D.Mich.
1983), summarily aff'd 746 F.2d 1475 (6th
Cir. 1984), cert. denied 473 U.S. 909 (1985)
(discharge of police officer for cohabitation
and adultery—acts prohibited by state
law—reversed as violation of right of sexual privacy and damages awarded) (Chief
Justice Burger and Justices White and
Rehnquist dissented from the denial of certiorari), and Erb v. Iowa State Bd. of Public
Instruction, 216 N.W.2d 339 (Iowa 1974)
(teacher who committed adultery held
"morally fit to teach"), with Hollenbaugh

v. Carnegie Free Library, 578 F.2d 1374 (3d
Cir. 1978) (upholding dismissal of state library employees for adulterous cohabitation), cert. denied 439 U.S. 1052 (1978)
(Justice Marshall dissented from the denial
of certiorari; Justice Brennan would have
granted the writ).

87. Poe v. Ullman, 367 U.S. at 547 (dissenting opinion) (original emphasis). Thus
the state could conceivably discourage the
use of contraceptives by granting tax subsidies and be subject only to minimal scrutiny, but it could not, without more compelling justification, wield the bludgeon of
criminal sanctions against such conduct.
Id. at 548. Compare Roe v. Wade, 410 U.S.
113 (1973), with Maher v. Roe, 432 U.S. 464
(1977). Both cases are discussed in § 15–
10, supra.

88. One commentator has speculated
that, as the gay and lesbian community
becomes an increasingly public sector of
our society, it will become necessary to
legitimate that community in order to govern it effectively: "Perhaps something like
marriage will have to be recognized for
homosexual couples, not because *they* need
it for their happiness (though they may),
but because *society* needs it to avoid the
insecurity and instability generated by the
existence in its midst of a permanent and
influential subculture outside the law."
Grey, supra note 28, at 97. See also Note,

approbation or notions of normality cannot constitutionally provide the criterion for arriving at a defensible level of generality for a concept of sexual intimacy, there is no convincing basis for excluding an enlarged circle of consensual partners from the realm of protected conduct.[89] It seems likely that *no* unconventional form of consensual human sexuality can be flatly excluded from the protected sphere *solely* on the ground that it is thought by the majority not to draw on the historically deepest wellsprings of human feeling. The moral flux evident in the forms of sexual and other intimate relationships should be seen "neither as the effluent of social sickness nor as the flow of convention from one dominant associational mode to another; it is rather the proliferation of acceptable forms of intimate association. Looking at our associational patterns in [recent decades], we have seen the future, and it diversifies."[90]

We must consider, finally, in what sense secrecy is an intrinsic element in sexual privacy. Surely it is not if "secrecy" is sacrificed by any failure to shield sexual activity from contemporaneous or later discovery by others.[91] Such a notion of privacy partakes too much of vernacular connotations and gives recognition to the value of seclusion while slighting values of sexual autonomy and self-definition.[92] The latter value is of particular importance with respect to lesbians and gay men for whom the mundane aspects of life—such as changing the gender of pronouns when referring to a lover or companion—pose a constant temptation to be false to the self. The choice about whether to "come out of the closet" can be of unsurpassed significance to homosexuals, since doing so can entail enormous social and economic disadvantages,[93] while declining to do so can exact an enormous price in fulfillment and self-esteem.

"The Legality of Homosexual Marriage," 82 Yale L.J. 573 (1973).

89. Cf. Lovisi v. Slayton, 539 F.2d 349 (4th Cir. 1976), cert. denied sub nom. Lovisi v. Zahradnick, 429 U.S. 977 (1976) (no constitutional protection where married couple joined by a third person). See note 91, infra. A more intimate and on-going group sex arrangement that includes no "strangers as onlookers," 539 F.2d at 351, is not necessarily foreclosed by Lovisi.

90. Karst, "The Freedom of Intimate Association," 89 Yale L.J. 624, 660 (1980).

91. But see Lovisi v. Slayton, supra note 89, where the lower courts upheld the conviction of a husband and wife for engaging in oral sex with each other. The right of privacy was held waived by the fact that a third party, a "stranger" who had answered a magazine "personals" advertisement placed by the couple, observed the acts and took photographs. The prosecution arose when the photos fell into the hands of the wife's children, who lived with their mother and stepfather but wished to see them in jail so that they could reside with their father. See 363 F.Supp. 620, 626 n.3 (E.D.Va. 1973). The pictures were eventually taken to school and displayed in an impromptu "show-and-tell" by the children, who alleged that *they* had operated the camera. The sodomy conviction seems to have been a fall-back prosecution when an arguably more appropriate conviction—for child abuse—fell apart because of a technical defect in the jury charge.

92. The participation of a physician or pharmacist in matters of contraception or abortion does not in any way diminish the constitutional protection afforded such aspects of sexuality. See § 15–10, supra.

93. The disadvantages of having the world discover that one is gay are canvassed in Rivera, "Our Straight-Laced Judges: The Legal Position of Homosexual Persons in the United States," 30 Hastings L.J. 798 (1979). The Court has so far been content to let stand cases directly or indirectly visiting injury on lesbians and gays who come out or are found out. See, e.g., Rowland v. Mad River Local School District, 730 F.2d 444 (6th Cir. 1984) (upholding dismissal of bisexual teacher predicated solely on the fact that she revealed her sexual orientation to some fellow staff, in

We thus return to where this chapter began—to the paradox of a right invoked by those who would enmesh themselves within society while laying claim to their own personalities; who would reach out to those around them while making intimate associations on their own terms. Our system of ordered liberty values individual autonomy, and any regime that would value individuals must at least tolerate—if not celebrate—diversity among the myriad personalities who breathe life into the abstractions we call liberty and community. Justice Blackmun closed his dissenting opinion in *Bowers v. Hardwick* with the hope that the Court would soon reconsider its holding and recognize "that depriving individuals of the right to choose for themselves how to conduct their intimate relationships poses a far greater threat to the values most deeply rooted in our nation's history than tolerance of nonconformity could ever do." [94] Before that hope is too readily dismissed as a dissenter's wishful thinking, we should recall that Justice Brandeis' formulation of the right of privacy as the "right to be let alone"—the most frequently quoted words in the jurist's privacy lexicon—was also penned in dissent.[95]

the face of a jury finding that her mention of her bisexuality did not in any way interfere with school operations), cert. denied 470 U.S. 1009 (1985) (Brennan and Marshall, JJ., dissented from the denial of certiorari; Powell, J., took no part in the decision); Gish v. Board of Educ. of Paramus, 145 N.J.Super. 96, 366 A.2d 1337 (1976) (per curiam) (upholding the dismissal of a public school teacher who had refused to undergo a psychiatric exam after becoming active in a gay rights organization), cert. denied 74 N.J. 251, 377 A.2d 658 (1977), cert. denied 434 U.S. 879 (1977); Gaylord v. Tacoma School Dist. No. 10, 88 Wn.2d 286, 559 P.2d 1340 (1977) (upholding school board decision to presume a homosexual teacher "immoral" and thus unfit to teach), cert. denied 434 U.S. 879 (1977). Cf. Hollenbaugh v. Carnegie Free Library, 578 F.2d 1374 (3d Cir. 1978) (upholding dismissal of state library employees for adulterous cohabitation), cert. denied 439 U.S. 1052, 1054 (1978) (Marshall, J., dissenting from the denial of certiorari) (library "apparently did not object to furtive adultery, but only to petitioners' refusal to hide their relationship. In essence, respondents sought to force a standard of hypocrisy on their employees and fired those who declined to abide by it."). But cf. One Eleven Wines & Liquors, Inc. v. Division of Alcoholic Beverage Control, 50 N.J. 329, 235 A.2d 12, 18 (1967) (state may not, without more, revoke liquor licenses of those who permit homosexuals to patronize their licensed premises; "[s]o long as their public behavior violates no legal proscriptions, [homosexuals] have the undoubted right to congregate in public").

94.   106 S.Ct. at 2856.

95.   Olmstead v. United States, 277 U.S. 438, 478 (1928).

Chapter 16

MODEL VI—THE MODEL OF EQUAL PROTECTION

§ 16–1. Overview of Equal Protection Analysis

Concerns of equality and even-handedness in governmental action have been evident in earlier contexts, as in Model I's limits on state discrimination against outsiders,[1] and in Model V's limits on governmental discrimination against the unorthodox idea or the unpopular group.[2] But the ideal of equality expresses aspirations so basic as to demand major attention on its own terms. Indeed, the notion that equal justice under law may serve as indirect guardian of virtually all constitutional values is evidenced by more than a maxim carved in marble on the United States Supreme Court. That notion, expressed with growing frequency and even stridency throughout this century, wars with the idea that equality is liberty's great enemy and can be purchased only at an unacceptable price to freedom.

Whether treating equality as prized because of its indirect role in enhancing freedom, regarding it as a crucial but independent variable, or viewing it as dangerous because of its asserted tension with liberty, constitutional thought and adjudication have made equal protection too central, particularly in the decades following the collapse of *Lochner* and of Model II,[3] to allow its treatment as anything less than a constitutional model in its own right.

Model VI, the model of equal protection, has occasionally been embraced as less intrusive of majoritarian political choice than model V, the model of preferred rights.[4] Neither in theory nor in operation, however, can a norm of equality be given real content without imposing significant constraints upon the substantive choices that political majorities and their representatives might feel strongly inclined to make. As with the models of settled expectations (Model III)[5] and governmental regularity (Model IV),[6] that of equality makes non-circular commands and imposes non-empty constraints only to the degree that we are willing to posit substantive ideals to guide collective choice.

§ 16–1

1. See Chapter 6.

2. See Chapters 11–15.

3. See Chapter 8.

4. See, e.g., Justice Jackson's concurring opinion in Railway Express Agency, Inc. v. N.Y., 336 U.S. 106, 112 (1949) ("Invalidation of a statute or an ordinance on due process grounds leaves ungoverned and ungovernable conduct which many people find objectionable. Invocation of the equal protection clause, on the other hand, does not disable any governmental body from dealing with the subject at hand."). See also Gunther, "Foreword: In Search of Evolving Doctrine on a Changing Court: A Model for a Newer Equal Protection," 86 Harv.L.Rev. 1, 41–43 (1972).

5. See Chapter 9.

6. See Chapter 10.

The textual source of those constraints and ideals has ordinarily been the fourteenth amendment's equal protection clause,[7] but in matters of race both the thirteenth [8] and the fifteenth [9] amendments have done service in addition to the fourteenth. Requirements of voting equality have also found support in the original body of the Constitution.[10] Moreover, the due process clauses of the fifth [11] and fourteenth [12] amendments have also been held to yield norms of equal treatment indistinguishable from those of the equal protection clause.[13] Although most of this chapter is couched in terms of the equal protection clause of the fourteenth amendment, it is worth stressing that no single clause or provision is the exclusive fount of doctrine in this area, and that principles of equal treatment have emerged in ways fairly independent of particular constitutional phrases. What must be explicated here is thus truly a model—a way of looking at constitutional issues generally—and not simply a section of the document.[14]

Having referred to norms and principles of "equal treatment," we can sharpen understanding of the equal protection idea by distinguishing between equality of treatment, and treatment as an equal.[15] The *right to equal treatment* [16] holds with respect to a limited set of interests—like voting—and demands that every person have the same access to these interests as every other person. Note that this right to equal treatment clearly does not operate with respect to all interests; any such universal demand for sameness would prevent government from discriminating in the public interest. On the other hand, the *right to*

7. U.S. Const. amend. XIV, § 1: "No State shall . . . deny to any person within its jurisdiction the equal protection of the laws."

8. U.S. Const., amend. XIII, § 1: "Neither slavery nor involuntary servitude, except as a punishment for crime whereof the party shall have been duly convicted, shall exist within the United States, or any place subject to their jurisdiction."

9. U.S. Const. amend. XV, § 1: "The right of citizens of the United States to vote shall not be denied or abridged by the United States or by any State on account of race, color, or previous condition of servitude."

10. See, e.g., U.S. Const., art. I, § 2: "The House of Representatives shall be composed of Members chosen every second Year *by the People* of the several States. . . ." (emphasis added).

11. See, e.g., Bolling v. Sharpe, 347 U.S. 497 (1954) (invalidating racial segregation in public schools of District of Columbia as violative of due process guaranteed by fifth amendment).

12. See, e.g., Boddie v. Connecticut, 401 U.S. 371 (1971) (holding violative of due process guaranteed by fourteenth amend-

ment state's denial of judicial access to indigents seeking divorce).

13. See Bolling v. Sharpe, supra note 11, at 499: "[T]he concepts of equal protection and due process, both stemming from our American ideal of fairness, are not mutually exclusive. . . . [D]iscrimination may be so unjustifiable as to be violative of due process". See also Buckley v. Valeo, 424 U.S. 1, 93 (1976) (upholding as constitutional Federal Election Campaign Act's allocation of federal tax revenues for campaign funding): "Equal protection analysis in the Fifth Amendment area is the same as that under the Fourteenth Amendment."

14. Note also the Supreme Court's insistence that determinations of unconstitutional discrimination must "never be confined to historic notions of equality." Harper v. Virginia Bd. of Elections, 383 U.S. 663, 669 (1966).

15. The formulation in this paragraph owes much to the admirably lucid account in Dworkin, "Social Sciences and Constitutional Rights: The Consequences of Uncertainty," 6 J. Law & Educ. 3, 10–11 (1977).

16. This right is considered in §§ 16–7 through 16–12, infra.

treatment as an equal [17] holds with regard to all interests and requires government to treat each individual with equal regard as a person. This is not to say that every political outcome which operates to an individual's disadvantage should be deemed to deny treatment as an equal, but only to single out for special scrutiny and probable invalidation those disadvantageous political judgments which seem likely to reflect a preference based on prejudice.[18]

With respect to each of these aspects of equality, a distinction should be made between two basic ways in which the constitutional norm can be violated. First, equality can be denied when government classifies so as to distinguish, in its rules or programs, between persons who should be regarded as similarly situated in terms of the relevant equal protection principles. For example, individuals living in the same county might be classified as eligible or ineligible to vote based on their length of residence (an alleged denial of equality of treatment with respect to voting), or individuals might be classified as eligible or ineligible for attendance at a particular public school based on their race (an alleged denial of treatment as equals).

Second, equality can be denied when government *fails* to classify, with the result that its rules or programs do *not* distinguish between persons who, for equal protection purposes, should be regarded as differently situated. So it was with the majestic equality of French law, which Anatole France described as forbidding rich and poor alike to sleep under the bridges of Paris. Thus, voters might be required to come to the polls personally regardless of their physical capacity to do so (an alleged denial of equality of treatment in voting as to the handicapped or hospitalized, for example), or children might be compelled to pay for their own transportation to and from school regardless of their economic ability to do so, and regardless of the likely effects of such a rule on racial separation in the public schools (an alleged denial of equality of treatment with respect to education and also of treatment

---

17. This right is discussed in §§ 16–13 through 16–34, infra.

18. Cf. City of Cleburne v. Cleburne Living Center, 473 U.S. 432, 455 (1985) (Stevens, J., joined by Burger, C.J., concurring) (striking down municipal requirement of a special use permit for operation of a group home for the mentally retarded) ("I cannot believe that a rational member of this disadvantaged class could ever approve of the discriminatory application of the city's ordinance in this case.").

This analysis of equal protection principles focuses on the claims of *individuals* to governmental treatment of a particular sort. In contrast, some commentators have argued that groups, especially those racial groups which have historically been subordinated in our society and whose political power is severely circumscribed, should be treated as "natural classes" to whom redistribution is owed. See, e.g., Fiss, "Groups and the Equal Protection Clause," 5 Phil. & Pub.Aff. 107, 148–56

(1976): Van Dyke, "Justice as Fairness: For Groups?" 69 Am.Pol.Sci.Rev. 607, 614 (1975). Critics of this theory have stressed the function of the group as "proxy" for the individual, emphasizing that discrimination has operated to the disadvantage of particular persons, and concluding that it is individuals alone who deserve reparation. See, e.g., Brest, "The Supreme Court, 1975 Term—Foreword: In Defense of the Antidiscrimination Principle," 90 Harv.L. Rev. 1, 48–52 (1976). One need not agree that the political theory underlying our Constitution necessarily opts for liberal individualism over more organic and communitarian notions even with respect to such rights as those of associations, see id. at 49, in order to find puzzling the proposition that a ban on denying "to any person . . . the equal protection of the laws," U.S. Const. amend. XIV, § 1, must be *more* concerned with justice to groups as collective wholes than with justice to individual human beings.

as equals without regard to income or race).[19] As the Supreme Court observed in *Jenness v. Fortson*,[20] "sometimes the greatest discrimination can lie in treating things that are different as though they were exactly alike."

Deprivations of equality by governmental classification and thus different treatment are frequently described as de jure discriminations; deprivations attributable to failure to classify and hence treat differently are usually described as de facto discriminations. Although the latter have generally been more resistant to successful constitutional attack,[21] particularly when the attack has claimed denial of the right to be treated as an equal,[22] *any* governmental discrimination must be tested against the fundamental requirements of equal protection.[23] The rest of this chapter examines those requirements.

§ 16–2. The Basic Requirement of Minimum Rationality

The Supreme Court, from its earliest examination of socioeconomic regulation, has considered that equal protection demands reasonableness in legislative and administrative classifications. The Court's original conception of the "reasonableness" required, however, was very limited: no regulatory provision was repugnant to equal protection as long as it "place[d] under the same restrictions, and subject[ed] to like penalties and burdens, all who . . . [were] embraced by its prohibi-

19. Note, however, that non-classification, that is, government's omission to draw lines, is especially hard to challenge on the ground that it deprives persons of the right to be treated as equals; in our tradition, that right has usually been viewed as only a formal requirement. See, e.g., Clune, "The Supreme Court's Treatment of Wealth Discriminations Under the Fourteenth Amendment," 1975 S.Ct.Rev. 289, 290–93 (arguing the arbitrary nature of this form of legalism).

20. 403 U.S. 431, 442 (1971) (upholding state elections laws that imposed ballot-access requirements on minor political parties different from those imposed on major parties).

21. The relatively more immune position of de facto discriminations is traceable, at bottom, to a reluctance—diminishing over the long run but still very much a reality—to recognize and especially to enforce affirmative governmental duties to redress disadvantages or injuries not thought to be actively engineered by government itself. See, e.g., Harris v. McRae, 448 U.S. 297 (1980) (upholding government refusal to pay for medically-necessary abortions for poor women, 'and observing that the government was not responsible for the poverty that constituted the barrier to the women's full exercise of abortion rights). But see Tribe, "The Abortion Funding Conundrum: Inalienable Rights, Affirmative Duties, and the Dilemma of Dependence," 99 Harv.L.Rev. 330, 336–37 (1985) (arguing

that the unavailability of abortion to poor women follows from their lack of funds *only* by virtue of the government's affirmative decision to treat this particular medical procedure as a purely private commodity governed by the market—a decision rendered suspect by the government's simultaneous decision to take childbirth for the very same poor women off the private market by funding the necessary medical care within a comprehensive medical benefits program).

22. Note that the equal protection command has generally been interpreted as focusing on legislative and administrative classifications. Statutes characteristically classify: that is, they do not apply universally. The constraints imposed by the norm of equality, as we shall see, operate in part to ensure some degree of "fit" between classifications and objectives. See §§ 16–2 through 16–5, infra. See also § 16–32, infra.

23. Note that in Keyes v. School Dist. No. 1, 413 U.S. 189 (1973), the Supreme Court reaffirmed the distinction between de jure and de facto racial segregation. See § 16–18, infra. Justice Powell, dissenting and concurring in part, would have eliminated the distinction as one which "long since has outlived its time," id. at 217, 219, adding that "the facts deemed necessary to establish de jure discrimination present problems of subjective intent which the courts cannot fairly resolve." Id. at 225.

tions; thus recognizing and preserving the principle of equality among those engaged in the same [regulated activities.]"[1] But this narrow view of nondiscriminatory application within the established class was soon discarded as empty of content, since persons or activities treated differently by government could for that very reason be deemed not "the same." Unaccompanied by any independent measure of when persons or acts were inherently equivalent, the original test afforded virtually no scope for review. To provide content, equal protection came to be seen as requiring "some rationality in the nature of the class singled out,"[2] with "rationality" tested by the classification's ability to serve the purposes intended by the legislative or administrative rule: "The courts must reach and determine the question whether the classifications drawn in a statute are reasonable in light of its purpose. . . ."[3]

This theory of rationality as governing the relation between means and ends assumes that all legislation must have a legitimate public purpose or set of purposes based on some conception of the general good.[4] Without such a requirement of legitimate public purpose, it would seem useless to demand even the most perfect congruence between means and ends, for each law would supply its own indisputable—and indeed tautological—fit: if the means chosen burdens one group and benefits another, then the means perfectly fits the end of burdening just those whom the law disadvantages and benefitting just those whom it assists.

But rejecting such circular justification as insufficient to distinguish "law" from "special, partial and arbitrary exertions of power"[5] has not meant closely scrutinizing public purposes. Within very broad limits, courts have traditionally exhibited extreme deference to the legislative definition of "the general good," either out of judicial sympathy for the difficulties of the legislative process, or out of a belief in judicial restraint generally.[6] In the unique case of

§ 16–2

1. Powell v. Pennsylvania, 127 U.S. 678, 687 (1888).

2. Rinaldi v. Yeager, 384 U.S. 305, 308–09 (1966).

3. McLaughlin v. Florida, 379 U.S. 184, 191 (1964). Whether the idea of equality is itself empty of content—whether it does more than provide a vehicle for enforcing independently derived but often not openly defended constitutional norms—has been much debated. See, e.g., Westen, "The Empty Idea of Equality," 95 Harv.L.Rev. 537 (1982); Burton, "Comment on 'Empty Ideas': Logical Positivist Analysis of Equality and Rules," 91 Yale L.J. 1136 (1982); Westen, "On 'Confusing Ideas': Reply," 91 Yale L.J. 1153 (1982); Chemerinsky, "In Defense of Equality: A Reply to Professor Westen," 81 Mich.L.Rev. 575 (1983); Michelman, "The Meanings of Legal Equality," 3 Harv. BlackLetter J. 24, 27 n.10 (1986) (criticizing Professor Wes-

ten's view because "a norm that directs us towards universalization of rights—or towards a universalistic conception of the very idea of a right—seems to me not very empty.").

4. See generally the seminal article of Tussman & tenBroeck, "The Equal Protection of the Laws," 37 Cal.L.Rev. 341 (1949).

5. Hurtado v. California, 110 U.S. 516, 535–36 (1884). See the excellent Note, "Legislative Purpose, Rationality, and Equal Protection," 82 Yale L.J. 123 (1972).

6. For important departures from this normal deferential role, see the significance played by "rationality" in the judicial invalidation of legislation during the Lochner era, Chapter 8, supra; in judicial "strict scrutiny" of suspect classifications and classifications burdening fundamental rights in §§ 16–7 through 16–20, infra; and in judicial "intermediate review," §§ 16–24 to 16–34, infra.

Morey v. Doud,[7] which held unconstitutional an Illinois regulatory statute exempting the American Express Company from its provisions governing "currency exchanges," the Court accepted the legislature's statutory objective: "to afford the public continuing protection." [8] The Court's invalidation of the statute was based rather on the conclusion that the legislature's exemption of a particular business entity, and not of a generic category, was irrational.[9] And when the Supreme Court overruled *Morey* less than twenty years later in *City of New Orleans v. Dukes*,[10] the Court nevertheless assessed the challenged statutory exemptions without questioning the legitimate and general objective served by the ordinance as a whole.[11]

In recent years, the Supreme Court has occasionally found what it labeled as the purposes behind economic legislation *themselves* to be illegitimate and hence the "rationality" test to be unsatisfied. In *Zobel v. Williams* [12], which invalidated as irrational a statutory scheme in which Alaska distributed income from its natural resources to state residents based upon the year in which their residency was established, the Court held, quite remarkably, that rewarding citizens for past contributions simply does not qualify as a "legitimate state purpose." [13] *Zobel* was followed in *Hooper v. Bernalillo County Assessor* [14], which struck down as irrational a New Mexico law granting a tax exemption to Vietnam Veterans only if they had resided in the state prior to a specified date arguably related to the conclusion of the Vietnam war.[15] Such cases, however, seem more the result of dissatisfaction with the

7. 354 U.S. 457 (1957), overruled by City of New Orleans v. Dukes, 427 U.S. 297 (1976).

8. 354 U.S. at 466 (emphasis omitted).

9. Id. at 467. While the legislature may have reasonably found that American Express was in no need of regulation at the time of the law's enactment, there was no assurance that the Company would not need regulation in the future. Cf. §§ 10–4 to 10–6, supra.

10. 427 U.S. 297 (1976).

11. Id. at 303–06. The ordinance, allegedly "an economic regulation aimed at enhancing the vital role of the French Quarter's tourist-oriented charm in the economy of New Orleans," contained a "grandfather provision" exempting two identifiable vendors from its ban on push-cart selling. Id. at 300. Noting that Morey was "essentially indistinguishable" from the case at hand, id. at 306, the Court nonetheless held that "[t]he city could reasonably decide" that the two exempted vendors "had themselves become part of the distinctive character and charm that distinguishes the Vieux Carre." Id. at 305.

12. 457 U.S. 55 (1982). Chief Justice Burger wrote for the Court, joined by Justices Brennan, White, Marshall, Blackmun, Powell and Stevens. Justices Brennan and O'Connor also filed separate concurrences.

13. Id. at 63. The Court offered no response to Justice O'Connor's compelling observation that "[a] desire to compensate citizens for their prior contributions is neither inherently invidious nor irrational. Under some circumstances, the objective may be wholly reasonable. Even a generalized desire to reward citizens for past endurance particularly in a state where years of hardship only recently have produced prosperity, is not innately improper." Id. at 73 (O'Connor, J., concurring in the judgment) (footnote omitted). Justice O'Connor agreed with the Court's result on a persuasive if novel theory based on the privileges and immunities clause of article IV. See § 6–35, supra; see also § 16–8, infra. Justice Rehnquist dissented.

14. 472 U.S. 612 (1985). Chief Justice Burger wrote for the Court, joined by Justices Brennan, White, Marshall and Blackmun. Justice Powell took no part in the decision of the case. Justice Stevens dissented, joined by Justices Rehnquist and O'Connor.

15. The statute predicated eligibility for the exemption on residence in New Mexico prior to May 8, 1976—one year and one day after the date designated by President Ford as the last day of the "Vietnam era". The latter date is used by the Federal Government to determine eligibility for

existing tools of equal protection analysis for dealing with "fixed permanent distinctions between . . . classes of concededly bona fide residents, based on how long they have been in the State," [16] than of any overall shift in the Court's scrutiny of how well various purposes fit legislatively chosen means.[17] The traditional deference *both* to legisla-

veterans' benefits. See id. at 616–617 n. 5.

16. Zobel v. Williams, 457 U.S. at 59; see Hooper v. Bernalillo County Assessor 472 U.S. at 621. See also Williams v. Vermont, 472 U.S. 14, (1985), discussed in § 16–4, infra, at note 14. These are distinct from *durational* residency requirements imposing a threshold waiting period on those seeking benefits, which are discussed in § 16–8, infra. The Court in Zobel and Hooper engaged in a peculiarly free-form version of equal protection analysis, deciding that the classifications could not be sustained under a covertly tightened variety of minimum rationality, in order to avoid expressly deciding whether heightened scrutiny was warranted. A plurality of the Court criticized this disingenuous method in Attorney General of New York v. Soto-Lopez, 106 S.Ct. 2317 (1986), which found the fundamental right to interstate travel implicated by a somewhat similar residency requirement. See § 16–8, infra. The plurality there concluded that "[t]he logical first question to ask when presented with an equal protection claim, and the one we usually ask first, is what level of review is appropriate. . . . It is true . . . that in *Hooper* and *Zobel*, the Court did not follow this same logical sequence of analysis. We think that the better approach is that which the Court has employed in other equal protection cases—to inquire first as to the proper level of scrutiny and then to apply it." 106 S.Ct. at 2323 n.6 (opinion of Brennan, J., joined by Marshall, Blackmun & Powell, JJ.) (citations omitted).

17. See § 16–3 infra. In a case *not* involving the "permanent classes" problem posed by Zobel and Hooper, a closely divided Court also found the public purpose behind a statute to be illegitimate in Metropolitan Life Insurance Co. v. Ward, 470 U.S. 869 (1985), striking down an Alabama tax on out-of-state insurance companies on the ground that "a state may not constitutionally favor its own residents by taxing corporations at a higher rate solely because of their residence", id. at 878, and reasoning that encouraging investments through a discriminatory tax "serves no legitimate state purpose." Id. at 882.

This type of discriminatory taxation would normally be invalidated under the commerce clause, see Chapter 6, supra. However, in the McCarran-Ferguson Act, Congress expressly lifted the commerce clause bar to state regulation burdening or discriminating against interstate commerce in the insurance field. Unable, therefore, to rely on the commerce clause, appellants challenged the statute on equal protection grounds. Because they waived any right to be heard on the rationality of the relationship between the statute's means and its ends, 470 U.S. at 874, the Court was faced with the artificial question of the legitimacy of the public purposes upheld by the lower court. As the majority described it, the only purposes at issue—although others might be adduced on remand, id. at 875 n.5—were (1) "promoti[ng] domestic business *by discriminating against nonresident competitors*", and (2) encouraging local investment "*by discrimination*", id. at 882 (emphasis added)—aims the majority readily dismissed as equivalent to a bare desire to injure unrepresented outsiders so as to benefit one's own constituents, id at 878, the very paradigm of a constitutionally forbidden objective. See generally Sunstein, "Naked Preferences and the Constitution," 84 Colum.L. Rev. 1689 (1984). It is doubtful that Metropolitan Life will be generative of much significant doctrine—although it did divide the Court along lines that may be of enduring interest. Justice Powell, writing for the majority, was joined by Chief Justice Burger and by Justices White, Blackmun, and Stevens; Justice O'Connor, writing in dissent, was joined by the unlikely alignment of Justices Brennan, Marshall and Rehnquist.

In a case decided just 11 weeks after Metropolitan Life without Justice Powell's participation—Northeast Bancorp, Inc. v. Board of Governors of the Federal Reserve System, 472 U.S. 159 (1985)—the Court unanimously upheld, against challenges from banks within and outside New England, statutes of Massachusetts and Connecticut permitting the acquisition of an in-state bank by an out-of-state bank holding company, provided that its principal place of business is in one of the other New England states, and that the other state accords equivalent reciprocal privileges to the enacting state's banking organizations. In a concurring opinion, Justice O'Connor expressed the view that Northeast Bancorp was indistinguishable from Metropolitan Life for equal protection purposes, id. at 178, suggesting that the Northeast Bancorp ruling may have confined the holding of Metropolitan Life to its peculiar

because its efficacy was dubious and its goals insubstantial—the hallmarks of heightened scrutiny. But at least the reasons for such closer review, however labeled, were more forthrightly described in *Plyler* than they were in *Zobel, Hooper* or *Cleburne*.[16]

This sporadic move away from near-absolute deference to legislative judgment seems to be a judicial response to statutes creating distinctions among classes of residents based on factors the Court evidently regards as in some sense "suspect" but appears unwilling to label as such.[17] While there may be grounds for the reluctance to proliferate new categories of classifications overtly triggering closer scrutiny, its *covert* use under the minimum rationality label presents dangers of its own. The lack of openly acknowledged criteria for heightened scrutiny permits arbitrary use of the type of inquiry undertaken in *Cleburne*,[18] for which courts will remain essentially unaccountable. With no articulated principle guiding the use of this more searching inquiry, even routine economic regulations may from time to time succumb to a form of review reminiscent of the *Lochner* era.[19] A far better approach would subject to heightened review only those classifications determined to be quasi-suspect after explicit judicial debate over the reasons for so regarding them—reasons amply present in the instance of zoning out the mentally retarded[20] but not necessarily in all of the other instances recently subjected to covertly heightened scrutiny. The resulting protection would not be left to the manipulable discretion of judges operating with multiple standards of review all masquerading as "minimum rationality". For all the remaining forms of economic regulation, the minimum rationality test would continue to govern under the traditional, deferential "conceivable basis" test—as, for the most part it still does[21]—as a means of

---

16. While the Plyler Court noted that, under San Antonio Independent School Dist. v. Rodriguez, 411 U.S. 1 (1973), discussed in §§ 16–52, 16–58, infra, public education is not a fundamental right requiring heightened scrutiny, see § 16–7, infra, it did find education unusually "important" in "maintaining our basic institutions", 457 U.S. at 221. The Court in Plyler accordingly concluded that "the discrimination contained in [this legislation] can hardly be considered *rational* unless it furthers some substantial goal of the State." Id. at 224 (emphasis added).

17. See the analysis of Zobel and Hooper in § 16–2, supra.

18. See Cleburne, 473 U.S. at 458 (Marshall, J., concurring in the judgment in part and dissenting in part) ("[P]erhaps the method employed [in Cleburne] must hereafter be called 'second order' rational basis review. . . .").

19. See id. at 432; see Chapter 8, supra.

20. See § 16–31, infra.

21. See, e.g., Exxon Corp. v. Eagerton, 462 U.S. 176, 196 (1983) (upholding Alabama royalty owner exemption from oil and gas severance tax because legislature "could reasonably have determined" that the exemption would encourage investment in oil or gas production); Texaco, Inc. v. Short, 454 U.S. 516, 539 & n.36 (1982) (upholding an exception from Indiana's Mineral Lapse Act, for owners of 10 or more mineral interests in one county, from the automatic lapsing of a severed mineral interest within a statutorily prescribed period because the lower court found that "'[t]he legislature could reasonably have concluded that those meeting the criteria . . . include those most likely to . . . actually produce minerals"); Western & Southern Life Insurance Co. v. State Board of Equalization, 451 U.S. 648, 672 (1981) (upholding a retaliatory California tax intended to deter other states from imposing excessive taxes on California insurers because "the Equal Protection Clause is satisfied if we conclude that the California Legislature *rationally could have believed* that the retaliatory tax would promote its objective") (emphasis in original); Minnesota v. Clover Leaf Creamery Co., 449 U.S. 456, 466 (1981) (upholding Minnesota ban on plastic nonreturnable milk containers be-

upholding all but the most brazenly and blatantly irrational governmental measures.

§ 16–4.　The Pros and Cons of Approximation: Underinclusiveness and Overinclusiveness

Parallel to its concern that the political process be allowed primacy in defining the ends to be served, the Court has recognized the legislative need for approximation in choosing the means of serving them. Because "[t]he problems of government are practical ones and may justify, if they do not require rough accommodations," [1] a demand for "mathematical nicety" [2] is implausible: instead, the Constitution invalidates only that governmental choice which is "clearly wrong, a display of arbitrary power, not an exercise of judgment." [3]

cause the legislature "could rationally have decided" that its ban would foster use of environmentally desirable alternatives) (emphasis omitted); United States Railroad Retirement Board v. Fritz, 449 U.S. 166, 179 (1980) (upholding provision of the Railroad Retirement Act of 1974 preserving dual benefits for some employees who qualified for both social security and railroad benefits in such a way that, for example, an employee who had completed as many as 24 years of railroad service but had not worked on the railroad in 1974 would lose the dual benefits, while the dual benefits of an employee who had worked 10 years but who had performed *any* railroad service in 1974 would be preserved, because "there are plausible reasons for Congress' action"); McGowan v. Maryland, 366 U.S. 420, 425–426 (1961) (upholding statutory prohibition of selected activities on Sundays because "[a] statutory discrimination will not be set aside if any state of facts reasonably may be conceived to justify it").

Four Justices have supported the proposition that the Court ought not to accept "conceivable" bases which did not actually motivate the legislature, and which are merely *post hoc* justifications. See United States Railroad Retirement Board v. Fritz 449 U.S. at 184 (Brennan, J. dissenting); Schweiker v. Wilson 450 U.S. 221, 245 (1981) (Powell, J., dissenting, joined by Brennan, Marshall & Stevens, JJ.) ("In my view, the Court should receive with some skepticism post hoc hypothesis about legislative purpose, unsupported by legislative history. When no indication of legislative purpose appears other than the current position of the Secretary [of Health and Human Services], the Court should require that the classification bear a 'fair and substantial relation' to the asserted purpose"); see also Bowen v. Owens, 106 S.Ct. 1881, 1887 (1986) (Marshall, J., dissenting). This understanding of a limitation on the conceivable basis test as a com-

ponent of *minimum* rationality review has never been accepted by a majority of the Court. See Fritz, 449 U.S. at 177 n.10 ("The comments in the dissenting opinion . . . are just that: comments in a dissenting opinion."). Any limit placed on the Court's imagination vis-a-vis legislative purpose must be recognized as a tightened form of scrutiny. Refusing to consider any post hoc justifications for a challenged measure should be distinguished from considering only those justifications offered in litigation by those engaged in the measure's defense. These approaches—and others serving to constrain the set of purposes to which a court may refer in assessing the validity of a challenged government action—entail distinctive strengths and weaknesses canvassed in § 16–32, infra, where all such approaches are examined for what they manifestly are—namely, techniques of heightened judicial scrutiny.

§ 16–4

1. Metropolis Theater Co. v. Chicago, 228 U.S. 61, 69 (1913); cf. Vance v. Bradley, 440 U.S. 93, 108 (1979) ("We accept such imperfection because it is in turn rationally related to the secondary objective of legislative convenience.").

2. Lindsley v. Natural Carbonic Gas Co., 220 U.S. 61, 78 (1911).

3. Mathews v. DeCastro, 429 U.S. 181, 185 (1976) (upholding provision of Social Security Act according "wife's insurance benefits" to wives living with husbands, but not to divorced wives) (quoting Helvering v. Davis, 301 U.S. 619, 640 (1937)). The Court has been particularly explicit about this deference in cases concerning classifications in the Social Security Act. See, e.g., Bowen v. Owens, 106 S.Ct. 1881 (1986); Califano v. Boles, 443 U.S. 282 (1979); Califano v. Jobst, 434 U.S. 47, 53 (1977) ("General rules are essential if a fund of this magnitude is to be administered with a modicum of efficiency, even

"Underinclusiveness" is one such variant of approximation which the Court may invalidate as too arbitrarily departing from "mathematical nicety." [4]   Underinclusive classifications do not include all who are similarly situated with respect to a rule, and thereby burden less than would be logical to achieve the intended government end. In defense of underinclusiveness it has been argued that piecemeal legislation is a pragmatic means of effecting needed reforms, where a demand for completeness may lead to total paralysis: "The State [is] not bound to deal alike with all . . . classes, or to strike at all evils at the same time or in the same way." [5]   Under this rationale, the Supreme Court in *Williamson v. Lee Optical* [6] upheld an Oklahoma law which subjected opticians to a regulatory system from which sellers of ready-to-wear glasses were exempted: "Evils in the same field may be of different dimensions and proportions, requiring different remedies. Or so the legislature may think. . . . Or the reform may take one step at a time, addressing itself to the phase of the problem which seems most acute to the legislative mind." [7]

In further defense of underinclusiveness as a political device, it may be said that statutory classifications which appear underinclusive when viewed in light of a single legislative objective often appear more precise when it is assumed that the legislature sought to achieve more than one purpose simultaneously. Thus in *Railway Express Agency, Inc. v. New York*, [8] Justice Douglas' majority opinion identified only traffic safety as the purpose of a city statute banning all vehicular advertising except that connected with the business of the vehicle's owner. Rationalizing the regulation, although difficult, was possible: "The local authorities may well have concluded that those who advertise their own wares on their trucks do not present the same traffic problem in view of the nature or extent of the advertising which they use." [9]   As Justice Jackson pointed out, however, the city may have entertained an additional purpose when distinguishing between "doing in self-interest and doing for hire," regarding it as "one thing to tolerate action for those who act on their own and . . . another thing to permit the same action to be promoted for a price." [10]

On the other hand, the ordinary judicial tolerance of underinclusiveness may well invite legislatures to avoid the full political consequences of their actions, for "nothing opens the door to arbitrary action so effectively as to allow . . . officials to pick and choose only a few to

though such rules inevitably produce seemingly arbitrary consequences in some individual cases.").

4. See generally Tussman & tenBroeck, "The Equal Protection of the Laws," 37 Cal.L.Rev. 341, 348–51 (1949). In practice, only rarely does the Court invalidate underinclusive legislation as unconstitutionally arbitrary. For one such case, see O'Brien v. Skinner, 414 U.S. 524 (1974) (overturning state statute allowing incarcerated persons to vote by absentee ballot only if confined in county where not resident); cf. McDonald v. Board of Election Comm'rs., 394 U.S. 802 (1969) (upholding state statute failing to provide absentee balloting for pretrial detainees but not necessarily preventing them from voting altogether).

5. Semler v. Dental Examiners, 294 U.S. 608 (1935).

6. 348 U.S. 483 (1955).

7. Id. at 489.

8. 336 U.S. 106 (1949).

9. Id. at 110.

10. Id. at 116 (Jackson, J., concurring).

whom they will apply legislation and thus to escape the political retribution that might be visited upon them if larger numbers were affected." [11] Thus even the flexibility promoted by attributing several purposes to a law or rule must have some limits. The exemption invalidated in *Smith v. Cahoon* [12] of "any transportation company engaged exclusively in the transporting [of] agricultural, horticultural, dairy or other farm products and . . . fish" from a state regulation of transportation companies,[13] for example, could have been rationalized as blending the double purposes of encouraging traffic safety and subsidizing agricultural production. Yet the Court, declining to test the classification by all conceivable purposes, found "not . . . the slightest justification" for an agricultural exemption from a statute "designed to safeguard the public with respect to the use of the highways." [14] The Court may have been influenced in this decision by a suspicion of legislation providing no "notice" to those whom the rule could have been expected to concern; such legislation could only increase the obstacles to public participation in the political process, and therefore detract from the possibility for legislative accountability.[15] Ultimately, though, this is not a sufficient justification for the

11. Id. at 112–13. A parallel danger exists when benefits are extended to classes which are underinclusive with respect to the purposes of the legislation. In benefitting a smaller group than would be logical in light of a law's purposes, the legislature may have chosen to exclude the politically powerless for no better reason than that it fears reprisal from this group less than from others. As with other underinclusive measures, however, such classifications are normally upheld despite this potential political defect. See, e.g., Bowen v. Owens, 106 S.Ct. 1881, 1886 (1986) (upholding provision of the Social Security Act extending survivor's benefits to remarried widows and widowers, but not to remarried divorcees who outlive their spouses, since in "decid[ing] to create some exceptions to the marriage rule, [Congress] was not required to take an all-or-nothing approach"); Schweiker v. Wilson, 450 U.S. 221, 238 (1981) (upholding provision of some Supplemental Security Income benefits to needy aged, blind and disabled persons between the ages of 21 and 64 in public institutions only in those facilities receiving Medicaid funds for their care, inasmuch as "[t]he limited gratuity represents a partial solution to a far more general problem.").

12. 283 U.S. 553 (1931).

13. Id. at 557.

14. Id. at 567. See Ely, "Legislative and Administrative Motivation in Constitutional Law," 79 Yale L.J. 1205, 1225–26 (1970) (suggesting that, in Cahoon, the Court's inquiry focused upon the statute's relation only to those purposes typically associated with legislation of the sort at issue). That there continue to be limits on the Court's willingness to tolerate underinclusiveness even in economic legislation became clear in Williams v. Vermont, 472 U.S. 14 (1985), overturning a Vermont automobile use tax which gave credit for out-of-state sales or use tax payments only to car registrants who were Vermont residents at the time the out of state tax was paid. The Court, in an opinion by Justice White, joined by Chief Justice Burger and by Justices Brennan, Marshall and Stevens—despite the objection of Justice Blackmun, joined by Justices Rehnquist and O'Connor—made no attempt to rationalize the classification as acceptably underinclusive. See id. at 34 (Blackmun, J. dissenting) ("A tax classification does not violate the demands of equal protection simply because it may not perfectly identify the class of people it wishes to single out"). Instead, the majority held that "the choice of a proxy criterion . . . cannot be so casual as this, particularly when a more precise and direct classification is easily drawn." Id. at 23 n.8. In all likelihood, Williams v. Vermont is best explained as one of the growing series of residency-related decisions covertly employing heightened scrutiny. See § 16–2, supra, text at notes 16–17.

15. While an analysis based on a desire for political accountability may seem equally applicable to Railway Express, supra note 8, that case is distinguishable, for a rule that would ordinarily arouse one group was not used there to affect the interest of totally unexposed groups. For another example where sufficient "notice" may have influenced judicial tolerance of

Court's action in *Cahoon*. Even with a far more comprehensive constitutional theory of how lawmaking should be structured than is yet available,[16] it hardly seems defensible to invalidate legislative action based solely on speculation as to the degree to which differently affected groups became aware of a pending measure. It would trivialize the Constitution to suggest that equal protection includes a requirement that could readily be satisfied by sending enough postcards to all potentially concerned parties. Some state constitutions purport to require that laws deal with one subject at a time. No similar requirement—one that would cast doubt on the validity of the myriad unrelated riders routinely attached to tax and other congressional bills—can be found in, or should be read into, the United States Constitution.

"Overinclusiveness," a second variant of legislative approximation for which a classification may be overturned,[17] poses less danger than underinclusiveness, at least from the viewpoint of political accountability, for overinclusiveness does not ordinarily *exempt* potentially powerful opponents from a law's reach. On the other hand, an overinclusive law may well *burden* a politically powerless group which would have been spared if it had enough clout to compel normal attention to the relevant costs and benefits. In *New York Transit Authority v. Beazer*,[18] for example, the Court upheld a flat Transit Authority (TA) ban on the employment of users of all narcotic drugs—including methadone— despite the district court's conclusion that about 75% of patients who have been in a methadone treatment program for at least a year are "free from illicit drug use," [19] and that no "rational" reason exists for excluding such methadone users from non-safety-sensitive jobs. The Court asserted, implausibly, that the regulation did not "circumscribe a class of persons characterized by some unpopular trait or affiliation",[20] and therefore that it did not "create or reflect any special likelihood of bias on the part of the ruling majority".[21] The classification was held to be acceptably over-inclusive: "[A]ny special rule short of total exclusion that TA might adopt is likely to be less precise—and will assuredly be more costly—than the one that it currently enforces. If eligibility is marked at an intermediate point—whether after one year of treatment or later—the classification will inevitably discriminate between employees or applicants equally or almost equally apt to achieve full recovery. . . . By contrast, the 'no drugs' policy now enforced by TA is supported by the legitimate inference that as long as a treatment program (or other drug use) continues, a degree of uncer-

---

underinclusiveness, see City of New Orleans v. Dukes, 427 U.S. 297 (1976), discussed in § 16–2, supra.

16. See Chapter 17, infra.

17. Often the Supreme Court evaluates overbroad classifications without explicitly invoking equal protection, but by examining the constitutional constraints imposed by the character of the activities burdened, as in United States v. Robel, 389 U.S. 258 (1967) (invalidating restrictions on first amendment rights on grounds of "overbreadth"). See Chapter 12, supra.

18. 440 U.S. 568 (1979). Justice Stevens wrote the opinion of the Court, which was joined by Chief Justice Burger and Justices Stewart, Blackmun and Rehnquist. Justice Powell concurred in part and dissented in part. Justice Brennan wrote a dissent as did Justice White, who was joined by Justice Marshall. See the further discussion of Justice White's dissent in § 17–2, infra.

19. Id. at 576 n.10.

20. Id. at 593.

21. Id.

tainty persists. Accordingly, an employment policy that postpones eligibility until the treatment program has been completed, rather than accepting an intermediate point on an uncertain line, is rational. It is neither unprincipled nor invidious in the sense that it implies disrespect for the excluded subclass." [22]

Because overinclusive classifications by definition burden some who are not similarly situated with respect to the purposes of a rule, they may of course be challenged as denying equal protection.[23] But as in the case of underinclusiveness, it has been argued with success—as *Beazer* well illustrates—that legislative resort to somewhat overinclusive classifications is legitimate as a prophylactic device to insure the achievement of statutory ends: "We must remember that the machinery of government would not work if it were not allowed a little play in its joints." [24] On essentially this rationale, the Court in *Dandridge v. Williams* [25] upheld a regulation of the Maryland Department of Public Welfare which placed an absolute welfare limit of $250 monthly per family, regardless of the family's size or actual need. The Court accepted the state's defense for its regulation in terms of the "legitimate interest in encouraging employment," over the response that "in some [recipient] families there may be no person who is employable," for, as the Court concluded, "the Equal Protection Clause does not require that a State must choose between attacking every aspect of a problem or not attacking the problem at all." [26]

22. Id. at 590–592 (footnotes omitted). Whether or not this observation is correct when applied to the category of drug users at issue in Beazer, it seems unlikely to be an accurate description of many, if not most, programs designed to screen various medically identifiable groups out of employment, housing, schooling or other similar settings. Particularly when public concern reaches panic proportions over such issues as drug abuse and AIDS (acquired immune deficiency syndrome), as appears to be the case in the 1980s, it is critical that courts display heightened sensitivity to the risk that overly sweeping measures, defended on grounds of safety or efficiency, might in fact rest upon, and in turn reinforce, stigmatizing stereotypes about the persons injured. In City of Cleburne v. Cleburne Living Center, 473 U.S. 432 (1985), discussed in § 16–3, supra and § 16–31, infra, Justice Stevens, concurring, offered a similar observation when he proposed that restrictions on handicapped individuals be tested by asking whether they could be made to seem justifiable from the perspective of those who are restricted. See Cleburne, 473 U.S. at 455 (Stevens, J., concurring).

23. Borrowing language ordinarily used elsewhere, see, e.g., Chapters 6, 12, and 14, supra, it could be said that less restrictive

alternatives exist for overinclusive classifications.

24. Bain Peanut Co. v. Pinson, 282 U.S. 499, 501 (1931) (Holmes, J.).

25. 397 U.S. 471 (1970).

26. Id. at 486. It should be noted that the Supreme Court has sometimes had occasion to examine statutory classifications whose alleged arbitrariness is revealed by the combination of both underinclusiveness and overinclusiveness. See, e.g., Vance v. Bradley, 440 U.S. 93, 108 (1979) (upholding mandatory Foreign Service retirement age of 60, despite absence of any mandatory retirement age for Civil Service employees, even those who serve abroad) ("Even if the classification involved here is to some extent both underinclusive and overinclusive . . . it is nevertheless the rule that in a case like this 'perfection is by no means required' "); Rinaldi v. Yeager, 384 U.S. 305, 310 (1966) (upholding a law "imposing a financial obligation for the cost of judicial appeals only upon inmates of institutions," despite the fact that, in doing so, the "state inevitably burdens many whose appeals, though unsuccessful, were not frivolous, and leaves untouched many whose appeals may have been frivolous indeed").

§ 16–5. Rationality and Restraint: Beyond Pluralism

The Madisonian ideal of law as the expression of a general public good stands in sharp opposition to the pluralist notion that law aspires merely to satisfy the preferences of ad hoc interest groups.[1] Whether or not judicially enforced, this ideal of law as rationally embodying a shared social vision may serve to broaden the perceived responsibilities of lawmakers and administrators in fulfilling their constitutional oaths.

The role of courts in reminding others of this ideal should not be underestimated. Even when judges stress the virtues of deference to choices made by the political branches—particularly in such spheres as zoning, taxation, and economic distribution or regulation[2]—and even when they do not act in a spirit of suspicion that some illegitimate prejudice or other flaw has poisoned the political process by which the public interest, or the general good, has been defined, the very fact that judges continue to speak in the language of rationality, requiring some demonstration that the government's actions bear a discernable relationship to a defensible vision of the public good, reaffirms the possibility of a politics that transcends special-interest deals and bargains, and of a polity that builds on civic virtue and public-spiritedness rather than one that wallows entirely in the exchange of private benefits and burdens. To the degree that the Constitution in general, and the fourteenth amendment in particular, embody efforts to transcend such factionalism and to elevate public law above private interest, the judicial role in insisting upon rationality serves to reinforce a major constitutional aspiration.

§ 16–6. Equal Protection Strict Scrutiny

There is a case to be made for a significant degree of judicial deference to legislative and administrative choices in some spheres. Yet the idea of strict scrutiny acknowledges that other political choices—those burdening fundamental rights, or suggesting prejudice against racial or other minorities—must be subjected to close analysis in order to preserve substantive values of equality and liberty. Although strict scrutiny in this form ordinarily appears as a standard for judicial review, it may also be understood as admonishing lawmakers and regulators as well to be particularly cautious of their *own* purposes and premises and of the effects of their choices.

When expressed as a standard for judicial review, strict scrutiny is, in Professor Gunther's formulation, "strict" in theory and usually "fatal" in fact.[1] In only one episode did the Supreme Court uphold an *explicit* racial discrimination, for example, after applying strict scruti-

---

§ 16–5

1. See generally H. Kariel, The Decline of American Pluralism (1961); Michelman, "Politics and Values or What's Really Wrong with Rationality Review?" 13 Creighton L.Rev. 487 (1979); Sunstein, "Interest Groups in American Public Law," 38 Stan.L.Rev. 28 (1985).

2. See, e.g., Village of Belle Terre v. Boraas, 416 U.S. 1, 9 (1974); Lehnhausen v. Lake Shore Auto Parts Co., 410 U.S. 356, 365 (1973); Jefferson v. Hackney, 406 U.S. 535, 546 (1972); see also the cases discussed in § 16–4, note 3, supra.

§ 16–6

1. Gunther, "The Supreme Court, 1971 Term—Foreword: In Search of Evolving Doctrine on a Changing Court: A Model for a Newer Equal Protection," 86 Harv.L. Rev. 1, 8 (1972).

ny.[2] That episode culminated in *Korematsu v. United States*,[3] which sustained a military order excluding Americans of Japanese origin from designated West Coast areas following Pearl Harbor; the decision represents the nefarious impact that war and racism can have on institutional integrity and cultural health. Similarly, there are very few cases which strictly scrutinize and yet uphold instances of impaired fundamental rights.[4]

Because most constitutional theorizing in recent decades has focused, if somewhat nearsightedly, on this judicial-review aspect of strict scrutiny and on associated issues of institutional competence, the tendency has been to explain the occasions for strict scrutiny solely in terms of reasons to avoid deference to politics. This "political process" theme was prominent as early as Justice Stone's renowned footnote in *United States v. Carolene Products Co.*,[5] where he speculated that "legislation which restricts those *political processes* which can ordinarily be expected to bring about repeal of undesirable legislation, [may] be subjected to more exacting judicial scrutiny under the general prohibitions of the Fourteenth Amendment than are most other types of legislation. [Citing cases involving restrictions on voting, speech, assembly] . . . [And] similar considerations [may] enter into the review of statutes directed at particular religious, . . . or national, . . . or racial minorities . . . .: . . . prejudice against discrete and insular minorities may be a special condition, which tends seriously to curtail the operation of those *political processes* ordinarily to be relied upon to protect minorities, and which may call for a correspondingly more searching judicial inquiry.. . . ."[6]

As this focus has developed, strict scrutiny as a judicial device has taken two quite different directions. The first entails restructuring the political decision-making process itself, usually through reapportionment, but occasionally through facial invalidation of schemes for political change loaded against certain groups or interests. Such was the

2. In the context of affirmative action, however, the Court has upheld an explicitly racial classification as acceptable even under purportedly strict scrutiny. See Sheet Metal Workers' Local 28 v. EEOC, 106 S.Ct. 3019, 3053 (1986) (opinion of Brennan, J., joined by Marshall, Blackmun & Stevens, JJ.); id. at 3054–3055 (Powell, J., concurring in part and concurring in the judgment). It seems doubtful that the Court in Sheet Metal Workers' Local 28 was, in fact, applying a level of scrutiny as "strict" as that usually employed in cases of non-remedial racially discriminatory classifications. See the discussion of affirmative action in § 16–22, infra.

3. 323 U.S. 214 (1944), discussed in § 16–14, infra. See also Hirabayashi v. United States, 320 U.S. 81 (1943) (upholding military curfew on persons of Japanese ancestry in West Coast during early months of World War II).

4. Marston v. Lewis, 410 U.S. 679 (1973), and Burns v. Fortson, 410 U.S. 686 (1973), are perhaps the purest examples in the equal protection area. The per curiam decisions in those cases accepted the states' judgments that a 50-day durational voter residency requirement was "necessary" to promote the states' "important interest in accurate voter lists." 410 U.S. at 681. See also Buckley v. Valeo, 424 U.S. 1, 25 (1976) (strictly scrutinizing but upholding federal ceiling on contributions to political campaigns); Roe v. Wade, 410 U.S. 113, 155, 163–64 (1973) (strictly scrutinizing but upholding state bans on post-viability abortion).

5. 304 U.S. 144 (1938).

6. Id. at 152–53 n.4 (emphasis added). For a powerful critique of the Carolene theory, see Brilmayer, "*Carolene*, Conflicts, And the Fate of the 'Inside-Outsider,' " 134 U.Pa.L.Rev. 1291 (1986).

approach taken by the Supreme Court in *Reitman v. Mulkey*,[7] where the Court invalidated a state constitutional provision purporting to withdraw the state from entanglement in private housing discrimination, and in *Hunter v. Erickson*,[8] where the Court struck down as unconstitutional a municipal regulation providing that the city council could implement no ordinance dealing with racial discrimination in housing without majority approval by the city's voters. *Hunter* was followed in *Washington v. Seattle School District No. 1*,[9] invalidating a popularly enacted state law which effectively prohibited local public school authorities from busing children involuntarily for purposes of integration absent a court order, because the law "uses the racial structure of an issue to define the governmental decisionmaking structure, and thus imposes substantial and unique burdens on racial minorities." [10]   In reaching its conclusion, the Court found that the law "removes the authority to address a racial problem—and only a racial problem—from the existing decisionmaking body, in such a way as to burden minority interests." [11]   While this approach may seem radical in its degree of intrusion into apparently legislative provinces, it actually involves little continuing supervision once the new structure of decision has been set in place.

The second approach involves leaving the political process intact but striking down particular political outcomes as insufficiently justified, either for their looseness of fit between means and ends, or for the weakness of the interest they purport to serve. Often, for example, the governmental interest in efficiency, convenience, or cost-saving may be cited in support of a challenged rule: strict scrutiny would include judicial wariness of interests such as these which can so easily and indiscriminately be invoked, and which almost never point uniquely to a challenged political choice. This second variety of strict scrutiny may appear less radical than the first in the sense that it leaves the political system as it finds it. On the other hand, it is arguably more intrusive in that it can quite readily lead to a continuing process of judicial revision of political outcomes at the behest of losers in the political process.

That is perhaps why the device of strict scrutiny is most powerfully employed for the examination of political outcomes challenged as injurious to those groups in society which have occupied, as a conse-

---

7. 387 U.S. 369 (1967), discussed in § 16–17, infra.

8. 393 U.S. 385 (1969), discussed in § 16–17, infra.

9. 458 U.S. 457 (1982).

10. Id. at 470.

11. Id. at 474. Note that, in Crawford v. Los Angeles Board of Education, 458 U.S. 527 (1982), handed down the same day as Seattle School District No.1, the Court upheld a popularly adopted amendment to the California Constitution prohibiting all involuntary busing of schoolchildren other than busing which a court would *have* to order under "federal decisional law."

Crawford was distinguished from Seattle School District No.1 on the ground that, unlike the state law at issue there, the California amendment did not distort the political process for racial reasons, but served only to modify the state constitution's equal protection clause substantively insofar as it had been held to prohibit even de facto segregation: "[H]aving gone beyond the requirements of the Federal Constitution, the State was free to return in part to the standard prevailing generally throughout the United States." Id. at 542. The author was counsel for the losing schoolchildren in Crawford.

quence of widespread, insistent prejudice against them, the position of perennial losers in the political struggle. While difficult problems are posed by treating certain groups as special clients or wards of the federal judiciary, it will be seen that the notion of invidious classification—that is, classification to the unjustified disadvantage of "discrete and insular minorities"—shares a close and complex relationship with notions of fundamental rights.[12] As long as this is so, extreme care must be taken not to discredit one to the unwitting derogation of the other.

§ 16–7. Inequalities Bearing on Fundamental Rights

Legislative and administrative classifications are to be strictly scrutinized and thus held unconstitutional absent a compelling governmental justification if they distribute benefits or burdens in a manner inconsistent with fundamental rights. For the purpose of equal protection analysis, classifications may create inequalities bearing on fundamental rights in two distinct ways.

First, inequalities with respect to a liberty, property, or other interest, such as the interest in securing a judicial decree of divorce,[1] or in receiving welfare benefits,[2] may be structured in such a way as to deter or penalize the exercise of a right independently protected against governmental interference. This is frequently one of the effects of state and federal durational residency requirements,[3] which discriminate against all individuals who have recently moved into the discriminating jurisdiction, and in that sense are said to penalize the exercise of the constitutional right to travel interstate. Second, and more intrinsic to the concept of equal protection, the inequalities may impinge directly on access to, or levels of, a right deemed fundamental in the specific sense that departures from equality in its availability or enjoyment are suspect. Such inequalities are particularly injurious when they interfere with either of the two major sources of political and legal legitimacy—namely, voting [4] and litigating [5]—or with the exercise of intimate personal choices.[6]

12. See, e.g., §§ 16–12, 16–25, infra.

§ 16–7

1. See, e.g., Sosna v. Iowa, 419 U.S. 393 (1975), discussed in § 16–8, infra.

2. See, e.g., Shapiro v. Thompson, 394 U.S. 618 (1969), discussed in §§ 16–8, 16–50, infra.

3. See § 16–8, infra.

4. See §§ 16–10, 16–46 to 16–48, infra. See also Chapter 13, supra.

5. See §§ 16–11, 16–45, infra.

6. See, e.g., Loving v. Virginia, 388 U.S. 1, 12–13 (1967), discussed in § 15–20, supra, and § 16–15, infra; Skinner v. Oklahoma, 316 U.S. 535 (1942), discussed in §§ 15–10, supra, and 16–12, infra; Zablocki v. Redhail, 434 U.S. 374 (1978), discussed in § 15–20, supra, and § 16–52, infra.

While the Court has explicitly found education *not* to be a fundamental right for equal protection purposes, see San Antonio Independent School Dist. v. Rodriquez, 411 U.S. 1, 28–39 (1973), discussed in §§ 16–52, 16–58, infra, its importance in "maintaining our basic institutions, and the lasting impact of its deprivation on the life of the child" has been held to justify heightened scrutiny—in fact if not in name—of classifications bearing upon at least the minimum availability of basic education. Plyler v. Doe, 457 U.S. 202, 221 (1982). See id. at 224 ("In light of these countervailing costs, the discrimination contained in [the legislation] can hardly be considered rational unless it furthers some substantial goal of the state.").

§ 16–8. The Fundamental Right to Interstate Travel

Shapiro v. Thompson [1] is widely considered the classic case illustrating the first way in which inequalities may bear on fundamental rights—that is, by penalizing the exercise of a right independently protected against government interference. In that case, the Supreme Court held unconstitutional state and federal provisions denying welfare benefits to individuals who had resided in the administering jurisdictions less than one year. Absent a compelling justification, which the Court found lacking, families could not be "denied welfare aid upon which may depend [their] ability . . . to obtain the very means to subsist," solely because they were members of a class which could not satisfy a one-year residency requirement.[2] Such denial would operate impermissibly to qualify the guarantee implicit in the Constitution that "all citizens be free to travel throughout the length and breadth of our land." [3]

In *Shapiro* the Warren Court made its earliest major statement of the "fundamental rights" strand of equal protection strict scrutiny. As Justice Marshall pointed out in a later decision, "it is irrelevant whether . . . denial of welfare is [a] . . . potent deterrent to travel. *Shapiro* did not rest upon a finding that denial of welfare actually deterred travel. . . . In *Shapiro* we explicitly stated that the compelling-state-interest test would be triggered by 'any classification which serves to *penalize* the exercise of [the right to travel]. . . .' " [4] At the

§ 16–8

1. 394 U.S. 618 (1969).

2. Id. at 627.

3. Id. at 629. See § 15–15, supra. There is no agreement on the exact source of the right to interstate travel. The Shapiro court itself found that "[w]e have no occasion to ascribe this source of the right to travel interstate to a particular constitutional provision." Id. at 630. Two possible sources are (1) the commerce clause, see Edwards v. California, 314 U.S. 160, 173 (1941) (striking down a state law under which "bring[ing] or assist[ing] in bringing into the state any indigent person who is not a resident of the State" was made a misdemeanor as "an unconstitutional barrier to interstate commerce"), and (2) the privileges or immunities clause of the fourteenth amendment, see id. at 178 (Douglas, J., dissenting) ("The right to move freely from State to State is an incident of national citizenship protected by the privileges or immunities clause of the Fourteenth Amendment against state interference."); see also Shapiro, 394 U.S. at 666–69 (Harlan, J., dissenting).

Justice O'Connor has suggested that the right derives from the privileges and immunities clause of article IV, discussed in § 6–35, supra. See Zobel v. Williams, 457 U.S. 55, 78–81 (1982) (O'Connor, J., concurring in the judgment) (discussing historical origins of privileges and immunities clause

and its ability to provide a theoretical foundation for many of the Court's prior right to travel opinions). The Court relied on the privileges and immunities clause of article IV in Ward v. Maryland, 79 U.S. (12 Wall.) 418 (1870), holding that it "plainly and unmistakably secures and protects the right of a citizen of one State to pass into any other State of the Union for the purpose of engaging in lawful commerce, trade, or business, without molestation; to acquire personal property; [and] to take and hold real estate . . ." id. at 430; see also Paul v. Virginia, 75 U.S. (8 Wall.) 168, 180 (1869) (the privileges and immunities clause of article IV gives the citizens of each state "the right of free ingress into other States and egress from them"). For a recent argument that no definitive textual source for the right need be found, see Zobel v. Williams, 457 U.S. at 67 (Brennan, J., concurring) ("[I]f, finding no citable passage in the Constitution to assign as its source, some might be led to question the independent vitality of the principle of free interstate migration, I find its unmistakable essence in that document that transformed a loose confederation of States into one Nation.").

4. Dunn v. Blumstein, 405 U.S. 330, 339–40 (1972) (quoting Shapiro, 394 U.S. at 634) (overturning state and local durational residency requirements for voting) (emphasis added in Dunn). For a discussion of

same time, the Court articulated what Justice Harlan feared was "an exception which threaten[ed] to swallow the standard equal protection rule": [5] "I must reiterate that I know of nothing which entitles this Court to pick out particular human activities, characterize them as 'fundamental,' and give them *added* protection under an unusually stringent equal protection test." [6] Even more disturbing to Harlan was what he saw as the Court's "cryptic suggestion . . . that the 'compelling interest' test [was] applicable merely because the result of the classification may [have been] to deny the appellees 'food, shelter, and other necessities of life.' " [7]

As subsequent decisions demonstrated, Justice Harlan's fear of the Court's "cryptic suggestion" proved to be exaggerated, for the Burger Court was at least reluctant to impose affirmative governmental obligations to redress economic inequalities.[8] On the other hand it seems correct to say that the fundamental right to travel interstate is sufficiently protected, for example, under the due process clause,[9] or, as other opinions have suggested, under the privileges or immunities clause of the fourteenth amendment.[10] And even if the majority's assertion is accepted that the right to travel is a fundamental one whose protection against penalization the equal protection clause demands, it is difficult to see this definition borne out by the line of cases which have followed *Shapiro.*

In *Memorial Hospital v. Maricopa County,*[11] the Supreme Court held unconstitutional a state statute requiring a year's residence in a county before an indigent could receive non-emergency medical care at county expense. Although the Court acknowledged that a showing of *deterrence* from travelling by the challenged restriction was not only lacking but also unnecessary,[12] the Court relied heavily on its conclusion that the *penalty* inflicted was very severe: "[Diseases], if untreated for a year, may become all but irreversible paths to pain, disability, and even loss of life." [13] Employing this same approach, the Court later upheld a state university regulation conditioning student eligibility for reduced tuition on one year's residence instate,[14] and also sustained the

---

the penalization aspect of durational residence requirements, see note 13, infra.

5. Shapiro, 394 U.S. at 661 (Harlan, J., dissenting).

6. Id. at 662 (emphasis added).

7. Id. at 661.

8. See, e.g., Dandridge v. Williams, 397 U.S. 471 (1970). For an analysis of the Supreme Court's application of equal protection analysis to the "basic necessities of life," see §§ 16–35 to 16–37, 16–43, 16–45, 16–49 to 16–54, 16–56 to 16–59, infra.

9. Shapiro, 394 U.S. at 661–62 (Harlan, J., dissenting).

10. Id. at 666–69 (Harlan, J., dissenting); see note 3, supra. See Chapter 7, supra.

11. 415 U.S. 250 (1974).

12. Id. at 257.

13. Id. at 261. In a sense, of course, the residency requirements in Shapiro and its progeny might neither deter potential migrants, who eventually will get the higher benefits, nor penalize them, since they are not being denied something they would have received had they not migrated. See McCoy, "Recent Equal Protection Decisions—Fundamental Right to Travel or 'Newcomers' as a Suspect Class?", 28 Vand.L.Rev. 987, 996–999 (1975) ("[F]ailing to offer benefits that would make the state a more attractive place does not in any ordinary sense constitute penalizing those who travel [or] inhibiting [those who do not]"). Still, the Court places heavy emphasis on the rhetoric of "penalization" in cases such as these.

14. Starns v. Malkerson, 401 U.S. 985 (1971), aff'g without opinion 326 F.Supp. 234 (D.Minn. 1970). But cf. Vlandis v.

constitutionality of a state statute conditioning petition for divorce upon satisfaction of a one-year residency requirement.[15] The distinction between the cases focused on the severity of the penalization inflicted: there was no showing of "any dire effects" on the nonresident student equivalent to those noted in *Shapiro*;[16] nor did the prospective divorcee suffer "total deprivation, . . . but only delay."[17] Although an equal protection theory based on deterrence might depend on severity of deprivation, penalty theory should trigger special judicial protection the moment any penalty, even one conceded as not very severe, is occasioned by exercise of a right.[18] Because these cases may thus be understood more readily as revolving about the issues of welfare and poverty, and not truly about the fundamental right to travel, they will be addressed in the poverty context in § 16–50.[19]

Kline, 412 U.S. 441 (1973) (overturning as violative of due process state's use for tuition purposes of "irrebuttable presumption" of students' nonresidence), discussed in § 16–34, infra.

15. Sosna v. Iowa, 419 U.S. 393 (1975). By contrast to those cases imposing durational residence requirements, the Court has upheld the use of bona fide residence requirements imposing no fixed waiting period as a condition for the receipt of benefits. See McCarthy v. Philadelphia Civil Serv. Comm'n, 424 U.S. 645 (1976) (per curiam) (upholding Philadelphia regulation that employees of the city be residents of the city as well). In Martinez v. Bynum, 461 U.S. 321 (1983), the Court upheld a Texas law denying free public education to any child living apart from his parent, guardian or other person having lawful control of him whose presence in the school district is "for the primary purpose of attending the public free schools." Unlike McCarthy, Martinez suggests that there are legitimate and illegitimate *reasons* for interstate migration, and calls into question the premises behind the Court's statement in Shapiro that a mother who considers the level of public assistance when moving into a state, "is no less deserving than a mother who moves into a particular state to take advantage of its better educational facilities." Shapiro, 394 U.S. at 631–632. The Martinez Court distinguished between a child with no other "reason for being [in the district] but his desire to attend school"—who can be required to pay tuition—and a child with an intention to make his home in the district, even if "the desire to make the new home is motivated solely by the desire to attend school"—who can not. Martinez, 461 U.S. at 332. In practical fact, this may limit the Court's holding to circumstances, like those in Martinez, where the excluded child has conceded his intention to leave after the state has provided a service of limited duration. See id. at 332 n.15.

The Court has also upheld a Georgia statute which transforms willful child abandonment from a misdemeanor into a felony when accompanied by departure from the state. Jones v. Helms, 452 U.S. 412, 422–423 (1981) ("[A]lthough a simple penalty for leaving a State is plainly impermissible, if departure aggravates the consequences of conduct that is otherwise punishable, the State may treat the entire sequence of events . . . as more serious than its separate components") (footnote omitted).

16. Starns, 326 F.Supp. at 238.

17. Sosna, 419 U.S. at 410.

18. A one dollar fine for choosing to be critical of government, for example, would be as clearly suspect as a one thousand dollar fine. It would indeed be an odd "fundamental right" whose exercise government could penalize just a *bit* without any special justification. Cf. Griffin v. California, 380 U.S. 609, 614 (1965) (holding comment on criminal defendant's refusal to testify violative of due process); Raley v. Ohio, 360 U.S. 423, 438 (1959). See § 11–5, supra.

19. The Court has, in fact, in recent years refused to find the fundamental right to interstate travel implicated in two cases in which statutes served to create fixed, permanent distinctions between classes of bona fide residents based on the date of establishment of residence. See Zobel v. Williams, 457 U.S. 55 (1982); Hooper v. Bernalillo County Assessor, 472 U.S. 612 (1985), both discussed in § 16–2, supra. Under the type of analysis used in Memorial Hospital and Sosna, these cases would seem to impose a large "penalty"; unlike Sosna, the plaintiffs in Zobel and Hooper were "irretrievably foreclosed from obtaining" what they sought. See Sosna, 419 U.S. at 406. However, the Court in Zobel and Hooper, in order to avoid deciding whether heightened scrutiny was warranted, struck down the classifications by

§ 16–9. Intersection of Model V "Preferred Rights" and Model VI "Equality of Rights"

The equal protection clause is more than a vehicle for strict scrutiny of government action penalizing the exercise of independently-derived constitutional rights. Inequalities may trigger strict scrutiny in a second way, by impinging directly on access to, or levels of, those rights deemed fundamental in the sense that departures from equality in their availability are suspect. Even cases of this sort may nonetheless involve variations on the general theme of unwarranted government interference with what under Model V are known as preferred personal freedoms—such as expression, association, assembly, and privacy.[1] For example, in *San Antonio Independent School District v. Rodriguez*,[2] the Court sustained against equal protection attack public school finance schemes using local property taxation as a base and thereby forcing districts with lower property values to make more effort than others in order to raise the same amount of money per pupil for educational purposes. Yet the Court alluded in dictum to the possibility that an absolute minimum of educational benefits may be demanded of government in order to avoid inequalities in the right to speak or to vote: "Even if it were conceded that *some identifiable quantum of education is a constitutionally protected prerequisite* to the meaningful exercise of either [the right to speak or the right to vote], we have no indication that the present levels of educational expenditures in Texas provide an education that falls short. Whatever merit appellees' argument might have if a State's financing system occasioned *an absolute denial of educational opportunities* to any of its children, that argument provides no basis for finding an interference with fundamental rights where only relative differences in spending levels are involved and where . . . no charge fairly could be made that the system fails to provide each child with an opportunity to acquire the basic minimal skills necessary for the enjoyment of the rights of speech and of full participation in the political process." [3]

But an absolute denial of public education was at issue in *Plyler v. Doe*,[4] where the Court reviewed a Texas law barring the children of

purporting to apply minimum scrutiny, as described in §§ 16–2, 16–3, supra. See Zobel, 457 U.S. at 60–61 ("[I]f the statutory scheme cannot pass even the minim[um rationality] test . . . we need not decide whether any enhanced scrutiny is called for."). A plurality of the Court criticized this method in Attorney General of New York v. Soto-Lopez, 106 S.Ct. 2317 (1986), concluding that the fundamental right to interstate travel was implicated by a New York civil service preference given to veterans only if they entered the armed forces while residing in New York. 106 S.Ct. at 2324 (opinion of Brennan, J., joined by Marshall, Blackmun & Powell, JJ.).

The Shapiro line of cases might best be explained by a concern about discrimination between groups of new residents. The Court used heightened scrutiny for dura-

tional requirements burdening only poor newcomers in their ability to receive services provided by the state. See § 16–50, infra. Cf. Edwards v. California, 314 U.S. 160, 174 (1941) (striking down an "attempt by a State to prohibit the transportation of indigent non-residents into its territory"), discussed in § 16–36, infra.

§ 16–9

1. See Chapters 11–15, supra. Skinner v. Oklahoma, 316 U.S. 535 (1942), involving a constitutional challenge to Oklahoma's Habitual Criminal Sterilization Act, is the prototype case of this sort, and is treated separately in § 16–12, infra.

2. 411 U.S. 1 (1973).

3. Id. at 36–37 (emphasis added).

4. 457 U.S. 202 (1982).

illegal aliens from attending public schools. The Court declared that education is not a fundamental right, but "neither is it merely some governmental 'benefit' indistinguishable from other forms of social welfare legislation." [5] And even though *illegal* aliens are not a suspect class,[6] their *children*—who are here through no fault of their own—are entitled to constitutional protection. The Court considered the "inestimable toll of th[e] deprivation [of basic education] on the social, economic, intellectual, and psychological well-being of the individual, and the obstacle it poses to individual achievement," and found it impossible "to reconcile the cost or the principle of a status-based denial of basic education with the framework of equality embodied in the Equal Protection Clause." [7] No rationale advanced by the state could justify "creation and perpetuation of a subclass of illiterates within our boundaries." [8]

The Court in *Police Department of Chicago v. Mosley* [9] enunciated the same principle, that the existence of a constitutionally protected right may form the basis for the enforcement, against selective state interference, of a constitutional norm of equality—in that case, equal treatment of different speakers—under the equal protection clause. As in the cases dealing with interstate travel,[10] equal protection analysis was not crucial in *Mosley*; first amendment or due process analysis would have sufficed.[11] Yet the equal protection conclusion of the Court is worth noting: despite the close connection between assuring unimpeded personal choice and preventing governmental selectivity with respect to who may speak, be educated, or otherwise participate in society's basic structures, mere differences in *relative levels* of governmental support provided to various groups need not automatically trigger the same concern.[12] Indeed, the Supreme Court has indicated that neither the importance of a governmental service, nor even the fact that the service touches on a sphere of personal choice protected from undue collective intrusion,[13] will invariably trigger the equal

5. Id. at 221.

6. Id. at 223. This aspect of the case is discussed in § 16–23, infra.

7. Id. at 222.

8. Id. at 230.

9. 408 U.S. 92, 96 (1972), discussed in Chapter 12, supra.

10. See § 16–8, supra.

11. See Carey v. Brown, 447 U.S. 455, 471–72 (1980) (Stewart, J., concurring). The Court has, however, continued to turn to the equal protection clause to strike down laws that discriminate among speakers based on the subject matter of their expression. See id. at 470–71 (opinion of the Court).

12. See Regan v. Taxation With Representation, 461 U.S. 540 (1983), where the Court upheld over first amendment and equal protection challenges a federal law permitting veterans' organizations, but no other tax exempt groups, to engage in legislative lobbying. The Court noted that Congress enjoys wide latitude in writing the tax laws, and a merely rational purpose will suffice to justify a congressional decision to subsidize one voice while declining to subsidize all others, since there is no right to a government subsidy for one's expression. Id. at 546–47. In Perry Educ. Assn. v. Perry Local Educators' Assn., 460 U.S. 37 (1983), the Court found no equal protection violation in a school board's decision to allow only the union which was the teachers' exclusive bargaining representative, and not a rival teachers' union, access to the interschool mail system. That system was not a public forum, and the grant of a special access privilege to the established union therefore violated no fundamental right of the opposing labor organization. Id. at 54.

13. See, e.g., the cases upholding government refusals to subsidize abortions, Maher v. Roe, 432 U.S. 464 (1977); Harris v. McRae, 448 U.S. 297 (1980); Williams v.

protection strict scrutiny that absolute deprivation of the service, visited selectively, would occasion. The Court has so held in its failure to raise to constitutional stature the right to housing [14] and welfare [15] as well as in its treatment of education in *Rodriguez* [16] and *Plyler*. Yet this conclusion overlooks the possibility that even relative deprivations may well be employed to usurp the ability of individuals to make personal choices in spheres presumptively beyond majoritarian intrusion. Furthermore, the distinction between "absolute" and "relative" deprivations seems all but meaningless in the context of interests—like the right to vote or to acquire skills—which become effective exclusively or largely in competitive settings. Finally, it is at least arguable that the Court's denial of strict judicial scrutiny for such cases of clear inequality in governmental provision of services important in the achievement of personal freedom has the especially harsh effect of overlooking indivious discrimination against the poor.[17]

§ 16–10. The Fundamental Right to Equal Voting Opportunity

Cases involving departures from equality in the availability of fundamental rights at times submerge the concern about government interference with personal liberty, making the consideration of equality as such paramount. Such cases, involving the right to vote and the right to litigate, share with the first amendment and due process cases discussed above a core structural idea that the right at stake is really one to equal participation in governmental and societal decision-making.

In the area of voting, it is clear that government has wide discretion, at least at the state and local levels, to avoid granting public participation through the franchise—by employing appointed officials instead of elected ones, for example. It is this aspect which most sharply distinguishes what the Court has done in the context of Model V due process, by isolating islands of preferred rights whose exercise the government *must* protect or provide in some basic degree, from what it has done under the aegis of Model VI equal protection: here, the Court focuses not on whether the state has sufficiently respected a right but on whether the state has evenly extended, in accord with some substantive norm of equality, those rights that it has *chosen* to grant. Thus, while the Supreme Court has never required a state to hold elections for any particular office,[1] "once the franchise is granted

Zbaraz, 448 U.S. 358 (1980), discussed in Chapter 15.

14. See Lindsey v. Normet, 405 U.S. 56, 74 (1972).

15. See Dandridge v. Williams, 397 U.S. 471, 485 (1970) (denying strict scrutiny of state welfare scheme despite its involvement with "the most basic economic needs of impoverished human beings").

16. 411 U.S. at 33 ("the key to discovering whether education is 'fundamental' is not to be found in . . . the relative societal significance of education").

17. See §§ 16–52 to 16–59, infra.

§ 16–10

1. Left open in Sailors v. Board of Education, 387 U.S. 105 (1967), was the question whether a state *must* provide for election, rather than appointment, of officers performing "legislative" as opposed to merely "administrative" functions. The difficulty of drawing any such functional line has led lower courts to hold that a state has no such federal constitutional duty. See, e.g., People ex rel. Younger v. El Dorado, 5 Cal.3d 480, 96 Cal.Rptr. 553, 487 P.2d 1193 (1971). Cf. Rodriguez v. Popular Democratic Party, 457 U.S. 1 (1982) (upholding Puerto Rican statute pro-

to the electorate, lines may not be drawn that are inconsistent with the Equal Protection Clause of the Fourteenth Amendment." [2] Such "inconsistent lines" may be found in state laws effecting unequal absolute deprivations of the right to vote,[3] or in state laws responsible for only marginal, relative inequalities in the distribution of the right to vote.[4] On the other hand, the Supreme Court has not demanded that voting schemes be strictly majoritarian,[5] or that they disregard residence [6] or criminal status [7] for enfranchisement.

§ 16–11. The Fundamental Right to Equal Litigation Opportunity

The Court's treatment of the right of access to meaningful adjudication [1] illustrates the principle that decision-making processes made essential by the government must not simultaneously be denied because of poverty to those who are obliged to rely upon such processes. As is the case with voting, government has wide discretion, at least at the state level, to replace entirely a system where disputes are settled by litigation, providing a system of mediation in its stead, and government certainly has wide discretion to decide how protracted a system of litigation to furnish. Yet while a state is not, for example, required by the Constitution to provide a system of appellate review at all,[2] if it does in fact grant defendants an appeal by right from a criminal conviction, it cannot do so "in a way that discriminates against some convicted defendants on account of their poverty." [3] In defining such

viding that interim legislative vacancies be filled by appointment by the political party of the previous incumbent rather than by special election). Various federal offices, of course, are expressly made elective by the Constitution itself. See generally Chapter 13, supra, on questions of voting and election-related rights.

2. Harper v. Virginia Bd. of Elections, 383 U.S. 663, 665 (1966) (invalidating state poll tax).

3. See, e.g., Kramer v. Union Free School Dist. No. 15, 395 U.S. 621 (1969) (overturning state statute restricting voting in school district elections to parents of school-children, and property-owners). But see Holt Civic Club v. Tuscaloosa, 439 U.S. 60 (1978) (upholding state "police jurisdiction" statutes extending municipal police, sanitary, and business-licensing power to three mile zone beyond municipal boundaries, while denying vote in municipal elections to those affected by this extraterritorial power); Ball v. James, 451 U.S. 355 (1981) (upholding state law restricting voting in elections for water district directors to property owners, and giving those owners voting power proportional to the number of acres owned).

4. See, e.g., Reynolds v. Sims, 377 U.S. 533, 568 (1964): "[A]n individual's right to vote for state legislators is unconstitutionally impaired when its weight is in a substantial fashion diluted when compared with votes of citizens living in other parts of the State." See also Davis v. Bandemer, 106 S.Ct. 2797 (1986) (political gerrymandering may violate the equal protection clause if the redistricting in fact disadvantages members of the target party at the polls).

5. See, e.g., Gordon v. Lance, 403 U.S. 1 (1971) (upholding state requirement that municipal bonded indebtedness not be incurred without approval of 60% of voters in referendum election); Lucas v. Forty-Fourth Gen. Assembly, 377 U.S. 713 (1964) (striking down state apportionment scheme despite majority approval thereof).

6. The assumption underlying the deference to geography seems to be a notion of freedom of residence. See Chapters 13 and 15, supra.

7. See, e.g., Richardson v. Ramirez, 418 U.S. 24 (1974) (upholding state disenfranchisement of convicted felons).

§ 16–11

1. For a fuller discussion of the right of access to the criminal justice system and to courts in general, see §§ 16–38 to 16–41, 16–43 to 16–45, 16–51, 16–53 to 16–54, 16–56 to 16–57, infra.

2. See McKane v. Durston, 153 U.S. 684 (1894).

3. See Griffin v. Illinois, 351 U.S. 12, 18 (1956).

unconstitutional discrimination against criminal defendants, the Supreme Court has held that equal protection assures equal access only within the sphere that the state's own system makes basic; thus, not all advantages accorded the rich in the system of criminal justice have been treated as establishing that the system discriminates against indigent defendants. While a state cannot condition direct appellate review of criminal conviction upon a defendant's ability to purchase a transcript of his trial proceedings,[4] and while a state must provide counsel for all indigent defendants challenging their criminal convictions as of right,[5] no norm of equality is held to be violated by the state's refusal to provide counsel for defendants attempting to invoke discretionary review.[6]

Analyzing the right of equal access to civil adjudication of disputes in somewhat similar fashion, the Supreme Court has severely limited the extent to which such equal access may validly be claimed. On the rationale that "the legitimacy of the State's monopoly over techniques of final dispute settlement" becomes questionable when an indigent claimant is denied full access to the judicial proceeding which is "the only effective means of resolving the dispute at hand,"[7] the Supreme Court in *Boddie v. Connecticut*[8] held unconstitutional a state law conditioning a judicial decree of divorce upon the claimant's ability to pay court fees and costs. Yet the Court refused to extend this reasoning to indigents' "voluntary" petitions in bankruptcy: finding bankruptcy "not the only method available to a debtor for the adjustment of his legal relationship with his creditors,"[9] the Court in *United States v. Kras*[10] upheld a state filing fee requirement conditioning access to judicial discharge in bankruptcy. And in *Ortwein v. Schwab*,[11] the Court repeated its conclusion from *Kras* that, without a " 'fundamental interest that is gained or lost depending on the availability' of the relief sought,"[12] no violation of due process or equal protection is committed by conditioning civil litigants' access to courts upon fee payment, and upheld a state filing fee requirement conditioning access to appellate court review of agency reductions in welfare payments.

The Court has suggested that only in a case like *Boddie*, where the state makes judicial decision the exclusive lawful means of resolving the underlying dispute, is the state responsible for excluding a group from a necessary forum for dispute-resolution. Yet the state's rules of contract, and its laws against forcible self-help, make judicial decision the only lawful mechanism for securing a binding determination against a recalcitrant opponent in *any* case.[13] That divorce may be

---

4. Id.

5. Douglas v. California, 372 U.S. 353 (1963).

6. Ross v. Moffitt, 417 U.S. 600 (1974).

7. Boddie v. Connecticut, 401 U.S. 371, 375–76 (1971).

8. Id.

9. United States v. Kras, 409 U.S. 434, 445 (1973).

10. Id.

11. 410 U.S. 656 (1973) (per curiam).

12. Id. at 659, quoting Kras, 409 U.S. at 445.

13. In Schlagenhauf v. Holder, 379 U.S. 104 (1964), for example, the Court extended from plaintiffs to defendants its former determination that a party making certain allegations about his or her physical condition must submit to medical examination. Refusing to treat the situation of plaintiffs as distinguishable on the basis that they

unique in preventing non-judicial settlement even when the parties both seek the same thing seems true enough, but quite irrelevant. Moreover, if the Court in *Boddie* was serious in its assertion that a basic form of binding conflict-resolution in society—adjudication— should not be closed to any group in advance, and hence should not be put beyond the reach of the poor, its decisions in *Kras* and *Ortwein* seem unjustifiable in opposing the "fundamentality" of the marriage relationship [14] to the allegedly "lesser constitutional significance" of the debtor-creditor,[15] or the welfare recipient-welfare administrator,[16] relationships. Certainly the Court's decision in *NAACP v. Button*,[17] upholding the NAACP's furnishing of legal services to plaintiffs in NAACP-sponsored litigation, as well as its subsequent decisions enlarging the freedom to associate for the purpose of litigating,[18] would seem to support a theory of equal protection based on an ideal that binding decision mechanisms not be structured so as to exclude any identifiable group, no matter what claims the group seeks to advance.

§ 16–12. Rights Deemed Fundamental Because of Feared Invidious Discrimination

The decision to treat a right as fundamental for equal protection purposes may be influenced by, and may even represent a surrogate for, a concern that allowing government to exercise centralized, discretionary choice with respect to the right will invite prejudiced action, oppressing powerless or despised minorities. This concern colored the Court's decision in *Skinner v. Oklahoma*,[1] where for the first time constitutional recognition of a fundamental right was held by the Supreme Court to mandate a norm of equal distribution precluding government selectivity in the absence of a compelling justification. In *Skinner* the Court invalidated a state law providing for the sterilization of persons convicted two or more times of "felonies involving moral turpitude"; expressly exempted from the terms of the statute were such offenses as embezzlement and violation of revenue acts.[2] Recognizing procreation as "fundamental to the very existence and survival of the race," the Court invoked "strict scrutiny of the classification" to strike down the law: [3] "Sterilization of those who commit grand larceny, with immunity for those who are embezzlers, is a clear, pointed, unmistakable discrimination. . . . We have not the slightest basis for inferring that that [discrimination] has any significance in eugenics, nor that the inherita-

---

had come into court voluntarily and thus "waived" their right to resist such an examination, the Court reasoned that, if the "plaintiff is prevented or detered from [obtaining judicial] redress, the loss is thereby forced on him to the same extent as if the defendant were prevented or deterred from defending against the action" since the injury to the plaintiff, for which suit is brought, is "an involuntary act on his part." Id. at 114.

14. Boddie, 401 U.S. at 383.

15. Kras, 409 U.S. at 444–45.

16. Ortwein, 410 U.S. at 659.

17. 371 U.S. 415 (1963).

18. See § 12–26, supra, and §§ 16–45, 16–54, infra.

§ 16–12

1. 316 U.S. 535 (1942).

2. Id. at 536–37.

3. Id. at 541.

bility of criminal traits follows the neat legal distinctions which the law has marked between these two offenses." [4]

Clearly prominent in the Court's consideration of the statute in *Skinner* was its concern to protect within the realm of personal autonomy "one of the basic civil rights of man," [5] the right to reproduce. Yet the Court's opinion makes evident an even greater preoccupation with the notion that the state's classifications had been promulgated with their harshest effect against a relatively powerless minority, that of lower-class, as opposed to white-collar, criminals: "The power to sterilize, if exercised, . . . [i]n evil or reckless hands . . . can cause races or types which are inimical to the dominant group to wither and disappear." [6] While not willing to characterize the group discriminated against as automatically deserving the protection of special judicial scrutiny, the Court combined allusion to the invidiousness of discrimination against the class with discussion of the fundamental right involved. Indeed, since that right—personal autonomy in reproductive matters—had not previously been held fundamental, it seems likely that the *Skinner* Court was moved to give the right such a status, and thereby to assure the most rigorous scrutiny of future governmental intrusions into the reproductive realm,[7] in large part *because* of fear about the invidiously selective and ultimately genocidal way in which governmental control over that realm might tend to be exercised—a fear illustrated by the facts of *Skinner* itself.

On this understanding of the case, it stands for an extraordinarily powerful proposition: equal protection analysis demands strict scrutiny not only of classifications that penalize rights already established as fundamental for reasons unrelated to equality,[8] and of classifications that unequally distribute access to established rights whose very fundamentality resides in a norm of equal availability,[9] but also of classifications unequally distributing access to choices that ought to be placed beyond government's reach—and in that sense be deemed fundamental—because, in government's hands, control over those choices would pose too great a danger of majoritarian oppression or enduring subjugation.

Although the classification of many rights as "fundamental" or "preferred" for purposes of Model V might be similarly analyzed—even speech is put presumptively beyond government's control in part to prevent majorities from imposing their view on dissenting minorities [10]—*Skinner* is the leading instance in which a new star appears to

---

4. Id. at 541–42.

5. Id. at 541.

6. Id. See also Justice Jackson's concurring opinion: "There are limits to the extent to which a legislatively represented majority may conduct biological experiments at the expense of the dignity and personality and natural powers of a minority—even those who are guilty of what the majority define as crimes." Id. at 546.

7. See § 15–10, supra. Skinner is also discussed in § 16–22, note 25, infra.

8. See, e.g., the right to interstate travel, in §§ 15–15, 16–8, supra.

9. See, e.g., the right to equal opportunity to vote or to litigate, in §§ 16–10, 16–11, supra.

10. See Justice Jackson's opinion for the Court in West Virginia State Bd. of Educ. v. Barnette, 319 U.S. 624, 641 (1943) (holding unconstitutional a school board regulation requiring students to salute American flag), discussed in § 15–5, supra. See also Justice Stone's treatment of two cases generally cited for their first amend-

have been added to the firmament of preferred freedoms primarily because of concerns about invidious discrimination and majoritarian domination.[11]　Such concerns of course move to center stage once we are prepared to treat the classification employed by government as so plainly invidious or prejudiced that, quite without regard to the nature of the choice burdened or the interest unequally distributed, strict scrutiny seems required if any semblance of equal justice under law is to be preserved.　The theory of invidious or suspect classification, developed below in §§ 16–13 through 16–21, thus takes us beyond *Skinner* to a realm in which, even without finding a fundamental right, our tolerance for inequality will be at low ebb.

§ 16–13.　Suspect Classifications and Forms of Invidious Government Action

The core idea of equal protection strict scrutiny, as we have seen above in the context of fundamental rights analysis, is to subject governmental choices to close inspection in order to preserve substantive values of equality and autonomy.　We have observed that strict scrutiny as a judicial device may lead to restructuring the political decision-making process itself, as through facial invalidation of voting schemes weighted against certain groups in society;[1] or it may lead to striking down specific outcomes of the established political process as insufficiently justified, especially given the character of the groups burdened.　The central concern has been to root out any action by government which, in Justice Stone's phrase, is tainted by "prejudice against discrete and insular minorities," the sort of prejudice "which tends . . . to curtail the operation of those political processes ordinarily to be relied upon to protect minorities" in our society.[2]　Thus far, the cases have limited such strict scrutiny to instances of prejudice operating to the detriment of racial and ancestral groups; succeeding sections

ment implications, in United States v. Carolene Products Co., 304 U.S. 144, 152–53 n.4 (1938) (indicating "more exacting scrutiny" may enter review of statutes "directed at particular religious, Pierce v. Society of Sisters, . . . or national, Meyer v. Nebraska, . . . minorities"). Pierce v. Society of Sisters, 268 U.S. 510 (1925), upheld a parochial school's suit to enjoin enforcement of a state statute making it a misdemeanor for parents to fail to send their children to public school; Meyer v. Nebraska, 262 U.S. 390 (1923), held unconstitutional a state ban on the teaching of German in public schools. See § 15–6, supra.

11. Cf. Plyler v. Doe, 457 U.S. 202 (1982), where the Court struck down a Texas law denying public education to the children of illegal aliens—even though illegal aliens are not a suspect class and even though education is not a fundamental right, id. at 223—because the law would perpetuate a " 'shadow population' of illegal migrants," id. at 218, an "underclass," id. at 219, a "subclass of illiterates," id. at

230, a "permanent caste of undocumented resident aliens, encouraged . . . to remain here as a source of cheap labor, but nevertheless denied the benefits that our society makes available to citizens and lawful residents," id. at 218–19.

§ 16–13

1. See § 16–10, supra.

2. United States v. Carolene Products Co., 304 U.S. 144, 152–53 n.4 (1938) (dictum).　This aspect of Carolene Products has been developed into a comprehensive theory of judicial review, see J. Ely, Democracy and Distrust (1980), which has in turn spawned an extensive body of criticism.　See, e.g., Brilmayer, "Carolene, Conflicts, and the Fate of the 'Inside-Outsider,' " 134 U.Pa.L.Rev. 1291 (1986); Ackerman, "Beyond Carolene Products," 98 Harv.L.Rev. 713 (1985); Tribe, "The Puzzling Persistence of Process-Based Constitutional Theories," 89 Yale L.J. 1063 (1980).

of this chapter will elaborate these and related categories of governmental action deemed suspiciously prejudicial.

§ 16–14. Facially Invidious Discrimination: Racial and Ancestral Minorities and the Special Case of Indian Tribes

The classic case for identifying government's treatment of a group as prejudiced appears in those legislative and administrative promulgations which on their face officially disadvantage members of racial or ancestral minorities as such.[1] A clear example of such facial discrimination was invalidated by the Court in *Strauder v. West Virginia*,[2] where a black defendant had been convicted of murder by a jury from which blacks had been barred by a state law providing that only "white male persons who are twenty-one years of age and who are citizens of this State" were eligible to serve as jurors. The Court rightly saw the equal protection clause as declaring at least "that all persons, whether colored or white, shall stand equal before the laws of the States, and, in regard to the colored race, for whose protection the amendment was primarily designed, that no discrimination shall be made against them by law because of their color . . . ."[3]

As *Strauder* illustrates, the Court has long held a suspicion of legislation cast in terms that seem likely to reflect stereotyped prejudice. Ironically, the Court first explicitly referred to race as a "suspect" criterion in the one justly infamous episode in which the Court *upheld* as "compellingly justified" an overtly racial discrimination.[4] In *Korematsu v. United States*,[5] the Court held constitutional the incarceration and dispossession of all persons of Japanese ancestry on the West Coast following Pearl Harbor, citing "the judgment of the military authorities and of Congress that there were disloyal members of that population, whose number and strength could not be precisely and quickly ascertained."[6] Accordingly, the Court found that the judgment that "exclusion of the whole group [was] a military imperative answer[ed] the contention that the exclusion was in the nature of group punishment based on antagonism to those of Japanese origin."[7]

§ 16–14

1. Besides the fourteenth amendment, it is important to note that the thirteenth and fifteenth amendments, see §§ 5–13 and 5–14, supra, both voice strong constitutional prohibitions against discriminatory racial classification and arm Congress with broad enforcement powers.

2. 100 U.S. 303 (1879).

3. Id. at 307.

4. The Court has also held that race-based classifications designed to remedy past discrimination—"benign" race-based classifications—can be upheld as serving a compelling state interest. See Local 28, Sheet Metal Workers' Int'l Ass'n v. E.E. O.C., 106 S.Ct. 3019 (1986). See also § 16–22, infra.

5. 323 U.S. 214 (1944). See also Hirabayashi v. United States, 320 U.S. 81 (1943)

(upholding West Coast curfew against persons of Japanese ancestry).

6. 323 U.S. at 218.

7. Id. at 219. Especially memorable was General DeWitt's remarkable argument that the subversive threat posed by Americans of Japanese descent on the West Coast was confirmed by the sinister absence of any overtly subversive activities in that area after Pearl Harbor. J. DeWitt, Final Report: Japanese Evacuation From the West Coast, 1942, at 34 (1943, released 1944). Justice Murphy, in a strong dissent from "this legalization of racism" in Korematsu, found it "difficult to believe that reason, logic or experience could be marshalled in support of [the] assumption" on which the exclusion order was based—namely, that "*all* persons of Japanese ancestry may have a dangerous tendency to commit sabotage and espio-

In the American experience, the closest historical precedent for the Japanese incarcerations came 104 years earlier, in 1838: the forcible removal [8] of some 13,000 Cherokee Indians [9] from the ancestral territory of the Cherokee Nation to what is now the state of Oklahoma.[10] The removal was conducted in accordance with a fraudulent treaty between the United States and the Cherokee Nation.[11] Execution of the removal ultimately entailed a military roundup of nearly 17,000 Cherokees, more than 11,000 of whom were locked for months in hastily constructed army stockades or existing military forts. Approximately 2,500 Cherokee people died in the roundup and the stockades. Another 1,500

nage." 323 U.S. at 235, 242. (Emphasis added.) See generally Rostow, "The Japanese American Cases: A Disaster," 54 Yale L.J. 489 (1945). Detailed reports of incidents of arson and intimidation against Japanese Americans during this period may be found in N.Y. Times, Jan. 11, 1945, at p. 4, col. 7; id., Jan. 21, 1945, at p. 4, col. 3.

8. The Cherokee Removal was one phase of a broad national strategy to induce the powerful Indian tribes of the southern United States to relocate west of the Mississippi. The goal was to open their land to American settlement and to free the federal government from the political and financial costs of enforcing treaty and statutory obligations to protect the integrity of the tribes' boundaries from unauthorized entry by American citizens. F. Prucha, American Indian Policy in the Formative Years: The Indian Trade and Intercourse Acts, 1790–1834, at 213–249 (1962); F. Prucha, Documents of United States Indian Policy 39, 44–57, 71 (1975); see Indian Removal Act of May 28, 1830, 4 Stat. 1830 (authorizing the President to attempt to secure treaties with the southern tribes to effect their consensual removal to the west). The Cherokee, Choctaw, Creek, Seminole, and Chicasaw tribes were each removed west of the Mississippi under treaties negotiated pursuant to the Removal Act. See generally G. Foreman, Indian Removal (1932) (a classic study of the mechanics of the Indian removal policy and its impact on the affected tribes). Remnants of these tribes evaded removal. Some were subsequently recognized as separate tribes. See e.g. United States v. John, 437 U.S. 634 (1978).

The remainder of § 16–14 focuses more closely on constitutional aspects of federal Indian law than is customary in treatments of this sort, largely because the topic seems so much more important than its customary neglect might suggest.

For a thorough and scholarly treatment of federal Indian law, See F. Cohen, Handbook of Federal Indian Law (1982 ed.).

9. See G. Foreman, supra note 8 at 312; G. Fleischmann, The Cherokee Removal, 1838, at 70–73 (1971).

10. For a succinct account of United States-Cherokee relations after removal, see Choctaw Nation v. State of Oklahoma, 397 U.S. 620 (1970) (holding that Choctaw and Cherokee nations now hold fee simple title and mineral rights to certain land underlying the navigable portion of the Arkansas River pursuant to the original removal treaties); United States v. Cherokee Nation of Oklahoma, 107 S.Ct. 1487 (1987) (damage to Cherokee Nation's rights in Arkansas River from Federal Government's exercise of navigational servitude not compensable either as Fifth Amendment taking or as breach of Government's recognized fiduciary duty to Indian tribes).

11. The fraud was concealed from no one. The instrument, Treaty of New Echota, 1835, 7 Stat. 478 (Dec. 24, 1835), was "negotiated" on behalf of the Cherokee Nation without the knowledge or authorization of its elected leadership. The Cherokee Nation was "represented" at the treaty session by no more than one hundred Cherokee voters out of a population of some 19,000; none of the Cherokees present at the session held any official capacity in the government of the Cherokee Nation. See G. Fleischmann, The Cherokee Removal, 1838, 34–37, 72 (1971); G. Foreman, Indian Removal 269–270 (1932). See also Preamble to Treaty of New Echota, 1835, 7 Stat. 478, 473–479 (Dec. 29, 1835). It should be noted that the general rule applicable to allegedly fraudulent but ratified treaties with foreign nations has been applied with equal force to treaties with the Indian tribes: courts have not gone behind ratified treaties to inquire into the circumstances surrounding their negotiation. See Fellows v. Blacksmith, 60 U.S. 366, 372 (1856); F. Cohen, Handbook of Federal Indian Law 34 (1942 ed.).

died on the removal trek west,[12] known to the Cherokee people as the "Trail of Tears."[13]

Although the impact of these programs on the "relocated" Japanese-American and Cherokee people was in many respects similar,[14] at least one feature sharply distinguished the incidents: the incarceration orders challenged in *Korematsu* were directed at a discrete geographical segment of Japanese-American individuals purely on the basis of their national ancestry, as the product of an overtly unilateral political and military judgment by the national government. In contrast, the Cherokee removal orders were at least formally the product of bilateral political relations, however distorted, between the United States and the Cherokee Nation and were issued to enforce compliance with the terms of a ratified if fraudulent treaty by which the Cherokee people, as a polity rather than a class racially or ancestrally defined, became bound in their collective national capacity to remove to the west.[15]

The distinction drawn here between the two episodes rests on a conception of Indian tribes as self-governing political communities which retain inherent, if diminished, powers of sovereignty.[16] The basic contours of this conception of Indian tribes as "domestic dependent nations" under the "protection" of the United States were established by Chief Justice Marshall writing for the Court in *Cherokee Nation v. State of Georgia*.[17] The Chief Justice more fully developed this conception and its jurisdictional implications in *Worcester v. State of Georgia*:[18] "The Indian nations had always been considered as distinct, independent political communities, retaining their original

12. G. Foreman, supra note 8, at 290, 300, 312. Foreman's 1932 account describes the stockades as "Concentration Camps." See id. at 290, 300. See also G. Fleischmann, supra note 9, at 54, 70–72.

13. G. Foreman, supra note 8, at 294. See D. Benford, Tsali (1972). Note that the practice of forcibly removing Indian tribes from their homelands and confining tribal members to prescribed reservations under often dictatorial and arbitrary federal administrative control continued well into the 1890's: "Although there never was any statutory authority for confining Indians on reservations, administrators relied on the magic word 'wardship' to justify the assertion of such authority." F. Cohen, Handbook of Federal Indian Law 173, 181 (1942 ed.), and cases there cited. See generally D. Brown, Bury My Heart at Wounded Knee (1972); Andrist, The Long Death: The Last Days of the Plains Indians (1969).

14. Compare the accounts of systematic looting, physical brutality and grave robbing sustained by the Cherokees incident to their initial capture and interment. G. Foreman, supra note 8, at 286–290. Cf. note 7, supra.

15. See Art. 16 of the Treaty of New Echota, 1835, 7 Stat. 428 (Dec. 29, 1835).

16. Merrion v. Jicarilla Apache Tribe, 455 U.S. 130, 148, n.14 (1982) ("Because the Tribe retains all inherent attributes of sovereignty that have not been divested by the Federal Government, the proper inference from silence . . . is that the sovereign power to tax remains intact."); Iowa Mutual Ins. Co. v. LaPlante, 107 S.Ct. 971, 978 (1987) ("Tribal authority over the activities of non-Indians on reservation lands is an important part of tribal sovereignty . . . Civil jurisdiction over such activities presumptively lies in the tribal courts unless affirmatively limited by a specific treaty provision or federal statute"); but see Montana v. United States, 450 U.S. 544 (1981); See also F. Cohen, Handbook of Federal Indian Law, 232, 257 (1982 ed.).

17. 30 U.S. (5 Pet.) 1, 16–17 (1831). This action was brought by the Cherokee Nation to prevent interference with its territory and citizens by the State of Georgia and by Georgia citizens. The Court held that the Cherokee Nation was a "domestic dependent nation" under "protection" of the United States rather than a "foreign nation" within the meaning of art. III, § 2, and dismissed the action for want of jurisdiction.

18. 31 U.S. (6 Pet.) 515, 559–562 (1832). This action was brought on behalf of Reverend Worcester, who had been jailed by

natural rights, as the undisputed possessors of the soil. The very term, 'nation,' so generally applied to them, means 'a people distinct from others.' The constitution, by declaring treaties already made, as well as those to be made, to be the supreme law of the land, has adopted and sanctioned the previous treaties with the Indian nations, and consequently admits their rank among those powers who are capable of making treaties . . .

"The Cherokee nation, then, is a distinct community, occupying its own territory, with boundaries accurately described, in which the laws of Georgia can have no force, and . . . no right to enter, but with the assent of the Cherokees themselves, or in conformity with treaties, and with the acts of congress. The whole intercourse between the United States and this nation, is, by our constitution and laws, vested in the government of the United States."

In *Williams v. Lee*,[19] the Court declared that the broad principles established in *Worcester v. State of Georgia* remained the law, although as "modified . . . where essential tribal relations were not involved and where the rights of Indians would not be jeopardized."[20] The Court then enunciated a new test for resolution of conflicting state-tribal claims of regulatory authority over on-reservation transactions:[21] "Essentially, absent governing acts of Congress, the question has always been whether [a state] action infringed on the right of reservation Indians to make their own laws and be ruled by them." In holding that Arizona courts have no jurisdiction to hear a civil action brought by a non-Indian against a tribal Indian arising from a transaction on the Navajo Reservation,[22] the Court stated:[23] "There can be no doubt that to allow the exercise of state jurisdiction here would infringe on the right of the Indians to govern themselves. It is immaterial that respondent is not an Indian. He was on the Reservation and the transaction with an Indian took place there . . . The cases in this Court have consistently guarded the authority of Indian governments over their reservations."

Judicial decisions and actions of Congress[24] subsequent to *Williams v. Lee* manifest continued adherence by the Nation to the core of *Worcester* and to related doctrines which lie at the foundation of the law governing United States-Indian relations. In brief, those doctrines establish: (1) the political conception of Indian tribes[25] as governments

Georgia authorities for residing in the Cherokee Nation without securing a license as required by a Georgia statute. Id. at 523, 529. The Court held the statute void as applied to the Cherokee.

19. 358 U.S. 217 (1959).

20. Id. at 219.

21. Id. at 220. The Court has recently reaffirmed the Williams test. Iowa Mutual Ins. Co. v. LaPlante, 107 S.Ct. 971 (1987). See also White Mountain Apache Tribe v. Bracker, 448 U.S. 136, 143 (1980); Moe v. Confed. Salish and Kootenai Tribes, 425 U.S. 463, 483 (1976); Fisher v. District Ct., 424 U.S. 382, 387 (1976) (per curiam) (dic-

tum); United States v. Mazurie, 419 U.S. 544, 558 (1975).

22. Williams, 358 U.S. at 217–218.

23. Id. at 223.

24. See, e.g., the Menominee Restoration Act of Dec. 22, 1973, 87 Stat. 170; Indian Self-Determination and Education Assistance Act of Jan. 4, 1974, Pub.L. 93–638, 88 Stat. 2203; Indian Civil Rights Act of April 11, 1968, 82 Stat. 77.

25. The Supreme Court has never established a generic federal common law definition of the term "Indian Tribe" for purposes of federal Indian law. See F. Cohen, Handbook of Federal Indian Law,

having inherent powers and attributes of sovereignty [26]—powers which may with certain exceptions [27] and subject to certain limits [28] be exer-

268–273 (1942 ed.). A definition frequently drawn on by the courts in construing the term is one used without qualification in several federal statutes: "a body of Indians of the same or similar race, united in a community under one leadership or government, and inhabiting a particular though sometimes ill-defined territory." United States v. Candelaria, 271 U.S. 432, 442 (1926) (Indian Non-Intercourse Acts), quoting Montoya v. United States, 180 U.S. 261, 266 (1901) (Indian Depradation Act); Joint Tribal Council of Passamaquoddy Tribes v. Morton, 388 F.Supp. 649, 659 (D.Me.1975), aff'd 528 F.2d 370 (1st Cir. 1975) (Indian Non-Intercourse Acts).

26. Recent cases recognizing that Indian tribes are diminished sovereigns retaining their own political and judicial institutions include Iowa Mutual Ins. Co. v. LaPlante, 107 S.Ct. 971, 977–978 (1987); National Farmers Union Insurance Co. v. Crow Tribe of Indians, 471 U.S. 845 (1985); Kerr-McGee Corp. v. Navajo Tribe, 471 U.S. 195 (1985); Merrion v. Jicarilla Apache Tribe, 455 U.S. 130, 137 (1982); United States v. Wheeler, 435 U.S. 313, 323–24 (1978); United States v. Antelope, 430 U.S. 641, 645 (1977); Fisher v. District Court, 424 U.S. 382, 390 (1976); United States v. Mazurie, 419 U.S. 544, 557 (1975); Morton v. Mancari, 417 U.S. 535, 554 (1974).

27. In Oliphant v. Suquamish Indian Tribe, 435 U.S. 191 (1978), the Court held that the Suquamish Tribal Court did not retain criminal jurisdiction to try and punish non-Indians for offenses committed within tribal territorial jurisdiction. Such power was held inconsistent with the tribes' dependent status and a century of federal legislation conferring jurisdiction on the federal courts to handle such prosecutions. Id. 204.

National Farmers Union Ins. Co. v. Crow Tribe of Indians, 471 U.S. 845 (1985), rejected the notion that Oliphant precluded the exercise of tribal court jurisdiction over non-Indian defendants in civil lawsuits arising within tribal territorial jurisdiction. Iowa Mutual Ins. Co. v. Lamplant, 107 S.Ct. 971 (1987), affirmed tribal civil jurisdiction over such cases absent a specific federal statute or treaty to the contrary.

In Rice v. Rehner, 463 U.S. 713, 722 (1983), the Court held that liquor regulation was not a fundamental attribute of sovereignty retained by the tribes in part because "tradition simply has not recognized a sovereign immunity or inherent authority in favor of liquor regulation by Indians." Instead, the Court found in 18

U.S.C. § 1161 a governing act of Congress authorizing the states to require federally licensed Indian traders to obtain state liquor licenses in order to sell liquor on Indian reservations for off-premises consumption, and found that Congress had authorized a comparable state role in the area of liquor regulation since the earliest days of the Nation.

In California v. Cabazon Band of Mission Indians, 107 S.Ct. 1083 (1987), the Court refused to extend Rice v. Rehner beyond its unique subject matter (regulation of the use and distribution of liquor on Indian reservations), finding no comparable basis for allowing state regulation of gambling on Indian reservations.

A different kind of limit on tribal power was suggested in Escondido Mutual Water Company v. La Jolla, 466 U.S. 765, 787–88 n.30 (1984) ("[I]t is highly questionable whether the Bands have inherent authority to prevent a federal agency from carrying out its statutory responsibility since such authority would seem to be inconsistent with their status.") (dictum).

28. Congress has substantially circumscribed both state and tribal criminal jurisdiction by enactment of statutes which have been construed to render certain enumerated major offenses to be within the exclusive jurisdiction of the Federal Government when committed in "Indian Country" by Tribal Indians (see 18 U.S.C. § 1153 as amended). See United States v. John, 437 U.S. 634 (1978) (leaving undecided "the more disputed question whether Section 1153 also was intended to pre-empt tribal jurisdiction"). Congress has also preempted the application of state law in "Indian Country" in respect of all crimes except those where both the victim and the defendant are not tribal Indians. See, e.g., State of New York ex rel. Ray v. Martin, 326 U.S. 496 (1946). The exercise of tribal government powers has also been more generally circumscribed by Congress, both substantively and procedurally, by the Indian Civil Rights Act, §§ 201–203 of the Act of April 11, 1968, 82 Stat. 77 (codified at 25 U.S.C. §§ 1301–1303). Santa Clara Pueblo v. Martinez, 436 U.S. 49, 59 (1978) (holding that the Act neither conferred a private right of action upon persons subjected to tribal action contrary to its projections, nor abrogated tribal sovereign immunity from civil lawsuits, thus placing the burden of enforcing the Act squarely upon the tribal courts). These rulings were in part the product of the Court's reluctance to allow the federal courts to interfere with tribal autonomy and self-

cised as against all persons and in respect of all conduct affecting Tribal Indians within a tribe's territorial jurisdiction [29] free of state interference except as expressly provided to the contrary by treaty or act of Congress; [30] (2) the principle of the legal equality of races, and the

government and the authority of tribal courts over reservation affairs. Iowa Mutual Insurance Co. v. LaPlante, 107 S.Ct. 971, 976–977 (1987) (question whether federal law has divested tribal courts of jurisdiction to subject non-Indians to civil trial in particular case is to be decided in first instance by tribal court, not by diversity proceeding in federal district court); accord, National Farmers Union Insurance Co. v. Crow Tribe of Indians, 471 U.S. 845 (1985) (as to federal question proceeding in federal district court challenging jurisdiction of Crow tribal court over civil action involving non-Indian defendants).

29. See, e.g., Iowa Mutual Ins. Co. v. LaPlante, 107 S.Ct. 971 (1987) (upholding Blackfeet tribal court jurisdiction to subject non-Indian defendant to civil trial arising from auto accident on reservation causing injury to tribal members, absent federal statute or treaty to the contrary); National Farmers Union Ins. Co. v. Crow Tribe of Indians, 471 U.S. 845 (1985) (rejecting notion that Oliphant decision foreclosed Crow Tribal Court jurisdiction to subject Montana School District to civil trial arising from motorcycle injury to minor tribal member on state-owned school lands within reservation boundaries); Merrion v. Jicarilla Apache Tribe, 455 U.S. 130 (1982) (upholding tribal power to tax oil and gas production on tribal lands by non-Indian lessees as an essential attribute of inherent tribal sovereignty); Fisher v. District Court, 424 U.S. 382, 391 (1976) (upholding the exclusive jurisdiction of tribal court over child custody disputes on the reservation between Indians and finding such jurisdiction to derive "not from the race of the [Indian] plaintiff but rather from the quasi-sovereign status of the Northern Cheyenne Tribe under federal law"); United States v. Mazurie, 419 U.S. 544, 556–558 (1975) (upholding delegation to Indian tribes of congressional regulatory authority over on-reservation liquor sales because the tribes, as "unique aggregations possessing attributes of sovereignty", are not simply private associations, and have "independent tribal authority" to regulate the conduct of non-Indians, on fee-patented land within reservation borders "insofar as concern[s] their transactions [there] with Indians"); but see Rice v. Rehner, 463 U.S. 713, 722 (1983).

30. "Our cases, . . . have not established an inflexible per se rule precluding state jurisdiction over tribes and tribal members in the absence of express congres-

sional consent. '[U]nder certain circumstances a State may validly assert authority over the activities of nonmembers on a reservation, and . . . in exceptional circumstances a State may assert jurisdiction over the on-reservation activities of tribal members'," California v. Cabazon Band of Mission Indians, 107 S.Ct. 1083 (1987) (citations omitted) (quoting New Mexico v. Mescalero Apache Tribe, 462 U.S. 324, 331–332 (1983)). However, in the special area of state taxation of Indian tribes and tribal members the Court has adopted a per se rule prohibiting such taxation. Id. at 1091 n.17.

Congressional preemption and infringement of sovereignty create two "independent barriers to the assertion of state regulatory authority over tribal reservations and members." White Mountain Apache Tribe v. Bracker, 448 U.S. 136, 143 (1980). In White Mountain Apache Tribe, the Court outlined its unique method of preemption analysis in the context of Indian affairs. This analysis "calls for a particularized inquiry into the nature of the state, federal, and tribal interests at stake . . . to determine whether, in the specific context, the exercise of state authority would violate federal law," id. at 145, or "stand as an obstacle to the accomplishment of the full purposes and objectives of Congress", Ramah Navajo School Board, Inc. v. Bureau of Revenue of New Mexico, 458 U.S. 832, 845 (1982), quoting Hines v. Davidowitz, 312 U.S. 52, 67 (1941). With regard to Indian affairs, state law may be preempted even in the absence of any explicit congressional statement in light of "traditional notions of Indian self-government . . . [that] have provided an important 'backdrop' against which vague or ambiguous federal enactments must always be measured." White Mountain Apache Tribe v. Bracker, supra, at 143 (citation omitted).

This recent reliance on preemption has provided Indians some protection from the adverse economic effects of state regulation of non-Indians on reservations, see, e.g., Ramah Navajo School Board v. Bureau of Revenue of New Mexico, 458 U.S. 832 (1982) (federal law preempts state tax imposed on gross receipts of a construction company received from a Tribal school board for building an on-reservation school for Indian children in furtherance of the federal policy of increasing Indian control of Indian education); White Mountain Apache Tribe, 448 U.S. at 143 (federal law

concomitant doctrines (a) that Congress has no greater authority to legislate in respect of individuals of the American Indian race,[31] solely on account of their race, than it has in regard to persons of any other race,[32] (b) that Congress' Indian affairs powers are properly exercised to restrict individual conduct or to preempt state action only with respect to or on behalf of Indian tribes or "dependent Indian communities" [33] and individuals of the American Indian race who remain affiliated with such tribes or communities,[34] and (c) that any state or federal action directed at persons of the American Indian race as a racially defined class is subject to strict scrutiny to prevent invidious discrimination just as in the case of government action directed at any other racial minority; [35] (3) the principle that Congress has plenary and preemptive

preempts imposition of Arizona motor carrier license and use fuel taxes on non-Indians engaged in on-reservation logging and hauling of Indian timer); Three Affiliated Tribes v. Wold Engineering, 106 S.Ct. 2305 (1986) (federal law preempts North Dakota requirement that Tribe waive its sovereign immunity and have any civil disputes in state court to which it is a party adjudicated under state law in order to avail itself of state court jurisdiction); New Mexico v. Mescalero Apache Tribe, 462 U.S. 324 (1983) (barring enforcement of state hunting and fishing laws as against non-Indians on Mescalero Indian Reservation); California v. Cabazon Band of Mission Indians, 107 S.Ct. 1083 (1987) (prohibiting enforcement of state gambling laws as against non-Indians and tribal operators of on-reservation bingo and gaming enterprises). This balancing test sometimes upholds concurrent state regulatory authority on reservations where no substantial tribal interest is implicated (such an interest will typically be found lacking when the enterprise the state seeks to regulate or tax does not involve the creation and sale of "new value" on the reservation, id. at 1093); where a significant state interest involving off-reservation effects is shown; and where no federal law or policy to the contrary exists. Moe v. Confederated Salish and Kootenai Tribes, 425 U.S. 463 (1976), and Washington v. Confederated Tribes of the Colville Indian Reservation, 447 U.S. 134 (1980), both upheld collection of state sales taxes generated by on-reservation cigarette sales to non-Indians, rather than allow the Indians "to market an exemption from state taxation to persons who would normally do their business elsewhere." California v. Cabazon Bank of Mission Indians, 107 S.Ct. at 1093.

31. What is said in this section in respect to individuals of the American Indian race—whether or not they remain affiliated with an Indian tribe—generally applies with equal force to Alaskan natives. See United States v. Native Village of Unalakleet, 411 F.2d 1255 (Ct.Cl. 1969); F.

Cohen, Handbook of Federal Indian Law 734–764 (1982 ed.).

32. Cohen, "Indians are Citizens," 1 The Am.Ind. 12, 14–16 (1944) (". . . the individual Indian can . . . for all legal purposes cease to be an Indian whenever he wants to do so. He can do this most simply by giving up his tribal membership. . . . Once an Indian has severed his tribal relations he no longer comes within the scope of [Congress's Indian Affairs Powers]."); United States ex rel. Standing Bear v. Crook, 25 F.Cas. 695 (C.C.D. Neb. 1879). See Craig v. Boren, 429 U.S. 190, 209 n.22 (1976) (laws which single out individuals of the American Indian race as a class for special adverse treatment are of "questionable constitutionality") (dictum).

33. The Court has often used the phrase "dependent Indian Community" interchangeably with the terms "Indian Tribe" or "dependent Indian Tribe." See, e.g., Bryan v. Itasca Cty., Minn., 426 U.S. 373, 375, 392 (1976), quoting Alaska Pacific Fisheries v. United States, 248 U.S. 78, 89 (1918).

34. In United States v. Antelope, 430 U.S. 641, 647 n.7 (1977), the Court stated that enrollment in an Official Tribe is not an absolute requirement for federal jurisdiction, at least where the Indian defendant lived on the reservation and "maintained tribal relations with the Indians thereon". Antelope thus acknowledges that an individual of the American Indian race may be deemed an "Indian" for regulatory purposes in federal Indian law either by virtue of his formal political affiliation with a non-terminated Indian tribe, or by virtue of his residential, cultural, or social affiliation with such a tribe or Indian community.

35. United States v. Antelope, 523 F.2d 400, 403–406 (9th Cir. 1975) (when Tribal Indians "are put at a serious racially based disadvantage" by federal statute, their "rights to due process and equal protection under the Fifth Amendment require that

power over Indian affairs,[36] subject to the Bill of Rights and other constitutional limitations; [37] (4) the existence of a trust relationship between the United States and the Indian Tribes—a relationship binding the nation to the highest fiduciary standards in meeting its "unique obligation toward the Indians"; [38] (5) the rule that "in respect of distinctly Indian Communities the questions whether, to what extent, and for what time they shall be recognized and dealt with as dependent tribes requiring the guardianship and protection of the United States are to be determined by Congress, and not by the Courts," [39] and the related proposition that courts retain authority to determine whether any given community or body of people is so distinctly Indian that Congress may today deal with it or on its behalf as an Indian Tribe; [40] (6) the binding force of ratified United States-Indian treaties [41] and

they not be treated worse than similarly situated non-Indians"; proper test on review is strict scrutiny), rev'd on other grds., 430 U.S. 641 (1977) (holding that the federal statute under review did not single out Tribal Indians for adverse treatment on account of their race and that the statutory scheme did not impose a disparate burden on Tribal Indians as compared to non-Indians); Piper v. Big Pine School District, 193 Cal. 664, 226 P. 926, 928, 929 (1924); see Craig v. Boren, 429 U.S. 190, 209 n.22 (1976) (dictum). Nothing in these rules prevents Congress from extending remedial benefits or services to individuals of the American Indian race as a racial group, or defining the term "Indian" by reference to race for such benign purposes or for other purposes so long as the federal action "can be tied rationally to the fulfillment of Congress' unique obligation toward the Indians." Morton v. Mancari, 417 U.S. 535, 555 (1974); see also United States v. John, 437 U.S. 634 (1978); Delaware Tribal Business Committee v. Weeks, 430 U.S. 73 (1977); Maynor v. Morton, 510 F.2d 1254, 1256 (D.C.Cir. 1975).

36. United States v. Sioux Nation of Indians, 448 U.S. 371, 407–412 (1980); See Antoine v. Washington, 420 U.S. 194, 204–205 (1975); Morton v. Mancari, 417 U.S. 535, 551 (1974). Congress' power over Indian affairs has been given negative effect (compare Chapter 6, supra) such that, even absent affirmatively preemptive congressional action, the states are often held barred from legislation with respect to "Indian Affairs." see, e.g., McClanahan v. Arizona Tax Comm'n, 411 U.S. 164 (1973); California v. Cabazon Band of Mission Indians, 107 S.Ct. 1083 (1987). For the special rules governing preemption in "Indian Affairs", see note 30, supra.

37. The fifth amendment prohibition against uncompensated takings of private property by the federal government extends to protect the property interests of Indian tribes and individual tribal Indians, without regard to the nature of the proper-

ty interests involved—e.g., treaty right, statutory grant, common law property interest, or recognized aboriginal land rights. Hodel v. Irving, 107 S.Ct. 2076 (1987) (federal statute prohibiting devise and descent of certain small, fractionated shares of Indian allotments held a fifth amendment taking requiring just compensation); United States v. Sioux Nation of Indians, 448 U.S. 371 (1980) (1877 statute breached Fort Laramie Treaty of 1868 and effected fifth amendment taking of treaty land, necessitating just compensation); See Northern Cheyenne Tribe v. Hollowbreast, 425 U.S. 649, 655 (1976); Tee-Hit-Ton Indians v. United States, 348 U.S. 272, 277–278 & n.9 (1955).

38. Delaware Tribal Bus. Comm. v. Weeks, 430 U.S. 73, 85 (1977), quoting Morton v. Mancari, 417 U.S. 535, 555 (1974). See United States v. Mitchell, 463 U.S. 206, 225–228 (1983) (Indians damaged by United States' breaches of special duties assumed by it per statutes and regulations enacted in furtherance of "general trust relationship between the United States and the Indian people" have right to sue the United States for resulting money damages).

39. United States v. Sandoval, 231 U.S. 28, 46 (1913); United States v. John, 437 U.S. 634 (1978) (Congress retained power to deal with small band of Mississippi Choctaws who evaded removal to Oklahoma as Indian Tribe despite long lapses of federal supervision); South Carolina v. Catawba Indian Tribe, 106 S.Ct. 2039 (1986) (Congressional redefinition of federal relationship with Catawba Indians ended their special status as Indians under federal law).

40. "Congress may [not] bring a community or body of people within the range of [its Guardianship] power by arbitrarily calling them an Indian Tribe." United States v. Sandoval, supra at 46.

41. An excellent analysis of the effect of time on Indian treaties is C. Wilkinson,

bilateral agreements as against both the treaty parties and third parties, including states, so long as such treaties or agreements have not been abrogated by further treaty or by act of Congress,[42] and the principle that the Indian tribes retain aboriginal[43] rights to their ancestral lands until and unless those rights have been extinguished pursuant to federal law, and have a federal right of action to sue for recovery of unextinguished aboriginal interests and other recognized interests in land.[44]

§ 16–15. "Separate But Equal" Discrimination

More complex than laws that discriminate on their face against racial or ancestral groups is the case of discriminatory legislation that officially separates racial or ancestral minorities, although on terms of superficial equality. The Court first endorsed the provision of "equal but separate accommodations for the white and colored races" in *Plessy v. Ferguson*,[1] where it upheld Louisiana's racial segregation of railroad passengers. The Court rejected the argument that legislatively compelled apartheid stamped blacks with a badge of inferiority: "If this be so, it is not by reason of anything found in the act, but solely because the colored race chooses to put that construction upon it."[2] After all, the Court reasoned, if a state legislature dominated by blacks—a phenomenon not unknown in the south during Reconstruction[3]—were to enact precisely the same segregation law, surely whites "would not acquiesce in th[e] assumption" that this law "relegate[d] the white race to an inferior position."[4]

The willfully blind eye that the *Plessy* Court turned to what was obviously a law "enacted for the purpose of humiliating citizens of the

American Indians, Time and the Law (1987); see also Wilkinson & Volkman, "Judicial Review of Indian Treaty Abrogation: 'As Long as Water Flows, or Grass Grows upon the Earth'—How Long a Time is That?", 63 Cal.L.Rev. 601 (1975).

42. See, e.g., Antoine v. Washington, 420 U.S. 194 (1975); Washington Dept. of Game v. Puyallup Tribe, 414 U.S. 44 (1973). Compare United States v. Dion, 106 S.Ct. 2216 (1986) (containing a detailed statement of the standard used in determining whether a subsequent federal statute will be deemed to have abrogated an Indian Treaty right). Where Congress does abrogate an Indian treaty or agreement or repeal a statute guaranteeing rights to a tribe or tribal members, compensation is required under the fifth amendment takings clause. Hodel v. Irving, 107 S.Ct. 2076 (1987); United States v. Sioux Nation of Indians, 448 U.S. 371 (1980); See Tee-Hit-Ton Indians v. United States, 348 U.S. 272, 277–78 & n.9 (1955).

43. Amoco Production Co. v. Village of Gambell, Alaska, 107 S.Ct. 1396, 1399 and n.4 (1987); Tee-Hit-Ton Indians v. United States, 348 U.S. 272, 277–278 and n.9 (1955).

44. Oneida County, N.Y. v. Oneida Indian Nation of New York, 470 U.S. 226 (1985) (conveyances of Indian lands without congressional consent void ab initio; Indian tribes have a federal common law right to sue for recovery of lands conveyed without federal consent); accord, Wilson v. Omaha Indian Tribe, 442 U.S. 653 (1979); and see Mountain States Tel. & Tel. v. Pueblo of Santa Anna, 472 U.S. 237 (1985) (Federal Executive approval of conveyance of Indian lands not effective to validate transfer unless authorized by Congress).

§ 16–15

1. 163 U.S. 537, 540 (1896).

2. Id. at 551.

3. Of course, the domination by the "colored race" to which the Court alluded was usually if not always a sham: southern state legislatures were in fact controlled by white carpetbaggers who manipulated the black representatives they put into office.

4. Id.

United States of a particular race," [5] was replaced in this century by more honest and more realistic judicial perceptions. In *Loving v. Virginia*,[6] for example, the Supreme Court struck down a Virginia law making it illegal for any white person in the state to marry outside the Caucasian race.[7] The Court correctly found irrelevant the fact that both parties to such an illegal marriage were equally punished: "The fact that Virginia prohibits only interracial marriages involving white persons demonstrates that the racial classifications must stand on their own justification, as measures designed to maintain White Supremacy." [8] The Court discerned no compelling justification for the law.

The same realization that apparent symmetry in treatment created only a shallow illusion of equality prompted the Court in *Brown v. Board of Education* [9] to overturn legally-compelled segregation in public schools. Expressly rejecting the contrary language in *Plessy*,[10] the Court finally embraced the notion that "[s]eparate educational facilities are inherently unequal": [11] "To separate [children] from others of

5. Id. at 563 (Harlan, J., dissenting).

6. 388 U.S. 1 (1967).

7. The law contained a romantic exception allowing whites to marry "persons with less than one-sixteenth 'of the blood of the American Indian'" in order "'to recognize as an integral and honored part of the white race the descendants of John Rolfe and Pocahontas. . . .'" Id. at 5 n. 4. A few years after the Loving decision was handed down, the state tourist board adopted "Virginia is for lovers" as its official motto.

8. Id. at 11. The title of the law was "An Act to Preserve Racial Integrity," yet it extended only to the integrity of the white race. Other races were free to intermarry. Id. at 11 n.11. Cf. McLaughlin v. Florida, 379 U.S. 184, 196 (1964) (holding unconstitutional state statute prohibiting habitual occupation of a room at night by unmarried interracial couples).

The Court, in a strange dialogue with the Supreme Court of Appeals of Virginia, had refused to consider the antimiscegenation issue in 1955, when it was presented to the Court on appeal. See Naim v. Naim, 197 Va. 80, 87 S.E.2d 749 (1955), judgment vacated and cause remanded for clarification of record, 350 U.S. 891 (1955) (per curiam); decree aff'd 197 Va. 734, 90 S.E.2d 849 (1956) (per curiam); appeal dismissed for want of "properly presented federal question," 350 U.S. 985 (1956). Whether there was any principled justification for the Supreme Court's dismissal in Naim was the subject of a debate between Professors Bickel and Gunther. Bickel argued in favor of the Court's power to decline the exercise of jurisdiction, especially in the political context presented at the time of Naim. A. Bickel, The Least Dangerous Branch 174 (1962). Gunther at-

tacked this argument for judicial discretion as without legal basis. Gunther, "The Subtle Vices of the 'Passive Virtues': A Comment on Principle and Expediency in Judicial Review," 64 Colum.L.Rev. 1, 12 (1964).

9. 347 U.S. 483 (1954) (Brown I). The Supreme Court's decision considering a remedy for this racial segregation, Brown v. Board of Educ., 349 U.S. 294 (1955) (Brown II), is discussed in § 16–18, infra. See also Bolling v. Sharpe, 347 U.S. 497 (1954) (holding racial segregation in District of Columbia public schools denial of fifth amendment due process).

10. 347 U.S. at 494–95. Plessy had relied on school segregation laws as an example of legislation permissibly reflecting the social inequality of the races. 163 U.S. at 544–45.

11. 347 U.S. at 495. In several cases prior to Brown I, the Court struck down racial graduate school segregation without explicitly examining the "separate but equal" doctrine. In each case, inequality was found in that specific benefits available to white students were not available to blacks. See, e.g., Sweatt v. Painter, 339 U.S. 629 (1950) (overturning state ban on admission of blacks to state law school where state's alternative law school for blacks offered inferior opportunity for law study); Sipuel v. Board of Regents, 332 U.S. 631 (1948) (requiring admission of qualified black applicant to state's only law school, where state had denied admission solely on ground of race); Missouri ex rel. Gaines v. Canada, 305 U.S. 337 (1938) (holding that state which provides legal education within state for white students must furnish same for blacks, although not necessarily in same schools). For an excellent analysis of the history of Brown I, see R. Kluger, Simple Justice (1976).

similar age and qualifications solely because of their race generates a feeling of inferiority as to their status in the community that may affect their hearts and minds in a way unlikely ever to be undone." [12]

The holding in *Brown I* has been defended on a number of grounds. The first posits that blacks learn better when exposed to whites and therefore have a right to sit at desks next to white schoolchildren. Whatever its empirical merits,[13] this line of reasoning contains a distasteful echo of the argument pressed by the plaintiff in *Plessy*, that he had a right to sit amongst whites in the white railway coach because the "reputation of belonging to the dominant race, in this instance the white race," was a property right of which he could not constitutionally be deprived.[14] Plainly, neither that rationale nor its modern incarnations will do.

A second justification for the decision in *Brown I* focuses on the notion that "separate" facilities are likely to be tangibly unequal, despite appearances,[15] because only the presence of white children can persuade prejudiced school authorities to provide quality education.[16] Although that premise may in some instances be empirically sound, it was expressly abjured in *Brown* itself. There were findings in the lower courts that the black and white schools involved were equal, or in

12. 347 U.S. at 494. The Court noted that this finding was "amply supported by modern authority," citing in footnote the works of seven sociologists. See id. at 494–95 & n.11. The Court's reliance on social science evidence, as well as the reliability of the evidence itself, has been severely criticized. See, e.g., Cahn, "Jurisprudence," 30 N.Y.U.L.Rev. 150 (1955); Goodman, "De Facto School Segregation: A Constitutional and Empirical Analysis," 70 Calif.L.Rev. 275 (1972). The Court has held segregation in other public facilities unconstitutionally discriminatory: see, e.g., Lee v. Washington, 390 U.S. 333 (1968) (per curiam) (prisons; Court reserved question of constitutionality of segregation for maintenance of prison security); Johnson v. Virginia, 373 U.S. 61 (1963) (per curiam) (courtrooms); Turner v. Memphis, 369 U.S. 350 (1962) (per curiam) (municipal airport restaurant); State Athletic Comm'n v. Dorsey, 359 U.S. 533 (1959) (per curiam) (state-regulated athletic contests); New Orleans City Park Improvement Assoc. v. Detiege, 358 U.S. 54 (1958) (per curiam) (parks); Gayle v. Browder, 352 U.S. 903 (1956) (per curiam) (buses); Holmes v. Atlanta, 350 U.S. 879 (1955) (per curiam) (golf courses); Mayor of Baltimore v. Dawson, 350 U.S. 877 (1955) (per curiam) (beaches).

13. During the 1970s the most impressive gains on standardized reading tests were scored by black elementary students in the southeast, where desegregation had its first and greatest impact. National Assessment of Educational Progress, Three National Assessments of Progress in Read-

ing Performance, 1970–1980 (Rep. No. 11–R–01, Apr. 1981). Studies of particular school communities under busing orders show that in most cases black achievement and I.Q. test scores increase significantly while white student performance is unchanged or slightly improved. R. Crain & R. Mahard, Desegregation Plans That Raise Black Achievement: A Review Of The Research 35–45 (1982). Metropolitan or countywide desegregation plans are accompanied by the most striking black gains. Id. It is thought that these results reveal the value of classrooms that are mixed across socioeconomic or class lines as well as across racial lines. See Taylor, "Brown, Equal Protection, and the Isolation of the Poor," 95 Yale L.J. 1700, 1710–11 (1986). The salutary effects of integrated public education are lasting. Black students who attend desegregated schools are more likely to graduate from high school, to graduate from mixed-race colleges, and, over all, to escape the social pathology that afflicts the black urban underclass. Id. at 1711 & n.40. In one sense, or course, these studies may be taken to demonstrate the concrete impact of the stigma of inferiority of which the Court spoke in Brown I.

14. 163 U.S. at 549.

15. See, e.g., Larson, "The New Law of Race Relations," 1969 Wisc.L.Rev. 470, 482.

16. See, e.g., Bell, "School Litigation Strategies for the 1970's: New Phases in the Continuing Quest for Quality Schools," 1970 Wisc.L.Rev. 257, 291–92.

the process of being made equal, "with respect to buildings, curricula, qualifications and salaries of teachers, and other 'tangible' factors." [17] The Court therefore wisely declined to ground its decision on the empirical inequality of the particular segregated schools at issue.[18]

The most obvious rationale for the holding in *Brown I* is also the most persuasive. Racial separation by force of law conveys strong social stigma and perpetuates both the stereotypes of racial inferiority and the circumstances on which such stereotypes feed. Its social meaning *is* that the minority race is inferior. As Justice Harlan rightly asked in his dissent in *Plessy*: "What can more certainly arouse race hate, what more certainly create and perpetuate a feeling of distrust between these races, than state enactments, which, in fact, proceed on the ground that colored citizens are so inferior and degraded that they cannot be allowed to sit in public coaches occupied by white citizens?" [19] The harm justifying the Court's desegregation ruling, on this view, resided less in apartheid's mutual separation of the races than in its allowing one race to enjoy full communal life in society, while effectively ostracizing members of another race. Professor Charles Black has put it most eloquently: "[I]f a whole race of people finds itself confined within a system which is set up and continued for the very purpose of keeping it in an inferior station, and if the question is then propounded whether such a race is being treated 'equally,' I think we ought to exercise one of the sovereign prerogatives of philosophers—that of laughter. The only question remaining (after we get our laughter under control) is whether the segregation system answers to this description. Here I must confess to a tendency to start laughing all over again." [20]

Professor Alexander Bickel argued that, if the Court in *Brown I* had seen itself as bound by the legislative history showing the immediate objectives which the fourteenth amendment addressed, it could not correctly have applied the amendment to public school segregation—a common phenomenon even in northern states at the time of the amendment's ratification. The Court, however, "was able to avoid the dilemma because the record of history . . . left the way open to, in fact invited, a decision based on the moral and material state of the nation in 1954, not 1866." [21] This is not to say that, in light of modern and more enlightened values, the Court in *Brown I* radically reinterpreted the norm of equality found in the fourteenth amendment to create a new basic right that the amendment authors would have rejected. Rather, the Court in 1954 understood, as the *Plessy* Court in 1896 did not, that racial segregation in public schools and other public facilities in fact subjugates blacks, despite its appearance of symmetry, because it stands for and reenforces white supremacy—a regime we

17.   347 U.S. at 492.

18.   Id. Nor did Brown I reject the proposition, implicit in Plessy, that separate and *unequal* schools would deny equal protection. See note 29, infra.

19.   163 U.S. at 560 (Harlan, J., dissenting).

20.   Black, "The Lawfulness of the Segregation Decisions," 69 Yale.L.J. 421, 424 (1960).

21.   Bickel, "The Original Understanding and the Segregation Decision," 69 Harv.L.Rev. 1, 64–65 (1955).

now recognize to be utterly at odds with the concept of "equal protection of the laws." It was not the concept embodied in the equal protection clause that changed between 1896 and 1954, but only our relevant perceptions and understandings.[22]

Professor Herbert Wechsler instead suggested that the rationale of *Brown I* must be found in its declaration of the associational right of black children to attend the same schools as whites. For Wechsler, "assuming equal facilities, the question posed by state-enforced segregation is not one of discrimination at all. Its human and its constitutional dimensions lie . . . in the denial by the state of freedom to associate. . . ."[23] At least one Supreme Court decision is consistent with this thesis. In *Trafficante v. Metropolitan Life Insurance Co.*,[24] a group of white tenants, who charged that defendant owner's racially discriminatory renting practices relegated them to a white ghetto and denied them the benefits of living in an integrated community, were granted standing to sue.[25]

Although *Brown I* was likewise defensible partly on a freedom-of-association rationale, Professor Wechsler erred when he argued that *no* other principle supported the decision, and when he concluded that the decision was therefore insupportable for those who would not be willing to follow the associational rationale to its logical conclusion—namely, that *integration* "forces an association upon those for whom it is unpleasant or repugnant".[26] Professor Wechsler is correct that integration coerces some associational choices—*but so does segregation*.[27] The difference is that racial segregation by law denies the basic human right to be treated as an equal—a distinct claim that Professor Wechsler overlooks.[28] The fourteenth amendment declares the fundamental importance of equality; that value is sufficient to trump whatever power a state might otherwise have to impose racial separation in order to promote the associational preferences of some of its citizens.

22. See R. Dworkin, Law's Empire 359–69, 387–89 (1986).

23. Wechsler, "Toward Neutral Principles of Constitutional Law," 73 Harv.L. Rev. 1, 34 (1959).

24. 409 U.S. 205 (1972).

25. Petitioners were granted standing under § 801(a) of the Civil Rights Act of 1968. Id. at 209. The Supreme Court reversed the appellate court's holding that standing could be granted only to "direct victims" of discriminatory practices.

26. Wechsler, 73 Harv.L.Rev. at 34.

27. The elder Justice Harlan recognized the implications of apartheid for freedom of association in 1896: "If a white man and a black man choose to occupy the same public conveyance on a public highway, it is their right to do so, and no government, proceeding alone on grounds of race, can prevent it without infringing the personal liberty of each." 163 U.S. at 557 (Harlan, J., dissenting). The majority in Plessy countered that, even though the "object of the [fourteenth] amendment was undoubtedly to enforce the absolute equality of the two races before the law, . . . in the nature of things it could not have been intended . . . to enforce . . . a commingling of the two races upon terms unsatisfactory to either." Id. at 544. Compare Coppage v. Kansas, 236 U.S. 1, 17–18 (1915) (state may not intervene in labor-capital contract negotiations to redress imbalance of bargaining power, because such inequalities are "but the normal and inevitable result" of the exercise of the right to contract itself), discussed in § 8–4, supra.

28. For criticism of Wechsler's position, see Pollak, "Racial Discrimination and Judicial Integrity: A Reply to Professor Wechsler," 108 U.Pa.L.Rev. 1 (1959).

It remains true, however, that judicial rejection of the "separate but equal" talisman [29] seems to have been accompanied by a potentially troublesome lack of sympathy for racial separateness as a possible expression of group solidarity. In *Norwood v. Harrison*,[30] for example, the Court held unconstitutional a Mississippi program in which textbooks were purchased by the State and loaned to students in both public and private schools, including private schools with racially discriminatory policies.[31] The Court asserted that a "state's constitutional obligation requires it to steer clear, not only of operating the old dual system of racially segregated schools, but also of giving significant aid to institutions that practice racial or other invidious discrimination."[32] Although the Court admitted that private racial discrimination might in some contexts be characterized as an exercise of freedom of association protected by the first amendment, it concluded that this "private bias," unlike such activities as the running of religious schools, is not affirmatively valued by the Constitution [33] and thus cannot serve to justify public aid that would otherwise be impermissible.

Although the result in *Norwood* seems correct,[34] the Court's treatment of the case as one involving freedom of association may be criticized. In *Norwood*, the school children whose associational freedom was allegedly curtailed were obviously dominated in their associational behavior by their parents; [35] the case thus presented no occasion to consider the validity of a state decision to tolerate or even foster pluralism and diversity by extending various forms of assistance neutrally to groups of adults banding together for social purposes on an all-black (or perhaps even an all-white) basis or on some other basis that

29. But see Gomperts v. Chase, 404 U.S. 1237, 1240–41 (1971) (Douglas, J., sitting as Circuit Justice) (denying preliminary injunction in school desegregation case) ("Plessy v. Ferguson has not yet been overruled on its mandate that separate facilities be equal. . . ."). Of course, where racial integration is not attainable, the *minimum* requirement is that the facilities and resources available to the minority be *equal* to those available to the majority.

30. 413 U.S. 455 (1973).

31. The Court had not yet decided Runyon v. McCrary, 427 U.S. 160 (1976) (holding that 42 U.S.C. § 1981 prohibits private, commercially operated, nonsectarian schools from denying admission to blacks and that, as so construed, § 1981 is a permissible exercise of Congress' power to enforce the thirteenth amendment), discussed in §§ 5–13, and 15–20, supra.

32. Norwood, 413 U.S. at 467. This obligation arguably supports construing the federal tax laws to withhold even indirect subsidies for segregated private schools and colleges. See Bob Jones University v. United States, 461 U.S. 574 (1983).

33. 413 U.S. at 469–70, distinguishing Board of Educ. v. Allen, 392 U.S. 236, 244–45 (1968).

34. The Norwood Court purported to "assume that the State's textbook aid to private school" had been "motivated by . . . a sincere interest in the educational welfare of all Mississippi children," 413 U.S. at 466, but the decision was plainly marked by awareness that the "creation and enlargement of [the private schools themselves] occurred simultaneously with major events in the desegregation of public schools." Id. at 457. Cf. Griffin v. County School Bd., 377 U.S. 218 (1964). See also Gilmore v. Montgomery, 417 U.S. 556, 567 (1974) (upholding propriety of federal court's enjoining municipality from permitting use of public parks by private segregated schools that allegedly discriminated on basis of race; city engaged in this "elaborate subterfuge" to circumvent prior court order mandating establishment of unitary school system).

35. Cf. Pierce v. Society of Sisters, 268 U.S. 510, 532, 535 (1925), where the Court not only conspicuously passed over "the right of the child to influence the parents' choice of a school," but also seemingly opined that the child is entirely the creature of "those who nurture him and direct his destiny." See § 16–31, infra.

could not be employed by government itself.[36]   *Norwood* should not be seen as disposing of such a case, especially given the importance racial solidarity and exclusivity can have for associations organized to promote the interests of oppressed minorities.[37]

§ 16–16.   "Neutral" Governmental Reflection of Private Prejudice

The odious doctrine of "separate but equal" was interred in *Brown v. Board of Education*,[1] and the fraudulent equality of a symmetrical prohibition on interracial marriage was exposed in *Loving v. Virginia*.[2] But the Supreme Court has occasionally deferred to apparently "symmetrical" governmental action, especially when such action represents a decision in one of the areas traditionally reserved to legislative discretion—as, for example, the allocation of resources from the public fisc.   In *Palmer v. Thompson*,[3] for example, the Court upheld the decision of the Jackson, Mississippi, City Council to close its public swimming pools after they had been ordered desegregated by a federal district court.   The Court, accepting the city's defense that "the pools were closed because the city council felt they could not be operated safely and economically on an integrated basis," [4] concluded that, since there was no proof of "state action affecting blacks differently from whites," [5] the city's decision could not be invalidated simply on a showing that one of the motives underlying it was "ideological opposition to racial integration." [6]

36. Such self-enforced separation could hardly be characterized as inflicting the pervasive stigmatizing effect which the Court found persuasive in invalidating the segregation in Brown I. But cf. Moose Lodge No. 107 v. Irvis, 407 U.S. 163 (1972), discussed in Chapter 18, infra. If Moose Lodge was wrong in allowing private clubs with state liquor licenses to practice racial discrimination, it was because the state's decision to limit the number of licenses made it responsible for injury to racial minorities and not because the state's tolerance of private discrimination was unacceptable.

37. But the Norwood decision nonetheless stands as a vital reminder that the inclusion of serious injury to racial minorities in an otherwise protected context—there, injury to the black children of excluded families in the context of parental control over child rearing—cannot automatically immunize such injury from governmental control and certainly cannot entitle it to affirmative public support. Runyon v. McCrary, 427 U.S. 160 (1976), purported to leave open the validity of § 1981 as applied to prohibit racial segregation by private schools which invoke religious reasons for such discrimination. But if religious motives do not automatically immunize from government regulation acts inflicting physical harm on nonconsenting outsiders, see Chapter 14, supra, such mo-

tives should not automatically render immune those acts whose injurious impact is less physically observable but whose tendency to exclude minorities from housing, education, or employment may nonetheless work grave harm. Direct financial aid to institutions that practice racial discrimination should be particularly suspect regardless of the religious origin of such discrimination. Accord, Bob Jones University v. United States, supra note 32 (unanimously rejecting a religious exemption to the statutory ban on tax benefits to segregated schools).

The less intimate and more attenuated the association—and the more the association affects the public realm and access to the privileges and opportunities available in that realm—the greater the state's power to regulate an organization's exclusionary practices. See Roberts v. United States Jaycees, 468 U.S. 609, 620–24 (1984), discussed in § 15–17, supra.

§ 16–16

1.   347 U.S. 483 (1954) (Brown I).

2.   388 U.S. 1 (1967).

3.   403 U.S. 217 (1971).

4.   Id. at 225.

5.   Id.

6.   Id. at 224.

Yet the obviously plausible suspicion of racist intention should have been sufficient in *Palmer* to trigger scrutiny at least strict enough to compel rejection of the city officials' explanation. Justice White pointed out in dissent that "the only evidence in [the] record [was] the conclusions of the officials themselves, unsupported by even a scintilla of added proof." [7] Furthermore, the effect of the closing was anything but racially neutral, for it seems clear that more whites than blacks had alternative places to swim in Jackson once the public pools were closed.[8] Given the appropriate showing that the closings would have this racially unequal impact, the burden should have been placed on the government to justify the closing in racially neutral terms. Finally, the "justification" offered by the city and uncritically accepted by the *Palmer* majority was itself racially prejudiced. The supposed difficulty of operating the city's pools on a racially integrated basis rested on nothing but a belief that prejudiced private attitudes would persist and that the city could properly shape its policies to reflect those attitudes. Just as no such argument was allowed to prevail in *Brown I*, and just as the Court has specifically held that states may not facilitate private prejudice in racial matters,[9] so it should have held in

7. Id. at 260.

8. Note also that even if there had been symmetry in this regard, Loving v. Virginia, 388 U.S. 1 (1967), and Brown v. Board of Educ., 347 U.S. 483 (1954), discussed in § 16–15, supra, point to the psychological and symbolic impact as a relevant effect; moreover, even before the Palmer decision, the Court had held acts arguably neutral in impact violative of the fourteenth amendment on the ground of non-neutral *motives*: see, e.g., Griffin v. County School Bd., 377 U.S. 218 (1964) (holding that county ordered to desegregate public schools may not close them to prevent racial mixing). If Griffin is thought to rest on the differential impact implicit in the county's use of public funds to subsidize the segregated private schools with which the public schools were replaced, then the city's awareness that closing its pools would leave more whites than blacks with alternative places to swim provides a nearly parallel element in Palmer.

9. See, e.g., Norwood v. Harrison, 413 U.S. 455 (1973) (state may not indirectly subsidize racial discrimination in private schools), discussed in § 16–15 supra. In Anderson v. Martin, 375 U.S. 399 (1964), the Court held unconstitutional an amendment to Louisiana's election law requiring the designation of each candidate's race on nomination papers and ballots. The Court found that "by directing the citizen's attention to the single consideration of race or color, the State indicate[d] that a candidate's race or color [was] an important—perhaps paramount—consideration in the citizen's choice, which may decisively [have] influence[d] the citizen to cast his

ballot along racial lines." Id. at 402. Therefore, despite the labeling provision's superficially equal application to all races, and thus its superficially nondiscriminatory nature, the effect of the classification was inevitably discriminatory, "in light of 'private attitudes and pressures' towards Negroes at the time of its enactment." Id. at 403. Cf. NAACP v. Alabama, 357 U.S. 449, 462 (1958) (state may not compel disclosure of association's membership list where doing so would expose members to persecution and threaten survival of association).

However, neither the Court's sensitivity in Anderson to the potential for a prejudiced society's abuse of racial information, nor a recognition of the possibly demeaning nature of a demand for such information, moved the Court to the same degree of vigilance in a case involving a state statute requiring recitation of the spouses' race in divorce decrees. The Court in Tancil v. Woolls, 379 U.S. 19 (1964) (per curiam), aff'g 230 F.Supp. 156 (E.D.Va.1964), approved without opinion a federal district court decision holding that "the securing and chronicling of racial data for identification or statistical use violates no constitutional privilege. . . . Vital statistics, obviously, are aided by denotation in the divorce decrees of the race of the parties." 230 F.Supp. at 158. In a per curiam order issued simultaneously with its order in Tancil, the Court affirmed the district court's invalidation of laws requiring separate lists of blacks and whites in voting, tax, and property records. Hamm v. Virginia Bd. of Elections, 230 F.Supp. 156 (E.D.Va.1964). Note, however,

Palmer that the state's action was racially prejudiced—in its effect, in its purpose, and even in its avowed justification.

The Court's capitulation to racial animus in *Palmer* was retrograde motion. More than half a century before, in *Buchanan v. Warley*,[10] the Court had invalidated a Kentucky law forbidding blacks to buy homes in white neighborhoods, emphatically rejecting the argument that the proposed segregation would "promote the public peace by preventing race conflicts." [11] Having lost its way in *Palmer*, the Supreme Court recovered its constitutional compass in *Palmore v. Sidoti*.[12] A divorced white father sought to remove his 3-year-old daughter from the custody of his white ex-wife when she married a black man. The state court counselor recommended a change in custody because "[t]he life [petitioner] has chosen for herself and for her child [is] a life-style unacceptable to the father *and to society*." [13] The state court ruled that the best interests of the child would be served by transferring custody to the father: "This Court feels that despite the strides that have been made in bettering relations between the races in this country, it is inevitable that [the girl] will, if allowed to remain in her present situation . . . suffer from the social stigmatization that is sure to come." [14]

The Supreme Court acknowledged the persistence of racial prejudice in American society and admitted that there was indeed a risk of adverse impact on the child, but unanimously ruled that these considerations could not constitute grounds for a custody decision: "The Constitution cannot control such prejudices but neither can it tolerate them. Private biases may be outside the reach of the law, but the law cannot, directly or indirectly, give them effect." [15]

§ 16–17. The Application of Equal Protection Principles to a State's Entire Legal and Governmental Apparatus

In the century that has passed since the ratification of the fourteenth amendment, equal protection of the law has become a pervasive constitutional value. On a horizontal axis, the mandate of equality governs state action by all branches of government; before the close of the nineteenth century, the equal protection clause had been applied

that government may plausibly defend its information-gathering as neither unduly subject to abuse, nor excessively demeaning when the information is gathered in a good-faith "affirmative action" effort to eliminate discrimination. See § 16–22, infra.

10. 245 U.S. 60 (1917).

11. Id. at 81.

12. 466 U.S. 429 (1984).

13. Id. at 431 (original emphasis).

14. Id. (emphasis omitted).

15. Id. The Court then relied upon a quotation from Justice White's dissenting opinion in Palmer v. Thompson. Compare Brown v. North Carolina, 107 S.Ct. 423, 424 (1986) (O'Connor, J., concurring in denial of certiorari): "That the Court will not tolerate prosecutors' racially discriminatory use of the peremptory challenge, in effect, is a special rule of relevance, a statement about what this Nation stands for, rather than a statement of fact."

In a world where the "color line" still matters a great deal, it would be a mistake to take Palmore as a straight repudiation of Palmer and to assume that this settles the matter once and for all. As my colleague Randall Kennedy has shown in an article as disillusioning as it is perceptive, the Supreme Court's vindication of the Constitution's pledge of racial justice has been far too uneven over the years to permit any such assumption. See Kennedy, "Race Relations Law and the Tradition of Celebration: The Case of Professor Schmidt," 86 Colum.L.Rev. 1622 (1986).

not only to discriminatory legislation, but to discriminatory executive, administrative, and judicial behavior as well. These varieties of governmental action may be invalidated as invidious under the analyses described above. But they may also display prejudice at a more fully disguised level, as when, for example, no official use is made of race or ancestry as a criterion, but the record leaves race or ancestry as in fact the only plausible explanatory factor. In *Yick Wo v. Hopkins*,[1] for example, the Supreme Court reversed a conviction under a municipal ordinance "fair on its face and impartial in appearance,"[2] which prohibited the construction of wooden laundries without a license. The Court found that under the law, licensors' decisions were entirely discretionary, and that while all but one of the eighty non-Chinese applicants had received licenses, all two hundred Chinese applicants had been denied. The Court therefore concluded: "The fact of this discrimination is admitted. No reason for it is shown, and the conclusion cannot be resisted, that no reason for it exists except hostility to the race and nationality to which the petitioners belong, and which in the eye of the law is not justified."[3]

The actions of state courts and judicial officers are likewise subject to the restraints of the equal protection clause. Sometimes the illicit racial discrimination is displayed for all to see. In *Ex parte Virginia*,[4] a Virginia county court judge was accused of excluding blacks from grand and petit jury service in violation of federal law. In *Palmore v. Sidoti*,[5] a state family court was reversed for removing a child from her mother's custody on the ground that the mother (who was white) had married a black man.

But the *Yick Wo* case illustrates a problem commonplace in the judicial as well as the administrative context: purposeful and invidious discrimination must often be inferred from statistical data regarding the operation of a facially neutral law or requirement. Discrimination in jury selection, for example, has frequently been demonstrated by reliance on statistics showing a racially discriminatory pattern of administration. In *Hernandez v. Texas*,[6] the Supreme Court overturned the criminal conviction of a Mexican-American who alleged that "persons of Mexican descent were systematically excluded from service as jury commissioners, grand jurors, and petit jurors, although there were such persons fully qualified to serve residing in [the County of his

§ 16–17

1. 118 U.S. 356 (1886).

2. Id. at 373.

3. Id. at 374. It is possible that Yick Wo was decided on facts that never occurred. Before the Supreme Court, the municipality vehemently denied that it had admitted to discrimination. The city insisted that only two of the 80 non-Chinese laundry owners had applied for permits and that many of the non-Chinese owners had also been arrested for operating in non-conforming buildings. If the facts were really as the city, and not the Court, described them, then the fourteenth amendment was first extended to discrimination against racial or ancestral groups other than blacks in a rather inappropriate case. This would make Yick Wo an ironic inversion of the subsequent decision in Korematsu v. United States, 323 U.S. 214 (1944), discussed in § 16–14, supra, where the Court refused to acknowledge the blatant racial animus presented by the facts of the case.

4. 100 U.S. 339 (1879).

5. 466 U.S. 429 (1984), discussed in § 16–16, supra.

6. 347 U.S. 475 (1954).

conviction]." [7]   While the petitioner acknowledged that the system of jury selection was "fair on its face and capable of being utilized without discrimination," [8] the Court upheld his claim of discrimination against Mexican-Americans on a showing that that group constituted a separate class, and that the law as applied singled out that class for different treatment not based on some reasonable, racially neutral classification. [9]

The taint on the criminal justice system wrought by exclusionary practices at the grand jury stage is not cured by a subsequent fair trial before a petit jury untainted by racial discrimination. [10]   Nor will the Constitution tolerate a regime in which the state's judicial branch draws up petit jury lists pursuant to unbiased procedures only to have the executive branch, in the person of the prosecutor, wield its peremptory challenges to strike all black jurors when a black defendant is on trial. [11]

The norm of equal protection also operates along a vertical axis, governing the ways in which states may allocate decision-making power up and down the governmental hierarchy. Invidious discrimination along these lines is not always easily discernible. But the Supreme Court has recognized the existence of, and acted to remedy, prejudiced laws that masquerade as instances of democratic redistributions of authority. In *Reitman v. Mulkey*, [12] for example, the Court invalidated a California constitutional provision prohibiting any interference, by the State or any of its agencies or subdivisions, with "the right of any person . . . to decline to sell, lease or rent [any part or all of his real] property to such person or persons as he, in his absolute discretion, chooses." [13]   The Court accepted the California Supreme Court's characterization of the constitutional provision as not merely repealing existing laws forbidding private racial discrimination, but affirmatively authorizing racial discrimination in the housing market and establish-

---

7. Id. at 476–477.

8. Id. at 478–479.

9. Id. at 478.

10. Vasquez v. Hillery, 474 U.S. 254 (1986).

11. Batson v. Kentucky, 106 S.Ct. 1712 (1986). Batson overruled Swain v. Alabama, 380 U.S. 202 (1965). Other jury selection decisions involving discrimination include Castaneda v. Partida, 430 U.S. 482 (1977) (statistical evidence makes out prima facie case of discrimination against Mexican-Americans in grand jury selection process, even where three of five jury commissioners in charge of selection are themselves Mexican-American, because discrimination can make those who are subjugated think less of themselves or alienate them from their own kind); Peters v. Kiff, 407 U.S. 493 (1972) (upholding white defendants' due process challenge to exclusion of blacks from juries); Alexander v. Louisi-

ana, 405 U.S. 625 (1972) (prima facie case established where jury commissioners used questionnaires and cards indicating race of potential jurors); Turner v. Fouche, 396 U.S. 346 (1970) (prima facie case established where blacks comprised 60% of general population and 37% of jury lists); Carter v. Jury Comm'n, 396 U.S. 320 (1970) (persons excluded from juries on alleged basis of race have standing to sue for declaratory and injunctive relief); Norris v. Alabama, 294 U.S. 587 (1935) (history of exclusion of blacks from juries not adequately justified by mere assertion of officials' good faith); Neal v. Delaware, 103 U.S. 370 (1880) (criminal conviction overturned where blacks excluded from jury on state presumption that blacks lacked adequate intelligence and integrity).

12. 387 U.S. 369 (1967).

13. Id. at 371.

ing the right to discriminate as "one of the basic policies of the State."[14]

In *Reitman*, the California constitutional provision's attempt to withdraw the State from entanglement in private housing discrimination triggered a severe burden of governmental explanation and justification. The transparent focus of a regulation on racial discrimination, its superficially neutral terms notwithstanding, prompted the same standard of review in *Hunter v. Erickson*.[15] In *Hunter*, the Court invalidated a city charter amendment, adopted pursuant to a popular initiative, that provided that the city council could implement no ordinance dealing with racial, religious, or ancestral discrimination in housing without the approval of a majority of the city's voters.[16] The Court reasoned that, "although the law on its face treat[ed] Negro and white, Jew and gentile in an identical manner, the reality [was] that the law's impact [fell] on the minority,"[17] for it was those who would obviously benefit from laws barring racial, religious or ancestral discriminations, and thus it was minorities whom the amendment deliberately disadvantaged: "The majority needs no protection against discrimination. . . ."[18] Even more than other forms of disadvantage, hurdles imposed in the political process itself on groups traditionally the subjects of prejudice must therefore be strictly scrutinized, and ordinarily invalidated.[19]

Transfers of power involving direct democracy have been a popular ploy for electoral majorities which sensed that their governments were becoming too aggressive in combating racial segregation. In 1978 the Seattle School District ordered extensive busing to counteract the racially segregative effects of a neighborhood school policy. In response, the electorate of the State of Washington passed Initiative 350, which prohibited the assignment of pupils to other than the closest schools. A number of broad exceptions allowed pupil reassignment to meet students' special educational needs and to avert overcrowding, but busing for racial purposes was permitted only in the event that it was required by the fourteenth amendment pursuant to court order.[20] In what the Court's majority characterized as an "extraordinary"[21] move, the Seattle school board went to court and invoked the fourteenth amendment to defend its busing program from this state assault.

14. Id. at 381. For an insightful analysis of Reitman, see Black, "The Supreme Court, 1966 Term—Foreword: State Action, Equal Protection, and California's Proposition 14," 81 Harv.L.Rev. 69 (1965).

15. 393 U.S. 385 (1969).

16. The Court's decision should not be read as casting doubt on the constitutionality of requirements of more than majority approval in other settings. See, e.g., Gordon v. Lance, 403 U.S. 1 (1971) (upholding state requirement of super-majority approval before municipal assumption of bonded indebtedness).

17. 393 U.S. at 391.

18. Id. Compare the discussion of affirmative action in § 16–22, infra.

19. But see James v. Valtierra, 402 U.S. 137 (1971) (holding wealth classifications insufficient to trigger strict scrutiny), discussed in § 16–58, infra.

20. Washington v. Seattle School Dist. No. 1, 458 U.S. 457 (1982).

21. Id. at 459.

In *Washington v. Seattle School District No. 1*,[22] a sharply divided Court[23] held that Initiative 350 was unconstitutional. The Court concluded that the principle of *Hunter v. Erickson* disposed of the case in a straightforward fashion.[24] Just as the charter amendment in *Hunter* selectively removed the power to eliminate housing discrimination from the Akron city council and placed it in the hands of the city's electorate, so Initiative 350 stripped the Seattle School District of the authority to remedy de facto racial segregation and gave it to the voters of the entire State of Washington. Although the initiative was neutral on its face, the Court had "little doubt that [it] was drawn for racial purposes."[25] Since it was riddled with exceptions to allow almost every other conceivable purpose for busing, "the initiative expressly require[d] those championing school integration to surmount a considerably higher hurdle than those seeking comparable legislative action."[26] By selecting out a form of legislative action of particular interest to racial minorities and removing it to a different and less accessible level of government, the Washington initiative changed the rules of the game and put minorities at a distinct disadvantage.[27]

The facts in the companion case, *Crawford v. Board of Education of Los Angeles*,[28] were similar; but the result was not. In the wake of state court decisions holding that the equal protection clause of the California constitution outlawed de facto as well as de jure segregation, California voters ratified Proposition 1, a constitutional amendment that stripped state courts of the power to order busing to remedy school segregation except when a federal court would be permitted to do so under the fourteenth amendment.[29] When asked whether this change constituted an impermissible shift in political structure like those in *Hunter* and *Seattle*, the Supreme Court answered "no" with only a single dissenting vote.[30] Justice Powell, who authored the dissent in *Seattle* and who had lamented the use of busing as a response to de facto segregation,[31] wrote the opinion of the Court in *Crawford*. He concluded that *Hunter v. Erickson* was not relevant since Proposition 1 was a change not in legal remedies but in substantive legal rights.[32] The voters of California had simply changed the state constitution that the courts enforce, and there is nothing in the equal protection clause that prohibits the states from changing their minds and stepping back

22. 458 U.S. 457 (1982).

23. The vote was 5–4. Justice Blackmun's opinion for the Court was joined by Justices Brennan, Marshall, White and Stevens. Justice Powell's dissent was joined by Chief Justice Burger and Justices Rehnquist and O'Connor.

24. Id. at 470.

25. Id. at 471.

26. Id. at 474.

27. The Court noted that Washington could have reserved to state officials control over all pupil assignments, but once it had chosen to decentralize authority it had

to do so without according different treatment to racial issues. Id. at 476–80 & n.23.

28. 458 U.S. 527 (1982).

29. Id. at 532.

30. Justice Marshall was the sole dissenter. The author of this treatise argued the Crawford case in the Supreme Court on behalf of the plaintiffs who challenged Proposition 1.

31. See, e.g., Estes v. Dallas NAACP, 444 U.S. 437 (1980) (Powell, J., dissenting from denial of certiorari).

32. 458 U.S. at 540.

to the reduced level of protection guaranteed by the fourteenth amendment.[33]

In fact, the change wrought by Proposition 1 was strikingly analogous to that wrought by Initiative 350 or by the *Hunter* charter amendment. In *Crawford* the shift in authority was from the courts to the state legislature or the electorate; in *Seattle*, from the local school board to the state legislature or electorate; and in *Hunter*, from the city council to the city electorate. The majority and concurring opinions in *Crawford* misconstrued the impact of Proposition 1 because of confusion over just what "right" was at issue. What was at stake was not some sort of derivative "right to invoke a judicial busing remedy," [34] but a state-guaranteed "right to be free from racial isolation in the public schools." [35] As the majority repeatedly admitted,[36] Proposition 1 did not remove from the state courts or the local school boards the state constitutional obligation to root out *de facto* segregation; it merely stripped the courts of the power to use mandatory pupil reassignment as a tool. That change left the substantive right in place but removed the remedy to a different level of government. After the adoption of Proposition 1, the only method of enforcing the duty to eliminate racial isolation, in the face of school board opposition, was to petition either the state legislature or the electorate as a whole. As Justice Marshall put it, "Clearly, the rules of the game have been significantly changed. . . ." [37]

No matter how one views the role of state courts, the fact remains that they are always subservient to the relevant constitution. If the state constitution is amended as it was in *Crawford*, then the important question is whether the resulting change in the substantive law is itself in compliance with the federal constitution. If a state has a system of open-ended, judicially enforceable civil rights—dealing with everything from race to speech to educational finance—which are not mere copies of their fourteenth amendment counterparts, may the state pick the right to end racially isolated public education out of this dynamic system and relegate *it alone* to the status of a federal facsimile? The answer to that question should be the same as the answer to the

---

33. Justice Blackmun, the author of the Court's opinion in the Seattle case, argued in a concurring opinion (joined by Justice Brennan) that, unlike Initiative 350, California's Proposition 1 did not work a change in the structure of the political process—it "simply repeal[ed] the right to invoke a judicial busing remedy." 458 U.S. at 546. Those who sought busing in California were not ousted from a decision-making or policy-making forum; the substantive law that the state courts were to apply had simply been changed. Justice Blackmun based this conclusion on the notion that courts do not create rights, they merely enforce them. See id. Such a Blackstonian view of what courts do has not been entirely persuasive since the early nineteenth century. Moreover, in the very same Term, Justice Blackmun himself responded to the assertion that state courts are mere oracles by characterizing them as "a coequal part of the State's sovereign decision-making apparatus. . . ." FERC v. Mississippi, 456 U.S. 742, 763 n.27 (1982). As Dean Choper put it, if Justice Blackmun thinks California courts do not create constitutional rights, "he ought to come to California more often." J. Choper, Y. Kamisar & L. Tribe, 4 Supreme Court Trends & Developments 44 (1983); see id. at 45–46.

34. 458 U.S. at 546 (Blackmun, J., concurring); see id. at 544 (opinion of the Court).

35. Id. at 557 (Marshall, J., dissenting).

36. 458 U.S. at 535, 544.

37. Id. at 555 (Marshall, J., dissenting).

question whether the state could, in the first place, establish dynamic judicial protection for all rights *except* the right to end de facto racial segregation in its schools. For California to take three steps forward and then one race-specific step back is the same as selectively omitting that particular step at the outset.

The clearest precedent for suggesting that a state may not do *that* is *Shelley v. Kraemer*,[38] where the Supreme Court established that the equal protection clause governs even the edifice of the common law— and is thus applicable to state law in the broadest sense of the term. At issue in *Shelley* were Missouri's rules for judicial enforcement of contracts restraining alienability of property.[39] Restraints on alienability were generally disfavored by the common law of Missouri (as of other states), but racially restrictive covenants were included within a special subclass of restraints that the state's courts would *not* set aside. The Supreme Court's decision to strike down the Missouri courts' enforcement of racially restrictive covenants meant that the fourteenth amendment required Missouri to make judicial invalidation of private agreements causing racial segregation *just as available* as judicial invalidation of other disfavored restraints on the free alienability of real property. If *Shelley v. Kraemer* is correct, then *Crawford* seems wrong, inasmuch as it upholds a system of laws that selectively omits just such judicial protection against racial isolation—in schooling rather than in housing.[40]

§ 16–18. The Developing Law of School Desegregation Remedies

In *Brown v. Board of Education (Brown II)*,[1] the Supreme Court announced its decision, postponed for further argument in *Brown I*,[2] concerning the problem of appropriate relief.[3] "Because of their prox-

---

38. 334 U.S. 1 (1948), discussed in Chapter 18, infra.

39. Such contracts were not self-executing; they required judicial review and enforcement.

40. Unless a showing could have been made in Shelley that a discriminatory purpose lay behind the challenged rule, see Washington v. Davis, 426 U.S. 229 (1976), discussed in § 16–19, infra—a showing that the plaintiffs could not make persuasively in Crawford—Shelley survives as precedent after Davis *only* if the Missouri law that selectively omitted judicial protection against racial segregation could be deemed *facially* discriminatory and thus invalid even without any proof of discriminatory intent.

§ 16–18

1. 349 U.S. 294 (1955).

2. The Court had requested further argument on a number of questions, see 347 U.S. 483, 495–96 n.3 (1954).

3. Note that this section and the section which follows deal with pupil assignment remedies. By no means, however, have

either the litigants or the courts restricted their examination of equal protection violations in education to the issue of pupil segregation. The Supreme Court has ruled, for example, that students are entitled to challenge faculty segregation, Rogers v. Paul, 382 U.S. 198 (1965), and has upheld the imposition of formulas setting specific quotas for teaching assignments in order to ensure that the racial composition of each school's teaching staff equals the racial composition of all teachers in the entire system, United States v. Montgomery County Bd. of Educ., 395 U.S. 225 (1969). As the Third Circuit has held, "proper integration of faculties is as important as proper integration of schools themselves." Porcelli v. Titus, 431 F.2d 1254, 1257 (1970), cert. denied 402 U.S. 944 (1971). See also Milliken v. Bradley (II), 433 U.S. 267 (1977) (federal court may order school board to institute comprehensive programs for reading and communication skills, in-service training, testing, counseling and career guidance, as part of school desegregation decree; neither tenth nor eleventh amendment prevents federal court from ordering state officials found

imity to local conditions and the possible need for further hearings," [4] the federal district courts were delegated primary responsibility to supervise the "transition to a system of public education freed of racial discrimination." [5] The district courts were to be guided in this task by traditional equitable principles, and could take into account "the public interest in the elimination of [obstacles to desegregation] in a systematic and effective manner." [6] However, the Supreme Court, insisting that public school officials make a "prompt and reasonable start toward full compliance" with *Brown I*,[7] placed upon them the burden of showing any need for delay, and required the district courts to effect the necessary transition "with all deliberate speed." [8]

The Court's "all deliberate speed" standard described a remedy unusual in its imprecision.[9] And for some time after its promulgation, the Supreme Court offered no elaboration, leaving enforcement of the desegregation requirement to the lower courts and community politics.[10] Finally, in *Cooper v. Aaron*,[11] in an opinion signed separately by all nine justices,[12] the Court spoke out against the open and violent resistance which *Brown* was encountering in the South. In that case, the Court held that a federal district court could not grant a request of the Little Rock, Arkansas school board for a two and one-half year delay in implementing a court-approved desegregation program. The school board had sought delay because of "extreme public hostility" towards desegregation engendered by the Governor of Arkansas, who dispatched units of the Arkansas National Guard to block the school board's planned desegregation of a local high school.[13] The Court ruled that it would not hear "those immediately in charge of the school . . . assert their own good faith as a legal excuse for delay. . . . [C]onstitutional rights . . . [were] not to be sacrificed or yielded to the violence and disorder which . . . followed upon the actions of the Governor." [14]

responsible for constitutional violations to pay appropriate share of the costs of implementing the remedy).

4. 349 U.S. at 299.

5. Id.

6. Id. at 300.

7. Id.

8. Id. at 301.

9. Cf. A. Bickel, The Least Dangerous Branch 247 (1962); see also McKay, "'With All Deliberate Speed': A Study of School Desegregation," 31 N.Y.U.L.Rev. 991 (1956). The Court's rejection of petitioner's request for immediate relief in favor of the "all deliberate speed" approach engendered severe criticism. See, e.g., R. Carter, The Warren Court: A Critical Analysis 46, 52–57 (R. Sayler, B. Boyer, & R. Gooding, eds. 1969). It has been reported that the "all deliberate speed" standard was worked into the amicus brief of the United States by a former law clerk of Justice Frankfurter in response to that Justice's privately expressed concerns

about putting together a majority in Brown. See Elman & Silber, "The Solicitor General's Office, Justice Frankfurter, and Civil Rights Litigation, 1946–1960: An Oral History," 100 Harv.L.Rev. 817, 827–30 (1987). If the report is historically accurate, it signals a distressing ethical lapse.

10. As a result, delay in implementation was inevitable. Southern resistance took form in judicial hostility, legislative evasion, and popular expression of dissatisfaction. See generally, H. Rodgers and C. Bullock, Law and Social Change, Ch. 4 (1972); Bickel, "The Decade of School Desegregation: Progress and Prospects," 64 Colum.L.Rev. 193 (1964).

11. 358 U.S. 1 (1958).

12. Of the nine, Justices Brennan, Whittaker and Stewart and joined the Court since the decision in Brown II.

13. 358 U.S. at 9–10. The Governor's blockade had been broken only after the intervention of federal troops. Id. at 12.

14. Id. at 16.

In *Goss v. Board of Education*,[15] the Court expressed further impatience with the pace at which *Brown II* was being enforced. In *Goss*, the Court invalidated a procedure which allowed students initially assigned on the basis of school zone boundaries to transfer from a school where their race was in the minority to a school where their race was a majority. In voiding the plan, which the Court characterized as working only toward "perpetuation of segregation,"[16] the Court remarked that, in the years since the first *Brown* decision, the context in which *Brown* was to be interpreted had been "significantly altered."[17] And one year later, in *Griffin v. County School Board*,[18] the Court stated that "[t]here has been entirely too much deliberation and not enough speed" in enforcing the constitutional rights declared in *Brown*.[19]

Not until the Court's decision in *Green v. County School Board*[20] was the Court's emphasis on immediate action given substantive content.[21] There, focusing on the effects rather than the purpose and good faith of desegregation efforts, the Court rejected New Kent County's "freedom-of-choice" plan for desegregation permitting all students to choose the school in which they would enroll. Although refusing to rule that freedom-of-choice would be an inadequate remedy for school desegregation in every case, the Court held that, given the merely token desegregation produced by the county's plan in the three years of its operation, this particular plan "fail[ed] to provide meaningful assurance of prompt and effective disestablishment of a dual system."[22] The Court cast on the school board the burden "to come forward with a plan that promises realistically to work and promises realistically to work *now*."[23]

In the aftermath of *Green*, questions remained as to what techniques could be utilized by federal courts to implement the "at once" requirement. In *Swann v. Charlotte-Mecklenburg Board of Education*,[24]

---

15. 373 U.S. 683 (1963).

16. Id. at 686.

17. Id. at 689.

18. 377 U.S. 218 (1964).

19. Id. at 229. Litigation to desegregate the Prince Edward County school had begun thirteen years before. Rather than comply with the Supreme Court's decision to desegregate, which had been announced as consolidated with the judgment in Brown I, the county had closed its public schools. At the same time, however, it contributed grants of public funds to white children to attend private schools. In Griffin, the Court struck down the county's scheme as unconstitutionally intended to oppose desegregation. Id. at 231. See also Bradley v. School Bd., 382 U.S. 103, 105 (1965) (per curiam).

20. 391 U.S. 430 (1968).

21. In the interim, Congress had demonstrated its own concern with the lack of progress in school desegregation by enacting the Civil Rights Act of 1964, including provisions to deal with the problem through various federal agencies. See 42 U.S.C. §§ 2000 et seq.

22. 391 U.S. at 438.

23. Id. at 439. The Court's decision, requiring not only cessation of discriminatory activities, but actual disestablishment of a dual school system, in effect supported HEW guidelines issued under the 1964 Civil Rights Act, and upheld somewhat earlier in the lower courts. For HEW's "General Statement of Policies," see Price v. Denison Independent School Dist., 348 F.2d 1010, 1015 (5th Cir. 1965); see also United States v. Jefferson County Bd. of Educ., 372 F.2d 836 (5th Cir. 1966), aff'd en banc 380 F.2d 385 (5th Cir. 1967) (promulgating model decree based on HEW guidelines and binding on all district courts in circuit), cert. denied 389 U.S. 840 (1967); Dunn, "Title VI, the Guidelines and School Desegregation in the South," 53 Va.L.Rev. 42 (1967).

24. 402 U.S. 1 (1971).

the Supreme Court attempted to define broad guidelines structuring the use of pupil assignment devices as techniques for desegregating dual school systems. First the Court held that while "[t]he constitutional command to desegregate schools does not mean that every school in every community must always reflect the racial composition of the school system as a whole," [25] mathematical ratios could serve as "a useful starting point in shaping a remedy to correct past constitutional violations." [26] Further, the Court found that while a desegregation plan was not necessarily invalid if it allowed "some small number of one-race, or virtually one-race, schools within a district," [27] the existence of such schools called for close scrutiny: "[I]n a system with a history of segregation, the need for remedial criteria of sufficient specificity to assure a school authority's compliance with its constitutional duty warrants a presumption against schools that are substantially disproportionate in their racial composition." [28] Moreover, district courts were empowered to take "affirmative action in the form of remedial altering of attendance zones . . . to achieve truly nondiscriminatory [pupil] assignments." [29] Finally, the Court ruled that local authorities could use bus transportation as "a tool of school desegregation," while conceding the validity of objections to transportation of students when "the time or distance of travel is so great as to either risk the health of the children or significantly impinge on the educational process." [30]

Even after *Swann*, numerous school systems followed a procedure of totally restructuring school district lines, hoping to avoid *Brown*'s full impact. In *Wright v. Council of the City of Emporia*,[31] the Supreme Court reviewed the circumstances under which a federal court could enjoin local officials from carving out a new school district from an existing one which had not yet completed the process of dismantling a segregated system.[32] Specifically, the Court approved district court action based not so much on the magnitude of the changes in racial composition produced by dividing a county-wide school system into a

25. Id. at 24.

26. Id. at 25.

27. Id. at 26.

28. Id.

29. Id. at 28.

30. Id. at 30–31. In a companion case to Swann, the Court affirmed a lower court's invalidation of a state statute prohibiting assignment or involuntary busing of students on account of race to achieve a racial balance. See North Carolina v. Swann, 402 U.S. 43 (1971), for further discussion of busing as a remedy, see § 16–19, infra. In reaction to Swann, several dozen constitutional amendments addressed to school desegregation and busing were proposed in Congress. See "School Busing: Hearings Before Subcomm. No. 5 of the House Comm. on the Judiciary," 92d Cong., 2d Sess., ser. 32, pt. 3, at xii–xiii (1972). The executive branch supervised significant changes in the federal role in civil rights enforcement. See, e.g., Adams v. Richardson, 356 F.Supp. 92 (D.D.C. 1973) aff'd per curiam 480 F.2d 1159, 1161 (D.C. Cir. 1973) (ordering HEW to take "appropriate action to end segregation in public educational institutions receiving federal funds"). Among legal commentators, perhaps Professor Owen Fiss's reaction was the most favorable. See Fiss, "The Charlotte-Mecklenburg Case: Its Significance for Northern School Desegregation," 38 U.Chi.L.Rev. 697 (1971).

31. 407 U.S. 451 (1972).

32. See also the companion case decided with Wright, United States v. Scotland Neck Bd. of Educ., 407 U.S. 484 (1972) (relying on substantial statistical disparity in racial composition of two proposed school systems, Court overturned legislative creation of new school district as unconstitutionally impeding school desegregation process).

city system and a county system, as on the apparent consequences of the changes: [33] among other factors, the district court had found that announcement of the redistricting plan just prior to the implementation of a plan desegregating the former school system constituted an invitation to "white flight." [34]

Most judicial action dealing with school desegregation in the twenty years after *Brown I* focused on the South, where state legislatures before 1954 explicitly permitted or required the operation of dual school systems. *Keyes v. School District No. 1* [35] was the Supreme Court's first decision on school desegregation in the North. Justice Brennan's majority opinion in *Keyes* made clear that only de jure segregation, that is, "a current condition of segregation resulting from intentional state action," [36] constitutes a violation of equal protection. In *Keyes*, the Supreme Court directed a federal district court to base its decision as to whether Denver, Colorado maintained a system of de jure school segregation upon an analysis of policies and practices with respect to such factors as the location, size, and physical condition of schools.[37] Further, the Court announced that "a predicate for . . . finding . . . the existence of a dual school system" would be established where it could be shown that "school authorities [had] carried out a systematic program of segregation affecting a substantial portion of the students, schools, teachers, and facilities within the school system." [38] Finally,

33. It has been suggested that the Court couched its decision in terms of effect, rather than purpose, in a desire to avoid confrontation with the principles enunciated in Palmer v. Thompson, 403 U.S. 217 (1971), discussed in § 16–16, supra. See "The Supreme Court, 1971 Term," 86 Harv.L.Rev. 50, 62 (1972).

34. As the Supreme Court summarized the lower court's findings, the newly-created city school system would not only have a lower percentage of black students than the previous county-wide system, but would utilize the superior facilities previously restricted to whites in the days of the county's dual school system. Correspondingly, the surviving remnant of the county system would have a larger percentage of black students than the previous system, and would be required to use the inferior facilities previously allotted to blacks under the dual system. Wright, 407 U.S. at 463–66.

Note that, although school systems have had little success in evading desegregation through secession, private schools and academies with all-white enrollments mushroomed after Brown. But state and local governments attempting to aid these private schools have been successfully challenged in the courts. See, e.g., Gilmore v. Montgomery, 417 U.S. 556 (1974) (upholding federal court injunction barring city from permitting use of public recreational facilities by private segregated school groups); Norwood v. Harrison, 413 U.S.

455 (1973) (prohibiting state from lending textbooks to students in private segregated schools, under program providing books to all public and private school children). And Runyon v. McCrary, 427 U.S. 160 (1976), held that 42 U.S.C. § 1981 prohibits even privately-owned, non-subsidized white-only schools. See § 5–13, supra. In Bob Jones University v. United States, 461 U.S. 574 (1983), the Court sustained the IRS policy of denying tax exempt status to private colleges and schools that practice racially discriminatory admissions standards, whether on the basis of their religious doctrine or otherwise: "the government has a fundamental, overriding interest in eradicating racial discrimination in education," and this interest "substantially outweighs whatever burden denial of tax benefits places on petitioners' exercise of their religious beliefs." Bob Jones, 461 U.S. at 604. See Chapter 14, supra.

35. 413 U.S. 189 (1973).

36. Id. at 205.

37. Id. at 201–03.

38. Id. at 201. As the Court restated its holding, "a finding of intentionally segregative board actions in a meaningful portion of a school system . . . creates a presumption that other segregated schooling within the system is not adventitious." Id. at 208. Note also the Court's conclusion that the district court erred in separating blacks and Mexican-Americans for

of the substantive violation of the plaintiff's rights: "Once the nature of the defendant's wrong is determined—defeat of plaintiff's expectations, retention of a benefit, or frustration of a reliance interest—the relief follows as a matter of course." [10]   But in a school desegregation case, the remedy takes the form of a judicial decree restructuring an institution and, often, establishing a continuing regime of oversight. Myriad particular circumstances must be taken into account by the district judge in framing the affirmative injunction, thereby drastically expanding the discretionary component of the relief. As Professor Abram Chayes has argued, "This discretion makes it impossible to identify a unique remedial regime that follows ineluctably from and is measured by the determination of substantive liability." [11]

By demanding a tight fit between the remedy and the narrowly-defined right in the face of extensive de jure segregation, the Court for the first time rationalized a segregated result in a case where a constitutional violation had been found to exist. The Court offered no explanation in *Milliken* for why it thought district boundaries were sacrosanct [12]—a conclusion especially puzzling in the wake of the Court's repeated rulings that neighborhood school assignments enjoy no such sacred status as emblems of local autonomy and community control of public schools. The plaintiffs were to be trapped within the city's boundaries, without even an opportunity to demand that those boundary lines be justified as either rational or innocently nonrational. [13] Thus *Milliken* became the first case in which the Supreme Court overruled a desegregation decree, only three years after *Swann*—the case in which the Court had first reviewed such a decree and upheld the sweeping remedial power of the federal district courts. [14]

With its emphasis on the significance of local control over the operation of schools, [15] and its caution regarding the essentially political character of the role played by federal courts in devising and enforcing metropolitan school desegregation, [16] *Milliken* signaled the Supreme Court's mounting hesitation in the school desegregation area. That trend was confirmed by the Court's opinion in *Pasadena City Board of Education v. Spangler*, [17] which held that a school board that has

10. Chayes, "Foreword: Public Law Litigation and the Burger Court," 96 Harv.L. Rev. 4, 45 (1982).

11. Id. at 46.

12. 418 U.S. at 741–42.

13. See Freeman, "Legitimizing Racial Discrimination Through Antidiscrimination Law: A Critical Review of Supreme Court Doctrine," 62 Minn.L.Rev. 1049, 1109 (1978).

14. For a comprehensive and enlightening account of the Milliken litigation by the plaintiffs' counsel, see R. Dimond, Beyond Busing: Inside the Challenge to Urban Segregation (1985).

15. See 418 U.S. at 741–44. Cf. Justice White's dissenting opinion, id. at 778–79 (criticizing majority's "talismanic invocation" of desirability of local control and

suggesting that control by a community of parents is possible as long as their children attend the same school, whether or not they all happen to live in the school's immediate neighborhood); see also Justice Marshall's dissenting opinion, id. at 793–97 (emphasizing actuality of "[c]entralized state control" over education). Note that some black leaders attribute a different significance to local control over the operation of schools, arguing that predominantly black-populated and black-controlled local schools may better serve black community interests than will the lengthy and troublesome process of desegregation. See Professor Derrick Bell's careful survey of alternatives to integrated schools in Race, Racism and American Law, ch. 7 (2d ed. 1980).

16. See 418 U.S. at 743–44.

17. 427 U.S. 424 (1976).

initially complied with a court desegregation order specifying the proportion of minority students permitted in each of its schools cannot be required to alter attendance zones each year in response to local population changes. Justice Rehnquist's majority opinion measured the district court's continued jurisdiction to supervise student assignments against dicta in *Swann v. Charlotte-Mecklenburg Board of Education.*[18] Conceding that the Pasadena Board may not have achieved the unitary school system mandated by *Swann,*[19] the Court held nonetheless that the district court had fully performed its function by once implementing a "racially neutral attendance pattern";[20] the Court found no authority for the district court's attempting to ensure the maintenance of a desired racial mix "in perpetuity."[21]

The notion advanced in *Spangler* that prior unconstitutional discrimination can be erased by single moves marks a drawing-back from desegregation cases advocating broad equitable power in the district courts to supervise the removal of "all vestiges" of state-imposed discrimination.[22] Another avenue for showing the appropriateness of interdistrict remedies, through an inference of racial motivation behind suburban refusals to build low income housing and to zone areas for high density,[23] has also been significantly, though not completely, blocked by the Supreme Court.[24] In *Hills v. Gautreaux,*[25] the Court upheld the authority of a federal court to require a federal housing agency to correct the effects of its inner-city constitutional violations by undertaking remedial efforts on a metropolis-wide scale. At the same time, however, the Court confirmed its decision in *Milliken v. Bradley,*[26] indicating that an interdistrict remedy in a school desegregation case could touch only school districts which had either themselves committed or been affected by a constitutional violation.

In *Gautreaux*, the Court found insufficient evidence to support the conclusion that maintenance of a racially discriminatory program of public housing in the inner city of Chicago by the Department of Housing and Urban Development (HUD) had produced a segregative impact on the suburbs sufficient to form the basis, under *Milliken*, for a judicial remedy including those suburbs.[27] Nevertheless, the Court

---

18. 402 U.S. 1 (1971).

19. See 427 U.S. at 436.

20. Id. at 436–37.

21. Id. But see Justice Marshall's dissenting opinion. Id. at 441–44.

22. See, e.g., Swann v. Charlotte-Mecklenburg Bd. of Educ., 402 U.S. 1, 15 (1971); Green v. County School Bd., 391 U.S. 430, 437–38 & n.4 (1968).

23. This approach recognizes that the various agencies of government are not autonomous entities whose actions effect separate and independent results. See Kushner & Werner, "Metropolitan Desegregation after Milliken v. Bradley: The Case for Land Use Litigation Strategies," 24 Cath.U.L.Rev. 187 (1975). The largely statutory law of housing, voting, and employment discrimination is beyond the

scope of this book. The impact of Title VII (Equal Employment Opportunity) of the Civil Rights Act of 1964, 42 U.S.C. §§ 2000e et seq.; of Title VIII (Fair Housing) of the Civil Rights Act of 1968, id. §§ 3601 et seq.; of the Voting Rights Act of 1965, id. §§ 1971 et seq.; and of earlier legislation, is discussed in light of federal judicial interpretations in D. Bell, Race, Racism and American Law, ch. 7 (2d ed. 1980).

24. See Village of Arlington Heights v. Metropolitan Housing Dev't Corp., 429 U.S. 252 (1977).

25. 425 U.S. 284 (1976).

26. 418 U.S. 717 (1974).

27. 425 U.S. at 294–95 n.11. The role of governmental institutions other than school boards in fostering residential segre-

concluded that *Milliken* did not bar metropolitan relief in *Gautreaux*.[28] While it is not entirely clear why the Court thought a metropolitan remedy appropriate in the absence of a showing that the entire metropolitan area had been affected by HUD's unconstitutional conduct,[29] *Gautreaux* does make clear that the Court will apply a high standard of proof for the *Milliken* test of "inter-district violation or effect." Moreover, the Court's reiteration of caution against remedies with "coercive effect" on local governmental units [30] implies increased difficulties for plaintiffs seeking broad desegregation decrees across district lines.

Finally, the Court has indicated its unwillingness to allow lower court reliance on the disproportionate impact doctrine in cases of school desegregation. In *United States v. Texas Education Agency*,[31] the Fifth Circuit invoked the traditional doctrine of tort law that a person "intends the natural and foreseeable consequences of his actions" [32] to create a presumption that a school district that is segregated in fact is intentionally segregated. In view of that rule, as well as a showing that it was the city school authorities' official policy to assign students to schools closest to their homes and that the city had a definitely segregated housing pattern, the court held that plaintiffs had established a prima facie case of de jure segregation of Mexican-Americans.[33] But the Supreme Court remanded the case [34] for reconsideration in light of its 1976 decision in *Washington v. Davis*.[35] In *Davis* the Court interpreted a number of its recent decisions as establishing "the basic equal protection principle that the invidious quality of a law claimed to be racially discriminatory must ultimately be traced to a racially discriminatory purpose." [36] Despite disparate impact on an acknowledged suspect class, the government need meet only the rational basis standard in the absence of a showing that an intent to create the disparate impact at issue in fact animated the promulgation of the challenged rule or policy.[37]

School integration cases decided in the wake of *Washington v. Davis* at first appeared to continue the trend of retrenchment begun in *Milliken I*. In *Dayton Bd. of Educ. v. Brinkman*,[38] the Court voted

gation, and the details of the Gautreaux litigation in particular, are canvassed in R. Dimond, Beyond Busing: Inside the Challenge to Urban Segregation (1985).

28. The Court remanded the case to the District Court for consideration of the nature and scope of the remedial order to be entered. Id. at 306.

29. It may be possible to understand the Court's result by applying the analysis developed in Keyes v. School Dist. No.1, 413 U.S. 189 (1973), where the Court approved a district-wide remedy on the basis of evidence showing a less than district-wide violation. See "The Supreme Court, 1975 Term," 90 Harv.L.Rev. 56, 226–28 (1976). Moreover, as the Court stressed, the remedy in Gautreaux did not automatically entail ordering local housing, school, or other public authorities to restructure their operations or even to alter their poli-

cies. 425 U.S. at 303–06; cf. Milliken v. Bradley, 418 U.S. at 742–43 n.20; but see 418 U.S. at 793–97 (Marshall, J., dissenting). See also National League of Cities v. Usery, 426 U.S. 833 (1976), discussed in Chapter 5, supra.

30. 425 U.S. at 305.

31. 532 F.2d 380 (5th Cir. 1976) (Wisdom, J.).

32. Id. at 388.

33. Id. at 389–92.

34. Austin Independent School Dist. v. United States, 429 U.S. 990 (1976) (mem.).

35. 426 U.S. 229 (1976).

36. Id. at 240.

37. Davis and its implications are discussed at greater length in § 16–20, infra.

38. 433 U.S. 406 (1977).

8–0 [39] to vacate a school desegregation decree and remand for reconsideration in light of *Davis*. The Court held that the sweeping remedy ordered by the district court was unjustified by the evidence of what the lower courts called a "cumulative violation" of the equal protection clause.[40] Evidence of racial imbalance in Dayton's schools was not enough to establish a violation without a showing that the school board had acted with the intent to segregate.[41] The situation in *Dayton* was complicated by the fact that, shortly after the school board had admitted to segregationist practices, the newly elected membership of that body voted to rescind its *mea culpa*. The lower courts deemed that rescission to be a violation of the fourteenth amendment in itself, but the Supreme Court, speaking through Justice Rehnquist, opined that such a conclusion was of "dubious merit." [42] Such a rescission could constitute a violation only if the school board had at the time been under an affirmative constitutional duty to desegregate; if there were no duty to make a resolution admitting guilt, it could not be a violation to rescind the same.

In *Dayton* the Court once again insisted on "a geometric congruence of right and remedy." [43] The district court was instructed on remand to "determine how much incremental segregative effect [the school board's isolated] violations had on the racial distribution of the Dayton school population as presently constituted, when that distribution is compared to what it would have been in the absence of such constitutional violations. The remedy must be designed to redress that difference. . . . ." [44]

Yet when the *Dayton* case reached the Supreme Court for the second time, the Court upheld the judgment of the court of appeals that the district court had erred in failing to find that the school board had perpetuated a dual school system. *Dayton II* [45] was a companion case to *Columbus Bd. of Educ. v. Penick*.[46] Justice White, author of the Court's opinion in *Washington v. Davis*, wrote for the Court in both cases.

In *Dayton II* a sharply divided Court [47] agreed with the appellate court's conclusion that, because the board had operated an intentionally segregated dual school system at the time *Brown v. Bd. of Education* [48] was decided in 1954, it was under a continuing affirmative duty to eradicate the effects of that system.[49] The apparent barrier to systemwide relief posed by *Dayton I* was overcome by resort to *Keyes v. School District No.1*,[50] where the Court had held that isolated acts of official discrimination were sufficient to shift to the school board the

---

39. Justice Marshall took no part in the case.

40. 433 U.S. at 418.

41. Id. at 413.

42. Id. at 413–14.

43. Chayes, "Foreword: Public Law Litigation and the Burger Court," 96 Harv.L. Rev. 4, 49 (1982).

44. 433 U.S. at 420.

45. Dayton Bd. of Educ. v. Brinkman, 443 U.S. 526 (1979).

46. 443 U.S. 449 (1979).

47. Justice White was joined by Justices Brennan, Marshall, Blackmun, and Stevens. Justice Stewart, joined by Chief Justice Burger, dissented. Justices Powell and Rehnquist also filed dissenting opinions.

48. 347 U.S. 483 (1954).

49. 443 U.S. at 536–37.

50. 413 U.S. 189 (1973).

burden of proving that the remainder of its decision-making was untainted by racial animus. Since the school board was, unsurprisingly, unable to meet that onerous burden, the Court was able to bootstrap the board's isolated discriminatory acts to justify a finding that the discrimination was systemwide, which in turn provided the basis for systemwide relief.[51]

The decision in *Columbus Board of Education v. Penick* blurred the line between de facto and de jure segregation. Again writing for the Court,[52] Justice White found a violation of the fourteenth amendment even though the City of Columbus had had no statutorily-mandated segregation in this century. Although disparate racial impact and foreseeable consequences do not, without more, establish a constitutional violation, they are nevertheless fertile ground for drawing inferences of segregative intent.[53] Justice White explicitly endorsed the district court's understanding of his opinion for the Court in *Washington v. Davis*,[54] and agreed that the practices employed by the Columbus school board could not "reasonably be explained without reference to racial concerns." [55] While the Court claimed [56] to be applying the reasoning of *Keyes v. School District No.1*,[57] an argument can be made that the *Columbus* Court in fact relaxed the standards set forth in *Keyes* for imposing systemwide remedies on the basis of inferred causal links between particular past and present practices and the actual racial composition of particular schools.[58] The scope of remedies acceptable to the Supreme Court thus varies with the shifting of the tenuous majorities that have often attended school desegregation cases. Arguably, the only consistent message the foregoing precedents bear is that there is no reliable way to reason from the "right" to an integrated school system established by *Brown I* to the contours of the remedy appropriate in any particular set of circumstances.[59]

The firmness with which the Supreme Court has nonetheless asserted its rationales for limiting the reach of judicial remedies in the school desegregation field—the neighborhood school policy, the respect for district lines, the de jure requirement, the necessity of proven

---

51. Dayton II, 443 U.S. at 537. The right-remedy link forged in Milliken I was just as easily decoupled in Milliken II, Milliken v. Bradley, 433 U.S. 267 (1977). Denied the power to impose an interdistrict remedy in Milliken I, the district judge augmented his desegregation plan for the Detroit school district with educational enrichment programs and required the State of Michigan to foot half the bill. The state objected to the scope of the decree, arguing that, "since the constitutional violation . . . was the unlawful segregation of students on the basis of race, the court's decree must be limited to remedying unlawful pupil assignments." Id. at 281. The Supreme Court simply disagreed, quoting Milliken I while stepping around it: "the remedy does not 'exceed' the violation if the remedy is tailored to cure 'the condi-

tion that offends the Constitution.'" Id. at 282.

52. The majority comprised the same Justices who constituted the majority in Dayton II, but Chief Justice Burger and Justice Stewart concurred in the judgment.

53. Columbus, 443 U.S. at 464–65.

54. Id. at 464.

55. Id. at 461.

56. Id. at 467–68.

57. 413 U.S. 189 (1973).

58. See 443 U.S. at 490–91, 500–01, 506–07 (Rehnquist, J., dissenting).

59. See Chayes, "Foreword: Public Law Litigation and the Burger Court," 96 Harv. L.Rev. 4, 50–51 (1982).

discriminatory intent—is unfortunate.[60] The arguments in favor of the Court's expanding, rather than contracting, the judicial role seem powerful even with respect to de facto segregation.[61] The harms of both de facto and de jure discrimination are similar, if not identical: racially specific harm to members of politically less-powerful minority groups, with discriminatory intent much more often present than provable, and with even truly unintended racial consequences often reflecting unconscious bias and blindness traceable to a legacy of racial subordination initially decreed by law. Until our society's widespread racial prejudice recedes, or until minority members acquire sufficient political leverage to ensure fully equal justice through the political process, judicially compelled integration may be the only acceptable response to the high probability of governmental prejudice and corruption behind all segregation.[62]

Most unfortunate of all is the Court's unwillingness even to consider—let alone to counteract—the role of government agencies other than school boards in promoting and perpetuating the residential segregation that will inevitably undermine the effort to eliminate racial isolation in the public schools.[63] Unless the local, state and federal agencies whose policies and programs contribute to residential segregation are held responsible and made to bear their share of the financial and other burdens of achieving integration, school boards, whether cooperative or not, will appear to be hapless scapegoats, and the children who are bused about will seem mere pawns in a game that always ends in a draw.[64] If all vestiges of racial isolation in the public schools are to be "eliminated root and branch," [65] the federal courts will require discretion to formulate remedies as complex, continuing and wide-ranging as the problem they confront.

Little can be said in reply to Justice Marshall's trenchant observation that, from *Milliken* onward, the Court has invoked its opposition to

60. See Professor Owen Fiss's discussion of what he terms the Court's hesitant and flawed move towards a result-oriented approach in the second decade after Brown, in "The Fate of an Idea Whose Time has Come: Antidiscrimination Law in the Second Decade After Brown v. Board of Education," 41 U.Chi.L.Rev. 742 (1974).

61. See Goodman, "De Facto School Segregation: A Constitutional and Empirical Analysis," 60 Cal.L.Rev. 275 (1972).

62. See Professor Ronald Dworkin's argument that uncertainty about causation is insufficient to justify denying constitutional remedy to de facto segregation. Dworkin, "Social Sciences and Constitutional Rights: the Consequences of Uncertainty," 6 J. of L. & Educ. 3 (1977).

63. The Court may eventually be forced to confront the problem it has been ducking ever since Swann. In late 1985 a district court held the City of Yonkers, New York, its school board and its Community Development Agency liable on *both* school and housing segregation claims: "It is indisputable that a hypothetical single state agency which controls the operation of, and engages in the racial segregation of, both housing and schools—by confining for racial reasons the city's subsidized housing to one section of the city, while simultaneously adhering to a neighborhood school policy of student assignment—can be held liable for such conduct. It is inconceivable that state action may be fractionalized such that two state agencies could be permitted collectively to engage in precisely the same conduct, yet avoid legal accountability for the identical result." United States v. Yonkers Bd. of Educ., 611 F.Supp. 730 (S.D.N.Y. 1985).

64. See Days, Book Review, "School Desegregation Law in the 1980's: Why Isn't Anybody Laughing?" 95 Yale L.J. 1737, 1753–64 (1986).

65. Green v. County School Bd., 391 U.S. 430, 438 (1968); Swann v. Bd. of Educ., 402 U.S. 1, 15 (1971).

political management by the federal judiciary in school cases in the service of a politics of its own, reflecting more a "perceived public mood" than "neutral principles of law." [66] "In the short run, it may seem to be the easier course to allow our great metropolitan areas to be divided up each into two cities—one white, the other black—but it is a course, I predict, our people will ultimately regret." [67]

Even if the twists and turns the law has taken from *Green* and *Swann* to *Columbus/Dayton II* could be satisfactorily explained in purely doctrinal or precedential terms, it would remain a fact that the evolution of school desegregation law reflects a deep-seated frustration on the part of the Supreme Court.[68] The Justices are mindful that, a quarter of a century after *Brown I*, many school districts had not even begun meaningful desegregation efforts. But several of the Court's members evidently harbor at least a nagging suspicion that the passage of time has ingrained residential segregation so deeply into the urban landscape that the solution to the problem lies beyond the power of school boards *and* federal courts.

66. Milliken v. Bradley, 418 U.S. at 814 (Marshall, J., dissenting).

67. Id. at 814–15 (Marshall, J., dissenting).

68. Sometimes the Court reveals as much about its current uncertainty or future direction by the cases it declines to hear as by the cases it decides. In 1980, the Court narrowly denied certiorari in Delaware State Bd. of Ed. v. Evans, 446 U.S. 923 (1980), and in Estes v. Dallas NAACP, 444 U.S. 437 (1980). In Evans, the district court had ordered dissolution of eleven independent school boards and the substitution of a single, court-appointed board for an entire metropolitan county. Justice Rehnquist, joined by Justices Stewart and Powell, dissented, bitterly criticizing the lack of detailed findings of segregative impact to support "a countywide remedy more Draconian than any other approved by this Court." 446 U.S. at 923. In Estes, where the Court dismissed its writ of certiorari as improvidently granted, Justice Powell filed a lengthy dissent, joined by Justices Stewart and Rehnquist, in which he bemoaned the lost opportunity to confront the problem of busing orders which stimulate resegregation. Justice Powell argued that busing to remedy de facto segregation often results in white flight, thereby converting "one-race schools" into "one-race school systems," 444 U.S. at 450, and complained that lower courts were ignoring the ban on additional remedies absent further segregation by the state set out in Pasadena City Bd. of Ed. v. Spangler, 427 U.S. 424 (1976). See 444 U.S. at 448–49.

In 1986, the Court again denied certiorari in two cases, thereby declining to resolve an apparent circuit conflict on whether school systems may abandon court-ordered busing plans after they have achieved unitary status. See 107 S.Ct. 420 (1986). There were no dissenting opinions, although Justice White would have granted the writ in both cases. In one of those cases, Riddick v. School Bd., 784 F.2d 521 (4th Cir. 1986), the circuit court had allowed the Norfolk school board to scrap busing and return a third of the system's elementary schools to one-race status. The court of appeals imposed on those who would continue busing the burden of proving that the adoption of a neighborhood school student assignment plan, ten years after unitary status had been achieved and court supervision had ceased, had been racially motivated. The court of appeals found that Norfolk's goal of creating enough majority-white schools to stem white flight was legitimate. Dowell v. Board of Ed., 795 F.2d 1516 (10th Cir. 1986), the other case the Supreme Court declined to hear, grew out of the Oklahoma City school board's unilateral abandonment of the court-ordered busing plan that had been the basis for a 1977 judicial finding that the system had achieved unitary status. The court of appeals, stressing the duty "not only to achieve, but to maintain" desegregation, ordered the district court to force the resumption of busing unless the board proved that it had led to "extreme and unexpected" hardship.

§ 16–20. The Problem of Discriminatory Purpose: When Reservations About Remedies Masquerade as Questions About the Existence of Constitutional Violations

The Supreme Court's reservations about the efficacy and legitimacy of intrusive federal injunctive remedies may have first surfaced in the school desegregation context,[1] but they influence all equal protection clause jurisprudence in fundamental—if sometimes subtle—ways. Indeed, these concerns may be the wellspring of the doctrine of discriminatory purpose established in *Washington v. Davis*.[2]

The doctrine that facially race-neutral governmental action will be strictly scrutinized only if it is discriminatory in *both* impact and purpose began to emerge in the Supreme Court's decisions in *White v. Regester*[3] and *Jefferson v. Hackney*.[4] In *Regester* the Court reviewed the use of multimember districts in a reapportionment plan for the House of the Texas Legislature, concluding, from the "totality of the circumstances,"[5] that such districts were "being used invidiously to cancel out or minimize the voting strength" of blacks and Mexican-Americans in several counties.[6] The low incidence of successful candidates from these groups, their depressed socioeconomic status, and the residue of a long history of official discrimination combined to persuade the Court that the apportionment plan was insufficient to represent the minority populations.[7]

Jefferson v. Hackney dealt not with allegations of bias in the structure of the political process but with claims of prejudice in a specific political outcome. Recipients of Aid to Families With Dependent Children (AFDC) challenged the system whereby Texas, in allocating its welfare funds among persons with acknowledged needs, covered

§ 16–20

1. See Milliken v. Bradley (Milliken I), 418 U.S. 717 (1974), discussed in § 16–19, supra.

2. 426 U.S. 229 (1976). Justice White delivered the opinion of the Court, joined by Chief Justice Burger and Justices Blackmun, Powell, Rehnquist and Stevens, and joined in great part by Justice Stewart. Justice Stevens filed a concurring opinion to stress his belief that the "line between discriminatory purpose and discriminatory impact is not nearly as bright, and perhaps not quite as critical, as the reader of the Court's opinion might assume." Id. at 254. Justice Brennan, joined by Justice Marshall, dissented without reaching the constitutional issues. Justice Brennan disagreed with the Court's application of statutory civil rights standards to the case since, as the Court agreed, id. at 238–39, it was "plain error" to apply statutory standards because the complaint was filed before Title VII of the Civil Rights Act was made applicable to public employers and was never amended to include a claim under that or any other statutory provision. Id. at 257 (Brennan, J., dissenting).

3. 412 U.S. 755 (1973). Justice White delivered the opinion of the Court, which was unanimous with respect to the racial vote-dilution claims discussed here.

4. 406 U.S. 535 (1972). Justice Rehnquist wrote for the Court, joined by Chief Justice Burger and Justices White, Blackmun, and Powell, and joined in part by Justice Stewart. Justice Douglas, joined by Justice Brennan, dissented from the Court's analysis of federal welfare statutes. Justice Marshall, joined by Justice Brennan, also dissented on statutory grounds, and expressed doubts that the state decision to under-fund AFDC programs was unrelated to the race of the recipients; 87% of the recipients were blacks or chicanos, and the record was replete with admissions that AFDC was funded at a lower level than other aid programs because it was politically unpopular. Id. at 575 (Marshall, J., dissenting).

5. 412 U.S. at 769.

6. Id. at 765. See Chapter 13, supra.

7. Id. at 766–70.

a lower percentage of "need" for AFDC recipients than for recipients of aid for the aged and infirm. The claimed violation of equal protection was that the short-changed AFDC recipients, in comparison to the other recipient groups, were disproportionately black or Mexican-American.[8] Justice Rehnquist's opinion for the Court, applying "the traditional standard of review,"[9] rejected plaintiffs' "naked statistical argument,"[10] and held that a statistical deviation alone would not suffice to invite close judicial scrutiny; otherwise, "each difference in treatment among the grant classes [would be rendered suspect], however lacking in racial motivation and however . . . rational the treatment might be."[11] As with a governmental decision to develop a luxurious shopping mall instead of low-rent housing, the fact that a different choice in *Jefferson* might have given more aid to minorities imposed only the most minimal burden of explanation. The Court blanched at the thought of "second-guess[ing] state officials charged with the difficult responsibility of allocating limited public welfare funds among the myriad of potential recipients."[12]

While it might have been possible to limit the holding of *Jefferson* to the special context of resource-allocation decisions,[13] this possibility was foreclosed by the Court's opinion in *Washington v. Davis*. That case involved a challenge to a verbal skills examination known as Test 21, used by the District of Columbia police department to screen applicants for its training program. Unsuccessful black applicants alleged that the test, which had a failure rate four times as high for blacks as for whites, violated the equal protection component of the fifth amendment due process clause.[14] Citing a number of its recent equal protection decisions including *Jefferson v. Hackney*, the Court announced "the basic equal protection principle that the invidious quality of a law claimed to be racially discriminatory must ultimately be traced to a racially discriminatory purpose."[15] Test 21 on its face was neutral with respect to race; therefore, absent proof that the test was chosen with a design to produce racially disproportionate results, blacks could no more cry foul than could the white applicants who also failed.[16] Disparate impact on an acknowledged suspect class, without more, required only judicial review under the rational basis standard. In truth, even rationality was not demanded: *no* evidence was offered to show that Test 21 related to qualities or abilities relevant to police work, or that it correlated with job performance after the completion of training.[17] It was sufficient for the *Davis* majority that Test 21 was

---

8. 406 U.S. at 538.

9. Id. at 549. The Court found it "not irrational for the State to believe that the young are more adaptable than the sick and elderly, especially because the latter have less hope of improving their situation in the years remaining to them." Id.

10. Id. at 548.

11. Id.

12. Id. at 551 (citation omitted).

13. Cf. Dandridge v. Williams, 397 U.S. 471 (1970) (upholding a "reasonable" state program imposing $250 monthly ceiling on AFDC grants to individual families, regardless of family size or need). See §§ 16–51, 16–52, 16–57, infra.

14. 426 U.S. at 237.

15. Id. at 240.

16. Id. at 246.

17. 426 U.S. at 262 (Brennan, J., dissenting); see also Davis v. Washington, 512 F.2d 956, 963 n.38 (D.C.Cir. 1975).

said to be effective in predicting whether applicants would be able to pass the training examinations given at the end of the course [18]—even though *everyone* passed because, as a matter of policy, any recruit having difficulty was given assistance until he succeeded.[19]

The precise weight that evidence of disproportionate impact on one race should receive was left uncertain. Nor did the Court give many clues as to just what sort of proof it expected of the precise role of prejudiced motives in a given governmental action. Yet the Supreme Court reaffirmed its deferential stand in *Village of Arlington Heights v. Metropolitan Housing Development Corp.*[20] In *Arlington Heights*, a non-profit real estate developer who had contracted to purchase a tract of land in order to build racially integrated low- and moderate-income housing filed suit for injunctive relief, alleging that the local authorities' refusal to change the tract from a single-family to a multi-family zoning classification was racially discriminatory. Citing *Washington v. Davis*, the Supreme Court reiterated its ruling that proof of racially discriminatory intent or purpose is required to show a violation of the equal protection clause.[21] Noting that the "historical background of the [governmental] decision is one evidentiary source" for determining whether invidious discriminatory purpose was a motivating factor,[22] the Court found that, although the impact of the Village's decision "[did] arguably bear more heavily on racial minorities, . . . there [was] little about the sequence of events leading up to the decision that would spark suspicion."[23] Instead, the Court accepted the "neutral" motive offered by the Village based on the Village's "undeniabl[e] commit[ment] to single-family homes as its dominant residential land

18. 426 U.S. at 251 n.17. The Court also remarked that any inference of racial prejudice in use of the test was negated by the affirmative efforts of the police department to recruit blacks. Id. at 246.

19. 426 U.S. at 263 n.7 (Brennan, J., dissenting). As one commentator summed it up: "[T]here was no proof that the test given at the end of the training program measured anything taught in that program, even assuming that the program was related to future performance as a police officer. The most that was established was that [Test 21] correlated with another test, which in itself is hardly surprising. But that other test may or may not measure something, which something, even if measured, may or may not have anything to do with the job for which the training program is supposed to prepare those who pass [Test 21]." Freeman, "Legitimizing Racial Discrimination Through Antidiscrimination Law: A Critical Review of Supreme Court Doctrine," 62 Minn.L.Rev. 1049, 1116 (1978).

20. 429 U.S. 252 (1977). Justice Powell wrote the opinion of the Court, joined by Chief Justice Burger and Justices Stewart, Blackmun, and Rehnquist. Justice Mar-

shall, joined by Justice Brennan, concurred in part, dissenting only from the Court's decision to apply the Washington v. Davis test to the record before it, rather than remanding for further proceedings. Id. at 271–72. Justice White, author of the Court's opinion in Davis, dissented on similar grounds. Id. at 272. For detailed analysis of the issues involved in litigation over segregated housing, see R. Dimond, Beyond Busing: Inside the Challenge to Urban Segregation (1985) (discussing Hills v. Gautreaux, 425 U.S. 284 (1976)); McGee, "Illusion and Contradiction in the Quest for a Desegregated Metropolis," 1976 U.Ill.L. Forum 948 (1976).

21. 429 U.S. at 264–65.

22. Id. at 267.

23. Id. at 269. Contrast Palmer v. Thompson, 403 U.S. 217 (1971), discussed in § 16–16, supra. Although the formal obituary has not yet been published, Palmer has been quietly but unmistakably buried. See, e.g., the Court's treatment of Palmer in Hunter v. Underwood, 471 U.S. 222, 232 (1985); Palmore v. Sidoti, 466 U.S. 429, 433 (1984); Washington v. Davis, 426 U.S. 229, 243 (1976).

use." [24]   Accordingly, the Court held that respondents had failed to carry their burden of proof, and that any inference of discriminatory "ultimate effect" was without independent constitutional significance. [25]

Just what constituted a "discriminatory purpose" remained less than obvious. The Court began to formulate a more precise definition in *Personnel Administrator of Massachusetts v. Feeney.* [26] A female state employee challenged the civil service's absolute veterans' preference, which had the inevitable effect—since military service is a male province—of benefitting men almost exclusively. The Court admitted that it "would be disingenuous to say that the adverse consequences of this legislation for women were unintended, in the sense that they were not volitional or in the sense that they were not foreseeable." [27] But an invidious intent to discriminate constitutes more than mere volition or an awareness of inevitable consequences. The Court ruled that discriminatory purpose "implies that the decisionmaker . . . selected or reaffirmed a particular course of action at least in part 'because of', not merely 'in spite of,' its adverse effects upon an identifiable group." [28] This does not mean that the foreseeability of disparate impact is irrelevant to the intent inquiry. The Court noted that, if a facially-neutral rule or policy inevitably has adverse consequences on a group, one may draw "a strong inference that the adverse effects were desired." [29] Practical results can therefore be cogent evidence of what the government "is up to." [30] In the school desegregation context, for example, the Court has observed that "[a]dherence to a particular policy or practice, 'with full knowledge of the predictable effects of such adherence upon racial imbalance in a school system, is one factor among many others which may be considered by a court in determining whether an inference of segregative intent should be drawn.' " [31]

The discriminatory purpose requirement was expressly extended to the fifteenth amendment in *City of Mobile v. Bolden,* [32] which involved a challenge to a multimember district apportionment plan for Mobile's

---

24. 429 U.S. at 269. For a critique of the "neutrality" of such a rationale, see § 16–58, infra.

25. 429 U.S. at 271.

26. 442 U.S. 256 (1979).

27. Id. at 278.

28. Id. at 279 (emphasis added). Justice Marshall, joined by Justice Brennan, dissented. Justice Marshall noted that the veterans' preference had for 70 years contained an exception for those jobs "especially calling for women," and the state legislature—well aware of what it was doing—had thereby created a gender-based civil service hierarchy, with women relegated to low-paying clerical and secretarial jobs. Id. at 285. "Such a statutory scheme both reflects and perpetuates precisely the kind of archaic assumptions about women's roles which we have previously held invalid." Id.

29. Id. at 279 n.25.

30. Id. at 279 n.24. See also Washington v. Davis, 426 U.S. at 254 (Stevens, J., concurring) (implying that, in practice, the meaning of the discriminatory intent requirement will turn on how great a statistical disparity is required to trigger a burden of explanation, and how readily the Court will accept such explanations as the state may offer).

31. Columbus Bd. of Educ. v. Penick, 443 U.S. 449, 465 (1979). There, the Court affirmed the trial court's conclusion that the Columbus school board's practices "could not 'reasonably be explained without reference to racial concerns.' " Id. at 461. See also Dayton Bd. of Educ. v. Brinkman (Dayton II), 443 U.S. 526, 537–38 (1979). These cases are discussed in § 16–19, supra.

32. 446 U.S. 55 (1980).

city commissioners. Comparing the facts to those of *White v. Regester*,[33] the district court found an unconstitutional dilution of black voting strength and ordered the replacement of the city commission form of government by a mayor and a 9-member city council elected from single-member districts.[34] The Supreme Court reversed. A plurality of the Court [35] held that racial prejudice is a necessary ingredient of a fifteenth amendment violation: [36] "where the character of a law is readily explainable on grounds apart from race, as would nearly always be true where, as here, an entire system of local governance is brought into question, disproportionate impact alone cannot be decisive. . . ." [37]

Justice White, the author of the Court's opinions in both *Regester* and *Davis*, dissented, arguing that the plurality had completely ignored the principle that "an invidious discriminatory principle can be inferred from objective factors." [38] In *Mobile*, as in *Regester*, the plaintiffs adduced evidence of a dearth of successful minority candidates,[39] a pattern of persistent governmental neglect and prejudice,[40] and a history of statewide official racial discrimination.[41] By refusing to consider all of these factors together, instead viewing them seriatim and in isolation, the plurality failed to follow the "totality of circumstances" test established in *Regester* to ensure that the "design and impact" of a challenged electoral plan be appraised "in the light of past and present reality, political and otherwise." [42]

Regardless of what precisely is needed to establish the existence of a discriminatory purpose, it seems singularly inappropriate to apply the test at all in voting rights cases. As Justice Marshall pointed out in

33. 412 U.S. 755 (1973).

34. Bolden v. Mobile, 423 F.Supp. 384 (S.D.Ala.1976).

35. Justice Stewart wrote for himself, Chief Justice Burger, and Justices Powell and Rehnquist.

36. 446 U.S. at 62. Relief was denied under the fourteenth amendment on the same ground. Id. at 66–67.

37. Id. at 70. Justice Stevens concurred in the judgment on the ground that no constitutional violation had been established, arguing that the "objective effects of the political decision" rather than the subjective intent of the decisionmakers should be sufficient to establish a violation. Id. at 90. Justice Stevens has consistently argued that inquiries into government intent tend to be both unrealistic and irrelevant. See, e.g., his concurrence in Washington v. Davis, 426 U.S. 229, 253 (1976) ("A law conscripting clerics should not be invalidated because an atheist voted for it.").

38. Mobile v. Bolden, 446 U.S. at 95 (White, J., dissenting). In separate dissents, Justices Brennan and Marshall agreed that the plaintiffs had demonstrated discriminatory intent. See id. at 94

(Brennan, J., dissenting); id. at 138–39 (Marshall, J., dissenting).

39. Mobile, 446 U.S. at 73; Regester, 412 U.S. at 766.

40. Mobile, 446 U.S. at 73; Regester, 412 U.S. at 768.

41. Mobile, 446 U.S. at 74; Regester, 412 U.S. at 766.

42. Regester, 412 U.S. at 769–70. See Mobile, 446 U.S. at 102 (White, J., dissenting). Justice White's application of the standards set out in his own prior opinions for the Court subsequently prevailed in Rogers v. Lodge, 458 U.S. 613 (1982), where a district court order dividing a county into single-member districts for the election of county commissioners was upheld 6–3 (Justices Powell, Rehnquist and Stevens dissented). The Court upheld an inference of invidious discriminatory purpose on the basis of evidence very similar to that adduced in Regester and Mobile. Although this apparent loosening of the standards for determining discriminatory intent is by no means unwelcome, the primary lesson to be drawn from Rogers v. Lodge may instead be that the doctrine of Washington v. Davis, whatever its vices, cannot lay claim to the virtue of consistency.

dissent in *Mobile v. Bolden*, the challenge to the city's electoral scheme did not fall under the suspect classification category of fourteenth amendment review, but was instead a fundamental rights claim.[43] In such cases, evidence of discriminatory intent has long been deemed irrelevant.[44] Certainly the Court has never hesitated to condemn "neutral" laws that had an unacceptably adverse impact upon such rights as free speech,[45] freedom of political association,[46] or freedom of religion.[47] Proof of impermissible motive should hardly be a necessary element of a prima facie case of unconstitutional vote dilution, since the denial of something to which a person has a substantive constitutional right is no less illegal just because it may have been unintentional.

In *City of Memphis v. Greene*,[48] the Supreme Court had an opportunity to decide whether the thirteenth amendment's prohibition of slavery requires a showing that the challenged action was motivated by racial animus. In response to a petition from the residents of an affluent, all-white neighborhood that had been developed years before as an exclusive white enclave,[49] Memphis closed off traffic on the neighborhood's main street precisely at the point where it adjoined a black neighborhood. Black neighbors whose travel into the central part of the city was forced to detour around the closed neighborhood alleged that the street-closing was a monument to racism, and as such constituted a badge of slavery in violation of the thirteenth amendment.[50]

In an opinion by Justice Stevens,[51] the Supreme Court expressly left open the question of whether disparate racial impact by itself could establish a violation of the thirteenth amendment, because the street closing "could not, in any event, be fairly characterized as a badge or

---

43. 446 U.S. at 114 (Marshall, J., dissenting).

44. 446 U.S. at 120–21 (Marshall, J., dissenting). See also id. at 135 (a risk of hidden governmental discrimination may be insufficient to overcome judicial deference to decisions about the distribution of benefits or payments from the public fisc, but that risk is intolerable when the right to vote is at stake).

45. See, e.g., Schneider v. Irvington, 308 U.S. 147 (1939).

46. See, e.g., NAACP v. Button, 371 U.S. 415 (1963).

47. See, e.g., Wisconsin v. Yoder, 406 U.S. 205 (1972). See also Eisenberg, "Disproportionate Impact and Illicit Motive: Theories of Constitutional Adjudication," 52 N.Y.U.L.Rev. 36, 165–66 (1977) (arguing that a disparate impact test is more appropriate in the context of race than religion, since (1) blacks cannot escape calumny by changing their beliefs, (2) the establishment clause puts a limit on governmental concessions to religion that has no parallel

in the race context, and (3) no religious group has ever been victimized in this country to the degree blacks have been).

48. 451 U.S. 100 (1981).

49. Id. at 137 (Marshall, J., dissenting).

50. The plaintiffs also alleged a violation of 42 U.S.C. § 1982, which protects the right of blacks to buy, lease, and hold property on the same terms as whites. The Court dismissed the uncontroverted expert testimony that the closing would lower property values in the black neighborhood and cause an increase in racially-motivated police harassment of black property owners, 451 U.S. at 117–18; see id. at 146–47 (Marshall, J., dissenting), and denied statutory relief, explaining that being forced to make a detour does not constitute impairment of the property interests protected by § 1982. Id. at 120–24.

51. He was joined by Chief Justice Burger and Justices Stewart, Powell and Rehnquist. Justice White concurred in the judgment. Justice Marshall dissented, joined by Justices Brennan and Blackmun.

incident of slavery."[52]   The Court blithely declared that the mere inconvenience of a traffic detour was a "routine burden of citizenship,"[53] hardly a restraint on liberty comparable to the reduction of human beings to the status of chattel. Even if almost all of the citizens affected by a particular street closing, because of the racial homogeneity of many urban neighborhoods, happened to be black, "regard[ing] an inevitable consequence of that kind as a form of stigma so severe as to violate the thirteenth amendment would trivialize the great purpose of that charter of freedom."[54]

While the majority in *Memphis* never said that racial prejudice was an essential element of a thirteenth amendment claim, it nevertheless engaged in a detailed review of the record and concluded that there was no evidence that the city council was trying to discriminate against blacks.[55]   In concluding that the street was closed off not to protect a white enclave, but to enhance the safety and tranquility of what just happened to be an all-white neighborhood, the Court overlooked the facts that Memphis had never before closed a street for traffic control purposes, that the city gave no notice to the black neighbors of the proposed closing and refused to allow them access to the planning commission file on the issue, and that the city violated its own unambiguous procedures by processing the closing application without the consent of all the property owners abutting the street.[56]   Furthermore, white residents who opposed the closing testified that those urging erection of the barrier to block off access from the adjoining black neighborhood explained that there was a need to eliminate the "undesirable traffic" on the street,[57] and more than a thousand black citizens petitioned the city council about their concern that closing the street would wall them out of the community.[58]   In a depressing lapse that echoed the invidious rationale of *Plessy v. Ferguson*,[59] the *Memphis* majority dismissed the harm suffered by the black neighbors as being of merely "symbolic significance."[60]

52.   451 U.S. at 126. See id. at 128–29. The Court also found it unnecessary to decide whether the thirteenth amendment by itself outlaws more than formal slavery. But there is no doubt that the enforcement clause of the amendment at least empowers Congress to regulate both the public and private spheres in order to root out the legacies of slavery. Id. at 125 & nn.38, 39; Runyon v. McCrary, 427 U.S. 160, 170 (1976); Jones v. Alfred H. Mayer Co., 392 U.S. 409, 440–41 (1968). See § 5–13, supra.

53.   451 U.S. at 129.

54.   Id. at 128.

55.   See id. at 106–08, 113–16 & nn.22–27, 126. But see Justice Marshall's compelling appraisal of the evidence that led the Sixth Circuit Court of Appeals to strike down the closing as an intentional racist act. Id. at 138–44 (Marshall, J., dissenting).

56.   Id. at 142–43 & n.8 (Marshall, J., dissenting).

57.   451 U.S. at 115–16 n.26; see id. at 141–42 & n.7 (Marshall, J., dissenting).

58.   Id. at 143 n.9 (Marshall, J., dissenting).

59.   163 U.S. 537, 551 (1896) ("We consider the underlying fallacy of the plaintiff's argument to consist in the assumption that the enforced separation of the two races stamps the colored race with a badge of inferiority. If this be so, it is not by reason of anything found in the act, but solely because the colored race chooses to put that construction upon it.").

60.   451 U.S. at 128. Even the district court, which had ruled for the city, conceded that " '[o]bviously, the black people north of [the white neighborhood] . . . are being told to stay out of the subdivision.' " Id. at 139 (Marshall, J., dissenting) (quoting district court transcript).

In essence, *Washington v. Davis* announced that henceforth every lawsuit involving constitutional claims of racial discrimination directed at facially race-neutral rules would be conducted as a search for a bigoted decision-maker. This "perpetrator perspective" [61] sees contemporary racial discrimination not as a social phenomenon—the historical legacy of centuries of slavery and subjugation—but as the misguided, retrograde, almost atavistic behavior of individual actors in an enlightened, egalitarian society. If such actors cannot be found—and the standards for finding them are tough indeed—then there has been no violation of the equal protection clause.

This is not to say that every case which has applied the intent requirement has necessarily reached the wrong result, or that every equal protection challenge to a facially race-neutral government act is doomed by *Washington v. Davis*. For example, in *Hunter v. Underwood*,[62] the Supreme Court unanimously [63] struck down a provision of the Alabama Constitution that disenfranchised people convicted of crimes of moral turpitude—a category that, curiously, included vagrancy and passing bad checks but excluded second-degree manslaughter and assault on a police officer.[64] Plaintiffs proved that the provision had a racially disparate impact: it had disenfranchised approximately ten times as many blacks as whites.[65] In accord with *Davis* and *Arlington Heights*, the Court then inquired into evidence of racial animus, and found that the provision had been adopted in 1901 by an Alabama Constitutional Convention convened with a self-professed mandate " 'to establish white supremacy in this state.' " [66] The convention's suffrage committee had relied on the experience of white plantation owners in carefully selecting crimes thought to be more commonly committed by blacks.[67] The Court, in an opinion by Justice Rehnquist, unanimously rejected the proposition that the existence of an allegedly permissible motive—here, the state's even-handed desire to disenfranchise all poor people, whether black or "white trash"—"trumps any proof of a parallel impermissible motive." [68]

What distinguishes *Underwood* from the other progeny of *Washington v. Davis* is that the facts of the case allowed the Court to find a racially motivated government actor without pointing the finger at anyone who was *alive*: the men who adopted the disenfranchisement clause in 1901 were long dead in 1985. To a Court that often proceeds as if America has entered a brave, new, color-blind age, labeling post-Reconstruction southern leaders as racists must have been a relatively painless exercise in legal anthropology.[69]

61. See Freeman, supra note 19 at 1052–54.

62. 471 U.S. 222 (1985).

63. Justice Powell did not participate in the case.

64. Id. at 225.

65. Id. at 227.

66. Id. at 229.

67. Id. at 231.

68. Id. In advancing this argument, Alabama relied on Palmer v. Thompson, 403 U.S. 217, 224 (1971), and Michael M. v. Superior Court, 450 U.S. 464, 472 n.7 (1981) (plurality opinion).

69. One of the more egregious cases of the Court's blithe assumption that a new age of racial equality has arrived is Bazemore v. Friday, 106 S.Ct. 3000 (1986). The North Carolina Agricultural Extension Service had a formal policy of

Yet there is more to the doctrine of discriminatory purpose than naive or wishful thinking about the current state of race relations. The talisman of discriminatory intent symbolizes the Supreme Court's trepidation about embracing the highly intrusive structural remedies that may be required to root out the entrenched results of racial subjugation. From the very beginning, the problem of remedies in racial segregation cases has given the Court pause—so much so, that the Court limited itself in *Brown v. Board of Education (Brown I)* [70] to determining whether there had been a violation of equal protection, with the question of remedy being left for separate argument and resolution in *Brown II*.[71] The gravitational pull of traditional thinking is strong: the remedial "decree cannot bespeak judicial choice but must embody the voice of the law. Any significant divergence between the contours of the entitlement and the relief granted represents an improper exercise of judicial power, a departure from the rule of law itself." [72] The application of this approach to segregation and other race cases is problematic. Just what does an "entitlement" to "equal protection of the laws" mean? [73] And how does a court go about framing a decree that will provide it? Racial segregation cases in particular—and public law litigation in general [74]—threaten to sever the traditional ties that bind rights to remedies, and to cast the courts adrift on a sea of discretion.[75]

This quandary did not stay the Court's hand in *Hunter v. Underwood*. The right violated by the Alabama Constitution's disenfranchisement provision was clear enough: the right not to be deprived of the franchise on the basis of one's color. The remedy was equally straightforward: strike down the offending provision and order the

segregating its 4H Clubs prior to the enactment of the Civil Rights Act of 1964. Under Title VI of that act, the Department of Agriculture issued a regulation requiring North Carolina and other states administering similar programs to "take affirmative action to overcome the effects of prior discrimination." Id. at 3015 (Brennan, J., dissenting). North Carolina did nothing beyond terminating its formal policy of segregation and announcing that, henceforth, children could join 4H Clubs of their own choosing; unsurprisingly, nearly all of the clubs remained single-race. In a breezy three-paragraph opinion, the Supreme Court held 5–4 that the state's policy of passive nonobstructionism constituted "affirmative action" and was all that the statute and the Constitution required. Id. at 3013 (White, J., joined by Chief Justice Burger and Justices Powell, Rehnquist and O'Connor). In dissent, Justice Brennan (joined by Justices Marshall, Blackmun and Stevens) called the majority's reasoning "feeble," id. at 3014, and reminded the Court that 4H Clubs were organized in the public schools, which were

segregated by law in North Carolina until the early 1960s. The state was therefore under an affirmative duty to eradicate the effects of de jure segregation "root and branch," and a passive policy of voluntary programs had never before been held sufficient to meet that constitutional obligation. Id. at 3016. As Justice Brennan put it, the majority endorsed the proposition that "the state can be conclusively determined to have fulfilled its duty as long as no black can point to a blatant discriminatory act." Id. at 3019.

70.   347 U.S. 483 (1954).

71.   Brown v. Bd. of Educ., 349 U.S. 294 (1955).

72.   Chayes, "Foreword: Public Law Litigation and the Burger Court," 96 Harv.L. Rev. 4, 46–47 (1982).

73.   This question is discussed in § 16–21, infra.

74.   See Chayes, supra note 72, at 46–51.

75.   This problem is discussed in the context of school desegregation cases in § 16–19, supra.

state to register on the voter rolls members of the plaintiff class who so request and otherwise qualify.[76]

Providing relief in *Underwood* was thus a simple matter of lopping off an excrescence on the state constitution—like removing a wart. The remedial problem is of greater magnitude when major exploratory surgery is in the offing. *Milliken v. Bradley (Milliken I)*,[77] for example, involved a desegregation suit against the Detroit public schools. The problem was caused not only by the policies of the Detroit school board, but also by residential segregation promoted by the government: the Michigan courts enforced racially restrictive covenants in real estate contracts until the very day in 1948 that the Supreme Court ruled the practice unconstitutional;[78] the state agencies responsible for licensing real estate brokers encouraged discrimination against black realtors and home buyers;[79] police consistently failed to stop white mobs from hounding black residents from their new homes in white neighborhoods;[80] and local, state and federal housing agencies endorsed and encouraged racial separation throughout the Detroit metropolitan area.[81] The district court concluded that this complex pattern of wide-ranging segregative activity compelled a remedy that would reach beyond Detroit's city limits to include surrounding school districts. But the Supreme Court balked and remanded the case for formulation of a less comprehensive and intrusive remedy.[82]

Washington v. Davis itself illustrates the remedial challenge posed by many equal protection cases. The reason black applicants failed the police department's Test 21 at a disproportionate rate was no mystery: as a group, blacks possessed disproportionately substandard language skills; and that, in turn, was caused by the fact that they had had disproportionately substandard education. As residents of the District of Columbia in the 1950s and '60s, the black applicants had attended segregated schools and grown up in a segregated society. The combined pressure of continuing, if not always conscious, patterns of pervasive racial prejudice in the interrelated "gateway" areas of housing, employment, and education disproportionately forced blacks to remain at the lowest stratum of society. The Supreme Court was understandably daunted by the prospect of attempting to remedy years of deprivation and disadvantage by dealing solely with a police department admission test where that sad legacy of racial oppression happened to come to a head.

The Court's perception of how much *ad hoc* judicial action can hope to achieve in a reluctant society is not the only factor at work here. In those cases where the Court has invoked the discriminatory intent

---

76. Hunter v. Underwood, 471 U.S. at 225.

77. 418 U.S. 717 (1974).

78. Shelley v. Kraemer, 334 U.S. 1 (1948); McGee v. Sipes, id. (the companion case from Detroit).

79. See Days, Book Review, "School Desegregation Law in the 1980's: Why Isn't Anybody Laughing?" 95 Yale L.J. 1737, 1755 (1986).

80. Id.

81. Id. at 1755–56; Bradley v. Milliken, 345 F.Supp. 914, 932–33 & n.20 (E.D.Mich. 1972). For an insider's account of the Milliken litigation, see R. Dimond, Beyond Busing: Inside the Challenge to Urban Segregation (1985).

82. Milliken I is discussed in § 16–19, supra.

requirement, the remedies sought often posed the risk that the federal courts would become deeply enmeshed in the machinery of state and local government, reviewing equal protection challenges to seemingly neutral government choices about the allocation of public funds,[83] the zoning of land in residential neighborhoods,[84] the elimination of traffic problems,[85] and the very structure of local government.[86]

The Supreme Court may be forgiven for being taken aback by this prospect; the institutional concerns about such a role for the judiciary are serious and legitimate. But the Court may not be forgiven for the way it has elided the problem rather than facing up to it. The proper course would have been to confront the remedial challenge head on: either grit the teeth and get to work fixing the inequality, no matter what it takes, or swallow hard and acknowledge that the constitutional wrong cannot be judicially put right.[87] The Court did neither, instead declaring that no substantive constitutional violation existed: no matter how great the imposition on a particular class, the equal protection clause has not been offended so long as there is no showing of discriminatory intent. If no racially motivated government actor can be identified, the actual circumstances of racial disadvantage—unemployment, inadequate education, poverty, and political powerlessness—are to be regarded as mere unfortunate conditions, not as consequences of racial discrimination. Those conditions are then readily rationalized, "by treating them as historical accidents or products of a malevolent fate, or, even worse, by blaming the victims as inadequate to function in the good society." [88]

This avoidance tactic—subsuming issues about the propriety and efficacy of judicial remedies in the question of whether a constitutional violation exists—is not just intellectual self-deception. There is a very real difference between saying "There is a violation here but institutional considerations prevent us from providing a remedy," and saying "There is no violation." [89] The fact that the federal judiciary has sound reasons for not directly[90] enforcing a constitutional norm does not mean that the norm does not apply to the case in question.[91] A right to equal protection of the laws, even if not perfectly enforceable in court,

---

83. See Jefferson v. Hackney, 406 U.S. 535 (1972).

84. See Village of Arlington Heights v. Metropolitan Housing Dev. Corp., 429 U.S. 252 (1977).

85. See City of Memphis v. Greene, 451 U.S. 100 (1981).

86. City of Mobile v. Bolden, 446 U.S. 55 (1980).

87. See Tribe, "Unravelling National League of Cities: The New Federalism and Affirmative Rights to Essential Government Services," 90 Harv.L.Rev. 1065, 1088 (1977) (the obviously great institutional difficulties of framing appropriate relief may sometimes entail a conclusion that a judicially cognizable remedy simply is not available).

88. Freeman, supra note 19, at 1103.

89. Cf. City of Mobile v. Bolden, 446 U.S. 55, 80 (1980) (Blackmun, J., concurring in the result) (finding a violation of equal protection but voting to reverse on the ground that the remedy—complete restructuring of a city's form of government—"was not commensurate with the sound exercise of judicial discretion").

90. In some instances, only indirect vindication of the substantive value is possible—for example, through the policing of procedural safeguards. See Tribe, supra note 87 at 1089 (indirect vindication of a right to basic human needs for survival); Michelman, "In Pursuit of Constitutional Welfare Rights: One View of Rawls' Theory of Justice," 121 U.Pa.L.Rev. 962 (1973) (same).

91. The most familiar instance in which courts make this distinction is the

remains a right legally valid to its full conceptual limits; federal judicial decisions which stop short of those limits merely indicate the boundaries of the federal courts' role in vindicating that right.[92]

The significance of this distinction, of course, is that federal judges are not the only officials sworn to uphold the Constitution. The President and Congress, as well as the governments of the states and their political subdivisions, are equally obliged to serve constitutional values and, therefore, to make good on the promise of the Civil War amendments even when institutional concerns stop the judiciary from enforcing the norms contained in those amendments to their conceptual limits.[93] And officers of state government, regardless of the branch in which they serve, are not restrained by the principles of federalism that may hinder a federal court's ability to enforce a decree.[94] But this reservoir of alternative fora in which a citizen may petition for the equality guaranteed by the fourteenth amendment is likely to dry up if the Supreme Court allows its institutional concerns about remedies to dictate a holding that the citizen in fact has not been denied equal protection. Such a holding might in some circumstances bind the other branches of government,[95] and would in any event let them off the hook—the body charged with ultimately interpreting the Constitution would have spoken, and that would probably be the end of the matter. In contrast, a judicial declaration that the plaintiff's rights have been violated, but in a manner that the federal courts cannot remedy, leaves the other branches of government, both state and federal, free to step in where the federal judiciary dared not tread.

The ominous significance of discouraging other governmental bodies from vindicating the right of equality should not be underestimated. "The federal courts comprise a crucial bulwark against evulsive depredations of constitutional values; but against scattered erosion they are relatively powerless." [96] The courts were most effective in dismantling overt apartheid when there were Jim Crow laws to strike down and

political question doctrine. See Sager, "Fair Measure: The Legal Status of Underenforced Constitutional Norms," 91 Harv.L.Rev. 1212, 1224–26 (1978). That doctrine is discussed in § 3–13, supra.

92. See Tribe, supra note 87, at 1088–90; Sager, supra note 91, at 1221.

93. The notion that being legally obligated means being vulnerable to external—in most cases, judicial—enforcement is a superficial bromide. See H. L. A. Hart, The Concept of Law 113 (1961). Justices of a jurisdiction's highest court, for example, are routinely understood to be obliged to comply with legal standards, even though they cannot be forced to do so except through the less than effective means of impeachment (or, in the case of elected jurists, recall). See H. L. A. Hart, supra, at 138–42; Fried, "Two Concepts of Interests: Some Reflections on the Supreme Court's Balancing Test," 76 Harv.L. Rev. 755, 760 (1963) ("It is altogether fallacious to conclude from the unreviewability

of an exercise of judgment that there are no proper limits to confine that judgment, or to conclude from the absence of a remedy for abuse that there can be no abuse.").

94. The courts in some states may play a role vis-a-vis the other branches of government that differs markedly from the limited, interstitial role of the federal courts. See Mosk, "The Law of the Next Century: The State Courts," in American Law: The Third Century 213, 220–25 (B. Schwartz ed. 1976). Such tribunals should by no means be limited in their enforcement of federal constitutional rights by the institutional concerns which influence their federal counterparts. See Minnesota v. Clover Leaf Creamery Co., 449 U.S. 456, 477–85 (1981) (Stevens, J., dissenting); Sager, supra note 91, at 1255–57.

95. But see Katzenbach v. Morgan, 384 U.S. 641 (1966), discussed in § 5–14, supra. See also Sager, supra note 91, at 1229–42.

96. Sager, supra note 91, at 1263.

"whites only" signs to tear up. The contemporary symptoms of inertial and unconscious racial prejudice are more subtle, and eradicating them will require not only the ad hoc, episodic efforts of the judiciary, but also the more flexible and continuous tools possessed by the executive and the legislature for systematically bringing about systemic change.[97]

§ 16–21. Making Sense of the Equal Protection Clause: A Right Not to Be Subjugated

The words of the equal protection clause do not, by themselves, tell us as much as we might wish. The central concept of the clause, equality, requires the specification of substantive values before it has full meaning.[1] To declare that no state shall "deny to any person within its jurisdiction the equal protection of the laws" is more to proclaim a delphic edict than to state an intelligible rule of decision. Not even those committed to Justice Black's strict textual approach to the Constitution could make much sense of the equal protection clause standing alone. The opacity of the clause cries out for a mediating principle, and some variety of antidiscrimination principle is usually supplied.[2]

---

97. Consider McCleskey v. Kemp, 107 S.Ct. 1756 (1987), where the Court rejected an equal protection challenge to the Georgia capital sentencing process, brought by a black man convicted of murdering a white man, alleging racial discrimination in administration of that process. A statistical study revealed significant disparities in imposition of the death sentence based on the race of the murderer and of the victim: murder defendants of either race who killed white victims were more than four times as likely to receive the death penalty as were defendants with black victims; black defendants with white victims had the greatest likelihood of being sentenced to death. In an opinion by Justice Powell, joined by Chief Justice Rehnquist and Justices White, O'Connor, and Scalia, the Court followed Washington v. Davis and insisted that petitioner McCleskey "prove that the decisionmakers in *his* case"—the prosecutor and the jury—"acted with discriminatory purpose." Id. at 1766 (original emphasis). The Court declared itself unwilling to assume that "what is unexplained is invidious." Id. at 1778.

The Court stressed that McCleskey's statistical argument challenged the central role of the jury as "the conscience of the community," id. at 1776 n.32, and the Court balked at endorsing "wide-ranging arguments that basically challenge the validity of capital punishment in our multi-racial society." Id. at 1781. The majority concluded that such systemic arguments are best addressed to legislatures, while courts are better suited to "determine on a case-by-case basis whether these laws are applied consistently with the Constitu-

tion." Id. at 1781. The McCleskey opinion arguably left room for Congress, exercising its enforcement power under § 5 of the fourteenth amendment, to regulate state death penalty procedures that, whether intentionally or not, whether consciously or unconsciously, discriminate against the black murderers of white victims and against the black victims of white murderers. Cf. Katzenbach v. Morgan, 384 U.S. 641 (1966); Rome v. United States, 446 U.S. 156 (1980), discussed in § 5–14, supra.

§ 16–21

1. See Westen, "The Empty Idea of Equality," 95 Harv.L.Rev. 537 (1982); Karst, "Why Equality Matters," 17 Ga.L. Rev. 245, 289 (1983); Westen, "The Meaning of Equality in Law, Science, Math and Morals: A Reply," 81 Mich.L.Rev. 604 (1983). But see Michelman, "The Meanings of Legal Equality," 3 Harv. Black-Letter J. 24, 27 n.10 (1986) (criticizing Professor Westen's view because "a norm that directs us toward universalization of rights—or towards a universalistic conception of the very idea of a right—seems to me not very empty.").

2. See Fiss, "Groups and the Equal Protection Clause," 5 Phil. & Public Affairs 107, 108 (1976). Perhaps the best explication of this mediating principle is Brest, "Foreword: In Defense of the Antidiscrimination Principle," 90 Harv.L.Rev. 1 (1976).

A separate school of thought interprets the equal protection clause as a judicial mandate to patch up representative democracy by strictly scrutinizing, and sometimes invalidating, those government ac-

The central conceptual problem of the antidiscrimination principle is evident in its very terminology. Discrimination is "an act based on prejudice," and its essential elements are therefore an actor and a decision based on invidious rather than rational grounds. When mediated by an antidiscrimination principle, the fourteenth amendment [3] becomes a tool for overturning those injurious legislative acts, judicial decisions, and executive or administrative choices that are motivated by racial or other unacceptable types of bias. The focus under this approach is on the perpetrator of prejudiced action.

The Supreme Court embraced this antidiscrimination principle in *Washington v. Davis* [4] and its progeny. In *Davis*, the Court noted that Test 21 disproportionately burdened black police applicants, but it found no evidence that the administators who formulated and adopted the test acted out of racial animosity.[5] Similarly, in *City of Mobile v. Bolden*,[6] it was obvious that the multimember district electoral plan all but foreclosed the election of minority candidates, but the Court discerned among the legislators who enacted the plan no intent to freeze blacks out of politics. In each case the Court first acknowledged a disparate impact on the minority group and then looked to the intent of the perpetrator (the actor), rather than to the impact on the victim (who was acted on).[7]

A more promising theme in equal protection doctrine may well be an antisubjugation principle, which aims to break down legally created or legally reenforced systems of subordination that treat some people as second-class citizens. The core value of this principle is that all people have equal worth. When the legal order that both shapes and mirrors our society treats some people as outsiders or as though they were worth less than others, those people have been denied the equal protection of the laws.[8] The "citizenship clause of the fourteenth amendment . . . does not allow for degrees of citizenship":[9] no citizen is "more equal" than any other. The antisubjugation principle is more

---

tions that burden "discrete and insular minorities." See United States v. Carolene Products Co., 304 U.S. 144, 152 n.4 (1938); J. Ely, Democracy and Distrust (1980). The most fundamental flaws in this approach, both with respect to its pretentions to having solved the problem of the legitimacy of judicial review in a democratic regime, as well as with respect to its analysis of equal protection as such, have been quite thoroughly explored in the literature. See Brilmayer, "Carolene, Conflicts, and the Fate of the 'Inside-Outsider,'" 134 U.Pa.L.Rev. 1291 (1986); Ackerman, "Beyond Carolene Products," 98 Harv.L.Rev. 713 (1985); Tribe, "The Puzzling Persistence of Process-Based Constitutional Theories," 89 Yale L.J. 1063 (1980).

3. Or the fifteenth, and perhaps the thirteenth. See City of Mobile v. Bolden, 446 U.S. 55 (1980), and City of Memphis v. Greene, 451 U.S. 100 (1981), discussed in § 16–20, supra.

4. 426 U.S. 229 (1976).

5. See § 16–20, supra.

6. 446 U.S. 55 (1980), discussed in § 16–20, supra.

7. The serious difficulties with this focus on the perpetrator are explored in § 16–20.

8. See Plyler v. Doe, 457 U.S. 202, 217 n.14 (1982) (fourteenth amendment designed to abolish "class or caste" treatment), discussed in § 16–23, infra.

9. Zobel v. Williams, 457 U.S. 55, 69 (1982) (Brennan, J., joined by Marshall, Blackmun and Powell, JJ., concurring). See Karst, supra note 1, at 248 (principle of equal citizenship is "presumptively violated when the organized society treats someone as an inferior, as part of a dependent caste, or as a nonparticipant"). See also Karst, "Foreword: Equal Citizenship Under the Fourteenth Amendment," 91 Harv. L.Rev. 1 (1977).

concerned with the burdens government action imposes on suspect groups than with what prejudices lurk in the hearts and minds of government actors. The goal of the equal protection clause is not to stamp out impure thoughts, but to guarantee a full measure of human dignity for all.[10] The Constitution may be offended not only by individual acts of racial discrimination, but also by government rules, policies or practices that perennially reenforce the subordinate status of any group.[11] Mediated by the antisubjugation principle, the equal protection clause asks whether the particular conditions complained of, examined in their social and historical context, are a manifestation or a legacy of official oppression.

The antisubjugation principle is faithful to the historical origins of the Civil War amendments. Under *Dred Scott v. Sandford*,[12] blacks were not deemed citizens—as though they were not counted among the "People of the United States" in the Constitution's preamble—because they were "a subordinate and inferior class of beings, who had been subjugated by the dominant race." The Civil War amendments were drafted specifically to overturn that odious hierarchy.[13] The notion that one race is, or ought to be, subordinate to another is "at war with the one class of citizenship created by the thirteenth, fourteenth, and fifteenth amendments."[14] In *Strauder v. West Virginia*,[15] the first postbellum racial discrimination case to reach the Supreme Court, Justice Strong recognized for a unanimous Court that subjugation was the very evil that the equal protection clause was meant to remedy: the clause is an "exemption from legal discriminations implying inferiority," which are "steps toward reducing [blacks] to the condition of a subject race."[16] The import of the Court's denunciation of subjugation in *Strauder* is all the more telling because the law at issue, which barred blacks from jury duty, had been enacted eight years after the Civil War not by a state assembly full of former slave owners in a confederate backwater, but by the legislature of a *free* state that had fought with the Union.

Even at the nadir of fourteenth amendment jurisprudence, an undercurrent of judicial opinion remained true to the promise of equality. Dissenting from the spurious concept of "separate but equal" in *Plessy v. Ferguson*,[17] the elder Justice Harlan wrote that the Constitution recognizes "no superior, dominant, ruling class of citizens. There is no caste here."[18] When the Supreme Court finally vindicated

---

10. Cf. Palmore v. Sidoti, 466 U.S. 429, 431 (1984) (reversing order removing custody of child when white mother married black man): "Private biases may be outside the reach of the law, but the law cannot, directly or indirectly, give them effect." See § 16–16, supra.

11. Professor Owen Fiss refers to this as the "group-disadvantaging principle," Fiss, supra note 2, at 108, 148–56, but it is important to recognize that one need not accept notions of "group rights," or reject individualistically grounded conceptions of rights, to embrace the principle.

12. 60 U.S. (19 How.) 393, 404–05 (1856).

13. See tenBroek, The Antislavery Origins of the Fourteenth Amendment 192–95 (1951).

14. Bell v. Maryland, 378 U.S. 226, 252 (1964) (Douglas, J., concurring).

15. 100 U.S. 303 (1880).

16. Id. at 308.

17. 163 U.S. 537 (1896), discussed in § 16–15, supra.

18. Id. at 559. See § 16–22, infra.

Justice Harlan half a century later by outlawing legally segregated schools in *Brown v. Board of Education*,[19] it did so partly to avert the imposition upon black children of practical barriers to success,[20] but primarily to prevent the stigma of inferiority that separation inevitably brands on those whom society deems untouchable.[21] When the Court struck down miscegenation laws in *Loving v. Virginia*,[22] it did not strike a blow for freedom of association so much as it repudiated official acceptance of the obnoxious eugenic theory that intermarriage between blacks and whites pollutes the Aryan gene pool and threatens "White Supremacy."[23]

The drive to terminate subordination of particular groups has also animated decisions outside the context of race. The Court invoked the equal protection clause in *Skinner v. Oklahoma*[24] to invalidate a state law that required sterilization of recidivist felons but exempted those convicted of such white-collar crimes as tax fraud, embezzling, and political corruption.[25] The Constitution cannot tolerate class legislation embodying the repugnant premise that middle-class crooks who have had the opportunity to commit genteel crimes make better breeding stock than do chicken thieves and other less sophisticated felons.[26] *Plyler v. Doe*[27] held that Texas could not deny public education to the children of illegal immigrants because doing so would convert the members of that group into "a discrete underclass"[28] and "promote the creation and perpetuation of a subclass of illiterates."[29] And in *Mississippi University for Women v. Hogan*,[30] the Court struck down the

19. 347 U.S. 483 (1954). See § 16–15, supra.

20. Id. at 494.

21. Id. at 493.

22. 388 U.S. 1 (1967). See § 16–15, supra.

23. Id. at 11. In addition, the Court did affirm that such laws impermissibly abridged the fundamental, if nowhere expressly stated, constitutional right to choose a spouse. Id. at 12, discussed in Ch. 15, supra. The realization that the Court, in cases such as Brown and Loving, was attacking the stigma and oppression that result from apartheid—and not the denial of a black child's "right" to learn arithmetic with white children—answers the old riddle posed by the advocates of "neutral principles." See, e.g., Wechsler, "Toward Neutral Principles of Constitutional Law," 73 Harv.L.Rev. 1 (1959). For as Professor Robert Cover once observed, "the apparently neutral structural characteristics of the Constitution had never been neutral concerning race." See Cover, "The Origins of Judicial Activism in the Protection of Minorities," 91 Yale L.J. 1287, 1308 (1982). See § 16–15, supra.

24. 316 U.S. 535 (1942).

25. Id. at 542.

26. Skinner demonstrates that construction of the fourteenth amendment as a guarantee against subjugation dissolves the less enlightening doctrinal rubrics and links cases decided under the equal protection clause with those that vindicate the substantive liberty element of the due process clause. See § 16–12, supra. The Court has itself noted this convergence. See Schlesinger v. Ballard, 419 U.S. 498, 500 n.3 (1975); Bolling v. Sharpe, 347 U.S. 497, 499 (1954). Roe v. Wade, 410 U.S. 113 (1973), which upheld a woman's liberty to control her own body in matters of procreation, could have been decided under the equal protection clause on the basis of the antisubjugation principle: arguably, any group whose members may be compelled by the dominant gender to serve as incubators has been reduced to a position of servitude. See § 15–10, supra.

27. 457 U.S. 202 (1982).

28. Id. at 234 (Blackmun, J., concurring).

29. Id. at 230 (Brennan, J., for the Court); see id. at 239 (Powell, J., concurring); id. at 242, 254 (Burger, C.J., dissenting). The Court reached this holding without deeming education a fundamental right. Id. at 221 (opinion of the Court). See § 16–9, supra.

30. 458 U.S. 718 (1982).

single-sex admissions policy of a state nursing school because it "reflect[ed] archaic and stereotypic notions" of the "proper" roles of men and women and thereby perpetuated the relegation to women to inferior status.[31]   The antidiscrimination approach to equal protection cannot alone explain the decision in *Hogan*, for the Court denounced the single-sex policy both because it *discriminated* against men and because it reenforced the *subjugation* of women.[32]

An antidiscrimination principle may be sufficient to contend with the deprivations of equal protection that result from "isolated instances of impropriety" or "transitory hysteria."[33]   But the subjugation of blacks, women, and other groups that persists today is usually neither isolated nor hysterical. Indeed, for purely practical reasons, even an informal and subtle caste system could not long endure if it were necessary to visit conscious, personalized discrimination on every member of the victimized group on a regular basis. Regimes of sustained subordination therefore generate "devices, institutions, and circumstances that impose burdens or constraints on the target group without resort to repeated or individualized discriminatory actions."[34]   People draw lines and attribute differences as a way of ordering social existence—of deciding who may occupy what place and play which roles.[35] In order to justify the institution of slavery, white society differentiated the role of chattel servant by describing it in terms of the most obvious distinguishing feature of the people who were forced to play it, thus equating race and role.[36]   This equation survived the Civil War and Reconstruction. It did so not just by inertia, but because the role that society allowed blacks remained significantly unchanged; so the need to justify the role by differentiating it persisted.[37]   The dominant, white race continued to see not the role but the group: "inferior" blacks capable of nothing better anyway. The inequities that persist in American society have survived this long because they have become ingrained in our modes of thought;[38] the Supreme Court recognized a century ago that "habitual" discriminations are the hardest to eradicate.[39]

The antidiscrimination principle harbors a fundamental gap because it identifies but one mechanism of subjugation: the purposeful, affirmative adoption or use of rules that disadvantage the target group. Government officials cannot be held accountable to the constitutional norm of equality unless they "selected or reaffirmed a particular course of action at least in part '*because of*,' not merely 'in spite of,' its adverse effects upon an identifiable group."[40]   This overlooks the fact that

---

31. Id. at 725, 726.

32. See id. at 723. 729–30 & n.15. See §§ 16–26, 16–27, infra.

33. Cover, supra note 23, at 1316.

34. Schnapper, "Perpetuation of Past Discrimination," 96 Harv.L.Rev. 828, 834 (1983).

35. See Tribe, supra note 2, at 1073–74.

36. See W. Jordan, White Over Black (1968).

37. See C. Van Woodward, The Strange Career of Jim Crow (2d ed. 1966).

38. See J. Kovel, White Racism: A Psychohistory 60–66 (1971).

39. Strauder v. West Virginia, 100 U.S. 303, 306 (1880).

40. Personnel Administrator of Massachusetts v. Feeney, 442 U.S. 256, 279 (1979) (emphasis added).

minorities can also be injured when the government is "only" indifferent to their suffering or "merely" blind to how prior official discrimination contributed to it and how current official acts will perpetuate it.

For example, it is possible, although not necessarily plausible, that those who established the challenged electoral scheme in *City of Mobile v. Bolden* [41] simply gave no thought to how multimember districts would synergize with previous official discrimination to deny blacks a voice in government. It is also possible that the Memphis City Council closed off a thoroughfare through an all-white enclave merely "in spite of" the racial insult the closing conveyed to thousands of neighboring black residents, rather than "because of" it.[42] When asked by a group of white citizens to erect a traffic barrier between their neighborhood and the adjoining black community, maybe the city council just did not think about black feelings and interests at all. Perhaps the nineteenth century Louisiana lawmakers who decided to minister to the sensibilities of their white constituents by mandating segregated railway coaches simply never gave a thought to how this would affect Homer Plessy.[43] But surely that cannot make a decisive constitutional difference.[44] If government is barred from enacting laws with an eye to invidious discrimination against a particular group, it should not be free to visit the same wrong whenever it happens to be looking the other way. If a state may not club minorities with its fist, surely it may not indifferently inflict the same wound with the back of its hand.

The pseudo-scienter requirement that *Washington v. Davis* grafted onto the fourteenth amendment is therefore utterly alien to the basic concept of equal justice under law. The burden on those who are subjugated is none the lighter because it is imposed inadvertently. Granted, even a dog can tell the difference between being kicked and being tripped over. But if one is first dragged toward the boot and then stumbled over often enough, the pains and bruises become indistinguishable from those inflicted by kicking: the effect is the same, no matter how understanding the victim tries to be.

Whereas the antidiscrimination principle looks inward to the perpetrator's state of mind, the antisubjugation principle looks outward to the victim's state of existence. In *Washington v. Davis* the Supreme Court feared that adoption of a disparate impact test for equal protection analysis would threaten a whole panoply of socioeconomic and fiscal measures that inevitably burden the average poor black more than the average affluent white.[45] That might be a concern if all resource allocations that had a statistically differential impact by race

---

41. 446 U.S. 55 (1980).

42. See City of Memphis v. Greene, 451 U.S. 100 (1981).

43. See Plessy v. Ferguson, 163 U.S. 537 (1896).

44. Under traditional psychoanalytic theory, one would anticipate that much, if not most, irrational prejudice operates at a level below the conscious mind. The legitimacy of the Washington v. Davis approach is therefore seriously in doubt. See Law-

rence, "The Id, the Ego, and Equal Protection: Reckoning With Unconscious Racism," 39 Stan.L.Rev. 317, 329–44 (1987). A mode of constitutional inquiry heavily dependent on the search for evidence of conscious discriminatory intent is likely to be even less successful than the quest for the Grail. The proper place for such quixotic endeavors is literature, not law.

45. 426 U.S. at 248 & n.14.

were automatically subject to strict scrutiny. But there is a difference between an admittedly implausible affirmative duty to help subjugated groups by every means possible including handouts from the public fisc,[46] and a governmental responsibility not to sanction tests, rules, practices and policies that predictably and avoidably perpetuate the inferior position of a group originally relegated to that position by a ruthless regime of official discrimination and exploitation.

The antisubjugation principle thus does not argue for adopting disparate impact as a *per se* rule; strict judicial scrutiny would be reserved for those government acts that, given their history, context, source, and effect, seem most likely not only to perpetuate subordination but also to reflect a tradition of hostility toward an historically subjugated group, or a pattern of blindness or indifference to the interests of that group. This "test plainly would require intuitive judgments, but judgments resting on correlations between observable events, without explanations as to cause, are not necessarily unsound." [47] There is a common-sense appeal, for example, in the notion that a government decision to combat traffic congestion by walling a white enclave off from a black neighborhood, or to zone a white neighborhood for large lots that exclude the possibility of low-income housing, is more likely to be the product of racial animus or indifference than is a decision to subsidize a shopping mall project.

It also makes sense to distinguish between an inherently arbitrary practice like the drawing of electoral district boundaries—which may not need to be justified in rational terms [48]—and a presumably rational practice like testing.[49] Those who challenged Test 21 in *Davis* amply demonstrated racially disproportionate impact. And the probability of a link between the higher failure rate for blacks and the District of Columbia's history of de jure school segregation is obvious.[50] More intensive inquiry was therefore in order, and the police department should have been required to defend its use of Test 21 in rational, race-neutral terms. An admission test that fails to correlate with either job performance or success in the training program [51] is a manifestly artificial barrier. Use of such a test is therefore suspicious, raising an inference that selection of the test was, at best, tainted by unacceptable government indifference to blacks. The antisubjugation principle also informs the constitutional inquiry by expanding the scope of relevant considerations. Given the aura of white supremacy implicit in main-

46. See Tribe, "The Abortion Funding Conundrum: Inalienable Rights, Affirmative Duties, and the Dilemma of Dependence," 99 Harv.L.Rev. 330, 332–35 (1985).

47. Dworkin, "Social Sciences and Constitutional Rights: the Consequences of Uncertainty," 6 J. of Law & Educ. 3, 4–6 (1977) (defending the use of "interpretive," as opposed to "causal," judgments to support judicial decisions).

48. See, e.g., Wright v. Rockefeller, 376 U.S. 52 (1964). The Court relied on Wright to justify its refusal to require a meaningful explanation for the testing policy challenged in Washington v. Davis. See 426 U.S. at 240.

49. For an intricate and ingenious argument that impermissible motive should be the touchstone of constitutional invalidity in situations where government is free to be arbitrary or random but not in situations where government is required to act according to rational criteria, see Ely, "Legislative and Administrative Motivation in Constitutional Law," 79 Yale L.J. 1205 (1970).

50. See § 16–20, supra.

51. See id.

taining a predominantly white police force in a predominantly black city like Washington, D.C., one may fairly ask: is it more important for police officers to converse in the Queen's English, or to be sympathetic to the problems and needs of the community and capable of relating to—not alienating—those whom they police?

The antidiscrimination principle has an undeniable subliminal allure. Conceiving of governmental racial prejudice as the work of aberrant individuals is more appealing than acknowledging that it is the virulent vestige of centuries of official subjugation, for it allows us to believe that a color-blind society is already upon us. But "[w]e ought not delude ourselves that the deep faith that race should never be relevant has completely triumphed over the painful social reality that, sometimes, it may be." [52] As Justice Brennan put it in his forceful dissent from the Court's decision to turn the other way at evidence of racism in the administration of the death penalty, "we remain imprisoned by the past as long as we deny its influence in the present." [53]

§ 16–22. Affirmative Action: Governmental Attention to Race and Gender in Redressing Past Injury, Combatting Persistent Prejudice, or Pursuing Goals of Diversity and Integration

Despite the suggestion that our Constitution should be "color-blind," [1] it has long been recognized that this is a misleading metaphor. Just as race has played a crucial role in our nation's past, so it must play a role in the present—whether to eradicate racial distinctions from our future, or to overcome the lingering effects of racial discrimination, or to achieve racial pluralism and diversity without racial domination. There is no doubt that courts must often take explicit account of race—and of the different circumstances of persons of different races—both in formulating adequate remedies for unlawful past discrimination and in assessing the constitutionality of classifications favoring racial minorities.[2] No member of the Supreme Court has supposed that such racial

52. Brown v. North Carolina, 107 S.Ct. 423, 424 (1986) (O'Connor, J., concurring in the denial of certiorari).

53. McCleskey v. Kemp, 107 S.Ct. 1756 (1987) (Brennan, J., joined by Marshall, Blackmun, and Stevens, JJ., dissenting).

§ 16–22

1. Plessy v. Ferguson, 163 U.S. 537, 552, 559 (1896) (Harlan, J., dissenting).

2. In North Carolina v. Swann, 402 U.S. 43 (1971), where the Court unanimously invalidated a state anti-busing law which flatly prohibited assignment of students on the basis of race, Chief Justice Burger emphasized for all nine Justices that race "must be considered" not only in determining whether a constitutional violation exists, but also in formulating its remedy. Id. at 46. See also Local 28, Sheet Metal Workers Int'l Assoc. v. Equal Employment

Opportunity Comm'n, 106 S.Ct. 3019 (1986), and United States v. Paradise, 107 S.Ct. 1053 (1987), discussed infra, where the Court upheld district court decrees ordering race-specific affirmative action in circumstances of "egregious" discrimination. In Paradise, Justice Stevens concurred in the judgment, arguing that the relevant guidelines for remedying segregation had been established by the Court's unanimous opinion in Swann v. Charlotte-Mecklenburg Bd. of Ed., 402 U.S. 1 (1971). Since the record in Paradise "disclose[d] an egregious violation of the equal protection clause . . . [i]t follows that the district court has broad and flexible authority to remedy the wrongs resulting from this violation." 107 S.Ct. at 1077. Even if the remedy "employs mathematical ratios," no different standard of review is required. Id. See also Swann, 402 U.S. at 25.

preferences are always invalid.[3]   In some instances, indeed, the Court has required the very opposite of color blindness.[4]   And in others the Court has at least *tolerated* color-consciousness because forbidding it would defeat the struggle against racism and its invidious effects.[5] Moreover, as Justice Powell wrote for a plurality of the Court in *Wygant v. Jackson Board of Education*,[6] the Court has recognized that, "[a]s part of this Nation's dedication to eradicating racial discrimination, innocent persons may be called upon to bear some of the burden of the remedy." [7]   Thus it is not a decisive objection to a voluntarily adopted racial preference favoring non-whites that some or even all of the white individuals disfavored by it have themselves been guilty of no discriminatory act.   The Court has also accepted the proposition that affirmative attention to race in such a context may sometimes be expressed quantitatively through the use of numerical goals and set-asides for racial minorities.[8]

3.   See, e.g., Regents of the University of California v. Bakke, 438 U.S. 265, 315 (1978) (opinion of Powell, J.) (approving under some circumstances minority preferences to achieve academic diversity); id. at 362 (opinion of Brennan, White, Marshall and Blackmun, JJ.) (approving minority preferences to remedy minority under-representation); Fullilove v. Klutznick, 448 U.S. 448, 484 (1980) (plurality opinion of Burger, C.J., joined by White and Powell, JJ.) (approving minority preferences used to remedy past discrimination); id. at 528 (Stewart, J. joined by Rehnquist, J. dissenting) (same, if past discrimination was committed by the body adopting the remedial preferences); id. at 553 (Stevens, J., dissenting) (approving preferences for the purpose of correcting for minorities' past competitive disadvantage).

4.   In Swann, supra note 2, the Court held that the anti-busing statute "exploit[ed] an apparently neutral form to control school assignment plans by directing that they be 'color-blind': that requirement, against the background of segregation, would render illusory the promise of Brown." Id. at 45–46.   See also Local 28 of Sheet Metal Workers, V.E.E.O.C., 106 S.Ct. 3019 (1986); Strauss, "The Myth of Colorblindness," 1986 S.Ct. Rev. 99, 114 (arguing that prohibiting the use of even accurate racial generalizations that disadvantage blacks—as even the rule announced in Brown does—is itself very much like affirmative action in that it may disadvantage innocent people and in that it definitely draws attention to race: "we do not have a choice between colorblindness and race-consciousness; we only have a choice between different forms of race-consciousness.").

5.   In dictum in Swann v. Charlotte-Mecklenburg Bd. of Educ., 402 U.S. 1, 16 (1971), the Court approved school officials' regard to race for the purpose of correcting *de facto*—and therefore not unconstitution-

al—segregation, as falling within the broad discretionary powers of local school authorities.   The Court has subsequently upheld various forms of voluntarily adopted governmental affirmative action plans.   See, e.g., Regents of University of California v. Bakke, 438 U.S. 265 (1978); Fullilove v. Klutznick, 448 U.S. 448 (1980).

6.   106 S.Ct. 1842 (1986) (Powell, J. joined by Burger, C.J. and Rehnquist, J.).

7.   Id. at 1850; see also Fullilove, 448 U.S. at 484 (plurality opinion of Burger, C.J., joined by White and Powell, JJ.).   The notion of "innocent" persons being victims of "reverse discrimination" is symptomatic of the perpetrator perspective on the fourteenth amendment, discussed in §§ 16–20 and 16–21, supra.   The battle against racism is conceived not as an assault on an endemic social malady, but as culling out of the herd those blameworthy individuals who account for the remaining, isolated acts of discrimination in an otherwise color-blind society.   The fault concept that inheres in this approach creates, by implication, a class of innocents who need feel no moral, let alone personal responsibility for the conditions associated with racial discrimination.   See Freeman, "Legitimizing Racial Discrimination Through Antidiscrimination Law: A Critical Review of Supreme Court Doctrine," 62 Minn.L.Rev. 1049, 1054–55 (1978).   The morality of the perpetrator perspective could be said to have a remarkably limited range: it conveys no sense that we are collectively responsible for our society's shortcomings or that we must all shoulder the burden of redressing them.

8.   See Local 28 of Sheet Metal Workers' Int'l Assoc. v. E.E.O.C., 106 S.Ct. 3019, 3037 (1986) (plurality opinion of Brennan, J., joined by Marshall, Blackmun, and Stevens, JJ.); Fullilove, 448 U.S. at 484–89 (plurality opinion of Burger, C.J., joined by White and Powell, JJ.); United Steelwork-

Yet the Court's cases express considerable unease about such racially explicit set-asides, and about measures that visit focused burdens on individuals because of their non-minority racial status. For reasons never fully explained—reasons to be explored in this section—the Court has seemingly regarded *all* such governmental uses of explicit racial classification as constitutionally problematic to *some* degree, regardless of whether the particular classification at issue appears to reflect any stigmatizing prejudice that has distorted the fairness of the political process that produced the classification,[9] and regardless of whether the classification operates to reinforce anything resembling a racial caste system in which some races permanently dominate others. Indeed, every member of the Court seems to think that at least some form of heightened scrutiny is appropriate; no justice has endorsed minimal scrutiny of race-based preferences.[10] But the Court has yet to agree on how searching its review of affirmative action need be.[11]

ers v. Weber, 443 U.S. 193 (1979) (majority opinion by Brennan, J., joined by Stewart, White, Marshall and Blackmun, JJ.).

9. Following Justice Stone's observation in United States v. Carolene Products Co., 304 U.S. 144 (1938), that a "more searching judicial inquiry" is provoked by "prejudice *against* discrete and insular minorities," id. at 152–53 n.4 (dictum) (emphasis added), judicial distrust of political processes may not be pertinent when a discrete and insular minority is benefitted, rather than burdened, by government action. When a predominantly white public body chooses to confer a comparative advantage on racial minorities while comparatively disadvantaging all white applicants, a court on review would have to assure itself only that this was indeed the purpose and effect of the choice in question, and that the choice did not deliberately conceal any discrimination against a racial, ethnic, or other minority. See note 39 infra. Once having been so assured, the judiciary would lack the usual reasons to subject the choice to the sort of scrutiny that makes sense when prejudice against insular minorities seems to be present, and when the political process accordingly seems unworthy of deference. When the group (or coalition of groups) in control of the political process adopts classifications which protect or benefit a minority and burden the majority group, the usual reasons are absent for regarding the governmental choice with suspicion, and therefore for strictly scrutinizing the results: "A white majority is unlikely to disadvantage itself for reasons of racial prejudice; nor is it likely to be tempted either to underestimate the needs and deserts of whites relative to those of others, or to overestimate the costs of devising an alternative classification that would extend to certain whites the advantages generally extending to Blacks." Ely, "The Constitutionality of Re-

verse Discrimination," 41 U.Chi.L.Rev. 723, 735 (1974). See Sullivan, "The Supreme Court, 1986 Term—Comment: Sins of Discrimination: Last Term's Affirmative Action Cases," 100 Harv.L.Rev. 78, 96–97 (1986) (arguing that voluntary affirmative action should not provoke the same degree of judicial suspicion as might similar court-ordered measures, and criticizing Justice Powell's opinion in Wygant as "convert[ing] . . . concern for *restraining* government into a doctrine that would bar even the willing extension of benefits to blacks at whites' expense") (emphasis in original). Invalidating affirmative action because it may disadvantage some whites reads into the equal protection clause a new right for members of the white majority to be judicially protected from losing out in the give and take of politics.

Of course, the entirely plausible idea that whites are unlikely to be prejudiced against whites as such does not at all imply that members of a minority group can be counted on to treat others in the same group with fairness. See, e.g., Castaneda v. Partida, 430 U.S. 482, 496–97, 498–500 (1977) (prima facie case of intentional discrimination in county grand jury selection process established on showing Mexican-Americans constituted 79% of the population and only 39% of those summoned for jury service; state could not rebut prima facie case with evidence that Mexican Americans enjoyed "governing majority" status in county). Justice Marshall, concurring, emphasized that "members of minority groups frequently respond to discrimination and prejudice by attempting to disassociate themselves from the group, even to the point of adopting the majority's negative attitudes toward the minority." Id. at 1284.

10.–11. See notes 10–11 on page 1524.

Despite its unease, the Court has approved the application of classificatory criteria in affirmative action that would be "suspect," and would almost certainly be invalidated, if used for purposes of discrimination against individuals of a minority race. This should come as no surprise, even to those who believe that all individuals have a presumptive right not to be burdened because of such immutable and usually irrelevant factors as their race. For the usually irrelevant may at times be highly relevant, and the fact that racial classifications have often served, in our own history and throughout the world, to denigrate the equal worth and human dignity of those set apart by them hardly means that such classifications necessarily and always play this invidious role.

Indeed, the notion that *all* racial classifications—the ostensibly and evidently benign no less than the overtly malign—are *equally* "suspect" is not supported by constitutional text, principle, or history. It was the justly infamous 1944 decision in *Korematsu v. United States* [12] that gave the first explicit articulation of the doctrine of suspectness for racial classifications. In *Korematsu*, the Court upheld the government's forced relocation of Japanese-American citizens to concentration camps. Before announcing its result, the Supreme Court proclaimed that "*all* legal restrictions which curtail the civil rights of a single racial group are immediately suspect. . . . Courts must subject them to the most rigid scrutiny." [13] Yet even in *Korematsu* the Court held that the *purpose* of strict scrutiny for racial classifications is to detect whether they reflect "pressing public necessity" or merely "racial antagonism." [14] Racial antagonism, of course, is hardly the motive of today's minority set-aside programs.

Nor does Justice Harlan's oft-quoted but rarely examined declaration in *Plessy v. Ferguson* [15] that "[o]ur constitution is color-blind" support the view that the Supreme Court should act as if race had to be

---

10. See Wygant, 106 S.Ct. at 1852–53 (O'Connor, J., concurring in part and concurring in the judgment) (reviewing approaches of various members of the Court, ranging from requiring that a classification bear a substantial relation to important governmental interests to requiring "the most exacting judicial examination") (quoting Bakke, 438 U.S. at 361–62 (opinion of Powell, J.)).

Several state courts have upheld, on the reduced justification of reasonableness, benign or protective color-consciousness in voluntary school integration programs. In School Committee v. Board of Education, 352 Mass. 693, 227 N.E.2d 729 (1967), appeal dism'd 389 U.S. 572 (1968), for example, the Supreme Judicial Court of Massachusetts stated that "it would be the height of irony if the racial imbalance act [challenged by plaintiffs], enacted as it was with the laudible purpose of achieving equal educational opportunities, should . . . founder on unsuspected shoals in the Fourteenth Amendment." Id. at 698, 227

N.E.2d at 733 (footnote omitted). Instead, the court found that, since "the means were reasonably related to the [proper] objective" of the statute, the statute was constitutionally sound. Id. See also Tometz v. Board of Educ., 39 Ill.2d 593, 237 N.E.2d 498 (1968) (upholding, on test of reasonableness, state statute requiring school boards to alter district boundaries, on basis of pupil race, for purposes of elimination of de facto segregation); Balaban v. Rubin, 14 N.Y.2d 193, 250 N.Y.S.2d 281, 199 N.E.2d 375 (1964), cert. denied 379 U.S. 881 (1964) (upholding, on test of reasonableness, school officials' zoning plan based, inter alia, on pupil race).

11. See Wygant, 106 S.Ct. at 1849; Sheet Metal Workers, 106 S.Ct. at 3052–53.

12. 323 U.S. 214 (1944).

13. Id. at 216 and accompanying text.

14. 323 U.S. at 216.

15. 163 U.S. 537 (1896).

excluded from all governmental and legal classifications; Justice Harlan's dissent in *Plessy* supports treating classifications as fully "suspect" only when those classifications denigrate someone's equal worth on racial grounds—as by reinforcing the legacy of slavery. Consider Justice Harlan's reference to color blindness in the context of his preceding five sentences:

> The white race deems itself to be the dominant race in this country. *And so it is*, in prestige, in achievements, in education, in wealth and in power. So, I doubt not, it will continue to be for all time, if it remains true to its great heritage and holds fast to the principles of constitutional liberty. But in the view of the Constitution, in the eye of the law, there is in this country no superior, dominant, ruling class of citizens. There is no caste here. Our Constitution is color-blind. . . .[16]

Even for this late nineteenth-century proponent of white dominance, it appears that the color-blind ideal was only shorthand for the concept that the fourteenth amendment prevents our law from enshrining and perpetuating white supremacy.[17] To say that any such constitutional vice is shared, automatically or even presumptively, by race-specific minority set-asides is surely far-fetched—even for those who would urge a prophylactic constitutional barrier to all but the most compellingly justified uses of race in government programs of affirmative action.

The principle that race may be taken into account by a government body at least for the purpose of remedying past racial discrimination reasonably believed, by that body, to have distorted the situation that it would otherwise confront seems compatible not only with the text but with the historical intent of the framers of the fourteenth amendment. Such affirmative action is compatible with the framers' intent regardless of whether that intent is defined in specific terms, by examining the practices those framers evidently deemed compatible with the amendment,[18] or in general terms, by explicating the concept of equality that the framers seemingly enacted into law.[19] Viewing the fourteenth amendment as requiring *all* race distinctions to be condemned as instances of inequality derives less from any genuine analysis of what the fourteenth amendment has ever meant than from the most sweeping and activist reading of the decision that justly stands as the most celebrated embodiment of fourteenth amendment theory: *Brown*

16. Id. at 559 (emphasis added).

17. Perhaps it is anachronistic and even unfair to stress too heavily the manifest racism in Justice Harlan's full statement. Like most "southern gentlemen" of the nineteenth century, Justice Harlan—a former slave owner and, originally, an opponent of the thirteenth amendment—was certainly a product of his time. See Filler, "John M. Harlan," in 2 The Justices of the United States Supreme Court 1789–1969: Their Lives and Major Opinions 1282 (L. Friedman and F. Israel eds. 1969). Yet it is hardly less anachronistic, or more fair, to wrench Justice Harlan's words out of their original context and to invoke them as a talisman against all color-consciousness in government action.

18. For example, the framers of the fourteenth amendment created a Freedmen's Bureau to assist former slaves. In practice, under the 1865 Act, most of the Bureau's programs applied only to black Freedmen; in addition, the 1866 Act contained explicitly race-conscious measures. See Schnapper, "Affirmative Action and the Legislative History of the Fourteenth Amendment," 71 Va.L.Rev. 753, 761, 772–73 (1985).

19. See R. Dworkin, Law's Empire 393–97 (1986).

v. Board of Education.[20]   According to that activist reading, *Brown* revises the fourteenth amendment principle at its most basic level by directing the courts, in light of modern and more enlightened values, to create a general right never to be disadvantaged by law on account of one's race—or perhaps to be so disadvantaged only upon a showing of the strictest national necessity.[21]   Such a reading of *Brown* creates a right that the fourteenth amendment's language does not really suggest and that the fourteenth amendment's authors—authors who did not regard even racial segregation in public schools as offensive to the amendment—would certainly not have endorsed.   *Brown* is better understood not as having assigned a new constitutional principle to the fourteenth amendment, but rather as having embraced, in light of a changed understanding of the social meaning of segregation, the central principle for which the fourteenth amendment always stood.   The 1954 Court in *Brown* saw, as the 1896 Court in *Plessy* did not, that racial segregation by law in public schools and other public facilities in fact subjugated blacks, despite its superficial appearance of symmetry and equality, because it stood for white supremacy and therefore denied individuals in the minority "equal protection" of the laws.[22]   So regarded, *Brown* reflects a change in perceptions and understandings of racial segregation, rather than a change in the underlying legal principle.

Deprived of any support in the landmark *Brown* ruling, proponents of the view that "benign" racial classifications are no less suspect if part of an affirmative action program than they are if part of a system of apartheid [23] must resort to a form of judicial activism and creative constitutionalism many of them deplore in other settings: they must argue that our Constitution's overall commitment to treating people as

---

20. 347 U.S. 483 (1954).

21. See, e.g., Reynolds, "Individualism v. Group Rights: The Legacy of Brown," 93 Yale L.J. 995, 997–98 (1984). In Assistant Attorney General Reynolds' view, the Court in Brown "acknowledged with eloquent simplicity that the equal protection clause requires governmental race neutrality in all public activities." In "Rites of Passage: Race, the Supreme Court, and the Constitution," 46 U.Chi.L.Rev. 775, 783 (1979), Professor Van Alstyne similarly asserts that, "during the two years following Brown, . . . a line of per curiam decisions appeared . . . to enact Harlan's view that the Civil War Amendments altogether 're-moved the race line from our governmental systems.'" (quoting Plessy, 163 U.S. at 555 (Harlan, J., dissenting). According to Van Alstyne, "from 1954 to 1974, the Supreme Court's unambiguous 'lesson' . . . seemed to be that race was . . . constitutionally withdrawn from the incorrigible temptations of governmental use." Id. at 790–91. See also A. Bickel, The Morality of Consent 132–34 (1975); Posner, "The DeFunis Case and the Preferential Treatment of Minorities," 1974 Sup.Ct.Rev. 1, 25.

22. The Court in Brown did *not* argue that the wrong to black students under segregation was equally suffered by whites. For blacks, the legally enforced separation was a virtual badge of slavery. A racial distinction that favored rather than stigmatized or excluded minorities thus need not suffer the constitutional infirmity recognized by the Court in Brown.

23. Solicitor General Charles Fried argued in Wygant that "[w]hether a Plessy is ejected from a railroad coach because he is one-eighth black or because he is seven-eighths white, the concrete harm to him is much the same." Brief of the United States as Amicus Curiae Supporting Petitioners at 21, Wygant v. Jackson Bd. of Educ., 106 S.Ct. 1842 (1986). These wrongs are *not* self-evidently the same when properly viewed—as the Court in Brown viewed the harm of racial separation—in terms of racist stigma. See 347 U.S. at 494. Against an historical background of race hierarchy in which whites have been dominant and blacks oppressed, excluding Mr. Plessy because he was black reinforced a legacy of slavery in a way that excluding him for his whiteness could not.

individuals without regard to their ancestry [24] permits of no distinction among various governmental uses of a person's race to deprive that person of an otherwise available benefit or opportunity. All are equally bad—unless, perhaps, they simply serve to "make whole" the proven victims of racial discrimination by depriving proven discriminators of their race-specific ill-gotten gains—because all treat persons less as individuals than as members of hereditarily defined, immutable classes.[25]

Such an implied right to individualized treatment [26] does appear to have constitutional roots and has indeed been recognized, albeit un-

24. See, e.g., the clause in article III of the Constitution that guarantees that "no Attainder of Treason shall work corruption of the blood"—i.e., that no person convicted of treason would thereby be legally disqualified to leave property to his heirs.

25. The position that all racial classifications are equally suspect shares with the Court's opinion in Skinner v. Oklahoma, 316 U.S. 535 (1942), a premise that people's immutable characteristics should not be viewed as facts relevant to social ordering, even when that ordering is conducted not by the judiciary but by an electorally accountable body such as a legislature. The Court in Skinner applied strict scrutiny to invalidate Oklahoma's Habitual Criminal Sterilization Act on the ground that its burden on the fundamental right to procreate was unsupported by any compelling justification. Justice Douglas perceived dangerous potential in the Act because, "in evil or reckless hands," the power to sterilize "can cause races or types which are inimical to the dominant group to whither and disappear." Id. at 541. The Act, which provided for sterilization of only those felons convicted of "crimes involving moral turpitude", was also inimical to fair treatment of persons as individuals because it "la[id] an unequal hand on those who ha[d] committed intrinsically the same quality of offense and steriliz[ed] the one and not the other," making "as invidious a discrimination as if it had selected a particular race or nationality for oppressive treatment." Id. Using affirmative action to fit individuals into a social blueprint, not by virtue of individual characteristics bearing some relation to personal responsibility but instead in accordance with elected officials' visions of how bloodlines should be woven together to create a preferred social fabric, clashes with the belief that racial representation within our social institutions should evolve more organically from individual choices. Legislative planning with attention to race has a discomforting resonance with the kind of genetic engineering that the Court identified in the sterilization law it struck down in Skinner.

It would, however, be an overreaction to invalidate all explicit, affirmative attention to race on the basis of the concern raised in Skinner that mere constitutional permission to consider immutable characteristics might in practice be used in a discriminatory way to create a permanent underclass. There are obvious distinctions between the eugenic overtones of policies that unfavorably consider genetic theories of criminality in the context of permission to procreate and policies that favorably consider race in order to eradicate racism. Even apart from those distinctions, the concerns raised in Skinner may not argue against but may indeed argue for quantitative affirmative action measures. Fears of genetic engineering are at bottom fears that governmental discretion will invade too deeply, and often on hidden grounds, into private choice; integrationist goals and quotas, in contrast, have the virtue of leaving *less* discretion in the hands of government decisionmakers and making the racial factor in decisions more explicit and therefore more publicly accountable.

26. In his separate opinion in Bakke, Justice Powell suggested that an individual may have a right to be treated by the government as a unique and not a fungible being. See 438 U.S. at 318; see also Carey v. Piphus, 435 U.S. 247 (1978), discussed in § 10–7, supra. Nothing but Justice Powell's aversion to mass process as such stands between the individualized consideration of race he would deem permissible, and the governmental focus on the racial proportions within a group as a whole that he deems violative of the fourteenth amendment. "The denial to respondent of [his] right to individualized consideration without regard to his race," Justice Powell wrote in Bakke, "is the principal evil of petitioner's special admissions program." Id. at 318 n.52. Justice Powell found unconstitutional the fact that U.C.-Davis had set aside sixteen places for which only disadvantaged *minorites* were considered; this indicated to each white applicant that he would not be considered for any of these places—for the sole reason that "he was not of the right color." Id. at 318. Consti-

evenly, in the Supreme Court's decisions striking down various "disabilities on the illegitimate [as] contrary to the basic concept of our system that burdens should bear some relationship to individual responsibility." [27] But that concept has not led the Court uniformly to apply strict scrutiny even in all cases of legal disabilities imposed upon illegitimates, despite the usual irrelevance of legitimacy and its history as a "source of social opprobrium." [28] Invoking the individual responsibility concept to subject to the strictest scrutiny those stigmatizing classifications that reflect only a habitual prejudice against certain categories of persons—"a tradition of thinking of [them] as less deserving" than others [29]—hardly implies doing so when the classifications used are neither stigmatizing nor the knee-jerk products of a habitual premise of lesser worth for those disadvantaged.

Accordingly, from its first major collision with the issue [30] in *Regents of the University of California v. Bakke*,[31] the Supreme Court

tutionally distinguishable, Justice Powell reasoned, was any program that, for justifiable reasons (such as the diversity of a student body), treated "race or ethnic background . . . as a 'plus' in a particular applicant's file," id. at 317, without telling any applicant, black or white, that some seats were totally beyond that applicant's reach. The alternative kind of program suggested by Justice Powell, unlike one that set aside a number of slots for which whites were wholly ineligible, "treats each applicant as an individual in the admissions process." Id. at 318.

The four justices who were prepared to uphold the U.C.-Davis program in its entirety reasoned that explicitly setting aside a fixed number of places for minorities was constitutionally indistinguishable from giving individuals an edge because of their minority status—an edge that could mean that the same number of places would end up being filled by minorities anyway. Id. at 378 (opinion of Brennan, White, Marshall, and Blackmun, JJ.). See also id. at 406 (Blackmun, J.). If process had constitutional significance only because of results, the conclusion of these four justices would seem inescapable, as would the often-voiced view that a program that "adds points" for minority race is simply a less candid version of an explicit set-aside. Id. at 378. In a constitutional world concerned only with outcomes, the theory that underlay Justice Powell's vote—and thus the result in Bakke, although not the views of any other justice individually—would indeed seem indefensible.

But ours is not such a world. To be kicked is not the same as to be tripped over. That the Court, because of Justice Powell's sensitivity to this point, did not embrace numerical quotas as willingly as it approved affirmative action of a more individualized sort smacks of raw politics

only to the unduly cynical: there *is* a difference between the individualized approach that five justices indicated they would approve on a record like that in the Bakke case, and the quotas that no majority could be mustered to approve without a more compelling case than could be gleaned from the Bakke record. But the difference is visible through the lens of the Constitution only if one admits the intrinsic significance of process as such as a fourteenth amendment value. See § 10–7, supra.

27. Lalli v. Lalli, 439 U.S. 259, 265 (1978), discussed in § 16–24, infra.

28. Mathews v. Lucas, 427 U.S. 495, 523 (1976) (Stevens, J., joined by Brennan and Marshall, JJ., dissenting) discussed in § 16–24, infra.

29. Id. at 523.

30. For prior close encounters, see United Jewish Organizations v. Carey, 430 U.S. 144 (1977); DeFunis v. Odegaard, 416 U.S. 312 (1974) (per curiam). In United Jewish Organizations, the Court approved, in the context of legislative redistricting, numerical targets defined by race in order to assure fair representation for the minority. In upholding the use of such race-specific targets so long as they did not deprive whites of the franchise or unfairly dilute their political power, several justices thought it crucial that there was "no racial slur or stigma with respect to whites or any other race," id. at 166 (White, J., joined by Rehnquist and Stevens, JJ.); that no "racial insult or injury [was intended] to those whites who are adversely affected," id. at 179 (Brennan, J., concurring); and that the plan did not represent "purposeful discrimination against white voters." Id. at 180 (Stewart, J., joined by Powell, J.,

31. See note 31 on page 1529.

has quite properly rejected so extreme a version of individualism as a basis for striking down governmental programs reasonably tailored to address racial realities in our society. Thus the Court in *Bakke* ruled, 5–4, that state educational institutions need not be color-blind in confronting the realities of race with "a properly devised admissions program."[32] The Court struck down, also by a 5–4 vote, the particular admissions program before it, which set aside a specific number of places for which only disadvantaged minorities could compete.[33] The Court thus upheld the kind of affirmative action program used by most American colleges and universities, and disallowed only the unusually

concurring). In DeFunis v. Odegaard, a precursor to Bakke that presented an analogous affirmative action issue, DeFunis, a white applicant, claimed that he had been discriminated against on account of his race in the admissions process of the University of Washington Law School. The Washington Supreme Court had rejected DeFunis' claim. Although the United States Supreme Court ultimately found DeFunis' case moot because he had been admitted to the Law School during the pendency of the case and would graduate with a law degree regardless of the Court's decision, Justice Douglas dissented from the finding of mootness and therefore reached the merits of the case. He concluded that a state could constitutionally set "minority applicants apart for separate processing," but only in order to "make more certain that racial factors [did] not militate against an applicant or on his behalf." 416 U.S. at 334, 336 (emphasis omitted). See also id. at 348 (Brennan, J., joined by Douglas, White, and Marshall, JJ., dissenting).

31. 438 U.S. 265 (1978). Justices Powell, Brennan, White, Marshall, and Blackmun formed a majority to uphold the affirmative use of racial classifications in admissions decisions. Four justices would have upheld the U.C. Davis program under the equal protection clause on the ground that the program was designed to serve an important interest in "remedying the effects of past racial discrimination," id. at 362 (opinion of Brennan, J., joined by White, Marshall, and Blackmun, JJ.), but Justice Powell did not agree that U.C.-Davis' set-aside of a specific number of places was sufficiently justified under the equal protection clause. Id. at 315–20. Four justices in Bakke did not reach the constitutional issue, but simply found that the program violated Title VI of the Civil Rights Act of 1964, 42 U.S.C. §§ 2000d–2000d–4 (1976), inasmuch as that statute expressly barred excluding anyone from a federally funded program "on account of race," and Bakke had indisputably been excluded, on account of his race, from the federally-funded special admissions pro-

gram at the University of California at Davis. Id. at 412–21 (Stevens, J., concurring in the judgment in part and dissenting in part, joined by Burger, C.J., and Stewart and Rehnquist, JJ.). Each of those justices had previously approved some form of affirmative action. See Califano v. Webster, 430 U.S. 313 (1977) (per curiam) (upholding constitutionality of social security retirement benefits formula providing higher payments to women than to men with equal past earnings); United Jewish Organizations v. Carey, 430 U.S. 144, 144, 180 (1977) (Justices Rehnquist and Stevens joining plurality opinion and Justice Stewart concurring to uphold constitutionality of race-conscious reapportionment plan enhancing nonwhite minority voting strength); Kahn v. Shevin, 416 U.S. 351 (1974) (Chief Justice Burger and Justices Stewart and Rehnquist joining majority opinion upholding statute allowing property tax exemption for widows but not for widowers). See "The Supreme Court, 1977 Term," 92 Harv.L.Rev. 57, 131–48 (1978), for a full statement of facts and the differing opinions expressed in the Bakke case. See also Ely, "The Supreme Court, 1977 Term—Foreword: On Discovering Fundamental Values," 92 Harv.L.Rev. 5, 9 n.33 (1978).

32. 438 U.S. at 320 (opinion of Powell, J., joined by White, Brennan, Marshall and Blackmun, JJ.).

33. Justice Powell alone wrote that U.C.-Davis' set-aside of a specific number of places was invalid under the fourteenth amendment. 438 U.S. at 315–20. Justice Stevens, joined by Chief Justice Burger and Justices Stewart and Rehnquist, found that the U.C. Davis program violated Title VI and thus formed a majority with Justice Powell for the judgment invalidating the program and affirming the judgment ordering Bakke admitted. Id. at 408–21. The other four justices that had joined Justice Powell to form a majority upholding explicit affirmative consideration of race in admissions would have upheld U.C.-Davis' numerical set-aside. Id. at 378–79.

mechanical approach taken by the Medical School of the University of California at Davis.

Four of the justices in the five-member majority in *Bakke* favored an intermediate level of judicial scrutiny.[34] Only Justice Powell was prepared to subject state educational programs disadvantaging whites to precisely the same degree of scrutiny as programs disadvantaging blacks,[35] and only he held the Davis quota violative of equal protection.[36] While recognizing that calling a classification "benign" or "compensatory" does not necessarily make it so,[37] the other four justices in the majority found that a program like that at U.C.-Davis which met four tests should be subject only to intermediate review.[38] The four tests were: (1) that no fundamental right be involved; (2) that the disadvantaged class not have the "traditional indicia of suspectness . . . as to command extraordinary protection from the majoritarian political process"; [39] (3) that race be relevant to the goal sought; and (4) that the classification never be based on a presumption of racial

34. Id. at 359 (opinion of Brennan, J., joined by White, Marshall, and Blackmun, JJ.).

35. Justice Powell suggested in a footnote to his opinion that affirmative action in some cases may not need to be understood as racial *preference* at all, but may instead be justified as merely eliminating the distorting effects of racism that may have entered into decisionmaking and produced a racially unrepresentative outcome. See 438 U.S. at 306 n.43. Justice Powell did not find such a justification sufficient to sustain a judgment for the U.C.-Davis program at issue in Bakke, however, because he found "[n]othing in the record . . . suggest[ing] either that any of the quantitative factors considered by the medical school were culturally biased or that petitioners' special admissions program was formulated to correct for any such biases." Id. But given that the parties in Bakke were a white opponent of the University's minority set-aside and the University itself, it is hardly surprising that the record lacked any indication of reliance by the University on racially biased factors. Even if some bias were shown, Justice Powell would find reserving a fixed number of places—rather than according a more discretionary, individualized preference to minorities—"inexplicable" as a means to correct for that bias. Id. But the fact that the set-aside in Bakke was numerical does not convert into impermissible group reparation a program that Justice Powell suggested might otherwise be viewed as granting no special preference. To employ a numerical measure of the success of an affirmative action program is only to approximate what an unbiased system would produce—assuming that ability to succeed in medical school is not inherently linked to race.

36. 430 U.S. at 320. It is disturbing that, while the Court has not applied strict scrutiny to explicit discrimination against women, see § 16–26, infra; against the young or old, see § 16–31, infra; or against aliens, see § 16–23, infra, Justice Powell was willing to apply such scrutiny on behalf of a white male who not merely vicariously but individually had enjoyed a full measure of "power, authority and goods." See Wasserstrom, "Racism, Sexism and Prefential Treatment: An Approach to the Topics," 24 U.C.L.A.L.Rev. 581, 584–603 (1977).

37. 438 U.S. at 358–59 (opinion of Brennan, White, Marshall and Blackmun, JJ.).

38. Id. at 357–76.

39. Id. at 357 (quoting San Antonio Independent School District v. Rodriguez, 411 U.S. 1 (1973), discussed in § 16–9, supra; §§ 16–52, 16–58, infra. Justices Brennan, White, Marshall and Blackmun recognized that such protection might be needed by white ethnic minorities. But they maintained that, because the U.C.-Davis program did not on its face discriminate against any white ethnic group, members of such groups would have no constitutional claim unless they could show discriminatory intent under Washington v. Davis, 426 U.S. 229 (1976), discussed in § 16–20, supra. See 438 U.S. at 358 n.35. Because the Court in Davis held that a policy not explicitly distinguishing blacks did not trigger equal protection strict scrutiny even though it had a disproportionately adverse impact on blacks as a group, it would be ironic indeed if mere adverse impact on a *white* subgroup were enough to invalidate an affirmative action plan, or even to trigger strict scrutiny.

inferiority, nor promote racial hatred or separatism.[40]   When these four tests are met, Justices Brennan, White, Marshall and Blackmun said they would require only that an important purpose for the classification be articulated, and that the classification be used reasonably in light of its objectives.[41]

Although the Court struck down what it viewed as an unnecessarily rigid 16% set-aside in *Bakke*, the Court subsequently has both mandated numerical quotas as part of affirmative action remedies for persistent racial discrimination and upheld quantitative affirmative action programs when voluntarily adopted.   In *United Steelworkers of America v. Weber*,[42] the Court upheld against a Title VII challenge a private affirmative action plan negotiated by an employer and a labor union that reserved 50 percent of the openings in craft-training programs for black workers until the percentage of black craft workers was commensurate with their representation in the local labor force. The Court voted 5–2 that the challenged affirmative action set-aside did not constitute discrimination on the basis of race, but rather, because it was designed "to break down old patterns of racial segregation and hierarchy," [43] legitimately aided in the elimination of racial discrimination.   Unlike Justice Powell in *Bakke*, the Court in *Weber* did not view the set-aside of a specific number of places as unfairly denying opportunities to individual whites.   The plan did not "unnecessarily trammel the interests of white employees" because it did not "require the discharge of white workers and their replacement with new black hirees," nor "create an absolute bar to the advancement of white employees" who still might fill the remaining places in the craft

40. Id. at 357 (opinion of Brennan, White, Marshall and Blackmun, JJ.) (quoting Carolene Products, 304 U.S. at 152 n.4).

41. Id. at 359. These Justices found that the U.C.-Davis program's objective was to remedy past societal discrimination, and they found this purpose sufficient since the University had a "sound basis for concluding that minority underrepresentation [in the medical profession was] substantial and chronic, and that the handicap of past discrimination was impeding access of minorities to the medical school." Id. at 369. That the racial classifications used were reasonable in light of U.C.-Davis's objectives was confirmed, in the view of these four justices, by two characterizations of that program. First, the program did not operate to stigmatize whites or to relegate them to second-class citizenship. Id. at 374–75. Second, there was no evidence that the program in fact hurt the minorities it was supposed to help: it did not set a ceiling on their numbers, nor did it treat them as less capable than white students; once minority students were admitted, they had to meet the same standards set for white students in their course work. Id. at 375–76.

Three of the four justices who concurred in Bakke to articulate an intermediate standard of equal protection review for affirmative race-based preferences again concurred in Fullilove on similar grounds. See 448 U.S. at 517–21 (Marshall, J., joined by Brennan and Blackmun, JJ., concurring). Justice White, however, departed in Fullilove from his earlier understanding in Bakke and, together with Justice Powell, joined the plurality opinion by Chief Justice Burger which asserted that "[a]ny preference based on racial or ethnic criteria must necessarily receive a most searching examination to make sure that it does not conflict with constitutional guarantees." 448 U.S. at 491.

42. 443 U.S. 193 (1979) (majority opinion of Brennan, J., joined by Stewart, White, Marshall, and Blackmun, JJ.); see id. at 209 (Blackmun, J., concurring); id. at 216 (Burger, C.J., dissenting); id. at 219 (Rehnquist, J., joined by Burger, C.J., dissenting). Justices Powell and Stevens took no part in consideration or decision of this case.

43. Weber, 443 U.S. at 208. The plan was upheld as not violative of Title VII of the Civil Rights Act of 1964, 42 U.S.C. § 2000e-2(a) & (d).

training program not reserved for black workers. The Court also focused on the fact that the plan was temporary, and was "not intended to maintain racial balance, but simply to eliminate manifest racial imbalance." [44]

Even if, as a matter of statutory construction, the majority in *Weber* had been wrong and the view of Justice Rehnquist in dissent had prevailed to hold that Title VII should be read to preclude affirmative action,[45] construing Title VII that way might be unconstitutional. For the equal protection component of the fifth amendment's due process clause might forbid Congress from passing laws that selectively hinder private attempts to redress racial discrimination. In *Hunter v. Erickson*,[46] the Court struck down a city charter amendment requiring the electorate—rather than the city council alone—to approve provisions addressing racial discrimination in housing because the structural impact of the law would be to hinder minorities seeking open housing. The law in *Hunter* was superficially symmetrical.[47] But because the Constitution and other federal laws already independently forbade laws that would *invite* racial discrimination in housing, the only additional goal and effect of the new law was to frustrate legal efforts to *redress* racial discrimination.[48] Similarly, Justice Rehnquist in *Weber* would have read Title VII as prohibiting the use of *all* race-conscious employment practices. But on that reading, Title VII—like the law in *Hunt-*

---

44. Id. at 208. In order to avoid the spectre of impermissible "social engineering," the Court in Weber strained to characterize as limited those circumstances in which racial balancing might be warranted. But it is difficult to imagine what a distinction between maintaining racial balance and avoiding racial imbalance might mean in practice. By drawing such a distinction, the Court cannot mean to imply that even voluntary affirmative action such as that at issue in Weber must be viewed as a one-shot effort, so that recurring racial imbalance would fail to justify ongoing efforts at rectification. Indeed, in Local 28 of Sheet Metal Workers International Assoc. v. E.E.O.C., 106 S.Ct. 3019 (1986), the Court upheld a court-ordered affirmative action quota specifically as a means to measure *over time* the union's performance in eliminating discrimination. See id. at 3056; id. at 3056 (Powell, J., concurring in part and concurring in the judgment) (characterizing the union membership goal as "a benchmark against which [the district court] could measure [the union's] progress in eliminating discriminatory practices").

To condemn as social engineering the programs devised by *political* bodies is to invoke an inapposite assumption regarding the limitations on the role of the *judiciary* in forming social policy. *Upholding* a voluntary affirmative action plan does not *adopt* that plan or its underlying premises as a model of what is constitutionally mandatory, but merely confirms that the justifications for affirmative action deemed adequate by those who chose the particular plan are constitutionally permissible. Moreover, to seek racial balance is not necessarily to engage in social engineering for its own sake. Plans designed to achieve racially balanced union memberships, medical or law school classes, employment ranks or teaching staffs need not be invalidated as the programs of meddling social engineers even if the Constitution were deemed to include something akin to an "anti-engineering" principle. For such balance approximates the racial proportions that an unbiased system would naturally produce. To view the effort to achieve proportional racial balance as social engineering—rather than as an attempt to approximate the allocation of individuals most likely to have occurred but for a history of slavery and racism—is to assume that the tastes and abilities that lead to success in various fields are inherently linked to race. See supra note 35. Policies resting on such an assumption, and not those the Court resists as "social engineering," are inconsistent with equal treatment without regard to race.

45. Id. at 219 (Rehnquist, J., joined by Burger, C.J., dissenting).

46. 393 U.S. 385 (1969), discussed in § 16–17, supra.

47. Id. at 390.

48. Id. at 391.

er—was only superficially neutral, since federal law already forbade *invidious* racial discrimination in private economic intercourse.[49] Thus, reading Title VII as barring all remedial uses of race in private agreements would add the same sort of legal obstacles to efforts in seeking equal access for minorities which the Court found to violate equal protection in *Hunter v. Erickson.*

In *Fullilove v. Klutznick,*[50] the Court again confronted the constitutionality of a minority quota analogous to the one condemned in *Bakke. Fullilove* contained no statutory issue, however, so all the Justices reached the constitutional question. The 6–3 decision firmly established the legitimacy of affirmative action by upholding a provision of a federal public works employment program that set aside 10% of its total funds for minority business enterprises (MBEs). Chief Justice Burger, in his opinion announcing the judgment of the Court, concluded that Congress had the power to regulate the practices of prime contractors on federally funded projects in this way under either the spending power or the commerce power because there was a "rational basis for Congress to conclude that the subcontracting practices of prime contractors could perpetuate the prevailing impaired access by minority businesses" even if those prime contractors could not be "shown responsible for any violation of antidiscrimination laws."[51] Chief Justice Burger repudiated the contention that Congress must act in a wholly color-blind manner,[52] and held not only that "innocent parties" may be constitutionally required to "share the burden" of affirmative action designed to "cure the effects of prior discrimination,"[53] but also that Congress was free to impose such a burden on the "assumption that in the past some non-minority businesses have reaped competitive benefit over the years" from the free ride resulting from "the virtual exclusion of minority firms from these contracting opportunities."[54]

The holding in *Fullilove* at first appears to be a closely confined one. The Court stressed that the affirmative action program at issue was modest, characterizing it as a temporary "pilot project" within a "flexible" administrative scheme,[55] and further observing that the "bur-

49. See, e.g., Jones v. Alfred H. Mayer Co., 392 U.S. 409 (1968) (holding that 42 U.S.C. § 1982 prohibits racial discrimination in the sale of private homes); McDonald v. Santa Fe Trail Transp. Co., 427 U.S. 273 (1976); Johnson v. Railway Express Agency, 421 U.S. 454 (1975) (holding that 42 U.S.C. § 1981 prohibits racial discrimination by private employers).

50. 448 U.S. 448 (1980). Chief Justice Burger, joined by Justices White and Powell, wrote for the plurality. Justice Marshall filed an opinion concurring in the judgment, in which Justices Brennan and Blackmun joined. The concurring justices treated their joint opinion in Bakke as dispositive of what was "not even a close [question]." 448 U.S. at 519 (Marshall, J., concurring in the judgment). Thus, with the addition of Chief Justice Burger, the five members of the Court who had voted

to uphold affirmative action in Bakke did so again in Fullilove. Justice Stewart, who had voted with the majority in Weber, dissented in Fullilove, joined by Justice Rehnquist. Justice Stevens also filed a dissenting opinion.

51. Id. at 475 (plurality opinion of Burger, C.J.).

52. Id. at 482.

53. Id. at 484.

54. Id. at 485.

55. Id. at 481–82, 487–89. Unlike the rigid allocation of sixteen places in the medical school class under the Davis minority admissions program, the 10% set-aside in Fullilove was subject to several other exemptions and could be waived by the Secretary of Commerce. There were, according to Chief Justice Burger, proce-

den" it imposed on non-minority businesses was "relatively light." [56]
The Court also repeatedly stressed that Congress had "abundant evidence" of discrimination with which to justify the MBE set-aside.[57] Yet the fact that the evidence was relatively meager and largely derivative [58] and that the administrative guidelines were less flexible than some members of the Court evidently wanted to believe [59] suggests that *Fullilove's* limiting factors may be illusory.

Taken together, *Bakke, Weber,* and *Fullilove* might be thought to suggest the disturbing conclusion that the Court seems more willing to uphold quantitative, race-specific affirmative action plans when the result disrupts "only" the prospective expectations of blue-collar tradesmen than when the result affects opportunities in elitist institutions such as medical schools—institutions in which meritocracy supposedly still thrives.[60] But when white employees' expectations of retaining their current jobs—rather than their prospective hopes for new employment or business opportunities such as those in *Weber* and *Fullilove*— are at stake, they have received the same sympathy from the Court as did the white applicants to U.C.-Davis.[61]

dures for challenging and excluding from participation those MBEs whose competitive position could be shown not to have been adversely affected by past discrimination. Id. at 482.

56. Id. at 484. The Court had made the same observation in Weber, 443 U.S. at 208–09. In addition, Chief Justice Burger opined that Congress did not discriminate against any disadvantaged group by excluding it from the program. See Fullilove, 448 U.S. at 485–86.

57. Id. at 477–78.

58. All the evidence of past discrimination to which Chief Justice Burger referred came from past hearings on other legislation, 448 U.S. at 465–66. None of it was actually mentioned during the brief discussion on the floor of Congress. 448 U.S. at 550 n.25 (Stevens, J., dissenting). The minority set-aside was offered as a floor amendment, id. at 458 (opinion of Burger, C.J.), and no specific hearings on the set-aside were ever held: its consideration by Congress was "perfunctory." Id. at 549–50 & n.25 (Stevens, J. dissenting). See Days, "Fullilove," 96 Yale L.J. 451, 464 (1987) (stating that "[o]ne can only marvel at the fact that the minority set-aside provision [upheld in Fullilove] was enacted into law without hearing or committee reports, and with only token opposition").

59. For all of the detailed attention that Chief Justice Burger's opinion devoted to the administrative guidelines, they simply do not support the reading he gave them. The concept of "unjust participation" on which he relied so heavily, 448 U.S. at 472, 488, is nowhere defined in the guidelines, which provide no means for assessing whether an MBE has indeed been

the victim of discrimination, but only a procedure for challenging the participation of businesses that are not really minority-owned. See J. Choper, Y. Kamisar & L. Tribe, 2 Supreme Court Trends & Developments 67–69 (1981). See 448 U.S. at 492–95 app. (opinion of Burger, C.J.) for the text of the regulations.

60. See Fallon, "To Each According to His Ability, From None According to His Race: The Concept of Merit in the Law of Antidiscrimination," 60 B.U.L.Rev. 815, 864–76 (1980).

61. Expressing its concern for white workers' expectations of competitive job seniority, the Court in Firefighters Local Union No. 1784 v. Stotts, 467 U.S. 561 (1984) (opinion of White, J., joined by Burger, C.J., and Powell, Rehnquist, and O'Connor, JJ.), rejected a district court's modification of a consent decree between the Memphis Fire Department and black firefighters. The decree had been entered in a Title VII case challenging as discriminatory the city's pattern of hiring firefighters, but it protected blacks only at the hiring and promotion stages. When budget constraints forced the Department to lay off firefighters, the district court modified the decree to enjoin the Department from applying its seniority system in a manner that would result in a disproportionate number of minority workers being laid off. The Sixth Circuit Court of Appeals upheld the District Court's action, but the Supreme Court reversed. Despite broad dicta to the effect that Title VII would preclude laying off comparatively senior white employees on behalf of others who have not been proved to be actual victims of discrimination, the Court's holding rested on the

Concern for the settled expectations of white workers played a decisive part in the Court's decision in *Wygant v. Jackson Board of Education*.[62] In *Wygant* the school board, in a collective bargaining agreement with black teachers, had attempted to provide newly hired blacks with protection against layoffs. Acting at the behest of white teachers laid off because of the collective bargaining agreement, the Supreme Court invalidated the agreement on the basis that the layoff provision was not an appropriate means to meet even a compelling state interest.[63]

Because, according to the *Wygant* plurality, no arguably relevant state interest could have justified the school district's layoff plan, the Court did not need to consider whether the board's asserted interests—in providing minority role models for the increasing proportion of black students in the school district and in counteracting the effects of the societal discrimination that accounted for the underrepresentation of black teachers in Jackson—could ever support affirmative action. Although the plurality in dictum rejected the role-model and societal-discrimination justifications that the lower courts had adopted,[64] five justices nonetheless confirmed that a state interest in promoting racial diversity might well be sufficient to warrant the use of a racial classification in furtherance of that interest.[65]

narrow ground that the district court did not have power to modify the consent decree as it had because neither the decree's express terms nor its purposes indicated that it should be modified to affect layoffs. Because resolution of the question of whether layoffs imposed an impermissible burden on white workers under Title VII was not necessary to the Court's holding, Justice Stevens criticized the Court for engaging in a "wholly advisory" discussion of Title VII. Stotts, 467 U.S. at 590 (Stevens, J., concurring in the judgment).

62. 106 S.Ct. 1842 (1986) (plurality opinion of Powell, J., joined by Burger, C.J., and Rehnquist, J.); see id. at 1852 (O'Connor, J., concurring in part and concurring in the judgment), id. at 1857 (White, J., concurring in the judgment).

63. 106 S.Ct. at 1852.

64. 106 S.Ct. at 1847–48. The plurality suggested that an affirmative action program that implied that black students might uniquely benefit from the presence of black teachers as role models could itself lead to a racist system reminiscent of the "separate but equal" system sanctioned in Plessy v. Ferguson. Id. at 1848. Justice Stevens pointed out, however, that "[t]here is a critical difference between a decision to *exclude* a member of a minority race because of his skin color and a decision to *include* more members of a minority in a school faculty for that reason." Id. at 1869 (Stevens, J., dissenting) (emphasis in original). Justice Stevens in part based this distinction on his view that exclusion, un-

like inclusion, "may give rise to the belief that there is some significant difference between [persons of different races]." Id. Yet even if inclusion of additional minority teachers through affirmative action *does* imply that black teachers are different from white teachers, the more important point is that those differences are embraced rather than denigrated by affirmative action. The role-model theory may indeed suggest that some black teachers might share a cultural heritage with black students that no white teacher does, that some black students might be more readily encouraged to emulate black teachers than white, and that black teachers might communicate the worth of blacks to *all* members of the school community, white as well as black, more effectively than white teachers. Cf. Bakke, 438 U.S. at 314 (opinion of Powell, J.) (stating that students of different backgrounds may contribute uniquely to medical school and to the medical profession). The implication that there may be relevant differences between black and white teachers that make black teachers in some respects uniquely qualified to teach are not, however, inconsistent with the conclusion that race cannot constitutionally impair "a person's right to share in the blessings of a free society." 106 S.Ct. at 1869 (Stevens, J., dissenting).

65. 106 S.Ct. at 1853 (O'Connor, J., concurring in part and concurring in the judgment) (stating that the Court may in the future find sufficient other interests in addition to diversity); id. at 1862 (Marshall,

Wygant suggests a distinction between the permissibility of affirmative action in hiring and in layoffs, but it does not invalidate *a priori* all plans that provide affirmative action protection against minority layoffs. Three justices in the *Wygant* plurality explicitly distinguished the burden on innocent whites imposed by a hiring plan from that imposed by a layoff scheme.[66] But Justice O'Connor, who provided the fourth vote for the plurality in *Wygant*, avoided generalizing about the permissibility of affirmative action in layoffs, concluding instead that the hiring goal protected by the layoff provision at issue was wrongly keyed to an irrelevant disparity between the percentages of minority teachers and minority students, rather than to the probative disparity between the percentages of qualified teachers in the relevant labor pool and on the school district's teaching staff.[67]

The *Wygant* Court's concern for the burden that layoff protection imposes on innocent white workers seems exaggerated. That burden cannot be distinguished in a principled way from the burdens on whites' expectations of employment and promotion that the Court has more readily permitted.[68] The fact that implementing preferences in layoffs may be viewed as causing harms more focused and intrusive than those caused by preferences in allocating limited economic opportunities in the first place [69] should not be deemed to make otherwise acceptable affirmative action violative of equal protection. To be sure, burdening vested employment rights of white workers might well amount to a taking for a public purpose and thus require just compensation.[70] But interpreting equal protection to require a balancing of hardships imposed on white workers by affirmative action plans against benefits derived from such plans itself invites social engineering [71] of the very sort that the Court so often condemns.[72] Distinguishing between otherwise justified affirmative action plans on the basis of the degree of sacrifice they extract from equally innocent white workers unnecessarily confounds takings and equal-protection analyses and

J., joined by Brennan and Blackmun, JJ., dissenting); id. at 1867, 1868 (Stevens, J., dissenting).

66. 106 S.Ct. at 1851–52 (Powell, J., joined by Burger, C.J., and Rehnquist, J.). These justices noted, however, that layoff protection may be a necessary remedy for identifiable victims of past discrimination. Id. at 1852 n.12. See id. at 1857–58 (White, J., concurring) (making same distinction). See also United States v. Paradise, 107 S.Ct. 1053, 1073 (1987) (plurality opinion of Brennan, J., joined by Marshall, Blackmun and Powell, JJ.) (noting that racial promotion quota does not require layoffs of the sort that concerned the Wygant plurality and opining that postponement of a promotion "imposes a lesser burden still").

67. 106 S.Ct. at 1857 (O'Connor, J., concurring in part and concurring in the judgment).

68. The Court has approved affirmative action programs that required no layoffs of white workers, concluding that they did

not "disproportionately harm the interests, or unnecessarily trammel the rights, of innocent individuals," Paradise, 107 S.Ct. at 1073 (plurality opinion). See also Fullilove, 448 U.S. at 484–85; Weber, 443 U.S. at 208.

69. See Wygant, 106 S.Ct. at 1851–52 (Powell, J., joined by Chief Justice Burger and Rehnquist, J.); Stotts, 467 U.S. at 574–76, 578–79; Fallon & Weiler, "Conflicting Models of Racial Justice," 1984 S.Ct.Rev. 1, 58.

70. See Hawaii Housing Authority v. Midkiff, 467 U.S. 229 (1984), discussed in § 9–2, supra; Vulcan Pioneers v. New Jersey Department of Civil Serv., 588 F.Supp. 716 (D.N.J. 1984) (requiring layoffs to protect affirmative action goals but compensating for their loss those whose seniority is thereby sacrificed), vacated in light of Stotts 588 F.Supp. 732 (D.N.J. 1984).

71. See Sullivan, supra note 9 at 95.

72. See supra note 44.

subordinates the achievement of racial justice to whatever pattern of economic distribution our discriminatory past happens to have produced.

Although compensation to innocent workers whose economic interests are "taken" by a government-instituted affirmative action plan may sometimes be necessary, the case for such compensation seems weakest when the burdened whites are fairly represented by the body that *voluntarily gives* affirmative action benefits—at least if public compensation is required principally as a means of assuring that the transfer of economic benefits actually serves an overriding public purpose.[73] Moreover, because white expectations formed within a discriminatory historical context are likely to be inflated, if not wholly unfounded, the level of compensation necessary to relieve whites of the burdens properly attributable to affirmative action should be gauged accordingly.

Regardless of whether compensation for individuals burdened by affirmative action might be forthcoming, courts have required that judicially mandated programs have a remedial purpose. But in reviewing voluntary affirmative action plans—such as those in *Bakke, Weber, Fullilove* and *Wygant*—the Court has at times maintained a needlessly restrictive focus on past discrimination that is appropriate only when the Court itself awards, or permits lower federal courts to award, affirmative action as a remedy.[74] Demanding that voluntary affirmative action be upheld only insofar as it remedies what Professor Kathleen Sullivan has aptly described as past "sins of discrimination" [75] is problematic in part because it "dooms affirmative action to further challenge even while legitimating it." [76] Remedial justifications for affirmative action legitimate it by promising that affirmative action will require present sacrifice only to make up for past wrong, and will bestow benefits only to compensate for past injustice. Such justifications doom affirmative action as well, however, by subjecting even voluntary plans to challenges that they should not be required to meet. Focusing on past discrimination invites litigation over how that discrimination may be shown,[77] over whether minorities who were not

---

73. See supra § 9–2.

74. See, e.g., Bakke 438 U.S. at 362 (opinion of Brennan, White, Marshall, & Blackmun, JJ.) (stating that the 16% set-aside should have been upheld as a "remedy [for] the effects of past societal discrimination"); Weber, 443 U.S. at 208 (opinion of Brennan, J. joined by Stewart, White, Marshall, and Blackmun, JJ.) (upholding affirmative action plan "designed to break down old patterns of racial segregation and hierarchy"); Fullilove, 448 U.S. at 528 (Stewart, J., joined by Rehnquist, J., dissenting) (stating that court-ordered affirmative action can be upheld "only where its sole purpose is to eradicate the actual effects of illegal race discrimination"); Wygant, 106 S.Ct. at 1847 (opinion of Powell, J., Burger, C.J., Rehnquist, & O'Connor, JJ.) (stating that some forms of affirmative

action might be tolerated to remedy "prior discrimination by the governmental unit involved").

75. See Sullivan, supra note 9.

76. Id. at 92.

77. Compare Wygant, 106 S.Ct. at 1849 n.5 (opinion of Powell, J., joined by Chief Justice Burger, Rehnquist, and O'Connor, JJ.) (requiring a formal judicial finding of past discrimination by a governmental unit proposing an affirmative action plan), with id. at 1858 (O'Connor, J., concurring in part and concurring in the judgment) (suggesting that a public body need only have a "firm basis for determining that affirmative action is warranted," and that the burden of proving any inadequacy of that basis remains with the plaintiff who challenges the affirmative action plan).

themselves the victims of proven discrimination should be allowed to benefit from affirmative action, and over whether non-minorities who might in the absence of affirmative action have received some of the benefit it allocates should be made to sacrifice in order to remedy wrongs that they did not commit.[78]

As Professor Sullivan has stressed, however, voluntary affirmative action is often justifiable more to pursue a vision of the future than to eradicate a spectre of the past.[79] Some forward-looking visions have appeared in the cases. In *Bakke*, Justice Powell found compelling an interest in promoting future diversity within the student body.[80] In *Fullilove*, Justice Stevens approved of the purpose of "facilitating and encouraging the participation by minority business enterprises in the economy"; [81] in *Wygant* he agreed with the school board and the lower courts that an integrated faculty would "advance the public interest in educating children for the future," and that a finding of past discrimination was therefore unnecessary.[82] And in *Johnson v. Santa Clara Transportation Agency*,[83] a majority of the Court upheld an affirmative action plan designed to promote women to jobs from which they have traditionally been excluded.

The Supreme Court has not circumscribed affirmative action as closely as a purely remedial analysis would require. Under both the Constitution and Title VII, the Court has upheld affirmative action plans that benefit minority members who were not proven victims of past discrimination.[84] Burdens on innocent whites have also sometimes

See id. at 1858 (Marshall, Blackmun, and Brennan, JJ., dissenting) (finding fault with the plurality for deciding the merits based on an inadequate factual record, and therefore "too quickly assum[ing] the absence of a legitimate factual predicate . . . for affirmative action").

78. The Court might justify such sacrifice on the basis that whites never deserved in the first place to develop expectations contingent on a racist *status quo*, cf. R. Nozick, Anarchy, State and Utopia 174–82 (1974), thus far, the Court has not done so.

79. Justice Stevens, concurring in Johnson v. Santa Clara Transportation Agency, quoted at length and explicitly embraced Professor Sullivan's argument that forward-looking considerations can provide sufficient justification for voluntary affirmative action. See 107 S.Ct. 1442, 1460 (1987). But see Days, supra note 58. Professor Days argues that voluntary affirmative action programs should be justified by even more extensive showings of past discrimination than the Court has demanded in pre-1987 cases. In his view, "more than good motives should be required when government seeks to allocate its resources by way of an explicit racial classification system. It must be shown that such a system is responsive to findings of racial discrimination, is designed to redress that problem,

and is employed only as long as is necessary to achieve its remedial objective." Id. at 483–84.

80. 438 U.S. at 314, 317–18. Justice Powell was not concerned with removing the taint of past discrimination, but with ensuring a better future by bringing to the medical school more "experiences, outlooks and ideas that enrich the training of its student body," and by providing society with medical school graduates "better equip[ped] . . . to render with understanding their vital service to humanity." Id. at 314.

81. 448 U.S. at 542–43. Justice Stevens dissented solely on the ground that the affirmative action plan at issue was not narrowly tailored to that or any other legitimate goal.

82. 106 S.Ct. at 1867 (Stevens, J., dissenting).

83. 107 S.Ct. 1442 (1987).

84. See id. at 1450–51 (majority opinion of Brennan, J., joined by Marshall, Blackmun, Powell and Stevens, JJ.); Local 28, Sheet Metal Workers' Int'l Assoc. v. E.E. O.C., 106 S.Ct. 3019, 3054 (1986) (plurality opinion of Brennan, J., joined by Marshall, Blackmun, and Stevens, JJ.) (stating that "six members of the Court agree that a district court may, in appropriate circumstances, order preferential relief benefit-

been deemed necessary.[85] But because the Court continues in some instances to evaluate even non-remedial affirmative action with reference to a remedial paradigm, its deviations from that paradigm to benefit victims and burden innocent third parties may seem aberrant and imperfectly justified.[86]

In *Local 28, Sheet Metal Workers International Association v. Equal Employment Opportunity Commission*,[87] the Court upheld against both Title VII and equal protection challenges a numerical quota for union membership despite the fact that "whites seeking admission into the union may be denied benefits extended to their nonwhite counterparts," [88] and that the plan extended relief to blacks and Hispanics who were not "actual victims" of the union's discrimination.[89] The plan at issue in *Sheet Metal Workers* was court-ordered rather than voluntarily adopted, but the justices in the majority nonetheless treated the affirmative action plan as clearly valid. Still disagreeing over the appropriate standard of review for such plans, the Court nonetheless held that the numerical membership goal was a necessary remedy for the union's persistent discriminatory admissions practices and repeated contempt of court orders to cease that discrimination.[90] As Justice Powell wrote in his concurrence, "[i]t would be difficult to find defendants more

ting individuals who are not the actual victims of discrimination as a remedy for violations of Title VII"); Local No.93, Int'l Assoc. of Firefighters v. Cleveland, 106 S.Ct. at 3072 (majority opinion of Brennan, J., joined by Marshall, Blackmun, Powell, Stevens, and O'Connor, JJ.) (stating that "the voluntary action available to employers and unions seeking to eradicate race discrimination may include reasonable race-conscious relief that benefits individuals who were not actual victims of discrimination").

85. See Wygant, 106 S.Ct. at 1850 (plurality opinion of Powell, J., joined by Burger, C.J., and Rehnquist, J.).

86. See Sullivan, supra note 9 at 95. Professor Sullivan argues that, within a remedial, or "sin-based," paradigm, the Court has justified benefits to non-victims only by "shift[ing] the focus of correction from compensating victims to reforming sinners." Id. at 93. Such a shift adds support to claims by innocent third parties that, if affirmative action is justified as punishment, they should not be implicated. The Court has only partially responded to such "claims of innocence" by striking down programs that it views as unnecessarily rigid or intrusive. Although the Court has thus required that lesser burdens to whites be tolerated, see Fullilove, 448 U.S. at 514–15 (Powell, J., concurring); Weber, 443 U.S. at 208 (majority opinion of Brennan, J., joined by Stewart, White, Marshall, and Blackmun, JJ.), "viewing white sacrifice as a matter of degree cannot dis-

pel the perception of innocence that the paradigm of sin sets up—a perception that makes even lesser sacrifices seem unfair." Sullivan at 95.

87. 106 S.Ct. 3019 (1986) (plurality opinion of Brennan, J., joined by Marshall, Blackmun, and Stevens, JJ.); see id. at 3054 (Powell, J., concurring in part and concurring in the judgment), id. at 3057 (O'Connor, J., concurring in part and dissenting in part), id. at 3062 (White, J., dissenting), id. at 3063 (Rehnquist, J., joined by Burger, C.J., dissenting).

88. Id. at 3052.

89. Id. at 3034. Justice Brennan wrote for the plurality that the text and legislative history of § 706(g)'s prohibition on court-ordered admission of individuals who had been "refused admission . . . for any reason other than discrimination," 106 S.Ct. at 3035 (quoting Title VII of the Civil Rights Act of 1964, 42 U.S.C. § 2000e–5(g)), merely sustained unions' and employers' prerogative to reject workers for cause, and did not preclude them from being required to admit other qualified minority nonvictims. See id.

90. The United States had obtained the orders—including both membership goals and fines against the union to be placed in a fund to subsidize the recruitment of minority apprentices—in a suit against the union under Title VII of the Civil Rights Act of 1964, 42 U.S.C. §§ 2000e–2000h. See 106 S.Ct. at 3026, 3030.

determined to discriminate against minorites." [91]   Because other remedial measures had clearly failed, the Court concluded that the plan's "marginal" and "temporary" burdens on whites were necessary to combat the union's discrimination.[92]   The plurality echoed the distinction suggested in *Wygant* between laying off white workers and spreading less focused affirmative action burdens among whites when it emphasized that the affirmative action plan in *Sheet Metal Workers* "did not disadvantage *existing* union members." [93]   It also stressed the flexibility of the plan in accommodating "legitimate excuses" for failure to comply, and adjusting the deadline for compliance where necessary.[94] Indeed, the degree of flexibility that the Court describes in the plan makes it sound like it may be an inadequate response to the union's intransigent racism.

Another court-ordered numerical affirmative action plan was upheld in *United States v. Paradise*.[95]   A plurality of the Court outlined the relevant considerations for determining whether race-conscious remedies may be judicially imposed: "the necessity for the relief and the efficacy of alternative remedies, the flexibility of the duration of the relief, including the availability of waiver provisions; the relationship of the numerical goals to the relevant labor market; and the impact of the relief on the rights of third parties." [96]   After reviewing the district court's order requiring that 50% of Alabama state police promotions go to black officers until a given rank was 25% black or until the department implemented an acceptable promotion plan, the plurality concluded that the one-for-one promotion requirement "d[id] not disproportionately harm the interests, or unnecessarily trammel the rights, of innocent individuals." [97]   The 50% black promotion requirement was "flexible in application," could "be waived if no qualified black candidates [were] available," and did not apply if "external forces, such as budget cuts, necessitate a promotion freeze." [98]   The plan did not require "the layoff or discharge of white employees," but instead merely postponed some white promotions—a "diffuse burden" even less onerous than the denial of future employment occasioned by a racial hiring goal.[99]   Most significantly, the one-for-one requirement, imposed by the district court in 1984—twelve years after it found pervasive

---

91. 106 S.Ct. at 3055 (Powell, J., concurring).

92. 106 S.Ct. at 3052, 53 (plurality opinion); see id. at 3055–57 (Powell, J., concurring in part and concurring in the judgment).

93. 106 S.Ct. at 3053 (emphasis in original).

94. See id. at 3051 & n.49. Justice Powell supplied the fifth vote upholding the plan because it was not a rigid "means to achieve a racial balance," but a flexible gauge to "assist a court in determining whether discrimination has been eradicated." Id. at 3056 (Powell, J., concurring).

95. 107 S.Ct. 1053 (1987). Justice Brennan announced the opinion of the Court in a plurality opinion joined by Justices Marshall, Blackmun, and Powell. Justice Stevens concurred in the judgment on the ground that an "egregious" violation of the equal protection clause had been established and that the district court had not abused its discrimination in ordering relief that included a numerical hiring program for black officers. Id. at 1077. See note 2, supra. Justice O'Connor, joined by Chief Justice Rehnquist and Justice Scalia, dissented.

96. Id. at 1067 (plurality opinion).

97. Id. at 1073.

98. Id. at 1070.

99. Id. at 1073.

discrimination within the Alabama state police [100]—was "ephemeral:" "the term of its application [wa]s contingent upon the department's own conduct. The requirement endures only until the department comes up with a procedure that does not have a discriminatory impact on blacks—something the department was enjoined to do in 1972 and expressly promised to do by 1980." [101]

In upholding an affirmative action plan embodied in a consent decree between black and Hispanic firefighters and the City of Cleveland, the Court in *Local Number 93, International Association of Firefighters v. Cleveland* [102] found inapplicable to voluntary affirmative action measures the remedial limitations posed by § 706(g) of Title VII. The firefighters had sued the city in a class action alleging racially discriminatory hiring, assignment, and promotion policies. The parties settled and entered into a consent decree establishing an affirmative action plan.[103]

The Court in *Firefighters* drew the distinction—albeit in the context of a Title VII decision—that it had failed to make in *Wygant* between voluntary and court-ordered affirmative action.[104] The majority favored greater latitude for voluntary affirmative action plans than might be allowable if the plans were judicially mandated: "We have on numerous occasions recognized that Congress intended voluntary compliance to be the preferred means of achieving the objectives of Title VII." [105] And the majority quoted the conclusion in *Weber* that:

> It would indeed be ironic if a law triggered by a Nation's concern over centuries of racial injustice and intended to improve the lot of those who had "been excluded from the American dream for so long" constituted the first legislative prohibition of all voluntary,

---

100. Id. at 1062.

101. Id. at 1070. This built-in self-destruct mechanism for the promotion quota was crucial in convincing the plurality that the requirement that one black be promoted for every white officer who was promoted was "not a disguised means to achieve racial balance." Id at 1071. See also id. at 1066 n.20 ("The one-for-one mechanism was employed not to punish the department's failure to achieve a racial balance, but to remedy the department's refusal to fulfill the commitment made in the consent decrees to implement a promotion procedure without adverse impact on blacks and to eradicate the effects of its past delay and discrimination.").

102. 106 S.Ct. 3063 (1986) (majority opinion by Brennan, J., joined by Marshall, Blackmun, Powell, and Stevens, JJ.); see id. at 3080 (O'Connor, J., concurring), id. at 3082 (Rehnquist, J., joined by Burger, C.J., dissenting).

103. Petitioner, a white-dominated labor union, had intervened in the district court and strongly objected to the decree, but the Court held that the intervening

union's consent was not required for the decree to be approved.

104. Justice Brennan wrote for five members of the Court that there is no material distinction between voluntary affirmative action measures and those adopted by the consent of the parties in order to avert a trial. The majority emphasized that the important distinction is instead between a consent decree and a judicial order: "it is the agreement of the parties, rather than the force of law upon which the complaint was originally based, that creates the obligations embodied in a consent decree." Id. at 3076. Whether affirmative action plans created by consent decrees are viewed as voluntary because they represent the consent of the parties, or as mandatory because they are judicially acknowledged, the general point remains that voluntary affirmative action plans should not be inhibited by the separation-of-powers concerns that limit the judiciary from fashioning affirmative action plans justified by forward-looking rather than narrower remedial concerns.

105. Id. at 3072.

private, race-conscious efforts to abolish traditional patterns of racial segregation and hierarchy.[106]

In recognizing that women, too, have historically been excluded from many job categories, six members of the Court in *Johnson v. Transportation Agency* [107] upheld a voluntarily adopted affirmative action plan designed to increase the representation of women in jobs in which they have traditionally been underrepresented. Choosing among seven employees rated "well qualified" for promotion to the position of road dispatcher, the Agency under its affirmative action plan promoted a woman, Diane Joyce, over the petitioner, a white man. If it is more important to an employer to promote a qualified woman to a job classification in which all of the 238 positions had previously been held by men than it is to select a man who scored two points higher in a subjectively-graded interview, the Court held that Title VII does not prohibit that promotion.

The *Johnson* majority broadly reaffirmed the holding of *Weber* that an employer need only point to a " 'manifest imbalance' that reflected underrepresentation of women in 'traditionally segregated job categories' " [108] in order to justify its affirmative action plan. The Court specified that, in determining whether there is a "manifest imbalance" in an employer's skilled work force, the relevant comparison is between the percentages of women and minorities in skilled job categories and their percentages in the qualified labor force.[109] The existence of such an imbalance itself "provides assurance both that sex or race will be taken into account in a manner consistent with Title VII's purpose of eliminating the effects of employment discrimination, and that the interests of those employees not benefitting from the plan will not be unduly infringed." [110] The validity under Title VII of the Agency's

---

106. Id. (quoting Weber, 443 U.S. at 204).

107. 107 S.Ct. 1442, 1450–51 (1987). (majority opinion of Brennan, J., joined by Marshall, Blackmun, Powell, and Stevens, JJ.); see id. at 1459–60, (Stevens, J., concurring); id. at 1461–62, (O'Connor, J., concurring in the judgment).

108. Id. at 1452 (majority opinion) (quoting Weber, 443 U.S. at 197). The dissenters in Johnson would overrule Weber. See id. at 1472 (Scalia, J., joined by Rehnquist, C.J., dissenting); id. at 1465 (White, J., dissenting). Even if Weber were not abandoned, Justice Scalia saw no reason to extend its holding to encompass public as well as private employers. Id. at 1475 (Scalia, J., joined by Rehnquist, C.J., dissenting).

109. Id. at 1452. Where a job does not require special training, the relevant comparison is with the percentage of minorities or women in the area labor market or in the general population. Id. (citing Teamsters v. United States, 431 U.S. 324 (1977); Weber v. United Steelworkers, 443 U.S. 193 (1979)).

110. Johnson, 107 S.Ct. at 1452. The majority left open the question of how small the relevant imbalance might be and still qualify as "manifest," but did specify that it need not be so great as to amount to a *prima facie* case of discrimination. The majority expressed concern that requiring a showing amounting to a *prima facie* case would invite Title VII suits against employers by the intended beneficiaries of their affirmative action plans, and would thus deter the employers from taking voluntary steps to eliminate discrimination. Id. at 1452–53.

Justice O'Connor disagreed, however, arguing that affirmative action—under both Title VII and the equal protection clause alike—must rest on a "firm basis," such as "a statistical disparity sufficient to support a *prima facie* claim under Title VII by the employed beneficiaries of the affirmative action plan." Id. at 1461 (O'Connor, J., concurring in the judgment). She argued that the basis for voluntary affirmative action must be stronger than the "societal discrimination" that had failed to justify the affirmative action plan in Wygant. But because the total absence of women in

voluntary affirmative action plan thus did not depend on any showing that Joyce had been a victim of past discrimination, or even that the Agency had in the past discriminated against women generally.

In finding that historical underrepresentation can at least count for something, the majority in *Johnson* removed many remaining doubts about the validity of voluntary, forward-looking affirmative action. The decision did not require affirmative consideration of race or sex in employment decision-making, nor did it set those factors apart as trumps over other relevant qualifications. In establishing long-term hiring goals aimed at increasing the representation of women in skilled craft classifications, the Santa Clara Transportation Agency had merely included underrepresentation of women among "a host of practical factors" that employers were to consider in pursuing affirmative action goals.[111] The Agency's plan did not set aside positions for women, but "require[d] women to compete with all other qualified applicants." [112] Because the Agency director was authorized to select among all qualified applicants, the Court found that the choice to promote a qualified woman over the petitioner "unsettled no legitimate firmly rooted expectation" on his part.[113]

Although the majority in *Weber* had emphasized that the temporary nature of the 50% set-aside for minority contractors was a factor important to the validity of that plan,[114] the majority in *Johnson* held that the lack of any express end date was not fatal to a plan containing no numerical set-aside.[115] The Agency referred to the percentage of women in the labor market not as a rigid goal, but as a "benchmark" for measuring its progress in opening up traditionally segregated job categories.[116] The manner in which the plan upheld in *Johnson* permitted the Agency to take account of the sex and race of employees as factors in promotion decisions represented "a moderate, flexible, case-by-case approach to effectuating a gradual improvement in the representation of minorities and women in the Agency's work force." [117] The plan "was intended to *attain* a balanced work force, not to maintain one." [118]

the Transportation Agency's skilled craft positions would have supported a *prima facie* case brought by the excluded women, she found that sufficient to support the Agency's plan. Id. at 1465.

111. Id. at 1455 (majority opinion). See also id. at 1465 (O'Connor, J., concurring in the judgment) (approving of consideration of sex as a " 'plus' factor"). Justice Scalia in dissent emphasized the district court's finding that gender was "the determining factor" in the disputed promotion decision, id. at 1469 (Scalia, J., joined by Rehnquist, C.J., and White, J., dissenting), as if to suggest that that finding belied the majority's observation that the Agency's affirmative action plan allowed many factors to be considered. To be sure, if an employee's sex tips the scale in a given case, it may

appear to be the only factor that mattered to that particular outcome. But Joyce's other qualifications were equally necessary to her promotion, and the alternative of *never* allowing sex to be *determinative* amounts to excluding it from being considered at all.

112. Id. at 1455 (majority opinion).

113. Id.

114. Id. at 1456.

115. Id.

116. Id.

117. See supra note 44 and accompanying text.

118. See Johnson, 107 S.Ct. at 1456 (emphasis in original).

The arguments that a majority of the Court has found persuasive in upholding the plans challenged under Title VII in *Bakke*, *Weber*, *Firefighters*, and *Johnson* suggest that reasonably tailored forms of voluntary affirmative action should be upheld under the equal protection clause as well. A lower level of judicial scrutiny in cases reviewing voluntary affirmative action would place on a par with other political choices the efforts of public bodies to eradicate the effects of a racist and sexist past and to build a future that more completely embodies the equal protection guarantee and its vision of a diverse society freed of racial and sexual domination.[119]

§ 16-23. Discrimination Against Aliens: Broadening the Concept of Suspect Classification

We have seen above[1] that strict scrutiny may reveal particular outcomes of the political process as insufficiently justified, especially in light of the character of the groups burdened by the governmental choice. The central concern has been to root out any action by government which, in Justice Stone's phrase, is tainted by a "prejudice against discrete and insular minorities," the sort of prejudice "which tends . . . to curtail the operation of those political processes ordinarily to be relied upon to protect minorities" in our society.[2] As we shall see in this section, the Supreme Court has extended this guarantee of equal protection beyond the fourteenth amendment's historical origins as a safeguard against racial discrimination, and has declared alienage to be a suspect criterion forbidden to state government absent a showing of compelling justification.[3]

---

119. In his concurring opinion in Paradise, Justice Stevens drew a distinction between the standard of review for court-ordered affirmative action, where a constitutional violation has been found, and that for non-judicial (voluntary, executive, or legislative) affirmative action efforts, which involve no proven violations of law. *Only* in the latter case must "the governmental decisionmaker who would make race-conscious decisions . . . overcome a strong presumption against them." 107 S.Ct. at 1078. Justice Stevens' evident (and laudable) purpose was to rebut the government's argument that, even in the wake of a finding of discrimination, "the judge's discretion is constricted by a 'narrowly tailored to achieve a compelling government interest' standard." Id. at 1077. But the implication that affirmative action efforts voluntarily adopted by employers, unions, and state and local government agencies are *more* suspect than those ordered by federal courts is unfortunate, even if unintended. See Johnson, 107 S.Ct. at 1459-60 (rejecting that view in the context of affirmative action for promotion of women, challenged under Title VII). Such organizations should be *more* free to engage in remedial efforts, not less, since they are not bound by the institutional and

federalism concerns that restrain the federal judiciary when it orders individuals or institutions to take actions they would not voluntarily take. See id. at 1451-52 n.8. Moreover, officers of state and local government, like federal judges, are sworn to uphold the Constitution; they, too, have an obligation to make good on the fourteenth amendment's grand promise of equality under law. It would be a tragic irony if the Court were to evolve a doctrine discouraging employers and states from taking the initiative to redress racial discrimination—a doctrine wherein race-conscious remedies that a federal court has commanded someone to employ are easier to defend than are race-conscious measures that someone has voluntarily adopted.

§ 16-23

1. See §§ 16-13 to 16-21, supra.

2. United States v. Carolene Products Co., 304 U.S. 144, 152-53 n.4 (1938) (dictum).

3. Note that "alienage" as used here refers to noncitizenship: to be an alien is not necessarily to be of any particular national origin. The Supreme Court has assimilated discrimination based on specific national origin to racial or ancestral dis-

Although occasionally the Court explains the identification of a suspect criterion or classification simply by repeating Justice Stone's phrase,[4] the Court has isolated particular factors—in addition to the obvious factor of political underrepresentation—which demonstrate a group's "discrete and insular" character. Significantly, the Supreme Court has often stressed the link between a history of prejudice and the existence of "an immutable characteristic determined solely by the accident of birth."[5] Further, the Court has treated as suspect those criteria which are so unlikely to prove relevant to any legitimate governmental purpose that their adverse use by government probably signals a bare desire to disadvantage a politically weak or unpopular group. Because such a desire "cannot constitute a *legitimate* governmental interest,"[6] it is appropriate that government's use of such criteria trigger judicial suspicion and thus close scrutiny.

In terms of these factors, it would be difficult to decide that laws treating aliens less favorably than citizens should be subject to full strict scrutiny. Because aliens are ordinarily eligible to become citizens, alienage, unlike race, sex, and in some instances extreme poverty, is not an unalterable trait. That aliens do not vote might be seen as demonstrating their lack of political power; but, at least if it is alien disenfranchisement that is being challenged, it would seem oddly circular to rely on the very practice challenged to establish the propriety of so strictly scrutinizing it as to make very probable its invalidation. And, as Justice Stevens pointed out in *Hampton v. Mow Sun Wong*,[7] overriding national interests such as "the need for undivided loyalty in certain sensitive positions"[8] may well be relevant to governmental determinations at the federal level.[9]

Yet it is clear that aliens have historically[10] suffered from prejudice and bias and, as "an identifiable class of persons . . ., are already subject to disadvantages not shared by the remainder of the

---

crimination. See Hernandez v. Texas, 347 U.S. 475 (1954) (overturning criminal conviction on allegation of state's systematic exclusion of Mexican-Americans from jury service); accord, Castaneda v. Partida, 430 U.S. 482 (1977). Cf. Espinoza v. Farah Mfg. Co., 414 U.S. 86 (1973) (private employer's refusal to hire aliens held not to constitute discrimination on basis of "national origin" in violation of Title VII of Civil Rights Act of 1964).

4. See, e.g., Graham v. Richardson, 403 U.S. 365, 372 (1971).

5. See Frontiero v. Richardson, 411 U.S. 677, 686 (1973), discussed in § 16–26, infra. The Court's concern for a characteristic's immutability may well stem in part from the notion that political majorities can be trusted least when they act to burden minority groups to which they never belonged and from which they will always be excluded.

6. United States Dep't of Agriculture v. Moreno, 413 U.S. 528, 534 (1973) (emphasis added).

7. 426 U.S. 88 (1976) (overturning, on fifth amendment due process grounds, Civil Service Commission's exclusion of aliens from federal competitive civil service).

8. Id. at 104.

9. For more detailed treatment of alienage as a semi-suspect criterion for classification, see §§ 16–32 to 16–34, infra.

10. Note the Supreme Court's use of history as a criterion in its determination of suspect classifications. See, e.g., San Antonio Independent School Dist. v. Rodriguez, 411 U.S. 1, 28 (1973) (sustaining against equal protection attack public school finance scheme using local property taxation as base) (among "traditional indicia of suspectness" is that class have been "subjected to . . . a history of purposeful unequal treatment"), in § 16–7, supra. See also Mathews v. Lucas, 427 U.S. 495, 520 (1976) (upholding denial of automatic social security survivor's benefits to illegitimate children) (Stevens, J., dissenting) ("a traditional classification is more likely to be used without pausing to consider its

community." [11]   While the "national security" may provide a justification for exclusion of aliens from sensitive *federal* posts,[12] no such rationale exists to warrant treating alienage as anything less than a suspect classification in challenges to *state* or *local* use of the criterion.[13]

In *Truax v. Raich*,[14] the Court struck down a state law prohibiting employers of more than five persons from hiring any more than twenty percent aliens. In response to the state's argument that " 'the employment of aliens unless restrained was a peril to the public welfare,' " [15] the Court held that so general a justification for any state regulation of alien employment was impermissible, given Congress' plenary power to control the admission of aliens: [16] "[The] authority to deny to aliens the opportunity of earning a livelihood when lawfully admitted to the State would be tantamount to . . . the right to deny them entrance. . . . [T]he practical result would be that those lawfully admitted to the country under the authority of . . . Congress . . . would be segregated in such of the States as chose to offer hospitality." [17]

justification than is a newly created classification").

11. Hampton v. Mow Sun Wong, 426 U.S. 88, 102 (1976).

12. Petitioners in Mow Sun Wong argued that the broad exclusion of aliens might facilitate executive negotiation of foreign treaties by making possible the offer of employment opportunities to foreigners in exchange for reciprocal concessions, and that reserving the federal service for citizens provided incentive for aliens to qualify for naturalization. Id. at 104. The Court found these arguments interesting, but beyond the properly delegated range of concerns of the Civil Service Commission (CSC), limited as those concerns were to matters like efficiency. As to that concern, the Court entertained the government's argument that the blanket exclusion of aliens avoided "the trouble and expense of classifying those positions which properly belong in executive or sensitive categories." Id. Nevertheless, the Court refused to sustain so large a deprivation of liberty imposed upon a group so much like a discrete and insular minority on a basis so hypothetical, inasmuch as the CSC had neither shown that its action had followed a real finding of "the relative desirability of a simple exclusionary rule," nor demonstrated that the administrative burden of establishing job classifications "would be a particularly onerous task for an expert in personnel matters." Id. at 115.

Note that the Court reserved the question whether Congress or the President could explicitly decide to exclude all noncitizens from the federal civil service. Id. at 116. And see President Ford's subsequent

Order requiring citizenship for federal employment, Exec. Order No.11,935, 41 Fed. Reg. 37, 301 (1976) (to be codified in 5 C.F.R. § 7.4). It is likely, however, that the due process clause of the fifth amendment, which the Court has held to yield a norm of equal protection indistinguishable from that of the fourteenth amendment, see Bolling v. Sharpe, 347 U.S. 497 (1954), would invalidate even congressional or presidential discrimination against resident aliens as such where no substantial justification could be shown. Cf. Mathews v. Diaz, 426 U.S. 67, 81–84 (1976) (upholding federal Medicare program conditioning alien's eligibility for participation on 5 years' continuous residence in United States) (Court deferred to Congress' decision to establish five-year line on the ground of its substantial justification; without "principled basis" for such discrimination, legislative classification would fail). But see § 5–16, supra, with respect to Congress' nearly plenary control over immigration.

13. See 426 U.S. at 100–01.

14. 239 U.S. 33 (1915).

15. Id. at 41.

16. Under art. I, § 8, Congress exercises exclusive authority over the admission, exclusion, and deportation of aliens; under the supremacy clause of art. VI, the states may not interfere with such federal authority.

17. 239 U.S. at 42. Truax also seems understandable as an expression of Lochner-era solicitude for the employer's liberty of property and contract. See Chapter 8, supra.

Nevertheless, the Supreme Court asserted in dictum that, despite this overarching congressional power, the "special public interest" in state regulation of a wide variety of governmental concerns justified less favorable state treatment of noncitizens.[18] And subsequently, in *Heim v. McCall*,[19] the Court upheld a state requirement that public contractors employ only United States citizens.[20] In *Terrace v. Thompson*,[21] the Court upheld a state statute forbidding aliens to own land for the purpose of farming. And in *Clarke v. Deckebach*,[22] the Court held it compatible with equal protection for a city to prohibit aliens from operating pool and billiard rooms.

Later decisions greatly reduced the scope of the "special public interest" doctrine, as a consequence both of a broadened interpretation of Congress' plenary authority, and of a judicial recognition that alienage itself constituted a suspect criterion. In *Oyama v. California*,[23] the Court invalidated California's Alien Land Law, which forbade aliens ineligible for citizenship from owning or transferring agricultural land, and which provided that any property acquired in violation of the statute would escheat as of the date of acquisition or transfer. Certain lands recorded in the name of a minor American citizen escheated to the state under the statute because the lands had been paid for by his father, a Japanese alien ineligible for naturalization. As the Court held, "This case presents a conflict between the state's right to formulate a policy of landholding within its bounds and the right of American citizens to own land anywhere in the United States. When these two rights clash, the rights of a citizen may not be subordinated merely because of his father's [ineligibility for citizenship]."[24] And in *Takahashi v. Fish and Game Commission*,[25] the Court rejected a state's claim of "special public interest" in conserving fish in its coastal waters by barring issuance of commercial fishing licenses to persons ineligible for citizenship. Holding that congressional legislation made clear that "the power of a state to apply its laws exclusively to its alien inhabitants as a class [was to be] confined within narrow limits,"[26] the Court found the state's proprietary interest inadequate to prevent "lawfully admitted aliens within its borders from earning a living in the same way that other state inhabitants earn their living."[27]

By the 1970's, the Court was insisting that states were generally powerless to treat aliens as a distinct class for reasons of federal supremacy and that such treatment also amounted to invidious discrimination. Thus, in *Graham v. Richardson* the Court invalidated state

---

18. Id. at 39–40 (citing governmental concerns in "regulation or distribution of the public domain, or of the common property or resources," "devolution of real property," and public employment).

19. 239 U.S. 175 (1915).

20. See also Crane v. New York, 239 U.S. 195 (1915) (upholding criminal conviction under state statute prohibiting employment of aliens by public contractors).

21. 263 U.S. 197 (1923).

22. 274 U.S. 392 (1927).

23. 332 U.S. 633 (1948).

24. Id. at 647.

25. 334 U.S. 410 (1948).

26. Id. at 420. The Court cited 8 U.S.C. § 41 (current version at 42 U.S.C. § 1981): "All persons within the jurisdiction of the United States shall have the same right in every State and Territory . . . to the full and equal benefit of all laws and proceedings . . . as is enjoyed by white citizens. . . ." 334 U.S. at 419.

27. 334 U.S. at 418–19.

statutes denying welfare benefits to resident aliens,[28] and in *Sugarman v. Dougall* the Court invalidated a statutory prohibition against employment of aliens in the state competitive civil service.[29] Similarly the Court has ruled that resident aliens may not be excluded from law practice,[30] or from practice as licensed civil engineers.[31]

The Court's unanimous opinion in *Graham* constituted the high-water mark of judicial protection of aliens. Thereafter the margin for applying scrict scrutiny to all alienage classifications narrowed steadily.[32] *Nyquist v. Mauclet*[33] was the beginning of the end. Although the holding was a definite and significant advance for aliens, the vote was 5–4.[34] The New York statute at issue denied college financial aid to those aliens who would not affirm their intent to apply for citizenship as soon as they were eligible. Even though the law therefore denied aid only to those aliens who were committed to keeping their foreign citizenship, a majority of the Court found the proposition that any discrimination against aliens is suspect so well established that the principle was invoked to protect a group which voluntarily preferred its disenfranchised, alien status. The Court stressed that encouraging naturalization was an impermissible purpose for a *state*—since Congress has plenary authority in such matters—and it was therefore irrelevant that the New York law hurt only those who stubbornly clung to their foreign citizenship.[35] That note resonated with the long-standing view that Congress alone sets immigration policy, and that state laws which might interfere are void under the supremacy clause of article VI.

The tide finally turned against alienage as a suspect classification in *Foley v. Connelie*,[36] where six Justices[37] voted to uphold a New York law that required police officers to be American citizens. The Court declared that, while it had previously applied strict scrutiny to discrimination against aliens, such searching review was appropriate only where state action "struck at the noncitizens' ability to exist in the community" by denying them important benefits or the right to engage

28. 403 U.S. 365, 376 (1971) ("There can be no 'special public interest' in tax revenues to which aliens have contributed on an equal basis with the residents of the State"); see also id. at 378 ("State laws that restrict the eligibility of aliens for welfare benefits merely because of their alienage conflict with overriding national policies in an area constitutionally entrusted to the Federal Government").

29. 413 U.S. 634, 642–43 (1973) (while statute rested on legitimate state interests in having loyal employees and in establishing state's own form of government, statute was "neither narrowly confined nor precise in its application," and therefore failed).

30. In re Griffiths, 413 U.S. 717, 729 (1973) (rejecting as insufficiently substantial the state interest in maintaining high professional standards, and denying argument that "status of holding a license to practice law place[s] one so close to the core of the political process as to make [one] a formulator of government policy").

31. Examining Board v. De Otero, 426 U.S. 572 (1976).

32. Justice Rehnquist, who joined the Court after Graham, was the sole dissenter in Sugarman v. Dougal. He was joined in dissenting from the decision in Griffiths by Chief Justice Burger.

33. 432 U.S. 1 (1977).

34. Chief Justice Burger and Justices Stewart, Powell and Rehnquist dissented.

35. 432 U.S. at 9–10.

36. 435 U.S. 291 (1978).

37. The previous dissenters were joined by Justice White to make the new majority; Justice Blackmun concurred in the result.

in ordinary trades or professions.[38] The Court took its doctrine from Justice Blackmun's opinion for the majority in *Sugarman v. Dougall*, where he wrote that the power of the state "to preserve the basic conception of a political community" justifies its reservation of the franchise and the right to hold "elective and important nonelective" state offices to full-fledged members of the polity.[39] The controversial aspect of *Foley* was the Court's use of that doctrine to characterize service as a police officer as "participation in our democratic political institutions." [40] The dissent aptly observed that reading the *Sugarman* exception for "officers who participate directly in the formulation, execution or review of broad public policy" [41] as embracing state highway patrolmen effectively allows the exception to swallow the rule.[42]

Since the *Foley* Court stressed the coercive physical authority wielded by the policy,[43] one would infer that it meant to distinguish that authority from the more mundane state power exercised by such functionaries as school teachers and clerks. But *Ambach v. Norwick* [44] demonstrated just how expansive the government function exception could be by upholding a New York law barring aliens from employment as public school teachers. The Court distinguished its invalidation in *In re Griffiths* [45] of a similar law banning aliens from the practice of law on the ground that lawyers are private citizens, whereas public school teachers fulfill an important public function. The majority quoted rhetoric about the role of public education in training citizens and perpetuating values and remained unimpressed by the dissent's observation that lawyers fulfill an equally important governmental function as officers of the court.[46]

After *Foley* and *Ambach*, the Court's holding in *Cabell v. Chavez-Salido* [47] that refusing aliens employment as probation officers is "a necessary consequence of the community's process of political self-definition" came as no surprise. In his opinion for the Court, Justice White wrote that California could rationally decide that probation officers—who were included in the statutory definition of "peace officers"—were so endowed with the "sovereign's power to exercise coercive force" that they must be citizens.[48] The problem is that there were more than 70 positions which California statutorily designated "peace

38. 435 U.S. at 294–95. Cf. § 6–35, supra, discussing the Court's protection of such opportunities for American non-residents under the privileges and immunities clause of article IV, § 2.

39. Sugarman v. Dougall, 413 U.S. 634, 647 (1973). Cf. McCarthy v. Philadephia Civil Service Comm'n, 424 U.S. 645 (1976) (per curiam) (rejecting equal protection challenge to municipal residency requirement for municipal employees).

40. Foley, 435 U.S. at 295.

41. 413 U.S. at 637.

42. Foley, 435 U.S. at 304 (Marshall, J., joined by Brennan and Stevens, JJ., dissenting).

43. 435 U.S. at 297–98.

44. 441 U.S. 68 (1979). Justice Powell wrote for the Court, joined by Chief Justice Burger and Justices Stewart, White, and Rehnquist. Justice Blackmun filed a dissenting opinion, joined by Justices Brennan, Marshall, and Stevens.

45. 413 U.S. 717 (1973).

46. 441 U.S. at 88–89 (Blackmun, J., dissenting). Cf. Supreme Court of New Hampshire v. Piper, 470 U.S. 274 (1985) (invalidating under privileges and immunities clause a law requiring state residence for admission to state bar, noting that a lawyer "is not an 'officer' of the state in any political sense").

47. 454 U.S. 432 (1982).

48. 454 U.S. at 445–46.

officers"; the category apparently expanded as more and more state employees persuaded the legislature to classify them thus in order to garner superior group insurance benefits.[49] Therefore, bringing all of California's "peace officers" within the *Sugarman* exception required the Court to keep a straight face while declaring that state furniture and bedding inspectors and government office messengers [50] are "important nonelective officers" who "perform functions that go to the heart of representative government." [51] Both *Sugarman* and *Foley* denounced state imposition of citizenship requirements that "sweep indiscriminately" without regard to the positions involved,[52] yet the *Cabell* Court found no difficulty in holding that a law that includes toll takers and cemetery sextons—but not state supreme court justices—is not "so broad and haphazard as to belie the state's claim that it is only attempting to ensure that an important function of government be in the hands of those having the 'fundamental legal bonds of citizenship.' " [53]

If the level of scrutiny applied in *Cabell* gives new meaning to the term "minimum rationality," [54] the result reached the same Term in *Toll v. Moreno* [55] confirms that state alienage classifications that impinge on access to government benefits must meet a higher standard. The Court held that the University of Maryland could not deny in-state tuition status to a particular class of aliens domiciled in the state.[56] Although *Toll v. Moreno* might appear to be a relatively straightforward application of *Nyquist v. Mauclet*, the case was not decided on equal protection grounds. Instead, the Court held that the Maryland rule violated the supremacy clause by imposing an additional burden on aliens to whom Congress had explicitly accorded special treatment.[57]

49. Id. at 451–52 & n.5 (Blackmun, J., dissenting).

50. These are among the positions included in the "peace officer" laundry list of California Penal Code § 1031(a). See 454 U.S. at 451 (Blackmun, J., dissenting).

51. 454 U.S. at 440, quoting Sugarman, 413 U.S. at 647.

52. Sugarman, 413 U.S. at 643; Foley, 435 U.S. at 296–97 n.5.

53. 454 U.S. at 442.

54. The appropriate standard of review in alienage cases where the political function exception does not apply continues to be strict scrutiny, under which a challenged law must advance a compelling state purpose by the least restrictive means available. Bernal v. Fainter, 467 U.S. 216 (1984). In Bernal, this standard was employed by eight members of the Court—Justice Rehnquist dissented—to strike down a Texas law requiring notaries public to be American citizens. The Court found the duties of such officials to be clerical and ministerial, rather than responsibilities going "to the heart of representative government." In contrast to the abject deference that followed from the Court's superficial reading of California statutes in Cabell, the Bernal Court was not swayed by the fact that notaries are designated as public officers by the Texas Constitution itself.

55. 458 U.S. 1 (1982). Justice Brennan wrote for the Court, joined by Justices White, Marshall, Blackmun, Powell, and Stevens. Justice Blackmun also filed a concurring opinion. Justice O'Connor concurred in part and dissented in part. Justice Rehnquist, joined by Chief Justice Burger, dissented.

56. Specifically, resident aliens holding G–4 visas: non-immigrant aliens whose families were employed by international organizations based in Washington, D.C.

57. 458 U.S. at 17. Several commentators have suggested that the Court's alienage cases are better understood and justified in terms of the supremacy clause than the fourteenth amendment. See, e.g., Perry, "Modern Equal Protection: A Conceptualization and Appraisal," 76 Colum.L. Rev. 1023 (1979); Choper, "Discrimination Against Aliens," in J. Choper, Y. Kamisar & L. Tribe, 4 Supreme Court Trends and Developments (1983). Justice Brennan,

The most interesting and yet most problematic alienage case in recent years is *Plyler v. Doe*.[58] A Texas law denied state funds to school districts for the education of children who were not legally admitted into the United States, and empowered local school authorities to refuse to enroll such children. A sharply divided Court [59] held that the law denied the children who were its targets the equal protection of the laws. In his opinion for the Court, Justice Brennan announced at the outset that although the undocumented aliens in question were, by definition, in the country unlawfully, they were nevertheless "persons" under the fourteenth amendment and therefore entitled to equal protection.[60] Their status as illegal aliens was not, however, irrelevant to the question of the appropriate level of judicial scrutiny. The Court expressly declined to characterize illegal aliens as a suspect class, in part because their membership in the statutory classification at issue was the result of a wholly voluntary—indeed, criminal—act.[61] But Justice Brennan carefully distinguished the adult illegal aliens who were responsible for their presence in the United States, from the children they had brought with them who were the victims of the Texas law. The majority found it difficult to conceive of a rational justification for discriminating against children on the basis of a legal characteristic over which they had little if any control.[62]

The *Plyler* majority was constrained by the Court's decision in *San Antonio School District v. Rodriguez* [63] from declaring public education to be a right guaranteed by the Constitution, but the majority nonetheless made it clear that public education was not just another governmental benefit either. Public education might not be a "fundamental right," but it plays a "fundamental role in maintaining the fabric of our society." [64] Writing for the *Plyler* majority, Justice Brennan then mated this not-quite-fundamental right with this not-quite-suspect class to produce a hybrid equal protection test: in order to be considered

---

writing for the Court in Toll v. Moreno, noted this trend in the literature. 458 U.S. at 12 n.16. The argument is plausible and would certainly help to explain why state classifications denying aliens benefits receive strict scrutiny while congressional acts which do the same thing are only subject to the rational basis test. Yet is it hard to avoid the suspicion that the explicit adoption of statutory preemption as the basis of decision in Toll v. Moreno was seen by some members of the Court as a way of reaching the desired result without putting any strain on an equal protection clause whose strength has been sapped by recent precedents. The danger inherent in this sort of tactical retreat from substantive to structural grounds is that the constitutional guarantees will atrophy into an even weaker state, ultimately leaving the Constitution incapable of rising to meet new challenges to our system of ordered liberty.

58. 457 U.S. 202 (1982).

59. Justices Brennan, Marshall, Blackmun, Powell and Stevens found the law

unconstitutional. Chief Justice Burger, joined by Justices White, Rehnquist and O'Connor, dissented.

60. 457 U.S. at 210. The Court also rejected the hair-splitting argument that aliens unlawfully residing within a state may be deemed not to be "within its jurisdiction," as the fourteenth amendment uses that phrase, and therefore not to be entitled to the equal protection of the laws. As the Court pointed out, the equal protection clause was written into the fourteenth amendment precisely to eradicate the sort of "caste-based and invidious class-based legislation" that Texas had enacted. Id. at 211–13.

61. Id. at 219 n.19.

62. Id. at 220. See § 16–32, infra. Cf. government classifications based on illegitimate birth, discussed in § 16–23, infra.

63. 411 U.S. 1, 28–39 (1973), discussed in §§ 16–9, 16–52, 16–58.

64. 457 U.S. at 221.

"rational", the Texas education law would have to further a "substantial" state interest.[65]

This curious new species of equal protection review proved to have real bite. The *Plyler* majority used it to dispatch all three major objectives offered by Texas: the state's interests in deterring illegal immigration, in maintaining its fiscal ability to provide quality education to its citizens, and in reserving scarce educational resources for those who are most likely to stay in the state and promote its quality of life. While colorable, these goals were held to be in no rational way substantially furthered by "promoting the creation and perpetuation of a subclass of illiterates." [66] The Court emphasized that, whether Texas liked it or not, there exists within America's borders a "shadow population" of millions of illegal aliens. A policy of denying basic education to these people, coupled with the realities of enforcing the immigration laws, raised in the Court's mind "the specter of a permanent caste of undocumented resident aliens" [67]—a "discrete underclass" [68] that it could hardly be "rational" for the state to create.[69]

Although the majority opinion discussed federal immigration law,[70] the decision in *Plyler*, unlike that in *Toll v. Moreno*, did not rely on the supremacy clause to do the work of the fourteenth amendment. Indeed, it would have been extremely difficult to do so: it may not be hard to find a conflict with federal policy when a state imposes burdens on aliens whom Congress has welcomed into the country,[71] but it is another thing altogether to find such a conflict when the very presence of the aliens in question is itself a federal crime.

Moreover, even if it were more doctrinally satisfying to decide *Plyler v. Doe* under the supremacy clause, there could be no satisfaction in thereby granting to Congress the power to decide that no money should be spent on educating alien children even if there were no effective means of deporting them. Nothing about Congress' special role with respect to immigration and naturalization should necessarily make Congress more free than Texas to inflict permanent harm upon long-term residents of the United States for reasons that are wholly beyond their control. The equal protection component of the fifth amendment binds Congress just as the fourteenth amendment binds the states. And if equality under the law means anything, it surely means that the government may not treat the helpless children of illegal aliens as untouchables and condemn them to lives of peonage.[72]

---

65. Id. at 224.

66. Id. at 230 (opinion of the Court); id. at 234 (Blackmun, J., concurring); id. at 241 (Powell, J., concurring).

67. Id. at 219.

68. Id. at 234 (Blackmun, J., concurring).

69. Id. at 220 (opinion of the Court). See § 16–3, supra.

70. The Court suggested that a different result might obtain if Congress had articulated a policy of discouraging illegal immigration by denying undocumented aliens benefits, because such a policy might be construed as authorizing the action taken by Texas. Id. at 224–26.

71. The immigration reforms enacted in the closing days of the 99th Congress in 1986 would presumably preempt state efforts to disadvantage aliens on whom Congress had chosen to confer amnesty and legal status.

72. See the discussion of anti-subjugation as a mediating principle for the equal protection clause, in § 16–21, supra.

In his dissenting opinion, Chief Justice Burger predicted that, because it rested on "such a unique confluence of theories and rationales," the Court's opinion in *Plyler v. Doe* would come to stand for little beyond the result in the case itself.[73] He may well be correct. Some may find it comforting that, when it is confronted by a truly horrendous prospect, a majority of the Court will show its heart to be in the right place. But others will quite properly wish that the Court's head had proven equal to its heart and that a sturdier analytic foundation had been provided for the result reached. For now, it remains to be seen whether the hybrid analysis that gave birth to the result in *Plyler* will prove to be sterile,[74] or will instead contribute to the evolving law of intermediate scrutiny.[75]

§ 16–24. Discrimination Against Illegitimates

The effort to expand the category of suspect classifications beyond race has to some extent reached classifications involving illegitimacy. Unlike alienage, however, illegitimacy has never been pronounced a "suspect" criterion. Still, we shall see in this section that, when dealing with illegitimacy-based classifications, the Supreme Court has properly, if not always consistently or coherently, exercised a significantly closer scrutiny than the "minimum rationality" standard would warrant.

In *Levy v. Louisiana*,[1] the Supreme Court first struck down as unconstitutional a state statute discriminating against illegitimates. The Court invalidated provisions of the Louisiana wrongful death statute excluding illegitimates from the class of children entitled to recover for a parent's death. While the opinion purported to apply a rationality standard,[2] it nonetheless quite plainly subjected the statute to some version of strict scrutiny. Whether such scrutiny followed from the involvement of a fundamental right or from the presence of a suspect classification was unclear: "The rights asserted here involve the intimate, familial relationship between a child and his own mother. . . . Why should the illegitimate child . . . be denied correlative rights which other citizens enjoy?"[3] In any case, the Court stressed the fact that discrimination against illegitimates resulted "when no

73. 457 U.S. at 243 (Burger, C.J., dissenting); see id. at 239 (Powell, J., concurring) (heightened standard of review appropriate in these "unique circumstances").

74. In Martinez v. Bynum, 461 U.S. 321 (1983), the Court voted 8–1 to uphold another provision of the Texas Education Code that permitted school districts to deny tuition-free education to minors living apart from their parents or guardians for the primary purpose of attending Texas schools. The plaintiff, an American citizen but the child of non-resident aliens, challenged the law on its face, so the Court rendered no judgment on the constitutionality of the law as applied to him. Id. at

330 n.10; id. at 333 (Brennan, J., concurring). The Court held that there was a rational basis for the bona fide residence requirement, id. at 329–30, and cited Plyler v. Doe only for the propositions that schools have a right to set residence criteria, id. at 327–28, and that public education is not a fundamental right, id. at 328 n.7.

75. See §§ 16–31 to 16–33, infra.

§ 16–24

1. 391 U.S. 68 (1968).

2. See id. at 71.

3. Id.

action, conduct, or demeanor of theirs [was] possibly relevant to the harm that was done the [deceased parent]." [4]

Similarly, in *Weber v. Aetna Casualty & Surety Co.*,[5] the Court held that a state may not deprive dependent illegitimate children of recovery for the death of their father under the state's workmen's compensation law. Again a strict standard seems to have been applied by the Court, but the precise basis for doing so was unclear, for the Court cited both the "fundamental personal rights" endangered by the classification, and the invidiousness of discrimination resting on "status of birth." [6] Nevertheless, as in *Levy*, the Court treated as determinative the inability of both parent and child to reverse the burdens imposed by illegitimacy.[7]

In *Labine v. Vincent*,[8] however, the Court distinguished *Levy* and upheld a state law denying acknowledged illegitimate children the right to share equally with legitimate children in the estate of an intestate father. Noting the state's legitimate "power to make laws for distribution of property," the Court emphasized "that this [was] not a case, like *Levy*, where the State has created an insurmountable barrier to [the] illegitimate child." [9] Rather, the Court pointed out that the father could have executed a will naming the illegitimate child as beneficiary, thereby removing any bar to inheritance by the child; this tenuous distinction from the situation in which being born illegitimate would place the child under a disability removable by no one enabled the Court to uphold the discrimination. Although not expressly overruling *Labine*, the Court more recently stressed, in *Trimble v. Gordon*,[10]

---

4. Id. at 72. See also the companion case of Glona v. American Guarantee & Liability Ins. Co., 391 U.S. 73 (1968), holding the same Louisiana statute invalid as applied to a mother's damage suit for the alleged wrongful death of her illegitimate child. Acknowledging the state's legitimate interest in "dealing with 'sin,'" the Court nevertheless found "no possible rational basis" for assuming the statute served this interest." Id. at 75. See also Stanley v. Illinois, 405 U.S. 645 (1972) (invalidating a state rule that automatically deprived unwed fathers of their children upon the mother's death). See also Caban v. Mohammed, 441 U.S. 380 (1979) (overturning state law which gave mother of illegitimate child veto power in adoption proceeding, while the child's natural father, although he enjoyed a close relationship with the child, was given only the right to show that the adoption would not be in the best interest of the child). But cf. Quilloin v. Walcott, 434 U.S. 246 (1978) (unanimously rejecting an equal protection challenge to a state rule that gave the natural father of a legitimate child absolute veto over adoption of the child by the natural mother's husband, but used a "best interest of the child" standard when such an adoption was opposed by an illegitimate child's father who had not sought custody

of the child prior to the disputed adoption proceedings); Lehr v. Robertson, 463 U.S. 248 (1983) (upholding statute which granted more procedural rights to mother of illegitimate child than to father who failed to create a substantial relationship with the child).

5. 406 U.S. 164 (1972).

6. Id. at 172, 176.

7. See id. at 171 & n.9 (under state law, acknowledgment of children by parents incapable of contracting marriage at time of conception was prohibited; decedent in instant case was married at time of claimant-children's conception).

For cases relying on Levy and Weber, see New Jersey Welfare Rights Org. v. Cahill, 411 U.S. 619, 621 (1973) (per curiam) (holding unconstitutional state welfare program denying benefits to households with only illegitimate children); Gomez v. Perez, 409 U.S. 535, 538 (1973) (per curiam) (overturning state law granting only legitimate children judicially enforceable right to support from their natural fathers).

8. 401 U.S. 532 (1971).

9. Id. at 539.

10. 430 U.S. 762, 773 (1977).

that since "illegitimate children can affect neither their parents' conduct nor their own status," the "focus on the presence or absence of an insurmountable barrier is . . . an analytical anomaly;" accordingly, the Court struck down an Illinois statute which allowed illegitimate children to inherit by intestate succession only from their mothers while legitimate children could inherit by intestate succession from either parent.[11]   Particularly given "the difference in the rights of illegitimate children in the estates of their mothers and their fathers," the Illinois law, unlike that of Louisiana, was not even "consistent with a theory of social opprobrium regarding the parents' relationships and with a measured, if misguided, attempt to deter illegitimate relationships."[12]   Despite this valiant effort to distinguish *Labine*, the four Justices who dissented in *Trimble* on the ground that the case was in fact "constitutionally indistinguishable"[13] should probably be deemed correct in their assessment: *Labine v. Vincent* did not survive *Trimble*.

But if *Trimble sub silentio* overruled *Labine*, the see-saw teetered back the other way in *Lalli v. Lalli*,[14] when Justice Powell joined the four *Trimble* dissenters to all but repudiate his own opinion in the earlier case.[15]

In *Lalli* an illegitimate would-be heir challenged a New York law which barred children born out of wedlock from inheriting from their fathers unless paternity had been declared in a judicial proceeding during his life.[16]   Justice Powell distinguished the Illinois law struck down in *Trimble* on the ground that it required not only the acknowledgement of paternity by the father, but also the marriage of the child's parents, as an absolute precondition to inheritance.[17]   In contrast, the "discrete procedural demands"[18] of the New York statute were satisfied so long as a judicial declaration of paternity was made before the father's death.   Because the New York law recognized a " 'middle ground between the extremes of complete exclusion and case-by-case determination of paternity,' "[19] it was justified by the state's interest in quick and accurate distributions of property following a man's intestate demise.[20]   Furthermore, unlike the Illinois inheritance scheme, New

11. The Court correctly observed that "focusing on the steps that an intestate might have taken . . . loses sight of the essential question: the constitutionality of discrimination against illegitimates in a state intestate succession law." Id. at 774. Thus alternatives available to persons other than the illegitimate child have *no* "constitutional significance . . . in this case." Id.

12. Id. at 768 n.13.

13. Id. at 777 (Burger, C.J., joined by Stewart, Blackmun, and Rehnquist, JJ.).

14. 439 U.S. 259 (1978).

15. Justice Powell was joined by Chief Justice Burger and Justice Stewart. Justice Rehnquist concurred in the judgment on the basis of his Trimble dissent, 439 U.S. at 276, and Justice Blackmun would have affirmed the judgment below on the basis of Labine by overruling Trimble. Id. at 276–77.

16. The law also required that the proceeding be commenced before the child was two years old, but since no proceeding had ever been initiated in the instant case, the Court had no occasion to decide whether that limitation violated the equal protection clause. 439 U.S. at 267 n.5. In light of Pickett v. Brown, 462 U.S. 1 (1983), discussed infra at note 44, it is highly unlikely that the Court would uphold such a brief statute of limitations.

17. 439 U.S. at 266. In Illinois, not even a *judicial* declaration of paternity sufficed to allow inheritance. Id. at 267.

18. Id. at 268.

19. 439 U.S. at 266, quoting Trimble v. Gordon, 430 U.S. at 770–71.

20. Id. at 268–69.

York's exhibited no intent " 'to discourage illegitimacy, to mold human conduct or to set societal norms.' " [21]

The inconsistency between *Trimble* and *Lalli* may be explained by examining the standard of review applied in each case. Although Justice Powell claimed in *Lalli* to be employing the same "substantial relation" test he had used in his opinion for the Court in *Trimble* [22]—a standard of "stricter," [23] if "less than strictest scrutiny" [24]—in fact he required only that the statute's relation to the state's interests not be so "tenuous that it lacks the *rationality* contemplated by the 14th Amendment." [25]   This retreat to a perfunctory review of classifications based on illegitimacy caused the plurality in *Lalli* to misconstrue the Court's holding in *Trimble*. Deta Trimble, as an illegitimate daughter, was not *completely* foreclosed from inheriting from her father because her father could have made out a will or married her mother. Yet the *Trimble* Court held that to "focus on the presence or absence of an insurmountable barrier is . . . an analytical anomaly" since "illegitimate children can affect neither their parents' conduct nor their own status." [26]   The plurality in *Lalli* noted that requiring a mother to go to court to establish the paternity of her illegitimate child is less burdensome than requiring her and the child's father to marry. But that observation is wholly irrelevant because the *Trimble* Court focused on the burdens imposed on the *child*, not on the parents. Robert Lalli, at the tender age of two,[27] was no more capable of making his parents take a trip to court than was Deta Trimble of making her parents take a trip to the altar.[28]

Justice Powell's comment that the Court was not concerned with the "fairness" of the New York inheritance law [29] is all too descriptive of the result in *Lalli*. Because his parents failed to obtain a judicial decree, the Supreme Court denied Robert Lalli his share of his father's estate despite the concession by all interested parties that Robert was indeed Mario Lalli's son.[30]   While purporting to adhere to precedent,

21. Id. at 267–68 (citation omitted).

22. 439 U.S. at 265 (citing, inter alia, Trimble v Gordon).

23. Trimble, 430 U.S. at 762, quoting Weber v. Aetna Casualty & Surety Co., 406 U.S. 164, 172 (1972).

24. Trimble, 430 U.S. at 762, quoting Mathews v. Lucas, 427 U.S. 495, 510 (1976).

25. 439 U.S. at 273 (emphasis added).

26. 430 U.S. at 770, 773–74.

27. The New York law required the proceeding to establish paternity to be brought during gestation or within two years of the child's birth. See 439 U.S. at 267 n.5.

28. In Mathews v. Lucas, 427 U.S. 495 (1976), the Supreme Court held that, when an illegitimate child *could* surmount the statutory burden, a lower standard of scrutiny would be applied. The Lucas Court accordingly upheld a Social Security Act provision governing surviving children's

insurance benefits under which illegitimate children were deprived of procedural benefits that eased the evidentiary task of certain legitimate children—but were not wholly prevented from succeeding in that task. While it may be understandable for the Court to permit government to place on illegitimate children burdens which are not absolute and which seem at least rationally linked to legitimate governmental interests, Justice Stevens in dissent rightly warned that, because of the "social opprobrium" long associated with illegitimacy, all classifications based on legitimacy should trigger the closest judicial scrutiny. Id. at 523.

29. Lalli, 439 U.S. at 273.

30. 439 U.S. at 277 (Brennan, J., dissenting, joined by White, Marshall, and Stevens, JJ.); id. at 272 (opinion of Powell, J.). Mario Lalli had made it known that Robert was his son, had provided financial support for Robert, and had formally ac-

the Court thus failed to vindicate its often-voiced belief that "imposing disabilities on the illegitimate child is contrary to the basic concept of our system that burdens should bear some relationship to individual responsibility." [31]

The Court again applied the rationality standard to another case concerning the classification of illegitimate children in the same Term it decided *Lalli*. In *Califano v. Boles*,[32] the Court upheld a provision of the Social Security Act which granted "mother's benefits" to a deceased male wage earner's widow or divorced wife, but not to the mother of his illegitimate children. To anyone unsophisticated in the nuances of family law, such a distinction would appear to discriminate against illegitimate offspring. In his opinion for the Court, however, Justice Rehnquist [33] pointed out that even illegitimate children receive "child's benefits," and that "mother's benefits" were not meant to be basic child support but to compensate mothers for the economic dislocation of losing the family bread-winner.[34] A lower level of scrutiny was therefore appropriate, and the Court found that Congress could "reasonably conclude that a woman who has never been married to the wage earner is far less likely to be dependent upon the wage earner at the time of his death." [35] Justice Marshall argued convincingly in dissent that the "mother's benefit's" program, "both in purpose and effect, is a form of assistance to children," [36] so that the denial of those benefits impermissibly discriminated against illegitimate children.

In *Mills v. Habluetzel*,[37] the mother of an illegitimate child did what Robert Lalli was made to wish his mother had done: bring suit to establish paternity. A Texas court held that Lois Mills' suit, brought when her child was 19 months old, was barred by the special one-year statute of limitations for paternity suits filed on behalf of illegitimate children. In an opinion by Justice Rehnquist, the Supreme Court unanimously held that the law violated the equal protection clause.[38] If a state provides legitimate children with an enforceable right of support from their parents, declared the Court, it must provide to illegitimate children a parallel right of support which is "more than illusory." [39] Justice Rehnquist noted that "it requires little experience

---

knowledged his paternity in a document giving permission for Robert to marry.

31. Lalli, 439 U.S. at 265; Trimble, 430 U.S. at 769–70; Mathews, 427 U.S. at 505; Weber, 406 U.S. at 175.

32. 443 U.S. 282 (1979).

33. He was joined by Chief Justice Burger and Justices Stewart, Powell, and—curiously enough—Stevens.

34. Id. at 294.

35. Id. at 289. See also Bowen v. Owens, 106 S.Ct. 1881 (1986), discussed in § 16-2, supra, in note 18.

36. 443 U.S. at 303. He was joined by Justices Brennan, White, and—in a curious balance to Justice Stevens' anomalous vote—Justice Blackmun.

37. 456 U.S. 91 (1982).

38. Justice O'Connor filed a concurring opinion, in which Chief Justice Burger, and Justices Brennan, Blackmun and Powell (Part I) joined. Justice Powell also filed a brief statement concurring in the judgment but declined to join the opinion of the Court.

39. 456 U.S. at 97. Prior to the Court's decision in Gomez v. Perez, 409 U.S. 535 (1973), Texas recognized no duty on the part of a natural father to support his illegitimate offspring, and even allowed him to assert illegitimacy as a defense to prosecution for criminal nonsupport. 456 U.S. at 93. The Texas Legislature's first response to Gomez—the creation of a voluntary procedure by which fathers could legitimate their children—was held by the Texas Court of Civil Appeals to be inadequate. See In the Interest of R___ V___

to appreciate the obstacles to [paternity] suits that confront unwed mothers during the child's first year." [40]   Although the problems of proof in paternity suits " 'are not to be lightly brushed aside,' " they do not "justify a period of limitation which so restricts [support] rights as effectively to extinguish them." [41]

Although Justice Rehnquist's opinion for the Court suggested that, because of the unique problems of proving paternity, the support rights of illegitimate children need not necessarily be identical to those accorded legitimate offspring,[42] a separate majority of the Court endorsed Justice O'Connor's conclusion that the practical obstacles which made the one-year support opportunity illusory could just as easily render longer statutory periods meaningless.[43]   Given the position of this second majority in *Habluetzel*, the disposition in the Court's next term of a challenge to Tennessee's two-year statute of limitations for paternity suits was predictable.   In an opinion joined by all nine members of the Court, Justice Brennan held in *Pickett v. Brown* [44] that the equal protection principles discussed in the *Habluetzel* opinions required the Court to strike down the two-year limitation.[45]   Justice Brennan took particular note of the fact that Tennessee, like Texas, tolled most actions during a child's minority and even provided that paternity suits on behalf of those illegitimate children who were likely to become public charges could be brought up until the child's 18th birthday.[46]   The state's willingness to deal with litigation long after the fact in these situations made its purported concern about "stale evidence" in paternity suits brought on behalf of non-penurious minors appear somewhat spurious.

§ 16–25. Gender Discrimination: The Early Acceptance of Prejudiced Laws

We have seen that the Supreme Court treats state classification by race, national origin, or, in some cases, alien status or illegitimacy, as suspect and therefore subject to strict scrutiny. The reasons are not hidden: There has been a long history of prejudice against non-citizens and against illegitimates as well as against racial and national minorities—a history of continuing subordination. Moreover, although aliens sometimes become citizens, and illegitimates may be legitimized,

M——, 530 S.W.2d 921, 923 (Tex.Civ.App. 1975).

40.   456 U.S. at 100.

41.   Id. at 101.

42.   Id. at 97.

43.   Id. at 102.   (O'Connor, J., concurring, joined in relevant part by Chief Justice Burger and by Justices Brennan, Blackmun, and Powell). Justice O'Connor wrote that the state's own interests "in ensuring that genuine claims for child support are not denied," id. at 104, "coupled with the Texas Legislature's efforts to deny illegitimate children any significant opportunity to prove paternity and thus obtain child support," id. at 104–05, makes it "fair

to question whether the burden on illegitimates is designed to advance permissible state interests." Id. at 105. She added that the "risk that the child will find himself without financial support from his natural father seems as likely throughout his minority as during the first year of his life," id. at 106—making highly suspicious the fact that a paternity suit is one of the very few Texas causes of action not tolled throughout the plaintiff's minority. Id. at 105 (O'Connor, J., concurring); accord, id. at 106 (Powell, J., concurring).

44.   462 U.S. 1 (1983).

45.   Id. at 11.

46.   Id. at 12.

neither transformation is the result of unilateral choice, and the linking of historic prejudice to that circumstance—magnified in the case of race or national origin by the complete inability to transform one's condition at all and by the fact that the condition is rarely relevant to any constitutionally permissible goal of government—appears to tie together all the decisions in which a classification has been deemed suspect. Thus the stereotyping that has been singled out as unjust in Model VI has involved habitually treating individuals as less worthy or, in any event, less suited for certain roles, by virtue of rarely relevant traits that, if not immutable, are at least not alterable by simple acts of will.

While it may seem immediately apparent to some that gender-based governmental discrimination shares this unjust-stereotyping flaw,[1] until the early 1970's the Supreme Court routinely upheld sexually discriminatory laws whenever they could be rationally related to government purposes reflecting the traditional views of the "proper" relationship between men and women in American society.[2] In Justice Bradley's words, "Man is, or should be, woman's protector and defender. . . . The paramount destiny and mission of woman are to fulfill the noble and benign offices of wife and mother. This is the law of the Creator."[3] Accordingly, because "the constitution of the United States [did] not confer the right of suffrage upon any one, . . . the constitutions and laws of the several States which commit[ted] that important trust to men alone [were] not necessarily void."[4] Similarly, in *Muller v. Oregon*[5] the Court upheld a state statute limiting the hours women were permitted to work: "That woman's physical structure and the performance of maternal functions place her at a disadvantage in the struggle for subsistence is obvious. . . . Differentiated by these mat-

---

§ 16-25

1. Justice Stevens, dissenting in Mathews v. Lucas, 427 U.S. 495, 520-21 (1976), said it most concisely: "Habit, rather than analysis, makes it seem acceptable and natural to distinguish between male and female . . .; for too much of our history there was the same inertia in distinguishing between black and white. But that sort of stereotyped reaction may have no rational relationship—other than pure prejudicial discrimination—to the stated purpose for which the classification is being made." See also Califano v. Goldfarb, 430 U.S. 199, 222 (1977) (Stevens, J., concurring).

2. By no means was this attitude confined to the highest circle of the American judiciary. Thomas Jefferson believed that "were our state a pure democracy there would still be excluded from our deliberations women, who, to prevent deprivation of morals and ambiguity of issues, should not mix promiscuously in gatherings of men." M. Gruberg, Women in American Politics 4 (1960).

3. Bradwell v. Illinois, 83 U.S. (16 Wall.) 130, 141 (1872) (upholding state pro-

hibition of law practice by women) (Bradley, J., concurring in the judgment). Contrast Justice Bradley's view, in the same volume of the United States Reports, that the fourteenth amendment prevents a state from requiring butchers to ply their trade through a state-run monopoly, much less barring them from their trade altogether: "[I]n my judgment, the right of any citizen to follow whatever lawful employment he chooses to adopt (submitting himself to all lawful regulations) is one of his most valuable rights, and one which the legislature of a State cannot invade. . . ." The Slaughter-House Cases, 83 U.S. (16 Wall.) 36, 113-14 (1873) (Bradley, J., dissenting). Evidently, Justice Bradley's exclusive use of male pronouns was not merely a matter of stylistic convention.

4. Minor v. Happersett, 88 U.S. (21 Wall.) 162 (1875), overruled in 1920 by U.S. Const. amend. XIX ("the right of citizens of the United States to vote shall not be denied or abridged by the United States or by any State on account of sex.").

5. 208 U.S. 412 (1908).

ters from the other sex, she is properly placed in a class by herself, and legislation designed for her protection may be sustained, even when like legislation is not necessary for men and could not be sustained." [6]

While the Court justified the limitation of women's working hours by reference to the perceived social and biological need to limit the participation of women in the labor force,[7] the Court initially struck down women's minimum wage laws, which could not so easily be assimilated to sexist assumptions about the nature and role of women: "[W]hile the physical differences must be recognized in appropriate cases, and legislation fixing hours or conditions of work may properly take them into account, we cannot accept the doctrine that women of mature age, *sui juris*, require or may be subjected to restrictions upon their liberty of contract which could not lawfully be imposed in the case of men under similar circumstances." [8] In *West Coast Hotel Co. v. Parrish*,[9] however, the Court overturned these earlier decisions, and held valid a state statute establishing minimum wages for women. The Court asked, "What can be closer to the public interest than the health of women and their protection from unscrupulous and overreaching employers? And if the protection of women is a legitimate end of the exercise of state power, how can it be said that the requirement of the payment of a minimum wage fairly fixed to meet the very necessities of existence is not an admissible means to that end?" [10]

Even while recognizing the "vast changes in the social and legal position of women," [11] the Supreme Court continued its role as benevolent protector. Thus in *Goesaert v. Cleary* [12] the Court upheld a state statute prohibiting the licensing of women as bartenders unless a woman applicant was the wife or daughter of the male owner of the bar in which she would work. Assuming without question that the state

6. Id. at 421–22. The rationale for treating women differently had rested largely on claims of divine intention in the 1830's and 1840's; although that approach was reflected in some judicial opinions as late as the 1870's, and echoes into the 1970's, the dominant defense of "protective" laws and practices by the late 19th and early 20th centuries was cast along physiological lines. The physiological rationale for special treatment of women, however thin its evidentiary base, fit well for several decades with sterilization laws and similar state attempts to shape the population's genetic future. For a fuller discussion of Muller in the context of its Lochner-era setting, see Chapter 8, supra.

7. See, e.g., Radice v. New York, 264 U.S. 292, 294 (1924) (upholding state statute prohibiting employment of women in restaurants between 10 p.m. and 6 a.m.) (Court accepts state's argument that prohibition prevents impairment of woman's "peculiar and natural functions").

8. Adkins v. Children's Hospital, 261 U.S. 525, 553 (1923) (overturning District of Columbia's minimum wage act authorizing

fixing of minimum wage standards for women). Note Justice Holmes' dissenting opinion in Adkins: "Muller v. Oregon, I take it, is as good law today as it was in 1908. It will need more than the Nineteenth Amendment [enacted since *Muller*] to convince me that there are no differences between men and women, or that legislation cannot take those differences into account." Id. at 569–70 (Holmes, J., dissenting). See also Morehead v. New York ex rel. Tipaldo, 298 U.S. 587 (1936) (overturning state minimum wage act for women).

9. 300 U.S. 379 (1937).

10. Id. at 398. Note that the Court rejected the claim that the law constituted an "arbitrary discrimination" by its exclusion of coverage for men, reasoning that the legislature was not required to recognize all cases of harm. Id. at 400.

11. Goesaert v. Cleary, 335 U.S. 464, 465–66 (1948), disapproved in Craig v. Boren, 429 U.S. 190, 210 n.23 (1976).

12. 335 U.S. 464 (1948).

could prohibit all women from working as bartenders,[13] Justice Frankfurter concluded that, given the legitimate state interest in establishing preventive measures to combat the "moral and social problems" to which bartending by women might give rise,[14] the legislature was reasonable in believing that "the oversight assured through ownership of a bar by a barmaid's husband or father minimize[d] hazards that [might] confront a barmaid without such protecting oversight." [15] Similarly, in *Hoyt v. Florida*,[16] the Warren Court unanimously approved a state law which included men on the jury list unless they requested an exemption, but exempted women unless they volunteered. The recent "enlightened emancipation of women" notwithstanding, the Court found the state's classification reasonable in light of the fact that "woman is still regarded as the center of home and family life." [17]

§ 16–26. Gender Discrimination: The Emerging Condemnation of Explicit Sex-Role Stereotyping Under an Intermediate Standard of Review

Not until its decision in *Reed v. Reed* [1] did the Supreme Court finally withdraw from its posture of utmost deference to political judgments respecting the role of women. In *Reed*, the Court unanimously invalidated an Idaho statute requiring, as between persons "equally entitled" to administer a decedent's estate, that "males . . . be preferred to females." [2] Although the Court purported to apply its traditional test of "rational relationship," it did state that "[t]o give a mandatory preference to members of either sex over members of the other, merely to accomplish the elimination of hearings on the merits, [was] to make the very kind of arbitrary legislative choice forbidden by [equal protection]." [3] As Professor Gerald Gunther commented, "It is difficult to understand [the *Reed*] result without an assumption that some special sensitivity to sex as a classifying factor entered into the analysis. . . . Only by importing some special suspicion of sex-related means . . . can the result be made entirely persuasive." [4]

---

13. Id. at 465.

14. Id. at 466.

15. Id. But see Seidenberg v. McSorleys' Old Ale House, Inc., 317 F.Supp. 593 (S.D.N.Y.1970) (overturning tavern owner's exclusion of female patrons); Sailer Inn, Inc. v. Kirby, 5 Cal.3d 1, 95 Cal. Rptr. 329, 485 P.2d 529 (1971) (invalidating state statutory prohibition against female bartenders). The Court in Goesaert did not even consider the possibility that the bar might be *owned* by a *woman*. Justice Frankfurter's opinion for the Court was too busy being amused by the "beguiling" subject of barmaids—and too busy recalling the "sprightly and ribald" alewife of old England—to indulge in much hard thinking about the case before the Court. Goesaert, 335 U.S. at 465.

16. 368 U.S. 57 (1961).

17. Id. at 61–62. Contrast Taylor v. Louisiana, 419 U.S. 522, 531 (1975) (state jury-selection system operating to exclude women from jury service invalidated on sixth amendment grounds): "[w]omen are sufficiently numerous and distinct from men and . . . if they are systematically eliminated from jury panels, the Sixth Amendment's fair cross-section requirement cannot be satisfied." See also Duren v. Missouri, 439 U.S. 357 (1979) (striking down a state law that gave women who so requested an automatic exemption from jury service).

§ 16–26

1. 404 U.S. 71 (1971).

2. Id. at 73.

3. Id. at 76.

4. Gunther, "The Supreme Court, 1971 Term: Foreword: In Search of Evolving Doctrine on a Changing Court: A Model for a New Equal Protection," 86 Harv.L. Rev. 1, 34 (1972).

And in *Frontiero v. Richardson*,[5] decided some 17 months later, a plurality of four Justices made such a suspicion explicit.[6] Holding unconstitutional, under the due process clause of the fifth amendment, federal statutes providing that spouses of male members of the armed services were "dependents" for purposes of obtaining military benefits, but that spouses of female members were not "dependents" unless in fact dependent on their wives for over one-half of their support, the plurality found "at least implicit support" in *Reed* for declaring classifications based on sex suspect.[7] The Court's plurality expressly rejected the sufficiency of the argument that the statutory scheme's classification served administrative convenience, and described the effect of the scheme as " 'romantic paternalism'," operating to "put women not on a pedestal, but in a cage." [8]

Relying only in part on *Frontiero*, a unanimous Court in *Weinberger v. Wiesenfeld* [9] invalidated a provision of the Social Security Act awarding survivor's benefits to widows, but not widowers, responsible for dependent children. Citing the "indistinguishable" provision struck down in *Frontiero*,[10] the Court noted that "the Constitution . . . forbids the gender-based differentiation that results in the efforts of female workers required to pay social security taxes producing less protection for their families than is produced by the efforts of men." [11] Further, without expressly invoking strict scrutiny, the Court asserted that "the mere recitation of a benign, compensatory purpose [was] not an automatic shield which protect[ed] against any inquiry into the actual purposes underlying [the] statutory scheme." [12] Given what the Court found to be the actual statutory purpose—to enable the surviving parent to remain at home to care for a child—the gender-based classification was held "entirely irrational." [13] The Court expressed an added objection to the statute's anti-male aspect: "It is no less important for a child to be cared for by its sole surviving parent when that parent is male rather than female. And a father, no less than a mother, has a constitutionally protected right to the 'companionship, care, custody, and management' of 'the children he has sired and raised, [which] undeniably warrants deference and, absent a powerful countervailing interest, protection.' *Stanley v. Illinois*, 405 U.S. 645, 651 (1972). Further, to the extent that women who work when they have sole responsibility for children encounter special problems, it would seem

---

5. 411 U.S. 677 (1973).

6. Justices Douglas, Marshall and White joined Justice Brennan's plurality opinion, announcing the judgment of the Court. Justice Stewart concurred in the judgment but did not join the plurality opinion, finding simply that the statutes "work[ed] an invidious discrimination." Id. at 691. Justice Powell, joined by Chief Justice Burger and Justice Blackmun, also concurred only in the Court's judgment, finding it unnecessary to decide whether sex was a suspect classification, pending consideration by the States of the proposed Equal Rights Amendment. Id. at 692. See § 16–30, infra.

7. 411 U.S. at 682.

8. Id. at 684. Frontiero made plain that Reed could not be circumvented merely by giving individual women an opportunity to rebut the presumption that their spouses were the wage-earners and they were the dependents.

9. 420 U.S. 636 (1975).

10. Id. at 642.

11. Id. at 645.

12. Id. at 648.

13. Id. at 651.

that men with sole responsibility for children will encounter the same childcare related problems."[14]   Thus, the legislation acted to reinforce sex-based stereotypes, and in general inhibited the exercise, by both men and women, of liberty in the choice of social roles.[15]

The Court again invoked its approach from *Reed* in *Stanton v. Stanton*,[16] finding it illegitimate for government to assume that social roles are functions of gender.   In *Stanton* the Court, by a vote of 7–1, held irrational a Utah statute providing for a parental support obligation for sons until age 21, but for daughters only until age 18.   After commenting that it was "unnecessary" to decide whether the classification was suspect, the Court invalidated the discrimination on the ground that "a child, male or female, is still a child.   No longer is the female destined solely for the home and the rearing of the family, and only the male for the marketplace and the world of ideas. . . .   If a specified age of minority is required for the boy in order to assure him parental support while he attains his education and training, so, too, it is for the girl.   To distinguish between the two on educational grounds is to be self-serving: if the female is not to be supported so long as the male, she hardly can be expected to attend school as long as he does, and bringing her education to an end earlier coincides with the role-typing society has long imposed."[17]

The court's insistence that legislatures recognize that "the times they are a'changing" is ably illustrated by *Craig v. Boren*,[18] which invalidated state statutes prohibiting the sale of 3.2% beer to males under the age of 21 and females under the age of 18.   While the government offered in defense a variety of statistical surveys intended to demonstrate a high correlation between gender and alcohol-related traffic accidents, the Court rejected the evidence as establishing "an unduly tenuous 'fit.'"[19]   The Court further noted that "[t]he very social steretypes that find reflection in age differential laws . . . are likely substantially to distort the accuracy of these comparative statistics.

14. Id. at 652.

15. See "The Supreme Court, 1974 Term," 89 Harv.L.Rev. 47, 101 (1975).

16. 421 U.S. 7 (1975). Justice Blackmun wrote for the majority. Justice Rehnquist dissented. See id. at 18 (arguing that the appeal should be dismissed for procedural reasons).

17. Id. at 14–15. On remand, the Utah Supreme Court disregarded the U.S. Supreme Court's mandate to decide how Utah was to eliminate the discrimination between the genders, and held instead that the age of majority statute was constitutional as applied to females. Stanton v. Stanton, 552 P.2d 112 (Utah 1976). On appeal, the U.S. Supreme Court vacated the judgment and remanded once again for further proceedings. See 429 U.S. 501 (1977). In the interim, the Utah Legislature amended the statute to provide 18 years as the age of majority for both sexes. See id. at 501 n.2.

18. 429 U.S. 190 (1976). Justice Brennan wrote the opinion for a 7–2 Court. Justices Powell, Stevens, Stewart and Blackmun each filed separate concurring opinions. Chief Justice Burger and Justice Rehnquist each filed a dissenting opinion.

19. Id. at 202. In the relevant age group, the proportion of males arrested for driving under the influence was 2%—an order of magnitude greater than the proportion of female offenders (.18%). Id. at 201. But these figures prove only that maleness and youth correlate better with drunk driving than do femaleness and youth, and do not change the fact that fully 98% of those in the disadvantaged group did not commit the behavior at which the traffic safety law was aimed. As the Court explained, "if maleness is to serve as a proxy for drinking and driving, a correlation of 2% must be considered an unduly tenuous 'fit.'" Id. at 201–02.

Hence 'reckless' young men who drink and drive are transformed into arrest statistics, whereas their female counterparts are chivalrously escorted home." [20] Openly adopting for the first time a judicial standard of review based on intermediate scrutiny, the Court found the state's showing inadequate to prove that "sex represents a legitimate, accurate proxy for the regulation of drinking and driving." [21]

Applying this intermediate standard of review, the Court has continued to show little tolerance for legislative classifications that presume that women have no responsibilities outside the home or no role in supporting their families. *Califano v. Westcott* [22] held that a provision of the Social Security Act violated the equal protection component of the fifth amendment due process clause by providing benefits to the dependent children of unemployed fathers but not those of unemployed mothers. *Orr v. Orr* [23] invalidated laws that authorized Alabama's courts to impose alimony obligations only on men. In his opinion for the Court, Justice Brennan declared it well settled that a state has no authority to prefer "an allocation of family responsibilities under which the wife plays a dependent role." [24] And in *Kirchberg v. Feenstra*,[25] the Court unanimously struck down a Louisiana law which gave a husband, "as 'head and master' of property jointly owned with his wife, the unilateral right to dispose of such property without his spouse's consent." [26]

It is no surprise that many of these sex discrimination cases were brought by male plaintiffs, since legislative assumptions about traditional sex roles often impinge on the rights of both men and women. For example, Alabama's rule requiring alimony payments only of men derogated women—by assuming that they play no role in bringing home the bacon—while simultaneously limiting the family roles available to men—by assuming that men do not stay home to fry the bacon, and hence have no need of support payments from a former spouse. The Court likewise demonstrated solicitude for male pursuit of non-traditional family roles in *Caban v. Mohammed*,[27] where it struck down a New York law which gave unwed mothers, but not unwed fathers, the power unilaterally to block adoption of their children by simply with-

---

20. Id. at 202 n.14.

21. Id. at 204. See § 16–32, infra. Given this intermediate standard, no explicitly gender-based occupational disqualification can be upheld without the clearest showing that a gender-neutral criterion would leave a serious problem unsolved. For an illustration of what purported to be such a showing, see Dothard v. Rawlinson, 433 U.S. 321, 335–36 & n.22, (1977) (women may be denied positions as contact guards for violent male sex offenders in maximum security prison of state whose prison system has a history of rampant violence; record showed attacks on women in the state's prisons), discussed in § 16–28, infra.

22. 443 U.S. 76 (1979). Justice Blackmun delivered the opinion of the Court, in which Justices Brennan, White, Marshall, and Stevens joined. Justice Powell con-

curred in part and dissented in part, joined by Chief Justice Burger and Justices Stewart and Rehnquist.

23. 440 U.S. 268 (1979). Justice Brennan wrote for the six-member majority. Justice Powell filed a dissenting opinion, as did Justice Rehnquist, who was joined by Chief Justice Burger. The dissenters did not reach the merits.

24. 440 U.S. at 279–80.

25. 450 U.S. 455 (1981).

26. Id. at 456.

27. 441 U.S. 380 (1979). Justice Powell wrote the opinion of the Court, in which Justices Brennan, White, Marshall, and Blackmun joined. Justice Stewart and Justice Stevens dissented; Justice Stevens' dissent was joined by Chief Justice Burger and Justice Rehnquist.

holding consent. In his opinion for the Court, Justice Powell criticized the assumption that fathers are "invariably less qualified and entitled than mothers to exercise a concerned judgment as to the fate of their children." [28]

It is clear that the laws invalidated in these cases, from *Reed* to *Caban*, shared an important characteristic in terms of impact on behavior: All either prevented, or economically discouraged, departures from "traditional" sex roles, freezing biology into social destiny. And government's almost uniform argument [29] in justification of these laws emphasized the economy achieved by the accurate and therefore "rational" assumption of traditional male and female inclinations and capacities. The Supreme Court's thoughtful response to this argument has recognized the argument's essence as self-fulfilling prophecy: The "accuracy" of government's assumption is derived in some significant degree from the chill on sex-role experimentation and change generated by the classifications themselves. While that may have been thought permissible as late as 1948, when the Court declared that "the Constitution does not require legislatures to reflect . . . shifting social standards," [30] thirty years later the Court decidedly came to view "shifting social standards" as controlling.[31]

§ 16–27. "Benign" Gender Discrimination

The argument usually offered by government to justify gender classifications revolves about administrative economy. But sometimes the state seeks justification in a statute's supposedly "benign" or "protective" purpose "to compensate female beneficiaries as a group for the economic difficulties which still confront women who seek to

28. Id. at 394; see id. at 389, 392. The majority expressly noted that the equal protection clause would not preclude the state from withholding adoption veto power from those unwed fathers who had never come forward to participate in rearing their children. Lehr v. Robertson, 463 U.S. 248 (1983), involved just such a case. In an opinion by Justice Stevens joined by Chief Justice Burger and Justices Brennan, Powell, Rehnquist, and O'Connor, the Court there upheld a New York law guaranteeing all mothers but only certain classes of "putative fathers" the right to veto an adoption and to receive notice of adoption proceedings. The Court distinguished Caban v. Mohammed on the ground that the father there had admitted paternity and helped raise the child, whereas the plaintiff in Lehr had never supported his child, never offered to marry the mother, and never entered his name in the state "putative father registry," which would have entitled him to notice of the adoption proceeding. Justice White, joined by Justices Marshall and Blackmun, dissented. Cf. Parham v. Hughes, 441 U.S. 347 (1979)

(upholding law that allowed the mother, but not the father, of an illegitimate child to sue for the child's wrongful death, reasoning that parents were not similarly situated since only fathers could legitimate children born out of wedlock by use of another state procedure), discussed in § 16–28, infra.

29. For the exceptional argument based on "benignity" of the discrimination, see § 16–27, infra.

30. Goesaert v. Cleary, 335 U.S. 464, 466 (1948).

31. See Justice Stevens' dissenting opinion in Mathews v. Lucas, 427 U.S. 495, 520–21 (1976): "Habit, rather than analysis, makes it seem acceptable and natural to distinguish between male and female . . .; for too much of our history there was the same inertia in distinguishing between black and white. But that sort of stereotyped reaction may have no rational relationship—other than pure prejudicial discrimination—to the stated purpose for which the classification is being made."

support themselves and their families." [1] In *Kahn v. Shevin* [2] the Court embraced its old doctrine of benign preferences [3] to uphold as "compensatory" a Florida law that granted widows a special $500 property tax exemption as a supposedly reasonable means of relieving the financial impact of the loss of a spouse "upon the sex for which that loss imposes a disproportionately heavy burden." [4] Although the law had been enacted in 1885 to create a sweeping, permanent and separate legal status for all widows on the assumption that all wives are dependent upon their husbands for support, the state defended its law as "an affirmative step toward alleviating the effects of past economic discrimination against women." [5] The Court, in a 6–3 opinion by Justice Douglas, conducted a discourse on female socialization and, after comparing employment and wage data for men and women, endorsed the state's position under *Reed v. Reed*'s "fair and substantial" relation standard of review. [6]

Citing *Kahn*, the Court by a 5–4 margin again rejected a male's claim of unconstitutional gender discrimination in *Schlesinger v. Ballard*, [7] upholding the military's "up or out" policy under which women were given 13 years to be promoted, but men twice passed over for promotion were subject to mandatory discharge. The Court concluded that this federal policy reflected "not archaic and overbroad generalizations, but, instead, the demonstrable fact that male and female line officers in the Navy are not similarly situated with respect to opportunities for professional service." [8] But the legislative history offered no support for the "benign" purpose the majority imagined for the law: redressing differential opportunities for promotion created by laws limiting female service on most navy ships. [9]

Kahn and *Ballard* are not the most unimpeachable of precedents. [10] Within a few months after *Ballard*, in *Weinberger v. Wiesenfeld*, [11] the

---

§ 16–27

1. Weinberger v. Wiesenfeld, 420 U.S. 636, 648 (1975) (unanimously rejecting this defense).

2. 416 U.S. 351 (1974).

3. Note Kahn's favorable reference to Muller v. Oregon, 208 U.S. 412 (1908), discussed in § 16–25, supra, as permitting a gender classification based on the "special physical structure of women." 416 U.S. at 356 n.10.

4. 416 U.S. at 355.

5. Id. at 358 (Brennan, J., dissenting).

6. Id. at 353–54. The opinion was joined by Chief Justice Burger and Justices Stewart, Blackmun, Powell, and Rehnquist. Justices Brennan and Marshall, finding no compelling governmental interest under the Frontiero plurality test discussed in § 16–26, supra, dissented. Id. at 357–60. Justice White in dissent argued that the sole state justification for the failure to exempt needy widowers—perhaps including the widower who challenged the law—was "administrative efficiency," an

insufficient rationale under both Reed and Frontiero. Id. at 360–62.

7. 419 U.S. 498 (1975). Justice Stewart's opinion for the Court was joined by Chief Justice Burger and Justices Blackmun, Powell, and Rehnquist.

8. Id. at 508.

9. Id. Four Justices refused to indulge the notion that the differential treatment of women was taken in response to differential opportunities for promotion, believing instead that the difference was based on technical administrative reasons that had outlived their usefulness. Id. at 517–18 (Brennan, J., joined by Douglas and Marshall, JJ., dissenting); id. at 521 (White, J., dissenting).

10. Justice Stevens has indicated that he might vote to overrule Kahn, which was decided before he joined the Court. See Califano v. Goldfarb, 430 U.S. 199, 224 (1977) (Stevens, J., concurring in the judgment).

---

11. See note 11 on page 1567.

Supreme Court unanimously rejected benign purposes supplied by hindsight or afterthought.[12] And subsequent cases have established that carefully tailored remedial provisions cast in terms of gender will be upheld only if they were in fact adopted for remedial reasons rather than out of "romantic paternalism," [13] and if they are in fact substantially well fitted to their remedial goals.

In *Califano v. Goldfarb*,[14] a closely divided Court invalidated a Social Security provision that paid survivor benefits to widowers only if they could show substantial reliance on the deceased's income, while paying benefits to widows without regard to such dependence. The Court found no basis other than administrative convenience and sexist stereotyping for the law's presumption that wives alone are dependent on their spouses.[15] As Justice Stevens wrote in his concurring opinion, "It is fair to infer that habit, rather than analysis or actual reflection, made it seem acceptable to equate the terms 'widow' and 'dependent surviving spouse.' That kind of automatic reflex is far different from . . . a legislative decision to favor females in order to compensate for past wrongs." [16] Finding just such a legislative decision to provide compensation, the Court, again dividing 5–4, upheld in *Califano v. Webster* [17] a Social Security benefit formula that generated uniformly higher payments for retired female wage-earners than for males who appeared to be similarly situated. The formula did so by permitting women to exclude more low-earning years than males could in calculating their average past earnings. The Court concluded that the legislative history revealed a decision to treat women more favorably solely in order to remedy prior wage discrimination, and noted that amendments to the law provided that this remedy would be phased out as the need for it diminished in light of the passage of federal anti-discrimination legislation.[18]

11. 420 U.S. 636 (1975) (striking down social security law granting survivor's benefits to widows but not to widowers).

12. The Court determined the purpose of the challenged Social Security law to be "provid[ing] children deprived of one parent with the opportunity for the personal attention of the other," id. at 648–49. Hence there was no reason—beyond blatant gender-role stereotyping—to provide survivor benefits to mothers with dependent children but not to fathers with such children.

13. Califano v. Webster, 430 U.S. 313, 320 (1977) (per curiam).

14. 430 U.S. 199 (1977). Justice Brennan's plurality opinion was joined by Justices White, Marshall, and Powell. Justice Stevens concurred in the judgment. Justice Rehnquist dissented, joined by Chief Justice Burger and Justices Stewart and Blackmun.

15. Id. at 217 & n.18.

16. Id. at 222. The four dissenters in Goldfarb, belatedly disturbed at what had happened in the unanimous decision two years earlier in Weinberger v. Wiesenfeld, 420 U.S. 636 (1975), admitted that there was authority to support the Court's result. 430 U.S. at 224–25 (Rehnquist, J., dissenting). But they sought to distinguish Wiesenfeld as involving a social insurance provision that "flatly denied" benefits to surviving widowers, whereas the provision under attack in Goldfarb "does not totally foreclose widowers, but simply requires from them a proof of dependency which is not required from similarly situated widows." Id. at 229.

17. 430 U.S. 313 (1977) (per curiam).

18. See id. at 320 & n.9 (noting that 1972 amendment's equalization of treatment followed such congressional reforms as the Equal Pay Act, which " 'have lessened the economic justification for the more favorable benefit computation formula' "). It is strongly arguable, however, that "compensation" for past wrongs, and particularly lump-sum compensation, should be less tolerantly regarded than measures actually broadening equality of opportunity in the future; a cash bonus for widows, as in Kahn v. Shevin, supra, and

The Court has placed a premium on avoiding unnecessary generalizations in allegedly benign gender discrimination. The blanket state rule against imposing alimony obligations on women which the Court struck down in *Orr v. Orr* [19] could not be justified as an attempt to compensate needy women for past discrimination during marriage while avoiding burdensome individualized hearings on need, since the necessity of holding individual hearings on alimony in any event made the gender classification wholly gratuitous.[20] Similarly, in *Wengler v. Druggists Mutual Insurance Co.*,[21] the Court employed "heightened scrutiny" [22] to strike down a Missouri workers' compensation law that required a widower but not a widow to prove dependence on the spouse in order to qualify for benefits. Evidence that women have a lower economic status than men, which was deemed sufficient to justify the discriminatory tax exemption for widows in *Kahn v. Shevin*,[23] was held inadequate to support the Missouri law. The state could assess need on an individual basis or grant benefits to all widows and widowers, but it could not arbitrarily assume that a woman's income is less important to her family than her husband's.[24] Although it did not expressly overrule *Kahn, Wengler* relegated it to a footnote, finding it "in no way dispositive of the case at bar." [25]

These cases, and others in which the defense of benign discrimination was raised, were brought by men seeking to be treated as women, whether with respect to access to traditional female family roles,[26] or with respect to financial support from one's spouse,[27] or otherwise. These male plaintiffs did not wish to have the preferential treatment of women terminated; rather, they wished to have the preference extended to themselves. The male plaintiffs who unsuccessfully challenged

perhaps (although less clearly) even a more favorable formula for retired female workers, as in Califano v. Webster, does less actually to remedy past inequity or present prejudice, and perhaps more to perpetuate lingering stereotypes, than would, say, a policy of preferentially admitting or hiring women for places in education or employment. See United Jewish Organizations of Williamsburgh v. Carey, 430 U.S. 144, 173–74 & n.3 (1977) (Brennan, J., concurring). See also "The Supreme Court, 1974 Term," 89 Harv.L.Rev. 47, 95 (1975). Cf. Sullivan, "Sins of Discrimination: Last Term's Affirmative Action Cases," 100 Harv.L.Rev. 78, 96 (1986) (suggesting purposes for affirmative action other than compensation for past wrongs, such as promoting social progress for disadvantaged groups or aspiring to a more integrated future).

19. 440 U.S. 268 (1979).

20. Id. at 282.

21. 446 U.S. 142 (1980).

22. Id. at 152.

23. 416 U.S. 351 (1974).

24. 446 U.S. at 151. The Court's observation that there might be cases in which

administrative convenience would justify gender discrimination even under heightened scrutiny was wholly gratuitous, since the Court had, at that time, never upheld a gender classification on that basis. Rostker v. Goldberg, 453 U.S. 57 (1981), where the Court subsequently upheld the constitutionality of male-only draft registration, does not really qualify as an administrative convenience case. The Court there held that, since Congress had found that any future draft "would be characterized by a need for combat troops" and that "women as a group . . . are not eligible for combat," there was an obvious and sound basis for registering only men. Id. at 76.

25. 446 U.S. at 148 n.4.

26. E.g., Weinberger v. Wiesenfeld, 420 U.S. 636 (1975) (man seeking "mother's benefits" as surviving parent of an infant).

27. E.g., Orr v. Orr, 440 U.S. 268 (1979) (man seeking to overturn law allowing courts to order alimony payments only to women); Wengler v. Druggists Mutual Ins. Co., 446 U.S. 142 (1980) (man seeking workers' compensation death benefits provided by state to widows).

the male-only draft registration law in *Rostker v. Goldberg*,[28] given their druthers, would probably have preferred to share women's exemption from the draft rather than to require the registration of women. And the plaintiffs who won *Craig v. Boren*[29] did not seek a regime in which women aged 18–20, like their male counterparts, were denied the right to buy beer, but a regime in which young males would have the same access to alcohol that women enjoyed. In this respect, most gender benign-discrimination cases differ from the analogous race reverse-discrimination cases, where white plaintiffs do not so much seek to be treated as blacks—for example, with respect to affirmative action employment opportunities—as they seek to have the preferential treatment of blacks terminated, since it constitutes a barrier to the positions they seek.[30]

In this difference lies support for the Supreme Court's application of at least an intermediate standard of equal protection scrutiny to all gender classifications, even those challenged as a burden on men. Chief Justice Rehnquist has consistently dissented on this issue, arguing that the minimum rationality standard is appropriate because men have suffered from no history of discrimination or disadvantage, and therefore are not "in need of the special solicitude of the courts."[31] Although this historical fact is of relevance in deciding the appropriate standard of review in challenges brought by white males to remedial preferences for blacks,[32] it is immaterial to choosing the proper standard for evaluating legislative reinforcement of restrictive sex roles. For while our laws and institutions no longer value distinctive race roles, they still promote—with vast popular support—distinctive and restrictive gender roles. And while the history of racial discrimination litigation constitutes a one-way model of desired access—blacks seeking the status and privileges accorded to whites[33]—the Supreme Court's sex discrimination cases reveal a two-way street:[34] women asking to be

28. 453 U.S. 57 (1981).

29. 429 U.S. 190 (1976).

30. See Kay, "Models of Equality," 1985 Univ.Ill.L.Rev. 39, 45–47, 75–77 (1985). An exception to this generalization—an exception that may become far more common—is Johnson v. Santa Clara Transportation Agency, 107 S.Ct. 1442 (1987), where the Court upheld a voluntarily-adopted affirmative action plan that allowed gender to be considered as one factor in promotions to positions, such as dispatcher, in which women have been significantly underrepresented. The plan was challenged under Title VII by a male employee who was passed over for a promotion that went to a less senior female employee. See § 16–22, supra.

31. Michael M. v. Superior Court, 450 U.S. 464 (1981); see also Craig v. Boren, 429 U.S. 190, 218–19 (1976) (Rehnquist, J., dissenting).

32. Perhaps curiously, Chief Justice Rehnquist has been willing to invoke the equal protection clause to strike down affirmative action programs that burden white males. See, e.g., Fullilove v. Klutznick, 448 U.S. 448, 523 (1980) (joining the dissent of Justice Stewart); United States v. Paradise, 107 S.Ct. 1053, 1080 (1987) (joining the dissent of Justice O'Connor); cf. Johnson v. Transportation Agency, 107 S.Ct. 1442, 1465 (1987) (joining the Title VII dissent of Justice Scalia).

33. With respect to racial role-typing, blacks wished access to the dignity and power that went with roles which were the exclusive province of whites, but there were never any roles dominated by blacks to which whites wished access—because the only role ever exclusively occupied or even dominated by blacks was that of slave.

34. See Kay, supra note 30, at 45–46.

treated like men, typically in the commercial realm,[35] and men asking to be treated like women, primarily in the sphere of family life.[36] Thus, in contrast to the racial context, where privileged whites cannot plausibly contend that their challenge to a racial classification benefitting disadvantaged blacks will in fact redound to the benefit of blacks,[37] men can legitimately argue that dismantling a regime of legislatively-reinforced gender roles offers the prospect for a two-way flow of enhanced liberty, opportunity and power for both sexes.[38] Sauce for the gander may well be sauce for the goose.

Obviously, it is not the case that "*all* discriminations between the sexes ultimately redound to the detriment of females, [simply] because they tend to reinforce 'old notions' restricting the roles and opportunities of women." [39] If that were so, it would be a strong argument for strict scrutiny of all gender classifications. But it is precisely because many, but not all, differences in treatment predicated on gender in fact injure women while purporting to favor them that such classifications must be examined for more than minimum rationality, even when challenges to them are brought by privileged males.

Consider *Mississippi University for Women v. Hogan*,[40] where a male would-be nursing student challenged the state school's single-sex admissions policy. The proffered justification was more than plausible on its face: providing a remedial haven for women from the hierarchy of domination in the "man's world" of higher education.[41] But in her

35. See, e.g., Roberts v. United States Jaycees, 468 U.S. 609 (1984) (women protected by Minnesota Human Rights Act against exclusion from important private business organization on basis of sex); Turner v. Department of Employment Security, 423 U.S. 44 (1975) (invalidating state law making pregnant women ineligible for unemployment compensation during months before and after childbirth); Cleveland Bd. of Educ. v. LaFleur, 414 U.S. 632 (1974) (invalidating school disctrict's mandatory maternity leave rules).

36. See, e.g., Quilloin v. Walcott, 434 U.S. 246 (1978) (natural father who had never lived with son not entitled to object to adoption by child's step-father); Caban v. Mohammed, 441 U.S. 380 (1979) (children who have lived in relationship with natural father may not be adopted without his consent); Stanley v. Illinois, 405 U.S. 645 (1972) (father of illegitimate child suing to be considered for custody award).

37. The possible exception, to the extent it deserves credence in particular circumstances, is a challenge by whites to preferential treatment for blacks on the ground, inter alia, that such favoritism constitutes condescending and stigmatizing paternalism which actually impedes black progress and diminishes the value of black achievement.

38. For example, in Weinberger v. Wiesenfeld, 420 U.S. 636 (1975), the Social Se-

curity Act's program of providing survivor's benefits to widows with dependent children but not to widowers was challenged by a man as discrimination denying men the same opportunity to stay at home to care for their children—discrimination that valued motherhood over fatherhood. Id. at 652. The Court also noted, however, that the law injured female workers required to pay social security taxes, since their contributions produced less income protection for their families than the identical contributions of male workers produced. Id. at 645.

39. Craig v. Boren, 429 U.S. 190, 220 n. 2 (1976) (Rehnquist, J., dissenting) (emphasis added).

40. 458 U.S. 718 (1982).

41. For a discussion of the alleged advantages to women of single-sex education, see, e.g., Carnegie Comm'n on Higher Education, Report on Opportunities for Women in Higher Education (1975). Justice Powell took note of this study and others in his dissenting opinion in Hogan. 458 U.S. at 738. In Vorcheimer v. School District of Philadelphia, 430 U.S. 703 (1977) (per curiam), an evenly-divided Court upheld an otherwise coeducational school system's maintenance of sexually segregated high schools for academic high achievers. The only mention of the Vorcheimer case by any of the opinions in Hogan was in a footnote in the opinion of the Court, which

opinion for the Court, Justice O'Connor [42] demanded an "exceedingly persuasive justification" for Mississippi's refusal to admit men to one of its nursing schools.[43] And upon closer inspection the state's defense became transparent: the school's policy of allowing men to audit and fully participate in classes and to enroll in its continuing education courses, and uncontroverted evidence that admitting men to nursing classes affected neither teaching style nor female performance,[44] "fatally undermine[d] its claim that women . . . in the school of nursing are adversely affected by the presence of men." [45] Moreover, the supposedly benign discrimination against men in admissions in fact injured women by "perpetuat[ing] the stereotyped view of nursing as an exclusively woman's job" and thereby depressing nurses' wages.[46] The nature of sex discrimination claims in our role-ridden society thus manifestly requires sensitive and searching judicial inquiry.

§ 16–28. The Tangled Web of Gender Discrimination: Using One Discriminatory Practice to Justify Another

The easiest targets in the assault on gender discrimination are laws, such as that struck down in *Kirchberg v. Feenstra*,[1] that blatantly relegate women to a subordinate role in society. Less obvious are sex-specific classifications based on allegedly accurate statistical differences; yet *Frontiero v. Richardson* [2] and its successors have established a rule that the law cannot use gender as a statistical proxy, even in a rebuttable way, in those instances where courts perceive no inherently relevant difference that gender as such makes. Differences that are obviously attributable to social conventions that the judges themselves have come to perceive as arbitrary and outmoded—and therefore as mere cultural artifacts supporting only contingent statistical correlations—are insufficient to justify explicit legal differentiation between the sexes. But when a gender classification is so woven into the entire social understanding of women that it reflects what the judiciary itself still perceives as a genuine gender difference, the plot begins to thicken.

When confronted with a multi-level matrix of intersecting discriminatory practices, a court may be forced to choose among (1) eliminating

stated that the question of "separate but equal" higher education for men and women was not before the Court because Mississippi maintained no other single-sex university. 458 U.S. at 720 n.1.

42. She was joined by Justices Brennan, White, Marshall and Stevens. Justice Powell, joined by Justice Rehnquist, dissented. Chief Justice Burger and Justice Blackmun also filed dissenting opinions.

43. 458 U.S. at 731.

44. Id.

45. Id. at 730.

46. Id. at 729–30 & n.15. Because its idiosyncratic facts made Hogan an easy case once meaningful scrutiny had been conducted, the case should not be regarded as a definitive ruling on the viability of the

"separate but equal" argument in the context of sex discrimination. Indeed, the Hogan majority expressly noted that that issue was not before the Court. Id. at 720 n. 1.

§ 16–28

1. 450 U.S. 455 (1981) (unanimously striking down a law giving every husband, as "head and master" of the household, unilateral power to dispose of property owned jointly with his wife), discussed in § 16–26, supra.

2. 411 U.S. 677 (1973) (striking down even a rebuttable statutory presumption that female spouses of military service personnel are dependents, while male spouses are not), discussed in § 16–26, supra.

the multiple layers and lines of discrimination insofar as all are fairly implicated in the case at bar, (2) striking down one layer or line while allowing the inequality created by the others to remain, or (3) allowing the particular discriminatory practice that has been challenged to be justified by other such practices or by underlying layers of invidious gender subordination. In too many instances, the Court has taken the third course.

Among the clearest examples is *Parham v. Hughes*,[3] where the Court upheld a Georgia law that allowed the mother, but not the father, of an illegitimate child to sue for the child's wrongful death. A plurality[4] concluded that mothers and fathers of illegitimate children were not "similarly situated" because—under a different Georgia statute—the father, but not the mother, could legitimate a child born out of wedlock by voluntary, unilateral use of a specified state procedure.[5] The Court refused to evaluate this underlying discrimination, whereby Georgia defined illegitimate children as all those—and only those— whom the *father* refused to acknowledge, thereby assuring that men and men alone need never suffer whatever stigma accompanies parenthood of an illegitimate child. Instead, the plurality relied on this discrimination against women to justify another against men. The lapse in the plurality's logic was glaring. As Justice White pointed out in dissent, "That only fathers *may* resort to the legitimization process cannot dissolve the sex discrimination in *requiring* them to. Under the plurality's bootstrap rationale, a state could require that women, but not men, pass a course in order to receive a taxi license, simply by limiting admission to the course to women."[6]

In *Rostker v. Goldberg*,[7] the Court used the government's policy of excluding women from combat service to uphold the congressional decision to require only men to register for the draft: since only men could be sent into battle, the sexes were not similarly situated with regard to conscription.[8] If the Court had been willing to evaluate carefully this underlying exclusionary policy, it might have seen the invalidity of restricting registration requirements to men. Indeed, even without such an exercise, the invalidity of male-only registration might have emerged from closer attention to the alleged link between that underlying policy with respect to *combat* and the challenged rule with respect to *registration*. For the evidence made clear[9] that mere registration of women would have had no deleterious effect on preparation for war, particularly since such registration would not foreclose any

3. 441 U.S. 347 (1979).

4. Justice Stewart wrote for the Court, joined by Chief Justice Burger and Justices Rehnquist and Stevens. Justice Powell concurred in the judgment.

5. Id. at 355–56.

6. Id. at 361–62 (White, J., joined by Brennan, Marshall and Blackmun, JJ., dissenting) (original emphasis).

7. 453 U.S. 57 (1981).

8. Id. at 78–79. Justice Rehnquist wrote for the Court, joined by Chief Justice

Burger and Justices Stewart, Blackmun, Powell, and Stevens. Justice White and Justice Marshall filed dissenting opinions, in which Justice Brennan joined.

9. Id. at 99 (Marshall, J., joined by Brennan, J., dissenting) ("All four service chiefs agreed that there are no military reasons for refusing to register women, and uniformly advocated requiring registration of women").

option concerning the actual composition of any draft or the issue of combat service: combat-ineligible men, including those physically unable to serve and conscientious objectors, routinely had to register on precisely this basis. That fact should probably have ended the debate. For, as Justice Marshall observed in dissent, the relevant inquiry "is not whether a *gender-neutral* classification would substantially advance important governmental interests. Rather, the question is whether the gender-based classification is itself substantially related to the achievement of the asserted governmental interest." [10]

In his opinion for the Court, Justice Rehnquist turned equal protection analysis on its head by arguing that the government did not *need* women to achieve military readiness, and therefore was free to discriminate against women by conducting an all-male draft.[11] Since gender classifications "carry the inherent risk of reinforcing sexual stereotypes about the 'proper place' of women and their need for special protection," [12] it is incumbent on the government to prove that it *must* discriminate in order to achieve its goal, not merely that it *can* achieve the goal *despite* discrimination. The legislative history of the male-only registration law embodied precisely the kinds of beliefs about sex roles which the Court has disapproved in other cases: Congress had expressed deep concern about "unpredictable reactions to the fact of female conscription" and the "broader implications" of "a young father remaining at home with the family in a time of national emergency. . . ." [13]

Rostker is perhaps best understood as a "military affairs" case.[14] Under all the doctrinal rubrics, from free speech [15] to equal protection,[16] to free exercise of religion,[17] the executive and legislative branches have always been accorded special deference by the Supreme Court in matters touching upon national defense. But *Rostker* can also be seen as yet another instance of courts invoking a legacy of female subordination to men to justify further gender discrimination. By being excluded from the draft and barred from service in many of the military capacities open to men, including combat, women lose major economic opportunities [18] and are effectively denied equal status as citizens with full civic obligations commensurate with those of male members of the society. In return, women are spared exposure to that traditional *bete*

---

10. Id. at 94 (Marshall, J., dissenting) (original emphasis).

11. 453 U.S. at 81–82. Justice White's dissent offers a cogent alternative view of the record, id. at 83–85, and reminds the Court that its administrative convenience rationale, id. at 81 (opinion of the Court), had never before been sufficient justification for naked gender discrimination. Id. at 85 (White, J., joined by Brennan, J., dissenting).

12. Orr v. Orr, 440 U.S. 268, 283 (1979).

13. S.Rep.No.826, 96th Cong., 2d Sess., reprinted in 1980 U.S. Code Cong. & Ad. News 2612, 2649.

14. See 453 U.S. at 64–68 & n.6.

15. See, e.g., Brown v. Glines, 444 U.S. 348 (1980), discussed in § 12–24, supra.

16. See, e.g., Korematsu v. United States, 323 U.S. 214 (1944).

17. See, e.g., Goldman v. Weinberger, 475 U.S. 503 (1986), discussed in § 14–13, supra.

18. In addition to a military career itself, such exclusion limits the access of women to incidents of service such as the veterans' hiring preference in public employment. See Personnel Administrator of Massachusetts v. Feeney, 442 U.S. 256 (1979), discussed in § 16–20, supra.

noir, the threat of sexual molestation at the hands of the enemy or their own male comrades, thereby perpetuating an image of women less as hardy citizens willing and able to pull their own weight than as vulnerable creatures who must be sequestered at home for their own safety.[19] Asked not what they can do for their country, women are *told* what their countrymen will do for them.

Another striking case of the law compelling women to trade liberty for protection against men is *Dothard v. Rawlinson*,[20] holding that Alabama did not violate Title VII of the Civil Rights Act by excluding women from employment as prison guards in all-male maximum security penitentiaries that housed a significant number of sex offenders. The Court noted that the Alabama prison environment was "characterized by 'rampant violence' and a 'jungle atmosphere,' "[21] and concluded that both sex offenders and other inmates would be all too likely to rape female prison guards and thereby impair prison security.[22] The *Dothard* majority saw the policy of refusing to hire female prison guards not as a sexist cultural artifact but as an accurate reflection of *biological* difference: Dianne Rawlinson's "very womanhood" made her unsuitable for a job that required people who could not be heterosexually raped.[23] As Justice Marshall pointed out in dissent, denying Rawlinson a job because her mere presence would incite sexual assaults "regrettably perpetuates one of the most insidious of the old myths about women—that women, wittingly or not, are seductive sexual objects."[24]

It is perverse to justify discrimination against women on the basis of their vulnerability to rape, since rape itself is both a tool and a symptom of male subjugation of women. Permitting male sexual violence to deny women jobs is akin to sanctioning a heckler's veto: punishing the speaker for the sins of the audience. In fact, it is far worse, for while a speaker may sometimes intend to provoke the heckler, no court should be allowed to assume that women encourage rapists. Few misogynist shibboleths are more repugnant than the phrase, "she wanted it."[25] Alabama would rather deny women jobs than control the violence of its prison population,[26] and the Court's

---

19. In fact, statistics on American military women reveal performance equal or superior to that of their male counterparts. See 453 U.S. at 91 n.8, 98–99 & n.13. (Marshall, J., dissenting). Yet the legislative history of the draft registration bill discloses congressional fears about "the performance of sexually mixed units." S.Rep.No.826, 96th Cong., 2d Sess., reprinted in 1980 U.S. Code Cong. & Ad. News 2612, 2649.

20. 433 U.S. 321 (1977). Justice Stewart delivered the opinion of the Court, joined by Justices Powell and Stevens, and in substantial part by Chief Justice Burger and Justices Brennan, Marshall, Blackmun, and Rehnquist. Justice Rehnquist also filed an opinion concurring in the judgment, joined by Chief Justice Burger and Justice Blackmun. Justice Marshall

concurred in part and dissented in part, joined by Justice Brennan. Justice White dissented.

21. Id. at 334.

22. Id. at 335–36.

23. Id. at 336.

24. Id. at 345 (Marshall, J., joined by Brennan, J., concurring in part and dissenting in part).

25. See S. Estrich, Real Rape (1987).

26. The prison conditions that the Court used to justify Rawlinson's exclusion from employment had shortly before been found to violate the eighth amendment. Pugh v. Locke, 406 F.Supp. 318, 329, 331 (M.D.Ala.1976); see also Dothard, 433 U.S. at 342 (Marshall, J., concurring in part and dissenting in part).

acceptance of that choice perpetuates an inferior role for women both symbolically and pragmatically.

A final example of this trade-off phenomenon is found in the Court's narrowly-divided decision to uphold California's statutory rape law in *Michael M. v. Superior Court.*[27] The statute made it a crime for males of any age to engage in non-marital intercourse with females under 18; there was no similar proscription of non-marital sex between women and male minors. The Court understood the issue to be whether it was fair to prosecute Michael M. under a law that subjected him to punishment solely on the basis of his gender.

Justice Rehnquist, writing for the plurality, concluded that the law legitimately served to deter unwed teenage pregnancies.[28] With reference to that goal, the plurality concluded, the discrimination against Michael M. was in fact no discrimination at all: because the "risk of pregnancy itself constitutes a substantial deterrence to young females," whereas "no similar sanction deters males," imposing a criminal penalty solely on men "serves to roughly 'equalize' the deterrents on the sexes."[29]

The dissenting Justices concluded that the state's actual purpose for punishing only the male sexual participant was to protect the chastity of young women under archaic notions of moral virtue,[30] and they found it particularly indefensible to punish Michael M. under a statute that discriminated between male and female on the basis of nothing but "irrational prejudice"[31] and "outmoded sexual stereotypes."[32]

What may be most striking about the case is that all nine members of the Court saw it exclusively in terms of the reasonableness of the discrimination against males, focusing on the accuracy with which anatomical and physiological differences between men and women could support the challenged distinction in legal treatment. Examined through a different lens, however, the California statutory rape law might have been seen to discriminate not so much against Michael M.,

---

27. 450 U.S. 464 (1981). Justice Rehnquist authored the opinion of the plurality, joined by Chief Justice Burger and Justices Stewart and Powell. Justice Blackmun concurred in the judgment, while Justice Brennan, joined by Justices White and Marshall, and Justice Stevens filed dissenting opinions.

28. 450 U.S. at 470–71. Justice Blackmun found the Court's belated recognition that unwanted pregnancy is a major social problem to be "gratifying"—but surprising, given the decisions in, e.g., Maher v. Roe, 432 U.S. 464 (1977); Harris v. McRae, 448 U.S. 297 (1980); and H.L. v. Matheson, 450 U.S. 398 (1981). See Michael M., 450 U.S. at 481–82 (Blackmun, J., concurring in the judgment); id. at 498 (Stevens, J., dissenting).

29. 450 U.S. at 473. The plurality added that exempting females encourages them to report such rapes. Id. at 473–74.

But see note 33, infra. Justice Rehnquist had evidently become accustomed to thinking about pregnancy in terms of deterrence. In Carey v. Population Services Int'l, 431 U.S. 678 (1977), he had approved of denying teenagers contraceptives in order to deter them from having sex by increasing the risks of pregnancy and venereal disease. Id. at 718–19 (Rehnquist, J., dissenting). Cf. id. at 715–16 (Stevens, J., concurring) (exacerbating the health risks inherent in sex as a means of deterring it is "irrational and perverse").

30. 450 U.S. at 494–96 & nn.9–10 (Brennan, J., joined by White and Marshall, JJ., dissenting). Among other things, the law obviously applied to girls not yet capable of becoming pregnant.

31. Id. at 501 (Stevens, J., dissenting).

32. Id. at 496 (Brennan, J., dissenting).

as against his female partner, who could have been prosecuted for aiding and abetting.[33] California proscribes all sex involving underage, unwed females, but not all sex involving underage, unwed males. Unmarried, adolescent women are denied the sexual freedom accorded to men, and they are given in exchange only a weak statutory protection against male sexual aggression.[34] This sort of judicially-compelled contract borders on the unconscionable.

A judicial role in dismantling the system of subordination of women that is built into the law would require courts to examine such "contracts" carefully, rejecting those that merely trade one invidious practice for another. But the Supreme Court's willingness to uphold ameliorative laws in proper circumstances should not give way to a fetish about gender distinctions as illegitimate per se, or to an obsession with the symbolism of paternalism.[35] Instead, what is needed is a

33. The record revealed that 14% of the juveniles arrested for acts made unlawful by California's statutory rape law are female. Id. at 477 & n.5 (Stewart, J., concurring).

34. Sharon, the victim in Michael M., "let [Michael] do what he wanted" only after he hit her repeatedly in the face. 450 U.S. at 483–85 n.* (Blackmun, J., concurring). To deal with this criminal conduct, California employed a statute that, prior to the Michael M. litigation, had consistently been understood by the state's courts in terms of protecting the virtue of young and unsophisticated girls from the perils of their own judgment. See 450 U.S. at 494–96 & nn.9–10 (Brennan, J., dissenting); Freedman, "Sex Equality, Sex Differences, and the Supreme Court," 92 Yale L.J. 913, 932 n.104 (1984).

35. For example, a sex-specific statutory rape law might still be grounded on the theory that women and men are not similarly situated with respect to sexual relations, although not in the sense the Court supposed in Michael M. Because of the prevalence of coercive male sexual initiation toward women, and the lack of meaningful consent on the part of women in many situations, male and female may sometimes be, in fact, dissimilarly situated with regard to sex. See, e.g., MacKinnon, "Introduction to Symposium on Sexual Harassment," 10 Cap.Univ.L.Rev. v–vi n.21 (1981). To pretend that men and women are similarly situated in such matters and therefore to demand formally symmetrical treatment of underage males and females as a means of eradicating "outmoded sexual stereotypes" would be to deny women the equal protection of the laws by failing to provide them with the legal protection against men which they may well need as women. Cf. Jenness v. Fortson, 403 U.S. 431, 442 (1971) ("Sometimes the grossest discrimination can lie in treating things that are different as though they were exactly alike").

Examples of the inequality inherent in the symmetrical treatment approach abound. In AFSCME v. Washington, 770 F.2d 1401 (9th Cir.1985), the court of appeals held that the State of Washington did not violate Title VII by basing its pay scales on the "competitive" market rather than on a theory of comparable worth absent proof that the state participated in the market system with the intent to discriminate against female employees in setting wages and salaries. There is no injustice in allowing female, as well as male, wage rates to be determined by the market. This holding is obviously uninformed by the fact that the supposedly "competitive" market that has established low wage rates for jobs in such female employment ghettoes as administration, personnel and secretarial services has been shaped from the very beginning by laws and practices that limit women to these low-paying, low-status jobs. In Vinson v. Taylor, 760 F.2d 1330 (D.C.Cir. 1985) (denying rehearing en banc), Judge Bork, joined by Judge Starr and Judge (now Justice) Scalia, dissented from the proposition that sexual harassment is sex discrimination under Title VII. These jurists were so mired in mechanical notions of symmetrical treatment—as were the precedents they were applying—that they manufactured a bizarre paradox:

"It is 'discrimination' if a man makes unwanted sexual overtures to a woman, a woman to a man, a man to another man, or a woman to another woman. But this court has twice stated that Title VII does not prohibit sexual harassment by a 'bisexual superior [because] the insistence upon sexual favors would . . . apply to male and female employees alike.' Thus, this court holds that only the differentiating libido runs afoul of Title VII, and bisexual harassment, how-

sensitivity to the possibility that eradicating stereotypes, and refusing to reinforce irrelevant differences between men and women, may not be enough. The law must be prepared to act to make those stereotypes *less* accurate reflectors of our world, by affirmatively combating the inequities that result when we all too casually allow biological differences to justify the imposition of legal disabilities on women.

§ 16–29. Equal Protection and "Real" Gender Differences: The Case of Pregnancy

The previous section examined the difficulty the Supreme Court has had in perceiving unlawful gender discrimination when differential treatment under the law is predicated on what the Court deems a genuine, more than merely statistical or conventional, difference between the sexes. This problem of perception is most acute when the basis for disparate treatment of men and women is pregnancy.

Although explicit gender discrimination has been upheld because only women can become pregnant,[1] the fact that pregnancy occurs only in women has not led the Court to treat pregnancy-based lines as the gender-specific classifications they clearly are. Indeed, the Court does not always perceive such cases as even involving questions of equal protection. In *Cleveland Bd. of Education v. LaFleur*,[2] the Court reviewed two mandatory maternity leave policies that excluded pregnant teachers from the classroom even though they were able and willing to continue working. The circuit courts of appeals had treated the issue as squarely one of equal protection,[3] but the Supreme Court chose to invalidate the school board policies on due process grounds, as impermissible irrebuttable presumptions about a pregnant woman's capacity to work that unduly burdened the teacher's fundamental decision to bear a child.[4]

ever blatant and however offensive and disturbing, is legally permissible."
Id. at 1333 n.7 (original emphasis) (citations omitted). This view fails to perceive that the all too common phenomenon of sexual harassment of women, who usually lack the power to object without incurring reprisal, can constitute sex discrimination even if the symmetrical scenarios—women harassing men or other women, bisexuals harassing anyone—seem less plausible a focus for legal concern. The important point that must not be obscured is that, in a society where women are subordinated by being treated as sexual objects, sexual harassment of women by *anyone*, regardless of sexual preference or orientation, is in invidious practice that must be discouraged. On appeal, the Supreme Court unanimously held that sexual harassment in the workplace can constitute a violation of Title VII. Meritor Savings Bank v. Vinson, 106 S.Ct. 2399 (1986).

§ 16–29

1. See Michael M. v. Superior Court, 450 U.S. 464 (1981), discussed in § 16–28, supra.

2. 414 U.S. 632 (1974). Justice Stewart wrote for the Court, joined by Justices Brennan, White, Marshall, and Blackmun. Justice Douglas and Justice Powell concurred in the result. Justice Rehnquist, joined by Chief Justice Burger, dissented.

3. They differed, however, in their resolution of the issue. The Sixth Circuit accepted the argument that a mandatory maternity leave policy was a classification based on sex, LaFleur v. Cleveland Bd. of Education, 465 F.2d 1184, 188 (6th Cir. 1972), while the Fourth Circuit ruled that no sex discrimination was involved because the rule, since it dealt exclusively with pregnancy, "d[id] not apply to women in an area in which they compete with men." Cohen v. Chesterfield County School Bd., 474 F.2d 395, 397 (4th Cir. 1973) (en banc).

4. 414 U.S. at 644–48. See § 16–34, infra.

Five months after *LaFleur*, the Court applied equal protection analysis to the pregnancy issue in *Geduldig v. Aiello*.[5] California's disability insurance system covered a host of conditions, many expensive and voluntary, that applied to both sexes, as well as some health problems and medical procedures unique to men, such as prostatitis and circumcision,[6] but excluded normal pregnancy and childbirth. Invoking the minimum rationality standard of *Williamson v. Lee Optical Co.*,[7], the Court held that the equal protection clause did not require the "sacrifice[ ]" of California's "policy determination[s]" as to benefit levels, employee contribution rates, and the risks to be insured.[8] The issue of gender discrimination was dismissed in a footnote, where the Court declared that "[t]he lack of identity between the excluded disability and gender as such under this insurance program becomes clear upon the most cursory analysis":[9] "The California insurance program does not exclude anyone from benefit eligibility because of gender but merely removes one physical condition—pregnancy—from the list of compensable disabilities . . . The program divides potential recipients into two groups—pregnant women and nonpregnant persons. While the first group is exclusively female, the second includes members of both sexes."[10]

This analysis—so artificial as to approach the farcical—was extended to cases under Title VII of the Civil Rights Act[11] in *General Electric Co. v. Gilbert*,[12] despite the promulgation by the Equal Employment Opportunity Commission of guidelines construing Title VII to mandate pregnancy coverage.[13] The Court thereby denied relief to female employees whose disability plan paid benefits for nonoccupational health problems but not for absence due to pregnancy, taking as the centerpiece of its analysis *Geduldig*'s dichotomy between pregnant and nonpregnant persons. The majority conceded that pregnancy is unique to women, but distinguished it from other health-related temporary disabilities because it is "often a voluntarily undertaken and desired condition."[14] Justice Stevens exposed the odd characterization upon which both *Geduldig* and *Gilbert* turned: the challenged insurance

5. 417 U.S. 484 (1974). Justice Stewart wrote for the Court, joined by Chief Justice Burger and Justices White, Blackmun, Powell, and Rehnquist. Justices Brennan, Marshall and Douglas dissented.

6. Id. at 501 (Brennan, J., joined by Douglas and Marshall, JJ., dissenting).

7. 348 U.S. 483, 489 (1955), discussed in Chapter 8, supra.

8. 417 U.S. at 494.

9. Id. at 497 n.20.

10. Id. at 496–97 n.20.

11. 42 U.S.C. § 2000e–2(a)(1).

12. 429 U.S. 125 (1976). Justice Rehnquist wrote for the Court, joined by Chief Justice Burger and Justices Stewart, White and Powell. Justice Stewart filed a concurring statement. Justice Blackmun concurred in part. Justices Brennan, Marshall, and Stevens dissented.

13. The Court found the statute's "plain meaning" to be otherwise. See id. at 145. But cf. Chevron U.S.A. Inc. v. NRDC, Inc., 467 U.S. 837, 860–65 (1984) (there can be a wide range of plausible judicial interpretations even of a statute which defines its own terms).

14. Just *how* voluntary may of course depend on the validity of restrictive abortion laws. In this regard, compare Justice Rehnquist's dissenting opinion in Roe v. Wade, 410 U.S. 113, 173 (1973). And vasectomy, which is at least as "voluntarily undertaken" as pregnancy, was covered by the General Electric plan. For an analysis of just how similar pregnancy is to the disabling conditions covered by the California plan in Geduldig, which was in turn much like the plan in Gilbert, see Bartlett, "Pregnancy and the Constitution: The Uniqueness Trap," 62 Cal.L.Rev. 1532, 1561–63 (1974).

plans did not divide " 'potential recipients into two groups—pregnant women and nonpregnant persons.' Insurance programs, company policies, and employment contracts all deal with future *risks* rather than historic facts. The classification is between persons who face a risk of pregnancy and those who do not." [15]

Purporting to apply the same analysis, the Court, again in an opinion by Justice Rehnquist, reached the opposite result in *Nashville Gas Co. v. Satty*.[16] Nashville Gas not only required pregnant employees to take a leave of absence without pay, it also deprived them upon return to work of their accumulated seniority.[17] The Court distinguished *Gilbert* on the ground that General Electric's plan merely denied women a benefit, while the plan in *Satty* imposed a burden exclusively on women by compelling forfeiture of seniority.[18] Justice Stevens wisely observed in his concurrence that such a distinction is at best problematic.[19]

The Court cut back on the full implications of its holding in *Geduldig* and *Gilbert* in *City of Los Angeles v. Manhart*[20] and *Arizona Governing Committee v. Norris*.[21] *Manhart* held that Title VII prevented a city from deducting higher pension fund contributions from female employees' paychecks, even though they could be expected, as a group, to live longer and hence to collect more pension benefits than male employees. The Court insisted that such distinctions, like other employment decisions, be made on an individual basis, not by use of gender as a statistical proxy—however accurate.[22] *Norris* was the flip side of the coin: the Court there held that, under Title VII, employers and insurance companies could not pay lower monthly annuity retirement benefits to women than men on the basis of statistical projections of longer lives for women as a class. Implicit in these decisions is the recognition that gender sometimes denotes, as a valid statistical generalization, biological differences which in certain contexts put women as

15. 429 U.S. at 161 n.5 (Stevens, J., dissenting) (original emphasis). Unsurprisingly, no Justice denied that only women are at risk of becoming pregnant.

16. 434 U.S. 136 (1977). Justice Powell, joined by Justices Brennan and Marshall, concurred in the result and in part. Justice Stevens concurred in the judgment.

17. Id. at 137–38.

18. Id. at 142.

19. Id. at 154 n.4. Professor Catharine MacKinnon has astutely noted: "It is hard to avoid the impression that the real distinction here is that granting seniority credit is a cheap concession which mainly benefits some workers over others, while paying disability benefits is expensive for employers." Sexual Harassment of Working Women: A Case of Sex Discrimination 113 (1979).

20. 435 U.S. 702 (1978). Justice Stevens wrote for the Court, joined by Justices Stewart, White, and Powell. Justice Blackmun concurred in part and concurred in the judgment. Chief Justice Burger, joined by Justice Rehnquist, concurred in part and dissented in part. Justice Marshall concurred in part and dissented in part. Justice Brennan did not take part in the case.

21. 463 U.S. 1073 (1983) (per curiam). Justice Marshall, joined by Justices Brennan, White, and Stevens, and in part by Justice O'Connor, filed an opinion concurring in the judgment in part. Justice Powell, joined by Chief Justice Burger and Justices Blackmun and Rehnquist, filed an opinion dissenting in part and concurring in part, in which Justice O'Connor joined in part. Justice O'Connor also filed a concurring opinion.

22. 435 U.S. at 710.

a group at a disadvantage that women as individuals should not be forced to suffer.

This is an important step toward understanding that the characteristic injury of sex discrimination lies not in the failure to be treated on a gender-blind basis, but rather in being deprived of liberty or opportunity *because* one is a woman, or *because* one is a man. Yet it is only one step. *Norris* and *Manhart* rejected the use against individual women of generalizations that are undeniably accurate about women as a group: "women live longer than men." This is an advance beyond, but not radically different from, the Court's prior rejection of the use of generalizations about women's roles, where those generalizations took the form of stereotypes that are—or at least at the time arguably were—accurate about women as a group: "women play a much larger role than men in the rearing of children." [23] Although use of such actuarial realities as the generalization that women live longer is unacceptable when it results in disadvantaging individual women on the basis of their gender, even if it does not reinforce an outmoded and artificial cultural restriction on women's lives, the two concerns are alike in that each involves judicial repudiation of a generalization about women, whether a function of biology or of culture, that will not always be accurate with respect to the particular women to whom it is applied. This may mean that, under Title VII, an assumption that all women become incapable of working when they become pregnant cannot be deployed to force all pregnant school teachers to take a leave of absence.[24] But it does not mean that governments, employers, or other decision-makers are precluded from treating women differently from men with respect to pregnancy, for such classifications or generalizations are deemed under *Geduldig* to be keyed to pregnancy itself, not to gender. Moreover, one generalization that is always accurate, at least so far, is that only women can become pregnant.

In response to lobbying by more than 300 groups, from feminists and labor unions to church organizations,[25] Congress enacted the Pregnancy Discrimination Act ("PDA") of 1978, amending Title VII to include pregnancy classifications within the statutory definition of sex discrimination.[26] In thus overturning *General Electric v. Gilbert*, Congress repudiated the Court's notions of Title VII's "plain meaning" [27] and in essence endorsed the opinions of Justice Stevens in *Gilbert* and *Satty* that criticized the formalistic distinction between "pregnant and nonpregnant persons." [28] The Supreme Court subsequently conceded

---

23. See, e.g., Weinberger v. Wiesenfeld, 420 U.S. 636 (1975), and other Social Security benefit cases discussed in § 16–27, supra.

24. Cf. Cleveland Bd. of Education v. LaFleur, 414 U.S. 632 (1974) (invalidating such an irrebuttable presumption on due process grounds). The two lawsuits culminating in LaFluer were filed before March 24, 1972, the date on which Title VII was extended to state agencies and schools. See Pub.L. 92–261, 86 Stat. 103 (1972).

25. J. Gelb & M. Palley, Women And Public Policies 159–60 (1982).

26. 42 U.S.C. § 2000(e)(k) (1978). ("The terms 'because of sex' or 'on the basis of sex' include, but are not limited to, because of or on the basis of pregnancy, childbirth, or related medical conditions").

27. 429 U.S. at 145.

28. S.Rep. No.331, 95th Cong., 1st Sess. 2–3 (1977); H.Rep. No.948, 95th Cong., 2d Sess. 2 (1977), reprinted in 1978 U.S. Code Cong. & Admin. News at 4750.

that, for statutory purposes, "discrimination based on a woman's pregnancy is, on its face, discrimination because of her sex." [29]

There has been much conflict even within the feminist legal community itself over the implications of the PDA. Many scholars and advocates interpret the PDA as mandating that pregnant women receive the same treatment as other workers: no more, no less.[30] Others contend that the PDA should be read as forbidding even neutral employment practices that have a disparate impact on pregnant women, and as requiring employers to provide reasonable leave and reemployment opportunities to pregnant women even if they do not provide disability leave to employees for other reasons.[31] The disagreement is more a matter of strategy than theory: those who would read the PDA narrowly evidently believe that women can gain more from pressing claims in common with all workers than from seeking special treatment for pregnancy that might perpetuate restrictive stereotypes about the "weaker sex." [32] The issue of whether the PDA preempts state laws that require employers to provide maternity leave or benefits regardless of any other disability plans or policies they may have was settled against preemption by *California Federal Savings & Loan Ass'n v. Guerra*,[33] where the Court read the PDA as preventing covered employers from discriminating *against* pregnant employees but leaving them free to provide benefits unique to pregnant employees if they choose to do so, or are forced by state laws to do so.[34] But the more

29. Newport News Shipbuilding & Dry Dock Co. v. E.E.O.C., 462 U.S. 669, 684 (1983) (holding that an employer that had amended its health insurance plan in response to the PDA violated the PDA by providing the husbands of female employees a specified level of hospitalization coverage for *all* conditions while providing the wives of male employees such coverage *except* for pregnancy-related conditions, thereby discriminating against married male employees and in favor of married female employees).

30. See, e.g., Williams, "The Equality Crisis: Some Reflections on Culture, Courts, and Feminism," 7 Women's L.Rep. 175, 193–98 (1982).

31. See, e.g., 1 A. Larson, Employment Discrimintion § 38.22 at 8–34 to 8–35 (1985); Note, "Sexual Equality Under the Pregnancy Discrimination Act," 83 Colum. L.Rev. 690, 693 (1983); Betty Friedan, quoted in Lewin, "Pregnancy-Leave Suit Has Divided Feminists," The New York Times, p. 52 (June 28, 1986).

32. For a discussion of the danger to working women posed by the prospect of special treatment, see Bartlett, "Pregnancy and the Constitution: The Uniqueness Trap," 62 Calif.L.Rev. 1532, 1533 (1974).

33. 107 S.Ct. 683 (1987). The Court subsequently held, in a unanimous opinion by Justice O'Connor, that the Federal Unemployment Tax Act merely prohibits

states from singling out pregnancy for unfavorable treatment under their unemployment compensation programs, and does not mandate preferential treatment for pregnant workers who leave their jobs. Therefore, the act did not preempt a Missouri statute that denied benefits to all workers who left their jobs for reasons not directly attributable to the work or to the employer, whether because of illness, pregnancy, or other temporary disabilities. Wimberly v. Labor and Industrial Relations Comm'n, 107 S.Ct. 821, 825 (1987).

34. On Justice Scalia's concurring rationale, state laws that require employers to give pregnant workers leave with guaranteed reinstatement are not preempted if they say nothing as to how employers may treat other similarly situated workers, but *might* be preempted if they purport to require or even to permit employers to *deny* the same benefits to such other workers. See 107 S.Ct. at 697 (reasoning that this issue was not presented by the California law, which purported to do nothing of the sort). The majority opinion of Justice Marshall, joined by Justices Brennan, Blackmun, Stevens, and O'Connor, concluded that even laws of the latter sort are not preempted. See id. at 692–94; see also id. at 696–97 (Stevens, J., concurring in part). Justice White, joined in dissent by Chief Justice Rehnquist and Justice Powell, indeed read the California law as purporting to authorize employers to deny the

fundamental question of how to reconcile equality under the law with the unique phenomenon of pregnancy is not likely to be answered soon.

Apart from the problem of perpetuating negative stereotypes, it is understandable that many may hesitate to endorse a rule requiring special treatment of pregnant women. After all, minimizing the legal consequences of irrelevant physical differences between groups of people has long been a standard approach under the equal protection clause, whether the groups involved are blacks and whites or men and women. This "equal treatment" or "assimilationist" [35] model of equal protection requires that the law treat all alike—as if they were fungible—on the premise that there are no real differences among them. That model has worked fairly well in promoting racial equality, since the difference on which discrimination in that context is based is literally only skin deep. And the "equal treatment" model has worked quite well in eradicating gender discrimination predicated less on anatomy than on invidious and outmoded stereotypes.[36] But an approach to the equal protection clause that is dominated by formal comparisons between classes of people thought to be similarly situated is inadequate to the task of ferreting out inequality when a court confronts laws dealing with reproductive biology, since such laws, by definition, identify ways in which women and men are definitely *not* similarly situated.[37]

The Supreme Court failed to perceive the discrimination at work in *Geduldig v. Aiello* precisely because the Court was mired in formalism. The Court explained that California's disability program passed constitutional muster despite its exclusion of pregnancy coverage because "[t]here is no risk from which men are protected and women are not. Likewise, there is no risk from which women are protected and men are not." [38] The first statement is true enough, since men cannot become pregnant, and the second is equally true, since women were not protected against loss of work due to pregnancy. But so what? In looking only for a neat relationship between means and ends, and in admiring the symmetrical precision of California's classification, the Court treated the concept of equality under the law as if it were a matter of aesthetics rather than ethics.[39] Equality is a substantive concept, and it is not in every circumstance achieved by formal symmetry.

benefits at issue to all but pregnant employees. See id. at 701–02 & n.12.

35. See Kay, "Models of Equality," 1985 U.Ill.L.Rev. 39, 40–41 (1985); Law, "Rethinking Sex and the Constitution," 132 U.Pa.L.Rev. 955, 1010 (1984).

36. See generally Kay, supra note 35.

37. See Minow, "When Difference Has Its Home: Group Homes for the Mentally Retarded, Equal Protection and Legal Treatment of Difference," 22 Harv.C.R.—C.L.L.Rev. 111, 120–22 (1987); Minow, "Book Review: Rights of One's Own," 98 Harv.L.Rev. 1084, 1092 & n.25 (1985).

38. 417 U.S. at 496–97.

39. Even judged on its own terms, the Court's evaluation of when men and women are and are not similarly situated with respect to pregnancy is both inconsistent and unsatisfactory. In Michael M. v. Superior Court, 450 U.S. 464 (1981), where the Court upheld California's male-only statutory rape law, the imposition of criminal sanctions only on the male participant in underage, non-marital sex was justified as a legislative effort to balance the deterrent to illegitimate teenage childbirth which nature imposes on women in the form of pregnancy. Id. at 472–73. Risk of pregnancy was a gender-based distinction in Michael M. because "only women may become pregnant," id. at 471, while in

Deeming "special treatment" of pregnant women a violation of the rule of "equal treatment" for all, and deeming sameness of treatment without regard to pregnancy enough to meet the demands of "equal treatment," begs the question of what equality under law *means* when men and women are decidedly unequal with respect to such a significant biological fact.[40] Laws based on reproductive differences between men and women should be treated as posing a problem distinct from classifications based on gender as such.[41] For, as Professor Sylvia Law has written, "pregnancy, abortion, . . . and creation of another human being *are* special—very special. Women have these experiences. Men do not." [42] In *Geduldig* and *Gilbert*, the Supreme Court recognized pregnancy's "unique characteristics," [43] but used them as a basis to characterize disability due to pregnancy as an "extra," an "additional risk unique to women." [44] Additional, that is, to men's health needs. But the choice of men and *their* needs as the touchstone for equal protection analysis is neither natural nor necessary. An even more fundamentally biased assumption is that pregnancy ought to be characterized as a disability at all. It may be a uniquely male myopia which looks upon the capacity to bring human life into the world as a *dis*ability. What sense is there in treating an often joyous and sought after condition, essential to the survival of humanity, as something akin to a hernia? Might there not be different reasons for requiring employers to support the reproductive process, perhaps even in ways, or to an extent, that they are not required to support those who are ill or injured?

To ignore woman's unique role in human reproduction is to allow women to lay claim to equality only insofar as they are like men.[45] Yet the Court's refusal to countenance laws that freeze men out of the nurturing role of parent [46] demonstrates that woman can be the standard by which the freedom of men is judged, and the reference by which equality for all human beings is given content. Of course, the

---

Geduldig that risk was not gender-based because women as well as men may be nonpregnant. 417 U.S. at 496–97 n.20. Professor MacKinnon has demonstrated that these results are not only inconsistent, but inverted:

"Not all statutorily underage girls are even 'potentially pregnant' since many have not reached puberty; not all underage girls who have intercourse conceive (the plaintiff in Michael M. for example); not all (or even most) unwed mothers are underage; male sterility is not a defense; and not all underage children at risk of intercourse are girls. By contrast, as a matter of rational fit between gender, the characteristic, and its applications, all 'persons' at risk of noncoverage for pregnancy disabilities are women and all who would receive benefits would be both pregnant and female."

MacKinnon, "Introduction to Symposium on Sexual Harassment," 10 Cap.U.L.Rev. vi n.21 (1981).

40. A fine exploration of this controversy can be found in Williams, "Equality's Riddle: Pregnancy and the Equal Treatment/Special Treatment Debate," 13 N.Y.U.Rev.L. & Soc. Change 325 (1984–85).

41. See Law, supra note 35 at 1005, 1007–1013; Kay, "Equality and Difference: The Case of Pregnancy," 1 Berkeley Women's L.J. 1, 21–24 (1985). Cf. MacKinnon, Sexual Harassment of Working Women: A Case of Sex Discrimination 116–17 (1979).

42. Law, supra note 35, at 1007.

43. Geduldig, 417 U.S. at 496 n.20.

44. Gilbert, 429 U.S. at 139 n.17.

45. Law, supra note 35 at 1007.

46. See, e.g., Weinberger v. Wiesenfeld, 420 U.S. 636 (1975) (invalidating Social Security law that denied so-called "mother's benefits" to widowers with small children).

ultimate goal must be to transcend the mere exchange of traditional gender roles. For the fundamental problem is not the Court's inability to see man and woman's essential sameness, but its willingness to transmute woman's "real" biological difference to woman's disadvantage. The Court itself has recognized that the requirement that similarly situated people be treated alike does not exhaust the idea of equality: "Sometimes the grossest discrimination can lie in treating things that are different as though they were exactly alike." [47]

Many women who engage in reproductive activity, unlike any men who do so, become pregnant and may as a consequence be temporarily unable to continue working—either physically unable to do so (something less often true than some laws presuppose [48]), or unable to do so consistent with the wish to nurture one's child. Analysis of laws, policies, and practices that discriminate on the basis of pregnancy, rather than on the basis of gender per se, is therefore better advanced by the concept of equality of opportunity than by notions of identical treatment. [49] In the workplace, this comports with Title VII's purpose of achieving "equality of employment opportunities." [50] The opportunity in question is the privilege of keeping one's job while engaging in reproductive and parenting activity. The proper comparison in *Geduldig*, therefore, was not between pregnant women and all other, nonpregnant workers, but between female employees who had engaged in reproductive behavior and male workers who had done likewise. [51] If no man loses his job or his seniority as a result of this activity, neither should any woman. A program of pregnancy leave and benefits removes this inequity. In the Court's own formal logic: there would be no risk from which women are protected and men are not (since both male and female workers would be protected from disability due to reproductive activity); likewise, there would be no risk from which men are protected and women are not (unlike the program upheld in *Geduldig*). [52] This outcome possesses all the indicia of formal equality that the Court admired in *Geduldig*, and it is preferable to the result actually reached in that case because it does not subordinate women by

47. Jenness v. Fortson, 403 U.S. 431, 442 (1971) (Stewart, J., for the Court) (upholding state election laws that imposed ballot-access requirements on minor political bodies different from those imposed on major political parties). See also Williams v. Rhodes, 393 U.S. 23 (1968); Brown v. Socialist Workers Campaign Committee, 459 U.S. 87 (1982).

48. See, e.g., Cleveland Bd. of Education v. LaFleur, 414 U.S. 632 (1974).

49. See Kay, supra note 41 at 26.

50. Griggs v. Duke Power Co., 401 U.S. 424, 429 (1971); California Federal Savings & Loan Ass'n v. Guerra, 107 S.Ct. 683, 693 (1987) (quoting Griggs).

51. As Professor Herma Kay has explained, the relevant reference group "should be limited to persons who have engaged in reproductive behavior while continuing to work. That group is divided into two sub-groups, persons who will require medical care and who may at times be temporarily disabled as a result of that reproductive conduct and persons who will not. The first group of persons is exclusively female, while the second is exclusively male." Kay, supra note 41 at 30. See id. at 31, 35.

52. Although a man's work performance will be unaffected by his reproductive activity in the vast majority of cases, some men experience during their mate's pregnancy what is known as the couvade syndrome, which amounts to a variety of sympathetic pregnancy symptoms in the male including nausea, vomiting, indigestion and abdominal swelling. Studies indicate that job impairment and income loss from couvade syndrome are negligible. See Kay, supra note 41 at 27 n.141.

requiring them, but not men, to choose between work and children—between the paradigmatically public and private roles that men are more free to combine.[53]

In one sense, discrimination based on pregnancy is no different from discrimination based on skin color, because in each case the origin of the discrimination is not the physical characteristic itself, but the social and legal significance that we choose to attribute to it. Pregnancy may look more like a genuine, meaningful difference than pigmentation from a late-20th century perspective, but it is merely a more modern example of the consistent confusion of biology with the social consequences of biology.[54] The latter, unlike the former, are *not* immutable, however deep (and even universal) may be the cultural patterns in which these social consequences appear and reappear. The concept of "equal protection of the laws" should be understood to mean that woman's possession of a second X-chromosome cannot translate into laws and institutions that make women second-class citizens.

§ 16–30. Gender Discrimination and the Equal Rights Amendment

The Supreme Court's failure to articulate clearer and more sensitive principles in the area of gender discrimination than those expressed in its opinions to date may be explained in part by the Court's reluctance to overstep what it conceives to be the bounds between constitutional interpretation and constitutional amendment. While the decision to treat racial discrimination as highly suspect is firmly rooted in the most orthodox interpretations of constitutional history, the same is not true of gender discrimination. Indeed Justice Miller in *The Slaughter-House Cases* stated the Court's great "doubt . . . whether any action of a State not directed by way of discrimination against the Negroes as a class, or on account of their race, [would] ever be held to come within the purview of [the fourteenth amendment]."[1] Although Miller proved a poor prophet, the doubt he expressed casts a shadow over most extensions of the equal protection principle. It is true that three other Justices joined in Justice Brennan's plurality opinion in *Frontiero v. Richardson*[2] concluding that, given the immuta-

---

53. Employment leave for both mothers *and* fathers of newborn children is guaranteed by law in most industrialized nations. The United States is, as it were, the odd man out in this respect. Legislation introduced in Congress in the late 1980s would rectify this situation.

54. See L. Tribe, Constitutional Choices 241–42, 244–45 (1985). Cf. Dred Scott v. Sandford, 60 U.S. (19 How.) 393, 407 (1857) (blacks were "regarded as being of an inferior order, and altogether unfit to associate with the white race, either in social or political relations; and so far inferior, that they had no rights which the white man was bound to respect; . . . [the negro was] an ordinary article of merchandise"); Bradwell v. Illinois, 83 U.S. (16 Wall.) 130, 141 (1872) (Bradley, J., joined by Swayne

and Field, JJ., concurring in the judgment) ("a woman had no legal existence separate from her husband, who was regarded as her head and representative in the social state . . . The paramount destiny and mission of woman are to fulfil [sic] the noble and benign offices of wife and mother. This is the law of the Creator.").

§ 16–30

1. 83 U.S. (16 Wall.) 36, 81 (1873).

2. 411 U.S. 677 (1973). Justice Brennan was joined by Justices Douglas, Marshall, and White. For an indication of Justice Stevens' seemingly parallel views, see Mathews v. Lucas, 427 U.S. 495, 516–23 (1976) (Stevens, J., dissenting); Califano v. Goldfarb, 430 U.S. 199, 222–24 (1977).

bility of sex, its history as a basis for irrational discrimination, and the views of Congress, sex should be regarded as a suspect criterion. But in a concurring opinion, three other Justices contended that, given the pendency of the Equal Rights Amendment, the Court should not "appear unnecessarily to decide sensitive issues of broad social and political importance at the very time they are under consideration within the prescribed constitutional processes." [3]

Section 1 of the Equal Rights Amendment (ERA), passed by Congress on March 22, 1972, and submitted to the legislatures of the states for ratification as the twenty-seventh amendment to the Constitution, would have declared that "[e]quality of rights under the law shall not be denied or abridged by the United States or by any State on account of sex." [4] As Professor (now Judge) Ruth Ginsburg has argued, such an amendment would add to our fundamental law a principle under which the judiciary would be encouraged to develop a more coherent pattern of gender-discrimination doctrines. And it could help bring an end to the "legislative inertia that keeps discriminatory laws on the books despite the counsel of amendment opponents that removal or revision of these laws is 'the way.' " [5] In addition, § 2 of the amendment, which would have given Congress "the power to enforce by appropriate legislation" the amendment's substantive provisions, would have foreclosed any argument that Congress has less extensive powers to proscribe various forms of sex discrimination than to prohibit parallel instances of race discrimination under the fourteenth amendment. Finally, the psychological impact of such an amendment's passage would be of major importance: "The expression of a national commitment by formal adoption of a constitutional amendment will give strength and purpose to efforts to bring about a far-reaching change which, for some, may prove painful." [6]

On June 30, 1982, the time allotted for ratification of the ERA ended before the measure had gained approval by a sufficient number of states.[7] But since the ERA had been introduced in every session of

---

3. 411 U.S. at 691, 692 (Powell, J., joined by Burger, C.J., and Blackmun, J., concurring).

4. H.R.J.Res.No.208, 92d Cong., 2d Sess. (1972). The operative language of the original ERA, drafted by Alice Paul in 1923, had an admirable and more affirmative clarity: "Women and men shall have equal rights throughout the United States and in every place subject to its jurisdiction."

5. Ginsburg, "Gender in the Supreme Court: The 1973 and 1974 Terms," 1975 Sup.Ct.Rev. 1, 23–24. See also Elsen, Coogan & Ginsburg, "Men, Women, and the Constitution: The Equal Rights Amendment," 10 Colum.J.L. & Soc.Prob. 77, 94 (1973) (arguing that major legislative revision will not occur without impetus of ERA).

6. Brown, Emerson, Falk & Freedman, "The Equal Rights Amendment: A Constitutional Basis for Equal Rights for Women," 80 Yale L.J. 871, 884 (1971).

7. By 1978, the ERA had been ratified by 35 states, only three short of the three-fourths required by Article V to amend the Constitution. Concerned that additional ratifications might not be obtained by March 22, 1979, the original expiration date, Congress conducted extensive hearings and extended the period to June 30, 1982. H.J.Res. 638 was signed into law on October 20, 1978. See generally H.R.Rep. No.95–1405, 95th Cong., 2d Sess. 1–12 (1978). Three of those 35 states voted to rescind their ratifications, but it would probably have been up to Congress to decide, if 38 states had ratified by the deadline, whether to count the three rescinding states toward the required 38, notwithstanding their legislative change of mind. Although a federal district court ruled that rescinded ratifications cannot be counted and that the extension voted by Congress was unconstitutional, Idaho v. NOW, 529 F.Supp. 1107 (D.Idaho 1981), the Supreme Court stayed that ruling, 455 U.S. 918

Congress from 1923 to 1972, the defeat of 1982 could not stop the struggle.[8] Indeed, the ERA was reintroduced on January 6, 1987, as Senate Joint Resolution Number 1 and House Joint Resolution Number 1 of the 100th Congress, with nearly half the Senate and over 160 members of the House as co-sponsors. It seems probable that this ERA, or its functional equivalent, will one day be passed by Congress and ratified by the states. The concept of equality before the law regardless of gender has simply become too much a part of our culture for the ultimate outcome to be much in doubt. Therefore, a few words are in order on the subject of how an Equal Rights Amendment might be interpreted and applied when it eventually assumes its place in the Constitution.

Advocacy on behalf of the ERA, in several important respects, stressed the relative insignificance of the proposed amendment's departure from contemporaneous constitutional equality doctrine.[9] While attempting to appease those who feared the ramifications of equality before the law regardless of gender, proponents of the amendment may have made it more vulnerable to the criticism that its supposedly incremental addition to the jurisprudence of equality was not worth the bother. If an ERA is not read to prohibit some gender classifications entirely, and to demand heightened scrutiny of classifications that have a differential and deleterious impact on one sex regardless of intent, the value of the amendment could well be questioned. Commands of equality that can be avoided by a showing of a government interest, and commands that require one to identify an intentional perpetrator of discrimination,[10] are particularly ineffective when, for example, one discriminatory practice is justified by reference to another,[11] or when a legal distinction between the sexes is made to appear natural, inevitable or otherwise necessary because it is enmeshed in the legal and social legacy of female subordination to men.[12]

(1982), and the case was mooted later that year when the extended period for ratification expired. 459 U.S. 809 (1982). See Chapter 3, supra.

8. An enlightening historical comparison can be drawn to the nineteenth amendment, which gave women the vote. The ratification of that amendment in 1920 was the culmination of 72 years of political struggle, including 56 state referendum campaigns, 480 legislative campaigns to get state suffrage amendments submitted, 47 state constitutional convention campaigns, 277 state party convention campaigns, 30 national party convention campaigns to get suffrage planks written into the party platforms and 19 campaigns addressed to 19 successive Congresses to get the amendment submitted to the states. See National NOW Times at 5 (Winter 1987).

9. See Brown, Emerson, Falk and Freedman, "The Equal Rights Amendment: A Constitutional Basis for Equal Rights for Women," 80 Yale L.J. 871, 898–99, 895–96 (1971). The Yale article, which was intended to be and was treated as a legislator's guide to the proposed amendment, see Law, "Rethinking Sex and the Constitution," 132 U.Pa.L.Rev. 955, 975 & n.68 (1984), interpreted the ERA as not precluding legislation that regulates physical characteristics unique to one sex, and did not discuss what principles should apply under the ERA to laws regulating such physical characteristics as pregnancy. Of particular concern to ERA advocates was debunking the notions that passage of the ERA would erase all distinctions between the sexes, leading, for example, to unisex public bathrooms.

10. See §§ 16–20, 16–21, supra.

11. See, e.g., Parham v. Hughes, 441 U.S. 347 (1979), discussed in § 16–28, supra.

12. See, e.g., Dothard v. Rawlinson, 433 U.S. 321 (1977); Michael M. v. Superior Court, 450 U.S. 464 (1981), discussed in § 16–28, supra.

Since similar treatment of dissimilarly situated individuals may also constitute invidious discrimination,[13] debate over the present or any future ERA must decide whether its principles will be understood to apply to regulations of sex-specific physical characteristics, particularly those that limit individual control of reproduction. Regulation pertaining to abortion and pregnancy, for example, was carefully disassociated from the now-defeated ERA in order to improve its chances for ratification,[14] and that same separation was evident in hearings when the ERA was reintroduced.[15] This approach to sexual equality may have much to recommend it as a matter of politics, but it presents fundamental problems that cannot forever escape resolution.[16]

In any event, this sort of false legal modesty should not be allowed to prevent any eventually ratified ERA from achieving its goal of sexual equality through methods not expressly advocated or specifically anticipated in its legislative history. It is the rule, rather than the exception, for the principles underlying constitutional amendments ultimately to be applied in ways not precisely envisioned by their framers, who were necessarily acting within a particular legal and social context.[17] As Justice White noted in *Gertz v. Robert Welch, Inc.*,[18] libel laws that placed the burden upon the speaker to prove the truth of his statements coexisted with the first amendment for almost two hundred years.[19] And the necessity of developing an understanding of racial equality deeper than that held by those who wrote and ratified the fourteenth amendment is now a truism.[20] Likewise, the constitutional understanding of equality before the law regardless of sex should not be a prisoner of the perceptions and fears of the 1980s and 1990s.

§ 16–31. Age-Based and Disability-Based Discrimination: New Horizons for Semi-Suspect Classifications

We have seen thus far that the equal protection technique of strict scrutiny operates in large part as an anti-majoritarian safeguard which views with suspicion all public actions tending to burden "discrete and insular" minorities.[1] If the system of coalitions and elections functioned properly at the political level, it is at least arguable that no such

---

13. See § 16–29, supra.

14. See Law, supra note 9, at 981–82, 986–87.

15. See "The Impact of the Equal Rights Amendment Upon Abortion Rights: Hearings Before the Subcomm. on the Constitution of the Senate Comm. on the Judiciary," 98th Cong., 2d Sess. 6–8, 65 (1984).

16. See § 16–29, supra. See also Law, supra note 9, at 1037–40.

17. The constitutional command that may come closest to a direct and dispositive tie to the past is the seventh amendment's guarantee of the common law right to jury trial, which has been interpreted to preserve that right as it existed in 1791. Yet even in that context the courts have had to adapt the understandings of the past to discern the amendment's meaning in con-

temporary situations. See Atlas Roofing Co. v. Occupational Safety and Health Review Comm'n, 430 U.S. 442 (1977) (no right to jury trial in government-initiated penalty proceeding paralleling common law private litigation remedies).

18. 418 U.S. 323, 380 (1974) (White, J., dissenting).

19. But see Anderson v. Liberty Lobby, Inc., 106 S.Ct. 2505 (1986), discussed in § 12–13, supra.

20. See, e.g., Brown v. Board of Education, 347 U.S. 483 (1954), discussed in § 16–15, supra.

§ 16–31

1. United States v. Carolene Prods. Co., 304 U.S. 144, 152–53 n.4 (1938) (dictum).

powerless minorities would exist; but if one assumes inadequate coalition-formation and incomplete electoral representation, or pervasive prejudice, then every group that finds itself disadvantaged by a public choice potentially qualifies for anti-majoritarian solicitude as "discrete" and "insular."[2] Children ideally illustrate the difficulty. If the universality of the childhood experience—all of us were children once—could guarantee empathy from adult lawmakers despite the absence of children from legislative assemblies, there would be no occasion to regard children as an isolated and unrepresented minority in need of special protection; but if adults instead look with contempt at a stage they have "outgrown" and will never re-enter, then every privilege withheld by legislators or administrators from the young must become a source of suspicion. Yet judicially treating age-based classifications as suspect for this reason is easily reconcilable only with the ideal of an ultimately "child-blind" society.[3] Aspiring to a society that gives children a special place, instead of one that ignores their distinctiveness, does not fit well with a demand that all public actions setting children apart be halted unless specially justified to the satisfaction of a suspicious arbiter.[4]

At the same time, a tenaciously-held principle of many in our society—a principle with undeniable constitutional roots—is that each person should be treated as an individual rather than as a statistic or as a member of a group—particularly of a group the individual did not knowingly choose to join. Yet the ideal we have come to revere as the "rule of law" points away from individualized treatment and suggests instead the decision of particular cases in accord with general rules, promulgated in advance, that identify as dispositive certain readily ascertainable and separable facets of the "total" situation. Again, the tale is well told by children. To assume that *this* 17-year-old is unfit to vote, to work, to choose his or her own school, simply because *most* persons of like age have certain characteristics is to condemn by association, by statistical stereotype, by what the Supreme Court in a number of recent decisions has invalidated as "conclusive presumptions."[5] Yet, to tailor all determinations to the individual case would be to encourage

2. "It would hardly take extraordinary ingenuity for a lawyer to find 'insular and discrete' minorities at every turn in the road." Sugarman v. Dougall, 413 U.S. 634, 657 (1973) (Rehnquist, J., dissenting).

3. In the somewhat analogous case of racial classification, it may be nothing but the long-term ideal of a "color-blind" Constitution, Plessy v. Ferguson, 163 U.S. 537, 559 (1896) (Harlan, J., dissenting), that makes strict judicial scrutiny of laws discriminating against racial minorities acceptable as something other than insulting paternalism; and it may well be only the "color-blind" ideal that makes "benign" racial discrimination tolerable as an intermediate step toward ultimate neutrality. See § 16–22, supra. Gender-based discriminations are much more likely to reflect prejudice and work injustice than discriminations based on age and should therefore trigger stricter scrutiny. See §§ 16–25 to 16–30, supra.

4. As a temporary tactic, "thinking of minors as a class which may be victimized in [distinct] ways," Kaimowitz, "Legal Emancipation of Minors in Michigan," 19 Wayne L.Rev. 23, 45 (1972), might be helpful; but as a longer-term strategy, thinking in this way could run counter to the deepest wellsprings of the movement for justice to children, a movement that proceeds less from a sense of the historically-rooted oppression of a group properly classified as such than from a sense that, in some settings, classification as a substitute for thought may *itself* work grave injustice—as when a person's status as infant, child, or adolescent is invoked as a sufficient justification for allowing others to speak, while the person most intimately affected remains unheard and often essentially unseen.

5. See § 16–34, infra.

arbitrary choices, choices that depart from the goal of treating similar cases similarly, and choices that could well conceal substantively impermissible grounds of decision.

This much, at least, the notions of "suspect classifications" and "conclusive presumptions" have in common: both seem easiest to apply when the issue involves the exercise of a right we have come to regard as constitutionally "fundamental," such as the right to bodily integrity or the right to be heard in one's own defense.[6] Children need not be recognized as a disadvantaged minority for all purposes in order to suspect the lawmaker whose only excuse for a deprivation that would be intolerable as to adults is that "only children" are affected. And conclusive presumptions need not be abandoned wholesale in order to concede that readily disprovable generalizations about children—like all other measures for which "less restrictive alternatives" exist [7]—cannot suffice to justify what would, absent the fact of childhood, constitute an action beyond the power of the state.[8]

6. See Chapter 15, supra.

7. See, e.g., § 12–23, supra.

8. "[W]hatever may be their precise impact, neither the Fourteenth Amendment nor the Bill of Rights is for adults alone." In re Gault, 387 U.S. 1, 13 (1967). See, e.g., Planned Parenthood of Central Missouri v. Danforth, 428 U.S. 52 (1976) (minor's right to abortion); Goss v. Lopez, 419 U.S. 565 (1975) (procedural due process); Tinker v. Des Moines School Dist., 393 U.S. 503 (1969) (freedom of expression). But a somewhat less rigorous test applies to state restrictions inhibiting the personal choices of minors; a "significant" state interest "not present in the case of an adult" will suffice in lieu of a "compelling justification." Carey v. Population Services International, 431 U.S. 678, 693 & n.15 (1977) (plurality opinion of Brennan, J., joined by Stewart, Marshall, Blackmun, JJ., on this issue) (finding insufficient state interest to justify ban on sale of contraceptives to persons under 16); cf. id. at 702–703 (White, J., concurring) (finding insufficient proof that ban on sale to minors measurably deters sex among young teenagers); id. at 715–716 (Stevens, J., finding the state's means of deterrence—exposing children to risk of pregnancy and disease—irrational and perverse).

When the arena of controversy is located within the family itself and when the child or someone acting on his or her behalf seeks the aid of government against a parent in asserting a constitutional right, the issue obviously becomes more complex, since it now presents a difficult problem of allocating roles as between the family and the state. See, e.g., Bellotti v. Baird, 443 U.S. 622 (1979) (invalidating parental consent and judicial authorization requirements restricting even a mature minor's right to an abortion). Justice Powell's plurality opinion noted that "[t]he guiding role of parents

in the upbringing of their children justifies limitations on the freedom of minors." Id. at 637. But it remains true that a ruling against the child in a case involving an otherwise "fundamental right" should not turn on the circumstance of childhood itself. If governmental action on the child's behalf would seriously disrupt the on-going internal processes of a basically harmonious family unit, one may well conclude that government should not intervene. In such a case, however, it is not the fact of childhood but the overriding values of family autonomy and integrity that would be thought to justify governmental abstention, just as they might justify such abstention when the party seeking the state's help is an adult. One doctrinal counterpart of this proposition may be the principle that associational considerations help to establish the boundaries of the "state action" concept in the first instance. See Henkin, "Shelley v. Kraemer: Notes for a Revised Opinion," 110 U.Pa.L. Rev. 473 (1972). Thus, routine cases of parental discipline in an essentially successful family whose continuation is mutually desired will properly be treated as raising no real constitutional issue even when the state extends various forms of incidental support to parental authority; in these cases, it may well be said, the state simply should not be deemed responsible for how such authority is exercised, with the result that constitutional constraints will not apply. See Chapter 18, infra. But when a family is in disintegration or at the threshold of collapse—as when an adolescent persistently seeks complete emancipation and is willing, in return, to relieve his or her parents of reciprocal obligations—then it seems wrong to exonerate the state of responsibility for such coercive parental measures as it permits even by its inaction. Once a person is capable of survival away from home and insists, after sustained re-

What emerges is a principle that at first may seem unexceptionable: Whenever it is agreed that government must provide a convincing justification for depriving a person of certain kinds of liberty or opportunity, highly generalized appeals to the characteristics of "the young" will not do. Insofar as the deprivation is to be justified by reference to immaturity and its supposed consequences, nothing less than demonstrable incapacity to make acceptable use of the opportunity in question should suffice.[9] But "demonstrable incapacity" may, in fact, ask for too much. In no area of constitutional controversy has our legal system *wholly* repudiated rules of thumb, even where such rules, in some of their applications, would be guilty of overkill. Not even in its heyday did the doctrine of first amendment overbreadth go so far.[10] If this is so, then why not a bit of "overkill" with respect to children? The opportunity to vote is central to our constitutional scheme; deprivations of that opportunity must be strictly scrutinized by the judiciary and must be invalidated unless precisely and powerfully justified.[11] But surely it does not follow that every *infant* must be accommodated at the polls unless and until the state comes forward with particularized proof of the specific infant's incapacity?

It may be that overly generalized appeals to "youth" cannot suffice when otherwise fundamental rights are at stake; but fully particularized findings about each affected individual cannot be required either, at least as a matter of course. So long as the "fit" between an appropriate purpose and the circumscribing of a right is sufficiently close in light of the values affected,[12] there is no basis in the general run of cases for demanding anything more. The "general run of cases," however, may conceal quite a different sort of problem. A court perceiving systemically unresponsive institutions affecting important even if not fundamental rights in areas of shifting standards might hold that law and policy must be developed on an individualized, case-by-case basis, unconfined by rules of thumb. At least some aspects of childhood and of children's roles in

flection, upon a complete break, to permit his or her parents to "hold on" arguably shares few of the characteristics of voluntary association. Likewise, appeals to romantic notions of the unity of the family as a basis for validating parental authority and lowering the level of constitutional protection for minors seem misplaced when the family unit has been fractured because of the child's involuntary institutionalization. Yet Chief Justice Burger, writing for the Court in Parham v. J.R., 442 U.S. 584 (1979) (Georgia's procedures for commitment of juveniles to state institutions comport with minimum due process requirements), alluded to interests of family unity and smooth-functioning parental authority in upholding Georgia's juvenile commitment procedures—procedures which denied a minor the right to a full-fledged adversary hearing before being committed at the behest of his parents: ". . . historically [the law] has recognized that natural bonds of affection lead parents to act in the best interests of their children." Id. at 602. The majority also argued that an adversary hearing with parents and child on opposite sides would undermine "the parent-child relationship." See id. at 610. Justice Brennan, concurring in part and dissenting in part, pointed out that "the parent-child dispute at issue here cannot be characterized as involving only a routine child-rearing decision made within the context of an ongoing family relationship . . . [H]ere a break in family autonomy has actually resulted in the parents' decision to surrender custody of their child to a state mental institution." Id. at 631.

9. See, e.g., Bellotti v. Baird, 443 U.S. 622 (1979), supra note 8; Planned Parenthood v. Danforth, 428 U.S. 52, 72–75 (1976) (invalidating absolute parental veto over abortion by a minor), discussed in § 15–10, supra.

10. See § 12–28, supra.

11. See §§ 13–10 to 13–16, and 16–10, supra.

12. See § 16–34, infra.

contemporary American society—for example, their sex roles and economic roles—seem to involve the sort of "moral flux" this formulation requires; as to such aspects, this "anti-rigidity" doctrine would point to individualized determination of at least some child-related controversies involving important rights or liberties.[13]

Even in the absence of peculiar institutional rigidity, a prohibition against conclusive presumptions adversely affecting children might be derivable simply from the status of children as a group sharing *most* of the characteristics of a discrete and insular minority, while having needs so special as to make the goal of a "child-blind" society quite unthinkable. A halfway constitutional position for children as a "semi-discrete minority," and for childhood as a "semi-suspect classification," could thus take the form of a rule that all age-based lines, and all governmental allocations of responsibility or opportunity dependent upon the circumstance of youth, are "semi-suspect" in the limited sense that there must be an opportunity, absent strong justification for denying it, for a child to *rebut* any implied or asserted age-based incapacity. Unlike a rule treating age as a fully suspect criterion, which would result in completely invalidating all but the most compellingly justifiable age-based lines, the suggested doctrine would have the effect only of making such lines ordinarily permeable to rebuttal; judicial suspicion would, in effect, focus not on the legislative act of making childhood *relevant*—an act as consistent with genuine concern as with stereotyped contempt—but rather on the act of making childhood *conclusive*. The doctrine would thus preserve childhood as a legal category, with the concomitant protections typically flowing from such categorization,[14] while creating a way out for the unusually mature, capable, or independent young person.[15]

But one serious objection to this line of analysis may require its modification. Invalidating age-based conclusive presumptions on so broadly applicable a ground leaves the legislative and administrative processes with little flexibility in accommodating conflicting ends and allocating scarce resources among analogously underrepresented interests. For every "qualified" sixteen-year-old who enters junior college after a special hearing to win an exemption from an eighteen-year-old minimum, the state might argue, there will have to be an admittedly less qualified but probably more needy eighteen-year-old (more eighteen-year-olds have families and need jobs requiring further education) who is excluded. If courts are to deny legislatures and other governmental institutions the power to act upon premises such as these, the legitimacy of their intervention may thus have to turn on more than a claim that a "semi-suspect" criterion like age warrants judicial intrusion—not least because the resulting controversies will ordinarily implicate not one minority, but several. Yet the use of a criterion like youth, when *coupled* with a showing that the line irrebuttably drawn operates to

13. See § 17–3, infra.

14. One must, of course, be alert to the risk that supposed "protections" are in reality something else. See, e.g., § 16–27, supra.

15. See Tribe, "Childhood, Suspect Classifications, and Conclusive Presumptions: Three Linked Riddles," 39 Law & Contemp. Probs. 8 (1975).

abridge or burden an interest that adults would find protected as an important aspect of liberty,[16] might suffice to support judicial intervention of the form discussed here.

Lines based on old age require a separate analysis but ought to support a similar conclusion. Like at least some discriminations against youth (those that increase the likelihood of long-term disabilities, as in the case of some juvenile delinquency proceedings), discriminations against the very old may appear, from the perspective of those imposing them, to be of more limited duration than they appear from the perspective of those who experience their impact, particularly since a disability is most burdensome if one cannot look forward (ever) to losing it.[17] It is true that, as to discriminations against the aged, there exists at least the political safeguard that legislators and administrators might expect someday to experience the consequences of their current choices to withhold benefits from the old. But if persons are regarded as poor representatives of their own future selves (as well they might be), then the efficacy of this safeguard is dubious at best. Indeed, if people tend to discount the future more heavily than most persons in the abstract would find desirable, then the prospect of becoming old, although most legislators share it, will not induce a level of legislative empathy that would make treatment of the elderly as a "semi-discrete" minority unnecessary.[18]

16. Compare Hampton v. Mow Sun Wong, 426 U.S. 88, 102–03 (1976) (treating interest in federal civil service employment as an "interest in liberty" important enough to warrant more than minimal scrutiny of its "wholesale" deprivation for aliens).

17. Some commentators have argued that the young deserve less constitutional protection than the old since all were young once, and all the young can look forward to outgrowing their disability. See, e.g., Eglit, "Of Age and the Constitution," 57 Chicago Kent L.Rev. 859, 905 (1981). This analysis, however, is troubling for at least two reasons. First, it overlooks the fact that the young require *more* protection than the old to the degree that legislators feel constrained by the realization that they will have to endure the consequences of any burden they place on the old. Second, it may be an oversimplification to say that burdens become acceptable if one knows that they will be relieved in the future. Not only do some die young, but, in the eyes of someone suffering a disability throughout childhood, even a theoretical certainty that the tide will turn cannot be equated with the likelihood, in a political system without bias and with properly functioning coalitions, that gains and losses will be more or less evenly distributed at *all* times. Thus the logic that courts need not closely supervise the workings of such a political system because, on the whole, burdens will be balanced by benefits, should not be woodenly applied to deprivations directed against children. If telling children that they must simply wait their turn for adult status and privileges is justifiable, this must be because the legal disabilities they suffer as children are warranted on the merits and not the other way around; otherwise, *no* degree or form of legal deprivation visited upon the young could be deemed constitutionally problematic.

18. But see Massachusetts Bd. of Retirement v. Murgia, 427 U.S. 307 (1976) (per curiam), in which the Supreme Court upheld, on traditional "minimum rationality" grounds, a state statute mandating retirement at age 50 for state uniformed police. While admitting that the state could have chosen "to determine fitness more precisely through individualized testing after age 50," id. at 316, the Court refused to find those over age 50 a "discrete and insular" group: "[Old age] marks a stage that each of us will reach if we live out our normal span." Id. at 313–14. Justice Marshall, dissenting, would have invalidated the statute on application of a "flexible equal protection standard" utilizing a "heightened" level of scrutiny. Id. at 325. In Vance v. Bradley, 440 U.S. 93 (1979), the Court considered an equal protection challenge to a mandatory retirement rule for federal employees covered by the Foreign Service retirement system—a challenge that stressed the absence of any comparable requirement for federal Civil Service employees. Following what it said was the standard of review applied in Murgia, the Court rejected the constitution-

Discriminations against handicapped persons should also be susceptible to the kind of "semi-suspect" treatment outlined above for age-based discriminations. While pressure from the handicapped themselves has resulted in state and federal action to remove landscape and architectural barriers to disabled persons previously barred from employment in or enjoyment of buildings and parks,[19] discriminations which the handicapped have suffered and may continue to suffer are not readily recognized or gauged. Bias against the disabled is difficult to detect because it is often hidden behind rules neutral on their face.[20] Only

al challenge in Bradley. Justice White, writing for the Court, explained the propriety of minimum rationality review by noting that "[t]he Constitution presumes that, absent some reason to infer antipathy, even improvident decisions will eventually be rectified by the democratic process and that judicial intervention is generally unwarranted no matter how unwisely we may think a political branch has acted." Id. at 97. Justice Marshall dissented in Bradley along the lines of his dissent in Murgia. Id. at 112–115.

Despite the claim of consistency with Murgia, the approach in Bradley—the relatively detailed examination of the way in which the retirement system rationally furthered both "promotion opportunities through the selection-out process," see id. at 98–102, and the maintenance of a corps of foreign service officers able to endure "overseas duty under difficult and often hazardous conditions," see id. at 103–108—suggests that the Court may have been applying a more stringent form of review than the typical minimum rationality analysis exemplified in Murgia. See also City of Cleburne v. Cleburne Living Center, 473 U.S. 432, 455–57 (1985) (Marshall, J., joined by Brennan and Blackmun, JJ., concurring in the judgment and dissenting in part, suggesting that the Court had applied heightened equal protection review in the guise of traditional minimum rationality in striking down a zoning ordinance as applied to a home for the mentally retarded). See § 16–32, and § 16–33, infra.

It is true that, in Cleburne Living Center, the Court, in refusing to treat the mentally retarded as a quasi-suspect class, said that the legislative attention which the mentally retarded had received belied "a continuing antipathy and a corresponding need for more intrusive oversight by the judiciary." Id. at 442. The same could be said of the old. But this formulation, were it to become central to the Court's equal protection analysis, would put disadvantaged groups in an untenable position since legislative efforts to ease their disability would jeopardize the level of judicial protection extended to them. Constitutional protection should not be a zero-sum enterprise. Thus it should not undercut the case for significant

judicial scrutiny that there have indeed been major legislative gains for the elderly, at least with respect to employment discrimination. Since passage of the Age Discrimination in Employment Act (ADEA) of 1967, 29 U.S.C. §§ 621 et seq., Congress has repeatedly strengthened the act through a series of amendments extending its coverage to state and local governments, see E.E.O.C. v. Wyoming, 460 U.S. 226 (1983) (sustaining the extension of the ADEA to state governments in the face of a tenth amendment attack), and raising the mandatory retirement age for state, local and private employees from 65 to 70. See Age Discrmination in Employment Act Amendments of 1978, § 3(a), 92 Stat. 189, 29 U.S.C. § 631(b).

The most dramatic strengthening of the act, an amendment signed into law by President Reagan on November 1, 1986, eliminated mandatory retirement at any age for employees covered by the act. See H.R. 4154, 99th Cong., 2nd Session, 132 Cong. Rec. 11,280–81 (1986). As a practical matter, after this latest amendment, and in light of the fact that the act applies to state and local governments as well as to all private employers having at least 20 workers, nearly all plaintiffs will henceforth rely on the ADEA and not the equal protection clause as a source of protection from age discrimination in employment. Yet, notwithstanding the availability of powerful legislative protection against age discrimination in employment, the equal protection clause should still be deemed relevant for older persons complaining of other kinds of deprivations.

19. See, e.g., Education for All Handicapped Children Act, 20 U.S.C. §§ 1401 et seq.; Rehabilitation Act of 1973, 29 U.S.C. §§ 701 et seq. (prohibiting federally-funded institutions from excluding handicapped persons from programs or facilities solely on basis of handicap); Va. Code § 2.1–514 to 2.1–521.1 (barring architectural barriers to disabled in state buildings). See Krass, "The Right to Public Education for Handicapped Children: A Primer for the New Advocate," 1976 U.Ill.L. Forum 1016.

20. The most obvious case for heightened judicial scrutiny is governmental ac-

recently have legislatures and courts begun to realize that, intentionally

tion which, on its face, distinguishes between the disabled and the nondisabled to the detriment of the former. Yet, in one case of facial discrimination against the disabled, the Supreme Court resisted the explicit application of heightened scrutiny, although the Court apparently applied heightened review in the guise of minimum rationality. City of Cleburne v. Cleburne Living Center, 473 U.S. 432 (1985), involved an equal protection challenge to a zoning ordinance which, on its face, burdened the disabled by requiring a special use permit for the operation of a group home for the mentally retarded. Justice White's majority opinion rejected the holding of the lower court that mental retardation constituted a "quasi-suspect" classification and that an intermediate level of scrutiny should therefore be applied. The majority first maintained that, unlike race or gender, mental retardation often was a legitimate proxy: ". . . legislation thus singling out the retarded for special treatment reflects the real and undeniable differences between the retarded and others." Id. at 444. Second, the majority suggested that heightened judicial scrutiny might dampen legislative efforts to benefit the mentally retarded, since requiring the legislature to pass laws able to withstand heightened scrutiny "may lead it to refrain from acting at all." Id. In addition, the Court cited several legislative acts protective of the mentally retarded which supposedly negated "any claim that the mentally retarded are politically powerless in the sense that they have no ability to attract the attention of the lawmakers." Id. Finally, the Court expressed its unwillingness to recognize mental retardation as a quasi-suspect classification because of the apparently limitless implications of that holding, saying that "it would be difficult to find a principled way to distinguish a variety of other groups . . . who can claim some degree of prejudice." Id. at 444–47. Having disclaimed heightened judicial scrutiny, and applying what it said was traditional minimum rationality review, the Court invalidated the zoning ordinance as applied in the case at hand. See id. at 446–51. Justice Marshall, joined by Justices Brennan and Blackmun, concurring in the judgment in part and dissenting in part, suggested—convincingly, it should be said— that the Court had applied heightened judicial scrutiny sub silentio: "Cleburne's ordinance surely would be valid under the traditional rational basis test applicable to economic and commercial regulation." Id. at 455. Justice Marshall advocated the explicit application of heightened scrutiny in light of "the history of discrimination against the retarded and its continuing legacy," and the fact that what was at stake

was "a liberty so valued as the right to establish a home in the community, and so likely to be denied on the basis of irrational fears and outright hostility." Id. at 473.

Even assuming that Justice Marshall was correct and that the Court's majority was applying heightened scrutiny without admitting it, the harder question is whether disparate impact adverse to the handicapped in the absence of any facial discrimination of the sort present in Cleburne Living Center should suffice to trigger heightened judicial scrutiny. The Court's approach to this question in the context of § 504 of the Rehabilitation Act, 29 U.S.C. § 794 as amended, is illuminating. In Alexander v. Choate, 469 U.S. 287 (1985), the Court faced a challenge to a state decision to reduce from 20 to 14 days Medicaid coverage of hospital bills. Plaintiffs alleged that the reduction of coverage violated § 504 because of the disproportionate impact on the handicapped; historically, more handicapped than nonhandicapped persons had had hospital stays in excess of the 14-day cap. Since the 14-day rule was neutral on its face, was not alleged to reflect a discriminatory motive, and did not deny the handicapped meaningful access to Medicaid services, Justices Marshall wrote for the unanimous Court that the reduction did not discriminate against the handicapped within the meaning of § 504: "Assuming . . . that § 504 or its implementing regulations reach some claims of disparate-impact discrimination, the effect of Tennessee's reduction in annual inpatient coverage is not among them." Id. at 309. In elaborating the concept of meaningful access, the Court eschewed a reading of § 504 that would have required the equalization of burdens borne by the disabled and non-disabled. "Tennessee is not required to assure that its handicapped Medicaid users will be as healthy as its nonhandicapped users." Id. at 305–06.

Justice Marshall maintained that the concept of meaningful access was wholly consistent with the Court's holding in Southeastern Community College v. Davis, 442 U.S. 397 (1979) (college could properly refuse to admit a nurse with a substantial hearing impairment who requested that she have full-time, personal supervision whenever she attended patients and that she not be required to take clinical courses). While conceding that an institution might be required under § 504 to take some steps to remove exclusionary barriers to the disabled, the Court held in Davis that § 504 did not require "affirmative action" if it meant a "substantial modification of standards to accommodate a handicapped person." Id. at 413. Yet, although Choate and

or not, the disabled have been systematically excluded from and denied access to governmental privileges and benefits that *appear* to have been made available to all on equal terms.

Undoubtedly, some discrimination against the disabled is inadvertent, in the sense that it is the product of legislative blindness rather than prejudicial bias.[21] On the other hand, although neutral on their face, some rules which have a sharply discriminatory impact against the handicapped may be animated by an invidious hostility towards the disabled—a hostility analogous to the prejudice sometimes directed against racial minorities. The physical and mental impairments of the disabled have been the basis of their persistent social stigmatization and isolation, including the uninhibited exercise, in the not too distant past,

Davis are both centered on "the extent to which a grantee is required to make reasonable modifications in its programs for the needs of the handicapped," Choate at 299 & n.19, the cases follow two different tests in determining the reasonableness of modifications. The Court determined reasonableness in Davis by looking at the substantiality of the desired modifications and the burden those modifications would place on the program, not by looking at whether the handicapped person would actually have some minimal degree of "access" to the federally-funded program without the requested modifications. Indeed, in Davis, the handicapped person was denied access altogether when the Court refused to require the college to admit her. On the other hand, in Choate the Court concluded that "nothing in the record suggests that the handicapped in Tennessee will be unable to benefit meaningfully from the coverage they will receive under the 14-day rule." Choate at 302. This formulation suggests that reasonableness does depend upon some minimal degree of "access." Choate's formula, however, is not necessarily in conflict with Davis' if one reads meaningful access as a sufficient but not a necessary condition to a finding that § 504 is complied with. That is, if the access for the handicapped does satisfy the meaningful access standard, then the Court may not closely scrutinize an allegation that further accommodation can be effected without substantial modifications. If the access does *not* satisfy that standard, then this further allegation will be addressed. Under this reading of Choate and Davis, only when the access is denied altogether, or when access does not come up to a level deemed "meaningful," will the substantiality of potential modifications be an issue.

In its first interpretation of the Education of the Handicapped Act (20 U.S.C. §§ 1401 et seq.), the Court followed a line of analysis similar to that in Choate. Writing for the Court, Justice Rehnquist held that the failure of a school to provide a hearing-impaired student with a qualified sign language interpreter in all her classes did not violate the act. Hendrick Hudson District Board of Education v. Rowley, 458 U.S. 176 (1982). The Court held that, since the student, who had been furnished with a hearing aid and special tutors, derived some benefit from her education, as evidenced by her above average academic performance, the school had not deprived her of the "free appropriate public education" guaranteed by the act. The act required "sufficient support services to permit the child to benefit educationally from that institution," id. at 203, but did not require that the state "maximize the potential of each handicapped child commensurate with the opportunity provided nonhandicapped children." Id. at 200. Justice Blackmun, concurring in the judgment, interpreted the act to require equalization of burdens but thought that, when viewed as a whole, the child's program "offered her an educational opportunity substantially equal to that provided her nonhandicapped classmates." Id. at 211. Justice White, joined by Justices Brennan and Marshall, dissented on the ground that the act intended "to give handicapped children an educational opportunity commensurate with that given other children," id. at 214, and that "the basic floor of opportunity is, as the courts below recognized, intended to eliminate the effects of the handicap, at least to the extent that the child will be given an equal opportunity to learn if that is reasonably possible." Id. at 215. Yet, while only the five justices joining the majority opinion in Rowley were willing to accept the concept of meaningful access in the context of the Handicapped Education Act, all nine justices later endorsed the meaningful access test in interpreting § 504 of the Rehabilitation Act. See discussion of Choate, supra.

21. "Discrimination against the handicapped was perceived by Congress to be most often the product, not of invidious animus, but rather of thoughtlessness and indifference—of benign neglect." Alexander v. Choate, 469 U.S. at 295.

of institutionalization as a mechanism for segregating those handicapped persons whose disabilities even their families did not understand or accept.[22] Even when not physically isolated from society, disabled persons may experience painful ostracism in a culture that puts great weight on conformity to norms of appearance or performance that not all can meet.[23] But whatever the source of the discrimination against the disabled—whether from overtly invidious discrimination and stereotyping, or from an insidious blindness to the ramifications of rules that operate inexorably to exclude the disabled—the rationale for semi-suspect treatment of the handicapped is compelling. A history of continuous and pervasive deprivations and exclusions, the product of both legislative blindness and bias towards the disabled, justifies the exercise of heightened judicial scrutiny.

Even when the invisibility of the discrimination at issue is not a problem because that discrimination is apparent on the face of governmental action, there is a danger that discrimination against the disabled may be glossed over if the action is successfully cast as a response to the *effects* of the disability and not to the *fact* of the disability itself. For example, it has been urged that persons who carry a contagious disease are not discriminated against, within the meaning of the equal protection clause or of various anti-discrimination statutes, if the relevant governmental action is designed to protect third persons from the risks which those disabled persons may pose to those around them. By this logic, the government is not discriminating against the person who suffers the disability—and hence need not justify its action—if that action can plausibly be characterized as an attempt, however misguided or indeed irrational, to minimize the impact of the disability on third persons and not simply as a manifestation of some bias directed against the disabled as such. The obvious problem with this formulation is that virtually any discriminatory governmental action can be recast in equivalently "neutral" terms. In almost all cases, the burdens of a disability, while most directly and inescapably borne by the handicapped person, are also felt, although in different and more diffuse form, by non-disabled persons who come in contact with the disabled. Thus, for example, we all bear some risk that a blind person may inadvertently knock us down in the street. In light of that risk, government action restricting the opportunity of blind persons to move about freely in public could be characterized as a response to the effects of a person's blindness on the non-disabled rather than as a discrimination against blind persons per se.

Because virtually every imaginable governmental restriction imposed on the disabled could be similarly recast, a governmental action should not—simply by virtue of being recharacterized as a regulation of

---

22. See City of Cleburne v. Cleburne Living Center, 473 U.S. 432, 461, 463 (1985) (Marshall, J., dissenting), for a brief account of the history of deprivation and isolation suffered by just one class of the disabled, the mentally retarded.

23. See O'Connor v. Donaldson, 422 U.S. 563 (1975) (involuntary confinement of a nondangerous mentally ill patient when the patient is receiving no medical treatment for his mental illness violates due process), where the Court disparaged the idea that a state could confine a nondangerous mentally ill patient in order to avoid public unease from the "physically unattractive or socially eccentric." Id. at 575.

the effects and not of the fact of a disability—escape heightened scrutiny under the applicable anti-discriminatory statutory and constitutional provisions.[24] While the interests of third parties are certainly factors to be weighed in determining whether discriminatory governmental action can survive heightened scrutiny, the level of judicial scrutiny should not turn on pliable characterizations of the governmental action; otherwise, the protection to which the disabled are entitled under the statutory and constitutional framework might be largely eviscerated.

A different set of characterizations may also potentially function to obscure discrimination against various categories of the handicapped. As courts become more sympathetic to arguments that persons have a right to die with dignity and that the state interest in the preservation of life may sometimes be subordinated to an individual's right to die,[25] there is a possibility that doctrines which are intended to facilitate the exercise of this right will be exploited, either intentionally or unwittingly, to practice the most terrible discrimination against handicapped persons who require medical treatment to stay alive: [26] judgments that their disabilities are such that persons afflicted with them would be better off dead and thus should be "allowed" to die. The most pernicious discriminatory bias against the disabled that one can imagine—the desire of families or others to dispose of handicapped persons whom they

24. In School Bd. of Nassau County v. Arline, 107 S.Ct. 1123 (1987), the Court held that individuals with contagious diseases such as tuberculosis are handicapped within the meaning of § 504 of the Rehabilitation Act and that governmental burdens on these persons—such as being fired as a school teacher—may constitute prohibited discrimination. In an opinion for the Court joined by Justices White, Marshall, Blackmun, Powell, Stevens, and O'Connor, Justice Brennan noted that the Act recognized that "society's accumulated myths and fears about disability and disease are as handicapping as are the physical limitations that flow from actual impairment." Id. at 1129. Individualized findings as to the nature, duration, and severity of the risk of transmission are required to avert "discrimination on the basis of mythology," since the purpose of the act is to replace fearful, reflexive reactions with reasonable, medically sound judgments. Id. at 1129–30. This interpretation of the Act promises to become of increasing importance as the epidemic of Acquired Immune Deficiency Syndrome (AIDS) spreads. Chief Justice Rehnquist, joined by Justice Scalia, dissented.

25. Courts which formerly recognized a person's right to refuse "extraordinary" life-prolonging medical treatment have gone further, holding that the right to bodily integrity, grounded in a right to privacy, may extend, in some cases, to decisions about whether to accept ordinary life-sustaining treatment—including the supply of food and water. See, e.g., Brophy v. New England Sinai Hospital, 398 Mass. 417, 497

N.E.2d 626 (1986) (allowing the removal of the food and water supply from a patient who was in a persistent vegetative state after a showing that, before his illness, the patient had expressed a desire not to have his life prolonged in that manner). Brophy extended the holding of Superintendent of Belchertown State School v. Saikewicz, 373 Mass. 728, 370 N.E.2d 417 (1977) (holding that the "substituted judgment" doctrine, permitting a surrogate decisionmaker to determine the subjective intent of the patient when the patient is unable to express that intent for himself, is applicable in the case of a mentally retarded patient), that "extraordinary" life-prolonging medical treatment might lawfully be withheld. See § 15–11, supra.

26. As courts expand the scope of the right to die, and as that right is transformed from a right to refuse "extraordinary" medical treatment into a right to refuse even ordinary, life-sustaining treatment, and perhaps ultimately into a right, under some circumstances, to hasten death through some form of euthanasia, see § 15–11, supra, the condition of being near death may itself come to be seen as a disability which, without anything more, justifies an assertion of the right to die. If this is the case, then the condition of being near death might be considered a "handicap" for purposes of the discussion in the text, and thus the extra judicial solicitude which is urged on behalf of those who suffer mental and physical impairments might also be relevant for those who are handicapped only in the sense that they are near death.

simply consider undesirable—might be effectively disguised behind their requests, made in the name of the disabled's right to die, that medical treatment be withheld from the disabled. The right to die, in other words, may offer a convenient pretext for profoundly discriminatory decisionmaking.

If they are to ensure that decisions about medical treatment for the disabled are not driven by prejudice against the disabled,[27] court's must scrupulously adhere to the intent of the person who suffers the disability. A court faced with a decision about whether to permit the withholding of medical treatment should accordingly require a clear showing of the disabled's preference not to suffer the "bodily invasion" of the treatment.

The tension between the right to live and die with dignity,[28] and the right of the handicapped not to be discriminated against, is hardest to reconcile when there is no possibility for self-determination, as in the case of handicapped newborns. When the patient is unable to speak for herself, and when the subjective intent of the patient cannot be ascertained by referring to previously expressed preferences or other evidence strongly probative of intent,[29] medical treatment decisions by a surrogate decisionmaker—whether a parent, guardian, or the state—will always be susceptible to conflicting characterizations. A decision *not* to treat a person who is unable to make the decision himself might be celebrated as effectuating that person's right to die with dignity. Alternatively, such a decision might be condemned as discriminatory, at least in the sense that the decisionmaker undervalued the life of the handicapped person by overestimating the burden of the handicap. Since decisions not to treat will generally be open to attack on this ground, it might appear that the only effective way to ensure that this kind of discrimination is not at work would be to require treatment in all cases except those in which there is a clear showing that the handicap entails physical suffering that *no* person would ever choose to endure.

27. This prejudice against the disabled or incompetent need not take the form of malevolence. Guardians and family members (or even state officials) may genuinely believe that, if they were in the disabled's position, they would choose to discontinue medical treatment. But having persons who do not actually experience an affliction make judgments about the potential quality of life of the disabled is extremely perilous. "Other people may crudely misjudge the effect of handicaps and grossly undervalue the life of a handicapped person." Minow, "Beyond State Intervention in the Family: For Baby Jane Doe," 18 U.Mich.J. Law Reform 933, 961 (1985).

28. See § 15–11, supra.

29. Except in cases where the patient continues to be competent to express a preference, treatment decisions which are based on preferences that the disabled expressed *prior* to the onset of his or her disability may strain the concept of self-determination beyond coherence. Previously expressed preferences may be suspect for the same reason that the judgments of third persons are always suspect: it is hard to be confident that a person who does not experience a disability will be able to predict accurately the decision he would make if he actually were suffering the disability. We can never be certain that the person would not change his mind about the treatment decision after experiencing the disability. Still, following the patient's previously expressed preferences, although subject to some of the same deficiencies as third party judgments, is perhaps the best we can do in being faithful to the right to bodily integrity—a right which, after all, belongs to the individual patient, not to third parties. On the whole, it seems reasonable to expect that an individual's guess about what decision he or she would make if afflicted will come closer to what that person would decide after the disability than will any third party's prediction about what choice the patient would make.

But, ironically, this presumption in *favor* of treatment might itself be a form of discrimination against the disabled. For a presumption that decisions not to treat are always founded on an undervaluation of the handicapped's life would dramatically curtail the scope of the disabled's right to die. A prophylactic rule mandating treatment in all but the most exceptional cases of extraordinary pain, although solicitous of the handicapped in guaranteeing that conscious and unconscious biases against the handicapped would not distort treatment decisions, is discriminatory because it effectively forces *overvaluation* of life, forces treatment in cases where a disabled person would choose to die if he were able to express that choice, and thereby compromises a disabled's right to die.

Rather than prescribing flat prophylactic *or* presumptive rules, perhaps one should recognize a state responsibility to monitor medical treatment decisions, at least so far as is necessary to assure that they are not unduly shaped by conscious or unconscious bias against the handicapped.[30] Deciding upon a surrogate decisionmaker is itself problemat-

---

30. Courts have wisely avoided too rigid an approach to these medical treatment decisions. Critics could argue that the courts have abdicated responsibility for the hardest choices, but it seems altogether sensible for the courts to defer initially to the legislative process. If legislatures do not fashion an effective response, courts might consider taking on a more active role. The unwillingness of at least one court to rely on § 504 of the Rehabilitation Act to resolve the complex issues surrounding these medical treatment decisions seems wholly justifiable, since the statutory provision does not seem supple enough to sort out the countervailing interests that are at stake in these difficult cases. In United States v. University Hospital, 729 F.2d 144 (2d Cir.1984), the court of appeals rejected the argument that § 504 applies to medical treatment decisions concerning handicapped newborns. The court noted first that the language in § 504 referring to "otherwise qualified" handicapped individuals could not be meaningfully applied to treatment decisions concerning a newborn with multiple birth defects. Id. at 156. Moreover, an examination of congressional intent suggested that "Congress never contemplated that § 504 would apply to treatment decisions of this nature." Id. at 157. The Supreme Court seemed poised to address the Second Circuit's reasoning in Bowen v. American Hospital Association, 106 S.Ct. 2101 (1986). In that case, a plurality of the Court, in an opinion by Justice Stevens, joined by Justices Marshall, Blackmun, and Powell, concluded that four challenged regulations promulgated by the Secretary of the Department of Health and Human Services were not authorized by § 504 of the Rehabilitation Act. Applying an axiom of administrative law that an agency must "explain the rational and factual basis for its decision," id. at 2113, the plurality found, among other things, that the agency could not sustain its burden of justifying the challenged regulations since the Secretary produced no evidence that hospitals were withholding medical treatment on the basis of handicap. See id. at 2114–2117. The plurality emphasized that decisions *by parents* to withhold medical treatment were not within the ambit of § 504, since § 504 purported only to regulate discriminatory decisions made by institutions receiving federal funds. See id. at 2114–2115. The plurality never reached what the dissent called the "threshold statutory issue" whether § 504 gave the Secretary any authority to regulate medical treatment decisions regarding newborn infants. According to Justice White's dissent, the plurality avoided the threshold question "by first erroneously reading the decision below as enjoining only the enforcement of specific regulations and by then affirming on the basis that the promulgation of the regulations did not satisfy established principles of administrative law." Id. at 2123–2124. Justice White, joined by Justice Brennan and in part by Justice O'Connor, would have reversed the holding of the Second Circuit that § 504 did not grant the Secretary authority to regulate treatment decisions concerning handicapped newborns. In addition, while hesitant (without the benefit of further lower court deliberations) to reach the "subsidiary" question of the scope of the Secretary's authority under the statute, Justice White did express his disagreement with the plurality's conclusion that there was no rational basis for the agency action. See id. at 2128–2131.

ic.[31] But, regardless of who the ultimate decisionmaker is, the state should stand ready to provide some neutral inquiry into the basis of the treatment decision, exposing bias whenever it appears to be operating. Professor Martha Minow has urged that the state should ideally facilitate dialogue among the various interested third parties—including the parents or guardian, the hospital, and officials from the appropriate state agencies—and, in so doing, should strive to achieve a constructive interaction so that the decision can be made after the differing perspectives of these third parties have been thoroughly aired.[32]

§ 16–32. Cataloguing the Techniques of Intermediate Review: Assessing Importance, Demanding Close Fit, Altering Perspective, Requiring Current Articulation, Limiting Afterthought, and Permitting Rebuttal

Although indicating that he "would not welcome a further subdividing of equal protection analysis," Justice Powell, concurring in *Craig v. Boren*, acknowledged that "[t]here are valid reasons for dissatisfaction with the 'two-tier' approach that has been prominent in the Court's [equal protection] decisions in the past decade," and added that "candor compels the recognition that the relatively deferential 'rational basis' standard of review normally applied takes on a sharper focus when we address a gender-based classification."[1] The Justice might well have added that a growing range of cases, involving classifications other than gender and involving a number of important but not "constitutionally fundamental" interests, have likewise triggered forms of review in fact poised between the largely toothless invocation of minimum rationality and the nearly fatal invocation of strict scrutiny—intermediate forms of review which Justice Powell must have had in mind when he spoke of "sharper focus."[2] Since *Craig*, intermediate scrutiny has become a regular part of equal protection method.[3] What was once two-tiered

---

31. See Minow, supra note 27.

32. See id., arguing that the state should work to diminish mutual distrust among the interested third parties and that the debate be advanced beyond the current stage where the issues have been misleadingly framed in either/or terms of state intervention v. family autonomy.

§ 16–32

1. 429 U.S. 190, 210–11 n.* (1976).

2. See also Mississippi University for Women v. Hogan, 458 U.S. 718, 724 (1982) (Per O'Connor, J.) ("[T]he party seeking to uphold a statute that classifies individuals on the basis of their gender must carry the burden of showing an 'exceedingly persuasive justification' for the classification"); Michael M. v. Sonoma County Superior Court, 450 U.S. 464, 468 (1981) (opinion of Rehnquist, J.) ("[T]he traditional minimum rationality test takes on a somewhat 'sharper focus' when gender-based classifications are challenged."); cf. Justice White's concurring opinion in Vlandis v. Kline, 412 U.S. 441, 458 (1973) (concurring in judgment): "From [a large number of] cases, . . ., it is clear that we employ not just one, or two, but, as my Brother Marshall has so ably demonstrated, a 'spectrum of standards in reviewing discrimination allegedly violative of the Equal Protection Clause.'" The quotation was from Justice Marshall's dissent in San Antonio Independent School District v. Rodriguez, 411 U.S. 1, 98–99 (1973). See also Dandridge v. Williams, 397 U.S. 471, 519–20 (1970) (Marshall, J., dissenting).

3. See, e.g., Mississippi University for Women v. Hogan, 458 U.S. 718 (1982) (applying intermediate scrutiny to classification based on gender); Craig v. Boren, 429 U.S. 190 (1976) (same); Mills v. Habluetzel, 456 U.S. 91, 99 (1982) (applying intermediate scrutiny to classification based on illegitimacy).

analysis has now become three-tiered analysis.[4] Close review is not always candidly admitted by the court, see §§ 16–2, 16–3, supra, but whether employed overtly or covertly, the tools used by the court all are canvassed here for what they are—techniques of intermediate review. In § 16–33, we examine the circumstances that trigger such intermediate review; here we look more closely at precisely what is triggered when a "middle-tier" approach is employed.

The techniques encompassed by intermediate review, whether overtly or covertly applied, have been of six general types, as indicated by the title of this section. The first has been that of assessing importance— that is, insisting that the objectives served by a challenged classification or limitation on liberty be "important" even if they need not be as "compelling" as strict scrutiny would demand.[5] Thus, in *Reed v. Reed*, the objectives of "reducing the workload on probate courts" and "avoiding intra-family controversy,"[6] for example, "were deemed of insufficient importance to sustain use of an overt gender criterion in the appointment of [intestate] administrators."[7] More generally, it has become "obvious . . . that, as the Court's assessment of the weight and value of the individual interest escalates, the less likely it is that mere administrative convenience and avoidance of hearings or investigations will be sufficient to justify what otherwise would appear to be irrational discriminations."[8] The "establishment of prompt efficacious procedures to achieve legitimate state ends is a proper state interest worthy of cognizance in constitutional adjudication. But the Constitution recognizes higher values than speed and efficiency."[9] When "the interest at stake" is of great importance to the individual, "[a]ny fair balancing" of that interest "as opposed to what may be nothing more than a hypothetical justification, requires rejection of the argument of administrative convenience . . . ."[10] Indeed, an insistence on assessing the importance of the state interest by balancing it against the burdens imposed on the individual and on society—thereby rejecting the balance struck by the legislature—seems a hallmark of a new form of heightened scrutiny. This form was applied—but under the minimum rationality label—in

---

4. See City of Cleburne v. Cleburne Living Center, 473 U.S. 432, 439–42 (1985) (discussing the current structure of equal protection review).

5. It is axiomatic that the objectives served must be constitutionally legitimate. To the extent that such purposes as "a bare desire to harm a politically unpopular group", United States Department of Agriculture v. Moreno, 413 U.S. 528, 534 (1973), are inconsistent with the very idea of equal protection of the laws, there is nothing novel in rejection of laws the Court views as explicable only in terms of such illicit objectives. To the extent, however, that the Court's rejection of an objective as illegitimate reflects an unexplained refusal to credit goals that seem entirely compatible with norms of equal justice under law, it is hardly a technique of heightened scrutiny,

but an act of judicial fiat. See Zobel v. Williams, 457 U.S. 55 (1982); Hooper v. Bernalillo County Assessor, 472 U.S. 612 (1985), discussed in § 16–2, supra.

6. 404 U.S. 71, 76–77 (1971).

7. Craig v. Boren, 429 U.S. 190, 198 (1976) (rejecting statute prohibiting sale of 3.2% beer to under-21 males and under-18 females).

8. Vlandis v. Kline, 412 U.S. 441, 458–59 (1973) (White, J., concurring in judgment).

9. Stanley v. Illinois, 405 U.S. 645, 656 (1972).

10. Hampton v. Mow Sun Wong, 426 U.S. 88, 115–16 (1976) (rejecting Civil Service Commission rule excluding all aliens from federal competitive civil service).

Plyler v. Doe [11], where the Court, in overturning a Texas statute excluding the children of illegal immigrants from public education, rejected the asserted state purpose of improving the overall quality of state education by raising per pupil expenditures.[12] The Court concluded instead that the classification would "promot[e] the creation and perpetuation of a subclass of illiterates within our boundaries." [13]

The second technique has been that of demanding close fit—that is, requiring that the rules employed by government be "substantially related to achievement of . . . [the] objectives" invoked to defend those rules.[14] Thus, in *Craig v. Boren*, for example, "the protection of public health and safety" was plainly "an important function of state and local governments," [15] but the statistics—which "broadly establish that .18% of females and 2% of males in [the 18-to-20-year-old] age group were arrested" for driving while drunk—provided "an unduly tenuous 'fit' " to justify a gender-based rule regulating the sale of 3.2% beer to 18-to-20-year-olds.[16]

City of Cleburne v. Cleburne Living Center [17] illustrates a new and more modest form of the requirement of close fit. The Court struck down—but only as applied—a zoning ordinance requiring a special use permit for a group home for the mentally retarded. In reviewing the

---

11. 457 U.S. 202 (1982), discussed in §§ 16–3, 16–9, 16–23, supra, and § 16–58, infra.

12. 457 U.S. at 229.

13. Id. at 230.

14. Craig, 429 U.S. at 197.

15. Id. at 199–200.

16. Id. at 201, 202. The requirement of close fit can also be seen in Williams v. Vermont, 472 U.S. 14 (1985), discussed in § 16–4, supra (invalidating a Vermont automobile use tax which gave credit for out-of-state sales or use tax payments only to car registrants who were Vermont residents at the time the out-of-state tax was paid, because the classification was not sufficiently closely related to the goal of allowing users of out-of-state roads to pay only one state's use tax); cf., id. at 34 (Blackmun, J., dissenting) (arguing that the classification ought not to be overturned merely because of underinclusiveness), and in Caban v. Mohammed, 441 U.S. 380, 392–393 (1979) (invalidating a New York statute giving unmarried mothers, but not fathers, the power to veto the adoption of their child, because in cases such as the one before the Court, where the father had admitted paternity and participated in child-rearing, the classification was not substantially related to the state's proclaimed interest in promoting adoption); cf. id. at 407 (Stevens, J., dissenting) (arguing that differences between mothers and fathers during a child's infancy justify the classification because "[t]he mere fact that an otherwise valid general classification appears arbitrary in an isolated case is not a

sufficient reason for invalidating the entire rule"); see also Trimble v. Gordon, 430 U.S. 762, 770–71 (1977) (invalidating Illinois rule making it impossible for illegitimate children to inherit by intestate succession from their fathers; state "failed to consider the possibility of a middle ground between the extremes of complete exclusion and case-by-case determination of paternity;" for "at least some significant categories of illegitimate children of intestate men, inheritance rights can be recognized without jeopardizing the orderly settlement of estates or the dependability of titles to property passing under intestacy laws"); Hampton v. Mow Sun Wong, 426 U.S. 88, 101 n.20, 116 n.48 (1976) (suggesting that, although a flat ban on employment of aliens violates due process, "citizenship [might] be required as a qualification for appropriately defined classes of positions", and adding that even "the argument of administrative convenience . . . would adequately support a rather broad classification of positions reflecting the considered judgment of an agency expert in personnel matters"); Cleveland Board of Education v. LaFleur, 414 U.S. 632, 647 n.13 (1974) (indicating that, although due process invalidates a flat rule requiring pregnant teachers to take unpaid maternity leaves after fourth month of pregnancy, "maternity leave regulations requiring a termination of employment at some firm date during the last few weeks of pregnancy" might be justified).

17. 473 U.S. 432 (1985), discussed in § 16–3, supra.

law as applied, rather than on its face, the Court avoided substitution of its own generic judgment for the generic judgment of the legislature.[18]

Justice Stevens' concurrence in *Cleburne* indicates a third technique of intermediate review altogether, that of altering perspective by focusing on the challenged rule not from a perspective deferential to the legislative authority [19]—or from a perspective objectively neutral [20]—but from the perspective of the disadvantaged group itself.[21] This approach requires the judge to attempt to gain the perspective of a group to which he or she does not belong—no mean feat.[22]

The fourth technique has been that of requiring current articulation—that is, refusing to supply a challenged rule with a rationale, drawn from judicial imagination or even from the rule's history, where the rationale is not advanced in the litigation in the rule's defense.[23] That technique was employed in several due process cases before its

18. Of course, even the invalidation of a law as applied is a departure from traditional judicial deference. See, e.g., Caban v. Mohammed, 441 U.S. 380, 407 (1979) (Stevens, J., dissenting) (that a generically valid rule or classification "appears arbitrary in an isolated case" is unsurprising). The invalidation in Cleburne, however, must be distinguished from permitting rebuttal, discussed infra. In a case like Cleburne, the Court decides that the ordinance cannot be applied at all to the case before it, not that those affected must be given a hearing to demonstrate why the general rule should be waived administratively for them.

19. See the discussion of the normal requirement of minimum rationality in § 16–2, supra.

20. Cf. Justice O'Connor's concurrence in Wallace v. Jaffree, 472 U.S. 38, 74 (1985), in which she expands upon the argument she originally put forth in Lynch v. Donnelly, 465 U.S. 668, 690–93 (1984) (O'Connor, J., concurring), that the establishment clause would be violated by government action that fairly could be understood to have the effect of communicating a message of government endorsement or disapproval of religion: "The relevant issue is whether an *objective observer* . . . would perceive Alabama's moment of silence statute as an endorsement of prayer in public schools" Wallace v. Jaffree, 472 U.S. at 74 (O'Connor, J., concurring in the judgment) (emphasis added). See also Witters v. Washington Dept. of Serv. for the Blind, 106 S.Ct. 748, 755 (1986) (O'Connor, J., concurring in the judgment and concurring in part) ("No reasonable observer is likely to draw from the facts before us an inference that the state itself is endorsing a religious practice or belief.").

21. See Cleburne, 473 U.S. at 454 (Stevens, J., concurring) ("The differences between mentally retarded persons and those with greater mental capacity are obviously

relevant to certain legislative decisions . . . [E]ven a member of a class of persons defined as mentally retarded . . . could vote in favor of a law providing funds for special education and special treatment for the mentally retarded. . . . I cannot believe that a rational member of the disadvantaged class could ever approve of the discriminatory application of the city's ordinance in this case.").

22. For a sensitive discussion of the problems and potentialities of such attempts at shifting perspective, see Minow, "When Difference Has Its Home: Group Homes for the Mentally Retarded, Equal Protection, and Legal Treatment of Difference", 22 Harv.C.R.—C.L.L.Rev. 111 (1987).

23. See generally Gunther. "The Supreme Court, 1971 Term—Foreword: In Search of Evolving Doctrine on a Changing Court: A Model for a Newer Equal Protection," 86 Harv.L.Rev. 1 (1972). Professor Gunther's formulation of the approach is somewhat ambiguous. He occasionally suggests that the purposes to be considered are those expressed or at least entertained by the enacting legislature, see id. at 28, 44–46, but at some points he also suggests that the only purposes to be considered are those argued by the state's representatives in the lawsuit. See id. at 35, 47. The first of these formulations suggests a principle against validation by afterthought—a principle considered later in this section. It is the second formulation alone that bears on a requirement of current articulation. See also note 54, infra.

The requirement of current articulation, as a boundary on the judicial imagination, is a rejection of the traditional deference of the conceivable basis test discussed in § 16–3, supra. The limitation on the use of afterthought, discussed infra, which permits rejection even of currently preferred governmental objectives, likewise rejects traditional deference.

more systematic development in the equal protection area. For example, in *Griswold v. Connecticut*,[24] the Supreme Court struck down a state ban on the use of contraceptives in 1965 without ever adverting to the most obvious possible rationales for the ban: that sex without a childbearing purpose was immoral in itself, or that population expansion was needed. What was the reason for ignoring those rationales? Evidently that the state chose not to articulate them in the ban's defense,[25] a choice quite different from the one the state had made in 1961, when the Court refused to reach the merits of the ban in *Poe v. Ullman*.[26] And in *Cleveland Board of Education v. LaFleur*,[27] where the Court invalidated local school board rules requiring pregnant teachers to take unpaid maternity leaves for periods of several months before and after childbirth, the Court studiously avoided assessing the rules against the governmental purpose—not argued in appeal although suggested by the record—of preventing schoolchildren from seeing conspicuously pregnant teachers, whether to "save pregnant teachers from embarrassment at the hands of giggling schoolchildren" [28] or to keep thoughts of sex out of the classroom.[29] For the Court, the likely origins of the maternity-leave regulations merited a footnote about school board fears that students might believe their teacher had "swallowed a watermelon," and a remark about "the possible role of outmoded taboos in the adoption of the rules," [30] but the Court made no attempt to decide whether such purposes would be legitimate and sufficiently weighty if they were being currently advanced to defend the rules,[31] or to evaluate the "fit" between the rules and those purposes. In *LaFleur*, as in *Griswold*, the Court was spared the task of passing upon the adequacy of the most obviously close-fitting purposes for the rules under attack [32]—since those purposes were no longer being articulated in the rules' defense.

When the requirement of articulation is thus imposed, it will have special bite only when those responsible for enforcing a law or regulation, while under pressure to invoke it either routinely or occasionally, no longer share, or respond to a constituency that no longer shares, the values the law originally expressed. Even if pressed, officers of the state

---

24. 381 U.S. 479 (1965).

25. See id. at 505 (White, J., concurring) ("There is no serious contention that Connecticut thinks the use of artificial or external methods of contraception immoral or unwise in itself, or that the anti-use statute is founded upon any policy of promoting population expansion").

26. 367 U.S. 497 (1961); see id. at 545–53 (Harlan, J., dissenting) ("The State . . . asserts that . . . it considers the practice of contraception immoral in itself").

27. 414 U.S. 632 (1974).

28. Id. at 641 n.9.

29. Id.

30. Id. The Court quoted Green v. Waterford Board of Education, 473 F.2d 629, 635 (2d Cir. 1973): "Whatever may have been the reaction in Queen Victoria's time, pregnancy is no longer a dirty word."

31. Of course Justice Stewart's reference in the majority opinion to "outmoded taboos," 414 U.S. at 641 n.9, provided a hint of sorts, as did Justice Powell's separate observation that the "initial primacy" of these non-administrative rationales cast "a shadow over these cases," id. at 653 (concurring in result), but hints do not a holding make, and indeed the hinters themselves might have been influenced by the litigation strategy of the rule's defenders.

32. In both cases, the rules were so badly fitted to the currently *articulated* purposes (curbing extramarital sex in Griswold, maintaining capable and continuous classroom instruction in LaFleur) that their invalidation as irrational invasions of liberty became fairly simple.

may be unwilling to defend a contraceptive ban or a discrimination against illegitimates, say, in terms of the supposed immorality of non-procreative or extramarital sexual behavior; so few people may continue to share a belief in such immorality that state officials may simply be embarrassed to assert it as a justification. One may worry, particularly in the case of a *statute* attacked in this way, whether the handiwork of a lawmaking body should be so heavily dependent upon the willingness of the executive to advance the proper sustaining argument. But a legislature can defend its predecessors' enactments when the executive will not,[33] and if *no* current government spokesman is willing to do so, then it may be said both that the continuing legitimacy of the law is problematic[34] and that enforcing the law would offend the principle that laws, unlike naked commands, must be understandable to those affected.[35]

The fifth technique associated with intermediate review is that of limiting the use of afterthought. However weighty an objective, however closely it might fit the challenged rule, and however persuasively it is currently articulated by the rule's defenders, that objective should not be credited, once the rule is subjected to intermediate scrutiny, if there are convincing reasons to believe that the objective is being supplied purely by hindsight—as one of several "after-the-fact rationalizations"[36] invoked to justify a rule that was not in fact adopted with the objective in mind.[37] When either the nature of the classification challenged or the character of the deprivation attacked warrants intermediate scrutiny, "inquiry into the actual purposes" of the rule,[38] as illuminated by its language, its structure, and its history, warrants the rule's invalidation when it can be defended only with considerations that did not in fact contribute to its enactment.[39] This technique is most clearly seen in

---

33. See, e.g., Ely, "United States v. Lovett: Litigating the Separation of Powers," 10 Harv.C.R.—C.L.L.Rev. 1, 10–11 (1975).

34. Such a view presupposes that legitimacy turns on more than a law's proper enactment and the failure of succeeding legislatures to repeal it. Cf. Kennedy, "Legal Formality," 2 J. Legal Stud. 351 (1973). On this view, the legitimacy of a law poses a question for each generation to address anew. Its legitimacy does not inhere in the past alone; its locus is also the present and the future. And the measure of such legitimacy is not the momentary coincidence of alienated wills at the instant the social contract is struck but is instead the gradual evolution of shared values—values shared (not merely overlapping) as they could never be in a purely contractarian vision.

35. Note the close connection between this principle and the limits on government's use of irrebuttable presumptions, discussed in § 16–34, infra.

36. Cleveland Board of Education v. LaFleur, 414 U.S. 632, 653 (1974) (Powell, J., concurring in result). See also Vlandis v. Kline, 412 U.S. 441, 449 (1973).

37. See Bowen v. Owens, 106 S.Ct. 1881, 1887 (1986) (Marshall, J., dissenting, joined by Brennan, J.); Schweiker v. Wilson, 450 U.S. 221, 245 (1981) (Powell, J., dissenting, joined by Brennan, Marshall & Stevens, JJ.); United States Railroad Retirement Board v. Fritz, 449 U.S. 166, 184 (1980) (Brennan, J., dissenting, joined by Marshall, J.); id. at 180 (Stevens, J., concurring in the judgment), all discussed in § 16–3, supra. This type of limitation on judicial acceptance of conceivable bases is distinct from that achieved by requiring current articulation. See note 23, supra.

38. Weinberger v. Wiesenfeld, 420 U.S. 636, 648 (1975).

39. The Court has suggested in dictum that "if a rule were expressly mandated by Congress or the President," the Court "might presume that any interest which might rationally be served by the rule did in fact give rise to its adoption." Hampton v. Mow Sun Wong, 426 U.S. 88, 103 (1976) (refusing, however, to apply such a presumption in defense of rules promulgated by "the Civil Service Commission, the Postal Service, the General Services Administration, or the Department of Health, Education, and Welfare," id. at 105). But

Mississippi University For Women v. Hogan,[40] in which the Court rejected Mississippi's defense that its policy of permitting only women to attend a state nursing school was justified as compensating for discrimination against women. The Court held that "although the State recited a 'benign, compensatory purpose,' it failed to establish that the alleged objective is the actual purpose underlying the discriminatory classification."

In part, such a principle can be explained as enhancing political accountability: a legislature or agency that cannot count on the post-hoc rationalizations of those charged with responsibility to enforce and defend its enactments or promulgations might be motivated to ventilate more fully the considerations underlying those enactments.[41] It is conceivable, of course, that a lawmaking body realizing how much will be made of its stated reasons would be moved to generate a convincing record, but not to change its actual deliberations or its ultimate conclusions. But even if this occasionally occurs, it seems sound to resist upholding a significant deprivation of liberty or a substantial discrimination on a basis that did not occur to those responsible for the injury or on a basis that was not within their purview.[42] In a sense, such resistance deprives the enacting body of nothing it deliberately (and properly) sought but only of the windfall it would receive if the product of its work were to survive for reasons that played no proper role, and perhaps no role at all, in the enacting process. Moreover, if the only reason a rule is struck down is that its justification has been conceived only after the fact, re-enactment for the proper reason remains a possibility.[43] And from the perspective of the individual adversely affected by the results of a lawmaking process, justice requires at least some sensitivity to whether the process that produced a challenged rule was itself an example of the very evil to be avoided—such as "a traditional way of thinking about females" [44]—rather than a considered effort to overcome that evil—by carefully deciding, for example, "to compensate for past . . . discrimi-

subsequent decisions such as Califano v. Goldfarb, 430 U.S. 199 (1977), clearly hold that not even Congress is entitled to a presumption of the sort described when intermediate scrutiny is properly employed.

40. 458 U.S. 718, 730 (1982).

41. Compare McGautha v. California, 402 U.S. 183, 256, 259–65 (1971) (Brennan, J., joined by Douglas and Marshall, JJ., dissenting); see id. at 265: "[T]he protection against arbitrary and discriminatory action embodied in the Due Process Clause requires that state power be exerted only through mechanisms that assure that fundamental choices among competing state policies be explicitly made by some responsible organ of the State."

42. See, e.g., Hampton v. Mow Sun Wong, 426 U.S. 88, 115 (1976) (rejecting, as justifications for Civil Service Commission ban on federal employment of aliens, "interests which . . . are not . . . properly the business of the Commission" as well as interests properly its business but not the

subject of "any considered evaluation" by the Commission).

43. The "anti-afterthought" principle thus bears some resemblance to a "remand" to the legislature. Cf. A. Bickel, The Least Dangerous Branch 111–98 (1962); R. Keeton, Venturing To Do Justice (1969); J. Sax, Defending the Environment 175–92 (1971); Monaghan, "The Supreme Court, 1974 Term—Foreword: Constitutional Common Law," 89 Harv.L.Rev. 1 (1975). For further development of this theme, See, G. Calabresi, A Common Law for the Age of Statutes (1982).

44. Califano v. Goldfarb, 430 U.S. 199, 223 (1977) (Stevens, J., concurring in result). Justice Stevens has often expressed a concern about classifications which seem to be based on habitual or stereotypical thinking rather than upon any difference properly deemed relevant to the disparate treatment of the disadvantaged group. See, e.g., Michael M. v. Sonoma County Superior Court, 450 U.S. 464, 501 (1981) (Stevens, J.,

nation against women." [45]   Similarly, an employment discrimination against aliens promulgated after a "considered evaluation of the relative desirability of a simple exclusionary rule on the one hand, or the value . . . . of enlarging the pool of eligible employees on the other," [46] may be fairer than one promulgated for no reason beyond the habitual assumption that aliens are less worthy than citizens.[47]

Eisenstadt v. Baird [48] illustrates a somewhat less conventional and perhaps a less candid application of this "anti-afterthought" technique. The statutory scheme invalidated in that case made it more difficult for single persons to obtain contraceptives than for married persons to do so; in finding the discrimination irrational, the Court refused to measure it against the purpose, articulated in the state's argument to the Court and by the state courts, of discouraging premarital sexual intercourse, because "[i]t would be plainly unreasonable to assume that Massachusetts has prescribed pregnancy and the birth of an unwanted child as punishment for fornication." [49]   This was so partly because of the strange "scheme of values that assumption would attribute to the State," [50] and partly because "the ban on distribution of contraceptives to unmarried persons has at best a marginal relation to the proffered objective . . . Even on the assumption that the fear of pregnancy operates as a deterrent to fornication, the . . . statute is . . . so riddled with exceptions that deterrence of premarital sex cannot reasonably be regarded as its aim." [51]   The upshot is that, when the legislative history is unclear but is consistent with a currently articulated purpose,[52] power nonetheless reposes in the Court to deny that purpose serious consideration when it is implausible or perverse to suppose that the purpose in fact underlay the challenged legislation.[53]   In such a case, the Court may treat the purpose as though it were supplied simply by hindsight, even

---

dissenting) ("[T]he possibility that such a habitual attitude may reflect nothing more than an irrational prejudice makes it an insufficient justification for discriminatory treatment that is otherwise blatantly unfair."); cf. Mathews v. Lucas, 427 U.S. 495, 520–521 (1976) (Stevens, J., dissenting) (arguing that "th[e] tradition of disfavor [toward illegitimates]" demands that "the Court should be especially vigilant in examining any classification which involves illegitimacy").

45. Califano v. Webster, 430 U.S. 313, 318 (1977) (per curiam).

46. Hampton v. Mow Sun Wong, 426 U.S. 88, 115 (1976).

47. "Habit, rather than analysis, makes it seem acceptable and natural to distinguish between male and female, alien and citizen, legitimate and illegitimate." Mathews v. Lucas, 427 U.S. 495, 520 (1976) (Stevens, J., dissenting). To recognize that the acceptability of a tangible injury—loss of a job, for example—may depend on the *process by which*, and the *reasons for which*, the injury was inflicted, is simply to acknowledge the morally and legally obvious: being lynched is different from receiving a

fair trial, even if the "end result" looks the same.

48. 405 U.S. 438 (1972).

49. Id. at 448.

50. Id.

51. Id. at 448–49. A much more satisfactory rationale was suggested by Justice Stevens in Carey v. Population Services International, 431 U.S. 678, 712 (1977) (concurring opinion), reasoning that making contraceptives unavailable to unmarried teen-agers in order to underscore the state's disapproval of sexual conduct by unwed minors would be like forbidding the use of safety helmets to dramatize state disapproval of motorcycles: an utterly perverse means of either control or propaganda.

52. See 405 U.S. at 442.

53. See also Trimble v. Gordon, 430 U.S. 762, 768–69 n.13 (1977) (refusing to consider promotion of legitimate family relationships as a justification for a rule that prevented illegitimates from inheriting by intestate succession from their fathers, but allowed such intestate inheritance from mothers, since this "purpose is not apparent from the statute" and is hard to square with "the

though the record leaves that matter in some doubt.[54] As the Court put it in *Trimble v. Gordon*, whenever more than minimum rationality may be demanded, "the Equal Protection Clause requires more than the mere incantation of a proper state purpose." [55]

The sixth and final technique of intermediate review is to require that the legal scheme under challenge be altered so as to permit rebuttal in individual cases even if the scheme is not struck down altogether.[56] In *Craig v. Boren*, the Court summarized its approach in cases of intermediate scrutiny involving gender: "In light of the weak congruence between gender and the characteristic or trait that gender purported to represent, it was necessary that the legislatures choose either to realign their substantive laws in a gender-neutral fashion, or to adopt procedures for identifying those instances where the sex-centered generalization actually comported to fact." [57] As examples of the latter alternative, the Court identified *Stanley v. Illinois* [58] and *Cleveland Board of Education v. LaFleur*,[59] two of the "irrebuttable presumption" decisions considered below in § 16–34. In effect, the Court was signaling what had been suggested in *Weinberger v. Salfi* [60]—that the invalidation of irrebuttable presumptions was but one of several techniques included in intermediate scrutiny, and that the technique, far from representing a death-knell for the legislative use of per se rules, simply requires legislatures to proceed on a less wholesale basis, if possible, when certain sensitive matters are at stake.[61] If it is understood that this approach is taken only when the Court might otherwise have invalidated the legislation more sweepingly, it emerges not as a threat to legislative flexibility but as a restrained form of intervention compared with the more conventional form of total invalidation.[62]

All six of the techniques canvassed here respond to a perception that the all-or-nothing choice between minimum rationality and strict

---

difference in the rights of illegitimate children in the estates of their mothers and their fathers").

54. Professor Gunther's criticism of the Court's approach in Eisenstadt v. Baird, see "The Supreme Court, 1971 Term—Foreword: In Search of Evolving Doctrine on a Changing Court: A Model For a Newer Equal Protection," 86 Harv.L.Rev. 1, 34–36 (1972), treated the Court as guilty of a "peremptory rejection of proffered state purposes." Id. at 35. If the only proper form of intermediate scrutiny consisted of a rule limiting judicial consideration to currently "proffered" or articulated purposes, the criticism would be well founded. But if one accepts a principle against justification by afterthought, then it is not the case that *only* "a value-laden appraisal of the legitimacy of ends," id., could explain the Baird decision. See also note 23, supra.

55. 430 U.S. 762, 769 (1977).

56. Note that this differs from the technique of requiring close fit employed in Cleburne Living Center, discussed supra. Requiring individualization on the adminis-

trative level is not the same as simply striking down the classification as applied after reviewing the result of its application in a particular case. The former remedy results in a procedurally different legal regime for future cases; the latter merely provides one-shot relief.

57. 429 U.S. 190, 199 (1976).

58. 405 U.S. 645 (1972).

59. 414 U.S. 632 (1974).

60. 422 U.S. 749, 772–77 (1975).

61. When they are not, or when the group disadvantaged is in no way suspect, the Court has required no fine tuning. See, e.g., Lyng v. Castillo, 106 S.Ct. 2727 (1986) (upholding a classification which gives all close relatives who live together a lower food stamp allotment than more distant relatives or groups of unrelated persons who live together, because of an irrebuttable presumption that close relatives who live together purchase food as a group and dine together.)

62. See § 16–34, infra.

scrutiny ill-suits the broad range of situations arising under the equal protection clause, many of which are best dealt with neither through the virtual rubber-stamp of truly minimal review nor through the virtual death-blow of truly strict scrutiny, but through methods more sensitive to risks of injustice than the former and yet less blind to the needs of governmental flexibility than the latter. There may well be situations—gender discrimination is probably one [63]—in which the appropriate level of scrutiny is indeed strict rather than intermediate, and in which the availability of the "middle tier" serves to divert pressure that might otherwise develop for strict review. Yet it seems just as likely in such situations that the alternative, if intermediate review were to be foreclosed, would be retreat into a largely meaningless requirement of rationality.[64] In any event, there seems little likelihood that equal protection analysis will ever again be neatly separable into two dramatically polar forms of review; whatever formulas they announce, judges are understandably reluctant to constrain themselves with a method that leaves them no choice between total affirmation and total negation.[65]

§ 16–33. Identifying the Circumstances That Trigger Intermediate Review

During the Burger era, the Court increasingly departed from the use of minimum rationality, expanding the categories of classifications which are subjected to heightened scrutiny. Although the Court itself has not always been candid about its use of intermediate review,[1] this section describes those circumstances in which, whether overtly or covertly, the Court has employed some form of close review.

Broadly speaking, there are two circumstances that trigger heightened scrutiny. The first involves infringement of "important", although not necessarily "fundamental", rights or interests.[2] The extent to which the Court's scrutiny is heightened depends both on the nature of the interest and the degree to which it is infringed. Thus, in *Plyler v. Doe*,[3] the Court adopted a requirement that the state's goal be "substantial" when faced with a classification which served to deprive illegal alien children of any education, an interest which the Court explicitly held to be "importan[t]" in "maintaining our basic institutions".[4] Significant in the Court's decision to heighten scrutiny was the

---

63. See §§ 16–25 to 16–30, supra.

64. Compare §§ 16–2 to 16–5, supra.

65. Judges might reject this polarity by insisting on a finer subdivision, see, e.g., San Antonio Independent School District v. Rodriguez, 411 U.S. 1, 98–99 (1973) (Marshall, J., dissenting) (arguing that the Court "has applied a spectrum of standards in reviewing discrimination allegedly violative of the Equal Protection Clause"), or—at the other extreme—by rejecting subdivisions and tiers altogether. See, e.g., Craig v. Boren, 429 U.S. 190, 211–212 (1976) (Stevens, J., concurring) (arguing that the Court "actually appl[ies] a single standard in a reasonably consistent fashion").

§ 16–33

1. See §§ 16–2, 16–3, supra.

2. Those rights explicitly deemed fundamental for purposes of equal protection strict scrutiny are the right to interstate travel, see § 16–8, supra; the right to equal voting opportunity, see § 16–10, supra; and the right to equal litigation opportunity, see § 16–11, supra.

3. 457 U.S. 202 (1982), discussed in §§ 16–3, 16–23 supra.

4. 457 U.S. at 224. The Plyler Court noted that, under San Antonio Independent School District v. Rodriguez, 411 U.S. 1 (1973), public education is not a funda-

risk that such deprivation would serve to "creat[e] and perpetuat[e] . . . a subclass of illiterates within our boundaries".[5]

Likewise, in *Hampton v. Mow Sun Wong*,[6] infringement of the interest of aliens in employment in the federal competitive civil service was struck down specifically because of how broadly the "liberty" of aliens is restricted by their exclusion from such a large part of the economy.[7] By contrast, the Court in *New York Transit Authority v. Beazer*[8] reviewed only for minimum rationality, and casually upheld, a ban on the employment of all narcotic drug users, including methadone users, despite the district court's conclusion that no "rational" reason exists for excluding from non-safety-sensitive jobs those persons successfully maintained in a methadone treatment program for at least a year.[9] But the ban applied only to jobs with the New York City Transit Authority. One might envision heightened scrutiny and a different result if such a ban were instituted for all employment by the City of New York.

The Court has not always *referred* to the importance of the interest at stake when heightening its level of scrutiny, but it is hard to believe that importance was not at least a factor in the closer look taken by the Court where governmental deprivations affected the interest of the individual in receiving such subsistence benefits as food stamps.[10] That

---

mental right. See § 16–7, supra, §§ 16–52, 16–58, infra.

5. 457 U.S. at 230. When the Court originally held the interest in education not to be "fundamental", it suggested the possibility of stricter judicial scrutiny of an absolute deprivation of the interest in education—at least if public education were made available to the well-to-do on a tuition basis rather than simply being eliminated altogether. See Rodriguez, 411 U.S. at 25 n.60 ("If elementary and secondary education were made available by the State only to those able to pay a tuition assessed against each pupil, there would be a clearly defined class of 'poor' people—definable in terms of their inability to pay the prescribed sum—who would be absolutely precluded from receiving an education. That case would present a far more compelling set of circumstances for judicial assistance than the case before us today."). Cf. Vlandis v. Kline, 412 U.S. 441, 459 (1973) (White, J., concurring) (concluding that infringement on "the interest . . . of obtaining a higher education" by a one-year residency requirement violates equal protection).

6. 426 U.S. 88 (1976).

7. See id. at 102 ("The added disadvantage resulting from the enforcement of the rule—ineligibility for employment in a major sector of the economy—is of sufficient significance to be characterized as a deprivation of an interest in liberty."). The impact on employment may also help ex-

plain the Court's heightened review when governmental deprivations have impaired the interest of the individual in retaining a driver's license. See Bell v. Burson, 402 U.S. 535, 539 (1971) ("Once licenses are issued, as in petitioner's case, their continued possession may become essential in the pursuit of a livelihood."); cf. Dixon v. Love, 431 U.S. 105 (1977) (upholding summary license suspension for traffic safety reasons, based on number of prior traffic convictions, with hardship exceptions for persons depending on driver's license to earn their living.)

8. 440 U.S. 568 (1979), discussed in § 16–4, supra.

9. Id. at 578. The Court found that approximately 75% of patients who have been in a methadone treatment program for at least a year have no drug or alcohol problems. See id. at 576 n.10.

10. See United States Department of Agriculture v. Murry, 413 U.S. 508 (1973) (invalidating denial of food stamps to members of households containing dependents of taxpayers who are themselves ineligible for food stamps); New Jersey Welfare Rights Organization v. Cahill, 411 U.S. 619 (1973) (per curiam) (invalidating denial of state provision of financial assistance and other services to two-adult households with minor children only if they contained illegitimate children, two unmarried adults, or the child of only one adult not adopted by the other).

the Court has found it easy to ignore this precedent [11] is only further argument for conducting such heightened scrutiny more explicitly, and for articulating the criteria which are thought to make an interest "important".

The unusual importance of the interest in suitable housing at least arguably played a role in triggering intermediate review in *City of Cleburne v. Cleburne Living Center*,[12] where the Court subjected to covertly heightened scrutiny the city's denial of a use permit to a group of 13 mentally retarded men and women who wished to live in a group home in that city. In *Cleburne*, the Court was faced with at least the suggestion that the potential occupants of respondents' group home would be left without appropriate shelter.[13] The increasingly evident plight of the homeless in the 1980s, caused in large measure by deinstitutionalization, puts into high relief the importance of the interest in having a decent place to live, without being put to a choice between sleeping on sidewalks and seeking to be shelved in a warehouse.[14]

An examination of the interests whose impairment seems to have triggered intermediate review highlights a distinction between rights whose infringement serves to disempower,[15] and those whose infringement violates a norm of privacy or purely negative liberty. The latter give rise only to government obligations not to interfere with their exercise,[16] while the former may give rise to more affirmative obliga-

---

11. See Lyng v. Castillo, 106 S.Ct. 2727, 2729 (1986) (upholding as rational a statutory classification treating parents, children and siblings ["close relatives"] living together, but not more distant relatives or groups of unrelated persons living together, as a single "household" for purposes of reducing food stamp eligibility and benefits, despite the fact that "the loss or reduction of benefits will impose a severe hardship on a needy family, and may be especially harmful to the affected young children for whom an adequate diet is essential.").

12. 473 U.S. 432 (1985), discussed in §§ 16–3, 16–31, supra.

13. See City of Cleburne v. Cleburne Living Center, 473 U.S. 432 (1985), Brief for Respondents at 41 ("To accept the argument that retardation alone disqualifies one from living normally amongst the community of citizens would run contrary not only to the fundamental principle of the Equal Protection Clause but also be legislative trends and professional understandings. The nearly inevitable result of such a determination would be the reinstitutionalization of America's retarded people and increased efforts to isolate them from society.").

14. The Court has found the interest in housing not to be fundamental, see Lindsey v. Normet, 405 U.S. 56, 74 (1972). But the increase in numbers of the homeless has

since led to much litigation. At least one state has found a statutorily imposed affirmative duty to provide shelter. See Hodge v. Ginsberg, 303 S.E.2d 245 (W.Va. 1983). In addition, it has been argued that some state constitutional provisions may create an affirmative duty to provide shelter. See Note, "A Right to Shelter for the Homeless in New York State," 61 N.Y.U.L. Rev. 272 (1986) (arguing that the "affirmative duty to aid the needy" found under the New York Constitution should be extended to mandate provision of shelter to the homeless).

15. Denial of the ability to exercise these rights tends to lead to the creation of a permanent underclass. See, e.g., City of Cleburne v. Cleburne Living Center, 473 U.S. 432 (1985) (shelter); Plyler v. Doe, 457 U.S. 202 (1982) (education); Memorial Hospital v. Maricopa County, 415 U.S. 250 (1974) (medical services); United States Department of Agriculture v. Murry, 413 U.S. 508 (1973) (food); Shapiro v. Thompson, 394 U.S. 618 (1969) (welfare benefits).

16. See, e.g., Regan v. Taxation With Representation, 461 U.S. 540 (1983) (finding that Congress' decision not to subsidize the exercise of the first amendment right to lobby, even where it does provide tax benefits to qualifying veterans' groups who engage in lobbying, does not infringe that first amendment right, as long as the ability to lobby is itself not denied or penalized,

tions on the part of the state; classifications absolutely denying them are more closely scrutinized and more likely to be struck down.[17]

To the extent the Court views abortion rights as among the second group, it is not surprising that classifications indirectly impinging on levels of affordable access to those rights should not be subjected to specially heightened scrutiny.[18] However, the abortion rights recognized by the Court in *Roe v. Wade*[19] can perhaps best be understood primarily as rights whose impairment serves to disempower women.[20] Thus understood, classifications implicating support for abortion rights should trigger at least an intermediate level of review.[21]

A second broad circumstance in which intermediate review has been triggered involves government's use of sensitive, although not necessarily suspect, criteria of classification.[22] Rules discriminating against aliens are subjected to a judicial approach clearly more demanding than the basic requirement of minimum rationality and yet sometimes less demanding, particularly when federal laws or regula-

---

and therefore declining to apply a heightened form of scrutiny). See also Buckley v. Valeo, 424 U.S. 1 (1976) (upholding a statute providing public funding for candidates who enter primary campaigns, but not for candidates who do not run in party primaries).

17. See Tribe, "Unraveling National League of Cities: The New Federalism and Affirmative Rights to Essential Governmental Services," 90 Harv.L.Rev. 1065, 1084–1090 (1977) (arguing for incompletely enforceable individual rights against the government for certain basic services).

18. See Harris v. McRae, 448 U.S. 297, 316 (1980) (upholding, after minimal scrutiny, severe limitations on the use of federal funds to reimburse the cost of medically necessary abortions, because "although government may not place obstacles in the path of a woman's exercise of her freedom of choice, it need not remove those not of its own creation."); Maher v. Roe, 432 U.S. 464 (1977) (upholding, after minimal scrutiny, state decision to fund childbirth but not elective abortion), both discussed in § 15–10, supra.

19. 410 U.S. 113 (1973).

20. See Tribe, "Commentary—The Abortion Funding Conundrum: Inalienable Rights, Affirmative Duties, and the Dilemma of Dependence," 99 Harv.L.Rev. 330 (1985) (arguing that abortion rights are best seen as concerned with structuring power relationships to avoid the creation or perpetuation of hierarchy in which women are perennially subjugated).

21. Cf. Framingham Clinic, Inc. v. Board of Selectmen of Southborough, 373 Mass. 279, 367 N.E.2d 606 (1977) (subjecting to heightened scrutiny on the basis of Maher v. Roe, 432 U.S. 464 (1977), and invalidating for want of "acceptable justifi-

cation", a town zoning ordinance which prohibited abortion clinics but not clinics which offered other lawful medical procedures).

22. The traditional and paradigmatic suspect classifications are, of course, those based on race or national origin. See §§ 16–13 to 16–21, supra. Some cases of intermediate review combine sensitive criteria of classification with important liberties or benefits. See, e.g., City of Cleburne v. Cleburne Living Center, 473 U.S. 432 (1985) (mentally retarded persons cannot be deprived of housing); Plyler v. Doe, 457 U.S. 202 (1982) (illegal alien children cannot be deprived of education); Hampton v. Mow Sun Wong, 426 U.S. 88 (1976) (aliens cannot be deprived of federal civil service employment); United States Department of Agriculture v. Moreno, 413 U.S. 528 (1973) (households containing unrelated members cannot be deprived of food stamps); New Jersey Welfare Rights Organization v. Cahill, 411 U.S. 619 (1973) (per curiam) (households containing illegitimate children, two unmarried adults, or the child of only one adult not adopted by the other cannot be deprived of financial assistance and other services); Stanley v. Illinois, 405 U.S. 645 (1972) (unwed fathers cannot be deprived of child custody). In other intermediate review cases, an important liberty or benefit is at stake but no sensitive criterion is involved. See, e.g., United States Department of Agriculture v. Murry, 413 U.S. 508 (1973) (households containing dependents of ineligible persons cannot be deprived of foodstamps). And in still other intermediate review cases, a sensitive criterion is involved but no independently important liberty or benefit is at stake. See, e.g., Bernal v. Fainter, 467 U.S. 216 (1984) (aliens cannot be deprived of opportunity to be notaries public).

tions are involved,[23] than the scrutiny employed to review rules burdening racial and ancestral minorities.[24] Rules discriminating against illegitimates are now explicitly subjected to an intermediate form of heightened review.[25] Gender discrimination similarly occupies an intermediate position.[26] Likewise, the Court has implicitly subjected a classification based on mental retardation to intermediate review despite explicit efforts to deny that it was doing so.[27]

The Court has never provided a coherent explanation of the characteristics which, either overtly or covertly, trigger intermediate review.[28] Status as a supposedly "discrete and insular minorit[y]" [29] has been considered important, both in finding some classifications suspect,[30] and in evaluating other classifications to decide they are not suspect.[31] The

---

23. See Mathews v. Diaz, 426 U.S. 67 (1976).

24. See § 16–23, supra. Classifications based on alienage are operatively subjected to a form of intermediate scrutiny achieved by the Court formally finding that classifications based on alienage are sometimes "suspect" and subject to "strict scrutiny", see Graham v. Richardson, 403 U.S. 365 (1971) (subjecting to strict scrutiny and invalidating a citizenship requirement for receipt of welfare benefits), and sometimes, when a statute requires citizenship as a qualification for some governmental positions at least theoretically political in nature, subject only to minimum rationality. See, e.g., Cabell v. Chavez-Salido, 454 U.S. 432 (1982) (subjecting to rational basis review and upholding a citizenship requirement for probation officers); Ambach v. Norwick, 441 U.S. 68 (1979) (subjecting to rational basis review and upholding a citizenship requirement for public school teachers); Foley v. Connelie, 435 U.S. 291 (1978) (subjecting to rational basis review and upholding a citizenship requirement for state troopers); Sugarman v. Dougall, 413 U.S. 634 (1973) (subjecting to rational basis review and upholding a citizenship requirement for elective and important non-elective positions in state government). While this list might suggest the total evisceration of judicial scrutiny of classifications based on alienage, the use of heightened scrutiny does continue. See, e.g., Bernal v. Fainter, 467 U.S. 216 (1984) (subjecting to strict scrutiny and invalidating a citizenship requirement for notaries public).

25. The Court has enunciated a test under which, in order to be upheld, challenged illegitimacy-based classifications must be "substantially related to a legitimate state interest." Mills v. Habluetzel, 456 U.S. 91, 99 (1982). See § 16–24, supra.

26. The Court has enunciated a test under which, in order to be upheld, challenged gender-based classifications must be "substantially related" to an "important

governmental objective". Mississippi University for Women v. Hogan, 458 U.S. 718, 724 (1982) (citation omitted); Craig v. Boren, 429 U.S. 190, 197 (1976). See §§ 16–25 to 16–29, supra.

27. See City of Cleburne v. Cleburne Living Center, 473 U.S. 432 (1985), discussed in § 16–31, supra. It has also been argued that those classifications commonly understood as penalizing the right to travel, see § 16–8, supra, are actually instances in which the Court found newcomers to a state in some degree a suspect class, and thus subjected classifications which disadvantage them to heightened judicial review. See McCoy, "Recent Equal Protection Decisions—Fundamental Right to Travel or 'Newcomers' as a Suspect Class?," 28 Vand.L.Rev. 987 (1975).

28. Indeed, it has been argued that a more useful approach might do away with sharply differentiated levels of scrutiny altogether, replacing them with a more contextual examination of each classification. This approach is most clearly reflected in Justice Stevens' equal protection method. For a discussion of this jurisprudence, indicating ways in which such an approach is of value given recent developments in the Court's equal protection methodology, see Note, "Justice Stevens' Equal Protection Jurisprudence," 100 Harv.L.Rev. 1146 (1987).

29. United States v. Carolene Products Co., 304 U.S. 144, 152–153 n.4 (1938) (dictum).

30. See Graham v. Richardson, 403 U.S. 365, 372 (1971) (citing Carolene Products Co., 304 U.S. at 152–53 n.4) (finding alienage suspect).

31. See, e.g., Lyng v. Castillo, 106 S.Ct. 2727, 2729 (1986) (declining to subject to heightened scrutiny a classification based on close family relationship); Massachusetts Board of Retirement v. Murgia, 427 U.S. 307, 313 (1976) (per curiam) (declining to subject to heightened scrutiny a classification based on age); San Antonio Inde-

risk that particular classifications may serve to stereotype and stigmatize has also supplied a rationale for heightened scrutiny, particularly in the case of gender.[32] Personal immutability of characteristic is sometimes used by the Court to explain a requirement of heightened scrutiny, as in the case of illegitimacy.[33] Similarly, the Court has sometimes found the class's lack of responsibility for its own defining characteristic to be relevant.[34] Many of these factors were discussed by the Court when it decided to apply heightened scrutiny, despite ostensible application of the minimum rationality test, in evaluating a classification disadvantaging the mentally retarded in City of *Cleburne v. Cleburne Living Center*.[35] Likewise, in its most recent explanation of the indicia of suspectness that trigger heightened scrutiny, the Court in *Lyng v. Castillo* [36] held that the class composed of close relatives living together was not quasi-suspect because, "as a historical matter, [members of the class] have not been subjected to discrimination; they do not exhibit obvious, immutable, or distinguishing characteristics that define them as a discrete group; and they are not a minority or politically powerless." [37]

While the Court has increasingly hidden its uses of intermediate review behind a mask of minimum rationality, greater candor about what criteria trigger heightened scrutiny [38] might suggest that classifi-

pendent School District v. Rodriguez, 411 U.S. 1, 28 (1973) (declining to subject to heightened scrutiny a classification based on residence in a less wealthy school district). See generally J. Ely, Democracy and Distrust, 135–179 (1980).

32. See Kahn v. Shevin, 416 U.S. 351, 357 (1974) (Brennan, J., dissenting); Frontiero v. Richardson, 411 U.S. 677, 684–85 (1973) (plurality opinion). Stigma has also been suggested as a basis for heightened scrutiny in the case of "benign" discrimination. See, e.g., Regents of the University of California v. Bakke, 438 U.S. 265, 360 (1978) (opinion of Brennan, White, Marshall & Blackmun, JJ.), discussed in § 16–22, supra. It has been argued that substantive rather than purely process-based constitutional values support court protection of the victims of racial and ethnic prejudice, and that, in general, "procedural" failure cannot explain heightened review of government actions injuring various minorities. See Tribe, "The Puzzling Persistence of Process-Based Constitutional Theories," 89 Yale L.J. 1063 (1980); Ackerman, "Beyond *Carolene Products*," 98 Harv.L.Rev. 713, 742–746 (1985); Brilmayer, "*Carolene*, Conflicts, and the Fate of the 'Inside-Outsider'," 134 U.Pa.L. Rev. 1291 (1986).

33. See, e.g., Weber v. Aetna Casualty & Surety Co., 406 U.S. 164, 176 (1972) (suggesting that heightened scrutiny is triggered by invidious discrimination based on "status of birth"). See also Sugarman

v. Dougall, 413 U.S. 634, 657 (1973) (Rehnquist, J., dissenting) (arguing that suspectness should be found only in the case of classifications based upon "status . . . which cannot be altered by an individual" and that alienage should therefore not be found suspect).

34. See Mathews v. Lucas, 427 U.S. 495, 505 (1976) ("[T]he legal status of illegitimacy, however defined, is, like race or national origin, a characteristic determined by causes not within the control of the illegitimate individual, and it bears no relation to the individual's ability to participate in and contribute to society.").

35. 473 U.S. 432 (1985). In Cleburne, the Court, while declining to find mental retardation even "quasi-suspect", id. at 440, made reference to the history of " 'unfair and often grotesque mistreatment' of the retarded", id. at 437 (citing Cleburne Living Center v. Cleburne, 726 F.2d 191, 197 (5th Cir. 1984)), as well as to their sometime political powerlessness and the immutability of their situations, see id. at 443, before covertly subjecting the challenged classification to intermediate review.

36. 106 S.Ct. 2727 (1986).

37. Id. at 2729. For a thoughtful disaggregation of these often falsely lumped indicia, see Ackerman, supra note 32, at 718–40.

38. See § 16–3, supra.

cations based on age [39] and handicap [40] as well as mental illness or disability might require close review.[41]

Classifications based on sexual orientation certainly merit a searching judicial approach. Not only is the characteristic of homosexuality or heterosexuality central to the personal identities of those singled out by laws based on sexual orientation,[42] but homosexuals in particular seem to satisfy all of the Court's implicit criteria of suspectness. As subjects of age-old discrimination and disapproval, homosexuals form virtually a discrete and insular minority.[43] Their sexual orientation is in all likelihood "a characteristic determined by causes not within [their] control," [44] and is, if not immutable, at least "extremely difficult to alter." [45] Further, and in contrast with a characteristic like mental retardation, homosexuality bears no relation at all to the individual's ability to contribute fully to society.[46] Homosexuality should thus be added—and openly—to the list of classifications that trigger increased judicial solicitude.[47]

Although the Court has been less explicit about elaborating it, an additional consideration appears to have played a role from time to time in its decisions to intensify the level of scrutiny to an intermediate level. If a rule is imbedded in a setting characterized by institutional rigidity to change, so that shifting social and moral norms are less likely to be reflected in modifications of the rule, the propriety and

---

39. See § 16–31, supra. But see Massachusetts Board of Retirement v. Murgia, 427 U.S. 307 (1976) (declining to apply heightened judicial scrutiny to a classification based on age).

40. See § 16–31, supra.

41. Ironically, in declining to find the mentally retarded a quasi-suspect class, Justice White, writing for the Court, both revealed the Court's doctrinal inconsistency and provided a list of those classifications which, like mental retardation, would probably result in tacitly heightened review if the Court were to be more candid: "[I]f the large and amorphous class of the mentally retarded were deemed quasi-suspect . . . it would be difficult to distinguish a variety of other groups who have perhaps immutable disabilities setting them off from others, who cannot themselves mandate the desired legislative responses, and who can claim some degree of prejudice from at least part of the public at large. One need only mention in this respect only the aging, the disabled, the mentally ill and the infirm. We are reluctant to set out on that course, and we decline to do so." City of Cleburne v. Cleburne Living Center, 473 U.S. 432, 444 (1985).

42. See § 15–21, supra.

43. See J. Ely, Democracy and Distrust, 163 (1980) ("It is . . . a combination of the factors of prejudice and hideability that renders classifications that disadvantage homosexuals suspicious.").

44. Mathews v. Lucas, 427 U.S. 495, 505 (1976) (describing illegitimacy).

45. Note, "The Constitutionality of Laws Forbidding Private Homosexual Conduct," 72 Mich.L.Rev. 1613, 1626 (1974).

46. See Resolution of the American Psychiatric Association, December 15, 1973 ("[H]omosexuality *per se* implies no impairment in judgment, stability, reliability or general social or vocational capabilities. . . . In the reasoned judgment of most American psychiatrists today, homosexuality *per se* does not constitute any form of mental disease.").

47. See also generally Note, "The Constitutional Status of Sexual Orientation: Homosexuality as a Suspect Classification," 98 Harv.L.Rev. 1285 (1985); Note, "An Argument for the Application of Equal Protection Heightened Scrutiny to Classifications Based on Homosexuality," 57 S.Cal.L.Rev. 797 (1984).

The fact that the Court in Bowers v. Hardwick, 106 S.Ct. 2841 (1986), went out of its way to create a line between heterosexuals and homosexuals, where there was none in the challenged sodomy statute, merely to preserve prosecution of homosexuals under the law from constitutional infirmity, indicates how unlikely it is that homosexuality will be deemed quasi-suspect in the near future. But compare Brown v. Board of Education, 347 U.S. 483 (1954), with Plessy v. Ferguson, 163 U.S. 537 (1896).

probability of intermediate scrutiny both increase. That this should be so may seem entirely natural; yet it is worth adding a word, given the assumption of many that society's majoritarian lawmaking processes themselves adequately reflect evolving conceptions and ideals. To reject that assumption may be simply to accept certain elementary realities: in a society whose legislative and administrative processes of value-formation and conflict-resolution resemble less the ancient ideal of the polis [48] or even the Madisonian ideal of public-spirited transcendence of faction,[49] than the contemporary notion of pluralist compromise,[50] any suggestion that bartered rules are necessarily expressions of substantive consensus seems almost impossible to maintain.[51] Moreover, flux alone—the simple fact of change in views and values—may generate little pressure for change from one rule to the next when the rulemaker is in a position to block the coalescence of flux into a new consensus supporting repeal.

It has been argued [52] that this was indeed the case when the Supreme Court intervened to invalidate rules against custody by unwed fathers [53] and teaching by women late in pregnancy; [54] in both situations, the responsible decisionmakers could act to perpetuate habitual assumptions by blocking the exposure of their respective communities to the experiences that might have led them to conclude that unwed fathers could be capable parents and that teachers in late pregnancy could do well in the classroom.[55] More generally, intermediate review, in any of the six forms discussed in § 16–30, will be most appropriate when the legislative and administrative process seems systematically resistant to change. But it must be conceded that any theory that hopes to justify judicial activism in terms of supposedly improper resistance within the political process will either have to develop a

48. See Aristotle, The Politics Bk. II at 113–15, 119–25, Bk. VII at 225–61 (Penguin ed. Sinclair trans. 1962); E. Barker, The Political Thought of Plato and Aristotle 7 (Dover ed. 1959); H. Arendt, The Human Condition 13, 22–37 (1958).

49. See Sunstein, "Interest Groups in American Public Law," 38 Stan.L.Rev. 29 (1985).

50. See, e.g., A. Bentley, The Process of Government (1908); D. Truman, The Governmental Process (1951); R. Dahl, A Preface to Democratic Theory (1956); R. Dahl, Pluralist Democracy in the United States (1967).

51. Cf. New York Transit Authority v. Beazer, 440 U.S. 568, 609 n.15 (1979) (White, J., dissenting) ("Heroin addiction is a special problem of the poor, and the addict population is composed largely of racial minorities that the Court has previously recognized as politically powerless and historical subjects of majoritarian neglect. Persons on methadone maintenance have few interests in common with members of the majority, and thus are unlikely to have their interests protected, or even considered, in governmental decisionmaking.").

52. See Tribe, "Structural Due Process," 10 Harv.C.R.—C.L.L.Rev. 269, 315–17 (1975).

53. Stanley v. Illinois, 405 U.S. 645 (1976).

54. Cleveland Board of Education v. La-Fleur, 414 U.S. 632 (1974).

55. Similarly, the decisionmakers in City of Cleburne v. Cleburne Living Center, 473 U.S. 432 (1985), by denying a special use permit to a group home for the mentally retarded, effectively blocked exposure of their constitutents to a community including mentally retarded people. Had the Court not invalidated the ordinance as applied, the decision could well have helped to perpetuate the "irrational prejudice against the mentally retarded" that the Court suspected was the motive for denying the permit in the first instance. See id. at 450.

more coherent view of the internal structure of that process,[56] or will have to build upon an avowedly substantive, and not purely process-based, conception of legislative or administrative failure, one which incorporates independent substantive norms.[57]

§ 16–34. Intermediate Remedies: The Irrebuttable Presumption Doctrine

We saw in § 16–32 that a range of intermediate approaches may be employed when neither minimal nor strict review seems entirely appropriate. Section 16–33 canvassed the considerations that make intermediate review proper. In this section, we examine the most common intermediate *remedy*: that of requiring the decisionmaker to permit rebuttal in an individualized hearing and thus to allow exceptions to its general rules, transforming them from "irrebuttable presumptions" to burden-shifting devices.

It should be noted at the outset that, when intermediate review is employed, a variety of intermediate remedies might be considered. A court convinced that a rule no longer represents a meaningful consensus might refuse to enforce the rule unless and until it has been reenacted.[1] Or a court might insist that the lawmakers articulate more clearly their intention to achieve a particular result when that result seems to the court arguably unjust but may not be so clearly impermissible as to warrant outright invalidation.[2]

Another such intermediate remedy which the Supreme Court has recently begun to employ, and which may gain more currency, is to reverse the result of applying a challenged regime to the case before it while leaving the regime in place when it deems that result unjust, but is unprepared to announce general restrictions on the use of the regime in question—whether such restrictions would take the form of insisting that different substantive criteria be used, or demanding that individualized hearings be held. In *City of Cleburne v. Cleburne Living Center*,[3] for example, the Court struck down, as applied only to the case before it, the requirement of a special use permit for a group home for the mentally retarded. Faced with a challenge to the city's denial of such a special use permit, under a regime in which such group homes were required to seek permits while other similar uses (such as sanitaria, hospitals and homes for convalescents) were not,[4] the Court ruled neither that the city's use of mental retardation as a classification or a criterion was impermissible,[5] nor that the city must give each such group home an individualized opportunity to rebut the propriety of

---

56. See ch. 17, infra, for a modest beginning.

57. See Tribe, supra note 32. See also Brilmayer, supra note 32.

§ 16–34

1. See § 16–32, supra, at notes 34 and 43, and § 16–33, supra, at notes 47 to 49.

2. See, e.g., Kent v. Dulles, 357 U.S. 116 (1958); see § 5–17, supra, and Chapter 17, infra.

3. 473 U.S. 432 (1985), discussed in § 16–3, supra.

4. See id. at 447.

5. Cf., e.g., Craig v. Boren, 429 U.S. 190 (1976) (forbidding use of gender in state choice of drinking age).

requiring a special permit.[6] Rather, the Court took the unusual step of itself holding—as though its own appellate consideration of the case in effect constituted just such an individualized administrative hearing— that a special use permit could not constitutionally be required of the group home before it.[7] An administrative hearing already having been held by the city to decide whether a special use permit should issue, the Court might have thought it pointless hair-splitting to send the case back for yet another individualized proceeding at which those who wished to establish the group home would be given an opportunity to rebut the blanket rule mandating a permit.[8] Instead, the Court used the wild card of *certiorari* review to decide that, in the particular case, not even such an individualized hearing, given the possibility of an identical result, would be acceptable. This was in a sense a stronger remedy than requiring the state's regime to be made subject to individualized fine-tuning—but it was also weaker in the sense that it is less generalizable.

For the Court to treat individualized hearings or other ad hoc procedures as more of a problem than a solution is by no means unprecedented outside the equal protection context. Elsewhere, the Court has required the state to remove the burden of certain seemingly neutral bureaucratic procedures.[9] The Court's decision to strike down the very requirement of a special use permit as applied to this group home, rather than insisting that the city's procedure leave room for rebuttal, might reflect an unwillingness on the part of the Court to restructure the deliberative process of the city on behalf of the mentally retarded.[10] Or the Court's decision to eliminate the permit require-

6. Cf., e.g., the cases discussed in notes 8 to 21, infra.

7. See 473 U.S. at 448–51. The Court did *not* hold that the special permit should have been granted; it held that no application for a special permit should have been required.

8. Perhaps the Court in Cleburne was implicitly rejecting the reasons proffered by the city for its rejection of the group home's permit application, see id. at 448–51, and, wishing to avoid a new special use permit hearing, simply issued an order effectively permitting the group home to be built. But, if this were the case, the Court could simply have ruled the *denial* of a permit violative of equal protection, as did the court below. See Cleburne Living Center v. Cleburne, 726 F.2d 191, 201–02 (5th Cir. 1984).

9. See, e.g., Lovell v. Griffin, 303 U.S. 444 (1938) (invalidating a permit requirement for the distribution of any printed matter), discussed in § 12–38, supra and in § 17–3, infra. The Court has also invalidated unacceptably overinclusive "red tape" requirements insofar as they burden an important liberty or benefit. See, e.g., Federal Election Commission v. Massachusetts Citizens for Life, 107 S.Ct. 616, 624–25

(1986) (invalidating a section of the Federal Election Campaign Act, as applied to a non-profit "pro-life" advocacy organization, which prohibited corporations from making election-related political expenditures from general funds, because the prohibition impermissibly burdened political speech protected by the first amendment, even though the organization remained free to establish a separate fund of contributions donated for that purpose); Larson v. Valente, 456 U.S. 228, 253 and n.29 (1982) (invalidating part of a state law regulating charitable solicitations, which exempted only those religions which acquired over 50% of their contributions from members, in part because the requirement of registration and reporting of financial information, at least when imposed selectively, constituted an impermissible burden on the appellee Unification Church).

10. Because the mentally retarded should be regarded as a suspect or quasi-suspect class, see § 16–31, supra, some such restructuring, at a minimum, would have been an appropriate response to a challenge such as the one brought in Cleburne. The intermediate remedy of requiring the state at least to permit rebuttal has been employed only in circumstances

ment altogether in the case before it (but in no others) might reflect a judgment that the irrationality and prejudice reflected in the original denial of the permit [11] would leave any system incorporating individualized discretion too heavily weighted against this disadvantaged group.[12]

But individualized discretion is often a much-desired opportunity rather than a fearsome burden. Requiring that a rule be made permeable to rebuttal—that individuals subject to its terms be given such an opportunity to convince the relevant decisionmaker that they ought to prevail notwithstanding a generally rational per se rule—is best understood as one among several possible ways of proceeding when a rule seems unconstitutionally harsh in its remorseless enforcement but is not so clearly invalid in all possible applications as to warrant a simple adjudication of unconstitutionality.[13] As Justice Marshall explained in *United States Department of Agriculture v. Murry*, such an "analysis combines elements traditionally invoked in what are usually treated as distinct classes of cases, involving due process and equal protection. But the elements of fairness should not be so rigidly cabined." [14] Thus, "where the private interests affected are very important, and the governmental interest can be promoted without much difficulty by a well-designed hearing procedure," the Constitution sometimes "requires the Government to act on an individualized basis, with general propositions serving only as rebuttable presumptions or other burden-shifting devices." [15] At other times, when neither the interests affected nor the criteria employed are such as to warrant special concern,[16] "the fact that a litigant falls within the [government's] classification will be enough to justify its application. There is no reason . . . to categorize inflexibly the rudiments of fairness" to determine "whether individual-

---

in which intermediate or strict scrutiny is independently warranted. See infra.

11. See Cleburne, 473 U.S. at 450 ("The short of it is that requiring the permit in this case appears to rest on an irrational prejudice against the mentally retarded, including those who would occupy [this] facility. . . ."); id. at 455 (Stevens, J., concurring) ("The record convinces me that this permit was required because of the irrational fears of the neighboring property owners, rather than for the protection of the mentally retarded persons who would reside in respondent's home.").

12. In Lovell v. Griffin, 303 U.S. 444 (1938), supra note 9, the mere fact of governmental discretion—the idea that a license was required to distribute printed matter—was held an impermissible burden on the first amendment rights of those wishing to distribute such material, without even a showing that a permit would not have been granted. See id. at 451: "[T]he liberty of the press became initially a right to publish '*without* a license what formerly could be published only with

one.'" (emphasis in original) (citation omitted). Given no analogue to this first amendment history, the Court in Cleburne did not go so far as to say that the permit requirement could not be applied to any group of mentally retarded individuals. Rather, the Court chose to utilize an *ad hoc*, surgical, as-applied invalidation.

13. See, e.g., Trimble v. Gordon, 430 U.S. 762, 770–71 (1977) (explaining need "to consider the possibility of a middle ground between the extremes of complete exclusion and case-by-case determination of paternity"), discussed in §§ 16–24, 16–32, 16–33, supra. For a suggestion that age-based lines, unlike lines based on gender or legitimacy, should trigger "irrebuttable presumption" analysis only when unusually important interests are at stake, see § 16–31, supra.

14. 413 U.S. 508, 519 (1973) (concurring opinion), discussed in §§ 10–19 and 16–33, supra, and in § 16–50, infra.

15. Murry, 413 U.S. at 518 (Marshall, J., concurring).

16. See § 16–33, supra.

ized determination is required or categorical treatment is permitted by the Constitution." [17]

In a series of decisions stretching from the early 1940s to the late 1960s, the Supreme Court expressed its invalidation of various per se rules in opinions condemning the irrebuttable presumptions that such rules embodied. In 1942, Chief Justice Stone, concurring in *Skinner v. Oklahoma*,[18] wrote of the special injustice of automatically inflicting a harm as serious as sterilization upon an entire class of convicted individuals, "without opportunity to [each] individual to show that his [was] not the type of case which would justify resort to it." [19] In *Carrington v. Rash*, the Court in 1965 struck down a ban on voting by military personnel, condemning as an unfairly irrebuttable presumption the state's insistence that such personnel should never be treated as bona fide residents of the counties in which they were stationed.[20] In *United States v. Brown*, the Court in 1965 invalidated a federal statute forbidding all members of the Communist Party to hold labor union offices, on the ground that the prohibition automatically treated Communists as posing a threat, rather than leaving "to other tribunals" the task of sifting out the harmless from the dangerous.[21] In *Shapiro v. Thompson*, when the Court in 1969 struck down one-year waiting periods for new residents who applied for welfare, it did so in an opinion which in part condemned the "nonrebuttable presumptions" that new residents had migrated merely to exploit a state's superior welfare system.[22] More recently, the Court has required that a person whose driver's license is about to be suspended for failure to post a bond adequate to cover damages allegedly resulting from an accident be given an opportunity to present evidence of ultimate nonliability in order to prevent the suspension; [23] that a woman be given an opportunity to establish her ability to administer an estate; [24] that an illegitimate child be given an opportunity to prove economic dependence upon a deceased father for purposes of state workmen's compensation benefits; [25] that an unwed father be given a chance to prove his fitness as a parent in a custody proceeding; [26] that a student who applied to a state

17. Murry, 413 U.S. at 519 (Marshall, J., concurring). See § 17–3, infra.

18. 316 U.S. 535 (1942), discussed in § 16–12, supra.

19. 316 U.S. at 544 (Stone, C.J., concurring in result).

20. 380 U.S. 89, 96 (1965).

21. 381 U.S. 437, 454 n.29 (1965), discussed in §§ 10–4 to 10–6, supra. See also Aptheker v. Secretary of State, 378 U.S. 500 (1964); United States v. Robel, 389 U.S. 258 (1967).

22. 394 U.S. 618, 631 (1969).

23. Bell v. Burson, 402 U.S. 535 (1971).

24. Reed v. Reed, 404 U.S. 71, 76 (1971). In fact, Reed was not a "true" irrebuttable presumption decision since the Court has properly held that gender may not be given even a rebuttable, burden-shifting sig-

nificance in such matters as the distribution of economic benefits or social opportunities. See, e.g., Craig v. Boren, 429 U.S. 190, 210 n.24 (1976) (state may define "any cutoff age for the purchase and sale of 3.2 beer that it chooses, provided that the redefinition operates in a gender-neutral fashion"); see generally § 16–26, supra. Contrast illegitimacy, which may be given *rebuttable*, but not *irrebuttable*, significance. See, e.g., Mathews v. Lucas, 427 U.S. 495 (1976), discussed in § 16–24, supra.

25. Weber v. Aetna Casualty & Surety Co., 406 U.S. 164 (1972), discussed in § 16–24, supra. See also Jimenez v. Weinberger, 417 U.S. 628, 636 (1974).

26. Stanley v. Illinois, 405 U.S. 645 (1972).

university from out-of-state and who seeks reduced tuition as a resident must be given an opportunity to prove that he or she has become a bona fide resident; [27] that a person seeking food stamps but living with someone declared as a tax dependent by a non-needy individual be given a chance to prove that he is genuinely needy; [28] that a person who is refused public employment as an alien must at least have an opportunity for an individualized determination that noncitizenship would render the particular individual unsuited for the employment sought; [29] that a public school teacher beyond the fourth month of her pregnancy be given an opportunity to show that she is fit to continue teaching; [30] and that a woman seeking unemployment compensation be given a chance to demonstrate her ability to work, and hence her availability for employment (and thus her eligibility for compensation) in the period extending from 12 weeks before to 6 weeks after childbirth. [31]

In each of those instances, as with any rule described as an irrebuttable presumption, it would of course be possible to defend the challenged regulation on the ground that it "presumes" nothing but simply chooses one substantive policy over another. [32] For this reason, in fact, most commentators have regarded the Court's invocation of the irrebuttable presumption doctrine as analytically confused and ultimately unhelpful. [33] All the Court is really condemning when it invalidates an irrebuttable presumption, one may argue, is a substantive rule that it deems impermissibly overinclusive.

There is some truth in the criticism, but it also misses an important point. For when the Court strikes down a rule as fatally overinclusive, it *may* be suggesting that the state is forbidden to make *any use at all* of the factor that led to the rule's condemnation. [34] The special feature of an invalidation employing the irrebuttable presumption doctrine is that it ordinarily suggests, on the contrary, that the state may be free to use the factor *so long as it does not give that factor conclusive force.* Thus, precisely because the Court has applied the irrebuttable presumption doctrine only in situations where intermediate or strict scrutiny was independently warranted either by the involvement of a sensitive classification or by the presence of an

27. Vlandis v. Kline, 412 U.S. 441 (1973).

28. United States Department of Agriculture v. Murry, 413 U.S. 508 (1973).

29. Sugarman v. Dougall, 413 U.S. 634, 646–47 (1973). See also Hampton v. Mow Sun Wong, 426 U.S. 88, 101 n.20 (1976).

30. Cleveland Board of Education v. LaFleur, 414 U.S. 632 (1974). See also Crawford v. Cushman, 531 F.2d 1114 (2d Cir. 1976) (per Oakes, J.) (requiring that a pregnant United States Marine be afforded an opportunity to show that she is fit to continue her assigned military occupation in rebuttal to the presumption embodied in Marine regulations that any pregnant female in the Marine Corps is permanently unfit for duty).

31. Turner v. Department of Employment Security of Utah, 423 U.S. 44 (1975) (per curiam). But compare Geduldig v. Aiello, 417 U.S. 484 (1974), and General Electric Co. v. Gilbert, 429 U.S. 125 (1976), discussed in § 16–29, supra.

32. Compare the discussion of "tautological" defenses in bill of attainder adjudication, § 10–5, supra.

33. See, e.g., Note, "The Irrebuttable Presumption Doctrine in the Supreme Court," 87 Harv.L.Rev. 1534 (1974); Note, "Irrebuttable Presumptions: An Illusory Analysis," 27 Stan.L.Rev. 449 (1975).

34. See, e.g., note 24, supra.

important liberty or benefit,[35] that doctrine has become anything but

35. See § 16–33, supra. Contrast the decisions discussed in notes 18 to 31, supra, with such decisions as Usery v. Turner Elkhorn Mining Co., 428 U.S. 1, 23–24 (1976) (upholding federal law containing "irrebuttable presumption" of total disability for miners seeking compensation and clinically diagnosable as extremely ill with pneumoconiosis arising out of coal mine employment); Weinberger v. Salfi, 422 U.S. 749, 777 (1975) (upholding federal statute preventing widows and their children from receiving Social Security survivors' benefits unless the claimants' relationship to the deceased wage earner began more than nine months prior to his death); Mourning v. Family Publications Service, Inc., 411 U.S. 356, 377 (1973) (upholding application of truth-in-lending regulations to all agreements providing for payment in more than four installments). Such early decisions as Heiner v. Donnan, 285 U.S. 312 (1932) (invalidating conclusive presumption that gifts made within two years of donor's death were made in contemplation of death and thus taxable at higher rates), which invoked a doctrine against irrebuttable presumptions in the absence of what would now be deemed a basis for heightened scrutiny (i.e., for intermediate review), are plainly not good law today—despite the approving citation of those decisions in Vlandis v. Kline, 412 U.S. 441, 446 (1973). The difficulty of reconciling Vlandis, supra note 27; Bell v. Burson, 402 U.S. 535 (1971), supra note 23; and United States Department of Agriculture v. Murry, 413 U.S. 508 (1973), supra note 28, with Usery v. Turner Elkhorn Mining Co., Weinberger v. Salfi, and Mourning v. Family Publications, should not be underestimated. In Salfi, the Court attempted to distinguish Murry as a case in which the criterion employed bore "no rational relation to a legitimate legislative goal," but Justice Rehnquist, the author of the majority opinion in Salfi, had persuasively argued precisely the contrary in Murry itself. See Murry, 413 U.S. at 522–27 (dissenting opinion). Salfi's attempted distinction of Vlandis as a case in which the state "purported to be concerned with residency" but denied individuals "the opportunity to show factors bearing on that issue," 422 U.S. at 771 (but cf. Vlandis, 412 U.S. at 464–65 (Rehnquist, J., dissenting)) may be more successful, since in Vlandis the only alternative explanation—that the state was in reality seeking to separate new residents from old—had been supplied only as an afterthought and thus was appropriately rejected by the majority. See Vlandis, 412 U.S. at 449; see also § 16–33, supra. But if the interests at stake in Murry, Vlandis and Bell (food stamps, reduced col-

lege tuition, and use of a driver's license) were all important enough to trigger intermediate review, it is not easy to understand why the interest at stake in Salfi—survivor's benefits—was insufficiently important to trigger such review, particularly since a hearing on whether the marriage in Salfi was collusive did not seem impractical, and since the "presumption" of collusion involved a measure of social opprobrium. See Salfi, 422 U.S. at 804 (Brennan, J., joined by Marshall, J., dissenting). The Court's more recent distinction between social security disability benefits and welfare payments for purposes of procedural due process in Mathews v. Eldridge, 424 U.S. 319 (1976) (no right to pretermination hearing for disability benefits), see §§ 10–13, supra, and 16–56, infra, can perhaps explain Salfi—but it cannot explain Bell v. Burson or Vlandis v. Kline. Bell nonetheless remains potentially distinguishable as involving a troublesome delegation of ordinarily public authority to the private party who, by naming the level of damages required as security of the driver, could assure the suspension of the latter's license, and Vlandis as involving an arguably impermissible burden on the student's right to engage in interstate travel. But see Vlandis, 412 U.S. at 452–53 n.9 (reaffirming Court's support for its summary affirmance 401 U.S. 985 (1971), of Starns v. Malkerson, 326 F.Supp. 234 (D.Minn.1970), which had upheld a one year durational residency requirement for lower tuition at the state university). See also Sosna v. Iowa, 419 U.S. 393 (1975) (upholding one year residency requirement for obtaining a divorce). Moreover, it is possible to see in both Bell and Vlandis elements of "false advertising". See Bell, 402 U.S. at 541 ("we are not dealing . . . with a no-fault scheme. Since the [state] makes liability an important factor [in ultimate license denial], the State may not . . . eliminate consideration of that factor in its prior hearing"); Vlandis, 412 U.S. at 452 ("since [the state] *purports* to be concerned with residency in allocating the rates for tuition . . ., it is forbidden . . . to deny an individual the resident rates" without allowing the individual to establish residency) (emphasis added). If a state's misleading identification of its concerns is thought sufficiently incompatible with constitutional values of political accountability, cf. § 16–33, supra, and Chapter 17, infra, perhaps Bell and Vlandis were defensible.

The Salfi Court had no difficulty distinguishing such other irrebuttable presumption decisions as Stanley v. Illinois, 405 U.S. 645 (1972), and Cleveland Board of Education v. LaFleur, 414 U.S. 632 (1974),

an "engine of destruction for countless legislative judgments." [36] Instead, it has served only as a modest addition to the set of intermediate remedies where the alternative, in its absence, might have been a more drastic form of invalidation.[37]

In deciding when this particular remedy should be invoked in a case already shown to be appropriate for intermediate review,[38] one must take several factors into account.   First, one must ask how difficult it would in fact be to serve the government's legitimate interests, and to protect both privacy and even-handedness, while following an individualized hearing procedure.[39]   Second, one must assess the degree to which an individualized interchange between government agents and the affected individual would advance the cause of respecting personal dignity and individuality more than it would risk the dangers of personalized government.[40]   And third, one must evalu-

inasmuch as they involved government action "curtail[ing] important liberties cognizable under the Constitution."   422 U.S. at 785. Salfi, of course, did not involve the liberty interest in deciding whether, when, and whom to marry, because any claim that the duration-of-relationship rule in fact affected a particular marriage decision would in effect concede to the government the only issue to be addressed at any individualized hearing—i.e., whether the particular marriage was in fact entered into for purposes of obtaining social security benefits.

36. Weinberger v. Salfi, 422 U.S. 749, 772 (1975) (Rehnquist, J.). It was in Cleveland Board of Education v. LaFleur, 414 U.S. 632 (1974), that Justice Rehnquist most strongly expressed his fear that the doctrine could have that effect, id. at 657 (dissenting opinion); see also id. at 652 (Powell, J., concurring in result but expressing misgivings about the doctrine despite his prior decision to join in the Vlandis opinion, 412 U.S. 441 (1973)).

37. But in some cases, the more drastic alternative of ruling that a state may not employ a factor at all—even rebuttably—cf. note 24, supra, seems unlikely. Compare, e.g., Stanley v. Illinois, 405 U.S. 645 (1972) (unwed father cannot automatically be denied custody), with Mathews v. De Castro, 429 U.S. 181 (1976) (minimum rationality suffices to uphold government's different treatment of married and divorced women in allocating benefits upon retirement or disability of present or former husband). See Stanley, 405 U.S. at 654–65: "It may be . . . that most unmarried fathers are unsuitable and neglectful parents. . . . But . . . some are [not], [and] . . . Stanley . . . [should be] [g]iven the opportunity to make his case. . . ."   The Court thus seems to have assumed that a father's unwed status could properly be given weight as a device for shifting to him the burden of establish-

ing fitness. See also id. at 657 n.9. But the Court might well have ruled that, if the state did not take a mother's marital status into account, equal protection would require it not to take a father's into account either. Cf. id. at 658 & n.10 (denying fitness hearings to unwed fathers while granting them to unwed mothers violates equal protection).

38. It must be stressed that Weinberger v. Salfi, 422 U.S. 749 (1975), eliminated any doubt about whether such a showing was independently required as a prerequisite for invocation of the irrebuttable presumption doctrine: It is. See id. at 777.

39. Per se rules governing the age below which state officials will not intervene in a child's relation with his or her family absent some clear showing of abuse may serve to illustrate cases where individualized hearings could do more harm than good. It is not difficult, for example, to imagine situations where an inquiry into a particular child's maturity and ability to lead an independent life would cause serious disruption of an ongoing family. Cf. §§ 15–20, 16–31, supra.

40. Cf. § 10–7, supra. One might well regard individual human confrontation as an intrinsically more fitting response than rigid codification both to the predicament of moral uncertainty and to the involvement of ultimate matters of birth and death. See generally Tribe, "Structural Due Process," 10 Harv.Civ.Rts.—Civ.Lib.L. Rev. 269, 310–14 (1975). Such a concern seems to have played a role in the Supreme Court's invalidation of death sentences that states had made mandatory for all who committed a designated type of offense. The Court's opinion in Woodson v. North Carolina, 428 U.S. 280 (1976), treated such mandatory sentences as incompatible with the defendant's personal dignity, which precludes treating "all persons convicted of a designated offense not

ate the extent to which the responsiveness and accountability of the legal regime in question would be enhanced rather than compromised by the implementation of policy through the individualized application of relatively open-ended standards.[41]

§ 16–35. Equal or Minimal Protection: Poverty in Constitutional Law

Various majorities of the Warren Court were willing to join opinions which claimed that legislative classifications based on wealth, like those based on race, are "suspect" classifications triggering strict judicial scrutiny. As the Chief Justice wrote, wealth and race are "two factors which would independently render a classification highly suspect and thereby demand a more exacting judicial scrutiny." [1] Similarly, Justice Douglas wrote for the Court in *Harper v. Virginia Board of Elections*,[2] "Lines drawn on the basis of wealth or property, like those of race . . . are traditionally disfavored."

This sweeping language described a commitment to equal justice for rich and poor alike, a commitment that the Warren Court often elaborated and occasionally fulfilled in cases respecting the rights and opportunities of the poor. The general proposition that wealth classifications are always suspect, however, never accurately reflected the

as uniquely individual human beings, but as members of a faceless, undifferentiated mass to be subjected to the blind infliction of the penalty of death." Id. at 304. Accord, Stanislaus Roberts v. Louisiana, 428 U.S. 325 (1976) (per curiam) (invalidating mandatory death penalty for murder of on-duty police officer); Sumner v. Shuman, 107 S.Ct. 2716 (1987) (invalidating mandatory death penalty for prison inmate convicted of murder while serving life sentence without possibility of parole).

41. The Woodson decision, for example, supra note 40, also held mandatory death penalties incompatible with the preservation of an adequate "link between contemporary community values and the penal system." Id. at 295. To avoid arbitrariness, the sentencing authority must exercise a *guided* discretion, Furman v. Georgia, 408 U.S. 238 (1972), but to respect individual personality and serve as a catalyst to change, *discretion* must be present. See also Witherspoon v. Illinois, 391 U.S. 510, 519 & n.15 (1968) (jurors conscientiously opposed to capital punishment must be included at sentencing stage); but see Spaziano v. Florida, 468 U.S. 447, 462–63 (1984) (holding that a judge can override a jury's recommendation of life imprisonment and impose the death penalty, but "not denigrat[ing] the significance of the jury's role as a link between the community and the penal system").

In effect, the Supreme Court has held that the law's responsiveness and account-

ability, both to those it affects, see note 40, supra, and to those in whose name it is imposed, requires a structure of decision increasingly open to individual, purposive argument as the groups injured increasingly resemble discrete and insular minorities, or as the interests sacrificed increasingly parallel those otherwise entitled to special judicial protection from overbearing or insensitive majorities. In this light, it seems particularly significant that the Court's invalidation of the irrebuttable presumption in Cleveland Board of Education v. LaFleur, 414 U.S. 632 (1974), came in an opinion that criticized "the possible role of outmoded taboos" in the promulgation and persistence of the challenged restrictions on pregnant teachers. Id. at 641 n.9. See also Crawford v. Cushman, 531 F.2d 1114, 1125–26 (2d Cir. 1976), (Oakes, J.) (invalidating mandatory discharge of pregnant Marines, as violative of equal protection and also of due process, the latter because "[m]otherhood . . . is an area in which the need to reflect rapidly changing norms affecting important interests in liberty compels an individualized determination, one not bound by any preexisting rule of thumb within the zone of moral change").

§ 16–35

1. McDonald v. Board of Election Commissioners of Chicago, 394 U.S. 802, 807 (1969) (dictum).

2. 383 U.S. 663, 668 (1966).

law.[3] Although its sensitivity to the poor was evident in a wide range of cases, the Warren Court had in fact employed the stricter tier of equal protection doctrine to strike down only two sorts of laws disadvantaging the poor: laws denying indigents or non-freeholders the franchise, and laws limiting the access of indigents to various levels of a state's system of criminal justice.

Although it purported to endorse the major voting and criminal justice decisions of the Warren Court, the Burger Court's employment of wealth classification doctrine has been far more restrained. The spread of heightened review of wealth classifications into any new areas has been halted. Significantly, the Court has abandoned the ardent rhetoric of equal justice for the poor, rhetoric which promised more than even the Warren Court had delivered, and far more than the Burger Court was prepared to deliver in the name of equal protection of the laws. In conjunction with its deflation of rhetoric, the Court has recast what were originally equal protection and equal access cases in a new mold of "minimal protection"[4] and minimal access. The remodelling, which purports to preserve the holdings of the Warren Court's decisions while cutting away only the exaggerated language in which those holdings were clothed, has occasionally accomplished radical sacrifices of both the spirit and letter of the Warren Court's equal protection decisions. Finally, the imaginative compassion for the plight of the poor, which at least informed and perhaps generated so many of the Warren Court's holdings in tangential areas, has been replaced with a determined reluctance to tell the states how to deal with the problems of their poor.[5]

§ 16–36. The Early Emergence of Poverty as a Potentially Suspect Criterion for Legislative Discrimination

In *Edwards v. California*,[1] the Supreme Court struck down, as an unconstitutional barrier to interstate commerce, a California law making it a misdemeanor knowingly to bring a non-resident indigent into the state. In a stirring and often cited concurring opinion, Justice Jackson found the statute to represent an unconstitutional discrimination against indigents: "We should say now, and in no uncertain terms

---

3. Nonetheless, some lower federal courts took the Warren Court at its word. In Hobson v. Hansen, 269 F.Supp. 401, 513 (D.D.C.1967), aff'd sub nom. Smuck v. Hansen, 408 F.2d 175 (D.C.Cir. 1969), appeal dismissed 393 U.S. 801 (1968), Judge Skelly Wright treated wealth and race classifications as equivalents: "[The District of Columbia Public Schools] 'can no more discriminate on account of poverty than on account of religion, race, or color.'" His conjoining of wealth and race, however, has not been followed in the federal courts.

4. The term "minimal protection" used throughout this and the succeeding sections is intended to be descriptive of the Burger Court's retrenchment in the judicial struggle for equal justice which had

escalated during the tenure of the Warren Court. Compare the concept of "minimum protection," advanced in Michelman, "On Protecting the Poor Through the Fourteenth Amendment," 83 Harv.L.Rev. 7 (1969), reflecting a normative theory of "just wants" which the government has an affirmative duty to fulfill. See also § 15–9, supra.

5. For an excellent source of references and provocative questions in most of the major areas discussed in §§ 16–35 through 16–59, see B. Brudno, Poverty, Inequality, and the Law (1976).

§ 16–36
1. 314 U.S. 160 (1941).

that a man's mere property status, without more, cannot be used by a state to test, qualify, or limit his rights as a citizen of the United States. . . . The mere state of being without funds is a neutral fact—constitutionally an irrelevance, like race, creed, or color."[2]

Although resting its conclusion on the commerce clause, the majority opinion of Justice Byrnes reflected two concerns which recur consistently when the doctrinal focus of constitutional protection of the poor shifts to the equal protection clause of the fourteenth amendment. The first is reflected in the California law's stigmatizing judgment that indigents are undesirable. The State defended its law on the authority of language in *City of New York v. Miln*,[3] supporting state power "to provide precautionary measures against the moral pestilence of paupers [and] vagabonds." The *Edwards* Court expressly disavowed as unworthy of serious consideration the notion that indigency constitutes a "moral pestilence." "Poverty and immorality are not synonymous;"[4] legislative judgments equating them, therefore, cannot be sustained as rational.

The second element in *Edwards* which presaged future developments in equal protection doctrine was the State of California's unsuccessful assertion, in support of its law, that the recent influx of immigrants into California had imposed "staggering" fiscal and other burdens on the State.[5] The Court replied that the Constitution "was framed upon the theory that the peoples of the several states must sink or swim together, and that in the long run prosperity and salvation are in union and not division."[6] In the face of this noble vision, California's fear of financial drain was dismissed as "parochial."[7]

§ 16–37. Equal Justice for Rich and Poor Alike: The Basic Premises

Edwards v. California involved a state law which explicitly[1] and purposefully singled out and disadvantaged the poor. In the mid-1950's, the Court began striking down laws and practices, such as court-related fees,[2] which appeared neutral on their face but operated to disadvantage the poor. Guiding these decisions was a constitutional vision of equal justice for rich and poor alike. Just as poverty was viewed as an attribute no less arbitrary than race for purposes of legislative classification, so fees were seen as hardly less invidious than

---

2. Id. at 184–85.

3. 36 U.S. (11 Pet.) 102, 142 (1837) (upholding, against a preemption attack under the commerce clause, a New York statute requiring the master of every ship arriving in port to submit to the mayor the name, place of birth, last legal settlement, age, and occupation of each of the ship's passengers).

4. 314 U.S. at 177.

5. 314 U.S. at 173.

6. Id. at 174 (quoting Baldwin v. Seelig, 294 U.S. 511, 523 (1935)). See § 6–6, supra.

7. 314 U.S. at 174. For another early case reflecting implicit disapproval of wealth classifications, see Skinner v. Oklahoma, 316 U.S. 535 (1942), discussed in § 16–12, supra.

§ 16–37

1. 314 U.S. 160 (1941). Skinner v. Oklahoma, 316 U.S. 535 (1942), did so only implicitly.

2. See, e.g., Griffin v. Illinois, 351 U.S. 12 (1956).

grandfather clauses.[3] The two principles which led the Court in *Edwards* to reject the fencing out of indigents as a valid exercise of a state's police power—watchfulness for stigmatizing preconceptions about the poor, fortified by disregard of financial burdens on state treasuries—were marshalled by the Warren Court to mandate, in the name of equal protection of the laws, "an affirmative duty to lift the handicaps flowing from differences in economic circumstances." [4]

To be sure, not even that egalitarian-minded Court ever mandated such a duty across the board. Nor would the Constitution as enacted support such a duty, whatever some might think an *ideal* constitution would provide in this respect. But a limited duty to lift *some* of the handicaps of poverty in *some* circumstances is a different matter altogether.

In particular, "equal protection of the laws" could well be deemed incompatible with laws that are written so as to add insult—such as explicit exclusion from a community or from enjoyment of its benefits—to the injury that poverty itself entails in a money-based economy.

Although some such laws might be justified in fiscal or other seemingly non-invidious terms, the Warren Court's denigration of state fiscal justifications was crucial to its conclusion that classifications based on wealth are invidious. Such justifications always attend discrimination against the poor, even such purposeful discrimination as that of the California law struck down in *Edwards*; [5] if recognized as sufficient, fiscal justifications would effectively deny constitutional protection to the poor as a group.[6]

---

3. Id. at 17 n.11. See the discussion of such clauses in § 5–14, supra. But unlike grandfather clauses, a state's decision to charge a fee for a service or commodity rather than to provide it *gratis* is not completely devoid of non-invidious justification. A state might reasonably charge a fee for providing a trial transcript requisite to an appeal in order to husband scarce resources and to restrict the burden on its judicial machinery by deterring frivolous appeals. As Justice Harlan observed, "[a] policy of economy may be unenlightened, but it is certainly not capricious." Griffin, 351 U.S. at 37–38 (Harlan, J. dissenting). Because of the fiscal justification inherent in every wealth classification, many of which he was prepared to find persuasive, Justice Harlan, beginning with his dissent in Griffin v. Illinois, consistently warned against approaching constitutional protection of the poor in terms of equal protection. For the suggestion that Justice Harlan's recommended due process approach eventually triumphed in what throughout this section is referred to as "minimal protection", see Clune, "The Supreme Court's Treatment of Wealth Discriminations Under the Fourteenth Amendment," 1975 Sup.Ct.Rev. 289.

4. Griffin, 351 U.S. at 34 (Harlan J., dissenting). It is important to remember, however, that the Court invoked this duty only to justify intervention directed toward remedying the effects of poverty on access to *political* and *judicial* processes. Therefore, insofar as criticisms of the Warren Court are founded upon the inadvisability of widespread judicially mandated redistribution of wealth, see, e.g., Winter, "Poverty, Economic Equality, and the Equal Protection Clause," 1972 Sup.Ct.Rev. 41, they are aimed largely at a straw man.

5. See also James v. Valtierra, 402 U.S. 137, 143 n.4 (1971) (explaining that even federally subsidized low-income housing represents a substantial drain on any community in which it is built); Village of Arlington Heights v. Metropolitan Housing Development Corporation, 429 U.S. 252 (1977) (explaining that low-income housing development results in diminished property values).

6. See discussion of the partial fulfillment of this prophecy in the Burger Court's treatment of state fiscal justifications in §§ 16–51 to 16–59, infra.

Also crucial to the Court's suspicion of wealth classifications was its refusal to draw moral conclusions from the mere fact of poverty. The Court in *City of New York v. Miln*,[7] in calling poverty a "moral pestilence", had assumed that indigency was evidence of bad character, lack of industry and sloth. Imposition of fees as a screening device, whether for meritorious appeals or qualified voters, recapitulates this assumption, albeit in a somewhat muted form. A fee can be an effective screening device only if the decision whether or not to pay it is voluntary, or if inability to pay in itself identifies a quality sought to be screened out. The state's underlying assumption must be that no one of any ability need be poor who does not wish to be, and that poverty is thus a sign of moral or mental deficiency. The Court's rejection of this syllogism represented its own assumption that poverty is so often a result of circumstances beyond an individual's control that it can reflect only an individual's financial, and not moral or intellectual, worth.[8]

§ 16-38. Criminal Justice: Equal Access to State Court Review of Criminal Convictions

In *Griffin v. Illinois*,[1] the Supreme Court held under the combined mandate of the equal protection and due process clauses [2] that the state must provide indigent criminal appellants with a free transcript of trial proceedings when the bill of exceptions necessary for full appellate review could not be prepared absent such a transcript.[3] While due process may not require a state to provide any appellate review at all of criminal convictions,[4] once the state does establish an appellate system, that system must treat rich and poor alike. "There can be no equal justice where the kind of trial a man gets depends on the amount of money he has. Destitute defendants must be offered as adequate appellate review as defendants who have money enough to buy transcripts." [5]

The transcript fee charged in *Griffin* obviously served two purposes: financing production of the transcript, and restricting the burden on the state's appellate machinery by screening out appellants who

---

7. 36 U.S. (11 Pet.) 102, 142 (1837).

8. See, e.g., Goldberg v. Kelly, 397 U.S. 254, 265 (1970). For an alternative reading of the Warren Court's decisions affecting the poor, see Miller, "Social Justice and the Warren Court: A Preliminary Examination," 11 Pepperdine L.Rev. 473 (1984).

§ 16-38

1. 351 U.S. 12 (1956).

2. The opinion in Griffin, written by Justice Black, was joined by only a plurality of four justices. Justice Frankfurter concurred in a separate opinion which, although it chose equal protection as the constitutional rubric for the holding and recommended only prospective application, did not appear to differ in theory from the

plurality. See Willcox and Bloustein, "The Griffin Case—Poverty and the Fourteenth Amendment," 43 Cornell L.Q. 1, 11–12 (1957).

3. Although the transcript was not a legal prerequisite to appellate review, the state had conceded that it was necessary for "adequate" review. It is worth noting, therefore, in light of later characterizations of Griffin, e.g., Ross v. Moffitt, 417 U.S. 600, 607 (1974), discussed in § 16–51, infra, that under the Illinois system access to appellate review had not been completely foreclosed.

4. See McKane v. Durston, 153 U.S. 684, 687–88 (1894).

5. 351 U.S. at 19.

could not or chose not to pay the fee.[6] Yet the majority chose to ignore these possible justifications and held the fee irrational.[7] "In criminal trials a State can no more discriminate on account of poverty than on account of religion, race or color. Plainly [wealth] bears no rational relationship to a defendant's guilt or innocence. . . ."[8]

In *Douglas v. California*,[9] the question was whether the state had to provide indigent appellants with counsel for their first appeal as of right. In rejecting the state's intermediate solution of appointing counsel if the state appellate court determined that counsel would be helpful, the Supreme Court reaffirmed the equal protection holding of *Griffin*: "In either case [10] the evil is the same: discrimination against the indigent. For there can be no equal justice where the kind of an appeal a man enjoys 'depends on the amount of money he has.' "[11] The discretionary power of the state court to appoint counsel was held insufficient to satisfy due process: "When an indigent is forced to run this gantlet of a preliminary showing of merit, the right to appeal does not comport with fair procedure."[12]

The Court in *Griffin* was careful to note that the state was not necessarily required to provide a transcript in every instance where an indigent could not afford one, leaving room for the states to come up with "other means of affording adequate and effective appellate review to indigent defendants."[13] This leeway, however, turned out to be extremely narrow; in only one case did the Court actually find that such an alternative existed.[14] The various state attempts to test its boundaries provide an illuminating focus for testing at the same time the Warren Court's commitment to equal as opposed to minimal access to the states' systems of criminal justice.

In two cases decided the same day as *Douglas*, the Court rejected "gantlet" procedures with which the state had attempted to mitigate the overinclusiveness, with regard to indigents, of its transcript fees as a means of screening out frivolous appeals. In *Draper v. Washington* [15] the trial judge, and in *Lane v. Brown* [16] the court-appointed public defender, could grant or refuse a free transcript to the putative appel-

---

6. These are really two aspects of the resource allocation function served by pricing systems in general.

7. This indifference to state fiscal arguments should be contrasted with the discussion in § 16–51, infra.

8. 351 U.S. at 17.

9. 372 U.S. 353 (1963).

10. Denial of a free transcript or of appointed counsel.

11. Douglas, 372 U.S. at 355, quoting Griffin, 351 U.S. at 19.

12. 372 U.S. at 357. The dissenters in Douglas argued that Griffin did not control. Justice Harlan, joined by Justice Stewart, distinguished Douglas from the filing fee cases. Justice Clark, who had joined the plurality in Griffin, found the California "gantlet" procedure a fair

screening device since he thought most in forma pauperis appeals were frivolous anyway. The Court's "new fetish for indigency," he warned, "piles an intolerable burden on the State's judicial machinery." 372 U.S. at 359. Along similar lines, Justice Harlan added that the Constitution does not prohibit "a State, in seeking to redress economic imbalances at its bar of justice and to provide indigents with full review, from taking reasonable steps to guard against needless expense." Id. at 367.

13. 351 U.S. at 20.

14. Britt v. North Carolina, 404 U.S. 226 (1971).

15. 372 U.S. 487 (1963).

16. 372 U.S. 477 (1963).

lant depending on whether or not the appeal seemed to them frivolous.[17] Theoretically, the "gantlet" required of indigents is merely that their appeals not be frivolous.[18] The state in *Draper* argued that the price of the transcript operated as a similar screen against frivolous appeals by non-indigents, who "motivated by a 'sense of thrift' will choose not to appeal in exactly the same circumstances that an indigent will be denied a transcript."[19] The Court found this suggestion untenable, observing that indigents could appeal only if their claims were non-frivolous, while some non-indigents could and would appeal however frivolous their claims: "In *all* cases the duty of the State is to provide the indigent as adequate and effective an appellate review as that given appellants with funds—the State must provide the indigent defendant with means of presenting his contentions to the appellate court which are as good as those available to a non-indigent defendant *with similar contentions*."[20]

In *Anders v. California*,[21] the Court likewise sought to ensure that court-appointed counsel for indigent appellants pursue their clients' interests as zealously as would retained counsel, in situations where the merits of the appeal were questionable. Instead of the "no-merit" letter, on the basis of which the California Court had been willing to dismiss Anders' appeal, the Court held that a request for withdrawal must be accompanied by a brief referring to *anything* in the record which *might arguably* support the appeal, presumably on the assumption that retained counsel would make a similar all-out effort. The state court could then decide for itself whether the appeal was frivolous, presumably by the same standard as for any non-indigent appeal. This procedure "will assure penniless defendants the same rights and opportunities on appeal—as nearly as is practicable—as are enjoyed by those persons who are in a similar situation but who are able to afford the retention of private counsel."[22]

The Court's holdings in these gantlet cases plainly represented a deep commitment to equal justice for the poor, regardless of the merits of their claims. Justice Clark, joined by Justice Harlan, made a not completely unpersuasive counter-argument in *Coppedge v. United States*.[23] The majority in that case had held that for federal applications to appeal *in forma pauperis*, the burden of proving frivolity is on

---

17. In Draper the transcript was not a legal prerequisite to the appeal, and the dissenters argued that the appellant possessed a narrative account of the trial which was an adequate substitute for the transcript, 372 U.S. at 500–503. In Lane, the transcript was a prerequisite. Id. at 480. This distinction appears to have made no difference to the Court.

18. In fact it was suggested, without demonstration, that the system did not so operate, because the trial judge and public defender, both of whom were involved in the challenged proceedings, would be inherently biased and could not make an adequate judgment of frivolity. Id. at 485–86, 498 (concurring opinion). However,

there was no suggestion of such bias in Douglas, where another gantlet procedure was rejected, indicating that even a perfectly functioning screen for indigents was deemed unacceptable so long as frivolous non-indigents could acquire transcripts.

19. 372 U.S. at 495 n.4.

20. Draper, 372 U.S. at 496 (emphasis added).

21. 386 U.S. 738 (1967).

22. Id. at 745. See also Evitts v. Lucey, 469 U.S. 387 (1985) (criminal defendants have a right to *effective* assistance of counsel on appeal).

23. 369 U.S. 438 (1962).

the government, exactly as in motions to dismiss frivolous appeals brought by non-indigents. The purpose of this standard is "to assure equality of consideration for all litigants," [24] the same purpose that was at work in *Draper, Lane*, and *Anders*. The dissent could see "no constitutional impediment to asking one who seeks a free ride to show that he is not just a joyrider. Although a government that affords appellate review must pay the cost of meritorious indigent appeals, surely it may protect itself from frivolous ones . . . being 'subsidized and public moneys . . . needlessly spent.'" [25] Perhaps more sympathetically put, a state need not waste the public's money on the frivolous appeals of indigents merely because it allows wealthy individuals to waste theirs.[26] For the Warren Court, the reply lay in its sense that the risk or the appearance of marginal error could not be justified by the saving of even significant amounts of money. "When society acts to deprive one of its members of his life, liberty, or property, it takes its most awesome steps . . . The methods we employ in the enforcement of our criminal law have aptly been called the measures by which the quality of our civilization may be judged." [27]

Related to the Court's rejection of the various state gantlet alternatives was its persistence in refusing to require any showing of particularized need for the requested document. Such a showing is not required of non-indigents who can purchase transcripts at will; therefore equal justice requires a similar absence of barriers to the indigent's procurement of the transcript.[28] In these cases, the Court required a free transcript no matter how inessential to the appeal it might be. As in the gantlet cases, the underlying rationale must, at least in part, be prophylactic; the rule that indigents must be given the same time, tools, and attention as paying appellants may be based on a suspicion that judges and lawyers are likely to be somewhat more obtuse to the merits of indigents' claims than to those of nonindigents but that, with the sort of enforced seriousness imposed by cases like *Anders*, they might perceive an indigent's case more penetratingly. Counsel for nonindigents generally do not need the extra push. And the state when giving away transcripts might be a less than neutral judge of the claims presented by the objects of its involuntary charity.[29]

---

24. Id. at 447.

25. Id. at 460, quoting Griffin, 351 U.S. at 24 (Frankfurter, J., concurring).

26. See Draper, 372 U.S. at 496. See also Jones v. Barnes, 463 U.S. 745 (1983) (on appeal, appointed counsel need not raise every nonfrivolous claim suggested by the client); Pennsylvania v. Finley, 107 S.Ct. 1990 (1987) (because the federal constitutional right to appointed counsel extends only to a first appeal that a state chooses to provide as a matter of right and not to any further discretionary appeals or collateral postconviction proceedings, the procedures of Anders need not be followed beyond such first appeal).

27. Coppedge, 369 U.S. at 449, referring to Justice Shaefer of the Supreme Court of

Illinois, "Federalism and State Criminal Procedure," 70 Harv.L.Rev. 1, 26 (1956).

28. This liberality was consistently highlighted and attacked by the dissenters, who could not justify spending the states' money unless doing so accomplished some tangible good. See, e.g., Gardner v. California, 393 U.S. 367, 372 (1969). (Harlan, J., dissenting).

29. For other cases reaffirming the principles of Griffin and Douglas, see, e.g., Britt v. North Carolina, 404 U.S. 226 (1971) (petitioner's conviction for murder would not be reversed because state had failed to provide him a transcript of mistrial to use in his second trial a month later, when the trials were held in a small town where defense counsel was on friendly terms with

§ 16–39. Criminal Justice: Equalizing the "Price" of Liberty

In *Williams v. Illinois*,[1] the Supreme Court held that a convicted criminal could not be imprisoned for a period exceeding the statutory maximum as a substitute for payment of a fine, when nonpayment was involuntary due to indigency. The "statutory ceiling placed on imprisonment for any substantial offense [must] be the same for all defendants irrespective of their economic status".[2] Relying on *Williams*, the Court has also held that a state cannot revoke a defendant's probation, and thus imprison him, merely for failure to pay a fine—unless it can prove that the defendant failed to make "bona fide" efforts to seek employment or borrow money to pay the fine, or that alternative forms of punishment would not meet the state's interests.[3] Similarly in *Tate v. Short*[4] the state was prohibited from detaining an indigent one day for every $5 of traffic fines totalling $425, when according to statute the offenses were otherwise punishable only by fine and not by imprisonment: " '[T]he Constitution prohibits the State from imposing a fine as a sentence and then automatically converting it into a jail term solely because the defendant is indigent and cannot forthwith pay the fine in full.' "[5]

The Court had much earlier implied a similar principle in its explication of the eighth amendment's "excessive bail" prohibition in *Stack v. Boyle*;[6] bail must not be set at a figure higher than reasonably calculated to assure the presence of the accused at trial. Arriving at the correct figure requires, among other considerations, an assessment of the defendant's financial ability. Such individualized attention is designed to ensure that individuals of all degrees of wealth are treated

court reporter so that an acceptable alternative to the transcript had been available and an effective defense had been possible); Mayer v. City of Chicago, 404 U.S. 189 (1971) (indigent convicted on non-felony charges and sentenced to two fines entitled to complete transcript; he had established arguable need for the transcript and government had not met burden of showing that only a portion of the transcript or an alternative would suffice); Roberts v. La Vallee, 389 U.S. 40 (1967) (indigent granted writ of habeas corpus because state had failed to provide him with a free transcript of preliminary hearing for use at trial, even though there was no showing of what use might have been made of transcript); Smith v. Bennett, 365 U.S. 708 (1961) ($4.00 filing fee preventing indigents from petitioning for writ of habeas corpus held violative of equal protection).

The holdings of all the cases discussed in this section remain good law. See also Bounds v. Smith, 430 U.S. 817 (1977) (fundamental constitutional right of access to courts requires prison authorities to assist inmates in filing legal papers by providing adequate law libraries or adequate assistance from law-trained persons). Much of their language, however, and their underlying commitment to equal justice for rich and poor alike, have since been at least partially rejected. See § 16–51, infra.

§ 16–39

1. 399 U.S. 235 (1970).

2. Id. at 244.

3. Bearden v. Georgia, 461 U.S. 660, 668–69 (1983). The Court's holding rested on the presumption that the fine was originally determined "to be the appropriate and adequate penalty," and that it was thus unfair to alter the penalty because of the defendant's indigency alone. Id. at 667, 668 n.9. But both the majority and the concurring opinion noted that poverty cannot be allowed to immunize an indigent defendant from punishment. Id. at 669; id. at 675 (White, J., concurring in judgment, joined by Chief Justice Burger, and Justices Powell and Rehnquist).

4. 401 U.S. 395 (1971).

5. Id. at 398, quoting Morris v. Schoonfield, 399 U.S. 508, 509 (1970).

6. 342 U.S. 1 (1951).

equally with regard to their relative ability to pay and are thus charged a relatively equal price for their liberty.[7]

§ 16–40. Criminal Justice: Investigatory and Prosecutory Reform

Criminal procedure represents the most significant area in which concern for equal justice for the poor has found expression in constitutional guarantees other than those of equal protection. In this area it has been primarily the sixth amendment right to counsel in conjunction with the fifth amendment prohibition against compelled self-incrimination, both incorporated through the due process clause of the fourteenth amendment, that have generated restraints and affirmative duties upon the states' law enforcement machinery and personnel.

In *Gideon v. Wainwright*[1], the Court adopted a prophylactic rule requiring appointed counsel for every indigent criminal defendant accused of a felony. The "noble ideal" of "fair trials before impartial tribunals in which every defendant stands equal before the law," the Court explained, "cannot be realized if the poor man charged with crime has to face his accusers without a lawyer to assist him."[2] Important to the Court's conclusion were the facts that the states had established the necessity of counsel for effective advocacy by hiring lawyers to prosecute, just as solvent defendants had made the same point by retaining the best counsel they could afford. Denial of this universally recognized necessity to indigents resulted in an unevenly matched legal battle with the prosecuting government, and caused great disparity in the quality of defense available to the rich and poor. The guarantee of appointed counsel, which had been held to attach in felony cases at every critical prosecutorial stage,[3] was extended in *Argersinger v. Hamlin*[4] to all prosecutions which resulted in imprisonment for any term. This rule prohibiting any imprisonment imposed without the assistance of counsel[5] was adopted as a hedge against the "obsession for speedy dispositions, regardless of the fairness of the result,"[6] caused by the large volume of misdemeanor cases. Concur-

---

7. The very poor, who can advance no money at all and therefore may have nothing to offer as security for their presence at trial other than their personal liberty, may in effect have to pay a higher price than their solvent counterparts. But see the Federal Bail Reform Act of 1984, 18 U.S.C. § 3142 (providing for conditions of release pending trial, such as personal recognizance or custodial supervision, which do not operate unequally against indigents). Cf. Schilb v. Kuebel, 404 U.S. 357 (1971) (upholding Illinois bail statute against equal protection challenge that retaining 1% of unsecured bail bonds as costs discriminated against those without the means to obtain secured bail bonds).

§ 16–40

1. 372 U.S. 335 (1963). See A. Lewis, Gideon's Trumpet (1964).

2. 372 U.S. at 344.

3. Coleman v. Alabama, 399 U.S. 1 (1970) (preliminary hearing to determine if sufficient evidence existed to present case to grand jury and if so to fix bail); Mempa v. Rhay, 389 U.S. 128 (1967) (sentencing hearing which had been postponed subject to probation); United States v. Wade, 388 U.S. 218 (1967) (post-indictment line-up); White v. Maryland, 373 U.S. 59 (1967) (preliminary hearing at which a plea of guilty had been entered before a magistrate); Hamilton v. Alabama, 368 U.S. 52 (1961) (arraignment where certain defenses had to be pleaded or waived).

4. 407 U.S. 25 (1972).

5. Absent knowing and voluntary waiver. See Johnson v. Zerbst, 304 U.S. 458 (1938).

6. Argersinger, 407 U.S. at 34.

ring in the result, Justices Powell and Rehnquist warned of inadequate state resources and urged the thriftier approach whereby the trial court need appoint counsel only if the circumstances required it.[7] More recently, the Court held that an indigent defendant also has a right to the assistance of a psychiatrist at state expense if his sanity will be a significant factor at trial or during a capital sentencing proceeding.[8]

Particularly noteworthy in all of these cases is the Court's willingness to mandate what amounts to state purchase of *private services*— legal or medical—for private citizens. Although a constitutional duty to rescue an individual from his fate in the private market in those cases where the state is itself pursuing that individual is a far cry from a general duty to assist the poor in overcoming the limits of a fee-for-service economy, it does suggest that such a duty to the indigent may arise when the state bears some special responsibility for their predicament.[9] To be sure, many of the right-of-counsel cases do not focus on or even mention indigency.[10] That indigents were understood to be the primary beneficiaries of such rights in criminal prosecutions, however, was made clear in *Miranda v. Arizona*:[11] "In fact, were we to limit these constitutional rights to those who can retain an attorney, our decisions today would be of little significance. The cases before us as well as the vast majority of confession cases with which we have dealt in the past involve those unable to retain counsel." For this reason, the Court in *Miranda* included, as chief among the warnings which must be given to the accused prior to police questioning, the express information that the accused has a right to appointed counsel.[12]

7. Id. at 55–56. This case-by-case approach had been the rule of Betts v. Brady, 316 U.S. 455 (1942), overruled by Gideon, supra note 1. See also Gagnon v. Scarpelli, 411 U.S. 778 (1973) (Betts v. Brady-type rule adopted for appointment of counsel at probation and parole revocation hearings, in light of non-adversary nature of hearing and substantial cost to state); compare the rejection of analogous "gantlet" procedures in the cases discussed in § 16–38, supra.

8. Ake v. Oklahoma, 470 U.S. 68 (1985). The Court viewed its holding in Ake as consistent with "the belief that justice cannot be equal where, simply as a result of his poverty, a defendant is denied the opportunity to participate meaningfully in a judicial proceeding in which his liberty is at stake." Id. at 76. Justice Rehnquist dissented alone. Id. at 87 (arguing that the rule should be limited to "capital cases," and that "the entitlement is to an independent psychiatric evaluation, not to a defense consultant").

9. Cf. Boddie v. Connecticut, 401 U.S. 371 (1971), discussed in § 16–11, supra; Little v. Streater, 452 U.S. 1 (1981), discussed in § 16–49, infra; and Bounds v. Smith, 430 U.S. 817 (1977), discussed in §§ 10–18, 15–9, and 16–36, supra.

10. See, e.g., United States v. Wade, 388 U.S. 218 (1967); White v. Maryland, 373 U.S. 59 (1963); Powell v. Alabama, 287 U.S. 45 (1932).

11. 384 U.S. 436, 472 (1966). See also Wright, "Poverty, Minorities, and Respect for the Law," 1970 Duke L.J. 425, 434–37.

12. See also Escobedo v. Illinois, 378 U.S. 478 (1964). The Burger Court made significant but not enormous cutbacks in the area of criminal procedure. For major developments limiting the expansive holdings discussed in this section, see, e.g., Harris v. New York, 401 U.S. 222 (1971) (statements obtained in violation of Miranda are admissible to impeach an accused who takes the stand and testifies contrary to those statements); Kirby v. Illinois, 406 U.S. 682 (1972) (Wade held not to apply to pre-indictment line-ups); New York v. Quarles, 467 U.S. 649 (1984) (statements obtained in violation of Miranda admissible when those statements are responses to police questions asked out of concern for public safety); Oregon v. Elstad, 470 U.S. 298 (1985) (a prior unlawful interrogation resulting in a confession does not taint subsequent confession that comes after defendant receives Miranda warnings). But see Brewer v. Williams, 430 U.S. 387 (1977) (prisoner entitled to release on habeas corpus where officers made statements designed to induce confession after agreeing with defense attorney not to interrogate

§ 16–41. Criminal Justice: Recoupment Schemes

Several states have attempted to minimize the financial burden imposed by the duty to appoint counsel or provide a free transcript by recouping such costs from defendants once they become able to pay. While consistently approving the idea of such recoupment schemes, the Court rejected early attempts at recoupment which failed to meet the requisite standard of even-handedness. In *Rinaldi v. Yeager*,[1] a New Jersey scheme was invalidated because it fastened the duty of recoupment for transcript costs only on convicted appellants confined in institutions, excusing from recoupment those appellants given a suspended sentence, placed on probation, or sentenced to pay a fine, a distinction the Court found insufficient to pass the rationality test.[2] Similarly, *James v. Strange*[3] rejected the Kansas recoupment statute which "strips from indigent defendants the array of protective exemptions Kansas has erected for other civil judgment debtors . . . ." The Court found no rational justification for the state to "blight in such discriminatory fashion the hopes of indigents for self-sufficiency and self-respect."[4]

§ 16–42. Criminal Justice: Substantive Requirements of Specificity

In *Papachristou v. Jacksonville*,[1] the Supreme Court attacked the vestiges of the view that poverty and idleness were indications of unregeneracy,[2] by declaring vague and general vagrancy laws unconstitutional.[3] While identifying in such statutes the common vice of inadequate notice as to what conduct was prohibited, the Court found them rife with additional defects, including a particular threat to poor people, nonconformists, dissenters, and idlers.[4] Vagrancy laws represented the criminal aspects of the old poor laws which *Edwards v. California* had long since interred.[5]

accused); Edwards v. Arizona, 451 U.S. 477 (1981) (after a defendant invokes right to counsel, only a knowing and intelligent act can waive that right, and waiver is not established by a showing that the defendant responded to questions).

§ 16–41

1. 384 U.S. 305 (1966).

2. For the suggestion that a stricter standard was being imposed under the guise of rationality, see id. at 311 (Harlan, J., dissenting).

3. 407 U.S. 128 (1972).

4. Id. at 135, 141–42. The Burger Court subsequently approved as free from discriminatory infirmities a recoupment plan requiring repayment for appointed counsel by persons indigent at the time of trial but subsequently able to afford repayment. Fuller v. Oregon, 417 U.S. 40 (1974).

§ 16–42

1. 405 U.S. 156 (1972).

2. For an earlier rejection of that view, see Edwards v. California, 314 U.S. 160, 176–77 (1941), discussed in § 16–36, supra.

3. The Florida law struck down in Papachristou characterized as vagrants all "[r]ogues and vagabonds, or dissolute persons who go about begging, . . . or common drunkards, common night walkers, thieves, pilferers, or pickpockets, . . . persons wandering or strolling around from place to place without any lawful purpose or object, habitual loafers . . ., persons able to work but habitually living upon the earnings of their wives or minor children." 405 U.S. at 156–57 n.1. See also §§ 12–31, 15–14, supra.

4. 405 U.S. at 162, 170.

5. 314 U.S. 160 (1941). Interestingly, in striking down a California loitering statute on vagueness grounds, the Burger Court cited not the risk to *poor* persons but the possible harassment of "joggers" as a potential danger the statute presented. See Kolender v. Lawson, 461 U.S. 352, 360 (1983). One may perhaps be forgiven for

§ 16–43.　Civil Justice: A Judicial Hearing at a Meaningful Time

The commitment to equal justice for rich and poor alike expressed in *Griffin v. Illinois* [1] was articulated most clearly in the civil realm not in cases about access to civil courts [2] but rather in two holdings which ensured a fair judicial hearing before debtors' property could be seized. In *Sniadach v. Family Finance Corp.*,[3] the Court invalidated the Wisconsin wage garnishment scheme, under which a debtor's wages could be frozen by order of a court clerk upon the ex parte request of the creditor's lawyer.　Absence of a prior adversary hearing was held to be a violation of due process since prejudgment garnishment is a "taking which may impose tremendous hardship on wage earners with families to support".[4]　Equal protection concerns were also explicit: "For a poor man—and whoever heard of the wage of the affluent being attached?— to lose part of his salary often means his family will go without the essentials." [5]　Indeed the Court's frequent expressions of sympathy for the debtor victims of the statutes, "trapped in an easy credit nightmare" by exploitative, predatory creditors, drew sharp criticism from dissenting Justice Black,[6] who condemned such expressions as indications of the majority's personal preferences.　Perhaps they are better understood as responses to the presumption, implicit in the garnishment statute, that as between debtors and creditors, debtors are most often the parties at fault, a presumption which in turn rests upon a preconception of debtors generally as lazy, profligate, and faithless.

A similar presumption stigmatizing the debtor class was perhaps implicit in the summary repossession statutes struck down in *Fuentes v. Shevin.*[7]　Under the Florida and Pennsylvania statutes there challenged, sellers of goods under installment purchase contracts, upon an ex parte allegation of right to such goods and posting of a security bond, could obtain a writ of replevin ordering a state agent to seize the disputed property without notice or hearing to the purchaser, thereby allowing creditors to dispossess "uneducated, uninformed consumer[s] with little access to legal help." [8]　The possessory interest in household goods might be "essential to provide a minimally decent environment for human beings in their day-to-day lives." [9]　Debtors could not be deprived of that interest without an opportunity to tell their side of the

seeing in this shift at least a signal of the gentrification or "yuppification" of constitutional law in the 1980s.

§ 16–43

1.　351 U.S. 12 (1956), discussed in § 16–38, supra.

2.　The direct civil counterpart to Griffin, a challenge to a civil court filing or transcript fee, was never decided by the Warren Court.　But indications of a somewhat lesser commitment to equal justice in civil proceedings than in criminal proceedings may be seen in the Court's denial of certiorari in Sandoval v. Rattikin, 395 S.W.2d 889 (1965), cert. denied 385 U.S. 901 (1966) (Texas Court refused to grant a new trial when appointed Legal Aid Attorney carelessly failed to plead a good and sufficient defense on behalf of indigent clients who thereby lost their homestead); compare Anders v. California, 386 U.S. 738 (1967), in § 16–38, supra.

3.　395 U.S. 337 (1969).

4.　Id. at 340.　See also §§ 10–9, 10–14, supra.

5.　395 U.S. at 342 n.9.

6.　Id. at 344.

7.　407 U.S. 67 (1972).

8.　Id. at 83 n.13.

9.　Id. at 89.

story. The generalized presumption that the creditor's story was more trustworthy was not an adequate substitute for due process of law.

Although *Sniadach* and *Fuentes* were conceived as providing *procedural* protection for wage-earners and debtors, it is important to recognize how misleading this description is, and consequently how much more fundamental and substantive is the import of the decisions. In *Fuentes*, for example, the state law allowing for ex parte prejudgment replevin had been incorporated into the contract between debtor and creditor.[10] Mrs. Fuentes' interest in the stove and stereo had therefore been limited, from the inception of the contract, to an interest in uninterrupted possession only so long as Firestone chose not to exercise its summary repossession rights. By providing what it called procedural protection for her possessory interest, the Court in substance held that the state was not free to grant such a limited, uncertain property interest. Debtors under conditional sales contracts are constitutionally entitled to a full measure of quiet enjoyment. Prior to *Fuentes*, this full measure could be acquired through bargaining and only for a price, like all other contract terms, and thus had been virtually unattainable for the poor.[11]

In *Memphis Light, Gas, and Water Div. v. Craft*,[12] the Court extended its due process protections for the poor to include the principles that customers of a public utility are entitled to process before their power is cut off for non-payment of disputed bills. Writing for the majority, Justice Powell[13] found that a state statutory provision allowing the termination of utility services only "for cause" created a "property interest" in continuing service protected by the fourteenth amendment.[14] In deciding what process was due, the Court continued to rely on *Mathews v. Eldridge*,[15] and found the public interest in an immediate cut-off to be slight compared with the private hardship worked by lack of service, considering both the seriousness of the deprivation and the possibility of error.[16]

The Court specifically found that process was required *before* the termination of service, since the injury of a cut-off was irreparable, and since so little money would normally be involved that it would not be worth pursuing the matter in the courts after the fact.[17] The process required was not a hearing as such, but official notice and an opportunity to dispute the bill with utility employees, who had authority to settle the dispute.[18]

---

10. See Ogden v. Saunders, 25 U.S. (12 Wheat.) 213 (1827), discussed in Chapter 9, supra.

11. See § 16–53, infra, for subsequent limitations on the holdings in Sniadach and Fuentes.

12. 436 U.S. 1 (1978).

13. Justice Powell's opinion was joined by Justices Brennan, Stewart, White, Marshall and Blackmun.

14. 436 U.S. at 11–12.

15. 424 U.S. 319 (1976), discussed in § 10–13, supra.

16. 436 U.S. at 18.

17. Id. at 20–21.

18. For a discussion of Justice Stevens' dissenting opinion, see § 16–51, infra.

§ 16–44. Civil Justice: Equal Access to Divorce Proceedings Under the Due Process Clause

Boddie v. Connecticut[1] remains the only case in which the Supreme Court has denied states a right to charge filing fees to indigents seeking access to civil court. The plaintiffs were welfare recipients who sought a divorce but could not afford the requisite sixty dollars in court costs. Writing for the Court, Justice Harlan found the plaintiffs' exclusion from court to be a denial of due process,[2] rejecting the more open-ended equal protection analysis employed in *Griffin* and *Douglas*, the analogous criminal cases.[3] "[G]iven the basic position of the marriage relationship in this society's hierarchy of values and the concomitant state monopolization of the means for legally dissolving this relationship, due process does prohibit a state from denying, solely because of inability to pay, access to its courts to individuals who seek judicial dissolution of their marriages."[4]

Justice Harlan had long preferred to locate constitutional protection for the poor in the due process, rather than the equal protection clause.[5] Equal protection doctrine, which focuses on differential treatment of poor people as a class, contains no natural limiting principle which would readily distinguish access fees to divorce proceedings from tuition at a state university[6] or a fee charged for a fishing license.[7] Judicial intervention to redress poverty on the basis of equal protection is therefore in constant danger of becoming either wholesale or unprincipled, both of which Justice Harlan wanted to avoid. Due process analysis, on the other hand, seemed better suited to a case-by-case inquiry into the nature of the particular benefit sought and the circumstances of the particular indigent plaintiff.[8] Such an approach would

§ 16–44

1. 401 U.S. 371 (1971). See also § 10–18, supra.

2. For a chronicle of how the issues in Boddie developed and changed through the pre-trial, trial, and appellate stages, see LaFrance, "Constitutional Law Reform for the Poor: Boddie v. Connecticut," 1971 Duke L.J. 487.

3. See § 16–38, supra. Justices Douglas and Brennan concurred in the result in Boddie, urging equal access to courts in all civil cases for indigents under the equal protection clause. For the eventual significance of Justice Harlan's rejection of equal protection analysis, which he had urged since Griffin, and his attempt to protect the poor instead through the due process clause, see § 16–51, infra.

4. 401 U.S. at 374. The importance of the fundamental right of marriage to the Boddie holding was underscored in Zablocki v. Redhail, 434 U.S. 374 (1978), where the Court struck down as an impermissible burden on the right to marry a Wisconsin statute requiring a parent without child custody but with child support obligations to seek court approval before

remarrying. For a discussion of Zablocki, see § 15–20, supra, and § 16–52, infra. In Little v. Streater, 452 U.S. 1 (1981), discussed in § 16–51, infra, the Court arguably extended Boddie to the somewhat cognate context of paternity litigation.

5. See, e.g., Griffin v. Illinois, 351 U.S. 12, 34–36 (1956) (dissenting opinion).

6. This was Justice Harlan's example in Griffin, 351 U.S. at 35.

7. See Boddie, 401 U.S. at 385 (Douglas, J., concurring).

8. One of the crucial circumstances of the Boddie plaintiffs for Justice Harlan's purposes was that structurally they were in the position of defendants. The state's monopoly on marriage dissolution *forced* them to settle their claims in court. See Michelman, "The Supreme Court and Litigation Access Fees: The Right to Protect One's Rights—Part I", 1973 Duke L.J. 1153, 1158; see also Yarbrough v. Superior Court, 39 Cal.3d 197, 216 Cal.Rptr. 425, 702 P.2d 583 (1985) (equal access to courts may, in appropriate circumstances, require the state to provide counsel to indigent civil defendants).

leave the basic distribution of wealth intact while remedying the more egregious injustices suffered at the margins of that distributional system.[9]

§ 16–45. Equal Access to Courts Through Concerted Action

Filing fees and court costs represent only the first obstacles to equal access to civil courts. A second and often more substantial obstacle is the price of adequate legal representation, without which an indigent litigant may have paid a filing fee for the dubious privilege of going through the motions to a foregone defeat. "Laymen cannot be expected to know how to protect their rights when dealing with practised and carefully counseled adversaries . . ."[1] While the Supreme Court has never found a constitutional right to appointed counsel in civil cases,[2] the Court has made counsel in civil cases far more accessible to lower income groups by invalidating, as contrary to the first amendment freedom of association,[3] various state prohibitions against concerted legal action.

In *NAACP v. Button*,[4] the Court held unconstitutional, as applied to the NAACP, a Virginia law (1) prohibiting persons from advising others that their legal rights had been infringed and referring them to particular attorneys, and (2) prohibiting attorneys from taking on cases so initiated. The actions of the NAACP legal staff in soliciting and encouraging desegregation suits constituted association for the purpose of "political expression," and were therefore immune from state abridgement without compelling justification.[5] Subsequently, the Court expanded this right of association to protect a union's channeling of its members' legal claims under the Federal Safety Appliance and Employers Liability Acts to lawyers the union felt were legally and morally competent to handle such claims.[6] The Court also held constitutionally protected a union's salaried employment of an attorney to handle its members' claims under a State Workmen's Compensation Act.[7] What began in *Button* as a right of political expression analogous to access to the ballot thus developed into a broader first amendment right for groups to "unite to assert their legal rights as effectively and economically as practicable."[8]

9. See Clune, "Wealth Discrimination and the Fourteenth Amendment," 1975 Sup.Ct.Rev. 289. The fate of Justice Harlan's attempt to circumscribe the elements in Boddie which comprised the due process violation, state monopolization of marriage dissolution and the importance of marriage, is chronicled in § 16–51, infra.

§ 16–45

1. Brotherhood of Railway Trainmen v. Virginia, 377 U.S. 1, 7 (1964).

2. But see Yarbrough v. Superior Court, 39 Cal.3d 197, 216 Cal.Rptr. 425, 702 P.2d 583 (1985), discussed in § 16–44, note 8, supra.

3. See §§ 12–26, 16–11, supra. See also the Court's invalidation of state bans on

advertising of attorney's prices for routine legal services, in § 12–15, supra.

4. 371 U.S. 415 (1963).

5. Id. at 429.

6. Brotherhood of Railroad Trainmen v. Virginia, 377 U.S. 1 (1964).

7. United Mine Workers of America v. Illinois State Bar Association, 389 U.S. 217 (1967).

8. United Transportation Union v. State Bar of Michigan, 401 U.S. 576, 580 (1971) (Union's attempts to protect its members from excessive fees at hands of incompetent counsel in suits for damages under Federal Employees Liability Act, by means of recommending selected attorneys and securing commitment from them that

These decisions met with acrimonious dissents, accusing the majority of "cut[ting] deeply into one of the most traditional of state concerns, the maintenance of high standards within the state legal profession." [9] What the dissenters ignored and the majorities implicitly acknowledged, however, is that those "high standards" cherished by the state were available only at an equally high price. The states' failure to permit an alternative model of attorney-client relationship operated to foreclose the poor from meaningful assistance of counsel in civil cases, and it was this result that the Court held violated the first and fourteenth amendments.

§ 16–46. Equal Participation in the Political Process: Demise of the Poll Tax [1]

Structurally, *Harper v. Virginia Board of Elections*,[2] the first of the cases striking down wealth classifications within the states' distribution of the franchise, is strikingly like *Griffin*.[3] *Harper* involved a challenge to the Virginia poll tax. Like the right of appeal from criminal convictions, the franchise is not independently guaranteed by the Constitution. Nevertheless, again like the criminal appeal, granting the vote to some and denying it to others violates the equal protection clause.[4] Since "[w]ealth, like race, creed, or color, is not germane to one's ability to participate intelligently in the electoral process," the poll tax introduced "a capricious or irrelevant factor." [5] This finding of irrelevance, exactly as in *Griffin*, reflected the majority's refusal to recognize the obvious fiscal purposes served by the poll tax.

The majority's disregard of fiscal concerns and its categorical rejection of the poll tax as measuring "ability to participate intelligently in the electoral process" [6] appear to have been aimed at Virginia's proposed justification of the tax: ". . . the Virginia system affords a non-discriminatory objective test of minimum intelligence for ordering one's own affairs and participating in those of the state, requiring no more than a token payment of $1.50 . . ." [7] The State's brief went on to characterize the poll tax as "an elementary and objective intelligence test." [8] In other words, Virginia's system was based on the view that if

they would not charge more than 25% of recovery, held protected against state prohibition).

9. United Mine Workers, 389 U.S. at 225–26 (Harlan, J., dissenting).

§ 16–46

1. The decisions discussed in §§ 16–46 to 16–48 are explored more closely in Chapter 13, supra.

2. 383 U.S. 663 (1966), discussed in § 16–10, supra.

3. The major exception to this structural similarity lies in the remedies imposed. In Griffin v. Illinois, 351 U.S. 12 (1956), the Court required states to provide free transcripts only for indigents. In Harper, the poll tax was abolished in its entirety.

4. See § 16–10, supra.

5. 383 U.S. at 668. Compare the almost identical statement in Griffin v. Illinois, 351 U.S. 12, 17 (1956).

6. 383 U.S. at 668.

7. Brief for Commonwealth of Virginia at 5.

8. Id. at 38. Although the Commonwealth's Brief did not mention the revenue-raising function of the tax, Virginia's Tax Commissioner did mention this function as one of two subsidiary purposes of the tax at the trial in District Court. Id., in Appendix at 5. The major purpose advanced at trial was the intelligence test equivalent argued in the brief; the subsidiary purpose was keeping the registration rolls up to date. Finally, the Commissioner testified that all three of the current purposes were adopted subsequent to the

you can't scrape together $1.50 for a very important purpose, you're probably not smart enough, or at least you don't have enough business sense, to vote.

The intelligence test function claimed by the state in defending the poll tax gives the majority's treatment of the tax as creating a suspect classification more plausibility than it might seem to command on the surface. For the wealth discrimination was revealed as intentional, and not simply de facto. The whole *point* of the poll tax was to prevent the very poor from voting, viewing poverty as evidence of a complete lack of prudence about how to manage one's affairs. This legislative purpose in turn reflected an intolerant, and indeed hostile, attitude toward the poor, an attitude not entirely dissimilar to the equation of poverty and bad character which had been rejected as unacceptable in *Edwards v. California*.[9]

§ 16–47. Demise of Property Ownership as a Means of Voter Qualification

In *Cipriano v. Houma*,[1] the Court struck down a Louisiana law restricting to "property taxpayers" the right to vote in elections called to approve the issuance of revenue bonds by a municipal utility. Because the franchise was at stake, the Court applied the compelling governmental interest test and rejected the state's contention that the "special pecuniary interest"[2] of property owners justified the exclusion of non-property owners who were "as substantially affected and directly interested in the matter voted upon as those who are permitted to vote."[3] *Turner v. Fouche*,[4] decided a year later, struck down a limitation on school board membership to freeholders. This time a unanimous Court eschewed a determination of which level of scrutiny to apply, since the limitation was said to be wholly irrational; the ability to participate responsibly in educational decisions depends in no way on land ownership, nor does attachment to the community and its educational values.[5]

§ 16–48. Equal Access to the Ballot for Political Candidates

In *Bullock v. Carter*,[1] the Court struck down the Texas system of financing primary elections, under which the candidates themselves bore the election costs in the form of filing fees, often running to thousands of dollars per candidate. Although the system was not directed against any precisely defined class, and although some candi-

poll tax itself. The poll tax was written into the Virginia Constitution in 1902. "Many of the most vocal members of the Constitutional Convention at that time expressed approval of the capitation tax on the ground that it tend to retard or prevent voting by members of the Negro race." Id., in Appendix at 5.

9. 314 U.S. 160 (1941), discussed in § 16–36, supra.

§ 16–47

1. 395 U.S. 701 (1969) (per curiam).

2. Id. at 704.

3. Id. at 706. Accord, Phoenix v. Kolodziejski, 399 U.S. 204 (1970); see also Kramer v. Union Free School District, 395 U.S. 621 (1969). See §§ 13–10, 13–11, supra.

4. 396 U.S. 346 (1970).

5. Id. at 363–64. But see Salyer Land Co. v. Tulare Water District, 410 U.S. 719 (1973), discussed in § 16–58, infra.

§ 16–48

1. 405 U.S. 134 (1972).

dates representing poor people would undoubtedly be able to pay the fees assessed against them, "we would ignore reality were we not to recognize that this system falls with unequal weight on voters, as well as candidates, according to their economic status." [2]   Because the system had a "real and appreciable impact on the exercise of the franchise," and the impact was "related to the resources of the voters supporting a particular candidate," [3] the Court applied the heightened level of scrutiny used in *Harper*—i.e., inquiring whether the system was "reasonably necessary to the accomplishment of legitimate state objectives." [4]   The state's purposes in charging the costs of the primary to the candidates were two: limiting the ballot to a manageable size, and collecting revenues for financing the elections.   Limiting the primary ballot thus had a positive dimension only vaguely present in limiting the burden on a state's judicial machinery; an overloaded ballot confuses and discourages the voter and often works to thwart the will of the majority.   However, the means chosen was completely arbitrary. The filing fee did not measure a candidate's seriousness when the candidate was "*unable*, not simply *unwilling*" to pay.[5]   Furthermore, "even assuming that every person paying the large fees required by Texas law takes his own candidacy seriously, that does not make him a 'serious candidate' in the popular sense." [6]   The Court therefore found the filing fee "extraordinarily ill-fitted" [7] to the goal of limiting the ballot to serious candidates.

With regard to the fiscal goal, the Court was forced to admit the rationality of the scheme as a means of raising money for the primaries [8] but found that *this particular financing scheme* was not reasonably necessary.   Since the state required primary elections by law, "presumably . . . more to benefit the voters than the candidates," there was no particular justice in making the candidates subsidize it.[9] The Court found much more amenable some system of putting the burden on the taxpayers.[10]   "Without making light of the State's interest in husbanding its revenues, we fail to see such an element of necessity in the State's present means of financing primaries as to justify the resulting incursion on the prerogatives of voters." [11]

§ 16–49. Welfare Rights: The Guarantee of Distribution With an Even Hand and the Implicit Recognition of Affirmative Duties to the Poor

In *Goldberg v. Kelly*,[1] the Supreme Court held that states could not terminate an individual's welfare benefits prior to a quasi-judicial

2. Id. at 144.

3. Id.

4. Id. See Harper v. Virginia Board of Elections, 383 U.S. 663 (1966), discussed in §§ 16–10, 16–46, supra.

5. Bullock, 405 U.S. at 146 (emphasis in original).

6. Id.

7. Id.

8. The Court's recognition that *any* fee is reasonable as a financing measure (compare Griffin v. Illinois, 351 U.S. 12 (1956))

highlights the necessity of applying some heightened level of scrutiny, lest all fees be upheld as self-justifying.

9. Bullock, 405 U.S. at 148.

10. Although not in their capacity as voters, of course, in the form of a poll tax.

11. 405 U.S. at 149. Compare the remedy chosen in Lubin v. Panish, 415 U.S. 709 (1974), discussed in § 16–55, infra.

§ 16–49

1. 397 U.S. 254 (1970), discussed in § 10–9 and §§ 10–14 to 10–16, supra.

administrative hearing on the recipient's eligibility.[2] Such a hearing was required, in the face of the state's pleas against the financial burdens entailed, because of the pressing need for an accurate determination of non-eligibility: "[T]ermination of aid pending resolution of a controversy over eligibility may deprive an *eligible* recipient of the very means by which to live while he waits." [3]

Although decided on due process grounds, *Goldberg* contains the clearest and most direct exposition of the rationale behind the cases protecting the poor under the equal protection clause: "We have come to recognize that forces not within the control of the poor contribute to their poverty." [4] This recognition of the poor as innocent victims of social, economic, and legal forces represents the death blow to any connection of poverty with moral or mental deficiency.[5] And the same point of view generates at least one underpinning for an affirmative governmental duty of public assistance: "Welfare, by meeting the basic demands of subsistence, can help bring within the reach of the poor the same opportunities that are available to others to participate meaningfully in the life of the community . . . Public assistance, then, is *not mere charity*, but a means to 'promote the general Welfare, and secure the Blessings of Liberty to ourselves and our Posterity'." [6]

Like *Fuentes v. Shevin*,[7] the *Goldberg* decision cannot be properly understood as protecting purely procedural rights. Unless the Court were concerned to secure for welfare recipients a substantive right of some sort to the subsistence provided by the state, there would be no satisfactory reply to the contention that, having chosen to extend only benefits terminable without prior hearing, the state should not be compelled to enlarge the substance of what it has given.[8] Nor was *Goldberg* the sort of case in which the procedure guaranteed by the Court served significant participatory purposes apart from the welfare benefits themselves.[9] Not even the Court's subsequent limitations of the *Goldberg* principle [10] have altered the rule that welfare benefits cannot be arbitrarily terminated, a rule explicable only in terms of an underlying right to subsistence at least when a welfare program has been established.[11]

2. Note that, unlike Sniadach v. Family Finance Corp., 395 U.S. 337 (1967) and Fuentes v. Shevin, 407 U.S. 67 (1972), discussed in § 16–43, supra, no right to a *judicial* hearing was at stake in Goldberg.

3. Goldberg, 397 U.S. at 264.

4. Id. at 265.

5. But see United States v. Kras, 409 U.S. 434 (1973), discussed in § 16–51, infra, and Lassiter v. Dept. of Social Services, 452 U.S. 18 (1981), discussed in § 16–51, infra.

6. 397 U.S. at 264 (emphasis added).

7. 407 U.S. 67 (1972), discussed in § 16–43, supra, and § 16–53, infra.

8. See §§ 10–9 to 10–12, supra.

9. See §§ 10–7, 10–19, supra.

10. See § 16–56, infra.

11. See § 15–9, supra, and § 16–8, supra. The Court has not yet addressed the issue of Goldberg v. Kelly's relevance to applicants for welfare benefits. Some Justices, however, seem willing to do so. In dissenting from a denial of certiorari, Justice O'Connor, joined by Justices Brennan and Marshall, found the lack of due process protections to initial applicants for welfare benefits "unsettling in its implication that less fortunate persons in our society may arbitrarily be denied benefits that a state has granted as a matter of right." Gregory v. Pittsfield, 470 U.S. 1018 (1985). Keeping in mind the needs of the poor and the rationale of Goldberg, a distinction between applicants for welfare benefits and those already receiving them, where the state's positive law establishes an entitle-

§ 16–50. Welfare Distribution With an Even Hand—Criteria of Eligibility

A heightened standard of evenhandedness in dealing with the poor has been employed to strike down two classifications drawn in the Federal Food Stamp Act [1] and one classification in a state public assistance program.[2] The purposes of the Federal Food Stamp Act were to raise levels of nutrition among low-income households and strengthen the agricultural economy.[3] In *Moreno*, a congressional amendment denying assistance to households including one or more members unrelated to the rest was held "clearly irrelevant" to these purposes [4] because the amendment excluded "*only* those persons . . . so desperately in need of aid that they cannot even afford to alter their living arrangements so as to retain their eligibility." [5] In *Murry*, the

ment in both instances, seems utterly indefensible. See also § 10–9, supra.

§ 16–50

1. United States Department of Agriculture v. Moreno, 413 U.S. 528 (1973); United States Department of Agriculture v. Murry, 413 U.S. 508 (1973).

2. New Jersey Welfare Rights Organization v. Cahill, 411 U.S. 619 (1973). For arguments that the rationality test had been stiffened in these cases, see especially the dissenting opinions in Moreno, 413 U.S. at 545–47, and Cahill, 411 U.S. at 622–23.

3. 413 U.S. at 533. See also Rodway v. United States Department of Agriculture, 514 F.2d 809, 818–22 (D.C.Cir. 1975) (food stamp program must provide "nutritionally adequate" diet, and allotment schemes not meeting this goal are invalid).

4. 413 U.S. at 534.

5. Id. at 538 (emphasis in original). The Moreno claimants included a diabetic woman living with another woman and the latter's three children, as well as two women sharing living expenses to enable the daughter of one to attend a school for the deaf. In Lyng v. Castillo, 106 S.Ct. 2727 (1986), the Court upheld congressional amendments to the Federal Food Stamp Program that automatically treated parents, children, and siblings living together (unless one of the parents or siblings is elderly or disabled) as a single "household"—and hence as ineligible, even if they in fact neither purchase nor prepare meals as a single economic unit, for the increased food stamp allotment available in such factual circumstances to more distant relatives and unrelated persons who live together but can show that they do not eat together. Rather than discriminating against unrelated persons who live in a single home, as in Moreno, this measure in effect discriminated the other way around: the *family* that lived together was presumed to eat together, to its economic disadvantage in calculating food stamp allotments. The majority opinion by Justice Stevens, joined by Chief Justice Burger and Justices Blackmun, Powell, Rehnquist, and O'Connor, reasoned that the "disadvantaged class . . . comprised by parents, children, and siblings" could hardly be deemed a "'suspect' or 'quasi-suspect' class" since such "[c]lose relatives. . . . have not been subjected to discrimination; . . . do not exhibit obvious, immutable, or distinguishing characteristics that define them as a discrete group; and . . . are not a minority or politically powerless." Id. at 2729. It was entirely reasonable, the majority concluded, for Congress to decide "that limited funds would not permit the accommodation given distant relatives and unrelated persons to be stretched to embrace close relatives as well." Id. at 2732. "Finally, Congress might have reasoned that it would be somewhat easier for close relatives—again, almost by definition—to accommodate their living habits to a federal policy favoring common meal preparation than it would be for more distant relatives or unrelated persons to do so." Id. Justices Brennan and White, in separate dissents, would have found the challenged classifications "irrational" despite these considerations. Id.

For Justice Marshall, also dissenting separately, the decisive defect in the provisions at issue was their adverse impact upon "families whose resources are so low that they must rely on their relatives for shelter." Id. at 2733. By enforcing what "amount[s] to a conclusive presumption that [close relatives] living under the same roof do all of their cooking together," the regulations, in Justice Marshall's view, intrude upon "not merely . . . the important privacy interest in family living arrangements . . . but the even more vital interest in survival," inasmuch as some relatives who must live in the same house "cannot prepare meals together because of different work schedules" or because they

Court invalidated the Act's exclusion of households in which any member over eighteen years of age had been claimed, during the prior tax year, as a dependent on the federal income tax return of a taxpayer not a member of an eligible household. This exclusion was held to operate as an irrebuttable presumption, often contrary to fact, that the tax dependent's household was not needy and thus has access to nutritional adequacy.[6] Finally, New Jersey's denial of benefits to families with illegitimate children was held to violate equal protection. "[T]here can be no doubt that the benefits extended under the challenged Families of the Working Poor program are as indispensable to the health and well-being of illegitimate children as to those who are legitimate."[7]

That welfare criteria must be closely related to need also provides one plausible way to understand the so-called "right to travel" cases, in which the Court invalidated durational residency requirements for the receipt of welfare benefits[8] and free non-emergency medical care.[9] The right to travel rationale alone, under which the waiting periods are seen as deterrents or penalties for poor people desiring to start afresh in life but reluctant to move unless they are certain of a continuous source of income, cannot quite support these decisions; it is at least as great a deterrent to travel when the second state provides no welfare assistance to all, or offers significantly lower benefits although with no waiting period; yet the right to travel has, of course, not been read to require any minimum level of welfare benefits.[10] A large component of these decisions must therefore be the heightened level of evenhandedness, requiring disregard of non-need related factors such as length of residency, which the Court has at times imposed on programs purporting to provide for the needy.[11]

"lack sufficient plates and utensils to accommodate more than a few persons at once, or may have only one burner on their stove" and thus may entirely "lack the option of cooking and eating together." Id. The majority's observation that the challenged law worked no injury to "unrelated persons who live together for reasons of economy or health," id. at 2729, provided no answer to Justice Marshall's concern for those closely related persons as to whom "the regulation threatens . . . lives and health by denying . . . the minimal benefits provided to all other families of similar income and needs." Id. at 2733. The Court's unwillingness to force Congress to fine-tune the food stamp program to the degree necessary to accommodate Justice Marshall's entirely realistic concern was, of course, quite predictable—and may even have been defensible—in light of Dandridge v. Williams, 397 U.S. 471 (1970), discussed in §§ 10–12, 16–4, supra, and 16–57, infra.

6. The plaintiffs in Murry, for example, obtained no support whatever from the taxpayers claiming them as dependents;

see the discussion of irrebuttable presumptions in § 16–34, supra.

7. New Jersey Welfare Rights Organization v. Cahill, 411 U.S. 619, 621 (1973). See also § 16–24, supra.

8. Shapiro v. Thompson, 394 U.S. 618 (1969).

9. Memorial Hospital v. Maricopa County, 415 U.S. 250 (1974).

10. See the further discussion of these cases, in § 16–8, supra.

11. In Shapiro, the state admitted that it intended to exclude welfare recipients from other states—or at least those recipients who would enter the state solely to obtain larger benefits—in order to preserve its resources. The Court responded that fiscal justifications could not meet the compelling interest test. 394 U.S. at 627–33. Compare Edwards v. California, 314 U.S. 160 (1941), discussed in § 16–36, supra. See also § 16–49, supra. But see Batterton v. Francis, 432 U.S. 416 (1977) (state may deny welfare to families where father's unemployment is caused by participation in labor dispute). Perhaps the soundest ex-

§ 16–51.   Decline of Judicial Intervention on Behalf of the Poor: The Triumph of the State Fisc and the Sterilization of Griffin, Douglas and Boddie

In the three decades since it was decided, *Griffin v. Illinois* [1] has spawned roughly a dozen decisions reaffirming the states' duties to waive filing fees or provide free transcripts of proceedings to convicted or accused indigents seeking various avenues of relief. [2] *Douglas v. California*, [3] on the other hand, remained an inactive precedent until 1974, when the Burger Court effectively sterilized it in *Ross v. Moffitt*. [4] Cutting off *Douglas'* possibilities for future growth, *Ross* held that the state is not constitutionally required to appoint counsel for indigent state prisoners seeking discretionary state review or filing applications for United States Supreme Court review. In the course of so holding, the Court disengaged *Griffin* from *Douglas*, deftly rewove the *Griffin* transcript and filing fee decisions together as minimal access cases rather than equal protection cases, and neatly severed *Douglas* from this newly created body of law. Under this revised rationale, *Griffin* and its progeny "stand for the proposition that a State cannot arbitrarily cut off appeal rights for indigents while leaving open avenues of appeal for more affluent persons." [5] *Douglas*, by contrast, "undertook an examination of whether an indigent's access to the appellate system was adequate." [6] Furthermore, the suspect status of wealth classifications was neutralized in *Ross* by exactly the factors the Court refused to consider in *Griffin* and *Douglas*: The Court in *Ross* chose not to impose the cost of counsel for discretionary review on states which "find that other claims for public funds within or without the criminal justice system preclude the implementation of such a policy at the present time." [7]

An indication that similar considerations had contributed to the severely restricted holding on the right to access to civil courts in

planation of the Shapiro line of cases is that the state must offer a compelling justification for making welfare applicants, but not would-be users of those state benefits that are available to rich and poor alike, wait for a significant period after establishing their residency: "[A] state may no more try to fence out those indigents who seek higher welfare benefits than it may try to fence out indigents generally. Implicit in any such distinction is the notion that indigents who enter a state with the hope of securing higher welfare benefits are somehow less deserving than indigents who do not take this consideration into account. But we do not perceive why a mother who is seeking to make a new life for herself and her children should be regarded as less deserving because she considers, among other factors, the level of a State's public assistance. Surely such a mother is no less deserving than a mother who moves into a particular State in order to take advantage of its better educational facilities." Shapiro, 394 U.S. at 631–32. See also § 16–8, *supra*.

§ 16–51

1. 351 U.S. 12 (1956).

2. See, e.g., cases cited in § 16–38, note 29, *supra*.

3. 372 U.S. 353 (1963).

4. 417 U.S. 600 (1974).

5. Id. at 607. For an explanation of why Griffin and its progeny in fact stood for a great deal more than Ross allows, see § 16–38, *supra*.

6. Ross, 417 U.S. at 607.

7. Id. at 618. Several states had filed amicus curiae briefs threatening financial ruin. In accord with Ross is Pennsylvania v. Finley, 107 S.Ct. 1990 (1987) (state's decision to grant access to counsel for postconviction review does not require that counsel's actions comport with Anders v. California, 386 U.S. 738 (1967)), discussed in § 16–38, *supra*, at note 26.

Boddie v. Connecticut [8] is found in the Court's denial of certiorari soon after *Boddie* was decided in a handful of suits by indigents seeking free access to civil courts for a variety of purposes.[9] Justice Black dissented from the denial of certiorari on the ground that *Boddie*, from which he had dissented, could have rested on only one principle, "that the civil courts of the United States and each of the States belong to the people of this country and that no person can be denied access to those courts, either for a trial or an appeal, because he cannot pay a fee, finance a bond, risk a penalty, or afford to hire an attorney." [10] He had "no doubt that this country can afford to provide court costs and lawyers to Americans who are now barred by their poverty from resort to the law for resolution of their disputes." [11]

In *United States v. Kras*,[12] the Burger Court's departure from the equal justice model erected by the Warren Court became most poignantly evident. The great deference toward state fiscal justifications with which *Ross v. Moffitt* explicitly and the civil cases implicitly had already replaced the Warren Court's indifference to such matters was joined by the Burger Court's adoption of the very attitude toward the poor which the Warren Court's decisions had striven to banish. Kras, a particularly sympathetic indigent petitioner with a tale of woe laid out in full Dickensian detail,[13] sought escape from his unfortunate past and a new start in life via release in bankruptcy. The only obstacle was the $50 bankruptcy fee which Kras, according to the trial court's findings, was completely unable to pay, and which under the rule of *Boddie v. Connecticut* [14] he asked the Court to hold violative of due process. A closely divided Court rejected the claim by construing *Boddie* narrowly as requiring both that a fundamental interest be at stake and that the state's monopoly over resolution of disputes concerning that interest be complete.[15]

Unredeemed by the distinguishing characteristics of *Boddie*, therefore, the bankruptcy filing fee was merely another law in the "area of economics and social welfare," requiring only rational justification.[16] The Court then adopted the tautological position which had for so long suggested itself to dissenters and had so far been eschewed by the majority—i.e., that charging a fee is its own justification: Congress "sought to make the system self-sustaining and paid for by those who use it rather than by tax revenues drawn by the public at large." [17] Thus Kras, challenging the nature of the bankruptcy financing scheme,

---

8. 401 U.S. 371 (1971), discussed in §§ 16–11, 16–44, supra.

9. See, e.g., Meltzer v. C. Buck LeCraw & Co., 402 U.S. 954 (1971). Among the unheard cases was a suit by an indigent mother denied court-appointed counsel to defend her in a state civil suit to declare her an unfit mother and take away five of her seven children. Carter v. Kaufman, 8 Cal.App.3d 783, 87 Cal.Rptr. 678 (1970), cert. denied 402 U.S. 964 (1971). Accord, Lassiter v. Department of Social Services, 452 U.S. 18 (1981), discussed infra.

10. 402 U.S. at 955.

11. Id. at 956.

12. 409 U.S. 434 (1973).

13. The story included a blameless falling into debt, a pack of ruthless creditors, no income, no assets, a dependent wife and mother, and an infant child hospitalized with cystic fibrosis.

14. 401 U.S. 371 (1971).

15. See the critique of this rationale in § 16–11, supra.

16. Kras, 409 U.S. at 446.

17. Id. at 448.

was told that charging him was rational because it is *a* financing scheme, not because it is a *fair* one.

The Court's final remarks in *Kras* indicated one possible source of the Court's deference—or, more accurately, the absence of a factor which would have engendered a more critical stance. The $50 fee was payable, in extraordinary circumstances, in installments of $1.28 per week, which the Court found a pitiably small sum, "less than the price of a movie and little more than the cost of a pack or two of cigarettes." [18] If Kras were as serious as he claimed about his fresh start in life, Justice Blackmun opined, "this much available revenue should be within his able-bodied reach . . ." [19] This approached the "poverty as evidence of unworthiness" argument which even the dissenters in the Warren Court could barely bring themselves to articulate.[20] It traced the low-water mark of the twentieth century Supreme Court's battle against stigmatizing stereotypes of the poor.

The Court's rejection of claims of equal access to civil courts was consolidated in *Ortwein v. Schwab*,[21] where the Court, again dividing 5–4, refused to find an equal protection or due process violation in Oregon's requirement of a $25 appellate filing fee from an indigent seeking judicial review of an administrative reduction in his old-age assistance. Characterizing the case as arising in the area of economics and social welfare and as implicating no fundamental right and disadvantaging no suspect class, the Court applied the rational relation test in the same question-begging manner it had employed in *Kras*: "the purpose of the filing fee . . . is apparent. The Oregon Court system incurs operating costs, and the fee produces some small revenue to assist in offsetting those expenses." [22] The concerns of *Kras* were much muted in the per curiam opinion in *Ortwein*, but the Court's determination to draw the line, however arbitrarily, was no less evident. A central question in the case should have been, as the dissenters pointed out, whether there is a due process right to judicial review of administrative action.[23] Had this question been answered in the affirmative, the filing fee must have fallen; independent constitutional rights cannot be denied to indigents by means of a fee.[24] Only a negative answer to the judicial review question could have begun to justify the filing fee.[25] Evidently the Court was not willing to answer

18. Id. at 449.

19. Id.

20. See § 16–46, supra.

21. 410 U.S. 656 (1973) (per curiam). Justices Stewart, id. at 661, Douglas, id., Brennan, id. at 664, and Marshall, id. at 665, dissented.

22. Id. at 660.

23. See § 3–5, supra. This question is not entirely separate from the Boddie monopoly question, to which the Court in Ortwein also gave short shrift. According to the Court, the Goldberg-type hearing *already held* constituted a sufficient alternative to dispel the monopoly claim. This answer begs two questions. First, it was

the very integrity of that proceeding the plaintiff was challenging with a lack-of-substantial-evidence claim. Second, the "alternative" was itself a *state* monopolized, although not a *judicially* monopolized, settlement procedure. The appellants could not even theoretically obtain relief outside of the state's administrative machinery. See Comment, "The Heirs of Boddie: Court Access For Indigents after Kras and Ortwein," 8 Harv.Civ.Rts.—Civ. Lib.Rev. 571, 579 (1973).

24. See, e.g., Gideon v. Wainwright, 372 U.S. 335 (1963) (right to counsel).

25. Furthermore, even if an independent right to judicial review were not recognized, allowing the rich to utilize availa-

the due process question in the negative. Yet neither was the Court willing to say "yes" when such an answer would have required dipping into the states' treasuries.

Ortwein and *Kras* do as great an injustice to *Boddie v. Connecticut* as would the adoption of Justice Black's all-or-nothing approach.[26] In fact, these two cases effectively choose "nothing", leaving *Boddie* as a single, unprincipled exception to the otherwise blanket current rule that indigents have no constitutional right of access to civil courts.[27] Justice Harlan in *Boddie* obviously wanted to assure indigents access to civil courts in some important cases, while hesitating to impose upon the states the cost of filing fees and perhaps counsel for every indigent who could dream up a tort claim or find a lawyer to draw one up. But the Burger Court perpetuated Justice Harlan's frugality more consistently than his sense of fairness, treating nearly every claim of access to civil proceedings as a floodgate that must be kept closed at all costs.

On the same day in 1981, the Court took one step forward and one step back in a pair of decisions revealing the importance of the particular facts of a case in determining the doctrinal result. In *Little v. Streater*,[28] the Court expanded the opportunities for fair adjudication of paternity claims against indigents. Gloria Streater gave birth to a child out of wedlock and was compelled by the Connecticut Department of Social Services to bring a paternity suit in order to qualify her daughter for welfare benefits. A state attorney brought suit on Streater's behalf against the alleged father, Walter Little, who was indigent and was incarcerated in a state prison. Little requested blood tests of Streater and her child pursuant to state law, but his motion was denied because he lacked the money to pay for them. Under Connecticut law, the reputed father's testimony is insufficient to overcome the mother's prima facie case in a paternity suit.[29] Thus Little was declared to be the father and was ordered to pay child support.

The Supreme Court unanimously held Connecticut's refusal to pay for the blood tests to be a violation of the due process clause. In an opinion by Chief Justice Burger, the Court praised the unique exculpatory quality of blood grouping tests [30] and observed that compelling the state to pay for them in cases of indigency imposed no real financial burden on the public fisc.[31] The Court reasoned that, because the state played a "prominent role in the litigation," [32] it was responsible for

ble judicial review machinery while effectively excluding the poor still raises equal protection problems analogous to those in Griffin v. Illinois, 351 U.S. 12 (1956). See §§ 16–11, 16–38, supra.

26. See Meltzer v. C. Buck LeCraw & Co., 402 U.S. 954 (1971) (dissenting opinion).

27. It is hard to imagine many other cases fulfilling the strict monopoly definition imposed in Kras. But other matters of state-determined personal status in the domestic relations area, such as child custody or annulment, may be able to meet the test. See LaFrance, "Constitutional

Law Reform for the Poor: Boddie v. Connecticut," 1971 Duke L.J. 487, 535.

28. 452 U.S. 1 (1981).

29. Id. at 12.

30. The Court made a similar observation concerning the usefulness of blood test evidence in Pickett v. Brown, 462 U.S. 1 (1983), and relied in part on the fact that such evidence does not go stale to justify its condemnation of a two-year statute of limitations for paternity suits. See § 16–24, supra.

31. 452 U.S. at 14–16.

32. Id. at 6.

paying for the tests in order that the state's onerous evidentiary rule not deprive Little of a "meaningful opportunity to be heard." [33]

The Court's holding in *Streater* that the state must subsidize blood tests for an indigent man whose paternity is in question contrasts strikingly with its ruling in the companion case, *Lassiter v. Department of Social Services*,[34] that the state does *not* have to pay for a lawyer for an indigent woman whose child is being permanently taken away. In *Lassiter*, Justice Stewart wrote for a five-member majority [35] which held that Abby Gail Lassiter was not deprived of liberty without due process of law when North Carolina terminated her parental rights without providing counsel for her. Until one reaches the bottom line, reading Justice Stewart's opinion might lead one to expect the Court to reach the opposite conclusion. First, Justice Stewart declared that a parent's interest in not losing her child is "extremely important." [36] Second, he stated that North Carolina shared this interest in reaching an accurate determination of the best interests of the child and had only a weak pecuniary interest in avoiding the costs of appointed counsel.[37] Finally, Justice Stewart admitted that the incapacity of the parent and the complexity of termination hearings—with their frequent emphasis on psychiatric testimony—would often be great enough "to make the risk of an erroneous deprivation of the parent's rights insupportably high." [38] He recounted the fact that every previous state court decision on the question had held that due process requires appointment of counsel,[39] and he cited numerous studies which had urged the adoption of such a rule.[40] Justice Stewart went so far as to characterize the practice of providing counsel to indigents in termination proceedings as "enlightened and wise." [41]

Despite all this, the majority's conclusion was that an indigent is presumptively entitled to appointed counsel only when faced with the risk of being deprived of physical liberty,[42] and the petition alleged no neglect on which criminal charges could be based.[43] The majority held that the need for counsel in termination proceedings was best determined by appellate review on an ad hoc basis, and opined—after reading a cold record that had been compiled without the aid of counsel—that the case before the Court "presented no specially trouble-

33. Id. The "state action" aspects of this holding are discussed in § 18–7, infra.

34. 452 U.S. 18 (1981).

35. Chief Justice Burger and Justices White, Powell and Rehnquist joined Justice Stewart's majority opinion. Justices Blackmun, Brennan, Marshall and Stevens dissented.

36. 452 U.S. at 34.

37. Id. at 28.

38. Id. at 34.

39. Id. at 30.

40. Id. at 33–34.

41. Id. at 34.

42. Id. at 25–26. A contrary holding would have to be reconciled with Morrissey

v. Brewer, 408 U.S. 471 (1972) (no presumptive right to appointed counsel in parole revocation hearing); Gagnon v. Scarpelli, 411 U.S. 778 (1973) (probation revocation); Parham v. J.R., 442 U.S. 584 (1979) (civil commitment where no imprisonment results). The dissent noted that these hearings were less formal and adversarial than the one in issue because the state was not represented by counsel. See 452 U.S. at 44 (Blackmun, J., dissenting). And in Little v. Streater, which the Court decided the same day, the indigent defendant was not threatened with incarceration or having his child taken away, but only with paying child support.

43. 452 U.S. at 32.

some points of law, either procedural or substantive." [44]   As the dissent rightly pointed out, that conclusion parallels the infamous rule of *Betts v. Brady*,[45] which the Court had denounced two decades earlier.[46]

The real basis for *Lassiter* may lie in the singularly unsympathetic facts of the case. First, the petitioner made no effort to obtain counsel and never averred that she was indigent.[47] Second, Ms. Lassiter was hardly a model parent: she had pointedly refused to show up at the original hearing in 1975 when her infant son was first adjudged "neglected" and transferred to state custody; [48] she made no effort to contact her son or to inquire about him during the two years he was in foster care; [49] and, at the time of the termination hearing in 1978, she was serving a 40-year sentence for having murdered a man with a butcher knife.[50] The majority's detailed recitation of the facts of the murder, which it gleaned from the record of her criminal trial rather than from that of the termination proceeding, suggests that Lassiter's fitness as a mother, and not her right to counsel, was uppermost in the Justices' minds.[51] Nonetheless, one can only hope that the states and localities will heed the strong argument which the Court made in *favor* of a rule requiring states to furnish indigents with counsel in parental status hearings, or that any similar future cases that make their way to the Supreme Court will bear a less distracting and depressing set of facts.

The road the Court has travelled from *Boddie* to *Lassiter* has become increasingly narrow. The states are required to subsidize the most basic civil litigation costs of indigents only when: the state has a complete monopoly on resolution of the dispute, a fundamental interest is at stake, and the resulting financial burden on the state treasury would be light. Because these decisions contain so many escape hatches for a judiciary not particularly familiar with the plight of the dispossessed and understandably hesitant to spend the states' revenues, the fourteenth amendment provides only modest relief for poor people who seek a day in court.

---

44. Id.

45. 316 U.S. 455 (1942), overruled in Gideon v. Wainwright, 372 U.S. 335 (1963). See, e.g., Kamisar, "The Right of Counsel and the 14th Amendment: A Dialogue on the 'The Most Pervasive Right' of An Accused," 30 U.Chi.L.Rev. 1, 65–7 (1962).

46. 452 U.S. at 35–36 (Blackmun, J., dissenting).

47. Id. at 21–22.

48. 452 U.S. at 32–33.

49. Id. at 21.

50. Id. at 20 n.1.

51. The Court softened its tone one year later in a case where it held, 5–4, that due process requires a clear and convincing standard of proof in a termination hearing before a child can be taken away from a

natural parent on grounds of permanent neglect. See Santosky v. Kramer, 455 U.S. 745 (1982). In arriving at this conclusion, Justice Blackmun noted: "The fundamental liberty interest of natural parents in the care, custody, and management of their child does not evaporate simply because they have not been model parents." Id. at 753. Justice Rehnquist, in a dissent joined by Chief Justice Burger and Justices White and O'Connor, denounced the majority as having "moved us in [the] direction" of "a society where every aspect of [family] life [is] regulated by a single source of law." Id. at 770. The dissenters rejected both the Court's due process analysis and its inclination to displace with federal law the rule of states in structuring family relationships. See § 10–15, supra.

§ 16–52. Decline But Not Demise of Judicial Intervention on Behalf of the Poor: Minimal Protection of the Laws

In *Ross v. Moffitt*, the Court, spurred by its respect for state financial concerns, trimmed the *Griffin-Douglas* line of cases down to the bone and characterized what remained as a guarantee of minimal access to a state's criminal appellate system.[1] In *San Antonio Independent School District v. Rodriguez*,[2] the Burger Court attempted the same sort of comprehensive overview of its holdings on wealth classifications as a whole. In both cases, the Court is to be commended for achieving a significant degree of surface plausibility. Justice Powell in *Rodriguez* was even more successful than Justice Rehnquist in *Ross*, a feat all the more remarkable in that Justice Rehnquist was more fortunate in his precedents. As has been suggested, *Ross* was able to contract the *Griffin* line from equal to minimal protection so as to leave only one case, *Douglas v. California*, as an aberration.[3] The precedents facing Justice Powell were more recalcitrant, requiring more ingenuity from a Court seemingly determined to reach a particular result. *Rodriguez* involved an equal protection challenge to Texas' system of financing its public schools. Under the Texas system, the state guaranteed a minimum level of education for all the state's children, allocating to each school district roughly $220–225 per pupil. School districts were empowered to raise additional revenues through, and only through, a local property tax, which could not exceed a certain percentage of assessed property value.[4] The *Rodriguez* plaintiffs lived in the Edgewood School District, a property-poor district which by imposing the highest property tax rate in the metropolitan area[5] was able to raise just $26 per pupil beyond the state grant—an amount that, in addition to federal funds, gave the district a total of only $356 per student. The plaintiffs contrasted their educational budget with that of Alamo Heights, a property-rich district which, with a lower percentage tax[6] than Edgewood's, raised $333 per pupil, giving it a per pupil sum of $594. The gist of the challenge was that the gross disparity in educational spending, depending on whether a child lived in a property-rich or property-poor neighborhood, was directly caused by the state's choice of financing system and violated the right of the children in property-poor districts to equal protection of the laws.

The District Court had applied strict scrutiny and upheld the challenge.[7] In so doing, the Supreme Court held, the District Court had failed to recognize the "novelty" of the claim advanced. All prior

§ 16–52

1. 417 U.S. 600, 607 (1974).

2. 411 U.S. 1 (1973).

3. See § 16–51, supra.

4. 1.50%. See 411 U.S. at 67 (White J., dissenting).

5. 1.05%. Id. at 12.

6. .85%. Id. at 13.

7. In finding the wealth classification suspect, the District Court followed the California Supreme Court in Serrano v. Priest, 5 Cal.3d 584, 96 Cal.Rptr. 601, 487 P.2d 1241 (1971) (California's foundation grant scheme, whereby the major source of school revenues were derived from the local property tax, held violative of equal protection under both California and United States Constitutions), and the Federal Court for the District of Minnesota in Van Dusartz v. Hatfield, 334 F.Supp. 870 (1971) (adopting Serrano analysis). Rodriguez v. San Antonia Independent School District, 337 F.Supp. 280, 281 n.1 (W.D.Tex.1971).

wealth classification cases, the Court explained, had involved a precisely defined class of indigents; "because of their impecunity they were completely unable to pay for some desired benefit, and as a consequence, they sustained an absolute deprivation of a meaningful opportunity to enjoy that benefit." [8] The plaintiff class in *Rodriguez* was, on the other hand, "large, diverse, and amorphous." [9] "Indeed, there is reason to believe that the poorest families are not necessarily clustered in the poorest property districts." [10] Furthermore, the class, such as it was, suffered at best only a relative deprivation. The state ensured everyone at least a minimum level of funds for an adequate education. The fact that other children received a better than adequate education did not amount to state discrimination against a suspect class or state deprivation of a fundamental right. As a final blow to the equal protection claim, the Court argued that it was far from clear that even a relative deprivation had occurred, since the quality of education does not necessarily depend on the amount of money spent.[11] The Court then provided an example of "a far more compelling set of circumstances for judicial assistance than the case before us today." The example was a public school system which charged tuition, so that children of indigents were foreclosed from any education at all.[12]

All of the foregoing was advanced as requiring application of the minimum rationality test, rather than the compelling state interest test. However, the Court advanced another and independent set of reasons for relaxed review: the Court lacks expertise in the area of raising revenue and has traditionally deferred to legislative judgments. This argument for judicial reticence was said to be particularly potent when education, about which there are such deeply conflicting theories, is concerned. Finally, principles of federalism militate against the Court's invalidation of a financing system which exists in virtually every state.

The earlier discussion of the history of wealth classification holdings [13] indicates that the prize for "novelty" might more justly be awarded to the Supreme Court in *Rodriguez* than to the District Court. It is no more true that all prior wealth classification cases had involved precisely defined classes suffering absolute deprivations than it is that the Court had always deferred to state decisions on how to finance various programs. Even *Griffin v. Illinois* did not involve an absolute deprivation; and its progeny, including *Douglas v. California*, certainly did not.[14] In *Harper* the Court was very clear about telling the state

---

8. 411 U.S. at 20.

9. Id. at 28.

10. Id. at 23.

11. 411 U.S. at 43. The Court's uncertainty in this area was derived from various social science authorities, including C. Jencks, Inequality (1972); U.S. Office of Education, Equality of Educational Opportunity (1966) (the Coleman Report); and other authorities listed at 411 U.S. at 43 n. 1. For a critique of the Coleman Report and an attack on its utility in adjudication, see McDermott and Klein, "The Cost-Qual-

ity Debate in School Finance Litigation: Do Dollars Make a Difference?", 38 Law and Cont.Probs. 415 (1975). For the suggestion that use of social science data is likely to lead consistently to conservative "decisional paralysis," see Yudoff, "Equal Educational Opportunity and the Courts," 51 Tex.L.Rev. 411, 504 (1973).

12. 411 U.S. at 25 n.60.

13. See §§ 16–35 to 16–52, supra.

14. See Griffin v. Illinois, 351 U.S. 12 (1954), and Douglas v. California, 372 U.S.

how it could or could not finance part of its educational system.[15] Finally, in the most recent and homologous precedent, *Bullock v. Carter*, a case which involved no "discrete and precisely defined" class and only a relatively "unequal" impact rather than an absolute deprivation,[16] the same Court [17] had unanimously ordered the state to find a different, more equitable method of financing its primary elections.

However narrow the Court's reading of wealth classification precedents in *Rodriguez* may be,[18] its conclusion that the Court can guarantee only minimal, and not equal, access to state sponsored institutions, has taken very deep root. Cutbacks parallel to *Ross v. Moffitt* [19] are found in most of the major areas where the Court had earlier promised plenary protection and solicitude, as the succeeding sections will demonstrate.[20]

But the cutbacks have not been unmitigated. Unwilling in *Harris v. McCrae* to treat a denial of public funding even for medically necessary abortions as a decision discriminating against the poor,[21] the Court nonetheless struck down three years later a law requiring all second trimester abortions to be performed in full-service hospitals, reasoning that the additional costs imposed by that law unconstitutionally burdened "women's access to a relatively inexpensive, otherwise accessible, and safe abortion procedure." [22] There is little functional difference between a law that selectively refuses to subsidize one medical procedure (abortion), and a law that selectively escalates the cost of that procedure. The decision in *Akron* is important because the Court, by a 6–3 margin,[23] engaged in a "searching" review of the abortion ordinances and required Akron to show that they were justified by a "compelling state interest" [24] which was supported by the medical evidence, despite the fact that health and safety regulations have traditionally been accorded more judicial deference than social and economic legislation such as the Medicaid laws upheld in *Harris v. McCrae*. The Court may ultimately have to reexamine its basic assumptions about the legal implications of poverty if it is to resolve the tension between the holding in *McRae* that a state may put extreme pressure on an indigent woman's choice between birth and abortion by

353 (1963), discussed in §§ 16–38, 16–51, supra.

15. Virginia had financed its public schools in part through the revenues obtained from the poll tax, and was forced to find an alternative method when the tax was struck down in Harper v. Virginia, 383 U.S. 663, 664 n.1 (1966), discussed in §§ 16–10, 16–46, supra.

16. 405 U.S. 134, 144 (1972).

17. Although without the participation of Justices Powell and Rehnquist.

18. Note also the Court's rejection of education as a fundamental interest, crucial to its choice of minimal scrutiny, because "[i]t is not the province of this Court to create substantive constitutional rights in the name of guaranteeing equal protection of the laws." 411 U.S. at 33.

19. 417 U.S. 600 (1974), discussed in § 16–51, supra.

20. The decision in Rodriguez is further discussed, and an explanation for its treatment of precedent offered, in § 16–58, infra.

21. See 448 U.S. 297 (1980), discussed in § 15–10, supra.

22. Akron v. Akron Center for Reproductive Health, 462 U.S. 416, 438 (1983) (footnote omitted), discussed in § 15–10, supra.

23. Justice Powell wrote the opinion of the Court, joined by Chief Justice Burger and Justices Brennan, Marshall, Blackmun and Stevens. Justice O'Connor dissented, joined by Justices White and Rehnquist.

24. 462 U.S. at 427.

making only the latter prohibitively expensive, and the holding in *Akron* that the state may *not* exert that same kind of economic pressure by indirectly escalating the price of an abortion through health regulations.

The Court's decision in *Zablocki v. Redhail* [25] is further evidence of the distinction the Court evidently perceives between government treatment of the poor that affirmatively burdens them, even if only *de facto* (as in *Akron*) rather than by a wealth-based classification as such, and state action that merely declines to alleviate the burdens of penury in our legal system. The Wisconsin statute challenged in *Zablocki* required a parent without child custody but with court-ordered support obligations to obtain judicial approval before marriage. Approval was not forthcoming unless the parent had met his outstanding child support obligations, and unless the court first found that the children covered by the support order were "not then and [were] not likely thereafter to become public charges." [26] A nearly unanimous [27] Court held that the law violated the equal protection clause. In his opinion for the Court, Justice Marshall observed that a parent who was unemployed or had a low income, such as the father in this case, could not keep his child off the welfare rolls even if he met his support obligations; thus such a parent could never remarry under the state's law. The statute therefore worked an absolute deprivation of a fundamental right for certain poor people and, like the statute reviewed in *Boddie v. Connecticut*,[28] fell within the intersection of "fundamental rights" and "equality of rights." [29] Justice Marshall went even further, stating that many others would be effectively coerced by the law into foregoing their right to marry.[30]

Wisconsin's defense that its permission-to-marry requirement was a way to induce the marrying parent to obtain financial counseling before taking on new obligations was transparent: the statute neither provided for any counseling nor made permission to marry automatic after counseling.[31] A second justification for the law was that it acted as an incentive to parents to make support payments to their non-custodial children. Justice Marshall rejected this rationale as implausible with respect to parents too poor to provide adequate support to their prior children and unnecessary with respect to other parents, given the state's panoply of alternative means of directly enforcing support obligations.[32] The Court was unpersuaded by the further argument that the requirement protected the ability of marriage applicants to meet current support obligations by precluding them from incurring new ones. Justice Marshall found the argument overinclusive in that it assumed that the new spouse would be financially dependent on the

25. 434 U.S. 374 (1978).

26. Wis. Stat. §§ 245–10(1), (4), (5) (1973). See 434 U.S. at 375.

27. Justice Marshall wrote for the Court, joined by Chief Justice Burger and Justices Brennan, White, and Blackmun. Justice Rehnquist was the sole dissenter. Justices Stewart, Powell and Stevens each concurred in the judgment.

28. 401 U.S. 371 (1971).

29. See § 16–9, supra.

30. 434 U.S. at 387.

31. Id. at 388–89.

32. Id. at 389.

parent, and underinclusive in not applying to other kinds of new financial obligations which were equally likely to drain financial resources.[33]

Zablocki, like *Boddie*, should probably be understood as assuring equal protection to the poor only when an independently secured constitutional right is involved.[34] Only Justice Stevens abjured the discussion of a fundamental right to marry and founded his decision squarely and solely on wealth discrimination.[35] Yet *Zablocki* implicitly held that a state may be required in some circumstances to subsidize indigents in order that they have the opportunity to exercise their constitutional rights. For by striking down the law denying the right of marriage to parents whose children are currently or are likely to become public charges, the Court compelled Wisconsin to permit Zablocki's marriage while the state picked up any welfare tab for the support of his child. Wisconsin was no more responsible for Zablocki's indigency than Congress was for McRae's, yet eight Justices voted to force Wisconsin to allow Zablocki to exercise his right of marriage even though under state law he, like McRae, lacked sufficient funds to do so.

Similarly, when the denial by Texas of free enrollment to the children of illegal aliens was challenged on equal protection grounds, the Supreme Court held the law unconstitutional. The children in *Plyler v. Doe*,[36] were not only poor, they were aliens. Justice Brennan, writing for the Court, in effect cross-bred alienage, a sometimes "suspect" classification,[37] with poverty, a normally non-suspect classification, to produce a quasi-suspect class comprising the children of illegal aliens who had no control over their unlawful presence in this country.[38] Although *Plyler v. Doe* did not directly involve a classification based on wealth, all the Justices who voted to overturn the Texas law made it clear that what made the law constitutionally offensive was its tendency to "create and perpetuate" a distinct subclass of impoverished illiterates who would be denied the opportunity to participate in and contribute to society.[39]

The facts in *Plyler v. Doe* were highly sympathetic, and the case was decided by a process that looked more visceral than analytical: the conditions that would have resulted had the case gone the other way

---

33. Id. at 390. Instead of preventing a parent from incurring financial obligations to any children born of the contemplated marriage, Justice Marshall surmised that the result would be that such children would be born out of wedlock.

34. This was the first case in which the Court explicitly recognized a right to marry. See § 15–20, supra.

35. 434 U.S. at 403 (Stevens, J., concurring in the judgment). Justice Stewart ridiculed the majority's equal protection analysis as substantive due process in sheep's clothing. Id. at 391–92, 395–96 (Stewart, J., concurring in the judgment).

36. 457 U.S. 202 (1982), discussed in § 16–23, supra.

37. The Court has been quite consistent in applying heightened scrutiny to state laws denying significant benefits to aliens, if not to laws denying them some forms of public employment. See § 16–23, supra.

38. 457 U.S. at 220–24.

39. See id. at 230 (opinion of the Court by Brennan, J.); id. at 234 (Blackmun, J., concurring); id. at 239 (Powell, J., concurring). Even the dissent admitted that the law might have such an invidious effect. See id. at 254 (Burger, C.J., joined by Justices White, Rehnquist, and O'Connor, dissenting).

were simply unacceptable to a majority of the Court. That same special set of facts, of course, will make *Plyler* relatively easy to isolate in the future; the case will probably generate little enduring doctrine.[40] The one significant principle established by the case is that the state may not pursue policies which predictably create a permanent class of economically dispossessed and politically disadvantaged people and that, in some circumstances, such as those in *Plyler*, the state may have a duty to spend public money to avert the creation of a "permanent caste" of the discreet underclass.[41]

The Court endorsed a similar notion in *Zobel v. Williams*,[42] where eight Justices [43] voted to overturn Alaska's policy of distributing dividends from the state's mineral income fund to state residents on the basis of how long they had lived in Alaska. Chief Justice Burger, in his opinion for the Court, held that the distribution scheme violated the equal protection clause by creating "fixed, permanent distinctions between an ever-increasing number of perpetual classes." [44] Even though no "suspect" class was involved, and there was at stake no right more "fundamental" than the manifestly *non*-fundamental interest in an equal share of the state's mineral fund dividends, the Court applied a level of judicial review sufficiently demanding to overcome several plausible state justifications [45] while purporting to apply the minimum rationality test.[46]

The principle which appears to animate these diverse decisions is that the state may not actively go about dividing people into different economic classes, but that government is ordinarily free—unless it is allocating access to the franchise or some other independently fundamental right—to treat people differently on the basis of the economic classes into which "nature" or some supposedly "invisible hand" has sorted them. One failure of contemporary constitutional jurisprudence has been its inability to perceive the ways in which the law itself may be implicated in this distribution scheme. The principle of equality under the law is not offended by the mere fact that there are rich and poor, but *may* be offended by the wide-ranging legal and social significance which the law gives to this disparity in material wealth. The problem is not that X has more money than Y, but that the law allows X's superior position in the material sphere to translate into a superior position in other spheres as well. To put *everything*—health care, education, political power, personal autonomy, access to judicial relief—

---

40. See § 16–23, supra.

41. Plyler, 457 U.S. at 219.

42. 457 U.S. 55 (1982), discussed in § 6–35, supra.

43. Justice Rehnquist was the sole dissenter.

44. 457 U.S. at 59; see also id. at 70 (Brennan, J., concurring). Although Justice O'Connor concurred in the judgment on the ground that the Alaska law discriminated against recent arrivals, and hence violated a right to travel implicitly protected by the privileges and immunities clause

of art. iv, id. at 78, she agreed that the vice of the law was its creation of economic groups "liv[ing] on less favorable terms" than previous waves of residents. Id. at 75.

45. The Court dismissed one rationale, Alaska's desire to reward intangible contributions to the state, as wholly illegitimate, id. at 63. For a persuasive argument to the contrary, see Justice O'Connor's concurring opinion, id. at 72–73 & nn.1–2.

46. 457 U.S. at 60–61.

on an effectively cash basis is to create and perpetuate a world in which "all good things come to those who have the one best thing." [47] Such a regime arguably provides not the equal protection of the laws but the unequal hazard of the auction hall.

Recognizing this inequity and the law's role in producing it need represent no threat to meritocracy. Personal qualities and social goods have their own spheres of operation, which are governed by different principles of distribution: welfare to the needy, health care to the infirm, honors to the deserving, political influence to the persuasive, salvation to the pious, luxuries to those inclined and able to pay for them. [48] Injustice may result, however, when the distribution principle of one sphere, such as material wealth, is allowed to invade the spheres of other social goods and determine who gets what. The end result may be not just an inequitable distribution of social goods, but the subjugation of those people who do not possess that particular item by which all other social goods are valued. As Michael Walzer puts it: "Birth and blood, landed wealth, capital, education, divine grace, state power— all these have served at one time or another to enable some people to dominate others. Domination is always mediated by some set of social goods." [49]

The Court's reluctance to subject classifications based on wealth to consistently meaningful equal protection scrutiny may reflect not simply a commendable sense of judicial modesty in the face of ambiguous constitutional commands, but a less commendable failure to perceive that money, the currently dominant good, is converted into other social goods not by a natural process but by a sort of legal alchemy. [50] There was a time when the law denied blacks equal protection, unerringly translating skin color into status as master or slave. Today, this sort of mistaken attribution of legal significance to other "natural" differences is more subtle, but not much less invidious. The law fails to make women and men equal before the law when it automatically translates biology into social destiny, thereby denying women power over both their bodies and their futures. [51] In a similar fashion, the law at times mechanically transmutes indigency into a socioeconomic hierarchy in which the poor are bereft of shelter, sustenance and dignity. As Justice Blackmun reminded the majority in *Harris v. McCrae*: "there truly is another world 'out there,' the existence of which the Court . . . either chooses to ignore or fears to recognize; the cancer of poverty will continue to grow, and the lot of the poorest among us, once again, and still, is not to be bettered." [52]

47. M. Walzer, Spheres of Justice 11 (1983), discussed in L. Tribe, Constitutional Choices 242 (1985).

48. See M. Walzer, supra, at 18–20.

49. Id. at xiii.

50. See id. at 11. For a discussion of the changing place of welfare rights in our jurisprudence, see Simon, "Rights and Redistribution in the Welfare System," 38 Stan.L.Rev. 1431 (1986). Contrast Bork, "The Impossibility of Finding Welfare Rights in the Constitution," 1979 Wash. U.L.Q. 695, with Black, "Changing Concepts of Equality," 1979 Wash.U.L.Q. 741.

51. See § 16–29, supra.

52. 448 U.S. 297, 348–49 (1980) (Blackmun, J., dissenting).

§ 16–53. Fuentes v. Shevin Revisited

In *Mitchell v. W. T. Grant Co.*[1] the adversary hearing prior to seizure of disputed property guaranteed in *Fuentes v. Shevin*[2] was held not mandated by due process so long as certain procedural safeguards attended the creditor's ex parte application and a prompt post-seizure adversary hearing was made available. The Court was unwilling to let concern for the debtor upset the basic allocation of property rights, including the procedures guarding them, defined by state law.[3] "[W]e remain unconvinced that the impact on the debtor of deprivation of the household goods here in question overrides his inability to make the creditor whole for wrongful possession, the risk of destruction or alienation if notice and a prior hearing are supplied, and the low risk of a wrongful determination of possession through the procedures now employed."[4] The prior adversary hearing which was the heart of the *Fuentes* due process holding was cut back in light of the state's generalized fear that debtors cannot be trusted with the disputed property.[5]

In another due process case, Justice Stevens wrote a dissenting opinion that is not a model of sensitivity to the poor. His dissent in *Memphis Light, Gas & Water Div. v. Craft*[6] argued that, rather than hiring an attorney to handle a bill dispute, the customer threatened with a utility cut-off could easily avoid that injury by paying the disputed portion of the bill and then filing for a refund.[7] This, of course, assumes that a person can afford the extra expense—in this case, double billing for several months. Similarly, the majority opinion in *Flagg Brothers, Inc. v. Brooks*,[8] upholding a statute allowing a warehouse to sell an indigent's furniture to recover an unpaid bill, observed that the respondent could have begun a replevin proceeding. Dissenting in *Flagg Brothers*, Justice Marshall[9] pointed out that one must post bond for a writ of replevin, an impossible requirement for a poor woman recently evicted from her apartment.[10]

§ 16–54. Brotherhood of Railway Trainmen Restrained

The expansion of rights assertable through concerted action which the Court had protected against state interference in *NAACP v. But-*

---

§ 16–53

1. 416 U.S. 600 (1974).

2. 407 U.S. 67 (1972), discussed in § 16–43, supra.

3. But see North Georgia Finishing, Inc. v. Di-Chem, Inc., 419 U.S. 601 (1975). Mitchell and Di-Chem are also analyzed in § 10–14, supra.

4. Mitchell, 416 U.S. at 610.

5. For a touch of irony see North Georgia Finishing, Inc. v. Di-Chem, Inc., 419 U.S. 601, 614 (1975) (Blackmun, J., joined by Rehnquist, J., dissenting from the majority's invalidation of the Georgia garnishment statute on the strength of Sniadach and Fuentes; the dissenters objected to the application of these cases in the instant dispute between two corporations, since in Sniadach and Fuentes the unfair and unequal position of the debtors had required special solicitude).

6. 436 U.S. 1 (1978). In dissent, Justice Stevens was joined by Chief Justice Burger and Justice Rehnquist. For a discussion of the majority opinion, see § 16–43, supra.

7. 436 U.S. at 28.

8. 436 U.S. 149 (1978).

9. Justice Stevens also filed a dissenting opinion, which was joined by Justices White and Marshall. Justice Brennan did not participate in the decision.

10. 436 U.S. at 166–67 (Marshall, J., dissenting).

ton,[1] *Brotherhood of Railroad Trainmen v. Virginia*,[2] *United Mine Workers v. Illinois*,[3] and *United Transportation Union v. State Bar of Michigan*,[4] *progressing from exalted political rights to state workmen's compensation claims*,[5] *was abruptly halted in Garcia v. Texas State Board of Medical Examiners*.[6] The low-income minority plaintiffs had formed a health maintenance organization (HMO) which pooled its members' resources in order to provide them with low-cost, high-quality medical care, as an alternative to the prohibitively expensive fee-for-service health care which prevailed in Texas. The state enjoined the operation of the association, the directors of which were non-professional community members, for practicing medicine without a license; the federal district court rejected the applicability of the legal services precedents as preserving first amendment rights and refused to extend those precedents to protect the more mundane "non-constitutional" interest in health;[7] the Supreme Court summarily affirmed. Freedom of association as an adjunct to equal protection, combatting elitist exclusionary state regulatory schemes, was thus severely restricted.[8]

§ 16–55. Bullock v. Carter Restricted

The Court's decision in *Lubin v. Panish*[1], a 1974 case similar in principle to the 1972 decision in *Bullock v. Carter*,[2] dramatized the Court's movement toward minimal protection. Petitioner in *Lubin* challenged the California Election Code under which he was required to pay a filing fee of $701.60 in order to have his name placed on the ballot for nomination for membership on the Los Angeles County Board of Supervisors. Petitioner alleged that he was indigent and could not afford the fee. The Court explained in a footnote why *Bullock* did not dispose of the case: the fees in *Bullock* were "so patently exclusionary as to violate traditional equal protection concepts."[3] Although the Court's intended meaning in drawing this distinction is unclear, the cases did come before the Court in slightly different postures. *Lubin* was skeletally more like *Harper*[4] or *Griffin*;[5] it involved an indigent who wanted something for which the state sought a fee, in this case a place on the ballot. *Bullock*, in which the Court gave the candidate more favored treatment, was, oddly enough, more like *San Antonio Independent School District v. Rodriguez*,[6] in that a vague, not necessarily indigent, and altogether ill-defined group challenged an entire financing scheme by which it claimed to be relatively disadvantaged. But this difference in posture could ill account for the different solu-

§ 16–54

1. 371 U.S. 415 (1963).

2. 377 U.S. 1 (1964).

3. 389 U.S. 217 (1967).

4. 401 U.S. 576 (1971).

5. These cases are discussed in § 16–45, supra.

6. 421 U.S. 995 (1975), aff'g mem. 384 F.Supp. 434 (W.D.Tex.1974).

7. But see § 15–9, supra.

8. See also § 12–26, supra.

§ 16–55

1. 415 U.S. 709 (1974).

2. 405 U.S. 134 (1972), discussed in § 16–48, supra.

3. 415 U.S. at 715 n.4.

4. 383 U.S. 663 (1966), discussed in § 16–46, supra.

5. 351 U.S. 12 (1956), discussed in § 16–38, supra.

6. 411 U.S. 1 (1973), discussed in § 16–52, supra, and § 16–58, infra.

tions reached in *Lubin* and *Bullock*. In *Bullock*, the Court struck down the entire financing scheme so that all candidates were on the same footing, regardless of resources, with respect to any test the state might set up for gaining a place on the ballot. The Court's solution in *Lubin*, on the other hand, was (1) to waive the filing fee for indigents while allowing the state to retain it for all non-indigents, some of whom might find filing fees more of a burden than others; and (2) to permit the states to require an indigent to demonstrate the " 'seriousness' of his candidacy by persuading a substantial number of voters to sign a petition on his behalf." [7] This remedy is clearly geared to the Court's identification of *absolute deprivation* of access to the ballot as the crucial defect of the scheme.[8]

The holding of *Lubin* was that "ballot access must be *genuinely* open to all." [9] But the Court's suggestion of retaining the filing fee while offering an alternative avenue for indigents made clear that access need not be *equally* open to all. The middle class and rich may still write their checks and obtain a place on the ballot. Only the poor are required to run the gantlet of making a serious showing of support.

§ 16–56. Pre-termination Hearings: The Requirement of a Showing of Desperation

In *Mathews v. Eldridge* [1] the Court refused to extend *Goldberg v. Kelly* [2] to require a hearing on eligibility prior to the state's termination of social security disability benefits. *Goldberg*, the Court held, turned on the desperate situation of the mistakenly terminated welfare recipient during the period after benefits ceased but before eligibility was determined. A key distinguishing feature was that the hardship of deprivation "is generally likely to be less than in *Goldberg*, although the degree of difference can be overstated." [3] This distinction, expressed with so little conviction, was further weakened by the fact, mentioned only by the dissenters, that the hardship suffered in the case had been severe; because of the termination of benefits, the Eldridges' home and furniture had been repossessed, and the entire family forced to sleep in a single bed. Plainly, *Mathews* signalled a retreat from the *Goldberg* approach, that both justice and self-preservation required from an affluent society exacting standards of fairness and liberality toward its economically marginal members.[4]

§ 16–57. Rights Among the Poor: A Minimally Even Hand Suffices

When dealing with federal and state legislation regarding public assistance, an area where the basic necessities of survival hang in the

7. Lubin, 415 U.S. at 718–19.

8. The Court in Lubin was also harshly critical of the vast overinclusiveness and underinclusiveness of the fee as a means of ballot regulation. 415 U.S. at 717.

9. 415 U.S. at 719 (emphasis added).

§ 16–56

1. 424 U.S. 319 (1976).

2. 397 U.S. 254 (1970), discussed in § 16–49, supra.

3. 424 U.S. at 341.

4. Cf. Heckler v. Day, 467 U.S. 104 (1984) (refusing to impose deadlines for future social security disability determinations). See generally § 10–13 to 10–16, supra.

balance, the Warren Court consistently, and the Burger Court from time to time,[1] demanded somewhat more in the way of governmental justification and fairness than would be required under the traditionally toothless minimum rationality test employed to review other forms of economic regulation.[2] In *Dandridge v. Williams*,[3] however, welfare legislation was officially stripped of any preferential status and drawn back into the fold of "state regulation in the social and economic field," requiring only the most relaxed judicial scrutiny. Supreme Court review of welfare legislation since *Dandridge* has by no means been consistently deferential.[4] Nevertheless the *Dandridge* reluctance to intervene in welfare legislation represents a deep current in the concerns of the post-Warren era; the talismanic characterization of "state regulation in the social and economic field" lies poised and ready to spring any time the Court decides not to intervene, and poses a constant threat to challenges of inequalities and arbitrariness in public assistance laws.[5]

The assumption in *Dandridge* was that laws distributing welfare benefits do not "affect . . . freedoms guaranteed by the Bill of Rights,"[6] and that "the myriad of potential recipients" with claims to "limited public welfare funds"[7] represent a monolithic group among whom invidious distinctions are difficult to perceive. The wide berth

§ 16–57

1. See, e.g., the food stamp cases, United States Department of Agriculture v. Moreno, 413 U.S. 528 (1973); United States Department of Agriculture v. Murry, 413 U.S. 508 (1973). Both are discussed in § 16–50, supra.

2. See generally §§ 16–2 to 16–5, supra.

3. 397 U.S. 471 (1970) (upholding state's maximum grant provision in its Aid to Families with Dependent Children program whereby large families received less than their computed need).

4. See cases cited in note 1, supra. See also New Jersey Welfare Rights Organization v. Cahill, 411 U.S. 619 (1973).

5. See, e.g., Schweiker v. Wilson, 450 U.S. 221 (1981) (upholding denial of supplemental subsistence benefits to needy aged, blind, disabled persons in public institutions even though they were otherwise eligible for such benefits but for their institutionalization); Jefferson v. Hackney, 406 U.S. 535 (1972), discussed in § 16–20, supra; Richardson v. Belcher, 404 U.S. 78 (1971) (reduction in social security benefits to reflect Workmen's Compensation Awards but not benefits received from private insurance plans upheld as rational); cf. Wyman v. James, 400 U.S. 309 (1971) (upholding termination of welfare benefits to AFDC recipients who refuse warrantless home visit of caseworker for purpose of investigating eligibility). It seems noteworthy that, in Schweiker v. Wilson, supra, Justice Powell, dissenting in an opinion

joined by Justices Brennan, Marshall, and Stevens, could not avoid the conclusion that Congress had "thoughtlessly . . . applied a statutory classification developed to further legitimate goals of one welfare program to another welfare program serving entirely different needs. The result is an exclusion of wholly dependent people from minimal benefits, serving no Government interest. This irrational classification violates the equal protection component of the Due Process Clause of the Fifth Amendment." 450 U.S. at 239–40. Justice Blackmun's majority opinion, joined by Chief Justice Burger and Justices Stewart, White, and Rehnquist, offered no very compelling analysis in rejoinder, but instead chose simply to defer to Congress' judgment. See also Lyng v. Costillo, 106 S.Ct. 2727 (1986), discussed in § 16–50, supra, in note 5.

6. 397 U.S. at 484. This assumption prevails even when the lines drawn could be seen as incidentally operating to burden protected choices—like the choice to have additional children. Compare Dandridge v. Williams, 397 U.S. 471 (1970), with Cleveland Bd. of Educ. v. LaFleur, 414 U.S. 632 (1974). Indeed the same approach is taken even when the state's line is *intended* to influence how the poor decide to exercise a protected right. See, e.g., Maher v. Roe, 432 U.S. 464, 474 (1977) (upholding state choice to encourage childbirth by denying public funding for nontherapeutic abortions).

7. 397 U.S. at 487.

afforded legislative judgments is thus thought to result from the remoteness of such judgments from the fundamental interests and suspect classifications that are necessary to trigger strict scrutiny.

Yet the second of the *Dandridge* assumptions glosses over at least one danger in classifications *among* the poor that strict scrutiny of classifications discriminating *against* the poor had previously been employed to combat, the danger of stigmatizing stereotypes. In *Jefferson v. Hackney*,[8] the Court found not invidious the Texas scheme allotting a lower percentage [9] of calculated need to AFDC families than to recipients of aid to the blind, disabled and elderly,[10] since "the State may have concluded that the aged and infirm are the least able of the categorical grant recipients to bear the hardships of an inadequate standard of living." [11]   But even this justification carries with it a potentially stigmatizing judgment: the blind and disabled are needy because of physical causes beyond their control; AFDC families have no such excuse. Indeed, Justice Marshall in dissent noted that the record was replete with evidence that AFDC was politically unpopular, and that its recipients were in fact stigmatized and looked down on by the community.[12]   There is a genuine danger that the discounted grant to AFDC families will be interpreted by a citizenry already so inclined as a legislative judgment that such families deserve substantially less than they need; the differential must be borne by the families as a badge of their own fault.[13]

These dangers were most explicitly articulated in Justice Marshall's dissent in *New York State Department of Social Services v. Dublino*,[14] in which the majority held that New York's work rules, under which any recipient of public assistance was deemed to have refused suitable employment if he failed to file an appropriate certificate every two weeks, were not preempted by the Federal Work Incentive Program. The majority had held that a finding of preemption "could impair the capacity of the state government to deal effectively with the critical problem of mounting welfare costs and the increasing financial dependency of many of its citizens. New York has a legitimate interest in encouraging those of its citizens who can work to do so. . . ." [15] Justice Marshall answered: [16] "Because the recipients of public assistance generally lack substantial political influence,

---

8. 406 U.S. 535 (1972).

9. 75%.

10. 95%, 95%, and 100%, respectively.

11. 406 U.S. at 549.

12. Id. at 575. Compare United States Department of Agriculture v. Moreno, 413 U.S. 528, 534 (1973) (exclusion of commune households from food stamp assistance simply to burden politically unpopular groups would be an unconstitutional legislative purpose).

13. Furthermore, the state made no effort to show that AFDC recipients actually were better able to improve their situation or endure hardship, a proposition that appears quite susceptible of proof. See No-

wak, "Realigning the Standards of Review Under the Equal Protection Guarantee— Prohibited, Neutral, and Permissive Classifications," 62 Geo.L.J. 1071, 1119 (1974).

14. 413 U.S. 405, 423 (1973) (Marshall, J., joined by Brennan, J., dissenting).

15. Id. at 413. See also Batterton v. Francis, 432 U.S. 416 (1977) (states may limit AFDC aid to families of involuntarily unemployed); Ohio Bureau of Employment Services v. Hodory, 431 U.S. 471 (1977) (states may deny unemployment compensation to workers whose joblessness results from participation in a labor dispute).

16. 413 U.S. at 432 (dissenting opinion).

state legislators may find it expedient to accede to pressures generated by misconceptions [such as the 'myth' that welfare recipients have little desire to become self-supporting]."

Finally, neither judicially reinforced myths about the poor nor judicial reluctance to shape doctrine with a view to its impact on the poor are limited to the Court's review of legislation regarding welfare and public assistance. On the contrary, the Court in recent years has displayed a quite consistent lack of solicitude for the poor in such disparate spheres as the regulation of speech and registration for the draft. Thus, in upholding against first amendment challenges Los Angeles' ban on the posting of signs on public property, the Court attached no special significance to the fact that signposting is often the only feasible communication option for the poor.[17] And the Court similarly ignored the impact of a challenged law upon the poor as a group when it addressed a congressional regulation denying federal financial assistance to students who had not registered for the draft. In *Selective Service System v. Minnesota Public Interest Research Group*,[18] Chief Justice Burger, writing for the Court, tersely dismissed in a footnote the argument that Congress' approach to encouraging draft registration discriminated against the poor: the majority observed simply that the state "treats all nonregistrants alike, denying aid to both the poor and the wealthy." [19] As Justice Marshall hardly needed to point out in dissent,[20] the rich are rarely eligible for financial educational assistance.[21]

§ 16–58. A Right to What Money Can Buy: Understanding Valtierra, Rodriguez, and Salyer

The Burger Court's enormous reluctance to tell the states how to spend their scarce resources, and its willingness to tolerate—indeed occasionally its own adoption of—pejorative generalizations about the poor, explain many, but not all, of the Court's decisions cutting back constitutional protections in the poverty field. Several of its most crucial decisions contain lapses of logic, disregard or distortion of relevant precedent, and other indications that those decisions are impelled by considerations that never quite surface in the opinions.

---

17. See City Council of Los Angeles v. Taxpayers for Vincent, 466 U.S. 789, 812–13 n.30 (1984) (explaining that the Court's "special solicitude for forms of expression that are much less expensive than feasible alternatives and hence may be important to a large segment of the citizenry," citing Martin v. Struthers, 319 U.S. 141, 146 (1943), "has practical boundaries."). Cf. Martin v. Struthers, 319 U.S. at 146 (protecting "[d]oor to door distribution of circulars" as "essential to the poorly financed causes of the little people."); Schneider v. Irvington, 308 U.S. 147 (1939), discussed in §§ 12–7, 12–23, supra.

18. 468 U.S. 841 (1984).

19. Id. at 859 n.17.

20. Justice Brennan joined Justice Marshall's dissent but only on the basis that the statute violated the fifth amendment's proscription against self-incrimination. Justice Blackmun did not participate in the decision.

21. 468 at 877 (Marshall, J., dissenting). In a portion of his dissent not joined by Justice Brennan, Justice Marshall believed the statute "created a *de facto* classification based on wealth." Id. at 878. He criticized the Court's attitude as "superficial, indeed cavalier," and suggested that the majority had shown a " 'callous indifference to the realities of life for the poor.' " Id. at 876, quoting Flagg Brothers, Inc. v. Brooks, 436 U.S. 149, 166 (1978) (Marshall, J., dissenting).

This section attempts first to identify such examples and then to formulate a plausible theory which might link together and explain these cases.

In *James v. Valtierra*,[1] a group of low-income plaintiffs eligible for federally subsidized low-income housing challenged a recent amendment to the California Constitution, which provided that no low-rent housing project could be "developed, constructed, or acquired in any manner by a state public body until approved by a majority of voters at a community election."[2] A literal reading of the Warren Court's precedents would have made *Valtierra* seem an open and shut case. An almost identical amendment to the Akron City Charter, requiring that any fair housing ordinance had to be approved by a majority at a city election, had been struck down by the Supreme Court as a violation of equal protection in *Hunter v. Erickson*.[3] The obvious difference between the two amendments was that one discriminated on the basis of race, the other on the basis of wealth. But according to several of the Court's opinions, race and wealth were functionally equivalent as bases for legislative classification. Q.E.D.: The *Valtierra* amendment was unconstitutional.

Justice Black, writing for the Court, escaped the ineluctability of this logic by refusing to recognize either that the amendment constituted a wealth classification,[4] or that wealth classifications required any heightened judicial attention. As if writing on a clean slate rather than a complicated body of seemingly contrary precedent, the Court said, "[t]he present case could be affirmed only by extending *Hunter* [to wealth classification], and this we decline to do."[5] Justice Marshall objected sharply to the majority's unexplained and unprecedented shrinking from the wealth classification claim. "It is far to late in the day to contend that the Fourteenth Amendment prohibits only racial discrimination; and to me, singling out the poor to bear a burden not placed on any other class of citizens tramples the values the Fourteenth Amendment was designed to protect."[6] His point seems especially well taken since the challenged provision in *Valtierra* was an explicit, de jure wealth classification. The stigmatizing impact of a law allowing communities to band together and exclude poor people as such need

§ 16–58

1. 402 U.S. 137 (1971).

2. Id. at 139.

3. 393 U.S. 385 (1969).

4. See Justice Marshall's dissent for a persuasive showing that the amendment clearly *was* a wealth classification. The challenged article by its terms singled out low income people, defined as those "who lack the amount of income which is necessary . . . to enable them, without financial assistance, to live in decent, safe and sanitary dwellings, without overcrowding," to bear its burden. 402 U.S. at 144 (quoting California Constitution, Article XXXIV).

5. Id., at 141.

6. Id., at 145 (dissenting opinion). See also Justice Marshall's dissenting opinion in Selective Service System v. Minnesota Public Interest Research Group, discussed in § 16–57, supra. Perhaps the short shrift given the wealth classification claim can be explained partly by the opinion's evident regard for California's referendum tradition, demonstrating "devotion to democracy, not to bias, discrimination, or prejudice." Id. at 141. But see Village of Arlington Heights v. Metropolitan Housing Development Corp., 429 U.S. 252 (1977), discussed in § 16–20, supra.

hardly be spelled out.[7] The majority's seemingly studied disregard of these defects cries out for an explanation.

Section 16–52 identifies the questionable use of precedent by which the Court in *San Antonio Independent School District v. Rodriguez* demonstrated that all roads led to the minimum rationality test.[8] The Court's application of the test showed how crucial it was for upholding the Texas scheme that even slightly heightened scrutiny be avoided at all costs. For even the minimum rationality hurdle could be cleared only by the same absence of rigor which characterized the Court's choice of the test in the first place. The Court found that funding the public schools through local property taxes furthered the state's legitimate interest in preserving local control over education. Centralized funding, on the other hand, would lead to centralized legislative control. The Court's willingness to believe that local funding promotes local control might at first seem plausible enough.[9] But insofar as local control is a concomitant of local rather than centralized funding,[10] the Texas system afforded local control only to the property-rich districts.[11] In other words, the Court's proffered rational justification merely restated the equal protection problem; it renamed the rich districts' revenue-raising power "local control" without explaining what was rational about a system which extended such "control" to inhabitants of rich districts and denied it to inhabitants of poor districts.[12]

7. Compare Edwards v. California, 314 U.S. 160 (1941), discussed in § 16–36, supra.

8. 411 U.S. 1 (1973). Indeed it is not entirely clear why the plaintiff class, definable as inhabitants of property-poor districts unable to raise more than a negligible per student sum, did not fit even the Court's narrow, revisionist criteria for a wealth classification. Such a definition would have side-stepped the Court's exaggerated concern, derived mainly from a study of Connecticut school districts, that poor people might not live in property poor districts. Furthermore, even given this concern, it was at least shown that between 10% and 20% of the poorest and richest families lived in the poorest and richest districts, respectively. The Court did not adequately explain why the poorest inhabitants of the poorest districts were not an adequately defined class. See Clune, "Wealth Discrimination in School Finance," 68 Nw.U.L.Rev. 651 (1973); Coons, "Introduction: 'Fiscal Neutrality' After Rodriguez," 38 Law & Cont.Probs. 299 (1974).

9. For a more sophisticated prognosis that centralized funding could be expected to diminish local control, especially in the area of contract negotiations with teachers, see Simon, "The School Finance Decisions: Collective Bargaining and Future Finance Systems," 82 Yale L.J. 409 (1973).

10. The educational theorists who had developed and promoted the foundation grant scheme adopted in Texas actually defined local control as "the freedom to devote more money to the education of one's children." 411 U.S. at 49.

11. The funding in property-poor districts was overwhelmingly from centralized grants. See 411 U.S. at 64–67 (White, J., dissenting).

12. This critique of the Rodriguez opinion is not meant to suggest that the decision was insupportable. Its logic has both its supporters and its detractors. Compare Carrington, "Financing the American Dream: Equality and School Taxes," 73 Colum.L.Rev. (1973), and Goldstein, "Interdistrict Inequalities in School Financing: A Critical Analysis of Serrano v. Priest and its Progeny," 120 U.Pa.L.Rev. 504 (1973), with Yudoff, "Equal Educational Opportunity and the Courts," 51 Tex.L. Rev. 411 (1973), and Clune, "Wealth Discrimination in School Finance," 68 Nw. U.L.Rev. 651 (1973). Nonetheless the confidence with which the Court espoused conclusions that were at best debatable leads one to wonder whether unarticulated premises must not have been strongly guiding the Court's hand.

Finally in *Salyer Land Co. v. Tulare Water District*,[13] the line of cases striking down property qualifications for the franchise [14] came to an abrupt and inadequately explained halt. The Court upheld under the rational relation test the California Water Code, which extended eligibility to vote for the Board of Directors of Water Districts only to landowners, and in proportion to the assessed valuation of their land, excluding both non-property owning residents and all lessees of property within the District. The Court determined that the primary purpose of the Water District was to provide for the acquisition, storage, and distribution of water for farming in the Tulare Lake Basin. The costs of District projects were assessed against the land in proportion to the services provided. Any delinquent charge became a lien on the land. "In short, there is no way that the economic burdens of district operations can fall on residents *qua* residents, and the operations of the [water] districts primarily affect the land within their boundaries." [15]

The Court's limitation of interest in governmental decisions to those with a direct economic stake represented a radical departure from the more wide-ranging sorts of interests the Court had previously protected from disenfranchisement.[16] This departure seems unlikely to represent a broad or permanent shift in perspective [17] and was rendered especially peculiar in light of the obviously grave adverse effects that one of the non-landowning appellants had suffered as a result of a District decision. In the great flood of 1969, the Board had voted six to four to table a motion to divert flood waters from the Basin; as a consequence, 88,000 of the 193,000 acres in the Basin were flooded, leaving the appellant's residence 15½ feet below water.[18]

Nevertheless, in *Ball v. James*,[19] the Court fully transformed the *Salyer* holding into a one-acre-one-vote principle. While conceding that the Salt River District at issue in *James* was both larger and more encompassing than the contested water district in *Salyer*,[20] the majority employed a distinctly narrow definition of governmental services, suggesting that only those entities that provide "core services" are governmental, to find the District to be "essentially business enterprises,

13. 410 U.S. 719 (1973), discussed in § 13–11, supra.

14. See §§ 13–11, 13–15, 16–47, supra.

15. Salyer, 410 U.S. at 729.

16. See § 13–11, supra.

17. Note, for example, the Court's reaffirmation, in Town of Lockport v. Citizens for Community Action, 430 U.S. 259, 267 (1977), of the view that "nonproperty owners [must] also [be deemed for franchise purposes to] share in the tax burden when the tax on rental property or commercial businesses is passed on in the form of higher prices."

18. This event, described by Justice Douglas in dissent, 410 U.S. at 735–38, takes on a more sinister cast by virtue of the fact that the major landholder in the Basin, the J. G. Boswell Co., commanded 37,825 votes, enough to elect a majority of the Board. Apparently the Board's inaction in 1969 had resulted from the fact that the J. G. Boswell Co. had a long-term agricultural lease in the Buena Vista Lake Basin, and flooding it would have interfered with the planting, growing, and harvesting of crops.

19. 451 U.S. 355 (1981). The Salt River Project Agricultural Improvement and Power District under attack in James was a governmental entity that stored and delivered untreated water in Arizona. The Project, which was the second largest utility in Arizona, also subsidized its water operations by selling electricity to hundreds of thousands of people in an area larger than that encompassed by the water program. See § 13–11, supra.

20. Id. at 365.

created by and chiefly benefiting a specific group of landowners." [21] Thus, there was no constitutional infirmity in the District's limitation of the franchise to voters who owned land within the District and its apportionment of voting power according to the number of acres owned. Because the effect on the landowners was "disproportionately greater than the effect on those seeking the vote," the District's voting system was reasonably related to its statutory objectives. [22] The dissenters, [23] however, viewed the entity, including its tax-exempt status, eminent domain powers, and its authority to control the use and source of energy for the District, as sufficiently governmental to necessitate striking down the voting system as a violation of the fourteenth amendment. The dissenters were also persuaded by the fact that 98% of the District's operating income came from the generation of electricity, with much of the revenue coming from nonvoters, producing a situation in which the "landowning irrigators are getting a free ride at the expense of the users of electricity." [24]

Perhaps these cases, inadequately explained within their four corners, can be understood by reference to the consequences that contrary decisions would have entailed. Unlike the cases in which wealth discrimination challenges have been upheld, *Valtierra, Rodriguez, Salyer* and *James* involved not poor people asking the state to give them something they could not afford, but rather poor people asking rich people to share with them something the legislature had told the rich people they could enjoy. In *Salyer* and *James* the disputed benefit was political power; in *Valtierra*, land use; in *Rodriguez*, expensive schools for children.

There are at least two major ways to redistribute wealth. The first and most obvious is to take wealth or property from the rich and give it to the poor. This is the model of legislative action which the Court in effect forbade during the *Lochner* era. [25] The second is to reduce the category of desirable goods which wealth can purchase. This category has traditionally included, for example, pricey lawyers, access to courts, residence in exclusive neighborhoods with large lot requirements, fancy public schools, and political power. Some believe that the prospect of such desiderata has led people to work hard, live frugally, accumulate savings, and invest capital. Decisions requiring free transcripts or invalidating poll taxes obviously represent redistributions of a very minor sort. The amounts of money involved are small; more important, criminal appeals and the vote are not among the most cherished dreams of upward mobility. The ambitious working class family is far more likely to lighten its dreary hours with visions of a house far from

21. Id. at 368. As examples of "governmental powers," the majority listed laws "governing the conduct of citizens," the "maintenance of streets, the operation of schools, or sanitation, health, or welfare services." Id. at 366.

22. Id. at 371.

23. Justice White, joined by Justices Brennan, Marshall, and Blackmun, dissented. Justice Powell filed a concurring opinion stating that "[t]he authority and will of the Arizona legislature to control the electoral composition of the District are decisive for me in this case." Id. at 374 (Powell, J., concurring). Justice Stewart wrote for the Court, joined by Chief Justice Burger and Justices Powell, Rehnquist, and Stevens.

24. Id. at 384 (White, J., dissenting).

25. See Chapter 8, supra.

the fumes and dirt and crowding of the city, with a backyard and fresh air and only the shouts of playing children breaking the general tranquility.[26] The middle class family might dream of a four acre lot. Increased distance from the less fortunate seems to be a major incentive for upward mobility.[27] State legislatures often allow the wealthy to purchase such distance.[28] The Texas public education financing scheme went a step further and told the rich that they could spend, for the public education of their own children, all the money they chose to have taxed against them. The rich were thus permitted to create their own secure haven of privilege and exclusion. Judicial disruption of this pattern of upward mobility would have represented redistribution of a fundamental variety. *Salyer* and *James*, even if less justifiable, seem explicable along similar lines: the Burger Court was evidently unwilling to divest wealthy landowners of the political power they wielded by virtue of their land-holdings.

That the Court has become hesitant to upset existing distributions of wealth by restricting the pool of benefits which wealth can purchase is implicit in two landmark cases decided outside the context of wealth classifications. In *Village of Arlington Heights v. Metropolitan Housing Development Corporation* [29] and *Buckley v. Valeo*,[30] the Court reinforced existing distributions by preserving the price tag on two scarce and precious commodities which exist at all only so long as they are unequally distributed: distance from the poor and political power. *Arlington Heights* upheld the power of a predominantly white middle class suburb to exclude a low-income housing development when motivated by a desire "to protect property values and the integrity of the Village's zoning plan." [31] The Court's decision turned on the District Court's finding [32] that the Village's zoning decision was not motivated by *racial* discrimination. Perhaps because *James v. Valtierra* [33] might have appeared to foreclose the issue, *wealth* discrimination by itself was neither argued by the parties nor discussed by the courts. Nevertheless, a holding about wealth classification is implicit in the Court's tacit assumption that the purposeful exclusion of poor people is constitutionally permissible if it is in service of some fiscal interest, such as preserving property values or maintaining a wealthy tax base.[34] This exclusion had already been sanctioned in *Valtierra*; there, however, it

---

26. See, e.g., Village of Belle Terre v. Boraas, 416 U.S. 1, 9 (1974) (upholding state's power "to lay out zones where family values, youth values, and the blessings of quiet seclusion and clean air make the area a sanctuary for people").

27. See Clune, "Wealth Discrimination and the Fourteenth Amendment," 1975 Sup.Ct.Rev. 289, 294.

28. See Branfman, Cohen and Trubek, "Measuring the Invisible Wall: Land Use Controls and the Residential Patterns of the Poor," 82 Yale L.J. 483 (1973) (studies indicate that public land use controls promote income group clustering).

29. 429 U.S. 252 (1977), discussed in § 16–20, supra.

30. 424 U.S. 1 (1976), discussed in §§ 13–27 to 13–31, supra.

31. 429 U.S. at 259.

32. This finding was affirmed by the Court of Appeals for the Seventh Circuit in Metropolitan Housing Development Corporation v. Village of Arlington Heights, 517 F.2d 409, 412 (1975).

33. 402 U.S. 137 (1971).

34. Excluding the poor to preserve the tax base is not inherently stigmatizing; the town is saying, in effect, "We want to keep you out, not because you are *poor types*, but because *you have no money* for us to tax." The argument that the presence of poor people lowers property values is less neutral, since its thrust is that if poor

had been veiled by judicial deference to California's referendum tradition. *Arlington Heights* extracts the holding of *Valtierra* from this setting and stands it on its own feet: the Constitution permits the wealthy to keep their distance from the poor.[35]

In *Buckley v. Valeo*,[36] the Court struck down as violative of the first amendment those portions of the Federal Election Campaign Act Amendments of 1974 which imposed ceilings on independent expenditures on behalf of a candidate, personal funds spent by a candidate on his or her own behalf, and total expenditures by a candidate.[37] The Court treated controls of campaign spending as controls over communication as such, requiring the most rigorous review, rather than as regulations of aspects unrelated to the ideas communicated, ordinarily commanding a lesser degree of scrutiny.[38] This equation of spending and speech entailed an unusually activist judicial support of existing wealth distribution: by diverting political influence away from the rich, Congress had attempted a redistribution of political power very similar to the redistribution of educational revenues sought by the plaintiffs in *Rodriguez*, along "wealth-neutral" lines; political power, like education, would no longer be keyed quite so closely to concentrations of wealth. Deference to *legislative* judgments on distribution can hardly explain *Buckley*, which stands out conspicuously as one of the most interventionist decisions of a generally restrained Court. *Buckley* begins to suggest, on the other hand, a commitment to *existing* distributions deep enough to forestall even legislative changes.[39]

§ 16–59. Reconciling Room at the Top With Protection at the Bottom

What emerges from the decisions of the 1970's and 1980's,[1] then, is a wavering commitment to maintain for the poor access to criminal justice and the political process; a possible, but not openly professed or entirely consistent, belief in protection for the poor against the most severe forms of deprivation with respect to education, nutrition, and welfare; and a determined, occasionally even activist, though again not openly proclaimed, commitment to preserve for the non-poor ways of purchasing distance and distinction from the less fortunate—to pre-

---

people live in the town, rich people won't want to live there any more. The crucial point, however, is that both of these arguments are always *available* to suburbs seeking to exclude the poor, whether or not they are in fact *operative*. The Court's uncritical acceptance of those arguments precluded further inquiry, for the time being, into whether more invidious motivations actually impelled the exclusion.

35. Of course, Edwards v. California, 314 U.S. 160 (1941), discussed in § 16–36, supra, prohibits a whole state from keeping out the poor. It is worth wondering whether a distinction between states and municipalities in this respect is supportable. Cf. § 15–14, supra.

36. 424 U.S. 1 (1976).

37. The Court upheld, as an appropriate hedge against campaign finance corruption, certain dollar ceilings on individual contributions.

38. For a critique of this treatment, see Wright, "Politics and the Constitution: Is Money Speech?", 85 Yale L.J. 1001, 1005–8 (1976). The campaign finance decisions are discussed in §§ 13–27 to 13–31, supra.

39. Compare Chapter 8, supra.

§ 16–59

1. See §§ 16–51 to 16–58, supra.

serve, in effect, plenty of room at the top, without wholly abandoning protection at the bottom.

The vision animating this mix of aspirations is plainly not an egalitarian one, but it is not without its own elements of decency and concern; whatever the doctrinal strains, the Burger Court did not refuse lifelines to those about to drown, even if it threw them from a point perched safely above the disquieting signs of distress—a point from which the struggle to survive may not always be visible at all.[2]

How much *more* egalitarian an approach would be justifiable under the Constitution we have inherited—as an honest interpretation of that not altogether egalitarian document—is by no means clear. But another question looms as well: whether the equal protection of the laws can survive the transformation into minimal protection of the laws, with some of us very much more equal than others, remains to be seen. It will depend in part on just *how* minimal the protection provided at the bottom turns out to be. But it may also depend on the viability of a system that separates liberty from equality, and separates both from fraternity. And the problem has a final, disturbing dimension: So long as poverty and race remain so closely linked, the reminder that a nation cannot endure half slave and half free will echo with a haunting relevance.

2. See, e.g., Maher v. Roe, 432 U.S. 464 (1977) (states need not fund nontherapeutic abortions even if they do fund childbirth; majority treats such a government choice as analogous to government refusal to pay bus fares of children exercising right to attend private school or government refusal to pay for foreign language lessons of persons exercising right to learn such language), discussed in § 15–10, supra.

Chapter 17

MODEL VII—TOWARD A MODEL OF STRUCTURAL JUSTICE?

§ 17-1. The Relevance of Structure to Substance

It is possible, and may prove fruitful, to describe a final if perhaps subsidiary model of constitutional argument—one whose elements are drawn from themes and doctrines present in the first six models, but one that nonetheless seems distinctive in its potential reconnection of individual rights with institutional design.

We may begin by observing that all six of the constitutional models thus far examined have been concerned with ways of achieving substantive ends through various governmental structures and processes of choice. Whether by separating and dividing those structures into mutually checking centers of power, by insisting that certain spheres of choice be placed beyond the reach of governmental authority, by demanding that certain problems be affirmatively addressed by government, or by insisting on regularity and even-handedness in governmental action, each model has reflected a conception in which one or more features of the society's overall structure for making decisions serves to implement, and at times to mirror, some set of social ideals or values. From this perspective, a constitutional model designed to match decision structures with substantive human ends might seem indistinguishable from the models already set forth. Yet if such a model were to draw eclectically on all of the first six, seeking to achieve such ends as human freedom not through any *one* characteristic structure of choice but through that *combination* of structures that seems best suited to those ends *in a particular context*, then the model might indeed prove distinct from Models I through VI.

Rather than routinely treating freedom as best preserved, whatever the context, by strict separation of powers and federal-state division, as in Model I, or routinely treating it as best advanced, again whatever the context, by placement of specific subjects beyond governmental control, as in Models II and V, a model consciously concerned with contextually matching decisional structures to substantive ends—Model VII—might perceive freedom as best served in some contexts by putting a matter beyond governmental reach, and in others by precisely the opposite approach. This model would distill from all the others what is often a poorly disguised secret: that "neutral" principles of structure are worth embracing as constitutional precepts only to the extent that the substantive human realities they bring about help fulfill the constitutional design and that each prior model proved empty exactly to the degree that it sought to deny this truth.

Such a Model VII might comfortably embrace, for example, both *Skinner v. Oklahoma* [1] and *West Coast Hotel v. Parrish* [2] as establishing structures of choice best suited to serve the constitutionally central end of freedom, although in *Skinner* the structure mandated was one that *denied* government the power to select who would procreate—thereby leaving the matter to be shaped by personal choice—while in *Parrish* the structure accepted was one that *gave* government the power to impose contract terms—thereby taking a matter from the realm of personal determination. A judgment that constitutionally meaningful freedom precludes governmental decision in the first context is entirely consistent with a judgment that such freedom permits, and perhaps even mandates, governmental decision in the second.[3] Inescapable is the substantive question: given the relevant social and economic realities, which path now points away from domination in a constitutionally relevant sense?[4] So also a judgment that respect for unconventional ideas or choices of lifestyle precludes overly personalized government

§ 17–1

1. 316 U.S. 535 (1942) (invalidating compulsory sterilization of selected categories of convicted criminals). See generally Tribe, "Foreword: Toward a Model of Roles in the Due Process of Life and Law," 87 Harv.L.Rev. 1 (1973).

2. 300 U.S. 379 (1937) (upholding minimum wage law).

3. The Constitution mandates affirmative government action to protect constitutional rights in a number of contexts—usually when those rights both (1) are relational and systemic rather than solely individual and (2) "concern[ ] . . . capacities that persons are unable to exercise without assistance." Tribe, "The Abortion Funding Conundrum: Inalienable Rights, Affirmative Duties, and the Dilemma of Dependence," 99 Harv.L.Rev. 330, 333, 341–343 (1985). However, some of these affirmative constitutional duties may well be wholly or partly unenforceable by courts. Particularly likely to be incompletely enforceable are those open-ended duties whose fulfillment would require the government to spend large sums of money, primarily because courts are limited in two key institutional respects: the ability to manage resources and the ability to decide when such an open-ended duty has been faithfully discharged. The resulting limits on judicial enforcement of the underlying norms, cf. Sager, "Fair Measure: The Legal Status of Underenforced Constitutional Norms," 91 Harv.L.Rev. 1212 (1978), should redouble the attention given by the political branches to their constitutional oaths.

4. This substantive question also uncovers the real problem with Lochner v. New York, 198 U.S. 45 (1905), and why West Coast Hotel v. Parrish, 300 U.S. 379 (1937), properly overruled it. The problem was not primarily that the Court lacked the institutional capacity or competence to address the social or economic issues at stake; rather, the core problem with Lochner was that the Court erred in supposing that the pattern of economic power established by common-law contract and property arrangements must be taken as a reflection of natural justice in deciding which legislative interventions to condemn as violations of due process of law. Conversely, Parrish correctly recognized that many legislative rearrangements of common-law power relationships might reasonably attempt to combat economic subjugation and human domination. See § 8–7, supra. Indeed, the key error of decisions like Lochner lies in the way the Court often misconceives patterns reinforced by extant law as natural mirrors of justice. As Michael Walzer has argued, justice is offended less by the fact that some are rich and some are poor, than by the fact that the law attaches to this disparity in wealth a wide-ranging legal and social significance. See M. Walzer, Spheres of Justice 11–12 (1983). When the law either tolerates or requires a regime in which a group's superior position in the material sphere translates into a superior position in such other spheres as health care, education, political power, access to judical relief, and personal autonomy and safety, then the law creates and perpetuates a world in which "all good things come to those who have the one best thing." Id. at 11. See also L. Tribe, Constitutional Choices 242 (1985) (developing a parallel point with respect to the role of some laws in transmuting biological differences into social hierarchies).

action in a context where pamphleteers are being licensed[5] is consistent with a judgment that the same respect for the unconventional compels highly individualized adjudication where custody decisions affecting unmarried males,[6] or employment decisions affecting pregnant females,[7] are at stake.[8] Again inescapable is the substantive question: given the cultural and bureaucratic realities, which path currently points toward the freedom protected by the relevant constitutional provisions?[9]

Indeed, a fairly common characteristic of the evolution of a substantive constitutional ideal is that its "optimal" structural embodiment is likely to undergo significant change from one era to the next. Sensitivity to the substantive ideals implicit in various structural prescriptions is needed if this sort of transformation is to be traced, but once such sensitivity exists the trajectory of change may become apparent.

Consider, for example, the principles and rules through which the judiciary has protected persons from political oppression by the national government. Long before substantive first amendment doctrines began their explicit growth, the Supreme Court advanced values implicit in those doctrines through decisions of a structural character. When the Jefferson Administration allowed the Alien and Sedition Act of 1798 to lapse in 1801 but then prosecuted newspaper editors for the common-law crime of seditious libel, the Marshall Court intervened in 1812 to hold, in *United States v. Hudson & Goodwin*,[10] that there can exist no federal common law of crimes—that the national government can invoke the power to convict and imprison publishers only pursuant to explicit legislation enacted by Congress. A Model I argument thus served to advance values of free expression. When Congress in the wake of the Civil War sought to bar practice in federal courts by attorneys refusing to swear that they had never engaged in hostility to the United States, the Court in 1866 intervened to hold in *Ex parte Garland*[11] that such punitive measures may not be visited by legislative decree upon persons so specified—that the ex post facto and bill of attainder clauses forbid such treatment. It was the bill of attainder clause that the Court again invoked both in 1946, to protect govern-

---

5. See, e.g., Lovell v. Griffin, 303 U.S. 444 (1938) (invalidating open-ended licensing ordinance as creating undue risk of censorship).

6. See Stanley v. Illinois, 405 U.S. 645 (1972) (unwed father must be given individualized opportunity to show he is a fit parent).

7. See Cleveland Board of Educ. v. La-Fleur, 414 U.S. 632 (1974), (school board must give pregnant teachers individualized opportunity to show fitness notwithstanding school rule requiring unpaid maternity leaves several months before expected childbirth).

8. See generally § 16–34, supra.

9. While this chapter discusses the structural model in constitutional terms, it is possible to apply a similar mode of analysis to statutes governing agencies. See, e.g., Rosenblatt, "Health Care Reform and Administrative Law: A Structural Approach," 88 Yale L.J. 243 (1978). In such a context, the structural question would become: given the cultural and bureacratic realities, which path currently points toward the realization of the relevant statutory goals? See id. at 251, 255–64, 331–336.

10. 11 U.S. (7 Cranch) 32 (1812). See also § 12–34, supra.

11. 71 U.S. (4 Wall.) 333 (1866). See also Cummings v. Missouri, 71 U.S. (4 Wall.) 277 (1866). Both cases are discussed in §§ 10–2, 10–4, supra.

ment employees from a Congress bent on barring them from federal positions for views that had made them the targets of congressional investigation [12], and in 1965, to protect members of the Communist Party from a congressional ban on their serving as officers or employees of labor unions.[13] This time it was Model IV through which freedom of speech and association were defended.[14]

Nor did the evolution of the preferred rights theory of Model V render useless the prior models of constitutional argument. In 1971, for example, it was partly the failure of Congress to authorize enjoining publication of national defense documents that the Supreme Court stressed, when it held that the Executive Branch could not obtain injunctions against publishing the Pentagon Papers,[15] just as the Court in *Hudson* had relied upon the government's failure to invoke an applicable federal statute, when it held that the Executive Branch could not punish certain publications after the fact.

This history suggests first, that not even the fully developed emergence of substantive doctrine can wholly replace attention to structure; and second, that the structural norms through which a substantive value is best preserved may be expected to vary over time and from one setting to the next. Taking our cue from these lessons, we might define Model VII as reconstituting Models I through VI by seeking particular decision structures for particular substantive purposes in particular contexts, while avoiding generalizations about which decisional pattern is best suited, on the whole, to which substantive aims.[16] This "model of structural justice" would borrow from each of the prior models its insights about the substantive tendencies of specific structural arrangements; but it would repudiate each prior model by refusing to regard those tendencies as inhering in one structure rather than another, without regard to context, time, or place. In some cases, the greatest threat to freedom of speech might be traceable to overreaching by the executive branch; in others, to a legislature's political vindictiveness; in still others, to governmental insensitivity to expressional values. In some cases, the greatest threat to economic freedom might be traceable to a concentration of governmental power; in others, to governmental abdication in favor of private wealth. In its maturity, Model VII might

---

12. United States v. Lovett, 328 U.S. 303 (1946), discussed in § 10–4, supra.

13. United States v. Brown, 381 U.S. 437 (1965), discussed in §§ 10–4 to 10–6, supra.

14. In some individual cases, some members of the Court rely on Model I while others use Model IV arguments to protect persons from political oppression. See, e.g., INS v. Chadha, 462 U.S. 919 (1983), discussed in Chapter 4, supra. In that case, the majority held that the House of Representatives could not "veto" the Attorney General's decision to suspend the deportation of six aliens, because, even if authorized by a properly passed statute, the legislative veto-power conflicts with separation of powers principles. But Justice Powell stressed Model IV concerns, arguing that the House's isolation of six

individuals for deportation in essence violated the bill of attainder clause's prohibition of "trial by legislature." See 462 U.S. at 959, 962 (Powell, J., concurring in the judgment).

15. New York Times v. United States, 403 U.S. 713 (1971) (per curiam), discussed in § 12–34, supra, and in § 17–2, infra.

16. On the treachery of such generalizations, see Kennedy, "Form and Substance in Private Law Adjudication," 89 Harv.L.Rev. 1685, 1703–04 (1976). Cf. Unger, "The Critical Legal Studies Movement," 96 Harv.L.Rev. 563, 567–73 (1983). Contrast A. Cox, The Role of the Supreme Court in American Government 114 (1976) (insisting that only a "virtually absolute and enduring principle" can qualify as a source of a constitutional right).

identify criteria linking particular structure-substance pairings to specific aspects of each social and historical setting in which such pairings occur; in its early development, Model VII can at best hint at such criteria.[17]

§ 17–2. Two Ways in Which Structure May Be Relevant: Rules and Principles

In understanding two distinct ways in which structural concerns may be brought to bear on a substantive constitutional analysis, it is useful to compare *United States v. Hudson & Goodwin*[1] to *New York Times v. United States*,[2] and to compare *Panama Refining Co. v. Ryan*[3] to *Hampton v. Mow Sun Wong*.[4] In *Hudson & Goodwin*, the Supreme Court, undoubtedly for reasons related to freedom of speech and press, reversed a conviction on the ground that a federal criminal law must be embodied in an Act of Congress and cannot rest solely on an executive policy or a judicial rule. In *New York Times v. United States*, the Court, again to protect freedom of speech and press, dissolved a prior restraint in a decision giving weight to Congress' failure to authorize suppression of such publications as the ones involved in that case. Thus *Hudson & Goodwin* established a formal requirement that federal crimes be legislatively defined while five Justices in *New York Times v. United States* treated as relevant, but not dispositive, the fact that no congressional authorization had supported the government's attempt at civil suppression.[5] Although the difference between the decisions could be described as a matter of degree, that would obscure a fundamental point: in the first case, the Court was prepared to formulate its conclusion as a *rule about decision-making structure*. In the second, the Court was prepared to *consider* the structure of decision that had given rise to the action challenged, and even to state a *principle* under which it could treat the process of decision as a factor bearing on the action's substantive validity, but not yet to announce a rule-like formula to guide legislative structuring in the future.

Similarly, in *Panama Refining Co. v. Ryan*,[6] the Supreme Court struck down a congressional delegation of lawmaking authority to the executive, holding that the challenged delegation had gone beyond the bounds of Congress' power to abdicate responsibility for substantive policy choice; Congress was thereby told how it would have to enact laws

---

17. The Model of Structural Justice should not be confused with Charles Black's method of structural inference. See his Structure and Relationship in Constitutional Law 3–32 (1969). The latter, which moves significantly beyond simple textual exegesis as a mode of constitutional argument, may form a helpful *part* of Model VII analysis, but focuses much less on substantive context than Model VII must. In particular, Professor Black's search for elements "inherent" in our form of government, see, e.g., id. at 40, is distinctly more Platonic in cast than the core of what is contemplated here. But cf. id. at 46–47.

§ 17–2

1. 11 U.S. (7 Cranch) 32 (1812).

2. 403 U.S. 713 (1971) (per curiam). See id. at 720 (Douglas, J., joined by Black, J., concurring); id. at 730 (Stewart, J., joined by White, J., concurring); id. at 740 (White, J., joined by Stewart, J., concurring); id., at 740, 743–47 (Marshall, J., concurring).

3. 293 U.S. 388 (1935).

4. 426 U.S. 88 (1976).

5. See note 2, supra. See also Cantwell v. Connecticut, 310 U.S. 296, 307–08, 311 (1940).

6. 293 U.S. 388 (1935).

in the future.[7] In *Hampton v. Mow Sun Wong*,[8] on the other hand, the Supreme Court's decision to strike down a Civil Service Commission

7. See also decisions like United States v. Brown, 381 U.S. 437 (1965), setting bounds on the allowable degree of legislative specification when punitive measures are involved, discussed in §§ 10–4 to 10–6 and in § 17–1, supra. Rules governing permissible lawmaking are typically (1) of the Brown type, specifying bounds on the *form* a law may take (neither so specific as to single out identifiable persons for punishment, nor so general as to afford either inadequate notice to the law's targets and/or insufficiently focused debate among its initial proponents and opponents); or (2) of the Panama Refining type, insisting on assurance of a policy's promulgation *by a sufficiently accountable body.* Not only a legislative assembly but also the community as a whole, acting through a public referendum, is such a body for some purposes, see Eastlake v. Forest City Enterprises, Inc., 426 U.S. 668 (1976), but a group of private citizens exercising delegated authority in an open-ended way within the community is not. See Furman v. Georgia, 408 U.S. 238 (1972), discussed in § 17–3, infra. See also Larkin v. Grendel's Den, Inc., 459 U.S. 116 (1982) (state may not delegate to churches the power to effectively veto applications for liquor liscenses), discussed in Chapter 14, supra; Carter v. Carter Coal Co., 298 U.S. 238 (1936), discussed in § 5–17, supra; see also Eubank v. Richmond, 226 U.S. 137 (1912), cited with approval in Eastlake, 426 U.S. at 677–78. Cf. McBain, "Law-Making by Property Owners," 36 Pol.Sci.Q. 617, 640–41 (1921): "[T]he owners of property in a block . . . are not an organized political unit."

Although these rules may usefully be bifurcated into the Brown or Panama Refining types, there may be some rules which overlap both categories. For example, at first glance, the Court's void-for-vagueness doctrine apparently specifies only the form that a law must take: "a penal statute [must] define the criminal offense with sufficient difiniteness that ordinary people can understand what conduct is prohibited. . . ." Kolender v. Lawson, 461 U.S. 352, 357 (1983). However, recent decisions recognize "that the more important aspect of the vagueness doctrine [more important than its role in assuring fair notice] 'is . . . the requirement that a legislature establish minimal guidelines to govern law enforcement'" in order to avoid "vest[ing] virtually complete discretion in the hands of the police." Id. at 358, quoting Smith v. Goguen, 415 U.S. 566, 574 (1974). This focus demonstrates that the form of the statute is important primarily because the legislature, rather than the executive branch, must make the discretionary policy choice about which actions are criminal. Hence, like Panama

Refining, Kolender disapproves legislative action which excessively delegates discretion to the executive.

It may be that decisions insisting that at least some types of governmental action be taken only by bodies officially accountable to the constituencies most significantly affected could rest more comfortably on article IV, § 4's guarantee of a "republican form of government" than on "due process" notions. See also § 5–23, supra (resting states'-rights notions on this guarantee). For an illuminating analysis of the differences between "legislative" (representative) and "plebiscitory" (directly democratic) decisionmaking, stressing the role of consensus-formation in preventing decision processes from readily overriding intensely felt minority views, see Wolfinger & Greenstein, "The Repeal of Fair Housing in California: An Analysis of Referendum Voting," 62 Am. Pol.Sci.Rev. 753 (1968). Despite occasional Supreme Court insensitivity to the distinction, see Eastlake v. Forest City Enterprises, supra, government bodies in America have not, by and large, been direct democracies. Our system has instead chosen representative government in most matters as a way of guarding against "rashness, precipitancy, and misguided zeal; and to protect the minority against the injustice of the majority." Rice v. Foster, 4 Del. (4 Harr.) 479, 487 (1847). See also Sirico, "The Constitutionality of the Initiative and Referendum," 65 Iowa L.Rev. 637 (1980); Bessette, "Deliberative Democracy: The Majority Principle in Republican Government," in How Democratic Is the Constitution? 102, 104–05 (1980); Note, "Constitutional Constraints on Initiative and Referendum," 32 Vand.L.Rev. 1143 (1979); Cf. Wood, "Democracy and the Constitution," in How Democratic Is the Constitution? 1, 8–9 (1980) ("folly of democracy" was thought to be representatives responding too readily to their constituents); Cf. E. Burke, Works 89, 96 (7th ed. 1881) (the representative betrays his constituents if he sacrifices his judgment to their opinions). But see Opinions of the Justices, 160 Mass. 586, 593, 594–95, 36 N.E. 488, 491–92 (1894) (Holmes, J., dissenting); Note, "The Judiciary and Popular Democracy: Should Courts Review Ballot Measures Prior to Elections?" 53 Fordham L.Rev. 919 (1985); Liebmann, "Delegation to Private Parties in American Constitutional Law," 50 Ind.L.J. 650, 669 (1975). See generally, D. Magleby, Direct Legislation: Voting on Ballot Propositions in the United States (1984); R. Goldwin & W. Schambra, How Democratic Is the Constitution? (1980); Freedman, "Delegation of Powers and Institutional Competence," 43 U.Chi.L.Rev. 307 (1976).

8. 426 U.S. 88 (1976).

regulation barring federal employment of aliens presented neither Congress nor the Commission with a formal requirement for the structuring of future decisions. Instead, the Court simply treated as *relevant* the circumstance that the broad employment disability challenged by aliens in that case had been promulgated by an agency to which neither Congress nor the President had openly and clearly entrusted the sorts of foreign policy concerns that alone might have furnished persuasive justification for the rule.[9] The agency was not found to have acted beyond its statutory mandate; that it might promulgate precisely the regulation challenged was sufficiently contemplated by Congress to rule out any holding that the choice was not statutorily authorized. Nor was the statutory mandate itself deemed too broad to comply with constitutional prohibitions on standardless delegation.[10] Either of those conclusions could have been expressed as a formal requirement for similar regulatory decisions in the future. Instead, how this rule had been made counted against its validity—but not in a manner giving rise to a recipe for future rule-making.[11]

9. Efficiency concerns, also argued in defense of the rule, *had* clearly been entrusted to the agency. But these provided no sufficient justification because the agency invoked them only as an afterthought; the record showed no actual agency determination, at the time the rule was adopted, that the rule would be more "efficient" than a less sweeping ban. See § 16–32, supra. In stressing these factors, the Supreme Court was plainly (and properly) influenced by the disconcerting ease with which conversation-stopping rationales either as ubiquitous and potentially trivial as "efficiency" or as distinctive and potentially momentous as "foreign diplomacy" can be invoked to rescue a challenged rule or policy. Accountable lawmaking would be ill-served by ready judicial acquiescence in such impenetrable forms of justification. But note the Court's greater willingness to uphold on efficiency grounds rules promulgated directly by *legislatures*, even where the rules burden important (though non-fundamental) interests or impinge on groups having some similarity to disadvantaged minorities. Compare, e.g., Massachusetts Bd. of Retirement v. Murgia, 427 U.S. 307 (1976) (upholding legislatively enacted mandatory retirement age of 50 for state police), discussed in § 16–31, supra. But see Nyquist v. Mauclet, 432 U.S. 1, 10–11 & n.13 (1977) (invalidating state legislation limiting higher education financial aid to citizens and resident aliens seeking U.S. citizenship; purpose of encouraging naturalization held "not a permissible one for a State," and not wholly consistent with the statute's history).

10. See § 5–17, supra.

11. See also Florida Lime & Avocado Growers, Inc. v. Paul, 373 U.S. 132, 150–51 (1963), discussed in §§ 6–25 to 6–27, supra, treating as relevant to the nationally preemptive effect of certain federal regulations the fact that they had been drafted by a self-interested group of Florida avocado growers and handlers rather than by lawmakers or officers with a nationwide constituency. But see United States Railroad Retirement Bd. v. Fritz, 449 U.S. 166 (1980). In dissent, Justice Brennan suggested that the Court's equal protection analysis should take into account that Congress was likely misled about the effects of the complex legislation at issue in Fritz by the outside parties who drafted it and "whose self-serving interest . . . destroys any basis for attaching weight to their statements." See 449 U.S. at 182, 189, 193 (Brennan, J., dissenting). The majority rejected the argument out of hand, stating that "we disagree with the District Court's conclusion that Congress was unaware of what it accomplished or that it was misled by the groups that appeared before it. If this test were applied literally to every member of any legislature . . . there would be very few laws which would survive it." 449 U.S. 166, at 179. Under the majority's approach, the injured group's only recourse is a new appeal to the legislative forum. Id. & n.12.

Justice Stevens has also argued that "the character of [congressional] procedures [should] be considered relevant to the decision whether the legislative process has . . . [violated the equal protection component of] due process . . . [w]henever Congress creates a classification . . . subject to strict scrutiny." Fullilove v. Klutznick, 448 U.S. 448, 550–51 (1980) (Stevens, J., dissenting). Thus, Justice Stevens would invalidate a statute where it "cannot fairly be characterized as a 'narrowly tailored' racial classification because it simply raises too many serious questions that Congress failed to answer or even to address in a responsible way." Id. at 552. See also Wygant v. Jackson Bd. of Education, 106 S.Ct. 1842,

This structural concern over the constitutional authority and competence of the decisionmaker was also relevant to the pivotal opinion of Justice Powell in *Regents of University of California v. Bakke*.[12] He there rejected the Regents' assertion that the University's affirmative action program remedied the effects of prior societal discrimination. Highly relevant to his rejection was the fact that findings of past discrimation were not made by either the "legislature or a responsible administrative agency."[13] The Regents were "in no position to make[ ] such findings," since "isolated segments of our vast governmental structures are not competent to make those decisions, at least in the absence of legislative mandates and legislatively determined criteria."[14]

Both the *Panama Refining* approach and that of *Hampton v. Mow Sun Wong* and *Bakke* put pressure on legislatures and/or agencies to reconsider the invalidated provision from a fresh perspective, and both approaches leave open the possibility that the Court may uphold a somewhat revised provision if such reconsideration leads to its enactment either in an altered form, or in the same form but by a different body.[15] Thus both approaches bear some similarity to the notion of "remand to the legislature" often advocated by constitutional and common-law commentators.[16] The idea is not new; what seems new is the

1869–70 & n.10 (1986) (Stevens, J., dissenting) (affirmative action agreement between school and union, which would retain minority teachers over more senior white teachers during layoff periods, should be upheld in part because "the procedures for adopting th[e] provision were scrupulously fair.").

12. 438 U.S. 265 (1978) (delivering Court's judgment but writing only for himself). See § 16–22, supra.

13. Id. at 305.

14. Id. at 309. See also New York City Transit Authority v. Beazer, 440 U.S. 568, 609–10 n.15 (1979) (White, J., joined by Marshall, J., dissenting). The Transit Authority excluded from employment all former heroin addicts then receiving methadone treatment. While arguing that the Authority's regulation violated equal protection, Justice White noted that "[s]ome weight should . . . be given to . . . [the fact that p]etitioners are not directly accountable to the public, are not the type of official body that normally makes legislative judgments of fact such as those relied upon by the majority today, and are by nature more concerned with business efficiency than with other public policies for which they have no direct responsibility." Id. See § 16–4, supra.

The Court uses similar reasoning when deciding whether to grant a party state-action immunity from the federal antitrust laws. In determining whether active state supervision is a prerequisite to the immunity, the Court has distinguished between local governmental bodies, whose processes are normally open to public input and

whose actions are presumptively accountable to a political electorate, and private associations or other similar entities, whose processes are not so open and whose actions are not so accountable. See Town of Hallie v. Eau Claire, 471 U.S. 34, 46 (1985) (municipality need not be supervised by state to obtain immunity); Southern Motor Carriers Rate Conference v. United States, 471 U.S. 48, 57 & n.20, 1729 (1985) (rate bureaus composed of private common carriers must be supervised by state to obtain immunity). Both cases are discussed further in § 6–26, supra.

15. In fact, in response to the Mow Sun Wong decision, President Ford issued an executive order which generally barred employment of aliens in the federal competitive civil service but gave the Civil Service Commission discretion to make exceptions to the rule. See Exec. Order No. 11,935, 5 C.F.R. § 7.4 at 14 (1979), reprinted in 5 U.S.C. § 3301 at 384 (1976). The order has been upheld by several circuit courts. See Mow Sun Wong v. Campbell, 626 F.2d 739 (9th Cir. 1980); Jalil v. Campbell, 590 F.2d 1120 (D.C. Cir. 1978), cert. denied, 450 U.S. 959 (1981); Vergara v. Hampton, 581 F.2d 1281 (7th Cir. 1978), cert. denied 441 U.S. 905 (1979).

16. See, e.g., G. Calabresi, A Common Law for the Age of Statutes (1982); A. Bickel, The Least Dangerous Branch 111–198 (1962); R. Keeton, Venturing to do Justice (1969); J. Sax, Defending the Environment 175–192 (1971); Monaghan, "The Supreme Court, 1974 Term—Foreword: Constitutional Common Law," 89 Harv.L.Rev. 1 (1975); Tribe, "Structural Due Process," 10 Harv.

eagerness of the modern Court to embrace it, whether through narrowing construction,[17] or through outright constitutional invalidation, as in *Hampton v. Mow Sun Wong*.[18]

In a parallel vein, the Court has with growing frequency found itself not quite prepared to pull out the heavy artillery of strict (and almost invariably fatal) scrutiny under Model V or Model VI—but nonetheless prepared, as a form of intermediate review, to reject justifications for a government action where those justifications had not actually been considered by the governmental entity that took the action in question.[19] In such cases, the Court treats decision-making structure as relevant in the second, weaker sense of *Hampton v. Mow Sun Wong*. For example, in *Mississippi University for Women v. Hogan*, the Supreme Court struck down a nursing school's refusal to admit men, in part because, "although the State recited a 'benign, compensatory purpose,' it failed to establish that the alleged objective is the *actual purpose* underlying the discriminatory classification." [20] This heightened scrutiny revealed that the nursing school's exclusion of men, far from compensating for discriminatory barriers faced by women,[21] "tends to perpetuate the stereotyped view of nursing as an exclusively women's job." [22] Since the reflection of

Civ.Rts.—Civ.Lib.L.Rev. 269, 314–318 (1976). But see Mikva, "The Shifting Sands of Legal Topography" (Book Review), 96 Harv.L.Rev. 534 (1982) (reviewing G. Calabresi, A Common Law for the Age of Statutes (1982)). But neither in Hampton nor in Panama Refining, unlike some of the "legislative remand" proposals, could a simple re-enactment of the provision, by the same government body that initially promulgated it, automatically save it in a subsequent judicial challenge.

17. See, e.g., National Cable Television Ass'n. v. United States, 415 U.S. 336 (1974) (construing FCC's statutory authority as not encompassing power to impose on regulated operators fees unrelated to benefits they received; doubt as to Congress' constitutional authority to delegate taxing power resolved by refusing to find such power in the FCC unless and until Congress clearly purports to delegate it). See also Kent v. Dulles, 357 U.S. 116 (1958) (construing congressional statute as not having delegated constitutionally problematic authority to deny passports to Communists). Cf. Chief Justice (then Justice) Rehnquist's opinions in both American Textile Mfrs. Institute, Inc. v. Donovan, 452 U.S. 490, 543–48 (1981) (Rehnquist, J., joined by Burger, C.J., dissenting), and Industrial Union Dept. v. American Petroleum Institute, 448 U.S. 607, 671–88 (1980) (Rehnquist, J., concurring in judgment), arguing that OSHA's power to promulgate standards for toxic-substance levels in the workplace should be limited to "setting safe standards or no standard at all," because Congress improperly delegated its legislative duty to decide whether OSHA may or should use cost-benefit analyisis in setting those standards). Id. at 688.

18. 426 U.S. 88 (1976). See also New York Times v. United States, 403 U.S. 713 (1971) (per curiam).

19. See, e.g., Mississippi University for Women v. Hogan, 458 U.S. 718, 730 (1982); Weinberger v. Wiesenfeld, 420 U.S. 636 (1975); Eisenstadt v. Baird, 405 U.S. 438 (1972). See § 16–32, supra. See also Bowen v. Owens, 106 S.Ct. 1881, 1889 (1986) (Marshall, J., joined by Brennan, J., dissenting); Schweiker v. Wilson, 450 U.S. 221, 244–245 & n.6 (1981) (Powell, J., joined by Brennan, Marshall, and Stevens, JJ., dissenting); United States Railroad Retirement Bd. v. Fritz, 449 U.S. 166, 187, 188 (1980) (Brennan, J., joined by Marshall, J., dissenting); Delaware Tribal Business Committee v. Weeks, 430 U.S. 73, 96–98 (1977) (Stevens, J., dissenting). The "efficiency" justification in Hampton v. Mow Sun Wong was also in this category. See note 9, supra. Cf. Shaffer v. Heitner, 433 U.S. 186, 215–16 (1977).

20. 458 U.S. 718, 730 (1982) (emphasis added), discussed in § 16–27, supra.

21. Statistics indicated that women have always dominated the nursing field, obtaining more than 90% of the nursing degrees conferred both in Mississippi and nationwide. Id. at 729 & n.14.

22. Id. at 729. See also Califano v. Goldfarb, 430 U.S. 199, 217 (1977) (while invalidating the Social Security Act's less favorable treatment of widowers than of widows, the Court found it important that the differential treatment resulted not, as the government asserted, from a "deliberate congressional intention to remedy the arguably greater needs of [widows]," but from "archaic and overbroad" generalizations

such stereotypes in legal categories that tie anatomy to destiny is the very evil to which doctrine in this area is directed, surely it is appropriate for substantive outcomes to be sensitive to whether the governmental process that produced the challenged exclusion was itself an example of the very evil to be avoided. A decision such as *Hogan*, like *Hampton v. Mow Sun Wong* but unlike *Panama Refining Co. v. Ryan*,[23] cannot be employed to extract a useful "rule" about how the lawmaking process must proceed in the future if its results are to be sustained; but it does express principled concerns with the link between political process and legal outcome—concerns surfacing with mounting frequency in the cases.

§ 17–3. Two Levels at Which Structural Analysis Plays a Role: Due Process of Lawmaking and Due Process of Law-applying

Cutting across the distinction between structural considerations expressible as rules for decisionmaking and structural considerations expressible only as principles bearing on particular substantive outcomes[1] is a more significant dichotomy, one which identifies two different levels of governmental choice. All of the examples considered in § 17–2 involved structural considerations bearing on the *initial formulation* of a governmental provision or regulation; the concern was with what might be termed "due process of lawmaking"[2]—*who* promulgated the provision, *to what ends*, and *in what manner*.[3] No less significant is "due process of law-applying" in the eventual enforcement of the provision or regulation—its application to particular entities or persons. At this level, too, concerns with *who* does the applying, *why*, and *how*, may be expressed in structural terms, and again such concerns may take the form either of rules about permissible structures or of principles shaping the analysis of specific outcomes.[4]

about women), discussed in §§ 16–26 to 16–30, supra.

23. 293 U.S. 388 (1935).

§ 17–3

1. See § 17–2, supra.

2. The phrase is Oregon Supreme Court Justice Hans Linde's. See his "Due Process of Lawmaking," 55 Nebraska L.Rev. 197 (1976) (adopting, however, a far more limited notion of such legislative due process than that espoused here). See also Justice Stevens' dissenting opinion in Delaware Tribal Business Committee v. Weeks, 430 U.S. 73, 96–98 & n.11 (1977).

3. A word should be said here about a body of principles obviously linked to Model VII but not dealt with directly in this chapter. I have in mind those principles that speak explicitly to the mechanisms through which law is made in our society—principles governing the veto power, or the seating of elected representatives, or the opportunity to participate in hearings disposing of one's interests, or the right to vote on a proposed government action or for one's preferred candidate for an elective office, or the division of lawmaking authority among the federal branches or between the national and state levels of government. Because such principles have not ordinarily been developed in response to concerns about the *substance* of whatever law is ultimately produced by the structure that the principles establish, it has seemed best to deal with principles of this sort under such separate headings as governmental regularity, see Chapter 10, or rights of political participation, see Chapter 13. Constitutional doctrines limiting the delegation of power are dealt with elsewhere, see § 5–17, for the same reason—but they nonetheless play a role in this chapter, see § 17–2, largely because they provide instructive points of comparison.

4. For a discussion of how structural concerns can cut across the lawmaking/law-applying dichotomy, see Tribe, "Structural Due Process," 10 Harv.Civ.Rts.—Civ.Lib.L. Rev. 269, 290, 303–21 (1976).

Rules governing permissible structures of enforcement may take the form of requirements that actions adversely affecting identified persons be taken through processes other than popular vote,[5] with safeguards for meaningful participation by the affected individuals.[6] Unfortunately, this assurance of participatory process is generally afforded only on an all-or-nothing basis: caught on the wrong side of overly formalistic distinctions between government rule-making and rule-applying,[7] relatively small and distinct groups are allowed no input other than the right to vote for political candidates, even where the government isolates them with decisions specifically vital to the lives of each of their members.[8]

5. See §§ 10–4 & 10–5, supra.

6. See §§ 10–7–10–19, supra.

7. Generally, parties have the right to be heard (and other adjudicatory due-process rights) when a rule is ultimately applied, but not when it is first made. See Bi-Metallic Invest. Co. v. State Board of Equalization, 239 U.S. 441 (1915) (no right of all affected property-owners to be heard personally before agency promulgates county-wide increase in property valuations for tax purposes). However, there are some exceptions. See, e.g., Thompson v. Washington, 497 F.2d 626 (D.C. Cir. 1973). Tenants in a low-rent housing project sought the right to participate in the consideration of rent increases under the National Housing Act and the due process clause. "Informed" by the due-process interests potentially at stake but avoiding decision upon constitutional grounds, the court interpreted the National Housing Act to establish a right to be heard. In distinguishing Bi-Metallic, the court stated: "[T]he determination which emerges from the governmental process under scrutiny here is not so individualized. We do not, however, regard this difference as determinative. We believe the correct approach is to ascertain whether tenants can make relevant contribution to the issues presented for decision, notwithstanding the fact that they apply to a potentially large class." Id. at 638 n.42. Moreover, in analyzing the process due, the court observed that "because the number of tenants potentially involved is quite large, we must be careful to shape procedures to protect the tenants' interests that avoid their becoming unduly burdensome." Id. at 639. While settling for hearings of the type prescribed by the Administrative Procedure Act, the court noted that additional safeguards might be required in other specific contexts. Id. at 641. Cf. § 17–3, infra; Tribe, supra note 4, at 268. But see Harlib v. Lynn, 511 F.2d 51 (7th Cir. 1975).

8. See, e.g., O'Bannon v. Town Court Nursing Center, 447 U.S. 773, 786, 789 n.22 (1980) (when a group of elderly patients from a nursing home sought an evidentiary hearing on the home's decertification and their forced transfer, the Court held that the individuals had "no right to participate in the enforcement proceedings" because decertification was "not the same . . . as a decision to transfer a particular patient,"), discussed in §§ 10–7 & 10–19, supra. The Court could better approximate due process concerns with less stress on formal distinctions and more insight into potential models of representational participation. See § 10–19, supra; J. Mashaw, Bureaucratic Justice 200–201 (1983); C. Edley, Judicial Governance 22, 60, 118, 390–95 (June, 1986 manuscript) (forthcoming); cf. O'Bannon, 447 U.S. at 790 (Blackmun, J., concurring).

In some contexts, the Court could achieve representational participation more consonant with the aims of due process by scrutinizing more closely those decisionmaking structures which ultimately set the rules regarding who will be heard by the primary decisionmaker and how. Two distinct structural concerns arise: (1) the structure of the *substantive* decisionmaking process—the participational question here is to what extent are individuals or groups represented in the substantive decisions which directly affect their lives? (2) the structure of the *structural* decisionmaking process—the participational question here is to what extent are individuals or groups represented in the decision about the level at which they may participate in the forming of the substantive decision? The answer to this second question colors the answer to the first. Thus, the less accountable the structural decisionmaking body is to the disaffected group, the more suspect is the denial of participation to that group. See Minnesota State Bd. for Community Colleges v. Knight, 465 U.S. 271, 294 (1984) (Marshall, J., concurring) (the Court should "be more suspicious when a state legislature instructs college administrators to listen to some faculty members and not others . . . [because a]dministrators are more accountable to slighted faculty members than are state legislatures.").

Rules regarding the structures of enforcement may also set boundaries on executive discretion in order to confine its implicit dangers.[9] Or they may, at the other extreme, insist on leaving room for rebuttal and discretionary adjustment where mandatory, per se rules are either too insensitive to personal differences in matters of great moment, or too impervious to changing values and conceptions to represent a fair expression of the continuing consent of the governed.[10] It is beyond the scope of this chapter to offer here a full theory of structural rules at either level; my sole purpose here is to underscore the growing significance of judicial decisions understandable only on the premise that such a theory is possible.

Finally, the way in which a provision is enforced may be deemed relevant, although not in the dispositive sense suggested by a structural rule about permissible enforcement mechanisms. Consider, for example, the occasional refusal of the Supreme Court to entertain justifications considered by the legislature or agency initially promulgating a rule but no longer pressed in its defense.[11] Such a refusal to credit bases for action that are not currently articulated to those who are adversely affected (and to reviewing courts) is best understood as part of an attempt to assure law's continuing legitimacy. Particularly in cases close to the line of substantive invalidity, declining to uphold the enforcement of a law on a theory that its enforcers are unwilling to espouse serves a role analogous to the careful examination of actual enactment processes and purposes in cases like *Hampton v. Mow Sun Wong*[12] and *Mississippi University for Women v. Hogan*.[13]

Indeed, even when a case is close to *no* clearly marked substantive constitutional boundary, values of responsiveness and accountability, from enactment through enforcement, may be enhanced by judicial decisions that focus on how the lawmaking and law-applying processes have in fact functioned, or failed to function, in a particular case.[14] At least one example of the confluence of these structural concerns is

9. See, e.g., Kolender v. Lawson, 461 U.S. 352, 358 (1983) (criminal statute requiring an individual to provide "credible and reliable" identification to police is void for vagueness, because "the statute vests virtually complete discretion in the hands of the police to determine whether the suspect has satisfied the statute. . . ."). See also Lovell v. Griffin, 303 U.S. 444 (1938). Cf. Furman v. Georgia, 408 U.S. 238 (1972) (totally discretionary imposition of death penalty held cruel and unusual punishment).

10. See § 16–34, supra (discussing irrebuttable presumption doctrine). Even when a court does not expressly reject the application of per se rules, it may reject, as ostensibly irrational, rules which ultimately reflect an improper governmental purpose. See Cleburne v. Cleburne Living Center, Inc., 473 U.S. 432, 450 (1985) (invalidating, as applied, an ordinance requiring a special permit for the operation of a group home for the mentally retarded, since the requirement, on the facts before the Court, "ap-

pear[ed] . . . to rest on an irrational prejudice against the mentally retarded").

11. See § 16–32, supra.

12. 426 U.S. 88 (1976), discussed in § 17–2, supra.

13. 458 U.S. 718, 730 (1982), discussed in § 17–2, supra.

14. In fact, these structural concerns may now be the states' only weapon of defense against congressional regulation of states as states. In Garcia v. San Antonio Metropolitan Transit Authority, 469 U.S. 528 (1985), the Court held that, while acting under the commerce power, Congress is not limited by how far its measures intrude upon state autonomy; rather, "the principal and basic limit on the federal commerce power is that inherent in all congressional action—the built-in restraints that our system provides through state participation in federal governmental action." Id. at 556. Hence, "[a]ny substantive restraint . . . must be tailored to compensate for possible

presented by the Court's treatment of the death penalty.[15] The lawmaking process fails constitutionally when a legislature effectively abdicates its responsibility to set the standards for deciding who should live and who should die for their crimes.[16] Absent specific standards, "[l]egislative 'policy' is . . . defined not by what is legislatively authorized but by what juries and judges do in exercising the discretion so regularly conferred upon them." [17] Hence, the Court held, such standardless death penalty statutes violate the eighth amendment.[18] The rules governing the process of applying the death penalty are similarly structural. First, the structure of the law-applying process is important to the Court's invalidation of mandatory death sentences.[19] Since the death penalty differs qualitatively from other sentences, the legislature may not retain complete power to decide who will die.[20] Instead, the decision requires discretion and a "process that accords . . . significance to relevant facets of the character and record of the individual offender or the circumstances of the particular offense." [21] Second, by invalidating jury-selection procedures which exclude potential jurors for cause "simply because they voiced a general objection to the death penalty," [22] the Court mandated a legal structure which linked the decision to impose the death penalty to contemporary community sentiments about capital punishment—sentiments which could evolve over time.[23] Thus, the Court not only created a process which respected fairness at the time of the Court's decision, it also shaped a process which both "incorporate[s] evolving visions of law and society into constitutional principle" and

failings in the national political process rather than to dictate a 'sacred province of state autonomy.' " Id. at 554.

15. See generally, McGautha v. California, 402 U.S. 183, 248–87 (1971) (Brennan, J., dissenting).

16. See Godfrey v. Georgia, 446 U.S. 420, 428 (1980) (plurality opinion of Stewart, Blackmun, Powell and Stevens, JJ.) ("[I]f a state wishes to authorize capital punishment it has a constitutional responsibility to tailor . . . its law in a manner that avoids the arbitrary and capricious infliction of the death penalty.").

17. Furman v. Georgia, 408 U.S. 238, 314 (1972) (White, J., concurring).

18. Furman v. Georgia, 408 U.S. 238. See also Gregg v. Georgia, 428 U.S. 153, 189 (1976) (opinion of Stewart, Powell, and Stevens, JJ.) ("*Furman* mandates that where discretion is afforded a sentencing body on a matter so grave as the determination of whether a human life should be taken or spared, that discretion must be suitably directed and limited so as to minimize the risk of wholly arbitrary and capricious action.").

19. See Woodson v. North Carolina, 428 U.S. 280 (1976); Roberts v. Louisiana, 428 U.S. 325 (1976).

20. Woodson, 428 U.S. at 305. A mandatory death sentence may not be imposed even for premeditated murders committed by persons under sentence of life imprisonment without possibility of parole. See Sumner v. Shuman, 107 S.Ct. 2716 (1987); cf. id. at 2728–29 (White, J., joined by Rehnquist, C.J., and Scalia, J., dissenting).

21. Id. at 304.

22. Witherspoon v. Illinois, 391 U.S. 510, 522 (1968).

23. As the Court stated, "[O]ne of the most important functions any jury can perform in making such a selection [of who should receive the ultimate penalty] is to maintain a link between contemporary community values and the penal system—a link without which the determination of punishment could hardly reflect the 'evolving standards of decency that mark the progress of a maturing society.' " Id. at 519 n.15, quoting Trop v. Dulles, 356 U.S. 86, 101 (1958) (plurality opinion). But see Spaziano v. Florida, 468 U.S. 447, 462–63 (1984). While "not denigrat[ing] the significance of the jury's role as a link between the community and the penal system," the Court held that a judge could override a jury's recommendation of life imprisonment and impose the death sentence.

"minimizes the justices' discretionary role in decreeing" the substance of the change.[24]

Despite the utility of analyzing constitutional questions through a structural lens, courts and commentators should not forget that a structural focus can sometimes be used as a subterfuge to "rig" a desired substantive outcome.[25] But such a practice not only lacks integrity, it lacks reliability. Take the death penalty cases for example. When the Court in *Gregg v. Georgia*[26] permitted a death sentence, *Furman v. Georgia*[27] was declared a failure by those who believed they could rely on structural concerns to achieve their desired outcome—the end to the death pealty. However, *Furman* "failed" in this manner only if structural concerns are valued solely for their usefulness in preordaining the desired substantive outcome. But structural concerns do not correlate perfectly with substantive outcomes. Hence, once states reworked the applicable structures,[28] the Court could arrive at a seemingly different substantive outcome because the core substantive question[29] had not been answered in the earlier decision. The key point is that, while realism compels recognition of the highly indeterminate nature of the link between structure and substance, it does not compel, or even permit, treating the link as nonexistent.

In the end, therefore, respect for both lawmaking and law-applying processes need not imply fanciful assumptions about their actual operation; it may indeed require greater realism.[30] And direct and open

---

24. Tribe, "Structural Due Process," 10 Harv.C.R.—C.L.L.Rev. 269, 293, 295–96 (1975).

25. See Brilmayer, "*Carolene*, Conflicts, and the Fate of the 'Inside-Outsider,'" 134 U.Pa.L.Rev. 1291 (1986). Professor Brilmayer assails analysis based on Justice Stone's famous footnote 4 in United States v. Carolene Products Co., 304 U.S. 144, 152 n.4 (1938), which suggests that the Court should scrutinize more closely legislation affecting "discrete and insular minorities" because those minorities may be foreclosed from participation in the political process. As Brilmayer demonstrates, Carolene analysis ultimately hides behind the mask of "policing the process of democratic decision-making," although it is actually seeking a specific substantive outcome—invalidation of discriminatory laws. Brilmayer, supra, at 1296, 1298. In fact, the Carolene approach is not really process-based at all; instead of inquiring about the process underlying legislation, Carolene proponents focus on the result. Instead of proving the defect in the legislative process directly, Carolene infers the defect from the discrimination itself. Id. at 1307–08. By invalidating only discriminatory rules, Carolene "fails to recognize that neutral rules . . . as well . . . might result from defective processes." Id. at 1308. By linking the structural and substantive problems so closely together, the Carolene theory not only disguised its substantive purpose, it

also implied that, if the substantive problem were solved, the underlying process problems must themselves be solved. Hence,

> "*Carolene's* cruelest hoax is its suggestion that, once the discriminatory rules are invalidated, our political process problems are over. But, as any excluded person surely realizes after putting the illusion of *Carolene* to one side, discriminatory rules are only a small part of a very large problem. They are only the first hurdle in a long road to political participation and equality."

Id. at 1334. But see Sunstein, "Interest Groups in American Public Law," 38 Stan. L.Rev. 29 (1985) (arguing that the Court should scrutinize all legislative classifications more closely in order to encourage legislative "deliberation.").

26. 428 U.S. 153 (1976).

27. 408 U.S. 238 (1972).

28. With legislatures providing allegedly adequate standards (but not mandatory death penalties).

29. That is, whether the death penalty was itself unconstitutional.

30. See United States Railroad Retirement Bd. v. Fritz, 449 U.S. 166, 179 (1980) (pointing out that members of Congress are often ignorant of the effects of legislation or misled by outside groups). See also Justice Stevens' discussion of "[r]espect for the legislative process" in Califano v. Goldfarb, 430

attention to actual process reduces the temptation to distort a law's clear meaning or to pervert various doctrines (such as those of vagueness and delegation) [31] in response to an undifferentiated dissatisfaction with the way in which a governmental decision came about, or with why it persists. Model VII analysis may provide more focused ways of dealing with such dissatisfaction.

U.S. 199, 221 (1977) (concurring in judgment).

31. See, e.g., Gunther, "The Subtle Vices of the 'Passive Virtues'—A Comment on Principle and Expediency in Judicial Review," 64 Colum.L.Rev. 1 (1964).

Chapter 18

THE PROBLEM OF STATE ACTION

§ 18–1. The Lessons of "Anti-doctrine"

Nearly all of the Constitution's self-executing, and therefore judicially enforceable, guarantees of individual rights shield individuals only from government action.[1] Accordingly, when litigants claim the protection of such guarantees, courts must first determine whether it is indeed government action—state or federal[2]—that the litigants are challenging.[3]

If litigants challenge a federal or state *statute*, such as a law mandating racial segregation of public schools, in a case where the validity of the statute is necessarily implicated, state action is obvious, and no formal inquiry into the matter is needed.[4] Similarly, the *rule of decision* expressly invoked or necessarily relied upon by a state's highest court—either to grant relief against one party[5] or to deny the

---

§ 18–1

1. The Bill of Rights, the first eight amendments to the Constitution, on their face constrain only the conduct of the federal government, and to the extent of their incorporation in the fourteenth amendment due process clause, see § 11–2, supra, also limit state governments. Similarly, the prohibitions found in article I, §§ 9 and 10, as well as the guarantees of the fifteenth, nineteenth, twenty-fourth and twenty-sixth amendments, restrain only federal and state government action. The fourteenth amendment due process and equal protection clauses limit only state action. Congress may protect the privileges or immunities of national citizenship by regulating private conduct, see § 5–14, supra, but the fourteenth amendment grants courts the power to protect such rights only from state action. The thirteenth amendment's prohibitions of slavery encompass both governmental and private action. See Civil Rights Cases, 109 U.S. 3, 20 (1883). Although the Supreme Court has held that the thirteenth amendment grants Congress potentially broad power to regulate private conduct, see Jones v. Alfred H. Mayer Co., 392 U.S. 409 (1968), discussed in § 5–13, supra, the Supreme Court has directly invoked the amendment only to strike down state peonage laws imprisoning individuals for breaching labor contracts, see, e.g., Pollock v. Williams, 322 U.S. 4 (1944); Bailey v. Alabama, 219 U.S. 219 (1911), and has indicated that, for purposes of judicial enforcement, it will define "slavery" quite narrowly. See Palmer v. Thompson, 403 U.S. 217,

226–27 (1971); Memphis v. Greene, 451 U.S. 100 (1981).

2. Throughout this chapter, the words "state action" will denote action by *any* level of government, from local to national.

3. This requirement of state action should not be understood to support the conclusion that, as a substantive constitutional matter, the state owes no *affirmative* duties to its people. That the state has no duty to provide law and order or to supply the material conditions necessary to the full exercise of constitutional rights may or may not be so. See Tribe, "The Abortion Funding Conundrum: Inalienable Rights, Affirmative Duties, and the Dilemma of Dependence," 99 Harv.L.Rev. 330 (1985). But—given the universal recognition "that the line between action and inaction, between inflicting and failing to prevent the infliction of harm" is less than clear, Bowers v. DeVito, 686 F.2d 616, 618 (7th Cir.1982)—the absence of the alleged duty certainly does not follow from the principle that the Constitution addresses only the government. To the degree that the state "action" doctrine subliminally suggests otherwise, it is a subterfuge for substantive choices the authors of the document did not necessarily make one way or the other.

4. See, e.g., Brown v. Board of Education, 347 U.S. 483 (1954).

5. See, e.g., New York Times Co. v. Sullivan, 376 U.S. 254 (1964) (state rule that publishers of defamatory falsehoods are strictly liable in tort); Shelley v. Kraemer, 334 U.S. 1 (1948) (state rule that contractu-

relief sought by another party [6]—constitutes "state action" reviewable on the merits by the Supreme Court. Occasionally, however, litigants claim the protection of constitutional rights in circumstances where state action—in the sense of state responsibility for the litigants' injuries—is less apparent. The Supreme Court, for example, has had to decide whether a privately owned and operated electrical monopoly, subject to state protection and regulation, must comply with the requirements of procedural due process when cutting off service to nonpaying customers; [7] whether a privately owned "company town" can invoke the aid of state trespass laws to keep evangelizing Jehovah's Witnesses off its streets; [8] and whether the existence of a state statute saying that those to whom personal belongings have been entrusted may sell those belongings in order to recoup unpaid storage fees makes the warehouse owners into state actors subject to the constraints of procedural due process. [9]

The difference between these last cases and the school segregation case is plain. In these cases, it is not so much the basic government action to which litigants object: no one contended in these cases that government should not protect and regulate monopolies, punish trespassers, or permit creditors to protect their interests. Rather, the litigants, objecting to the acts of private parties, sought to portray as support or tacit approval what might be characterized as mere governmental acquiescence in certain acts, in order to obtain federal judicial assistance in discouraging the objectionable private activity. In deciding whether the litigants would indeed obtain that judicial assistance, the Supreme Court had to determine whether government inaction, acquiescence, or tolerance could fairly be judged to be tacit ratification of a challenged private choice or, perhaps, delegation of a public responsibility to a private party; if so, whether all such governmental silence or acceptance was itself a form of "state action"; and if not, whether any criteria exist for distinguishing varieties of inaction. [10]

al restraints on alienation of real property, at least if they are racially restrictive covenants, will be enforced); Barrows v. Jackson, 346 U.S. 249 (1953) (state rule that sellers of real property who violate racially restrictive covenants are liable for damages).

6. See, e.g., Martinez v. California, 444 U.S. 277 (1980) (state rule that parole board members are immune from damages liability for actions of parolees); cf. Burton v. Wilmington Parking Authority, 365 U.S. 715, 726–27 (1961) (Stewart, J., concurring) (state rule that restaurant proprietor may refuse service on the basis of race), discussed in § 18–3, note 13, infra.

7. See Jackson v. Metropolitan Edison, Co., 419 U.S. 345 (1974) (holding due process inapplicable). See §§ 18–5, 18–7, infra.

8. See Marsh v. Alabama, 326 U.S. 501 (1946) (holding that it cannot). See § 18–5, infra.

9. See Flagg Brothers, Inc. v. Brooks, 436 U.S. 149 (1978) (holding that it does not); cf. Lugar v. Edmondson Oil Co., 457 U.S. 922 (1982) (private party authorized by statute to attach and sequester disputed property acts under color of law, and is thus suable as a state actor under 42 U.S.C. § 1983, provided the state both permits the party to resolve the dispute without judicial supervision and provides a state official to assist the party in the attachment).

10. A fourth consideration is also sometimes relevant: the target of the remedy sought by the litigant challenging an alleged state action. It might appear from the cases that a litigant has a measurably better chance of persuading the Supreme Court that it is "state action" to which the litigant objects if it is a government actor, and not an apparently private actor, who would be the target of the relief that the litigant seeks. Compare, e.g., Shelley v. Kraemer, 334 U.S. 1 (1948) (litigant seeks

The Court has gone about this task frequently enough over the years to develop a body of case law to which it can look in resolving new controversies, and to develop catch phrases such as "public function" and "nexus" in terms of which it can characterize various situations. But despite the precedents, and despite the vocabulary, the Supreme Court has not succeeded in developing a body of state action "doctrine," a set of rules for determining whether governmental or private actors are to be deemed responsible for an asserted constitutional violation. The Court itself has acknowledged the stubborn individuality of the state action cases. "[F]ormulating an infallible test" of state action, the Court has said, is "an impossible task." [11] "Only by sifting facts and weighing circumstances can the nonobvious involvement of the State in private conduct be attributed its true significance." [12] Professor Charles Black no doubt spoke for the consensus in concluding that, viewed doctrinally, the state action cases are "a conceptual disaster area." [13]

Against this background, it might seem that any discussion of state action could begin and end with Wittgenstein: "Whereof one cannot

to prevent court from enforcing racially restrictive covenant; Supreme Court finds state action), with, e.g., Jackson v. Metropolitan Edison Co., 419 U.S. 345 (1974) (litigant seeks to require privately owned utility to continue electrical service; Supreme Court finds no state action); also compare Lugar v. Edmondson Oil Co., 457 U.S. 922 (1982) (litigant seeks injunctive and damages relief against private party authorized by statute to attach and sequester disputed property *with* sheriff's assistance but *without* state judicial supervision; Supreme Court holds private party to be state actor), with Flagg Brothers, Inc. v. Brooks, 436 U.S. 149 (1978) (litigant seeks declaratory, injunctive and damages relief against private warehouse owners authorized by statute to sell her stored property to recoup disputed storage fees *without any trace of overt official involvement*; Supreme Court finds no state action). The relevance of the remedial target to the state action inquiry, however, can easily be overstated, and there are obvious counterexamples. Compare, e.g., Moose Lodge No. 107 v. Irvis, 407 U.S. 163 (1972) (litigant seeks to require government agency to revoke liquor license of racially discriminatory private club; Supreme Court finds no state action), with, e.g., Burton v. Wilmington Parking Authority, 365 U.S. 715, 726 (1961) (action for declaratory and injunctive relief naming as defendants both racially discriminatory private restaurant and state agency owning building within which restaurant operates; Supreme Court finds state action, specifically holding that "the proscriptions of the Fourteenth Amendment must be complied with by the lessee as certainly as though they were binding covenants written into the agree-

ment itself"). Moreover, it need not be the case that a court's remedial responsibilities will be rendered complex, cf. Gilligan v. Morgan, 413 U.S. 1, 5–8 (1973), if relief runs against a private rather than a governmental actor. In Burton, for example, an order to the restaurant not to discriminate was plainly a simpler form of relief to administer than an order to the government agency to evict the restaurant. This is not to say that the relief sought is irrelevant to the state action inquiry. Plainly, it has some psychological effect. Furthermore, the character of the relief sought may be one indicator of the decision-making level at which a litigant must direct an attack in order to challenge state action, and is thus a pertinent factor in determining the litigant's success on the merits. Finally, targeting an apparently private actor as the defendant in a suit under 42 U.S.C. § 1983 might prevent the relevant state action—the rule of law empowering the seemingly private defendant to inflict the challenged injury—from being sufficiently implicated in the litigation. See, e.g., Flagg Brothers v. Brooks, supra (state law authorizing private self-help not directly implicated in § 1983 action because that law was never invoked by a state court as a basis for denying the plaintiff relief against self-help).

11. Reitman v. Mulkey, 387 U.S. 369, 378 (1967).

12. Burton v. Wilmington Parking Authority, 365 U.S. 715, 722 (1961).

13. Black, "The Supreme Court, 1966 Term—Foreword: 'State Action,' Equal Protection, and California's Proposition 14," 81 Harv.L.Rev. 69, 95 (1967).

speak, thereof one must be silent." Chaos, however, may itself be a form of order. If the usual premise is reversed—if the state action cases are assumed *not* to reveal any general rule, and if the inquiry is redirected to consider *why* this anarchy prevails—it is possible to construct an "anti-doctrine," an analytical framework which, in explaining why various cases differ from one another, paradoxically provides a structure for the solution of state action problems. In a metaphor: the way out of the forest is through the trees.

§ 18–2.　The Dialectic of Purpose and the Inevitable Indeterminacy of Contemporary State Action "Doctrine"

The source of the failure of contemporary state action doctrine lies in the interplay of the purposes which such a doctrine would serve if it were available. The state action requirement, it is generally thought,[1] furthers two primary purposes. First, by exempting private action from the reach of the Constitution's prohibitions, it stops the Constitution short of preempting individual liberty—of denying to individuals the freedom to make certain choices, such as choices of the persons with whom they will associate. Such freedom is basic under any conception of liberty, but it would be lost if individuals had to conform their conduct to the Constitution's demands. Second, the state action requirement reinforces the two chief principles of division which organize the governmental structure that the Constitution creates: federalism and the separation of powers.[2] By limiting the scope of the rights which the Constitution guarantees, the state action requirement limits the range of wrongs which the federal judiciary may right in the absence of congressional action, and thus creates a zone of action which, in the absence of valid congressional legislation, is reserved to the states unencumbered by the constraints of federal supremacy.

Plainly, these purposes coexist only in tension. It is not possible to preserve maximum space simultaneously for individual choice and for state or congressional regulation: to the extent the states or Congress act, the space left to individual discretion is narrowed. The tension, however, is resolvable. Two accommodations are possible. On the one hand, it is possible to say that the state action requirement creates a space for state and congressional regulation, except insofar as the specific requirements of individual liberty constrain such regulation. Alternatively, it may be said that the state action requirement recognizes a background of individual liberty, except insofar as particular state or congressional regulations limit that liberty.

State action doctrine will be more or less coherent depending upon which of these formulations is adopted. The first formulation presumes the existence of a developed conception of individual liberty which serves to limit the scope of possible government action; the second formulation treats liberty as the range of choices left to the individual when government has not acted. Under the first formula-

§ 18–2

1. See, e.g., Burke & Reber, "State Action, Congressional Power and Creditors' Rights: An Essay on the Fourteenth Amendment," 46 So.Cal.L.Rev. 1003, 1014–17 (1973).

2. See §§ 1–2, 2–2, 2–3, supra.

tion, it is possible to distinguish among government decisions to act, government decisions not to act, and government decisions prohibited because they would usurp choices that must be left to private individuals. By contrast, under the second formulation, there exist only government decisions to act and government decisions to abstain.

The state action inquiry is far more discriminating under the first formulation. For the most difficult state action questions are those which require the Supreme Court to judge whether government should be held accountable for its failure to act—whether government acquiescence in or authorization of private action amounts to ratification of that action and is therefore subject to constitutional challenge—even in a suit brought against the private actor, deemed to be wielding power "under color of law." Under the first formulation, the Court can without difficulty hold that government acquiescence does *not* amount to "state action" whenever affirmative government action, whether to the same or opposite effect as the acquiesced-in private conduct, would usurp a necessarily private decision, and thus improperly limit the sphere of individual liberty. Moreover, if affirmative government action would *not* infringe individual liberty in a given case, then there is no barrier to seeing even mere government tolerance of private conduct as a government decision not to act so as to prevent that conduct—as "state action" at least in that limited sense—and thus as subject to constitutional scrutiny to determine whether the state's failure to prevent the conduct at issue amounts to a breach of the state's constitutional duty. Indeed, if the conception of liberty is sufficiently developed to define a sphere of private autonomy free from both governmental *and* private infringement, a government decision not to protect individuals from private infringements will plainly be a species of unconstitutional state action.

The second formulation, however, suggests no similar solution to the problem of government inaction. This formulation may suggest that all inaction should be viewed as reflecting decisions not to act, thus ratification, and thus "state action." But the second formulation also offers no barrier to a precisely opposite interpretation of the state action requirement, one which sees all inaction as simply that—"inaction" and thus not "state action." The one thing the second formulation does *not* do is suggest any general criteria for distinguishing among kinds of government inaction. To the extent that state action doctrine depends upon the existence of such criteria, therefore, this second synthesis of the policies which would underlie such doctrine contributes nothing to the doctrine's development.

The two accommodations of the purposes underlying the state action requirement differ with regard to the conceptions of individual liberty which they presuppose. The first treats liberty affirmatively as capable of definition without reference to government action, and thus as capable of defining the proper limit of such action. The second, by contrast, treats liberty negatively, as simply a residue of private choice left untouched by government regulation. For analytical purposes, it is possible to speak of these two conceptions as alternatives. In its state action decisions, however, the Supreme Court has not enjoyed the luxury of selecting between these alternatives. For the rise and fall of substantive due process under Model II,[3] as a doctrine incorporating within the Constitution a delineation of private and public responsibility more comprehensive than that defined by the Constitution's several guarantees of individual rights, has inevitably affected the Court's state action decisions. The state action cases suggest reliance upon an affirmative conception of liberty as a basis for reconciling the purposes underlying the state action requirement, and thus as a basis for distinguishing at the doctrinal level among forms of government inaction, only in that era in which the Court's substantive due process decisions similarly reveal adherence to a unified, affirmative theory of liberty.[4]

The *Civil Rights Cases*,[5] the Supreme Court's first full-dress treatment of the fourteenth amendment's state action requirement,[6] provides a noteworthy illustration of the role of an affirmative theory of liberty in shaping state action doctrine.[7] The Civil Rights Act of 1875 [8] declared illegal all racially motivated interference by private individuals with the exercise by other individuals of their right to make use of "the accommodations, advantages, facilities, and privileges of inns, public conveyances, and theatres. . . ."[9] The Court held this statute to be unconstitutional on its face:[10] congressional power under § 5 of the fourteenth amendment, Justice Bradley's majority opinion concluded, was confined to enforcing § 1's prohibitions of "state action."[11] Significantly, however, the Court did not deny Congress all power to regulate private conduct under the fourteenth amendment. In some circumstances, the majority opinion implied, a state's failure to regulate private conduct could constitute "state action" justifying federal intervention.

Justice Bradley's opinion did not deny that individuals had a right to make use of public accommodations, a right which other individuals could not limit on racial grounds.[12] Rather, the majority assumed that

---

3. See §§ 8–2 to 8–6, supra.

4. See §§ 8–2 to 8–4, supra.

5. 109 U.S. 3 (1883).

6. The Supreme Court had previously discussed the fourteenth amendment's state action requirement in less detail in a number of cases. See, e.g., United States v. Harris, 106 U.S. 629, 637–40 (1883); Ex parte Virginia, 100 U.S. 339, 346–47 (1880); Virginia v. Rives, 100 U.S. 313, 318 (1880); United States v. Cruikshank, 92 U.S. 542, 554–55 (1876).

7. The connection between the Supreme Court's nineteenth century development of the state action requirement and substantive due process doctrine is also explored in Nerken, "A New Deal for Fourteenth Amendment Rights Protection: Challenging the Doctrinal Bases of the Civil Rights Cases and State Action Theory," 12 Harv.Civ.Rts.—Civ.Lib.L.Rev. 297 (1977). Nerken takes a somewhat different approach from that developed here, connecting substantive due process and state action as derivatives of assumptions underlying the contract clause and arguing that, given the realities of racial discrimination in the post-bellum era, the contract clause's assumption of ordinarily enforceable state-recognized rights was irrelevant in the fourteenth amendment setting. Nerken ultimately concludes that, like substantive due process, the state action requirement should be seen as a relic of a bygone age. This chapter does not go nearly so far.

8. 18 Stat. 336.

9. 109 U.S. at 9–10.

10. See H. Friendly, The Dartmouth College Case and the Public-Private Penumbra 13 (1968).

11. See 109 U.S. at 9–10.

12. See id. at 19.

state courts would protect this right as a matter of course unless a state had affirmatively denied its courts the power to extend such protection.[13] The Supreme Court assumed, in other words, that the right to nondiscriminatory treatment was an aspect of an individual's common law liberty.[14] If a state legislature denied state courts the power to protect such common law liberty, the Supreme Court implied the legislature would act unconstitutionally;[15] Congress, however, erred in failing to key the applicability of its statute to the existence of such unconstitutional state action. "It applies equally to cases arising in States which have the justest laws respecting the personal rights of citizens, and whose authorities are ever ready to enforce such laws, as

13. See id. at 17: "The wrongful act of an individual, unsupported by any such authority, is simply a private wrong or a crime of that individual; an invasion of the rights of the injured party, it is true, whether they affect his person, his property, or his reputation: but if not sanctioned in some way by the State, or not done under State authority, his rights remain in full force, and may presumably be vindicated by resort to the laws of the State for redress."

14. In a concurring opinion in Bell v. Maryland, 378 U.S. 226, 286 (1964), Justice Goldberg argued that the framers of the fourteenth amendment intended the amendment to guarantee a right of racially equal access to public accommodations. This argument somewhat overstates the historical evidence. See id. at 335–41 (Black, J., dissenting). But the evidence does clearly suggest that, at the time of the adoption of the fourteenth amendment, "civil rights" were understood to be rights pre-existing the amendment, and that, in contemporary view, the function of the fourteenth amendment, and specifically of the equal protection clause, was to guarantee racially equal access to those rights, in much the same way that the fifteenth amendment guaranteed racially equal access to the right to vote, but did not itself confer that right. The specific evidence includes statements by legislators during debates on the Civil Rights Act of 1866, the act that the fourteenth amendment was drafted to authorize. See, e.g., Cong. Globe, 39th Cong., 1st Sess., 599 (Sen. Trumbull), 1115–19 (Rep. Wilson), 1832–37 (Rep. Lawrence), App. 288–89, 290–92 (Rep. Shellabarger); see also Bell v. Maryland, supra, at 294 (Goldberg, J., concurring); 6 C. Fairman, Reconstruction and Reunion 1864–88, at 1172–1204 (1971), as well as the language of the first Supreme Court decisions construing the amendment itself. See, e.g., Ex parte Virginia, 100 U.S. 339, 344–45 (1880); Strauder v. West Virginia,

100 U.S. 303, 307–08 (1880); Neal v. Delaware, 103 U.S. 370, 386 (1881). Although, as Justice Goldberg demonstrates, a persuasive argument can be made that common law rights included a right of access to public accommodations at the time of the adoption of the fourteenth amendment, see 378 U.S. at 297 & n.17, legislative debate on the Civil Rights Act of 1866, at least, suggests that the drafters of the fourteenth amendment were not themselves certain of the exact content of such common law rights. See C. Fairman, supra; see also 378 U.S. at 336–38 (Black, J., dissenting).

15. This proposition is stated somewhat more explicitly in United States v. Cruikshank, 92 U.S. 542, 555 (1876): "The equality of the rights of citizens is a principle of republicanism. Every republican government is in duty bound to protect all its citizens in the enjoyment of this principle, if within its power. That duty was originally assumed by the States; and it still remains there. The only obligation resting upon the United States is to see that the States do not deny the right. This the amendment guarantees, but no more." The most straightforward nineteenth century development of this proposition is probably that of Judge Woods in United States v. Hall, 26 Fed.Cas. 79 (Cas.No. 15,282) (C.C.S.D.Ala.1871). Judge Woods concluded that under the fourteenth amendment Congress could adopt legislation "to protect the fundamental rights of citizens of the United States against unfriendly or insufficient state legislation, for the fourteenth amendment not only prohibits the making or enforcing of laws which shall abridge the privileges of the citizen, but prohibits the states from denying to all persons within its jurisdiction the equal protection of the laws. Denying includes inaction as well as action, and denying the equal protection of the laws includes the omission to protect, as well as the omission to pass laws for protection." Id. at 81.

to those which have arisen in States that may have violated the prohibitions of the amendment." [16]

The *Civil Rights Cases* thus suggested that government tolerance of private action could be "state action" if the private action infringed common law liberty, and hence was not itself within the sphere of individual liberty. *Buchanan v. Warley* [17] and *Corrigan v. Buckley* [18] illustrate the second corollary of an affirmative theory of liberty: government tolerance of private action which falls within the sphere of the actor's protected liberty is *not* "state action." In *Buchanan*, the Supreme Court held unconstitutional a municipal ordinance denying persons of one race the right to occupy any house located on a block peopled in the majority by persons of another race. The Court did not hold the ordinance unconstitutional simply because its object was racial segregation. Racial segregation, Justice Day's opinion indicated, was a legitimate government objective insofar as it did not deny individuals equal rights [19] and did not entail a condition associated with the distribution of government privileges.[20] The ordinance in question, however, infringed individuals' property rights, "the free use, enjoyment, and disposal of a person's acquisitions without control or diminution. . . ." [21] Since the right to property was a right to "free use," the racial segregation ordinance did not so much preserve equal rights as equally deny rights. The Court conceded that a state, within the exercise of its police power, could limit property rights.[22] The fourteenth amendment, however, prohibited the states from abridging prop-

16. 109 U.S. at 14. It should be remembered that, while the chief present significance of the Civil Rights Cases lies in the analytical framework of Justice Bradley's opinion, with its suggestion that state tolerance of at least some private conduct might be state action, the decision in its own time, and for many subsequent years, was significant chiefly for its result: the invalidation of the Civil Rights Act of 1875 and the consequent denial to the federal government of any power to prevent the emergence of "Jim Crow" *apartheid* in the South. This result was plainly wrong, not only morally and politically, but as a matter of constitutional law. Justice Bradley's majority opinion offered no response to Justice Harlan's argument in dissent that § 1 of the fourteenth amendment, in granting *state* citizenship to "[a]ll persons born or naturalized in the United States," afforded Congress a constitutional basis for guaranteeing to all state citizens an equal right to common law protections. In effect, Justice Harlan treated the fourteenth amendment as itself the sort of "legislation" which the majority had suggested would be constitutional, finding support for his interpretation of the state citizenship clause as an affirmative grant of congressional power in the fact that, between the adoption of the thirteenth amendment and

the fourteenth, several states had announced that freed slaves were not entitled to the common law rights shared by other state residents, but rather possessed only those rights affirmatively granted to them by state legislation. See 109 U.S. at 43–48 (Harlan, J., dissenting). Moreover, Justice Bradley's majority opinion neither explained why this interpretation was inappropriate, nor sought to justify its facial, rather than as-applied, scrutiny of the statute, notwithstanding the fact that in one of the cases before the Court but not the others, a state (Tennessee) had specifically repealed its common law rule of equal access, see Bell v. Maryland, 378 U.S. 226, 306 n.25 (1964) (Goldberg, J., concurring), thus making the Civil Rights Cases an ideal vehicle for demonstrating both proper and improper applications of the Civil Rights Act.

17. 245 U.S. 60 (1917).

18. 271 U.S. 323 (1926).

19. See 245 U.S. at 79, distinguishing Plessy v. Ferguson, 163 U.S. 537 (1896).

20. See 245 U.S. at 79, distinguishing Berea College v. Kentucky, 211 U.S. 45 (1908).

21. 245 U.S. at 74.

22. See id. at 74–75.

erty rights on racial grounds.[23] The ordinance therefore did not fall within the police power and thus violated substantive due process.[24]

The *Buchanan* opinion was ambiguous: although framing its analysis in terms of substantive due process doctrine, at a critical juncture the opinion invoked equal protection notions in order to explain why the challenged ordinance did not fall within the police power. Taken in isolation, therefore, the opinion was susceptible of two interpretations. If the substantive due process theme were taken as decisive, *Buchanan* would suggest that the vice of the ordinance was that it infringed a zone of private choice, a zone which government presumably could not invade to promote either racial segregation or racial integration. Alternatively, if the equal protection emphasis were decisive, *Buchanan* would suggest that the vice of the ordinance was that it denied certain opportunities to blacks (or to whites) because of their race—that, just as individuals possessed a right to equal access to public accommodations, a right not challenged in the *Civil Rights Cases*, so too individuals possessed a right to equal access to property. In *Corrigan v. Buckley*,[25] the Court resolved *Buchanan's* ambiguity in favor of the substantive due process interpretation. Plaintiff in *Corrigan* sought to enjoin defendants from consummating a transfer of property in violation of a racially restrictive covenant. Defendants argued, however, that judicial enforcement of the covenant would be unconstitutional: if a legislature could not mandate racially restricted land transfers, a court could not do so either.[26] The Supreme Court rejected defendants' argument, finding that it did not even rise to the level of a substantial federal question.[27] Neither the fourteenth amendment nor the fifth amendment (the case arose in the District of Columbia) "prohibited private individuals from entering into contracts respecting the control and disposition of their property. . . ."[28] In sum, there was no state action.

If *Buchanan* rested upon the premise that individuals, as a matter of common law liberty (at least after the adoption of the fourteenth amendment), possessed a racially equal right to property, then *Corrigan's* "no state action" conclusion would have been inexplicable. Under the logic of the *Civil Rights Cases*, the District of Columbia courts' failure to enforce such a right would have qualified as state action. But if *Buchanan* rested upon the substantive due process premise that individuals were free to decide how and to whom they would dispose of their property, then *Corrigan's* conclusion was perfectly straightforward. There was no state action because the District of Columbia courts, as much as any legislature, lacked the authority to decide with whom a propertyholder should deal; that was a matter of private choice.

Since at least 1937, the Supreme Court has abandoned any attempt to enforce as a matter of due process a general division of responsibility

---

23. See id. at 75–79.

24. See id. at 82, citing Otis v. Parker, 187 U.S. 606, 609 (1903); Booth v. Illinois, 184 U.S. 425, 429 (1902).

25. 271 U.S. 323 (1926).

26. See id. at 324.

27. Id. at 331.

28. Id. at 330.

between governmental and private actors.[29] Contemporary substantive due process doctrine holds that, in the ordinary case, government may limit individual liberty to whatever extent it finds, or rationally could find, justifiable.[30] In resolving state action questions, therefore, the Court has not been able to resort to a unified, affirmative theory of liberty in order to reconcile the tension between the premises of the state action requirement, or to decide when government tolerance of private conduct amounts to "state action." Not surprisingly, therefore, many of the Court's recent state action decisions, insofar as they purport to articulate and apply an autonomous state action doctrine, appear peculiarly unpersuasive.

In *Shelley v. Kraemer*,[31] for example, the Supreme Court held that state courts acted in violation of the equal protection clause if they granted injunctive relief to litigants seeking to enforce privately negotiated racially restrictive covenants. The Court appeared to find the requisite state action in the fact that the state courts had indeed enforced the covenants;[32] but such reasoning, consistently applied, would require individuals to conform their private agreements to constitutional standards whenever, as almost always, the individuals might later seek the security of potential judicial enforcement. Some nineteen years after *Shelley*, in *Reitman v. Mulkey*,[33] the Court held that the equal protection clause prevented a state from amending its constitution to recognize a right of private property holders to dispose of their property to whomever they might choose. The Court concluded that the constitutional amendment improperly "encouraged"[34] private racial discrimination; the Court did not explain, however, why a failure on the part of the state to pass any civil rights legislation in the first instance would not have amounted to similar encouragement.[35]

The questions these cases raised would not have appeared particularly difficult prior to 1937. *Shelley* was simply *Corrigan v. Buckley* revisited:[36] to reach the *Shelley* conclusion, a pre-1937 court would have needed only to reinterpret *Buchanan v. Warley* as recognizing a racially equal right to property as an aspect of post-fourteenth amend-

---

29. See §§ 8–5 to 8–7, supra.

30. See, e.g., Ferguson v. Skrupa, 372 U.S. 726 (1963); Williamson v. Lee Optical Co., 348 U.S. 483 (1955). See § 8–7, supra. In §§ 18–3 to 18–7, infra, we consider the degree to which the existence of "preferred rights" or special claims to equality in the post-1937 period, see Chapters 11 to 16, supra, modifies the analysis.

31. 334 U.S. 1 (1948). See § 18–6, infra.

32. See id. at 20.

33. 387 U.S. 369 (1967).

34. See id. at 381.

35. See id. at 394–95 (Harlan, J., dissenting).

36. In Shelley, the Supreme Court attempted to distinguish Corrigan by finding that the defendants in that case had challenged only the racially restrictive covenants, and not the validity of judicial enforcement of such covenants. See 334 U.S. at 8–9. This finding is flatly inconsistent with the Court's own summary of defendants' argument, a summary which accompanied the Corrigan opinion. See 271 U.S. at 324–25. The Court in Corrigan did note procedural defects with defendants' argument, see id. at 331, as the Shelley Court emphasizes, but the Corrigan Court also found that the argument was "lacking in substance." Id. In so finding, the Court had interpreted defendants' challenge to judicial enforcement as a procedural due process challenge, a reinterpretation so curious in light of defendants' plain invocation of Buchanan that it reinforces the conclusion that the Court simply saw no independent judicial action as involved in enforcement of a private covenant.

ment common law liberty, and then apply the analysis of the *Civil Rights Cases*. *Reitman* raised essentially the same question considered in the *Civil Rights Cases*: a pre-1937 court would not have found state action to be the difficult question in *Reitman*; rather, the central issue would have been whether the state had the power to limit property rights by passing the repealed civil rights legislation in the first place.

To contemporary commentators, however, *Shelley* and *Reitman* appear as highly controversial decisions. In neither case, a commonly voiced view has it, is the Court's finding of state action supported by any reasoning which would suggest that "state action" is a meaningful requirement rather than a nearly empty or at least extraordinarily malleable formality.[37] Of course, as several recent Supreme Court decisions indicate, the state action requirement is plainly *not* an "empty formality." [38] What is empty is the concept of state action "doctrine." Because the Supreme Court does not currently have access to a general theory of liberty allocating public and private responsibility, the Court can no longer derive doctrinal rules from any accommodation of the premises underlying the state action requirement. To the extent that the Court has nonetheless *attempted* to produce a state action doctrine, it is not surprising that its efforts have yielded little which does not appear to be too readily manipulable to be called doctrine: doctrine in this context is inevitably cut off from its roots. Those who simply criticize the Court's attempts are thus both correct and irrelevant. Plainly, the state action decisions fail as doctrine; the question is, do they make sense as anything else?

§ 18–3. The State Action Requirement in a Pluralist Jurisprudence of Rights

The preceding section examined the concept of state action "doctrine," identified the characteristics of substantive constitutional law which such a concept presupposes, and explored the consequences for that concept of the absence of such characteristics. We saw that a coherent and autonomous body of state action doctrine cannot exist in the absence of an affirmative theory of liberty capable in general of distinguishing situations in which a government has *decided* not to act from situations in which government has not acted because it *cannot* constitutionally act. Traditional substantive due process doctrine in Model II reflected just such a theory; indeed, its underlying structure was even more powerful, identifying situations in which government *had* to act, and thus situations in which government inaction was clearly a form of unconstitutional state action.

---

37. The standard critique of Shelley is definitively stated in Wechsler, "Toward Neutral Principles of Constitutional Law," 73 Harv.L.Rev. 1, 29–31 (1959). The Reitman opinion has been criticized even by defenders of its result. See, e.g., Karst & Horowitz, "Reitman v. Mulkey: A Telophase of Substantive Equal Protection," 1967 Sup.Ct.Rev. 39, 55; see also A. Bickel, The Supreme Court and the Idea of Progress 65–70 (1970).

38. See, e.g., Blum v. Yaretsky, 457 U.S. 991 (1982); Rendell-Baker v. Kohn, 457 U.S. 830 (1982); Polk County v. Dodson, 454 U.S. 312 (1982); Flagg Bros., Inc. v. Brooks, 436 U.S. 149 (1978); Jackson v. Metropolitan Edison Co., 419 U.S. 345 (1974); Moose Lodge No.107 v. Irvis, 407 U.S. 163 (1972).

The current constitutional universe, however, is only partly described by noting the absence of a unifying theory of liberty, reflected in an overarching doctrine of substantive due process.[1] Contemporary constitutional law recognizes and protects individual rights without reference to a single, necessarily procrustean theory of liberty. Rights instead give legal expression to a series of distinct if related values which the Supreme Court has found to be implicit in the constitutional plan.[2] These values take the form of a series of judgments: about the identity of those choices which are peculiarly individual and thus shielded from government frustration or usurpation;[3] about the dimensions of individual difference which government must generally ignore;[4] and about the required structural characteristics of government decision-making processes.[5]

Nor is the current status of the state action requirement fully revealed by the observation that the requirement yields no coherent doctrine. Unitary state action doctrine cannot coexist with a pluralist jurisprudence of rights, but to abandon the concept of unitary doctrine is not to give up all possibility of explaining the Supreme Court's state action decisions. The "anti-doctrinal" assumption that state action decisions should give effect to the values which underlie the specific rights litigants assert need not preclude an analysis which treats state action problems as comparable in form if not in resolution. On this view, the state action requirement performs a function more complex than the threshold role which a unitary doctrine would assign to it. The state action requirement fixes a frame of reference. The substantive constitutional right at issue initially determines the parameters of this frame. Ultimately, however, it is the frame itself which determines the relevance of the right to the inquiry.

Despite its seeming complexity, at bottom this approach to the state action requirement rests upon a quite straightforward differentiation of two clearly distinct questions. First, there is the question of *whether the actors who make a particular decision are government actors or private actors.* Insofar as harms inflicted by government are thought to be distinguishable for that very reason from similar harms inflicted by others, cases turning on the characterization of an actor as private or governmental properly depend upon external factors and symbols no less than upon the government's internal criteria for identifying agents as its own. Second, there is the question of *whether federal or state law can validly distribute authority between governmental and private actors as it purports to do.* In a sense, this is *the* fundamental question of constitutional law; the state action inquiry does not so much answer it as insure that, in particular cases, the question is correctly framed.

State action analysis draws this distinction between the conduct of government or private actors as such, and the rules which authorize or mandate their conduct, because contemporary constitutional jurispru-

1. Contrast §§ 8–2 to 8–4, supra.

2. See Chapter 11, supra.

3. See Chapters 12 to 15, supra.

4. See Chapter 16, supra.

5. See Chapter 17, supra.

dence generally draws such a distinction. The Constitution's protections of individual rights ordinarily address government in its rulemaking and rule-applying capacity, either by setting constraints on the substantive rules which government may formulate or by regulating the procedures through which government formulates and administers those rules. The motives of particular actors, even clearly governmental actors, are rarely a matter of constitutional concern, at least insofar as it is possible to restrict the rules which the actors make and enforce, or the procedures through which they act.[6]

Constitutional rights define the characteristics of unconstitutional state action. To the extent that such rights impose restraints on governmental *rules* and not on governmental *actors* per se, the state action inquiry must initially focus on the task of *identifying the governmental rule implicated in a particular case*, and *not* on the task of determining *whether or not a particular actor is a governmental actor*. Indeed, the constitutional right which a litigant invokes structures the state action inquiry even more specifically: By defining the elements of an individual's substantive claim, a right necessarily identifies the features of a government rule which would render the rule unconstitutional. The state action inquiry, therefore, is a search not simply for a government rule, but for *a government rule possessing the forbidden characteristics identified by the particular right the litigant invokes*.

It is at this level that the state action inquiry, although framed in terms fixed by the constitutional right which a litigant invokes, may in turn determine the ultimate relevance of that right. In some cases, it may not be difficult to identify a rule which appears to possess unconstitutional features and is obviously government-formulated. Thus, in *Reitman v. Mulkey*,[7] at least as *Hunter v. Erickson*[8] demonstrated in retrospect, there plainly existed a government-formulated racially discriminatory classification: the state constitutional amendment at issue in that case[9] discriminated against minority groups who sought the protection of fair housing legislation since, to achieve their goal, these groups would have to obtain repeal of the amendment, and then proceed through the legislative process, while groups seeking other legislation needed only to resort to the state legislature.[10] In other

---

6. For the exceptions that underscore the rule, see §§ 12–6, 14–9, 16–20, supra. Even in those situations, it was *institutional* motive rather than any *individual's* personal attitudes that mattered for constitutional purposes.

7. 387 U.S. 369 (1967), discussed in § 18–2, supra.

8. 393 U.S. 385 (1969). Hunter held that a city charter amendment violated the fourteenth amendment's equal protection clause inasmuch as it required fair housing legislation, but no other legislation, to be approved by a majority of the voters before going into effect. See § 16–20, supra.

9. The constitutional amendment, California's famous Proposition 14, provided that: "Neither the State nor any subdivision or agency thereof shall deny, limit or abridge, directly or indirectly, the right of any person, who is willing or desires to sell, lease or rent any part or all of his real property, to decline to sell, lease or rent such property to such person or persons as he, in his absolute discretion, chooses." 387 U.S. at 371.

10. This argument is essentially Professor Black's. See Black, "The Supreme Court, 1966 Term—Foreword: 'State Action,' Equal Protection, and California's Proposition 14," 81 Harv.L.Rev. 69, 82 (1967).

cases, however, the only apparently unconstitutional rule may be the product of a private actor's decision. Thus, in *Burton v. Wilmington Parking Authority*,[11] it was a private restauranteur, and not the government parking authority that leased him space, who formulated the rule that no blacks would be served.

In these latter cases, the state action requirement dictates that the rule subject to constitutional scrutiny be restated at the decision-making level at which a government actor is responsible for its formulation. In *Burton*, for example, the parking authority was clearly responsible for the decision to lease restaurant space without requiring the restaurant operator to agree not to discriminate on the basis of race. Expressed at that level, the decision may not appear unconstitutional. But as Justice Clark's majority opinion in *Burton* demonstrated, the parking authority had "so far insinuated itself into a position of interdependence"[12] with the restaurant operator that the restaurant had to be regarded as a joint venture between the public authority and the private operator; as a result, the parking authority—a government agency—could be held equally responsible with the restauranteur for the latter's decision to discriminate.[13]

---

11. 365 U.S. 715 (1961).

12. 365 U.S. at 725. In particular, the parking authority benefitted by the private operator's discriminatory policies—both by attracting parking customers, and by charging a higher rent than might otherwise have been possible. It was also relevant that the restaurant was visually indistinguishable from a public entity, complete with the symbolically significant flag displayed over its entrance.

13. On this view, *Burton* can be understood as entailing an inference of purposeful racial discrimination by government. Cf. *Lombard v. Louisiana*, 373 U.S. 267 (1963) (government discriminated purposefully by inviting property-owners to invoke facially neutral trespass laws against blacks during sit-ins at restaurants). See §§ 16–15, 16–16, 16–17, supra.

No such unconstitutional government act was found in *San Francisco Arts & Athletics, Inc.* ("SFAA") v. United States Olympic Committee, 107 S.Ct. 2971 (1987), where the Court reviewed a challenge to the Olympic Committee's decision to deny organizers of a gay athletic event license to use the word "Olympic." Although the Committee enjoyed a congressional grant of exclusive licensing power over that word, there was no evidence that the federal government could or did exercise any influence over the Committee's enforcement of that power. Id. at 2986 n.29. *Burton's* dwindling precedential power is illustrated by the fact that the majority mentioned the case only in a short footnote—evidently added only after the Court's entire omission of the case had been pointed out by the dissent, see id. at

2991 n. 12 (Brennan, J., dissenting)—even though *Burton* formed a central part of the SFAA's state action argument. Although the financial fortunes of the Committee and the federal government do not appear to have been tied together by the licensing of the word "Olympic" in the way that the restaurant and the parking authority were linked by the financial advantages of the former's discriminatory policies, compare *Burton*, 365 U.S. at 861, with *Olympic*, 107 S.Ct. at 2992 & nn. 13, 15 (Brennan, J., dissenting), the dissenters may have had the better of the argument with respect to the symbolic link between the Olympic Committee and the government. In *Burton*, the Court had found it significant that the restaurant and the public parking garage were linked in the public's eye by such things as the fact that the American and state flags flew from mastheads on the roof, see 365 U.S. at 859–61. Justice Brennan, joined by Justice Marshall, with Justices O'Connor and Blackmun in accord, 107 S.Ct. at 2987, argued in SFAA that the public image of the Olympic Committee was even more strongly bound up with the federal government, the national honor, and Old Glory. See id. at 2992 & n.14 (Brennan, J., dissenting). Yet this argument was insufficient in the eyes of the majority even to warrant a direct rebuttal. See 107 S.Ct. at 2986 n. 29.

The only surviving explanation of the result in *Burton* may be that found in Justice Stewart's concurrence. In upholding the restaurant's right to deny service to the plaintiff solely because of his race, the Supreme Court of Delaware relied upon a state law permitting any restaurant

In other situations, the process of restatement which the state action inquiry requires may alter the outcome of a case. A decision by a government actor to eject all black individuals who come on government premises would plainly be unconstitutional; but if the racist actor is in fact a private individual, and if the only government choice takes the form of a racially neutral decision to enforce the trespass laws at the request of any private property owner, a litigant may be unable to point to any decision which is *both* government-made *and* susceptible to successful constitutional challenge.[14]

For example, in *Polk County v. Dodson*,[15] the Supreme Court held that a state-paid public defender was not acting as a state agent when she decided not to prosecute a criminal defendant's appeal on the ground that it was frivolous. Since she was acting on the *defendant's* behalf as *his* defense lawyer—"a private function, traditionally filled by retained counsel, for which state office and authority are not needed"— the decision was held not to be attributable to the state.[16] Yet, since

proprietor to refuse to serve "persons whose reception or entertainment would be offensive to the major part of his customers . . . ." 24 Del.Code 1501. Since the only thing allegedly "offensive" about the plaintiff was his race, "[t]he highest court of Delaware ha[d] thus construed this legislative enactment as authorizing discriminatory classification based exclusively on color. Such a law . . . [is] clearly violative of the fourteenth amendment." 365 U.S. at 726–27 (Stewart, J., concurring). See § 18–1, note 6, supra. Nothing in SFAA v. United States Olympic Committee, undermines this aspect of Burton. See § 18–7, note 22, infra.

14. The question whether unconstitutional government action can be found in such circumstances was raised in a series of "sit-in" cases which the Supreme Court decided in 1963 and 1964. See Bouie v. Columbia, 378 U.S. 347 (1964); Bell v. Maryland, 378 U.S. 226 (1964); Robinson v. Florida, 378 U.S. 153 (1964); Barr v. Columbia, 378 U.S. 146 (1964); Griffin v. Maryland, 378 U.S. 130 (1964); Avent v. North Carolina, 373 U.S. 375 (1963); Gober v. Birmingham, 373 U.S. 374 (1963); Lombard v. Louisiana, 373 U.S. 267 (1963); Peterson v. Greenville, 373 U.S. 244 (1963). In every case, however, the Court managed to avoid the issue. See Paulsen, "The Sit-in Cases of 1964: 'But Answer Came There None,' " 1964 Sup.Ct.Rev. 137; Lewis, "The Sit-in Cases: Great Expectations," 1963 Sup.Ct.Rev. 101.

15. 454 U.S. 312 (1981). See § 18–7, infra, at note 9.

16. Id. at 319. See also Ferri v. Ackerman, 444 U.S. 193, 204 (1979) (although court-appointed counsel serves pursuant to state authorization and in furtherance of the constitutional requirement of the sixth amendment, her duty is not to the public

at large but to her client). Cf. Cuyler v. Sullivan, 446 U.S. 335 (1980). In reviewing a habeas corpus petition which alleged that, unbeknownst to the state, a conflict of interest on the part of defendant's retained counsel impaired defendant's sixth amendment rights, the Court in Cuyler deemed it irrelevant that the "conduct of retained counsel does not involve state action," id. at 342: under the sixth amendment, "the state's conduct of a criminal trial itself implicates the state in the defendant's conviction." Id. at 344.

The precise nature of the right at issue was equally integral to the state action analysis in Colorado v. Connelly, 107 S.Ct. 515 (1986), where a schizophrenic defendant experiencing "command hallucinations" walked up to a policeman and confessed to a murder, then later sought to suppress the confession as involuntary due to his mental state. No police misconduct or pressure was alleged, but the lower court "found that the very admission of the evidence in a court of law was sufficient state action" to implicate the due process clause. Id. at 519. Deeming the core of a due process involuntary confession claim to be "a substantial element of coercive police conduct," id. at 520, the Supreme Court reversed: "Absent police conduct causally related to the confession, there is simply no basis for concluding that any state actor has deprived a criminal defendant of due process of law." Id. It would be misleading to say that there was state action in Cuyler but not in Connelly; the point, rather, is that the state has a strict affirmative duty to assure that an accused be adequately assisted by counsel at any criminal trial, but no similar duty to assure that a confession used at trial was voluntarily offered. Cf. Burdeau v. McDowell, 256 U.S. 465 (1921) (conviction need not be

the public defender was on the state payroll and was acting as the defendant's lawyer at the state's behest, it would perhaps have been sounder for the Court to hold that the decision to drop a trifling appeal was in fact made by a state actor, but implicated no constitutionally troublesome rule or criterion. As the Court itself noted, *all* lawyers have a professional duty not to clog the courts with frivolous appeals.[17]

The remaining sections of this chapter will consider the implications of this approach for certain traditional puzzles in the state action field. The aim will be to demonstrate that, although the approach outlined here appears to be quite far removed from the rhetoric of the Supreme Court's state action decisions, it is generally [18] consistent with the Court's results, and often reveals why the Court found its decisions difficult.

§ 18-4. State Action and "Color of Law"

Insofar as it addresses states (or the national government), the Constitution speaks not only to the abstract legal entities we know as "the State" or as "the United States" but also to those institutions, and indeed individuals, that wield state power—those who, in other words, act "under color of law." At first glance, the approach set forth in § 18-3, with its emphasis on *government rules* or *decisions*, more than on the *status* of individuals as private or government *actors*, appears inconsistent with this axiom—and with the long line of cases that hold that the acts of a single government official, even if taken in violation of state law, may still constitute unconstitutional state action,[1] or action "under color of law" in violation of federal civil rights statutes.[2] Such a conclusion, however, would be mistaken. An individual government official can formulate and act on a rule that is illegal as a matter of state law without thereby forfeiting his state office, altering the conclusion that he acts as an agent of the state, or terminating the state's accountability for his conduct in that representative capacity. The argument set out above can thus accommodate situations in which the rule that is the subject of constitutional challenge is void as a matter of non-constitutional law as well.

It is important, however, not to overstate the significance of the Supreme Court's decisions that the ultra vires acts of individual government officials can amount to unconstitutional state action. *Home Tel.*

---

reversed because evidence used by state was obtained through unlawful private seizure of accused's property).

17. Polk County, 454 U.S. at 323 & n.14 (citing ABA Standards for Criminal Justice).

18. But not uniformly. See § 18-7, infra.

§ 18-4

1. See, e.g., Snowden v. Hughes, 321 U.S. 1, 11 (1944); Iowa-Des Moines National Bank v. Bennett, 284 U.S. 239, 244, 246 (1931); Home Tel. & Tel. Co. v. Los Angeles, 227 U.S. 278 (1913). The early cases

are collected in Barnett, "What is 'State' Action Under the Fourteenth, Fifteenth, and Nineteenth Amendments of the Constitution?" 24 Ore.L.Rev. 227 (1945).

2. See, e.g., Adickes v. Kress & Co., 398 U.S. 144, 152 (1970) (42 U.S.C. § 1983); Monroe v. Pape, 365 U.S. 167, 172 (1961) (same); Screws v. United States, 325 U.S. 91, 108 (1945) (18 U.S.C. § 242). For most purposes, the inquiry whether challenged conduct is "under color of law" within the meaning of 42 U.S.C. § 1983 is the same as the inquiry whether the challenged conduct is "state action." Lugar v. Edmondson Oil Co., 457 U.S. 922, 928–32 (1982).

& Tel. Co. v. Los Angeles [3] states the central proposition of these cases: "The theory of the [F]ourteenth Amendment is that where an officer or other representative of a State in the exercise of the authority with which he is clothed misuses the power possessed to do a wrong forbidden by the Amendment, inquiry concerning whether the State has authorized the wrong is irrelevant. . . ." [4] This conclusion reflects the fact that "the provisions of the Amendment . . . are addressed, of course, to the States, but also to every person whether natural or juridical who is the repository of state power," [5] as well as the absurdity of the contrary conclusion: "a state officer cannot on the one hand as a means of doing a wrong forbidden by the Amendment proceed upon the assumption of the possession of state power and at the same time for the purpose of avoiding the application of the Amendment, deny the power and thus accomplish the wrong." [6] But this conclusion also contains an important limitation: "one who is in possession of state power" must use that power "to the doing of the wrongs which the Amendment forbids. . . ." [7]

The decision which *Home Tel. & Tel. Co.* took to be the "leading case," [8] *Ex parte Young*,[9] implicitly indicated the significance of this limitation. There, the Supreme Court held that state rate-making legislation was unconstitutional on its face since it permitted railroads to obtain judicial review of rates only as defendants in criminal prosecutions. *Ex parte Young* did not hold that the state attorney general's threat of prosecution was by itself unconstitutional; it was the scheme as a whole, of which the threat was a part, that violated due process. More recently, in *Ingraham v. Wright*,[10] the Supreme Court made explicit what was only implicit in *Ex parte Young*: there are some constitutional prohibitions that the acts of individual government officials cannot in isolation violate. These prohibitions concern themselves with more systematic government activity and thus, in their light, individual acts simply cannot rise to the level of a constitutional violation. *Ingraham* involved a suit brought by students against a public school principal alleging that the principal did not afford the students procedural due process before authorizing corporal punishment. The Court did not deny that the principal was a state actor acting "under color of law" but refused to judge the principal's acts in isolation and, noting that the students had a common-law right to an after-the-fact damages action if corporal punishment were excessive or improper, held that availability of this subsequent hearing satisfied the requirements of due process.

Whether or not *Ingraham's* conclusion is correct on the merits,[11] it underscores the inevitable plurality of even the "color of law" cases.

---

3. 227 U.S. 278 (1913).

4. Id. at 287.

5. Id. at 286.

6. Id. at 288.

7. Id. at 287.

8. See id. at 294.

9. 209 U.S. 123 (1908). See § 3–27, supra.

10. 430 U.S. 651 (1977).

11. See § 10–14, supra, criticizing Ingraham and also criticizing Paul v. Davis, 424 U.S. 693 (1976) (no federal due process right to hearing when police officer erroneously disseminates accusation of crime).

Police officers may be deemed to deprive prisoners of life without due process of law by beating them to death,[12] to infringe the right of protection from unreasonable searches and seizures by breaking into homes without warrants,[13] or to deny individuals the equal protection of the laws by arresting them for associating in racially mixed groups,[14] even when the state forbids such acts and provides remedies against them. This is not to say, however, that all constitutional provisions are susceptible of violation by government officials acting individually.[15] In this context, as in all others, the existence of unconstitutional state action depends upon the characteristics that the specific constitutional guarantee at issue fixes as relevant.

§ 18–5. The "Public Function" Cases

When the state "merely" authorizes a given "private" action— imagine a green light at a street corner authorizing pedestrians to cross if they wish—that action cannot automatically become one taken under "state authority" in any sense that makes the Constitution applicable. Which authorizations have that Constitution-triggering effect will necessarily turn on the character of the decision-making responsibility thereby placed (or left) in private hands. However described, there must exist a category of responsibilities regarded at any given time as so "public" or "governmental" that their discharge by private persons, pursuant to state authorization even though not necessarily in accord with state direction, is subject to the federal constitutional norms that would apply to public officials discharging those same responsibilities. For example, deciding to cross the street when a police officer says you may is *not* such a "public function;" but authoritatively deciding who is free to cross and who must stop *is* a "public function" whether or not the person entrusted under state law to perform that function wears a police uniform and is paid a salary from state revenues or wears civilian garb and serves as a volunteer crossing guard. As one might expect, a series of Supreme Court decisions articulates this "public function" theory.[1]

Because the approach taken here holds that the state action requirement serves to frame constitutional questions at the decision-making level at which government actors are responsible for the conduct in dispute, this approach might also appear inconsistent with the Supreme Court's "public function" decisions. In these cases, the Court has held that the actions of seemingly private actors may be

---

12. See Screws v. United States, 325 U.S. 91 (1945).

13. See Monroe v. Pape, 365 U.S. 167 (1961).

14. See Adickes v. Kress & Co., 398 U.S. 144 (1970).

15. The requirements of procedural due process and of just compensation seem the clearest instances of norms ordinarily addressed to legal systems as a whole rather

than to individual government actors. See generally § 10–14, supra.

§ 18–5

1. E.g., Smith v. Allwright, 321 U.S. 649 (1944); Marsh v. Alabama, 326 U.S. 501 (1946); Evans v. Newton, 382 U.S. 296 (1966); Amalgamated Food Employees Local 590 v. Logan Valley Plaza, 391 U.S. 308 (1968); Jackson v. Metropolitan Edison Co., 419 U.S. 345 (1974).

inherently governmental,[2] and thus subject to constitutional limitation, notwithstanding the absence of overt state responsibility for the specific choices challenged. To the extent that they make use of a public function analysis, the Court's opinions in these cases focus attention on the governmental or private status of particular actors, treating that status as fixed ultimately by constitutional law.[3]

It is in analyzing these cases, however, that the approach taken in this chapter proves most useful. The public function decisions are troublesome precisely to the extent that they purport to apply independent constitutional standards in distinguishing governmental from private actors. But no satisfactory criteria currently exist to determine what is or is not inherently governmental for this purpose.[4] If these decisions are recast as raising questions of whether government actors can constitutionally decide to leave certain kinds of decisions to private actors, analysis of the cases becomes much more straightforward.

Despite this evident lack of criteria, it is not impossible to analyze an activity or function with a view to deciding whether a particular substantive norm or a specific procedural safeguard must attend performance of the activity or function even by a private person or institution. For example, given the powerful case for the view that the state exists largely to resolve private disputes,[5] and especially given the peculiar risks that harm will be too often inflicted and too acutely felt if its imposition in the purported resolution of such disputes is not surrounded by special procedural safeguards,[6] it may be convincingly

---

2. Thus, in Evans v. Newton, 382 U.S. 296, 299 (1966), the Supreme Court spoke of "powers or functions governmental in nature. . . ." More recently, the Court attempted to describe public functions both more precisely and more narrowly as "powers traditionally exclusively reserved to the State." Jackson v. Metropolitan Edison Co., 419 U.S. 345, 352 (1974).

3. "[W]here private individuals or groups are endowed by the State with powers or functions governmental in nature, they become agencies or instrumentalities of the State and subject to its constitutional limitations." Evans, 382 U.S. at 299.

4. Compare, e.g., Jackson v. Metropolitan Edison Co., 419 U.S. 345 (1974) (provision of electrical service held not a public function), with, e.g., Evans v. Newton, 382 U.S. 296 (1966) (provision of park treated as public function). Cf. Garcia v. San Antonio Metro. Transit Authority, 469 U.S. 528, 543–46 (1985) (concluding that the distinction between "traditional" governmental functions and proprietary functions was both unworkable in practice and unsound in principle, since it is inconsistent with federalism's basic tenet that states should be free to experiment with "any activity that their citizens choose for the common weal").

One of the few clear rules in this regard is that a private entity does not become a

state actor simply because it may have been created by the government. In San Francisco Arts & Athletics, Inc. v. United States Olympic Committee, 107 S.Ct. 2971 (1987), the Court held that the Olympic Committee was not a state actor simply because it had been chartered by Congress and granted an exclusive right to license use of the word "Olympic." Id. at 2985. After all, every corporation operates under a government charter, and every trademark owner enjoys exclusive rights pursuant to common or statutory law, yet the conduct of either actor remains private. Id. The Court further found that neither the conduct nor the coordination of amateur athletic contests—the Olympic Committee's business—constituted "a traditional governmental function." Id. "most fundamentally," the Court concluded that the government could not be held responsible for the Committee's choice of how to enforce its exclusive right because the Committee operated independent of the federal government, id. at 2986 & n.27, and there was no evidence that the government "coerced or encouraged the [Committee] in the exercise of its right." Id. at 2986.

5. See, e.g., R. Nozick, Anarchy, State and Utopia (1974).

6. See Michelman, "The Supreme Court and Litigation Access Fees: The Right to

argued that a state legal regime that permits private individuals to employ self-help with immunity in the coercive resolution of disputes over life, liberty, or property is constitutionally defective unless that same regime provides, for example, for adversary, trial-type hearings before or promptly after the use of such self-help.[7] Although such a conclusion may be expressed by saying that coercive dispute-resolution is inherently governmental and therefore is a "public function," it seems more illuminating to focus on the rule of law under which a particular form or instance of dispute-resolution occurs. It is doubtful, for example, that vigilante justice—in the form of physical punishment meted out by a mob—would be subject to the requirements of the fourteenth amendment on a "public function" theory in a state whose legal system clearly condemns such private "punishment" and provides effective remedies against its infliction. But when a state's statutory or common law purports to *authorize* private self-help, and provides a defense to civil or criminal liability on the part of those who take matters into their own hands by restricting liberty or seizing property, such individuals should probably be deemed to exercise state power sufficient to support suing them directly under 42 U.S.C. § 1983.[8]

The Supreme Court's opinions in the White Primary Cases [9] illustrate the alternative approaches. In *Smith v. Allwright*,[10] the Court considered the fifteenth amendment implications of the Texas Democratic Party's refusal to admit black Texans to membership, so as to allow black Texans to vote in its primary election. The Court's opinion, concluding that there was a fifteenth amendment violation, offered two theories in support of that holding. On the one hand, the Democratic Party itself violated the fifteenth amendment in denying blacks the right to vote in its primary. The Court refused to accept "Texas' decision that the exclusion is produced by private or party action." [11] Instead, the Court independently concluded that Texas law made primary elections an integral part of the state's overall electoral scheme, placed initial responsibility for primary election management upon political parties, and subjected the parties' election management to close regulation. Thus, the Court found, in managing the primaries the parties performed "a state function," [12] and must therefore comport with the fifteenth amendment in fixing voter eligibility. Alternatively, the *Smith* opinion argued, it was the state, and not the Democratic Party, which violated the fifteenth amendment. A state leaves itself vulnerable to a charge of purposeful racial discrimination if its gives primary elections central importance in its electoral scheme and yet casts "its electoral process in a form which permits a private organization to practice racial discrimination in the election." [13] The fact that

Protect One's Rights—Part II," 1974 Duke L.J. 527, 568–70.

7. See §§ 18–6, infra, and 10–14, supra.

8. But see Flagg Bros., Inc. v. Brooks, 436 U.S. 149 (1978) (no state action where privately-owned warehouse uses state statutory self-help provision to sell individual's stored property to recover unpaid storage fees), discussed in § 18–6, infra.

9. The White Primary Cases are discussed against a background of other election cases in § 13–23, supra.

10. 321 U.S. 649 (1944).

11. Id. at 662.

12. Id. at 660; see also id. at 663.

13. Id. at 664.

the state otherwise so closely regulates party management of primary elections suggests that the state, by pointedly failing to regulate voter eligibility for such primaries, "endorses, adopts and enforces the discrimination against Negroes. . . ."[14]

Terry v. Adams[15] revealed a similar duality. There, the issue was the constitutionality of a pre-primary election which white voters held among themselves avowedly in order to render a racially open primary election meaningless. The Supreme Court held that the pre-primary scheme was unconstitutional, but divided in its reasoning. Justice Clark's concurring opinion concluded that the pre-primary association itself acted unconstitutionally: "When a state structures its electoral apparatus in a form which devolves upon a political organization the uncontested choice of public officials, that organization itself, in whatever disguise, takes on those attributes of government which draw the Constitution's safeguards into play."[16] Justice Black's opinion announcing the Court's decision, however, held that it was government toleration of the pre-primary which violated the fifteenth amendment: "It violates the Fifteenth Amendment for a state . . . to permit within its borders the use of any device that produces an equivalent of the prohibited [racially discriminatory] election."[17]

Of the two approaches which the White Primary Cases reveal, the public function analysis appears to be the less convincing and the more artificial. In *Smith* and *Terry*, the Court persuasively demonstrated that state electoral schemes accorded an important role to political parties. The Court, however, could not explain its equation of an important role with a "governmental" role. On the other hand, *Smith* and *Terry* probably characterized correctly the purpose of the Texas legislature: state tolerance of privately run, racially discriminatory primaries reflected a purposeful state decision to maintain a racially discriminatory electoral system. Moreover, even if such a characterization was doubtful, it revealed the fundamental constitutional issue in these as in other fifteenth amendment cases: the extent to which courts may rely upon indirect circumstantial proof of purposeful racial discrimination.[18]

The first amendment public function cases suggest a similar pattern. Ironically, the first decision in this line, *Marsh v. Alabama*,[19] although it coined the phrase,[20] was not on its own terms a true "public function" decision. In *Marsh*, the Supreme Court reversed a state trespass conviction incurred by a Jehovah's Witness who distributed religious literature in a company town in contravention of the wishes of the town's owners, who invoked the state trespass law to enforce their prohibition. Justice Black's majority opinion did not concern itself, as a genuine public function opinion would have, with whether the streets of the town's central business district should be deemed "public property," in the sense of being open to the public, as a matter of constitution-

---

14. Id.

15. 345 U.S. 461 (1953).

16. Id. at 484.

17. Id. at 469.

18. See § 16–20, supra.

19. 326 U.S. 501 (1946).

20. See id. at 506.

al law.[21] Instead, the majority saw as the pertinent issue whether a state could protect private property rights by allowing company town owners to invoke trespass laws even though, in so doing, the state would deny residents of such towns [22] free speech rights which the state could not otherwise deny—simply because company town residents must inevitably exercise those rights on private property. Justice Black found no basis in the first amendment for such differential treatment of free speech rights: "Whether a corporation or a municipality owns or possesses the town the public in either case has an identical interest in the functioning of the community in such manner that the channels of communication remain free." [23] The state's interest in protecting the private property rights of the town owners failed to justify the differential treatment: free speech rights "occupy a preferred position." [24] Moreover, Justice Black observed, "[t]he more an owner, for his advantage, opens up his property for use by the public in general, the more do his rights become circumscribed by the statutory and constitutional rights of those who use it." [25]

The next case in the series, *Amalgamated Food Employees Local 590 v. Logan Valley Plaza*,[26] is a true public function case: in form the opinion purports to decide whether the state can, through use of its trespass power, delegate to a shopping center owner the power to exclude union picketers; in substance, however, the opinion keys its holding that the state cannot do so to an analysis of whether the shopping center is constitutionally public or private property. To this end, Justice Black's observation about the inverse relationship between property's public use and its private status, which was not in fact central to the argument in *Marsh*, becomes decisive in *Logan Valley*, shaping the very statement of the holding in the latter case: members of the public may "exercise their First Amendment rights on the premises in a manner and for a purpose generally consonant with the use to which the property was put."[27]

Although the *Logan Valley* opinion asserted in dictum that the shopping center was "clearly the functional equivalent of the business district . . . in *Marsh*," [28] it did not purport to decide whether the public could exercise first amendment rights in a shopping center to the same extent as in a downtown business district.[29] In *Lloyd Corp. v. Tanner*,[30] the Court rejected *Logan Valley's* dictum, and held that first

---

21. Nor did Marsh establish, for example, that the individuals charged with managing the streets had to be selected as public officials would. See Chapter 13, supra.

22. And those who wished to communicate with such residents.

23. 326 U.S. at 507. See §§ 12–19, 12–23, 12–24, 12–25, supra.

24. 326 U.S. at 509.

25. Id. at 506. If state law permitted the company town's owners to imprison the Jehovah's Witness by themselves rather than with the aid of state police and state courts, the owners ought to be subject to suit under 42 U.S.C. § 1983. At the very least, a state court's refusal to grant relief against the owners in a false imprisonment suit would be reviewable on the merits, see § 18–1, supra, and § 18–6, infra, and would violate the same first amendment principles as those vindicated by the Court in Marsh.

26. 391 U.S. 308 (1968).

27. Id. at 319–20.

28. Id. at 318.

29. See id. at 320 n.9.

30. 407 U.S. 551 (1972).

amendment rights were indeed circumscribed in the shopping center context: individuals could not, for example, distribute anti-war leaflets in a shopping center in the absence of the owner's consent. In limiting *Logan Valley*, however, the *Lloyd* Court did not depart from the earlier opinion's logic. Emphasizing that "First Amendment activity" must be "related to the shopping center's operations," [31] the *Lloyd* opinion explained that the shopping center operator could deny entry to anti-war protesters, but not to union picketers, because there was "no relationship, direct or indirect," between anti-war protest and "the business of the shopping center," [32] as there could be if union picketing was at issue; moreover anti-war protesters, unlike union picketers, possessed "adequate alternative means of communication. . . ." [33]

In thus rigorously adhering to *Logan Valley's* public function analysis, *Lloyd* created an apparent anomaly insofar as first amendment doctrine was concerned: the existence of first amendment rights in the shopping center context depended upon the conformity of an individual's purpose with the shopping center's function, and thus ultimately depended upon the content of the message which the individual wished to communicate. Recognizing that such content-conditioning is itself problematic under the first amendment,[34] the Supreme Court in *Hudgens v. NLRB* [35] concluded that a shopping center must be a first amendment forum for purposes of all communications or none. Curiously, instead of making for itself the choice between "all" and "none," the *Hudgens* Court noted that *Lloyd* had rejected *Logan Valley's* suggestion that a shopping center was in all respects the functional equivalent of a downtown business district, concluded that *Lloyd* had therefore overruled *Logan Valley* insofar as the latter decision was relevant, and ultimately held that *Lloyd* was stare decisis.[36] In so doing, the *Hudgens* Court unfortunately continued to give effect to public function reasoning even while repudiating that reasoning's prior conclusion. The "functional equivalence" test determined only whether particular property was private or public for a particular purpose as a matter of constitutional law. If the *Hudgens* Court had framed the question as *Marsh* originally did, the issue would have been whether a state, in choosing to enforce what it deemed private property rights, denied some individuals free speech rights without adequate justification.[37] The relevant inquiry would not have been whether the property was public or private, but whether state-protected freedom of speech in

---

31. Id. at 562.

32. Id. at 564.

33. Id. at 567.

34. See §§ 12–3, 12–19, supra. But see § 12–25, supra, for a response to that difficulty in the shopping center context.

35. 424 U.S. 507 (1976).

36. "It matters not that some Members of the Court may continue to believe that the *Logan Valley* case was rightly decided. Our institutional duty is to follow until changed the law as it now is, not as some Members of the Court might wish it to be.

And in the performance of that duty we make clear now, if it was not clear before, that the rationale of *Logan Valley* did not survive the Court's decision in the *Lloyd* case." Id. at 518.

37. Cf. PruneYard Shopping Center v. Robins, 447 U.S. 74 (1980) (no unconstitutional taking of property or abridgment of free speech rights of property owners where state construes its constitution to prohibit privately-owned shopping center from excluding people who wish to engage in nondisruptive expressive activity).

the shopping center context was required in order to secure first amendment values. The outcome of this latter inquiry may not be clear,[38] but an analysis along the lines proposed here would have been more likely to focus properly upon the free speech and other constitutional interests which the decision would ultimately affect.

§ 18–6. Common Law as a Subject of State Action Theory: The Role of Constitutional Rights in Fixing the Relevant Level of Analysis

To this point, analysis of traditional state action issues has required reference only to an outline of a reformulated state action inquiry. This section, however, examines the operation of such an inquiry in greater detail. The aim is not simply to describe in a general way the changed perspective which this chapter's form of state action analysis brings to bear on certain traditional questions. Rather, this section will attempt to operate *within* that perspective in considering certain chronically unresolved state action issues.

All three of the issues discussed here concern the common law. The general proposition that common law is state action—that is, that the state "acts" when its courts create and enforce common law rules— is hardly controversial: [1] "It would be a narrow conception of jurisprudence to confine the notion of 'laws' to what is found written on the statute books, and to disregard the gloss which life has written upon it. Settled state practice cannot supplant constitutional guarantees, but it can establish what is state law." [2] Nonetheless, in different contexts, courts have come to very different conclusions about the necessity for judging common law rules in light of constitutional limitations. In the line of decisions which begins with *New York Times Co. v. Sullivan,*[3] the Supreme Court, at least in reviewing the results of state court adjudications, has shown no hesitation whatsoever about subjecting common law defamation and privacy rules to first amendment scrutiny.[4] Next, *Shelley v. Kraemer*[5] held that a state court could not, consistent with the equal protection clause, enforce a racially restrictive covenant satisfying the state's common law standards. Writing for the Court, Chief Justice Vinson did not satisfactorily articulate the reasoning that underlay *Shelley's* holding; courts and commentators

---

38. See § 12–25, supra.

§ 18–6

1. See, e.g., cases collected in Barnett, "What is 'State' Action Under the Fourteenth, Fifteenth, and Nineteenth Amendments of the Constitution?" 24 Ore.L.Rev. 227 (1945).

2. Nashville, Chattanooga & St. Louis Ry. v. Browning, 310 U.S. 362, 369 (1940) (Frankfurter, J., for a unanimous Court). See also Adickes v. Kress & Co., 398 U.S. 144, 171 (1970) (state law includes custom "having the force of law").

3. 376 U.S. 254 (1964), discussed in §§ 12–12 to 12–14, supra.

4. See, e.g., New York Times Co. v. Sullivan, 376 U.S. at 265: "Although this is a civil lawsuit between private parties, the Alabama courts have applied a state rule of law which petitioners claim to impose invalid restrictions on their constitutional freedoms of speech and press. It matters not that that law has been applied in a civil action and that it is common law only, though supplemented by statute. . . . The test is not the form in which state power has been applied but, whatever the form, whether such power has in fact been exercised."

5. 334 U.S. 1 (1948).

have characteristically viewed *Shelley* with suspicion.[6] Finally, a majority of the lower federal courts that considered the question prior to the Supreme Court's decision in *Flagg Brothers, Inc. v. Brooks*[7] held that the Uniform Commercial Code's codification of the private common law right of self-help repossession[8] is not state action subject to procedural due process scrutiny,[9] at least in a suit against the private creditor under 42 U.S.C. § 1983. The leading pre-*Flagg Brothers* case, *Adams v. Southern California First National Bank*,[10] specifically emphasized the U.C.C.'s status as a mere codification of the common law rule; by implication, *Adams* seemed to hold that the common law rule is not itself state action.[11] So it was perhaps unsurprising when the Supreme Court, in *Flagg Brothers v. Brooks*, found no state action in conduct taken pursuant to the U.C.C. by a privately-owned business.

Ms. Brooks and her family were evicted from their apartment, and the city marshal arranged for the storage of their possessions in Flagg Brothers' warehouse. Ms. Brooks authorized storage of her household goods because she had no practical alternative, even though she found the price exorbitant. After a series of disputes with Flagg Brothers over the claimed storage fees, she was told to pay up or her furniture would be sold. She sought relief in a federal court under 42 U.S.C. § 1983, claiming the right to an opportunity to be heard on the amount owed prior to the sale of her belongings.

The Supreme Court apparently assumed that, if the sale of property were conducted by state officials without providing the owner a hearing, that sale would violate the due process clause. But the Court held that a private warehouseman's proposed sale of bailed goods to recover unpaid storage fees, even pursuant to the New York U.C.C. self-help provision, was not an action attributable to the state. Justice Rehnquist began his state action inquiry for the *Flagg Brothers* majority by focusing not on the governmental *rules* implicated by the particular right asserted by Ms. Brooks, but on whether public or private *actors* were responsible for her injury. There had been no trace of overt official involvement—and this was sufficient[12] to distinguish *Flagg Brothers* from prior cases where the challenged statute had required the clerk of the court to issue a summons at the request of the creditor's lawyer[13] or to make out a writ of replevin, upon the creditor's demand, for seizure of the property by the sheriff.[14] But the signifi-

---

6. See, e.g., Bell v. Maryland, 378 U.S. 226, 329–32 (1964) (Black, J., dissenting); Wechsler, "Toward Neutral Principles of Constitutional Law," 73 Harv.L.Rev. 1, 29–31 (1959).

7. 436 U.S. 149 (1978).

8. U.C.C. § 9–503.

9. See Alexander, "Cutting the Gordian Knot: State Action and Self-Help Repossession," 2 Hast.L.Q. 893, 893–95 n.3 (1975).

10. 492 F.2d 324 (9th Cir. 1973), cert. denied 419 U.S. 1006 (1974). But see id. at 340–42 (Hufstedler, J., dissenting); Shirley v. State National Bank of Connecticut, 493

F.2d 739, 745–47 (2d Cir. 1974) (Kaufman, J., dissenting); Watson v. Branch County Bank, 380 F.Supp. 945, 961–73 (W.D.Mich. 1974) (Fox, C. J.) (finding state responsibility for self-help repossession), rev'd mem. 516 F.2d 902 (6th Cir. 1975).

11. See 492 F.2d at 330.

12. 436 U.S. at 157.

13. Sniadach v. Family Finance Corp., 395 U.S. 337, 338–39 (1969), discussed in § 16–43, supra.

14. Fuentes v. Shevin, 407 U.S. 67, 70–71 (1972), discussed in §§ 16–43, 16–53, supra. See also North Georgia Finishing Co. v. Di-Chem, Inc., 419 U.S. 601, 607 (1975)

cance Justice Rehnquist attributed to the absence of overt official involvement made due process review turn on whether the legislative scheme happened to require the private party to enlist the participation of some minor functionary exercising merely ministerial powers. Since what was wrong in prior due process cases was that the state had not reserved *enough* control over the use of coercive force, it would be perverse for the Court to conclude that the scheme in *Flagg Brothers* was *less* constitutionally infirm because the state withdrew even its clerical rubber stamp and freed creditors to dispose of debtors' property without any mediation or intervention by public authorities.[15]

Ms. Brooks' argument that the sale by the warehouseman itself became a state act because of what the state's laws had done was doomed by the Court's restrictive "public function" doctrine.[16] The mere fact that an actor *might* or *could* invoke the state law as a *defense* if and when sued in state court, the Supreme Court evidently believed, does not mean that the state law is at issue in the federal suit brought by that actor.[17] In a sense, the Court decided that the U.C.C. self-help provision was *never directly implicated* in Ms. Brooks' § 1983 suit: the mere *existence* of that provision did not convert the private creditor's act, which was all the plaintiff had actually challenged, into an act of the State of New York.

Justice Rehnquist made a telling observation in a footnote to his opinion for the Court: "There is no reason . . . to believe that the [plaintiff] could not . . . seek resort to the New York Courts . . . to . . . prevent the [challenged] surrender[ ] of [her] property."[18] Had Ms. Brooks sought such injunctive relief against Flagg Brothers and been denied it by a state court on the ground that the state U.C.C. provision barred the relief sought, that ruling by the courts of New York would *itself* have constituted challengeable state action[19]—unless common law rules, and their statutory codifications, do not qualify as "state action" at all.

In sorting out the underlying issues, it is helpful to begin analysis by considering *New York Times Co. v. Sullivan* and *Shelley v. Kraemer* in conjunction. How is it that common law adjudication is so obviously state action in the first case and so obscurely state action in the second? At first glance, it might appear that the crucial distinction between the two cases lies in the fact that *Sullivan* sounds in tort and *Shelley* essentially in contract. Rules of tort law, this argument would have it, are quite plainly that: government-made rules. By contrast, contract law, so it is said, consists simply of rules by which courts identify

(court clerk issued writ of garnishment solely on basis of creditor's affidavit).

15. See 436 U.S. at 174–75 (Stevens, J., joined by White and Marshall, JJ., dissenting). Yet this is precisely the path chosen by the Court, as confirmed by Lugar v. Edmondson Oil Co., 457 U.S. 922, 941–42 (1982), which held that the mere initiation of a defective state attachment procedure is sufficient to convert a private creditor into a state actor, so long as the procedure involves even the most trivial joint participation with ministerial state functionaries.

16. See § 18–5, supra.

17. See Louisville & Nashville R.R. v. Mottley, 211 U.S. 149 (1908) (no federal jurisdiction of case where only federal issue is a defense based on federal law which might be invoked by defendant).

18. 436 U.S. at 161 n.11.

19. See § 18–1, supra.

enforceable contracts; the substance of the agreements which courts enforce is the product of the parties' will and not the state's. In an era in which contract and tort merge, however, this distinction is hardly satisfactory.[20] Contract law plainly encompasses rules which either define the substantive acceptability of contracts or which fill in missing contractual provisions, in addition to the more or less traditional rules defining the process of contract formation and the operation of available remedies.[21] Moreover, tort law, as it is currently conceptualized, revives and revises traditional notions of commutative justice: liability rules, at least in part, are not externally imposed codes of conduct, but represent an initial allocation of risk arranged to facilitate negotiation of consensual arrangements which reflect individuals' own views as to proper risk-sharing.[22]

A better way of comparing the two cases starts with the constitutional rights asserted in each case. In *Sullivan*, a newspaper, as defendant in a libel action, relied on the free press clause of the first amendment. By its terms, the first amendment was not an absolute bar to the libel action: "Calculated falsehood," at least, is not protected by the first amendment.[23] Yet the character of the first amendment right at stake persuaded the Court that the requisite "breathing space" for speech could be "purchased only by allowing some constitutionally unprotected defamatory falsehoods to go unpunished." [24] Both to avoid an unacceptable level of erroneous suppression of truthful speech and to avoid an unacceptably high level of self-censorship, it was thought necessary to impose procedural limits on permissible forms of defamation recovery under state law.[25] Thus the nature of the right involved in *New York Times v. Sullivan* directed inquiry to the procedural defects of the state's scheme of common law remedies. In *Shelley*, on the other hand, a purchaser of real estate, as defendant in an action to enforce a restrictive covenant, relied on the equal protection clause of the fourteenth amendment. As conventionally understood, the clause commanded governmental neutrality with respect to such matters as race.[26] And, on the surface at least, the required neutrality seemed to be satisfied by the argument that the state's courts were simply enforcing blindly the terms of a contract restricting the sale of land. Again, the nature of the right involved focused the inquiry—but this time, so long as the right was deemed satisfied by neutrality, and so long as the state's policy was characterized as neutral, the inquiry appeared to hit a dead end without turning up any constitutional violation.

It was for this reason that *Shelley* was and remains a more problematic case than *Sullivan*. If it was rightly decided, as there is

20. See generally G. Gilmore, The Death of Contract (1974).

21. Even these background rules have been understood, ever since the fall of Model II, to reflect positive governmental choices. See §§ 8–5 to 8–7, supra.

22. See generally G. Calabresi, The Costs of Accidents: A Legal and Economic Analysis (1970).

23. Garrison v. Louisiana, 379 U.S. 64, 75 (1964).

24. New York Times Co. v. Sullivan, 376 U.S. 254, 271–72 (1964).

25. See §§ 12–12, 12–13, 12–23, 12–33, supra.

26. See §§ 16–13 to 16–20, supra.

every reason to believe it was, the reason is either that neutrality does not suffice in matters of racial segregation in housing,[27] or that the state's contract and property rules, including elaborate doctrines designed to limit the enforceability of restraints on the alienation of land, were not in fact neutral in their enforcement of *racial* restraints on alienation while treating many other restraints as unenforceable.[28] The issue, in this formulation, becomes a matter for resolution in terms of the substantive rules of equal protection—rules that must obviously take into account the absence of any countervailing value of privacy when restrictive covenants, rather than a homeowner's preferences with respect to personal guests, are being enforced.[29] The approach to state action advocated in this chapter provides no sudden solution to that (or any other) problem of substantive constitutional law; its mission is simply to reveal how the search for state action, properly conducted, ends by identifying the precise substantive constitutional issue to be addressed. The purpose here has thus been more to identify the right questions than to supply the answers.

§ 18–7. The Positive State as a Subject of State Action Theory: The Role of Governmental Carrots and Sticks in Fixing the Relevant Level of Analysis

As we saw in our prior consideration of *Burton v. Wilmington Parking Authority*,[1] a situation of pervasive interdependence between a government actor and a private actor may make it appropriate to focus not on the substantively acceptable governmental decision to leave particular choices to the private actor, but on the substantively unacceptable way in which those choices are exercised in the specific case. Put more broadly, the level of decision that is subject to constitutional challenge will vary with the character of government's involvement, so that the more government gains (and the more it appears to gain) by the way in which a choice is made, the clearer is the case for treating the choice as one for which government bears responsibility. In this way, analysis in a case like *Burton* shifts from the level of the rule that tells the lessee, "serve whomever you wish," to the level of the rule adopted by the lessee himself: "whites only."

27. That neutrality does not suffice in matters of racial segregation in education, at least, was settled by Norwood v. Harrison, 413 U.S. 455 (1973), discussed in § 16–15, supra, at notes 30–37. But see Evans v. Abney, 396 U.S. 435 (1970) (fourteenth amendment not violated by judicial ruling that racially restrictive trust failed when the trust property, a park, could no longer be used "for whites only" as testator had decreed); In re Girard College Trusteeship, 391 Pa. 434, 138 A.2d 844 (1958), cert. denied 357 U.S. 570 (1958) (allowing substitution of private trustees to maintain school for whites in accord with testator's wish), rejected in Pennsylvania v. Brown, 392 F.2d 120 (3d Cir. 1968), cert. denied 391 U.S. 921 (1968). See generally § 16–20, supra.

28. See, e.g., Restatement of Property § 406 (1944). See the analysis in § 16–17, supra.

29. See, e.g., Henkin, "Shelley v. Kraemer: Notes for a Revised Opinion," 110 U.Pa.L.Rev. 473 (1962). In accord with Shelley is Barrows v. Jackson, 346 U.S. 249 (1953) (fourteenth amendment bars award of damages for breach of racially restrictive covenant).

§ 18–7

1. 365 U.S. 715 (1961). See § 18–3, supra.

The state's responsibility for the private decisions it influences is illustrated by *Little v. Streater*,[2] where the Supreme Court unanimously held that Connecticut was obliged to pay for blood-grouping tests requested by the indigent defendant in a paternity suit because of the state's "considerable and manifest" involvement in the suit:[3] the plaintiff mother was compelled by Connecticut's welfare laws to bring suit against the father of her illegitimate child if she wished to receive benefits; the state attorney general was a party to the action and had the power to disapprove any settlement; the plaintiff's lawyer was paid by the state; and any support payments awarded by the court were to be paid directly to the state.[4]

Despite the temporary reinvigoration of the *Burton* "symbiosis" analysis in *Streater*, the Court subsequently refused to find state action in two cases where the state had insinuated itself into the operations of private organizations. Both the nursing homes involved in *Blum v. Yaretsky*,[5] and the special school involved in *Rendell-Baker v. Kohn*,[6] received the vast bulk of their funding from the government[7] and were heavily regulated by the state as well.[8] Yet the Court did not find governmental responsibility for the *specific decisions* complained of in either case.

In *Blum v. Yaretsky*, several Medicaid patients had challenged their involuntary transfer or discharge from their nursing homes. In his opinion for the Court, Justice Rehnquist concluded that the decision to discharge or reassign a particular patient was a medical judgment about the patient's health needs made by a private physician,[9] to which the state merely reacted by lowering or terminating Medicaid benefits accordingly.[10]

Writing for the Court in *Rendell-Baker v. Kohn*, Chief Justice Burger could not see how extensive regulation and almost exclusive funding by Massachusetts implicated that state in the decision of the director of the New Perspectives School to fire one of its teachers for opposing school policy. Although the school was under contract to fulfill the state statutory obligation of several cities to provide special

---

2. 452 U.S. 1 (1981).

3. Id. at 9. Although the Court did not cite Burton, it had no difficulty in finding state action while treating Streater as a case of equal access to the courts.

4. Id.

5. 457 U.S. 991 (1982).

6. 457 U.S. 830 (1982).

7. Yaretsky, 457 U.S. at 1011; Rendell-Baker, 457 U.S. at 840.

8. Yaretsky, 457 U.S. at 1004; Rendell-Baker, 457 U.S. at 841.

9. 457 U.S. at 1008 & n.19. This may be the seed of a new "medical question" doctrine that even the decision of a doctor on the state payroll may not be state action—by analogy to the attorney-client relationship that was isolated from state involvement in Polk County v. Dodson, 454

U.S. 312, 320–21 (1981), discussed in § 18–3, supra. Justice Blackmun, the member of the Court with the greatest legal experience in medical matters, took strong exception to the Court's analysis in Polk County and to its use of doctor-patient cases. See id. at 330–31 & n.2 (dissenting opinion).

10. 457 U.S. at 1005. Justice Brennan argued in a cogent dissent that the decision to discharge was anything but a "private medical decision," since the doctor merely filled in numerical scores of "medical need" in accord with carefully delineated state criteria on a highly detailed state form. The very notion of different levels of nursing care was a product of state money-saving policies, not medical practice, which made physicians agents of the state cost-control program. See id. at 1016–27 (Brennan, J., dissenting).

schooling for troubled students and was extensively regulated by the state in that capacity,[11] there was hardly any regulation of personnel matters.[12] And even if state funds accounted for 99% of the school's operating budget,[13] the Chief Justice concluded that this in no way affected the relationship between the school and its faculty.[14] Director Kohn's decision to fire Rendell-Baker for siding with students in a school policy battle, however much it might stifle free speech, simply did not constitute action under color of state law.[15] The Court in each of these cases found it significant that the plaintiffs had not challenged any particular state rules as such: no state rules dealing with personnel discipline or dismissal existed in *Rendell-Baker*,[16] and the particular state rules about adjusting Medicaid benefits were not being directly challenged in *Yaretsky*.[17]

There are occasions, of course, on which a careful analysis will make it unnecessary to move to this more specific level of decision, as where the government's seemingly more general rule is *itself* constitutionally objectionable. As we saw in our analysis of the shopping center cases,[18] the constitutional objection (successful or otherwise) must be directed in those cases to the very fact that private property owners are delegated authority to constrict opportunities for communication to a large segment of the would-be speakers' desired audience.[19] So too, when government creates a situation of scarcity, whether by conferring territorial monopoly power or by issuing a limited number of licenses and forbidding performance of a designated service without a license, the very decision to permit the monopolist or the licensee to deny service at his discretion—a decision unmistakably the government's—is arguably unconstitutional insofar as it causes injury that would not have occurred in the absence of government's restriction of the market, and that would be forbidden to government as a matter of explicit choice. Thus both *Jackson v. Metropolitan Edison Co.*,[20] if read as holding that an electric company is not bound to observe procedural due process in terminating service notwithstanding the government's delegation of monopoly power, and *Moose Lodge No. 107 v. Irvis*,[21] if read as holding that a private club's racial discrimination in serving liquor is not affected by the equal protection clause notwithstanding the government's limitation of the availability of liquor licenses, seem difficult if not impossible to defend in principled terms. Both decisions become at least arguably defensible, however, if they are read to hold only that neither the club sued in *Moose Lodge* nor the electric company sued in *Jackson* acted "under color of law." But if the plaintiff in the former case had sued the members of the Pennsylvania

---

11. 457 U.S. at 823–33 & n.1.

12. Id. at 833, 842–43.

13. Id. at 832.

14. Id. at 840–41.

15. It is possible that Rendell-Baker could constitutionally have been fired even if she were a public employee, since her speech may have concerned office and personnel grievances rather than questions of "public concern." See Connick v. Myers,

461 U.S. 138 (1983), discussed in § 12–18, supra.

16. 457 U.S. at 833, 841; id. at 844 (White, J., concurring).

17. 457 U.S. at 1003.

18. See § 18–5, supra.

19. See § 12–25, supra.

20. 419 U.S. 345 (1974).

21. 407 U.S. 163 (1972).

liquor control board rather than the Moose Lodge, he could have directly charged the board members with suborning racism and aggravating its impact by handing out the privilege of a scarce liquor license without regard to the licensee's racist practices. Similarly, the plaintiff in *Jackson* probably should have sued not Metropolitan Edison but the members of the public utility commission that gave Met Ed a monopoly and thereby put it in a position to cut plaintiff off from all electrical power without first providing due process.[22]

Although Justice Marshall, dissenting in *Jackson*, is surely right that "[t]he values of pluralism and diversity are simply not relevant when the private company is the only electric company in town," [23] such values are at least relevant in assessing the substantive constitutionality of the governmental delegation in *Moose Lodge*. But the claim in that case was not that the equal protection clause required the state to prevent racial discrimination in every private club; [24] the claim was only that the state violated equal protection when it helped to *intensify* the harm caused by such discrimination by permitting it to occur in the delivery of a service that the state licensed, and forbade to those who were unlicensed. Whether equal protection doctrine should be construed to reach this result is perhaps debatable; [25] that the

22. In each such hypothetical case the critical point is that the entity sued—the liquor board or the utility commission—had been delegated the power to control access to a widely desired or even essential commodity—a liquor license or electrical power. In contrast, the alleged state actor in San Francisco Arts & Athletics, Inc. ("SFAA") v. United States Olympic Committee, 107 S.Ct. 2971 (1987)—i.e., the Olympic Committee—enjoyed congressionally delegated power merely to control use of the word "Olympic." It would have been a very different case if Congress had ceded to the Committee the power to control the conduct of all American involvement in international amateur athletic contests. Moreover, it is clear that, if the plaintiffs in either Moose Lodge or Jackson had first sought and been denied relief in the state courts, those state judicial rulings would themselves have constituted state action reviewable on appeal or by certiorari by the Supreme Court. See § 18–1, note 6, and § 18–6, supra. In Olympic Committee, the Court declined to address the question whether the entry of a federal injunction at the Committee's behest, denying the SFAA's use of the word "Olympic," constituted sufficient governmental action to require constitutional inquiry into the Committee's motivation in seeking the injunction, because the SFAA had not presented that theory of state action—arguably based on Shelley v. Kraemer, 334 U.S. 1 (1948)—in its petition for certiorari.

23. 419 U.S. at 372–73.

24. The Court did reach and decide one substantive constitutional question in

Moose Lodge, holding that a Pennsylvania law compelling a liquor licensee to comply with its own racially restrictive charter and bylaws denies equal protection. Although that substantive holding seems sound, in reaching it the Court—in an opinion by Justice Rehnquist—relied on an expansive misreading of Shelley v. Kraemer: "Shelley . . . makes it clear that the application of state sanctions to enforce [a discriminatory private rule] would violate the fourteenth amendment." 407 U.S. at 179. This common misconstruction of Shelley, see, e.g., Kennedy, "The Stages of Decline of the Public/Private Distinction," 130 U.Pa.L.Rev. 1349, 1352 (1982), assumes that the fourteenth amendment requires the states to outlaw all private acts of racism whenever the private party might ultimately seek the security of judicial enforcement—a common circumstance indeed. If Shelley ever stood for such a bold proposition, it certainly does no longer, for in Washington v. Davis, 426 U.S. 229 (1976), and its progeny the Court declared that disparate adverse impact on a racial minority is insufficient to make a facially neutral rule or practice unconstitutional or even suspect. A more accurate reading of Shelley—and one that survives Washington v. Davis—is offered in § 16–21, supra.

25. The primary obstacles to finding an equal protection violation in the state's decision to issue a limited number of liquor licenses without assuring non-discriminatory service by each licensee are two: (1) the difficulty of demonstrating a significant net impact on minority drinking opportunities, and (2) the requirement of proving a

state's delegation should have been subject to scrutiny under the equal protection clause, despite the Court's apparent holding to the contrary in the context of a § 1983 suit against the private lodge, seems reasonably clear.

When the state has little realistic choice other than to issue licenses, as in the case of allocating technologically scarce frequencies in the electromagnetic spectrum, the situation differs precisely because it can no longer be said, when a licensee withholds a service or denies access, that the denied individual can trace his or her injury to government's regulatory involvement.[26] In a case like *Moose Lodge*, the black person denied service by one of the state's liquor licensees could at least argue that, but for the licensing scheme, he would have had greater access to the very service withheld in that case. But in a case like *Columbia Broadcasting System v. Democratic National Committee*,[27] the individual or group denied time to broadcast an editorial advertisement by one of the FCC's licensees cannot show that, but for the FCC's involvement, such time would have been available. Indeed, but for the FCC's involvement, the situation might have been one of sheer chaos—with no effective broadcasting network at all.

In such a case, it is far more difficult to claim that the FCC's failure to insist that television licensees accept paid editorial advertisements should be treated as analogous, for first amendment purposes, to an FCC decree that such advertisements must be rejected. In either case, the FCC's position represents a governmental choice that should be subject to first amendment scrutiny. But in the first case, unlike the second, the choice may be defended in terms of the substantive first amendment values advanced by leaving editorial discretion to broadcast licensees, subject only to such regulations as those of the fairness doctrine.[28] Unlike *Moose Lodge*, where the supposed values of associational privacy and pluralism in the realm of social life were separable from the government's licensing presence, the situation in *Columbia Broadcasting System* was such that the values of decentralized broadcaster choice might have been unattainable but for the government's regulatory role.

Despite these differences between *Moose Lodge* and *Columbia Broadcasting System*, it is important to perceive that the distinctions noted here go to the *merits* and *not to the threshold question whether government has made any decision that is subject to at least nonfrivolous attack under the Constitution*. In both cases, government's regulatory policy—a mix, as always, of acts and omissions—constituted government action which should have been subject to testing, in a

discriminatory governmental purpose if mere inattention to the adverse racial consequences of licensing bigots is deemed insufficient to establish a denial of equal protection. See Washington v. Davis, 426 U.S. 229 (1976), discussed in §§ 16–20 and 16–21, supra. The second obstacle could be overcome if such inattention to discrimination based on race, coupled with attention to other sorts of allegedly immoral or anti-

social behavior, were deemed to be facially race-specific. Cf. Shelley v. Kraemer, 334 U.S. 1 (1948), discussed in § 18–6, supra.

26. See § 12–25, supra.

27. 412 U.S. 94 (1973), discussed in § 12–25, supra.

28. See 412 U.S. at 146–47 (White, J., concurring); id. at 147–48 (Blackmun, J., joined by Powell, J., concurring).

procedurally suitable context, for its consistency with the underlying norms made relevant by the right allegedly violated. To decide, in either of these cases, that the Constitution creates a zone within which government should be free simply to leave the disputed choice in private hands, is to make a defensible decision—but it is a decision about the substantive reach of specific constitutional commands rather than a decision about whether the government has *done* anything to which the Constitution speaks.[29]

Thus, if constitutional law is understood as a snapshot of the deepest norms by which we govern our political lives, the state action problem is its negative. It is a problem, or rather a series of problems, whose solutions must currently be sought in perceptions of what we do not believe particular constitutional provisions should be read to control. This conclusion should not seem too surprising. For in the end, is it not fitting that a book about the Constitution should close by studying what the Constitution is not about?

29. The Supreme Court's establishment clause cases provide among the best illustrations of a substantive approach to state action. In Larkin v. Grendel's Den, Inc., 459 U.S. 116 (1982), for example, the Court struck down the state's delegation to churches of a power to veto nearby liquor license applications; a license applicant had relied on 42 U.S.C. § 1983 to sue the local liquor license officials entrusted with enforcing the church's veto pursuant to the state law. Had the church itself been sued under § 1983, a powerful argument could have been made that its wielding of the state-delegated veto, especially in conjunction with local officials, cf. Lugar v. Edmondson Oil Co., 457 U.S. 922, 941–42 (1982), rendered the church a party acting "under color of law."

Many of the establishment clause cases concern whether various government benefits—in the form of financial aid, tax exemptions, or whatever—constitute improper government support for organized religion. See, e.g., § 14–9, supra. The Court's decisions in this area are open to many criticisms; at the least, however, it can be said that the Court has avoided the temptation to distinguish a threshold question of state action, ostensibly filtering out only peripheral government involvements with religion, from the substantive inquiry under the establishment clause itself. For example, in Corporation of the Presiding Bishop v. Amos, 107 S.Ct. 2862 (1987), which upheld over an establishment clause attack an exemption for religious organizations from Title VII's bar on discrimination in employment on the basis of religion— one broad enough to cover even employees of their nonprofit secular arms—the Court

stressed that, although the exemption made it easier for religious organizations to advance their principles by pressing employees to conform, the government *itself* had not thereby advanced religion through its *own* actions. Id. at 2868–69 & n.15. Even if, as Justice O'Connor suggested in concurring in the judgment, this was a distinction without a difference, see id. at 2874, at least the majority did not treat the indirect *nature* of the government benefit to religion—as a threshhold matter—as preventing the establishment clause from applying at all on the theory that only private advancement of religion was involved. Rather, the majority recognized that facilitation of private behavior *could* be state action, and that the establishment clause therefore applied.

The establishment clause cases thus provide a model for analysis of the state action problems lower federal courts are beginning to discover in resolving other constitutional challenges to government benefit programs. For example, the true issue in a case like Jackson v. Statler Foundation, 496 F.2d 623 (2d Cir. 1974), cert. denied 420 U.S. 927 (1975), is not whether a tax exemption is governmental aid, and thus state action, but rather whether the exemption, regarded as a tax expenditure, so implicates the federal government in a private foundation's activities that, as a matter of substantive equal protection law, the government becomes a partner in the foundation's purposeful racial discrimination. Cf. Burton v. Wilmington Parking Authority, 365 U.S. 715 (1961), discussed in § 18–3, supra. See also Brown, "State Action Analysis of Tax Expenditures," 11 Harv. Civ.Rts.—Civ.Lib.L.Rev. 97 (1976).

Appendix

THE JUSTICES OF THE SUPREME COURT *

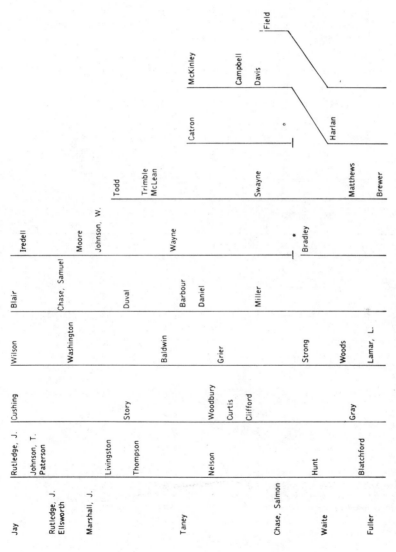

* Catron died in 1865, Wayne in 1867; their positions were abolished by Congress to prevent their being filled by President Johnson; a new position was created in 1869, which traditionally has been regarded as a re-creation of Wayne's seat.

* Adapted, with permission of John J. Cound, from W. Lockhart, Y. Kamisar, J. Choper, and S. Shiffrin, Constitutional Law: Cases—Comments—Questions, Appendix A (6th ed. 1986).

1890
1892
1893
1894
1895
1898
1902
1903
1906
1909
1910
1912
1914
1916
1921
1922
1923
1925
1930
1932
1937
1938
1939
1940
1941
1943
1945
1946
1949
1953
1955
1956
1957
1958
1962
1965
1966
1967
1968
1969
1970
1972
1975
1981
1986

McKenna
Stone
Jackson, R.
Harlan
Rehnquist
Scalia

Pitney
Sanford
Roberts
Burton
Stewart
O'Connor

Hughes
Clarke
Sutherland
Reed
Whittaker
White, B.

Shiras
Day
Butler
Murphy
Clark
Marshall, T.

Brown
Moody
Lamar, J.
Brandeis
Douglas
Stevens

Jackson, H.
Peckham
Lurton
McReynolds
Byrnes
Rutledge
Minton
Brennan

Holmes
Cardozo
Frankfurter
Goldberg
Fortas
Blackmun

White, E.
Van Devanter
Black
Powell

White, E.
Taft
Hughes
Stone
Vinson
Warren
Burger
Rehnquist

1890
1892
1893
1894
1895
1898
1902
1903
1906
1909
1910
1912
1914
1916
1921
1922
1923
1925
1930
1932
1937
1938
1939
1940
1941
1943
1945
1946
1949
1953
1955
1956
1957
1958
1962
1965
1966
1967
1968
1969
1970
1972
1975
1981
1986

** Fuller died in 1910, and White was named Chief Justice. Hughes resigned in 1941, and Stone was named Chief Justice.

TABLE OF AUTHORITIES

References are to Pages. Only the page at which an authority is
first cited within a section is noted.

1723

INDEX *

References are to Pages

* I thankfully acknowledge the extraordinary efforts, in the preparation of this index, of Kenneth Chesebro, J.D., Harvard Law School, 1986; Jonathan Massey, J.D., Harvard Law School, 1988; and Peter Rubin, J.D., Harvard Law School, 1988.

University Textbook Series

December, 1987

Especially Designed for Collateral Reading

HARRY W. JONES
Directing Editor
Professor of Law, Columbia University

ADMINISTRATIVE LAW AND PROCESS (1985)
Richard J. Pierce, Jr., Dean and Professor of Law, University of Pittsburgh.
Sidney A. Shapiro, Professor of Law, University of Kansas.
Paul R. Verkuil, President and Professor of Law, College of William and Mary.

ADMIRALTY, Second Edition (1975)
Grant Gilmore, Professor of Law, Yale University.
Charles L. Black, Jr., Professor of Law, Yale University.

ADMIRALTY AND FEDERALISM (1970)
David W. Robertson, Professor of Law, University of Texas.

AGENCY (1975)
W. Edward Sell, Dean of the School of Law, University of Pittsburgh.

BUSINESS ORGANIZATION AND FINANCE, Second Edition (1986)
William A. Klein, Professor of Law, University of California, Los Angeles.
John C. Coffee, Jr., Professor of Law, Columbia University.

CIVIL PROCEDURE, BASIC, Second Edition (1979)
Milton D. Green, Professor of Law Emeritus, University of California, Hastings College of the Law.

COMMERCIAL TRANSACTIONS, INTRODUCTION TO (1977)
Hon. Robert Braucher, Associate Justice, Supreme Judicial Court of Massachusetts.
Robert A. Riegert, Professor of Law, Cumberland School of Law.

CONFLICT OF LAWS, COMMENTARY ON THE, Third Edition (1986) with 1987 Supplement
Russell J. Weintraub, Professor of Law, University of Texas.

CONSTITUTIONAL LAW, AMERICAN, Second Edition (A TREATISE ON) (1988)
Laurence H. Tribe, Professor of Law, Harvard University.

CONTRACT LAW, THE CAPABILITY PROBLEM IN (1978)
Richard Danzig.

CORPORATE TAXATION (1987)
Howard E. Abrams, Professor of Law, Emory University.
Richard L. Doernberg, Professor of Law, Emory University.

CORPORATIONS, Second Edition (1971)
Norman D. Lattin, Professor of Law, University of California, Hastings College of the Law.

UNIVERSITY TEXTBOOK SERIES—Continued

CORPORATIONS IN PERSPECTIVE (1976)
Alfred F. Conard, Professor of Law, University of Michigan.

CRIMINAL LAW, Third Edition (1982)
Rollin M. Perkins, Professor of Law, University of California, Hastings College of the Law.
Ronald N. Boyce, Professor of Law, University of Utah College of Law.

CRIMINAL PROCEDURE, Second Edition (1986) with 1987 Supplement
Charles H. Whitebread, II, Professor of Law, University of Southern California.
Christopher Slobogin, Associate Professor of Law, University of Florida.

ESTATES IN LAND & FUTURE INTERESTS, PREFACE TO, Second Edition (1984)
Thomas F. Bergin, Professor of Law, University of Virginia.
Paul G. Haskell, Professor of Law, University of North Carolina.

EVIDENCE: COMMON SENSE AND COMMON LAW (1947)
John M. Maguire, Professor of Law, Harvard University.

EVIDENCE, STUDENTS' TEXT ON THE LAW OF (1935)
The late John Henry Wigmore, Northwestern University.

JURISPRUDENCE: MEN AND IDEAS OF THE LAW (1953)
The late Edwin W. Patterson, Cardozo Professor of Jurisprudence, Columbia University.

LEGAL CAPITAL, Second Edition (1981)
Bayless Manning.

LEGAL RESEARCH ILLUSTRATED, 1987 Edition with 1985 Assignments Supplement and Assignment Update
J. Myron Jacobstein, Professor of Law, Law Librarian, Stanford University.
Roy M. Mersky, Professor of Law, Director of Research, University of Texas.

LEGAL RESEARCH, FUNDAMENTALS OF, 1987 Edition with 1985 Assignments Supplement and Assignment Update
J. Myron Jacobstein, Professor of Law, Law Librarian, Stanford University.
Roy M. Mersky, Professor of Law, Director of Research, University of Texas.

PROCEDURE, THE STRUCTURE OF (1979)
Robert M. Cover, Professor of Law, Yale University.
Owen M. Fiss, Professor of Law, Yale University.

PROPERTY, Second Edition (1975)
John E. Cribbet, Dean of the Law School, University of Illinois.

TAXATION, FEDERAL INCOME, Fourth Edition (1985) with 1987 Supplement
Marvin A. Chirelstein, Professor of Law, Columbia University.

TORTS, Second Edition (1980)
Clarence Morris, Professor of Law, University of Pennsylvania.
C. Robert Morris, Professor of Law, University of Minnesota.

WILLS AND TRUSTS, THE PLANNING AND DRAFTING OF, Second Edition (1979) with 1982 Supplement
Thomas L. Shaffer, Professor of Law, University of Notre Dame.

WILLS, TRUSTS AND ADMINISTRATION, PREFACE TO (1987)
Paul G. Haskell, Professor of Law, University of North Carolina.

†